January 9–12, 2013
Berkeley, California, USA

Association for
Computing Machinery

Advancing Computing as a Science & Profession

ITCS'13

Proceedings of the 2013 ACM Conference on
Innovations in Theoretical Computer Science

Sponsored by:

ACM SIGACT

Supported by:

Akamai and Simons Foundation

Association for
Computing Machinery

Advancing Computing as a Science & Profession

The Association for Computing Machinery
2 Penn Plaza, Suite 701
New York, New York 10121-0701

Notice to Past Authors of ACM-Published Articles
ACM intends to create a complete electronic archive of all articles and/or other material previously published by ACM. If you have written a work that has been previously published by ACM in any journal or conference proceedings prior to 1978, or any SIG Newsletter at any time, and you do NOT want this work to appear in the ACM Digital Library, please inform permissions@acm.org, stating the title of the work, the author(s), and where and when published.

ISBN: 978-1-4503-1859-4 (Digital)

ISBN: 978-1-4503-2087-0 (Print)

Additional copies may be ordered prepaid from:

ACM Order Department
PO Box 30777
New York, NY 10087-0777, USA

Phone: 1-800-342-6626 (USA and Canada)
+1-212-626-0500 (Global)
Fax: +1-212-944-1318
E-mail: acmhelp@acm.org
Hours of Operation: 8:30 am – 4:30 pm ET

Printed in the USA

Preface

The papers in this volume were presented at the 4th *Innovations in Theoretical Computer Science (ITCS 2013)* conference, sponsored by the ACM Special Interest Group on Algorithms and Computation Theory (SIGACT). The conference was held in Berkeley, California, USA, January 9–12, 2013.

The program committee consisted of Mark Braverman (Princeton University), Shuchi Chawla (University of Wisconsin), Julia Chuzhoy (TTI-Chicago), Yevgeniy Dodis (New York University), Andrew Drucker (MIT and IAS), Uriel Feige (Weizmann Institute), Ravi Kannan (Microsoft Research India), Robert Kleinberg (Chair, Cornell University), Eyal Kushilevitz (Technion), S. Muthukrishnan (Rutgers University), Ronitt Rubinfeld (MIT and Tel Aviv University), Atri Rudra (University at Buffalo), Adam Smith (Pennsylvania State University), Santosh Vempala (Georgia Tech), and Andrew Yao (Tsinghua University).

The call for papers attracted 123 submissions worldwide. The program committee accepted 49 papers that cover a wide range of topics in theoretical computer science, including algorithms, complexity, cryptography, learning, data privacy, quantum computing, and relations between computing and the biological and social sciences.

The program committee selected two papers for the Best Student Paper award: "Properties and Applications of Boolean Function Composition" by Avishay Tal, and "Time Hierarchies for Sampling Distributions" by Thomas Watson.

I wish to thank the organizing committee, consisting of Berkeley professors Satish Rao (Chair), Christos Papadimitriou, and Umesh Vazirani, for all of their help. Special thanks go to Adrienne Griscti from ACM and Lisa Tolles from Sheridan Communications, for creating the conference proceedings. I am also grateful to the many individuals who assisted in reviewing the submitted papers.

Above all, I thank the authors for contributing their work to ITCS 2013. As you read these proceedings, I trust you will find that their papers present a varied and stimulating perspective on current and future directions for theoretical computer science research.

Robert Kleinberg
ITCS 2013 Program Chair
Cornell University, Ithaca, NY, USA

Table of Contents

Session 5

Session Chair: Friday, January 11, 2013 – 8:40-8:50

Session 6

Friday, January 11, 2013 – 10:35AM-10:45AM

Session 7

Friday, January 11, 2013 – 2:00PM-2:10PM

Session 8
Friday, January 11, 2013 – 3:55PM-4:05PM

Session 9
Saturday, January 12, 2013 – 8:30AM-8:40AM

Session 10
Saturday, January 12, 2013 – 10:45AM-10:55AM

Session 11
Saturday, January 12, 2013 – 2:00PM-2:10PM

ITCS 2013 Conference Organization

Program Chair: Robert Kleinberg *(Cornell University)*

Local Arrangements Chair: Satish Rao *(University of California, Berkeley)*

Organizing Committee: Christos Papadimitriou *(University of California, Berkeley)*
Satish Rao *(University of California, Berkeley)*
Umesh Vazirani *(University of California, Berkeley)*

Steering Committee Chair: Shafi Goldwasser *(MIT and Weizmann Institute)*

Steering Committee: Sanjeev Arora *(Princeton University)*
Manuel Blum *(Carnegie Mellon University)*
Bernard Chazelle *(Princeton University)*
Oded Goldreich *(Weizmann Institute)*
Shafi Goldwasser *(Massachusetts Institute of Technology and Weizmann Institute)*
Richard Karp *(University of California, Berkeley)*
Ueli Maurer *(ETH Zürich)*
Silvio Micali *(Massachusetts Institute of Technology)*
Peter Bro Miltersen *(Aarhus University)*
Christos Papadimitriou *(University of California, Berkeley)*
Michael Rabin *(Harvard University)*
Madhu Sudan *(Microsoft Research)*
Leslie Valiant *(Harvard University)*
Umesh Vazirani *(University of California, Berkeley)*
Avi Wigderson *(Princeton University)*
Andrew Yao *(Tsinghua University)*

Program Committee: Mark Braverman *(Princeton University)*
Shuchi Chawla *(University of Wisconsin)*
Julia Chuzhoy *(Toyota Technological Institute at Chicago)*
Yevgeniy Dodis *(New York University)*
Andrew Drucker *(Massachusetts Institute of Technology and IAS)*
Uriel Feige *(Weizmann Institute)*
Ravi Kannan *(Microsoft Research India)*
Robert Kleinberg *(Cornell University)*
Eyal Kushilevitz *(Technion)*
S. Muthukrishnan *(Rutgers University)*
Ronitt Rubinfeld *(Massachusetts Institute of Technology and Tel Aviv University)*
Atri Rudra *(University at Buffalo)*
Adam Smith *(The Pennsylvania State University)*
Santosh Vempala *(Georgia Tech)*
Andrew Yao *(Tsinghua University)*

Additional Reviewers:

Jacob Abernethy
Divesh Aggarwal
Amitanand Aiyer
Saeed Alaei
Albert Atserias
Hagit Attiya
Per Austrin
Tess Avitabile
Nikhil Bansal
Siddharth Barman
Rida Bazzi
Paul Beame
Chris Beck
Eli Ben-Sasson
Anand Bhaskar
Arnab Bhattacharyya
Nir Bitansky
Eric Blais
Avrim Blum
Andrej Bogdanov
Adam Bouland
Anne Broadbent
Yang Cai
Ran Canetti
Keren Censor-Hillel
Deeparnab Chakrabarty
Ning Chen
Po-An Chen
Flavio Chierichetti
Alessandro Chiesa
Giulio Chiribella
Tsz Chiu Kwok
Eden Chlamtac
Roger Colbeck
Holger Dell
Amit Deshpande
Benjamin Doerr
Shaddin Dughmi
Alina Ene
Pedro Felzenszwalb
Dario Fiore
Felix Fischer
Lisa Fleischer
Michael Forbes
Luke Friedman
Rafael Frongillo
Hu Fu
Ariel Gabizon
Chaya Ganesh
Rong Ge
Konstantinos Georgiou
Sevag Gharibian
Michael Gofman
Sasha Golovnev
Parikshit Gopalan
Sergey Gorbunov
Vipul Goyal
Navin Goyal
Fabrizio Grandoni
Elena Grigorescu
Joshua Grochow
Bach Ha
Moritz Hardt
Dennis Hofheinz
Nicholas Hopper
Nicole Immorlica
Yuval Ishai
Patrick Jaillet
Abhishek Jain
Prateek Jain
Madhav Jha
Yael Tauman Kalai
Satyen Kale
Jonathan Katz
Kristian Kersting
Subhash Khot
Adam Klivans
Robert Krauthgamer
Michael Krivelevich
Amit Kumar
Silvio Lattanzi
Stefano Leonardi
Reut Levi
Allison Lewko
Jian Li
Adriana Lopez-Alt
Brendan Lucier
Mohammad Mahdian
Mohammad Mahmoody
David Malec
Bodo Manthey
Andrew McGregor
Vahab Mirrokni
Ankur Moitra
Benjamin Moseley
Yoram Moses
Steven Myers
Arkadi Nemirovski

Additional Reviewers (continued):

Thanh Nguyen
Jakob Nordstrom
Adam O'Neill
Tatsuaki Okamoto
Joel Oren
Claudio Orlandi
Abraham Othman
Shayan Oveis Gharan
Renato Paes Leme
Denis Pankratov
Periklis Papakonstantinou
Rafael Pass
Valerio Pastro
Chris Peikert
Krzysztof Pietrzak
Toni Pitassi
Kirk Pruhs
Tsvetomira Radeva
Prasad Raghavendra
Vijaya Ramachandran
Vibhor Rastogi
Kenneth Regan
Oded Regev
Lev Reyzin
Heiko Roglin
Dana Ron
Noga Ron-Zewi
Alon Rosen
Benjamin Rossman
Guy Rothblum
Sushant Sachdeva
Shubhangi Saraf
C. Seshadhri
Asaf Shapira
Yaoyun Shi
Amir Shpilka
Hava Siegelmann
Balasubramanian Sivan
Aleksandrs Slivkins
Nikhil Srivatsava
John Steinberger
Noah Stephens-Davidowitz
David Steurer
Scott Summers
Jukka Suomela
Chaitanya Swamy
Pingzhong Tang
Moshe Tennenholtz
Aris Tentes
Justin Thaler
Pushkar Tripathi
Jonathan Ullman
Chris Umans
Seeun Umboh
Salil Vadhan
Paul Valiant
Virginia Vassilevska Williams
Michael Viderman
Aravindan Vijayaraghavan
Jan Vondrak
Andrew Wan
John Watrous
Thomas Watson
Hoeteck Wee
S. Matthew Weinberg
Omri Weinstein
Daniel Wichs
Jens Witkowski
Xiaodi Wu
Yi Wu
Lirong Xia
David Xiao
Ning Xie
Sergey Yekhanin
Morteza Zadimoghaddam
Shengyu Zhang
Yuan Zhou
Anastatios Zouzias
Uri Zwick

ITCS 2013 Sponsor & Supporters

Sponsor: SIGACT

Supporters: Akamai

SIMONS FOUNDATION

Massive Online Teaching to Bounded Learners

Brendan Juba*
Harvard University
School of Engineering and Applied Sciences
33 Oxford St.
Cambridge, MA 02138
bjuba@alum.mit.edu

Ryan Williams†
Stanford University
Computer Science Department
353 Serra Mall
Stanford, CA 94305
rrw@cs.stanford.edu

ABSTRACT

We consider a model of teaching in which the learners are consistent and have bounded state, but are otherwise arbitrary. The teacher is non-interactive and "massively open": the teacher broadcasts a sequence of examples of an arbitrary target concept, intended for every possible on-line learning algorithm to learn from. We focus on the problem of designing interesting teachers: *efficient* sequences of examples that lead all capable and consistent learners to learn concepts, regardless of the underlying algorithm used by the learner. We use two measures of teaching efficiency: the number of mistakes made by the worst-case learner, and the maximum length of the example sequence needed for the worst-case learner. Our results are summarized as follows:

• Given a uniform random sequence of examples of an n-bit concept function, learners (capable of consistently learning the concept) with $s(n)$ bits of state are guaranteed to make only $O(n \cdot s(n))$ mistakes and exactly learn the concept, with high probability. This theorem has interesting corollaries; for instance, every concept c has a sequence of examples can teach c to all capable consistent on-line learners implementable with $s(n)$-size circuits, such that every learner makes only $\tilde{O}(s(n)^2)$ mistakes. That is, all resource-bounded algorithms capable of consistently learning a concept can be simultaneously taught that concept with few mistakes, on a single example sequence.

We also show how to efficiently generate such a sequence of examples on-line: using Nisan's pseudorandom generator, each example in the sequence can be generated with polynomial-time overhead per example, with an $O(n \cdot s(n))$-bit initial seed.

• To justify our use of randomness, we prove that any non-trivial derandomization of our sequences would imply new circuit lower bounds. For instance, if there is a deterministic $2^{n^{O(1)}}$ time algorithm that generates a sequence of examples, such that all consistent and capable polynomial-size circuit learners learn the all-zeroes concept *with less than 2^n mistakes*, then $\mathsf{EXP} \not\subset \mathsf{P/poly}$.

• We present examples illustrating that the key differences in our model – our focus on mistakes rather than the total number of examples, and our use of a state bound – must be considered together to obtain our results.

• We show that for every consistent $s(n)$-state bounded learner $\mathcal{A}$, and every n-bit concept that $\mathcal{A}$ is capable of learning, there is a custom "tutoring" sequence of only $O(n \cdot s(n))$ examples that teaches $\mathcal{A}$ the concept. That is, in principle, there are *no slow learners*, only *bad teachers*: if a state-bounded learner is capable of learning a concept at all, then it can always be taught that concept quickly via some short sequence of examples.

Categories and Subject Descriptors

F.1.3 [**Computation by Abstract Devices**]: Complexity Measures and Classes; I.2.6 [**Artificial Intelligence**]: Learning—*Concept learning*

Keywords

derandomization, on-line learning, semantic communication, teaching

1. INTRODUCTION

In 1960, Hans Freudenthal [11] proposed a non-interactive message called LINCOS, which attempts to teach the "whole bulk of our knowledge" in a way that can be easily understood by any intelligent being. Using regularities in the message itself, the message presents a long sequence of examples for each concept, starting with basic concepts such as equality (of natural numbers), gradually building up a vocabulary of arithmetic, and then proceeding onwards to more complex concepts using the existing vocabulary. Freudenthal's intent was to broadcast this message into outer space, to teach alien civilizations about humanity.

Inspired by this remarkable (but perhaps a bit zany) work, we ask a more grounded question: can concepts be taught to *every* capable and bounded computational device in a non-interactive way? This sort of question is "dual" to the usual type of problem that arises so often in theoretical computer science, where we wish to design an algorithm that is "useful"

*Supported by ONR grant number N000141210358 and NSF Grant CCF-0939370. This author was also affiliated with MIT CSAIL during the course of this work.

†Supported in part by a David Morgenthaler II Faculty Fellowship, and NSF Grant CCF-1212372 (Exploiting Duality between Algorithms and Complexity).

on a large class of data. Here we have a problem of *data design*: presenting an arrangement of data that is useful to a large class of algorithms. We wish to design, once and for all, a sequence of inputs and outputs so that no matter *who* or *what* observes the behavior (including future observers we haven't conceived of), so long as its complexity is bounded, the observer will discover the structure of the underlying process. Is this possible, even in principle? What are the constraints involved?

To properly formalize these questions, we consider a new variant of teaching model in which the learners are of limited computational complexity (and consistent), but otherwise arbitrary. A vast array of teaching models already exist in the literature (cf. Section 1.2); most of these works have either considered models in which either the learner is assumed to be more sophisticated, or the teacher and learner are designed as a pair. Our study is most closely related to the well-known work on teaching dimension by Goldman and Kearns [12] and Shinohara and Miyano [26], which studies the number of examples needed to identify each concept in a given class. Our work can be seen as a complexity-theoretic extension of the work on teaching dimension, focused on efficient learners. (See Section 2 for more comparison.) The model we consider retains a complexity-theoretic "universal" flavor along the lines of Goldreich, Juba, and Sudan [14]: we wish to design sequences of examples for efficiently teaching an *unknown* but capable bounded-state learner.

1.1 Our Results

We first observe that the number of examples required to teach some very simple concepts for very simple learners can be maximally large. (The precise definitions we use are recalled in Section 2.) Let AC^0-LINEAR be the class of on-line learning algorithms whose functionality is computable by AC^0 circuits of size $O(n)$; more precisely, the learner's predictions and hypothesis updates are computable with AC^0 circuits of $O(n)$ size (as a consequence, the learner's hypotheses is stored among at most $O(n)$ bits of state).

THEOREM 1.1. (TEACHING SIMPLE LEARNERS REQUIRES MANY EXAMPLES.) *There is a concept class $\mathcal{H}$ such that for all n, there is a concept $h_n \in \mathcal{H}$ such that, for every sequence s_n of n-bit examples that allow all AC^0-LINEAR learners to identify c, the length of s_n equals 2^n.*

Hence we cannot measure learning efficiency by the number of examples, without further constraints. Furthermore, we observe that existing results on PAC-learning readily imply methods for *approximately* teaching concepts to many bounded learners. However, if we instead focus on exact learning, and consider the number of *mistakes* made by learners, we enter interesting territory. We find that there are simple, efficient (per round, on-line) universal teaching strategies for learners with bounded state. Informally, we say that a learning algorithm is *$s(n)$-bounded* if, in learning any n-bit concept function, the maximum length of its state descriptions is $s(n)$. (Full definitions will come later.)

THEOREM 1.2. (EXACT LEARNING WITH FEW MISTAKES FROM RANDOM EXAMPLES.) *For all concepts $h : \{0,1\}^n \to \{0,1\}$ and $\delta > 0$, every consistent $s(n)$-bounded $\mathcal{A}$ for h learns h and makes at most $O(s(n)(n+\log\frac{1}{\delta}))$ mistakes with probability at least $1-\delta$, when the instances of length n are chosen uniformly at random.*

Theorem 1.2 has interesting corollaries; for example, any concept that is consistently learnable by some subset of the $s(n)$-size circuits can be learned all such circuits simultaneously, with $\tilde{O}(s(n)^2)$ mistakes by any learner, just by broadcasting uniform random examples (Corollary 3.1). Our use of the probabilistic method begs the question of whether such a sequence can be generated efficiently, with little to no randomness. As a partial answer, we confirm that Nisan's pseudorandom generator [22] for space-bounded computation can be used to obtain an efficient teaching strategy that uses few bits of randomness.

THEOREM 1.3. (FEW MISTAKES FROM LOW RANDOMNESS.) *Using a block length of $\Theta(s(n)+n+\log\frac{1}{\delta})$ (and $k = O(n+\log\frac{1}{\delta})$), Nisan's pseudorandom generator produces a sequence of $2^{O(n)}$ random bits for which with probability $1-\delta$ over the seed $h_1, \dots, h_k, x$, any consistent learning algorithm that is $s(n)$-bounded on a given concept exactly identifies that concept and makes at most $O(s(n)(n+\log\frac{1}{\delta}))$ mistakes.*

So using $O(s(n)\cdot n)$ random bits, we can generate $2^{O(n)}$ examples such that any learning algorithm consistent on h can be taught h with at most $O(s(n)\cdot n)$ mistakes on the examples, with high probability. This still does not answer the question of whether we can eliminate randomness entirely. We show that a *deterministic* exponential time algorithm for generating a sequence with similar properties would imply strong circuit lower bounds for EXP.

THEOREM 1.4. (DETERMINISTIC SEQUENCES TEACHING ALL LEARNERS IMPLIES CIRCUIT LOWER BOUNDS.) *Let $\mathcal{F}$ be a class of functions from $\mathbb{N}$ to $\mathbb{N}$. Suppose there is a deterministic $t(n)$ time algorithm M such that for all $s(n) \in \mathcal{F}$ and all sufficiently large n, $M(1^n)$ prints a sequence S of examples of the empty concept $h : \{0,1\}^n \to \{0\}$ such that every consistent $s(n)$-size circuit learner $\mathcal{A}$ for h learns h and makes less than 2^n mistakes on the sequence S. Then there are problems solvable in $t(n)$ time that do not have circuits of size $s(n)$, for all $s(n) \in \mathcal{F}$ and almost every n.*

To illustrate, let $\mathcal{F}$ contain all functions of the form $f(n) = 2^{\delta n}$ and let $t(n) = 2^{O(n)}$. Suppose there is an $\varepsilon > 0$ and a $2^{O(n)}$ time algorithm which (for all n) prints a sequence such that all consistent learners implementable with $2^{\varepsilon n}$-size circuits learn the empty concept with less than 2^n mistakes. Then Theorem 1.4 implies E lacks $2^{\varepsilon n}$ size circuits (almost everywhere), which by Impagliazzo and Wigderson [16] implies $\mathsf{P} = \mathsf{BPP}$. (In contrast, Theorem 1.2 says that a uniform random sequence would teach all such learners with less than $2^{3\varepsilon n}$ mistakes.) For another example, let $\mathcal{F}$ contain all polynomials and let $t(n) = 2^{n^k}$ for a fixed k. Then any 2^{n^k} time algorithm which prints a sequence teaching all polynomial-size circuit learners the empty concept with less than 2^n mistakes implies $\mathsf{EXP} \not\subset \mathsf{P/poly}$. Hence our teaching model provides another case where non-trivial derandomization of a simple random process implies strong circuit lower bounds [15, 18]. Theorem 1.4 also clarifies why we consider our "data design" problem to be dual to algorithm design: positive solutions to the data design problem entail negative solutions to some circuit design problems.

Another natural question is whether we could remove the dependence on the state size $s(n)$ in the above bounds. We prove that this dependency is inherent:

THEOREM 1.5. (LEARNERS WITH LARGE SPACE CAN MAKE MANY MISTAKES.) *For every integer $s \in [n, 2^n]$, there is a concept class $\mathcal{H}$, a concept $h \in \mathcal{H}$ and a consistent on-line learning algorithm $\mathcal{A}$ for $\mathcal{H}$, computed by a uniform family of AC^0 circuits of size $O(s \cdot n)$ using s-bit states, such that for every sequence of examples of c, $\mathcal{A}$ makes at least $s - 1$ mistakes before identifying c.*

Finally, we consider a slightly relaxed objective. Suppose we have chosen both a concept h and a particular algorithm $\mathcal{A}$ capable of learning the concept. Can $\mathcal{A}$ be taught h quickly? A variant of our analysis in Theorem 3.1 establishes that there is always a short sequence of examples that forces any given state-bounded learner to identify any concept it is capable of learning:

THEOREM 1.6. (SHORT SEQUENCES OF EXAMPLES FOR EXACT IDENTIFICATION.) *For every concept class $\mathcal{H}$, every $h \in \mathcal{H}$, and every consistent $s(n)$-bounded learner $\mathcal{A}$ for $\mathcal{H}$, there is a sequence of examples of length $O(n \cdot s(n))$ after which $\mathcal{A}$ identifies h.*

1.2 Existing models of teaching

Although we will try to review the main threads of research here, we advise the interested reader to consult the recent survey of Balbach and Zeugmann [6]. The oldest model of teaching, described by Freivalds et al. [10] is a variant of inductive inference (featuring little to no emphasis on computational complexity) in which the learner is given a carefully selected set of "good instances." Balbach and Zeugmann [4] considered a different sort of inductive-inference model in which a neighborhood structure is imposed on the space of concepts, and they study the structural properties of such learning—for example, they consider a variant in which the teacher may view the learner's hypothesis.

The highly influential notion of teaching dimension was independently introduced and studied by Shinohara and Miyano [26] and by Goldman and Kearns [12]. While we will discuss the relationship of our work to teaching dimension further in Section 2, a brief summary is warranted here, as it motivated most subsequent work. The underlying goal is to select minimum sets of examples so that a target concept can be uniquely identified out of the class of possible concepts; the maximum size of such a set (over all concepts in the class) is called the teaching dimension of that concept class. (The definition may also be cast in terms of consistent learning, a point we return to in Section 2.) Although the definition is highly natural and has spawned much interesting work, its consequences are unfortunately counterintuitive. For instance, the set $\mathcal{CONJ}$ of non-contradictory conjunctions over n variables has polynomial-size teaching dimension, but when the empty (always false) concept is included in $\mathcal{CONJ}$, the teaching dimension jumps to 2^n, i.e., *every* example must be presented to the learner.

In follow-up work, Anthony et al. [2] consider (among other results) the *average* teaching dimension (under the uniform measure over concepts), where the above undesirable effect disappears. In a similar vein, Balbach and Zeugmann [5] consider an "average" learner modeled by a MDP that chooses its concept at random from the space of consistent concepts; they also restrict the number of states in the MDP.

A different direction concerns models in which the teacher and learner are designed together. The main obstacle in such a model is that somehow the teacher must "honestly" teach the class to the learner, and not "collude" by coordinating an encoding of the concepts, and thus directly sending an encoding of the target concept, e.g., by either requiring that the learner still operate correctly with an adversarial teacher (as in Jackson and Tomkins [17]), by requiring that the learner still identify the concept correctly when (e.g.) additional examples are inserted into the teaching set (as in Goldman and Mathias [13] and Mathias [21]), or by giving the teacher and learner different representations of the concept (as in Angluin and Kriķis [1]).

Another recent direction assumes a helpful and powerful teacher who provides a *minimal* set of examples necessary for learning a concept, so the learner can eliminate competing concepts based on the size of the teaching set [3, 28]. Naturally, the strange behavior of the learner on the contradictory concept also vanishes in this model (and in fact, this concept has a teaching set of size $O(1)$), but only under the troublesome assumption that the learner "knows" the optimal size of teaching sets—troublesome because Servedio [25] showed that the optimal size of teaching sets (in the traditional sense) is NP-hard to compute, so it is doubtful that these more sophisticated notions of teaching dimension could be computed easily.

1.3 Compression in learning and other structural learning themes

Our main results can be seen as a variant on the theme that learning algorithms which compress the data well must necessarily learn efficiently. At the most basic level, we note in Section 3 that a standard hypothesis-size analysis in PAC-learning establishes the existence of short teaching sequences for approximate concept identification. A more general result for the PAC model, starting from an arbitrary compression scheme, was the content of the well-known work by Blumer et al. [7] on Occam's razor. The difference here is that we start with a stronger algorithm – a consistent on-line learning algorithm rather than a consistent batch algorithm (or mere "compression scheme") – but then show that the given algorithm learns exceptionally well, obtaining *exact* rather than approximate identification in a mistake-bounded model. The "moral" that compression implies generalization is certainly a common thread across these results. Relationships between compression schemes and learnability were also considered by Littlestone and Warmuth [20], and further developed by Floyd and Warmuth [9], but there the learner was restricted to remember a list of examples that "compressed" the given sample; Floyd [8] also studied on-line algorithms in a similar vein. Our learners are not restricted to store information in any particular form.

Our analysis, which considers the performance of an online learning algorithm on independent examples from an arbitrary distribution, is thus also vaguely related to constructions that convert on-line learning algorithms to batch PAC-learning algorithms (cf. [19, 24]). Here, we analyze an on-line model and obtain mistake bounds for exact identification from random examples, rather than extracting an approximately good hypothesis in the batch model from an (on-line) algorithm.

2. PRELIMINARIES AND DEFINITIONS

We first recall some standard terminology for on-line learning algorithms.

DEFINITION 2.1 (ON-LINE LEARNING ALGORITHMS). *An* on-line learning algorithm *is specified by a pair of algorithms,* EVAL *and* UPDATE, *and an initial* state $\sigma_0 \in \{0,1\}^*$ *which may depend on the instance length n. Learning of a* target concept $h : \{0,1\}^n \to \{0,1\}$ *from a* concept class $\mathcal{H}$ *proceeds in a sequence of* trials*: given the current* state *of the algorithm* $\sigma \in \{0,1\}^*$ *and the current* instance $x \in \{0,1\}^*$, EVAL(σ, x) *produces a* prediction $p \in \{0,1\}$. *The subsequent state of the algorithm is output by* UPDATE$(\sigma, x, p, h(x))$ *for a* reinforcement *value* $h(x)$. *If* $p \neq h(x)$, *then we say that the algorithm has made a* mistake. *The* mistake bound *of an algorithm for a concept class* $\mathcal{H}$ *and fixed size n is given by the maximum number of mistakes over all* $h \in \mathcal{H}$ *and (infinite) sequences of n-bit instances.*

Let $\mathcal{C}$ *be a class of algorithms. We say that an on-line learning algorithm is* $\mathcal{C}$-bounded *if the algorithms* EVAL *and* UPDATE *are given by algorithms from* $\mathcal{C}$. *If* $\mathcal{C}$ *is a class of non-uniform circuits, we require that for each* $n \in \mathbb{N}$ *that the algorithms* EVAL *and* UPDATE *on instances of length n are given by circuits from* $\mathcal{C}$ *having n-bit inputs.*

We say that a learning algorithm is consistent on $\mathcal{H}$ *if, for every n and every* $h \in \mathcal{H}$, *after every sequence of instances* $x_1, \ldots, x_t \in \{0,1\}^n$ *of h, the algorithm is in a state* σ *such that* EVAL$(\sigma, x_i) = h(x_i)$ *for all i.*

The algorithm is said to have identified *or* learned *h if the algorithm is in a state* σ *such that for every subsequent sequence of instances* $x_1, \ldots, x_t \in \{0,1\}^n$ *the algorithm correctly predicts* $h(x_i)$ *for all i.*

Finally, the algorithm is a learner for *h if there is a sequence of instances after which the algorithm identifies h.*

The most relevant learning concept to our present work is that of teaching dimension.

DEFINITION 2.2 (TEACHING DIMENSION). *Given a concept class* $\mathcal{H}$, *a* teaching sequence *for an* $h \in \mathcal{H}$ *is a list of examples such that all consistent learners for* $\mathcal{H}$ *identify h after receiving those examples. The* minimum teaching length *for an* $h \in \mathcal{H}$ *is the minimum number n of examples in any teaching sequence for h. The* teaching dimension *of* $\mathcal{H}$ *is the maximum over all* $h \in \mathcal{H}$ *of the minimum teaching length for h.*

Therefore, the teaching dimension specifies the minimum number of examples needed for any consistent learner to distinguish any concept in $\mathcal{H}$ from all other concepts. This concept is quite similar to the notion of teaching that we consider; the two major differences are that we only consider learners with bounded state complexity, and we will focus on the number of mistakes rather than the number of examples in order to achieve meaningful generic bounds. The tutoring sequences considered in Section 4 are different from the teaching sequences in the above definition, in that they are tailored to a specific learner and they take into account the learner's complexity.

As noted earlier, the teaching dimension model [12, 26] has some counterintuitive properties, namely that some very simple concepts are maximally hard to teach, i.e., it requires specifying the entire domain. An example we will use is:

DEFINITION 2.3 (SINGLETONS AND EMPTY CONCEPT). *For each* $y \in \{0,1\}^n$, *the* singleton *concept for y is given by the function that evaluates to 1 at y and 0 everywhere else; the class of singletons is thus the set of all singleton concepts. The* empty *concept is the constant all-0 function.*

We define $\mathcal{S}$ to be the concept class consisting of all singleton concepts and the empty concept, for all n.

3. TEACHING CONSISTENT LEARNERS OF BOUNDED COMPLEXITY

Can we find sequences of examples that force every simple consistent learning algorithm to identify the target hypothesis? For *approximate* identification (i.e., standard PAC guarantees) this is immediate: the standard counting analysis shows that for learners that find consistent hypotheses of size at most $s(n)$, presenting $O(\frac{1}{\epsilon}(s(n) + \log\frac{1}{\delta}))$ random examples suffices to guarantee that any such learner arrives at a $1-\epsilon$-accurate hypothesis with probability $1-\delta$. Our hope is that the introduction of a "simple" requirement on the learners might reduce the complexity of (exact) teaching. In one sense, we can show that this *cannot* be true. The concept class $\mathcal{S}$ from the previous section, which is hard to learn in the usual (Goldman-Kearns-Shinohara-Miyano) teaching model, remains hard under severe complexity restrictions on learners. Recall from the Introduction that AC^0-LINEAR is the class of on-line learning algorithms whose functionality is computable by AC^0 circuits of size $O(n)$.

REMINDER OF THEOREM 1.1 *For all n, let* $h_n : \{0,1\}^n \to \{0,1\}$ *be the all-zeroes concept (i.e., the empty concept). For every sequence* s_n *of n-bit examples that allow all* AC^0-LINEAR *learners to identify* h_n, *the length of* s_n *equals* 2^n.

Note the length of the sequence cannot exceed 2^n: once all examples have been seen, the concept is certainly identified. Hence we only have to prove a lower bound of at least 2^n.

PROOF. Consider the following class of learners $\mathcal{L}$: for each $z \in \{0,1\}^n$, the initial hypothesis for $L_z \in \mathcal{L}$ is the singleton concept for z, which is used for prediction until either L_z makes a mistake on z, or L_z makes a mistake on some other y. In the former case, L_z switches to the empty concept; in the latter case, L_z switches to the singleton concept for y. Finally, if the current hypothesis is the empty concept, and L_z makes a mistake on some y, then L_z switches to the singleton for y.

Observe that for all $z \in \{0,1\}^n$, the learner L_z is consistent for the concept class $\mathcal{S}$, and every L_z can be implemented with linear size depth-2 circuits which output states of length at most $n+1$. The first n bits of the state are used to represent a singleton concept, and the last bit of the state is 1 if and only if the current hypothesis is the empty concept. The algorithm UPDATE for L_z works as follows: if the label of the current example is 1, then the first n bits of state are switched to the current example and the last bit of state is set to 0. If the label is 0 and the current example equals z, then the last bit of state is set to 1. This behavior can be easily implemented with an OR of ANDs of $O(n)$ size. The algorithm EVAL just tests if the input equals the first n bits of state (and that the last bit of state is 0), which can be done with a linear size depth-2 circuit.

Note that for any sequence s_n of length less than 2^n, there must be some $z \in \{0,1\}^n$ that does not appear in the sequence. Then the learner L_z, after reading the sequence s_n, still has not identified the empty concept (it will make a mistake on z). □

Rather than being discouraged, let us consider other measures of the complexity of teaching. Notice that

1. The learners L_z constructed above only make at most two mistakes.
2. For every learner L_z, there is a one-example sequence after which L_z identifies the target concept.

In the following sections, we show that some version of these nice properties hold of low-complexity learners *in general* for state-bounded learners, and for arbitrary concepts that they can learn.

3.1 Sequences guaranteeing few mistakes for state-bounded learners

Another measure of the quality of a teaching strategy is the number of mistakes that the learners make. Here, we show how to construct strategies for which *every* consistent learner with bounded state makes at most a polynomial number of mistakes in its space bound and the size of the examples.

DEFINITION 3.1 (SPACE-BOUNDED LEARNER). *Let* $\mathcal{A} = (\texttt{EVAL}, \texttt{UPDATE})$ *be an on-line learning algorithm, and let* $s : \mathbb{N} \to \mathbb{N}$. $\mathcal{A}$ *is* $s(n)$-bounded *if, on all length-n instances, the length of the initial state of* $\mathcal{A}$ *is at most* $s(n)$*, and all outputs of* UPDATE *(on all length-n instances and all states of length at most* $s(n)$*) have length at most* $s(n)$.

That is, an $s(n)$-bounded learner always stores its hypothesis and its general summary of the n-bit examples it has seen, using at most $s(n)$ bits. We note that consistent learning by simple memorization of examples can always be performed (i.e., for any concept) in space $s(n) = 2^n$, whereas consistent learning of an n-bit concept $\mathcal{H}_n$ requires $s(n) \geq \log|\mathcal{H}_n|$. Thus, for any concept class, there is some well-defined space complexity of consistent learning; our results will only be of interest for concept classes for which this complexity is $o(2^n/n)$. Note that there are several examples in the literature of consistent on-line learning algorithms with polynomially bounded state, such as the learning algorithms we have described for learning singletons, learning constant-degree polynomials over F_2, and the elimination algorithm for learning conjunctions (analyzed by Valiant [27] in the original work on PAC-learning) which also lends to learning k-CNF formulas.

The core of our analysis is the following theorem, giving a mistake bound for consistent on-line learning algorithms when presented with i.i.d. examples (as opposed to adversarial). A key point is that the quality of the final hypothesis improves *exponentially* with the number of mistakes—this will ensure that we can get exact identification of a concept in a polynomial number of mistakes.

THEOREM 3.1. (RANDOM EXAMPLES TEACH CONSISTENT BOUNDED LEARNERS WITH FEW MISTAKES.) *For every concept* $h : \{0,1\}^n \to \{0,1\}$, $\varepsilon > 0$, $\delta > 0$, *distribution D over examples of length n, and consistent* $s(n)$*-bounded learner* $\mathcal{A}$ *for h, the following holds. Given random labeled examples drawn from D, after* $\mathcal{A}$ *makes at most* $O(s(n)(\log\frac{1}{\varepsilon} + \log\frac{1}{\delta}))$ *mistakes on the examples, the hypothesis of* $\mathcal{A}$ *agrees with h on all but an* ε*-fraction of D, with probability at least* $1 - \delta$.

The proof requires a couple of useful definitions.

DEFINITION 3.2 (CONFIGURATIONS AND KNOWLEDGE). *Given an* $s(n)$*-bounded learning algorithm* $\mathcal{A}$*, and a concept* $h : \{0,1\}^n \to \{0,1\}$*, we define the* configuration graph of $\mathcal{A}$ *on h to be a directed graph in which the vertices correspond to the* $O(2^{s(n)})$ *states of the algorithm, and there is an edge from a state* σ_i *to a state* σ_j *labeled by* $x \in \{0,1\}^n$ *provided that* $\texttt{UPDATE}(\sigma_i, x, \texttt{EVAL}(\sigma_i, x), h(x)) = \sigma_j$.

For a given concept h and algorithm $\mathcal{A}$*, we say that a state* σ knows (the label of) $x \in \{0,1\}^n$ *if there is a path from the initial state* σ_0 *to* σ *such that some edge in the path is labeled by* x.

Note that there may be many paths between configurations of the algorithm; on a given teaching sequence, the algorithm only takes one of these paths, but the final configuration "knows" the labels of *all* of the examples on *all* of the paths. The key property of our "knowledge" definition is the following:

PROPOSITION 1. *For any on-line learning algorithm that is consistent on h and is in a state* σ *that knows an instance* x*, we have* $\texttt{EVAL}(\sigma, x) = h(x)$. *Furthermore, all states* $\tilde{\sigma}$ *reachable from* σ *must also know* x.

Next, we show that after making $s(n)$ mistakes, the fraction of instances not known by the algorithm drops by a constant fraction. For a distribution D, we say that a subset $S \subseteq D$ is a *ρ-fraction of D* provided that $\Pr_{x \in D}[x \in S] = \rho$.

LEMMA 3.1. *Suppose that the algorithm* $\mathcal{A}$ *is in a state* σ_t *that knows all but a* ρ*-fraction of D. Then, after a sequence of trials in which instances are drawn from D and* $\mathcal{A}$ *makes* $s(n)$ *mistakes,* $\mathcal{A}$ *enters a state* σ_{t+1} *that knows all but a* $(3/4 \cdot \rho)$*-fraction of D, with probability at least* $1 - 2^{-s(n)}$.

PROOF. Consider any state $\tilde{\sigma}$ that is reachable from a path from σ_t on which $s(n)$ mistakes occur, and that knows less than a $(1 - 3/4 \cdot \rho)$-fraction of D. Since σ_t knows a $(1-\rho)$-fraction of D, and all mistakes made by $\mathcal{A}$ starting from σ_t must fall in the ρ-fraction that σ_t does not know, this means that the $s(n)$ mistakes leading to $\tilde{\sigma}$ must have all been drawn from a set that has conditional probability at most $1/4$, out of the instances that σ_t does not know. The probability that we hit such a set of conditional probability at most $1/4$ $s(n)$ times (for our $s(n)$ mistakes) is at most $2^{-2s(n)}$. Therefore the probability that we reach $\tilde{\sigma}$ from σ_t (assuming we make $s(n)$ mistakes) is at most $2^{-2s(n)}$. Taking the union bound over all (at most $2^{s(n)}$) such states $\tilde{\sigma}$, the probability that we reach some state that does not know at least a $(1 - 3/4 \cdot \rho)$-fraction of D is at most $2^{-s(n)}$. □

The final ingredient in the proof of Theorem 3.1 is the following probabilistic inequality, which can be derived from Chernoff-Hoeffding bounds:

THEOREM 3.2. *Let* $X_1, \ldots, X_t$ *be independent Bernoulli random variables such that* $E[X_i] \geq 1/2$ *for all i, let* $\delta > 0$*, and let* $s \in \mathbb{N}$. *Then for* $t = 3s + 3\log(1/\delta)$ *trials,* $\Pr[\sum_{i=1}^{t} X_i < s] \leq \delta$.

The proof of Theorem 3.2 is in the appendix. Now we can complete the proof of Theorem 3.1:

PROOF OF THEOREM 3.1. Let $\mathcal{A}$ and h be as in the theorem statement. Until $\mathcal{A}$ has correctly labeled every instance correctly (in which case we are done), $\mathcal{A}$ reduces the fraction of D that it does not know by a $(3/4)$-factor, after every sequence of examples from D in which it makes $s(n)$ mistakes, with probability at least $1-2^{-s(n)}$ (independently on each such sequence). This $1-2^{-s(n)}$ probability event only has to occur $u = (\log 1/\varepsilon)/\log(4/3)$ times, in order for the fraction of D that $\mathcal{A}$ does not know to drop below ε. Letting $t = 3 \cdot u + 3\log(1/\delta)$ and applying Theorem 3.2, we find that after $t \cdot s(n) = O(s(n)(\log 1/\delta + \log 1/\varepsilon))$ mistakes, the probability that $\mathcal{A}$ knows all but an ε-fraction of D is at least $1-\delta$. □

Exact learning from Theorem 3.1.

It is now straightforward to construct the desired teaching strategies for state-bounded consistent learners: we only need to present the learner with i.i.d. examples from a distribution for which the minimum probabilities are relatively large (at most exponentially small). Of course, the uniform distribution meets these needs optimally:

REMINDER OF THEOREM 1.2 *For every concept $h : \{0,1\}^n \to \{0,1\}$ and $\delta > 0$, every consistent $s(n)$-bounded $\mathcal{A}$ for h makes at most $O(s(n)(n + \log \frac{1}{\delta}))$ mistakes with probability at least $1-\delta$, when the instances of length n are chosen uniformly at random.*

PROOF. Since the instance space has size 2^n, once the algorithm is in a state that is correct on all but a ε-measure set under the uniform distribution for $\varepsilon < 2^{-n}$, the algorithm must label every instance correctly. The claim thus follows immediately from Theorem 3.1. □

Theorem 1.2 only guarantees that the sequence of examples selected by the strategy works for a particular learner with high probability. Of course, when the probability is exponentially close to 1, we can obtain a *fixed* sequence that guarantees a polynomial mistake bound for *all* of the learners from some finite class. Let $\mathsf{SIZE}[s(n)]$ denote the class of all circuit families $\{C_n\}$ such that C_n has bounded fan-in and $s(n)$ size.

COROLLARY 3.1. *For every concept $h : \{0,1\}^n \to \{0,1\}$ and every size bound $s(n) \geq n$, there is a sequence of examples of h such that every $\mathsf{SIZE}[s(n)]$-bounded learner for h makes at most $O(s(n)^2 \log s(n))$ mistakes.*

PROOF. First, note that if the learning algorithm is computable by a circuit of size $s(n)$, its states must have length at most $s(n)$. Second, note that there are at most $S = s(n)^{O(s(n))}$ circuits of size $s(n)$. Therefore, by taking $\delta < 1/S$, we find by Theorem 1.2 that a random sequence of examples guarantees that every consistent learner for h with states of size $s(n)$ makes at most $O(s(n)(n+\log S))$ mistakes with probability $> 1-1/S$. By taking a union bound over all S circuits, we find that every circuit makes a number of mistakes not exceeding $O(s(n)(n+\log S)) \leq O(s(n)^2 \log s(n))$ with nonzero probability, hence some sequence of examples suffices. □

Finally, before moving on, we note that some polynomial dependence on the space bound (hypothesis size) is essentially inevitable in the mistake bound of any teaching sequence for learners given any reasonable complexity bound. Recall that $\mathcal{S}$ is the class consisting of all singleton and empty concepts.

REMINDER OF THEOREM 1.5 *For every integer $s \in [n, 2^n]$, there is a consistent on-line learning algorithm $\mathcal{A}$ for the concept class $\mathcal{S}$ computed by a uniform family of AC^0 circuits of size $O(s \cdot n)$ using s-bit states, such that for every sequence of examples of the empty concept, $\mathcal{A}$ makes at least $s-1$ mistakes before identifying the empty concept.*

PROOF. We describe our "adversarial" learning algorithm $\mathcal{A}$. Fix a lexicographic ordering on strings, and divide the space of $\{0,1\}^n$ into $s-1$ intervals of equal length in which the first $s-2$ intervals all have length $\lfloor 2^n/(s-1) \rfloor$ (and the final interval contains the rest). If $\mathcal{A}$ ever sees an example y such that $h(y) = 1$, then it switches to the singleton for y as its concept. Otherwise, $\mathcal{A}$ represents its concept by a bit-vector of length $s-1$, corresponding to each of these intervals. Initially the bits are all set to 1, and if $\mathcal{A}$ sees an example falling in an interval with its corresponding bit set to 1, `EVAL` predicts 1, otherwise it predicts 0. When the `UPDATE` algorithm sees an example z for which $h(z) = 0$ in an interval with a bit previously set to 1, that bit is set to 0. (All other bits remain unchanged.) We observe that this $\mathcal{A}$ is consistent on the class of singletons with the empty concept—once it sees a 1, it always predicts the singleton correctly (and likewise correctly labels all of the other points it previously saw labeled 0), and until that point, every example it sees labeled 0 will subsequently be predicted to be 0 (along with the rest of the interval it belongs to). We also observe that the lexicographic comparisons can be carried out in uniform AC^0, and that the hypotheses of $\mathcal{A}$ can be represented in s bits as required. Finally, observe that until $\mathcal{A}$ has received an example from each of the $s-1$ intervals, $\mathcal{A}$ does not identify the empty concept. □

On the efficiency of teaching.

Although we noted in Theorem 1.1 that teaching concepts such as even the singletons and empty concept may involve presenting exponentially many examples, there is a sense in which the teaching sequences of Theorem 1.2 *are* efficiently generated. Namely, if we consider an on-line communication model such as the one introduced by Goldreich, Juba, and Sudan [14], then as our teaching strategy simply chooses an n-bit example uniformly at random on each round, our strategy is a (randomized) linear-time on-line universal teaching strategy (for space-bounded consistent learners) that achieves polynomial error complexity (in n and the learners' space bound).

3.2 Sequences guaranteeing few mistakes from Nisan's generator

We have already noted that the teaching sequences we consider must be exponentially long in order to guarantee that *every* consistent algorithm identifies the target concept. Nevertheless, we might hope to improve the construction of such sequences in Theorem 1.2 by reducing the number of random bits they require. As stated, Theorem 1.2 requires exponentially many random bits. However, given that the sequences are uniform-random and the learners have bounded state, one might anticipate that Nisan's pseudorandom generator for space-bounded computation [22] could generate sequences with similar properties, from a short random seed. Although Nisan's analysis says nothing about such a property of the entire string – it only considers the probability that the algorithm ends up in an accepting state

– we can confirm that it also generates sequences suitable for our purposes. We prove:

REMINDER OF THEOREM 1.3 *Using a block length of* $\Theta(s(n)+n+\log\frac{1}{\delta})$ *(and* $k = O(n+\log\frac{1}{\delta})$*), Nisan's pseudorandom generator produces a sequence of* $2^{O(n)}$ *random bits for which with probability* $1-\delta$ *over the seed* $h_1,\ldots,h_k,x$*, any consistent learning algorithm that is* $s(n)$*-bounded on a given concept exactly identifies that concept and makes at most* $O(s(n)(n+\log\frac{1}{\delta}))$ *mistakes.*

Nisan's pseudorandom generator.

We recall that Nisan's generator uses a family of pairwise-independent hash functions H taking b bits to b bits, i.e., satisfying the property that for x_1, x_2, y_1, and y_2 in $\{0,1\}^b$, for a uniformly chosen $h \in H$, $\Pr_h[h(x_1) = y_1 \text{ and } h(x_2) = y_2] = 2^{-2b}$; we know that these can be constructed from $O(b)$ random bits by, e.g., multiplying by a random Toeplitz matrix and adding a random vector. The construction is then a recursive construction, in which G_k takes a b-bit seed and k hash functions: $G_0(x) = x$, and

$$G_k(x, h_1, \ldots, h_k) = G_{k-1}(x, h_1, \ldots, h_{k-1})G_{k-1}(h_k(x), h_1, \ldots, h_{k-1})$$

i.e., concatenating the output of G_{k-1} on x with G_{k-1} on $h_k(x)$. So, the generator stretches $O(kb)$ bits to $b2^k$ bits. We refer to b as the *block length* of the generator (observe that the sequence is a concatenation of blocks of length b obtained by hashing x with the many various subsets of $h_1,\ldots,h_k$).

As is well known, Nisan's generator is also time-efficient in an on-line sense: after the initial choice of seed and k hash functions, the ith block (out of 2^k) of the generator's output may be computed by taking, for each jth bit in the binary representation of i that is a 1, the hash function h_j, and applying them to the seed in order. Thus, by keeping a k-bit counter of the blocks, the sequence of examples can be computed on-line in time polynomial in n and $s(n)$. So, Theorem 1.3 also yields an efficient on-line universal teaching strategy with polynomial error complexity.

Our starting point is the following lemma encapsulating the abstract version of the analysis of Nisan's generator. For convenience, given $\delta > 0$, for each $k, b \in \mathbb{N}$ and pairs of states i and j of a given (learning) algorithm, we will define events $B^{h_1,\ldots,h_k}_{i,j}$ that $G_k(x, h_1,\ldots,h_k)$ takes state i to state j, and events $A^k_{i,j}$ that a sequence of 2^k uniformly chosen blocks of b bits takes state i to state j.

LEMMA 3.2 (LEMMA 2 OF NISAN [22]). *Let any space-*$s(n)$ *algorithm that reads its input* n *bits at a time from a read-once input tape be given. Let* H *be a family of pairwise-independent hash functions on* b *bits,* $\delta > 0$*, and* $k \in \mathbb{N}$*. Then with probability at least* $1 - \frac{k2^{6s(n)}}{\delta^2}2^{-b}$ *over* $h_1,\ldots,h_k$ *chosen from* H*,*

$$\|\,[\Pr[A^k_{i,j}]] - [\Pr[B^{h_1,\ldots,h_k}_{i,j}]]\,\|_1 \le (2^k - 1)\delta$$

Now, instead of merely examining the probability that $h_1,\ldots,h_k$ take state i to state j (as Nisan does), we will also examine the probability that the algorithm makes a given number of mistakes, m. Ultimately, we will argue that the *joint distribution* over final states and number of mistakes remains close (in ℓ_1-distance) when the output of Nisan's pseudorandom generator is substituted for the uniform random bits; we do this by noting that the algorithm could be modified to keep count of the number of mistakes that it makes in an n-bit counter (using total space $s(n)+n$) and then the distribution over states of this modified algorithm captures the joint distribution over states of the original algorithm and total number of mistakes. Then by a union bound over the various sources of error, we obtain a general analysis of the quality of Nisan's pseudorandom generator for generating easy sequences of examples:

THEOREM 3.3. (NISAN'S PSEUDORANDOM GENERATOR PRODUCES EASY SEQUENCES.) *Using a block length of* $\Theta(s(n)+n+\log\frac{1}{\delta^*}+\log R)$ *rounded to a multiple of* n *(and* $k = \log R/b$*), Nisan's pseudorandom generator produces a sequence of* R *random bits for which with probability* $1-\delta^*$ *over the seed* $h_1,\ldots,h_k,x$*, for any consistent learning algorithm that is space-*$s(n)$ *bounded on a given concept, the distribution over states and total number of mistakes of the learning algorithm induced by the generator for the concept is* δ^**-close to the distribution induced by the uniform distribution over* R *bits in* ℓ_1*.*

PROOF. Given any consistent space-$s(n)$ bounded learning algorithm A for a given concept, consider the algorithm A' with states given by pairs (σ, m) where σ is a state of A and m is an integer, which simulates A and keeps count of the number of mistakes A makes in the second component; note that since A is consistent, it can never make more than 2^n mistakes (since the concept is then identified) and hence A' uses at most $s(n)+n$ bits of state.

By Lemma 3.2, for this block length, with probability $1-\delta^*$ over the choice of hash functions and seed, the pseudorandom generator produces a sequence of R random bits such that the statistical distance over final states of A' is δ^*-close to the distribution over states of A' on R uniformly chosen bits; as A' behaves identically to A, by considering the two components of the states of A', we find that the joint distribution over final states of A and total number of mistakes made by A is therefore δ^*-close to the distribution over states and mistakes of A on R uniformly chosen bits. The theorem follows. □

In particular, we can get exact identification sequences, establishing the main theorem of this section:

PROOF OF THEOREM 1.3. By the coupon collector's bound, the expected number of uniformly random examples needed to include every example is $O(n2^n)$, and by Markov's inequality, the probability that this exceeds $\Omega(\frac{1}{\delta}n2^n)$ is at most $\delta/3$. So, using $R = O(\frac{1}{\delta}n^2 2^n)$ random bits, the algorithm enters a state that knows the entire domain with probability $1-\delta$ (and therefore exactly identifies the concept). By Theorem 1.2, the algorithm makes more than $O(s(n)(n+\log\frac{1}{\delta}))$ mistakes with probability at most $\delta/3$. By a union bound over these two events, we find that on R uniform bits, the algorithm enters a state that identifies the concept and makes at most $O(s(n)(n+\log\frac{1}{\delta}))$ mistakes with probability at least $1-(2/3)\delta$. Therefore, Theorem 3.3 guarantees that for the stated block length, the probability that the algorithm fails to identify the concept or makes more than $O(s(n)(n+\log\frac{1}{\delta}))$ mistakes on the output of the generator is greater by at most $\delta/3$. □

3.3 Deterministic sequences guaranteeing few mistakes implies circuit lower bounds

We now turn to the question of whether the random seed can be removed entirely in generating a sequence which teaches all bounded consistent learners a concept. We show that a deterministic sequence achieving any reduction in the mistake bound to less than 2^n for all bounded learners implies circuit lower bounds:

REMINDER OF THEOREM 1.4 *Let $\mathcal{F}$ be a class of functions from $\mathbb{N}$ to $\mathbb{N}$. Suppose there is a deterministic $t(n)$ time algorithm M such that for all $s(n) \in \mathcal{F}$ and all sufficiently large n, $M(1^n)$ prints a sequence S of examples of the empty concept $h : \{0,1\}^n \to \{0\}$ such that every consistent $s(n)$-size circuit learner $\mathcal{A}$ for h learns h and makes less than 2^n mistakes on the sequence S. Then there are problems solvable in $t(n)$ time that do not have circuits of size $s(n)$, for all $s(n) \in \mathcal{F}$ and almost every n.*

PROOF. By contradiction. Suppose there is a deterministic algorithm that runs in $t(n)$ time and prints a sequence S of examples for the empty concept h with the hypothesized property. Further suppose that for every problem solvable in time $t(n)$ there is an $s(n) \in \mathcal{F}$ such that the problem has circuits of size $s(n)$, for infinitely many input lengths n. First note that all 2^n strings must appear among in S, otherwise some $O(n)$-size circuit learner which learns the class $\mathcal{S}$ of singletons with the empty concept will not be able to distinguish h from some singleton concept (cf. Theorem 1.1). This also implies that $t(n) \geq 2^n$.

We define a "bad" on-line algorithm $\mathcal{A}$ for learning h as follows. First, order the n-bit strings by the order in which they first appear in the sequence S, and re-index the strings as $x_1, x_2, \ldots, x_{2^n}$. (That is, x_1 is the first instance in S, x_2 is the next distinct instance, x_3 is the one after that, and so on. Since every string must appear somewhere in S, this is indeed an ordering on all n-bit strings.)

- The states of $\mathcal{A}$ are the integers from 0 to 2^n, and the initial state is 0.
- Given an example $(x, 0)$ on which a mistake was been made:
  `UPDATE` the state to be the integer i such that $x = x_i$.
- $\texttt{EVAL}(i, x)$ predicts 0 if $x = x_j$ for some $j \in [1, i]$, otherwise it predicts 1.

That is, in the initial state 0, all examples are classified as 1, but if $\mathcal{A}$ makes a mistake on example x, x must have the label 0. $\mathcal{A}$ rectifies this by increasing the state to i such that $x = x_i$.

It is easy to verify that, assuming every language in time $t(n)$ has circuits of size $s(n) \in \mathcal{F}$ for infinitely many n, the above `UPDATE` and `EVAL` functions can be implemented with $O(s(n))$-size circuits for some $s(n) \in \mathcal{F}$ and some sufficiently large n – this follows because the sequence S can be generated in $t(n)$ time.

Observe that $\mathcal{A}$ is consistent for h: the state i always increases with each mistake, and when we make a mistake on x_i, we increase the state to some $j \geq i$ such that this never happens again. However, on the sequence S, $\mathcal{A}$ makes 2^n mistakes: it predicts every example it sees to have label 1, until all 2^n examples have appeared in S. That is, the state i must equal 2^n in order for $\mathcal{A}$ to correctly label all examples as 0, but when $\mathcal{A}$ receives examples in the sequence S, the state i increases only by 1 for each mistake that is made.

Therefore $\mathcal{A}$ is consistent for the empty concept, and it learns the empty concept, but on the sequence S of examples generated by 1^n, $\mathcal{A}$ makes 2^n mistakes. This contradicts the assumption that all consistent learners with size-$s(n)$ circuits make fewer than 2^n mistakes on S. □

Note it is not hard to show that $\mathcal{A}$ actually learns the empty concept from a uniform random sequence of examples with only $O(n)$ mistakes, with high probability, confirming our earlier results. Moreover, it is easy to quickly teach $\mathcal{A}$ the empty concept: simply give it the *last* example $(x_{2^n}, 0)$.

4. SHORT TUTORING SEQUENCES

Finally, we consider the problem of generating short sequences of examples tailored to a given learner and given concept that lead the learner to exactly identify the concept. We will informally refer to these as *tutoring sequences*. Although the motivation for considering such sequences is somewhat different from that we discussed for the "massive on-line" teaching models, one can think of it as a communication model that reveals a sense in which a weaker receiver may be easier to communicate with.

The technique from Theorem 3.1 also easily yields a probabilistic (nonconstructive) proof of existence of such sequences, which have *length* that is only polynomially related to the learner's state complexity. This is in stark contrast to the earlier setting, where the lengths of sequences were forced to be exponential.

REMINDER OF THEOREM 1.6 *For every concept class $\mathcal{H}$, every $h \in \mathcal{H}$, and every consistent $s(n)$-bounded learner $\mathcal{A}$ for $\mathcal{H}$, there is a sequence of examples of length $O(n \cdot s(n))$ after which $\mathcal{A}$ identifies h.*

PROOF. The argument is quite similar to Theorem 3.1: we again consider the configuration graph of the algorithm, and will argue that the set of examples the algorithm does not know shrinks exponentially. We first state an appropriately modified version of Lemma 3.1 (assuming the uniform distribution, along the lines of Theorem 1.2):

CLAIM 1. *Suppose that the on-line algorithm is in a state σ_t that knows all but a ρ-fraction of $\{0,1\}^n$. Then, after a sequence of $s(n)$ instances chosen uniformly at random from the set of instances that σ_t does not know, the algorithm enters a state σ_{t+1} that knows all but a $(3/4 \cdot \rho)$-fraction of $\{0,1\}^n$, with probability at least $1 - 2^{-s(n)}$.*

The proof is essentially the same as Lemma 3.1. Now, since the algorithm reaches such a state with nonzero probability, we can in particular fix a sequence of $s(n)$ examples for which the remaining instances decreases by a factor of 3/4; thus, after $\log_2(4/3) \cdot n$ of these sequences of $s(n)$ examples, the algorithm identifies the target concept as needed. □

5. CONCLUSION

We have introduced a new model of teaching that attempts to teach all "worst-case learners" a concept with a single sequence of labeled examples, and have established that the number of mistakes made by consistent learners on random examples are only polynomially related to the learner's state complexity. Several interesting questions arise naturally, and we describe a few below.

The most immediate question is: how tight is the connection between mistakes and state complexity? The lower bound in Theorem 1.5 only provides an $\Omega(s(n))$ lower bound on the number of mistakes, whereas our constructions all achieve mistake bounds of $O(s(n) \cdot n)$. Is this extra factor of n essential (say, for constant probability of success)?

Of course, our results analyze the mistake bound just in terms of the state bound of the (consistent) algorithm. In the standard (batch) PAC model, analyses based on representation sizes have been very useful, e.g., for analyzing Rivest's algorithm for learning decision lists [23]. Our analysis may not be very useful for many learning algorithms, because they do not satisfy such a strong "consistency" condition (it is often the case that an algorithm may initially label an example correctly, and later switch to a hypothesis that labels it incorrectly). Is it possible to generalize the class of learning algorithms further and achieve similar results? Perhaps our work can help give a novel analysis of some interesting on-line learning algorithms.

We have found another setting where uniform random bits do the job, but generating similar bits deterministically would entail circuit lower bounds. Could we build a sequence for ACC-circuit learners in such a way that we separate EXP from ACC? Does EXP $\not\subset$ P/poly imply the existence of good deterministic teaching sequences?

6. ACKNOWLEDGEMENTS

We are grateful to Manuel Blum for having introduced us to LINCOS. We thank Varun Kanade for a useful discussion.

7. REFERENCES

[1] D. Angluin and M. Kriķis. Learning from different teachers. *Mach. Learn.*, 51(2):137–163, 2003.

[2] M. Anthony, G. Brightwell, and J. Shawe-Taylor. On specifying Boolean functinos by labelled examples. *Discrete Applied Mathematics*, 61(1):1–25, 1995.

[3] F. J. Balbach. Measuring teachability using variants of the teaching dimension. *Theoret. Comput. Sci.*, 397(1–3):94–113, 2008.

[4] F. J. Balbach and T. Zeugmann. Teaching learners with restricted mind changes. In *Proc. 16th ALT*, volume 3734, pages 474–489. Springer, 2005.

[5] F. J. Balbach and T. Zeugmann. Teaching randomized learners. In *Proc. 19th COLT*, volume 4005, pages 229–243. Springer, 2008.

[6] F. J. Balbach and T. Zeugmann. Recent developments in algorithmic teaching. In *Proc. 3rd Int'l Conf. on Language and Automata Theory and Applications*, pages 1–18, 2009.

[7] A. Blumer, A. Ehrenfeucht, D. Haussler, and M. K. Warmuth. Occam's razor. *Inf. Process. Lett.*, 24:377–380, 1987.

[8] S. Floyd. *On space-bounded learning and the Vapnik-Chervonenkis dimension.* PhD thesis, University of California, Berkeley, Berkeley, CA, 1989.

[9] S. Floyd and M. Warmuth. Sample compression, learnability, and the Vapnik-Chervonenkis dimension. *Mach. Learn.*, 21:269–304, 1995.

[10] R. Freivalds, E. B. Kinber, and R. Wiehagen. On the power of inductive inference from good examples. *Theoret. Comput. Sci.*, 110(1):131–144, 1993.

[11] H. Freudenthal. *LINCOS: Design of a language for cosmic intercourse.* North-Holland, Amsterdam, 1960.

[12] S. A. Goldman and M. J. Kearns. On the complexity of teaching. *J. Comput. Syst. Sci.*, 50(1):20–31, 1995.

[13] S. A. Goldman and H. D. Mathias. Teaching a smarter learner. *J. Comput. Syst. Sci.*, 52(2):255–267, 1996.

[14] O. Goldreich, B. Juba, and M. Sudan. A theory of goal-oriented communication. *J. ACM*, 59(2):8:1–8:65, 2012.

[15] R. Impagliazzo, V. Kabanets, and A. Wigderson. In search of an easy witness: Exponential time vs. probabilistic polynomial time. *Journal of Computer and System Sciences*, 65(4):672–694, 2002.

[16] R. Impagliazzo and A. Wigderson. P=BPP unless E has subexponential circuits: Derandomizing the XOR lemma. In *Proc. 29th STOC*, pages 220–229, 1997.

[17] J. Jackson and A. Tomkins. A computational model of teaching. In *Proc. 5th COLT*, pages 319–326, 1992.

[18] V. Kabanets and R. Impagliazzo. Derandomizing polynomial identity tests means proving circuit lower bounds. *Computational Complexity*, 13(1-2):1–46, 2004.

[19] N. Littlestone. From on-line to batch learning. In *Proc. COLT'89*, pages 269–284, 1989.

[20] N. Littlestone and M. K. Warmuth. Relating data compression and learnability. Unpublished manuscript, 1986.

[21] H. D. Mathias. A model of interactive teaching. *J. Comput. Syst. Sci.*, 54(3):487–501, 1997.

[22] N. Nisan. Pseudorandom generators for space-bounded computation. *Combinatorica*, 12(4):449–461, 1992.

[23] R. L. Rivest. Learning decision lists. *Mach. Learn.*, 2(3):229–246, 1987.

[24] D. Schuurmans and R. Greiner. Sequential PAC learning. In *Proc. 8th COLT*, pages 377–384, 1995.

[25] R. A. Servedio. On the limits of efficient teachability. *Inf. Process. Lett.*, 79(6):267–272, 2001.

[26] A. Shinohara and S. Miyano. Teachability in computational learning. *New Generation Comput.*, 8(4):337–347, 1991.

[27] L. G. Valiant. A theory of the learnable. *Communications of the ACM*, 18(11):1134–1142, 1984.

[28] S. Zilles, S. Lange, R. Holte, and M. Zinkevich. Models of cooperative teaching and learning. *JMLR*, 12:349–384, 2012.

APPENDIX

A. TAIL BOUND DERIVATION

Here we prove:

REMINDER OF THEOREM 3.2 *Let $X_1, \ldots, X_t$ be independent Bernoulli random variables such that $E[X_i] \geq 1/2$ for all i, let $\delta > 0$, and let $s \in \mathbb{N}$. Then for $t = 3s + 3\log(1/\delta)$ trials, $\Pr[\sum_{i=1}^{t} X_i < s] \leq \delta$.*

The theorem will follow from a calculation using Hoeffding's inequality (a.k.a. the additive Chernoff bound).

THEOREM A.1. *Let $X_1, \ldots, X_t$ be independent Bernoulli random variables such that $E[X_i] \geq 1/2$ for all i, and*

$$E\left[\frac{1}{t}\sum_{i=1}^{t} X_i\right] = \mu.$$

Then for any $\epsilon > 0$,

$$\Pr\left[\frac{1}{t}\sum_{i=1}^{t} X_i < \mu - \epsilon\right] \leq \exp(-2t\epsilon^2)$$

To prove our inequality, we want to compute the number of trials t so that at least s of these X_i come up 1, with probability $1 - \delta$. Naturally, in $2s$ trials, we have at least s in expectation; we will calculate the number of additional trials a needed to guarantee at least s with probability $1-\delta$. That is, we want a such that the probability that fewer than s out of the $2s + a$ trials come up 1 is at most δ. Plugging in Hoeffding's inequality, we find that a satisfying

$$\exp\left(-2(2s+a)\left(\frac{a}{2(2s+a)}\right)^2\right) = \exp\left(\frac{-a^2}{2(2s+a)}\right) \leq \delta$$

suffices. As $a > 0$ increases, the LHS decreases, so we merely need to find the smallest a that suffices. We note that equality holds when

$$\ln\frac{1}{\delta} = \frac{a^2}{2(2s+a)}$$
$$0 = a^2 - 2a\ln\frac{1}{\delta} - 4s\ln\frac{1}{\delta}$$

which has the solutions

$$a = \frac{2\ln\frac{1}{\delta} \pm \sqrt{4\ln^2\frac{1}{\delta} + 16s\ln\frac{1}{\delta}}}{2} = \ln\frac{1}{\delta} \pm \sqrt{\ln^2\frac{1}{\delta} + 4s\ln\frac{1}{\delta}}.$$

To simplify the expression for a, we recall that $\sqrt{x^2+y^2} \leq x + y$ and $\sqrt{xy} \leq (x+y)/2$ for non-negative x and y, and obtain:

$$\begin{aligned} a &= \ln\frac{1}{\delta} + \sqrt{\ln^2\frac{1}{\delta} + 4s\ln\frac{1}{\delta}} \\ &\leq \ln\frac{1}{\delta} + \ln\frac{1}{\delta} + 2\sqrt{s\ln\frac{1}{\delta}} \\ &\leq \ln\frac{1}{\delta} + \ln\frac{1}{\delta} + s + \ln\frac{1}{\delta} \end{aligned}$$

Therefore, $t = 2s + a \leq 3s + 3\ln(1/\delta)$ trials suffice.

Learning Mixtures of Spherical Gaussians: Moment Methods and Spectral Decompositions

[Extended Abstract] *

Daniel Hsu
Microsoft Research New England
dahsu@microsoft.com

Sham M. Kakade
Microsoft Research New England
skakade@microsoft.com

ABSTRACT

This work provides a computationally efficient and statistically consistent moment-based estimator for mixtures of spherical Gaussians. Under the condition that component means are in general position, a simple spectral decomposition technique yields consistent parameter estimates from low-order observable moments, without additional minimum separation assumptions needed by previous computationally efficient estimation procedures. Thus computational and information-theoretic barriers to efficient estimation in mixture models are precluded when the mixture components have means in general position and spherical covariances. Some connections are made to estimation problems related to independent component analysis.

Categories and Subject Descriptors

I.2.6 [**Learning**]: Parameter learning

General Terms

Algorithms, Theory

Keywords

Mixtures of Gaussians; mixture models; method of moments; spectral decomposition

1. INTRODUCTION

The Gaussian mixture model [25, 26] is one of the most well-studied and widely-used models in applied statistics and machine learning. An important special case of this model (the primary focus of this work) restricts the Gaussian components to have spherical covariance matrices; this probabilistic model is closely related to the (non-probabilistic) k-means clustering problem [21].

*A full version of this paper is available at http://arxiv.org/abs/1206.5766

ITCS'13, January 9–12, 2013, Berkeley, California, USA.

The mixture of spherical Gaussians model is specified as follows. Let w_i be the probability of choosing component $i \in [k] := \{1, 2, \dots, k\}$, let $\mu_1, \mu_2, \dots, \mu_k \in \mathbb{R}^d$ be the component mean vectors, and let $\sigma_1^2, \sigma_2^2, \dots, \sigma_k^2 \geq 0$ be the component variances. Define

$$w := [w_1, w_2, \dots, w_k]^\top \in \mathbb{R}^k, \quad A := [\mu_1|\mu_2|\cdots|\mu_k] \in \mathbb{R}^{d\times k};$$

so w is a probability vector, and A is the matrix whose columns are the component means. Let $x \in \mathbb{R}^k$ be the (observed) random vector given by

$$x := \mu_h + z,$$

where h is the discrete random variable with $\Pr(h = i) = w_i$ for $i \in [k]$, and z is a random vector whose conditional distribution given $h = i$ (for some $i \in [k]$) is the multivariate Gaussian $\mathcal{N}(0, \sigma_i^2 I)$ with mean zero and covariance $\sigma_i^2 I$.

The estimation task is to accurately recover the model parameters (component means, variances, and mixing weights) $\{(\mu_i, \sigma_i^2, w_i) : i \in [k]\}$ from independent copies of x.

This work gives a procedure for efficiently and exactly recovering the parameters using a simple spectral decomposition of low-order moments of x, under the following condition.

Condition 1 (Non-degeneracy). *The component means span a k-dimensional subspace (*i.e.*, the matrix A has column rank k), and the vector w has strictly positive entries.*

The proposed estimator is based on a spectral decomposition technique [9, 23, 3], and is easily stated in terms of exact population moments of the observed x. With finite samples, one can use a plug-in estimator based on empirical moments of x in place of exact moments. These empirical moments converge to the exact moments at a rate of $O(n^{-1/2})$, where n is the sample size. Sample complexity bounds for accurate parameter estimation can be derived using matrix perturbation arguments. Since only low-order moments are required by the plug-in estimator, the sample complexity is polynomial in the relevant parameters of the estimation problem.

Related work.

The first estimators for the Gaussian mixture models were based on the method-of-moments, as introduced by Pearson [25] (see also [20] and the references therein). Roughly speaking, these estimators are based on finding parameters under which the Gaussian mixture distribution has moments approximately matching the observed empirical moments. Finding these parameters typically involves solving systems of multivariate polynomial equations, which is typically computationally challenging. Besides this, the order of the moments of some of the early moment-based estimators were either growing with the dimension d or the number of components k, which is undesirable because the empirical estimates of such high-order moments may only be reliable when the sample size is exponential in d or k. Both the computational and sample complexity issues have been addressed in recent years, at least under various restrictions. For instance, several distance-based estimators require that the component means be well-separated in Euclidean space, by at least some large factor times the directional standard deviation of the individual component distributions [13, 5, 14, 27, 10], but otherwise have polynomial computational and sample complexity. Some recent moment-based estimators avoid the minimum separation condition of distance-based estimators by requiring either computational or data resources exponential in the number of mixing components k (but not the dimension d) [6, 19, 22] or by making a non-degenerate multi-view assumption [3].

By contrast, the moment-based estimator described in this work does not require a minimum separation condition, exponential computational or data resources, or non-degenerate multiple views. Instead, it relies only on the non-degeneracy condition discussed above together with a spherical noise condition. The non-degeneracy condition is much weaker than an explicit minimum separation condition because the parameters can be arbitrarily close to being degenerate, as long as the sample size grows polynomially with a natural quantity measuring this closeness to degeneracy (akin to a condition number). Like other moment-based estimators, the proposed estimator is based on solving multivariate polynomial equations, although these solutions can be found efficiently because the problems are cast as eigenvalue decompositions of symmetric matrices, which are efficient to compute.

Recent work from [22] demonstrates an information-theoretic barrier to estimation for general Gaussian mixture models. More precisely, they construct a pair of one-dimensional mixtures of Gaussians (with separated component means) such that the statistical distance between the two mixture distributions is exponentially small in the number of components. This implies that in the worst case, the sample size required to obtain accurate parameter estimates must grow exponentially with the number of components, even when the component distributions are non-negligibly separated. A consequence of the present work is that natural non-degeneracy conditions preclude these worst case scenarios. The non-degeneracy condition in this work is similar to one used for bypassing computational (cryptographic) barriers to estimation for hidden Markov models [9, 23, 17, 3].

Finally, it is interesting to note that similar algebraic techniques have been developed for certain models in independent component analysis (ICA) [11, 8, 18, 12, 4] and other closely related problems [15, 24]. In contrast to the ICA setting, handling non-spherical Gaussian noise for mixture models appears to be a more delicate issue. These connections and open problems are further discussed in Section 3.

2. MOMENT-BASED ESTIMATION

This section describes a method-of-moments estimator for the spherical Gaussian mixture model.

The following theorem is the main structural result that relates the model parameters to observable moments.

THEOREM 1 (OBSERVABLE MOMENT STRUCTURE). *Assume Condition 1 holds. The average variance $\bar{\sigma}^2 := \sum_{i=1}^k w_i\sigma_i^2$ is the smallest eigenvalue of the covariance matrix $\mathbb{E}[(x - \mathbb{E}[x])(x - \mathbb{E}[x])^\top]$. Let $v \in \mathbb{R}^d$ be any unit norm eigenvector corresponding to the eigenvalue $\bar{\sigma}^2$. Define*

$$M_1 := \mathbb{E}[x(v^\top(x - \mathbb{E}[x]))^2],$$
$$M_2 := \mathbb{E}[x \otimes x] - \bar{\sigma}^2 I,$$
$$M_3 := \mathbb{E}[x \otimes x \otimes x] - \sum_{i=1}^{d}(M_1 \otimes e_i \otimes e_i + e_i \otimes M_1 \otimes e_i + e_i \otimes e_i \otimes M_1)$$

(where $\otimes$ denotes tensor product, and $\{e_1, e_2, \dots, e_d\}$ is the coordinate basis for $\mathbb{R}^d$). Then

$$M_1 = \sum_{i=1}^{k} w_i\ \sigma_i^2\mu_i, \qquad M_2 = \sum_{i=1}^{k} w_i\ \mu_i \otimes \mu_i,$$
$$M_3 = \sum_{i=1}^{k} w_i\ \mu_i \otimes \mu_i \otimes \mu_i.$$

REMARK 1. *We note that in the special case where $\sigma_1^2 = \sigma_2^2 = \cdots = \sigma_k^2 = \sigma^2$ (i.e., the mixture components share a common spherical covariance matrix), the average variance $\bar{\sigma}^2$ is simply σ^2, and M_3 has a simpler form:*

$$M_3 = \mathbb{E}[x \otimes x \otimes x] - \sigma^2 \sum_{i=1}^{d}(\mathbb{E}[x] \otimes e_i \otimes e_i + e_i \otimes \mathbb{E}[x] \otimes e_i + e_i \otimes e_i \otimes \mathbb{E}[x]).$$

There is no need to refer to the eigenvectors of the covariance matrix or M_1.

PROOF OF THEOREM 1. We first characterize the smallest eigenvalue of the covariance matrix of x, as well as all corresponding eigenvectors v. Let $\bar{\mu} := \mathbb{E}[x] = \mathbb{E}[\mu_h] = \sum_{i=1}^k w_i\mu_i$. The covariance matrix of x is

$$\mathbb{E}[(x - \bar{\mu}) \otimes (x - \bar{\mu})] = \sum_{i=1}^{k} w_i \left((\mu_i - \bar{\mu}) \otimes (\mu_i - \bar{\mu}) + \sigma_i^2 I\right) = \sum_{i=1}^{k} w_i\ (\mu_i - \bar{\mu}) \otimes (\mu_i - \bar{\mu})\ +\ \bar{\sigma}^2 I.$$

Since the vectors $\mu_i - \bar{\mu}$ for $i \in [k]$ are linearly dependent ($\sum_{i=1}^k w_i(\mu_i - \bar{\mu}) = 0$), the positive semidefinite matrix $\sum_{i=1}^k w_i(\mu_i - \bar{\mu}) \otimes (\mu_i - \bar{\mu})$ has rank $r \leq k - 1$. Thus, the $d - r$ smallest eigenvalues are exactly $\bar{\sigma}^2$, while all other eigenvalues are strictly larger than $\bar{\sigma}^2$. The strict separation of eigenvalues implies that every eigenvector corresponding to $\bar{\sigma}^2$ is in the null space of $\sum_{i=1}^k w_i(\mu_i - \bar{\mu}) \otimes (\mu_i - \bar{\mu})$; thus $v^\top(\mu_i - \bar{\mu}) = 0$ for all $i \in [k]$.

Now we can express M_1, M_2, and M_3 in terms of the parameters w_i, μ_i, and σ_i^2. First,

$$M_1 = \mathbb{E}[x(v^\top(x - \mathbb{E}[x]))^2] = \mathbb{E}[(\mu_h + z)(v^\top(\mu_h - \bar{\mu} + z))^2] = \mathbb{E}[(\mu_h + z)(v^\top z)^2] = \mathbb{E}[\mu_h\sigma_h^2],$$

where the last step uses the fact that $z|h \sim \mathcal{N}(0, \sigma_h^2 I)$, which implies that conditioned on h, $\mathbb{E}[(v^\top z)^2|h] = \sigma_h^2$ and

$\mathbb{E}[z(v^\top z)^2|h] = 0$. Next, observe that $\mathbb{E}[z \otimes z] = \sum_{i=1}^k w_i \sigma_i^2 I = \bar{\sigma}^2 I$, so

$$\begin{aligned} M_2 &= \mathbb{E}[x \otimes x] - \bar{\sigma}^2 I \\ &= \mathbb{E}[\mu_h \otimes \mu_h] + \mathbb{E}[z \otimes z] - \bar{\sigma}^2 I \\ &= \mathbb{E}[\mu_h \otimes \mu_h] = \sum_{i=1}^k w_i \; \mu_i \otimes \mu_i. \end{aligned}$$

Finally, for M_3, we first observe that

$$\begin{aligned} \mathbb{E}[x \otimes x \otimes x] = \mathbb{E}[\mu_h \otimes \mu_h \otimes \mu_h] + \mathbb{E}[\mu_h \otimes z \otimes z] \\ + \mathbb{E}[z \otimes \mu_h \otimes z] + \mathbb{E}[z \otimes z \otimes \mu_h] \end{aligned}$$

(terms such as $\mathbb{E}[\mu_h \otimes \mu_h \otimes z]$ and $\mathbb{E}[z \otimes z \otimes z]$ vanish because $z|h \sim \mathcal{N}(0, \sigma_h^2 I)$). We now claim that $\mathbb{E}[\mu_h \otimes z \otimes z] = \sum_{i=1}^d M_1 \otimes e_i \otimes e_i$. This holds because

$$\begin{aligned} \mathbb{E}[\mu_h \otimes z \otimes z] &= \mathbb{E}\big[\mathbb{E}[\mu_h \otimes z \otimes z|h]\big] \\ &= \mathbb{E}\left[\mathbb{E}\left[\sum_{i,j=1}^d z_i z_j \; \mu_h \otimes e_i \otimes e_j \middle| h\right]\right] \\ &= \mathbb{E}\left[\sum_{i=1}^d \sigma_h^2 \; \mu_h \otimes e_i \otimes e_i\right] \\ &= \sum_{i=1}^d M_1 \otimes e_i \otimes e_i, \end{aligned}$$

crucially using the fact that $\mathbb{E}[z_i z_j|h] = 0$ for $i \neq j$ and $\mathbb{E}[z_i^2|h] = \sigma_h^2$. By the same derivation, we have $\mathbb{E}[z \otimes \mu_h \otimes z] = \sum_{i=1}^d e_i \otimes M_1 \otimes e_i$ and $\mathbb{E}[z \otimes z \otimes \mu_h] = \sum_{i=1}^d e_i \otimes e_i \otimes M_1$. Therefore,

$$\begin{aligned} M_3 &= \mathbb{E}[x \otimes x \otimes x] \\ &\quad - \big(\mathbb{E}[\mu_h \otimes z \otimes z] + \mathbb{E}[z \otimes \mu_h \otimes z] + \mathbb{E}[z \otimes z \otimes \mu_h]\big) \\ &= \mathbb{E}[\mu_h \otimes \mu_h \otimes \mu_h] = \sum_{i=1}^k w_i \mu_i \otimes \mu_i \otimes \mu_i \end{aligned}$$

as claimed. □

Theorem 1 shows the relationship between (some functions of) the observable moments and the desired parameters. A simple estimator based on this moment structure is given in the following theorem. For a third-order tensor $T \in \mathbb{R}^{d \times d \times d}$, we define the matrix

$$T(\eta) := \sum_{i_1=1}^d \sum_{i_2=1}^d \sum_{i_3=1}^d T_{i_1,i_2,i_3} \eta_{i_3} \; e_{i_1} \otimes e_{i_2}$$

for any vector $\eta \in \mathbb{R}^d$.

Theorem 2 (Moment-based estimator). *The following can be added to the results of Theorem 1. Suppose $\eta^\top \mu_1, \eta^\top \mu_2, \ldots, \eta^\top \mu_k$ are distinct and non-zero (which is satisfied almost surely, for instance, if η is chosen uniformly at random from the unit sphere in $\mathbb{R}^d$). Then the matrix*

$$M_{\mathrm{GMM}}(\eta) := M_2^{\dagger 1/2} M_3(\eta) M_2^{\dagger 1/2}$$

is diagonalizable (where † denotes the Moore-Penrose pseudoinverse); its non-zero eigenvalue / eigenvector pairs $(\lambda_1, v_1), (\lambda_2, v_2), \ldots, (\lambda_k, v_k)$ satisfy $\lambda_i = \eta^\top \mu_{\pi(i)}$ and $M_2^{1/2} v_i = s_i \sqrt{w_{\pi(i)}} \mu_{\pi(i)}$ for some permutation π on $[k]$ and signs $s_1, s_2, \ldots, s_k \in \{\pm 1\}$. The μ_i, σ_i^2, and w_i are recovered (up to permutation) with

$$\begin{aligned} \mu_{\pi(i)} &= \frac{\lambda_i}{\eta^\top M_2^{1/2} v_i} M_2^{1/2} v_i, \\ \sigma_i^2 &= \frac{1}{w_i} e_i^\top A^\dagger M_1, \\ w_i &= e_i^\top A^\dagger \mathbb{E}[x]. \end{aligned}$$

Proof. By Theorem 1,

$$\begin{aligned} M_1 &= A \operatorname{diag}(\sigma_1^2, \sigma_2^2, \ldots, \sigma_k^2) w, \\ M_2 &= A \operatorname{diag}(w) A^\top, \\ M_3(\eta) &= A \operatorname{diag}(w) D_1(\eta) A^\top, \end{aligned}$$

where $D_1(\eta) := \operatorname{diag}(\eta^\top \mu_1, \eta^\top \mu_2, \ldots, \eta^\top \mu_k)$.

Let $USR^\top$ be the thin SVD of $A \operatorname{diag}(w)^{1/2}$ ($U \in \mathbb{R}^{d \times k}$, $S \in \mathbb{R}^{k \times k}$, and $R \in \mathbb{R}^{k \times k}$), so $M_2 = US^2U^\top$ and $M_2^{\dagger 1/2} = US^{-1}U^\top$ since $A \operatorname{diag}(w)^{1/2}$ has rank k by assumption. Also by assumption, the diagonal entries of $D_1(\eta)$ are distinct and non-zero. Therefore, every non-zero eigenvalue of the symmetric matrix $M_{\mathrm{GMM}}(\eta) = UR^\top D_1(\eta) RU^\top$ has geometric multiplicity one. Indeed, these non-zero eigenvalues λ_i are the diagonal entries of $D_1(\eta)$ (up to some permutation π on $[k]$), and the corresponding eigenvectors v_i are the columns of $UR^\top$ up to signs:

$$\lambda_i = \eta^\top \mu_{\pi(i)} \quad \text{and} \quad v_i = s_i U R^\top e_{\pi(i)}.$$

Now, since

$$\begin{aligned} M_2^{1/2} v_i &= s_i \sqrt{w_{\pi(i)}} \mu_{\pi(i)}, \\ \frac{\lambda_i}{\eta^\top M_2^{1/2} v_i} &= \frac{\eta^\top \mu_{\pi(i)}}{s_i \sqrt{w_{\pi(i)}} \eta^\top \mu_{\pi(i)}} = \frac{1}{s_i \sqrt{w_{\pi(i)}}}, \end{aligned}$$

it follows that

$$\mu_{\pi(i)} = \frac{\lambda_i}{\eta^\top M_2^{1/2} v_i} M_2^{1/2} v_i, \quad i \in [k].$$

The claims regarding σ_i^2 and w_i are also evident from the structure of M_1 and $\mathbb{E}[x] = Aw$. □

An efficiently computable plug-in estimator can be derived from Theorem 2. We provide one such algorithm (called LearnGMM) in Appendix C; for simplicity, we restrict to the case where the components share the same common spherical covariance, *i.e.*, $\sigma_1^2 = \sigma_2^2 = \cdots = \sigma_k^2 = \sigma^2$. The following theorem provides a sample complexity bound for accurate estimation of the component means. Since only low-order moments are used, the sample complexity is polynomial in the relevant parameters of the estimation problem (in particular, the dimension d and the number of mixing components k). It is worth noting that the polynomial is quadratic in the inverse accuracy parameter $1/\varepsilon$; this owes to the fact that the empirical moments converge to the population moments at the usual $n^{-1/2}$ rate as per the central limit theorem.

Theorem 3 (Finite sample bound). *There exists a polynomial* poly$(\cdot)$ *such that the following holds. Let M_2 be the matrix defined in Theorem 2, and $\varsigma_t[M_2]$ be its t-th largest singular value (for $t \in [k]$). Let $b_{\max} := \max_{i \in [k]} \|\mu_i\|_2$ and $w_{\min} := \min_{i \in [k]} w_i$. Pick any $\varepsilon, \delta \in$*

(0, 1). *Suppose the sample size n satisfies*

$$n \geq \text{poly}\Big(d, k, 1/\varepsilon, \log(1/\delta), 1/w_{\min}, \varsigma_1[M_2]/\varsigma_k[M_2], b_{\max}^2/\varsigma_k[M_2], \sigma^2/\varsigma_k[M_2], \Big).$$

Then with probability at least $1-\delta$ over the random sample and the internal randomness of the algorithm, there exists a permutation π on $[k]$ such that the $\{\hat{\mu}_i : i \in [k]\}$ returned by LEARNGMM *satisfy*

$$\|\hat{\mu}_{\pi(i)} - \mu_i\|_2 \leq \Big(\|\mu_i\|_2 + \sqrt{\varsigma_1[M_2]}\Big)\varepsilon$$

for all $i \in [k]$.

It is also easy to obtain accuracy guarantees for estimating σ^2 and w. The role of Condition 1 enters by observing that $\varsigma_k[M_2] = 0$ if either $\text{rank}(A) < k$ or $w_{\min} = 0$, as $M_2 = A \operatorname{diag}(w) A^\top$. The sample complexity bound then becomes trivial in this case, as the bound grows with $1/\varsigma_k[M_2]$ and $1/w_{\min}$. Finally, we also note that LEARNGMM is just one (easy to state) way to obtain an efficient algorithm based on the structure in Theorem 1. It is also possible to use, for instance, simultaneous diagonalization techniques [7] or orthogonal tensor decompositions [2] to extract the parameters from (estimates of) M_2 and M_3; these alternative methods are more robust to sampling error, and are therefore recommended for practical implementation.

3. DISCUSSION

Multi-view methods and a simpler algorithm in higher dimensions.

Some previous work of the authors on moment-based estimators for the Gaussian mixture model relies on a non-degenerate multi-view assumption [3]. In this work, it is shown that if each mixture component i has an axis-aligned covariance $\Sigma_i := \operatorname{diag}(\sigma_{1,i}^2, \sigma_{2,i}^2, \ldots, \sigma_{d,i}^2)$, then under some additional mild assumptions (which ultimately require $d > k$), a moment-based method can be used to estimate the model parameters. The idea is to partition the coordinates $[d]$ into three groups, inducing multiple "views" $x = (x_1, x_2, x_3)$ with each $x_t \in \mathbb{R}^{d_t}$ for some $d_t \geq k$ such that x_1, x_2, and x_3 are conditionally independent given h. When the matrix of conditional means $A_t := [\mathbb{E}[x_t|h=1]|\mathbb{E}[x_t|h=2]|\cdots|\mathbb{E}[x_t|h=k]] \in \mathbb{R}^{d_t \times k}$ for each view $t \in \{1,2,3\}$ has rank k, then an efficient technique similar to that described in Theorem 2 will recover the parameters. Therefore, the problem is reduced to partitioning the coordinates so that the resulting matrices A_t have rank k.

In the case where each component covariance is spherical ($\Sigma_i = \sigma_i^2 I$), we may simply apply a random rotation to x before (arbitrarily) splitting into the three views. Let $\tilde{x} := \Theta x$ for a random orthogonal matrix $\Theta \in \mathbb{R}^{d \times d}$, and partition the coordinates so that $\tilde{x} = (\tilde{x}_1, \tilde{x}_2, \tilde{x}_3)$ with $\tilde{x}_t \in \mathbb{R}^{d_t}$ and $d_t \geq k$. By the rotational invariance of the multivariate Gaussian distribution, the distribution of $\tilde{x}$ is still a mixture of spherical Gaussians, and moreover, the matrix of conditional means $\tilde{A}_t := [\mathbb{E}[\tilde{x}_t|h=1]|\mathbb{E}[\tilde{x}_t|h=2]|\cdots|\mathbb{E}[\tilde{x}_t|h=k]] \in \mathbb{R}^{d_t \times k}$ for each view $\tilde{x}_t$ has rank k with probability 1. To see this, observe that a random rotation in $\mathbb{R}^d$ followed by a restriction to d_t coordinates is simply a random projection from $\mathbb{R}^d$ to $\mathbb{R}^{d_t}$, and that a random projection of a linear subspace of dimension k (in particular, the range of A) to $\mathbb{R}^{d_t}$ is almost surely injective as long as $d_t \geq k$. Therefore it is sufficient to require $d \geq 3k$ so that it is possible to split $\tilde{x}$ into three views, each of dimension $d_t \geq k$. To guarantee that the k-th largest singular value of each $\tilde{A}_t$ is bounded below in terms of the k-th largest singular value of A (with high probability), we may require d to be somewhat larger: $O(k \log k)$ certainly works (see Appendix B), and we conjecture $c \cdot k$ for some $c > 3$ is in fact sufficient.

Spectral decomposition approaches for ICA.

The Gaussian mixture model shares some similarities to a standard model for independent component analysis (ICA) [11, 8, 18, 12]. Here, let $h \in \mathbb{R}^k$ be a random vector with independent entries, and let $z \in \mathbb{R}^k$ be multivariate Gaussian random vector. We think of h as an unobserved signal and z as noise. The observed random vector is

$$x := Ah + z$$

for some $A \in \mathbb{R}^{k \times k}$, where h and z are assumed to be independent. (For simplicity, we only consider square A, although it is easy to generalize to $A \in \mathbb{R}^{d \times k}$ for $d \geq k$.)

In contrast to this ICA model, the spherical Gaussian mixture model is one where h would take values in $\{e_1, e_2, \ldots, e_k\}$, and the covariance of z (given h) is spherical.

For ICA, a spectral decomposition approach related to the one described in Theorem 2 can be used to estimate the columns of A (up to scale), without knowing the noise covariance $\mathbb{E}[zz^\top]$. Such an estimator can be obtained from Theorem 4 using techniques commonplace in the ICA literature; its proof is given in Appendix A for completeness.

THEOREM 4. *In the ICA model described above, assume $\mathbb{E}[h_i] = 0$, $\mathbb{E}[h_i^2] = 1$, and $\kappa_i := \mathbb{E}[h_i^4] - 3 \neq 0$ (i.e., the excess kurtosis is non-zero), and that A is non-singular. Define $f \colon \mathbb{R}^k \to \mathbb{R}$ by*

$$f(\eta) := 12^{-1}\big(m_4(\eta) - 3m_2(\eta)^2\big)$$

where $m_p(\eta) := \mathbb{E}[(\eta^\top x)^p]$. Suppose $\phi \in \mathbb{R}^k$ and $\psi \in \mathbb{R}^k$ are such that $\frac{(\phi^\top \mu_1)^2}{(\psi^\top \mu_1)^2}, \frac{(\phi^\top \mu_2)^2}{(\psi^\top \mu_2)^2}, \ldots, \frac{(\phi^\top \mu_k)^2}{(\psi^\top \mu_k)^2} \in \mathbb{R}$ are distinct. Then the matrix

$$M_{\mathrm{ICA}}(\phi, \psi) := \big(\nabla^2 f(\phi)\big)\big(\nabla^2 f(\psi)\big)^{-1}$$

is diagonalizable; the eigenvalues are $\frac{(\phi^\top \mu_1)^2}{(\psi^\top \mu_1)^2}, \frac{(\phi^\top \mu_2)^2}{(\psi^\top \mu_2)^2}, \ldots, \frac{(\phi^\top \mu_k)^2}{(\psi^\top \mu_k)^2}$ and each have geometric multiplicity one, and the corresponding eigenvectors are $\mu_1, \mu_2, \ldots, \mu_k$ (up to scaling and permutation).

Again, choosing ϕ and ψ as random unit vectors ensures the distinctness assumption is satisfied almost surely, and a finite sample analysis can be given using standard matrix perturbation techniques [3]. A number of related deterministic algorithms based on algebraic techniques are discussed in [12]. Recent work in [4] provides a finite sample complexity analysis for an efficient estimator based on local search.

Non-degeneracy.

The non-degeneracy assumption (Condition 1) is quite natural, and its has the virtue of permitting tractable and consistent estimators. Although previous work has typically tied it with additional assumptions, this work shows that they are largely unnecessary.

One drawback of Condition 1 is that it prevents the straightforward application of these techniques to certain problem domains (*e.g.*, automatic speech recognition (ASR), where the number of mixture components is typically enormous, but the dimension of observations is relatively small; alternatively, the span of the means has dimension $< k$). To compensate, one may require multiple views, which are granted by a number of models, including hidden Markov models used in ASR [17, 3], and combining these views in a tensor product fashion [1]. This increases the complexity of the estimator, but that may be inevitable as estimation for certain non-singular models is conjectured to be computationally intractable [23].

4. ACKNOWLEDGEMENTS

We thank Dean Foster and Anima Anandkumar for helpful insights. We also thank Rong Ge and Sanjeev Arora for discussions regarding their recent work on ICA.

5. REFERENCES

[1] E. S. Allman, C. Matias, and J. A. Rhodes. Identifiability of parameters in latent structure models with many observed variables. *The Annals of Statistics*, 37(6A):3099–3132, 2009.

[2] A. Anandkumar, R. Ge, D. Hsu, S. M. Kakade, and M. Telgarsky. Tensor decompositions for learning latent variable models, 2012. Manuscript.

[3] A. Anandkumar, D. Hsu, and S. M. Kakade. A method of moments for mixture models and hidden Markov models. In *COLT*, 2012.

[4] S. Arora, R. Ge, A. Moitra, and S. Sachdeva. Provable ICA with unknown Gaussian noise, and implications for Gaussian mixtures and autoencoders. In *NIPS*, 2012.

[5] S. Arora and R. Kannan. Learning mixtures of arbitrary Gaussians. In *STOC*, 2001.

[6] M. Belkin and K. Sinha. Polynomial learning of distribution families. In *FOCS*, 2010.

[7] A. Bunse-Gerstner, R. Byers, and V. Mehrmann. Numerical methods for simultaneous diagonalization. *SIAM Journal on Matrix Analysis and Applications*, 14(4):927–949, 1993.

[8] J.-F. Cardoso and P. Comon. Independent component analysis, a survey of some algebraic methods. In *IEEE International Symposium on Circuits and Systems Circuits and Systems Connecting the World*, 1996.

[9] J. T. Chang. Full reconstruction of Markov models on evolutionary trees: Identifiability and consistency. *Mathematical Biosciences*, 137:51–73, 1996.

[10] K. Chaudhuri and S. Rao. Learning mixtures of product distributions using correlations and independence. In *COLT*, 2008.

[11] P. Comon. Independent component analysis, a new concept? *Signal Processing*, 36(3):287–314, 1994.

[12] P. Comon and C. Jutten. *Handbook of Blind Source Separation: Independent Component Analysis and Applications*. Academic Press. Elsevier, 2010.

[13] S. Dasgupta. Learning mixutres of Gaussians. In *FOCS*, 1999.

[14] S. Dasgupta and L. Schulman. A probabilistic analysis of EM for mixtures of separated, spherical Gaussians. *Journal of Machine Learning Research*, 8(Feb):203–226, 2007.

[15] A. M. Frieze, M. Jerrum, and R. Kannan. Learning linear transformations. In *FOCS*, 1996.

[16] D. Hsu, S. M. Kakade, and T. Zhang. An analysis of random design linear regression, 2011. arXiv:1106.2363.

[17] D. Hsu, S. M. Kakade, and T. Zhang. A spectral algorithm for learning hidden Markov models. *Journal of Computer and System Sciences*, 78(5):1460–1480, 2012.

[18] A. Hyvärinen and E. Oja. Independent component analysis: algorithms and applications. *Neural Networks*, 13(4–5):411–430, 2000.

[19] A. T. Kalai, A. Moitra, and G. Valiant. Efficiently learning mixtures of two Gaussians. In *STOC*, 2010.

[20] B. G. Lindsay and P. Basak. Multivariate normal mixtures: a fast consistent method. *Journal of the American Statistical Association*, 88(422):468–476, 1993.

[21] J. B. MacQueen. Some methods for classification and analysis of multivariate observations. In *Proceedings of the fifth Berkeley Symposium on Mathematical Statistics and Probability*, volume 1, pages 281–297. University of California Press, 1967.

[22] A. Moitra and G. Valiant. Settling the polynomial learnability of mixtures of Gaussians. In *FOCS*, 2010.

[23] E. Mossel and S. Roch. Learning nonsingular phylogenies and hidden Markov models. *Annals of Applied Probability*, 16(2):583–614, 2006.

[24] P. Q. Nguyen and O. Regev. Learning a parallelepiped: Cryptanalysis of GGH and NTRU signatures. *Journal of Cryptology*, 22(2):139–160, 2009.

[25] K. Pearson. Contributions to the mathematical theory of evolution. *Philosophical Transactions of the Royal Society, London, A.*, page 71, 1894.

[26] D. M. Titterington, A. F. M. Smith, and U. E. Makov. *Statistical analysis of finite mixture distributions.* Wiley, 1985.

[27] S. Vempala and G. Wang. A spectral algorithm for learning mixtures of distributions. In *FOCS*, 2002.

APPENDIX

A. CONNECTION TO INDEPENDENT COMPONENT ANALYSIS

PROOF OF THEOREM 4. It can be shown that

$$m_2(\eta) = \mathbb{E}[(\eta^\top Ah)^2] + \mathbb{E}[(\eta^\top z)^2],$$
$$m_4(\eta) = \mathbb{E}[(\eta^\top Ah)^4] - 3\mathbb{E}[(\eta^\top Ah)^2]^2 + 3m_2(\eta)^2.$$

By the assumptions,

$$\begin{aligned}\mathbb{E}[(\eta^\top Ah)^4] &= \sum_{i=1}^{k}(\eta^\top \mu_i)^4\mathbb{E}[h_i^4] + 3\sum_{i\neq j}(\eta^\top \mu_i)^2(\eta^\top \mu_j)^2 \\ &= \sum_{i=1}^{k}\kappa_i(\eta^\top \mu_i)^4 + 3\sum_{i,j}(\eta^\top \mu_i)^2(\eta^\top \mu_j)^2 \\ &= \sum_{i=1}^{k}\kappa_i(\eta^\top \mu_i)^4 + 3\mathbb{E}[(\eta^\top Ah)^2]^2,\end{aligned}$$

and therefore

$$f(\eta) = 12^{-1}\left(\mathbb{E}[(\eta^\top Ah)^4] - 3\mathbb{E}[(\eta^\top Ah)^2]^2\right) = 12^{-1}\sum_{i=1}^{k}\kappa_i(\eta^\top \mu_i)^4.$$

The Hessian of f is given by

$$\nabla^2 f(\eta) = \sum_{i=1}^{k}\kappa_i(\eta^\top \mu_i)^2\mu_i\mu_i^\top.$$

Define the diagonal matrices

$$K := \mathrm{diag}(\kappa_1, \kappa_2, \ldots, \kappa_k),$$
$$D_2(\eta) := \mathrm{diag}((\eta^\top\mu_1)^2, (\eta^\top\mu_2)^2, \ldots, (\eta^\top\mu_k)^2)$$

and observe that

$$\nabla^2 f(\eta) = AKD_2(\eta)A^\top.$$

By assumption, the diagonal entries of $D_2(\phi)D_2(\psi)^{-1}$ are distinct, and therefore

$$M_{\mathrm{ICA}}(\phi,\psi) = (\nabla^2 f(\phi))(\nabla^2 f(\psi))^{-1} = AD_2(\phi)D_2(\psi)^{-1}A^{-1}$$

is diagonalizable, and every eigenvalue has geometric multiplicity one. □

B. INCOHERENCE AND RANDOM ROTATIONS

The multi-view technique from [3] can be used to estimate mixtures of product distributions, which include, as special cases, mixtures of Gaussians with axis-aligned covariances $\Sigma_i = \mathrm{diag}(\sigma_{1,i}^2, \sigma_{2,i}^2, \ldots, \sigma_{d,i}^2)$. Spherical covariances $\Sigma_i = \sigma_i^2 I$ are, of course, also axis-aligned. The idea is to randomly partition the coordinates $[d]$ into three groups, inducing multiple "views" $x = (x_1, x_2, x_3)$ with each $x_t \in \mathbb{R}^{d_t}$ for some $d_t \geq k$ such that x_1, x_2, and x_3 are conditionally independent given h. When the matrix of conditional means $A_t := [\mathbb{E}[x_t|h=1]|\mathbb{E}[x_t|h=2]|\cdots|\mathbb{E}[x_t|h=k]] \in \mathbb{R}^{d_t\times k}$ for each view $t \in \{1,2,3\}$ has rank k, then an efficient technique similar to that described in Theorem 2 will recover the parameters (for details, see [3, 2]).

It is shown in [3] that if A has rank k and also satisfies a mild incoherence condition, then a random partitioning guarantees that each A_t has rank k, and lower-bounds the k-th largest singular value of each A_t by that of A. The condition is similar to the spreading condition of [10].

Define $\mathrm{coherence}(A) := \max_{i\in[d]}\{e_i^\top \Pi_A e_i\}$ to be the largest diagonal entry of the ortho-projector Π_A to the range of A. When A has rank k, we have $\mathrm{coherence}(A) \in [k/d, 1]$; it is maximized when $\mathrm{range}(A) = \mathrm{span}\{e_1, e_2, \ldots, e_k\}$ and minimized when the range is spanned by a subset of the Hadamard basis of cardinality k. Roughly speaking, if the matrix of conditional means has low coherence, then its full-rank property is witnessed by many partitions of $[d]$; this is made formal in the following lemma.

LEMMA 1. *Assume A has rank k and that* $\mathrm{coherence}(A) \leq (\varepsilon^2/6)/\ln(3k/\delta)$ *for some $\varepsilon, \delta \in (0,1)$. With probability at least $1-\delta$, a random partitioning of the dimensions $[d]$ into three groups (for each $i \in [d]$, independently pick $t \in \{1,2,3\}$ uniformly at random and put i in group t) has the following property. For each $t \in \{1,2,3\}$, the matrix A_t obtained by selecting the rows of A in group t has full column rank, and the k-th largest singular value of A_t is at least $\sqrt{(1-\varepsilon)/3}$ times that of A.*

For a mixture of spherical Gaussians, one can randomly rotate x before applying the random coordinate partitioning. This is because if $\Theta \in \mathbb{R}^{d\times d}$ is an orthogonal matrix, then the distribution of $\tilde{x} := \Theta x$ is also a mixture of spherical Gaussians. Its matrix of conditional means is given by $\tilde{A} := \Theta A$. The following lemma implies that multiplying a tall matrix A by a random rotation Θ causes the product to have low coherence.

LEMMA 2 ([16]). *Let $A \in \mathbb{R}^{d\times k}$ be a fixed matrix with rank k, and let $\Theta \in \mathbb{R}^{d\times d}$ be chosen uniformly at random among all orthogonal $d\times d$ matrices. For any $\eta \in (0,1)$, with probability at least $1-\eta$, the matrix $\tilde{A} := \Theta A$ satisfies*

$$\mathrm{coherence}(\tilde{A}) \leq \frac{k + \sqrt{2k\ln(d/\eta)} + 2\ln(d/\eta)}{d\left(1 - 1/(4d) - 1/(360d^3)\right)^2}.$$

Take η from Lemma 2 and ε, δ from Lemma 1 to be constants. Then the incoherence condition of Lemma 1 is satsified provided that $d \geq c\cdot(k\log k)$ for some positive constant c.

C. LEARNING ALGORITHM AND SKETCH OF FINITE SAMPLE ANALYSIS

In this section, we state and sketch an analysis of a learning algorithm based on the estimator from Theorem 2, which assumed availability of exact moments of x. The full analysis is provided in the full version of the paper. The proposed algorithm only uses a finite sample to estimate moments, and also explicitly deals with the eigenvalue separation condition assumed in Theorem 2 via internal randomization.

C.1 Notation

For a matrix $X \in \mathbb{R}^{m\times m}$, we use $\varsigma_t[X]$ to denote the t-th largest singular value of a matrix X, and $\|X\|_2$ to denote its spectral norm (so $\|X\|_2 = \varsigma_1[X]$).

For a third-order tensor $Y \in \mathbb{R}^{m\times m\times m}$ and $U, V, W \in \mathbb{R}^{m\times n}$, we use the notation $Y[U,V,W] \in \mathbb{R}^{n\times n\times n}$ to denote the third-order tensor given by

$$Y[U,V,W]_{j_1,j_2,j_3} = \sum_{1\leq i_1,i_2,i_3\leq m} U_{i_1,j_1}V_{i_2,j_2}W_{i_3,j_3}Y_{i_1,i_2,i_3}$$

for all $j_1, j_2, j_3 \in [n]$. Note that this is the analogue of $U^\top XV \in \mathbb{R}^{n\times n}$ for a matrix $X \in \mathbb{R}^{m\times m}$ and $U, V \in \mathbb{R}^{m\times n}$. For $Y \in \mathbb{R}^{m\times m\times m}$, we use $\|Y\|_2$ to denote its operator (or supremum) norm $\|Y\|_2 := \sup\{|Y[u,v,w]| : u, v, w \in \mathbb{R}^m, \|u\|_2 = \|v\|_2 = \|w\|_2 = 1\}$.

C.2 Algorithm

The proposed algorithm, called LEARNGMM, is described in Figure 1. The algorithm essentially implements the decomposition strategy in Theorem 2 using plug-in moments. To simplify the analysis, we split our sample (say, initially of size $2n$) in two: we use the first half for empirical moments ($\hat{\mu}$ and $\widehat{M}_2$) used in constructing $\hat{\sigma}^2$, $\widehat{M}_2$, $\widehat{W}$, and $\widehat{B}$; and we use the second half for empirical moments ($\widehat{W}^\top\underline{\hat{\mu}}$ and $\underline{\widehat{M}}_3[\widehat{W},\widehat{W},\widehat{W}]$ used in constructing $\widehat{M}_3[\widehat{W},\widehat{W},\widehat{W}]$. Observe that this ensures $\widehat{M}_3$ is independent of $\widehat{W}$.

Let $\{(x_i, h_i) : i \in [n]\}$ be n i.i.d. copies of (x,h), and write $S := \{x_1, x_2, \ldots, x_n\}$. Let $\underline{S}$ be an independent copy of S.

Furthermore, define the following moments and empirical moments:

$$\mu := \mathbb{E}[x], \qquad \mathcal{M}_2 := \mathbb{E}[xx^\top],$$
$$\mathcal{M}_3 := \mathbb{E}[x \otimes x \otimes x], \qquad \hat{\mu} := \frac{1}{|\mathcal{S}|}\sum_{x \in \mathcal{S}} x,$$
$$\widehat{\mathcal{M}}_2 := \frac{1}{|\mathcal{S}|}\sum_{x \in \mathcal{S}} xx^\top, \qquad \underline{\widehat{\mathcal{M}}_3} := \frac{1}{|\underline{\mathcal{S}}|}\sum_{x \in \underline{\mathcal{S}}} x \otimes x \otimes x,$$
$$\underline{\hat{\mu}} := \frac{1}{|\underline{\mathcal{S}}|}\sum_{x \in \underline{\mathcal{S}}} x.$$

So $\mathcal{S}$ represents the first half of the sample, and $\underline{\mathcal{S}}$ represents the second half of the sample.

C.3 Structure of the moments

We first recall the basic structure of the moments μ, $\mathcal{M}_2$, and $\mathcal{M}_3$ as established in Theorem 2; for simplicity, we restrict to the special case where $\sigma_1^2 = \sigma_2^2 = \cdots = \sigma_k^2 = \sigma^2$.

LEMMA 3.

$$\mu = \sum_{i=1}^k w_i \mu_i, \qquad \mathcal{M}_2 = \sum_{i=1}^k w_i \mu_i \mu_i^\top + \sigma^2 I,$$
$$\mathcal{M}_3 = \sum_{i=1}^k w_i \mu_i \otimes \mu_i \otimes \mu_i$$
$$+ \sigma^2 \sum_{j=1}^d \Big(\mu \otimes e_j \otimes e_j + e_j \otimes \mu \otimes e_j + e_j \otimes e_j \otimes \mu \Big).$$

C.4 Concentration behavior of empirical quantities

In this subsection, we prove concentration properties of empirical quantities based on $\mathcal{S}$; clearly the same properties hold for $\underline{\mathcal{S}}$.

Let $\mathcal{S}_i := \{x_j \in \mathcal{S} : h_j = i\}$ and $\hat{w}_i := |\mathcal{S}_i|/|\mathcal{S}|$ for $i \in [k]$. Also, define the following (empirical) conditional moments:

$$\mu_i := \mathbb{E}[x|h = i], \qquad \mathcal{M}_{2,i} := \mathbb{E}[xx^\top|h = i],$$
$$\mathcal{M}_{3,i} := \mathbb{E}[x \otimes x \otimes x|h = i], \qquad \hat{\mu}_i := \frac{1}{|\mathcal{S}_i|}\sum_{x \in \mathcal{S}_i} x,$$
$$\widehat{\mathcal{M}}_{2,i} := \frac{1}{|\mathcal{S}_i|}\sum_{x \in \mathcal{S}_i} xx^\top, \qquad \widehat{\mathcal{M}}_{3,i} := \frac{1}{|\mathcal{S}_i|}\sum_{x \in \mathcal{S}_i} x \otimes x \otimes x.$$

LEMMA 4. *Pick any $\delta \in (0, 1/2)$. With probability at least $1 - 2\delta$,*

$$|\hat{w}_i - w_i| \le \sqrt{\frac{2w_i(1 - w_i)\ln(2k/\delta)}{n}} + \frac{2\ln(2k/\delta)}{3n}, \quad \forall i \in [k];$$
$$\left(\sum_{i=1}^k (\hat{w}_i - w_i)^2 \right)^{1/2} \le \frac{1 + \sqrt{\ln(1/\delta)}}{\sqrt{n}}.$$

LEMMA 5. *Pick any $\delta \in (0, 1)$ and any matrix $R \in \mathbb{R}^{d \times r}$ of rank r.*

1. *First-order moments: with probability at least $1 - \delta$,*

$$\|R^\top(\hat{\mu}_i - \mu_i)\|_2 \le \sigma \|R\|_2 \sqrt{\frac{r + 2\sqrt{r\ln(k/\delta)} + 2\ln(k/\delta)}{\hat{w}_i n}}$$

for all $i \in [k]$.

LEARNGMM

1. Using the first half of the sample, compute empirical mean $\hat{\mu}$ and empirical second-order moments $\widehat{\mathcal{M}}_2$.
2. Let $\hat{\sigma}^2$ be the k-th largest eigenvalue of the empirical covariance matrix $\widehat{\mathcal{M}}_2 - \hat{\mu}\hat{\mu}^\top$.
3. Let $\widehat{M}_2$ be the best rank-k approximation to $\widehat{\mathcal{M}}_2 - \hat{\sigma}^2 I$
$$\widehat{M}_2 := \arg \min_{X \in \mathbb{R}^{d \times d} : \mathrm{rank}(X) \le k} \|(\widehat{\mathcal{M}}_2 - \hat{\sigma}^2 I) - X\|_2$$
which can be obtained via the singular value decomposition.
4. Let $\widehat{U} \in \mathbb{R}^{d \times k}$ be the matrix of left orthonormal singular vectors of $\widehat{M}_2$.
5. Let $\widehat{W} := \widehat{U}(\widehat{U}^\top \widehat{M}_2 \widehat{U})^{\dagger 1/2}$, where $X^\dagger$ denotes the Moore-Penrose pseudoinverse of a matrix X.
Also define $\widehat{B} := \widehat{U}(\widehat{U}^\top \widehat{M}_2 \widehat{U})^{1/2}$.
6. Using the second half of the sample, compute whitened empirical averages $\widehat{W}^\top \underline{\hat{\mu}}$ and third-order moments $\underline{\widehat{\mathcal{M}}_3}[\widehat{W}, \widehat{W}, \widehat{W}]$.
7. Let $\widehat{M}_3[\widehat{W}, \widehat{W}, \widehat{W}] := \underline{\widehat{\mathcal{M}}_3}[\widehat{W}, \widehat{W}, \widehat{W}] - \hat{\sigma}^2 \sum_{i=1}^d \big((\widehat{W}^\top \underline{\hat{\mu}}) \otimes (\widehat{W}^\top e_i) \otimes (\widehat{W}^\top e_i) + (\widehat{W}^\top e_i) \otimes (\widehat{W}^\top \underline{\hat{\mu}}) \otimes (\widehat{W}^\top e_i) + (\widehat{W}^\top e_i) \otimes (\widehat{W}^\top e_i) \otimes (\widehat{W}^\top \underline{\hat{\mu}}) \big)$.
8. Repeat the following steps t times (where $t := \lceil \log_2(1/\delta) \rceil$ for confidence $1 - \delta$):
   (a) Choose $\theta \in \mathbb{R}^k$ uniformly at random from the unit sphere in $\mathbb{R}^k$.
   (b) Let $\{(\hat{v}_i, \hat{\lambda}_i) : i \in [k]\}$ be the eigenvector/eigenvalue pairs of $\widehat{M}_3[\widehat{W}, \widehat{W}, \widehat{W}\theta]$.

   Retain the results for which $\min\big(\{|\hat{\lambda}_i - \hat{\lambda}_j| : i \ne j\} \cup \{|\hat{\lambda}_i| : i \in [k]\}\big)$ is largest.
9. Return the parameter estimates $\hat{\sigma}^2$,
$$\hat{\mu}_i := \frac{\hat{\lambda}_i}{\theta^\top \hat{v}_i} \widehat{B} \hat{v}_i, \quad i \in [k],$$
$$\hat{w} := [\hat{\mu}_1 | \hat{\mu}_2 | \cdots | \hat{\mu}_k]^\dagger \hat{\mu}.$$

Figure 1: Algorithm for learning mixtures of Gaussians with common spherical covariance.

2. *Second-order moments: with probability at least* $1-\delta$,

$$\|R^\top(\widehat{\mathcal{M}}_{2,i}-\mathcal{M}_{2,i})R\|_2 \le \sigma^2\|R\|_2^2 \left(\sqrt{\frac{128(r\ln 9+\ln(2k/\delta))}{\hat{w}_i n}}+\frac{4(r\ln 9+\ln(2k/\delta))}{\hat{w}_i n}\right) + 2\sigma\|R^\top\mu_i\|_2\|R\|_2\sqrt{\frac{r+2\sqrt{r\ln(2k/\delta)}+2\ln(2k/\delta)}{\hat{w}_i n}}$$

for all $i\in[k]$.

3. *Third-order moments: with probability at least* $1-\delta$,

$$\|(\widehat{\mathcal{M}}_{3,i}-\mathcal{M}_{3,i})[R,R,R]\|_2 \le \sigma^3\|R\|_2^3 \sqrt{\frac{108e^3\lceil r\ln 13+\ln(3k/\delta)\rceil^3}{\hat{w}_i n}} + 3\sigma^2\|R^\top\mu_i\|_2\|R\|_2^2 \left(\sqrt{\frac{128(r\ln 9+\ln(3k/\delta))}{\hat{w}_i n}}+\frac{4(r\ln 9+\ln(3k/\delta))}{\hat{w}_i n}\right) + 3\sigma\|R^\top\mu_i\|_2^2\|R\|_2 \sqrt{\frac{r+2\sqrt{r\ln(3k/\delta)}+2\ln(3k/\delta)}{\hat{w}_i n}}$$

for all $i\in[k]$.

We now bound the accuracy of $\hat{\mu}$, $\widehat{\mathcal{M}}_2$, and $\widehat{\mathcal{M}}_3$ in terms of the accuracy of the conditional moments and the $\hat{w}_i$.

LEMMA 6. *Fix a matrix* $R\in\mathbb{R}^{d\times r}$. *Define* $\mathcal{B}_{1,R}:=\max_{i\in[k]}\|R^\top\mu_i\|_2$, $\mathcal{B}_{2,R}:=\max_{i\in[k]}\|R^\top\mathcal{M}_{2,i}R\|_2$, $\mathcal{B}_{3,R}:=\max_{i\in[k]}\|\mathcal{M}_{3,i}[R,R,R]\|_2$, $\mathcal{E}_{1,R}:=\max_{i\in[k]}\|R^\top(\hat{\mu}_i-\mu_i)\|_2$, $\mathcal{E}_{2,R}:=\max_{i\in[k]}\|R^\top(\widehat{\mathcal{M}}_{2,i}-\mathcal{M}_{2,i})R\|_2$, $\mathcal{E}_{3,R}:=\max_{i\in[k]}\|\widehat{\mathcal{M}}_{3,i}[R,R,R]-\mathcal{M}_{3,i}[R,R,R]\|_2$, *and* $\mathcal{E}_w:=(\sum_{i=1}^k(\hat{w}_i-w_i)^2)^{1/2}$. *Then*

$$\|R^\top(\hat{\mu}-\mu)\|_2 \le (1+\sqrt{k}\mathcal{E}_w)\mathcal{E}_{1,R}+\sqrt{k}\mathcal{B}_{1,R}\mathcal{E}_w;$$
$$\|R^\top(\widehat{\mathcal{M}}_2-\mathcal{M}_2)R\|_2 \le (1+\sqrt{k}\mathcal{E}_w)\mathcal{E}_{2,R}+\sqrt{k}\mathcal{B}_{2,R}\mathcal{E}_w;$$
$$\|(\widehat{\mathcal{M}}_3-\mathcal{M}_3)[R,R,R]\|_2 \le (1+\sqrt{k}\mathcal{E}_w)\mathcal{E}_{3,R}+\sqrt{k}\mathcal{B}_{3,R}\mathcal{E}_w.$$

C.5 Estimation of σ^2, M_2, and M_3

The covariance matrix can be written as $\mathcal{M}_2-\mu\mu^\top$, and the empirical covariance matrix can be written as $\widehat{\mathcal{M}}_2-\hat{\mu}\hat{\mu}^\top$. Recall that the estimate of σ^2, denoted by $\hat{\sigma}^2$, is given by the k-th largest eigenvalue of the empirical covariance matrix $\widehat{\mathcal{M}}_2-\hat{\mu}\hat{\mu}^\top$; and that the estimate of M_2, denoted by $\widehat{M}_2$, is the best rank-k approximation to $\widehat{\mathcal{M}}_2-\hat{\sigma}^2 I$. Of course, the singular values of a positive semi-definite matrix are the same as its eigenvalues; in particular, $\hat{\sigma}^2=\varsigma_k[\widehat{\mathcal{M}}_2-\hat{\mu}\hat{\mu}^\top]$.

LEMMA 7 (ACCURACY OF $\hat{\sigma}^2$ AND $\widehat{M}_2$).

1. $|\hat{\sigma}^2-\sigma^2|\le\|\widehat{\mathcal{M}}_2-\mathcal{M}_2\|_2+2\|\mu\|_2\|\hat{\mu}-\mu\|_2+\|\hat{\mu}-\mu\|_2^2$.
2. $\|\widehat{M}_2-M_2\|_2\le 4\|\widehat{\mathcal{M}}_2-\mathcal{M}_2\|_2+4\|\mu\|_2\|\hat{\mu}-\mu\|_2+2\|\hat{\mu}-\mu\|_2^2$.

LEMMA 8 (ACCURACY OF $\widehat{M}_3$). *For any matrix* $R\in\mathbb{R}^{d\times r}$,

$$\begin{aligned}&\|\widehat{M}_3[R,R,R]-M_3[R,R,R]\|_2\\ &\le \|\widehat{\mathcal{M}}_3[R,R,R]-\mathcal{M}_3[R,R,R]\|_2\\ &\quad+3\|R\|_2^2(\|R^\top(\hat{\mu}-\mu)\|_2+\|R^\top\mu\|_2)\\ &\qquad(\|\widehat{\mathcal{M}}_2-\mathcal{M}_2\|_2+2\|\mu\|_2\|\hat{\mu}-\mu\|_2+\|\hat{\mu}-\mu\|_2^2)\\ &\quad+\sigma^2\|R\|_2^2\|R^\top(\hat{\mu}-\mu)\|_2.\end{aligned}$$

C.6 Properties of projection and whitening operators

Recall that $\widehat{U}\in\mathbb{R}^{d\times k}$ is the matrix of left orthonormal singular vectors of $\widehat{M}_2$, and let $\widehat{S}\in\mathbb{R}^{k\times k}$ be the diagonal matrix of corresponding singular values. Analogously define U and S relative to M_2.

Define $\mathcal{E}_{M_2}:=\|\widehat{M}_2-M_2\|_2/\varsigma_k[M_2]$. The following lemma can be shown using standard matrix perturbation arguments.

LEMMA 9 (PROPERTIES OF PROJECTION OPERATORS). *Assume* $\mathcal{E}_{M_2}\le 1/3$. *Then*

1. $(1+\mathcal{E}_{M_2})S\succeq\widehat{U}^\top\widehat{M}_2\widehat{U}=\widehat{S}\succeq(1-\mathcal{E}_{M_2})S\succ 0$.
2. $\varsigma_k[\widehat{U}^\top U]\ge\sqrt{1-(9/4)\mathcal{E}_{M_2}^2}>0$.
3. $\varsigma_k[\widehat{U}^\top M_2\widehat{U}]\ge(1-(9/4)\mathcal{E}_{M_2}^2)\varsigma_k[M_2]>0$.
4. $\|(I-\widehat{U}\widehat{U}^\top)UU^\top\|_2\le(3/2)\mathcal{E}_{M_2}$.

Recall that $\widehat{W}=\widehat{U}(\widehat{U}^\top\widehat{M}_2\widehat{U})^{\dagger 1/2}$. We now show that $\widehat{W}$ indeed has the effect of whitening M_2.

LEMMA 10 (PROPERTIES OF WHITENING OPERATORS). *Define* $W:=\widehat{W}(\widehat{W}^\top M_2\widehat{W})^{\dagger 1/2}$. *Assume* $\mathcal{E}_{M_2}\le 1/3$. *Then*

1. $\widehat{W}^\top M_2\widehat{W}$ *is symmetric positive definite,* $W^\top M_2 W=I$, *and* $W^\top A\operatorname{diag}(w)^{1/2}$ *is orthogonal.*
2. $\|\widehat{W}\|_2\le\frac{1}{\sqrt{(1-\mathcal{E}_{M_2})\varsigma_k[M_2]}}$.
3. $\|(\widehat{W}^\top M_2\widehat{W})^{1/2}-I\|_2\le(3/2)\mathcal{E}_{M_2}$,
   $\|(\widehat{W}^\top M_2\widehat{W})^{-1/2}-I\|_2\le(3/2)\mathcal{E}_{M_2}$,
   $\|\widehat{W}^\top A\operatorname{diag}(w)^{1/2}\|_2\le\sqrt{1+(3/2)\mathcal{E}_{M_2}}$,
   $\|(\widehat{W}-W)^\top A\operatorname{diag}(w)^{1/2}\|_2\le(3/2)\sqrt{1+(3/2)\mathcal{E}_{M_2}}\mathcal{E}_{M_2}$.

We now show the effect of applying the whitening matrix $\widehat{W}$ to the tensor M_3. Define $\widehat{T}:=\widehat{M}_3[\widehat{W},\widehat{W},\widehat{W}]$ and $T:=M_3[W,W,W]$, both symmetric tensors in $\mathbb{R}^{k\times k\times k}$. Also, define

$$\widehat{T}[u]:=\widehat{M}_3[\widehat{W},\widehat{W},\widehat{W}u]$$

and

$$T[u]:=M_3[W,W,Wu],$$

both symmetric matrices in $\mathbb{R}^{k\times k}$.

LEMMA 11 (TENSOR STRUCTURE). *Define*

$$v_i:=W^\top A\operatorname{diag}(w)^{1/2}e_i$$

for all $i\in[k]$. *The tensor* T *can be written as*

$$T=\sum_{i=1}^k\frac{1}{\sqrt{w_i}}v_i\otimes v_i\otimes v_i$$

where the vectors $\{v_i : i\in[k]\}$ *are orthonormal. Furthermore, the eigenvectors of* $T[u]$ *are* $\{v_i : i\in[k]\}$ *and the corresponding eigenvalues are* $\{u^\top W^\top\mu_i : i\in[k]\}$.

LEMMA 12 (TENSOR ACCURACY). *Assume $\mathcal{E}_{M_2} \leq 1/3$. Then*

$$\|\widehat{T} - T\|_2 \leq \|\widehat{M_3}[\widehat{W}, \widehat{W}, \widehat{W}] - M_3[\widehat{W}, \widehat{W}, \widehat{W}]\|_2 + \frac{6}{\sqrt{w_{\min}}} \mathcal{E}_{M_2}.$$

C.7 Eigendecomposition analysis

Using Lemma 11 and Lemma 12, it is possible to show that an approximate orthogonal tensor decomposition of $\widehat{T}$ approximately recovers the v_i and $1/\sqrt{w_i}$. Computing such a decomposition is a bit more involved, but can be achieved efficiently [2]. A simpler-to-state randomized approach involving just an eigendecomposition has the same effect, albeit with worse final sample complexity; we analyze this method for sake of simplicity.

Define

$$\gamma := \frac{1}{2\sqrt{w_{\max}}\sqrt{ek}\binom{k+1}{2}} \tag{1}$$

where $w_{\max} := \max_{i \in [k]} w_i$.

LEMMA 13 (RANDOM SEPARATION). *Let $\theta \in \mathbb{R}^k$ be a random vector distributed uniformly over the unit sphere in $\mathbb{R}^k$. Let $Q := \{e_i - e_j : \{i,j\} \in \binom{k}{2}\} \cup \{e_i : i \in [k]\}$. Then*

$$\Pr\Big[\min_{q \in Q} |\theta^\top W^\top A q| > \gamma\Big] \geq \frac{1}{2}$$

where the probability is taken with respect to the distribution of θ.

Let $\mathcal{E}_T := \|\widehat{T} - T\|_2/\gamma$. Let $\theta_1, \theta_2, \ldots, \theta_t$ be the random unit vectors in $\mathbb{R}^k$ drawn by the algorithm. Define $\widehat{T}[\theta_{t'}] := \widehat{M_3}[\widehat{W}, \widehat{W}, \widehat{W}\theta_{t'}]$ and $T[\theta_{t'}] := M_3[W, W, W\theta_{t'}]$. Also, let $\Delta(t') := \min\{|\lambda_i - \lambda_j| : i \neq j\} \cup \{|\lambda_i| : i \in [k]\}$ for the eigenvalues $\{\lambda_i : i \in [k]\}$ of $T[\theta_{t'}]$, and let $\widehat{\Delta}(t') := \min\{|\hat{\lambda}_i - \hat{\lambda}_j| : i \neq j\} \cup \{|\lambda_i| : i \in [k]\}$ for the eigenvalues $\{\hat{\lambda}_i : i \in [k]\}$ of $\widehat{T}[\theta_{t'}]$.

LEMMA 14 (EIGENVALUE GAP). *Pick any $\delta \in (0,1)$. If $t \geq \log_2(1/\delta)$, then with probability at least $1-\delta$, the trial $\hat{\tau} := \arg\max_{t' \in [t]} \widehat{\Delta}(t')$ satisfies*

$$\widehat{\Delta}(\hat{\tau}) \geq \gamma - 2\mathcal{E}_T\gamma.$$

We now just consider the trial $\hat{\tau}$ retained by the algorithm. Let $\{(v_i, \lambda_i) : i \in [k]\}$ be the eigenvector/eigenvalue pairs of $T[\theta_{\hat{\tau}}]$, and let $\{(\hat{v}_i, \hat{\lambda}_i) : i \in [k]\}$ be the eigenvector/eigenvalue pairs of $\widehat{T}[\theta_{\hat{\tau}}]$.

LEMMA 15 (EIGENDECOMPOSITION). *Assume the $1-\delta$ probability event in Lemma 14 holds, and also assume that $\mathcal{E}_T \leq 1/4$. Then there exists a permutation π on $[k]$ and signs $s_1, s_2, \ldots, s_k \in \{\pm 1\}$ such that, for all $i \in [k]$,*

$$\|v_i - s_i \hat{v}_{\pi(i)}\|_2 \leq 4\sqrt{2}\mathcal{E}_T$$
$$|\lambda_i - \hat{\lambda}_{\pi(i)}| \leq \mathcal{E}_T\gamma.$$

C.8 Overall error analysis

Define

$$\kappa[M_2] := \varsigma_1[M_2]/\varsigma_k[M_2],$$
$$\epsilon_0 := \Big(5.5\mathcal{E}_{M_2} + 7\mathcal{E}_T\Big)/\sqrt{w_{\min}},$$
$$\epsilon_1 := \frac{1}{\gamma\sqrt{w_{\min}}}\Bigg(\frac{1.25\|M_2\|_2^{1/2}\epsilon_0/\sqrt{w_{\min}}}{\varsigma_k[M_2]^{1/2}} + 2\mathcal{E}_{M_2} + \gamma\sqrt{w_{\min}}\mathcal{E}_T\Bigg).$$

LEMMA 16 (ERROR BOUND). *Assume the $1-\delta$ probability event of Lemma 14 holds, and also assume that $\mathcal{E}_{M_2} \leq 1/3$, $\mathcal{E}_T \leq 1/4$, and $\epsilon_1 \leq 1/3$. Then there exists a permutation π on $[k]$ such that*

$$\|\hat{\mu}_{\pi(i)} - \mu_i\|_2 \leq 3\|\mu_i\|_2\epsilon_1 + 2\|M_2\|_2^{1/2}\epsilon_0, \quad i \in [k].$$

The proof of Theorem 3 now follows by combining the error bounds in Lemma 4, Lemma 5, Lemma 6, Lemma 7, Lemma 8, Lemma 10, Lemma 12, and Lemma 16 together with the probabilitistic analysis of Lemma 14.

Low-weight Halfspaces for Sparse Boolean Vectors

Philip M. Long
NEC Labs America
plong@nec-labs.com

Rocco A. Servedio
Columbia University
rocco@cs.columbia.edu

ABSTRACT

For $S \subseteq \{0,1\}^n$, a Boolean function $f : S \rightarrow \{-1,1\}$ is a *halfspace over* S if there exist $w \in \mathbb{R}^n$ and $\theta \in \mathbb{R}$ such that $f(x) = \text{sign}(w \cdot x - \theta)$ for all $x \in S$. We give bounds on the size of integer weights $w_1, \ldots, w_n \in \mathbb{Z}$ that are required to represent halfspaces over Hamming balls centered at 0^n, i.e. halfspaces over $S = \{0,1\}^n_{\leq k} \stackrel{\text{def}}{=} \{x \in \{0,1\}^n : x_1 + \cdots + x_n \leq k\}$. Such weight bounds for halfspaces over Hamming balls have immediate consequences for the performance of learning algorithms in the increasingly common scenario of learning from very high-dimensional categorical examples which are such that only a small number of features are active in each example.

We give upper and lower bounds on weight both for exact representation (when $\text{sign}(w \cdot x - \theta)$ must equal $f(x)$ for every $x \in S$) and for ε-approximate representation (when $\text{sign}(w \cdot x - \theta)$ may disagree with $f(x)$ for up to an ε fraction of points $x \in S$). Our results show that extremal bounds for exact representation are qualitatively rather similar whether the domain is all of $\{0,1\}^n$ or the Hamming ball $\{0,1\}^n_{\leq k}$, but extremal bounds for approximate representation are qualitatively very different between these two domains.

Categories and Subject Descriptors

F.1.3 [**Theory of Computation**]: Computation by Abstract Devices—*Complexity measures and classes*

General Terms

Theory

Keywords

Linear threshold functions, halfspaces, Boolean functions, Boolean hypercube

1. INTRODUCTION AND MOTIVATION

Many machine learning problems involve data with Boolean features. For example, news articles may be classified based on which words they contain, and analogous "bag of visual words" representations have become popular for image classification as well. In many such modern machine learning problems, the set of all possible features is extremely large but each example has only a small number of active features. For example, in a search engine scenario the set of all possible features might be the set of all words that appear in any query, while the active features in a given example might be the much smaller set of words appearing in that query. In such a setting, the space of all possible examples is contained in a Hamming ball centered at the origin $\{0,1\}^n_{\leq k}$ where $k \ll n$. It is intuitively clear that limiting the domain in this way may make learning easier; studying the complexity of learning over such domains can potentially lend insight useful for the design of practical algorithms for learning in such settings.

Let S be a subset of the Boolean hypercube $\{0,1\}^n$. We say that a Boolean function $f : S \rightarrow \{-1,1\}$ is a *halfspace over* S if there exist $w \in \mathbb{R}^n$ and $\theta \in \mathbb{R}$ such that $f(x) = \text{sign}(w \cdot x - \theta)$ for all $x \in S$. The pair (w, θ) is an *integer representation* of f if $w \in \mathbb{Z}^n$. The *weight* of an integer representation is $\max_{i=1,\ldots,n} |w_i|$. The weight of a halfspace f over S is the smallest weight of any integer representation which computes f correctly on all $x \in S$.

In this paper we give a detailed study of the weight of halfspaces, both exact and approximate, over *Hamming balls of radius* k, i.e. we study halfspaces over the domain

$$S = \{0,1\}^n_{\leq k} \stackrel{\text{def}}{=} \{x \in \{0,1\}^n : x_1 + \cdots + x_n \leq k\}.$$

The weight of an integer halfspace is closely related to the "margin" by which it classifies examples in S. Since halfspaces play a central role in machine learning, and the margin of a halfspace H is an important measure of the difficulty of learning H, we are naturally motivated to understand the weight of halfspaces over Hamming balls as an initial step toward understanding the impact of sparsity in feature vectors on learning complexity.

Many researchers have studied the weight of halfspaces over the entire Boolean cube (corresponding to taking $S = \{0,1\}^n$), see e.g. [10, 9, 12, 4, 13, 11, 14, 8, 6, 1, 16, 3]. Upper and lower bounds have been obtained both for exact representation as described above, and for a relaxed scenario in which the integer-weight halfspace $\text{sign}(w \cdot x - \theta)$ need only ε-approximate the function f (i.e. we allow $\Pr_{x \in S}[\text{sign}(w \cdot x - \theta) \neq f(x)]$ to be at most ε for some given approximation parameter $\varepsilon > 0$). We describe these previous results in detail in Section 1.1.

1.1 Previous Work and Our Results

In this section we review prior work on the weight of halfspaces (all of the previous work that we are aware of deals with halfspaces over the entire Boolean cube $\{0,1\}^n$), and state our results for halfspaces over the Hamming ball $\{0,1\}^n_{\leq k}$.

Prior work on exact representation of halfspaces over $\{0,1\}^n$. It has been known at least since the 1960s [10] that every halfspace over $\{0,1\}^n$ has weight at most $n^{O(n)}$ (this fact has been rediscovered several times, see e.g. [7, 12]). Since there are $2^{\Omega(n^2)}$ halfspaces over $\{0,1\}^n$ a counting argument shows that there exist halfspaces over $\{0,1\}^n$ that require weight $2^{\Omega(n)}$, and specific halfspaces that require weight $2^{\Omega(n)}$ have been known for decades [9, 5]. [6] exhibited a specific halfspace that has weight $n^{\Omega(n)}$ and his construction was subsequently refined by [1]. So the weight of exact representations of halfspaces over all of $\{0,1\}^n$ is by now quite well understood.

Our results on exact representation of halfspaces over $\{0,1\}^n_{\leq k}$. We give an essentially complete picture of the weight of halfspaces over Hamming balls $\{0,1\}^n_{\leq k}$ for all values of k. First, it is easy to see that for $k \in \{0,1\}$ every halfspace over $\{0,1\}^n_{\leq k}$ has an integer representation of weight 1. For $k = 2$, by analyzing a greedy construction we show (Theorem 2) that every halfspace over $\{0,1\}^n_{\leq 2}$ has weight $O(n)$, and we observe that a simple explicit halfspace has weight $\Theta(n)$.

Things get more interesting beyond $k = 2$. Using a linear programming argument, we show (Theorem 1) that for every $k \geq 3$, every halfspace over $\{0,1\}^n_{\leq k}$ has an integer representation of weight $(k+2)^{(n+1)/2}$, and we show that already for $k = 3$ there is a simple explicit halfspace for which any integer representation must have weight $2^{\Omega(n)}$. Our main lower bound result for exact representation (Theorem 4) is a general lower bound showing that for every $k \geq 3$, there is an explicit halfspace over $\{0,1\}^n_{\leq k}$ that requires integer weight $k^{\Omega(n)}$. This is established via a construction that carefully combines Håstad's halfspace [6] with a "decision list" type construction. Our lower bound shows that our upper bound on the weight of halfspaces over $\{0,1\}^n_{\leq k}$ is essentially the best possible.

Prior work on approximation over $\{0,1\}^n$. The lower bound of [6] immediately implies that there is an n-variable halfspace f over $\{0,1\}^n$ which is such that any halfspace $\text{sign}(w \cdot x - \theta)$ which satisfies $\Pr_{x \in \{0,1\}^n}[\text{sign}(w \cdot x) \neq f(x)] \leq \varepsilon$ must have weight $1/\varepsilon^{\Omega(\log\log(1/\varepsilon))}$. [16] showed that every n-variable halfspace over $\{0,1\}^n$ can be ε-approximated by a halfspace of weight $\sqrt{n} \cdot 2^{\tilde{O}(1/\varepsilon^2)}$, and showed an $\Omega(\sqrt{n})$ lower bound for constant ε. The upper bound was subsequently improved (as a function of ε) to weight $n^{3/2} \cdot 2^{\tilde{O}(1/\varepsilon^{2/3})}$ by [3], and very recently [2] have further improved the upper bound to $\sqrt{n} \cdot (1/\varepsilon)^{O(\log^2(1/\varepsilon))}$.

Our results on approximation over $\{0,1\}^n_{\leq k}$. We study the weight required to ε-approximate halfspaces over $\{0,1\}^n_{\leq k}$, i.e. given a halfspace f we now allow the integer-weight halfspace $\text{sign}(w \cdot x - \theta)$ to disagree with $f(x)$ on an ε fraction of all points in $\{0,1\}^n_{\leq k}$. (For the informal discussion here k should be viewed as "small" compared to n; precise bounds on k are given in the actual detailed theorem statements.) As our main positive result (Theorem 5), we show that for every halfspace f over $\{0,1\}^n_{\leq k}$ there is a halfspace that ε-approximates f and has integer weights each of which is at most $k^{O(k/\varepsilon)}$, independent of n. This proof combines linear programming arguments with upper bounds on the edge boundary of monotone Boolean-valued functions over the discrete domain $\{1,\ldots,t\}^k$.

As our main negative result (Theorem 7), we show that for any constant $k \geq 3$ there is a simple explicit halfspace f (the "decision list" halfspace, which we denote DL) which is such that any ε-approximator of f over $\{0,1\}^n_{\leq k}$ must have weight $k^{\Omega(1/\varepsilon^{1/(k-1)})}$. This shows that an inverse exponential dependence on $1/\varepsilon$ is necessary in any upper bound.

Finally, we give a detailed analysis of the specific "decision list" halfspace DL and show (Theorem 8) that for this particular function the general weight upper bound of Theorem 5 can be strengthened to $k^{O(k/\sqrt{\varepsilon})}$. This shows that strengthening the analysis of the DL function that is given in Theorem 7 will not be enough to improve that lower bound to match the general upper bound of Theorem 5.

Discussion. Our results show that (as long as $k \geq 3$) the extremal bounds on the weights required for exact representation of halfspaces are fairly similar whether the domain is $\{0,1\}^n_{\leq k}$ or $\{0,1\}^n$; in the former case the "right" weight bound is $k^{\Theta(n)}$, while in the latter case it is $n^{\Theta(n)}$. For ε-approximate representation, though, our results show that there are two interesting qualitative differences between the "right" weight bounds for the two domains. First, our $k^{O(k/\varepsilon)}$ upper bound (independent of n) for $\{0,1\}^n_{\leq k}$ stands in contrast with the $\Omega(\sqrt{n})$ lower bound of [16] for $\{0,1\}^n$; so for Hamming balls *no* dependence on n is necessary in the weights, whereas for the Boolean cube a polynomial dependence is required. Second, our $k^{\Omega(1/\varepsilon^{1/(k-1)})}$ lower bound shows that for any fixed constant k, some halfspaces over $\{0,1\}^n_{\leq k}$ require any ε-approximator to have weights that are *exponential* in $1/\varepsilon$. This is in sharp contrast with the recent [2] upper bound, which shows that over $\{0,1\}^n$ it is always possible to construct an ε-approximating halfspace with integer weights that are only quasipolynomial in $1/\varepsilon$.

Preliminaries. Note that under the correspondence $-1 \leftrightarrow 0$, $1 \leftrightarrow 1$ an integer-weight halfspace $\text{sign}(w \cdot x - \theta)$ over the hypercube $\{-1,1\}^n$ corresponds to an integer-weight halfspace $\text{sign}(2w \cdot x - (\theta + w_1 + \cdots + w_n))$ over the hypercube $\{0,1\}^n$. So we may work either over the Hamming ball $\{0,1\}^n_{\leq k} = \{x \in \{0,1\}^n : x_1 + \cdots + x_k \leq k\}$ of the 0/1 hypercube, or over the Hamming ball $\{-1,1\}^n_{\leq k} = \{x \in \{-1,1\}^n : x_1 + \cdots + x_k \leq -n + 2k\}$ of the $+1/-1$ hypercube; weight bounds obtained for one domain will carry over to the other one with at most a factor of 2 difference. Similarly we may also work over $\{-1,1\}^n_{\geq n-k} = \{x \in \{-1,1\}^n : x_1 + \cdots + x_k \geq n - 2k\}$; sometimes this will be the most convenient.

Some more useful observations: If $\text{sign}(w \cdot x - \theta)$ is a halfspace with integer coefficients over any subset $S \subseteq \{-1,1\}^n$ or $S \subseteq \{0,1\}^n$, then it is easy to see that w.l.o.g. we may modify the threshold θ to be of the form (integer $+\frac{1}{2}$). We also note that if $\text{sign}(w \cdot x - \theta)$ is an integer-weight halfspace with such a threshold that computes a function f

over $\{-1,1\}^n_{\leq k}$, then $\text{sign}(-w \cdot x + \theta)$ is a halfspace of the same weight computing $-f$ over $\{-1,1\}^n_{\leq k}$; so to bound the weight of f over $\{-1,1\}^n_{\leq k}$ it is enough to bound the weight of $-f$.

Finally, we establish some useful notation. We write $[n]$ to denote the set $\{1,\ldots,n\}$. For $i \in [n]$ we write e_i to denote the unit vector in $\mathbb{R}^n$ whose only nonzero entry is a 1 in the i-th coordinate. We let $DL(x)$ denote the "decision list" halfspace over $\{0,1\}^n$ that is defined as follows: $DL(x)$ equals $(-1)^i$, where i is the largest index such that $x_i = 1$. To see that $DL(x)$ is a halfspace, we observe that it can be represented as $DL(x) = \text{sign}(\sum_{i=1}^n (-2)^i x_i)$.

2. UPPER BOUNDS FOR EXACT REPRESENTATION

We start with a general upper bound. The proof (see Appendix A) is a straightforward modification of standard integer weight upper bound arguments for halfspaces over $\{0,1\}^n$ (see e.g. [10, 6]) adapted to the domain $\{0,1\}^n_{\leq k}$.

THEOREM 1. *For $3 \leq k \leq n$, every halfspace over $\{0,1\}^n_{\leq k}$ has weight at most $(k+2)^{(n+1)/2}$.*

We note that the proof given above actually holds for all $k \geq 1$ (not just $k \geq 3$ as in the theorem statement), but much stronger bounds are possible for $k = 1, 2$. For $k = 1$, it is easy to see that every halfspace over $\{0,1\}^n_{\leq 1}$ has an integer representation of weight 1. For $k = 2$ Theorem 1 only gives an upper bound that is exponential in n, but the true upper bound for $k = 2$ is actually linear in n:

THEOREM 2. *Every halfspace f over $\{0,1\}^n_{\leq 2}$ has weight $O(n)$.*

The proof of Theorem 2 is in Appendix B. Before giving the proof, here is some some high-level intuition. Since we are working over $\{0,1\}^n_{\leq 2}$, intuitively in order to set the weight v_j of variable x_j correctly the "only constraint that matters" is how many of the other $n-1$ variables x_i are such that $f(e_i + e_j) = 1$. The proof shows that a suitable greedy approach of setting the weights can satisfy all these constraints taking all the weights to be $O(n)$ in absolute value.

We note that for odd n the decision list halfspace $DL(x) = \text{sign}(\sum_{i=1}^n (-2)^i x_i)$ requires integer weight at least $(n-1)/2$ over $\{0,1\}^n_{\leq 2}$, and thus the $O(n)$ upper bound of Theorem 2 is tight up to a constant factor. To see this, suppose that $\text{sign}(v \cdot x - \theta)$ has integer weights and computes DL correctly over $\{0,1\}^n_{\leq 2}$. By considering inputs of the form e_i where i ranges from 1 to n we see that $v_i \geq \theta$ for i even and $v_i < \theta$ for i odd. By considering inputs of the form $e_i + e_{i+1}$ we see that $v_1 > v_3 > v_5 > \cdots > v_n$ and $v_2 < v_4 < v_6 < \cdots < v_{n-1}$, so there are n distinct integer weights and the largest magnitude weight must be at least $(n-1)/2$ as claimed.

3. LOWER BOUNDS FOR EXACT REPRESENTATION

In this section we give lower bounds on the weight required to exactly represent various halfspaces over $\{-1,1\}^n_{\leq k}$ for $k \geq 3$. We first note that simple counting arguments do not give very good lower bounds (see Appendix C for details).

An exponential lower bound for a simple function. We now observe that even for $k = 3$ a simple halfspace gives an exponential lower bound. In Appendix C we prove:

PROPOSITION 3. *The function $DL(x)$ has weight $2^{\Omega(n)}$ over $\{0,1\}^n_{\leq 3}$.*

Proposition 3 gives an exponential lower bound but in general it does not match the $k^{O(n)}$ upper bound provided by Theorem 1, since the DL function has weight 2^n over the whole boolean cube. As our main lower bound result for exact representation we match the upper bound of Theorem 1 (up to an absolute constant in the exponent) and prove the following:

THEOREM 4. *Let k be an integer of the form $k = 2^\ell$, and let $n = rk + 1$ for some integer r. There is a halfspace G (defined explicitly below) over $\{-1,1\}^n_{\geq n-2k-1}$ for which the weight of any integer representation over $\{-1,1\}^n_{\geq n-2k-1}$ is at least $2^{(n \log k)/2 - O(n)}$, i.e. $k^{\Omega(n)}$.*

We recall that in [6] Håstad gave an explicit halfspace over $\{-1,1\}^k$ and proved that its weight over $\{-1,1\}^k$ is $k^{\Theta(k)}$. Our construction builds on his construction; indeed our $n = (rk+1)$-variable halfspace may be viewed as r copies of Håstad's halfspace "concatenated" in a careful way (the exact meaning of this will be clearer when we describe our construction in detail below).

Setup. First some notational preliminaries: since $k = 2^\ell$ we may view a k-bit string as a function from $\{-1,1\}^\ell$ to $\{-1,1\}$, and for f a k-bit string and $j \in \{0,\ldots,k-1\}$ we write $f(j)$ to denote the j-th coordinate of such a string. For $f, g \in \{-1,1\}^k$ we write (f,g) to denote the inner product $\sum_{j=0}^{k-1} f(j)g(j)$. Note that for $f, g \in \{-1,1\}^k$ we have $|(f,g)| \leq k$.

Following the notation from [6], for $\alpha \subseteq [\ell] = \{1,\ldots,\ell\}$ let φ_α denote the parity function $\varphi_\alpha(x) = \prod_{i\in\alpha} x_i$ over the variables in α. Again following [6], let $\alpha_0,\ldots,\alpha_{k-1}$ be an ordering of subsets of $[\ell]$ such that $|\alpha_i| \leq |\alpha_{i+1}|$ and the symmetric difference $\alpha_i \Delta \alpha_{i+1}$ always satisfies $|\alpha_i \Delta \alpha_{i+1}| \leq 2$. Note that α_0 is the empty set and thus φ_{α_0} is the k-bit string consisting of all 1's, while for each $j = 1,\ldots,k-1$ we have that φ_{α_j} is a k-bit string with exactly half of its entries -1.

Writing $f : \{-1,1\}^\ell \to \{-1,1\}$ in terms of its Fourier representation as $f(j) = \sum_{i=0}^{k-1} \hat{f}(\alpha_i)\varphi_{\alpha_i}(j)$ we see that

$$(f, \varphi_{\alpha_i}) = k\hat{f}(\alpha_i),$$

so we may view each inner product (f, φ_{α_i}) as a scaled Fourier coefficient of f.

For $f \in \{-1,1\}^n$ we decompose f by writing it as

$$(b, f^1, \ldots, f^r)$$

where $b \in \{-1,1\}$ and each f^i is a k-bit string. We sometimes refer to f^i as the "i-th block" of f and we write $f^i(j)$ to denote the j-th coordinate of the i-th block of f.

The construction. Let $G : \{-1,1\}^n_{\geq n-2k-1} \to \{-1,1\}$ denote the n-variable function

$$G(b, f^1, \ldots, f^r) \stackrel{\text{def}}{=} \text{sign}\left(b + \sum_{i=1}^{r}\sum_{j=1}^{k-1}(k+1)^{k(i-1)+j}(f^i, \varphi_{\alpha_j})\right).$$

(Note that the inner sum starts with $j = 1$ and not 0; this will be important later.) Since each $(f^i, \varphi_{\alpha_j})$ is a (± 1)-weighted sum of the coordinates of f^i, it is clear that G

is a halfspace with weight at most $k^{O(n)}$. We will show that any integer-weight halfspace for G over $\{-1,1\}^n_{\leq n-2k-1}$ must have some weight that is at least $k^{\Omega(n)}$.

To get some more intuition for the function G, note that for a block f^i we have that $(f^i, \varphi_{\alpha_1}) = \cdots = (f^i, \varphi_{\alpha_{k-1}}) = 0$ if and only if f^i is one of the two inputs $(1, \ldots, 1)$ or $(-1, \ldots, -1)$ (this is because the constant $+1$ function and the constant -1 function are the only two Boolean functions that have all nonconstant Fourier coefficients equal to zero). So in words, given an input $f = (b, f^1, \ldots, f^r)$ the value $G(f)$ is obtained as follows: If any block is neither constantly $+1$ nor constantly -1, let i be the largest such block, and output the sign of the Fourier coefficient $\widehat{f^i}(\alpha_j)$ where j is the largest index such that $\widehat{f^i}(\alpha_j)$ is nonzero. Otherwise output the bit b.

The high-level intuition behind the lower bound is as follows. Consider a single block i and fix all other bits in other blocks $i' \neq i$ to be 1. By fixing the bit b appropriately, the function G computes exactly Håstad's halfspace over the k variables in block i. (We recall that Håstad's k-variable halfspace F over a k-bit input string $f \in \{-1,1\}^k$ is $F(f) = \text{sign}((f, \varphi_{\alpha_j}))$ where j is the largest index such that $(f, \varphi_{\alpha_j}) \neq 0$; equivalently,

$$F(f) = \text{sign}\left(\sum_{i=0}^{k-1} (k+1)^i (f, \varphi_{\alpha_i})\right)$$

gives an explicit representation of the halfspace F.) So applying Håstad's weight lower bound for his halfspace F, intuitively the variables in block i should require integer weights growing as $k^{\Omega(k)}$. Since higher blocks dominate lower blocks in G and there are $r = (n-1)/k$ blocks, intuitively a $k^{\Omega(k)}$ growth factor within each of $(n-1)/k$ blocks means that overall the weights should grow as $(k^{\Omega(k)})^{(n-1)/k} = k^{\Omega(n)}$.

Unfortunately, this simple reasoning is not quite right when applied to the actual weights w^i_j of the input variables $f^i(j)$. This is because in Håstad's halfspace all integer coefficients must be large but they do not actually increase by much; in fact, the integer coefficients of all k variables in Håstad's function can be taken to be within a factor of 2 of each other. But as we shall see the reasoning of the previous paragraph is essentially correct when a different representation is used, namely when it is applied to the "Fourier transformed" weights v^i_j that are the coefficients of $(f^i, \varphi_{\alpha_j})$ (see Equation (10) below), and this suffices to give the desired overall weight bound. We will show that the v^i_j's must grow very rapidly, and hence some v^i_j must be large, and consequently some w^i_j must be large.

The analysis. See Appendix D for the actual analysis and proof of Theorem 4.

4. PRELIMINARIES ON APPROXIMATING HALFSPACES OVER HAMMING BALLS

Let f be a halfspace over a domain S. We say that f has an *ε-approximator of weight W over S* if there is an integer vector $(v_1, \ldots, v_n) \in \mathbb{Z}^n$ with $\max_i |v_i| \leq W$ and a threshold $\theta \in \mathbb{R}$ such that

$$\Pr_{x \in S}[\text{sign}(v \cdot x - \theta) \neq f(x)] \leq \varepsilon,$$

where the probability is with respect to a uniform choice of x from S. In the rest of this paper we prove upper and lower bounds on the weight of ε-approximators over the Hamming ball $\{0,1\}^n_{\leq k}$, where k is viewed as "small" compared to n.

Related work. In [3] it was shown that for any fixed $p \in (0,1)$ and any halfspace f over $\{0,1\}^n$, there is an ε-approximating halfspace $\text{sign}(w \cdot x - \theta)$ of weight $n \cdot 2^{\tilde{O}_p(1/\varepsilon^2)}$ for f with respect to the product distribution $\mathcal{D}_p$, i.e.

$$\Pr_{x \sim \mathcal{D}_p}[\text{sign}(w \cdot x - \theta) \neq f(x)] \leq \varepsilon.$$

Here the distribution $\mathcal{D}_p$ is the product distribution over $\{0,1\}^n$ such that each coordinate x_i of a draw from $\mathcal{D}_p$ is independently set to be 1 with probability p. The "$\tilde{O}_p$" in the exponent of the weight bound hides a dependence on p.

For constant $p \in (0, 1/2)$ the distribution $\mathcal{D}_p$ is somewhat similar to the uniform distribution on $\{0,1\}^n_{\leq pn}$ since both distributions are spread much of their weight equally over strings of weight pn. In contrast, we give upper and lower bounds that depend only on k and ε, independent of n, but our bounds require that k be "small" relative to n. Thus the main difference seems to be that the [3] results may be viewed as addressing the case where k is "large" (linear in n) while our results may be viewed as addressing the case where k is "small."

In proving our upper and lower bounds it will often be simpler for us to work with "nice" distributions which are close to the uniform distribution over $\{0,1\}^n_{\leq k}$. In Appendix E we prove some simple observations which we will use in the following sections:

Observation 1. *Let $\mathcal{D}$ denote the uniform distribution over $\{0,1\}^n_{\leq k}$ and let $\mathcal{D}_1$ denote the uniform distribution over $\{0,1\}^n_{=k}$, the set of all strings with exactly k ones. The total variation distance $\|\mathcal{D} - \mathcal{D}_1\|_1$ between $\mathcal{D}$ and $\mathcal{D}_1$ is at most $4k/n$.*

Moreover, let $\mathcal{D}_2$ denote the distribution over $[k]^n$ defined as follows: a draw of $x \sim \mathcal{D}_2$ is obtained by taking x to be $e_{i_1} + e_{i_2} + \cdots + e_{i_k}$ where each of $i_1, \ldots, i_k$ is drawn independently and uniformly from $[n]$. Then the total variation distance $\|\mathcal{D} - \mathcal{D}_2\|_1$ is at most $(k^2 + 4k)/n$.

We close this section with the following notation which will be useful later. Let $Z_{n,k}$ denote the set

$$Z_{n,k} = \{x = (x_1, \ldots, x_n) \in \mathbb{Z}^n : x_i \geq 0 \text{ for all } i \text{ and } x_1 + \cdots + x_n = k\}.$$

Let $\Phi : [n]^k \to Z_{n,k}$ denote the mapping $\Phi(a) = \sum_{i=1}^k e_{a_i}$. Thus a draw of $x \sim \mathcal{D}_2$ is obtained by drawing a uniformly from $[n]^k$ and setting $x = \Phi(a)$.

5. UPPER BOUND FOR APPROXIMATING HALFSPACES

In this section we prove our main positive result on approximating halfspaces over $\{0,1\}^n_{\leq k}$ using small weights, which is the following:

Theorem 5. *Let f be any halfspace over $\{0,1\}^n_{\leq k}$. Let ε, k satisfy $\frac{k^2}{n} \leq c\varepsilon$ where $c > 0$ is a (small) universal constant. Then there is an ε-approximator for f over $\{0,1\}^n_{\leq k}$ that has weight $k^{O(k/\varepsilon)}$.*

As noted in the introduction, it is easy to see that there are halfspaces over the entire Boolean cube $\{0,1\}^n$ that require weight $\Omega(\sqrt{n})$ for ε-approximation even when ε is (say)

1/5; an example of such a halfspace is $\text{sign}(x_1 + x_2 + \cdots + x_{n-1} + nx_n)$ (see [16] for the proof). In contrast, Theorem 5 shows that over Hamming balls of any constant radius, every halfspace can be approximated to any constant accuracy using weights that are independent of n.

Here is some intuition before the formal proof. The proof works by showing that every halfspace can be approximated to within $\varepsilon/2$ with respect to the distribution $\mathcal{D}_2$ (this is sufficient to establish the theorem by Observation 1). To $\varepsilon/2$-approximate an arbitrary halfspace f with respect to $\mathcal{D}_2$, the argument proceeds as follows. After sorting the weights, we first define a collection of $t = O(k/\varepsilon)$ "key coordinates" in $\{1,\ldots,n\}$ (these are just t coordinates which are evenly spaced out in $\{1,\ldots,n\}$). Then we define a set $S \subset Z_{n,k}$ of "key inputs," which are the elements of $Z_{n,k}$ that have nonzero entries only in the key coordinates. Using a linear programming argument, we show that there is a halfspace h' that depends only on the t key coordinates, has weight $k^{O(t)}$, and agrees with f on all key inputs. An additional crucial property of h' is that its weights are sorted in the same order as the weights of f. We then define an n-variable halfspace h by basing the weights of the other $n-t$ non-key coordinates in a natural way on the weights that h assigns to the key coordinates. We use the sortedness of the weights of h' to characterize the error points of h. Finally, we upper bound the error of h by using this characterization together with a simple upper bound on the edge-boundary of monotone Boolean-valued functions over the domain $[t]^k$.

Proof of Theorem 5. We first note that if $k \in \{0,1\}$ then there is a weight-1 exact representation of f, so we henceforth assume that $k \geq 2$.

Let $w_1,\ldots,w_n,\theta'$ be a weight representation of f over $\{0,1\}^n_{\leq k}$, so $f(x) = \text{sign}(w \cdot x - \theta')$ for all $x \in \{0,1\}^n_{\leq k}$. We may assume that each w_i is an integer and that θ' is of the form (integer $+1/2$). Additionally, we may assume that the weights are sorted $w_1 \leq \cdots \leq w_n$, since if this is not the case we can rename variables to make this condition hold. We use the representation w, θ' to extend the domain of f to all of $\mathbb{R}^n$, i.e. we define $f(x) = \text{sign}(w \cdot x - \theta')$ for all $x \in \mathbb{R}^n$.

Key coordinates and key inputs. Let $t = O(k/\varepsilon)$. Note that if $t \geq n$ then by Theorem 1 in fact there is an exact representation for f over $\{0,1\}^n_{\leq k}$ that has weight $k^{O(k/\varepsilon)}$; thus we may assume that $t < n$. In fact, by the assumptions on ε, k and n in the statement of the theorem we may assume that $k \leq n/t$; this will be useful later.

We define the set $KC \subset [n], |KC| = t$ of "key coordinates" to be a fixed set

$$KC = \{\text{key}_1 = 1, \text{key}_2, \ldots, \text{key}_t = n\}$$

of values in $[n]$ that are equally spaced as much as possible, i.e. for all $j, j' \in [t-1]$ we have $\text{key}_{j+1} - \text{key}_j = \text{key}_{j'+1} - \text{key}_{j'} \pm 1$.

We next define the set $KI \subset Z_{n,k}$ of "key inputs" as

$$KI = \{x \in Z_{n,k} : \text{ for all } i, \text{ if } x_i > 0 \text{ then } i \in KC\},$$

so $x \in Z_{n,k}$ is a key input if and only if all of its nonzero coordinates are key coordinates.

A low-weight halfspace h that agrees with f on all key inputs. Our next step is to establish the existence of a low-weight halfspace that depends only on the key coordinates and agrees with f on all key inputs. This is done via a linear programming argument quite similar to the proof of Theorem 1.

LEMMA 6. *There is a halfspace $h'(x) = \text{sign}(v' \cdot x - \theta)$ with the following properties: (1) For each $i \notin KC$ we have $v'_i = 0$ (so h depends only on the key coordinates); (2) For each $i \in KC$ we have that v'_i is an integer satisfying $|v'_i| \leq k^{O(t)}$; (3) For each $j \in [t-1]$ we have $v'_{\text{key}_j} \leq v'_{\text{key}_{j+1}}$; and (4) $h'(x) = f(x)$ for every key input $x \in KI$.*

PROOF. We obtained the desired integer weights $(v'_i)_{i \in KC}$ and the threshold θ as the solution to a linear program, which we now describe. Each key input $x \in KI$ defines a linear constraint $f(x) \cdot \left(\sum_{i \in KC} v'_i x_i - \theta\right) \geq 1$ over the $t+1$ variables $(v'_i)_{i \in KC}, \theta$. The linear program additionally contains $t-1$ constraints of the form $v'_{\text{key}_j} \leq v'_{\text{key}_{j+1}}$ for all $j \in [t-1]$. This is a feasible linear program, since taking $v'_i = 2w_i$ for all $i \in KC$, $v'_i = 0$ for all $i \notin KC$, and $\theta = 2\theta'$ is a feasible solution. (To see that this works, observe that for any $x \in KI$ the total value of $w \cdot x$ is entirely contributed by coordinates in KC.) It is clear that any feasible solution satisfies items (1), (3) and (4) of the Lemma, so it remains only to show that there is a feasible solution satisfying the weight bound (2). This follows from the same arguments used in the proof of Theorem 1 with trivial modifications (the fact that there are now $t+1$ unknowns in the linear program leads to the claimed bound of $k^{O(t)}$ rather than $k^{O(n)}$ as was the case in Theorem 1). □

Filling in the other weights. We now define the halfspace h that has weights for all coordinates (not just the key coordinates). The halfspace h is defined as $h(x) = \text{sign}(v \cdot x - \theta)$ in a very natural way as follows: for each key coordinate $i \in KC$ we take $v_i = v'_i$. For each non-key coordinate $i \notin KC$, let j be such that $\text{key}_{j-1} < i < \text{key}_j$, i.e. key_j is the first key coordinate immediately after i; we take $v_i = v'_{\text{key}_j}$. For example, if $v' = (1/4, 0, 0, 1/3, 0, 1/2)$ then $v = (1/4, 1/3, 1/3, 1/3, 1/2, 1/2)$. Note that the weights v_i satisfy $v_1 \leq v_2 \leq \cdots \leq v_n$; this will be useful later.

We will show that this halfspace $h(x)$ is the ε-approximator for f claimed in the theorem statement. It is clear that the weight of h is at most $k^{O(t)} = k^{O(k/\varepsilon)}$ as desired; it remains to show that $\Pr_{x \sim \mathcal{D}_2}[h(x) \neq f(x)] \leq \varepsilon/2$, or equivalently, that at most an $\varepsilon/2$ fraction of points $a \in [n]^k$ have $h(\Phi(a)) \neq f(\Phi(a))$.

Bounding $\Pr_{a \in [n]^k}[h(\Phi(a)) \neq f(\Phi(a))]$. We define a function $\text{up} : [n-1] \to KC$ as follows: $\text{up}(i) = \text{key}_j$ where key_j is the smallest element of KC satisfying $i < \text{key}_j$. Similarly we define $\text{down} : [n-1] \to KC$ as $\text{down}(i) = \text{key}_j$ where key_j is the largest element of KC satisfying $\text{key}_j \leq i$. Each $i \in [n-1]$ has $\text{up}(i) = \text{down}(i) + 1$.

For any $a \in [n-1]^k$ we define the "upper key neighbor" of a and "downward key neighbor" of a as

$$\text{ukn}(a) = (\text{up}(a_1), \ldots, \text{up}(a_k)) \in (KC)^k,$$
$$\text{dkn}(a) = (\text{down}(a_1), \ldots, \text{down}(a_k)) \in (KC)^k$$

respectively. It is easy to see that for each $a \in [n-1]^k$, both $\Phi(\text{ukn}(a))$ and $\Phi(\text{dkn}(a))$ are key inputs. Thus Lemma 6 ensures that $\text{sign}(v \cdot \Phi(\text{ukn}(a)) - \theta) = \text{sign}(w \cdot \Phi(\text{ukn}(a)) - \theta')$ for all $a \in [n-1]^k$, and likewise for $\Phi(\text{dkn}(a))$.

We next observe that by the monotonicity of the weights $v_1, \ldots, v_n$, we have that every $a \in [n-1]^k$ satisfies

$$v \cdot \Phi(\text{dkn}(a)) \leq v \cdot \Phi(a) \leq v \cdot \Phi(\text{ukn}(a)).$$

Consequently if $a \in [n-1]^k$ is such that $\text{sign}(v \cdot \Phi(\text{dkn}(a)) - \theta) = \text{sign}(v \cdot \Phi(\text{ukn}(a)) - \theta)$, then $\text{sign}(v \cdot \Phi(a) - \theta)$ must equal the same value, and hence for such an a we have

$$\begin{aligned} &\text{sign}(w \cdot \Phi(\text{dkn}(a)) - \theta') \\ &= \text{sign}(v \cdot \Phi(\text{dkn}(a)) - \theta) = \text{sign}(v \cdot \Phi(a) - \theta) \\ &= \text{sign}(v \cdot \Phi(\text{ukn}(a)) - \theta) = \text{sign}(w \cdot \Phi(\text{ukn}(a)) - \theta') \quad (1) \end{aligned}$$

By monotonicity of the weights $w_1, \ldots, w_n$ we have that $w \cdot \Phi(\text{dkn}(a)) \le w \cdot \Phi(a) \le w \cdot \Phi(\text{ukn}(a))$, so, if (1) holds, all the quantities in (1) above are also equal to $\text{sign}(w \cdot \Phi(a) - \theta')$. Thus we have shown that if $a \in [n-1]^k$ is such that $\text{sign}(v \cdot \Phi(\text{dkn}(a)) - \theta) = \text{sign}(v \cdot \Phi(\text{ukn}(a)) - \theta)$, then $\text{sign}(v \cdot \Phi(a) - \theta) = \text{sign}(w \cdot \Phi(a) - \theta')$, i.e. $h(\Phi(a)) = f(\Phi(a))$. We observe that at most a k/n fraction of all inputs $a \in [n]^k$ have $a_i = n$ for any i; by the conditions on k, ε and n in the statement of the theorem, k/n may be assumed to be at most $\varepsilon/4$. So to finish the proof of the theorem, it suffices to show the following, which we refer to as statement (*):

(*): At most an $\varepsilon/4$ fraction of all points $a \in [n-1]^k$ have $\text{sign}(v \cdot \Phi(\text{dkn}(a)) - \theta) = -1$ and $\text{sign}(v \cdot \Phi(\text{ukn}(a)) - \theta) = 1$.

We first note that for any two elements $i, j \in [t-1]$ we have $|\text{down}^{-1}(\text{key}_i)|, |\text{down}^{-1}(\text{key}_j)| \in \{\lfloor n/t \rfloor, \lfloor n/t \rfloor + 1\}$ and we recall from the bounds on t stated at the beginning of the proof that consequently $|\text{down}^{-1}(i)|, |\text{down}^{-1}(j)| \ge k$. As a result, for any two vectors $(i_1, \ldots, i_k) \in [t-1]^k$ and $(j_1, \ldots, j_k) \in [t-1]^k$, we have that the two sets

$$\{a \in [n-1]^k : \text{down}(a_\ell) = i_\ell \text{ for all } \ell = 1, \ldots, k\} \quad \text{and}$$
$$\{b \in [n-1]^k : \text{down}(b_\ell) = j_\ell \text{ for all } \ell = 1, \ldots, k\}$$

have sizes that differ by at most a multiplicative factor of $(1 + \frac{1}{k})^k < 3$. Hence to establish (*) it suffices to show that at most a $\varepsilon/12$ fraction of all vectors $(i_1, \ldots, i_k) \in [t-1]^k$ have

$$\text{sign}(v \cdot \Phi(\text{key}_{i_1}, \ldots, \text{key}_{i_k}) - \theta) = -1$$
$$\text{and } \text{sign}(v \cdot \Phi(\text{key}_{i_1+1}, \ldots, \text{key}_{i_k+1}) - \theta) = 1.$$

We define a Boolean-valued function $F : [t-1]^k \to \{-1, 1\}$ as follows:

$$F(i_1, \ldots, i_k) = \text{sign}\left(v \cdot \Phi(\text{key}_{i_1}, \ldots, \text{key}_{i_k}) - \theta\right).$$

The monotonicity of the weights $v_{\text{key}_1}, \ldots, v_{\text{key}_{t-1}}$ implies that F is a monotone non-decreasing function over $[t-1]^k$: if $r, s \in [t-1]^k$ satisfy $r_i \le s_i$ for all $i \in [k]$ then it cannot be the case that $F(r) = 1$ and $F(s) = -1$. Now we upper bound the desired probability using a union bound:

$$\begin{aligned} &\Pr_{(i_1,\ldots,i_k)\in[t-1]^k}[F(i_1, \ldots, i_k) \ne F(i_1+1, \ldots, i_k+1)] \le \\ &\quad \Pr_{(i_1,\ldots,i_k)\in[t-1]^k}[F(i_1, \ldots, i_k) \ne F(i_1+1, i_2, \ldots, i_k)] + \\ &\quad \Pr_{(i_1,\ldots,i_k)\in[t-1]^k}[F(i_1+1, i_2, \ldots, i_k) \\ &\qquad\qquad \ne F(i_1+1, i_2+1, i_3, \ldots, i_k)] \\ &\qquad\qquad + \cdots + \\ &\quad \Pr_{(i_1,\ldots,i_k)\in[t-1]^k}[F(i_1+1, \ldots, i_{k-1}+1, i_k) \\ &\qquad\qquad \ne F(i_1+1, \ldots, i_k+1)]. \end{aligned}$$

By the monotonicity of F, each of the k probabilities on the RHS is at most $1/(t-1)$ (since fixing all the values of the other $k-1$ coordinates, there can be at most one setting of the remaining free coordinate which causes the value of F to change). For a suitable choice of the hidden constant in $t = O(k/\varepsilon)$, we have that $1/(t-1) \le \varepsilon/(12k)$. Thus the RHS above is at most $\varepsilon/12$ as desired. This concludes the proof of Theorem 5. □

6. LOWER BOUNDS FOR APPROXIMATING HALFSPACES

Recall that the n-variable halfspace DL is defined as

$$DL(x) = \text{sign}(\sum_{i=1}^{n} (-2)^i x_i).$$

Our main result in this section is a lower bound on the weight of any ε-approximator for DL:

THEOREM 7. *Let $k \ge 3$ and $\varepsilon \ge 4k/n$. Then any ε-approximator for DL over $\{0,1\}^n_{\le k}$ must have weight at least* $k^{\Theta(1)/\varepsilon^{1/(k-1)}-1}$.

Discussion. It is easy to see that for all ε, the function DL has an ε-approximator over $\{0,1\}^n$ of weight $O(1/\varepsilon)$. So Theorem 7 shows that for a specific natural function, taking k to be constant and letting ε vary, getting an ε-approximator over the Hamming ball $\{0,1\}^n_{\le k}$ (for k constant) requires weights that are *exponentially* larger than the weights required for ε-approximation over the entire Boolean cube. Theorem 7 is also in sharp contrast with the recent upper bound of [2] which shows that there is always an ε-approximator over the entire Boolean cube which has weight at most quasipoly$(1/\varepsilon)$ (as a function of ε).

6.1 Proof Sketch of Theorem 7

Since the proof of Theorem 7 is somewhat involved we give an outline here; please see Appendix F for a detailed proof. At a very high level, the idea is that in order for an LTF $\text{sign}(v \cdot x - \theta)$ to be a good approximator for DL, it should be the case that (roughly speaking) $v_i > 0$ for even i, $v_i < 0$ for odd i, and the magnitudes of the weights $|v_i|$ increase sharply with i; the essence of the proof is to show that if any of these conditions are "badly violated" then $\text{sign}(v \cdot x - \theta)$ must disagree with DL on many inputs.

In more detail, let $\text{sign}(v \cdot x - \theta)$ be an arbitrary integer weight halfspace which is a 2ε-approximator for DL with respect to $\mathcal{D}_1$ (by Observation 1 it suffices to consider such approximators). We first show (Claim 17) that without loss of generality we may assume that the threshold θ is 0 and the weights v_i are positive for even i and negative for odd i. This is not too difficult; the bulk of our work is to show that overall the magnitudes of the weights must increase significantly from smallest to largest, and thus the largest magnitude weight must be very large (since the smallest magnitude weight has magnitude at least 1). To do this, we consider the weights in order of increasing magnitude and consider disjoint "blocks" of the smallest-magnitude weights, the next-smallest-magnitude weights, and so on. We show (Lemma 18) that either there are large weights, or else almost all of the blocks are "pure," meaning that they either consist almost entirely of positive (even-index) weights, or consist almost entirely of negative (odd-index) weights. Finally, the argument concludes by showing that if almost all of the blocks are "pure" as described above, then in fact the halfspace must err on a significant fraction of all inputs.

7. AN UPPER BOUND FOR APPROXIMATING DECISION LISTS

At this point we have established that every halfspace over $\{0,1\}^n_{\le k}$ can be ε-approximated using weight $k^{O(k/\varepsilon)}$, and that for the DL halfspace any ε-approximator must use weight $k^{\Theta(1)/\varepsilon^{1/(k-1)}-1}$. It is a natural goal to close the gap between these upper and lower bounds; while we have not yet succeeded in doing this, in Appendix G we give a detailed analysis of the DL halfspace and prove a stronger $k^{O(k/\sqrt{\varepsilon})}$ upper bound for it. This tells us that if the $k^{O(k/\varepsilon)}$ upper bound of Theorem 5 is in fact the "right answer," then any lower bound proof establishing this must use a halfspace other than DL.

THEOREM 8. *Let ε, k, n satisfy $\varepsilon = \omega(k^2/n)$. Then there is an ε-approximator for the function DL over $\{0,1\}^n_{\le k}$ that has weight $k^{O(k/\sqrt{\varepsilon})}$.*

8. CONCLUSION

We have studied exact and approximate representations of halfspaces over the Hamming ball $\{0,1\}^n_{\le k}$, giving upper and lower bounds on the weight of such representations. While our upper and lower bounds are fairly close, there are still several open questions that naturally suggest themselves for followup work. In particular, our Theorem 5 gives a weight upper bound of $k^{O(k/\varepsilon)}$ which is independent of n but depends super-exponentially on k; we suspect that it may be possible to improve this dependence on k. Even for fixed k there is a gap between our upper bound, which is exponential in ε^{-1}, and our lower bound, which is exponential in $\varepsilon^{-1/(k-1)}$. It would be interesting to close this gap.

Finally, a broader goal for future work is to explore the implications of our newly established weight bounds on the effectiveness of various margin-based learning algorithms over $\{0,1\}^n_{\le k}$.

APPENDIX

A. PROOF OF THEOREM 1

Fix f to be any halfspace over $\{0,1\}^n_{\le k}$. Each point x in $\{0,1\}^n_{\le k}$ with $f(x) = y \in \{-1,1\}$ provides a linear constraint

$$y(w_1x_1 + \cdots + w_nx_n + w_{n+1}) \ge 1$$

over the weights $w_1, \ldots, w_{n+1}$ which define the halfspace $f(x) = \text{sign}(w_1x_1 + \cdots + w_nx_n + w_{n+1})$. Since f is a halfspace the above system of $\sum_{j=0}^{k}\binom{n}{j}$ linear inequalities over variables $w_1, \ldots, w_{n+1}$ is feasible. A standard result in the theory of linear programming (see e.g. [10, 6]) implies that there is a subset of $n+1$ of the above inequalities which is such that if each inequality is replaced with equality, the resulting set of $n+1$ equalities defines a unique weight vector $(w_1, \ldots, w_{n+1}) \in \mathbb{R}^{n+1}$ which is a feasible solution to the entire set of $\sum_{j=0}^{k}\binom{n}{j}$ inequalities. In other words, there is a representation $\text{sign}(w \cdot x + w_{n+1})$ computing f where $(w_1, \ldots, w_{n+1}) \in \mathbb{R}^{n+1}$ is the solution to a linear system

$$Aw = b$$

where $b \in \{-1,1\}^{n+1}$ and A is an $(n+1)\times(n+1)$ 0/1 matrix in which the first n entries of each row have at most k ones and the last entry is 1. Let $\frac{\det(A_i)}{\det(A)}$ be the expression for a solution w_i using Cramer's rule. Since scaling the components of w by the same constant factor does not affect the behavior of f, setting each $w_i = \det(A_i)$ also works. Fix an arbitrary i, let $B = A_i$, and let $B_1, \ldots, B_{n+1}$ be the columns of B. Hadamard's inequality gives $\det(B) \le \prod_{j=1}^{n+1} \|B_j\|$, where $\|B_j\|$ denotes the 2-norm of the B_j viewed as a vector in $\mathbb{R}^{n+1}$. Let ℓ_j be the number of nonzero components in B_j; since these components are all ± 1, we have $\|B_j\| = \sqrt{\ell_j}$, so that $\det(B) \le \prod_{j=1}^{n+1}\sqrt{\ell_j}$. Each row of B has at most $k+2$ nonzero components, so $\sum_{j=1}^{n+1}\ell_j \le (k+2)(n+1)$. Since $\prod_{j=1}^{n+1}\sqrt{\ell_j}$ is maximized subject to $\sum_{j=1}^{n+1}\ell_j \le (k+2)(n+1)$ when $\ell_j = k+2$ for all j, we have $w_i = \det(B) \le (k+2)^{(n+1)/2}$. So f can be realized using integer weights of at most this magnitude.

B. PROOF OF THEOREM 2

Since f is a halfspace over $\{0,1\}^n_{\le 2}$, it has some representation as $f(x) = \text{sign}(w \cdot x - \theta)$ where $w_1, \ldots, w_n, \theta$ are real numbers. We will use this representation to construct an integer-weight representation $\text{sign}(v \cdot x - \theta')$ that agrees with f on all points in $\{0,1\}^n_{\le 2}$ and where each $|v_i| \le O(n)$.

By negating f if necessary (which does not change the integer weight required for a representation) we may assume that $f(0^n) = -1$. This means that $\text{sign}(-\theta) = -1$ and thus we have $\theta > 0$.

We may suppose without loss of generality that $w_1 < \cdots < w_n$ and all n weights $w_1, \ldots, w_n$ are nonzero (since if the weights do not satisfy these conditions they can be reordered and perturbed to satisfy them). We note that if $w_n < 0$ then every input $x \in \{0,1\}^n_{\le 2}$ (and indeed every input in $\{0,1\}^n$) has $w \cdot x \le 0 < \theta$; in this case f is the constant-(-1) function and f trivially has a representation of weight 0. Thus we assume going forth that $w_n > 0$.

Let $\ell \in \{1, \ldots, n\}$ be such that $w_{\ell-1} < 0 < w_\ell$ (so $\ell = 1$ if $w_1 > 0$). Now,

- Let $w' \in \mathbb{R}^{n+1}$ be $(w_1, \ldots, w_{\ell-1}, 0, w_\ell, \ldots, w_n)$.
- For each $x \in \{0,1\}^n_{=2}$, let
$$x' \in \{0,1\}^{n+1}_{=2} = (x_1, \ldots, x_{\ell-1}, 0, x_\ell, \ldots, x_n).$$
- For each $x \in \{0,1\}^n_{=1}$, let
$$x' \in \{0,1\}^{n+1}_{=2} = (x_1, \ldots, x_{\ell-1}, 1, x_\ell, \ldots, x_n).$$
- When $x = 0^n$, let $x' \in \{0,1\}^{n+1}$ be $(0, \ldots, 0)$.

Note that, for all $x \in \{0,1\}^n_{\le 2}$, $\text{sign}(w' \cdot x' - \theta) = \text{sign}(w \cdot x - \theta)$, and, for all x except 0^n, x' has exactly two ones. Furthermore, if we have a weight vector $v \in \mathbb{R}^{n+1}$ such that $v_\ell = 0$, if we define $\hat{v} \in \mathbb{R}^n$ by $\hat{v} = (v_1, \ldots, v_{\ell-1}, v_{\ell+1}, v_{n+1})$, then, for all $x \in \{0,1\}^n_{\le 2}$ and all real θ, we have $\text{sign}(v \cdot x' - \theta) = \text{sign}(\hat{v} \cdot x - \theta)$. So, our problem reduces to the problem of finding a vector $v \in \mathbb{R}^{n+1}$ with small integer weights for which $v_\ell = 0$ and there is a θ' such that

$$\text{sign}(v \cdot x - \theta') = \text{sign}(w' \cdot x - \theta)$$

for all $x \in \{0^{n+1}\} \cup \{0,1\}^{n+1}_{=2}$.

Now let us define an $(n+1) \times (n+1)$ matrix

$$(M(i,j))_{i,j \in \{1,\ldots,n+1\}}$$

with entries in $\{-1,1\}$ as follows. The matrix M will be symmetric, i.e. $M(i,j) = M(j,i)$. It will also be monotone increasing within each row and column, i.e. for each value i, the string $M(i,1)\ldots M(i,n+1)$ will be of the form $(-1)^r(1)^{n+1-r}$ for some $r \in \{0,\ldots,n+1\}$. Here is how M is defined:

- For $\{i,j\} \subset \{1,\ldots,n+1\}$ we have $M(i,j) = 1$ if and only if $\text{sign}(w' \cdot (e_i + e_j)) = 1$.
- Define $M(\ell,\ell) = -1$ (recall that $f(0^n) = -1$), and define the other diagonal values, $M(i,i)$ for $i \neq \ell$, as follows. For $i > 1$ simply set $M(i,i)$ equal to $M(i,i-1)$. For $i = 1$ set $M(1,1)$ equal to $M(1,2)$.

For example, if

$$w = (-3,-5/2,1,4/3,6,7), \theta = 1/2 \tag{2}$$

then

$$w' = (-3,-5/2,0,1,4/3,6,7)$$

and

$$M = \begin{pmatrix} -1 & -1 & -1 & -1 & -1 & 1 & 1 \\ -1 & -1 & -1 & -1 & -1 & 1 & 1 \\ -1 & -1 & -1 & 1 & 1 & 1 & 1 \\ -1 & -1 & 1 & 1 & 1 & 1 & 1 \\ -1 & -1 & 1 & 1 & 1 & 1 & 1 \\ 1 & 1 & 1 & 1 & 1 & 1 & 1 \\ 1 & 1 & 1 & 1 & 1 & 1 & 1 \end{pmatrix}.$$

It is easy to check that, in general, the matrix M is indeed symmetric. By virtue of the fact that $w_1 < \cdots < w_{\ell-1} < 0 < w_{\ell+1} < \cdots < w_n$, we have that M is monotone increasing within each row and column. Finally, the construction of M ensures that it faithfully reflects the structure of f over $\{0,1\}^n_{\leq 2}$, in the following sense. Suppose we can define weights $v_1 \leq \ldots \leq v_{n+1}$ and a threshold θ' with $v_\ell = 0$ such that

$$M(i,j) = 1 \quad \text{if and only if} \quad v_i + v_j \geq \theta'. \tag{3}$$

Then the halfspace

$$\text{sign}(v_1x_1 + \cdots + v_{\ell-1}x_{\ell-1} + v_{\ell+1}x_{\ell+1} + \cdots + v_{n+1}x_{n+1} - \theta')$$

correctly computes f over $\{0,1\}^{n+1}_{\leq 2}$, and therefore correctly solves the original problem. (In fact (3) is stronger than what is needed – all of the correct classifications are already enforced by the off-diagonal elements, with the exception of 0^n, whose correct classification is enforced by the constraint associated with $M(\ell,\ell)$.)

In the rest of the proof we will construct the desired $v_1,\ldots,v_{n+1}$ satisfying (3) where

$$v_1 \leq \cdots \leq v_{\ell-1} \leq v_\ell = 0 \leq v_{\ell+1} \leq \cdots \leq v_{n+1}, \tag{4}$$

each v_i is an integer, and each v_i satisfies $|v_i| \leq O(n)$.

Going forth the following notation will be useful: we write M_i to denote the i-th row of M, which we view as an $(n+1)$-character string $M(i,1)\ldots M(i,n+1)$ over the alphabet $\{-1,1\}$, and is, of course, the same as the i-th column of M.

We may assume that M is not the $(n+1) \times (n+1)$ identically-(-1) matrix (since if it is then f is the constant-(-1) function over $\{0,1\}^n_{=2}$), so in particular the bottom right entry $M(n+1,n+1)$ equals 1. On the other hand, we know that the $M(\ell,\ell)$ entry is -1. Since M is monotone increasing within each row and column, and is symmetric, the only way that M could have all its rows $M_1 = \cdots = M_{n+1}$ equal to each other is if M were either the identically $+1$ or identically -1 matrix. Since M is neither of these matrices, there are at least two distinct rows in M.

The weights $v_1,\ldots,v_{n+1}$ are constructed in a greedy stage-wise fashion that we now describe. We partition the set $\{1,\ldots,n+1\}$ into $2 \leq A \leq n+1$ intervals $I_1,\ldots,I_A$ in the following way. The interval I_1 is $\{1,\ldots,i_1\}$ where i_1 is such that rows $1,\ldots,i_1$ satisfy $M_1 = \cdots = M_{i_1} \neq M_{i_1+1}$. Let j_1 be such that $M_1 = \cdots = M_{i_1} = (-1)^{n+1-j_1}1^{j_1}$. Then interval I_2 is $\{i_1+1,\ldots,i_2\}$ where similarly i_2 is such that $M_{i_1+1} = \cdots = M_{i_2} \neq M_{i_2+1}$. As before j_2 denotes the value such that $M_{i_1+1} = \cdots = M_{i_2} = (-1)^{n+1-j_2}1^{j_2}$ (note that $j_2 > j_1$). Continuing in this way we get intervals $I_1,\ldots,I_A$ and values $0 \leq j_1 < \cdots < j_A \leq n+1$, where the right endpoint of I_A is $n+1$. If $a < b$ are both in the same interval I_i then our construction will assign the same weight to v_a and v_b.

Returning to the example shown in (2), we have

- $I_1 = \{1,2\}$, $I_2 = \{3\}$, $I_3 = \{4,5\}$, $I_4 = \{6,7\}$, and
- $i_1 = 2$, $i_2 = 3$, $i_3 = 5$, $i_4 = 7$, and
- $j_1 = 2$, $j_2 = 4$, $j_3 = 5$, $j_4 = 7$.

Fix any index $i \in \{1,\ldots,A\}$ and consider any element $a \in I_i$. We have that $M(a, n+2-j_i) = 1$ while $M(a, n+1-j_i) = -1$. The idea of our construction is that we will maintain

$$v_a + v_{n+2-j_i} = C \text{ and } v_a + v_{n+1-j_i} = C - 1, \tag{5}$$

where C is a fixed integer (the same across all $i \in \{1,\ldots,A\}$ and all $a \in I_i$). Together with (4) this ensures that (3) holds as required, taking $\theta' = C - 1/2$.

In the first stage we set the weights "at the ends" and in subsequent stages we "work our way in toward the middle." More precisely, in the first stage we start with the first interval I_1. We take $v_1 = \cdots = v_{i_1} = \alpha$, and consequently to obey the description in the previous paragraph v_{n+2-j_1} must equal $C - \alpha$ (in fact we set all of v_{n+2-j_1} through v_{n+1} to equal $C - \alpha$) and v_{n+1-j_1} must equal $C - 1 - \alpha$ (we will explain how α is set below). Moving on to the second interval I_2, we set $v_{i_1+1} = \cdots = v_{i_2} = \alpha + 1$, and we set all of v_{n+2-j_2} through v_{n+1-j_1} to $C - (\alpha+1)$ (note that this setting of v_{n+1-j_1} is consistent with the way it was set when we were dealing with the first interval I_1).

During the first stage, the set of indices that get their weights set to $C - \alpha$ is exactly I_A. Each of their columns has a 1 in the first row of M, and, since M is monotone, each of their columns has all 1's, and so they all have the same columns. Since M is symmetric, they also have the same rows. However, $n+1-j_1$ is not in I_A, because column $n+1-j_1$ has a -1 in the first row. Similarly, in the second round (if there is a second round), the indices in I_{A-1} are exactly the indices whose values are set to $C - \alpha - 1$.

From here let us divide our analysis into cases, depending on whether A is even or odd.

If A is even, after $A/2$ iterations, all of the weights have been determined, and to ensure that the second of the constraints of (5) holds when $i = A/2$, we need

$$\alpha + A/2 = (C - \alpha - A/2) - 1. \quad (6)$$

If A is odd, in iteration number $(A+1)/2$, we want to set the weights of $I_{(A+1)/2}$ both to $\alpha + (A+1)/2$ and $C - (\alpha + (A+1)/2)$, so

$$\alpha + (A+1)/2 = (C - \alpha - (A+1)/2),$$

which is equivalent to (6). Recall that we also need $v_\ell = 0$. Let t be the index for which $\ell \in I_t$. Since $v_\ell = \alpha + (t-1)$, we need $\alpha = -(t-1)$, and then setting $C = A - 2t - 1$ satisfies all of the constraints.

We have constructed $v_1, \ldots, v_{n+1}$ that satisfy (4) where each v_i is an integer. It follows easily from the construction that each $|v_i|$ is at most $O(n)$, and the theorem is proved.

C. ANALYSIS OF DECISION LISTS

Counting arguments. We first show that straightforward counting arguments do not give good bounds. Let $N(n,k)$ denote $\sum_{i=0}^{k}\binom{n}{i}$, the number of points in $\{-1,1\}^n_{\leq k}$ (note that $N_k \leq (en/k)^k$). Since the VC dimension of halfspaces over $\{-1,1\}^n_{\leq k}$ is known to be $n+1$, the Sauer-Shelah lemma [15, 17] says that there are at most

$$\sum_{j=0}^{n+1}\binom{N_k}{j} \leq \sum_{j=0}^{n+1}\binom{(en/k)^k}{j} \leq \left(\frac{e(en/k)^k}{n+1}\right)^{n+1}$$

halfspaces over $\{-1,1\}^n_{\leq k}$. A standard counting argument says that if there are more than C^n halfspaces over a given domain $S \subseteq \{-1,1\}^n_{\leq k}$, then some halfspace over S must require integer weight $\Omega(C)$. So the strongest weight lower bound that can be obtained from this kind of counting argument is $O((en/k)^k/n)$. This is actually quite weak; we will see that much stronger lower bounds can be obtained for explicit functions.

Proof of Observation 3. Let $\mathrm{sign}(v \cdot x - \theta)$ be a representation of DL over $\{0,1\}^n_{\leq 3}$. As noted in the preliminaries we may assume θ is of the form (integer $+\frac{1}{2}$) so its magnitude is at least 1/2.

Since $DL(0^n) = \mathrm{sign}(0 - \theta)$ is $+1$ we have that $\theta < 0$. Writing each v_i as $w_i\theta$ we may divide through by $|\theta|$ and re-express $\mathrm{sign}(v \cdot x - \theta)$ as $\mathrm{sign}(w \cdot x + 1)$. Here the w_i's may not be integers, but since $|\theta| \geq 1/2$ it suffices to show that $|w_n| = 2^{\Omega(n)}$.

Since $DL(e_j) = -1$ for j odd we have $w_j < -1$ for j odd, and since $DL(e_{k-1} + e_k) = 1$ for k even we have $w_k \geq -w_{k-1} - 1$ and thus $w_k > 0$ for even k. For even $k \geq 4$, since $DL(e_k + e_{k-1} + e_{k-3}) = 1$ we have

$$|w_k| = w_k \geq -w_{k-1} - w_{k-3} - 1 = |w_{k-1}| + |w_{k-3}| - 1, \quad (7)$$
for even $k \geq 4$.

For odd $k \geq 5$, since $DL(e_k + e_{k-1} + e_{k-3}) = -1$ we have $w_k < -w_{k-1} - w_{k-3} - 1$, and since w_k is negative for odd k and positive for even k this means

$$|w_k| > |w_{k-1}| + |w_{k-3}| + 1 \qquad \text{for odd } k \geq 5 \quad (8)$$

An easy induction using the inequalities (7) and (8) and the initial condition $w_j < -1$ for j odd gives that $|w_n| = 2^{\Omega(n)}$. □

D. PROOF OF THEOREM 4

Our goal is to prove the following which immediately gives Theorem 4. (Throughout this section β denotes the constant $\log_2(3/2)$.)

THEOREM 9. *If*

for all $f \in \{-1,1\}^n_{\geq n-2k-1}$,
$$G(f) = \mathrm{sign}\left(\sum_{i=1}^{r}\sum_{j=0}^{k-1} w_j^i f^i(j) + w_0 b - \theta\right) \quad (9)$$

where each w_j^i *and* w_0 *is an integer, then for some* $j \in \{0, \ldots, k-1\}$ *we have*

$$w_j^r \geq (e^{-4k^\beta} 2^{(k\log k)/2 - k})^{(n-1)/k}/k.$$

Following [6], the main step is to prove the following:

THEOREM 10. *Suppose that*

$$G(f) = \mathrm{sign}\left(\sum_{i=1}^{r}\sum_{j=0}^{k-1} v_j^i (f^i, \varphi_{\alpha_j}) + v_0 b - t\right)$$
for all $f = (b, f^1, \ldots, f^r) \in \{-1,1\}^n_{\geq n-2k-1}$ (10)

where each v_j^i *and* v_0 *is an integer. Then*

$$v_{k-1}^r \geq (e^{-4k^\beta} 2^{(k\log k)/2 - k})^{(n-1)/k}.$$

To show that Theorem 10 implies Theorem 9 we use the following claim which is a simple consequence of Fourier analysis (see Lemma 2.3 of [6]):

CLAIM 11. *For any* $f \in \{-1,1\}^k$ *and any* $(w_0, \ldots, w_{k-1}) \in \mathbb{R}^k$, *setting*

$$v_a = \frac{1}{k}\sum_{j=0}^{k-1} w_j \varphi_{\alpha_a}(j) \quad \text{for each } a \in \{0, \ldots, k-1\},$$

we have that $\sum_{j=0}^{k-1} w_j f(j) = \sum_{a=0}^{k-1} v_a (f, \varphi_{\alpha_a})$

Proof of Theorem 9 using Theorem 10: Suppose that $\{w_j^i\}, w_0, \theta$ satisfy (9). By Claim 11, for all

$$f \in \{-1,1\}^n_{\geq n-2k-1}$$

we have that

$$G(f) = \mathrm{sign}\left(\sum_{i=1}^{r}\sum_{a=0}^{k-1} v_a^i (f^i, \varphi_{\alpha_a}) + w_0 b - \theta\right)$$

where $v_a^i = \frac{1}{k}\sum_{j=0}^{k-1} w_j^i \varphi_{\alpha_a}(j)$. We have that kv_a^i is an integer for all i, a and so by Theorem 10 we get that $kv_{k-1}^r \geq (e^{-4k^\beta} 2^{(k\log k)/2 - k})^{(n-1)/k}$, i.e.

$$\sum_{j=0}^{k-1} w_j^r \varphi_{\alpha_{k-1}}(j) \geq (e^{-4k^\beta} 2^{(k\log k)/2 - k})^{(n-1)/k},$$

which gives Theorem 9 since $|\varphi_{\alpha_{k-1}}(j)| = 1$ for all j. □

D.1 Proof of Theorem 10

Throughout this section $\{v_j^i\}, v_0, t$ are as in (10). Since all weights are integers we may assume that t is of the form integer$+\frac{1}{2}$.

We begin with some straightforward claims that will be useful later.

CLAIM 12. *We have $v_0 \geq 1$. Moreover, for each $i \in [r-1]$ we have $v_0 \geq \sum_{i' \notin \{i,i+1\}, i' \in [r]} v_0^{i'} - t$.*

PROOF. First we observe that for $b \in \{-1,1\}$ we have $G(b, \varphi_{\alpha_0}, \ldots, \varphi_{\alpha_0}) = b$, which follows from the fact that $(\varphi_{\alpha_0}, \varphi_{\alpha_i}) = 0$ for all $i \neq 0$. By (10) this means that we have $\text{sign}(v_0 b + \sum_{i=1}^r v_0^i - t) = b$ so it must be the case that $v_0 > 0$ and since v_0 is an integer this means $v_0 \geq 1$. Furthermore, taking $b = -1$ we find that $v_0 > \sum_{i=1}^r v_0^i - t$.

For the second part of the claim, fix any $i \in [r-1]$ and consider the input $f = (-1, f^1, \ldots, f^r)$ where $f^{i'} = \varphi_{\alpha_0}$ for $i' \notin \{i, i+1\}$ and $f^{i'} = -\varphi_{\alpha_0}$ for $i' \in \{i, i+1\}$. This input f has $2k+1$ bits that are -1 (this is the only place in the proof where we use an input with this many -1 bits) and since $G(f) = -1$ and also

$$G(f) = \text{sign}\left(-v_0 + \sum_{i' \notin \{i,i+1\}, i' \in [r]} v_0^{i'} - v_0^i - v_0^{i+1} - t\right)$$

we have that $v_0 > \sum_{i' \notin \{i,i+1\}, i' \in [r]} v_0^{i'} - v_0^i - v_0^{i+1} - t$. Averaging this with the earlier inequality $v_0 > \sum_{i=1}^r v_0^i - t$ gives the second statement of the claim. □

CLAIM 13. *For every $i \in [r], j \in [k-1]$ we have $v_j^i > v_0$ (in particular, all these weights are positive).*

PROOF. Fix $i \in [r], j \in [k-1]$. For $\varepsilon, b \in \{-1,1\}$ consider the input $f = (b, f^1, \ldots, f^r) \in \{-1,1\}^n$ defined by $f^i = \varepsilon \varphi_{\alpha_j}$ and $f^{i'} = \varphi_{\alpha_0}$ for $i' \neq i$. Since every φ_{α_j} for $j \geq 1$ corresponds to the truth table of a parity function over some nonempty subset of ℓ bits, the string f has either $k/2$ or $k/2+1$ entries that are -1 (depending on whether b is $+1$ or -1). By the definition of G we have $G(f) = \text{sign}(b + (k+1)^{k(i-1)+j}\varepsilon) = \varepsilon$, and, referring to (10), we have $G(f) = \text{sign}(\varepsilon v_j^i + v_0 b + \sum_{i \neq i' \in [r]} v_0^{i'} - t)$. When b is $\text{sign}(\sum_{i \neq i' \in [r]} v_0^{i'} - t)$ and $\epsilon = -b$ this implies that $v_j^i \geq v_0 + |\sum_{i \neq i' \in [r]} v_0^{i'} - t|$ which implies $v_j^i \geq v_0$. □

The proof uses two main lemmas. The first lemma says that weights do not get smaller as we pass from the i-th to the $(i+1)$-st block:

LEMMA 14. *For every $i \in [r-1]$ and every $j \in [k-1]$ we have $v_j^{i+1} \geq v_{k-1}^i$.*

PROOF. Fix $i \in [r-1], j \in [k-1]$. Consider the input $f = (-1, f^1, \ldots, f^r) \in \{-1,1\}^n$ defined by $f^i = -\varphi_{\alpha_{k-1}}$, $f^{i+1} = \varphi_{\alpha_j}$ and $f^{i'} = \varphi_{\alpha_0}$ for $i' \notin \{i, i+1\}$. This f has exactly $k+1$ entries that are -1 and the definition of G implies that $G(f) = 1$. So $G(f) = \text{sign}(v_j^{i+1} - v_{k-1}^i + \sum_{i' \notin \{i,i+1\}, i' \in [r]} v_0^{i'} - v_0 - t) = 1$, which implies that

$$v_j^{i+1} \geq v_{k-1}^i - \sum_{i' \notin \{i,i+1\}, i' \in [r]} v_0^{i'} + v_0 + t \geq v_{k-1}^i,$$

where the final inequality follows from the second statement of Claim 12. □

The crucial lemma for us is Lemma 16, which says that the v_j^i weights grow quite significantly (by a factor of $k^{\Omega(k)}$) from the "beginning" to the "end" of each block i. Because of the way the function G has been set up we will be able to show this by a reduction to a weight lower bound that Håstad proves for his halfspace over $k = 2^\ell$ variables.

DEFINITION 15. *Let t_0 be the index of the first set in the enumeration of subsets of $[\ell]$ such that α_{t_0} has size 2.*

LEMMA 16. *For every $i \in [r]$ we have*

$$v_{k-1}^i \geq e^{-4k^\beta} 2^{(k \log k)/2 - k} \cdot v_{t_0}^i.$$

PROOF. Fix any $i \in [r]$. Consider the $(k+1)$-variable function defined as

$$\begin{aligned} & A(b, f^i) \\ & \stackrel{\text{def}}{=} G(b, \varphi_{\alpha_0}, \ldots, \varphi_{\alpha_0}, f^i, \varphi_{\alpha_0}, \ldots, \varphi_{\alpha_0}) \qquad (11) \\ & = \text{sign}\left(v_0 b + \sum_{j=0}^{k-1} v_j^i (f^i, \varphi_{\alpha_j}) + \sum_{i \neq i' \in [r]} k v_0^{i'} - t\right) (12) \end{aligned}$$

where in line (11) f^i appears in the i-th of the r blocks and all other blocks are set to φ_{α_0}. The equality (12) holds because for each $i' \neq i$ we have that $(\varphi_{\alpha_0}, \varphi_{\alpha_j})$ is 0 for $j \neq 0$ and is k for $j = 0$. For every $(b, f^i) \in \{-1,1\}^{k+1}$ the corresponding input to G in (11) has at most $k+1$ variables set to -1, so by the definition of G we have that

$$A(b, f^i) = \begin{cases} F_k(f^i) & \text{if } f \text{ is neither } \varphi_{\alpha_0} \text{ nor } -\varphi_{\alpha_0} \\ b & \text{if } f^i \text{ is either } \varphi_{\alpha_0} \text{ or } -\varphi_{\alpha_0} \end{cases} \qquad (13)$$

where F_k is Håstad's function on k variables, $F_k(f^i) = \text{sign}((f^i, \varphi_{\alpha_j}))$ where j is the largest index such that

$$(f, \varphi_{\alpha_j}) \neq 0.$$

Recall that since φ_{α_0} is the constant 1 function, we have $(f^i, \varphi_{\alpha_0}) = \sum_{j=0}^{k-1} f^i(j)$. Thus (13) gives us that

$$A\left(\text{sign}\left(\sum_{j=0}^{k-1} f^i(j)\right), f^i\right) = F_k(f^i) \quad \text{for all } f^i \in \{-1,1\}^k.$$

Now it is clear that flipping the value of b changes the value of $A(b, f^i)$ only if f^i is either φ_{α_0} or $-\varphi_{\alpha_0}$. By (12) this implies that for all $f^i \notin \{\varphi_{\alpha_0}, -\varphi_{\alpha_0}\}$ we must have

$$|v_0| < \left|\sum_{j=0}^{k-1} v_j^i (f^i, \varphi_{\alpha_j}) + \sum_{i \neq i' \in [r]} k v_0^{i'} - t\right|.$$

But this means that the k-variable function $A' : \{-1,1\}^k \to \{-1,1\}$

$$\begin{aligned} A'(f^i) \stackrel{\text{def}}{=} \text{sign} & \left(v_0 \left(\frac{1}{k} \sum_{j=0}^{k-1} f^i(j) \right) \right. \\ & \left. + \sum_{j=0}^{k-1} v_j^i (f^i, \varphi_{\alpha_j}) + \sum_{i \neq i' \in [r]} k v_0^{i'} - t \right) \qquad (14) \end{aligned}$$

must equal $F_k(f^i)$ for all $f^i \in \{-1,1\}^k$, because $\frac{1}{k} \sum_{j=0}^{k-1} f^i(j)$ is always at most 1 in magnitude and equals sign $\left(\sum_{j=0}^{k-1} f^i(j)\right)$

when f^i is φ_{α_0} or $-\varphi_{\alpha_0}$. Scaling the argument to sign$(\cdot)$ by a factor of k in (14), we get

$$\text{sign}\left(v_0 \sum_{j=0}^{k-1} f^i(j) + k\left[\sum_{j=0}^{k-1} v_j^i(f^i, \varphi_{\alpha_j}) + \sum_{i \neq i' \in [r]} kv_0^{i'} - t\right]\right),$$

a halfspace over $\{-1,1\}^k$ that computes precisely Håstad's function F_k. As Håstad notes (Lemma 2.2 of his paper) we may remove the constant term $k(\sum_{i\neq i' \in [r]} kv_0^{i'} - t)$ without changing the function. Recalling again that $(f^i, \varphi_{\alpha_0}) = \sum_{j=0}^{k-1} f^i(j)$, we rewrite the resulting expression for $A'(f^i)$ as

$$A'(f^i) = \text{sign}\left(\sum_{j=0}^{k-1} v_j'(f^i, \varphi_{\alpha_j})\right)$$

where v_j' equals kv_j^i for $j \neq 0$ and equals $kv_0^t + v_0$ for $j = 0$. Since these coefficients are all integers, we are in precisely the situation of Håstad's Theorem 2.4. The proof of that theorem explicitly establishes (see the second to last highlighted equation on p. 489) that $v_{k-1}' \geq e^{-4k^\beta} 2^{(k \log k)/2 - k} \cdot v_{t_0}'$, and the lemma is proved. □

Applying Lemmas 14 and 16 repeatedly and taking j in Lemma 14 to be t_0 each time, we get that

$$v_{k-1}^r \geq (e^{-4k^\beta} 2^{(k \log k)/2-k})^{(n-1)/k} v_{t_0}^1$$

which is at least $(e^{-4k^\beta} 2^{(k \log k)/2-k})^{(n-1)/k}$ since $v_{t_0}^1$ is at least 1 by Claim 13. This proves Theorem 10. □

E. PROOF OF OBSERVATION 1

For the first claim, if $k > n/4$ then the claimed bound is trivially true so we assume that $k < n/4$. We recall that $\binom{n}{j-1}/\binom{n}{j} = j/(n-j+1)$, and that this is at most 1/2 for $j \leq n/4$. So induction gives us that $\binom{n}{k-2} \leq \frac{1}{2}\binom{n}{k-1}$, $\binom{n}{k-3} \leq \frac{1}{4}\binom{n}{k-1}$, and so on, so

$$|\{0,1\}^n_{\leq k-1}| \leq \sum_{j=0}^{k-1} \frac{1}{2^j} \times |\{0,1\}^n_{=k-1}| \leq 2|\{0,1\}^n_{=k-1}|.$$

and hence

$$\frac{|\{0,1\}^n_{\leq k-1}|}{|\{0,1\}^n_{\leq k}|} \leq \frac{2|\{0,1\}^n_{=k-1}|}{|\{0,1\}^n_{\leq k}|} \leq \frac{2|\{0,1\}^n_{=k-1}|}{|\{0,1\}^n_{=k}|} = \frac{2\binom{n}{k-1}}{\binom{n}{k}} \leq 4k/n. \quad (15)$$

So, the total variation distance between $\mathcal{D}$ and $\mathcal{D}_1$ is

$$\sum_{x:\mathcal{D}(x)>\mathcal{D}_1(x)} (\mathcal{D}(x) - \mathcal{D}_1(x)) = \frac{|\{0,1\}^n_{\leq k}| - |\{0,1\}^n_{=k}|}{|\{0,1\}^n_{\leq k}|} = \frac{|\{0,1\}^n_{\leq k-1}|}{|\{0,1\}^n_{\leq k}|} \leq 4k/n.$$

For the second claim, let dup be the event that $x_i > 1$ for some i. We have

$$\mathcal{D}_2(\text{dup}) = \sum_{i=1}^{k-1} \frac{i}{n} \leq \frac{k(k-1)}{2n}. \quad (16)$$

Conditioned on the event $(\neg\text{dup})$, the distribution $\mathcal{D}_2$ is identical to $\mathcal{D}_1$. Thus for any event E we have

$$\begin{aligned}
&|\mathcal{D}_1(E) - \mathcal{D}_2(E)| \\
&= |\mathcal{D}_1(E) - \mathcal{D}_2(E \mid \neg\text{dup})\mathcal{D}_2(\neg\text{dup}) \\
&\qquad - \mathcal{D}_2(E \mid \text{dup})\mathcal{D}_2(\text{dup})| \\
&\leq |\mathcal{D}_1(E) - \mathcal{D}_2(E \mid \neg\text{dup})\mathcal{D}_2(\neg\text{dup})| + \mathcal{D}_2(\text{dup}) \\
&= |\mathcal{D}_1(E) - \mathcal{D}_1(E)\mathcal{D}_2(\neg\text{dup})| + \mathcal{D}_2(\text{dup}) \\
&= \mathcal{D}_1(E) \cdot (1 - \mathcal{D}_2(\neg\text{dup})) + \mathcal{D}_2(\text{dup}) \\
&\leq 1 - \mathcal{D}_2(\neg\text{dup}) + \mathcal{D}_2(\text{dup}) = 2\mathcal{D}_2(\text{dup}) \\
&\leq \frac{k(k-1)}{n},
\end{aligned}$$

by (16). So $\|\mathcal{D}_2 - \mathcal{D}_1\|_1 \leq \frac{k(k-1)}{n}$ which together with the first claim and the triangle inequality for variation distance gives the desired bound.

F. PROOF OF THEOREM 7

Let $\varepsilon \geq 4k/n$, and assume that sign$(v \cdot x - \theta)$ is an integer-weight halfspace which is a 2ε-approximator for DL with respect to $\mathcal{D}_1$. (Recall that $\mathcal{D}_1$ is the uniform distribution over $\{0,1\}^n_{=k}$.) We will show that if no $|v_i|$ exceeds $k^{\Theta(1)/\varepsilon^{1/(k-1)}-1}$ then sign$(v \cdot x - \theta)$ cannot be a 2ε-approximator for DL.

We first observe that if $\varepsilon > 1000^{-k}$ then the claimed lower bound holds trivially, so we assume henceforth that $\varepsilon \leq 1000^{-k}$. Note that together with the lower bound on ε in the theorem's premises this means that we may assume $k \leq \log n$; such an upper bound on k will be useful later.

Claim 17. *We may assume without loss of generality that all of the following conditions hold:*

1. $\theta = 0$;
2. *each coordinate v_i is a nonzero integer;*
3. $v_i > 0$ *for i even and* $v_i < 0$ *for i odd.*

Proof. We first show how to obtain conditions (1) and (2) at the cost of only a multiplicative-factor increase of $\Theta(k)$ in the weights (this factor of $\Theta(k)$ corresponds to the "-1" at the end of the exponent of the weight bound of Theorem 7). Then we show how to further obtain condition (3) at the cost only of decreasing n from its original value down to some $n' \in [n/2, n]$ and of increasing ε from its original value by at most a factor of 2.

As noted in the preliminaries we may assume that θ is of the form (integer)+1/2. Let $u \in \mathbb{R}^n$ denote the vector $u = (1, \ldots, 1)$. It is easy to verify that the halfspace sign$((2kv - 2\theta u) \cdot x)$ agrees with sign$(v \cdot x - \theta)$ on every $x \in \{0,1\}^n_{=k}$, because for $x \in \{0,1\}^n_{=k}$ we have

$$(2kv - 2\theta u) \cdot x = 2kv \cdot x - 2k\theta = 2k(v \cdot x - \theta).$$

Next, we observe that since $2kv_i$ is even and 2θ is odd, we have that each coordinate of $(2kv - 2\theta u)$ is a nonzero integer. Thus we have achieved conditions (1) and (2) at the cost of at most a $\Theta(k)$ multiplicative factor for each weight.

So, let us suppose that sign$(v \cdot x)$ achieves conditions (1) and (2); we now deal with the signs of the weights. Let $P \subseteq [n]$ be the set of positive weights, $P \stackrel{\text{def}}{=} \{i : v_i > 0\}$, and $N = [n] \setminus P$ be the set of negative weights $N = \{i : v_i < 0\}$.

Let $E \subset [n]$ denote the set $\{2, 4, \ldots, 2\lfloor n/2 \rfloor\}$ of even indices and $O = [n] \setminus E$ denote the set of odd indices in $[n]$.

We claim that we have $|N \cap E| \le \frac{n}{200k}$ and $|P \cap O| \le \frac{n}{200k}$. To see why this must be true, suppose $|N \cap E| > \frac{n}{200k}$. Then there are at least $\frac{n}{200k} \cdot (\frac{n}{200k} - 1) \cdots (\frac{n}{200k} - (k-1))$ inputs $x \in \{0,1\}^n_{=k}$ of the form $x = e_{i_1} + \cdots + e_{i_k}$ where $i_1, \ldots, i_k$ are distinct and all belong to $N \cap E$. For each such x we have $v \cdot x < 0$ (because all the weights which contribute to $v \cdot x$ are negative) but $DL(x) = 1$ (because all the bits that are set to 1 in x are in even coordinates), and hence $\mathrm{sign}(v \cdot x)$ is in error on each such x. This means that $\mathrm{sign}(v \cdot x)$ has error rate at least

$$\frac{\frac{n}{200k} \cdot (\frac{n}{200k} - 1) \cdots (\frac{n}{200k} - (k-1))}{\binom{n}{k}} > \frac{\left(\frac{n}{200k} - (k-1)\right)^k}{\binom{n}{k}}. \tag{17}$$

From our bounds on ε, k and n, the quantity (17) is $\gg 2\varepsilon$; but this contradicts the assumption that $\mathrm{sign}(v \cdot x)$ is a 2ε-approximator of f over $\{0,1\}^n_{=k}$. Thus it must indeed be the case that $|N \cap E| \le \frac{n}{200k}$. The same argument works for $P \cap O$. Thus, we have established that indeed $|N \cap E| \le \frac{n}{200k}$ and $|P \cap O| \le \frac{n}{200k}$.

So an overwhelming majority of the even i lie in P and an overwhelming majority of the odd i lie in N. Let G' be defined as $G' = (P \cap E) \cup (N \cap O)$; intuitively, G' is the set of "good" indices i for which v_i has the "right" sign. The preceding paragraph gives us that $|G'| \ge (1 - \frac{1}{100k})n$.

Viewing the elements of G' as being sorted in increasing order, it may be the case that G' contains multiple consecutive even elements or multiple consecutive odd elements, i.e. we could have $G' = \{1, 3, 5, 7, 8, 10, 11, 14, \ldots\}$ and the first 4 points in G' would all belong to O. Let G be the subset of G' obtained by going through the points of G' from smallest to largest and greedily keeping the first (odd, even, odd, even, ...) points of alternating parity that we encounter (so if G' were as in the above example we would have $G' = \{1, 8, 11, 14, \ldots\}$). For a point i (like 3 in the above example) to be discarded from G', it must be the case that $i - 1$ does not belong to G'. Since at most $\frac{n}{100k}$ points do not belong to G', we have that the number of points in G' that are discarded in constructing G from G' is at most $\frac{n}{100k}$. Thus overall we have that $|G| \ge (1 - \frac{1}{50k})n$. Consequently, of the $\binom{n}{k}$ points in $\{0,1\}^n_{=k}$, at least

$$\prod_{j=0}^{k-1} \left(\left(1 - \frac{1}{50k}\right) n - j \right) > \left(\left(1 - \frac{1}{50k}\right) n - (k-1) \right)^k$$

of them are of the form $x = \sum_{j=1}^k e_{i_j}$ where all k of the distinct indices $i_1, \ldots, i_k$ belong to G. By the upper bound on k given in the statement of the theorem, this is at least half of the points in $\{0,1\}^n_{=k}$. Let us restrict the halfspace $\mathrm{sign}(v \cdot x)$ to the domain $\{0,1\}^G_{=k}$. Even if all the error points of $\mathrm{sign}(v \cdot x)$ were to lie in $\{0,1\}^G_{=k}$, since $\mathrm{sign}(v \cdot x)$ has error rate at most 2ε over $\{0,1\}^n_{=3}$, it must have error rate at most 4ε over $\{0,1\}^G_{=k}$. Moreover, since the points in G (going from smallest to largest) alternate parity (odd, even, odd, even, ...) we have that DL over the domain $\{0,1\}^G$ is completely isomorphic to DL over the domain $\{0,1\}^{|G|}$. Thus it suffices to analyze the halfspace $\mathrm{sign}(v \cdot x)$ over the domain $\{0,1\}^{|G|}_{=k}$. As claimed in the first paragraph of the proof the number of variables has gone down by at most a factor of 2 (from n to $|G|$) and the error bound has at most doubled from 2ε to 4ε, so the claim is proved. □

Using the above claim, for the rest of the proof we assume that the halfspace $\mathrm{sign}(v \cdot x)$ satisfies conditions (1)-(3). Next, as described in the overview at the start of this subsection, we divide the weights into disjoint blocks according to their magnitudes and show that almost all the blocks are "pure" (almost entirely comprised of even-indexed weights, or almost entirely comprised of odd-indexed weights).

Fix $\pi : [n] \to [n]$ to be a permutation which sorts the weights $v_1, \ldots, v_n$ in increasing order of magnitude, i.e. $0 < |v_{\pi(1)}| \le |v_{\pi(2)}| \le \cdots \le |v_{\pi(n)}|$. (If the weights v_i have all distinct magnitudes then there is a unique such permutation π, and otherwise we fix any such π.) Let $b \stackrel{\text{def}}{=} \Theta(1)/\varepsilon^{1/(k-1)}$. If any weight has $|v_i| > (k/2)^{b/1000}$ then we are done, so we assume that each i has $|v_i| \le (k/2)^{b/1000}$. We partition $[n]$ into b blocks $S_1, \ldots, S_b$ whose sizes are as nearly even as possible, i.e.

$$S_1 = \{\pi(1), \ldots, \pi(|S_1|)\}, \ldots, S_b = \{\pi(n - |S_b| + 1), \ldots, \pi(n)\}$$

where there is a fixed value $s \approx n/b$ such that $|S_i| \in \{s, s+1\}$ for all $1 \le i \le b$. Note that S_1 consists of the smallest-magnitude weights, S_2 consists of the next-smallest-magnitude weights, and so on.

We say that a block S_i is *pure* if at least $\frac{999}{1000}$ of the coefficients $(v_j)_{j \in S_i}$ have the same sign; equivalently, S_i is pure if at least this fraction of the elements of S_i have the same parity (almost all are even, or almost all are odd). We say that a pure block is "pure odd" ("pure even") if $\frac{999}{1000}$ of its elements are odd (even). A block which is not pure is said to be *impure*.

We have the following lemma:

LEMMA 18. *At least $\frac{998}{1000}b$ blocks are pure.*

PROOF. We introduce a different notion, that of a block being "narrow," and use this notion to prove the lemma. We show that at least $\frac{999}{1000}$ of all blocks are narrow, and that at most $\frac{1}{1000}$ of all blocks are both narrow and impure; this gives the lemma.

For a block S_j let $R_j \ge 1$ denote the ratio (largest magnitude of any weight in the block)/(smallest magnitude of any weight in the block), i.e. $R_j = |v_{\pi(i_1)}|/|v_{\pi(i_2)}|$ where $\pi(i_1), \pi(i_2) \in S_j$ and $|v_{\pi(i_1)}| \le |v_{\pi(i')}| \le |v_{\pi(i_2)}|$ for all $\pi(i') \in S_j$. (Note that this ratio is well defined for all $j = 1, \ldots, b$ because each weight v_i is nonzero.) We say that a block S_j is *narrow* if $R_j \le k/2$.

We first show that at least $\frac{999}{1000}b$ blocks are narrow. Recall that $|v_{\pi(n)}| \le (k/2)^{b/1000}$. Since $|v_{\pi(n)}| \ge |v_{\pi(n)}|/|v_{\pi(1)}| \ge \prod_{i=1}^b R_i$ it must be the case that at least $\frac{999}{1000}b$ blocks are narrow, since otherwise we would have $\prod_{i=1}^b R_i > (k/2)^{b/1000}$.

We next claim that if more than $b/1000$ blocks S_i are both narrow and impure then we have $\Pr_{x \in \{0,1\}^n_{=k}}[\mathrm{sign}(v \cdot x) \ne DL(x)] > 2\varepsilon$. To see this, fix any block ℓ that is both narrow and impure. Consider an input $x = \sum_{j=1}^k e_{i_j}$ chosen uniformly from $\{0,1\}^n_{=k}$ conditioned on $i_1, \ldots, i_k$ all belonging to S_ℓ. Some sign – either positive or negative – must constitute the majority of the largest $\frac{1}{2000}$ elements of $\{v_i\}_{i \in S_\ell}$; say that sign is positive. With probability at least $\frac{1}{4000}$ the element v_{i_k} will belong to this positive subset of the $\frac{1}{2000}$ largest elements of $\{v_i\}_{i \in S_\ell}$. On the other hand, the smallest $(1 - \frac{1}{2000})$ of the elements of $\{v_i\}_{i \in S_\ell}$ must also contain at least $\frac{1}{2000} \cdot |S_\ell|$ negative elements, (because S_ℓ is impure), and with probability $\frac{1}{2^{O(k)}}$ the elements $v_{i_1}, \ldots, v_{i_{k-1}}$ will all belong to this set of negative elements. Thus, under the conditioning on x described above, with probability at least $1/2^{O(k)}$ we have that

$$(-1)^{i_1} = \cdots = (-1)^{i_{k-1}} \neq (-1)^{i_k}, \quad (18)$$

i.e. $i_1, \ldots, i_{k-1}$ all have the same parity (odd or even) but i_k has the opposite parity (even or odd respectively). However, since S_ℓ is narrow, the magnitude of v_{i_k} can be at most $k/2$ times the minimum magnitude of any of $v_{i_1}, \ldots, v_{i_{k-1}}$. Since $k \geq 3$, it follows that we have that $\text{sign}(v \cdot x) = (-1)^{i_1}$; but this is incorrect since $DL(x) = (-1)^{i_k}$ (because i_k is the largest value in $i_1, \ldots, i_k$). Thus, conditioned on $i_1, \ldots, i_k$ all belonging to S_ℓ, we have that x is classified incorrectly by $\text{sign}(v \cdot x)$ with probability at least $1/2^{O(k)}$. The probability (over a random $x \in \{0,1\}^n_{=k}$) that all k coordinates of x belong to S_ℓ is at least $\Theta(1)/b^k$. Assuming that at least $b/1000$ blocks are both narrow and impure, we get that overall the error rate $\Pr_{x \in \{0,1\}^n_{=k}}[\text{sign}(v \cdot x) \neq DL(x)]$ is at least

$$\frac{b}{1000} \cdot \frac{\Theta(1)}{b^k} \cdot \frac{1}{2^{O(k)}},$$

which exceeds 2ε by our choice of b.

From the above paragraph, we may conclude that at most $b/1000$ blocks S_i are both narrow and impure. Since at least $\frac{999}{1000}b$ blocks are narrow, at least $\frac{998}{1000}b$ of the b blocks are both narrow and pure, and Lemma 18 is proved. □

At this point we have shown that at least 998/1000 of the b blocks are pure. Let $\text{pure}_1 < \text{pure}_2 < \cdots < \text{pure}_{b'}$ be the indices of the pure blocks, where from the above lemma we have $b' \geq \frac{998}{1000}b$. To conclude the proof we now show that if there are so many pure blocks then the error of $\text{sign}(v \cdot x)$ must exceed 2ε.

The following terminology will be useful: Given an index $\kappa \in [n-1]$ we define the "up-shift" $up(\kappa)$ to be $up(\kappa) = \kappa + 1$. For a set $S \subset [n]$ we define $up(S)$ to be the set

$$up(S) = \{j + 1 : j \in S\}.$$

It is clear that $|up(S)| = |S|$ for all S, and that if a ρ fraction of S is even (odd) then a ρ fraction of $up(S)$ is odd (even).

Consider any $\ell \in \{1, \ldots, b'\}$ for which S_{pure_ℓ} is a pure even block. (There are at least $\frac{49}{100}$ such ℓ's, since half of all indices are odd and half are even and 99.8% of all indices belong to a pure block.) We say that S_{pure_ℓ} is *upshift-decreasing* if at least $\frac{45}{100}$ of the elements $j \in S_{\text{pure}_\ell}$ are even and have $up(j) \in S_{\ell'}$ for some $\ell' < \text{pure}_\ell$, and we say that S_{pure_ℓ} is *upshift-increasing* if at least $\frac{45}{100}$ of the elements $j \in S_{\text{pure}_\ell}$ are even and have $up(j) \in S_{\ell'}$ for some $\ell' > \text{pure}_\ell$. Since (at least) 99.9% of the elements $j \in S_{\text{pure}_\ell}$ are even, and thus have $up(j)$ odd, at least 99.8% of the elements $j \in S_{\text{pure}_\ell}$ are even and have $up(j)$ in some block S_k with $k \neq \text{pure}_\ell$, so S_{pure_ℓ} must be either upshift-decreasing or upshift-increasing.

We consider two cases:

Case I: at least half of all pure even blocks S_{pure_ℓ} are upshift-decreasing. In this case, there are at least $\frac{49}{200}b$ pure even upshift-decreasing blocks S_{pure_ℓ}.

For S_{pure_ℓ} a pure even upshift-decreasing block, let

$$G_{\text{pure}_\ell} \subset S_{\text{pure}_\ell}$$

denote the set

$$G_{\text{pure}_\ell} = \{j \in S_{\text{pure}_\ell} : j \text{ is even and } up(j) \in S_{\ell'} \text{ for some } \ell' < \text{pure}_\ell\}$$

so $|G_{\text{pure}_\ell}| \geq \frac{4}{10} \cdot \frac{n}{b}$ (since $|S_{\text{pure}_\ell}| \approx \frac{n}{b}$). Let L_{pure_ℓ} denote the lower half of the elements in G_{pure_ℓ} and $U_{\text{pure}_\ell} = G_{\text{pure}_\ell} \setminus L_{\text{pure}_\ell}$ denote the upper half of the elements (so for every $\alpha \in L_{\text{pure}_\ell}$ and $\beta \in U_{\text{pure}_\ell}$ we have $\alpha < \beta$). We have $|L_{\text{pure}_\ell}|, |U_{\text{pure}_\ell}| \geq \frac{2}{10} \cdot \frac{n}{b}$.

Fix an ℓ such that S_{pure_ℓ} is a pure even upshift-decreasing block. Consider the set of all inputs $x = e_{i_1} + \cdots + e_{i_k} \in \{0,1\}^n_{=k}$ for which $i_1, \ldots, i_{k-1}$ all belong to L_{pure_ℓ} and i_k belongs to $up(U_{\text{pure}_\ell})$. By the cardinality bounds of the previous paragraph there are at least

$$\left(\frac{2}{10} \cdot \frac{n}{b}\right) \cdot \prod_{j=0}^{k-2} \left(\frac{2}{10} \cdot \frac{n}{b} - j\right)$$

possible such outcomes for x, so the probability that a random $x \in \{0,1\}^n_{=k}$ is of this sort is at least $\frac{1}{2^{\Theta(k)}} \cdot \frac{1}{b^k}$. For such an x we have that $v_{i_1}, v_{i_2}, \ldots, v_{i_{k-1}} > 0$ (since $i_1, \ldots, i_{k-1}$ are even), $v_{i_k} < 0$ (since i_k is odd), and $|v_{i_1}|, \ldots, |v_{i_{k-1}}| \geq |v_{i_k}|$ (since i_k belongs to S'_ℓ for some $\ell' < \text{pure}_\ell$ and

$$i_1, \ldots, i_{k-1}$$

all belong to S_{pure_ℓ}). These conditions together give that $\text{sign}(v \cdot (e_{i_1} + \cdots + e_{i_k})) = +1$. But since we have $i_k \in up(U_{\text{pure}_\ell})$ and $i_1, \ldots, i_{k-1} \in L_{\text{pure}_\ell}$, it must be the case that $i_1, \ldots, i_{k-1} < i_k$; since i_k is odd this means $DL(x) = -1$, so $\text{sign}(v \cdot x)$ is incorrect on such x. Taking a union bound across all $\frac{49}{200}b$ possibilities for ℓ that make S_{pure_ℓ} a pure even upshift-decreasing block, we get that overall

$$\Pr_{x \in \{0,1\}^n_{=k}}[\text{sign}(v \cdot x) \neq DL(x)] \geq \frac{49}{200}b \cdot \frac{1}{2^{\Theta(k)}b^k}$$

which is larger than 2ε.

We now turn to

Case II: at least half of all pure even blocks S_{pure_ℓ} are upshift-increasing, so there are at least $\frac{49}{200}b$ pure even upshift-increasing blocks S_{pure_ℓ}. Recall that in a upshift-increasing block, at least $\frac{4}{10}$ of the elements $j \in S_{\text{pure}_\ell}$ are even and have $up(j) \in S_{\ell'}$ for some $\ell' > \text{pure}_\ell$.

This analysis of this case is quite similar to Case I; the difference is that we consider a slightly different event. For S_{pure_ℓ} a pure even upshift-increasing block, let $G_{\text{pure}_\ell} \subset S_{\text{pure}_\ell}$ denote the set

$$G_{\text{pure}_\ell} = \{j \in S_{\text{pure}_\ell} : j \text{ is even and } up(j) \in S_{\ell'} \text{ for some } \ell' > \text{pure}_\ell\}$$

[1] so $|G_{\text{pure}_\ell}| \geq \frac{4}{10} \cdot \frac{n}{b}$. As before, let L_{pure_ℓ} denote the lower half of the elements in G_{pure_ℓ} and $U_{\text{pure}_\ell} = G_{\text{pure}_\ell} \setminus L_{\text{pure}_\ell}$ denote the upper half of the elements (so for every $\alpha \in L_{\text{pure}_\ell}$ and $\beta \in U_{\text{pure}_\ell}$ we have $\alpha < \beta$). As before, we have $|L_{\text{pure}_\ell}|, |U_{\text{pure}_\ell}| \geq \frac{2}{10} \cdot \frac{n}{b}$.

Fix an ℓ such that S_{pure_ℓ} is a pure even upshift-increasing block. Consider the set of all inputs $x = e_{i_1} + \cdots + e_{i_k} \in \{0,1\}^n_{=k}$ for which $i_1, \ldots, i_{k-1}$ all belong to $up(L_{\text{pure}_\ell})$ and i_k belongs to U_{pure_ℓ}.[2] As in Case I there are at least

$$\left(\frac{2}{10} \cdot \frac{n}{b}\right) \cdot \prod_{j=0}^{k-2} \left(\frac{2}{10} \cdot \frac{n}{b} - j\right)$$

possible such outcomes for x, so the probability that a random $x \in \{0,1\}^n_{=k}$ is of this sort is at least $\frac{1}{2^{\Theta(k)}} \cdot \frac{1}{b^k}$. For such

[1]Note that in Case I we had "$\ell' < \text{pure}_\ell$" where now we have "$\ell' > \text{pure}_\ell$" in the definition of G_{pure_ℓ}

[2]Note the difference from Case I.

an x we have that $v_{i_k} > 0$ (since i_k is even), $v_{i_1}, \ldots, v_{i_{k-1}} < 0$ (since $i_1, \ldots, i_{k-1}$ are all odd), and $|v_{i_1}|, \ldots, |v_{i_{k-1}}| \geq |v_{i_k}|$ (since $i_1, \ldots, i_{k-1}$ belong to S_{ℓ_1} and S_{ℓ_2} respectively for some $\ell_1, \ell_2 > \text{pure}_\ell$ whereas A belongs to S_{pure_ℓ}). These conditions together give that $\text{sign}(v \cdot (e_{i_1} + \cdots + e_{i_k})) = -1$. But since we have $i_k \in U_{\text{pure}_\ell}$ and $i_1, \ldots, i_{k-1} \in up(L_{\text{pure}_\ell})$ it must be the case that $i_k > i_1, \ldots, i_{k-1}$; since i_k is even this means $DL(x) = +1$, so $\text{sign}(v \cdot x)$ is incorrect on such an x. The rest of the argument (analyzing the probability) proceeds exactly as in Case I: taking a union bound across all $\frac{49}{200}b$ possibilities for ℓ that make S_{pure_ℓ} a pure even upshift-increasing block, we get that overall

$$\Pr_{x \in \{0,1\}^n_{=k}} [\text{sign}(v \cdot x) \neq DL(x)] \geq \frac{49}{200} b \cdot \frac{1}{2^{\Theta(k)} b^k}$$

which is larger than 2ε. We are done in Case II, and done with the proof of Theorem 7.

G. PROOF OF THEOREM 8

Recall that the obvious halfspace representation for DL as

$$\text{sign}(\sum_{i=1}^{n} (-2)^i x_i)$$

has weight 2^n. We first present a simple construction with an easy analysis that gives an $\varepsilon/2$-approximator of weight $k^{O(k/\varepsilon)}$ under distribution $\mathcal{D}_2$ (this yields an ε-approximator over $\{0,1\}^n_{\leq k}$ by Observation 1 and our choice of ε). This of course only recovers the general result of Theorem 5, but then we will sharpen this DL-specific simple construction and analysis to prove the theorem.

We assume that ε is of the form 1/integer and we define $r \stackrel{\text{def}}{=} k/\varepsilon$. Note that $r < n$ by the assumed lower bound on ε.

We partition $[n]$ into r blocks $S_1, \ldots, S_r$ whose sizes are as nearly even as possible, i.e.

$$S_1 = \{1, \ldots, |S_1|\}, \ldots, S_r = \{n - |S_r| + 1, \ldots, n\}$$

where there is a fixed value $s \approx n/r$ such that $|S_i| \in \{s, s+1\}$ for all $1 \leq i \leq r$. For $j \in [n]$ let $bl(j) \in [r]$ denote the index of the block $S_{bl(j)}$ that contains j. For $1 \leq j \leq n$ let $w_j \stackrel{\text{def}}{=} (-1)^j (2k)^{bl(j)}$. It is clear that $\max_{j \in [n]} |w_j| = (2k)^r = (2k)^{k/\varepsilon}$.

We claim that $\text{sign}(w \cdot x)$ is an $O(\varepsilon)$-approximator for $DL(x)$ over $\mathcal{D}_2$. To establish this, consider an input $x = e_{i_1} + \cdots + e_{i_k}$ drawn from $\mathcal{D}_2$, i.e. $(i_1, \ldots, i_k)$ is drawn uniformly from $[n]^k$. Let $b^\star$ denote $\max\{bl(i_1), \ldots, bl(i_k)\}$. Since the weights increase by a factor of $2k$ between successive blocks, it is easy to see that if there is precisely one index $j \in [k]$ for which $bl(i_j) = b^\star$, then $\text{sign}(w \cdot x) = (-1)^{\max\{i_1, \ldots, i_k\}}$ agrees with the value $DL(x)$. So we have that $\Pr_{x \sim \mathcal{D}_2}[\text{sign}(w \cdot x) \neq DL(x)]$ is at most the probability that there are at least two distinct indices $j_1, j_2 \in [k]$ such that $bl(i_{j_1}) = bl(i_{j_2}) = b^\star$. It is clear that for each $\ell \in [r]$, the probability that both (none of $bl(i_1), \ldots, bl(i_k)$ lie in $[\ell+1, \ldots, r]$) and (at least two of $bl(i_1), \ldots, bl(i_k)$ equal ℓ) is at most

$$O(1) \cdot \left(\frac{\ell}{r}\right)^k \cdot \frac{k^2}{\ell^2}.$$

Summing over $\ell = 1, \ldots, r$ we get that $\Pr_{x \sim \mathcal{D}_2}[\text{sign}(w \cdot x) \neq DL(x)]$ is at most

$$\sum_{\ell=1}^{r} O(1) \cdot \frac{k^2}{r^k} \cdot \ell^{k-2} = O\left(\frac{k}{r}\right) = O(\varepsilon)$$

by our choice of $r = k/\varepsilon$. This concludes the initial simple construction and analysis.

We now build on the above simple construction to prove Theorem 8. The idea is to have the magnitude of the weights increase gradually within each block while keeping the sign of each weight correct as in the earlier construction. This lets us argue that in order for an input to be misclassified, it must have the "top two" bits that are set to 1 being quite close to each other, as well as a third input bit set to 1 that is also close to these top two. This more stringent condition lets us give a stronger bound on the probability of failure, which lets us use smaller weights to achieve an overall failure probability of ε.

We now take $r = k/\sqrt{\varepsilon}$. As before we may assume this is an integer which is less than n. We define r blocks of variables $S_1, \ldots, S_r$ and $bl(\cdot)$ as before.

We define integer weights $w_1, \ldots, w_n$ as follows. For each j the sign of w_j is $(-1)^j$. The magnitude of the weights is defined as follows: first, $|w_1| = (2k)^r$. If the first weight in block S_i (say its index is $\alpha_i + 1$) has $|w_{\alpha_i+1}| = C$, then the magnitudes of weights increase linearly in that block from C to $(2k)C$, i.e. for $j \in \{1, \ldots, |S_i|\}$ we have

$$|w_{\alpha_i+j}| = C + C \cdot \left\lceil \frac{(2k-1) \cdot j}{|S_i|} \right\rceil$$

so the final weight in block S_i has magnitude $|w_{\alpha_i+|S_i|}| = (2k)C$. If the final weight $w_{\alpha_i+|S_i|}$ of block S_i has magnitude $(2k)C$ then the first weight $w_{\alpha_i+|S_i|+1} = w_{\alpha_{i+1}+1}$ of the next block has magnitude $(4k^2)C$ (so there is a factor-of-$(2k)$ increase in the weights between each pair of successive blocks). It is clear that all weights are integers and that the largest one has magnitude $|w_n| \leq (2k)^r \cdot (2k)^{2r} = k^{O(r)}$. The halfspace we consider is $\text{sign}(w \cdot x)$.

Consider an input $x = e_{i_1} + \cdots + e_{i_k}$ drawn from $\mathcal{D}_2$, so $(i_1, \ldots, i_k)$ is drawn uniformly from $[n]^k$. As before let $b^\star$ denote $\max\{bl(i_1), \ldots, bl(i_k)\}$. As before, the only way that it is possible for $\text{sign}(w \cdot x)$ to disagree with $DL(x)$ is if there is some $\ell \in [r]$ such that both (none of $bl(i_1), \ldots, bl(i_k)$ lie in $[\ell+1, \ldots, r]$) and (at least two of $bl(i_1), \ldots, bl(i_k)$ equal ℓ). (Our subsequent analysis will impose even more conditions that must be satisfied in order for $\text{sign}(w \cdot x)$ to be incorrect on x.)

Fix any $\ell \in [r]$. The probability that both

none of $bl(i_1), \ldots, bl(i_k)$ lie in $[\ell+1, \ldots, r]$

and

at least two of $bl(i_1), \ldots, bl(i_k)$ equal ℓ

is at most k^2 times the probability that both

none of $bl(i_1), \ldots, bl(i_k)$ lie in $[\ell+1, \ldots, r]$

and

$bl(i_1) = bl(i_2) = \ell$;

let us condition on this event. Let us write $i_1 = \alpha_\ell + j_1$ and $i_2 = \alpha_\ell + j_2$; we have that j_1, j_2 are selected independently and uniformly from $\{1, \ldots, |S_\ell|\} \approx \{1, \ldots, n/r\}$. This means that $||w_{i_1}| - |w_{i_2}||$ is essentially distributed as

$$\left| w_{\alpha_\ell+1} \cdot \frac{(2k-1)\cdot(j_1 - j_2)}{|S_\ell|} \right|$$

(we have omitted ceiling operators for readability; it is easy to check that this omission does not significantly affect the subsequent analysis), and consequently x is classified incorrectly only if at least one of the $k-2$ values $(|w_{i_j}|)_{j=3,\ldots,k}$ is at least $\left| w_{\alpha_\ell+1} \cdot \frac{(j_1-j_2)}{|S_\ell|} \right|$, for otherwise the cumulative effect of the other $k-2$ weights would not be large enough to offset the effect of w_{i_1} and w_{i_2}.

Let $c \in \{0, 1, \ldots, \}$ be such that

$$|j_1 - j_2|/|S_\ell| \in ((2k)^{-(c+1)}, (2k)^{-c}].$$

Since every possible outcome for $|j_1 - j_2|$ (where j_1, j_2 are drawn independently from $\{1, \ldots, |S_\ell|\}$ has probability at most $O(1)/|S_\ell|$, we have that for each c the value $\Pr[|j_1 - j_2|/|S_\ell| \in ((2k)^{-(c+1)}, (2k)^{-c}]$ is at most $O((2k)^{-c})$. Because the weights increase by a factor of $2k$ between successive blocks, this means that the only way that $|w_{i_j}|$ can be at least $\left| w_{\alpha_\ell+1} \cdot \frac{(j_1-j_2)}{|S_\ell|} \right|$ is if $bl(i_j)$ belongs to $\{\ell - c - 1, \ell - c, \ldots, \ell\}$ (recall that because of our conditioning we have $bl(i_j) \leq \ell$). Because of the conditioning described earlier, for each fixed $j \in \{3, \ldots, k\}$ this occurs with probability $O(1+c)/\ell$. Taking a union bound over $k-2$ different j's, the probability that any $|w_{i_j}|$ is as large as would be necessary to cause an error is at most $O((1+c)k)/\ell$.

Putting all the pieces together and summing over all possible values $\ell = 1, \ldots, r$, we have that

$$\begin{aligned}
&\Pr_{x\sim\mathcal{D}_2}[\text{sign}(w \cdot x) \neq DL(x)] \\
&\leq \sum_{\ell=1}^{r} O(1) \cdot \left(\frac{\ell}{r}\right)^k \frac{k^2}{\ell^2} \cdot \sum_{c=0}^{\infty} O((2k)^{-c}) \cdot \frac{O((1+c)k)}{\ell} \\
&= O(1) \cdot \frac{k^3}{r^k} \sum_{\ell=1}^{r} \ell^{k-3} \sum_{c=0}^{\infty} \frac{1+c}{(2k)^c} \\
&= O(1) \cdot \frac{k^2}{r^2}
\end{aligned}$$

which is $O(\varepsilon)$ by our choice of r. The theorem is proved.

H. REFERENCES

[1] N. Alon and V. H. Vu. Anti-Hadamard Matrices, Coin Weighing, Threshold Gates, and Indecomposable Hypergraphs. *Journal of Combinatorial Theory, Series A*, 79(1):133–160, 1997.

[2] A. De, I. Diakonikolas, V. Feldman, and R. Servedio. Near-optimal solutions for the Chow Parameters Problem and low-weight approximation of halfspaces. *STOC*, 2012.

[3] I. Diakonikolas and R. Servedio. Improved approximation of linear threshold functions. In *Proc. 24th Annual IEEE Conference on Computational Complexity (CCC)*, pages 161–172, 2009.

[4] M. Goldmann, J. Håstad, and A. Razborov. Majority gates vs. general weighted threshold gates. *Computational Complexity*, 2:277–300, 1992.

[5] S. Hampson and D. Volper. Linear function neurons: structure and training. *Biological Cybernetics*, 53:203–217, 1986.

[6] J. Håstad. On the size of weights for threshold gates. *SIAM Journal on Discrete Mathematics*, 7(3):484–492, 1994.

[7] J. Hong. On connectionist models. Technical Report Technical Report 87-012, Dept. of Computer Science, University of Chicago, 1987.

[8] W. Maass and G. Turan. How fast can a threshold gate learn? In *Computational Learning Theory and Natural Learning Systems: Volume I: Constraints and Prospects*, pages 381–414. MIT Press, 1994.

[9] M. Minsky and S. Papert. *Perceptrons: an introduction to computational geometry*. MIT Press, Cambridge, MA, 1968.

[10] S. Muroga, I. Toda, and S. Takasu. Theory of majority switching elements. *J. Franklin Institute*, 271:376–418, 1961.

[11] P. Orponen. Neural networks and complexity theory. In *Proceedings of the 17th International Symposium on Mathematical Foundations of Computer Science*, pages 50–61, 1992.

[12] P. Raghavan. Learning in threshold networks. In *First Workshop on Computational Learning Theory*, pages 19–27, 1988.

[13] A. Razborov. On small depth threshold circuits. In *Proceedings of the Third Scandinavian Workshop on Algorithm Theory (SWAT)*, pages 42–52, 1992.

[14] M. Saks. Slicing the hypercube. In Keith Walker, editor, *Surveys in Combinatorics 1993*, pages 211–257. London Mathematical Society Lecture Note Series 187, 1993.

[15] N. Sauer. On the density of families of sets. *Journal of Combinatorial Theory (Series A)*, 13:145–147, 1972.

[16] R. Servedio. Every linear threshold function has a low-weight approximator. *Comput. Complexity*, 16(2):180–209, 2007.

[17] S. Shelah. A combinatorial problem; stability and order for models and theories in infinitary languages. *Pacific J. Math.*, 41:247–261, 1972.

Learnability of DNF with Representation-Specific Queries

Liu Yang
Machine Learning Department
Carnegie Mellon University
liuy@cs.cmu.edu

Avrim Blum
Department of Computer Science
Carnegie Mellon University
avrim@cs.cmu.edu

Jaime Carbonell
Language Technologies Institute
Carnegie Mellon University
jgc@cs.cmu.edu

ABSTRACT

We study the problem of PAC learning the class of DNF formulas with a type of natural pairwise query specific to the DNF representation. Specifically, given a pair of positive examples from a polynomial-sized sample, we consider boolean queries that ask whether the two examples satisfy at least one term in common in the target DNF, and numerical queries that ask how *many* terms in common the two examples satisfy. We provide both positive and negative results for learning with these queries under both uniform and general distributions.

For boolean queries, we show that the problem of learning an arbitrary DNF target under an arbitrary distribution is no easier than in the traditional PAC model. However, on the positive side, we show that under the uniform distribution, we can properly learn any DNF formula with $O(\log(n))$ relevant variables, any DNF formula where each variable appears in at most $O(\log(n))$ terms, and any DNF formula having at most $2^{O(\sqrt{\log(n)})}$ terms. Under general distributions, we show that 2-term DNFs are efficiently properly learnable as are disjoint DNFs.

For numerical queries, we show we can learn arbitrary DNF formulas under the uniform distribution; in the process, we give an algorithm for learning a sum of monotone terms from labeled data only. Numerical-valued queries also allow us to properly learn any DNF with $O(\log(n))$ relevant variables under arbitrary distributions, as well as DNF having $O(\log(n))$ terms, and DNF for which each example can satisfy at most $O(1)$ terms.

Other possible generalizations of the query include allowing the algorithm to ask the query for an arbitrary number of examples from the sample at once (rather than just two), or allowing the algorithm to ask the query for examples of its own construction; we show that both of these generalizations allow for efficient proper learnability of arbitrary DNF functions under arbitrary distributions.

Categories and Subject Descriptors

F.2.0 [**Theory of Computation**]: Analysis of Algorithms and Problem Complexity—*General*

ITCS'13, January 9–12, 2013, Berkeley, California, USA.

General Terms

Algorithms, Theory

Keywords

Learning DNF, PAC Learnability, Efficient Learning, Queries

1. INTRODUCTION

Consider a bank aiming to use machine learning to identify new instances of financial fraud. To do so, the bank would ask financial experts to label past transactions as fraudulent or not, and then run a learning algorithm on the resulting labeled data. However, this learning problem might be quite difficult because of the existence of multiple intrinsic types of fraud, with each positive example perhaps involving multiple types of fradulent behavior. For instance, the fraud may involve identity theft, unauthorized account access, security-code violations, overdraft and/or insider security breaches. That is, the target concept would be in the general case a DNF formula, a class for which no efficient algorithms are known.

Yet in such cases, perhaps the experts performing the labeling could be called on to provide a bit more information. In particular, suppose that given two positive examples of fraud, the experts could indicate whether or not the two examples are *similar* in the sense of having at least one intrinsic type of fraud (at least one term) in common, such as both involving unauthorized account access, or both involving internal blockage of account monitoring (inside job). Or perhaps the experts could indicate *how* similar the examples are (how many terms in common they satisfy), stating the number of common ways in which the fraud occurred. This is certainly substantially more information. Can it be used to learn DNF formulas and their natural subclasses efficiently?

Fraud detection is just one of many potential applications of DNF learning in which pairwise queries are natural. Others applications include medical multi-factor medical diagnosis, where patients suffer from several ailments and a full diagnosis is required to select optimal treamtent, and not aggravate one condition while treating another.

In our work, we study the problem of learning DNF formulas and other function classes using such pairwise, representation-dependent queries. Specifically, we consider queries of the form, "Do these two positive examples satisfy at least one term in common in the target DNF formula?" (we call these *boolean similarity queries*) and "How many terms in common do these two positive examples satisfy?" (we call these *numerical similarity queries*).

These queries must be over data in a labeled sample drawn from the distribution; we assume membership queries are *not* allowed. Our motivation comes from scenarios such as fraud detection, where the boolean-vector representation of an example is just a projection of the actual data object (the fraudulent transaction), so that the human oracle cannot necessarily make sense of artificially-constructed boolean vectors, as they need to observe the actual data objects in order to answer the query. Similarly, in the problem of drug design, the span of constructable examples is highly constrained, so that general membership queries may not be feasible.

We show, for these types of queries, a number of both positive and negative results for learning DNF formulas and interesting subclasses of them. For example, we show that under the uniform distribution, with the boolean-valued queries, we can properly learn any DNF with $O(\log(n))$ relevant variables, any DNF where each relevant variable appears in at most $O(\log(n))$ terms, and any DNF having at most $2^{O(\sqrt{\log(n)})}$ terms. Under arbitrary distributions, we can properly learn 2-term DNF and disjoint DNF, but we find that the general problem of learning an arbitrary DNF target under an arbitrary distribution is no easier than in the traditional PAC model. With numerical queries, under the uniform distribution we can learn arbitrary DNF formulas, and under arbitrary distributions we can can properly learn any DNF with either $O(\log(n))$ relevant variables, $O(\log(n))$ terms, or for which each example can satisfy at most $O(1)$ terms.

Our model can also be viewed in the context of the paradigm of learning with kernels. A kernel is a pairwise numerical similarity function over examples that is presumed to be available at both training and test time. However, suppose this kernel is computationally expensive to run, or even is a human expert, and so will not be available when the learned hypothesis is fielded. Can one use this kernel to produce a good hypothesis defined only over the base features? Our model can be viewed as addressing this question in the context of DNF, for a particular type of kernel function.

1.1 Model

In this setting, we suppose there is a DNF formula $f : \{0,1\}^n \to \{-1,+1\}$, where $f = T_1 \vee \ldots \vee T_t$ for conjunctions $T_i : \{0,1\}^n \to \{-1,+1\}$. There is additionally a distribution D over $\{0,1\}^n$; some of our results deal specifically with D uniform, while others leave D to be arbitrary. The learning algorithm is given parameters ϵ and δ, and is allowed access to a $poly(n)$-sized i.i.d. sample of data points (examples) $x_1, x_2, \ldots, x_{poly(n)}$ drawn from D, along with their target labels $f(x_1), f(x_2), \ldots, f(x_{poly(n)})$.

The algorithm can additionally make certain *queries*, which vary in type among the results below. The two main types of queries we study are boolean-valued queries and numerical-valued queries, defined as follows. For any x_i, x_j in the data set, the boolean-valued query $k(x_i, x_j)$ takes value 1 if $\exists \ell \leq t$ such that $T_\ell(x_i) = T_\ell(x_j) = 1$, and otherwise takes value 0. Similarly, for any x_i, x_j in the data set, the numerical-valued query

$$K(x_i, x_j) = \sum_{\ell \leq t} I[T_\ell(x_i) = T_\ell(x_j) = 1].$$

Thus, the boolean-valued query indicates whether the two examples satisfy some term in common, while the numerical-valued query indicates the precise number of terms they satisfy in common.

We say it is possible to learn a family of DNF formulas H with a given type of query if there exists an algorithm that uses the random data and the given type of query and, for any $f \in H$, in time polynomial in n, $1/\epsilon$, and $\log(1/\delta)$, produces a classifier $h : \{0,1\}^n \to \{-1,+1\}$ such that, with probability at least $1-\delta$, $err(h) = P_{x\sim D}(h(x) \neq f(x)) \leq \epsilon$. We further say it is possible to *properly* learn H with the given type of query if there exists such an algorithm for which h is guaranteed to be an element of H.

Note that we do not allow membership queries in our main results below (membership queries allow an algorithm to generate its own example and ask the oracle the label of it). We do have one general result (learning arbitrary DNF under arbitrary distributions) based on an analogue of membership queries in this model (see Appendix A).

1.2 Related Work

There have been many positive results on learning $poly(n)$-term DNF formulas with membership queries. Two landmark results are [Ang88] showing that monotone DNF formulas can be properly learned under arbitrary distributions using membership queries, and [Jac94] giving an efficient membership-query algorithm for the (improper) learning of DNF formulas under the uniform distribution.

The problem of learning DNF from random examples without queries has remained open over decades since Valiant introduced the PAC (Probably Approximately Correct) learning model [Val84]. It is not known whether we can efficiently learn DNF from random examples alone and there are known hardness results for properly learning DNF. In fact, [PV88] showed that even 2-term DNF formulas are not properly learnable from labeled data alone unless NP = RP. The fastest algorithms so far for learning $poly(n)$-term DNF formulas in the PAC model requires time $2^{\tilde{O}(n^{1/3})}$ [KS01].

For the problem of PAC learning DNF formulas under the uniform distribution, no polynomial-time algorithms are known. The fastest known algorithm for learning $poly(n)$-term DNF under the uniform distribution requires time $n^{O(\log n)}$ [Ver90]. At the heart of this problem lies the problem of efficiently learning k-juntas (an arbitrary boolean function depending on an unknown set of only k out of n boolean variables) for $k = O(\log n)$. The best known algorithm for learning k-juntas from uniform random examples is given by [Val12], building on [MOS04], which requires time roughly $n^{0.6k}$.

Some partial positive results have been obtained for special cases of monotone DNF formulas. [Ser04] provided an algorithm that learns any $2^{O(\sqrt{\log n})}$-term monotone DNF under the uniform distribution to any constant accuracy in $poly(n)$ time, and [OS07] gave an algorithm that learns any monotone boolean function under the uniform distribution to any constant accuracy, in time polynomial in n and in the *decision tree size* of the target function.

Recent work on restricted access learning [WDYR12] of DNF is related to our work at the high level: both our work and [WDYR12] give the learner more power with the goal of being able to learn DNF using this extra power.

1.3 Our Results

We begin with a somewhat surprising negative result: that learning general DNF formulas under arbitrary distributions from boolean similarity queries is as hard as PAC-learning DNF formulas without them. This result uses the equivalence between group learning, weak learning, and strong learning.

Under the uniform distribution, we show that if we are allowed to ask numerical pairwise queries, we can efficiently learn *arbitrary* DNF formulas. If we are restricted to boolean-valued queries, we can properly learn any DNF formula for which each variable appears in $O(\log(n))$ terms, as well as any DNF formula with $O(\log(n))$ relevant variables. We can also learn any DNF having at most $2^{O(\sqrt{\log n})}$ terms. Specifically, we use Servedio's results [Ser04] in the context of learning the $k(x_i, \cdot)$ DNF, which is a monotone DNF after appropriate transformation of the feature space; if we do this for enough random x_i points, the $\max_i k(x_i, \cdot)$ function will agree with the target DNF with high probability.

For the more general case of learning under arbitrary distributions, we show that with numerical-valued queries we can properly learn any DNF formula having $O(\log(n))$ terms, or any DNF formula having $O(\log(n))$ relevant variables. In this case, with boolean-valued queries, we can easily learn disjoint DNF (a class that contains decision trees). We in addition show that we can properly learn any "parsimonious" DNF formula (a formula for which no term can be deleted without appreciably changing the function) as well as any 2-term DNF, a class known to be NP-Hard to properly learn from labeled data alone.

If we are allowed to ask "Do these k examples satisfy any term in common?" for arbitrary (poly-sized) k, we can even properly learn arbitrary DNF formulas under arbitrary distributions.

2. HARDNESS RESULTS

To illustrate why pairwise similarity queries do not trivialize the DNF learning problem, we begin with two hardness results.

THEOREM 2.1. *Learning DNF from random data under arbitrary distributions with boolean similarity queries is as hard as learning DNF from random data under arbitrary distributions with only the labels (no queries).*

PROOF. [Kea89] and [KLV94] proved that "group learning" is equivalent to "weak learning".

In group learning, at each round we are given $poly(n)$ examples that are either all iid from D^+ or all iid from D^- (i.e. all positive or all negative) and our goal is to identify which case it is. Subsequently, Schapire [Sch90] proved that weak-learning is equivalent to strong-learning. So, if DNF is hard to PAC-learn, then DNF is also hard to group-learn.

Now, consider the following reduction from group-learning DNF in the standard model to learning DNF in the boolean similarity queries model. In particular, given an algorithm $\mathcal{A}$ for learning from a polynomial number of examples in the boolean similarity queries model, we show how to use $\mathcal{A}$ to group-learn as follows:

Given a set S of $m = poly(n)$ examples $x_1, x_2, ..., x_m$ (we will use $m = tn$ where t is the number of terms in the target), construct a new example by just concatenating them together. So overall we now have nm variables. We present this concatenated example to $\mathcal{A}$ with label equal to the label of S. If $\mathcal{A}$ makes a similarity query between two positive examples $[x_1, x_2, ..., x_m]$ and $[x'_1, x'_2, ..., x'_m]$, we simply output *yes* (i.e., that they do indeed share a term in common).

We now argue that with high probability, the labels and our responses to $\mathcal{A}$ are all fully consistent with some DNF formula of size mt. In particular, we claim they will be consistent with a target function that is just the OR of m copies of the original target function.

First of all, note that the OR of m copies of the original target function will produce the correct labels since by assumption either all $x_i \in S$ are positive or all $x_i \in S$ are negative. Next, we claim that whp, any two of these concatenated positive examples will share a term in common. Specifically, if the original DNF formula has t terms, then for two random positive examples from D^+ there is probability at least $1/t$ that they share a common term. So, the chance of failure for two concatenated examples is at most $(1 - 1/t)^m$. (Because the only way that two of these big concatenated examples $[x_1, x_2, ..., x_m]$ and $[x'_1, x'_2, ..., x'_m]$ can fail to share a term in common is if x_1 and x'_1 fail, x_2 and x'_2 fail, etc.). Setting $m = tn$, the probability of failure for any given query is at most $1/e^n$. Applying the union bound over all polynomially-many pairs of positive examples in $\mathcal{A}$'s sample yields that with high probability all our responses are consistent. Therefore, by assumption, $\mathcal{A}$ will produce a low-error hypothesis under the distribution over concatenated examples, which yields a low-error hypothesis for the group-learning problem. □

We can extend the above result to "approximate numerical" queries that give the correct answer up to a $1 \pm \tau$ factor, for some constant $\tau > 0$ (or even $\tau \geq 1/poly(n)$).

THEOREM 2.2. *Learning DNF from random data under arbitrary distributions with approximate-numerical-valued queries is as hard as learning DNF from random data under arbitrary distributions with only the labels (no queries). Specifically, if C is the number of terms x_i and x_j satisfy in common, the oracle returns a value in the range $[(1-\tau)C, (1+\tau)C]$.*

PROOF. Assume we have an algorithm $\mathcal{A}$ that learns to error $\epsilon/2$ given an oracle for approximate numerical queries.

Now we do the reduction from group learning as before, forming higher-dimensional examples by concatenating groups $x_1, \cdots, x_m$, all of the same class, but this time with $m = 2n(t^4)(1+\tau/2)^2/\tau^2$. Suppose, for now, that we know for the original DNF formula, the expected number of terms α that two random positive examples would have in common (we discharge this assumption later). In that case, when queried by $\mathcal{A}$ for the similarity between two positive examples x, x', we simply answer with the closest integer to αm. As before, we argue that with high probability, our answers are consistent with a DNF formula g consisting of just m shifted copies of the original DNF.

Note that for a random pair of the concatenated examples composed of positive sub-examples, the expected number of terms in common in g is $m\alpha$. Furthermore, the number of terms in common is a sum of m independent samples of the original random variable of mean α, each of which is bounded in the range $[0, t]$. So Hoeffding's inequality implies that with probability

$$1 - 2e^{-2m^2\alpha^2(\tau/2)^2/(m(t^2)(1+\tau/2)^2)} \geq 1 - 2e^{-n}$$

(since $\alpha \geq 1/t$), the number C of terms in common satisfies $|C - m\alpha| \leq m\alpha(\tau/2)/(1+\tau/2)$, which implies $(1-\tau/2)C \leq m\alpha \leq (1+\tau/2)C$.

Thus, for a $poly(n)$-sized sample of data points, with high probability, all of the pairs of positive concatenated examples have the nearest integer to $m\alpha$ within these factors of their true number of terms in common. It therefore suffices to respond to $\mathcal{A}$'s similarity queries with the nearest integer to $m\alpha$.

Now the only difficulty is that we do not know α. So we just try all positive integers i from 1 to mt and then use a validation set to select among the hypotheses produced. That is, we run $\mathcal{A}$ on the constructed data set and respond to all similarity queries with a single value i, getting back a classifier for these concatenated examples, and then repeat for each i. Then we take $O((1/\epsilon)\log(mt/\delta))$ additional higher-dimensional samples (with labels) and choose the classifier among these mt returned classifiers, having the smallest number of mistakes on that validation set. At least one of these mt values of i is the closest integer to $m\alpha$, so at least one of these mt classifiers is $\epsilon/2$-good, and our validation set will identify one whose error is at most ϵ. So we can use this classifier to identify whether a random m-sized group of examples is composed of all positives or all negatives, with error rate ϵ: i.e., we can do group learning.

If the algorithm A only has a "high probability" guarantee of success, we can repeat this several times with independent data sets, to boost the confidence that there will be a good classifier among those we choose from at the end, and slightly increase the size of the validation set to compensate for this larger number of classifiers. □

3. LEARNING DNF UNDER THE UNIFORM DISTRIBUTION

In this section, we investigate the problem of learning DNF under a uniform distribution on $\{0,1\}^n$. We begin with a result showing how to learn general DNF formulas from numerical similarity queries. For boolean similarity queries, we show how to learn several natural classes of DNF formulas, including $2^{O(\sqrt{\log n})}$-term DNF, DNF with $O(\log n)$ relevant variables (juntas), and DNF formulas in which each variable appears in at most $O(\log n)$ terms. First, however, we give an algorithm for learning a sum of monotone terms in the standard (no queries) PAC model under the uniform distribution.

3.1 A useful subroutine: Learning a sum of monotone terms

In this section we give an algorithm for learning a sum of monotone terms over the uniform distribution (without pairwise queries). That is, the target is a (not necessarily boolean) function $f(x) = T_1(x) + T_2(x) + \ldots + T_t(x)$ where the T_i are monotone conjunctions (outputting 1 if x satisfies T_i and 0 if x does not) and $t = poly(n)$. This will then be used in our algorithm for learning general DNF formulas over the uniform distribution from pairwise queries.

THEOREM 3.1. *We can efficiently learn a sum of t monotone terms over the uniform distribution, without pairwise queries, using time and samples $poly(t, n, 1/\epsilon)$.*

PROOF. Let $f(x) = T_1(x) + T_2(x) + \ldots + T_t(x)$ denote the target function. Our algorithm is based on the following facts:

1. The Fourier representation (using the parity basis) for a single term T (viewed as a $\{0,1\}$ function) has a particularly simple form. In particular, $\hat{T}_S = \mathbb{E}[T(x)\phi_S(x)] = 0$ if $S \not\subseteq T$ and $\hat{T}_S = 2^{-|T|}(-1)^{|S|+1}$ if $S \subseteq T$. See, e.g., [BFJ+94].
2. This implies that for any given set S, the associated Fourier coefficient of f is $\hat{f}_S = (-1)^{|S|+1}\sum_{i:S\subseteq T_i} 2^{-|T_i|}$. This further implies that if $S' \subseteq S$, then $|\hat{f}_{S'}| \geq |\hat{f}_S|$. Note that we are using here the fact that the T_i are monotone, so that all terms inside the summation have the same sign.
3. Since for each term T_i, its L_1 length in the Fourier representation is exactly 1, we have $L_1(f) \leq t$. This implies that for any given threshold θ there are at most t/θ coefficients of magnitude at least θ.

We can use the above facts to identify all Fourier coefficients of f of magnitude at least $\theta = \epsilon/(8t)$ in time polynomial in n, t, and $1/\epsilon$ as follows.

We begin by examining each parity function of size 1 and estimating its Fourier coefficient from data (up to accuracy $\theta/4$). We place all coefficients of magnitude at least $\theta/2$ into a list L^1.

For $j = 2, 3, \ldots$ we repeat the following: for each parity function ϕ_S in list L^{j-1} and each $x_i \notin S$, estimate the Fourier coefficient of $S_i = S \cup \{x_i\}$. If the estimated value is at least $\theta/2$ then add it to list L^j (if it is not in the list already). Note that by observation (2) above, we maintain by induction that list L^j contains all parity functions of size j whose coefficients have magnitude at least θ.

Lastly, note that by observation (3), each list L^j can have length at most $O(t/\theta)$, so the overall total time is polynomial in n, t, and $1/\theta$.

We now construct a function g consisting of the weighted sum of parities for all coefficients identified in the above procedure. Since g includes all coefficients of f of magnitude at least $\epsilon/(8L_1(f))$, this implies that we have

$$\langle f-g, f-g\rangle \leq \sum_{S:|\hat{f}_S|<\epsilon/(8L_1(f))} (\hat{f}_S)^2 \leq \epsilon/8$$

[Man94]. The above assumes we have measured the large Fourier coefficients precisely; adding in measurement error, by measuring coefficients to $poly(t/\epsilon)$ accuracy, we have $\langle f-g, f-g\rangle \leq \epsilon/4$. In particular, this implies that $\mathbb{E}[(f(x)-g(x))^2] \leq \epsilon/4$. Finally, we output the function $h(x) = [g(x)]$ where "[.]" is rounding to the nearest integer. Each mistake of h on some example x implies that $(f(x)-g(x))^2 \geq 1/4$, so h has error at most ϵ with respect to f. □

Feldman, Kothari, and Vondrak (personal communication) have recently independently proven a result related to this theorem. Note that the above result holds just as well for *unate* sums of terms (a sum of terms in which no variable appears both positively and negatively). In particular, the only place where monotonicity was used in the proof was in observation (2), which applies just as well to unate sums, since they still have the property that $|\hat{f}_S| = \sum_{i:S\subseteq T_i} 2^{-|T_i|}$, implying that if $S' \subseteq S$, then $|\hat{f}_{S'}| \geq |\hat{f}_S|$. Therefore, we have:

THEOREM 3.2. *We can efficiently learn a unate sum of t terms over the uniform distribution, using time and samples $poly(t, n, 1/\epsilon)$.*

In the case that all terms T_i have size at most $s = O(\log(t/\epsilon))$, we can convert the above procedure into a proper learning algorithm by setting the threshold θ to $O(1/2^s)$ and outputting terms for the maximal sets S found having large Fourier coefficients.

3.2 Learning DNF over the uniform distribution from numerical pairwise queries

We now use Theorem 3.2 to learn general DNF formulas over the uniform distribution from numerical pairwise queries.

THEOREM 3.3. *Under the uniform distribution, with numerical pairwise queries, we can learn any $poly(n)$-term DNF.*

PROOF. Let t be the number of terms in the target. Sample $m = O((t/\epsilon)\log(t/\epsilon\delta))$ "landmark" points $x_1, x_2, \ldots, x_m$. If x_i is a positive example, define $F_i(\cdot) = K(x_i, \cdot)$, where K is the pairwise numerical query function. That is, $F_i(x)$ is the sum-of-terms function for the target DNF formula in which all terms not satisfied by x_i have been removed. This sum-of-terms is unate, since every variable that appears must be in agreement with x_i. Therefore, we can use Theorem 3.2 to learn a hypothesis $h_i(x)$ with error at most $\epsilon/(2m)$ with respect to F_i.

We now combine all hypotheses h_i produced to a single boolean function h defined as: $h(x) = 0$ if $h_i(x) = 0$ for all i, else $h(x) = 1$. By the union bound, h has error at most $\epsilon/2$ with respect to the function f' consisting of all terms of the target satisfied by at least one landmark x_i. Finally, the number of landmarks is sufficiently large that f' has error at most $\epsilon/2$ with respect to the target, so by the triangle inequality, h has error at most ϵ with respect to the target. □

3.3 Learning DNF over the uniform distribution from boolean pairwise queries

DEFINITION 3.4. *Fix a constant $c \in (0, \infty)$. We say a term T in the target DNF is "relatively distinct" if it contains a variable v*

which occurs in at most $c\log(n)$ *other terms. We say* v *is a witness to* T *being relatively distinct.*

DEFINITION 3.5. *For a term* T *in the target DNF, and a variable* v *in* T*, we say* v *is "sometimes nonredundant" for* T *if, given a random example that satisfies* T*, there is at least an* ϵ *probability that every term in the target DNF that the example satisfies also contains* v.

THEOREM 3.6. *Suppose no term in the target DNF is logically entailed by any other term in the target DNF, every term* T *is relatively distinct, and that some variable* v *that is a witness to* T *being relatively distinct is sometimes nonredundant for* T*. Then we can properly learn any monotone DNF of this type under a uniform distribution on* $\{0,1\}^n$ *with boolean pairwise queries.*

PROOF. By Lemma 4.1, it suffices to show that every term having at least $\epsilon/(2t)$ probability of being satisfied will, with high probability, have some example satisfying only that term, given a polynomial-sized data set.

Consider a given term T in the target DNF, and choose the v that witnesses relative distinctness which is sometimes nonredundant. Note that every other term in the target DNF contains some variable not present in T, and in particular this is true for the (at most) $c\log(n)$ terms containing v. So under the conditional distribution given that T is satisfied and that v is nonredundant, with probability at least $2^{-c\log(n)} = n^{-c}$, none of these other terms containing v are satisfied, so that T is the only term satisfied. Thus, since T has probability at least $\epsilon/(2t)$ of being satisfied, and v has probability at least ϵ of being nonredundant given that T is satisfied, we have that with probability at least $(\epsilon^2/t)n^{-c}$, a random example satisfies T and no other terms in the target DNF.

Since this is the case for all terms in the target, a sample of size $O((t/\epsilon^2)n^c\log(t/\delta))$ guarantees every term has some example satisfying only that term, with probability at least $1-\delta$. □

We can also consider the class of DNF formulas having only a small number of relevant variables. In this context, it is interesting to observe that if the ith variable is irrelevant, then $P(k(x,y) = 1 \text{ and } x_i \neq y_i) = P(k(x,y) = 1 \text{ and } x_i = y_i)$, where x and y are independent uniformly-distributed samples, and $k(x,y) = 1$ iff x and y are positive examples that satisfy at least one term in common. However, as the following lemma shows, this is not true for relevant variables.

LEMMA 3.7. *For* x *and* y *independent uniformly-distributed examples, if the target function has* r *relevant variables, and the* i^{th} *variable is relevant to the target function, then* $P(k(x,y) = 1$ *and* $x_i = y_i) - P(k(x,y) = 1$ *and* $x_i \neq y_i) \geq (1/4)^r$.

PROOF. For each pair (x,y) with $x_i \neq y_i$, there is a unique corresponding pair (x',y) with $x'_j = x_j$ for $j \neq i$, and $x'_i = y_i$. Let M_i be the number of x,y pairs with $x_i \neq y_i$ and $k(x,y) = 1$. Then note that for every x,y pair with $x_i \neq y_i$ and $k(x,y) = 1$, we also have $k(x',y) = 1$, since whatever term x and y satisfy in common cannot contain variable i anyway, so flipping that feature in x does not change whether x and y share a term or not. In particular, this implies the number of x,y pairs with $x_i = y_i$ and $k(x,y) = 1$ is at least M_i. However, we can also argue it is strictly larger, as follows. By definition of "relevant", each of the 2^r settings of the relevant variables corresponds to an equivalence class of feature vectors, all of which have the same label, and if that label is positive, then all of which have the same profile. Since variable i is relevant, at least one of the 2^r settings of the relevant variables yields an equivalence class of positive examples whose profile contains only terms with variable i in them (these are positive examples such that flipping variable i makes them negative). The probability that both x and y (chosen at random) are in this equivalence class is $(1/4)^r$. Note that for the (x,y) pairs of this type, we have $k(x,y) = 1$; however, if we flip feature x_i, then x would become negative, and hence $k(x,y)$ would no longer be 1; this means this (x,y) pair is not included among those M_i pairs constructed above by flipping x_i starting from some (x,y) with $x_i \neq y_i$ and $k(x,y) = 1$. So $P(k(x,y) = 1 \text{ and } x_i = y_i) - P(k(x,y) = 1 \text{ and } x_i \neq y_i) \geq (M_i/4^n + (1/4)^r) - M_i/4^n = (1/4)^r$. □

THEOREM 3.8. *Under the uniform distribution, with boolean pairwise queries, we can properly learn any DNF having* $O(\log(n))$ *relevant variables.*

PROOF. We can use the property in Lemma 3.7 to design an algorithm as follows. For each i, sample $\Omega(8^r\log(n/\delta))$ random pairs (x,y), and evaluate $k(x,y)$ for each pair. Then calculate the difference of empirical probabilities (fraction of pairs (x,y) for which $k(x,y) = 1$ and $x_i = y_i$ minus fraction of pairs (x,y) for which $k(x,y) = 1$ and $x_i \neq y_i$). If this difference is $> (1/2)(1/4)^r$, decide variable i is relevant, and otherwise decide variable i is irrelevant. By Hoeffding and union bounds, with probability $1-\delta/2$, this will find exactly the r relevant variables. Now enumerate all $2^r = \text{poly}(n)$ possible conjunctions that can be formed from using all of these r relevant variables. Considering this as a 2^r-dimensional feature space, take $\Omega((2^r/\epsilon)log(1/\delta))$ random labeled data points and learn a disjunction over this 2^r-dimensional feature space; since the VC dimension of this set of disjunctions is 2^r, the usual PAC analysis implies this will learn an ϵ-good disjunction with probability $1-\delta/2$. A union bound implies both stages (finding variables and learning the disjunction) will succeed with probability at least $1-\delta$. □

An alternative approach to the second stage in the proof would be to take $\Omega(2^r\log(2^r/\delta))$ random samples, so that with probability at least $1-\delta/2$, we have at least one data point satisfying each of the 2^r possible conjunctions on the relevant variables; then for each of the conjunctions, we check the label of the example that satisfies it, and if that label is positive, we include that conjunction as a term in our DNF, and otherwise we do not include it. This has the property that, altogether, with probability $1-\delta$, we construct a DNF that has error rate *zero*.

Another family of DNF studied in the literature are those with a sublinear number of terms. Specifically, [Ser04] proved that the class of $2^{O(\sqrt{\log n})}$-term *monotone* DNF are learnable under the uniform distribution from labeled data alone. As the following theorem states, we can extend this result to include general $2^{O(\sqrt{logn})}$-term DNF (including non-monotone) given access to our boolean pairwise queries.

THEOREM 3.9. *Under the uniform distribution, with boolean pairwise queries, we can learn any* $2^{O(\sqrt{\log n})}$*-term DNF (supposing* ϵ *to be a constant).*

First, we review some known results from [Ser04]. For any function $g : \{0,1\}^n \to \{-1,+1\}$, define the $g_{i,1}$ and $g_{i,0}$ functions by the property that any x with $x_i = 1$ has $g_{i,1}(x) = g(x)$, and $g_{i,0}(x) = g(y)$, where $y_j = x_j$ for $j \neq i$ and $y_i = 0$. Then define the influence function $I_i(g) = P(g_{i,0}(x) \neq g_{i,1}(x))$. [Ser04] developed a procedure, FindVariable, which uses a poly$(n, 1/\gamma, \log(1/\eta))$ number of random labeled samples, labeled according to any monotone DNF g having at most t terms, and with probability $1-\eta$, returns a set S of variables (indices in $\{1,\ldots,n\}$) such that every $i \notin S$ has $I_i(g) \leq \gamma$ and every $i \in S$ has $I_i(g) \geq \gamma/2$ and the ith variable is contained in some term in g with at most $\log \frac{32tn}{\gamma}$ variables in it.

Furthermore, [Ser04] showed that, for any t-term DNF f, if we are provided with a set $S_f \subseteq \{1,\ldots,n\}$ such that every $i \notin S_f$ has $I_i(f) \leq \epsilon/4n$, then we can learn f in time polynomial in n, $|S_f|^{O(\log \frac{t}{\epsilon} \log \frac{1}{\epsilon})}$, and $\log(1/\delta)$. In particular, for $|S_f| = O(t \log \frac{tn}{\epsilon})$ and $t = 2^{O(\sqrt{\log n})}$, this is polynomial in n (though not necessarily in ϵ). Given the set S_f, the learning procedure simply estimates the Fourier coefficients for small subsets of S_f.

PROOF OF THEOREM 3.9. To prove Theorem 3.9, we consider the following procedure. First draw m random labeled examples $x^{(1)},\ldots,x^{(m)}$. Then, for each $j \leq m$, define $k_j(\cdot) = k(x^{(j)},\cdot)$. Now note that, if we define $\varphi_j(y) = (\varphi_{j1}(y),\ldots,\varphi_{jn}(y))$ by $\varphi_{ji}(y) = 2I[y_i = x_i^{(j)}] - 1$, then we can represent $k_j(\cdot) = (k'_j(\varphi_j(\cdot)) + 1)/2$, where k'_j is a monotone DNF (mapping into $\{-1,+1\}$); specifically, the terms in k'_j correspond to the terms in the target satisfied by $x^{(j)}$, except none of the literals are negated. We then run FindVariable for each of these k'_j, with $\gamma = \epsilon/m$ and $\eta = \delta/2m$. Let S_f denote the union (over $j \leq m$) of the returned sets of variables. It remains only to show this S_f satisfies the requirements for the procedure of [Ser04], including the size requirement.

Taking $m = \Omega(\frac{ct}{\epsilon} \log \frac{t}{\delta})$, with probability at least $1-\delta/4$, every term in the target having probability at least $\epsilon/2ct$ will have at least one of the m examples satisfying it. Suppose this event happens. In particular, this means $\text{error}(\max_j k_j) < \epsilon/2c$. Note that

$$\begin{aligned} I_i(f) &= P(f_{i,0}(x) \neq f_{i,1}(x)) \\ &\leq 2P(\max_j k_j(x) \neq f(x)) + \\ &\quad P((\max_j k_j)_{i,0}(x) \neq (\max_j k_j)_{i,1}(x)) \\ &< \epsilon/c + \sum_j P((k'_j)_{i,0}(x) \neq (k'_j)_{i,1}(x)) \\ &= \epsilon/c + \sum_j I_j(k'_j). \end{aligned}$$

Thus, by a union bound, with probability $1-\delta/2$, any variable $i \notin S_f$ has $I_i(f) < \epsilon/c + m\gamma$, and any variable $i \in S_f$ appears in a term in some k'_j of size at most $\log \frac{32tn}{\gamma}$, and therefore also appears in a corresponding term of this size in f. Suppose this happens. Letting $c = 8n$ and $\gamma = \epsilon/8nm$, we have that any $i \notin S_f$ has $I_i(f) < \epsilon/4n$, while any $i \in S_f$ appears in a term of size at most $\log \frac{256tn^2m}{\epsilon} = O(\log \frac{tn\log(1/\delta)}{\epsilon})$. In particular, this implies $|S_f| = O(t \log \frac{tn \log(1/\delta)}{\epsilon})$, and S_f satisfies the requirements of the method of [Ser04].

Thus, running the procedure from [Ser04] with confidence parameter $\delta/4$, a union bound implies the total probability of successfully producing an ϵ-good classifier is at least $1-\delta$. The above process of constructing S_f is clearly polynomial-time. Then, if $t = 2^{O(\sqrt{\log n})}$, the procedure of [Ser04] runs in time polynomial in n, $\log(1/\delta)$, and $|S_f|^{O(\log(t/\epsilon)\log(1/\epsilon))}$, which is polynomial in n and $\log(1/\delta)$ (though not necessarily in ϵ). □

One interesting observation is that the above is a general reduction. In particular, given any method for learning monotone DNF under the uniform distribution in time $\text{poly}(n, 1/\epsilon, \log(1/\delta))$ from random labeled data, we have a method for learning general DNF under the uniform distribution in time $\text{poly}(n, 1/\epsilon, \log(1/\delta))$ using boolean-valued queries: simply sample $O(t/\epsilon)$ random examples x_i, and for each learn the monotone (with respect to x_i) DNF $k(x_i,\cdot)$ to error ϵ^2/t, and return the resulting estimate of the hypothesis $\max_i k(x_i,\cdot)$. This points out that one advantage of learning with boolean-valued queries is that it allows us to convert results that hold for monotone DNF into results that hold for general DNF, due to the monotone landmark DNFs that compose to form the target function.

4. LEARNING DNF UNDER GENERAL DISTRIBUTIONS : POSITIVE RESULTS

Our methods are described below, split based on the type of query they use (boolean vs numerical). We will see that the method for boolean queries (called the "neighborhood method" below) is effective for any *parsimonious* DNF: a target DNF for which, on the given data set, removing any term from the target DNF would change the label of some example in the data. Note that ordinarily one can assume without loss of generality that a DNF target is parsimonious, but that is not the case with pairwise queries. The method based on numerical-valued queries (called the "common profiles approach" below) will turn out to be effective under conditions on the target DNF that imply *common profiles*; that is, if we partition the data into equivalence classes based on equality of the set of all terms they satisfy in the target DNF, then each equivalence class has $poly(n)$ examples in it; for instance, this is the case as long as we are guaranteed there are at most a $poly(n)$ number of such equivalence classes (independent of the number of data points).

4.1 Methods

4.1.1 The Neighborhood Method

We refer to the following simple procedure as the "neighborhood method". Take $m = \text{poly}(n, 1/\epsilon, \log(1/\delta))$ samples. First, among the positive examples, query all pairs (with the boolean-valued query) to construct a graph, in which examples are adjacent if they satisfy a term in common. For each positive example, construct a minimal conjunction consistent with that example and all of its neighbors (i.e., the consistent conjunction having largest number of literals in it). Next, discard any of these conjunctions that make mistakes on any negative examples. Then sequentially remove any conjunction c_1 such that some other remaining conjunction c_2 subsumes it (contains a subset of the variables). Form a DNF from the remaining conjunctions. Produce this resultant DNF as the output hypothesis.

LEMMA 4.1. *Suppose the target DNF has $t = \text{poly}(n)$ terms. For an appropriate (t-dependent) polynomial sample size m, the neighborhood method will, with probability at least $1-\delta$, produce an ϵ-accurate DNF if, for each term T_i in the target DNF having a probability of satisfaction at least $\epsilon/2t$, there is at least a $p = 1/\text{poly}(n, 1/\epsilon)$ probability that a random example satisfies term T_i and no other term (we call such an example a "nice seed" for T_i).*

PROOF. Under these conditions we have that

$$m = O((1/p)\log(t/\delta) + (t/\epsilon)\log(1/\epsilon\delta))$$

samples suffice to guarantee each T_i with probability of satisfaction at least $\epsilon/2t$ has at least one nice seed, with probability at least $1-\delta/2$.

In the second phase, we remove any conjunction inconsistent with the negative examples. The conjunctions guarnateed by the above argument survive this pruning due to their minimality, and the fact that they are learned from a set of examples that actually are consistent with some term in the target DNF (due to the nice seed). The final pruning step, which removes any redundancies in the set of conjunctions, leaves at most t conjunctions.

The terms that do not have nice seeds compose at most $\epsilon/2$ total probability mass, and m is large enough so that with probability at least $1 - \delta/4$, at most a $3\epsilon/4$-fraction of the data satisfy these terms. Thus, since the result of the neighborhood method is a DNF formula with at most t terms, which correctly labels a $1 - 3\epsilon/4$ fraction of the m examples, the standard PAC bounds imply that with probability at least $1 - \delta/4$, the resulting DNF has error rate at most ϵ. A union bound over the above events implies this holds with probability at least $1 - \delta$. □

4.1.2 The Common Profile Approach

In the case of numerical queries, we have some additional flexibility in designing a method. In this context, we refer to the following procedure as the "common profiles approach".

Consider a sample of $m = \text{poly}(n, 1/\epsilon, \log(1/\delta))$ random labeled examples, and for each pair of positive examples x, y, we request the number $K(x, y)$ of terms they satisfy in common; we additionally request $K(x, x)$ for each positive example x. For each positive example x, we identify the set S of examples y such that the numerical value of $K(x, y)$ is equal $K(x, x)$. So these points satisfy at least all the terms x satisfies. For each such set S, we learn a minimal conjunction consistent with these examples. Then for each of these conjunctions, if it is a specialization of some other one of the conjunctions, we discard it. Then we form our hypothesis DNF with the remaining conjunctions as the terms.

For any example x, relative to a particular target DNF, we refer to the "profile" of x as the set of terms T_i in the target DNF satisfied by x.

LEMMA 4.2. *If the target DNF has at most* $p = \text{poly}(n)$ *possible profiles, then the common profile approach, with an appropriate (p-dependent) sample size* m*, will with probability at least* $1 - \delta$*, produce a DNF having error rate at most* ϵ*.*

PROOF. Note that this procedure produces a DNF that correctly labels the entire data set, since $K(x, y) = K(x, x)$ implies x and y have the same profiles, so that in particular the set S has some term in common to all the examples. If there are only a $\text{poly}(n)$ number of possible profiles, then the above will only produce at most as many distinct terms in its hypothesis DNF, so that a sufficiently large $\text{poly}(n)$-sized data set will be sufficient to guarantee good generalization error. Specifically, $m = O((pn/\epsilon)\log(1/\epsilon\delta))$ examples are enough to guarantee with probability at least $1 - \delta$, any DNF consistent with the data having at most p terms will have error rate at most ϵ, so this is sufficient for the common profile approach. □

4.2 Positive Results

THEOREM 4.3. *If it happens that the target DNF is parsimonious (no redundant terms) for some random* $\Omega((tn/\epsilon)\log(1/\epsilon) + (1/\epsilon)\log(1/\delta))$*-sized data set (for any distribution), then we can efficiently produce a DNF consistent with it having at most* t *terms using boolean-valued queries.*

PROOF. Parsimonious, in this case, means that we cannot remove any terms without changing some labels. But this means that every term has some example that satisfies only that term (i.e., a nice seed). So as described in the proof of Lemma 4.1 above, the "neighborhood method," produces a DNF with terms for the neighborhoods of each of these nice seeds, which in the parsimonious case, covers all of the positive examples. □

COROLLARY 4.4. *We can properly learn any 2-term DNF with boolean-valued queries.*

PROOF. Take $O((n/\epsilon)\log(1/\epsilon) + (1/\epsilon)\log(1/\delta))$ random labeled examples and make the boolean query for all pairs of positive examples. First, find a minimal conjunction consistent with all of the positive examples; if this conjunction does not misclassify any negative examples, return it. By classic PAC bounds, a conjunction consistent with this many random labeled examples will, with probabiliy at least $1-\delta$, have error rate at most ϵ. Otherwise, if this conjunction misclassifies some negatives, then we are assured the target DNF is parsimonious for this data set, and thus Theorem 4.3 guarantees we can efficiently identify a 2-term DNF consistent with it using the boolean-valued queries. Again, the classic PAC bounds imply the sample size is large enough to, with probability at least $1 - \delta$, guarantee that any consistent 2-term DNF has error rate at most ϵ. □

Corollary 4.4 gives a concrete result where using this type of query overturns a known hardness result for supervised learning.

COROLLARY 4.5. *With numerical-valued queries, we can properly learn any DNF having* $O(\log(n))$ *relevant variables, under arbitrary distributions.*

PROOF. These targets have $\text{poly}(n)$ possible profiles, so the common profiles approach will be successful. □

COROLLARY 4.6. *If the target DNF has only* $O(\log(n))$ *terms, then we can efficiently properly learn from random data under any distribution using numerical-valued queries.*

PROOF. There are only $\text{poly}(n)$ number of possible profiles, so the "common profiles" approach will work. □

The above result is interesting particularly because proper learning (even for 2-term DNF) is known to be hard from labeled data alone.

COROLLARY 4.7. *If the target DNF has* $t = \text{poly}(n)$ *terms, and is such that any example can satisfy at most* $O(1)$ *terms, then we can efficiently properly learn from random data using numerical-valued queries.*

PROOF. There are at most $\text{poly}(t) = \text{poly}(n)$ possible profiles, so the "common profiles" approach will work. □

COROLLARY 4.8. *If the DNF is such that any example can satisfy at most* 1 *term (a so-called "disjoint" DNF), then we can efficiently properly learn from random data using boolean-valued queries.*

PROOF. A numerical query whose value can be at most 1 is just a boolean query anyway. □

In particular, Decision Trees can be thought of as a DNF where each example satisfies at most 1 term.

5. MORE POWERFUL QUERIES

If we can ask about k-tuples of examples (do they all jointly satisfy a term in common?), we have the following result:

THEOREM 5.1. *If we can use query sets of arbitrary sizes (instead of just 2 points), then under any distribution we can efficiently properly learn DNF using boolean-valued queries from random data.*

PROOF. We take any set of examples and ask the oracle the number of terms all examples in the set have in common. Let S be the query set. The idea is to greedily add the examples to S while keeping some terms in common.

Algorithm:

0. Input : dataset D
1. Initialize S to be an empty set
2. **Do**{
3. **Do**{
4. $r_{\max} \leftarrow 0$
5. For each example x in the dataset D
6. add x to the set S
7. query the combined set S, and let $r = Oracle(S)$, $r_{\max} \leftarrow \max\{r_{\max}, r\}$
8. If $r = 0$, remove x from S, and otherwise leave it in S and remove x from D
9. } **Until**($r_{max} = 0$)
10. Learn a "most-specific" conjunction from S and add that term to the hypothesis DNF
11. Reset S to empty set
12. }**Until** ($|D| = 0$)

Each time we add a term to the DNF, the examples in S satisfy some term in the target DNF, because we only add each example if by adding it S still has at least one term in common. So the "most-specific" conjunction consistent with S (i.e., the one with most literals in it, still labeling all of S positive) will not misclassify any negative point as positive. Since whenever we add a new term, there were no additional examples in D that could have satisfied a term in common with the examples in S, after adding the term we have removed from D all examples that satisfy the term S has in common. Therefore, the number of terms in our learnt DNF is at most the number of terms T in the true DNF. If the total number of examples is $\gg nT$ (and say T is $poly(n)$), it will get us a DNF that has at most T terms and correctly labels a $poly(n) \gg nT$ sized dataset. Since the training dataset size is much larger than the size of the classifier, by the Occam bound, the learnt DNF will have small generalization error. □

6. OPEN QUESTIONS

- Is it possible to efficiently learn an arbitrary DNF from random data under the uniform distribution with boolean-valued queries?
- Is it possible to efficiently learn an arbitrary DNF from random data under arbitrary distributions with numerical-valued queries? To establish this, in light of the general reduction used to prove Theorem 3.9, it would suffice to show that the class of sums of monotone terms are efficiently learnable from random data under arbitrary distributions. Or, alternatively, can Theorem 2.2 be extended to apply to *exact* numerical queries?

Acknowledgments

Liu Yang would like to extend her sincere thanks to Ryan O'Donnell for his feedback and Steven Rudich for his counseling on Fourier techniques. This work was supported in part by NSF grant IIS-1065251 and a Google Core AI grant.

7. REFERENCES

[Ang88] D. Angluin. Queries and Concept Learning. *Machine Learning*, 2(4):319–Ð342, 1988.

[BFJ+94] A. Blum, M. Furst, J. Jackson, M. Kearns, Y. Mansour, and S. Rudich. Weakly Learning DNF and Characterizing Statistical Query Learning using Fourier Analysis. In *Proceedings of the 26th annual ACM symposium on Theory of computing (STOC)*, pages 253–262, 1994.

[Jac94] J. Jackson. An Efficient Membership-Query Algorithm for Learning DNF with Respect to the Uniform Distribution. In *Proceedings of the 35th Annual Symposium on Foundations of Computer Science (FOCS)*, pages 42–53, 1994.

[Kea89] M. Kearns. *The Computational Complexity of Machine Learning*. PhD thesis, Department of Computer Science, Harvard University, 1989.

[KLV94] M. Kearns, M. Li, and L. Valiant. Learning Boolean Formulas. *J. ACM*, 41:1298–1328, 1994.

[KS01] A. Klivans and R. Servedio. Learning DNF in Time $2^{\tilde{O}(n^{1/3})}$. In *Proceedings of the 33rd Symposium on Theory of Computing (STOC)*, pages 258–265, 2001.

[Man94] Y. Mansour. Learning Boolean Functions via the Fourier Transform. pages 391Ð–424, 1994.

[MOS04] E. Mossel, R. O'Donnell, and R. Servedio. Learning Juntas AKA Learning Functions of k Relevant Variables. *Journal of Computer and System Sciences*, 69(3):421–434, 2004.

[OS07] R. O'Donnell and R. Servedio. Learning Monotone Decision Trees in Polynomial Time. *SIAM Journal on Computing*, 37:827–844, 2007.

[PV88] L. Pitt and L. Valiant. Computational Limitations on Learning from Examples. *J. ACM*, 35:965–984, October 1988.

[Sch90] R. E. Schapire. The Strength of Weak Learnability. *Machine Learning*, 5:197–227, July 1990.

[Ser04] R. A. Servedio. On Learning Monotone DNF under Product Distributions. *Information and Computation*, 193:57–74, 2004.

[Val84] L. Valiant. A Theory of the Learnable. *Communications of the ACM,*, 27:1134Ð–1142, 1984.

[Val12] G. Valiant. Finding correlations in subquadratic time, with applications to learning parities and juntas with noise. In *FOCS*, 2012.

[Ver90] K. Verbeurgt. Learning DNF under the Uniform Distribution in Quasi-Polynomial Time. In *Proceedings of the 3rd Annual Workshop on Computational Learning Theory (COLT)*, pages 314–326, 1990.

[WDYR12] A. Wigderson, Z. Dvir, A. Yehudayoff, and A. Rao. Restriction access. In *Proceedings of the 3rd Innovations in Theoretical Computer Science (ITCS)*, pages 19–33, 2012.

APPENDIX

A. QUERYING WITH POINTS OF OUR OWN CONSTRUCTION

THEOREM A.1. *If we can construct our own feature vectors in addition to getting random data, then under any distribution we can efficiently properly learn DNF using boolean-valued queries.*

PROOF. Suppose we can adaptively construct our own examples. Suppose the target DNF has $T = poly(n)$ terms. Oracle(x,

x') gives the number of terms that x and x' have in common. For any x, let x_{-i} be x but with the ith bit flipped. Let $\bar{x}$ be the negative of x.

Below is an algorithm. **Move**(x, x') moves x' away from x by one bit, while trying to maintain at least one common term. **LearnTerm**(x) returns a term in the target function.

Move(x, x')
    $x'' \leftarrow \bar{x}$
    For $i = 1, 2, ..., n$ s.t. $x_i = x'_i$
    If (Oracle(x, x'') $\leq$ Oracle(x, x'_{-i}))
        $x'' \leftarrow x'_{-i}$
    Return x''

LearnTerm(x)
    Replicate x to get x'
    While (Oracle(x, Move(x, x')) $! = \emptyset$)
        $x' \leftarrow$ Move(x, x')
    Let $I \leftarrow \{i : Oracle(x, x'_{-i}) = \emptyset\}$
    Return x_I (i.e. a conjunction with the literals indexed by I, either positive or negative so that x satisfies it)

LearnDNF
    Initialize all-negative DNF $\hat{h}$
    Take $M = poly(n) \gg nT$ random examples S
    For each $x \in S$
        If Oracle(x,x) > 0 (positive example) and $\hat{h}(x)$ = negative
            Add term LearnTerm(x) to $\hat{h}$
    Return $\hat{h}$ (a DNF with at most T terms, consistent with all M examples)

When we reach x' such that we can't flip any more bits (not already flipped) without making it so they don't satisfy any terms in common anymore, then the bits these two have in common must form a term in the target DNF, so LearnTerm(x) should still find a term in the target DNF. □

Can Theories be Tested? A Cryptographic Treatment of Forecast Testing

Kai-Min Chung*
Department of Computer Science
Cornell University
chung@cs.cornell.edu

Edward Lui
Department of Computer Science
Cornell University
luied@cs.cornell.edu

Rafael Pass†
Department of Computer Science
Cornell University
rafael@cs.cornell.edu

ABSTRACT

How do we test if a weather forecaster actually knows something about whether it will rain or not? Intuitively, a "good" forecast test should be *complete*—namely, a forecaster knowing the distribution of Nature should be able to pass the test with high probability, and *sound*—an uninformed forecaster should only be able to pass the test with small probability.

We provide a comprehensive cryptographic study of the feasibility of complete and sound forecast testing, introducing various notions of both completeness and soundness, inspired by the literature on interactive proofs. Our main technical result is an incompleteness theorem for our most basic notion of computationally sound and complete forecast testing: If Nature is implemented by a polynomial-time algorithm, then every complete polynomial-time test can be passed by a completely uninformed polynomial-time forecaster (i.e., a computationally-bounded "charlatan") with high probability. We additionally study alternative notions of soundness and completeness and present both positive and negative results for these notions.

Categories and Subject Descriptors

F.1.2 [**Theory of Computation**]: Modes of Computation—*Interactive and reactive computation*

*Chung is supported in part by a Simons Foundation postdoctoral fellowship.

†Pass is supported in part by an Alfred P. Sloan Fellowship, Microsoft New Faculty Fellowship, NSF CAREER Award CCF-0746990, NSF Award CCF-1214844, NSF Award CNS-1217821, AFOSR YIP Award FA9550-10-1-0093, and DARPA and AFRL under contract FA8750-11-2-0211. The views and conclusions contained in this document are those of the authors and should not be interpreted as representing the official policies, either expressed or implied, of the Defense Advanced Research Projects Agency or the US government.

ITCS'13, January 9–12, 2013, Berkeley, California, USA.

General Terms

Theory, Economics

Keywords

Forecast testing; incompleteness; multiplicative weights

1. INTRODUCTION

Forecasting plays an important role in many parts of society and in many fields, such as economics and the sciences. One example is weather forecasting, where a weather forecaster tries to predict the weather in future days (e.g., the forecaster may predict that the next day is sunny with 80% probability and rainy with 20% probability) over a sequence of days. How can we evaluate if such a forecaster actually knows something about the weather?

More generally, forecasting is used by many firms, investors, and governments to make decisions based on the forecasts of variables such as demand, stock prices, unemployment rates, and energy consumption. Also, entire industries, such as management consulting and financial advising, are dedicated to the business of supplying forecasts. In the sciences, theories and models also supply forecasts (i.e., predictions) of the outcome of experiments and natural processes. One way of evaluating forecasts is the use of a scoring rule, which assigns a numerical score to a (probabilistic) forecast based on the forecast and the observed outcome (e.g., see [Bri50, Bic07, GR07]), and the score of a sequence of forecasts is typically the average score of the forecasts. Strictly proper scoring rules (see [Bic07, GR07]) incentivize forecasters to report forecasts equal to their personal beliefs (instead of gaming the system). Another way of evaluating a sequence of forecasts is seeing how well "calibrated" the forecasts are; roughly speaking, the forecasts are well-calibrated if when we consider the periods where the forecasts predict an outcome o with probability close to p, we have that the empirical frequency of outcome o during these periods is close to p (e.g., see [Daw82]). For example, if we consider the days where a weather forecaster predicts something close to "30% rainy" and compute the proportion of these days that were actually rainy, then the proportion should be close to 30%.

For concreteness, let us consider weather forecasting specifically, and suppose Nature generates weather sequences according to some distribution. Can we use scoring rules, calibration, or some other method to determine whether a forecaster actually knows (or even just approximately knows)

Nature's distribution for generating weather? More specifically, can one design a *forecast test* that passes forecasters that have accurate knowledge about Nature's distribution, but fails ignorant forecasters that have no knowledge about Nature's distribution? Such a test is an algorithm that takes a sequence of n forecasts and n outcomes generated by a forecaster and Nature (respectively) over n days, and either passes or fails the forecasting; the forecasts made by the forecaster each day are distributions over outcomes (e.g., 80% sunny and 20% rainy).

A good test should at least be passable (with high probability) by an informed forecaster that knows Nature's distribution and forecasts the correct conditional probabilities each day (otherwise, the test is not very useful, since it does not distinguish good forecasters from bad/ignorant forecasters). We call such a property *completeness.*

DEFINITION 1 (COMPLETENESS OF A TEST (INFORMAL)). *A test is said to be* complete *if an informed forecaster that knows Nature's distribution can pass the test with high probability.*

A good test should at the very least also fail (with decent probability) every ignorant forecaster (i.e., a "charlatan") that has no knowledge about Nature's distribution. We call such a property *soundness.*

DEFINITION 2 (SOUNDNESS OF A TEST (INFORMAL)). *A test is said to be* sound *if for every forecaster P that has no (a priori) knowledge of Nature's distribution, P fails the test with decent probability.*

One of the central contributions of this paper is to provide formal definitions of completeness and soundness for forecast testing (inspired by the literature on interactive proofs initiated by Goldwasser, Micali and Rackoff [GMR89] and Babai and Moran [BM88]) and to study the feasibility of such tests. But before turning to our own treatment, let us briefly review the intriguing literature on this topic.

In [San03], Sandroni showed a surprising incompleteness theorem: Any test that is complete (in a particular well-defined way) cannot even satisfy very weak notions of soundness. That is, for any test that passes an informed forecaster that forecasts the correct conditional probabilities each day, there exists an *ignorant* cheating forecaster that passes the test with the same probability as the informed forecaster (who *knows* Nature's distribution). (See [DF06, OS09, OS06, FV98, Leh01, VS03] for related work.) Let us briefly review the proof of this elegant result (which follows a proof technique by Hart). Sandroni's proof uses the minimax theorem and roughly works as follows. Consider a two-player zero-sum game between a forecaster and Nature. The forecaster chooses a forecasting scheme, while Nature chooses a weather generating distribution. The forecaster's payoff is the probability that the test passes the chosen forecasting scheme. Since the test is complete, if the forecaster knows Nature's distribution, then the forecaster can choose a forecasting scheme that has high payoff. Thus, for every mixed strategy of Nature, there exists a forecaster strategy that yields high payoff. By the minimax theorem, there exists a mixed forecaster strategy that yields high payoff no matter what strategy Nature uses; that is, the forecaster passes the test with high probability no matter what Nature's distribution is. Thus, a completely ignorant forecaster (i.e., a charlatan) can pass the test with high probability.

Forecast testing with computational restrictions. Even though Sandroni's proof ([San03]) exhibits an ignorant cheating forecaster that can pass the test, it is not clear whether the cheating forecaster can be found efficiently. Since the game is exponentially large in the sense that both the forecaster and Nature have (at least) exponentially many pure strategies, there is little hope in finding the cheating forecaster efficiently. This leads to the question of whether computational restrictions on the forecaster can help us design a test that is both complete and sound for reasonable notions of completeness and soundness.

Some initial positive results along these lines appear in the work of Fortnow and Vohra [FV09]: it shows the existence of a particular (polynomial-time computable) test and a particular polynomial-time algorithm for Nature such that a forecaster that forecasts the correct conditional probabilities will pass the test, but an uninformed *efficient* (i.e., polynomial-time) forecaster can only pass the test with negligible probability. This result thus suggests that at the very least, Sandroni's universal cheating strategy does not hold for *every* Nature distribution, as long as we restrict to computationally bounded forecasters. The idea is as follows: the algorithm for Nature generates large random primes p and q and outputs one bit of (pq, p, q) per day. Assuming that one cannot factor the product of two large random primes efficiently, it follows that an *efficient* forecaster cannot make decent forecasts and thus cannot pass the test with decent probability.

1.1 Our Treatment of Forecast Testing

The result of Fortnow and Vohra gives some hope that meaningful forecast testing may actually be possible. However, observe that an *efficient* forecaster that *knows* the algorithm for Nature cannot even pass the test of Fortnow and Vohra. This is because their algorithm for Nature keeps *hidden state* in the sense that after generating p and q, the algorithm remembers p and q for use in future days. A forecaster that knows the algorithm for Nature would still not know the hidden state (p, q), so the forecaster would be unable to efficiently make good forecasts. Thus, the test of Fortnow and Vohra does not satisfy completeness with respect to informed *efficient* forecasters. If we aim to provide a computational treatment of forecast testing, it is imperative that the test satisfies a notion of completeness also with respect to *efficient* forecasters (knowing Nature); towards this, we thus consider Natures with *publicly observable state.*

Natures with publicly observable state. In general, if Nature's algorithm keeps hidden state, then even if a forecaster knows Nature's algorithm, it might be computationally intractable for the forecaster to learn Nature's distribution for the next day. Thus, to ensure that an informed forecaster who knows Nature's algorithm can efficiently pass the test, we consider algorithms for Nature as efficient Turing machines that keep no hidden state, and on input a history of outcomes, outputs a distribution over outcomes for the next day. Note that in this model, an informed forecaster can simply run Nature's algorithm to learn the next day's distribution. (One can also consider a slightly more complicated model where we allow Nature to also output state information that is publicly observable and of polynomial length; our results still hold in this model, but for simplicity, we will mainly work with the simpler model.)

Our computational incompleteness theorem. One of our main results is to restore the strong impossibility result of Sandroni ([San03]) in the computationally bounded setting; that is, we show the following:

THEOREM 1 (INFORMALLY STATED). *Any efficient test that is complete cannot even satisfy very weak notions of soundness with respect to efficient forecasters. That is, for any efficient test that is complete, and for any polynomial bound $t(\cdot)$, there exists a universal uniform* efficient *cheating forecaster that passes the test with high probability for every uniform Nature algorithm that runs in time $t(\cdot)$.*

Recall that Sandroni ([San03]) used the minimax theorem to show the existence of a (possibly inefficient) universal cheating forecaster in the corresponding zero-sum game. A natural approach to showing the above theorem is to show that such a universal cheating forecaster is actually efficient and that we can find it efficiently. Note that when Nature algorithms are polynomial-time Turing machines, by a standard enumeration argument, it suffices to consider polynomially many such machines as pure strategies of Nature in the game.[1]

Thus, it seems that the game is now of polynomial size, and one can find a universal mixed strategy for the forecaster efficiently using linear programming. However, Nature still has exponentially many mixed strategies, each of which may have a different "good response", resulting in super-polynomially many strategies for the forecaster. Thus, the linear programming approach may yield a complex mixed strategy over super-polynomially many pure strategies, and so the universal cheating forecaster may not be efficient.

Another possible strategy is for the forecaster to run an experts algorithm that roughly guarantees that the forecaster's payoff is almost as good as the payoff of the best forecaster. However, these algorithms and results consider a scenario where the forecaster receives some payoff on each day, and it is only guaranteed that the forecaster's payoff on average (over the days) is almost as good as that of the best forecaster. This does not fit our scenario where we consider *general* tests that may not necessarily assign some payoff/score to the forecaster on each day; in particular, the test may fail the forecaster if the forecaster does not do well near the beginning. One can also consider forecasters that try to learn Nature's algorithm over time; however, it may take many days to learn Nature's algorithm, and by then, the forecaster may have already failed the test.

Our approach. In general, our result does not follow from a straight-forward application of known results on experts/learning algorithms. However, we do use a multiplicative weights algorithm, which can be used to approximately find the minimax strategies of two-player zero-sum games (e.g., see [FS99]). Unlike the linear programming approach, a multiplicative weights algorithm can efficiently yield an approximate minimax strategy for the forecaster that only has polynomial support. The multiplicative weights algorithm roughly works as follows. A zero-sum game between a row player and a column player is played for a certain number of rounds. In the first round, the column player chooses the uniform mixed strategy, and then the row player chooses a "good response" (a pure strategy) that yields high payoff. In the next round, the column player updates it's mixed strategy using a multiplicative update rule that depends on the row player's strategy in the previous round. The row player again chooses a good response that yields high payoff. By repeating this procedure for polynomially many rounds, the row player obtains a sequence of good responses such that the uniform distribution over the multiset of good responses yields high payoff no matter what strategy the column player chooses. In our setting, the row player is the forecaster and the column player is Nature.

There are some issues that need to be resolved. Firstly, finding a good response for the forecaster involves running Nature's mixed strategy, but Nature's mixed strategy depends on the forecaster's strategy in the previous round. This recursion may potentially lead to a blow up in the algorithm's running time. However, using the fact that Nature only has polynomially many strategies, we can approximate Nature's current mixed strategy by just keeping track of the weights for each of the possible Turing machines. This guarantees that the time complexity needed to implement any mixture over Nature strategies is always a priori bounded, which prevents a blow-up in running time. Another issue is that the forecaster needs to efficiently find a good response to Nature's mixed strategy. This is done by using the informed forecaster P from the completeness property of the test; however, P only needs to work for Nature algorithms that have no hidden state, but a mixture over Nature strategies is normally implemented as a Nature algorithm that keeps hidden state. We overcome this problem by considering a non-uniform stateless Nature algorithm that uses Bayesian updating to essentially simulate Nature's mixed strategy, and we then use the informed forecaster P for this stateless Nature algorithm instead. After resolving these issues, we get a universal uniform efficient cheating forecaster.

Let us also point out that it is crucial for our proof that Nature is modeled as a uniform polynomial-time algorithm, as opposed to a non-uniform algorithm. Our technique easily extends to the case where Nature is a polynomial-time machine with $\log n$ bits of advice, but as we show in our full paper, the ideas of Fortnow and Vohra [FV09] can be used to show the existence of a complete test for polynomial-time Natures with polylog n bits of advice that no universal efficient cheater can pass (except with negligible probability).

1.2 Restricted Natures

In light of our computational incompleteness theorem for forecast testing, we investigate other alternative approaches (other than computational restrictions) to get complete and sound forecast testing. A crucial component of both Sandroni's and our impossibility result is that the strategy set of Nature is convex. Thus, a natural approach to circumvent these results would be to only require completeness with respect to a non-convex subclass of Nature distributions. Towards this, we consider Nature distributions that are slightly "biased", in the sense that for at least e.g., 10% of days, the weather is $> 60\%$ likely to be rainy or $> 60\%$ likely to be sunny, and completeness only needs to hold with respect to biased Nature distributions. In this setting, we are able to design a simple complete test that satisfies the

[1] Recall that a polynomial-time Turing machine M is a single (fixed-sized, independent of the input length) Turing machine that, on inputs of length n, takes $poly(n)$ computational steps. Thus, if we enumerate the first n Turing machines in a list, M will always be in the list as long as n is sufficiently large.

following notion of soundness[2] (inspired by the classic notion of soundness of an interactive proof [GMR89, BM88]):

DEFINITION 3 (SOUNDNESS OF A TEST (INFORMAL)). *A test is said to be* sound (resp., computationally sound) with respect to a class $\mathcal{N}$ of Nature algorithms *if every uninformed forecaster (resp., uninformed efficient forecaster) will fail the test with high probability over a uniformly random Nature algorithm in* $\mathcal{N}$.

We show the following:

THEOREM 2 (INFORMALLY STATED). *There exists a linear-time computable test that is complete with respect to biased Nature algorithms, and is sound with respect to a class of biased polynomial-size Nature algorithms.*

Our notion of a "biased" Nature, as well as the above theorem, are closely related to a recent result by Olszewski and Sandroni [OS09].[3] The main differences are that our test is simpler and more efficient, our notion of soundness is stronger, and our analysis is significantly simpler and can provide a concrete bound on the soundness error as a function of the number of days. Our test T computes a score s_i for each day i with forecast p_i as follows: if the outcome is 1, $s_i = p_i - 1/2$; otherwise, $s_i = 1/2 - p_i$. The test T accepts if and only if the total score is greater than a certain threshold. We show that T satisfies the restricted completeness and soundness by a martingale analysis using Azuma's inequality.

1.3 Towards Stronger Notions of Soundness

In our opinion, the above notion of soundness is still relatively weak. Ideally, we would want a notion of soundness similar to the cryptographic notion of a proof of knowledge [FS89, BG92, MP07]: roughly speaking, we only want a forecaster to be able to pass the test if the forecaster's predictions are close to the actual distribution of Nature, on average over the days. We refer to this notion of soundness as *strong soundness.*

DEFINITION 4 (STRONG SOUNDNESS (INFORMAL)). *A test is said to be* strongly sound (resp., computationally strongly sound) with respect to a class $\mathcal{N}$ of Nature algorithms *if for every Nature $N \in \mathcal{N}$, with high probability, if a forecaster (resp., efficient forecaster) manages to pass the test, then the forecasts made by the forecaster are close to the Nature N's actual distribution, on average over the days.*

Unfortunately, we demonstrate that achieving this strong notion of soundness cannot be done, even in the setting of computationally-bounded forecasters, and even when only requiring completeness to hold for biased computationally-efficient Natures.

[2]As far as we can tell, this notion of soundness is significantly stronger than previous notions of soundness considered in the literature on forecast testing; there, the typical notion of soundness only requires that for each uninformed forecaster, there exists some Nature for which the test will fail the forecaster with high probability.

[3]At the time of writing the first version of this paper, we were unaware of this result. We thank Lance Fortnow for pointing us to it.

THEOREM 3 (INFORMALLY STATED). *Any test that is complete with respect to biased Nature algorithms is not computationally strongly sound with respect to some class of biased polynomial-time Nature algorithms with n bits of non-uniform advice. If we additionally assume the existence of a problem in the complexity class* E *with exponential circuit complexity*[4]*, then the same holds even if Nature algorithms are uniform and efficient.*

The idea behind Theorem 3 is quite straight-forward. Consider a Nature that outputs rain with probability 0.7 on each day independently. By completeness, a forecaster outputting 0.7 on each day will pass the test with high probability. Now, if we select a "deterministic" Nature (that on each day either outputs rain with probability 1, or sun with probability 1) at random such that the probability of rain on each day is 0.7 independently, then the same forecaster will still pass the test with high probability, although it outputs an incorrect prediction on every day (which contradicts strong soundness). Such a "deterministic" Nature requires n bits of non-uniform advice (namely, the rain/sun sequence); nevertheless, by relying on derandomization techniques, these n bits can be generated using an appropriate Nisan-Wigderson type pseudorandom generator ([NW94]) using only $O(\log n)$ bits of random seed. By enumerating over all polynomially many possible seeds, we can make Nature uniform and efficient.

The above argument has other implications. Consider the following commonly used method for checking the accuracy of a theory of some physical phenomenon. The theory outputs a single prediction and next this prediction is evaluated on multiple supposedly independent samples (using e.g., some statistical test such as a t-test or a χ^2-test). For example, a theory may predict the movement of a particle, and we can evaluate the prediction on multiple supposedly independent samples. When the samples are indeed independent, the soundness of the evaluation/test follows from elementary statistical theory. However, when independence cannot be safely assumed, in order for this method to be actually sound, we need to check that the samples are actually independent[5]. It is not hard to see that the above argument can be used to show that checking independence is impossible.

The above discussion motivates our last relaxation of the problem of forecast testing. We further restrict both the completeness and the soundness conditions to only hold with respect to Natures that already satisfy some notion of independence over each consecutive (non-overlapping) segment of k days. More specifically, for each segment i, conditioned on the outcomes before segment i, the outcomes in segment i are pairwise independent and have the same marginal distribution. We refer to such Natures as *k-segment Natures.* These Natures can capture the testing of scientific theories, where predictions are evaluated on multiple independent or pairwise independent trials/samples. In this setting, we present a simple test that achieves both completeness and strong soundness.

[4]This is a standard complexity-theoretic assumption from the literature on derandomization (e.g., see [IW97]).

[5]There are various method used in practice, such as permuting the data, using sliding windows, etc.

THEOREM 4 (INFORMALLY STATED). *There exists a linear-time computable test that is both complete and strongly sound with respect to k-segment Natures.*

The test is straight-forward: On each segment of k days, compute the distance between the empirical probability of outcome 1 and the forecaster's prediction on the first day of the segment. If the average distance (over the segments) is sufficiently small, the test accepts; otherwise, the test rejects. To analyze the test, we use Chebyshev's inequality to analyze the distance in each segment, and then we use Azuma's inequality to analyze the average distance over the segments.

1.4 Outline of Our Results

Our model for forecast testing can be found in Section 2, and our definitions of soundness can be found in Section 2.1. Our computational incompleteness theorem (Theorem 1) can be found in Section 3. Our feasibility result for biased Natures (Theorem 2) can be found in Section 4. Our computational strong soundness impossibility result for biased Natures (Theorem 3) can be found in Section 5. Lastly, our strong soundness feasibility result for k-segment Natures (Theorem 4) can be found in Section 6. All missing proofs, as well as our other results, can be found in the full version of this paper.

2. PRELIMINARIES AND DEFINITIONS

Let $\mathcal{O}$ be any finite set representing possible *outcomes*, and let $\Delta(\mathcal{O})$ be the set of all probability distributions over $\mathcal{O}$. A *forecast* is a distribution over $\mathcal{O}$, i.e., an element of $\Delta(\mathcal{O})$. Given a vector $\vec{v} = (v_1, \ldots, v_n)$ and a positive integer $i \leq n+1$, let $\vec{v}_{<i}$ be the vector $(v_1, \ldots, v_{i-1})$. Given a positive integer $k \in \mathbb{N}$, let $[k] = \{1, \ldots, k\}$.

A *nature* is a deterministic Turing machine N such that on input 1^n and a history $\vec{o}_{<i}$ of outcomes for days 1 through $i-1$, N outputs a distribution over $\mathcal{O}$ representing the likelihood of each outcome for day i. For generality, we allow natures to be non-uniform and take an advice string as auxiliary input. A class of natures $\mathcal{N} = \{\mathcal{N}_n\}_{n\in\mathbb{N}}$ is a sequence of sets of natures $\mathcal{N}_n$; we often omit the index n when the context is clear. A *forecaster* is a probabilistic interactive Turing machine P such that on input 1^n and a history $\vec{o}_{<i}$ of outcomes for days 1 through $i-1$, P outputs a forecast for day i.

Given a forecaster P, a nature N, and a positive integer n, let $(P, N)(1^n)$ be the output of the following experiment: For $i = 1, \ldots n$ do: $p_i \leftarrow P(1^n, \vec{o}_{<i})$; $O_i \leftarrow N(1^n, \vec{o}_{<i})$; $o_i \leftarrow O_i$; End for; Output $((p_1, \ldots, p_n), (o_1, \ldots, o_n))$. The forecaster P can be *stateful* throughout the experiment; in particular, P can keep track of the forecasts that it has made so far. Nature is always given the history of outcomes as well as any (non-uniform) advice it had at the beginning of the experiment, but nature is not allowed to keep any hidden (unobservable) state for use in future days. $(P, N)(1^n)$ represents an n-day experiment where the forecaster P tries to make good forecasts of the outcomes generated by the nature N.

We can also consider an alternative model where nature can keep track of state, but the state is publicly observable (since otherwise even a good forecaster that knows the algorithm of nature would not be able to make good forecasts). In our full paper, we describe such a model where nature also outputs state information on each day, and a history now includes the outcome as well as the state for each day in the past. We refer to this alternative model as "the model of Nature with publicly observable state", and we refer to the earlier simpler model as "the simple Nature model". In this paper, we will mainly work with the simple Nature model for simplicity. However, all of our technical results still hold in the other model.

A (forecast) *test* is a (possibly probabilistic) Turing machine T such that on input $(\vec{p}, \vec{o}) \in (\Delta(\mathcal{O}))^n \times \mathcal{O}^n$ representing a sequence of forecasts and outcomes, T outputs a bit in $\{0, 1\}$ to indicate whether the test accepts or rejects, with 1 being accept. A test is only meaningful if it passes (with high probability) a forecaster that knows the distribution of nature (otherwise, the test is not very useful, since it does not distinguish good forecasters from bad/ignorant forecasters). Borrowing terminology from interactive proofs [GMR89, BM88], we call this property *completeness.*

Our definition of completeness considers a "canonical forecaster" that knows the nature algorithm. Given a nature N, the *canonical forecaster for* N is the forecaster P_N that, on input $(1^n, \vec{o}_{<i})$, runs N on input $(1^n, \vec{o}_{<i})$ to get a distribution O_i, and then outputs O_i as its forecast. Given a nature N, we will use P_N to denote the canonical forecaster for N. We now formally define what it means for a test T to be *complete.*

DEFINITION 5 (COMPLETENESS OF A TEST). *A test T is said to be* complete with completeness error $\epsilon(\cdot)$ *if for every nature N and every $n \in \mathbb{N}$, we have*

$$\Pr[T((P_N, N)(1^n)) = 1] \geq 1 - \epsilon(n),$$

where P_N is the canonical forecaster for N, and the probability is over the random coins of T and the experiment $(P_N, N)(1^n)$.

2.1 Definitions of Soundness

In this section, we present several definitions of soundness with varying levels of strength. Let T be any test. We would like the test T to satisfy some notion of *soundness*, i.e., a forecaster without knowledge of nature should not be able to pass the test with decent probability. A very weak notion of soundness is that there is no universal forecaster that passes the test with decent probability no matter what nature is.

DEFINITION 6 (WEAK SOUNDNESS OF A TEST). *Let $\mathcal{N}$ be any set of natures. A test T is said to be* weakly sound (resp., computationally weakly sound) with soundness error $\epsilon(\cdot)$ with respect to $\mathcal{N}$ *if for every forecaster (resp., efficient forecaster) P, there exists an $N \in \mathcal{N}$ such that for sufficiently large $n \in \mathbb{N}$, we have*

$$\Pr[T((P, N)(1^n)) = 1] \leq \epsilon(n),$$

where the probability is over the random coins of T and the experiment $(P, N)(1^n)$.

Weak soundness has been the typical notion of soundness used in the literature. However, this notion of soundness is very weak, and it does not even prevent the existence of a cheating forecaster that actually passes the test for most natures in $\mathcal{N}$. Ideally, if a forecaster does not know any information about Nature beyond being in a certain class $\mathcal{N}$, then the test should reject the forecaster with high probability for most natures in $\mathcal{N}$. We formalize this stronger soundness property in the following definition.

DEFINITION 7 (SOUNDNESS OF A TEST). *Let $\mathcal{N}$ be any class of natures. A test T is said to be* sound (resp., computationally sound) *with respect to $\mathcal{N}$ if for every forecaster (resp., efficient forecaster) P, there exists a negligible function*[6] *$negl(\cdot)$ such that for every $n \in \mathbb{N}$, we have that at least a $(1 - negl(n))$-fraction of the natures $N \in \mathcal{N}$ satisfy*

$$\Pr[T((P,N)(1^n)) = 1] \leq negl(n),$$

where the probability is over the random coins of T and the experiment $(P,N)(1^n)$.

We note that the above soundness definition is still weak in the following sense. It is possible that a sound test T passes some $(P,N)(1^n)$ with high probability, but the forecast $\vec{p}$ produced by P may be still poor in the sense that for most of the days $i \in [n]$, p_i is actually statistically far from the true distribution $N(1^n, \vec{o}_{<i})$ of the nature N. Ideally, we would like a good test T to prevent such possibilities, which is formalized by the following definition of strong soundness similar to the cryptographic notion of a proof of knowledge [FS89, BG92, MP07].

DEFINITION 8 (STRONG SOUNDNESS OF A TEST). *Let $\mathcal{N}$ be any class of natures. A test T is said to be (ϵ, δ)-strongly* sound (resp., computationally (ϵ,δ)-strongly sound) *with respect to $\mathcal{N}$ if for every forecaster (resp., efficient forecaster) P, every $n \in \mathbb{N}$, and every nature $N \in \mathcal{N}$, the following event B occurs with probability at most $\epsilon(n)$ over the randomness of the experiment $(P,N)(1^n)$ and the test T: Let $(\vec{p}, \vec{o})$ be the output of $(P,N)(1^n)$; then, the event B is defined to be the event where both of the following conditions hold:*

- $T(\vec{p}, \vec{o}) = 1$
- $\frac{1}{n}\sum_{i=1}^{n} ||p_i - N(1^n, \vec{o}_{<i})||_1 > \delta(n)$.

In other words, the event B says that the test T accepts but the average statistical distance between the forecasts and the true distributions is greater than $\delta(n)$.

3. A UNIVERSAL EFFICIENT CHEATING FORECASTER

In this section, we formalize and prove our computational incompleteness theorem (Theorem 1) for forecast testing: For any efficient complete test, there exists a universal uniform efficient cheating forecaster that passes the test without any knowledge of nature's distribution.

THEOREM 5. *Let $t(\cdot)$ be any polynomial, and let $\mathcal{N}$ be the collection of all uniform natures whose running time is bounded by $t(\cdot)$. Let $p(\cdot)$ be any positive polynomial.*

Let T be any efficient (PPT) test that is complete with completeness error $\epsilon(\cdot)$. Then, there exists a universal uniform efficient cheating forecaster C for T that runs in time $poly(n, t(n), p(n))$ such that for every nature $N \in \mathcal{N}$ and every sufficiently large $n \in \mathbb{N}$, we have

$$\Pr[T((C,N)(1^n)) = 1] \geq 1 - \epsilon(n) - \frac{1}{p(n)},$$

where the probability is over the random coins of T and the experiment $(C,N)(1^n)$.

[6]A function $f : \mathbb{N} \to \mathbb{R}^+$ is *negligible* if it decays faster than any inverse polynomial function, i.e., for every $c \in \mathbb{N}$, we have $f(n) \leq \frac{1}{n^c}$ for sufficiently large $n \in \mathbb{N}$.

We now prove Theorem 5. We will construct a uniform forecaster C running in time $poly(n, t(n), p(n))$ such that for every uniform nature N running in time $t(n)$, we have that for sufficiently large $n \in \mathbb{N}$,

$$\Pr[T((C,N)(1^n)) = 1] \geq 1 - \epsilon(n) - O\left(\frac{1}{p(n)}\right).$$

Since $p(\cdot)$ is an arbitrary positive polynomial, this is sufficient for proving Theorem 5.

High-level description of the universal cheating forecaster C. Let $M_1, M_2, M_3, \ldots$ be any enumeration of the set of all uniform natures, and let M_1', M_2', $M_3', \ldots$ be the corresponding sequence where M_i' is the same as M_i except that after $t(n)$ steps, M_i' stops and deterministically outputs any fixed distribution over $\mathcal{O}$.

At a high level, the forecaster C finds a "good set" of forecasting machines $\{P_1, \ldots, P_L\}$ using a multiplicative weights algorithm ([FS99]), and then chooses one of them uniformly at random and uses the chosen machine to make forecasts in the interactive game *for all n days.*

In the multiplicative weights algorithm of the forecaster C, C simulates L rounds (repetitions) of a zero-sum game between a forecaster F and "Nature", where the payoff for the forecaster is the probability that the forecaster passes the test T. In each round i, Nature chooses a mixed strategy $N^{(i)}$ over its pure strategies (nature machines) $\{M_1', \ldots, M_n'\}$, and then F chooses a forecasting machine $P_i := P_i(N^{(i)})$ that hopefully "does well" against Nature's mixed strategy $N^{(i)}$, i.e., F's expected payoff $\mathbb{E}[\Pr[T((P_i, N^{(i)})(1^n)) = 1]]$ is high. In the first round, Nature chooses the uniform distribution $N^{(1)}$ over $\{M_1', \ldots, M_n'\}$, and after each round i, Nature updates its mixed strategy to get $N^{(i+1)}$ in a manner similar to the multiplicative weights algorithm described in [FS99].

We later show that by using an analysis similar to that in [FS99], we can show that the forecaster C does well against all nature machines in $\{M_1', \ldots, M_n'\}$ if in every round i, the chosen forecasting machine P_i does well against Nature's mixed strategy $N^{(i)}$. To achieve the latter condition, the forecaster C makes use of the completeness of the test T, which guarantees that the canonical forecaster P_N for a nature N does well against N. However, the forecaster C cannot simply choose P_i to be the canonical forecaster $P_{N^{(i)}}$ for $N^{(i)}$, since $N^{(i)}$ is a *mixture* of nature machines, not a single nature machine N. (A mixture of nature machines may be captured by a single nature machine that keeps hidden state, but nature machines are stateless by definition and the completeness of T only holds for stateless nature machines.)

The forecaster C overcomes this problem by letting P_i be the canonical forecaster $P_{B(N^{(i)})}$ for $B(N^{(i)})$, where $B(N^{(i)})$ is essentially a "stateless version" of $N^{(i)}$ that uses Bayesian updating. Using the fact that completeness holds for all natures[7], we have that $P_i = P_{B(N^{(i)})}$ does well against the nature $B(N^{(i)})$. We show that the output distribution of the nature $B(N^{(i)})$ and the mixed-strategy nature $N^{(i)}$ are essentially the same in the (single-round) forecasting experiment, so P_i also does well against the mixed-strategy nature $N^{(i)}$, as required. (Due to the fact that $B(N^{(i)})$ uses

[7]In fact, it suffices for completeness to hold for non-uniform polynomial-time natures.

Bayesian updating, $B(N^{(i)})$ might actually only be an approximation of the mixed-strategy nature $N^{(i)}$; however, by making the error polynomially small, the result still holds.)

The universal cheating forecaster C. Let $M_1, M_2, M_3, \ldots$ be any enumeration of the set of all uniform natures, and let $M_1', M_2', M_3', \ldots$ be the corresponding sequence where M_i' is the same as M_i except that after $t(n)$ steps, M_i' stops and deterministically outputs any fixed distribution over $\mathcal{O}$.

On input 1^n, C proceeds as follows:

1. Let $L = \Theta(p(n)^2 \ln n)$ and $\beta = \frac{1}{1+\sqrt{(2\ln n)/L}}$.

2. **Multiplicative weights algorithm:**

   Let $N^{(1)}$ be the uniform distribution over $\{M_1', \ldots, M_n'\}$.

   For $i = 1, \ldots, L$ **do:**

   (a) **Choosing a forecaster P_i that does well against $N^{(i)}$:**

   Let $P_i = P_{B(N^{(i)})}$ be the canonical forecaster for the nature $B(N^{(i)})$, where B is the (non-uniform) nature that takes the weights of a distribution $N^{(i)}$ over $\{M_1', \ldots, M_n'\}$ as advice and, on input a history $\vec{o}_{<k}$, updates the distribution $N^{(i)}$ using Bayesian updating (by conditioning on the history $\vec{o}_{<k}$), samples a nature M_j' from the updated distribution, and then outputs $M_j'(1^n, \vec{o}_{<k})$.

   (b) **Weight update:**

   Let $N^{(i+1)}(M_j') \sim \beta^{\widehat{\mu}(P_i, M_j')} \cdot N^{(i)}(M_j')$, where $\widehat{\mu}(P_i, M_j')$ is an approximation of

   $$\begin{aligned}\mu(P_i, M_j') &:= \Pr[T((P_i, M_j')(1^n)) = 1] \\ &= \mathbb{E}[T((P_i, M_j')(1^n))]\end{aligned}$$

   by taking the average of $\Theta(p(n)^2 \ln(Lnp(n)))$ samples of $T((P_i, M_j')(1^n))$.

   End for

3. Choose $i \leftarrow \{1, \ldots, L\}$ uniformly at random.

4. Use the machine P_i to make forecasts in the interactive game for all n days.

We now continue with the formal proof of Theorem 5. It can be easily verified that C runs in time $poly(n, t(n), p(n)) = poly(n, t(n))$. Let N be any uniform nature with running time bounded by $t(n)$.

CLAIM 1. *For every sufficiently large $n \in \mathbb{N}$, we have*

$$\Pr[T((C, N)(1^n)) = 1] \geq 1 - \epsilon(n) - O\left(\frac{1}{p(n)}\right).$$

To prove the theorem, it suffices to prove the above claim. Fix a sufficiently large integer n such that the nature N appears in $\{M_1, \ldots, M_n\}$. We note that the nature N also appears in $\{M_1', \ldots, M_n'\}$, since the running time of N is bounded by $t(n)$. Given a forecaster F and a nature M, let $\mu(F, M)$ be defined by

$$\mu(F, M) = \Pr[T((F, M)(1^n)) = 1].$$

Given a forecaster F and a distribution $N^{(i)}$ over natures, let

$$\begin{aligned}\mu(F, N^{(i)}) &:= \mathbb{E}_{M \sim N^{(i)}}[\mu(F, M)] \\ &= \sum_{M \in Supp(N^{(i)})} N^{(i)}(M) \cdot \mu(F, M).\end{aligned}$$

We note that $\widehat{\mu}(P_i, M_j')$ in the forecasting algorithm C above is an approximation of $\mu(P_i, M_j')$. Let

$$\widehat{\mu}(P_i, N^{(i)}) = \sum_{k=1}^{n} N^{(i)}(M_k') \cdot \widehat{\mu}(P_i, M_k').$$

Then $\widehat{\mu}(P_i, N^{(i)})$ is an approximation of $\mu(P_i, N^{(i)})$. We first prove a lemma that gives a lower bound on $\frac{1}{L}\sum_{i=1}^{L} \widehat{\mu}(P_i, M_j')$ for a fixed nature M_j' in $\{M_1', \ldots, M_n'\}$.

LEMMA 1. *For every nature $M_j' \in \{M_1', \ldots, M_n'\}$, if we run the forecaster $C(1^n)$, then (with probability 1) we have*

$$\frac{1}{L}\sum_{i=1}^{L} \widehat{\mu}(P_i, M_j') \geq \frac{1}{L}\sum_{i=1}^{L} \widehat{\mu}(P_i, N^{(i)}) - O\left(\frac{1}{p(n)}\right)$$

The proof of Lemma 1 is very similar to the analysis of the multiplicative weights algorithm found in [FS99]. In [FS99], the multiplicative weights algorithm updates the weights in $N^{(i)}$ using the exact value of $\mu(P_i, M_j')$; here, we only have an approximation $\widehat{\mu}(P_i, M_j')$ of $\mu(P_i, M_j')$, but with minor changes, the analysis in [FS99] can still be used to show Lemma 1. We now prove a lemma that gives a lower bound on $\frac{1}{L}\sum_{i=1}^{L} \mu(P_i, M_j')$ for every nature M_j' in $\{M_1', \ldots, M_n'\}$.

LEMMA 2. *For every nature $M_j' \in \{M_1', \ldots, M_n'\}$, if we run the forecaster $C(1^n)$, then with probability $1 - O(\frac{1}{p(n)})$ over the random coins of C, $C(1^n)$ internally generates $N^{(1)}$, $\ldots$, $N^{(L)}$ and $P_1, \ldots, P_L$ such that*

$$\frac{1}{L}\sum_{i=1}^{L} \mu(P_i, M_j') \geq \frac{1}{L}\sum_{i=1}^{L} \mu(P_i, N^{(i)}) - O\left(\frac{1}{p(n)}\right).$$

The proof of Lemma 2 follows from Lemma 1, the Chernoff bound, and a union bound. We will now show that $\mu(C, N) = \Pr[T((C, N)(1^n)) = 1] \geq 1 - \epsilon(n) - O(\frac{1}{p(n)})$. Since $N \in \{M_1', \ldots, M_n'\}$, we have by Lemma 2 that with probability $1 - O(\frac{1}{p(n)})$ over the random coins of C, $C(1^n)$ internally generates $N^{(1)}, \ldots, N^{(L)}$ and $P_1, \ldots, P_L$ such that $\frac{1}{L}\sum_{i=1}^{L} \mu(P_i, N) \geq \frac{1}{L}\sum_{i=1}^{L} \mu(P_i, N^{(i)}) - O(\frac{1}{p(n)})$. Since C chooses a machine in $\{P_1, \ldots, P_L\}$ uniformly at random to use in the n-day experiment, to show that $\Pr[T((C, N)(1^n)) = 1] \geq 1 - \epsilon(n) - O(\frac{1}{p(n)})$, it suffices to show that we always have $\mu(P_i, N^{(i)}) \geq 1 - \epsilon(n) - O(\frac{1}{p(n)})$ for every $i \in [L]$.

Fix $i \in [L]$. Let B be the (non-uniform) nature described in Step 2a of the description of C: $B(N^{(i)})$ takes the weights of the distribution $N^{(i)}$ over $\{M_1', \ldots, M_n'\}$ as advice and, on input a history $\vec{o}_{<k}$, updates the distribution $N^{(i)}$ using Bayesian updating (by conditioning on the history $\vec{o}_{<k}$), samples a nature M_j' from the updated distribution, and then outputs $M_j'(\vec{o}_{<k})$. We note that $P_i = P_{B(N^{(i)})}$ by definition, so it suffices to show

$$\mu(P_{B(N^{(i)})}, N^{(i)}) \geq 1 - \epsilon(n) - O\left(\frac{1}{p(n)}\right). \quad (1)$$

By definition of completeness of T, we have

$$\mu(P_{B(N^{(i)})}, B(N^{(i)})) \geq 1 - \epsilon(n). \quad (2)$$

Let us first assume for simplicity that $B(N^{(i)})$ can do the Bayesian updating exactly without any precision error. Then, we have $\mu(P_{B(N^{(i)})}, N^{(i)}) = \mu(P_{B(N^{(i)})}, B(N^{(i)}))$. To see this, we first view the "nature" $N^{(i)}$ in $\mu(P_{B(N^{(i)})}, N^{(i)})$ as a stateful nature that first chooses a machine M'_j according to the distribution $N^{(i)}$, and then uses M'_j to generate (distributions over) outcomes for all n days. Then, we note that for the first day, the output distribution of $B(N^{(i)})$ is the same as that of $N^{(i)}$. It is easy to verify by induction that for every $k \in [n]$, the output distribution of $B(N^{(i)})$ for the first k days is the same as that of $N^{(i)}$. This shows that $\mu(P_{B(N^{(i)})}, N^{(i)}) = \mu(P_{B(N^{(i)})}, B(N^{(i)}))$, so by (2) we have $\mu(P_{B(N^{(i)})}, N^{(i)}) = \mu(P_{B(N^{(i)})}, B(N^{(i)})) \geq 1 - \epsilon(n)$. Thus, (1) holds, as required.

Let us finally show that even if $B(N^{(i)})$ cannot do the Bayesian updating exactly, as long as $B(N^{(i)})$ uses at least $O(n)$ (significant) bits of precision in its computation of probabilities, B can ensure that the updated distribution obtained from Bayesian updating has at most $O(\frac{1}{2^n}) \leq O(\frac{1}{n^2 p(n)})$ relative error pointwise. This ensures that the updated distribution has an L_1-error of at most $O(\frac{1}{np(n)})$. Then, the output distribution of $B(N^{(i)})$ for all n days has an L_1-error of at most $O(\frac{1}{p(n)})$. Thus, we have

$$\left|\mu(P_{B(N^{(i)})}, N^{(i)}) - \mu(P_{B(N^{(i)})}, B(N^{(i)}))\right| \leq O\left(\frac{1}{p(n)}\right),$$

so

$$\begin{aligned}\mu(P_{B(N^{(i)})}, N^{(i)}) &\geq \mu(P_{B(N^{(i)})}, B(N^{(i)})) - O\left(\frac{1}{p(n)}\right)\\ &\geq 1 - \epsilon(n) - O\left(\frac{1}{p(n)}\right),\end{aligned}$$

where the second inequality follows from (2). Thus, (1) still holds, as required.

This completes the proof of Theorem 5. The proof of Theorem 5 can be easily extended so that the theorem holds even if Nature is modeled as a non-uniform Turing machine with $O(\log n)$ bits of non-uniform advice; in our full paper, we show that the ideas from Fortnow and Vohra [FV09] can be used to show that this is tight.

4. FEASIBILITY FOR BIASED NATURES

In this section, we investigate the possibility of achieving a positive result for forecast testing by imposing restrictions on the completeness condition. We will show that if we only require the completeness property to hold for a slightly restricted class of natures (as opposed to all possible distributions over outcomes), then we can obtain a meaningful forecast test that satisfies this restricted completeness and the soundness property as defined in Definition 7 of Section 2.1. Furthermore, our forecast test is simple and efficient. For simplicity, we shall focus on the case of two possible outcomes, i.e. $\mathcal{O} = \{0, 1\}$, and hence a forecast in $\Delta(\mathcal{O})$ can be denoted by a probability $p \in [0, 1]$ of the outcome being 1.

Informally, we say that a nature N is (α, β)-biased if for at least an α-fraction of the days, the probability p of outcome 1 is β-biased, i.e., $|p - 1/2| \geq \beta$.

Definition 9. *A nature N is (α, β)-biased if on input 1^n, for every possible n-day outcome $\vec{o} \in \{0, 1\}^n$, the following holds: For at least an α-fraction of $i \in [n]$, we have $|N(1^n, \vec{o}_{<i}) - 1/2| \geq \beta$.*

For example, suppose outcomes 1 and 0 denote raining and sunny respectively; a nature N being $(.1, .1)$-biased means that at least 10% of days are either 60% likely to be raining or 60% likely to be sunny, which seems to be a very reasonable assumption on the nature. (See [OS09] for a class of natures that is similar to our class of (α, β)-biased natures.)

For every constants $\alpha, \beta \in [0, 1]$, we will present a simple (deterministic) forecast test T that satisfies completeness with respect to all (α, β)-biased natures (including inefficient and non-uniform ones) and the soundness property (with respect to a class of non-uniform natures). We now define completeness with respect to biased natures.

Definition 10. *A test T is (α, β)-*restricted complete* if for every (α, β)-biased nature N and every $n \in \mathbb{N}$, we have*

$$\Pr[T((P_N, N)(1^n)) = 1] \geq 1 - negl(n),$$

where P_N is the canonical forecaster for N.

As a sanity check, we note that by considering (α, β)-restricted completeness, we get around the impossibility result in Section 3 and in [San03]. The reason is that a mixture of (α, β)-biased natures may not be a (α, β)-biased nature. Therefore, the (α, β)-restricted completeness does not imply that the zero-sum game defined in Section 3 and [San03] has value close to 1, and hence the constructed universal cheating forecaster C may only pass the test with poor probability. We proceed to present our formal theorem.

Theorem 6. *For every constants $\alpha, \beta \in (0, 1]$, there exists a deterministic and efficient forecast test that satisfies (α, β)-restricted completeness, and soundness with respect to the class $\mathcal{N}_{det}$ of natures with deterministic outcomes.*

We now present the desired forecast test T. On input $(\vec{p}, \vec{o}) \in (\Delta(\{0, 1\}))^n \times \{0, 1\}^n$, T does the following.

- For every $i \in [n]$, let

$$s_i = \begin{cases} p_i - 1/2 & \text{if } o_i = 1, \\ 1/2 - p_i & \text{if } o_i = 0. \end{cases}$$

- Compute $s = \sum_i s_i$, and accept iff $s \geq \alpha\beta^2 n$.

In other words, T computes some score s_i for each day, and accepts if the total score is sufficiently large. In our full paper, we show that the test T satisfies (α, β)-restricted completeness, as well as soundness with respect to the class $\mathcal{N}_{det}$ of natures with deterministic outcomes.

5. IMPOSSIBILITY OF ACHIEVING STRONG SOUNDNESS

In this section, we demonstrate that achieving strong soundness (as formally defined in Definition 8 of Section 2.1) is impossible, even in the setting of computationally-bounded forecasters, and even when only requiring completeness to hold for (α, β)-biased and computationally-efficient natures. Our result for the setting of computationally-efficient natures uses derandomization techniques from complexity theory and is based on mild complexity-theoretic assumptions.

Towards formally stating our result, we first present the necessary preliminaries as follows.

Preliminaries on derandomization. The main tool we will use is a complexity-theoretic *pseudorandom generator* (PRG) that "fools" bounded size circuits [NW94, IW97]. Let U_n denote the uniform distribution over $\{0,1\}^n$. Informally, a pseudorandom generator $G : \{0,1\}^d \to \{0,1\}^m$ is a function that takes a short d-bit uniform seed $z \leftarrow U_d$ and stretches it to a long m-bit pseudorandom string $G(z)$ that "looks like" an m-bit uniformly random string. Here, "looks like" means that for any bounded size circuit C, the probability that C outputs 1 on uniformly random input U_m is roughly the same as the probability that C outputs 1 on pseudorandom input $G(U_d)$.

Definition 11. *A function $G : \{0,1\}^d \to \{0,1\}^m$ is a (s,ϵ)-pseudorandom generator if for every circuit $C : \{0,1\}^m \to \{0,1\}$ of size at most s,*

$$|\Pr[C(U_m) = 1] - \Pr[C(G(U_d)) = 1| \leq \epsilon.$$

The existing construction of a pseudorandom generator that we use is (necessarily) based on the (unproven) complexity-theoretic assumption of the existence of problems that are solvable in exponential time but has exponential circuit complexity. We first provide the necessary definitions in order to state the pseudorandom generator that we will use later.

Definition 12. *The complexity class E consists of all languages L that can be decided by a deterministic Turing machine M in time $O(2^{cn})$ for some constant $c \in \mathbb{N}$; that is, for every $x \in \{0,1\}^*$, M on input x terminates in time $O(2^{c|x|})$ and $M(x) = 1$ iff $x \in L$.*

Definition 13. *Let L be a language. The circuit complexity of L on input length n is the size of the smallest circuit C_n that decides L on input length n, i.e., for every $x \in \{0,1\}^n$, $C_n(x) = 1$ iff $x \in L$.*

The following pseudorandom generator was first achieved by Impagliazzo and Wigderson [IW97] based on a construction from Nisan and Wigderson [NW94].

Theorem 7. *[IW97] Assume the existence of a language $L \in$ E with circuit complexity $2^{\gamma n}$ for every input length $n \in \mathbb{N}$ and some constant $\gamma > 0$. Then for every $m \in \mathbb{N}$, there exists an $(m, 1/m)$-pseudorandom generator $G : \{0,1\}^{O(\log m)} \to \{0,1\}^m$. Furthermore, G is computable in uniform poly(m) time.*

Our impossibility result for strong soundness. We are now ready to formally state our impossibility result.

Theorem 8. *Let $\alpha \in (0,1], \beta \in (0, 1/2]$ be constants. For every efficient forecast test T that satisfies (α,β)-restricted completeness, T is not computationally $(1-negl(n), (1/2) - \alpha\beta)$-strongly sound with respect to (α,β)-biased natures.*

Furthermore, if we assume the existence of a language $L \in$ E with circuit complexity $2^{\gamma n}$ for every input length $n \in \mathbb{N}$ and some constant $\gamma > 0$, then T is not computationally $(1 - 1/n, (1/2) - \alpha\beta)$-strongly sound with respect to uniform and efficient *(α,β)-biased natures.*

6. FEASIBILITY OF STRONG SOUNDNESS FOR K-SEGMENT NATURES

In this section, we consider natures that output pairwise independent samples with the same marginal distribution in each segment of k consecutive non-overlapping days. We refer to such natures as *k-segment natures.* We show that for such natures, we can achieve complete and strongly sound forecast testing (see Definition 8 in Section 2.1 for the definition of strong soundness). For simplicity, we consider the case of two possible outcomes, i.e. $\mathcal{O} = \{0,1\}$, and thus a forecast in $\Delta(\mathcal{O})$ can be represented by the probability $p \in [0,1]$ of the outcome being 1.

We first give the definition of a k-segment nature. Roughly speaking, a k-segment nature is a nature that groups the days into consecutive non-overlapping segments of k days, and within each segment, the k samples obtained from the nature are pairwise independent and have the same marginal distribution (when conditioned on the outcomes in the previous segments). Such natures can capture the testing of scientific theories, where predictions are evaluated on multiple independent or pairwise independent trials/samples.

Definition 14 (k-segment nature). *Let $k \in \mathbb{N}$. A nature N is said to be a* k-segment nature *if on input 1^{nk}, if we group the days into n consecutive non-overlapping segments each containing k days, and if we let $o_{<i}$ denote the outcomes that occur before segment i, and if we let $q_{i,j}$ denote the output of N on day j of segment i, then for each segment $i \in [n]$ and every $o_{<i}$, the following holds:*

- *The random variables $\{q_{i,1}|_{o_{<i}}, \ldots, q_{i,k}|_{o_{<i}}\}$ are pairwise independent, where $q_{i,j}|_{o_{<i}}$ is the random variable $q_{i,j}$ conditioned on $o_{<i}$.*
- *There exists a $q_i \in [0,1]$ such that $\mathbb{E}[q_{i,j} \mid o_{<i}] = q_i$ for every $j \in [k]$.*

We now define completeness with respect to k-segment natures.

Definition 15. *Let $k \in \mathbb{N}$. A test T is said to be* complete with respect to k-segment natures *if there exists a negligible function $\epsilon(\cdot)$ such that for every k-segment nature N and every $n \in \mathbb{N}$, we have*

$$\Pr[T((P_N, N)(1^{nk})) = 1] \geq 1 - \epsilon(nk),$$

where P_N is the canonical forecaster for N, and the probability is over the random coins of T and the experiment $(P_N, N)(1^{nk})$.

The definition of strong soundness can be found in Definition 8 of Section 2.1. We now formally state our feasibility result.

Theorem 9. *Let $k \in \mathbb{N}$. Then, there exists a deterministic and efficient forecast test T that satisfies the following properties:*

- *T is complete with respect to k-segment natures.*
- *T is (ϵ,δ)-strongly sound with respect to k-segment natures, where ϵ is a negligible function, and $\delta(n) = O(\frac{1}{k^{1/3}} + \frac{1}{n^{1/3}})$.*

We now present the desired forecast test T. On input $(\vec{p}, \vec{o}) \in (\Delta(\{0,1\}))^{nk} \times \{0,1\}^{nk}$, T does the following:

- For each segment $i \in [n]$, compute the average $\widehat{q}_i$ of the outcomes in segment i.
- Compute $\frac{1}{n}\sum_{i=1}^{n}|p_i - \widehat{q}_i|$, where p_i is the forecast in $\vec{p}$ for the first day of segment i.
- Output 1 (accept) if $\frac{1}{n}\sum_{i=1}^{n}|p_i - \widehat{q}_i| \leq \frac{2}{k^{1/3}} + \frac{1}{n^{1/3}}$; otherwise, output 0 (reject).

In our full paper, we show that the test T satisfies the properties described in Theorem 9.

7. ACKNOWLEDGMENTS

We thank Bobby Kleinberg and Lance Fortnow for helpful discussions.

8. REFERENCES

[BG92] Mihir Bellare and Oded Goldreich, *On defining proofs of knowledge*, CRYPTO '92, 1992, pp. 390–420.

[Bic07] J. Eric Bickel, *Some comparisons among quadratic, spherical, and logarithmic scoring rules*, Decision Analysis **4** (2007), no. 2, 49–65.

[BM88] László Babai and Shlomo Moran, *Arthur-Merlin games: a randomized proof system, and a hierarchy of complexity class*, J. Comput. Syst. Sci. **36** (1988), no. 2, 254–276.

[Bri50] Glenn W. Brier, *Verification of forecasts expressed in terms of probability*, Mon. Wea. Rev. **78** (1950), no. 1, 1–3.

[Daw82] A. P. Dawid, *The well-calibrated bayesian*, Journal of the American Statistical Association **77** (1982), no. 379, pp. 605–610.

[DF06] Eddie Dekel and Yossi Feinberg, *Non-bayesian testing of a stochastic prediction*, Review of Economic Studies **73** (2006), no. 4, 893–906.

[FS89] Uriel Feige and Adi Shamir, *Zero knowledge proofs of knowledge in two rounds*, CRYPTO, 1989, pp. 526–544.

[FS99] Yoav Freund and Robert E. Schapire, *Adaptive game playing using multiplicative weights*, Games and Economic Behavior **29** (1999), no. 1, 79–103.

[FV98] Dean P. Foster and Rakesh V. Vohra, *Asymptotic calibration*, Biometrika **85** (1998), no. 2, 379–390.

[FV09] Lance Fortnow and Rakesh V. Vohra, *The complexity of forecast testing*, Econometrica **77** (2009), no. 1, 93–105.

[GMR89] Shafi Goldwasser, Silvio Micali, and Charles Rackoff, *The knowledge complexity of interactive proof systems*, SIAM Journal on Computing **18** (1989), no. 1, 186–208.

[GR07] Tilmann Gneiting and Adrian E. Raftery, *Strictly proper scoring rules, prediction, and estimation*, Journal of the American Statistical Association **102** (2007), 359–378.

[IW97] Russell Impagliazzo and Avi Wigderson, *P = BPP if E requires exponential circuits: derandomizing the XOR lemma*, Proceedings of the twenty-ninth annual ACM symposium on Theory of computing, STOC '97, ACM, 1997, pp. 220–229.

[Leh01] Ehud Lehrer, *Any inspection is manipulable*, Econometrica **69** (2001), no. 5, pp. 1333–1347 (English).

[MP07] Silvio Micali and Rafael Pass, *Precise zero knowledge*, 2007.

[NW94] Noam Nisan and Avi Wigderson, *Hardness vs randomness*, J. Comput. Syst. Sci. **49** (1994), no. 2, 149–167.

[OS06] W Olszewski and A Sandroni, *Counterfactual predictions*, 2006.

[OS09] Wojciech Olszewski and Alvaro Sandroni, *Strategic manipulation of empirical tests*, Math. Oper. Res. **34** (2009), no. 1, 57–70.

[San03] Alvaro Sandroni, *The reproducible properties of correct forecasts*, International Journal of Game Theory **32** (2003), no. 1, 151–159.

[VS03] Vladimir Vovk and Glenn Shafer, *Good randomized sequential probability forecasting is always possible, the game-theoretic probability and finance project, http://probabilityandfinance.com, working paper*, the Journal of the Royal Statistical Society B **67** (2003), 747–763.

Multiplicative Updates in Coordination Games and the Theory of Evolution

[Working Paper Abstract]

Erick Chastain
Department of Computer Science
Rutgers University
erickc@cs.rutgers.edu

Adi Livnat
Department of Biological Sciences
Virginia Tech
adi@vt.edu

Christos Papadimitriou
Department of EECS, Division of Computer Science
University of California, Berkeley
christos@cs.berkeley.edu

Umesh Vazirani
Department of EECS, Division of Computer Science
University of California, Berkeley
vazirani@cs.berkeley.edu

In this paper we point out a new and unexpected connection between three fields: Evolution Theory, Game Theory, and Algorithms.

In particular, we study the standard equations of population genetics for Evolution, in the presence of recombination (sex), focusing on the important special case of *weak selection* [1, 2] in which all fitness values are assumed to be close to one another. Weak selection is the mathematical regime capturing the widely accepted *Neutral Theory* proposed by Kimura in the 1970s [3], hypothesizing that evolution proceeds for the most part not by substantial increases in fitness but by essentially random drift. We show that in this regime evolution through natural selection and sex is tantamount to a game played through the multiplicative weight updates game dynamics [4]. The players of the game are the genes (genetic loci), the strategies available to each player are the alleles of the gene, and the probabilities whereby a player plays a strategy is the strategy's frequency in the population. The utility to each player/gene of each strategy profile is the fitness of the corresponding genotype (organism). That is, the game is a coordination game between genes, in which the players' interests are perfectly aligned. Importantly, the utility maximized in this game, as well as the amount by which each allele is boosted, is precisely the allele's *mixability*, or average fitness, a quantity recently proposed in [5] as a novel concept that is crucial in understanding natural selection under sex, thus providing a rigorous demonstration of that insight.

We also establish a result regarding the maintenance of genetic diversity (multiplicity of alleles per gene). We prove that the equilibria in two-person coordination games are likely to have large supports, and thus genetic diversity need not suffer much at equilibrium. Establishing large supports involves answering through a novel technique the following question: what is the probability that for a random square matrix A (with entries drawn independently from smooth distributions that are symmetric around zero) both systems $Ax = 1$ and $A^T y = 1$ have positive solutions? The proof is through a simple potential function argument. Both the question and the technique may be of broader interest.

It has often seemed astonishing — even to experienced students of Evolution, Darwin included — that the crude mechanism of natural selection is responsible for producing the dazzling variety of Life around us. The present mathematical connection of Evolution with the multiplicative weight updates algorithm — a technique that has surprised our field time and again with its fantastic effectiveness and versatility — may carry some explanatory force in this regard.

ITCS'13, January 9–12, 2013, Berkeley, California, USA.
ACM 978-1-4503-1859-4/13/01.

Categories and Subject Descriptors

F.0 [**Theory of Computation**]: General; F.2.2 [**Analysis of Algorithms and Problem Complexity**]: Miscellaneous

General Terms

Theory, Economics

Keywords

Algorithmic Game Theory, Multiplicative Weight Updates, Theory of Evolution

1. REFERENCES

[1] T. Nagylaki. The evolution of multilocus systems under weak selection. *Genetics*, 134(2):627–647, 1993.

[2] T. Nagylaki, J. Hofbauer, and P. Brunovský. Convergence of multilocus systems under weak epistasis or weak selection. *Journal of mathematical biology*, 38(2):103–133, 1999.

[3] J.F. Crow and M. Kimura. Evolution in sexual and asexual populations. *American Naturalist*, pages 439–450, 1965.

[4] S. Kale. *Efficient algorithms using the multiplicative weights update method*. PhD thesis, University Microfilms International, P. O. Box 1764, Ann Arbor, MI, 48106, USA, 2007.

[5] A. Livnat, C. Papadimitriou, J. Dushoff, and M.W. Feldman. A mixability theory for the role of sex in evolution. *Proceedings of the National Academy of Sciences*, 105(50):19803–19808, 2008.

Making Evolution Rigorous- The Error Threshold

Nisheeth K. Vishnoi
Microsoft Research, Bangalore, India
nisheeth.vishnoi@gmail.com

Categories and Subject Descriptors

F.m [**Theory of Computation**]: Miscellaneous

Keywords

Evolution, Quasispecies Model, Error Thresholds

Introduction.

In a series of influential papers Eigen and his coworkers [Eig71, EMS88] introduced the quasispecies model, a remarkably clean mathematical model that captured the error-prone evolution of molecules such as RNA and addressed the origins-of-life question. It was argued, see [Eig93], that an important property of such a model is the existence of an *error threshold, i.e.*, a replication error rate below which genetic information is intact and above which it is destroyed. Besides the insights the quasispecies model provides on the emergence of life, it has had a powerful impact on design of drug strategies for RNA-viruses such as Foot-and-Mouth-Disease, Poliovirus and even RNA *retroviruses* such as HIV. In all these cases, the error threshold phenomena is leveraged to attempt to mutate the virus to death, see [Vis]. While the existence of error thresholds for specific settings has been verified by computer simulations, a mathematical proof of this phenomena did not exist. Problematically, one can construct pathological examples for which no non-trivial error threshold exists. The main contribution of this work is to rigorously study error thresholds in the quasispecies model of evolution, identify a class of biologically relevant parameters and prove the existence of a sharp error threshold in such cases. Our analysis benefits from viewing the quasispecies model as an evolutionary process on the hypercube which permits the use of simple yet powerful techniques from linear algebra and Fourier analysis. The rest of this abstract presents a description of the quasispecies model, the error threshold and outlines our contribution.

The Quasispecies Model.

We describe the quasispecies model for discrete-time evolution of strings of length L comprising of two building blocks 0 and 1. Thus, the model considers L-bit strings, $\{0,1\}^L$, and is parametrized by an *error* or *mutation rate* μ and a *fitness function* or *landscape* $a:\{0,1\}^L \mapsto \mathbb{Z}_{\geq 1}$. The mutation rate indicates the per-bit copying error during reproduction and for a string $\sigma \in \{0,1\}^L$, its fitness $a_\sigma \stackrel{\text{def}}{=} a(\sigma)$ captures its survivability with respect to an environment. The process starts with a distribution over $\{0,1\}^L$ and it iterates deterministically applying the tenets of reproduction-selection-mutation. In the reproduction stage each σ produces a_σ copies of itself, in the selection stage we normalize, obtaining a new distribution over $\{0,1\}^L$, and finally, mutation occurs. The eventual outcome of the evolutionary process is not a single string (*i.e.*, a species), rather it is an invariant distribution, justifying the term *quasispecies*. In this sense, it is a first-order approximation to Darwinian survival-of-the-fittest evolution.

Suppose $\mathbf{m}(0)$ is the starting distribution over the population at time 0 and, more generally, let $m_\sigma(t)$ denote the fraction of the population of σ at time t. If reproduction were error-free then $m_\sigma(t+1)$ would be proportional to $a_\sigma m_\sigma(t)$. Instead, with errors, for every string τ, $a_\tau m_\tau(t)\mu^{d_H(\sigma,\tau)}(1-\mu)^{L-d_H(\sigma,\tau)}$ (fractional) copies[1] of σ are produced (without normalization) where $d_H(\sigma,\tau)$ is the Hamming distance between σ and τ. This deterministic process is the expectation of the randomized copying process where each bit of τ flips independently with probability μ. This process can be described by the following coupled difference equations:

$$\forall \sigma \in \{0,1\}^L, \quad m_\sigma(t+1) \stackrel{\text{def}}{=} \frac{\sum_{\tau\in\{0,1\}^L} m_\tau(t) a_\tau Q^\mu_{\tau\sigma}}{\sum_{\tau\in\{0,1\}^L} m_\tau(t) a_\tau}. \qquad (1)$$

Here, $Q^\mu_{\sigma\tau} \stackrel{\text{def}}{=} \mu^{d_H(\sigma,\tau)}(1-\mu)^{L-d_H(\sigma,\tau)} = Q^\mu_{\tau\sigma}$. If we let A be the diagonal matrix with $A_{\sigma\sigma} \stackrel{\text{def}}{=} a_\sigma$, then the evolutionary equation above can be succinctly expressed in the matrix form as

$$\mathbf{m}(t+1) \stackrel{\text{def}}{=} \frac{Q^\mu A\mathbf{m}(t)}{\|A\mathbf{m}(t)\|_1} = \frac{(Q^\mu A)^{t+1}\mathbf{m}(0)}{\|A\mathbf{m}(t)\|_1}. \qquad (2)$$

The population determined by $\mathbf{v}^\mu$ marks the culmination of the evolutionary process and is the quasispecies for the evolution.

The Error Threshold.

If μ is close to 0 then one would expect $\mathbf{v}^\mu$ to have its mass concentrated on sequences of high fitness but not entirely on the fittest or *master* sequence. On the other hand note that if $\mu = 1/2$, then $v^\mu_\sigma = 1/2^L$ for all σ. This conforms with the intuition that if each bit, during copying, can be 0 or 1 with probability $1/2$, then no genetic information can be retained by the quasispecies. Interestingly, Eigen and his coworkers observed that when the fitness landscape is single-peaked, *i.e.*, the master sequence has fitness above 1 while the rest have fitness 1, this phenomena occurs much below $\mu = 1/2$, in fact around $1/L$. This led them to hypothesize that there exists a particular mutation rate (below $1/2$) beyond which all the 2^L strings become nearly-equally abundant. They called this critical mutation rate the *error threshold* as, beyond this rate the master sequence's genetic information is lost, and called this transition an

[1]The population is assumed to be infinite justifying fractions.

ITCS'13, January 9–12, 2013, Berkeley, California, USA.
ACM 978-1-4503-1859-4/13/01.

error catastrophe; the mutation induced loss of genetic information. Subsequently error threshold has been observed empirically for many other fitness functions, see [DSV12].

The notion of an error threshold is widely recognized, however no consensus exists on its definition; see Wilke [Wil05]. Since $\mathbf{v}^\mu$ will hardly ever be $\mathscr{U}$, the uniform distribution on $\{0,1\}^L$, the goal is to find the smallest μ such that $\mathbf{v}^\mu$ is *close* to $\mathscr{U}$. To define the error threshold one needs a function that measures closeness. Since both the uniform distribution and $\mathbf{v}^\mu$ are probability distributions, we can use the most prevalent way in probability to measure closeness: $\|\mathbf{v}^\mu - \mathscr{U}\|_1 \stackrel{\text{def}}{=} \sum_{\tau\in\{0,1\}^L} |v^\mu_\tau - 1/2^L|$. We define $\mu_\star(\varepsilon) \stackrel{\text{def}}{=} \min\{\mu \in (0,1) : \|\mathbf{v}^\mu - \mathscr{U}\|_1 \le \varepsilon\}$. As noted before, when $\mu = 1/2$, the steady state vector $\mathbf{v}^\mu$ is *exactly* $\mathscr{U}$. Hence, $\mu_\star(\varepsilon) \le 1/2$ for all $\varepsilon > 0$. Thus, we will focus on μ in $(0, 1/2]$.

Finally, the notion of error catastrophe is important in antiviral drug-design as several important viruses are RNA viruses and their evolution can be captured to the first order by the quasispecies model. From the virus' point of view, a high mutation rate implies greater diversity, which in turn could mean greater adaptability and greater ability to escape the hosts immune responses and pressure from drug therapy. At the same time, too high a mutation rate induces a loss of genetic information. Thus, if we could increase the mutation rate past the error threshold, we would severely compromise the virus' identity. Intriguingly, this strategy is already employed by the body which can produce antibodies that increase mutation rate. Artificially, this effect can also be accomplished by mutagenic drugs such as ribavirin, see [Vis].

What Makes the Quasispecies Model Hard?.

Given L, a, and ε, we wish to analytically determine[2] the smallest value of μ for which the vector $\mathbf{v}^\mu$ comes ε-close to the uniform distribution in the ℓ_1 norm. The matrix Q^μ is well studied in TCS and is often referred to as the *noisy hypercube* matrix. *All* its eigenvalues and eigenvectors can be written explicitly in terms of the parameters μ and L. Additionally, A is a diagonal matrix whose eigenvectors and eigenvalues are explicit. Hence, it may be tempting to believe that the eigenvalues and eigenvectors for $Q^\mu A$ can be easily determined. The problem is that A is not explicit (it is given as input) and the fact that it is a diagonal matrix is superfluous (we could always make either matrix diagonal). Thus, since the eigenspaces interact in a complex manner, the largest eigenvector of $Q^\mu A$ does not seem to be derivable in closed form from the spectral data of Q^μ and A. In short, the Boolean function a, which gives the quasispecies model the ability to elegantly capture complex evolutionary interactions, turns out to be the reason this process is difficult to analyze.

Our Contribution.

It seems difficult to analytically determine the error threshold when the fitness landscape, a, is arbitrary. Indeed, even the existence of a low error threshold in the simple-sounding, single-peak landscape was only argued heuristically by Eigen and his coworkers. We first present a class of fitness functions which generalize Eigen's single-peak model and is implicit in almost all biological settings where the quasispecies model is being deployed. First, consider how one obtains a fitness function. In applications L is at least a few thousand and, for HIV-1, about 10000. Hence, it is not possible to expect $2^L = 2^{10000}$ distinct numbers as input. Moreover, experimentally obtaining each of these numbers is a laborious and expensive process. Typically, the fitness is estimated for a number of strings which are considered to carry genetic information and the rest are assumed to be 1. Additionally, it can be argued that the fitness function has little to no dependance on L. Hence, a reasonable model is one where at most k strings have fitness $1 < a_\sigma \le c$ and the rest have fitness 1 and where k, c are relatively small compared to 2^L. This leads us to the following definition.

DEFINITION. ((c,k)-FINITE AND BOUNDED LANDSCAPE) *Let c and k be positive integers. A (c,k)-finite and bounded landscape is a fitness function $a : \{0,1\}^L \mapsto \mathbb{Z}_{\ge 1}$ such that there exist $\sigma_1, \ldots, \sigma_k$ with $1 < a_{\sigma_i} \le c$ and for all $\sigma \notin \{\sigma_1, \ldots, \sigma_k\}$, $a_\sigma = 1$.*

Note that when $k = 1$ this is equivalent to Eigen's single-peak landscape model. For (c,k)-finite and bounded landscapes we prove the following theorem.

MAIN THEOREM. *For a given L, (c,k)-finite and bounded fitness landscape and small enough $\varepsilon > 0$,*

$$\Omega\left(\frac{1}{L}\ln\frac{c}{\varepsilon}\right) \le \mu_\star(\varepsilon) \le O\left(\frac{1}{L}\ln\frac{ckL}{\varepsilon}\right).$$

Thus, consistent with *in vitro* and *in silico* observations, a sharp error threshold exists for (c,k)-finite and bounded landscapes much below $1/2$. As one might expect, the sharpness of the error threshold deteriorates as c and k increase. One way to interpret ℓ_1 closeness is the following. If the probability vector $\mathbf{v}^\mu$ is ε close to the uniform distribution in the ℓ_1 norm, then the number of indices σ, for which $|v^\mu_\sigma - 1/2^L| \ge \varepsilon/C$ is at most C. A quantitatively similar threshold can also be shown for closeness in ℓ_2 and average fitness, and is implicit in our work. The average fitness, defined to be $\sum_\sigma v^\mu_\sigma a_\sigma$, is always at least 1, and an error catastrophe is said to occur if it drops below $1+\varepsilon$. Note that both ℓ_2 and average are weaker notions of convergence: It can happen that $\mathbf{v}^\mu$ normalized to have ℓ_2 norm 1 is ε close to the corresponding uniform distribution but its distance in ℓ_1 norm is $\varepsilon \cdot 2^{L/2}$. Similarly, the largest eigenvalue being at most $1+\varepsilon$ (it has to be at least 1) gives a bound on ℓ_1 closeness which is not useful as such. The proof appears in the full version of this work and can be found here[3].

References

[DSV12] Narendra Dixit, Piyush Srivastava, and Nisheeth K. Vishnoi. A finite population model of molecular evolution: Theory and computation. *Journal of Computational Biology*, 19(10):1176–1202, 2012.

[Eig71] M. Eigen. Selforganization of matter and the evolution of biological macromolecules. *Die Naturwissenschaften*, 58:456–523, 1971.

[Eig93] M. Eigen. The origin of genetic information: Viruses as models. 135:37–47, 1993.

[EMS88] M. Eigen, J. McCaskill, and P. Schuster. Molecular quasi-species. *J. Phys. Chem.*, 92:6881–6891, 1988.

[TBVD12] Kushal Tripathi, Rajesh Balagam, Nisheeth K. Vishnoi, and Narendra M. Dixit. Stochastic simulations suggest that HIV-1 survives close to its error threshold. *PLoS Computational Biology*, 8(9):e1002684, 2012.

[Vis] Nisheeth K. Vishnoi. Evolution without sex, drugs and Boolean functions. *http://research.microsoft.com/en-us/um/people/nvishno.*

[Wil05] Claus Wilke. Quasispecies theory in the context of population genetics. *BMC Evolutionary Biology*, 5(1):44, 2005.

[2] Often computing $\mu_\star(\varepsilon)$ suffices, see e.g. [DSV12, TBVD12]. However, analytical answers are useful as they provide the ability to ask if-then questions and understand for what parameters the error threshold occurs much below $1/2$.

[3] `http://research.microsoft.com/en-us/um/people/nvishno/Site/Publications_files/VError.pdf`

On the Convergence of the Hegselmann-Krause System

Arnab Bhattacharyya[*]
DIMACS
Rutgers University
arnabb@dimacs.rutgers.edu

Mark Braverman[†]
Computer Science Dept.
Princeton University
mbraverm@cs.princeton.edu

Bernard Chazelle[‡]
Princeton University and
Collège de France
chazelle@cs.princeton.edu

Huy L. Nguyễn[§]
Computer Science Dept.
Princeton University
hlnguyen@princeton.edu

ABSTRACT

We study convergence of the following discrete-time non-linear dynamical system: n agents are located in $\mathbb{R}^d$ and at every time step, each moves synchronously to the average location of all agents within a unit distance of it. This popularly studied system was introduced by Krause to model the dynamics of opinion formation and is often referred to as the *Hegselmann-Krause model*. We prove the first polynomial time bound for the convergence of this system in arbitrary dimensions. This improves on the bound of $n^{O(n)}$ resulting from a more general theorem of Chazelle [4]. Also, we show a quadratic lower bound and improve the upper bound for one-dimensional systems to $O(n^3)$.

Categories and Subject Descriptors

F.2.2 [**Nonnumerical Algorithms and Problems**]: Geometrical problems and computations

General Terms

Algorithms, Theory

Keywords

Hegselmann-Krause system, opinion dynamics, convergence

[*]Research done while at Princeton University and Center for Computational Intractability, supported by NSF Grants CCF-0832797, 0830673, and 0528414.

[†]Research supported in part by an Alfred P. Sloan Fellowship, an NSF CAREER award, and a Turing Centenary Fellowship.

[‡]This work was supported in part by NSF grants CCF-0832797, CCF-0963825, and CCF-1016250.

[§]Supported in part by NSF CCF-0832797 and a Gordon Wu fellowship.

1. INTRODUCTION

Lately, there has been a surge of attention given to network-based dynamical systems, in which agents interact according to local rules via a dynamic communication graph [7]. Much of the previous work has focused on the exogenous case, where the communication topology is decoupled from the evolution of the system. We refer interested readers to [3] for a good overview of research in this area. In the more common, endogenous version, the communication graph changes over time according to the current states. The feedback loop between dynamics and topology creates considerable difficulties, and efforts have been underway to build an algorithmic calculus within the broad framework of *influence systems* [5]. This work investigates the complexity of *Hegselmann-Krause systems* (abbreviated as HK system from now on), a popular model of opinion dynamics that has proven highly influential over the years [1, 8, 9, 11, 13] and stands as the archetype of a diffusive influence system [6]. In the d-dimensional version of the model, each agent has an opinion represented as a point in $\mathbb{R}^d$. Two agents are neighbors if they are within unit distance from each other. At every time step, each agent moves synchronously to the mass center of its neighbors.

HK systems are known to converge [10, 12, 16], meaning that they eventually come to a full stop. The convergence time has been bounded by $n^{O(n)}$ time and conjectured to be polynomial [4]. In the case $d = 1$, it was shown to be $O(n^5)$ [14] and later improved to $O(n^4)$ [18]. The contribution of this work is threefold: first, we prove that the convergence time is indeed polynomial in n, regardless of the dimension; second, we lower the one-dimensional bound from $O(n^4)$ to $O(n^3)$; third, we establish a quadratic lower bound, which improves the known bound of $\Omega(n)$ [14]. We also consider noisy variants of the model.

The bidirectionality of the system plays a crucial role in the proof, as it should. Indeed, it is known from [5] that allowing different radii and averaging weights for the agents can prevent the convergence of the communication graph. Our proofs are an elementary mix of geometric and algebraic techniques. Much of the current technology for HK systems centers around products of stochastic matrices. This work injects a geometric perspective that, we believe, will be necessary for further progress on the more difficult directional case.

2. PRELIMINARIES

We formally define the discrete-time *HK system in dimension d* as follows. There are n agents. For every $t \in \mathbb{Z}^{\geqslant 0}$ and for every $i \in [n]$, the *position* of agent i at time t is $\mathbf{x}_i(t) \in \mathbb{R}^d$. The positions at $t = 0$ are given and, thereafter, are updated synchronously according to the following rule:

$$\mathbf{x}_i(t+1) = \frac{\sum_{j:\|\mathbf{x}_i(t)-\mathbf{x}_j(t)\|\leqslant 1} \mathbf{x}_j(t)}{\sum_{j:\|\mathbf{x}_i(t)-\mathbf{x}_j(t)\|\leqslant 1} 1} \tag{1}$$

Here, $\|\cdot\|$ denotes the Euclidean norm. We say that agents i and j are *neighbors* at time t if $\|\mathbf{x}_i(t) - \mathbf{x}_j(t)\| \leqslant 1$, and we denote the *neighborhood* at time t of agent i by $\mathcal{N}_i(t) = \{j : i \text{ and } j \text{ neighbors at time } t\}$. Note that if $i \in \mathcal{N}_j(t)$, then $j \in \mathcal{N}_i(t)$. Also for a given $\mathbf{x} \in \mathbb{R}^d$, we define the *weight of* $\mathbf{x}$ *at time* t to be $w_t(\mathbf{x}) = |\{i : \mathbf{x}_i(t) = \mathbf{x}\}|$. Note that at any given t, $0 \leqslant w_t(\mathbf{x}) \leqslant n$ for all $\mathbf{x} \in \mathbb{R}^d$ and that the sum of all weights equals n. Also, let the *weight of agent i at time t* denote $w_t(\mathbf{x}_i(t))$. The weight of an agent is monotonically non-decreasing with time. The system is said to have *converged* at time t if $\mathbf{x}_i(t+1) = \mathbf{x}_i(t)$ for all $i \in [n]$.

In the case of one dimension, one can observe that order is preserved:

Proposition 2.1 (Lemma 2 in [11]). *The HK system in dimension 1 preserves order of positions. That is, for any $i, j \in [n]$, if $x_i(0) \leqslant x_j(0)$, then $x_i(t) \leqslant x_j(t)$ for all $t > 0$.* □

For this reason, in one dimension, we can number the agents from 1 to n such that $x_1(t) \leqslant x_2(t) \leqslant \cdots \leqslant x_n(t)$ for all $t \geqslant 0$. The one-dimensional system also has the following decomposability property:

Proposition 2.2 (Proposition 2 in [3]). *Suppose $d = 1$. If at time t, and for some $i \in [n]$, $|x_{i+1}(t) - x_i(t)| > 1$, then for all $t' > t$ also, $|x_{i+1}(t') - x_i(t')| > 1$. So, the system can be decomposed into two subsystems, one consisting of agents $\{1, \ldots, i\}$ and the other of agents $\{i+1, \ldots, n\}$, each evolving independently after time t.* □

Therefore, if at time t, an agent has no neighbor strictly to its left and no neighbor strictly to its right, it never moves subsequently, and we say that the agent has *frozen* at time t.

This decomposability property is not true in higher dimensions. For instance, consider the two-dimensional HK system with agents at positions $(0, 0)$, $(1, 0)$ and $(1/2, 1)$; the third agent does not neighbor any other agent at $t = 0$, but this is not so at $t = 1$.

3. CONVERGENCE IN ONE DIMENSION

Theorem 3.1. *The HK system in 1 dimension converges within $O(n^3)$ time steps.*

Proof. Recall that we number the agents such that $x_i(t) \leqslant x_{i+1}(t)$ for all t and all $i \in [1, n-1]$. Suppose the system has not already converged at time t, and let $\ell(t)$ denote the leftmost non-frozen agent, i.e., the least $\ell \geqslant 1$ such that $\{x_i(t) : i \in \mathcal{N}_\ell(t)\} \neq \{x_\ell(t)\}$. Note that at time t, agent $\ell(t)$ must have at least one neighbor strictly to its right and no neighbor strictly to its left (because any neighbor strictly to the left would violate minimality of ℓ).

The following lemma is the heart of our proof.

Lemma 3.2. *For every $t \geqslant 0$, by time $t + 2$, agent $\ell(t)$ increases in weight, or gets frozen, or moves to the right by at least $\frac{1}{2n^2}$.*

Proof. Fix t, let $\ell = \ell(t)$, and let $r = \min\{j : x_j(t) > x_\ell(t)\}$ be the leftmost agent that is strictly right of agent ℓ. Agent r is a neighbor of ℓ because ℓ has at least one neighbor strictly to its right. If $\mathcal{N}_\ell(t) = \mathcal{N}_r(t)$, agent ℓ at time $t+1$ moves to the same location as agent r does and increases its weight. So, suppose otherwise. Since ℓ has no neighbor strictly to its left, r also does not have any neighbor strictly left of ℓ. Hence, there must exist $s \in \mathcal{N}_r(t) \setminus \mathcal{N}_\ell(t)$ strictly to the right of r.

We now show $x_r(t+1) \geqslant x_\ell(t) + \frac{1}{n}$. Observe that $x_s(t) - x_\ell(t) > 1$. So, if $\delta = x_r(t) - x_\ell(t)$ and $k = |\mathcal{N}_r(t)|$, then agent r moves to the left by at most:

$$\frac{\delta \cdot (k-1) - (1-\delta) \cdot 1}{k} = \delta - \frac{1}{k} \leqslant \delta - \frac{1}{n}$$

If $x_\ell(t+1) \geqslant x_\ell(t) + \frac{1}{2n}$, we are already done. Otherwise, $x_r(t+1) - x_\ell(t+1) \geqslant \frac{1}{2n}$. By Proposition 2.2, agent ℓ still has no neighbor strictly to its left at time $t+1$. If $x_r(t+1) - x_\ell(t+1) > 1$, then agent ℓ gets frozen at time $t+1$. Otherwise, $\frac{1}{2n} \leqslant x_r(t+1) - x_\ell(t+1) \leqslant 1$, and so:

$$x_\ell(t+2) - x_\ell(t+1) \geqslant \frac{1}{2n|\mathcal{N}_\ell(t+1)|} \geqslant \frac{1}{2n^2}$$

□

We can assume $x_n(0) - x_1(0) \leqslant n$ without loss of generality, because otherwise, by Proposition 2.2, the system can be decomposed into independently evolving subsystems. So, $x_n(t) - x_1(t) \leqslant n$ for all t. Now, apply Lemma 3.2 at $t = 0, 2, 4, \ldots$ as long as the system has not converged and $\ell(t)$ exists. $\ell(t)$ can increase in weight only at most n times. Also, because $\ell(t)$ is non-decreasing with t, $x_{\ell(t+2)}(t+2) \geqslant x_{\ell(t)}(t+2)$ and, hence, the third case in Lemma 3.2 can occur only at most $2n^3$ times. Thus, after $t > 2(n + 2n^3)$, Lemma 3.2 cannot be applied, and the system must have converged.

3.1 Noisy neighborhoods

In this subsection, we study an extension to a noisy version of the HK model. We consider the following system HK_η where $\eta \in (0, 1)$ is a parameter. There are n agents, and each agent has an associated *left-neighborhood parameter* η_i that is in the interval $(0, \eta)$. The positions at $t = 0$ are given, and then, the positions are updated according to the following rule:

$$x_i(t+1) = \frac{\sum_{j:-1+\eta_i \leqslant x_j(t)-x_i(t) \leqslant 1} x_j(t)}{\sum_{j:-1+\eta_i \leqslant x_j(t)-x_i(t) \leqslant 1} 1} \tag{2}$$

One can interpret the η_i's as noise acting on the left side of each agent's neighborhood. We can prove the following extension of Theorem 3.1 to HK_η.

Theorem 3.3. *For fixed $\eta \in (0, 1)$, the HK_η system converges within $O(n^3)$ time steps.*

PROOF. The proof proceeds similarly to that of Theorem 3.1. We say that agent j is a neighbor of agent i at time t if $-1+\eta_i \leqslant x_j(t)-x_i(t) \leqslant 1$. Conceptually, the main complicating issue is that being neighbors is no longer a symmetric relation. Also, Proposition 2.1 is no longer true as order may not be preserved by the dynamics.

Let $\ell(t)$ denote the leftmost agent at time t that neighbors at least one agent positioned strictly to its right. Notice that this implies there is no k such that $0 < x_{\ell(t)} - x_k \leqslant 1$, because agent k would neighbor $\ell(t)$ and hence violate the minimality of $\ell(t)$. We prove the following analog of Lemma 3.2.

LEMMA 3.4. *For every $t \geqslant 0$, by time $t+2$, agent $\ell(t)$ increases in weight, or gets frozen, or moves to the right by at least $\frac{1}{2n^2}$.*

PROOF. Let $\ell=\ell(t)$ and let r be the leftmost neighbor of ℓ. If $x_r(t)-x_\ell(t) > 1-\eta_r$, then $x_\ell(t+1) > {}^{(1-\eta_r)}/_n \geqslant {}^{(1-\eta)}/_n$, and we are already done. So, assume otherwise.

Then, agent ℓ is a neighbor of agent r. Since ℓ has no neighbor strictly to its left within a distance of 1, r also has no neighbor strictly to the left of ℓ. Now, we can use the same argument as in the proof of Lemma 3.2 to argue that either agent ℓ freezes at time $t+1$ or at time $t+2$, it moves to the right by at least $\frac{1}{2n^2}$. □

The rest of the proof can be finished in exactly the same way as the proof of Theorem 3.1.

By symmetry, Theorem 3.3 also applies when the right side of each agent's neighborhood is perturbed and the left side is fixed. The case when both sides are perturbed remains open; convergence for such heterogeneous HK systems is conjectured [15].

4. CONVERGENCE IN HIGH DIMENSIONS

In this section, we consider the HK system in d dimensions with n agents and $d \geqslant 2$. We show that the convergence time is polynomial in both n and d.

The proof follows from a sequence of lemmas. The first lemma asserts that there is some vector $\mathbf{a}$ such that taking the projection of agents on $\mathbf{a}$ does not bring two non-neighbors too close together.

LEMMA 4.1. *For every t, there exists a unit vector $\mathbf{a}$ such that for any two agents i,j, we have $\left|\mathbf{a}\cdot\frac{\mathbf{x}_i(t)-\mathbf{x}_j(t)}{\|\mathbf{x}_i(t)-\mathbf{x}_j(t)\|}\right| = \Omega(n^{-2}d^{-1})$.*

PROOF. Let $\mathbf{d}_{i,j} = \frac{\mathbf{x}_i(t)-\mathbf{x}_j(t)}{\|\mathbf{x}_i(t)-\mathbf{x}_j(t)\|}$. We can view $\mathbf{d}_{i,j}$ as a point on S^{d-1}, the unit ball in $\mathbb{R}^d$. The set of points on S^{d-1} with dot product with $\mathbf{d}_{i,j}$ of absolute value at most $O(n^{-2}d^{-1})$ has area $\frac{\pi^{(d-2)/2}}{n^2 d\cdot\Gamma((d-2)/2)}$. The area of S^{d-1} is $\frac{2\pi^{d/2}}{\Gamma(d/2)}$. There are $\binom{n}{2}$ pairs i,j, and so, by a volume argument, there exists a point $\mathbf{a}\in S^{d-1}$ such that for all i and j, $|\mathbf{d}_{i,j}\cdot\mathbf{a}| = \Omega(n^{-2}d^{-1})$. □

The next lemma analyzes the one-dimensional system formed by projecting onto $\mathbf{a}$ and shows a lower bound on the total movement in each step.

LEMMA 4.2. *Assume that at time t, the system has not converged. One of the following cases happens.*

- *Two agents move to the same location at time $t+1$.*
- *Some agent moves by at least $\Omega(n^{-4}d^{-1})$.*

PROOF. Let $\mathbf{a}$ be a unit vector satisfying Lemma 4.1 and j be the agent with minimum $\mathbf{x}_j(t)\cdot\mathbf{a}$ among agents with neighbor at time t. Consider two cases.

Case 1.

j has a neighbor i such that $(\mathbf{x}_i(t)-\mathbf{x}_j(t))\cdot\mathbf{a} = \Omega(n^{-3}d^{-1})$. Because $(\mathbf{x}_k(t)-\mathbf{x}_j(t))\cdot\mathbf{a} \geqslant 0\ \forall k$, j must move by $\Omega(n^{-4}d^{-1})$.

Case 2.

All neighbors i of j satisfy $(\mathbf{x}_i(t)-\mathbf{x}_j(t))\cdot\mathbf{a} = O(n^{-3}d^{-1})$. If none of them has any neighbor that is not j or j's neighbors, then they all move to the same location at time $t+1$. Otherwise, some neighbor i of j has a neighbor k that is not a neighbor of j. Then $(\mathbf{x}_k(t)-\mathbf{x}_j(t))\cdot\mathbf{a} = \Omega(n^{-2}d^{-1})$. We have

$$
\begin{aligned}
&\mathbf{x}_i(t+1)\cdot\mathbf{a}\\
\geqslant&\mathbf{x}_i(t)\cdot\mathbf{a} + \frac{(\mathbf{x}_k(t)-\mathbf{x}_j(t))\cdot\mathbf{a} + (n-1)(\mathbf{x}_j(t)-\mathbf{x}_i(t))\cdot\mathbf{a}}{n}\\
\geqslant&\mathbf{x}_i(t) + \Omega(n^{-3}d^{-1})
\end{aligned}
$$

Thus i moves by at least $\Omega(n^{-3}d^{-1})$. □

We now use the following special case of a result from [17] to show the existence of a potential function which is strictly decreasing as long as some agent moves. The proof is included for completeness.

THEOREM 4.3 ([17], THEOREM 2). *Let $f^t_{i,j}:\mathbb{R}^d\times\mathbb{R}^d\to\mathbb{R}$ be defined as follows: $f^t_{i,j}(\mathbf{z},\mathbf{z}') = \|\mathbf{z}-\mathbf{z}'\|^2$ if $\|\mathbf{x}_i(t)-\mathbf{x}_j(t)\| < 1$ and $f^t_{i,j}(\mathbf{z},\mathbf{z}')=1$ otherwise. Let*

$$V(t) = \sum_{i,j\in[n]} f^t_{i,j}(\mathbf{x}_i(t),\mathbf{x}_j(t))$$

Then V is non-increasing along the trajectory of the system. In fact:

$$
\begin{aligned}
&V(t)-V(t+1)\\
&\geqslant \sum_{i,j:f^t_{i,j}\neq 1} f^t_{i,j}(\mathbf{x}_i(t+1)-\mathbf{x}_i(t),\mathbf{x}_j(t)-\mathbf{x}_j(t+1))\\
&\geqslant \sum_i 4\|\mathbf{x}_i(t+1)-\mathbf{x}_i(t)\|^2
\end{aligned}
$$

PROOF. First, notice that $f^{t+1}_{i,j}(\mathbf{x}_i(t+1),\mathbf{x}_j(t+1)) \leqslant f^t_{i,j}(\mathbf{x}_i(t+1),\mathbf{x}_j(t+1))\ \forall i,j$. Next, we will show

$$
\begin{aligned}
&\sum_{i,j} f^t_{i,j}(\mathbf{x}_i(t),\mathbf{x}_j(t)) - f^t_{i,j}(\mathbf{x}_i(t+1),\mathbf{x}_j(t+1))\\
=&\sum_{i,j\in[n]:f^t_{i,j}\neq 1} f^t_{i,j}(\mathbf{x}_i(t+1)-\mathbf{x}_i(t),\mathbf{x}_j(t)-\mathbf{x}_j(t+1))
\end{aligned}
$$

Let $F:(\mathbb{R}^d)^n\times(\mathbb{R}^d)^n\to\mathbb{R}$ be defined as $F(\mathbf{x},\mathbf{y}) = \sum_{i,j:f_{i,j}\neq 1} f^t_{i,j}(\mathbf{x}_i,\mathbf{y}_j)$. Then $\mathbf{x}(t+1) = \operatorname{argmin}_{\mathbf{y}} F(\mathbf{x}(t),\mathbf{y})$. We can also view F as 2 matrices A,B and $F(\mathbf{x},\mathbf{y}) = \mathbf{x}^T A\mathbf{x} + \mathbf{y}^T A\mathbf{y} - 2\mathbf{x}^T B\mathbf{y}$ where A,B are symmetric and A

is positive semidefinite. We have $\mathbf{x}(t+1) = A^{-1}B\mathbf{x}(t)$.

$$\begin{aligned}&F(\mathbf{x},\mathbf{x}) - F(A^{-1}B\mathbf{x}, A^{-1}B\mathbf{x})\\ =&2\mathbf{x}^T(BA^{-1}(A-B)A^{-1}B + A - B)\mathbf{x}\\ =&2\mathbf{x}^T(BA^{-1}B - BA^{-1}BA^{-1}B + A - B)\mathbf{x}\\ =&2\mathbf{x}^T(I - BA^{-1})(A+B)(I - A^{-1}B)\mathbf{x}\\ =&F((I - A^{-1}B)\mathbf{x}, -(I - A^{-1}B)\mathbf{x})\end{aligned}$$

□

THEOREM 4.4. *The system converges in* poly(n, d) *time.*

PROOF. There are at most n time steps where two agents move to the same place. In all other time steps, by Lemma 4.2, some agent moves by at least $\Omega(n^{-4}d^{-1})$. We have $V(0) \leqslant n^2$ and $V(t) \geqslant 0\ \forall t$. Therefore, by Theorem 4.3, the number of time steps before the system converges is $O(n^{10}d^2)$. □

5. LOWER BOUND

In this section, we give an instance of an HK system that requires $\Omega(n^2)$ steps to converge. Our example is in two dimensions, and we know of no example that takes longer time even when the number of dimensions is large. The previous best lower bound on the convergence time [14] was $\Omega(n)$, which is achieved by n points on a line with unit distance spacing between each pair of consecutive points. This is still the worst example we know of in one dimension.

Our lower bound is achieved by the following system. There are n agents in the system and initially, they are located at vertices of a regular n-gon with side length $l_1 = 1$. Label the agents clockwise around the polygon from 0 to $n-1$. Let O be the center of the polygon and A_i be the location of agent i. For notational convenience, all index computation is done modulo n (so if $i = 0$ then A_{i-1} is A_{n-1}).

THEOREM 5.1. *The system described above requires at least* $\Omega(n^2)$ *steps to converge.*

PROOF. We will prove by induction that for all $t \leqslant n^2/28$, A_i's are vertices of a regular n-gon with side length $l_t \geqslant (1 - \frac{14}{n^2})^t$.

By the initial state of the system, the invariant holds for $t = 1$. Assume that it holds before step $t = k$, we will show it holds before step $t = k + 1 \leqslant n^2/28$.

We analyze the movement of agent i from A_i to A'_i in one step (see Figure 1). Note that $\angle A_iOA_{i+1} = \frac{2\pi}{n}$. For any $j \notin \{i-1, i, i+1\}$, we have

$$\begin{aligned}A_iA_j &= \frac{OA_i \sin(\angle OA_iA_j)}{\sin(\angle A_iOA_j)}\\ &\geqslant \frac{OA_i \sin(\frac{4\pi}{n})}{\sin(\frac{\pi(n-4)}{2n})}\\ &= \frac{l_t \sin(\frac{\pi(n-2)}{2n}) \sin(\frac{4\pi}{n})}{\sin(\frac{2\pi}{n}) \sin(\frac{\pi(n-4)}{2n})}\\ &\geqslant 2l_k\left(1 - \frac{\pi^2}{2n^2}\right)\left(1 - \frac{4\pi^2}{n^2}\right)\\ &> 1\end{aligned}$$

Thus, for $j \notin \{i-1, i, i+1\}$, agents i and j are not neighbors. A_i moves to the centroid of A_i, A_{i-1}, A_{i+1} and by symmetry,

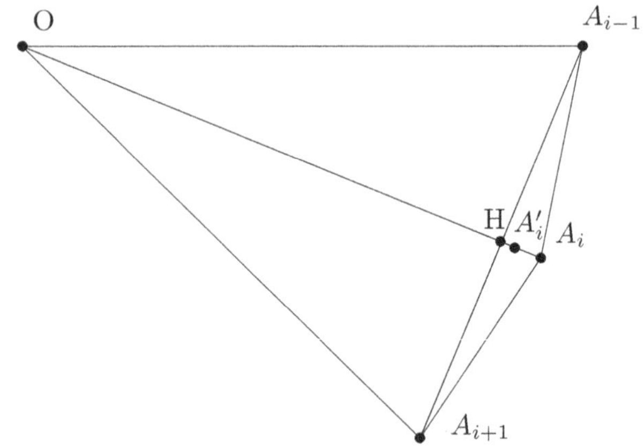

Figure 1: In one time step, agent i moves from A_i to A'_i, the centroid of A_i, A_{i-1}, A_{i+1}

the locations of the agents are vertices of a new regular n-gon centered at O and with a smaller side length l_{k+1}. We have

$$\begin{aligned}l_{k+1} &= \frac{OA'_i}{OA_i} l_k\\ &= \left(1 - \frac{2HA_i}{3OA_i}\right) l_k\\ &= \left(1 - \frac{2l_k \sin(\frac{\pi}{n}) \sin(\frac{2\pi}{n})}{3l_k \sin(\frac{\pi(n-2)}{2n})}\right) l_k\\ &\geqslant \left(1 - \frac{14}{n^2}\right) l_k\end{aligned}$$

Thus, the system requires at least $n^2/28$ steps to converge. □

6. DISCUSSION

In this paper, we analyzed the convergence rate of the homogeneous HK system in arbitrary dimensions. The system is shown to converge in polynomial time, but can take at least a quadratic number of steps in the worst case. Getting tight bounds on the convergence time of the system, even in just one dimension, remains an interesting open problem.

A particularly interesting challenge is to analyze the heterogeneous version of the HK system, i.e. when the neighborhood radii of all the agents are not necessarily the same [15]. New ideas are needed to understand the behavior of this system in particular, and directional systems in general. Our analysis of a noisy variant of homogeneous HK system is a step towards studying more complicated directional systems.

Beyond convergence rate, the behavior of the homogeneous HK system is still full of mysteries. Most notable perhaps is the 2R conjecture [2]: when agents are drawn uniformly at random on an interval, they converge to clusters at distance close to twice the minimum possible inter-cluster distance. Resolving this conjecture remains well beyond our understanding of the system.

7. ACKNOWLEDGMENTS

We thank Behrouz Touri for bringing reference [18] to our attention.

8. REFERENCES

[1] R. Axelrod. The dissemination of culture: a model with local convergence and global polarization. *Journal of Conflict Resolution*, 1997. Reprinted in "The complexity of cooperation," Princeton University Press, Princeton, 1997.

[2] V. D. Blondel, J. M. Hendricx, and J. N. Tsitsiklis. On the 2R conjecture for multi-agent systems. In *European Control Conference*, pages 2996–3000, July 2007.

[3] V. D. Blondel, J. M. Hendricx, and J. N. Tsitsiklis. On Krause's multi-agent consensus model with state-dependent connectivity. *IEEE Transactions on Automatic Control*, 54(11), Nov. 2009.

[4] B. Chazelle. The total s-energy of a multiagent system. *SIAM J. Control and Optimization*, 49(4):1680–1706, 2011.

[5] B. Chazelle. The dynamics of influence systems. *arXiv:1204.3946v2*, 2012. Prelim. version in Proc. 53rd FOCS, 2012.

[6] B. Chazelle. Natural algorithms and influence systems. *CACM Research Highlights*, 2012.

[7] D. A. Easley and J. M. Kleinberg. *Networks, Crowds, and Markets - Reasoning About a Highly Connected World*. Cambridge University Press, 2010.

[8] S. Fortunato. On the consensus threshold for the opinion dynamics of krause-hegselmann. *International Journal of Modern Physics C*, 16(2):259–270, 2005.

[9] R. Hegselmann and U. Krause. Opinion dynamics and bounded confidence: models, analysis and simulation. *J. Artificial Societies and Social Simulation*, 5(3), 2002.

[10] J. M. Hendrickx and V. D. Blondel. Convergence of different linear and non-linear Vicsek models. In *Proc. 17th International Symposium on Mathematical Theory of Networks and Systems (MTNS2006)*, pages 1229–1240, July 2006.

[11] U. Krause. A discrete nonlinear and non-autonomous model of consensus formation. In *Proc. Commun. Difference Equations*, pages 227–236, 2000.

[12] J. Lorenz. A stabilization theorem for dynamics of continuous opinions. *Physica A: Statistical Mechanics and its Applications*, 355(1):217–223, 2005.

[13] J. Lorenz. Continuous opinion dynamics under bounded confidence: a survey. *International Journal of Modern Physics C*, 16(18):1819–1838, 2007.

[14] S. Martínez, F. Bullo, J. Cortés, and E. Frazzoli. On synchronous robotic networks – Part ii: Time complexity of rendezvous and deployment algorithms. *IEEE Transactions on Automatic Control*, 52(12):2214–2226, Dec. 2007.

[15] A. Mirtabatabaei and F. Bullo. Opinion dynamics in heterogeneous networks: convergence, conjectures and theorems. *arXiv:1103.2829v2*, Mar. 2011. To appear in SIAM J. Control Optim.

[16] L. Moreau. Stability of multiagent systems with time-dependent communication links. *IEEE Transactions on Automatic Control*, 50(2):169 – 182, Feb. 2005.

[17] M. Roozbehani, A. Megretski, and E. Frazzoli. Lyapunov analysis of quadratically symmetric neighborhood consensus algorithms. In *CDC*, pages 2252–2257, 2008.

[18] B. Touri and A. Nedic. Discrete-time opinion dynamics. In *Signals, Systems and Computers (ASILOMAR), 2011 Conference Record of the Forty Fifth Asilomar Conference on*, pages 1172 –1176, Nov. 2011.

Is Privacy Compatible with Truthfulness?

David Xiao
LIAFA
CNRS, Université Paris 7
Paris, France
dxiao@liafa.univ-paris-diderot.fr

ABSTRACT

In the area of privacy-preserving data mining, a differentially private mechanism intuitively encourages people to share their data because they are at little risk of revealing their own information. However, we argue that this interpretation is incomplete because external incentives are necessary for people to participate in databases, and so data release mechanisms should not only be differentially private but also compatible with incentives, otherwise the data collected may be false. We apply the notion of *truthfulness* from game theory to this problem. In certain settings, it turns out that existing differentially private mechanisms do not encourage participants to report their information truthfully.

On the positive side, we exhibit a transformation that takes truthful mechanisms and transforms them into differentially private mechanisms that remain truthful. Our transformation applies to games where the type space is small and the goal is to optimize an insensitive quantity such as social welfare. Our transformation incurs only a small additive loss in optimality, and it is computationally efficient. Combined with the VCG mechanism, our transformation implies that there exists a differentially private, truthful, and approximately efficient mechanism for any social welfare game with small type space.

We also study a model where an explicit numerical cost is assigned to the information leaked by a mechanism. We show that in this case, even differential privacy may not be strong enough of a notion to motivate people to participate truthfully. We show that mechanisms that release a perturbed histogram of the database may reveal too much information. We also show that, in general, any mechanism that outputs a synopsis that resembles the original database (such as the mechanism of Blum et al. (STOC '08)) may reveal too much information.

Categories and Subject Descriptors

F.0 [**Theory**]: General

Keywords

differential privacy, mechanism design

1. INTRODUCTION

As our world becomes ever more digitized and connected, concerns about the privacy of our personal information have become increasingly pressing. With various organizations collecting, accessing, and storing individuals' data, our desire to fully take advantage of the data has come into stark tension with the equally important desire to keep information about various aspects of our lives private, including for example our medical histories and our demographic information.

Understanding and resolving this tension has been a longstanding goal in the statistics and data analysis literature [5, 16]. More recently, the theoretical computer science community has provided definitions and a rigorous treatment of this question [7, 8, 11, 3, 12], culminating in the definition and study of differential privacy [11, 8]. See [9] for a more complete overview of the area and further references.

Differential privacy guarantees the following: a (randomized) data release mechanism is ε-differentially private if, for any input database, any participant i in the database, and any possible output of the release mechanism s, the presence or absence of participant i causes at most a multiplicative e^{ε} change in the probability of the mechanism outputting s. The question is whether one can achieve privacy while at the same time preserving some notion of utility, since one could always build a trivially private (but not very useful) mechanism that outputs a constant value without looking at the input data. The advantage of working with the rigorous definition provided by differential privacy is that one can now show that certain tasks can be done with formal guarantees of utility and privacy [2, 3, 24, 27, 15, 29].

For a problem where one can achieve both meaningful utility and differential privacy, the differential privacy guarantee is interpreted as follows: since the output distribution of the mechanism is barely affected by the presence or absence of participant i in the above very precise and very strong sense, therefore the release mechanism leaks very little private information about participant i, and participant i should feel comfortable entering his data in the database.

Differential privacy and incentives.

In this paper we investigate this interpretation. The first question we pose is why do individuals want to participate in a database at all? If individuals are indeed concerned about the privacy of their information, then they must receive some incentive to participate in order to counteract the preference for guarding their information private.

It seems hard to imagine individuals submitting private data to an organization that gives them no incentive whatsoever (interpreting "incentive" broadly). For example, individuals do not willingly submit their information to marketing companies selling something they have no interest in (unless they are incentivized by money or the chance of winning a prize). On the other hand, when something can be gained, such as the pleasure or connection to friends offered by Facebook or by using email hosted on Google, individuals do readily reveal private information. Approaching incentives from the point of view of game theory, we therefore posit that for any database where the information being collected is sensitive, there must be an associated game whose outcome incentivizes the individuals to participate in the database.

We will study the most general setting of incentives in the following two senses: (1) the incentives of the individual may be incompatible with each other and with the incentives of the database curator, and (2) the individuals may be able to lie about their data if it is to their advantage. See Section 2.4.1 for a discussion of work that uses different assumptions.

2. OUR RESULTS

The main contribution of this paper is conceptual: we advocate combining the study of differential privacy and game-theoretic incentives into the following natural and coherent model. We also prove some general positive results in this model showing that one can achieve differential privacy in an incentive-compatible way, and we give negative results showing that additional care must be taken when assigning explicit costs to privacy.

2.1 Our model

The differential privacy setting.

There is a database curator who solicits information from individuals and puts them into a database. Each row of the database contains the information of one individual. The curator then applies some *release mechanism* to the database in order to produce an output, which is then published. We assume that there is some *quality metric* that determines how good the output of the release mechanism is. The database curator wants to use a mechanism that produces high quality outputs, but the individuals wish for the output to be differentially private, and these two may be in tension.[1]

The mechanism design setting.

We next give an informal introduction to the game-theoretic setting of mechanism design, and we then relate it to the problem of differential privacy (more precise definitions appear in Section 3). In order to make things slightly more concrete, for each notion that we introduce, we state what it would be in the case of an auction for a single item.

In mechanism design, there are n players, each of whom has some private information called his *type* (*e.g.* in a single-item auction, each player's type would be how much he values the item), and there is a space of possible outcomes (*e.g.* a choice of winner and a price). Each of the n players has a *individual utility function* that determines the amount of utility a player gets from each possible outcome (*e.g.* the difference between the price and his valuation if the player wins the auction, or 0 if he loses). The goal of each individual in participating in the game is to optimize his individual utility. There is also a "global utility" function that determines the overall quality of the outcome (*e.g.* the social welfare, which is just the sum of the individual utilities of all the players).

A mechanism is a (possibly randomized) function mapping each possible setting of the players' types to an outcome. The main problem studied in mechanism design is to build mechanisms that satisfy the following two properties:

Efficiency For any choice of the players' types, the expected global utility of the output of the mechanism should be close to the optimal global utility.[2]

Truthfulness For any choice of the players' types, no single player, say player i, can report a false type so that (if all other players remain honest) the mechanism gives an outcome with greater expected utility to player i than if player i had reported honestly.

Since individual utilities may not be aligned with the global utility, it turns out that implementing even very simple functionalities satisfying the two criteria above simultaneously is non-trivial. For example, the study of the single-item auction led to the Vickrey 2nd-price auction mechanism.

The combined model.

We can now see how the differential privacy setting can be comfortably re-stated using game-theoretic terminology. An individual is a player, and each individual's private information is his type. The database is just the concatenation of all players' types. The database release mechanism is just a mechanism in the game-theoretic sense. The quality metric is the global utility of the game, and therefore "accurate" release mechanisms correspond to "efficient" game-theoretic mechanisms. In addition to the above, the *individual* utility functions now may also affect players' behaviors.

Truthfulness is essential not only because it is a standard game-theory notion, but also because privacy does not make sense without truthfulness. If the data being collected were misreported, it would be of little use to the database curator. Moreover, protecting the privacy of false data seems superfluous.

Also, recall that in differential privacy, the concern is that if there is too little privacy then individuals may choose not to participate in a database. In the game theoretic setting, truthfulness and participation are closely related: one can always extend a game to have a "$\perp$" type that represents non-participation, and have a player deviate to the "$\perp$" type to represent non-participation. Conversely, a player who reports a type that is independent of his true type is in some sense choosing not to participate. In the rest of this paper, we will focus on truthfulness, with the understanding that non-participation is a specific kind of deviation from truthfulness.

[1] As is typical in the differential privacy literature, we treat the database curator as a trusted third party, who is allowed to see the individuals' private information.

[2] Throughout this paper, *efficiency* refers to the game-theoretic notion. Computational efficiency will be explicitly stated as such.

Roadmap.

We will see that mechanisms that seem satisfactory when privacy is studied in isolation are not necessarily satisfactory when truthfulness is also explicitly considered.

We will look at the relationship between differential privacy and truthfulness in two frameworks. The first is to construct mechanisms that are truthful, efficient, and whose output satisfies differential privacy. In this model, privacy is not given an explicit numerical value, but is simply an additional property of the mechanism. We call such mechanisms PTE, and we show the first PTE mechanisms by exhibiting a transformation from truthful and efficient mechanisms into PTE mechanisms for games where the type space is small and where the global utility is insensitive to any particular player's type and depends only on the number of players who have each type.

The second framework is where the value of privacy is explicitly quantified. We will assign a non-zero cost to the amount of information leaked by a mechanism, and we ask when does the cost of revealing information overwhelm the utility a player gets from the game. We will show that when privacy has a non-zero cost, even differentially private mechanisms may not motivate individuals to reveal their true information.

While the first framework may seem overly simple by not quantifying privacy loss, the techniques developed there have subsequently been shown to apply to the second framework as well (see Section 2.4.2).

2.2 Private, truthful, and efficient (PTE) mechanisms

The Exponential Mechanism is not necessarily truthful.

Our first result revisits the question of whether or not the Exponential Mechanism is truthful. Nissim et al. [31] already exhibited a counter-example showing that the Exponential Mechanism is not truthful. However, the counter-example they give is somewhat artificial because it is easy to see that *no* efficient and truthful mechanism exists for their game (even without considering privacy). We believe the following Theorem 2.1 highlights the drawback of the Exponential Mechanism in sharper relief than the counter-example of [31], because the LINE-1-FAC game we consider *does* have a truthful and efficient mechanism. In fact, we will see that there even exists a PTE mechanism for LINE-1-FAC.

We consider the well-studied 1-facility location on a line game, denoted LINE-1-FAC, which is a special case of the k-facility problem [31, 26, 1] and also of the single-peaked preference games [28, 33]. In the LINE-1-FAC game, each player has a point on the interval $[0, 1]$ and the mechanism is supposed to output $s \in [0, 1]$. Each individual wants to minimize their distance to s, while the mechanism wants to minimize the sum of all the individuals' distances to s. This game *does* have a truthful and efficient mechanism without money, namely outputting the left-most median player's point [28]. We prove:

THEOREM 2.1. *For LINE-1-FAC, the Exponential Mechanism with any privacy $\varepsilon > 0$ is not truthful.*

Transforming a truthful and efficient mechanism into a private, truthful, and efficient mechanism.

Our main positive technical result is a transformation for a large class of games that converts truthful and efficient mechanisms into PTE mechanisms.

More precisely, we work with the relaxed notion of (ε, η)-differential privacy [10], which, in addition to the e^ε multiplicative difference, also allows an additive error η, usually taken to be negligible, in the difference between the output distributions of two databases. Our transformation takes any truthful and efficient mechanism and transforms it into a (ε, η)-differentially private, truthful, and δ-efficient mechanism, where δ is an additive approximation error that depends on ε, η. Formal definitions are deferred to Section 3.

These are the first PTE mechanisms exhibited for non-trivial games. Furthermore, our transformation preserves other properties such as computational efficiency and moneylessness, and it applies to *all* games with small type space. Therefore, applying our transformation to the VCG mechanism gives a PTE mechanism for *all* social welfare games with small type space.

As throughout this paper, we will assume in the following that the utility functions of each user is bounded in $[-1, 1]$, and that the global utility function is bounded between $[-n, n]$. In particular, this means that it is interesting to obtain mechanisms that are δ-efficiency for $\delta = o(n)$.

The transformation.

The idea of the transformation is based on the ideas for privately releasing histogram data [11]. Suppose the type space of the game is a finite set of size q. For player inputs $\underline{t} = (t_1, \ldots, t_n)$ where t_i is the type of the i'th player, we will let $\underline{h}$ denote the histogram with q entries, one for each possible type, and where $h_j = |\{i \mid t_i = j\}|$, the number of players who have type j.

Suppose each individual player's utility function is $v(t, s)$ where t is the player's type and s is an outcome of the game; suppose that v lies in the interval $[-1, 1]$. Suppose that the global utility function $w(\underline{t}, s)$ is anonymous (*i.e.* it depends only on the histogram $\underline{h}$ and not on player identities), and is insensitive: namely if $\underline{h}, \underline{h}'$ are close in ℓ_1 distance then for all outcomes s it holds that $|w(\underline{h}, s) - w(\underline{h}', s)|$ is small. For example, the social welfare function, which is just the sum of the individual players' utilities, is an example of such a global utility function. Without loss of generality, we can assume that all mechanisms for games with such global utility functions need only depend on the histogram of player types, rather than looking at the individual players' types. (We show this in Appendix A.)

At a high level, our transformation from truthful and efficient to PTE works by constructing the histogram of inputs, adding independent noise distributed according to the two-sided geometric distribution to each of the entries of the histogram, and then running the original truthful and efficient mechanism on the perturbed histogram. Care must be taken that the noise does not create negative entries into the histogram; simply truncating negative entries to 0 does not give truthful mechanisms. We show a way to achieve this in Section 4. Our procedure gives the following theorem.

THEOREM 2.2 (INFORMAL). *Let $\varepsilon, \eta > 0$. Let G be a game with a type space of size q and where the global utility function depends only on the histogram and is insensitive to individual players' types. Let M be a truthful and δ-approximately efficient mechanism. Then there ex-*

ists a truthful mechanism M' for the game G that is (ε, η)-differentially private and is δ'-approximately efficient for $\delta' \approx \delta$. Furthermore, if M is computationally efficient then so is M', and if M is moneyless then so is M'.

We note that our transformation is applicable to many settings where small type space is natural: for example, in some auction settings, the bids are discretized so there are only a few possible values of bids; in surveys or questionnaires, the questions are often multiple-choice and therefore take on only a few values. In the following we choose to highlight two particularly interesting applications of our transformation.

Application to LINE-1-FAC.

We will show that using a simple rounding procedure and then applying Theorem 2.2 to a mechansim for the discretized version of the LINE-1-FAC game, we can give a PTE mechanism for LINE-1-FAC.

COROLLARY 2.3. *For all $\varepsilon, \eta > 0$, there exists an (ε, η)-differentially private, truthful, and $O(n^{1/2} \log(n/\eta)/\varepsilon)$ approximately efficient mechanism for LINE-1-FAC.*

Applying our transformation to this game highlights two features: first, although the Exponential Mechanism is not truthful when applied to this game, our transformation shows there does exist a private, truthful, and efficient mechanism for this game. Second, although our main transformation applies to games with small finite type space, our mechanism for LINE-1-FAC shows that in certain cases one can suitably discretize large or infinite type spaces and then apply our transformation.

PTE mechanism for all *social welfare games with small type space.*

In fact, because the VCG mechanism gives a general truthful and perfectly efficient mechanism (using money) for all social welfare games, *i.e.* games optimizing the sum of the individuals' utilities, our main theorem implies the following:

COROLLARY 2.4. *Fix $\varepsilon, \eta > 0$. For any game G with n players and where the type space has size q, and where the goal is to optimize social welfare, there is a truthful mechanism for G that is (ε, η)-differentially private and is $O(q \log(q/\eta)/\varepsilon)$-approximately efficient.*

2.3 The value of privacy

Prior work (including the results outlined in the previous section) studied privacy and utility as orthogonal features. For example, in the above we showed that one could achieve a truthful (with respect to utility functions that do not consider privacy) and efficient mechanism that simultaneously satisfied differential privacy. However, if one really believes that participants value their privacy, then this should explicitly be taken into account in their utility functions. Not only does this allow us to quantify *how much* participants value their privacy, it also allows us to model tradeoffs between utility and privacy. That is, participants may be willing to sacrifice some of the utility they reap from a game by reporting a false type and thereby protecting their privacy. Vice versa, participants may be willing to sacrifice their privacy if by doing so they gain a larger utility from the outcome of the game. We will show that it is possible even for PTE mechanisms to leak too much information to achieve truthfulness in games where there exists a tradeoff between utility and privacy.

2.3.1 Quantifying privacy

The first task is to define a measure of how much information a mechanism leaks. One natural condition that the information cost should satisfy is that it should be 0 if a player reports a type that is independent of his honest type, since this means that the output of the mechanism does not contain information about his type, and so should not compromise his privacy. This criterion implies that information cost cannot *solely* be a function of the player's type and the outcome of the game, because the notion "independent of the honest type" is inherently a statement about how the player behaves on *all* possible values of his type. As a thought experiment, fix any type t, and consider the following two strategies: first is the truthful strategy, and second the strategy that always outputs t regardless of what the player's actual type is. Then, in the case that the player's actual type is t, the two strategies give exactly the same output, but intuitively the truthful strategy might reveal information about the player's type while the constant t strategy does not.

Therefore our measure of information cost cannot be expressed as a modification of a "traditional" utility function that depends solely on the player's type and outcome. Instead, we work with a measure that depends on the player's strategy over all possible types.

We let $\mathsf{IC}_M(\sigma, \underline{t}, i)$ denote the information cost to player i of the strategy σ, given that the (true) input is $\underline{t} = (t_1, \ldots, t_n)$ and that the mechanism is M. A strategy σ is simply a function mapping types to distributions over types, so that if player i has true type t, then to use strategy σ he will sample $t' \leftarrow \sigma(t)$ and declare t' to the mechanism.

In general the information cost can be highly application-specific, and so we prefer to state our results without fixing a specific information cost function. Rather, our results hold for any information cost function that satisfies the following assumptions:

Players can hide their data: for any strategy σ that is independent of its input (*i.e.* $\sigma(t) = \sigma(t')$ for all t, t'), then for all $i, \underline{t}$ it holds that $\mathsf{IC}_M(\sigma, \underline{t}, i) = 0$.

Cost reflects differential privacy: roughly, this condition requires that, if ε is the minimal value such that M is a ε-differentially private mechanism, the information cost cannot be much lower than ε.

We formalize the assumptions above in Section 5. We already justified the first assumption above. Intuitively, the second assumption simply means that the amount of differential privacy (the ε) is "dominated" by the application-specific information cost. In contexts where the information cost did not satisfy the second condition, presumably this means that we have application-specific knowledge about what privacy concerns are relevant, and so it would be more sensible to study mechanisms that target directly the information cost specific to the application rather than trying to use differential privacy as a generic tool.

In Appendix C we give some candidate definitions of information cost.

Tradeoffs between the value of the game and the value of privacy.

Given an information cost function, we would like to explicitly incorporate it into the utility of the player. Let us use the word "game value" or simply "value" to denote the benefit that the player extracts from the outcome of the game without taking into account privacy, and we will let overall utility be the game value minus the information cost, and we will say that such a utility is privacy-sensitive.

2.3.2 *Releasing histograms for* LINE-1-FAC

Our first negative result draws on the LINE-1-FAC game once again. Corollary 2.3 says that a PTE mechanism for LINE-1-FAC exists, let us denote it by M (see Algorithm 4.10 for the definition of the mechanism). In order to understand the following result, we first give a rough description of M: M first rounds the positions of the players to discrete points, then constructs a histogram of the players' rounded locations, perturbs the histogram, and finally outputs the median point of the perturbed histogram. Suppose now that, instead of outputting the median, the mechanism outputs "more than necessary" and also publishes the entire perturbed histogram of the players' locations as well. Call this mechanism $\hat{M}$. We believe that $\hat{M}$, represents a plausible situation in the real world: an agency gathers data for a single explicit purpose, for example to decide where to build a hospital so as best to serve local residents, but then publishes the entire perturbed histogram data so that it may be of use to other agencies that may want to use it in a different way.

$\hat{M}$ is actually PTE: truthfulness and efficiency remain because the facility location output is the same as M, while privacy also remains because the perturbation of the histogram was designed to render the entire histogram differentially private. However, we show in Theorem 5.6 that if we set the parameters so that the mechanism is $(2\varepsilon, \eta)$-differentially private, then the information cost is greater than ε. On the other hand, we show in Theorem 5.3 that there exist situations where the amount of value that a player loses by ignoring his true type and declaring a fixed type, say 0, is at most $e^{-\Omega(n)}$. This implies the following:

THEOREM 2.5 (INFORMAL). *The PTE mechanism for LINE-1-FAC given by $\hat{M}$ is untruthful when one takes into account the information cost.*

2.3.3 *Releasing synopses.*

We prove a more general theorem about the information cost of any mechanism that publishes information that can be useful for many different count queries: if Q is the type space of the players and $F : Q \to \{0,1\}$, then we define the count query $\overline{F}(\underline{t}) = \frac{1}{n}\sum_{i=1}^{n} F(t_i)$. For example, in the case of a census, F might be the set of households with two children, and $\overline{F}(\underline{t})$ would be the fraction of all households that have two children.

We say that a mechanism M is a synopsis generator for a class of predicates $\mathcal{C}$ if, given an input database $\underline{t}$, it outputs a data structure $M(\underline{t})$ from which we can deduce $\overline{F}(\underline{t})$ for many $F \in \mathcal{C}$. It was shown by Blum et al. [3] that it is possible to construct differentially private and accurate synopsis generators. Subsequent work has extended this to achieve better parameters [13, 21].

Here we show that good synopsis generators must leak information:

THEOREM 2.6 (INFORMAL, SEE THEOREM 5.11). *If M is a good synopsis generator for a rich class of predicates, and IC_M reflects differential privacy, then for almost all databases, the information cost of revealing a synopsis generated from that database is $\Omega(1)$ with respect to at least one player.*

This shows that synopsis generators such as the one proposed by Blum et al. [3] must inherently reveal a lot of information some player's type, and furthermore, that they must leak information on "most" databases (more precisely, we will show that for any database, there is a nearby one where some player has a high information cost). Interestingly, the proof uses a construction of a combinatorial design to show that, for every $\underline{t}$, there exists an exponentially large family of $\underline{t}'$ that differ little from $\underline{t}$ such that one of them has a player with large information cost.

This theorem leads to the following consequences: consider a mechanism M that publishes an output that (a) incentives players' participation by giving them some value and (b) includes a good synopsis. If the value to each player diminishes by very little (say vanishingly small) when a player mis-reports his type, but the information cost is constant (as is implied by Theorem 2.6), then the mechanism cannot be truthful. Namely, individuals will prefer to lie because by declaring, say, a constant value, they will gain in information cost more than enough to compensate for their loss in value. This may hold even if M is differentially private. As a specific instantiation, we prove that if a mechanism M approximately solves the 1-facility location problem over any metric space and simultaneously releases a synopsis, then M cannot be truthful. See Section 5.2 for formal statements.

2.4 Comparison with related work

Since the original version of this manuscript appeared in January 2011 [35], in the following discussion we separate "previous work" and "subsequent work" according to that date.

2.4.1 *Previous work.*

There has already been a fruitful interaction between game theory and the study of differential privacy. The first work combining the two is the "Exponential Mechanism" of McSherry and Talwar [27], which achieves privacy, *approximate* truthfulness, and efficiency. Approximate truthfulness says that the amount any player can gain by announcing a false type is small (but possibly positive). Approximate truthfulness is in fact a consequence of differential privacy, which says that any one player's type can only affect the output distribution of the mechanism by a little. McSherry and Talwar [27] interpret approximate truthfulness to mean that the player might as well announce his type honestly, since he has little incentive to deviate. They also show that their mechanism achieves good efficiency (assuming the players behave truthfully).

Unfortunately, the approach suffers from the following two drawbacks, first observed by Nissim et al. [31]. First, in the Exponential Mechanism, *all* possible strategies of any individual player lead to approximately the same output distribution of the mechanism. If one accepts the interpretation that players are indifferent to small changes in their utility, then intuitively privacy may even motivate players to *lie*: players are indifferent to the small amount of utility from the game outcome that is lost by lying, but they would prefer to lie because that would reduce the amount of information leaked by the mechanism about their private type. (We will formalize this concern in Section 5, see also the discussion in Section 2.3.) Thus, it seems that approximate truthfulness cannot substitute for standard truthfulness when privacy is desired.

Second, Nissim et al. [31] showed that the Exponential Mechanism is *not* truthful for a game based on digital goods auctions, and therefore the relaxation to approximate truthfulness is inherently necessary. (As we mentioned, we show that Exponential Mechanism is not truthful also for the LINE-1-FAC game.)

Nissim et al. [31] go on to show that by combining the Exponential Mechanism with a "Gap Mechanism" that incentivizes honesty, one can get a fully truthful mechanism. They apply this mechanism to give a truthful and approximately efficient mechanism for the k-facility problem on a line, which is a more general version of the 1-facility problem on a line that we will study in this paper. Unfortunately, their mechanism is not differentially private, because the Gap Mechanism relies on constraining the post-actions of the players, and this constraint reveals the types of the players in a very non-private way.

Ghosh and Roth [18] consider a question that is related but orthogonal to our work: they consider *verified* databases where each player has private information that a database owner wants to gather. Their mechanism allows each player i to declare a pricing function $c_i : \mathbb{R} \to \mathbb{R}$ such that $c_i(\varepsilon)$ represents the minimal payment that player i would require to submit his information to a database that is then published via an ε-differentially private sanitization mechanism. Their mechanism uses these pricing functions to compute a value of ε and payment values that are paid out to each player such that enough of them are incentivized to participate to make the outcome of the sanitizer accurate. More follow-up works in this direction have appeared recently [32, 17, 25]. The main difference with our model is that in this line of work, it is assumed that the players' private information will be accurately reported, and they may *only* lie about how much they value their privacy. In contrast, our model focuses on deviations resulting from players reporting false private information, but does not explicitly consider players' lying about their valuation of their privacy.

Feigenbaum et al. [14] study how to keep information private even from the database owner, *i.e.* before running sanitization. We do not study this problem here and treat the database owner as a trusted party. We note however that, using standard cryptographic assumptions and protocols, one can replace a trusted database owner by a secure multiparty computation among the individuals.

2.4.2 Subsequent work

Subsequent to the initial version of this manuscript, Chen et al. [4] showed that it is possible to build truthful mechanisms even when the players' utilities explicitly take into account the cost of information leaked, thus answering affirmatively one of the open questions posed in the initial version of this manuscript. Their result holds for a general class of information costs. Some of their mechanisms are inspired by the TE-to-PTE transformation (Theorem 4.3) presented in this paper.

Huang and Kannan [23] resolve another problem posed in the original version of this manuscript: they show that one can alter the VCG mechanism to give a PTE mechanism for *any* social welfare game. This bypasses the restriction of our transformation to small type spaces. We note that their result is nevertheless incomparable to ours in certain respects, because it inherently uses payments and so cannot be used to construct moneyless mechanisms, and their mechanism is not necessarily computationally efficient (although for certain specific games they acheive computational efficiency).

Nissim et al. [30] show that under certain assumptions about the distribution of information costs of a population and assuming that the mechanism can restrict the reactions of individuals, one can build truthful mechanisms that take into account the players' information costs.

3. PRELIMINARIES

We let $[q] = \{1, \ldots, q\}$. We identify sets S with the uniform distribution over the set. For a distribution X, we write $x \leftarrow X$ to denote a random sample from that distribution. We let underlined variables $\underline{x}$ denote vectors and x_i the i'th coordinate in the vector. For $\underline{x} \in \mathbb{R}^n$, we let $\|\underline{x}\|_1 = \sum_{i=1}^n |x_i|$ denote the ℓ_1 norm and $\|\underline{x}\|_\infty = \max_i |x_i|$ the ℓ_∞ norm.

Games.

A game with n players consists of the type space Q, a space S of possible outcomes of the game, a valuation function $v : Q \times S \to [-1, 1]$, and a global utility function $w : Q^n \times S \to \mathbb{R}$. The valuation function v determines the private utilities of the players. When Q is finite, we let $|Q| = q$. For $i \in [n]$, for $t_1, \ldots, t_n$, we let $\underline{t}^{-i}$ denote the vector with $n-1$ entries given by $t_1, \ldots, t_{i-1}, t_{i+1}, \ldots, t_n$. Define $\underline{h}(\underline{t}) \in \mathbb{Z}^q$ the histogram of the input, where $h_j = |\{i \mid t_i = j\}|$. We assume *w.l.o.g.* that the type space has a special $\perp$ type, and any player that declares this special type is ignored. (Namely, an input with n players, k of whom have type $\perp$, is treated as an input to the game with $n-k$ players with those k players removed.)

We define the following properties of games:

1. A game is *anonymous* if it has an anonymous global utility function: let w be its global utility function, then there is a function w' such that for all $\underline{t}, s$, it holds that $w(\underline{t}, s) = w'(\underline{h}(\underline{t}), s)$. In such cases, we abuse notation and write $w(\underline{h}, s)$ to mean $w(\underline{t}, s)$ where $\underline{h} = \underline{h}(\underline{t})$.
2. An anonymous global utility function is *insensitive* if for all integers k, $\|\underline{h} - \underline{h}'\|_1 \leq k$ implies that for all s, $|w(\underline{h}, s) - w(\underline{h}', s)| \leq k$.
3. The *social welfare* is $w(\underline{t}, s) = \sum_{i=1}^n v(t_i, s)$. It is anonymous and insensitive.

Mechanisms.

A mechanism M is a (randomized) function that takes types $t_1, \ldots, t_n$ for all of the players and samples an outcome $(s, p) \leftarrow M(t_1, \ldots, t_n)$ where $s \in S$ is the game outcome and $p : Q \to \mathbb{R}$ is a function determining payments. Namely, any player with type t must pay $p(t)$ to the mechanism (since we only consider anonymous games, payments only depend on the type and not the identity of the player). Each player tries to maximize $v(t_i, s) - p(t_i)$ where (s, p) is the outcome of the game.

We say that M is *moneyless* if $p \equiv 0$ for all inputs and random coins. We are concerned with asymptotic analysis, so M must be be able to handle any number of players n.

A player strategy σ is a function mapping the type space Q to distributions over Q. If a player uses strategy σ, this means given a true type t, the player samples from $t' \leftarrow \sigma(t)$ and reports t' to the mechanism.

1. We say a mechanism M is *truthful* if for every player $i \in [n]$, and for all $\underline{t}$ and all strategies σ, it holds that[3]

$$\mathbb{E}_{(s,p)\leftarrow M(\underline{t})} M[v(t_i, s) - p(t_i)] \geq \mathbb{E}_{t'_i \leftarrow \sigma(t_i),(s,p)\leftarrow M(\underline{t}^{-i},t'_i)}[v(t_i, s) - p(t'_i)]$$

2. We say a mechanism is $\delta(n)$-*efficient* if for all inputs $\underline{t}$ on n players, it holds that

$$\mathbb{E}_M[w(\underline{t}, M(\underline{t}))] \geq \max_{s\in S} w(\underline{t}, s) - \delta(n)$$

Observe that our definition of efficiency allows for an *additive* error. In contrast, most work in the mechanism design literature on approximate mechanisms deal with *multiplicative* error. However, additive error is more suitable when working with differential privacy.

Differential privacy.

A mechanism M is (ε, η)-*differentially private* if for all $i \in [n]$, all $\underline{t} \in Q^n$, all $t' \in Q$, and all subsets U of the output space of M, it holds that $\Pr[M(\underline{t}) \in U] \leq e^{\varepsilon} \Pr[M(\underline{t}^{-i}, t') \in U] + \eta$. Typically we think of $\varepsilon > 0$ being a small constant and η as being $o(1)$, preferably negligible.

Definition 3.1 (PTE mechanisms). *A mechanism M for a game define by private valuation functions $v : Q \to [-1, 1]$ and global utility function $w : Q^n \to \mathbb{R}$ is $(\varepsilon, \eta, \delta)$-PTE if it is (ε, η)-differentially private, truthful (with respect to private valuations v), and δ-efficient (with respect to global utility w).*

Useful distributions.

We will frequently write $\alpha = e^{-\varepsilon}$. Let $\mathcal{G}_\varepsilon$ denote the geometric distribution over the integers, with probability mass function $f(x) = \frac{1-\alpha}{1+\alpha}\alpha^{|x|}$. Let $\mathcal{H}_{\varepsilon,\tau,q}$ be the following distribution: sample $\underline{\zeta} \leftarrow \mathcal{G}_\varepsilon^q$. If $\|\underline{\zeta}\|_\infty > \tau$, output 0, otherwise output $\underline{\zeta}$.

It is straightforward to calculate that for $\zeta \leftarrow \mathcal{G}_\varepsilon$:

$$\Pr[|\zeta| \geq \tau] = \frac{2\alpha^\tau}{1+\alpha} \tag{3.1}$$

Lemma 3.2. *For all $i, j \in [q]$ and $U \subseteq \mathbb{Z}^q$, for $\underline{\zeta}'$ sampled from $\mathcal{H}_{\varepsilon,\tau,q}$ it holds that:*

$$\Pr[\underline{\zeta}' \in U] \leq e^{2\varepsilon} \Pr[e_i - e_j + \underline{\zeta}' \in U] + \tfrac{2q\alpha^\tau}{1+\alpha}$$

where e_i denotes the i'th standard basis vector.

For completeness we provide a proof in Section B.1.

[3]Observe that the value is calculated according to the true type t_i on both sides, but the payment is calculated according to the declared type (t_i in one case, t'_i in the other). This is because the payment is what the mechanism asks the player to play, and this is a function of the *declared* type.

Negative binomial distribution.

The negative binomial distribution $\mathcal{NB}_{q,\varepsilon}$ is defined using the probability mass function

$$f(x) = \binom{x+q-1}{q-1} \cdot (1 - e^{-\varepsilon})^q e^{-\varepsilon x}$$

Fact 3.3 (*e.g.* [34]). *We note the following:*

1. *The sum of q two-sided random geometric variables $\sum_{j=1}^q \zeta_j$, where each ζ_j is distributed according to $\mathcal{G}_\varepsilon$, is distributed identically to $Y - Y'$ where both Y, Y' are independent and identically distributed according to the $\mathcal{NB}_{q,\varepsilon}$.*[4]

2. *Suppose Y is distributed according to $\mathcal{NB}_{q,\varepsilon}$. Then $\Pr[Y \geq t] = \Pr[Z \leq q]$ where Z is a binomial random variable for an experiment with $q+t$ trials and success probability $(1 - e^{-\varepsilon})$ for each trial.*

4. PTE MECHANISMS

4.1 The Exponential Mechanism not truthful for LINE-1-FAC

Definition 4.1. *The **LINE-1-FAC** game is defined as follows. The player types are $t_i \in [0, 1]$. The outcome of the game is a point $s \in [0, 1]$. The utility function is $v(t, s) = -|t - s|$ and the global utility is the social welfare: $w(\underline{t}, s) = \sum_{i\in[n]} v(t_i, s) = -\sum_{i\in[n]} |t_i - s|$.*

The moneyless mechanism that outputs the median (breaking ties say by picking the left median point) of the $\{t_1, \ldots, t_n\}$ is truthful and achieves optimal social welfare for this game [28].

We now prove Theorem 2.1, the fact that the Exponential Mechanism is not truthful for LINE-1-FAC.

Proof of Theorem 2.1. For $n = 2$, set $t_1 = 0, t_2 = 2/3$. (This can easily be extended to an arbitrary even number of players n by placing $n/2$ players at 0 and $(n/2 - 1)$ players at 1, and one player at $2/3$.)

Claim 4.2. *For all $\varepsilon > 0$, if player 2 declares 1 then his utility under the Exponential Mechanism is $-5/18$, while if he declares $2/3$ then his utility is strictly less than $-5/18$.*

Proof of Claim 4.2. The Exponential Mechanism M_{Exp} generates an output s according to the density function $f(s) = \frac{e^{\varepsilon w(\underline{t},s)}}{\int_0^1 e^{\varepsilon w(\underline{t},s)}ds}$. One can compute that the expected utility of player 2 if he reports 1 is $-\int_0^1 |2/3 - s|ds = -5/18$, since in this case there are exactly half the players at 0 and at 1 and so the social welfare function (and hence the mechanism's output) is uniform over $[0, 1]$.

If player 2 is truthful, then the social welfare equals $w(\underline{t}, s) = -s - |2/3 - s|$. The idea is that this welfare decreases as s increases past $2/3$, and so the Exponential Mechanism will give lower weight to the points in $[2/3, 1]$. This will hurt player 2 and he will get worse utility than if he declared that he was at 1.

[4]This follows from the fact that a two-sided geometric random variable is identical to the difference between two one-sided geometric random variables, and the sum of one-sided geometric random variables is a negative binomial.

We formalize this and analyze the Exponential Mechanism for a truthful player 2. The expected utility of player 2 is:

$$V \stackrel{def}{=} \mathbb{E}_{s \leftarrow M_{\mathsf{Exp}}(0,2/3)}[v(2/3, s)] = \frac{-\int_0^1 e^{-\varepsilon(s+|2/3-s|)}|2/3-s|ds}{\int_0^1 e^{-\varepsilon(s+|2/3-s|)}ds}$$

We claim that for all $\varepsilon > 0$, it holds that $V < -5/18$. This is equivalent to proving

$$0 < -V - 5/18 = \frac{\int_0^1 e^{-\varepsilon(s+|2/3-s|)} \cdot (|2/3-s| - 5/18)ds}{\int_0^1 e^{-\varepsilon(s+|2/3-s|)}ds}$$

Observe that the denominator is positive, so it suffices to prove that the numerator is positive for all $\varepsilon > 0$. Evaluating the integral we obtain that

$$\int_0^1 e^{-\varepsilon(s+|2/3-s|)} \cdot (|2/3-s| - 5/18)ds = e^{-2\varepsilon/3}\left(\frac{1}{27} + \frac{9 - 5\varepsilon - e^{-2\varepsilon/3}(\varepsilon+9)}{36\varepsilon^2}\right) \quad (4.1)$$

Since $e^{-2\varepsilon/3} > 0$ so we can multiply the LHS of Equation 4.1 by $36\varepsilon^2 e^{2\varepsilon/3}$ and simplify, and it suffices to prove that

$$\tfrac{4\varepsilon^2}{3} + 9 - 5\varepsilon - e^{-2\varepsilon/3}(\varepsilon+9) > 0 \quad (4.2)$$

For large $\varepsilon \gg 0$ the RHS of Equation 4.2 is dominated by the quadratic term. For instance it is easy to check that for all $\varepsilon > 1$, it holds that $e^{-2\varepsilon/3} < 0.52$ and so:

$$\tfrac{4\varepsilon^2}{3} + 9 - 5\varepsilon - e^{-2\varepsilon/3}(\varepsilon+9) > \tfrac{4\varepsilon^2}{3} + 9 - 5\varepsilon - 0.52(\varepsilon+9) \quad (4.3)$$

$$> \tfrac{4\varepsilon^2}{3} - 4.48\varepsilon + 4.32 \quad (4.4)$$

$$> 0 \quad (4.5)$$

where the final inequality can be deduced by the fact that the quadratic polynomial in Equation 4.4 has no real roots and is non-negative. Therefore we can restrict our attention to the case $\varepsilon \leq 1$. Using the Taylor expansion of the exponential, we know that $e^{-2\varepsilon/3} \leq 1 - \frac{2\varepsilon}{3} + \frac{2\varepsilon^2}{9} - \frac{4\varepsilon^3}{81} + \frac{2\varepsilon^4}{243}$ for $\varepsilon \leq 1$, therefore Equation 4.2 can be rewritten as:

$$\begin{aligned}
&\tfrac{4\varepsilon^2}{3} + 9 - 5\varepsilon - e^{-2\varepsilon/3}(\varepsilon+9) \\
&\geq \tfrac{4\varepsilon^2}{3} + 9 - 5\varepsilon - (1 - \tfrac{2\varepsilon}{3} + \tfrac{2\varepsilon^2}{9} - \tfrac{4\varepsilon^3}{81} + \tfrac{2\varepsilon^4}{243})(\varepsilon+9) \\
&= \tfrac{4\varepsilon^2}{3} + 9 - 5\varepsilon - \varepsilon - 9 + \tfrac{2\varepsilon^2}{3} + 6\varepsilon - \tfrac{2\varepsilon^3}{9} - 2\varepsilon^2 \\
&\quad + \tfrac{4\varepsilon^4}{81} + \tfrac{4\varepsilon^3}{9} - \tfrac{2\varepsilon^5}{243} - \tfrac{2\varepsilon^4}{27} \\
&= \tfrac{2\varepsilon^3}{9} - \tfrac{2\varepsilon^4}{81} - \tfrac{2\varepsilon^5}{243} \\
&> \varepsilon^3(\tfrac{2}{9} - \tfrac{2}{27} - \tfrac{2}{27}) \\
&> 0
\end{aligned}$$

where in the last two lines we use the fact that $\varepsilon \leq 1$. ■

4.2 Transformation from TE to PTE

We now exhibit a generic transformation that converts a truthful and efficient mechanism M into a PTE mechanism M'. We assume M satisfies the following: on input $\underline{t}$, M computes its output depending only on $\underline{h} = \underline{h}(\underline{t})$ (and never looks at the entries of $\underline{t}$ individually). (This is without loss of generality for anonymous games, see Appendix A.)

> Input: types $t_1, \ldots, t_n \in [q]$. Auxiliary input: ε, η privacy parameters. Set $\tau = O(\log(q/\eta)/\varepsilon)$.
>
> 1. Sample $\underline{\zeta} \leftarrow \mathcal{H}_{\varepsilon,\tau,q}$
> 2. Construct $\underline{h}' = \underline{h} + \underline{\zeta} + \tau \cdot \underline{1}$, where $\underline{1}$ is the all 1 vector.
> 3. Output $M(\underline{h}')$.
>
> ALGORITHM 4.4. *PTE mechanism based on a truthful and efficient mechanism M.*

THEOREM 4.3. *Let G be a game with type space of size q and whose global utility function is anonymous and insensitive. Suppose G has a truthful and δ-efficient histogram mechanism M and that δ is non-decreasing.*[5]

Then for all $\varepsilon, \eta > 0$, G also has a $(2\varepsilon, \eta, \delta')$-PTE mechanism M', where $\delta'(n) = \delta(n+O(q\log(q/\eta)/\varepsilon))+O(q\log(q/\eta)/\varepsilon)$. M' is given by Algorithm 4.4. Note that if M is computationally efficient, so is M', and if M is moneyless, so is M'.

PROOF OF THEOREM 4.3. Let M be the truthful and δ-efficient mechanism. By Equation 3.1 and the union bound, we can set $\tau = O(\log(q/\eta)/\varepsilon)$ such that

$$\Pr_{\underline{\zeta} \leftarrow \mathcal{G}_\varepsilon^q}[\|\underline{\zeta}\|_\infty > \tau] < \frac{2qe^{-\varepsilon\tau}}{1+e^{-\varepsilon}} = \eta \quad (4.6)$$

In Algorithm 4.4 we construct a mechanism M' (using τ set as just mentioned) that is private, truthful, and δ'-approximately efficient. We prove that M' is PTE:

Truthfulness.

Fix an input $\underline{t}$. We claim that for every choice of $\underline{\zeta}$, the mechanism is truthful. We run M on the histogram $\underline{h}' = \underline{h} + \underline{\zeta} + \tau \cdot \underline{1}$. Because $\underline{\zeta}$ is sampled from $\mathcal{H}_{\varepsilon,\tau,q}$, it holds for every $t \in Q$ that $h'_t \geq h_t \geq 0$. Suppose that, for this fixing of $\underline{\zeta}$, there is a deviation that benefits some player, *i.e.* there exists i and σ such that

$$\mathbb{E}_{(s,p)\leftarrow M(\underline{h}')}[v(t_i, s) - p(t_i)] < \mathbb{E}_{t'\leftarrow\sigma(t_i),(s,p)\leftarrow M(\underline{h}'-e_{t_i}+e_{t'})}[v(t_i, s) - p(t')]$$

where $e_t \in \mathbb{Z}^q$ is the t'th standard basis vector. Then this is also a deviation on the input $\underline{h}'$ for the original M, which contradicts the fact that M is truthful.

Efficiency.

Let $\underline{\zeta}$ be sampled from $\mathcal{H}_{\varepsilon,\tau,q}$ and observe that $\|\underline{\zeta}\|_\infty \leq \tau$. For any input $\underline{t}$ define $\underline{h} = \underline{h}(\underline{t})$ and the modified histogram $\underline{h}' = \underline{h}(\underline{t}) + \underline{\zeta} + \tau \cdot \underline{1}$. Observe that $|\underline{h} - \underline{h}'|_1 \leq 2q\tau$. By the insensitivity of w, it holds that for all possible outcomes of the game s', it holds that $|w(\underline{h}', s') - w(\underline{h}, s')| \leq 2q\tau$.

[5]This is a technical condition to simplify the expression for δ'; for any interesting δ we can artificially increase it as some points to make it satisfy this property.

Therefore it holds that:

$$\begin{aligned}\mathbb{E}_M[w(\underline{h}, M(\underline{h}'))] &\geq \mathbb{E}_M[w(\underline{h}', M(\underline{h}'))] - 2q\tau & (4.7)\\ &\geq \max_{s'} w(\underline{h}', s') - 2q\tau - \delta(n + 2q\tau) & (4.8)\\ &\geq w(\underline{h}', s_0) - 2q\tau - \delta(n + 2q\tau) & (4.9)\\ &\geq \max_{s} w(\underline{h}, s) - 4q\tau - \delta(n + 2q\tau) & (4.10)\end{aligned}$$

In Equation 4.8 we use the efficiency of M, the fact that $\underline{h}'$ corresponds to a game with at most $n + 2q\tau$ players, and that $\delta(n) \in [0, 2n]$ is non-decreasing. In Equation 4.10 s_0 denotes the outcome that maximizes $w(\underline{h}, s)$.

Applying Equation 4.10 to the expected utility of M', one obtains the following:

$$\begin{aligned}\mathbb{E}_{M'}[w(\underline{t}, M'(\underline{h}))] &= \mathbb{E}_{\varsigma \leftarrow \mathcal{H}_{\varepsilon,\tau,q}, M}[w(\underline{t}, M(\underline{h}'))]\\ &\geq \max_{s} w(\underline{t}, s) - \delta(n + 2q\tau) - 4q\tau\end{aligned}$$

Privacy.

Observe that Algorithm 4.4 is just perturbing the histogram according to the distribution $\mathcal{H}_{\varepsilon,\tau,q}$. Therefore, from Lemma 3.2, we know that for any adjacent $\underline{h}, \underline{h}^*$, it holds that for all subsets $U \subseteq \mathbb{Z}^q$ that

$$\Pr[\underline{h} + \underline{\varsigma}' \in U] \leq e^{2\varepsilon} \Pr[\underline{h}^* + \underline{\varsigma}' \in U] + \tfrac{2qe^{-\varepsilon\tau}}{1+e^{-\varepsilon}}$$

Since by our choice of τ we know that $\frac{2qe^{-\varepsilon\tau}}{1+e^{-\varepsilon}} \leq \eta$, this shows the mechanism is $(2\varepsilon, \eta)$-differentially private. ■

Note that one popular alternative way of perturbing the histogram, by adding noise according to $\mathcal{G}_\varepsilon$ to each bin of the histogram and then truncating negative bins to 0, does not seem to guarantee truthfulness. The problem is that the truncation process is non-linear, and so it is unclear how to prove that a deviation in the perturbed game implies a deviation in the original game.

4.3 LINE-1-FAC has a PTE mechanism

We show that although the Exponential Mechanism is not truthful for LINE-1-FAC (Definition 4.1), there does exist a mechanism that is truthful, differentially private, and approximately efficient. This mechanism is given in Algorithm 4.10. The idea is to reduce LINE-1-FAC to a game D-L1F ("discrete one-facility on a line") with a small type space, and then to give a private, truthful, and efficient mechanism for D-L1F using Theorem 4.3.

4.3.1 The D-L1F game

Definition 4.5. *The D-L1F$_\gamma$ game is defined as follows. Assume that $\gamma > 0$ is such that $q = 1/\gamma + 1$ is an integer. The player types are $t_i \in [q]$. Output of mechanism is $s \in [q]$. Utility function is $v(t, s) = -\gamma|t - s|$. Global utility is social welfare: $w(\underline{t}, s) = \sum_{i=1}^n v(t_i, s)$.*

Theorem 4.7. *There is a truthful and perfectly efficient mechanism for D-L1F$_\gamma$.*

The mechanism is given in Algorithm 4.6. We may apply Theorem 4.3, we obtain:

Corollary 4.8. *For all $\varepsilon, \eta > 0$, D-L1F$_\gamma$ has a $(\varepsilon, \eta, \delta)$-PTE mechanism for $\delta = O(\log(\frac{1}{\gamma\eta})/(\gamma\varepsilon))$.*

Input: histogram of player types $\underline{h}$. Let $n = \sum_{j=1}^q h_j$.

1. Output the minimal $s \geq 1$ such that $\sum_{j=1}^s h_j \geq \frac{n}{2}$.

Algorithm 4.6. *Truthful and efficient mechanism for D-L1F*

The proof of Theorem 4.7 is a special case of the proof that the median mechanism is truthful and efficient for single-peaked preferences. For completeness, we give a proof in Section B.2.

4.3.2 PTE mechanism for LINE-1-FAC using D-L1F$_\gamma$

Theorem 4.9. *For any $\gamma, \varepsilon, \eta > 0$, the mechanism of Algorithm 4.10 is $(2\varepsilon, \eta)$-differentially private, truthful, and δ-efficient for the LINE-1-FAC game, where $\delta = n\gamma + O(\frac{1}{\gamma\varepsilon}\log(\frac{1}{\gamma\eta}))$.*

As an example setting, pick $\gamma = n^{-1/2}$, which implies $\delta = O(n^{1/2}\log(n/\eta)/\varepsilon)$.

Proof of Theorem 4.9. $(2\varepsilon, \eta)$-differential privacy follows immediately from Theorem 4.3. Efficiency is also straightforward, because the overall error is at most the discretization error, which is bounded by γ for each player, plus the error from M', which is bounded by $O(\frac{1}{\gamma\varepsilon}\log(\frac{1}{\gamma\eta}))$.

Truthfulness. Truthfulness must be argued more carefully because the rounding process might cause unexpected problems. By symmetry, it suffices to consider player 1.

Fix $t_1, \underline{t}^{-1}$, and t^*. We will show that the player can gain no utility from declaring t^* when his actual type is t_1. Fix any choice of random coins $\underline{\varsigma}$ used by M'. Let $\underline{h}' = \underline{h}(\underline{t}) + \underline{\varsigma} + \tau \cdot \underline{1}$ and $\underline{h}^* = \underline{h}(\underline{t}^{-1}, t^*) + \underline{\varsigma} + \tau \cdot \underline{1}$. Let $s = M(\underline{h}')$ and $s^* = M(\underline{h}^*)$. From the proof of truthfulness of Algorithm 4.6, we observe that M has the following property (which is stronger than truthfulness): either $s = s^*$ or $|\hat{t}_1 - s| \leq |\hat{t}_1 - s^*| - 1$. (Namely, it is impossible for $s^* \neq s$ and yet $|\hat{t}_1 - s| = |\hat{t}_1 - s^*|$.)

In the case where $s = s^*$ then there is clearly no advantage to lying, so suppose $|\hat{t}_1 - s| \leq |\hat{t}_1 - s^*| - 1$. Observe that the rounding process guarantees that for all $t \in [0, 1]$, $|t - \gamma\hat{t}| \leq \gamma/2$. Therefore we may write

$$\begin{aligned}|t_1 - \gamma s| &\leq \gamma|\hat{t}_1 - s| + \gamma/2\\ &\leq \gamma(|\hat{t}_1 - s^*| - 1) + \gamma/2\\ &\leq |t_1 - \gamma s^*|\end{aligned}$$

This again implies that there is no advantage to declaring t^*, and so since for every choice of $\underline{\varsigma}$ the mechanism is truthful, it follows that the overall mechanism is truthful. ■

4.4 Application to the VCG mechanism

Corollary 2.4, stating that all social welfare games with small type space have a PTE mechanism, follows from applying Theorem 4.3 to the VCG mechanism (which is truthful and perfectly efficient for all social welfare games).

Observe that the privacy holds with respect to the outcome of the game s and the payment function p that maps

Input: player types $t_1, \dots, t_n \in [0,1]$. Assume for simplicity that $1/\gamma$ is an integer.

1. Discretize $[0,1]$ into $q = 1/\gamma + 1$ intervals: $[0, \gamma/2), [\gamma/2, (1 + 1/2)\gamma), \dots, [(j - 1/2)\gamma, (j + 1/2)\gamma), \dots, [(q - 1/2)\gamma, 1]$.
2. Assign player i the proxy type $\hat{t}_i = j$ such that t_i falls into the j'th interval.
3. Let M denote the mechanism for D-L1F$_\gamma$ given by Theorem 4.7. Let M' be the corresponding $(2\varepsilon, \eta)$-differentially private, truthful, and efficient mechanism, given by Corollary 4.8. Run $M'(\hat{t}_1, \dots, \hat{t}_n)$ to obtain $s \in [q]$.
4. Output γs.

ALGORITHM 4.10. *$(2\varepsilon, \eta)$-differentially private, truthful, and efficient mechanism for LINE-1-FAC.*

types to payments. In particular, we assume that the payments of individual players are not revealed publicly. Clearly, privacy would not hold if outside observers learned that, say, player i made payment $p(t_i)$. This is unavoidable, but it seems reasonable that the actual payment of each player can be kept secret *e.g.* by transmitting the payment using cryptographic techniques or some other secure channel. One can also ensure that the player and curator do not try to underpay/overcharge by using proofs that the mechanism was computed correctly and that amount paid is correct by using traditional cryptographic techniques (*e.g.* NIZK proofs).

5. THE VALUE OF PRIVACY

We now explore a model that assigns non-negative costs to the information leaked by mechanisms about the private types of the players. As argued in the introduction, we assume the information cost to player i depends on the mechanism M, the strategy σ used by player i, and the types of all players $\underline{t}$. In addition we will allow the information cost with respect to a small approximation factor $\eta \geq 0$, which we motivate below. Therefore, the information cost is a function of the form $\mathsf{IC}_M^\eta(\sigma, \underline{t}, i)$. We will sometimes write IC_M to denote IC_M^0. Our formal assumptions about the information cost are:

ASSUMPTION 5.1. *We make the following assumptions about the η-approximate information cost:*

Players can hide their data: *if σ is independent of its input (*i.e. *$\sigma(t) = \sigma(t')$ for all t, t'), then for all $i, \underline{t}$ it holds that $\mathsf{IC}_M^\eta(\sigma, \underline{t}, i) = 0$.*

Cost reflects differential privacy: *for the truthful (*i.e. *identity) strategy* Id:

$$\mathsf{IC}_M^\eta(\mathsf{Id}, \underline{t}, i) \geq \Omega\left(\max_{t' \in Q} \max_B \log \frac{\Pr[M(\underline{t}^{-i}, t) \in B] - \eta}{\Pr[M(\underline{t}^{-i}, t') \in B](1 - \eta)}\right) \tag{5.1}$$

where the maximum of B is taken over all subsets such that $\Pr[M(\underline{t}^{-i}, t) \in B] > \eta$.

The intuition behind these assumptions was discussed in Section 2.3.1. The formal definition of the assumption that cost reflects differential privacy (Equation 5.1) intuitively says that the cost is at least how much more likely the true type t is than any other type t' after having observed the output of the mechanism. This is precisely the kind of difference in probability captured by differential privacy. In fact, one natural definition of information cost in the case where we have no further application-specific criteria is precisely the RHS of Equation 5.1 (see Appendix C).

We now mention the role of η. When we study (ε, η)-differentially private mechanisms, we will set η in the assumption to roughly match the η in (ε, η)-differential privacy. This is intuitively natural, since without this η the mechanism's output may have small fluctuations in probability that create large (but intuitively unmeaningful) information costs. For ε-differential privacy, we set $\eta = 0$.

To combine the information cost with the value derived by players from a game, we use the following

$$u_i(\sigma, \underline{t}) = \mathbb{E}_{t' \leftarrow \sigma(t), s \leftarrow M(\underline{t}^{-i}, t')}[v(t_i, s)] - \nu_i \mathsf{IC}_M(\sigma, \underline{t}, i) \tag{5.2}$$

Here, we have weighted the information cost with a factor ν_i that expresses how much the individual values his privacy relative to the value of the game.

REMARK 5.2. *In Equation 5.2, ν_i models the weight of player i's privacy, and for simplicity we assume that the ν_i are fixed and known (Ghosh and Roth [18] study mechanisms where these valuations are private). Intuitively $1/\nu_i$ represents how many bits must be leaked for player i to lose a constant amount of utility. $\nu_i = \Omega(1/\log|Q|)$ is a realistic setting, and would mean a constant cost is incurred if a constant* fraction *of bits is leaked. Signficantly smaller values of ν_i would model a situation in which the player assigns significant cost* only *when his type is essentially* completely *revealed by the mechanism. In particular, we may safely assume that the weights to satisfy $\nu_i = 2^{-o(n)}$, since otherwise the amount of utility that the player places on privacy is so small that explicitly modelling the value of privacy loses relevance.*

5.1 Releasing histograms for LINE-1-FAC

Recall that Corollary 2.3 says that by applying our transformation (Theorem 4.3) to a discretized version of the median mechanism for the LINE-1-FAC game, we can give a PTE mechanism for the LINE-1-FAC game. An explicit description of this mechanism is given in Algorithm 4.10, let us call this mechanism M'.

Here we show that, on certain databases, no single player can heavily influence the outcome of M'. $(2\varepsilon, \eta)$-differential privacy implies that being untruthful can hurt the value of a player by at most $2\varepsilon + \eta$. It turns out that for this particular mechanism M', there exist inputs for which the loss is much smaller.

THEOREM 5.3. *Fix any $\varepsilon > 0$ and any $\eta > 0$ such that $\eta = 2^{-o(\sqrt{n}/\log n)}$ (*i.e. *η is not too small). Then for n large enough, for all i, there exists $\underline{t}^{-i} \in [0,1]^{n-1}$ such that for all $t_i, t_i' \in [0,1]$, it holds that:*

$$\mathbb{E}_{s \leftarrow M'(\underline{t})}[v(t_i, s)] - \mathbb{E}_{s \leftarrow M'(\underline{t}^{-i}, t_i')}[v(t_i, s)] \leq e^{-(1 - e^{-\varepsilon})^2 n} \tag{5.3}$$

PROOF. To simplify our notation, suppose that the number of players is $n+1$ rather than n. By our choice of γ, Algorithm 4.10 divides $[0,1]$ into $q = n^{1/2}$ intervals.

We study the case $i = 1$, as symmetry will imply that the same argument works for all choices of i. The setting of player types $\underline{t}^{-1}$ is simply to put n players at location 0.

Recall that M' functions by building a histogram of the players' locations, generating noise $\underline{\varsigma} \leftarrow \mathcal{H}_{\varepsilon,\tau,q}$ where $\tau = O(\log(q/\eta)/\varepsilon)$, adding $\underline{\varsigma} + \tau \cdot \underline{1}$ to the histogram, and then running the deterministic mechanism M of Algorithm 4.6. Notice that for our choice of $\underline{t}^{-1}$, there is no rounding necessary. Let us rewrite the LHS of Equation 5.3 as:

$$\mathbb{E}_{\underline{\varsigma}}[v(t_1, M(\underline{h}(\underline{t}) + \underline{\varsigma} + \tau \cdot \underline{1})) - v(t_1, M(\underline{h}(\underline{t}^{-1}, t_1') + \underline{\varsigma} + \tau \cdot \underline{1}))] \tag{5.4}$$

The main observation is that for most choices of $\underline{\varsigma}$, M gives the same output regardless of what player 1 declares as its value. To state this more formally, define

$$\underline{h}^{-1} = \underline{h}(\underline{t}^{-1}) + \underline{\varsigma} + \tau \cdot \underline{1} \tag{5.5}$$

$$n' = (n+1) + \sum_{j=1}^{q} \varsigma_j + q\tau \tag{5.6}$$

The value in Equation 5.4 is upper-bounded by the probability over ς that $M(\underline{h}(\underline{t})+\underline{\varsigma}+\tau\cdot\underline{1}) \neq M(\underline{h}(\underline{t}^{-1}, t_1')+\underline{\varsigma}+\tau\cdot\underline{1})$. Call this event B. B occurs only when there exists $k \in [q]$ such that $\sum_{j=1}^{k} (\underline{h}^{-1})_j = \lceil n'/2 - 1 \rceil$.

CLAIM 5.4. $\Pr[B] \leq e^{-(1-\alpha)^2 n}$

Since we argued above that $\mathbb{E}_{\underline{\varsigma}}[v(t_1, M(\underline{h}(\underline{t}) + \underline{\varsigma} + \tau \cdot \underline{1})) - v(t_1, M(\underline{h}(\underline{t}^{-1}, t_1') + \underline{\varsigma} + \tau \cdot \underline{1}))] \leq \Pr_{\underline{\varsigma}}[B]$, this claim implies the theorem. ∎

PROOF OF CLAIM 5.4. Observe that $\Pr_{\underline{\varsigma} \leftarrow \mathcal{H}_{\varepsilon,q,\tau}}[B]$ can be written as:

$$\Pr_{\underline{\varsigma} \leftarrow \mathcal{H}_{\varepsilon,q,\tau}} \left[\|\underline{\varsigma}\|_\infty \leq \tau \wedge \exists k, \sum_{j=1}^{k} (\underline{h}^{-1})_j = \lceil n'/2 - 1 \rceil \right] \tag{5.7}$$

$$= \Pr_{\underline{\varsigma} \leftarrow \mathcal{G}_\varepsilon^q} \left[\|\underline{\varsigma}\|_\infty \leq \tau \wedge \exists k, \sum_{j=1}^{k} (\underline{h}^{-1})_j = \lceil n'/2 - 1 \rceil \right] \tag{5.8}$$

$$\leq \Pr_{\underline{\varsigma} \leftarrow \mathcal{G}_\varepsilon^q} \left[\exists k, \sum_{j=1}^{k} (\underline{h}^{-1})_j = \lceil n'/2 - 1 \rceil \right] \tag{5.9}$$

$$\leq \sum_{k=1}^{q} \Pr_{\underline{\varsigma} \leftarrow \mathcal{G}_\varepsilon^q} \left[\sum_{j=1}^{k} (\underline{h}^{-1})_j = \lceil n'/2 - 1 \rceil \right] \tag{5.10}$$

where Equation 5.8 holds because by definition the distribution of $\underline{\varsigma} \leftarrow \mathcal{H}_{\varepsilon,q,\tau}$ is exactly the same as $\mathcal{G}_\varepsilon^q$ under the condition $\|\underline{\varsigma}\|_\infty \leq \tau$.

Observe that, by the definition of $\underline{h}^{-1}$ and n', we may rewrite Equation 5.10 to obtain:

$$\Pr_{\underline{\varsigma}}[B] \leq \sum_{k=1}^{q} \Pr_{\underline{\varsigma}} \left[\sum_{j=1}^{k} (\underline{h}(\underline{t}^{-1})_j + \varsigma_j) = -b + \right. \tag{5.11}$$

$$\left. \sum_{j=k+1}^{q} (\underline{h}(\underline{t}^{-1})_j + \varsigma_j) + (q-2k)\tau \right] \tag{5.12}$$

where $b = 1$ if n' is even and $b = 0$ if n' is odd. Let us consider $b = 0$ (the other case follows by the same argument). By construction there are n players at position 0, so it follows that $h_1 = n$ and $h_j = 0$ for all $j > 1$. Therefore the RHS of Equation 5.12 equals

$$\Pr_{\underline{\varsigma}} \left[n + \sum_{j=1}^{k} \varsigma_j = \sum_{j=k+1}^{q} \varsigma_j + (q-2k)\tau \right]$$

Since $\mathcal{G}_\varepsilon$ is symmetric therefore ς_j is distributed identically as $-\varsigma_j$, and combined with the above we may deduce:

$$\Pr_{\underline{\varsigma}}[B] \leq \sum_{k=1}^{q} \Pr_{\underline{\varsigma}} \left[\sum_{j=1}^{q} \varsigma_j = n - (q-2k)\tau \right] \tag{5.13}$$

We will prove the following lemma.

LEMMA 5.5. *For all $k \in [q]$ and sufficiently large n, it holds that*

$$\Pr_{\underline{\varsigma}} \left[\sum_{j=1}^{q} \varsigma_j = n - (q-2k)\tau \right] \leq e^{-1.9(1-\alpha)^2 n}$$

Applying this lemma to Equation 5.13 we obtain $\Pr_{\underline{\varsigma}}[B] \leq q e^{-1.9(1-\alpha)^2 n}$, which, for large n, is bounded by $e^{-(1-\alpha)^2 n}$. ∎

We now turn to proving Lemma 5.5 The key point is the characterization of the sum of q two-sided geometric random variables given in Fact 3.3: $\sum_{j=1}^{q} \varsigma_j$ is distributed identically to $Y - Y'$ where Y, Y' are independent $\mathcal{NB}_{q,\varepsilon}$ variables.

PROOF OF LEMMA 5.5. We will prove the following slightly stronger inequality:

$$\Pr_{\underline{\varsigma}} \left[\sum_{j=1}^{q} \varsigma_j \geq n - (q-2k)\tau \right] \leq e^{-1.9(1-\alpha)^2 n}$$

By Fact 3.3 it holds that $\sum_{j=1}^{q} \varsigma_j$ is distributed identically to $Y - Y'$ as stated in Fact 3.3. Furthermore, since both Y, Y' are non-negative, $Y - Y' \geq n - (q-2k)\tau$ implies that $Y \geq n - (q-2k)\tau$. Therefore it suffices to bound $\Pr[Y \geq n - (q-2k)\tau]$. Furthermore, it suffices to consider just the case $k = 0$, which is the worst possible.

To summarize, it suffices to bound the probability $\Pr[Y \geq n - q\tau]$ where Y is a $\mathcal{NB}_{q,\varepsilon}$ variable. We apply the second point of fact Fact 3.3, which says that this probability is equal to the probability $\Pr[Z \leq q]$ where Z is a binomial random variable with $n - q\tau + q$ trials and success probability $1 - e^{-\varepsilon} = 1 - \alpha$. We can apply the Hoeffding bound for binomial variables and the fact that $q = \sqrt{n}$ and $\tau = o(\sqrt{n})$ (which follows from our hypothesis that $\eta = 2^{-o(\sqrt{n})/\log n}$) to conclude that, for sufficiently large n:

$$\Pr[Z \leq q] \leq e^{-2((1-\alpha)(n-q\tau)-\alpha q)^2/(n-q\tau+q)} \leq e^{-1.9(1-\alpha)^2 n} \tag{5.14}$$

∎

Releasing the histogram leaks information.

Recall that M' discretizes the input into q intervals, samples $\underline{\varsigma} \leftarrow \mathcal{H}_{\varepsilon,\tau,q}$, computes the perturbed histogram $\underline{h}' = \underline{h}(\underline{t}) + \underline{\varsigma} + \tau \cdot \underline{1}$, and outputs the median point of $\underline{h}'$.

We consider a slight modification of this mechanism: in addition to outputting the facility location, it also outputs the perturbed histogram $\underline{h}'$. Call this modified mechanism

$\hat{M}$, and notice that $\hat{M}$ remains PTE: privacy holds because the perturbed histogram is $(2\varepsilon, \eta)$-differentially private, while truthfulness and efficiency remain (with respect just to the game value, before taking into account the information cost) because the facility location output is the same as what M' would have output. As mentioned in the introduction, we believe this represents a common practice: the database curator gathers the data using one particular incentive for the individuals, but in addition to the outcome of the game, he publishes some auxiliary information about the individuals' types that may be useful in the future for some other goal not necessarily related to the incentives used for the original database.

THEOREM 5.6. *$\forall \varepsilon, \eta > 0$, suppose $\hat{M}$ is run with $(2\varepsilon, \eta)$-differential privacy. Then there exists $\eta' \leq \eta$ such that for any $\mathsf{IC}^{\eta'}_{\hat{M}}$ satisfying Assumption 5.1, for all inputs $\underline{t} \in Q^n$ and all $i \in [n]$, $\mathsf{IC}^{\eta'}_{\hat{M}}(\mathsf{Id}, \underline{t}, i) = \Omega(\varepsilon)$.*

PROOF. $\hat{M}$ outputs a histogram perturbed by $\zeta \leftarrow \mathcal{H}_{\varepsilon,\tau,q}$. Given any database $\underline{t}$, construct the histogram $\underline{h}(\underline{t})$. The following Lemma 5.7 says that for the setting $\eta' = \Pr[\|\zeta\|_\infty > \tau] \leq \eta$, for any player i, there exists $t' \neq t_i$ and B such that

$$\varepsilon < \log \frac{\Pr[\hat{M}(\underline{t}) \in B] - \eta'}{\Pr[\hat{M}(\underline{t}^{-i}, t') \in B]}$$

Theorem 5.6 then follows since Assumption 5.1 states that the information cost is at least the RHS (up to constant factors). ■

LEMMA 5.7. *Fix any q a positive integer, $\underline{h} \in \mathbb{Z}^q$, $i \in [q]$. Let e_k denote the k'th standard basis vector. Suppose $\underline{\zeta}$ is sampled according to the distribution $\mathcal{H}_{\varepsilon,\tau,q}$, where τ satisfies $\Pr_{\zeta \leftarrow \mathcal{G}^q_\varepsilon}[\|\zeta\|_\infty > \tau] = \eta'$. Then for all $j \in [q]$, $j \neq i$, there exists $B \subseteq \mathbb{Z}^q$ such that:*

$$\log \frac{\Pr[\underline{h} + e_i + \underline{\zeta} \in B] - \eta'}{\Pr[\underline{h} + e_j + \underline{\zeta} \in B]} > \varepsilon$$

PROOF. Let $B = \{\underline{h}' \mid h'_i > h_i\}$. Letting $\alpha = e^{-\varepsilon}$, we calculate that:

$$\Pr_{\underline{\zeta} \leftarrow \mathcal{H}_{\varepsilon,\tau,q}}[\underline{h} + e_i + \underline{\zeta} \in B] \quad (5.15)$$

$$= \Pr_{\underline{\zeta} \leftarrow \mathcal{H}_{\varepsilon,\tau,q}}[\underline{\zeta}_i \geq 0] \quad (5.16)$$

$$= \Pr_{\underline{\zeta} \leftarrow \mathcal{G}^q_\varepsilon}[\|\underline{\zeta}\|_\infty > \tau] + \Pr_{\underline{\zeta}_i \leftarrow \mathcal{G}_\varepsilon}[\tau \geq \underline{\zeta}_i \geq 0] \quad (5.17)$$

$$= \eta' + \left(\tfrac{1-\alpha}{1+\alpha}\right) \sum_{j=0}^{\tau} \alpha^j \quad (5.18)$$

$$> \eta' + \left(\tfrac{1-\alpha}{1+\alpha}\right) e^\varepsilon \sum_{j=1}^{\tau} \alpha^j \quad (5.19)$$

Above, Equation 5.17 holds because by the definition of $\mathcal{H}_{\varepsilon,\tau,q}$ (see Section 3), $\underline{\zeta}_i \geq 0$ can occur one of two ways: either we sampled $\underline{\zeta}' \leftarrow \mathcal{G}^q_\varepsilon$ and got $\|\underline{\zeta}'\|_\infty > \tau$ so we set $\underline{\zeta} = 0$, or else we sampled $\underline{\zeta}' \leftarrow \mathcal{G}^q_\varepsilon$ and got $\underline{\zeta}'_i \geq 0$ and we set $\underline{\zeta} = \underline{\zeta}'$. Similarly, we can deduce that:

$$\Pr_{\underline{\zeta} \leftarrow \mathcal{H}_{\varepsilon,\tau,q}}[\underline{h} + e_j + \underline{\zeta} \in B] = \Pr_{\underline{\zeta} \leftarrow \mathcal{H}_{\varepsilon,\tau,q}}[\underline{\zeta}_i \geq 1]$$
$$< \left(\tfrac{1-\alpha}{1+\alpha}\right) \sum_{j=1}^{\tau} \alpha^j$$

Therefore, we may conclude that

$$\frac{\Pr_{\underline{\zeta} \leftarrow \mathcal{H}_{\varepsilon,\tau,q}}[\underline{h} + e_i + \underline{\zeta} \in B] - \eta'}{\Pr_{\underline{\zeta} \leftarrow \mathcal{H}_{\varepsilon,\tau,q}}[\underline{h} + e_j + \underline{\zeta} \in B]} > e^\varepsilon$$

■

Combining Theorem 5.3 and Theorem 5.6, we conclude that the following gives a deviation showing that $\hat{M}$ is *not* truthful when one uses the tradeoff utility of Equation 5.2 (for reasonable settings of ν_i).

COROLLARY 5.8 (FORMALIZATION OF THEOREM 2.5). *Fix $\varepsilon > 0$ and $\eta = 2^{-o(\sqrt{n}/\log n)}$, and let $\hat{M}$ be the $(2\varepsilon, \eta)$-differentially private mechanism described above. There exists $\eta' \leq \eta$ such that the following holds for any $\mathsf{IC}^{\eta'}_{\hat{M}}$ satisfying Assumption 5.1 up to η approximation: if there exists a player i such that $\nu_i = \omega(e^{-(1-e^{-\varepsilon})^2 n})$. Let σ_0 be the strategy that always outputs 0. Then, there exists $i \in [n], \underline{t}^{-i} \in [0,1]^{n-1}$ such that for all $t_i \in [0,1]$, $\underline{t} = (\underline{t}^{-i}, t_i)$ satisfies $u_i(\mathsf{Id}, \underline{t}) < u_i(\sigma_0, \underline{t})$.*

PROOF. Fix i such that $\nu_i = \omega(e^{-(1-\varepsilon)^2 n})$. Let $\underline{t}^{-i}$ be the input guaranteed to exist by Theorem 5.3. Using the definition of u_i (Equation 5.2) and applying Theorem 5.3, we have that for all $t_i \in [0,1]$:

$$\begin{aligned} u_i(\mathsf{Id}, \underline{t}) &< \mathbb{E}_{(s,\underline{h}') \leftarrow \hat{M}(\underline{t}^{-i},0)}[v(t_i, s)] + e^{-(1-e^{-\varepsilon})^2 n} - \nu_i \varepsilon \\ &< \mathbb{E}_{(s,\underline{h}') \leftarrow \hat{M}(\underline{t}^{-i},0)}[v(t_i, s)] - \nu_i \cdot \mathsf{IC}_{\hat{M}}(\sigma_0, \underline{t}, i) \\ &= u_i(\sigma_0, \underline{t}) \end{aligned}$$

where we used the fact that $e^{-(1-e^{-\varepsilon})^2 n} - \nu_i \varepsilon < 0 = \mathsf{IC}_{\hat{M}}(\sigma_0, \underline{t}, i)$ (using Assumption 5.1). ■

This proves that, under the hypotheses of Corollary 5.8, not only is there $\underline{t}^{-i}$ such that player i would prefer not to tell the truth on some possible values of t_i (which we may view as "weakly" untruthful), but there is $\underline{t}^{-i}$ such that player i would *always* prefer to lie about his input for all values of t_i (which we may view as "strongly" untruthful).

5.2 Releasing synopses

Synopsis generators give a summary of the database that is accurate with respect to a specific set of count queries. Let $\mathcal{C}$ be a class of predicates on Q, *i.e.* functions mapping $Q \to \{0,1\}$. For $F \in \mathcal{C}, \underline{t} \in Q^n$, we define $\overline{F}(\underline{t}) = \frac{1}{n}\sum_{i=1}^n F(t_i)$.

DEFINITION 5.9. *M is a (γ, ρ)-synopsis generator on n-player inputs with respect to a class $\mathcal{C}$ if there is a real-valued function $P(s, F)$ such that, for all $\underline{t} \in Q^n$, it holds that:*

$$\Pr_{(s,p) \leftarrow M(\underline{t})}[\max_{F \in \mathcal{C}} |\overline{F}(\underline{t}) - P(s, F)| \leq \gamma] \geq 1 - \rho$$

Blum et al. [3] showed that, if $n = \tilde{O}(\frac{d \log |Q|}{\varepsilon \gamma^3})$ where d denotes the VC-dimension of $\mathcal{C}$, then there exists M that is a (γ, ρ)-synopsis generator with respect to $\mathcal{C}$ and also ε-differentially private (subsequent work [13, 21] improved the parameters).

5.2.1 Synopsis generators reveal information

Intuitively, it makes sense that if the synopsis must be accurate for a very rich class of predicates, then it must also be that the synopsis reveals a lot of information about the database. This is what we formalize next, by using the VC-dimension as a quantification of the "richness" of the class of predicates.

DEFINITION 5.10. *The* VC-dimension *of a class of predicates* $\mathcal{C}$ *is the largest* d *such that there exist* $X = \{t_1, \ldots, t_d\} \subseteq Q$ *and* $D = 2^d$ *functions* $F_1, \ldots, F_D$ *such that the* F_i *classify* X *in all possible ways,* i.e. *for all* $b_1, \ldots, b_d \in \{0,1\}$*, there exists* $j \in D$ *such that* $F_j(t_i) = b_i$*. We say that* X *is the* shattering set *for* $\mathcal{C}$*, or that* $\mathcal{C}$ *shatters* X*.*

THEOREM 5.11. *Fix any* $\gamma \in (0, \frac{1}{5}), \rho \in (0,1)$*. Suppose* M *is a mechanism that is a* (γ,ρ)*-synopsis generator on* n*-player inputs with respect to* $\mathcal{C}$*, which has VC dimension* d*. Suppose that* IC_M *satisfies Assumption 5.1. Then for all* $\underline{t} \in Q^n$*, there exists* $\underline{t}' \in Q^n$ *and* $i \in [n]$ *such that* $\underline{t}, \underline{t}'$ *differ in at most* $4\gamma n$ *entries and such that* $\mathsf{IC}_M(\mathsf{Id}, \underline{t}', i) \geq \min(\Omega(\frac{d}{\gamma n}), \Omega(1))$*.*

The intuition is the following: define the ball of radius γ induced by $\underline{t}$ in the outcome space, $B_\gamma(\underline{t}) = \{s \in S \mid \|P(s) - \overline{\mathcal{C}}(\underline{t})\|_\infty \leq \gamma\}$. We use a combinatorial design to construct a set of databases $T \subseteq Q^n$ of size $|T| \geq 2^{\Omega(d')}$ where $d' = \min(d, \gamma n)$, such that each $\underline{t}' \in T$ differ from $\underline{t}$ in at most $4\gamma n$ coordinates, and $B_\gamma(\underline{t}') \cap B_\gamma(\underline{t}'') = \varnothing$ for all $\underline{t}', \underline{t}'' \in T$. By the pigeon-hole principle, there exists $\underline{t}' \in T$, such that $\Pr[M(\underline{t}) \in B_\gamma(\underline{t}')] \leq 2^{-\Omega(d')}$. Since $\Pr[M(\underline{t}') \in B_\gamma(\underline{t}')] \geq 1 - \rho$ because M is a (γ,ρ)-synopsis generator, one of the hybrid databases between $\underline{t}, \underline{t}'$ must exhibit a large jump in the probability of giving an outcome in $B_\gamma(\underline{t}')$, and this gives a large information cost.

This proof is related to the packing arguments found in [22, 20, 6]; however, it is incomparable, as it gives quantitatively weaker bounds but it gives the additional property that, given *any* database, we can produce a *nearby* database that leaks a large amount of information. This last property was not present in previous lower bounds and is essential in the following applications.

PROOF OF THEOREM 5.11. By the definition of VC dimension, there exists a shattering set of size d. To simplify notation, let us name the shattering set $[d]$. The definition of VC dimension implies that for every $X \subseteq [d]$, there exists $F_X \in \mathcal{C}$ such that $F_X(t) = 1$ if $t \in X$ and $F_X(t) = 0$ if $t \in [d] \setminus X$. F_X can behave arbitrarily outside $[d]$.

Let $P(s) = (P(s,F))_{F \in \mathcal{C}}$ be the vector containing all estimates of counts. Let $\overline{\mathcal{C}}(\underline{t}) = (\overline{F}(\underline{t}))_{F \in \mathcal{C}}$. Let $B_\gamma(\underline{t}) = \{s \in S \mid \|P(s) - \overline{\mathcal{C}}(\underline{t})\|_\infty \leq \gamma\}$ be the γ-ball induced by $\underline{t}$ in the output space of the mechanism.

LEMMA 5.12. *There exists an absolute constant* $K > 0$ *such that for any* $1/5 > \gamma > 0$*, and for all* $\underline{t} \in Q^n$*, there exists a set* $T \subseteq Q^n$ *satisfying:*

1. $|T| \geq 2^{d'/K}$ *where* $d' = \min(d, 12\gamma n)$*.*
2. *For all* $\underline{t}' \in T$*, there are exactly* $4\gamma n$ *coordinates* i *such that* $t'_i \neq t_i$*.*
3. *For all* $\underline{t}', \underline{t}'' \in T$*, it holds that* $B_\gamma(\underline{t}') \cap B_\gamma(\underline{t}'') = \varnothing$*.*

We first assume the lemma is true to prove the theorem. Let T be a set as guaranteed by Lemma 5.12. By the first and third properties, there exists $\underline{t}'' \in T$ such that

$$\Pr[M(\underline{t}) \in B_\gamma(\underline{t}'')] \leq 2^{-d'/K} \tag{5.20}$$

Fix such a $\underline{t}''$.

Let Z denote the set of $4\gamma n$ coordinates on which $\underline{t}$ and $\underline{t}''$ differ. Now consider the hybrids $\underline{t}^{(0)}, \ldots, \underline{t}^{(4\gamma n)}$ where $\underline{t}^{(i)}$ agrees with $\underline{t}''$ on the first i coordinates in Z, and agrees with $\underline{t}$ on the last $4\gamma n - i$ coordinates in Z (and it agrees with both on the coordinates outsize Z). Clearly $\underline{t}^{(0)} = \underline{t}$ and $\underline{t}^{(4\gamma n)} = \underline{t}''$.

Let $\mathsf{wt}(i) = -\log \Pr[M(\underline{t}^{(i)}) \in B_\gamma(\underline{t}'')]$. We know that $\mathsf{wt}(0) \geq d'/K$ by Equation 5.20, and we know that $\mathsf{wt}(4\gamma n) \leq \log \frac{1}{1-\rho} \leq O(1)$ because M is a (γ,ρ)-synopsis generator, $\underline{t}'' = \underline{t}^{(4\gamma n)}$, and we assume that ρ is constant. Therefore we have

$$\tfrac{d'}{K} - O(1) \leq \mathsf{wt}(0) - \mathsf{wt}(4\gamma n) = \sum_{i=1}^{4\gamma n} \mathsf{wt}(i-1) - \mathsf{wt}(i)$$

By an averaging argument, there must exist i such that

$$\begin{aligned}\mathsf{wt}(i-1) - \mathsf{wt}(i) &\geq \tfrac{1}{4\gamma n}(\tfrac{d'}{K} - O(1)) \\ &= \Omega(\tfrac{d'}{\gamma n}) = \min(\Omega(\tfrac{d}{\gamma n}), \Omega(1))\end{aligned}$$

Furthermore, by the definition of wt and Assumption 5.1 about the information cost IC_M, it therefore holds that

$$\mathsf{IC}_M(\mathsf{Id}, \underline{t}^{(i)}, j_i) \geq \Omega(\mathsf{wt}(i-1) - \mathsf{wt}(i))$$

where j_i on the LHS equals the i'th element of Z and is the only coordinate that differs between $\underline{t}^{(i)}, \underline{t}^{(i-1)}$. Therefore, we deduce that

$$\mathsf{IC}_M(\mathsf{Id}, \underline{t}^{(i)}, j_i) \geq \min(\Omega(\tfrac{d}{\gamma n}), \Omega(1))$$

■

PROOF OF LEMMA 5.12. Let $\underline{h}(\underline{t})$ be the histogram of $\underline{t}$. Let us assume that $h_1 \leq h_2 \leq \ldots \leq h_d$ (for notational convenience and without loss of generality, since the names of the coordinates are immaterial and one could just rearrange them to satisfy this property).

Let $d'' \leq d$ be the largest integer such that $\sum_{i=1}^{d''} h_i \leq (1-4\gamma)n$. Either $d'' = d$, or else $d'' < d$ and we can deduce that:

$$\begin{aligned} n \geq \sum_{i=1}^{d} h_i &= \sum_{i=1}^{d''+1} h_i + \sum_{i=d''+2}^{d} h_i & (5.21)\\ &> (1-4\gamma)n + (d - d'' - 1)\frac{(1-4\gamma)n}{d''+1} & (5.22)\\ \Rightarrow \quad d'' &\geq (1-4\gamma)d & (5.23)\end{aligned}$$

Here we used the definition of d'' and the fact that the h_i are non-decreasing, meaning that h_i for $d \geq i > d''+1$ must satisfy $h_i \geq (1-4\gamma)n/(d''+1)$.

Set $d' = \min(d'', 12\gamma n)$. We first construct U which is a combinatorial design over $[d']$. Namely, $|U| \geq 2^{\Omega(d')}$ and each pair $X, Y \in U$ have small intersection.

1. Initially $U = \varnothing$, so pick an arbitrary $X \subseteq [d']$ of size $d'/3$. Add X to U.
2. If there exists $X \subseteq [d']$ such that $|X \cap Y| < d'/6$ for all $Y \in U$, then add X to U, otherwise halt and output U.

It is clear from the construction that, for all $X, Y \in U$, it holds that $|X \cap Y| < d'/6$. We show that U is exponentially large:

$$|U| \geq e^{2/18^2 \cdot d'/3} \tag{5.24}$$

This is a consequence of the Hoeffding inequality. Suppose we have already added i elements to U. We show that if $i < e^{2/18^2 \cdot d'/3}$ then there exists another subset that can be added. We use the probabilistic method by showing that the probability that a random subset X of $[d']$ with size $d'/3$ does not satisfy the desired property is strictly smaller than 1.

$$\Pr_{X \leftarrow \binom{[d']}{d'/3}} [\exists Y \in U, |X \cap Y| \geq d'/6]$$
$$< e^{2/18^2 \cdot (d'/3)} \Pr[|X \cap Y| \geq d'/6] < 1$$

where we use the Hoeffding inequality (the version for sampling without replacement) in the final inequality (*i.e.* sampling $d'/3$ elements without replacement from among $[d']$, where the elements in Y are marked 1 and the rest are marked 0).

Let K be the smallest constant so that $|U| \geq 2^{d'/K}$. We now construct T using U. Let $X \in U$, then define $\underline{t}_X \in Q^n$ as follows. Let $X_1, \ldots, X_{d'/3} \in [d']$ be the elements of X, say sorted in increasing order.

1. Initialize $i = 1$ and $j = 1$. (i will take value between $1, \ldots, n$ and j between $1, \ldots d'/3$).

2. Initialize $\underline{t}_X = \underline{t}$.

3. Do the following while $j \leq d'/3$:

   (a) Take the first $12\gamma n/d'$ individuals after and including the i'th individual in $\underline{t}_X$ whose values lie in $Q \setminus [d']$, and change their values to X_j.

   (b) Set i to be the individual after the last individual modified in the previous step, and increment j.

Observe two facts: first, we never "run out" of individuals to modify, since our choice of $d' \leq d''$ and Equation 5.23 ensure that the number of players with value in $Q \setminus [d']$ is at least $4\gamma n$. Second, $\frac{12\gamma n}{d'} \geq 1$ so in each iteration we modify at least one player.

We prove that $T = \{\underline{t}_X \mid X \in U\}$ satisfies the properties of the lemma. First, it is clear that if $X \neq Y$ then $\underline{t}_X \neq \underline{t}_Y$, and therefore $|T| \geq 2^{d/K}$. The second property holds because we modify $12\gamma n/d'$ individuals in each iteration, and there are $d'/3$ iterations.

To prove the third property, let $\underline{t}_X, \underline{t}_Y \in T$ be two distinct elements of T. Let $F_X \in \mathcal{C}$ be a function satisfying $F_X(x) = 1$ if $x \in X$ and $F_X(x) = 0$ if $x \in [d'] \setminus X$ (and F_X can behave arbitrarily outside $[d']$). Such F_X exists because $X \subseteq [d'] \subseteq [d]$ and $[d]$ is shattered by $\mathcal{C}$. Let $Z \subseteq [n]$ be the first $4\gamma n$ coordinates of $\underline{t}$ taking value in $Q \setminus [d']$. It holds that:

$$|\overline{F}_X(\underline{t}_X) - \overline{F}_X(\underline{t}_Y)| = \frac{1}{n}\left|\sum_{i=1}^{n}(F_X((\underline{t}_X)_i) - F_X((\underline{t}_Y)_i))\right|$$

Observe that $\underline{t}$ and $\underline{t}_X$ are identical outside of Z. Therefore,

$$\begin{aligned}|\overline{F}_X(\underline{t}_X) - \overline{F}_X(\underline{t}_Y)| &= \frac{1}{n}\left|\sum_{i\in Z} F_X((\underline{t}_X)_i) - \sum_{i \in Z} F_X((\underline{t}_Y)_i)\right| \\ &= \tfrac{1}{n}\left|\,|Z| - \tfrac{12\gamma n}{d'} \cdot |X \cap Y|\,\right| \\ &> \tfrac{1}{n}(4\gamma n - \tfrac{12\gamma n}{d'} \cdot \tfrac{d'}{6}) \\ &= 2\gamma\end{aligned}$$

Suppose now for the sake of contradiction that $\exists s \in B_\gamma(\underline{t}_X) \cap B_\gamma(\underline{t}_Y)$. This means that $\|\overline{C}(\underline{t}_X) - P(s)\|_\infty \leq \gamma$ and $\|\overline{C}(\underline{t}_Y) - P(s)\|_\infty \leq \gamma$. But by the triangle inequality, this would imply that:

$$\begin{aligned}2\gamma &< |\overline{F}_X(\underline{t}_X) - \overline{F}_X(\underline{t}_Y)| \\ &\leq |\overline{F}_X(\underline{t}_X) - P(s)| + |P(s) - \overline{F}_X(\underline{t}_Y)| \\ &\leq 2\gamma\end{aligned}$$

which is a contradiction, and therefore $B_\gamma(\underline{t}_X) \cap B_\gamma(\underline{t}_Y) = \varnothing$. ■

5.2.2 *Non-reactive mechanisms*

As in Section 5.1, we would like to use Theorem 5.11 to infer that if the database owner publishes a synopsis rather than just the outcome of the game (in the hopes that the synopsis may be useful for other purposes), then individuals may prefer to lie because their gain in information cost outweighs their loss in value derived from the outcome. Intuitively this happens if by deviating, a player cannot lose too much value. We now formalize this.

DEFINITION 5.13. *M is (β, γ)-non-reactive if there exists $\underline{t} \in Q^n$ such that for all $\underline{t}'$ that differ from $\underline{t}$ in at most γn coordinates, for every $i \in [n]$ and $t'' \in Q$, it holds that $\mathbb{E}[v(t'_i, M(\underline{t}'))] \leq \mathbb{E}[v(t'_i, M((\underline{t}')^{-i}, t''))] + \beta$.*

The following is an easy corollary of Theorem 5.11.

COROLLARY 5.14. *Fix any $\gamma \in (0, \frac{1}{5}), \rho \in (0,1)$. If M is a (γ, ρ)-synopsis generator for $\mathcal{C}$ of VC-dimension d. Let $\nu = \min_i \nu_i$ and suppose that M is also $(o(\frac{\nu d'}{\gamma n}), 4\gamma)$-non-reactive, where $d' = \min(d, \gamma n)$. Then there exists $\underline{t} \in Q^n, i \in [n]$ and a strategy $\sigma(t)$ that is independent of t such that $u_i(\mathsf{Id}, \underline{t}) < u_i(\sigma, \underline{t})$.*

PROOF. By the definition of non-reactive, let $\underline{t} \in Q^n$ be such that for all $\underline{t}'$ differing from $\underline{t}$ in at most $4\gamma n$ coordinates, for all $i \in [n], t'' \in Q$, it holds that

$$\mathbb{E}[v(t'_i, M(\underline{t}'))] \leq \mathbb{E}[v(t'_i, M((\underline{t}')^{-i}, t''))] + o(\tfrac{\nu d}{\gamma n})$$

By Theorem 5.11, one of these $\underline{t}'$ satisfies $\mathsf{IC}(\mathsf{Id}, \underline{t}', i) \geq \Omega(\frac{d}{\gamma n})$. Therefore, if we let σ be the strategy that outputs an arbitrary constant value in $x \in Q$ (and therefore by Assumption 5.1 it holds that $\mathsf{IC}_M(\sigma, \underline{t}', i) = 0$), we may write:

$$\begin{aligned}u_i(\mathsf{Id}, \underline{t}') &\leq \mathbb{E}[v(t'_i, M(\underline{t}'))] - \nu \cdot \mathsf{IC}(\mathsf{Id}, \underline{t}', i) \\ &< \mathbb{E}[v(t'_i, M((\underline{t}')^{-i}, x))] + o(\tfrac{\nu d}{\gamma n}) - \Omega(\tfrac{\nu d}{\gamma n}) \\ &< \mathbb{E}[v(t'_i, M((\underline{t}')^{-i}, x))] - \nu \cdot \mathsf{IC}(\sigma, \underline{t}', i) \\ &= u_i(\sigma, \underline{t}')\end{aligned}$$

Therefore, M is not truthful. ■

In particular, Corollary 5.14 holds even if M is differentially private as long as the VC-dimension of $\mathcal{C}$ is large. Blum et al. [3] prove that it is possible for M to be ε-differentially private and still be a (γ, ρ)-synopsis generator for a class of predicates with VC-dimension $d = \Omega(\frac{\gamma^3 \varepsilon n}{\log |Q| \log(1/\rho)})$. If in addition $|Q| = \text{poly}(n)$ and $\nu = \Omega(1/\log |Q|)$ (which by Remark 5.2 constitutes a realistic setting of parameters), and M is $(o(1/\log n), 4\gamma)$-non-reactive, then M cannot be truthful.

5.2.3 The 1-facility location game on arbitrary bounded metric spaces

In fact, mechanisms may be quite non-reactive because intuitively the influence of a single individual on the outcome may diminish rapidly as there are more players. As a concrete example of such a class of mechanisms, we show that any efficient mechanism for a 1-facility location game over an arbitrary bounded metric space must be non-reactive. Let (Q, d) be a general bounded metric space, normalized so that

$$\max_{t,t' \in Q} \mathsf{d}(t, t') \leq 1$$

The general 1-facility location game is defined similarly to LINE-1-FAC, except that the type space is Q rather than just $[0, 1]$.

THEOREM 5.15. *Suppose M is a δ-efficient mechanism for the 1-facility location game over a bounded metric space (Q, d). Then for any $\gamma \in (0, \frac{1}{2})$, it holds that M is $(\frac{2\delta}{(1-2\gamma)n-2}, \gamma)$-non-reactive.*

Therefore, we can construct the following deviation showing that M cannot be truthful if it is efficient for the 1-facility location on a metric space game and is also a good synopsis generator.

COROLLARY 5.16. *Let $\gamma \in (0, \frac{1}{10}), \rho \in (0, 1)$. Suppose M is a δ-efficient mechanism for the 1-facility location game on a bounded metric space, and also M is a (γ, ρ)-synopsis generator for $\mathcal{C}$ of VC-dimension d. Suppose that IC_M satisfies Assumption 5.1.*

Let $\nu = \min_i \nu_i$. If $\delta = o(\nu d')$ where $d' = \min(d, \gamma n)$, then there exists $\underline{t} \in Q^n, i \in [n]$ and a strategy $\sigma(t)$ that is independent of t such that $u_i(\mathsf{Id}, \underline{t}) < u_i(\sigma, \underline{t})$.

For example, the above theorem applies for the choice of parameters $d = \Omega(\frac{\gamma^3 \varepsilon n}{\log |Q| \log(1/\rho)})$, $\delta = n^{0.99}$, $|Q| = \text{poly}(n)$, and $\nu = \Omega(1/\log |Q|)$.

Corollary 5.16 applies to a much broader setting than Corollary 5.8 in terms of the games considered. However, even when applied to LINE-1-FAC, Corollary 5.16 gives an incomparable result. Whereas Corollary 5.8 applies to the specific mechanism (Algorithm 4.10) studied in this paper, Theorem 5.15 holds for *any* efficient mechanism. On the other hand, Corollary 5.8 is better quantitatively, and also applies when only a histogram of the discretization of the player types is released, which may contain less information than a synopsis. (One can reconstruct the histogram from a synopsis if $\mathcal{C}$ is sufficiently rich, see for example Theorem 4.1 of [12].)

PROOF OF THEOREM 5.15. Let $\underline{t} \in Q^n$ be the vector where all coordinates have value x for an arbitrary $x \in Q$. Fix $\underline{t}' \in Q^n$ different from $\underline{t}$ in at most $m < n/2$ coordinates, *i.e.* m coordinates of $\underline{t}'$ are not equal to x. Suppose for convenience of notation that these are the first coordinates $t_1, \ldots, t_m$. We know that, by picking $s = x$, it is possible to achieve welfare $w(\underline{t}', x) \geq -\sum_{i=1}^m \mathsf{d}(x, t_i')$, and therefore by the δ-efficiency of the mechanism, it holds that

$$\delta \geq w(\underline{t}', x) - \mathbb{E}_{s \leftarrow M(\underline{t}')}[w(\underline{t}', s)] \tag{5.25}$$

$$\geq -\sum_{i=1}^m \mathsf{d}(x, t_i') \tag{5.26}$$

$$+ \mathbb{E}_{s \leftarrow M(\underline{t}')}\left[(n-m) \cdot \mathsf{d}(s, x) + \sum_{i=1}^m \mathsf{d}(s, t_i')\right] \tag{5.27}$$

$$= \mathbb{E}_{s \leftarrow M(\underline{t}')}\left[(n-2m) \cdot \mathsf{d}(s, x)\right] \tag{5.28}$$

$$+ \mathbb{E}_{s \leftarrow M(\underline{t}')}\left[\sum_{i=1}^m (\mathsf{d}(s, t_i') + \mathsf{d}(s, x) - \mathsf{d}(x, t_i'))\right] \tag{5.29}$$

$$\geq \mathbb{E}_{s \leftarrow M(\underline{t}')}\left[(n-2m) \cdot \mathsf{d}(s, x)\right] \quad \text{(triangle inequality)} \tag{5.30}$$

$$\Rightarrow \mathbb{E}_{s \leftarrow M(\underline{t}')}[\mathsf{d}(s, x)] \leq \frac{\delta}{n - 2m} \tag{5.31}$$

For any $y \in Q$, we may write the following, using the triangle inequality and Equation 5.31:

$$\mathbb{E}_{s \leftarrow M(\underline{t}')}[v(y, s)] = -\mathbb{E}_{s \leftarrow M(\underline{t}')}[\mathsf{d}(y, s)] \tag{5.32}$$

$$\leq -\mathbb{E}_{s \leftarrow M(\underline{t}')}[\mathsf{d}(y, x) - \mathsf{d}(s, x)] \tag{5.33}$$

$$= -\mathsf{d}(y, x) + \mathbb{E}_{s \leftarrow M(\underline{t}')}[\mathsf{d}(s, x)] \tag{5.34}$$

$$\leq v(y, x) + \tfrac{\delta}{n-2m} \tag{5.35}$$

$$\mathbb{E}_{s \leftarrow M(\underline{t}')}[v(y, s)] = -\mathbb{E}_{s \leftarrow M(\underline{t}')}[\mathsf{d}(y, s)] \tag{5.36}$$

$$\geq -\mathbb{E}_{s \leftarrow M(\underline{t}')}[\mathsf{d}(y, x) + \mathsf{d}(s, x)] \tag{5.37}$$

$$= -\mathsf{d}(y, x) - \mathbb{E}_{s \leftarrow M(\underline{t}')}[\mathsf{d}(s, x)] \tag{5.38}$$

$$\geq v(y, x) - \tfrac{\delta}{n-2m} \tag{5.39}$$

If $\underline{t}'$ differs from $\underline{t}$ in at most γn coordinates, then for every i, it holds that $((\underline{t}')^{-i}, t'')$ differs from $\underline{t}$ in at most $\gamma n + 1$ coordinates. Therefore we can apply Equation 5.35 and Equation 5.39 for $m = \gamma n + 1$ to obtain:

$$\mathbb{E}[v(t_i', M(\underline{t}'))] \leq v(t_i', x) + \tfrac{\delta}{(1-2\gamma)n-2}$$
$$\leq \mathbb{E}[v(t_i', M((\underline{t}')^{-i}, t''))] + \tfrac{2\delta}{(1-2\gamma)n-2}$$

■

6. CONCLUSIONS

In this paper we argued that the study of privacy must be coupled with the study of the incentives that motivate people to reveal private data. To study this question, we introduced a model combining differential privacy with truthfulness and efficiency. We constructed a general transformation that takes a truthful and efficienct mechanism and builds a PTE mechanism. We showed that when privacy is given an explicit numerical cost, even PTE mechanisms (which at first may seem to give us everything we want) are not necessarily sufficient. Our work has already spurred several follow-up works [4, 30, 23], and there are many interesting remaining open questions. For example, is it always possible for each problem to create a PTE mechanism that has as good efficiency as a mechanism that is not private? Another question, more empirical, is to explore what are good models for information cost functions and how we may be able to use a better understanding of these functions to achieve better parameters.

7. ACKNOWLEDGMENTS

Part of this work was done while the author was visiting Microsoft Research Asia. The author would like to thank Pinyan Lu and Yajun Wang for their collaboration at the initial stages of this work. The author also thanks Salil Vadhan, Aaron Roth, and Yiling Chen for useful discussions, and the anonymous reviewers for their comments. The author was supported by the French ANR Defis program under contract ANR-08-EMER-012.

References

[1] Noga Alon, Michal Feldman, Ariel D. Procaccia, and Moshe Tennenholtz. Strategyproof approximation of the minimax on networks. *Mathematics of Operations Research*, 35(3):513–526, 2010.

[2] Boaz Barak, Kamalika Chaudhuri, Cynthia Dwork, Satyen Kale, Frank Mcsherry, and Kunal Talwar. Privacy, accuracy, and consistency too: a holistic solution to contingency table release. In *Proc. of 26th PODS*, pages 273–282, 2007.

[3] Avrim Blum, Katrina Ligett, and Aaron Roth. A learning theory approach to non-interactive database privacy. In *Proc. 40'th STOC*, pages 609–618, 2008.

[4] Yiling Chen, Stephen Chong, Ian A. Kash, Tal Moran, and Salil P. Vadhan. Truthful mechanisms for agents that value privacy. *CoRR*, abs/1111.5472, 2011.

[5] T. Dalenius. Towards a methodology for statistical disclosure control. *Statistik Tidskrift*, 5:429–444, 1977.

[6] Anindya De. Lower bounds in differential privacy. In *TCC*, pages 321–338, 2012.

[7] Irit Dinur and Kobbi Nissim. Revealing information while preserving privacy. In *In PODS*, pages 202–210. ACM Press, 2003.

[8] Cynthia Dwork. Differential privacy. In *In Proc. ICALP*, pages 1–12. Springer, 2006.

[9] Cynthia Dwork. Differential privacy: A survey of results. In Manindra Agrawal, Dingzhu Du, Zhenhua Duan, and Angsheng Li, editors, *Theory and Applications of Models of Computation*, volume 4978 of *Lecture Notes in Computer Science*, pages 1–19. Springer Berlin / Heidelberg, 2008.

[10] Cynthia Dwork, Krishnaram Kenthapadi, Frank Mcsherry, and Moni Naor. Our data, ourselves: Privacy via distributed noise generation. In *In EUROCRYPT*, pages 486–503. Springer, 2006.

[11] Cynthia Dwork, Frank Mcsherry, Kobbi Nissim, and Adam Smith. Calibrating noise to sensitivity in private data analysis. In *In Proc. of the 3rd TCC*, pages 265–284. Springer, 2006.

[12] Cynthia Dwork, Moni Naor, Omer Reingold, Guy N. Rothblum, and Salil Vadhan. On the complexity of differentially private data release: Efficient algorithms and hardness results. In *Proc. 41'st STOC*, STOC '09, pages 381–390. ACM, 2009.

[13] Cynthia Dwork, Guy N. Rothblum, and Salil P. Vadhan. Boosting and differential privacy. In *FOCS*, pages 51–60, 2010.

[14] Joan Feigenbaum, Aaron D. Jaggard, and Michael Schapira. Approximate privacy: foundations and quantification (extended abstract). In *Proc. 11th EC*, EC '10, pages 167–178, New York, NY, USA, 2010. ACM.

[15] Dan Feldman, Amos Fiat, Haim Kaplan, and Kobbi Nissim. Private coresets. In *Proc. 41st STOC*, STOC '09, pages 361–370, New York, NY, USA, 2009. ACM.

[16] I. Fellegi. On the question of statistical confidentiality. *J. of the Amer. Stat. Assoc.*, 67:7–18, 1972.

[17] Lisa K. Fleischer and Yu-Han Lyu. Approximately optimal auctions for selling privacy when costs are correlated with data. In *Proceedings of the 13th ACM Conference on Electronic Commerce*, EC '12, pages 568–585, New York, NY, USA, 2012. ACM.

[18] Arpita Ghosh and Aaron Roth. Selling privacy at auction. In *Proc. 12th EC*, EC '11, pages 199–208, New York, NY, USA, 2011. ACM. ISBN 978-1-4503-0261-6.

[19] Arpita Ghosh, Tim Roughgarden, and Mukund Sundararajan. Universally utility-maximizing privacy mechanisms. In *Proc. 41'st STOC*, STOC '09, pages 351–360. ACM, 2009.

[20] Moritz Hardt. *A Study of Privacy and Fairness in Sensitive Data Analysis.* PhD thesis, Princeton University, 2011.

[21] Moritz Hardt and Guy N. Rothblum. A multiplicative weights mechanism for privacy-preserving data analysis. In *Proc. 51'st FOCS*, pages 61–70, Washington, DC, USA, 2010. IEEE Computer Society. doi: 10.1109/FOCS.2010.85.

[22] Moritz Hardt and Kunal Talwar. On the geometry of differential privacy. In *Proc. 42nd STOC*, pages 705–714, New York, NY, USA, 2010. ACM. ISBN 978-1-4503-0050-6. doi: 10.1145/1806689.1806786.

[23] Zhiyi Huang and Sampath Kannan. The exponential mechanism for social welfare: Private, truthful, and nearly optimal. In *Proc. FOCS '12*, 2012. To appear. Available at `http://arxiv.org/abs/1204.1255`.

[24] Shiva Prasad Kasiviswanathan, Homin K. Lee, Kobbi Nissim, Sofya Raskhodnikova, and Adam Smith. What can we learn privately? In *Proc. 49th FOCS*, pages 531–540, Washington, DC, USA, 2008. IEEE.

[25] Katrina Ligett and Aaron Roth. Take it or leave it: Running a survey when privacy comes at a cost. *CoRR*, abs/1202.4741, 2012.

[26] Pinyan Lu, Xiaorui Sun, Yajun Wang, and Zeyuan Allen Zhu. Asymptotically optimal strategy-proof mechanisms for two-facility games. In *Proceedings of the 11th ACM conference on Electronic commerce*, EC '10, pages 315–324. ACM, 2010.

[27] Frank McSherry and Kunal Talwar. Mechanism design via differential privacy. In *Proceedings of the 48th Annual Symposium on Foundations of Computer Science*. Citeseer, 2007.

[28] H. Moulin. On strategy-proofness and single peakedness. *Public Choice*, 35:437–455, 1980.

[29] Kobbi Nissim, Sofya Raskhodnikova, and Adam Smith. Smooth sensitivity and sampling in private data analysis. In *Proc. 39th STOC*, pages 75–84, 2007.

[30] Kobbi Nissim, Claudio Orlandi, and Rann Smorodinsky. Privacy-aware mechanism design. In *Proceedings of the 13th ACM Conference on Electronic Commerce*, EC '12, pages 774–789, New York, NY, USA, 2012. ACM.

[31] Kobbi Nissim, Rann Smorodinsky, and Moshe Tennenholtz. Approximately optimal mechanism design via differential privacy. In *Proceedings of the 3rd Innovations in Theoretical Computer Science Conference*, ITCS '12, pages 203–213, New York, NY, USA, 2012. ACM. ISBN 978-1-4503-1115-1.

[32] Aaron Roth and Grant Schoenebeck. Conducting truthful surveys, cheaply. In *Proceedings of the 13th ACM Conference on Electronic Commerce*, EC '12, pages 826–843, New York, NY, USA, 2012. ACM.

[33] J. Schummer and R. V. Vohra. Mechanism design without money. In N. Nisan, T. Roughgarden, E. Tardos, and V. Vazirani, editors, *Algorithmic Game Theory*, chapter 10, pages 243–266. Cambridge University Press, 2007.

[34] M. R. Spiegel. *Theory and Problems of Probability and Statistics*. McGraw-Hill, 1992.

[35] David Xiao. Is privacy compatible with truthfulness? Cryptology ePrint Archive, Report 2011/005, 2011. `http://eprint.iacr.org/`.

APPENDIX

A. MECHANISMS ONLY NEED TO CONSIDER THE HISTOGRAM

Suppose that G is an anonymous game, *i.e.* the global utility function is symmetric and all players have the same private utility functions. Suppose M is an arbitrary mechanism, possibly looking at individual types. We transform it into a mechanism M' that considers only the histogram according to Algorithm A.1.

M' is efficient because for all π it holds that the histogram of $\hat{\underline{t}}$ is exactly $\underline{h}$. Since the outcome of M is efficient on $\hat{\underline{t}}$, therefore the outcome is efficient for $\underline{h}$.

To see that M' is truthful, suppose that there were an input $\underline{h}$ with a possible deviation. Namely, there exists $\underline{t} \in Q^n, i \in [n], t'_i \in [n]$ such that $\mathbb{E}[u(t_i, M'(\underline{h}(\underline{t}^{-i}, t'_i)))] > \mathbb{E}[u(t_i, M'(\underline{h}(\underline{t})))]$. Let $\underline{h} = \underline{h}(\underline{t})$ and let $\underline{h}' = \underline{h}(\underline{t}^{-i}, t'_i)$. We will show using a (subtle) averaging argument that this implies that there is a deviation that allows some player to improve his utility for the original mechanism M.

> Input: histogram $\underline{h}$ with m coordinates. Let $n = \sum_{i=1}^m h_i$.
>
> 1. Select a random permutation $\pi : [n] \to [n]$.
> 2. For $i = 1$ to n, set $\hat{t}_{\pi(i)} = \min\{j \mid \sum_{k=1}^j h_k \geq i\}$. Let $\hat{\underline{t}}$ denote this setting of $\hat{t}_1, \dots, \hat{t}_n$.
> 3. Run $M(\hat{t}_1, \dots, \hat{t}_n)$.
>
> ALGORITHM A.1. *Converting an arbitrary mechanism to one looking only at histogram.*

Since we need only consider the case $t'_i \neq t_i$, we may define the following two quantities:

$$c = \sum_{k=1}^{t_i} h_k$$

$$c' = \sum_{k=1}^{t'_i} h_k$$

Namely, c is the number of players with type at most t_i (assuming the types are ordered $1, \dots, q$), and likewise for c' with respect to t'_i.

Define the following cyclic permutation over n elements σ:

$$\sigma = \begin{cases} (c, c-1, \dots, c'+1) & \text{if } c' < c \\ (c, c+1, \dots, c') & \text{if } c' > c \end{cases}$$

Let M'_π be the mechanism of Algorithm A.1 with fixed permutation π. Then the assumption that $\underline{t}, i, t'_i$ constitutes a deviation for M' is equivalent to saying:

$$\mathbb{E}_{\pi \leftarrow S_n}[u(t_i, M'_{\pi\circ\sigma}(\underline{h}'))] > \mathbb{E}_{\pi \leftarrow S_n}[u(t_i, M'_\pi(\underline{h}))] \qquad \text{(A.1)}$$

where S_n is the symmetric group over n elements.

By an averaging argument, there must exist π such that

$$\mathbb{E}[u(t_i, M'_{\pi\circ\sigma}(\underline{h}'))] > \mathbb{E}[u(t_i, M'_\pi(\underline{h}))] \qquad \text{(A.2)}$$

where the expectation is only over the random coins used to run an execution of the original mechanism M.

We claim that this gives us a deviation for the original mechanism M. Let $\hat{t}_1 \dots \hat{t}_n$ be the types that M' constructs using histogram $\underline{h}$ and permutation π, and let $\hat{\hat{t}}_1, \dots, \hat{\hat{t}}_n$ be the types that M' constructs using histogram $\underline{h}'$ and permutation $\pi \circ \sigma$. Let $\ell = \pi(c)$.

CLAIM A.2. *For all $j \in [n]$, $j \neq \ell$ it holds that $\hat{t}_j = \hat{\hat{t}}_j$. Also it holds that $\hat{t}_\ell = t_i$ and $\hat{\hat{t}}_\ell = t'_i$.*

First observe that this gives a deviation for the original mechanism M, since plugging into Equation A.2 we get that

$$\mathbb{E}[u(\hat{t}_\ell, M(\hat{\underline{t}}^{-\ell}, \hat{\hat{t}}_\ell))] > \mathbb{E}[u(\hat{t}_\ell, M(\hat{\underline{t}}))]$$

where the randomness is only over the coins of M.

We now prove Claim A.2. Let us first consider the case that $c' < c$. We divide the analysis into the following cases:

1. For all $j \in \{\pi(1), \dots, \pi(c')\}$: Fix any $z \in \{1, \dots, c'\}$. By the definition of σ and our assumption that $c' < c$, it holds that $z = \sigma(z)$. Therefore, since the $\underline{h}, \underline{h}'$ have the same counts for each type strictly smaller than t'_i, and $\underline{h}'_{t'_i} = \underline{h}_{t'_i} + 1$, it follows from the construction that $\hat{t}_{\pi(z)} = \hat{\hat{t}}_{\pi\circ(z)} = \hat{\hat{t}}_{\pi(z)}$.

2. For all $j \in \{\pi(c'+1), \pi(c'+2), \dots, \pi(c-1)\}$: Fix any $z \in \{c'+1, c'+2, \dots, c-1\}$. By the definition of σ and our assumption that $c' < c$, it holds that $z = \sigma(z+1)$. Therefore, since the $\underline{h}, \underline{h}'$ have the same counts for each type strictly smaller than t'_i, since $\underline{h}'_{t'_i} = \underline{h}_{t'_i} + 1$, and since $\underline{h}, \underline{h}'$ have the same counts on all types strictly between t'_i and t_i, it follows from the construction that $\hat{t}_{\pi(z)} = \hat{\hat{t}}_{\pi\circ\sigma(z+1)} = \hat{\hat{t}}_{\pi(z)}$.

3. For all $j \in \{\pi(c+1), \pi(c+2), \dots, \pi(n)\}$: Fix any $z \in \{c+1, c+2, \dots, n\}$. By the definition of σ and our assumption that $c' < c$, it holds that $z = \sigma(z)$. Therefore, since $\underline{h}, \underline{h}'$ have the same total number of elements whose type is strictly smaller than $c+1$, and since for each type between $c+1, n$ the two histograms have the same counts, it follows from the construction that $\hat{t}_{\pi(z)} = \hat{\hat{(t)}}_{\pi\circ\sigma(z)} = \hat{\hat{(t)}}_{\pi(z)}$.

4. For $\ell = \pi(c)$: By the definition of c, it holds that $\hat{t}_{\pi(c)} = t_i$. Observe that $\underline{h}, \underline{h}'$ have identical counts for all types strictly smaller than t'_i and $\underline{h}'_{t'_i} = \underline{h}_{t'_i} + 1$. By the definition of σ and our assumption that $c' < c$, it holds that $\sigma(c'+1) = c$. Therefore, it holds that $\hat{\hat{t}}_{\pi(c)} = \hat{\hat{t}}_{\pi\circ\sigma(c'+1)} = \hat{t}_{\pi(c')} = t'_i$.

We can repeat essentially the same analysis for the case that $c' > c$. (Observe that this case is not exactly symmetric with the previous case; in particular, in this case σ is a cycle of length $|c - c'| + 1$, while in the previous case it was of length $|c - c'|$. This is because of an asymmetry in our construction: the types $\hat{t}_j$ are created reading the histogram from left to right.) We divide the analysis into the following cases:

1. For all $j \in \{\pi(1), \pi(2), \dots, \pi(c-1)\}$: Fix any $z \in \{1, \dots, c-1\}$. By the definition of σ and our assumption that $c < c'$, it holds that $z = \sigma(z)$. Therefore, since the $\underline{h}, \underline{h}'$ have the same counts for each type strictly smaller than t_i, and $\underline{h}'_{t_i} = \underline{h}_{t_i} - 1$, it follows from the construction that $\hat{t}_{\pi(z)} = \hat{\hat{t}}_{\pi\circ(z)} = \hat{\hat{t}}_{\pi(z)}$.

2. For all $j \in \{\pi(c+1), \pi(c+2), \dots, \pi(c')\}$: Fix any $z \in \{c+1, \dots, c'\}$. By the definition of σ and our assumption that $c < c'$, it holds that $z = \sigma(z-1)$. Therefore, since the $\underline{h}, \underline{h}'$ have the same counts for each type strictly smaller than t_i, since $\underline{h}'_{t_i} = \underline{h}_{t_i} - 1$, and since $\underline{h}, \underline{h}'$ have the same counts on all types strictly between t_i and t'_i, it follows from the construction that $\hat{t}_{\pi(z)} = \hat{\hat{t}}_{\pi\circ\sigma(z-1)} = \hat{\hat{t}}_{\pi(z)}$.

3. For all $j \in \{\pi(c'+1), \pi(c'+2), \dots, \pi(n)\}$: Fix any $z \in \{c'+1, c'+2, \dots, n\}$. By the definition of σ and our assumption that $c < c'$, it holds that $z = \sigma(z)$. Therefore, since $\underline{h}, \underline{h}'$ have the same total number of elements whose type is strictly smaller than c', and since for each type between $c'+1, n$ the two histograms have the same counts, it follows from the construction that $\hat{t}_{\pi(z)} = \hat{\hat{(t)}}_{\pi\circ\sigma(z)} = \hat{\hat{(t)}}_{\pi(z)}$.

4. For $\ell = \pi(c)$: By the definition of c, it holds that $\hat{t}_{\pi(c)} = t_i$. By the definition of c' and σ and by our assumption that $c < c'$ (which is equivalent to saying $t_i < t'_i$), it holds that $\sigma(c') = c$ and furthermore the total count of elements of types at most t'_i is equal in $\underline{h}$ and $\underline{h}'$. Therefore it holds that $\pi\hat{(c)} = \hat{\hat{t}}_{\pi\circ\sigma(c')} = \hat{t}_{\pi(c')} = t'_i$.

B. OMITTED PROOFS

B.1 Proof of Lemma 3.2

PROOF OF LEMMA 3.2. From [11, 19], it holds for all $U \subseteq \mathbb{Z}^q$ that

$$\Pr[\underline{\zeta} \in U] \leq e^{2\varepsilon} \Pr[e_i - e_j + \underline{\zeta} \in U] \tag{B.1}$$

Our situation is almost the same, except our perturbed histogram has the following distribution: sample $\underline{\zeta} \leftarrow \mathcal{G}^q_\varepsilon$ and check whether $\|\underline{\zeta}\|_\infty > \tau$. If so, set $\underline{\zeta}' = 0$, otherwise set $\underline{\zeta}' = \underline{\zeta}$.

Let $X_a = \{\underline{x} \in \mathbb{Z}^q \setminus \{0\}, \|\underline{x}\|_\infty \leq a\}$, the set of all non-zero points with infinity norm at most a. We will use the observation that, by the definition of ζ', for all $\underline{x} \in X_\tau$, it holds that $\Pr[\underline{\zeta} = \underline{x}] = \Pr[\underline{\zeta}' = \underline{x}]$, and also $\Pr[\underline{\zeta} = 0] \leq \Pr[\underline{\zeta}' = 0]$.

Fix an arbitrary set U, and divide up U into three disjoint parts: $U_0 = U \cap \{0\}$, $U_1 = U \cap X_{\tau-1}$, and $U_2 = U \setminus U_0 \setminus U_1$. We reason about each of the three separately. Let $\alpha = e^{-\varepsilon}$.

1. By the definition of ζ', $\Pr[\underline{\zeta}' = 0] = \Pr[\zeta = 0] + \Pr[\|\zeta\|_\infty > \tau]$. Therefore, Equation B.1 and the fact that $-e_i + e_j \in X_\tau$ imply that

   $$\begin{aligned}\Pr[\zeta = 0] &\leq e^{2\varepsilon} \Pr[e_i - e_j + \zeta = 0] \\ &= e^{2\varepsilon} \Pr[e_i - e_j + \zeta' = 0]\end{aligned}$$

   Along with Equation 3.1, this implies that

   $$\Pr[\underline{\zeta}' = 0] \leq e^{2\varepsilon} \Pr[e_i - e_j + \zeta' = 0] + \tfrac{2q\alpha^{\tau+1}}{1+\alpha}$$

2. Using Equation B.1, it holds that

   $$\begin{aligned}\Pr[\underline{\zeta}' \in U_1] &= \Pr[\underline{\zeta} \in U_1] &\text{(B.2)} \\ &\leq e^{2\varepsilon} \Pr[e_i - e_j + \underline{\zeta} \in U_1] &\text{(B.3)}\end{aligned}$$

   Since $U_1 \subseteq X_{\tau-1}$, it holds that the shifted set $U_1 - e_i + e_j$ is contained in the set $X_\tau \cup \{0\}$. Therefore it follows that

   $$\Pr[e_i - e_j + \underline{\zeta} \in U_1] \leq \Pr[e_i - e_j + \underline{\zeta}' \in U_1]$$

   which, combined with Equation B.3 implies

   $$\Pr[\underline{\zeta}' \in U_1] \leq e^{2\varepsilon} \Pr[e_i - e_j + \underline{\zeta}' \in U_1]$$

3. Since $\underline{\zeta}'$ takes range in $[-\tau, \tau]^q$, we have that

$$\begin{aligned}\Pr[\underline{\zeta}' \in U_2] &= \Pr[\|\underline{\zeta}\|_\infty = \tau] \\ &\leq \frac{2q(1-\alpha)\alpha^\tau}{1+\alpha} \\ &\leq e^{2\varepsilon} \Pr[e_i - e_j + \underline{\zeta}' \in U_2] + \frac{2q(1-\alpha)\alpha^\tau}{1+\alpha}\end{aligned}$$

Combining all three sets gives us

$$\begin{aligned}\Pr[\underline{\zeta}' \in U] &\leq e^{2\varepsilon} \Pr[e_i - e_j + \underline{\zeta}' \in U] \\ &\quad + \frac{2q(1-\alpha)\alpha^\tau + 2q\alpha^{\tau+1}}{1+\alpha}\end{aligned}$$

which in turn implies the lemma. ■

B.2 Proof of Theorem 4.7

PROOF OF THEOREM 4.7. The mechanism is listed in Algorithm 4.6.

Truthfulness. Since the the players are symmetric, it suffices just to consider the truthfulness of player 1. Fix $\underline{t}^{-1} = (t_2, \ldots, t_n)$. Let $\underline{h} = \underline{h}(\underline{t})$.

For all j it holds that $h_j \geq 0$. Furthermore, because player 1 is in column t_1, it holds that $h_{t_1} \geq 1$.

The mechanism's output is the minimal $s \geq 1$ such that $\sum_{j=1}^{s} h_j \geq n/2$. Let s be the output of the mechanism, and we consider what happens when t_1 declares some other value t^*. Let $\underline{h}^*$ be the histogram that is identical to $\underline{h}$ everywhere, except $h^*_{t_1} = h_{t_1} - 1 \geq 0$ and $h^*_{t^*} = h_{t^*} + 1$. Let s^* be the minimal s such that $\sum_{j=1}^{s^*} h^*_j \geq n/2$, namely the output of the mechanism on input $(\underline{t}^{-1}, t^*)$. We analyze the following cases, using the fact that both $\underline{h}, \underline{h}^*$ are non-negative:

1. $t_1 < s$. Because for all $s' < s$ it holds that $\sum_{j=1}^{s'} h^*_j \leq \sum_{j=1}^{s-1} h_j < n/2$, it follows that $s^* \geq s$. Since $t_1 < s$, this implies that $v(t_1, s^*) \leq v(t_1, s)$. Furthermore, observe that if $s^* > s$ then $v(t_1, s^*) \leq v(t_1, s) - 1$.

2. $t_1 = s$: in this case player 1's utility is 0, which cannot be improved (since for this game the utility is a non-positive number). Furthermore, if $s^* \neq s$ then $v(t_1, s^*) \leq -1 \leq v(t_1, s) - 1$.

3. $t_1 > s$: Because it holds that $\sum_{j=1}^{s} h^*_j \geq \sum_{j=1}^{s} h_j \geq n/2$, therefore $s^* \leq s$. Since $t_1 > s$, this implies that $v(t_1, s^*) \leq v(t_1, s)$. Furthermore, if $s^* < s$ then $v(t_1, s^*) \leq v(t_1, s) - 1$.

Therefore, regardless of the value of t_1, it holds that $v(t_1, s^*) \leq v(t_1, s)$, and therefore player 1 has no incentive to misreport his type. Furthermore, if $s^* \neq s$ then $v(t_1, s^*) \leq v(t_1, s) - 1$.

Efficiency. Let s be the output of the mechanism. We prove the utility is greater for s than for all other s'.

CLAIM B.1. *For any histogram $\underline{h}$ and $s = M(\underline{h})$, and for all $s' \in [q]$, it holds that $\sum_{j=1}^{q} h_j |j - s'| \geq \sum_{j=1}^{q} h_j |j - s|$.*

Recalling that $v(t, s) = -\gamma |t - s|$, this immediately implies that $w(\underline{t}, s') \leq w(\underline{t}, s)$ for all s'.

We now prove the claim. First consider $s' < s$. Split the summation $\sum_{j=1}^{q} h_j |j - s'|$ into three parts:

$$\sum_{j=1}^{q} h_j |j - s'| = \sum_{j \leq s'} h_j(s' - j) + \sum_{s' < j < s} h_j(j - s') + \sum_{s \leq j \leq q} h_j(j - s') \tag{B.4}$$

We will bound each of the three terms. The following hold:

$$\sum_{j \leq s'} h_j(s' - j) = \sum_{j \leq s'} h_j(s - j) - (s - s') \sum_{j \leq s'} h_j \tag{B.5}$$

$$\sum_{s \leq j} h_j(j - s') = \sum_{s \leq j} h_j(j - s) - (s' - s) \sum_{s \leq j} h_j \tag{B.6}$$

$$\begin{aligned}\sum_{s' < j < s} h_j(j - s') &= \sum_{s' < j < s} h_j(s - j) - \sum_{s' < j < s} h_j(s + s' - 2j) \\ &\geq \sum_{s' < j < s} h_j(s - j) - (s - s') \sum_{s' < j < s} h_j\end{aligned} \tag{B.7}$$

The first two equalities follow by definition; Equation B.7 is justified by the inequality $s + s' - 2j < s - s'$ and the fact that the h_j are non-negative.

Applying Equation B.5 Equation B.6, Equation B.7 to Equation B.4, we obtain

$$\sum_{j=1}^{q} h_j |j - s'| \geq (s - s') \left(\sum_{s \leq j} h_j - \sum_{j < s} h_j \right) + \sum_{j=1}^{q} h_j |j - s| \tag{B.8}$$

Since $s - s' > 0$, $\sum_{j=1}^{q} h_j = n$, and, by the definition of s it holds that $\sum_{j<s} h_j < n/2$, it follows that the first term on the RHS of Equation B.8 is positive. This implies the claim for the case $s' \leq s$.

The case for $s' \geq s$ follows similarly, resulting in the inequality

$$\sum_{j=1}^{q} h_j |j - s'| \geq (s' - s) \left(\sum_{s < j} h_j - \sum_{j \leq s} h_j \right) + \sum_{j=1}^{q} h_j |j - s|$$

Now, using the fact that $s' \geq s$ and by the definition of s, it holds that $\sum_{s<j} h_j \leq n/2$, we can similarly conclude that the claim also holds in this case. ■

C. FURTHER DISCUSSION ABOUT INFORMATION COST DEFINITION

In [4, 30], a subtle point is raised about the definition of information cost. In our work, we assume that the information cost is zero if the player reports a type that is independent of his true type, and this requires that the information cost depend on the strategy used by the player. Intuitively, this models what an adversary, knowing the strategy the player used, would deduce about the players' private information after seeing the output of the mechanism. This based on the following rationality argument: if the adversary knows that the players will behave strategically, then in analyzing the adversary we should use a measure where the adversary assumes that the players played their optimal strategy when trying to learn private information from the output of the mechanism. In contrast, Chen et al. [4], Nissim et al. [30] argue that one should use a measure where the adversary tries to learn private information assuming that the players reported truthfully. We believe that both points of view have merit, and which view to take depends on whether, in a particular context, the adversary assumes that the players played strategically or not.

C.1 Max-divergence based candidate

We propose two possible measure of information cost. The first uses the following general information-theoretic measure, which is essentially a "max-divergence" measure between the output distributions of the mechanism on different player inputs (shifted slightly to be non-negative). The max-divergence was introduced in the context of differential privacy by Dwork et al. [13], and we refer the reader there for a discussion. We work with the η-approximate notion here in order to prevent the information cost from being artificially large (or even infinite) due to some low-probability events.

DEFINITION C.1. *The η-approximate max-divergence information cost of strategy σ to player i on input $\underline{t}$ and for mechanism M is denoted $\mathsf{IC}_M^{\eta}(\sigma, \underline{t}, i)$ and defined as*

$$\max_{t' \in Q} \max_{\substack{B \subseteq S \times \mathbb{R}^n \\ \Pr[M(\underline{t}^{-i}, \sigma(t)) \in B] > \eta}} \log \frac{\Pr[M(\underline{t}^{-i}, \sigma(t)) \in B] - \eta}{\Pr[M(\underline{t}^{-i}, \sigma(t')) \in B](1-\eta)}$$

We write IC_M to denote IC_M^0.

Observe that this definition satisfies Assumption 5.1. A simple calculation shows that if a mechanism is (ε, η)-differentially private, then it holds that $\mathsf{IC}_M(\sigma, \underline{t}, i) \leq \varepsilon + \log \frac{1}{1-\eta}$ for all $\sigma, \underline{t}, i$. Note that typically we will take η to be negligible and so we can consider $\log \frac{1}{1-\eta} \approx 0$.

C.2 Mutual information based candidate

If one puts a probability distribution T on player i's input, then one can measure the information cost using the following natural measure based on information cost, which appeared in previous versions of this paper:

DEFINITION C.2. *The mutual-information-based information cost of strategy σ to player i on input $\underline{t}$ with prior distribution on inputs T and with respect to mechanism M is:*

$$\mathsf{IC}_M(\sigma, \underline{t}, i) = I(T; M(\underline{t}^{-i}, \sigma(T)))$$

The definition satisfies the first part of Assumption 5.1, namely that players can hide their data. However, this definition does not satisfy the second part, namely that cost reflects differential privacy (Equation 5.1). This is because this definition is inherently Bayesian, whereas Equation 5.1 requires some worst-case properties. Our impossibility results about releasing histograms do generalize to this measure (Corollary 5.8) although with a more involved proof, while as far as we know our impossibility results on synopsis generators (Corollary 5.16) do not extend to this measure.

Differentially Private Data Analysis of Social Networks via Restricted Sensitivity

Jeremiah Blocki Avrim Blum Anupam Datta Or Sheffet
Canegie Mellon University
5000 Forbes Ave
Pittsburgh, PA 15213
{jblocki@cs, avrim@cs, danupam@andrew, osheffet@cs}.cmu.edu*

ABSTRACT

We introduce the notion of *restricted sensitivity* as an alternative to global and smooth sensitivity to improve accuracy in differentially private data analysis. The definition of restricted sensitivity is similar to that of global sensitivity except that instead of quantifying over all possible datasets, we take advantage of any beliefs about the dataset that a querier may have, to quantify over a restricted class of datasets. Specifically, given a query f and a hypothesis $\mathcal{H}$ about the structure of a dataset D, we show generically how to transform f into a new query $f_{\mathcal{H}}$ whose global sensitivity (over all datasets including those that do not satisfy $\mathcal{H}$) matches the restricted sensitivity of the query f. Moreover, if the belief of the querier is correct (i.e., $D \in \mathcal{H}$) then $f_{\mathcal{H}}(D) = f(D)$. If the belief is incorrect, then $f_{\mathcal{H}}(D)$ may be inaccurate.

We demonstrate the usefulness of this notion by considering the task of answering queries regarding social-networks, which we model as a combination of a graph and a labeling of its vertices. In particular, while our generic procedure is computationally inefficient, for the specific definition of $\mathcal{H}$ as graphs of bounded degree, we exhibit efficient ways of constructing $f_{\mathcal{H}}$ using different projection-based techniques. We then analyze two important query classes: *subgraph counting queries* (e.g., number of triangles) and *local profile queries* (e.g., number of people who know a spy and a computer-scientist who know each other). We demonstrate that the restricted sensitivity of such queries can be significantly lower than their smooth sensitivity. Thus, using restricted sensitivity we can maintain privacy whether or not $D \in \mathcal{H}$, while providing more accurate results in the event that $\mathcal{H}$ holds true.

*This research was supported in part by CyLab at Carnegie Mellon University under grants DAAD19-02-1-0389 and W911NF-09-1-0273 from the Army Research Office, the National Science Foundation under grants CCF-1101215 and CCF-1116892, the NSF Science and Technology Center TRUST, and an NSF Graduate Fellowship, as well as by the MSR-CMU Center for Computational Thinking.

ITCS'13, January 9–12, 2013, Berkeley, California, USA.

Categories and Subject Descriptors

I.1.2 [**Algorithms**]: Analysis of Algorithms; K.4.1 [**Public Policy Issues**]: Privacy

General Terms

Algorithms, Theory

Keywords

Differential Privacy, Social Networks

1. INTRODUCTION

The social networks we inhabit have grown significantly in recent decades with digital technology enabling the rise of networks like Facebook that now connect over 900 million people and house vast repositories of personal information. At the same time, the study of various characteristics of social networks has emerged as an active research area [10]. Yet the fact that the data in a social network might be used to infer sensitive details about an individual, like sexual orientation [15], is a growing concern among social networks' participants. Even in an 'anonymized' unlabeled graph it is possible to identify people based on graph structures [3]. In this paper, we study the feasibility of and design efficient algorithms to release statistics about social networks (modeled as graphs with vertices labeled with attributes) while satisfying the semantic definition of differential privacy [8, 9].

A differentially private mechanism guarantees that any two neighboring data sets (i.e., data sets that differ only on the information about a single individual) induce similar distributions over the statistics released. For social networks, we consider two notions of neighboring or adjacent networks: (1) *edge adjacency* stipulating that adjacent graphs differ in just one edge or in the attributes of just one vertex; and (2) *vertex adjacency* stipulating that adjacent networks differ on just one vertex—its attributes or *any number* of edges incident to it.

For any given statistic or query, its global sensitivity measures the maximum difference in the answer to that query over all pairs of neighboring data sets [9]; global sensitivity provides an upper bound on the amount of noise that has to be added to the actual statistic in order to preserve differential privacy. Since the global sensitivity of certain types of queries can be quite high, the notion of smooth sensitivity was introduced to reduce the amount of noise that needs to be added while still preserving differential privacy [18].

However, a key challenge in the differentially private analysis of social networks is that for many natural queries, both global and smooth sensitivity can be very large. In the vertex adjacency model, consider the query "How many people in G_1 are a doctor or are friends with a doctor?" Even if the answer is 0 (e.g., there are no doctors in the social network) there is a neighboring social network G_2 in which the answer is n (e.g., pick an arbitrary person from G_1, relabel him as a doctor, and connect him to everyone). Even in the edge adjacency model, the sensitivity of queries may be high. Consider the query "How many people in G_1 are friends with two doctors who are also friends with each other?" In G_1 the answer may be 0 even if there are two doctors that everyone else is friends with (e.g, the doctors are not friends with each other), but the answer jumps to $n-2$ in a neighboring graph G_2 (e.g, if we simply connect the doctors to each other). In fact, even the first query can have high sensitivity in the edge-adjacency model if we just relabel a high-degree vertex as a doctor.

Yet, while these examples respect the mathematical definitions of neighboring graphs and networks, we note that in a real social network no single individual is likely to be directly connected with everyone else. Suppose that in fact a querier has some such belief $\mathcal{H}$ about the given network ($\mathcal{H}$ is a subset of all possible networks) such that its query f has low sensitivity restricted only to inputs and deviations within $\mathcal{H}$. For example, the querier may believe the following hypothesis ($\mathcal{H}_k$): the maximum degree of any node in the network is at most $k = 5000 \ll n \approx 9 \times 10^8$ (e.g, after reading a study on the anatomy of Facebook [21]). Can one in that case provide accurate answers in the event that indeed $G \in \mathcal{H}$ and yet preserve privacy no matter what (even if $\mathcal{H}$ is not satisfied)?

In this work, we provide a positive answer to this question. We do so by introducing the notion of *restricted sensitivity*, which represents the sensitivity of the query f over only the given subset $\mathcal{H}$, and providing procedures that map a query f to an alternative query $f_{\mathcal{H}}$ s.t. f and $f_{\mathcal{H}}$ identify over the inputs in $\mathcal{H}$, yet the global sensitivity of $f_{\mathcal{H}}$ is comparable to just the restricted sensitivity of f. Therefore, the mechanism that answers according to $f_{\mathcal{H}}$ and adds Laplace random noise preserves privacy for *all* inputs, while giving good estimations of f for inputs in $\mathcal{H}$.

While our general scheme for devising such $f_{\mathcal{H}}$ is inefficient and requires that we construct a separate $f_{\mathcal{H}}$ for each query f, we also design a complementary *projection-based* approach. A projection of $\mathcal{H}$ is a function mapping all possible inputs (e.g., all possible n-node social networks) to inputs in $\mathcal{H}$ with the property that any input in $\mathcal{H}$ is mapped to itself. Therefore, a projection μ allows us to define $f_{\mathcal{H}}$ for any f, simply by composing $f_{\mathcal{H}} = f \circ \mu$. Moreover, if this projection μ satisfies certain smoothness properties, which we define in Section 4, then this function $f_{\mathcal{H}}$ will have its global sensitivity—or at least its smooth sensitivity over inputs in $\mathcal{H}$—comparable to only the restricted sensitivity of f. In particular, for the case $\mathcal{H} = \mathcal{H}_k$ (the assumption that the network has degree at most $k \ll n$), we show we can *efficiently* construct projections μ satisfying these conditions, therefore allowing us to efficiently take advantage of low restricted sensitivity. These results are given in Section 4 and summarized in Table 1.

The next natural question is: how much advantage does restricted sensitivity provide, compared to global or smooth sensitivity, for natural query classes and natural sets $\mathcal{H}$? In Section 5 we consider two natural classes of queries: local profile queries and subgraph counting queries. A local profile query asks how many nodes v in a graph satisfy a property which depends only on the immediate neighborhood of v (e.g, queries relating to clustering coefficients and bridges [10], or queries such as "how many people know two spies who don't know each other?"). A subgraph counting query asks how many copies of a particular subgraph P are contained in the network (e.g., number of triangles involving at least one spy). For the case $\mathcal{H} = \mathcal{H}_k$ for $k \ll n$ we show that the restricted sensitivity of these classes of queries can indeed be much lower than the smooth sensitivity. These results, presented in Section 5, are summarized in Table 2.

1.1 Related Work

Easley and Kleinberg provide an excellent summary of the rich literature on social networks [10]. Previous literature on differentially-private analysis of social networks has primarily focused on the edge adjacency model in unlabeled graphs where sensitivity is manageable [1]. Triangle counting queries can be answered in the edge adjacency model by efficiently computing the smooth sensitivity [18], and this result can be extended to answer other counting queries [16]. [14] shows how to privately approximate the degree distribution in the edge adjacency model. The Johnson-Lindenstrauss transform can be used to answer all cut queries in the edge adjacency model [5].

The approach taken in the work of Rastogi et al. [19] on answering subgraph counting queries is the most similar to ours. They consider a bayesian adversary whose prior (background knowledge) is drawn from a distribution. Leveraging an assumption about the adversary's prior they compute a high probability upper bound on the local sensitivity of the data and then answer by adding noise proportional to that bound. Loosely, they assume that the presence of an edge does not presence of other edges more likely. In the specific context of a social network this assumption is widely believed to be false (e.g., two people are more likely to become friends if they already have common friends [10]). The privacy guarantees of [19] only hold if these assumptions about the adversaries prior are true. By contrast, we always guarantee privacy even if the assumptions are incorrect.

A relevant approach that deals with preserving differential privacy while providing better utility guarantees for nice instances is detailed in the work of Nissim et al [18] who define the notion of smooth sensitivity. In their framework, the amount of random noise that the mechanism adds to a query's true ansewr is dependent on the extent for which the input database is "nice" – having small *local sensitivity*. As we discuss later, in social networks many natural queries (e.g., local profile queries) even have high local and smooth sensitivity.

2. PRELIMINARIES

2.1 Differential Privacy

We adopt the framework of differential privacy. We use $\mathcal{D}$ to denote the set of all possible datasets. Intuitively, we say

[1]Kasiviswanathan, Nissim, Raskhodnikova and Smith have independently been exploring and developed an analysis for node level privacy using an approach similar to ours (personal communication, 2012).

	Adjacency	Hypothesis	Query	Sensitivity	Efficient
Theorem 9	Any	Any	Any	$GS_{f_{\mathcal{H}}} = RS_f(\mathcal{H})$	No
Theorem 14	Edge	$\mathcal{H}_k$	Any	$GS_{f_{\mathcal{H}}} = 3RS_f(\mathcal{H})$	Yes
Theorem 18	Vertex	$\mathcal{H}_k$	Any	$S_{f_{\mathcal{H}}} = O(1) \times RS_f(\mathcal{H}_{2k})$	Yes

Table 1: Summary of Results. GS **= global sensitivity,** RS **= restricted sensitivity, and** S **= smooth bound of local sensitivity.**

	Subgraph Counting Query P		Local Profile Query	
Adjacency	Smooth	Restricted	Smooth	Restricted
Edge	$\|P\|\ k^{\|P\|-1}$	$\|P\|\ k^{\|P\|-1}$	$k+1$	$k+1$
Vertex	$O\left(n^{\|P\|-1}\right)$	$\|P\|\ k^{\|P\|-1}$	$n-1$	$2k+1$

Table 2: Worst Case Smooth Sensitivity over $\mathcal{H}_k$ **vs. Restricted Sensitivity** $RS_f(\mathcal{H}_k)$**.**

two datasets $D, D' \in \mathcal{D}$ are *neighbors* if they differ on the details of a single individual. (See further discussion in Definitions 6 and 7.) We denote the fact that D' is a neighbor of D using $D' \sim D$. We define the *distance* $d(D, D')$ between two databases $D, D' \in \mathcal{D}$ as the minimal non-negative integer k s.t. there exists a path $D_0, D_1, \ldots, D_k$ where $D_0 = D$, $D_k = D'$ and for every $1 \le i \le k$ we have that $D_{i-1} \sim D_i$. Given a subset $\mathcal{D}' \subset \mathcal{D}$ we denote the distance of a database D to $\mathcal{D}'$ as $d(D, \mathcal{D}') = \min_{D' \in \mathcal{D}'} d(D, D')$.

Definition 1. *[8] A mechanism A is (ϵ, δ)-differentially private if for every pair of neighboring datasets $D, D' \in \mathcal{D}$ and every subset $S \subseteq Range(A)$ we have that* $\Pr[A(D) \in S] \le e^{\epsilon} \Pr[A(D') \in S] + \delta$.

Intuitively differential privacy guarantees that an adversary has a very limited ability to distinguish between the output of $A(D)$ and the output of $A(D')$. A query is a function $f : \mathcal{D} \to \mathbb{R}$ mapping the dataset to a real number.

Definition 2. *The* local sensitivity *of a query f at a dataset D is $LS_f(D) = \max_{D' \sim D} |f(D) - f(D')|$.*

Definition 3. *The* global sensitivity *of a query f is $GS_f = \max_{D \in \mathcal{D}} LS_f(D)$.*

The Laplace mechanism $A(D) = f(D) + Lap(GS_f/\epsilon)$ preseves $(\epsilon, 0)$-differential privacy [9]. This mechanism provides useful answers to queries with low global sensitivity. The primary challenge in the differentially private analysis of social networks is the high global sensitivity of many queries. The local sensitivity $LS_f(D)$ may be significantly lower than the global sensitivity GS_f. However, adding noise proportional to $LS_f(D)$ does not preserve differential privacy because the noise level itself may leak information. A clever way to circumvent this problem is to smooth out the noise level [18].

Definition 4. *[18] A β-smooth upper bound on the local sensitivity of a query f is a function $S_{f,\beta}$ which satisfies (i) $\forall D \in \mathcal{D}, S_{f,\beta}(D) \ge LS_f(D)$, and (ii) $\forall D, D' \in \mathcal{D}$ it holds that $S_{f,\beta}(D) \le \exp(-\beta d(D, D')) S_{f,\beta}(D')$.*

It is possible to preserve privacy while adding noise proportional to a β-smooth upper bound on the sensitivity of a query. For example, the mechanism $A(D) = f(D) + Lap\left(\frac{2S_{f,\beta}(D)}{\epsilon}\right)$, with $\beta = -\epsilon/2 \ln \delta$ preserves (ϵ, δ)-differential privacy [18]. To evaluate A efficiently one must present an algorithm to efficiently compute the β-smooth upperbound $S_{f,\beta}(G)$, a task which is by itself often non-trivial.

2.2 Graphs and Social Networks

Our work is motivated by the challenges posed by differentially private analysis of social networks. As always, a graph is a pair of a set of vertices and a set of edges $G = \langle V, E \rangle$. We often just denote a graph as G, referring to its vertex-set or edge-set as $V(G)$ or $E(G)$ resp. A key aspect of our work is modeling a social network as a *labeled* graph.

Definition 5. *A social network (G, ℓ) is a graph with labeling function $\ell : V(G) \to \mathbb{R}^m$. The set of all social networks is denoted $\mathcal{G}$.*

The labeling function ℓ allows us to encode information about the nodes (e.g., age, gender, occupation). For convenience, we assume all social networks are over the same set of vertices, which is denotes as V and has size n, and so we assume $|V| = n$ is public knowledge.[2] Therefore, the graph structures of two social networks are equal if their edge-sets are identical. Similarly, we also fix the dimension m of our labeling.

Defining differential privacy over the labeled graphs $\mathcal{G}$ requires care. What does it mean for two labeled graphs $G_1, G_2 \in \mathcal{G}$ to be neighbors? There are two natural notions: edge-adjacency and vertex adjacency.

Definition 6 (Edge-adjacency). *We say that two social networks (G_1, ℓ_1) and (G_2, ℓ_2) are neighbors if either (i) $E(G_1) = E(G_2)$ and there exists a vertex u such that $\ell_1(u) \ne \ell_2(u)$ whereas for every other $v \ne u$ we have $\ell_1(v) = \ell_2(v)$ or (ii) $\forall v, \ell_1(v) = \ell_2(v)$ and the symmetric difference $E(G_1) \triangle E(G_2)$ contains a single edge.*

In the context of a social network, differential-privacy w.r.t edge-adjacency can, for instance, guarantee that an adversary will not be able to distinguish whether a particular individual has friended some specific pop-singer on Facebook. However, such guarantees do not allow a person to pretend to listen only to high-end indie rock bands, should that person have friended numerous pop-singers on Facebook. This motivates the stronger vertex-adjacency neighborhood model.

Definition 7 (Vertex-adjacency). *We say that two social networks (G_1, ℓ_1) and (G_2, ℓ_1) are neighbors if there exists a vertex v_i such that $G_1 - v_i = G_2 - v_i$ and $\ell_1(v_j) = \ell_2(v_j)$ for every $v_j \ne v_i$.*

[2] Adding or removing vertices could be done by adding one more dimension to the labeling, indicating whether a node is active or inactive.

where for a graph G and a vertex v we denote $G - v$ as the result of removing every edge in $E(G)$ that touches v.

It is evident that any two social networks that are edge-adjacent are also vertex-adjacent. Preserving differential privacy while guaranteeing good utility bounds w.r.t vertex-adjacency is a much harder task than w.r.t edge-adjacency.

Distance.

Given two social networks (G_1, ℓ_1) and (G_2, ℓ_2), recall that their distance is the minimal k s.t. one can form a path of length k, starting with (G_1, ℓ_1) and ending at (G_2, ℓ_2), with the property that every two consecutive social-networks on this path are adjacent. Given the above two definitions of adjacency, we would like to give an alternative characterization of this distance.

First of all, the set $U = \{v : \ell_1(v) \neq \ell_2(v)\}$ dictates $|U|$ steps that we must take in order to transition from (G_1, ℓ_1) to (G_2, ℓ_2). It is left to determine how many adjacent social-networks we need to transition through until we have $E(G_1) = E(G_2)$. To that end, we construct the difference-graph whose edges are the symmetric difference of $E(G_1)$ and $E(G_2)$. Clearly, to transition from (G_1, ℓ_1) to (G_2, ℓ_2), we need to alter every edge in the difference graph. In the edge-adjacency model, a pair of adjacent social networks covers precisely a single edge, and so it is clear that the distance $d\big((G_1, \ell_1), (G_2, \ell_2)\big) = |U| + |E(G_1) \triangle E(G_2)|$. In the vertex-adjacency model, a single vertex can cover all the edges that touch it, and so the distance between the graphs $G_1 - U$ and $G_2 - U$ is precisely the *vertex cover* of the difference graph. Denoting this vertex cover as $VC(G_1 - U \triangle G_2 - U)$ we have that $d\big((G_1, \ell_1), (G_2, \ell_2)\big) = |U| + |VC(G_1 - U \triangle G_2 - U)|$. It is evident that computing the distance of between any two social-networks in the vertex-adjacency model is a NP-hard problem.

To avoid cumbersome notation, from this point on we omit the differentiation between graphs and social networks, and denote networks as graphs $G \in \mathcal{G}$.

3. RESTRICTED SENSITIVITY

We now introduce the notion of restricted sensitivity, using a hypothesis about the dataset D to restrict the sensitivity of a query. A hypothesis $\mathcal{H}$ is a subset of the set $\mathcal{D}$ of all possible datasets (so in the context of social networks, $\mathcal{H}$ is a set of labeled graphs). We say that $\mathcal{H}$ is true if the true dataset $D \in \mathcal{H}$. Because the hypothesis $\mathcal{H}$ may not be a convex set we must consider all pairs of datasets in $\mathcal{H}$ instead of all pairs of adjacent datasets as in the definition of global sensitivity.

DEFINITION 8. *For a given notion of adjacency among datasets, the* restricted sensitivity *of f over a hypothesis $\mathcal{H} \subset \mathcal{D}$ is*

$$RS_f(\mathcal{H}) = \max_{D_1, D_2 \in \mathcal{H}} \Big(\frac{|f(D_1) - f(D_2)|}{d(D_1, D_2)}\Big) .$$

To be clear, $d(D_1, D_2)$ denotes the length of the shortest-path in $\mathcal{D}$ between D_1 and D_2 (not restricting the path to only use $D \in \mathcal{H}$) using the given notion of adjacency (e.g., edge-adjacency or vertex-adjacency). That is, we restrict the set of databases for which we compute the sensitivity, but we do not re-define the distances.

Observe that $RS_f(\mathcal{H})$ may be smaller than $LS_f(D)$ for some $D \in \mathcal{H}$ if D has a neighbor $D' \notin \mathcal{H}$. In fact we often have $LS_f(D) \geq |f(D) - f(D')| \gg RS_f(\mathcal{H})$. As an immediate corollary, in such cases $RS_f(\mathcal{H})$ will be significantly lower than $S_{f,\beta}(D)$, a β-smooth upper bound on $LS_f(D)$.

4. USING RESTRICTED SENSITIVITY TO REDUCE NOISE

To achieve differential privacy while adding noise proportional to $RS_f(\mathcal{H})$ we must be willing to sacrifice accuracy guarantees for datasets $D \notin \mathcal{H}$. Our goal is to create a new query $f_{\mathcal{H}}$ such that $f_{\mathcal{H}}(D) = f(D)$ for every $D \in \mathcal{H}$ ($f_{\mathcal{H}}$ is accurate when the hypothesis is correct) and $f_{\mathcal{H}}$ either has low global sensitivity or low β-smooth sensitivity over datasets $D \in \mathcal{H}$. In this section, we first give a non-efficient generic construction of such $f_{\mathcal{H}}$, showing that it is always possible to devise $f_{\mathcal{H}}$ whose global sensitivity equals *exactly* the restricted sensitivity of f over $\mathcal{H}$. We then show how for the case of social networks and for the hypothesis $\mathcal{H}_k$ that the network has bounded degree, we can construct functions $f_{\mathcal{H}_k}$ having approximately this property, efficiently.

4.1 A General Construction

We now show how given $\mathcal{H}$ to generically (but not efficiently) construct $f_{\mathcal{H}}$ whose global sensitivity *exactly* equals the restricted sensitivity of f over $\mathcal{H}$.

THEOREM 9. *Given any query f and any hypothesis $\mathcal{H} \subset \mathcal{D}$ we can construct a query $f_{\mathcal{H}}$ such that*

1. *$\forall D \in \mathcal{H}$ it holds that $f_{\mathcal{H}}(D) = f(D)$, and*

2. *$GS_{f_{\mathcal{H}}} = RS_f(\mathcal{H})$*

PROOF. For each $D \in \mathcal{H}$ set $f_{\mathcal{H}}(D) = f(D)$. Now fix an arbitrary ordering of the set $\{D : D \notin \mathcal{H}\}$, and denote its elements as $D_1, D_2, \ldots, D_m$, where m is the size of the set. For every $D \notin \mathcal{H}$ we define the value of $f_{\mathcal{H}}(D)$ inductively. Denote $\mathcal{T}_i = \mathcal{H} \bigcup \{D_1, ..., D_i\}$. Initially, we are given the values of every $D \in \mathcal{T}_0$. Given $i > 0$, we denote $\Delta_i = RS_{f_{\mathcal{H}}}(\mathcal{T}_i)$. We now prove one can pick the value $f_{\mathcal{H}}(D_i)$ in a way that preserves the invariant that $\Delta_{i+1} = \Delta_i$. By applying the induction m times we conclude that

$$RS_f(\mathcal{H}) = \Delta_0 = \Delta_m = RS_{f_{\mathcal{H}}}(\mathcal{D}) = GS_{f_{\mathcal{H}}} .$$

Fix $i > 0$. Observe that

$$\Delta_{i+1} = \max\left(\Delta_i, \left(\max_{D \in \mathcal{T}_i} \frac{|f_{\mathcal{H}}(D) - f_{\mathcal{H}}(D_{i+1})|}{d(D, D_{i+1})}\right)\right)$$

so to preserve the invariant it suffices to find any value of $f_{\mathcal{H}}(D_{i+1})$ that satisfies that for every $D \in \mathcal{T}_i$ we have $|f_{\mathcal{H}}(D) - f_{\mathcal{H}}(D_{i+1})| \leq \Delta_i \cdot d(D, D_{i+1})$. Suppose for contradiction that no value exists. Then there must be two intervals

$$[f_{\mathcal{H}}(D_1^*) - \Delta_i \cdot d(D_1^*, D_{i+1}),\ f_{\mathcal{H}}(D_1^*) + \Delta_i \cdot d(D_1^*, D_{i+1})]$$
$$[f_{\mathcal{H}}(D_2^*) - \Delta_i \cdot d(D_2^*, D_{i+1}),\ f_{\mathcal{H}}(D_2^*) + \Delta_i \cdot d(D_2^*, D_{i+1})]$$

which don't intersect. This would imply that

$$\frac{|f_{\mathcal{H}}(D_1^*) - f_{\mathcal{H}}(D_2^*)|}{d(D_1^*, D_2^*)} \geq \frac{|f_{\mathcal{H}}(D_1^*) - f_{\mathcal{H}}(D_2^*)|}{d(D_{i+1}, D_1^*) + d(D_{i+1}, D_2^*)} > \Delta_i$$

which contradicts the fact that Δ_i is the restricted sensitivity of $\mathcal{T}_i$. □

4.2 Efficient Procedures for $\mathcal{H}_k$ via Projection Schemes

Unfortunately, the construction of Theorem 9 is highly inefficient. Furthermore, this construction deals with one query at a time. We would like to a-priori have a way to efficiently devise $f_{\mathcal{H}}$ for any f. In this section, the way we devise $f_{\mathcal{H}}$ is by constructing a *projection* – a function $\mu : \mathcal{D} \to \mathcal{H}$ with the property that $\mu(D) = D$ for every $D \in \mathcal{H}$. Such μ allows us to canonically convert *any* f into $f_{\mathcal{H}}$ using the naïve definition $f_{\mathcal{H}} = f \circ \mu$. Below we discuss various properties of projections that allow us to derive "good" $f_{\mathcal{H}}$-s. Following each property, we exhibit the existence of such projections μ for the specific case of social networks and $\mathcal{H} = \mathcal{H}_k$, the class of graphs of degree at most k.

Definition 10. *The class $\mathcal{H}_k$ is defined as the set $\{G \in \mathcal{G} : \forall v,\ \deg(v) \leq k\}$.*

In many labeled graphs, it is reasonable to believe that $\mathcal{H}_k$ holds for $k \ll n$ because the degree distributions follow a power law. For example, the number of telephone numbers receiving t calls in a day is proportional to $1/t^2$, and the number of web pages with t incoming links is proportional to $1/t^2$ [17, 7, 10]. For these networks it would suffice to set $k = O(\sqrt{n})$. The number of papers that receive t citations is proportional to $1/t^3$ so we could set $k = O(\sqrt[3]{n})$ [10]. While the degrees on Facebook don't seem to follow a power law, the upper bound $k = 5,000$ seems reasonable [21]. By contrast, Facebook had approximately $n = 901,000,000$ users in June, 2012 [1].

4.2.1 Smooth Projection

The first property we discuss is perhaps the simplest and most coveted property such projection can have – smoothness. Smoothness dictates that there exists a global bound on the distance between any two mappings of two neighboring databases.

Definition 11. *A projection $\mu : \mathcal{D} \to \mathcal{H}$ is called* c-smooth *if for any two neighboring databases $D \sim D'$ we have that $d(\mu(D), \mu(D')) \leq c$.*

Lemma 12. *Let $\mu : \mathcal{D} \to \mathcal{H}$ be a c-smooth projection (i.e., for every $D \in \mathcal{H}$ we have $\mu(D) = D$). Then for every query f, the function $f_{\mathcal{H}} = f \circ \mu$ satisfies that $GS_{f_{\mathcal{H}}} \leq c \cdot RS_f(\mathcal{H})$.*

Proof.

$$\begin{aligned} GS_{f_{\mathcal{H}}} &= \max_{D_1 \sim D_2} |f_{\mathcal{H}}(D_1) - f_{\mathcal{H}}(D_2)| \\ &= \max_{D_1 \sim D_2} |f(\mu(D_1)) - f(\mu(D_2))| \cdot 1 \\ &\leq \max_{D_1 \sim D_2} |f(\mu(D_1)) - f(\mu(D_2))| \frac{c}{d(\mu(D_1), \mu(D_2))} \\ &\leq c \cdot \max_{D_1, D_2 \in \mathcal{H}} \frac{|f(D_1) - f(D_2)|}{d(D_1, D_2)} \\ &= c \cdot RS_f(\mathcal{H}) \end{aligned}$$

□

As we now show, for $\mathcal{H} = \mathcal{H}_k$ and for distances defined via the edge-adjacency model, we can devise an efficient smooth projection.

Claim 13. *In the edge-adjacency model, there exists an efficiently computable 3-smooth projection to $\mathcal{H}_k$.*

The proof of the claim is deferred to the appendix. The high-level idea is to fix a canonical ordering over all edges and then define μ to delete an edge e if and only if there is a vertex v such that (1) e is incident to v and (2) e is not one of the first k edges incident to v. This is then used to achieve the smoothness guarantee. An immediate corollary of Lemma 12 and Claim 13 is the following theorem.

Theorem 14. *(Privacy wrt Edge Changes) Given any query for social networks f, the mechanism that uses the projection μ from Claim 13, and answers the query using $A(f, G) = f(\mu(G)) + Lap(3 \cdot RS_f(\mathcal{H}_k)/\epsilon)$ preserves $(\epsilon, 0)$ privacy for any graph G.*

Now, it is evident that this mechanism has the guarantee that for every $G \in \mathcal{H}_k$ it holds that $\Pr[\,|A(f,G) - f(G)| \leq O(RS_f(\mathcal{H}_k)/\epsilon)] \geq 2/3$. Furthermore, if the querier "lucked out" to ask a query f for which $f(G)$ and $f(\mu(G))$ are close (say, identical), then the same guarantee holds for such G as well. Note however that we *cannot reveal* to the querier whether $f(G)$ and $f(\mu(G))$ are indeed close, as such information might leak privacy.

4.2.2 Projections and Smooth Distances Estimators

Unfortunately, the smooth projections do not always exist, as the following toy-example demonstrates. Fix n graphs, where $d(G_i, G_j) = |i - j|$ for $1 \leq i, j \leq n$, and let $\mathcal{H} = \{G_1, G_n\}$. Because $\mu(G_1) = G_1$ and $\mu(G_n) = G_n$, then there must exist some value i such that $\mu(G_i) \neq \mu(G_{i+1})$, thus every μ cannot be c-smooth for $c < n$.

Note that smooth projections have the property that they also provide a c-approximation of the distance of D to $\mathcal{H}$. Meaning, for every D we have that $d(D, \mathcal{H}) \leq d(D, \mu(D)) \leq c \cdot d(D, \mathcal{H})$. In the vertex adjacency model, however, it is evident that we cannot have a $O(1)$-smooth projection since, as we show in the appendix, it is NP-hard to approximate $d(G, \mathcal{H}_k)$ (see Claim 23), but there does exists an efficient approximation scheme (see Claim 24) of the distance. Yet, we show that it is possible to devise a somewhat relaxed projection s.t. the distance between a database and its mapped image is a smooth function. To that end, we relax a little the definition of projection, allowing it to map instances to some predefined $\bar{\mathcal{H}} \supset \mathcal{H}$.

Definition 15. *Fix $\bar{\mathcal{H}} \supset \mathcal{H}$. Let μ be a projection of $\mathcal{H}$, so μ is a mapping $\mu : \mathcal{D} \to \bar{\mathcal{H}}$ that maps every element of $\mathcal{H}$ to itself ($\forall D \in \mathcal{H}$ we have that $\mu(D) = D$). A* c-smooth distance estimator *is a function $\hat{d}_\mu : \mathcal{D} \to \mathbb{R}$ that satisfies all of the following. (1) For every $D \in \mathcal{H}$ it is defined as $\hat{d}_\mu(D) = 0$. (2) It is lower bounded by the distance of D to its projection: $\forall D \in \mathcal{D}$, $\hat{d}_\mu(D) \geq d(D, \mu(D))$. (3) Its value over neighboring databases changes by at most c: $\forall D \sim D'$, $\left|\hat{d}_\mu(D) - \hat{d}_\mu(D')\right| \leq c$.*

It is simple to verify that for every $D \in \mathcal{D}$ we have that $\hat{d}_\mu(D) \leq c \cdot d(D, \mathcal{H})$ (using induction on $d(D, \mathcal{H})$). We omit the subscript when μ is specified.

The following lemma suggests that a smooth distance estimator allows us to devise a good smooth-upper bound on the local-sensitivity, thus allowing us to apply the smooth-sensitivity scheme of [18].

Lemma 16. *Fix $\bar{\mathcal{H}} \supset \mathcal{H}$ and let $\mu : \mathcal{D} \to \bar{\mathcal{H}}$ be a projection of $\mathcal{H}$. Let $\hat{d} : \mathcal{D} \to \mathbb{R}$ be an efficiently computable c-smooth* *distance estimator. Then for every query f, we can define the composition $f_{\mathcal{H}} = f \circ \mu$ and define the function*

$$S_{f_{\mathcal{H}},\beta}(D) = \max_{d\in\mathbb{Z}, d\geq \hat{d}(D)} e^{\left(-\frac{\beta}{c}\left(d-\hat{d}(D)\right)\right)} (2d+c+1)\cdot RS_f\left(\bar{\mathcal{H}}\right)$$

Then $S_{f_{\mathcal{H}},\beta}$ is an efficiently computable β-smooth upper bound on the local sensitivity of $f_{\mathcal{H}}$. Furthermore, define g as the function $g(x) = \begin{cases} 2\frac{1}{x}e^{-1+\frac{c+1}{2}x}, & 0 \leq x \leq \frac{2}{c+1} \\ c+1, & x > \frac{2}{c+1} \end{cases}$. Then for every D it holds that

$$S_{f,\beta}(D) \leq \exp(\tfrac{\beta}{c}\hat{d}(D)) \cdot g(\beta/c) RS_f(\bar{\mathcal{H}})$$

The proof of Lemma 16 is deferred to the appendix. Like in the edge-adjacency model, we now exhibit a projection and a smooth distance estimator for the vertex-adjacency model.

CLAIM 17. *In the vertex-adjacency model, there exists a projection $\mu : \mathcal{G} \to \mathcal{H}_{2k}$ and a 4-smooth distance estimator $\hat{d}$, both of which are efficiently computable.*

To construct μ and $\hat{d}$ we start with the linear program that determines a "fractional distance" from a graph to $\mathcal{H}_k$. This LP has $n + \binom{n}{2}$ variables: x_u which intuitively represents whether x_u ought to be removed from the graph or not, and $w_{u,v}$ which represents whether the edge between u and v remains in the projected graph or not. We also use the notation $a_{u,v}$, where $a_{uv} = 1$ if the edge $\{u, v\}$ is in G; otherwise $a_{uv} = 0$.

$$\begin{aligned} \min \textstyle\sum_{v\in V} x_v \quad & s.t. \\ & (1)\ \forall v,\ x_v \geq 0 \\ & (2)\ \forall u,v,\ w_{u,v} \geq 0 \\ & (3)\ \forall u,v,\ a_{uv} \geq w_{uv} \geq a_{uv} - x_u - x_v \\ & (4)\ \forall u, \textstyle\sum_{v\neq u} w_{u,v} \leq k \end{aligned}$$

To convert our fractional solution $(\bar{x}^*, \bar{w}^*)$ to a graph $\mu(G) \in \mathcal{H}_{2k}$ we define $\mu(G)$ to be the graph we get by removing every edge $(u,v) \in E(G)$ whose either endpoint has weight $x_u^* > 1/4$ or $x_v^* \geq 1/4$. We define our distance estimator as $\hat{d}(G) = 4\sum_u x_u^*$. In the appendix we show that μ and $\hat{d}$ satisfy the conditions of claim 17.

As before, combining Lemma 16 with Claim 17 gives the following theorem as an immediate corollary.

THEOREM 18. *(Privacy wrt Vertex Adjacency) Given any query for social networks f, the mechanism that uses the projection μ from Claim 13 and the β-smooth upper bound of Lemma 16, and answers the query using $A(f,G) = f(\mu(G)) + Lap(2 \cdot S_{f_{\mathcal{H}},-\epsilon/2\ln\delta}(G)/\epsilon)$ preserves (ϵ,δ) privacy for any graph G.*

Again, it is evident from the definition that the algorithm has the guarantee that for every $G \in \mathcal{H}_k$ it holds that $\Pr[\,|A(f,G) - f(G)| \leq O(g(\frac{\epsilon}{8\ln(1/\delta)})RS_f(\mathcal{H}_{2k})/\epsilon)] \geq 2/3$.

5. RESTRICTED SENSITIVITY AND $\mathcal{H}_K$

Now that we have constructed the machinery of restricted sensitivity, we compare the restricted sensitivity over $\mathcal{H}_k$ with smooth sensitivity for specific types of queries, in order to demonstrate the benefits of our approach. In a nutshell, restricted sensitivity offers a significant advantage over smooth sensitivity whenever $k \ll n$. I.e., we show that there are queries f s.t. for some $G \in \mathcal{H}_k$ it holds that $RS_f(\mathcal{H}_k) \ll S_{f,\beta}(G)$.

We now define two types of queries. First, let us introduce some notation. A profile is a function that maps a vertex v in a social network (G,ℓ) to $[0,1]$. Given a set of vertices $\{v_1, v_2, \ldots, v_t\}$, we denote by $G[v_1, v_2, \ldots, v_t]$ the social network derived by restricting G and ℓ to these t vertices. We use $G_v = G[\{v\} \cup \{w \,|(v,w) \in E(G)\}]$ to denote the social network derived by restricting G and ℓ to v and its neighbors. A *local* profile satisfies the constraint $p(v,(G,\ell)) = p(v,G_v)$.

DEFINITION 19. *A (local) profile query*

$$f_p(G,\ell) = \sum\nolimits_{v\in V(G)} p(v,(G,\ell))$$

sums the (local) profile p accross all nodes.

Local profile queries are a natural extension of predicates to social networks, which can be used to study many interesting properties of a social network like clustering coefficients[22, 17, 4], local bridges [10, 12] and 2-betweeness [11]. Further dissussion can be found in section C in the appendix. Claim 20 bounds the restricted sensitivity of a local profile query over $\mathcal{H}_k$ (e.g., in the vertex adjacency model a node v can at worst affect the local profiles of itself, its k old neighbors and its k new neighbors). A formal proof of Claim 20 is deferred to the appendix.

CLAIM 20. *For any local profile query f, we have that $RS_f(\mathcal{H}_k) \leq 2k+1$ in the vertex adjacency model, and $RS_f(\mathcal{H}_k) \leq k+1$ in the edge adjacency model.*

By contrast the smooth sensitivity of a local profile query may be as large as $O(n)$ even for graphs in $\mathcal{H}_k$. Consider the local profile query "how many people are friends with a spy?" The $n-1$-star graph G_1 in which a spy v is friends with everyone is adjacent to the empty graph $G_0 \in \mathcal{H}_k$. Therefore, any smooth upper bound $S_{f,\beta}$ must have $S_{f,\beta}(G) \geq n-1$. It is also worth observing that the assumption $G \in \mathcal{H}_k$ does not necessarily shrink the range of possible answers to a local profile query f (e.g., there are graphs $G \in \mathcal{H}_k$ in which everyone is friends with a spy).

Subgraph queries allows us to ask questions such as "how many triplets of people are all friends when two of them are doctors and the other is a pop-singer?" or "how many paths of length 2 are there connecting a spy and a pop-singer over 40?" The average clustering coefficient of a graph can be computed from the number of triangles and 2-stars in a graph.

DEFINITION 21. *A subgraph counting query $f = \langle H, \bar{p}\rangle$ is given by a connected graph H over t vertices and t predicates $p_1, p_2, \ldots, p_t$. Given a social network (G,ℓ), the answer to $f(G,\ell)$ is the size of the set*

$$\{v_1, v_2, \ldots, v_t : G[v_1, v_2, \ldots, v_t] = H \text{ and } \forall i,\ \ell(v_i) \in p_i\}$$

The smooth sensitivity of a subgraph counting query may be as high as $O\left(n^{t-1}\right)$ in the vertex adjacency model. Let $f = \langle H, \bar{p}\rangle$ be a subgraph counting query where H is a t-star and each predicate p_i is identically true. Let G_1 be a n-star

$(f(G_1) = \binom{n}{c-1})$. Then in the vertex adjacency model there is a neighboring graph G_2 with no edges $(f(G_2) = 0)$. We have that $LS_f(G_2) \geq \binom{n}{t-1}$. Observe that $G_2 \in \mathcal{H}_k$. In the appendix we show that the smooth sensitivity of $f = \langle K_3, \bar{p} \rangle$ is *always* greater than n when each predicate p_i is identically true (see claim 25). By contrast Claim 22 bounds the restricted sensitivity of subgraph counting queries. The proof is deferred to the appendix.

CLAIM 22. *Let $f = \langle H, \bar{p} \rangle$ be subgraph counting query and let $t = |H|$ then $RS_f(\mathcal{H}_k) \leq tk^{t-1}$ in the edge adjacency model and in the vertex adjacency model.*

While the assumption $G \in \mathcal{H}_k$ may shrink the range of a subgraph counting query f, the restricted sensitivity of f will typically be much smaller than this reduced range. For example, if $f(G)$ counts the number of triangles in G then $f(G) \leq nk^2$ for any $G \in \mathcal{H}_k$, while $RS_f(\mathcal{H}_k) \leq 3k^2 \ll nk^2$.

6. FUTURE QUESTIONS/DIRECTIONS

Efficient Mappings: While we can show that there doesn't exist an efficiently computable $O(1)$-smooth projection $\mu : \mathcal{G} \to \mathcal{H}_k$, we don't know whether the construction of Claim 17 can be improved. Meaning, there could be a mapping $\mu : \mathcal{G} \to \bar{\mathcal{H}}$ for some $\bar{\mathcal{H}} \supset \mathcal{H}_k$, whether the solution itself, the set of vertices that dominate the removed edges, is smooth. In other words, Is there an efficiently computable mapping $\mu : \mathcal{G} \to \bar{\mathcal{H}} \subset \mathcal{H}_k$ which satisfies $|d(\mu(G_1), G_1) - d(\mu(G_2), G_2)| \leq c$ for some constant c?
Multiple Queries: We primarily focus on improving the accuracy of a single query f. Could the notion of restricted sensitivity be used in conjunction with other mechanisms (e.g., BLR [6], Private Multiplicative Weights mechanism [13], etc.) to accurately answer an entire class of queries?
Alternate Hypotheses: We focused on the specific hypothesis $\mathcal{H}_k$. What other natural hypthothesis could be used to restrict sensitivity in private data analysis? Given such a hypothesis $\mathcal{H}$ can we efficiently construct a query f_H with low global sensitivity or with low smooth sensitivity over datasets $D \in \mathcal{H}$?

7. REFERENCES

[1] Facebook newsroom: Statistics. `http://newsroom.fb.com/Key-Facts`, 2012. Retrieved 6/29/2012.
[2] N. Alon, D. Moshkovitz, and S. Safra. Algorithmic construction of sets for k-restrictions. *ACM Transactions on Algorithms (TALG)*, 2(2):153–177, 2006.
[3] L. Backstrom, C. Dwork, and J. Kleinberg. Wherefore art thou r3579x?: anonymized social networks, hidden patterns, and structural steganography. In *Proceedings of the 16th international conference on World Wide Web*, pages 181–190. ACM, 2007.
[4] P.S. Bearman and J. Moody. Suicide and friendships among american adolescents. *Journal Information*, 94(1), 2004.
[5] J. Blocki, A. Blum, A. Datta, and O. Sheffet. The johnson-lindenstrauss transform itself preserves differential privacy. In *Proceedings of the 53rd annual IEEE Symposium on Foundations of Computer Science*. IEEE, 2012.
[6] A. Blum, K. Ligett, and A. Roth. A learning theory approach to non-interactive database privacy. In *Proceedings of the 40th annual ACM Symposium on Theory of computing*, STOC '08, pages 609–618, New York, NY, USA, 2008. ACM.
[7] A. Broder, R. Kumar, F. Maghoul, P. Raghavan, S. Rajagopalan, R. Stata, A. Tomkins, and J. Wiener. Graph structure in the web. *Computer Networks*, 33(1):309–320, 2000.
[8] C. Dwork. Differential privacy. *Automata, languages and programming*, pages 1–12, 2006.
[9] C. Dwork, F. Mcsherry, K. Nissim, and A. Smith. Calibrating noise to sensitivity in private data analysis. In *In Proceedings of the 3rd Theory of Cryptography Conference*, pages 265–284. Springer, 2006.
[10] D. Easley and J. Kleinberg. *Networks, crowds, and markets*. Cambridge Univ Press, 2010.
[11] L.C. Freeman. Centrality in social networks conceptual clarification. *Social networks*, 1(3):215–239, 1979.
[12] M.S. Granovetter. *Getting a job: A study of contacts and careers*. University of Chicago Press, 1995.
[13] M. Hardt and G.N. Rothblum. A multiplicative weights mechanism for privacy-preserving data analysis. In *2010 IEEE 51st Annual Symposium on Foundations of Computer Science*, pages 61–70. IEEE, 2010.
[14] M. Hay, C. Li, G. Miklau, and D. Jensen. Accurate estimation of the degree distribution of private networks. In *ICDM*, pages 169–178, 2009.
[15] C. Jernigan and B.F.T. Mistree. Gaydar: Facebook friendships expose sexual orientation. *First Monday*, 14(10), 2009.
[16] V. Karwa, S. Raskhodnikova, A. Smith, and G. Yaroslavtsev. Private analysis of graph structure. *PVLDB*, 4(11):1146–1157, 2011.
[17] M.E.J. Newman. The structure and function of complex networks. *SIAM review*, pages 167–256, 2003.
[18] K. Nissim, S. Raskhodnikova, and A. Smith. Smooth sensitivity and sampling in private data analysis. In *Proceedings of the thirty-ninth annual ACM Symposium on Theory of Computing*, pages 75–84. ACM, 2007.
[19] V. Rastogi, M. Hay, G. Miklau, and D. Suciu. Relationship privacy: output perturbation for queries with joins. In *Proceedings of the twenty-eighth ACM SIGMOD-SIGACT-SIGART symposium on Principles of database systems*, pages 107–116. ACM, 2009.
[20] R. Raz and S. Safra. A sub-constant error-probability low-degree test, and a sub-constant error-probability pcp characterization of np. In *Proceedings of the twenty-ninth annual ACM Symposium on Theory of Computing*, pages 475–484. ACM, 1997.
[21] J. Ugander, B. Karrer, L. Backstrom, and C. Marlow. The anatomy of the facebook social graph. *Arxiv preprint arXiv:1111.4503*, 2011.
[22] D.J. Watts and S.H. Strogatz. Collective dynamics of Śsmall-worldŠnetworks. *Nature*, 393(6684):440–442, 1998.

APPENDIX

A. MISSING PROOFS

Reminder of Claim 13. *In the edge-adjacency model, there exists an efficient way to compute a 3-smooth projection μ to $\mathcal{H}_k$.*

Proof of Claim 13. We construct our smooth-projection μ by first fixing a canonical ordering over all possible edges. Let $e_1^v, ..., e_t^v$ denote the edges incident to v in canonical order. For each edge $e = \{u, v\}$ we delete e if and only if (i) $e = e_j^v$ for $j > k$ or (ii) $e = e_j^u$ for $j > k$ (Intuitively for each v with $\deg(v) \geq k$ we keep this first k edges incident to v and flag the other edges for deletion). If $G \in \mathcal{H}_k$ then no edges are deleted, so $\mu(G) = G$. Suppose that G_1, G_2 are neighbors differing on one edge $e = \{x, y\}$ (wlog, say that e is in G_1). Observe that for every $v \neq x, y$, the same set of edges incident to v will be deleted from both G_1 and G_2. In fact, if $\mu(G_1)$ does not contain e then $\mu(G_1) = \mu(G_2)$. Otherwise, if e is not deleted we may assume then there may be at most one edge e_x (incident to x) and at most one edge e_y (incident to y) that were deleted from $\mu(G_1)$ but not from $\mu(G_2)$. Hence, $d(\mu(G_1), \mu(G_2)) \leq 3$. □

Reminder of Lemma 16. *Fix $\bar{\mathcal{H}} \supset \mathcal{H}$ and let $\mu : \mathcal{D} \to \bar{\mathcal{H}}$ be a projection of $\mathcal{H}$. Let $\hat{d} : \mathcal{D} \to \mathbb{R}$ be an efficiently computable c-smooth distance estimator. Then for every query f, we can define the composition $f_{\mathcal{H}} = f \circ \mu$ and define the function*

$$S_{f_{\mathcal{H}},\beta}(D) = \max_{d\in\mathbb{Z}, d\geq \hat{d}(D)} e^{\left(-\frac{\beta}{c}(d-\hat{d}(D))\right)} (2d+c+1)\cdot RS_f\left(\bar{\mathcal{H}}\right)$$

Then $S_{f_{\mathcal{H}},\beta}$ is an efficiently computable β-smooth upper bound on the local sensitivity of $f_{\mathcal{H}}$. Furthermore, define g as the function $g(x) = \begin{cases} 2\frac{1}{x}e^{-1+\frac{c+1}{2}x}, & 0 \leq x \leq \frac{2}{c+1} \\ c+1, & x > \frac{2}{c+1} \end{cases}$. Then for every D it holds that

$$S_{f,\beta}(D) \leq \exp(\tfrac{\beta}{c}\hat{d}(D)) \cdot g(\beta/c) RS_f(\bar{\mathcal{H}})$$

Proof of Lemma 16. First, we show that indeed $S_{f_{\mathcal{H}},\beta}$ is an upper bound on the local sensitivity of $f_{\mathcal{H}}$. Fix any $D \in \mathcal{D}$ and indeed

$$\begin{aligned}
LS_{f_{\mathcal{H}}}(D) &= \max_{D'\sim D} \left|f_{\mathcal{H}}(D) - f_{\mathcal{H}}(D')\right| \\
&= \max_{D'\sim D} \left|f(\mu(D)) - f(\mu(D'))\right| \\
&\leq \max_{D'\sim D} RS_f(\bar{\mathcal{H}}) \cdot d(\mu(D), \mu(D')) \\
&\leq \max_{D'\sim D} RS_f(\bar{\mathcal{H}}) \cdot \\
&\qquad (d(D, \mu(D)) + d(D, D') + d(D', \mu(D'))) \\
&\leq RS_f(\bar{\mathcal{H}}) \cdot (\hat{d}(D) + 1 + \max_{D'\sim D} \hat{d}(D')) \\
&\leq RS_f(\bar{\mathcal{H}}) \cdot (2\hat{d}(D) + c + 1) \\
&\leq \max_{d\geq \hat{d}(D)} e^{-\beta c\left(d-\hat{d}(D)\right)} (2d+c+1) RS_f\left(\bar{\mathcal{H}}\right) \\
&= S_{f_{\mathcal{H}},\beta}(D) \ .
\end{aligned}$$

Next we prove that $S_{f_{\mathcal{H}},\beta}$ is β-smooth. Let D_1 and D_2 be two neighboring databases, and wlog assume $\hat{d}(D_2) \leq \hat{d}(D_1)$. Then

$$\begin{aligned}
&\frac{S_{f_{\mathcal{H}},\beta}(D_1)}{S_{f_{\mathcal{H}},\beta}(D_2)} \\
&= \frac{\max_{d\geq \hat{d}(D_1)} e^{\left(-\frac{\beta}{c}(d-\hat{d}(D_1))\right)} (2d+c+1) RS_f\left(\bar{\mathcal{H}}\right)}{\max_{d\geq \hat{d}(D_2)} e^{\left(-\frac{\beta}{c}(d-\hat{d}(D_2))\right)} (2d+c+1) RS_f\left(\bar{\mathcal{H}}\right)}
\end{aligned}$$

Let d_0 be the value of d on which the maximum of numerator is obtained. Then

$$\begin{aligned}
&\frac{S_{f_{\mathcal{H}},\beta}(D_1)}{S_{f_{\mathcal{H}},\beta}(D_2)} \\
&= \frac{\exp\left(-\frac{\beta}{c}\left(d_0 - \hat{d}(D_1)\right)\right)(2d_0+c+1) RS_f\left(\bar{\mathcal{H}}\right)}{\max_{d\geq \hat{d}(D_2)} \exp\left(-\frac{\beta}{c}\left(d - \hat{d}(D_2)\right)\right)(2d+c+1) RS_f\left(\bar{\mathcal{H}}\right)} \\
&\leq \frac{\exp\left(-\frac{\beta}{c}\left(d_0 - \hat{d}(D_1)\right)\right)(2d_0+c+1) RS_f\left(\bar{\mathcal{H}}\right)}{\exp\left(-\frac{\beta}{c}\left(d_0 - \hat{d}(D_2)\right)\right)(2d_0+c+1) RS_f\left(\bar{\mathcal{H}}\right)} \\
&= \exp\left(-\tfrac{\beta}{c}(\hat{d}(D_2) - \hat{d}(D_1))\right) \leq \exp(\beta)
\end{aligned}$$

where the last inequality uses the smoothness property, i.e. that $\hat{d}(D_2) - \hat{d}(D_1) \geq -c$.

Finally, we wish to prove the global upper bound on $S_{f_{\mathcal{H}},\beta}$, i.e., that for every $D \in \mathcal{D}$

$$S_{f_{\mathcal{H}},\beta}(D) \leq \exp(\tfrac{\beta}{c}\hat{d}(D)) \cdot g(c/\beta) RS_f\left(\bar{\mathcal{H}}\right) \ .$$

Fix D and define $h(x) = \exp\left(-\frac{\beta}{c}x\right)(2x+c+1)$, so that $S_{f_{\mathcal{H}},\beta} = \exp\left(\frac{\beta}{c}\hat{d}(D)\right) RS_f(\bar{\mathcal{H}}) \cdot \max_{d\geq d_0} h(d)$. Taking the derivative of h we have

$$h'(x) = e^{-\frac{\beta}{c}x}\left(-2x\tfrac{\beta}{c} - \beta - \tfrac{\beta}{c} + 2\right)$$

which means that $h(x)$ is maximized at $x_0 = \frac{c}{\beta} - \frac{c+1}{2}$. In the case that $x_0 < 0$ (i.e. for $\beta/c > \frac{2}{c+1}$) we can upper bound the function $h(x)$ with $h(0) = c+1$ for every $x \geq 0$. Otherwise, we have that $h(x) \leq h(x_0)$ for every $x \geq 0$, and indeed $h(x_0) = 2\frac{c}{\beta}e^{-1+\frac{\beta}{c}\cdot\frac{c+1}{2}} = g(\beta/c)$.

To conclude the proof, observe that computing $S_{f_{\mathcal{H}},\beta}(D)$ is just a simple optimization once $\hat{d}(D)$ is known, much like the derivation done above. So since $\hat{d}$ is efficiently computable, we have that $S_{f_{\mathcal{H}},\beta}$ is efficiently computable. □

Reminder of Claim 17. *In the vertex-adjacency model, there exists a projection $\mu : \mathcal{G} \to \mathcal{H}_{2k}$ and a 4-smooth distance estimator $\hat{d}$, both of which are efficiently computable.*

Proof of Claim 17. We first prove that μ is a projection mapping every graph to a graph in $\mathcal{H}_{2k}$. Suppose that some $v \in G$ has degree $\geq 2k$, then clearly $x_v^* \leq 1/4$, for otherwise we would have removed all of the edges touching v. Observe that every edge we keep has $w_{u,v}^* \geq 1 - 1/4 - 1/4 = 1/2$. Consequently, we can have at most $2k$ edges with $w_{u,v} \geq \frac{1}{2}$ because of the constraint $\sum_u w_{u,v} \leq k$. So there are at most $2k$ edges incident to v in $\mu(G)$.

Now, let us prove that $\hat{d}$ satisfies all of the requirements of a 4-smooth distance estimator. First, if $G \in \mathcal{H}_k$ then the optimal solution of the LP is the all zero vector, so $\hat{d}(G) = 0$ for all graphs of max-degree $\leq k$. Secondly, observe that in the process of computing $\mu(G)$, every edge that is removed from G can be "charged" to a vertex v with $x_v^* \geq 1/4$. If follows that

$$d(G, \mu(G)) \leq \sum_{v: x_v^* \geq 1/4} 1 \leq \sum_{v: x_v^* \geq 1/4} 4x_v^* \leq 4 \sum_v x_v^* = \hat{d}(G) .$$

Lastly, fix any neighboring $G_1, G_2 \in \mathcal{G}$, and let v be the vertex whose edges differ in G_1 and G_2. Clearly, if $\bar{x}^*$ is a solution for $LP(G_1)$, then we set $y_v = 1$ for $i = 1...d$ and $y_v = x_v^*$ otherwise. Now $\vec{y}$ is a feasible (not necessarily optimal) solution to $LP(G_2)$. It is simple to infer that

$$\begin{aligned}\hat{d}(G_2) - \hat{d}(G_1) &= \hat{d}(G_2) - 4\sum_u x_u^* \\ &\leq 4\sum_u y_u - 4\sum_u x_u^* \leq 4\sum_u |(y_u - x_u^*)| \\ &= 4|y_v - x_v^*| \leq 4\end{aligned}$$

□

Reminder of Claim 20. *For any local profile query f, we have that $RS_f(\mathcal{H}_k) \leq 2k+1$ in the vertex adjacency model and $RS_f(\mathcal{H}_k) \leq k+1$ in the edge adjacency model.*

Proof of Claim 20. Consider a local profile query f_p.

(Label change) Let $G_1, G_2 \in \mathcal{H}$ be two graphs with the same exact edge set, but with labeling functions ℓ_1, ℓ_2 that are different on a single vertex. Let v be the vertex whose label differs on G_1 and G_1, and let N_v denote the set of its (at most k) neighbors. Then for every $u \notin \{v\} \cup N_v$ we have that $p(u, (G_1, \ell_1)) = p(u, (G_2, \ell_2))$. Hence, $|f_p(G_1) - f_p(G_2)| \leq |\{v\} \cup N_v| \leq k+1$.

(Vertex Adjacency) Let $G_1, G_2 \in \mathcal{H}$ be any two neighboring labeled graphs such that $G_1 - v = G_2 - v$. Let N_v^1 (resp. N_v^2) denote the neighborhood of v then for any $y \notin N_v^1 \cup N_v^2$ we have that $p(y, (G_1, \ell_1)) = p(y, (G_2, \ell_2))$. Hence, $|f_p(G_1) - f_p(G_2)| \leq |N_v^1 \cup N_v^2 \cup \{v\}| \leq 2k+1$.

(Edge Adjacency) Let $G_1, G_2 \in \mathcal{H}$ be any two neighboring labeled graphs. Wlog, there is an edge $e = \{u, v\}$ such that $E(G_1) = E(G_2) \cup \{e\}$. In order to have a vertex y s.t. $p(y, (G_1, \ell_1)) \neq p(y, (G_2, \ell_2))$ we need that the edge e appears in graph we get by restricting the social network to set of y and its neighbors. It follows that the only vertices whose local profile can change are in the union $\{u, v\} \cup (N_u \cap N_v)$. Hence, $|f(G_1) - f(G_2)| \leq |\{u\} \cup \{v\}| + |N_u \setminus \{v\}| \leq 2 + k - 1 = k+1$. □

Reminder of Claim 22. *Let $f = \langle H, \bar{p} \rangle$ be subgraph counting query and let $t = |H|$ then*

$$RS_f(\mathcal{H}_k) \leq tk^{t-1}$$

in the edge adjacency model and in the vertex adjacency model.

Proof of Claim 22. (Sketch) Let $G_1, G_2 \in \mathcal{H}_k$ be neighbors and let v be a vertex such that $G_1 - v = G_2 - v$, and let N_i denote the neighbors of v in G_i. Any copy of H which occurs in G_1 but not in G_2 must contain v. Because H is connected we can bound the number of G_1 copies of H. We can start with v, and we pick one of the t vertices of H to be mapped to v. Denote this vertex as v_0. Now, we proceed inductively. We pick a vertex $v \in H$, connected to the set $\{v_0, v_1, \ldots, v_{i-1}\}$. The vertex v_i must be assigned to a vertex in G which is incident to some specific vertex of the i vertices that we already mapped. Because we have bounded degree, then there are at most k options from which to choose v_i. We obtain the bound: $f(G_1) - f(G_2) \leq t\prod_{i=1}^{t-1} k = tk^{t-1}$. □

B. ADDITIONAL CLAIMS

Claim 23. *(Privacy wrt Vertex Adjacency) Unless $P = NP$ there is no efficiently computable mapping $\mu : \mathcal{G} \to \mathcal{H}_k$ such that*

1. *$\forall G \in \mathcal{H}_k, \mu(G) = G$.*
2. *$\forall G \in \mathcal{G}, d(G, \mu(G)) \leq O(\ln(k)\, d(G, \mathcal{H}_k))$.*

Proof. (Sketch) Our reduction is from the minimum set cover problem. It is NP-hard to approximate the minimum set cover problem to a factor better than $O(\log n)$ [20, 2]. Given a set cover instance with sets $S_1, ..., S_m$ and universe $U = \{x_1, ..., x_n\}$ we set $m_i = |\{j : x_i \in S_j|$ and $k = n+1$. We construct our labeled graph G as follows:

1. Add a node for each S_i.
2. Add a node for each x_j.
3. Add the edge $\{x_j, S_i\}$ if and only if $x_j \in S_i$.
4. For each x_i, create $k+1-m_i$ fresh nodes $y_1, ..., y_{k-m_i}$ and add each edge $\{y_j, x_i\}$.

Intuitively each node x_j has $k+1$ incident edges. By deleting all of the edges incident to the node S_i we can fix all of the nodes $x \in S_i$. Hence, $d(G, (\mathcal{H}_k))$ corresponds exactly to the size of the minimum set cover. □

Claim 24. *(Privacy wrt Vertex Adjacency) There is an efficiently computable projection $\mu : \mathcal{G} \to \mathcal{H}_k$ such that for every $G \in \mathcal{G}$ it holds that $d(G, \mu(G)) \leq (\ln(2d^2 + kd))\, d(G, \mathcal{H}_k)$,*

Proof. (Sketch) We use a greedy algorithm to create μ. Define the potential of a graph G as follows

$$\phi(G) = \sum_{v \in G : \deg(v) \geq k} (\deg(v) - k) .$$

Our algorithm μ starts by guessing a value d for $d(G, \mathcal{H}_k)$ and deleting any vertex with degree $\geq k+d+1$ (these vertices *must* be deleted because the degree will be at least $k+1$ after deleting d other vertices). Then μ repeatedly picks the vertex v with the highest potential and eliminates all incident edges, where the potential of a vertex v is $\phi(G) - \phi(G-v)$. Let ϕ_i denote the potential after round i (ϕ_0 is the potential after deleting vertices with degree $\geq k+d+1$). Observe that $\phi_0 \leq 2d^2 + kd$ if d is correct because (i) there are d vertices we can delete to drop the potential to 0 and (2) deleting a single vertex v decreases the potential by at most $\deg(v) + \deg(v) - k \leq 2d + k$. Also observe that in any round there always exists some vertex whose removal decreases the potential by at least $(1 - 1/d)\, \phi_i$ so we have $\phi_i \leq \phi_{i-1}\left(1 - \frac{1}{d}\right)$. Once $i \geq d \ln(2d^2 + dk + d)$ we have $\phi_i \leq 1$. □

The reduction in Claim 24 might be used to produce a function $f_{\mathcal{H}}(G) = \mu(f(G))$ with low smooth-sensitivity over the nice graphs $\mathcal{H}_k$. Unfortunately, we don't know of any efficient algorithm to compute the smooth upper bound for such $f_{\mathcal{H}}$.

Claim 25. *Let $f = \langle K_3, \bar{p} \rangle$ be a subgraph counting query with predicates p_i that are identically true. In the vertex adjacency model for any β smooth upper bound on the local sensitivity of f and any graph G we have*

$$S^*_{f^P, \beta}(G) \geq \exp(-2\beta)(n-2) .$$

PROOF. Let G be given. Pick $v_1, v_2 \in V(G)$ and let G_1 be obtained from G by adding all possible edges incident to v_1 and let G_2 be obtained from G_1 by deleting all edges incident to v_2. Finally, let G_3 be obtained from G_2 by adding all possible edges incident to v_2. Now the local sensitivity of f at G_2 is at least $n-2$,

$$\begin{aligned} LS_f(G_2) &= \max_{G':d(G_2,G')=1} \left| f(G_2) - f(G') \right| \\ &\geq f(G_3) - f(G_2) \geq n-2 \end{aligned}$$

Plugging this lower bound into the definition of β smooth sensitivity we obtain the required result:

$$S^*_{f^P,\beta}(G) \geq e^{-\beta d(G,G_2)} LS_{f^P}(G_2) \geq e^{-2\beta}(n-2)$$

□

C. LOCAL PROFILE QUERIES

Local profile queries are a natural extension of predicates to social networks, which can be used to study many interesting properties of a social network like clustering coefficients, local bridges and 2-betweeness). The clustering coefficient $c(v)$ [22, 17] of a node v (e.g., the probability that two randomly selected friends of v are friends with each other) has been used to identify teenage girls who are more likely to consider suicide[4]. One explanation, is that it becomes an inherent source of stress if a person has many friends who are not friends with each other [10]. Observe that $c(v)$ *is* a local profile query. An edge $\{v, w\}$ is a local bridge if its endpoints have no friends in common. A local profile could score a vertex v based on the number local bridges incident to v. A marketing agency may be interested in identifying nodes that are incident to many local bridges because local bridges "provide their endpoints with access to parts of the network - and hence sources of information - that they would otherwise be far away from [10]." For example, a 1995 study showed that the best job leads often come from aquaintances rather than close friends [12]. 2-betweeness (a variant of betweeness [11]) measures the centrality of a node. We say that the 2-betweeness of a vertex v is the probability that the a randomly chosen shortest path between two randomly chosen neighbors of v $x, y \in G_v$ goes through v.

Characterizing the Sample Complexity of Private Learners*

Amos Beimel
Dept. of Computer Science
Ben-Gurion University
beimel@cs.bgu.ac.il

Kobbi Nissim
Dept. of Computer Science
Ben-Gurion University &
Harvard University
kobbi@cs.bgu.ac.il

Uri Stemmer
Dept. of Computer Science
Ben-Gurion University
stemmer@cs.bgu.ac.il

ABSTRACT

In 2008, Kasiviswanathan el al. defined *private learning* as a combination of PAC learning and differential privacy [16]. Informally, a private learner is applied to a collection of labeled individual information and outputs a hypothesis while preserving the privacy of each individual. Kasiviswanathan et al. gave a generic construction of private learners for (finite) concept classes, with sample complexity logarithmic in the size of the concept class. This sample complexity is higher than what is needed for non-private learners, hence leaving open the possibility that the sample complexity of private learning may be sometimes significantly higher than that of non-private learning.

We give a combinatorial characterization of the sample size sufficient and necessary to privately learn a class of concepts. This characterization is analogous to the well known characterization of the sample complexity of non-private learning in terms of the VC dimension of the concept class. We introduce the notion of *probabilistic representation* of a concept class, and our new complexity measure RepDim corresponds to the size of the smallest probabilistic representation of the concept class.

We show that any private learning algorithm for a concept class $\mathcal{C}$ with sample complexity m implies $\mathrm{RepDim}(\mathcal{C}) = O(m)$, and that there exists a private learning algorithm with sample complexity $m = O(\mathrm{RepDim}(\mathcal{C}))$. We further demonstrate that a similar characterization holds for the database size needed for privately computing a large class of optimization problems and also for the well studied problem of private data release.

Categories and Subject Descriptors

K.4.1 [**Computers and Society**]: Public Policy Issues—*Privacy*; F.2.m [**Analysis of Algorithms and Problem Complexity**]: Miscellaneous

*Research partially supported by the Israel Science Foundation (grants No. 938/09 and 2761/12) and by the Frankel Center for Computer Science.

General Terms

Theory

Keywords

Differential privacy, PAC learning, Sample complexity, Probabilistic Representation

1. INTRODUCTION

Motivated by the observation that learning generalizes many of the analyses applied to large collections of data, Kasiviswanathan el al. [16] defined in 2008 *private learning* as a combination of probably approximately correct (PAC) learning [19] and differential privacy [11]. A PAC learner is given a collection of labeled examples (sampled according to an unknown probability distribution and labeled according to an unknown concept) and generalizes the labeled examples into a hypothesis h that should predict with high accuracy the labeling of fresh examples taken from the same unknown distribution and labeled with the same unknown concept.

The privacy requirement is that the choice of h preserves differential privacy of sample points. Intuitively this means that this choice should not be significantly affected by any particular sample. Differential privacy is increasingly accepted as a standard for rigorous privacy and recent research has shown that differentially private variants exists to many analyses. We refer the reader to surveys of Dwork [9, 10].

The sample complexity required for learning a concept class $\mathcal{C}$ determines the amount of *labeled* data needed for learning a concept $c \in \mathcal{C}$. It is well known that the sample complexity of learning a concept class $\mathcal{C}$ (non-privately) is proportional to a complexity measure of the class $\mathcal{C}$ knowns as the VC-dimension [20, 6, 13]. Kasiviswanathan et al. [16] proved that a private learner exists for every *finite* concept class. The proof is via a generic construction that exhibits sample complexity logarithmic in the size of the concept class. The VC-dimension of a concept class is bounded by this quantity (and significantly lower for some interesting concept classes), and hence the results of [16] left open the possibility that the sample complexity of private learning may be significantly higher than that of non-private learning.

In analogy to the characterization of the sample complexity of (non-private) PAC learners via the VC-dimension, we give a combinatorial characterization of the sample size sufficient and necessary for private PAC learners. Towards obtaining this characterization, we introduce the notion of *probabilistic representation* of a concept class. We note that our characterization, as the VC-dimension characterization, ignores the computation required by the learner. Some of our algorithms are, however, computationally efficient.

1.1 Related Work

We start with a short description of prior work on the sample complexity of private learning. To simplify the exposition, we ignore dependencies on the error, confidence and privacy parameters by considering them constants for this and the following section. The dependency on these parameters would be made explicit in the later sections of the paper.

Recall that the sample complexity of non-private learners for a class of functions $\mathcal{C}$ is proportional to the VC-dimension of the class [6, 13] – a combinatorial measure of the class that is equal to the size of the largest set of inputs that is shattered by the class. This characterization, as ours, ignores the computation required by the learner.

Kasiviswanathan et al. [16] showed, informally, that every finite concept class $\mathcal{C}$ can be learned privately (ignoring computational complexity). Their construction is based on the exponential mechanism of McSherry and Talwar [17], and the $O(\ln |\mathcal{C}|)$ bound on sample complexity results from the union bound argument used in the analysis of the exponential mechanism. Computationally efficient learners were shown to exist by Blum et al. [4] for all concept classes that can be efficiently learned in the *statistical queries* model. Kasiviswanathan et al. [16] showed an example of a concept class – the class of parity functions – that is not learnable in the statistical queries model but can be learned privately and efficiently. These positive results suggest that many "natural" computational learning tasks that are efficiently learned non-privately can be learned privately and efficiently.

Beimel et al. [3] studied the sample complexity of private learning. They examined the concept class of point functions $\texttt{POINT}_d$ where each concept evaluates to one on exactly one point of the domain and to zero otherwise. Note that the VC-dimension of $\texttt{POINT}_d$ is one. Beimel et al. proved lower bounds on the sample complexity of *properly* and privately learning the class $\texttt{POINT}_d$ (and related classes), implying that the VC dimension of a class does not characterize the sample complexity of private proper learning. On the other hand, they observed that the sample complexity can be improved for *improper* private learners whenever there exists a smaller hypothesis class $\mathcal{H}$ that represents $\mathcal{C}$ in the sense that for every concept $c \in \mathcal{C}$ and for every distribution on the examples, there is a hypothesis $h \in \mathcal{H}$ that is close to c. Using the exponential mechanism to choose among the hypotheses in $\mathcal{H}$ instead of $\mathcal{C}$, the sample complexity is reduced to $\ln |\mathcal{H}|$ (this is why the *size* of the representation $\mathcal{H}$ is defined to be $\ln |\mathcal{H}|$). For some classes this can dramatically improve the sample complexity, e.g., for the class $\texttt{POINT}_d$ (defined in Example 3.2), the sample complexity is improved from $O(\ln |\texttt{POINT}_d|) = O(d)$ to $O(\ln d)$. Using other techniques, Beimel et al. showed that the sample complexity of learning $\texttt{POINT}_d$ can be reduced even further to $O(1)$, hence showing the largest possible gap between proper and non proper private learning. Such a gap does not exists for non-private learning.

Chaudhuri and Hsu [7] studied the sample complexity needed for private learning infinite concept classes when the data is drawn from a continuous distribution. They showed that under these settings there exists a simple concept class for which any proper learner that uses a finite number of examples and guarantees differential privacy fails to satisfy accuracy guarantee for at least one data distribution. This implies that the results of Kasiviswanathan et al. [16] do not extend to infinite hypothesis classes. Interestingly, our results imply an improper private algorithm for an infinite extension of the class $\texttt{POINT}$ (that is, a class over the natural numbers of all boolean functions that return 1 on exactly one number).

Chaudhuri and Hsu [7] also study learning algorithms that are only required to protect the privacy of the labels (and do not necessarily protect the privacy of the examples themselves). They prove upper bounds and lower bounds on the sample complexity of such algorithms. In particular, they prove a lower bound on the sample complexity using the doubling dimension of the disagreement metric of the hypothesis class with respect to the unlabeled data distribution. This result does not imply our characterization as the privacy requirement in protecting the labels is much weaker than protecting the sample point and the label.

A line of research (started in [18]) that is very relevant to our paper is boosting learning algorithms, that is, taking learning algorithms that have a big classification error and producing a learning algorithm with small error. Dwork et al. [12] show how to privately boost accuracy, that is, given a *private* learning algorithms that have a big classification error, they produce a *private* learning algorithm with small error. In Lemma 3.14, we show how to boost the accuracy α for probabilistic representations. This gives an alternative private boosting, whose proof is simpler. However, as it uses the exponential mechanism, it is (generally) not computationally efficient.

1.2 Our Results

Beimel et al. [3] showed how to use a representation of a class to privately learn it. We make an additional step in improving the sample complexity by considering a *probabilistic* representation of a concept class $\mathcal{C}$. Instead of one collection $\mathcal{H}$ representing $\mathcal{C}$, we consider a list of collections $\mathcal{H}_1, \ldots, \mathcal{H}_r$ such that for every $c \in \mathcal{C}$ and every distribution on the examples, if we sample a collection $\mathcal{H}_i$ from the list, then with high probability there is a hypothesis $h \in \mathcal{H}_i$ that is close to c. To privately learn $\mathcal{C}$, the learning algorithm first samples $i \in \{1, \ldots, r\}$ and then uses the exponential mechanism to select a hypothesis from $\mathcal{H}_i$. This reduces the sample complexity to $O(\max_i \ln |\mathcal{H}_i|)$; the *size* of the probabilistic representation is hence defined to be $\max_i \ln |\mathcal{H}_i|$.

We show that for $\texttt{POINT}_d$ there exists a probabilistic representation of size $O(1)$. This results in a private learning algorithm with sample complexity $O(1)$, matching a different private algorithm for $\texttt{POINT}_d$ presented in [3]. Our new algorithm offers some improvement in the sample complexity compared to the algorithm of [3] when considering the learning and privacy parameters. Furthermore, our algorithm can be made computationally efficient without making any computational hardness assumptions, while the efficient version in [3] assumes the existence of one-way functions. Finally, it is conceptually simpler and in particular it avoids the sub-sampling technique used in [3].

One can ask if there are private learning algorithms with smaller sample complexity than the size of the smallest probabilistic representation. We show that the answer is no —

the size of the smallest probabilistic representation is a lower bound on the sample complexity. Thus, the size of the smallest probabilistic representation of a class $\mathcal{C}$, which we call the *representation dimension* and denote by $\text{RepDim}(\mathcal{C})$, characterizes (up to constants) the sample size necessary and sufficient for privately learning the class $\mathcal{C}$. We also show that for concepts defined over a finite domain, the difference between the sizes of the best deterministic and probabilistic representation is bounded. Namely, that if $\mathcal{C}$ is a concept class over the domain $\{0,1\}^d$, then there exists a deterministic representation of $\mathcal{C}$ of size $O(\text{RepDim}(\mathcal{C}) + \ln d)$. Thus, for classes whose smallest deterministic representation is of size $\omega(\ln d)$, the size of the smallest deterministic representation characterizes the sample complexity of private learning of the class.

The notion of probabilistic representation applies not only to private learning, but also to optimization problems. We consider a scenario where there is a domain X, a database S of m records, each taken from the domain X, a set of solutions $\mathcal{F}$, and a quality function $\text{q} : X^* \times \mathcal{F} \rightarrow [0,1]$ that we wish to maximize. If the exponential mechanism is used for (approximately) solving the problem, then the size of the database should be $\Omega(\ln|\mathcal{F}|)$ in order to achieve a reasonable approximation. Using our notions of a representation of $\mathcal{F}$ and of a probabilistic representation of $\mathcal{F}$, one can reduce the size of the minimal database without paying too much in the quality of the solution. Interestingly, a similar notion to representation, called "solution list algorithms", was considered in [2] for constructing secure protocols for search problems while leaking only a few bits on the input. Curiously, their notion of leakage is very different from that of differential privacy.

We give two examples of such optimization problems. First, an example inspired by [2]: each record in the database is a clause with exactly 3 literals and we want to find an assignment satisfying at least 7/8 fraction of the clauses while protecting the privacy of the clauses. A construction of [2] yields a deterministic representation for this problem where the size of the database can be much smaller. Using a probabilistic representation, we can give a good assignment even for databases of constant size. This example is a simple instance of a scenario, where each individual has a preference on the solution and we want to choose a solution maximizing the number of individuals whose preference are met, while protecting the privacy of the preference. Another example of optimization is sanitization, where given a database we want to publish a synthetic database, which gives a similar utility as the original database while protecting the privacy of the individual records of the database. Using our techniques, we study the minimal database size for which sanitization gives reasonable performance with respect to a given family of queries.

Open Problem. We still do not know the relation between this dimension and the VC dimension. By Sauer's Lemma, if $\mathcal{C}$ is a concept class over $\{0,1\}^d$, then the number of functions in $\mathcal{C}$ is at most $\exp(d \cdot \text{VC}(\mathcal{C}))$. By [16], there is a private learning algorithm for $\mathcal{C}$ whose sample size is $O(d \cdot \text{VC}(\mathcal{C}))$, thus, the probabilistic representation dimension of $\mathcal{C}$ is $O(d \cdot \text{VC}(\mathcal{C}))$. We do not know if there is a class $\mathcal{C}$ such that $\text{RepDim}(\mathcal{C}) \gg \text{VC}(\mathcal{C})$. A candidate for such separation appears in [1].

2. PRELIMINARIES

Notation. We use $O_\gamma(g(n))$ as a shorthand for $O(h(\gamma) \cdot g(n))$ for some non-negative function h. Given a set $\mathcal{B}$ of cardinality r, and a distribution $\mathcal{P}$ on $\{1, 2, \ldots, r\}$, we use the notation $b \in_{\mathcal{P}} \mathcal{B}$ to denote a random element of $\mathcal{B}$ chosen according to $\mathcal{P}$.

2.1 Preliminaries from Privacy

A database is a vector $S = (z_1, \ldots, z_m)$ over a domain X, where each entry $z_i \in S$ represents information contributed by one individual. Databases S_1 and S_2 are called *neighboring* if they differ in exactly one entry. An algorithm preserves differential privacy if neighboring databases induce nearby outcome distributions. Formally,

Definition 2.1 (Differential Privacy [11]). *A randomized algorithm A is ϵ-differentially private if for all neighboring databases S_1, S_2, and for all sets $\mathcal{F}$ of outputs,*

$$\Pr[A(S_1) \in \mathcal{F}] \leq \exp(\epsilon) \cdot \Pr[A(S_2) \in \mathcal{F}]. \quad (1)$$

The probability is taken over the random coins of A.

An immediate consequence of the definition is that for *any* two databases $S_1, S_2 \in X^m$, and for all sets $\mathcal{F}$ of outputs,

$$\Pr[A(S_1) \in \mathcal{F}] \geq \exp(-\epsilon m) \cdot \Pr[A(S_2) \in \mathcal{F}].$$

2.2 Preliminaries from Learning Theory

Let $X_d = \{0,1\}^d$. A concept $c : X_d \rightarrow \{0,1\}$ is a function that labels *examples* taken from the domain X_d by either 0 or 1. A *concept class* $\mathcal{C}$ over X_d is a class of concepts mapping X_d to $\{0,1\}$.

PAC learning algorithms are given examples sampled according to an unknown probability distribution $\mathcal{D}$ over X_d, and labeled according to an unknown *target* concept $c \in \mathcal{C}$. The *generalization error* of a hypothesis $h : X_d \rightarrow \{0,1\}$ is defined as

$$\text{error}_{\mathcal{D}}(c, h) = \Pr_{x \in_{\mathcal{D}} X_d}[h(x) \neq c(x)].$$

For a labeled sample $S = (x_i, y_i)_{i=1}^m$, the *empirical error* of h is

$$\text{error}_S(h) = \frac{1}{m}|\{i : h(x_i) \neq y_i\}|.$$

Definition 2.2. *An α-*good *hypothesis for c and $\mathcal{D}$ is a hypothesis h such that* $\text{error}_{\mathcal{D}}(c, h) \leq \alpha$.

Definition 2.3 (PAC Learning [19]). *Algorithm A is an (α, β)-*PAC learner *for a concept class $\mathcal{C}$ over X_d using hypothesis class $\mathcal{H}$ and sample size m if for all concepts $c \in \mathcal{C}$, all distributions $\mathcal{D}$ on X_d, given an input of m samples $S = (z_1, \ldots, z_m)$, where $z_i = (x_i, c(x_i))$ and x_i are drawn i.i.d. from $\mathcal{D}$, algorithm A outputs a hypothesis $h \in \mathcal{H}$ satisfying*

$$\Pr[\text{error}_{\mathcal{D}}(c, h) \leq \alpha] \geq 1 - \beta.$$

The probability is taken over the random choice of the examples in S according to $\mathcal{D}$ and the coin tosses of the learner A.

Definition 2.4. *An algorithm satisfying Definition 2.3 with $\mathcal{H} \subseteq \mathcal{C}$ is called a* proper *PAC learner; otherwise it is called an* improper *PAC learner.*

2.3 Private Learning

As a private learner is a PAC learner, its outcome hypothesis should also be a good predictor of labels. Hence, the privacy requirement from a private learner is not that an application of the hypothesis h on a new sample (pertaining to an individual) should leak no information about the sample.

DEFINITION 2.5 (PRIVATE PAC LEARNING [16]). *Let A be an algorithm that gets an input $S = (z_1, \dots, z_m)$. Algorithm A is an $(\alpha, \beta, \epsilon)$-*PPAC learner *for a concept class C over X_d using hypothesis class $\mathcal{H}$ and sample size m if*

PRIVACY. *Algorithm A is ϵ-differentially private (as formulated in Definition 2.1);*

UTILITY. *Algorithm A is an (α, β)-*PAC learner *for C using $\mathcal{H}$ and sample size m (as formulated in Definition 2.3).*

2.4 The Exponential Mechanism

We next describe the exponential mechanism of McSherry and Talwar [17]. We present its private learning variant; however, it can be used in more general scenarios. The goal here is to chooses a hypothesis $h \in \mathcal{H}$ approximately minimizing the empirical error. The choice is probabilistic, where the probability mass that is assigned to each hypothesis decreases exponentially with its empirical error.

> Inputs: a privacy parameter ϵ, a hypothesis class $\mathcal{H}$, and m labeled samples $S = (x_i, y_i)_{i=1}^m$.
>
> 1. $\forall h \in \mathcal{H}$ define $q(S, h) = |\{i : h(x_i) = y_i\}|$.
> 2. Randomly choose $h \in \mathcal{H}$ with probability
>
> $$\frac{\exp(\epsilon \cdot q(S,h)/2)}{\sum_{f\in\mathcal{H}} \exp(\epsilon \cdot q(S,f)/2)}.$$

PROPOSITION 2.6. *Denote $\hat{e} \triangleq \min_{f\in\mathcal{H}}\{\text{error}_S(f)\}$. The probability that the exponential mechanism outputs a hypothesis h such that $\text{error}_S(h) > \hat{e} + \Delta$ is at most $|\mathcal{H}| \cdot \exp(-\epsilon\Delta m/2)$. Moreover, The exponential mechanism is ϵ differentially private.*

2.5 Concentration Bounds

Let $X_1, \dots, X_n$ be independent random variables where $\Pr[X_i = 1] = p$ and $\Pr[X_i = 0] = 1 - p$ for some $0 < p < 1$. Clearly, $\mathbb{E}[\sum_i X_i] = pn$. Chernoff and Hoeffding bounds show that the sum is concentrated around this expected value:

$$\Pr\left[\sum_i X_i > (1+\delta)pn\right] \le \exp\left(-pn\delta^2/3\right) \quad \text{for } \delta > 0,$$
$$\Pr\left[\sum_i X_i < (1-\delta)pn\right] \le \exp\left(-pn\delta^2/2\right) \quad \text{for } 0 < \delta < 1,$$
$$\Pr\left[\left|\sum_i X_i - pn\right| > \delta\right] \le 2\exp\left(-2\delta^2/n\right) \quad \text{for } \delta \ge 0.$$

The first two inequalities are known as the multiplicative Chernoff bounds [8], and the last inequality is known as the Hoeffding bound [15].

3. THE SAMPLE COMPLEXITY OF PRIVATE LEARNERS

In this section we present a combinatorial measure of a concept class C that characterizes the sample complexity necessary and sufficient for privately learning C. The measure is a *probabilistic representation* of the class C. We start with the notation of deterministic representation from [3].

DEFINITION 3.1 ([3]). *A hypothesis class $\mathcal{H}$ is an α-representation for a class C if for every $c \in C$ and every distribution $\mathcal{D}$ on X_d there exists a hypothesis $h \in \mathcal{H}$ such that $\text{error}_{\mathcal{D}}(c, h) \le \alpha$.*

EXAMPLE 3.2 ($\texttt{POINT}_d$). *For $j \in X_d$, define $c_j : X_d \to \{0,1\}$ as $c_j(x) = 1$ if $x = j$, and $c_j(x) = 0$ otherwise. Define $\texttt{POINT}_d = \{c_j\}_{j\in X_d}$. In [3] it was shown that for $\alpha < 1/2$, every α-representation for $\texttt{POINT}_d$ must be of cardinality at least d, and that an α-representation $\mathcal{H}_d$ for $\texttt{POINT}_d$ exists where $|\mathcal{H}_d| = O(d/\alpha^2)$.*

The above representation can be used for non-private learning, by taking a big enough sample and finding a hypothesis $h \in \mathcal{H}_d$ minimizing the empirical error. For *private* learning it was shown in [3] that a sample of size $O_{\alpha,\beta,\epsilon}(\log|\mathcal{H}_d|)$ suffices, with a learner that employs the exponential mechanism to choose a hypothesis from $\mathcal{H}_d$.

DEFINITION 3.3. *For a hypothesis class $\mathcal{H}$ we denote $\text{size}(\mathcal{H}) = \ln|\mathcal{H}|$. We define the Deterministic Representation Dimension of a concept class C as*

$$\text{DRepDim}(C) = \min\left\{ \text{size}(\mathcal{H}) : \mathcal{H} \ \tfrac{1}{4}\text{-represents } C\right\}.$$

EXAMPLE 3.4. *By the results of [3], stated in the previous example,* $\text{DRepDim}(\texttt{POINT}_d) = \theta(\ln(d))$.

We are now ready to present the notion of a probabilistic representation. The idea behind this notion is that we have a list of hypothesis classes, such that for every concept c and distribution $\mathcal{D}$, if we sample a hypothesis class from the list, then with high probability it contains a hypothesis that is close to c.

DEFINITION 3.5. *Let $\mathcal{P}$ be a distribution over $\{1, 2, \dots, r\}$, and let $\mathscr{H} = \{\mathcal{H}_1, \mathcal{H}_2, \dots, \mathcal{H}_r\}$ be a family of hypothesis classes (every $\mathcal{H}_i \in \mathscr{H}$ is a set of boolean functions). We say that $(\mathscr{H}, \mathcal{P})$ is an (α, β)-probabilistic representation for a class C if for every $c \in C$ and every distribution $\mathcal{D}$ on X_d:*

$$\Pr_{\mathcal{P}}[\exists h \in \mathcal{H}_i \ s.t.\ \text{error}_{\mathcal{D}}(c,h) \le \alpha] \ge 1 - \beta.$$

The probability is over randomly choosing a set $\mathcal{H}_i \in_{\mathcal{P}} \mathscr{H}$.

EXAMPLE 3.6 ($\texttt{POINT}_d$). *In Section 7 we construct for every α and every β a pair $(\mathscr{H}, \mathcal{P})$ that (α, β)- probabilistically represents the class $\texttt{POINT}_d$, where $\mathscr{H}$ contains all the sets of at most $\frac{4}{\alpha}\ln(1/\beta)$ boolean functions.*

DEFINITION 3.7. *Let $\mathscr{H} = \{\mathcal{H}_1, \mathcal{H}_2, \dots, \mathcal{H}_r\}$ be a family of hypothesis classes. We denote $|\mathscr{H}| = r$, and $\text{size}(\mathscr{H}) = \max\{\ln|\mathcal{H}_i| : \mathcal{H}_i \in \mathscr{H}\}$. We define the Representation Dimension of a concept class C as*

$$\text{RepDim}(C) = \min\left\{ \text{size}(\mathscr{H}) \ : \begin{array}{c} \exists\mathcal{P} \ s.t.\ (\mathscr{H},\mathcal{P}) \text{ is a} \\ (\frac{1}{4},\frac{1}{4})\text{-probabilistic} \\ \text{representation for } C \end{array} \right\}.$$

EXAMPLE 3.8 ($\texttt{POINT}_d$). *The size of the probabilistic representation mentioned in Example 3.6 is $\ln(\frac{4}{\alpha}\ln(1/\beta))$. Placing $\alpha = \beta = \frac{1}{4}$, we see that the Representation Dimension of $\texttt{POINT}_d$ is constant.*

3.1 Equivalence of (α,β)-Probabilistic Representation and Private Learning

We now show that $\text{RepDim}(\mathcal{C})$ characterizes the sample complexity of private learners. We start by showing in Lemma 3.9 that an (α,β)-probabilistic representation of $\mathcal{C}$ implies a private learning algorithm whose sample complexity is the size of the representation. We then show in Lemma 3.12 that if there is a private learning algorithm with sample complexity m, then there is probabilistic representation of $\mathcal{C}$ of size $O(m)$; this lemma implies that $\text{RepDim}(\mathcal{C})$ is a lower bound on the sample complexity. Recall that $\text{RepDim}(\mathcal{C})$ is the size of the smallest probabilistic representation for $\alpha=\beta=1/4$. Thus, to complete the proof we show in Lemma 3.14 that a probabilistic representation with $\alpha=\beta=1/4$ implies a probabilistic representation for arbitrary α and β.

LEMMA 3.9. *If there a exists pair $(\mathscr{H},\mathcal{P})$ that (α,β)-probabilistically represents a class $\mathcal{C}$, then for every ϵ there exists an algorithm A that $(6\alpha,4\beta,\epsilon)$-PPAC learns $\mathcal{C}$ with a sample size $m=O\left(\frac{1}{\alpha\epsilon}(\text{size}(\mathscr{H})+\ln(\frac{1}{\beta}))\right)$.*

PROOF. Let $(\mathscr{H},\mathcal{P})$ be an (α,β)-probabilistic representation for the class $\mathcal{C}$, and consider the following algorithm A:

Inputs: $S=(x_i,y_i)_{i=1}^m$, and a privacy parameter ϵ.
1. Randomly choose $\mathcal{H}_i \in_{\mathcal{P}} \mathscr{H}$.
2. Choose $h\in\mathcal{H}_i$ using the exp. mechanism with ϵ.

By the properties of the exponential mechanism, A is ϵ-differentially private. We will show that with sample size $m=O\left(\frac{1}{\alpha\epsilon}(\text{size}(\mathscr{H})+\ln(\frac{1}{\beta}))\right)$, algorithm A is a $(6\alpha,4\beta)$-PAC learner for $\mathcal{C}$. Fix some $c\in\mathcal{C}$ and $\mathcal{D}$, and define the following 3 good events:

E_1 $\mathcal{H}_i$ chosen in step 1 contains at least one hypothesis h s.t. $\text{error}_S(h)\le 2\alpha$.

E_2 For every $h\in\mathcal{H}_i$ s.t. $\text{error}_S(h)\le 3\alpha$, it holds that $\text{error}_{\mathcal{D}}(c,h)\le 6\alpha$

E_3 The exponential mechanism chooses an h such that $\text{error}_S(h)\le \alpha+\min_{f\in\mathcal{H}_i}\{\text{error}_S(f)\}$.

We first show that if those 3 good events happen, algorithm A returns a 6α-good hypothesis. Event E_1 ensures the existence of a hypothesis $f\in\mathcal{H}_i$ s.t. $\text{error}_S(f)\le 2\alpha$. Thus, event $E_1\cap E_3$ ensures algorithm A chooses (using the exponential mechanism) a hypothesis $h\in\mathcal{H}_i$ s.t. $\text{error}_S(h)\le 3\alpha$. Event E_2 ensures therefore that this h obeys $\text{error}_{\mathcal{D}}(c,h)\le 6\alpha$.

We will now show that those 3 events happen with high probability. As $(\mathscr{H},\mathcal{P})$ is an (α,β)-probabilistic representation for the class $\mathcal{C}$, the chosen $\mathcal{H}_i$ contains a hypothesis h s.t. $\text{error}_{\mathcal{D}}(c,h)\le\alpha$ with probability at least $1-\beta$; by the Chernoff bound with probability at least $1-\exp(-m\alpha/3)$ this hypothesis has empirical error at most 2α. Event E_1 happens with probability at least $(1-\beta)(1-\exp(-m\alpha/3))>1-(\beta+\exp(-m\alpha/3))$, which is at least $(1-2\beta)$ for $m\ge\frac{3}{\alpha}\ln(1/\beta)$.

Using the Chernoff bound, the probability that a hypothesis h s.t. $\text{error}_{\mathcal{D}}(c,h)>6\alpha$ has empirical error $\le 3\alpha$ is less than $\exp(-m\alpha 3/4)$. Using the union bound, the probability that there is such a hypothesis in $\mathcal{H}_i$ is at most $|\mathcal{H}_i|\cdot\exp(-m\alpha 3/4)$. Therefore, $\Pr[E_2]\ge 1-|\mathcal{H}_i|\cdot\exp(-m\alpha 3/4)$. For $m\ge\frac{4}{3\alpha}(\ln(\frac{|\mathcal{H}_i|}{\beta}))$, this probability is at least $(1-\beta)$.

The exponential mechanism ensures that the probability of event E_3 is at least $1-|\mathcal{H}_i|\cdot\exp(-\epsilon\alpha m/2)$ (see Section 2.4), which is at least $(1-\beta)$ for $m\ge\frac{2}{\alpha\epsilon}\ln(\frac{|\mathcal{H}_i|}{\beta})$.

All in all, by setting $m=\frac{3}{\alpha\epsilon}(\text{size}(\mathscr{H})+\ln(\frac{1}{\beta}))$ we ensure that the probability of A failing to output a 6α-good hypothesis is at most 4β. □

We will demonstrate the above lemma with two examples:

EXAMPLE 3.10 (EFFICIENT LEARNER FOR $\texttt{POINT}_d$). *As described in Example 3.6, there exists an $(\mathscr{H},\mathcal{P})$ that $(\alpha/6,\beta/4)$-probabilistically represents the class $\texttt{POINT}_d$, where $\text{size}(\mathscr{H})=O_{\alpha,\beta,\epsilon}(1)$. By Lemma 3.9, there exists an algorithm that (α,β,ϵ)-PPAC learns $\mathcal{C}$ with sample size $m=O_{\alpha,\beta,\epsilon}(1)$.*

The existence of an algorithm with sample complexity $O(1)$ was already proven in [3]. Moreover, assuming the existence of oneway functions, their learner is efficient. Our constructions yields an efficient learner, without assumptions. To see this, consider again algorithm A presented in the above proof, and note that as $\text{size}(\mathscr{H})$ is constant, step 2 could be done in constant time. Step 1 can be done efficiently as we can efficiently sample a set $\mathcal{H}_i\in_{\mathcal{P}}\mathscr{H}$. In Claim 7.1 we initially construct a probabilistic representation in which the description of every hypothesis is exponential in d. The representation is than revised using pairwise independence to yield a representation in which every hypothesis h has a short description, and given x the value $h(x)$ can be computed efficiently.

EXAMPLE 3.11 ($\texttt{POINT}_{\mathbb{N}}$). *Consider the class $\texttt{POINT}_{\mathbb{N}}$, which is exactly like $\texttt{POINT}_d$, only over the natural numbers. By results of [7, 3], it is impossible to properly PPAC learn the class $\texttt{POINT}_{\mathbb{N}}$. Our construction can yield an (inefficient) improper private learner for $\texttt{POINT}_{\mathbb{N}}$ with $O_{\alpha,\beta,\epsilon}(1)$ samples. The details are deferred to Section 7.*

The next lemma shows that a private learning algorithm implies a probabilistic representation. This lemma can be used to lower bound the sample complexity of private learners.

LEMMA 3.12. *Let $\alpha\le 1/4$. If there exists an algorithm A that $(\alpha,\frac{1}{2},\epsilon)$-PPAC learns a concept class $\mathcal{C}$ with a sample size m, then there exists a pair $(\mathscr{H},\mathcal{P})$ that $(1/4,1/4)$-probabilistically represents the class $\mathcal{C}$ such that $\text{size}(\mathscr{H})=O(m\epsilon\alpha)$.*

PROOF. Let A be an $(\alpha,\frac{1}{2},\epsilon)$-PPAC learner for the class $\mathcal{C}$ using hypothesis class $\mathcal{F}$ whose sample size is m. Without loss of generality, we can assume that $m\ge\frac{3\ln(4)}{4\alpha}$ (since A can ignore part of the sample). For a target concept $c\in\mathcal{C}$ and a distribution $\mathcal{D}$ on X_d, we define

$$G^\alpha_{\mathcal{D}}=\{h\in\mathcal{F}:\text{error}_{\mathcal{D}}(c,h)\le\alpha\}.$$

Fix some $c\in\mathcal{C}$ and a distribution $\mathcal{D}$ on X_d, and define the following distribution $\tilde{\mathcal{D}}$ on X_d:

$$\Pr_{\tilde{\mathcal{D}}}[x]=\begin{cases}1-4\alpha+4\alpha\cdot\Pr_{\mathcal{D}}[x], & x=0^d.\\ 4\alpha\cdot\Pr_{\mathcal{D}}[x], & x\ne 0^d.\end{cases}$$

Note that for every $x\in X_d$,

$$\Pr_{\tilde{\mathcal{D}}}[x]\ge 4\alpha\cdot\Pr_{\mathcal{D}}[x]. \qquad (2)$$

As A is an $(\alpha, \frac{1}{2})$-PAC learner, it holds that

$$\Pr_{\tilde{\mathcal{D}},A}\left[A(S) \in G_{\tilde{\mathcal{D}}}^{\alpha}\right] \geq \frac{1}{2},$$

where the probability is over A's randomness and over sampling the examples in S (according to $\tilde{\mathcal{D}}$). In addition, by inequality (2), every hypothesis h with $\text{error}_{\mathcal{D}}(c,h) > 1/4$ has error strictly greater than α under $\tilde{\mathcal{D}}$:

$$\text{error}_{\tilde{\mathcal{D}}}(c,h) \geq 4\alpha \cdot \text{error}_{\mathcal{D}}(c,h) > \alpha.$$

So, every α-good hypothesis for c and $\tilde{\mathcal{D}}$ is a $\frac{1}{4}$-good hypothesis for c and $\mathcal{D}$. That is, $G_{\tilde{\mathcal{D}}}^{\alpha} \subseteq G_{\mathcal{D}}^{1/4}$. Therefore, $\Pr_{\tilde{\mathcal{D}},A}\left[A(S) \in G_{\mathcal{D}}^{1/4}\right] \geq \frac{1}{2}$.

We say that a database S of m labeled examples is *good* if the unlabeled example 0^d appears in S at least $(1-8\alpha)m$ times. Let S be a database constructed by taking m i.i.d. samples from $\tilde{\mathcal{D}}$, labeled by c. By the Chernoff bound, S is good with probability at least $1-\exp(-4\alpha m/3)$. Hence,

$$\Pr_{\tilde{\mathcal{D}},A}\left[(A(S) \in G_{\mathcal{D}}^{1/4}) \wedge (S \text{ is good})\right] \geq \frac{1}{2} - \exp(-4\alpha m/3) \geq \frac{1}{4}.$$

Therefore, there exists a database S_{good} of m samples that contains the unlabeled sample 0^d at least $(1-8\alpha)m$ times, and $\Pr_A\left[A(S_{\text{good}}) \in G_{\mathcal{D}}^{1/4}\right] \geq \frac{1}{4}$, where the probability is only over the randomness of A. All of the examples in S_{good} (including the example 0^d) are labeled by c.

For $\sigma \in \{0,1\}$, denote by $\vec{0}_\sigma$ a database containing m copies of the example 0^d labeled as σ. As A is ϵ-differentially private, and as the target concept c labels the example 0^d by either 0 or 1, for at least one $\sigma \in \{0,1\}$ it holds that

$$\begin{aligned}\Pr_A[A(\vec{0}_\sigma) \in G_{\mathcal{D}}^{1/4}] &\geq \exp(-8\alpha\epsilon m) \cdot \Pr_A\left[A(S_{\text{good}}) \in G_{\mathcal{D}}^{1/4}\right] \\ &\geq \exp(-8\alpha\epsilon m) \cdot 1/4. \end{aligned} \tag{3}$$

That is, $\Pr_A[A(\vec{0}_\sigma) \notin G_{\mathcal{D}}^{1/4}] \leq 1 - \frac{1}{4}e^{-8\alpha\epsilon m}$. Now, consider a set $\mathcal{H}$ containing the outcomes of $4\ln(4)e^{8\alpha\epsilon m}$ executions of $A(\vec{0}_0)$, and the outcomes of $4\ln(4)e^{8\alpha\epsilon m}$ executions of $A(\vec{0}_1)$. The probability that $\mathcal{H}$ does not contain a $\frac{1}{4}$-good hypothesis for c and $\mathcal{D}$ is at most $(1-\frac{1}{4}e^{-8\alpha\epsilon m})^{4\ln(4)e^{8\alpha\epsilon m}} \leq \frac{1}{4}$. Thus, $\mathscr{H} = \{\mathcal{H} \subseteq \mathcal{F} : |\mathcal{H}| \leq 2 \cdot 4\ln(4)e^{8\alpha\epsilon m}\}$, and $\mathcal{P}$, the distribution induced by $A(\vec{0}_0)$ and $A(\vec{0}_1)$, are a $(1/4, 1/4)$-probabilistic representation for the class $\mathcal{C}$. Note that the value $c(0^d)$ is unknown, and can be either 0 or 1. Therefore the construction uses the two possible values (one of them correct).

It holds that $\text{size}(\mathscr{H}) = \max\{\ \ln|\mathcal{H}| : \mathcal{H} \in \mathscr{H}\ \} = \ln(8\ln(4)) + 8\alpha\epsilon m = O(m\epsilon\alpha)$. □

Lemma 3.14 shows how to construct a probabilistic representation for an arbitrary α and β from a probabilistic representation with $\alpha = \beta = 1/4$; in other words we boost α and β. The proof of this lemma is combinatorial. It allows us to start with a private learning algorithm with constant α and β, move to a representation, use the combinatorial boosting, and move back to a private algorithm with small α and β. This should be contrasted with the private boosting of [12] which is algorithmic and more complicated (however, the algorithm of Dwork et al. [12] is computationally efficient).

We first show how to construct a probabilistic representation for arbitrary β from a probabilistic representation with $\beta = 1/4$.

CLAIM 3.13. *For every concept class $\mathcal{C}$ and for every β, there exists a pair $(\mathscr{H}, \mathcal{P})$ that $(1/4, \beta)$-probabilistically represents $\mathcal{C}$ where* $\text{size}(\mathscr{H}) \leq \text{RepDim}(\mathcal{C}) + \ln\ln(1/\beta)$.

PROOF. Let $\beta < 1/4$, and let $(\mathscr{H}^0, \mathcal{P}^0)$ be a $(\frac{1}{4}, \frac{1}{4})$- probabilistic representation for $\mathcal{C}$ with $\text{size}(\mathscr{H}^0) = \text{RepDim}(\mathcal{C}) \triangleq k_0$ (that is, for every $\mathcal{H}_i^0 \in \mathscr{H}^0$ it holds that $|\mathcal{H}_i^0| \leq e^{k_0}$). Denote $\mathscr{H}^0 = \{\mathcal{H}_1^0, \mathcal{H}_2^0, \ldots, \mathcal{H}_r^0\}$, and consider the following family of hypothesis classes:

$$\mathscr{H}^1 = \left\{\mathcal{H}_{i_1}^0 \cup \cdots \cup \mathcal{H}_{i_{\ln(1/\beta)}}^0 \ : \ 1 \leq i_1 \leq \cdots \leq i_{\ln(1/\beta)} \leq r\right\}.$$

Note that for every $\mathcal{H}_i^1 \in \mathscr{H}^1$ it holds that $|\mathcal{H}_i^1| \leq \ln(1/\beta)e^{k_0}$ and so $\text{size}(\mathscr{H}^1) \triangleq k_1 \leq k_0 + \ln\ln(1/\beta)$. We will now show an appropriate distribution $\mathcal{P}^1$ on $\mathscr{H}^1$ s.t. $(\mathscr{H}^1, \mathcal{P}^1)$ is a $(\frac{1}{4}, \beta)$-probabilistic representation for $\mathcal{C}$. To this end, consider the following process for randomly choosing an $\mathcal{H}^1 \in \mathscr{H}^1$:

1. Denote $M = \ln(1/\beta)$
2. For $i = 1, \ldots, M$:
   Randomly choose $\mathcal{H}_i^0 \in_{\mathcal{P}_0} \mathscr{H}^0$.
3. Return $\mathcal{H}^1 = \bigcup_{i=1}^M \mathcal{H}_i^0$.

The above process induces a distribution on $\mathscr{H}^1$, denoted as $\mathcal{P}^1$. As $\mathscr{H}^0$ is a $(\frac{1}{4}, \frac{1}{4})$-probabilistic representation for $\mathcal{C}$, we have that

$$\begin{aligned}&\Pr_{\mathcal{P}^1}\left[\nexists h \in \mathcal{H}^1 \ s.t.\ \text{error}_{\mathcal{D}}(c,h) \leq 1/4\right] = \\ &= \prod_{i=1}^{M} \Pr_{\mathcal{P}^0}\left[\nexists h \in \mathcal{H}_i^0 \ s.t.\ \text{error}_{\mathcal{D}}(c,h) \leq 1/4\right] \leq \\ &\leq \left(\frac{1}{4}\right)^M \leq \beta.\end{aligned}$$

□

LEMMA 3.14. *For every concept class $\mathcal{C}$, every α, and every β, there exists $(\mathscr{H}, \mathcal{P})$ that (α, β)-probabilistically represents $\mathcal{C}$ where*

$$\text{size}(\mathscr{H}) = O\Big(\ln(\frac{1}{\alpha}) \cdot \big(\text{RepDim}(\mathcal{C}) + \ln\ln\ln(\frac{1}{\alpha}) + \ln\ln(\frac{1}{\beta})\big)\Big).$$

PROOF. Let $\mathcal{C}$ be a concept class, and let $(\mathscr{H}^1, \mathcal{P}^1)$ be a $(\frac{1}{4}, \beta/T)$-probabilistic representation for $\mathcal{C}$ (where T will be set later). By Claim 3.13, such a representation exists with $\text{size}(\mathscr{H}^1) \triangleq k_1 \leq \text{RepDim}(\mathcal{C}) + \ln\ln(T/\beta)$. We use $\mathscr{H}^1$ and $\mathcal{P}^1$ to create an (α, β)- probabilistic representation for $\mathcal{C}$. We begin with two notations:

1. For T hypotheses $h_1, \ldots, h_T$ we denote by $\text{maj}_{h_1,\ldots,h_T}$ the majority hypothesis. That is, $\text{maj}_{h_1,\ldots,h_T}(x) = 1$ if and only if $|\{h_i : h_i(x) = 1\}| \geq T/2$.

2. For T hypothesis classes $\mathcal{H}_1, \ldots, \mathcal{H}_T$ we denote
$$\text{MAJ}(\mathcal{H}_1, \ldots, \mathcal{H}_T) = \left\{\text{maj}_{h_1,\ldots,h_T} \ : \ \forall_{1 \leq i \leq T}\ h_i \in \mathcal{H}_i\right\}.$$

Consider the following family of hypothesis classes:

$$\mathscr{H} = \left\{\text{MAJ}(\mathcal{H}_{i_1}, \ldots, \mathcal{H}_{i_T}) \ : \ \mathcal{H}_{i_1}, \ldots, \mathcal{H}_{i_T} \in \mathscr{H}^1\right\}.$$

Moreover, denote the distribution on $\mathscr{H}$ induced by the following random process as $\mathcal{P}$:

> For $j = 1, \ldots, T$:
> Randomly choose $\mathcal{H}_{i_j} \in_{\mathcal{P}^1} \mathscr{H}^1$
> Return $\text{MAJ}(\mathcal{H}_{i_1}, \ldots, \mathcal{H}_{i_T})$.

Next we show that $(\mathscr{H}, \mathcal{P})$ is an (α, β)-probabilistic representation for $\mathcal{C}$: For a fixed pair of a target concept c and a distribution $\mathcal{D}$, randomly choose $\mathcal{H}_{i_1}, \ldots, \mathcal{H}_{i_T} \in_{\mathcal{P}^1} \mathscr{H}^1$. We now show that with probability at least $(1-\beta)$ the set $\text{MAJ}(\mathcal{H}_{i_1}, \ldots, \mathcal{H}_{i_T})$ contains at least one α-good hypothesis for $c, \mathcal{D}$.

To this end, denote $\mathcal{D}_1 = \mathcal{D}$ and consider the following thought experiment, inspired by the Adaboost Algorithm of [14]:

> For $t = 1, \ldots, T$:
>
> 1. Fail if $\mathcal{H}_{i_t}$ does not contain a $\frac{1}{4}$-good hypothesis for $c, \mathcal{D}_t$.
> 2. Denote by $h_t \in \mathcal{H}_{i_t}$ a $\frac{1}{4}$-good hypothesis for $c, \mathcal{D}_t$.
> 3. $\mathcal{D}_{t+1}(x) = \begin{cases} 2\mathcal{D}_t(x), & \text{if } h_t(x) \neq c(x). \\ \left(1 - \frac{\text{error}_{\mathcal{D}_t}(c,h_t)}{1-\text{error}_{\mathcal{D}_t}(c,h_t)}\right)\mathcal{D}_t(x), & \text{otherwise.} \end{cases}$

Note that as $\mathcal{D}_1$ is a probability distribution on X_d; the same is true for $\mathcal{D}_2, \mathcal{D}_3, \ldots, \mathcal{D}_T$. As $(\mathscr{H}^1, \mathcal{P}^1)$ is a $(\frac{1}{4}, \beta/T)$-probabilistic representation for $\mathcal{C}$, the failure probability of every iteration is at most β/T. Thus (using the union bound), with probability at least $(1-\beta)$ the whole thought experiment will succeed, and in this case we show that the error of $h_{\text{fin}} = \text{maj}_{h_1,\ldots,h_T}$ is at most α.

Consider the set $R = \{x : h_{\text{fin}}(x) \neq c(x)\} \subseteq X_d$. This is the set of points on which at least $T/2$ of $h_1, \ldots, h_T$ err. Next consider the partition of R to the following sets:

$$R_t = \left\{x \in R \,:\, \left(h_t(x) \neq c(x)\right) \wedge \left(\forall_{i>t}\, h_i(x) = c(x)\right)\right\}.$$

That is, R_t contains the points $x \in R$ on which h_t is last to err. Clearly $\mathcal{D}_t(R_t) \leq 1/4$, as R_t is a subset of the set of points on which h_t errs. Moreover,

$$\begin{aligned}
\mathcal{D}_t(R_t) &\geq \mathcal{D}_1(R_t) \cdot 2^{T/2} \cdot \left(1 - \frac{\text{error}_{\mathcal{D}_t}(c,h_t)}{1 - \text{error}_{\mathcal{D}_t}(c,h_t)}\right)^{t-T/2} \\
&\geq \mathcal{D}_1(R_t) \cdot 2^{T/2} \cdot \left(1 - \frac{1/4}{1-1/4}\right)^{t-T/2} \\
&\geq \mathcal{D}_1(R_t) \cdot 2^{T/2} \cdot \left(1 - \frac{1/4}{1-1/4}\right)^{T/2} \\
&= \mathcal{D}(R_t) \cdot \left(\frac{4}{3}\right)^{T/2},
\end{aligned}$$

so,

$$\mathcal{D}(R_t) \leq \mathcal{D}_t(R_t) \cdot \left(\frac{4}{3}\right)^{-T/2} \leq \frac{1}{4} \cdot \left(\frac{4}{3}\right)^{-T/2}.$$

Finally,

$$\text{error}_{\mathcal{D}}(c, h_{\text{fin}}) = \mathcal{D}(R) = \sum_{t=T/2}^{T} \mathcal{D}(R_t) \leq$$
$$\leq \frac{T}{2} \cdot \frac{1}{4} \cdot \left(\frac{4}{3}\right)^{-T/2} = \frac{T}{8} \cdot \left(\frac{4}{3}\right)^{-T/2}.$$

Choosing $T = 14\ln(\frac{2}{\alpha})$, we get that $\text{error}_{\mathcal{D}}(c, h_{\text{fin}}) \leq \alpha$. Hence, $(\mathscr{H}, \mathcal{P})$ is an (α, β)-probabilistic representation for $\mathcal{C}$. Moreover, for every $\mathcal{H}_i \in \mathscr{H}$ we have that $|\mathcal{H}_i| \leq \left(e^{k_1}\right)^T$, and so

$$\begin{aligned}
\text{size}(\mathscr{H}) &\leq k_1 \cdot T \leq \left(\text{RepDim}(\mathcal{C}) + \ln\ln(T/\beta)\right)T \\
&= O\Big(\ln(\frac{1}{\alpha}) \cdot \left(\text{RepDim}(\mathcal{C}) + \ln\ln\ln(\frac{1}{\alpha}) + \ln\ln(\frac{1}{\beta})\right)\Big).
\end{aligned}$$

□

The next theorem states the main result of this section – RepDim characterizes the sample complexity of private learning.

THEOREM 3.15. *Let $\mathcal{C}$ be a concept class. $\widetilde{\Theta}_\beta\left(\frac{\text{RepDim}(\mathcal{C})}{\alpha\epsilon}\right)$ samples are necessary and sufficient for the private learning of the class $\mathcal{C}$.*

PROOF. Fix some $\alpha \leq 1/4, \beta \leq 1/2$, and ϵ. By Lemma 3.14, there exists a pair $(\mathscr{H}, \mathcal{P})$ that $(\frac{\alpha}{6}, \frac{\beta}{4})$-represent class $\mathcal{C}$, where $\text{size}(\mathscr{H}) = O\Big(\ln(1/\alpha) \cdot \big(\text{RepDim}(\mathcal{C}) + \ln\ln\ln(1/\alpha) + \ln\ln(1/\beta)\big)\Big)$. Therefore, by Lemma 3.9, there exists an algorithm A that $(\alpha, \beta, \epsilon)$-PPAC learns the class $\mathcal{C}$ with a sample size

$$m = O_\beta\left(\frac{1}{\alpha\epsilon}\ln(\frac{1}{\alpha}) \cdot \left(\text{RepDim}(\mathcal{C}) + \ln\ln\ln(\frac{1}{\alpha})\right)\right).$$

For the lower bound, let A be an $(\alpha, \beta, \epsilon)$-PPAC learner for the class $\mathcal{C}$ with a sample size m, where $\alpha \leq 1/4$ and $\beta \leq 1/2$. By Lemma 3.12, there exists an $(\mathscr{H}, \mathcal{P})$ that $(\frac{1}{4}, \frac{1}{4})$-probabilistically represents the class $\mathcal{C}$ and $\text{size}(\mathscr{H}) = \ln(8) + \ln\ln(4) + 8\alpha\epsilon m$. Therefore, by definition, $\text{RepDim}(\mathcal{C}) \leq \ln(8\ln(4)) + 8\alpha\epsilon m$. Thus,

$$m \geq \frac{1}{8\alpha\epsilon} \cdot \left(\text{RepDim}(\mathcal{C}) - \ln(8\ln(4))\right) = \Omega\left(\frac{\text{RepDim}(\mathcal{C})}{\alpha\epsilon}\right).$$

□

4. FROM A PROBABILISTIC REPRESENTATION TO A DETERMINISTIC REPRESENTATION

In this section we will establish a connection between the (probabilistic) representation dimension of a class and its deterministic representation dimension.

OBSERVATION 4.1. *Let $(\mathscr{H}, \mathcal{P})$ be an (α, β)-probabilistic representation for a concept class $\mathcal{C}$. Then, $\mathcal{B} = \bigcup_{\mathcal{H}_i \in \mathscr{H}} \mathcal{H}_i$ is an α-representation of $\mathcal{C}$.*

PROOF. As $(\mathscr{H}, \mathcal{P})$ is an (α, β)-probabilistic representation for $\mathcal{C}$, for every c and every $\mathcal{D}$

$$\Pr_{\mathcal{P}}[\exists h \in \mathcal{H}_i \;\; s.t \;\; \text{error}_{\mathcal{D}}(c, h) \leq \alpha] \geq 1 - \beta > 0.$$

The probability is over choosing a set $\mathcal{H}_i \in_{\mathcal{P}} \mathscr{H}$. In particular, for every c and every $\mathcal{D}$ there exists an $\mathcal{H}_i \in \mathscr{H}$ that contains an α-good hypothesis. □

The simple construction in Observation 4.1 may result in a very large deterministic representation. For example, in Claim 7.1 we show an $(\mathscr{H}, \mathcal{P})$ that (α, β)- probabilistically represents the class $\texttt{POINT}_d$, where $\mathscr{H}$ contains all the sets of at most $\frac{4}{\alpha}\ln(\frac{1}{\beta})$ boolean functions. While $\bigcup_{\mathcal{H}_i \in \mathscr{H}} \mathcal{H}_i = 2^{X_d}$ is indeed an α-representation for $\texttt{POINT}_d$, it is extremely over-sized.

We will show that it is not necessary to take the union of all the $\mathcal{H}_i$'s in $\mathscr{H}$ in order to get an α-representation for $\mathcal{C}$. As $(\mathscr{H}, \mathcal{P})$ is an (α, β)-probabilistic representation, for every c and every $\mathcal{D}$, with probability at least $1 - \beta$ a randomly chosen $\mathcal{H}_i \in_{\mathcal{P}} \mathscr{H}$ contains an α-good hypothesis. The straight forward strategy here is to first boost β as in Claim 3.13, and then use the union bound over all possible $c \in \mathcal{C}$ and over all possible distributions $\mathcal{D}$ on X_d. Unfortunately, there are infinitely many such distributions, and the proof will be somewhat more complicated.

Definition 4.2. *Let $\mathscr{H} = \{\mathcal{H}_1, \mathcal{H}_2, \ldots, \mathcal{H}_r\}$ be a family of hypothesis classes, and $\mathcal{P}$ be a distribution over $\{1, \ldots, r\}$. We will denote the following non private algorithm as Learner$(\mathscr{H}, \mathcal{P}, m, \gamma)$:*

> *Input: a sample $S = (x_i, y_i)_{i=1}^m$.*
> 1. *Randomly choose $\mathcal{H}_i \in_{\mathcal{P}} \mathscr{H}$.*
> 2. *If for every $h \in \mathcal{H}_i$ $\text{error}_S(h) > \gamma$, then fail.*
> 3. *Return $h \in \mathcal{H}_i$ minimizing $\text{error}_S(h)$.*

We will say that Learner$(\mathscr{H}, \mathcal{P}, m, \gamma)$ is β-successful for a class $\mathcal{C}$ over X_d, if for every $c \in \mathcal{C}$ and every distribution $\mathcal{D}$ on X_d, given an input sample drawn i.i.d. according to $\mathcal{D}$ and labeled by c, algorithm Learner fails with probability at most β.

Claim 4.3. *If $(\mathscr{H}, \mathcal{P})$ is an (α, β)-probabilistic representation for a class $\mathcal{C}$, then, for $m \geq \frac{3}{\alpha}\ln(1/\beta)$, algorithm Learner$(\mathscr{H}, \mathcal{P}, m, 2\alpha)$ is 2β-successful for $\mathcal{C}$.*

Proof. We will show that with probability at least $1-2\beta$, the set $\mathcal{H}_i$ (chosen in Step 1) contains at least one hypothesis h s.t. $\text{error}_S(h) \leq 2\alpha$. As $(\mathscr{H}, \mathcal{P})$ is an (α, β)-probabilistic representation for class $\mathcal{C}$, the chosen $\mathcal{H}_i$ will contain a hypothesis h s.t. $\text{error}_{\mathcal{D}}(c, h) \leq \alpha$ with probability at least $1 - \beta$; by the Chernoff bound with probability at least $1 - \exp(-m\alpha/3)$ this hypothesis has empirical error at most 2α. The set $\mathcal{H}_i$ contains a hypothesis h s.t. $\text{error}_S(h) \leq 2\alpha$ with probability at least $(1 - \beta)(1 - \exp(-m\alpha/3)) > 1 - (\beta + \exp(-m\alpha/3))$, which is at least $(1 - 2\beta)$ for $m \geq \frac{3}{\alpha}\ln(1/\beta)$. □

Claim 4.4. *Let $\mathscr{H}$ be a family of hypothesis classes, and $\mathcal{P}$ a distribution on it. Let γ, β and m be such that $m \geq \frac{4}{\gamma}(\text{size}(\mathscr{H}) + \ln(\frac{1}{\beta}))$. If Learner$(\mathscr{H}, \mathcal{P}, m, \gamma)$ is β-successful for a class $\mathcal{C}$ over X_d, then there exists $\widehat{\mathscr{H}} \subseteq \mathscr{H}$ and a distribution $\widehat{\mathcal{P}}$ on it, s.t. Learner$(\widehat{\mathscr{H}}, \widehat{\mathcal{P}}, m, \gamma)$ is a $(2\gamma, 3\beta)$-PAC learner for $\mathcal{C}$ and $\left|\widehat{\mathscr{H}}\right| = \frac{d \cdot m}{\beta^2}$.*

Proof. For every input $S = (x_i, y_i)_{i=1}^m$, denote by p_S the probability of Learner$(\mathscr{H}, \mathcal{P}, m, \gamma)$ failing on step 2 (the probability is only over the choice of $\mathcal{H}_i \in_{\mathcal{P}} \mathscr{H}$ in the first step). As Learner$(\mathscr{H}, \mathcal{P}, m, \gamma)$ is β-successful,

$$\Pr_{\mathcal{P}, \mathcal{D}}\left[\text{Learner}(\mathscr{H}, \mathcal{P}, m, \gamma) \text{ fails}\right] = \sum_S \Pr_{\mathcal{D}}[S] \cdot p_S \leq \beta.$$

Consider the following process, denoted by Proc, for randomly choosing a multiset $\widetilde{\mathscr{H}}$ of size t (t will be set later):

> For $i = 1, \ldots, t$:
> Randomly choose $\mathcal{H}_i \in_{\mathcal{P}} \mathscr{H}$
> Return $\widetilde{\mathscr{H}} = (\mathcal{H}_1, \mathcal{H}_2, \ldots, \mathcal{H}_t)$.

Denote by $\mathcal{U}_t$ the uniform distribution on $\{1, 2, \ldots, t\}$. As before, for every input $S = (x_i, y_i)_{i=1}^m$, denote by $\widetilde{p_S}$ the probability of Learner$(\widetilde{\mathscr{H}}, \mathcal{U}_t, m, \gamma)$ failing on its second step (again, the probability is only over the choice of $\mathcal{H}_i \in_{\mathcal{U}_t} \widetilde{\mathscr{H}}$ in the first step). Using those notations:

$$\Pr_{\mathcal{U}_t, \mathcal{D}}\left[\text{Learner}(\widetilde{\mathscr{H}}, \mathcal{U}_t, m, \gamma) \text{ fails}\right] = \sum_S \Pr_{\mathcal{D}}[S] \cdot \widetilde{p_S}.$$

Fix a sample S. As the choice of $\mathcal{H}_i \in_{\mathcal{U}_t} \widetilde{\mathscr{H}}$ is uniform,

$$\widetilde{p_S} = \frac{\left|\left\{\mathcal{H}_i \in \widetilde{\mathscr{H}} \,:\, \forall h \in \mathcal{H}_i \ \text{error}_S(h) > \gamma\right\}\right|}{\left|\widetilde{\mathscr{H}}\right|}.$$

Using the Hoeffding bound,

$$\Pr_{Proc}\left[|\widetilde{p_S} - p_S| \geq \beta\right] \leq 2e^{-2t\beta^2}.$$

The probability is over choosing the multiset $\widetilde{\mathscr{H}}$. There are at most $2^{m(d+1)}$ samples of size m (as every entry in the sample is an element of X_d, concatenated with a label bit). Using the union bound over all possible samples S,

$$\Pr_{Proc}\left[\exists S \text{ s.t. } |\widetilde{p_S} - p_S| \geq \beta\right] \leq 2^{m(d+1)} \cdot 2 \cdot e^{-2t\beta^2}.$$

For $t \geq \frac{m \cdot d}{\beta^2}$ the above probability is strictly less than 1. This means that for $t = \frac{m \cdot d}{\beta^2}$ there exists a multiset $\widehat{\mathscr{H}}$ such that $|\widehat{p_S} - p_S| \leq \beta$ for every sample S. We will show that for this $\widehat{\mathscr{H}}$, Learner$(\widehat{\mathscr{H}}, \mathcal{U}_t, m, \gamma)$ is a $(2\gamma, 3\beta)$-PAC learner. Fix a target concept $c \in \mathcal{C}$ and a distribution $\mathcal{D}$ on X_d. Define the following two good events:

E_1 Learner$(\widehat{\mathscr{H}}, \mathcal{U}_t, m, \gamma)$ outputs a hypothesis h such that $\text{error}_S(h) \leq \gamma$.

E_2 For every $h \in \mathcal{H}_i$ s.t. $\text{error}_S(h) \leq \gamma$, it holds that $\text{error}_{\mathcal{D}}(c, h) \leq 2\gamma$.

Note that if those two events happen, Learner$(\widehat{\mathscr{H}}, \mathcal{U}_t, m, \gamma)$ returns a 2γ-good hypothesis for c and $\mathcal{D}$. We will show that those two events happen with high probability. We start by bounding the failure probability of Learner$(\widehat{\mathscr{H}}, \mathcal{U}_t, m, \gamma)$.

$$\begin{aligned}
&\Pr_{\mathcal{U}_t, \mathcal{D}}\left[\text{Learner}(\widehat{\mathscr{H}}, \mathcal{U}_t, m, \gamma) \text{ fails}\right] \\
&= \sum_S \Pr_{\mathcal{D}}[S] \cdot \widehat{p_S} \\
&\leq \sum_S \Pr_{\mathcal{D}}[S] \cdot (p_S + \beta) \\
&= \Pr_{\mathcal{P}, \mathcal{D}}\left[\text{Learner}(\mathscr{H}, \mathcal{P}, m, \gamma) \text{ fails}\right] + \beta \leq 2\beta.
\end{aligned}$$

When Learner$(\widehat{\mathscr{H}}, \mathcal{U}_t, m, \gamma)$ does not fail, it returns a hypothesis h with empirical error at most γ. Thus, $\Pr[E_1] \geq 1 - 2\beta$.

Using the Chernoff bound, the probability that a hypothesis h with $\text{error}_{\mathcal{D}}(c, h) > 2\gamma$ has empirical error $\leq \gamma$ is less than $\exp(-m\gamma/4)$. Using the union bound, the probability that there is such a hypothesis in $\mathcal{H}_i$ is at most $|\mathcal{H}_i| \cdot \exp(-m\gamma/4)$. Therefore, $\Pr[E_2] \geq 1 - |\mathcal{H}_i| \cdot \exp(-m\gamma/4)$. For $m \geq \frac{4}{\gamma}\ln(\frac{|\mathcal{H}_i|}{\beta})$, this probability is at least $(1-\beta)$.

All in all, the probability of *Learner*$(\mathscr{H}, \mathcal{P}, m, \gamma)$ failing to output a 2γ-good hypothesis is at most 3β. □

THEOREM 4.5. *If there exists a pair* $(\mathscr{H}, \mathcal{P})$ *that* (α, β)-*probabilistically represents a class* $\mathcal{C}$ *over* X_d *(where* $|\mathscr{H}|$ *might be very big), then there exists a pair* $(\widehat{\mathscr{H}}, \widehat{\mathcal{P}})$ *that* $(4\alpha, 6\beta)$-*probabilistically represents* $\mathcal{C}$, *where* $\widehat{\mathscr{H}} \subseteq \mathscr{H}$ *, and*

$$\left|\widehat{\mathscr{H}}\right| = \frac{3d}{4\alpha\beta^2}\left(\text{size}(\mathscr{H}) + \ln(\frac{1}{\beta})\right).$$

PROOF. Let $(\mathscr{H}, \mathcal{P})$ be an (α, β)-probabilistic representation for a class $\mathcal{C}$. Set $m = \frac{3}{\alpha}(\text{size}(\mathscr{H}) + \ln(\frac{1}{\beta}))$. By Claim 4.3, *Learner*$(\mathscr{H}, \mathcal{P}, m, 2\alpha)$ is 2β-successful for class $\mathcal{C}$. By Claim 4.4, there exists an $\widehat{\mathscr{H}} \subseteq \mathscr{H}$ and a distribution $\widehat{\mathcal{P}}$ on it, such that *Learner*$(\widehat{\mathscr{H}}, \widehat{\mathcal{P}}, m, 2\alpha)$ is a $(4\alpha, 6\beta)$-PAC learner for $\mathcal{C}$ and $\left|\widehat{\mathscr{H}}\right| = \frac{d \cdot m}{4\beta^2} = \frac{3d}{4\alpha\beta^2}(\text{size}(\mathscr{H}) + \ln(\frac{1}{\beta}))$.

Assume towards contradiction that $(\widehat{\mathscr{H}}, \widehat{\mathcal{P}})$ does not $(4\alpha, 6\beta)$-represent $\mathcal{C}$. So, there exist a concept $c \in \mathcal{C}$ and a distribution $\mathcal{D}$ s.t., with probability strictly greater than 6β, a randomly chosen $\mathcal{H}_i \in_{\widehat{\mathcal{P}}} \widehat{\mathscr{H}}$ does not contain a 4α-good hypothesis for $c, \mathcal{D}$. Therefore, for those c and $\mathcal{D}$, *Learner*$(\widehat{\mathscr{H}}, \widehat{\mathcal{P}}, m, 2\alpha)$ will fail to return a 4α-good hypothesis with probability strictly greater than 6β. □

THEOREM 4.6. *For every class* $\mathcal{C}$ *over* X_d *there exists a* $\frac{1}{4}$-*representation* $\mathcal{B}$ *such that* $\text{size}(\mathcal{B}) = O(\ln(d) + \text{RepDim}(\mathcal{C}))$.

PROOF. By Lemma 3.14, there exists a pair $(\mathscr{H}, \mathcal{P})$ that $(\frac{1}{16}, \frac{1}{12})$-probabilistically represents $\mathcal{C}$ such that $\text{size}(\mathscr{H}) = O(\text{RepDim}(\mathcal{C}))$. Using Theorem 4.5, there exists a pair $(\widehat{\mathscr{H}}, \widehat{\mathcal{P}})$ that $(\frac{1}{4}, \frac{1}{2})$-probabilistically represents $\mathcal{C}$, such that $\text{size}(\widehat{\mathscr{H}}) = \text{size}(\mathscr{H})$ and

$$\left|\widehat{\mathscr{H}}\right| = O\left(d \cdot \text{size}(\mathscr{H})\right).$$

We can now use Observation 4.1 and construct the set $\mathcal{B} = \bigcup_{\mathcal{H}_i \in \widehat{\mathscr{H}}} \mathcal{H}_i$ which is a $\frac{1}{4}$-representation for the class $\mathcal{C}$. In addition,

$$|\mathcal{B}| = O\left(\left|\widehat{\mathscr{H}}\right| \cdot e^{\text{size}(\mathscr{H})}\right) = O\left(d \cdot \text{size}(\mathscr{H}) \cdot e^{\text{size}(\mathscr{H})}\right).$$

Thus, $\text{size}(\mathcal{B}) = \ln|\mathcal{B}| = O(\ln(d) + \text{RepDim}(\mathcal{C}))$. □

COROLLARY 4.7. *For every concept class* $\mathcal{C}$ *over* X_d, $\text{DRepDim}(\mathcal{C}) = O(\ln(d) + \text{RepDim}(\mathcal{C}))$.

COROLLARY 4.8. *There exists a constant* N *s.t. for every concept class* C *over* X_d *where* $\text{DRepDim}(\mathcal{C}) \geq N\log(d)$, *the sample complexity that is necessary and sufficient for privately learning* $\mathcal{C}$ *is* $\Theta_{\alpha,\beta}(\text{DRepDim}(\mathcal{C}))$.

5. PROBABILISTIC REPRESENTATION FOR PRIVATELY SOLVING OPTIMIZATION PROBLEMS

The notion of probabilistic representation applies not only to private learning, but also to a broader task of optimization problems. We consider the following scenario:

DEFINITION 5.1. *An* optimization problem OPT *over a universe* X *and a set of solutions* $\mathcal{F}$ *is defined by a quality function* $q : X^* \times \mathcal{F} \to [0,1]$. *Given a database* S, *the task is to choose a solution* $f \in \mathcal{F}$ *such that* $q(S, f)$ *is maximized.*

Notation. We will refer to the optimization problem defined by a quality function q as OPT_q.

DEFINITION 5.2. *An* α-good *solution for a database* S *is a solution* s *such that* $q(S,s) \geq \max_{f\in\mathcal{F}}\{q(S,f)\} - \alpha$.

Given an optimization problem OPT_q, one can use the exponential mechanism to choose a solution $s \in \mathcal{F}$. In general, this method achieves a reasonable solution only for databases of size $\Omega(\log|\mathcal{F}|/\epsilon)$. To see this, consider a case where there exists a database S of m records such that exactly one solution $t \in \mathcal{F}$ has a quality of $q(S,t) = 1$, and every other $f \in \mathcal{F}$ has a quality of $q(S,f) = 1/2$. The probability of the exponential mechanism choosing t is:

$$\Pr[t \text{ is chosen}] = \frac{\exp(\epsilon m/2)}{(|\mathcal{F}| - 1) \cdot \exp(\epsilon m/4) + \exp(\epsilon m/2)}.$$

Unless

$$m \geq \tfrac{4}{\epsilon}\ln(|\mathcal{F}| - 1) = \Omega(\tfrac{1}{\epsilon}\ln|\mathcal{F}|), \tag{4}$$

the above probability is strictly less than 1/2. Using our notations of probabilistic representation, it might be possible to reduce the necessary database size.

Consider using the exponential mechanism for choosing a solution s, not out of $\mathcal{F}$, but rather from a smaller set of solutions $\mathcal{B}$. Roughly speaking, the factor of $\ln|\mathcal{F}|$ in requirement (4) will now be replaced with $\ln|\mathcal{B}|$, which corresponds to size of the representation. Therefore, the database size m should be at least $\ln|\mathcal{B}|/\epsilon$. So m needs to be bigger than the size of the representation by at least a factor of $1/\epsilon$.

In the following analysis we will denote this required gap, i.e., $m/\ln|\mathcal{B}|$, as Δ. We will see that the existence of a private approximation algorithm implies a probabilistic representation with $1 < \Delta \approx \frac{1}{\epsilon}$, and that a probabilistic representation with $\Delta > 1$ implies a private approximation algorithm. Bigger Δ corresponds to better privacy; however, it might be harder to achieve.

DEFINITION 5.3. *Let* OPT_q *be an optimization problem over a universe* X *and a set of solutions* $\mathcal{F}$. *Let* $\mathcal{B}$ *be a set of solutions, and denote* $\text{size}(\mathcal{B}) = \ln|\mathcal{B}|$. *We say that* $\mathcal{B}$ *is an* α-*deterministic representation of* OPT_q *for databases of* m *elements if for every* $S \in X^m$ *there exists a solution* $s \in \mathcal{B}$ *such that* $q(S,s) \geq \max_{f\in\mathcal{F}}\{q(S,f)\} - \alpha$.

DEFINITION 5.4. *Let* $\mathcal{B}$ *be an* α-*deterministic representation of* OPT_q *for databases of* m *elements. Denote* $\Delta \triangleq \frac{m}{\text{size}(\mathcal{B})}$. *If* $\Delta > 1$, *then we say that* the ratio *of* $\mathcal{B}$ *is* Δ.

An α-deterministic representation $\mathcal{B}$ with ratio Δ is required to support all the databases of $m = \Delta \cdot \text{size}(\mathcal{B})$ elements. That is, for every $S \in X^m$, the set $\mathcal{B}$ is required to contain at least one α-good solution.

Fix $S \in X^m$. Intuitively, Δ controls the ratio between m and number of bits needed to represent an α-good solution for S. As $\mathcal{B}$ contains an α-good solution for S, and assuming $\mathcal{B}$ is publicly known, this solution could be represented with $\ln|\mathcal{B}| = \text{size}(\mathcal{B}) = m/\Delta$ bits.

DEFINITION 5.5. *Let* OPT_q *be an optimization problem over a universe* X *and a set of solutions* $\mathcal{F}$. *Let* $\mathcal{P}$ *be a distribution over* $\{1, 2, \ldots, r\}$, *and let* $\mathscr{B} = \{\mathcal{B}_1, \mathcal{B}_2, \ldots, \mathcal{B}_r\}$ *be a family of solution sets for* OPT_q. *We denote* $\mathrm{size}(\mathscr{B}) = \max\{\, \ln |\mathcal{B}_i| : \mathcal{B}_i \in \mathscr{B}\,\}$. *We say that* $(\mathscr{B}, \mathcal{P})$ *is an* (α, β)*-probabilistic representation of* OPT_q *for databases of* m *elements if for every* $S \in X^m$:

$$\Pr_{\mathcal{P}}\left[\exists s \in \mathcal{B}_i \text{ s.t. } q(S,s) \geq \max_{f\in\mathcal{F}}\{q(S,f)\} - \alpha\right] \geq 1-\beta.$$

DEFINITION 5.6. *Let* $(\mathscr{B}, \mathcal{P})$ *be an* (α, β)*-probabilistic representation of* OPT_q *for databases of* m *elements. Denote* $\Delta \triangleq \frac{m}{\mathrm{size}(\mathscr{B})}$. *If* $\Delta > 1$, *then we say that the* ratio *of the representation is* Δ.

DEFINITION 5.7. *An optimization problem* OPT_q *is* bounded *if* $\Big||S_1| \cdot q(S_1, f) - |S_2| \cdot q(S_2, f)\Big| \leq 1$ *for every solution* f *and every two neighboring databases* S_1, S_2.

We are interested in approximating bounded optimization problems, while guaranteeing differential privacy:

DEFINITION 5.8. *Let* OPT_q *be a bounded optimization problem over a universe* X *and a set of solutions* $\mathcal{F}$. *An algorithm* A *is an* $(\alpha, \beta, \epsilon)$-private approximation algorithm *for* OPT_q *with a database of* m *records if:*

1. *Algorithm* A *is* ϵ*-differentially private (as formulated in Definition 2.1);*
2. *For every* $S \in X^m$, *algorithm* A *outputs with probability at least* $(1-\beta)$ *a solution* s *such that* $q(S, s) \geq \max_{f\in\mathcal{F}}\{q(S, f)\} - \alpha$.

EXAMPLE 5.9 (SANITIZATION). *Consider a class of predicates* C *over* X. *A database* S *contains points taken from* X. *A predicate query* Q_c *for* $c \in C$ *is defined as* $Q_c(S) = \frac{1}{|S|} \cdot |\{x_i \in S : c(x_i) = 1\}|$. *Blum et al. [5] defined a sanitizer (or data release mechanism) as a differentially private algorithm that, on input a database* S, *outputs another database* $\hat{S}$ *with entries taken from* X. *A sanitizer* A *is* (α, β)*-useful for predicates in the class* C *if for every database* S *it holds that*

$$\Pr_A\left[\forall c \in C \;\; |Q_c(S) - Q_c(\hat{S})| \leq \alpha\right] \geq 1-\beta.$$

This scenario can be viewed as a bounded optimization problem: The solutions are sanitized databases. For an input database S *and and a sanitized database* $\hat{S}$, *the quality function is*

$$q(S, \hat{S}) = 1 - \max_{c\in C}\left\{|Q_c(S) - Q_c(\hat{S})|\right\}.$$

To see that this optimization problem is bounded, note that for every two neighboring databases S_1, S_2 *of* m *elements, and every* $c \in C$ *it holds that* $|Q_c(S_1) - Q_c(S_2)| \leq \frac{1}{m}$. *Therefore, for every sanitized database* f,

$$
\begin{aligned}
& m \cdot |q(S_1, f) - q(S_2, f)| \\
&= m \cdot \left|\max_{c\in C}\{|Q_c(S_1) - Q_c(f)|\} - \max_{c\in C}\{|Q_c(S_2) - Q_c(f)|\}\right| \\
&\leq 1
\end{aligned}
$$

The next two lemmas establish an equivalence between a private approximation algorithm and a probabilistic representation for a bounded optimization problem.

LEMMA 5.10. *Let* OPT_q *be a bounded optimization problem over a universe* X. *If there exists a pair* $(\mathscr{B}, \mathcal{P})$ *that* (α, β)*-probabilistically represents* OPT_q *for databases of* m *elements, s.t. the ratio of* $(\mathscr{B}, \mathcal{P})$ *is* $\Delta > 1$, *then for every* $\hat{\alpha}, \hat{\beta}, \epsilon$ *satisfying*

$$\Delta \geq \frac{2}{\epsilon\hat{\alpha}}\left(1 + \frac{\ln(1/\hat{\beta})}{\mathrm{size}(\mathscr{B})}\right),$$

there exists an $\big((\alpha+\hat{\alpha}), (\beta+\hat{\beta}), \epsilon\big)$*-approximation algorithm for* OPT_q *with a database of size* m.

PROOF. Consider the following algorithm A:

> Inputs: a database $S \in X^m$, and a privacy parameter ϵ.
>
> 1. Randomly choose $\mathcal{B}_i \in_{\mathcal{P}} \mathscr{B}$.
> 2. Choose $s \in \mathcal{B}_i$ using the exponential mechanism, that is, with probability
>
> $$\frac{\exp(\epsilon \cdot m \cdot q(S,s)/2)}{\sum_{f\in\mathcal{B}_i}\exp(\epsilon \cdot m \cdot q(S,f)/2)}.$$

By the properties of the exponential mechanism, A is ϵ-differentially private. Fix a database $S \in X^m$, and define the following 2 bad events:

E_1 The set $\mathcal{B}_i$ chosen in step 1 does not contain a solution s s.t. $q(S,s) \geq \max_{f\in\mathcal{F}}\{q(S,f)\} - \alpha$.

E_2 The solution s chosen in step 2 is such that $q(S,s) < \max_{t\in\mathcal{B}_i} q(S,t) - \hat{\alpha}$.

Note that if those two bad events do not occur, algorithm A outputs a solution s such that $q(S,s) \geq \max_{f\in\mathcal{F}}\{q(S,f)\} - \alpha - \hat{\alpha}$. As $(\mathscr{B}, \mathcal{P})$ is an (α, β)-probabilistic representation of OPT_q for databases of size m, event E_1 happens with probability at most β. By the properties of the exponential mechanism, the probability of event E_2 is bounded by $|\mathcal{B}_i| \cdot \exp(-\epsilon m\hat{\alpha}/2)$. As $m = \Delta\,\mathrm{size}(\mathscr{B})$, this probability is at most

$$
\begin{aligned}
\Pr[E_2] &\leq \mathrm{size}(\mathscr{B}) \cdot \exp(-\epsilon m \hat{\alpha}/2) \\
&= \mathrm{size}(\mathscr{B}) \cdot \exp(-\epsilon\Delta\,\mathrm{size}(\mathscr{B})\hat{\alpha}/2) \\
&\leq \mathrm{size}(\mathscr{B}) \cdot \exp\left(-\left(1 + \frac{\ln(1/\hat{\beta})}{\mathrm{size}(\mathscr{B})}\right)\mathrm{size}(\mathscr{B})\right) \\
&= \mathrm{size}(\mathscr{B}) \cdot \exp(-\,\mathrm{size}(\mathscr{B}) - \ln(1/\hat{\beta})) = \hat{\beta}.
\end{aligned}
$$

Therefore, algorithm A outputs an $(\alpha + \hat{\alpha})$-good solution with probability at least $(1 - \beta - \hat{\beta})$. □

LEMMA 5.11. *Let* OPT_q *be an optimization problem. If there exists an* $(\alpha, \beta, \epsilon)$*-private approximation algorithm for* OPT_q *with a database of* m *records, then for every* $\hat{\beta}$ *satisfying*

$$\Delta \triangleq \frac{m}{\ln(\frac{1}{1-\beta}) + \ln\ln(\frac{1}{\hat{\beta}}) + m \cdot \epsilon} > 1,$$

there exists a pair $(\mathscr{B}, \mathcal{P})$ *that* $(\alpha, \hat{\beta})$*-probabilistically represents* OPT_q *for databases of* m *elements, where the ratio of the representation is* Δ.

PROOF. Let A be an (α,β,ϵ)-private approximation algorithm for OPT_q, with a sample size m. Fix an arbitrary input database $S \in X^m$. Define G as the set of all solutions s, possibly outputted by A, such that $q(S,s) \geq \max_{f\in\mathcal{F}}\{q(S,f)\} - \alpha$. As A is an (α,β,ϵ)-approximation algorithm, $\Pr_A[A(S) \in G] \geq 1-\beta$. As A is ϵ-differentially private, $\Pr_A\left[A(\vec{0}) \in G\right] \geq (1-\beta)e^{-m\epsilon}$, where $\vec{0}$ is a database with m zeros. That is, $\Pr_A\left[A(\vec{0}) \notin G\right] \leq 1-(1-\beta)e^{-m\epsilon}$. Now, consider a set $\mathcal{B}$ containing the outcomes of $\Gamma \triangleq \frac{1}{1-\beta}\ln(\frac{1}{\beta})e^{m\epsilon}$ executions of $A(\vec{0})$. The probability that $\mathcal{B}$ does not contain a solutions $s \in G$ is at most $(1-(1-\beta)e^{-m\epsilon})^{\Gamma} \leq \hat{\beta}$. Thus, $\mathscr{B} = \{\mathcal{B} \subseteq support(A) : |\mathcal{B}| \leq \Gamma\}$, and $\mathcal{P}$, the distribution induced by $A(\vec{0})$, are an $(\alpha,\hat{\beta})$-probabilistic representation of OPT_q for databases with m elements. Moreover, the ratio of the representation is

$$\frac{m}{\mathrm{size}(\mathscr{B})} = \frac{m}{\max\{\ln|\mathcal{B}| : \mathcal{B}\in\mathscr{B}\}} = \frac{m}{\ln(\frac{1}{1-\beta}) + \ln\ln(\frac{1}{\beta}) + m\epsilon} = \Delta.$$

□

5.1 Exact 3SAT

Consider the following bounded optimization problem, denoted as $\mathrm{OPT}_{\mathrm{E3SAT}}$: The universe X is the set of all possible clauses with exactly 3 different literals over n variables, and the set of solutions $\mathcal{F}$ is the set of all possible 2^n assignments. Given a database $S = (\sigma_1, \sigma_2, \ldots, \sigma_m)$ containing m E3CNF clauses, the quality of an assignment $a \in \mathcal{F}$ is

$$q(S,a) = \frac{|\{i : a(\sigma_i) = 1\}|}{m}.$$

Aiming at the (very different) objective of secure protocols for search problems, Beimel et al. [2] defined the notation of solution-list algorithms, which corresponds to our notation of deterministic representation. We next rephrase their results using our notations.

$R1$ For every $\alpha > 0$ and every $\Delta > 1$, there exists a set $\mathcal{B}$ that $(\alpha+1/8)$-deterministically represents $\mathrm{OPT}_{\mathrm{E3SAT}}$ for databases of size $m = O\big(\Delta(\ln\ln(n) + \ln(1/\alpha))\big)$, and a ratio of Δ.

$R2$ Let $\alpha < 1/2$ and $\Delta > 1$. For every set $\mathcal{B}$ that α- deterministically represents $\mathrm{OPT}_{\mathrm{E3SAT}}$ for databases of size m with a ratio of Δ, it holds that $m = \Omega(\ln\ln(n))$.

Using ($R1$) and a deterministic version of Lemma 5.10, for every $\alpha,\beta,\epsilon > 0$, there exists an $\big((1/8+\alpha),\beta,\epsilon\big)$- approximation algorithm for $\mathrm{OPT}_{\mathrm{E3SAT}}$ with a database of $m = O_{\alpha,\beta,\epsilon}(\ln\ln(n))$ clauses. By ($R2$), this is the best possible using a deterministic representation.

We can reduce the necessary database size, using a probabilistic representation. Fix a clause with three different literals. If we pick an assignment at random, then with probability at least 7/8 it satisfies the clause. Now, fix any exact 3CNF formula. If we pick an assignment at random, then the expected fraction of satisfied clauses is at least 7/8. Moreover, for every $0 < \alpha < 7/8$, the fraction of satisfied clauses is at least $(7/8-\alpha)$ with probability at least $\frac{\alpha}{\alpha+1/8}$. So, if we pick $t = \frac{\ln(1/\beta)}{\ln(\alpha+1/8)+\ln(1/\alpha)}$ random assignments, the probability that none of them will satisfy at least $(7/8-\alpha)m$ clauses is at most $\left(\frac{\alpha}{\alpha+1/8}\right)^t = \beta$. So, for every $\Delta > 1$,

$$\mathscr{B} = \{\mathcal{B} : \mathcal{B} \text{ is a set of at most } t \text{ assignments}\},$$

and $\mathcal{P}$, the distribution induced on $\mathscr{B}$ by randomly picking t assignments, are an $\big((1/8+\alpha),\beta\big)$-probabilistic representation of $\mathrm{OPT}_{\mathrm{E3SAT}}$ for databases of size $\Delta\cdot\ln(t)$ and a ratio of Δ. By Lemma 5.11, for every ϵ there exists an $\big((1/8+\alpha),\beta,\epsilon\big)$-approximation algorithm for $\mathrm{OPT}_{\mathrm{E3SAT}}$ with a database of $m = o_{\alpha,\beta,\epsilon}(1)$ clauses.

6. EXTENSIONS

6.1 (ϵ,δ)-Differential Privacy

The notation of ϵ-differential privacy was generalized to (ϵ,δ)-differential privacy, where the requirement in inequality (1) is changed to

$$\Pr[A(S_1)\in\mathcal{F}] \leq \exp(\epsilon)\cdot\Pr[A(S_2)\in\mathcal{F}] + \delta.$$

The proof of Lemma 3.12 remains valid even if algorithm A is only (ϵ,δ)-differential private for

$$\delta \leq \tfrac{1}{8}e^{-8\alpha\epsilon m}(1-e^{-\epsilon}). \tag{5}$$

To see this, note that inequality (3) changes to

$$\begin{aligned}
&\Pr_A\left[A(\vec{0})\in G\right] \geq \\
&\geq \left(\left(\left(\Pr_A[A(S)\in G]\cdot e^{-\epsilon} - \delta\right)e^{-\epsilon} - \delta\right)\cdots\right)e^{-\epsilon} - \delta \\
&\geq \frac{1}{4}e^{-8\alpha\epsilon m} - \delta\left(\sum_{i=0}^{8\alpha m-1} e^{-i\epsilon}\right) \\
&\geq \frac{1}{4}e^{-8\alpha\epsilon m} - \delta\left(\frac{1}{1-e^{-\epsilon}}\right) \geq \frac{1}{8}e^{-8\alpha\epsilon m}.
\end{aligned}$$

The rest of the proof remains almost intact (only minor changes in the constants). With that in mind, we see that the lower bound showed in Theorem 3.15 for ϵ-differentially private (that is, with $\delta = 0$) learners also applies for (ϵ,δ)-differentially private learners satisfying inequality (5). That is, every such learner for a class $\mathcal{C}$ must use $\Omega\left(\frac{\mathrm{RepDim}(\mathcal{C})}{\alpha\epsilon}\right)$ samples.

When using (ϵ,δ)-differential privacy, δ should be negligible in the security parameter, that is, in d – the representation length of elements in X_d. Therefore, using (ϵ,δ)-differential privacy instead of ϵ-differential privacy cannot reduce the sample complexity for PPAC learning a concept class $\mathcal{C}$ whenever $\mathrm{RepDim}(\mathcal{C}) = O(\log(d))$.

6.2 Probabilistic Representation Using a Hypothesis Class

We will now consider a generalization of our representation notations that can be useful when considering PPAC learners that use a specific hypothesis class. In particular, those notation can be useful when considering proper-PPAC learners, that is, a learner that learns a class $\mathcal{C}$ using a hypothesis class $\mathcal{B} \subseteq \mathcal{C}$.

DEFINITION 6.1. *We define the α-Deterministic Representation Dimension of a concept class $\mathcal{C}$ using a hypothesis* *class $\mathcal{B}$ as*

$$\mathrm{DRepDim}_\alpha(\mathcal{C},\mathcal{B}) = \min\left\{ \mathrm{size}(\mathcal{H}) : \begin{array}{c} \mathcal{H}\subseteq\mathcal{B} \textit{ is an} \\ \alpha\textit{-representation} \\ \textit{for class } \mathcal{C} \end{array}\right\}.$$

Note that $\mathrm{DRepDim}_{\frac{1}{4}}(\mathcal{C}, 2^{X_d}) = \mathrm{DRepDim}(\mathcal{C})$. The dependency on α in the above definition is necessary: if $\mathcal{C}$ is not contained in $\mathcal{B}$ then for every small enough α, the hypothesis class $\mathcal{B}$ itself does not α-represents $\mathcal{C}$ (and therefore no subset $\mathcal{H} \subseteq \mathcal{B}$ can α-represent $\mathcal{C}$). Moreover, when considering the notations of representation using a hypothesis class, our boosting technique for α does not work (as the boosting uses more complex hypotheses).

Example 6.2. *Beimel et al. [3] showed that for every $\alpha < 1$, every subset $\mathcal{H} \subsetneq$ $\mathtt{POINT}_d$ does not α-represent the class $\mathtt{POINT}_d$. Therefore,* $\mathrm{DRepDim}_\alpha(\mathtt{POINT}_d, \mathtt{POINT}_d) = \theta(d)$ *for every $\alpha < 1$.*

Definition 6.3. *A pair $(\mathscr{H}, \mathcal{P})$ is an (α,β)-probabilistic representation for a concept class C using a hypothesis class $\mathcal{B}$ if:*

1. *$(\mathscr{H}, \mathcal{P})$ is an (α,β)-probabilistic representation for the class C, as formulated in Definition 3.5.*
2. *Every $\mathcal{H}_i \in \mathscr{H}$ is a subset of $\mathcal{B}$.*

Note that whenever $\mathcal{B} = 2^{X_d}$, this definition is identical to Definition 3.5. Using this general notation, we can restate Lemma 3.9 and Lemma 3.12 as follows:

Lemma 6.4. *If there exists a pair $(\mathscr{H}, \mathcal{P})$ that (α,β)- probabilistically represents a class $\mathcal{C}$ using a hypothesis class $\mathcal{B}$, then for every ϵ and every γ there exists an algorithm A that $(\alpha+\gamma, 3\beta, \epsilon)$-PPAC learns $\mathcal{C}$ using $\mathcal{B}$ and a sample size $m = O((\mathrm{size}(\mathscr{H}) + \ln(\frac{1}{\beta}))\max\{\frac{1}{\gamma\epsilon}, \frac{1}{\gamma^2}\})$.*

Note that in the above lemma the resulting algorithm A has accuracy $(\alpha+\gamma)$ as opposed to 6α in lemma 3.9, where γ is arbitrary. While in section 3 we did not mind the multiplicative factor of 6 in the accuracy parameter (as we could boost it back), replacing it with an additive factor of γ might be of value in this section as our boosting technique for the accuracy parameter does not work here. As an example, consider a representation with $\alpha = \frac{1}{10}$. Without boosting capabilities, this change makes the difference between the ability to generate an algorithm with $\alpha = \frac{6}{10}$, or an algorithm with $\alpha = \frac{1}{10} + \frac{1}{1000}$.

Lemma 6.5. *If there exists an algorithm A that $(\alpha, \frac{1}{2}, \epsilon)$-PPAC learns a concept class $\mathcal{C}$ using a hypothesis class $\mathcal{B}$ and a sample size m, then there exists a pair $(\mathscr{H}, \mathcal{P})$ that $(\alpha, 1/4)$-probabilistically represents the class $\mathcal{C}$ using the hypothesis class $\mathcal{B}$ where* $\mathrm{size}(\mathscr{H}) = O(m\epsilon)$.

Definition 6.6. *We define the α-Probabilistic Representation Dimension of a concept class $\mathcal{C}$ using a hypothesis class $\mathcal{B}$ as*

$$\mathrm{RepDim}_\alpha(\mathcal{C},\mathcal{B}) = \min\left\{ \mathrm{size}(\mathscr{H}) : \begin{array}{c} \exists\mathcal{P} \textit{ s.t. } (\mathscr{H},\mathcal{P}) \\ \textit{is an } (\alpha,\frac{1}{4})\textit{-prob.} \\ \textit{representation} \\ \textit{for } \mathcal{C} \textit{ using } \mathcal{B} \end{array}\right\}.$$

Example 6.7. *Beimel et al. [3] showed that for every $\alpha < 1$, every proper-PPAC learner for $\mathtt{POINT}_d$ requires $\Omega((d + \log(1/\beta))/(\epsilon\alpha))$ labled examples. Using Lemma 6.4, we get that* $\mathrm{RepDim}_\alpha(\mathtt{POINT}_d, \mathtt{POINT}_d) = \Omega(d)$.

We still do not know the relation between the representation dimension of a concept class and its VC dimension. However, the above example shows a strong separation between the VC dimension of the class $\mathtt{POINT}_d$ and $\mathrm{RepDim}_\alpha(\mathtt{POINT}_d, \mathtt{POINT}_d)$.

7. A PROBABILISTIC REPRESENTATION FOR POINTS

Example 3.6 states the existence of a constant size probabilistic representation for the class $\mathtt{POINT}_d$. We now give the construction.

Claim 7.1. *There exists an (α,β)-probabilistic representation for $\mathtt{POINT}_d$ of* size $\ln(4/\alpha) + \ln\ln(1/\beta)$. *Furthermore, each hypothesis h in each $\mathcal{H}_i$ has a short description and given x, the value $h(x)$ can be computed efficiently.*

Proof. Consider the following set of hypothesis classes

$$\mathscr{H} = \left\{ \mathcal{H} \subseteq 2^{X_d} \; : \; |\mathcal{H}| \le \frac{4}{\alpha}\ln(\frac{1}{\beta}) \right\}.$$

That is, $\mathcal{H} \in \mathscr{H}$ if $\mathcal{H}$ contains at most $\frac{4}{\alpha}\ln(\frac{1}{\beta})$ boolean functions. We will show an appropriate distribution $\mathcal{P}$ s.t. $(\mathscr{H}, \mathcal{P})$ is an (α,β)-probabilistic representation of the class $\mathtt{POINT}_d$. To this end, fix a target concept $c_j \in \mathtt{POINT}_d$ and a distribution $\mathcal{D}$ on X_d (remember that j is the unique point on which $c_j(j) = 1$). We need to show how to randomly choose an $\mathcal{H} \in_R \mathscr{H}$ such that with probability at least $(1-\beta)$ over the choice of $\mathcal{H}$, there will be at least one $h \in \mathcal{H}$ such that $\mathrm{error}_\mathcal{D}(c_j, h) \le \alpha$. Consider the following process for randomly choosing an $\mathcal{H} \in \mathscr{H}$:

> 1. Denote $M = \frac{4}{\alpha}\ln(\frac{1}{\beta})$
> 2. For $i = 1, \ldots, M$ construct hypothesis h_i as follows:
>   For each $x \in X_d$ (independently):
>   Let $h_i(x) = 1$ with probability $\alpha/2$,
>   and $h_i(x) = 0$ otherwise.
> 3. Return $\mathcal{H} = \{h_1, h_2, \ldots, h_M\}$.

The above process induces a distribution on $\mathscr{H}$, denoted as $\mathcal{P}$. We will next analyze the probability that the returned $\mathcal{H}$ does not contain an α-good hypothesis. We start by fixing some i and analyzing the expected error of h_i, conditioned on the event that $h_i(j) = 1$. The probability is taken over the random coins used to construct h_i.

$$\mathop{\mathbb{E}}_{h_i}\left[\mathrm{error}_\mathcal{D}(c_j, h_i) \;\middle|\; h_i(j) = 1\right] =$$

$$= \mathop{\mathbb{E}}_{h_i}\left[\mathop{\mathbb{E}}_{x\in\mathcal{D}}\left[|c_j(x) - h_i(x)|\right] \;\middle|\; h_i(j) = 1\right]$$

$$= \mathop{\mathbb{E}}_{x\in\mathcal{D}}\left[\mathop{\mathbb{E}}_{h_i}\left[|c_j(x) - h_i(x)| \;\middle|\; h_i(j) = 1\right]\right] \le \frac{\alpha}{2}.$$

Using Markov's Inequality,

$$\Pr_{h_i}\left[\mathrm{error}_\mathcal{D}(c_j, h_i) \ge \alpha \;\middle|\; h_i(j) = 1\right] \le \frac{1}{2}.$$

So, the probability that h_i is α-good for c_j and $\mathcal{D}$ is:

$$\Pr_{h_i}[\mathrm{error}_{\mathcal{D}}(c_j,h_i)\le\alpha]\ge$$

$$\ge\Pr_{h_i}[h_i(j)=1]\cdot\Pr_{h_i}\left[\mathrm{error}_{\mathcal{D}}(c_j,h_i)\le\alpha\;\middle|\;h_i(j)=1\right]$$

$$\ge\frac{\alpha}{2}\cdot\frac{1}{2}=\frac{\alpha}{4}.$$

Thus, the probability that $\mathcal{H}$ fails to contain an α-good hypothesis is at most $(1-\frac{\alpha}{4})^M$, which is less than β for our choice of M. This concludes the proof that $(\mathscr{H},\mathcal{P})$ is an (α,β)-probabilistic representation for $\mathtt{POINT}_d$.

When a hypothesis $h_i()$ was constructed in the above random process, the value of $h_i(x)$ was independently drawn for every $x\in X_d$. This results in a hypothesis whose description size is $O(2^d)$, which in turn, will result in a non efficient learning algorithm. We next construct hypotheses whose description is short. To achieve this goal, we note that in the above analysis we only care about the probability that $h_i(x)=0$ given that $h_i(j)=1$. Thus, we can choose the values of h_i in a pairwise independent way, e.g., using a random polynomial of degree 2. The size of the description in this case is $O(d)$. □

OBSERVATION 7.2. *Consider the class* $\mathtt{POINT}_{\mathbb{N}}$*, defined in Example 3.11. The above construction can be adjusted to yield an (inefficient) improper private learner for* $\mathtt{POINT}_{\mathbb{N}}$ *with* $O_{\alpha,\beta,\epsilon}(1)$ *samples. The only adjustments necessary are in the construction of the* (α,β)*-probabilistic representation. Specifically, we need to specify how to randomly draw a boolean function* h *over the natural numbers, such that for every* $x\in\mathbb{N}$ *the probability of* $h(x)=1$ *is* $\alpha/2$*, and the values of* h *on every two distinct points in* $\mathbb{N}$ *are independent. This can be done easily, as a random real number could be interpreted as a random function over* $\mathbb{N}$.

8. REFERENCES

[1] A. Beimel, H. Brenner, S. P. Kasiviswanathan, and K. Nissim. Bounds on the sample complexity for private learning and private data release. Full version of [3], in submition, 2012.

[2] A. Beimel, P. Carmi, K. Nissim, and E. Weinreb. Private approximation of search problems. *SIAM J. Comput.*, 38(5):1728–1760, 2008.

[3] A. Beimel, S. P. Kasiviswanathan, and K. Nissim. Bounds on the sample complexity for private learning and private data release. In *7th Theory of Cryptography Conference*, pages 437–454, 2010.

[4] A. Blum, C. Dwork, F. McSherry, and K. Nissim. Practical privacy: The SuLQ framework. In *PODS*, pages 128–138. ACM, 2005.

[5] A. Blum, K. Ligett, and A. Roth. A learning theory approach to non-interactive database privacy. In *STOC*, pages 609–618. ACM, 2008.

[6] A. Blumer, A. Ehrenfeucht, D. Haussler, and M. K. Warmuth. Learnability and the Vapnik-Chervonenkis dimension. *Journal of the Association for Computing Machinery*, 36(4):929–965, 1989.

[7] K. Chaudhuri and D. Hsu. Sample complexity bounds for differentially private learning. *Journal of Machine Learning Research - COLT 2011 Proceedings*, 19:155–186, 2011.

[8] H. Chernoff. A measure of asymptotic efficiency for tests of a hypothesis based on the sum of observations. *Ann. Math. Statist.*, 23:493–507, 1952.

[9] C. Dwork. The differential privacy frontier. In O. Reingold, editor, *TCC*, volume 5444 of *LNCS*, pages 496–502. Springer, 2009.

[10] C. Dwork. A firm foundation for private data analysis. *Commun. of the ACM*, 54(1):86–95, 2011.

[11] C. Dwork, F. McSherry, K. Nissim, and A. Smith. Calibrating noise to sensitivity in private data analysis. In S. Halevi and T. Rabin, editors, *TCC*, volume 3876 of *LNCS*, pages 265–284. Springer, 2006.

[12] C. Dwork, G. N. Rothblum, and S. P. Vadhan. Boosting and differential privacy. In *51th Annual IEEE Symposium on Foundations of Computer Science*, pages 51–60, 2010.

[13] A. Ehrenfeucht, D. Haussler, M. J. Kearns, and L. G. Valiant. A general lower bound on the number of examples needed for learning. *Inf. Comput.*, 82(3):247–261, 1989.

[14] Y. Freund and R. E. Schapire. A decision-theoretic generalization of on-line learning and an application to boosting. *Journal of Computer and System Sciences*, 55(1):119 – 139, 1997.

[15] W. Hoeffding. Probability inequalities for sums of bounded random variables. *Journal of the American Statistical Association*, 58(301):13–30, 1963.

[16] S. P. Kasiviswanathan, H. K. Lee, K. Nissim, S. Raskhodnikova, and A. Smith. What can we learn privately? In *48th Annual IEEE Symposium on Foundations of Computer Science*, pages 531–540. IEEE Computer Society, 2008.

[17] F. McSherry and K. Talwar. Mechanism design via differential privacy. In *48th Annual IEEE Symposium on Foundations of Computer Science*, pages 94–103. IEEE, 2007.

[18] R. E. Schapire. The strength of weak learnability. *Mach. Learn.*, 5(2):197–227, 1990.

[19] L. G. Valiant. A theory of the learnable. *Communications of the ACM*, 27:1134–1142, 1984.

[20] V. N. Vapnik and A. Y. Chervonenkis. On the uniform convergence of relative frequencies of events to their probabilities. *Theory of Probability and its Applications*, 16:264, 1971.

Barriers in Cryptography with Weak, Correlated and Leaky Sources

Daniel Wichs
IBM Research, T.J. Watson Center
1101 Kitchawan Rd
Yorktown Heights, NY 10598
wichs@cs.nyu.edu

ABSTRACT

There has been much recent progress in constructing cryptosystems that maintain their security without requiring uniform randomness and perfect secrecy. These schemes are motivated by a diverse set of problems such as providing resilience to side-channel *leakage*, using *weak physical sources* of randomness as secret keys, and allowing *deterministic encryption* for high-entropy messages.

Nevertheless, despite this progress, some basic and seemingly achievable security properties have eluded our reach. For example, we are unable to prove the security of basic tools for manipulating weak/leaky random sources, such as as *pseudo-entropy generators* and *seed-dependent computational condensers*. We also do not know how to prove leakage-resilient security of any cryptosystem with a *uniquely determined* secret key. In the context of deterministic encryption we do not have a standard-model constructions achieving the strongest notion of security proposed by Bellare, Boldyreva and O'Neill (CRYPTO '07), that would allow us to encrypt arbitrarily correlated messages of sufficiently large individual entropy.

We provide broad black-box separation results, showing that the security of such primitives cannot be proven under virtually *any* standard cryptographic hardness assumption via a reduction that treats the adversary as a *black box*. We do so by formalizing the intuition that "the only way that a reduction can simulate the correctly distributed view for an attacker is to know all the secrets, in which case it does not learn anything useful from the attack". Such claims are often misleading and clever way of getting around them allow us to achieve a wealth of positive results with imperfect/leaky randomness. However, in this work we show that this intuition can be formalized and that it indeed presents a real barrier for the examples given above.

Categories and Subject Descriptors

F.0 [**Theory of Computation**]: General

General Terms

Theory

Keywords

Cryptography, Black-Box Seperation

1. INTRODUCTION

We look at several related scenarios involving imperfect randomness and secrecy. Although the motivation behind studying these scenarios differs greatly from one to another, the technical means of achieving and analyzing security are strikingly similar between them.

LEAKAGE-RESILIENT CRYPTOGRAPHY. Motivated by the prevalence of various physical *side-channel attacks*, the study of leakage-resilient cryptography strives to construct cryptosystems that maintain their security even if the attacker can observe some partial leakage related to the secret key of the cryptosystem. By now, many different formal models of leakage-resilience have been proposed in the literature – see e.g., [ISW03, MR04, DP08, AGV09, DHLW10a, BKKV10, GR12] and references therein. Perhaps the most basic model, sometimes also called the *bounded-leakage or memory-leakage model* was proposed by Akavia, Goldwasser and Vaikuntanathan [AGV09]. This model allows the attacker to learn any adversarially chosen information about the secret key, as long as the amount of information is not too large. More specifically, a cryptosystem is *ℓ-leakage-resilient*, if its security is maintained even if the attacker can choose any efficient *leakage function* $\mathsf{Leak} : \{0,1\}^* \to \{0,1\}^\ell$ and gets to observe the resulting value $\mathsf{Leak}(sk)$. In the past few years, we have seen a vast number of positive results (e.g., [AGV09, ADW09a, NS09, KV09, ADN$^+$10, GKPV10, BG10, DHLW10b, BSW11, BHK11, HL11] etc.) showing how to construct many such leakage resilient schemes including encryption, signatures and various related primitives, under various (standard) computational assumptions.

CRYPTOGRAPHY WITH WEAK SOURCES. The study of cryptography with *weak randomness* aims to build cryptosystems whose security is maintained even if their secret keys are chosen from some efficiently samplable but otherwise unspecified/adversarial distribution of sufficient min-entropy. This can model various physical sources whose distributions are complex and we know little about them (e.g., password or biometrics). The connection between weak and leaky randomness can be made formal in the information-theoretic setting: conditioned on ℓ-bits of leakage, a uniformly random source can loose at most ℓ bits of entropy. However, such connections are lost in the computational setting since, even if a leakage function is efficiently computable, the distribution of secret keys conditioned on some fixed leakage may not be efficiently samplable. Nevertheless, most of the known positive results for leakage-resilient cryptography do also carry over to the setting of weak randomness.

DETERMINISTIC ENCRYPTION AND CORRELATED SOURCES. The issue of imperfect randomness also occurs in the context of *deterministic encryption* [BBO07, BFOR08, BFO08, BS11, FOR12]. In such encryption schemes, we assume that the messages being encrypted already contain some reasonable amount of entropy, allowing us to make the encryption procedure itself deterministic without sacrificing security. The original work of Bellare, Boldyreva and O'Neill [BBO07], which introduced deterministic encryption, suggested that such schemes should be able to securely encrypt multiple distinct messages that come from any arbitrarily correlated distribution, as long as each message individually has sufficient entropy. A corresponding scheme satisfying this notion was then constructed in the *random oracle model*, and achieving this notion in the standard model was left as a major open question. Subsequent works showed how to realize a *weaker* notions of security in the standard model, by assuming that each message contains some fresh entropy conditioned on all others, but the question of achieving the strongest notion of security remains open. Similar issues of maintaining security under correlated random inputs also come up in several related contexts [RS09, HLO10, GOR11] that do not explicitly deal with deterministic encryption.

1.1 The "Paradox" of Cryptography with Imperfect Randomness

One of the challenges in proving the security of cryptosystems with imperfect (weak/leaky/correlated) sources is having the reduction generate a correctly distributed view for the attacker. Let us look at a simple case study, using the notion of "*leakage resilient one-way functions*" as an example. Such a function f should have the property that, if we choose x at random and give the attacker $y = f(x)$, then it should be hard for the attacker to find a preimage $x' \in f^{-1}(y)$, *even* if the attacker can observe some arbitrary (but sufficiently short) leakage $\mathsf{Leak}(x)$ about the input x. Now imagine we have some candidate construction f and want to prove it secure via a *reduction* from some hard problem. Then the reduction needs to run the attacker and give it a correctly distributed pair $(y, \mathsf{Leak}(x))$. But, it seems that the only way for the reduction to generate a pair of this form is to *already* know x, in which case there is seemingly no point in running the attacker, since it won't yield anything new that the reduction doesn't already know! Similar issues appear to come up in cryptography with weak/correlated sources, where the only way for the reduction to ensure that the attacker gets correctly distributed view is to seemingly just sample all of the secrets itself, in which case the attacker won't produce anything useful that the reduction doesn't already know. We call the above intuition the *"useless attacker paradox"*.

OVERCOMING THE PARADOX. Of course, the above paradox is not very formal (as highlighted by the excessive use of the word "seemingly"), and fortunately breaks down on deeper scrutiny. For example, in the case of leakage-resilient one-way functions, even if the reduction produces a correctly distributed pair $(y, \mathsf{Leak}(x))$ by choosing x on its own, the attacker may respond with some other preimage $x' \neq x$, which may not be known to the reduction. Indeed, this loophole can be turned into a positive result, showing that any collision-resistant (and even just second-preimage resistant) function f is already a leakage-resilient one-way function (see e.g., [ADW09b]). In general, the process of explicitly considering the "useless attacker paradox" and seeing where it may break down, is often a good way to arrive at many of the positive results in this area.

FORMALIZING THE PARADOX IN SPECIAL CASES. Nevertheless, despite the success of cryptographic constructions in overcoming the seeming paradox in many cases, there are several important primitives which have eluded the grasp of provably secure constructions so far. In this work, we examine and formalize the "useless attacker paradox" and show that it indeed does present a real barrier in these important instances. For example, returning to our case-study of leakage-resilient one-way functions, let us add an additional requirement that the function f is *injective*. Then, for any given y, there is a unique value $\mathsf{Leak}(x)$ that the attacker expects to see and a unique x that the attacker will produce. Therefore the reduction really is stuck: either it doesn't know x, in which case it will not be able to provide a correctly distributed leakage $\mathsf{Leak}(x)$ to the attacker, or it does know x, in which case the attacker's unique output is useless. In this work we manage to formalize such intuition into a broad *black-box separation result* for several important primitives as highlighted below.

1.2 Our Results

SIMULATABLE ATTACKERS ARE USELESS. Our first result is to formalize the "useless attacker paradox". We say that an *inefficient* attack $\mathcal{A}$ against some cryptographic scheme is *simulatable* if there exists an *efficient* simulator Sim such that getting oracle access to $\mathcal{A}$ is indistinguishable from getting oracle access to Sim. Notice tat the mere existence of an inefficient attack against a cryptographic scheme is usually not interesting or surprising, but the existence of a *simulatable* attack turns out to have an interesting consequence. In particular, we show that the existence of a simulatable attack against some scheme implies that the security of the scheme cannot be proven via a *black-box reduction* from a large class of assumptions modeled as *cryptographic games* between an attacker and challenger. This captures essentially all standard assumptions in cryptography (factoring, CDH, DDH, RSA, LWE etc.).

The intuition is simple - anything a reduction could do with the help of $\mathcal{A}$, it could do efficiently on its own by running Sim. More concretely, assume that some `scheme` has a simulatable attack $\mathcal{A}$ with corresponding simulator Sim, and that there is a black-box reduction $\mathcal{R}$ proving the security of this `scheme` based on some `assumption`. Then the reduction $\mathcal{R}^{\mathcal{A}}$ must be able to use oracle access to $\mathcal{A}$ to break the security of the `assumption`. But since $\mathcal{A}$ and Sim are indistinguishable, there is also an efficient attack $\mathcal{R}^{\mathsf{Sim}}$ that breaks the security of the `assumption` efficiently, contradicting its hardness.

Notice that this type of a black-box separation shows that the security of a *concrete scheme* cannot be proven from a large class of *concrete assumptions* via a reduction that *treats the attacker as a black box.* This is different from most black-box separations in the literature (e.g., [IR89, Sim98, GKM$^+$00, GMR01, RTV04]) which show that some *target primitive* (e.g., key-agreement) cannot be constructed from an *arbitrary instance of some source primitive* (e.g., a one-way function) if the *construction treats the source primitive as a black box.* Several prior black box separations in the literature [DOP05, HH09, GW11, Pas11, DHT12] for completely unrelated notions have the same flavor as the one in this work and rely on a similar notion of a "simulatable attack". One of the contributions of this work is to abstract out this useful technique.

SIMULATABLE ATTACKS FOR IMPERFECT RANDOMNESS. At first, it may seem that the existence of an inefficient simulatable attack $\mathcal{A}$ against some $\mathtt{scheme}$ would simply imply that the $\mathtt{scheme}$ is insecure – if the inefficient $\mathcal{A}$ breaks the security of the $\mathtt{scheme}$ and Sim is indistinguishable from $\mathcal{A}$, then the efficient simulator Sim should also break the security of the $\mathtt{scheme}$. Indeed, the above holds for all schemes whose security can itself be modeled as a cryptographic game. However, this is not the case for the security definitions involving leakage or imperfect randomness that we consider in this work.

For example, in the case of leakage, a valid attacker $\mathcal{A}$ is required to consist of two independent (non-communicating) components $\mathcal{A} = (\mathsf{Leak}, \mathsf{Break})$ and the security game consists of *two stages*: in the first stage the attacker generates leakage $z = \mathsf{Leak}(sk)$ on the secret key sk, and in the second stage the attacker Break attempts to break security (e.g., invert a one-way function of sk) given the leakage z. The attacker $\mathcal{A}$ cannot keep any state in between these two stages. The simulator Sim simulating $\mathcal{A}$, however, may not satisfy these structural requirements of the definition - it is allowed to simulate queries to Leak and Break in a coordinated manner while keeping some state. In other words, the efficient simulator Sim will not have the structure of a valid attack on leakage-resilient security of the scheme and therefore does not contradict its security. A similar phenomenon occurs in security definitions involving weak/correlated sources of randomness, where an attacker $\mathcal{A} = (\mathsf{Sam}, \mathsf{Break})$ consists of two independent components: a sampling algorithm Sam that defines some adversarial distribution and a Break component which attempts to break security when the secrets are sampled according to Sam.

It is precisely because the security definitions involving imperfect sources of randomness consist of multi-stage games with multi-component attackers $\mathcal{A}$, that makes them *different* from standard *cryptographic game* assumptions (e.g., DDH, RSA, LWE etc.) and gives us the opportunity to prove such broad black-box separations.[1] Note that by describing the attacker as consisting of two independent components in a multi-stage game, we are assuming that a black-box reduction treats both components – including the leakage function or the adversarial distribution – as a black box. This type of reduction was also called a *strongly* black-box reduction in the work of [HH09], but we can really think of it as the natural notion of a black-box reduction when dealing with a multi-component attacker.

[1]This distinction between security definitions involving multi-stage and single-stage games is also prominent in the work of [RSS11] in the context of indifferentiabiliy.

PRIMITIVES WITH SIMULATABLE ATTACKS. Our main result is to look at several cryptographic primitives involving imperfect randomness and show that *every* candidate scheme for these primitives has a simulatable attack against it. Therefore, there is no instantiation of these primitives that can be proven secure via a black-box reduction from any cryptographic game assumption. Our results fall into three categories.

***Unique Witnesses*:** We begin by considering *one-way relations with unique witnesses*, which generalizes the example of injective one-way functions and cryptosystems (encryption, signature etc.) where every public key has a unique secret key. We show that there is always an inefficient simulatable attack against *leakage-resilient one-wayness* of such relations when the attacker can observe leakage of super-logarithmic size, and therefore one cannot prove the leakage-resilient security of such schemes via black-box reductions from standard assumptions. Similar separations also apply to security with *weak randomness* in place of leakage-resilience.

***Deterministic Encryption, Correlated Inputs*:** We also consider a strong notion of deterministic encryption from Bellare et al. [BBO07], which allows us to deterministically encrypt distinct messages $m_1, \ldots, m_t$ chosen from any distribution that places sufficient entropy on each individual m_i, but otherwise allows the messages to be arbitrarily correlated. The definition of security aims to ensure that the ciphertexts $c_i = \mathsf{Enc}_{pk}(m_i)$ do not reveal essentially any information about the messages. The work of [BBO07] gives a construction of this strong security notion in the random oracle model. Subsequent works [BFOR08, BFO08, BS11, FOR12] were only able to achieve a weaker security notion, where each message m_i must have fresh entropy conditioned on all the others. Here, we focus on the strong notion of security where the messages can be arbitrarily correlated, and we show a simulatable-attack against this notion for any candidate scheme, thus deriving a broad black-box separation result. In fact, our result generalizes to any function family $\{f_{pk}\}$ (even one without a decryption trapdoor), and shows black-box impossibility of proving the one-wayness of $(f_{pk}(m_1), \ldots, f_{pk}(m_t))$ when the distinct inputs $m_1, \ldots, m_t$ can come from an arbitrarily correlated distribution, even if each individual value m_i has high entropy.

***Entropy Generation and Condensation*:** Lastly, we consider basic tools for manipulating entropy of weak/leaky sources. The first such tool is a *pseudo-entropy generator* which takes a random seed x from a weak or leaky distribution and outputs a longer value $y = \mathsf{PEG}(x)$ such that the computational entropy of y is greater than that of x. This tool is used as a building block in several leakage-resilient primitives and was initially explored by Dziembowski and Pietrzak [DP08]. The second such tool is a (seed-dependent) *condenser* which takes a value x from a weak distribution and outputs a shorter value $y = \mathsf{Cond}(x)$ such that the entropy-loss of y (the difference between the length of y and its entropy) is smaller than that of x. This tool was explored in the recent work of Dodis et al. [DRV12]. The only known constructions of these primitives require exponential hardness assumptions and we show that this is necessary under black-box reductions.

2. PRELIMINARIES

NOTATION. Let n be the security parameter. A function $\mu(n)$ is negligible, denoted $\mu(n) = \mathsf{negl}(n)$, if $\mu(n) = 1/n^{\omega(1)}$. We also use $\mathsf{poly}(n)$ to denote $n^{O(1)}$. If X is a probability distribution or a random variable then $x \leftarrow X$ denotes the process of sampling a value x at random according to X. If S is a set then $s \xleftarrow{\$} S$ denotes sampling s according to the *uniformly random* distribution over the set S. We let $[n]$ denote the set $\{1, \ldots, n\}$.

ENTROPY. The *min-entropy* of a random variable X is $\mathbf{H}_\infty(X) \stackrel{\text{def}}{=} -\log(\max_x \Pr[X = x])$. This is a standard notion of entropy used in cryptography, since it measures the worst-case predictability of X. We often find it useful to work with a generalized version of min-entropy, called *average conditional min-entropy*, defined by[DORS08] as

$$\begin{aligned}\mathbf{H}_\infty(X|Z) &\stackrel{\text{def}}{=} -\log\left(\mathop{\mathbf{E}}_{z\leftarrow Z}\left[\ \max_x \Pr[X = x|Z = z]\ \right]\right)\\ &= -\log\left(\mathop{\mathbf{E}}_{z\leftarrow Z}\left[2^{-\mathbf{H}_\infty(X|Z=z)}\right]\right)\end{aligned}$$

This measures the best guess for X by an adversary that may observe an *average-case* correlated variable Z. That is, for all (inefficient) functions $\mathcal{A}$, we have $\Pr[\mathcal{A}(Z) = X] \le 2^{-\mathbf{H}_\infty(X|Z)}$ and there exists some $\mathcal{A}$ which achieves equality. The following lemma says that conditioning on ℓ bits of information, the min-entropy drops by at most ℓ bits.

LEMMA 2.1 ([DORS08]). *Let X, Y be random variables where Y takes on values in a set of size at most 2^ℓ. Then $\mathbf{H}_\infty(X|Y) \ge \mathbf{H}_\infty(X) - \ell$.*

3. CRYPTOGRAPHIC GAMES AND BLACK-BOX REDUCTIONS

CRYPTOGRAPHIC GAMES. We begin by defining a general notion of cryptographic games between a challenger and an attacker. Cryptographic games are used to capture the security requirements of most cryptographic primitives, as well as to define the standard hardness assumptions that we rely on in cryptography.

DEFINITION 3.1 ([HH09]). *A cryptographic game $\mathcal{G} = (\Gamma, c)$ is defined by a (possibly inefficient) random system Γ, called the* challenger, *and a constant $c \in [0, 1)$. On security parameter n, the challenger $\Gamma(1^n)$ interacts with some attacker $\mathcal{A}(1^n)$ and outputs a bit b. We denote this interaction by $b = (\mathcal{A}(1^n) \leftrightarrows \Gamma(1^n))$. The* advantage *of an attacker $\mathcal{A}$ in the game $\mathcal{G}$ is defined as*

$$\mathbf{Adv}^{\mathcal{A}}_{\mathcal{G}}(n) \stackrel{def}{=} \Pr[\ (\mathcal{A}(1^n) \leftrightarrows \Gamma(1^n)) = 1\ ] - c.$$

A cryptographic game $\mathcal{G}$ is secure *if for all* PPT *attackers $\mathcal{A}$, the advantage $\mathbf{Adv}^{\mathcal{A}}_{\mathcal{G}}(n)$ is negligible.*

We say that a (possibly inefficient) attacker $\mathcal{A}$ *successfully breaks the security of $\mathcal{G}$* if the advantage $\mathbf{Adv}_{\mathcal{G}}(\mathcal{A})$ is *not* negligible. When $c = 0$, the above definition of cryptographic games captures *search problems* such as the one-way hardness of factoring, the discrete logarithm problem, etc. When $c = \frac{1}{2}$, it captures *decisional problems* such as DDH. Note that cryptographic games may be highly interactive and may not even have any a-priori bound on the number of rounds of interaction between $\mathcal{A}, \Gamma$. For example, the security of RSA signatures when instantiated with some concrete hash function family would qualify as a cryptographic game assumption. Lastly, we mention that the work of [GW11] defined a more restricted notion of cryptographic games (called "falsifiable assumptions") where the challenger is also required to be efficient. We do *not* rely on this requirement in the current work. Essentially all common assumptions used in cryptography fall under the framework of cryptographic games.

We define a cryptographic game $\mathcal{G}$ to be *δ-exponentially secure* for some constant $\delta > 0$ if for all $\mathcal{A}(1^n)$ running in time $2^{O(n^\delta)}$ the advantage $\mathbf{Adv}^{\mathcal{A}}_{\mathcal{G}}(n) = 2^{-\Omega(n^\delta)}$.

CRYPTOGRAPHIC SECURITY PROPERTIES BEYOND GAMES. The above definition captures most standard cryptographic security notions. However, not all cryptographic properties can be defined via the above template. For example, various definitions involving leakage resilience and weak randomness consider an attacker that consists of two independent (non-communicating) components rather than a single monolithic attacker as needed for cryptographic games. In addition, they can make additional restriction, such as requiring that the adversary defines a distribution of high min-entropy, which cannot easily be checked by a challenger. Therefore, we also give a very general definition of an arbitrary *cryptographic property* $\mathcal{C}$ as a mapping which assigns to each attacker $\mathcal{A}$ some real number $\mathbf{Adv}^{\mathcal{A}}_{\mathcal{C}}(n)$ indicating how successful $\mathcal{A}$ is in breaking the property. We say that $\mathcal{C}$ is secure if for *all* PPT attackers $\mathcal{A}$, the advantage $\mathbf{Adv}^{\mathcal{A}}_{\mathcal{C}}(n)$ is negligible in the security parameter. Although this definition is very general, and most security properties of this type are not very meaningful, it captures several useful notions which we can't easily capture by cryptographic games. In this work, we will only consider several concrete and meaningful instances of "cryptgoraphic properties" involving leakage-resilience and weak/correalated randomness.

BLACK-BOX REDUCTIONS. We now define the concept of a *black-box reduction.* Almost all proofs in cryptography have the form of a black-box reductions and hence this captures a meaningful notion. Since the focus of this work is on black-box separations, we want to define as *weak* of a definition as possible. For simplicity, we will therefore assume that any attacker given to the reduction has advantage $\ge \frac{1}{2}$ (rather than insisting that the reduction works for all attackers with any non-negligible advantage).

DEFINITION 3.2. *Let $\mathcal{C}$ be some cryptographic property and let $\mathcal{G}$ be a cryptographic game. A* black-box reduction *deriving the security of $\mathcal{C}$ from the security of $\mathcal{G}$ is an oracle-access* PPT *machine $\mathcal{B}^{(\cdot)}$ for which there are some constants $c, N_0 > 0$ such that, for all integers $n \ge N_0$ and all (possibly inefficient, non-uniform) oracles $\mathcal{A}_n$ with $\mathbf{Adv}^{\mathcal{A}_n}_{\mathcal{C}}(n) \ge \frac{1}{2}$, we have $\mathbf{Adv}^{\mathcal{B}^{\mathcal{A}_n}}_{\mathcal{G}}(n) \ge n^{-c}$.*
We also define black-box reductions deriving the security of $\mathcal{C}$ from the δ-exponential security of $\mathcal{G}$, by allowing $\mathcal{B}^{(\cdot)}$ to run in time $2^{O(n^\delta)}$ and insisting that $\mathbf{Adv}^{\mathcal{B}^{\mathcal{A}_n}}_{\mathcal{G}}(n) \ge 2^{-o(n^\delta)}$.

Remarks on the Definition: In general, the attacker can be a stateful and interactive machine, in which case a black-box reduction can also use *rewinding access* rather than just *oracle access* to the attacker. However, for the security properties $\mathcal{C}$ considered in this work, the attacker is always (without loss of generality) stateless and hence we will safely ignore the issue of rewinding in this work.

Notice that, although we weaken the definition by insisting that the advantage of that attacker $\mathcal{A}$ given to the reduction is at least a half (for all n), we also do strengthen the definition by insisting that the reduction $\mathcal{B}(1^n)$ has a *noticeable* advantage $\geq n^{-c}$ for *every* large-enough n, rather than just insisting on some *non-negligible* advantage. Furthermore, we assume that on security parameter n, the reduction only queries the attacker $\mathcal{A}_n$ on the *same* security parameter n. This may incur some loss of generality, but all the known reductions in the literature that we are aware of are of this type. In particular, their advantage on every security parameters is related by some fixed polynomial to that of the attacker on the *same* security parameter. A less restrictive definition would say that for any $\mathcal{A}$ with $\mathbf{Adv}_{\mathcal{C}}^{\mathcal{A}}(n) \geq 1/2$ we would have $\mathbf{Adv}_{\mathcal{G}}^{\mathcal{B}^{\mathcal{A}}}(n)$ being non-negligible. Proving separations for the less restrictive definition often introduces many subtleties which detract from the main ideas of the result, but it is relatively easy to extend all our proofs to this less restrictive definition as well.

4. BLACK-BOX SEPARATIONS VIA A SIMULATABLE ATTACK

We now describe a general technique for proving strong black-box separation results. Let $\mathcal{C}$ be some cryptographic property (e.g. the leakage-resilience security of some candidate construction). The main idea of the technique is to construct an inefficient but otherwise valid and successful attacker $\mathcal{A}$ against $\mathcal{C}$, along with an efficient simulator Sim so that no oracle-access machine can distinguish interaction with $\mathcal{A}$ and interaction with Sim. Usually, the efficient simulator is *not* going to be a valid attack against $\mathcal{C}$ since it will fail to satisfy some of the required structure. Therefore, the existence of such attack and simulator does not in-itself show the *insecurity* of $\mathcal{C}$ since the attacker $\mathcal{A}$ is valid but inefficient while the simulator Sim is efficient but not valid. However, it will show the impossibility of a black-box reduction proof of security for $\mathcal{C}$.

DEFINITION 4.1. *A $\varepsilon(n)$-*simulatable attack *on a cryptographic property $\mathcal{C}$ consists of: (1) an ensemble of (possibly inefficient) stateless non-uniform attackers $\{\mathcal{A}_{n,h}\}_{n\in\mathbb{N},h\in\mathcal{H}_n}$ where $\mathcal{H}_n$ are some finite sets, and (2) a stateful* PPT *simulator* Sim. *We require that the following two properties hold:*

- *For each $n \in \mathbb{N}, h \in \mathcal{H}_n$, the (inefficient) attacker $\mathcal{A}_{n,h}$ successfully breaks the security of $\mathcal{C}$ with advantage $\mathbf{Adv}_{\mathcal{C}}^{\mathcal{A}_{n,h}}(n) = 1$.*
- *For every (possibly inefficient) oracle access machine $\mathcal{M}^{(\cdot)}$ making at most $q = q(n)$ queries to its oracle:*

$$\left| \begin{array}{l} \Pr[\mathcal{M}^{\mathcal{A}_{n,h}}(1^n) = 1] \\ -\Pr[\mathcal{M}^{\mathsf{Sim}(1^n)}(1^n) = 1] \end{array} \right| \leq \mathsf{poly}(q(n))\varepsilon(n)$$

where the probability is over $h \xleftarrow{\$} \mathcal{H}_n$ and the random coins of $\mathcal{M}, \mathsf{Sim}$. In other words, oracle access to $\mathcal{A}_{n,h}$ for a random h is indistinguishable from that to Sim.

We omit the $\varepsilon(n)$ and just say "simulatable attack" as shorthand for an $\varepsilon(n)$-simulatable attack with some negligible $\varepsilon(n) = \mathsf{negl}(n)$.

The following theorem shows that the existence of a simulatable attack against some cryptographic notion $\mathcal{C}$ implies that there is no black-box reduction deriving the security of $\mathcal{C}$ from *any* secure cryptographic game $\mathcal{G}$.

THEOREM 4.2. *If there exists a simulatable attack against some cryptographic notion $\mathcal{C}$ and there is a black-box reduction showing the security of $\mathcal{C}$ from the security of some cryptographic game $\mathcal{G}$, then $\mathcal{G}$ is* not *secure. Furthermore, for any constant $\delta > 0$, if there exists an $(\varepsilon(n) = 2^{-\omega(n^\delta)})$-simulatable attack against $\mathcal{C}$ and there is a black-box reduction from the δ-exponential security of $\mathcal{G}$, then $\mathcal{G}$ is* not *δ-exponentially secure.*

PROOF. Let $\mathcal{B}$ be the black-box reduction showing the security of $\mathcal{C}$ from that of $\mathcal{G} = (\Gamma, c)$. Let $\{A_{n,h}\}_{n\in\mathbb{N},h\in\mathcal{H}_n}$ and Sim be the simulatable attack as in Definition 4.1. Then, by the definition of a black-box reduction, there is some polynomial $p(\cdot)$ and some $N_0 \in \mathbb{N}$ such that for every $n \geq N_0$ and all $h \in \mathcal{H}_n$ we have

$$\mathbf{Adv}_{\mathcal{G}}^{\mathcal{B}^{\mathcal{A}_{n,h}}}(n) = \Pr\left[(\mathcal{B}^{\mathcal{A}_{n,h}}(1^n) \leftrightarrows \Gamma(1^n)) = 1\right] - c \geq 1/p(n)$$

where the probability is over the coins of $\mathcal{B}, \Gamma, \mathcal{A}_{n,h}$. Now, since the above holds for all $h \in \mathcal{H}_n$, we can also take the probability over a random h to get:

$$\Pr_{h\leftarrow\mathcal{H}_n}\left[(\mathcal{B}^{\mathcal{A}_{n,h}}(1^n) \leftrightarrows \Gamma(1^n)) = 1\right] - c \geq 1/p(n) \qquad (1)$$

We can now group the reduction $\mathcal{B}$ and the challenger Γ together as a single oracle access machine $\mathcal{M}^{(\cdot)} \stackrel{\text{def}}{=} (\mathcal{B}^{(\cdot)}(1^n) \leftrightarrows \Gamma(1^n))$. Since $\mathcal{B}$ is polynomial-time, there must be some polynomial upper bound $q(n)$ on the number of queries made by $\mathcal{B}$ to its oracle. We use the simulator from Definition 4.1 to get

$$\left| \begin{array}{l} \Pr_{h\xleftarrow{\$}\mathcal{H}_n}\left[(\mathcal{B}^{\mathcal{A}_{n,h}}(1^n) \leftrightarrows \Gamma(1^n)) = 1\right] \\ -\Pr\left[(\mathcal{B}^{\mathsf{Sim}(1^n)}(1^n) \leftrightarrows \Gamma(1^n)) = 1\right] \end{array} \right| \leq \mathsf{negl}(n) \qquad (2)$$

Now, combining equations (1) and (2), we get

$$\begin{aligned} \mathbf{Adv}_{\mathcal{G}}^{\mathcal{B}^{\mathsf{Sim}}}(n) &= \Pr\left[(\mathcal{B}^{\mathsf{Sim}(1^n)}(1^n) \leftrightarrows \Gamma(1^n)) = 1\right] - c \\ &\geq 1/p(n) - \mathsf{negl}(n). \end{aligned}$$

Therefore $\mathcal{B}^{\mathsf{Sim}}$ has non-negligible advantage against the game $\mathcal{G}$. Furthermore, the running time of $\mathcal{B}^{\mathsf{Sim}}$ is polynomial since both $\mathcal{B}$ and Sim are PPT machines. Therefore, there is a polynomial-time attack against $\mathcal{G}$ with a non-negligible advantage.

The second part of the argument for δ-exponential security goes the same way by replacing the *polynomial* $p(n)$ with $p(n) = 2^{o(n^\delta)}$ the value $\mathsf{negl}(n)$ with

$$q(n)\varepsilon(n) \leq 2^{O(n^\delta)}2^{-\omega(n^\delta)} \leq 2^{-\omega(n^\delta)}.$$

□

5. UNIQUE-WITNESS ONE-WAY RELATIONS

A *one-way relation* $\mathcal{R} = (\mathsf{Gen}, \mathsf{Ver})$ consists of a PPT sampling algorithm $(y, x) \leftarrow \mathsf{Gen}(1^n)$ that samples an *instance* $y \in \{0,1\}^{m(n)}$ along with a *witness* $x \in \{0,1\}^{k(n)}$, and a deterministic poly-time verification algorithm $\mathsf{Ver}(y, x) \in \{0,1\}$ checks whether the pair (y, x) satisfies the relation. For correctness, we require that $\mathsf{Ver}(y, x) = 1$ for all (y, x) output by $\mathsf{Gen}(1^n)$. Intuitively, one-wayness says that given a randomly generated instance y it should be hard to find a valid witness x' such that $\mathsf{Ver}(y, x') = 1$. Leakage-resilient one-wayness requires that the above holds even if the attacker can gets some leakage on the original witness x.

DEFINITION 5.1 (LR-OWR). *We say that a relation* $\mathcal{R} = (\mathsf{Gen}, \mathsf{Ver})$ *is an* $\ell(\cdot)$-leakage-resilient one-way relation (ℓ-LR-OWR) *if for every* PPT *attacker* $\mathcal{A} = (\mathsf{Leak}, \mathsf{Break})$ *such that the output domain of* $\mathsf{Leak}(1^n, \cdot)$ *is* $\{0,1\}^{\ell(n)}$*, we have:*

$$\Pr\left[\mathsf{Ver}(y, x') = 1 \;\middle|\; \begin{array}{c} (y, x) \leftarrow \mathsf{Gen}(1^n) \\ z \leftarrow \mathsf{Leak}(1^n, x), \\ x' \leftarrow \mathsf{Break}(1^n, y, z) \end{array} \right] = \mathsf{negl}(n).$$

We say that the relation has unique witnesses *if for every* $y \in \{0,1\}^{m(n)}$ *there exists* at most a single $x \in \{0,1\}^{k(n)}$ *such that* $\mathsf{Ver}(y, x) = 1$.

Remarks. The idea of leakage-resilient one-way relations is implicit in essentially all leakage-resilient cryptosystems since, for example, the relation between public and secret keys has to satisfy this definition. One simple observation is that *any* standard one-way relation without leakage is also secure against $\ell = O(\log(n))$ bits of leakage, since such small amount of leakage can just be guessed with good probability. Actually, this "guessing argument" even allows us to prove security for larger values of $\ell(n) = O(n^\delta)$, if we assume the δ-exponential security of the one-way relation without leakage.[2] Most of the work on leakage-resilient cryptosystems (starting with [AGV09]) is about clever ways of beating this trivial "guessing argument" and achieving leakage-resilience for large polynomial values of $\ell(n)$ without making exponential hardness assumptions. For example, [ADW09b] describes a very simple construction of an $\ell(n)$-leakage-resilient one-way functions/relations for *any* arbitrarily large polynomial $\ell(n)$, under only the assumption that standard one-way functions exist.[3]

When it comes to one-way relations with *unique witnesses*, we can construct these in the setting without leakage assuming the existence of injective one-way functions. Therefore, we can also apply the "guessing argument" to get such relations with leakage $\ell = O(\log(n))$ under the same assumption, or $\ell = O(n^\delta)$ under a δ-exponential version. However, unlike the previous case without unique witnesses, we do not know of any clever techniques that beat the trivial guessing argument and allow for larger values of ℓ without exponential assumptions. Here, we show that indeed this is impossible under black-box reductions from cryptographic-game assumptions. In other words, we show that the trivial "guessing argument" is essentially tight.

THEOREM 5.2. *For any relation* $\mathcal{R} = (\mathsf{Gen}, \mathsf{Ver})$ *with unique witnesses, and for any leakage-bound* $\ell(\cdot)$*, there exists a* $2^{-\ell(n)}$*-simulatable attack against the* ℓ*-LR-OWR security of* $\mathcal{R}$*.*

PROOF IDEA. We construct an inefficient attacker $\mathcal{A} = (\mathsf{Leak}, \mathsf{Break})$ where $z = \mathsf{Leak}(x)$ is just a random function with ℓ-bit output and $\mathsf{Break}(y, z)$ does an exhaustive search over all possible values to find an x' s.t. $\mathsf{Ver}(y, x') = 1$ and $\mathsf{Leak}(x') = z$: if it finds one, it outputs x' and else $\perp$. Now the only way that the reduction can get something useful from $\mathsf{Break}(y, z)$ is by giving it the correct value $z = \mathsf{Leak}(x)$ for the unique witness x of y (if any exists). But the only way that it can come up with such value is by having previously made a call to $\mathsf{Leak}(x)$ *or by guessing it.* Therefore, we can have a simulator Sim that keeps state and responds to "leak" queries x with random ℓ-bit outputs and to "break" queries (y, z) by checking if the correct witness was given in a previous "leak" query. The simulation matches the outputs of $\mathcal{A}$ up to the $q2^{-\ell}$ probability of the reduction guessing the correct leakage z without querying it within the its q queries to the Break oracle. We translate this idea into a formal proof below.

Proof of Theorem 5.2. Let $\mathcal{H}_n$ be the set of all functions $h : \{0,1\}^{k(n)} \to \{0,1\}^{\ell(n)}$. We define an inefficient class of attackers $\{\mathcal{A}_{n,h} = (\mathsf{Leak}_{n,h}, \mathsf{Break}_{n,h})\}_{n \in \mathbb{N}, h \in \mathcal{H}_n}$ as follows:

$\mathsf{Leak}_{n,h}$ **:** On input x, output $h(x)$.

$\mathsf{Break}_{n,h}$**:** On input (y, z), do an exhaustive search to find $x \in \{0,1\}^{k(n)}$ such that $\mathsf{Ver}(y, x) = 1$. If such x is found and $h(x) = z$ output x, else output $\perp$.

It is easy to see that for each $h \in \mathcal{H}_n$, the attacker $\mathcal{A}_{n,h}$ inefficiently breaks the ℓ-LR one-wayness security of $\mathcal{R} = (\mathsf{Gen}, \mathsf{Ver})$ with advantage 1.

The more interesting property is the second part of the definition showing that, when $h \xleftarrow{\$} \mathcal{H}_n$ is chosen as a uniformly random function, getting oracle access to $\mathcal{A}_{n,h} = (\mathsf{Leak}_{n,h}, \mathsf{Break}_{n,h})$ is *useless* and can be efficiently simulated. Recall that we must construct a simulator $\mathsf{Sim}(1^n)$ such that for any (possibly inefficient) probabilistic oracle-access machine $\mathcal{M}^{(\cdot)}(1^n)$ making at most $q(n)$ queries in total to its oracle(s), we have:

$$\left| \begin{array}{l} \Pr_{h, \mathsf{coins}(\mathcal{M})}[\mathcal{M}^{(\mathsf{Leak}_{n,h}, \mathsf{Break}_{n,h})}(1^n) = 1] \\ - \Pr_{\mathsf{coins}(\mathcal{M}, \mathsf{Sim})}[\mathcal{M}^{\mathsf{Sim}(1^n)}(1^n) = 1] \end{array} \right| \leq q(n) 2^{-\ell(n)}. \tag{3}$$

The simulator $\mathsf{Sim}(1^n)$ is stateful and randomized, and gets to respond to both "leak" and "break" queries in a coordinated manner (as compared to $\mathcal{A}_{n,h} = (\mathsf{Leak}_{n,h}, \mathsf{Break}_{n,h})$ which is stateless and responds to leakage and break queries independently). The simulator works as follows:

- Initialization: Initialize the set $Q := \emptyset$.
- Leakage: On a *leakage* query x, check if, for some z there is already a tuple $(x, z) \in Q$ and, if so, return z. Else select $z \xleftarrow{\$} \{0,1\}^{\ell(n)}$ at random, add the tuple (x, z) to Q and output z.

[2]This "guessing argument" can also be used to similarly prove the leakage-resilience of most other primitives (e.g., signatures, CPA encryption, etc.) with similar parameters.

[3]All these positive results even achieve a stronger definition where the leakage function $\mathsf{Leak}(1^n, x, y)$ also gets the statement y as an input. Since the focus here is on a negative result, we use the weaker and simpler definition stated above.

- Break: On a *break* query (y, z), check if there is a tuple $(x, \hat{z}) \in Q$ for the (unique) witness x s.t. $\mathsf{Ver}(y, x) = 1$. If so, and $\hat{z} = z$ return x. Else return $\perp$.

We now want to show indistinguishability of oracle access to $(\mathsf{Leak}_{n,h}, \mathsf{Break}_{n,h})$ when $h \xleftarrow{\$} \mathcal{H}_n$ is random, and oracle access to $\mathsf{Sim}(1^n)$. First, let us define an event E which occurs if, during the execution $\mathcal{M}^{(\mathsf{Leak}_{n,h}, \mathsf{Break}_{n,h})}(1^n)$, the machine $\mathcal{M}$ makes some "break" query (y, z) such that there has been no prior "leak" query on the unique x for which $\mathsf{Ver}(y, x) = 1$, and the oracle outputs x. Then the query that causes E to occur must "guess" the random value $z = h(x)$ for the unique witness x for which $\mathsf{Ver}(y, x) = 1$. The probability that this occurs in any of the $q = q(n)$ queries made by $\mathcal{M}$ is at most $q(n)2^{-\ell(n)}$. Now as a hybrid experiment, let us consider the oracle Hyb that works just like $(\mathsf{Leak}_{n,h}, \mathsf{Break}_{n,h})$ but, on any "break" query that causes E to occur, it just automatically responds with $\perp$. Then

$$\left| \begin{array}{l} \Pr[\mathcal{M}^{(\mathsf{Leak}_{n,h}, \mathsf{Break}_{n,h})}(1^n) = 1] \\ \quad - \Pr[\mathcal{M}^{\mathsf{Hyb}}(1^n) = 1] \end{array} \right| \leq \Pr[E] \leq q(n)2^{-\ell(n)}.$$

Lastly, we claim that

$$\Pr_{\text{coins}(\mathcal{M}),h}[\mathcal{M}^{\mathsf{Hyb}}(1^n) = 1] = \Pr_{\text{coins}(\mathcal{M},\mathsf{Sim})}[\mathcal{M}^{\mathsf{Sim}(1^n)}(1^n) = 1].$$

In particular, the simulator $\mathsf{Sim}(1^n)$ and Hyb work the same way, except that the simulator chooses the outputs of h "on-the-go" as needed to answer leakage queries and break queries. Together the two equations above prove equation (3), concluding the proof. □

As an immediate corollary of the above theorem and Theorem 4.2 we get the following result.

Corollary 5.3. *For any $\ell(n) = \omega(\log(n))$, if there is a black-box reduction showing the ℓ-LR-OWR security of a relation $\mathcal{R}$ with unique witnesses based on the security of some cryptographic game $\mathcal{G}$, then $\mathcal{G}$ is not secure. Moreover, for any $\ell(n) = n^\delta$ with constant $\delta > 0$, if there is such a black-box reduction based on the δ'-exponential security of $\mathcal{G}$ with $\delta' < \delta$ then $\mathcal{G}$ is not δ'-exponentially secure.*

This essentially says that the only way to get $\ell(n)$-leakage-resilience is to assume the $\ell(n)$-exact security of some cryptographic game, meaning that the "guessing" argument is essentially optimal in proving leakage-resilience for unique-witness one-way relations.

Consequences and Implications. Since one-way relations are implicit in all constructions of more advanced cryptosystems, the above theorem gives several interesting implications. Most obviously, it implies similar separations for leakage-resilient *injective* one-way functions and permutations since they immediately give us one-way relations with unique witnesses. Interestingly, the separation does *not* extend to the leakage-resilience of injective *function families* $\mathcal{F} = \{f_{pk}\}$ where each function in the family is described by some $pk \leftarrow \mathsf{Gen}(1^n)$. This is because the corresponding relation $\{(pk, y), x \ : \ y = f_{pk}(x)\}$ with instances (pk, y) and witnesses x does not necessarily have unique witnesses – there may be "invalid" keys pk which are *not* in the support of Gen for which f_{pk} is not injective. Indeed, the notion of *lossy (trapdoor) functions* [PW08] can be used to construct such injective function families $\mathcal{F}$ with arbitrarily high polynomial leakage ℓ under standard assumptions (DDH, LWE, and others). However, if we were to insist that the function family $\mathcal{F}$ is *certifiably injective*, meaning that we can efficiently verify that pk is a "valid" public key for which the function $f_{pk}(\cdot)$ is injective, then the resulting relation does have unique witnesses and the separation result kicks in. A similar phenomenon occurs in essentially all leakage-resilient *public-key* cryptosystems (e.g., encryption, signatures) where we insist that there is a unique secret key for every public-key. If we insist that the valid public keys of the scheme are efficiently recognizable, then the resulting relation between public and secret keys has unique witnesses and our separation result applies. As another corollary, we also get a similar separation for leakage-resilient *unique signatures* [Lys02] where, for every public key pk (even an adversarially chosen one) and message m, there should be a unique signature that verifies for pk.

Lastly in Appendix Appendix A, we show a similar separation for injective one-way functions where, instead of allowing the attacker to observe leakage on the input x, we allow the attacker to choose any efficiently samplable *weak source* of sufficient min-entropy from which the input x is then sampled. The style of the separation and its parameters are very similar to the leakage case.

6. DETERMINISTIC ENCRYPTION AND CORRELATED INPUT SECURITY

We start with a notion of a one-way function family which is secure against correlated inputs. The definition closely follows that of Goyal et al. [GOR11]. Let

$$\mathcal{F} \stackrel{\text{def}}{=} \{ \ f_{pk} \ : \ \{0,1\}^{k(n)} \to \{0,1\}^{m(n)} \ : \ pk \in \{0,1\}^{p(n)}\}_{n \in \mathbb{N}}$$

be some family of efficiently computable functions keyed by a public pk. Let $pk \leftarrow \mathsf{Gen}(1^n)$ be a PPT sampling algorithm for choosing pk. We say that $(\mathcal{F}, \mathsf{Gen})$ is an *injective function family* if for *every pk in the support of* Gen the function f_{pk} is *injective*. Note that we make no requirements on f_{pk} for other values of pk which are not in the support of Gen. In this section, we focus on an adversary that can observe evaluations $f_{pk}(x_1), \ldots, f_{pk}(x_t)$ for several adversarially distributed correlated inputs $x_1, \ldots, x_t$. We only place the restriction that (1) the distribution of $(x_1, \ldots, x_t)$ is independent of pk, (2) each input x_i individually has high entropy and (3) the inputs are distinct. We ask for a simple one-wayness property, that the attacker should be unable to recover all of the x_i values. Under the above restrictions on the distribution, this one-wayness property appears achievable and simple positive results exist in the random oracle model. On the other hand, in this work, we show that one cannot prove this security property for any actual scheme using black-box reductions. We note that the work of [GOR11] shows interesting positive results under further restrictions on the adversarial input distribution (e.g., the inputs are related by some bounded-degree polynomial).

Relation to One-Wayness with Weak Keys. Note that we do not require that the set of valid pk to be efficiently recognizable. In particular, there may be other values pk (not in the support of Gen) such that the functions f_{pk} are *not* injective. Therefore the relation $\{((pk, y), x) \ : \ f_{pk}(x) = y\}$ may not have *unique witnesses* and the results from the previous section and from Appendix A do not apply in any meaningful way to $\mathcal{F}$. Indeed, if $\mathcal{F}$ is a lossy trapdoor function family, we are able to prove that (e.g.) the functions f_{pk}

remain one-way when evaluated on a single input x, even if x comes from an adversarial source of sufficient min-entropy.

RELATION TO DETERMINISTIC ENCRYPTION. The work of [BBO07] studies a somewhat harder problem in the context of *deterministic encryption* where the functions $f_{pk}(x)$ are used as encryptions of the message x. In that context, one needs to make an additional requirement that pk can be sampled with a *decryption trapdoor sk* allowing the recovery of x from $f_{pk}(x)$. Furthermore, the security definition of deterministic encryption is fairly subtle but certainly (and significantly) stronger than one-wayness property that we consider here. The work of [BBO07] was able to achieve this strong notion of security in the *random-oracle model*, assuming the existence of any standard semantically-secure (randomized) public-key encryption scheme. In particular, it shows that $f_{pk}(x) \stackrel{\text{def}}{=} \mathsf{Enc}_{pk}(x; H(x))$ satisfies this definition when H is modeled as a random oracle. This gave a deterministic encryption scheme which could be used to encrypt any message distribution satisfying properties (1),(2) and (3) above. Subsequent work on deterministic encryption [BFOR08, BFO08, BS11] gives constructions in the standard model, but only for more restricted message distributions where each new message contains some fresh entropy conditioned on the previous ones. Our results therefore imply that some such restrictions on the message distribution are necessary if one wants to prove deterministic encryption security (or even just one-wayness) via black-box reductions.

DEFINING CORRELATION RESILIENCE. Let us now make the above definition formal. An algorithm $\mathsf{Sam}(1^n)$ that samples $t(n)$-tuples $\mathbf{x} = (x_1, \dots, x_t)$ with $x_i \in \{0,1\}^{k(n)}$ produces a *(t, ℓ)-legal correlated distribution* if it satisfies:

- *Distinct Inputs:* For any tuple output by Sam we have $x_i \neq x_j$ for all $i \neq j$.
- *Individual Entropy:* We have $\mathbf{H}_\infty(X_i) \geq k(n) - \ell(n)$, where X_i is a random variable for the ith component x_i produced by $\mathsf{Sam}(1^n)$.

DEFINITION 6.1. *We say that $(\mathcal{F}, \mathsf{Gen})$ is $(t(n), \ell(n))$-correlation-resilient one way (CROW) if for any* PPT *attacker $\mathcal{A} = (\mathsf{Sam}, \mathsf{Break})$ such that Sam it a (t,ℓ)-legal correlated distribution, we have:*

$$\Pr\left[\mathbf{x}' = \mathbf{x} \;\middle|\; \begin{array}{c} pk \leftarrow \mathsf{Gen}(1^n), \\ \mathbf{x} = (x_1, \dots, x_t) \stackrel{\$}{\leftarrow} \mathsf{Sam}(1^n), \\ \mathbf{y} = (f_{pk}(x_1), \dots, f_{pk}(x_t)), \\ \mathbf{x}' \leftarrow \mathsf{Break}(1^n, pk, \mathbf{y}) \end{array}\right] = \mathsf{negl}(n).$$

We say that $(\mathcal{F}, \mathsf{Gen})$ is ℓ-CROW if it is (t,ℓ)-CROW for all polynomial $t(n)$.

THEOREM 6.2. *For any injective function family $(\mathcal{F}, \mathsf{Gen})$ with input size $k(n)$ there exists an $\varepsilon(n)$-simulatable attack against its (t,ℓ)-CROW security for any $\ell(n) > \log(t(n))$ with $\varepsilon(n) \leq 2^{-(t(n)-2k(n))/2+1}$.*

Proof Intuition. We choose $\bar{h}$ to be a random function which maps 'short'($\approx k$ bit) values z to 'long' tuples $\mathbf{x} = (x_1, \dots, x_t)$, and define the inefficient sampler $\mathbf{x} \leftarrow \mathsf{Sam}(1^n)$ by having it choose z at random and output $\bar{h}(z)$. With some additional restrictions on the structure of $\bar{h}$, we can ensure that this always yields a (t,ℓ)-legal correlated distribution over the choice of z. Now assume the reduction makes several "Sample" queries and then comes up with some pk and some $\mathbf{y} = (y_1, \dots, y_k)$. Then we claim that one of the following must hold: either (1) the function $f_{pk}(\cdot)$ is extremely degenerate and (say) half of all inputs x will map to the same output $y = f_{pk}(x)$, or (2) it is extremely unlikely (over the choice of $\bar{h}$) that there is some new value z, which wasn't used by a prior sample query, such that $\mathbf{x} = \bar{h}(z)$ is a pre-image of $\mathbf{y}$ under f_{pk}. The reason is that there are only a few choice of z, each corresponding to some long tuple $\mathbf{x} = (x_1, \dots, x_t)$ which is uniformly random over the choice of $\bar{h}$. Therefore its extremely unlikely that even one such new z will correspond to a preimage of $\mathbf{y}$ unless f_{pk} is degenerate. So, unless pk is degenerate, getting access to a breaker $\mathsf{Break}(pk, \mathbf{y})$ that does exhaustive search over z to find a preimage $\mathbf{x} = \bar{h}(z)$ is not useful since it will only return preimages that were previously given by Sam. On the other hand, we can efficiently test if pk is degenerate and so can allow $\mathsf{Break}(pk, \mathbf{y})$ to just fail on degenerate pk while maintaining the ability to simulate it. We formalize this intuition in a formal proof.

Proof of Theorem 6.2. We use $t = t(n), k = k(n)$ etc. as shorthand. Let $k' \stackrel{\text{def}}{=} k - \lceil \log(t) \rceil$ and identify tuples $x = (i, x') \in [t] \times \{0,1\}^{k'}$ as members of $\{0,1\}^k$ in the natural way. For every $n \in \mathbb{N}$ let $\mathcal{H}_n$ be the family of all functions $h : [t(n)] \times \{0,1\}^{k'(n)} \rightarrow \{0,1\}^{k'(n)}$ such that, for every $i \in [t]$, the projected function $h_i(z) \stackrel{\text{def}}{=} h(i,z)$ is a *permutation* over $\{0,1\}^{k'}$. For any such $h \in \mathcal{H}_n$, we also implicitly define the function $\bar{h}(\cdot) : \{0,1\}^{k'} \rightarrow \{0,1\}^{k \times t}$ defined by

$$\bar{h}(z) \stackrel{\text{def}}{=} ((1, h_1(z)), \dots, (t, h_t(z))).$$

For any $h \in \mathcal{H}_n$, we define an inefficient class of attackers $\mathcal{A}_{n,h} = (\mathsf{Sam}_{n,h}, \mathsf{Break}_{n,h})$ as follows:

$\mathsf{Sam}_{n,h}$: On input 1^n, sample $z \stackrel{\$}{\leftarrow} \{0,1\}^{k'}$, and output the vector $\mathbf{x} = (x_1, \dots, x_t) = \bar{h}(z)$.

$\mathsf{Break}_{n,h}$: On input $(1^n, pk, \mathbf{y} = (y_1, \dots, y_t))$:

1. First check that $f_{pk}(\cdot)$ is *non-degenerate* by performing the following check for each $i \in [t]$: Sample $r = 2t$ random distinct points $x'_1, \dots, x'_r$ from $\{0,1\}^{k'}$ and compute $y'_j = f_{pk}((i, x'_j))$ for $j = 1, \dots, r$. If $y'_1, \dots, y'_r$ are not all distinct, output $\perp$.
2. Do an exhaustive search over $z \in \{0,1\}^{k'}$ for one that satisfies $\bar{h}(z) = \mathbf{x} = (x_1, \dots, x_t)$ such that $f_{pk}(x_i) = y_i$ for all $i \in [t]$. When the first such z is found, output the corresponding $\mathbf{x}$ and if no such z exists output $\perp$.

Firstly, we check that for each $h \in \mathcal{H}$, the attacker $\mathcal{A}_h = (\mathsf{Sam}_{n,h}, \mathsf{Break}_{n,h})$ breaks the (t,ℓ)-CROW security of $(\mathcal{F}, \mathsf{Gen})$ with advantage 1. Notice that the distribution

$$\mathbf{x} = (x_1, \dots, x_t) \leftarrow \mathsf{Sam}_{n,h}(1^n)$$

is a (t,ℓ)-legal correlated distribution since: (a) the value $x_i = (i, h_i(z))$ have entropy $k' = k - \lceil \log(t) \rceil \geq k - \ell$ over a random choice of z since h_i is a permutation and (b) $x_i \neq x_j$ for $i \neq j$. Moreover, when calling $\mathsf{Break}_{n,h}$ on $pk \leftarrow \mathsf{Gen}(1^n)$ the non-degeneracy check always passes since f_{pk} is injective.

Hence $\mathsf{Break}_{n,h}$ will succeed in recovering the unique preimage $\mathbf{x}$ of $\mathbf{y}$ under f_{pk} with probability 1.

We now want to show that, when $h \xleftarrow{\$} \mathcal{H}_n$ is chosen uniformly at random, getting oracle access to $\mathcal{A}_h = (\mathsf{Sam}_{n,h}, \mathsf{Break}_{n,h})$ is *not very useful* and can be efficiently simulated.

We construct our simulator $\mathsf{Sim}(1^n)$ as follows:

Initialization: Initialize the set $Q := \emptyset$.

Sam: On a *sample* query, select random $z \xleftarrow{\$} \{0,1\}^{k'}$. If there is a value $(z, \mathbf{x})$ in Q output $\mathbf{x}$. Else, for $i \in [t]$, let Q_i be the set of all x s.t. there is a tuple of the form $(z, \mathbf{x} = (\cdots, (i,x), \cdots)) \in Q$. Choose $\{x_i \xleftarrow{\$} \{0,1\}^{k'} \setminus Q_i\}_{i \in [t]}$, set $\mathbf{x} = ((1,x_1), \ldots, (t, x_t))$, add $(z, \mathbf{x})$ to Q, and output $\mathbf{x}$.

If $|Q| \geq 2^{k'}/4$ then "fill in" the rest of Q by choosing $\mathbf{x}$ as above sequentially for every $z \in \{0,1\}^{k'}$ which is not in Q yet.[4]

Break: On a *break* query $(pk, \mathbf{y} = (y_1, \ldots, y_t))$.

- First check that $f_{pk}(\cdot)$ is *non-degenerate* using the same process as the oracle $\mathsf{Break}_{n,h}$. That is, for each $i \in [t]$, sample $r = 2t(n)$ random distinct points $x'_1, \ldots, x'_r$ from $\{0,1\}^{k'}$ and compute $y'_j = f_{pk}((i, x'_j))$ for $j = 1, \ldots, r$. If $y'_1, \ldots, y'_r$ are not all distinct, output $\perp$.
- Check if there is a tuple $(z, \mathbf{x} = (x_1, \ldots, x_t)) \in Q$ such that $f_{pk}(x_i) = y_i$ for all $i \in [t]$. If so, output $\mathbf{x}$, else output $\perp$.

For the analysis of the simulation, we define a public-key pk as *degenerate* if there is some $i \in [t], y \in \{0,1\}^m$ such that $\Pr_{x' \xleftarrow{\$} \{0,1\}^{k'}}[f_{pk}((i,x')) = y] \geq \frac{1}{2}$. In other words pk is degenerate if f_{pk} is very much non-injective and half all values of the form (i, x') map to the same y. Let δ be the probability that the non-degeneracy test passes for some degenerate pk. Then this only occurs if during the ith iteration of the test, at most 0 or 1 of the x'_j values map to $f_{pk}(i, x'_j) = y$. This occurs with probability $\delta \leq 2^{-r} + r2^{-r+1} \leq 2^{-t}$.

We now want to show indistinguishability of oracle access to $(\mathsf{Sam}_{n,h}, \mathsf{Break}_{n,h})$ when h is random, and oracle access to $\mathsf{Sim}(1^n)$:

$$\left| \begin{array}{l} \Pr[\mathcal{M}^{(\mathsf{Sam}_{n,h}, \mathsf{Break}_{n,h})}(1^n) = 1] \\ \quad - \Pr[\mathcal{M}^{\mathsf{Sim}(1^n)}(1^n) = 1] \end{array} \right| \leq q(n) 2^{-(t-2k)/2+1}. \tag{4}$$

First, let us define an event E which occurs if, during the execution $\mathcal{M}^{(\mathsf{Sam}_{n,h}, \mathsf{Break}_{n,h})}(1^n)$ with $h \xleftarrow{\$} \mathcal{H}_N$ random, the machine $\mathcal{M}$ makes some "Break" query $(pk, \mathbf{y})$ and:

- It gets a response $\mathbf{x} \neq \perp$ such that $\mathbf{x}$ was *not* the outputs of a previous "Sam" query.
- The number of previous "Sam" queries made by $\mathcal{M}$ is $< 2^{k'}/4$.

[4]The work here is polynomial in the size of the simulator's current state. In other words, amortized over the number of queries, this only takes a polynomial amount of work per query.

Now we claim that the simulation error (the left-hand side of (4)) is at most $\Pr[E]$. To see this, we can define an attacker $\mathcal{A}'_{n,h} = (\mathsf{Sam}'_{n,h}, \mathsf{Break}'_{n,h})$ which acts like $\mathcal{A}_{n,h}$ but outputs $\perp$ on any query that makes E occur. Then we claim that the responses of $\mathcal{A}'_{n,h}$ for $h \leftarrow \mathcal{H}_n$ and $\mathsf{Sim}(1^n)$ are identical since the only (syntactic) difference between them is that $\mathsf{Sim}(1^n)$ chooses the outputs of the function h "on-the-go" for the first $2^{k'}/4$ queries to "Sam". Therefore, we are only left to find an upper bound on $\Pr[E]$.

Let E_i be the event that the ith "Break" query makes E occur. Let D_i be the even that the value pk contained in the ith query $(pk, \mathbf{y})$ is degenerate. Then, $\Pr[E_i \wedge D_i] \leq \Pr[E_i \mid D_i] \leq \delta \leq 2^{-t}$. To calculate $\Pr[E_i \wedge \neg D_i]$, let Z be the set of all values $z \in \{0,1\}^{k'}$ used during previous "sample" queries before query i. Then, conditioned on the view of the attacker prior to the ith query, for each $z \notin Z$, the values of $\{h_j(z)\}_{j \in [t]}$ are mutually uniformly random over the sets $S_j = \{0,1\}^{k'} \setminus h_j(Z)$ of size $|S_j| = 2^{k'} - |Z|$. Moreover, if pk is non-degenerate then at most a $\left(\frac{1}{2} \cdot \frac{2^{k'}}{|S_j|}\right)$ fraction of the values $x \in S_j$ can satisfy $f_{pk}((j,x)) = y$ for any given y. Therefore, since we can assume $|Z| \leq 2^{k'}/4$, we get:

$$\begin{aligned} & \Pr[E_i \wedge \neg D_i] \\ \leq\; & \Pr[E_i \mid \neg D_i] \\ \leq\; & \Pr_h\left[\ \exists z \in \{0,1\}^{k'} \setminus Z \text{ s.t. } \forall j \in [t] : h_j(z) = y_j\ \right] \\ \leq\; & 2^{k'} \left(\frac{2^{k'}}{2 \cdot (2^{k'} - |Z|)} \right)^t \\ \leq\; & 2^{k'} (\frac{2}{3})^t \leq 2^k (\frac{4}{9})^{k + (t-2k)/2} \leq 2^{-(t-2k)/2} \end{aligned}$$

So the statistical distance of the simulation is bounded by

$$\begin{aligned} \Pr[E] \;&\leq\; \sum_{i=1}^{q(n)} \Pr[E_i] \\ &\leq\; q(n)(2^{-(t-2k)/2} + 2^{-t}) \leq q(n) 2^{-(t-2k)/2+1} \end{aligned}$$

which concludes the proof of the theorem. □

As an immediate corollary of the above theorem and Theorem 4.2 we get the following.

COROLLARY 6.3. *Let $(\mathcal{F}, \mathsf{Gen})$ be an injective function family with input size $k(n)$:*

- *If $t(n) \geq 2k(n) + \omega(\log(n))$, $\ell(n) > \log(t(n))$ then there is no black-box reduction showing (t, ℓ)-CROW security of $(\mathcal{F}, \mathsf{Gen})$ based on the security of some cryptographic game $\mathcal{G}$, unless $\mathcal{G}$ is insecure.*
- *If $t(n) \geq 2k(n) + n^\delta$, $\ell(n) > \log(t(n))$, then there is no black-box reduction showing (t, ℓ)-CROW security of $(\mathcal{F}, \mathsf{Gen})$ based on the δ-exponential security of $\mathcal{G}$, unless $\mathcal{G}$ is not δ-exponentially secure.*
- *There is no black-box reduction showing ℓ-CROW security of $(\mathcal{F}, \mathsf{Gen})$ for $\ell(n) = \omega(\log(n))$ under the δ-exponential security of some game $\mathcal{G}$ for some $\delta > 0$, unless $\mathcal{G}$ is not δ-exponentially secure.*

7. PSEUDO-ENTROPY GENERATION

If x is a random string, and the attacker may get some ℓ-bit leakage $z = \mathsf{Leak}(x)$ about x, then the *conditional entropy* of x conditioned on z may go down by as much as ℓ bits (see Lemma 2.1). Here we ask if we can "increase" the *computational entropy* of x by applying some deterministic function $y = \mathsf{PEG}(x)$, called a *pseudo-entropy generator* (PEG). Since the leakage z may contain (say) the first ℓ bits of y, the conditional computational entropy of y conditioned on z is at most $|y|-\ell$ (under any reasonable definition). However, if $|y| > |x|$, it is possible that the function PEG *increases* the amount of conditional computational entropy from $|x| - \ell$ possibly all the way to $|y| - \ell$. Indeed, when $\ell = 0$, this is exactly the role of a *pseudorandom generator*. Therefore a PEG generalizes the notion of a pseudorandom generator to weaker entropy requirements on both the input and output. The existence of PEGs with essentially optimal parameters follows easily in the random-oracle model. In the standard model, there has been much interesting work, starting with [DP08, RTTV08], showing that *any* pseudorandom generator is also a PEG for small values of $\ell = O(\log(n))$, or for larger value $\ell = n^\delta$ assuming exponential security. Unlike the trivial "guessing argument" used to prove such bounds for leakage-resilient one-way relations, showing the above is highly non-trivial. We now ask if there are clever constructions of PEGs which provably beat the above bounds and allow us to prove security for $\ell = \omega(\log(n))$ under standard (non-exponential) assumptions. We show that the answer is negative if we restrict ourselves to black-box reductions.

We now give a formal definition of PEGs. Since the focus is on negative results, we give a weak definition using a weak variant of *conditional metric entropy* [BSW03]. We also only require that the PEG increases computational entropy by a single bit, from $|x| - \ell$ to $|x| - \ell + 1$.

DEFINITION 7.1. *Let*

$$\mathsf{PEG} = \{\mathsf{PEG}_n : \{0,1\}^{k(n)} \to \{0,1\}^{m(n)}\}_{n\in\mathbb{N}}$$

be a function ensemble with $m(n) > k(n)$. We say that it is an $\ell(\cdot)$-leaky pseudo-entropy generator *(ℓ-LPEG) if the following holds. For every* PPT *attacker $\mathcal{A} = (\mathsf{Leak}, \mathsf{Dist})$ such that the output domain of $\mathsf{Leak}(1^n, \cdot)$ is $\{0,1\}^{\ell(n)}$, there exists some pair of (correlated and not necessarily efficiently samplable) random variables $\{(Y_n, Z_n)\}_{n\in\mathbb{N}}$ of high* statistical *conditional entropy $\mathbf{H}_\infty(Y_n \mid Z_n) \geq k(n) - \ell(n) + 1$ and the distinguishing advantage $\mathbf{Adv}^{\mathcal{A}}_{LPEG}(n) \leq \mathsf{negl}(n)$ where*

$$\mathbf{Adv}^{\mathcal{A}}_{LPEG}(n) \stackrel{\text{def}}{=} \left| \begin{array}{l} \Pr_{x \stackrel{\$}{\leftarrow} \{0,1\}^{k(n)}} [\mathsf{Dist}(1^n, \mathsf{PEG}(x), \mathsf{Leak}(x)) = 1\,] \\ \quad - \Pr_{(y,z)\leftarrow(Y_n,Z_n)} [\mathsf{Dist}(1^n, y, z) = 1] \end{array} \right|.$$

THEOREM 7.2. *For any function* PEG *and for any $\ell(\cdot)$, there exists a $(\varepsilon(n) = 2^{-\ell(n)})$-simulatable attack against the ℓ-LPEG security of* PEG .

Proof Intuition. We define the inefficient simulatable attack $\mathcal{A} = (\mathsf{Leak}, \mathsf{Dist})$ as follows. The function $\mathsf{Leak}(x)$is defined by a uniformly random function $h : \{0,1\}^{m(n)} \to \{0,1\}^{\ell(n)}$ and just outputs $h(\mathsf{PEG}(x))$. On the other hand $\mathsf{Dist}(y, z)$ outputs 1 iff there is a seed x with $y = \mathsf{PEG}(x)$ and $h(y) = z$. Now Dist will always output 1 on pseudorandom inputs with correct leakage, but for any distribution (Y, Z) with sufficient statistical conditional entropy, it will often output 0 since there will not be a seed x explaining the tuple. Therefore this is a valid attack. On the other hand, the only way that a reduction can call $\mathsf{Dist}(y, z)$ and get output 1 for any "new" y for which it did not make a prior call to $\mathsf{Leak}(x)$ with $x \in \mathsf{PEG}^{-1}(y)$, is if the reduction guesses the random ℓ-bit value $h(y)$, which occurs with probability $2^{-\ell}$. Therefore, we can efficiently simulate the attack for the reduction.

Proof of Theorem 7.2. Define $\mathcal{Y}_n \stackrel{\text{def}}{=} \{\mathsf{PEG}(x) : x \in \{0,1\}^{k(n)}\} \subseteq \{0,1\}^{m(n)}$. Let $\mathcal{H}_n$ be the family of all functions $h : \{0,1\}^{m(n)} \to \{0,1\}^{\ell(n)}$ which are *almost regular over* $\mathcal{Y}_n$, meaning that for all $z \in \{0,1\}^{\ell(n)}$ we have $|h_n^{-1}(z) \cap \mathcal{Y}_n| \leq 2^{k(n)-\ell(n)}$. We define an inefficient class of attackers $\mathcal{A}_{n,h} = (\mathsf{Leak}_{n,h}, \mathsf{Dist}_{n,h})$ with respect to $h \in \mathcal{H}_n$ as follows:

$\mathsf{Leak}_{n,h}$: On input $x \in \{0,1\}^{k(n)}$ output $h_n(\mathsf{PEG}(x))$.

$\mathsf{Dist}_{n,h}$: On input y, z, first check that $h(y) = z$ and output 0 if not. Otherwise, do an exhaustive search to find $x \in \{0,1\}^{k(n)}$ such that $\mathsf{PEG}(x) = y$. If x exists output 1 else output 0.

We show that this attack has advantage 1/2. Firstly, given any fixed $h \in \mathcal{H}_n$, we have

$$\Pr_{x \stackrel{\$}{\leftarrow} \{0,1\}^{k(n)}} [\mathsf{Dist}_{n,h}(1^n, \mathsf{PEG}(x), \mathsf{Leak}_{n,h}(x)) = 1] = 1. \quad (5)$$

Secondly, given any r.v. (Y_n, Z_n) with $\mathbf{H}_\infty(Y_n \mid Z_n) \geq k(n) - \ell(n) + 1$, we claim

$$\begin{aligned} \Pr_{(y,z) \stackrel{\$}{\leftarrow} (Y_n,Z_n)} [\mathsf{Dist}_{n,h}(1^n, y, z) = 1] &\leq \Pr[y \in h_n^{-1}(z) \cap \mathcal{Y}_n] \\ &\leq \frac{1}{2}. \end{aligned} \quad (6)$$

To see the last inequality, let $\mathcal{B}(z)$ be an inefficient predictor that, given z, outputs $y \stackrel{\$}{\leftarrow} h^{-1}(z) \cap \mathcal{Y}_n$. Then

$$\begin{aligned} 2^{-k(n)+\ell(n)-1} &\geq \Pr[\mathcal{B}(z) = y] \\ &\geq \Pr[y \in h_n^{-1}(z) \cap \mathcal{Y}_n] 2^{-k(n)+\ell(n)} \end{aligned}$$

where the left inequality follows from the definition of the conditional min-entropy (Y_n, Z_n), while the right follows by analyzing the strategy of $\mathcal{B}$. This proves equation (6), which together with (5) shows that $\mathcal{A}_{n,h}$ successfully attacks the $\ell(\cdot)$-LPEG security of PEG with advantage $\geq 1/2$.

Now let us show that, when $h \stackrel{\$}{\leftarrow} \mathcal{H}_n$ is chosen uniformly at random, getting oracle access to $\mathcal{A}_{n,h} = (\mathsf{Leak}_{n,h}, \mathsf{Dist}_{n,h})$ can be efficiently simulated. The simulator $\mathsf{Sim}(1^n)$ works as follows:

- Initialization: Initialize the set $Q := \emptyset$.
- Leakage: On a *leakage* query x check if there is already a tuple $(\mathsf{PEG}(x), z) \in Q$ and, if so, return z. Else select $z \stackrel{\$}{\leftarrow} \{0,1\}^{\ell(n)}$ at random, add the tuple $(\mathsf{PEG}(x), z)$ to Q and output z.
- Distinguish: On a *distinguish* query (y, z), check if $(y, z) \in Q$ – if so return 1 else return 0.

We now want to show indistinguishability of oracle access to $(\mathsf{Leak}_{n,h}, \mathsf{Dist}_{n,h})$, and oracle access to $\mathsf{Sim}(1^n)$. That is, for every $\mathcal{M}$ making at most $q(n)$ queries to its oracle, we want to show:

$$\left| \begin{array}{c} \Pr[\mathcal{M}^{(\mathsf{Leak}_{n,h},\mathsf{Dist}_{n,h})}(1^n) = 1] - \\ \Pr[\mathcal{M}^{\mathsf{Sim}(1^n)}(1^n) = 1] \end{array} \right| \leq \frac{(q^2(n) + q(n))}{2^{\ell(n)}}. \quad (7)$$

First let us define a hybrid oracle Hyb which works just like $\mathcal{A}_h = (\mathsf{Leak}_{n,h}, \mathsf{Dist}_{n,h})$ but instead of selecting $h \xleftarrow{\$} \mathcal{H}_n$, it selects a uniformly random function $\tilde{h} : \{0,1\}^{m(n)} \to \{0,1\}^{\ell(n)}$, without insisting that it is almost regular. We claim that the statistical distance between q queries to $\mathcal{A}_h$ and Hyb is bounded by $q^2/2^\ell$. This is because, conditioned on the values of any i prior (distinct) queries to $\tilde{h}$ (resp. h), for any new input $y \in \mathcal{Y}_n$ and any $Z \subseteq \{0,1\}^\ell$ we have $\Pr[\tilde{h}(y) \in Z] = |Z|2^{-\ell}$ and $\Pr[h(y) \in Z] = \frac{|Z|2^{k-\ell} - i_Z}{2^k} = |Z|2^{-\ell} - i_Z/2^k$ where i_Z is the number of prior queries for which the response was in Z. Therefore the statistical distance between the responses to the ith query is at most $q2^{-k} \leq q(n)2^{-\ell}$. Under a hybrid argument over the q queries we get the bound $q^2 2^{-\ell}$ as desired.

We define an event E which occurs if, during the execution $\mathcal{M}^{\mathsf{Hyb}}(1^n)$, the machine $\mathcal{M}$ makes some "distinguish" query (y, z) such that it never made a prior leakage query on x with $\mathsf{PEG}(x) = y$, and it gets a response 1. Then, conditioned on E not occurring, the oracles Hyb and $\mathsf{Sim}(1^n)$ are identically distributed, and therefore we can bound the difference in (7) by $\Pr[E] + q^2 2^{-\ell}$. On the other hand, the query (y, z) that causes E to occur must "guess" the random value $z = \tilde{h}(y)$ which is uniformly random and of size $\ell(n)$. The probability that this occurs in any of the $q = q(n)$ queries made by $\mathcal{M}$ is at most $\Pr[E] \leq q(n)2^{-\ell(n)}$. Together these two bounds give us (7) and prove the theorem.

As an immediate corollary of the above theorem and Theorem 4.2 we get the following separation.

COROLLARY 7.3. *For any $\ell(n) = \omega(\log(n))$, if there is a black-box reduction showing the ℓ-LPEG security of some function* PEG *based on the security of some cryptographic game $\mathcal{G}$, then $\mathcal{G}$ is not secure. Moreover, for any $\ell(n) = n^\delta$ with constant $\delta > 0$, if there is a reduction based on the δ'-exponential security of $\mathcal{G}$ with $\delta' < \delta$ then $\mathcal{G}$ is not δ'-exponentially secure.*

We mention that the work of [BHK11] gives positive results for an interesting related notion called "leaky pseudo-entropy functions", which does not satisfy our definition of PEGs (Definition 7.1) and therefore does not contradict our barrier. In particular, although "pseudo-entropy functions" never increase the total amount of pseudo-entropy, they ensure that the output of the function at any point is unpredictable even give its outputs at many other points.

8. ENTROPY CONDENSATION

Another tool studied in the context of manipulating weak sources of randomness is a *condenser*, originally defined in the information theoretic setting by [RR99], with the aim of increasing the *entropy rate* of a source X, defined as the ratio of its entropy to bit size. Unfortunately, much like randomness extractors, such information theoretic condensers for general sources require a random seed chosen independently of the source X. The recent work of [DRV12] suggested an interesting idea of building condensers for a restricted class of *efficiently samplable* sources, which are essentially the only sources we need to worry about in cryptography. Although these condensers (may) still require a seed, the source X can now depend on the seed. Intuitively, such condensers may be plausible since, the only way that an efficient high-entropy distribution on the inputs results in a lower-than-expected entropy distribution on the outputs is if it has a higher-then-expected probability of collisions, which may be hard to achieve efficiently. Indeed, [DRV12] showed that such condensers can be constructed from *collision-resistant hash functions* with sufficient (exponential) security, and gave several interesting cryptographic applications of such condensers. Here we show that, if we want black-box reductions, than there is no clever construction of such condensers which avoids the reliance on exponential security assumptions. In other words, the construction of [DRV12] is essentially tight. Let

$$\mathsf{Cond} = \{\mathsf{Cond}_n : \{0,1\}^{k(n)} \times \{0,1\}^{d(n)} \to \{0,1\}^{m(n)}\}_{n \in \mathbb{N}}$$

be some function ensemble with $m(n) < k(n)$. We use the notation $\mathsf{Cond}_s(x)$ in place of $\mathsf{Cond}(x, s)$ and call the value s a *seed*.

DEFINITION 8.1 (SEED-DEPENDENT CONDENSER). *We say that* Cond *is a $t(\cdot)$-condenser if for all* PPT *distributions* $\mathsf{Sam}(1^n, s)$ *over* $\{0,1\}^{k(n)}$ *satisfying*

$$\mathbf{H}_\infty(\mathsf{Sam}(1^n, s)) \geq k(n) - m(n) + t(n)$$

for all $s \in \{0,1\}^{d(n)}$, we have

$$\mathbf{H}_\infty(\mathsf{Cond}_S(\mathsf{Sam}(1^n, S)) \mid S) \geq t(n) + 1,$$

where S is a uniformly random seed in $\{0,1\}^{d(n)}$.

A condenser is regular *if, for every $s \in \{0,1\}^{d(n)}, y \in \{0,1\}^{m(n)}$ we have $|\{x : \mathsf{Cond}_s(x) = y\}| = 2^{k(n)-m(n)}$.*

Notice that the function Cond which just outputs the first m bits of its input x and ignores the seed s entirely already has output entropy $\geq t$ if the input entropy is $\geq k - m + t$. This is because cutting the last $k - m$ bits of the input can decrease its entropy by at most $k - m$. Therefore, our definition of a condenser only requires us to beat the above trivial construction by only a single bit!

THEOREM 8.2. *For any* Cond *which is regular, and for any $t(\cdot)$, there exists an $2^{-t(n)}$-simulatable attack against the $t(n)$-condenser security of* Cond.

PROOF. Let $H \subseteq \{0,1\}^{m(n)}$ be a sets of size $|H| = 2^{t(n)}$. Let $\mathcal{H}_n$ be the set of all such H. We define an inefficient class of attackers $\mathsf{Sam}_{n,H}$ with respect to the ensemble $H \xleftarrow{\$} \mathcal{H}_n$ as follows:

$\mathsf{Sam}_{n,H}$: On input $s \in \{0,1\}^{d(n)}$, choose a random $y \xleftarrow{\$} H$ and a random pre-image $x \xleftarrow{\$} \{x : \mathsf{Cond}_s(x) = y\}$. Output x.

Firstly, fix any $H \in \mathcal{H}_n$ and define $X_s \stackrel{\text{def}}{=} \{x : \mathsf{Cond}_s(x) \in H\}$. Then, by regularity, $|X_s| = 2^{k(n)-m(n)+t(n)}$. Moreover, the output of $\mathsf{Sam}_{n,H}(1^n, s)$ is just a random sample from X_s and therefore has entropy $\mathbf{H}_\infty(\mathsf{Sam}(1^n, s)) = k(n) - m(n) + t(n)$. On the other hand, for any s, the output of $\mathsf{Cond}_s(\mathsf{Sam}(1^n, s)) \in H$ is contained in a set of size $2^{t(n)}$ and therefore $\mathbf{H}_\infty(\mathsf{Cond}_S(\mathsf{Sam}(1^n, S)) \mid S) = t(n)$. Together, this shows that $\mathsf{Sam}_{n,H}$ is a successful attacker against the $t(n)$-condenser security of Cond.

The simulator $\mathsf{Sim}(1^n)$ simply responds to any query s with a uniformly random value $x \xleftarrow{\$} \{0,1\}^{k(n)}$. We need to show that the simulation is good – namely, that for any (possibly inefficient) probabilistic oracle-access machine $\mathcal{M}^{(\cdot)}(1^n)$ making at most $q(n)$ queries in total to its oracle(s), we have:

$$\left| \begin{array}{c} \Pr[\mathcal{M}^{\mathsf{Sam}_{n,H}}(1^n) = 1] \\ -\Pr[\mathcal{M}^{\mathsf{Sim}(1^n)}(1^n) = 1] \end{array} \right| \leq \frac{2q^2(n)}{2^{t(n)}} \quad (8)$$

Let us define a hybrid oracle Hyb which works just like $\{\mathsf{Sam}_{n,H} : H \xleftarrow{\$} \mathcal{H}\}$ but it remembers the set Q of values y chosen in prior "sample" queries and makes sure that each new query is answered with a fresh $y \xleftarrow{\$} H \setminus Q$. Let E be the event that, during the execution of $\mathcal{M}^{\mathsf{Sam}_H}$ with $H \xleftarrow{\$} \mathcal{H}_n$, some two distinct queries were answered with the same choice of $y \xleftarrow{\$} H$. The, conditioned on E not occurring, the oracles $\mathsf{Sam}_{n,H}$ and Hyb are statistically the same, and therefore the distance between them is bounded by $\Pr[E] \leq q^2(n)2^{-t(n)}$. Let E' be the event that, during the execution of $\mathcal{M}^{\mathsf{Sim}(1^n)}(1^n)$, two queries to Sim map to the same y. Then conditioned on E' not occurring, the oracles Hyb and Sim are statistically the same since on each query s both oracles respond with a random preimage $\mathsf{Cond}_s^{-1}(y)$ for a uniformly random fresh y. Therefore the statistical distance between them is at most $\Pr[E'] \leq q^2(n)2^{-m(n)} \leq q^2(n)2^{-t(n)}$. This proves equation (8) and concludes the proof. □

As an immediate corollary of the above theorem and Theorem 4.2 we get the following.

COROLLARY 8.3. *For any $t(n) = \omega(\log(n))$, if there is a black-box reduction showing the t-condenser security of any regular candidate function* Cond *based on the security of some cryptographic game $\mathcal{G}$, then $\mathcal{G}$ is not secure. Moreover, for any $t(n) = n^\delta$ with constant $\delta > 0$, if there is a reduction based on the δ'-exponential security of $\mathcal{G}$ with $\delta' < \delta$ then $\mathcal{G}$ is not δ'-exponentially secure.*

9. CONCLUSIONS AND OPEN PROBLEMS

In this work, we consider several cryptographic security notions involving weak, leaky and correlated sources of randomness. These notions cannot be naturally expressed in terms of cryptographic games between an attacker and an adversary, and we show a broad black-box separation, that their security does not follow from that of any standard cryptographic game. One open problem is to apply our approach to other primitives whose security is not expressed as a cryptographic game. Another open problem is to come up with reductions that do not treat the attacker as a black box. One such approach by Barak et al. [BHHI10] has been used in the context of KDM secure encryption, cleverly circumventing the black-box separation of Haitner and Holenstein [HH09] by treating a component of the adversary in a non-black-box way. It does not seem that this technique could apply to the primitives discussed in this work, but it remains an interesting open problem to look for some such approach.

10. ACKNOWLEDGEMENTS

We thank Yael Tauman Kalai for suggesting the problem of *pseudo-entropy generators*, which lead us to the results of this work. We also thank Yael, Iftach Haitner and Yevgeniy Dodis for many enlightening discussions on the topics and results of this work.

11. REFERENCES

[ADN+10] Joël Alwen, Yevgeniy Dodis, Moni Naor, Gil Segev, Shabsi Walfish, and Daniel Wichs. Public-key encryption in the bounded-retrieval model. In Henri Gilbert, editor, *Advances in Cryptology - EUROCRYPT 2010*, volume 6110 of *Lecture Notes in Computer Science*, pages 113–134. Springer, 2010.

[ADW09a] Joël Alwen, Yevgeniy Dodis, and Daniel Wichs. Leakage-resilient public-key cryptography in the bounded-retrieval model. In Halevi [Hal09], pages 36–54.

[ADW09b] Joël Alwen, Yevgeniy Dodis, and Daniel Wichs. Survey: Leakage resilience and the bounded retrieval model. In *ICITS*, pages 1–18, 2009.

[AGV09] Adi Akavia, Shafi Goldwasser, and Vinod Vaikuntanathan. Simultaneous hardcore bits and cryptography against memory attacks. In Omer Reingold, editor, *Sixth Theory of Cryptography Conference — TCC 2007*, volume 5444 of *Lecture Notes in Computer Science*. Springer-Verlag, 2009.

[BBO07] Mihir Bellare, Alexandra Boldyreva, and Adam O'Neill. Deterministic and efficiently searchable encryption. In Alfred Menezes, editor, *CRYPTO*, volume 4622 of *Lecture Notes in Computer Science*, pages 535–552. Springer, 2007.

[BFO08] Alexandra Boldyreva, Serge Fehr, and Adam O'Neill. On notions of security for deterministic encryption, and efficient constructions without random oracles. In Wagner [Wag08], pages 335–359.

[BFOR08] Mihir Bellare, Marc Fischlin, Adam O'Neill, and Thomas Ristenpart. Deterministic encryption: Definitional equivalences and constructions without random oracles. In Wagner [Wag08], pages 360–378.

[BG10] Zvika Brakerski and Shafi Goldwasser. Circular and leakage resilient public-key encryption under subgroup indistinguishability - (or: Quadratic residuosity strikes back). In Tal Rabin, editor, *CRYPTO*, volume 6223 of *Lecture Notes in Computer Science*, pages 1–20. Springer, 2010.

[BHHI10] Boaz Barak, Iftach Haitner, Dennis Hofheinz, and Yuval Ishai. Bounded key-dependent message security. In *EUROCRYPT*, pages 423–444, 2010.

[BHK11] Mark Braverman, Avinatan Hassidim, and Yael Tauman Kalai. Leaky pseudo-entropy functions. In Bernard Chazelle, editor, *ICS*, pages 353–366. Tsinghua University Press, 2011.

[BKKV10] Zvika Brakerski, Jonathan Katz, Yael Kalai, and Vinod Vaikuntanathan. Overcomeing the hole in the bucket: Public-key cryptography against resilient to continual memory leakage. In *FOCS* [IEE10], pages 501–510.

[BS11] Zvika Brakerski and Gil Segev. Better security for deterministic public-key encryption: The auxiliary-input setting. In Phillip Rogaway, editor, *CRYPTO*, volume 6841 of *Lecture Notes in Computer Science*, pages 543–560. Springer, 2011.

[BSW03] Boaz Barak, Ronen Shaltiel, and Avi Wigderson. Computational analogues of entropy. In Sanjeev Arora, Klaus Jansen, José D. P. Rolim, and Amit Sahai, editors, *RANDOM-APPROX*, volume 2764 of *Lecture Notes in Computer Science*, pages 200–215. Springer, 2003.

[BSW11] Elette Boyle, Gil Segev, and Daniel Wichs. Fully leakage-resilient signatures. In Paterson [Pat11], pages 89–108.

[Cra12] Ronald Cramer, editor. *Theory of Cryptography - 9th Theory of Cryptography Conference, TCC 2012, Taormina, Sicily, Italy, March 19-21, 2012. Proceedings*, volume 7194 of *Lecture Notes in Computer Science*. Springer, 2012.

[DHLW10a] Yevgeniy Dodis, Kristiyan Haralambiev, Adriana López-Alt, and Daniel Wichs. Cryptography against continuous memory attacks. In *FOCS* [IEE10], pages 511–520.

[DHLW10b] Yevgeniy Dodis, Kristiyan Haralambiev, Adriana López-Alt, and Daniel Wichs. Efficient public-key cryptography in the presence of key leakage. In Masayuki Abe, editor, *ASIACRYPT*, volume 6477 of *Lecture Notes in Computer Science*, pages 613–631. Springer, 2010.

[DHT12] Yevgeniy Dodis, Iftach Haitner, and Aris Tentes. On the instantiability of hash-and-sign rsa signatures. In Cramer [Cra12], pages 112–132.

[DOP05] Yevgeniy Dodis, Roberto Oliveira, and Krzysztof Pietrzak. On the generic insecurity of the full domain hash. In *CRYPTO*, pages 449–466, 2005.

[DORS08] Yevgeniy Dodis, Rafail Ostrovsky, Leonid Reyzin, and Adam Smith. Fuzzy extractors: How to generate strong keys from biometrics and other noisy data. *SIAM Journal on Computing*, 38(1):97–139, 2008.

[DP08] Stefan Dziembowski and Krzysztof Pietrzak. Leakage-resilient cryptography. In *49th Symposium on Foundations of Computer Science*, pages 293–302, Philadelphia, PA, USA, October 25–28 2008. IEEE Computer Society.

[DRV12] Yevgeniy Dodis, Thomas Ristenpart, and Salil P. Vadhan. Randomness condensers for efficiently samplable, seed-dependent sources. In Cramer [Cra12], pages 618–635.

[FOR12] Benjamin Fuller, Adam O'Neill, and Leonid Reyzin. A unified approach to deterministic encryption: New constructions and a connection to computational entropy. In Cramer [Cra12], pages 582–599.

[FV11] Lance Fortnow and Salil P. Vadhan, editors. *Proceedings of the 43rd ACM Symposium on Theory of Computing, STOC 2011, San Jose, CA, USA, 6-8 June 2011*. ACM, 2011.

[GKM$^+$00] Yael Gertner, Sampath Kannan, Tal Malkin, Omer Reingold, and Mahesh Viswanathan. The relationship between public key encryption and oblivious transfer. In *41st Annual Symposium on Foundations of Computer Science*, pages 325–335, Redondo Beach, California, November 2000. IEEE.

[GKPV10] Shafi Goldwasser, Yael Tauman Kalai, Chris Peikert, and Vinod Vaikuntanathan. Robustness of the learning with errors assumption. In Andrew Chi-Chih Yao, editor, *ICS*, pages 230–240. Tsinghua University Press, 2010.

[GMR01] Yael Gertner, Tal Malkin, and Omer Reingold. On the impossibility of basing trapdoor functions on trapdoor predicates. In *42nd Annual Symposium on Foundations of Computer Science*, Las Vegas, Nevada, October 2001. IEEE.

[GOR11] Vipul Goyal, Adam O'Neill, and Vanishree Rao. Correlated-input secure hash functions. In Ishai [Ish11], pages 182–200.

[GR12] Shafi Goldwasser and Guy N. Rothblum. How to compute in the presence of leakage. *Electronic Colloquium on Computational Complexity (ECCC)*, 19:10, 2012.

[GW11] Craig Gentry and Daniel Wichs. Separating succinct non-interactive arguments from all falsifiable assumptions. In Fortnow and Vadhan [FV11], pages 99–108.

[Hal09] Shai Halevi, editor. *Advances in Cryptology - CRYPTO 2009*, volume 5677 of *LNCS*. Springer-Verlag, 2009.

[HH09] Iftach Haitner and Thomas Holenstein. On the (im)possibility of key dependent encryption. In Reingold [Rei09], pages 202–219.

[HL11] Shai Halevi and Huijia Lin. After-the-fact leakage in public-key encryption. In Ishai [Ish11], pages 107–124.

[HLO10] Brett Hemenway, Steve Lu, and Rafail Ostrovsky. Correlated product security from any one-way function and the new notion of decisional correlated product security. Cryptology ePrint Archive, Report 2010/100, 2010. `http://eprint.iacr.org/`.

[IEE10] IEEE. *51th Symposium on Foundations of Computer Science*, Las Vegas, NV, USA, October 23–26 2010.

[IR89] Russell Impagliazzo and Steven Rudich. Limits on the provable consequences of one-way permutations. In D. S. Johnson, editor, *Proceedings of the Twenty First Annual ACM Symposium on Theory of Computing*, pages 44–61, Seattle, Washington, 15–17 May 1989.

[Ish11] Yuval Ishai, editor. *Theory of Cryptography -*

8th Theory of Cryptography Conference, TCC 2011, Providence, RI, USA, March 28-30, 2011. Proceedings, volume 6597 of *Lecture Notes in Computer Science*. Springer, 2011.

[ISW03] Yuval Ishai, Amit Sahai, and David Wagner. Private circuits: Securing hardware against probing attacks. In Dan Boneh, editor, *Advances in Cryptology—CRYPTO 2003*, volume 2729 of *LNCS*. Springer-Verlag, 2003.

[KV09] Jonathan Katz and Vinod Vaikuntanathan. Signature schemes with bounded leakage resilience. In Mitsuru Matsui, editor, *Advances in Cryptology—ASIACRYPT 2009*, LNCS. Springer-Verlag, 2009. To Appear.

[Lys02] Anna Lysyanskaya. Unique signatures and verifiable random functions from the dh-ddh separation. In Moti Yung, editor, *CRYPTO*, volume 2442 of *Lecture Notes in Computer Science*, pages 597–612. Springer, 2002.

[MR04] Silvio Micali and Leonid Reyzin. Physically observable cryptography (extended abstract). In Naor [Nao04], pages 278–296.

[Nao04] Moni Naor, editor. *First Theory of Cryptography Conference — TCC 2004*, volume 2951 of *LNCS*. Springer-Verlag, February 19–21 2004.

[NS09] Moni Naor and Gil Segev. Public-key cryptosystems resilient to key leakage. In Halevi [Hal09], pages 18–35.

[Pas11] Rafael Pass. Limits of provable security from standard assumptions. In Fortnow and Vadhan [FV11], pages 109–118.

[Pat11] Kenneth G. Paterson, editor. *Advances in Cryptology - EUROCRYPT 2011 - 30th Annual International Conference on the Theory and Applications of Cryptographic Techniques, Tallinn, Estonia, May 15-19, 2011. Proceedings*, volume 6632 of *Lecture Notes in Computer Science*. Springer, 2011.

[PW08] Chris Peikert and Brent Waters. Lossy trapdoor functions and their applications. In Cynthia Dwork, editor, *STOC*, pages 187–196. ACM, 2008.

[Rei09] Omer Reingold, editor. *Theory of Cryptography, 6th Theory of Cryptography Conference, TCC 2009, San Francisco, CA, USA, March 15-17, 2009. Proceedings*, volume 5444 of *Lecture Notes in Computer Science*. Springer, 2009.

[RR99] Ran Raz and Omer Reingold. On recycling the randomness of states in space bounded computation. In Jeffrey Scott Vitter, Lawrence L. Larmore, and Frank Thomson Leighton, editors, *STOC*, pages 159–168. ACM, 1999.

[RS09] Alon Rosen and Gil Segev. Chosen-ciphertext security via correlated products. In Reingold [Rei09], pages 419–436.

[RSS11] Thomas Ristenpart, Hovav Shacham, and Thomas Shrimpton. Careful with composition: Limitations of the indifferentiability framework. In Paterson [Pat11], pages 487–506.

[RTTV08] Omer Reingold, Luca Trevisan, Madhur Tulsiani, and Salil P. Vadhan. Dense subsets of pseudorandom sets. In *FOCS*, pages 76–85. IEEE Computer Society, 2008.

[RTV04] Omer Reingold, Luca Trevisan, and Salil Vadhan. Notions of reducibility between cryptographic primitives. In Naor [Nao04], pages 1–20.

[Sim98] Daniel R. Simon. Finding collisions on a one-way street: Can secure hash functions be based on general assumptions. In Kaisa Nyberg, editor, *Advances in Cryptology—EUROCRYPT 98*, volume 1403 of *LNCS*. Springer-Verlag, May 31–June 4 1998.

[Wag08] David Wagner, editor. *Advances in Cryptology - CRYPTO 2008, 28th Annual International Cryptology Conference, Santa Barbara, CA, USA, August 17-21, 2008. Proceedings*, volume 5157 of *Lecture Notes in Computer Science*. Springer, 2008.

APPENDIX

A. WEAK-DISTRIBUTION RESILIENT ONE-WAY FUNCTIONS

Let $\mathcal{F} \stackrel{\text{def}}{=} \{ f_{pk} : \{0,1\}^{k(n)} \to \{0,1\}^{m(n)} \}_{n\in\mathbb{N}}$ be a family of efficiently computable functions keyed by a public $pk \leftarrow \mathsf{Gen}(1^n)$.

Definition A.1. *Let* $(\mathcal{F}, \mathsf{Gen})$ *be as above. A probabilistic sampling algorithm* Sam *is called* $\ell(\cdot)$-weak *if the distribution* $\mathsf{Sam}(1^n)$ *induces a distribution over* $\{0,1\}^{k(n)}$ *such that* $\mathbf{H}_\infty(\mathsf{Sam}(1^n)) \geq k(n) - \ell(n)$. *We say that* $(\mathcal{F}, \mathsf{Gen})$ *is an* $\ell(\cdot)$-weakness resilient one-way function *if for any PPT algorithms* $\mathcal{A} = (\mathsf{Sam}, \mathsf{Break})$ *such that* Sam *is* $\ell(n)$*-weak, we have*

$$\Pr\left[f_{pk}(x') = y \;\middle|\; \begin{array}{c} pk \leftarrow \mathsf{Gen}(1^n), \\ x \xleftarrow{\$} \mathsf{Sam}(1^n), \\ y = f_{pk}(x) \\ x' \leftarrow \mathsf{Break}(1^n, pk, y) \end{array} \right] = \mathsf{negl}(n).$$

Definition A.2. *We say that the function family* $\mathcal{F}$ *is* recognizably injective *if there is an efficient algorithm* Ver *such that* $\mathsf{Ver}(pk) = 1$ *iff* f_{pk} *is injective.*

Theorem A.3. *Let* $(\mathcal{F}, \mathsf{Gen})$ *be any recognizably injective function family. Then there is a* $2^{-\ell(n)}$ *simulatable attack against the* ℓ*-weakness-resilient one-wayness of the family.*

Proof. Let $H \subseteq \{0,1\}^{k(n)}$ be a set of size $|H| = 2^{k(n)-\ell(n)}$ and let $\mathcal{H}_n$ consist of all such sets. We define two (inefficient) oracles $\mathsf{Sam}_{n,H}, \mathsf{Break}_{n,H}$ with respect to $H \in \mathcal{H}$ as follows:

Sam_H : On input 1^n, output a random $x \xleftarrow{\$} H$.

Break_H: On input (pk, y), verify that $\mathsf{Ver}(pk) = 1$ and output $\perp$ if not. Else do an exhaustive search to find $x \in H$ such that $f_{pk}(x) = y$. If no such x exists output $\perp$ and else output x.

Firstly, it is easy to see that for any $H \in \mathcal{H}_n$, the above oracles break ℓ-WR one-wayness of $(\mathcal{F}, \mathsf{Gen})$ with advantage 1. This is because the entropy of the distribution $\mathsf{Sam}_{n,H}(1^n)$ is always exactly $k(n) - \ell(n)$ and for any $x \xleftarrow{\$} \mathsf{Sam}_{n,H}(1^n, s)$, we have $\mathsf{Break}_{n,H}(1^n, s, f_s(x)) = x$.

Now we show that when H is chosen uniformly at random from $\mathcal{H}_n$, then getting oracle access to $(\mathsf{Leak}^H, \mathsf{Break}_{n,H})$ is *not very useful*. In particular, access to such oracles can be efficiently simulated up to a small statistical distance. The simulator $\mathsf{Sim}(1^n)$ must respond to "sample" queries and to "break" queries and it does so as follows:

1. Initialization: Set $Q := \emptyset$.
2. Sample: With probability $p = \frac{|Q|}{2^{k(n)-\ell(n)}}$ output a random $x \xleftarrow{\$} Q$. Otherwise choose $x \xleftarrow{\$} \{0,1\}^{k(n)}$, add the tuple x to Q, and output x.
3. Break: On a *break* query (pk, y), first verify (efficiently) that $\mathsf{Ver}(pk) = 1$ and output $\perp$ if the check fails. Else check if there is some $x \in Q$ such that $f_{pk}(x) = y$ and, if so, output it and else output $\perp$.

We wish to show that the simulation is good and for any oracle-access (possibly inefficient) $\mathcal{M}$ making at most $q(n)$ queries to its oracle, we have:

$$\left| \begin{array}{c} \Pr[\mathcal{M}^{(\mathsf{Sam}_{n,H}, \mathsf{Break}_{n,H})}(1^n) = 1] \\ - \Pr[\mathcal{M}^{\mathsf{Sim}(1^n)}(1^n) = 1] \end{array} \right| \leq \frac{q(n)}{2^{\ell(n)}}.$$

First, let us define the event E to be the event that during the execution $\mathcal{M}^{(\mathsf{Sam}_{n,H}, \mathsf{Break}_{n,H})}(1^n)$, the machine $\mathcal{M}$ makes a "break" query (pk, y) such that $y \neq f_{pk}(x)$ for any x returned by a prior "sample" query, and the response from the oracle is *not* $\perp$. The conditioned on E not occurring, the experiments are the same, since we can think of $\mathsf{Sim}(1^n)$ as just choosing the values of H "on-the-go" as it answers its sample queries. Therefore the statistical distance between the real game and the simulation is bounded by $\Pr[E]$ which is the probability that the query (pk, y) satisfies that its unique preimage $x = f_{pk}^{-1}(y) \in H$, which is the probability of the attacker being able to guess a new value in H after $\leq q$ queries, which is bounded by $\Pr[E] \leq q(n)2^{-\ell(n)}$ as we wanted to show. □

On the Possibilities and Limitations of Pseudodeterministic Algorithms

[Extended Abstract]

Oded Goldreich*
Weizmann Institute of Science
Rehovot, Israel
oded.goldreich@weizmann.ac.il

Shafi Goldwasser†
MIT
Cambridge, MA, USA
Weizmann Institute of Science
Rehovot, Israel
shafi@csail.mit.edu

Dana Ron‡
Tel Aviv University
Tel Aviv, Israel
danar@eng.tau.ac.il

ABSTRACT

We study the possibilities and limitations of pseudodeterministic algorithms, a notion put forward by Gat and Goldwasser (2011). These are probabilistic algorithms that solve search problems such that on each input, with high probability, they output the same solution, which may be thought of as a canonical solution. We consider both the standard setting of (probabilistic) polynomial-time algorithms and the setting of (probabilistic) sublinear-time algorithms. Some of our results are outlined next.

In the standard setting, we show that pseudodeterministic algorithms are more powerful than deterministic algorithms if and only if $\mathcal{P} \neq \mathcal{BPP}$, but are weaker than general probabilistic algorithms. In the sublinear-time setting, we show that if a search problem has a pseudodeterministic algorithm of query complexity q, then this problem can be solved deterministically making $O(q^4)$ queries. This refers to total search problems. In contrast, for several natural promise search problems, we present pseudodeterministic algorithms that are much more efficient than their deterministic counterparts.

Categories and Subject Descriptors

F.1.3 [**Complexity Measures and Classes**]: Relations among complexity classes; F.2 [**Analysis of Algorithms and Problem Complexity**]: Nonnumerical Algorithms and Problems

*Supported by the Israel Science Foundation (grant no. 1041/08).

†Supported by DARPA (contract no. FA8750-11-2-0225), NSF (contract no. CCF-1018064) and Simons investigator award.

‡Supported by the Israel Science Foundation (grant no. 246/08).

General Terms

Theory

Keywords

Search problems, BPP, ZPP, unique solutions, sublinear-time computations

1. INTRODUCTION

In [5], Gat and Goldwasser initiated a study of probabilistic (polynomial-time) search algorithms that, with high probability, output the same solution. That is, for a fixed binary relation R, such algorithms associate a canonical solution, denoted $s(x)$, with any instance x such that, with overwhelmingly high probability, on input x the algorithm outputs $s(x)$.

Algorithms that satisfy the foregoing condition are called pseudodeterministic[1], because they essentially offer the same functionality as deterministic algorithms; that is, they produce a fixed (canonical) output for each possible input (except with negligible error probability). In contrast, arbitrary probabilistic algorithms that solve search problems may output different solutions when presented with the same input (but using different internal coin tosses); that is, on input x, with overwhelmingly high probability, the output is arbitrarily distributed among all valid solutions for x (e.g., it may be uniformly distributed).

Pseudodeterministic algorithms have the appealing feature that they (typically) yield the same result, when invoked on the same input. Thus if two parties invoke the algorithm on the same input at different times and locations (and using different sources of randomness), they are still guaranteed to obtain the same result, except very rarely. Needless to say, the lack of such agreement is a drawback of standard probabilistic algorithms.

The notion of a canonical solution is quite natural, and has appeared in various contexts such as the notion of canonical labeling of graphs, cf. [1]. Furthermore, probabilistic algorithms that find canonical solutions for natural problems (for which no deterministic algorithms is known) were implicit in work of Lenstra and de Smit [14].

[1]We mention that pseudodeterministic polynomial-time algorithms were also called Bellagio algorithms (in [5]).

In addition to defining pseudodeterministic algorithms and presenting pseudodeterministic polynomial-time algorithms for several natural search problems (which were previously known to be solvable probabilistically), Gat and Goldwasser [5] characterized the class of search problems having such algorithms. They showed that a search problem has a polynomial-time pseudodeterministic algorithm if and only if solving the search problem is reducible in deterministic polynomial-time to some set in $\mathcal{BPP}$ (see Theorem 2.2).

Many questions come to mind: Do polynomial-time pseudodeterministic algorithms exist for all search problems that can be solve in probabilistic polynomial-time? Or, to the other extreme, do polynomial-time pseudodeterministic algorithms exist only for search problems that can be solved in deterministic polynomial-time? And what happens in the context of sublinear time and query complexity?

The latter question is appealing since probabilism is essential to any sublinear-time algorithm that solves a "non-degenerate problem". Thus, unlike in the context of polynomial-time, there are a huge number of probabilistic sublinear-time algorithms (cf., the property testing literature). Furthermore, many property testing algorithms yield algorithms that solve related search problems (e.g., finding a k-partition with few violating edges [8]), and in all cases that come to mind these algorithms are not pseudodeterministic. An intriguing question is whether this is inherent.

1.1 Our results

In the current work, we advance the understanding of probabilistic algorithms for finding canonical solutions, considering both the standard context of polynomial-time algorithms and the context of sublinear-time algorithms. In both cases, we explore the possibilities and limitations of such algorithms, but the results provided in the sublinear case are more natural.

The standard context (of PPT algorithms). The characterization of the class of search problems having pseudodeterministic algorithms (in terms of P-reducibility[2] to $\mathcal{BPP}$ (i.e., Theorem 2.2)) implies that pseudodeterministic algorithms may exceed the scope of deterministic algorithms only if $\mathcal{BPP} \neq \mathcal{P}$. We first show that this necessary condition is also sufficient; in other words, if pseudodeterministic algorithms do not exceed the scope of deterministic algorithms, then $\mathcal{BPP} = \mathcal{P}$. On the other hand, we show that there exist search problems that can be solved in probabilistic polynomial-time but have no pseudodeterministic algorithms. Thus, in the context of solving search problems in polynomial-time, *pseudodeterministic algorithms are more powerful than deterministic algorithms if and only if $\mathcal{P} \neq \mathcal{BPP}$, but are weaker than general probabilistic algorithms.*

We also discuss a zero-error version of the notion of pseudodeterministic algorithms; that is, these algorithms never output a solution that differs from the canonical one (but they may rather halt, with small probability, while providing a special error indication). We show that this class equals the class of search problems that are P-reducible to $\mathcal{ZPP}$.

The context of sublinear-time algorithms. We show several limitations on the scope of finding canonical solutions in probabilistic sublinear number of queries. Firstly, this is not possible for problems that have instances of linear sensitivity (i.e., search problems R having infinitely many instance x such that the set of solutions associated with x does not intersect the set of solutions associated with most strings obtained by flipping one bit of x). Note that many natural search problems have such instances. Secondly, with respect to non-adaptive algorithms, finding canonical solutions probabilistically is not easier than doing so deterministically. Lastly, even when adaptivity is allowed, finding canonical solutions probabilistically is not *significantly easier* than doing so deterministically. In particular, if this can be done in a constant or poly-logarithmic number of queries, then it can be done so deterministically. In general, the speed-up offered by probabilism (over determinism) is at most polynomial.

The aforementioned negative result implies a huge gap between probabilistic algorithms and pseudodeterministic ones: There exist search problems that are solved probabilistically in a constant number of queries but have no pseudodeterministic algorithm of sublinear query complexity. We also demonstrate the existence of a three-way separation between probabilism, pseudodeterminism, and determinism: There exist problems in which the query complexities are $O(1)$, n^c for some $c \in (0,1)$, and $\Omega(n)$, respectively.

The above negative results leave some room for sublinear-time pseudodeterministic algorithms. Firstly, pseudodeterministic algorithms may be somewhat faster than their deterministic counterparts, provided that they are adaptive and that the search problem has no instances of linear sensitivity. Secondly, the negative results refer to *total search problems*; that is, the search algorithm is required to work for all possible inputs (and not for a subset of them). In contrast, strong "disconnectivity" of the (promise) set of legitimate inputs allows probabilistic algorithms to find canonical solutions much more efficiently than deterministic ones. Several natural cases are presented in Section 4, and include search problems for graphs in the adjacency matrix model and in the incidence lists model. We discuss one, referring to the adjacency matrix model, next.

Suppose that we are presented with a huge graph G that is obtained by a blow-up of some small unknown graph H (i.e., each vertex of H is replaced by a cluster of $m \in [M, 2M]$ vertices and edges of H are replaced by complete bipartite graphs). That is, G has some underlying structure (captured by H), and we are interested in finding this underlying structure (or finding substructures in it). Then, a pseudodeterministic algorithm may have complexity related to the size of H, whereas the complexity of any deterministic algorithm will be related to the size of G.

1.2 Organization

In Section 2 we present the basic definitions as well as the characterization result of [5], which are the starting point of our study. In Section 3, we consider the standard context of polynomial-time algorithms, whereas in Section 4 we consider the context of sublinear time and query algorithms. Finally, in Section 5, we discuss a zero-error version of the notion of pseudodeterministic algorithms.

2. BACKGROUND

Our starting point is the following notion, explicitly introduced by Gat and Goldwasser [5]. As usual, the definition

[2] A P-reduction is a deterministic polynomial-time Turing reduction.

refers to a fixed error probability (of 1/3), and the ramification for other error bounds is straightforward.

DEFINITION 2.1. (finding canonical solutions and pseudodeterministic algorithms [5]):[3] *Let* $R \subseteq \{0,1\}^* \times \{0,1\}^*$ *be a binary relation, and let* $R(x) = \{y : (x,y) \in R\}$ *and* $S_R = \{x : R(x) \neq \emptyset\}$. *Suppose that the empty string is never a solution; that is,* $\lambda \notin R(x)$ *for all* x. *A* (possibly probabilistic) *algorithm A* finds canonical solutions with respect to R *if there exists a function* $s : \{0,1\}^* \to \{0,1\}^*$ *such that the following conditions hold:*

1. *For every* $x \in S_R$ *it holds that* $s(x) \in R(x)$, *whereas* $s(x) = \lambda$ *for every* $x \in \{0,1\}^* \setminus S_R$.
2. *For every* $x \in \{0,1\}^*$, *it holds that* $\Pr[A(x) = s(x)] \geq 2/3$.

The function s is called a canonical solution function for R *and A is called a* pseudodeterministic algorithm for R.

In the context of polynomial-time algorithms, Definition 2.1 is robust in the sense that replacing the threshold 2/3 by either $0.5 + 1/\text{poly}(|x|)$ or $1 - \exp(-\text{poly}(|x|))$ yields the same class (via standard error reduction). In other settings (where the complexity measures are more refined), the same error reduction applies, but one should bear in mind its cost (e.g., going from error probability of 1/3 to error probability δ costs a multiplicative factor of $O(\log(1/\delta))$ in all complexities). Also, any deterministic algorithm for finding solutions w.r.t R finds canonical solutions w.r.t R.

Of course, a probabilistic (polynomial-time) algorithm for finding canonical solutions w.r.t R is of interest only if it is (significantly) faster than the known deterministic algorithm (e.g., if no deterministic (polynomial-time) algorithms are known for finding solutions w.r.t R). Gat and Goldwasser presented several such examples as well as established the following necessary and sufficient condition for such algorithms:

THEOREM 2.2. (a characterization [5]): *A relation R has a pseudodeterministic polynomial-time algorithm if and only if finding solutions w.r.t R is P-reducible to some set in* $\mathcal{BPP}$, *where a* P-reduction *is a deterministic polynomial-time Turing reduction.*

In particular, if $\mathcal{BPP} = \mathcal{P}$, then the existence of a probabilistic polynomial-time algorithm for finding canonical solutions w.r.t R implies that (canonical) solutions w.r.t R can be found by a deterministic polynomial-time algorithm.

PROOF. The first direction is proved by using the P-reduction as an algorithm, while providing answers to its queries via a BPP algorithm (of sufficiently low error probability). This yields a probabilistic algorithm that outputs the same (canonical) solution whenever all the emulated answers are correct. For the opposite direction, suppose that algorithm A finds canonical solutions w.r.t R, and consider the set S such that $(x, i, b) \in S$ if and only if $\Pr[A(x)_i = b] \geq 2/3$, where $A(x)_i$ denotes the ith bit in the output $A(x)$. Then, (i) the set S is a BPP set (since it is essentially decided by $A(x)$), and (ii) finding solutions w.r.t R is P-reducible to S. ■

[3] An alternative formulation may refer to R' such that for every x it holds that $R'(x) \neq \emptyset$ and either $\lambda \notin R'(x)$ or $R'(x) = \{\lambda\}$. Indeed, $R'(x) = R(x)$ if $x \in S_R$ and $R'(x) = \{\lambda\}$ otherwise.

Note: A zero-error version of Definition 2.1 and a corresponding chractaterization (in terms of $\mathcal{ZPP}$) are discussed in Section 5.

3. THE STANDARD CONTEXT (OF PPT ALGORITHMS)

In this section we consider the standard setting of polynomial-time algorithms.

3.1 Possibilities and impossibilities

Theorem 2.2 implies that relations for which canonical solutions can be found in probabilistic polynomial-time but not in deterministic polynomial-time may exist only if $\mathcal{BPP} \neq \mathcal{P}$. We observe that this necessary condition is also sufficient.

PROPOSITION 3.1. (on the non-triviality of pseudodeterministic algorithms): *If* $\mathcal{BPP} \neq \mathcal{P}$, *then there exists a search problem that has a pseudodeterministic polynomial-time algorithm but does not have a deterministic polynomial-time algorithm. Furthermore, for every* $S \in \mathcal{BPP}$, *there exists a relation R such that (1) deciding S is P-reducible to finding solutions w.r.t R, and (2) canonical solutions w.r.t R can be found in probabilistic polynomial-time.*

PROOF. The main claim follows from the furthermore claim. To see this consider, for every $S \in \mathcal{BPP}$, the relation R that is guaranteed by the furthermore claim, and suppose (towards the contradiction) that whenever canonical solutions can be found in probabilistic polynomial-time they can also be found in deterministic polynomial-time. Then, S is in $\mathcal{P}$ (by combining the guaranteed P-reduction of S to R with the deterministic algorithm for finding solutions w.r.t R).

We now turn to the furthermore claim itself. This claim is proved by observing that any decision problem in $\mathcal{BPP}$ is essentially a search problem that has a pseudodeterministic polynomial-time algorithm. Specifically, for any $S \in \mathcal{BPP}$, consider the relation

$$R = \{(x, 1) : x \in S\} \cup \{(x, 0) : x \in \{0,1\}^* \setminus S\} \quad (1)$$

Clearly, S is P-reducible to solving R, which has unique solutions, which in turn can be found probabilistically (by running the decision procedure for S). Needless to say, various syntactic requirements regarding R can be met by simple modifications; for example, if solutions have to be longer than the input and non-unique, then one may use $R'(x) = \{\sigma^{|x|}\alpha : \sigma \in R(x) \;\&\; \alpha \in \{0,1\}^{|x|}\}$. ■

An impossibility result. On the other hand, there exist search problems that can be solved in probabilistic polynomial-time but for which canonical solutions cannot be found in probabilistic polynomial-time.

PROPOSITION 3.2. (search problems solvable in PPT, but not pseudodeterministically): *There exists a search problem R such that R can be solved in probabilistic polynomial-time but no probabilistic algorithm can find canonical solutions w.r.t R.*

PROOF. Let $K(z)$ denote the Kolmogorov complexity of z, and consider the binary relation

$$R = \{(x, y) : |y| = 2|x| \ \& \ K(y) > 2|x| - 7\}. \quad (2)$$

(Indeed, the solutions to x only depend on the length of x.) Then, on the one hand, solutions w.r.t R can be found in probabilistic polynomial-time (by just generating uniformly distributed $2|x|$-bit long strings, and hitting a valid solution with probability at least 99%). But, on the other hand, no probabilistic algorithm can find canonical solutions w.r.t R, because a probabilistic t-time algorithm A that finds a canonical solution y with probability greater than half yields a deterministic (indeed, $\exp(t)$-time) algorithm that (on input x) finds this y (which implies $K(y) \leq O(1) + |x|$, in contradiction to $K(y) > 2|x| - 7$). ■

On problems with unique solution. Clearly, for any relation R having unique solutions (i.e., $|R(x)| \leq 1$ for every x), the unique solutions are canonical (i.e., whenever $R(x) = \{y\}$ we must use $s(x) = y$). Thus, a probabilistic algorithm that finds solutions w.r.t R, actually finds canonical solutions w.r.t R. Many such algorithms are known, especially in the domain of computational number theory (e.g., finding (the smallest) square root modulo a given prime, or the subexponential-time algorithms for factoring and discrete logarithms). Hence, while we are still interested in new probabilistic algorithms that solve natural search problems with unique solutions (and, in general, in any new probabilistic algorithms that solve natural computational problems), such algorithms are not necessarily "good" examples for the concept of finding canonical solutions.

3.2 On BPP-search problems

A natural class of "BPP search problems" (studied in [7]) refers to the class of all search problems that can be solved in probabilistic polynomial-time and for which solutions can be recognized in probabilistic polynomial-time.

DEFINITION 3.3. (BPP-search problems): *A relation R is a* BPP-search problem *if (1) the set R is in $\mathcal{BPP}$, and (2) there exists a probabilistic polynomial-time algorithm A such that for every $x \in S_R$ it holds that* $\Pr[A(x) \in R(x)] \geq 2/3$.

(There is no need to require that for every $x \notin S_R$ it holds that $\Pr[A(x) = \lambda] \geq 2/3$, since (by using the algorithm of Item (1)) we can guarantee that wrong solutions are output with probability at most 1/3.) Note that the relation used in Proposition 3.2 is not a BPP-search problem (since it does not satisfy the first condition (i.e., it is not recognizable in probabilistic polynomial-time)). A natural question is whether every BPP-search problem has a polynomial-time pseudodeterministic algorithm. We note that a positive answer would follow if the "promise problem version of BPP", denoted pr$\mathcal{BPP}$, were P-reducible to $\mathcal{BPP}$ itself. This is the case since Goldreich [7] showed that BPP-search problems are P-reducible to pr$\mathcal{BPP}$, whereas by Theorem 2.2 every search problem that is P-reducible to $\mathcal{BPP}$ has a a polynomial-time pseudodeterministic algorithm.[4] On the other hand, a negative answer must assume that pr$\mathcal{BPP}$ is not solvable in deterministic polynomial-time.

Not being able to resolve the above question, we present a search problem that is "semi-complete" with respect to the class of BPP-search problems in the sense that (i) if this problem has a polynomial-time pseudodeterministic algorithm, then so does any problem in the class, and (ii) the problem itself is "somewhat related" to this class.[5]

The problem we present is "generic" and is thus denoted G: For a Boolean circuit C, let $P_C(y) \stackrel{\text{def}}{=} \Pr_z[C(yz)=1]$, where $|z| = |y|$ (i.e., we assume that C takes an even number of input bits, and denote a generic prefix by y and suffix by z). Then, $G(C) \stackrel{\text{def}}{=} \{y : P_C(y) \geq 2/3\}$ if $\Pr_r[P_C(r) \geq 2/3] \geq 2/3$, and $G(C) \stackrel{\text{def}}{=} \emptyset$ otherwise; that is,

$$G \stackrel{\text{def}}{=} \{(C, y) : P_C(y) \geq 2/3 \ \& \ \Pr_r[P_C(r) \geq 2/3] \geq 2/3\}. \quad (3)$$

This search problem can be solved by merely selecting a random r, since $\Pr_r[P_C(r) \geq 2/3] \geq 2/3$ for any $C \in S_C$. Thus, G satisfies the second condition of Definition 3.3. It is unclear whether G satisfies the first condition, but it does satisfy a weak version of this condition: One can distinguish in probabilistic polynomial-time between pairs (C, y) in G and pairs (C, y) such that either $P_C(y) < 0.66$ or $\Pr_r[P_C(r) > 0.66] < 0.66$. Furthermore, the set G is recognizable in exponential time.[6] Hence, we say that this problem is *semi-complete*.

PROPOSITION 3.4. *Every BPP-search problem is P-reducible to G.*

Thus, if G has a polynomial-time pseudodeterministic algorithm, then we obtain such an algorithm for any BPP-search problem: Invoke the P-reduction and answer its queries using the pseudodeterministic algorithm guaranteed for G, and check the solution before outputting it (i.e., if it is invalid, then we output a special indicator). This is done after applying an error reduction such that the G-solver provides the canonical solution with overwhelmingly high probability. Thus, when the reduction is invoked on a yes-instance, then it yields a canonical solution, and otherwise (by the additional checking) it outputs a special indicator (as required in Definition 2.1).

PROOF. For any BPP-search problem R, we show a P-reduction of R to G. Fixing R, let V and F be the probabilistic polynomial-time algorithms guaranteed by the two conditions of Definition 3.3 (i.e., V recognizes valid instance solution pairs, whereas F finds valid solutions). Assume, without loss of generality, that each of these algorithms uses the same number of coins (on the respective inputs). Then, given an input x, consider the circuit C_x that represents the computation of $V(x, F(x))$; that is, $C_x(r, r')$ is the output

[4]We note that, in contrast to Theorem 2.2, a P-reduction of BPP-search problems to pr$\mathcal{BPP}$ (and, in particular, the one in [7]) does not seem to yield an algorithm for finding canonical solutions: The problem is that queries that violate the promise may yield arbitrary answers, which may possibly lead the search to different solutions.

[5]Indeed, it would have been better to present a problem in BPP-search that is complete under P-reductions, but this seems as difficult as presenting a problem in $\mathcal{BPP}$ that is complete under P-reductions.

[6]Moreover, if G is not a BPP-search problem, then this is due to a separation of $\mathcal{BPP}$ from $\mathcal{EXP}$, which in turn implies that $\mathcal{BPP}$ can be solved in *average* subexponential time [13] (and ditto for BPP-search problems [7]).

of V on input (x, s) and coins r', where s is the output of F on input x and coins r. (By the above, $|r'| = |r|$.) Note that $p_{C_x}(r) = \Pr_{r'}[C_x(r, r) = 1] = \Pr[V(x, F(x; r)) = 1]$, where $F(x; r)$ denotes the output of F on input x and coins r.

Note that if $x \in S_R$, then $\Pr_r[p_{C_x}(r) \geq 2/3] \geq 2/3$, which implies that $G(C_x) \neq \emptyset$. On the other hand, $G(C_x) \subseteq \{r : F(x; r) \in R(x)\}$, since $r \in G(C_x)$ implies $p_{C_x}(r) \geq 2/3$. Hence, a P-reduction of R to G may proceed as follows. On input x, it constructs the circuit C_x, invokes the G-solver to obtain a solution, denoted r, for C_x w.r.t G, and outputs $F(x; r)$. ∎

4. THE CONTEXT OF SUBLINEAR-TIME ALGORITHMS

Let us now turn to the sublinear-time model. In this context, the algorithm is given oracle access to the input, and is only provided with the input's length as explicit input. Thus, the computation of machine M with oracle access to x is captured by the notation $M^x(|x|)$.

4.1 Limitations

We show several limitations on scope of finding canonical solutions in probabilistic sublinear-time. Firstly, this is not possible for problems that have instances of linear sensitivity (i.e., search problems R having infinitely many $x \in S_R$ such that $|\{i \in [|x|] : R(x) \cap R(x \oplus e_i) = \emptyset\}| = \Omega(|x|)$, where $e_i = 0^{i-1}10^{|x|-i}$). Note that many natural search problems have such instances (e.g., the number of connected components in a graph may change if a single edge is added in any of many possible ways). Secondly, finding canonical solutions probabilistically is not significantly easier than doing so deterministically. In particular, if this can be done in a constant or poly-logarithmic number of queries, then it can be done so deterministically.

THEOREM 4.1. (on the limitations of sublinear-time algorithms): *Let R be an arbitrary search problem such that $S_R = \{0,1\}^*$ and M be a probabilistic machine that makes at most $q(n)$ queries on any n-bit long input.*

1. *If for every function $f : \{0,1\}^* \to \{0,1\}^*$ there exists an x such that either $f(x) \notin R(x)$ or $|\{i \in [|x|] : f(x) \neq f(x \oplus e_i)\}| > 3q(|x|)$, then M fails to find canonical solutions w.r.t R. In particular, if there exists an x such that $|\{i \in [|x|] : R(x) \cap R(x \oplus e_i) = \emptyset\}| > 3q(|x|)$, then M fails to find canonical solutions w.r.t R.*

2. *If M is non-adaptive and finds canonical solutions w.r.t R, then canonical solutions w.r.t R can be found deterministically by making at most $3q(n)$ non-adaptive queries.*

3. *If M finds canonical solutions w.r.t R, then canonical solutions w.r.t R can be found deterministically by making at most $\min(28q(n)^4, 27\ell(n)q(n)^3)$ queries* (possiblly adaptively), *where $\ell(n) = \lceil \log_2 |\cup_{x \in \{0,1\}^n} R(x)| \rceil$.*

The condition $S_R = \{0,1\}^*$ can be assumed, without loss of generality, since, for any R', we may consider R such that $R(x) = \{1y : y \in R'(x)\}$ if $x \in S_{R'}$ and $R(x) = \{0^{|x|}\}$ otherwise (cf. Footnote 3). The polynomial blow-up in Item 3 is inherent, since the deterministic query complexity is greater than $\Omega(q(n)^{1.3})$ even in the special case of decision problems (which correspond to search problems with unique solutions in $\{0,1\}$). This follows from a gap between the probabilistic and deterministic decision tree complexity [17] (see also [16]). Item 3 is established by using an upper bound on the very same question, which asserts that the deterministic decision tree complexity is at most cubic in the probabilistic complexity [15].

PROOF. Consider an arbitrary probabilistic machine M, and let $Q(x)$ denote a random variable that represents the set of queries made by $M^x(|x|)$; that is, for every coin sequence ω, let $Q_\omega(x)$ denote the set of queries made by $M^x(|x|, \omega)$, and let $Q(x) \leftarrow Q_\omega(x)$ for a uniformly selected ω. Then, $H(x) \stackrel{\text{def}}{=} \{i \in [|x|] : \Pr[i \in Q(x)] \geq 1/3\}$ has cardinality at most $3q(n)$. The basic observation is that if $\Pr[i \in Q(x)] < 1/3$, then, for every y, it holds that $|\Pr[M^x(|x|) = y] - \Pr[M^{x \oplus e_i}(|x|) = y]| < 1/3$.

The first item is proved by considering all possible functions f that may serve as a canonical solution function w.r.t R; that is, $f(x) \in R(x)$ for all x's. For each such function f, we are guaranteed (by the hypothesis) that there exists an x such that $|\{i \in [|x|] : f(x) \neq f(x \oplus e_i)\}| > 3q(|x|)$. Fixing such an x, it follows that there exists an $i \in [|x|]$ such that $f(x) \neq f(x \oplus e_i)$ and $\Pr[i \in Q(x)] < 1/3$ (since there are at least $3q(n) + 1$ indices that satisfy the first condition and at most $3q(n)$ violate the second). In such a case, it holds that $\Pr[M^{x \oplus e_i}(|x|) = f(x)] > \Pr[M^x(|x|) = f(x)] - 1/3$, which implies that $\Pr[M^{x \oplus e_i}(|x|) = f(x \oplus e_i)] < (4/3) - \Pr[M^x(|x|) = f(x)]$. It follows that f cannot be the canonical solution function of M, since either $\Pr[M^x(|x|) = f(x)] < 2/3$ or $\Pr[M^{x \oplus e_i}(|x|) = f(x \oplus e_i)] < 2/3$. Given that the same argument holds with respect to any possible canonical solution function (w.r.t R), it follows that M has no such function (which means that it is not a pseudodeterministic algorithm for R).

Turning to the second item, we observe that, in the non-adaptive case, $H(x)$ depends only on the length of x, and so we may define $H_n \stackrel{\text{def}}{=} H(1^n)$ and note that $H(x) = H_n$ for all $x \in \{0,1\}^n$. We claim that every $x, x' \in \{0,1\}^n$ that agree on bit locations H_n must admit the same canonical solution. Once this claim is proven, the second item follows, because a non-adaptive deterministic machine may just query the oracle on positions in H_n, set the other input bits arbitrarily, and decide accordingly (by emulating all possible executions of the probabilistic algorithm internally).

The foregoing claim (i.e., inputs that agree on bits in H_n must admit the same canonical solution) is proved by considering a "Hamming walk" from x to x' (i.e., considering a sequence $x = v_1, v_2, \ldots, v_t = x'$ such that each pair (v_i, v_{i+1}) differ in a single bit), and using $\Pr[M^{v_{i+1}}(n) = y] > \Pr[M^{v_i}(n) = y] - 1/3$. Specifically, suppose that y is a canonical solution found by M^x (i.e., $\Pr[M^x(n) = y] \geq 2/3$), then y must also be a canonical solution for v_2 (since $\Pr[M^{v_2}(n) = y] > 1/3$), and the same holds for $v_3, \ldots, v_t$ (since if y is a canonical solution for v_i, then $\Pr[M^{v_i}(n) = y] \geq 2/3$, which implies $\Pr[M^{v_{i+1}}(n) = y] > 1/3$, which in turn implies that y is a canonical solution for v_{i+1}).

Turning to the third item, we define $S_n = \{s(x) : x \in \{0,1\}^n\}$, where $s : \{0,1\}^* \to \{0,1\}^*$ describes the canonical solutions used by M. We shall prove (below) that $|S_n| < 2^{q(n)+1}$. Now, consider an arbitrary (deterministic) *binary decision tree* T_n *of depth* $q(n)+1$ *for the set* S_n, where each internal node v of the tree is associated with some subset $S_v \subseteq S_n$ as well as a partition of this subset into two equals subsets, denoted (S_v^0, S_v^1) associated with its children (i.e., if the children are v_0 and v_1, then $S_{v_\sigma} = S_v^\sigma$ for each $\sigma \in \{0,1\}$). Machine M can be used to decide each of the corresponding "bits" (since it actually yields the entire value of $s(\cdot)$). Formally, for every internal node v of T_n, we consider an oracle machine M_v, derived from M, that probabilistically decides the corresponding bit (i.e., $M_v^x(n) = \sigma$ if and only if $s(x) \in S_v^\sigma$) by making at most $q(n)$ queries (to x).[7] Replacing M_v by a deterministic counterpart (denoted M'_v) that is guaranteed by Nisan's result [15], we obtain a deterministic algorithm that (on input x) finds $s(x)$ by making at most $(q(n)+1)\cdot 27q(n)^3$ queries. (That is, our algorithm goes down T_n by using the various machines M'_v to make the relevant decisions.)

It is thus left to show that $|S_n| < 2^{q(n)+1}$. For each $y \in S_n$, let $\chi_y(\omega) = 1$ if there exists an input $x \in \{0,1\}^n$ such that machine M outputs y on input x when using coins ω, and $\chi_y(\omega) = 0$ otherwise. Clearly, $\sum_y \chi_y(\omega) \leq 2^{q(n)}$, for any ω, and so $\sum_y \Pr[\chi_y(\omega)=1] \leq 2^{q(n)}$. Assuming towards the contradiction that $|S_n| \geq 2^{q(n)+1}$, we obtain an $x \in \{0,1\}^n$ such that $\Pr[\chi_{s(x)}(\omega)=1] \leq 1/2$, which implies $\Pr[M^x(n) = s(x)] \leq 1/2$ (in violation of the correctness of M). The theorem follows. ■

Corollary 4.2. (Corollary to Theorem 4.1): *There exist search problems that can be solved probabilistically in a constant number of queries, but have no pseudodeterministic algorithm of sublinear query complexity.*

Proof. Consider, for example, the search problem $R \stackrel{\text{def}}{=} \{(x,v) : |\mathtt{wt}(x) - v| < |x|/10\}$, where $\mathtt{wt}(x)$ is the Hamming weight of x. Clearly, R can be solved probabilistically with a constant number of queries, and we shall use Item 1 of Theorem 4.1 to show that it has no pseudodeterministic algorithm that makes less than $|x|/4$ queries. Towards this end, we have to show that the hypothesis of Item 1 (of Theorem 4.1) holds for $q(n) = n/4$. Indeed, let f be a function such that $f(x) \in R(x)$ holds for every x. Starting at $x_0 = 0^n$, we seek an x such that $|\{i \in [|x|] : f(x) \neq f(x \oplus e_i)\}| > 3n/4$. We call such an x unstable. We proceed in $n/4$ iterations such that (in the jth iteration) if the current x_{j-1} is not unstable, then we select x_j in $N_j \stackrel{\text{def}}{=} \{x_{j-1} \oplus e_i : i \in [n] \;\&\; \mathtt{wt}(x_{j-1} \oplus e_i) = \mathtt{wt}(x_{j-1})+1\}$ such that $f(x_j) = f(x_{j-1})$, which is possible since the set N_j has cardinality $n - j + 1 > 3n/4$. As long as the process goes on, we have $f(x_j) = f(x_0)$, which implies that we must find a string that is unstable (since $R(x_0) \subseteq [0, 0.1n]$, whereas $R(x_{n/4}) \subseteq [0.15n, 0.35n]$). ■

Proposition 4.3. (probabilism vs pseudodeterminism vs determinism): *There exists a search problem R such that*

1. *R can be solved probabilistically in a constant number of queries;*
2. *R has a pseudodeterministic algorithm of query complexity $n^{0.76}$, but no pseudodeterministic algorithm of query complexity $n^{0.33}$;*
3. *R cannot be solved deterministically in sublinear query complexity.*

Proof. By [17, 16], there exists a Boolean function, denoted b, that cannot be computed deterministically in a sublinear number of queries but can be computed probabilistically (with error probability at most 1/3) in $n^{0.76}$ queries; Let $R = R_1 \cup R_2$, where $R_1 = \{(x, b(x)) : x \in \{0,1\}^*\}$ and $R_2 = \{(x,i) \in \{0,1\}^* \times \mathbb{N} : |i - 10\rho(x)| \leq 1\}$, where $\rho(x) = \mathtt{wt}(x)/|x|$. (Assume that $v \in R_2(x)$ is encoded by several bits and so is different from the single bit solution to R_1.) Then, R can be solved probabilistically in a constant number of queries (via R_2) and has a pseudodeterministic algorithm of query complexity $n^{0.76}$ (via R_1). To see that R cannot be solved deterministically in a sublinear number of queries, note that we may "force" the solver to solve R_1. Specifically, consider a (sublinear-query) deterministic algorithm that on some input x outputs a solution y. Then, y cannot be in $R_2(x)$, because this algorithm also outputs y on any string x' that agrees with x on the $o(n)$ queries bits (whereas $R_2(x) \cap R_2(x) = \emptyset$ for some of these x'). Lastly, the lower bound on the query complexity of pseudodeterministic algorithms for R follows by combining the deterministic lower bound with Item 3 of Theorem 4.1, while using $|\cup_{x \in \{0,1\}^n} R(x)| < 15$. ■

Discussion. Theorem 4.1 leaves some room for sublinear-time probabilistic algorithms for finding canonical solutions. Such algorithms may be somewhat faster than their deterministic counterparts, provided that they are adaptive and that the search problem has no instances of linear sensitivity. Even in these cases, the speed-up offered by probabilism (over determinism) is at most polynomial, but on the other hand polynomial differences do matter (also in the sublinear-time context, cf., e.g., [11]).

Theorem 4.1 refers to *total search problems*; that is, the searching algorithm is required to work for all possible inputs (and not for a subset of them). The claim of Item 2 holds whenever the set of legitimate inputs is sufficiently connected (w.r.t the Boolean lattice).[8] In contrast, disconnectivity of this (promise) set allow probabilistic algorithms to find canonical solutions more efficiently than deterministic ones.

The role of a promise can be demonstrated by considering the problem of estimating the fraction of 1-values in a binary string. As shown in the proof of Corollary 4.2, no sublinear-time probabilistic algorithm can find a canonical solution w.r.t the relation $R \stackrel{\text{def}}{=} \{(x,v) : |\mathtt{wt}(x) - v| < |x|/10\}$. However, if we restrict the set of admissible x's to those that satisfy $\mathtt{wt}(x) \in \{i \cdot (|x|/10) \pm s : i \in [10], s \in [|x|/30]\}$, then

[7]In the next line, we consider M_v as a depth $q(n)$ probabilistic decision tree. This tree should not be confused with the tree T_n introduced above.

[8]The claim of Item 1 holds when modified to the promise set (i.e., x and the $x \oplus e_i$'s have to satisfy the promise). Regarding Item 2, consider, for example, the promise problem that consists of finding a 1-entry in a string x that contains a majority of 1-entries. Clearly, this promise problem can be solved probabilistically with a constant number of queries, but cannot be solved deterministically in less than $|x|/2$ queries. By an extension of Item 2 of Theorem 4.1, this problem cannot be solved by a non-adaptive pseudodeterministic algorithm that makes less than $|x|/6$ queries. The claim extends to adaptive algorithms by observing that any adaptive pseudodeterministic algorithm for this problem can be converted into a non-adaptive one, while maintaining the query complexity (cf. [2]).

canonical solutions w.r.t the resulting promise problem can be found by a constant-time probabilistic algorithm. More interesting examples are presented next.

4.2 Possibilities

In light of Theorem 4.1, we focus on search problems with a promise. The promise consists of several "instance regions" such that only (distant) regions can be associated with different canonical solutions. That is, the allowed instances are partitioned into sets $I_1, \ldots, I_M \subset \{0,1\}^n$ such that the canonical solution for each I_j is the same and strings in different I_j's are far apart.

The above formulation is closely related to error correcting codes, and it suggests that we may get search problems for which canonical solutions can be found in sublinear-time by considering locally decodable codes. Specifically, we consider codes that stretch k-bit messages into n-bit codewords, which are at relative distance $\delta > 0$. (Recall that local decodability means that each message bit can be correctly recovered (with probability 2/3) from a corrupted codeword (at error rate $\delta/3$) by making few queries to that codeword.) Two concrete proposals follow.

1. Recall that for $n = \text{poly}(k)$ local decodability is feasible with poly-logarithmic many queries (and some constant $\delta > 0$). Let $\ell = \text{poly}(\log n)$. Then, considering only strings $w \in \{0,1\}^n$ that are $\delta/3$-close to the code, we define a relation R such that $y \in R(w)$ if y is an ℓ-bit (consecutive) substring of x and w is $\delta/3$-close to an encoding of x.

   Canonical solutions w.r.t this relation can be found probabilistically by making poly-logarithmically many queries. For example, by invoking the local decoder ($O(\log\log n)$ times) to recover each bit position $i \in \{1, \ldots, \ell\}$. Note that we have intentionally defined R in a way that avoids having unique solutions.

2. Recall that for $n = 2^k$ local decodability is feasible with a constant number of queries (and $\delta = 1/2$). Indeed, this refers to the Hadamard code. Then, considering only strings that are 0.24-close to the code, we define a relation R such that $y \in R(w)$ if $w \in \{0,1\}^n$ is 0.24-close to an encoding of y. Canonical solutions w.r.t this relation can be found probabilistically by making logarithmically many queries (indeed, the double-logarithmic overhead involved in error reduction can be avoided; see [6, Sec. 2.5.2, Fn. 11]).[9]

   Indeed, as defined, R has unique solutions.

Both search problems can be generalized so that the sought solutions are not the strings denoted y, but rather search problems regarding y; that is, for any R as above and any search problem R', consider composed search problem R'' such that $z \in R''(w)$ if $y \in R(w)$ and $z \in R'(y)$. Indeed, if canonical solutions can be found w.r.t R' (by a standard probabilistic algorithm), then canonical solutions w.r.t R'' can be found in a number of queries that equals the number of queries needed for finding canonical solutions w.r.t R.

[9]The idea is to self-correct $O(k)$ positions in the codeword, where these positions correspond to an auxiliary good (and linear) error correcting code, and capitalize on the fact that it suffices to correctly recover each such auxiliary bit with constant probability.

The above examples refer to somewhat artificial objects (i.e., (corrupted) codewords w.r.t some error correcting codes). As in the context of property testing, the real question is whether we can present examples that refer to natural objects, under a natural representation. It seems that natural examples arise in the case of huge structures that are based on some small substructure. We consider such cases in two natural models of graphs.[10]

4.2.1 *Graph problems in the adjacency matrix representation*

A very natural model of direct access to graphs refers to providing oracle access to their adjacency predicate; that is, a query of the form (u, v) is answered by 1 if there exists an edge between vertices u and v in the graph, and by 0 otherwise. In the context of sublinear-time algorithms, this model is most suitable for dense graphs (cf. [8]).

In this model, a natural notion of a small substructure is provided by the notion of graph blow-up. Indeed, the notion of a graph blow-up yields natural examples of problems for which canonical solutions can be found in probabilistic constant time (but not in deterministic sublinear-time).

Graph blow-up. Recall that a blow-up of a graph $H = ([n], L)$ is a graph $G = ([N], E)$ obtained by replacing each vertex $i \in [n]$ of H by a (non-empty) subset $C_i \subset [N]$ (which may be called a cloud or a cluster) such that $(C_1, \ldots, C_n)$ is a partition of $[N]$, and placing a complete bipartite graph between C_i and C_j if and only if $(i,j) \in L$. That is, if $(i,j) \notin L$, then there will be no edges between C_i and C_j (and, in particular, there are no edges within each C_i). One usually looks at balanced blow-ups, in which all clouds are of the same size, but we may look at ϵ-balanced blow-up in which each cloud contains at least an ϵ fraction of the vertices (i.e., $|C_i| \geq \epsilon N$ for each $i \in [n]$). Finally, call H irreducible if it is not a blow-up of any smaller graph.

Now, consider an arbitrary (solvable) search problem R for graphs (e.g., finding spanning forests, shortest paths trees, Eulerian or Hamiltonian cycles, maximum matching, minimum vertex cover, etc). Define a parameterized search problem $\mathcal{BL}_{k,\epsilon}(R)$ as follows:

Input: A graph $G = ([N], E)$ that is an ϵ-balanced blow-up of some irreducible k-vertex graph.

Valid solution: Any solution y for a graph H (i.e., $(H, y) \in R$), where H is a k-vertex graph such that G is an ϵ-balanced blow-up of H.

(Indeed, this is a promise problem, and it is parameterized by k and ϵ.) Note that ϵ-balanced blow-ups provide a reasonable model for some types of clustering situations; the search problems R relate to the structure that underlies these clusters.

PROPOSITION 4.4. (pseudodeterministic algorithms for $\mathcal{BL}_{k,\epsilon}(R)$): *For every R, k, and $\epsilon > 0$ as above, canonical solutions w.r.t $\mathcal{BL}_{k,\epsilon}(R)$ can be found by a probabilistic algorithm that makes $O(\epsilon^{-1} \log k)^2$ adjacency queries.*

Typically (i.e., ignoring pathological cases such as $\epsilon \geq 1/k$ or a trivial R), no deterministic algorithm making $N/4$ queries can find solutions w.r.t $\mathcal{BL}_{k,\epsilon}(R)$, since such an algorithm may never encounter any vertex of the smallest cloud.

[10]Interestingly, similar substructures were used in the (different) context of [9].

PROOF. Consider a randomized algorithm that uniformly selects a set S of $O(\epsilon^{-1}\log k)$ vertices in G, queries all vertex pairs, finds the unlabeled irreducible graph H such that the induced subgraph of G (i.e., G_S) is a blow-up of H, labels H in a canonical way, and finds a solution by running a deterministic algorithm on H. Note that the graph H that emerges from the sample is unlabeled and it is crucial for our application to obtain a canonical labeling of it (since the labeling will effect the solution found for H). However, a canonical labeling of a k-vertex graph can always be found deterministically in time $k!$ (e.g., by finding the lexicographically first representation among all possible labeling of H).

The analysis amounts to observing that, with high probability, the initial sample S will hit each cloud of the graph G, since G is an ϵ-balanced blow-up of some (irreducible) k-vertex graph. The irreducibility condition guarantees that, in that case, the graph H is uniquely determined by G_S (i.e., the subgraph of G induced by S). ∎

Note. It is possible to relax the formalism in various ways, while maintaining the result (i.e., a pseudodeterministic algorithm of poly(k/ϵ) query complexity). For example, we may allow the input to be any graph that can be obtained from an ϵ-balanced blow-up of some irreducible k-vertex graph by changing at most $\epsilon N/6$ of the neighbors of each vertex.[11]

4.2.2 *Graph problems in the incidence-lists representation*

A standard model of direct access to graphs refers to providing oracle access to their incidence function; that is, a query of the form (v, i) is answered by the ith neighbor of v if v has at least i neighbors, and by 0 otherwise. In the context of sublinear-time algorithms, this model is most suitable for bounded-degree graphs (cf. [10]).

In this model, a natural notion of a small substructure is provided by the notion of recurring connected components; for example, we may consider graphs that consist of connected components of bounded size, and further restrict the graphs such that each subgraph either appears in very few connected component or appears in many such components. Indeed, this notion yields natural examples of problems for which canonical solutions can be found in probabilistic constant time (but not in deterministic sublinear-time).

Specifically, consider an arbitrary search problem R for graphs, and define a parameterized search problem $\mathcal{RP}_{k,\epsilon}(R)$ as follows:

Input: A graph $G = ([N], E)$ that consists of connected components such that (1) each connected component is of size at most k, and (2) each connected component is isomorphic to a a number of connected components that is either greater than ϵN or smaller than $\epsilon N/2$.

Valid solution: Any solution y for a graph H (i.e., $(H, y) \in R$), where H is isomorphic to at least ϵN connected components of G. (If there is no such H, then the solution is a special symbol.)

[11] In such a case, vertices that belong to the same cloud will differ on at most $\epsilon N/3$ neighbors, while vertices that belong to different clouds will differ on at least $2\epsilon N/3$ neighbors. Note that if we can change $\epsilon N/2$ neighbors of $2\epsilon N$ vertices, then the graph H may no longer uniquely recovered from G.

PROPOSITION 4.5. (pseudodeterministic algorithms for $\mathcal{RP}_{k,\epsilon}(R)$): *For every R, k, and $\epsilon > 0$ as above, canonical solutions w.r.t $\mathcal{RP}_{k,\epsilon}(R)$ can be found by a probabilistic a algorithm that makes $\widetilde{O}(k^2/\epsilon)$ incidence queries.*

Typically (i.e., ignoring pathological cases such as $\epsilon \geq 1/k$ or a trivial R), no deterministic algorithm making $\epsilon N/4$ queries can find solutions w.r.t $\mathcal{BL}_{k,\epsilon}(R)$, since such an algorithm cannot distinguish subgraphs that are isomorphic to at least ϵN connected components from subgraphs that are isomorphic to less than $\epsilon N/2$ such components.

PROOF. Consider a randomized algorithm that samples $\widetilde{O}(\epsilon^{-1}\log k)$ vertices in G, and explores their connected component (by making at most k^2 incidence queries). The algorithm also estimates the number of connected components (in G) that are isomorphic to each k'-vertex possible graph, for k', such that all estimates are correct in the sense discussed below. Next, among the graphs that had an estimate above $3\epsilon N/4$, the algorithm selects one graph (in a canonical fashion), and labels it (canonically, as in the proof of Proposition 4.4). Finally, it finds the desired canonical solution by running a deterministic algorithm on this graph.

The analysis amounts to observing that, with high probability, the initial sample will provide adequately good estimates of the various subgraphs that appear as connected components. Specifically, note that by taking $O(\epsilon^{-1}\log(1/\delta))$ one can estimate with probability at least $1 - \delta$ the frequency of events such that events that have frequency below $\epsilon/2$ (resp., at least ϵ) are judged to have frequency below $3\epsilon/4$ (resp., above $3\epsilon/4$). ∎

Note. It is possible to generalize the formalism and extend the results in various ways. For example, we may consider search problems R that refer to sets of graphs (e.g., we may seek a sequence of solutions such that each solution correspond to one of the graphs). Alternatively, we may consider highly connected components that are connected via a structure of lower connectivity (e.g., the superstructure may be a ring or a two-dimensional grid and its nodes may be 5-connected graphs).

4.3 On the class of graph problems having pseudodeterministic algorithms

The examples presented in Section 4.2 correspond to search problems that refer to small substructures of graphs. We claim that this is no coincidence in the sense that pseudodeterministic algorithms of low query complexity may exist only for problems that are defined in terms of the frequency in which various small graphs appear as induced subgraphs. Our discussion is restricted to "search problems regarding graphs" and to algorithms that access graphs via their adjacency predicate (i.e., as in §4.2.1).

A natural notion of "search problems regarding graphs" corresponds to binary relations R such that if $y \in R(G)$ then y is a solution for any graph that is isomorphic to G. For example, $R(G)$ may consist of approximate values of a graph parameter such as the diameter or the conductance of G. (Other examples are the classes of problems $\mathcal{BL}_{k,\epsilon}(\cdot)$ and $\mathcal{RP}_{k,\epsilon}(\cdot)$ considered in Section 4.2.) This notion of search problems extends the standard notion of decision problems for graphs (a.k.a graph properties).[12] The natural promise problem version of this notion couples such search problems with promises that are graph properties (i.e., G satisfies the promise P if and only if each graph that is isomorphic to G satisfies P).

DEFINITION 4.6. (search promise problem for graphs): *A* search promise problem for graphs (for short, graph problem) *is a pair (P, R) such that P is a graph property and R is closed under isomorphism in the sense that if G and G' are isomorphic, then $R(G) = R(G')$.*

For a graph $G = ([N], E)$ and a set of vertices $S \subseteq [N]$, we denote by G_S the subgraph of G induced by S. By $\binom{[N]}{k}$ we denote the set of all k-subsets of $[N]$.

THEOREM 4.7. *Let $\Pi = (P, R)$ be a search promise problem for graphs. Then, Π has a pseudodeterministic algorithm of query complexity q if and only if there exists k that is polynomially related to q and a function f such that for every $G = ([N], E) \in P$ there exists a $y \in R(G)$ such that $\Pr_{S\in\binom{[N]}{k}}[f(N, G_S) = y] \geq 2/3$. In particular, if Π has a pseudodeterministic algorithm then $k = 18q$ will do, whereas if such a k and f exist then Π has a pseudodeterministic algorithm of query complexity $q = \binom{k}{2}$.*

The function f associates a candidate solution with each k-vertex graph such that a large fraction of all induced k-vertex subgraphs of each $G \in P$ are associated with the same candidate solution (which is in $R(G)$). The search problem Π has a poly(k)-query pseudodeterministic algorithm if and only if such a function f exists.

PROOF. Suppose that there exists k and a function f such that for every $G = ([N], E) \in P$ there exists a $y \in R(G)$ such that $\Pr_{S\in\binom{[N]}{k}}[f(N, G_S) = y] \geq 2/3$. Then, a pseudodeterministic algorithm of query complexity $q = \binom{k}{2}$ is obtained by just sampling k vertices at random in the graph, obtaining the induced subgraph, denoted G', and outputting $f(N, G')$.

To prove the opposite direction, we follow the transformation[13] of [12, Sec. 4], while observing that its steps are still applicable. Loosely speaking, in [12, Sec. 4] it is shown that any q-query property tester (in the adjacency matrix model) can be transformed into one that takes a random sample of $2q$ vertices, queries the induced subgraph, and decides based on that subgraph. Here we show that this transformation applies also in the case of pseudodeterministic algorithms for graph problems (as in Definition 4.6). The point is that a canonical solution that is output with probability at least 2/3 can be treated as a decision bit. The following steps correspond to the transformation of [12, Sec. 4] (and the specific pointers are included as a source of additional details).

Step 1: Obtaining a vertex-uncovering algorithm (first part of [12, Lem. 4.1]).

A vertex-uncovering algorithm proceeds in iterations such that in each iteration a new vertex v is selected (possibly based on prior answers) and queries of the form (v, u) are made for each u that was selected in prior iterations. The transformation here is rather generic. Each query (v_1, v_2) is emulated by two iterations of the vertex-uncovering algorithm, which means that the query complexity may get squared. Actually it is more important to note that the number of vertices selected, denoted k_1, is at most twice the original query complexity.

Step 2: Obtaining an algorithm that inspects a random induced subgraph (second part of [12, Lem. 4.1]).

This step consists of observing what happens when we let the algorithm query a random isomorphic copy of the input graph. The original analysis relies on the fact that the algorithm's decision should remain valid also in this case, and this reasoning holds in our setting as well. Specifically, if the pseudodeterministic algorithm outputs y (with probability at least 2/3) as canonical solution for the graph $G \in P$, then the algorithm must output y with probability at least 2/3 when given an isomorphic copy of G.

Step 3: Obtaining a sample-independent output [12, Sec. 4.2.1].

In the context of [12], the output is a decision, but again the analysis generalizes. The issue at hand is that the original algorithm selects a random k_1-set of vertices S uniformly, and given that it saw the induced subgraph α, it outputs y with probability $q_{S,\alpha}(y)$. Instead, when seeing the induced subgraph α, the new algorithm outputs y with probability $q_\alpha(y) \stackrel{\text{def}}{=} \mathrm{E}_S[q_{S,\alpha}(y)]$, which is independent of the selected sample S. Note that if $G \in P$, then there exists a y such that $\mathrm{E}_S[q_{S,\pi(G)_S}(y)] \geq 2/3$, for every relabeling π of the graph G. Noting that $\pi(G)_S = G_{\pi(S)}$, for a random permutation π, it holds that $\mathrm{E}_{S,\pi}[q_{S,G_{\pi(S)}}(y)] \geq 2/3$, which implies that $\mathrm{E}_{S,S'}[q_{S,G_{S'}}(y)] \geq 2/3$. But this means that $\mathrm{E}_{S'}[q_{G_{S'}}(y)] \geq 2/3$, which means that the new algorithm satisfies the pseudodeterministic requirement.

Step 4: Obtaining an isomorphism-oblivious output [12, Sec. 4.2.2].

Step 3 established that the output depends only on the induced subgraph seen, and here we claim that it is oblivious of the labeling of this subgraph. The analysis is similar to the one underlying Step 3.

Step 5: Obtaining an output that is determined by the induced subgraph [12, Sec. 4.2.3].

Step 4 established that the output depends only on the unlabeled induced subgraph, but this dependence may take a probabilistic form; that is, seeing a subgraph H causes the algorithm to output y with probability $p_H(y)$. Our goal is to have the output be uniquely determined as a function of the (unlabeled) induced subgraph. Following [12], we assume that the algorithm

[12]One may also consider search problems of a different type in which solutions are sets of vertices and it is required that $S \in R(G)$ if and only if $\{\pi(v) : v \in S\}$ is a solution to the graph $\pi(G)$ (i.e., the relabelling of G under the permutation π). For example, $R(G)$ may consist of all triples of vertices that form a triangle in G. For further discussion, see the end of this section.

[13]This transformation of [12, Sec. 4] is often referred to as a "canonization" procedure, yielding a "canonical" tester. But this notion of "canonical" has nothing to do with the notion of canonical solutions.

has error probability less than 1/6 (i.e., the probability that it outputs the canonical solution is at least 5/6). This assumption can be enforced by error reduction (but the number of vertices increases from k_1 to $9k_1$). At this point, we introduce a new algorithm that, upon seeing the subgraph H, outputs y if $p_H(y) > 1/2$ (and outputs nothing if $\max_y\{p_H(y)\} \leq 1/2$). Since the original algorithm outputs canonical solutions with probability at least 5/6, for every $G \in P$, it holds that $\mathrm{E}_S[p_{G_S}(y)] \geq 5/6$ for the canonical solution $y \in R(G)$. Therefore, $\Pr_S[p_{G_S}(y) > 1/2] \geq 2/3$. Define $f_N(H) = y$ if $p_H(y) > 1/2$ (and $f_N(H) = \perp$ if no such y exists).

We now obtain the desired function f: For any k-vertex graph H, define $f(N, H) = f_N(H)$. By Step 5, we know that for every $G = ([N], E) \in P$ there exists a $y \in R(G)$ such that $\Pr_{S\in\binom{[N]}{k}}[f(N, G_S) = y] \geq 2/3$. The theorem follows. ∎

A different type of graph problems. In continuation to Footnote 12, we stress that Definition 4.6 only covers one type of graph problems; that is, graph problems for which solutions are values that are invariant under isomorphism of the input graph. In contrast, one may consider a more general type of graph problems, which we call labeled graph problems. In these problems solutions are triples (v, S, f) where v is a value (as in Definition 4.6), S is a set of vertices and $f : S \to \{0,1\}^*$ such that the following ("graph nature") condition holds: *If (v, S, f) is a solution for graph G, then $(v, \{\pi(u) : u \in S\}, f \circ \pi^{-1})$ is a solution for the graph that results from G by applying the vertex relabeling π.* A natural question about such labeled graph problems is whether they have pseudodeterministic algorithms of complexity that is smaller than that of deterministic algorithms.

5. SAFELY FINDING CANONICAL SOLUTIONS

An even stronger notion than finding canonical solutions is finding such solutions without ever outputting an alternative solution (but rather allowing a small probability of having no output).

DEFINITION 5.1. (safely finding canonical solutions): *Let R, $R(x)$ and S_R be as in Definition 2.1. A* (possibly probabilistic) *algorithm A* safely finds canonical solutions with respect to R *if there exists a function $s : \{0,1\}^* \to \{0,1\}^*$ such that the following conditions hold:*

1. *As in Definition 2.1, for every $x \in S_R$ it holds that $s(x) \in R(x)$, whereas $s(x) = \lambda$ for every $x \in \{0,1\}^* \setminus S_R$.*
2. *For every $x \in \{0,1\}^*$, it holds that $\Pr[A(x) = s(x)] \geq 2/3$ and $A(x) \in \{s(x), \perp\}$ always holds.*

Definition 5.1, which is implicit in Gat's thesis [4], is robust in the sense that replacing the threshold 2/3 by either $1/\mathrm{poly}(|x|)$ or $1 - \exp(-\mathrm{poly}(|x|))$ yields the same class (via standard error reduction). Indeed, this class of search problems is reminiscent of the class $\mathcal{ZPP}$ of decision problems recognized with zero-error probability. In fact:

THEOREM 5.2. (Theorem 2.2, adapted): *A relation R has a probabilistic polynomial-time algorithm that safely finds canonical solutions w.r.t it if and only if finding solutions w.r.t R is P-reducible to some set in $\mathcal{ZPP}$.*

(The proof of Theorem 5.2 mimics the proof of Theorem 2.2.) Thus, the difference between finding canonical solutions and safely finding canonical solutions is reflected in the difference between $\mathcal{BPP}$ and $\mathcal{ZPP}$. This fact becomes even more evident when considering the set associated with any canonical solution function $s : \{0,1\}^* \to \{0,1\}^*$ for R. Specifically, let $S_s = \{(x, i, b) : s(x)_i = b\}$, where $s(x)_i$ denotes the ith bit of $s(x)$. The actual contents of the proofs of Theorems 2.2 and 5.2 is captured by the following proposition.

PROPOSITION 5.3. *A relation R has a probabilistic polynomial-time algorithm that finds* (resp., safely finds) *canonical solutions w.r.t it if and only if there exists a canonical solution function $s : \{0,1\}^* \to \{0,1\}^*$ for R such that the corresponding set S_s is in $\mathcal{BPP}$* (resp., in $\mathcal{ZPP}$).

Indeed, R has a deterministic polynomial-time algorithm that (safely) finds (canonical) solutions w.r.t it if and only if S_s is in $\mathcal{P}$.

PROOF. The first direction (from S_s to finding s-canonical solutions) is proved by using the standard P-reduction of computing s to deciding S_s; that is, on input x, for all $i \leq \mathrm{poly}(|x|)$ and $b \in \{0,1\}$, make the query (x, i, b) and constract $s(x)$ accordingly.[14] In particular, when using a ZPP algorithm for S_s and obtaining a failure notification, the search algorithm outputs $\perp$. For the opposite direction (i.e., from finding s-canonical solutions to S_s), recall that deciding S_s is P-reducible to computing s, which is turn is done by an algorithm that finds s-canonical solutions w.r.t R. Likewise, when using a safe finder, a failure notification makes the decider issue a similar notification. ∎

6. REFERENCES

[1] Laszlo Babai and Eugene M. Luks. Canonical Labeling of Graphs. In proceedings of *15th STOC*, pages 171–183, 1983.

[2] Ziv Bar-Yossef, Ravi Kumar, and D. Sivakumar, Sampling Algorithms: Lower Bounds and Applications. In proceedings of *33rd STOC*, pages 266–275, 2001.

[3] Harry Buhrman and Ronald de Wolf. Complexity measures and decision tree complexity: a survey. *Theoretical Computer Science*, Vol. 288(1), pages 21–43, 2002.

[4] Eran Gat. On the canonization of probabilistic algorithms. M.Sc. Thesis, Weizmann Institute of Science, 2009.

[5] Eran Gat and Shafi Goldwasser. Probabilistic Search Algorithms and their Cryptographic Applications. ECCC TR11-136, 2011.

[6] Oded Goldreich. *Foundations of Cryptography – Basic Tools*. Cambridge University Press, 2001.

[7] Oded Goldreich. In a World of P=BPP. ECCC TR10-135, 2010.

[14] As in the proof of Theorem 2.2, the oracle S_s is implemented by a BPP (resp., ZPP) algorithm of sufficiently low error probability.

[8] Oded Goldreich, Shafi Goldwasser, and Dana Ron. Property testing and its connection to learning and approximation. *Journal of the ACM*, pages 653–750, July 1998.

[9] Oded Goldreich, Michael Krivelevich, Ilan Newman, and Eyal Rozenberg. Hierarchy Theorems for Property Testing. *Computational Complexity*, Vol. 21 (1), pages 129–192, 2012.

[10] Oded Goldreich and Dana Ron. Property Testing in Bounded Degree Graphs. *Algorithmica*, Vol. 32 (2), pages 302–343, 2002.

[11] Oded Goldreich and Dana Ron. A Sublinear Bipartitness Tester for Bounded Degree Graphs. *Combinatorica*, Vol. 19 (3), pages 335–373, 1999.

[12] Oded Goldreich and Luca Trevisan. Three theorems regarding testing graph properties. *Random Structures and Algorithms*, Vol. 23 (1), pages 23–57, 2003.

[13] Russell Impagliazzo and Avi Wigderson. Randomness vs. Time: De-Randomization under a Uniform Assumption. In proceedings of *39th FOCS*, pages 734–743, 1998.

[14] Hendrik Lenstra and Bart de Smit. Standard Models for Finite Fields. Lecture in *Foundations of Computational Mathematics*, 2008. Slides avialable from `http://www.damtp.cam.ac.uk/user/na/FoCM/FoCM08/Talks/Lenstra.pdf`

[15] Noam Nisan. CREW PRAMs and and decision trees. *SIAM Journal on Computing*, Vol. 20(6), pages 999–1007, 1991.

[16] Michael Saks and Avi Wigderson. Probabilistic Boolean decision trees and the complexity of evaluation game trees. In proceedings of *27th FOCS*, pages 29–38, 1986.

[17] Marc Snir. Lower Bounds on Probabilistic Linear Decision Trees. *Theoretical Computer Science*, Vol. 38, pages 69–82, 1985.

Evasiveness Through A Circuit Lens

[Extended Abstract] *

Raghav Kulkarni
Centre for Quantum Technologies, Singapore
Singapore
kulraghav@gmail.com

ABSTRACT

A function $f : \{0,1\}^n \to \{0,1\}$ is called *evasive* if its decision tree complexity is maximal, i.e., $D(f) = n$. The long-standing Anderaa-Rosenberg-Karp (ARK) Conjecture asserts that every non-trivial monotone graph property is evasive. The Evasiveness Conjecture (EC) is a generalization of ARK Conjecture from monotone graph properties to arbitrary monotone transitive Boolean functions.

In this paper we study a weakening of the Evasiveness Conjecture called Weak Evasivenss Conjecture (weak-EC). The weak-EC asserts that every non-trivial monotone transitive Boolean function must have $D(f) \geq n^{1-\epsilon}$, for every $\epsilon > 0$. The purpose of this note is to make some remarks on weak-EC that hint towards a plausible attack on EC.

First we observe that weak-EC is equivalent to EC. Further we observe that ruling out only certain simple (monotone-NC^1) counter-examples to weak-EC suffices to confirm EC in its whole generality. Finally we rule out some simple counter-examples to weak-EC (AC^0 : unconditionally; and monotone-TC^0 : under a conjecture of Benjamini, Kalai, and Schramm on their noise stability).

We also investigate an analogue of weak-EC for the stronger model of *parity decision trees* and provide a counter-example to this seemingly stronger version under a conjecture of Montanaro and Osborne.

Categories and Subject Descriptors

F.2.0 [**Theory of Computation**]: ANALYSIS OF ALGORITHMS AND PROBLEM COMPLEXITY—*General*; F.1.3 [**Theory of Computation**]: COMPUTATION BY ABSTRACT DEVICES—*Complexity Measures and Classes*

General Terms

Algorithms, Theory

Keywords

Decision Tree Complexity, Evasiveness Conjecture, Monotone Graph Properties, Circuit Complexity

*Research at the Centre for Quantum Technologies is funded by the Singapore Ministry of Education and the National Research Foundation. No qubits were harmed during the preparation of this article. At the time of submission of this article the author was at LIAFA Paris 7, partially supported by the French ANR Defis program under contract ANR-08- EMER-012 (QRAC project) and the European Commission IST STREP Project Quantum Computer Science (QSC) 25596.

ITCS'13, January 9–12, 2013, Berkeley, California, USA.

1. INTRODUCTION

The *decision tree model* aka *query model* [3], perhaps due to its simplicity and fundamental nature, has been extensively studied over decades; yet it remains far from being completely understood.

Fix a Boolean function $f : \{0,1\}^n \to \{0,1\}$. A deterministic decision tree D_f for f takes $x = (x_1, \ldots, x_n)$ as an input and determines the value of $f(x_1, \ldots, x_n)$ using queries of the form " is $x_i = 1$? ". Let $C(D_f, x)$ denote the cost of the computation, that is the number of queries made by D_f on input x. The *deterministic decision tree complexity* of f is defined as $D(f) = \min_{D_f} \max_x C(D_f, x)$.

The function f is called *evasive* if $D(f) = n$, i.e., one must query all the variables in worst case in order to determine the value of the function.

1.1 The Anderaa-Rosenberg-Karp Conjecture

A natural theme in the study of decision tree complexity is to exploit the structure within f to prove strong lower bounds on its query complexity. A classic example is the following conjecture attributed to Anderaa, Rosenberg, and Karp, asserting the *evasiveness* of monotone graph properties:

Conjecture 1.1 (ARK Conjecture). *(cf. [6]) Every non-trivial monotone graph property is evasive.*

Since its origin around 1975, the ARK Conjecture has caught the imagination of generations of researchers resulting in beautiful mathematical ideas; yet - to this date - remains unsolved. A major breakthrough on ARK Conjecture was obtained by Kahn, Saks, and Sturvevant [6] via their novel *topological approach.* They settled the conjecture when the number of vertices of the graphs is a power of prime number. The topological approach subsequently turned out useful for solving some other variants and speccial cases of the conjecture. For example: Yao confirms the variant of the conjecture for monotone properties of bipartite graphs [19]. More recently, building on Chakraborty, Khot, and Shi's work [4], Babai et. al. [1] show that under some well-known conjectures in number theory, *forbidden subgraph* property - containment of a fixed subgraph in the graph - is evasive.

1.2 The Evasiveness Conjecture

The key feature of monotone graph properties is that they are sufficiently *symmetric*. In particular, they are *transitive* Boolean functions, i.e., there is a transitive group acting on the set of variables under which the function remains invariant. A natural question was raised: how much *symmetry* is necessary in order to guarantee the evasiveness? The following generalization (cf. [10]) of ARK Conjecture asserts that only transitivity suffices.

CONJECTURE 1.2 (EVASIVENESS CONJECTURE (EC)). *If f is a non-trivial monotone transitive Boolean function then f is evasive.*

The above conjecture is known to hold when the number of variables is a power of prime number [15]. The general case remains widely open.

1.3 The Weak Evasiveness Conjecture

'Whether or not one can save a single query?' might appear to some a bit obscure question as we are usually content with a loose bound on the complexity (say up to a constant or poly-logarithmic factor). The ARK Conjecture holds up to a constant factor [6] and one may raise the following:

CONJECTURE 1.3 (WEAK EVASIVENESS CONJECTURE). *If $\{f_n\}$ is a sequence of non-trivial monotone Boolean functions then for every $\epsilon > 0$*

$$D(f_n) \geq n^{1-\epsilon}.$$

The best known lower bond in this context is $D(f) \geq R(f) \geq n^{2/3}$, which follows from the work of O'Donell et. al. [14]. The purpose of this paper is to make some remarks on the weak-EC in connection with EC.

1.4 Our remarks on the Weak EC

Loosely speaking, we attempt to test the following hypothesis: *computationally simple* monotone transitive functions are *weakly evasive.* Our simple but crucial observation is that with an appropriate quantification of *computational simplicity* and of *weak evasiveness*, the above hypothesis becomes equivalent to the EC itself! Our main contribution is in formulating the above hypothesis in terms of circuit complexity and then verifying it partially. More concretely, we observe:

- The weak-EC is equivalent to the EC (Section 3).
- Furthermore, it suffices to prove weak-EC only for certain simple functions, namely monotone-NC^1 functions (Section 3).
- Finally, the weak-EC holds for AC^0 functions (Section 4); and for monotone-TC^0 functions (Section 5) assuming their noise-stability [2].

We note that the EC for AC^0 functions is widely open. The *forbidden subgraph* property is in AC^0 but it is only known to be evasive under some number theoretic conjectures [1].

2. PRELIMINARIES

Stronger variants of decision tree

A bounded error randomized decision tree R_f is a probability distribution over all deterministic decision trees such that for every input, the expected error of the algorithm is bounded by some fixed constant less than 1/2. The cost $C(R_f, x)$ is the highest possible number of queries made by R_f on x, and the *bounded error randomized decision tree complexity* of f is $R(f) = \min_{R_f} \max_x C(R_f, x)$.

A *parity decision tree* may query " is $\sum_{i \in S} x_i \equiv 1 \pmod 2$? " for an arbitrary subset $S \subseteq [n]$. We call such queries *parity queries.* For a parity decision tree P_f for f, let $C(P_f, x)$ denote the number of parity queries made by P_f on input x. The *parity decision tree complexity* of f is

$$D_{\oplus}(f) = \min_{P_f} \max_x C(P_f, x).$$

Note that $D_{\oplus}(f) \leq D(f)$ as " is $x_i = 1$? " can be treated as a parity query.

Parity decision trees were introduced by Kushilevitz and Mansour [7] in the context of learning Boolean functions by estimating their Fourier coefficients. Recently they came in light in the study of the communication complexity of XOR functions [18].

Variance, influence, and average depth

Let μ_p denote the p-biased distribution on the Boolean cube, i.e., each co-ordinate is independently chosen to be 1 with probability p. The *variance* of a Boolean function is $\text{Var}(f,p) := 4 \cdot \Pr_{x \leftarrow \mu_p}(f(x) = 0) \Pr_{x \leftarrow \mu_p}(f(x) = 1)$. The *influence* of the ith variable under μ_p is $\text{Inf}_i(f,p) := \Pr_{x \leftarrow \mu_p}(f(x) \neq f(x \oplus e_i))$. The *total influence* aka *average sensitivity* of f is $\text{Inf}(f,p) := \sum_i \text{Inf}_i(f,p)$.

Let $f : \{0,1\}^n \to \{0,1\}$. Let T_f be a deterministic decision tree for f. Let $d(T_f, x)$ denote the number of queries that T_f makes on input x. The average depth of T is $\Delta(T_f, p) := \mathbb{E}_{x \leftarrow \mu_p} d(T_f, x)$, and the average depth of f under μ_p is $\Delta(f,p) := \min_{T_f} \Delta(T_f, p)$.

Critical probability and threshold interval

We say that f is *balanced with repect to μ_p* if:

$$1 - 1/3 \leq \text{Var}(f,p) \leq 1 + 1/3.$$

We call f *balanced* if f is balanced with respect to $\mu_{1/2}$. The *critical probability* of f is $p_c(f) := p$ such that $\text{Var}(f,p) = 1$, i.e., $\Pr_{x \leftarrow \mu_p}(f(x) = 1) = 1/2$. If f is a monotone Boolean function then $p_c(f)$ is well-defined. Moreover, the critical probability can not be too small:

PROPOSITION 2.1. *If f is a non-trivial monotone Boolean function on n variables then*

$$p_c(f) = \Omega(1/n).$$

The threshold interval of f is $I := \{q \in [0,1] \mid 1 - 1/3 \leq \text{Var}(f,q) \leq 1 + 1/3\}$. Let p be the critical probability of f. The threshold window of f, denoted by $t(f)$, is the largest real number such that $[p-t, p+t]$ is contained in the threshold interval of f.

The threshold window can not be too small either:

PROPOSITION 2.2. *If f is a non-trivial monotone Boolean function on n variables then:*

$$t(f) = \Omega(1/n).$$

Polynomial degree and sparsity

Let $f_\pm : \{-1,1\}^n \to \{-1,1\}$ be represented by the following polynomial with real coefficients: $f_\pm(z_1,\ldots,z_n) = \sum_{S\subseteq[n]} \widehat{f}(S)\prod_{i\in S} z_i$. The above polynomial is unique and it is called the Fourier expansion of f. The $\widehat{f}(S)$ are called the Fourier coefficients of f. The *polynomial degree* of f is $\deg(f) := max\{|S| \mid \widehat{f}(S) \neq 0\}$. The *sparsity* of a Boolean function f is $||\widehat{f}||_0 := |\{S \mid \widehat{f}(S) \neq 0\}|$. It is known that $\deg(f) \leq D(f)$ and $\log ||\widehat{f}||_0 \leq D_\oplus(f)$.

3. EQUIVALENCE OF WEAK-EC AND EC

OBSERVATION 3.1. *Conjecture 1.2 is equivalent to Conjecture 1.3.*

Proof: Firstly Conjecture 1.2 $\Rightarrow$ Conjecture 1.3 is obvious as the later is a weakening of the former.

Now we prove Conjecture 1.3 $\Rightarrow$ Conjecture 1.2 by contrapositive.

Suppose there is a counter-example $g : \{0,1\}^T \to \{0,1\}$ to Conjecture 1.2 then one can construct a counter-example $\{f_n\}$ to Conjecture 1.3.

For $n = T^k$, construct g_k recursively from g.

$$g_1 := g,$$

$$g_k := g(g_{k-1},\ldots,g_{k-1}).$$

Note that g_k is a non-trivial monotone transitive function on $n = T^k$ variables. Moreover: $D(g_k) \leq (T-1)^k = T^{k\cdot(\log(T-1)/\log T)} = n^{\log(T-1)/\log T}$. The first inequality follows because $D(g(h,\ldots,h)) \leq D(g)\cdot D(h)$.

Let $1-\delta := \log(T-1)/\log T$. Since T is a constant $\delta > 0$ is a constant. We have $D(g_k) \leq n^{1-\delta}$ for a constant $\delta > 0$.

Now our counter-example $\{f_n\}$ to the Weak Evasiveness Conjecture would be as follows: if $n = T^k$ for some k then choose $f_n = g_k$; otherwise choose f_n to be (say) the OR function on n variables.

□

We note that the above construction fails to prove the equivalence of 'ARK and weak-ARK' as the recursive function no longer remains a graph property. However, the recursive construction still preserves the transitivity. A glance at the above proof also yields the following:

OBSERVATION 3.2. *If Conjecture 1.2 is false then there is a counter-example $\{f_n\}$ to Conjecture 1.3 such that $\{f_n\}$ is in monotone-NC^1.*

4. REFUTING AC^0 COUNTER-EXAMPLES TO WEAK-EC

The main ingredient of our proof is a well known inequality by O'Donell et. al. [14] that relates maximum influence to the average depth. The second ingredient that we use is another well known result by Linial, Mansour, and Nissan [9] that gives upper bound on the total influence of AC^0 functions (using the Switching Lemma). In order to make these two ingredients fit together in our context, we need (as a technicality) a simple but crucial transformation. Our transformation modifies a monotone Boolean function so that it becomes balanced with only constant increase in the depth. This allows us to derive a good (nearly linear) lower bound on the query complexity of balanced AC^0 functions. Then we infer the desired bound for non-balanced case via composition theorems for query complexity.

4.1 A transformation to balance the monotone functions

The idea is to *simulate* its critical probability by a monotone circuit and our crucial observation is that only a constant depth monotone circuit suffices. More specifically, we replace each variable of f by a read-once formula of depth 2 (OR of ANDs) that outputs 1 with probability sufficiently close to the critical probability of f so that the composed function is balanced.

Our construction works in two steps: first we make the function sufficiently unbalanced and then we balance the sufficiently unbalanced function.

Unbalancing the function only to help in balancing it later

Given a monotone Boolean function f on n variables we construct (A.1) another monotone Boolean function f_U on $N = n^3$ variables such that:

$$p_c(f_U) = O(\log N/N^{2/3}).$$

The function f_U is defined as follows:

$$f_U := f(g,\ldots,g),$$

where $g : \{0,1\}^{n^2} \to \{0,1\}$ is the OR function on n^2 variables:

$$g(y_1,\ldots,y_{n^2}) := \bigvee_{i=1}^{n^2} y_i.$$

Simulating the critical probability of unbalanced functions

Let f be a monotone Boolean function on n variables such that:

$$p_c(f) = o(1/\sqrt{n}).$$

We construct another balanced monotone Boolean function f_B as follows:

$$f_B := f(g,\ldots,g),$$

where

$$g((x_{ij})) := \bigvee_{i=1}^{m}\bigwedge_{j=1}^{k} x_{ij}$$

where $k = \lceil 3\log n\rceil$ and m is the integer minimizing $|p_c(f) - \frac{m}{2^k}|$.

Our goal is to show that g *approximates* the critical probability of f well enough so that the composite function $f_B = f(g,\ldots,g)$ is balanced.

More formally, let q be the probability that g outputs 1 under the uniform distribution. Our goal will be to show that $q \in [p_c(f) - t(f), p_c(f) + t(f)]$. The crucial fact that we use is that both the critical probability and the threshold window can not be too small.

First note that: $|p_c(f) - \frac{m}{2^k}| \leq 1/2^k$. Since $p_c(f) \geq 1/n$ and $k = \lceil 3\log n\rceil$, we have $1/2^k \leq p_c(f)^2$, and $m/2^k \leq p_c(f) + p_c(f)^2 \leq 2\cdot p_c(f)$.

Next note that: $q = 1 - (1 - 1/2^k)^m = 1 - \frac{m}{2^k} \pm \epsilon$, where $\epsilon \leq (m/2^k)^2 \leq 4\cdot p_c(f)^2$.

Now we use the assumption $p_c(f) = o(1/\sqrt{n})$ together with Proposition 2.2 ($t(f) \geq 1/n$) to conclude: $\epsilon = o(t(f))$.

Since $m/2^k \leq p_c(f) + p_c(f)^2 = p_c(f) + o(t(f))$, we have: $q = p_c(f) \pm \gamma$, where $\gamma = o(t(f))$. Hence:

LEMMA 4.1. *If f is a monotone Boolean function on n variables such that $p_c(f) = o(1/\sqrt{n})$ then f_B is balanced.*

4.2 AC^0 transitive monotone functions are weakly evasive

THEOREM 4.2 (O'DONELL ET AL.). *(Corollary 1.2 in [14])*

$$\max_i\{\mathrm{Inf}_i(f,p)\} \geq \frac{\mathrm{Var}(f,p)}{\Delta(f,p)}.$$

COROLLARY 4.3. *If f is transitive then*

$$R(f) \geq \Delta(f,p) \geq \frac{\mathrm{Var}(f,p)\cdot n}{\mathrm{Inf}(f,p)}.$$

The first inequality follows from Yao's min-max principle.

THEOREM 4.4 (LINIAL, MANSOUR, AND NISAN [9]). *If $\{f_n\}$ is a sequence of functions on n variables having circuits of size $M(n)$ and depth $d(n)$ then:*

$$\mathrm{Inf}(f,1/2) = O((\log M)^d).$$

Thus from Corollary 4.3 we have:

LEMMA 4.5. *If $\{f_n\}$ is a sequence of balanced transitive Boolean function on n variables having circuit of size M and depth d then:*

$$R(f) = \Omega(n/(\log M)^d).$$

THEOREM 4.6. *If f is a monotone transitive Boolean function on n variables having a circuit of size M and depth d then:*

$$D(f) \geq R(f) \geq \Omega\left(\frac{n}{(\log M)^{d+4}}\right).$$

Proof: Let $F := (f_U)_B$, i.e., F is obtained from f by first making it unbalanced f_U and then making f_U balanced. Note that $F = f(g,\dots,g)$ for some monotone transitive g on $K = n^{O(1)}$ variables. Thus: F has the following properties: (a) F is a monotone transitive function on $N = nK = n^{O(1)}$ variables, (b) F is balanced, and (c) F has a circuit of size $M \cdot n^{O(1)}$ and depth $d+3$. Thus from Lemma 4.5 we have: $R(F) = \Omega(N/(\log M + \log n)^{d+3})$. Since $R(f(g,\dots,g)) \leq R(f)\cdot R(g)\cdot O(\log n)$, and $R(g) \leq K$ we get the desired lower bound on $R(f)$ and hence on $D(f)$. □

5. REFUTING TC^0 COUNTER-EXAMPLES

THEOREM 5.1 (O'DONELL ET AL.). *(Theorem A.1 in [14]) If $f: \{0,1\}^n \to \{-1,1\}$ is a Boolean function on n variables and $g: \{0,1\}^n \to \mathbb{R}$ is a function such that there is an anti-chain $\mathcal{S} \subseteq 2^{[n]}$ (no member is a subset of another) with $\widehat{g}(S) = 0$ for all $S \notin \mathcal{S}$; then*

$$\mathrm{Cov}[f,g]^2 \leq \mathrm{Var}(f)\cdot\sum_{i=1}^{n}\delta_i(\mathcal{T})\,\mathrm{Inf}_i(g),$$

where $\mathrm{Cov}[f,g] := \mathbb{E}[f\cdot g] - \mathbb{E}[f]\cdot\mathbb{E}[g]$, δ_i is the probability (over the uniform distribution of the inputs) that the randomized decision tree $\mathcal{T}$ for f queries the variable i, and $\mathrm{Inf}_i(g) := \sum_{i\in S}|S|\cdot\widehat{g}(S)^2$.

The *noise sensitivity* of f under noise μ_δ, denoted by $NS_\delta(f)$ is $\Pr(f(x) \neq f(x\oplus\eta))$, where η is drawn according to μ_δ and x is drawn uniformly at random. It is convenient to write $NS_\delta(f) = (1-\mathrm{Stab}_{1-2\delta}(f))/2$, where $\mathrm{Stab}_{1-2\delta}(f)$ is called *noise stability* under δ noise. Moreover: $\mathrm{Stab}_{1-2\delta}(f) = \sum_S (1-2\delta)^{|S|}\widehat{f}(S)^2$. Benjamini, Kalai, and Schramm [2] conjecture:

CONJECTURE 5.2 (BKS CONJECTURE). *If f is computed by a monotone threshold circuit of size $M(n)$ and depth $d(n)$ then for $\delta(n) = (\log M(n))^{-\Omega(d(n))}$,*

$$\mathrm{Stab}_{1-2\delta(f)} \geq 2/3.$$

We can combine Conjecture 5.2 with Theorem 5.1 along the lines of the previous section to obtain the following (A.2):

THEOREM 5.3. *If f is a monotone transitive function on n variables computed by a monotone threshold circuit of size $M(n)$ and depth $d(n)$ then assuming Conjecture 5.2 we have*

$$D(f) \geq R(f) \geq \Omega(n/(\log M(n))^{100d(n)}).$$

6. A STRONGER VERSION OF WEAK-EC

Our results for AC^0 and TC^0 functions in fact hold for the randomized decision trees complexity. However the 'weak-EC for $R(f)$' is false as demonstrated by the recursive ternary majority function [16], which is in monotone-NC^1. So far we are unable to extend our results in the previous sections to monotone-NC^1 for deterministic decision trees (hence to settle the weak-EC). This motivates us to explore the stronger deterministic variants of weak-EC in the hope of finding a counter-example. In this section we consider a stronger deterministic model of decision trees called *parity decision trees*. The model is certainly more powerful than the ordinary decision trees as demonstrated by the parity function. In the case of monotone functions, the majority on 3 bits has parity decision tree of depth 2 whereas the ordinary decision tree must query all 3 variables. [1]However it is unclear whether or not the parity queries help significantly under the restriction of monotonicity. In this light we explore:

CONJECTURE 6.1 (PARITY-WEAK-EC). *If $\{f_n\}$ is a sequence of non-trivial monotone transitive Boolean functions on n variables then for every $\epsilon > 0$,*

$$D_\oplus(f) \geq \Omega(n^{1-\epsilon}).$$

The best known lower bound is $D_\oplus(f) \geq n^{1/2}$. We provide a counter-example to the above conjecture assuming the following:

[1]In fact, [5] shows that the majority on n variables requires exactly $n-\nu(n)+1$ parity queries, where $\nu(n)$ is the number of 1s in the binary representation of n.

CONJECTURE 6.2 (MONTANARO AND OSBORNE). *(cf. Conjecture 7 in [11]) For any Boolean function f,*

$$D_{\oplus}(f) = O(\log ||\widehat{f}||_0).$$

Our main observation is the following lemma (A.3):

LEMMA 6.3. *There exists a non-trivial monotone transitive evasive Boolean function on n variables such that*

$$\deg(f) \leq n^{1-\Omega(1)}.$$

Now we use the folklore fact: $\log ||\widehat{f}||_0 = O(\deg(f))$ to conclude that assuming Conjecture 6.2, the Conjecture 6.1 is false.

7. OPEN ENDS

7.1 Conditional/unconditional extensions

It seems that we are able to translate the circuit lower bound tools for certain classes (e.g. upper bound on the average sensitivity of AC^0) to lower bound their query complexity using monotonicity and transitivity. Would it be possible to do the same for other tools (e.g. Karchmer-Wigderson games) may be using the topological consequences of non-evasiveness?

If one can refute TC^0 counter-examples to weak-EC unconditionally then disproving EC would be at least as difficult as separating NC^1 from TC^0.

7.2 EC $\equiv$ weak-EC - with further restrictions

The equivalence of weak-EC and EC holds even under suitable restrictions and this equivalence may be useful. For example: for the functions that are transitive under some solvable group. Another example is when the number of distinct prime factors on n is bounded by a constant.

7.3 Gap between CC and Log-rank for monotone functions

To the best of our knowledge, we note the first monotone function with a super-linear gap between $D(f)$ and $\deg(f)$. Nissan and Wigderson [13] used earlier such examples for non-monotone functions [12] to produce a super-linear gap between the communication complexity and the log-rank. No such super-linear gap is noted for monotone functions. Does our example help in finding such a gap? Or does montonicity not allow such a gap?

7.4 The weak-parity-EC for AC^0 functions

In [8] it is shown that the Fourier spectrum of AC^0 functions is *dense*, i.e., $\log ||\widehat{f}||_0 = \widetilde{\Omega}(\deg(f))$. [2] A consequence is that for AC^0 transitive (possibly non-monotone) functions $D_{\oplus}(f) \geq n^{\Omega(1)}$. Is $D_{\oplus}(f) = \widetilde{\Omega}(n)$, more strongly: if f is non-trivial AC^0 transitive function on n variables then $\deg(f) \stackrel{?}{=} \widetilde{\Omega}(n)$.

7.5 Parity trees for monotone functions

Does there exist a monotone Boolean function f with super-linear gap between $D(f)$ and $D_{\oplus}(f)$? A negative answer disproves the conjecture of Montantaro and Osborne [11].

[2]The $\widetilde{\Omega}$ hides the multiplicative poly-logarithmic factor in Ω notation.

8. REFERENCES

[1] László Babai, Anandam Banerjee, Raghav Kulkarni, Vipul Naik: Evasiveness and the Distribution of Prime Numbers. STACS 2010: 71-82

[2] Itai Benjamini, Gil Kalai, and Oded Schramm: Noise sensitivity of Boolean functions and its application to percolation

[3] Harry Buhrman, Ronald de Wolf: Complexity measures and decision tree complexity: a survey. Theor. Comput. Sci. 288(1): 21-43 (2002)

[4] Amit Chakrabarti, Subhash Khot, Yaoyun Shi: Evasiveness of Subgraph Containment and Related Properties. SIAM J. Comput. 31(3): 866-875 (2001)

[5] Thomas P. Hayes, Samuel Kutin, Dieter van Melkebeek: The Quantum Black-Box Complexity of Majority. Algorithmica 34(4): 480-501 (2002)

[6] Jeff Kahn, Michael E. Saks, Dean Sturtevant: A topological approach to evasiveness. Combinatorica 4(4): 297-306 (1984)

[7] Eyal Kushilevitz, Yishay Mansour: Learning Decision Trees Using the Fourier Spectrum. SIAM J. Comput. 22(6): 1331-1348 (1993)

[8] Raghav Kulkarni, Miklos Santha: Query complexity of matroids. Electronic Colloquium on Computational Complexity (ECCC) 19: 63 (2012)

[9] Nathan Linial, Yishay Mansour, Noam Nisan: Constant Depth Circuits, Fourier Transform, and Learnability. J. ACM 40(3): 607-620 (1993)

[10] Frank H. Lutz: Some Results Related to the Evasiveness Conjecture. Comb. Theory, Ser. B 81(1): 110-124 (2001)

[11] Ashley Montanaro, Tobias Osborne: On the communication complexity of XOR functions CoRR abs/0909.3392: (2009)

[12] Noam Nisan, Mario Szegedy: On the Degree of Boolean Functions as Real Polynomials. Computational Complexity 4: 301-313 (1994)

[13] Noam Nisan, Avi Wigderson: On Rank vs. Communication Complexity. Combinatorica 15(4): 557-565 (1995)

[14] Ryan O'Donnell, Michael E. Saks, Oded Schramm, Rocco A. Servedio: Every decision tree has an influential variable. FOCS 2005: 31-39

[15] Ronald L. Rivest, Jean Vuillemin: On Recognizing Graph Properties from Adjacency Matrices. Theor. Comput. Sci. 3(3): 371-384 (1976)

[16] Michael E. Saks, Avi Wigderson: Probabilistic Boolean Decision Trees and the Complexity of Evaluating Game Trees FOCS 1986: 29-38

[17] Yaoyun Shi, Zhiqiang Zhang: Communication Complexities of XOR functions CoRR abs/0808.1762: (2008)

[18] Zhiqiang Zhang, Yaoyun Shi: On the parity complexity measures of Boolean functions. Theor. Comput. Sci. 411(26-28): 2612-2618 (2010)

[19] Andrew Chi-Chih Yao: Monotone Bipartite Graph Properties are Evasive. SIAM J. Comput. 17(3): 517-520 (1988)

APPENDIX

A.

A.1 Unbalancing

PROPOSITION A.1.

$$p_c(f_U) = O(\log N/N^{2/3}).$$

Proof: Let

$$\alpha_p := \Pr_{x \leftarrow \mu_p}(f_U(x) = 1).$$

Since f_U is monotone increasing, $\alpha_0 = 0$ and $\alpha_1 = 1$. Moreover: α_p is a monotone increasing function of p.

Let g_i denote a copy of g so that we can write $f_U = f(g_1, \ldots, g_n)$.

Since f is monotone increasing, we have:

$$\alpha_p \geq \Pr_{x \leftarrow \mu_p}[(\forall i)(g_i = 1)].$$

In other words:

$$\alpha_p \geq 1 - \Pr_{x \leftarrow \mu_p}[(\exists i)(g_i = 0)].$$

Applying the union bound, we get:

$$\alpha_p \geq 1 - n \cdot \Pr_{x \leftarrow \mu_p}(g = 0).$$

In particular, for $q := \ln(2n)/n^2$, we have: $\alpha_q \geq 1/2$. Since α_p is monotone increasing, the critical probability is at most q.

□

A.2 monotone-TC^0

To refute the monotone-TC^0 counter examples to weak-EC we procede as follows: given a transitive function in monotone-TC^0, first we transform it into a balanced function F (as in the previous section) by simulating its critical probability by an OR-AND function. We will need a stronger guarantee, namely: $\Pr(F = 1) = 1/2 \pm \alpha$ where $\alpha = o((\log n)^{-100d})$, which can be obtained by the same method described in previous section.

Now let $G := T_{1-2\delta}(F) := \sum_S (1-2\delta)^{|S|} \widehat{F}(S)$. Note that for $\delta = (1/\log n)^{d+4}$, we have: $\mathbb{E}[F \cdot G] = \operatorname{Stab} F \geq 2/3$ by Kalai's conjecture.

In order to apply Theorem 5.1 we need the Fourier spectrum of G to be supported on an anti-chain. For this we consider $G^* = \sum_{|S|=k} \widehat{G}(S)$, where k is such that $\mathbb{E}[F \cdot G^*] \geq (\log n)^{2d}$. Note that such a k exists because G has $\Omega(1)$ Fourier weight on the first $(\log n)^{2d}$ layers.

Now note that $\mathbb{E}[F] = \mathbb{E}[G^*] = O(\alpha)$ and $\operatorname{Cov}[F, G^*] \geq 1/(\log n)^{2d} - \alpha^2 = \Omega(1/(\log n)^{2d})$.

Now from Theorem 5.1 we have: $\max_i \delta_i(F) \cdot \sum_i \operatorname{Inf}_i(G^*) \geq \Omega(1/(\log n)^{2d})$.

It is easy to see that $\sum_i \operatorname{Inf}_i(G^*) = O((\log n)^{2d}$ since the higher Fourier coefficients of G become negligible. Moreover: since F is transitive we can assume: $\max_i \delta_i = \Delta/N$ where N is the number of variables of F. This gives a nearly linear (up to poly logarithmic factor) lower bound on $\Delta(F)$. In the same manner as the one used for the AC^0 functions, we can now infer nearly linear lower bound on the randomized query complexity of f from here.

Benjamini, Kalai, and Schramm [2] conjecture the noise stability for monotone functions computed by (not necessarily monotone) TC^0 circuits as well. However they comment that the conjecture for monotone-TC^0 is more believable.

A.3 Gap between $D(f)$ and $\deg(f)$ for monotone functions

We use a specific example of Lutz [10] together with a theorem of Kahn, Saks, and Sturtevant [6] that show that non-trivial monotone graph properties of 6-vertex graphs are evasive.

PROPOSITION A.2 (LUTZ, FIG. 2 IN [10]). *There is a non-trivial monotone graph property $f : \{0,1\}^{\binom{6}{2}} \to \{0,1\}$ of 6-vertex graphs such that $\widehat{f}([n]) = 0$, i.e., $\deg(f) < 15$.*

THEOREM A.3 (KAHN, SAKS, AND STURTEVANT [6]). *If $f : \{0,1\}^{\binom{6}{2}} \to \{0,1\}$ is a non-trivial monotone graph property of 6-vertex graphs then $D(f) = 15$.*

Combining Proposition A.2 with Theorem A.3 we have:

COROLLARY A.4. *There exists a monotone Boolean function f on 15 variables such that*

$$D(f) = 15 \text{ and } \deg(f) \leq 14.$$

THEOREM A.5. *There exists a monotone Boolean function f on $n = 15^k$ variables such that:*

$$n = D(f) = \deg(f)^{1+\Omega(1)}.$$

Proof: Construct $f (= f_k)$ recursively from g.

$$f_1(\cdot) = g(\cdot),$$

$$f_k(\cdot) = g(f_{k-1}(\cdot), \ldots, f_{k-1}(\cdot)).$$

It is easy to see that $\deg(f) \leq 14^k$; whereas $D(f) = 15^k$ follows from $D(g(h, \ldots, h)) = D(h) \cdot D(g)$. □

The Garden-Hose Model

Harry Buhrman
CWI, University of Amsterdam
h.buhrman@cwi.nl

Serge Fehr
Centrum Wiskunde & Informatica (CWI) Amsterdam
s.fehr@cwi.nl

Christian Schaffner
University of Amsterdam, CWI
c.schaffner@uva.nl

Florian Speelman
CWI, University of Amsterdam
f.speelman@cwi.nl

ABSTRACT

We define a new model of communication complexity, called the *garden-hose model*. Informally, the garden-hose complexity of a function $f : \{0,1\}^n \times \{0,1\}^n \to \{0,1\}$ is given by the minimal number of water pipes that need to be shared between two parties, Alice and Bob, in order for them to compute the function f as follows: Alice connects her ends of the pipes in a way that is determined solely by her input $x \in \{0,1\}^n$ and, similarly, Bob connects his ends of the pipes in a way that is determined solely by his input $y \in \{0,1\}^n$. Alice turns on the water tap that she also connected to one of the pipes. Then, the water comes out on Alice's or Bob's side depending on the function value $f(x,y)$.

We prove almost-linear lower bounds on the garden-hose complexity for concrete functions like inner product, majority, and equality, and we show the existence of functions with exponential garden-hose complexity. Furthermore, we show a connection to classical complexity theory by proving that all functions computable in log-space have polynomial garden-hose complexity.

We consider a *randomized* variant of the garden-hose complexity, where Alice and Bob hold pre-shared randomness, and a *quantum* variant, where Alice and Bob hold pre-shared quantum entanglement, and we show that the randomized garden-hose complexity is within a polynomial factor of the deterministic garden-hose complexity. Examples of (partial) functions are given where the quantum garden-hose complexity is logarithmic in n while the classical garden-hose complexity can be lower bounded by n^c for constant $c > 0$.

Finally, we show an interesting connection between the garden-hose model and the (in)security of a certain class of *quantum position-verification* schemes.

Categories and Subject Descriptors

E.4 [**Coding and Information Theory**]: Formal models of communication

Keywords

communication complexity; garden-hose model; position-based quantum cryptography

1. INTRODUCTION

The garden-hose model.

On a beautiful sunny day, Alice and Bob relax in their neighboring gardens. It happens that their two gardens share s water pipes, labeled by the numbers $1, 2, \ldots, s$. Each of these water pipes has one loose end in Alice's and the other loose end in Bob's garden. For the fun of it, Alice and Bob play the following game. Alice uses pieces of hose to locally connect some of the pipe ends that are in her garden with each other. For example, she might connect pipe 2 with pipe 5, pipe 4 with pipe 9, *etc.* Similarly, Bob locally connects some of the pipe ends that are in his garden; for instance pipe 1 with pipe 4, *etc.* We note that no T-pieces (nor more complicated constructions), which connect two or more pipes to one (or vice versa) are allowed. Finally, Alice connects a water tap to one of her ends of the pipes, e.g., to pipe 3 and she turns on the tap. Alice and Bob observe which of the two gardens gets sprinkled. It is easy to see that since Alice and Bob only use simple one-to-one connections, there is no "deadlock" possible and the water will indeed eventually come out on one of the two sides. Which side it is obviously depends on the respective local connections.

Now, say that Alice connects her ends of the pipes (and the tap) not in a *fixed* way, but her choice of connections depends on a private bit string $x \in \{0,1\}^n$; for different strings x and x', she may connect her ends of the pipes differently. Similarly, Bob's choice which pipes to connect depends on a private bit string $y \in \{0,1\}^n$. These strategies then specify a function $f : \{0,1\}^n \times \{0,1\}^n \to \{0,1\}$ as follows: $f(x,y)$ is defined to be 0 if, using the connections determined by x and y respectively, the water ends up on Alice's side, and $f(x,y)$ is 1 if the water ends up on Bob's side.

Switching the point of view, we can now take an *arbitrary* Boolean function $f : \{0,1\}^n \times \{0,1\}^n \to \{0,1\}$ and ask: How can f be computed in the garden-hose model? How do Alice and Bob have to choose their local connections, and how many water pipes are necessary for computing f in the garden-hose model? We stress that Alice's choice for which pipes to connect may only depend on x but not on y, and vice versa; this is what makes the above questions non-trivial.

In this paper, we introduce and put forward the notion of *garden-hose complexity*. For a Boolean function $f : \{0,1\}^n \times \{0,1\}^n \to \{0,1\}$, the garden-hose complexity $GH(f)$ of f is defined to be the minimal number s of water pipes needed to compute f in the garden-hose model. It is not too hard to see that $GH(f)$ is well defined (and finite) for any function $f : \{0,1\}^n \times \{0,1\}^n \to \{0,1\}$.

This new complexity notion opens up a large spectrum of natural problems and questions. What is the (asymptotic or exact) garden-hose complexity of natural functions, like equality, inner product *etc.*? How hard is it to compute the garden-hose complexity in general? How is the garden-hose complexity related to other complexity measures? What is the impact of randomness, or entanglement? Some of these questions we answer in this work; others remain open.

Lower and upper bounds.

We show a near-linear $\Omega(n/\log(n))$ lower bound on the garden-hose complexity $GH(f)$ for a natural class of functions $f : \{0,1\}^n \times \{0,1\}^n \to \{0,1\}$. This class of functions includes the mod-2 inner-product function, the equality function, and the majority function. For the former two, this bound is rather tight, in that for these two functions we also show a linear upper bound. For the majority function, the best upper bound we know is quadratic. Recently, Margalit and Matsliah improved our upper bound for the equality function with the help of the IBM SAT-Solver [23] to approximately $1.448n$, and the question of how many water pipes are necessary to compute the equality function in the garden-hose model featured as April 2012's "Ponder This" puzzle on the IBM website[1]. The *exact* garden-hose complexity of the equality function is still unknown, though; let alone of other functions.

By using a counting argument, we show the existence of functions with *exponential* garden-hose complexity, but so far, no such function is known explicitly.

Connections to other complexity notions.

We show that every function $f : \{0,1\}^n \times \{0,1\}^n \to \{0,1\}$ that is *log-space computable* has polynomial garden-hose complexity. And, vice versa, we show that every function with polynomial garden-hose complexity is, up to local pre-processing, log-space computable. As a consequence, we obtain that the set of functions with polynomial garden-hose complexity is exactly given by the functions that can be computed by arbitrary local pre-processing followed by a log-space computation.

We also point out a connection to communication complexity by observing that, for any function $f : \{0,1\}^n \times \{0,1\}^n \to \{0,1\}$, the *one-way communication complexity* of f is a lower bound on $GH(f)\log(GH(f))$.

Randomized and quantum garden-hose complexity.

We consider the following natural variants of the garden-hose model. In the *randomized* garden-hose model, Alice and Bob additionally share a uniformly random string r, and the water is allowed to come out on the wrong side with small probability ε. Similarly, in the *quantum* garden-hose model, Alice and Bob additionally hold an arbitrary entangled quantum state and their wiring strategies can depend on the outcomes of measuring this state before playing the garden-hose game. Again, the water is allowed to come out on the wrong side with small probability ε. Based on the observed connections of the garden-hose complexity to log-space computation and to one-way communication complexity, we can show that the resulting notion of *randomized* garden-hose complexity $GH_\varepsilon(f)$ is polynomially related to $GH(f)$. For the resulting notion of *quantum* garden-hose complexity $GH_\varepsilon^Q(f)$, we can show a separation (for a partial function) from $GH_\varepsilon(f)$.

[1]`http://ibm.co/I7yvMz`

Application to quantum position-verification.

Finally, we show an interesting connection between the garden-hose model and the (in)security of a certain class of *quantum position-verification* schemes. The goal of position-verification is to verify the geographical position *pos* of a prover P by means of sending messages to P and measuring the time it takes P to reply. Position-verification with security against collusion attacks, where different attacking parties collaborate in order to try to fool the verifiers, was shown to be impossible in the classical setting by [11], and in the quantum setting by [5], if there is no restriction put upon the attackers. In the quantum setting, this raises the question whether there exist schemes that are secure in case the attackers' quantum capabilities are limited.

We consider a simple and natural class of quantum position-verification schemes; each scheme $\mathsf{PV}^f_{\text{qubit}}$ in the class is specified by a Boolean function $f : \{0,1\}^n \times \{0,1\}^n \to \{0,1\}$. These schemes may have the desirable property that the more classical resources the honest users use to faithfully execute the scheme, the more quantum resources the adversary needs in order to break it. It turns out that there is a one-to-one correspondence between the garden-hose game and a certain class of attacks on these schemes, where the attackers teleport a qubit back and forth using a supply of EPR pairs. As an immediate consequence, the (quantum) garden-hose complexity of f gives an upper bound on the number of EPR pairs the attackers need in order to break the scheme $\mathsf{PV}^f_{\text{qubit}}$. As a corollary, we obtain the following interesting connection between proving the security of quantum protocols and classical complexity theory: If there is an f in P such that there is no way of attacking scheme $\mathsf{PV}^f_{\text{qubit}}$ using a polynomial number of EPR pairs, then P $\neq$ L. Vice versa, our approach may lead to practical secure quantum position-verification schemes whose security is based on classical complexity-theoretical assumptions such as P is different from L. However, so far it is still unclear whether the garden-hose complexity by any means gives a *lower bound* on the number of EPR pairs needed; this remains to be further investigated.

2. THE GARDEN-HOSE MODEL

2.1 Definition

Alice and Bob get n-bit input strings x and y, respectively. Their goal is to "compute" an agreed-upon Boolean function $f : \{0,1\}^n \times \{0,1\}^n \to \{0,1\}$ on these inputs, in the following way. Alice and Bob have s water pipes between them, and, depending on their respective classical inputs x and y, they connect (some of) their ends of the pipes with pieces of hose. Additionally, Alice connects a water tap to one of the pipes. They succeed in computing f in the garden-hose model, if the water comes out on Alice's side whenever $f(x,y) = 0$, and the water comes out on Bob's side whenever $f(x,y) = 1$.

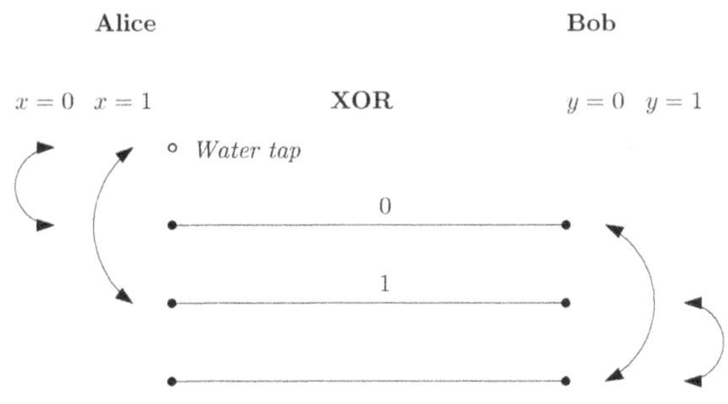

Figure 1: Computing the XOR function in the garden-hose model using three water pipes. If Alice's input bit x is 0, she connects the water tap to the first water pipe labeled "0". In case $x=1$, she connects the tap to the second pipe labeled "1".

Note that it does not matter out of which pipe the water flows, only on which side it flows. What makes the game non-trivial is that Alice and Bob must do their "plumbing" based on their local input only, and they are not allowed to communicate. We refer to Figure 1 for an illustration of computing the XOR function in the garden-hose model.

We formalize the above description of the garden-hose game, given in terms of pipes and hoses *etc.*, by means of rigorous graph-theoretic terminology. However, we feel that the above terminology captures the notion of a garden-hose game very well, and thus we sometimes use the above "watery" terminology. We start with a balanced bi-partite graph $(A \cup B, E)$ which is 1-regular and where the cardinality of A and B is $|A| = |B| = s$, for an arbitrary large $s \in \mathbb{N}$. We slightly abuse notation and denote both the vertices in A and in B by the integers $1, \dots, s$. If we need to distinguish $i \in A$ from $i \in B$, we use the notation i^A and i^B. We may assume that E consists of the edges that connect $i \in A$ with $i \in B$ for every $i \in \{1, \dots, s\}$, i.e., $E = \{\{i^A, i^B\} : 1 \le i \le s\}$. These edges in E are the *pipes* in the above terminology. We now extend the graph to $(A_\circ \cup B, E)$ by adding a vertex 0 to A, resulting in $A_\circ = A \cup \{0\}$. This vertex corresponds to the *water tap*, which Alice can connect to one of the pipes. Given a Boolean function $f : \{0,1\}^n \times \{0,1\}^n \to \{0,1\}$, consider two functions $E_{A_\circ}$ and E_B; both take as input a string in $\{0,1\}^n$ and output a set of edges (without self loops). For any $x, y \in \{0,1\}^n$, $E_{A_\circ}(x)$ is a set of edges on the vertices $A_\circ$ and $E_B(x)$ is a set of edges on the vertices B, so that the resulting graphs $(A_\circ, E_{A_\circ}(x))$ and $(B, E_B(y))$ have maximum degree at most 1. $E_{A_\circ}(x)$ consists of the *connections* among the pipes (and the tap) on Alice's side (on input x), and correspondingly for $E_B(y)$. For any $x, y \in \{0,1\}^n$, we define the graph $G(x,y) = (A_\circ \cup B, E \cup E_{A_\circ}(x) \cup E_B(y))$ by adding the edges $E_{A_\circ}(x)$ and $E_B(y)$ to E. $G(x,y)$ consists of the pipes with the connections added by Alice and Bob. Note that the vertex $0 \in A_\circ$ has degree at most 1, and the graph $G(x,y)$ has maximum degree at most two 2; it follows that the maximal path $\pi(x,y)$ that starts at the vertex $0 \in A_\circ$ is uniquely determined. $\pi(x,y)$ represents the flow of the water, and the endpoint of $\pi(x,y)$ determines whether the water comes out on Alice or on Bob's side (depending on whether the final vertex is in $A_\circ$ or in B).

Definition 2.1. *A* garden-hose game *is given by a graph function $G : (x,y) \mapsto G(x,y)$ as described above. The number of pipes s is called the* size *of G, and is denoted as $s(G)$.*

A garden-hose game G is said to compute *a Boolean function $f : \{0,1\}^n \times \{0,1\}^n \to \{0,1\}$ if the endpoint of the maximal path $\pi(x,y)$ starting at 0 is in $A_\circ$ whenever $f(x,y) = 0$ and in B whenever $f(x,y) = 1$.*

Definition 2.2. *The deterministic* garden-hose complexity *of a Boolean function $f : \{0,1\}^n \times \{0,1\}^n \to \{0,1\}$ is the size $s(G)$ of the smallest garden-hose game G that computes f. We denote it by $GH(f)$.*

2.2 Upper and Lower Bounds

In this section, we present upper and lower bounds on the number of pipes required to compute some particular (classes of) functions in the garden-hose model. We first give a simple upper bound on $GH(f)$ which is implicitly proven in the attack on Scheme II in [18].

Proposition 2.3. *For every Boolean function $f : \{0,1\}^n \times \{0,1\}^n \to \{0,1\}$, the garden-hose complexity $GH(f)$ is at most $2^n + 1$.*

Proof. We identify $\{0,1\}^n$ with $\{1, \dots, 2^n\}$ in the natural way. For $s = 2^n + 1$ and the resulting bipartite graph $(A_\circ \cup B, E)$, we can define $E_{A_\circ}$ and E_B as follows. $E_{A_\circ}(x)$ is set to $\{(0, x)\}$, meaning that Alice connects the tap with the pipe labeled by her input x. To define E_B, group the set $Z(y) = \{a \in \{0,1\}^n : f(a,y) = 0\}$ arbitrarily into disjoint pairs $\{a_1, a_2\} \cup \{a_3, a_4\} \cup \ldots \cup \{a_{\ell-1}, a_\ell\}$ and set $E_B(y) = \{\{a_1, a_2\}, \{a_3, a_4\}, \dots, \{a_{\ell-1}, a_\ell\}\}$. If $\ell = |Z(y)|$ is odd so that the decomposition into pairs results in a left-over $\{a_\ell\}$, then a_ℓ is connected with the "reserve" pipe labeled by 2^n+1.

By construction, if $x \in Z(y)$ then $x = a_i$ for some i, and thus pipe $x = a_i$ is connected on Bob's side with pipe a_{i-1} or a_{i+1}, depending on the parity of i, or with the "reserve" pipe, and thus $\pi(x,y)$ is of the form $\pi(x,y) = (0, x^A, x^B, v^B, v^A)$, ending in $A_\circ$. On the other hand, if $x \notin Z(y)$, then pipe x is not connected on Bob's side, and thus $\pi(x,y) = (0, x^A, x^B)$, ending in B. This proves the claim. □

We notice that we can extend this proof to show that the garden-hose complexity $GH(f)$ is at most $2^{D(f)+1} - 1$, where $D(f)$ is the deterministic communication complexity of f. See Appendix A for a sketch of the method.

Definition 2.4. *We call a function f* injective for Alice, *if for every two different inputs x and x' there exists y such that $f(x,y) \neq f(x',y)$. We define* injective for Bob *in an analogous way: for every $y \neq y'$, there exists x such that $f(x,y) \neq f(x,y')$ holds.*

Proposition 2.5. *If f is injective for Bob or f is injective for Alice, then*[2]

$$GH(f)\log(GH(f)) \ge n\,.$$

Proof. We give the proof when f is injective for Bob. The proof for the case where f is injective for Alice is the same. Consider a garden-hose game G that computes f. Let s be its size $s(G)$. Since, on Bob's side, every pipe is connected to at most one other pipe, there are at most $s^s = 2^{s\log(s)}$ possible choices for $E_B(y)$, i.e., the set of connections on Bob's side. Thus, if $2^{s\log(s)} < 2^n$, it follows from the pigeonhole principle that there must exist y and y' in $\{0,1\}^n$ for which $E_B(y) = E_B(y')$, and thus for which $G(x,y) =$

[2]All logarithms in this paper are with respect to base 2.

$G(x, y')$ for all $x \in \{0,1\}^n$. But this cannot be since G computes f and $f(x,y) \neq f(x,y')$ for some x due to the injectivity for Bob. Thus, $2^{s\log(s)} \geq 2^n$ which implies the claim. □

We can use this result to obtain an almost linear lower bound for several functions that are often studied in communication complexity settings such as:

- Bitwise inner product: $\mathrm{IP}(x,y) = \sum_i x_i y_i \pmod 2$
- Equality: $\mathrm{EQ}(x,y) = 1$ if and only if $x = y$
- Majority: $\mathrm{MAJ}(x,y) = 1$ if and only if $\sum_i x_i y_i \geq \lceil \frac{n}{2} \rceil$

The first two of these functions are injective for both Alice and Bob, while majority is injective for inputs of Hamming weight at least $n/2$, giving us the following corollary.

COROLLARY 2.6. *The functions bitwise inner product, equality and majority have garden-hose complexity in* $\Omega(\frac{n}{\log(n)})$.

By considering the water pipes that actually get wet, one can show a lower bound of n pipes for equality [25]. On the other hand, we can show upper bounds that are linear for the bitwise inner product and equality, and quadratic in case of majority. We refer to [29] for the proof of the following proposition.

PROPOSITION 2.7. *In the garden-hose model, the equality function can be computed with* $3n+1$ *pipes, the bitwise inner product with* $4n+1$ *pipes and majority with* $(n+2)^2$ *pipes.*

In general, garden-hose protocols can be transformed into (one-way) communication protocols by Alice sending her connections $E_{A_\circ}(x)$ to receiver Bob, which will require at most $GH(f)\log(GH(f))$ bits of communication. Bob can then locally compute the function by combining Alice's message with $E_B(y)$ and checking where the water exits.[3] We summarize this observation in the following proposition.

PROPOSITION 2.8. *Let* $D^1(f)$ *denote the deterministic one-way communication complexity of* f. *Then,*

$$D^1(f) \leq GH(f)\log(GH(f)) .$$

As a consequence, lower bounds on the communication complexity carry over to the garden-hose complexity (up to logarithmic factors). Notice that this technique will never give lower bounds that are better than linear, as problem in communication complexity can always be solved by sending the entire input to the other party. It is an interesting open problem to show super-linear lower bounds in the garden-hose model, e.g. for the majority function.

PROPOSITION 2.9.
There exist functions $f : \{0,1\}^n \times \{0,1\}^n \to \{0,1\}$ *for which* $GH(f)$ *is exponential.*

PROOF. The existence of functions with an exponential garden-hose complexity can be shown by a simple counting argument. There are $2^{2^{2n}}$ different functions $f(x,y)$. For a given size $s = s(G)$ of G, for every $x \in \{0,1\}^n$, there are at most $(s+1)^{s+1}$ ways to choose the connections $E_{A_\circ}(x)$ on Alice's side, and thus there are at most $((s+1)^{s+1})^{2^n} = 2^{2^n(s+1)\log(s+1)}$ ways to choose the function $E_{A_\circ}$. Similarly for E_B, there are at most $2^{2^n s\log(s)}$ ways to choose E_B. Thus, there are at most $2^{2\cdot 2^n(s+1)\log(s+1)}$ ways to choose G of size s. Clearly, in order for every function f to have a G of size s that computes it, we need that $2\cdot 2^n(s+1)\log(s+1) \geq 2^{2n}$, and thus that $(s+1)\log(s+1) \geq 2^{n-1}$, which means that s must be exponential. □

2.3 Polynomial Garden-Hose Complexity and Log-Space Computations

A family of Boolean functions $\{f_n\}_{n\in\mathrm{N}}$ is *log-space computable* if there exists a deterministic Turing machine M and a constant c, such that for any n-bit input x, M outputs the correct output bit $f_n(x)$, and at most $c \cdot \log n$ locations of M's work tapes are ever visited by M's head during computation.

DEFINITION 2.10. *We define* $\mathrm{L}_{(2)}$, *called* logarithmic space with local pre-processing, *to be the class of Boolean functions* $f(x,y)$ *for which there exists a Turing machine* M *and two* arbitrary *functions* $\alpha(x), \beta(y)$, *such that*[4] $M(\alpha(x),\beta(y)) = f(x,y)$ *and* $M(\alpha(x),\beta(y))$ *runs in space logarithmic in the size of the original inputs* $|x|+|y|$.

This definition can be extended in a natural way by considering Turing machines and circuits corresponding to various complexity classes, and by varying the number of players. For example, a construction as in Proposition 2.3 and a similar reasoning as in Proposition 2.14 below can be used to show that every Boolean function is contained in $\mathrm{PSPACE}_{(2)}$. As main result of this section, we show that our newly defined class $\mathrm{L}_{(2)}$ is equivalent to functions with polynomial garden-hose complexity. We leave it for future research to study intermediate classes such as $\mathrm{AC}^0_{(2)}$ which are related to the polynomial hierarchy of communication complexity [1].

THEOREM 2.11. *The set of functions* f *with polynomial garden-hose complexity* $GH(f)$ *is equal to* $\mathrm{L}_{(2)}$.

The two directions of the theorem follow from Theorem 2.12 and Proposition 2.14.

THEOREM 2.12. *If* $f : \{0,1\}^n \times \{0,1\}^n \to \{0,1\}$ *is log-space computable, then* $GH(f)$ *is polynomial in* n.

PROOF SKETCH, FULL PROOF IN APPENDIX B.1.
Let M be the deterministic log-space Turing machine deciding $f(x,y) = 0$. Using techniques from [19], M can be made *reversible* incurring only a constant loss in space. As M is a log-space machine, it has at most polynomially many configurations. The idea for the garden-hose strategy is to label the pipes with those configurations of the machine M where the input head of M "switches sides" from the x-part of the

[3]In fact, garden-hose protocols can even be transformed into communication protocols in the more restrictive *simultaneous-message-passage* model, where Alice and Bob send simultaneous messages consisting of their connections $E_{A_\circ}(x)$ and $E_B(y)$ to the referee who then computes the function. The according statements of Propositions 2.8, 2.19 and 2.20 can be derived analogously.

[4]For simplicity of notation, we give two arguments to the Turing machine whose concatenation is interpreted as the input.

input to the y-part or vice versa. Thanks to the reversibility of M, the players can then use one-to-one connections to wire up (depending on their individual inputs) the open ends of the pipes on their side, so that eventually the water flow corresponds to M's computation of $f(x,y)$. □

In the garden-hose model, we allow Alice and Bob to locally pre-process their inputs before computing their wiring. Therefore, it immediately follows from Theorem 2.12 that any function f in $L_{(2)}$ has polynomial garden-hose complexity, proving one direction of Theorem 2.11.

We saw in Proposition 2.9 that there exist functions with large garden-hose complexity. However, a negative implication of Theorem 2.12 is that proving the existence of a *polynomial-time computable* function f with exponential garden-hose complexity is at least as hard as separating L from P, a long-standing open problem in complexity theory.

COROLLARY 2.13. *If there exists a function $f:\{0,1\}^n \times \{0,1\}^n \to \{0,1\}$ in P that has super-polynomial garden-hose complexity, then $P \neq L$.*

It remains to prove the other inclusion of Theorem 2.11.

PROPOSITION 2.14. *Let $f:\{0,1\}^n \times \{0,1\}^n \to \{0,1\}$ be a Boolean function. If $GH(f)$ is polynomial (in n), then f is in $L_{(2)}$.*

PROOF. Let G be the garden-hose game that achieves $s(G) = GH(f)$. We write s for $s(G)$, the number of pipes, and we let $E_{A_\circ}$ and E_B be the underlying edge-picking functions, which on input x and y, respectively, output the connections that Alice and Bob apply to the pipes. Note that by assumption, s is polynomial. Furthermore, by the restrictions on $E_{A_\circ}$ and E_B, on any input, they consist of at most $(s+1)/2$ connections.

We need to show that f is of the form $f(x,y) = g(\alpha(x),\beta(y))$, where α and β are arbitrary functions $\{0,1\}^n \to \{0,1\}^m$, $g:\{0,1\}^m \times \{0,1\}^m \to \{0,1\}$ is log-space computable, and m is polynomial in n. We define α and β as follows. For any $x,y \in \{0,1\}^n$, $\alpha(x)$ is simply a natural encoding of $E_{A_\circ}(x)$ into $\{0,1\}^m$, and $\beta(y)$ is a natural encoding of $E_B(y)$ into $\{0,1\}^m$. In the hose-terminology we say that $\alpha(x)$ is a binary encoding of the connections of Alice, and $\beta(y)$ is a binary encoding of the connections of Bob. Obviously, these encodings can be done with m of polynomial size. Given these encodings, finding the endpoint of the maximum path $\pi(x,y)$ starting in 0 can be done with logarithmic space: at any point during the computation, the Turing machine only needs to maintain a pointer to the position of the water and a binary flag to remember on which side of the input tape the head is. Thus, the function g that computes $g(\alpha(x),\beta(y)) = f(x,y)$ is log-space computable in m and thus also in n. □

2.4 Randomized Garden-Hose Complexity

It is natural to study the setting where Alice and Bob share a common random string and are allowed to err with some probability ε. More formally, we let the players' local strategies $E_{A_\circ}(x,r)$ and $E_B(y,r)$ depend on the shared randomness r and write $G_r(x,y) = f(x,y)$ if the resulting garden-hose game $G_r(x,y)$ computes $f(x,y)$.

DEFINITION 2.15. *Let r be the shared random string. The* randomized garden-hose complexity *of a Boolean function $f:\{0,1\}^n \times \{0,1\}^n \to \{0,1\}$ is the size $s(G_r)$ of the smallest garden-hose game G_r such that $\forall x,y: \Pr_r[G_r(x,y) = f(x,y)] \geq 1-\varepsilon$. We denote this minimal size by $GH_\varepsilon(f)$.*

In Appendix B.2, we show that the error probability can be made exponentially small by repeating the protocol a polynomial number of times.

PROPOSITION 2.16. *Let $f:\{0,1\}^n \times \{0,1\}^n \to \{0,1\}$ be a function such that $GH_\varepsilon(f)$ is polynomial in n, with error $\varepsilon \leq \frac{1}{2} - n^{-c}$ for a constant $c > 0$. For every constant $d > 0$ there exists a polynomial $q(\cdot)$ such that $GH_{2^{-n^d}}(f) \leq q(GH_\varepsilon(f))$.*

Using this result, any randomized strategy can be turned into a deterministic strategy with only a polynomial overhead in the number of pipes.

PROPOSITION 2.17. *Let $f:\{0,1\}^n \times \{0,1\}^n \to \{0,1\}$ be a function such that $GH_\varepsilon(f)$ is polynomial in n and $\varepsilon \leq \frac{1}{2} - n^c$ for a constant $c > 0$. Then there exists a polynomial $q(\cdot)$ such that $GH(f) \leq q(GH_\varepsilon(f))$.*

PROOF SKETCH. By Proposition 2.16 there exists a randomized garden-hose protocol $G_r(x,y)$ of size $q(GH_\varepsilon(f))$ with error probability at most 2^{-2n-1}. The probability for a random string r to be wrong for all inputs is at most $2^{2n} \cdot 2^{-2n-1} < 1$. In particular, there exists a string $\hat{r}$ which works for every input (x,y). □

Using this Proposition 2.17, we conclude that the lower bound from Proposition 2.9 carries over to the randomized setting.

COROLLARY 2.18.
There exist functions $f:\{0,1\}^n \times \{0,1\}^n \to \{0,1\}$ for which $GH_\varepsilon(f)$ is exponential.

With the same reasoning as in Proposition 2.8, we get that lower bounds on the randomized one-way communication complexity with public shared randomness carry over to the randomized garden-hose complexity (up to a logarithmic factor).

PROPOSITION 2.19. *Let $R_\varepsilon^{1,\text{pub}}(f)$ denote the minimum communication cost of a one-way-communication protocol which computes f with an error ε using public shared randomness. Then, $R_\varepsilon^{1,\text{pub}}(f) \leq GH_\varepsilon(f)\log(GH_\varepsilon(f))$.*

For instance, the linear lower bound $R_\varepsilon^{pub}(IP) \in \Omega(n)$ from [12] for the inner-product function yields $GH_\varepsilon(IP) \in \Omega(\frac{n}{\log n})$.

2.5 Quantum Garden-Hose Complexity

Let us consider the setting where Alice and Bob share an arbitrary entangled quantum state besides their water pipes. Depending on their respective inputs x and y, they can perform local quantum measurements on their parts of the entangled state and wire up the pipes depending on the outcomes of these measurements. We denote the resulting *quantum garden-hose complexity* with $GH^Q(f)$ in the deterministic case and with $GH_\varepsilon^Q(f)$ if errors are allowed.

With the same reasoning as in Proposition 2.8, we get that lower bounds on the entanglement-assisted one-way communication complexity carry over to the quantum garden-hose complexity (up to a logarithmic factor).

PROPOSITION 2.20. *For $\varepsilon \geq 0$, let $Q_\varepsilon^1(f)$ denote the minimum cost of an entanglement-assisted one-way communication protocol which computes f with an error ε. Then, $Q_\varepsilon^1(f) \leq GH_\varepsilon^Q(f)\log(GH_\varepsilon^Q(f))$.*

For instance, the lower bound $Q^1_\varepsilon(IP) \in \Omega(n)$ which follows from results in [13] gives $GH^Q_\varepsilon(IP) \in \Omega(n/\log n)$. For the disjointness function, $Q^1_\varepsilon(DISJ) \in \Omega(\sqrt{n})$ from [26] implies $GH^Q_\varepsilon(DISJ) \in \Omega(\sqrt{n}/\log n)$.

In Appendix D, we present partial functions which give a separation between the quantum and classical garden-hose complexity in the deterministic and in the randomized setting.

THEOREM 2.21. *There exist partial Boolean functions f and g such that*

1. $GH^Q(f) \in O(\log n)$ *and* $GH(f) \in \Omega(\frac{n}{\log n})$,
2. $GH^Q_\varepsilon(g) \in O(\log n)$ *and* $GH_\varepsilon(g) \in \Omega(\frac{\sqrt{n}}{\log n})$.

3. APPLICATION TO POSITION-BASED QUANTUM CRYPTOGRAPHY

The goal of *position-based cryptography* is to use the geographical position of a party as its only "credential". For example, one would like to send a message to a party at a geographical position *pos* with the guarantee that the party can decrypt the message only if he or she is physically present at *pos*. The general concept of position-based cryptography was introduced by Chandran, Goyal, Moriarty and Ostrovsky [11].

A central task in position-based cryptography is the problem of *position-verification*. We have a *prover* P at position *pos*, wishing to convince a set of *verifiers* $V_0, \ldots, V_k$ (at different points in geographical space) that P is indeed at that position *pos*. The prover can run an interactive protocol with the verifiers in order to convince them. The main technique for such a protocol is known as distance bounding [3]. In this technique, a verifier sends a random nonce to P and measures the time taken for P to reply back with this value. Assuming that the speed of communication is bounded by the speed of light, this technique gives an upper bound on the distance of P from the verifier.

The problem of secure position-verification has been studied before in the field of wireless security, and there have been several proposals for this task ([3, 27, 30, 7] [9, 28, 31, 8]). However, [11] shows that there exists no protocol for secure position-verification that offers security in the presence of *multiple colluding* adversaries. In other words, the set of verifiers cannot distinguish between the case when they are interacting with an honest prover at *pos* and the case when they are interacting with multiple colluding dishonest provers, none of which is at position *pos*.

The impossibility result of [11] relies heavily on the fact that an adversary can locally store all information he receives *and* at the same time share this information with other colluding adversaries, located elsewhere. Due to the quantum no-cloning theorem, such a strategy will not work in the quantum setting, which opens the door to secure protocols that use quantum information. The quantum model was first studied by Kent et al. under the name of "quantum tagging" [17, 18]. Several schemes were developed [18, 21, 10, 22, 20] and proven later to be insecure. Finally in [5] it was shown that in general no unconditionally secure quantum position-verification scheme is possible. Any scheme can be broken using a double exponential amount of EPR pairs in the size of the messages of the protocol. Later, Beigi and König improved in [2] the double exponential dependence to single exponential making use of port-based teleportation [15, 16].

Due to the exponential overhead in EPR pairs, the general no-go theorem does not rule out the existence of quantum schemes that are secure for all practical purposes. Such schemes should have the property that the protocol, when followed honestly, is feasible, but cheating the protocol requires unrealistic amounts of resources, for example EPR pairs or time.

3.1 A Single-Qubit Scheme

Our original motivation for the garden-hose model was to study a particular quantum protocol for secure position verification, described in Figure 2. The protocol is of the generic form described in Section 3.2 of [5]. In Step 0, the verifiers prepare challenges for the prover. In Step 1, they send the challenges, timed in such a way that they all arrive at the same time at the prover. In Step 2, the prover computes his answers and sends them back to the verifiers. Finally, in Step 3, the verifiers verify the timing and correctness of the answer.

As in [5], we consider here for simplicity the case where all players live in one dimension, the basic ideas generalize to higher dimensions. In one dimension, we can focus on the case of two verifiers V_0, V_1 and an honest prover P in between them.

We minimize the amount of quantum communication in that only one verifier, say V_0, sends a qubit to the prover, whereas both verifiers send classical n-bit strings $x, y \in \{0,1\}^n$ that arrive at the same time at the prover. We fix a publicly known Boolean function $f : \{0,1\}^n \times \{0,1\}^n \to \{0,1\}$ whose output $f(x,y)$ decides whether the prover has to return the qubit (unchanged) to verifier V_0 (in case $f(x,y) = 0$) or to verifier V_1 (if $f(x,y) = 1$).

0. V_0 randomly chooses two n-bit strings $x, y \in \{0,1\}^n$ and privately sends y to V_1. V_0 prepares an EPR pair $(|0\rangle_V|0\rangle_P + |1\rangle_V|1\rangle_P)/\sqrt{2}$. If $f(x,y) = 0$, V_0 keeps the qubit in register V. Otherwise, V_0 sends the qubit in register V privately to V_1.
1. V_0 sends the qubit in register P to the prover P together with the classical n-bit string x. V_1 sends y so that it arrives at the same time as the information from V_0 at P.
2. P evaluates $f(x,y) \in \{0,1\}$ and routes the qubit to $V_{f(x,y)}$.
3. V_0 and V_1 accept if the qubit arrives in time at the correct verifier and the Bell measurement of the received qubit together with the qubit in V yields the correct outcome.

Figure 2: Position-verification scheme $\mathsf{PV}^f_{\text{qubit}}$ using one qubit and classical n-bit strings.

The motivation for considering this protocol is the following: As the protocol uses only one qubit which needs to be correctly routed, the honest prover's quantum actions are trivial to perform. His main task is evaluating a classical Boolean function f on classical inputs x and y whose bit size n can be easily scaled up. On the other hand, our results suggest that the adversary's job of successfully attacking the protocol becomes harder and harder for larger input strings x, y.

3.2 Connection to the Garden-Hose Model

In order to analyze the security of the protocol $\mathsf{PV}^f_{\text{qubit}}$, we define the following communication game in which Alice and Bob play the roles of the adversarial attackers of $\mathsf{PV}^f_{\text{qubit}}$. Alice starts with an unknown qubit $|\phi\rangle$ and a classical n-bit string x while Bob holds the n-bit string y. They also share some quantum state $|\eta\rangle_{AB}$ and both players know the Boolean function $f : \{0,1\}^n \times \{0,1\}^n \to \{0,1\}$. The players are allowed one round of simultaneous classical communication combined with arbitrary local quantum operations. When $f(x,y) = 0$, Alice should be in possession of the qubit $|\phi\rangle$ at the end of the protocol and on $f(x,y) = 1$, Bob should hold it.

As a simple example consider the case where $f(x,y) = x \oplus y$, the XOR function, with 1-bit inputs x and y. Alice and Bob then have the following way of performing this task perfectly by using a pre-shared quantum state consisting of three EPR pairs (three ebits). Label the first two EPR pairs 0 and 1. Alice teleports[5] $|\phi\rangle$ to Bob using the pair labeled with her input x. This yields measurement result $i \in \{0,1,2,3\}$, while Bob teleports his half of the EPR pair labeled y to Alice using his half of the third EPR pair while obtaining measurement outcome $j \in \{0,1,2,3\}$. In the round of simultaneous communication, both players send the classical measurement results and their inputs x or y to the other player. If $x \oplus y = 1$, i.e. x and y are different bits, Bob can apply the Pauli operator σ_i to his half of the EPR pair labeled $x = y \oplus 1$, correctly recovering $|\phi\rangle$. Similarly, if $x \oplus y = 0$, it is easy to check that Alice can recover the qubit by applying $\sigma_i \sigma_j$ to her half of the third EPR pair.

If Alice and Bob are *constrained* to the types of actions in the example above, i.e., if they are restricted to teleporting the quantum state back and forth depending on their classical inputs, there is a one-to-one correspondence between attacking the position-verification scheme $\mathsf{PV}^f_{\text{qubit}}$ and computing the function f in the garden-hose model. The quantum strategy for attacking $\mathsf{PV}^f_{\text{qubit}}$ in the example above exactly corresponds to the strategy depicted in Figure 1 for computing the XOR-function in the garden-hose model.

More generally, we can translate any strategy of Alice and Bob in the garden-hose model to a perfect quantum attack of $\mathsf{PV}^f_{\text{qubit}}$ by using one EPR pair per pipe and performing Bell measurements where the players connect the pipes.

Our hope is that also the converse is true: if many pipes are required to compute f (say we need super-polynomially many), then the number of EPR pairs needed for Alice and Bob to successfully break $\mathsf{PV}^f_{\text{qubit}}$ with probability close to 1 by means of an *arbitrary* attack (not restricted to Bell measurements on EPR pairs) should also be super-polynomial.

The examples of (partial) functions from Theorem 2.21 show that the classical garden-hose complexity $GH(f)$ does not capture the amount of EPR pairs required to attack $\mathsf{PV}^f_{\text{qubit}}$. It is conceivable that one can show that arbitrary attacks can be cast in the quantum garden-hose model and hence, the quantum garden-hose complexity $GH^Q_\varepsilon(f)$ (or a variant of it[6]) correctly captures the amount of EPR pairs required to attack $\mathsf{PV}^f_{\text{qubit}}$. We leave this question as an interesting problem for future research.

[5]See Appendix C.1 for a brief introduction to quantum teleportation.

[6]In addition to the number of pipes, one might have to account for the size of the entangled state as well.

We stress that for this application, any polynomial lower bound on the number of required EPR pairs is already interesting.

3.3 Lower Bounds on Quantum Resources to Perfectly Attack $\mathsf{PV}^f_{\text{qubit}}$

In Appendix E, we show that for a function that is injective for Alice or injective for Bob (according to Definition 2.4), the dimension of the quantum state the adversaries need to handle (including possible quantum communication between them) in order to attack protocol $\mathsf{PV}^f_{\text{qubit}}$ perfectly has to be of order at least linear in the classical input size n. In other words, they require at least a logarithmic number of qubits in order to successfully attack $\mathsf{PV}^f_{\text{qubit}}$.

THEOREM 3.1. *Let f be injective for Bob. Assume that Alice and Bob perform a perfect attack on protocol PV^f_{qubit}. Then, the dimension d of the overall state (including the quantum communication) is in $\Omega(n)$.*

In the last subsection, we show that there exist functions for which perfect attacks on $\mathsf{PV}^f_{\text{qubit}}$ requires the adversaries to handle a polynomial amount of qubits.

THEOREM 3.2. *For any starting state $|\psi\rangle$ of dimension d, there exists a Boolean function f on inputs $x, y \in \{0,1\}^n$ such that any perfect attack on PV^f_{qubit} requires d to be exponential in n.*

These results can be seen as first steps towards establishing the desired relation between classical difficulty of honest actions and quantum difficulty of the actions of dishonest players. We leave as future work the generalization of these lower bounds to the more realistic case of imperfect attacks and also to more relevant quantities like some entanglement measure between the players (instead of the dimension of their shared state).

4. CONCLUSION AND OPEN QUESTIONS

The garden-hose model is a new model of communication complexity. We connected functions with polynomial garden-hose complexity to a newly defined class of log-space computations with local pre-processing. Alternatively, the class $\mathrm{L}_{(2)}$ can also be viewed as the set of functions which can be decided in the simultaneous-message-passing (SMP) model where the referee is restricted to log-space computations. Many open questions remain. Can we find better upper and lower bounds for the garden-hose complexity of the studied functions? The constructions given in [29] still leave a polynomial gap between lower and upper bounds for many functions. It would also be interesting to find an explicit function for which the garden-hose complexity is provably super-linear or even exponential, the counting argument in Proposition 2.9 only shows the existence of such functions. It is possible to extend the basic garden-hose model in various ways and consider settings with more than two players, non-Boolean functions or multiple water sources. Furthermore, it is interesting to relate our findings to very recent results about space-bounded communication complexity [4].

Garden-hose complexity is a tool for the analysis of a specific scheme for position-based quantum cryptography. This scheme requires the honest prover to work with only a single qubit, while the dishonest provers potentially have to manipulate a large quantum state, making it an appealing scheme to further examine. The garden-hose model captures the power of attacks that only use teleportation, giving upper bounds for the general scheme, and lower bounds when restricted to these attacks.

An interesting additional restriction on the garden-hose model would involve limiting the computational power of Alice and Bob. For example to polynomial time, or to the output of quantum circuits of polynomial size. Bounding not only the amount of entanglement, but also the amount of computation with a realistic limit might yield stronger security guarantees for the cryptographic schemes.

5. ACKNOWLEDGMENTS

HB is supported by an NWO Vici grant and the EU project QCS. FS is supported by the NWO DIAMANT project. CS is supported by an NWO Veni grant. We thank Louis Salvail for useful discussions about the protocol $\mathsf{PV}^f_{\text{qubit}}$.

6. REFERENCES

[1] L. Babai, P. Frankl, and J. Simon. Complexity classes in communication complexity theory. In *Foundations of Computer Science, 1986., 27th Annual Symposium on*, pages 337–347, 1986.

[2] S. Beigi and R. König. Simplified instantaneous non-local quantum computation with applications to position-based cryptography. *New Journal of Physics*, 13(9):093036, 2011.

[3] S. Brands and D. Chaum. Distance-bounding protocols. In *EUROCRYPT'93*, pages 344–359. Springer, 1994.

[4] J. Brody, S. Chen, P. A. Papakonstantinou, H. Song, and X. Sun. Space-bounded communication complexity. to appear at ITCS 2013, 2012.

[5] H. Buhrman, N. Chandran, S. Fehr, R. Gelles, V. Goyal, R. Ostrovsky, and C. Schaffner. Position-based quantum cryptography: Impossibility and constructions. In P. Rogaway, editor, *Advances in Cryptology - CRYPTO 2011*, volume 6841 of *Lecture Notes in Computer Science*, pages 429–446. Springer Berlin / Heidelberg, 2011.

[6] H. Buhrman, R. Cleve, and A. Wigderson. Quantum vs. classical communication and computation. In *Proceedings of the thirtieth annual ACM symposium on Theory of computing*, STOC '98, pages 63–68, New York, NY, USA, 1998. ACM.

[7] L. Bussard. *Trust Establishment Protocols for Communicating Devices.* PhD thesis, Eurecom-ENST, 2004.

[8] S. Capkun, M. Cagalj, and M. Srivastava. Secure localization with hidden and mobile base stations. In *IEEE INFOCOM*, 2006.

[9] S. Capkun and J.-P. Hubaux. Secure positioning of wireless devices with application to sensor networks. In *IEEE INFOCOM*, pages 1917–1928, 2005.

[10] N. Chandran, S. Fehr, R. Gelles, V. Goyal, and R. Ostrovsky. Position-based quantum cryptography. arXiv:1005.1750v2, May 2010.

[11] N. Chandran, V. Goyal, R. Moriarty, and R. Ostrovsky. Position based cryptography. In *CRYPTO 2009*, pages 391–407. Springer, 2009.

[12] B. Chor and O. Goldreich. Unbiased bits from sources of weak randomness and probabilistic communication complexity. *SIAM J. Comput.*, 17(2):230–261, Apr. 1988.

[13] R. Cleve, W. v. Dam, M. Nielsen, and A. Tapp. Quantum entanglement and the communication complexity of the inner product function. In *Selected papers from the First NASA International Conference on Quantum Computing and Quantum Communications*, QCQC '98, pages 61–74. Springer-Verlag, 1998.

[14] D. Gavinsky, J. Kempe, I. Kerenidis, R. Raz, and R. de Wolf. Exponential separations for one-way quantum communication complexity, with applications to cryptography. In *Proceedings of the thirty-ninth annual ACM symposium on Theory of computing*, STOC '07, pages 516–525, New York, NY, USA, 2007. ACM.

[15] S. Ishizaka and T. Hiroshima. Asymptotic teleportation scheme as a universal programmable quantum processor. *Phys. Rev. Lett.*, 101(24):240501, Dec 2008.

[16] S. Ishizaka and T. Hiroshima. Quantum teleportation scheme by selecting one of multiple output ports. *Phys. Rev. A*, 79(4):042306, Apr 2009.

[17] A. Kent, W. Munro, T. Spiller, and R. Beausoleil. Tagging systems, 2006. US patent nr 2006/0022832.

[18] A. Kent, W. J. Munro, and T. P. Spiller. Quantum tagging: Authenticating location via quantum information and relativistic signaling constraints. *Phys. Rev. A*, 84:012326, Jul 2011.

[19] K.-J. Lange, P. McKenzie, and A. Tapp. Reversible space equals deterministic space. In *Proceedings of Computational Complexity. Twelfth Annual IEEE Conference*, pages 45–50. IEEE Comput. Soc, Apr. 1997.

[20] H.-K. Lau and H.-K. Lo. Insecurity of position-based quantum-cryptography protocols against entanglement attacks. *Phys. Rev. A*, 83(1):012322, Jan 2011.

[21] R. A. Malaney. Location-dependent communications using quantum entanglement. *Phys. Rev. A*, 81(4):042319, Apr 2010.

[22] R. A. Malaney. Quantum location verification in noisy channels. In *GLOBECOM'10*, pages 1–6, 2010. arXiv:1004.4689v1.

[23] O. Margalit and A. Matsliah. Mage - the CDCL SAT solver developed and used by IBM for formal verification `http://ibm.co/P7qNpC`. personal communication, 2012.

[24] M. A. Nielsen and I. L. Chuang. *Quantum Computation and Quantum Information.* Cambridge university press, 2000.

[25] K. Pietrzak. personal communication, 2011.

[26] A. A. Razborov. Quantum communication complexity of symmetric predicates. *Izvestiya Mathematics*, 67(1):145–159, 2003.

[27] N. Sastry, U. Shankar, and D. Wagner. Secure verification of location claims. In *WiSe'03*, pages 1–10, 2003.

[28] D. Singelee and B. Preneel. Location verification using secure distance bounding protocols. In *IEEE MASS'10*, 2005.

[29] F. Speelman. Position-based quantum cryptography and the garden-hose game. Master's thesis, University of Amsterdam, 2011. arxiv:1210.4353.

[30] A. Vora and M. Nesterenko. Secure location verification using radio broadcast. In *OPODIS'04*, pages 369–383, 2004.

[31] Y. Zhang, W. Liu, Y. Fang, and D. Wu. Secure localization and authentication in ultra-wideband sensor networks. *IEEE Journal on Selected Areas in Communications*, 24:829–835, 2006.

APPENDIX

A. UPPER BOUND BY COMMUNICATION COMPLEXITY

We show that the garden-hose complexity $GH(f)$ of any function f is at most $2^{D(f)+1} - 1$, where $D(f)$ is the deterministic communication complexity of f.

Consider a protocol where Alice and Bob alternate in sending one bit. The pipes between Alice and Bob are labeled with all possible non-empty strings of length up to $D(f)$, with one extra reserve pipe.

Let $A_v(x)$ be the bit Alice sends after seeing transcript $v \in \{0,1\}^*$ given input x and let $B_v(x)$ be the bit Bob sends after a transcript v on input y. (Since Alice and Bob alternate, Alice sends a bit on even length transcripts, while Bob sends when the transcript has odd length.) Alice connects the tap to 0 or 1 depending on the first sent bit. Then, Alice makes connections

$$\{\{v, vA_v(x)\} | v \in \{0,1\}^* \text{ with } |v| \text{ even and } 1 \leq |v| \leq D(f)\}.$$

Here $vA_v(x)$ is the concatenation of v and $A_v(x)$. Bob's connections are given by the set

$$\{\{v, vB_v(x)\} \, | v \in \{0,1\}^* \text{ with } |v| \text{ odd and } 1 \leq |v| \leq D(f)\}.$$

Now, for all transcripts of length $D(f)$, Alice knows the function outcome. (Assume $D(f)$ is even for simplicity.) For those $2^{D(f)}$ pipes she can route the water to the correct side by connecting similar outcomes, as in the proof of Proposition 2.3, using one extra reserve pipe. This brings the total used pipes to $1 + \sum_{i=1}^{D(f)} 2^i = 2^{D(f)+1} - 1$. The correctness can be verified by comparing the path of the water to the communication protocol: the label of the pipe the water is in, when following it through the pipes for r "steps", is exactly the same as the transcript of the communication protocol when executing it for r rounds.

B. PROOFS

B.1 Proof of Theorem 2.12

THEOREM 2.12 *If $f : \{0,1\}^n \times \{0,1\}^n \rightarrow \{0,1\}$ is log-space computable, then $GH(f)$ is polynomial in n.*

PROOF. Let M be a deterministic Turing machine deciding $f(x,y) = 0$. We assume that M's read-only input tape is of length $2n$ and contains x on positions 1 to n and y on positions $n+1$ to $2n$. By assumption M uses logarithmic space on its work tapes.

In this proof, a *configuration* of M is the location of its tape heads, the state of the Turing machine and the content of its work tapes, excluding the content of the read-only input tape. This is a slightly different definition than usual, where the content of the input tape is also part of a configuration. When using the normal definition (which includes the content of all tapes), we will use the term *total configuration*. Any configuration of M can be described using a logarithmic number of bits, because M uses logarithmic space.

A Turing machine is called *deterministic*, if every total configuration has a unique next one. A Turing machine is called *reversible* if in addition to being deterministic, every total configuration also has a unique predecessor. An $S(n)$ space-bounded deterministic Turing machine can be simulated by a reversible Turing machine in space $O(S(n))$ [19]. This means that without loss of generality, we can assume M to be a reversible Turing machine, which is crucial for our construction. Let M also be *oblivious*[7] in the tape head movement on the input tape. This can be done with only a small increase in space by adding a counter.

Alice's and Bob's perfect strategies in the garden-hose game are as follows. They list all configurations where the head of the input tape is on position n coming from position $n+1$. Let us call the set of these configurations C_A. Let C_B be the analogous set of configurations where the input tape head is on position $n+1$ after having been on position n the previous step. Because M is oblivious on its input tape, these sets depend only on the function f, but not on the input pair (x, y). The number of elements of C_A and C_B is at most polynomial, being exponential in the description length of the configurations. Now, for every element in C_A and C_B, the players label a pipe with this configuration. Also label $|C_A|$ pipes ACCEPT and $|C_B|$ of them REJECT. These steps determine the number of pipes needed, Alice and Bob can do this labeling beforehand.

For every configuration in C_A, with corresponding pipe p, Alice runs the Turing machine starting from that configuration until it either accepts, rejects, or until the input tape head reaches position $n+1$. If the Turing machine accepts, Alice connects p to the first free pipe labeled ACCEPT. On a reject, she leaves p unconnected. If the tape head of the input tape reaches position $n+1$, she connects p to the pipe from C_B corresponding to the configuration of the Turing machine when that happens. By her knowledge of x, Alice knows the content of the input tape on positions 1 to n, but not the other half. Alice also runs M from the starting configuration, connecting the water tap to a target pipe with a configuration from C_B depending on the reached configuration.

Bob connects the pipes labeled by C_B in an analogous way: He runs the Turing machine starting with the configuration with which the pipe is labeled until it halts or the position of the input tape head reaches n. On accepting, the pipe is left unconnected and if the Turing machine rejects, the pipe is connected to one of the pipes labeled REJECT. Otherwise, the pipe is connected to the one labeled with the

[7]A Turing machine is called *oblivious*, if the movement in time of the heads only depend on the length of the input, known in advance to be $2n$, but not on the input itself. For our construction we only require the input tape head to have this property.

configuration in C_A, the configuration the Turing machine is in when the head on the input tape reached position n.

In the garden-hose game, only one-to-one connections of pipes are allowed. Therefore, to check that the described strategy is a valid one, the simulations of two different configurations from C_A should never reach the same configuration in C_B. This is guaranteed by the reversibility of M as follows. Consider Alice simulating M starting from different configurations $c \in C_A$ and $c' \in C_A$. We have to check that their simulation can not end at the same $d \in C_B$, because Alice can not connect both pipes labeled c and c' to the same d. Because M is reversible, we can in principle also simulate M backwards in time starting from a certain configuration. In particular, Alice can simulate M backwards starting with configuration d, until the input tape head position reaches $n+1$. The configuration of M at that time can not simultaneously be c and c', so there will never be two different pipes trying to connect to the pipe labeled d.

It remains to show that, after the players link up their pipes as described, the water comes out on Alice's side if M rejects on input (x,y), and that otherwise the water exits at Bob's. We can verify the correctness of the described strategy by comparing the flow of the water directly to the execution of M. Every pipe the water flows through corresponds to a configuration of M when it runs starting from the initial state. So the side on which the water finally exits also corresponds to whether M accepts or rejects. □

B.2 Proof of Proposition 2.16

PROPOSITION 2.16 *Let $f : \{0,1\}^n \times \{0,1\}^n \to \{0,1\}$ be a function such that $GH_\varepsilon(f)$ is polynomial in n, with error $\varepsilon \leq \frac{1}{2} - n^{-c}$ for a constant $c > 0$. For every constant $d > 0$ there exists a polynomial $q(\cdot)$ such that $GH_{2^{-n^d}}(f) \leq q(GH_\varepsilon(f))$.*

PROOF. The new protocol $G'_r(x,y)$ takes the majority of $k = 8n^{2c+d}$ outcomes of $G_{r_i}(x,y)$ where $r_1,\dots,r_k$ are k independent and uniform samples of the random string. We have to establish (i) that taking the majority of k instances of the original protocol indeed gives the correct outcome with probability at least $1 - 2^{-n^d}$ and (ii) that $G'_r(x,y)$ requires only polynomial pipes.

(i) Let X_i be the random variable that equals 1 when $G_{r_i}(x,y) = f(x,y)$ and 0 otherwise. Note that the X_i are independent and identically distributed random variables with expectation $E[X_i] \geq 1 - \varepsilon =: p$. Whenever $\sum_{i=1}^k X_i \geq \frac{k}{2}$ the protocol gives the correct outcome. Use the Chernoff bound to get

$$\Pr\left[\sum_{i=1}^k X_i < (1-\zeta)pk\right] \leq e^{-\frac{\zeta^2}{2}pk}$$

for any small ζ. Picking $\zeta = n^{-c}$, so that $(1-\zeta)pk$ is still greater than $\frac{k}{2}$, and filling in k, we can upper bound the probability of failure by

$$e^{-\frac{8n^{2c+d}}{2n^{2c}}p} \leq 2^{-n^d}$$

(ii) In Theorem 2.12 we show that any log-space computable function can be simulated by a polynomial-sized garden-hose strategy. Thus, if checking the majority of k garden-hose strategies can be done in logarithmic space (after local pre-computations by Alice and Bob), then $G'_r(x,y)$ can be computed using a polynomial number of pipes.

Let $A_i = E_{A_\circ}(x, r_i)$ be the local wiring of Alice for strategy G on input x with randomness r_i, and let $B_i = E_B(y, r_i)$. Alice locally generates $(A_1,\dots,A_k)$ and Bob locally generates $(B_1,\dots,B_k)$. In the proof of Proposition 2.14 it was shown that simulating the outcome of a single garden-hose strategy (A_i, B_i) can be done in logarithmic space. Here we follow the same construction, but instead of getting the outcome of a single strategy we simulate all k strategies. This can still be done in logarithmic space, since we can re-use the memory needed to simulate each of the k strategies. To find the majority, we need to add a counter to keep track of the simulation outcomes, using only an extra $\log k$ bits of space. □

C. QUANTUM PRELIMINARIES

For Appendices D and E, we assume that the reader is familiar with basic concepts of quantum information theory. We refer to [24] for an introduction and merely fix some notation here.

C.1 Quantum Teleportation

An important example of a 2-qubit state is the *EPR pair*, which is given by $|\Phi\rangle_{AB} = (|0\rangle_A|0\rangle_B + |1\rangle_A|1\rangle_B)/\sqrt{2} \in \mathcal{H}_A \otimes \mathcal{H}_B = \mathbb{C}^2 \otimes \mathbb{C}^2$ and has the following properties: if qubit A is measured in the computational basis, then a uniformly random bit $x \in \{0,1\}$ is observed and qubit B collapses to $|x\rangle$. Similarly, if qubit A is measured in the Hadamard basis, then a uniformly random bit $x \in \{0,1\}$ is observed and qubit B collapses to $H|x\rangle$.

The goal of quantum teleportation is to transfer a quantum state from one location to another by only communicating classical information. Teleportation requires pre-shared entanglement among the two locations. To teleport a qubit Q in an arbitrary unknown state $|\psi\rangle_Q$ from Alice to Bob, Alice performs a Bell-measurement on Q and her half of an EPR pair, yielding a classical measurement outcome $k \in \{0,1,2,3\}$. Instantaneously, the other half of the corresponding EPR pair, which is held by Bob, turns into the state $\sigma_k|\psi\rangle$, where $\sigma_0, \sigma_1, \sigma_2, \sigma_3$ denote the four Pauli-corrections $\{\mathbb{I}, X, Z, XZ\}$, respectively. The classical information k is then communicated to Bob who can recover the state $|\psi\rangle$ by performing σ_k on his EPR half.

D. SEPARATIONS BETWEEN QUANTUM AND CLASSICAL GARDEN-HOSE COMPLEXITY

D.1 Deterministic Setting

Using techniques from [6], we show a separation between the garden-hose model and the quantum garden-hose model in the deterministic setting for the function EQ', defined as:

$$EQ'(x,y) = \begin{cases} 1 & \text{if } \Delta(x,y) = 0\,, \\ 0 & \text{if } \Delta(x,y) = n/2\,, \end{cases}$$

where $\Delta(x,y)$ denotes the Hamming distance between two n-bit strings x and y. We show that the zero-error quantum garden-hose complexity of EQ' is logarithmic in the input length.

THEOREM D.1. $GH^Q(EQ') \in O(\log n)$.

PROOF. Alice and Bob start with the fully entangled quantum state of $\log n$ qubits, i.e. with $\frac{1}{\sqrt{n}}\sum_{i=0}^{n-1}|i\rangle|i\rangle$. Counting indices of the input bits from 0 to $n-1$, Alice gives a phase of -1 to state $|i\rangle$ whenever $x_i = 0$ and Bob does the same thing with his half when the bit $y_i = 0$, yielding the state

$$\frac{1}{\sqrt{n}}\sum_{i=0}^{n-1}(-1)^{x_i+y_i}|i\rangle|i\rangle\,.$$

After both Alice and Bob perform a Hadamard transformation on their qubits, we obtain

$$\frac{1}{n\sqrt{n}}\sum_{i}\sum_{a,b}(-1)^{x_i+y_i}(-1)^{a\cdot i}(-1)^{b\cdot i}|a\rangle|b\rangle\,.$$

So the probability $p_{a,b}$ of obtaining outcome a, b when measuring in the computational basis is

$$p_{a,b} = \frac{1}{n^3}\left|\sum_{i}(-1)^{x_i+y_i+(a+b)\cdot i}\right|^2$$

If $x = y$, then $p_{a,b} = 0$ wherever $a \neq b$. If $\Delta(x, y) = n/2$, then $p_{a,b} = 0$ wherever $a = b$. It follows that $EQ'(x, y) = EQ(a, b)$ — determining the equality of the n-bit strings x and y is equivalent to computing the equality of the $\log(n)$-bit strings a and b. The garden-hose protocol for equality needs a number of pipes that is linear in the input size. After the quantum steps above, Alice and Bob can use $O(\log n)$ water pipes to compute $EQ(a, b)$. □

We can also show that the deterministic classical garden-hose complexity has an almost-linear lower bound.

THEOREM D.2. $GH(EQ') \in \Omega(\frac{n}{\log n})$

PROOF. Theorem 1.7 of [6] shows that the zero-error classical communication complexity of EQ' is lower bounded by $\Omega(n)$. The statement then follows from Proposition 2.8. □

D.2 Randomized Setting

The Noisy Perfect Matching problem (NPM) is a variant of the Boolean Hidden Matching introduced in [14] where they prove an exponential gap between the classical one-way communication complexity and the quantum one-way communication complexity of NPM. We adapt the given quantum one-way protocol to our setting, showing that the quantum garden-hose complexity is only logarithmic. This gives a separation between the classical and quantum garden-hose complexity of a partial function in the randomized setting.

The NPM problem is described as follows:[8]

Alice's input: $x \in \{0,1\}^{2n}$.

Bob's input: a perfect matching M on $\{1, \ldots, 2n\}$ and a string $w \in \{0,1\}^n$. The matching M consists of n edges, $e_1 = (i_1, j_1), \ldots, e_n = (i_n, j_n)$.

Promise: $\exists b \in \{0,1\}$ such that $\Delta(M \cdot x \oplus b^n, w) \leq n/3$, where $\Delta(\cdot,\cdot)$ is the Hamming distance and the k-th bit of the n-bit string $M \cdot x$ equals $x_{i_k} \oplus x_{j_k}$.

Function value: b.

Informally, the question asked is whether the parity on the edges of M, where the vertices are entries of x, is close to the parities specified by w, or not.

[8]For this example, we deviate from the earlier convention of giving two n-bit strings as input to the players.

THEOREM D.3. $GH^Q(\text{NPM}) \in O(\log n)$.

PROOF. Alice and Bob use $\log(2n)$ EPR pairs as quantum state $|\psi\rangle = \frac{1}{\sqrt{2n}}\sum_{i=0}^{2n-1}|i\rangle|i\rangle$. Alice inserts her input bits $x = x_0 \ldots x_{2n-1}$ as phases of the shared superposition, yielding the shared state

$$\frac{1}{\sqrt{2n}}\sum_{i=0}^{2n-1}(-1)^{x_i}|i\rangle_A|i\rangle_B\,.$$

Bob performs the following measurement: he uses projectors $P_k = |i_k\rangle\langle i_k|_B + |j_k\rangle\langle j_k|_B$ corresponding to the n edges. As they form a perfect matching, we have $\sum_{k=1}^{n} P_k = I$ and $P_k P_{k'} = \delta_{kk'}P_k$, so $\{P_k\}_k$ is a valid orthogonal measurement. Let us denote Bob's measurement outcome by ℓ. Setting $i := i_\ell$ and $j := j_\ell$, the post-measurement state is

$$(-1)^{x_i}|i\rangle_A|i\rangle_B + (-1)^{x_j}|j\rangle_A|j\rangle_B\,.$$

Alice then performs a Hadamard transform $H^{\otimes 2n} \otimes I$ on her part of the state, resulting in

$$\sum_{a=0}^{2n-1}|a\rangle_A\left[(-1)^{x_i+a\cdot i}|i\rangle_B + (-1)^{x_j+a\cdot j}|j\rangle_B\right].$$

Alice measures her register in the computational basis and obtains outcome a. Bob performs a Hadamard gate on basis states $|i\rangle_B$ and $|j\rangle_B$, that is, $H_{i,j} = \frac{1}{2}(|i\rangle\langle i|_B + |i\rangle\langle i|_B + |j\rangle\langle j|_B - |j\rangle\langle j|_B)$, resulting in the state

$$|a\rangle_A\left(\frac{1}{2}\left[(-1)^{x_i+a\cdot i} + (-1)^{x_j+a\cdot j}\right]|i\rangle_B + \frac{1}{2}\left[(-1)^{x_i+a\cdot i} - (-1)^{x_j+a\cdot j}\right]|j\rangle_B\right).$$

and measures in the computational basis. He gets outcome i if and only if $x_i \oplus a \cdot i = x_j \oplus a \cdot j$ which is equivalent to $x_i \oplus x_j = a \cdot (i \oplus j)$. In case $x_i \oplus x_j \neq a \cdot (i \oplus j)$, Bob gets outcome j.

In the garden-hose game played after the measurements, Alice and Bob perform the garden-hose protocol for the inner-product function described in [29] with a and $i \oplus j$ as their respective inputs. The protocol can be easily adapted so that at the end of it, the water will be in one particular pipe (known to Bob) on Bob's side if $a \cdot (i \oplus j) = 0$, let us call this pipe 0-pipe. The water will be in another "1-pipe" (known to Bob) if $a \cdot (i \oplus j) = 1$. Furthermore, Bob knows from his second measurement outcome if they are computing $x_i \oplus x_j$ or $x_i \oplus x_j \oplus 1$. In the first case, Bob looks at the ℓ-th bit of w and leaves the 0-pipe open if $w_\ell = 1$ and routes the 1-pipe to Alice, and if $w_\ell = 0$ he keeps the 1-pipe open and sends back the 0-pipe. This strategy computes the function value $w_\ell \oplus x_i \oplus x_j$, with ℓ uniformly random in $\{1, \ldots, n\}$. The promise guarantees that it gives the correct value b with probability at least $\frac{2}{3}$. The second case (when Bob knows that $a \cdot (i \oplus j) \neq x_i \oplus x_j$) is handled by the "inverse" strategy. □

THEOREM D.4. $GH_\varepsilon(\text{NPM}) \in \Omega(\frac{\sqrt{n}}{\log n})$.

PROOF. Combining the lower bound on the classical one-way communication complexity from [14] of $\Omega(\sqrt{n})$ with Proposition 2.19 gives the statement. □

E. LOWER BOUNDS ON QUANTUM RESOURCES FOR A PERFECT ATTACK

We show that for a function that is injective for Alice or injective for Bob (according to Definition 2.4), the dimension of the state the adversaries need to handle (including possible quantum communication between them) in order to attack protocol $\mathsf{PV}^f_{\text{qubit}}$ perfectly has to be of order at least linear in the classical input size n. We start by showing two lemmas. The actual bound is shown in Section E.3.

In the last subsection, we show that there exist functions for which perfect attacks on $\mathsf{PV}^f_{\text{qubit}}$ requires the adversaries to handle a polynomial amount of qubits.

E.1 Localized Qubits

Assume we have two bipartite states $|\psi^0\rangle$ and $|\psi^1\rangle$ with the property that $|\psi^0\rangle$ allows Alice to locally extract a qubit and $|\psi^1\rangle$ allows Bob to locally extract the same qubit. Intuitively, these two states have to be different.

More formally, we assume that both states consist of five registers $R, A, \tilde{A}, B, \tilde{B}$ where registers R, A, B are one-qubit registers and $\tilde{A}$ and $\tilde{B}$ are arbitrary. We assume that there exist local unitary transformations $U_{A\tilde{A}}$ acting on registers $A\tilde{A}$ and $V_{B\tilde{B}}$ acting on $B\tilde{B}$ such that[9]

$$U_{A\tilde{A}}|\psi^0\rangle_{RA\tilde{A}B\tilde{B}} = |\beta\rangle_{RA} \otimes |P\rangle_{\tilde{A}B\tilde{B}} \qquad (1)$$

$$V_{B\tilde{B}}|\psi^1\rangle_{RA\tilde{A}B\tilde{B}} = |\beta\rangle_{RB} \otimes |Q\rangle_{A\tilde{A}\tilde{B}}\,, \qquad (2)$$

where $|\beta\rangle_{RA} := (|00\rangle_{RA} + |11\rangle)_{RA})/\sqrt{2}$ denotes an EPR pair on registers RA and $|P\rangle_{\tilde{A}B\tilde{B}}$ and $|Q\rangle_{A\tilde{A}\tilde{B}}$ are arbitrary pure states.

LEMMA E.1. *Let $|\psi^0\rangle, |\psi^1\rangle$ be states that fulfill* (1) *and* (2). *Then,*

$$|\langle\psi^0|\psi^1\rangle| \leq 1/2\,.$$

PROOF. Multiplying both sides of (1) with $U^\dagger_{A\tilde{A}}$ and multiplying (2) with $V^\dagger_{B\tilde{B}}$, we can write

$$\begin{aligned}
|\langle\psi^0|\psi^1\rangle| &= |\langle\beta|_{RA}\langle P|_{\tilde{A}B\tilde{B}}\, U_{A\tilde{A}}\, V^\dagger_{B\tilde{B}}\, |\beta\rangle_{RB}|Q\rangle_{A\tilde{A}\tilde{B}}| \\
&= |\langle\beta|_{RA}\langle P'|_{\tilde{A}B\tilde{B}}|\beta\rangle_{RB}|Q'\rangle_{A\tilde{A}\tilde{B}}| \\
&= |\langle P'|_{\tilde{A}B\tilde{B}}\langle\beta|_{RA}|\beta\rangle_{RB}|Q'\rangle_{A\tilde{A}\tilde{B}}|\,,
\end{aligned}$$

where we used that $U_{A\tilde{A}}$ and $V_{B\tilde{B}}$ commute and defined $|P'\rangle_{\tilde{A}B\tilde{B}} := V_{B\tilde{B}}|P\rangle_{\tilde{A}B\tilde{B}}$ and $|Q'\rangle_{A\tilde{A}\tilde{B}} := U_{A\tilde{A}}|Q\rangle_{A\tilde{A}\tilde{B}}$. The last equality is just rearranging terms that act on different registers.

Note that writing out the partial inner product between $|\beta\rangle_{RA}$ and $|\beta\rangle_{RB}$ gives

$$\langle\beta|_{RA}|\beta\rangle_{RB} = \frac{1}{2}\left(\langle 0|_A|0\rangle_B + \langle 1|_A|1\rangle_B\right)\,,$$

where the operator in the parenthesis "transfers" a qubit from register A to register B. Hence,

$$\begin{aligned}
|\langle\psi^0|\psi^1\rangle| &= |\langle P'|_{\tilde{A}B\tilde{B}}\frac{1}{2}\left(\langle 0|_A|0\rangle_B + \langle 1|_A|1\rangle_B\right)|Q'\rangle_{A\tilde{A}\tilde{B}}| \\
&= \frac{1}{2}\cdot|\langle P'|_{\tilde{A}B\tilde{B}}|Q'\rangle_{B\tilde{A}\tilde{B}}| \\
&\leq \frac{1}{2}\,,
\end{aligned}$$

where the last step follows from the fact that the inner product between any two unit vectors on the same registers can be at most 1. □

E.2 Squeezing Many Vectors in a Small Space

For the sake of completeness, we reproduce here an argument similar to [24, Section 4.5.4] about covering the state space of dimension d with patches of radius ε.

LEMMA E.2. *Let $\mathcal{B}$ be a set of 2^n distinct unit vectors in a complex Hilbert space of dimension d, with pairwise absolute inner product at most $1/2$. Then, the dimension d has to be in $\Omega(n)$.*

PROOF. For any two vectors $|v\rangle, |w\rangle$, we can rotate the space such that $|v\rangle = |0\rangle$ and $|w\rangle = \cos\theta|0\rangle + \sin\theta|1\rangle$ for two orthogonal vectors $|0\rangle$ and $|1\rangle$. The *Euclidean distance* between $|v\rangle$ and $|w\rangle$ can be expressed as

$$\begin{aligned}
\big|\,|v\rangle - |w\rangle\,\big| &= |(1-\cos\theta)|0\rangle - \sin\theta|1\rangle| \\
&= \sqrt{(1-\cos\theta)^2 + \sin^2\theta} \\
&= \sqrt{1 - 2\cos\theta + \cos^2\theta + \sin^2\theta} \\
&= \sqrt{2}\sqrt{1-\cos\theta}\,.
\end{aligned}$$

If $|v\rangle$ and $|w\rangle$ have absolute inner product at most $1/2$, we have that $|\cos\theta| \leq 1/2$ and hence $\big|\,|v\rangle - |w\rangle\,\big| \geq 1$. Therefore, the vectors in $\mathcal{B}$ have pairwise Euclidean distance at least 1. The set of unit vectors $|w\rangle$ with Euclidean distance at most δ from $|v\rangle$ is called *patch of radius δ around $|v\rangle$*. It follows that patches of radius $1/2$ around every vector in the set $\mathcal{B}$ do not overlap.

The space of all d-dimensional state vectors can be regarded as the real unit $(2d-1)$-sphere, because the vector has d complex amplitudes and hence $2d$ real degrees of freedom with the restriction that the sum of the squared amplitudes is equal to 1. Notice that the Euclidean distance between complex vectors $|v\rangle$, $|w\rangle$ remains unchanged if we regard these vectors as points of the real unit $(2d-1)$-sphere.

The surface area of a patch of radius $1/2$ near any vector is lower bounded by the volume of a $(2d-2)$-sphere of radius ε where ε is a constant slightly less than $1/2$.[10]. We use the formula $S_k(r) = 2\pi^{(k+1)/2}r^k/\Gamma((k+1)/2)$ for the surface area of a k-sphere of radius r, and $V_k(r) = 2\pi^{(k+1)/2}r^{k+1}/[(k+1)\Gamma((k+1)/2)]$ for the volume of a k-sphere of radius r. The total surface area of all patches, which is at least $2^n \cdot V_{2d-2}(\varepsilon)$, is not more than the total surface of the whole sphere $S_{2d-1}(1)$. Inserting the formulas, we get

$$2^n \cdot 2\pi^{d-\frac{1}{2}}\frac{\varepsilon^{2d-1}}{(2d-1)\,\Gamma(d-\frac{1}{2})} \leq 2\pi^d\frac{1}{\Gamma(d)}$$

Using the fact that $\frac{\Gamma(d-\frac{1}{2})}{\Gamma(d)} \leq \frac{1}{d}$, we conclude that

$$2^n \leq \sqrt{\pi}(2-\frac{1}{d})\varepsilon^{-(2d-1)} \leq 2\sqrt{\pi}\varepsilon^{-(2d-1)}\,.$$

As $\varepsilon < 1/2$, we obtain that d has to be in $\Omega(n)$. □

E.3 The Lower Bound

We consider perfect attacks on protocol $\mathsf{PV}^f_{\text{qubit}}$ from Figure 2. We allow the players one round of simultaneous

[9]We always assume that these transformations act as the identities on the registers we do not specify explicitly.

[10]The patch is a "bent" version of this volume.

quantum communication which we model as follows. Let $|\psi\rangle_{RA\tilde{A}A_C B\tilde{B}B_C}$ be the pure state after Alice received the EPR half from the verifier. The one-qubit register R holds the verifier's half of the EPR-pair, the one-qubit register A contains Alice's other half of the EPR-pair, the register $\tilde{A}$ is Alice's part of the pre-shared entangled state and the register A_C holds the qubits that will be communicated to Bob. The registers $B\tilde{B}B_C$ belong to Bob where B holds one qubit and $\tilde{B}$ is Bob's part of the entangled state and the B_C register will be sent to Alice. We denote by q_A the total number of qubits in registers $\tilde{A}$ and A_C and by q_B the total number of qubits in $\tilde{B}$ and B_C. The overall state is thus a unit vector in a complex Hilbert space of dimension $d := 2^{2+q_A+1+q_B}$.

In the first step of their attack, Alice performs a unitary transform U^x depending on her classical input x on her registers $A\tilde{A}A_C$. Similarly, Bob performs a unitary transform V^y depending on y on registers $B\tilde{B}B_C$. After the application of these transforms, the communication registers A_C and B_C and the classical inputs x and y are exchanged. A final unitary transform (performed either by Alice or Bob) depending on both x, y "unveils" the qubit either in Alice's register A or in Bob's register B.

THEOREM E.3. *Let f be injective for Bob. Assume that Alice and Bob perform a perfect attack on protocol PV^f_{qubit}. Then, the dimension d of the overall state (including the quantum communication) is in $\Omega(n)$.*

PROOF. We assume that the player's actions are unitary transforms as described before the theorem.

We investigate the set $\mathcal{B}$ of overall states after Bob performed his operation, but *before* Alice acts on the state. These states depend on Bob's input $y \in \{0,1\}^n$,

$$\mathcal{B} := \left\{ V^y_{B\tilde{B}B_C} |\psi\rangle_{RA\tilde{A}A_C B\tilde{B}B_C} : y \in \{0,1\}^n \right\} .$$

We claim that for any two different n-bit strings $y \neq y'$, the corresponding two vectors $V^y|\psi\rangle$ and $V^{y'}|\psi\rangle$ in $\mathcal{B}$ have an absolute inner product of at most $1/2$.

Due to the injectivity of f, there exists an input x for Alice such that $f(x,y) \neq f(x,y')$. Applying Alice's unitary transform U^x to both vectors does not change their inner product, i.e.

$$|\langle\psi|(V^y)^\dagger V^{y'}|\psi\rangle| = |\langle\psi|(V^y)^\dagger (U^x)^\dagger U^x V^{y'}|\psi\rangle| .$$

As $f(x,y) \neq f(x,y')$, the qubit has to end up on different sides. Formally, there exist unitary transforms $K_{A\tilde{A}B_C}$ and $L_{B\tilde{B}A_C}$ that "unveil" the qubit in register A or B respectively. Hence, we can apply Lemma E.1 to prove the claim that the two vectors $V^y|\psi\rangle$ and $V^{y'}|\psi\rangle$ have an absolute inner product of at most $1/2$. In particular, all of the vectors in $\mathcal{B}$ are distinct. Applying Lemma E.2 yields the theorem. □

E.4 Functions For Which Perfect Attacks Need a Large Space

Using similar arguments as above, we can show the existence of functions for which perfect attacks require polynomially many qubits.

THEOREM E.4. *For any starting state $|\psi\rangle$ of dimension d, there exists a Boolean function on inputs $x, y \in \{0,1\}^n$ such that any perfect attack on PV^f_{qubit} requires d to be exponential in n.*

We believe that the statement with the reversed order of quantifiers is true as well (but our current proof does not suffice for this purpose), so that we can guarantee the existence of one particular function (independent of the starting state) for which perfect attacks require large states.

PROOF SKETCH. We consider covering the sphere with K patches of vectors whose pairwise absolute inner product is larger than $\frac{\sqrt{3}}{2}$ (which corresponds to an Euclidean distance of $\varepsilon = \sqrt{2}\sqrt{1+\sqrt{3}/2} \approx 0.52$). This partitioning also induces a partitioning on all possible unitary operations of Alice and Bob. We say that two actions A and A' are in the same patch if they take the starting state $|\psi\rangle$ to the same patch. In other words, if two actions are in the same patch then

$$|\langle\psi|A'^\dagger A|\psi\rangle| \geq \frac{\sqrt{3}}{2}.$$

Claim. Given two actions of Alice A, A' coming from the same patch i, and two actions of Bob B, B' coming from the same patch j, the inner product between $BA|\psi\rangle$ and $B'A'|\psi\rangle$ has magnitude at least $\frac{1}{2}$.

PROOF OF THE CLAIM. Since Alice and Bob act on different parts of the state, their actions commute. Write $|\psi_A\rangle := A'^\dagger A|\psi\rangle$ and $|\psi_B\rangle := B^\dagger B'|\psi\rangle$. Then the inner product can be written as

$$\langle\psi|A'^\dagger B'^\dagger BA|\psi\rangle = \langle\psi|B'^\dagger BA'^\dagger A|\psi\rangle = \langle\psi_B|\psi_A\rangle$$

Note that

$$|\langle\psi|\psi_A\rangle| = |\langle\psi|A'^\dagger A|\psi\rangle| \geq \frac{\sqrt{3}}{2},$$

so the angle θ between $|\psi_A\rangle$ and $|\psi\rangle$ is at most $\arccos\frac{\sqrt{3}}{2} = \frac{\pi}{6}$. The same holds for the angle between $|\psi_B\rangle$ and $|\psi\rangle$. We can upper bound the total angle between $|\psi_A\rangle$ and $|\psi_B\rangle$ by the sum of these angles, giving a total angle of at most $\frac{\pi}{3}$. This corresponds to a lower bound on the inner product of $\cos\frac{\pi}{3} = \frac{1}{2}$. □

So there exists no pair of combined actions AB and $A'B'$, with A and A' in patch i and B and B' in patch j, such that the qubit ends up on Alice's side for AB and on Bob's side for $A'B'$. Therefore, the combination of i and j completely determines the destination of the qubit and hence the output of the function. If K denotes the number of patches, then there are K^{2^n} possible strategies for Alice and K^{2^n} possible strategies for Bob. Hence, the number of combined strategies (possibly resulting in different functions) is at most $K^{2\cdot 2^n}$.

It is shown in [24, Section 4.5.4] that we need at least $K = \Omega(\frac{1}{\varepsilon^{d-1}})$ patches. Using the same counting argument as in Proposition 2.9, we have that

$$2^{2^{2n}} \geq \Omega\left(\frac{1}{\varepsilon^{(d-1)2\cdot 2^n}}\right),$$

from which follows that for some function, d has to be exponential in n. □

Space-Bounded Communication Complexity

Joshua Brody
Aarhus University
Aarhus, Denmark
joshua.e.brody@gmail.com

Shiteng Chen
ITCS/IIIS, Tsinghua University
Beijing, China
shitengchen@gmail.com

Periklis A. Papakonstantinou
ITCS/IIIS, Tsinghua University
Beijing, China
papakons@tsinghua.edu.cn

Hao Song
ITCS/IIIS, Tsinghua University
Beijing, China
hao.song42@gmail.com

Xiaoming Sun
Institute of Computing Technology, CAS
Beijing, China
xiaoming.sun@gmail.com

ABSTRACT

In the past thirty years, Communication Complexity has emerged as a foundational tool to proving lower bounds in many areas of computer science. Its power comes from its generality, but this generality comes at a price—no superlinear communication lower bound is possible, since a player may communicate his entire input. However, what if the players are limited in their ability to recall parts of their interaction?

We introduce memory models for 2-party communication complexity. Our general model is as follows: two computationally unrestricted players, Alice and Bob, each have $s(n)$ bits of memory. When a player receives a bit of communication, he "compresses" his state. This compression may be an arbitrary function of his current memory contents, his input, and the bit of communication just received; the only restriction is that the compression must return at most $s(n)$ bits. We obtain memory hierarchy theorems (also comparing this general model with its restricted variants), and show super-linear lower bounds for some explicit (non-boolean) functions.

Our main conceptual and technical contribution concerns the following variant. The communication is one-way, from Alice to Bob, where Bob controls two types of memory: (i) a large, *oblivious* memory, where updates are only a function of the received bit and the current memory content, and (ii) a smaller, *non-oblivious/general* memory, where updates can be a function of the input given to Bob. We exhibit natural protocols where this semi-obliviousness shows up. For this model we also introduce new techniques through which certain limitations of space-bounded computation are revealed. One of the main motivations of this work is in understanding the difference in the use of space when computing the following functions: Equality (EQ), Inner Product (IP), and connectivity in a directed graph (REACH). When viewed as communication problems, EQ can be decided using 0 non-oblivious bits (and $\log_2 n$ oblivious bits), IP requires exactly 1 non-oblivious bit, whereas for REACH we obtain the same lower bound as for IP and conjecture that the actual bound is $\Omega(\log^2 n)$. In fact, proving that 1 non-oblivious bit is required becomes technically sophisticated, and the question even for 2 non-oblivious bits for any explicit boolean function remains open.

ITCS'13, January 9–12, 2013, Berkeley, California, USA.

Categories and Subject Descriptors

F.1.2 [**Computation by Abstract Devices**]: Modes of Computation—*interactive and reactive computation*

Keywords

communication complexity; space-bounded; memory-bounded

1. INTRODUCTION

In computer science research most lower bounds have an information theoretic nature, but for a few exceptions (e.g. time/space hierarchy theorems, and the recent ACC^0 lower bound [26]). These lower bounds amount to showing that there is an "information cost we must pay" if we wish to correctly complete the task. This is commonly proved either implicitly, or by a reduction an information theoretic setting such as the communication complexity. The Communication Complexity model, originally introduced by Yao [27], is almost information theoretic by definition. (In fact, establishing a strong formal connection between communication complexity and information theory is itself an active area of research; see e.g., [11, 4, 5] for more details.) In its simplest form two computationally unbounded players, Alice (who holds an input x) and Bob (who holds y), aim to evaluate a function $f(x, y)$ by communicating as little as possible. This is an area of intense research activity, has autonomous existence, and finds several applications in diverse areas such as circuit complexity ([16, 23]), VLSI design ([1, 28]), data structure lower bounds ([21, 22, 20]) streaming algorithms ([2, 15, 25, 12, 13]), and property testing ([7]) to name a just a few.

When lower bounds are derived by a reduction from communication complexity, the quality of the lower bound is bounded by the corresponding communication lower bound.

In particular, in the classical communication complexity setting no super-linear communication lower bound is possible, as one player may simply send his entire input to the other.

To put things in context, consider the following example from streaming algorithms. Let REACH(G, s, t) be the problem that, given a directed graph G, determines if t is reachable from s. For a graph of n vertices and a machine with working memory $O(\log n)$, classical communication complexity techniques show that the number of passes must be $\Omega(\frac{n}{\log n})$. However, if one believes the conjecture that REACH cannot be computed in logarithmic space, the actual lower bound on the number of passes should be infinite.

What if we modify the original communication complexity model in a way that Alice and Bob can use only a small amount, say $O(\log n)$, of memory between steps of communication? In this setting, when players receive a bit of communication, they may spend an arbitrary amount of computation deciding what to save in their memory; however, they still must *compress* the information they know at each step; i.e., they must take their $s(n)$ bits of memory and the communication just received and again save only $s(n)$ bits of memory. In this case super-linear communication lower bounds are possible, and furthermore common reduction arguments (including the one mentioned above) go through *intact*. Being able to prove such lower bounds sounds too good to be true. Simply restricting the memory of the players corresponds to a model at least as strong as width-bounded branching programs and depth-bounded circuits. Although slightly super-linear communication lower bounds is within the reach of known techniques, showing lower bounds that shed actual light on the limitations of space-bounded computation seems non-trivial. In this paper we obtain strong lower bounds for explicit non-boolean functions in the general model, and for explicit boolean functions in a certain restricted model. We discuss this restriction in Section 1.2 and view it as an important part of our conceptual contribution.

1.1 Background

Lam, Tiwari and Tompa [19] were the first to study tradeoffs between communication and space requirements when computing functions in the *straight-line protocols* model. Alternatively, a straight-line protocol can be modeled as a pebble game on an arithmetic or boolean circuit. On the arithmetic model, they proved communication-space tradeoffs for matrix multiplication and polynomial convolution, through a detailed analysis of the structure of arithmetic circuits computing bilinear forms; i.e. the results rely heavily on the specifics of arithmetic circuits. On the other hand, the tradeoff for matrix-vector multiplication in their one-way boolean model follows a more generic information theoretic technical approach. Beame, Tompa and Yan [6] took a step further, introducing the more general *communicating branching programs* model. Adopting earlier techniques of Borodin et al. [9, 8] on branching programs into the communication setting, they showed stronger communication-space tradeoffs for matrix-vector multiplication and other functions.

In [19] and [6], techniques from classical computational complexity literature were modified to find application in the more powerful communication setting. Our motivation is in the opposite direction. We introduce a conceptually simple, purely information theoretic model. This choice of the model is not only a matter of elegance. First, given that currently we understand very little about computation itself it is not clear that there is any gain by bounding the players computationally. Second, this level of generality makes more transparent possible applications.

Besides [19, 6] and follow-ups of those (see e.g. [17, 18] by Klauck et. al.), some recent papers appear to be relevant to our approach. Impagliazzo and Williams [14] studied a variant of communication complexity where players share synchronized access to a common clock. They showed that with the help of this synchronized clock, it is sometimes possible to save communication. This clock resembles a special type of memory we study in this paper called "oblivious memory". The *garden-hose* model, introduced recently by Buhrman et al. [10], also resembles several characteristics of the space-bounded communication complexity model we study here. If fact, if we denote the *garden-hose complexity* defined in [10] of a function f as $GH(f)$, and the minimum space requirement to compute the function f in our space-bounded communication model as $s(f)$, then there are constants $c \in (0, 1)$ and $d \in \mathbb{N}^+$ that satisfies the following relation for every boolean function f

$$c \cdot 2^{s(f)} \leq GH(f) \leq 2^{2s(f)+2} + d$$

1.2 Oblivious Memory Updates – Compressing Interaction Obliviously

In addition to considering communication problems where players have limited space, we wish to understand an aspect of how space gets used in computing different functions of interest, e.g. the equality function EQ, inner product IP, and REACH.

Consider a one-way space-bounded protocol for computing equality in the two-party communication setting. Alice sends her input $x \in \{0, 1\}^n$ bit-by-bit to Bob. Bob in turn compares each bit x_i to the corresponding bit y_i of his input $y \in \{0, 1\}^n$. If Bob discovers a mismatch he outputs 0 and the protocol halts. Otherwise Bob halts after n bits of communication and outputs 1. We emphasize that in this protocol the players only need to maintain a counter which increases independent of their inputs.

A similar strategy also applies to the inner product function IP, where players receive n-bit strings and must compute their inner product modulo 2. Again, Alice and Bob keep counters incremented at each step, and Alice sends x to Bob bit-by-bit. This time, Bob keeps an additional bit to store the intermediate result. Namely, at step k Bob maintains a single bit containing the value $\sum_{i=1}^{k} x_i y_i$.

While both functions can be computed with $n + O(1)$ bits of communication and $\log_2 n + O(1)$ bits of work memory (optimal in the sense that both functions have deterministic communication complexity n), there is a difference in the way Bob uses his work memory. In the protocol for equality, the content of Bob's memory remains independent of his input, while in the protocol for inner product, the extra bit Bob uses depends on y. We will call the part of Bob's work memory whose content does not depend on y as "oblivious", and the part of Bob's work memory whose content does depend on y as "non-oblivious" or "general".

How about functions that have been conjectured to be hard for reasonably large space in the Turing Machine world? For example, we conjecture that the function REACH(G, s, t) requires $\Omega(\log^2 n)$ *non*-oblivious bits, unless the oblivious memory is large enough to hold Alice's entire input. Interestingly, so far we were only able to prove that at least 1 non-oblivious bit is required, and in fact just proving such a bound becomes challenging.

Apart from the above natural semi-oblivious protocols there are more high-level reasons this two-type memory merits consideration. By allowing a large enough oblivious memory we can realize protocols where players are able to perform simple tasks such as counting and communicating small parts of the information given in their input. This allows us to consider a weaker "type" of memory and attempt to study the general one *in isolation*. Note that if we instead only had non-oblivious memory then on one hand memory size lower bounds of e.g. $\frac{\log_2 n}{3}$ are trivial (even counting is impossible in this amount of space), whereas lower bounds for slightly larger memory directly imply strong circuit lower bounds. Even proving lower bounds for a smaller number of non-oblivious bits turns out to be a daunting task. One reason is because oblivious bits are present, and oblivious bits aren't as weak as one might think. For instance, in Section 3, we show that you cannot replace oblivious memory by a slightly smaller amount of non-oblivious memory.

1.3 Our Techniques and a Roadmap to Our Results

In this work, we define the space-bounded communication complexity model and give upper bounds for many interesting problems. Importantly, we also provide lower bounds and create new proof techniques tailored to space-bounded communication. Our results are organized as follows. In Section 3 we give several robust memory hierarchy theorems. In particular, we show:

THEOREM 1. (MEMORY HIERARCHY THEOREM, INFORMALLY STATED). *For all $s(n)$, there are functions computable using a $(s(n) + log(n))$-space communication protocol that cannot be computed by any $s(n)$-space communication protocol.*

We also show a direct-sum type of upper bound, where oblivious protocols can be combined without losing the oblivious nature of the protocol. For example, this shows that 2-output-bit equality (where each player has two strings, and players must determine whether each pair is equal) can be computed with a logarithmic amount of oblivious memory. We present additional interesting examples of space-bounded protocols in Section 4.

In Section 5, we show a non-computability result for the general memory model for explicit functions with large outputs. Our first such function, ALL-EQ, computes equality on every subset of bits. The output of ALL-EQ is thus 2^n bits long. By using ideas from combinatorial designs, we create another function EQ-WITH-DESIGN$_k$ whose output is polynomial in the number of input bits. We show that computing this function is also hard in the space-bounded communication model.

THEOREM 2. (LOWER BOUNDS FOR NON-BOOLEAN FUNCTIONS, INFORMALLY STATED). *Computing* ALL-EQ *requires $\Omega(n)$ space in the space-bounded communication model. Computing* EQ-WITH-DESIGN$_k$ *requires $\Omega(k \log n)$ space.*

Both lower bounds are close to their respective known upper bounds. A significant part of this work refers to new model-specific techniques we devised to prove lower bounds. The most involved such technique is in the proof that computing Inner Product requires non-oblivious memory.

THEOREM 3. *Any one-way oblivious protocol for* IP *requires $\Omega(n)$ space.*

Proving this theorem using standard communication lower bound techniques is not possible, as these techniques do not account for the space used by players. To that end, we develop a way to combine the standard notion of a communication matrix with an accounting of the current state of memory at any point in time in a space-bounded protocol. We analyze how the output decision is made based on the changing state of memory through the course of a protocol and argue that with limited space, little progress can be made. To show this, we introduce a geometric/covering notion of progress. Making this precise, and quantifying the details is technical and involved. We develop these concepts in depth in Section 6 and provide a full proof in Section 10.

2. THE SPACE-BOUNDED COMMUNICATION COMPLEXITY MODEL

For this paper, we focus on two-player deterministic protocols. Unless otherwise specified, we assume Alice and Bob receive inputs $x, y \in \{0,1\}^n$ and wish to compute a boolean function $f : \{0,1\}^n \times \{0,1\}^n \to \{0,1\}$.

In this section, we formally define the space-bounded communication complexity model as well as some variants. A player is space-bounded if he has a variable $M \in \{0,1\}^s$ corresponding to a limited amount of memory. A player's actions are defined by a *transition function*

$$T : \{0,1\} \times \{0,1\}^n \times \{0,1\}^s \to \{0,1\}^s \times \{0,1\} \times \{0,1,\perp\},$$

where $T(b, x, m) = (m', b', h)$ means the player, given input x, old memory contents m, and after receiving a bit of communication b, sets his memory contents to m', sends b' to the other player, and if $h \neq \perp$, the player halts and outputs h. A protocol is space-bounded when both players are space-bounded. Thus, a protocol can be described by a tuple (T_A, T_B).

DEFINITION 4. *A* space-bounded communication protocol $\mathcal{P}$ *with s bits of memory is a tuple (T_A, T_B) where $T_A, T_B : \{0,1\} \times \{0,1\}^n \times \{0,1\}^s \to \{0,1\}^s \times \{0,1\} \times \{0,1,\perp\}$, and in this paper, we use $M_A, M_B \in \{0,1\}^s$ to denote the content of Alice's and Bob's local memory, respectively. We say that $\mathcal{P}$ computes f if for all x, y, with the initial state $M_A = M_B = 0^s$, both players halt and output $f(x, y)$. The* communication cost *of $\mathcal{P}$ is the maximum total number of bits communicated over all inputs.*

Remark.

Note that no restriction is placed on the computational power required to compute T_A and T_B. In particular, players may use an arbitrary amount of time *or space* to compute T_A or T_B. Nevertheless, between steps of communication, memory remains bounded.

It is helpful to consider how players interact during the course of a protocol. Initialily, Alice and Bob receive inputs x and y and initialize their memory to zero. Communication proceeds in a number of steps, where Alice receives b_B from Bob and applies

$$(M_A, b_A, h_A) \leftarrow T_A(b_B, x, M_A) \ .$$

Alice then sends b_A to Bob, who computes

$$(M_B, b_B, h_B) \leftarrow T_B(b_A, y, M_B) \ .$$

completing a step of communication. (Initially, Alice sets b_B to zero.) Players proceed until each halts and outputs $f(x,y)$.

We are particularly interested in bounds on the minimum amount of space required to compute a function, and in which classes of functions are computable in limited space.

DEFINITION 5. $\mathsf{SPACECC}(s)$ *is the set of boolean functions computed by a space-bounded communication protocol using s bits of space.*

2.1 One-Way Semi-Oblivious Protocols

As mentioned in the introduction, we believe it is interesting to consider memory that is oblivious when communication is one-way.

DEFINITION 6. *In a* one-way *protocol, Alice feeds a stream of bits to Bob, but Bob cannot communicate back. Each of them has s bits of memory. The protocol halts as soon as Bob gives an answer and halts, even if Alice chooses to continue.* $\mathsf{SPACECC}_{\rightarrow}(s)$ *is the set of boolean functions computable with one-way protocols using s bits of space.*

In an oblivious protocol, Alice is space-bounded as before, but Bob's memory is further restricted.

DEFINITION 7. *In a one-way* semi-oblivious *protocol, Bob has two variables* $M_B^f \in \{0,1\}^{s_f}$ *and* $M_B^o \in \{0,1\}^{s_o}$ *and transition functions*

$$T_B^f : \{0,1\}\times\{0,1\}^n\times\{0,1\}^{s_f}\times\{0,1\}^{s_o} \rightarrow \{0,1\}^{s_f}\times\{0,1,\perp\}$$

and

$$T_B^o : \{0,1\} \times \{0,1\}^{s_o} \rightarrow \{0,1\}^{s_o}$$

The total amount of space used by Bob is $s_f + s_o$*. The protocol is* oblivious *if* $s_f = 0$*.*

$\mathsf{SPACECC}^{\mathsf{o}}_{\rightarrow}(s)$ *is the set of all functions computable by oblivious protocols where each player uses s bits of space.*

Bob uses T^f and T^o in the natural way. Note that updates to a player's oblivious memory are independent of both his input and his non-oblivious memory. Also note that in an oblivious protocol, the function T_B^f serves the purpose of deciding Bob's final answer (and that purpose only).

2.2 Space-Bounded Communication as Communicating State Machines.

It is natural to view a space-bounded communication protocol as the interaction between communicating state machines. In this view, Alice and Bob construct state machines $\mathcal{M}_x$ and $\mathcal{M}_y$ during a preprocessing stage. Each machine has a state for each possible memory configuration, plus two additional halt states YES and NO. From each non-halt state, there are 0 and 1 edges corresponding to the bit received from the other player. Each edge is further labeled by the output bit sent to the other player. Note that players construct different state machines on different inputs, since their behavior during a protocol differs on different inputs.

3. BASIC PROPERTIES

We give a list of basic properties of our space-bounded communication model and its variants. Observe that, as in other common space-bounded computation models, if a protocol runs for long enough then it repeats a configuration and does not halt.

PROPOSITION 8. *Let $\mathcal{P}$ be a communication protocol where each players has an input of length n and memory space $s(n)$. Furthermore, the protocol always halts. Then, on every input* $(x,y) \in \{0,1\}^n\times\{0,1\}^n$ *$\mathcal{P}$ runs in at most* $2^{2s(n)+1}$ *steps, or in other words, the communication cost is at most* $2^{2s(n)+1}$.

3.1 Memory Hierarchy Theorem

A natural, initial question for these memory models is whether more space can be used to compute more functions.

THEOREM 9. *For any* $s(n) < \frac{n}{5}$*, almost every boolean function (on two n-bit inputs) that can be computed with one-way oblivious protocol of work memory size* $s(n)+\log n$*, is not computable by any protocol (not necessarily oblivious) of work memory size* $s(n)$*.*

To prove this theorem, we will first prove Lemma 10 and Lemma 11 below.

LEMMA 10. *The number of different boolean functions (on inputs from* $\{0,1\}^n\times\{0,1\}^n$*) that can be computed with protocols with memory size* $s(n)$ *is at most* $2^{(4+s(n))\cdot 2^{n+s(n)+2}}$.

LEMMA 11. *The number of different boolean functions (on inputs from* $\{0,1\}^n\times\{0,1\}^n$*) that can be computed with one-way oblivious protocols of work memory size* $s(n)$ $(s(n) \le n)$ *is at least* $2^{2^{n+s(n)}}$.

PROOF OF THEOREM 9. This follows immediately by comparing the lower bound on the number of boolean functions computable by one-way oblivious protocols of memory size $s(n)+\log n$ (Lemma 11) and the upper bound on the number of boolean functions computable by two-way general protocols of memory size $s(n)$ (Lemma 10). □

Note that this implies two hierarchy theorems, one for the general (not necessarily one-way or oblivious) space-bounded communication model, and one for the one-way oblivious model.

COROLLARY 12. *For any* $s(n) < \frac{n}{5}$,

$$\mathsf{SPACECC}(s(n)) \subsetneq \mathsf{SPACECC}(s(n) + \log n).$$

COROLLARY 13. *For any* $s(n) < \frac{n}{5}$,

$$\mathsf{SPACECC}^{\mathsf{o}}_{\rightarrow}(s(n)) \subsetneq \mathsf{SPACECC}^{\mathsf{o}}_{\rightarrow}(s(n) + \log n).$$

3.2 Parallel repetitions of one-way Oblivious Protocols

Let us revisit the one-way oblivious protocol for equality (Section 1.2). First, observe that the protocol may halt at different steps for different input pairs (x,y). This can be shown to be essential (see Section 11). Now, consider the question of computing the non-boolean "2-bit EQ". In this problem Alice is given two n-bit strings x_1, x_2, and Bob is given y_1, y_2, and we want to find out if x_1 is equal to y_1, and simultaneously, if x_2 is equal to y_2. Interestingly, we do not need an extra non-oblivious bit to compute this 2-bit EQ. In fact, there is a more general property according to which we can compose "parallel" oblivious protocols on independent inputs.

PROPOSITION 14. *For a pair of boolean functions f_1 and f_2, if each is a function on two n-bit inputs, $f_1, f_2 : \{0,1\}^n \times \{0,1\}^n \to \{0,1\}$, and can be computed by a one-way oblivious protocol with space-bound $s_1(n), s_2(n)$ and communication cost $c_1(n), c_2(n)$, then the composite function $f(x,y) = (f_1(x,y), f_2(x,y))$ can be computed with a one-way oblivious protocol with space-bound $s_1(n) + 3s_2(n) + 1$ and communication cost $c_1(n) \cdot (c_2(n) + 2)$.*

4. EXAMPLE PROTOCOLS

In this section, we briefly present some space-bounded protocols for two natural problems on directed graphs. We defer proofs of the theorems in this section to Section 8.

Depth First Search on a Tree.

The input to this problem is a directed binary tree $T = (V, E)$ with distinguished vertices $s, t \in V$, and we wish to determine which vertex is reached first in a depth-first lexicographic traversal of T. We refer to this problem as DFS-TREE and define DFS-TREE$(T, s, t) = 1$ if and only if s precedes t. In the space-bounded communication version, Alice and Bob are given different sides of a fixed vertex cut $A \uplus B = V$. Alice receives all edges leaving vertices in A, and Bob receives all edges leaving vertices in B.

THEOREM 15. DFS-TREE $\in \mathsf{SPACECC}(\log n + \log\log n + O(1))$.

Note that while the space in the protocol achieving Theorem 15 is extremely limited, it requires worst-case communication $\Omega(n^2 \log(n))$, close to the theoretical maximum of $\Theta(n^2 \log^2 n)$ given by Proposition 8 and Theorem 15. We are interested in knowing if this is required, or if in general it is possible to *compress* communication close to this maximal bound. More generally we ask if there is a general scheme to bring the worst case communication cost of a space-bounded communication protocol down to $2^{s+o(s)}$ (from 2^{2s}).

Reachability.

The input for this problem is again a directed graph $G = (V, E)$, with distinguished vertices s, t. Define

$$\text{REACH}(G, s, t) := \begin{cases} 1 & \text{if } \exists \text{ an } s \rightsquigarrow t \text{ path in } G \\ 0 & \text{otherwise} \end{cases}$$

In the space-bounded communication version of this problem, players are again given different sides of a fixed vertex cut $A \uplus B = V$. Alice gets as input all edges in A; Bob gets as input all edges in B, and both players see all crossing edges. Let C_A denote the set of vertices in A adjacent to some vertex in B. Define C_B analogously. $C_A \cup C_B$ thus defines the boundary of the cut. Finally, let $C := \{s, t\} \cup C_A \cup C_B$, and let $c = |C|$. The performance of all of our protocols highly depend on c.

THEOREM 16. *REACH(G, s, t) can be computed (i) using $O(\log^2 c)$ space and $2^{O(\log^2 c)}$ communication, (ii) using $O(c)$ space and $O(c^2)$ communication, (iii) with a one-way protocol that uses $O(c^2)$ space and $O(c^2)$ communication, and (iv) with a one-way protocol that uses $O(c)$ space and $O(c^3)$ communication.*

5. LOWER BOUND FOR EXPLICIT NON-BOOLEAN FUNCTIONS

We give lower bounds for two explicit non-boolean functions $f : \{0,1\}^n \times \{0,1\}^n \to \{0,1\}^m$. Note that some care must be made when discussing space-bounded communication for such functions. When the number of output bits is large, space lower bounds become trivial if we require players to output the entire function at once. Instead, we modify the model so players can output a *subset* of the output bits at any step. As long as the entire function is eventually output, and the answers are consistent, we say the protocol computes f.

DEFINITION 17. *A space-bounded communication protocol $\mathcal{P}$ computing $f : \{0,1\}^n \times \{0,1\}^n \to \{0,1\}^m$ using s bits of space is a tuple (T_A, O_A, T_B, O_B), with*

- *transition functions $T_A, T_B : \{0,1\} \times \{0,1\}^n \times \{0,1\}^s \to \{0,1\}^s \times \{\text{HALT}, \bot\}$,*
- *output functions $O_A, O_B : \{0,1\} \times \{0,1\}^n \times \{0,1\}^s \to \{0,1,*\}^m$.*

We use $M_A, M_B \in \{0,1\}^s$ to denote Alice and Bob's memory, respectively. $\mathcal{P}$ computes f if (i) both players halt on all inputs, (ii) for all $j \in [m]$, some player correctly outputs $f_j(x,y)$, and (iii) no player incorrectly outputs $f_j(x,y)$.

In this definition, if, e.g., the jth bit of $O_A(b, x, m)$ is $v \neq *$, then Alice outputs $f_j(x,y) = v$. Note that we allow players to (correctly) output bits of f multiple times. This allows players to compute f without having to remember which bits have already been computed.

Our first non-boolean function ALL-EQ : $\{0,1\}^n \times \{0,1\}^n \to \{0,1\}^{2^n}$ computes equality on all *subsets* of bits. Let $\{I_1, \ldots, I_{2^n}\}$ enumerate all possible subsets of $\{1, \ldots, n\}$. Then, the ith output bit of ALL-EQ is defined as:

$$\text{ALL-EQ}_i(x, y) := \begin{cases} 1 & \text{if } \forall j \in I_i,\ x_j = y_j \\ 0 & \text{otherwise} \end{cases}$$

The function EQ-WITH-DESIGN$_k$ is similarly defined, except that instead of using all 2^n the subsets of $\{1, 2, \ldots, n\}$, we use a combinatorial design containing only p^k many such subsets, where p is a prime number satisfying $p^2 = n$,[1] and k is any positive integer. This family of subsets satisfies the following two properties: each subset has size p, and the intersection of any two subsets has size at most k.[2]

[1]We assume for simplicity that n is always the square of some prime number. Strictly speaking, it suffices to choose a prime number between $\lceil\sqrt{n}\rceil$ and $2\lceil\sqrt{n}\rceil$. Bertrand's postulate guarantees this is possible.

[2]A specific construction utilizes the one-to-one correspondence between $\mathbb{F}_p \times \mathbb{F}_p$ ($\mathbb{F}_p$ being the prime field of size p) and $\{1, 2, \ldots, n\}$. Consider all polynomials of degree at most $k-1$ on $\mathbb{F}_p$, they are all of the form $q(x) = a_{k-1}x^{k-1} + a_{k-2}x^{k-2} + \ldots + a_1 x + a_0$. There are p^k such polynomials, each of them can determine a subset of $\mathbb{F}_p \times \mathbb{F}_p$ of size p, namely $\{(0, q(0)), (1, q(1)), \ldots, (p-1, q(p-1))\}$. These corresponds to a family $\{I_i\}_{i=1,2,\ldots,p^k}$ of subsets of $\{1, 2, \ldots, n\}$ which we can use to define EQ-WITH-DESIGN$_k$.

THEOREM 18. *For any* $s(n) < \log_2(1.5) \cdot n - 2$, ALL-EQ $\notin$ $\mathsf{SPACECC}(s(n))$. ALL-EQ $\in \mathsf{SPACECC}(n + O(1))$.

THEOREM 19. *For any fixed positive integer* k, *positive number* ϵ, *and any* $s(n) < (\frac{1}{2} - \epsilon) k \log(n)$, *we have* EQ-WITH-DESIGN$_k$ $\notin \mathsf{SPACECC}(s(n))$ *and* EQ-WITH-DESIGN$_k \in \mathsf{SPACECC}\left(\frac{1}{2}(k+1)\log(n) + O(1)\right)$.

In this section, we sketch the proof of Theorem 18, which is technically simpler. The proof of Theorem 19 uses similar techniques and appears in Section 9.

As explained in Section 2.2, given a space-bounded communication protocol $\mathcal{P}$, for every possible input x to Alice, she has a corresponding state machine $\mathcal{M}_x$, and for every possible input y to Bob, he has a corresponding state machine $\mathcal{M}_y$. Connecting $\mathcal{M}_x$ and $\mathcal{M}_y$, let $\pi(\mathcal{M}_x, \mathcal{M}_y)$ denote the resulting computational history, and $\pi(\mathcal{M}_x, \mathcal{M}_y)|_{\mathsf{out}}$ the outputs of Alice and Bob. Using $\|\pi_A(\mathcal{M}_x, \mathcal{M}_y)|_{\mathsf{out}}\|_1$ and $\|\pi_B(\mathcal{M}_x, \mathcal{M}_y)|_{\mathsf{out}}\|_1$ to denote the number of 1 output bits produced by Alice and Bob respectively.

LEMMA 20. *If there is a protocol* $\mathcal{P}$ *that correctly computes* ALL-EQ, *then among the state machines* $\{\mathcal{M}_x\}_{x \in \{0,1\}^n}$ *and* $\{\mathcal{M}_y\}_{y \in \{0,1\}^n}$, *one of the following statements must hold*

- $\exists x \in \{0,1\}^n$, *such that*
$$\sum_{y \in \{0,1\}^n} \|\pi_A(\mathcal{M}_x, \mathcal{M}_y)|_{\mathsf{out}}\|_1 \geq \frac{3^n}{2}$$
- $\exists y \in \{0,1\}^n$, *such that*
$$\sum_{x \in \{0,1\}^n} \|\pi_B(\mathcal{M}_x, \mathcal{M}_y)|_{\mathsf{out}}\|_1 \geq \frac{3^n}{2}$$

PROOF OF THEOREM 18. We show the contrapositive. Suppose that there is a protocol $\mathcal{P}$ with memory size bound $s(n)$ that correctly computes ALL-EQ. Assume without loss of generality that the clause of x in Lemma 20 is true, and the input value that makes this condition true is $x_0 = 0^n$.

First let's introduce some notation, for two n-bit strings x and y, we denote the hamming distance between x and y as $H(x,y)$, and $D(x,y) = n - H(x,y)$, is the number of positions at which the corresponding bits are the same. $\|x\|_1$ is the number of 1 bits in x.

Consider the states in $\mathcal{M}_{x_0}$, for every state $\gamma \in \{0,1\}^{s(n)}$ and every possible communication bit $b \in \{0,1\}$, denote the edge leading out of γ labelled b as $e(\gamma, b)$, denote the number of 1 output bits produced at $e(\gamma, b)$ as $o^1(\gamma, b)$, and denote the set of $y \in \{0,1\}^n$ such that $\pi(\mathcal{M}_{x_0}, \mathcal{M}_y)$ passes through edge $e(\gamma, b)$ as $Y(\gamma, b)$. For every $y \in Y(\gamma, b)$, $\|\text{ALL-EQ}(x_0, y)\|_1 \geq o^1(\gamma, b)$, thus $2^{D(x_0,y)} \geq o^1(\gamma, b)$, i.e. $D(x_0, y) \geq \log_2 o^1(\gamma, b)$. That means $|Y(\gamma, b)| \leq 2^n / o^1(\gamma, b)$.

On the other hand,

$$\begin{aligned}
&\sum_{y \in \{0,1\}^n} \|\pi_A(\mathcal{M}_{x_0}, \mathcal{M}_y)|_{\mathsf{out}}\|_1 \\
= &\sum_{\gamma \in \{0,1\}^{s(n)}} \sum_{b \in \{0,1\}} \sum_{y \in Y(\gamma, b)} o^1(\gamma, b) \\
= &\sum_{\gamma \in \{0,1\}^{s(n)}} \sum_{b \in \{0,1\}} |Y(\gamma, b)| \cdot o^1(\gamma, b) \\
\leq \; & 2^{s(n)} \cdot 2 \cdot 2^n
\end{aligned}$$

Therefore $3^n/2 \leq 2^{s(n)} \cdot 2 \cdot 2^n$, which implies $s(n) \geq \log_2(1.5) \cdot n - 2$. □

6. EQUALITY, INNER PRODUCT, REACHABILITY, AND BEYOND...

When not viewed as communication problems, the computational complexity for equality (EQ) is EQ $\in \mathsf{AC}^0$, for inner product IP $\in \mathsf{NC}^1$ but not in AC^0, and for REACH we know that it can be done non-deterministically in $O(\log n)$ space (see e.g. [3] for definitions and conjectures). A famous conjecture states that REACH $\notin \mathsf{NC}^1$, in fact REACH $\notin$ $\mathsf{LogSPACE}$. We wish to understand (at least partly) the difference in the use of space when computing these three functions, and we ask this question in our semi-oblivious model. We have already seen the following protocols.

THEOREM 21. EQ $\in \mathsf{SPACECC}^{\mathsf{o}}_{\rightarrow}(\log_2 n)$, IP *is computable with* 1 *non-oblivious bit and* $\lceil \log_2 n \rceil$ *oblivious bits, and* REACH $\in \mathsf{SPACECC}(O(\log^2 n))$.

Our most technically involved contribution is the following theorem, which states that the IP protocol is space-optimal; i.e. we need this one non-oblivious bit.

THEOREM 22. IP $\notin \mathsf{SPACECC}^{\mathsf{o}}_{\rightarrow}(n/7)$.

We observe that IP can be reduced to REACH through local preprocessing, implying that REACH also requires 1 non-oblivious bit. We conjecture that REACH requires $\Omega(\log^2 n)$ non-oblivious bits. Even the more modest goal of showing that REACH requires 2 non-oblivious bits is open.

The proof of Theorem 22 is given in Section 10. Below we attempt to flesh-out a more general, model-specific technique, which also serves as a high-level description of this argument.

Overview of the IP *lower bound.*

Let us first recall the concept of *communication matrix* from classical communication complexity. We organize the correct answers of the function being computed on all possible input pairs (x, y) in a matrix where rows are associated with x and columns with y, and the (x, y) position contains the value of $f(x, y)$. A *monochromatic rectangle* is a submatrix where f has the same value for each entry.

The only property of IP that our proof technique uses is the fact that all the monochromatic rectangles in the communication matrix of IP have a relatively small size bound (for two n-bit inputs, this bound is 2^{n+1}). In fact, the same proof works for every function enjoying this property.

The Progress Measure. We use the number of columns that are "partially solved" after a certain number of steps as a progress measure. A column is called "partially solved" after t steps if after t steps the protocol has output the correct value and halted on at least one position in this column. Since the number of steps in a halting protocol is bounded, if we obtain an upper bound on the amount of progress in a single step then we can conclude that at the end of the protocol run, the number of "partially solved" columns can not reach 2^n (the number of columns in the matrix). Handling this progress measure appropriately is a subtle technical issue.

Bands and the protocol matrix. Note that in a one-way oblivious protocol we can think of Alice as uploading Bob's memory.[3] If we fix the value Alice uploads to Bob's memory in a particular step (plus the one bit of communication of that step), we are actually fixing a subset of possible value of x, and therefore a subset of rows in the communication matrix. We call such a subset of rows as a "band". That means to capture the current state of Bob's memory, we only need to look at those "bands". In each step, Bob makes his output decision based solely on his current memory state, communication bit (which collectively correspond to a "band" in the communication matrix) and his input y (which corresponds to a column in the matrix).

The Stepwise Upper Bound on Progress. If a "band" is too "narrow" (containing too few rows), we can somehow ignore it as being insignificant. On the other hand, if a "band" is too "wide" (containing too many rows), its contribution to the progress measure we discussed above is limited, due to the monochromatic rectangle size bound. That limit implies the desired upper bound on progress to complete the proof. Note that without excluding the narrow bands (and showing that there can't be too many) the argument breaks down.

What's left to be done?

Conceptually, we introduce memory models for communication complexity, and technically we give model-specific, non-trivial arguments giving leverage to these new models. Many questions raised in this work are left open. Closing the $\log n$ gap between the levels of the memory hierarchies is one such question.

An important open question is towards devising a technique for showing explicit space lower bounds for 2 or more non-oblivious bits. How far can we push such a lower bound for REACH?

One issue we haven't touched at the current stage of development is what happens in the presence of randomness. Studying such variants opens the possibility for answering some restricted forms of open questions in Communication Complexity itself; e.g. proving strong direct-sum theorems but in a space-bounded setting.

Finally, there are all sorts of questions relating these new models to open problems in Computational Complexity. How does the semi-oblivious model relate to circuit complexity classes such as AC and P/poly? We know that oblivious refinements of the Karchmer-Wigderson games do not provide something meaningful (a discussion about this will appear in the full version), but other possibilities are open. In general we would like to know if there are any other, genuine applications of the semi-oblivious model in other areas? One can easily devise contrived settings where oblivious memory is relevant, but how about the natural settings people actually care about?

7. PROOFS OF THE BASIC PROPERTIES

PROOF OF PROPOSITION 8. With the two players in protocol $\mathcal{P}$ combined (both M_A and M_B), they have $2s(n)$ bits of memory, plus the bit received by Alice at the beginning of a step, the system would have at most $2^{2s(n)+1}$ different configurations in total. Therefore, if $\mathcal{P}$ makes more than $2^{2s(n)+1}$ a configuration is repeated and $\mathcal{P}$ never halts. □

[3]See Lemma 23 in Section 10.

PROOF OF LEMMA 10. According to Definition 4, a space-bounded protocol $\mathcal{P}$ is defined by functions T_A and T_B. For input size n and space-bound $s(n)$, the number of such function tuples is at most $2^{(4+s(n))\cdot 2^{n+s(n)+2}}$, each corresponds to one protocol. Each protocol can correctly compute at most one boolean function if any. Hence the conclusion. □

PROOF OF LEMMA 11. Any boolean function that only depends on the first $s(n)$ bits of Alice's input x is computable by such protocols. The protocol works as follows:

Alice and Bob both increment the content of their respective memory simultaneously step by step. Alice sends 0 to Bob until the content of Alice's memory coincides the first $s(n)$ bits of x, at which time Alice sends 1. Upon receiving a 1, Bob computes the final answer.

The number of such boolean functions (that depend only on the first $s(n)$ bits of Alice's input) is $2^{2^{n+s(n)}}$. This gives a lower bound on the number of boolean functions computable by such class of protocols. □

PROOF OF PROPOSITION 14. Suppose the protocols for solving f_1 and f_2 are $\mathcal{P}_1 = (T_{A,1}, T^o_{B,1}, T^f_{B,1})$ (with Alice and Bob's memory denoted as $M_{A,1}$ and $M_{B,1}$ respectively), and $\mathcal{P}_2 = (T_{A,2}, T^o_{B,2}, T^f_{B,2})$ (with Alice and Bob's memory denoted as $M_{A,2}$ and $M_{B,2}$ respectively), respectively. Now we construct a protocol $\mathcal{P}$ for solving f. In this protocol, Alice has a $s_1(n)$-bit memory that corresponds to $M_{A,1}$, a $s_2(n)$-bit memory that corresponds to $M_{A,2}$, and an additional counter C_A of $2s_2(n)+1$ bits long. Similarly for Bob, we have $s_1(n)$-bit $M_{B,1}$, $s_2(n)$-bit $M^o_{B,2}$, $2s_2(n)+1$-bit C_B. And the protocol $\mathcal{P}$ works as follows (shown in Algorithm 1 and 2):

Algorithm 1: Algorithm for solving $f(x,y) = (f_1(x,y), f_2(x,y))$, Alice's part

```
M_{A,1} ⟵ 0^n;
while YES do
    Alice simulate one step of P_1 by carrying out T_{A,1},
    sending the computed bit to Bob;
    M_{A,2} ⟵ 0^n;
    C_A ⟵ 0;
    while C_A ≤ c_2(n) + 1 do
        Alice simulate one step of P_2 by carrying out
        T_{A,2}, sending the computed bit to Bob;
        increment C_A;
    end
end
```

It's easy to verify that if both $\mathcal{P}_1$ and $\mathcal{P}_2$ are one-way oblivious protocols with the specified parameters, $\mathcal{P}$ presented above is also a one-way oblivious protocol with the required parameters. Note that according to Proposition 8, if C_A and C_B are both $2s_2(n)+1$ bits long, they can count to $c_2(n)+1$. □

8. EXAMPLE PROTOCOLS

PROOF OF THEOREM 15. First, we consider an algorithm for solving this problem within $2\log(n)+O(1)$ bits of memory (see Algorithm 3). We emphasize that this algorithm is not the standard DFS algorithm. Later, we convert this algorithm into a space-bounded communication protocol.

Algorithm 2: Algorithm for solving $f(x,y) = (f_1(x,y), f_2(x,y))$, Bob's part

```
M_{B,1} ⟵ 0^n;
while YES do
    Bob simulate one step of P_1 by receiving one bit
    from Alice and carrying out T^o_{B,1};
    M_{B,2} ⟵ 0^n;
    C_B ⟵ 0;
    while C_B ≤ c_2(n) + 1 do
        Bob simulate one step of P_2 by receiving one bit
        from Alice and carrying out T^o_{B,2};
        if both T^f_{B,1} and T^f_{B,2} give definitive output
        answers (not ⊥) then
            Bob gives the answer and halts;
        end
        increment C_B;
    end
end
```

Algorithm 3: Space Efficient Algorithm for Solving the Decision Version of DFS

```
if s = t then output 0;
s' ⟵ s;
s_d ⟵ 0;
while s' ≠ r do
    if s' = t then output 1;
    t' ⟵ t;
    repeat
        t' ⟵ ParentOf(t');
        if t' = s' then output s_d;
    until t' = r;
    if s' = LeftChildOf(ParentOf(s')) then
        s_d ⟵ 0;
    else
        s_d ⟵ 1;
    end
    s' ⟵ ParentOf(s');
end
output s_d
```

In this algorithm, we only need to remember at any point in time the value of s', t' and s_d. In the space-bounded communication model, we construct a protocol where each player has $\log(n) + \log(\log(n)) + O(1)$ space, divided into three parts.

- Each player uses $\lceil \log(n) \rceil$ bits of memory to store s' *or* t'. When ever Alice maintains s', Bob keeps t', and vice versa. Whenever say, Alice needs to perform some operation on s' but currently holds t', she will inform Bob that she wants to exchange s' for t', and they will exchange with the help of the second chunk of memory.
- Alice and Bob use the second chunk of $\lceil \log(\lceil \log(n) \rceil) \rceil$ bits of memory for an index into the first $\lceil \log(n) \rceil$ bits of memory. When they need to exchange or compare s' and t', they do so bitwise, using the index to remember which bit they are exchanging or comparing.
- An additional $O(1)$ bits per player is for housekeeping; e.g., to remember which step of the algorithm they are executing, who hold s' and who holds t', etc.

□

In the worst case scenario, the tree is highly imbalanced. Both s' and t' traverse $\Omega(n)$ vertices before they meet near the root of the tree, and furthermore, their traversal bounces back and forth between A and B, and so Alice and Bob end up exchange s' and t' in every step. In this case, the communication complexity of the protocol is $\Theta(n^2 \log(n))$. Given the space bound $s(n) = \log(n) + \log(\log(n)) + O(1)$, this communication complexity is close to the theoretical upper bound given by Proposition 8, which is $2^{2s(n)+2} = \Theta(n^2 \log^2 n)$. We are very interested to know if this close to $2^{2s(n)+2}$ worst case communication cost is "compressible", meaning the worst case communication cost can be brought down.

Proof of Theorem 16. We give several different protocols for $\text{Reach}(G,s,t)$. Recall that in this problem, the inputs consists of a directed graph $G = (V,E)$ and distinguished vertices s,t. $\text{Reach}(G,s,t)$ outputs 1 if there exists an $s \rightsquigarrow t$ path in G.

In the communication version of this problem, Alice and Bob are again given different sides of a fixed vertex cut $A \uplus B = V$. Alice gets as input all edges in A; Bob gets as input all edges in B, and both players see all crossing edges. Let C_A denote the set of vertices in A adjacent to some vertex in B. Define C_B analogously. $C_A \cup C_B$ thus defines the boundary of the cut. Finally, let $C := \{s,t\} \cup C_A \cup C_B$, and let $c = |C|$. Given an instance G,s,t, let c denote the total number of vertices on the boundary of the cut. The performance of all of our protocols highly depend on c.

Our first protocol Savitch emulates Savitch's Theorem [24]. Note that if s and t are indeed connected in G, then trivially, there exists a path from s to t that uses at most c crossing edges. The key intuition in Savitch's Theorem is the following

> If u,v are connected using at most k crossing edges, then there exists w such that (i) u and w are connected using at most $k/2$ crossing edges and (ii) w and v are connected using at most $k/2$ crossing edges.

This intuition leads to a recursive algorithm at the heart of Savitch's Theorem—determine if u, v are reachable using at most k edges by recursively deciding if e.g. u, w are reachable using at most $k/2$ edges. In the protocol that emulates this theorem, Alice and Bob recursively implement this algorithm. This algorithm has $\log(c)$ depth. At each level of the algorithm, Alice and Bob use $O(\log c)$ space to iterate through w. At the bottom level of recursion, $O(c)$ communication occurs as players communicate whether e.g. w is reachable from u by crossing the cut zero times. The performance of SAVITCH is captured by the following theorem. Thus, SAVITCH costs $O(\log^2 c)$ space and uses $c^{O(\log c)}$ total communication.

In our second protocol BITVECTOR, Alice and Bob iteratively maintain a vector $V \in \{0,1\}^c$, which represents which vertices on the boundary of the cut are reachable by s. For example, suppose $s \in A$. Alice then initializes V_u to be 1 for all u on her side of the cut boundary that are reachable from s. She sets $V_u := 0$ for all u on Bob's side of the cut boundary and for all u on her side that are not directly reachable from s. Bob then sets $V_w := 1$ for all w on his side of the cut boundary that are reachable from some u such that $V_u = 1$, again using only the vertices he sees. This proceeds iteratively until wither players learn that $\text{REACH}(G, s, t) = 1$, or until V doesn't change between messages. At this point, players output $\text{REACH}(G, s, t) = 0$ and halt the protocol. Overall, BITVECTOR uses $O(c)$ space and $O(c^2)$ total communication.

This protocol is called MATRIX and is similar to the protocol BITVECTOR. This time, Alice constructs the "induced adjacency matrix" of C. Specifically, she sets $(u, v) = 1$ if v is reachable from u using only edges seen by Alice. Bob updates this matrix in a similar way—he sets $(u, v) = 1$ if there is a u, v path using only (i) the edges seen by Bob and (ii) paths seen by Alice. Note that this gives Bob enough information to compute $\text{REACH}(G, s, t)$ directly. In particular, MATRIX uses a single round of communication. MATRIX is a one-way protocol that uses $O(c^2)$ space and $O(c^2)$ total communication.

Our last reachability protocol is called MATRIXMULT. It is a one-way protcol that is similar in spirit to MATRIX, but uses less space, albeit the cost of a blowup in total communication.

Let M_A, M_B be the reachability matricies given Alice and Bob's inputs; e.g., $A_{uv} = 1$ if there is a $u \rightsquigarrow v$ path using only edges Alice sees. Let $M := M_A \vee M_B$ be the bitwise OR of these matrices. Alice and Bob solve REACH by computing the matrix product $M^* := M^{c+1}$ and outputting M^*_{st}. This value is 1 if there is an s, t path that crosses the cut only c times. The intuition behind the MATRIXMULT protocol is that M^*_{st} can be computed in a space-efficient manner. Specifically, Alice first sends the row of M_A containing s. Then, she sends all of A to Bob, column by column. This allows Bob to compute the row s of M^2. If Bob had enough space to store all of A, we would be done. Instead, Alice sends A to Bob $O(c)$ times, each time sending the elements column by column. In this way, Bob iteratively computes only row s of M^*. Thus, MATRIXMULT is a one-way protocol that uses $O(c)$ space and $O(c^3)$ total communication. □

9. PROOFS FOR LOWER BOUND RESULT OF ALL-EQ AND EQ-WITH-DESIGN

PROOF OF LEMMA 20. Using the notation we introduced in the proof of Theorem 18, for two n-bit strings x and y, we denote the hamming distance between x and y as $H(x, y)$, and $D(x, y) = n - H(x, y)$, is the number of positions at which the corresponding bits are the same. $\|x\|_1$ is the number of 1 bits in x.

It's easy to see that

$$\|\text{ALL-EQ}(x, y)\|_1 = 2^{D(x,y)}$$

By definition, if a protocol $\mathcal{P}$ correctly computes ALL-EQ, then for every possible pair of inputs (x, y),

$$\|\pi_A(\mathcal{M}_x, \mathcal{M}_y)|_{\text{out}}\|_1 + \|\pi_B(\mathcal{M}_x, \mathcal{M}_y)|_{\text{out}}\|_1 \geq \|\text{ALL-EQ}(x, y)\|_1.$$

Since $\mathcal{P}$ correctly computes ALL-EQ, then we have

$$\sum_{x\in\{0,1\}^n} \sum_{y\in\{0,1\}^n} (\|\pi_A(\mathcal{M}_x, \mathcal{M}_y)|_{\text{out}}\|_1 + \|\pi_B(\mathcal{M}_x, \mathcal{M}_y)|_{\text{out}}\|_1) \geq \sum_{x\in\{0,1\}^n} \sum_{y\in\{0,1\}^n} |\text{ALL-EQ}(x, y)|$$

On the other hand

$$\begin{aligned} &\sum_{x\in\{0,1\}^n} \sum_{y\in\{0,1\}^n} \|\text{ALL-EQ}(x, y)\|_1 \\ = &\sum_{x\in\{0,1\}^n} \sum_{y\in\{0,1\}^n} 2^{D(x,y)} \\ = &\sum_{x\in\{0,1\}^n} \sum_{j=0}^{n} \left(\sum_{y\in\{y_0|D(x,y)=j\}} 2^{D(x,y)} \right) \\ = &\sum_{x\in\{0,1\}^n} \sum_{j=0}^{n} \binom{n}{j} 2^j = \sum_{x\in\{0,1\}^n} 3^n = 2^n \cdot 3^n \end{aligned}$$

Thus

$$\sum_{x\in\{0,1\}^n} \sum_{y\in\{0,1\}^n} \|\pi_A(\mathcal{M}_x, \mathcal{M}_y)|_{\text{out}}\|_1 + \sum_{y\in\{0,1\}^n} \sum_{x\in\{0,1\}^n} \|\pi_B(\mathcal{M}_x, \mathcal{M}_y)|_{\text{out}}\|_1 \geq 2^n \cdot 3^n$$

Therefore

- either

$$\sum_{x\in\{0,1\}^n} \sum_{y\in\{0,1\}^n} \|\pi_A(\mathcal{M}_x, \mathcal{M}_y)|_{\text{out}}\|_1 \geq 2^{n-1} \cdot 3^n$$

- or,

$$\sum_{y\in\{0,1\}^n} \sum_{x\in\{0,1\}^n} \|\pi_B(\mathcal{M}_x, \mathcal{M}_y)|_{\text{out}}\|_1 \geq 2^{n-1} \cdot 3^n$$

Then, by averaging, we have

- either $\exists x \in \{0,1\}^n$, such that

$$\sum_{y\in\{0,1\}^n} \|\pi_A(\mathcal{M}_x, \mathcal{M}_y)|_{\text{out}}\|_1 \geq \frac{3^n}{2}$$

- or, $\exists y \in \{0,1\}^n$, such that

$$\sum_{x\in\{0,1\}^n} \|\pi_B(\mathcal{M}_x, \mathcal{M}_y)|_{\text{out}}\|_1 \geq \frac{3^n}{2}$$

□

PROOF OF THEOREM 19. For the upper bound part, we give the following straightforward protocol: Alice and Bob each has two counters, one $\lceil k \log p \rceil$ bits long, to enumerate through the p^k subsets in the function definition; another one, $\lceil \log p \rceil$ bits long, to enumerate through the bits in a particular subset. In each step, they look at the counters, and compare the corresponding bits in their inputs x and y.

For the lower bound part, we show the contrapositive. Suppose that there is a protocol $\mathcal{P}$ with memory size bound $s(n)$ that correctly computes EQ-WITH-DESIGN. Using the notation introduced in the previous proof, we have

$$\sum_{x\in\{0,1\}^n}\sum_{y\in\{0,1\}^n}(\|\pi_A(\mathcal{M}_x,\mathcal{M}_y)|_{\text{out}}\|_1+\|\pi_B(\mathcal{M}_x,\mathcal{M}_y)|_{\text{out}}\|_1)$$
$$=\sum_{x\in\{0,1\}^n}\sum_{y\in\{0,1\}^n}|\text{EQ-WITH-DESIGN}(x,y)|$$

Suppose the family of subsets of $\{1,2,\ldots,n\}$ we use to define EQ-WITH-DESIGN is $\{I_i\}_{i=1,2,\ldots,p^k}$. We have

$$\begin{aligned}&\sum_{y\in\{0,1\}^n}\sum_{x\in\{0,1\}^n}|\text{EQ-WITH-DESIGN}(x,y)|\\ =&\sum_{y\in\{0,1\}^n}\sum_{x\in\{0,1\}^n}|\{i\mid EQ_{I_i}(x,y)=1\}|\\ =&\sum_{y\in\{0,1\}^n}\sum_{i\in\{1,2,\ldots,p^k\}}|\{x\mid EQ_{I_i}(x,y)=1\}|\\ =&\sum_{y\in\{0,1\}^n}\sum_{i\in\{1,2,\ldots,p^k\}}2^{p^2-p}\\ =&\ 2^n\cdot p^k\cdot 2^{p^2-p}\end{aligned}$$

By averaging like we did in the proof of Lemma 20, we have

- either $\exists x\in\{0,1\}^n$, such that
$$\sum_{y\in\{0,1\}^n}\|\pi_A(\mathcal{M}_x,\mathcal{M}_y)|_{\text{out}}\|_1\geq 2^{p^2-p-1}\cdot p^k$$
- or, $\exists y\in\{0,1\}^n$, such that
$$\sum_{x\in\{0,1\}^n}\|\pi_B(\mathcal{M}_x,\mathcal{M}_y)|_{\text{out}}\|_1\geq 2^{p^2-p-1}\cdot p^k$$

Again, like we did in the proof of Theorem 18, we assume, without loss of generality, that the clause of x above is true, and the input value that makes this condition true is $x_0=0^n$.

$$\sum_{y\in\{0,1\}^n}\|\pi_A(\mathcal{M}_{x_0},\mathcal{M}_y)|_{\text{out}}\|_1\geq 2^{p^2-p-1}\cdot p^k \quad (1)$$

And for every state $\gamma\in\{0,1\}^{s(n)}$ in the corresponding state machine $\mathcal{M}_{x_0}$, and for every possible communication bit $b\in\{0,1\}$, we likewise denote the edge leading out of γ labelled b as $e(\gamma,b)$, denote the number of 1 output bits produced at $e(\gamma,b)$ as $o^1(\gamma,b)$, and denote the set of $y\in\{0,1\}^n$ such that $\pi(\mathcal{M}_{x_0},\mathcal{M}_y)$ passes through edge $e(\gamma,b)$ as $Y(\gamma,b)$.

$$\begin{aligned}&\sum_{y\in\{0,1\}^n}\|\pi_A(\mathcal{M}_{x_0},\mathcal{M}_y)|_{\text{out}}\|_1\\ =&\sum_{\gamma\in\{0,1\}^{s(n)}}\sum_{b\in\{0,1\}}\sum_{y\in Y(\gamma,b)}o^1(\gamma,b)\\ =&\sum_{\gamma\in\{0,1\}^{s(n)}}\sum_{b\in\{0,1\}}|Y(\gamma,b)|\cdot o^1(\gamma,b)\end{aligned}\quad (2)$$

In addition, we define

$$\alpha(t)=\min_{\substack{i_1,i_2,\ldots,i_t\in\{1,2,\ldots,p^k\}\\ i_1,i_2,\ldots,i_t\text{ are all different}}}\left|\bigcup_{j=1}^{t}I_{i_j}\right|,$$

then $\forall\gamma\in\{0,1\}^{s(n)},\forall b\in\{0,1\}$,

$$o^1(\gamma,b)\cdot|Y(\gamma,b)|\leq\max_{t\in\{1,2,\ldots,p^k\}}t\cdot 2^{p^2-\alpha(t)} \quad (3)$$

And clearly we have

- $\alpha(t)$ is non-decreasing for $t\in\{1,2,\ldots,p^k\}$. In particular, for $t\in\{1,2,\ldots,p/2k\}$, $\alpha(t)$ is strictly increasing
- $\forall t\in\{1,2,\ldots,p^k\}\quad \alpha(t)\geq tp-\binom{t}{2}k$

Therefore for $t\in\{1,2,\ldots,p/2k\}$, $t\cdot 2^{p^2-\alpha(t)}$ is strictly decreasing.

$$\begin{aligned}&\max_{t\in\{1,2,\ldots,p^k\}}t\cdot 2^{p^2-\alpha(t)}\\ =&\max(\max_{t\in\{1,2,\ldots,p/2k\}}t\cdot 2^{p^2-\alpha(t)},\max_{t\in\{p/2k,p/2k+1,\ldots,p^k\}}t\cdot 2^{p^2-\alpha(t)})\\ \leq&\max(t\cdot 2^{p^2-\alpha(t)}|_{t=1},\left(\max_{t\in\{p/2k,p/2k+1,\ldots,p^k\}}t\right)\\ &\cdot\left(\max_{t\in\{p/2k,p/2k+1,\ldots,p^k\}}2^{p^2-\alpha(t)}\right))\\ =&\max(2^{p^2-p},p^k\cdot\left(2^{p^2-\alpha(t)}\right)|_{t=p/2k})\\ \leq&\max(2^{p^2-p},p^k\cdot 2^{p^2(1-7/16k)})\\ =&\ 2^{p^2-p}\end{aligned}$$

Combine this with (1), (2), and (3), we have

$$\begin{aligned}2^{s(n)+1}\cdot 2^{p^2-p}&\geq 2^{s(n)+1}\cdot\max_{t\in\{1,2,\ldots,p^k\}}t\cdot 2^{p^2-\alpha(t)}\\ &\geq\sum_{\gamma\in\{0,1\}^{s(n)}}\sum_{b\in\{0,1\}}|Y(\gamma,b)|\cdot o^1(\gamma,b)\\ &=\sum_{y\in\{0,1\}^n}\|\pi_A(\mathcal{M}_{x_0},\mathcal{M}_y)|_{\text{out}}\|_1\\ &\geq 2^{p^2-p-1}\cdot p^k\end{aligned}$$

Therefore $2^{s(n)+1}\geq p^k/2$, $s(n)\geq(\frac{1}{2}-\epsilon)k\log(n)$ for any positive number ϵ and $p=\sqrt{n}$. □

10. PROOF OF THE INNER PRODUCT NON-COMPUTABILITY RESULT

LEMMA 23. *Given a one-way semi-oblivious protocol $\mathcal{P}$ with Bob's oblivious work memory of size $s(n)$, there is a family of functions $\{K_i\}_{i\in\mathbb{N}^+}:\{0,1\}^n\rightarrow\{0,1\}^{s(n)}\times\{0,1\}$,* *such that for any positive integer $i \in \mathbb{N}^+$, and $x \in \{0,1\}^n$, $K_i(x)$ correctly computes the value of (M_B^o, b_A) at step i, in which M_B^o is the content of Bob's oblivious work memory if Alice and Bob executes $\mathcal{P}$ on input x and some $y \in \{0,1\}^n$, b_A is the bit Alice sends to Bob in such an execution.*

PROOF. This follows immediately by Definition 7, where the value of M_B^o and b_A rely only on functions T_A and T_B^o. Both functions operate only on input x, independent of y. We conclude with an obvious induction. □

PROOF OF THEOREM 22. We show that if a correct protocol for IP has no non-oblivious bits then the number of oblivious bits $s(n) \geq \frac{n}{7}$. Assume otherwise that $s(n) < \frac{n}{7}$. Let $\mathcal{P}$ be a one-way oblivious protocol for IP of memory size $s(n)$. By definition only Bob using T_B^f is able to compute the correct answer to the given input.

By Lemma 23 there's a family of functions $\{K_i\}$ on $x \in \{0,1\}^n$ that would affect Bob's decision (in the sense that Bob's final output only depends on y and the output of K_i, if we denote the output of $K_i(x)$ as t, then T_B^f can be written as $T_B^f(y,t)$).

We construct a set $\mathcal{X} \subseteq \{0,1\}^n$ through the following process (Algorithm 4)

Algorithm 4: Construct $\mathcal{X} \subseteq \{0,1\}^n$

$\mathcal{X} \longleftarrow \{0,1\}^n$;
while $\exists t \in \{0,1\}^{s(n)+1}, i \in \{1,2,\ldots,2^{2s(n)+2}\}$ *such that* $|K_i^{-1}(t) \cap \mathcal{X}| < 2^{3s(n)+6}$ **do**
  $\mathcal{X} \longleftarrow \mathcal{X} \setminus K_i^{-1}(t)$;
end

The following simple observations imply that this procedure terminates with a non-empty set $\mathcal{X}$ if $s(n) < n/7$.

- Any pair of (t,i) would be chosen at most once, $(t,i) \in \{0,1\}^{s(n)+1} \times \{1,2,\ldots,2^{2s(n)+2}\}$, thus there would be at most $2^{s(n)+1}(1+2^{2s(n)+2})$ iterations of the loop.
- During each iteration of the loop, the cardinality of $\mathcal{X}$ would decrease by at most $2^{3s(n)+6}$, since $\mathcal{X} \setminus K_i^{-1}(t) = \mathcal{X} \setminus (K_i^{-1}(t) \cap \mathcal{X})$ and $|K_i^{-1}(t) \cap \mathcal{X}| < 2^{3s(n)+6}$.

That means in the end the cardinality of set $\mathcal{X}$ is at least $2^n - 2^{3s(n)+6}2^{s(n)+1}(1+2^{2s(n)+2})$, which is positive given $s(n) < \frac{n}{7}$ and n is large enough.

Since $\mathcal{P}$ computes IP on $\{0,1\}^n \times \{0,1\}^n$ then it also computes IP on inputs from $\mathcal{X} \times \{0,1\}^n$. By inspection on the process which constructs $\mathcal{X}$, for every $t \in \{0,1\}^{s(n)+1}$ and $i \in \{1,2,\ldots,2^{2s(n)+2}\}$, we have either $|K_i^{-1}(t) \cap \mathcal{X}| \geq 2^{3s(n)+6}$ or $|K_i^{-1}(t) \cap \mathcal{X}| = 0$, define

$$\Gamma := \{(i,t) \mid |K_i^{-1}(t) \cap \mathcal{X}| \geq 2^{3s(n)+6}\}$$

Now consider the execution of the the protocol $\mathcal{P}$ on domain $\mathcal{X} \times \{0,1\}^n$. For $i \in \{1,2,\ldots,2^{2s(n)+2}\}$, define $Y_i := \{y \mid \exists x \in \mathcal{X}$ such that $\mathcal{P}$ have halted on (x,y) before step $i\}$.

For $(i,t) \in \Gamma, j \in \{0,1\}$, define

$$L_{i,t}^{(j)} := \{y \mid y \notin Y_i \text{ and } T_B^f(y,t) = j\}$$

By definition we have

$$|Y_{i+1}| \leq |Y_i| + \sum_{t \in \{t' \mid (i,t') \in \Gamma\},\ j \in \{0,1\}} |L_{i,t}^{(j)}| \quad (4)$$

Since $\mathcal{P}$ gives correct answer for every pair $(x,y) \in \mathcal{X} \times \{0,1\}^n$, this means that for every $(i,t) \in \Gamma$ and every $y \in L_{i,t}^{(0)}$, we know $y \notin Y_i$, then

$$x \perp y, \quad \text{for every } x \in K_i^{-1}(t) \cap \mathcal{X}$$

In linear algebra terms, every vector in $L_{i,t}^{(0)}$ is orthogonal to a set of at least $2^{3s(n)+6}-1$ different non-zero vectors (in a n-dimensional space), and is thus orthogonal to the subspace spanned by these vectors. This subspace is of dimension at least $3s(n)+6$. Therefore $|L_{i,t}^{(0)}| \leq \frac{2^n}{2^{3s(n)+6}}$.

Similarly for any $y \in L_{i,t}^{(1)}$, we have

$$\forall x \in K_i^{-1}(t) \cap \mathcal{X} \quad \text{IP}(x,y) = 1$$

We know that $K_i^{-1}(t) \cap \mathcal{X} \neq \emptyset$, choose some $x_0 \in K_i^{-1}(t) \cap \mathcal{X}$, we have

$$\forall x \in (K_i^{-1}(t) \cap \mathcal{X}) \setminus \{x_0\} \quad x - x_0 \perp y$$

Again, we claim that every vector in $L_{i,t}^{(1)}$ is orthogonal to a set of at least $2^{3s(n)+6}-1$ different non-zero vectors (in a n-dimensional space), therefore $|L_{i,t}^{(1)}| \leq \frac{2^n}{2^{3s(n)+6}}$.

Substitute the upper bound we just obtained for $|L_{i,t}^{(0)}|$ and $|L_{i,t}^{(1)}|$ into equation (4) and considering the fact that $|Y_0| = 0$, we have

$$|Y_i| \leq i \cdot \frac{2^n}{2^{3s(n)+6}} \cdot 2 \cdot 2^{s(n)+1}$$

$$|Y_{2^{2s(n)}+1}| \leq (2^{2s(n)+2}+1) \cdot \frac{2^n}{2^{3s(n)+6}} \cdot 2 \cdot 2^{s(n)+1} < 2^n$$

That is, after $2^{2s(n)+2}+1$ steps, $Y_{2^{2s(n)+2}+1} \neq \{0,1\}^n$, there exist input pairs $(x,y) \in \mathcal{X} \times \{0,1\}^n$ on which the protocol $\mathcal{P}$ has not halted, and therefore (according to Proposition 8) it never halts. □

11. ONE-WAY OBLIVIOUS PROTOCOLS FOR EQ

PROPOSITION 24. *There is no one-way oblivious protocol that can correctly solve* EQ *within space size $s(n) < n-1$ and halt at the same step for all input pairs $(x,y) \in \{0,1\}^n \times \{0,1\}^n$.*

PROOF. We prove this by contradiction. Suppose there is such a protocol $\mathcal{P}$, which halts at some step i_0 for every input pair (x,y) and correctly computes EQ. As we have shown in Lemma 23 in Section 10, Alice has this "upload function" K_{i_0} for step i_0. Since K_{i_0} takes a n-bit input, but gives a $(s(n)+1)$-bit output, $s(n)+1 < n$, there must be two different $x_1 \neq x_2$, such that $K_{i_0}(x_1) = K_{i_0}(x_2)$.

On the other hand, $\mathcal{P}$ correctly computes EQ, that means

$$T_B^f(x_1, K_{i_0}(x_1)) = \text{EQ}(x_1,x_1) = 1$$
$$T_B^f(x_1, K_{i_0}(x_2)) = \text{EQ}(x_1,x_2) = 0$$

This contradicts with the fact that T_B^f is a deterministic function and $K_{i_0}(x_1) = K_{i_0}(x_2)$. □

12. ACKNOWLEDGEMENTS

The authors would like to thank Paul Beame, Mark Braverman, Michael Saks, Chengu Wang and Arkadev Chattopadhyay for helpful discussions on this topic.

The 3rd author would like to express his gratitude to Matei David and Anastasios Sidiropoulos for many stimulating discussions back in 2008.

The authors acknowledge support from the National Natural Science Foundation of China and the Danish National Research Foundation for the Institute for Theoretical Computer Science and the Sino-Danish Center for the Theory of Interactive Computation, within which this work was performed. The Sino-Danish Center for the Theory of Interactive Computation is supported in part by the National Natural Science Foundation of China Grant 61061130540. The authors also acknowledge support from the Center for Research in Foundations of Electronic Markets (CFEM), supported by the Danish Strategic Research Council.

The first author also acknowledges support of the Danish Council for Independent Research grant LOBO 438146.

The second, third and fourth author also acknowledge support of the National Basic Research Program of China Grant 2011CBA00300, 2011CBA00301, the National Natural Science Foundation of China Grant 61033001, 61061130540, 61073174, 61150110582.

The last author also acknowledges support of the National Natural Science Foundation of China Grant 61170062, 61222202.

13. REFERENCES

[1] A. V. Aho, J. D. Ullman, and M. Yannakakis. On notions of information transfer in VLSI circuits. In *Proceedings of the 15th Annual ACM Symposium on Theory of Computing*, pages 133–139, 1983.

[2] N. Alon, Y. Matias, and M. Szegedy. The space complexity of approximating the frequency moments. *Journal of Computer and System Sciences*, 58(1):137–147, 1999. Preliminary version in *Proceedings of the 28th Annual ACM Symposium on Theory of Computing*, pages 20–29, 1996.

[3] S. Arora and B. Barak. *Computational Complexity: A Modern Approach.* Cambridge University Press, 2009.

[4] Z. Bar-Yossef, T. S. Jayram, R. Kumar, and D. Sivakumar. An information statistics approach to data stream and communication complexity. *Journal of Computer and System Sciences*, 68(4):702–732, 2004.

[5] B. Barak, M. Braverman, X. Chen, and A. Rao. How to compress interactive communication. In *Proceedings of the 41st Annual ACM Symposium on Theory of Computing*, pages 67–76, 2010.

[6] P. Beame, M. Tompa, and P. Yan. Communication-space tradeoffs for unrestricted protocols. In *Proceedings of the 31st Annual Symposium on Foundations of Computer Science*, pages 420–428, 1990.

[7] E. Blais, J. Brody, and K. Matulef. Property testing lower bounds via communication complexity. In *Proceedings of the 26th Annual IEEE Conference on Computational Complexity*, pages 210–220, 2011.

[8] A. Borodin and S. Cook. A time-space tradeoff for sorting on a general sequential model of computation. *SIAM Journal on Computing*, 11(2):287–297, 1982.

[9] A. Borodin, M. J. Fischer, D. G. Kirkpatrick, N. A. Lynch, and M. Tompa. A time-space tradeoff for sorting on non-oblivious machines. *Journal of Computer and System Sciences*, 22(3):351–364, 1981.

[10] H. Buhrman, S. Fehr, C. Schaffner, and F. Speelman. The garden-hose game: A new model of computation, and application to position-based quantum cryptography. *CoRR*, abs/1109.2563, 2011.

[11] A. Chakrabarti, Y. Shi, A. Wirth, and A. C. Yao. Informational complexity and the direct sum problem for simultaneous message complexity. In *Proceedings of the 42nd Annual Symposium on Foundations of Computer Science*, pages 270–278, 2001.

[12] A. Gál and P. Gopalan. Lower bounds on streaming algorithms for approximating the length of the longest increasing subsequence. In *Proceedings of the 48th Annual Symposium on Foundations of Computer Science*, pages 294–304, 2007.

[13] M. M. Halldórsson, X. Sun, M. Szegedy, and C. Wang. Streaming and communication complexity of clique approximation. In *Proceedings of the 39th International Colloquium on Automata, Languages, and Programming*, pages 449–460, 2012.

[14] R. Impagliazzo and R. Williams. Communication complexity with synchronized clocks. In *Proceedings of the 25th Annual IEEE Conference on Computational Complexity*, pages 259–269, 2010.

[15] P. Indyk and D. Woodruff. Tight lower bounds for the distinct elements problem. In *Proceedings of the 45th Annual Symposium on Foundations of Computer Science*, pages 283–289, 2003.

[16] M. Karchmer and A. Wigderson. Monotone circuits for connectivity require super-logarithmic depth. In *Proceedings of the 20th Annual ACM Symposium on Theory of Computing*, pages 539–550, 1988.

[17] H. Klauck. Quantum and classical communication-space tradeoffs from rectangle bounds. In *Proceedings of the 24th International Conference on Foundations of Software Technology and Theoretical Computer Science*, pages 384–395, 2004.

[18] H. Klauck, R. Spalek, and R. D. Wolf. Quantum and classical strong direct product theorems and optimal time-space tradeoffs. In *Proceedings of the 45th Symposium on Foundations of Computer Science*, pages 12–21, 2004.

[19] T. W. Lam, P. Tiwari, and M. Tompa. Tradeoffs between communication and space. In *Proceedings of the 21st Annual ACM Symposium on Theory of Computing*, pages 217–226, 1989.

[20] K. G. Larsen. The cell probe complexity of dynamic range counting. In *Proceedings of the 44th Annual ACM Symposium on Theory of Computing*, pages 85–94, 2012.

[21] P. B. Miltersen, N. Nisan, S. Safra, and A. Wigderson. On data structures and asymmetric communication complexity. In *Proceedings of the 27th Annual ACM Symposium on Theory of Computing*, pages 103–111, 1995.

[22] M. Pătraşcu and M. Thorup. Time-space trade-offs for predecessor search. In *Proceedings of the 38th Annual ACM Symposium on Theory of Computing*, pages 232–240, 2006.

[23] R. Raz and A. Wigderson. Monotone circuits for

matching require linear depth. *Journal of the ACM*, 39(3):736–744, 1992.

[24] W. J. Savitch. Relationships between nondeterministic and deterministic tape complexities. *Journal of Computer and System Sciences*, 4(2):177–192, 1970.

[25] X. Sun and D. P. Woodruff. The communication and streaming complexity of computing the longest common and increasing subsequences. In *Proceedings of the 18th Annual ACM-SIAM Symposium on Discrete Algorithms*, pages 336–345, 2007.

[26] R. Williams. Non-uniform ACC circuit lower bounds. In *Proceedings of the 26th Annual IEEE Conference on Computational Complexity*, pages 115–125, 2011.

[27] A. C. Yao. Some complexity questions related to distributive computing. In *Proceedings of the 11th Annual ACM Symposium on Theory of Computing*, pages 209–313, 1979.

[28] A. C. Yao. The entropic limitations of VLSI computations. In *Proceedings of the 13th Annual ACM Symposium on Theory of Computing*, pages 308–311, 1981.

Towards An Optimal Query Efficient PCP?

Subhash Khot
NYU and U. Chicago
khot@cims.nyu.edu *

Muli Safra
Tel Aviv University
safra@cs.tau.ac.il

Madhur Tulsiani
TTI-Chicago
madhurt@ttic.edu

ABSTRACT

We construct a PCP based on the hyper-graph linearity test with 3 free queries. It has near-perfect completeness and soundness strictly less than $\frac{1}{8}$. Such a PCP was known before only assuming the Unique Games Conjecture, albeit with soundness arbitrarily close to $\frac{1}{16}$.

At a technical level, our main contribution is constructing a new outer PCP which is "robust" against bounded degree polynomials, and showing that it can be composed with the hyper-graph linearity test with 3 free queries. We believe this outer PCP may be useful in obtaining the optimal query vs. soundness tradeoff for PCPs.

Categories and Subject Descriptors

F.2.8 [**Analysis of Algorithms and Problem Complexity**]: Nonnumerical Algorithms and Problems

General Terms

Theory

Keywords

Constraint Satisfaction Problems, PCPs

1. INTRODUCTION

Testing procedures for certain classes of boolean functions have been extremely useful towards constructing Probabilistically Checkable Proofs (PCPs) for NP. Two classes of boolean functions that are most relevant from the PCP viewpoint are the class of linear functions and the class of dictator functions.

A function $f : \{0,1\}^n \mapsto \{0,1\}$ is called linear if there is some $\alpha \in \{0,1\}^n$ such that $f(x) = \alpha \cdot x = \sum_{i=1}^{n} \alpha_i x_i$ (all computations are over $GF(2)$). Blum, Luby and Rubinfeld [5] suggested the following test: pick two inputs $x, y \in \{0,1\}^n$ uniformly at random and accept iff $f(x) + f(y) = f(x+y)$. They analyzed the test combinatorially and subsequently a Fourier analytic approach led to the following theorem (see for instance [11]).

THEOREM 1.1. *The BLR Test*

- *has perfect completeness, meaning if f is linear, the test passes with probability 1.*
- *has soundness $\frac{1}{2}$, in the sense that if the test passes with probability $\frac{1}{2} + \varepsilon$, then f has a non-negligible Fourier coefficient.*

We note that the soundness characterization in terms of existence of a non-negligible Fourier coefficient is the most relevant from PCP viewpoint. Here non-negligible means a constant that is independent of the dimension n. In the above theorem, there is in fact a Fourier coefficient with magnitude $\Omega(\varepsilon)$, but we will ignore a specific dependence since it typically is less important in PCP applications. The BLR test and its generalizations have found many applications, e.g. in the (original) proof of the PCP Theorem [9, 4, 3], Håstad's 3-bit PCP [11], and the "query efficient" PCPs [21] that are the focus of this paper.

A generalization of the BLR test is the *hyper-graph linearity test* (HLT) with k free queries[1], $k \geq 2$: pick k inputs $x_1, \ldots, x_k \in \{0,1\}^n$ uniformly at random and accept iff

$$\forall S \subseteq \{1, \ldots, k\}, |S| \geq 2, \quad f\left(\sum_{i \in S} x_i\right) = \sum_{i \in S} f(x_i).$$

A variant of the HLT is the *graph linearity test* (GLT) where the above test is carried out only for the $\binom{k}{2}$ sets S with $|S| = 2$. Clearly both GLT and HLT have perfect completeness, meaning a linear function passes the test with probability 1. Samorodnitsky and Trevisan [21] showed (see also [12]) that the GLT has soundness $2^{-\binom{k}{2}}$ (in the sense of Theorem 1.1) and the soundness does not improve with the HLT. Both these are remarkable facts! In the GLT, each of the $\binom{k}{2}$ queries in addition to the k free queries *cuts down* the soundness by a factor half, and afterwards, all the other queries in HLT put together (all those corresponding to sets with $|S| > 2$) do not help at all. Specifically, [21] exhibits a function f that passes the HLT with probability $2^{-\binom{k}{2}}$

*Research supported by NSF CAREER grant CCF-0833228, NSF Expeditions grant CCF-0832795, NSF Waterman Award and BSF grant 2008059.

[1] A set of queries is called "free" if the answer to every other query is determined by the answers to these "free" queries.

ITCS'13, January 9–12, 2013, Berkeley, California, USA.

and has no non-negligible Fourier coefficient. On the other hand, if the acceptance probability exceeds $2^{-\binom{k}{2}}$, even in the GLT, the function must have a non-negligible Fourier coefficient.

After one designs a linearity test (or a dictatorship test), the next question from the PCP viewpoint is whether the test can translated to a full-fledged PCP. One expects the PCP to have near-perfect completeness, the same acceptance predicate as the test and (ideally) the same soundness as the test. Indeed, the BLR test can be translated to a PCP, namely the celebrated 3-bit PCP of Håstad [11], and so can be the GLT test [21, 8] (the first paper gets down to soundness $2^{-k^2/4}$ for even k and the latter to the "correct" bound of $2^{-\binom{k}{2}}$). We would like to emphasize that this translation is often highly non-trivial and as we will see later, there are tests, especially for the class of dictatorship functions, that are currently known to translate to PCPs only assuming the Unique Games Conjecture [14]. When a PCP construction is viewed as an inapproximability result for a *constraint satisfaction problem* (CSP), these results imply that is it hard to distinguish whether the CSP on the "GLT predicate" has optimum $1 - o(1)$ or at most $2^{-\binom{k}{2}} + o(1)$. The GLT predicate is a predicate on $k + \binom{k}{2}$ variables where the last $\binom{k}{2}$ variables are pairwise sums of the first k variables and negated variables are allowed in the CSP. Another application to inapproximability is a much simpler proof of Håstad's $n^{1-\varepsilon}$ inapproximability result for clique [10]. For the clique application one desires a PCP whose *amortized free bit complexity* is arbitrarily small. Indeed, for the [21, 8] PCP, this parameter, defined as the ratio of the number of free queries to the logarithm of the inverse soundness, is $\approx \frac{k}{\binom{k}{2}}$ which becomes arbitrarily small as k gets larger[2].

After successfully translating the GLT to a PCP, it is natural (and fruitful) to further investigate the HLT. As we already mentioned, the HLT, when viewed as a linearity test, gets stuck at the soundness threshold of $2^{-\binom{k}{2}}$, i.e. there are functions with no non-negligible Fourier coefficient but pass the HLT with probability $2^{-\binom{k}{2}}$. One approach to get around this barrier is to use the HLT as a dictatorship test instead (and this is how the BLR Test and the GLT are actually used in [11, 21, 8], but the way these tests are used, the distinction between a linearity test and a dictatorship test is hazy). A function $f : \{0,1\}^n \mapsto \{0,1\}$ is called a dictatorship if $f(x) = x_i$ for some $i \in [n]$. In other words, the ith co-ordinate has *influence* 1 where influence of a co-ordinate is the probability that flipping that co-ordinate flips the value of the function on a random input. The HLT (and similarly the BLR Test and the GLT) can be adapted into a dictatorship test, called the *hyper-graph dictatorship test* (HDT), where the test is the same except that a small noise is added to each query.[3] Viewed now as a dictatorship test, the soundness barrier of $2^{-\binom{k}{2}}$ is broken, as shown in [22]! Specifically,

THEOREM 1.2. *The HDT*

- *has near-perfect completeness, meaning if f is a dictatorship, it passes the test with probability close to 1.*
- *has soundness $2^{-(2^k-k-1)}$, in the sense that if the test passes with probability slightly above this threshold, then f has a co-ordinate with non-negligible influence*[4]

Note that the threshold $2^{-(2^k-k-1)}$ indicates that each of the $2^k - k - 1$ queries (corresponding to sets $S \subseteq \{1, \dots, k\}, |S| \geq 2$) in addition to the k free queries *cuts down* the soundness by a factor half. HDT is a remarkable test and it would be even more remarkable if it were to translate into a PCP. In addition to being an interesting PCP in its own right, it would have (at least) two applications to inapproximability: firstly, for the the Max-K-CSP problem, it would be NP-hard to distinguish whether a CSP on $K = 2^k - 1$ variables has optimum $1 - o(1)$ or at most $2^{-(2^k-k-1)} + o(1)$, which would essentially match the best known algorithm for the problem [7]. Secondly, it would be NP-hard to approximate the independent set problem on degree d graphs within factor $d/\text{polylog}(d)$ [22].

However, one knows how to translate HDT to a PCP only assuming the Unique Games Conjecture [22]. This is the case for many other dictatorship tests, perhaps the *Max-Cut Test* being the most prominent example. Therein, we know a two-query test that "works" and analyzed via the Majority Is Stablest Theorem [17], but one knows how to translate the test to a PCP and obtain optimal inapproximability result for Max-Cut only assuming the UGC [15].

Since the UGC, if true, remains out of reach of current techniques, it is worth-while to attempt proving (at least some of) the implications of UGC without relying on it. This paper may be viewed as a modest step in this direction for the specific problem of Max-K-CSP and the related HLT test.

Fix the number of free queries to $k = 3$. Let us call the corresponding GLT and HLT predicates as 3GLT and 3HLT. Note that 3GLT is a predicate on 6 variables (x, y, z, a, b, c) which is True iff $a = x + y, b = y + z, c = x + z$. Similarly, 3HLT is a predicate on 7 variables (x, y, z, a, b, c, d) which is True iff in addition $d = x + y + z$. As mentioned before, 3GLT is known to be NP-hard with gap $(1 - o(1), \frac{1}{8} + o(1))$ [8] and 3HLT is known to be Unique Games hard with gap $(1 - o(1), \frac{1}{16} + o(1))$ [22]. The predicate 3HLT has one additional "query" and the UGC tells us that this query helps bring the soundness down to $\frac{1}{16}$ from $\frac{1}{8}$. However, without relying on UGC, we didn't know whether this additional query helps at all. Our main result is to show that it does:

THEOREM 1.3. *There exists a constant $s < \frac{1}{8}$ such that for an arbitrarily small constant $\varepsilon > 0$, it is NP-hard to distinguish whether the CSP on 3HLT predicate has optimum at least $1 - \varepsilon$ or at most $s + \varepsilon$.*

The constant s for which we can prove the above theorem is $\frac{1}{8} - \frac{1}{320}$.

[2]The results in [21] are stated in terms of the *amortized query complexity* which is the ratio of the number of queries to the logarithm of the inverse soundness, and is $1 + O(\frac{1}{k})$ for the PCPs in [21, 8]

[3]Dictatorship functions form a restricted sub-class of linear functions. Thus a dictatorship test is required to "kill" not just the non-linear functions but also the linear functions with a "large support". The purpose of introducing noise is precisely to "kill" the latter.

[4]There is an issue of influence versus the *low-degree influence* which we omit from this discussion.

Techniques

At a high level, our approach is to revisit the analysis of HLT and not get *discouraged* by lack of a non-negligible Fourier coefficient. A non-negligible Fourier coefficient would allow us to conclude that the boolean function f is correlated with a linear function. We instead conclude that the function is close (in Hamming distance) to a unique quadratic polynomial and hence the function may be *decoded uniquely* to a quadratic polynomial. This constitutes the so-called *Inner PCP*. To integrate it inside a full PCP however requires an *Outer PCP* that is *robust against quadratic polynomials.* We construct such an Outer PCP from scratch (it is robust against degree d polynomials for any fixed d). In the following, we give a more detailed overview of the techniques.

Consider the HLT with three free queries. Given a function $f : \{0,1\}^n \mapsto \{0,1\}$:

- Pick inputs $x, y, z \in \{0,1\}^n$ uniformly at random.
- Accept iff:

$$\begin{aligned} f(x+y) &= f(x) + f(y)\,, \\ f(y+z) &= f(y) + f(z)\,, \\ f(x+z) &= f(x) + f(z)\,, \\ f(x+y+z) &= f(x) + f(y) + f(z)\,. \end{aligned}$$

A (by-now) standard way to analyze such a test is to think of the function f as $\{1,-1\}$ valued and *arithmetize* the acceptance predicate:

$$\frac{1+f(x)f(y)f(x+y)}{2} \cdot \frac{1+f(y)f(z)f(y+z)}{2} \cdot \frac{1+f(x)f(z)f(x+z)}{2} \cdot \frac{1+f(x)f(y)f(z)f(x+y+z)}{2}.$$

The above expression equals 1 if the test accepts and 0 otherwise and thus the acceptance probability equals its expectation over the choice of x, y, z. The expression can be written as a sum of 16 terms, with the constant term equal to $\frac{1}{16}$. Fourteen of the terms, after taking expectation over x, y, z, can be written in terms of Fourier coefficients either as $\sum_\alpha \widehat{f}(\alpha)^3$ or as $\sum_\alpha \widehat{f}(\alpha)^4$. This step is standard and allows us to conclude that if either of these fourteen terms is non-negligible, then f must have a non-negligible Fourier coefficient. Moreover f may be *decoded* into a small list of non-negligible Fourier coefficients. In this sense, these fourteen terms may be "handled well" in the PCP setting (if and when we get to the PCP) and hence may be assumed to be arbitrarily small. The only "troublesome term" is the last one:

$$\mathop{\mathbb{E}}_{x,y,z}\left[f(x)f(y)f(z)f(x+y)f(y+z)f(x+z)f(x+y+z)\right].$$

Indeed, if f is a quadratic polynomial (or to be precise, a quadratic phase $(-1)^{g(x)}$ where g is a quadratic polynomial, since we are now thinking of f as being $\{1,-1\}$ valued), the above expectation equals 1 whereas there are quadratic phase functions that have no non-negligible Fourier coefficient. Still, for a small enough constant $\theta \in (0, \frac{1}{20})$, it was shown by Alon et al. [1] that if the above expectation is at least $1-\theta$, then f is $(1-\theta)$ close in Hamming distance to a quadratic phase function, which then may be taken as a unique decoding of f. Thus we may upper bound the "troublesome term" by $1-\theta$ and get an overall soundness of $\frac{1}{16} + \frac{1}{16}(1-\theta) = s < \frac{1}{8}$.

The next issue is whether the decoding to a quadratic polynomial can be integrated with an appropriate Outer PCP. The known Outer PCPs are obtained by parallel repetition of a basic "equation versus variable" game and this basic game is not robust enough towards this end. We design a new game that is robust against low degree polynomials. Its description is a bit cumbersome and non-intuitive, so we elaborate it in some detail.

Let us first describe the standard "equation versus variable" game. One starts with a hard instance of 3LIN problem: a set of variables $x_1, \ldots, x_n$ and equations $E_1, \ldots, E_m$ over $GF(2)$ with each equation containing three variables. It is known [11] that distinguishing between a gap $(1-o(1), \frac{1}{2}+o(1))$ is NP-hard. For the ease of exposition, assume that all right hand sides of the equations are zero (this would actually make the instance trivial, but the right hand sides serve as "offsets" that can easily be incorporated via "folding"). The basic game consists of two provers and a verifier. The verifier picks a random equation, say $E_\ell : x_i + x_j + x_k = 0$. The first prover is asked to furnish values of two variables in the equation, say x_i and x_j (and given the equation). The second prover is asked to furnish the value of one of the three variables chosen at random (without revealing the equation). The verifier accepts iff the two provers' answers are consistent on variables x_i, x_j and on the variable x_k, the sum of the values of variables x_i, x_j furnished by the first prover equals the value of variable x_k furnished by the second prover. The value of the game is the maximum probability with which the provers can make the verifier accept. It is easily checked that the hardness of 3LIN translates to hardness of distinguishing whether the value of the game is $1-o(1)$ or bounded away from 1.

Let us now reformulate the above game so as to incorporate the notion of robustness against low degree polynomials. Let $r = 2$. We first describe the reformulated game in abstract and then show how it indeed is a reformulation of the above game.

- The question to the first prover is an index $\ell \in [m]$. His answer is a linear function $f_\ell : \{0,1\}^r \mapsto \{0,1\}$.
- The verifier chooses a random non-zero input $z \in \{0,1\}^r$. Depending on the index ℓ and input z, the verifier calculates an index $t \in [n]$.
- The question to the second prover is the index $t \in [n]$. His answer is a single bit, say y_t.
- The verifier accepts iff $f_\ell(z) = y_t$.

It is intended that $y_t = x_t$ in a supposedly almost-satisfying assignment to the 3LIN instance. The function f_ℓ is intended to be the linear function

$$f_\ell(z_1, z_2) = x_i \cdot z_1 + x_j \cdot z_2,$$

where the index ℓ identifies the equation $E_\ell : x_i + x_j + x_k = 0$. After choosing ℓ and non-zero $z \in \{0,1\}^r$, verifier calculates the index t as: if $z =$ "10", $t = i$, if $z =$ "01", $t = j$, and if $z =$ "11", $t = k$. Note that the input z is not revealed to either of the provers. It is clear that the game is a simple reformulation of the game before and hence the hardness of its gap-version holds.

With the reformulated version, it is now straightforward to introduce the notion of robustness. We prove that it is NP-hard to distinguish whether the value of the game is

$1 - o(1)$ (and the first prover furnishes linear functions as required) or whether the value of the game is bounded away from 1 even if the first prover is allowed to furnish functions $f_\ell : \{0,1\}^r \mapsto \{0,1\}$ that are degree d polynomials. I.e. the soundness is robust even against degree d polynomials. Our result holds with $r = d+1$ and the soundness is $1 - 2^{-O(d)}$. A formal statement of the result appears as Theorem 3.1 and proved in Section 3. The proof is a rather significant and non-intuitive variant (in authors' opinion) of Håstad's 3-bit PCP and instead of attempting to give some intuition here, the reader is referred directly to Section 3.

The Outer PCP is now obtained by a *smooth* parallel repetition of the basic robust game. The term *smooth* refers to a variant of the parallel repetition where the actual game is played only on a small fraction of co-ordinates and on the remaining co-ordinates, the same question is sent to both provers. As demonstrated in [16], when Hadamard Code (i.e. table of values of a linear function) is "plugged in" at the Inner PCP level, the smoothness of the parallel repetition game ensures the so-called *subcode covering* property. In short, the property says that the code (or rather the encoding space) corresponding to a fixed question to the "larger" prover is almost uniformly covered by the codes (or rather the encoding spaces) of the questions to the "smaller" prover. This property is very convenient (and essential towards the result in [16]) and we make use of it as well.

Related and Future Work

The question of obtaining a PCP with $2^k - 1$ queries and the optimal soundness of $2^{-(2^k - k - 1)}$ (without relying on the UGC) which was the motivating application for our construction, was subsequently resolved by a beautiful result of Chan [6]. Implicit in his construction, is also a PCP similar to ours, which is robust against degree-d polynomials. However, our PCP construction still leads to several other questions which might be interesting for future work.

We construct a PCP based on the 3HLT predicate with soundness strictly below $\frac{1}{8}$. A natural (and very interesting in authors's opinion) question is whether the soundness of this particular PCP can be pushed arbitrarily close to $\frac{1}{16}$, matching the UGC-based result. At the Outer PCP level, one may use the same Outer PCP as herein: a smooth parallel repetition of the basic robust game. At the Inner PCP level however we can no longer appeal to unique decoding to a quadratic polynomial and a naive appeal to list decoding does not work because the list would be too large. If a function has a non-negligible correlation with a a linear polynomial, i.e. has a non-negligible Fourier coefficient, then the list decoding consists of making a list of all non-negligible Fourier coefficients, and since the sum of squares of the Fourier coefficients is 1, the list is bounded (by $O(1/\varepsilon^2)$ if the correlation is ε). For the class of quadratic polynomials, we (fortunately) do have a theorem [20] stating that if the expectation

$$\mathop{\mathbb{E}}_{x,y,z}\left[f(x)f(y)f(z)f(x+y)f(y+z)f(x+z)f(x+y+z)\right]$$

is non-negligible, then $f : \{0,1\}^n \mapsto \{1,-1\}$ must be correlated with a quadratic polynomial (or rather a quadratic phase). Unfortunately however, the list of all quadratic phases with which f may have a non-negligible correlation could be as large as $2^{O(n)}$. This seems like an insurmountable difficulty from the PCP viewpoint, a priori at least. The authors however do have some indications that there might be a way to bypass this difficulty.

The nature of our PCP also leads to a natural question about a variant of parallel repetition. We formulate is as a concrete problem in Section 7. The resolution of this problem would provide an alternate approach to the construction of optimal query efficient PCPs, bypassing the above difficulty.

2. PRELIMINARIES AND DEFINITIONS

2.1 Fourier Analysis

The vector space of all functions $f : \{0,1\}^n \mapsto \mathbb{R}$ has an orthonormal basis $\{\chi_\alpha \mid \alpha \in \{0,1\}^n\}$ where the inner product between two functions $f, g : \{0,1\}^n \to \mathbb{R}$ is defined as $\langle f, g\rangle := \mathbb{E}_x[f(x)g(x)]$. Hence, every $f : \{0,1\}^n \mapsto \mathbb{R}$ can be expressed uniquely as $f = \sum_{\alpha\in\{0,1\}^n} \widehat{f}(\alpha)\,\chi_\alpha$. The coefficients $\widehat{f}(\alpha) \in \mathbb{R}$ are called Fourier coefficients and are defined by: $\widehat{f}(\alpha) = \langle f, \chi_\alpha\rangle = \mathbb{E}_x\left[f(x)\overline{\chi_\alpha(x)}\right]$. By Parseval's identity, $\sum_\alpha |\widehat{f}(\alpha)|^2 = \|f\|_2^2 = \mathbb{E}_x\left[|f(x)|^2\right]$. In particular, for a function taking values in $\{-1,1\}$, the sum of squared absolute values of all its Fourier coefficients equals 1.

DEFINITION 2.1. *Let $f : \{0,1\}^n \mapsto \{-1,1\}$ be a Boolean function. We define the* influence *of the ith variable in f as the probability over all inputs that changing the ith bit changes the value of f.*

$$\mathsf{Inf}_i(f) := \mathop{\mathbb{P}}_{x\in\{0,1\}^n}\left[f(x) \neq f(x+e_i)\right] = \sum_{\substack{\alpha\in\{0,1\}^n\\ \alpha_i=1}} |\widehat{f}(\alpha)|^2 .$$

Here e_i represents the input with 1 only in the ith position. The influence for $f : \{0,1\}^n \to \{0,1\}$ is also defined as the same probability as above.

For $\eta > 0$, let $\mu \sim_\eta \{0,1\}^n$ denote sampling $\mu \in \{0,1\}^n$ from a distribution with each bit independently set to 1 with probability η and 0 with probability $1-\eta$. For a function $f : \{0,1\}^n \mapsto \{-1,1\}$, it's noise stability at noise η is given by

$$\mathop{\mathbb{E}}_{\substack{x\in\{0,1\}^n\\ \mu\sim_\eta\{0,1\}^n}}\left[f(x)f(x+\mu)\right] = \sum_\alpha (1-2\eta)^{|\alpha|}\cdot|\widehat{f}(\alpha)|^2 ,$$

where $|\alpha|$ denotes the number of 1s in α.

2.2 Hellinger and Statistical Distance

The squared Hellinger distance between distributions D_1 and D_2 over a discrete probability space $\mathcal{A}$ is

$$\begin{aligned} H^2(D_1, D_2) &:= \frac{1}{2}\sum_{a\in\mathcal{A}}\left(\sqrt{D_1(a)} - \sqrt{D_2(a)}\right)^2 \\ &= 1 - \sum_{a\in\mathcal{A}}\sqrt{D_1(a)D_2(a)}. \end{aligned}$$

It is clear that $1 - H^2(\cdot,\cdot)$ is multiplicative for product distributions D_1^k, D_2^k on space $\mathcal{A}^k$, i.e.

$$1 - H^2(D_1^k, D_2^k) = (1 - H^2(D_1, D_2))^k.$$

The statistical distance between D_1 and D_2 is:

$$\Delta(D_1, D_2) := \frac{1}{2}\sum_{a\in\mathcal{A}}|D_1(a) - D_2(a)| .$$

We have the standard inequality:

LEMMA 2.2.

$$H^2(D_1, D_2) \le \Delta(D_1, D_2) \le \sqrt{2} \cdot H(D_1, D_2).$$

2.3 Label Cover and 2 Prover 1 Round Games

DEFINITION 2.3. *An instance $\mathcal{L}$ of* Label Cover *with projection property is defined by a tuple $(U, V, E, \Sigma_1, \Sigma_2, \Pi)$. Here, (U, V, E) is a bipartite graph, $R_1 \ge R_2$ are natural numbers (called alphabet sizes) and $\Pi = \{\pi_{uv}\}_{(u,v)\in E}$ is a collection of projection functions $\pi_{uv} : [R_1] \mapsto [R_2]$. A labeling is pair of maps $A : U \mapsto [R_1]$, $B : V \mapsto [R_2]$. We say that an edge $e = (u, v)$ is* satisfied *by the labeling if $\pi_{uv}(A(u)) = B(v)$. We define:*

$$\mathsf{Opt}(\mathcal{L}) := \max_{\substack{A:U\to[R_1]\\ B:V\to[R_2]}} \mathop{\mathbb{P}}_{(u,v)\in E} [\pi_{uv}(A(u)) = B(v)] \ .$$

It is known that for all $\delta > 0$, there exist R_1, R_2 such that it is NP-hard to decide if for a given label cover instance with alphabet sizes R_1, R_2, $\mathsf{Opt}(\mathcal{L}) = 1$ or $\mathsf{Opt}(\mathcal{L}) < \delta$. This result also holds for the special case of instances in which the bipartite graph (U, V, E) is regular on both sides.

DEFINITION 2.4. *A* 2P1R Game *$\mathcal{G}(U, V, \mu, \mathcal{R}, \mathcal{S}, \{\pi_{uv}\})$ consists of sets of questions U, V and sets of answers $\mathcal{R}, \mathcal{S}$ for the two provers respectively, a distribution μ on the set of question pairs $U \times V$ and for every question pair (u, v) in the support of μ, a predicate $\pi_{uv} : \mathcal{R} \times \mathcal{S} \mapsto \{0, 1\}$ that defines the pairs of accepting answers. A strategy of provers is a map $\varphi : V \mapsto \mathcal{R}, \varphi : U \mapsto \mathcal{S}$. The value of the strategy φ is:*

$$\mathsf{Val}(\varphi, \mathcal{G}) := \mathop{\mathbb{P}}_{(u,v)\sim\mu} [\pi_{uv}(\varphi(u), \varphi(v)) = 1] \ .$$

The value of the game $\mathsf{Val}(\mathcal{G})$ is the maximum value of any prover strategy. A Projection Game is one where for every answer of the first prover, there is exactly one accepting answer of the second prover. For a projection game, the predicate π_{uv} can be thought of as a map $\pi_{uv} : \mathcal{R} \mapsto \mathcal{S}$ and the accepting answers are of the form $(r, \pi_{uv}(r))$ for $r \in \mathcal{R}$. For a projection game, $|\mathcal{S}| \le |\mathcal{R}|$.

A 2P1R Game is best viewed as a game between the two provers and a verifier. The verifier picks a random question pair (u, v) from the distribution μ, asks one question each to the two prover respectively, and accepts if and only if the provers' answers satisfy the predicate π_{uv}. The probability of acceptance of the verifier is same as the value of a provers' strategy. Each bipartite label cover instance can be viewed as a 2P1R Game where the verifier picks a random edge $(u, v) \in E$, and the questions sent to the two provers are the vertices u and v. The acceptance predicate is the same as the projection π_{uv} for the edge.

DEFINITION 2.5. *Given a 2P1R Game $\mathcal{G}(U, V, \mu, \mathcal{R}, \mathcal{S}, \{\pi_{uv}\})$, the k-wise repeated game is*

$$\mathcal{G}^{\otimes k}(U^k, V^k, \mu^k, \mathcal{R}^k, \mathcal{S}^k, \{\pi^k_{\mathbf{uv}}\}),$$

where for $\mathbf{u} = (u_1, \ldots, u_k)$ and $\mathbf{v} = (v_1, \ldots, v_k)$, $\pi^k_{\mathbf{uv}} := \wedge_{i=1}^k \pi_{u_i v_i}$.

We state below Raz's Parallel Repetition Theorem along with the recent improvements (and simplifications) by Holenstein and Rao.

THEOREM 2.6. **([19, 13, 18])** *There exists an absolute constant $c > 0$ such that for a 2P1R Game $\mathcal{G}$ with answer sets $\mathcal{R}, \mathcal{S}$ and $\mathrm{val}(\mathcal{G}) = 1 - \varepsilon$,*

$$\mathsf{Val}(\mathcal{G}^k) \le (1 - \varepsilon^3)^{ck/\log(|\mathcal{R}||\mathcal{S}|)}.$$

For a Projection Game, the bound of $(1 - \varepsilon^2)^{ck}$ holds.

2.4 Linear vs. Degree-d Labeling

We will, in fact, consider label cover instances in which the labels on one side are functions. These will have the property that in the YES case one can satisfy almost all constraints with labels corresponding to linear functions, while in the NO case it not possible to satisfy many constraints even with labels corresponding to degree-d polynomials (for technical reasons, we only argue about polynomials with no constant term). We define the problem below.

DEFINITION 2.7. *An instance of* Linear vs. Degree-d Label-Cover *with parameters $\eta, \gamma > 0$ is a graph (U, V, E) and a set of (possibly weighted) constraints. A label for each vertex $u \in U$ is a function $F_u : \{0, 1\}^{d+1} \to \{0, 1\}$ and a label for each $v \in V$ is a bit $A(v) \in \{0, 1\}$. Each constraint is indexed by a tuple (u, v, x) for $x \in \{0, 1\}^{d+1} \setminus \{0^{d+1}\}$ and is of the form*

$$F_u(x) = A(v) + c_{uv,x} \mod 2 \,,$$

for $c_{uv,x} \in \mathbb{F}_2$. The goal is to distinguish between the cases:

- YES*: $\exists A : V \to \{0, 1\}$ and homogeneous linear functions $\{F_u : \{0, 1\}^{d+1} \to \{0, 1\}\}_{u\in U}$ satisfying $1 - \eta$ fraction of the constraints.*
- NO*: $\forall A : V \to \{0, 1\}$, any collection of degree-d polynomials $\{F_u : \{0, 1\}^{d+1} \to \{0, 1\}\}_{u\in U}$ (with $F_u(0) = 0\ \forall u$) satisfies at most $1 - \gamma$ fraction of the constraints.*

REMARK 2.8. *The instances of* Linear vs. Degree-d Label-Cover *we will consider will have the additional property that for all $u \in U$ and all $x, x' \in \{0, 1\}^{d+1} \setminus \{0^{d+1}\}$, the total weight of the constraints involving the pair (u, x) will be the same as the weight of the constraints involving the pair (u, x'). This assumption is not crucial, but it makes the PCP construction a little simpler.*

It is perhaps also useful to view Linear vs. Degree-d Label-Cover as a gap version of a constraint satisfaction problem, where the hardness result involves two kinds of constraints. Let $L : \{0, 1\}^{2^{d+1}} \to \{0, 1\}$ be a predicate on 2^{d+1} variables which is 1 iff the input corresponds to the evaluation table of a linear function in $d + 1$ variables. Let $D : \{0, 1\}^{2^{d+1}} \to \{0, 1\}$ be a similar predicate which is 1 iff the input corresponds to the table of a polynomial of degree at most D.

Then an instance of Linear vs. Degree-d Label-Cover as above can be considered as a constraint satisfaction problem, where each constraint is imposed on the 2^{d+1} values of the form $A(v)$ corresponding to all the inputs of a single function F_u (after shifting the values $A(v)$ by appropriate constants $c_{uv,x}$). The goal is to distinguish between the cases when $1 - \eta$ fraction of the constraints can be satisfied even when we consider each constraint to be the predicate L, and when not even $1 - \gamma$ fraction of the constraints can be satisfied even when we take the constraints to be predicate D (the accepting assignments for which are a superset of those for L).

3. HARDNESS OF LINEAR VS. DEGREE-d LABELING

We now give a reduction from Label Cover to the Linear vs. Degree-d Label-Cover problem as defined in Definition 2.7. We will prove the following theorem:

THEOREM 3.1. *For any $d \geq 1$, there exists $\gamma = 2^{-O(d)}$ such that for any $\eta \in (0, \gamma)$, the Linear vs. Degree-d Label-Cover problem with parameters η and γ is NP-hard.*

Let (U, V, R_1, R_2, Π) be an instance of Label Cover where $\Pi = \{\pi_{uv}\}_{(u,v) \in E}$ is a collection of projections $\pi_{uv} : [R_1] \to [R_2]$. Assume the constraint graph is regular on both sides. To prove the hardness of Linear vs. Degree-d Label-Cover with parameters η, γ, we will need δ for the Label Cover instance to be less than $\eta \cdot 2^{-\Omega(d)} / \sqrt{\gamma}$.

Reduction from Label-Cover..

Identify $\{0,1\}^{d+1}$ with $2^{[d+1]}$ in the canonical way and for $y_1, y_2, \ldots, y_t \in [d+1]$, let $\mathbb{1}_{\{y_1, \ldots, y_t\}} \in \{0,1\}^{d+1}$ denote the string which has 1s only in the positions corresponding to $y_1, \ldots, y_t$.

For $u \in U, v \in V$ and $S_1 \subseteq \{0,1\}^{R_1}, S_2 \subseteq \{0,1\}^{R_2}, |S_1| = |S_2| = d+1$, we will impose constraints on functions $F_{u,S_1} : \{0,1\}^{d+1} \to \{0,1\}$, $F_{v,S_2} : \{0,1\}^{d+1} \to \{0,1\}$, $A_u : \{0,1\}^{R_1} \to \{0,1\}$ and $A_v : \{0,1\}^{R_2} \to \{0,1\}$. Thus, for the resulting instance of Linear vs. Degree-d Label-Cover, the left vertices will be of the form (u, S_1) and (v, S_2) for $u \in U, v \in V$ and $S_1 \subseteq \{0,1\}^{R_1}, S_2, \subseteq \{0,1\}^{R_2}, |S_1| = |S_2| = d+1$. The labels for these vertices are functions from $\{0,1\}^{d+1}$ to $\{0,1\}$. The right vertices are of the form (u, x) and (v, y) for $u \in U, v \in V, x \in \{0,1\}^{R_1}$ and $y \in \{0,1\}^{R_2}$. The labels for these vertices are bits. The collection of labels for the vertices (u, x) for all x (and similarly (v, y) for all y) can be viewed as a function $A_u : \{0,1\}^{R_1} \to \{0,1\}$ and we write the constraints for the values of such functions.

REMARK 3.2. *We will write our constraints assuming that the functions A_u and A_v are* folded *for all u, v i.e., they satisfy $A_u(x + \mathbf{1}) = A_u(x) + 1$ (and similarly for A_v) where $\mathbf{1}$ denotes the all-1s string. This is implemented by requiring the labeling A_u to be specified only for half the inputs in $\{0,1\}^{R_1}$ (say with the first bit 0) and constructing the value for the remaining inputs using the above relation. This is what results in the constants $c_{uv,x}$ in the constraints.*

We also assume $A_u(0) = A_v(0) = 0$ for all u, v. This will be true for the labeling we give in the YES *case. Also, any labeling can be modified to satisfy this without significantly affecting the number of satisfies constraints.*

We include the following types of constraints with equal probability:

1. For each $u \in U$, select a random set $S \subseteq \{0,1\}^{R_1}$ with $|S| = d+1$ and a random $T \subseteq S$, $T \neq \emptyset$, and include the constraint:

$$F_{u,S}(\mathbb{1}_T) = A_u\left(\sum_{y \in T} y\right).$$

Similarly, for each $v \in V$, $S \subseteq \{0,1\}^{R_2}$ with $|S| = d+1$ and $T \subseteq S, T \neq \emptyset$, include the constraint:

$$F_{v,S}(\mathbb{1}_T) = A_v\left(\sum_{z \in T} z\right).$$

2. For each $u \in U$, select a random $S \subseteq \{0,1\}^{R_1}$ with $|S| = d+1$, $T \subseteq S, T \neq \emptyset$ and $\mu \sim_\eta \{0,1\}^{R_1}$. Include the constraint [5]:

$$F_{u,S}(\mathbb{1}_T) = A_u\left(\sum_{y \in T} y + \mu\right).$$

Similarly, for each $v \in V$, $S \subseteq \{0,1\}^{R_2}$ with $|S| = d+1$, $T \subseteq S, T \neq \emptyset$ and $\mu \sim_\eta \{0,1\}^{R_2}$, include:

$$F_{v,S}(\mathbb{1}_T) = A_v\left(\sum_{z \in T} z + \mu\right).$$

3. For each edge $(u, v) \in E$, pick $y_1, \ldots, y_d \in \{0,1\}^{R_1}$ and $z \in \{0,1\}^{R_2}$. Let $\pi_{uv}^{-1}(z) \in \{0,1\}^{R_1}$ denote the string obtained by copying appropriate bits of z. Let $S = \{y_1, \ldots, y_d, y_1 + \ldots + y_d + \pi_{uv}^{-1}(z)\}$. Include the constraint

$$F_{u,S}(\mathbb{1}_S) = A_v(z).$$

Also, for each $T \subseteq S$, $1 \leq |T| \leq d$, include the constraint

$$F_{u,S}(\mathbb{1}_T) = A_u\left(\sum_{y \in T} y\right).$$

Note that some of the constraints of type (3) are the same as constraints of type (1). However, type (1) constraints would have small total weight for special sets S of the form $\{y_1, \ldots, y_d, y_1 + \ldots + y_d + \pi_{uv}^{-1}(z)\}$, whereas constraints of type (3) are exclusively for sets of this form, and thus have large total weight.

3.1 Completeness

Let $\mathcal{L} : U \cup V :\to \Sigma_1 \cup \Sigma_2$ be a labeling which satisfies all the constraints in the Label-Cover instance. Choose the functions A_u, A_v to be dictator functions according to $\mathcal{L}$. For each u and $S \subseteq \{0,1\}^{R_1}$, let let $F_{u,S}$ be the linear function defined as $F_{u,S}(x) = \sum_{y \in S} x_y \cdot A_u(y) \mod 2$, where we think of x being in $\{0,1\}^S$. We define $F_{v,S}$ similarly. We now verify the completeness for each type of constraints.

1. Since $F_{u,S}$ and A_u are both linear, for any set $T \subseteq S$ we have

$$F_{u,S}(\mathbb{1}_T) = \sum_{y \in S} \mathbb{1}_T(y) \cdot A_u(y) = \sum_{y \in T} A_u(y) = A_u\left(\sum_{y \in S} y\right).$$

A similar argument holds for any $v \in V$.

2. Since A_u (similarly A_v) is a dictator function, with

[5] We will need to use these constraints only for singletons sets T. However, we include them for all non-empty T to maintain the property that all non-zero inputs to the functions $F_{u,S}$ are equally likely to appear in a constraint, as discussed in Remark 2.8.

probability $1-\eta$ over the choice of μ, we have

$$\begin{aligned} F_{u,S}(\mathbb{1}_T) &= \sum_{y \in S} \mathbb{1}_T(y) \cdot A_u(y) \\ &= \sum_{y \in T} A_u(y) \\ &= A_u\left(\sum_{y \in T} y\right) \\ &= A_u\left(\sum_{y \in T} y + \mu\right). \end{aligned}$$

Hence, a $1-\eta$ fraction of constraints of this type are satisfied.

3. By linearity of $F_{u,S}$ and A_u, we get

$$\begin{aligned} & F_{u,S}\left(\mathbb{1}_{y_1,\ldots,y_d,y_1+\ldots+y_d+\pi_{uv}^{-1}(z)}\right) \\ &= \sum_{i=1}^{d} A_u(y_i) + A_u(y_1+\ldots+y_d+\pi_{uv}^{-1}(z)) \\ &= A_u(\pi_{uv}^{-1}(z)), \end{aligned}$$

which is equal to $A_v(z)$ since A_u and A_v are dictator functions according to a labeling satisfying the constraint on the edge (u,v). The rest of the type (3) constraints are satisfied simply as type (1) constraints.

Thus, if the starting instance of Label-Cover is satisfiable, there exist linear functions $\{F_{w,S}\}_{w\in U\cup V, |S|=d+1}$ satisfying at least $1-\eta$ fraction of the constraints.

3.2 Soundness

Suppose there exist functions $\{F_w, A_w\}_{w\in U\cup V}$ satisfying $1-\gamma$ fraction of the constraints. Also, the functions $\{F_{w,S}\}_{w\in U\cup V, |S|=d+1}$ are degree-d polynomials.

For at least $1-3\sqrt{\gamma}$ fraction of the edges (u,v) we have that at least $1-\sqrt{\gamma}$ fraction of the constraints of type (1) and (2) are satisfied for u and v, and that at least $1-\sqrt{\gamma}$ fraction of constraints of type (3) are satisfied. For the rest of the argument, we fix such an edge (u,v) and drop the subscript from the projection π_{uv},

Using the fact that $1-\sqrt{\gamma}$ fraction of the constraints of type (1) are satisfied and that each $F_{u,S}$ is a degree-d polynomial over $\{0,1\}^{d+1}$, the following claim gives that A_u must also be close to a degree-d polynomial over $\{0,1\}^{R_1}$.

Claim 3.3. *With probability $1-O(2^d\sqrt{\gamma})$ over the choice of the tuples $(y_1,\ldots,y_{d+1})$, the function A_u must satisfy*

$$\sum_{I\subseteq[d+1]} A_u\left(\sum_{i\in I} y_i\right) = 0.$$

Proof. Note that if the tuple $(y_1,\ldots,y_{d+1})$ has $y_i = y_j$ for any $i \neq j$ then the expression on the left is identically 0. Hence, we only need to prove the claim when $y_1,\ldots,y_{d+1}$ are all distinct.

Since the functions $F_{u,S}$ and A_u satisfy $1-\sqrt{\gamma}$ fraction of the constraints of type (1), we have

$$\mathop{\mathbb{P}}_{|S|=d+1, T\subseteq S}\left[F_{u,S}(\mathbb{1}_T) = A_u\left(\sum_{y\in T} y\right)\right] \geq 1-\sqrt{\gamma},$$

Where we have also included $T=\emptyset$ since $F_{u,S}(0)=0$ by assumption and $A_u(0)=0$ by assumption. By averaging, we get

$$\mathop{\mathbb{P}}_{|S|=d+1}\left[\mathop{\mathbb{P}}_{T\subseteq S}\left[F_{u,S}(\mathbb{1}_T) = A_u\left(\sum_{y\in T} y\right)\right] \geq 1-2^{-(d+2)}\right]$$
$$\geq 1-\sqrt{\gamma}\cdot 2^{d+2}.$$

This means that for a large fraction of the subsets S, the constraint is satisfied for all $T\subseteq S$, since the number of subsets is only 2^{d+1}. Since picking a set $S\subseteq\{0,1\}^{R_1}$ with $|S| = d+1$ is the same as picking $d+1$ *distinct* elements $y_1,\ldots,y_{d+1}$, we have for $S=\{y_1,\ldots,y_{d+1}\}$

$$\mathop{\mathbb{P}}_{y_1,\ldots,y_{d+1}}\left[\forall T\subseteq S \quad F_{u,S}(\mathbb{1}_T) = A_u\left(\sum_{y\in T} y\right)\right]$$
$$\geq 1-\sqrt{\gamma}\cdot 2^{d+2}.$$

Also, since each $F_{u,S}$ is a degree-d polynomial, $\sum_{T\subseteq S} F_{u,S}(\mathbb{1}_T) = 0$ for *every* $S=\{y_1,\ldots,y_{d+1}\}$. Combining this with the above, we get that

$$\mathop{\mathbb{P}}_{y_1,\ldots,y_{d+1}}\left[\sum_{T\subseteq\{y_1,\ldots,y_{d+1}\}} A_u\left(\sum_{y\in T} y\right) = 0\right]$$
$$\geq 1-\sqrt{\gamma}\cdot 2^{d+2},$$

which proves the claim. ■

By [1], there exits a degree-d polynomial $\tilde{A}_u$ which is at distance at most $2^{O(d)}\sqrt{\gamma}$ from A_u. Similarly, A_v is close to a degree-d polynomial $\tilde{A}_v$. We will need to show that these polynomials can have only few relevant variables (variables with non-zero influence). We need the following lower bound on the influence of a relevant variable.

Claim 3.4. *Let $P:\{0,1\}^R\to\{0,1\}$ be a degree-d polynomial over $\mathbb{F}_2$ and let the $\mathsf{Inf}_i(P) > 0$. Then $\mathsf{Inf}_i(P) \geq 2^{-(d-1)}$.*

Proof. This simply follows by noting that $\mathsf{Inf}_i(P)$ is the probability that the degree $d-1$ polynomial $P(y+e_i) - P(y)$ is non-zero. Since $\mathsf{Inf}_i(P) > 0$, the polynomial is nontrivial and hence must be non-zero with probability at least $2^{-(d-1)}$. ■

With probability $1-\sqrt{\gamma}\cdot 2^{d+1}$ over the choice of y, $S\ni y$ and μ, we have that $F_{u,S}(\mathbb{1}_y) = A_u(y+\mu)$ (since they form at least a $2^{-(d+1)}$ fraction of the type (2) constraints). Also with probability $1-\sqrt{\gamma}\cdot 2^{d+1}$ we have $F_{u,S}(\mathbb{1}_y) = A_u(y)$ (since these form a $2^{-(d+1)}$ fraction of the type (1) constraints). Thus, with probability at least $1-2^{d+2}\sqrt{\gamma}$, $A_u(y) = A_u(y+\mu)$. We then have that for $\tilde{A}_u$,

$$\mathop{\mathbb{P}}_{y,\mu}\left[\tilde{A}_u(y) = \tilde{A}_u(y+\mu)\right] \geq 1-2^{O(d)}\cdot\sqrt{\gamma},$$

and similarly for $\tilde{A}_v$. However, since $\tilde{A}_u$ and $\tilde{A}_v$ are degree-d polynomials and highly resistant to noise by the above, the following claim gives that they cannot have too many variables with non-zero influence.

CLAIM 3.5. *Let P be a degree-d polynomial over $\mathbb{F}_2^R$ with at least t variables having non-zero influence. Let y be uniform in $\{0,1\}^R$ and $\mu \sim_\eta \{0,1\}^R$. Then*

$$\mathop{\mathbb{P}}_{y,\mu}\left[P(y) = P(y+\mu)\right] \leq 1 - \frac{1}{2^{d+1}} + \frac{(1-2\eta)^{t/2^d}}{2^{d+1}}.$$

PROOF. Let the polynomial P have *exactly* t variables with non-zero influence. Let f denote the function $f(y) = (-1)^{P(y)}$. Note that

$$\begin{aligned}\mathop{\mathbb{P}}_{y,\mu}\left[P(y) = P(y+\mu)\right] &= \frac{1}{2} + \frac{1}{2}\cdot \mathop{\mathbb{E}}_{y,\mu}\left[f(y)f(y+\mu)\right]\\ &= \frac{1}{2} + \frac{1}{2}\cdot \sum_{\alpha\in\{0,1\}^R} (1-2\eta)^{|\alpha|}\hat{f}(\alpha)^2\end{aligned}$$

Since $\sum_\alpha (\hat{f}(\alpha))^2 = \mathbb{E}_y\left[f^2(y)\right] = 1$, we can think of these values as giving a distribution, say $\mathcal{D}$, on the vectors α. We want to upper bound the quantity $\mathbb{E}_{\alpha\sim\mathcal{D}}\left[(1-2\eta)^{|\alpha|}\right]$. We have by Claim 3.4 that

$$\begin{aligned}\sum_{i\in[R]} \mathsf{Inf}_i(f) &= \sum_{\alpha\in\{0,1\}^R} |\alpha|\cdot(\hat{f}(\alpha))^2\\ &= \mathop{\mathbb{E}}_{\alpha\sim\mathcal{D}}\left[|\alpha|\right] \geq \frac{t}{2^{d-1}}.\end{aligned}$$

On the other hand, we also know that since P (and hence f) has exactly t relevant variables, $\mathcal{D}$ is supported only on vectors α of size at most t. Thus, we have that $\mathbb{P}_{\alpha\sim\mathcal{D}}\left[|\alpha| \geq \frac{t}{2^d}\right] \geq \frac{1}{2^d}$. This gives the required bound as

$$\mathop{\mathbb{E}}_{\alpha\sim\mathcal{D}}\left[(1-2\eta)^{|\alpha|}\right] \leq \left(1 - \frac{1}{2^d}\right)\cdot 1 + \frac{1}{2^d}\cdot(1-2\eta)^{t/2^d}.$$

■

Thus, both $\tilde{A}_u$ and $\tilde{A}_v$ can have at most $t \leq \sqrt{\gamma}\cdot\frac{2^{O(d)}}{\eta}$ variables with non-zero influence.

We now consider constraints of type (3) which are satisfied with probability $1-\sqrt{\gamma}$.

CLAIM 3.6. *With probability $1 - 2^{O(d)}\sqrt{\gamma}$ over the choice of $y_1,\ldots,y_d \in \{0,1\}^{R_1}$ and $z \in \{0,1\}^{R_2}$, we have that*

$$\sum_{\substack{T\subseteq[d+1]\\ 1\leq|T|\leq d}} A_u\left(\sum_{i\in T} y_i\right) = A_v(z),$$

where we take $y_{d+1} = y_1 + \ldots + y_d + \pi^{-1}(z)$.

PROOF. The proof is virtually identical to that of Claim 3.3. Let S be a random set chosen by picking $y_1,\ldots,y_d \in \{0,1\}^{R_1}$ and $z \in \{0,1\}^{R_2}$ at random and taking $S = \{y_1,\ldots,y_d,y_{d+1}\}$ with $y_{d+1} = y_1+\ldots+y_d+\pi^{-1}(z)$. As in Claim 3.3, we have that the probability over the choice of S, that $F_{u,S}$ satisfies

$$\forall T\subseteq S, T\neq S\ F_{u,S}(\mathbb{1}_T) = A_u\left(\sum_{y\in T} y\right) \quad\text{and}$$

$$F_{u,S}(\mathbb{1}_S) = A_v(z)$$

is at least $1-\sqrt{\gamma}\cdot 2^{d+2}$. However, since $F_{u,S}$ is a degree d polynomial with $F_{u,S}(0) = 0$, we have that for any $S = \{y_1,\ldots,y_{d+1}\}$, $\sum_{T\subseteq S, T\neq\emptyset} F_{u,S}(\mathbb{1}_T) = 0$. Thus, with probability $1-\sqrt{\gamma}\cdot 2^{d+2}$ over the choice of S as above, we have that

$$\sum_{\substack{T\subseteq[d+1]\\ 1\leq|T|\leq d}} A_u\left(\sum_{i\in T} y_i\right) + A_v(z) = 0,$$

which proves the claim. ■

Note that we cannot simplify the left hand side in the above equation using Claim 3.3 since the $d+1$ elements $y_1,\ldots,y_{d+1}$ are not independent elements of $\{0,1\}^{R_1}$. However, we can replace A_u by $\tilde{A}_u$ and then simplify the LHS as it holds for *every* $y_1,\ldots,y_{d+1}$ that

$$\sum_{\substack{T\subseteq[d+1]\\ 1\leq|T|\leq d}} \tilde{A}_u\left(\sum_{i\in T} y_i\right) = \tilde{A}_u\left(\sum_{i=1}^{d+1} y_i\right).$$

However, $y_1+\ldots+y_{d+1} = \pi^{-1}(z)$. We then have with probability $1-2^{O(d)}\sqrt{\gamma}$ over the choice of $z\in\{0,1\}^{R_2}$ that

$$\tilde{A}_u(\pi^{-1}(z)) = \tilde{A}_v(z).$$

But $\tilde{A}_u(\pi^{-1}(z)) - \tilde{A}_v(z)$ is a degree-d polynomial in z. If $2^{O(d)}\sqrt{\gamma} \leq 2^{-d}$, then the above implies that the polynomial must be *always* 0 i.e.

$$\tilde{A}_u(\pi^{-1}(z)) = \tilde{A}_v(z) \quad \forall z\in\{0,1\}^{R_2}.$$

Thus, if $\mathsf{Inf}_i(\tilde{A}_v) > 0$ then $\exists j\in\pi^{-1}(i)$ such that $\mathsf{Inf}_j(\tilde{A}_u) > 0$. If we construct the unique polynomials $\tilde{A}_u$ and $\tilde{A}_v$ close to A_u and A_v and randomly pick the index of a variable with non-zero influence it gives a labeling satisfying the edge with probability $1/t$, where t is the maximum number of relevant variables in either of these polynomials. By Claim 3.5, t is at most $2^{O(d)}\sqrt{\gamma}/\eta$. This gives a labeling which in expectation satisfies $(1-3\sqrt{\gamma})\cdot\frac{1}{t} = 2^{-O(d)}\eta/\sqrt{\gamma}$ fraction of the constraints of the label cover instance. By choosing the parameter δ for the Label-Cover instance to be smaller than $\eta/2^{O(d)}$, we can conclude that if the Label-Cover instance we start from is such that at most δ-fraction of the constraints are satisfiable, then one cannot have degree-d polynomials satisfying $1-\gamma$ fraction of the constraints for Linear vs. Degree-d labeling, with $\gamma = 2^{-O(d)}$.

4. THE OUTER PCP

We will construct an outer PCP starting with an instance of Linear vs. Degree-d Label-Cover and performing (smooth) parallel repetition. Let $\Phi = (U,V,E)$ be an instance of Linear vs. Degree-d Label-Cover with parameters $\eta,\gamma > 0$. This can be equivalently thought of as a two-prover game in which the verifier picks a constraint indexed by (u,v,x) and sends u to the first prover and v to the second prover. We define the two-prover game corresponding to the outer PCP according to the following procedure:

- The verifier picks constraints $(u_1,v_1,x'_1),\ldots,(u_k,v_k,x'_k)\in\Phi$.
- The question sent to the first prover is $\mathbf{u} = (u_1,\ldots,u_k)$.
- The question sent to the second prover is $\mathbf{w} = (w_1,\ldots,w_k)$ where each $w_i = u_i$ with probability $1-\beta$ and v_i with probability β. Let $R_{\mathbf{w}} \stackrel{\text{def}}{=} \{i\in[k] : w_i = u_i\}$ and let $|\mathbf{w}|$ denote $|R_{\mathbf{w}}|$.

- The provers are required to respond with functions $F_{\mathbf{u}} : \{0,1\}^{(d+1)k} \rightarrow \{0,1\}$ and $G_{\mathbf{w}} : \{0,1\}^{(d+1)|\mathbf{w}|+(k-|\mathbf{w}|)} \rightarrow \{0,1\}$. We think of each input x to $F_{\mathbf{u}}$ as $x = (x_1, \ldots, x_k)$ where each $x_i \in \{0,1\}^{d+1}$. Similarly, we think of an input y to $G_{\mathbf{w}}$ as $y = (y_1, \ldots, y_k)$ where $y_i \in \{0,1\}^{d+1}$ if $i \in R_{\mathbf{w}}$ and $y_i \in \{0,1\}$ otherwise.

- Let $F_{\mathbf{u}}|_i$ denote the function on $d+1$ bits obtained by setting all inputs to $F_{\mathbf{u}}$ except the ith one to 0 i.e., $F_{\mathbf{u}}|_i(z) = F_{\mathbf{u}}(x_1, \ldots x_k)$ where $x_j = z$ if $j = i$ and $x_j = 0$ otherwise. Define $G_{\mathbf{w}}|_i$ similarly. The verifier accepts if the following conditions are satisfied:

$$F_{\mathbf{u}}|_i(z) = G_{\mathbf{w}}|_i(z) \qquad \forall i \in R_{\mathbf{w}}, \forall z \in \{0,1\}^{d+1}$$
$$F_{\mathbf{u}}|_i(x'_i) = G_{\mathbf{w}}|_i(1) + c_{u_i v_i, x'_i} \qquad \forall i \notin R_{\mathbf{w}}$$

where the inputs x'_i for $i \notin R_{\mathbf{w}}$ are picked initially as part of the constraints.

Let $\mathcal{G}(\Phi, k, \beta)$ denote the above two-prover game with parameters k, β, starting from an instance Φ of Linear vs. Degree-d Label-Cover. Let $\mathsf{Val}^{(l)}(\mathcal{G}(\Phi, k, \beta))$ denote the maximum acceptance probability of the verifier over the prover strategies where all the functions are degree-l polynomials.

Completeness

LEMMA 4.1. *Let the instance Φ of* Linear vs. Degree-d Label-Cover *be such that there exists a labeling $A : V \rightarrow \{0,1\}$ and linear functions $\{F_u\}_{u \in U}$ satisfying $1 - \eta$ fraction of the constraints. Then $\mathsf{Val}^{(1)}(\mathcal{G}(\Phi, k, \beta)) \geq 1 - k\eta$.*

PROOF. The provers define the functions $F_{\mathbf{u}}$ and $G_{\mathbf{w}}$ as

$$F_{\mathbf{u}}(x_1, \ldots, x_k) \stackrel{\text{def}}{=} F_{u_1}(x_1) + \ldots + F_{u_k}(x_k)$$
$$G_{\mathbf{w}}(y_1, \ldots, y_k) \stackrel{\text{def}}{=} \sum_{i \in R_{\mathbf{w}}} F_{u_i}(y_i) + \sum_{i \notin R_{\mathbf{w}}} y_i \cdot A(v_i).$$

By definition of the functions, for any pair of questions $(\mathbf{u}, \mathbf{w})$ generated by the verifier, the answers of the provers always satisfy $F_{\mathbf{u}}|_i(z) = G_{\mathbf{w}}|_i(z)$ for all $i \in R_{\mathbf{w}}, z \in \{0,1\}^{d+1}$. Moreover, with probability at least $1 - k\eta$ over the choice of the initial constraints $(u_1, v_1, x'_1), \ldots, (u_k, v_k, x'_k) \in \Phi$, it is true that for all $i \in [k]$, $F_{u_i}(x'_i) = A(v_i) + c_{u_i v_i, x'_i}$. Then the answers of the provers also satisfy $F_{\mathbf{u}}|_i(x'_i) = G_{\mathbf{w}}|_i(1) + c_{u_i v_i, x'_i}$ for all $i \notin R_{\mathbf{w}}$. ■

Soundness

LEMMA 4.2. *Let the instance Φ of* Linear vs. Degree-d Label-Cover *be such any labeling $A : V \rightarrow \{0,1\}$ and degree-d polynomials $\{F_u\}_{u \in U}$ satisfy at most $1 - \gamma$ fraction of the constraints. Then $\mathsf{Val}^{(d)}(\mathcal{G}(\Phi, k, \beta)) \leq (1 - \gamma^2)^{\Omega(\beta k)}$.*

PROOF. Let the prover strategy make the verifier accept with probability s. Note that constraints checked by the verifier are only on the polynomials obtained by setting all inputs except one (x_i for some $i \in [k]$) to zero. Thus, if $F_{\mathbf{u}}$ and $G_{\mathbf{w}}$ are a pair of degree-d polynomials which make the verifier accept, then so do the polynomials $F'_{\mathbf{u}}$ and $G'_{\mathbf{w}}$ obtained by dropping all the monomials involving bits from two different inputs x_i and x_j for $i \neq j$. Also, the constant terms in both $F_{\mathbf{u}}$ and $G_{\mathbf{w}}$ must be the same for the verifier to accept and we can drop these in $F'_{\mathbf{u}}$ and $G'_{\mathbf{w}}$.

For all $(x_1, \ldots, x_k)$ and $(y_1, \ldots, y_k)$, we can then write $F'_{\mathbf{u}}$ and $G'_{\mathbf{w}}$ as

$$F'_{\mathbf{u}}(x_1, \ldots, x_k) = F_{u_1}(x_1) + \ldots + F_{u_k}(x_k)$$
$$G'_{\mathbf{w}}(y_1, \ldots, y_k) = G_{w_1}(y_1) + \ldots + G_{w_k}(y_k),$$

where $F_{u_1}, \ldots, F_{u_k}$ and $G_{w_1}, \ldots, G_{w_k}$ are degree-d polynomials with $F_{u_i}(0) = G_{w_i}(0) = 0 \; \forall i$. Since the above pair is accepted by the verifier, it must be true that $F_{u_i} = G_{w_i}$ for $i \in R_{\mathbf{w}}$. Also, for $i \notin R_{\mathbf{w}}$, since G_{w_i} is a homogeneous function on a 1-bit input, it must be of the form $A(v_i) \cdot y_i$. Moreover, if v_i was chosen according to a constraint indexed by (u_i, v_i, x'_i), then $A(v_i)$ must satisfy $F_{u_i}(x'_i) = A(v_i) + c_{u_i v_i, x'_i}$.

Thus, the prover strategy also gives a strategy for game obtained by parallel repetition of Φ, when viewed as a two-prover game, which makes the verifier accept with probability s. However, as argued in [16], then we must have $s \leq (1 - \gamma^2)^{\Omega(\beta k)}$, which completes the proof. As in [16], we consider the set of *useful* coordinates, which are the coordinates $i \notin R_{\mathbf{w}}$. With probability at least $1 - 2^{-\Omega(\beta k)}$, the number of useful coordinates is at least $\beta k/2$. The repeated game restricted to questions with at least $\beta k/2$ useful coordinates is a convex combination of sub-games, in each of which the basic game corresponding to Φ is repeated at least $\beta k/2$ times. By Theorem 2.6, each such sub-game has value at most $(1 - \gamma^2)^{\Omega(\beta k)}$ and hence so does the game $\mathcal{G}(\Phi, k, \beta)$. ■

5. THE INNER PCP

The inner PCP we will simply use the Hypergraph Test with 7 queries as described by Samorodnitsky and Trevisan [22]. Given a function $f : \{0,1\}^m \rightarrow \{-1,1\}$, the test $\mathsf{HypergraphTest}(f)$ picks $x, y, z \in \{0,1\}^m$ at random and accepts if and only if

$$f(x+y) = f(x) \cdot f(y),$$
$$f(y+z) = f(y) \cdot f(z),$$
$$f(z+x) = f(z) \cdot f(x),$$
$$\text{and} \quad f(x+y+z) = f(x) \cdot f(y) \cdot f(z).$$

Let $s(f)$ denote the probability that $\mathsf{HypergraphTest}(f)$ accepts. We can write $s(f)$ as

$$s(f) = \mathop{\mathbb{E}}_{x,y,z}\left[\begin{array}{c}\left(\frac{1+f(x)f(y)f(x+y)}{2}\right)\left(\frac{1+f(y)f(z)f(y+z)}{2}\right) \\ \times\left(\frac{1+f(z)f(x)f(z+x)}{2}\right)\left(\frac{1+f(x)f(y)f(z)f(x+y+z)}{2}\right)\end{array}\right]$$

We can also write $s(f)$ as a multilinear polynomial in the values of f since $f(x)^2 = 1$ for $f : \{0,1\}^m \rightarrow \{-1,1\}$. We define $s(f)$ for a function f taking values in $[-1,1]$ to be the expectation of the corresponding multilinear polynomial. We will also need the following (well-known) concentration result for Lipschitz functions, which follows from Azuma's inequality:

LEMMA 5.1 (THEOREM 7.4.2 IN [2]). *Let $\mathbf{F} = \mathbf{F}(X_1, \ldots, X_N)$ be a function in random variables $X_1, \ldots, X_N$ taking value ± 1, which is C-Lipschitz in each of the variables i.e., for any $i \in [N]$, $x_1, \ldots, x_N \in \{-1,1\}$ and $x'_i \in \{-1,1\}$, $|\mathbf{F}(x_1, \ldots, x_i, \ldots, x_N) - \mathbf{F}(x_1, \ldots, x'_i, \ldots, x_N)| \leq C$.*

Then

$$\mathbb{P}[|\mathbf{F} - \mathbb{E}[\mathbf{F}]| > \gamma] \leq \exp\left(-\gamma^2/(2C^2N)\right).$$

The following is easy to prove using the results from [1].

LEMMA 5.2. *Let* $f : \{0,1\}^m \to [-1,1]$ *be such that* $s(f) > \frac{1}{8} - \frac{1}{320} + \varepsilon$. *Then,*

- *there exists* $\alpha \in \{0,1\}^m$ *such that* $\left|\hat{f}(\alpha)\right| \geq \frac{\varepsilon}{2}$, *or*
- *there exists a quadratic polynomial* $q : \{0,1\}^m \to \{0,1\}$ *such that* $\mathbb{E}_x\left[f(x)(-1)^{q(x)}\right] \geq \frac{9}{10} - \varepsilon$.

PROOF. We first argue that we can take f to be Boolean. Given an f as above, consider a random function $\tilde{f}$ such that for each $x \in \{0,1\}^m$, $\tilde{f}(x) = 1$ with probability $(1+f(x))/2$ and -1 with probability $(1-f(x))/2$. Thus, for each x, $\mathbb{E}\left[\tilde{f}(x)\right] = f(x)$.

The quantity $s(\tilde{f})$ is a degree-7 polynomial in the 2^m random variables $\left\{\tilde{f}(x)\right\}_{x\in\{0,1\}^m}$ with expectation $s(f)$ (since we wrote s as a multilinear polynomial in the values of f). Also, it is C-Lipschitz with $C = 7/2^n$. Thus, by Lemma 5.1, the probability that $\left|s(f) - s(\tilde{f})\right| > \varepsilon/4$ is at most $\exp(-\Omega_\varepsilon(2^m))$. Also, the correlation of $\tilde{f}$ with any quadratic polynomial q is $\mathbb{E}_x\left[\tilde{f}(x)(-1)^{q(x)}\right]$, which is a linear polynomial in the values of $\tilde{f}$, with expectation $\mathbb{E}_x\left[f(x)(-1)^{q(x)}\right]$. The probability that the correlation differs from it's expected value by more than $\varepsilon/2$ for *any* quadratic polynomial is at most $2^{m^2} \cdot \exp -\Omega_\varepsilon(2^m)$. Since the set of quadratic polynomials also includes all linear functions, this also gives that with high probability, all Fourier coefficients of $\tilde{f}$ are within an additive $\varepsilon/4$ of the corresponding Fourier coefficients of f. Thus, up to a change of an additive $\varepsilon/4$ in the correlations and the quantity $s(f)$, we can replace the function f by a "good" $\tilde{f}$. We this assume f takes values in $\{-1,1\}$ in the argument below.

Expanding the terms and changing variables to simply, we can re-write $s(f)$ as

$$\begin{aligned} s(f) &= \frac{1}{16} + \frac{7}{16}\cdot \mathop{\mathbb{E}}_{x,y}[f(x)f(y)f(x+y)] \\ &\quad + \frac{7}{16}\cdot \mathop{\mathbb{E}}_{x,y,z}[f(x)f(y)f(x+z)f(y+z)] \\ &\quad + \frac{1}{16}\cdot s^*(f) \\ &= \frac{1}{16} + \frac{7}{16}\sum_\alpha (\hat{f}(\alpha))^3 + \frac{7}{16}\sum_\alpha (\hat{f}(\alpha))^4 + \\ &\quad \frac{1}{16}\cdot s^*(f), \end{aligned}$$

where $s^*(f)$ denotes the term

$$\mathop{\mathbb{E}}_{x,y,z}[f(x)f(y)f(z)f(x+y)f(y+z)f(z+x)f(x+y+z)].$$

If $s(f) \geq \frac{1}{8} - \frac{1}{320} + \varepsilon$, then we must have $\sum_\alpha (\hat{f}(\alpha))^3 \geq \varepsilon$, $\sum_\alpha (\hat{f}(\alpha))^4 \geq \varepsilon$ or $s^*(f) > 1 - \frac{1}{20}$. The first two cases both imply

$$\begin{aligned} \max_\alpha \left|\hat{f}(\alpha)\right| &= \max_\alpha \left|\hat{f}(\alpha)\right| \cdot \sum_\alpha (\hat{f}(\alpha))^2 \\ &\geq \sum_\alpha \left|\hat{f}(\alpha)\right| \cdot (\hat{f}(\alpha))^2 \geq \varepsilon. \end{aligned}$$

On the other hand Alon et al. [1] show that for $f : \{0,1\}^m \to \{-1,1\}$, if $s^*(f) > 1 - \nu$ for $\nu \leq \frac{1}{20}$, then there exists a quadratic function $q : \{0,1\}^m \to \{0,1\}$ such that $\mathbb{E}_x\left[f(x)(-1)^{q(x)}\right] \geq 1 - 2\nu$. Using $\nu = 1/20$ and adjusting all correlations for the loss of $\varepsilon/4$ in passing from f to $\tilde{f}$ gives the required result. ■

6. THE COMPOSED PCP

We instantiate the outer PCP with $d = 2$. The final proof comprises of the tables of functions $\{G_{\mathbf{w}}\}_{\mathbf{w}\in(U\cup V)^k}$. The verifier chooses a random $\mathbf{u} \in U^k$ and performs $\mathsf{HypergraphTest}(\tilde{F}_{\mathbf{u}})$, where $\tilde{F}_{\mathbf{u}}$ is a *virtual* function described below. To query $\tilde{F}_{\mathbf{u}}$ on an input $x = (x_1, \ldots, x_k) \in \{0,1\}^{3k}$, the verifier generates a random $\mathbf{w} \in (U \cup V)^k$ and $y = (y_1, \ldots, y_k) \in \{0,1\}^{3|\mathbf{w}|+(k-|\mathbf{w}|)}$ and queries $G_{\mathbf{w}}(y)$. The tuple $\mathbf{w}$ is generated by taking $w_i = u_i$ for each $i \in R_{\mathbf{w}}$, generating a string $x'_i \in \{0,1\}^3$ for each $i \notin R_{\mathbf{w}}$ and taking w_i as $v_i \sim (u_i, x'_i)$, where this notation denotes taking a random constraint (u_i, v_i, x'_i) (with probability proportional to weights) involving the pair (u_i, x'_i) and choosing the corresponding v_i. Below we describe the distribution of $(\mathbf{w}, y, x')$ given an input x.

Suppose that we have already (randomly) chosen the set $R_{\mathbf{w}}$. Recall that the intended solution is

$$\begin{aligned} F_{\mathbf{u}}(x_1, \ldots, x_k) &\stackrel{\text{def}}{=} F_{u_1}(x_1) + \ldots + F_{u_k}(x_k) \\ G_{\mathbf{w}}(y_1, \ldots, y_k) &\stackrel{\text{def}}{=} \sum_{i\in R_{\mathbf{w}}} F_{u_i}(y_i) + \sum_{i\notin R_{\mathbf{w}}} y_i \cdot A(v_i), \end{aligned}$$

where $F_{u_1}, \ldots, F_{u_k}$ are polynomials with $F_{u_i}(0) = 0\ \forall i$. Thus, to obtain $F_{\mathbf{u}}$ from the function $G_{\mathbf{w}}$, we simply want to take $y_i = x_i$ if $i \in R_{\mathbf{w}}$. Also, for $i \notin R_{\mathbf{w}}$, $x_i \neq 000$ and $v_i \sim (u_i, x_i)$, $F_{u_i}(x_i)$ and $A(v_i)$ must be related as $F_{u_i}(x_i) = A(v_i) + c_{u_i v_i, x_i}$. Thus, if $i \notin R_{\mathbf{w}}$ and $x_i \neq 000$, the verifier must choose $x'_i = x_i$, $v_i \sim (u_i, x'_i)$ and $y_i = 1$. The contribution of the intended solution in the ith coordinate is then $A(v_i)$ and the verifier can add $c_{u_i v_i, x'_i}$ for this coordinate to obtain the (intended) contribution from the ith coordinate of $F_{\mathbf{u}}$.

However, when $i \notin R_{\mathbf{w}}$ and $x_i = 000$, the verifier has more freedom in choosing v_i. Suppose we choose *any* $x'_i \neq 000$ and $v_i \sim (u_i, x'_i)$ (recall that constraints (u_i, v_i, x'_i) are only defined for $x'_i \neq 000$). If y_i is chosen to be 0, then the contribution from the ith coordinate of $G_{\mathbf{w}}(y)$ is $y_i \cdot A(v_i) = 0$, and so is $F_{u_i}(0)$ for the intended solution. Thus, when $i \notin R_{\mathbf{w}}$ and $x_i = 000$, we take $y_i = 0$ and choose x'_i randomly from $\{0,1\}^3 \setminus \{000\}$. Note that this does *not* complete the description of the sampling process since $\mathbb{P}[i \in R_{\mathbf{w}} \mid x_i]$ might (and will) depend on the value of x_i.

From the above description, given the tuple $(\mathbf{w}, y, x')$, we can uniquely identify the input x i.e. there exists a map φ such that $\varphi(\mathbf{w}, y, x') = x$ given for the ith coordinate by

$$x_i = (\varphi(\mathbf{w}, y, x'))_i = \begin{cases} y_i & \text{if } i \in R_{\mathbf{w}} \\ x'_i & \text{if } i \notin R_{\mathbf{w}} \text{ and } y_i = 1 \\ 000 & \text{otherwise} \end{cases}$$

We will now define a distribution $\mathcal{D}_{\mathbf{u}}$ on the tuples $(\mathbf{w}, y, x')$ (for a fixed $\mathbf{u}$) such that y is uniformly distributed in $\{0,1\}^{3|\mathbf{w}|+(k-|\mathbf{w}|)}$ and $\varphi(\mathbf{w}, y, x')$ is close to the uniform distribution on $\{0,1\}^{3k}$. Given an input x, the verifier will simply sample a tuple $(\mathbf{w}, y, x')$ from $\mathcal{D}_{\mathbf{u}}$ conditioned on

$\varphi(\mathbf{w}, y, x') = x$. Given the tuple, the function $\tilde{F}_{\mathbf{u}}$ is taken to be

$$\tilde{F}_{\mathbf{u}}(x) = G_{\mathbf{w}}(y) + \sum_{i \notin R_{\mathbf{w}}} y_i \cdot c_{u_i v_i, x'_i}.$$

We now describe the distribution $\mathcal{D}_{\mathbf{u}}$. For a fixed $\mathbf{u} \in U^k$, we sample a tuple $(\mathbf{w}, y, x')$ according to $\mathcal{D}_{\mathbf{u}}$ by performing the following process for each $i \in [k]$:

- with probability $1 - \beta$, set $w_i = u_i$ and sample $y_i \in_R \{0,1\}^3$.
- with probability $\beta/2$, take $y_i = 1$, $x'_i \in_R \{0,1\}^3 \setminus \{000\}$ and $w_i = v_i \sim (u_i, x'_i)$.
- with probability $\beta/2$, take $y_i = 0$, $x'_i \in_R \{0,1\}^3 \setminus \{000\}$ and $w_i = v_i \sim (u_i, x'_i)$.

Let $\varphi(\mathcal{D}_{\mathbf{u}})$ denote the distribution on $\{0,1\}^{3k}$ obtained by sampling $(\mathbf{w}, y, x')$ according to $\mathcal{D}_{\mathbf{u}}$ and then computing $\varphi(\mathbf{w}, y, x')$. We show that it is very close to the uniform distribution on $\{0,1\}^{3k}$, denoted by $\mathcal{U}_{3k}$.

Claim 6.1. $\Delta(\varphi(\mathcal{D}_{\mathbf{u}}), \mathcal{U}_{3k}) = O(\beta\sqrt{k})$.

Proof. It is easy to see that $\varphi(\mathcal{D}_{\mathbf{u}})$ is also a product distribution. For each $i \in [k]$,

$$\mathop{\mathbb{P}}_{x \sim \mathcal{D}_{\mathbf{u}}}[x_i = 000] = \frac{1-\beta}{8} + \frac{\beta}{2} = \frac{1}{8} + \frac{3\beta}{8}$$

$$\mathop{\mathbb{P}}_{x \sim \mathcal{D}_{\mathbf{u}}}[x_i = b] = \frac{1-\beta}{8} + \frac{\beta}{2} \cdot \frac{1}{7} = \frac{1}{8} - \frac{3\beta}{56} \quad \forall b \neq 000.$$

Let $\mathcal{D}_i$ denote the distribution of x_i when x is sampled according to $\varphi(\mathcal{D}_{\mathbf{u}})$. By the above, we can bound the squared Hellinger distance of $\mathcal{D}_i$ and $\mathcal{U}_3$, the uniform distribution on 3 bits as

$$\begin{aligned} H^2(\mathcal{D}_i, \mathcal{U}_3) &= 1 - \sum_{b \in \{0,1\}^3} \sqrt{\frac{1}{8} \cdot \mathcal{D}_i(b)} \\ &= 1 - \sqrt{\frac{1}{8} \cdot \left(\frac{1}{8} + \frac{3\beta}{8}\right)} - 7\sqrt{\frac{1}{8} \cdot \left(\frac{1}{8} - \frac{3\beta}{56}\right)} \\ &= O(\beta^2). \end{aligned}$$

By multiplicativity of $1 - H^2(\cdot,\cdot)$ for product distributions, we get

$$1 - H^2(\varphi(\mathcal{D}_{\mathbf{u}}), \mathcal{U}_{3k}) \geq (1 - O(\beta^2))^k \geq 1 - O(\beta^2 k).$$

Finally, using the relationship between statistical and Hellinger distance gives

$$\Delta(\varphi(\mathcal{D}_{\mathbf{u}}), \mathcal{U}_{3k}) \leq \sqrt{2}H(\varphi(\mathcal{D}_{\mathbf{u}}), \mathcal{U}_{3k}) = O(\beta\sqrt{k})$$

as claimed. ■

It is also easy to observe that if $\mathbf{u}$ is chosen with probability proportional to the weight of constraints incident on it, then the distribution of the pair $(\mathbf{u}, \mathbf{w})$ is the same as in the outer PCP.

Claim 6.2. *Let $\mathbf{u} \in U^k$ be sampled with probability proportional to the weight of constraints (in the outer PCP) incident on it and let $(\mathbf{w}, y, x')$ be sampled according to $\mathcal{D}_{\mathbf{u}}$. Then the distribution of the pair $(\mathbf{u}, \mathbf{w})$ is the same as the questions of the verifier in $\mathcal{G}(\Phi, k, \beta)$.*

Proof. By definition of $\mathcal{D}_{\mathbf{u}}$, the distribution is a product distribution over the coordinates. It only remains to analyze the distribution of a pair of questions (u_i, w_i) in a single coordinate. With probability $1 - \beta$, $w_i = u_i$ and with probability β, $w_i = v_i \sim (u_i, x'_i)$ for a random x'_i i.e. it is a random constraint incident on u_i. This is exactly the same as the distribution of questions for the game $\mathcal{G}(\Phi, k, \beta)$. ■

We can now analyze the composed PCP.

6.1 Completeness

Lemma 6.3. *Let $\mathsf{Val}^{(1)}(\mathcal{G}(\Phi, k, \beta)) \geq 1 - \eta$. Then there exists a proof that the verifier accepts with probability at least $1 - 7\eta$.*

Proof. Let $\{F_{\mathbf{u}}\}_{\mathbf{u} \in U^k}$ and $\{G_{\mathbf{w}}\}_{\mathbf{w} \in (U \cup V)^k}$ be a family of linear functions which make the verifier in $\mathcal{G}(\Phi, k, \beta)$ accept with probability $1 - \eta$. Since any pair of functions $F_{\mathbf{u}}, G_{\mathbf{w}}$ satisfying the constraint corresponding to the pair of questions $(\mathbf{u}, \mathbf{w})$ must have the same constant term, we can assume that all the polynomials have constant term 0. We can then write the functions for each $\mathbf{u}$ and $\mathbf{w}$ as a sum of linear functions

$$\begin{aligned} F_{\mathbf{u}}(x_1, \ldots, x_k) &= F_{u_1}(x_1) + \ldots + F_{u_k}(x_k) \\ G_{\mathbf{w}}(y_1, \ldots, y_k) &= G_{w_1}(y_1) + \ldots + G_{w_k}(y_k). \end{aligned}$$

Let the proof for the final verifier consist of the tables $G_{\mathbf{w}}$ as above. By Claim 6.2, the distribution of the pairs $(\mathbf{u}, \mathbf{w})$ generated by the final verifier is the same as that in the game $\mathcal{G}(\Phi, k, \beta)$ and thus, for any x, $\mathbb{P}_{\mathbf{u},r}\left[F_{\mathbf{u}}(x) = \tilde{F}_{\mathbf{u}}(x)\right] \geq 1 - \eta$, where r is the randomness used in sampling a random $G_{\mathbf{w}}$ to read the value of $\tilde{F}_{\mathbf{u}}$. Recall that the verifier performs $\mathsf{HypergraphTest}(\tilde{F}_{\mathbf{u}})$ which reads the value of $\tilde{F}_{\mathbf{u}}$ on 7 inputs. By the above, we have that with probability at least $1 - 7\eta$, all the 7 values read by HypergraphTest agree with the function $F_{\mathbf{u}}$. However, if all 7 values read by HypergraphTest agree with $F_{\mathbf{u}}$, then the verifier will accept since $F_{\mathbf{u}}$ is linear. ■

6.2 Soundness

Lemma 6.4. *Let $\{G_{\mathbf{w}}\}_{\mathbf{w} \in (U \cup V)^k}$ be a proof that makes the verifier accept with probability at least $1/8 - 1/320 + \varepsilon$. Let $\mathcal{G}(\Phi, k, \beta)$ denote the game constructed by the outer verifier as before with β, k chosen so that $\beta\sqrt{k} = o(\varepsilon)$. Then $\mathsf{Val}^{(2)}(\mathcal{G}(\Phi, k, \beta)) \geq \varepsilon^6/2^{18}$.*

Proof. Let $s(f)$ be the expression for the probability of acceptance of HypergraphTest(f) as defined in Section 5. Let $\tilde{F}_{\mathbf{u}} : \{0,1\}^{3k} \to \{0,1\}$ be the (random) function queried by the verifier as above. Then,

$$\mathbb{P}[\text{Verifier accepts}] = \mathop{\mathbb{E}}_{\mathbf{u}}\left[s\left((-1)^{\tilde{F}_{\mathbf{u}}}\right)\right].$$

If r is the randomness used by the verifier in sampling $\tilde{F}_{\mathbf{u}}$, let $H_{\mathbf{u}}$ denote the real-valued function

$$\begin{aligned} H_{\mathbf{u}}(x) &= \mathop{\mathbb{E}}_{r}\left[(-1)^{\tilde{F}_{\mathbf{u}}(x)}\right] \\ &= \mathop{\mathbb{E}}_{(\mathbf{w}, y, x') | x}\left[(-1)^{G_{\mathbf{w}}(y) + \sum_{i \notin R_{\mathbf{w}}} y_i \cdot c_{u_i v_i, x'_i}}\right]. \end{aligned}$$

Since the verifier uses fresh randomness for sampling $\tilde{F}_{\mathbf{u}}(x)$ for each input x, we can re-write the acceptance probability of the verifier as

$$\mathbb{P}\,[\text{Verifier accepts}] \;=\; \mathop{\mathbb{E}}_{\mathbf{u}}\left[s\left(H_{\mathbf{u}}\right)\right].$$

Since the verifier accepts with probability $\frac{1}{8}-\frac{1}{320}+\varepsilon$, we have

$$\mathop{\mathbb{E}}_{\mathbf{u}}\left[s(H_{\mathbf{u}})\right] \geq \frac{1}{8}-\frac{1}{320}+\varepsilon$$
$$\Rightarrow \quad \mathop{\mathbb{P}}_{u}\left[s(H_{\mathbf{u}}) \geq \frac{1}{8}-\frac{1}{320}+\frac{\varepsilon}{2}\right] \geq \frac{\varepsilon}{2}$$

By Lemma 5.2, for each $\mathbf{u}$ with $s(H_{\mathbf{u}}) \geq \frac{1}{8}-\frac{1}{320}+\frac{\varepsilon}{2}$, either there exists an $\alpha_{\mathbf{u}} \in \{0,1\}^{3k}$ such that $\left|\hat{H}_{\mathbf{u}}(\alpha_{\mathbf{u}})\right| \geq \frac{\varepsilon}{4}$ or there exists a quadratic function $q_{\mathbf{u}}$ such that $\mathbb{E}_x\left[H_{\mathbf{u}}(x)(-1)^{q_{\mathbf{u}}(x)}\right] \geq \frac{9}{10}-\frac{\varepsilon}{2}$. Thus we have

$$\mathop{\mathbb{P}}_{\mathbf{u}}\left[\max_{\alpha}\left\{\left|\hat{H}_{\mathbf{u}}(\alpha)\right|\right\} \geq \frac{\varepsilon}{4}\right] \geq \frac{\varepsilon}{4} \quad \text{or}$$
$$\mathop{\mathbb{P}}_{\mathbf{u}}\left[\exists q_{\mathbf{u}} \text{ such that } \mathop{\mathbb{E}}_{x}\left[H_{\mathbf{u}}(x)(-1)^{q_{\mathbf{u}}(x)}\right] \geq \frac{9}{10}-\frac{\varepsilon}{2}\right] \geq \frac{\varepsilon}{4}.$$

We first consider the case that a significant fraction of the functions $H_{\mathbf{u}}$ have a large Fourier coefficient.

Claim 6.5. *Let* $\mathbb{P}_{\mathbf{u}}\left[\max_{\alpha}\left\{\left|\hat{H}_{\mathbf{u}}(\alpha)\right|\right\} \geq \frac{\varepsilon}{4}\right] \geq \frac{\varepsilon}{4}$. *Then* $\mathsf{Val}^{(1)}(\mathcal{G}(\Phi,k,\beta)) \geq \varepsilon^6/2^{18}$.

Proof. Let $\mathbf{u}$ be such that $\left|\hat{H}_{\mathbf{u}}(\alpha)\right| \geq \frac{\varepsilon}{4}$ for some $\alpha \in \{0,1\}^{3k}$. We will show that there exists a prover strategy which satisfies a significant fraction of constraints incident on all such $\mathbf{u}$. We give the argument for the case when $\hat{H}_{\mathbf{u}}(\alpha) \geq \frac{\varepsilon}{4}$. The argument for the case when the value is negative is identical. By assumption, we have

$$\mathop{\mathbb{E}}_{x\sim\mathcal{U}_{3k}}\left[H_{\mathbf{u}}(x)(-1)^{\alpha\cdot x}\right] \;\geq\; \frac{\varepsilon}{4}.$$

By Claim 6.1, the distribution $\mathcal{U}_{3k}$ is very close to the distribution $\varphi(\mathcal{D}_{\mathbf{u}})$. Hence, we also have

$$\mathop{\mathbb{E}}_{x\sim\varphi(\mathcal{D}_{\mathbf{u}})}\left[H_{\mathbf{u}}(x)(-1)^{\alpha\cdot x}\right] \;\geq\; \frac{\varepsilon}{4}-O(\beta\sqrt{k}) \;\geq\; \frac{\varepsilon}{8}$$

since $\beta\sqrt{k}=o(\varepsilon)$. Using the definition of the function $H_{\mathbf{u}}$ we have

$$\mathop{\mathbb{E}}_{\substack{x\sim\varphi(\mathcal{D}_{\mathbf{u}})\\(\mathbf{w},y,x')|x}}\left[(-1)^{G_{\mathbf{w}}(y)+\sum_{i\notin R_{\mathbf{w}}} y_i\cdot c_{u_iv_i,x_i'}+\alpha\cdot x}\right] \geq \frac{\varepsilon}{8},$$

which implies

$$\mathop{\mathbb{E}}_{(\mathbf{w},y,x')\sim\mathcal{D}_{\mathbf{u}}}\left[(-1)^{G_{\mathbf{w}}(y)+\sum_{i\notin R_{\mathbf{w}}} y_i\cdot c_{u_iv_i,x_i'}+\alpha\cdot\varphi(\mathbf{w},y,x')}\right] \geq \frac{\varepsilon}{8}$$

since sampling $x \sim \varphi(\mathcal{D}_{\mathbf{u}})$ and $(\mathbf{w},y,x')$ from $\mathcal{D}_{\mathbf{u}}$ conditioned on $\varphi(\mathbf{w},y,x')=x$ is the same as sampling the tuple $(\mathbf{w},y,x')$ from $\mathcal{D}_{\mathbf{u}}$ and taking $x=\varphi(\mathbf{w},y,x')$. The above gives that with probability at least $\varepsilon/16$ over the choice of $\mathbf{w}$ and x', we have that

$$\mathop{\mathbb{E}}_{y|(\mathbf{w},x')}\left[(-1)^{G_{\mathbf{w}}(y)+\sum_{i\notin R_{\mathbf{w}}} y_i\cdot c_{u_iv_i,x_i'}+\alpha\cdot\varphi(\mathbf{w},y,x')}\right] \geq \frac{\varepsilon}{16}.$$

Note that according to the distribution $\mathcal{D}_{\mathbf{u}}$, given the tuple $(\mathbf{w},x')$, y is distributed uniformly in $\{0,1\}^{3|\mathbf{w}|+(k-|\mathbf{w}|)}$.

We can now analyze the inner expression. We can write $\alpha\cdot\varphi(\mathbf{w},y,x')$ as $\sum_{i\in R_{\mathbf{w}}}\alpha_i\cdot(\varphi(\mathbf{w},y,x'))_i+\sum_{i\notin R_{\mathbf{w}}}\alpha_i\cdot(\varphi(\mathbf{w},y,x'))_i$ where α_i denotes the 3 bits of α in the positions $(3i-2,3i-1,3i)$ and $(\varphi(\mathbf{w},y,x'))_i$ denotes the corresponding 3 bits of $x=\varphi(\mathbf{w},y,x')$. For $i\in R_{\mathbf{w}}$, we have $x_i=y_i$. Also, for $i\notin R_{\mathbf{w}}$, $x_i=000$ if $y_i=0$ and x_i' if $y_i=1$. Thus, we can write $\alpha\cdot\varphi(\mathbf{w},y,x')$ as

$$\alpha\cdot\varphi(\mathbf{w},y,x') \;=\; \sum_{i\in R_{\mathbf{w}}}\alpha_i\cdot y_i+\sum_{i\notin R_{\mathbf{w}}} y_i\cdot(\alpha_i\cdot x_i').$$

Consider a pair $(\mathbf{w},x')$ for which the inner expectation is large. Grouping the terms in the expectation, we can re-write it as

$$\mathop{\mathbb{E}}_{y|(\mathbf{w},x')}\left[(-1)^{G_{\mathbf{w}}(y)+\sum_{i\notin R_{\mathbf{w}}} y_i\cdot(\alpha_i\cdot x_i'+c_{u_iv_i,x_i'})+\sum_{i\in R_{\mathbf{w}}} y_i\cdot\alpha_i}\right]$$

Since y is uniformly distributed, the above expression gives that $\mathbb{E}_y\left[(-1)^{G_{\mathbf{w}}(y)}(-1)^{\overline{\alpha}\cdot y}\right] \geq \frac{\varepsilon}{16}$ where $\overline{\alpha}\in\{0,1\}^{3|\mathbf{w}|+(k-|\mathbf{w}|)}$ is defined as

$$\overline{\alpha}_i \;=\; \begin{cases}\alpha_i & \text{for } i\in R_{\mathbf{w}}\\ \alpha_i\cdot x_i'+c_{u_iv_i,x_i'} & \text{for } i\notin R_{\mathbf{w}}\end{cases}$$

This implies that for a question pair $(\mathbf{u},\mathbf{w})$ if the first prover answers with the linear function $L_{\mathbf{u}}(x)=\alpha\cdot x$ and the second prover answers with the linear function $L_{\mathbf{w}}(x)=\overline{\alpha}\cdot y$, then their answers satisfy

$$L_{\mathbf{u}}|_i(z)=\alpha_i\cdot z=\overline{\alpha}_i\cdot z=L_{\mathbf{w}}|_i(z) \qquad \forall i\in R_{\mathbf{w}},\forall z\in\{0,1\}^3$$
$$L_{\mathbf{u}}|_i(x_i')=\alpha_i\cdot x_i'=\overline{\alpha}_i+c_{u_iv_i,x_i'}=L_{\mathbf{w}}|_i(1)+c_{u_iv_i,x_i'} \qquad \forall i\notin R_{\mathbf{w}}$$

which are all the constraints checked by the outer verifier. Thus, the strategy for the provers is simply as follows. Given a $\mathbf{u}$, the first prover gives a linear function $\alpha\cdot x$ for a random α such that $\left|\hat{H}_{\mathbf{u}}\right| \geq \frac{\varepsilon}{4}$. Similarly, given a $\mathbf{w}$, the second prover answers with the function $\overline{\alpha}\cdot y$ for a random $\overline{\alpha}$ such that $\mathbb{E}_y\left[(-1)^{G_{\mathbf{w}}(y)}(-1)^{\overline{\alpha}\cdot y}\right] \geq \frac{\varepsilon}{16}$. The probability that they choose a consistent pair $(\alpha,\overline{\alpha})$ is at least $\frac{\varepsilon^2}{16}\cdot\frac{\varepsilon^2}{256}=\frac{\varepsilon^4}{2^{12}}$. Thus, the probability that they make the outer verifier accept over the choice of the pair $(\mathbf{u},\mathbf{w})$ is at least $\frac{\varepsilon}{4}\cdot\frac{\varepsilon}{16}\cdot\frac{\varepsilon^4}{2^{12}}=\frac{\varepsilon^6}{2^{18}}$. ∎

The argument for the second case is almost identical.

Claim 6.6. *Let*

$$\mathop{\mathbb{P}}_{\mathbf{u}}\left[\exists q_{\mathbf{u}} \text{ such that } \mathop{\mathbb{E}}_{x}\left[H_{\mathbf{u}}(x)(-1)^{q_{\mathbf{u}}(x)}\right] \geq \frac{9}{10}-\frac{\varepsilon}{2}\right] \geq \frac{\varepsilon}{4}$$

Then $\mathsf{Val}^{(2)}(\mathcal{G},k,\beta) \geq \varepsilon^2/4$.

Proof. Let $\mathbf{u}$ be such that $\mathbb{E}_{x\sim\mathcal{U}_{3k}}\left[H_{\mathbf{u}}(x)(-1)^{q(x)}\right] \geq \frac{9}{10}-\frac{\varepsilon}{2}$ for some quadratic function q. As before, this gives

$$\mathop{\mathbb{E}}_{x\sim\varphi(\mathcal{D}_{\mathbf{u}})}\left[H_{\mathbf{u}}(x)(-1)^{q(x)}\right] \;\geq\; \frac{9}{10}-\varepsilon,$$

which implies that the expectation

$$\mathop{\mathbb{E}}_{(\mathbf{w},y,x')\sim\mathcal{D}_{\mathbf{u}}}\left[(-1)^{G_{\mathbf{w}}(y)+\sum_{i\notin R_{\mathbf{w}}} y_i\cdot c_{u_iv_i,x_i'}+q(\varphi(\mathbf{w},y,x'))}\right]$$

is at least $9/10 - \varepsilon$. Hence, we have that with probability at least ε over the choice of $\mathbf{w}$ and x',

$$\mathop{\mathbb{E}}_{y}\left[(-1)^{G_{\mathbf{w}}(y)+\sum_{i\notin R_{\mathbf{w}}} y_i \cdot c_{u_i v_i, x'_i} + q(\varphi(\mathbf{w},y,x'))}\right] \geq \frac{9}{10} - 2\varepsilon\,.$$

Now, given x', we can interpret $q(\varphi(\mathbf{w},y,x'))$ as a polynomial in y. Let $q' : \{0,1\}^{3|\mathbf{w}|+(k-|\mathbf{w}|)} \to \{0,1\}$ be the quadratic polynomial in y obtained as follows. Replace the 3 bits corresponding to the input x_i in q by the 3 bits corresponding to y_i for $i \in R_{\mathbf{w}}$. Also, for $i \notin R_{\mathbf{w}}$, let x_{i1}, x_{i2}, x_{i3} be the 3 bits corresponding to x_i. Replace them by $y_i x'_{i1}, y_i x'_{i2}, y_i x'_{i3}$ where $x'_{i1}, x'_{i2}, x'_{i3}$ are the 3 bits of x'_i.

Let $\overline{q}$ denote the polynomial $q' + \sum_{i\notin R_{\mathbf{w}}} y_i \cdot c_{u_i v_i, x'_i}$. It is easy to check that

$$q|_i(z) = \overline{q}|_i(z) \qquad \forall i \in R_{\mathbf{w}}, \forall z \in \{0,1\}^3$$
$$q|_i(x'_i) = q'|_i(1) = \overline{q}|_i(1) + c_{u_i v_i, x'_i} \qquad \forall i \notin R_{\mathbf{w}}\,.$$

Thus, in this case, given $\mathbf{u}$, the first prover answers with the *unique* quadratic polynomial q such that $\mathbb{E}_x\left[H_{\mathbf{u}}(x)(-1)^{q(x)}\right] \geq \frac{9}{10} - \varepsilon$, and the second prover, given $\mathbf{w}$, answers with the *unique* quadratic polynomial $\overline{q}$ such that $\mathbb{E}_y\left[(-1)^{G_{\mathbf{w}}(y)(-1)^{\overline{q}(y)}}\right] \geq \frac{9}{10} - 2\varepsilon$. If $\mathbf{u}, \mathbf{w}$ are as above, then q and $\overline{q}$ satisfy the required conditions and the verifier accepts. Hence, this strategy makes the verifier accept with probability at least $(\varepsilon/4) \cdot \varepsilon = \varepsilon^2/4$. ∎

Since $\mathsf{Val}^{(2)}(\mathcal{G}(\Phi,k,\beta)) \geq \mathsf{Val}^{(1)}(\mathcal{G}(\Phi,k,\beta))$, we have $\mathsf{Val}^{(2)}(\mathcal{G}(\Phi,k,\beta)) \geq \varepsilon^6/2^{18}$ in both cases. ∎

6.3 Choice of Parameters

We require that $\beta\sqrt{k} = o(\varepsilon)$ and the soundness of the outer PCP, which is $(1-\gamma^2)^{\Omega(\beta k)}$ is less than $\varepsilon^6/2^{18}$. Since we are working with $d = 2$, we have $\gamma = \Omega(1)$ and so this means that we require $\beta k = \Omega(\log(1/\varepsilon))$. Choosing $k = \Omega((1/\varepsilon^3) \cdot \log^2(1/\varepsilon))$ and $\beta = O(\varepsilon^3/\log(1/\varepsilon))$ meets both these conditions. Finally, we choose the parameter η for the Linear vs. Degree-d Label-Cover problem to be $O(\varepsilon/k)$ so that the completeness of the composed PCP is $1-\varepsilon$.

7. PARALLEL REPETITION OF LINEAR VS. DEGREE-D PCPS

Let Φ be an instance of Linear vs. Degree-d Label-Cover as defined in Definition 2.7. Consider a new instance of Linear vs. Degree-d Label-Cover defined by the following two-prover game:

- The verifier picks constraints $(u_1, v_1, x'_1), \ldots, (u_k, v_k, x'_k) \in \Phi$.
- The question sent to the first prover is $\mathbf{u} = (u_1, \ldots, u_k)$.
- The question sent to the second prover is $\mathbf{v} = (v_1, \ldots, v_k)$.
- The first prover is required to respond with a degree-d polynomial $F_{\mathbf{u}} : \{0,1\}^{(d+1)k} \to \{0,1\}$ and the second prover responds with a bit $A(\mathbf{v}) \in \{0,1\}$. The verifier accepts if

$$F_{\mathbf{u}}(x'_1, \ldots, x'_k) = A(\mathbf{v}) + c_{u_1 v_1, x'_1} + \ldots + c_{u_k v_k, x'_k}\,.$$

Note that the label for $\mathbf{u} = (u_1, \ldots, u_k)$ is now a single polynomial, which is supposed to be the XOR of the polynomials $F_{u_1}, \ldots, F_{u_k}$. Similarly, the label for $\mathbf{v}$ is supposed to be the XOR of $A(v_1), \ldots, A(v_k)$.

It is natural to ask that if any degree-d labeling can satisfy (say) at most $s = 1 - 2^{-O(d)}$ fraction of constraints in Φ, then does the fraction of constraints satisfiable in the new instance obtained above decrease to $1/2 + \exp(-\Omega_s(r))$. Note that since the first prover is required to prove a single polynomial $F_{\mathbf{u}}$ in $(d+1)k$ variables, which might involve cross-terms between the inputs $x_1, \ldots, x_k$, the above does not follow from known results on parallel repetition.

If it is indeed possible to reduce the soundness of the Linear vs. Degree-d Label-Cover label cover to a value arbitrarily close to $1/2$ as above, then one can in fact avoid the complication of going through the smoothed parallel repetition approach in the outer PCP. In our current proof, both provers are required to decode a degree-2 polynomial in a way that the polynomial of the second prover is a projection of the polynomial of the first prover. We are unable to do this unless there is only a unique choice of the quadratic polynomial for each prover.

However, using the above instance of Linear vs. Degree-d Label-Cover, one can instead apply the HLT directly the functions $F_{\mathbf{u}}$ by only reading the corresponding values for $A(\mathbf{v})$. Then, if the table of values $A(\mathbf{v})$ satisfies the verifier in the composed PCP with probability more than $1/16$, the first prover can find functions $F_{\mathbf{u}}$ which are polynomials of degree at most 2 (by using the table $A(\mathbf{v})$), which satisfy significantly more than half of the constraints in the instance above. We omit the details of the analysis.

We believe that if the parallel repetition as above can indeed be used to reduce the soundness even for degree-d labeling then an appropriate modification of our PCP might even give an alternate proof of the soundness guarantee of $2^{-(2^{d+1}-(d+1)-1)}$ with $2^{d+1}-1$ queries.

8. REFERENCES

[1] N. Alon, T. Kaufman, M. Krivelevich, S. Litsyn, and D. Ron. Testing Reed-Muller codes. *IEEE Transactions on Information Theory*, 51(11):4032–4039, 2005.

[2] N. Alon and J. Spencer. *The Probabilistic Method.* Wiley, 2008.

[3] S. Arora, C. Lund, R. Motawani, M. Sudan, and M. Szegedy. Proof verification and the hardness of approximation problems. *Journal of the ACM*, 45(3):501–555, 1998.

[4] S. Arora and S. Safra. Probabilistic checking of proofs : A new characterization of NP. *Journal of the ACM*, 45(1):70–122, 1998.

[5] M. Blum, M. Luby, and R. Rubinfeld. Self-testing/correcting with applications to numerical problems. *J. Comput. Syst. Sci.*, 47(3):549–595, 1993.

[6] S. O. Chan. Inapproximability of Abelain subgroup CSPs vis direct sum. Manuscript, 2012.

[7] M. Charikar, K. Makarychev, and Y. Makarychev. Near-optimal algorithms for unique games. In *Proc. ACM Symposium on the Theory of Computing*, pages 205–214, 2006.

[8] L. Engebretsen and J. Holmerin. More efficient queries in pcps for np and improved approximation hardness

of maximum csp. *Random Struct. Algorithms*, 33(4):497–514, 2008.

[9] U. Feige, S. Goldwasser, L. Lovász, S. Safra, and M. Szegedy. Interactive proofs and the hardness of approximating cliques. *Journal of the ACM*, 43(2):268–292, 1996.

[10] J. Hastad. Clique is hard to approximate within $n^{1-\varepsilon}$. *Acta Mathematica*, 182:105–142, 1999.

[11] J. Hastad. Some optimal inapproximability results. *Journal of ACM*, 48:798–859, 2001.

[12] J. Hastad and A. Wigderson. Simple analysis of graph tests for linearity and PCP. In *Proc. 16th IEEE Conference on Computational Complexity*, 2001.

[13] T. Holenstein. Parallel repetition: simplifications and the no-signaling case. In *Proc. ACM Symposium on the Theory of Computing*, pages 411–419, 2007.

[14] S. Khot. On the power of unique 2-prover 1-round games. In *Proc. 34th ACM Symposium on Theory of Computing*, 2002.

[15] S. Khot, G. Kindler, E. Mossel, and R. O'Donnell. Optimal inapproximability results for MAX-CUT and other 2-variable CSPs? *SIAM J. Comput.*, 37(1):319–357, 2007.

[16] S. Khot and M. Safra. A two prover one round game with strong soundness. In *Proceedings of the 52nd IEEE Symposium on Foundations of Computer Science*, pages 648–657, 2011.

[17] E. Mossel, R. O'Donnell, and K. Oleszkiewicz. Noise stability of functions with low influences: invariance and optimality. In *Proc. 46th IEEE Symposium on Foundations of Computer Science*, pages 21–30, 2005.

[18] A. Rao. Parallel repetition in projection games and a concentration bound. In *Proc. ACM Symposium on the Theory of Computing*, pages 1–10, 2008.

[19] R. Raz. A parallel repetition theorem. *SIAM J. of Computing*, 27(3):763–803, 1998.

[20] A. Samorodnitsky. Low-degree tests at large distances. In *Proceedings of the 39th ACM Symposium on Theory of Computing*, pages 506–515, 2007.

[21] A. Samorodnitsky and L. Trevisan. A PCP characterization of NP with optimal amortized query complexity. In *Proc. 32nd ACM Symposium on Theory of Computing*, pages 191–199, 2000.

[22] A. Samorodnitsky and L. Trevisan. Gowers uniformity, influence of variables, and PCPs. In *Proc. 38th ACM Symposium on Theory of Computing*, 2006.

A Characterization of Approximation Resistance for Even k-Partite CSPs

Per Austrin*
Aalto Science Institute and
KTH Royal Institute of Technology
austrin@kth.se

Subhash Khot†
New York University and
University of Chicago
khot@cims.nyu.edu

ABSTRACT

A constraint satisfaction problem (CSP) is said to be *approximation resistant* if it is hard to approximate better than the trivial algorithm which picks a uniformly random assignment. Assuming the Unique Games Conjecture, we give a characterization of approximation resistance for k-partite CSPs defined by an even predicate.

Categories and Subject Descriptors

F.2.0 [**Theory of Computation**]: Analysis of Algorithms and Problem Complexity

General Terms

Theory

Keywords

approximation resistance, unique games conjecture

1. INTRODUCTION

In the past 20 years, there has been a significant amount of work done on understanding the approximability of various *constraint satisfaction problems* (CSPs).

For the purposes of this paper, a CSP is defined by a k-ary predicate $P : \{-1, 1\}^k \to \{0, 1\}$ over a Boolean alphabet.[1] An instance consists of a set of *constraints*, each of which dictates that P applied to some list of k literals should be satisfied (a literal is a variable or the negation of a variable). The objective is to find an assignment to the variables so as to maximize the number of satisfied constraints. Two well-known examples are MAX k-SAT (where P is the disjunction of the k input bits) and MAX k-LIN (where P is the parity of the k input bits).

Essentially every MAX CSP is NP-hard (the exception being when P only depends on one of its input bits). In terms of approximability, it is easy to see that choosing a uniformly random assignment to the variables, without even looking at the instance, yields an approximation ratio of $|P^{-1}(1)|/2^k$, where $|P^{-1}(1)|$ is the number of inputs in $\{-1, 1\}^k$ that satisfy P.

Improving upon this trivial algorithm turns out to be surprisingly difficult. In a groundbreaking paper, Goemans and Williamson [GW95] used semidefinite programming (SDP) to give improved approximation algorithms for MAX 2-SAT and MAX 2-LIN. SDP was soon used to give better approximation algorithms for many other problems as well, but for some CSPs, perhaps most prominently MAX 3-SAT and MAX 3-LIN, no improvement over the random assignment algorithm was found. Then, in a new breakthrough, Håstad [Hås01] showed that such an improvement would not be possible: approximating MAX 3-SAT within $7/8 + \epsilon$ or MAX 3-LIN within $1/2 + \epsilon$ for some $\epsilon > 0$ is NP-hard. In other words, MAX 3-SAT and MAX 3-LIN have the remarkable property that the completely mindless random assignment algorithm is optimal!

CSPs which have this property – that they are NP-hard to approximate within $|P^{-1}(1)|/2^k + \epsilon$ – are called *approximation resistant.* Following Håstad's initial result, many more CSPs have been shown to be approximation resistant [GLST98, ST00, EH08, Has05]. Fairly quickly, a complete characterization of approximation resistance for predicates of arity three was found: $P : \{-1, 1\}^3 \to \{0, 1\}$ is approximation resistant if and only if P accepts all inputs of odd parity, or if it accepts all inputs of even parity [Hås01, Zwi98].

However, the next small case, predicates of arity 4, is still not completely classified, and it is not at all clear whether there is a nice, clean characterization. We would like to emphasize that by a characterization we mean a necessary and sufficient condition. Modulo symmetries, there are 400 non-constant predicates of arity 4. Hast [Has05] showed 275 of these to be approximable, 79 of them to be approximation resistant, and left the status of the remaining 46 open.

In recent years, progress has been made on our understanding of approximation resistance under the assumption of the *Unique Games Conjecture* (UGC) [Kho02]. The first

*Work done while at the University of Toronto. Supported by NSERC.

†Research supported by NSF Expeditions grant CCF-0832795, NSF Waterman Award and BSF grant 2008059.

[1] As is common, the input bits are written in the $\{-1, 1\}$ notation with -1 interpreted as logical True and 1 as logical False. Also "parity" corresponds to taking product of the bits: odd parity means the product is -1 and even parity means the product is 1.

ITCS'13, January 9–12, 2013, Berkeley, California, USA.

author and Mossel [AM09] proved that assuming the UGC, P is approximation resistant if there exists an unbiased pairwise independent distribution over $\{-1,1\}^k$ supported on $P^{-1}(1)$. Using this condition, it can be shown that as $k \to \infty$, an overwhelming fraction of all predicates are in fact approximation resistant [AH11]. A somewhat more (complicated and) general sufficient condition is known [AH12]. As in [AM09], this condition is in terms of the biases and pairwise correlations of distributions supported on P. At this point, it seems unlikely that there is a clean characterization (necessary and sufficient), but one can hope that approximation resistance is at least decidable.

Relevant here is the work of Raghavendra [Rag08], which shows assuming the UGC that for any CSP, its approximability threshold is determined by the integrality gap of a natural SDP relaxation for the problem. Furthermore, Raghavendra and Steurer [RS09] show that this integrality gap can be approximated to within an additive error ϵ (in time doubly exponential in ϵ).

This "almost" shows that it is decidable to determine whether a CSP is approximation resistant. However, as we have no a priori bound on the error ϵ needed, it only shows that it is recursively enumerable to determine whether a CSP is approximable. Note that, for every k there is a smallest gap ϵ_k such that any approximable predicate P on k bits can be approximated within at least $|P^{-1}(1)|/2^k + \epsilon_k$. If this number ϵ_k can be computed, approximation resistance would be decidable, but it is possible (though seemingly unlikely) that ϵ_k tends to 0 faster than any computable function.

1.1 Our Contribution

The strength of [Rag08], namely that it works in a blackbox fashion for any CSP, is in some sense a weakness in this setting, as it is not explicit and does not give any insight into what structural properties cause a predicate to be approximation resistant. In this paper, we make progress towards an explicit characterization of approximation resistance. We restrict the class of CSPs we study in two ways.

1. We only consider *k-partite* instances. In a k-partite instance, the variables are grouped into k layers, and in each constraint, the literal passed as the i'th argument to P comes from the i'th layer.

2. We only consider P which are *even*. P is even if $P(x) = P(-x)$ for every $x \in \{-1,1\}^k$, where $-x$ denotes bitwise negation of x.

We refer to this as the MAX PARTCSP(P) problem. Our main contribution is an explicit necessary and sufficient characterization (assuming the UGC) of when MAX PARTCSP(P) is approximation resistant. As in the case of [AM09] and its generalizations, our condition is based on the existence of certain distributions μ over the set of satisfying assignments of P and furthermore the conditions on these distributions depend only on their pairwise correlations $\mathbb{E}_\mu[x_i x_j]$.

In order to properly state the characterization, we need to make a few definitions.

DEFINITION 1.1. *Let $G = (S, E)$ be a multigraph with vertex set $S \subseteq [k]$ and no self-loops. For a correlation matrix $\rho \in \mathbb{R}^{k\times k}$ we define $\rho(G) = \prod_{ij\in E} \rho_{ij}$. For a distribution Λ over $k \times k$ correlation matrices we define $\Lambda(G) = \mathbb{E}_{\rho\in\Lambda}[\rho(G)]$.*

The key part of our definition is the existence of distributions Λ over correlation matrices each of which arises from a distribution over $P^{-1}(1)$ – we refer to these as P-supported correlation matrices – such that $\Lambda(G)$ vanishes on certain graphs. Specifically:

DEFINITION 1.2. *Let Λ be a distribution over $k \times k$ correlation matrices. We say that Λ is m-vanishing on P if:*

1. *Λ is a distribution over P-supported correlation matrices.*

2. *For every $S \subseteq [k]$ such that $\hat{P}(S) \neq 0$, and every odd-degree multigraph G on S with at most m edges, it holds that $\Lambda(G) = 0$.*

Here $\hat{P}(S)$ denotes the Fourier coefficient of the predicate P on the set S (i.e. the coefficient of the monomial $\prod_{i\in S} x_i$ when P is written as a multi-linear polynomial). Now we can state our main result.

THEOREM 1.3. *Assuming the UGC, MAX PARTCSP(P) is approximation resistant if and only if for every positive integer m there exists a distribution Λ which is m-vanishing on P.*

Note that if there is a pairwise independent distribution supported on P, i.e., if the identity matrix is P-supported, then taking Λ to be the singleton distribution on the identity matrix is m-vanishing on P for every m. As such, this characterization generalizes the sufficient condition of [AM09].

Given m and P, it is fairly easy to prove that the existence of an m-vanishing Λ on P is decidable. Hence the condition of Theorem 1.3 is recursively enumerable. We feel that this characterization is promising with respect to decidability. For instance, it is quite possible that one can show some explicit upper bound on the largest value of m that one needs to check, which would immediately give decidability. We also remark that, even though we do not prove it here, the characterization in Theorem 1.3 is equivalent to saying that there is a distribution Λ which is m-vanishing on P for all m simultaneously.

1.2 Proof Ideas

We now briefly and informally outline the main ideas of the proof of Theorem 1.3.

Algorithm.

Suppose there is no m-vanishing distribution Λ for some m. By LP duality, there are then constants $\{\gamma_G\}$ such that $\sum_G \gamma_G \rho(G) > \delta$ for all P-supported ρ, where the sum is over all odd-degree G on at most m edges. Now, assume we are given a solution to the basic SDP relaxation for MAX PARTCSP(P) with value 1 (in reality it will only have value close to 1 but this is just a small technicality). Then for each constraint we have a local distribution μ and since the SDP value is 1 its correlation matrix ρ is P-supported. The basic idea is, very loosely, to design a rounding algorithm which, given some graph G, finds an assignment with value $|P^{-1}(1)|/2^k + \rho(G)$. Picking a random G with probability proportional to $|\gamma_G|$ then gives an assignment with value $|P^{-1}(1)|/2^k + \Omega(\delta)$.

To get an assignment with value $|P^{-1}(1)|/2^k + \rho(G)$, the idea is to do as follows. For simplicity, suppose $V(G) = [k]$

and consider the monomial $\prod_{i=1}^{k} x_i$. We can construct the solution iteratively edge by edge, as follows. Initially, set all $x_i = 1$ (corresponding to the empty graph). Then, for an edge $e = (i, j)$, pick a standard Gaussian vector $\mathbf{g}_e$, and multiply x_i (resp. x_j) by $\langle \mathbf{g}_e, \mathbf{v}_i \rangle$ (resp. $\langle \mathbf{g}_e, \mathbf{v}_j \rangle$), where $\mathbf{v}_i$ and $\mathbf{v}_j$ are the vectors in the SDP solution corresponding to x_i and x_j. This operation has the effect of multiplying $\mathbb{E}[\prod_{i\in[k]} x_i]$ by a factor $\langle \mathbf{v}_i, \mathbf{v}_j \rangle = \rho_{ij}$ where ρ_{ij} is the correlation between i and j in the local distribution on $x_1, \ldots, x_k$. Repeating this for all edges of the graph, we get $\mathbb{E}[\prod_{i\in[k]} x_i] = \rho(G)$, and we can make sure that all other non-constant monomials have expectation 0, meaning that we get an advantage of $\rho(G)$ over $|P^{-1}(1)|/2^k + \rho(G)$.

To wrap this up and get the formal proof, there are som additional technicalities to account for: the values assigned by the above rounding are not Boolean-valued, we need to deal with negated literals, and we need to take the magnitude of the Fourier coefficients $\hat{P}(S)$ of P into consideration. The formalization of the "monomial rounding" described above is given in Lemma 4.1 in Section 4.1 and its use to give a non-trivial algorithm for MAX PARTCSP(P) is then described in Section 4.3.

Hardness.

As is by now standard, the task of proving hardness boils down to constructing a *dictatorship test* using the predicate P. The dictatorship test gets oracle access to k functions $f_1, \ldots, f_k : \{-1, 1\}^n \to \{-1, 1\}$, and the question is whether $f_1 = f_2 = \ldots = f_k$ are all equal to some dictatorship function. The test operates by picking k inputs $x_1, \ldots, x_k$ and then accepts iff $P(f_1(x_1), f_2(x_2), \ldots, f_k(x_k)) = 1$. The restriction to only using P as the acceptance predicate is what gives us hardness for MAX CSP(P) rather than an arbitrary CSP, and the restriction that we have k different functions and make one query to each, instead of a single function, is precisely what gives us hardness for MAX PARTCSP(P) instead of MAX CSP(P).

Such a test is completely specified by the distribution of $(x_1, \ldots, x_k)$. To specify this we choose some very large m and use the m-vanishing distribution Λ guaranteed to exist. To sample $(x_1, \ldots, x_k)$, we do as follows: first sample a P-supported correlation matrix ρ according to Λ, and let μ be some P-supported distribution with correlation matrix ρ. Then, for each $i \in [n]$ we sample the i'th coordinate $(x_1^i, \ldots, x_k^i)$ independently from μ. The completeness of the test follows by μ being P-supported. The soundness follows using the invariance principle: first, we show that if the functions $f_1, \ldots, f_k$ have low influence the acceptance probability (appropriately arithmetized) can be well approximated by a multilinear polynomial in Gaussian variables with the same second moments as x. Since higher moments of Gaussian variables are determined by their covariance matrix, this multilinear polynomial (and therefore also the acceptance probability) can be expressed as a function of the covariance matrix, i.e., ρ, and it turns out that all terms except for the constant $|P^{-1}(1)|/2^k$ are of the form $\rho(G)$ for some odd-degree graph G on less than m edges. Hence taking the expectation over $\rho \sim \Lambda$, all non-constant terms vanish.

Source of the various restrictions.

It may be instructive to point out where the various restrictions we impose come into play.

k-partiteness. The fact that we know for each variable what "role" it will play is critical in allowing us to obtain the algorithm. In particular, in the "monomial rounding" described above, it is important that any given variable corresponds to some given vertex of the graph G that we are using (the vertices of G correspond to layers of the CSP instance). If a vertex could appear as several different vertices of G (i.e., in several different layers), it is not clear how to round it in such a way that the different occurences don't interfere with each other.

Even predicates. This restriction is in some sense minor and more technical in nature. It allows us to assume that the distributions μ supported on $P^{-1}(1)$ are unbiased, which simplies may arguments. That said, it is not clear exactly how to generalize the present characterization to a general P.

Odd-degree graphs. The reason why the characterization only involves odd-degree graphs is essentially the presence of negated literals. First, in the algorithm it turns out that it is *necessary* for the graphs to be odd-degree, as this essentially ensures that we don't have cancellations when dealing with negated literals. Second, in the hardness result it turns out that it is *sufficient* for the graphs to have odd-degree, because the functions f_i we are testing can be assumed to be odd by the standard technique of folding, which is implemented by introducing negated literals.

1.3 Discussion

On the unnecessity of pairwise independence.

It is known that there are approximation resistant predicates which do not support a pairwise independent distribution. A basic such example is the predicate $GLST$: $\{-1, 1\}^4 \to \{0, 1\}$ defined by

$$GLST(x_1, x_2, x_3, x_4) = \begin{cases} x_2 \neq x_3 & \text{if } x_1 = -1 \\ x_2 \neq x_4 & \text{if } x_1 = 1 \end{cases}.$$

This predicate was shown to be approximation resistant by Guruswami et al. [GLST98], but there is no pairwise independent distribution supported on its accepting assignments – indeed it is not difficult to check that $x_2x_3 + x_2x_4 + x_3x_4 < 0$ for all accepting inputs. In [AH12], Theorem VIII.6, a generalization of the pairwise independence condition was given which also covers the $GLST$ predicate and in fact as far as we are aware cover all currently known examples of approximation resistant predicates.

The condition of Theorem 1.3 *essentially* generalizes the condition of [AH12]. We say "essentially" because Theorem VIII.6 of [AH12] in some cases allows for a condition referred to as $\{i, j\}$-negativity, and it is not clear that this condition is captured by Theorem 1.3. The only example given in [AH12] using the $\{i, j\}$-negativity condition is not an even predicate, so it is possible that this is a distinction between even P and general P. On the other hand, it appears that for the example given in [AH12], one can prove approximation resistance without using $\{i, j\}$-negativity so it is not completely clear whether allowing this adds any new predicates. Another possibility is that this is a distinction between MAX CSP(P) and MAX PARTCSP(P), because the proof in [AH12] that $\{i,j\}$-negativity suffices does not extend to partite instances. In short, the situation is a bit of a mystery and may warrant further study.

On Max PartCSP(P) *vis-à-vis* Max CSP(P).

It is not known whether Max PartCSP(P) behaves differently from Max CSP(P) with respect to approximation resistance. Almost all proofs of approximation resistance for Max CSP(P), including NP-hardness results such as [Hås01, EH08], can be adjusted to produce k-partite instances, thereby also showing approximation resistance for Max PartCSP(P).

However, one exception is the general result of Raghavendra [Rag08], where it is not at all clear how to achieve this. If it were the case that the reduction of [Rag08] can be adjusted to produce partite instances, our restriction to k-partite instances would have been without loss of generality (assuming the UGC), but as matters stand, this can not be deduced.

Another exception is the hardness derived in [AH12] from the $\{i,j\}$-negativity condition mentioned above.

1.4 Outline

In Section 2 we introduce notation and terminology used throughout the paper and state some known theorems that we need. In Section 3 we describe how to decide whether an m-vanishing distribution exists. We then proceed to prove Theorem 1.3, giving an algorithm in Section 4 and proving hardness in Section 5.

2. NOTATION AND DEFINITIONS

As is common, for convenience of notation we use $\{-1,1\}$ for Boolean values rather than $\{0,1\}$. Throughout, P denotes a k-ary predicate $P:\{-1,1\}^k \to \{0,1\}$ which we assume to be *even*, i.e., $P(x)=P(-x)$ for all x.

We say a distribution μ over $\{-1,1\}^k$ is *P-supported* if $\text{supp}(\mu) \subseteq P^{-1}(1)$. Similarly a correlation matrix $\rho \in \mathbb{R}^{k\times k}$ is P-supported if there is a P-supported μ such that $\rho_{ij} = \mathbb{E}_\mu[x_i x_j]$ for all i,j. Note that since P is even, any P-supported distribution can without loss of generality be assumed to be *unbiased*, i.e., satisfying $\mathbb{E}_\mu[x_i]=0$ for all i, as far as its correlation matrix is concerned (since we can spread the probability mass equally on any pair of assignments x and $-x$ without affecting the correlation matrix).

For the purposes of this paper, a *multigraph* is a graph G which may have multiple edges but no self-loops. A multigraph has *odd degree* if every vertex of the graph has odd degree (when edges are counted with multiplicities). A key role in our characterization is played by multigraphs G whose vertex set is some subset $S \subseteq [k]$, we refer to this as a *multigraph on S*.

We write S^n for the n-dimensional unit sphere (i.e., the set of unit vectors in $\mathbb{R}^{n+1}$, and for two vectors $\mathbf{u},\mathbf{v} \in \mathbb{R}^n$ we write $\langle \mathbf{u},\mathbf{v}\rangle$ for their standard inner product.

2.1 Partite Max-CSP and its SDP relaxation

An instance Ψ of Max PartCSP(P) has $k\cdot n$ Boolean variables indexed by $[k]\times[n]$. Each constraint is of the form $P(b_1 x_{1,j_1}, b_2 x_{2,j_2}, \ldots, b_k x_{k,j_k})$ for some indices $j_1,\ldots,j_k$ and some signs $b_1,\ldots,b_k \in \{-1,1\}$.

We use the following notation. The constraints of an instance are (T_1,P_1), (T_2,P_2), ..., where $T_i \subseteq [k]\times[n]$ are the set of variables that the i'th constraint depends on – exactly one from each layer – and $P_i:\{-1,1\}^{T_i} \to \{0,1\}$ is P applied to the variables of T_i, possibly with some variables negated.

We say that Ψ is *α-satisfiable* if there is an assignment to the variables which satisfies an α fraction of all the constraints.

The basic SDP relaxation is described in Figure 1. It has as variables a vector $\mathbf{v}_{i,j} \in S^{n\cdot k}$ for every variable $x_{i,j}$, and an unbiased distribution μ_i over $\{-1,1\}^{T_i}$ for each constraint (T_i,P_i). The fact that this is a relaxation follows from the following observation: for any global integral assignment $\sigma \in \{-1,1\}^{k\cdot n}$, let $\mathcal{D}$ be the uniform distribution over the pair of integral assignments σ and $-\sigma$. Let μ_i be the restrictions of $\mathcal{D}$ to the respective sets T_i and $\mathbf{v}_{i,j}=\sigma_{i,j}$ be a 1-dimensional vector. Then it is easy to see that this is a feasible solution to the SDP and its objective is same as the fraction of constraints satisfied by σ (or $-\sigma$). Here we use the evenness of the predicate.

2.2 The Unique Games Conjecture

In this section, we state the formulation of the Unique Games Conjecture that we will use.

Definition 2.1. *An instance $\Lambda=(U,V,E,\Pi,[L])$ of the* Unique Games *problem consists of an unweighted bipartite multigraph $G=(U\cup V,E)$, a set Π of* constraints, *and a set $[L]$ of* labels. *For each edge $e\in E$ there is a constraint $\pi_e \in \Pi$, which is a permutation on $[L]$. The goal is to find a* labeling $\ell: U\cup V\to[L]$ *of the vertices such that as many edges as possible are satisfied, where an edge $e=(u,v)$ is said to be satisfied by ℓ if $\ell(v)=\pi_e(\ell(u))$.*

Definition 2.2. *Given an instance $\Lambda=(U,V,E,\Pi,[L])$ of Unique Games, let $\mathsf{Opt}(\Lambda)$ denote the maximum fraction of simultaneously satisfied edges of Λ by any labeling, i. e.,*

$$\mathsf{Opt}(\Lambda) := \frac{1}{|E|}\max_{\ell:U\cup V\to[L]} |\{\, e : \ell \text{ satisfies } e\,\}|.$$

Conjecture 2.3. *([Kho02]) For every $\gamma>0$, there is an integer L such that, for Unique Games instances Λ with label set $[L]$ it is NP-hard to distinguish between*

- $\mathsf{Opt}(\Lambda) \geq 1-\gamma$
- $\mathsf{Opt}(\Lambda) \leq \gamma$.

2.3 Analytic Tools

Any Boolean function $f:\{-1,1\}^n \to \mathbb{R}$ can be written uniquely as a multilinear polynomial

$$f(x) = \sum_{T\subseteq[n]} \hat{f}(T)\chi_T(x),$$

where $\hat{f}(T)$ are the Fourier coefficients of f and $\chi_T(x) = \prod_{i\in T} x_i$. As such, f can be viewed as a multilinear polynomial $f:\mathbb{R}^n\to\mathbb{R}$ and this is the view we commonly take. We write $f^{\leq d}$ for the part of f that is of degree $\leq d$, i.e., $f^{\leq d}(x) = \sum_{|S|\leq d}\hat{f}(S)\chi_S(x)$.

Fact 2.4.

$$\mathbb{E}[f(X)] = \hat{f}(\emptyset) \qquad \text{Var}[f(X)] = \sum_{T\neq\emptyset}\hat{f}(T)^2,$$

where the expectations are over a uniform X in $\{-1,1\}^n$.

$$\begin{array}{lll}
\textbf{Maximize} & \sum_i \mathop{\mathbb{E}}_{x\sim\mu_i}[P_i(x)] & \\
\textbf{Subject to} & \mu_i \text{ is an unbiased distribution over } \{-1,1\}^{T_i} & \text{for every } i \\
& \mathbf{v}_{i,j} \in S^{n\cdot k} & \text{for all } (i,j)\in[k]\times[n] \\
& \mu_i|_T = \mu_j|_T & \text{where } T = T_i\cap T_j \\
& \langle \mathbf{v}_{i_1,j_1}, \mathbf{v}_{i_2,j_2}\rangle = \mathop{\mathbb{E}}_{x\sim\mu_l}[x_{i_1,j_1}x_{i_2,j_2}] & \text{for all } (i_1,j_1),(i_2,j_2)\in T_l
\end{array}$$

Figure 1: SDP relaxation of Max PartCSP(P).

DEFINITION 2.5. *The* influence *of the i'th variable on f is*

$$\mathrm{Inf}_i(f) = \sum_{T\ni i} \hat{f}(T)^2,$$

and the low-degree influence is

$$\mathrm{Inf}_i^{\leq d}(f) = \mathrm{Inf}_i(f^{\leq d}) = \sum_{\substack{T\ni i\\ |T|\leq d}} \hat{f}(T)^2.$$

As is common, the main analytic tool in our hardness result is the invariance principle [MOO10, Mos10]. In particular, we have the following theorem.

THEOREM 2.6. *For every k, $\epsilon > 0$ there is a $\delta > 0$ such that the following holds.*

Let μ be an unbiased distribution over $\{-1,1\}^k$ satisfying $\min_{x\in\{-1,1\}^k}\mu(x) \geq \epsilon$, X be a random $k\times n$ matrix over $\{-1,1\}$ with each column distributed according to μ, independently, and G be a random $k\times n$ matrix of standard Gaussians with the same covariance structure as X.

Then for any k multilinear polynomials $f_1,\ldots,f_k : \mathbb{R}^n \to \mathbb{R}$ with $\mathrm{Inf}_j^{\leq 1/\delta}(f_i) \leq \delta$ and $\mathrm{Var}[f_i] \leq 1$ for all $i\in[k]$, $j\in[n]$, we have

$$\left|\mathop{\mathbb{E}}_X\left[\prod_{i=1}^k f_i(X_i)\right] - \mathop{\mathbb{E}}_G\left[\prod_{i=1}^k f_i^{\leq 1/\delta}(G_i)\right]\right| \leq \epsilon.$$

Theorem 2.6 can be derived using Theorem 4.2 and Lemma 6.2 of [Mos10]: using Lemma 6.2 therein it follows that $\mathbb{E}_X\left[\prod_{i=1}^k f_i(X_i)\right]$ is close to $\mathbb{E}_X\left[\prod_{i=1}^k f_i^{\leq 1/\delta}(X_i)\right]$ for sufficiently small δ. Then we can use Theorem 4.2 on the functions $\{f_i^{\leq 1/\delta}\}$. In Theorem 4.2, the values of $f_i^{\leq 1/\delta}(X_i)$ and $f_i^{\leq 1/\delta}(G_i)$ are truncated to the range $[0,1]$. By scaling this holds with $[0,1]$ replaced by some interval $[-B,B]$. It is not too hard to show that for sufficiently large B (as a function of k and ϵ) truncation to the interval $[-B,B]$ does not change $\mathbb{E}[\prod_{i=1}^k f_i^{\leq 1/\delta}(X_i)]$ (resp. $\mathbb{E}[\prod_{i=1}^k f_i^{\leq 1/\delta}(G_i)]$) by more than ϵ.

2.4 Products of Gaussians

We need the following Lemma about the expectation of a product of gaussians in terms of their pairwise correlations.

LEMMA 2.7. *Let r be an integer and let $g_1,\ldots,g_r$ be gaussians with mean 0, variance 1, and covariance matrix ρ. Then*

$$\mathbb{E}\left[\prod_{i=1}^r g_i\right] = \sum_M \prod_{ij\in M} \rho_{ij},$$

where M ranges over all perfect matchings of the complete graph on r vertices (if r is even there are $(r-1)!!$ terms and if r is odd the expectation is 0).

3. DECIDABILITY OF M-VANISHING DISTRIBUTIONS

PROPOSITION 3.1. *Given P and m, the existence of a Λ which is m-vanishing on P is decidable.*

PROOF. There are $M \leq 2^k \cdot k^{2m}$ graphs $G_1,\ldots,G_M$ of interest namely graphs with at most m edges supported on some vertex set $S\subseteq[k]$. We need to decide whether there is a distribution Λ on P-supported correlation matrices such that

$$\mathop{\mathbb{E}}_{\rho\in\Lambda}[(\rho(G_1),\ldots,\rho(G_M))] = \mathbf{0}.$$

By Carathéodory's theorem this implies that Λ can be assumed to have support at most M. Each ρ in the support of Λ can be represented using $|P^{-1}(1)| + k^2 + 1$ real variables, representing a distribution μ over $P^{-1}(1)$, its correlation matrix ρ, and finally its probability under Λ. The constraints that each ρ is the correlation matrix of the corresponding μ and that $\Lambda(G_i) = 0$ for every G_i can be written as a finite number of polynomial equations in the $M(|P^{-1}(1)|+k^2+1)$ variables.[2] In other words the set of m-vanishing Λ of support size $\leq M$ form an algebraic set, so determining whether such Λ exists boils down to determining whether this algebraic set is non-empty, which is decidable [Tar51]. □

4. ALGORITHM

In this section we give an approximation algorithm with approximation ratio strictly larger than $|P^{-1}(1)|/2^k$ for predicates P which do not satisfy the condition of Theorem 1.3. Thus, there exists an m such that for every distribution Λ (over P-supported correlation matrices), there is an odd-degree multigraph G over $S\subseteq[k]$ with at most m edges such that $\hat{P}(S)\neq 0$ and $\Lambda(G)\neq 0$. For the rest of this section, fix this value of m.

4.1 Rounding Monomials

First, we give an algorithm which will allow us to "pick up" a contribution proportional to $\rho(G)$ for any monomial, where ρ is the correlation matrix of the local distribution (given by the SDP) on that monomial and G is any graph. Lemma 4.1

[2]The variables representing probabilities need to be non-negative. This can be effected by taking them to be squares of respective variables.

below formalizes the high-level idea given in Section 1.2. Recall that the variables of the CSP are partitioned into k layers, there are n variables in each layer, and the SDP relaxation is as in Figure 1.

LEMMA 4.1. *Let $S \subseteq [k]$ be a set of layers, G be an odd-degree multigraph on S, and $\tau > 0$. Then for all sufficiently large $B \geq \text{poly}(\log 1/\tau)$ (where the polynomial depends only on G) there is a polynomial time algorithm which, given an SDP solution as in Figure 1 outputs an assignment $\alpha : S \times [n] \to [-1, 1]$ to the layers of S such that the following holds.*

Let $V : S \to [n]$ be any choice of variables, one from each layer in S. Then

$$\mathbb{E}\left[\prod_{i\in S} \alpha_{i,V(i)}\right] = \frac{\rho(G)}{B^{|S|}} \pm \tau,$$

where ρ is the correlation matrix defined by the SDP solution on these k variables, i.e., $\rho_{i_1,i_2} = \langle \mathbf{v}_{i_1,V(i_1)}, \mathbf{v}_{i_2,V(i_2)} \rangle$.

PROOF. The algorithm works as follows. For each edge $e \in E(G)$, pick a standard Gaussian vector $\mathbf{g}_e$, independently. For a vertex $u \in V(G)$, let $E(u) \subseteq E(G)$ denote the set of edges incident on u. For a variable $x_{i,j}$ such that $i \in S$, set

$$\beta_{i,j} = \prod_{e\in E(i)} \langle \mathbf{g}_e, \mathbf{v}_{i,j} \rangle .$$

Then, set

$$\alpha_{i,j} = \begin{cases} \frac{\beta_{i,j}}{B} & \text{if } |\beta_{i,j}| \leq B \\ 0 & \text{otherwise.} \end{cases}$$

Fix $V : S \to [n]$ as in the statement. Now let us analyze $\mathbb{E}[\prod_{i\in S} \alpha_{i,V(i)}]$. Note that without the truncation when $|\beta_{i,V(i)}|$ exceeds B, the expectation would be exactly equal to (where in the second step below we use the independence of the Gaussians to move the expectation inside the product)

$$\begin{aligned}\mathbb{E}\left[\frac{1}{B^{|S|}}\prod_{i\in S}\beta_{i,V(i)}\right] &= \frac{1}{B^{|S|}}\mathbb{E}\left[\prod_{i\in S}\prod_{e\in E(i)}\langle \mathbf{g}_e, \mathbf{v}_{i,V(i)}\rangle\right] \\ &= \frac{1}{B^{|S|}}\prod_{(a,b)=e\in E(G)}\mathbb{E}\left[\langle \mathbf{g}_e, \mathbf{v}_{a,V(a)}\rangle \langle \mathbf{g}_e, \mathbf{v}_{b,V(b)}\rangle\right] \\ &= \frac{1}{B^{|S|}}\prod_{(a,b)\in E(G)}\langle \mathbf{v}_{a,V(a)}, \mathbf{v}_{b,V(b)}\rangle = \frac{\rho(G)}{B^{|S|}}.\end{aligned}$$

Thus we want to bound the expectation of

$$\left|\prod_{i\in S}\frac{\beta_{i,V(i)}}{B} - \prod_{i\in S}\alpha_{i,V(i)}\right|$$

by τ. This can be shown to be of order $m \cdot \exp(-B^{2/m}/2)$, because each $\beta_{i,V(i)}$ is a product of at most $|E(G)| \leq m$ independent gaussians. Thus setting B of order $(\log 1/\tau)^{m/2}$ we get the desired error bound. □

4.2 Setup for the Algorithm

Let $M \leq 2^k \cdot k^{2m}$ be the number of odd-degree graphs on some $S \subseteq [k]$ with $\hat{P}(S) \neq 0$ and at most m edges, and let $G_1, \ldots, G_M$ be these graphs. Further write $S_t = V(G_t) \subseteq [k]$ for the vertex set of G_t. For a correlation matrix $\rho \in \mathbb{R}^{k\times k}$, let $q(\rho)$ be the vector

$$q(\rho) = (\rho(G_1), \rho(G_2), \ldots, \rho(G_M)) \in \mathbb{R}^M,$$

and let $Q \subseteq \mathbb{R}^M$ be the convex hull of the set of points $\{q(\rho) : \rho \text{ is } P\text{-supported}\}$.

Note that a Λ such that $\Lambda(G_i) = 0$ for all $1 \leq i \leq M$ is precisely a convex combination Λ of ρ's such that $\mathbb{E}_{\rho\sim\Lambda}[q(\rho)] = \mathbf{0}$. In other words since P does not satisfy the condition of Theorem 1.3 we have that Q does not contain the origin. Furthermore Q is compact and so we can find a separating hyperplane $(\gamma_1, \ldots, \gamma_M)$ such that $\sum_{t=1}^M \gamma_t \rho(G_t) > \delta$ for every P-supported ρ and some universal constant δ (depending only on P).

Now let $\tau = \frac{\delta}{4M}$ and set $B = \text{poly}(\log 1/\tau)$ large enough to make Lemma 4.1 work for all the graphs $G_1, \ldots, G_M$. In our algorithm, we are going to choose one $t \in [M]$ at random and then the algorithm is going to focus solely on the terms involving layers S_t. More precisely, as we shall see in the next section, t should be chosen with probability proportional to $\left|\frac{\gamma_t}{\hat{P}(S_t)}\right| \cdot B^{|S_t|}$. In order for this to make sense, we therefore need that

$$\sum_{t=1}^{M}\left|\frac{\gamma_t}{\hat{P}(S_t)}\right| \cdot B^{|S_t|} \leq 1. \tag{1}$$

Fortunately, we can assume without loss of generality that this holds: since $B^{|S_t|} \leq B^k$ depends sub-linearly (in fact even poly-logarithmically) on $1/\tau$, dividing each γ_t by some factor $f > 1$ causes δ and τ to also be divided by f, which in turn changes $B^{|S_t|}$ to $\text{poly}\log(f/\tau) = o(fB^{|S_t|})$, so that the sum in the left hand side of (1) decreases by a factor which is super-constant in f. Hence choosing f a sufficiently large constant, we can make (1) hold.

4.3 The Rounding Algorithm

We are now ready to describe the algorithm. Without loss of generality, we may assume that we are given a $(1-\epsilon)$-satisfiable MAX PARTCSP(P) instance where $\epsilon > 0$ is some sufficiently small constant (depending on P) to be determined later. If the instance is not $(1-\epsilon)$-satisfiable then a random assignment already gives an approximation ratio of $\frac{|P^{-1}(1)|}{2^k(1-\epsilon)}$.

By Markov's inequality, for at least a $1-\sqrt{\epsilon}$ fraction of constraints (T_i, P_i) we have $\mathbb{E}_{x\sim\mu_i}[P_i(x)] \geq 1-\sqrt{\epsilon}$. In other words, μ_i has a $1-\sqrt{\epsilon}$ fraction of its mass on $P_i^{-1}(1)$.

CLAIM 4.2. *Given a correlation matrix $\rho \in \mathbb{R}^{k\times k}$ of a distribution which is $(1-\sqrt{\epsilon})$-supported on $P^{-1}(1)$, there is a P-supported correlation matrix ρ' such that $|\rho(G) - \rho'(G)| \leq \sqrt{\epsilon}2^m$ for every G on m edges.*

Thus, setting $\epsilon < \frac{\delta^2}{4\cdot 2^m}$ we have that $\sum_i \gamma_i \rho(G_i) > \delta/2$ for all correlation matrices of distributions which are $(1-\sqrt{\epsilon})$-supported on $P^{-1}(1)$.

Now the rounding algorithm is as in Figure 2.

Now, fix the value of t chosen in step 1, and let $\alpha_{i,j}$ be the rounded value to the variable $x_{i,j}$ as in Lemma 4.1 and $\tilde{\alpha}_{i,j}$ be equal to $\alpha_{i,j}$ or its negation after the third step above. The assignment $\tilde{\alpha}$ is in $[-1,1]^{n\times k}$ but as the objective function is multilinear it can be greedily adjusted to an integral assignment in $\{-1,1\}^{n\times k}$ without decreasing the objective value, so it suffices to study $\tilde{\alpha}$. Let $S \subseteq [k]$ be some set of layers and $V : S \to [n]$ be any choice of variables from these

1. Pick $t \in [M]$ with probability $\left|\frac{\gamma_t}{\hat{P}(S_t)}\right| \cdot B^{|S_t|}$.
2. Using Lemma 4.1, round the variables in layers in S_t using graph G_t. For every other layer, set all the variables in that layer to 0.
3. If $\text{sign}(\gamma_t \hat{P}(S_t)) = -1$, then select an odd sized subset A of S_t at random, else select an even sized subset A of S_t at random. Flip the sign of all variables in layers in A.

Figure 2: Rounding algorithm for Max PartCSP(P)

layers. Observe that for every $S \neq S_t$,

$$\mathop{\mathbb{E}}_{\alpha}\left[\prod_{i\in S} \tilde{\alpha}_{i,V(i)}\right] = 0.$$

To see this, note that if $S \not\subseteq S_t$, then the variables in layers $S \setminus S_t$ are set to 0. On the other hand if $S \subset S_t$, then we flip the signs of a random set of layers of either odd or even size. As the distribution over which layers get flipped is $(|S_t|-1)$-wise independent, the layers of any $S \subset S_t$ get flipped completely uniformly.

On the other hand, by Lemma 4.1 and the way the signs are flipped in the third step, if $S = S_t$ we have

$$\mathop{\mathbb{E}}_{\alpha}[\prod_{i\in S} \tilde{\alpha}_{i,V(i)}] = \text{sign}(\gamma_t \hat{P}(S_t)) \cdot \frac{\rho(G_t)}{B^{|S_t|}} \pm \tau.$$

Thus, taking the expectation of $\mathbb{E}_\alpha[\prod_{i\in S} \tilde{\alpha}_{i,V(i)}]$ over $t \in [M]$ chosen according to Step 1, we have

$$\begin{aligned}
&\mathop{\mathbb{E}}_{t}\left[\mathop{\mathbb{E}}_{\alpha}[\prod_{i\in S} \tilde{\alpha}_{i,V(i)}]\right] \\
&= \sum_{t:S_t=S}\left|\frac{\gamma_t}{\hat{P}(S_t)}\right| \cdot B^{|S_t|}\left(\text{sign}(\gamma_t \hat{P}(S_t)) \cdot \frac{\rho(G_t)}{B^{|S_t|}} \pm \tau\right) \\
&= \sum_{t:S_t=S} \frac{\gamma_t}{\hat{P}(S_t)}\rho(G_t) \pm \tau
\end{aligned}$$

Now we can analyze the probability that any specific constraint is satisfied. Let (T_i, P_i) be a constraint involving one variable from each layer which is $(1-\sqrt{\epsilon})$-satisfied by the SDP solution. In other words, $\mathbb{E}_{x\sim\mu_i}[P_i(x)] \geq 1-\sqrt{\epsilon}$. Write $V : [k] \to [n]$ for the variables involved (i.e., $T_i = \{(i', V(i')) : i' \in [k]\}$) and write

$$P_i(x) = P(b_1 x_{1,V(1)}, \ldots, b_k x_{k,V(k)})$$

for some signs $b_1, \ldots, b_k \in \{-1, 1\}$.

We also associate the domain of P_i with $\{-1,1\}^k$ in the obvious way. As such, it is easy to verify that the Fourier coefficient $\hat{P}_i(S)$ for $S \subseteq [k]$ satisfies $\hat{P}_i(S) = \hat{P}(S)\chi_S(b)$. Furthermore, let $\tilde{\mu_i}$ be the distribution over $\{-1,1\}^k$ obtained by sampling from μ_i and performing coordinatewise multiplication by b, and let ρ (resp. $\tilde{\rho}$) denote the correlation matrix of μ_i (resp. $\tilde{\mu_i}$). Then, for any graph G we have

$$\begin{aligned}
\rho(G) &= \prod_{(a,a')\in E} \rho_{a,a'} = \prod_{(a,a')\in E} \tilde{\rho}_{a,a'}\chi_{\{a,a'\}}(b) \\
&= \tilde{\rho}(G) \cdot \chi_{\text{Odd}(G)}(b)
\end{aligned}$$

where $\text{Odd}(G)$ denotes the set of odd-degree vertices of G. In particular for $G = G_t$ all vertices have odd degree so $\text{Odd}(G_t) = S_t$. Using this and noting that $\tilde{\mu_i}$ is $(1-\sqrt{\epsilon})$-supported on satisfying assignments of P we see that

$$\sum_t \gamma_t \rho(G_t)\chi_{S_t}(b) = \sum_t \gamma_t \tilde{\rho}(G_t) > \delta/2.$$

We then have the following, where the expectation below is taken over all the random choices of the algorithm (including that of $t \in [M]$).

$$\begin{aligned}
&\mathbb{E}[P_i(\tilde{\alpha}_{1,V(1)}, \cdots, \tilde{\alpha}_{k,V(k)})] \\
&= \hat{P}_i(\emptyset) + \sum_{\substack{\emptyset\neq S\subseteq[k] \\ \hat{P}_i(S)\neq 0}} \hat{P}_i(S)\,\mathbb{E}[\prod_{i\in S}\tilde{\alpha}_{i,V(i)}] \\
&= \hat{P}(\emptyset) + \sum_{\substack{\emptyset\neq S\subseteq[k] \\ \hat{P}(S)\neq 0}} \hat{P}(S)\chi_S(b) \sum_{t:S_t=S} \frac{\gamma_t}{\hat{P}(S_t)}\rho(G_t) \pm \tau \\
&= \hat{P}(\emptyset) + \sum_{t=1}^{M} \gamma_t \rho(G_t)\chi_{S_t}(b) \pm \tau M > \hat{P}(\emptyset) + \frac{\delta}{4}.
\end{aligned}$$

Thus the total fraction of constraints satisfied by the algorithm is in expectation at least $(1-\sqrt{\epsilon})(\hat{P}(\emptyset) + \delta/4)$ which is at least $\hat{P}(\emptyset) + \delta/8$ assuming $\epsilon < (\delta/8)^2$.

In other words, the algorithm finds a solution with value at least $\hat{P}(\emptyset) + \delta/8$ on all instances with value at least $1-\epsilon$. Combining this with a random assignment gives an approximation better than $\hat{P}(\emptyset)$ for any instance, and concludes the proof of approximability of MAX PARTCSP(P).

5. HARDNESS

In this section we show that any P which satisfies the condition of Theorem 1.3 is approximation resistant, assuming the UGC. As usual, we prove hardness by designing an appropriate dictatorship test, which is given in Section 5.1, followed by the (standard) hardness reduction in Section 5.2.

5.1 Dictatorship Test

THEOREM 5.1. *Let P satisfy the condition of Theorem 1.3. Then for every k and $\epsilon > 0$ there exists a $\delta > 0$ such that the following holds for all n.*

There is a randomized algorithm $\mathcal{T}$ which, given oracle access to k odd functions $f_1, \ldots, f_k : \{-1,1\}^n \to [-1,1]$, produces k queries $X_1, \ldots, X_k \in \{-1,1\}^n$ such that

(Yes) *If $f_1(x) = f_2(x) = \ldots = f_k(x) = x_i$ are the same dictator function, then $\mathbb{E}[P(f_1(X_1), \ldots, f_k(X_k))] \geq 1-\epsilon$.*

(No) *If all f_i's have $\text{Inf}_j^{\leq 1/\delta}(f_i) \leq \delta$ for all $j \in [n]$ then $\mathbb{E}[P(f_1(X_1), \ldots, f_k(X_k))] \leq \hat{P}(\emptyset) + \epsilon$*

Input: functions $f_1, \ldots, f_k : \{-1,1\}^n \to [-1,1]$

Output: accept/reject

1. Pick a random $\rho \sim \Lambda$.
2. Let η be an unbiased P-supported distribution with correlation matrix ρ (if there are many such η pick an arbitrary one in a deterministic fashion).
3. Let $\mu = (1-\epsilon)\eta + \epsilon U_k$.
4. Pick a random $k \times n$ matrix X where each column is sampled independently according to μ.
5. Accept with probability $P(f_1(X_1), \ldots, f_k(X_k))$.

Figure 3: Dictatorship Test

Let $m = k \cdot n$ and let Λ be a distribution over P-supported correlation matrices which is m-vanishing on P. Let U_k be the uniform distribution over $\{-1,1\}^k$. The tester $\mathcal{T}$ is described in Figure 3.

That the completeness is $1-\epsilon$ follows immediately from $\operatorname{supp}(\eta) \subseteq P^{-1}(1)$.

Let us then analyze the soundness. The acceptance probability can be written as

$$\begin{aligned}\Pr[\mathcal{T} \text{ accepts}] &= \mathop{\mathbb{E}}_{\rho\sim\Lambda}\left[\mathop{\mathbb{E}}_{X\sim\mu}[P(f_1(X_1), \ldots, f_k(X_k))]\right] \\ &= \hat{P}(\emptyset) + \mathop{\mathbb{E}}_{\rho}\left[\sum_{S\neq\emptyset} \hat{P}(S) \mathop{\mathbb{E}}_{X}[\prod_{i\in S} f_i(X_i)]\right]. \quad (2)\end{aligned}$$

Let ρ' be the correlation matrix of μ. Note that $\rho' = (1-\epsilon)\rho + \epsilon I$. Fix the value of ρ for the moment, and let G be a random $k \times n$ matrix of standard Gaussians with the same covariances as X (i.e., the columns are independent and in the j'th column we have $\mathbb{E}[G_{i,j}G_{i',j}] = \rho'_{i,i'} = (1-\epsilon)\rho_{i,i'}$ for $i \neq i'$).

Next, set δ small enough so that Theorem 2.6 gives that if $\mathrm{Inf}_j^{\leq 1/\delta}(f_i) \leq \delta$ for all $i \in [k]$, $j \in [n]$ then

$$\left|\mathop{\mathbb{E}}_{X}[\prod_{i\in S} f_i(X_i)] - \mathop{\mathbb{E}}_{G}[\prod_{i\in S} f_i^{\leq 1/\delta}(G_i)]\right| \leq \epsilon/2^k \quad (3)$$

for all S. Define $f'_i = f^{\leq 1/\delta}$. We need to understand expressions of the form $\mathbb{E}_G[\prod_{i\in S} f'_i(G_i)]$ for $S \subseteq [k]$. Expanding $f'_i = \sum_{T\subseteq[n]} \hat{f}'(T)\chi_T$ and applying Lemma 2.7, we obtain

$$\begin{aligned}\mathop{\mathbb{E}}_{G}\left[\prod_{i\in S} f'_i(G_i)\right] &= \sum_{\{T_i\}_{i\in S}} \prod_{i\in S} \hat{f}'_i(T_i) \prod_{j=1}^{n} \mathbb{E}\left[\prod_{i:j\in T_i} G_{ij}\right] \\ &= \sum_{\{T_i\}_{i\in S}} \prod_{i\in S} \hat{f}'_i(T_i) \prod_{j=1}^{n} \sum_{M_j\in\mathcal{M}(\{i:j\in T_i\})} \prod_{i,i'\in M_j} \rho'_{i,i'}, \quad (4)\end{aligned}$$

where we write $\mathcal{M}(S)$ for the set of perfect matchings on the complete graph with vertex set S.

For a choice $\mathbf{T} = \{T_i\}_{i\in S}$ of T_i's, let $c(\mathbf{T}) = \prod_{i\in S} \hat{f}'_i(T_i)$. Further, for a choice of matchings $\mathbf{M} = (M_1, \ldots, M_n)$ let $H(\mathbf{M})$ denote the multigraph being the union of $M_1, \ldots, M_n$. With a slight abuse of notation, write $\mathcal{M}(\mathbf{T})$ for the set of $\mathbf{M}$'s for a given $\mathbf{T}$; i.e., $\mathcal{M}(\mathbf{T}) = \{(M_1, \ldots, M_n) : M_j \in \mathcal{M}(\{i : j \in T_i\})$. With all this cumbersome notation in place, the equation above simplifies to

$$(4) = \sum_{\mathbf{T}} \sum_{\mathbf{M}\in\mathcal{M}(\mathbf{T})} c(\mathbf{T})\rho'(H(\mathbf{M})), \quad (5)$$

where $\mathbf{T}$ ranges over all $\{T_i \subseteq [n]\}_{i\in S}$. Note that since f_i (and therefore also f'_i) is odd, we can restrict the sum to $\mathbf{T}$ such that each $|T_i|$ is odd, implying that $H(\mathbf{M})$ is always odd degree.

Plugging (5) into (3), we have

$$\left|\mathop{\mathbb{E}}_{X}[\prod_{i\in S} f_i(X_i)] - \sum_{\mathbf{T}} \sum_{\mathbf{M}\in\mathcal{M}(\mathbf{T})} c(\mathbf{T})\rho'(H(\mathbf{M}))\right| \leq \epsilon/2^k$$

Finally, plugging this into (2) and using the identity $\rho' = (1-\epsilon)\rho + \epsilon I$ yields

$$\begin{aligned}&\Pr[\mathcal{T} \text{ accepts}] \\ &\leq \hat{P}(\emptyset) + \mathop{\mathbb{E}}_{\rho}\left[\sum_{S\neq\emptyset}\left(\hat{P}(S)\sum_{\mathbf{T}} \sum_{\mathbf{M}\in\mathcal{M}(\mathbf{T})} c(\mathbf{T})\rho'(H(\mathbf{M})) + \epsilon/2^k\right)\right] \\ &\leq \hat{P}(\emptyset) + \epsilon + \\ &\qquad \sum_{S\neq\emptyset} \hat{P}(S) \sum_{\mathbf{T}} \sum_{\mathbf{M}\in\mathcal{M}(\mathbf{T})} c(\mathbf{T})(1-\epsilon)^{|E(H(\mathbf{M}))|} \mathop{\mathbb{E}}_{\rho}[\rho(H(\mathbf{M}))] \\ &= \hat{P}(\emptyset) + \epsilon,\end{aligned}$$

where the last equality follows by the m-vanishing property of Λ: $H(\mathbf{M})$ has at most $n|S|/2 < nk = m$ edges, and so for each S either $\hat{P}(S) = 0$ or $\mathbb{E}_\rho[\rho(H(\mathbf{M}))] = \Lambda(H(\mathbf{M})) = 0$.

5.2 Hardness Reduction

Given the dictatorship test as in Theorem 5.1, a UGC-based hardness reduction can be designed in a standard manner. Some care needs to be taken however to ensure that the CSP instance produced by the reduction is k-partite. As is standard, we present the reduction as a Probabilistically Checkable Proof (PCP) for NP whose acceptance predicate matches the predicate P, has completeness $1-o(1)$ and soundness $\frac{|P^{-1}(1)|}{2^k} + o(1)$.

The PCP is based on the conjectured NP-hard instance $\Lambda = (U, V, E, \Pi, [L])$ of Unique Games as in Definition 2.1. Let L and γ be as in Conjecture 2.3. The PCP proof consists of k layers where the bits in the i'th layer correspond to

$V_i \times \{-1,1\}^L$ and V_i is a copy of the "right hand side" V of the UG instance. For any $v_i \in V_i (= V)$, the set of bits $\{v_i\} \times \{-1,1\}^L$ correspond to the bits of the long code of the label of v_i. In a "correct" proof, the assignment to these bits corresponds to a dictatorship function $f(x) = x_j$ where $j \in [L]$ is the intended label of v_i.

For a function $g : \{-1,1\}^L \to \{-1,1\}$ and a permutation $\pi : [L] \to [L]$, let $g \circ \pi^{-1} : \{-1,1\}^L \to \{-1,1\}$ denote the function defined as $g \circ \pi^{-1}(x) = g(x_{\pi^{-1}(1)}, \ldots, x_{\pi^{-1}(L)})$. The PCP verifier proceeds as in Figure 4.

5.2.1 Completeness

Let $\ell : U \cup V \to [L]$ be a labeling to the UG instance that satisfies $1-\gamma$ fraction of its edges. For every $v_i \in V_i (= V)$, let g_i be the long code of $\ell(v_i)$, i.e. $g_i(x) = x_{\ell(v_i)}$. With probability at least $1 - k\gamma$, all k edges $(u, v_1), \ldots, (u, v_k)$ are satisfied by the labeling and whenever this holds, the dictatorship test accepts with probability $1-\epsilon$. The latter conclusion follows by observing that if $\pi_i(\ell(u)) = \ell(v_i)$ for every $1 \le i \le k$, then in the PCP test above,

$$f_i(x) = g_i \circ \pi_i^{-1}(x) = g_i(x_{\pi_i^{-1}(1)}, \ldots, x_{\pi_i^{-1}(L)})$$
$$= x_{\pi_i^{-1}(\ell(v_i))} = x_{\ell(u)},$$

and hence $f_1, \ldots, f_k$ are identical dictatorship functions.

5.2.2 Soundness

Assume that the soundness of the UG instance is at most γ which is chosen to be sufficiently small beforehand. Fix any layer i in the PCP proof and let $g_{i,v}$ be the supposed long code corresponding to the vertex v (in the i'th layer). For any $u \in U$, define the function $f_{i,u}$ which is the average of functions over the neighbors of u after appropriate permutation:

$$f_{i,u}(x) = \mathop{\mathbb{E}}_{v:(u,v)\in E}\left[g_{i,v} \circ \pi_{(u,v)}^{-1}(x)\right].$$

Note that $f_{i,u}$ are $[-1,1]$-valued. By a standard argument, we may assume that for all but $\sqrt{\gamma}$ fraction of $u \in U$, the function $f_{i,u}$ has no coordinate that has degree $1/\delta$ influence δ (referred to as a low-influence function for brevity).

Otherwise, suppose that for $\sqrt{\gamma}$ fraction of u, $f_{i,u}$ has a coordinate that has degree $1/\delta$ influence δ. For brevity, call any such coordinate simply as an influential coordinate. The set of all influential coordinates has size bounded by $1/\delta^2$. Assign this bounded set as the set of candidate labels for u. For any influential coordinate $j \in [L]$, since $f_{i,u}$ is an average of $g_{i,v} \circ \pi_{(u,v)}^{-1}$ over neighbors of u, by an averaging argument, for at least $\delta/2$ fraction of the neighbors, $\pi_{(u,v)}(j)$ is influential for $g_{i,v}$. All influential coordinates of $g_{i,v}$ are assigned as the candidate labels for v. Now define a (randomized) labeling that selects one label at random from the candidate set of each vertex. The argument sketched implies that this labeling satisfies $\sqrt{\gamma} \cdot \delta/2 \cdot \delta^4$ fraction of the UG edges. This is a contradiction if the soundness γ was chosen to be sufficiently small to begin with.

Hence except with probability at most $k\sqrt{\gamma}$, the PCP verifier chooses $u \in U$ such that the k functions $f_{i,u}$, one in each layer, are all low influence functions. Whenever this holds, the analysis of the dictatorship test implies that the verifier accepts with probability at most $\frac{|P^{-1}(1)|}{2^k} + \epsilon$. One only needs to observe that for a fixed u, the verifier picks its random neighbor in each layer and hence running the test on these random neighbors (one in each layer) has the same effect as running the test on the (possibly non-boolean) averaged functions (again, one in each layer). Formally, fixing u,

$$\mathop{\mathbb{E}}_{v_1,\ldots,v_k}\left[\mathop{\mathbb{E}}_{\mathcal{T}}[P(g_{1,v_1} \circ \pi_1^{-1}(X_1), \ldots, g_{k,v_k} \circ \pi_k^{-1}(X_k))]\right]$$
$$= \mathop{\mathbb{E}}_{\mathcal{T}}\left[P(\mathop{\mathbb{E}}_{v_1}[g_{1,v_1} \circ \pi_1^{-1}(X_1)], \ldots, \mathop{\mathbb{E}}_{v_k}[g_{k,v_k} \circ \pi_k^{-1}(X_k)])\right]$$
$$= \mathop{\mathbb{E}}_{\mathcal{T}}[P(f_{1,u}(X_1), \ldots, f_{k,u}(X_k))].$$

6. ACKNOWLEDGEMENTS

We are grateful to Johan Håstad for many insightful discussions throughout this work, and to the anonymous referees for their helpful suggestions.

7. REFERENCES

[AH11] P. Austrin and J. Håstad. Randomly supported independence and resistance. *SIAM Journal on Computing*, 40:1–27, 2011.

[AH12] P. Austrin and J. Håstad. On the Usefulness of Predicates. In *IEEE Conference on Computational Complexity (CCC)*, 2012.

[AM09] P. Austrin and E. Mossel. Approximation resistant predicates from pairwise independence. *Computational Complexity*, 18:249–271, 2009.

[EH08] L. Engebretsen and J. Holmerin. More efficient queries in PCPs for NP and improved approximation hardness of maximum CSP. *Random Structures and Algorithms*, 33:497–514, 2008.

[GLST98] V. Guruswami, D. Lewin, M. Sudan, and L. Trevisan. A tight characterization of NP with 3 query PCPs. In *Proceedings of 39th Annual IEEE Symposium on Foundations of Computer Science*, pages 8–17, Palo Alto, 1998. IEEE.

[GW95] M. Goemans and D. Williamson. Improved approximation algorithms for maximum cut and satisfiability problems using semidefinite programming. *Journal of the ACM*, 42:1115–1145, 1995.

[Hås01] J. Håstad. Some optimal inapproximability results. *Journal of ACM*, 48:798–859, 2001.

[Has05] G. Hast. *Beating a random assignment.* KTH, Stockholm, 2005. Ph.D Thesis.

[Kho02] S. Khot. On the power of unique 2-prover 1-round games. In *Proceedings of 34th ACM Symposium on Theory of Computating*, pages 767–775, 2002.

[MOO10] E. Mossel, R. O'Donnell, and K. Oleszkiewicz. Noise stability of functions with low influences: invariance and optimality. *Annals of Mathematics*, 171(1):295–341, 2010.

[Mos10] E. Mossel. Gaussian bounds for noise correlation of functions. *GAFA*, 19:1713–1756, 2010.

[Rag08] P. Raghavendra. Optimal Algorithms and Inapproximability Results For Every CSP? In *ACM Symposium on Theory of Computing (STOC)*, 2008.

[RS09] P. Raghavendra and D. Steurer. How to Round Any CSP. In *IEEE Symposium on Foundations*

1. Pick a random vertex $u \in U$.
2. Pick k random neighbors of u, namely $v_1, \ldots, v_k \in V$.
3. Let $g_1, \ldots, g_k$ be the functions (supposed long codes) for $v_1 \in V_1, \ldots, v_k \in V_k$ respectively.
4. Let $f_1, \ldots, f_k$ be the permuted versions of $g_1, \ldots, g_k$ respectively, i.e., $f_i = g_i \circ \pi_i^{-1}$, $\pi_i = \pi_{e_i=(u,v_i)}$ for $1 \leq i \leq k$.
5. Run the dictatorship test as in Theorem 5.1 on $(f_1, \ldots, f_k)$.

Figure 4: PCP Verifier

of Computer Science (FOCS), pages 586–594, 2009.

[ST00] A. Samorodnitsky and L. Trevisan. A PCP characterization of NP with optimal amortized query complexity. In *Proceedings of the 32nd Annual ACM Symposium on Theory of Computing*, pages 191–199, 2000.

[Tar51] A. Tarski. A decision method for elementary algebra and geometry. *Bulletin of the American Mathematical Society*, 59, 1951.

[Zwi98] U. Zwick. Approximation algorithms for constraint satisfaction problems involving at most three variables per constraint. In *Proceedings 9th Annual ACM-SIAM Symposium on Discrete Algorithms*, pages 201–210. ACM, 1998.

On the Optimality of Semidefinite Relaxations for Average-Case and Generalized Constraint Satisfaction

Boaz Barak
Microsoft Research New England
Cambridge, MA, USA
boaz@boazbarak.org

Guy Kindler*
Hebrew University
Jerusalem, Israel
gkindler@cs.huji.ac.il

David Steurer†
Cornell University
Ithaca, NY, USA
dsteurer@cs.cornell.edu

ABSTRACT

This work studies several questions about the optimality of semidefinite programming (SDP) for constraint satisfaction problems (CSPs).

First we propose the hypothesis that the well known Basic SDP relaxation is actually optimal for random instances of constraint satisfaction problems for *every* predicate. This unifies several conjectures proposed in the past, and suggests a unifying principle for the average-case complexity of CSPs. We provide several types of indirect evidence for the truth of this hypothesis, and also show that it (and its variants) imply several conjectures in hardness of approximation including polynomial factor hardness for the densest k subgraph problem and hard instances for the Sliding Scale Conjecture of Bellare, Goldwasser, Lund and Russell (1993).

Second, we observe that for every predicate P, the basic SDP relaxation achieves the same approximation guarantee for the CSP for P and for a more general problem (involving not just Boolean but constrained vector assignments), which we call the *Generalized CSP* for P. Raghavendra (2008) showed that it is Unique Games-hard to approximate the CSP for P better than this guarantee. We show that it is **NP**-hard to approximate the Generalized CSP for P better than this guarantee.

Categories and Subject Descriptors

F.2.0 [**Theory of Computation**]: Analysis of Algorithms and problem complexityGeneral
; G.1.6 [**Mathematics of Computing**]: Optimization—*Convex Programming*

General Terms

Theory

Keywords

Constraint satisfaction problems, semidefinite programming, unique games conjecture, average-case complexity

*Supported by grants from the Israel Science Foundation and the Israel Binational Science Foundation.

†Most of the work done while at Microsoft Research New England.

1. INTRODUCTION

Some of the most appealing results in algorithms and computational complexity are *meta algorithms* or *meta reductions* that characterize the complexity not just of a single problem but a whole family of them. Some canonical examples for meta algorithms include the Ellipsoid algorithm, that applies for all convex problems admitting efficient separation and membership oracles [GLS81], and Robertson and Seymour's algorithm deciding every minor-closed graph property in polynomial time [RS95, RS04]. One example for a meta reduction is the work of Lewis and Yannakakis [Yan78, LY80] showing that for large a class of properties, finding the largest subgraph satisfying the property is **NP** hard.

Perhaps the nicest case is when we have a complimentary meta-algorithm and meta-reduction, thus obtaining a *meta characterization* that determines exactly the complexity of any computational problem inside some family. The *Dichotomy Conjecture* of Feder and Vardi [FV98] is aimed at achieving exactly such a characterization for the determining the satisfiability of constraint satisfaction problems (CSPs), and much exciting progress has been made on it [Sch78, HN90, Bul02, BK09]. In the context of approximation algorithms, Raghavendra [Rag08] gave, assuming Khot's Unique Games Conjecture (UGC) [Kho02b], a meta-characterization of the approximation threshold of all CSPs. In particular he showed that for every CSP it is Unique Games-hard to beat the approximation guarantee achieved by a simple semidefinite programming relaxation known as Basic Sdp.

Recent works, however, have raised some doubts concerning the UGC. In particular, while the UGC asserts that a certain computational problem known as Unique Games is **NP**-hard, it was shown that this problem can be solved in subexponential time [ABS10], and in fact there is a candidate algorithm that might solve it much faster than that [BBH+12]. Indeed, showing a distribution of plausibly hard instances for Unique Games appears to be a challenging problem [AKK+08, BHHS11, KMM11]. These works form a strong motivation for basing optimality results on conjectures that are weaker than, or at least different from, the UGC.[1] Moreover, as all of the above meta-characterization results are in the context of *worst-case* complexity, and the question of whether such characterizations can be proven, or are even true, in the context of *average-case complexity*, has not been addressed to our knowledge.

This paper shows some results in the above mentioned directions. Specifically, we study optimality results in two settings:

Average-case complexity We put forward the hypothesis that among polynomial time approximation algorithms, Basic Sdp is optimal for *random CSPs*. We show that this conjecture (and its extentions) would have some interesting consequences for hardness of approximation, and give some indirect evidence supporting it. While proving this hypothesis is beyond current techniques in complexity, there are many plausible ways to *refute* it, and we argue that studying this and similar conjectures is a good approach to make progress on average-case complexity.

Generalized CSPs We show that, assuming $\mathbf{P} \neq \mathbf{NP}$, Basic Sdp is in fact optimal for a class of problem that we call *generalized CSPs*. At a very high level, given a predicate P, the *generalized CSP* corresponding to P involves applying P not just on variables and their negations but an arbitrary linear functions of the variables (which are allowed now to be not just bits but certain real vectors). The definition of generalized CSP is motivated by the observation that Basic Sdp does not really distinguish between generalized CSPs and real ones. Thus in particular for every predicate P, Basic Sdp yields the same approximation on the generalized CSP for P that it yields for the CSP of P. (For example, Basic Sdp yields the same factor 0.87... approximation for Generalized Max-Cut as the one it achieves for the standard Max-Cut, and while it is an open question whether this factor can be improved for Max-Cut, our results imply that it is **NP**-hard to beat for the generalized version.)

We now give more details on our results.

1.1 Average-case complexity

For a predicate $P\colon \{\pm 1\}^K \to \{0,1\}$, an instance $\mathfrak{I}$ of CSP(P) is a set of K-tuples of literals over the variables $x_1, \ldots, x_n$. The *value* of $\mathfrak{I}$, denoted val($\mathfrak{I}$), is the maximum, over all assignments to the variables, of the fraction of tuples that satisfy P. We say that an algorithm A is a *relaxation* for CSP(P) if $\text{val}(\mathfrak{I}) \leqslant A(\mathfrak{I})$ for all instances $\mathfrak{I}$ of CSP(P). Some examples for relaxations are obtained by linear and convex programs for CSP(P), including the canonical algorithm Basic Sdp considered by [Rag08], but in general a relaxation is any algorithm that always upper bounds the true value. A *random instance* of CSP(P) is obtained by selecting m random K-tuples of literals for some parameter $m = m(n)$.[2] The following conjecture states that Basic Sdp is essentially the optimal polynomial time upper-certificate on *random* instances of CSP(P).

RCSP Hypothesis (*SDP optimality hypothesis for refuting CSPs, informal*) Let $P\colon \{\pm 1\}^K \to \{0,1\}$ be a predicate and let $\varepsilon > 0$. For every polynomial time relaxation A for CSP(P), it holds that for random instance $\mathfrak{I}$ of CSP(P), almost always $A(\mathfrak{I}) \geqslant \text{Basic Sdp}(\mathfrak{I}) - \varepsilon$.

(The R in RCSP can stand for either "refutation" or "random".)

While it is clear what a *disproof* of the RCSP Hypothesis would consist of, given the state of art in computational complexity it seems unlikely that it will be *proven* (or even derived from well studied worst-case conjectures such as $\mathbf{P} \neq \mathbf{NP}$ [BT06]) in the foreseeable future. Nevertheless, there are still several approaches to obtain *evidence* for its veracity:

- *(Reductions)* It may be possible to derive the RCSP Hypothesis from a more well-studied *average case* conjectures/hypothesis such as Feige's Hypothesis [Fei02] about refuting random 3SAT, or conjectures about the hardness of learning parity with noise [GKL88, BFKL93].

  We show a partial result in this direction, observing that Feige's results can be restated as showing that his hypothesis implies the RCSP Hypothesis for the case of predicates of arity at most 3.

- *(Integrality gaps)* If the RCSP Hypothesis is true, then in particular stronger mathematical relaxations than Basic Sdp such as its extension to various hierarchies will not give better results than Basic Sdp on random instances. Confirming this prediction can be thought of as evidence for the RCSP Hypothesis.

  We observe that the results of Benabbas, Georgiou, Magen, and Tulsiani [BGMT12] can be adapted to show this prediction for the relaxation obtained by augmenting Basic Sdp with $\Omega(n)$ rounds of the Sherali-Adams hierarchy, while Tulsiani's work [Tul09] shows that for particular families of predicates, the same holds for $\Omega(n)$ rounds of the Lasserre hierarchy.

- *(Worst-case hardness of approximation results)* As was observed in the past, average-case assumptions such as the RCSP Hypothesis imply worst-case hardness of approximation results. Confirming such predictions again can be thought of as providing evidence for the hypothesis.

  One can view the classic result of Håstad [Hås01] as some hardness of approximation on this form, for the case of predicates such as k-XOR and k-SAT. Our results on generalized CSP's (see below) are also in this flavor.

Beside being an attractive hypothesis in its own right, we also show that the RCSP Hypothesis implies the conjecture that predicates supporting pairwise independent distributions are approximation resistant.[3] This was shown based on the Unique Games Conjecture by [AM09], so our results gives an alternative basis for that statement. We also consider generalizations of the RCSP Hypothesis to larger alphabet and broader sets of parameters, and show that these generalizations yield hard instances for the "Sliding Scale" conjecture

[1]We note such optimality results will have to differ from those of Raghavendra's theorem since his meta-characterization also implies the UGC.

[2]Unless specified otherwise, m will equal cn for some sufficiently large constant c. Also note that our definition considers tuples of *literals* (i.e., variables or their negations) and not just un-negated variables.

[3]We say that a distribution D over a product set S^k is *pairwise independent* if for every $i \neq j$ in $[k]$, the projection $D_{i,j}$ is the uniform distribution over $S \times S$. This notion is also sometimes known as "pairwise uniform".

of [BGLR93] (including its projection game variant [Mos11]), as well as instances for the problem of obtaining a polynomial approximation for the densest κ-subgraph problem (see also [BCC+10, AAM+11]).

REMARK 1.1. *Traditionally in computational complexity it is not very common to consider "meta-conjectures" such as the* **RCSP** *Hypothesis, that posit the hardness of a large family of problems. Complexity theorists naturally prefer the more pleasing "meta-reductions" showing that hardness of a single problem implies the hardness of a large family. This approach has been particularly successful in the study of* worst-case *complexity, where researchers have been able to base the difficulty of an astounding number of problems based on the single assumption that 3SAT can't be solved efficiently. However, such reductions have been much more rare in average case complexity. Indeed, it seems that reductions are inherently problematic in this context, as they tend to use various "gadgets" and other transformations that result in the output of the reduction not being the natural distribution over the instances of the target problem. Thus in the context of average-case complexity we propose that such meta-conjectures, positing the optimality of a certain type of algorithm for a large family of problems, may be the right way to go forward in establishing at least some more intuition as to where lies the boundary between hardness and easiness.*

On a broader level, there are two general approaches in theoretical Computer Science to cope with the fact that many our basic questions remain unsolved. One very useful approach is to try to make the weakest possible conjectures, with the hope of eventually getting rid of them altogether. The other approach, which the **RCSP** *Hypothesis belongs to, is to start with the most simple and broad hypotheses possible and to see what they imply, thereby giving a "large target" for attempts at refutations. Finding refutations for such hypotheses can obviously be very instructive, directing research to more plausible directions. On the other hand, if many refutations attempts fail, this can also be quite useful, as it may reveal a general principle of nature which could be true even if a proof for it is very far from our reach. Finally, we note that as bold as the* **RCSP** *Hypothesis seems, it can be strengthened even further, both quantitatively and qualitatively; see Section 3.4.*

1.2 Generalized CSP

Raghavendra [Rag08] showed how an efficient approximation can be attained for every CSP (contraint satisfaction problem), using an associated SDP which we call the BASIC SDP. In this paper we define a generalized version of each such CSP, for which the same BASIC SDP can still be applied, achieving the same approximation factor. For this generalized CSP, we show that beating the performance of the BASIC SDP relaxation is **NP**-hard. This is in contrast to Raghavendra's result [Rag08] mentioned above, who showed a much stronger conclusion —tightness of BASIC SDP on *standard* CSPs— but under a much stronger assumption, namely the unique games conjecture. Our work draws on the techniques of [KKMO04, MOO05, Rag08] developed in the context of the unique games conjecture, and thus shows that even if this conjecture turns out to be false, both the techniques and at least some parts of the results obtained by works relying on it can still be salvaged. Adapting the above techniques to the case of **NP**-hardness is similar both in flavor and in techniques to the work of [GRSW12], where UGC-hardness was replaced by **NP**-hardness for a class of geometric problems rather than CSPs.[4]

Let $P : \{\pm 1\}^K \to \{0,1\}$ be a predicate. Our starting point is the observation that the BASIC SDP algorithm for CSP(P) actually obtains the same guarantee to a more general problem that we call the *generalized CSP* for P, denoted GCSP(P). The definition of GCSP(P) is a bit subtle (see more below), but roughly speaking it involves placing additional constraints on the assignment that can be enforced by semidefinite programming. Given the way we tailor the definition to BASIC SDP, it is perhaps not surprising that this relaxation achieves the exact same approximation for GCSP(P) as CSP(P). What is more surprising is that now we are able to prove that this approximation guarantee is *optimal*, and cannot be improved upon by any efficient algorithm unless **P** = **NP**. (See §4 for details and Subsection 4.5 for proofs.)

THEOREM 1.2. *For every $c, s \in \mathbb{R}$ with $0 < s < c < 1$ and predicates $P\colon \{\pm 1\}^K \to \{0,1\}$, the promise problem (c,s)-Gap* GCSP(P) *is either* **NP***-hard or solvable in polynomial time (by* BASIC SDP*). Furthermore,* BASIC SDP *solves (c,s)-Gap* GCSP(P) *if and only if it solves (non-generalized) (c,s)-Gap* CSP(P).

Defining generalized CSP.

We now give more details about the definition of generalized CSPs. The definition is closely tied to the BASIC SDP algorithm (see Section 2), and so we start by reviewing it. Let $P : \{\pm 1\}^K \to \{0,1\}$ be a predicate, and let $\mathfrak{I}$ be an instance of CSP(P) over n variables. An *assignment* to $\mathfrak{I}$ is a Boolean vector $x \in \{\pm 1\}^n$ and the *value* of x, denoted val(x), is the fraction of the constraints it satisfies. The BASIC SDP algorithm optimizes over a larger convex set $\mathcal{X}$, (which we call the set of *SDP assignments*) which embeds inside it all the Boolean vectors. For an SDP assignment X, we denote by sval(X) be the value that the SDP outputs on X. One can define a canonical rounding algorithm that maps every SDP assignment $X \in \mathcal{X}$ into a Boolean assignment $x \in \{\pm 1\}^n$ [Rag08], and we define rval(X) to be the value of this Boolean assignment. (If X was already *integral*, i.e., (isomorphic to) a single Boolean assignment x then the rounding algorithm just returns x, and hence rval(X) = sval(X) = val(x).) So, an equivalent way to phrase the problem CSP(P) is that we want to find the maximum of rval(X) over $X \in \mathcal{X}$, while the BASIC SDP algorithm can find the maximum of sval(X) over the same set. That is, instead of considering the goal of CSP(P) as finding a good Boolean assignment, we think of it as finding a "well roundable" / near-integral SDP assignment.

For every $X \in \mathcal{X}$, we have that

$$\alpha\, \mathrm{sval}(X) \leqslant \mathrm{rval}(X) \leqslant \mathrm{sval}(X)\,, \tag{1.1}$$

where α is called the *integrality gap ratio* of the program. Clearly, BASIC SDP is an α-approximation for CSP(P). But because (1.1) holds pointwise for every $X \in \mathcal{X}$, one can see that even if we placed additional linear and semidefinite constraints on X, thus restricting the set $\mathcal{X}$ into some subset $\mathcal{X}'$, then BASIC SDP still yields an α approximation for this more general program. This general problem is the generalized CSP problem. That is, an instance to GCSP(P) consists of a set of K-tuples of literals, as well as some additional constraints that we place on the SDP solutions X, and the goal is to find a "well roundable" / near-integral SDP solution meeting those constraints.

[4]We note that in [Rag08], the term "generalized CSP" was used for constraints which are real-valued rather than Boolean valued. Our notion is different, as we consider Boolean valued constraints where the variables which appear in them are real-valued.

Are generalized CSP natural? We think that the mere fact that GCSP(P) has the same approximation as CSP(P) but it is **NP**-hard to beat already shows that this problem is non-trivial. But one may wonder if the generalized CSP problem is also interesting on its own right. While the definition of the problem is indeed closely tied to the BASIC SDP algorithm, we believe that it also of some independent interest. One way to think about SDP assignment is as distributions over Boolean assignment, while the additional constraints posit certain correlations between the random variables comprising this distribution (e.g., a typical such constraint for generalized MAX CUT will require that if i and j are in the left side of the cut, then k is also likely to be on that side). One can imagine that solving a CSP with such weak side constraints could be useful in some applications.[5]

Evidence for the Unique Games Conjecture?

The UGC implies BASIC SDP is optimal for Generalized CSPs. Our results confirm this prediction of this conjecture, and hence can be interpreted as giving evidence for the truth of the UGC. However, there is also evidence that Generalized CSPs are strictly harder computationally than (non-generalized) CSPs: Our **NP**-hardness reductions from smooth LABEL COVER to Generalized CSPs have linear running time. There is some evidence that smooth LABEL COVER (with the parameters that we need) is exponentially hard (see Remark 3.8), which would imply that it is exponentially hard to beat the approximation guarantee of BASIC SDP for Generalized CSPs. In contrast, for some (non-generalized) CSPs, it is known how to beat the approximation of BASIC SDP in subexponential time [ABS10].

1.3 Our techniques

In this section we outline some of the techniques used in the proof of Theorem 1.2— optimality of BASIC SDP for generalized CSP's— which is our most technical result. We focus on the case of the *generalized* MAX CUT problem, which we also deal with more formally later, in Subsection 4.3. Going from generalized MAX CUT to generalized CSPs of other types follows quite closely the transition made in [Rag08] from (non-generalized) MAX CUT to other (non-generalized) CSPs. Both our construction and the proof are generalizations of the UNIQUE GAMES- hardness of the MAX CUT problem [KKMO07, MOO10], and readers familiar with that result as well as [Rag08] should see the similarities. We also use techniques similar to the ones from [GRSW12].

We begin by describing the (c, s)-gap generalized MAX CUT problem. As described above, this is the problem of finding an SDP solution which satisfies not just the constraints that result from the MAX CUT instance but also additional linear constraints, and has a high expected value when rounded. The goal in generalized MAX CUT is to find such an SDP solution which is rounded to the best possible integral solution by the standard rounding procedure. Specifically, the (c, s)-gap problem is that of distinguishing between the case where there exists an SDP solution that is rounded to a integral solution with value c, and the case where no SDP solution which satisfies the additional linear constraints get expected integral value greater than s.

The BASIC SDP algorithm for max-cut is the well known Goemans-Williamson SDP [GW95], which can be thought of as maximizing the sum of $\mathbb{E}\,\frac{1-y_iy_j}{2}$ over all edges (i, j) in the input graph, where (if the graph has m vertices) $y_1, \ldots, y_m$ are Gaussian random variables satisfying $\mathbb{E}\,|y_i|^2 = 1$ for all i.[6] The rounding function of this SDP is simply obtained by taking the sign of the Gaussians (which would of course not lose anything if they were degenerate random variables with variance zero), and hence one way to phrase the (non generalized) MAX CUT problem is that the aim is to find Gaussian variables $y_1, \ldots, y_m$ maximizing the sum of $\mathbb{E}\,\frac{1-\mathrm{sign}(y_i)\,\mathrm{sign}(y_j)}{2}$ over all edges (i, j).

For the (c, s)-gap generalized MAX CUT problem, we want to optimize the SDP solution under additional constraints, and in particular we allow the instance to require some linear constraints on the correlations between these Gaussians. A natural way in which this can be achieved is that the instance specifies that each gaussian y_i must be a linear combination of some other gaussian variables. Another way to say the same thing is that an instance of generalized MAX CUT will consists of a graph on m vertices where each vertex is identified with some linear function from $\mathbb{R}^n$ to $\mathbb{R}$. Thus, now we aim to find Gaussians $x_1, \ldots, x_n$ that maximize the sum of $\mathbb{E}\,\frac{1-\mathrm{sign}(a(x))\,\mathrm{sign}(b(x))}{2}$ over all edges (a, b). This leads us to the following definition:

DEFINITION 1.3. *(c, s)-gap generalized* MAX CUT *is the following promise problem: Given a distribution over pairs of linear functions (a, b) over $\mathbb{R}^n$, distinguish between the following cases:*

YES: *there exists $x \in \{0, 1\}^n$ such that $a(x) \in \{\pm 1\}$ for all linear forms a appearing in $\mathfrak{I}$ and $\mathbb{P}_{(a,b)\sim\mathfrak{I}}\,\{a(x) \neq b(x)\} \geqslant c$,*

NO: *for every n-dimensional random vector x whose coordinates are jointly Gaussian, which satisfies $\mathbb{E}_x\, xx^T \geqslant 0$ and $\mathbb{E}\,a(x)^2 = 1$ for all linear forms a appearing in $\mathfrak{I}$, we have $\mathbb{E}_x\,\mathbb{P}_{(a,b)\sim\mathfrak{I}}\,\{\mathrm{sign}(a(x)) \neq \mathrm{sign}(b(x))\} \leqslant s$.*[7]

To make the connection to other CSPs more apparent, we state our result for generalized MAX CUT in a generic way as follows.

THEOREM 1.4. *Let $c, s \in \mathbb{R}$ with $0 < s < c < 1$ and $c \geqslant 0.845$.*[8] *If there exists a (c, s) SDP-gap instance (with respect to the Goemans-Williamson* MAX CUT *SDP) for (non-generalized)* MAX CUT, *then (c, s)-gap generalized* MAX CUT *is* **NP**-*hard. On the other hand, if (c, s)-gap* MAX CUT *is solvable by the Goemans-Williamson* MAX CUT *algorithm, then so is the (c, s) generalized* MAX CUT *gap problem.*

As the generalized MAX CUT problem is obtained by linear constraints on an SDP solution, it's not hard to show that for pairs (c, s) where the Goemans-Williamson algorithm solved MAX CUT it will also solve generalized MAX CUT. Let us therefore see how a (c, s) integrality gap for MAX CUT translates to an **NP**-hardness result.

[5]Note that the constraints are weak rather than precise linear relations between the variables, since the rounding function can introduce some errors.

[6]The above description is equivalent to the more common description of the program with vectors, since every vector v_i can be associated with a Gaussian random variable y_i obtained by taking $\langle v_i, g\rangle$ for a random Gaussian, and visa versa. (To generate non-symmetric Gaussian variables one can introduce an additional vector v_0 and identify it with the Gaussian variable that is identically 1.)

[7]Note that the requirement that $\mathbb{E}_x\, xx^T \geqslant 0$ is another linear constraint on the correlation matrix. For showing the problem is easy we can generalize to all such linear constraints, but our hardness proof only requires this one.

[8]In this range of c the Goemans-Williamson rounding is optimal for BASIC SDP of MAX CUT

The projection test.

In [Rag08], it is explained how to transform an integrality gap instance of a CSP into a long-code test for a function $f : \{-1,1\}^R \to \{0,1\}$. For the specific case of Max Cut, this reduction was shown by [KKMO04] and works as follows: Pick a random edge (i,j) from the instance, and choose ρ to be the correlation between the Gaussian vectors x_i and x_j supplied by the SDP solution for the instance. Then pick $a, b \in \{-1,1\}^k$ to be random Boolean vectors with correlation ρ between the coordinates a_i and b_i for each i, and accepts if $f(a) \neq f(b)$. To get **NP**-hardnes, though, it is not enough to consider a dictatorship test – we need a test for projections, namely one that works for two functions on *different domains* $f : \{-1,1\}^{d \cdot R} \to \{0,1\}$ and $g : \{-1,1\}^R \to \{0,1\}$, with a given projection function $\pi : [d \cdot R] \to [R]$. Oversimplifying, the test should verify that f is an i dictatorship for some i, that g is a j dictatorship, and that $\pi(i) = j$. However, because the functions have so different domains, natural attempt at a test makes the distribution of the larger input a be very far from the uniform distribution, and instead depend strongly on the particular projection π. On an intuitive level this is a bad thing, since the function f might be very far from a dictator globally, but agree with a dictator on this particular distribution. Indeed, no such test is known.

Our solution to this problem, which follows a similar approach to [GRSW12], is to use the additional linear constraints to bypass this issue. Roughly speaking, one can define a simple linear map L_π that takes a function $f : \{\pm 1\}^{dR} \to \mathbb{R}$ and maps it into a function $f' : \{\pm 1\}^R \to \mathbb{R}$ such that if f is an i dictatorship then f' is a $\pi(i)$ dictatorship. Indeed, the map L_π is defined by simply requiring it to satisfy this property for the dictatorships, and extending it linearly to all other functions. In our problem we can enforce this kind of linear relation between f and f', and so at least are in the position where we can syntactically apply the same test on f' and g, which are now on the same domain.

However, there is a host of technical issues that must be overcome to show the test actually works. To prove soundness for this test, we need to show a that (very roughly speaking) the map L_π has the property that if $L_\pi f$ is close to a dictator (or more accurately, has an influential coordinate) then so is the original function f. It's very easy to show that this is not generally true, and that for every π one can come up with a function f that is far from a dictator but $L_\pi f$ is very close to one. Indeed, one example would be to fix some $j_0 \in [R]$ and take f to be the sum over all $i \in \pi^{-1}(j_0)$ of the ith dictator. However, here is where (as in [GRSW12]) the technical property of *smoothness* comes to the rescue. This property means that for every function f which is a sum of dictatorships, with non-negative weight w_i for the ith dictatorship, if we look at a "typical" projection π that will arise in our reduction, then the the sum of the weights in each of the "buckets" $\pi^{-1}(j)$ will be roughly the same. Now some additional complications arise since in our cases these "weights" may be negative, and in fact are not even numbers but actually vectors. Here we use some properties of moments of Gaussians, together with the condition on non-negative correlations, to argue that cancelations will not be an issue. The above is clearly only a very rough outline of the proof, which is given in Section 4.

2. PRELIMINARIES

A *Gaussian vector* (over some $\mathbb{R}$-vector space) is a vector-valued random variable with coordinates drawn from a joint Gaussian distribution. We do not assume symmetry. In particular, the mean of a Gaussian vector is not necessarily the 0 vector.

Boolean CSPs.

Let $P\colon \{\pm 1\}^K \to \{0,1\}$ be a Boolean predicate. A CSP(P) instance $\mathfrak{I}$ with variable set $V = [n]$ is specified by a collection of ordered K-tuples of literals. We identity K-tuple of literals with functions $S\colon \{\pm 1\}^V \to \{\pm 1\}^K$ such that each output bit $S(x)_i$ depends on at most one coordinate of $x \in \{\pm 1\}^V$. The value of an assignment $x \in \{\pm 1\}^V$ is defined as $\mathfrak{I}(x) = \mathbb{E}_{S \in \mathfrak{I}} P(S(x))$. We denote the maximum value of an assignment by $\text{opt}(\mathfrak{I}) = \max_{x \in \{\pm 1\}^V} \mathfrak{I}(x)$.

Basic SDP Relaxation.

For every CSP(P) instance $\mathfrak{I}$, we associate a semidefinite program Basic Sdp($\mathfrak{I}$). A *solution* for Basic Sdp($\mathfrak{I}$) consists of an n-dimensional Gaussian vector x and a collection of distributions $\{\mu_S\}_{S \in \mathfrak{I}}$ over $\{\pm 1\}^K$. The solution is *feasible* if for every $S \in \mathfrak{I}$, the first two moments of the distributions $S(x)$ and μ_S match. (Here, we extend S to $\mathbb{R}^n$ in a multilinear way.) Concretely, every K-variate quadratic[9] polynomial Q satisfies $\mathbb{E}_x Q(S(x)) = \mathbb{E}_{\mu_S} Q$. The *value* of such a solution is defined as $\mathbb{E}_{S \in \mathfrak{I}} \mathbb{E}_{\mu_S} P \circ S$. We denote the maximum value of Basic Sdp($\mathfrak{I}$) by opt(Basic Sdp($\mathfrak{I}$)). For brevity, we will often drop opt($\cdot$) and use Basic Sdp($\mathfrak{I}$) also to refer to the optimal value of the SDP relaxation.

Since a feasible Gaussian vector x is supposed to model (a distribution over) points in $\{\pm 1\}^n$, its diagonal second moments are $\mathbb{E}_x x_1^2 = \ldots = \mathbb{E}_x x_n^2 = 1$. We refer to this constraint as *normalization condition*.

For $0 < s < c < 1$, we say that Basic Sdp achieves a (c,s)-approximation for CSP(P) if every CSP(P) instance $\mathfrak{I}$ with Basic Sdp($\mathfrak{I}$) $\geqslant c$ also satisfies opt($\mathfrak{I}$) $\geqslant s$.

3. THE SDP OPTIMALITY HYPOTHESIS FOR RANDOM CSPS

In this section we formulate more precisely the RCSP Hypothesis, and show some of the evidence supporting it, as well as its implications. We also consider some extensions of the hypothesis to higher alphabet, and non-constant parameters, and discuss their implications.

3.1 Random CSPs

For every n, m and $P\colon \{\pm 1\}^K \to \{0,1\}$, we let $\text{CSP}_{n,m}(P)$ denote the distribution over instances of CSP(P) obtained by taking m random K-tuples over n variables. We let $\underline{\text{val}}(P)$ denote the expected value a random assignment gives to a CSP(P) instance, namely $\underline{\text{val}}(P) = \mathbb{E}\, P(U_K)$ where U_K is the uniform distribution over $\{\pm 1\}^K$. We note the simple fact that the optimal value of random instances of CSP(P) is asymptotically equal to the value obtained by a random assignment:

Lemma 3.1. *For every K, ε, δ there is $c = c(K, \varepsilon, \delta)$ such that for all $P\colon \{\pm 1\}^K \to \{0,1\}$ and $m \geqslant cn$, if $\mathfrak{I}$ is chosen at random from $\text{CSP}_{n,m}(P)$ then a.s. $\underline{\text{val}}(\mathfrak{I}) \leqslant \text{val}(\mathfrak{I}) \leqslant \underline{\text{val}}(\mathfrak{I}) + \varepsilon$.*

Proof. Since val($\mathfrak{I}$) is the maximum value over all assignments, clearly $\underline{\text{val}}(\mathfrak{I}) \leqslant \text{val}(\mathfrak{I})$ for all $\mathfrak{I}$. Now for the other direction, we claim that for sufficiently large c, with high probability over the choice of the m tuples $S_1, \ldots, S_m$, we will

[9]Here, quadratic means degree *at most* 2.

have that for *every* $x \in \{\pm 1\}^n$, the distribution $D = D_{\{S_i\},x}$ obtained by taking $i \leftarrow_R [m]$ and outputting $(y_1, \dots, y_K) = S_i(x)$ is ε-close to the uniform distribution in statistical distance, thus concluding the proof. This will follow from a simple concentration+union bound argument. Using the Vazirani XOR Lemma, it suffices to show that for every fixed vector $a = (a_1, \dots, a_K) \in \{0,1\}^K$ and fixed x, the probability over the choice of the S_i's that **(*)** $|\sum_{i \in [m]} \prod_{j=1}^K S_i(x)_j^{a_j} - m/2| \geqslant m\varepsilon/2^K$ is less than $\delta 2^{-n}$. But because the S_i's are chosen independently at random, and in particular the negation pattern added to them is random, for every x the random variables $b_1, \dots, b_m$ where $b_i = \prod_{j=1}^K S_i(x)_j^{a_j}$ are unbiased and independent, and hence the probability of **(*)** is at most $\exp(-\varepsilon^2 m/4)$ which can be made sufficiently small by taking c large enough. □

3.2 Characterizing the SDP value of CSP(P)

We now make a simple, but very useful observation, that has been implicitly made in other works as well [AM09]— the value that Basic Sdp returns on random instances of CSP(P) is equal to the maximum of $\mathbb{E}\,P(D)$ taken over all pairwise independent distributions D over $\{\pm 1\}^K$.

Theorem 3.2. *Let $P\colon \{\pm 1\}^K \to \{0,1\}$, and let $\overline{\mathrm{val}}(P)$ equal the maximum of $\mathbb{E}\,P(D)$ over all pairwise independent distributions D over $\{\pm 1\}^K$. Then:*

1. *For every instance $\mathfrak{I}$ of* CSP(P), Basic Sdp($\mathfrak{I}$) $\geqslant \overline{\mathrm{val}}(P)$.
2. *For every $\varepsilon, \delta > 0$, there is $c = c(K, \varepsilon, \delta)$ such that if $\mathfrak{I}$ is a random instance of* CSP(P) *with n variables and at least cn tuples, then with probability $1-\delta$,* Basic Sdp($\mathfrak{I}$) $\leqslant \overline{\mathrm{val}}(P) + \varepsilon$.

Proof. Let $\mathfrak{I}$ be a CSP(P) instance, consisting of m tuples of literals $S_1, \dots, S_m$ over the variables $x_1, \dots, x_n$. A Basic Sdp *assignment* for $\mathfrak{I}$ consists of n random variables $X_1, \dots, X_n$ (that can be thought of as real vectors over some sample space Ω), and m distributions $\mu_1, \dots, \mu_m$, each over $\{0,1\}^K$ (and hence can be given by 2^K numbers in $[0,1]$ summing to 1). The distribution μ_i is "supposed" to correspond to the restriction of the random variables $X_1, \dots, X_n$ to the literals in S_i, but the only constraints that it needs to satisfy is that it agrees with this distribution up to the first two moments. That is, if we let $(Y_1, \dots, Y_K)$ be the distribution $S_i(X_1, \dots, X_n)$, and let $(Z_1, \dots, Z_K)$ be distributed according to μ_i, then for all $j, j' \in [K]$, $\mathbb{E}\,Y_j Y_{j'} = \mathbb{E}\,Z_j Z_{j'}$, and $\mathbb{E}\,Y_j = \mathbb{E}\,Z_j$. The value of the assignment is $\mathbb{E}_i\,\mathbb{E}\,P(\mu_i)$, and the value Basic Sdp($\mathfrak{I}$) is the maximum of this value over all assignments.

1. Let D be the pairwise independent distribution that achieves $\overline{\mathrm{val}}(P)$, letting $X_1, \dots, X_n$ be orthogonal unit vectors, and let $\mu_i = D$ for all i, then we get a valid Basic Sdp assignment that demonstrates that Basic Sdp(P) $\geqslant \overline{\mathrm{val}}(P)$.
2. Suppose that there is a Basic Sdp assignment $X_1, \dots, X_n$, $\mu_1, \dots, \mu_m$ that achieves $\overline{\mathrm{val}}(P) + \varepsilon$. Let μ be the distribution over $\{\pm 1\}^K$ obtained by taking $i \in_r [m]$ and $(y_1, \dots, y_K) \in_r \mu_i$. We denote the resulting distribution by $(Y_1, \dots, Y_K)$. Then $\mathbb{E}\,P(\mu) = \overline{\mathrm{val}}(P) + \varepsilon$ which means that μ is *not* pairwise independent. In particular we get that there must be either **(i)** $j \in [K]$ such that $|\mathbb{E}\,Y_j| > \varepsilon'$ or **(ii)** some $j \neq j' \in [K]$ such that $|\mathbb{E}\,Y_j Y_{j'}| > \varepsilon'$ for some $\varepsilon' = \Omega(\varepsilon/k^2) > 0$. But, if c is big enough then both **(i)** and **(ii)** are highly unlikely. First, it's easy to see for c large enough we would have that all but small fraction of the vertices, the number of times they appear in the jth coordinate positively will be up to some $1 \pm \varepsilon'$ factor the same as the number of times in that coordinate negatively, thus ruling out **(i)**. Second, if we consider the 2XOR game obtained by taking for every tuple S_i the constraint that the product of the jth and j'^{th} literals is 1 (or -1), then it is a random 2XOR game, and it is known that (since the underlying graph will be an expander) the Basic Sdp value of this game will tend to 0 with c, thus ruling out **(ii)**.

□

We can now restate the RCSP Hypothesis:

RCSP Hypothesis. (*SDP optimality hypothesis for refuting* CSP's, *formal version*) Let $P\colon \{\pm 1\}^K \to \{0,1\}$ be a predicate, let $\Delta > 0$ and let $m(n)$ be some function such that $m(n) \leqslant \Delta n$. Then for every polynomial time relaxation A for CSP(P) and $\varepsilon, \delta > 0$, we have that for all sufficiently large n

$$\mathbb{P}[A(\mathfrak{I}) \leqslant \overline{\mathrm{val}}(\mathfrak{I}) - \varepsilon] < \delta\,,$$

where this probability is over $\mathfrak{I}$ chosen from $\mathrm{CSP}_{n,m(n)}(P)$.

Combining Lemma 3.1 with Theorem 3.2, we see that the RCSP Hypothesis implies that predicates supporting a pairwise independent distribution are *approximation resistant* in the sense of [AH12]. That is, for every predicate $P\colon \{\pm 1\}^K \to \{0,1\}$, if there exists a pairwise independent distribution D whose support is contained in $P^{-1}(1)$, then for every $\varepsilon > 0$ there is no polynomial-time algorithm B to distinguish, given an instance $\mathfrak{I}$ of CSP(P), between the case **YES** that $\mathrm{val}(\mathfrak{I}) = 1 - \varepsilon$ and the case **NO** that $\mathrm{val}(\mathfrak{I}) \leqslant \overline{\mathrm{val}}(\mathfrak{I}) + \varepsilon$. Indeed, if there was such an algorithm B then we could construct a relaxation algorithm A contradicting the RCSP Hypothesis by simply having $A(\mathfrak{I})$ output $1 - \varepsilon$ if $B(\mathfrak{I})$ ="NO", and $A(\mathfrak{I})$ output 1 otherwise.

3.3 Some evidence for the SDP optimality hypothesis

The RCSP Hypothesis is fairly bold, in the sense that it posits average-case hardness of a large family of problems, and so we would like to investigate whether it can actually be true. There are two types of evidence for such an hypothesis— (a) we could show that the hypothesis (or at least variants of it) is implied by seemingly weaker or more well studied conjectures, and (b) we could verify some of the *predictions* it makes, that is independently prove some the hypothesis' implications. As discussed in Section 1.1, we offer evidence of both types for this hypothesis. While we believe more investigations are merited, we believe these results do suggest that the RCSP Hypothesis may be true.

3.3.1 Relation to Feige's Hypothesis

Feige made the hypothesis [Fei02] that for every $\varepsilon > 0$ there is no algorithm that can certify that the value of a random 3SAT instance (i.e., taken from $\mathrm{CSP}_{n,O(n)}(OR)$ in our notation) is smaller than $1 - \varepsilon$. Though he didn't phrase it in those terms, Feige's results show that his Hypothesis 2 implies the special case of the RCSP Hypothesis for 3-ary predicates. Specifically, Theorem 2 in [Fei02] shows that under his Hypothesis 2, for every predicate $P\colon \{\pm 1\}^3 \to \{0,1\}$, it is hard, given a random $\mathfrak{I} \in \mathrm{CSP}_{n,O(n)}(P)$ to certify that $\mathrm{val}(\mathfrak{I}) \leqslant b(P)/4$, where b is the number of $x \in P^{-1}(1)$ such that $x_1x_2x_3 = +1$ (or -1, if that number is greater). However, it is not hard to show that for a 3-ary predicate P, $\overline{\text{val}}(P) = b(P)/4$.

In fact, Feige's work can be used to show that for *every* non-trivial predicate $P\colon \{\pm1\}^3 \to \{0,1\}$ (i.e., where $\underline{\text{val}}(P) < \overline{\text{val}}(P)$), the special case of the RCSP Hypothesis for P implies the hypothesis for all 3-ary predicates. For completeness we show a full proof of this result for the case of XOR.

Theorem 3.3. *Suppose that RCSP holds for the 3XOR predicate then it holds also for every other predicate $P\colon \{\pm1\}^3 \to \{\pm1\}$.*

Proof. For this proof it will be convenient to extend our notion of predicates to general functions $P\colon \{\pm1\}^3 \to \mathbb{R}$ (and not just those that have output in $\{0,1\}$). Note that the SDP value, as well as the notions of $\underline{\text{val}}$, $\overline{\text{val}}$, val easily extend to this case. In particular, it will be convenient to define the predicate 3XOR as simply outputting the product $x_1x_2x_3$ of its inputs. (The 0/1 definition of 3XOR is $P_0(x_1,x_2,x_3) = (x_1x_2x_3 - 1)/2$, but clearly if you can refute one then you can refute the other and so the two definitions are equivalent in computational difficulty.)

Let $P\colon \{\pm1\}^3 \to \{0,1\}$ be some predicate, and write P as a multilinear polynomial in the variables x_1,x_2,x_3 of the form $ax_1x_2x_3 + P'(x_1,x_2,x_3) + b$ where $a,b \in \mathbb{R}$ and P' has no constant term and degree at most 2. Suppose that there is an algorithm A that can certify that a random instance $\mathfrak{I}$ of CSP(P) has $\text{val}_P(\mathfrak{I}) \leqslant \overline{\text{val}}(P) - \varepsilon$ (where $\text{val}_P(\mathfrak{I})$ denotes the value of the set of tuples $\mathfrak{I}$ when thought of as an instance of CSP(P)). We'll construct an algorithm B that can certify that $\text{val}_{3XOR}(\mathfrak{I}) \leqslant 1-\varepsilon'$ for some $\varepsilon' > 0$ that tends to zero with ε. The algorithm B will first certify that $|\text{val}_{P'}(\mathfrak{I})| < \varepsilon/2$ using Basic Sdp (which can be done since since for every $f : \{\pm1\}^3 \to \mathbb{R}$ of degree at most 2 without a constant term, $\underline{\text{val}}(f) = \overline{\text{val}}(f) = 0$). Now this means that for every assignment x,

$$\mathop{\mathbb{E}}_{S \leftarrow_R \mathfrak{I}} P(S(x)) \in a \mathop{\mathbb{E}}_{S \leftarrow_R \mathfrak{I}} 3XOR(S(x)) + c \pm \varepsilon/2\,.$$

Assume $a < 0$ (the other case is symmetric). Thus, if we want to certify that $\text{val}_{3XOR}(\mathfrak{I}) \leqslant 1 - \varepsilon/2$, it suffices to certify that $\text{val}_P(-\mathfrak{I}) \leqslant |a| + c - \varepsilon$, where $-\mathfrak{I}$ is obtained by flipping all signs in the literals of $\mathfrak{I}$. Indeed, otherwise, if $\text{val}_{3XOR}(\mathfrak{I}) \geqslant 1 - \varepsilon/2$, then $\text{val}_P(-\mathfrak{I})$ would have been at least $|a|(1-\varepsilon/2) + c - \varepsilon/2 \geqslant |a| + c - \varepsilon$, since it's easy to see that $c \leqslant 1$. So the result follows by showing that $\overline{\text{val}}(P) \leqslant |a| + c$, which holds since for every pairwise independent distribution D over $\{\pm1\}^3$, $EP'(D) = 0$, while $|E_{x \leftarrow_R D} x_1x_2x_3| \leqslant 1$. (In fact, $\overline{\text{val}}(P) = |a| + c$, as demonstrated by the distribution $(x_1, x_2, -x_1x_2)$.) □

3.3.2 Integrality gaps

If the RCSP Hypothesis is true, then on random CSP instances, Basic Sdp can't be beat by even much more powerful algorithms. Thus, one way to get more evidence for our hypothesis is to verify this prediction for some particular algorithms. Specifically, we will be interested in semidefinite programming *hierarchies*, which are systematic way of strengthening Basic Sdp to obtain tighter relaxations (see the survey [Lau03]). We observe that prior works, though not phrased in those terms, establish particular predictions of the RCSP Hypothesis:

Theorem 3.4 (Implicit in [BGMT12]). *For every $P\colon \{\pm1\}^K \to \{0,1\}$, $\varepsilon > 0, \Delta \in \mathbb{N}$, there exists $\delta > 0$ such that for sufficiently large n, if $\mathfrak{I}$ is drawn randomly from $\text{CSP}_{n,\Delta n}(P)$, with probability at least $1 - \varepsilon$, the program obtained by augmenting* Basic Sdp *with δn levels of the Sherali-Adams hierarchy outputs at least $\overline{\text{val}}(P) - \varepsilon$.*

Proof. Benabbas Georgiou Magen Tulsiani (Theorem 4.3 in [BGMT12]) proved that this holds for the case that $\overline{\text{val}}(P) = 1$ (i.e., when there is a pairwise independent distribution supported on $P^{-1}(1)$). However, the proof easily extends to the general case. □

For the stronger SDP hierarchy of Lasserre, this is not yet currently known. However, it is known for the special case of *subspace predicates*, which are predicates $P\colon \{\pm1\}^K \to \{0,1\}$ such that if we identify $\{\pm1\}^K$ with $\mathbb{F}_2^K$ in the obvious way, then P^{-1} is an affine subspace. For such a predicate, let $d(P)$ be the minimum weight of the dual subspace to $P^{-1}(1)$. In other words, this is minimum number of variables in a linear equation over $x_1,\ldots,x_K$ that is satisfied by all $x \in P^{-1}(1)$. It's not hard to see that if $d(P) \geqslant 3$ then $\overline{\text{val}}(P) = 1$. Tulsiani (Theorem 4.3 in [Tul09]) showed for such P, $\Omega(n)$ rounds of the Lasserre hierarchy give value 1 on random instances of CSP(P).

3.3.3 Hardness of approximation results

Another consequence of the RCSP Hypothesis would be some *worst-case* hardness of approximation results. Since a random instance of CSP(P) has value roughly $\underline{\text{val}}(P)$, any approximation algorithm that can distinguish between instances with this value and instances with value $\overline{\text{val}}(P) - o(1)$ would refute the hypothesis. Thus, another way to increase confidence in the hypothesis would be to derive these predictions based on more standard and widely believed assumptions such as $\mathbf{P} \neq \mathbf{NP}$. We were not able to prove this result, which is of course interesting in its own right. However our results on generalized CSP can be viewed as making some progress for confirming these type of predictions.

Remark 3.5. *Note that if the Unique Games Conjecture was true, then Raghavendra's Theorem of course implies that it's* **NP***-hard to beat* Basic Sdp. *However, we don't consider this as strong evidence for the RCSP Hypothesis. First, as mentioned, it is not at all clear that the UGC is true. Second, even if true, the UGC seems not to say much about* random *or even* pseudorandom *instances, for which algorithms beating the UGC's predictions are known (indeed* Basic Sdp *itself can sometime work better than the worst case on such instances [AKK+08]). Furthermore, it is known that* Unique Games*-hardness cannot establish* $\exp(\Omega(n))$ *or* $\exp(n^{1-o(1)})$ *hardness for a problem, while the integrality gaps suggest that it may even be hard to beat* Basic Sdp *on random instances in subexponential time.*

3.4 Extensions of the RCSP Hypothesis and their applications

While there is more evidence for "vanilla" version of the RCSP Hypothesis, there are several natural ways to quantitatively strengthen it that are not known to be false, and some of these, if true, will have interesting applications.

Super polynomial running time.

While the hypothesis is stated equating "efficient" with polynomial time, it seems just as valid to assume that there is no $\exp(n^{o(1)})$-time algorithm that beats Basic Sdp. In fact, current integrality gaps support even the conjecture that beating Basic Sdp on random instances will take at least $\exp(\Omega(n))$ time, where the constant in the Ω notation may depend on the parameters (accuracy parameter ε, predicate arity parameter K, clause to variable ratio parameter Δ).

Non binary alphabet.

A very natural extension is to consider predicates over alphabet $q > 2$. One way to represent them is as $P\colon R^K \to \{0,1\}$, where R is a ring of size q (or perhaps a field if q is a prime or prime power). Following prior works on integrality gaps and proof complexity [Tul09], we'll use the convention that a *literal* y_i would correspond to not just a variable x_i or its negation (which has no meaning here) but it would be a *shift* of x_i by some arbitrary $a \in R$ (where for $R = \mathbb{F}_2$, $a = 0$ corresponds to taking the variable, and $a = 1$ corresponds to negating it). This preserves the property that a random instance of CSP(P) would have value roughly $\underline{\mathrm{val}}(P)$.

Super constant parameters.

While the conjecture is stated for parameters (such as accuracy ε, arity K, and clause to variable ratio Δ) that are constant, it may very well hold for values of these parameters (as well as the alphabet size parameter q mentioned above) that are *super-constant* functions of n. In particular, current knowledge seems consistent with the conjecture being true for $K, \Delta, q, 1/\varepsilon$ all being up to some value n^δ for some small $\delta > 0$. Such versions of the conjecture can be used to derive much stronger hardness of approximation results.

Remark 3.6 (*Determining thresholds for parameters*). *It is an interesting question whether SDP's can be used to predict the precise hardness thresholds for these parameters. A case in point is the value of the clause to variable ratio Δ for refuting random 3XOR (or 3SAT) instances. The best polynomial-time algorithms known work for Δ that is at least (roughly) $\sqrt{n}$.*[10] *This is not done by* Basic Sdp *(that always outputs at least $\overline{\mathrm{val}}(P)$ for any predicate P) but can be achieved by a polynomial-time extension of* Basic Sdp. *(One example is an algorithm that would work for $\Delta > \sqrt{n}$ is an SDP we call "local Lasserre" where one adds for every subset S of variables that appear in some tuple/clause, a vector that is supposed to correspond to $\prod_{i \in S} x_i$, with the appropriate consistency constraints.) Thus, one could hope to make a stronger SDP optimality conjecture that will pinpoint the right value of Δ. A more tricky question is whether SDP's can help pinpoint the minimum possible value for our "completeness parameter" ε. While setting ε to be an arbitrary small constant seems to keep the problem hard, and maybe we can even set it equal to $n^{-\delta}$ for some small $\delta > 0$, we do not know of a very principled way to hypothesize the right hardness threshold for ε. Consider again the case of 3XOR: although for $\varepsilon = 0$ the problem can be easily solved via Gaussian elimination, even very strong SDP's such as $\Omega(n)$ rounds of the Lasserre hierarchy cannot recover this algorithm, and hence do not yield a prediction on the right bound for ε. A related question is in what cases taking $\varepsilon = 0$ (i.e., "perfect completeness") still keeps the problem hard. Clearly having the predicate be* non-linear *(under any encoding of the alphabet) is a necessary requirement, but it is not clear that it is a sufficient one.*

[10] Interestingly, Feige, Kim and Ofek [FKO06] gave *non-deterministic* algorithm for refuting random 3XOR or 3SAT instances with $\Delta \sim n^{0.4}$. However, there is no efficient algorithm that matches their performance, and moreover their algorithm was for the case that ε is smaller than $n^{-0.2}$.

Decision version of the RCSP *Hypothesis.*

There is also a natural way to *qualitatively* strengthen the RCSP Hypothesis. For any **NP** promise set $(\mathcal{Y}, \mathcal{N})$ (where there is always a certificate/witness to certify that $x \notin \mathcal{N}$), given distributions $\mathcal{D}_Y, \mathcal{D}_N$ over these sets, one can define three variants of average-case computational problems: **(i)** The *decision problem* is to distinguish, given an input x drawn randomly from either $\mathcal{D}_Y$ or $\mathcal{D}_N$, which is the case with success noticeably larger than 1/2. **(ii)** The *search problem* is to find, given x drawn from $\mathcal{D}_Y$ the witness that certifies that it is at least not in $\mathcal{N}$. **(iii)** The *refutation problem* is to certify, given x drawn from $\mathcal{D}_N$, that x is not in $\mathcal{Y}$, by giving an algorithm that never outputs "NO" on $x \in \mathcal{Y}$, and typically outputs "NO" on x from $\mathcal{D}_N$.

The decision problem is obviously easier than the refutation and search problem, which are in general incomparable, although in some cases search to decision reductions are also known. We formulate now a decisional version of the RCSP hypothesis, which posits that its hard to distinguish between random CSPinstances, and instances in which we "planted" a solution:

DCSP Hypothesis. (*SDP optimality hypothesis for deciding CSPs, informal*) Let D_0 be a pairwise independent distribution over $\{\pm 1\}^K$ and let $\varepsilon, \delta > 0$ and $\Delta > 1$. Let $\mathrm{CSP}_{n,m,k}$ be the uniform distribution of taking m random K-tuples of literals over n variables, and let $\mathcal{D}_Y(n, m, k, D_0, \varepsilon)$ be the distribution over such tuples that is output by the following process:

1. Pick $x_0 \leftarrow_R \{\pm 1\}^n$.
2. For $i = 1 \ldots m$, the ith tuple S is chosen as follows. With probability ε, S is chosen to be a random K-tuple of literals. With probability $1 - \varepsilon$, we pick random $d \leftarrow_R D_0$, and pick S to be a random K-tuple of literals *conditioned on* $S(x_0) = d$.

Then for every polynomial-time algorithm A, if n is sufficiently large and $m = \Delta n$ it holds that

$$\left|\mathbb{E}\, A(\mathrm{CSP}_{n,m,k}) - \mathbb{E}\, A(\mathcal{D}_Y(n, m, k, D_0, \varepsilon)\right| < \delta\,.$$

Note that the DCSP Hypothesis talks about pairwise independent distributions over $\{\pm 1\}^K$, instead of predicates. This is in some sense necessary, since naive planting of a satisfying assignment, without ensuring that the induced distribution over tuples is pairwise independent, would make it easy even for Basic Sdp to detect the difference between the NO and YES cases. We show in the appendix that the DCSP Hypothesis implies the RCSP Hypothesis (as is the expected relation between decisional and refutation assumption). We also show that if one restricts to the case of "atomic" pairwise independent distributions (i.e., those that are not convex combinations of other pairwise independent distributions), then the variant of the DCSP for such distributions is equivalent to the variant of the RCSP Hypothesis for *non-Boolean* predicates P that output a value in $[0, 1]$.

Other distributions.

Another potential approach to strengthen the RCSP Hypothesis is to consider distributions other than the uniform one on instances. The integrality gap results do not need the instances to be random, but only require them to have sufficient expansion properties. However, since these integrality gaps can also apply to a distribution concentrated on a single input (that thus can never be hard), they cannot be blindly taken to be evidence of hardness. Still, while we do not explore this direction in the current work, it is possible that a much more general version of the RCSP Hypothesis holds, where every input satisfying a particular condition, randomly perturbing it would result in a distribution on hard instances. Indeed, conjectures of a somewhat similar type for Max-3XOR and learning parity with noise were raised by Alekhnovich, see Conjecture 2 in [Ale03], though to our knowledge they have not received much investigation. Such an hypothesis, if true, would be an interesting dual to the notion of "smoothed complexity" [ST04]— here perturbing an input would result in a hard instance, rather than an easy one.

3.5 Applications of the RCSP Hypothesis

The RCSP Hypothesis on its own is a very interesting statement about average-case complexity, but it also has some implications for hardness of approximation, and perhaps cryptography. Here are some examples:

Max K-AND.

Feige hypothesized that it is hard to certify that a random Max-K-AND formula has value less than $2^{-c\sqrt{K}}$ for some $c > 0$ (see Hypothesis 3 in [Fei02]). He showed that this hypothesis implies some hardness of approximation results for the 2-catalog problem, while [AAM+11] showed it implies hardness of approximation for the densest K subgraph problem. The RCSP Hypothesis posits much bolder hardness of approximation for this problem, since it's easy to see that $\overline{\text{val}}(K - AND)$ is equal to the maximum, over any $d \in \{\pm1\}^K$ and pairwise distribution D over $\{\pm1\}^K$, of the probability that $D = d$. In particular, if $K = 2^\ell - 1$ then, if we identify every $a \in [K]$ with a nonzero linear function over $\mathbb{F}(2)^\ell$, then the pairwise independent distribution obtained by choosing $b \leftarrow_R \mathbb{F}(2)^\ell$ and outputting the vector $(a(x))_{a\in[K]}$ demonstrates that $\overline{\text{val}}(K - AND) \geqslant 2^{-\ell} = 1/(K + 1)$. Thus, the RCSP Hypothesis posits that it is hard to distinguish random K-AND instances, which have value 2^{-K}, from instances with value $1/(K + 1)$. These are much stronger parameters than those hypothesized by Feige (though of course, such worst-case hardness of approximation does hold if the Unique Games Conjecture is true).

Label cover, sliding scale, densest κ-subgraph.

The large alphabet variant of the RCSP Hypothesis also implies hardness for random instances of the label cover problem. Recall that in this problem one is given a collection of triples (i, j, π) where $i \in [n']$, $j \in [n]$ and π is a function from $[Q]$ to $[q]$, and the value of an assignment $y \in [Q]^{n'}$ and $x \in [q]^n$ is the fraction of triples (i, j, π) such that $\pi(y_i) = x_j$. In particular, for every set of projections $\pi_1, \ldots, \pi_K$ mapping $[Q]$ to $[q]$, one can consider the predicate $P\colon [q]^K \to \{0, 1\}$ such that $P(x_1, \ldots, x_K)$ if there exists $y \in [Q]$ such that $\pi_i(y) = x_i$ for all i. A random instance of CSP(P) corresponds to a random instance of the label cover problem, and it is not hard to show that (assuming the parameters are chosen appropriately) every assignment of this label cover instance will have polynomially small value (see Lemma 3.7 below).[11] The RCSP hypothesis implies that it is hard to distinguish such instances from those where one can satisfy $1 - \varepsilon$ fraction of the triples. In particular, if we take K, q, Δ that can grow as large as n^δ for some small $\delta > 0$, we get the hardness of approximation predicted by (an imperfect completeness variant of) the "sliding scale conjecture" of Bellare et al. [BGLR93] and in fact, since the corresponding instances are projections, this also applies for the projection game variant proposed by Moshkovitz [Mos11]. Similarly, we can show that this variant of the RCSP Hypothesis also implies it's hard to approximate the densest κ-subgraph problem to some polynomial factor.

[11]Note that this is a stronger statement than the fact that every assignment $x \in [q]^n$ will satisfy at most this fraction of the constraints corresponding to the K-sary predicate P.

Lemma 3.7. *Let $\mathfrak{I}$ be a label cover instance chosen as above with parameters $Q, q, K, \Delta \geqslant 100$ satisfying that for some $0 < \mu < 1/(20K^{1/4})$, $Q < q^{\mu K/4}$, $2^{16\log(1/\mu)} < q$. Then with high probability, every assignment to $\mathfrak{I}$ satisfies at most 2μ fraction of the triples.*

Proof. Let us consider for a fixed assignment $x \in [q]^n$, what is the probability over the random choices of the Δn tuples (and in fact just the shifts) there exists some $y \in [Q]^{\Delta n}$ that such that for at least a μ fraction of the $i \in [\Delta n]$, there will be at least a μ fraction of the $j \in [K]$ with the constraint between y_i and the jth member of the tuple satisfied. The probability that it is possible to satisfy a μ fraction of any particular K-tuple is upper bounded by

$$\binom{K}{\mu k} Q q^{-\mu K} \leqslant 2^{2\log(1/\mu)\mu K} q^{-\mu K/4} \leqslant q^{-\mu K/8} ,$$

under our assumptions. Thus the probability that more than $\mu\Delta n$ of these tuples will be μ-satisfied is bounded by

$$2^{\Delta n} q^{-\mu^2 K \Delta n/8} \leqslant q^{-\sqrt{K}\Delta n} ,$$

since $\sqrt{K}\Delta \gg 1$, we can do a union bound over all q^n possible assignments. □

Remark 3.8. *Because a random CSP over the alphabet $[q]$ involves random shifts, the corresponding label cover instance will be* smooth *with a smoothness parameter that tends to zero as K tends to infinity. Also, if the image of the projections $\pi_1, \ldots, \pi_K$ is a linear code over $\mathbb{F}_q^K$ with dual distance at least 3, then the results of Tulsiani [Tul09] imply that this instance is hard to certify for $\Omega(n)$ rounds of the Lasserre program, just supporting the conjecture that it is in fact* exponentially hard *to certify.*

Lemma 3.9. *Suppose that the RCSP Hypothesis holds with $\Delta = \text{polylog}(n)$ and $q, k = n^\delta$ for some $\delta > 0$, then there is some $\delta' > 0$ such that there is no $n^{\delta'}$ polynomial-time algorithm for the densest κ-subgraph problem.*

Proof sketch. The proof closely follows the work of Bhaskara, Charikar, Guruswami, Vijayaraghavan and Zhou [BCV+12] who gave Lasserre integrality gaps for the densest κ-subgraph problem with similar parameters. Their proof was obtained in fact by reducing a random instance of a particular CSP into an instance of the densest subgraph problem (the CSP is of the same form as the one used to obtain random instances of label cover above, and the graph is essentially the label-extended graph of the label cover instance). In fact in our case the proof is easier since we don't need to carry out the completeness proof for vector assignments but only for actual assignments. They showed that for a random CSP(P) with for an appropriately chosen K-CSP P over the alphabet q, the resulting graph will have the property that every κ-sized subgraph has average degree $\tilde{O}(K/q)$, while if P had a satisfying assignment, there will be a κ-sized subgraph with average degree $\tilde{\Omega}(K)$. The only thing we need to do to complete the proof is to note that the same still holds even if P had an assignment that satisfied, say, 0.9 fraction of its clauses. □

Public key cryptography? The DCSP Hypothesis readily yields a one way function and hence private key cryptography. An intriguing question is whether it can yield stronger cryptographic primitives and in particular *public key cryptography*. This is of significance since we currently have very few candidates for public key systems, and the most well studied of them can be broken efficiently by quantum computers, and thus increasing the public key crypto "gene pool" has been recognized as an important problem (e.g., see the discussion in [ABW10]). A public key cryptosystem based on the DCSP Hypothesis would arguably be the first scheme for which we have at least somewhat "principled" reasons for arguing about its security. Applebaum, Barak and Wigderson [ABW10] made a step in that direction by giving public key cryptosystems based on hardness of random CSPs and the hardness of planted version of the densest k subgraph problem. In fact, their assumptions can be seen as an instantiation of the RCSP Hypothesis but with very strong parameters, in particular requiring not just polynomially large parameters, but also control on the particular polynomial and relation between them. Reducing those assumptions, or at least finding principled ways to justify them, would be welcome progress.

4. OPTIMALITY OF BASIC SDP FOR GENERALIZED CSPS

In this section we formally state and prove our harndess-of-approximation results for generalized Max Cut and generalized distribution matching, and also for any generalized CSP. The results are stated in Subsection 4.1, in Subsection 4.2 we define the label-cover problem and the generic rounding scheme of [Rag08] in a language that suits our needs. We also define there a dictatorship test and its properties. We then prove **NP**-hardness for the generalized Max-Cut and generalized distribution matching problems in Subsection 4.3 and Subsection 4.4 respectively, and in Subsection 4.5 we deal with all other generalized CSPs. The hardness proofs all rely on a theorem we prove in Subsection 4.6, which shows how to decode an assignment for a smooth label-cover instance from an assignment for its composition with a dictatorship test which has non-negligible influences, which in turn relies on an observation concerning smooth projections that appears in Subsection 4.7. Finally in Subsection 4.8 we deal with a technical issue of the sign function not having the Lipchitz property, and in Subsection 4.9 we cite the special case of the Invariance Principle that we use in Subsection 4.4.

4.1 Results

Our general approach for proving meta-characterizations of generalizations of CSPs is quite versatile. We restrict ourselves to three representative examples (listed in order of increasing generality).

Generalized Max Cut.

This problem is motivated by the Basic Sdp for Max Cut and the Goemans-Williamson (GW) rounding algorithm [GW95]. A solution to the Basic Sdp for Max Cut assigns a Gaussian variable with second moment[12] 1 to every vertex of the graph. (The variables have a jointly Gaussian distribution.) The GW rounding algorithm draws a sample from this Gaussian distribution and assigns to each vertex the sign of its sampled value. This rounding algorithm achieves an approximation factor $\alpha_{GW} \approx 0.878$ in the worst case. However, for integral Basic Sdp solution (i.e., the Gaussian variables are constant), the GW rounding algorithm has no loss. Hence, the Max Cut problem is equivalent to finding a Basic Sdp solution that maximizes of the expected value of output of the GW rounding algorithm. In Generalized Max Cut, we have this same objective but with additional restrictions on the Basic Sdp solutions (satisfying certain linear inequalities). Algorithmically, it is still easy to optimize over Basic Sdp solutions that satisfy the additional restrictions. Since the GW rounding applies to any Basic Sdp solution (as opposed to just optimal ones, say), it has the same approximation guarantee for Generalized Max Cut as for (non-generalized) Max Cut. We will show that for all $\varepsilon > 0$, it is **NP**-hard to find Basic Sdp solutions with these restrictions such that the GW rounding achieves for this solution an approximation factor of at least $\alpha_{GW} + \varepsilon$.

The kind of restrictions on Basic Sdp solutions we need for our hardness reductions are fairly simple: We require that the Gaussian variables for the vertices are linear forms $a(x)$ of an auxiliary Gaussian vector x with nonnegative second-moment matrix $\mathbb{E}\, xx^T \geqslant 0$. At this point, it is convenient to identify the vertices of the graph with these linear forms. The following summarizes the formal statement of Generalized Max Cut.

Problem 4.1 ((c,s)-Gap Generalized Max Cut). *Given a collection $\mathfrak{I}$ of pairs (a,b) of linear forms on $\mathbb{R}^n$, distinguish the cases,*

YES: *there exists $x \in \mathbb{R}^n_+$ such that $a(x) \in \{\pm 1\}$ for all linear forms a appearing in $\mathfrak{I}$ and*

$$\mathop{\mathbb{P}}_{(a,b)\sim\mathfrak{I}} \{a(x) \neq b(x)\} \geqslant c\,,$$

NO: *for every n-dimensional Gaussian vector x with $\mathbb{E}_x\, xx^T \geqslant 0$ and $\mathbb{E}\, a(x)^2 = 1$ for all linear forms a appearing in $\mathfrak{I}$, we have*

$$\mathop{\mathbb{E}}_{x}\ \mathop{\mathbb{P}}_{(a,b)\sim\mathfrak{I}} \{\mathrm{sign}\circ a(x) \neq \mathrm{sign}\circ b(x)\} \leqslant s\,.$$

We can think of the promise in the **YES** case as an integral Basic Sdp solution with value c (for $\mathfrak{I}$ as a graph on linear forms) generated by the nonnegative vector x in a linear way. In this case, the expected value of the GW rounding would be c.

The promise in the **NO** case is that for every Basic Sdp solution (for $\mathfrak{I}$ as a graph on linear forms) that is linearly generated by a Gaussian vector x with nonnegative second moment matrix $\mathbb{E}_x\, xx^T \geqslant 0$, the expected value of the GW rounding algorithm is at most s.

The following theorem shows a strong dichotomy for the complexity of (c,s)-Gap Generalized Max Cut, determined exactly by the approximation guarantee of the GW rounding algorithm.

Theorem 4.2. *For all $c,s \in \mathbb{R}$ with $0 < s < c < 1$ and $c \geqslant 0.845$,[13] the promise problem (c,s)-Gap Generalized* Max Cut *is*

[12]Here, we mean raw moment $\mathbb{E}\, X^2$ (as opposed to central moment $\mathbb{E}\, X^2 - (\mathbb{E}\, X)^2$).

[13]In this range of c, GW rounding is optimal for Basic Sdp of Max Cut.

either **NP**-*hard or solvable in polynomial time (by* Basic Sdp*). Furthermore,* Basic Sdp *succeeds if and only if GW rounding achieves a* (c, s)-*approximation for* Max Cut, *i.e.*, $s \leqslant \arccos(1 - 2c)/\pi$.

We like to mention an interesting known **NP**-hardness result in the context of Max Cut and the GW rounding. This result follows from techniques in [GRSW12] and was communicated to us by Prasad Raghavendra. (Here, we view SDP solutions as assignments of unit vectors to vertices and we think of the GW rounding as partitioning the vertices/vectors via a random hyperplane through the origin. This view is equivalent to ours.) The result is that given a Basic Sdp solution for a Max Cut instance, it is **NP**-hard to find a hyperplane that achieves a strictly better approximation factor for this Basic Sdp solution than a random hyperplane. We are not aware of any formal relations between this result and ours. Since for this result, the Basic Sdp solution is part of the input, the corresponding computational problem is not a generalization of Max Cut.

Generalized Distribution Matching.

For this example, we think about CSPs in a predicate-independent way (similar to the DCSP hypothesis in Subsection 3.4). Given a collection K-tuples of literals, the question is what kind of distributions over $\{\pm 1\}^K$ can be generated by assigning Boolean values to the variables and outputting the values of a random K-tuple of literals from the collection.

For a distribution D over $\{\pm 1\}^K$, the following formalizes this problem in the generalized setting. (Here, a collection of K-tuples of literals is generalized to a collection of linear maps from $\mathbb{R}^n$ to $\mathbb{R}^K$.)

Problem 4.3 (Generalized D-Distribution Matching). *Given a collection* $\mathfrak{I}$ *of linear maps* $A\colon \mathbb{R}^n \to \mathbb{R}^K$, *distinguish the cases,*

YES: *there exists* $x \in \mathbb{R}^n_+$ *such that* D *is* $o(1)$-*close to the distribution* $\{Ax\}$, *where* A *is drawn at random from* $\mathfrak{I}$. *(Furthermore,* $Ax \in \{\pm 1\}^K$ *for all* $A \in \mathfrak{I}$.*)*

NO: *for all Gaussian distributions over vectors* $x \in \mathbb{R}^n$ *with* $\mathbb{E}_x xx^T \geqslant 0$ *and* $\mathbb{E}_x \|Ax\|^2 \leqslant 1$ *for all* $A \in \mathfrak{I}$, *we have* $\mathbb{E}_x Q(Ax) \leqslant o(1)$ *for all normalized*[14] *multilinear polynomials* Q *with no constant term.*

(Here, $o(1)$ is a function going sufficiently slowly to 0 with the instance size, for concreteness say $1/\log\log\log n$. We could introduce another parameter to absorb the $o(1)$ term. This change would have little effect on our results.)

The **NO** promise roughly says that only distributions close to uniform can be generated by the collection $\mathfrak{I}$ (no matter the assignment x).

We show the following characterization of the complexity of D-distribution matching. (Assuming the Unique Games Conjecture, this characterization is known even for non-generalized distribution matching [AH12].)

Theorem 4.4. *For every distribution* D *over* $\{\pm 1\}^K$, *the promise problem* D-*distribution matching is either* **NP**-*hard or solvable in polynomial time (by* Basic Sdp*). Furthermore,* Basic Sdp *succeeds if and only if* D *is not pairwise-uniform.*

[14]Since the dimension of the space is constant, the choice of the norm is not important.

Generalized Boolean CSPs.

Let $P\colon \{\pm 1\}^K \to \{0, 1\}$ be a Boolean predicate. For $c, s \in \mathbb{R}$ with $0 < s < c < 1$, we consider a generalization of (c, s)-Gap CSP(P). The definition of the problem is based on the generic rounding algorithm for Basic Sdp (see §4.2 for details). Given an Gaussian vector x as part of a Basic Sdp solution for a CSP(P) instance $\mathfrak{I}$, the rounding scheme (with accuracy parameter η) computes an assignment for $\mathfrak{I}$ with value $\mathrm{rval}_{\mathfrak{I},\eta}(x)$. If Basic Sdp achieves a (c, s)-approximation for CSP(P), then for every feasible Basic Sdp solution x with value at least c for $\mathfrak{I}$, we have $\mathrm{rval}_{\mathfrak{I},\eta}(x) \geqslant s - \eta$ (see Theorem 4.8). For all fixed accuracy parameters $\eta > 0$, the running time of the rounding scheme is polynomial. In fact, the running time stays polynomial even for slightly subconstant η, say $\eta = 1/\log\log\log n$. We will use this choice later to eliminate η as a parameter.

In Generalized CSP(P), the goal is (roughly speaking) to find a Basic Sdp solution x satisfying certain simple additional constraints so as to maximize $\mathrm{rval}_\eta(x)$ (the value achieved by the generic rounding scheme applied to x).

Problem 4.5 ($(c, s)_\eta$-Gap Generalized CSP(P)). *Given a* CSP(P) *instance* $\mathfrak{I}$ *with variable set* $[n]$ *and a simple cone*[15] C *of* n-*by*-n *matrices, distinguish the cases,*

YES *there exists a* Basic Sdp *solution* x *with value at least* c *for* $\mathfrak{I}$ *and second-moment matrix* $\mathbb{E}_x xx^T \in C$ *such that achieves* $\mathrm{rval}_{\mathfrak{I},\eta}(x) \geqslant c$.

NO *there exists* no Basic Sdp *solution* x *for* $\mathfrak{I}$ *with second-moment matrix* $\mathbb{E}_x xx^T \in C$ *such that the rounding scheme achieves* $\mathrm{rval}_{\mathfrak{I},\eta}(x) \geqslant s - \eta$.

By design, Basic Sdp solves $(c, s)_\eta$-Gap Generalized CSP(P) for all $\eta > 0$ if it achieves a (c, s)-approximation for (non-generalized) CSP(P). The following shows a strong dichotomy for the complexity of $(c, s)_\eta$-Gap Generalized CSP(P).

Theorem 4.6. *For all* $c, s \in \mathbb{R}$ *with* $0 < s < c < 1$ *and every predicate* $P\colon \{\pm 1\}^K \to \{0, 1\}$, *the promise problem* $(c, s)_\eta$-*Gap Generalized* CSP(P) *is either* **NP**-*hard, for small enough* $\eta > 0$, *or solvable in polynomial time for all* $\eta > 0$ *(by* Basic Sdp*). Furthermore,* Basic Sdp *solves* $(c, s)_\eta$-*Gap Generalized* CSP(P) *for all* $\eta > 0$ *if and only if* Basic Sdp *solves (non-generalized)* (c, s)-*Gap* CSP(P).

We remark that the theorem above also holds for slightly subconstant η, say $\eta = 1/\log\log\log n$. For this choice of η, the quantification of the parameter η in the theorem statement above is not needed.

4.2 Preliminaries (continued)

In this section, we continue the preliminaries of Section 2 and define basic notions about Label Cover, smoothness, and SDP rounding.

Label-Cover.

A Label Cover instance $\mathcal{W}$ with vertex set V and alphabets $[d \cdot R]$ and $[R]$ is specified by a distribution over triples (u, v, π) with $u, v \in V$ and $\pi\colon [d \cdot R] \to [R]$. We may assume that the instance $\mathcal{W}$ is left-regular, so that every vertex u participates in the same number of constraints of the form

[15]Here, we say a cone $C \subseteq \mathbb{R}^{n \times n}$ is *simple* if it is the projection of a cone $C' \subseteq R^{n' \times n'}$ with $C' = \{Y \mid Y \succeq 0, \langle A_1, Y\rangle \geqslant 0, \ldots, \langle A_m, Y\rangle \geqslant 0\}$ and $n' + m \leqslant \mathrm{poly}(n)$. In particular, the cone C' can be described by a small semidefinite program.

(u, v, π). The value of an assignment $x \in [d \cdot R]^V$ is defined as the probability

$$\mathcal{W}(x) \stackrel{\text{def}}{=} \mathop{\mathbb{P}}_{(u,v,\pi),(u',v',\pi')\sim\mathcal{W}} \{\pi(x_v) = \pi'(x_{v'}) \mid u = u'\}$$

(It is more common to define the value of $\mathcal{W}$ for pairs of assignments $x \in [d \cdot R]^V$, $y \in [R]^V$ as the probability that $y_u = \pi(x_v)$ over $(u, v, \pi) \sim \mathcal{W}$. For our purposes, the two definitions are equivalent, but the first one is more convenient.)

Smoothness.

We say that a label cover instance as above is σ-smooth if for every $v_0 \in V$ and any two labels $i, j \in [d \cdot R]$, the values of a random projection on V have probability at most σ to coincide on i and j. That is, it is σ smooth if

$$\mathop{\mathbb{P}}_{(u,v,\pi),(u',v',\pi')\sim\mathcal{W}} \{\pi(i) = \pi'(j) \mid v = v' = v_0\} \leqslant \sigma$$

It was first shown in [Kho02a] that smooth label cover is NP-hard to approximate. The following theorem is a simplification of Theorem 3.5 from [GRSW12].

THEOREM 4.7. *For every constants $\sigma, \varepsilon > 0$ there exist d, R such that the following holds. Given an instance of* LABEL COVER *over alphabets $[d \cdot R]$ and $[R]$ which is σ smooth, it is NP-hard to distinguish between the case where the value of the instance is 1 and the case where its value is at most ε.*

(We remark that the theorem remains true with parameters σ and ε slightly subconstant [MR08].)

Generic Rounding Scheme

Let $\mathfrak{I}$ be an n-variable instance of CSP(P) for some K-ary boolean predicate P. Let x be an n-dimensional Gaussian vector, e.g., as part of a feasible solution to BASIC SDP($\mathfrak{I}$)). For a one-dimensional odd[16] rounding function $\phi\colon \mathbb{R} \to [-1, 1]$, we define

$$\mathfrak{I}(x, \phi) \stackrel{\text{def}}{=} \mathop{\mathbb{E}}_{x} \mathop{\mathbb{E}}_{S\sim\mathfrak{I}} P\big(\phi\,(S(x)_1), \ldots, \phi\,(S(x)_K)\big)\,.$$

Since ϕ is odd, there always exists an integral assignment $x' \in \{\pm 1\}^n$ with value $\mathfrak{I}(x') \geqslant \mathfrak{I}(x, \phi)$. (It is equivalent to apply the rounding functions to variables as opposed to literals.) For an L-dimensional odd rounding function $\phi\colon \mathbb{R}^L \to [-1, 1]$, we define

$$\mathfrak{I}(x, \phi) \stackrel{\text{def}}{=} \mathop{\mathbb{E}}_{X=(x^{(1)},\ldots,x^{(L)})} \mathop{\mathbb{E}}_{S\sim\mathfrak{I}} P\big(\phi\,(S(X)_1), \ldots, \phi\,(S(X)_K)\big)\,.$$

Here, $x^{(1)}, \ldots, x^{(L)}$ are independent samples drawn according to the distribution of x. We think of X as a L-by-n matrix. Recall that S encodes a K-tuple of literals. We extend S to matrices in the natural way. If the kth literal in S is the ith variable with sign σ_k, we set $S(X)_k = \sigma_k \cdot x_i$, where x_i is the ith column of X.

The idea of generic rounding schemes is to enumerate an ε-net of constant-dimensional rounding functions and show that for every CSP(P) instance, one rounding function achieves a value arbitrarily close to the integrality gap of BASIC SDP for CSP(P).

For every $\eta > 0$, there exists a $O_\eta(1)$-sized set N_η of $O_\eta(1)$-dimensional odd rounding functions with Lipschitz constant $O_\eta(1)$ such that the following theorem holds. (We can assume the rounding functions to be odd because we allow negations in instances of CSP(P). We will also assume that N_η contains the sign function for all $\eta > 0$.)

[16]Here, odd means $\phi(-x) = -\phi(x)$.

THEOREM 4.8 ([RAG08], SEE ALSO [RS09] FOR A DIRECT PROOF). *Suppose* BASIC SDP *achieves a (c, s)-approximation for* CSP(P) *with $0 < s < c < 1$. If $\mathfrak{I}$ is a* CSP(P) *instance and x is a Gaussian vector, that corresponds to a feasible solution for* BASIC SDP($\mathfrak{I}$) *with value at least c, then for every $\eta > 0$,*

$$\operatorname{rval}_{\mathfrak{I},\eta}(x) \stackrel{\text{def}}{=} \max_{\phi\in N_\eta} \mathfrak{I}(x, \phi) \geqslant s - \eta\,.$$

We will refer to $\operatorname{rval}_{\mathfrak{I},\eta}(x)$ as the value achieved by the generic rounding scheme for instance $\mathfrak{I}$ and SDP solution x at accuracy η. (For this work, the precise construction of the sets N_η will not be important.)

For our results on Generalized CSPs, we will be interested in Gaussian vectors that satisfy certain linear equalities and linear inequalities. Adding additional Gaussian variables p makes it easier to express these linear constraints. In our setting, the original Gaussian variables x will be linear transforms of the new variables p, so that $x = Tp$ for a linear map T. Then, we can express $\mathfrak{I}(x, \phi)$ in terms of p (considering one-dimensional rounding functions ϕ for simplicity),

$$\mathfrak{I}(x, \phi) = \mathop{\mathbb{E}}_{p} \mathop{\mathbb{E}}_{S\sim\mathfrak{I}} P\big(\phi\,(S(Tp)_1), \ldots, \phi\,(S(Tp)_K)\big)$$

For every $S \in \mathfrak{I}$, we can combine S and T into a linear map A. We will denote the resulting collection of the linear maps as $\mathfrak{I}'$ and write

$$\mathfrak{I}'(p, \phi) = \mathop{\mathbb{E}}_{p} \mathop{\mathbb{E}}_{A\sim\mathfrak{I}'} P\big(\phi\circ(Ap)\big)\,.$$

(Here, $\phi\circ(\cdot)$ means that we apply ϕ coordinate-wise.) By construction, $\mathfrak{I}'(p, \phi) = \mathfrak{I}(x, \phi)$. (Also for multi-dimensional rounding functions.) We will refer to $\mathfrak{I}'$ as a GCSP(P) instance.

Generic Dictatorship Tests for Boolean Predicates

In this section, we recall definitions and results about dictatorship tests, that we need for our reductions. In particular, we give a formal statement of Raghavendra's result that for every predicate P, there exist dictatorship tests using P with guarantees arbitrarily close to the integrality gap of BASIC SDP for CSP(P).

Let $P\colon \{\pm 1\}^K \to \{0, 1\}$ be a K-ary Boolean predicate and let $\mathcal{D}$ be a mixtures of distributions D over $\{\pm 1\}^K$. (Formally, we think of $\mathcal{D}$ as a distribution over distributions). The mixture $\mathcal{D}$ specifies a family of dictatorship test gadgets.

DEFINITION 4.9 (DICTATORSHIP TEST GADGET). *For a mixture $\mathcal{D}$ of distributions D over $\{\pm 1\}^K$, the R-dimensional dictatorship test gadget $\mathfrak{I}_{\mathcal{D}}$ for* CSP(P) *is an instance of* CSP(P) *with variable set $[K] \times \{\pm 1\}^R$ (K disjoint copies of $\{\pm 1\}^R$). An assignment $F = (f^{(1)}, \ldots, f^{(K)})$ with $f^{(k)}\colon \{\pm 1\}^R \to \{\pm 1\}$ has the following value for $\mathfrak{I}_{\mathcal{D}}$,*

$$\mathfrak{I}_{\mathcal{D}}(F) = \mathop{\mathbb{E}}_{D\sim\mathcal{D}} \mathop{\mathbb{E}}_{D^R} P(f^{(1)}(x^{(1)}), \ldots, f^{(K)}(x^{(K)}))\,.$$

(Here, we think of D^R as a distribution over matrices $X = (x^{(1)}, \ldots, x^{(K)})$ with columns $x^{(k)} \in \{\pm 1\}^R$ and each row drawn independently from D.) We extend $\mathfrak{I}_{\mathcal{D}}$ to assignments with range $[-1, 1]$ in a multilinear way.

To avoid dealing with negations or multiple predicates, we will only consider symmetric assignments $F = (f^{(1)}, \ldots, f^{(K)})$ so that $f^{(k)}(-x) = -f^{(k)}(x)$. It is a standard argument that this assumption is without loss of generality. (For example, one can think of $[K] \times \{\pm 1\}^R$ as the set of literals and $[K] \times \{\pm 1\}^{R-1}$ as the set of free variables.)

For a probability space Ω over $\{\pm 1\}$ and a function $f\colon \Omega^R \to \mathbb{R}$, let $\mathrm{Inf}_{\Omega,r} f$ denote the *ε-noisy influence* of coordinate r on f,

$$\mathrm{Inf}_{\Omega,\varepsilon,r} f \stackrel{\mathrm{def}}{=} \mathop{\mathbb{E}}_{x_{-r}\sim\Omega^{[R]\setminus\{r\}}} \mathop{\mathrm{Var}}_{x_r\sim\Omega} T_{\Omega,\varepsilon} f(x)$$

Here, $T_{\Omega,\varepsilon}$ is the ε-noise operator for functions on Ω^R, so that $T_{\Omega,\varepsilon} f(x)$ is the expected value of $f(y)$ with y obtained from x by resampling every coordinate from Ω with probability ε.

For a tuple of functions $F = (f^{(1)}, \ldots, f^{(K)})$ with $f^{(k)}\colon \mathbb{R}^R \to \mathbb{R}$, we define the ε-noisy influence of coordinate r with respect to the mixture $\mathcal{D}$,

$$\mathrm{Inf}_{\mathcal{D},\varepsilon,r} F \stackrel{\mathrm{def}}{=} \mathop{\mathbb{E}}_{D\sim\mathcal{D}} \sum_{k\in[K]} \mathrm{Inf}_{D_k,\varepsilon,r} f^{(k)} .$$

Here, D_k denotes the marginal of the kth coordinate in the distribution D over $\{\pm 1\}^K$. We say that F is ε-quasirandom if $\mathrm{Inf}_{\mathcal{D},\varepsilon,r} F \leqslant \varepsilon$ for all $r \in [R]$. (Typically, quasirandomness is defined differently, separating the noise parameter and the influence parameter. However, this definition is qualitatively equivalent to our, because influences decrease monotonically with noise.)

Definition 4.10. *We say that $\mathcal{D}$ has* quasirandom soundness s *if there exists $\varepsilon > 0$ such that $\mathfrak{I}_{\mathcal{D}}(F) \leqslant s$ for all ε-quasirandom assignments $F = (f, \ldots, f)$ with $f\colon \{\pm 1\}^R \to [-1, 1]$ (and all $R \in \mathbb{N}$).*

(With our definition, the set of all values $s \in (0, 1)$ such that $\mathcal{D}$ has quasirandom soundness s forms an open interval.)

A (c, s) dictatorship test.

We say that the mixture $\mathcal{D}$ is a (c, s)-dictatorship test distribution if $\mathbb{E}_{\mathcal{D}} P \geqslant c$ and if it has quasirandom soundness s. The parameter c indeed corresponds to the completeness of the associated dictatorship tests, because for every $R \in \mathbb{N}$ and every dictator $\chi_{\{r\}}$, the CSP(P) instance $\mathfrak{I}_{\mathcal{D}}$ has value at least $\mathfrak{I}_{\mathcal{D}}(\chi_{\{r\}}, \ldots, \chi_{\{r\}}) = \mathbb{E}_{\mathcal{D}} P \geqslant c$.

The following theorem is a special case of the main ingredient in Raghavendra's Theorem.[17] (The general version of the theorem applies also to (collections of) predicates over larger alphabets.)

Theorem 4.11 ([Rag08]). *For every Boolean predicate $P\colon \{\pm 1\}^K \to \{0, 1\}$ and every $c, s \in \mathbb{R}$ with $0 < s < c < 1$, either* Basic Sdp *achieves a (c, s)-approximation for* CSP(P) *or there exists a (c, s)-dictatorship test distribution for P.*

4.3 Generalized Max Cut

In this section, we describe our reduction from Label Cover to Generalized Max Cut. We show completeness and soundness of the reductions. At the end of the section, we use the reduction to prove Theorem 4.2.

Let $P\colon \{\pm 1\}^2 \to \{0, 1\}$ be the Max Cut predicate, so that $P(x, y) = 1$ if and only if $x \neq y$. (We consider here the variant of Max Cut with negations. This problem is sometimes called XOR games.) The multilinear extension of P is $P(x, y) = (1 - xy)/2$.

Let D be a distribution over $\{\pm 1\}^2$ with mean 0. (We will use this distribution as a dictatorship test distribution. For the parameter range of Max Cut which we are interested at the moment, such a distribution (as opposed to a mixture) can achieve optimal dictatorship testing parameters [KKMO04, MOO05].)

Let $\mathcal{W}$ be a Label Cover instance with vertex set V and alphabets $[d \cdot R]$ and $[R]$. Let $\mathfrak{I}_D$ be the dictatorship test gadget on $\{\pm 1\}^R \dot\cup \{\pm 1\}^R$ corresponding to the test distribution D (see Definition 4.9). The *composition* of $\mathcal{W}$ and $\mathfrak{I}_D$ is a Generalized Max Cut instance $\mathfrak{I}_{\mathcal{W},D}$ over $\mathbb{R}^{V\times[d\cdot R]}$. For a Gaussian vector p over $\mathbb{R}^{V\times[d\cdot R]}$ and a rounding function $\phi\colon \mathbb{R} \to [-1, 1]$ (e.g., $\phi = \mathrm{sign}$), the value of $\mathfrak{I}_{\mathcal{W},D}$ is defined as

$$\mathfrak{I}_{\mathcal{W},D}(p, \phi) \stackrel{\mathrm{def}}{=} \mathop{\mathbb{E}}_{p} \mathop{\mathbb{E}}_{u} \mathop{\mathbb{E}}_{(v,\pi),(v',\pi')\sim\mathcal{W}|u} \mathfrak{I}_D(\phi \circ (H_{v,\pi} p), \phi \circ (H_{v',\pi'} p)) .$$

Here, $H_{v,\pi}$ with $v \in V$ and $\pi\colon [d \cdot R] \to [R]$ is a linear map from $\mathbb{R}^{V\times[d\cdot R]}$ to the set of functions $f\colon \{\pm 1\}^R \to \mathbb{R}$,

$$H_{v,\pi}(p) := \sum_{i\in[d\cdot R]} p_{v,i} \chi_{\{\pi(i)\}} .$$

Completeness.

Suppose there exists an assignment $x \in [d \cdot R]^V$ satisfying all constraints of $\mathcal{W}$. (Hence, there exists $y \in [R]^V$ such that $y_u = \pi(x_v)$ for all $(u, v, \pi) \in \mathcal{W}$.) Let $p \in \mathbb{R}^{V\times[d\cdot R]}$ be the $\{0, 1\}$-indicator of this assignment, so that $p_{v,i} = 1$ if $x_v = i$ and $p_{v,i} = 0$ otherwise. Then, $H_{v,\pi} p = \chi_{\pi(x_v)}$ and

$$\mathfrak{I}_{\mathcal{W},D}(p, \mathrm{id}) = \mathop{\mathbb{E}}_{u\in V} \mathfrak{I}_D(\chi_{\{y_u\}}, \chi_{\{y_u\}}) = \mathop{\mathbb{E}}_{D} P .$$

(Since we defined $\mathfrak{I}_{\mathcal{W},D}$ only for Gaussian vectors, we can think here of p as a constant Gaussian vector.)

Soundness.

Suppose p is a Gaussian vector over $\mathbb{R}^{V\times[d\cdot R]}$ with $\mathbb{E}_p pp^T \succcurlyeq 0$ and $\mathbb{E}_p(H_{v,\pi} p(y))^2 = 1$ for all $y \in \{\pm 1\}^R$. (The latter is the normalization condition for generalized Max Cut.)

Since $\mathfrak{I}_D$ is block-multilinear (with respect to the two copies of $\{\pm 1\}^R$),

$$\mathfrak{I}_{\mathcal{W},D}(p, \phi) = \mathop{\mathbb{E}}_{p} \mathop{\mathbb{E}}_{u} \mathfrak{I}_D(f_u, f_u) ,$$

where $f_u = \mathbb{E}_{(v,\pi)\sim\mathcal{W}|u}\, \phi \circ (H_{v,\pi} p)$.

Suppose that D has quasirandom soundness s so that $\mathfrak{I}_D(f, f) \leqslant s$ for all ε_1-quasirandom functions $f\colon \{\pm 1\}^R \to [-1, 1]$. Also suppose that $\mathcal{W}(p, \phi) \geqslant s + \varepsilon_2$ for some $1/\varepsilon_3$-Lipschitz odd rounding function $\phi\colon \mathbb{R} \to [-1, 1]$. (The sign function is not Lipschitz, but we can approximate it by such functions without significant change of the objective value, see Subsection 4.8.) Let ε be the minimum of $\{\varepsilon_1, \varepsilon_2, \varepsilon_3\}$.

If f is not ε-quasirandom, then $\sum_r (\mathrm{Inf}_r f)^2 \geqslant \varepsilon^2$. Hence, $\mathfrak{I}_{\mathcal{W},D}(p, \phi) \geqslant s + \varepsilon$ together with the quasirandom soundness of D implies

$$\varepsilon^3 \leqslant \mathop{\mathbb{E}}_{p} \mathop{\mathbb{E}}_{u} \sum_r (\mathrm{Inf}_r f_u)^2 \leqslant O(1/\varepsilon^2) \mathop{\mathbb{E}}_{p} \mathop{\mathbb{E}}_{u} \sum_r \left(\mathbb{E}_{(v,\pi)\sim\mathcal{W}|u} \mathrm{Inf}_r H_{v,\pi} p\right)^2 .$$

(The last step uses convexity of influences and the fact that ϕ is $1/\varepsilon$-Lipschitz.) In case the smoothness σ of $\mathcal{W}$ satisfies $\sigma = o(\varepsilon^5)$, Theorem 4.15 (influence decoding from smoothly folded functions) allows us to conclude that there exists an assignment for $\mathcal{W}$ with value poly(ε).

[17] Raghavendra's Theorem is usually stated with allowing an arbitrarily small slack $\varepsilon > 0$ between the parameters for the Basic Sdp and the dictatorship test. We can argue that it is not necessary to allow this slack explicitly. If Basic Sdp does not achieve a (c, s)-approximation for CSP(P), there exists some $\varepsilon > 0$ such that it also does not achieve a $(c + \varepsilon, s - \varepsilon)$-approximation.

Since for all $\eta > 0$ it is **NP**-hard to distinguish between the case that a label cover instance $\mathcal{W}$ has value 1 and the case that it has value and smoothness at most η, we showed the following theorem.

THEOREM 4.12. *If there exists a (c,s)-dictatorship test distribution for* MAX CUT, *then $(c, s+\varepsilon)$-Gap Generalized* MAX CUT *is* **NP**-*hard for all $\varepsilon > 0$.*

PROOF OF THEOREM 4.2. Let $c, s \in \mathbb{R}$ with $0 < s < c < 1$ and $c \geqslant 0.845$. If GW rounding achieves a (c,s)-approximation, it is clear that BASIC SDP solves (c,s)-Gap Generalized MAX CUT. On the other hand, if GW rounding algorithm does not achieve a (c,s)-approximation for MAX CUT, then the BASIC SDP relaxation for MAX CUT does not achieve a (c,s)-approximation. (Here, we use that GW rounding is optimal in our range of c.) In this case, there exists $\varepsilon > 0$ such that BASIC SDP also does not achieve a $(c, s-\varepsilon)$-approximation for MAX CUT. Hence, by Theorem 4.11, there exists a $(c, s-\varepsilon)$-dictatorship test distribution for MAX CUT. By the above theorem, we conclude that $(c, (s-\varepsilon)+\varepsilon)$-Gap Generalized MAX CUT is **NP**-hard, as desired. □

4.4 Generalized Distribution Matching

In this section, we describe our reduction from LABEL COVER to Generalized distribution matching (Problem 4.3). We show completeness and soundness of the reductions. At the end of the section, we use the reduction to prove Theorem 4.4.

The reduction has the same flavor as the reduction for Generalized MAX CUT. One difference is that we can avoid rounding functions.

Let D be a pairwise independent distribution over $\{\pm 1\}^K$. Let Q be a K-variate normalized multilinear polynomial. (We don't assume that Q is a predicate, i.e., its range over $\{\pm 1\}^K$ is not necessarily $\{0,1\}$. We extend our notations for K-ary predicates to K-variate polynomials in the natural way.)

Let $\mathcal{W}$ be a LABEL COVER instance with vertex set V and alphabets $[d \cdot R]$ and $[R]$. Let $\mathfrak{I}_{D,Q}$ denote the dictatorship test gadget over $[K] \times \{0,1\}^R$ for CSP(Q) corresponding to the test distribution D, see Definition 4.9. (In this section, we will be interested in the behavior of $\mathfrak{I}_{D,Q}$ for all polynomials Q as above.) Let $\mathfrak{I}_{\mathcal{W},D,Q}$ be the composition of $\mathcal{W}$ and $\mathfrak{I}_{D,Q}$, a generalized CSP(Q) instance over $\mathbb{R}^{V\times[d\cdot R]}$. For a Gaussian vector p over $\mathbb{R}^{V\times[d\cdot R]}$, define its value as

$$\mathfrak{I}_{\mathcal{W},D,Q}(p) \overset{\text{def}}{=} \mathop{\mathbb{E}}_{p}\mathop{\mathbb{E}}_{u\in V}\mathop{\mathbb{E}}_{(v^{(1)},\pi^{(1)}),\ldots,(v^{(K)},\pi^{(K)})\sim\mathcal{W}|u} \mathfrak{I}_{D,Q}(H_{v^{(1)},\pi^{(1)}}p, \ldots, H_{v^{(K)},\pi^{(K)}}p).$$

As in the previous section, $H_{v,\pi}$ with $v \in V$ and $\pi\colon [d\cdot R] \to [R]$ is a linear map from $\mathbb{R}^{V\times[d\cdot R]}$ to the set of functions $f\colon \{\pm1\}^R \to \mathbb{R}$ with $H_{v,\pi}(p) := \sum_{i\in[d\cdot R]} p_{v,i}\chi_{\{\pi(i)\}}$.

Since $\mathfrak{I}_{D,Q}$ is block-multilinear (across the K copies of $\{\pm1\}^R$), the expression for $\mathfrak{I}_{\mathcal{W},D,Q}(p)$ simplifies to

$$\mathfrak{I}_{\mathcal{W},D,Q}(p) = \mathop{\mathbb{E}}_{p}\mathop{\mathbb{E}}_{u} \mathfrak{I}_{D,Q}(f_u, \ldots, f_u),$$

where $f_u = \mathbb{E}_{(v,\pi)\sim\mathcal{W}|u} H_{v,\pi}p$.

Completeness.

If there exists a satisfying assignment $x \in [d\cdot R]^V$ for $\mathcal{W}$, then for the $\{0,1\}$-indicator $p \in \mathbb{R}^{V\times[d\cdot R]}$ of x,

$$\mathfrak{I}_{\mathcal{W},D,Q}(p) = \mathop{\mathbb{E}}_{D} Q.$$

Since this identity holds for all Q, the promise of the **YES** case for Problem 4.3 (Generalized D-distribution Matching) is satisfied.

Soundness.

Let p be a Gaussian vector p with $\mathbb{E}_p pp^T \geqslant 0$ and $\mathbb{E}_p(H_{v,\pi}p(y))^2 \leqslant 1$ for all $y \in \{\pm1\}^R$. (The latter corresponds up to poly(K) factors to the normalization condition of Problem 4.3.) The invariance principle (in particular, the version in Theorem 4.18) implies

$$\mathfrak{I}_{\mathcal{W},D,Q}(p) \leqslant O_K(1)\cdot \mathop{\mathbb{E}}_{p}\mathop{\mathbb{E}}_{u}\Big(\sum_r (\mathrm{Inf}_r\, f_u)^2\Big)^{1/4} \cdot (1 + \|f_u\| + \ldots \|f_u\|^K).$$

(Recall that the f_u's are linear functions on $\{\pm1\}^R$.) By Theorem 4.15, the expectation of $\sum_r (\mathrm{Inf}_r\, f_u)^2$ is at most $\mathrm{opt}(\mathcal{W})^{\Omega(1)}$ (assuming sufficient smoothness of $\mathcal{W}$). Hence, by Cauchy–Schwarz, $\mathfrak{I}_{\mathcal{W},D,Q}(p) \leqslant O_K(1)\cdot \mathrm{opt}(\mathcal{W})^{\Omega(1)} \cdot (\mathbb{E}_p \mathbb{E}_u \sum_{k=0}^{K-1} \|f_u\|^{4k})^{1/4}$. Using estimates on Gaussian moments, we can bound also the last factor by $O_K(1)$. We conclude that if $\mathcal{W}$ has optimal value and smoothness $o(1)$, then $\mathfrak{I}_{\mathcal{W},D,Q}$ satisfies the promise of the **NO** case of Problem 4.3 for all normalized multilinear polynomials Q.

Together with known **NP**-hardness results for LABEL COVER [MR08], our reductions shows the following hardness for Generalized D-distribution matching.

THEOREM 4.13. *If D is pairwise independent, then Generalized D-distribution matching is* **NP**-*hard.*

PROOF OF THEOREM 4.4. If D is not pairwise independent, there exists $\varepsilon > 0$ and a quadratic polynomial P such that $\mathbb{E}_D P = \varepsilon$. The BASIC SDP finds a Gaussian x vector such that the first two moments of D and the distribution $\{Ax\}_{A \leftarrow_R \mathfrak{I}}$ match. Hence, it follows that $\mathbb{E}_x P(Ax) = \varepsilon$, contradicting the **NO** promise.

On the other hand, if D is pairwise independent, then the theorem above shows that the problem is **NP**-hard. □

4.5 Generalized CSPs

In this section, we describe our reduction from LABEL COVER to Generalized CSPs (Problem 4.3). We show completeness and soundness of the reductions. At the end of the section, we use the reduction to prove Theorem 4.6.

Again the flavor of the reduction is similar to the one for Generalized MAX CUT. The main difference is that we have to deal with multi-dimensional rounding functions and more general dictatorship distributions.

Let $P\colon \{\pm1\}^K \to \{0,1\}$ be a K-ary Boolean predicate. Let $\mathcal{D}$ be a mixture of distributions D over $\{\pm1\}$. (This mixture will serve for our dictatorship gadget.)

Let $\mathcal{W}$ be a LABEL COVER instance with vertex set V and alphabets $[d\cdot R]$ and $[R]$. Let $\mathfrak{I}_{\mathcal{D}}$ denote the dictatorship test gadget over $[K]\times\{0,1\}^R$ for CSP(P) corresponding to the mixture $\mathcal{D}$ (see Definition 4.9). Let $\mathfrak{I}_{\mathcal{W},\mathcal{D}}$ be the composition of $\mathcal{W}$ and $\mathfrak{I}_{D,Q}$, a generalized CSP(P) instance over $\mathbb{R}^{V\times[d\cdot R]}$. For a Gaussian vector p over $\mathbb{R}^{V\times[d\cdot R]}$ and an L-dimensional rounding function $\phi\colon \mathbb{R}^L \to [-1,1]$, define its value as

$$\mathfrak{I}_{\mathcal{W},\mathcal{D}}(p,\phi) \overset{\text{def}}{=} \mathop{\mathbb{E}}_{\boldsymbol{p}}\mathop{\mathbb{E}}_{u\in V}\mathop{\mathbb{E}}_{(v^{(1)},\pi^{(K)}),\ldots,(v^{(K)},\pi^{(K)})\sim\mathcal{W}|u} \mathfrak{I}_{\mathcal{D}}(\phi\circ(H_{v^{(1)},\pi^{(1)}}\boldsymbol{p}), \ldots, \phi\circ(H_{v^{(K)},\pi^{(K)}}\boldsymbol{p})).$$

Here, $\boldsymbol{p}$ denotes a L-by-$V\times[d\cdot R]$ Gaussian matrix, each row independently drawn from the distribution of the Gaussian vector p. As in the previous section $H_{v,\pi}$, with $v \in V$ and $\pi\colon [d \cdot R] \to [R]$, takes a vector in $\mathbb{R}^{V\times[d\cdot R]}$ and defines a corresponding function $f\colon \{\pm1\}^R \to \mathbb{R}$ with $H_{v,\pi}p := \sum_{i\in[d\cdot R]} p_{v,i}\chi_{\{\pi(i)\}}$. We extend $H_{v,\pi}$ to matrices, so that $H_{v,\pi}\boldsymbol{p} :: \{\pm1\}^R \to \mathbb{R}^L$ is the vector-valued function $\sum_{i\in[d\cdot R]} \boldsymbol{p}_{v,i} \cdot \chi_{\{\pi(i)\}}$. After composition with a rounding function, $\phi \circ (H_{v,\pi}\boldsymbol{p})$ is a function on $\{\pm1\}^R$ with range $[-1,1]$.

Since $\mathfrak{I}_{\mathcal{D}}$ is block-multilinear (across the K copies of $\{\pm1\}^R$), the expression for $\mathfrak{I}_{\mathcal{W},D,Q}(p)$ simplifies to

$$\mathfrak{I}_{\mathcal{W},\mathcal{D}}(p) = \mathop{\mathbb{E}}_{p}\mathop{\mathbb{E}}_{u} \mathfrak{I}_{\mathcal{D}}(f_u,\ldots,f_u),$$

where $f_u = \mathbb{E}_{(v,\pi)\sim\mathcal{W}|u}\, \phi \circ (H_{v,\pi}\boldsymbol{p})$.

Completeness.

If p is the $\{0,1\}$-indicator of a satisfying assignment for $\mathcal{W}$ (which we can think of as a constant Gaussian vector), then $\mathfrak{I}_{\mathcal{W},\mathcal{D}}(p,\phi) = \mathbb{E}_{\mathcal{D}} P$ for any rounding function ϕ with $\phi(1,\ldots,1) = 1$ and $\phi(-1,\ldots,-1) = -1$. Hence, $\mathfrak{I}_{\mathcal{W},\mathcal{D}}$ satisfies the **YES** promise of Problem 4.5 ((c,s)-Gap Generalized CSP(P)) with $c = \mathbb{E}_{\mathcal{D}} P$.

Soundness.

Suppose p is a Gaussian vector over $\mathbb{R}^{V\times[d\cdot R]}$ with $\mathbb{E}_p pp^T \succcurlyeq 0$ and $\mathbb{E}_p(H_{v,p}p(y))^2 = 1$ for all $y \in \{\pm1\}^R$. (The latter corresponds to the normalization condition for solutions to Basic Sdp($\mathfrak{I}_{\mathcal{W},\mathcal{D}}$).

Suppose that $\mathcal{D}$ has quasirandom soundness s so that $\mathfrak{I}_{\mathcal{D}}(f,\ldots,f) \leqslant s$ for all ε_1-quasirandom functions $f\colon \{\pm1\}^R \to [-1,1]$ and that $\mathfrak{I}_{\mathcal{W},\mathcal{D}}(p,\phi) \geqslant s + \varepsilon_2$ for an odd L-dimensional rounding function ϕ with Lipschitz constant $1/\varepsilon_3$. Let ε be the minimum of $\{\varepsilon_1,\varepsilon_2,\varepsilon_3\}$. Using similar arguments as for Generalized Max Cut, it follows that

$$\mathop{\mathbb{E}}_{p}\mathop{\mathbb{E}}_{u}\sum_{r}\left(\mathbb{E}_{(v,\pi)\sim\mathcal{W}|u} \operatorname{Inf}_{\mathcal{D},r} H_{v,\pi}p\right)^2 \geqslant (\varepsilon/LK)^{O(1)}.$$

Since $H_{v,\pi}p$ is linear, it is easy to verify that $\operatorname{Inf}_{\mathcal{D},r} H_{v,\pi}p \leqslant K \cdot \operatorname{Inf}_r H_{v,\pi}p$. (The latter influence is with respect to the usual uniform distribution on $\{\pm1\}$.)

Using Theorem 4.15 (influence decoding for smoothly folded functions), we can conclude that if $\mathcal{W}$ has optimal value and smoothness $(\varepsilon/LK)^{O(1)}$, then $\mathfrak{I}_{\mathcal{W},\mathcal{D}}$ satisfies the **NO** promise of Problem 4.5 (with soundness $s + \eta + \varepsilon$).

We can conclude the following theorem.

Theorem 4.14. *If there exists a (c,s)-dictatorship test for* CSP(P), *then $(c, s+\eta+\varepsilon)_\eta$-Gap Generalized* CSP($P$) *is* **NP**-*hard for all $\varepsilon,\eta > 0$.*

Proof of Theorem 4.6. Let $c, s \in \mathbb{R}$ with $0 < c < s < 1$. If Basic Sdp achieves a (c,s)-approximation for CSP(P), Theorem 4.8 implies that Basic Sdp also solves $(c,s)_\eta$-Gap Generalized CSP(P).

Otherwise, if Basic Sdp does not achieve a (c,s)-approximation for CSP(P), it does also not achieve a $(c, s-\varepsilon_0)$-approximation for some $\varepsilon_0 > 0$. Theorem 4.11 implies that there exists a $(c, s-\varepsilon_0)$-dictatorship test distribution for CSP(P). Then, the above theorem shows that for all $\eta < \varepsilon_0$, the problem $(c,s)_\eta$-Gap Generalized CSP(P) is **NP**-hard. □

4.6 Influence Decoding from Smoothly Folded Functions

Let V be a set of vertices and let $[d \cdot R]$ and $[R]$ be alphabets. For $v \in V$ and $\pi\colon [d\cdot R] \to [R]$, let $H_{v,\pi}$ be the linear map from $\mathbb{R}^{V\times[d\cdot R]}$ to the set of functions $f\colon \{\pm1\}^R \to \mathbb{R}$,

$$H_{v,\pi}p := \sum_{i\in[d\cdot R]} p_{v,i} \cdot \chi_{\{\pi(i)\}}.$$

Theorem 4.15. *Let $\mathcal{W}$ be a label cover instance with vertex set V, alphabets $[d\cdot R]$ and $[R]$, and smoothness σ. Let p be a Gaussian vector over $\mathbb{R}^{V\times[d\cdot R]}$ with $\mathbb{E}_p pp^T \succcurlyeq 0$. Assume that $\mathbb{E}_p(H_{v,\pi}p(y))^2 \leqslant 1$ for all $y \in \{\pm1\}^R$ and pairs (v,π) that appear in $\mathcal{W}$. (This assumption corresponds to the normalization condition for the assignment p.)*

Suppose $\varepsilon = \mathbb{E}_p \mathbb{E}_{u\in V} \sum_{r\in[R]}(\mathbb{E}_{(v,\pi)\sim\mathcal{W}|u} \operatorname{Inf}_r H_{v,\pi}p)^2$ and $\sigma \ll \varepsilon$. Then, there exists an assignment for $\mathcal{W}$ with value poly(ε).

Proof. We write $p = p' + p''$ with $p'_{v,i} = p_{v,i}$ if $\|p_{v,i}\|^2 > \eta$ and $p'_{v,i} = 0$ otherwise. (The parameter η is determined later.) Our strategy is to show that the contribution of p'' to ε is negligible. The random vector p' turns out to be sparse, which makes it easy to decode an assignment for $\mathcal{W}$ from it.

Let $P_\pi\colon \mathbb{R}^{d\cdot R} \to \mathbb{R}^R$ be as in Subsection 4.7. Then,

$$\begin{aligned}\varepsilon &= \mathop{\mathbb{E}}_{p}\mathop{\mathbb{E}}_{u}\sum_{r}\left(\mathbb{E}_{(v,\pi)|u}(P_\pi p_v)_r^2\right)^2\\ &\leqslant O(1)\cdot \mathop{\mathbb{E}}_{p}\mathop{\mathbb{E}}_{u}\sum_{r}\left(\mathbb{E}_{(v,\pi)|u}(P_\pi p'_v)_r^2\right)^2 + O(1)\cdot \mathop{\mathbb{E}}_{p}\mathop{\mathbb{E}}_{(u,v,\pi)}\sum_{r}(P_\pi p''_v)_r^4.\end{aligned}$$

(In the last step, we use triangle inequality to separate the contributions of p and p'', and we bound the term for p'' using convexity.) Using Lemma 4.16, we can bound the expectation of the term $\sum_r(P_\pi p''_v)_r^4$ (setting $a = p''_v$ and $b = P_\pi p''_v$ in the notation of the lemma),

$$\mathop{\mathbb{E}}_{p}\mathop{\mathbb{E}}_{(u,v,\pi)}\sum_{r}(P_\pi p''_v)_r^4 \leqslant O(1)\cdot \mathop{\mathbb{E}}_{v}\sum_i\|p''_{v,i}\|^4 + O(\sigma)\cdot \mathop{\mathbb{E}}_{v}\|\textstyle\sum_i p''_{v,i}\|^4.$$

By construction, $\|p''_{v,i}\|^2 \leqslant \eta$ for all $v \in V$ and $i \in [d\cdot R]$. Since $\mathbb{E}_p pp^T \succcurlyeq 0$ (and thus $\mathbb{E}_p(p'')(p'')^T \succcurlyeq 0$), we have $\sum_i\|p''_{v,i}\|^2 \leqslant \|\sum_i p''_{v,i}\| \leqslant \|\sum_i p_{v,i}\|$ for all $v \in V$. Using the assumption $\mathbb{E}_p(H_{v,\pi}p(y))^2 \leqslant 1$ for all $y \in \{\pm1\}^R$ (and again $\mathbb{E}_p pp^T \succcurlyeq 0$), we can bound $\|\sum_i p_{v,i}\| \leqslant 1$. Hence, we can bound the total contribution of p'' by

$$\mathop{\mathbb{E}}_{p}\mathop{\mathbb{E}}_{(u,v,\pi)}\sum_{r}(P_\pi p''_v)_r^4 \leqslant O(\eta+\sigma).$$

It follows that the contribution of p' is at least $\varepsilon' := \mathbb{E}_p \mathbb{E}_u \sum_r(\mathbb{E}_{(v,\pi)|u}(P_\pi p'_v)_r^2)^2 \geqslant \Omega(\varepsilon) - O(\eta+\sigma)$. Consider the assignment $x \in [d\cdot R]^V$ for $\mathcal{W}$ obtained by assigning $x_v = i$ with probability at least $\|p_{v,i}\|^2$ independently for every $v \in V$. (Since $\sum_i\|p_{v,i}\|^2 \leqslant 1$ for all $v \in V$, such a distribution over assignments x exists.) The expected value of this assignment for $\mathcal{W}$ is at least

$$\mathop{\mathbb{E}}_{x}\mathcal{W}(x) \geqslant \mathop{\mathbb{E}}_{u}\sum_{r}\left(\mathop{\mathbb{E}}_{(v,\pi)|u}\sum_{r\in\pi^{-1}(r)}\|p_{v,i}\|^2\right)^2$$

Our goal is to upper bound the contribution of p' in terms of this expected value of x,

$$\begin{aligned}\varepsilon' &= \mathop{\mathbb{E}}_{p}\mathop{\mathbb{E}}_{u}\sum_{r}(\mathbb{E}_{(v,\pi)|u}(P_\pi p'_v)_r^2)^2\\ &\leqslant O(1)\cdot \mathop{\mathbb{E}}_{u}\sum_{r}\left(\mathbb{E}_{(v,\pi)|u}\left\|\textstyle\sum_{i\in\pi^{-1}(r)} p'_{v,i}\right\|^2\right)^2 \quad (*)\\ &\leqslant O(1/\eta^2)\cdot \mathop{\mathbb{E}}_{u}\sum_{r}\left(\mathbb{E}_{(v,\pi)|u}\textstyle\sum_{i\in\pi^{-1}(r)}\|p'_{v,i}\|^2\right)^2 \quad (**)\\ &\leqslant O(1/\eta^2)\mathop{\mathbb{E}}_{x}\mathcal{W}(x).\end{aligned}$$

Step (*) uses that $\{P_{v,\pi}p_v\}$ are jointly Gaussian and thus $\mathbb{E}_p(P_{v,\pi}p_v)_r^2(P_{v',\pi'}p_{v'})_r^2 \leqslant O(1)\cdot\mathbb{E}_p(P_{v,\pi}p_v)_r^2\cdot\mathbb{E}_p(P_{v',\pi'}p_{v'})_r^2$. Step (**) uses that every random vector p'_v has at most $1/\eta$ coordinates that are not identically zero and therefore, $\|\sum_{i\in\pi^{-1}(r)} p'_{v,i}\|^2 \leqslant 1/\eta \cdot \sum_{i\in\pi^{-1}(r)}\|p'_{v,i}\|^2$.

We conclude that there exists an assignment for $\mathcal{W}$ with value at least $\Omega(\eta^2\cdot\varepsilon')$. (Recall $\varepsilon' = \Omega(\varepsilon) - O(\eta+\sigma)$.) Since we assumed $\sigma \ll \varepsilon$, we can choose $\eta = \Omega(\varepsilon)$ such that $\varepsilon' = \Omega(\varepsilon)$. Hence, $\mathcal{W}$ has optimal value at least $\Omega(\varepsilon^3)$. □

4.7 Smooth Distributions over Functions

For $d, R \in \mathbb{N}$, consider the alphabets $\Sigma = [R]$ and $\Sigma' = [d\cdot R]$. Let $\mathcal{D}$ be a σ-*smooth* distribution over functions $\pi\colon \Sigma' \to \Sigma$, that is, for all $i, j \in \Sigma'$, the probability of collision is at most $\mathbb{P}_{\pi\sim\mathcal{D}}\{\pi(i) = \pi(j)\} \leqslant \sigma$.

For a function $\pi\colon \Sigma' \to \Sigma$, we define H_π to be the linear operator that maps a vector $a \in \mathbb{R}^{\Sigma'}$ to the functional $H_\pi a = \sum_{i\in\Sigma'} a_i y_{\pi(i)}$. Similarly, for a function $\pi\colon \Sigma' \to \Sigma$, let $P_\pi\colon \mathbb{R}^{\Sigma'} \to \mathbb{R}^{\Sigma}$ be the linear operator with $P_\pi a = \sum_{i\in\Sigma'} a_i e_{\pi(i)}$, where $e_1, \ldots, e_R$ is the standard basis of $\mathbb{R}^\Sigma$.

Lemma 4.16. *Let a be an Gaussian vector over $\mathbb{R}^{\Sigma'}$ with $\mathbb{E}_a aa^T \succcurlyeq 0$. Let b be a jointly distributed random vector over $\mathbb{R}^\Sigma$ obtained by sampling a function $\pi \sim \mathcal{D}$ and outputting $P_\pi a$. Then,*

$$\mathop{\mathbb{E}}_b \textstyle\sum_r b_r^4 \leqslant O(1)\cdot \sum_i \|a_i\|^4 + O(\sigma)\cdot\|\sum_i a_i\|^4 .$$

Here, $\|X\| = (\mathbb{E}\, X^2)^{1/2}$ denotes the L_2-norm of a random variable X.

Proof. Conditioned on π, each b_r is a Gaussian variable. Hence, its fourth moment $\mathbb{E}_{b|\pi} b_r^4$ is proportional to the square of its second moment,

$$\begin{aligned}\mathop{\mathbb{E}}_b \sum_r b_r^4 &= O(1) \mathop{\mathbb{E}}_{\pi\sim\mathcal{D}} \textstyle\sum_{r\in\Sigma} \left\|\sum_{i\in\pi^{-1}(r)} a_i\right\|^4 \\ &= O(1) \textstyle\sum_{i,j,k,\ell\in\Sigma'} (\mathop{\mathbb{E}}_a a_i a_j)(\mathop{\mathbb{E}}_a a_k a_\ell)\cdot \mathbb{P}_{\pi\sim\mathcal{D}}\left\{\pi(i) = \pi(i) = \pi(j) = \pi(k)\right\} \\ &\leqslant \textstyle\sum_{i\in\Sigma'}\|a_i\|^4 + \sigma\cdot\left\|\sum_{i\in\Sigma'} a_i\right\|^4\end{aligned}$$

The last step uses that $\mathcal{D}$ is σ-smooth and that $\mathbb{E}_a aa^T \succcurlyeq 0$. □

4.8 Lipschitz Approximation of Sign

In this section, we show that for the purpose of the §4.3 it is possible to approximate the rounding function sign by a Lipschitz function $\phi\colon \mathbb{R} \to [-1, 1]$. For our approximation, we will use the piece-wise linear function $\phi_\varepsilon(x) := \mathrm{sign}(x)$ for $|x| > \varepsilon$ and $\phi_\varepsilon(x) := x/\varepsilon$ for $|x| \leqslant \varepsilon$. The function ϕ_ε is $1/\varepsilon$-Lipschitz.

For convenience of the reader, we will use similar notation as in §4.3. Let $\mathfrak{I}$ be a Max Cut instance with vertex set $\{\pm1\}^R$ (our dictatorship test gadget). Let f be Gaussian function on $\{\pm1\}^R$ (that is, the values $\{f(x)\}_{x\in\{\pm1\}^R}$ have a joint Gaussian distribution). Suppose $\mathbb{E}_f f(x)^2 = 1$ for all $x \in \{\pm1\}^R$.

Lemma 4.17.

$$\mathop{\mathbb{E}}_f \mathfrak{I}(\mathrm{sign}\circ f) = \mathop{\mathbb{E}}_f \mathfrak{I}(\phi_\varepsilon \circ f) \pm O(\sqrt{\varepsilon}) .$$

Proof. Since $\mathfrak{I}(\cdot)$ is a quadratic form with bounded eigenvalues, it is enough to show $\mathbb{E}_f\|\mathrm{sign}\circ f - \phi_\varepsilon\circ f\|^2 \leqslant O(\varepsilon)$. We can verify by direct calculation,

$$\begin{aligned}\mathop{\mathbb{E}}_f\|\mathrm{sign}\circ f - \phi_\varepsilon\circ f\|^2 &= \mathop{\mathbb{E}}_{x\in\{\pm1\}^R}\mathop{\mathbb{E}}_f(\mathrm{sign}(f(x)) - \phi_\varepsilon(f(x)))^2 \\ &\leqslant \mathop{\mathbb{E}}_{x\in\{\pm1\}^R}\mathop{\mathbb{P}}_f\{|f(x)| \leqslant \varepsilon\} = O(\varepsilon) .\end{aligned}$$

□

4.9 Pairwise Independence and Invariance Principle

In this section, we state a special case of the invariance principle [MOO05].

Let D be a pairwise independent distribution on $\{\pm1\}^K$. For $R \in \mathbb{N}$, let Δ_D be the following multilinear form on functions $f^{(1)}, \ldots, f^{(K)}\colon \{\pm1\}^R \to \mathbb{R}$,

$$\Delta_D(f^{(1)}, \ldots, f^{(K)}) \stackrel{\mathrm{def}}{=} \mathop{\mathbb{E}}_{D^R} f^{(1)} \cdots f^{(K)} .$$

(Here, we think of D^R as a distribution over vectors $x^{(1)}, \ldots, x^{(K)} \in \{\pm1\}^R$, each coordinate drawn independently from D.)

Theorem 4.18 ([MOO05, AM09]). *] Let $f\colon \{\pm1\}^R \to \mathbb{R}$ be a function of degree at most d and $\mathbb{E}\, f = 0$. Then,*

$$\Delta_D(f, \ldots, f) \leqslant O_{K,d}(1)\cdot\max_r(\mathrm{Inf}_r f)^{1/2}\|f\|^{K-1} .$$

Acknowledgements

We thank Avi Wigderson for some useful pointers on meta algorithmic results.

5. REFERENCES

[AAM+11] Noga Alon, Sanjeev Arora, Rajsekar Manokaran, Dana Moshkovitz, and Omri Weinstein, *Inapproximability of densest k-subgraph from average case hardness*, 2011, Manuscript.

[ABS10] Sanjeev Arora, Boaz Barak, and David Steurer, *Subexponential algorithms for unique games and related problems*, FOCS, 2010, pp. 563–572.

[ABW10] Benny Applebaum, Boaz Barak, and Avi Wigderson, *Public-key cryptography from different assumptions*, STOC, 2010, pp. 171–180.

[AH12] Per Austrin and Johan Håstad, *On the usefulness of predicates*, IEEE Conference on Computational Complexity, 2012, To appear.

[AKK+08] Sanjeev Arora, Subhash Khot, Alexandra Kolla, David Steurer, Madhur Tulsiani, and Nisheeth K. Vishnoi, *Unique games on expanding constraint graphs are easy*, STOC, 2008, pp. 21–28.

[Ale03] Michael Alekhnovich, *More on average case vs approximation complexity*, FOCS, IEEE Computer Society, 2003, pp. 298–307.

[AM09] Per Austrin and Elchanan Mossel, *Approximation resistant predicates from pairwise independence*, Computational Complexity **18** (2009), no. 2, 249–271.

[BBH+12] Boaz Barak, Fernando G.S.L. Brandão, Aram Harrow, Jonathan Kelner, David Steurer, and Yuan Zhou, *Hypercontractivity, sum-of-squares proofs, and their applications*, STOC, 2012, To appear.

[BCC+10] Aditya Bhaskara, Moses Charikar, Eden Chlamtac, Uriel Feige, and Aravindan Vijayaraghavan, *Detecting high log-densities: an $O(n^{1/4})$ approximation for densest k-subgraph*, STOC, 2010, pp. 201–210.

[BCV+12] Aditya Bhaskara, Moses Charikar, Aravindan Vijayaraghavan, Venkatesan Guruswami, and Yuan Zhou, *Polynomial integrality gaps for strong SDP relaxations of densest k-subgraph*, SODA, 2012, pp. 388–405.

[BFKL93] Avrim Blum, Merrick L. Furst, Michael J. Kearns, and Richard J. Lipton, *Cryptographic primitives based on hard learning problems*, CRYPTO, Lecture Notes in Computer Science, vol. 773, Springer, 1993, pp. 278–291.

[BGLR93] Mihir Bellare, Shafi Goldwasser, Carsten Lund, and Alexander Russell, *Efficient probabilistically checkable proofs and applications to approximations*, STOC, 1993, pp. 294–304.

[BGMT12] Siavosh Benabbas, Konstantinos Georgiou, Avner Magen, and Madhur Tulsiani, *SDP gaps from pairwise independence*, 2012, Manuscript.

[BHHS11] Boaz Barak, Moritz Hardt, Thomas Holenstein, and David Steurer, *Subsampling mathematical relaxations and average-case complexity*, SODA, SIAM, 2011, pp. 512–531.

[BK09] Libor Barto and Marcin Kozik, *Constraint satisfaction problems of bounded width*, FOCS, IEEE Computer Society, 2009, pp. 595–603.

[BT06] Andrej Bogdanov and Luca Trevisan, *On worst-case to average-case reductions for np problems*, SIAM J. Comput. **36** (2006), no. 4, 1119–1159, Preliminary version in FOCS '03.

[Bul02] Andrei A. Bulatov, *A dichotomy theorem for constraints on a three-element set*, FOCS, IEEE Computer Society, 2002, pp. 649–658.

[Fei02] Uriel Feige, *Relations between average case complexity and approximation complexity*, IEEE Conference on Computational Complexity, 2002, p. 5.

[FKO06] Uriel Feige, Jeong Han Kim, and Eran Ofek, *Witnesses for non-satisfiability of dense random 3CNF formulas*, FOCS, 2006, pp. 497–508.

[FV98] Tomás Feder and Moshe Y. Vardi, *The computational structure of monotone monadic snp and constraint satisfaction: A study through datalog and group theory*, SIAM J. Comput. **28** (1998), no. 1, 57–104.

[GKL88] Oded Goldreich, Hugo Krawczyk, and Michael Luby, *On the existence of pseudorandom generators*, CRYPTO, Lecture Notes in Computer Science, vol. 403, Springer, 1988, pp. 146–162.

[GLS81] Martin Grötschel, László Lovász, and Alexander Schrijver, *The ellipsoid method and its consequences in combinatorial optimization*, Combinatorica **1** (1981), no. 2, 169–197.

[GRSW12] Venkatesan Guruswami, Prasad Raghavendra, Rishi Saket, and Yi Wu, *Bypassing UGC from some optimal geometric inapproximability results*, SODA, 2012, pp. 699–717.

[GW95] Michel X. Goemans and David P. Williamson, *Improved approximation algorithms for maximum cut and satisfiability problems using semidefinite programming*, J. ACM **42** (1995), no. 6, 1115–1145, Preliminary version in STOC '94.

[Hås01] Johan Håstad, *Some optimal inapproximability results*, J. ACM **48** (2001), no. 4, 798–859.

[HN90] Pavol Hell and Jaroslav Nesetril, *On the complexity of h-coloring*, J. Comb. Theory, Ser. B **48** (1990), no. 1, 92–110.

[Kho02a] Subhash Khot, *Hardness results for coloring 3 -colorable 3 -uniform hypergraphs*, FOCS, IEEE Computer Society, 2002, pp. 23–32.

[Kho02b] ———, *On the power of unique 2-prover 1-round games*, STOC, 2002, pp. 767–775.

[KKMO04] Subhash Khot, Guy Kindler, Elchanan Mossel, and Ryan O'Donnell, *Optimal inapproximability results for Max-Cut and other 2-variable CSPs?*, FOCS, 2004, pp. 146–154.

[KKMO07] Subhash Khot, Guy Kindler, Elchanan Mossel, and Ryan O'Donnell, *Optimal inapproximability results for Max-Cut and other 2-variable CSPs?*, SIAM Journal on Computing **37** (2007), no. 1, 319–357.

[KMM11] Alexandra Kolla, Konstantin Makarychev, and Yury Makarychev, *How to play unique games against a semi-random adversary: Study of semi-random models of unique games*, FOCS, 2011, pp. 443–452.

[Lau03] Monique Laurent, *A comparison of the sherali-adams, lovász-schrijver, and lasserre relaxations for 0-1 programming*, Math. Oper. Res. **28** (2003), no. 3, 470–496.

[LY80] John M. Lewis and Mihalis Yannakakis, *The node-deletion problem for hereditary properties is np-complete*, J. Comput. Syst. Sci. **20** (1980), no. 2, 219–230.

[MOO05] Elchanan Mossel, Ryan O'Donnell, and Krzysztof Oleszkiewicz, *Noise stability of functions with low influences invariance and optimality*, FOCS, 2005, pp. 21–30.

[MOO10] E. Mossel, R. O'Donnell, and K. Oleszkiewicz., *Noise stability of functions with low influences: invariance and optimality*, Annals of Mathematics **171** (2010), no. 1, 295–341.

[Mos11] Dana Moshkovitz, *The projection games conjecture and the NP-hardness of* $\ln n$*-approximating set-cover*, Electronic Colloquium on Computational Complexity (ECCC) **18** (2011), 112.

[MR08] Dana Moshkovitz and Ran Raz, *Two query PCP with sub-constant error*, FOCS, 2008, pp. 314–323.

[Rag08] Prasad Raghavendra, *Optimal algorithms and inapproximability results for every CSP?*, STOC, 2008, pp. 245–254.

[RS95] Neil Robertson and Paul D. Seymour, *Graph minors. XIII. The disjoint paths problem*, J. Comb. Theory, Ser. B **63** (1995), no. 1, 65–110.

[RS04] ———, *Graph minors. XX. Wagner's conjecture*, J. Comb. Theory, Ser. B **92** (2004), no. 2, 325–357.

[RS09] Prasad Raghavendra and David Steurer, *How to round any CSP*, FOCS, 2009, pp. 586–594.

[Sch78] Thomas J. Schaefer, *The complexity of satisfiability problems*, STOC, 1978, pp. 216–226.

[ST04] Daniel A. Spielman and Shang-Hua Teng, *Smoothed analysis of algorithms: Why the simplex algorithm usually takes polynomial time*, J. ACM **51** (2004), no. 3, 385–463.

[Tul09] Madhur Tulsiani, *CSP gaps and reductions in the Lasserre hierarchy*, STOC, 2009, pp. 303–312.

[Yan78] Mihalis Yannakakis, *Node- and edge-deletion np-complete problems*, STOC, ACM, 1978, pp. 253–264.

On the Power of Many One-Bit Provers

Per Austrin*
Aalto Science Institute and KTH Royal Institute of Technology
austrin@kth.se

Johan Håstad†
School of Computer Science and Communication
KTH Royal Institute of Technology
johanh@nada.kth.se

Rafael Pass‡
Department of Computer Science
Cornell University
rafael@cs.cornell.edu

ABSTRACT

We study the class of languages, denoted by $\mathsf{MIP1}[k, 1-\epsilon, s]$, which have k-prover games where each prover just sends a *single* bit, with completeness $1-\epsilon$ and soundness error s. For the case that $k = 1$ (i.e., for the case of interactive proofs), Goldreich, Vadhan and Wigderson (*Computational Complexity'02*) demonstrate that SZK exactly characterizes languages having 1-bit proof systems with"non-trivial" soundness (i.e., $1/2 < s \leq 1 - 2\epsilon$). We demonstrate that for the case that $k \geq 2$, 1-bit k-prover games exhibit a significantly richer structure:

- (Folklore) When $s \leq \frac{1}{2^k} - \epsilon$, $\mathsf{MIP1}[k, 1-\epsilon, s] = \mathsf{BPP}$;
- When $\frac{1}{2^k} + \epsilon \leq s < \frac{2}{2^k} - \epsilon$, $\mathsf{MIP1}[k, 1-\epsilon, s] = \mathsf{SZK}$;
- When $s \geq \frac{2}{2^k} + \epsilon$, $\mathsf{AM} \subseteq \mathsf{MIP1}[k, 1-\epsilon, s]$;
- For $s \leq 0.62k/2^k$ and sufficiently large k, $\mathsf{MIP1}[k, 1-\epsilon, s] \subseteq \mathsf{EXP}$;
- For $s \geq 2k/2^k$, $\mathsf{MIP1}[k, 1, 1-\epsilon, s] = \mathsf{NEXP}$.

As such, 1-bit k-prover games yield a natural "quantitative" approach to relating complexity classes such as BPP,SZK,AM, EXP, and NEXP. We leave open the question of whether a more fine-grained hierarchy (between AM and NEXP) can be established for the case when $s \geq \frac{2}{2^k} + \epsilon$.

*Work partially done while at the University of Toronto. Supported by NSERC.

†Supported by ERC advanced grant 226203.

‡Supported in part by a Alfred P. Sloan Fellowship, Microsoft New Faculty Fellowship, NSF CAREER Award CCF-0746990, AFOSR YIP Award FA9550-10-1-0093, and DARPA and AFRL under contract FA8750-11-2- 0211. The views and conclusions contained in this document are those of the authors and should not be interpreted as representing the official policies, either expressed or implied, of the Defense Advanced Research Projects Agency or the US government.

Categories and Subject Descriptors

F.1.2 [**Theory of Computation**]: Modes of Computation—*Interactive and reactive computation*

General Terms

Theory

Keywords

multi-prover interactive proofs, laconic provers

1. INTRODUCTION

We study the expressiveness of k-prover games (introduced by Ben-Or et al. [BOGKW88]), where each prover sends a *single* bit. Let $\mathsf{MIP1}[k, 1-\epsilon, s]$ denote the class of languages having a k-prover game where each prover sends a single bit, completeness $1 - \epsilon$, and soundness error s. Throughout the paper, we think of k as a constant and ϵ as an arbitrarily small constant. Clearly, for a fixed k, as s increases the corresponding complexity class can only become larger. We are interested in understanding to what extent the complexity class grows, and whether the growth is "smooth" or if threshold phenomena occur.

When the soundness error is "too small", only trivial languages can have such games. In particular, provers sending random bits succeed with probability at least $(1-\epsilon)2^{-k}$, placing the language of any protocol with smaller soundness in BPP.

THEOREM 1.1 (FOLKLORE, IMPLICIT IN [BGS98]). *For every $k \geq 1$, $\epsilon > 0$, we have*

$$\mathsf{MIP1}[k, 1-\epsilon, 1/2^k - \epsilon] = \mathsf{BPP}$$

An interesting result by Goldreich, Vadhan and Wigderson [GVW02] shows that when $k = 1$ (i.e., for interactive proofs [GMR89, BM88]), whenever the soundness is "non-trivial", then $\mathsf{MIP1}[1, 1-\epsilon, s]$ characterizes SZK, the class of languages having statistical zero-knowledge proofs. We here focus on the case when $k \geq 2$. As we shall see, in this setting, 1-bit k-prover games contains a richer variety of complexity classes. We take a first step towards characterizing these classes.

Our first result is a simple generalization of the result of [GVW02]: we show that when $\frac{1}{2^k} + \epsilon \leq s < \frac{2}{2^k} - \epsilon$, then $\mathsf{MIP1}[k, 1-\epsilon, s]$ characterizes SZK.

THEOREM 1.2. *For every $k \geq 2$, $\epsilon > 0$, and $1/2^k + \epsilon < s < 2/2^k - \epsilon$, we have*

$$\mathsf{MIP1}[k, 1-\epsilon, s] = \mathsf{SZK}.$$

Our main result next shows that when the soundness becomes just slightly higher than $2/2^k$, MIP1s appear to become significantly more powerful; in particular, they contain all of AM.

THEOREM 1.3 (MAIN THEOREM). *For every $k \geq 2$ and $\epsilon > 0$*

$$\mathsf{AM} \subseteq \mathsf{MIP1}[k, 1-\epsilon, 2/2^k + \epsilon]$$

For instance, when $k = 2$, our MIP1 has soundness error $\frac{1}{2}+\epsilon$. This result should be compared to Håstad's 3-bit PCP [Hås01] that achieves the same soundness error. Since every 1-bit k-prover game yields a k-bit PCP, our MIP1 yields a 2-bit PCP for AM with soundness error $1/2+\epsilon$; in contrast, the PCP resulting from our MIP1 is exponentially long, whereas Håstad's PCP is polynomially long. Nonetheless, as we shall see shortly, our MIP1 construction heavily relies on Håstad's PCP.

We leave open the question of whether $\mathsf{MIP1}[k, 1-\epsilon, 2/2^k + \epsilon]$ contains even richer complexity classes than AM. As a first step towards this question, we note that EXP is an upper bound on this class.

THEOREM 1.4. *For all sufficiently large k, $\epsilon > 0$, $s \leq \frac{0.62k}{2^k}(1-\epsilon)$ we have*

$$\mathsf{MIP1}[k, 1-\epsilon, s] \subseteq \mathsf{EXP}.$$

This holds also for $k = 3$ and $s \leq 1/2 - \epsilon$.

Finally, we prove that for $k \geq 3$ and sufficiently high soundness error, k-prover 1-bit MIP1s capture all of NEXP. This follows by using the PCP analogue of the classic MIP = NEXP result [BFL91]. We sharpen the parameters by using more modern PCP machinery and then observing that the PCPs we use can be turned in to MIP1 at no cost. In particular using the recent results by Chan [Cha12], we get

THEOREM 1.5. *For every $\epsilon > 0$ and $s = 2^{\lceil \log(k+1) \rceil}/2^k + \epsilon \leq 2k/2^k + \epsilon$,*

$$\mathsf{MIP1}[k, 1-\epsilon, s] = \mathsf{NEXP}.$$

Taken together, these results demonstrate that k-prover games provide a natural "quantitative" way to relate complexity classes such as BPP, SZK, AM, EXP and NEXP.

We leave open the question of whether $\mathsf{MIP1}[k, 1-\epsilon, s]$ contains an even more fine grained hierarchy of complexity classes in the regime where $s \geq 2/2^k + \epsilon$.

1.1 Related work

The work most closely related to our is the work by Goldreich, Vadhan and Wigderson [GVW02] mentioned above which in turn builds on a work by Goldreich and Håstad [GH98]; just as we do, both these works investigate the complexity of interactive proofs with "laconic" provers. We have taken the question to an extreme in one direction (namely we focus only on provers that send a single bit); on the other hand, we have generalized the question by considering multi-prover interactive proofs, rather than just a single prover (as is the main focus in the above-mentioned works).

The large literature on PCP characterizations of NP (e.g., [AS98, ALM+98, BGLR94, BGS98, GLST98, ST00] and many others) is clearly also very related. As mentioned, a k-prover MIP1 yields a k-query PCP with the same soundness error, but of exponential length; typically, the PCP literature focuses on polynomial-length proofs. Nonetheless, we rely on both PCPs and techniques from this literature (most notably Fourier analysis) to analyze our proof system.

We also mention the recent work by Drucker [Dru11] that provides a PCP-type characterization of AM; his result is incomparable to our main theorem as he focuses on polynomial-length PCP proofs.

1.2 Outline

In Section 2 we present some definitions and background material that we use. In Section 3 we prove Theorem 1.2 for the SZK range. Our main result Theorem 1.3 is proved in Section 4. The Theorems 1.4 and 1.5 are proved in Section 5. Finally, we end with discussing some avenues for future work in Section 6.

2. PRELIMINARIES

2.1 Laconic Proof systems

We assume familiarity with multi-prover interactive proofs and probabilistically checkable proofs.

DEFINITION 2.1. *$\mathsf{IP}[k, c, s]$ denotes the class of problems having an two message protocol where the first message is sent by the Verifier and where the prover sends at most k bits and where the proof has soundness s and completeness c.*

DEFINITION 2.2. *$\mathsf{MIP1}[k, c, s]$ denotes the set of languages having a Multi-prover Interactive Proof System with k provers, each sending a single bit, soundness s, completeness c. The questions to the k provers are asked simultaneously. In other words, all questions are formulated before any answer is recieved.*

FACT 2.3. *For every $k \geq 1$, $0 \leq s < c \leq 1$, we have*

$$\mathsf{IP}[k, c, s] \subseteq \mathsf{MIP1}[k, c, s].$$

When constructing MIP1 it is convenient to rely on efficient PCPs. There are general translations from PCPs to MIP1s (one is given in [BGS98]) if one accepts a slight loss in the parameters. In the cases we are interested in, however, by a slight extension of the analysis we can turn the PCP directly into a MIP1 without any loss in parameters.

2.2 Statistical Zero Knowledge

For our characterization of the SZK range, we only need to rely on the following result of [GVW02] relating SZK to laconic IP systems.

THEOREM 2.4 ([GVW02], THEOREM 3.1). *For every c, s such that $1 > c^2 > s > c/2 > 0$, it holds that $\mathsf{IP}[1, c, s] = \mathsf{SZK}$.*

2.3 Fourier Analysis of Boolean Functions

For two vectors $x, y \in \{0,1\}^n$ we write $x \oplus y$ for their pointwise sum modulo 2. Given $a \in \{0,1\}^n$ we write $\chi_a : \{0,1\}^n \to \mathbb{R}$ for the *character* (which is in fact a linear function) $\chi_a(x) = (-1)^{\sum_{i=1}^n a_i x_i}$.

Any Boolean function $f : \{0,1\}^n \to \mathbb{R}$ can be uniquely decomposed as a linear combination of characters

$$f(x) = \sum_{a \in \{0,1\}^n} \hat{f}(a)\chi_a(x),$$

where $\hat{f}(a) = \mathbb{E}_x[f(x)\chi_a(x)]$ are the *Fourier coefficients* of f.

We recall Plancherel's equality: for any $f : \{0,1\}^n \to \mathbb{R}$, we have

$$\sum_a \hat{f}(a)^2 = \mathbb{E}_x[f(x)^2].$$

2.4 Inapproximability of Linear Equations

Our proof system for AM is based on the optimal inapproximability result for linear equations mod 2 by Håstad [Hås01], defined next.

DEFINITION 2.5. *An instance Ψ of* MAX 3-LIN-2 *consists of a set of equations in n variables $x_1, \ldots, x_n$ over $\{0,1\}$. Each equation is of the form $\chi_l(x) = b$ for some $l \in \{0,1\}^n$ of weight 3 and some $b \in \{-1,1\}$. We denote by $\mathrm{Opt}(\Psi) \in [0,1]$ the maximum fraction of equations satisfied by any assignment to x.*

THEOREM 2.6 ([HÅS01]). *For every $\epsilon > 0$, given a* MAX 3-LIN-2 *instance Ψ, it is NP-hard to determine whether $\mathrm{Opt}(\Psi) \le 1-\epsilon$ or whether $\mathrm{Opt}(\Psi) \ge \frac{1+\epsilon}{2}$.*

3. THE SZK RANGE

THEOREM 3.1. *For every $k \ge 1$, $\epsilon > 0$, we have*

$$\mathsf{IP}[k, 1-\epsilon, 1/2^k + \epsilon] \supseteq \mathsf{SZK}.$$

PROOF. Follows by repetition of the protocol from Theorem 2.4 and the fact that there is no problem with parallel repetition for one-prover proof systems. □

PROPOSITION 3.2. *For every $k \ge 1$, $0 \le s \le c \le 1$, we have*

$$\mathsf{MIP1}[k, c, s] \subseteq \mathsf{IP}[1, c, 2^{k-1}s].$$

PROOF. Given a MIP1 protocol $(V, P_1, \ldots, P_k)$ for a language L, we construct a single-prover protocol (V', P') as follows. The verifier V' runs V to generate k messages $x_1, \ldots, x_k$, and sends x_1 to the prover P'. The prover P' acts as P_1 and responds with an answer $y_1 \in \{0,1\}$. V' accepts iff there are bits $y_2, \ldots, y_k$ such that the original verifier V accepts on the transcript $(x_1, \ldots, x_k, y_1, \ldots, y_k)$. Clearly, the completeness of (V', P') is at least that of the original protocol. For the soundness, suppose that there is a strategy for P' that makes the verifier accept with probability s'. Construct a strategy for the original protocol by having P_1 act as P' and $P_2, \ldots, P_k$ return random answers. Clearly, these provers make V accept with probability at least $s'/2^{k-1}$, implying $s' \le 2^{k-1}s$ as desired. □

THEOREM 3.3. *For every $k \ge 1$, and every $\epsilon > 0$ it holds that*

$$\mathsf{MIP1}[k, 1-\epsilon, 2/2^k(1-2\epsilon)] \subseteq \mathsf{SZK}$$

PROOF. We have

$$\begin{aligned}\mathsf{MIP1}[k, 1-\epsilon, 2/2^k(1-2\epsilon)] &\subseteq \mathsf{IP}[1, 1, 1-\epsilon, 1-2\epsilon] \\ &\subseteq \mathsf{SZK},\end{aligned}$$

where the first inclusion is by Proposition 3.2 and the second is by Theorem 2.4. □

4. PROOF SYSTEMS FOR AM

First we note that, at a cost of an arbitrarily small loss in soundness and completeness, we may restrict ourselves to proof systems for NP.

LEMMA 4.1. *If $\mathsf{NP} \subseteq \mathsf{MIP1}[k, c, s]$ then for every $\epsilon > 0$ it holds that $\mathsf{AM} \subseteq \mathsf{MIP1}[k, c-\epsilon, s+\epsilon]$*

PROOF. Let $L \in \mathsf{AM}$. We remind the reader that this is equivalent to the existence of a language $L' \in \mathsf{NP}$ such that $x \in L$ iff $(x, r) \in L'$ with high probability for a random string r (of an appropriate polynomial length). Without loss of generality, we may assume that the protocol for L has completeness $1-\epsilon$ and soundness ϵ. The MIP1 verifier for L simply sends Arthur's random string r to each of the k provers and then executes the MIP1 protocol assumed to exist for $L' \in \mathsf{NP}$.

If $x \in L$ then with probability $1-\epsilon$ over r we have $(x, r) \in L'$ in which case the provers convince the verifier with probability $\ge c$.

On the other hand $x \notin L$ then the probability that the provers accept is at most $\Pr_r[(x,r) \in L'] + \Pr[(x,r) \notin L'] \Pr[\text{accept} \mid (x,r) \notin L'] \le \epsilon + s$. □

4.1 Warm-up: the case of 2 provers

We start off with the case of only 2 provers, as this case is somewhat simpler than the general case, and will be used to obtain the general case.

THEOREM 4.2. *For every $\epsilon > 0$*

$$\mathsf{NP} \subseteq \mathsf{MIP1}[2, 1-\epsilon, 1/2+\epsilon].$$

PROOF. We reduce from the MAX 3-LIN-2 problem. Given is a MAX 3-LIN-2 instance Ψ, on n variables $x_1, \ldots, x_n$ and m linear equations $\{l_i(x_i) = b_i\}_{i \in [m]}$.

The provers are expected to provide oracle access to the Hadamard encoding of a $(1-\epsilon)$-satisfying assignment $x \in \{0,1\}^n$. In other words, the verifier will give each prover a vector $a \in \{0,1\}^n$ and expects in response the value of the linear function $\chi_a(x) \in \{-1,1\}$.

The verifier proceeds as follows:

1. Pick a random equation $\chi_l(x) = b$ in Ψ
2. Pick random $y \in \{0,1\}^n$
3. Check that $P_2(y) \cdot P_1(l \oplus y) = b$

It is easy to see that there is a strategy for the provers which makes the verifier accept with probability at least $\mathrm{Opt}(\Psi)$. More interestingly, we will now prove that, $\mathrm{Opt}(\Psi)$ is *exactly* the maximum acceptance probability, over any strategy for P_1 and P_2.

We can then write the acceptance probability of the verifier as

$$\Pr[\text{Verifier accepts}] = \mathop{\mathbb{E}}_{\substack{y \in \{0,1\}^n \\ (l,b) \in \Psi}} \left[\frac{1 + bP_1(l \oplus y)P_2(y)}{2} \right]. \quad (1)$$

Replacing the two functions by their Fourier expansion we need to analyze

$$\sum_{a,a'} \hat{P}_1(a)\hat{P}_2(a') \mathop{\mathbb{E}}_{y,(l,b)}[b\chi_a(l \oplus y)\chi_{a'}(y)].$$

All terms with $a \neq a'$ have expectation 0 and furthermore we have

$$\left| \mathop{\mathbb{E}}_{(l,b)} [b\chi_a(l)] \right| \leq 2\,\mathrm{Opt}(\Psi) - 1,$$

as the assignment given by a satisfies at most an $\mathrm{Opt}(\Psi)$ fraction of the equations and at least a fraction $1 - \mathrm{Opt}(\Psi)$ as its negation does not satisfy more than a $\mathrm{Opt}(\Psi)$ fraction. We conclude that (1) is bounded by

$$\frac{1 + \sum_a |\hat{P}_1(a)\hat{P}_2(a)|(2\,\mathrm{Opt}(\Psi) - 1)}{2}.$$

Finally note that, by Cauchy-Schwarz,

$$\sum_a |\hat{P}_1(a)\hat{P}_2(a)| \leq \left(\sum_a \hat{P}_1^2(a)\right)^{1/2} \left(\sum_a \hat{P}_2^2(a)\right)^{1/2} = 1$$

and this finishes the argument. □

4.2 The general case

We have

THEOREM 4.3. *For every $k \geq 2$, $\epsilon > 0$, we have*

$$\mathsf{NP} \subseteq \mathsf{MIP1}[k, 1-\epsilon, 2/2^k + \epsilon].$$

PROOF. As before, we design a MIP1 system for linear equations. Given is a MAX 3-LIN-2 instance Ψ, in which either $\mathrm{Opt}(\Psi) \geq 1 - \epsilon_0$, or $\mathrm{Opt}(\Psi) \leq \frac{1+\epsilon_0}{2}$, where ϵ_0 will be chosen small enough to get the completeness and soundness bound that we want.

The verifier again expects all the k provers to provide answers to the Hadamard coding of the good assignment, and it then does the obvious generalization of the $k = 2$ case:

1. Pick $k - 1$ random equations $l_j(x) = b_j$, $1 \leq j \leq k - 1$
2. Pick random $y \in \{0, 1\}^n$
3. Check that $P_j(l_j \oplus y) \cdot P_k(y) = b_j$ for every $1 \leq j \leq k-1$

It is clear that the completeness is at least $(1 - \epsilon_0)^{k-1} \geq 1 - k\epsilon_0$. Thus, as long as $\epsilon_0 \leq \epsilon/k$, we have the desired completeness.

Let us now study the soundness, i.e., the maximum possible acceptance probability of verifier, given that $\mathrm{Opt}(\Psi) \leq \frac{1+\epsilon_0}{2}$.

We say that prover P_j *succeeds* if $P_j(l_j \oplus y) \cdot P_k(y) = b_j$. From the analysis of the previous theorem, we know that the probability that P_j succeeds is at most $\frac{1+\epsilon_0}{2}$. Thus, if the events that the different provers succeed were independent, we would obtain the desired soundness of $\approx 2^{1-k}$. However, *a priori*, it may be that the success events of the provers are very correlated, e.g., it could be that if one succeeds then they all succeed.

To cope with this, we need to obtain a more robust version of the previous analysis. Let $\frac{1+\delta_j(y)}{2}$ be the probability that P_j succeeds given that y is chosen. We have the following lemma.

LEMMA 4.4. $\mathbb{E}_y[\delta_j^2(y)] \leq \epsilon_0^2$.

PROOF. We have $\delta_j(y) = \mathbb{E}_{(l,b)}[bP_k(y)P_j(l \oplus y)]$ and thus

$$\mathop{\mathbb{E}}_y[\delta_j^2(y)] = \mathop{\mathbb{E}}_{(l,b),(l',b'),y} [bb'P_j(l \oplus y)P_j(l' \oplus y)].$$

Similarly to the case $k = 2$ we replace the function by its Fourier expansion and we are left to analyze

$$\sum_{a,a'} \hat{P}_j(a)\hat{P}_j(a') \mathop{\mathbb{E}}_{y,(l,b),(l',b')} [bb'\chi_a(l + y)\chi_{a'}(l' + y)].$$

Again we only have nonzero terms when $a = a'$. For these terms it easy to see that

$$\left| \mathop{\mathbb{E}}_{(l,b),(l',b')} [bb'\chi_a(l)\chi_a(l')] \right| \leq (2\,\mathrm{Opt}(\Psi) - 1)^2 = \epsilon_0^2.$$

Using $\sum_a \hat{P}_j(a)^2 = 1$, the lemma follows. □

Lemma 4.4 implies that the fraction of y such that $\delta_j(y) \geq \sqrt{\epsilon_0}$ is bounded by ϵ_0.

We conclude that the, for the y chosen, the probability that $\delta_j(y) \geq \sqrt{\epsilon_0}$ for any j is bounded by $k\epsilon_0$. On the other hand if $\delta_j(y) \leq \sqrt{\epsilon_0}$ for all values of j the probability that the verifier accepts is bounded by $(\frac{1+\sqrt{\epsilon_0}}{2})^{k-1}$. We conclude that the overall probability that the verifier accepts is bounded by

$$k\epsilon_0 + \left(\frac{1 + \sqrt{\epsilon_0}}{2}\right)^{k-1},$$

and choosing ϵ_0 sufficiently small, this is bounded by $2^{1-k} + \epsilon$.

5. THE HIGH END – EXP AND NEXP RESULTS

In this section we prove Theorems 1.4 and 1.5. These are essentially just "blow-ups" of corresponding approximation algorithms and inapproximability results.

THEOREM 5.1 (THEOREM 1.4 RESTATED). *For all sufficiently large k, $\epsilon > 0$, $s \leq \frac{0.62k}{2^k}(1 - \epsilon)$ we have*

$$\mathsf{MIP1}[k, 1 - \epsilon, s] \subseteq \mathsf{EXP}.$$

This holds also for $k = 3$ and $s \leq 1/2 - \epsilon$.

PROOF. Let $L \in \mathsf{MIP1}[k, 1 - \epsilon, s]$ with $s \leq \frac{0.62k}{2^k}(1 - \epsilon)$. Given an instance, the task of determining whether $x \in L$ boils down to finding the best joint strategy for the k provers. If the verifier uses r random bits she can send at most 2^r different queries to each prover, thus the optimal strategy can be described by $k \cdot 2^r = 2^{\mathsf{poly}\,|x|}$ bits. Further, for each outcome of the verifier's randomness, the acceptance criterion is a constraint on some k bits of the strategy. In other words, what we have is an exponentially large Max k-CSP instance. The value of this instance can be approximated in time polynomial in its size to within a factor $0.62k/2^k$ by the algorithm of Makarychev and Makarychev [MM12]. For the case $k = 3$ we use the 1/2-approximate Max 3-CSP algorithm of Zwick [Zwi98]. □

Next we show that if the soundness is sufficiently large, exponential-size k-query PCP systems can express every language in NEXP.

THEOREM 5.2. *For $t = 2^{\lceil \log_2(k+1) \rceil}$ ($k + 1$ rounded up to the next power of 2) we have*

$$\mathsf{MIP1}[k, 1 - \epsilon, t/2^k + \epsilon] = \mathsf{NEXP}.$$

This immediately implies Theorem 1.5.

PROOF SKETCH. The proof follows from a upscaling of the recent PCP of Chan [Cha12] that gives a predicate of arity k which has t accepting configurations and which is approximation resistant.

In a standard PCP, the verifier runs in polynomial time, uses a logarithmic number of random coins and reads a constant number of bits in a polynomial size proof and verifies an NP-statement. We are currently interested in the situation where the crucial parameters, except the running time of the verifier, are exponentially larger.

To be more precise we are interested in a polynomial time verifier, that uses a polynomial number of random coins and gets one bit each from k different provers that respond to questions of polynomial length.

As is convenient for us, Chan already analyzed his PCP in the k-partite situation where each bit is read from a separate table. This model is exactly the same as a k-prover model and hence this difference is only syntactical.

It remains to address the question on how to make the upscaled verifier run in polynomial time. This amounts to saying that a verifier of an NEXP statement runs in polynomial time. This was explicitly needed in [BFL91] but this paper predates the PCP-Theorem. The fact that this is true also for upscaled versions of the PCP-Theorem has been explicitly stated in [BGS98] and [BSGH+05]. The intuitive reason that this is true is that the verifier only needs to ensure that some bits in a suitable encoding of the inputs are correct and this takes polynomial time in the size of the input but not the other parameters of the proof. □

6. CONCLUDING REMARKS

There are a number of interesting avenues for further work. In this paper we focused solely on the case of almost perfect completeness and each prover sending exactly 1 bit. Obviously, understanding what happens with the expressiveness of these systems for other completeness values (in particular perfect completeness) and slightly less laconic provers would be very interesting. By simple extensions of the methods used in this paper it is possible to get some results but it would be interesting to see if perfect completeness could lead to a significantly different situation in any range of parameters.

There is also a specific question more directly related to the current paper. There is a huge gap between our lower bound AM and upper bound EXP for soundness $s = 2/2^k + \epsilon$. It seems quite plausible that an upper bound for this range of s should be PSPACE rather than EXP – proving this essentially boils down to proving that there is a $\delta > 0$ such that bipartite instances of Max 2-CSP can be approximated within a factor $1/2 + \delta$ in polylog-space (and not necessarily polynomial time). We hope that the recent algorithms for Max Cut, in particular [KS11], can be adapted to achieve this.

Even if this turns out to be true, whether the correct class here is AM or PSPACE or something in between we have little intuition about.

Acknowledgment. We are grateful to Salil Vadhan for pointing out a simple proof of the lower bound given in Theorem 1.2 rather than the more complicated proof with worse parameters that we originally had. We are also grateful to Madhu Sudan and Or Meir for discussions on how to blow-up PCPs.

7. REFERENCES

[ALM+98] Sanjeev Arora, Carsten Lund, Rajeev Motwani, Madhu Sudan, and Mario Szegedy. Proof verification and the hardness of approximation problems. *J. ACM*, 45(3):501–555, 1998.

[AS98] Sanjeev Arora and Shmuel Safra. Probabilistic checking of proofs: A new characterization of NP. *J. ACM*, 45(1):70–122, 1998.

[BFL91] László Babai, Lance Fortnow, and Carsten Lund. Non-deterministic exponential time has two-prover interactive protocols. *Computational Complexity*, 1:3–40, 1991.

[BGLR94] Mihir Bellare, Shafi Goldwasser, Carsten Lund, and Alexander Russell. Efficient probabilistic checkable proofs and applications to approximation. In *STOC*, page 820, 1994.

[BGS98] Mihir Bellare, Oded Goldreich, and Madhu Sudan. Free bits, PCPs, and nonapproximability-towards tight results. *SIAM J. Comput.*, 27(3):804–915, 1998.

[BM88] László Babai and Shlomo Moran. Arthur-Merlin games: A randomized proof system, and a hierarchy of complexity classes. *J. Comput. Syst. Sci.*, 36(2):254–276, 1988.

[BOGKW88] Michael Ben-Or, Shafi Goldwasser, Joe Kilian, and Avi Wigderson. Multi-prover interactive proofs: How to remove intractability assumptions. In *STOC*, pages 113–131, 1988.

[BSGH+05] Eli Ben-Sasson, Oded Goldreich, Prahladh Harsha, Madhu Sudan, and Salil Vadhan. Short PCPs verifiable in polylogarithmic time. In *Proceedings of the 20th Annual IEEE Conference on Computational Complexity*, CCC '05, pages 120–134, Washington, DC, USA, 2005. IEEE Computer Society.

[Cha12] Siu On Chan. Approximation Resistance from Pairwise Independent Subgroups. *Electronic Colloquium on Computational Complexity (ECCC)*, 19:110, 2012.

[Dru11] Andrew Drucker. A PCP characterization of AM. In *ICALP (1)*, pages 581–592, 2011.

[GH98] Oded Goldreich and Johan Håstad. On the complexity of interactive proofs with bounded communication. *Inf. Process. Lett.*, 67(4):205–214, 1998.

[GLST98] Venkatesan Guruswami, Daniel Lewin, Madhu Sudan, and Luca Trevisan. A tight characterization of np with 3 query PCPs. In *FOCS*, pages 8–17, 1998.

[GMR89] Shafi Goldwasser, Silvio Micali, and Charles Rackoff. The knowledge complexity of interactive proof systems. *SIAM J. Comput.*, 18(1):186–208, 1989.

[GVW02] Oded Goldreich, Salil P. Vadhan, and Avi Wigderson. On interactive proofs with a laconic prover. *Computational Complexity*, 11(1-2):1–53, 2002.

[Hås01] Johan Håstad. Some Optimal Inapproximability Results. *Journal of the ACM*, 48(4):798–859, 2001.

[KS11] Satyen Kale and C. Seshadhri. Combinatorial approximation algorithms for maxcut using random walks. In *ICS*, pages 367–388, 2011.

[MM12] Konstantin Makarychev and Yury Makarychev. Approximation Algorithm for Non-Boolean MAX k-CSP. To appear in APPROX, 2012.

[ST00] Alex Samorodnitsky and Luca Trevisan. A PCP characterization of NP with optimal amortized query complexity. In *STOC*, pages 191–199, 2000.

[Zwi98] Uri Zwick. Approximation algorithms for constraint satisfaction problems involving at most three variables per constraint. In *SODA*, pages 201–210, 1998.

Approaching Utopia: Strong Truthfulness and Externality-Resistant Mechanisms

Amos Fiat [*]
Tel Aviv University
fiat@tau.ac.il

Anna R. Karlin [†]
University of Washington
karlin@cs.washington.edu

Elias Koutsoupias [‡]
University of Oxford and
University of Athens
elias@cs.ox.ac.uk

Angelina Vidali [§]
Duke University
vidali@cs.duke.edu

"And verily it is naturally given to all men to esteem their own inventions best."
— Sir Thomas More, in *Utopia*, Book 1, 1516 AD.

ABSTRACT

We introduce and study strongly truthful mechanisms and their applications. We use strongly truthful mechanisms as a tool for implementation in undominated strategies for several problems, including the design of externality resistant auctions and a variant of multi-dimensional scheduling.

Categories and Subject Descriptors

F.2.m [**Theory of Computation**]: Analysis of Algorithms and problem Complexity—*Miscellaneous*

General Terms

Algorithms, Economics, Theory

Keywords

algorithmic game theory, mechanism design

[*]Partially supported by a grant from the Israeli Science Foundation, 822/10, and a grant via the Google Inter-University Center from Electronic Auctions and Markets.

[†]Supported by NSF CCF-1016509.

[‡]Partially supported by the European Union Seventh Framework Programme FP7, grant 284731 (UaESMC), and by the ESF-NSRF research program Thales (AGT).

[§]Work has been funded by the Vienna Science and Technology Fund (WWTF) through project 2010-002 while the author was at the University of Vienna.

ITCS'13, January 9–12, 2013, Berkeley, California, USA.

1. INTRODUCTION

1.1 Externalities

Mechanisms with externalities, and specifically altruism and spite, but also others ("the joy of winning", "malice"), have been studied at length in the literature. Experiments seem to indicate that both altruism and spite have an observable effect, and various theoretical models have been proposed to deal with this issue.

We quote higher authority (Cooper and Fang [16]) in the context of 2nd price auctions:
"We found that small and medium overbids are more likely to occur when bidders perceive their rivals to have similar values, supporting a modified 'joy of winning' hypothesis but large overbids are more likely to occur when bidders believe their opponents to have much higher values, consistent with the 'spite' hypothesis."

A partial list of (experimental and theoretical) references dealing with externalities is [20, 22, 23, 19, 9, 25, 26, 5, 31, 9, 24, 16, 14, 13, 11, 12]. The questions addressed in previous work primarily deal with the impact of externalities on the equilibria, e.g., observing that externalities such as "the joy or winning" or "spite" lead to overbidding in some auction mechanisms, or that externalities modeled as altruism lead to more-or-less balanced outcomes in the ultimatum game, although neither of these phenomena would be considered "reasonable" if one assumes no externalities. In recent years, the price of anarchy as impacted by such externalities has also been the subject of much research, *e.g.*, malice in congestion games [26, 5, 31].

In this paper we consider a somewhat different goal: we seek to devise mechanisms that *overcome* externalities. As a basic motivating example consider an auction selling a single item. The Vickrey second-price auction is dominant strategy incentive compatible. But, try to imagine that the bidders who lose are spiteful towards the winner (although this is really hard to believe). They may have reason to increase their bid so as to increase the payment by the winning agent.

Even more worrisome — say that the only spiteful losers are those who took part in the various experimental psychology studies cited above, and they did so only so as to mislead the researchers. In fact, we who reside in Utopia will never, ever, encounter spite. This is a fact, but it does *not* imply that everyone *believes* that it is so, it does *not* imply that everyone believes that everyone believes that it is so, it does *not* imply that this is common knowledge. Ergo, just the *concept* of spite (transmitted via the apple from the Garden of Eden), even if in fact there *are no* spiteful bidders, implies that bidders may have an incentive not to bid truthfully in the VCG mechanism.

So, why not define the agent type to include all possible externalities and then run VCG? There are two problems here: (1) It is impossible; payments to one agent impact the utility of another, we are no longer in the quasi-linear setting, (2) Ignoring the former concern (*i.e.*, impossibility), what social welfare are we optimizing? Is it our goal to pander to the spiteful masses? Offer them bread and circuses? Execute the winners during the lunch break of the Gladiatorial games? There are indications from the lives of the Caesars that this may actually maximize (spiteful) social welfare.

So, the very existence of the concept of spite seems to threaten the fundamentals of mechanism design.

To address these issues, we study an alternative utility model: We assume that agents have two utility functions, a *base utility*, and an *externality-modified utility* which is a linear combination of other agent utilities. Variants of this model appear in Ledyard [22], Levine [23], Chen and Kempe [14, 13, 11], and many other papers. The PhD thesis of Chen [11] includes numerous relevant papers.

1.2 Externality Resistant Mechanisms

We present a new type of private value mechanism, rVCG. Assume that it is common knowledge that no one is willing to lose more than (say) $\gamma = 5$ cents so as to increase another's payment by \$1. Now:

1. Agents using the rVCG mechanism are sure that the following two values are approximately equal:
   - The utility they obtain under rVCG, in an imperfect world, where externalities are real, and demons roam the earth.
   - The utility they would have obtained under VCG, in an imaginary, Utopian world, where externalities did not exist. (See Theorem 2).

   I.e., given a bound, γ, on the altruism/spite, the rVCG mechanism approximates Utopia, as promised in the title.[1]

2. On the other hand, irrespective of how infinitesimally small $\gamma > 0$ may be, a losing bidder in a second-price auction, may, out of spite, even infintesimally small spite, reduce the winner's profit to zero. (This holds in the more general VCG mechanism as well).

1.3 Strongly Truthful Mechanisms

To achieve externality resistant mechanisms we make use of strongly truthful mechanisms. These are mechanisms where it is not only a weakly dominant strategy to be truthful but where one gets punished for lying. The goal in the design of strongly truthful mechanisms is to increase the punishment as much as possible. Strongly truthful mechanisms are related to strongly convex mechanisms, analogous to the connection between truthful mechanisms and convex utility functions, (see, *e.g.*, Archer and Kleinberg, [3, 2]).

For bounded domains, we give (optimal) strongly truthful mechanisms, in this case, the punishment for the lie $\tilde{v} = v+\delta$ is $O(\delta^2)$.

For unbounded domains, we give a mechanism that is *relatively strongly truthful* where the lie is measured as a fraction of the truth, and the punishment for the lie $\tilde{v} = (1+\alpha)v$, where $\alpha \in \Theta(1)$, is $v/\log^{1+\epsilon} v$.

Strongly truthful mechanisms can also be used in mechanisms for multi-dimensional problems such as makespan minimization for unrelated machines, see below.

This idea of combining multiple mechanisms to boost truthfulness appears in [29], where it is used to derive truthful mechanisms for some problems via differential privacy. It also appears implicitly in the context of scoring rules [10, 7], and in the related responsive lotteries [17] so as to determine the true utility of an outcome. However, we are unaware of previous attempts to quantify the quality of such devices, nor are we aware of other attempts to apply them towards externality resistance or for multidimensional problems.

In the appendix we describe transformations between strongly truthful mechanisms and proper scoring rules. This automatically implies transformations between strongly truthful mechanisms, market scoring rules, responsive lotteries, and market maker pricing algorithms to provide liquidity for prediction markets [18, 32, 15]. Strongly truthful mechanisms are also related to Bregman divergence [1], a concept similar to strong convexity.

1.4 The Solution Concept

Adapting a solution concept from Babaioff, Lavi and Pavlov, [6], from approximation problems to arbitrary predicates, we say that a mechanism M is an algorithmic implementation of a predicate P in undominated strategies, if, for all agents i, there exists a set of strategies, D_i, such that

1. The output of M satisfies P, for any combination of strategies from $\prod_j D_j$, and,

2. For all i, for any agent i strategy, $s \notin D_i$, there exists some strategy $s' \in D_i$ that is strictly better for agent i than strategy s, irrespective of what strategies are chosen by the other agents.

I.e., predicate P is implemented by a mechanism in undominated strategies, if, in the game defined by the mechanism, and as long as no agent chooses a strategy that is obviously dominated (for arbitrary assumptions about the types of other agents, *e.g.*, values, bids, externalities), predicate P holds for the outcome of the mechanism.

In the context of externality resistant auctions, as long as agents do not bid stupidly (do not use a strategy that is obviously dominated), externality resistance holds.

In fact, any strategy that entails bidding "too far away" from the truth is dominated by bidding truthfully, where "too far away" for agent i is a function of her own externalities γ_{ij} (see Section 3 for a definition of these externalities). Moreover, agents can efficiently determine that bidding far from the truth is dominated by truthful bidding. Thus, D_i is contained in the set of all bids whose distance from the truth is not too big. Note that we don't make any claim on the precise strategies that will be adapted by the agents.

[1] Admittedly, the bound γ has to be very small in order to truly approximate Utopia.

1.5 Other Applications

We can also use strongly truthful mechanisms to achieve goals such as minimizing the makespan in a multi dimensional machine scheduling problem, the infamous Nisan-Ronen problem, see [28, 21, 4].

This magic is achieved by changing the problem, and allowing one to repeatedly assign the same job to a machine. So, choosing to verify the truthfullness of the agent types can be done by choosing at random, with some small probability, a target agent, and using strongly truthful mechanisms to punish the agent for misrepresentation of his type.

Given a sufficiently large punishment, all agents will have incentive to stick close to the truth. So, with high probability, the mechanism will achieve a close approximation to the minimum makespan in undominated strategies. We leave the details for the full version of the paper.

This is quite general and can be used in other multi-dimensional settings where one can boost truth extraction by repetition.

2. STRONGLY TRUTHFUL MECHANISMS

A key ingredient in our constructions is the notion of a *strongly truthful mechanism.* In this section, we define strongly truthful mechanisms for single dimensional problems and one agent. As discussed below, these definitions and results extend to multi-dimensional and multi-agent settings.

Consider a single dimensional agent with private value (type) v for receiving a good or service. A direct revelation mechanism takes as input some (possibly false) value, $\tilde{v}$, computes a payment, $p(\tilde{v})$, and allocates the good to the agent with probability $a(\tilde{v})$.

The standard quasilinear utility of an agent whose true value is v, but reports value $\tilde{v}$ (possibly different from v), is denoted by

$$u_v(\tilde{v}) = v \cdot a(\tilde{v}) - p(\tilde{v}). \quad (1)$$

We also define

$$u(v) = u_v(v),$$

i.e., the utility to the agent with value v when truthfully reporting $\tilde{v} = v$.

In this setting, it follows from Myerson [27], that a mechanism is truthful in expectation if and only if

- the allocation probability function $a(v)$ is monotone nondecreasing, and
- the payment function is

  $$p(v) = va(v) - \int_0^v a(x)dx + p(0),$$

  for some constant $p(0)$. (We will take $p(0) = 0$ herein).

It follows from the above and from Equation 1 that

$$\begin{aligned} u_v(\tilde{v}) &= v \cdot a(\tilde{v}) - \tilde{v} \cdot a(\tilde{v}) + \int_0^{\tilde{v}} a(x)dx \\ &= (v - \tilde{v}) \cdot a(\tilde{v}) + \int_0^{\tilde{v}} a(x)dx. \end{aligned}$$

Thus, for truthful in expectation mechanisms, it must be that

1. The utility function $u(v)$ is convex (the integral of a nondecreasing function).
2. The allocation function $a(v) = u'(v)$ (where u is differentiable).
3. Any convex function $u(v)$ whose subgradient, $u'(v)$, lies in the range $[0, 1]$, can be interpreted as the utility function for an associated truthful in expectation mechanism.
4. Ergo, if restricting oneself to truthful in expectation mechanisms, one can describe a mechanism using utility functions or allocation functions interchangeably. (Up to additive constants).

We seek to strengthen the notion of truthfulness in expectation so that the greater the deviation from the truth, the greater the loss in utility.

To this end, we define c-strongly truthful mechanisms as follows:

Definition 1. A mechanism with utility function u is called c-strongly truthful if for every v and $\tilde{v}$:

$$u_v(v) - u_v(\tilde{v}) \geq \frac{1}{2}c\,|\tilde{v} - v|^2. \quad (2)$$

This definition enables us to extend the connection between truthfulness and convexity to strongly truthful mechanisms. For this, recall the standard notion of strong convexity. For a differentiable function $f(x)$, convexity is equivalent to:

$$\forall x, x' \quad f(x) - f(x') \geq f'(x') \cdot (x - x').$$

The following notion is also standard [8]:

Definition 2. Let $m \geq 0$. A function f is called m-strongly convex if and only if for every x, x':

$$f(x) - f(x') \geq f'(x') \cdot (x - x') + \frac{1}{2}m\,|x - x'|^2 \quad (3)$$

By defining strong truthfulness as in Equation (2) the following proposition holds:

Lemma 1. *A mechanism with utility function $u(v)$ is m-strongly truthful if and only if $u(v)$ is m-strongly convex.*

Proof. Applying equation (1) to $u_v(\tilde{v})$ and $u_{\tilde{v}}(\tilde{v})$, we get

$$u_{\tilde{v}}(\tilde{v}) - u_v(\tilde{v}) = u'(\tilde{v}) \cdot (\tilde{v} - v).$$

It follows that

$$\begin{aligned} u_v(v) - u_v(\tilde{v}) &= u_v(v) - u_{\tilde{v}}(\tilde{v}) + u'(\tilde{v}) \cdot (\tilde{v} - v) \quad (4) \\ &= u(v) - u(\tilde{v}) + u'(\tilde{v}) \cdot (\tilde{v} - v) \end{aligned}$$

Since by definition, the mechanism is m-strongly truthful if and only if $u_v(v) - u_v(\tilde{v}) \geq \frac{1}{2}m\,|\tilde{v} - v|^2$, we derive that the mechanism is m-strongly truthful if and only if $u(v) - u(\tilde{v}) + u'(\tilde{v}) \cdot (\tilde{v} - v) \geq \frac{1}{2}m\,|\tilde{v} - v|^2$, which is precisely the definition that $u(v)$ is m-strongly convex. □

Remark: All of the definitions in this section extend naturally to multi-dimensional agents. Indeed, the three equivalent definitions of a doubly differentiable function being convex (the standard one, cycle monotonicity, and the Hessian being positive semidefinite) have analogues when discussing truthful multidimensional mechanisms over convex domains [8, 30]. Similarly, the equivalent notions of strong-convexity and strong truthfulness extend mutatis mutandis.

It follows from the above theorem that the question of finding the strongest truthful mechanism is an extremal question about strongly convex functions whose partial derivatives satisfy appropriate constraints that capture the constraints of the allocation probabilities (for example, for the single item case the constraint is the derivative of the utility is in $[0, 1]$).

2.1 Strongly Truthful Mechanisms for Single Agent, Single Item Auctions

Consider the case in which we want to find the strongest truthful mechanism for a single player and one item. (We will use this in the next section.) To start, assume that the agent's value is bounded: $v \in [L, H]$. For this case, we define the *linear mechanism*:

Definition 3. The linear mechanism for the single player and single item setting has allocation rule $a(v) = (v - L)/(H - L)$, and applies when the player's value is known to be in the range $[L, H]$.

THEOREM 1. *The linear mechanism for a player whose value v satisfies $v \in [L, H]$ is a $1/(H - L)$-strongly truthful mechanism. No other mechanism is m-strongly truthful for $m \geq 1/(H - L)$.*

PROOF. It is straightforward to check that for the linear mechanism, the utility function $u(v)$ is $\frac{(v-L)^2}{2(H-L)}$. We can directly verify that Equation (3) in the definition of strong convexity holds with equality for all v, with $m = 1/(H - L)$. Indeed, we derive the following equivalences

$$u(z) - u(y) = u'(y) \cdot (z - y) + \frac{1}{2} m |z - y|^2$$

$$\frac{(z - L)^2}{2(H - L)} - \frac{(y - L)^2}{2(H - L)} = \frac{y - L}{H - L}(z - y) + \frac{1}{2}\frac{1}{H - L}(z - y)^2$$

$$\frac{(z - y)(z + y - 2L)}{2(H - L)} = \frac{(z - y)(2(y - L) + (z - y))}{2(H - L)};$$

the last equality clearly holds.

We now show that this is the strongest truthful mechanism. From the definition of strong convexity for the extreme values of the domain, we get

$$u(H) - u(L) \geq u'(L)(H - L) + \frac{1}{2} m(H - L)^2$$

$$u(L) - u(H) \geq u'(H)(L - H) + \frac{1}{2} m(L - H)^2$$

Adding these two, we get that

$$(H - L)(u'(H) - u'(L)) \geq m(H - L)^2$$

Since $u'(L)$, and $u'(H)$ are in $[0, 1]$ (they represent allocations), we get that $m \leq 1/(H - L)$. □

Remarks:

- There is a direct connection between single-agent truthful mechanisms and scoring rules (see e.g., [7]). Indeed, one can define a notion of *strongly proper scoring rules* that is analogous to a strongly truthful mechanism. We note that the mechanism just described is in fact the well-known quadratic scoring rule.
- Definition 3 and Theorem 1 can easily be generalized to the case of one player and many items with additive valuations. In this case the utility is $u(v) = \sum_{j=1}^{m} \frac{(v_j - L)^2}{2(H-L)}$, for which $m = \frac{1}{n(H-L)}$.

2.2 Relative strong truthfulness

If we want to consider unbounded domains, it follows from Theorem 1 that no m-strongly truthful mechanism exists with $m > 0$.

For such domains, it may be useful to define a notion of relative strong truthfulness as follows:

Definition 4. We say a mechanism M is $f(v, \alpha)$-relatively truthful if, for all $\tilde{v}$ such that $\tilde{v} \notin [v(1 - \alpha), v(1 + \alpha)]$

$$\frac{u_v(v) - u_v(\tilde{v})}{u_v(v)} \geq f(v, \alpha).$$

For example, it is easy to show that the single agent mechanism with allocation rule $a(v) = 1 - \frac{1}{\ln v} + \frac{1}{\ln^2 v}$ (and payment $p(v) = \frac{v}{\ln^2(v)}$) satisfies $f(v, \alpha) = \Omega(\frac{\alpha^2}{\log^2 v})$. Slightly better mechanisms that approach $f(v, \alpha) = \Omega(\frac{\alpha^2}{\log v})$ exist[2].

3. EXTERNALITY RESISTANT AUCTIONS

In this section, we consider how strongly truthful, or truth-extraction mechanisms can be used to help cope with spiteful or altruistic bidders. Our goal is to ensure that a bidder participating in, say, an auction for a single item, does not need to worry about her competitor purposely bidding high just so as to make her pay a lot.

We consider the setting where an auctioneer wishes to maximize social welfare, and each agent has a value v_i for being one of the winners in the auction. Of course, in the standard version of this setting, the mechanism of choice would be the VCG mechanism.

As we have already discussed however, the VCG mechanism is entirely vulnerable to spiteful agents. Before explaining the alternative we propose, we define a utility model for externalities that captures precisely what we mean when we speak about spiteful and altruistic agents.

In the *externality-modified* setting, agent i's type t_i consists of

- v_i, her value for service; and
- a set of externality parameters γ_{ij} for all $j \neq i$. Intuitively, γ_{ij} represents how much agent i cares about the utility of agent j. A large, negative value means that i is significantly motivated by the desire to decrease agent j's utility, whereas a large, positive value means that i seeks to increase agent j's utility. A value of zero means that i is indifferent towards j.

[2]The following sequence of mechanisms are defined for every $k > 1$ and approach $f(v, \alpha) = \Omega(\frac{\alpha^2}{\log v})$:

$$p(v) = \frac{v}{\ln^k v} \qquad a(v) = 1 - \frac{1}{(k-1)\ln^{k-1} v} + \frac{1}{\ln^k v}$$

$$p(v) = \frac{v}{\ln v \ln^k \ln v} \qquad a(v) = 1 - \frac{1}{(k-1)\ln v \ln^{k-1} \ln v} + \frac{1}{\ln v \ln^k \ln v}$$

and so on.

Let $\mathcal{M}$ be an arbitrary mechanism for the single-parameter allocation problem under consideration. The mechanism takes as input a bid b_i from each agent (which is equal to v_i if the mechanism is truthful) and produces as output an allocation $\mathbf{x}$, where x_i is the probability that agent i receives service, and payments $\mathbf{p}$, with p_i the expected payment by agent i. Note that both $x_i = x_i(\mathbf{b})$ and $p_i = p_i(\mathbf{b})$ are functions of the bids. The allocation selected must satisfy the feasibility constraints of the setting, however, we do assume, that having only a single arbitrary agent receive service is feasible.

Given bids $\mathbf{b}_{-i}$ of all players except player i, the *base (standard) utility* of agent i, when her bid is b_i and her type is $t_i = (v_i, \{\gamma_{i1}, \ldots, \gamma_{in}\})$, is denoted by $u_{v_i}^{\mathcal{M}}(b_i, \mathbf{b}_{-i})$ and is defined as

$$u_{v_i}^{\mathcal{M}}(b_i, \mathbf{b}_{-i}) = v_i\, x_i(\mathbf{b}) - p_i(\mathbf{b}). \quad (5)$$

Notice that this utility depends only on v_i and not on the rest of agent i's private information (agent i's externality parameters γ_{ij}). This is why we subscript the utility by v_i instead of t_i.

We define the *externality-modified* utility $\widehat{u}_{t_i}^{\mathcal{M}}$ of agent i when the types of the agents are $\mathbf{t}$ and the bids are $\mathbf{b}$ as

$$\widehat{u}_{t_i}^{\mathcal{M}}(\mathbf{b}, \mathbf{t}_{-i}) = u_{v_i}^{\mathcal{M}}(b_i, \mathbf{b}_{-i}) + \sum_{j \neq i} \gamma_{ij}\, u_{v_j}^{\mathcal{M}}(b_j, \mathbf{b}_{-j}). \quad (6)$$

This model (and variants thereof) have been used previously in several papers, e.g. [23, 11].

Note that

- Because the externality-modified utility defined above depends, not only on the bids (or actions) of other agents, b_{-i}, but also on their types, we add the t_{-i} as an argument to the utility function, which is atypical. (Of course the only part of t_{-i} the utility depends on is v_{-i}.)
- The value of t_{-i} is, in general, unknown to agent i, so agent i will be, in general, unable to compute her externality modified utility $\widehat{u}_{t_i}^{\mathcal{M}}(\mathbf{b}, \mathbf{t}_{-i})$.
- We will be particularly interested in cases where the mechanism $\mathcal{M}$ that is being run is VCG, and then use $u_{v_i}^{\text{VCG}}(\mathbf{b})$ to denote the standard utility of agent i when her value is v_i, the reported bids are $\mathbf{b}$ and the mechanism being run is VCG.

Our goal is to design a mechanism that is *externality-resistant*, in the following sense:

- The mechanism approximately maximizes social welfare.
- Despite the fact that each agent bids to maximize their externality-modified utility, each agent ends up with a base utility that is approximately what it would have been had all agents bid so as to maximize their base utility. Thus, non-spiteful agents are not harmed by the presence of spiteful agents. Furthermore, the auctioneer's revenue is not harmed by the presence of altruistic agents.

An immediate difficulty that arises is the fact that our utility model is non-quasi linear. Our approach is to consider a weaker solution concept, *implementation in undominated strategies,* formally defined as follows.

In a game of incomplete information, a strategy for an agent is a function mapping types to actions. We say that a strategy s_i' for agent i is *dominated* by strategy s_i if for all types t_i for agent i, and for all possible types t_{-i} and all possible actions

$$b_{-i} = s_{-i}(t_{-i})$$

of the other agents, the utility of agent i satisfies:

$$u_{t_i}(s_i(t_i), b_{-i}, t_{-i}) \geq u_{t_i}(s_i'(t_i), b_{-i}, t_{-i}).$$

A strategy s_i for agent i is *undominated* if it is not dominated.

We say that a mechanism implements a predicate P in undominated strategies, if whenever agents are limited to playing undominated strategies, it must be that predicate P holds.

We consider the following simple variant of VCG, which we call *externality-resistant* VCG or rVCG , for short. The rVCG mechanism, with n agents participating, is parameterized by a value δ, $0 \leq \delta \leq 1$, and works as follows:

- Ask the n agents for their values/bids.
- With probability δ/n single out the i-th agent and run the truth extraction mechanism (denoted by TE) on him.
- With probability $1-\delta$, run VCG.

Our main theorem is the following:

THEOREM 2. *Consider any single-parameter allocation setting in which the n agents true values v_i are all in the range $[0, 1]$. Let γ denote $\max_{ij} \gamma_{ij}$. Then, for any n, δ, ϵ, and γ_{ij} such that*

$$\gamma < \frac{\epsilon\, \delta}{8\,(1-\delta)^2 n^3},$$

mechanism rVCG *above implements the following predicate in undominated strategies:*

For all agents i, and for all types $\mathbf{t}$, the base utility obtained under the rVCG *mechanism is close to the base utility obtained by agent i when all agents bid truthfully under the "standard" VCG mechanism. Specifically, for $\mathbf{b}$ undominated,*

$$u_{v_i}^{\text{rVCG}}(\mathbf{b}) \geq (1-\delta) u_{v_i}^{\text{VCG}}(\mathbf{v}) - \epsilon.$$

In the proof below, we use the following notation and definitions:

- For any set of bids $\mathbf{b}$, let $\text{MSW}(\mathbf{b})$ denote the maximum social welfare achievable with respect to the bids $\mathbf{b}$, i.e.

  $$\text{MSW}(\mathbf{b}) = \max_a \sum_j b_j(a),$$

  where the maximum runs over all possible allocations a.
- We define $\text{MSW}_{v_i}(b_i, \mathbf{b}_{-i})$ to be the maximum social welfare *experienced* by agent i, when agent i bids b_i, whereas her true value is v_i, and all other agents bid $\mathbf{b}_{-i}$. Thus,

  $$\text{MSW}_{v_i}(b_i, \mathbf{b}_{-i}) = v_i(a^*) + \sum_{j \neq i} b_j(a^*),$$

  where $a^* = \text{argmax}_a \sum_j b_j(a)$.

- The definitions of MSW and MSW_{v_i} will allow us to compare utilities that involve actual values and bids, in a clean way . For example, when agent i bids b_i, her true value is v_i, all agents but i bid $\mathbf{b}_{-i}$, then, the utility of agent i under VCG with Clarke Pivot Payments is

$$u_{v_i}^{\text{VCG}}(\mathbf{b}) = \text{MSW}_{v_i}(b_i, \mathbf{b}_{-i}) - \text{MSW}(\mathbf{b}_{-i}).$$

We can now turn to the proof of the theorem.

Proof. We assume that agents would like to maximize their externality-modified utility:

$$\widehat{u}_{t_i}^{\text{rVCG}}(\mathbf{b}, \mathbf{t}_{-i}) = (1-\delta)\widehat{u}_{t_i}^{\text{VCG}}(\mathbf{b}, \mathbf{t}_{-i}) + \frac{\delta}{n}\left(u_{v_i}^{\text{TE}}(b_i) + \sum_{j\neq i}\gamma_{ij}u_{v_j}^{\text{TE}}(b_j)\right), \quad (7)$$

where

$$\widehat{u}_{t_i}^{\text{VCG}}(\mathbf{b}, \mathbf{t}_{-i}) = u_{v_i}^{\text{VCG}}(\mathbf{b}) + \sum_{j\neq i}\gamma_{ij}\left(u_{v_j}^{\text{VCG}}(\mathbf{b})\right). \quad (8)$$

We say an agent is *standard* if $\gamma_{ij} = 0$ for all j. Such an agent doesn't care about the utility of others. For standard agents, the base utility and the externality-modified utility are the same. In addition, because VCG is dominant strategy truthful, it is a dominant strategy for the standard agents to bid truthfully.

So, we only need to understand how non-standard agents will bid. To this end, fix an agent i of type t_i and the bids $\mathbf{b}_{-i}$ and types $\mathbf{t}_{-i}$ of the other agents.

Suppose that the VCG part of rVCG is executed. Then agent i's externality-modified utility $\widehat{u}_{t_i}^{\text{VCG}}(b_i, \mathbf{b}_{-i}, \mathbf{t}_{-i})$ is defined by equation (8). We have

$$u_{v_j}^{\text{VCG}}(\mathbf{b}) = \text{MSW}_{v_j}(b_j, \mathbf{b}_{-j}) - \text{MSW}(\mathbf{b}_{-j})$$

and

$$u_{v_j}^{\text{VCG}}(b_j, v_i, \mathbf{b}_{-ij}) = \text{MSW}_{v_j}(b_j, v_i, \mathbf{b}_{-ij}) - \text{MSW}(v_i, \mathbf{b}_{-i,j}).$$

We want to compute the diference between agent i's externality modified utility when agent i bids b_i and when agent i bids v_i. We first observe that when we fix the bids $\mathbf{b}_{-i}$ of all agents except agent i, the maximum social welfare experienced by agent i is achieved when she is truthful. Specifically,

$$\text{MSW}_{v_i}(b_i, \mathbf{b}_{-i}) \leq \text{MSW}(v_i, \mathbf{b}_{-i}).$$

To see this, let $a^* = \text{argmax}_a\{v_i(a) + \sum_{j\neq i} b_j(a)\}$ be the allocation which optimizes the maximum social welfare experienced by agent i when she tells the truth; similarly, let $\overline{a}^* = \text{argmax}_a\{\sum_j b_j(a)\}$, be the allocation which optimizes the maximum social welfare experienced by agent i when she bids b_i. Then $\text{MSW}(v_i, \mathbf{b}_{-i}) = v_i(a^*) + \sum_j b_j(a^*) \geq v_i(\overline{a}^*) + \sum_j b_j(\overline{a}^*) = \text{MSW}_{v_i}(b_i, \mathbf{b}_{-i})$

We can now bound the difference between agent i's externality modified utility when agent i bids b_i and when agent i bids v_i with respect to $\eta_i = |b_i - v_i|$, the lie of agent i.

$$\begin{aligned}
&\widehat{u}_{t_i}^{\text{VCG}}(b_i, \mathbf{b}_{-i}, \mathbf{t}_{-i}) - \widehat{u}_{t_i}^{\text{VCG}}(v_i, \mathbf{b}_{-i}, \mathbf{t}_{-i}) \\
&= \text{MSW}_{v_i}(b_i, \mathbf{b}_{-i}) - \text{MSW}(v_i, \mathbf{b}_{-i}) \\
&+ \sum_{j\neq i}\gamma_{ij}\left(\text{MSW}_{v_j}(b_j, \mathbf{b}_{-j}) - \text{MSW}_{v_j}(b_j, v_i, \mathbf{b}_{-ij})\right) \\
&+ \sum_{j\neq i}\gamma_{ij}\left(\text{MSW}(v_i, \mathbf{b}_{-i,j}) - \text{MSW}(b_i, \mathbf{b}_{-i,j})\right) \\
&\leq 2\sum_{j\neq i}\gamma_{ij}\eta_i \\
&\leq 2(n-1)\gamma_i\eta_i, \qquad (9)
\end{aligned}$$

where $\gamma_i = \max_j \gamma_{ij}$.

On the other hand,

$$\widehat{u}_{v_i}^{\text{TE}}(v_i) - \widehat{u}_{v_i}^{\text{TE}}(b_i) \geq \frac{1}{2}m(b_i)|b_i - v_i|^2 \geq \frac{1}{2}\eta_i^2, \quad (10)$$

assuming valuations in the range $[0, 1]$ and the use of the linear TE algorithm. Combining inequalities (9) and (10), we have

$$\begin{aligned}
&\widehat{u}_{t_i}^{\text{rVCG}}(b_i, \mathbf{b}_{-i}, \mathbf{t}_{-i}) - \widehat{u}_{t_i}^{\text{rVCG}}(v_i, \mathbf{b}_{-i}, \mathbf{t}_{-i}) \\
&\quad \leq (1-\delta)2(n-1)\gamma\eta_i - \frac{\delta}{2n}\eta_i^2.
\end{aligned}$$

Consider any bid b_i for which $\eta_i = |b_i - v_i|$ has

$$(1-\delta)2(n-1)\gamma\eta_i - \frac{\delta}{2n}\eta_i^2 < 0.$$

Then the strategy of bidding truthfully dominates the strategy of bidding this b_i. Thus, for all undominated strategies, it must be that agent i bids a value b_i which satisfies:

$$0 \leq \widehat{u}_{t_i}^{\text{rVCG}}(b_i, \mathbf{b}_{-i}, \mathbf{t}_{-i}) - \widehat{u}_{t_i}^{\text{rVCG}}(v_i, \mathbf{b}_{-i}, \mathbf{t}_{-i}),$$

implying that she will choose η_i so that

$$0 \leq (1-\delta)2(n-1)\gamma\eta_i - \frac{\delta}{2n}\eta_i^2,$$

and thus

$$\eta_i \leq \frac{4(1-\delta)}{\delta}n^2\gamma. \quad (11)$$

In other words, *lying about v_i by more than the right-hand side of Equation (11) is a strategy dominated by the truth-telling strategy.*

From this, we can show that the utility of an agent in rVCG is close to the standard utility of VCG when all agents play undominated strategies. First notice that since the agents declare values with $\eta = \max_i \eta_i$ from their true values, we have

$$\begin{aligned}
&u_{v_\ell}^{\text{VCG}}(v_\ell, \mathbf{v}_{-\ell}) - u_{v_\ell}^{\text{VCG}}(b_\ell, \mathbf{b}_{-\ell}) \\
&= (\text{MSW}_{v_i}(v_i, \mathbf{v}_{-i}) - \text{MSW}(\mathbf{v}_{-i})) \\
&\quad - (\text{MSW}_{v_i}(b_i, \mathbf{b}_{-i}) - \text{MSW}(\mathbf{b}_{-i})) \\
&\leq (\text{MSW}_{v_i}(v_i, \mathbf{v}_{-i}) - \text{MSW}_{v_i}(b_i, \mathbf{b}_{-i})) \\
&\quad - (\text{MSW}(\mathbf{v}_{-i}) - \text{MSW}(\mathbf{b}_{-i})) \\
&\leq 2n\eta.
\end{aligned}$$

We can now conclude that for any agent ℓ who participates in rVCG, if all agents play undominated strategies, then:

$$\begin{aligned}
&u_{v_\ell}^{\text{rVCG}}(b_\ell, \mathbf{b}_{-\ell}) \\
&= (1-\delta)u_{v_\ell}^{\text{VCG}}(b_\ell, \mathbf{b}_{-\ell}) + \frac{\delta}{n}u_{v_\ell}^{\text{TE}}(b_\ell) \\
&= (1-\delta)(u_{v_\ell}^{\text{VCG}}(v_\ell, \mathbf{v}_{-\ell}) - (u_{v_\ell}^{\text{VCG}}(v_\ell, \mathbf{v}_{-\ell}) - u_{v_\ell}^{\text{VCG}}(b_\ell, \mathbf{b}_{-\ell}))) \\
&+ \frac{\delta}{n}u_{v_\ell}^{\text{TE}}(b_\ell) \\
&\geq (1-\delta)\left(u_{v_\ell}^{\text{VCG}}(v_\ell, \mathbf{v}_{-\ell}) - 2n\eta\right) \\
&\geq (1-\delta)u_{v_\ell}^{\text{VCG}}(v_\ell, \mathbf{v}_{-\ell}) - \frac{8(1-\delta)^2}{\delta}n^3\gamma.
\end{aligned}$$

□

The following two corollaries are immediate:

COROLLARY 1. *When* rVCG *is used and all agents play undominated strategies, the social welfare of the outcome a^* selected satisfies*

$$\sum_i v_i(a^*) \geq \text{MSW}(\mathbf{v}) - n\eta.$$

COROLLARY 2. *When* rVCG *is used and all agents play undominated strategies, the profit of the auctioneer is at least his profit from running VCG with truthful agents minus $2n\eta$.*

4. DISCUSSION

In this paper, we have introduced a number of concepts and taken first steps towards understanding and applying these concepts. Clearly though, we have only scratched the surface.

For example, the basic tool of strongly truthful mechanisms may have some potential, but there is clearly much left to be understood. What is the right way to define strong truthfulness? What mechanisms achieve optimal relative strong truthfulness? What is the tradeoff between the "strength" of the truthfulness and the social welfare that can be achieved?

We explored a new utility model for externalities in the context of mechanism design and sought to design mechanisms that protect agents from these externalities. Our mechanism has some externality-resistance, however, the externality parameters have to be extremely small in order for our mechanism to be effective. Is it possible to do better? More concretely, our mechanism tolerates externality parameters of value $\gamma = O(1/n^3)$. Are there mechanisms that tolerate higher values of γ? In the opposite direction, can we show a bound on the maximum γ?

What happens if we use a different solution concept? Also, while we chose to optimize for "base utility", that is not the only goal one might consider. One could optimize for social welfare with respect to the externality modified utilities. To what extent is this possible? Is this a reasonable goal? *I.e.*, should the goal of the mechanism be to encourage spite?

APPENDIX

A. STRONG TRUTHFULNESS AND SCORING RULES

In this appendix, we develop the connection between strongly truthful single-agent mechanisms and "strongly proper" scoring rules [10, 7]. As mentioned above, this immediately relates strongly truthful mechanisms to a host of seemingly unrelated problems.

A.1 The setting

We consider the following setting:

- There is a set of $n+1$ events, (call them events 0 through n) one of which will happen.
- The agent (forecaster) has a belief vector $\mathbf{p}$ as to which event will happen, where p_i is the probability that event i happens. $p_0 = 1 - \sum_{1\leq i\leq n} p_i$.
- The mechanism takes as input a postulated belief vector $\tilde{\mathbf{p}}$, and uses a scoring rule to determine the "payments" or "scores". Specifically, the scoring rule says for each outcome i, the "payment" or "score" the agent gets is $s_i(\tilde{\mathbf{p}})$.
- The agent proposes $\tilde{\mathbf{p}}$ and obtains utility
$$\sum_{0\leq i\leq n} p_i s_i(\tilde{\mathbf{p}}).$$
- The scoring rule is strictly proper if reporting $\tilde{\mathbf{p}} = \mathbf{p}$ strictly maximizes his utility.

A.2 Translating Mechanisms to Scoring Rules

Let M be a mechanism that takes as input an agent's valuations $x_1, \ldots, x_n$ for n alternatives. We assume $x_i \geq 0$ for all i and that $\sum_i x_i \leq 1$. The mechanism has allocation probabilities $a_i(\mathbf{x})$ and a payment rule $P(\mathbf{x})$.

We convert this to a scoring rule $S(M)$ as follows: Given vector $\mathbf{p}$ representing the probabilities $p_1, \ldots, p_n$ of outcomes (with $p_0 = 1 - \sum_i p_i$), let $s_i(\mathbf{p}) = a_i(\mathbf{p}) - P(\mathbf{p})$, and let $s_0(\mathbf{p}) = -P(\mathbf{p})$.

PROPOSITION 1. *If M is strictly truthful (i.e., it is strictly optimal to be truthful), then $S(M)$ is strictly proper.*

PROOF. By definition, the payoff to the agent when using the scoring rule and reporting $\tilde{\mathbf{p}}$ is

$$\sum_{1\leq i\leq n} p_i s_i(\tilde{\mathbf{p}}) + \left(1 - \sum_{1\leq i\leq n} p_i\right) s_0(\tilde{\mathbf{p}})$$

This is the same as

$$\begin{aligned}
\sum_{1\leq i\leq n} p_i\left(a_i(\tilde{\mathbf{p}}) - P(\tilde{\mathbf{p}})\right) - \left(1 - \sum_{1\leq i\leq n} p_i\right) P(\tilde{\mathbf{p}}) \\
= \sum_i p_i a_i(\tilde{\mathbf{p}}) - P(\tilde{\mathbf{p}}).
\end{aligned}$$

and thus the incentives for the scoring rule are identical to the incentives for the mechanism. □

A.3 Translating Scoring Rules to Mechanisms

Let S be a non-trivial scoring rule. We assume that the s_i's are of bounded absolute value. We show how to convert this to a mechanism:

Define the constants C_0 and C as follows:

$$C_0 = \max_{\mathbf{p}} |s_i(\mathbf{p}) - s_0(\mathbf{p})|$$

and

$$C = \max_{\mathbf{p}} \sum_{1 \le i \le n} \left(s_i(\mathbf{p}) - s_0(\mathbf{p}) + C_0 \right).$$

Since the scoring rule is non-trivial, the payments (scores) are not constant and therefore $C > 0$. Notice that $s_i(\mathbf{p}) - s_0(\mathbf{p}) + C_0 \ge 0$ and that

$$\sum_{i \le i \le n} \left(\frac{s_i(\mathbf{p}) - s_0(\mathbf{p}) + C_0}{C} \right) \le 1.$$

The mechanism $M(S)$ is now defined as follows.

- The mechanism takes as input the values x_i for each of the alternatives $1 \le i \le n$. We assume that $x_i \ge 0$ for all i and that $\sum_{1 \le i \le n} x_i \le 1$.
- Define $a_i(\mathbf{x}) = \left(s_i(\mathbf{x}) - s_0(\mathbf{x}) + C_0 \right) / C$. As observed above, $\sum_i a_i(\mathbf{x}) \le 1$ and $a_i(\mathbf{x}) \ge 0$.
- Define $P(\mathbf{x}) = -\left(s_0(\mathbf{x}) + (1 - \sum_i x_i) C_0 \right) / C$

PROPOSITION 2. *If S is strictly proper, then $M(S)$ is strictly truthful.*

PROOF. The utility of an agent playing this mechanism and reporting $\mathbf{x}$ is

$$\left(\sum_i x_i a_i(\mathbf{x}) \right) - P(\mathbf{x}).$$

This is the same as

$$\sum_i x_i \frac{\left(s_i(\mathbf{x}) - s_0(\mathbf{x}) + C_0 \right)}{C} + \frac{\left(s_0(\mathbf{x}) + \left(1 - \sum_i x_i\right) C_0 \right)}{C},$$

which is

$$\sum_i x_i \frac{\left(s_i(\mathbf{x}) + C_0 \right)}{C} + \left(1 - \sum_i x_i \right) \frac{\left(s_0(\mathbf{x}) + C_0 \right)}{C}.$$

If S is strictly proper then, it is strictly proper under the translation by C_0 and scaling by C. Thus the utility of the agent in the mechanism is strictly maximized by reporting truthfully. □

A.4 Strong truthfulness

Let us define $m(x)$-strongly proper scoring rules as follows:

Definition 5. A scoring rule with scores $s_i(\mathbf{p})$ is $m(\mathbf{p})$-strongly proper if for every $\mathbf{p}$, $\tilde{\mathbf{p}}$

$$u(\mathbf{p}, \mathbf{p}) - u(\mathbf{p}, \tilde{\mathbf{p}}) \ge \frac{1}{2} m(\tilde{\mathbf{p}}) \, ||\mathbf{p} - \tilde{\mathbf{p}}||^2,$$

where

$$u(\mathbf{p}, \tilde{\mathbf{p}}) = \sum_i p_i s_i(\tilde{\mathbf{p}}).$$

THEOREM 3.

- *Let M be an $m(\mathbf{x})$-strongly truthful mechanism. Then $S(M)$ is an $m(x)$-strongly proper scoring rule.*
- *Let S be an $m(\mathbf{p})$-strongly proper mechanism. Then $M(S)$ is an $m(x)/C$ strongly truthful mechanism.*

PROOF. The first part is immediate from the fact that utilities are precisely preserved under the transformation from mechanisms to scoring rules. For the second part, suppose that for scoring rule S

$$u^S(\mathbf{p}, \mathbf{p}) - u^S(\mathbf{p}, \tilde{\mathbf{p}}) \ge \frac{1}{2} m(\tilde{\mathbf{p}}) \, ||\mathbf{p} - \tilde{\mathbf{p}}||^2,$$

Then by the construction above

$$u^{M(S)}(\mathbf{x}, \mathbf{x}) - u^{M(S)}(\mathbf{x}, \tilde{\mathbf{x}}) = \frac{u^S(\mathbf{x}, \mathbf{x}) - u^S(\mathbf{x}, \tilde{\mathbf{x}})}{C} \ge \frac{1}{2} \frac{m(\tilde{\mathbf{x}})}{C} \, ||\mathbf{x} - \tilde{\mathbf{x}}||^2.$$

□

A.5 Application to some standard scoring rules

- Logarithmic scoring rule: the translation doesn't work because C_0 is unbounded.
- Quadratic scoring rule: $s_i(\mathbf{p}) = 1 + 2p_i - ||\mathbf{p}||^2$. Then $s_1(p) - s_0(p) = 2(p - (1-p)) = 4p - 2$ which is between -2 and 2. Thus $C_0 = 2$ and $C = 4$. This translates into $a(x) = x$, which has $m(x) = 1$.
- Spherical scoring rule: $s_i(\mathbf{p}) = p_i / ||\mathbf{p}||$. Then $s_1(p) - s_0(p) = (2p - 1)/\sqrt{p^2 + (1-p)^2}$ which is between -1 and 1. Thus $C_0 = 1$ and $C = 2$. This translates into

$$a(x) = \frac{1}{2} + \frac{2x - 1}{2\sqrt{x^2 + (1-x)^2}}.$$

The $m(x)$ value is half that of the spherical rule.

B. REFERENCES

[1] J. Abernethy and R. Frongillo. A characterization of scoring rules for linear properties. In *Proceedings of the 25th Conference on Learning Theory*, 2012.

[2] Aaron Archer and Robert Kleinberg. Characterizing truthful mechanisms with convex type spaces. *SIGecom Exchanges*, 7(3), 2008.

[3] Aaron Archer and Robert Kleinberg. Truthful germs are contagious: a local to global characterization of truthfulness. In *ACM Conference on Electronic Commerce*, pages 21–30. ACM, 2008.

[4] Itai Ashlagi, Shahar Dobzinski, and Ron Lavi. An optimal lower bound for anonymous scheduling mechanisms. In *ACM Conference on Electronic Commerce (EC)*, pages 169–176, 2009.

[5] Moshe Babaioff, Robert Kleinberg, and Christos H. Papadimitriou. Congestion games with malicious players. In *Proceedings of the 8th ACM conference on Electronic commerce*, EC '07, pages 103–112, New York, NY, USA, 2007. ACM.

[6] Moshe Babaioff, Ron Lavi, and Elan Pavlov. Single-value combinatorial auctions and implementation in undominated strategies. In *SODA*, pages 1054–1063. ACM Press, 2006.

[7] J. Eric Bickel. Some comparisons among quadratic, spherical, and logarithmic scoring rules. *Decision Analysis*, 4(2):49–65, 2007.

[8] S.P. Boyd and L. Vandenberghe. *Convex optimization.* Cambridge Univ Pr, 2004.

[9] F. Brandt, T. Sandholm, and Y. Shoham. Spiteful bidding in sealed-bid auctions. In *Proceedings of IJCAI'07*, 2007.

[10] Glenn W. Brier. Verification of forecasts expressed in terms of probability. *Mon. Wea. Rev.*, 78:1–3, 1950.

[11] Po-An Chen. The effects of altruism and spite on games. *PhD Thesis, University of Southern California*, 59(4):757–75, October 2011.

[12] Po-An Chen, Bart de Keijzer, David Kempe, and Guido Schäfer. The robust price of anarchy of altruistic games. In *WINE*, volume 7090 of *Lecture Notes in Computer Science*, pages 383–390. Springer, 2011.

[13] Po-An Chen and David Kempe. Altruism, selfishness, and spite in traffic routing. In *Proceedings of the 9th ACM conference on Electronic commerce*, EC '08, pages 140–149, New York, NY, USA, 2008. ACM.

[14] Po-An Chen and David Kempe. Bayesian auctions with friends and foes. In *Algorithmic Game Theory*, volume 5814 of *Lecture Notes in Computer Science*, pages 335–346. Springer Berlin / Heidelberg, 2009.

[15] Yiling Chen. A utility framework for bounded-loss market makers. In *In Proceedings of the 23rd Conference on Uncertainty in Artificial Intelligence*, pages 49–56, 2007.

[16] David J. Cooper and Hanming Fang. Understanding overbidding in second price auctions: An experimental study. *The Economic Journal*, 118(532):1572–1595, 2008.

[17] Uriel Feige and Moshe Tennenholtz. Responsive lotteries. In *SAGT*, volume 6386 of *Lecture Notes in Computer Science*, pages 150–161. Springer, 2010.

[18] Robin Hanson. Logarithmic market scoring rules for modular combinatorial information aggregation. *The Journal of Prediction Markets*, 1(1):3–15, 2007.

[19] Philippe Jehiel, Benny Moldovanu, and Ennio Stacchetti. Multidimensional mechanism design for auctions with externalities. *Journal of Economic Theory*, 85(2):258–293, 1999.

[20] John H. Kagel, Ronald M. Harstad, and Dan Levin. Information impact and allocation rules in auctions with affiliated private values: A laboratory study. *Econometrica*, 55(6):pp. 1275–1304, 1987.

[21] Ron Lavi and Chaitanya Swamy. Truthful mechanism design for multi-dimensional scheduling via cycle monotonicity. In *ACM Conference on Electronic Commerce (EC)*, pages 252–261, 2007.

[22] John O. Ledyard. Public goods: A survey of experimental research. Public Economics 9405003, EconWPA, May 1994.

[23] David K. Levine. Modeling altruism and spitefulness in experiments. *Review of Economic Dynamics*, 1(3):593 – 622, 1998.

[24] Emiel Maasland and Sander Onderstal. Auctions with financial externalities. *Economic Theory*, 32(3):551–574, September 2007.

[25] John Morgan, Ken Steiglitz, and George Reis. The spite motive and equilibrium behavior in auctions. *The B.E. Journal of Economic Analysis & Policy*, 0(1):5, 2003.

[26] Thomas Moscibroda, Stefan Schmid, and Roger Wattenhofer. The price of malice: A game-theoretic framework for malicious behavior in distributed systems. *Internet Mathematics*, 6(2):125–155, 2009.

[27] Roger B. Myerson. Optimal auction design. *Mathematics of Operations Research*, 6(1):58–73, 1981.

[28] Noam Nisan and Amir Ronen. Algorithmic mechanism design. *Games and Economic Behavior*, 35:166–196, 2001.

[29] Kobbi Nissim, Rann Smorodinsky, and Moshe Tennenholtz. Approximately optimal mechanism design via differential privacy. In *Proceedings of the 3rd Innovations in Theoretical Computer Science Conference*, ITCS '12, pages 203–213, New York, NY, USA, 2012. ACM.

[30] R.T. Rockafellar. *Convex analysis*, volume 28. Princeton Univ Pr, 1997.

[31] Aaron Roth. The price of malice in linear congestion games. In *WINE*, volume 5385 of *Lecture Notes in Computer Science*, pages 118–125. Springer, 2008.

[32] Justin Wolfers and Eric Zitzewitz. Prediction markets. Working Paper 10504, National Bureau of Economic Research, May 2004.

Parametric Digital Auctions

[Working Paper]*

Pablo Daniel Azar
MIT, CSAIL
Cambridge, MA, 02139
azar@csail.mit.edu

Silvio Micali†
MIT, CSAIL
Cambridge, MA, 02139
silvio@csail.mit.edu

ABSTRACT

We study revenue maximization for digital auctions, where there are infinitely many copies of a good for sale. There are n buyers, each of whom is interested in obtaining one copy of the good. The buyers' private valuations are drawn from a joint distribution $\boldsymbol{F}$. The seller does not know this distribution. The only information that she has are the mean μ_i and variance σ_i^2 of each buyer i's marginal distribution F_i. We call such auctions *parametric auctions.*

We construct a deterministic parametric auction that, for a wide class of distributions, guarantees a constant fraction of the optimal revenue achievable when the seller precisely knows the distribution $\boldsymbol{F}$. Furthermore, our auction is a posted price mechanism and it is *maximin optimal* among all such mechanisms. That is, it is the posted price mechanism that maximizes revenue in the worst case over an adversarial choice of the distribution.

Categories and Subject Descriptors

J.4 [**Computer Applications**]: Social and Behavioral Science—*Economics*

General Terms

Economics

Keywords

Approximately Optimal Auctions, Robust Optimization

1. INTRODUCTION

In a Bayesian auction of a digital good, there is one good for sale, available in an unlimited number of copies, and n buyers, each interested in buying one copy of the good. Each buyer i has a value v_i for the good, and the vector $(v_1, ..., v_n)$ is drawn from a joint distribution $\boldsymbol{F}$.

There are many real-world examples of such a setting, including but not limited to, selling music online, selling copies of a computer program, and giving non-exclusive licenses for a patent.

How much revenue can we guarantee to the seller in such a setting? If $\boldsymbol{F}$ is a product distribution and the seller knows $\boldsymbol{F}$, then an adaptation of Myerson's optimal auction [2] guarantees the maximum revenue that any incentive compatible mechanism can obtain.

We work with strictly weaker assumptions. Namely,

1. *$\boldsymbol{F}$ is an arbitrary joint distribution*; and
2. *The seller only knows the mean μ_i and standard deviation σ_i of each buyer i's marginal distribution F_i.*

We call such an auction a *parametric auction.* For a digital goods setting we construct a parametric auction $\mathbb{A}$, that simultaneously

(i) achieves a significant fraction of the optimal revenue, and

(ii) is *maximin optimal* among all parametric posted price mechanisms.

That is, our auction is a posted price mechanism and, for any other parametric posted price mechanism A, and for every pair of parameter vectors $(\mu_1, ..., \mu_n)$ and $(\sigma_1, ..., \sigma_n)$, there exists a distribution $\boldsymbol{F}$ —whose marginals have the given parameters— for which our $\mathbb{A}$ obtains strictly more revenue than A.

Since $\mathbb{A}$ is a *deterministic posted price mechanism,* it is dominant strategy truthful and very practical to implement. Furthermore, because we only require knowledge of the first two moments of the distribution, the seller can easily learn the information that she needs from a limited amount of data, while it may be infeasible to learn the whole distribution $\boldsymbol{F}$.

2. OUR RESULTS

We denote by $Rev(OPT, \boldsymbol{F})$ the optimal revenue achievable by a truthful auction which has knowledge of the distribution $\boldsymbol{F}$. For any auction A and distribution $\boldsymbol{F}$, the *competitive ratio of A* is given by

$$\frac{Rev(A, \boldsymbol{F})}{Rev(OPT, \boldsymbol{F})}.$$

*A full version of this working paper is available at `http://people.csail.mit.edu/azar/wp-content/uploads/2012/11/ParametricDigitalMechanisms.pdf`

†Supported by MIT-SkTech Grant # 019683-081

ITCS'13, January 9–12, 2013, Berkeley, California, USA.
ACM 978-1-4503-1859-4/13/01.

A parametric lower bound on the competitive ratio..

We construct a digital auction $\mathbb{A}$ that is competitive with the optimal auction. The competitive ratio is constant in the number of players and *does not rely on* any kind of symmetry, independence, or regularity of the distribution $\boldsymbol{F}$. However, it will be a function of the ratios $\frac{\mu_i}{\sigma_i}$. This is intuitive because if σ_i is very large compared with μ_i, then the seller has very little information about F_i, and one cannot expect her to collect significant revenue from player i.

More concretely, for any distribution $\boldsymbol{F}$ with parameter vectors $\boldsymbol{\mu}, \boldsymbol{\sigma}$ and for any player i our auction satisfies

$$\frac{Rev_i(\mathbb{A}, \boldsymbol{F})}{Rev_i(OPT, \boldsymbol{F})} \geq \rho(\frac{\mu_i}{\sigma_i})$$

where $\rho(\cdot)$ is a function of $\frac{\mu_i}{\sigma_i}$ with the following properties:

- $\rho(\frac{\mu_i}{\sigma_i})$ is always positive when μ_i, σ_i are positive.
- When each F_i has a monotone increasing hazard rate, $\rho(\frac{\mu_i}{\sigma_i}) > 10.5\%$.

More generally, for any constant c and any c-informative distribution F with mean μ and standard deviation σ, we will have $\rho(\frac{\mu}{\sigma}) > \rho(c)$. Since for any mechanism A we have $Rev(A, \boldsymbol{F}) = \sum_i Rev_i(A, \boldsymbol{F})$, we will be able to conclude that, as long as the marginals $F_1, ..., F_n$ are c-informative distributions, our auction $\mathbb{A}$ will have a competitive ratio bounded below by a constant

$$\frac{Rev(\mathbb{A}, \boldsymbol{F})}{Rev(OPT, \boldsymbol{F})} \geq \rho(c).$$

A parametric upper bound on the competitive ratio for posted price mechanisms.

It is a priori possible that one could obtain more than a constant fraction of the optimal revenue. That is, an auctioneer who knows only the first and second moments of the distribution $\boldsymbol{F}$ could guarantee a profit arbitrarily close to optimal as the number n of players grows very large. We show that this is impossible if we restrict the auctioneer to use posted price mechanisms. That is, for any parametric posted price mechanism A, and any parameter vectors $\boldsymbol{\mu}, \boldsymbol{\sigma}$ there exists a distribution $\boldsymbol{F}$ with the given parameters such that

$$\frac{Rev_i(A, \boldsymbol{F})}{Rev_i(OPT, \boldsymbol{F})} \leq \psi(\frac{\mu_i}{\sigma_i})$$

where $\psi(\cdot)$ is a function of $\frac{\mu_i}{\sigma_i}$ with the following properties

- $\psi(\frac{\mu_i}{\sigma_i}) < 1$
- $\lim_{\frac{\mu_i}{\sigma_i} \to \infty} \psi(\frac{\mu_i}{\sigma_i}) = 1$
- $\lim_{\frac{\mu_i}{\sigma_i} \to 0} \psi(\frac{\mu_i}{\sigma_i}) = 0.$

That is, our upper bound on the competitive ratio is a constant less than one when $\frac{\mu_i}{\sigma_i}$ is constant. When μ_i is much larger than σ_i, then the upper bound is meaningless (indeed, as μ_i becomes large, the revenue of our parametric auction $\mathbb{A}$ approaches the optimal auction). When σ_i is much larger than μ_i, no parametric posted price mechanism can obtain any significant fraction of the optimal revenue. For these mechanisms, this result formalizes our intuition that a very large standard deviation implies an "uninformative" distribution from which we can not guarantee any revenue.

Maximin Optimality and the Digital Auction $\mathbb{A}$..

As said above, our digital auction $\mathbb{A}$ is competitive with the optimal auction, where the competitive ratio depends on $\frac{\mu_i}{\sigma_i}$. Examining the competitive ratio is a meaningful way to give revenue guarantees when the full distribution is not known. However, there can be a multiplicity of parametric auctions which achieve a constant competitive ratio, and it may be difficult to decide which one is the "best." Any definition of optimality for parametric auctions needs to take into account the uncertainty that the seller has over the joint distribution $\boldsymbol{F}$. Since this is a *worst-case uncertainty*, our definition of optimality for parametric mechanisms is based on worst-case revenue maximization.

DEFINITION 1. *Let $\mathcal{M}$ be a class of mechanisms and let $\mathcal{D}_{\boldsymbol{\mu},\boldsymbol{\sigma}}$ be the class of distributions which have parameter vectors $\boldsymbol{\mu}$ and $\boldsymbol{\sigma}$. An auction A^* is* maximin optimal *for $\mathcal{M}$ if $A^* \in \mathcal{M}$ and, given parameter vectors $\boldsymbol{\mu}$ and $\boldsymbol{\sigma}$ we have,*

$$A^* = \underset{A \in \mathcal{M}}{\operatorname{argmax}} \min_{\boldsymbol{F} \in \mathcal{D}_{\boldsymbol{\mu},\boldsymbol{\sigma}}} Rev(A, \boldsymbol{F}).$$

We highlight that, in the definition, A^* is the *unique* mechanism maximizing worst-case revenue. We show that $\mathbb{A}$ is maximin optimal for the class of parametric posted price mechanisms.

3. CONCLUSION AND FUTURE WORK

In a Bayesian setting, it is important to construct auctions that are as detail-free as possible while still guaranteeing good revenue. In this paper, we focused on a seller auctioning who has knowledge of the means and variances of players' valuations and who wants to auction a digital good. These however, are not the only parameters that can be helpful in constructing parametric auctions, or the only environments of interest. In particular, the authors, together with Daskalakis and Weinberg [1] have extended this model to use the median and other quantiles as parameters, and have constructed approximately optimal parametric auctions for matroid environments where the players' distributions are independent and regular. For downward closed environments, an analogous result applies when the distributions have a monotone hazard rate. In the future, we plan to construct auctions that use higher order moments and covariances in order to guarantee more revenue in more general settings, including auctions with multidimensional types.

4. REFERENCES

[1] P. Azar, C. Daskalakis, S. Micali and S.M. Weinberg. Optimal and Efficient Parametric Auctions. In *Proceedings of the twenty-fourth annual ACM-SIAM symposium on Discrete algorithms. Society for Industrial and Applied Mathematics, 2013.*

[2] R.B. Myerson. Optimal auction design. *Mathematics of operations research*, 6(1):58, 1981.

Learning and Incentives in User-Generated Content: Multi-Armed Bandits with Endogenous Arms

Arpita Ghosh
Cornell University
Ithaca, NY, USA
arpitaghosh.work@gmail.com

Patrick Hummel*
Google Inc.
Mountain View, CA, USA
phummel@google.com

ABSTRACT

Motivated by the problem of learning the qualities of user-generated content on the Web, we study a multi-armed bandit problem where the number and success probabilities of the arms of the bandit are *endogenously* determined by strategic agents in response to the incentives provided by the learning algorithm. We model the contributors of user-generated content as attention-motivated agents who derive benefit when their contribution is displayed, and have a cost to quality, where a contribution's quality is the probability of its receiving a positive viewer vote. Agents strategically choose whether and what quality contribution to produce in response to the algorithm that decides how to display contributions. The algorithm, which would like to eventually only display the highest quality contributions, can only learn a contribution's quality from the viewer votes the contribution receives when displayed. The problem of inferring the relative qualities of contributions using viewer feedback, to optimize for overall viewer satisfaction over time, can then be modeled as the classic multi-armed bandit problem, *except* that the arms available to the bandit and therefore the achievable regret are endogenously determined by strategic agents — a good algorithm for this setting must not only quickly identify the best contributions, but also *incentivize* high-quality contributions to choose amongst in the first place.

We first analyze the well-known UCB algorithm $\mathcal{M}_{\text{UCB}}$ [Auer *et al.* 2002] as a *mechanism* in this setting, where the total number of potential contributors or arms, K, can grow with the total number of viewers or available periods, T, and the maximum possible success probability of an arm, γ, may be bounded away from 1 to model malicious or error-prone viewers in the audience. We first show that while $\mathcal{M}_{\text{UCB}}$ can incentivize high-quality arms and achieve strong sublinear equilibrium regret when $K(T)$ does not grow too quickly with T, it incentivizes very low quality contributions when $K(T)$ scales proportionally with T. We then show that modifying the UCB mechanism to explore a randomly chosen restricted subset of $\sqrt{T}$ arms provides excellent incentive properties — this modified mechanism achieves strong sublinear regret, which is the regret measured against the *maximum* achievable quality γ, in *every* equilibrium, for all ranges of $K(T) \leq T$, for all possible values of the audience parameter γ.

*This work was completed while the authors were affiliated with Yahoo! Research.

ITCS'13, January 9–12, 2012, Berkeley, California, USA.

Categories and Subject Descriptors

J.4 [**Computer Applications**]: Social & Behavioral Sciences

General Terms

Economics

Keywords

Attention economics; Endogenous arms; Game theory; Multi-armed bandits; Quality of online content; User-generated content (UGC)

1. INTRODUCTION

User-generated content, such as reviews on sites like Yelp and Amazon, answers on online Q&A forums like Y! Answers, Quora or StackOverflow, comments on news stories or blogs, and user-created videos on YouTube or articles, for example, on Associated Content, are now ubiquitous on the web. This user-generated content (UGC) spans a vast spectrum of qualities — a small number of comments on an article (*e.g.*, on Slashdot) or answers to a question might be very thoughtful and well-written, while others range all the way from mediocre to junk. A website that hosts such user-generated content would like to sort through these contributions and selectively present only the best few contributions to each viewer to optimize her experience. However, websites typically cannot directly observe the qualities of contributions, but rather must learn their qualities from feedback from these same viewers — in most UGC settings, a viewer can provide feedback about the contributions they see, for example, by using thumbs-up style buttons. How should a website decide which contributions to display to each viewer so as to quickly learn the contributions' qualities, while still ensuring the best possible viewer experience overall?

The simplest abstraction of the problem of inferring the relative qualities of contributions, each of which can be thought of as a biased coin whose success probability is this unknown quality, while maximizing the number of successes obtained over time, is the classic multi-armed bandit problem [1]. However, unlike in the standard multi-armed bandit setting, the set of contributions, or arms available to the bandit, is not a fixed, exogenous quantity — rather, the contributions are produced by users who have a choice about *whether* to produce a contribution (for example, whether to write an article or review, or to answer a question), as well as about its *quality*, *i.e.*, how much effort to put into the contribution. Since these users would all like their contributions to be seen by a large number of viewers[1], how contributions are explored and displayed now constitutes a *mechanism* for allocating attention, which might affect the incentives of contributors to participate, as well as the quality of their contributions.

We therefore have a multi-armed bandit problem where the number and success probabilities of arms of the bandit are now *endogenously* determined in response to the incentives provided by the learning algorithm to agents. A good mechanism in this setting not only needs to quickly identify and exploit the best arms, but also must *incentivize* high quality arms, or contributions, in the first place. What algorithms provide strong incentives to users to participate and make high-quality contributions, and then also quickly identify the best content?

Our contributions. We model and analyze the problem of learning the qualities of user-generated content, when this content is produced by strategic, attention-motivated agents with a cost to quality. Our model leads to a new version of the multi-armed bandit problem with *endogenous* arms, where the number and success probabilities of the arms presented to the bandit are not fixed apriori, but rather are determined by the incentives provided by the explore-exploit algorithm.

We begin by analyzing the well-known UCB algorithm [1] $\mathcal{M}_{\mathrm{UCB}}$ for the multi-armed bandit problem as a *mechanism*, in a setting where the maximum success probability of an arm, γ, may be bounded away from 1 — this models an important factor in the context of user-generated content, namely the presence of voters in the online audience who (either deliberately or accidentally) vote down even the best contributions. We find that while the UCB mechanism is able to incentivize high-quality arms and achieve strong sublinear regret (Definition 2.2) when the number of potential contributors $K(T)$ does not grow too quickly with the number of viewers T, it fails miserably when $K(T)$ scales up with T, which is a natural regime of interest in the UGC setting where often many viewers are also potential contributors — when $\lim_{T\to\infty} \frac{T}{K(T)} = r$, *all* contributors produce very low quality content under $\mathcal{M}_{\mathrm{UCB}}$, leading to poor regret.

We then investigate a modification of the UCB mechanism, motivated by another bandit algorithm $\mathcal{M}_{1-\mathrm{FAIL}}$ [6] that is designed to achieve good performance (algorithmically) in the large K regime. This mechanism $\mathcal{M}_{1-\mathrm{FAIL}}$ itself does not suffice, since while it produces strong sublinear regret for $\gamma = 1$, it is not robust to any down-voting errors by the audience, and fails to achieve strong sublinear regret for *any* $\gamma < 1$, when $K(T)$ grows proportionately with T. However, modifying the UCB mechanism to explore a randomly chosen restricted subset of $\sqrt{T}$ arms as in $\mathcal{M}_{1-\mathrm{FAIL}}$, but using the UCB index, provides excellent incentive and robustness properties — this modified mechanism achieves strong sublinear regret, which is the regret measured against the *maximum* achievable quality γ, in *every* equilibrium, for all ranges of $K(T) \leq T$, for all possible values of the audience parameter γ.

Related work. There is now an enormous literature on algorithms for learning in the multi-armed bandit setting which is too large to describe properly in this paper; see, for example, [19] and references therein for a nice overview. A large part of this literature addresses settings with a fixed and finite set of arms. In the context of user-generated content with unknown quality, however, the number of contributions, or arms, is potentially related to the number of viewers, or periods available for exploration, since a page with a larger number of viewers potentially also has a larger number of contributors. Our setting is therefore most closely related to the models that do not assume there is a fixed finite number of arms, as in [6], [21], and [22]. All of these papers take a purely algorithmic approach to the learning problem, and so do not address a situation where the number and success probabilities of the arms are *endogenously* determined in response to the incentives created by the learning algorithm.

There is a small but growing literature that addresses incentives in the multi-armed bandit setting. [2], [3], [9], [10], and [14] study multi-armed bandit problems in the context of online advertising with strategic advertisers, and investigate the design of truthful mechanisms when the system must learn the (unknown) click-through rates of ads. The strategic choice of the agents in these papers are the agents' *bids*, rather than the click-through rates of the arms that are learned by the mechanism. [5] considers questions related to endogenous pricing decisions of firms when these decisions may influence whether consumers explore other firms and the consumers face a multi-armed bandit problem. [7] addresses incentives to explore in a multi-armed bandit problem when agents will learn from other agents' explorations and agents potentially have an incentive to free ride. [15] considers questions related to how agents would choose to explore when an agent's payoff depends in part on how many other agents chose to explore the same arm. Lastly, [20] and [23] consider models of worker job search and job quitting decisions in the context of a multi-armed bandit problem. However, none of these papers studies a multi-armed bandit setting in which the success probabilities of the arms themselves are endogenously chosen by strategic agents.

There is a growing body of work on incentives and strategic behavior in the context of online user-generated content [8, 11, 12, 13, 16, 17]. [8] considers incentives for users to contribute content soon rather than delaying their contributions in the context of online Q&A sites; however, this work does not address questions related to the qualities of the contributions. [12] investigates incentives to contribute user-generated content when users are motivated by points rather than attention, and [11] and [13] address the question of incentivizing high-quality user-generated content in a model very similar to that used in this paper. However,

[1]In addition to attention (*i.e.*, number of views) being a direct psychological incentive, there are settings, such as Associated Content, where the author of an article is paid according to the number of views her article receives, so that attention might also translate to a direct monetary incentive.

this work does not consider the incentives provided to agents in the process of learning or estimating the qualities of their contributions, nor does it attempt to use as small a number of viewers as possible to estimate the qualities of contributions before the best contribution is identified. This aspect of maximizing viewer welfare is captured by the *regret* measure which is used to quantify the performance of the mechanisms we study in this paper.

2. MODEL AND PRELIMINARIES

In this section, we present a model for the problem of learning the unknown qualities of user-generated contributions to achieve the best overall viewer experience, when contributors are strategic, and viewers provide feedback on the quality of the contributions that are displayed to them. The outline of the model is as follows: (i) Contributors decide on whether, and with how much effort, to write a contribution, based on how often their contribution is likely to be displayed by the algorithm (ii) Viewers vote on contributions, and the learning mechanism would like to use these votes to find the best, or top few, contributions and eventually display only these top contributions to viewers (iii) The mechanism's performance is measured by its equilibrium regret, which measures the regret based on the elicited qualities of contributions displayed in equilibrium against the best possible quality a contributor could have chosen. The model is described in detail below. (We note that this model does not attempt to capture every nuance of the UGC setting, and hope that it will provide a building block to address other aspects of the problem of learning qualities in the UGC setting, such as sequential contributions, or the fact that a viewer may not always provide feedback on the contribution she sees; see §5 for a discussion.)

Content. We define the *quality* q of a contribution as the probability that a viewer will like the contribution, *i.e.*, rate it positively as 'good' or 'useful' or give it a thumbs-up; such ratings and thumbs-up buttons are widely used for feedback with online user-generated content. Since q is a probability, it must lie between 0 and 1. The qualities q_i of contributions are not directly observable (*i.e.*, are initially unknown) to the system, which can only infer these qualities from the viewer ratings.

There is a stream of T users, each of whom views contributions. For clarity of exposition, we begin by assuming that each user will be shown exactly one contribution (we later show how to extend all our results to displaying multiple contributions in §4.2). Each user provides feedback on the quality of the contribution he sees by giving it either a positive or negative vote.

We would like to model the fact that an audience of viewers need not be perfect: for example, it is possible that there are viewers who will always vote a contribution as bad no matter how good the contribution is, or that viewers make errors when rating contributions. A simple way to model such imperfect viewer populations is via an upper bound γ on the probability of receiving a positive vote from a random member of the audience. That is, we constrain the qualities of contributions as

$$q \in [0, \gamma],$$

where $\gamma \leq 1$ is the probability that a contribution of the highest possible quality receives a positive vote. When $\gamma = 1$, no segment of the viewer population makes errors or maliciously rates contributions negatively, so that a contribution of the highest possible quality always receives a positive vote from every viewer. A good mechanism should provide incentives that are robust to such realistic imperfections in the voting population, *i.e.*, that do not fail for audiences with $\gamma < 1$.[2]

Contributors. There is a pool of potential contributors, or agents, of size $K = K(T)$. The dependence of K on T reflects the fact that as the number of viewers for a site grows, the number of potential contributors can grow as well.

Each of the $K(T)$ potential contributors is a *strategic* agent who chooses whether to participate and the quality of her contribution (if participating) to maximize her expected payoff given the potential costs and benefits from contributing. We denote the probability that agent i decides to contribute by β_i and the quality she chooses when contributing by q_i. Since agents may decide whether or not to participate probabilistically, the number of actual contributors, which we denote by $k(T)$, is a random variable whose distribution depends on the total number of potential contributors K as well as their participation probabilities $\beta_1, \ldots, \beta_K$. Naturally, $k(T) \leq K(T)$.

If an agent chooses not to contribute, then she incurs no cost but also receives no benefit, so her net payoff is 0. An agent who contributes has a cost to quality which depends on her type, and derives benefit from attention, as described next.

The *cost* incurred by a contributor depends on the quality of the content she chooses to produce. To model the fact that different agents might have different abilities, *i.e.*, need to exert different levels of effort to produce the same quality contribution, we suppose that each agent can be one of several possible types τ in some finite set $\mathcal{T}$, each of which corresponds to a different cost function. An agent's type τ is an independent and identically distributed draw from a distribution ρ over $\mathcal{T}$ such that the probability an agent is type τ is ρ_τ.

The cost of producing content of quality q for an agent of type τ is $c_\tau(q)$, which is an increasing function of q (*i.e.*, producing higher quality content is more costly). We make the following assumptions on the functions c_τ:

1. The cost function c_τ is continuously differentiable in q for all $q < \gamma$ and all τ.
2. $c_\tau(0) > 0$.
3. $\lim_{q \to \gamma} c_\tau(q) = \infty$ for all τ.

The assumption that $c_\tau(0) > 0$ captures the fact that entry is endogenous, *i.e.*, participating and producing the contribution of even the lowest possible quality requires more effort than not participating at all. The assumption that $\lim_{q \to \gamma} c_\tau(q) = \infty$, as in [11] and [13], says that producing content of the highest possible quality, which corresponds to making *every* viewer that votes accurately happy, is nearly

[2]One could further generalize the model by assuming that there may be some viewers who make errors by rating contributions positively, so the lowest possible quality contribution is greater than 0. However, all our results continue to hold with this change to the model, since the analysis never uses the fact that the lowest possible quality contribution is 0.

impossible.[3] (We note that the assumption that $c_\tau(q) \to \infty$ is not required for our main result (Theorem 4.3), showing that the modified UCB mechanism $\mathcal{M}_{\text{UCB-MOD}}$ achieves strong sublinear regret, to hold; rather, the result holds despite this assumption.)

Agents derive *benefit* from attention, *i.e.*, when their contribution is displayed to a viewer. The total benefit to an agent is the total number of viewers who see her contribution. Recall that there are a total of T such viewers, *i.e.*, T is the total number of times contributions will be displayed. Let t denote a generic time period between 1 and T. We use n_i^t to denote the number of views contributor i receives until the t-th period, so that n_i^T is the total number of views, or the total amount of attention received by contribution i.

We note here that our results will also hold when agents only derive value from positive feedback to the contribution, *i.e.*, from $q_i n_i^T$ rather than n_i^T alone — informally, this is because it is easier to incentivize agents to produce higher qualities when they value positive feedback than when they only value views.

The payoff of an agent who chooses quality q_i is the difference between the number of views she obtains, n_i^T (which can depend, in general, on the number and qualities of other contributors in addition to q_i), and her cost. Thus an agent's expected payoff from participating with quality q_i if the agent's type is τ is

$$u_i = E[n_i^T(q_i, q_{-i}, k(T))] - c_\tau(q_i).$$

Mechanism. A *mechanism* in this setting determines which contribution to display for each $t \leq T$, and therefore the values of n_i^t, $t = 1, \ldots, T$, for all contributions i. The mechanism can choose which contribution to display based on the values of T, k (the number of contributions received), as well as the estimates of the qualities of these contributions from the (random) votes received by each contribution, and the number of times each contribution has been displayed so far (n_i^t). (We note again that the generalization to displaying multiple contributions, as is typically the case in real UGC applications, is presented in §4.2.)

The mechanism would like to eventually identify the highest quality contribution based on its estimates of qualities from the viewer votes, and then show this best contribution to every viewer. We next discuss how we measure performance — unlike in traditional multi-armed bandit settings, the performance of a mechanism here must be measured not only by how quickly the mechanism identifies and exploits the best contribution, but also on the qualities of the contributions it is able to *elicit* in equilibrium in the first place.

Solution Concept. In response to the incentives provided by the mechanism, agents strategically choose their contribution probabilities β_i and qualities q_i to maximize their utility. We use the solution concept of a free-entry Bayes-Nash equilibrium to determine the qualities and number of contributions (*i.e.*, arms), that will be elicited by the mechanism. Since agents' payoff functions are symmetric in the parameters of the game for all agents with the same type τ, we focus throughout on symmetric equilibria: in a symmetric equilibrium, all agents with the same type participate with the same probability and follow the same strategy of quality choices conditional on participating.

A *symmetric mixed strategy Bayes-Nash equilibrium* is a set of probabilities β_τ and distributions F_τ over qualities q, such that if agents' types are drawn according to the distribution ρ and all agents of type τ contribute with probability β_τ and choose a quality drawn from the CDF $F_\tau(q)$ conditional on contributing, then no agent can increase her expected payoff by deviating from this strategy given the uncertainty the agent faces about the precise realization of the other agents' types. That is, no agent can profitably deviate by changing either her probability of participation or the distribution of qualities with which she is contributing.

Equilibrium Regret. The notion of regret, which is the difference between the optimal cumulative reward (here, maximum possible viewer upvotes from all viewers) and the achieved cumulative reward (actual upvotes on the displayed contributions), is a natural measure of performance for our setting. We measure the performance of a mechanism that decides how to display contributions via its regret with respect to the *highest* possible qualities that could have potentially been chosen by agents:

Definition 2.1 (Strong regret). *Consider a mechanism $\mathcal{M}$, and suppose $\mathcal{M}$ has a symmetric mixed-strategy equilibrium (β_τ, F_τ). Recall that $\gamma \leq 1$ is the highest possible quality that an agent may choose. The strong regret of the mechanism $\mathcal{M}$ in this equilibrium is*

$$R(T) = \gamma T - E[\sum_{t=1}^{T} q_t],$$

where q_t is the quality of the contribution that is displayed in period t, and the expectation is over the randomness in the mechanism as well as over the random choices of agents choosing qualities from distribution F_τ in this mixed-strategy equilibrium.

We will be particularly interested in the performance of the mechanisms we consider in the limit as $T \to \infty$, as is common in the literature on explore-exploit algorithms which attempt to minimize asymptotic regret (*e.g.* [1]) as well as in prior work on incentivizing user-generated content [11, 13]. The diverging attention regime is arguably the most important for the user-generated content setting: first, these are the situations where delivering high quality content matters the most from the perspective of viewer welfare. Second, the popular sites are the ones that draw the most attention-motivated contributors, as well as the ones that tend to attract contributions of varying quality. Indeed, tremendously large amounts of attention are not uncommon for popular content on the web; for instance, the most popular YouTube videos have been viewed over a hundred million times and even days-old trending videos have hundred of thousands of views, numbers that clearly belongs to the diverging attention regime. Other instances of user-generated content with

[3]While this model assumes that an agent knows his or her own cost function, since agents do not know the types of the other agents, agents face uncertainty about the cost functions of the other agents. However, the assumption that an agent knows his cost for making a contribution of quality q is not important for any of the analysis. If an agent faced uncertainty about how costly it would be for him to make a contribution of quality q, all the analysis in the paper would go through by simply replacing known costs with expected costs.

diverging T include reviews of products, comments on popular articles, or answers on online Q&A sites that are viewed by many people over a long period of time. The notion of strong sublinear equilibrium regret, defined below, captures the performance of a mechanism in the diverging T regime, in all symmetric equilibria of the mechanism.

Definition 2.2 (Strong sublinear equilibrium regret). *A mechanism $\mathcal{M}$ has strong sublinear equilibrium regret if $R(T) = o(T)$, i.e., $\lim_{T\to\infty} \frac{R(T)}{T} = 0$, in every symmetric equilibrium of $\mathcal{M}$.*

Since the qualities q are *endogenously* determined, a mechanism must be evaluated not only by whether it quickly learned which contribution is best, but also the contribution qualities that the mechanism is able to elicit: for a mechanism to have strong sublinear equilibrium regret, it must both be able to elicit some contributions with qualities that tend to γ, as well as quickly learn which are these contributions.

2.1 Preliminaries

Here we briefly state the necessary conditions for a set of participation probabilities and quality distributions $(\beta_\tau, F_\tau(q))$, in which all agents of type τ contribute with probability $\beta_\tau \in [0, 1]$ and chooses quality drawn from the distribution $F_\tau(q)$ upon participating, to constitute an equilibrium to a mechanism. These conditions, summarized below, can be derived using the same analysis as in [11]:

1. If $\beta_\tau = 0$, the expected benefit from participating for an agent of type τ must be no greater than the expected cost.
2. If $\beta_\tau \in (0, 1)$, the expected benefit from participating for an agent of type τ must equal the expected cost.
3. If $\beta_\tau = 1$, the expected benefit from participating for an agent of type τ must be no smaller than the expected cost.
4. For any q in the support of F_τ, no agent of type τ can obtain a strictly larger payoff by choosing some other quality $q' \in [0, 1)$ instead of q upon participating, given that the remaining agents use the strategy $(\beta_\tau, F_\tau(q))$.

The equilibrium conditions essentially say that in addition to receiving nonnegative payoffs (Conditions 1 and 3) that cannot be improved by choosing a different distribution of qualities (Condition 4), it must be the case that if agents participate probabilistically, then the payoff to participation must be zero, since otherwise agents could increase their payoff by either always or never participating (Condition 2). This zero-payoff condition is a common feature in models with free entry.

3. UCB MECHANISM

In this section, we investigate the well-known UCB algorithm [1] as a *mechanism*, in which the number and success probabilities of the arms presented to the UCB algorithm are endogenously determined by strategic agents.

Let q_i^t denote the number of upvotes (or thumbs-ups) divided by the number of views that contribution i has received at time t, *i.e.*, the estimate of the quality of contribution i at time t. The UCB algorithm $\mathcal{M}_{\text{UCB}}$ proceeds as follows: it first displays all contributions once, and for each subsequent step t, it computes the value of the index $q_i^t + \sqrt{\frac{2\ln T}{n_i^t}}$ for each contribution i, and displays the contribution for which this index is the largest.

Before analyzing the performance of $\mathcal{M}_{\text{UCB}}$, we first need to address the question of the *existence* of an equilibrium. The following result assures us that $\mathcal{M}_{\text{UCB}}$ indeed possesses an equilibrium, allowing us to analyze the regret of $\mathcal{M}_{\text{UCB}}$ with the equilibrium set of contributions (*i.e.*, the equilibrium number and qualities of contributions) as input arms.

Theorem 3.1 (Equilibrium Existence). *There exists a symmetric mixed strategy equilibrium of $\mathcal{M}_{\text{UCB}}$ in which all contributors of type τ participate with probability β_τ and choose a quality drawn from the same cumulative distribution function $F_\tau(q)$ conditional on contributing.*

All results are proven in the appendix. It is worth noting that the proof of Theorem 3.1 does not depend in any way on the particulars of the mechanism $\mathcal{M}_{\text{UCB}}$. Instead, this proof simply appeals to fixed point arguments that would apply for virtually any reasonable mechanism. Since equilibrium existence would hold for virtually any mechanism with a virtually identical proof, we omit formal proofs of equilibrium existence for all other mechanisms considered in this paper, and simply note here that equilibria can be shown to exist in these settings with virtually identical arguments.

It is well known that the UCB algorithm achieves sublinear regret in a purely algorithmic sense [1]. We now proceed to analyze the behavior of $\mathcal{M}_{\text{UCB}}$ when treated as a mechanism with strategically determined arms. Recall that we assume throughout that $K(T)$, the number of potential contributors or arms, is less than or equal T, the number of viewers, or periods, available.

Our next theorem says that when the number of potential contributors $K(T)$ does not grow too quickly with T, there is no equilibrium in which agents choose qualities that remain bounded away from γ. This, together with Theorem 3.1 on the existence of equilibria, implies that when $K(T)$ grows adequately slowly, the UCB mechanism provides incentives for agents to participate with near-optimal quality in equilibrium, *i.e.*, $q \to \gamma$ in all equilibria. (Note that the number of potential participants $K(T)$ does not need to remain bounded as $T \to \infty$ — $K(T)$ can still diverge with T.)

Theorem 3.2. *Suppose $K(T)$ is such that $\lim_{T\to\infty} \frac{T}{K(T)\ln T} = \infty$. Then all agents participate in an equilibrium of $\mathcal{M}_{\text{UCB}}$ for sufficiently large T. Furthermore, for any fixed $q^* < \gamma$, the probability that an agent chooses quality $q \leq q^*$ in equilibrium goes to 0 in the limit as $T \to \infty$.*

Since every contributing agent chooses quality $q \to \gamma$ in every equilibrium as $T \to \infty$ and there are always contributing agents, it follows immediately that the UCB mechanism achieves strong sublinear regret for such $K(T)$. We summarize this in the following corollary.

Corollary 3.1. *Suppose $\lim_{T\to\infty} \frac{T}{K(T)\ln T} = \infty$. Then the UCB mechanism $\mathcal{M}_{\text{UCB}}$ achieves strong sublinear regret.*

However, as our next result shows, the UCB mechanism does not quite 'work' when the population of contributors scales proportionately with the number of viewers. In fact, not only does $\mathcal{M}_{\text{UCB}}$ fail to identify and exploit the best arm adequately quickly, it also manages to incentivize very low quality contributions — *every* agent who contributes chooses low quality contributions in *every* equilibrium of the mechanism.

We note that both regimes for the relative sizes of $K(T)$ and T are of interest in the context of user- generated content. In online Q&A sites such as Yahoo! Answers or StackOverflow, the number of users $K(T)$ who can answer a question is often significantly smaller than the number of users who consume the answer, possibly via a search engine. On the other hand, in settings like posts on discussion forums or comments on blogs where many consumers are also producers, the number of contributors may not be negligible compared to the number of viewers who consume the content, so that $K(T)/T$ is not vanishingly small.

Theorem 3.3. *Suppose that* $\lim_{T\to\infty} \frac{T}{K(T)} = r < \infty$. *Then for sufficiently large T, any equilibrium has the property that no agent of type τ makes a contribution with quality greater than* $q = c_\tau^{-1}(1 + c(0))$.

The proof (provided in the appendix) consists of two parts. (i) We first demonstrate that the incentives for *participation* provided to the agents are such that $\limsup_{T\to\infty} \frac{T}{E[k(T)]} < \infty$. (ii) We then show that if $\limsup_{T\to\infty} \frac{T}{E[k(T)]} < \infty$, the UCB algorithm is unable to identify and exploit the best arm, and gives all arms essentially the same amounts of attention, thereby providing incentives for poor *quality*. Note that here, the UCB mechanism fails in a purely algorithmic sense in addition to providing poor incentives — it fails to quickly identify and exploit the best contribution due to the large number of arms. We next address the question of designing a mechanism with good equilibrium regret.

4. IMPROVING EQUILIBRIUM REGRET

In this section, we address the problem of achieving strong sublinear regret for all $K(T)$. To do this, we borrow an idea from an explore-exploit algorithm $\mathcal{M}_{1-\text{FAIL}}$ [6, 19] that is designed specifically to achieve good regret for the infinite arms regime (in a purely algorithmic sense), and use it to develop a modification of the UCB mechanism which achieves strong sublinear equilibrium regret for all regimes of $K(T)$.

Before describing the modified UCB mechanism, we briefly describe the mechanism $\mathcal{M}_{1-\text{FAIL}}$ which motivates this modification. $\mathcal{M}_{1-\text{FAIL}}$ proceeds by first randomly selecting $\min\{\lfloor\sqrt{T}\rfloor, k(T)\}$ of the available contributions or arms and exploring each of these arms in turn, switching to a new arm as soon as the current arm receives a negative vote, unless this current arm has already received $\lfloor\sqrt{T}\rfloor$ or more positive votes. This continues until either all arms have received a negative vote, in which case the arm that received the largest number of positive votes is displayed for all remaining periods, or some arm receives $\lfloor\sqrt{T}\rfloor$ consecutive positive votes, in which case this arm is displayed for all remaining periods.

This algorithm $\mathcal{M}_{1-\text{FAIL}}$ itself does not, in fact, suffice for our setting with strategic contributors despite its excellent performance when arms are exogenously determined. While $\mathcal{M}_{1-\text{FAIL}}$ does achieve strong sublinear equilibrium regret when the audience parameter $\gamma = 1$ (*i.e.*, the maximum possible quality is $q = \gamma = 1$), this performance is not robust to any down-voting errors by the audience — $\mathcal{M}_{1-\text{FAIL}}$ fails to achieve strong sublinear equilibrium regret for *any* $\gamma < 1$ when $K(T)$ grows proportionally with T. We summarize the equilibrium regret behavior of the mechanism $\mathcal{M}_{1-\text{FAIL}}$ in the theorem below.

Theorem 4.1. *When* $\gamma = 1$, $\mathcal{M}_{1-\text{FAIL}}$ *achieves strong sublinear regret if there is some type τ for which* $c_\tau(q) = o(\sqrt{T})$ *when* $q = 1 - \Theta(\frac{1}{\ln T})$. *However, for any $\gamma < 1$, there exists some $q^* < \gamma$ such that the probability agents choose quality $q > q^*$ in equilibrium goes to zero in the limit as T goes to infinity when* $\lim_{T\to\infty} \frac{T}{K(T)} = r < \infty$.

Thus $\mathcal{M}_{1-\text{FAIL}}$ is extremely sensitive to the value of γ — agents do not produce qualities tending to γ in any equilibrium when $\lim_{T\to\infty} \frac{T}{K(T)} = r$ and $\gamma < 1$, so that $\mathcal{M}_{1-\text{FAIL}}$ cannot achieve strong sublinear regret in any equilibrium for *any* γ strictly less than 1. Thus, while providing an improvement over the UCB mechanism, $\mathcal{M}_{1-\text{FAIL}}$ does not perform well under all conditions when the arms are endogenously created by strategic agents responding to incentives of the mechanism. We now proceed with defining and analyzing the modified UCB mechanism.

4.1 The $\mathcal{M}_{\text{UCB-MOD}}$ Mechanism

We now analyze a modification of UCB which borrows the idea of exploring a restricted set of arms from $\mathcal{M}_{1-\text{FAIL}}$. The modified UCB mechanism $\mathcal{M}_{\text{UCB-MOD}}$ explores contributions using exactly the same index as the UCB mechanism, but differs from the UCB mechanism in that it explores from a smaller, randomly selected subset of arms when $K(T)$ is too large. This modified UCB mechanism $\mathcal{M}_{\text{UCB-MOD}}$ turns out to have extremely desirable incentive and learning properties: $\mathcal{M}_{\text{UCB-MOD}}$ achieves strong sublinear equilibrium regret for *all* values of $K(T)$ and the robustness parameter γ, with no restrictions on the cost functions c_τ.

Definition 4.1 ($\mathcal{M}_{\text{UCB-MOD}}$). *The modified UCB mechanism $\mathcal{M}_{\text{UCB-MOD}}$ first randomly selects a subset of size* $\min\{k(T), G(T)\}$ *of the available contributions, where $G(T)$ is some integer-valued function. The mechanism then explores these selected contributions using $\mathcal{M}_{\text{UCB}}$.*

As we will see, when $G(T)$ is chosen so that $\lim_{T\to\infty} G(T) = \infty$ and $G(T) = o(\frac{T}{\ln T})$, there is a balance between exploring enough contributions and not exploring too many contributions which provides the right incentives for achieving good equilibrium regret. We begin the equilibrium regret analysis with an easy algorithmic lemma, which says that every contribution that is explored by $\mathcal{M}_{\text{UCB-MOD}}$ except for the one with the highest quality receives precisely $\Theta(\ln T)$ views.

Lemma 4.1. *Consider the modified UCB algorithm $\mathcal{M}_{\text{UCB-MOD}}$ with $G(T) \to \infty$ and $G(T) = o(\frac{T}{\ln T})$, and any $\delta > 0$. Then, any contribution with quality satisfying $q_i \le q_{max}(T) - \delta$ receives $\Theta(\ln T)$ attention in expectation, where $q_{max}(T)$ is the quality of the highest-quality explored contribution.*

This result implies that an infinite number of agents (or all agents if $K(T)$ is bounded) will participate as $T \to \infty$ under $\mathcal{M}_{\text{UCB-MOD}}$, because if there are fewer than $G(T)$ participants, then an agent would strictly prefer contributing with any quality (and obtaining $\Omega(\ln T)$ attention) to not contributing.

The next theorem, which is the main component of the proof that $\mathcal{M}_{\text{UCB-MOD}}$ achieves strong sublinear equilibrium regret, says that the highest quality of an explored contribution in any equilibrium tends to γ as $T \to \infty$ with high probability, for appropriately chosen $G(T)$.

Theorem 4.2. *Suppose $G(T)$ is chosen so that $G(T) \to \infty$ and $G(T) = o(\frac{T}{\ln T})$. For any fixed $q^* < \gamma$, the probability that there is some agent explored by $\mathcal{M}_{\text{UCB-MOD}}$ who chooses quality $q > q^*$ goes to 1 as $T \to \infty$ in every equilibrium of $\mathcal{M}_{\text{UCB-MOD}}$.*

This result allows us to prove that the modified UCB mechanism $\mathcal{M}_{\text{UCB-MOD}}$ achieves strong sublinear equilibrium regret when $G(T)$ is as in Theorem 4.2:

Theorem 4.3. *Suppose $G(T) \to \infty$ and $G(T) = o(\frac{T}{\ln T})$. Then the modified UCB mechanism $\mathcal{M}_{\text{UCB-MOD}}$ achieves strong sublinear equilibrium regret for all values of γ and all $K(T) \leq T$.*

Note that the strong sublinear equilibrium regret property assures us that the regret of $\mathcal{M}_{\text{UCB-MOD}}$ with respect to the maximum achievable quality γ is sublinear in *every* equilibrium of $\mathcal{M}_{\text{UCB-MOD}}$, not just that there exists an equilibrium of $\mathcal{M}_{\text{UCB-MOD}}$ with this property.

The choice of $G(T)$, the maximum number of contributions explored by the modified UCB mechanism $\mathcal{M}_{\text{UCB-MOD}}$, can potentially have a significant effect on the incentives provided for both participation and quality. If $G(T)$ is large and the mechanism explores a larger number of contributions, then the expected benefit to having the highest quality contribution is correspondingly lower since $\mathcal{M}_{\text{UCB-MOD}}$ spends $\Theta(\ln T)$ time exploring each lower quality contribution. This leaves behind less attention for the highest quality contribution, so agents will have a relatively lower incentive to choose higher qualities. In addition, since agents produce lower quality content when the mechanism explores more contributions, it is relatively less costly to participate and play equilibrium strategies when the mechanism explores more contributions, so agents are more likely to participate when the mechanism explores more contributions. Thus a larger value of $G(T)$ provides incentives for larger participation but lower quality contributions, and vice versa, so varying $G(T)$ could enable one to achieve various points on the trade-off curve between participation and quality. We leave the problem of precisely quantifying this tradeoff as an open direction for future work.

4.2 Displaying Multiple Contributions

We have shown so far that the modified UCB mechanism $\mathcal{M}_{\text{UCB-MOD}}$ achieves strong sublinear equilibrium regret when each viewer sees a single contribution. We now show that this result also extends to the more realistic setting where each viewer is shown multiple contributions, as is typically the case with user-generated content.

Suppose that when shown multiple contributions, a viewer views the first contribution with probability p_1, the second with probability p_2, and so on, where $p_1 \geq p_2 \geq \ldots$ reflects the fact that viewers typically read contributions from the top to the bottom of a webpage so that a contribution displayed near the top of a webpage is more likely to be viewed than a contribution lower down on the page. (This model of viewing behavior by users is widely used in the online advertising literature as well, where ads are modeled as having a position-dependent clickability that decreases with their position down the page.) As before, we assume that a viewer rates every contribution she views.

We extend the mechanism $\mathcal{M}_{\text{UCB-MOD}}$ in the obvious way to displaying multiple contributions. Let $m \geq 1$ be the number of contributions to be displayed to each viewer. At every time period t, $\mathcal{M}_{\text{UCB-MOD}}$ displays the m contributions with the largest values of $q_i^t + \sqrt{\frac{2\ln T}{n_i^t}}$, displaying the contribution with the largest index most prominently (*i.e.*, in the top position), the contribution with the second-largest index next (in the second position), and so on.

We extend the notion of strong regret to mechanisms that display multiple contributions, also in the obvious way, as follows:

Definition 4.1. *The strong regret of a mechanism $\mathcal{M}$ which displays m contributions at each time t, in an equilibrium (β_T, F_T), is defined as*

$$R(T) = \sum_{j=1}^{m} p_j \gamma T - E[\sum_{t=1}^{T}\sum_{j=1}^{m} p_j q_{j,t}],$$

where $q_{j,t}$ is the quality of the contribution that is displayed in the jth most prominent position in period t, and $\gamma \leq 1$ is the highest possible quality that a contribution may have. A mechanism $\mathcal{M}$ has strong sublinear equilibrium regret if $R(T) = o(T)$, (i.e., $\lim_{T\to\infty} \frac{R(T)}{T} = 0$) in every symmetric equilibrium of $\mathcal{M}$.

This definition of strong regret differs from the original definition only in that it takes into account the qualities of all the displayed contributions and weighs them by the frequency with which they are viewed. Strong regret again compares the qualities of the displayed contributions relative to the optimal solution where every displayed contribution at every time t has the maximum possible quality γ. As before, the expectation is over the randomness in the mechanism as well as over the random choices of agents choosing qualities from the distribution F_T in this mixed-strategy equilibrium.

We now show that the results of Section 4.1 extend to this setting where the site owner displays $m \geq 1$ contributions at the same time to a viewer. First we note a lemma analogous to that in §4.1 which shows that all contributions except the best m contributions receive exactly $\Theta(\ln T)$ attention.

Lemma 4.2. *Consider the modified UCB algorithm $\mathcal{M}_{\text{UCB-MOD}}$ with $G(T) \to \infty$ and $G(T) = o(\frac{T}{\ln T})$, and any $\delta > 0$. Then any contribution with quality satisfying $q_i \leq q_m(T) - \delta$ receives $\Theta(\ln T)$ attention in expectation, where $q_m(T)$ is the quality of the mth-best explored contribution.*

As in §4.1, to prove that $\mathcal{M}_{\text{UCB-MOD}}$ achieves strong sublinear equillibrium regret, we must first show that enough agents will make high quality contributions in equilibrium. We use Lemma 4.2 above to show that there will almost certainly be at least m explored agents who choose arbitrarily high qualities in equilibrium:

Theorem 4.4. *Suppose $G(T) \to \infty$ and $G(T) = o(\frac{T}{\ln T})$. For any fixed $q^* < \gamma$, the probability that there are at least m agents who are explored by $\mathcal{M}_{\text{UCB-MOD}}$ and that choose quality $q > q^*$ goes to 1 as $T \to \infty$ in every equilibrium of $\mathcal{M}_{\text{UCB-MOD}}$.*

As before, Theorem 4.4 allows us to prove that the modified UCB mechanism also achieves strong sublinear equilibrium regret when displaying multiple contributions:

Theorem 4.5. *Suppose $G(T) \to \infty$ and $G(T) = o(\frac{T}{\ln T})$. Then the modified UCB mechanism $\mathcal{M}_{\text{UCB-MOD}}$ achieves strong sublinear equilibrium regret for all values of γ and all $K(T) \leq T$.*

5. DISCUSSION

In this paper, we modeled and investigated the problem of learning the qualities of user-generated content, which leads to a multi-armed bandit problem where the arms of the bandit are endogenously determined by the response of strategic agents to the incentives provided by the learning mechanism. There are a number of interesting directions for further work, consisting of both theoretical questions and mechanism design questions arising from more nuanced models; we discuss these below.

Our results show that a modification of the well-known UCB mechanism can achieve strong sublinear regret in all equilibria. What other learning algorithms can achieve this regret? We also note that we do not explicitly derive a quality-participation tradeoff as a function of $G(T)$ — this tradeoff can be particularly relevant in settings when m, the number of contributions to be displayed, is not fixed apriori but rather determined by a threshold on quality. An interesting family of open question is what classes of learning mechanisms provide strong incentives for eliciting arms with high success probabilities, and what mechanisms are optimal in terms of the quality-participation tradeoff.

Sequential Contributions. In our model, all agents simultaneously decide whether to contribute and the quality of their contribution if contributing in a Bayes-Nash equilibrium. This is a reasonable assumption, for instance, when it is too costly for an agent to look at all previous contributions and strategize about her own contribution based on this information (as in the case of, for example, popular news articles or blog posts which attract huge numbers of comments), or in settings like some Q&A forums where a number of answerers might be simultaneously working on the solution to a particular question (*e.g.*, in coding questions on StackOverflow). However, there are many other settings that are better suited to an alternative sequential model, in which different potential contributors arrive at different times and make decisions about their own contributions after viewing the existing set of contributions. The question of equilibrium contribution qualities in such a sequential model is an interesting, albeit possibly more challenging, direction for future work.

Enhancing the viewer model. Our model for multiple contributions assumes that the probability of viewing of contribution is independent of the qualities of the contributions displayed before it. However, in some settings a user may be more likely to want to continue to view contributions if they liked the first few contributions, whereas in other settings a user may be more likely to view additional contributions if their needs were not met by the previous contributions. Capturing these viewer behaviors in a model with multiple contributions and analyzing mechanisms to efficiently learn the qualities of contributions in these settings is another intriguing direction for further work.

Acknowledgments

We thank Anirban Dasgupta, Preston McAfee, Michael Schwarz, and the anonymous reviewers for helpful comments and discussions.

6. REFERENCES

[1] P. Auer, N. Cesa-Bianchi, P. Fischer, *Finite-Time Analysis of the Multiarmed Bandit Problem*, Machine Learning, 47, 235-256, 2002.

[2] M. Babaioff, R.D. Kleinberg, A. Slivkins, *Truthful Mechanisms with Implicit Payment Computation*, Proceedings of the 11th ACM Conference on Electronic Commerce (EC), 2010.

[3] M. Babaioff, Y. Sharma, A. Slivkins, *Characterizing Truthful Multi-Armed Bandit Mechanisms*, Proceedings of the 10th ACM Conference on Electronic Commerce (EC), 2009.

[4] J.G. Becker, D.S. Damianov, *On the Existence of Symmetric Mixed Strategy Equilibria*, Economics Letters, 90(1), 84-87, 2006.

[5] D. Bergemann, J. Välimäki, *Learning and Strategic Pricing*, Econometrica, 64(5), 1125-1149, 1996.

[6] D.A. Berry, R.W. Chen, A. Zame, D.C. Heath, L.A. Shepp, *Bandit Problems with Infinitely Many Arms*, Annals of Statistics, 25(5), 2103-2116, 1997.

[7] P. Bolton, C. Harris, *Strategic Experimentation*, Econometrica, 67(2), 349-374, 1999.

[8] Y. Chen, S. Jain, D. Parkes, *Designing Incentives for Online Question and Answer Forums*, Proceedings of the 10th ACM Conference on Electronic Commerce (EC), 2009.

[9] N.R. Devanur, S.M. Kakade, *The Price of Truthfulness for Pay-Per-Click Auctions*, Proceedings of the 10th ACM Conference on Electronic Commerce (EC), 2009.

[10] N. Gatti, A. Lazaric, F. Trovò, *A Truthful Learning Mechanism for Multi-Slot Sponsored Search Auctions with Externalities*, Proceedings of the 13th ACM Conference on Electronic Commerce (EC), 2012.

[11] A. Ghosh, P. Hummel, *A Game-Theoretic Analysis of Rank-Order Mechanisms for User-Generated Content*, Proceedings of the 12th ACM Conference on Electronic Commerce (EC), 2011.

[12] A. Ghosh, P. Hummel, *Implementing Optimal Outcomes in Social Computing: A Game-Theoretic Approach*, Proceedings of the 21st International World Wide Web Conference (WWW), 2012.

[13] A. Ghosh, R.P. McAfee, *Incentivizing High-Quality User-Generated Content*, Proceedings of the 20th International World Wide Web Conference (WWW), 2011.

[14] R. Gonen, E. Pavlov, *Brief Announcement: An Incentive-Compatible Multi-Armed Bandit Mechanism*, Proceedings of the 26th ACM Conference on Principles of Distributed Computing (PODC), 2007.

[15] R. Gummadi, R. Johari, J.Y. Yu, *Mean Field Equilibria of Multi Armed Bandit Games*, Proceedings of the 13th ACM Confernce on Electronic Commerce (EC), 2012.

[16] S. Jain, D. Parkes, *The Role of Game Theory in Human Computation Systems* (Position Paper), Proceedings of the 1st Human Computation Workshop (HCOMP), 2009.

[17] S. Jain, D. Parkes, *A Game-Theoretic Analysis of the ESP Game*, ACM Transactions on Economics and Computation (TEAC), in press.

[18] S.M. Kakade, I. Lobel, H. Nazerzadeh, *An Optimal Dynamic Mechanism for Multi-Armed Bandit Processes*, Working Paper.

[19] R.D. Kleinberg, *Online Decision Problems with Large Strategy Sets*, MIT Ph.D. Thesis, 2005.

[20] B.P. McCall, J.J. McCall, *A Sequential Study of Migration and Job Search*, Journal of Labor Economics, 5(4), 452-476, 1987.

[21] O. Teytaud, S. Gelly, M. Sebag, *Anytime Many-Armed Bandits*, Conférence d'Apprentissage, 2007.
[22] Y. Wang, J. Audibert, R. Munos, *Algorithms for Infinitely Many-Armed Bandits*, Proceedings of the 22nd Annual Conference on Neural Information Processing Systems (NIPS), 2008.
[23] W.K. Viscusi, *Job Hazards and Worker Quit Rates: An Analysis of Adaptive Worker Behavior*, International Economic Review, 20(1), 29-58, 1979.

APPENDIX

A. PROOFS OF RESULTS IN MAIN TEXT

Proof of Theorem 3.1: First note that no player in this game would ever choose a quality $q > \max_\tau\{c_\tau^{-1}(T)\}$, as a player could always obtain a strictly greater expected payoff by not participating. Thus any mixed strategy equilibrium to the game in which players are restricted to choosing $q \in [0, \max_\tau\{c_\tau^{-1}(T)\}]$ is also a mixed strategy equilibrium of the original game.

Now note that this modified game in which players are restricted to choosing $q \in [0, \max_\tau\{c_\tau^{-1}(T)\}]$ is a symmetric game in which each player has a pure strategy space that is compact and Hausdorff. Also note that each player's expected payoff in this modified game is continuous in the actions of the players. It thus follows from Theorem 1 of [4] that there exists a symmetric mixed strategy equilibrium of this modified game. This in turn implies that there is a symmetric mixed strategy equilibrium of the original game. □

Proof of Theorem 3.2: Suppose by means of contradiction that there exists some fixed $q^* < \gamma$ and some fixed probability $\pi > 0$ such that there are infinitely many values of T for which there is an equilibrium in which agents who participate choose quality $q \leq q^*$ with probability greater than or equal to π. Throughout the remainder of the proof, restrict attention to such values of T for which the probability (unconditional on the realizations of the agent's types τ) an agent who contributes chooses quality $q \leq q^*$ is greater than or equal to π. To establish a contradiction, we will show that for sufficiently large T, an agent can obtain a strictly greater expected utility by making a contribution of quality $q^*+\epsilon$ for some small $\epsilon \in (0, \gamma - q^*)$ than by making a contribution of quality $q \leq q^*$, *i.e.*, there exists a profitable deviation.

We first show that any contributing agent obtains $\Omega(\ln T)$ attention. Since $\frac{T}{K(T)} = \omega(\ln T)$, the contribution that receives the most attention receives $\omega(\ln T)$ attention. Thus the value of $q_i^t + \sqrt{\frac{2\ln T}{n_i^t}}$ for the contribution i that is explored the most tends to q_i as $t \to T$ and $T \to \infty$. Now if a contribution j is explored $o(\ln T)$ times, then the value of $q_j^t + \sqrt{\frac{2\ln T}{n_j^t}}$ tends to ∞ as $T \to \infty$. This implies that if a contribution j is explored $o(\ln T)$ times, then for sufficiently large t, $q_j^t + \sqrt{\frac{2\ln T}{n_j^t}} > q_i^t + \sqrt{\frac{2\ln T}{n_i^t}}$. This contradicts the possibility that i is explored $\omega(\ln T)$ times while j is only explored $o(\ln T)$ times, so it must be the case that each contribution j is explored $\Omega(\ln T)$ times, regardless of the qualities of the contributions.

Next we show that if an agent j contributes with quality $q_j = q^*+\epsilon$ for some small $\epsilon \in (0, \gamma - q^*)$ and some other agent i contributes with quality $q_i \leq q^*$, then there must exist some $\delta > 0$ such that the probability that $\frac{n_j^t}{n_i^t} > 1 + \delta$ goes to 1 in the limit as t goes to infinity. Suppose not, so that $\lim_{t\to\infty} \frac{n_j^t}{n_i^t} \leq 1$. Then $\lim_{T\to\infty} \lim_{t \to T} \sqrt{\frac{2\ln T}{n_j^t}} - \sqrt{\frac{2\ln T}{n_i^t}} \geq 0$ for large t and $q_i^t + \sqrt{\frac{2\ln T}{n_i^t}} < q_j^t + \sqrt{\frac{2\ln T}{n_j^t}}$ for large t. But since $q_i^t + \sqrt{\frac{2\ln T}{n_i^t}} < q_j^t + \sqrt{\frac{2\ln T}{n_j^t}}$ for sufficiently large t, there exists some threshold t^* such that i is not explored for any $t \geq t^*$, which contradicts the possibility that i is explored infinitely often. Therefore, there exists some $\delta > 0$ such that the probability that $\frac{n_j^t}{n_i^t} > 1 + \delta$ goes to 1 in the limit as t goes to infinity.

But this implies that if an agent deviates and contributes with quality $q^* + \epsilon$ for some small $\epsilon \in (0, \gamma - q^*)$, then the agent can obtain $\Omega(\ln T)$ more attention in expectation than when she contributes with quality no greater than q^*. Since q^* is bounded away from γ, the cost of this deviation, which is no greater than $c(q^* + \epsilon)$, remains bounded as $T \to \infty$ although the benefit from this deviation grows with $\Omega(\ln T)$ as $T \to \infty$. Thus for sufficiently large T, an agent can profitably deviate by contributing with quality $q^* + \epsilon$ for some small $\epsilon \in (0, \gamma - q^*)$ instead of using a quality no greater than q^*. This contradicts our assumption that the postulated sequence of equilibria exists and shows that for any fixed $q^* < \gamma$, the probability the agents choose quality $q \leq q^*$ in equilibrium must go to zero in the limit as T goes to infinity.

To complete the proof, we must show that all agents participate in equilibrium for sufficiently large T. To see that this holds, recall that regardless of the qualities of the contributions, an agent's expected benefit from participating is $\Omega(\ln T)$. But if an agent contributes with quality 0, the agent pays a fixed finite cost that remains bounded as $T \to \infty$. Thus for sufficiently large T, an agent always obtains a greater expected payoff from participating with quality 0 than not participating at all, and full participation must arise in equilibrium. □

Proof of Theorem 3.3: The proof consists of two parts. (i) We first demonstrate that the incentives for *participation* provided to the agents are such that $\limsup_{T\to\infty} \frac{T}{E[k(T)]} < \infty$ as well. (ii) We then show that if $\limsup_{T\to\infty} \frac{T}{E[k(T)]} < \infty$, the UCB algorithm is unable to identify and exploit the best arm, and gives all arms essentially the same amounts of attention, thereby providing incentives for poor *quality*.

(i) Consider a sequence of equilibria for the various values of T. Recall that the random variable $k(T)$ denotes the number of actual contributors of the $K(T)$ potential contributors, so that $E[k(T)] = \sum_\tau \beta_\tau(T)\rho_\tau K(T)$. We first show that $\limsup_{T\to\infty} \frac{T}{E[k(T)]} < \infty$ in this sequence by demonstrating that if this does not hold, a nonparticipating agent can profitably deviate by participating.

First note that if there is some subsequence of T such that there is an equilibrium for each T so that $\lim_{T\to\infty} \frac{T}{\sum_\tau \beta_\tau(T)\rho_\tau K(T)} = \infty$ holds in this subsequence, then any contributing agent must receive a diverging amount of attention in expectation in these equilibria in the limit as $T \to \infty$. To see why, note that the expected amount of attention received by the agent who receives the greatest amount of attention, say agent j, diverges in the limit as $T \to \infty$ since $\lim_{T\to\infty} \frac{T}{E[k(T)]} = \infty$. Thus if there is some contributing agent i who receives an amount of attention that remains bounded as $T \to \infty$, then $q_i^t + \sqrt{\frac{2\ln T}{n_i^t}} > q_j^t + \sqrt{\frac{2\ln T}{n_j^t}}$ for sufficiently large t and T. But this contradicts the possibility that the algorithm explores contribution j an infinite number of times in the limit as $T \to \infty$. Thus if $\lim_{T\to\infty} \frac{T}{E[k(T)]} = \infty$ along this subsequence, then any contributing agent must receive a diverging amount of attention in expectation in the limit of this sequence of equilibria.

But if any agent who participates receives a diverging amount of attention in expectation, irrespective of quality, in the limit of this sequence of equilibria, then an agent can profitably deviate by making a contribution of quality 0 and obtaining a diverging amount of attention instead of not participating at all for sufficiently large T in this subsequence. This contradiction implies that we must have $\limsup_{T\to\infty} \frac{T}{E[k(T)]} < \infty$ in any sequence of equilibria.

(ii) Next we show that if the number of arms presented to the UCB mechanism grows too quickly with T, as when $\limsup_{T\to\infty} \frac{T}{E[k(T)]} < \infty$, then for sufficiently large T the algorithm will first explore all contributions once, then explore each contribution a second time, and so on, until contributions have been displayed T times, regardless of the qualities of the contributions. To see this, note that if the algorithm displays contributions in this order and some contribution j has been displayed one more time than some other contribution i (*i.e.*. $n_j^t = n_i^t + 1$), then it is necessarily the case that $q_i^t + \sqrt{\frac{2\ln T}{n_i^t}} > q_j^t + \sqrt{\frac{2\ln T}{n_j^t}}$ for sufficiently large T. This holds because the fact that $n_j^t \leq \frac{T}{\sum_\tau \beta_\tau(T)\rho_\tau K(T)} + 1$ for large T implies there is some $s < \infty$ such that $n_j^t < s$ for all t and T, so $\sqrt{\frac{2\ln T}{n_i^t}} - \sqrt{\frac{2\ln T}{n_j^t}} \geq \sqrt{\frac{2\ln T}{s-1}} - \sqrt{\frac{2\ln T}{s}}$ for sufficiently large T. But $\sqrt{\frac{2\ln T}{s-1}} - \sqrt{\frac{2\ln T}{s}}$ becomes arbitrarily large as $T \to \infty$ since s is a constant independent of T, so $q_i^t + \sqrt{\frac{2\ln T}{n_i^t}} > q_j^t + \sqrt{\frac{2\ln T}{n_j^t}}$ for sufficiently large T. But since $q_i^t + \sqrt{\frac{2\ln T}{n_i^t}} > q_j^t + \sqrt{\frac{2\ln T}{n_j^t}}$ holds for large T whenever $n_j^t = n_i^t + 1$, if contribution j has been displayed one more time than contribution i, it is necessarily the case that contribution i must be explored at least once more before j is explored again for large T.

Thus no contribution ever obtains more than one extra unit of attention than any other contribution for sufficiently large T, irrespective of the contributions' qualities. But in this case, an agent of type τ would never choose a quality q such that $c_\tau(q) - c_\tau(0) > 1$. Thus for sufficiently large T, any equilibrium has the property that no agent of type τ makes a contribution with quality greater than $q = c_\tau^{-1}(1 + c(0))$. □

Proposition A.1. *If an agent changes her quality choice from q_i to $q_i + \epsilon$ for some small $\epsilon > 0$, then she obtains an additional success before her first failure with probability $\frac{\epsilon}{1-q_i}$.*

PROOF. Let $\{r_n\}_{n=1}^\infty$ denote an infinite sequence of random variables where each r_n is an independent and identically distributed draw from the uniform distribution on $[0, 1]$. Note that if an agent makes a contribution of quality q_i, then the probability she obtains a success on the nth draw is just the probability that $r_n \leq q_i$. Similarly, the probability of obtaining a success on the nth draw with a contribution of quality $q_i + \epsilon$ is just the probability that $r_n \leq q_i + \epsilon$.

Now let m denote the first draw where an agent with a contribution of quality q_i obtains a failure. Thus $r_n \leq q_i$ for all $n < m$ and $r_m > q_i$. If an agent makes a contribution with quality $q_i + \epsilon$ for some small $\epsilon > 0$, she also obtains a success for each of the first $m - 1$ draws (since $r_n \leq q_i + \epsilon$ for all $n < m$), and obtains a success on the mth draw if $r_m \leq q_i + \epsilon$. Since $r_m > q_i$, this agent obtains an additional success only if $r_m \in (q_i, q_i + \epsilon]$. The probability that $r_m \in (q_i, q_i + \epsilon]$ conditional on $r_m > q_i$ is $\frac{\epsilon}{1-q_i}$. Therefore, if an agent changes her quality choice from q_i to $q_i + \epsilon$ for some small $\epsilon > 0$, then she obtains an additional success before her first failure with probability $\frac{\epsilon}{1-q_i}$.

Proof of Theorem 4.1: First we illustrate that $\mathcal{M}_{1-\text{FAIL}}$ achieves strong sublinear regret in the case where $\gamma = 1$. To do this, let $\tilde{K}(T) = E[k(T)]$ denote the expected number of agents who participate in equilibrium. First consider the case where $\tilde{K}(T)$ remains bounded as $T \to \infty$. Note that if the 1-fail mechanism fails to achieve strong sublinear regret, there must be some $q^* < \gamma$ such that the probability all agents choose quality $q \leq q^*$ remains bounded away from zero in the limit as $T \to \infty$. In this case, if an agent i of type τ changes her quality choice from q_i to $q_i + \epsilon$ for some small $\epsilon > 0$, then she obtains an additional success before her first failure with probability $\Theta(\epsilon)$ by Proposition A.1. Furthermore, this change always has a probability bounded away from zero of affecting whether the agent obtains more successes before her first failure than any other agent (since there is a positive probability that all agents choose qualities $q_j \leq q^* < 1$). Now, if this change does affect whether the agent obtains more successes before her first failure than any other agent, then she obtains an additional $\Theta(T)$ units of attention. From this it follows that the expected benefits from making such a change are $\Theta(\epsilon T)$, so the derivative of an agent's benefit with respect to quality at q_i must be $b'(q_i) = \Theta(T)$. But the derivative of an agent's utility with respect to quality must be 0 at every quality in the support of an equilibrium distribution, *i.e.*, it is necessary that $c'_\tau(q_i) = \Theta(T)$ in equilibrium. Since $c'_\tau(q_i)$ remains bounded and finite in the limit as $T \to \infty$, this cannot hold for sufficiently large T. Thus the 1-fail mechanism achieves strong sublinear regret in this case.

Now consider the case where $\lim_{T\to\infty} \tilde{K}(T) = \infty$. Again, suppose by means of contradiction that the 1-fail mechanism fails to achieve strong sublinear regret. This implies that there is some $q^* < 1$ and some $\pi > 0$ such that $Pr(q_{win}^T \leq q^*) \geq \pi$ holds for an infinite number of T, where q_{win}^T denotes the quality that is chosen by the winning agent, *i.e.*, the agent who first has $\sqrt{T}$ consecutive successes or has the most successes before her first failure. Throughout the remainder of the proof, we restrict attention to values of T that satisfy $Pr(q_{win}^T \leq q^*) \geq \pi$.

First note that as $T \to \infty$, the probability that any agent who contributes with quality $q \leq q^*$ has $\sqrt{T}$ consecutive successes before her first failure goes to zero, so if $q_{win}^T \leq q^*$, then with probability arbitrarily close to 1, q_{win}^T is the quality chosen by the agent who has the most successes before her first failure.

Now if the mechanism explores $\min\{k(T), \lfloor\sqrt{T}\rfloor\}$ agents who all contribute with quality $q \leq q^*$, then the maximum number of consecutive successes that any such agent has before her first failure is $O(\ln T)$ with probability arbitrarily close to 1. To see this, first note that when restricting attention to $\min\{k(T), \lfloor\sqrt{T}\rfloor\}$ agents who contribute with quality $q \leq q^*$, this maximum number of successes will be largest when there are $\lfloor\sqrt{T}\rfloor$ agents and all of these agents contribute with quality $q = q^*$. Also note that if an agent contributes with quality q^*, then the probability the agent has less than r consecutive successes before her first failure is $1-(q^*)^r$. Therefore, the probability that all $\lfloor\sqrt{T}\rfloor$ agents with quality q^* explored by the mechanism have less than r consecutive successes before their first failure is $(1-(q^*)^r)^{\lfloor\sqrt{T}\rfloor}$. But for this probability to be bounded away from both zero and one, we must have $r = \Theta(\ln T)$. So if the mechanism explores $\min\{k(T), \lfloor\sqrt{T}\rfloor\}$ agents who contribute with quality $q \leq q^*$, then the maximum number of consecutive successes before the first failure in this group of $\min\{k(T), \lfloor\sqrt{T}\rfloor\}$ agents is $O(\ln T)$ with probability arbitrarily close to 1.

But if an agent contributes with quality q satisfying $\frac{1}{1-q} = \Theta(\ln T)$, then the expected number of successes this agent obtains before her first failure is $\Theta(\ln T)$. Therefore, if an agent contributes with quality q satisfying $\frac{1}{1-q} = \Theta(\ln T)$, then the probability this agent will have more consecutive successes before her first failure than $\min\{k(T), \lfloor\sqrt{T}\rfloor\}$ separate agents who contribute with quality $q \leq q^*$ remains bounded away from zero in the limit as $T \to \infty$. Thus if an agent contributes with quality q satisfying $\frac{1}{1-q} = \Theta(\ln T)$, then the expected amount of attention this agent obtains if the agent is explored is $\Theta(T)$.

But since $Pr(q_{win}^T \leq q^*) \geq \pi$ holds for an infinite number of T, it must be the case that the probability any given type contributes with quality $q > q^*$ goes to zero in the limit as $T \to \infty$. Thus if τ denotes some type for which $c_\tau(q) = o(\sqrt{T})$ when $q = 1 - \Theta(\frac{1}{\ln T})$, then for sufficiently large T, there is a positive probability that some agent of type τ does not contribute with quality $q > q^*$. Also, since $\tilde{K}(T) \to \infty$, the probability such an agent obtains more successes before her first failure than any other agent conditional on being explored goes to zero in the limit as $T \to \infty$. Thus if such an agent instead contributes with a quality q satisfying $\frac{1}{1-q} = \Theta(\ln T)$, then the expected additional amount of attention this agent obtains if she is explored is $\Theta(T)$.

Now the probability an agent who contributes is explored is $\Omega(\frac{1}{\sqrt{T}})$. Combining this with the result in the previous paragraph shows that if an agent of type τ contributes with a quality q satisfying $\frac{1}{1-q} = \Theta(\ln T)$ instead of using a quality $q \leq q^*$, then the agent obtains an expected additional amount of attention $\Omega(\sqrt{T})$. But since $c_\tau(q) = o(\sqrt{T})$ when $q = 1 - \Theta(\frac{1}{\ln T})$ and $\frac{1}{1-q} = \Theta(\ln T)$, it follows that the expected additional amount of attention an agent obtains from making this change exceeds the expected costs from making this change for sufficiently large T. Thus some agent would have a profitable deviation, giving a contradiction which establishes that the 1-fail mechanism achieves strong sublinear regret when $\gamma = 1$.

Next we show that if $\gamma < 1$ and $\lim_{T\to\infty} \frac{T}{K(T)} = r < \infty$, then there exists some $q^* < \gamma$ such that the probability agents choose quality $q > q^*$ in equilibrium goes to zero in the limit as T goes to infinity. First we show that $E[k(T)] = \sum_\tau \beta_\tau(T)\rho_\tau K(T) \to \infty$ in the limit as $T \to \infty$ by arguing that if only a finite number of agents participate, then an agent who is not participating could profitably deviate by participating with quality $\frac{\gamma}{2}$. Since there are only a finite number of competing agents, if an agent participates with this quality, the agent will always have a probability bounded away from zero of having more successes before her first failure than any other agent (even if all the other agents used quality γ). Thus it cannot be the case that $E[k(T)]$ stays bounded away from infinity in the limit as $T \to \infty$.

Now suppose by means of contradiction that there is no $q^* < \gamma$ such that the probability agents choose quality $q > q^*$ in equilibrium goes to zero as T goes to infinity. In this case, note that there exists some sequence $\{\hat{q}(T)\}_{T=1}^{\infty}$ such that $\lim_{T\to\infty} \hat{q}(T) = \gamma$ and $\lim_{T\to\infty} Pr(q_{win}^T > \hat{q}(T)) = 1$, where q_{win}^T denotes the quality that is chosen by the agent who first has $\sqrt{T}$ consecutive successes or has the most successes before her first failure.

To see why, note that as $T \to \infty$, the probability that any agent has $\sqrt{T}$ consecutive successes before her first failure goes to zero (since all agents choose some quality $q \leq \gamma < 1$), so with probability arbitrarily close to 1, q_{win}^T is the quality that is chosen by the agent who has the most successes before her first failure. Let $m(T)$ denote the number of successes obtained by an agent who has the most successes before her first failure. Since the mechanism explores an arbitrarily large number of agents as $T \to \infty$ (it explores $\min\{k(T), \sqrt{T}\}$ agents), $m(T)$, the highest number of consecutive successes amongst these explored agents, becomes unbounded with probability arbitrarily close to 1. But if $m(T)$ becomes unbounded, it is exponentially more likely that an agent with some high quality q_H will achieve $m(T)$ successes before her first failure than it is that an agent with some lower quality $q_L < q_H$ achieves $m(T)$ successes before her first failure. So if there are enough agents who participate with qualities in $[\hat{q}(T), \gamma]$ (which happens by assumption and since $E[k(T)] \to \infty$), then the probability the agent who has the most successes before her first failure has quality in $[\hat{q}(T), \gamma]$ goes to 1 as $T \to \infty$. Thus such a sequence $\{\hat{q}(T)\}_{T=1}^{\infty}$ exists.

Now consider the costs and benefits to participating with quality $q \in [\hat{q}(T), \gamma]$. Recall that the number of agents who participate with quality $q \in [\hat{q}(T), \gamma]$ becomes unbounded with probability arbitrarily close to 1 as $T \to \infty$, and let $F_T^\tau(q)$ denote the cumulative distribution function corresponding to the mixed strategy equilibrium quality choices of the agents of type τ who participate in the mechanism for a given T. Conditional on an agent participating with quality $q \in [\hat{q}(T), \gamma]$, the probability this agent is explored and obtains the most successes before her first failure is $\Theta(\frac{1}{\sum_\tau \beta_\tau(T)(1-F_T^\tau(\hat{q}(T)))\rho_\tau K(T)})$ since we have seen that the agent with the most successes before her first failure will almost certainly have quality $q \in [\hat{q}(T), \gamma]$ and (unconditional on the agents' precise quality choices and types) all agents who participate with qualities $q \in [\hat{q}(T), \gamma]$ have equal chances of being this agent. Also note that if an agent is explored and obtains the most successes before her first failure, then she obtains a benefit $\Theta(T)$. For this reason, conditional on contributing with quality $q \in [\hat{q}(T), \gamma]$, the expected benefit the agent obtains is $\Theta(\frac{T}{\sum_\tau \beta_\tau(T)(1-F_T^\tau(\hat{q}(T)))\rho_\tau K(T)})$.

Also note that we must have $\lim_{T\to\infty}\beta_\tau(T)=0$ for all τ: if there is some τ for which $\beta_\tau(T)$ remains bounded away from zero for an infinite number of T, then the expected benefits to contributing with a quality drawn randomly according to the mixed strategy equilibrium (unconditional on the agent's type) would be $\frac{T}{\sum_\tau \beta_\tau(T)\rho_\tau K(T)} = \Theta(\frac{T}{K(T)}) = \Theta(1)$ as $T\to\infty$. But the expected cost to contributing according to the mixed strategy equilibrium (unconditional on an agent's type and quality choice) would diverge as $T\to\infty$. Thus the costs to participating would exceed the benefits for sufficiently large T, and we could not have such an equilibrium in which there is some τ for which $\beta_\tau(T)$ remains bounded away from zero for an infinite number of T.

Since $\lim_{T\to\infty}\beta_\tau(T)=0$, we must have $\beta_\tau(T)<1$ for all τ for sufficiently large T. But if $\beta_\tau(T)<1$, *i.e.*, agents do not participate with probability 1, the zero payoff condition must apply, *i.e.*, the expected cost from participating equals the expected benefit for sufficiently large T. That is, we must have $E_\tau[E[c_\tau(q)|q\sim F_T^\tau(q)], q\in[\hat{q}(T),\gamma]] = \Theta(\frac{T}{\sum_\tau \beta_\tau(T)(1-F_T^\tau(\hat{q}(T)))\rho_\tau K(T)})$.

Now consider an agent who contributes with quality $q\in[\hat{q}(T),\gamma]$ and consider what happens when an agent changes her quality by ϵ for some small $\epsilon>0$. By Proposition A.1, this change increases the number of successes the agent obtains before her first failure with probability $\Theta(\epsilon)$ if the agent is explored. Also, this change can only affect whether the agent obtains additional attention after her first failure if the agent either had $m(T)$ or $m(T)-1$ successes. But the number of agents who obtain $m(T)$ or $m(T)-1$ successes stays bounded in the limit as $T\to\infty$ with probability arbitrarily close to 1. Combining this with the fact that (unconditional on the precise realization of the agents' qualities and types) all agents who contribute with quality $q\in[\hat{q}(T),\gamma]$ are equally likely to obtain $m(T)$ or $m(T)-1$ successes shows that the probability such an agent obtains $m(T)$ or $m(T)-1$ successes is $\Theta(\frac{1}{\sum_\tau \beta_\tau(T)(1-F_T^\tau(\hat{q}(T)))\rho_\tau K(T)})$. From this it follows that if an agent changes her quality by ϵ for some small $\epsilon>0$, the probability this affects whether she obtains additional attention after her first failure is $O(\frac{\epsilon}{\sum_\tau \beta_\tau(T)(1-F_T^\tau(\hat{q}(T)))\rho_\tau K(T)})$.

The expected additional benefit from increasing quality by ϵ is therefore $O(\frac{\epsilon T}{\sum_\tau \beta_\tau(T)(1-F_T^\tau(\hat{q}(T)))\rho_\tau K(T)})$, since if an agent wins as a result of making this change, then she obtains an additional $\Theta(T)$ attention and this happens with the probability derived above. Thus in order for agents to not be able to profitably deviate by making infinitesimal changes to their quality choices, it must be the case that $E_\tau[E[c'_\tau(q)|q\sim F_T^\tau(q)]|q\in[\hat{q}(T),\gamma]] = O(\frac{T}{\sum_\tau \beta_\tau(T)(1-F_T^\tau(\hat{q}(T)))\rho_\tau K(T)})$.

Combining this with the fact that $E_\tau[E[c_\tau(q)|q\sim F_T^\tau(q)]|q\in[\hat{q}(T),\gamma]] = \Theta(\frac{T}{\sum_\tau \beta_\tau(T)(1-F_T^\tau(\hat{q}(T)))\rho_\tau K(T)})$ shows that $\frac{E_\tau[E[c'_\tau(q)|q\sim F_T^\tau(q)]|q\in[\hat{q}(T),\gamma]]}{E_\tau[E[c_\tau(q)|q\sim F_T^\tau(q)]|q\in[\hat{q}(T),\gamma]]} = O(1)$. But for any set of distributions $F_T^\tau(q)$, it must be the case that $\lim_{T\to\infty}\frac{E_\tau[E[c'_\tau(q)|q\sim F_T^\tau(q)]|q\in[\hat{q}(T),\gamma]]}{E_\tau[E[c_\tau(q)|q\sim F_T^\tau(q)]|q\in[\hat{q}(T),\gamma]]} = \infty$ because $\lim_{q\to\gamma}\log c_\tau(q) = \infty$ for all τ, meaning $\lim_{q\to\gamma}\frac{d}{dq}\log c_\tau(q) = \lim_{q\to\gamma}\frac{c'_\tau(q)}{c_\tau(q)} = \infty$ for all τ. This gives a contradiction which shows that it must be the case that there exists some $q^*<\gamma$ such that the probability agents choose quality $q>q^*$ in equilibrium goes to zero in the limit as T goes to infinity. □

Proof of Lemma 4.1: Since no more than $G(T)$ contributions are explored for any given T, the contribution i that is displayed most often must receive at least $\frac{T}{G(T)}=\omega(\ln T)$ units of attention. Therefore, the value of $q_i^t+\sqrt{\frac{2\ln T}{n_i^t}}$ for this contribution i tends to q_i as $T\to\infty$.

Now if any contribution j is explored only $o(\ln T)$ times, then the value of $q_j^t+\sqrt{\frac{2\ln T}{n_j^t}}$ tends to ∞ as $T\to\infty$. For sufficiently large t and T, this would imply that $q_j^t+\sqrt{\frac{2\ln T}{n_j^t}} > q_i^t+\sqrt{\frac{2\ln T}{n_i^t}}$, which would in turn mean that there is some threshold t^* such that contribution i would never be explored for all $t\geq t^*$. Therefore, it cannot be the case that i is explored infinitely often while j is only explored $o(\ln T)$ times, so it must be the case that each contribution j is explored $\Omega(\ln T)$ times, regardless of the qualities of the contributions.

Now consider a contribution with quality $q_j\leq q_{max}(T)-\delta$. Note that it cannot be the case that this contribution receives $\omega(\ln T)$ units of attention: if this contribution receives $\omega(\ln T)$ units of attention, then $q_j^t+\sqrt{\frac{2\ln T}{n_j^t}}$ tends to q_j for large t in probability. But for a contribution i with quality $q_i=q_{max}(T)$, $q_i^t+\sqrt{\frac{2\ln T}{n_i^t}}$ tends to a value that is at least as large as q_i for large t in probability. Thus since $q_j\leq q_{max}(T)-\delta$, this would imply that $q_i^t+\sqrt{\frac{2\ln T}{n_i^t}} > q_j^t+\sqrt{\frac{2\ln T}{n_j^t}}$ for large t in probability. This in turn implies that there is some threshold t^* such that j is never explored for all $t\geq t^*$ in probability, meaning contribution j cannot be explored infinitely often. This contradicts the possibility that contribution j receives $\omega(\ln T)$ units of attention in expectation. Combining this with the result in the previous paragraph shows that any contribution with quality $q_j\leq q_{max}(T)-\delta$ obtains $\Theta(\ln T)$ units of attention in expectation. □

Proof of Theorem 4.2: Suppose not. Then there is some $q^*<\gamma$ such that there are infinitely many values of T for which the probability that an agent with quality $q>q^*$ is explored is less than or equal to π for some $\pi<1$. Throughout the remainder of the proof, we restrict attention to values of T in this subsequence.

Note that if an agent chooses quality $q_j>q^*+\epsilon$ for some $\epsilon>0$ and this agent's contribution is explored, then the agent obtains an expected amount of attention $\Theta(T)$. To see why, consider some other contribution i with quality $q_i<q^*$. This contribution i receives $O(\ln T)$ units of attention in expectation, because if i receives $\omega(\ln T)$ units of attention, then $q_i^t+\sqrt{\frac{2\ln T}{n_i^t}}$ tends to q_i for large t in probability, while $q_j^t+\sqrt{\frac{2\ln T}{n_i^t}}$ tends to a value that is greater than or equal to $q_j>q_i$. But this means there is some threshold t^* such that i is never explored for all $t\geq t^*$ in probability, meaning i cannot be explored infinitely often. This gives a contradiction which shows that i receives $O(\ln T)$ units of attention in expectation.

Therefore, if an agent chooses quality $q_j>q^*+\epsilon$ for some $\epsilon>0$ and this agent's contribution is explored and all other contributions that are explored have quality $q_i\leq q^*$, then the contributions with quality $q_i\leq q^*$ receive only a total of $O(\min\{G(T),k(T)\}\ln T)$ units of attention in expectation, so that agent j receives $\Theta(T)$ units of attention in expectation by our assumption on $G(T)$. But the probability that all other contributions that are explored have quality $q_i \leq q^*$ is at least $1 - \pi > 0$, *i.e.*, is bounded away from 0 for all T. Thus, conditional on being explored, this agent obtains an additional $\Theta(T)$ units of attention from this deviation, so that the expected additional benefit from deviating (unconditional on being explored) is $\Theta(\frac{\min\{G(T),k(T)\}T}{k(T)})$, which becomes unbounded as $T \to \infty$ since $k(T) \leq T$ and $G(T) \to \infty$.

This implies that if there is some subsequence such that the probability there is a contribution that is explored and has quality $q_i \geq q^*$ is no greater than π for some $\pi < 1$, then an agent can profitably deviate by choosing a quality $q_j > q^* + \epsilon$. Thus for any $q^* < \gamma$, the probability there is a contribution that is explored and has quality $q_i \geq q^*$ goes to 1 in the limit as $T \to \infty$. □

Proof of Theorem 4.3: Suppose by means of contradiction that $\mathcal{M}_{\text{UCB-MOD}}$ does not achieve strong sublinear regret. Then there exists some $\delta > 0$ such that the expected number of failures in $\mathcal{M}_{\text{UCB-MOD}}$ is at least $((1-\gamma)+\delta)T$ for sufficiently large T. In order for this to take place, it must be the case that $\mathcal{M}_{\text{UCB-MOD}}$ displays contributions with quality $q_i \leq \gamma - \delta$ on $\Theta(T)$ separate occasions.

Since there are no more than $G(T)$ contributions to be explored, there must be at least one contribution with quality $q_i \leq \gamma - \delta$ that is explored at least $\Theta(\frac{T}{G(T)})$ times, *i.e.*, $\omega(\ln T)$ times. For this contribution, $q_i^t + \sqrt{\frac{2\ln T}{n_i^t}}$ tends to q_i for large t in probability.

Now Theorem 4.2 guarantees that there will almost certainly be at least one explored contribution with quality arbitrarily close to γ in the limit as $T \to \infty$. That is, the highest quality contribution j explored by $\mathcal{M}_{\text{UCB-MOD}}$ has a quality q_j that tends to γ as $T \to \infty$.

For this contribution, $q_j^t + \sqrt{\frac{2\ln T}{n_j^t}}$ tends to a value that is no smaller than γ for large t in probability. But then $q_i^t + \sqrt{\frac{2\ln T}{n_i^t}} < q_j^t + \sqrt{\frac{2\ln T}{n_j^t}}$ for large t in probability. This implies that there is some threshold t^* such that contribution i is never explored for all $t \geq t^*$, which contradicts the possibility that the algorithm displays contribution i infinitely often. Therefore, it cannot be the case that $\mathcal{M}_{\text{UCB-MOD}}$ displays contributions with quality $q_i \leq \gamma - \delta$ on $\Theta(T)$ separate occasions in the limit as $T \to \infty$, and so the modified UCB mechanism achieves strong sublinear regret. □

Proof of Lemma 4.2: Since no more than $G(T)$ contributions are explored for any given T, the contribution i that receives the mth most attention must receive at least $\frac{p_m T}{G(T)} = \omega(\ln T)$ units of attention. Therefore, the value of $q_i^t + \sqrt{\frac{2\ln T}{n_i^t}}$ for this contribution i tends to q_i as $T \to \infty$.

Now if any contribution j receives only $o(\ln T)$ attention, then the value of $q_j^t + \sqrt{\frac{2\ln T}{n_j^t}}$ tends to ∞ as $T \to \infty$. For sufficiently large t and T, this would imply that $q_j^t + \sqrt{\frac{2\ln T}{n_j^t}} > q_i^t + \sqrt{\frac{2\ln T}{n_i^t}}$, which would in turn mean that there is some threshold t^* such that contribution i would never be explored for all $t \geq t^*$. Therefore, it cannot be the case that i receives an infinite amount of attention while j only receives $o(\ln T)$ attention, so it must be the case that each contribution j receives $\Omega(\ln T)$ attention, regardless of the qualities of the contributions.

Now consider a contribution with quality $q_j \leq q_m(T) - \delta$. Note that it cannot be the case that this contribution receives $\omega(\ln T)$ units of attention: if this contribution receives $\omega(\ln T)$ units of attention, then $q_j^t + \sqrt{\frac{2\ln T}{n_j^t}}$ tends to q_j for large t in probability. But for a contribution i with quality $q_i = q_m(T)$, $q_i^t + \sqrt{\frac{2\ln T}{n_i^t}}$ tends to a value that is at least as large as q_i for large t in probability. Thus since $q_j \leq q_m(T) - \delta$, this would imply that $q_i^t + \sqrt{\frac{2\ln T}{n_i^t}} > q_j^t + \sqrt{\frac{2\ln T}{n_j^t}}$ for large t in probability. This in turn implies that there is some threshold t^* such that j is never explored for all $t \geq t^*$ in probability, meaning contribution j cannot receive an infinite amount of attention. This contradicts the possibility that contribution j receives $\omega(\ln T)$ units of attention in expectation. Combining this with the result in the previous paragraph shows that any contribution with quality $q_j \leq q_m(T) - \delta$ obtains $\Theta(\ln T)$ units of attention in expectation. □

Proof of Theorem 4.4: Suppose not. Then there is some $q^* < \gamma$ such that there are infinitely many values of T for which the probability that at least m agents with quality $q > q^*$ are explored is less than or equal to π for some $\pi < 1$. Throughout the remainder of the proof, we restrict attention to values of T in this subsequence.

Note that if an agent chooses quality $q_j > q^* + \epsilon$ for some $\epsilon > 0$ and this agent's contribution is explored, then the agent obtains an expected amount of attention $\Theta(T)$. To see why, consider some other contribution i with quality $q_i < q^*$. This contribution i receives $O(\ln T)$ units of attention in expectation, because if i receives $\omega(\ln T)$ units of attention, then $q_i^t + \sqrt{\frac{2\ln T}{n_i^t}}$ tends to q_i for large t in probability, while $q_j^t + \sqrt{\frac{2\ln T}{n_i^t}}$ tends to a value that is greater than or equal to $q_j > q_i$. But this means there is some threshold t^* such that i is never explored for all $t \geq t^*$ in probability, meaning i cannot receive an infinite amount of attention. This gives a contradiction which shows that i receives $O(\ln T)$ units of attention in expectation.

Therefore, if an agent chooses quality $q_j > q^* + \epsilon$ for some $\epsilon > 0$ and this agent's contribution is explored and there are no more than m contributions that are explored that have quality $q_i \geq q^*$, then the contributions with quality $q_i \leq q^*$ receive only a total of $O(\min\{G(T), k(T)\}\ln T)$ units of attention in expectation, so that agent j receives $\Theta(T)$ units of attention in expectation by our assumption on $G(T)$. But the probability that there are no more than m contributions that are explored and have quality $q_i \geq q^*$ is at least $1 - \pi > 0$, *i.e.*, is bounded away from 0 for all T. Thus, conditional on being explored, this agent obtains an additional $\Theta(T)$ units of attention from this deviation, so that the expected additional benefit from deviating (unconditional on being explored) is $\Theta(\frac{\min\{G(T),k(T)\}T}{k(T)})$, which becomes unbounded as $T \to \infty$ since $k(T) \leq T$ and $G(T) \to \infty$.

This implies that if there is some subsequence such that the probability there are no more than m contributions that are explored that have quality $q_i \geq q^*$ is no greater than π for some $\pi < 1$, then an agent can profitably deviate by choosing a quality $q_j > q^* + \epsilon$. Thus for any $q^* < \gamma$, the probability there are at least m contributions that are explored that have quality $q_i \geq q^*$ goes to 1 in the limit as $T \to \infty$. □

Proof of Theorem 4.5: Suppose by means of contradiction that $\mathcal{M}_{\text{UCB-MOD}}$ does not achieve strong sublinear regret. Then there exists some $\delta > 0$ such that the expected number of failures in $\mathcal{M}_{\text{UCB-MOD}}$ is at least $(\sum_{j=1}^{m} p_j(1-\gamma)+p_m\delta)T$ for sufficiently large T. In order for this to take place, it must be the case that $\mathcal{M}_{\text{UCB-MOD}}$ displays contributions with quality $q_i \leq \gamma - \delta$ on $\Theta(T)$ separate occasions.

Since there are no more than $G(T)$ contributions to be explored, there must be at least one contribution with quality $q_i \leq \gamma - \delta$ that is explored at least $\Theta(\frac{T}{G(T)})$ times, *i.e.*, $\omega(\ln T)$ times. For this contribution, $q_i^t + \sqrt{\frac{2\ln T}{n_i^t}}$ tends to q_i for large t in probability.

Now Theorem 4.4 guarantees that there will almost certainly be at least m explored contribution with quality arbitrarily close to γ in the limit as $T \to \infty$. That is, the mth highest quality contribution j explored by $\mathcal{M}_{\text{UCB-MOD}}$ has a quality q_j that tends to γ as $T \to \infty$.

For this contribution, $q_j^t + \sqrt{\frac{2\ln T}{n_j^t}}$ tends to a value that is no smaller than γ for large t in probability. But then $q_i^t + \sqrt{\frac{2\ln T}{n_i^t}} < q_j^t + \sqrt{\frac{2\ln T}{n_j^t}}$ for large t in probability. This implies that there is some threshold t^* such that contribution i is never explored for all $t \geq t^*$, which contradicts the possibility that the algorithm displays contribution i infinitely often. Therefore, it cannot be the case that $\mathcal{M}_{\text{UCB-MOD}}$ displays contributions with quality $q_i \leq \gamma - \delta$ on $\Theta(T)$ separate occasions in the limit as $T \to \infty$, and so the modified UCB mechanism achieves strong sublinear regret. □

Welfare Maximization and the Supermodular Degree

Uriel Feige
Weizmann Institute of Science
Rehovot, Israel
uriel.feige@weizmann.ac.il

Rani Izsak
Weizmann Institute of Science
Rehovot, Israel
ran.izsak@weizmann.ac.il

ABSTRACT

Given a set of items and a collection of players, each with a nonnegative monotone valuation set function over the items, the welfare maximization problem requires that every item be allocated to exactly one player, and one wishes to maximize the sum of values obtained by the players, as computed by applying the respective valuation function to the bundle of items allocated to the player. This problem in its full generality is $\mathcal{NP}$-hard, and moreover, at least as hard to approximate as set-packing. Better approximation guarantees are known for restricted classes of valuation functions.

In this work we introduce a new parameter, the *supermodular degree* of a valuation function, which is a measure for the extent to which the function exhibits supermodular behavior. We design an approximation algorithm for the welfare maximization problem whose approximation guarantee is linear in the supermodular degree of the underlying valuation functions.

Categories and Subject Descriptors

F.1.3 [**Computation by Abstract Devices**]: Complexity Measures and Classes; F.2.2 [**Analysis of Algorithms and Problem Complexity**]: Nonnumerical Algorithms and Problems

General Terms

Algorithms; Theory

Keywords

approximation algorithms; combinatorial auctions; submodular functions

1. INTRODUCTION

The welfare maximization problem (also known as "combinatorial auction") is the following. There is a set of players and a set of indivisible items. Each player has its own (monotone non-decreasing) valuation for any subset of items. The goal is to distribute the items to the players while maximizing social welfare - the sum of values of all players, by their personal valuations. The welfare maximization problem is $\mathcal{NP}$-hard to approximate with any reasonable guarantee. For this reason past research considered restrictions on the class of set functions that may serve as valuation functions for the players. Lehmann, Lehmann and Nisan [15] considered *complement free* functions, which essentially means that a value of a set of items cannot exceed the sum of values of its parts. They presented a hierarchy of classes of complement free functions, and established constant factor approximations for the welfare maximization problem in some cases.[1] Subsequent work established constant factor approximation for all classes of complement free functions. This made it clear that the poor approximation guarantees for the general case must come from complementarities (sets whose value is larger than that of the sum of their parts). Recently, Abraham, Babaioff, Dughmi and Roughgarden [1] considered a restricted class of set functions strictly based on complementarities (in particular, no set is valued less than the sum of its parts). Among other results, they presented an algorithm with an approximation guarantee that is linear in a certain parameter related to the extent of these complementarities.

In the current work, similarly to [1], we express the approximation guarantees as a function of some parameter associated with the underlying set functions. The smaller this parameter is, the better the approximation guarantee. However, we depart from the practice of considering restricted classes of set functions – our parametrization can be applied to any set function. It is most advantageous (in the sense that our approximation guarantees are not bad whereas previous work does not apply to these set functions) when the set functions are basically submodular (offer decreasing marginal value, which is the discrete analog of convexity), but exhibit a limited amount of complementarities. As a simple example of how such functions may arise, consider shopping for shoes. Each additional pair of shoes may have decreasing marginal value, but within a pair of shoes, the left and right shoe are together worth more than the sum of values of each shoe on its own.

[1]There was earlier work with related results that used different terminology. For example, Fisher, Nemhauser and Wolsey [10] studied "the m-box problem" which is essentially the welfare maximization problem with monotone submodular valuation functions. Among their results there was a greedy approximation algorithm for a generalized version of this problem with approximation guarantee 1/2.

Specifically, we introduce two new (as far as we know) complexity measures of set functions. One is the *dependency degree*. Roughly speaking, this is the maximum number of items that may influence the marginal value of any item with respect to any possible subset of other items. The other is the *supermodular degree*. Roughly speaking, this is the dependency degree, taking into account only items that may *increase* the marginal value of an item. That is, "negative dependencies" do not increase the latter complexity measure. In particular, submodular functions might have arbitrary dependency degree, but their supermodular degree is 0. This measure can also be seen, in a sense, as the "degree of complementarity". We design two greedy approximation algorithms for the welfare maximization problem, each with approximation guarantee linear in the maximum of one of these measures over the set functions of the players.

2. PRELIMINARIES

We firstly define formally the welfare maximization problem:

Definition 1. An instance $\mathcal{I}(P, M, v)$ of the welfare maximization problem is the following:

- P is a set of n players $1, \ldots, n$.
- M is a set of m items $j_1, \ldots, j_m$.
- v is a vector of n valuation functions (set functions) $v_1, \ldots, v_n$, where $v_p : 2^M \to \mathbb{R}^+$ is the valuation function associated with the player $p \in P$.[2] For any $p \in P$, v_p is restricted to be monotone non-decreasing and with value 0 for the empty set (and hence also non-negative).

A feasible solution to $\mathcal{I}$ is a mapping $SOL : M \to P$, allocating each of the items to exactly one player. This mapping induces for each player $p \in P$ a set SOL_p of the items mapped to her. The utility/value of a player $p \in P$ is defined as $v_p(SOL_p)$. Our aim is to maximize the social welfare $v(SOL) \stackrel{\text{def}}{=} \sum_{p \in P} v_p(SOL_p)$.

2.1 Types of set functions without complementarities

We recall previously studied types of set functions without complementarities (see for example [15, 8]). Let S be a set and let $f : 2^S \to \mathbb{R}^+$ be a set function.

Definition 2. We say that f is submodular if for any $S'' \subseteq S' \subseteq S$ and $x \in S \setminus S'$, $f(x \mid S') \leq f(x \mid S'')$.

Definition 3. We say that f is fractionally subadditive if for every subset $S' \subseteq S$, subsets $T_i \subseteq S'$ and every coefficients $0 < \alpha_i \leq 1$ such that for any $x \in S'$, $\sum_{i: x \in T_i} \alpha_i \geq 1$, it holds that $f(S') \leq \sum_i \alpha_i f(T_i)$.

Definition 4. We say that f is subadditive or complement free if for every $S_1, S_2 \subseteq S$, $f(S_1 \cup S_2) \leq f(S_1) + f(S_2)$.

[2] We use $\mathbb{R}^+$ to indicate the set of all non-negative real numbers (that is, 0 is included).

2.2 Measuring dependencies

In this section we introduce complexity measures capturing dependencies of items in a groundset of a set function. For convenience, we treat the set functions as valuation functions of players of an instance of the welfare maximization problem (for notations only). Let M be a set, let $v_p : 2^M \to \mathbb{R}^+$ be a valuation function of player $p \in P$ and let $j \in M$. We firstly recall the following definition (see for example [15]):

Definition 5. Let $p \in P$ and let $j \in M$. The marginal valuation function $v_{p,j} : 2^{M \setminus \{j\}} \to \mathbb{R}^+$ is a function mapping each subset $S \subseteq M \setminus \{j\}$ to the marginal value of j given S:

$$v_{p,j}(S) \stackrel{\text{def}}{=} v_p(S \cup \{j\}) - v_p(S) \ .$$

We denote the marginal value $v_{p,j}(S)$ also by $v_p(j \mid S)$. For $S' = \{j_1, \ldots, j_{|S'|}\} \subseteq M$ and $S \subseteq M \setminus S'$ we also use either of the notations $v_p(j_1, \ldots, j_{|S'|} \mid S)$ or $v_p(S' \mid S)$ to indicate $v_p(S \cup S') - v_p(S)$.

Definition 6. The dependency set of j by v_p is the set of all items j' in M such that there exists $S \subseteq M \setminus \{j\}$ such that $v_p(j \mid S) \neq v_p(j \mid S \setminus \{j'\})$. For each such j', we say that j depends on j' by p and denote it by $j \to_p j'$, or by $j \stackrel{S}{\to}_p j'$ if we want to explicitly mention the set S. We denote the dependency set of j by v_p by $Dep_p(j)$. p or v_p may be omitted in any of the above, when it is clear from the context.

The relation '$\to$' is symmetric (see Appendix A), so we may also use the terminology "are dependent" and the notation '$\leftrightarrow$'.

Definition 7. The supermodular dependency set of j by v_p is the set of all items j' in M such that there exists $S \subseteq M \setminus \{j\}$ such that $v_p(j \mid S) > v_p(j \mid S \setminus \{j'\})$. Terminology and notations are the same as in Definition 6, but with the word "supermodular/ly" or with '+' as a superscript. Note that the relation '$\to^+$' is also symmetric (see Appendix A).

Definition 8. The dependency degree of v_p is defined as $DD(v_p) \stackrel{\text{def}}{=} \max_{j \in M} |Dep_p(j)|$. The supermodular dependency degree (or simply, the supermodular degree) of v_p is defined as $DD^+(v_p) \stackrel{\text{def}}{=} \max_{j \in M} |Dep^+_p(j)|$. The (supermodular) dependency degree of an instance of the welfare maximization problem is the maximum (supermodular) dependency degree among all valuation functions of the instance.

Note that any submodular set function has supermodular degree 0. Note also that $DD^+(f) \leq DD(f)$ for any set function f.

We also use the following definition:

Definition 9. Let f be a set function. The (supermodular) dependency graph of f is the following. There is a vertex for each item and an undirected edge for each pair of (supermodularly) dependent items.

2.3 Representing set functions

In the welfare maximization problem, the domain of the valuation functions is exponential in the number of items. We recall two possible approaches to cope with this. The first is using an explicit representation model (specifically, we recall a hypergraph representation; see [5], [4], [1]) and the second is using oracles, representing set functions by supporting queries with respect to them (see for example [3]).

2.3.1 A hypergraph representation

Every set function f can be represented in a unique way as a hypergraph in which the vertices are the items, vertices and hyperedges have weights associated with them, and the value $f(S)$ of a subset S of items equals the sum of all weights in the subgraph induced by the corresponding vertices. We observe that two items share a hyperedge in the hypergraph representation if and only if they are dependent, and that sharing a hyperedge of positive weight is a necessary condition but not sufficient for being supermodularly dependent.[3]

A succinct representation.

Let $f : 2^S \rightarrow \mathbb{R}^+$ be a set function and let $s \stackrel{\text{def}}{=} |S|$. In general, a succinct representation of f is any representation that takes space polynomial in s. For example, the hypergraph representation is succinct for any set function with dependency degree bounded by $\log s$ (and, of course, for some other set functions, as well).

2.3.2 Queries oracles

We recall the definitions of value and demand queries oracle. Let $f : 2^S \rightarrow \mathbb{R}^+$ be a set function.

Definition 10. Value queries are the following:
Input: A subset $S' \subseteq S$.
Output: $f(S')$.

Definition 11. Demand queries are the following:
Input: A cost function $c : S \rightarrow \mathbb{R}^+$.
Output: A subset $S' \subseteq S$ maximizing $f(S') - \sum_{j \in S'} c(j)$.

Note that demand queries are strictly stronger than value queries (see [3]).

Definition 12. Queries oracle for a type of queries for a given set function can answer queries of the respective type with respect to the given set function.

The notion of an oracle serves as an abstraction for a subroutine that computes an answer to the respective type of queries for a given set function. When we say that an algorithm uses a certain type of oracle, the running time of the algorithm is computed as if each query takes unit time to answer, regardless of the true running time of the underlying subroutine. This abstraction is most justified if for the underlying set function, answers to the respective query can indeed be computed efficiently. We remark that given a succinct hypergraph representation for a set function, one can efficiently answer value queries, whereas answering demand queries might be $\mathcal{NP}$-hard (see for example Theorem 1). We also remark that given a succinct hypergraph representation, one can construct the corresponding dependency graph and supermodular dependency graph.

[3]For example, consider the set function f that has value 0 on the empty set and 1 elsewhere. In its hypergraph representation every odd set of items forms a hyperedge of weight 1 and every even set of items forms a hyperedge of weight -1. Every two items share a positive hyperedge, but no two items are supermodularly dependent, since f is submodular.

2.4 Preliminary observations

2.4.1 $\mathcal{APX}$-hardness of the welfare maximization problem

PROPOSITION 1. *The welfare maximization problem is $\mathcal{APX}$-hard even if there are only three players who all have the same valuation function f, with $DD^+(f) = 0$ and $DD(f) = 3$.*

PROOF. It is known that the question of whether a 3-regular graph can be legally 3-colored is $\mathcal{NP}$-hard, and that it is $\mathcal{APX}$-hard to maximize the number of legally colored edges [16]. Given a 3-regular graph G, consider a set function f that has G as its hypergraph representation, with all vertices having value 3 and all edges having value -1. Associating a color with each player, the allocation that maximizes welfare is the one that minimizes the number of monochromatic edges. The proposition follows. □

2.4.2 Hardness of welfare maximization as a function of the dependency degree

Recall that the maximum weighted k-set packing problem is the following:

Definition 13. Let $G = (V, E, w)$ be a weighted k-uniform hypergraph (i.e. every hyperedge contains exactly k vertices) with set of vertices V, set of undirected edges E and edge weights function w. The maximum weighted k-set packing problem is to find a set of disjoint edges of maximum weight.

This problem is known to be $\mathcal{NP}$-hard for any $k > 2$ and is hard for approximation with guarantee $\Omega(\frac{\ln k}{k})$, even in the unweighted case, by a result of Hazan, Safra and Schwartz [14]. The best approximation guarantee known for it currently (as far as we know) is $(k+1)/2$, by an algorithm of Berman [2]. We show the following:

PROPOSITION 2. *There exists an approximation preserving reduction of the maximum weighted k-set packing problem to the welfare maximization problem with dependency degree at most $k - 1$.*

PROOF. The reduction is Reduction 2.1.

Reduction 2.1 k-set packing to welfare maximization with dependency degree at most $k - 1$

Input: An instance $\mathcal{I}_{SP}(V, E, w)$ of the maximum weighted k-set packing problem, with $V = \{v_1, \ldots, v_{|V|}\}$.
Output: An instance $\mathcal{I}(P, M, v)$ of the welfare maximization problem with dependency degree at most $k - 1$.

1: For each vertex $v_i \in V$, create an item $i \in M$.
2: For each hyper-edge $e = \{v_{e_1}, \ldots, v_{e_k}\} \in E$, create a player $p_e \in P$ with $v_p(S) = w(e)$ for any S such that $\{e_1, \ldots, e_k\} \subseteq S$ and $v_p(S) = 0$ otherwise.

It is easy to verify that any feasible solution for $\mathcal{I}_{SP}$ (the input of Reduction 2.1) has a corresponding feasible solution for $\mathcal{I}$ (the output of Reduction 2.1), with the same value, and vice versa, as desired. □

2.4.3 *An exact algorithm for dependency degree at most 1*

PROPOSITION 3. *The welfare maximization problem with dependency degree at most 1 admits an exact polynomial time algorithm.*

The main idea is to use symmetry of the dependency relation in order to reduce an instance of the welfare maximization problem to an instance of maximum weighted matching. The full reduction appears in Appendix C.

2.4.4 *Demand queries and the dependency degree*

THEOREM 1. *Given a hypergraph representation of any set function with dependency degree at most 2, demand queries may be answered in polynomial time (in the size of the hypergraph representation). Given a hypergraph representation of a set function with dependency degree at least 3, demand queries are generally $\mathcal{APX}$-hard to answer (with respect to the size of the hypergraph representation).*

PROOF. Let f be a set function. If $DD(f) \leq 2$, then each item depends on at most two other items. The dependency graph of f is of maximum degree 2 and hence its connected components are either isolated vertices, isolated paths or isolated cycles. On each such component, demand queries may be answered using dynamic programming.

To show hardness for set functions f with $DD(f) \geq 3$, we reduce from the problem of maximum independent set in 3-regular graphs. f is represented by the following hypergraph representation. Give each vertex value 3 and each edge value -1. The value of the answer to a demand query in which the cost of each vertex is 2 is equal to the size of the maximum independent set (it is worth taking a vertex only if it does not contribute an edge to the induced subgraph). Due to $\mathcal{APX}$-hardness of maximum independent set in 3-regular graphs, it is $\mathcal{APX}$-hard to answer demand queries, as well. □

2.5 Our main results

We view the notion of the supermodular degree and the study of its basic properties as an important contribution of our work. This notion is applicable to any set function, and its relevance to the welfare maximization problem is demonstrated by the following theorem.

THEOREM 2. *The welfare maximization problem with supermodular degree at most d admits a polynomial time greedy $\frac{1}{d+2}$-approximation algorithm. This algorithm requires a value queries oracle and a supermodular dependency graph.*

For the dependency degree we have a slightly better approximation guarantee, which is relevant only when the dependency degree and the supermodular degree are equal:

THEOREM 3. *The welfare maximization problem with dependency degree at most d admits a greedy $\frac{1}{d+1}$ approximation algorithm. Its running time is polynomial in the number of players and items and in 2^d. This algorithm requires a value queries oracle and a dependency graph.*

Proposition 2 implies that an improvement of our results by a multiplicative factor of more than roughly 2 would improve the current approximation guarantee for weighted k-set packing. Additionally, by a hardness result of Blumrosen and Nisan [3] of $O(\log m/m)$ for algorithms requiring only value queries oracle[4], our bounds are tight up to a multiplicative factor of $O(\log m)$, in the sense that general set functions have dependency degree (and supermodular degree) at most $m-1$.

2.6 Related work

The supermodular degree is a complexity measure for set functions, that ranges from 0 (for submodular set functions) to $m-1$ (where m is the number of items). Our main result is a greedy algorithm for the welfare maximization problem whose approximation guarantee increases linearly with the supermodular degree of the underlying set functions. Such a linear increase is to be expected, given the known reduction from set packing to the welfare maximization problem with single minded bidders, combined with the difficulty of approximating set packing ([14]). As far as we know, the notion of supermodular degree has not appeared in previous work. However, other related notions did appear, and in this section we discuss some of them.

Perhaps the simplest complexity measure for a set function is its support size, namely, the number of items that it depends on. This measure ranges from 1 to m. Moreover, simple greedy algorithms approximate the welfare maximization problem with guarantee equal to this measure, and known hardness results for the case of single minded bidders apply here as well. Hence the results that one can prove for the complexity measures of support size and supermodular degree are of a similar nature. However, as the supermodular degree of a function is not greater than its support size, and moreover, it is often much smaller (the gap being most dramatic for submodular functions), we view our results for supermodular degree as significantly more informative than the corresponding results for support size.

Lehmann, Lehmann and Nisan [15] proposed a hierarchy of classes of set functions based on notions of complement-freeness, and initiated a study of the complexity of the welfare maximization problem for these classes. For the lower classes (linear functions, and functions enjoying the *gross substitutes* property) the welfare maximization problem can be solved in polynomial time. For *submodular* functions, a constant approximation guarantee is possible and value queries suffice for this [15, 18] (and somewhat better constants are achievable using demand queries [9]). For XOS (later referred to as *fractionally subadditive* in [8]) and *subadditive* set functions there are approximation algorithms with constant approximation guarantees [6, 17, 8], but they require demand queries (value queries do not suffice [6]). The algorithm given in [15] for submodular functions is greedy,

[4]Our algorithms require also dependency graph / supermodular dependency graph. However, in the instance used by [3], it is trivial to construct both, since all the items supermodularly depend on each other (for infinitely many values of m). Alternatively, since the approximation hardness is $O(\log m/m)$, we may simply modify the valuations functions so that every two items are supermodularly dependent, by adding a positive hyperedge that contains all items. Details omitted.

and the greedy algorithm in the current paper can be viewed as an extension of the greedy algorithm of [15] to a setting that is not submodular. The classification of [15] does not distinguish between different classes of functions that are not subadditive, and hence unlike our supermodular degree measure, is applicable only to some classes of set functions, but not to set functions in general. Set functions not lying in the classification of [15] may have any supermodular degree between 1 and m and our algorithms for maximizing welfare distinguish among them in the approximation guarantees that they provide. Lehmann, Lehmann and Nisan [15] do suggest a way of extending their classification to additional functions, as follows. A function f can be called c-submodular, if for every (possibly empty) sets S and T and item x, the marginal value of x with respect to $S \cup T$ is at most c times larger that the marginal value of x with respect to S. (For submodular functions $c = 1$.) It is shown in [15] that the welfare maximization problem can be approximated with guarantee of $c + 1$ when the set functions are c-submodular. We note however that even functions on two items need not be c-submodular for any finite c (if one of the items has value 0 by itself but positive marginal value together with the other item).

Submodular functions play a central role in the definition of the supermodular degree. However, other classes within the hierarchy of [15] have no special significance in this respect. The supermodular degree does not distinguish between linear functions and arbitrary submodular functions – they both have supermodular degree 0. Functions in the [15] hierarchy which are not submodular may have arbitrarily large supermodular degree.[5]

Conitzer, Sandholm and Santi [5] introduce the representation of set functions via hypergraphs with positive and negative hyperedges (presented in Section 2.3. See also the work of Chevaleyre, Endriss, Estivie and Maudet [4], who defined independently a similar concept). They showed that even if each hyperedge has at most two vertices, the welfare maximization problem is $\mathcal{NP}$-hard. They did not consider approximation algorithms. Abraham, Babaioff, Dughmi and Roughgarden [1] consider supermodular functions which have no negative hyperedges in their hypergraph representation. Among other results, they give an algorithm approximating the welfare maximization problem within a value equal to the maximum cardinality of any hyperedge (which may be smaller than the supermodular degree). They prove that obtaining similar approximation guarantees in the presence of negative hyperedges is $\mathcal{NP}$-hard. This serves as an explanation of why their model forbids negative hyperedges. Our results are to some extent in disagreement with this conclusion of [1]. Given a hypergraph representation of a set function with a given supermodular degree, adding negative hyperedges cannot increase the supermodular degree (in fact, it may cause the supermodular degree to decrease) and hence will not hurt our bounds on the approximation guarantees. This discrepancy between our results and those of [1] is explained by our requirement that set functions are nondecreasing, whereas the hardness of approximation results presented in [1] used set functions that are sometimes decreasing.

[5]For example, partition the set of items into two disjoint sets, A and B. Let f_A be a linear function that gives value 1 to each item in A and 0 to each item in B. Let f_B be a linear function that gives value 1 to each item in B and 0 to each item in A. Let f be defined as $f(S) = \max[f_A(S), f_B(S)]$. This is an XOS function (according to the classification of [15]), but its supermodular degree is $\max[|A|, |B|] - 1$.

3. APPROXIMATION GUARANTEE LINEAR IN SUPERMODULAR DEGREE

In this section we prove Theorem 2. Our result may be seen as an extension of a work of Lehmann, Lehmann and Nisan [15], who presented a greedy 2-approximation algorithm for submodular set functions.

3.1 The algorithm

The algorithm is greedy. In a given iteration, for every player p and item j, let $D_p^+(j)$ denote the set of items not yet allocated that have supermodular dependency with j with respect to v_p. The algorithm computes the player p and item j for which the marginal value for p (given the items that p already has) of the set $j \cup D_p^+(j)$ is maximized, and allocates $j \cup D_p^+(j)$ to p. For a full description of the algorithm, see Algorithm 3.1.

Algorithm 3.1 Greedily Approximate Welfare Maximization with Guarantee Linear in supermodular degree

Input: An instance $\mathcal{I}(P, M, v)$ of the welfare maximization problem, a value queries oracle and a supermodular dependency graph for each of the valuation functions.

Output: A solution with approximation guarantee $\frac{1}{d+2}$, where d is the supermodular degree of $\mathcal{I}$.

1: $Unallocated \leftarrow M$, $Approx \leftarrow \emptyset$
2: **while** $Unallocated \neq \emptyset$ **do**
3: $MaxMarginalUtility \leftarrow -1$
4: **for all** $j \in Unallocated, p \in P$ **do**
5: **if** $v_p(j, Dep_p^+(j) \cap Unallocated \mid \{j' \in M \mid (j' \mapsto p) \in Approx\}) > MaxMarginalUtility$ **then**
6: $MaxMarginalUtility \leftarrow v_p(j, Dep_p^+(j) \cap Unallocated \mid \{j' \in M \mid (j' \mapsto p) \in Approx\})$
7: $BestAllocation \leftarrow (\{j\} \cup (Dep_p^+(j) \cap Unallocated) \mapsto p)$
8: $WinningPlayer \leftarrow p$, $AllocatedItem \leftarrow j$
9: **end if**
10: **end for**
11: $Approx \leftarrow Approx \cup BestAllocation$
12: $Unallocated \leftarrow Unallocated \setminus (AllocatedItem \cup Dep^+_{WinningPlayer}(AllocatedItem))$
13: **end while**

We show Algorithm 3.1 has approximation guarantee $1/(d+2)$, using a hybrid argument. This will prove Theorem 2.

Proof of Theorem 2. Let OPT be an optimal solution with value opt and let $APPROX$ be the output of Algorithm 3.1 with value approx. For iteration i of the loop at line 2 of Algorithm 3.1, let $APPROX_i$ be the allocations made at the first i iterations, let OPT_i be the allocations made by OPT for the items that have not been allocated yet and let $HYBRID_i = APPROX_i \cup OPT_i$ be a hybrid solution. Let $HYBRID_i^p$ and OPT_i^p be the allocations in $HYBRID_i$ and OPT_i (respectively) to player $p \in P$. Note that $HYBRID_0 = OPT$ and $HYBRID_t = APPROX$, where t is the total number of iterations. We prove the following lemma:

LEMMA 1. *Let i be an iteration of the loop at line 2 of Algorithm 3.1, let $j_1, \ldots j_{d'}$ be the items allocated at iteration i and let p^* be the player to whom they are allocated. Then,*

$$(d+2)(v_{p^*}(APPROX_i^{p^*}) - v_{p^*}(APPROX_{i-1}^{p^*}))$$
$$\geq \sum_{p=1}^{n} v_p(OPT_{i-1}^p \mid APPROX_{i-1}^p) -$$
$$\sum_{p=1}^{n} v_p(OPT_i^p \mid APPROX_i^p) \ .$$

That is, the value lost by any iteration is bounded by $d+2$ times the value gained by the same iteration.

PROOF. Let $x = v_{p^*}(APPROX_i^{p^*}) - v_{p^*}(APPROX_{i-1}^{p^*})$. Roughly speaking, we prove that:

1. For an item allocated to some $p' \neq p^*$ in OPT, the loss to the value of p' for not getting the item is at most x.
2. Having received items in the current iteration, the loss in marginal value of future items given to p^* is at most x.

The first "contributes" to the "damage" up to $(d+1) \cdot x$, since $d' \leq d+1$. The second "contributes" up to another x, and for any other player $HYBRID_{i-1} = HYBRID_i$. We prove the lemma formally. Let P' be the set of players $p' \neq p^*$ such that at least one of the items $j_1, \ldots, j_{d'}$ is allocated to p' in OPT_{i-1}. Let $p' \in P'$ and let $\hat{j}_1, \ldots, \hat{j}_{d''} \in \{j_1, \ldots, j_{d'}\}$ be all the items of $j_1, \ldots, j_{d'}$, allocated to p' by OPT_{i-1}. Then,

$$v_{p'}(OPT_{i-1}^{p'} \mid APPROX_{i-1}^{p'}) - v_{p'}(OPT_i^{p'} \mid APPROX_i^{p'})$$
$$= v_{p'}(\{\hat{j}_1, \ldots \hat{j}_{d''}\} \mid OPT_i^{p'} \cup APPROX_{i-1}^{p'})$$
$$= \sum_{k=1}^{d''} v_{p'}(\hat{j}_k \mid \bigcup_{k'=k+1}^{d''} \{\hat{j}_{k'}\} \cup OPT_i^{p'} \cup APPROX_{i-1}^{p'})$$
$$\leq d'' \cdot \max_{k=1}^{d''} v_{p'}(\hat{j}_k \mid \bigcup_{k'=k+1}^{d''} \{\hat{j}_{k'}\} \cup OPT_i^{p'} \cup APPROX_{i-1}^{p'})$$
$$\leq d'' \cdot \max_{k=1}^{d''} v_{p'}(\{\hat{j}_k\} \cup (Dep_{p'}^+(\hat{j}_k) \setminus \bigcup_{p \in P} APPROX_{i-1}^p) \mid$$
$$(\bigcup_{k'=k+1}^{d''} \{\hat{j}_{k'}\} \setminus Dep_{p'}^+(\hat{j}_k)) \cup OPT_i^{p'} \cup APPROX_{i-1}^{p'})$$
$$\leq d'' \cdot \max_{k=1}^{d''} v_{p'}(\{\hat{j}_k\} \cup (Dep_{p'}^+(\hat{j}_k) \setminus \bigcup_{p \in P} APPROX_{i-1}^p) \mid$$
$$APPROX_{i-1}^{p'})$$
$$\leq d'' \cdot v_{p^*}(j_1, \ldots, j_{d'} \mid APPROX_{i-1}^{p^*})$$
$$= d'' \cdot \left(v_{p^*}(APPROX_i^{p^*}) - v_{p^*}(APPROX_{i-1}^{p^*})\right)$$

where, the first equality follows by definitions and by observing that for any player $p \neq p^*$, $APPROX_{i-1}^p = APPROX_i^p$; the second by definitions. The first inequality is trivial; the second follows by monotonicity; the third by submodularity; the fourth by line 5 of Algorithm 3.1. The last equality follows by definitions. Since there are only $d' \leq d+1$ items allocated, and since for any player $p \notin P' \cup \{p^*\}$, $HYBRID_i^p = HYBRID_{i-1}^p$, we get,

$$(d+1)(v_{p^*}(APPROX_i^{p^*}) - v_{p^*}(APPROX_{i-1}^{p^*}))$$
$$\geq \sum_{p \in P \setminus \{p^*\}} (v_p(OPT_{i-1}^p \mid APPROX_{i-1}^p)$$
$$- v_p(OPT_i^p \mid APPROX_i^p)) \ . \qquad (1)$$

For player p^*, we have by monotonicity $v_{p^*}(HYBRID_i^{p*}) \geq v_{p^*}(HYBRID_{i-1}^{p*})$. Hence,

$$v_{p^*}(OPT_{i-1}^{p^*} \mid APPROX_{i-1}^{p^*}) + v_{p^*}(APPROX_{i-1}^{p^*})$$
$$\leq v_{p^*}(OPT_i^{p^*} \mid APPROX_i^{p^*}) + v_{p^*}(APPROX_i^{p^*})$$

and then,

$$v_{p^*}(OPT_{i-1}^{p^*} \mid APPROX_{i-1}^{p^*}) - v_{p^*}(OPT_i^{p^*} \mid APPROX_i^{p^*})$$
$$\leq v_{p^*}(APPROX_i^{p^*}) - v_{p^*}(APPROX_{i-1}^{p^*}) \ .$$

This and (1) prove Lemma 1. □

We use Lemma 1 to complete the proof of Theorem 2. Let x_i be the profit of Algorithm 3.1 at iteration i. Then, $\mathsf{approx} = \sum_{i=1}^t x_i$ and by Lemma 1, it is also true that $\mathsf{approx} \geq \mathsf{opt} - \sum_{i=1}^t (d+2) \cdot x_i + \sum_{i=1}^t x_i$. Therefore, $(d+2) \cdot \mathsf{approx} \geq \mathsf{opt}$. This proves Theorem 2. □

3.2 A tight example

The following example shows Algorithm 3.1 may return a solution with value arbitrarily close to $\frac{1}{d+2}$, which matches the upper bound we proved in Theorem 2.

EXAMPLE 1. *Let $\mathcal{I}(P, M, v)$ be an instance of the welfare maximization problem with players $P = \{1, 2\}$, items $M = \{j, j_1, \ldots, j_d, j'\}$ and valuation functions v_1 as in the hypergraph representation shown in Figure 1 below and $v_2(S) = |S \setminus \{j'\}|$, for any $S \subseteq M$. It is easy to observe the optimal solution gives all the items except j' to player 2 and j' to player 1. The value of this solution is $d+2$. On the other hand, Algorithm 3.1 gives all the items except j' to player 1, and gives j' to an arbitrary player. This solution has value of only $1 + d \cdot \varepsilon$, which tends to 1 as ε decreases.*

Figure 1: Valuation function of player 1

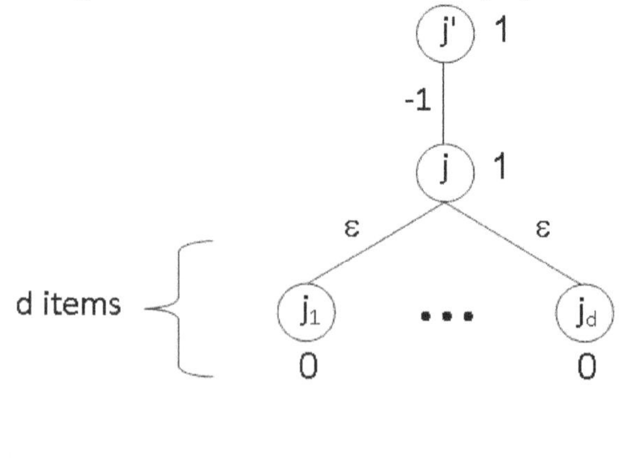

4. APPROXIMATION GUARANTEE LINEAR IN DEPENDENCY DEGREE

We discuss two possible alternatives for proving Theorem 3. One is adapting Algorithm 3.1, as we briefly discuss in this section and the other is presented in Appendix B. We sketch a possible adaptation of Algorithm 3.1. Recall that Algorithm 3.1 does the following in each iteration: for each player and item, it calculates the marginal value of the item and all its unallocated supermodular dependencies with respect to the allocated items of the player. A player and items with maximum value are selected. The modification here is twofold. Firstly, for each player and item, one considers not only the subset of *all* unallocated dependencies of the item, but *any possible subset* of unallocated dependencies. Secondly, one does not consider the marginal value of an item *together with its dependencies* with respect to the previously allocated items, but *only of the item*, with respect to the subset of dependencies under consideration and the previously allocated items, together. It can be shown that the "damage" for any player, caused by an allocation of a single item to another player, is bounded by the "profit" of the iteration "damaging" it, and also (unlike the case of supermodular dependency) that the player getting the allocation has no "damage" at all in future iterations.

The other alternative, fully presented in Appendix B, is designing a different greedy algorithm. This algorithm has the somewhat surprising property that when considering which items to add to a player, it completely ignores the items that the player already has (despite the fact that these items determine the marginal values for new items).

5. ACKNOWLEDGEMENTS

This research was supported by The Israel Science Foundation (grant No. 621/12).

6. REFERENCES

[1] I. Abraham, M. Babaioff, S. Dughmi, and T. Roughgarden. Combinatorial auctions with restricted complements. In *EC*, 2012.

[2] P. Berman. A $d/2$ approximation for maximum weight independent set in d-claw free graphs. *Nordic Journal of Computing*, 7:178–184, 2000. Preliminary version in SWAT'00.

[3] L. Blumrosen and N. Nisan. On the computational power of demand queries. *SIAM Journal on Computing*, 39:1372–1391, 2009.

[4] Y. Chevaleyre, U. Endriss, S. Estivie, and N. Maudet. Multiagent resource allocation in k-additive domains: preference representation and complexity. *Annals of Operations Research*, 163:49–62, 2008.

[5] V. Conitzer, T. Sandholm, and P. Santi. Combinatorial auctions with k-wise dependent valuations. In *AAAI*, pages 248–254, 2005.

[6] S. Dobzinski, N. Nisan, and M. Schapira. Approximation algorithms for combinatorial auctions with complement-free bidders. *Mathematics of Operations Research*, 35:1–13, 2010. Preliminary version in STOC'05.

[7] J. Edmonds. Maximum matching and a polyhedron with 0, 1-vertices. *Journal of Research of the National Bureau of Standards*, 69:125–130, 1965.

[8] U. Feige. On maximizing welfare when utility functions are subadditive. *SIAM Journal on Computing*, 39:122–142, 2009. Preliminary version in STOC'06.

[9] U. Feige and J. Vondrák. Approximation algorithms for allocation problems: Improving the factor of $1 - 1/e$. In *FOCS*, pages 667–676, 2006.

[10] M. L. Fisher, G. L. Nemhauser, and L. A. Wolsey. An analysis of approximations for maximizing submodular set functions - II. *Mathematical Programming Study*, 8:73–87, 1978.

[11] H. N. Gabow. *Implementation of algorithms for maximum matching on nonbipartite graphs*. PhD thesis, Stanford University, 1974.

[12] Z. Galil. Efficient algorithms for finding maximal matching in graphs. Technical report, Columbia University, New York, 1983.

[13] Z. Galil, S. Micali, and H. N. Gabow. An $O(EV \log V)$ algorithm for finding a maximal weighted matching in general graphs. *SIAM Journal on Computing*, 15:120–130, 1986.

[14] E. Hazan, S. Safra, and O. Schwartz. On the complexity of approximating k-set packing. *Computational Complexity*, 15:20–39, 2006.

[15] B. Lehmann, D. J. Lehmann, and N. Nisan. Combinatorial auctions with decreasing marginal utilities. *Games and Economic Behavior*, 55:270–296, 2006. Preliminary version in EC'2001.

[16] E. Petrank. The hardness of approximation: Gap location. *Computational Complexity*, 4:133–157, 1994.

[17] M. Schapira S. Dobzinski. An improved approximation algorithm for combinatorial auctions with submodular bidders. In *SODA*, pages 1064–1073, 2006.

[18] J. Vondrák. Optimal approximation for the submodular welfare problem in the value oracle model. In *STOC*, pages 67–74, 2008.

APPENDIX

A. SYMMETRY OF DEPENDENCY RELATIONS

LEMMA 2 (SYMMETRY). *Let $p \in P$ and let $j_1, j_2 \in M$ be such that $j_1 \rightarrow_p j_2$. Then $j_2 \rightarrow_p j_1$. In other words, the relation '$\rightarrow_p$' is symmetric.*

Note that the same is true for the relation $\rightarrow^+$ and that the proof is exactly the same.

PROOF. Let S be such that $j_1 \xrightarrow{S} j_2$. We show that

$$j_2 \xrightarrow{S \setminus \{j_2\} \cup \{j_1\}} j_1 .$$

From Definition 5, on one hand,

$$v(\{j_1\} \cup S) = v(j_1 \mid S) + v(j_2 \mid S \setminus \{j_2\}) + v(S \setminus \{j_2\}) ,$$

and on the other hand,

$$v(\{j_1\} \cup S) = \\ v(j_2 \mid S \setminus \{j_2\} \cup \{j_1\}) + \\ v(j_1 \mid S \setminus \{j_2\}) + v(S \setminus \{j_2\}) .$$

By subtracting $v(S \setminus \{j_2\})$, we get:

$$v(j_1 \mid S) + v(j_2 \mid S \setminus \{j_2\}) = v(j_2 \mid S \setminus \{j_2\} \cup \{j_1\}) + v(j_1 \mid S \setminus \{j_2\}) \ .$$

Since $j_1 \xrightarrow{S} j_2$ means $v(j_1 \mid S) \neq v(j_1 \mid S \setminus \{j_2\})$, we get $v(j_2 \mid S \setminus \{j_2\}) \neq v(j_2 \mid S \setminus \{j_2\} \cup \{j_1\})$. The latter is exactly the definition of $j_2 \xrightarrow{S \setminus \{j_2\} \cup \{j_1\}} j_1$, as desired. □

B. A GREEDY $\frac{1}{d+1}$-APPROXIMATION ALGORITHM FOR DEPENDENCY DEGREE AT MOST d

In this appendix we prove Theorem 3.

B.1 The algorithm

The algorithm is Algorithm B.1.

Algorithm B.1 Greedily Approximate Welfare Maximization with Guarantee Linear in Dependency Degree

Input: An instance $\mathcal{I}(P, M, v)$ of the welfare maximization problem, a value queries oracle and a dependency graph for each of the valuation functions.

Output: A solution with approximation guarantee $\frac{1}{d+1}$, where d is the dependency degree of $\mathcal{I}$.

```
1: Unallocated ← M, Approx ← ∅
2: while Unallocated ≠ ∅ do
3:   MaxMarginalUtility ← −1
4:   for all j ∈ Unallocated, p ∈ P, S' ⊆ (Dep_p(j) ∩ Unallocated) do
5:     if v_p(j | S') > MaxMarginalUtility then
6:       MaxMarginalUtility ← v_p(j | S')
7:       BestAllocation ← ({j} ∪ S' ↦ p)
8:       WinningPlayer ← p, AllocatedItem ← j, AllocatedOptimalDependencies ← S'
9:     end if
10:  end for
11:  Approx ← Approx ∪ BestAllocation
12:  Unallocated ← Unallocated \ (AllocatedItem ∪ AllocatedOptimalDependencies)
13:  Unallocated ← Unallocated \ Dep_WinningPlayer(AllocatedItem) {Discard also unallocated dependencies of j}
14: end while
```

Intuitively, Algorithm B.1 promises at each iteration that the most possibly contributing item will have its full contribution in the approximated solution. Thus, any mislocated item in an optimal solution cannot "damage" it in more than the benefit of the iteration "damaging" it. We conclude the approximation guarantee by observing no more than $d+1$ items are allocated at each iteration.

Few remarks are in place.

REMARK 1. *Algorithm B.1 does not look at all at the value of already allocated items (neither at new inspected items relatively to them nor at the whole sub-allocation). Note that an approach looking only at the marginal value with respect to already allocated items without looking on "forward" dependencies does not work.*[6]

[6]For example, we may have two items and two players, where the first player has set function $f(S) = |S|$ and the second has set function giving ∞ to both items together and 0 otherwise. An algorithm that looks only "backward" will allocate both items to player 1 and gain value 2 where an optimal solution has value ∞.

REMARK 2. *Algorithm B.1 discards unallocated dependencies (at line 13). This is to ensure any selected item will have its inspected marginal value. In other words, we ensure that the only dependencies of an item at the rest of the solution (i.e. the unallocated part) will be its optimal dependencies, as inspected at lines 4-10. Of course, because of monotonicity, we may add the "discarded" items to any player we wish (for example to the player we allocated to the rest or each item to its best possibility, in any order). The tight example we will show is tight also for any of these possibilities.*

PROOF OF THEOREM 3. Let OPT be an optimal solution with value opt and let $APPROX$ be an output of Algorithm B.1 with value approx. Let t be the number of iterations of the "while" loop at line 2 of the run created $APPROX$. We layer opt and approx by writing both of them by iterations of Algorithm B.1.

$$\mathsf{opt} = \sum_{i=1}^{t}\sum_{k=1}^{d+1} v_{p_{opt}(i,k)}\Big(j_{i,k} \mid OPT_{p_{opt}(i,k)} \setminus \bigcup_{i'=1}^{i-1}\bigcup_{k'=1}^{d+1}\{j_{i',k'}\} \setminus \bigcup_{k'=1}^{k}\{j_{i,k'}\}\Big) \quad (2)$$

$$\mathsf{approx} = \sum_{i=1}^{t}\sum_{k=1}^{d+1} v_{p_{app}(i)}\Big(j_{i,k} \mid APPROX_{p_{app}(i)} \setminus \bigcup_{i'=1}^{i-1}\bigcup_{k'=1}^{d+1}\{j_{i',k'}\} \setminus \bigcup_{k'=1}^{k}\{j_{i,k'}\}\Big) \quad (3)$$

where:

- $j_{i,k}$ is the kth item allocated at iteration i, where $j_{i,1}$ is the final item assigned at line 7 of this iteration, and the rest are ordered arbitrarily.
- $p_{opt}(i,k)$ is the player to whom the kth item of iteration i is allocated in OPT.
- $p_{app}(i)$ is the player to whom all the items of iteration i are allocated in $APPROX$ (all items of any iteration of Algorithm B.1 are allocated to the same player).

Note that for simplicity, equations are written assuming exactly $d+1$ items are allocated at each iteration. The proof is correct also without this assumption.

Let $i \in [1..t]$ and let $Unallocated_i$ be the items of $Unallocated$ at line 4 of Algorithm B.1 at iteration i. Then, since $M = \bigcup_{p=1}^{n}(OPT_p) = \bigcup_{p=1}^{n}(APPROX_p)$, we have:

$$Unallocated_i = \bigcup_{p=1}^{n}\Big(OPT_p \setminus \bigcup_{i'=1}^{i-1}\bigcup_{k'=1}^{d+1}\{j_{i',k'}\}\Big) = \bigcup_{p=1}^{n}\Big(APPROX_p \setminus \bigcup_{i'=1}^{i-1}\bigcup_{k'=1}^{d+1}\{j_{i',k'}\}\Big)$$

Therefore, for all $i \in [1..t]$, $k \in [1..d+1]$,

$$\bigcup_{p=1}^{n} \left(OPT_p \setminus \bigcup_{i'=1}^{i-1} \bigcup_{k'=1}^{d+1} \{j_{i',k'}\} \setminus \bigcup_{k'=1}^{k} \{j_{i,k'}\} \right) \subseteq Unallocated_i \; .$$

Then, by lines 4-10 and 13 of Algorithm B.1, for all $i \in [1..t]$, $k \in [1..d+1]$, $v_{p_{app}(i)}(j_{i,1} \mid APPROX_{p_{app}(i)} \setminus \bigcup_{i'=1}^{i-1} \bigcup_{k'=1}^{d+1} \{j_{i',k'}\} \setminus \{j_{i,1}\}) \geq v_{p_{opt}(i,k)}(j_{i,k} \mid OPT_{p_{opt}(i,k)} \setminus \bigcup_{i'=1}^{i-1} \bigcup_{k'=1}^{d+1} \{j_{i',k'}\} \setminus \bigcup_{k'=1}^{k} \{j_{i,k'}\})$.
Therefore and by invoking (2) and (3) together with monotonicity,

$$\begin{aligned}
&(d+1) \cdot \mathsf{approx} = \\
&(d+1) \cdot \sum_{i=1}^{t} \sum_{k}^{d+1} v_{p_{app}(i)}(j_{i,k} \mid \\
&\qquad APPROX_{p_{app}(i)} \setminus \bigcup_{i'=1}^{i-1} \bigcup_{k'=1}^{d+1} \{j_{i',k'}\} \setminus \bigcup_{k'=1}^{k} \{j_{i,k'}\}) \\
&\geq (d+1) \cdot \sum_{i=1}^{t} v_{p_{app}(i)}(j_{i,1} \mid \\
&\qquad APPROX_{p_{app}(i)} \setminus \bigcup_{i'=1}^{i-1} \bigcup_{k'=1}^{d+1} \{j_{i',k'}\} \setminus \{j_{i,1}\}) \\
&\geq \sum_{i=1}^{t} \sum_{k}^{d+1} v_{p_{opt}(i,k)}(j_{i,k} \mid \\
&\qquad OPT_{p_{opt}(i,k)} \setminus \bigcup_{i'=1}^{i-1} \bigcup_{k'=1}^{d+1} \{j_{i',k'}\} \setminus \bigcup_{k'=1}^{k} \{j_{i,k'}\}) \\
&= \mathsf{opt}
\end{aligned}$$

It is easy to see the running time of Algorithm B.1 is polynomial in $|M|, |P|$ and 2^c. This proves Theorem 3. ☐

B.1.1 An example justifying "discarding" items

We demonstrate the necessity of "discarding unused dependencies" as in line 13 of Algorithm B.1. Note that another approach is to look also on already allocated items, as described in Section 4.

EXAMPLE 2. *Let $|P| = 2$. Let the set functions be as follows: The valuation function of player 1 will be as in the hypergraph representation in Figure 2. The valuation function of player 2 will be $v_2(S) = |S|$.*

Intuitively, the idea is to cause Algorithm B.1 to "ruin" a marginal value of an already allocated item, when trying to gain a maximal marginal value for another item. The middle edge with value -1 does so, without breaking monotonicity.

We analyze the approximation guarantee for this instance for Algorithm B.1 with line 13 omitted (i.e. without "discarding unused dependencies"). On the first iteration the algorithm allocates either j_1 or j_2 to player 1 with their optimal dependencies. Assume without loss of generality it is j_1. The optimal dependencies of j_1 are $j_{1,1}, \ldots, j_{1,d-1}$ and the marginal value of j_1 with these dependencies is $1 + (d-1) \cdot \varepsilon$. On the second iteration, the algorithm allocates j_2 to player 1, together with its optimal dependencies (that has not been allocated yet) $j_{2,1}, \ldots, j_{2,d-1}$. The marginal value of j_2 with respect to these dependencies is also $1 + (d-1) \cdot \varepsilon$. But now,

Figure 2: Valuation function of player 1

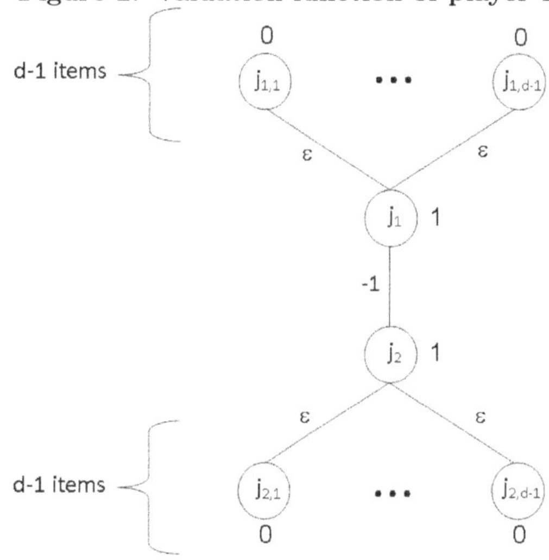

the marginal value of j_1 with respect to the rest of the items allocated to player 1 (which had not been allocated yet when it was allocated) is only $(d-1) \cdot \varepsilon$. The algorithm terminates after the second iteration with social welfare $1 + 2(d-1) \cdot \varepsilon$. On the other hand, allocating all the items to player 2 results in a social welfare of $2d$. For small enough ε the approximation guarantee is arbitrarily close to $1/2d$ which is much worse than the approximation guarantee of $1/(d+1)$ of Algorithm B.1.

Note that Algorithm B.1 (the unmodified version) does much better for this instance. It also chooses firstly j_1 (without loss of generality) with its optimal dependencies, but then does not inspect anymore any of its dependencies, including j_2. Therefore, assuming ε is small, it allocates $j_{2,1}, \ldots, j_{2,d-1}$ to player 2 and gains for them a value of $d-1$ in addition *to the marginal value* it indeed gained *for j_1. Thus, the approximated solution's total value Algorithm B.1 gains for this input is $1 + (d-1) \cdot \varepsilon + (d-1) = d + (d-1) \cdot \varepsilon$, which expresses an approximation guarantee of slightly more than $\frac{1}{2}$. Note that allocating j_2 to any of the players will do no harm (and allocating it to player 2 will even slightly help); just reinspecting it does the harm.*

B.2 A tight example

We now show the analysis of Algorithm B.1 is tight.

EXAMPLE 3. *Let $|P| = 2$ and let $|M| = m' \cdot (d+1)$ for some $m' \in \mathbb{N}$. We set an arbitrary ordering on the items and define m' subsets of items $S_1, \ldots S_{m'}$; the first set will be the first $d+1$ items, the second one will be the next $d+1$ items and so on. Let v be the following set functions for any $S \subseteq M$:*

- $v_1(S) = \sum_{i \in [1..m'],\, S_i \subseteq S} (1 + \varepsilon)$

  (meaning, $(1+\varepsilon)$ times the number of subsets S_i that are subsets of S).

- $v_2(S) = |S|$.

It is easy to see the marginal value of any item is maximized, when it is given to player 1 with all its dependen-

cies. Moreover, since at this way only whole subsets are allocated, this is the situation at any iteration of Algorithm B.1. Therefore, algorithm B.1 allocates all the items to player 1 and gains total value of $m' \cdot (1+\varepsilon)$. In contrast, the optimal solution is to allocate all the items to player 2 and to gain total value of m. Thus, the approximation guarantee for this instance is close as we with to $m/m' = 1/(d+1)$, and the analysis of Theorem 3 is indeed tight.

C. AN EXACT ALGORITHM FOR DEPENDENCY DEGREE AT MOST 1

In this appendix, we present a full reduction (Reduction C.1) of the welfare maximization problem with dependency degree at most 1 to the maximum weighted matching problem.

Reduction C.1

Input: An instance $\mathcal{I}(P, M, v)$ of the welfare maximization problem.
Output: An instance $\mathcal{I}_M(V, E, w)$ of the maximum weighted matching problem, with set of vertices V, set of undirected edges E and edge weights function w, such that each item $j \in M$ is represented by a corresponding vertex $v_j \in V$.
Reduction: For each item j, we have a vertex u_j. For each player p, we have the following. For each item j with $Dep_p(j) = \emptyset$, we have an auxiliary vertex u_j^p and an edge (u_j, u_j^p) with weight $v_p(\{j\})$, representing the possibility of allocating j to p. For each pair of items j, j', such that $j \leftrightarrow_p j'$, we have a single auxiliary vertex $u_{j,j'}^p$ and three edges: $(u_j, u_{j,j'}^p)$ with weight $v_p(\{j\})$, representing the possibility of allocating j to p without allocating j' to p; $(u_{j'}, u_{j,j'}^p)$ with weight $v_p(\{j'\})$, representing the possibility of allocating j' to p without allocating j to p; $(u_j, u_{j'})$ with weight $v_p(\{j, j'\})$, representing the possibility of allocating both j and j' to p. Note that both j and j' have no other dependencies, since the dependency degree is at most 1 and by Lemma 2. Note also that multiedges may be resolved, by choosing, without loss of generality, one edge with maximum weight for each pair of vertices.

The following observation is straightforward:

OBSERVATION 1.

- *Reduction C.1 is polynomial time computable.*
- *Every feasible solution for $\mathcal{I}_M$ induces a feasible solution for $\mathcal{I}$ with the same value, that may be computed in polynomial time.*
- *Every feasible solution for $\mathcal{I}$, induces a feasible solution for $\mathcal{I}_M$ with at least the same value.*

Therefore, we may use Reduction C.1 together with any exact polynomial time maximum weighted matching algorithm (see for example [7, 11, 12, 13]) to derive an exact polynomial time algorithm for the welfare maximization problem with dependency degree at most 1.

REMARK 3. *Note that Reduction C.1 does not work for $c > 1$. This is since we may have a player p with items j_1, j_2, j_3, such that $j_1 \leftrightarrow j_2 \leftrightarrow j_3$ (i.e. a "chain"). At this case, j_1, j_2 and j_3 may be allocated together to p, although this allocation does not induce a feasible matching.*

Reachability in Graph Timelines

Jakub Łącki
Institute of Informatics
University of Warsaw
Warsaw, Poland
j.lacki@mimuw.edu.pl

Piotr Sankowski
Institute of Informatics
University of Warsaw
Warsaw, Poland
sank@mimuw.edu.pl

ABSTRACT

In this paper we consider the problem of maintaining information about graphs with history – so called *graph timeline*. A graph timeline is a sequence of graphs $G_1, \ldots, G_t$, in which consecutive graphs are obtained from previous ones by small modifications, e.g., by adding or removing a single edge. We aim to devise algorithms that after some preprocessing are able to efficiently answer queries about the existence of paths in the entire timeline of the graph, or within some time interval. We consider two types of queries:

$\texttt{forall}(u, v, a, b)$ — query that checks if there exists a path from u to v in each of $G_a, \ldots, G_b$;

$\texttt{exists}(u, v, a, b)$ — query that checks if there exists a path from u to v in any of $G_a, \ldots, G_b$.

Our study is motivated by the recent intensive study of the evolution of graphs, and the question whether information about history can be efficiently aggregated. We show that for path queries this is, somewhat astonishingly, true. In some cases it is possible to preprocess graph timeline and answer such queries in almost optimal time.

First, we consider undirected graphs and timelines in which two consecutive graphs differ by addition or removal of a single edge. We show a randomized algorithm that requires $O(t \log t \log\log t \log n + m)$ preprocessing time and answers `forall` queries in $O(\log n \log\log t)$ time. Here, n is the number of vertices in the graph and m is the number of permanent edges, that is edges common to all graphs in the timeline. This algorithm can be derandomized at some cost in the running time. Second, we give a deterministic algorithm that needs $O(nt + m)$ preprocessing and answers `exists` queries in $O(1)$ time. Finally, for directed graphs, we consider timelines where two consecutive graphs differ by addition or removal of a set of edges incident to one vertex. In this case we, are able to propose a randomized algorithm that after $O(n^{\omega-1}t)$ preprocessing time can answer $\texttt{exists}(u, v, a, b)$ queries in $O(n)$ time and $\texttt{forall}(u, v, a, b)$ queries in $O(n + b - a)$ time.

ITCS'13, January 9–12, 2013, Berkeley, California, USA.

Categories and Subject Descriptors

G.2.2 [**Graph Theory**]: Graph algorithms; E.1 [**Data structures**]: Graphs and networks

General Terms

Algorithms, Theory

Keywords

dynamic graph algorithms; reachability; transitive closure; graph timeline

1. INTRODUCTION

In recently developed IT tools we are observing introduction of so called timelines, i.e., histories. In Apple TextEdit on OS X Lion there is no save button anymore. The system stores all versions of the file that can be scrolled through using timeline. Similarly, in Google Drive we can access the whole history of edits. This rises the question whether that kind of data can be stored and processed efficiently afterwards. Can one actually find which version of the TextEdit document contains a given word? Can we check whether some property of the document was true for a given time period? These problems can be solved by generating each version of the document explicitly and running an appropriate test. This, however, does seem to be a very inefficient solution.[1]

Here, we study the related question of maintaining a history of a graph. Our study is motivated by the ongoing study of the evolution of graphs, which is reflected by the wider and wider usage of so called historical graph snapshots (e.g., [14, 7]). This way of storing information about history of graphs has two disadvantages. First, it requires a lot of space, because each snapshot contains information about the entire graph. Second, in order to answer any type of query about the given snapshot one needs to process the whole graph. From applications point of view, it could be very useful to find more efficient solution that in the same time would use less memory. On the other hand, from theoretical point of view, it would be good to know whether the graph history can be somehow aggregated and represented in a more concise way. In this paper we concentrate on connectivity queries and show that a very efficient representation is possible. Somewhat astonishingly our representations are

[1]We note that for text documents the `exists` query can be solved efficiently – this requires a rather technical but simple modification to the very powerful technique in [1].

able not only to answer queries about single points in time, but about whole time intervals as well. We are able to answer queries regarding multiple graphs in the timeline in time almost independent on t. Such interval queries have never been considered before, and it would be very interesting to see whether more complex graph problems admit similar solutions.

We assume that we are given a graph with its history of changes, i.e., *a graph timeline*. The graph timeline G^t is a sequence of graphs $G_1, \ldots, G_t$ with the same set of vertices, where two consecutive graphs differ by addition or removal of a single edge, or of a vertex with its all incident edges. In the case of single edge changes G_{i+1} is obtained from G_i through one of the two operations:

`insert`(e) — inserts edge e into G_i, $E(G_{i+1}) = E(G_i) + e$;

`delete`(e) — deletes edge e from G_i, $E(G_{i+1}) = E(G_i) - e$.

The timeline G^t is either undirected or directed, which means that all graphs $G_1, \ldots, G_t$ are undirected or directed, respectively. We consider the following three types of queries that check if there exists a path from u to v:

`forone`(u, v, a) — in G_a;

`forall`(u, v, a, b) — in every graph $G_a, \ldots, G_b$;

`exists`(u, v, a, b) — in some graph $G_a, \ldots, G_b$.

Note that a `forone` query is a special case of both other queries.

Our aim is to devise an algorithm that uses as little time as possible to preprocess the timeline G^t and then answer the above queries. For example, a possible solution to the `forone` problem in undirected graphs is to compute connected components in every G_i and store this information. This requires $O(n^2t + m)$ preprocessing time and $O(nt)$ memory, but allows to respond to queries in $O(1)$ time. We show, however, that more efficient solutions are possible. In Section 3, we introduce a data structure called *connectivity history tree* (CHT) that after $O(t \log t \log\log t \log n + m)$ preprocessing time answers `forone` queries in $O(\log n \log\log t)$ time. In comparison to the straightforward solution the preprocessing time is improved by almost a linear factor, at a moderate cost of introducing nearly logarithmic time queries. Actually, the CHT is just a starting point and is a basis for devising a more powerful algorithm. While `forone` queries can be answered slightly faster by using different techniques, we describe how to extend the data structure, so that it responds to `forall` queries in the same time bounds (Section 4). We show a randomized algorithm that requires $O(t \log t \log\log t \log n + m)$ preprocessing time and answers queries in $O(\log n \log\log t)$ time. Hence, the ability to answer much more general interval queries comes at almost no cost. There is also a slightly slower, deterministic variant of the algorithm. For the resulting running times check Theorem 4.

Next, in Section 5, we consider `exists`(u, v, i, j) query in undirected graphs and give a deterministic algorithm that needs $O(nt)$ preprocessing time, but answers queries in constant time. Finally, in Section 6, we consider directed graphs. In this case, we allow slightly stronger updates – G_{i+1} can be obtained from G_i by adding or removing an arbitrary number of edges incident to one vertex. We propose a randomized algorithm that after $O(n^{\omega-1}t)$ preprocessing time[2] is able to answer `exists`(u, v, a, b) queries in $O(n)$ time and `forall`(u, v, a, b) queries in $O(n+b-a)$ time. The algorithm requires $O(nt)$ space. It is based on the dynamic matrix inverse algorithm with lookahead. An algorithm for this problem in the case of column updates was given in [16]. For our application we need to substantially extend it to rank-one updates – see Appendix B.

Our study is motivated by practical applications, and we believe that some of our algorithms might be of practical importance. For example, the `forall` algorithm in undirected graph is optimal up to logarithmic factors. Hence, the possibility of answering very powerful queries that can even concern the whole history of the graph is not very costly. Similarly, in directed graphs one change can alter the state of $\Omega(n)$ edges, so remembering the history of changes requires $\Omega(nt)$ memory. This bound matches the memory used by our algorithm, although the preprocessing time needs to be higher.

Related work.

Our study is related to dynamic algorithms, i.e., algorithms that maintain information about changing graphs and answer queries regarding the most recent version of the graph. However, in the case of dynamic graphs it seems that no existing algorithm for connectivity or reachability[3] is able to answer queries about the past. One can try to overcome this problem by running a dynamic algorithm and storing its full state after each update. This can be done with only a slight increase in the running time, by using persistent array data structure, which we later descrbie. If we use persistent array data structure of Kopelovitz[12] and the currently fastest known dynamic algorithm for connectivity [17], we obtain an algorithm that can answer `forone` queries in $O(\log n \log\log t / \log\log n)$ time and requires both $O(t \log\log t \log n (\log\log n)^3)$ space and preprocessing time. In contrast, our algorithms are able to answer more powerful `forall` queries in almost the same time bound.

On the other hand, in the case of directed graphs, using $O(n^2)$ time algorithms for reachability [4, 15] we can preprocess the timeline in $O(n^2t)$ time, computing the transitive closure matrix for each time moment in $O(n^2t)$ total space. This allows to answer `forone` queries in constant time. This solution requires more space and preprocessing time than ours, and it gives no way to handle `forall` and `exists` queries other than by executing a sequence of `forone` queries.

There is some also relation of our algorithms to offline dynamic algorithms, where both the sequence of changes and queries is known to the algorithm. Eppstein [6] has shown an algorithm that, given a sequence of updates in a weighted undirected graph, computes the minimum spanning tree for the graph after each update. The algorithm uses only $O(\log n)$ time to process each update operation. Its output is the sequence of changes in the minimum spanning tree. This can be combined with a data structure for dynamic trees (e.g. [9]) to obtain a data structure able to answer `forone` queries in a graph timeline in $O(\log n)$ time after preprocessing in $O(m + t \log n)$.

[2] $O(n^{\omega})$ is the time needed to multiply two $n \times n$ matrices.

[3] Connectivity is usually used to refer to reachability problem in undirected graphs.

2. PRELIMINARIES

Persistence.

A data structure is called *persistent* if the history of its changes is maintained and previous versions can be accessed for reading. A data structure is *fully persistent* if a new version can be created by altering any of the existing versions, not necessarily the most recent one. In this paper, we use *fully persistent arrays.* Such a data structure provides two operations:

- $\texttt{read}(A, i)$ – return the value of the i-th cell of array A,
- $\texttt{write}(A, i, x)$ – write x to the i-th cell of array A and return the newly created array (A remains unchanged).

Dietz [5] has described an algorithm that performs `write` operations in $O(\log\log c)$ amortized time and `read` operations in $O(\log\log c)$ worst-case time, where c is the upper bound both on the length of the array, as well as the number of operations performed on it. The running time of both operations was slightly improved by Kopelowitz [12] to $O(\log\log c)$ expected time.

Disjoint set data structure.

A *disjoint-set data structure* (DSDS) maintains a partition of a given set of size n into nonoverlapping subsets. Each of the subsets has one distinguished element called a *representative.* Initially every element is in a separate subset. The data structure supports the following two operations: $\texttt{find}(x)$ – return the representative of the set containing x; $\texttt{union}(x, y)$ – merge the sets, whose representatives are x and y.

We use union find algorithm that maintains a forest representing disjoint sets. For every element we store a pointer to its parent. By following these parent pointers we eventually reach the representative. Moreover, for each representative, we also store the size of its subtree (the number of elements in its set). Hence, a DSDS can be maintained in two arrays of length n. One array contains the parent pointers and the other one maintains the sizes. In some of our algorithms, these we will use fully persistent arrays to maintain them.

Merging two sets consists in making one representative a child of the other. We use *union by size* rule – when two sets are merged, the representative of the larger set becomes the representative of the union. However, we do not use path compression technique.[4] This guarantees that only a constant number of cells are changed after each operation, which we later make use of. As a result each `find` operation runs in $O(\log n)$ worst-case time, whereas a `union` operation in $O(1)$ worst-case time.

String hashing.

We use the *string hashing scheme* proposed by Rabin and Karp [11] which guarantees that w.h.p. two different strings are assigned different hashes. We heavily exploit the following property of hashes. Let x and y be two strings and let $h(z)$ denote the hash of a string z. Given any two of $h(x)$, $h(y)$ and $h(xy)$, the third one can be computed in constant time. Moreover, we assume that given any letter a, we can compute hash of a^n in constant time. All these operations require preprocessing that is linear in the length of the longest string that is represented with a hash.

[4]For the details of these techniques we refer the reader to [3].

Segment tree.

Let n be a power of 2. A *segment tree* over $[1, n]$ is a complete binary tree with n leaves numbered from left to right with integers from 1 to n. The ancestor of leaves $a, a+1, \ldots, b$, denoted by $v_{a\ldots b}$, aggregates information about an interval $[a, b]$. Each such interval (i.e. having a node associated with it) is called an *elementary interval.* We use the following well-known property of segment trees.

LEMMA 1. *Every interval $[a,b]$, where $1 \leq a \leq b \leq n$, can be partitioned in a unique way into a minimal number of $O(\log n)$ nonoverlapping elementary intervals of a segment tree over $[1, n]$.*

The decomposition can be obtained in a greedy way, e.g. by first finding the longest elementary interval contained in $[a, b]$ (it is uniquely defined) and then recursively decomposing the rest of $[a, b]$.

Graph timeline.

An *intersection* of two graphs $G_1 = (V, E_1)$ and $G_2 = (V, E_2)$ is a graph $G_1 \cap G_2 = (V, E_1 \cap E_2)$. Let $G^t = G_1, \ldots, G_t$ be a graph timeline. By m we denote the number of *permanent* edges, that is the edges from $G_1 \cap G_2 \cap \ldots \cap G_t$. There are $O(t)$ edges which are not permanent – we call them *temporary* edges. We say that an edge e is *alive* in the interval $[a, b]$ if e belongs to all of $E_a, E_{a+1}, \ldots, E_b$. In the following, we assume that for every edge there exists a maximal interval in which it is alive. If an edge connecting two vertices is removed and an identical edge is added later, we consider these two edges different objects.

3. CONNECTIVITY HISTORY TREE

We begin by describing a data structure that supports `forone` queries in undirected graphs. In the following section we will show how to extend it support interval queries as well.

DEFINITION 1. *Let t be a power of 2 and let G^t be graph timeline. A* connectivity history tree *(CHT) for G^t is a is a complete binary tree with t leaves numbered $1, 2, \ldots, t$ from left to right. Each node of the CHT contains a DSDS. A DSDS in node $v_{a\ldots b}$ represents connected components of $G_a \cap G_{a+1} \cap \ldots \cap G_b$.*

LEMMA 2. *The connectivity history tree can be computed in $O(m + t\log t\log\log t\log n)$ time. It uses $O(n + t\log t)$ space.*

PROOF. Observe that we can contract all permanent edges, as the vertices incident with them are connected in every graph in the timeline. To do this, we find the connected components determined by permanent edges, contract each such component to a single vertex and update the endpoints of temporary edges accordingly. These operations require $O(m+t)$ time. To simplify presentation, in the following we assume that the graph contains no permanent edges.

In order to compute the DSDS in every node of the tree, we make the DSDS *fully persistent.* As mentioned before, every DSDS consists of two arrays of length n. Hence, we can use the fully persistent array data structure to store these

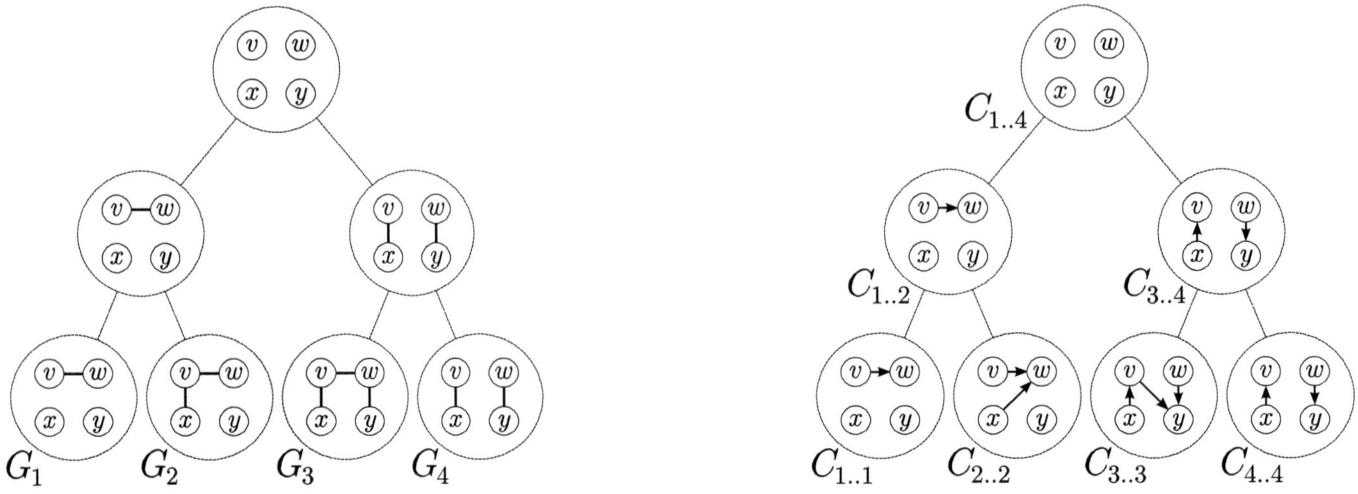

Figure 1: CHT of an example graph timeline (on the right) and the graphs represented by the DSDS in each node of the tree (on the left).

two arrays. This results in $O(\log\log t)$ amortized time overhead write operation and $O(\log\log t)$ worst-case time overhead on every read operation. Consequently, `find` operation requires $O(\log n \log\log t)$ time, whereas a union operation – $O(\log\log t)$ amortized time.[5]

Since there are now no permanent edges, the root of the CHT should contain a DSDS for a graph with no edges. The DSDS in any other node is computed from the structure stored in its parent. Assume that $C_{a\ldots b}$, that is the DSDS in node $v_{a\ldots b}$, has already been computed. We now compute the structures for its two immediate children, $C_{a\ldots(a+b-1)/2}$ and $C_{(a+b+1)/2\ldots b}$. Both these structures are obtained from $C_{a\ldots b}$ by adding some edges. In particular, to obtain the child $C_{a\ldots(a+b-1)/2}$, we add edges that are alive in $[a,(a+b-1)/2]$ (or in its super set), but are not alive in $[a,b]$.

The total number of these additions during the construction of the tree is bounded by $O(t\log t)$. To prove this, let us fix a temporary edge e. We show that it is added $O(\log t)$ times. Let $[l,r]$ be the maximal interval, in which e is alive. From Lemma 1 it follows that $[l,r]$ can be decomposed into $O(\log t)$ nonoverlapping elementary intervals. Observe that the nodes, where we add edge e during the construction of a DSDS, are exactly the nodes from the decomposition of $[l,r]$ into elementary intervals, so we conclude that there are $O(\log t)$ additions for any temporary edge. Each of the edge insertions requires $O(\log n\log\log t)$ amortized time. The total time of building the connectivity history tree is $O(m + t\log t\log\log t\log n)$.

We need $O(n)$ space to map the original endpoints of permament edges into vertices resulting from contracting them. After that, we perform $O(t\log t)$ write operations on a fully persistent array of length $O(n)$. As a result, the algorithm requires $O(n + t\log t)$ space. ☐

Observe that CHT contains union-find data structure for every graph in the timeline, so the CHT can answer `forone` queries in $O(\log n\log\log t)$ time. This construction can be generalized. We can build a similar tree, using any incremental, fully persistent dynamic data structure for graphs.

THEOREM 1. *Let G^t be a graph timeline. Assume that there exists an fully persistent incremental data structure that maintains some property of a graph, whose worst-case update time is $f(n,m)$ and which can be constructed for a given graph in $g(m,n)$ time. Then we can compute this data structure for every graph in the timeline in $O(g(m,n) + (t\log t)f(n,m))$ time.*

Note that it suffices to use an *incremental* data structure, although the timeline may include edge deletions. An easy consequence of this theorem an algorithm computing all-pairs distance matrices for all graphs in a timeline.

THEOREM 2. *Let G^t be a graph timeline of a directed graph and $t \geq \frac{n}{\log n}$. Then we can compute all-pairs distances matrices for every graph in G^t in $O(tn^2\log n)$ time.*

PROOF. Assume that we are given an all-pairs distance matrix A of a directed graph. After an edge uv of length d is inserted to this graph, the matrix can be updated in $\Theta(n^2)$ time, by simply setting $A[x,y] := \min(A[x,y], A[x,u] + d + A[v,y])$ for all pairs of vertices x,y. This data structure can be considered fully persistent, as the $\Theta(n^2)$ time suffices to copy the entire matrix. The distance matrix can also be constructed from scratch in $O(n^3)$ time, by using Floyd-Warshall algorithm [8].

We now split the timeline into blocks of $\frac{n}{\log n}$ consecutive graphs (with the last block possibly being smaller) and use the above Theorem for each block. The overall running time is $O(\frac{t\log n}{n}(n^3 + \frac{n}{\log n}\log(\frac{n}{\log n})n^2)) = O(tn^2\log n)$. ☐

It is also possible to compute all-pairs distances for all graphs in a timeline by using a dynamic algorithm that maintains the distance matrix. The fastest algorithm is due to Thorup [18] and handles each update in $O(n^2(\log n + \log^2\frac{m+n}{n}))$ time, which is equal to $O(n^2\log^2 n)$, if $m = \Omega(n^\alpha)$, for some constant $\alpha > 1$. In this case, our algorithm improves the time needed to compute one distance from $O(\log^2 n)$ to $O(\log n)$.

[5]More efficient fully persistent DSDS has been described by Italiano and Sarnak [10], but in the following we use some additional properties of the simple union-find algorithm.

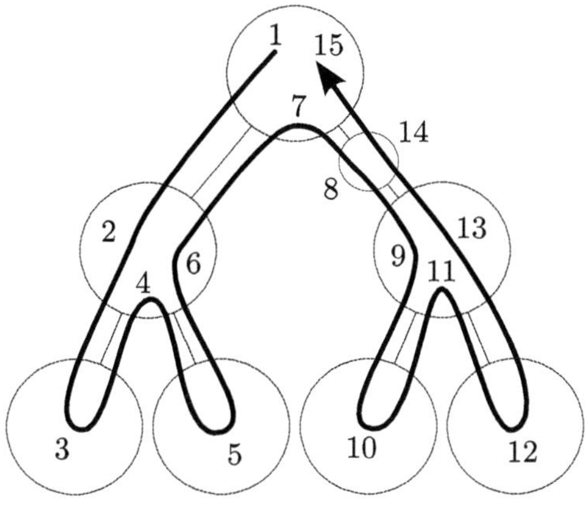

Figure 2: The order in which we visit the DSDSs in the CHT. In order to compute $C_{3...4}$ from $C_{1...4}$ two edges are added to the DSDS. The DSDS obtained by adding one edge is stored and associated with an edge between $v_{1...4}$ and $v_{3...4}$.

4. UNDIRECTED GRAPHS: FORALL QUERIES

In this section, we describe an algorithm that can handle `forall` queries efficiently after initial preprocessing. The first step in the algorithm consists in computing the CHT. However, in this case a slightly bigger data structure is required. Observe that when building the CHT, we add edges to $C_{a...b}$ in order to compute, e.g., $C_{a...(a+b-1)/2}$. Because the DSDS is fully persistent, after each such operation, we obtain a new version of the DSDS. In this algorithm, we use all these intermediate versions, so they are stored and associated with the edge connecting $v_{a...b}$ and $v_{a...(a+b-1)/2}$. Hence, the CHT contains $O(t \log t)$ incremental DSDSs that occupy $O(t \log t)$ total space. In particular it contains a DSDS $C_{i...i}$ that corresponds to G_i. In the following we denote it by C_i.

Let us denote by $p_i[x]$ an array in C_i that maps a vertex x to its parent (immediate ancestor) in C_i. If x is a representative, then $p_i[x] = x$. Moreover, we denote the representative of a vertex x in C_i by $r_i[x]$. Note that we use array notation, although the values $r_i[\cdot]$ are not stored explicitly in a DSDS.

In order to answer a $\texttt{forall}(x, y, a, b)$ query, we check whether the sequences $r_a[x] \dots r_b[x]$ and $r_a[y] \dots r_b[y]$ are equal. In the algorithm this is achieved by computing and comparing hashes of these sequences. The remaining part of this section gives the details of how to compute these hashes.

Preprocessing.

Consider an inorder (i.e., depth-first left-to-right) traversal of the CHT (see Figure 2). Each edge of the tree is traversed exactly twice, whereas an inner node is visited three times: first, when we entering from its parent, second, after visiting its left subtree and the last time after visiting its right subtree. Altogether, during the traversal, we visit each of the $O(t \log t)$ DSDSs from the tree a constant number of times. The structures associated with the edges of the CHT that we mentioned in the beginning of this section are visited in the order they were created when going down, and in reverse order, when going up.

Let $\tilde{G}_1, \tilde{G}_2, \dots, \tilde{G}_T$ denote the sequence of $T = O(t \log t)$ graphs that are represented by the DSDSs we encounter. Note that $\tilde{G}_{i+1}$ can be obtained from $\tilde{G}_i$ by adding or removing a single edge and that $G_1, G_2, \dots, G_t$ is a subsequence of $\tilde{G}_1, \tilde{G}_2, \dots, \tilde{G}_T$ (in the example shown in Figure 2 we have $G_1 = \tilde{G}_3$, $G_2 = \tilde{G}_5$, $G_3 = \tilde{G}_{10}$ and $G_4 = \tilde{G}_{12}$). Moreover, let $\tilde{C}_1, \tilde{C}_2, \dots, \tilde{C}_T$ be the sequence of the DSDSs, that we encounter during the traversal. By $\tilde{p}_i$ we denote the parent array in $\tilde{C}_i$ and by $\tilde{r}_i[x]$ – the representative of a vertex x in $\tilde{C}_i$.

Given the structures $\tilde{C}_1, \dots, \tilde{C}_T$, we can compute the sequences $\tilde{r}_i[x]$ and their hashes. However, our goal is a bit different, as we need to compute hashes of some fragments of $r_i[x]$, which is a *subsequence* of $\tilde{r}_i[x]$. Later on we show how to modify the algorithm for computing hashes over $\tilde{r}_i[x]$, so that it computes hashes of fragments of $r_i[x]$. It is essentially enough to skip elements of $\tilde{r}_i[x]$ that do not belong to $r_i[x]$. Thus, we now only use $\tilde{C}_1, \dots, \tilde{C}_T$ and show how to compute hashes of arbitrary fragments of $\tilde{r}_1[x], \dots, \tilde{r}_T[x]$.

The main reason for using $\tilde{C}_1, \dots, \tilde{C}_T$ is that each two consecutive structures are very similar to each other – they correspond to graphs that differ by a single edge. We say that i is a *critical moment* for x if $\tilde{p}_i[x] \neq \tilde{p}_{i+1}[x]$ or $i = 0$. Observe that $\tilde{C}_{i+1}$ is obtained from $\tilde{C}_i$ by performing or undoing a single union operation. This implies that $\tilde{p}_i[x]$ and $\tilde{p}_{i+1}[x]$ differ only in a single entry and for each $i \neq 0$ there is at most one critical moment. Thanks to that, it is possible to store all arrays $\tilde{p}_i[x]$ in a compact way: for each x we store a sorted list of critical moments. In the end, after $O(n + t \log t)$ preprocessing time, *all* sequences $\tilde{p}_i[x]$ are stored implicitly, in $O(n + t \log t)$ total space.

Let us now describe the process of computing hashes. In order to be able to obtain hashes of some subwords of $\tilde{r}_1[x] \dots \tilde{r}_T[x]$, we precompute selected prefix hashes. A *prefix hash* of vertex x of length k, denoted by $h(x, k)$, is a hash of $\tilde{r}_1[x] \dots \tilde{r}_k[x]$. Using the scheme from [11], given the hashes of $\tilde{r}_1[x] \dots \tilde{r}_{a-1}[x]$ and $\tilde{r}_1[x] \dots \tilde{r}_b[x]$, we can obtain the hash of $\tilde{r}_a[x] \dots \tilde{r}_b[x]$ in constant time.

The prefix hashes $h(x, k)$ are computed only for each critical moment k of vertex x. To perform the computation, we use the following three lemmas. We say that a vertex x is a root in some $\tilde{C}_k$ if x is a representative of its set in $\tilde{C}_k$ – the name comes from the fact that x is a root in the forest maintained in $\tilde{C}_k$.

The first lemma follows from the fact that a union operation affects only roots of two trees.

LEMMA 3. *Let $k > 0$ be a critical moment for a vertex x. Then $\tilde{p}_k[x]$ is a root in $\tilde{C}_k$. Moreover, x is a root in $\tilde{C}_k$ iff it is* not *a root in $\tilde{C}_{k+1}$.*

PROOF. Our goal is to prove that x is either a root in $\tilde{C}_k$ or a direct descendant of the root. Observe that the only change that can take place in a DSDS during a union operation is an insertion of a single edge that connects a representative to some other representative. In the sequence $\tilde{C}_1, \dots, \tilde{C}_T$, $\tilde{C}_{i+1}$ is obtained from $\tilde{C}_i$ by performing or undoing a single union operation. This means that if k is a critical moment ($\tilde{p}_k[x] \neq \tilde{p}_{k+1}[x]$) for x, then either: x is a root in $\tilde{C}_k$ and it gets connected to some other root in $\tilde{C}_{k+1}$ (so x is no longer a root in $\tilde{C}_{k+1}$); or x is a direct descendant of a root in $\tilde{C}_k$, and it becomes a root in $\tilde{C}_{k+1}$. In both cases $\tilde{p}_k[x]$ (the parent of x) is a root in $\tilde{C}_k$. □

In the next lemma we use the fact that if k' is the largest critical moment for x such that $k' < k$ then the elements $\tilde{p}_{k'+1}[x], \tilde{p}_{k'+2}[x], \ldots, \tilde{p}_k[x]$ are all equal. Hence, the hash $h(x, k')$ can be easily extended to $h(x, k)$.

LEMMA 4. *If x is a root in $\tilde{C}_k$ then the value of $h(x,k)$ can be computed in $O(\log\log t)$ time, given $h(y,k')$ for all pairs (y,k') such that $k' < k$ and k' is a critical moment for y.*

PROOF. We first show how to compute $h(x,k)$ in $O(\log t)$ time and speed the algorithm up. Let k' be the greatest critical moment of x lower than k. The value of k' can be found in $O(\log t)$ time using binary search. We will compute $h(x,k)$ by combining $h(x,k')$ and the hash of $\tilde{r}_{k'+1}[x], \tilde{r}_{k'+2}[x], \ldots, \tilde{r}_k[x]$. From the definition of k' it follows that $\tilde{p}_{k'+1}[x], \tilde{p}_{k'+2}[x], \ldots, \tilde{p}_k[x]$ are all equal to $\tilde{p}_k[x] = x$. Thus, we can simply compute the hash of $x^{k-k'}$ (x repeated $k - k'$ times) and combine it with $h(x,k')$. In this way we obtain $h(x,k)$.

We can speed up the computation of k' using persistent arrays. We compute and maintain a history of T versions of an array cm of size n. For each $i = 1, \ldots, T$ and a vertex x, the value of $cm[x]$ in version i of the array is the greatest critical moment of x that is lower than i. Computing cm requires $O(t \log t \log\log t)$ time. Initially, we fill cm with zeroes. After that, we iterate through all critical moments in ascending order and for each critical moment k of vertex x, we store k in $cm[x]$. Keeping all versions of the array allows us to compute the desired critical moments in $O(\log\log t)$ time. □

By joining together the above two lemmas one can obtain the following lemma.

LEMMA 5. *For any vertex x and any critical moment k, the value of $h(x,k)$ can be computed in $O(\log\log t)$ time, given $h(\tilde{p}_k[x],k)$ and $h(y,k')$ for all pairs (y,k') such that $k' < k$ and k' is a critical moment for y.*

PROOF. If $\tilde{p}_k[x] = x$, we can simply use Lemma 4, so from now on we assume that $\tilde{p}_k[x] \neq x$.

Let k' be the greatest critical moment lower than k. As in the previous proof, we will compute $h(x,k)$ by combining $h(x,k')$ and the hash of $S = \tilde{r}_{k'+1}[x], \tilde{r}_{k'+2}[x], \ldots, \tilde{r}_k[x]$. By the definition of the parent and representative, the sequence S is equal to $\tilde{r}_{k'+1}[\tilde{p}_{k'+1}[x]], \ldots, \tilde{r}_k[\tilde{p}_k[x]]$. Since there are no critical moments between k' and k, we infer that elements $\tilde{p}_{k'+1}[x], \tilde{p}_{k'+2}[x], \ldots, \tilde{p}_k[x]$ are all equal to $\tilde{p}_k[x]$. Thus S is equal to $\tilde{r}_{k'+1}[\tilde{p}_k[x]], \ldots, \tilde{r}_k[\tilde{p}_k[x]]$.

This means that the hash of S can be obtained from $h(\tilde{p}_k[x],k')$ and $h(\tilde{p}_k[x],k)$. By our assumption the latter is given, so it remains to obtain the former one.

Since x is not a root in $\tilde{C}_k$, it is also not a root in $\tilde{C}_{k'+1}$, but it *is* a root in $\tilde{C}_{k'}$ (by Lemma 3). Thus, in $\tilde{C}_{k'+1}$, x becomes a child of $\tilde{p}_{k'+1}[x]$. In the DSDSs we use, a node might only get connected to a root, so if x gets connected to $\tilde{p}_{k'+1}[x]$ in $\tilde{C}_{k'+1}$, then in the previous structure, $\tilde{C}_{k'}$, $\tilde{p}_{k'+1}[x]$ is a root. This means that $h(\tilde{p}_{k'+1}[x],k')$ can be computed in $O(\log\log t)$ time, by Lemma 4, but we know that $\tilde{p}_{k'+1}[x] = \tilde{p}_k[x]$, so this hash is equal to $h(\tilde{p}_k[x],k')$, which shows the desired. □

The above lemmas allow us to precompute the desired prefix hashes for critical moments efficiently, i.e., we simply compute $h(x,k)$ in the order of increasing values of k. For $k = 0$ and for each x, $h(x,0)$ is a hash of an empty sequence, so all of such hashes can be computed in $O(n)$ time. For $k > 0$, by Lemma 5, to compute $h(x,k)$, we need to know $h(\tilde{p}_k[x],k)$. As k is a critical moment, $\tilde{p}_k[x]$ is a root in $\tilde{C}_k$ (by Lemma 3), so we can use Lemma 4 to compute $h(\tilde{p}_k[x],k)$ in $O(\log\log t)$ time. As a result, every $h(x,k)$, where k is a critical moment for x, can be computed in $O(\log\log t)$ time. Therefore, computing all $O(t\log t)$ prefix hashes requires $O(n + t\log t \log\log t)$ time.

Answering queries.

In order to answer queries, we need to be able to compute hashes of arbitrary subwords of $\tilde{r}_1[x] \ldots \tilde{r}_T[x]$. Of course it suffices to describe how to compute $h(x,k)$ for arbitrary k.

We use Lemma 5, that reduces our problem to the problem to computing $h(x, \tilde{p}_k[x])$ (with an $O(\log\log t)$ overhead). In other words, computing a hash for x can be reduced to computing some hash for a parent of x. This value is then computed recursively. Since the depth of all trees in $\tilde{C}_k$ is bounded by $O(\log n)$, the recursion has $O(\log n)$ levels. On each level of the recursion we use Lemma 5, which requires $O(\log\log t)$ time. Thus, computing an arbitrary prefix hash requires $O(\log n \log\log t)$ time.

This allows us to hash arbitrary subwords of $\tilde{r}_1[x] \ldots \tilde{r}_T[x]$. However, as mentioned before, what we need are the hashes of subwords of $r_1[x] \ldots r_t[x]$. We now describe how to modify the algorithm, so that it computes the right hashes.

The only moment when we actually hash a fragment of a sequence is in the proof of Lemma 4, when we hash a word of the form x^l. In such case we only want to include the elements that are present in $r_1[x] \ldots r_t[x]$. Hence, given some fragment of $\tilde{r}_1[x] \ldots \tilde{r}_T[x]$, we need to know how many of its elements belong to $r_1[x] \ldots r_t[x]$. Denote by s_i the indices of $\tilde{r}_i$, which correspond to r_i, i.e., $r_i[x] = \tilde{r}_{s_i}[x]$. Thus, to count the number of elements in $\tilde{r}_a[x] \ldots \tilde{r}_b[x]$ that correspond to elements in $r_1[x] \ldots r_t[x]$, it suffices to count the number of elements of s_i that are between a and b. As s_i is an increasing sequence, whose values are bounded by $T = O(t\log t)$, we simply compute an array that for each j stores the number of elements of s_i that are smaller than j. This array allows to count the number of elements of s_i in any interval in constant time.

As a result we obtain the following theorem.

THEOREM 3. *There exists a randomized Monte Carlo data structure that, given a graph timeline G^t, after preprocessing in $O(m + t\log t \log\log t \log n)$ time can answer* `forall` *queries in $O(\log n \log\log t)$ time. It requires $O(n + t\log t)$ space.*

4.1 Deterministic algorithm

In this section we show a deterministic variant of the algorithm for answering `forall` queries. It uses a data structure for maintaining a family of dynamic sequences. This problem has been first solved by Mehlhorn *et. al* [13], and later the solution has been improved in [2]. Let us now describe this data structure briefly.

The operations performed on the data structure involve a pair of sequences. Let l be the length of the sequences involved in a single operation. Two sequences in the family can be joined or split in $O(\log l \log^* l)$ time, tested for equality in $O(1)$ time, and for any letter a and integer $k > 0$ the sequence a^k can be created in $O(1)$ time. The data structure can be used in place of prefix hashes. It allows us to maintain each desired prefix in the data structure.

During the process of computing the prefixes for all critical moments, an existing prefix is joined with a sequence in which all elements are equal. This is performed $O(t \log t)$ times and the length of the sequences involved in one operation is $O(t)$. Hence, by using the data structure it takes $O(\log t \log^* t)$ time to compute a single prefix, which gives $O(t \log^2 t \log^* t)$ time overhead for the whole process of computing hashes. This dominates the running time of the preprocessing phase.

However, the data structure allows us to answer queries in a simpler and effective way. After computing all prefixes, the data structure now contains a representation of sequences $r_1[v], \ldots, r_t[v]$ for each v. To answer a query, we need to compare $r_a[v] \ldots r_b[v]$ to $r_a[u] \ldots r_b[u]$, but both these sequences can be created with two split operations, each involving sequences of length $O(t)$. This requires $O(\log t \log^* t)$ time.

All results from this section are summarized in the following theorem.

THEOREM 4. *There exists a (deterministic) data structure that, given a graph timeline G^t, after preprocessing in $O(m + t \log^2 t \log^* t)$ time can answer* `forall` *queries in $O(\log t \log^* t)$ time. It requires $O(t \log^2 t \log^* t)$ space.*

5. UNDIRECTED GRAPHS: EXISTS QUERIES

In this section we describe an algorithm for answering `exists` queries in undirected graphs. The algorithm has considerably bigger running time than the one for answering `forall` queries. However, some increase in the running time is inevitable, since answering $\Omega(n^2)$ `exists` queries for a timeline of length $t = O(n^2)$ can be used to perform a multiplication of two $n \times n$ Boolean matrices. The details are given in Appendix A.

Preprocessing.

The algorithm is also based on the CHT for the given sequence of graphs. It precomputes, for all elementary intervals $[a, b]$, and all pairs of vertices u and v, the answer to an `exists`(u, v, a, b) query. Thus, by Lemma 1, the answer for a single query $[p, q]$ can be computed in $O(\log t)$ time by decomposing $[p, q]$ into $O(\log t)$ elementary intervals and combining the answers for these intervals. We later also show that this can be improved to constant time. Our techniques are similar to the one used by Eppstein [6].

As mentioned before, the algorithm begins by computing the CHT for the given sequence of graphs. By Lemma 2, this requires $O(m + t \log t \log \log t \log n)$ time. This time, however, we do not use persistent arrays to store DSDSs, and for each of the $O(t)$ nodes of the CHT create a new DSDS by copying $O(n)$ memory cells. This results in $O(nt)$ overhead, but we get rid of the $O(\log \log t)$ factor that comes from the use of fully persistent arrays. Hence the running time of this step is $O(m + t \log t \log n + nt)$, which can be bounded by $O(m + nt)$ under a mild assumption that $n = \Omega(\log t \log n)$. Observe that after contracting permanent edges we can dispose of all vertices which are not endpoints of any temporary edges, as they remain disconnected from the rest of the graph. After this step, we have that the number of temporary edges $t = \Omega(n)$.

Each node $v_{a \ldots b}$ of the CHT contains $C_{a \ldots b}$, which is a DSDS representing $G_a \cap \ldots \cap G_b$. In particular, for each $1 \le i \le t$ we have a DSDS C_i that represents G_i. For each $C_{a \ldots b}$, we compute the representatives $r_{a \ldots b}[x]$ of all elements x. Note that computing representatives of *all* elements in a given DSDS can be achieved in $O(n)$ time, since it suffices to traverse the forest representing the disjoint sets. This step requires $O(nt)$ time and from now on the representative of each vertex in every $C_{a \ldots b}$ can be found in $O(1)$ time.

Next, for each node $v_{a \ldots b}$ of the CHT, we compute a two-dimensional Boolean matrix $M_{a \ldots b}$ which contains answers to `exists`(u, v, a, b) queries for all pairs of vertices u, v. The matrix is indexed by vertices of the graph. We set $[M_{a \ldots b}]_{u,v} = 1$ if and only if u and v are connected in *any* of $G_a, \ldots, G_b$.

If $b - a > n$, then $M_{a \ldots b}$ is simply a $n \times n$ matrix. However, if $b - a \le n$, then the matrix has a more compact implicit representation, as some of its rows/columns are equal to each other. Consider the connected components of $G_a \cap G_{a+1} \cap \ldots \cap G_b$ (represented by $C_{a \ldots b}$). Vertices belonging to these components stay connected throughout the whole interval $[a, b]$. Hence, it suffices only to store rows and columns of $M_{a \ldots b}$ only for representatives of the sets in $C_{a \ldots b}$.

Furthermore, within $G_a, \ldots, G_b$ at most $b - a + 1$ edges are added or deleted. This means that at most $2(b - a + 1) = O(b - a)$ components of $G_a \cap G_{a+1} \cap \ldots G_b$ may become connected to other components within this time interval. It follows that we can limit our attention just to these $O(b - a)$ components, as the others stay disconnected from the rest in each of $G_a, \ldots, G_b$. As a result, it suffices to store an $O(b - a) \times O(b - a)$ matrix to implicitly represent $M_{a \ldots b}$. Using this representation, every value of $[M_{a \ldots b}]_{u,v}$ can be computed in constant time, using the $O(b - a) \times O(b - a)$ matrix and $C_{a \ldots b}$.

Additionally, for each node in the CHT, we define matrices $F_{a \ldots b}$ and $L_{a \ldots b}$. If $[M_{a \ldots b}]_{u,v} = 1$, then $[F_{a \ldots b}]_{u,v}$ is equal to the index of the first graph among $G_a, \ldots, G_b$, in which u and v are connected. Otherwise, $[F_{a \ldots b}]_{u,v}$ is set to ∞. The matrix $L_{a \ldots b}$ is defined similarly, but it contains indices of the last graph, in which the vertices are connected. Observe that both $F_{a \ldots b}$ and $L_{a \ldots b}$ can be represented implicitly, similarly to $M_{a \ldots b}$.

LEMMA 6. *The implicit representations of matrices $M_{a \ldots b}$, $F_{a \ldots b}$ and $L_{a \ldots b}$ for all elementary intervals $[a, b]$ can be computed in $O(nt)$ total time.*

PROOF. We focus on computing $M_{a \ldots b}$ and $F_{a \ldots b}$, but the description can easily be extended to $L_{a \ldots b}$. We first bound the total size of the implicit representations of all $M_{a \ldots b}$ and later show how to compute them efficiently. Let us assume w.l.o.g. that $t = 2^d$, so CHT has depth d and there are exactly 2^{d-i} nodes $v_{a \ldots b}$, for which $b - a + 1 = 2^i$. The total space for storing the matrices is

$$\sum_{i=0}^{d} 2^{d-i} \min(n, 2^i)^2 = \sum_{i=0}^{\lfloor \log n \rfloor} 2^{d-i} 2^{2i} + \sum_{\lfloor \log n \rfloor + 1}^{d} 2^{d-i} n^2$$
$$= 2^d \sum_{i=0}^{\lfloor \log n \rfloor} 2^i + 2^d n^2 \sum_{\lfloor \log n \rfloor + 1}^{d} 2^{-i}$$
$$= 2^d O(n) + 2^d O(n) = O(nt).$$

Note that we have used an assumption that $t \ge n$. However, in our case $t = \Omega(n)$, so the same bound can be derived.

The algorithm computes the matrices in the nodes of the CHT in a bottom-up fashion. The implicit representation of $M_{a...b}$ is its submatrix consisting of $O(\min(n, b-a))$ rows and columns. We show that each entry of each such submatrix can be computed in constant time. This follows trivially for matrices in the leaves of the CHT. On the other hand, if $v_{a...b}$ is an inner node, then $[M_{a...b}]_{u,v}$ is a bitwise `or` of $[M_{a...(a+b-1)/2}]_{u,v}$ and $[M_{(a+b+1)/2...b}]_{u,v}$, i.e., the corresponding cells in the children of $v_{a...b}$. Similarly, $[F_{a...b}]_{u,v}$ can be computed by taking a minimum of two respective values. Hence, computing all matrices requires time proportional to the total size of their implicit representations, equal to $O(nt)$. □

Answering queries.

After the preprocessing phase, a query regarding an interval $[a, b]$ can be answered by decomposing in into $O(\log t)$ elementary intervals. The matrices $M_{a...b}$ allow us to obtain the answer for every elementary interval in $O(\log t)$ time, so each query requires $O(\log t)$ total time. However, this can be also done faster. We show how use matrices $F_{a...b}$ and $L_{a...b}$ to improve the query time to $O(1)$.

Moreover, it is possible to extend the algorithm, so that it reports the graphs in which the two given vertices are connected. This can be done optimally, i.e., the graphs can be returned one by one, each with constant delay.

Let $par(x) := \max_i 2^i | x$ and $maxparity(a, b)$ be the number from the interval $[a, b]$ that maximizes the value of par.

LEMMA 7. *Let k be a fixed integer. After preprocessing in $O(k)$ time, it is possible to compute $maxparity(a, b)$ for any $1 \le a \le b \le k$ in constant time.*

PROOF. Observe that since $[a, b]$ is an interval, the value of $maxparity(a, b)$ is uniquely defined. This follows from the fact that if $par(x) = par(y)$ then $par((x + y)/2) > par(x)$. The pseudocode of an algorithm for computing $maxparity$ is given as Algorithm 5. `xor`, `and` and `not` denote bitwise operations, whereas $maxpower(x)$ is the greatest power of 2 that is not greater than x.

Algorithm 1 MAXPARITY(a, b)

Require: $1 \le a \le b$
1: **if** $a = b$ **then**
2:     **return** a
3: **else if** $a \le maxpower(b)$ **then**
4:     **return** $maxpower(b)$
5: **else**
6:     $d := maxpower(a$ `xor` $b)$
7:     $c := b$ `and` (`not` $(d-1)$)
8:     **if** $par(c) > par(a)$ **then**
9:         **return** c
10:    **else**
11:         **return** a
12:    **end if**
13: **end if**

We now prove its correctness. Let us denote the correct result of the function by M. The correctness of the first case is trivial. Consider the second case. Observe that $maxparity(b)$ is the number with the greatest value of par in the interval $[1, b]$. Moreover, in this case, this number lies in the interval $[a, b]$, from which we infer the desired.

Let us move to the third case. We have that $maxparity(b) < a < b$, so the binary representations of a and b have the same length. In the first step, d is computed. It is a number with just one bit lit — the most significant bit of all the bits that are different in a and b. Let $d = 2^{p-1}$, that is only p-th bit is lit in d. Because a is smaller than b, p-th bit is lit in b, but not in a. There are now two cases to consider.

1. M is divisible by $2d = 2^p$. Then p trailing bits of M are equal to 0. However, in $[a, b]$ there can be at most one number with p trailing zeroes, as other bits are common to a and b. It follows easily, that this can only happen when $M = a$, so we consider a one of the candidates for the answer.

2. M is not divisible by $2d$. In this case, we show that there exists a number in $[a, b]$ that is divisible by d, so it maximizes the value of $maxparity$. We claim that it is a number obtained from b by setting its $p - 1$ trailing bits to zeroes. Observe that this value is computed and assigned to c in the 7th line ($d - 1$ is a number consisting of p consecutive ones). Obviously c is divisible by $2^{p-1} = d$. Moreover $a < c$, as the most significant bit, in which they differ is the p-th one, which is lit in c.

Hence, it suffices to choose the better from among a and c. All the operations can be performed in constant time after $O(k)$ preprocessing, as the values of pri and $maxparity$ can be precomputed. □

Observe that it is possible to obtain the result of the above Lemma, by using a data structure that performs range minimum queries in constant time. However, such approach leads to a much more complicated algorithm.

When a query regarding an interval $[a, b]$ is issued, we compute $p = maxparity(a, b)$. Next, we find the nodes $v_{r...p}$ and $v_{p+1...s}$ with the minimal possible r and maximal possible s. Such nodes can be precomputed for all values of p in the beginning. We now claim that the interval $[a, b]$ is contained in $[r, s]$. Both these intervals contain p. We show that neither $r - 1$ nor s is contained in $[a, b]$. We use the following property of segment trees.

LEMMA 8. *Let T be a segment tree with n leaves. The set of elementary intervals consists of all such $[a, b]$ that $1 \le a \le b \le n$, $a = b - 2^k + 1$ and b is divisible by 2^k. The last two conditions can also be given as $b = a + 2^l - 1$ and $a - 1$ is divisible by 2^l.*

Hence, it follows that $r = p - 2^{par(p)} + 1$, so $r - 1 = p - 2^{par(p)}$. This is way $par(r - 1) > par(p)$, so $r - 1$ cannot belong to $[a, b]$. Similarly, $s = (p + 1) + 2^{par(p)} - 1 = p + 2^{par(p)}$, so s also does not belong to $[a, b]$.

To report a single graph, in which two given vertices are connected, it suffices to find the last graph among $G_r, \ldots, G_p$ and the first graph among $G_{p+1}, \ldots, G_s$, in which the vertices are connected. If the index of at least one of these graphs belongs to $[a, b]$, we get a graph G_j $(a \le j \le b)$, in which u and v are connected. The algorithm can then recurse on $[a, j-1]$ and $[j+1, b]$ to report further values. From the algorithm it follows that each value can be reported in constant time.

THEOREM 5. *There exists an $O(nt)$ size data structure that given the graph timeline G^t after preprocessing in $O(m+$*

nt) time can answer **exists** *queries in constant time. Moreover, the data structure can report indices of the graphs, in which u and v are connected, each with constant delay.*

6. DIRECTED REACHABILITY

In this section we describe an algorithm that is able to work with directed graphs. In the case of directed graphs we consider *vertex updates* – we assume that a single query can add or delete an arbitrary set of edges incident to a given vertex. We base our result on the following relation between matrix inverse and transitive closure.

Let $G = (V, E)$ be a directed n-vertex graph and let p be a prime number of order $\Theta(tn^4)$. A random adjacency matrix of G is the $n \times n$ matrix A such that:

$$A_{i,j}(G) = \begin{cases} \text{random element of } \mathbb{Z}_p & \text{if } (i,j) \in E, \\ 1 & \text{if } i = j, \\ 0 & \text{otherwise.} \end{cases}$$

THEOREM 6 (SANKOWSKI '04 [15]). *With probability* $\geq 1 - \frac{1}{n^3 t}$ *the following holds: there exists a path from i to j in G, iff* $(A(G))^{-1}_{i,j} \neq 0$.

This reduces the transitive closure problem to matrix inverse problem. Hence, we essentially need to show how to compute $A(G_i)^{-1}$ for all graphs G_i in the timeline. This will be done using a dynamic matrix inverse problem with *lookahead*. A lookahead of k operations means that the algorithm knows k future updates. For an $n \times n$ matrix A, we consider dynamic matrix problem for with rank-one operations:

update(i, u, v) – changes A to $A + uv^T$, where u and v are length n vectors;

query(u) – returns $A^{-1}u$, where u is length n vector.

The following theorem for any lookahead is proven in Appendix B. This is a generalization of the result from [16] that worked only for column updates. Column updates are not strong enough for our purposes.

THEOREM 7. *Given a lookahead of n operations, the dynamic matrix inverse problem for* $n \times n$ *matrix with nonsingular rank-one updates can be solved with the following costs:* **initialization** – $O(n^\omega)$ *arithmetic operations,* **update** *and* **query** – $O(n^{\omega-1})$ *arithmetic operations (amortized).*

Preprocessing.

Here, we assume that the length of the timeline t is multiple of n. We make this assumption for simplicity of presentation. When $n \geq t$ we can simply pad the sequence with empty updates. However, for $t < n$ one would need to adopt Theorem 7 to smaller lookahead. This would make the description of the running time considerably more complex.

Let A_i denote random adjacency matrix for graph G_i. Observe that changing edges incident to vertex w_i alters only w_i'th column and w_i'th row of the matrix. Hence, we know that there exist u_i and v_i such that $A_{i+1} = A_i + u_i e_{w_i}^T + e_{w_i} v_i^T$. The change of A_i can be represented as two rank-one updates. Again, for simplicity, we assume that in each time step matrix A_i undergoes only one rank-one update, i.e., we assume that there are u_i and v_i, such that $A_{i+1} = A_i + u_i v_i^T$.

First, we divide the graph timeline into phases of length n. The a'th phase, for $a = 1, \ldots, \frac{t}{n}$, is denoted by $\overline{G}_a$ and contains graphs $G_{n(a-1)+1}, \ldots, G_{na}$. For any two phases a and b we define a matrix $M_{a\ldots b}$, such that $[M_{a\ldots b}]_{u,v}$ is nonzero if and only if there is a path from u to v in any of $G_{n(a-1)+1}, \ldots, G_{nb}$. In our algorithm we compute and store the following data:

- for $i = 1, \ldots, t$ such that $n|i-1$ (that is for the beginning of each phase) we store A_i^{-1},
- for $i = 1, \ldots, t$, we store $\tilde{u}_i = A_i^{-1}u_i$, $\tilde{v}_i = (A_i^T)^{-1}v_i$, and $a_i = \frac{1}{1+v_i^T A_i^{-1} u_i}$,
- a segment tree $\overline{T}$ over phases $\overline{G}_i$,
- for each elementary interval $[a, b]$ in $\overline{T}$ we store a matrix $M_{a\ldots b}$.

Observe that storing this information requires $O(nt)$ memory. We assume that indexes for time moments require one word on the machine – this is standard assumption for the RAM model. Hence, elements of $\mathbb{Z}_p$ can be represented with $O(\log n + \log t)$ bits, and so require $O(1)$ space in the RAM model. We now argue that computing these information requires $O(n^{\omega-1}t)$ time. Matrices A_i^{-1} are computed every n operations, so the related cost is $O(n^\omega)\frac{t}{n}$. In order to compute $u_i' = A_i^{-1}u_i$ we use Theorem 7 applied to the sequence of changes, whereas in order to compute $v_i' = (A_i^T)^{-1}v_i$ we apply it to transposed matrix. To compute the matrices $M_{a\ldots b}$ we need the following lemma.

LEMMA 9. *For any phase a and any* $i \geq n(a-1)+1$ *we have*

$$A_i^{-1} = A_{n(a-1)+1}^{-1} - \sum_{j=n(a-1)+1}^{i-1} a_j \tilde{u}_j \tilde{v}_j^T.$$

PROOF. Recall Sherman-Morrison formula

$$(A + uv^T)^{-1} = A^{-1} - \frac{A^{-1}uv^TA^{-1}}{1 + v^TA^{-1}u}. \quad (1)$$

Hence, the statement of the lemma follows by applying the above formula to sequence of rank-one updates from $n(a-1)+1$ to $i-1$. □

We use the above observation to compute all the matrices $M_{a\ldots b}$ using batches of updates with fast matrix multiplication.

LEMMA 10. *The matrices* $M_{a\ldots b}$ *for all elementary intervals* $[a, b]$ *in* $\bar{T}$ *can be computed in* $O(n^{\omega-1}t)$ *time.*

PROOF. For a vector z let $\beta(z)$ be a vector defined as follows

$$\beta(z)_i = \begin{cases} 1 & \text{if } z_i \neq 0, \\ 0 & \text{otherwise.} \end{cases}$$

We first compute matrices $M_{a\ldots a}$ related to the leaves of the segment tree. In order to compute $M_{a\ldots a}$ we first find paths that exists at the beginning of the phase. By Theorem 6 they are represented by the matrix $A_{n(a-1)+1}^{-1}$. Next, we need to find paths that appeared latter on. Consider paths from a vertex $u \in V$ to vertex $v \in V$. By Lemma 9, if $[A_{n(a-1)+1}^{-1}]_{v,u}$ is zero then $[A_i^{-1}]_{u,v}$ is equal to $[-\sum_{j=n(a-1)+1}^{i-1} a_j \tilde{u}_j \tilde{v}_j^T]_{v,u}$.

Thus, $[A_i^{-1}]_{u,v}$ is nonzero for some $i = n(a-1)+1, \ldots, na-1$, if and only if there exists j such that $[a_j \tilde{u}_j \tilde{v}_j^T]_{v,u}$ is nonzero. This in turn means that $[\beta(\tilde{u}_j)\beta(\tilde{v}_j)^T]_{u,v}$ is nonzero. In order to check this condition for all $j = n(a-1)+1, \ldots, an-1$ and for all $u, v \in V$, we compute the matrix D_a defined as

$$D_a = \left(\beta(\tilde{u}_{n(a-1)+1})| \ldots |\beta(\tilde{u}_{na-1})\right) \cdot \left(\beta(\tilde{v}_{n(a-1)+1})| \ldots |\beta(\tilde{v}_{na-1})\right)^T.$$

This matrix can be computed using fast matrix multiplication $O(n^\omega)$ time, because the resulting numbers can be represented with $O(\log n)$ bits. Note that $[D_a]_{u,v} \neq 0$ if and only if there exists $j = n(a-1)+1, \ldots, na-1$ such that $[\beta(\tilde{u}_j)\beta(\tilde{v}_j)^T]_{u,v}$ is nonzero. Hence, computing $M_{a\ldots a}$ for the leaves of the segment tree takes $O(n^\omega \frac{t}{n})$ time. The matrices for other elementary intervals can be computed by taking `or` of two children matrices. This operation requires $O(n^2)$ time, and gives the total of $O(nt)$ time for the entire tree. □

Answering Queries.

Let us now consider the problem of answering queries. The procedure to answer an $\texttt{exists}(u, v, a, b)$ query is as follows:

- let a' be the smallest number such that $a'n \geq a$, let b' be the biggest number such that $b'n \leq b$,
- check the existence of path from u to v in $[a'n, b'n]$ using matrices $M_{a\ldots b}$ and Lemma 1 in $O(\log t)$ time,
- use Lemma 9 to compute $(A_j^{-1})_{u,v}$ for $j \in [a, a'] \cup [b', b]$ in $O(n)$ time,
- by Theorem 6 if for some $j \in [a, a'] \cup [b', b]$ we have that $(A_j^{-1})_{u,v} \neq 0$ there exists a path from u to v in G_j.

The procedure answering $\texttt{forall}(u, v, a, b)$ query is slightly easier:

- use Lemma 9 to compute $(A_j^{-1})_{u,v}$ for $j \in [a, b]$ in $O(n + b - a)$ time,
- by Theorem 6 if for all $j \in [a, a'] \cup [b', b]$ we have that $(A_j^{-1})_{u,v} \neq 0$ there always exists a path from u to v in time interval $[a, b]$.

THEOREM 8. *There exists an $O(nt)$ size randomized data structure that given a directed graph timeline after preprocessing in $O(n^{\omega-1}t)$ time can answer* `exists` *queries in $O(n)$ time and* `forall` *queries in $O(n + b - a)$ time. Answers to all queries are correct with probability at least $1 - \frac{1}{n}$.*

PROOF. The time complexities follow from the algorithms described above. Let us argue about the probability that the answers to all queries are correct. Observe that by Theorem 6 $(A_j^{-1})_{u,v}$ correctly encodes that there is a path from u to v in G_j with probability $\geq 1 - \frac{1}{n^3 t}$. There are n^2 elements in A_j^{-1} and j can take at most t values. Hence, all elements of the matrices A_j^{-1} are correct with probability at least $1 - \frac{1}{n}$. □

7. ACKNOWLEDGEMENTS

Jakub Łącki is a recipient of the Google Europe Fellowship in Graph Algorithms, and this research is supported in part by this Google Fellowship. Piotr Sankowski was partially supported by the ERC StG project PAAl no. 259515.

8. REFERENCES

[1] Stephen Alstrup, Gerth Stølting Brodal, and Theis Rauhe. Pattern matching in dynamic texts. In *Proccedings of the eleventh annual ACM-SIAM symposium on Discrete algorithms*, SODA '00, pages 819–828, Philadelphia, PA, USA, 2000. Society for Industrial and Applied Mathematics.

[2] Stephen Alstrup, Gerth Stølting Brodal, and Theis Rauhe. Pattern matching in dynamic texts. In *Proceedings of the eleventh annual ACM-SIAM symposium on Discrete algorithms*, SODA '00, pages 819–828, Philadelphia, PA, USA, 2000. Society for Industrial and Applied Mathematics.

[3] Thomas H. Cormen, Clifford Stein, Ronald L. Rivest, and Charles E. Leiserson. *Introduction to Algorithms.* McGraw-Hill Higher Education, 2nd edition, 2001.

[4] Camil Demetrescu and Giuseppe F. Italiano. Trade-offs for fully dynamic transitive closure on DAGs: breaking through the $O(n^2)$ barrier. *J. ACM*, 52(2):147–156, 2005.

[5] Paul F. Dietz. Fully Persistent Arrays. In *WADS*, pages 67–74, 1989.

[6] David Eppstein. Offline algorithms for dynamic minimum spanning tree problems. *J. Algorithms*, 17(2):237–250, 1994.

[7] Dennis Fetterly, Mark Manasse, Marc Najork, and Janet Wiener. A large-scale study of the evolution of web pages. WWW '03, pages 669–678. ACM, 2003.

[8] Robert W. Floyd. Algorithm 97: Shortest path. *Commun. ACM*, 5(6):345, 1962.

[9] Andrew V. Goldberg, Michael D. Grigoriadis, and Robert Endre Tarjan. Use of dynamic trees in a network simplex algorithm for the maximum flow problem. *Math. Program.*, 50:277–290, 1991.

[10] Giuseppe F. Italiano and Neil Sarnak. Fully persistent data structures for disjoint set union problems. In Frank K. H. A. Dehne, Jörg-Rüdiger Sack, and Nicola Santoro, editors, *WADS*, volume 519 of *Lecture Notes in Computer Science*, pages 449–460. Springer, 1991.

[11] Richard M. Karp and Michael O. Rabin. Efficient randomized pattern-matching algorithms. *IBM Journal of Research and Development*, 31(2):249–260, 1987.

[12] Tsvi Kopelowitz. On-line indexing for general alphabets via predecessor queries on subsets of an ordered list. *CoRR*, abs/1208.3798, 2012.

[13] Kurt Mehlhorn, R. Sundar, and Christian Uhrig. Maintaining Dynamic Sequences under Equality Tests in Polylogarithmic Time. *Algorithmica*, 17(2):183–198, 1997.

[14] Alexandros Ntoulas, Junghoo Cho, and Christopher Olston. What's new on the web?: the evolution of the web from a search engine perspective. WWW '04, pages 1–12. ACM, 2004.

[15] Piotr Sankowski. Dynamic Transitive Closure via

Dynamic Matrix Inverse (Extended Abstract). FOCS '04, pages 509–517. IEEE Computer Society, 2004.

[16] Piotr Sankowski and Marcin Mucha. Fast Dynamic Transitive Closure with Lookahead. *Algorithmica*, 56(2):180–197, February 2010.

[17] Mikkel Thorup. Near-optimal fully-dynamic graph connectivity. STOC '00, pages 343–350. ACM, 2000.

[18] Mikkel Thorup. Fully-dynamic all-pairs shortest paths: Faster and allowing negative cycles. In Torben Hagerup and Jyrki Katajainen, editors, *SWAT*, volume 3111 of *Lecture Notes in Computer Science*, pages 384–396. Springer, 2004.

APPENDIX

A. EXISTS QUERIES: LOWER BOUND

LEMMA 11. *Let G^t be a graph timeline, where $t = O(n^2)$. Moreover, let D be a data structure that supports* `exists` *queries. Then, initializing D and answering $\Omega(n^2)$ queries requires $\Omega(n^{\omega'})$ time, where ω' denotes the exponent of square Boolean matrix multiplication.*

PROOF. We show that a sequence of `exists` queries can be used to perform an $n \times n$ Boolean matrix multiplication. This is equivalent to showing that for an $2n \times 2n$ matrix A, we can compute $A \cdot A^T$. The reduction is the following. Assume that we are to compute $B \cdot C$, where B and C are $n \times n$ matrices. Then, we construct a $2n \times 2n$ matrix A as follows:

$$A = \begin{pmatrix} B & 0 \\ C^T & 0 \end{pmatrix}$$

Hence,

$$A \cdot A^T = \begin{pmatrix} B & 0 \\ C^T & 0 \end{pmatrix} \cdot \begin{pmatrix} B^T & C \\ 0 & 0 \end{pmatrix} = \begin{pmatrix} B \cdot B^T & B \cdot C \\ C^T \cdot B^T & C^T \cdot C \end{pmatrix}$$

In the following, for simplicity we assume that A is an $n \times n$ matrix. Denote its rows by $a_1, \ldots, a_n$. Let G_1 be an empty graph on $n+1$ vertices $w, v_1, \ldots, v_n$. We build the graph timeline $G_1, \ldots, G_t$ starting from G_1 and adding or deleting one edge at a time. First we connect w with v_i for each i such that $A_{i1} = 1$. These $O(n)$ edge additions are performed in an arbitrary order. Denote the obtained graph by G_{c_1}. It corresponds to the first column of the matrix A. Then, remove all the edges, again adding $O(n)$ new graphs to the timeline.

Repeat the same procedure for each column of the matrix A. As a result we obtain a timeline of length $O(n^2)$, which contains a subsequence $G_{c_1}, \ldots, G_{c_n}$. It is easy to see that two vertices are connected in some graph in the timeline iff they are connected in some G_{c_i}. Now, the following statements are equivalent:

- The answer to an $\texttt{exists}(v_j, v_k, 1, t)$ query is *yes*.
- Vertices v_j and v_k are connected in some graph in the timeline.
- Vertices v_j and v_k are connected in G_{c_i} for some $1 \le i \le n$.
- For some $1 \le i \le n$, $A_{ji} = A_{ki} = 1$.
- $a_j \cdot a_k = 1$.
- $[A \cdot A^T]_{jk} = 1$.

Thus, by issuing n^2 queries, we can compute $A \cdot A^T$. □

B. MATRIX INVERSE WITH LOOKAHEAD

In this section we recall the so called Sherman-Morrison formula, and introduce some notation used in our algorithms. We assume that the matrix remains non-singular during updates. The matrix A after the rank-one update is given by $A' = A + uv^T$. Thus, we can use Algorithm 2 for updating the inverse.

Algorithm 2 Sherman-Morrison update formula.

UPDATE-INVERSE(u, v):
$b := A^{-1}u$
$B := I - \frac{bv^T}{1+v^Tb}$
$A^{-1} := BA^{-1}$
$A := A + uv^T$

Observe that the computation of the vector b takes $O(n^2)$ arithmetic operations. Next, we compute matrix B in $O(n^2)$ operations. Finally, we have to perform the multiplication BA^{-1}. Due to the special structure of the matrix B this can be done in $O(n^2)$ operations. Observe, that this procedure allows to compute matrix determinant, as $\det(A + uv^T) = \det(A)(1 + v^Tb)$, and matrix adjoint, as $adj(A) = \det(A)A^{-1}$.

Update-only algorithm.

In this section we show a dynamic algorithm that supports updates in $O(n^{\omega(1,1,\epsilon)-\epsilon})$ operations, given a lookahead of n^ϵ updates. In the next section we describe how to extend it, so that it is able to answer queries.

We begin with presenting an algorithm computing the vector b introduced in Algorithm 2 for a sequence of $N = n^\epsilon$ updates in time $O(n^{\omega(1,1,\epsilon)})$[6]. We assume that $N \le n$ as larger values of N do not give speed improvement.

Let $(u_0, v_0), \ldots, (u_{N-1}, v_{N-1})$ be a sequence of N updates and consider the k-th update (u_k, v_k). The corresponding vectors b_k can be expressed as

$$b_k = B_{k-1}B_{k-2}\cdots B_0A^{-1}u_k,$$

This follows from formula on b in Algorithm 2 by plugging in the value of A just before the k-th update. Let us define

$$\mathcal{B}_p^q = B_{q-1}B_{q-2}\cdots B_p \quad \text{and} \quad b_k^{(q)} = \mathcal{B}_0^q A^{-1}u_k,$$

so that

$$b_k = b_k^{(k)} \quad \text{and} \quad b_k^{(0)} = A^{-1}u_k,$$

Now, the vectors $b_k^{(0)}$ can be computed for all $k = 0, \ldots, N-1$ during the initialization phase of the algorithm and then the $b_k^{(q)}$ for $q > 0$ can be computed once we know the corresponding $\mathcal{B}_0^q$. Note that for each k, we only compute $b_k^{(q)}$ for selected values of q.

The key to computing the $b_k^{(q)}$ vectors faster is to:

[6] $O(n^{\omega(\epsilon,\beta,\gamma)})$ is the time needed to multiply $n^\epsilon \times n^\beta$ matrix by $n^\beta \times n^\gamma$ matrix.

- compute them using $\mathcal{B}_p^q$-s for large $q-p$, rather than using B_r-s,
- compute many $b_k^{(q)}$-s using a single matrix multiplication.

Algorithm 3 shows how this can be done.

Algorithm 3 Update only algorithm

UPDATE-ONLY-INTERVAL(p, q):
  if $q-p=1$ then **return**
  let $m := \lfloor \frac{p+q}{2} \rfloor$
  UPDATE-ONLY-INTERVAL(p, m)
  $\left(b_m^{(m)}|\dots|b_{q-1}^{(m)}\right) := \mathcal{B}_p^m \left(b_m^{(p)}|\dots|b_{q-1}^{(p)}\right)$
  $\mathcal{B}_m^{m+1} := I - \frac{b_m^{(m)} v_m^T}{1+v_m^T b_m^{(m)}}$
  UPDATE-ONLY-INTERVAL(m, q)
  $\mathcal{B}_p^q := \mathcal{B}_m^q \mathcal{B}_p^m$

UPDATE-ONLY:
  $\left(b_0^{(0)}|\dots|b_{N-1}^{(0)}\right) := A^{-1}\left(u_0|\dots|u_{N-1}\right)$
  UPDATE-ONLY-INTERVAL$(0, N)$
  $A^{-1} := \mathcal{B}_0^N A^{-1}$

Before analyzing the complexity of the UPDATE-ONLY procedure we show that matrices $\mathcal{B}_p^q$ can be maintained in a way that speeds the computations up.

LEMMA 12. *There exist matrices U_p^q and V_p^q that have n rows and $q-p$ columns such that*

$$\mathcal{B}_p^q = I - U_p^q (V_p^q)^T,$$

consequently the result of the multiplication $\mathcal{B}_m^q \mathcal{B}_p^m$ can be computed in $O(n^{\omega(1,\epsilon,\epsilon)})$ operations for $n^\epsilon = q-p$.

PROOF. Observe that the statement is true in the case when $q-p=1$ because, we have $\mathcal{B}_m^{m+1} = I - \beta_m v_m^T$ for $\beta_m = \frac{b_m^{(m)}}{1+v_m^T b_m^{(m)}}$.

Now consider

$$\begin{aligned}
\mathcal{B}_p^q &= \mathcal{B}_m^q \mathcal{B}_p^m \\
&= (I - U_m^q (V_m^q)^T)(I - U_p^m (V_p^m)^T) \\
&= I - U_m^q \left[(V_m^q)^T - (V_m^q)^T U_p^m (V_p^m)^T \right] - U_p^m (V_p^m)^T \\
&= I - (U_m^q | U_p^m) \left(\left(V_m^q - V_p^m (U_p^m)^T V_m^q \right) | V_p^m \right)^T.
\end{aligned}$$

Hence we have

$$\begin{aligned}
U_p^q &= (U_m^q | U_p^m), \\
V_p^q &= \left(V_m^q - V_p^m (U_p^m)^T V_m^q | V_p^m \right),
\end{aligned}$$

so by induction both these matrices have $q-p$ columns.

Constructing U_p^q is easy, whereas in order to find V_p^q we need to compute $V_p^m((U_p^m)^T V_m^q)$. Observe that this multiplications when executed in the order given by brackets require $O(n^{\omega(1,\epsilon,1)} + n^{\omega(1,\epsilon,\epsilon)})$ operations. By dividing rectangular matrices into square ones we get that $O(n^{\omega(\epsilon,1,\epsilon)}) = O(n^{1-\epsilon} n^{\epsilon\omega})$. Similarly, $O(n^{\omega(1,\epsilon,\epsilon)}) = O(n^{1-\epsilon} n^{\epsilon\omega})$, and so $O(n^{\omega(1,\epsilon,1)} + n^{\omega(1,\epsilon,\epsilon)}) = O(n^{\omega(1,\epsilon,\epsilon)})$. □

Observe that thanks to the special structure of $\mathcal{B}_p^m$ in order to compute $\left(b_m^{(m)}|\dots|b_{q-1}^{(m)}\right)$ we need $O(n^{\omega(1,\epsilon,\epsilon)})$ operations, where $n^\epsilon = q-p$. The needed multiplication has exactly the same form as in the above proof.

We now analyze the complexity of the internal UPDATE-ONLY-INTERVAL procedure. For simplicity, we pad the sequence of updates with trivial updates, to guarantee that $N = 2^r$ for some $r \in \mathbb{N}$. This way $q-p$ is always a power of 2.

Let $T(x)$ denote the time required to perform UPDATE-ONLY-INTERVAL for a subsequence of updates of length x. We have

$$\begin{aligned}
T(2^k) &= 2T(2^{k-1}) + 2(n/2^{k-1})(2^{k-1})^\omega \\
&= 2T(2^{k-1}) + 2n2^{(k-1)(\omega-1)}.
\end{aligned}$$

By solving the above recurrence, we get

$$T(N) = O(nN^{\omega-1}) = O(n^{\omega(1,\epsilon,\epsilon)}).$$

Let us now analyze the UPDATE-ONLY procedure. The UPDATE-ONLY-INTERVAL call takes $T(N)$ time and both matrix multiplications take $O(n^{\omega(1,1,\epsilon)})$ time. These matrix multiplications are thus the most time consuming part of the algorithm and its time complexity is $O(n^{\omega(1,1,\epsilon)})$. The cost per update is $O(n^{\omega(1,1,\epsilon)-\epsilon})$.

Answering queries.

We now show how the UPDATE-ONLY algorithm can be modified to support queries. Notice that A^{-1} after k-th update is equal to $\mathcal{B}_0^k A^{-1}$. Hence, the value of `query` for u is equal to $\mathcal{B}_0^k A^{-1} u$ This is exactly the value of b_k we would get if $u_k = u$. Thus, the UPDATE-ONLY algorithm can be used to answer queries in the following way:

- if the k-th operation is a query for u, then it is substituted with an update ($u_k = u, v_k = 0$),
- these new updates do not modify A so they should be ignored in the computations of $\mathcal{B}_p^q$ matrices.

We get the following:

THEOREM 9. *Given a lookahead of n^ϵ operations. The dynamic matrix inverse problem with non-singular rank-one updates can be solved with the following costs:*

- `initialization` – *$O(n^\omega)$ arithmetic operations,*
- `update` *and* `query` – *$O(n^{\omega(1,1,\epsilon)-\epsilon})$ arithmetic operations (amortized).*

Runtime Guarantees for Regression Problems *

Hui Han Chin
CMU
hchin@cmu.edu

Aleksander Mądry †
EPFL
aleksander.madry@epfl.ch

Gary L. Miller
CMU
glmiller@cs.cmu.edu

Richard Peng ‡
CMU
yangp@cs.cmu.edu

ABSTRACT

We study theoretical runtime guarantees for a class of optimization problems that occur in a wide variety of inference problems. These problems are motivated by the LASSO framework and have applications in machine learning and computer vision.

Our work shows a close connection between these problems and core questions in algorithmic graph theory. While this connection demonstrates the difficulties of obtaining runtime guarantees, it also suggests an approach of using techniques originally developed for graph algorithms.

We show that most of these problems can be formulated as a grouped least squares problem, and give efficient algorithms for this formulation. Our algorithms rely on routines for solving quadratic minimization problems, which in turn are equivalent to solving linear systems. Some preliminary experimental work on image processing tasks are also presented.

Categories and Subject Descriptors

F.2 [**Theory of Computation**]: Analysis of Algorithms and Problem Complexity

Keywords

Image processing, Optimization, Regression

*Partially supported by the National Science Foundation under grant number CCF-1018463 and National Eye Institute (R01-EY01317-08, RO1-EY11289-22).

†Part of this work was done while at MIT and MSR New England

‡Partially supported by Natural Sciences and Engineering Research Council of Canada (NSERC) under grant number D-390928-2010, and by a Microsoft Fellowship. Part of this work was done while at MSR New England.

1. INTRODUCTION

The problem of recovering a clear signal from noisy data is an important problem in signal processing. One general approach to this problem is to formulate an objective based on required properties of the answer, and then return its minimizer via optimization algorithms. The power of this method was first demonstrated in image denoising, where the total variation minimization approach by Rudin, Osher and Fatemi [36] had much success. More recent works on sparse recovery led to the theory of compressed sensing [7], which includes approaches such as the least absolute shrinkage and selection operator (LASSO) objective due to Tibshirani [40]. These objective functions have proven to be immensely powerful tools, applicable to problems in signal processing, statistics, and computer vision. In the most general form, given vector $\mathbf{y}$ and a matrix $\mathbf{A}$, one seeks to minimize:

$$\min_{\mathbf{x}} ||\mathbf{y} - \mathbf{A}\mathbf{x}||_2^2 \quad \text{subject to: } |\mathbf{x}|_1 \leq c \tag{1.1}$$

It can be shown to be equivalent to the following by introducing a Lagrangian multiplier, λ:

$$\min_{\mathbf{x}} ||\mathbf{y} - \mathbf{A}\mathbf{x}||_2^2 + \lambda|\mathbf{x}|_1 \tag{1.2}$$

Many of the algorithms used to minimize the LASSO objective in practice are first order methods [33, 3], which updates a sequence of solutions using well-defined vectors related to the gradient. These methods are guaranteed to converge well when the matrix $\mathbf{A}$ is "well-structured". The formal definition of this well-structuredness is closely related to the conditions required by the guarantees given in the compressed sensing literature [7] for the recovery of a sparse signal. As a result, these methods perform very well on problems where theoretical guarantees for solution quality are known. This good performance, combined with the simplicity of implementation, makes these algorithms the method of choice for most problems.

However, LASSO type approaches have also been successfully applied to larger classes of problems. This has in turn led to the use of these algorithms on a much wider variety of problem instances. An important case is image denoising, where works on LASSO-type objectives predates the compressed sensing literature [36]. The matrices involved here are based on the connectivity of the underlying pixel structure, which is often a $\sqrt{n} \times \sqrt{n}$ square mesh. Even in a unweighted setting, these matrices tend to be ill-conditioned. In addition, the emergence of non-local formulations that can connect arbitrary pairs of vertices in the graph also highlights the need to handle problems that are traditionally considered ill-conditioned. We show in Appendix A that the broadest definition of LASSO problems include well-studied problems from algorithmic graph theory:

FACT 1.1. *Both the s-t shortest path and s-t minimum cut problems in undirected graphs can be solved by minimizing a LASSO objective.*

Although linear time algorithms for unweighted shortest path are known, finding efficient parallel algorithms for this has been a long-standing open problem. The current state of the art parallel algorithm for finding $1+\epsilon$ approximate solutions, due to Cohen [10], is quite involved. Furthermore, as the reductions done in Lemma A.1 are readily parallelizable, an efficient algorithm for LASSO minimization would also lead to an efficient parallel shortest path algorithm. This suggests that algorithms for minimizing LASSO objectives, where each iteration involve simple, parallelizable operations, are also difficult. Finding a minimum s-t cut with nearly-linear running time is also a long standing open question in algorithm design. In fact, there are known hard instances where many algorithms do exhibit their worst case behavior [20]. The difficulty of these problems and the non-linear nature of the objective are two of the main challenges in obtaining fast run time guarantees for grouped least squares minimization.

Previous run time guarantees for minimizing LASSO objectives rely on general convex optimization routines [6], which take at least $\Omega(n^2)$ time. As the resolution of images are typically at least 256×256, this running time is prohibitive. As a result, when processing image streams or videos in real time, gradient descent or filtering based approaches are typically used due to time constraints, often at the cost of solution quality. The continuing increase in problem instance size, due to higher resolution of streaming videos, or 3D medical images with billions of voxels, makes the study of faster algorithms an increasingly important question.

While the connection between LASSO and graph problems gives us reasons to believe that the difficulty of graph problems also exists in minimizing LASSO objectives, it also suggests that techniques from algorithmic graph theory can be brought to bear. To this end, we draw upon recent developments in algorithms for maximum flow [9] and minimum cost flow [13]. We show that relatively direct modifications of these algorithms allows us to solve a generalization of most LASSO objectives, which we term the **grouped least squares problem**. Our algorithm is similar to convex optimization algorithms in that each iteration of it solves a quadratic minimization problem, which is equivalent to solving a linear system. The speedup over previous algorithms come from the existence of much faster solvers for graph related linear systems [38], although our approaches are also applicable to situations involving other underlying quadratic minimization problems.

The organization of this paper is as follows: In Section 2 we provide a unified optimization problem that encompasses LASSO, fused LASSO, and grouped LASSO. We then discuss known applications of the grouped least squares minimization in Section 3 and other algorithms in Section 4. Section 5 shows an algorithm for approximating grouped least squares based on the maximum flow algorithm of Christiano et al. [9]. Some experimental results demonstrating the practical feasibility of this algorithm are discussed in Section 6. An alternate algorithm with better accuracy, but worse running time dependency on the number of groups is given in Appendix C.

2. BACKGROUND AND FORMULATIONS

The formulation of our main problem is motivated by the total variation objective from image denoising. This objective has its origin in the seminal work by Mumford and Shah [32]. There are two conflicting goals in recovering a smooth image from a noisy one, namely that it must be close to the original image, while having very little noise. The Mumford-Shah function models the second constraint by imposing penalties for neighboring pixels that differ significantly. These terms decrease with the removal of local distortions, offsetting the higher cost of moving further away from the input. However, the minimization of this functional is computationally difficult and subsequent works focused on minimizing functions that are close to it.

The total variation objective is defined for a discrete, pixel representation of the image and measures noise using a smoothness term calculated from differences between neighboring pixels. This objective leads naturally to a graph $G = (V, E)$ corresponding to the image with pixels. The original (noisy) image is given as a vertex labeling $\mathbf{s}$, while the goal of the optimization problem is to recover the 'true' image $\mathbf{x}$, which is another set of vertex labels. The requirement of $\mathbf{x}$ being close to $\mathbf{s}$ is quantified by $||\mathbf{x} - \mathbf{s}||_2^2$, which is the square of the L_2 norm of the vector that's identified as noise. To this is added the smoothness term, which is a sum over absolute values of difference between adjacent pixels' labels:

$$||\mathbf{x} - \mathbf{s}||_2^2 + \sum_{(u,v)\in E} |x_u - x_v| \tag{2.3}$$

This objective can be viewed as an instance of the fused LASSO objective [41]. As the orientation of the underlying pixel grid is artificially imposed by the camera, this method can introduce rotational bias in its output. One way to correct this bias is to group the differences of each pixel with its 4 neighbors, giving terms of the form:

$$\sqrt{(x_u - x_v)^2 + (x_u - x_w)^2} \tag{2.4}$$

where v and w are the horizontal and vertical neighbor of u.

Our generalization of these objectives is based on the key observation that $\sqrt{(x_u - x_v)^2 + (x_u - x_w)^2}$ and $|x_u - x_v|$ are both L_2 norms of vectors consisting of differences of values between adjacent pixels. Each such difference can be viewed as an edge in the underlying graph, and the grouping gives a natural partition of the edges into disjoint sets $S_1 \dots S_k$:

$$||\mathbf{x} - \mathbf{s}||_2^2 + \sum_{1\le i\le k} \sqrt{\sum_{(u,v)\in S_i} (x_u - x_v)^2} \tag{2.5}$$

When each S_i contain a single edge, this formulation is identical to the objective in Equation 2.3 since $\sqrt{(x_u - x_v)^2} =$

$|x_u - x_v|$. To make the first term resemble the other terms in our objective, we will take a square root of it – as we prove in Appendix D, algorithms that give exact minimizers for this variant still captures the original version of the problem. Also, the terms inside the square roots can be written as quadratic positive semi-definite terms involving $\mathbf{x}$. The simplified problem now becomes:

$$||\mathbf{x} - \mathbf{s}||_2 + \sum_{1 \le i \le k} \sqrt{\mathbf{x}^T \mathbf{L}_i \mathbf{x}} \tag{2.6}$$

We use $||\cdot||_{\mathbf{L}_i}$ to denote the norm induced by the PSD matrix $\mathbf{L}_i$, and rewrite each of the later terms as $||\mathbf{x}||_{\mathbf{L}_i}$. Fixed labels $\mathbf{s}_1 \dots \mathbf{s}_k$ an also be introduced for each of the groups, with roles similar to let $\mathbf{s} = \mathbf{s}_0$. As the L_2 norm is equivalent to the norm given by the identify matrix, $||\mathbf{x}-\mathbf{s}_0||_2$ is also a term of the form $||\mathbf{x} - \mathbf{s}_i||_{\mathbf{L}_i}$. These generalizations allows us to define our main problem:

DEFINITION 2.1. *The* **grouped least squares problem** *is:*

Input: $n \times n$ matrices $\boldsymbol{L}_1 \dots \boldsymbol{L}_k$ and fixed values $\boldsymbol{s}_1 \dots \boldsymbol{s}_k \in \Re^n$.

Output:

$$\min_{\boldsymbol{x}} \mathcal{OBJ}(\boldsymbol{x}) = \sum_{1 \le i \le k} ||\boldsymbol{x} - \boldsymbol{s}_i||_{\boldsymbol{L}_i}$$

Note that this objective allows for the usual definition of LASSO involving terms of the form $|\mathbf{x}_u|$ by having one group for each such variable with $\mathbf{s}_i = \mathbf{0}$. It is also related to group LASSO [44], which incorporates similar assumptions about closer dependencies among some of the terms. To our knowledge grouping has not been studied in conjunction with fused LASSO, although many problems such as the ones listed in Section 3 require this generalization.

2.1 Quadratic Minimization and Solving Linear Systems

Our algorithmic approach to the group least squares problem crucially depends on solving a related quadratic minimization problem. Specifically, we solve linear systems involving a weighted combination of the $\mathbf{L}_i$ matrices. Let $\mathbf{w}_1 \dots \mathbf{w}_k \in \Re^+$ denote weights, where $\mathbf{w}_i$ is the weight on the ith group. Then the quadratic minimization problem that we consider is:

$$\min_{\mathbf{x}} \mathcal{OBJ}2(\mathbf{x}, \mathbf{w}) = \sum_{1 \le i \le k} \frac{1}{\mathbf{w}_i} ||\mathbf{x} - \mathbf{s}_i||^2_{\mathbf{L}_i}$$

We will use OPT2($\mathbf{w}$) to denote the minimum value that is attainable. This minimizer, $\mathbf{x}$, can be obtained using the following Lemma:

LEMMA 2.2. *$\mathcal{OBJ}2(\boldsymbol{x}, \boldsymbol{w})$ is minimized for $\boldsymbol{x}$ such that*

$$\left(\sum_{1 \le i \le k} \frac{1}{\boldsymbol{w}_i} \boldsymbol{L}_i \right) \boldsymbol{x} = \sum_{1 \le i \le k} \frac{1}{\boldsymbol{w}_i} \boldsymbol{s}_i$$

Therefore the quadratic minimization problem reduces to a linear system solve involving $\sum_i \frac{1}{\mathbf{w}_i} \mathbf{L}_i$, or $\sum_i \alpha_i \mathbf{L}_i$ where α is an arbitrary set of positive coefficients. In general, this can be done in $O(n^\omega)$ time where ω is the matrix multiplication constant [39, 11, 42]. When $\mathbf{L}_i$ is symmetric diagonally dominant, which is the case for image applications and most graph problems, these systems can be approximately solved to ϵ accuracy in $\tilde{O}(m \log(1/\epsilon))$ [1] time, where m is the total number of non-zero entries in the matrices [37, 38, 25, 26], and also in $\tilde{O}(m^{1/3+\theta} \log(1/\epsilon))$ parallel depth [4]. There has also been work on extending this type of approach to a wider class of systems [2], with works on systems arising from well-spaced finite-element meshes [5], 2-D trusses [12], and certain types of quadratically coupled flows [21]. For the analysis of our algorithms, we treat this step as a black box with running time $T(n, m)$. Furthermore, to simplify our presentation we assume that the solves return exact answers, as errors can be brought to polynomially small values with an extra $O(\log n)$ overhead. We believe analyses similar to those performed in [9, 21] can be adapted if we use approximate solves instead of exact ones.

3. APPLICATIONS

A variety of problems ranging from computer vision to statistics can be formulated as grouped least squares. We describe some of them below, starting with classical problems from image processing.

3.1 Total Variation Minimization

As mentioned in Section 1, one of the earliest applications of these objectives was in the context of image processing. More commonly known as total variation minimization in this setting [8], various variants of the objective have been proposed with the anisotropic objective the same as Equation 2.3 and the isotropic objective being the one shown in Equation 2.5.

Obtaining a unified algorithm for isotropic and anisotropic TV was one of the main motivations for our work. Our results lead to an algorithm that approximately minimizes both variants in $\tilde{O}(m^{4/3}\epsilon^{-8/3})$ time. It's worth noting that this guarantee does not rely on the underlying structure of the of the graph. This makes the algorithm readily applicable to 3-D images or non-local models involving the addition of edges across the image . However, when the neighborhoods are those of a 2-D image, a $\log n$ factor speedup can be obtained by using the optimal solver for planar systems given in [24].

3.2 Denoising with Multiple Colors

Most works on image denoising deals with images where each pixel is described using a single number corresponding to its intensity. A natural extension would be to colored images, where each pixel has a set of c attributes (in the RGB case, $c = 3$). One possible analogue of $|x_i - x_j|$ in this case would be $||x_i - x_j||_2$, and this modification can be incorporated by replacing a cluster involving a single edge with clusters over the c edges between the corresponding pixels.

This type of approach can be viewed as an instance image reconstruction algorithms using Markov random fields. Instead of labeling each vertex with a single attribute, a

[1]We use $\tilde{O}(f(m))$ to denote $\tilde{O}(f(m) \log^c f(m))$ for some constant c.

set of c attributes are used instead and the correlation between vertices is represented using arbitrary PSD matrices. It's worth remarking that when such matrices have bounded condition number, it was shown in [21] that the resulting least squares problem can still be solved efficiently by preconditioning with SDD matrices, yielding a similar overall running time.

3.3 Poisson Image Editing

The Poisson Image Editing method of Perez, Gangnet and Blake [34] is a very popular method for image blending. This method aims to minimize the difference between the gradient of the image and a guidance field vector $\mathbf{v}$. We show here that the grouped least square problem can be used for minimizing objectives from this framework. The objective function given in equation (6) of [34]

$$\min_{f|\Omega} \sum_{(p,q)\cap\Omega\neq\emptyset} (f_p - f_q - v_{pq})^2, \text{ with } f_p = f_p^* \ \forall p \in \partial\Omega$$

comprises mainly of terms of the form:

$$(x_p - x_q - v_{pq})^2$$

This term can be rewritten as $((x_p - x_q) - (v_{pq} - 0))^2$. So if we let $\mathbf{s}_i$ be the vector where $s_{i,p} = v_{pq}$ and $s_{i,q} = 0$, and $\mathbf{L}_i$ be the graph Laplacian for the edge connecting p and q, then the term equals to $||\mathbf{x} - \mathbf{s}_i||^2_{\mathbf{L}_i}$. The other terms on the boundary will have x_q as a constant, leading to terms of the form $||x_{i,p} - s_{i,p}||_2^2$ where $s_{i,p} = x_q$. Therefore the discrete Poisson problem of minimizing the sum of these squares is an instance of the quadratic minimization problem as described in Section 2.1. Perez et al. in Section 2 of their paper observed that these linear systems are sparse, symmetric and positive definite. We make the additional observation here that the systems involved are also symmetric diagonally dominant. The use of the grouped least squares framework also allows the possibility of augmenting these objectives with additional L_1 or L_2 terms.

3.4 Clustering

Hocking et al. [19] recently studied an approach for clustering points in d dimensional space. Given a set of points $x_1 \dots x_n \in \Re^d$, one method that they proposed is the minimization of the following objective function:

$$\min_{y_1 \dots y_n \in \Re^d} \sum_{i=1}^{n} ||x_i - y_i||_2^2 + \lambda \sum_{ij} w_{ij} ||y_i - y_j||_2$$

Where w_{ij} are weights indicating the association between items i and j. This problem can be viewed in the grouped least squares framework by viewing each x_i and y_i as a list of d variables, giving that the $||x_i - y_i||_2$ and $||y_i - y_j||_2$ terms can be represented using a cluster of d edges. Hocking et al. used the Frank-Wolfe algorithm to minimize a relaxed form of this objective and observed fast behavior in practice. In the grouped least squares framework, this problem is an instance with $O(n^2)$ groups and $O(dn^2)$ edges. Combining with the observation that the underlying quadratic optimization problems can be solved efficiently allows us to obtain an $1+\epsilon$ approximate solution in $\tilde{O}(dn^{8/3}\epsilon^{-8/3})$ time.

4. PREVIOUS ALGORITHMIC RESULTS

Due to the importance of optimization problems motivated by LASSO there has been much work on efficient algorithms for them. We briefly describe some of the previous approaches for LASSO minimization below.

4.1 Second-order Cone Programming

To the best of our knowledge, the only algorithms that provide robust worst-case bounds for the entire class of grouped least squares problems are based on applying tools from convex optimization. In particular, it is known that interior point methods applied to these problems converge in $\tilde{O}(\sqrt{k})$ iterations with each iterations requiring solving a certain linear system [6, 17]. Unfortunately, computing these solutions is computationally expensive – the best previous bound for solving one of these systems is $O(m^\omega)$ where ω is the matrix multiplication exponent. This results in fairly large $O(m^{1/2+\omega})$ total running time and contributes to the popularity of first-order methods described above in practical scenarios. We will revisit this approach in Appendix C and show an improved algorithm for the inner iterations. However, its running time still has a fairly large dependency on k.

4.2 Graph Cuts

For the anisotropic total variation objective shown in Equation 2.3, a minimizer can be found by solving a large number of almost-exact maximum flow calls [14, 22]. Although the number of iterations can be large, these works show that the number of problem instances that a pixel can appear in is small. Combining this reduction with the fastest known exact algorithm for the maximum flow problem by Goldberg and Rao [16] gives an algorithm that runs in $\tilde{O}(m^{3/2})$ time.

It's worth mentioning that both of these algorithms requires extracting the minimum cut in order to construct the problems for subsequent iterations. As a result, it's not clear whether recent advances on fast approximations of maximum flow and minimum s-t cuts [9] can be used as a black box with these algorithms. Extending this approach to the non-linear isotropic objective also appears to be difficult.

4.3 Iterative Reweighted Least Squares

An approach similar to convex optimization methods, but has much better observed rates of convergence is the iterative reweighted least squares (IRLS) method. This method does a much more aggressive adjustment each iteration and to give good performances in practice [43].

4.4 First Order Methods

The method of choice in practice are first order methods such as [33, 3]. Theoretically these methods are known to converge rapidly when the objective function satisfies certain Lipschitz conditions. Many of the more recent works on first order methods focus on lowering the dependency of ϵ under these conditions. As discussed in Section 1 and Appendix A, this direction can be considered orthogonal to our guarantees as the grouped least squares problem is a significantly more general formulation.

5. APPROXIMATE ALGORITHM USING QUADRATIC MINIMIZATIONS

In this section, we show an approximate algorithm for the grouped least squares problem. The analyses of the algorithms is intricate, but is closely based on the approximate minimum cut algorithm given by Christiano et al. [9]. The main modifications that we make are presented in this section, while the full analysis is in Appendix B. A different algorithm based on the lossy generalized flow algorithm given in [13] is presented in Appendix C. It has better error dependencies, but also takes much more time for moderate number of groups. Both of these algorithms can be viewed as reductions to the quadratic minimization problems described in Section 2.1. As a result, they imply efficient algorithms for problems where fast algorithms are known for the corresponding least squares problems.

Recall that the minimum s-t cut problem - equivalent to an L_1-minimization problem - is a special case of the grouped least squares problem where each edge belongs to its own group(i.e., $k = m$). As a result, it's natural to extend the approach of [9] to the whole spectrum of values of k by treating each group as an 'edge'.

One view of the cut algorithm from [9] is that it places a weight on each group, and minimizes a quadratic, or L_2^2 problem involving terms of the from $\frac{1}{\mathbf{w}_i}||\mathbf{x} - \mathbf{s}_i||^2_{\mathbf{L}_i}$. Their algorithm then adjusts the weights based on the flow on each edge using the multiplicative weights update framework [1, 29]. This flow is in turn obtained from the dual of the quadratic minimization problem. We simplify this step by showing that the energy of the groups from the quadratic minimization problems can be directly used. Pseudocode of the algorithm is shown in Algorithm 1.

Algorithm 1 Algorithm for the approximate decision problem of whether there exist vertex potentials with objective at most OPT

ApproxGroupedLeastSquares

Input: PSD matrices $\mathbf{L}_1 \dots \mathbf{L}_k$, fixed values $\mathbf{s}_1 \dots \mathbf{s}_k$ for each group. Routine Solve for solving linear systems, width parameter ρ and error bound ϵ.

Output: Vector $\mathbf{x}$ such that $\mathcal{OBJ}(\mathbf{x}) \leq (1 + 10\epsilon)\text{OPT}$.

1: Initialize $\mathbf{w}_i^{(0)} = 1$ for all $1 \leq i \leq k$
2: $N \leftarrow 10\rho \log n\epsilon^{-2}$
3: **for** $t = 1 \dots N$ **do**
4: $\quad\mu^{(t-1)} \leftarrow \sum_i \mathbf{w}_i^{(t-1)}$
5: $\quad$Use Solve to compute a minimizer for the quadratic minimization problem where $\alpha_i = \frac{1}{\mathbf{w}_i^{(t-1)}}$, let this solution be $\mathbf{x}^{(t)}$
6: $\quad$Let $\lambda^{(t)} = \sqrt{\mu^{(t-1)}\mathcal{OBJ}2(\mathbf{x}^{(t)})}$
7: $\quad$Update the weight of each group:
$$\mathbf{w}_i^{(t)} \leftarrow \mathbf{w}_i^{(t-1)} + \left(\frac{\epsilon}{\rho}\frac{||\mathbf{x}^{(t)} - \mathbf{s}_i||_{\mathbf{L}_i}}{\lambda^{(t)}} + \frac{2\epsilon^2}{k\rho}\right)\mu^{(t-1)}$$
8: **end for**
9: $\bar{t} \leftarrow \arg\min_{0 \leq t \leq N} \mathcal{OBJ}(\mathbf{x}^{(t)})$
10: **return** $\mathbf{x}^{(\bar{t})}$

The main difficulty of analyzing this algorithm is that the analysis of minimum s-t cut algorithm of [9] relies strongly on the existence of a solution where $\mathbf{x}$ is either 0 or 1. Our analysis extends this potential function into the fractional setting via. a function based on the Kulback-Liebler (KL) divergence [28]. To our knowledge the use of this potential with multiplicative weights was first introduced by Freund and Schapire [15], and is common in learning theory. This function can be viewed as measuring the KL-divergence between $\mathbf{w}_i^{(t)}$ and $||\bar{\mathbf{x}} - \mathbf{s}_i||_{\mathbf{L}_i}$ over all groups, where $\bar{\mathbf{x}}$ an optimum solution to the grouped least squares problem. This term, which we denote as D_{KL} is:

$$D_{KL} = \sum_i ||\bar{\mathbf{x}} - \mathbf{s}_i||_{\mathbf{L}_i} \log\left(\frac{||\bar{\mathbf{x}} - \mathbf{s}_i||_{\mathbf{L}_i}}{\mathbf{w}_i^{(t)}}\right) \tag{5.7}$$

One way to interpret this function is that $||\mathbf{x} - \mathbf{s}_i||_{\mathbf{L}_i}$ and $\frac{1}{\mathbf{w}_i}||\mathbf{x}-\mathbf{s}_i||^2_{\mathbf{L}_i}$ are equal when $\mathbf{w}_i = ||\mathbf{x}-\mathbf{s}_i||_{\mathbf{L}_i}$. Therefore, this algorithm can be viewed as gradually adjusts the weights to become a scaled copy of $||\bar{\mathbf{x}}-\mathbf{s}_i||_{\mathbf{L}_i}$, and D_{KL} serves a way to measure this difference. It can be simplified by subtracting the constant term given by $\sum_i ||\bar{\mathbf{x}} - \mathbf{s}_i||_{\mathbf{L}_i^{(t)}} \log(||\bar{\mathbf{x}} - \mathbf{s}_i||_{\mathbf{L}_i^{(t)}})$ and multiplying by $-1/\text{OPT}$. This gives us our key potential function, $\nu^{(t)}$:

$$\nu^{(t)} = \frac{1}{\text{OPT}} \sum_i ||\bar{\mathbf{x}} - \mathbf{s}_i||_{\mathbf{L}_i} \log(\mathbf{w}_i^{(t)}) \tag{5.8}$$

It's worth noting that in the case of the cut algorithm, this function is identical to the potential function used in [9]. We show the convergence of our algorithm by proving that if the solution produced in some iteration is far from optimal, $\nu^{(t)}$ increases substantially. Upper bounding it with a term related to the sum of weights, $\mu^{(t)}$ allows us to prove convergence. The full proof is given in Appendix B.

To simplify the analysis, we assume that the guess that we're trying to solve the decision problem on, OPT, all entries of $\mathbf{s}$, and spectrum of $\mathbf{L}_i$ are polynomially bounded in n. That is, there exist some constant d such that $-n^d \leq \mathbf{s}_{i,u} \leq n^d$ and $n^{-d}\mathbf{I} \preceq \sum_i \mathbf{L}_i \preceq n^d\mathbf{I}$ where $\mathbf{A} \preceq \mathbf{B}$ means $\mathbf{B} - \mathbf{A}$ is PSD. Some of these assumptions can be relaxed via. analyses similar to Section 2 of [9].

Theorem 5.1. *On input of an instance of $\mathcal{OBJ}$ with edges partitioned into k sets. If all parameters polynomially bounded between n^{-d} and n^d, running* ApproxGroupedLeastSquares *with $\rho = 2k^{1/3}\epsilon^{-2/3}$ returns a solution $\boldsymbol{x}$ with such that $\mathcal{OBJ}(\boldsymbol{x}) \leq \max\{(1+10\epsilon)OPT, n^{-d}\}$ where OPT is the value of the optimum solution.*

The additive n^{-d} case is included to deal with the case where OPT $= 0$, or is close to it. We believe it should be also possible to handle this case by restricting the condition number of $\sum_i \mathbf{L}_i$.

6. EVIDENCE OF PRACTICAL FEASIBILITY

We performed a series of experiments using the approximate algorithm described in Section 5 in order to demonstrate its practical feasibility. Their running times that are slower than the state of the art methods, but nonetheless reasonable. This suggests the need of further experimental works on a more optimized version, which is outside of the scope of this paper.

The SDD linear systems that arise in the quadratic minimization problems were solved using the combinatorial multigrid (CMG) solver [23, 27]. One side observation confirmed by these experiments is that for the sparse SDD linear systems that arise from image processing, the CMG solver yields good results both in accuracy and running time.

6.1 Total Variational Denoising

Total Variational Denoising is the concept of applying Total Variational Minimization as denoising process. This was pioneered by Rudin, Osher and Fatemi [36] and is commonly known as the ROF image model [8]. Our approximate algorithm from Section 5 yields a simple way to solve the ROF model and most of its variants. In Figure 1, we present a simple denoising experiment using the standard image processing data set, 'Lenna'. The main goal of the experiment is to show that our algorithm is competitive in terms of accuracy, while having running times comparable to first-order methods. On a 512×512 grayscale image, we introduce Additive White Gaussian Noise (AWGN) at a measured Signal to Noise Ratio (SNR) of 2. AWGN is the most common noise model in photon capturing sensors from consumer cameras to space satellites systems. We compare the results produced by our algorithm with those by the Split Bregman algorithm from [18] and the Gauss-Seidel variation of the fixed point algorithm from [30]. These methods minimize an objective with L_2^2 fidelity term given in Equation 2.3 while we used the variant with L_2 fidelity shown in Equation 2.6. Also, the parameters in these algorithms were picked to give the best results for the objective functions being minimized. As a result, for measuring the qualities of output images we only use the L_2 and L_1 norms of pixel-wise differences with the original image.

Our experiments were conducted on a single core 64-bit Intel(R) Xeon(R) E5440 CPU @ 2.83GHz. The non-solver portion of the algorithm was implemented in Matlab(R). On images of size 256×256, 512×512 and 1024×1024, the average running times are 2.31, 9.70 and 47.61 seconds respectively. These running times are noticeably slower than the state of the art. However, it's worth noting is that on average 45% of the total running time is from solving the SDD linear systems using the CMG solver. The rest is mostly from reweighting edges and MATLAB function calls, which should be much faster in more optimized versions. More importantly, in all of our experiments the weights are observed to converge in under 15 iterations, even for larger images of size up to 3000×3000.

6.2 Image Processing

As exemplified by the denoising with colors application discussed in Section 3.2, the grouped least squares framework can be used for a wide range of image processing tasks. Some examples of such applications are shown in Figure 2. Our denoising algorithm can be applied as a preprocessing step to segmenting images of the retina obtained from Optical Coherence Tomography (OCT) scans. Here the key is to preserve the sharpness between the nerve fiber layers and this is achieve by using a L_1 regularization term. Variations of this formulation allows one to emulate a large variety of established image preprocessing applications. For example, introducing additional L_2 terms containing differences of neighboring pixels of a patch leads to the removal of boundaries, giving an overall blurring effect. On our examples, this leads to results similar to methods that apply a filter over the image, such as Gaussian blurring. Introducing such effects using an objective function has the advantage that it can be used in conjunction with other terms. By mixing and matching penalty terms on the groups, we can preserve global features while favoring the removal of small artifacts introduced by sensor noise.

Noisy Version
29.29E3, 8.85E6

Split Bregman
6.70E3, 1.89E6

Grouped Least Squares
5.99E3, 1.39E6

Fixed Point
6.64E3, 1.87E6

Figure 1: Outputs of various denoising algorithms on image with AWGN noise. Starting form top left in clock-wise order: noisy version, Split Bregman [18], Fixed Point [30], and Grouped Least Squares. Errors listed below each figure from left to right are L_2 and L_1 norms of differences with the original.

Examples of Poisson Image Editing mentioned in Section 3.3 are shown in Figure 3. The application is seamless cloning as described in Section 3 of [34], which aims to insert complex objects into another image. Given two images, they are blended by solving the discrete poisson equation based on a mix of their gradients and boundary values. We also added L_2 constraints on different parts of the image to give a smoother result. Below we show two examples produced by our algorithm with inputs on the left and results on the right. The input consists of locations of the foreground pictures over the background, along with boundaries (shown in red) around the objects in the foreground. These rough boundaries makes the blending of surrounding textures the main challenge, and our three examples (void/sky, sea/pool, snow/sand) are some representative situations. These examples also show that our approaches can be extended to handle multichannel images (RGB or multi-spectral) with only a few modifications.

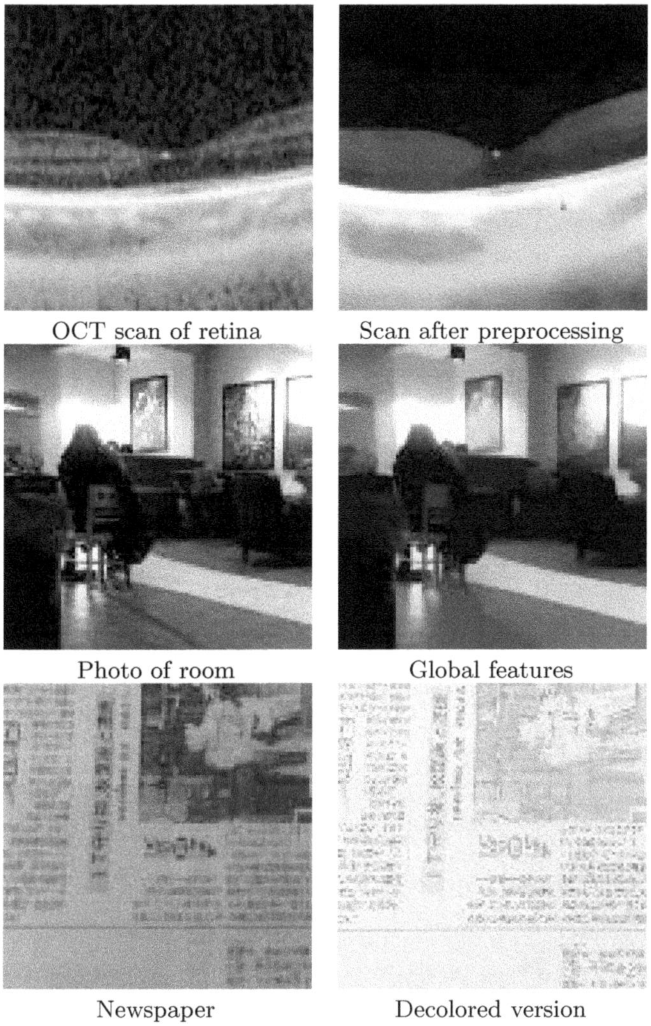

Figure 2: Applications to various image processing tasks. From top to bottom: image segmentation, global feature extraction / blurring, and decoloring.

Figure 3: Examples of seamless cloning using Poisson Image Editing

7. REMARKS

We believe that the ability of our algorithm to encompass many of the current image processing algorithms represents a major advantage in practice. It allows the use of a common data structure (the underlying graph) and subroutine (linear system solvers) for many different tasks in the image processing pipeline. Theoretically, the grouped least squares problem is also interesting as it represents an intermediate problem between linear and quadratic optimization.

The performances of our algorithms given in Section 5 and Appendix C depend on k, which is the number of groups in the formulation given in Definition 2.1. Two settings of k are helpful for comparison to previous works. When $k = 1$, the problem becomes the electrical flow problem, and the running time of both algorithms are similar to directly solving the linear system. This is also the case when there is a small (constant) number of groups. The other extremum is when each edge belongs to its own group, aka. $k = m$. Here our approximate algorithm is the same as the minimum s-t cut algorithm given in [9], but our analysis for our almost-exact algorithm gives a much worse running time. This is due to the interior point algorithm generating more complicated linear systems, and occurs when most groups contain a small number of edges. As a result, more work is needed on faster almost-exact algorithms for problems with intermediate values of k. One other consequence of this dependency on k is that although the problem with smaller number of groups is no longer captured by linear optimization, the minimum s-t cut problem – that still falls within the framework of linear optimization – is in some sense the hardest problem in this class. Therefore we believe that the grouped least squares problem is a natural interpolation between the L_1 and L_2^2 optimization, and has potential to be used as a subroutine in other algorithms.

The preliminary experimental results from Section 6 show that more aggressive reweightings of edges lead to much faster convergence than what we showed for our two algorithms. Although the running time from these experiments are slower than state of the art methods, we believe the results suggest that more thorough experimental studies with better tuned algorithms are needed. Also, the Mumford-Shah functional can be better approximated by non-convex functions [32]. Objectives as hinged loss often lead to better results in practice [35], but few algorithmic guarantees are known for them. Designing algorithms with strong guarantees for minimizing these objectives is an interesting direction for future work.

Acknowledgements

The authors would like to thank Jerome Darbon, Stanley Osher, Aarti Singh and Ryan Tibshirani for pointing them to works that are relevant to the grouped least squares framework, and also an anonymous reviewer of a previous submis-

[2]Image of Mars courtesy of NASA/JPL-Caltech/MSSS

sion of this paper for pointing out an alternate view of the proof of Theorem 5.1.

8. REFERENCES

[1] S. Arora, E. Hazan, and S. Kale. The multiplicative weights update method: a meta algorithm and applications. Technical report, Princeton University, 2005. 5

[2] H. Avron, G. Shklarski, and S. Toledo. On element SDD approximability. *CoRR*, abs/0911.0547, 2009. 2.1

[3] S. R. Becker, E. J. Candes, and M. Grant. Templates for convex cone problems with applications to sparse signal recovery. *MATHEMATICAL PROGRAMMING COMPUTATION*, 3:165, 2011. 1, 4.4

[4] G. E. Blelloch, A. Gupta, I. Koutis, G. L. Miller, R. Peng, and K. Tangwongsan. Near linear-work parallel SDD solvers, low-diameter decomposition, and low-stretch subgraphs. In *Proceedings of the 23rd ACM symposium on Parallelism in algorithms and architectures*, SPAA '11, pages 13–22, New York, NY, USA, 2011. ACM. 2.1

[5] E. G. Boman, B. Hendrickson, and S. A. Vavasis. Solving elliptic finite element systems in near-linear time with support preconditioners. *CoRR*, cs.NA/0407022, 2004. 2.1

[6] S. Boyd and L. Vandenberghe. *Convex Optimization*. Camebridge University Press, 2004. 1, 4.1, C, C.1

[7] J. Candes, E. Compressive sampling. *Proceedings of the International Congress of Mathematicians*, 2006. 1, 1

[8] T. Chan and J. Shen. *Image Processing And Analysis: Variational, Pde, Wavelet, And Stochastic Methods*. SIAM, 2005. 3.1, 6.1

[9] P. Christiano, J. A. Kelner, A. Mądry, D. Spielman, and S.-H. Teng. Electrical Flows, Laplacian Systems, and Faster Approximation of Maximum Flow in Undirected Graphs. In *Proceedings of the 43rd ACM Symposium on Theory of Computing (STOC)*, 2011. 1, 2.1, 4.2, 5, 5, 5, 7, B, B

[10] E. Cohen. Polylog-time and near-linear work approximation scheme for undirected shortest paths. *J. ACM*, 47(1):132–166, 2000. 1

[11] D. Coppersmith and S. Winograd. Matrix multiplication via arithmetical progressions. *J. Symbolic Computation*, 9:251–280, 1990. 2.1

[12] S. I. Daitch and D. A. Spielman. Support-graph preconditioners for 2-dimensional trusses. *CoRR*, abs/cs/0703119, 2007. 2.1

[13] S. I. Daitch and D. A. Spielman. Faster approximate lossy generalized flow via interior point algorithms. In *Proceedings of the 40th annual ACM symposium on Theory of computing*, STOC '08, pages 451–460, New York, NY, USA, 2008. ACM. 1, 5, A, C

[14] J. Darbon and M. Sigelle. Image restoration with discrete constrained total variation part i: Fast and exact optimization. *Journal of Mathematical Imaging and Vision*, 26(3):261–276, 2006. 4.2

[15] Y. Freund and R. E. Schapire. Adaptive game playing using multiplicative weights. *Games and Economic Behavior*, 29(1-2):79–103, October 1999. 5

[16] A. V. Goldberg and S. Rao. Beyond the flow decomposition barrier. *J. ACM*, 45:783–797, September 1998. 4.2

[17] D. Goldfarb and W. Yin. Second-order cone programming methods for total variation-based image restoration. *SIAM J. Sci. Comput*, 27:622–645, 2004. 4.1, C

[18] T. Goldstein and S. Osher. The split bregman method for l1-regularized problems. *SIAM J. Img. Sci.*, 2:323–343, April 2009. 6.1, 1

[19] T. Hocking, J.-P. Vert, F. Bach, and A. Joulin. Clusterpath: an algorithm for clustering using convex fusion penalties. In L. Getoor and T. Scheffer, editors, *Proceedings of the 28th International Conference on Machine Learning (ICML-11)*, ICML '11, pages 745–752, New York, NY, USA, June 2011. ACM. 3.4

[20] D. S. Johnson and C. C. McGeoch, editors. *Network Flows and Matching: First DIMACS Implementation Challenge*. American Mathematical Society, Boston, MA, USA, 1993. 1

[21] J. A. Kelner, G. L. Miller, and R. Peng. Faster approximate multicommodity flow using quadratically coupled flows. In *Proceedings of the 44th symposium on Theory of Computing*, STOC '12, pages 1–18, New York, NY, USA, 2012. ACM. 2.1, 3.2

[22] V. Kolmogorov and R. Zabih. What energy functions can be minimized via graph cuts. *IEEE Transactions on Pattern Analysis and Machine Intelligence*, 26:65–81, 2004. 4.2

[23] I. Koutis and G. Miller. The combinatorial multigrid solver. Conference Talk, March 2009. 6

[24] I. Koutis and G. L. Miller. A linear work, $O(n^{1/6})$ time, parallel algorithm for solving planar Laplacians. In *Proc. 18th ACM-SIAM Symposium on Discrete Algorithms (SODA 2007)*, 2007. 3.1

[25] I. Koutis, G. L. Miller, and R. Peng. Approaching optimality for solving sdd linear systems. In *Proceedings of the 2010 IEEE 51st Annual Symposium on Foundations of Computer Science*, FOCS '10, pages 235–244, Washington, DC, USA, 2010. IEEE Computer Society. 2.1

[26] I. Koutis, G. L. Miller, and R. Peng. A nearly-m log n time solver for sdd linear systems. In *Proceedings of the 2011 IEEE 52nd Annual Symposium on Foundations of Computer Science*, FOCS '11, pages 590–598, Washington, DC, USA, 2011. IEEE Computer Society. 2.1

[27] I. Koutis, G. L. Miller, and D. Tolliver. Combinatorial preconditioners and multilevel solvers for problems in computer vision and image processing. In *International Symposium of Visual Computing*, pages 1067–1078, 2009. 6

[28] S. Kullback and R. A. Leibler. On information and sufficiency. *Ann. Math. Statist.*, 22(1):79–86, 1951. 5

[29] N. Littlestone and M. K. Warmuth. The weighted majority algorithm. *Inf. Comput.*, 108(2):212–261, Feb. 1994. 5

[30] C. A. Micchelli, L. Shen, and Y. Xu. Proximity algorithms for image models: denoising. *Inverse Problems*, 27(4):045009, 2011. 6.1, 1

[31] K. Mulmuley, U. V. Vazirani, and V. V. Vazirani. Matching is as easy as matrix inversion. *Combinatorica*, 7(1):105–113, Jan. 1987. A

[32] D. Mumford and J. Shah. Optimal approximations by piecewise smooth functions and associated variational problems. *Communications on Pure and Applied Mathematics*, 42:577–685, 1989. 2, 7

[33] Y. NESTEROV. Gradient methods for minimizing composite objective function. CORE Discussion Papers 2007076, UniversitÃl' catholique de Louvain, Center for Operations Research and Econometrics (CORE), 2007. 1, 4.4

[34] P. Pérez, M. Gangnet, and A. Blake. Poisson image editing. *ACM Transactions on Graphics (SIGGRAPH'03)*, 22(3):313–318, 2003. 3.3, 6.2

[35] L. Rosasco, E. De, V. A. Caponnetto, M. Piana, and A. Verri. Are loss functions all the same. *Neural Computation*, 15, 2004. 7

[36] L. Rudin, S. Osher, and E. Fatemi. Nonlinear total variation based noise removal algorithm. *Physica D*, 1(60):259–268, 1992. 1, 1, 6.1

[37] D. A. Spielman and S.-H. Teng. Nearly-linear time algorithms for graph partitioning, graph sparsification, and solving linear systems. In *Proceedings of the 36th Annual ACM Symposium on Theory of Computing*, pages 81–90, June 2004. 2.1

[38] D. A. Spielman and S.-H. Teng. Nearly-linear time algorithms for preconditioning and solving symmetric, diagonally dominant linear systems. *CoRR*, abs/cs/0607105, 2006. 1, 2.1

[39] V. Strassen. Gaussian elimination is not optimal. *Numerische Mathematik*, 13:354–356, 1969. 2.1

[40] R. Tibshirani. Regression shrinkage and selection via the lasso. *Journal of the Royal Statistical Society (Series B)*, 58:267–288, 1996. 1

[41] R. Tibshirani, M. Saunders, S. Rosset, J. Zhu, and K. Knight. Sparsity and smoothness via the fused lasso. *Journal of the Royal Statistical Society Series B*, 67(1):91–108, 2005. 2

[42] V. Vassilevska Williams. Breaking the Coppersmith-Winograd barrier. In *Proceedings of the 44th symposium on Theory of Computing*, STOC '12, 2012. 2.1

[43] B. Wohlberg and P. Rodriguez. An iteratively reweighted norm algorithm for minimization of total variation functionals. *Signal Processing Letters, IEEE*, 14(12):948 -951, dec. 2007. 4.3

[44] M. Yuan and Y. Lin. Model selection and estimation in regression with grouped variables. *Journal of the Royal Statistical Society, Series B*, 68:49–67, 2006. 2

APPENDIX

A. PROOFS ABOUT GRAPH PROBLEMS AS MINIMIZING LASSO OBJECTIVES

In this section we give formal proofs that show the shortest path problem is an instance of LASSO and the minimum cut problem is an instance of fused-LASSO.

It's worth noting that our proofs do not guarantee that the answers returned are a single path or cut. In fact, when multiple solutions have the same value it's possible for our algorithm to return a linear combination of them. However, we can ensure that the optimum solution is unique using the Isolation Lemma of Mulmuley, Vazarani and Vazarani [31] while only incurring polynomial increase in edge lengths/weights. This analysis is similar to the one in Section 3.5 of [13] for finding a unique minimum cost flow, and is omitted here.

We prove the two claims in Fact 1.1 about shortest path and minimum cut separately in Lemmas A.1 and A.2.

LEMMA A.1. *Given a s-t shortest path instance in an undirected graph where edge lengths $\boldsymbol{l} : E \to \Re^+$ are integers between 1 and n^d. There is a LASSO minimization instance where all entries are bounded by $n^{O(d)}$ such that the value of the LASSO minimizer is within 1 of the optimum answer.*

Proof Our reductions rely crucially on the edge-vertex incidence matrix, which we denote using $\mathbf{B}$. Entries of this matrix are defined as follows:

$$\mathbf{B}_{e,u} = \begin{cases} -1 & \text{if u is the head of e} \\ 1 & \text{if u is the tail of e} \\ 0 & \text{otherwise} \end{cases} \tag{1.9}$$

We first show the reduction for shortest path. Then a path from s to t corresponds to a flow value assigned to all edges, $\mathbf{f} : E \to \Re$ such that $\mathbf{B}^T\mathbf{f} = \chi_{s,t}$. If we have another flow $\mathbf{f}'$ corresponding to any path from s to t, then this constraint can be written as:

$$||\mathbf{B}^T\mathbf{f} - \chi_{s,t}||_2 = \mathbf{0} \tag{1.10}$$

$$||\mathbf{B}^T(\mathbf{f} - \mathbf{f}')||_2 = \mathbf{0}$$

$$||\mathbf{f} - \mathbf{f}'||_{\mathbf{BB}^T} = \mathbf{0} \tag{1.11}$$

The first constraint is closer to the classical LASSO problem while the last one is within our definition of grouped least squares problem. The length of the path can then be written as $\sum_e l_e|f_e|$. Weighting these two terms together gives:

$$\min_{\mathbf{f}} \lambda||\mathbf{f} - \mathbf{f}'||^2_{\mathbf{BB}^T} + \sum_e l_e|f_e| \tag{1.12}$$

Where the maximum entry is bounded by $\max\{n^d, n^2\lambda\}$. Clearly its objective is less than the length of the shortest path, let this solution be $\bar{\mathbf{f}}$. Then since the total objective is at most n^{d+1}, we have that the maximum deviation between $\mathbf{B}^T\bar{\mathbf{f}}$ and $\chi_{s,t}$ is at most n^{d+1}/λ. Then given a spanning tree, each of these deviations can be routed to s or t at a cost of at most n^{d+1} per unit of flow. Therefore we can obtain $\mathbf{f}'$ such that $\mathbf{B}^T\mathbf{f}' = \chi_{s,t}$ whose objective is bigger by at most n^{2d+2}/λ. Therefore setting $\lambda = n^{2d+2}$ guarantees that our objective is within 1 of the length of the shortest path, while the maximum entry in the problem is bounded by $n^{O(d)}$. ∎

We now turn our attention to the minimum cut problem, which can be formulated as finding a vertex labeling $\mathbf{x}^{(vert)}$ where $\mathbf{x}^{(vert)}_s = 0$, $\mathbf{x}^{(vert)}_t = 1$ and the size of the cut, $\sum_{uv \in E} |\mathbf{x}^{(vert)}_u - \mathbf{x}^{(vert)}_v|$. Since the L_1 term in the objective can incorporate single variables, we use an additional vector $\mathbf{x}^{(edge)}$ to indicate differences along edges. The minimum cut problem then becomes minimizing $|\mathbf{x}^{(edge)}|$ subject to the constraint that $\mathbf{x}^{(edge)} = \mathbf{B}'\mathbf{x}^{(vert)'} + \mathbf{B}\chi_t$, where $\mathbf{B}'$ and $\mathbf{x}^{(vert)'}$ are restricted to vertices other than s and t and χ_t is the indicator vector that's 1 on t. The equality constraints can be handled similar to the shortest path problem by increasing the weights on the first term. One other issue is that $|\mathbf{x}^{(vert)'}|$ also appears in the objective term, and we handle this by scaling down $\mathbf{x}^{(vert)'}$, or equivalently scaling up $\mathbf{B}'$.

LEMMA A.2. *Given a s-t minimum cut instance in an undirected graph where edge weights $\mathbf{w} : E \rightarrow \Re^+$ are integers between 1 and n^d. There is a LASSO minimization instance where all entries are bounded by $n^{O(d)}$ such that the value of the LASSO minimizer is within 1 of the minimum cut.*

Proof
Consider the following objective, where λ_1 and λ_2 are set to n^{d+3} and n^2:

$$\lambda_1 ||\lambda_2 \mathbf{B}'\mathbf{x}^{(vert)'} + \mathbf{B}\chi_t - \mathbf{x}^{(edge)}||_2^2 + |\mathbf{x}^{(vert')}|_1 + |\mathbf{x}^{(edge)}|_1 \tag{1.13}$$

Let $\bar{\mathbf{x}}$ be an optimum vertex labelling, then setting $\mathbf{x}^{(vert')}$ to the restriction of $n^{-2}\bar{\mathbf{x}}$ on vertices other than s and t and $\mathbf{x}^{(edge)}$ to $\mathbf{B}\mathbf{x}^{(vert)}$ makes the first term 0. Since each entry of $\bar{\mathbf{x}}$ is between 0 and 1, the additive increase caused by $|\mathbf{x}^{(vert')}|_1$ is at most $1/n$. Therefore this objective's optimum is at most $1/n$ more than the size of the minimum cut.

For the other direction, consider any solution $\mathbf{x}^{(vert)'}, \mathbf{x}^{(edge)'}$ whose objective is at most $1/n$ more than the size of the minimum cut. Since the edge weights are at most n^d and s has degree at most n, the total objective is at most $n^{d+1} + 1$. This gives:

$$\begin{aligned} &||\lambda_2 \mathbf{B}'\mathbf{x}^{(vert)'} + \mathbf{B}\chi_t - \mathbf{x}^{(edge)}||_2^2 \leq n^{-1} \\ &||\lambda_2 \mathbf{B}'\mathbf{x}^{(vert)'} + \mathbf{B}\chi_t - \mathbf{x}^{(edge)}||_1 \\ \leq &||\lambda_2 \mathbf{B}'\mathbf{x}^{(vert)'} + \mathbf{B}\chi_t - \mathbf{x}^{(edge)}||_2 \leq n^{-1/2} \end{aligned} \tag{1.14}$$

Therefore changing $\mathbf{x}^{(edge)}$ to $\lambda_2 \mathbf{B}'\mathbf{x}^{(vert)'} + \mathbf{B}\chi_t$ increases the objective by at most $n^{-1/2} < 1$. This gives a cut with weight within 1 of the objective value and completes the proof. ∎

We can also show a more direct connection between the minimum cut problem and the fused LASSO objective, where each absolute value term may contain a linear combination of variables. This formulation is closer to the total variation objective, and is also an instance of the problem formulated in Definition 2.1 with each edge in a group.

LEMMA A.3. *The minimum cut problem in undirected graphs can be written as an instance of the fused LASSO objective.*

Proof Given a graph $G = (V, E)$ and edge weights **cost**, the problem can be formulated as finding a vertex labeling x such that $x_s = 0$, $x_t = 1$ and minimizing:

$$\sum_{uv \in E} \mathbf{cost}_{uv} |x_u - x_v| \tag{1.15}$$

∎

B. MULTIPLICATIVE WEIGHTS BASED APPROXIMATE ALGORITHM

In this section we show that the approximate algorithm described in Section 5 finds a solution close to the optimum. For readers familiar with the analysis of the Christiano et al. algorithm [9], the following mapping of terminology might be useful:

- edge $e \rightarrow$ group i.
- flow along edge $e \rightarrow$ value of $||\mathbf{x} - \mathbf{s}_i||_{\mathbf{L}_i}$.
- weight on edge $e \rightarrow$ weight of group i, $\mathbf{w}_i$.
- electrical flow problem $\rightarrow$ quadratic minimization problem (defined in Section 2.1)
- total energy of electrical flow / effective resistance $\rightarrow$ $\mathcal{OBJ}2(\mathbf{w})$.

We first show that if $\lambda^{(t)}$ as defined on Line 6 of Algorithm 1 is an upper bound for $\mathcal{OBJ}(\mathbf{x}^{(t)})$. This is crucial in its use the normalizing factor in our update step on Line 7.

LEMMA B.1. *In all iterations we have:*

$$\mathcal{OBJ}(\boldsymbol{x}^{(t)}) \leq \lambda^{(t)}$$

Proof By the Cauchy-Schwarz inequality we have:

$$\begin{aligned} (\lambda^{(t)})^2 &= \left(\sum_i \mathbf{w}_i^{(t-1)}\right)\left(\sum_i \frac{1}{\mathbf{w}_i^{(t-1)}} ||\mathbf{x}^{(t)} - \mathbf{s}_i||_{\mathbf{L}_i}^2\right) \\ &\geq \left(\sum_i ||\mathbf{x}^{(t)} - \mathbf{s}_i||_{\mathbf{L}_i}\right)^2 \\ &= \mathcal{OBJ}(\mathbf{x}^{(t)})^2 \end{aligned} \tag{2.16}$$

Taking square roots of both sides completes the proof. ∎

At a high level, the algorithm assigns weights $\mathbf{w}_i$ for each group, and iteratively reweighs them for N iterations. Recall that our key potential functions are $\mu^{(t)}$ which is the sum of weights of all groups, and:

$$\nu^{(t)} = \frac{1}{\text{OPT}} \sum_i ||\bar{\mathbf{x}} - \mathbf{s}_i||_{\mathbf{L}_i} \log(\mathbf{w}_i^{(t)}) \tag{2.17}$$

Where $\bar{\mathbf{x}}$ is a solution such that $\mathcal{OBJ}(\bar{\mathbf{x}}) = \text{OPT}$. We will show that if $\mathcal{OBJ}(\mathbf{x}^{(t)})$, or in turn $\lambda^{(t)}$ is large, then $\nu^{(t)}$ increases at a rate substantially faster than $\log(\mu^{(t)})$. These bounds, and the relations between $\mu^{(t)}$ and $\nu^{(t)}$ are summarized below:

LEMMA B.2. *1.*

$$\nu^{(t)} \leq \log(\mu^{(t)}) \tag{2.18}$$

2.

$$\mu^{(t)} \leq \left(1 + \frac{\epsilon(1+2\epsilon)}{\rho} t\right) \mu^{(t-1)} \tag{2.19}$$

and

$$\log(\mu^{(t)}) \leq \frac{\epsilon(1+2\epsilon)}{\rho} t + \log k \tag{2.20}$$

3. *If in iteration t,* $\lambda^{(t)} \geq (1+10\epsilon)OPT$ *and* $||\boldsymbol{x} - \boldsymbol{s}_i||_{L_i} \leq \rho \frac{w_i^{(t-1)}}{\mu^{(t-1)}} \lambda^{(t)}$ *for all groups i, then:*

$$\nu^t \geq \nu^{(t-1)} + \frac{\epsilon(1+9\epsilon)}{\rho} \tag{2.21}$$

The relationship between the upper and lower potentials can be established using the fact that $\mathbf{w}_i$ is non-negative:

Proof of Lemma B.2, Part 1:

$$\begin{aligned}
\nu^{(t)} =& \frac{1}{\text{OPT}} \sum_i ||\bar{\mathbf{x}} - \mathbf{s}_i||_{\mathbf{L}_i} \log(\mathbf{w}_i^{(t)}) \\
\leq& \frac{1}{\text{OPT}} \sum_i ||\bar{\mathbf{x}} - \mathbf{s}_i||_{\mathbf{L}_i} \log\left(\sum_j \mathbf{w}_j^{(t)}\right) \\
=& \log(\mu^{(t)}) \left(\frac{1}{\text{OPT}} \sum_i ||\bar{\mathbf{x}} - \mathbf{s}_i||_{\mathbf{L}_i}\right) \\
\leq& \log(\mu^{(t)})
\end{aligned} \tag{2.22}$$

■

Part 2 follows directly from the local behavior of the log function:

Proof of Lemma B.2, Part 2: The update rules gives:

$$\begin{aligned}
&\mu^{(t)} \\
=& \sum_i \mathbf{w}_i^{(t)} \\
=& \sum_i \mathbf{w}_i^{(t-1)} + \left(\frac{\epsilon}{\rho} \frac{||\mathbf{x}^{(t)} - \mathbf{s}_i||_{\mathbf{L}_i}}{\lambda^{(t)}} + \frac{2\epsilon^2}{k\rho}\right) \mu^{(t-1)} \\
&\text{by update rule on Line 7 of GroupedLeastSquares} \\
=& \mu^{(t-1)} + \frac{\epsilon}{\rho} \frac{\sum_i ||\mathbf{x}^{(t)} - \mathbf{s}_i||_{\mathbf{L}_i}}{\lambda^{(t)}} \mu^{(t-1)} + \sum_i \frac{2\epsilon^2}{k\rho} \mu^{(t-1)} \\
=& \mu^{(t-1)} + \frac{\epsilon}{\rho} \frac{\mathcal{OBJ}(\mathbf{x}^{(t)})}{\lambda^{(t)}} \mu^{(t-1)} + \frac{2\epsilon^2}{\rho} \mu^{(t-1)} \\
\leq& \mu^{(t-1)} + \frac{\epsilon}{\rho} \mu^{(t-1)} + \frac{2\epsilon^2}{\rho} \mu^{(t-1)} \qquad \text{By Lemma B.1} \\
=& \left(1 + \frac{\epsilon(1+2\epsilon)}{\rho}\right) \mu^{(t-1)}
\end{aligned} \tag{2.23}$$

Using the fact that $1 + x \leq \exp(x)$ when $x \geq 0$ we get:

$$\begin{aligned}
\mu^{(t)} \leq& \exp\left(\frac{\epsilon(1+2\epsilon)}{\rho}\right) \mu^{(t-1)} \\
\leq& \exp\left(t \frac{\epsilon(1+2\epsilon)}{\rho}\right) \mu^{(0)} \\
=& \exp\left(t \frac{\epsilon(1+2\epsilon)}{\rho}\right) k
\end{aligned}$$

Taking logs of both sides gives Equation 2.20.

■

This upper bound on the value of μ^t also allows us to show that the balancing rule keeps the w_i^ts reasonably balanced within a factor of k of each other. The following corollary can also be obtained.

Corollary B.3. *The weights at iteration t satisfy* $\mathbf{w}_i^{(t)} \geq \frac{\epsilon}{k} \mu^{(t)}$.

Proof

The proof is by induction on t. When $t = 0$ we have $\mathbf{w}_i^{(0)} = 1$, $\mu^{(0)} = k$ and the claim follows from $\frac{\epsilon}{k} k = \epsilon < 1$. When $t > 1$, we have:

$$\begin{aligned}
&\mathbf{w}_i^{(t)} \\
\geq& \mathbf{w}_i^{(t-1)} + \frac{2\epsilon^2}{k\rho} \mu^{(t-1)} \qquad \text{By line 7} \\
\geq& \left(\frac{\epsilon}{k} + \frac{2\epsilon^2}{k\rho}\right) \mu^{(t-1)} \qquad \text{By the inductive hypothesis} \\
=& \frac{\epsilon}{k} \left(1 + \frac{2\epsilon}{\rho}\right) \mu^{(t-1)} \\
\geq& \frac{\epsilon}{k} \left(1 + \frac{\epsilon(1+2\epsilon)}{\rho}\right) \mu^{(t-1)} \\
\geq& \frac{\epsilon}{k} \mu^{(t)} \qquad \text{By Lemma B.2, Part 2}
\end{aligned} \tag{2.24}$$

■

The proof of Part 3 is the key part of our analysis. The first order change of $\nu^{(t)}$ is written as a sum of products of $\mathbf{L}_i$ norms, which we analyze via. the fact that $\mathbf{x}^{(t)}$ is the solution of a linear system from the quadratic minimization problem.

Proof of Lemma B.2, Part 3:

We make use of the following known fact about the behavior of the log function around 1:

Fact B.4. *If* $0 \leq x \leq \epsilon$, *then* $\log(1+x) \geq (1-\epsilon)x$.

$$\begin{aligned}
&\nu^{(t)} - \nu^{(t-1)} \\
=& \frac{1}{\text{OPT}} \sum_{1 \leq i \leq k} ||\bar{\mathbf{x}} - \mathbf{s}_i||_{\mathbf{L}_i} \log\left(\mathbf{w}_i^{(t)}\right) \\
&- \frac{1}{\text{OPT}} \sum_{1 \leq i \leq k} ||\bar{\mathbf{x}} - \mathbf{s}_i||_{\mathbf{L}_i} \log\left(\mathbf{w}_i^{(t-1)}\right) \\
&\qquad \text{By Equation 2.17} \\
=& \frac{1}{\text{OPT}} \sum_{1 \leq i \leq k} ||\bar{\mathbf{x}} - \mathbf{s}_i||_{\mathbf{L}_i} \log\left(\frac{\mathbf{w}_i^{(t)}}{\mathbf{w}_i^{(t-1)}}\right) \\
\geq& \frac{1}{\text{OPT}} \sum_{1 \leq i \leq k} ||\bar{\mathbf{x}} - \mathbf{s}_i||_{\mathbf{L}_i} \log\left(1 + \frac{\epsilon}{\rho} \frac{||\mathbf{x}^{(t)} - \mathbf{s}_i||_{\mathbf{L}_i}}{\lambda^{(t)}} \frac{\mu^{(t-1)}}{\mathbf{w}_i^{(t-1)}}\right) \\
&\qquad \text{By update rule in line 7} \\
\geq& \frac{1}{\text{OPT}} \sum_{1 \leq i \leq k} ||\bar{\mathbf{x}} - \mathbf{s}_i||_{\mathbf{L}_i} \frac{\epsilon(1-\epsilon)}{\rho} \frac{||\mathbf{x}^{(t)} - \mathbf{s}_i||_{\mathbf{L}_i}}{\lambda^{(t)}} \frac{\mu^{(t-1)}}{\mathbf{w}_i^{(t-1)}} \\
&\qquad \text{Since } \log(1+x) \geq (1-\epsilon)x \text{ when } 0 \leq x \leq \epsilon \\
=& \frac{\epsilon(1-\epsilon)\mu_i^{(t-1)}}{\rho\text{OPT}\lambda^{(t)}} \sum_{1 \leq i \leq k} \frac{1}{\mathbf{w}_i^{(t-1)}} ||\bar{\mathbf{x}} - \mathbf{s}_i||_{\mathbf{L}_i} ||\mathbf{x}^{(t)} - \mathbf{s}_i||_{\mathbf{L}_i}
\end{aligned} \tag{2.25}$$

Since $\mathbf{L}_i$ forms a P.S.D norm, by the Cauchy-Schwarz inequality we have:

$$||\bar{\mathbf{x}} - \mathbf{s}_i||_{\mathbf{L}_i} ||\mathbf{x}^{(t)} - \mathbf{s}_i||_{\mathbf{L}_i}$$
$$\geq (\bar{\mathbf{x}} - \mathbf{s}_i)^T \mathbf{L}_i (\mathbf{x}^{(t)} - \mathbf{s}_i)$$
$$= ||\mathbf{x}^{(t)} - \mathbf{s}_i||^2_{\mathbf{L}_i} + (\bar{\mathbf{x}} - \mathbf{x})^T \mathbf{L}_i (\mathbf{x}^{(t)} - \mathbf{s}_i) \quad (2.26)$$

Recall from Lemma 2.2 that since $\mathbf{x}^{(t)}$ is the minimizer to $\mathcal{OBJ}2(\mathbf{w}^{(t-1)})$, we have:

$$\left(\sum_i \frac{1}{\mathbf{w}_i^{(t-1)}} \mathbf{L}_i\right) \mathbf{x}^{(t)} = \sum_i \frac{1}{\mathbf{w}^{(t-1)}} \mathbf{s}_i \quad (2.27)$$

$$\left(\sum_i \frac{1}{\mathbf{w}_i^{(t-1)}} \mathbf{L}_i\right) (\mathbf{x}^{(t)} - \mathbf{s}_i) = \mathbf{0} \quad (2.28)$$

$$(\bar{\mathbf{x}} - \mathbf{x}^{(t)})^T \left(\sum_i \frac{1}{\mathbf{w}_i^{(t-1)}} \mathbf{L}_i\right) (\mathbf{x}^{(t)} - \mathbf{s}_i) = 0 \quad (2.29)$$

Substituting this into Equation 2.25 gives:

$$\nu^{(t)} - \nu^{(t-1)}$$
$$\geq \frac{\epsilon(1-\epsilon)\mu_i^{(t-1)}}{\rho \mathrm{OPT} \lambda^{(t)}} \sum_i \frac{1}{\mathbf{w}_i^{(t-1)}} ||\mathbf{x}^{(t)} - \mathbf{s}_i||^2_{\mathbf{L}_i}$$
$$= \frac{\epsilon(1-\epsilon)}{\rho \mathrm{OPT} \lambda^{(t)}} \mu^{(t-1)} \mathcal{OBJ}2(\mathbf{w}, \mathbf{x}^{(t)})$$
$$= \frac{\epsilon(1-\epsilon)}{\rho \mathrm{OPT} \lambda^{(t)}} (\lambda^{(t)})^2$$

By definition of $\lambda^{(t)}$ on Line 6

$$\geq \frac{\epsilon(1-\epsilon)(1+10\epsilon)}{\rho}$$

By assumption that $\lambda^{(t)} > (1+10\epsilon)\mathrm{OPT}$

$$\geq \frac{\epsilon(1+8\epsilon)}{\rho} \quad (2.30)$$

Since the iteration count largely depends on ρ, it suffices to provide bounds for ρ over all the iterations. The proof makes use of the following lemma about the properties of electrical flows, which describes the behavior of modifying the weights of a group S_i that has a large contribution to the total energy. It can be viewed as a multiple-edge version of Lemma 2.6 of [9].

LEMMA B.5. *Assume that $\epsilon^2\rho^2 < 1/10k$ and $\epsilon < 0.01$ and let $\boldsymbol{x}^{(t-1)}$ be the minimizer for $\mathcal{OBJ}2(\mathbf{w}^{(t-1)})$. Suppose there is a group i such that $||\boldsymbol{x}^{(t-1)} - \boldsymbol{s}_i||_{\boldsymbol{L}_i} \geq \rho \frac{w_i^{(t-1)}}{\mu^{(t-1)}} \lambda^{(t)}$, then*

$$OPT2(\boldsymbol{w}^{(t)}) \leq \exp\left(-\frac{\epsilon^2\rho^2}{2k}\right) OPT2(\boldsymbol{w}^{(t-1)})$$

Proof

We first show that group i contributes a significant portion to $\mathcal{OBJ}2(\mathbf{w}^{(t-1)}, \mathbf{x}^{(t-1)})$. Squaring both sides of the given condition gives:

$$||\mathbf{x}^{(t-1)} - \mathbf{s}_i||^2_{\mathbf{L}_i}$$
$$\geq \rho^2 \frac{(\mathbf{w}_i^{(t-1)})^2}{(\mu^{(t-1)})^2} (\lambda^{(t)})^2$$
$$= \rho^2 \frac{(\mathbf{w}_i^{(t-1)})^2}{(\mu^{(t-1)})^2} \mu^{(t-1)} \mathcal{OBJ}2(\mathbf{w}^{(t-1)}, \mathbf{x}^{(t-1)}) \quad (2.31)$$
$$\frac{1}{\mathbf{w}_i^{(t-1)}} ||\mathbf{x}^{(t-1)} - \mathbf{s}_i||_{\mathbf{L}_i}$$
$$\geq \rho^2 \frac{\mathbf{w}_i^{(t-1)}}{\mu^{(t-1)}} \mathcal{OBJ}2(\mathbf{w}^{(t-1)}, \mathbf{x}^{(t-1)})$$
$$\geq \frac{\epsilon\rho^2}{k} \mathcal{OBJ}2(\mathbf{w}^{(t-1)}, \mathbf{x}^{(t-1)})$$

By Corollary B.3 (2.32)

Also, by the update rule we have $\mathbf{w}_i^{(t)} \geq (1+\epsilon)\mathbf{w}_i^{(t-1)}$ and $\mathbf{w}_j^{(t)} \geq \mathbf{w}_j^{(t-1)}$ for all $1 \leq j \leq k$. So we have:

$$\mathrm{OPT2}(\mathbf{w}^{(t)})$$
$$\leq \mathcal{OBJ}2(\mathbf{w}^{(t)}, \mathbf{x}^{(t-1)})$$
$$= \mathcal{OBJ}2(\mathbf{w}^{(t)}, \mathbf{x}^{(t-1)}) - (1 - \frac{1}{1+\epsilon}) ||\mathbf{x}^{(t-1)} - \mathbf{s}_i||^2_{\mathbf{L}_i}$$
$$\leq \mathcal{OBJ}2(\mathbf{w}^{(t)}, \mathbf{x}^{(t-1)}) - \frac{\epsilon}{2} ||\mathbf{x}^{(t-1)} - \mathbf{s}_i||^2_{\mathbf{L}_i}$$
$$\leq \mathcal{OBJ}2(\mathbf{w}^{(t)}, \mathbf{x}^{(t-1)}) - \frac{\epsilon^2\rho^2}{2k} \mathcal{OBJ}2(\mathbf{w}^{(t-1)}, \mathbf{x}^{(t-1)})$$
$$\leq \exp\left(-\frac{\epsilon^2\rho^2}{2k}\right) \mathcal{OBJ}2(\mathbf{w}^{(t-1)}, \mathbf{x}^{(t-1)}) \quad (2.33)$$

■

This means the value of the quadratic minimization problem can be used as a second potential function. We first show that it's monotonic and establish rough bounds for it.

LEMMA B.6. *$OPT2(\boldsymbol{w}^{(0)}) \leq n^{3d}$ and $OPT2(\boldsymbol{w}^{(t)})$ is monotonically decreasing in t.*

Proof By the assumption that the input is polynomially bounded we have that all entries of $\mathbf{s}$ are at most n^d and $\mathbf{L}_i \preceq n^d \mathbf{I}$. Setting $\mathbf{x}_u = 0$ gives $||\mathbf{x} - \mathbf{s}_i||_2 \leq n^{d+1}$. Combining this with the spectrum bound then gives $||\mathbf{x} - \mathbf{s}_i||_{\mathbf{L}_i} \leq n^{2d+1}$. Summing over all the groups gives the upper bound.

The monotonicity of $\mathrm{OPT2}(\mathbf{w}^{(t)})$ follows from the fact that all weights are decreasing. ■

Combining this with the fact that $\mathrm{OPT2}(\mathbf{w}^{(N)})$ is not low enough for termination gives our bound on the total iteration count.

Proof of Theorem 5.1: The proof is by contradiction. Suppose otherwise, since $\mathcal{OBJ}(\mathbf{x}^{(N)}) > \epsilon$ we have:

$$\lambda^{(N)} \geq (1+10\epsilon) n^{-d}$$
$$\geq 2n^{-d} \mathrm{OPT} \quad (2.34)$$

$$\sqrt{\mu^{(N)} \mathrm{OPT2}(\mathbf{w}^{(t)})} \geq 2n^{-d} \quad (2.35)$$

$$\mathrm{OPT2}(\mathbf{w}^{(t)}) \geq \frac{4}{n^{-2d} \mu^{(N)}} \quad (2.36)$$

Which combined with $\text{OPT2}(\mathbf{w}^{(0)}) \leq n^{3d}$ from Lemma B.6 gives:

$$\frac{\text{OPT2}(\mathbf{w}^{(0)})}{\text{OPT2}(\mathbf{w}^{(N)})} \leq n^{5d}\mu^{(N)} \tag{2.37}$$

By Lemma B.2 Part 2, we have:

$$\begin{aligned}
&\log(\mu^{(N)}) \\
\leq &\frac{\epsilon(1+\epsilon)}{\rho}N + \log k \\
\leq &\frac{\epsilon(1+\epsilon)}{\rho}10d\rho\log n\epsilon^{-2} + \log n \\
&\quad \text{By choice of } N = 10d\rho\log n\epsilon^{-2} \\
= &10(1+\epsilon)\epsilon^{-1}\log n + \log n \\
\leq &10d(1+2\epsilon)\epsilon^{-1}\log n \\
&\quad \text{when } \epsilon < 0.01
\end{aligned} \tag{2.38}$$

Combining with Lemma B.5 implies that the number of iterations where $||\mathbf{x}^{(t-1)} - \mathbf{s}_i||_{\mathbf{L}_i} \geq \rho\frac{\mathbf{w}_i^{(t-1)}}{\mu^{(t-1)}}\lambda^{(t)}$ for i is at most:

$$\begin{aligned}
&\log\left(\mu^{(N)}n^{5d}\right)/\left(\frac{\epsilon^2\rho^2}{2k}\right) \\
= &10d(1+3\epsilon)\epsilon^{-1}\log n/\left(\frac{2\epsilon^{2/3}}{k^{1/3}}\right) \\
&\quad \text{By choice of } \rho = 2k^{1/3}\epsilon^{-2/3} \\
= &8d\epsilon^{-5/3}k^{1/3}\log n \\
= &4d\epsilon^{-1}\rho\log n \leq \epsilon N
\end{aligned} \tag{2.39}$$

This means that we have $||\mathbf{x}^{(t-1)} - \mathbf{s}_i||_{\mathbf{L}_i} \leq \rho\frac{\mathbf{w}_i^{(t-1)}}{\mu^{(t-1)}}\lambda^{(t)}$ for all $1 \leq i \leq k$ for at least $(1-\epsilon)N$ iterations and therefore by Lemma B.2 Part 3:

$$\nu^{(N)} \geq \nu^{(0)} + \frac{\epsilon(1+8\epsilon)}{\rho}(1-\epsilon)N > \mu^{(N)} \tag{2.40}$$

Giving a contradiction. ∎

C. ALMOST-EXACT ALGORITHM USING INTERIOR POINT ALGORITHMS

We now show improved algorithms for solving the second order cone programming formulation given in [6, 17]. It was shown in [13] that in the linear case, as with graph problems such as maximum flow, minimum cost flow and shortest path, interior point algorithms reduce the problem to solving $\tilde{O}(m^{1/2})$ symmetrically diagonally dominant linear systems. The grouped least squares formulation creates artifacts that perturb the linear systems generated by the interior point algorithms, making the resulting system both more difficult to interpret and to solve. However, the iteration count of this approach also only depends on k, [17, 6], and has a better dependency on ϵ of $O(\log(1/\epsilon))$.

There are various ways to solve the grouped least squares problem using interior point algorithms. We follow the log-barrier method, as presented in Boyd and Vandenberghe [6] here for simplicity. This formulation defines one extra variable y_i for each group and enforces $y_i \geq ||\mathbf{x} - \mathbf{s}_i||_{\mathbf{L}_i}$ using the barrier function $\phi_i(\mathbf{x}, y_i) = \log(y_i^2 - ||\mathbf{x} - \mathbf{s}_i||_{\mathbf{L}_i}^2)$. Minimizing $t \cdot (\sum_i y_i)$ for gradually increasing values of t gives the following sequence of functions to minimize:

$$f(t, \mathbf{x}, \mathbf{y}) = t\sum_i y_i - \sum_i \log(y_i^2 - ||\mathbf{x} - \mathbf{s}_i||_{\mathbf{L}_i}^2) \tag{3.41}$$

Various interior point algorithms have been proposed, one commonality that they have is finding an update direction by solving a linear system. The iteration guarantees for recovering almost-exact solution can be characterized as follows:

LEMMA C.1. *(Section 11.5.3 from [6]) A solution that's within additive ϵ of the optimum solution can be produced in $\tilde{O}(k^{1/2}\log(1/\epsilon))$ steps, each of which requires solving a linear system involving $\nabla^2 f(t, \boldsymbol{x}, \boldsymbol{y})$ for some value of t, $\boldsymbol{x}$ and $\boldsymbol{y}$.*

Since the $t\sum_i y_i$ term is linear, it can be omitted from the Hessian, leaving $\sum_i \nabla^2\phi(\mathbf{x}, y_i)$. We then check that the barrier term y_i creates a low rank perturbation to the $\mathbf{L}_i$ term, which is the Hessian for $||\mathbf{x}-\mathbf{s}_i||_{\mathbf{L}_i}^2$. By taking Schur complements and applying the Sherman-Morrison-Woodbury identity on inverses for low rank perturbations, we arrive at the following observation.

THEOREM C.2. *Suppose there is an algorithm for solving linear systems of the form $\sum_i \alpha_i \boldsymbol{L}_i$ in $T(n, m)$ time where m. For any choice of $\boldsymbol{x}, \boldsymbol{y}$, a linear system involving the Hessian of $\phi(\boldsymbol{x}, \boldsymbol{y})$, $\nabla^2\phi(\boldsymbol{x}, \boldsymbol{y})$ can be solved in $O(k^\omega + kT(n, m) + k^2 n)$ time.*

Proof

We first consider the barrier function corresponding to each group, $\phi(\mathbf{x}, y_i)$. Its gradient is:

$$\begin{aligned}
\nabla\phi(\mathbf{x}, y_i) = &\nabla - \log\left(y_i^2 - (\mathbf{x} - \mathbf{s}_i)^T\mathbf{L}_i(\mathbf{x} - \mathbf{s}_i)\right) \\
= &\frac{2}{y_i^2 - ||\mathbf{x} - \mathbf{s}_i||_{\mathbf{L}_i}^2}\begin{bmatrix} \mathbf{L}_i(\mathbf{x} - \mathbf{s}_i) \\ -y_i \end{bmatrix}
\end{aligned} \tag{3.42}$$

and its Hessian, $\nabla^2\phi(\mathbf{x}, y_i)$, is:

$$\frac{2}{(y_i^2 - ||\mathbf{x} - \mathbf{s}_i||_{\mathbf{L}_i}^2)^2}\left[\begin{array}{c|c} \begin{array}{c}(y_i^2 - ||\mathbf{x} - \mathbf{s}_i||_{\mathbf{L}_i}^2)\mathbf{L}_i \\ +2\mathbf{L}_i(\mathbf{x} - \mathbf{s}_i)(\mathbf{x} - \mathbf{s}_i)^T\mathbf{L}_i\end{array} & 2y_i\mathbf{L}_i(\mathbf{x} - \mathbf{s}_i) \\ \hline 2y_i(\mathbf{x} - \mathbf{s}_i)^T\mathbf{L}_i & y_i^2 + ||\mathbf{x} - \mathbf{s}_i||_{\mathbf{L}_i}^2 \end{array}\right] \tag{3.43}$$

Since the variable y_i only appears in $\phi(\mathbf{x}, y_i)$, we may use partial Cholesky factorization to arrive at a linear system without it. The $n \times n$ matrix that we obtain is:

$$\begin{aligned}
&\mathbf{L}_i(y_i^2 - ||\mathbf{x} - \mathbf{s}_i||_{\mathbf{L}_i}^2) \\
&\quad + \left(2 - \frac{4y_i^2}{y_i^2 + ||\mathbf{x} - \mathbf{s}_i||_{\mathbf{L}_i}^2}\right)\mathbf{L}_i(\mathbf{x} - \mathbf{s}_i)(\mathbf{x} - \mathbf{s}_i)^T\mathbf{L}_i \\
= &(y_i^2 - ||\mathbf{x} - \mathbf{s}_i||_{\mathbf{L}_i}^2)\left(\mathbf{L}_i - \frac{2\mathbf{L}_i(\mathbf{x} - \mathbf{s}_i)(\mathbf{x} - \mathbf{s}_i)^T\mathbf{L}_i}{y_i^2 + ||\mathbf{x} - \mathbf{s}_i||_{\mathbf{L}_i}^2}\right)
\end{aligned} \tag{3.44}$$

Since $\phi(\mathbf{x},\mathbf{y}) = \sum_i \phi(\mathbf{x}, y_i)$, this partial Cholesky factorization of $\nabla^2\phi(\mathbf{x},\mathbf{y})$ can be written as:

$$\sum_i \alpha_i \mathbf{L}_i - \beta_i \mathbf{u}_i \mathbf{u}_i^T \tag{3.45}$$

Where $\mathbf{u}_i = \mathbf{L}_i(\mathbf{x} - \mathbf{s}_i)$ and α_i and β_i are scalars. We can simplify solving this system using the Sherman-Morrison-Woodbury formula:

FACT C.3. *(Sherman–Morrison–Woodbury formula)* *If A, U, C, V are $n \times n$, $n \times k$, $k \times k$ and $k \times n$ matrices respectively, then:*

$$(A + UCV)^{-1} = A^{-1} - A^{-1}U(C^{-1} + VA^{-1}U)^{-1}VA^{-1}$$

Here we have $\mathbf{A} = \sum_i \alpha_i \mathbf{L}_i$, $\mathbf{C} = -\mathbf{I}$, $\mathbf{U}$ being the k columns vectors $\sqrt{\beta_i}\mathbf{u}_i$ concatenated and $\mathbf{V} = \mathbf{U}^T$. So the linear system that we need to evaluate becomes:

$$\mathbf{A}^{-1} - \mathbf{A}^{-1}\mathbf{U}(\mathbf{U}^T\mathbf{A}^{-1}\mathbf{U} - \mathbf{I})^{-1}\mathbf{U}^T\mathbf{A}^{-1} \tag{3.46}$$

The system $\mathbf{A}^{-1}\mathbf{U}$ can be found using k solves in $\mathbf{A} = \sum_i \alpha_i \mathbf{L}_i$, which is equivalent to the quadratic minimization problem. Multiplying this by $\mathbf{U}$ can be done in $O(k^2 n)$ time and gives us $\mathbf{U}^T\mathbf{A}^{-1}\mathbf{U}$. This $k \times k$ system can in turn be solved in k^ω time. The other terms can be applied to vectors in either solves in $\mathbf{A}$ or matrix multiples in $\mathbf{U}$, taking $O(T(n,m) + kn)$ time. ∎

Combining this with the iteration count of $\tilde{O}(k^{1/2}\log(1/\epsilon))$ gives a total running time of $\tilde{O}((k^{\omega+1/2} + k^{3/2}T(n,m) + k^{5/2}n)\log(1/\epsilon))$.

D. OTHER VARIANTS

Although our formulation of $\mathcal{OBJ}$ as a sum of L_2 objectives differs syntactically from some common formulations, we show below that the more common formulation involving quadratic, or L_2^2 fidelity term can be reduced to finding exact solutions to $\mathcal{OBJ}$ using 2 iterations of ternary search. Most other formulations differs from our formulation in the fidelity term, but more commonly have L_1 smoothness terms as well. Since the anisotropic smoothness term is a special case of the isotropic one, our discussion of the variations will assume anisotropic objectives.

D.1 L_2^2 fidelity term

The most common form of the total variation objective used in practice is one with L_2^2 fidelity term. This term can be written as $||\mathbf{x} - \mathbf{s}_0||_2^2$, which corresponds to the norm defined by $\mathbf{I} = \mathbf{L}_0$. This gives:

$$\min_{\mathbf{x}} \quad ||\mathbf{x} - \mathbf{s}_0||_{\mathbf{L}_0}^2 + \sum_{1 \le i \le k} ||\mathbf{x} - \mathbf{s}_i||_{\mathbf{L}_i}$$

We can establish the value of $||\mathbf{x} - \mathbf{s}_0||_{\mathbf{L}_0}^2$ separately by guessing it as a constraint. Since the t^2 is convex in t, the following optimization problem is convex in t as well:

$$\min_{\mathbf{x}} \quad \sum_{1 \le i \le k} ||\mathbf{x} - \mathbf{s}_i||_{\mathbf{L}_i} ||\mathbf{x} - \mathbf{s}_0||_{\mathbf{L}_0}^2 \le t^2$$

Also, due to the convexity of t^2, ternary searching on the minimizer of this plus t^2 would allow us to find the optimum solution by solving $O(\log n)$ instances of the above problem.

Taking square root of both sides of the $||\mathbf{x} - \mathbf{s}_0||_{\mathbf{L}_0}^2 \le t^2$ condition and taking its Lagrangian relaxation gives:

$$\min_{\mathbf{x}} \max_{\lambda \ge 0} \sum_{i=1}^{k} ||\mathbf{x} - \mathbf{s}_i||_{\mathbf{L}_i} + \lambda(||\mathbf{x} - \mathbf{s}_0||_{\mathbf{L}_0} - t)$$

Which by the min-max theorem is equivalent to:

$$\max_{\lambda \ge 0} -\lambda t + \left(\min_{\mathbf{x}} \sum_{i=1}^{k} ||\mathbf{x} - \mathbf{s}_i||_{\mathbf{L}_i} + \lambda ||\mathbf{x} - \mathbf{s}_0||_{\mathbf{L}_0} \right)$$

The term being minimized is identical to our formulation and its objective is convex in λ when $\lambda \ge 0$. Since $-\lambda t$ is linear, their sum is convex and another ternary search on λ suffices to optimize the overall objective.

D.2 L_1 fidelity term

Another common objective function to minimize is where the fidelity term is also under L_1 norm. In this case the objective function becomes:

$$||\mathbf{x} - \mathbf{s}_0||_1 + \sum_i \sum_{1 \le i \le k} ||\mathbf{x} - \mathbf{s}_i||_{\mathbf{L}_i}$$

This can be rewritten as a special case of $\mathcal{OBJ}$ as:

$$\sum_u \sqrt{(x_u - s_u)^2} + \sum_i \sum_{1 \le i \le k} ||\mathbf{x} - \mathbf{s}_i||_{\mathbf{L}_i}$$

Which gives, instead, a grouped least squares problem with $m + k$ groups.

An Energy Complexity Model for Algorithms

Swapnoneel Roy*
Department of CSE
University at Buffalo, SUNY
Buffalo, NY, USA
sroy7@buffalo.edu

Atri Rudra†
Department of CSE
University at Buffalo, SUNY
Buffalo, NY, USA
atri@buffalo.edu

Akshat Verma
IBM Research - India
New Delhi, India
akshatverma@in.ibm.com

ABSTRACT

Energy consumption has emerged as a first class computing resource for both server systems and personal computing devices. The growing importance of energy has led to rethink in hardware design, hypervisors, operating systems and compilers. Algorithm design is still relatively untouched by the importance of energy and algorithmic complexity models do not capture the energy consumed by an algorithm.

In this paper, we propose a new complexity model to account for the energy used by an algorithm. Based on an abstract memory model (which was inspired by the popular DDR3 memory model and is similar to the parallel disk I/O model of Vitter and Shriver), we present a simple energy model that is a (weighted) sum of the time complexity of the algorithm and the number of "parallel" I/O accesses made by the algorithm. We derive this simple model from a more complicated model that better models the ground truth and present some experimental justification for our model. We believe that the simplicity (and applicability) of this energy model is the main contribution of the paper.

We present some sufficient conditions on algorithm behavior that allows us to bound the energy complexity of the algorithm in terms of its time complexity (in the RAM model) and its I/O complexity (in the I/O model). As corollaries, we obtain energy optimal algorithms for sorting (and its special cases like permutation), matrix transpose and (sparse) matrix vector multiplication.

Categories and Subject Descriptors

H.4 [**Information Systems Applications**]: Miscellaneous; D.2.8 [**Software Engineering**]: Metrics—*complexity measures, performance measures*

General Terms

Theory, Algorithms

Keywords

Energy Efficient Algorithms, Parallel Disk I/O model

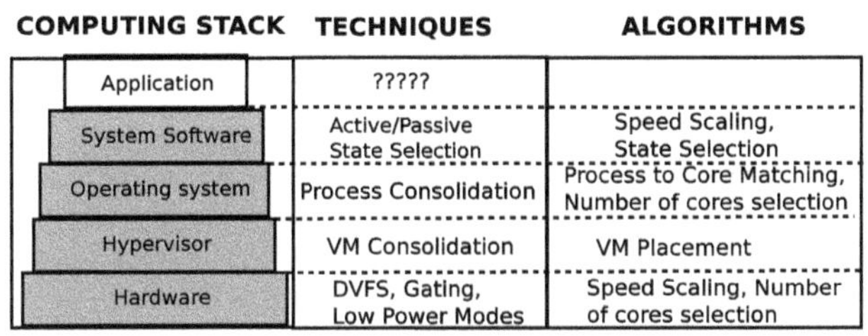

Figure 1: Overview of energy management across the computing stack. Layers in green incorporate energy-aware design.

1. INTRODUCTION

Energy has emerged as a first class computing resource in modern systems [37, 30]. Two trends have primarily led to the strong focus on reducing energy consumption. The first trend has been the ever-increasing energy consumption of data centers, which doubled between the years 2000 and 2006 [2]. Coupled with the growing awareness of the adverse impact on the environment due to data centers has led to a strong focus on energy management for server class systems. The second trend has been the explosive growth of personal computing devices like smartphones, handhelds, and notebooks, which run on batteries. Personal computing devices today perform a lot of computations and data transfer and energy conservation is a driving factor in the design of personal computing devices.

The focus on energy management has been cross-cutting across various computing disciplines including computer architecture (hardware design) [28], hypervisors [31], operating systems [27] and system software [11, 15]. Fig. 1 captures the various techniques developed to reduce energy consumption across the computing stack. One may note that energy management has not impacted application design, which includes the design of algorithms. Hardware and system engineers have treated the application as a black box and designed techniques to minimize energy without any modifications to this black box. This is not surprising since

*Supported in part by NSF grant CCF-0844796. Part of this work was done when the author was an intern at IBM Research - India.
†Supported in part by NSF CAREER award CCF-0844796.

application or algorithmic design is not their area of expertise. Interestingly, the focus of the algorithmic community has been on designing energy management algorithms in support of the energy management techniques developed by other computing disciplines [36, 7, 16]. We believe that the algorithmic community can make a more significant contribution by introducing energy-awareness in algorithm design. The central question explored in this paper is the following:

> *Should we redesign software applications using energy-optimal algorithms?*

Traditional algorithm design has mostly focused on minimizing time complexity (in the RAM model) and used polynomial time as a benchmark for efficient computation. With advances in computing technology, the algorithms community has refined the polynomial time model to better model these advances. The Input-Output (henceforth, I/O) model of Aggarwal and Vitter [5] was proposed to model the fact that problems of large size may not fit in main memory. This model has been refined over the years e.g., to include more realistic memory hierarchy in the form of cache oblivious algorithms [12] and parallel disks [34, 35]. Another popular recent model is that of data stream algorithms [26], which tries to model the fact that sequential access to disk memory is cheaper than random access to disk memory.

However, the energy consumed by a computational task is not covered by traditional algorithm design (nor by models mentioned above). There is a technological reason behind the relative lack of attention from algorithm community towards energy-aware algorithm design. Server models, developed as recently as 2004 (e.g., IBM Power5), were designed without energy awareness in mind and their power consumption was *work-oblivious*, i.e. they consumed the same power irrespective of the workload running on the server! It is only in the last decade that hardware architects have introduced techniques to ensure that circuitry not performing any operations at a given point in time consume minimal or no power.

In line with these change, ideal *work-proportional* energy models have been used recently for parallel algorithms, where a linear relationship is assumed between computational complexity and energy usage of an algorithm on a server running at a fixed frequency [22, 23]. This is diagonally opposite to work-oblivious energy models and do not model the complex memory circuitry.

We performed a number of experiments and observed that energy consumption is neither work-proportional nor work-oblivious. Fig. 2 shows the energy consumed by algorithms with *exactly* identical work and memory complexity (i.e. they are same even up to constants) on commodity laptop machines. The algorithms have been modified by changing their memory allocation on banks and the average power is measured to estimate the total energy consumed in completing a task. (See Section 6 for more details.) Energy estimated by work-proportional or work-oblivious models would be same for a given problem, i.e., max=min (represented by the flat line in the figure). We observe up to 225% higher energy usage for the same algorithm, highlighting a gap in existing complexity models. The platforms we used for our experiments had only 8 memory banks and do not support advanced fine-grained energy management techniques like per-core DVFS or per-bank refresh states [19]. We expect

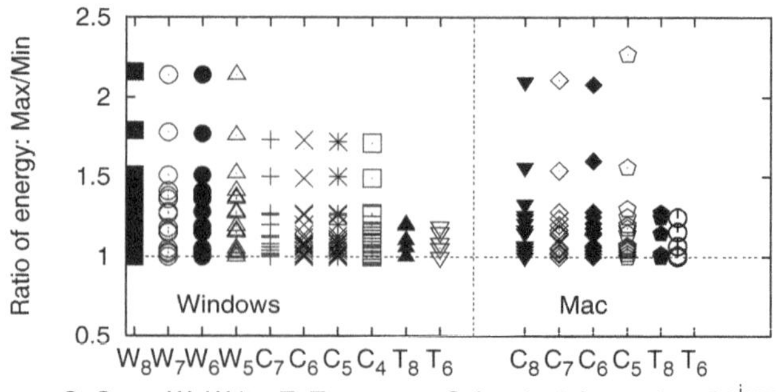

Figure 2: Impact of algorithm on energy. Each dot in the figure signifies the energy cost incurred by a given algorithm (among write, copy, and transpose) for a given input and access pattern.

the difference between variants of algorithms to increase on larger memory systems or emerging platforms.

A simple complexity model that captures the energy consumed by an algorithm can help design energy-efficient applications that can perform the same task, while consuming much less energy. An energy-aware design of applications will ensure that the entire computing stack from application to the hardware is energy efficient and has the potential to significantly reduce energy consumption of enterprise as well as personal computing devices. Designing such a model is tricky: it has to be simple enough so that it hides as much of the low level system detail to the algorithm design (so that the designed algorithms can be applied to various platforms) while on the other hand it should be a realistic enough to capture a lot of the ground truth.

System researchers have designed various models to estimate the power drawn by server systems. At high-level, they generalize the ideal work-proportional energy model of Korthikanti *et al.* [22, 23] by capturing memory activity as well as idle or leakage power. However, these models are typically based on system level parameters like CPU utilization, number of instructions dispatched, memory bandwidth etc. [9]. A recent study presented an application-aware model for estimating power drawn by server systems [21]. Even though the authors point out the requirement of capturing application behavior to accurately estimate power, the techniques treat an application as a black box and estimate the power based on empirical measurements. We believe that the lack of a simple yet realistic model of energy consumption at design time is one of the stumbling blocks for energy-aware algorithm design.

1.1 Our Results

Our main contribution is a simple energy complexity model for algorithms. Our model is based on the design of modern processors and memory elements. In particular, it turns out that a simple variation of the parallel disk I/O model [34, 35] (where the fast memory is not fully associative) models modern memory elements pretty well. Using this memory model, our final energy model for an algorithm $\mathcal{A}$ is a weighted linear combination of the work complexity of $\mathcal{A}$ (i.e. its time complexity in the traditional RAM model) and the number of "parallel" accesses to the memory. (We note that our memory model has some subtle differences from existing models such as the parallel disk I/O model and cache oblivious models: see the end of the section for a comparison.) To obtain our final energy model, we start with a fairly complex energy model and then use some simple reductions to reduce our energy complexity model to the two parameters above. We also present some simulation results to justify our energy model.

To the best of our knowledge, ours is the first work that naturally combines the work complexity and parallel I/O complexities into one. We also believe that the fact that our energy model is a simple combination of two well-studied models is a strength of our model as one can leverage existing techniques that have been developed for designing algorithms in these two models. Existing work in cache oblivious algorithms has focused on both of these parameters but existing literature in that model tries to optimize both these parameter *simultaneously*. By contrast, our model since it combines these two parameters, provides some flexibility. Indeed in our results, we use this freedom. For example, the problem of sorting N numbers has an optimal work complexity of $W(N) = \Theta(N \log N)$ (assuming a comparison model) and a parallel I/O complexity (where one has P parallel disks, each block has B items and the fast memory can hold P blocks) of $\mathcal{I}(N) = \Omega(\frac{N}{BP} \log_P N)$. Our energy model requires the algorithm to minimize the quantity $W(N) + BP \cdot \mathcal{I}(N)$. We briefly describe two examples that illustrate the two ends of the spectrum: one where $W(N)$ is the dominant term and the other where $\mathcal{I}(N)$ is the dominant term. First consider the sorting problem. Under the comparison model, for sorting we have $W(N) = \Theta(N \log N)$. On the other hand, (assuming the "k-way" mergesort algorithm can be fully parallelized), it is known that $\mathcal{I}(N)$ is $O(N/(PB) \log_k N)$. For optimal I/O complexity, one needs to pick $k = P$. However, in our case since $W(N)$ is the dominating term, even $k = 2$ (the "usual" mergesort algorithm) is also energy optimal. Second, consider the problem of permuting an array of elements under an implicitly specified permutation. This is a special case of the sorting problem and it is well known that for this problem $W(N) = \Theta(N)$. On the other hand, it is known that the I/O lower bound is the same as that of sorting. Thus, for the permuting problem, we have $\mathcal{I}(N) \geq \Omega(N/(PB) \log_P N)$. Thus, in this case to be energy optimal, we use the P-way mergesort algorithm (that is fully parallelized) to obtain the energy optimal algorithm for permuting. We are hopeful that this flexibility will enable the design of more algorithms that have the optimal energy complexity. Here we could like to point out that it is not enough to dovetail two algorithms one of which has a better work complexity and the other has a better I/O complexity and hope to have the "best of both worlds." See Appendix A for more.

We also believe that our model is complementary to the existing work on energy efficient algorithms [6]. In particular, one could potentially use our model to design the algorithmic tasks and then using the existing work to schedule each of these tasks so as to leverage the benefits of speed scaling and power-down mechanisms.

Our second key contribution is simulations of broad classes of algorithms. In particular, we present three simulations that convert algorithm designed for RAM and/or I/O model into ones that are suitable for our model. Our simulations do not change the work complexities but mildly blowup the parallel I/O complexity parameter. The first simulation result is a trivial one where the original algorithm already has a nice parallelizable memory access pattern and one gets the same work and I/O complexity as the original algorithm. The next two classes of algorithms are based on their memory access patterns. Informally, the first subclass, which we call *striped* algorithms run in phases where in each phase, the algorithm accesses a fixed number of "runs" of memory locations sequentially (e.g. the merge sort algorithm). We use the power of two choices [25] to simulate this class of algorithms. We also consider a much more general class of algorithms we call *bounded*, which has the minimal restriction of knowing which the memory locations it needs to allocate upfront and one that accesses at least a constant fraction of these allocated locations during its execution. The parameters for bounded algorithms are weaker than those of striped algorithm. We then apply these simulation results to obtain energy efficient algorithms for sorting, matrix transpose, matrix multiplication and matrix vector multiplication.

1.2 Proof Techniques

Finally, we present an overview of some of the proof techniques used to prove the simulation results. The idea for the simulation is fairly simple: we randomly permute (twice in the case of striped algorithms) the memory locations so that we can "batch" memory accesses into few parallel I/O accesses. This involves bounding the maximum load in a balls and bins game. For bounded algorithms, the resulting balls and bins problem is the traditional setup. For striped algorithms, the setup is the so called "parallel" balls and bins with two choices [25]. In this setup it is know that if the two choices for each ball can be coordinated than the maximum load is $O(1)$. In our case we have to be a bit careful to make sure that these choices can be made (centrally) in linear time. (This latter result is probably folklore– we present a proof in Appendix D.)

The main issue is how one stores this random permutation (since the corresponding map needs to be computed every time a memory location is accessed). We present two solutions. The first solution uses a lot of randomness and affects the work and I/O complexity negligibly. The second solution uses little randomness but has a mild effect on the work complexity. The first solution just divides up the memory locations into appropriate chunks and applies independent random permutations on each such chunk. These permutations are themselves stored in memory. This potentially could lead to the problem of ensuring that the accesses to the table entries themselves are sufficiently parallelizable. We overcome this by exploiting a fact that has been used before: the size of the table is much smaller than the input. This allows us to repeat each entry multiple times, which in turn allows for sufficient parallelizability.

For the second solution, a natural option is to reduce the randomness in the first solution by using a standard derandomization tool. An inspection of the proof implies that one only needs (roughly) $1/\text{poly}(P)$-almost P-wise independent random permutations to make the balls and bins argument go through. There exists good construction of such objects [17]. However, for reasons that will become clear shortly, we go through a slightly different route. We use the well-known P-wise independent random *strings* based on Reed-Solomon codes (which in turns are evaluations of low degree polynomials). Further, to make things easier, we first only map the locations to a random disk. To determine the location within a disk, we simply maintain a count of how many locations have already been mapped to the disk under consideration. (As before all this information is stored in a table.) To get a better work complexity, instead of using the naive polynomial evaluation algorithm, we use a recent efficient data structure for polynomial evaluation designed by Kedlaya and Umans [18]. In particular, if we had used the almost P-wise independent permutations from [17], we would have to pay roughly $O(P \log n)$ extra work overhead for each memory access in our simulations. By using the data structure from [18] we bring down the overhead to something $O(\text{poly} \log P \log n)$, which is why we chose the derandomization via Reed-Solomon codes.

1.3 Related Work

A lot of research has been carried out in the systems community to reduce energy consumption in diverse aspects of computing including design of server systems, voltage and frequency scaling, server consolidation, and storage energy management [11, 15, 27, 28, 31, 32]. These problems have also garnered a lot of attention in the theory community: see e.g. the recent survey by Albers [6], which gives an overview of the various threads of energy related research in the theory community. One of these techniques called speed scaling (which allows changing the speed of the processor in order to save energy) was defined about a decade and a half ago in the seminal paper of Yao et al. [36]. The last few years has seen a lot of activity in this area: see e.g. the paper by Bansal et al. [7]. Another approach is to dynamically power down a machine (or choose among multiple low power states) [16]. Both of these general approaches lead to scheduling problems in both the online and offline settings. However, in our opinion, the models proposed above for energy management though very nice, stop short of making energy minimization a primary goal of algorithm design like the I/O model made minimizing number of disk accesses a primary objective for algorithm design. The main impediment for pursuing this direction is a realistic model of energy consumption at the algorithm design. We believe that our model will complement this body of existing work.

Memory models with a small fast memory and a large slow memory have been studied for a long time. The I/O model [5] presents an external memory model, where accesses are made in blocks of size B to a fast memory of size M. Further, up to P parallel I/Os can be made simultaneously. Vitter and Shriver [34] extend this model with the restriction that the parallel I/Os can be made to P parallel disks only. This additional constraint introduces the aspect of data layout in the algorithm design, which ensures that blocks needed in parallel are written out to different disks. However, there is no associativity restriction and any block in slow memory can be mapped to any arbitrary block in the fast memory. Similar models have been proposed to model the number of cache misses in a 2-level cache-memory model with limited associativity [24]. A fundamental difference between our energy model and existing models is that in our model, we have a small value of M/B (equal to P) and an associativity of only 1 (every bank has exactly one sense amplifier and hence all blocks in slow memory have exactly one slot in fast memory that they can be mapped to).

Our model also has similarities with the cache oblivious model [12]. In this model, the goal is to minimize the number of cache misses (equivalent to the number of I/Os), while ensuring that the algorithm is also work optimal. Our model differs from this work in three ways: (i) The cache model assumes 'ideal cache' with high associativity whereas we have an associativity of 1 (ii) The tall cache assumption does not hold in our model due to small M/B and (iii) We aim to minimize a linear combination of work complexity and number of parallel I/Os whereas the cache oblivious model tries to minimize both the work complexity and the number of sequential I/Os without worrying about parallelism.

Parallel I/O algorithms naturally require a lookahead to read P blocks in parallel. Data oblivious algorithms are useful in this regard as they do not require a lookahead. We consider one data dependent problems in our work: sorting. For sorting, Goodrich recently presented an I/O optimal data oblivious algorithm [13]. However, it is non-trivial to ensure parallel access for the algorithm. Hence, in this work, we use prediction sequences [8] for ensuring lookahead as opposed to using data oblivious algorithms, which may be an alternate approach.

1.4 Extensions to our model

There are two obvious extensions to our energy model proposed in this work. First, since we wanted to follow the DDR3 memory architecture, each of the P disks has a cache that can only hold one block. A natural extension of this is to allow for the caches to be larger (this will mimic the "tall cache" assumption in the cache oblivious algorithms model). Our results easily extend to this more powerful model. We would like to point out that since our simulation results works for the much smaller caches (and the simulation only changes the disk memory accesses), they are more powerful and apply easily to the case when the cache sizes are larger. Another natural extension is to augment our energy model for multi-core machines. We leave this extremely interesting extension as future work.

2. DERIVATION OF AN ENERGY COMPLEXITY MODEL

The goal of our work is to define a model to capture the energy consumed by a modern server for executing an algorithm. In traditional data centers, servers perform the computation and I/O is handled separately by network attached storage. In this work, we focus only on server power, which includes the power drawn by processors and the server memory. Storage power is beyond the scope of this work.

2.1 Processor Power

The processor power drawn by a server can broadly be classified into the leakage power drawn by the processor clock and the power drawn by the processing elements. The processing power is determined by the number of operations performed by the processor. Hence, the computational energy consumed by a server for an algorithm $\mathcal{A}$ can broadly be captured as

$$E_{CPU}(\mathcal{A}) = P_{CLK}T(\mathcal{A}) + P_W W(\mathcal{A}) \quad (1)$$

where P_{CLK} is the leakage power drawn by the processor clock, $T(\mathcal{A})$ is the total time taken by the algorithm, and $W(\mathcal{A})$ is the total time taken by the non-I/O operations performed by the algorithm. (See (4) for the exact relation.) P_W is used to capture the power consumption per operation for the server.

2.2 Memory Elements

Modern memory is based on the *DDR* architecture [1]. Memory in this architecture is organized into a set of parallel banks. Each bank is arranged into a set of rows. Further, each bank has a sense amplifier in which exactly one row from the bank can be brought in. When a memory word needs to be read (or written), the row containing the word receives an ACT command. The ACT command activates the row and brings it into the sense amplifier. A column decoder is then used to identify the appropriate column of the row and a RD (or WR) command reads (or writes) the corresponding word from the sense amplifier. When the data is no longer needed, a PRE command writes back the sense amplifier into the row in the bank that the data belongs to. A memory clock is used to synchronize commands when the memory is activated.

A DDR memory may either be executing a command (e.g., ACT, PRE, RD, WR), be in power down mode, in a standby mode, or in an activated mode. A power down mode implies that no bank in the memory is being used and is not useful for algorithm design as it represents an input size of 0. When the memory is in the standby mode, each bank can individually be in an activated state (the sense amplifier has a row) or in a standby (precharged) state (the sense amplifier is empty). The time taken to activate a row in a bank is two orders of magnitude higher than the time taken to read a word. All banks can individually receive commands and execute these commands in parallel. Hence, memory access exhibits a parallel behavior (data in different banks can be parallely accessed) with a serial dependency (data in two rows of the bank can only be accessed in sequence).

We model the memory power as a sum of three components: (i) the first component P_{CKE} captures the leakage power drawn when the memory is in standby mode, but none of the banks are activated, (ii) the second component P_{STBY} captures the incremental cost over and above the leakage power for banks to be activated and waiting for commands, and (iii) the third component captures the incremental cost of various commands. The standby power needs to be computed for the duration that a bank is active and hence needs to be multiplied with the product of number of activations and the average activation time. Since ACT and PRE commands are always paired, we capture the energy cost of an ACT and a PRE command as E_{ACT}. Similarly, the cost of a RD or WR command is captured as $P_{RDWR}T_{RDWR}$. Hence, we model the memory power as

$$E_{MEM}(\mathcal{A}) = P_{CKE}T(\mathcal{A}) + P_{STBY}T_{ACT}(\mathcal{A})ACT(\mathcal{A}) + E_{ACT}ACT(\mathcal{A}) + (RD(\mathcal{A}) + WR(\mathcal{A})) \times T_{RDWR}P_{RDWR}. \tag{2}$$

where $ACT(\mathcal{A})$, $RD(\mathcal{A})$, $WR(\mathcal{A})$ denotes the number of activation cycles (ACT and PRE pair), the number of reads and writes respectively executed by an algorithm $\mathcal{A}$. $T_{ACT}(\mathcal{A})$ is the average time taken by one activation by $\mathcal{A}$.

2.3 Energy Complexity Model

We now present the energy complexity model, which is one of the key contributions of our work. (In what follows we will sometimes use equality instead of $\Theta(\cdot)$ to reduce clutter in some of the expressions.) We first combine the processor and memory power ((1) and (2) resp.) into a single model

$$E(\mathcal{A}) = P_{CLK}T(\mathcal{A}) + P_W W(\mathcal{A}) + P_{CKE}T(\mathcal{A}) + P_{STBY}T_{ACT}(\mathcal{A})ACT(\mathcal{A}) + E_{ACT}ACT(\mathcal{A}) + (RD(\mathcal{A}) + WR(\mathcal{A}))P_{RDWR}T_{RDWR}. \tag{3}$$

We can represent the time element in the energy equation as

$$T(\mathcal{A}) = W(\mathcal{A}) + ACT(\mathcal{A})T_{ACT}(\mathcal{A}) + (RD(\mathcal{A}) + WR(\mathcal{A})) \times T_{RDWR} \tag{4}$$

where T_{RDWR} is the number of processor cycles needed to execute a RD or WR command. T_{RDWR} has decreased over the years and is now a small constant (between 2 and 10) and can be taken out. Further, since every read and write corresponds to some work done, we can "charge" this work to the corresponding computational operations and thus, we can subsume this term in the work term. Hence, the overall time taken can be represented as

$$T(\mathcal{A}) = \Theta(W(\mathcal{A}) + ACT(\mathcal{A})T_{ACT}(\mathcal{A})). \tag{5}$$

Using the above value of $T(\mathcal{A})$ in (3) and using $T_{RDWR} = \Theta(1)$, we get

$$E(\mathcal{A}) = (P_{CLK} + P_{CKE})(W(\mathcal{A}) + ACT(\mathcal{A})T_{ACT}(\mathcal{A})) + P_W W(\mathcal{A}) + P_{STBY}T_{ACT}(\mathcal{A})ACT(\mathcal{A}) + E_{ACT}ACT(\mathcal{A}) + (RD(\mathcal{A}) + WR(\mathcal{A}))P_{RDWR}. \tag{6}$$

Since number of reads and writes are less than $W(\mathcal{A})$ and $P_{RDWR} < P_{CLK}$ (Fig. 4 provides a summary of typical values for these parameters), we subsume the last term in the first term.

$$E(\mathcal{A}) = (ACT(\mathcal{A})T_{ACT}(\mathcal{A}))P_{C_1} + W(\mathcal{A})P_{C_2} + E_{ACT}ACT(\mathcal{A}) \tag{7}$$

where P_{C_1} is $P_{CLK} + P_{CKE} + P_{STBY}$ and $P_{C_2} = P_{CLK} + P_{CKE} + P_W$. The average time taken for each activation $T_{ACT}(\mathcal{A})$ depends on the I/O parallelism of the algorithm. The activation cycle can be captured as a latency parameter L (e.g., in DDR3 typical value is 200 cycles) and can be amortized across all banks activated in parallel. For fully parallel access, the expected time to read turns out to be L/P. In modern processors with memory clocks approaching processor clock speeds, the best access to read PB blocks would be $O(PB)$ computations. Hence, $L = \Theta(PB)$ and $T_{ACT}(\mathcal{A}) = PB/k$, where k is the "average" I/O parallelism of the algorithm (or $ACT(\mathcal{A})/k$ is the number of parallel accesses made by the algorithm). Since $E_{ACT} < B \cdot P_{C_1}$ (Fig. 4 and B is typically 4096), we subsume the third term in the second term. Finally, for modern processors, $P_W < P_{CLK}$, which implies that $P_{C_1} = \Theta(P_{C_2})$, which in turn gives us our final model:

$$E(\mathcal{A}) = W(\mathcal{A}) + ACT(\mathcal{A})\frac{PB}{k} \tag{8}$$

Our energy model introduces a new term k or the average I/O parallelism for an algorithm. The other terms are either algorithm independent (P, B) or complexities that can

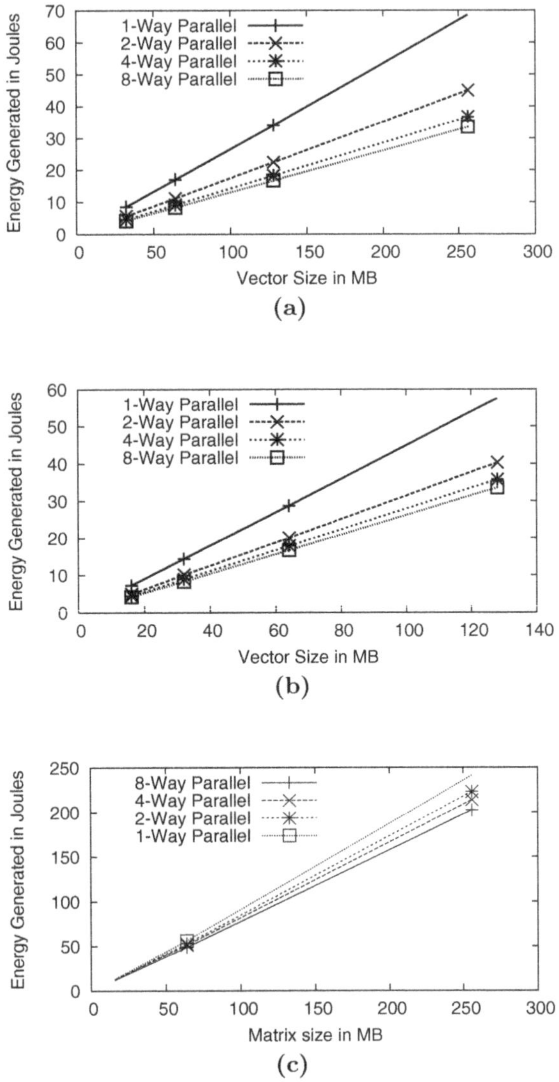

Figure 3: Energy consumed by (a) Write (b) Copy and (c) Matrix Transpose Workloads

be derived from known complexity models ($W(A)$ is work complexity and $ACT(A)$ can be derived from I/O complexity). The parameter k prevents direct application of known algorithms in other models and it is important to ascertain if the parameter is even needed in practice.

We conducted experiments with varying memory bank parallelism for some benchmarks, which are anecdotally known to be very frequent in applications. These include writing to a large vector, copying from one vector to another and matrix transpose. We also increase the work and I/O complexity by increasing the problem size for these operations and measured the energy. Each experiment is repeated 10 times and the means are reported in Fig. 3. More details of our experimental methodology as well as deviations from the average values is described in Section 6.

As expected from (8), we observe that energy increases linearly with increase in the work and I/O complexity for all three benchmarks (for fixed k). We observe that a 1-parallel layout (i.e. $k = 1$) consumes more than $2X$ energy, as compared to a 4-parallel layout (i.e. $k = 4$) for both *copy* and *write* benchmarks. We would also like to note that our benchmark code had overheads to ensure that our memory allocation provided the parallelism we wanted. This book-keeping of memory allocation was more significant for matrices as opposed to vectors and as a consequence, the difference is moderate for matrix transpose. Finally, for the benchmarks we evaluated, work complexity started to dominate beyond 4-parallel layout. Hence, the performance improvement of using 8 banks in parallel is not significant as compared to using 4 banks in parallel. In fact, as we show later, the tradeoff between work complexity and I/O parallelism is a salient attribute of our model. Since our goal is to minimize a function of these two parameters, we can afford to not optimize any parameter that does not impact the overall objective function for a specific algorithm. We next align our energy model with existing parallel I/O models.

3. OUR ENERGY MODEL

In this section, we present our abstract energy model. In our model, the energy consumption is very closely tied with the memory layout, so we begin with our model of memory.

We will have two levels of memory. The second level of memory (which we will call *main memory*) is divided into P *banks*: we will denote the banks by $\mathcal{M}_1, \ldots, \mathcal{M}_P$. The unit of memory access will be a *block*. The locations of a block in a bank will be called a *bank row*. The collection of all the banks rows with the same (relative) position in each bank will be called a *row*. Each block will contain B items. Each of the P banks has its own *cache*. In particular, we will denote $\mathcal{M}_i$'s cache by $\mathcal{C}_i$. $\mathcal{C}_i$ can only hold *one* block. Further, for any $i \in [P]$, only a block from $\mathcal{M}_i$ can be read into $\mathcal{C}_i$ and only the block in $\mathcal{C}_i$ can be written back into $\mathcal{M}_i$. With these constraints, an algorithm can manipulate the items in the caches $\mathcal{C}_1, \ldots, \mathcal{C}_P$ however it wants. (In other words, as long as it does not need to either read from the main memory or write to the main memory, the algorithm can consider $\mathcal{C}_1, \ldots, \mathcal{C}_P$ as one big cache with PB items in it.) The algorithm is allowed a constant number of extra registers as scratch space.

We emphasize that in our model

$$P < B. \tag{9}$$

In particular, P can be a few orders smaller than B. This for example is different from the *tall cache* assumption in the cache oblivious model, where we would have $P \geq B$.

Given the memory model, we are now ready to start defining our abstract energy model. To begin with, let $\mathcal{A}$ be the algorithm under consideration and let x be an arbitrary input. We define $W(\mathcal{A}, x)$ to be the *work* that algorithm $\mathcal{A}$ performs on input x (i.e. the run time of $\mathcal{A}$ on x without accounting for the time to transfer blocks from/to main memory with each basic computational step taking $\Theta(1)$ work).

Next we account for the memory accesses. Let $\mathcal{I}(\mathcal{A}, x)$ be the sequence of indices of the banks corresponding to the actual memory access for $\mathcal{A}$ in input x.[1] Starting from the

[1]Each memory access is defined by a bit that signifies whether it was a read or a write; the index of the bank that was accessed; and the bank row that was accessed. However, for this part of the model, we only need to consider the second component.

beginning of $\mathcal{I}(\mathcal{A}, x)$ we partition the sequence into maximal *batches*. We call a sequence of bank indices $b_1, \ldots, b_m$ to be a batch if (i) All the b_i's are distinct; and (ii) When $\mathcal{A}$ accesses the item corresponding to b_1, it also knows the location of the items corresponding to $b_2, \ldots, b_m$. The number m will be called the *lookahead* of $\mathcal{A}$ when it is accessing the item corresponding to b_1. Note that a batch can have size at most P. Let the resulting sequence of batches be defined as $\mathcal{T}(\mathcal{A}, x)$.

We would like to elaborate a bit on the second property: in general we allow $\mathcal{A}$ to have different lookahead for different item it accesses. We will also work with the following sub-class of algorithms

DEFINITION 1. *Let $\ell \geq 1$ be an integer. An algorithm $\mathcal{A}$ is said to have a* lookahead *of ℓ, if for every memory location it accesses, it knows the location of the next $\ell - 1$ memory locations.*

As an example, consider the case for $P = 4$: $\mathcal{I}(\mathcal{A}, x) = 1, 2, 2, 2, 3, 4, 1, 3, 1, 2, 4$, then if the algorithm has a look ahead of 4, then we have $\mathcal{T}(\mathcal{A}, x) = (1, 2), (2), (2, 3, 4, 1), (3, 1, 2, 4)$, and if the algorithm has a lookahead of 2, then we have $\mathcal{T}(\mathcal{A}, x) = (1, 2), (2), (2, 3), (4, 1), (3, 1), (2, 4)$.

Finally, the *batch complexity* of $\mathcal{A}$ on x is defined as $T(\mathcal{A}, x) = |\mathcal{T}(\mathcal{A}, x)|$.

We are now ready to define the *energy* consumed by $\mathcal{A}$ on x as $E(\mathcal{A}, x) = W(\mathcal{A}, x) + L \cdot T(\mathcal{A}, x)$, where L is a *latency* parameter with

$$L = \Theta(PB). \tag{10}$$

Given the size of the input N, we define the energy complexity of $\mathcal{A}$ as $E_{\mathcal{A}}(N) = \max_{x:|x|=N} E(\mathcal{A}, x)$, where we will drop $\mathcal{A}$ from the subscript if it is clear from the context. For a randomized algorithm, we consider its expected energy complexity.

4. SUFFICIENT CONDITIONS FOR EFFICIENT SIMULATION

In this section, we look at certain sub-class of algorithms for which we can do an efficient simulation in our model. To this end, we start with few definitions.

DEFINITION 2 (RUNS). *A sequence of memory locations is called a run if the locations can be partitioned into* stripes, *where each stripe consists of all the blocks in the same row in all the P memory banks.*

As an example, consider the case for $P = 4$ and consider the sequence of memory accesses:

$$0, 1, 2, 3, 8, 9, 10, 11, 4, 5, 6, 7, 12, 13, 14, 15, \tag{11}$$

where the index i goes to the ($i \mod 4$)th bank in row major form. Then this is a run with the stripes $(0, 1, 2, 3), (8, 9, 10, 11), (4, 5, 6, 7), (12, 13, 14, 15)$.

DEFINITION 3 (k-STRIPED ALGORITHM). *Let $k \geq 1$ be an integer. Call an algorithm* k-striped *if (1) One can divide the execution of the algorithm into phases, (2) In each phase the algorithm reads from at most k runs in memory and writes to one run*[2] *(and the runs are defined at the beginning of a phase); and (3) In each run it accesses the blocks in a sequential manner (i.e. row by row and within each row from the first bank to the last).*

[2]Our results can handle writing to a fixed constant many runs. However, it is easy to see that we can simulate such an algorithm with another one that just has one run with constant overhead in the parameters. Hence, we only explicitly consider the case have a single "write run."

As an example, consider the very simple algorithm of copying the contents of a vector $\mathbf{v}_1$ into another vector $\mathbf{v}_2$. Let $\mathbf{v}_1$ be allocated the sequence of indexes $0, 1, 2, 3, 8, 9, 10, 11$ and $\mathbf{v}_2$ be allocated the sequence of indexes $4, 5, 6, 7, 12, 13, 14, 15$, $P = 4$ and the memory location i goes to the ($i \mod 4$)th bank in a row major form. In this case we can have two phases in the algorithm. In the first phase we read the contents of run $(0, 1, 2, 3)$ and write it into run $(4, 5, 6, 7)$. In the second phase the contents of run $(8, 9, 10, 11)$ is written into run $(12, 13, 14, 15)$. Each run here consists of a single stripe and we read from exactly one run at each phase. Hence this algorithm in this case 1-striped.

DEFINITION 4 (BOUNDED ALGORITHM). *Call an algorithm* bounded *if (1) The algorithm only accesses blocks only within a run (and the run is defined/known at the beginning of the algorithm); and (2) The ratio of the size of the run to the number of memory access is upper bounded by a constant.*

We note that pretty much any reasonable algorithm will be a bounded algorithm. E.g. if an algorithm can earmark all its required space in one contiguous run and it does not "over-budget" by more than a constant factor, then it will be a bounded algorithm.

DEFINITION 5. *Let $\ell \geq 1$ be an integer. Then given an algorithm $\mathcal{A}$ and an input x, we call the sequence $\mathcal{I}(\mathcal{A}, x)$ to be* (ℓ, τ)-parallelizable *for some integer $1 \leq k \leq \ell$, if for every ℓ consecutive blocks in $\mathcal{I}(\mathcal{A}, x)$ has at most τ batches in it.*

E.g., the run in (11) is $(4, 1)$-parallelizable.

We first begin with a simple observation that any algorithm in the (parallel disk) I/O model can be easily modified to work in our model with a similar degree of parallelism and without incurring a penalty in the lookahead.

THEOREM 4.1. *Let $\mathcal{A}$ be an algorithm with lookahead ℓ in the parallel disk I/O model with $P - 1$ disks and $M = (P - 1)B$. Then there exists an algorithm $\mathcal{A}'$ with the same functional behavior as $\mathcal{A}$ such that for every x, we have*

$$|\mathcal{I}(\mathcal{A}', x)| \leq O\left(|\mathcal{I}(\mathcal{A}, x)|\right)$$

and

$$W(\mathcal{A}', x) \leq W(\mathcal{A}, x) + O(|\mathcal{I}(\mathcal{A}, x)| \cdot B).$$

Further, $\mathcal{A}'$ is bounded (k-striped respectively) if $\mathcal{A}$ is a bounded (k-striped resp.) algorithm. Finally, if $\mathcal{A}$ has a lookahead of ℓ, then so does $\mathcal{A}'$.

PROOF. Recall that the only way that the parallel disk I/O model differs from our memory model is that our P caches are associated with the P banks while the memory in the parallel I/O disk model is not associative. In our simulation, we will show that this is not a big restriction if we have one extra bank: the main idea is to use the cache of the extra bank as a temporary space. More precisely, we fix a map from the $(P - 1)B$ blocks in memory used by $\mathcal{A}'$ to the first $P - 1$ caches. (We also do the obvious map from the $P - 1$ disks to the $P - 1$ banks.) The only constraint on this map is that given any block's location for $\mathcal{A}$ we can immediately compute its location in the $P-1$ caches. For the rest of the proof, we will assume that this mapping has already been done. Next we define $\mathcal{A}'$. We will show how an arbitrary I/O in $\mathcal{A}$ can be simulated by a memory access in our model and $O(B)$ extra work per I/O, which proves the desired result. Assume that $\mathcal{A}$ needs to transfer a block b from bank i to the cache j. If $i=j$, then this can be done easily. If not, we first move the contents of the ith cache to the last cache, bring in the block b to the ith cache, move b from the ith cache to the jth cache and finally move back the contents of the last cache to cache i. Similarly one can simulate a write from one of the caches to one of the banks.

Finally, since $\mathcal{A}'$ has the same access pattern in the banks as $\mathcal{A}$ does (in the corresponding disks), it preserves the lookahead as well as the property of being striped/bounded as $\mathcal{A}$. □

We start with the following simple observation:

LEMMA 4.2. *If a sequence $\mathcal{I}(\mathcal{A},x)$ is (ℓ,τ) parallelizable, then $T(\mathcal{A},x)) \le \frac{|\mathcal{I}(\mathcal{A},x)|}{\ell}\cdot\tau$.*

PROOF. The sequence can be divided into $\frac{|\mathcal{I}(\mathcal{A},x)|}{\ell}$ blocks with ℓ bank indices in them. Further, as $\mathcal{I}(\mathcal{A},x)$ is (ℓ,τ)-parallelizable, each of these blocks have at most τ batches in them, which proves the claim. □

The above implies the following simple observation:

LEMMA 4.3. *Let $\mathcal{A}$ be an algorithm with lookahead $\ell = \Theta(P)$ such that for any input x, $\mathcal{I}(\mathcal{A},x)$ is $(\ell, O(1))$-parallelizable. If $\mathcal{A}$ is worst-case work-optimal and I/O optimal, then $\mathcal{A}$ is also energy optimal.*

PROOF. The main observation is simple: since there are P banks for any algorithm $\mathcal{A}'$ and input x, we have

$$T(\mathcal{A}',x) \ge \frac{|\mathcal{I}(\mathcal{A}',x)|}{P}.$$

Thus, Lemma 4.2 implies that for any given sequence, the number of batches is within a constant factor of the optimal. This implies that for any (large enough N), since the algorithm has worst-case optimal I/O complexity, $\max_{x:|x|=N} T(\mathcal{A},x)$ is worst-case optimal. Further, it is given that the algorithm is worst-case work optimal. Thus, the claim follows by the definition of $E_{\mathcal{A}}(N)$ (and the fact that the delay parameter L is independent of N). □

We are now ready to state and prove our first non-trivial sufficient condition:

THEOREM 4.4. *Let $1 \le k,\ell \le P$ be integers. Let $\mathcal{A}$ be a k-striped algorithm with lookahead ℓ. Then there exists a (randomized) algorithm $\mathcal{A}'$ with the same functional behavior as $\mathcal{A}$ (and uses up at most three times as much space as $\mathcal{A}$ does) such that for every x, we have $|\mathcal{I}(\mathcal{A}',x)| \le O(|\mathcal{I}(\mathcal{A},x)|)$, and $\mathcal{I}(\mathcal{A}',x)$ is (ℓ,τ)-parallelizable, where*

$$\mathbb{E}[\tau] \le O(1). \tag{12}$$

In particular, we have

$$\mathbb{E}\left[T(\mathcal{A}',x)\right] \le O\left(\frac{|\mathcal{I}(\mathcal{A},x)|}{\ell}\right). \tag{13}$$

Finally,

$$W(\mathcal{A}',x) \le O(W(\mathcal{A},x)). \tag{14}$$

PROOF. We first argue that the number of batches in $\mathcal{A}'$ is bounded. (13) follows from (12), Lemma 4.2 and the linearity of expectation. Thus, for the rest of the proof, we focus on proving (12).

We will design $\mathcal{A}'$ from $\mathcal{A}$ by using the power of two choices in the balls and bins framework. The main idea is the following: at the start of each phase we make two copies of the run. We divide each of the two copies into disjoint groups and (independently) reorder each group with a random permutation. When we need to read a block, we choose one that minimizes the "load." In particular, since $\mathcal{A}$ has a lookahead of ℓ the idea is to divide each group of ℓ memory locations into small number of batches. It turns out that this number of batches (which will determine τ) is exactly the maximum load in a balls and bins problem induced by the above process (which corresponds to a balls and bins problem with two choices). We now present the details.

We will show how $\mathcal{A}'$ simulates any arbitrary phase of $\mathcal{A}$ with the required properties. The claimed result then just follows by applying the same procedure to all the phases. For the rest of the proof, we will assume that $\mathcal{A}$ only uses the first $P/2$ banks and does not access any block in the last $P/2$ banks. (In general, this assumption might not be true but since $\mathcal{A}'$ does a step by step simulation of $\mathcal{A}$, one can always modify $\mathcal{A}'$ so that $\mathcal{A}$ effectively only uses the first $P/2$ banks.)

Fix any phase of $\mathcal{A}$ and consider the time when $\mathcal{A}$ is about to start the phase. The simulation proceeds in three steps.

Pre-Processing.

At the beginning of the current phase, $\mathcal{A}$ knows the run. Let m be the size of the run. For now, let us assume that

$$m \le 2^{2B/P} \tag{15}$$

$\mathcal{A}'$ will copy the run into fresh space (which is not used by $\mathcal{A}$). At the same time, for every block it stores the map between the old location and the new location. We now present the details.

Since $\mathcal{A}$ knows the run in the current phase, we'll assume w.l.o.g. that given the index of any block in the run, one can compute its actual location. Note that there are m/B blocks in the run (we'll assume that B divides m– this does not affect any of the asymptotic bounds later on). In particular, one can fit $g = \lfloor B/\log(m/B)\rfloor$ such indices into one bank row. (Note that (15) implies that $g \ge P/2$.) To compute the random map, we proceed as follows:

> Iterate the following $2(m/B)/(gP)$ times. In the $0 \le i < 2(m/B)/(gP)$ iteration, do the following *twice* (with independent randomness). Write the memory locations of the blocks indexed[3] by $i\cdot gP/2,\ldots,(i+1)\cdot gP/2-1$ into the last $P/2$ caches. Then using Knuth's Algorithm P (also known as the Fisher-Yates shuffle) [20] randomly permute the g contiguous groups of $P/2$ indices each in-place. (For different groups and iterations we use independent randomness. Note that we are permuting the $gP/2$ indices where relative positions of groups of sizes $P/2$ remains the same.) After the permutation, write all the $P/2$ cyclic shifts of the contents of the $P/2$ caches into

[3]Since everything in part of a run w.l.o.g., we will assume that these memory locations are also contiguous.

$P/2$ rows in fresh memory in the last $P/2$ banks (allocated for storing the random map).

(Note that each block gets permuted randomly twice. We will refer to these two random maps as the first and second random map. We'll see later why the $P/2$ cyclic shifts will be useful.)

Next we copy the actual contents of the run: we access the run row by row and then using the random map that we stored above we copy $P/2$ blocks at a time. In particular, we load the random maps for the m/B blocks in chunks of size $gP/2$ in the last $P/2$ caches (each of the $gP/2$ locations have $P/2$ copies: pick any arbitrary one). We then divide the $gP/2$ into chunks of size $P/2$ (i.e. we consider the maps for the first $P/2$ of the m/B blocks and so on). For each chunk we copy the corresponding blocks in the first $P/2$ banks into their corresponding locations in a fresh memory space (that is not used by $\mathcal{A}$). We do this for both the first and the second random maps.

We now argue about the contribution of the pre-processing step to $\mathcal{I}(\mathcal{A}', x)$. We first upper bound the number of new accesses. During the creation of the random map, in each of the $2m/(gBP)$ iterations, we add $2 \cdot P^2/4$ accesses, leading to a total of $mP/(gB) \leq 2m/B$ extra accesses. Further, each of the $P/2$ blocks that are written to one row form a single batch (for a total of $m/(BP)$ batches). For the copying part, for loading the random maps into the last $P/2$ caches, the number of extra accesses and batches can again be upper bounded by m/B and $m/(PB)$ respectively. Finally, we consider the copying part: we copy over m/B blocks in chunks of size $P/2$, so the number of extra accesses is again at most m/B. Further, while copying one chunk of $P/2$, note that by the assumption that these form a contiguous part of the run, when we randomly permute these $P/2$ elements, each such chunk forms exactly one batch.

Thus, overall, the preprocessing step adds $O(m/B)$ to accesses in $\mathcal{I}(\mathcal{A}', x)$. Further, these accesses are $(P/2, \tau)$ parallelizable, where τ satisfies (12). Recall that so far we have assumed that m satisfies (15). However, if this is not the case, we can just divide the run into consecutive chunks of size $2^{2B/P}$ and then apply the above procedure on each of these chunks. Note that doing so still preserves all the claimed bound (in terms of general value of m).

Since $\mathcal{A}$ is striped, it implies that m/B is $O(|\mathcal{I}(\mathcal{A}, x)|)$. Thus, overall this phase adds $O(|\mathcal{I}(\mathcal{A}, x)|)$ accesses with the required parallelizability property.

Simulation.

We now state how we simulate the actual computation steps of $\mathcal{A}$ in $\mathcal{A}'$: we will run the exact same steps as in $\mathcal{A}$ except when it does a memory read we access the "lighter loaded" of its two copies (according to the first and second random maps that we have stored). For memory writes since we have assumed that the algorithm writes to a single run in a sequential manner, we can easily simulate this step within the required resource parameters. Hence, for the rest of the description, we will focus on the simulation of the reads.

In particular, since $\mathcal{A}$ has a look-up of ℓ, $\mathcal{A}'$ will process the memory accesses of $\mathcal{A}$ in chunks of size $\ell \leftarrow \min(\ell, P/512)$ and perform the following two tasks:

- Load the two new locations of the ℓ blocks from the stored first and second random maps into the last $P/2$ caches.
- Think of the ℓ blocks as balls and the p banks as bins in the balls and bins framework in Section D. Then for each block pick the copy from either the first or second random map as dictated by the allocation algorithm in Section D.
- Using the location of the corresponding block from the previous step, one does the corresponding accesses into the ℓ blocks.

It is easy to see that each of the step above lead to at most ℓ memory accesses and thus, overall this step contributes $O(|\mathcal{I}(\mathcal{A}, x)|)$ number of accesses to $\mathcal{I}(\mathcal{A}', x)$. We now argue about the parallelizability of the accesses in this step. For the first step above, note that given the ℓ locations one can easily compute the corresponding indices into the random map. Given that each entry in random map is repeated $P/2$ times in all the last $P/2$ banks, implies that when we want to look up the new locations for the ℓ blocks, we pick the copies in such a way that all the ℓ accesses form a single block. For the second step above, Theorem D.2, implies that each of the chunk of ℓ accesses has $O(1)$ batches (in expectation). Thus, overall all the accesses in this step are (ℓ, τ)-parallelizable with τ as in (12), as desired.

Post-Processing.

In this step, we copy back blocks from the fresh memory to their original locations. To do this, we go over the old locations row by row, load the corresponding entries from (say the first) random map and then copy back the contents of the block in the new location to the original location.[4] It is easy to see that using the same arguments as in the pre-processing step, we add $O(|\mathcal{I}(\mathcal{A}, x)|)$ accesses with the required parallelizability property.

Finally, we argue (14). The inequality follows from the fact that the only ways $\mathcal{A}'$ differs from $\mathcal{A}$ are (i) Computing the random map– one needs $O(1)$ amount of work per entry in the random map (this includes the time taken to compute the random permutation– the Fischer-Yates shuffle can be implemented with $O(1)$ work per element); (ii) the copying of elements from the runs that are "active" in a phase to another portion in the memory using the random map– this just needs $O(1)$ work per elements in the run; (iii) while doing a memory access, one can has to compute its location from the random map, which again takes $O(1)$ work per element (here we use the fact that when computing the best of two choices we can compute the choices for the $\Theta(P)$ locations in time $O(P)$ due to Lemma D.1); and (iv) Undoing the random map for each block in the run, which again takes $O(1)$ work per element. The proof is complete by noting that the algorithm accesses each active element in each of the phases at least once. □

We now ready to state and prove our second non-trivial sufficient condition:

THEOREM 4.5. *Let $1 \leq \ell \leq P/2$ be an integer. Let $\mathcal{A}$ be a bounded algorithm with lookahead ℓ that uses space $S(x)$ for input x. Then there exists a (randomized) algorithm $\mathcal{A}'$ with the same functional behavior as $\mathcal{A}$ (and uses*

[4]Since we can do both reads and writes in a phase, we first copy back the runs that were read and then copy back the run that was written to– this way we ensure that the original locations after the phase is done has the correct value.

three times as much space as $\mathcal{A}$ does) such that for every x we have $|\mathcal{I}(\mathcal{A}',x)| \le O(|\mathcal{I}(\mathcal{A},x)|)$, and $\mathcal{I}(\mathcal{A}',x)$ is (ℓ,τ)-parallelizable, where

$$\mathbb{E}[\tau] \le O\left(\frac{\log P}{\log\log P}\right). \tag{16}$$

In particular, we have

$$\mathbb{E}\left[T(\mathcal{A}',x)\right] \le O\left(\frac{|\mathcal{I}(\mathcal{A},x)|\cdot\log P}{\ell\cdot\log\log P}\right). \tag{17}$$

Finally,

$$W(\mathcal{A}',x) \le O(W(\mathcal{A},x)). \tag{18}$$

PROOF. The proof is similar to that of Theorem 4.4 except that we randomize the blocks used by $\mathcal{A}$ differently: we just randomly permute each group of size $P/2$ once and then apply the balls and bins result from Section C. For the sake of completeness, next we present the details.

Using a similar argument as in the proof of Theorem 4.4, w.l.o.g., we can assume that

$$|S(x)| \le 2^{2B/P}. \tag{19}$$

Unlike before, $\mathcal{A}'$ does the random permuting before simulating any steps of $\mathcal{A}$. Thus, we will only need a preprocessing step (but no post-processing step). For the rest of the proof, we will assume that $\mathcal{A}$ only uses the first $P/2$ banks and does not access any block in the last $P/2$ banks. (In general, this assumption might not be true but since $\mathcal{A}'$ does a step by step simulation of $\mathcal{A}$, one can always modify $\mathcal{A}'$ so that $\mathcal{A}$ effectively only uses the first $P/2$ banks.)

Pre-Processing.

Note that since $\mathcal{A}$ is bounded, it knows the entire space that is going to use. For notational convenience, define $m = S(x)$. $\mathcal{A}'$ will copy this space into fresh space (which is not used by $\mathcal{A}$). At the same time, for every block it stores the map between the old location and the new location. We now present the details.

Since $\mathcal{A}$ knows the run it is going to use when executing itself on x, we'll assume w.l.o.g. that given the index of any block in the run, one can compute its actual location. Note that there are m/B blocks in the run (we'll assume that B divides m– this does not affect any of the asymptotic bounds later on). In particular, one can fit $g = \lfloor B/\log(m/B)\rfloor$ such indices into one bank row. (Note that (19) implies that $g \ge P/2$.) To compute the random map, we proceed as follows:

> Iterate the following $2(m/B)/(gP)$ times. In the $0 \le i < 2(m/B)/(gP)$ iteration, write the indices $i\cdot gP/2,\dots,(i+1)\cdot gP/2-1$ into the last $P/2$ caches. Then using Knuth's Algorithm P (also known as the Fisher-Yates shuffle) [20] randomly permute the $gP/2$ indices in-place. (For different iterations we use independent randomness.) After the permutation, write all the $P/2$ cyclic shifts of the contents of the $P/2$ caches into $P/2$ rows in fresh memory in the last $P/2$ banks (allocated for storing the random map).

(We'll see later why the $P/2$ cyclic shifts will be useful.)

Next we copy the actual contents of the run: we access the run row by row and then using the random map that we stored above we copy $P/2$ blocks at a time. In particular, we load the random maps for the m/B blocks in chunks of size $gP/2$ in the last $P/2$ caches (each of the $gP/2$ locations have $P/2$ copies: pick any arbitrary one). We then divide the $gP/2$ into chunks of size $P/2$ (i.e. we consider the maps for the first $P/2$ of the m/B blocks and so on). For each chunk we copy the corresponding blocks in the first $P/2$ banks into their corresponding locations in a fresh memory space (that is not used by $\mathcal{A}$).

We now argue about the contribution of the pre-processing step to $\mathcal{I}(\mathcal{A}',x)$. We first upper bound the number of new accesses. During the creation of the random map, in each of the $2m/(gBP)$ iterations, we add $P^2/4$ accesses, leading to a total of $mP/(2gB) \le m/B$ extra accesses. Further, each of the $P/2$ blocks that are written to one row form a single batch (for a total of $m/(BP)$ batches). For the copying part, for loading the random maps into the last $P/2$ caches, the number of extra accesses and batches can again be upper bounded by m/B and $m/(PB)$ respectively. Finally, we consider the copying part: we copy over m/B blocks in chunks of size $P/2$, so the number of extra accesses is again at most m/B. Further, while copying one chunk of $P/2$, we note that we're in the situation of the balls and bins problem considered in Section C and thus, Theorem C.1, implies that each such chunk will have at most $O(\log P/\log\log P)$ batches in expectation.

Thus, overall, the preprocessing step adds $O(m/B)$ accesses in $\mathcal{I}(\mathcal{A}',x)$. Further, these accesses are $(P/2,\tau)$ parallelizable, where τ satisfies (17). Since $\mathcal{A}$ is bounded, it implies that m/B is $O(|\mathcal{I}(\mathcal{A},x)|)$. Thus, overall this phase adds $O(|\mathcal{I}(\mathcal{A},x)|)$ accesses with the required parallelizability property.

Simulation.

We now state how we simulate the actual computation steps of $\mathcal{A}$ in $\mathcal{A}'$: the idea is as before– we'll run the exact same steps as in $\mathcal{A}$ except when it does a memory access we access its corresponding copy (according to the random map that we have stored). In particular, since $\mathcal{A}$ has a look-up of ℓ, $\mathcal{A}'$ will process the memory accesses of $\mathcal{A}$ in chunks of size ℓ and perform the following two tasks:

- Load the new locations of the ℓ blocks from the stored random map into the last $P/2$ caches.
- Using the location of the corresponding block in the fresh space (stored within the last $P/2$ caches), one does the corresponding access into the ℓ blocks.

It is easy to see that each of the step above lead to at most ℓ memory accesses and thus, overall this step contributes $O(|\mathcal{I}(\mathcal{A},x)|)$ number of accesses to $\mathcal{I}(\mathcal{A}',x)$. We now argue about the parallelizability of the accesses in this step. For the first step above, note that given the ℓ locations one can easily compute the corresponding indices into the random map. Given that each entry in random map is repeated $P/2$ times in all the last $P/2$ banks, implies that when we want to look up the new locations for the ℓ blocks, we pick the copies in such a way that all the ℓ accesses form a single block. For the second step above, Theorem C.1, implies that each of the chunk of ℓ accesses has $O(\log P/\log\log P)$ batches (in expectation). Thus, overall all the accesses in this step are (ℓ,τ)-parallelizable with τ as in (17), as desired.

Finally, we argue (18). The inequality follows from the fact that the only ways $\mathcal{A}'$ differs from $\mathcal{A}$ are (i) Computing the random map– one needs $O(1)$ amount of work per entry in the random map (this includes the time taken to compute the random permutation– the Fischer-Yates shuffle can be implemented with $O(1)$ work per element); (ii) the copying of elements from the run to another portion in the memory using the random map– this just needs $O(1)$ work per elements in the run; (iii) while doing a memory access, one can has to compute its location from the random map, which again takes $O(1)$ work per element.

□

Reducing the Amount of Randomness.

An inspection of the proofs of Theorems 4.4 and 4.5 reveals that $\mathcal{A}'$ needs a lot of random bits. In particular, if the algorithm uses S amounts of "active" space in a given run, then one needs $\Omega(S)$ space. In Appendix B, we show how using limited-wise independent sources based on Reed-Solomon codes, one can reduce the randomness to $O(P \log S)$ bits while pretty much maintaining the rest of the parameters.

5. COROLLARIES FOR SPECIFIC PROBLEMS

5.1 Inner Product

We start the simple problem of computing the inner product of two vectors of length N. Assuming both the vectors are stored in the same order in memory, the naive algorithm of getting $PB/2$ consecutive entries from each of the vectors from memory to the P caches (and keeping track of the current partial value of the inner product in a register) has the optimal work complexity of $O(N)$ as well as the optimal I/O complexity of $O(N/B)$. Further, it is easy to see that the above algorithm is $(P/2, 1)$-parallelizable. Thus by Lemma 4.3, we have the following result:

PROPOSITION 5.1. *The inner product problem can be solved with energy optimal complexity of* $\Theta(N)$.

We note that for this problem, having the tall cache assumption does not have any impact.

5.2 Sorting

It is easy to see that the k-way merge sort is a k-striped algorithm. However, since the algorithm is data dependent, the "traditional" merge sort algorithm does not good lookahead. Barve et al. [8] showed how to use a prediction sequence to get around this predicament and achieve a lookahead of $\Theta(P)$ (while not asymptotically changing the work or I/O complexity). For the sake of completeness the details are in Appendix F. The (modified) P-way merge sort has a work complexity of $O(N \log N)$ and an I/O complexity of $O\left(\frac{N}{B} \log_P(N/B)\right)$. Thus, Theorem 4.4 implies the following:

COROLLARY 5.2. *Sorting of N numbers can be done with the optimal $\Theta(N \log N)$ energy complexity.*

We would like to point out that we do not need Theorem 4.4 to prove the above corollary. We note that 2-way merge sort trivially is $(P/2, 1)$-parallelizable. Further, it is known that 2-way mergesort has I/O complexity of $O\left(\frac{N}{B} \log(N/B)\right)$. Thus, Lemma 4.2 then also proves the above corollary. Further, note that in this case having a larger cache can only make the I/O complexity smaller, which makes the time complexity component of the energy complexity dominate even more.

Using the optimal algorithm for sparse matrix-dense vector multiplication from [10] and the result above, we can also obtain energy optimal result for the sparse matrix-dense vector multiplication problem. (The algorithm in [10] uses sorting as a routine and the rest of the algorithm can be performed with linear scans, which are both work and I/O optimal as well as $(P, 1)$-parallelizable.) Indeed sorting is a basic primitive that is used in many I/O algorithms (see e.g. the book by Vitter [33]) and thus Corollary 5.2 would be applicable in many other problems.

5.3 Permuting

We now consider the problem of permuting a given vector of N items according to (an implicitly specified) permutation. Since this is a special case of sorting, we can use any sorting algorithm to solve this problem. However, one crucial way in which this problem differs from sorting is that the permuting problem has a work complexity of $\Theta(N)$. Further, it is known that the permuting problem has an I/O complexity of $\Omega\left(\min\left(N, \frac{N}{B} \log_M(N/B)\right)\right)$ [5]. This implies that the energy complexity of the permuting problem is $\Omega\left(N + \min\left(NB, N \log_M(N/B)\right)\right)$. Note that this implies that for this problem, the work complexity is the negligible part of the energy complexity (under the assumption that $N \geq MB$, which is reasonable even with the tall cache assumption). In other words, unlike the sorting problem, where even 2-way mergesort gave the optimal energy complexity algorithm, for the permuting problem, we need to use the (modified) P-way mergesort algorithm from Appendix F along with Theorem 4.4, to prove the following result:

COROLLARY 5.3. *Permuting of N numbers can be done with the optimal $\Theta(N \log_P(N/B))$ energy complexity.*

We remark that with larger cache size the logarithm term can be made smaller.

5.4 Matrix Transpose

The naive $\sqrt{N} \times \sqrt{N}$ matrix transpose algorithm has linear $O(N)$ work complexity but is not I/O-efficient and may require up to N I/Os. Even if the I/O sequence is $(P, 1)$ parallelizable, the batch complexity of the algorithm would be N/P, which is a factor of B times the optimal complexity. Under the assumption of tall cache, the algorithm in [5] that transposes sub-matrices can achieve a batch complexity of $N/(PB)$. In the absence of tall cache, [5] present an algorithm that has a tight I/O bound of $\Omega\left(\frac{N}{B}\frac{\log(M)}{\log(1+M/B)}\right)$.

The recursive matrix transpose algorithm alluded to above is a bounded algorithm and thus, one can apply Theorem 4.5 to it. However, the simulation in Theorem 4.5 suffers an overhead of $O(\log P / \log\log P)$ in its parallelizability, which does not give us the optimal result. Instead we notice that given the special structure of the algorithm we can make the algorithm $(P/2, 1)$-parallelizable (and without using any randomness). This makes sure we still have the optimal parallelized I/O complexity, which leads to the following optimal energy result (even though its work complexity is *not* optimal):

THEOREM 5.4. *The recursive Matrix Transpose algorithm is $(P/2, 1)$ parallelizable. Thus, the matrix transpose problem has an optimal energy complexity of* $\Theta(N \log_{(1+P)}(B/P))$.

We note that for larger cache size, we can get rid of the log factor. The proof is in Appendix E. The above result also implies the that matrix multiplication can be done with energy complexity $O(N^3)$. (The algorithm to compute $A \times B$ would be to first transpose B and then perform the natural N^2 inner products using the energy optimal algorithm from earlier in this section.)

6. EXPERIMENTAL SETUP

In this section, we present the experimental setup. For additional results, see Appendix G.

6.1 Energy Parameters

Parameter	Value
P_{RDWR}	$57mW$
P_{CLK}	$500mW$
P_{CKE}	$102mW$
E_{ACT}	$2.5nJ$
P_{STBY}	$16mW$

Figure 4: Energy Parameters for DDR3 RAM [1] and 1 Intel XScale CPU

Fig. 4 captures the values of various energy components for DDR3 memory. We use these values to derive the simple energy model used in this work.

6.2 Hardware Setup

We conducted our experiments on two different platforms. The first platform is a laptop with 2 Intel Xeon cores, each operating at a frequency of $2GHz$. The laptop has $2GB$ DDR2 memory with 8 banks and is running Windows 7. For running our experiments, we boot the machine in safe mode and run only a minimum set of basic OS services. This ensures that the power measured by us can be attributed primarily to the application being tested. We measured the power drawn by an application using the Joulemeter tool [4].

Our second platform is a Mac note book with 4 Intel cores, each operating at a frequency of 2 GHz. The machine has $4GB$ DDR3 memory with 8 banks and is running Mac OS X Lion 10.7.3. We repeated the copy and transpose experiments on this platform. We aborted most of the processes other than our programs while we executed it to ensure that the power measured by us can be attributed primarily to the application being tested. We measured the (total) power drawn using the Hardware Monitor tool [3].

6.3 Benchmark Algorithms

Our energy modeling experiment were driven using three benchmarks. Our first benchmark is Algorithm 1, which writes data into an integer vector along a specific access pattern. Our second benchmark (Algorithm 2) is inspired from the *dcopy* benchmark and copies a large integer vector into another. The third algorithm is a modified matrix transpose algorithm on an integer matrix.

Our goal in these experiments was to define an operating point with a fixed work compelxity and a fixed number of memory accesses. For this operating point, we would vary the allocation of data across the banks in such a way that the algorithm would have varying degrees of bank-parallelism (from 1 to 8). Since work complexity does not change due to data layout, the work complexity is preserved in our experiments by ensuring that we use identical code for all experiments. Having constant number of memory accesses across various data layouts is tricky. Further, memory controllers interleave memory across banks in a round robin fashion using a chunk size smaller than B called rs, complicating the problem further. In order to preserve memory complexity, we use a simple locality aware access pattern.

We elaborate with the example of vector copy. It is easy to see that the minimum number of I/Os needed to read a vector of size N is N/B. Ensuring that a 1-parallel access also uses N/B memory accesses is trivial. We read one bank and ensure that we read one bank row (B bytes from the same row) before moving to another row in the bank. For a p-parallel access, we read data from the p banks in parallel in chunks of size r, where $r < B$ and is set to rs. To ensure that we do not need to make multiple memory accesses for multiple chunks in the same bank row, we maintain locality of access within one bank. All elements from an open row are read before any data is read from any other other row in the given bank. Elements across different banks do not preserve locality and can be interleaved by the algorithm. It is easy to note that this property ensures that the number of memory accesses are still N/B. The same idea easily extends to the write experiment. The matrix transpose algorithm is performed using multiple runs of the matrix. We again ensure this property for each run individually.

We next describe details of the individual algorithms.

```
Input: A large vector V of integers of length N,
       integers G, C, and I
count = 0;
while count < G × C do
    i = 0, j = 0, k = 0;
    for i = 0 → N/(G×C) − 1 do
        j = count;
        for k = 0 → C − 1 do
            V[j + k] = I;
        end
        j+ = G × C;
    end
    count+ = C;
end
```

Algorithm 1: Writing into a large vector of integers

In Algorithm 1 and 2 we assume C divides N, and G divides C. In Algorithm 1, we group the input vector $\mathbf{V}$ into $\frac{N}{G}$ groups each of size G. The access is then done in the following way: At step i, we access the ith chunk of size C of each group sequentially. The elements of the current chunk are accessed sequentially and set to the integer I. The idea behind the algorithm is to ensure that the access defines various degrees of parallelism over the banks of the memory. As an example, we have a 1-way parallel access if we set G to be the number of banks in the memory, and C to be the round robin chunk size rs, which is allocated

```
Input: Two large vectors V_1 and V_2 of integers each
       of length N, integers G and C
count = 0;
while count < G × C do
    i = 0, j = 0, k = 0;
    for i = 0 → N/(G×C) − 1 do
        j = count;
        for k = 0 → C − 1 do
            V_2[j + k] = V_1[j + k];
        end
        j+ = G × C;
    end
    count+ = C;
end
```

Algorithm 2: Copying a large vector of integers into another

```
Input: An N × N matrix M of integers, integers P, r,
       and s
Output: Transposed matrix (φ_{r,P}(M))^T
Let A = φ_{r,P}(M)
Divide A into N^2/P^2 submatrices of size P × P
foreach P × P submatrix do
    Transpose the submatrix naively in place;
end
\* At this time all the submatrices are
transposed *\
foreach P × P submatrix do
    Swap it with its corresponding submatrix within A
    row-by-row;
end
```

Algorithm 3: Matrix transpose algorithm

per bank row at each allocation by the memory controller. In case the allocation is bank row wise across the banks, then C set to the bank row size (block size B), and G to the number of banks (P) gives us a 1-way parallel access. On the other hand setting $C = B$ and $G = 1$ leads to P-way parallel access. The work and I/O complexity of the algorithm does not change as we vary G, and C since we preserve the locality of access within each bank (elements within a bank are accessed sequentially ensuring that one row is written completely before we touch any other element on the same bank).

Algorithm 2 accesses two vectors defined in exactly the same way as in Algorithm 1. The difference here is we have two vectors on which this access pattern is defined, and data from the ith element of $\mathbf{V}_1$ is copied into the ith element of $\mathbf{V}_2$.

Algorithm 3 transposes an $N \times N$ matrix of integers. For this algorithm, we need to define a related map $\phi_{r,P}$ that maps an $N \times N$ matrix $\mathbf{M}$ into another matrix $\mathbf{A} \stackrel{\text{def}}{=} \phi_{r,P}(\mathbf{M})$ as follows. (The map ϕ depends on parameters P and r such that P divides r, Pr divides N and r is set to rs.) From $\mathbf{M}$, construct an $N \times N/r$ matrix $\mathbf{X}$ such that every r consecutive elements in any row in $\mathbf{M}$ constitute a single "mega"-element in the same row in $\mathbf{X}$. Now divide up $\mathbf{X}$ into $P \times P$ submatrices and transpose them in place to obtain the matrix $\mathbf{Y}$. (Note that by our choices of r, P and N, $\mathbf{Y}$ is also an $N \times N/r$ matrix.) The final matrix $\mathbf{A}$ is obtained from $\mathbf{Y}$ by simply "unpacking" each mega element in $\mathbf{Y}$ into r consecutive elements in the corresponding row in $\mathbf{A}$.

The central unit in this algorithm is a submatrix with P rows. The map vector ensures that this sub-matrix is hosted on p banks, where p can be varied from 1 to 8. The value of p dictates the degree of parallelism for the algorithm. We also process the sub-matrices in a row major fashion for the transpose step, which ensures the per-bank locality property required to preserve the number of memory accesses. For the swap step, the sub-matrices are picked in a row major fashion. This ensures locality property for the picked sub-matrices. The swap partners of the sub-matrices do not satisfy locality (only P elements out of B are read sequentially). However, P elements out of B are read across all the variants, leading to the same number of memory accesses for all the experiments.

Acknowledgments

We thank an anonymous reviewers from an earlier conference who pointed out to us that the usual 2-way mergesort suffices to prove Corollary 5.2. We also thank the anonymous ITCS reviewers whose comments helped improved the presentation of the paper.

7. REFERENCES

[1] Calculating memory system power for DDR3. http://download.micron.com/pdf/technotes/ddr3/TN41_-01DDR Power.pdf.

[2] Data center energy consumption trends. http://www1.eere.energy.gov/femp/program/dc_-energy_consumption.html.

[3] Hardware monitor. http://www.bresink.de/osx/HardwareMonitor.html.

[4] Joulemeter: Computational energy measurement and optimization. http://research.microsoft.com/en-us/projects/joulemeter/.

[5] A. Aggarwal and J. Vitter. The input/output complexity of sorting and related problems. In *Communications of the ACM. Volume 31, Number 9*, 1988.

[6] S. Albers. Energy-efficient algorithms. *Commun. ACM*, 53:86–96, May 2010.

[7] N. Bansal, T. Kimbrel, and K. Pruhs. Speed scaling to manage energy and temperature. *J. ACM*, 54(1), 2007.

[8] R. D. Barve, E. F. Grove, and J. S. Vitter. Simple randomized mergesort on parallel disks. *Parallel Computing*, 23(4-5):601–631, 1997.

[9] F. Bellosa. The benefits of event-driven enery accounting in power-sensitive systems. In *Proc. SIGOPS European Workshop*, 2000.

[10] M. A. Bender, G. S. Brodal, R. Fagerberg, R. Jacob, and E. Vicari. Optimal sparse matrix dense vector multiplication in the i/o-model. *Theory Comput. Syst.*, 47(4):934–962, 2010.

[11] J. Chase, D. Anderson, P. Thakar, A. Vahdat, and R. Doyle. Managing energy and server resources in hosting centers. In *Proc. ACM SOSP*, 2001.

[12] M. Frigo, C. E. Leiserson, H. Prokop, and S. Ramachandran. Cache-oblivious algorithms. In *Proceedings of the 40th Annual Symposium on*

Foundations of Computer Science, FOCS '99, pages 285–297, Washington, DC, USA, 1999. IEEE Computer Society.
[13] M. Goodrich. Data-oblivious external-memory algorithms for the compaction, selection, and sorting of outsourced data. In *Proceedings of SPAA*, 2011.
[14] A. Gupta. Balls and bins and the power of 2 choices, Spring 2009. http://www.cs.cmu.edu/afs/cs.cmu.edu/academic/class/15859m-s11/www/lectures/lect0202.pdf.
[15] T. Horvath, T. Abdelzaher, K. Skadron, and X. Liu. Dynamic voltage scaling in multitier web servers with end-to-end delay control. *IEEE Trans. Comput.*, 56(4):444–458, 2007.
[16] S. Irani, G. Singh, S. K. Shukla, and R. K. Gupta. An overview of the competitive and adversarial approaches to designing dynamic power management strategies. *IEEE Trans. Very Large Scale Integr. Syst.*, 13:1349–1361, December 2005.
[17] E. Kaplan, M. Naor, and O. Reingold. Derandomized constructions of k-wise (almost) independent permutations. *Algorithmica*, 55(1):113–133, 2009.
[18] K. S. Kedlaya and C. Umans. Fast polynomial factorization and modular composition. *SIAM Journal on Computing*, 40(6):1767–1802, 2011.
[19] W. Kim, M. S. Gupta, G.-Y. Wei, , and D. Brooks. System level analysis of fast, per-core dvfs using on-chip switching regulators. In *Proc. HPCA*, 2008.
[20] D. E. Knuth. *The Art of Computer Programming, Volume II: Seminumerical Algorithms.* Addison-Wesley, 1969.
[21] R. Koller, A. Verma, and A. Neogi. Wattapp: An application aware power meter for shared data centers. In *ICAC*, 2010.
[22] V. A. Korthikanti and G. Agha. Towards optimizing energy costs of algorithms for shared memory architectures. In *Proc. SPAA*, 2010.
[23] V. A. Korthikanti, G. Agha, and M. Greenstreet. On the energy complexity of parallel algorithms. In *Proc. ICPP*, 2011.
[24] K. Mehlhorn and P. Sanders. Scanning multiple sequences via cache memory. In *Algorithmica*, 2003.
[25] M. Mitzenmacher, A. W. Richa, and R. Sitaraman. The power of two random choices: A survey of techniques and results. In *in Handbook of Randomized Computing*, pages 255–312. Kluwer, 2000.
[26] S. Muthukrishnan. Data streams: Algorithms and applications. *Foundations and Trends in Theoretical Computer Science*, 1(2), 2005.
[27] R. Nathuji and K. Schwan. Virtualpower: coordinated power management in virtualized enterprise systems. In *Proc. ACM SOSP*, 2007.
[28] P. Ranganathan, P. Leech, D. Irwin, and J. Chase. Ensemble-level power management for dense blade servers. In *Proc. ISCA*, 2006.
[29] M. Thorup. Integer priority queues with decrease key in constant time and the single source shortest paths problem. *J. Comput. Syst. Sci.*, 69(3):330–353, 2004.
[30] A. Vahdat, A. Lebeck, and C. S. Ellis. Every joule is precious: the case for revisiting operating system design for energy efficiency. In *Proc. of ACM SIGOPS European workshop*, New York, NY, USA, 2000. ACM.
[31] A. Verma, G. Dasgupta, T. Nayak, P. De, and R. Kothari. Server workload analysis for power minimization using consolidation. In *Proc. Usenix ATC*, 2009.
[32] A. Verma, R. Koller, L. Useche, and R. Rangaswami. Srcmap: energy proportional storage using dynamic consolidation. In *Proc. of Usenix FAST*, 2010.
[33] J. S. Vitter. Algorithms and data structures for external memory, 2008.
[34] J. S. Vitter and E. A. M. Shriver. Algorithms for parallel memory I: Two-level memories. *Algorithmica*, 12(2/3):110–147, 1994.
[35] J. S. Vitter and E. A. M. Shriver. Algorithms for parallel memory II: Hierarchical multilevel memories. *Algorithmica*, 12(2/3):148–169, 1994.
[36] F. F. Yao, A. J. Demers, and S. Shenker. A scheduling model for reduced cpu energy. In *FOCS*, pages 374–382, 1995.
[37] H. Zeng, C. Ellis, A. Lebeck, and A. Vahdat. Ecosystem: Managing energy as a first class operating system resource. In *ASPLOS*, 2002.

APPENDIX

A. MORE ON THE ENERGY EQUATION

Recall that the equation for the energy consumed by any algorithm (Equation 8) is $E(\mathcal{A}) = W(\mathcal{A}) + ACT(\mathcal{A})\frac{PB}{k}$ where $W(\mathcal{A})$ and $ACT(\mathcal{A})$ are respectively the work and I/O complexities of algorithm $\mathcal{A}$, PB is the size of the cache, and k is the parallelization factor.

Now for some problem $\mathcal{P}$, let $\mathcal{A}_1$ and $\mathcal{A}_2$ be two algorithms such that one has the better work complexity and the other has the better I/O complexity. One natural question is whether simulating both $\mathcal{A}_1$ and $\mathcal{A}_2$ in parallel gives us "the best of both worlds." In other words if W_1 and W_2 and ACT_1 and ACT_2 respectively be the work and I/O complexities of $\mathcal{A}_1$ and $\mathcal{A}_2$, is the following true?

If both $\mathcal{A}_1$ and $\mathcal{A}_2$ have $k = 1$, then can running both the algorithms in parallel result in energy consumption of $O(\min(W_1, W_2) + PB \cdot \min(ACT_1, ACT_2))$?

We prove this to be not possible in general.

Problem ($\mathcal{P}$).

Let $C \subseteq \{0,1\}^n$ be a code with linear dimension and distance. The input to the problem are $L+1$ vectors $\mathbf{y}_1, \ldots, \mathbf{y}_{L+1} \in \{0,1\}^n$ such that $\mathbf{c} \in C$ is the unique closest codeword to $\mathbf{y}_1$ and $\sum_{i=1}^{L+1} \mathbf{y}_i = \mathbf{c}$. The goal is to decode $\mathbf{y}_1$ to $\mathbf{c}$. Also length of each vector $n = O(PB)$.

Algorithm 1 ($\mathcal{A}_1$).

We only use $\mathbf{y}_1$ and compute $\mathbf{c}$ via the exponential time nearest codeword algorithm. So $W_1(\mathcal{P}) = 2^{\Theta(PB)}$, and $ACT_1(\mathcal{P}) = \Theta(1)$.

Algorithm 1 ($\mathcal{A}_2$).

Read all $L + 1$ vectors, and compute $\sum_i \mathbf{y}_i = \mathbf{c}$. So $W_2(\mathcal{P}) = \Theta(Ln)$, and $ACT_2(\mathcal{P}) = \Theta(L)$.

We definitely need at least $\mathcal{A}_1$ or $\mathcal{A}_2$ to finish to make this dovetailing work properly. However, this implies that the energy would be $\Omega(LnPB)$ as opposed to the idealised goal of $O(Ln + PB)$, which is asymptotically smaller for large enough L.

B. REDUCING RANDOMNESS

THEOREM B.1. *Let $1 \le \ell \le P/2$ be an integer and let $0 < \delta < 1$ be a constant. Let $\mathcal{A}$ be a striped (bounded resp.) algorithm with lookahead ℓ and uses space $S(x)$ in input x. Then there exists a (randomized) algorithm $\mathcal{A}'$ that uses $O(P \log S(x))$ bits of randomness with the same functional behavior as $\mathcal{A}$ (and uses three times as much space as $\mathcal{A}$ does) such that for every x, we can attain the same parameters for $\mathcal{A}'$ in Theorem 4.4 (Theorem 4.5 resp.) except*

$$W(\mathcal{A}', x) \le O(W(\mathcal{A}, x)) + \text{poly}\log P \log^{1+\delta} S(x) \cdot |\mathcal{I}(\mathcal{A}, x)| + O((P \log S(x))^{1+\delta}). \quad (20)$$

The proof of the theorem above is the same as that of Theorem 4.4 (Theorem 4.5 resp.) except the part where we compute the table that stores the random map of the memory location to their "fresh location." Thus, we will only concentrate on this aspect of the simulation– the rest of the simulation remains the same.

We first start with the observation that the the property required from the random map is the following: for any ℓ memory accesses we want that they are thrown randomly into the P banks. In other words, all we need is a map $f : [S(x)] \to [P]$ such that the map is P-wise independent. This ensures that the balls and bins analyses in both Sections C and D go through and one can prove that the resulting access pattern the required bound on τ. However, there are two issues that need to be resolved.

First, using the same arguments as in proofs of Theorem 4.4, we can assume an upper bound on m. In particular, here we will assume that

$$m \le 2^{O(B^{1-\delta}/P)}. \quad (21)$$

First issue is that since we are only mapping the memory locations to banks, we need to decide on the bank row within the bank. For this purpose we do the obvious thing: for each of the P banks, we keep a counter of how many memory locations have already been assigned to that bank, which can then be used to easily determine the bank row for a given memory location. Since we will need this information later on during the simulation, for any memory location b, we save both $f(b)$ as well as the bank row "counter." Because of condition (21), this implies that all the P counters can be stored in one cache.

Second, we need to figure out how to compute the function f. The most well-known construction of P-wise independent *bits* is one based on BCH codes. However, for our purpose since we need P-wise independent vectors over $[P]$, we use the other common construction based on Reed-Solomon codes. In what follows, for simplicity, let us assume that P is a power of 2. We pick q to be the smallest power of 2 larger than m and do an arbitrary assignment of $[m]$ to elements of the field $\mathbb{F}_q$. Define R to be a random univariate polynomial over $\mathbb{F}_q$ of degree at most $P-1$ (this is the only place we will need random bits and we need $P \log q = O(P \log m)$ many such bits as desired). Then $f(b)$ is defined to be the least $\log P$ significant bits of $R(b)$ (where we think of $b \in \mathbb{F}_q$). It is well-known that this map has the required P-wise independence. Finally, to compute the map for every memory location b, we compute $R(b)$. If we do this naively, we will need $O(P \log q)$ time to evaluate the polynomial R at each memory location b. It turns out we can do better. Kedlaya and Umans [18] recently presented a data structure that given the coefficients of R build a data structure in time (and hence space) $O((P \log q)^{1+\delta})$ (for any constant δ) such that given this data structure, $R(b)$ can be evaluated at any b in time poly $\log P(\log q)^{1+\delta}$. The bound in (21) implies that computing the data structure from the coefficients of $R(X)$ can be done within one cache itself. The bounds on the construction and query time for the polynomial evaluation data structure then implies (20).

C. THE FIRST BALLS AND BINS PROBLEM

In this section, we will consider the following balls and bins framework:

> n balls are thrown into P bins (numbered from $0, \ldots, P-1$) as follows. For a parameter $g \ge 1$, divide up the n balls into $n/(gP)$ groups of gP balls each. For each group, randomly permute the gP balls in place. Then for a ball in location $0 \le i \le n-1$, place it in bin $i \mod p$.

C.1 Bounding the Maximum Load

We will prove the following bound on the maximum load on a bin (where we consider any arbitrary P balls):

THEOREM C.1. *Consider the random process above with $g \ge 2$. Now consider any arbitrary subset $S \subseteq [n]$ with $|S| = P$. Then with probability at least $1 - 1/P$, every bin has at most $O(\log P/\log\log P)$ balls from S in it.*

PROOF. Let ℓ be a parameter that we will fix later (to be $O(\log P/\log\log P)$). Fix an arbitrary bin $\mathcal{B}$. We will show that

$$\Pr[\mathcal{B} \text{ has at least } \ell \text{ balls from } S] \le \frac{1}{P^2}. \quad (22)$$

Note that (22) along with the union bound proves the claimed bound.

Fix an arbitrary subset of ℓ balls from S. Further, let b be one of these ℓ balls. We claim that

$$\Pr[b \text{ lands in } \mathcal{B} | S \setminus \{b\}] \le \frac{g}{gP - P} = \frac{1}{P} \cdot \frac{1}{1 - 1/g} \le \frac{2}{P}, \quad (23)$$

where we use $S \setminus \{b\}$ as shorthand for where the balls in $S \setminus \{b\}$ land and the last inequality follows from the assumption that $g \ge 2$.

First, we use the argument for the standard balls and bins problem to use (23) to prove (22). Indeed, (23) along with the union bound over all $\binom{P}{\ell}$ choices for the ℓ balls implies that

$$\Pr[\mathcal{B} \text{ has at least } \ell \text{ balls from } S] \le \binom{P}{\ell} \cdot \left(\frac{2}{P}\right)^\ell \le \left(\frac{2e}{\ell}\right)^\ell \le \frac{1}{P^2},$$

where in the above the second inequality follows by the bound $\binom{P}{\ell} \le (eP/\ell)^\ell$ and the last inequality follows by choosing $\ell \le O(\log P/\log\log P)$.

To complete the proof, we argue the first inequality in (23). Since the randomness used in different groups are independent, we can replace the conditional event by $S' \setminus \{b\}$, where $S' \subseteq S$ are the balls that lie in the same group as b. Note that in the random process, if b permuted to a location that is $\mathcal{B} \mod P$, then it lands in $\mathcal{B}$. In other words, within the random permutation of the group of b, this happens if it happens to land in one of the g locations that correspond to $\mathcal{B} \mod P$. As a mental exercise, think of the random permutation being done as follows: each of the at most $P-1$ balls in $S' \setminus \{b\}$ are thrown one after the other into (distinct) random bins. Let $g - g'$ of the special bins be occupied by some ball in $S' \setminus \{b\}$. Now when b is about to be thrown, there are at least $gP - P + 1$ bins to choose randomly from and we're interested in the event that it lands in one of the g' special bins that are vacant. Thus, this probability is upper bounded by

$$\frac{g'}{gP - P + 1} \leq \frac{g}{gP - P},$$

as desired. □

D. THE SECOND BALLS AND BINS PROBLEM

In this section, we will consider the following balls and bins framework:

> n balls are thrown into P bins (numbered from $0, \ldots, P-1$) as follows. For a parameter $g > 0$, divide up the n balls into $n/(gP)$ groups of gP balls each. For each group, randomly permute the gP balls twice. (The randomness is independent across groups and across the two permutations in each group.) For each ball $i \in [n]$, denote its two positions in the two permutations as i_1 and i_2.
>
> Let $S \subseteq [n]$ be of size $|S| = \frac{P}{512}$. Consider a graph $G = ([P], E)$ as follows. For each ball $i \in S$, add the edge $(i_1 \mod P+1, i_2 \mod P+1)$ to E. Now we assign each ball in S to a bin in $[P]$ as follows. Let $K \geq 3$ be a parameter. Consider the following iterative algorithm:
>
> 1. $G' \leftarrow G$.
> 2. While $|V(G')| > K$ do
>   (a) Let $T \subseteq V(G')$ be the set of all vertices with degree at most 5 in G'.
>   (b) Assign to bins in T, all its incident edges (or balls). If an edge is completely contained inside S, then assign it one of its end point arbitrarily.
>   (c) $V \leftarrow V(G') \setminus T$.
>   (d) G' is the induced sub-graph on V.
> 3. Assign edges in G' arbitrarily to the bins in $V(G')$.

Before we proceed, we record a lemma on the time complexity of the algorithm above that will be useful. The most obvious way to implement the above algorithm will be to use a priority queue to keep track of the degrees of the degree of vertices in G'. Using the best known implementation of priority queues (e.g. [29]) the above can be implemented in $O(P \log\log P)$ time. However, for our application we need $O(P)$ time and space. We are able to do so below by noting that we only care about vertices with degree at most 5 and not vertices with the minimum degree. Also the fact that the degrees are at most $P-1$ also helps.

Lemma D.1. *The algorithm above can be implemented in $O(P)$ time and $O(P)$ space.*

Proof. We will assume that the original graph G is given to us in adjacency list format. In particular, given a vertex $v \in [P]$, we can iterate over all its neighbors in $O(d_v)$ time, where d_v is the degree of v. We will have an array of doubly linked list called DEG, where for any $0 \leq d \leq P-1$, DEG$[d]$ contains the list of all vertices with degree exactly d in G'.[5] Finally, we have an array of pointers PTR, such that for every vertex $v \in [P]$, PTR$[v]$ points to actual location of v in the corresponding linked list in DEG (as well as keeping track of its current degree d_v). We will use the convention that PTR$[v]$ is null if $v \notin V(G')$. It is easy to check that all these data structures use $O(P)$ space and can be initialized in $O(P)$ time. (Recall that G has $O(P)$ edges.) Next we show we can implement the above algorithm in $O(P)$ time using these three data structures.

We will maintain a counter for $|V(G')|$ so the check in Step 2 can be computed in $O(1)$ time. Step 2(a) can be implemented in $O(|T|)$ time by just returning the linked lists DEG$[j]$ for $0 \leq j \leq 5$. For Step 2(b), we do the following. For each $v \in T$, we go through all its neighbors $u \in [P]$. We can check if $u \in V(G')$ by checking if PTR$[u]$ is null or not. If not, we assign the ball (v, u) to the bin v. Then using PTR$[u]$, we remove u from its current linked list, decrement d_u by one, add u to the head to the linked list for (the updated value of) d_u and change PTR$[u]$ to this new location. Since the linked lists are doubly linked, note that all this can be implemented in $O(1)$ time. To implement Step 2(c), for every $v \in T$, we set PTR$[v]$ to null.

It can be checked that the above implementation is correct and does $O(1)$ work per edge and vertex, which leads to the claimed $O(P)$ overall run time, as desired. □

D.1 Bounding the Maximum Load

We will prove the following bound on the maximum load on a bin.

Theorem D.2. *Consider the random process above with $g \geq 1/4$, $K \geq 3$ and any arbitrary subset $S \subseteq [n]$ with $|S| = \frac{P}{512}$. Then with probability at least $1 - 1/P$, every bin has at most $3 \cdot \max(K, 5)$ balls from S in it.*

It is not a priori clear that the algorithm in the random process above even terminates. We first state a lemma that will help us guarantee that and also help us prove Theorem D.2.

The following lemma has been proven in the case when $n = P$, $g = 1$ and the balls are assigned two bins at random (instead of using a random permutation.) See e.g. [14]. Here we present a straightforward generalization of that proof to our problem.

Lemma D.3. *Consider the graph G generated by S in the random process above. Then with probability at least $1 - \frac{1}{P^4}$, the following holds for every $U \subseteq V(G)$ with $|U| \geq K$. The average degree of the induced subgraph $G[U]$ is at most 5.*

[5] It turns out that we only need one entry for all degrees between 0 and 5 but we ignore this improvement as it only changes the constants.

We defer the proof of the above lemma for a bit and first prove Theorem D.2. Before that we prove two helpful lemmas.

LEMMA D.4. *Consider a fixed pair* $(b_1, b_2) \in [P]^2$ *with* $b_1 \neq b_2$ *and an arbitrary ball* $i \in S$. *The probability that the edge corresponding to* i *ends up at* (b_1, b_2) *is upper bounded by* $\frac{20}{P^2}$ *even when* conditioned *on where the remaining balls in* $S \setminus \{i\}$ *end up.*

PROOF. Assume that the choices for all balls in $S \setminus \{i\}$ have been made. Consider an arbitrary $j \in S \setminus \{i\}$. If j is in a different group than i (recall that $[n]$ is divided into groups of size gP), then the choice of edges for i and j are independent, which in turn implies that the location of such a j does not affect the probability that we want to bound. For the rest of the argument, we will only consider balls j that are in the same group as i.

For notational convenience define, $\bar{g} = \max(1, \lceil g \rceil)$. Now consider the case when $g_1 \leq \bar{g}$ (and $g_2 \leq \bar{g}$ resp.) balls j from the same group as i have $j_1 = b_1$ ($j_2 = b_2$ resp.). We consider the probability that $i_1 = b_1$ conditioned on the event above. Note that $i_1 = b_1$ can happen only if i happens to be one of the $\bar{g} - g_1$ locations in $[gP]$ that will lead to $i_1 = b_1$. Further, since everything in $S \setminus \{i\}$ has been assigned, there are $gP - |S| - 1$ locations in $[gP]$ that the first choice for i can land in. Thus, the probability that $i_1 = b_1$ (even conditioned on what happened with the balls in $S \setminus \{i\}$ is

$$\frac{\bar{g} - g_1}{gP - \frac{P}{512} - 1} \leq \frac{\bar{g}}{gP - \frac{2P}{512}} \leq \frac{1}{\frac{1}{4} - \frac{1}{256}} \cdot \frac{1}{P} \leq \frac{5}{P}.$$

One can make a similar argument to get the same bound as above for $i_2 = b_2$. Since the first and second choices for i are independent, we have that

$$\Pr[(i_1, i_2) = (b_1, b_2) | S \setminus \{i\}] \leq \frac{10}{P^2}.$$

Note that we also have to take into account the case that $(i_1, i_2) = (b_2, b_1)$, which again happens with probability at most $10/P^2$. The union bound completes the proof. □

LEMMA D.5. *With probability at least* $1 - \frac{1}{2P}$, *the graph* G *has at most* 3 *parallel edges for any vertex pair* (b_1, b_2).

PROOF. We will show that the probability that more than 3 balls $i \in S$ are assigned to a fixed bin pair (b_1, b_2) is at most $\frac{1}{2P^3}$. Taking union bound over the at most P^2 pairs completes the proof.

Now consider a fixed pair $(b_1, b_2) \in [P]^2$. Consider a fixed subset $T \subseteq S$ of size $|T| = 3$. By Lemma D.4, the probability that all balls in T are assigned (b_1, b_2) is at most $(20/P^2)^3$. Then taking the union bound over all possible choices of T, we get that the probability bound that we are after is upper bounded by

$$\binom{\frac{P}{512}}{3} \cdot \frac{20^3}{P^6} \leq \left(\frac{P}{512} \cdot \frac{20}{P^2}\right)^3 < \frac{1}{2P^3},$$

as desired. □

PROOF OF THEOREM D.2. Note that except for probability at most $\frac{1}{P^4} + \frac{1}{2P} < \frac{1}{P}$ (for $P \geq 2$), both Lemmas D.3 and D.5 are true. For the rest of proof, we will assume that this is indeed the case.

We will assume that each vertex pair in G has at most one edge. (By Lemma D.5, then whatever bound we prove can be safely multiplied by 3 to arrive at our final bound.)

W.l.o.g., we can assume that G has only one connected component. (If not, we can apply the subsequent argument to each component individually.)

Let $U \subseteq V(G)$ be the set of vertices (or bins) which form the connected component of G. If $|U| \leq K$, then by Step 3 of the assignment algorithm, we have that the maximum load in any bin in U is at most K (recall that because of Lemma D.5, we have assumed that each vertex pair has at most one edge between it). If $|U| > K$, then Lemma D.3 (and a Markov argument) implies that there is a bin $i \in [P]$ that has degree at most 5. Thus, Step 2(b) assigns a load of at most 5 to all such bins. We can argue the case for G' inductively. (Note since we remove assigned bins in Step 2(c), in all future iteration, this bin will not affect any of the future loads.) In this whole process we achieve a maximum load of $\max(K, 5)$. Lemma D.5 completes the proof. □

We finish by proving Lemma D.3.

PROOF OF LEMMA D.3. For notational convenience define $m = \frac{P}{512}$. Note that the proof is complete if we show that $G[U]$ has at most $5|U|/2$ edges.

Fix $k \geq K$ and let U be an arbitrary subset of size k. Then Lemma D.4 and the union bound (over the at most k^2 pairs in $U \times U$) shows that a fixed ball i lands in $G[U]$ is upper bounded by $\frac{20k^2}{P^2}$ (even conditioned on what happens with the rest of the balls). Then Lemma D.4 implies that the probability that any fixed subset T of $5k/2$ balls land in $G[U]$ is upper bounded by $\left(\frac{20k^2}{P^2}\right)^{5k/2}$. Then a union bound over all choices of T, implies that

$$\Pr[G[U] \text{ has } > 5k/2 \text{ edges}] \leq \binom{m}{\frac{5k}{2}} \cdot \left(\frac{5k}{P}\right)^{5k}.$$

The rest of the argument is the same as in [14] (with some minor changes in the values of the constants). □

E. MATRIX TRANSPOSE

We first present the standard I/O model algorithm for computing the transpose of a matrix, which has I/O complexity of $O(N/B \cdot \log_P(B/P))$ (and work complexity of $O(N \log_P(B/P))$. Then we will show how to modify this algorithm to also make it $(P/2, 1)$-parallelizable in a *deterministic* way.

The algorithm has three phases (where A is the $\sqrt{N} \times \sqrt{N}$ matrix, which is assumed to be stored in row major form in consecutive rows in the main memory). At the end of the first phase, all the $P \times P$ submatrices are correctly transposed. At the end of the second phase all the $B \times B$ submatrices are correctly transposed. The whole matrix is transposed after the end of the third phase. In particular,

- (PHASE 1) Divide up A in N/P^2 submatrices of size $P \times P$, bring them into the cache and transpose them in place.
- (PHASE 2) There are $\log_P(B/P) - 1$ many iterations. In the $2 \leq i \leq \log_P(B/P)$th such iteration, we correctly transpose the $P^i \times P^i$ submatrices within the $B \times B$ submatrices by swapping the $P^{i-1} \times P^{i-1}$ submatrices (within the same $P^i \times P^i$ submatrix) that are

counterparts. Two $P^{i-1} \times P^{i-1}$ submatrices D and E are counterparts if they should be swapped to make the resulting $P^i \times P^i$ submatrix correctly transposed.

- (PHASE 3) Swap the $B \times B$ submatrices with their counterparts (which are defined analogously to the counterparts from PHASE 2).

It is not too hard to verify that the algorithm above is correct. We now quickly argue the claimed I/O and work complexities of the algorithm above. In particular, we will argue that PHASE 1, PHASE 3 and each iteration in PHASE 2 takes $O(N/B)$ I/Os and $O(N)$ work, which immediately results in the claimed I/O and work complexity bounds.

- (PHASE 1) Load the $P \times B$ submatrices of A into the P caches and transpose the B/P submatrices of size $P \times P$ in place and write them back. It is easy to see that overall this phase takes $O(N/B)$ I/Os and has a work complexity of $O(N)$.
- (ith iteration in PHASE 2) Consider an arbitrary $B \times B$ submatrix of A. Now consider an arbitrary $P^i \times B$ submatrix (call it D) of this sub-matrix. Note that this has B/P^i many $P^i \times P^i$ submatrices within it. We arbitrarily fix such a $P^i \times P^i$ matrix (let us call it E) and state our operations. (One can easily verify that one can perform the same operations in parallel on the rest of the $P^i \times P^i$ submatrices of D.) Recall that we have to swap all the $P^{i-1} \times P^{i-1}$ submatrices in E with their counterparts. Divide up E into P submatrices (call them $F_1, \ldots, F_p$) of size $P^{i-1} \times P^i$. Note that when we swap the counterparts of size $P^{i-1} \times P^{i-1}$, we can swap them row by row. Further, for any fixed $j \in [P^{i-1}]$, note that all the jth rows of the $P^{i-1} \times P^{i-1}$ submatrices are themselves exactly contained in the jth rows of $F_1, \ldots, F_p$. Thus, we can implement this step, if we at the same time load the jth rows of $f_1, \ldots, F_p$ for every $j \in [P^{i-1}]$.

  It can be verified that the above can be implemented by reading and writing all the N/B blocks in A once and doing linear amount of work on them. Thus, this step needs $O(N/B)$ many I/Os and $O(N)$ work.
- (PHASE 3) Consider all the pairs of $B \times B$ submatrices of A that are counterparts. Note that these pairs can be swapped by swapping the corresponding rows. Thus, this step can also be done with $O(N/B)$ many I/Os and $O(N)$ work.

We note that the algorithm as stated above does not have the required $(P/2, 1)$-parallelizability but we will show shortly that a few modification suffice. In particular, we will argue that for each iterations/phases a simple *deterministic* cyclic shift of each row in the main memory will allow for the above algorithm to have the required parallelizability. For simplicity, we state the permutation for each of PHASE 1, PHASE 3 and each iteration in PHASE 2 separately. In the actual implementation of the algorithm, before each phase/iteration we perform the cyclic shifts and whenever we need to access a block we access the block from its new shifted position and once the iteration/phase has terminated, we undo the cyclic shift. These shifts are data independent and thus, do not need to be stored anywhere (and can be just computed from N, B, P and i). Thus this extra step for each phase/iteration will take $O(N/B)$ many I/Os and $O(N)$ work so asymptotically the claimed bounds on I/O and work complexity still hold (but now with a guaranteed $(P/2, 1)$-parallelizability). Next, we spell out the shifts:

- (PHASE 1) Consider any of the $P \times B$ submatrix that we consider. Note that if all the rows of this matrix are in different banks then the whole access will be $(P, 1)$-parallelizable. Thus, for this phase all we need to do is to make sure that this happens. Note that this can be easily computed given the location of the $P \times B$ submatrix within A and the different parameter values. (Further, these shifts for all the $P \times B$ submatrices can be applied in a consistent manner.)
- (ith iteration in PHASE 2) It can be verified that in this iteration, we need to swap corresponding rows between two $P^{i-1} \times B$ submatrices (let us call them X and Y). We note that if we can make sure that $P/2 \times B$ submatrices have all the $P/2$ rows in distinct banks, then all the P^{i-1} row swaps can be performed in a $(P/2, 1)$-parallelizable way. Again note that the shifts for X are completely determined by the location of X within A and other parameters. (Further, these shifts for the different $P^{i-1} \times B$ submatrices can be applied in a consistent manner.)
- (PHASE 3) This step is similar to that of PHASE 2. We must perform the shifts so that we can ensure that the rows of the $P/2 \times B$ submatrices are in distinct banks. Further, as before the shifts can be consistently applied and can be computed from the location of such submatrices in A and the parameters.

F. MERGE SORT

It is easy to see that the k-way merge sort is a k-striped algorithm. However, since the algorithm is data dependent, the "traditional" merge sort algorithm does not good lookahead. Next we see how to remedy this.

F.1 Achieving a $\Theta(P)$ lookahead

We will define a prediction sequence [8] that will allow the k-way merge sort to have lookahead of k. In particular, note that as long as we can show to successfully define a prediction sequence for the operation of merging k runs, then we would be done. We do so next.

We begin with a few definitions. We start with a definition to handle the case when in the middle of the merge algorithm, we have only have the partial "unmerged" part of the first block in the run.

DEFINITION 6. *A* merge run *is a usual run except the first block might have fewer than B items. Further, we call such a merge run* sorted *if all the elements when written down in the order of appearance in the run are in sorted order.*

For the rest of the section, we will establish the convention that if two items have the same value, then we break ties in the favor of the merged run with the smaller index. If both items are in the same merged run, then we break ties in favor of the item appearing earlier in the run. With this convention, w.l.o.g., we will assume that all the items in the runs have *distinct* values.

Next, we define a compressed representation of a block that will be crucial in our result.

DEFINITION 7. *Let block $\mathcal{B}$ in a sorted merge run be preceded by the block $(i_1, \ldots, i_m)$ (for some $m \le B$). Then we define the* label *of $\mathcal{B}$ to be i_m*

The following lemma is the crucial observation (and is well-known [8]):

LEMMA F.1. *Consider k sorted merge runs. Let T be blocks in the k merged runs where we drop the first block in each run. Let $\mathcal{L}$ be the blocks in T with the $3k$ smallest labels. Then the smallest kB elements in T are contained within the blocks in $\mathcal{L}$. Further, all the blocks in $\mathcal{L}$ that belong to the same run form a prefix of the run.*

PROOF. For national convenience let S denote the kB smallest elements in T. We first observe that S contained in at most $2k$ blocks. Note that there can be at most k blocks such that all of its B elements are in S. Further, since each of the merged runs are sorted, in each run only the last block can contribute less than B elements to S. Since there are k merged runs, this can contribute k more blocks, which leads to a total of at most $2k$ blocks that contain S.

Next we argue that if for any block $\mathcal{B}$ such that $\mathcal{B} \cap S \neq \emptyset$, then $\mathcal{B} \in \mathcal{L}$. For the sake of contradiction, assume that $\mathcal{B} \notin \mathcal{L}$. Note that for this to happen $\mathcal{B}$ has to be "displaced" by another block $\mathcal{B}' \in \mathcal{L}$ such that $\mathcal{B}' \cap S = \emptyset$. (Note that this has to happen as S is contained within $2k$ blocks and $|\mathcal{L}_e| = 3k$.) Now note that any block $\mathcal{B}''$ that comes after $\mathcal{B}'$ in the same run as $\mathcal{B}'$ cannot be in $\mathcal{L}$. Indeed, all elements in the block just before $\mathcal{B}$ are in S while none of the elements in $\mathcal{B}'$ are in S, which implies that the label of $\mathcal{B}$ has to be smaller than $\mathcal{B}''$. Thus, since $\mathcal{B}' \notin \mathcal{L}$, $\mathcal{B}'' \notin \mathcal{L}$. In particular, each merged run can have at most one block that can potentially displace some block $\mathcal{B}$ (such that $\mathcal{B} \cap S \neq \emptyset$). Thus, the total number of blocks that can potentially displace a legitimate block is at most $k-1$. However, $|\mathcal{L}| = 3k$, which implies that the remaining $2k+1$ blocks have to be filled in by blocks $\mathcal{B}$ such that $\mathcal{B} \cap S \neq \emptyset$ (recall we have argued that there are at most $2k$ such blocks).

The claim on all block in $\mathcal{L}$ for one run forming a prefix, note that a "gap" implies that a block with a larger label was included in $\mathcal{L}$ at the "expense" of a block with a smaller label, which is not possible. The proof is complete. □

LEMMA F.2. *Let $2 \leq k \leq P/6$. Given k runs each of which contain numbers in sorted order such that there are a total of N numbers among all the runs. Then there is an algorithm $\mathcal{A}$ that merges the k runs into one sorted run such that for any input k sorted runs (denoted by x):*

- *$\mathcal{A}$ is a k-striped algorithm with a lookahead of k.*
- *For any input x, $|\mathcal{I}(\mathcal{A}, x)| \leq O(N/B)$.*
- *For any input x, $W(\mathcal{A}, x) \leq O(N)$.*

PROOF. The algorithm $\mathcal{A}$ is the well known algorithm to merge k sorted lists (which is easy to see is k-striped) dovetailed with another algorithm that builds a prediction sequence (using Lemma F.1) that gives the final algorithm a lookahead of k. (It is not too hard to see that the "traditional" merge algorithm, which is data dependent, does not have any non-trivial lookahead in-built into it.)

We first assume that the input is present in the first $P/2$ banks: if not one can perform a scan of the input and transfer it to the first $P/2$ banks. It is easy to see that this transfer can be done in $O(N)$ time with $O(N/B)$ memory accesses and that this part has a lookahead of $P/2$ and is a 1-striped algorithm. We now present the algorithm in two steps. The first step will store the labels of all the blocks in the input, which would be used in the second step to do the actual merging.

We will use the last $P/6$ banks for enabling lookahead for $\mathcal{A}$. The remaining $P/3$ banks in the "middle" will be used to write out the merged output.

Pre-processing.

In this step, the algorithm makes a scan on the input (which recall is now in the first $P/2$ banks) and except for the first block in each of the k runs, stores the labels of all the blocks (in the same order as they appear in the input) in the last $P/6$ banks. It is easy to see that this phase needs $O(N/B)$ memory accesses. Further, this step is a k-striped algorithm with lookahead of $P/2 \geq k$.

Merging the runs.

At the beginning of this step we copy the head block of each run to k blocks in the middle $P/3$ caches.

Throughout this step, we will maintain the following invariants:

1. The first $P/2$ caches will contain $3k$ blocks from the input.
2. The last $P/6$ caches will maintain a table of size $k \times 6k$ of labels that will have enough information to predict the next $3k$ blocks that will be transferred to the first $P/2$ caches.
3. The middle $P/3$ caches will keep the "unused" part of the first block from each of the k runs as well function as a buffer for the next k blocks that need to be written to the output.

As mentioned above, we will maintain a table with one row for each of the k runs. Each row will always have at least $3k$ labels for the blocks from the corresponding run. (We initialize this table with the labels of the first $6k$ blocks in each run.)

This part of the algorithm will be divided into repetitions of a "reading" phase followed by "writing" phase. The writing phase is simple: once the buffer in the middle $P/3$ caches has accumulated the next k blocks in the sorted order, we write back those k blocks to the output.

The reading phase starts once a writing phase is over. Using the table stored in the last $P/6$ caches, we compute in $O(k)$ time, the top $3k$ blocks according to their labels. We then bring those $3k$ blocks from the first $P/2$ banks to the corresponding caches. Then we run the "traditional" merge algorithm on the k runs formed by the partial blocks stored in the middle $P/3$ caches followed by the k runs formed by these top $3k$ blocks (note that by Lemma F.1 these blocks form k sorted runs among themselves). We run the traditional merge algorithm till we have filled up the buffer for the next k blocks to be written to the output. Next, update the "head" blocks in each run in the middle $P/3$ caches if necessary. In the table in the last $P/6$ caches, for each run, we throw away the labels for the blocks that have been used up and been written to the output. If need be, we replenish the rows that have fewer than $3k$ entries and make sure we have $6k$ entries for the rows that we replenish.[6] At this point, the writing phase is triggered.

We first note that by Lemma F.1 that the above algorithm works: i.e., all the blocks that are needed to form the merged

[6]We note that the above is wasteful in the sense that some blocks in the first $P/2$ banks might be accessed more than once but we keep the above description as it makes stating the algorithm slightly simpler.

k output blocks for the writing phase are indeed accessed in the reading phase. Second, for every writing phase (which writes back k blocks), we access $3k$ blocks from the first $P/2$ banks. Further, we can in worst case access $6k^2$ labels for replenishing the table. Since each label is just one item, these are contained within

$$\frac{6k^2}{B} \leq \frac{6k^2}{P} \leq k$$

blocks (where the first inequality follows from (9) while the second inequality follows from the assumption that $k \leq P/6$). All of this implies that over all we access a total of $O(N/B)$ accesses for this step of the algorithm. By design, this step of $\mathcal{A}$ has a lookahead of k. Finally, it is easy to verify that this step is also k-striped.

Since both steps of $\mathcal{A}$ are k-striped and have lookahead of k, then so does $\mathcal{A}$, which proves the first two claimed properties. The final property follows by observing that both the steps have linear time complexity. □

G. ADDITIONAL RESULTS

G.1 Additional data for experiments on Windows

We present the variations in the energy readings for all the experiments of Figure 3 in Tables 1, 2, and 3.

G.1.1 Results on Macintosh

The copying and transpose experiments have been repeated on the Macintosh platform mentioned earlier Section 6. We present the results in Figure 5.

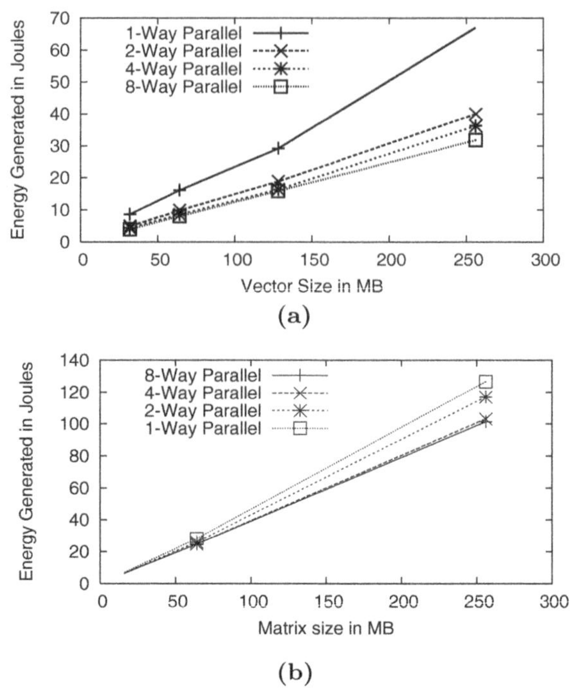

Figure 5: Energy consumed by (a) Copy and (b) Matrix Transpose Workloads on Macintosh

Algorithm	Vector or Matrix size	Degree of Parallelism	Max	Min	Avg
Write	$256MB$	1-Way	69.0374	68.4705	68.6285
Write	$256MB$	2-Way	45.7844	44.3620	45.0138
Write	$256MB$	4-Way	37.2824	34.7816	36.6009
Write	$256MB$	8-Way	34.1156	33.1847	33.4776
Write	$128MB$	1-Way	34.8290	33.6623	34.0199
Write	$128MB$	2-Way	23.2194	22.2575	22.4373
Write	$128MB$	4-Way	19.1495	18.0503	18.2758
Write	$128MB$	8-Way	17.4870	16.0016	16.7338
Write	$64MB$	1-Way	17.3420	16.8986	17.0549
Write	$64MB$	2-Way	11.4637	11.1825	11.1737
Write	$64MB$	4-Way	9.6474	9.0376	9.1379
Write	$64MB$	8-Way	8.9030	7.9290	8.3259
Write	$32MB$	1-Way	8.5935	8.4816	8.5057
Write	$32MB$	2-Way	5.8870	5.5657	5.6086
Write	$32MB$	4-Way	4.8235	4.3250	4.5704
Write	$32MB$	8-Way	4.5240	4.0340	4.1615

Table 1: Maximum, minimum, and average energy consumption in Joules for the write algorithm on various input sizes, and various degree of parallelism on Windows.

Algorithm	Vector or Matrix size	Degree of Parallelism	Max	Min	Avg
Integer copy	$128MB$	1-Way	58.9665	57.0488	57.5476
Integer copy	$128MB$	2-Way	41.3250	39.2921	40.2636
Integer copy	$128MB$	4-Way	36.8010	34.6318	35.7396
Integer copy	$128MB$	8-Way	34.5390	32.4379	33.5704
Integer copy	$64MB$	1-Way	29.2514	28.3649	28.681
Integer copy	$64MB$	2-Way	20.6575	19.6112	20.0854
Integer copy	$64MB$	4-Way	18.3955	17.3043	17.9162
Integer copy	$64MB$	8-Way	17.3420	16.2414	16.7388
Integer copy	$32MB$	1-Way	14.6255	14.2056	14.3898
Integer copy	$32MB$	2-Way	10.5264	9.8397	10.1326
Integer copy	$32MB$	4-Way	9.2025	8.6637	8.9552
Integer copy	$32MB$	8-Way	8.5935	8.0982	8.3288
Integer copy	$16MB$	1-Way	7.5400	7.1021	7.2384
Integer copy	$16MB$	2-Way	5.1234	4.9082	4.9764
Integer copy	$16MB$	4-Way	4.6785	4.4109	4.437
Integer copy	$16MB$	8-Way	4.3694	4.0716	4.2514

Table 2: Maximum, minimum, and average energy consumption in Joules for the copy algorithm on various input sizes, and various degree of parallelism on Windows

Algorithm	Vector or Matrix size	Degree of Parallelism	Max	Min	Avg
Transpose	$256MB$	1-Way	242.7729	235.7240	241.0828
Transpose	$256MB$	2-Way	222.9773	217.7890	222.8969
Transpose	$256MB$	4-Way	214.0016	209.0030	213.6227
Transpose	$256MB$	8-Way	203.2162	200.8830	202.0894
Transpose	$64MB$	1-Way	59.2514	58.3649	56.2803
Transpose	$64MB$	2-Way	53.3890	52.1630	53.0207
Transpose	$64MB$	4-Way	51.5910	51.5173	51.5272
Transpose	$64MB$	8-Way	48.8650	48.4010	48.8157
Transpose	$16MB$	1-Way	13.5400	13.1021	13.0929
Transpose	$16MB$	2-Way	12.9630	12.6730	12.8394
Transpose	$16MB$	4-Way	12.818	12.6730	12.6759
Transpose	$16MB$	8-Way	12.2380	11.7740	12.0524

Table 3: Maximum, minimum, and average energy consumption in Joules for the Transpose algorithm on various input sizes, and various degree of parallelism on Windows

Streaming Computations With a Loquacious Prover *

Hartmut Klauck
CQT and Nanyang Technological University
Singapore
hklauck@gmail.com

Ved Prakash
CQT
Singapore
ved_p@nus.edu.sg

ABSTRACT

We define a new model of data streaming algorithms that employ a prover/helper to outsource difficult computations in a verifiable way. While for the verifier the usual time (per symbol read) and space constraints of the data streaming model are in place, the prover has unbounded space. Both parties cannot look into the future (i.e., do not know data arriving later). Previous work on such models [9, 12, 14, 13] either severely restricted the *total* communication between the prover and the verifier, or extended the computation by a long annotation that has to be streamed from the prover to the verifier offline after the original stream has ended, delaying the computation of the result. We argue that restricting the total communication severely is unnatural and investigate a model that only bounds the communication *overhead*, i.e., the amount of communication sent from the prover to the verifier per symbol of the data stream. This allows for vastly more communication between prover and verifier while maintaining the online nature of the model (in particular long annotations sent after the stream has ended are not allowed).

Relaxing the communication requirement allows us to find simple algorithms for problems like the Longest Increasing Subsequence Problem (LIS), finding the Median, and for deciding whether the rank of a matrix is full or not. All our algorithms have a similar structure with phases whose length shrinks geometrically, and phase i being used to verify certain properties of the stream up to phase $i-1$ using re-streaming of parts of the previous stream. The challenge in each case is to tie the different phases together.

Furthermore, while in previous work [14, 13] it was shown that all problems in the class $\mathcal{NC}$ can be computed in a streaming model with a prover, this general purpose algorithm tends to be inefficient, and this as well as related algorithms based on arithmetization techniques suffer from the following bottleneck: they employ a final verification phase (taking place after the end of the stream), which uses polylogarithmic communication (essentially the only communication in the whole protocol), yet the prover needs to perform computations that take at least linear time during that phase. While we show that such a verification phase with a large number of communication rounds between the prover and the verifier is unavoidable for certain problems, most algorithms we describe in our model (for problems like Median or LIS or Rank) avoid this bottleneck.

*Research at the Centre for Quantum Technologies is funded by the Singapore Ministry of Education and the National Research Foundation. No qubits were harmed during the preparation of this article.

Categories and Subject Descriptors

G.3 [**Mathematics of Computing**]: PROBABILITY AND STATISTICS—*Probabilistic algorithms*; F.2.0 [**Theory of Computation**]: ANALYSIS OF ALGORITHMS AND PROBLEM COMPLEXITY—*General*; F.1.3 [**Theory of Computation**]: COMPUTATION BY ABSTRACT DEVICES —*Complexity Measures and Classes*

General Terms

Algorithms, Theory

Keywords

Proof Verification; Interactive Proofs; Delegating Computation; Data Streaming

1. INTRODUCTION

The investigation of data streaming algorithms is a research area with many highly relevant practical applications as well as an interesting underlying theory, featuring both algorithms and lower bounds. We refer to to [25] for a survey of this area. The main objective of data streaming algorithms is to process a massive data set arriving one at a time in an online fashion, i.e., with small time overhead, while at the same time minimizing the workspace used by the algorithm. Typical problems studied are statistics of the data, such as its frequency moments [4].

Since many interesting problems (like frequency moments larger than 2 [4, 10]) do not admit an efficient data streaming algorithm, one can study more powerful models for streaming models. Inspired by cloud computing applications a recent line of research papers [9, 12, 14, 13] has studied the situation where a helper processes the data stream for a client. While the client has the usual restrictions of data streaming algorithms (working online and using small space) the space restriction does not apply to the helper. In this situation the helper can certainly solve many important problems and communicate the result to the client, but an additional requirement is that the client should be able to *verify* the correctness of the result within his computational restrictions. The result announced by the helper is viewed as a claim which has to be verified according to the usual requirements in the theory of interactive proofs (see e.g. Chapter 8 in [5]). Throughout this paper we will refer to the helper as the prover, and to the client as the verifier.

The motivation for studying such models is as follows. While a device that processes a data stream might be severely limited (clearly in computation time, since it has to process the stream online, but also in the size of its workspace), internet companies that offer cloud computing services have built enormous data warehouses providing almost unlimited storage capacity. They could also offer much larger computational power. Hence it is natural to outsource the streaming computation by forwarding the stream to such a provider, and then receiving the processed answer. But can the results be trusted? The main concern in [9, 12, 14, 13] is that the results should be verifiable by an algorithm within the usual restrictions of data streaming algorithms, i.e., small space and online computation. One more important feature of these systems is that even though providers of cloud computing services might employ powerful computers and have large capacity, they cannot predict the future, i.e., don't have access to the future parts of the data stream.

[9, 12] study the situation in which the prover provides a (lengthy) annotation/proof to the verifier after the data stream has ended. The verifier processes the annotation in a streaming fashion. This corresponds to randomized checking of noninteractive proofs (in the theory of interactive proofs such systems are called Merlin Arthur games, because a powerful party that is not trusted (Merlin) sends a single message to a skeptical and computationally limited verifier (Arthur)).

Cormode et al. [13, 14] explored the situation when the proofs are fully interactive and gave very general algorithms for many problems. One of the main restrictions they place is that the total communication between prover and verifier should be very small, e.g. polylogarithmic in the length of the stream. Additionally of course the verifier has the usual streaming algorithm restrictions, and no one can see into the future.

In this paper we propose to relax the restriction on the total communication in place in previous work. We believe this to be an unnatural restriction. In fact, since the data stream does usually not originate with the provider processing it (the prover), giving the prover access can be understood as uploading of data. In practice uploading speed for most internet users is smaller by some factor than downloading speed. So why should the length of the messages from the prover be restricted massively? We find it more natural to restrict the communication *overhead*, i.e., the amount of communication exchanged per symbol on the data stream. In short, while the user/verifier uploads a symbol, he should also be able to download the next chunk of a proof, potentially even a constant factor larger than the coding length of the symbol. Furthermore, interactive proofs are known to be much more powerful than noninteractive proofs in most scenarios, so the user/verifier might as well upload short questions to the helper/prover.

Hence we consider a model for streaming computations with a prover, in which the verifier is very efficient, i.e., processes each symbol in polylogarithmic time and uses polylogarithmic space, whereas the prover is not space bounded, and uses some time $T(n)$ per symbol (the computation overhead). They may communicate after every symbol that is read from the stream (accessible to both) using $O(1)$ message exchanges of total length $C \cdot \log m$ when the symbols in the stream are from a size m universe. C is the communication overhead. The goal is to minimize both the communication and the computation overhead, under the condition that the verifier is as efficient as stated above.

What can we hope to gain from this relaxation of the model? First of all, in the model allowing only polylogarithmic total communication it is known that all functions in $\mathcal{NC}$ can be computed efficiently in the above sense [13]. So we might hope to find algorithms for problems not known to be in $\mathcal{NC}$. Beside this, the generic protocols for $\mathcal{NC}$ functions are complex and not well tuned to specific problems. One might wish for simpler and more efficient algorithms. Furthermore there is the following bottleneck in the algorithms described in [14, 13]. Their algorithms are based on classical interactive proof techniques and involve an additional verification phase after the stream has ended (or, once an output is required). This verification phase is quite short (polylogarithmic rounds and communication), but is in fact the only communication between prover and verifier performed at all. This implies that all the work of the prover that depends on random challenges sent from the verifier must essentially be done during this phase, i.e., a computation that is at least linear in the size of the stream (and often worse) must be squeezed into this short phase, in which no new inputs arrive, and the verifier is no more busy than usual. This leads to a huge computation bottleneck for the prover, which we hope to address with our model. Essentially the prover is almost completely idle before the onset of the verification phase, and then has to crank up his machines to perform exponentially more operations than the verifier during the verification phase.

Our main results are efficient streaming algorithms with a prover for computing the Median, approximating the longest increasing subsequence (LIS), and for determining whether a matrix has full rank. Our algorithms do not have additional verification phases after the end of the stream, or extravagant computation overheads for the prover. So in some sense we trade increased communication for simplicity and easier computation, while maintaining the full online nature of streaming. The results are stated in Section 4. On the other hand, in Section 7 we will investigate restrictions of our model, and show that certain problems that are as hard as the INDEX function in a very strong sense, cannot be computed fully online even in the presence of a powerful prover.

1.1 Previous Work

A model of streaming algorithms with a prover was first considered in [9] where the protocol between prover and verifier is not interactive, i.e., the prover produces a (long) annotation which he sends to the verifier after the stream has ended, who processes the annotation in a streaming fashion. The paper also shows lower bounds for tradeoffs between the length of the annotation and the workspace of the verifier, based on MA-communication complexity lower bounds. This line of work was continued in [12].

The mentioned model was extended by Cormode et al. [14, 13] by allowing multiple rounds of interaction between the prover and verifier. As a result of allowing multiple round interactions, they obtained exponentially cheaper protocols for some problems. They used a technique called linearization [27] which reduces the degree of the polynomial to be communicated but at the expense of allowing more rounds of communication.

Goldwasser, Kalai and Rothblum [19] proposed a delegation interactive protocol for log-space uniform $\mathcal{NC}$ circuits. Their protocols are presented formally in the streaming setting by Cormode, Mitzenmacher, and Thaler [13].

FACT 1. *Let f be a function that can be computed by a family of $O(\log(S(n)))$-space uniform arithmetic circuits of fan-in 2, size $S(n)$ and depth $d(n)$. Then in the streaming model with a prover where we allow multiple rounds of interaction, there is a protocol such that the verifier needs $O(\log(S(n)))$ bits of space and the total communication between the prover and the verifier is $d(n) \cdot \text{polylog}(S(n))$.*

If f can be solved in low parallel time, we have a efficient streaming protocol. In particular, if f is in L-uniform $\mathcal{NC}$, there is a protocol to compute f in the streaming model where the verifier's space is $O(\log n)$ and the total communication between the prover and the verifier is $\text{polylog}(n)$.

Canetti et al [7] showed some efficient delegation protocols where the client delegates the computation to several servers, of whom at least one server is honest. In this model, they showed a 1-round unconditionally sound delegation protocol for any function computable in L-uniform $\mathcal{NC}$.

We note that it is not known how to use arithmetization ideas like in Fact 1 for problems outside of $\mathcal{NC}$. Remarkably, it is not even clear how to extend this result to the class $\mathcal{RNC}$ of problems that have randomized polylogarithmic depth poly size circuits. The issue is that the verifier has to generate the random bits, which then need to be stored in the prover's space. It is not clear that the amount of random bits used by a circuit can in general be made as small as the number of input bits [1].

2. DEFINITIONS AND PRELIMINARIES

2.1 Streaming Algorithms

In this section we define our model of streaming computations with a helper/verifier.

We assume that in general the input is given as a data stream $x_1, \ldots, x_n$ of elements from a universe $\{1, \ldots, m\}$. For simplicity we will usually consider m, n such that $\log m = \Theta(\log n)$, and assume this here. The x_i are sometimes referred to as symbols.

In our model we consider two parties, the prover, and the verifier. Both parties are able to access the data stream one element at a time, consecutively, and synchronously, i.e., no party can look into the future with respect to the other one.

The verifier is a Turing machine that has space bounded by $poly(\log n)$, and processes each symbol in time $poly(\log n)$.

[1]Randomness can be removed by using nonuniformity, but this raises the issue that the verifier would have to be nonuniform as well.

The prover is a Turing machine that has unlimited workspace, and processes each symbol in some time $T(n)$ that will vary from problem to problem. Ideally we want $T(n)$ to be $poly(\log n)$ as well, but this would imply immediately that the problem at hand can be solved in quasilinear time (as the LIS, Median, and Frequency Moment problems indeed can be) but is too restrictive for some other problems, like computing the rank of a matrix.

Note that we indeed require the verifier to run in total time $n \cdot poly(\log n)$, and the prover to run in time $n \cdot T(n)$, but we furthermore require this time to be spread out evenly.

Prover and verifier communicate, under the following restrictions. For each symbol (i.e., right after that symbol has appeared on the stream) the verifier and prover can exchange $O(1)$ messages, each of length $C(m, n)$, where $C(m, n)$ is in general $O(\log mn)$. We refer to the constant factor as the communication overhead, because we think of x_i as a message of length $\log m$ sent from the verifier to the prover. Note that this allows the total communication from the prover to the verifier to exceed $n \log m$, so proofs can be long (and highly interactive), but must be produced online, i.e., before the stream has been seen completely, and the communication cannot contain very long messages between two consecutive symbols.

In short, the goal is to make the verifier extremely storage efficient and operate in an online fashion, offloading storage and computational load to the prover, while keeping the results verifiable. To fully describe algorithm in our model one also has to give instructions for the honest prover (since we are interested in his computation overhead).

We define correctness of a computation with regard to soundness and completeness as usual in the theory of interactive proofs, see for instance Chapter 8 in [5]. The completeness error is the probability over the random choices of the verifier that a correct claim is rejected by the verifier. The soundness error is the probability that an incorrect claim is accepted. The total error is the sum of the soundness and completeness errors.

2.2 Communication Complexity

For definitions of standard communication complexity modes we refer to [23]. The model of communication complexity we are interested in are *online* Arthur Merlin protocols. Here online refers to the fact that Alice sends only one message, and that Merlin cannot send messages to Alice.

DEFINITION 1. *In a k-round online Arthur Merlin protocol Alice receives input x, Bob receives input y, and Merlin sees x and y. Alice tosses a random coin r (which is seen by Bob and Merlin), and sends one message to Bob. Merlin and Bob engage in a conversation in which Merlin starts by sending a message M_1 to Bob (depending on r, x, y), Bob replies with a random challenge r_1, followed by another message from Merlin etc. until Merlin has sent k messages, and Bob (using more randomness) accepts or rejects.*

A protocol is correct, if for every 1-input there is a prover strategy such that with high probability the protocol accepts, and for every 0-input, no matter Merlin's strategy the protocol rejects with high probability. The cost of such a protocol is the sum of the lengths of the messages sent by Alice and by Merlin. The complexity $AM_k^o(f)$ is the cost of an optimal protocol.

In an online k-round Merlin Arthur protocol Merlin's first message cannot depend on Alice's randomness.

In particular 1-round online AM protocols there is one message from Alice to Bob, and one message from Merlin to Bob (which can depend on r), and in 1-round online MA protocols Merlin's message does not depend on r.

Furthermore in a strict 1-round AM protocol Bob cannot generate any randomness, and so all randomness is generated by Alice and is public, i.e., known by Merlin. The complexity is denoted $\widetilde{AM}^{o}_{1}(f)$.

We note that Aaronson and Wigderson [2] show online k-round MA protocols for problems like Disjointness, Inner Product, and Index with complexity $O(n^{1/(k+1)} \log n)$ for any k. This does not show that $\widetilde{AM}^{o}_{1}(\text{INDEX})$ is smaller than $O(n)$: the protocol for $k = 1$ relies on Alice using randomness that is unknown to Merlin.

2.3 Fingerprinting

In all of our algorithms fingerprinting plays a crucial role. The main application of this is quite simple: we wish to use the prover as a remote storage device in the spirit of cloud computing services, and we need to keep him honest, i.e., need to check that information he sends back is the same we deposited. While most fingerprinting schemes would work for that we also require another feature in some of our applications. We would like to have a fingerprint of a set, such that we can check equality with the same set, even when presented in a different order. Given a multiset presented as a stream $\sigma = \langle a_1, \cdots, a_n \rangle$, where each $a_i \in \{1, \ldots, M\}$, we compute the *set-fingerprint* of σ as follows: $\widetilde{FP}_q(r, \sigma) = \prod_{i=1}^{n} (r - a_i) \pmod{q}$, where q is a prime chosen as described below before the start of the streaming process. If n is not known in advance, an upper bound of n will suffice.

LEMMA 1. *Let $q \geq n/\delta$ be a prime for some given $0 < \delta < 1$ (we call $1 - \delta$ the reliability of the fingerprint) and choose r uniformly at random from $\mathbf{F}_q$. Given a stream σ of length n where each symbol is drawn from a universe of size M, the fingerprint $\widetilde{FP}_q(r, \sigma)$ can be computed using $O(\log M - \log \delta + \log n)$ bits of memory in a streaming fashion. Given another stream ς whose length is at most n and $\varsigma \neq \sigma$ (we say two streams are equal if and only if they are equal as multisets.), the collision probability*

$$\mathcal{P}\mathbf{r}_{r \in_R \mathbf{F}_q} \left[\widetilde{FP}_q(r, \sigma) = \widetilde{FP}_q(r, \varsigma) \right] \leq \delta.$$

This allows us to check the equality of two sets, even when the sets are presented in a different order.

In some cases we require the elements in the stream to be re-streamed in the same order as in the original stream. Given a stream $\sigma = \langle a_1, \cdots, a_n \rangle$, where each $a_i \in \{1, \ldots M\}$, compute

$$FP_q(r, \sigma) := \sum_{i=1}^{n} a_i \, r^i \qquad \pmod{q}.$$

for some prime q.

LEMMA 2. *Let $q \geq n/\delta$ be a prime for some given $0 < \delta < 1$ and choose r uniformly at random from $\mathbf{F}_q$. Given a stream σ of length n where each symbol is drawn from a universe of size M, the sequence-fingerprint $FP_q(r, \sigma)$ can be computed using $O(\log M - \log \delta + \log n)$ bits of memory in a streaming fashion. Given another stream ς whose length is at most n and $\varsigma \neq \sigma$, the collision probability*

$$\mathcal{P}\mathbf{r}_{r \in_R \mathbf{F}_q} \left[FP_q(r, \sigma) = FP_q(r, \varsigma) \right] \leq \delta.$$

For matrices, in the streaming model, we assume that the entries of $A \in M_{mn}(\mathbf{Z})$ are streamed row-wise(where $m \leq n$), i.e. the stream

$$\sigma = \langle a_{11}, \cdots, a_{1n}, a_{21}, \cdots, a_{2n}, \cdots, a_{m1}, \cdots, a_{mn} \rangle,$$

where each $a_{ij} \in [n]$. The verifier($\mathcal{V}$) choose a prime p such that $n^3 < p < 2n^3$. $\mathcal{V}$ then chooses x uniformly at random from $\mathbf{F}_p$(and keeps it private from $\mathcal{P}$) and computes the fingerprint of A as follows:

$$FP_p(x, A) := \sum_{i=1}^{m} \sum_{j=1}^{n} a_{ij} \, x^{(i-1)n+(j-1)} \qquad \pmod{p}. \quad (1)$$

Since the polynomial $FP_p(x, A) \in \mathbf{F}_p[X]$ has degree at most mn, for any $A' \neq A$, we have

$$\mathcal{P}\mathbf{r}_{x \in_R \mathbf{F}_p} \left[FP_p(x, A') = FP_p(x, A) \right] \leq \frac{mn}{p} < \frac{1}{n}.$$

3. WARMUP: MEDIAN

In this section we show how to compute the median of n numbers from a size n^2 universe arriving on a data stream, with the help of a prover. Recall that the median of $x_1, \ldots, x_n$ is the element with rank $n/2$ in the sorted sequence[2]. Our algorithm also serves as an introduction to the main ideas for our algorithms: splitting the input into geometrically shrinking phases, re-streaming parts of the data stream (usually during the next phase), and using some measure of progress that allows to restrict the length of the re-streaming.

While the Median problem is in $\mathcal{NC}$, and hence by Fact 1 there is a streaming algorithm with prover that uses only $O(\log n)$ space, this general algorithm has two drawbacks. First, there is an additional verification phase after the stream has ended, including a $O(\log n)$ round conversation between prover and verifier. Secondly, during this phase the prover has to perform a linear amount of computation, while being mostly idle while reading the stream. The algorithm given in this section increases the amount of communication between prover and verifier, but is substantially simpler than the algorithm of Fact 1, and does neither have an additional verification phase nor a large computation overhead for the prover. In the next subsection we show how to even remove the large amount of communication by combining the ideas from our algorithm and from Fact 1.

It is important to recall that the prover in our model is not clairvoyant, i.e., does not know the median in advance. Otherwise he could simply send the median to the verifier, who could store it, and then count all the elements on the stream that are smaller. But for a moment consider a setting, in which the prover and verifier are allowed to see the whole stream, and can exchange arbitrarily long messages after the end of the stream (the definition of our model does not allow this, since this would violate the communication overhead bound). In such a setting we can find a very simple algorithm as well: the verifier computes a fingerprint of the original stream while seeing the stream. Note that prime fingerprint has to be kept secret from the prover. The prover

[2]Throughout the rest of the paper we ignore floor and ceiling operations.

computes the median during the original stream, and then, after the stream has ended sends the median x to the verifier, and furthermore "re-streams" the whole original stream. The verifier can now operate as if in the clairvoyant model, and check if x is really the median of the re-streamed numbers. Furthermore the verifier must test, whether the prover faithfully re-streams, using his fingerprint.

In our median algorithm we try to emulate this approach, by "folding" the re-streaming of parts of the data stream into the original stream, maintaining small communication overhead. Since the prover does not know the median after, say $3n/4$ steps, he has to provide some partial information to the verifier.

Our algorithm is based on the following observation. Consider a stream of n numbers $x_n, \ldots, x_1$ with $0 \leq x_i \leq n^2$ for concreteness (for convenience x_n arrives first). After $n/2$ numbers have appeared on the stream, each of them could still be the median (due to $n/2$ numbers still appearing in the future). However, after we have seen $n(1 - 1/2^k)$ numbers at most $n/2^k$ of the numbers already seen are still candidates for becoming the median: all others either have rank smaller than $n/2 - n/2^k$ or larger than $n/2$ in the sorted sequence and are no longer candidates for being the median, no matter what the rest of the stream will look like.

The main idea is now to partition the stream in phases of length $n/2^k$ for $k = 1, \ldots, \log n$. Phase $k + 1$ is used to simulate the re-streaming idea described above. But note that during this phase we can only re-stream $O(n/2^k)$ elements, and not the whole previous stream. It is now very convenient, that there are only $n/2^k$ candidates left that are worth re-streaming. But this is not enough, because the verifier can only establish correctness of the re-streaming with his fingerprint if the whole stream he has computed the fingerprint from is repeated, not some selection from it.

We now describe the algorithm in detail. Denote by P_k the $k-th$ phase of the algorithm, as well as the numbers appearing on the stream in the k-th phase, i.e., $x_{n/2^{k-1}}, \ldots, x_{n/2^k+1}$. In the following let $FP()$ denote the fingerprint of a stream of length at most n with reliability $1 - \epsilon/\log n$. According to Lemma 2 such a fingerprint can be computed online with space $O(\log n - \log \epsilon)$ and has length $O(\log n - \log \epsilon)$.

- In P_1 the verifier computes the fingerprint $F_1 = FP(P_1)$ of the first $n/2$ numbers. The prover sorts the numbers. Let C_1 denote the first $n/2$ numbers in their original ordering.

- In P_2 the verifier computes the fingerprint $F_2 = FP(P_2)$ of the next $n/4$ numbers. The prover keeps sorting, and determines C_2, the sequence of numbers with ranks between $n/4$ and $n/2$ (relative to $P_1 \circ P_2$), in their original ordering. y_1 denotes the minimum of P_1 and z_k the maximum of P_1.

- In P_k for $k > 2$ the following happens. Let C_k denote the sequence of numbers with rank $n/2 - n/2^k$ up to $n/2$ in $P_1 \circ \cdots \circ P_k$ in their original ordering. At the beginning of P_k the verifier knows F_{k-1} (the fingerprint of P_{k-1}) and also the fingerprint of C_{k-2}. The prover knows C_{k-1}.

  1. The (honest) prover sends the elements y_{k-1} and z_{k-1} of C_{k-1} that have rank $n/2 - n/2^{k-1}$ and rank $n/2$ (relative to $P_1 \circ \cdots \circ P_{k-1}$).
  2. The prover re-streams C_{k-2} and P_{k-1}. The verifier checks the re-streaming of C_{k-2} and P_{k-1} against their fingerprints, and computes the fingerprints of the sequence C_{k-1} as well as of the sequence P_k. Note that C_{k-1} is easy to determine from $C_{k-2}, P_{k-1}, y_{k-1}, z_{k-1}$. Additionally the verifier checks that exactly $n/2 - n/2^{k-1} - 1$ elements of $x_n, \ldots, x_{n/2^{k-1}+1}$ are smaller than y_{k-1} and exactly $n/2 - 1$ are smaller than z_{k-1}. To do this he checks that exactly $n/2^{k-1}$ elements of C_{k-2} and P_{k-1} are between y_{k-2} and y_{k-2} and exactly $n/2^{k-2}$ between y_{k-2} and z_{k-1}.
  3. The re-streaming happens by sending 6 elements from C_{k-2} or P_{k-1} for every new element on the stream. Note that $|C_{k-2}| = 4n/2^k, |P_{k-1}| = 2n/2^k$ and $|P_k| = n/2^k$.
  4. At the end of P_k the prover determines the set C_k, which consists of all elements that have rank between $n/2 - n/2^k$ and $n/2$.

- When $n/2^k = O(1)$, then the verifier stores C_{k-1}, instead of fingerprinting it. He then stops talking to the prover, and instead sorts the remaining sequence himself (note that elements smaller than y_{k-1} or larger than z_{k-1} can be ignored). The verifier can determine the median at the end of the stream.

THEOREM 1. *The Median problem can be solved with communication overhead* $6 + o(1)$*, polylogarithmic time per symbol for both verifier and prover, and space* $O(\log n + \log(1/\epsilon))$ *verifier space, and error* ϵ.

PROOF. The communication overhead is shown to be 6 above, with the $o(1)$ accounting for the communication of the y_k and z_k. It is clear that this algorithm can be implemented using polylog time per symbol. The verifier at any given time needs to store at most two fingerprints, and a constant number of elements from the stream. Each fingerprint needs $O(\log n - \log \epsilon)$ bits of storage. □

3.1 Reducing the Communication

Since the median problem lies in $\mathcal{NC}$, the general algorithm of Fact 1 provides us with a solution to the problem in which prover and verifier communicate only $poly(\log n)$ bits. However, this comes at the expense of an additional verification phase after the end of the stream, during which there is also an exponential computation overhead for the prover. Here we explain how this can be remedied, by combining the above algorithm with arithmetization ideas used in the proof of Fact 1.

We keep the overall structure of our algorithm above. During $\log n$ phases we verify the rank of elements y_k and x_k using a small set of inputs C_{k-2} and P_{k-1} only. Verifying those ranks can be done by a circuit of polylogarithmic depth and size polynomial in $n/2^k$. Hence we can use the algorithm of Fact 1 during the next phase to simulate that circuit and perform the necessary verification. Both the computation time and the communication can be spread out over the next phase, leading to smaller computation overhead for the prover.

Hence in the case of the median problem the extra verification phase can be removed and the computation overhead of the prover lowered. We achieve a solution with polynomial computation overhead for the prover and the verifier, polylogarithmic total communication, and polylogarithmic space for the verifier.

4. STATEMENT OF MAIN RESULTS

In this section we state and explain our main results which are presented in more detail in the following three sections.

Our algorithms are much in the mold of the algorithm for Median described in Section 3. The main ingredients are re-streaming parts of the stream together with short annotations to allow the verifier to check the prover's claims. Each algorithm consists of phases P_ℓ whose length decreases by a factor of 2 with ℓ. Phase P_ℓ is used to re-stream data from earlier phases. But because the communication overhead is bounded by a constant we cannot re-stream all of the previous stream. So a measure of progress is needed that allows us to restrict the amount of data the prover has to present to the verifier. Let us reconsider the Median algorithm: the main observation was that the number of candidates for the median (among symbols that have so far been on the stream) shrinks by a factor of 2 each phase.

The next problem we tackle is the Longest Increasing Subsequence problem (LIS). Given a sequence/stream $x_1, \dots, x_n$ of elements from $\{1, \dots n^2\}$ (n^2 again chosen for concreteness) the length of the longest increasing subsequence $LIS(x)$ is the largest k such there exist $i_1 < \dots < i_k$ with $x_{i_j} \leq x_{i_{j+1}}$ for all $1 \leq j \leq k-1$.

We prove the following theorem:

THEOREM 2. *There is a streaming algorithm with a prover for computing a $1-\epsilon$-approximation to $LIS(x)$ using constant communication overhead (independent of n and ϵ), space $O(\log^2 n/\epsilon)$, and succeeds with probability $1-1/n$. The computation overhead of the prover is* polylog n.

While it is easy for a prover to provide a witness to a large increasing subsequence for the stream so far, the first problem is that the prover cannot see the future and hence cannot know which sequence is going to win. We resolve this issue by running a classic algorithm for the LIS problem on the prover side and keeping the prover honest by re-streaming certain permutations of the original stream during the phases. But, more importantly, the prover also needs to show that the LIS is smaller than his claim. For this we use a dual characterization of the value of the LIS.

We next consider the problem of checking whether an $n \times n$ integer matrix A containing integers of size n (for concreteness) has full rank over the reals (the matrix is streamed row by row, each entry being one symbol on the stream). It is known that even if we consider rank factorizations of $n \times n$ Boolean matrices, the factor matrices require numbers that are exponential. Hence we choose a large prime p and with high enough probability, the rank over $\mathbf{F}_p$ is equal to the rank over the reals. An important aspect of the protocol is the ability to verify matrix multiplications. We show that Freivalds' [17] algorithm can be implemented in the streaming model to verify matrix multiplications. We use the Hermite Normal form factorization over a finite field as the rank revealing factorization. Now, if we see a new row, x of A, we have to decide if it is linearly independent of the previous rows already seen. Let B be all the rows already seen and $\mathcal{C}_B$ be the row space of B. Viewed as a linear code, we have $\dim(\mathcal{C}_B) + \dim(\mathcal{C}_B^\perp) = n$, where $\mathcal{C}_B^\perp$ is the dual code of B, whose dimension shrinks as we see more and more rows of A. So as the protocol proceeds, we re-stream the dual code which gets smaller and smaller as the protocol proceeds. If the prover streams us a basis for $\mathcal{C}_B^\perp$, the verifier can use it to determine whether the membership $x \in B$ is true or false. Combining all these ideas, we have the following:

THEOREM 3. *Given a square matrix $A \in \mathcal{M}_n(\mathbf{Z})$ which is streamed row-wise, where $|a_{ij}| \leq n$, there is a streaming algorithm which can decide if A has full rank over the reals where the verifier uses $O(\log n)$ storage and the total communication overhead is constant with probability of failure $O\left(\frac{\log n}{n}\right)$.*

Finally, we consider the question of whether the additional verification phase present in the algorithms of [14, 13] is necessary, and, more general, how much interaction between prover and verifier is necessary. We show that for problems that have a specific reduction from the INDEX problem a lot of interaction is necessary.

THEOREM 4.
1. *Any data streaming algorithm with a prover for a problem that has a strict reduction from* INDEX *either has to use more than polylogarithmic communication overhead, or the verifier space is more than polylogarithmic, or there are at least $\Omega(\log n/\log\log n)$ communication rounds between prover and verifier after the end of the stream.*
2. *If a problem has a weak reduction from* INDEX, *then either more than polylogarithmic total communication is needed, or the verifier space is more than polylogarithmic, or there are at least $\Omega(\log n/\log\log n)$ communication rounds between prover and verifier.*

5. LONGEST INCREASING SUBSEQUENCE

5.1 The Problem

In this section we give an algorithm structurally similar to the algorithm from Section 3 to compute the Longest Increasing Subsequence of a data stream with the help of a prover. Given a sequence/stream $x_1, \dots, x_n$ of elements from $\{1, \dots n^2\}$ (n^2 again chosen for concreteness) the length of the longest increasing subsequence $LIS(x)$ is the largest k such there exist $i_1 < \dots < i_k$ with $x_{i_j} \leq x_{i_{j+1}}$ for all $1 \leq j \leq k-1$. This problem is not know to be in $\mathcal{NC}$ or $\mathcal{RNC}$, hence no streaming algorithm with prover following the techniques of Theorem 1 is known for the problem.

LIS is a natural and well-studied problem, for more information regarding this problem see the survey by Aldous and Diaconis [3]. LIS is also related to the distance to monotonicity problem (under the edit distance), see [20, 16]. There is a classical algorithm that computes $LIS(x)$, called *Patience Sort*.

The Patience Sort algorithm naturally works in the streaming model, but requires storage $O(k \log n)$ for $k = LIS(x)$, which is not efficient enough (e.g. for a random permutation one can expect $k \approx 2\sqrt{n}$ [3]). Gopalan et al. [20] describe a deterministic streaming algorithm (without prover) that uses space $O(\sqrt{n/\epsilon})$ to compute an $(1-\epsilon)$-approximation to $LIS(x)$. They also show that any randomized algorithm that computes $LIS(x)$ exactly in the streaming model requires linear space in the worst case. Gal et al. [18] as well as Ergün et al. [16] show deterministic lower bounds of the order $\Omega(\sqrt{n/\epsilon})$ for the space needed to compute a $(1-\epsilon)$-approximation to $LIS(x)$. Finally, Chakrabarti [8] argues that extending these lower bounds to the randomized case needs different techniques, so the best randomized lower bounds are still only logarithmic.

In this section we will show how to compute an $(1-\epsilon)$-approximation for $LIS(x)$ using polylog n verifier space in the presence of a prover in our model, i.e., with small communication overhead but large total communication.

5.2 Patience Sort

Patience Sort works as follows. The algorithm maintains an ordered set of sets (which we will call *stacks*) of elements. Stacks are named from 1 up to some number k, and should be imagined as being arranged from left to right. In the beginning we start with an empty set of stacks. As a new input x_i arrives, we find the leftmost stack such that the top (minimum) element of that stack is strictly larger than x_i, and put x_i on top of that stack. If no such stack exists, we start a new stack to the right of the existing stacks, and put x_i on top of that stack. Refer to [3] for the many interesting properties of this algorithm. Notice that the original version of Patience Sort only needs to maintain the top elements of all stacks used. We will refer to the number of the stack as arranged from left to right as the *name* of the stack. This is important, because in our algorithm we will not maintain all stacks but only a small subset of them, but we will keep their names intact.

It is easy to see that in the end the largest name of a stack (the rightmost stack) corresponds to $LIS(x)$. Further observations include that the sequence of elements on the top of the stacks (the sequence of stack minima) is increasing, but not necessarily an increasing subsequence. Each stack viewed from the bottom to the top is a strictly decreasing sequence (and indeed a subsequence of x).

Like our algorithm for computing the median, our algorithm for LIS works in $\log n$ phases, in which the prover re-streams part of the original stream, but in this case under various permutations. The main ingredient here is the following dual characterization of $LIS(x)$ in the spirit of Dilworth's theorem.

Definition 2. *A* descending chain *is a subsequence $x_{i_1} > \cdots > x_{i_l}$, where $1 \le i_1 < \cdots < i_l \le n$. For convenience we set $x_0 = \infty$ and $i_0 = 0$.*

The extension *of a descending chain is a sequence $y_1, \ldots, y_n$ such that $y_k = x_{i_j}$ for $i_j = \max\{i_j : i_j \le k\}$ for all $1 \le k \le n$.*

Two descending chains $x_{i_1} > \cdots > x_{i_l}$ and $x_{j_1} > \cdots > x_{j_m}$ cross, *if for their extensions y and z there are indices $u < v$ such that $y_u < z_u$ and $y_v > z_v$ or vice versa.*

Lemma 3. *$LIS(x) = k$ if and only if there is a partition of $x = x_1, \ldots, x_n$ into k descending chains, such that no two of the chains cross and that the chains can be ordered so that the smallest elements of the chains form an increasing sequence.*

Proof. If $LIS(x) = k$ then Patience Sort will find a partition x into exactly k descending chains (corresponding to the stacks maintained by the algorithm) whose smallest elements form an increasing sequence. These descending chains do not cross by construction: if two descending chains cross, then this means that an element that can fit on top of the left stack is placed on the stack further to the right at some point, which violates the algorithm.

Conversely, assume the minimum size of a partition with the above properties is k. The chains in the partitions are numbered 1 to k and we refer to lower numbered chains as being to the left of higher numbered chains.

First we observe that if we remove elements $x_l, \ldots, x_n$ from the chains the properties that the smallest elements of the chains form an increasing sequence remains true. To see this consider removing one element x_n. x_n must be the smallest element of some chain, because chains are subsequences. We remove the rightmost appearance of x_n if there are several elements equal to x_n which are smallest elements of chains. Clearly removing an element like this cannot make chains cross. Now suppose that the smallest elements of the resulting chains no longer form an increasing sequence. That means the smallest element of the chain to the right of the chain where we removed x_n is some x_j and $x_n < x_j < x_i$ where x_i is the new smallest element of the chain where we removed x_n. Let y denote the extension of the chain containing x_n and z the extension of the other chain.

Assume that $j < i < n$. In this case $y_j \ge y_i = x_i > x_j = z_j$. So assume that $i < j < n$. Then $y_j = y_i = x_i > x_j = z_j$. In both cases we have that $z_n = z_j = x_j > x_n = y_n$, so the chains cross, a contradiction.

We conclude that if we remove elements $x_l, \ldots, x_n$ from the chains the smallest elements of the chains, left to right, still form an increasing sequence.

We have to show that $LIS(x) = k$. To show $\le$ we simply observe that any partition into k descending chains is a witness for $LIS(x) \le k$. For the other direction take any partition into descending chains that do not cross and have increasing smallest elements. We construct an increasing subsequence of length k. Take the largest element of the rightmost chain, which is going to be the first (bottom) element of the chain. When this is x_j, we remove all elements $x_j, \ldots, x_n$. By the above argument we are left with $k-1$ chains that still have the desired properties. By induction we get an increasing subsequence of length $k-1$ that ends in the smallest element x_i of the rightmost chain (among $x_1, \ldots, x_{j-1}$). $x_i \le x_j$, because among $x_1, \ldots, x_j$ the element x_j is the smallest element of the rightmost chain. So we can find an increasing sequence of length k. □

The partition of x into k descending chains can easily be computed by modifying Patience Sort, so that it keeps all the elements on a stack, instead of only the top elements. Note that this increases the space usage, but this work will be done by the prover.

5.3 Intuition for the Algorithm

The idea of our protocol is that the (honest) prover runs Patience Sort, and convinces the verifier via re-streaming of certain permutations of sub-streams that he did so correctly. Let us consider a scenario, where this verification is allowed to take place after the original input stream has ended (this is not allowed in our model and considered here only for motivation). While the prover executes the Patience Sort algorithm during the original stream, he announces the stack number of each new element to the verifier. The verifier computes the set-fingerprint of the set of tuples i, x_i, l_i, where l_i is the announced stack number of elements x_i arriving at time i. This also implicitly checks, that each element of the stream is assigned to exactly one stack. After the original stream has ended, the prover re-streams this set in two different ways, making it possible for the verifier to check that Patience Sort was executed correctly.

The first re-streaming consists of all the i, x_i, l_i ordered by the stack numbers and then (inside every stack) by the sequence number i, i.e., the verifier gets to see the sequence as partitioned into the descending chains. If any chain is not descending, he will reject the computation. The set-fingerprint will allow him to check the re-streaming for correctness even though it is not in the original order. The verifier also tests that the minimum elements of all chains form an increasing sequence. For this he just needs to remember the smallest element of the current chain.

With the second re-streaming we want to check that none of the chains cross. If two chains cross, then two neighboring chains cross. So for all neighboring pairs of chains we check that they do not cross.

DEFINITION 3. *An* alignment *of two chains* $x_{i_1}, \ldots, x_{i_l}$ *and* $x_{j_1}, \ldots, x_{j_k}$ *is the sequence of all the elements of the two chains, sorted by their position in* x*, and accompanied by bits indicating whether elements belong to the first or the second sequence.*

The prover will re-stream all alignments of all pairs of neighboring chains. The verifier can now easily check that those pairs do not cross: crossing means that an element is added to the right chain even if it would fit into the left chain. The verifier can also easily construct the fingerprint of the set of i, x_i, l_i for their first and second appearance in the re-streaming (all chains except the first and the last are re-streamed twice). This fingerprint can be checked against the set-fingerprint the verifier knows.

In this way two re-streams would allow us to check the correctness of the Patience Sort execution, and allow for an exact computation of $LIS(x)$.

5.4 The Algorithm

As in the algorithm for Median in Section 3, we partition $\{1, \ldots, n\}$ into $\log n$ subsets of decreasing size, called the phases of the algorithm. Each phase is handled similarly to the above description (with the re-streaming taking place during the next phase). The main issue is how to connect the phases to check overall correctness. The first idea is to keep a fingerprint of the top of all stacks, i.e., the sequence visible to the sequential Patience Sort algorithm at all times. This allows to connect two phases, since all we need is to make sure that the tops of stacks are consistent across phases. However, the prover has to re-stream the k top elements to check consistency (the verifier does not have enough memory to store them), and usually at some time the phases become too short to do that (e.g. if $LIS(x) = \sqrt{n}$ and the phase length gets to $o(\sqrt{n})$). Note that we could simply stop at that point, since we achieved already some approximation. But in order to get a $(1-\epsilon)$-approximation one would have to stop when the current estimate for $LIS(x)$ is at least $1/\epsilon$ times the current phase length. This would mean that the re-streaming used until now requires the communication overhead to be at least $1/\epsilon$, which is not desirable. Instead we reduce the number of stacks to $O(\log(n)/\epsilon)$ and continue, still achieving a good approximation, but leaving the communication overhead independent of ϵ. Intuitively we keep stacks whose name is a multiple of $\epsilon k/\log n$ if k is the current largest stack name. This gives us an approximation error of ϵ, since the reduction in the number of stacks happens only at the end of a phase, and there are only $\log n$ phases. The error analysis is completely analogous to the one in [20].

Denote by P_ℓ the $\ell - th$ phase, i.e., $x_{n-n/2^{\ell-1}+1}, \ldots, x_{n-n/2^\ell}$. We now describe the algorithm in our usual model, i.e., without extra time for re-streaming at the end.

The algorithm keeps a variable k that contains the largest stack name used so far. It starts as $k = 0$. In phase P_1 the prover runs the Patience Sort algorithm, announcing for each element i, x_i the number s_i of the stack he is putting the element on to the verifier. The verifier computes the set-fingerprint of all the tuples i, x_i, s_i. We are using fingerprints with reliability $1 - 1/n^2$. The verifier increases k by one if necessary, and rejects, if the prover tries to increase k by more than 1.

In each phase P_ℓ for $\ell = 2, \ldots$ until $n/2^\ell < k$ the following happens. As before the prover will continue to run Patience Sort, and communicate the stack numbers, and the verifier will create a (new) set-fingerprint for the tuples i, x_i, s_i with $i \in P_\ell$. But furthermore the prover will use this phase to re-stream the permuted inputs from the previous phase. For $\ell = 2$ he re-streams the tuples i, x_i, s_i for $i \in P_{\ell-1}$ sorted by the third component (and for each value of the third component sorted by the first component). The verifier again takes the set-fingerprint of this sequence, and eventually checks it against the one computed in the previous phase. If the fingerprints do not agree he rejects and stops. Furthermore the verifier checks during this re-streaming that all stacks are indeed strictly decreasing sequences and that the minimal elements of all the stacks form an increasing sequence (if not he will reject). The verifier also computes the sequence-fingerprint of those elements, which is used to connect two neighboring phases.

As described above a second re-streaming of the elements from phase 1 is needed to check that neighboring stacks do not cross. So, the prover re-streams for all pairs of stacks their alignment (as defined above). If the two stacks cross the verifier rejects. To check consistency the verifier again computes the set fingerprints of the first and second occurrence of each the stacks and checks this fingerprint against the one from $P_{\ell-1}$. Finally, the verifier takes the sequence-fingerprints of the two occurrences of a stack in the re-streaming (except for the first and last stack) and checks that they are the same. This finishes the phase.

For $\ell > 2$ we need to make sure that the re-streaming for consecutive phases fit together. Furthermore we do not want to re-stream the whole stacks, because we need the length of the re-streaming in a phase to be within a constant factor of the length of the phase. Note that the only relevant point here is that top (minimal elements) of all stacks at the end of one phase coincides with the top of all stacks at the beginning of the next phase. Indeed the prover and verifier agree to discard all elements except the top of all stacks and re-streaming will only consider the elements that appeared in the previous phase.

Hence we modify the computations during a phase P_ℓ for $\ell \geq 3$ as follows. From phase $P_{\ell-1}$ we hold a sequence-fingerprint of the sequence of minimal elements of all the stacks at the end of $P_{\ell-2}$. Assume this sequence is $x_{i_1} \leq \cdots \leq x_{i_k}$. Then the re-streaming of phase P_ℓ concerns running Patience Sort on the sequence $x_{i_1}, \ldots, x_{i_k}$ followed by the inputs from phase $P_{\ell-1}$. These are $k + n/2^{\ell-1}$ elements. The verifier can now check that the first k elements are correct, and can compute the set-fingerprint of the re-streaming of $P_{\ell-1}$, as well as check the correct execution of Patience Sort.

Once we reach the point where $n/2^\ell < k$ we cannot continue the above, because the re-streaming of the top of the stacks is no longer possible with a small communication overhead. At this point we switch to approximation, similar to the deterministic streaming approximation algorithm from [20]. Say we have m stacks currently in use in the Patience Sort algorithm run by the prover. These have top elements $x_{i_1}, \ldots, x_{i_m}$ (i.e., the decreasing chains in the stacks end in those elements). We now choose $\log n/\epsilon$ stacks from 1 up to m (evenly spaced) and discard the remaining stacks. This operation is referred to as cleanup. Note that stacks do not change their names during cleanup and that we will never remove the stack with the largest name (which is k).

Assume the set of stack names is $S = \{j_1, \ldots, j_m\}$ and that $m > 2\log n/\epsilon$ and that $k = j_m$ is the largest stack number. The prover then sets S to $\{\lceil \epsilon/\log n \cdot k\rceil, \lceil 2\epsilon/\log n \cdot k\rceil, \ldots, k\}$, discarding the remaining stacks. The first time this happens S starts as $\{1, \ldots, k\}$, and the prover has to re-stream the sequence of top elements of all the stacks so that the verifier can compute the new sequence of top elements of the reduced set of stacks (and its fingerprint). This is still possible within constant overhead. The same needs to be done after any cleanup operation, but note that the number of stacks in phase ℓ can now never exceed $O(2\log n/\epsilon + n/2^\ell)$.

We claim that the cleanup operations each introduce error at most $\epsilon/\log n$. Also note, that this reduction step takes place every time $n/2^\ell$ exceeds the current k by a constant factor, because k may start to grow again after a cleanup, but that this happens at most once per phase. There are $\log n$ phases and hence at most that many cleanup operations and the total error is bounded by ϵ.

LEMMA 4. *The total error introduced by all the cleaning up steps is at most ϵ.*

PROOF. Each reduction step removes some of the stacks maintained by the Patience Sort algorithm. Consider sequences of some length l that ends in an element a from the universe $U = \{1, \ldots, n^2\}$. We denote by $P(l)$ the smallest element a of U such that there is an increasing subsequence of length l that ends in a. Note that Patience Sort computes $P(l)$ as the top (smallest) element of stack l.

For simplicity assume that a cleanup operation happens at the end of every phase. If the first few phases do not include a cleanup, then the error can only decrease. Denote by k_ℓ the maximum stack name after phase P_ℓ. We define $P'(l)$ to be $P(l)$ if stack l is in S, i.e., has not been discarded, and otherwise to be the smallest j such that $j > l$ and $j \in S$. With this definition $P'(l)$ is the smallest letter a such that our algorithm tracks an increasing subsequence that ends in a. Naturally, $P'(l) \geq P(l)$. Furthermore denote by $P'_t(l)$ and $P_t(l)$ the smallest element a such that there is a increasing subsequence of length l that ends in a among $x_1, \ldots, x_t$ in (P) the whole stream, and in (P') is the same when discarding stacks as described.

We will use the following claim, which basically states that at any time $t \leq \log n$ a slightly shorter sequence ending in a or a lesser element still exists. This claim is proved exactly like Lemma 2.2 in [20].

CLAIM 1.

$$P'_t(l - (t-1)\epsilon k_t/\log n) \leq P_t(l).$$

Note that there are at most $\log n$ phases and so in the end $P'((l-\epsilon)k) \leq P(l)$, where k is the final maximum name of any stack. This directly shows that in the end the error is at most ϵ. □

Finally, at some point $P_\ell < 10\log n/\epsilon$. At this point the prover still sends the sequence of top elements from all stacks, but then prover and verifier stop communicating. The prover starts with the given sequence (which fits into his memory), and runs Patience Sort himself with the remaining input.

We can now state the overall result of this section.

THEOREM 5. *There is a streaming algorithm with a prover for computing a $1-\epsilon$-approximation to $LIS(x)$ using constant communication overhead (independent of n and ϵ), space $O(\log^2 n/\epsilon)$, and succeeds with probability $1-1/n$. The computation overhead of the prover is* polylog n.

We note that the only source of error is a failure of fingerprinting, and that the underlying approximation is guaranteed if no fingerprinting operation fails.

6. RANK

In this section we consider the problem of checking whether an $n \times n$ integer matrix containing integers of size n (for concreteness) has full rank over the reals (the matrix is streamed row by row, each entry being one symbol on the stream).

Clarkson and Woodruff [11] studied the rank decision problem in the standard streaming model for turnstile updates. They showed that any streaming algorithm which succeeds with constant probability needs $\Omega(k^2)$ bits of space to determine if the rank of $A \in \mathcal{M}_n(\mathbf{Z})$ is at least k. They also gave a upper bound of $O(k^2 \log \frac{n}{\delta})$ bits of space needed for the failure probability to be at most δ. It follows from a reduction we describe in Section 7 that $\Omega(n^2)$ bits of space are needed to determine if $A \in \mathcal{M}_n(\mathbf{Z})$ is full rank in the time-series model [25].

We study the problem in our model. One issue we ran into immediately was that standard factorizations of even Boolean $n \times n$ matrices that reveal the rank (e.g., the QR factorization) require exponential size numbers as entries of the factor matrices. That means even if an honest prover tries to convince us by means of such a factorization, he cannot even tell us what the entries are in an efficient manner! However, probabilistic techniques come to our rescue, and it is possible to simply choose a large enough prime p, and test of the matrix has full rank over the field Z_p. On the other hand one has to be careful with standard concepts like orthogonality over a finite field, as we shall see below.

6.1 Verifying Matrix Multiplication in the Streaming Model

Suppose we are given $A \in \mathcal{M}_{mn}(\mathbf{F}_p)$ and we wish to verify if $A = BC$, where $B \in \mathcal{M}_m(\mathbf{F}_p)$ and $C \in \mathcal{M}_{mn}(\mathbf{F}_p)$. In the streaming model, we cannot store any of these matrices and compute the matrix multiplication and do the equality test. Even if the entries of B and C were streamed for us to verify the matrix multiplication, we would need to stream each row of B n times and each column of C n times. We first introduce a probabilistic algorithm for verifying matrix multiplication and use it to verify matrix multiplication in the streaming model, where we just need to stream the entries of B and C only once.

Freivalds [17] introduced a simple randomized algorithm to verify matrix multiplication using $O(n^2)$ multiplications and addition, using n bits of randomness. But the verifier cannot store this n bits of randomness. Kimbrel and Sinha [21] improved Freivalds' algorithm so that we only need to use $O(\log n)$ random bits. We introduce their algorithm below and show how we can use it to verify if $A = BC$ in the streaming model, where we are only allowed to stream A, B and C only once.

ALGORITHM 1.

1. *Choose a random integer y uniformly between* 1 *and* n^2.

2. *Choose a prime q such that $n^2 \leq q \leq 2n^2$. Let* $r = \left(y^0 \pmod q),\ y^1 \pmod q), \cdots,\ y^{n-1} \pmod q) \right)^T$.

3. *if $Ar = BCr$, then accept. Otherwise reject.*

Algorithm 1 uses $O(\log n)$ random bits. It is known that over any integral domain, every Vandermonde matrix of n distinct non-zero elements is nonsingular.(See [24] for details.) If $A \neq BC$, then there are only $n-1$ vectors r(out of n^2 vectors) such that $Ar = BCr$. The algorithm can only err when $A \neq BC$, and this happens with with probability at most $1/n$.

We now outline a streaming algorithm in which the verifier verifies the claim $A = BC$ over the field $\mathbf{F}_p$, where $p \geq n^2$.[3] First, as $\mathcal{V}$ sees the stream, he computes the fingerprint of A by (1) using a finite field of a suitable size. After seeing the stream, $\mathcal{P}$ will convince $\mathcal{V}$ that $A = BC$ is true over $\mathbf{F}_p$. First, the verifier chooses a random integer x_r uniformly between 1 and n^2. $\mathcal{P}$ will send the entries of C first to $\mathcal{V}$ as follows: He first sends the first row of C to the verifier. As soon as $\mathcal{V}$ sees $c_{1,j}$, he computes $r_j \in \mathbf{F}_q$, as in Algorithm 1. Note that this can be done by just storing the integer x_r. He computes $c_{1,j}r_j$ and adds this to $\sum_{i<j} c_{1,i}r_i$, which he has computed previously. If we let $y = Cr$, after seeing the first row of C, the verifier would have computed y_1. He first updates the fingerprint of y before sending y_1 back to the prover. Now the prover sends the second row of C. $\mathcal{V}$ can compute y_2 as he can generate the random bits, r_j by himself. He then updates the fingerprint of y before sending back y_2 to $\mathcal{P}$. After seeing all the rows of C, the verifier should have computed the fingerprint of y, which he stores. Note that the prover is holding on to the string y.

Now, $\mathcal{V}$ will compute $z = By$. They proceed as follows. The prover sends the entries of B row by row together with y, i.e. $\langle b_{i,1}, y_1, b_{i,2}, y_2, \cdots, b_{i,m}, y_m \rangle$ for $i = 1, \cdots, m$. With this, $\mathcal{V}$ can compute z_i and only accepts if the fingerprint of y agrees with the one calculated previously. As before, he updates the fingerprint of z and discard each of the z_i after updating its fingerprint. He can discard the fingerprint of y once he has computed the fingerprint of z. Similarly, he can compute the fingerprint of w, where $w = Ar$. When A is being re-streamed, its fingerprint is computed and compared with the one calculated previously. This completes the phase of verifying matrix multiplication. The verifier accepts only if both the fingerprints of w and z agree.

[3] So that Step 1 of Algorithm 1 can be carried out. We need to modify the algorithm slightly if $p < n^2$. But still, we need $O(\log n)$ bits of randomness and it errs with probability at most $1/n$. See [21] for details.

6.2 Hermite Normal Form of an Integer Matrix

Given an integer matrix, we would like to obtain an canonical representation of the matrix so that we can calculate important properties of the matrix, like its rank and determinant easily. One standard technique in linear algebra is to transform the matrix into row echelon form using Gaussian elimination. But this involves divisions over $\mathbf{Z}$, and the resulting reduced row echelon matrix need not be an integer matrix. There is an analogous notion of Gaussian elimination, which is called the Hermite normal form.

DEFINITION 4. *Let $A \in \mathcal{M}_{mn}(\mathbf{Z})$ with r nonzero rows. A is said to be in row Hermite normal form if the following conditions are satisfied:*

1. *The first r rows of A are nonzero.*

2. *For $1 \leq i \leq r$, let A_{i,j_i} be the first nonzero entry in the i-th row of A. Then $j_1 < j_2 < \cdots < j_r$.*

3. *$A_{i,j_i} > 0$ for all $1 \leq i \leq r$.*

4. *If $1 \leq k < i \leq r$, then $0 \leq A_{k,j_i} < A_{i,j_i}$.*

The entries A_{i,j_i} will be called the corner entries of A. Every integer matrix can be reduced to its Hermite normal form via row operations. See [28] for details. More preciously, we have the following.

LEMMA 5. *Let $A \in \mathcal{M}_{mn}(\mathbf{Z})$. Then there exist a unique matrix $H \in \mathcal{M}_{mn}(\mathbf{Z})$ which in in row Hermite normal form and $U \in \mathcal{GL}_m(\mathbf{Z})$ such that $UA = H$.*

The matrix factorization in Lemma 5 is rank revealing. But the entries in H and U can be exponential in the size of the entries of A. For details of "entry explosion" in the computation of Hermite normal form, the reader is referred to [15] and the references therein. In our model, we may not be able to communicate the entries of H and U. Thus we consider reducing the matrix modulo d to its Hermite normal form.

For any integer matrix A, we let $\bar{A}$ be the result of reducing all its entries modulo d.

DEFINITION 5. *A is said to be in row Hermite form modulo d if the following conditions are satisfied:*

1. *$A = \bar{A}$.*

2. *A is in row Hermite normal form over* $\mathbf{Z}$.

3. *The corner entries of A divide d.*

Similar to Lemma 5, given any $A \in \mathcal{M}_{mn}(\mathbf{Z})$, there exist a unique matrix $H \in \mathcal{M}_{mn}(\mathbf{Z_d})$ which in in row Hermite normal form modulo d and $U \in \mathcal{GL}_m(\mathbf{Z_d})$ such that $UA = H \pmod d$. The number of nonzero rows of H is called the d-rank of A.

For $A \in \mathcal{M}_{mn}(\mathbf{F}_p)$ where $m \leq n$, by considering the Hermite normal form factorization over $\mathbf{F}_p$ and permutating the columns of H, if necessary, we have

$$AP = U \overbrace{\begin{pmatrix} I_r & D \\ O & O \end{pmatrix}}^{\tilde{H}}$$

where $rank(A) = r$ over $\mathbf{F}_p$ and $U \in \mathcal{GL}_m(\mathbf{F}_p)$ and P is a $n \times n$ permutation matrix. We call this the Hermite normal form(HNF) factorization of A in standard form and $\tilde{H}$ is said to be in standard HNF. We define $\mathcal{C}_A$ to be the row space of A. The rows of $G := \begin{pmatrix} I_r & D \end{pmatrix}$ is a basis for $\mathcal{C}_A$. It is known that

$$\mathcal{C}_A^{\perp} := \{y \in \mathbf{F}_p \mid <x,y>= 0 \ \forall\, x \in C_A\}$$

has dimension $n-r$ and the columns of $H := \begin{pmatrix} -D \\ I_{n-r} \end{pmatrix}$ is a basis for $\mathcal{C}_A^{\perp}$, the dual code of A. In the literature of coding theory [30], G and H^T are called the generator and parity check matrix of the code $\mathcal{C}_A$ respectively.

6.3 The Result

Given a square matrix $A \in \mathcal{M}_n(\mathbf{Z})$ which is streamed row-wise, where $|a_{ij}| \leq n$, we wish to determine if A has full rank over the reals. Without loss of generality, we can assume that A has no zero rows. In Section 7 we show a reduction from the INDEX function which implies that this problem is hard for streaming algorithms without a prover, i.e., such algorithms would need space $\Omega(n^2)$. The problem is in $\mathcal{NC}$, so by Fact 1 there is an efficient streaming algorithm with prover, but our algorithm is much simpler and not based on arithmetization techniques (and does not have an extra verification phase after the end of the stream. Our algorithm does not have polylogarithmic time overhead for the prover, but finding an algorithm with that much efficiency would imply a quasilinear time algorithm for the problem, which is a major open problem. The time spend by the prover is, however, well spread out over the duration of the stream, and his work consists mostly of computing various matrix factorizations.

THEOREM 6. *Given a square matrix $A \in \mathcal{M}_n(\mathbf{Z})$ which is streamed row-wise, where $|a_{ij}| \leq n$, there is a streaming algorithm which can decide if A has full rank over the reals where the verifier uses $O(\log n)$ storage and the total communication overhead is constant with probability of failure $O\left(\frac{\log n}{n}\right)$.*

Our general approach is to compute that rank over a random prime p instead over the reals, in order to avoid blowing up the size of matrix entries, an often encountered problem with computing e.g. the QR factorization.

The following argument shows that if we choose a random prime p from a set of primes that is polynomial in n, the p-rank of A will be the same as the rank of A over the reals with high probability.

Let B be any $r \times r$ square submatrix of A. By the Hadamard bound for determinant, we have $|\det(B)| \leq (\sqrt{r}\,n)^r$. Hence, the number of of distinct prime factors for $\det(B)$ is at most $r(\log r + \log n) \leq 2n \log n$. Let $b = 2s \ln s$, where $s = 2n^2 \log n$. It is known that $\pi(n) > n/\ln n$ for $n \geq 17$, where $\pi(n)$ is the prime counting function. Since $\pi(b) > s$, if we choose a prime p randomly between $[1, b]$,

$$\mathcal{P}\mathbf{r}\left[\det(B) \equiv 0 \pmod{p}\right] \leq \frac{2n \log n}{2n^2 \log n} = \frac{1}{n}.$$

If the rank of A is k, there exist $\tilde{A}$, a $k \times k$ submatrix of A with nonzero determinant, and all $(k+1) \times (k+1)$ submatrices of A have zero determinant. If we choose p randomly between $[1, b]$, the probability that $\det(\tilde{A}) \not\equiv 0 \pmod{p}$ is at least $1 - 1/n$ and all $(k+1) \times (k+1)$ submatrices of A have zero determinant. As a result, with probability at least $1 - 1/n$, the p-rank of A is exactly k.

We introduce some notations first which will help us analyze the protocol. We let a_i to be the i-th row of A, $A^{(i)} := \text{span}\{a_1, \cdots, a_i\}$ and $W^{(i)} := (A^{(i)})^{\perp}$.

6.4 Protocol

The verifier and prover choose a prime[4] p randomly before seeing the stream. We will assume that the p-rank of A is equal to the rank of A over the reals. Before the entries are being streamed, the verifier chooses a prime $n^3 < q < 2n^3$ and then chooses x uniformly at random from $\mathbf{F}_q$(and keeps it private from $\mathcal{P}$). In phase 1, the verifier computes $FP_q(x, A_1)$, the fingerprint of A_1, which is a submatrix of A consisting of the first $n/2$ rows of A.

Phase 2 starts when $a_{n/2+1,1}$ is streamed and ends when $a_{3n/4,n}$ is streamed. In this phase, the verifier computes the fingerprint of A_2, which is a submatrix of A consisting of the next $n/4$ rows. In this phase, $\mathcal{P}$ informs $\mathcal{V}$ if A_1 is full rank. If A_1 is full rank, $\mathcal{P}$ and $\mathcal{V}$ verify the matrix multiplication

$$A_1 P_1 = U_1 \begin{pmatrix} I_{n/2} & H_1 \end{pmatrix}, \qquad (2)$$

which is the HNF factorization of A_1 in standard form. For the matrix in standard HNF, $\mathcal{P}$ should only stream the entries of H_1 and for each row of P_1, the prover should stream j such that $p_{i,j} = 1$. $\mathcal{V}$ should compute the fingerprints of U_1, H_1 and P_1 as they are streamed during the verification of the matrix multiplication. $\mathcal{P}$ should also convince $\mathcal{V}$ that U_1 and P_1 are invertible by verifying the matrix multiplication $U_1 U_1^{-1} = I$ and $P_1 P_1^T = I$ in the streaming model. Also, define $W_1 = \begin{pmatrix} -H_1 \\ I_{n/2} \end{pmatrix}$, whose column space is $W^{(n/2)}$. Note that the verifier has the fingerprint of W_1. They proceed to phase 3 if all fingerprints agree and the verifier accepts all the matrix multiplication verifications if A_1 is full rank.

If A_1 is not full rank, $\mathcal{P}$ and $\mathcal{V}$ will verify the matrix multiplication $xA_1 = 0$, where $0 \neq x \in \mathbf{F}_p^{n/2}$. In this case, the protocol terminates and $\mathcal{V}$ accepts only if the matrix multiplication verification passes.

Also during phase 2, for each $1 \leq i \leq n/4$, $\mathcal{P}$ determines if $a_{n/2+i} \in A^{(n/2+i-1)}$. If there exist an index $1 \leq i \leq n/4$ such that $a_{n/2+i} \in A^{(n/2+i-1)}$, $\mathcal{P}$ will inform $\mathcal{V}$ to stop. In this case, there exist $d \in \mathbf{F}_p^{i-1}$ such that $x := a_{n/2+i} + \sum_{j=1}^{i-1} d_j\, a_{n/2+j} \in A^{(n/2)}$. In this case, $\mathcal{P}$ and $\mathcal{V}$ will verify the matrix multiplication

$$\begin{pmatrix} d_1 & \cdots & d_{i-1} & 1 \end{pmatrix} \begin{pmatrix} a_{n/2+1} \\ \vdots \\ a_{n/2+i-1} \\ a_{n/2+i} \end{pmatrix} = x. \qquad (3)$$

$\mathcal{V}$ will keep the fingerprint of x as they verify 3. Now, they will verify $xW_1 = 0$ and the protocol terminates with $\mathcal{V}$ convinced that A is not full rank.

[4]Such a prime can be represented by $O(\log n)$ bits.

Otherwise, we have $a_{n/2+i} \notin A^{(n/2+i-1)}$ for all $1 \le i \le n/4$. Then for each such i, there exist a $z_i \in W^{(n/2+i-1)}$ such that $< a_{n/2+i}, z_i > \neq 0$. The prover computes all such z_i for $i = 1, \cdots, n/4$.

Phase 3 starts when $a_{3n/4+1,1}$ is streamed and ends when $a_{7n/4,n}$ is streamed. $\mathcal{V}$ will compute the fingerprint of A_3, which is a submatrix of A consisting of the next $n/8$ rows. In this phase, $\mathcal{P}$ will convince $\mathcal{V}$ that the first $3n/4$ rows of A are linearly independent by verifying the following matrix multiplications:

SUBROUTINE 1.

[(i)]

1. $A_2 \left[\, z_1 \cdots z_{n/4} \, \right] = L_2$ *for some* $L_2 \in \mathcal{GL}_{n/4}(\mathbf{F}_p)$ *which is lower triangular.*

2. $W_1 C_1 = \left[\, z_1 \cdots z_{n/4} \, \right]$ *for some* $C_1 \in \mathcal{M}_{n/2,n/4}(\mathbf{F}_p)$.

3. $A_2 W_2 = 0$, *where* $W_2 = \begin{pmatrix} H_2 \\ I_{n/4} \end{pmatrix}$ *whose column space is* $W^{(3n/4)}$.

4. $W_1 C_2 = W_2$ *for some* $C_2 \in \mathcal{M}_{n/2,n/4}(\mathbf{F}_p)$.

All the four steps can be done in parallel with $\mathcal{V}$ keeping the fingerprints of $[\, z_1 \cdots z_{n/4} \,]$ and H_2 to ensure that the right matrices are streamed in the different messages. They proceed as such in $O(\log n)$ phases to determine if A is full rank.

6.5 Proof of Completeness and Soundness of Protocol

Firstly, if A_1 is full rank, the matrix factorization (2) witnesses this and if A_1 is not full rank, such a factorization does not exist. Now consider the case where $B = \begin{pmatrix} A_1 \\ A_2 \end{pmatrix}$ is full rank. If the prover is honest, he can construct $\{z_i\}_{i=1}^{n/4}$ such that the diagonal entries of L_2 is non-zero. For $i < j$, since $a_{n/2+i} \in A^{(n/2+j-1)}$, it follows that L_2 is lower triangular. Moreover, span$\{\, z_1 \cdots z_{n/4} \,\} \subseteq W^{(n/2)}$, which is established in part (ii) of Subroutine 1.

Now, we argue that if B is not full rank, $\mathcal{P}$ cannot satisfy both (i) and (ii) in Subroutine 1 simultaneously. Let $a_{n/2+i}$ be such that $a_{n/2+i} \in A^{(n/2+i-1)}$. By means of contradiction, suppose $\mathcal{P}$ can choose a $x \in \mathbf{F}_p^n$ such that $< a_{n/2+i}, x > \neq 0$. Such an x belongs to $W^{(n/2)}$ and has to satisfy $< a_{n/2+j}, x >= 0$ for all $j = 1, \cdots, i-1$. This means $x \in W^{(n/2+i-1)}$, which contradicts $< a_{n/2+i}, x > \neq 0$.

If we know that rank of B is $3n/4$, then any $n/4$ dimensional subspace $V \subseteq \mathbf{F}_p^n$ which satisfy the requirements that the inner product with any row of A_2 and any vector in V is zero and that $V \subseteq W^{(n/2)}$ must be the dual code of B. Thus W_2 is the correct representation of the dual code of B.

If B is not full rank, it is clear that the honest prover can convince the verifier of this fact. If B is full rank, then for any b which is a row of A_2, there exist vectors c and d such that $b = c\,A_1 + d\,A_2 + \theta$ for some $\theta \notin \mathcal{C}_{A_1}$. Thus if B is full rank and the prover cheats, they will end up verifying a matrix multiplication which is not equal.

Inductively, it is clear that in phase 4, by streaming A_3 and W_2, they can determine if the rows of $\{A_i\}_{i=1}^3$ are linearly independent and they can construct W_3, the dual code generated by the rows of $\{A_i\}_{i=1}^3$. We do not need to stream the rows of A_1 and A_2 in this phase.

In each phase, we are using a constant number of Freivalds' technique to verify matrix multiplications. The protocol will err if either Freivalds' technique errs or when $\mathcal{P}$ streams an incorrect matrix whose fingerprint is the same as the original matrix. By the union bound, the probability of failure is $O\left(\frac{\log n}{n}\right)$.

6.6 Analysis of Space and Communication

For the whole protocol, $\mathcal{V}$ needs to store p, q and x. In each phase, $\mathcal{V}$ needs to store a constant number of fingerprints and $O(\log n)$ space to keep track of the rows of the matrix being streamed and to generate the random bits needed for matrix multiplication verification. Hence $\mathcal{V}$ needs $O(\log n)$ space in this protocol.

As we proceed to the next phase in the protocol, the size of the submatrix of A that we re-stream gets halved, and the dimension of the dual code also gets halved. Hence, the communication overhead is a constant. Also, we note that as the last row of A is being streamed, the verifier will be checking the correctness of the 1-dimensional space, which is the dual space of the first $n-1$ rows of A. As he checks the correctness of this 1-dimensional subspace, say spanned by v, he should also compute the inner product of the last row of A with v. This ensures that our protocol is fully online.

6.7 One Application to Determine if a Matrix is Full Rank

Given a graph $G = (V, E)$, a matching $M \subseteq E$ is a subset of the edges such that no two edges share a common vertex. A perfect matching is a matching such that exactly one edge of the matching is incident on each vertex of the graph. The decision problem of deciding whether a given graph G contains a perfect matching or not is known to be in the complexity class $\mathcal{RNC}$ but it is still open whether it belongs to NC or not. Our rank protocol can be used to determine if a graph G with even vertices has a perfect matching or not in our model, where the rows of A_G, the adjacency matrix of G are being streamed. As a result of Tutte's Theorem [29], we can replace each non-zero entry of A_G by a random integer from $\{1, \cdots, n^2\}$ and determine if the matrix is full rank. If the matrix has full rank, we conclude that with high probability, the graph has a perfect matching. Note that the random integer has to be chosen by the verifier for this to work.

7. A LOWER BOUND ON THE NUMBER OF ROUNDS

The streaming algorithms with prover in [14, 13] are based on techniques from interactive proofs in complexity theory. They share the feature that after the stream has ended a short ($O(\log n)$ round) verification phase takes place between the prover and verifier, i.e., the computation is not fully online in that sense that the answer can be given right away at the end of the stream. More importantly, the prover has to work very hard during this phase, computing certain polynomials depending on the previously hidden random bits of the verifier. This computation takes at least linear time in n, and is hence exponentially longer than the communication taking place during that phase. Is this additional phase really necessary? In section 3 we have shown that for the Median problem both the additional verification phase can be removed and the prover's computation overhead reduced to polynomial, even without requiring the prover to communicate more than $poly(\log n)$ bits in total.

In this section we show that for any problem that is as hard as the INDEX function in a very strong sense defined below, there have to be at least $\Omega(\log n/\log\log n)$ rounds of interaction between the prover and verifier, otherwise either the communication complexity during that last phase increases to above $poly(\log n)$ or the space complexity of the verifier increases to above $poly(\log n)$. Hence the extra verification phase is an inherent feature of protocols solving such problems, e.g., computing frequency moments. This is true for both our model and previous models that bound total communication. Our proof also shows that for many other problems (such as computing the rank) at least $\Omega(\log n/\log\log n)$ rounds are needed, or the total communication must increase to above $poly(\log n)$.

We show these result by investigating the *online* Arthur-Merlin communication complexity of INDEX. In the online one-way model of communication complexity, studied for instance in [9, 1], Bob receives a proof from Merlin as well as one message sent by Alice, while Alice receives no message from the prover. [9, 1] show similar lower bounds to ours for the Merlin-Arthur complexity, namely that INDEX has one-way online MA-complexity $\Omega(\sqrt{n})$. This is (almost) tight thanks to a protocol by Aaronson and Wigderson [2]. These bounds, however, only apply to protocols in which the proofs are noninteractive, i.e., Merlin sends a single message to Bob (and receives no message from Alice).

Our lower bound holds for online Arthur-Merlin protocols, in which Alice is allowed to challenge Merlin with a public random "question". Furthermore Bob and Merlin may exchange messages over several rounds. For detailed definitions see Section 2.2. The lower bound on the number of rounds we will show is based on the collapse of the AM-hierarchy in the theory of interactive proofs, combined with a simple direct argument for one round online AM-protocols.

We start by defining what it means for a streaming problem to be as hard as another streaming problem. Let P be a streaming problem, where we assume that inputs are streams of length n, where each symbol is from the same universe U_P. Similarly, denote by Q another streaming problem with input length m and universe U_Q.

DEFINITION 6. *We say that P strictly reduces to Q if there are functions $f_1, \ldots, f_n$ that map U_P to U_Q, $m = n$, and the output of Q on $f_1(x_1), \ldots, f_n(x_n)$ is the same as the output of P on $x_1, \ldots, x_n$.*

P weakly reduces to Q, if there are functions $f_1, \ldots, f_n$ that map U_P to $U_Q^{l_i}$, $\sum l_i = m$, and the output of Q on $f_1(x_1), \ldots, f_n(x_n)$ is the same as the output of P on $x_1, \ldots$ $\ldots x_n$.

Hence in a weak reduction one may inflate a single symbol into many. We give a few examples.

The function we reduce from is the INDEX function. In the communication complexity version of INDEX Alice receives an n-bit string x, and Bob an index i, and their task is to compute x_i. Note that Merlin sees x, i but he cannot talk to Alice in the online model. We also consider INDEX as a streaming problem, in which the first n elements on the stream are the bits of x, followed by i (which counts as one data symbol).

The infinity frequency moment F_∞ of a data stream consisting of elements from a universe U is the number of times the most frequent element appears on the stream.

1. There is a strict reduction from INDEX to $2-\epsilon$-approximating F_∞: map inputs x_j to $2j + x_j$ and then maps the index i to $2i + 1$. Clearly if INDEX$(x, i) = 1$ then F_∞ will be 2 for the image stream, else it will be 1.

2. There is a weak reduction from INDEX to Median: map all x_j to $2j+x_j$ and map i to $n-2i$ times the number 0 if $i \leq n/2$. Otherwise, if $i > n/2$, map i to $2i-n$ times the number $2n+2$. Our algorithm for Median implies that there can be no strict reduction from INDEX to Median.

3. Next we show that the problem of deciding whether the rank of a matrix has full rank or not has a weak reduction from INDEX. Consider INDEX, where $x \in \{0,1\}^{\frac{n^2}{4}}$ and $i \in \left[\frac{n^2}{4}\right]$. Define $X \in \mathcal{M}_{n/2}(\mathbf{R})$ whose entries are as follows: $X(r,c) = x_{\frac{n}{2}(r-1)+c}$ for $1 \leq r, c \leq n/2$. Suppose $x_i = X(s,t)$ for some $1 \leq s, t \leq n/2$. Also define $\tilde{Z} \in \mathcal{M}_{n/2}(\mathbf{R})$ such that $\tilde{Z}(t,s) = 1$ and all other entries of $\tilde{Z}$ are zero. Consider the following matrix
$$A = \begin{pmatrix} I_{n/2} & X \\ \tilde{Z} & I_{n/2} \end{pmatrix}.$$
It is easy to see that if $x_i = 1$, then rank(A) $= n - 1$. Otherwise, if $x_i = 0$, then A is full rank. Hence any streaming algorithm that decides if $A \in \mathcal{M}_n(\mathbf{R})$ is full rank or not (where the entries of A are streamed row-wise) also decides INDEX on $\Theta(n^2)$ input bits and we get a weak reduction from that problem.

We have the following obvious application of our reductions.

LEMMA 6. *1. If Problem P can be strictly reduced to problem Q and if every streaming algorithm with prover for P needs either more than $poly(\log n)$ space, or more than $t(n)$ rounds of communication between prover and verifier after the last symbol has been read, or more than $poly(\log n)$ communication after the last symbol has been read, then the same is true for Q.*

2. If P can be weakly reduced to Q and if every streaming algorithm with prover for P needs either more than $poly(\log n)$ space, or more than $t(n)$ rounds of communication between prover and verifier, or more than $poly(\log n)$ total communication, then so does Q.

Our main result in this section is that INDEX indeed needs either more than polylogarithmic space for the verifier, or at least $\Omega(\log n/\log\log n)$ rounds between prover and verifier after the last symbol has appeared on the stream, or more than polylogarithmic communication after i has appeared on the stream. Since the first and third possibilities are not allowed in our model we can conclude that there has to be a lot of interaction between prover and verifier in a special verification phase.

For any problem P, given a strict reduction from INDEX on size n strings, if we insist on $poly(\log n)$ communication overhead and space, this means that prover and verifier need a verification phase of $\Omega(\log n/ \log\log n)$ rounds after the end of the stream.

A weak reduction from INDEX suffices to show that for the models that bound total communication many rounds are needed, but those could potentially take place during the time the stream is observed, as can be seen in the algorithm in Section 3 for Median that has small total communication. Weak reductions do not imply anything for the model defined in this paper though, because we do not restrict the total communication.

We now turn to showing that INDEX is indeed a difficult problem. First let us consider the issue of public versus private coin randomness. A streaming algorithm with prover has a public coin, if all randomness used is from some source that is also accessible to the prover. I.e., when the verifier draws a random bit, this bit becomes known to the prover, but the prover cannot predict future random bits. This is opposed to a private coin algorithms, in which the verifier can hide random choices from the prover. Although all our algorithms are private coin, a general result from the theory of interactive proofs allows to convert every algorithm with private coin to a public coin algorithm, while increasing the space complexity and communication only polynomially, and increasing the number of rounds by only 2. For details on this standard construction see Chapter 8.2 in [5].

Once we have switched to a streaming algorithm with public coin randomness only, simulate the streaming algorithm by an online communication protocol. The general plan is as follows. A streaming algorithm with prover for INDEX can be simulated by a communication protocol in a pretty straightforward way. Here Alice receives x, Bob receives i, and there are two provers, MerlinA and MerlinB. MerlinA only sees x, and can only talk to Alice. MerlinB sees x, i, and will communicate with Bob. Alice and MerlinA simulate the streaming algorithm during x, and Bob and MerlinB take over afterwards. The protocol is one-way, i.e., Alice sends one message to Bob. It becomes clear immediately, that MerlinA is useless and can be removed, because he does not see anything that Alice doesn't see. Note that is does not matter how much the streaming verifier and prover communicate during x. Hence we arrive at a model where Alice sends one message to Bob, and one message to Merlin(B), then Merlin and Bob exchange messages. To simplify things further, we turn the original streaming algorithm into a public coin algorithm. This means that Alice's message to Merlin is unnecessary, and can be replaced by a public coin. Hence we will study the online Arthur Merlin communication complexity of INDEX.

At this point we can use a result by Babai and Moran [6] showing that a constant number of rounds of interaction between prover and verifier can be reduced to one round (i.e., that the AM hierarchy collapses). We need the following, more detailed statement for online AM protocols, which holds for all functions f.

LEMMA 7. *1.* $AM_k^o(f) \geq \Omega(\widetilde{AM}_1^o(f))^{1/(k+1)}$.

2. $MA_k^o(f) \geq \Omega(\widetilde{AM}_1^o(f))^{1/(k+1)}$.

LEMMA 8. $\widetilde{AM}_1^o(f) \geq \Omega(R^{A\to B}(f))$.

Due to the fact that $R^{A\to B}(\text{INDEX}) = \Omega(n)$ [22, 26] we get the following.

COROLLARY 1. $AM_k^o(\text{INDEX}) \geq \Omega(n^{1/(k+1)})$.
Every online k-round Arthur Merlin protocol for INDEX *with communication* polylog n *satisfies* $k \geq \Omega(\log n/ \log\log n)$.

Note that the online AM protocol for INDEX by Aaronson and Wigderson [2] can be modified to have $O(\text{polylog}\, n)$ communication and $O(\log n/ \log\log n)$ rounds, so this is strictly optimal.

We now state the main consequence for streaming algorithms.

THEOREM 7. *1. Any data streaming algorithm with prover for a problem that has a strict reduction from* INDEX *either has to use more than polylogarithmic communication overhead, or the verifier space is more than polylogarithmic, or there are at least* $\Omega(\log n/ \log\log n)$ *communication rounds between prover and verifier after the end of the stream.*

2. If a problem has a weak reduction from INDEX*, then either more than polylogarithmic total communication is needed, or the verifier space is more than polylogarithmic, or there are at least* $\Omega(\log n/ \log\log n)$ *communication rounds between prover and verifier.*

As an example let us consider the problem of approximating F_∞. We show now that the problem F_∞ can be 2-approximated, with $poly(\log n)$ total communication, verifier space, and fully online. To do so, we use the protocol from Fact 1. Assume the communication in that protocol is $O(\log^c n)$ for some constant c. We split the inputs $x_1, \ldots, x_n$ into a chunk of A of the first $n - \log^c n$ of the x_i, and the remaining x_i which go into B. During the streaming of B the communication of the protocol from Fact 1 takes place, in order to determine the most frequent element of A. Furthermore, the verifier can simply sort B in order to determine the most frequent element there. Finally, the verifier takes whichever element is more frequent, the one from A or the one from B, and outputs its frequency. Clearly, this number is a lower bound on F_∞, and never smaller than 1/2 times F_∞. So we get a 2-approximation. Note that this solution still requires a large computation overhead for the prover.

On the other hand, a $(2-\epsilon)$-approximation is not possible without an extra verification phase due to the above theorem, while by the results in [14] F_∞ can be computed exactly with such a phase, since it lies in $\mathcal{NC}$. Hence a 2-approximation can be computed without the extra verification phase (and hence fully online), but no better approximation, while exact computation is possible with such an extra verification phase.

PROOF PROOF OF LEMMA 7. Assume we are given an online AM-protocol with k rounds between Bob and Merlin. We will remove one round after another until we get a 1-round protocol, i.e., a protocol in which Alice, Merlin, Bob share a public coin r, Alice sends one message to Bob, Merlin sends one message to Bob, such that if $x_i = 1$ then with probability $1-\epsilon$ (over r) there is a message from Merlin that makes Bob accept, while if $x_i = 0$ then with probability $1-\epsilon$ no matter what Merlin sends, Bob will reject.

For a fixed input x, y let a denote the length of the message sent by Alice, and $m_1, \ldots, m_k$ the lengths of the messages M_i sent by Merlin. r is the coin used by Alice, and $r_1, \ldots, r_k$

the random strings used by Bob (all those are public, but r is generated in the beginning, and r_i after M_i has been sent. Then $a+m_1+\ldots+m_k \le c = AM_k^o(\textsc{Index})$ (where c is the complexity of the protocol).

We first wish to reduce the error to $1/2^{2m_k}$. This can be done by performing the whole protocol $O(m_k)$ times in parallel, i.e., Alice will send her message $O(m_k)$ times for different random strings, Merlin will send his first message several times (each time depending on the random strings chosen by Alice) etc. Note that parallel repetition is not an issue here. This increases the total communication to $O(m_k c)$.

Now consider the time after M_k has been sent. We change the protocol such that Bob sends r_k before M_k. Since $|M_k| = m_k$ by the union bound the probability that there is a message M_k for Merlin that makes Bob accept wrongly is at most 2^{-m_k}, even though Merlin knows Bob's last random string now.

Next we reduce the error to $1/2^{2m_{k-1}}$, again by parallel repetition, increasing the communication to $O(m_{k-1}m_k c)$. Again we can push Bob's last random choice one step ahead etc.

After k such steps we end up with a protocol as claimed, having communication $O(m_1 m_2 \cdots m_k c) = O(c^{k+1})$. □

Proof Proof of Lemma 8. We need to show $\widetilde{AM}_1^o(f) = \Omega(c)$, where c is the one-way randomized complexity of f. So consider a protocol, in which Alice, Bob, Merlin share a public coin, then Alice sends a message to Bob, and Merlin sends a message to Bob, who then decides. According to the Yao principle, for any probability distribution μ on the inputs we can fix the public coin, and find a protocol, in which Alice sends a message , Merlin sends a message to Bob, and Bob decides, and we allow error 1/3 under the given distribution.

Now, intuitively, Merlin has nothing of interest to say to Bob: since Bob can get no further information from Alice that is unknown to Merlin, there is nothing to check Merlin's claim against. We make this formal now.

Alice's messages partition the set of rows of the communication matrix (note that Alice acts deterministically). Bob knows the set of rows M that contains x, and he knows the column. Merlin tries to convince Bob that $x_i = 1$, and his message determines a subset M' of M (on which he sends that message). There is no way for Bob to check whether $x \in M'$, so he cannot trust Merlin's message.

Formally, we transform the given protocol in the following way. Given M, i Bob determines the probability of the set of $\{x', i : x' \in M \text{ and } x'_i = 1\}$ under μ conditioned on column i. If this is at least $1/2 \cdot \mu(M)$ he accepts, otherwise he rejects. He ignores Merlin's message. We claim that this protocol does at least as well as the original one. If that claim is true we can simply eliminate Merlin from the protocol.

Suppose there is a message m from Merlin, such that given M, i, m Bob will accept. In that case Merlin can simply always send m on inputs x', i with $x' \in M$, causing Bob to accept all such inputs. If the probability of 1-inputs conditioned on i is at least $1/2 \cdot \mu(M)$, then Bob will accept all x', i with $x' \in M$ and both protocols behave exactly the same. If on the other hand the probability is less than $\mu(M)/2$, then the modified protocol has less error than the original one.

So Bob never increases the error by simply ignoring Merlin, and we can turn our protocol into a deterministic one-way protocol with small error under μ. Appealing to the hard direction of the Yao principle we can find a randomized one-way protocol for f with at most the same communication and error as the protocol we started from.

□

8. CONCLUSIONS

In this paper we have proposed a new model of verifiable streaming computations, inspired by the cloud computing paradigm. Data streaming problems that are hard to solve for a streaming algorithm with small workspace might be solved by outsourcing computations to a more powerful party, the helper/prover, who must also process the stream online, but has no space restrictions. However, the results communicated by the prover should be verifiable by the streaming algorithm, within the usual restrictions of the model. Deviating from previous work we have proposed to not bound the total communication between prover and verifier, but only the communication overhead, i.e., the factor by which communication from prover to verifier is allowed to be larger than the size of the data elements on the stream (that can be thought of as being uploaded by the verifier to the prover). Since usually uploading is slower than downloading, this seems justifiable.

While previously efficient streaming algorithms with prover were known for all problems in $\mathcal{NC}$ (via a generic algorithm) we describe algorithms for Median, LIS, and deciding if the rank of a matrix is full, that are simple and would be easy to implement. Our algorithms do not require arithmetization techniques that lead to difficult computations for the prover, in particular in the final verification phase taking place after the end of the stream in the generic algorithm for all of $\mathcal{NC}$.

We have also addressed the problem of the necessity of the additional verification phase and have shown that this phase is unavoidable for problems that allow strict reductions from Index, e.g. computing frequency moments.

9. REFERENCES

[1] S. Aaronson. Qma/qpoly⊆ pspace/poly: De-merlinizing quantum protocols. In *IEEE Conference on Computational Complexity*, pages 261–273, 2006.

[2] S. Aaronson and A. Wigderson. Algebrization: A new barrier in complexity theory. *ACM Transactions on Computation Theory*, 1(1), 2009.

[3] D. Aldous and P. Diaconis. Longest increasing subsequences: From patience sorting to the baik-deift johansson theorem. *Bulleting of the American Mathematical Society*, 36:413–432, 1999.

[4] N. Alon, Y. Matias, and M. Szegedy. The space complexity of approximating the frequency moments. *Journal of Computer and System Sciences*, 58(1):137–147, 1999. Earlier version in STOC'96.

[5] S. Arora and B. Barak. *Complexity Theory: A Modern Approach*. Cambridge University Press, 2009.

[6] L. Babai and S. Moran. Arthur-merlin games: A randomized proof system, and a hierarchy of complexity classes. *J. Comput. Syst. Sci.*, 36(2):254–276, 1988.

[7] R. Canetti, B. Riva, and G. N. Rothblum. Practical delegation of computation using multiple servers. In *Proceedings of the 18th ACM conference on Computer*

and communications security, CCS '11, pages 445–454, New York, NY, USA, 2011. ACM.

[8] A. Chakrabarti. A note on randomized streaming space bounds for the longest increasing subsequence problem. *Information Processing Letters*, 112(7):261–263, 2012.

[9] A. Chakrabarti, G. Cormode, and A. Mcgregor. Annotations in data streams. In *Proceedings of the 36th International Colloquium on Automata, Languages and Programming: Part I*, ICALP '09, pages 222–234, Berlin, Heidelberg, 2009. Springer-Verlag.

[10] A. Chakrabarti, S. Khot, and X. Sun. Near-optimal lower bounds on the multi-party communication complexity of set disjointness. In *IEEE Conference on Computational Complexity*, 2003.

[11] K. L. Clarkson and D. P. Woodruff. Numerical linear algebra in the streaming model. In *Proceedings of the 41st annual ACM symposium on Theory of computing*, STOC '09, pages 205–214, New York, NY, USA, 2009. ACM.

[12] G. Cormode, M. Mitzenmacher, and J. Thaler. Streaming graph computations with a helpful advisor. In *Proceedings of the 18th annual European conference on Algorithms: Part I*, ESA'10, pages 231–242, Berlin, Heidelberg, 2010. Springer-Verlag.

[13] G. Cormode, M. Mitzenmacher, and J. Thaler. Practical verified computation with streaming interactive proofs. In *Proceedings of the 3rd Innovations in Theoretical Computer Science Conference*, ITCS '12, pages 90–112, New York, NY, USA, 2012. ACM.

[14] G. Cormode, J. Thaler, and K. Yi. Verifying computations with streaming interactive proofs. *Proc. VLDB Endow.*, 5(1):25–36, 2011.

[15] P. D. Domich, R. Kannan, and L. E. Trotter, Jr. Hermite normal form computation using modulo determinant arithmetic. *Math. Oper. Res.*, 12(1):50–59, Feb. 1987.

[16] F. Ergün and H. Jowhari. On distance to monotonicity and longest increasing subsequence of a data stream. In *SODA*, pages 730–736, 2008.

[17] R. Freivalds. Probabilistic machines can use less running time. In *IFIP Congress*, pages 839–842, 1977.

[18] A. Gal and P. Gopalan. Lower bounds on streaming algorithms for approximating the length of the longest increasing subsequence. In *FOCS*, pages 297–304, 2007.

[19] S. Goldwasser, Y. T. Kalai, and G. N. Rothblum. Delegating computation: interactive proofs for muggles. In *Proceedings of the 40th annual ACM symposium on Theory of computing*, STOC '08, pages 113–122, New York, NY, USA, 2008. ACM.

[20] P. Gopalan, T. Jayram, R. Krauthgamer, and R. Kumar. Estimating the sortedness of a data stream. In *SODA*, pages 318–327, 2007.

[21] T. Kimbrel and R. K. Sinha. A probabilistic algorithm for verifying matrix products using $o(n^2)$ time and $\log_2 n + o(1)$ random bits. *Inf. Process. Lett.*, 45(2):107–110, Feb. 1993.

[22] I. Kremer, N. Nisan, and D. Ron. On randomized one-round communication complexity. *Computational Complexity*, 8(1):21–49, 1999. Earlier version in STOC'95. Correction at `http://www.eng.tau.ac.il/~danar/Public/KNR-fix.ps`.

[23] E. Kushilevitz and N. Nisan. *Communication Complexity*. Cambridge University Press, 11 2006.

[24] S. Lang. *Algebra (3. ed.)*. Addison-Wesley, 1993.

[25] S. Muthukrishnan. Data streams: Algorithms and applications. *Foundations and Trends in Theoretical Computer Science*, 1(2), 2005.

[26] A. Nayak. Optimal lower bounds for quantum automata and random access codes. In *Proceedings of 40th IEEE FOCS*, pages 369–376, 1999. quant-ph/9904093.

[27] A. Shen. **IP = PSPACE**: Simplified proof. *J. ACM*, 39(4):878–880, Oct. 1992.

[28] C. C. Sims. *Computation with Finitely Presented Groups (Encyclopedia of Mathematics and its Applications)*. Cambridge University Press, 2010.

[29] W. T. Tutte. The factorization of linear graphs. *J. Lond. Math. Soc.*, 22:107–110, 1947.

[30] J. van Lint. *Introduction to Coding Theory (Graduate Texts in Mathematics)*. Springer, 3rd rev. and exp. ed. edition, 12 1998.

A Classical Leash for a Quantum System: Command of Quantum Systems via Rigidity of CHSH Games*

Ben W. Reichardt
University of Southern California

Falk Unger
Knight Capital Group

Umesh Vazirani
UC Berkeley

ABSTRACT

Can a classical experimentalist command an untrusted quantum system to realize arbitrary quantum dynamics, aborting if it misbehaves? If so, then we could realize the dream of device-independent quantum cryptography: using untrusted quantum devices to establish a shared random key, with security based on the correctness of quantum mechanics. It would also allow for testing whether a claimed quantum computer is truly quantum.

We prove a rigidity theorem for the famous Clauser-Horne-Shimony-Holt (CHSH) game, first formulated to provide a means of experimentally testing the violation of the Bell inequalities. The theorem shows that the only way for the two non-communicating quantum players to win many games played in sequence is if their shared quantum state is close to the tensor product of EPR states (Bell states) and their measurements are the optimal CHSH measurements on successive qubits. This theorem may be viewed as analogous to classical multi-linearity testing, in the sense that the outcome of local checks gives a characterization of a global object.

The rigidity theorem provides the basis of a technique by which a classical system can certify the joint, entangled state of a bipartite quantum system, as well as command the application of specific operators on each subsystem. This leads directly to a scheme for device-independent quantum key distribution. Control over the state and operators can also be leveraged to create more elaborate protocols for realizing general quantum circuits. In particular, it allows us to establish that a quantum interactive proof system with a classical verifier is as powerful as one with a quantum verifier, or $\mathsf{QMIP} = \mathsf{MIP}^*$.

Categories and Subject Descriptors

F.1 [**Computation by Abstract Devices**]: Miscellaneous

General Terms

Theory

Keywords

CHSH game; quantum computing; device independence; quantum key distribution; property testing; multi-prover interactive proof systems

1. REFERENCES

[1] Ben W. Reichardt, Falk Unger, and Umesh Vazirani. Classical command of quantum systems via rigidity of CHSH games. 2012, `arXiv:1209.0449 [quant-ph]`.

[2] Ben W. Reichardt, Falk Unger, and Umesh Vazirani. A classical leash for a quantum system: Command of quantum systems via rigidity of CHSH games. 2012, `arXiv:1209.0448 [quant-ph]`.

*An extended abstract for this paper, including proof sketches, is available at [1]. A full version of this paper, including all proofs, is available at [2].

ITCS'13, January 9–12, 2013, Berkeley, California, USA.
ACM 978-1-4503-1859-4/13/01.

Adversary Lower Bound for the k-sum Problem

Aleksandrs Belovs
University of Latvia
19 Raina Boulevard
Riga, Latvia
stiboh@gmail.com

Robert Špalek
Google Inc.
1600 Amphitheatre Parkway
Mountain View, CA, USA
rspalek@gmail.com

ABSTRACT

We prove a tight quantum query lower bound $\Omega(n^{k/(k+1)})$ for the problem of deciding whether there exist k numbers among n that sum up to a prescribed number, provided that the alphabet size is sufficiently large.

Categories and Subject Descriptors

F.2.2 [**Analysis of Algorithms and Problem Complexity**]: Nonnumerical Algorithms and Problems—*Computations on discrete structures*; H.2.4 [**Database Management**]: Systems—*Query processing*

General Terms

Algorithms

Keywords

Quantum query complexity, Knapsack packing problem, Orthogonal arrays

1. INTRODUCTION

Two main techniques for proving lower bounds on quantum query complexity are the polynomial method [6] developed by Beals *et al.* in 1998, and the adversary method [2] developed by Ambainis in 2000. Both techniques are incomparable. There are functions with adversary bound strictly larger than polynomial degree [3], as well as functions with the reverse relation.

One of the examples of the reverse relation is exhibited by the element distinctness function. The input to the function is a string of length n of symbols in an alphabet of size q, i.e., $x = (x_i) \in [q]^n$. We use notation $[q]$ to denote the set $\{1, \dots, q\}$. The element distinctness function evaluates to 0 if all symbols in the input string are pairwise distinct, and to 1 otherwise.

The quantum query complexity of element distinctness is $O(n^{2/3})$ with the algorithm given by Ambainis [5]. The tight lower bounds were given by Aaronson and Shi [1], Kutin [14] and Ambainis [4] using the polynomial method.

The adversary bound, however, fails for this function. The reason is that the function has 1-certificate complexity 2, and the so-called certificate complexity barrier [17, 18] implies that for any function with 1-certificate complexity bounded by a constant, the adversary method fails to achieve anything better than $\Omega(\sqrt{n})$.

In 2006 a stronger version of the adversary bound was developed by Høyer *et al.* [12]. This is the negative-weight adversary lower bound defined in Section 2. Later it was proved to be optimal by Reichardt *et al.* [16, 15]. Although the negative-weight adversary lower bound is known to be tight, it has almost never been used to prove lower bounds for explicit functions. The vast majority of lower bounds by the adversary method used the old nonnegative-weight version of this method. But since the polynomial method is known to be non-tight, a better understanding of the negative-weight adversary method would be very beneficial. In the sequel, we consider the negative-weight adversary bound only, and we will omit the adjective "negative-weight".

In this paper we use the adversary method to prove a lower bound for the following variant of the knapsack packing problem. Let $\mathbb{G}$ be a finite Abelian group, and $t \in \mathbb{G}$ be its arbitrary element. For a positive integer k, the *k-sum problem* consists in deciding whether the input string $x_1, \dots, x_n \in \mathbb{G}$ contains a subset of k elements that sums up to t. We assume that k is an arbitrary but fixed constant. The main result of the paper is the following

THEOREM 1. *For a fixed k, the quantum query complexity of the k-sum problem is* $\Omega(n^{k/(k+1)})$ *provided that* $|\mathbb{G}| \geq n^k$.

Clearly, the 1-certificate complexity of the k-sum problem is k, hence, it is also subject to the certificate complexity barrier that, for a variable k, states the nonnegative-weight adversary cannot prove a better lower bound than $\Omega(\sqrt{kn})$.

The result of Theorem 1 is tight thanks to the quantum algorithm based on quantum walks on the Johnson graph [5]. This algorithm was first designed to solve the k-distinctness problem. This problem asks for detecting whether the input string $x \in [q]^n$ contains k elements that are all equal. Soon enough it was realized that the same algorithm works for any function with 1-certificate complexity k [11], in particular, for the k-sum problem. The question of the tightness of this algorithm remained open for a long time. It was known to be tight for $k = 2$ due to the lower bound for the element distinctness problem. Now we know that it is not optimal for the k-distinctness problem if $k > 2$ [8]. However, Theorem 1 shows that, for every k, quantum walk on the Johnson graph

ITCS'13, January 9–12, 2012, Berkeley, California, USA.

is optimal for some functions with 1-certificate complexity k. Finally, we note that the k-sum problem is also interesting because of its applications in quantum Merkle puzzles [9, 13].

Actually, we get Theorem 1 as a special case of a more general result we are about to describe. The following is a special case of a well-studied combinatorial object:

Definition 1. Assume T is a subset of $[q]^k$ of size q^{k-1}. We say that T is an *orthogonal array of length* k iff, for every index $i \in [k]$ and for every vector $x_1, \dots, x_{i-1}, x_{i+1}, \dots, x_k \in [q]$, there exists exactly one $x_i \in [q]$ such that $(x_1, \dots, x_k) \in T$.

For $x = (x_i) \in [q]^n$ and $S \subseteq [n]$ let x_S denote the projection of x on S, i.e., the vector $(x_{s_1}, \dots, x_{s_\ell})$ where $s_1, \dots, s_\ell$ are the elements of S in the increasing order.

Assume each subset S of $[n]$ of size k is equipped with an orthogonal array T_S. The k-*orthogonal array* problem consists in finding an element of any of the orthogonal arrays in the input string. More precisely, the input $x \in [q]^n$ evaluates to 1 iff there exists $S \subseteq [n]$ of size k such that $x_S \in T_S$.

Consider the following two examples:

Example 1. Let $\mathbb{G}$ be a commutative group with q elements and $t \in \mathbb{G}$. $T = \{x \in \mathbb{G}^k : \sum_{i=1}^k x_i = t\}$ is an orthogonal array of length k. This choice corresponds to the k-sum problem of Theorem 1.

Example 2. $T = \{x \in [q]^2 : x_1 = x_2\}$ is an orthogonal array of length 2. This corresponds to the element distinctness problem from [7].

THEOREM 2. *For a fixed k and any choice of the orthogonal arrays T_S, the quantum query complexity of the k-orthogonal array problem is $\Omega(n^{k/(k+1)})$ provided that $q \geq n^k$. The constant behind big-Omega depends on k, but not on n, q, or the choice of T_S.*

The orthogonal array condition specifies that even if an algorithm has queried $k-1$ elements out of any k-tuple, it has the same information whether this k-tuple is a 1-certificate as if it has queried no elements out of it. Because of this, the search for a k-tuple as a whole entity is the best the quantum algorithm can do. Our proof of Theorem 2 is a formalization of this intuition.

Let us elaborate on the requirement on the size of the alphabet. It is easy to see that some requirement is necessary. Indeed, the k-sum problem can be solved in $O(\sqrt{n})$ queries if the size of $\mathbb{G}$ is $O(1)$, using the Grover search to find up to k copies of every element of $\mathbb{G}$ in the input string, and trying to construct t out of what is found. In some cases, e.g., when t is the identity element and k equals the order of the group, the problem becomes trivial if n is large enough.

The requirement on the size of the alphabet for the element distinctness problem is a subtle issue. The lower bounds by Aaronson and Shi [1] and Kutin [14] require the size of the alphabet to be at least $\Omega(n^2)$ that is the same that gives Theorem 2. However, later Ambainis [4] showed that the lower bound remains the same even if one allows the alphabet of size n. Reducing the alphabet size in Theorem 2 is one of our open problems.

2. ADVERSARY LOWER BOUND

In the paper we are interested in the quantum query complexity of solving the orthogonal array problem. For the definitions and main properties of quantum query complexity refer to, e.g., Ref. [10]. For the purposes of our paper, it suffices to work with the definition of the adversary bound we give in this section.

Compared to the original formulation of the negative-weighted adversary bound [12], our formulation has two differences. Firstly, in order to simplify notations we call an adversary matrix a matrix with rows labelled by positive inputs, and the columns—by the negative ones. It is a quarter of the original adversary matrix that completely specifies the latter. Secondly, due to technical reasons, we allow several rows to be labelled by the same positive input. All this is captured by the following definition and theorem.

Definition 2. Let f be a function $f\colon \mathcal{D} \to \{0,1\}$ with domain $\mathcal{D} \subseteq [q]^n$. Let $\widetilde{\mathcal{D}}$ be a set of pairs (x, a) with the property that the first element of each pair belongs to $\mathcal{D}$, and $\widetilde{\mathcal{D}}_i = \{(x,a) \in \widetilde{\mathcal{D}} : f(x) = i\}$ for $i \in \{0,1\}$. An *adversary matrix* for the function f is a non-zero real $\widetilde{\mathcal{D}}_1 \times \widetilde{\mathcal{D}}_0$ matrix Γ. And, for $i \in [n]$, let Δ_i denote the $\widetilde{\mathcal{D}}_1 \times \widetilde{\mathcal{D}}_0$ matrix defined by

$$\Delta_i[\![(x,a),(y,b)]\!] = \begin{cases} 0, & x_i = y_i; \\ 1, & \text{otherwise.} \end{cases}$$

THEOREM 3 (ADVERSARY BOUND). *In the notations of Definition 2, $Q_2(f) = \Omega(\mathrm{Adv}^{\pm}(f))$, where*

$$\mathrm{Adv}^{\pm}(f) = \sup_{\Gamma} \frac{\|\Gamma\|}{\max_{i \in n} \|\Gamma \circ \Delta_i\|} \tag{1}$$

with the maximization over all adversary matrices for f, $\|\cdot\|$ is the spectral norm, and $Q_2(f)$ is the quantum query complexity of f.

PROOF. In the original negative-weight adversary bound paper [12], Eq. (1) is proven when Γ is a real symmetric $\mathcal{D}\times\mathcal{D}$ matrix with the property $\Gamma[\![x,y]\!] = 0$ if $f(x) = f(y)$, and Δ_i are modified accordingly. We describe a reduction from the adversary matrix in our definition, Γ, to the adversary matrix Γ' in the definition of [12]. Also, let Δ'_i be the $\mathcal{D}\times\mathcal{D}$ matrix with $\Delta'_i[\![x,y]\!] = 1$ if $x_i \neq y_i$, and 0, otherwise.

At first, define $\overline{\Gamma}$ as

$$\overline{\Gamma} = \begin{pmatrix} 0 & \Gamma^* \\ \Gamma & 0 \end{pmatrix} .$$

Note that $\|\overline{\Gamma}\| = \|\Gamma\|$, and the spectrum of $\overline{\Gamma}$ is symmetric. Also, for all i, $\|\overline{\Gamma} \circ \overline{\Delta}_i\| = \|\Gamma \circ \Delta_i\|$, where $\overline{\Delta}_i$ is defined similarly to $\overline{\Gamma}$.

Let $\delta = (\delta_{x,a})$ be the normalized eigenvalue $\|\Gamma\|$ eigenvector of $\overline{\Gamma}$. For all $x, y \in \mathcal{D}$, let:

$$\delta'_x = \sqrt{\sum_{a:(x,a)\in\widetilde{\mathcal{D}}} \delta_{x,a}^2}$$

and

$$\Gamma'[\![x,y]\!] = \frac{1}{\delta'_x \delta'_y} \sum_{\substack{a:(x,a)\in\widetilde{\mathcal{D}} \\ b:(y,b)\in\widetilde{\mathcal{D}}}} \delta_{x,a}\delta_{y,b}\overline{\Gamma}[\![(x,a),(y,b)]\!].$$

Then it is easy to see that $\delta' = (\delta'_x)$ satisfies $\|\delta'\| = 1$ and $(\delta')^*\Gamma'\delta' = \delta^*\overline{\Gamma}\delta = \|\Gamma\|$, hence, $\|\Gamma'\| \geq \|\Gamma\|$.

And vice versa, if ε' is such that $\|\varepsilon'\| = 1$ and $(\varepsilon')^*(\Gamma' \circ \Delta'_i)\varepsilon' = \|\Gamma' \circ \Delta'_i\|$, let $\varepsilon_{x,a} = \delta_{x,a}\varepsilon'_x/\delta'_x$. Again, $\|\varepsilon\| = 1$ and $\varepsilon^*(\Gamma \circ \Delta_i)\varepsilon = (\varepsilon')^*(\Gamma' \circ \Delta'_i)\varepsilon'$, hence, $\|\Gamma' \circ \Delta'_i\| \le \|\Gamma \circ \Delta_i\| = \|\Gamma \circ \Delta_i\|$.

This means that Γ' provides at least as good adversary lower bound as Γ. □

3. PROOF

In this section we prove Theorem 2 using the adversary lower bound, Theorem 3. The idea of our construction is to embed the adversary matrix Γ into a slightly larger matrix $\widetilde{\Gamma}$ with additional columns. Then $\Gamma \circ \Delta_i$ is a submatrix of $\widetilde{\Gamma} \circ \Delta_i$, hence, $\|\Gamma \circ \Delta_i\| \le \|\widetilde{\Gamma} \circ \Delta_i\|$. (In this section we use Δ_i to denote all matrices defined like in Definition 2, with the size and the labels of the rows and columns clear from the context.) It remains to prove that $\|\widetilde{\Gamma}\|$ is large, and that $\|\Gamma\|$ is not much smaller than $\|\widetilde{\Gamma}\|$.

The proof is organized as follows. In Section 3.1 we define $\widetilde{\Gamma}$ in dependence on parameters α_m, in Section 3.2 we analyze its norm, in Sections 3.3 and 3.4 calculate $\|\widetilde{\Gamma} \circ \Delta_i\|$, in Section 3.5 optimize α_ms, and, finally, in Section 3.6 prove that the norm of the true adversary matrix Γ is not much smaller than the norm of $\widetilde{\Gamma}$.

3.1 Adversary matrix

Matrix $\widetilde{\Gamma}$ consists of $\binom{n}{k}$ matrices $\widetilde{G}_{s_1,\dots,s_k}$ stacked one on another for all possible choices of $S = \{s_1, \dots, s_k\} \subset [n]$:

$$\widetilde{\Gamma} = \begin{pmatrix} \widetilde{G}_{1,2,\dots,k} \\ \widetilde{G}_{1,2,\dots,k-1,k+1} \\ \cdots \\ \widetilde{G}_{n-k+1,n-k+2,\dots,n} \end{pmatrix}. \quad (2)$$

Each $\widetilde{G}_S$ is a $q^{n-1} \times q^n$ matrix with rows indexed by inputs $(x_1, \dots, x_n) \in [q]^n$ such that $x_S \in T_S$, and columns indexed by all possible inputs $(y_1, \dots, y_n) \in [q]^n$.

We say a column with index y is *illegal* if $y_S \in T_S$ for some $S \subseteq [n]$. After removing all illegal columns, $\widetilde{G}_S$ will represent the part of Γ with the rows indexed by the inputs having an element of the orthogonal array on S. Note that some positive inputs appear more than once in Γ. More specifically, an input x appears as many times as many elements of the orthogonal arrays it contains.

This construction may seem faulty, because there are elements of $[q]^n$ that are used as labels of both rows and columns in $\widetilde{\Gamma}$, and hence, it is trivial to construct a matrix $\widetilde{\Gamma}$ such that the value in (1) is arbitrarily large. But we design $\widetilde{\Gamma}$ in a specifically restrictive way so that it still is a good adversary matrix after the illegal columns are removed.

Let J_q be the $q \times q$ all-ones matrix. Assume $e_0, \dots, e_{q-1}$ is an orthonormal eigenbasis of J_q with $e_0 = 1/\sqrt{q}(1, \dots, 1)$ being the eigenvalue q eigenvector. Consider the vectors of the following form:

$$v = e_{v_1} \otimes e_{v_2} \otimes \cdots \otimes e_{v_n}, \quad (3)$$

where $v_i \in \{0, \dots, q-1\}$. These are eigenvectors of the Hamming Association Scheme on $[q]^n$. For a vector v from (3), the *weight* $|v|$ is defined as the number of non-zero entries in $(v_1, \dots, v_n)$. Let $E_k^{(n)}$, for $k = 0, \dots, n$, be the orthogonal projector on the space spanned by the vectors from (3) having weight k. These are the projectors on the eigenspaces of the association scheme. Let us denote $E_i = E_i^{(1)}$ for $i = 0, 1$.

These are $q \times q$ matrices. All entries of E_0 are equal to $1/q$, and the entries of E_1 are given by

$$E_1[\![x, y]\!] = \begin{cases} 1 - 1/q, & x = y; \\ -1/q, & x \ne y. \end{cases}$$

Elements of S in $\widetilde{G}_S$ should be treated differently from the rest of the elements. For them, we define a $q^{k-1} \times q^k$ matrix F_S. It has rows labelled by the elements of T_S and columns by the elements of $[q]^k$, and is defined as follows.

Definition 3. Let

$$E_{<k}^{(k)} = I - E_k^{(k)} = \sum_{i=0}^{k-1} E_i^{(k)} = \sum_{\substack{u = e_{u_1} \otimes \cdots \otimes e_{u_k} \\ |u| < k}} uu^*$$

be the projector onto the subspace spanned by the vectors of less than maximal weight. Let F_S be $\sqrt{q}$ times the submatrix of $E_{<k}^{(k)}$ consisting of only the rows from T_S.

Finally, we define $\widetilde{\Gamma}$ as in (2) with $\widetilde{G}_S$ defined by

$$\widetilde{G}_S = \sum_{m=0}^{n-k} \alpha_m F_S \otimes E_m^{(n-k)}, \quad (4)$$

where F_S acts on the elements in S and E_m acts on the remaining $n - k$ elements. Coefficients α_m will be specified later.

3.2 Norm of $\widetilde{\Gamma}$

LEMMA 1. *Let $\widetilde{\Gamma}$ be like in (2) with $\widetilde{G}_S$ defined as in (4). Then*

(a) $\|\widetilde{\Gamma}\| = \Omega(\alpha_0 n^{k/2})$,

(b) $\|\widetilde{\Gamma}\| = O(\max_m \alpha_m n^{k/2})$.

PROOF. Fix a subset S and denote $T = T_S$ and $F = F_S$. Recall that $E_{<k}^{(k)}$ is the sum of uu^* over all $u = e_{u_1} \otimes \cdots \otimes e_{u_k}$ with at least one u_j equal to 0, and F is the restriction of $E_{<k}^{(k)}$ to the rows in T.

For $u = e_{u_1} \otimes \cdots \otimes e_{u_k}$ and ℓ such that $u_\ell = 0$, let $u^{(\ell)}$ denote the $\sqrt{q}$ multiple of u restricted to the elements in T. The reason for the superscript is that we consider the following process of obtaining $u^{(\ell)}$: we treat T as $[q]^{k-1}$ by erasing the ℓ-th element in any string of T, then $u^{(\ell)}$ coincides on this set with u with the ℓ-th term removed.

In this notation, the contribution from uu^* to F equals $u^{(\ell_u)}u^*$, where ℓ_u is any position in u containing e_0. In general, we do not know how $u^{(\ell)}$s relate for different ℓ. However, we know that, for a fixed ℓ, they are all orthogonal; and for any ℓ, $(e_0^{\otimes k})^{(\ell)}$ is the vector $1/\sqrt{q^{k-1}}(1, \dots, 1)$.

Let us start with proving (a). We estimate $\|\widetilde{\Gamma}\|$ from below as $w^*\widetilde{\Gamma}w'$, where w and w' are unit vectors with all elements equal. In other words, $\|\widetilde{\Gamma}\|$ is at least the sum of all its entries divided by $\sqrt{\binom{n}{k}q^{2n-1}}$. In order to estimate the sum of the entries of $\widetilde{\Gamma}$, we rewrite (4) as

$$\widetilde{G}_S = \alpha_0 e_0^{\otimes(n-1)}(e_0^{\otimes n})^* + \sum_{u,v} \alpha_{|v|}(u^{(\ell_u)} \otimes v)(u \otimes v)^*, \quad (5)$$

where the summation is over all u and v such that at least one of them contains an element different from e_0. The sum of all entries in the first term of (5) is $\alpha_0 q^{n-1/2}$. The sum of each column in each of $(u^{(\ell_u)} \otimes v)(u \otimes v)^*$ is zero because at least one of $u^{(\ell_u)}$ or v sums up to zero. By summing over all $\binom{n}{k}$ choices of S, we get that $\|\widetilde{\Gamma}\| \geq \alpha_0 \sqrt{\binom{n}{k}} = \Omega(\alpha_0 n^{k/2})$.

In order to prove (b), express F_S as $\sum_{\ell=1}^k F_S^{(\ell)}$ with $F_S^{(\ell)} = \sum_{u \in U_\ell} u^{(\ell)} u^*$. Here $\{U_\ell\}$ is an arbitrary decomposition of all u such that U_ℓ contains only u with e_0 in the ℓ-th position. Define $\widetilde{G}_S^{(\ell)}$ as in (4) with F_S replaced by $F_S^{(\ell)}$, and $\widetilde{\Gamma}^{(\ell)}$ as in (2) with $\widetilde{G}_S$ replaced by $\widetilde{G}_S^{(\ell)}$.

Since all $u^{(\ell)}$s are orthogonal for a fixed ℓ, we get that

$$(\widetilde{G}^{(\ell)})^* \widetilde{G}^{(\ell)} = \sum_{u \in U_\ell, v} \alpha_{|v|}^2 (u \otimes v)(u \otimes v)^*,$$

thus $\|(\widetilde{G}^{(\ell)})^* \widetilde{G}^{(\ell)}\| = \max_m \alpha_m^2$. By the triangle inequality,

$$\|\widetilde{\Gamma}^{(\ell)}\|^2 = \left\|(\widetilde{\Gamma}^{(\ell)})^* \widetilde{\Gamma}^{\ell}\right\| = \left\|\sum_S (\widetilde{G}_S^{(\ell)})^* \widetilde{G}_S^{(\ell)}\right\| \leq \binom{n}{k} \max_m \alpha_m^2.$$

Since $\widetilde{\Gamma} = \sum_{\ell=1}^k \widetilde{\Gamma}^{(\ell)}$, another application of the triangle inequality finishes the proof of (b). □

3.3 Action of Δ_1

The adversary matrix is symmetric in all input variables and hence it suffices to only consider the entry-wise multiplication by Δ_1. Precise calculation of $\|\widetilde{\Gamma} \circ \Delta_1\|$ is very tedious, but one can get an asymptotically tight bound using the following trick. Instead of computing $\widetilde{\Gamma} \circ \Delta_1$ directly, we arbitrarily map $\widetilde{\Gamma} \overset{\Delta_1}{\longmapsto} \widetilde{\Gamma}_1$ such that $\widetilde{\Gamma}_1 \circ \Delta_1 = \widetilde{\Gamma} \circ \Delta_1$, and use the inequality $\|\widetilde{\Gamma}_1 \circ \Delta_1\| \leq 2\|\widetilde{\Gamma}_1\|$ that holds thanks to $\gamma_2(\Delta_1) \leq 2$ [15]. In other words, we change arbitrarily the entries with $x_1 = y_1$. We use the mapping

$$E_0 \overset{\Delta_1}{\longmapsto} E_0 \ , \qquad E_1 \overset{\Delta_1}{\longmapsto} -E_0 \ , \qquad I \overset{\Delta_1}{\longmapsto} 0 \ . \tag{6}$$

The projector $E_{<k}^{(k)}$ is mapped by Δ_1 as

$$E_{<k}^{(k)} = I - E_k^{(k)} \overset{\Delta_1}{\longmapsto} E_0 \otimes E_1^{\otimes(k-1)} \ .$$

It follows that

$$F \overset{\Delta_1}{\longmapsto} e_0^* \otimes E_1^{\otimes(k-1)} = \sum_{\substack{u = e_{u_1} \otimes \cdots \otimes e_{u_k} \\ u_0 = 0, |u| = k-1}} u^{(1)} u^* \ , \tag{7}$$

where $u^{(1)}$ is defined like in the proof of Lemma 1.

3.4 Norm of $\widetilde{\Gamma}_1$

LEMMA 2. *Let $\widetilde{\Gamma}$ be like in (2) with $\widetilde{G}_T$ defined as in (4), and map $\widetilde{\Gamma} \overset{\Delta_1}{\longmapsto} \widetilde{\Gamma}_1$ and $\widetilde{G}_T \overset{\Delta_1}{\longmapsto} (\widetilde{G}_T)_1$ using (6) and (7). Then*

$$\|\widetilde{\Gamma}_1\| = O(\max_m(\max(\alpha_m m^{(k-1)/2}, (\alpha_m - \alpha_{m+1}) n^{k/2}))).$$

PROOF. We have $\|\widetilde{\Gamma}_1\|^2 = \|\widetilde{\Gamma}_1^* \widetilde{\Gamma}_1\| = \|\sum_S (\widetilde{G}_S)_1^* (\widetilde{G}_S)_1\|$. Decompose the set of all possible k-tuples of indices into $\mathcal{S}_1 \cup \mathcal{S}_2$, where $\mathcal{S}_1$ are k-tuples containing 1 and $\mathcal{S}_2$ are k-tuples that don't contain 1. We upper-bound the contribution of $\mathcal{S}_1$ to $\|\widetilde{\Gamma}_1\|^2$ by $\max_m \alpha_m^2 \binom{m+k-1}{k-1}$ and the contribution of $\mathcal{S}_2$ by $\max_m (\alpha_m - \alpha_{m+1})^2 k \binom{n-1}{k}$, and apply the triangle inequality.

Let $v = e_{v_1} \otimes \cdots \otimes e_{v_n}$ with $|v| = m + k - 1$, and let $S \in \mathcal{S}_1$. Then, by (7),

$$(\widetilde{G}_S)_1 v = \begin{cases} \alpha_m v^{(1)}, & v_1 = 0 \text{ and } |v_S| = k-1, \\ 0, & \text{otherwise.} \end{cases}$$

Here $v^{(1)} = e_{v_2} \otimes \cdots \otimes e_{v_n}$ is v with the first term removed and $v_S = \bigotimes_{s \in S} e_{v_s}$.

For different v, these are orthogonal vectors, and hence v is an eigenvector of $(\widetilde{G}_S)_1^* (\widetilde{G}_S)_1$ of eigenvalue α_m^2 if $v_1 = 0$ and $|v_S| = k - 1$, and of eigenvalue 0 otherwise. For every v with $v_1 = 0$ and $|v| = m + k - 1$, there are $\binom{m+k-1}{k-1}$ sets $S \in \mathcal{S}_1$ such that $(\widetilde{G}_S)_1 v \neq 0$. Thus, the contribution of $\mathcal{S}_1$ is as claimed.

Now consider an $S \in \mathcal{S}_2$, that means $1 \notin S$.

$$\begin{aligned}
\widetilde{G}_S &= \sum_{m=0}^{n-k} \alpha_m F_S \otimes E_m^{(n-k)} \\
&= \sum_{m=0}^{n-k} \alpha_m F_S \\
&\qquad \otimes (E_0 \otimes E_m^{(n-k-1)} + E_1 \otimes E_{m-1}^{(n-k-1)}) \\
&\overset{\Delta_1}{\longmapsto} \sum_{m=0}^{n-k} \alpha_m F_S \otimes E_0 \otimes (E_m^{(n-k-1)} - E_{m-1}^{(n-k-1)}) \\
= (\widetilde{G}_S)_1 &= \sum_{m=0}^{n-k} (\alpha_m - \alpha_{m+1}) F_S \otimes E_0 \otimes E_m^{(n-k-1)} \ .
\end{aligned}$$

Therefore $(\widetilde{G}_S)_1$ is of the same form as $\widetilde{G}_S$, but with coefficients $(\alpha_m - \alpha_{m+1})$ instead of α_m and on one dimension less. We get the required estimate from Lemma 1(b).

Since $k = O(1)$, we get the claimed bound. □

3.5 Optimization of α_m

To maximize the adversary bound, we maximize $\|\widetilde{\Gamma}\|$ while keeping $\|\widetilde{\Gamma}_1\| = O(1)$. That means, we choose the coefficients $\{\alpha_m\}$ to maximize $\alpha_0 n^{k/2}$ (Lemma 1) so that, for every m, $\alpha_m \leq m^{(1-k)/2}$ and $\alpha_m \leq \alpha_{m+1} + n^{-k/2}$ (Lemma 2).

For every $r \in [n]$, $\alpha_0 \leq \alpha_r + rn^{-k/2} \leq r^{(1-k)/2} + rn^{-k/2}$. The expression on the right-hand side achieves its minimum, up to a constant, $\alpha_0 = 2\, n^{k(1-k)/(2(k+1))}$ for $r = n^{k/(k+1)}$. This corresponds to the following solution:

$$\alpha_m = \max\left\{2 - \frac{m}{n^{k/(k+1)}}, 0\right\} n^{\frac{k(1-k)}{2(k+1)}} \tag{8}$$

With this choice of α_m, $\|\widetilde{\Gamma}\| = \Omega(\alpha_0 n^{k/2}) = \Omega(n^{k/(k+1)})$.

3.6 Constructing Γ from $\widetilde{\Gamma}$

The matrix $\widetilde{\Gamma}$ gives us the desired ratio of norms of $\widetilde{\Gamma}$ and $\widetilde{\Gamma} \circ \Delta_i$. Unfortunately, $\widetilde{\Gamma}$ cannot directly be used as an adversary matrix, because it contains illegal columns y with $f(y) = 1$, that is, y that contain an element of the orthogonal array on $S \subset [n] : |S| = k$, i.e., $y_S \in T_S$. We show that after removing the illegal columns it is still good enough.

LEMMA 3. *Let Γ be the sub-matrix of $\widetilde{\Gamma}$ with the illegal columns removed. Then $\|\Gamma \circ \Delta_1\| \leq \|\widetilde{\Gamma} \circ \Delta_1\|$, and $\|\Gamma\|$ is still $\Omega(\alpha_0 n^{k/2})$ when $q \geq n^k$.*

PROOF. We estimate $\|\Gamma\|$ from below by $w^*\Gamma w'$ using unit vectors w, w' with all elements equal. Recall Equation (5):

$$\widetilde{G}_T = \alpha_0 e_0^{\otimes(n-1)}(e_0^{\otimes n})^* + \sum_{u,v} \alpha_{|v|}(u^{(\ell_u)} \otimes v)(u \otimes v)^* ,$$

where the summation is over all u and v such that at least one of them contains an element different from e_0. The sum of each column in each of $(u^{(\ell_u)} \otimes v)(u \otimes v)^*$ still is zero because at least one of $u^{(\ell_u)}$ or v sums up to zero. Therefore the contribution of the sum is zero regardless of which columns have been removed.

By summing over all $\binom{n}{k}$ choices of S, we get

$$\|\Gamma\| \geq w^*\Gamma w' = \sqrt{\binom{n}{k}} \alpha_0 \, (e_0^{\otimes n})_L^* w' ,$$

where e_L denotes the sub-vector of e restricted to L, and L is the set of legal columns. Since both e_0 and w' are unit vectors with all elements equal, and w' is supported on L, $(e_0^{\otimes n})_L^* w' = \sqrt{|L|/q^n}$.

Let us estimate the fraction of legal columns. The probability that a uniformly random input $y \in [q]^n$ contains an orthogonal array at any given k-tuple S is $\frac{1}{q}$. By the union bound, the probability that there exists such S is at most $\binom{n}{k}\frac{1}{q}$. Therefore the probability that a random column is legal is $\frac{|L|}{q^n} \geq 1 - \binom{n}{k}\frac{1}{q}$, which is $\Omega(1)$ when $q \geq n^k$. □

Thus, with the choice of α_m from (8), we have $\mathrm{Adv}^{\pm}(f) = \Omega(\alpha_0 n^{k/2}) = \Omega(n^{k/(k+1)})$. This finishes the proof of Theorem 2.

4. OPEN PROBLEMS

Our technique relies crucially on the n^k lower bound on the alphabet size. Can one relax this bound in some special cases? For example, element distinctness is nontrivial when $q \geq n$, but our lower bound only holds for $q \geq n^2$.

A tight $\Omega(n^{2/3})$ lower bound for element distinctness was originally proved by the polynomial method [1] by reduction via the collision problem. The k-collision problem is to decide whether a given function is $1:1$ or $k:1$, provided that it is of one of the two types. One can use an algorithm for element distinctness to solve the 2-collision problem, and thus the tight $\Omega(n^{1/3})$ lower bound for collision implies in [1] implies a tight lower bound for element distinctness. Unfortunately, the reduction doesn't go in both directions and hence our result doesn't imply any nontrivial adversary bound for k-collision. The simpler nonnegative-weight adversary bound is limited to $O(1)$ due to the property testing barrier. Roughly speaking, if every 0-input differs from every 1-input in at least an ε-fraction of the input, the nonnegative-weight adversary bound is limited by $O(\frac{1}{\varepsilon})$. How does an explicit negative-weight adversary matrix for an $\omega(1)$ lower bound look like?

The recent learning graph-based algorithm for k-distinctness [8] solves the problem in $O(n^{1-2^{k-2}/(2^k-1)})$ quantum queries, which is less than $O(n^{k/(k+1)})$ but more than the $\Omega(n^{2/3})$ lower bound by reduction from 2-distinctness. k-distinctness is easier than the k-sum problem considered in our paper because one can obtain nontrivial information about the solution from partial solutions, i.e., from ℓ-tuples of equal numbers for $\ell < k$. Can one use our technique to prove an $\omega(n^{2/3})$ lower bound for k-distinctness?

The k-sum problem is very structured in the sense that all k-tuples of the input variables, and all possible values seen on a $(k-1)$-tuple, are equal with respect to the function. The symmetry of this problem helped us to design a symmetric adversary matrix. The nonnegative-weight adversary bound gives nontrivial lower bounds for most problems, by simply putting most of the weight on hard-to-distinguish input pairs, regardless of whether the problem is symmetric or not. Can one use our technique to improve the best known lower bounds for some non-symmetric problems, for example, to prove an $\omega(\sqrt{n})$ lower bound for graph collision, $\omega(n)$ for triangle finding, or $\omega(n^{3/2})$ for verification of matrix products?

Acknowledgments

A.B. would like to thank Andris Ambainis, Troy Lee and Ansis Rosmanis for valuable discussions. We are grateful to Kassem Kalach for informing us about the applications of the k-sum problem in Merkle puzzles and for reporting on some minor errors in the early version of the paper, as well as to the anonymous reviewers for their suggestions on improving the presentation of the paper.

A.B. is supported by the European Social Fund within the project "Support for Doctoral Studies at University of Latvia" and by FET-Open project QCS.

5. REFERENCES

[1] S. Aaronson and Y. Shi. Quantum lower bounds for the collision and the element distinctness problems. *Journal of the ACM*, 51(4):595–605, 2004.

[2] A. Ambainis. Quantum lower bounds by quantum arguments. *Journal of Computer and System Sciences*, 64(4):750–767, 2002.

[3] A. Ambainis. Polynomial degree vs. quantum query complexity. In *Proceedings of the 44th IEEE FOCS*, pages 230–239, 2003.

[4] A. Ambainis. Quantum lower bounds for collision and element distinctness with small range. *Theory of Computing*, 1:37–46, 2005.

[5] A. Ambainis. Quantum walk algorithm for element distinctness. *SIAM Journal on Computing*, 37:210–239, 2007.

[6] R. Beals, H. Buhrman, R. Cleve, M. Mosca, and R. de Wolf. Quantum lower bounds by polynomials. *Journal of the ACM*, 48(4):778–797, 2001.

[7] A. Belovs. Adversary lower bound for element distinctness. Technical Report 1204.5074, arXiv, 2012.

[8] A. Belovs. Learning-graph-based quantum algorithm for k-distinctness. In *In Proc. of 53rd FOCS*, pages 207–216, 2012.

[9] G. Brassard, P. Høyer, K. Kalach, M. Kaplan, S. Laplante, and L. Salvail. Merkle puzzles in a quantum world. In *CRYPTO 2011*, volume 6841, page 391. Springer, 2011.

[10] H. Buhrman and R. de Wolf. Complexity measures and decision tree complexity: a survey. *Theoretical Computer Science*, 288:21–43, 2002.

[11] A. Childs and J. Eisenberg. Quantum algorithms for subset finding. *Quantum Information & Computation*, 5(7):593–604, 2005.

[12] P. Høyer, T. Lee, and R. Špalek. Negative weights

make adversaries stronger. In *Proceedings of the 39th ACM STOC*, pages 526–535, 2007.

[13] K. Kalach. Personal communication, 2012.

[14] S. Kutin. Quantum lower bound for the collision problem with small range. *Theory of Computing*, 1(1):29–36, 2005.

[15] T. Lee, R. Mittal, B. Reichardt, R. Špalek, and M. Szegedy. Quantum query complexity of the state conversion problem. In *Proceedings of 52nd IEEE FOCS*, pages 344–353, 2011.

[16] B. Reichardt. Reflections for quantum query algorithms. In *Proceedings of 22nd ACM-SIAM SODA*, pages 560–569, 2011.

[17] R. Špalek and M. Szegedy. All quantum adversary methods are equivalent. *Theory of Computing*, 2:1–18, 2006.

[18] S. Zhang. On the power of Ambainis lower bounds. *Theoretical Computer Science*, 339(2):241–256, 2005.

Stronger Methods of Making Quantum Interactive Proofs Perfectly Complete

Hirotada Kobayashi
National Institute of Informatics
Tokyo, Japan
hirotada@nii.ac.jp

François Le Gall
The University of Tokyo
Tokyo, Japan
legall@is.s.u-tokyo.ac.jp

Harumichi Nishimura
Nagoya University
Nagoya, Japan
hnishimura@is.nagoya-u.ac.jp

ABSTRACT

This paper presents stronger methods of achieving perfect completeness in quantum interactive proofs. First, it is proved that any problem in QMA has a two-message quantum interactive proof system of perfect completeness with constant soundness error, where the verifier has only to send a constant number of halves of EPR pairs. This in particular implies that the class QMA is necessarily included by the class $\mathrm{QIP}_1(2)$ of problems having two-message quantum interactive proofs of perfect completeness, which gives the first nontrivial upper bound for QMA in terms of quantum interactive proofs. It is also proved that any problem having an m-message quantum interactive proof system necessarily has an $(m+1)$-message quantum interactive proof system of perfect completeness. This improves the previous result due to Kitaev and Watrous, where the resulting system of perfect completeness requires $m+2$ messages if not using the parallelization result.

Categories and Subject Descriptors

F.1.2 [**Computation by Abstract Devices**]: Modes of Computation—*interactive and reactive computation*; F.1.3 [**Computation by Abstract Devices**]: Complexity Measures and Classes—*relations among complexity classes*

General Terms

Theory

Keywords

Computational complexity, quantum computing, interactive proof systems

1. INTRODUCTION

1.1 Background and Motivation

The classical complexity class MA of problems having Merlin-Arthur (MA) proof systems, first introduced by Babai [Bab85], is a natural probabilistic generalization of the class NP. Informally, in a Merlin-Arthur proof system, Arthur, a probabilistic polynomial-time verifier, first receives a message (a witness) from Merlin, an all-powerful but untrustworthy prover, and then checks with high probability the validity of Merlin's claim that the common input is a yes-instance of the problem.

Quantum Merlin-Arthur (QMA) proof systems are a generalization of the Merlin-Arthur proof systems to the quantum setting, whose notion was already discussed at an early stage of quantum computing research in a technical report by Knill [Kni96]. In this setting, Arthur now receives a quantum witness from Merlin and performs polynomial-time quantum computation to check with high probability whether the input is a yes-instance or not. The resulting complexity class is called QMA [Wat00] (originally called BQNP [Kit99, KSV02]), and has been central to the development of quantum complexity theory in that it plays a role similar to that NP plays in classical computation.

The standard way of defining MA and QMA allows two-sided bounded error: each yes-instance may be wrongly rejected with small probability (completeness error), while each no-instance may also be wrongly accepted with small probability (soundness error). If completeness error is zero, that is, any yes-instance is never wrongly rejected, the corresponding system is said to have *perfect completeness*. The versions of MA and QMA with perfect completeness are denoted by MA_1 and QMA_1, respectively.

Classically, it is known that any Merlin-Arthur proof system that may have two-sided bounded error can always be modified into another Merlin-Arthur proof system with one-sided bounded error of perfect completeness, i.e., $\mathrm{MA} = \mathrm{MA}_1$ holds [ZF87, GZ11]. This is a very nice property in that honest Merlin can always convince Arthur without error by providing a suitable witness for a yes-instance. A natural question to ask is whether the same property holds for quantum Merlin-Arthur proof systems as well, i.e., whether $\mathrm{QMA} = \mathrm{QMA}_1$ or not. This question still remains unsolved after many years of investigations. Besides its theoretical interest, answering this question by the affirmative would lead to many consequences. In particular, any computational problem complete for the class QMA_1, for instance the Quantum Satisfiability (QSAT) problems [Bra06], would immediately become complete for the class QMA as well. This would not only lead to a better understanding of QMA but also have potentials to significantly simplify and strengthen a possible quantum version of the celebrated PCP theorem [AS98, ALM$^+$98] that many researchers have

ITCS'13, January 9–12, 2012, Berkeley, California, USA.

been trying to establish [AALV09, AALV11, AE11], partly because one-sided error verifications are much easier to treat, and also because the QSAT problems are more direct quantum analogues of the SAT problems than the LOCAL HAMILTONIAN problems (note that the classical PCP theorem can be viewed as proving the NP-completeness of a special case of the 3SAT problem in which, for every no-instance, at most a constant fraction of clauses are simultaneously satisfiable).

As a barrier to affirmatively answering the QMA versus QMA_1 question, Aaronson [Aar09] constructed a quantum oracle relative to which QMA_1 is a proper subclass of QMA, which means that a "black-box" proof of $\mathrm{QMA} = \mathrm{QMA}_1$ cannot exist. Nevertheless, no classical oracle is known that separates QMA_1 from QMA, and the following recent results in some sense step towards an affirmative answer to the question: Nagaj, Wocjan, and Zhang [NWZ09] showed that perfect completeness is achievable for a special case of quantum Merlin-Arthur proof systems in which some real number related to the maximum acceptance probability of a given system can be exactly expressed with a bit string of polynomial length. More recently, Jordan, Kobayashi, Nagaj, and Nishimura [JKNN12] proved that the equality holds for quantum Merlin-Arthur proof systems *of classical witness*, that is, $\mathrm{QCMA} = \mathrm{QCMA}_1$ (or $\mathrm{MQA} = \mathrm{MQA}_1$ in a recently-proposed terminology [Wat09a, GSU11]) holds, assuming that the circuit of a verifier is exactly implementable with a gate set in which the Hadamard and any classical reversible transformations are performable without error. In particular, the latter result gives evidence that, if we put some natural assumption on a gate set, the quantum oracle barrier by Aaronson [Aar09] may not be an insurmountable obstacle when seeking the possibility of $\mathrm{QMA} = \mathrm{QMA}_1$, as the arguments in Ref. [Aar09] also lead to a quantum oracle that separates QCMA_1 from QCMA.

Quantum Merlin-Arthur proof systems may be viewed as a special case of more general quantum interactive proof systems, where the verifier and the prover may exchange messages using many rounds of communications. In their seminal paper, Kitaev and Watrous [KW00] showed that perfect completeness is achievable in quantum interactive proof systems. More precisely, with two additional messages, any quantum interactive proof system that may involve two-sided bounded error can be transformed into another quantum interactive proof system that has one-sided bounded error of perfect completeness. This in particular implies that $\mathrm{QMA} \subseteq \mathrm{QIP}_1(3)$, where $\mathrm{QIP}_1(3)$ is the class of problems having three-message quantum interactive proof systems of perfect completeness. Unfortunately, $\mathrm{QIP}_1(3)$ is already so powerful that it includes PSPACE [Wat03] (actually, $\mathrm{QIP}_1(3) = \mathrm{QIP} = \mathrm{PSPACE}$ [KW00, JJUW11], where QIP denotes the class of problems having general quantum interactive proofs). Accordingly, this only gives a weaker result for the upper bound of QMA, as QMA is known to be inside PP [KW00, Wat00, MW05] (in fact, a slightly stronger bound $\mathrm{QMA} \subseteq \mathrm{A_0PP} = \mathrm{SBQP}$ is known [Vya03, Kup09]).

1.2 Our Results and Their Meaning

This paper presents new general techniques to transform quantum interactive proof systems into those of perfect completeness, which increase the number of messages by just one. Our first result states that any problem in QMA has a two-message quantum interactive proof of perfect completeness.

THEOREM 1. $\mathrm{QMA} \subseteq \mathrm{QIP}_1(2)$.

Here $\mathrm{QIP}_1(2)$ is the class of problems having two-message quantum interactive proof systems of perfect completeness (with negligible soundness error). This gives the first nontrivial upper bound of QMA in terms of quantum interactive proofs, which has no relation known to the existing upper bound $\mathrm{A_0PP} = \mathrm{SBQP}$. Note that the inclusion $\mathrm{QMA} \subseteq \mathrm{QIP}(2)$ is indeed trivial for the two-sided error class $\mathrm{QIP}(2)$ of two-message quantum interactive proofs, but the inclusion here is by the one-sided error class $\mathrm{QIP}_1(2)$ and is nontrivial to prove.

In fact, we prove a much stronger result, which arguably steps towards settling the QMA versus QMA_1 question. Namely, we show that, to achieve perfect completeness with constant soundness error, the verifier in the two-message quantum interactive proof system has only to send a constant number of halves of EPR pairs to the prover. Or in other words, any problem in QMA has a quantum Merlin-Arthur proof system of perfect completeness with constant soundness error, in which Arthur and Merlin share a constant number of EPR pairs a priori. More formally, let $\mathrm{QMA}^{k\text{-EPR}}(c, s)$ denote the class of problems having quantum Merlin-Arthur proof systems with completeness c and soundness s, where Arthur and Merlin initially share k EPR pairs. Then we have the following containment.

THEOREM 2. *For any constant $s \in (0, 1]$, there exists a constant $k \in \mathbb{N}$ such that*

$$\mathrm{QMA} \subseteq \mathrm{QMA}^{k\text{-EPR}}(1, s).$$

Theorem 1 is an immediate consequence of Theorem 2, as one may view quantum Merlin-Arthur proof systems with shared EPR pairs as a special case of two-message quantum interactive proofs where the verifier first generates the EPR pairs and sends halves of them to the prover (and the parallel repetition of two-message quantum interactive proofs works perfectly [KW00]). Theorem 2 nevertheless appears to be much stronger than Theorem 1 since it shows that perfect completeness is achievable with just one additional message of a very restricted form (a constant number of halves of EPR pairs). To see this, let $\mathrm{QMA}^{\text{const-EPR}}$ be the class of problems having quantum Merlin-Arthur proof systems with a constant number of prior shared EPR pairs that may involve two-sided bounded error, and let $\mathrm{QMA}_1^{\text{const-EPR}}$ be that of perfect completeness. Then, indeed, the equality $\mathrm{QMA}^{\text{const-EPR}} = \mathrm{QMA}$ immediately follows from the result by Beigi, Shor, and Watrous [BSW11], as any quantum Merlin-Arthur proof system with a constant number of prior shared EPR pairs is a special case of two-message quantum interactive proofs *with short questions* (i.e., two-message quantum interactive proofs with the first message consisting of at most logarithmically many qubits). Therefore, we obtain the following characterization of QMA.

COROLLARY 3. $\mathrm{QMA}_1^{\text{const-EPR}} = \mathrm{QMA}^{\text{const-EPR}} = \mathrm{QMA}$.

This in particular implies that perfect completeness is achievable for the model of quantum Merlin-Arthur proof systems with a constant number of prior shared EPR pairs, a model that has computational power equivalent to QMA. Similar arguments further imply that perfect completeness is achievable even with the models of quantum Merlin-Arthur proof systems with a logarithmic number of prior shared EPR pairs and "short-question" two-message quantum interactive proof systems, as both of these have computational power equivalent to QMA.

The methodology developed in this paper essentially shows that, in order to obtain the inclusion $\mathrm{QMA} \subseteq \mathrm{QMA}_1$ (and thus immediately the equality $\mathrm{QMA} = \mathrm{QMA}_1$), it is sufficient to find a way of eliminating the need for the constant number of shared EPR pairs in our proof system. In fact, as will be clear with our proof structure, the constant number of shared EPR pairs are necessary only for the purpose of forcing a dishonest prover to send a witness that is close to some maximally entangled state of constant dimensions. Hence, some suitable procedure that tests if a given state of constant dimensions is sufficiently entangled or not may replace the shared EPR pairs to affirmatively answer the QMA versus QMA_1 question (if two-sided error is allowed, such a test is possible with quantum state tomography). Moreover, our construction gives another example of quantumly non-relativizing techniques for quantum interactive proofs, which again indicates that Aaronson's quantum oracle separation [Aar09] may not be an insurmountable barrier when proving that $\mathrm{QMA} = \mathrm{QMA}_1$ or its related results.

For general quantum interactive proof systems, we further present a method that makes any quantum interactive proof system perfectly complete by increasing the number of messages by just one. This improves the previous result due to Kitaev and Watrous [KW00], whose construction increases the number of messages by two, if not using their parallelization result. More precisely, for the class $\mathrm{QIP}(m)$ of problems having m-message quantum interactive proofs that may involve two-sided bounded error, and the class $\mathrm{QIP}_1(m)$ of problems having those of perfect completeness, we show the following.

THEOREM 4 (INFORMAL STATEMENT). *For any $m \geq 2$,*

$$\mathrm{QIP}(m) \subseteq \mathrm{QIP}_1(m+1).$$

In fact, if the number of messages in the original system is odd, our transformation does not increase it at all.

THEOREM 5 (INFORMAL STATEMENT). *For any odd $m \geq 3$,*

$$\mathrm{QIP}(m) \subseteq \mathrm{QIP}_1(m).$$

While the inclusions of Theorems 4 and 5 can also be obtained by using the parallelization results in Refs. [KW00, KKMV09], our techniques give a new and arguably more direct way of obtaining these results. Our construction actually works well even in the setting of quantum multi-prover interactive proof systems: it transforms any quantum k-prover interactive proof system into another quantum k-prover interactive proof system of perfect completeness by increasing the number of turns by just one in general, and without increasing it when the number of turns in the original system is odd. This much improves the previous result in Ref. [KKMV09], where the construction increases the number m of turns to $3m$ (i.e., by a factor of three), again without using their parallelization result. We refer to Theorems 25, 26, 33, and 34 in Section 7 for the precise statements of the results.

1.3 Organization of This Paper

Section 2 gives a high-level explanation of how Theorem 2 (i.e, the inclusion $\mathrm{QMA} \subseteq \mathrm{QMA}_1^{\text{const-EPR}}$) is proved. Section 3 presents an overview of the proof of Theorem 4 (i.e., the inclusion $\mathrm{QIP}(m) \subseteq \mathrm{QIP}_1(m+1)$). Section 4 provides basic notions and definitions that are used in this paper. Section 5 rigorously describes and analyzes the basic procedure called REFLECTION PROCEDURE, which is the fundamental technical tool throughout this paper. Section 6 then gives a full proof of Theorem 2. Finally, Section 7 proves the results on general quantum interactive proofs.

2. PROOF IDEA OF THEOREM 2

The purpose of this section is to give a high-level description of our construction that proves Theorem 2 (the inclusion $\mathrm{QMA} \subseteq \mathrm{QMA}_1^{\text{const-EPR}}$). We first describe the main idea in Subsection 2.1 and a simple protocol for a very special case. Then we explain in Subsection 2.2 how to make this simple protocol robust against any cheating strategy, by introducing additional tests. Finally, in Subsection 2.3, we present our complete protocol.

2.1 Underlying Ideas

For an input x, let V_x denote the verifier's quantum circuit in the original QMA proof system. The operator V_x acts on two quantum registers, one register A corresponding to the verifier's work space and another register M corresponding to the space that stores the witness from the prover. Let p_x denote the maximum acceptance probability, over all possible witnesses, of the verification procedure. From the definition of the class QMA one can assume that, for every yes-instance x it holds that $p_x \geq 1/2$, and for every no-instance x it holds that $p_x \leq 1/3$. As pointed out by Marriott and Watrous [MW05], the maximum acceptance probability p_x of V_x over all possible witnesses is the maximum eigenvalue of the Hermitian operator

$$M_x = \Pi_{\text{init}} V_x^\dagger \Pi_{\text{acc}} V_x \Pi_{\text{init}},$$

where Π_{init} is the projection onto the subspace spanned by states in which all the qubits in A are in state $|0\rangle$, and Π_{acc} is the projection onto the space spanned by the accepting states.

Reflection Procedure.

The basic idea of our protocol is to simulate a procedure that we call REFLECTION PROCEDURE, presented in details in Section 5. Roughly speaking, this procedure is viewed as performing a part of amplitude amplification [Gro96] on the original verification procedure, and is quite similar to the so-called quantum rewinding technique [Wat09b], the underlying idea of which dates back to the strong amplification method for QMA due to Marriott and Watrous [MW05]. Not surprisingly, our REFLECTION PROCEDURE can be analyzed in a way similar to the case of the strong amplification method for QMA due to Marriott and Watrous [MW05]. We refer to Figure 1 for a presentation of this procedure specialized to the case of QMA proof systems (a more general description of the procedure will be given in Figure 3 in Section 5).

Reflection Procedure

1. Receive a quantum register M. Prepare $|0\rangle$ in each of the qubits in a quantum register A. Apply V_x to the state in (A, M).

2. Perform a phase-flip (i.e., multiply -1 in phase) if the state in (A, M) belongs to the subspace corresponding to the projection Π_{acc}.

3. Apply $V_x^\dagger$ to (A, M).

4. Reject if the state in (A, M) belongs to the subspace corresponding to Π_{init}, and accept otherwise.

Figure 1: The Reflection Procedure (specialized to the case of QMA proof systems; see Figure 3 in Section 5 for the most general version of this procedure).

The Reflection Procedure has access to the unitary transformation V_x, receives a quantum state in register M, and has the following property:

1. If M_x has an eigenvalue $1/2$, then there exists a quantum state in M such that the procedure accepts with certainty.

2. If M_x has no eigenvalue in the interval $(\frac{1}{2} - \varepsilon, \frac{1}{2} + \varepsilon)$, then for any quantum state in M given, the procedure rejects with probability at least $4\varepsilon^2$.

This procedure would then enable us to transform the original QMA proof system into another QMA proof system with perfect completeness if we had exactly $p_x = 1/2$ for any yes-instance x. This nice property on the completeness of course does not necessarily hold in general.

We mention that the Reflection Procedure is actually slightly superior to the original quantum rewinding technique (for the purpose of achieving perfect completeness) in that it requires just two applications of V_x (more precisely, one application of V_x and one application of $V_x^\dagger$), instead of three. This property will be crucial for our analysis since the Reflection Procedure will ultimately be applied to a modified version of V_x that cannot be implemented directly by the verifier without the help of the prover.

Simple Protocol when p_x is Known.
In general, we only know that $p_x \geq 1/2$ for a yes-instance. Assume that the verifier can apply the matrix

$$W_q = \begin{pmatrix} \sqrt{1-q} & \sqrt{q} \\ \sqrt{q} & -\sqrt{1-q} \end{pmatrix}$$

acting on one qubit, where q is such that $0 \leq q \leq 1$ and $p_x q = 1/2$ (the value of q depends of course on the input x). Then, by performing in parallel the original verification test (which succeeds with probability p_x) and an additional test that applies W_q on a single qubit in the initial state $|0\rangle$ and measures it, we obtain a new verification procedure that accepts the input with probability exactly $p_x q = 1/2$ (where the new condition for acceptance is that the original test accepts *and* the additional single qubit contains 1). In particular, such a unitary transformation W_q always exists for any yes-instance x, and thus, this could achieve the perfect completeness if the verifier knew the probability $p_x \geq 1/2$.

The Hermitian operator corresponding to the case of applying in parallel these two tests can be represented by

$$M'_x = (\Pi_{\text{init}} \otimes |0\rangle\langle 0|)(V_x \otimes W_q)^\dagger \times (\Pi_{\text{acc}} \otimes |1\rangle\langle 1|)(V_x \otimes W_q)(\Pi_{\text{init}} \otimes |0\rangle\langle 0|),$$

which has $1/2$ as an eigenvalue for a yes-instance x. Moreover, it can be easily shown that, on a negative instance, the eigenvalues of this Hermitian operator are bounded away from $1/2$. Thus, the Reflection Procedure applied to the new verification test $V_x \otimes W_q$ transforms the original system into a perfect completeness system. This protocol of course works only when the verifier can apply W_q.

Reflection Simulation Test and Distillation Procedure.
The main problem with the protocol described above is that the verifier does not know in general the probability p_x, and is then not able to apply W_q. Informally, our basic idea to overcome this difficulty consists in asking the prover to send, along with the witness $|w\rangle$ of the original proof system, the unitary transformation W_q to the verifier, where $p_x q = 1/2$. Concretely, this is done by asking the prover to send two copies of the *Choi-Jamiołkowski state* associated with W_q, denoted by $|J(W_q)\rangle\rangle$ and defined as follows:

$$|J(W_q)\rangle\rangle = (I \otimes W_q)|\Phi^+\rangle = \sqrt{1-q}|\Phi^-\rangle + \sqrt{q}|\Psi^+\rangle,$$

where $|\Phi^+\rangle = \frac{1}{\sqrt{2}}(|00\rangle + |11\rangle)$, $|\Phi^-\rangle = \frac{1}{\sqrt{2}}(|00\rangle - |11\rangle)$ and $|\Psi^+\rangle = \frac{1}{\sqrt{2}}(|01\rangle + |10\rangle)$. By an analysis similar to the case of quantum teleportation, one can see that the state $|J(W_q)\rangle\rangle$ can be used to simulate one application of the unitary transformation W_q to any quantum state of a single qubit in a probabilistic manner; the application succeeds with probability $1/4$, and we know whether it succeeds or not.

Let us denote by M the register that is expected to contain the witness $|w\rangle$, and by S_1, S_1', S_2, and S_2' the four single-qubit registers that altogether are expected to contain the two copies of the Choi-Jamiołkowski state. On a yes-instance, an (honest) prover will then send the state

$$|w\rangle_{\mathsf{M}} \otimes |J(W_q)\rangle\rangle_{(\mathsf{S}_1,\mathsf{S}_1')} \otimes |J(W_q)\rangle\rangle_{(\mathsf{S}_2,\mathsf{S}_2')}.$$

With this state given, the verifier can simulate the desired QMA system with underlying verification procedure $V_x \otimes W_q$ with success probability $(1/4)^2 = 1/16$ (note that $W_q^\dagger = W_q$, and thus, one copy of $|J(W_q)\rangle\rangle$ is used to simulate the application of W_q, and another copy of it is used to simulate the application of $W_q^\dagger$). In case where the simulation fails, the verifier systematically accepts by giving up the simulation to keep perfect completeness. This is the core idea of the procedure Reflection Simulation Test described in Subsection 6.1.4, which is a key building block in our proof of Theorem 2.

In fact, we incorporate one more technique called Distillation Procedure, which is again based on the analysis of Ref. [MW05], and makes the analysis of our complete protocol significantly easier. In general, one of the main difficulties when analyzing the soundness with the simulation of the Reflection Procedure with the associated Hermitian operator M'_x above is that one has to care about the entanglement between the witness part in M and the part for the Choi-Jamiołkowski states in S_1, S_1', S_2, and S_2'. This could make the soundness analysis extremely hard, and in fact, the authors do not even know if the soundness can be proved without using the DISTILLATION PROCEDURE. The idea to settle this difficulty is that, instead of directly simulating the REFLECTION PROCEDURE above on a received state (that is expected to be a product state of a witness $|w\rangle$ and two copies of the Choi-Jamiołkowski state), one first performs the DISTILLATION PROCEDURE twice in sequence on the witness part (i.e., M) of the received state to produce a situation where one can perform a much simplified version of the REFLECTION PROCEDURE that does not even need to receive a witness. This new REFLECTION PROCEDURE has a very nice property that it does not significantly change the behavior of the original REFLECTION PROCEDURE, and its associated Hermitian operator acts over a space of just four dimensions and has a much simpler form:

$$(|0\rangle\langle 0| \otimes |0\rangle\langle 0|)(W_p \otimes W_q)^\dagger \\ \times (|1\rangle\langle 1| \otimes |1\rangle\langle 1|)(W_p \otimes W_q)(|0\rangle\langle 0| \otimes |0\rangle\langle 0|),$$

where $p = p_x^2/(2p_x^2 - 2p_x + 1)$ and $q = 1/(2p)$ (which is different from the value of q in the previous case with M_x'). More precisely, the two applications of the DISTILLATION PROCEDURE (described in Subsection 6.1.1) enable us to generate with high probability two identical copies of the single-qubit state

$$|\chi_p\rangle = \sqrt{1-p}|0\rangle + \sqrt{p}|1\rangle$$

from a given witness $|w\rangle$ (and one can know whether the generation of the two copies succeeded or not). The point is that, if the input were a no-instance, and the original soundness were very small, the generated state should be very close to $|0\rangle \otimes |0\rangle$, and could be analyzed as if it were unentangled with other qubits. Note that one can easily transform $|\chi_p\rangle$ into $|J(W_p)\rangle$, and thus one essentially obtains the desired two copies of the Choi-Jamiołkowski state corresponding to W_p after the two applications of the DISTILLATION PROCEDURE.

2.2 Towards the Actual Protocol

The main problem of the strategy described in the previous subsection is of course that, on a no-instance, a dishonest prover may not send the prescribed state. Actually, for a dishonest prover who sends a state of the form $|w\rangle \otimes |J(W_q)\rangle^{\otimes 2}$, then no matter which state $|w\rangle$ and no matter which value q the prover chooses, the soundness can be analyzed with a quite straightforward argument. The real issue lies in the case where a dishonest prover does not send a quantum state of the form $|w\rangle \otimes |J(W_q)\rangle^{\otimes 2}$, and especially when the state in $(\mathsf{S}_1, \mathsf{S}_1', \mathsf{S}_2, \mathsf{S}_2')$ is not a product state of two identical copies of a Choi-Jamiołkowski state.

To force a state in $(\mathsf{S}_1, \mathsf{S}_1', \mathsf{S}_2, \mathsf{S}_2')$ to be at least close to a mixture of two-fold products of an identical quantum state (which may be a mixed state), we modify the protocol so that we can use the finite quantum de Finetti theorem [KR05, CKMR07]. For this, the verifier now asks the prover to send not only two copies of $|J(W_q)\rangle$ but a larger number of copies of it: $|J(W_q)\rangle^{\otimes N}$ where N is large but still a constant. The expected witness sent by an honest prover is then

$$|w\rangle_{\mathsf{M}} \otimes |J(W_q)\rangle_{(\mathsf{S}_1,\mathsf{S}_1')} \otimes \cdots \otimes |J(W_q)\rangle_{(\mathsf{S}_N,\mathsf{S}_N')}.$$

The witness state in $(\mathsf{M}, \mathsf{S}_1, \mathsf{S}_1', \ldots, \mathsf{S}_N, \mathsf{S}_N')$ sent by a prover in a general case may of course not be of the form above, if the prover is dishonest. After the two applications of the DISTILLATION PROCEDURE with M, the verifier permutes the N pairs of registers $(\mathsf{S}_1, \mathsf{S}_1'), \ldots, (\mathsf{S}_N, \mathsf{S}_N')$ uniformly at random. This makes the state in $(\mathsf{S}_1, \mathsf{S}_1'), \ldots, (\mathsf{S}_N, \mathsf{S}_N')$ symmetric (i.e., invariant under any permutation of the N pairs of registers $(\mathsf{S}_1, \mathsf{S}_1'), \ldots, (\mathsf{S}_N, \mathsf{S}_N')$), and thus the quantum de Finetti theorem guarantees that the reduced state in $(\mathsf{S}_1, \mathsf{S}_1', \mathsf{S}_2, \mathsf{S}_2')$ of the resulting state after random permutation must be close to some mixture of two-fold product states

$$\sum_j \mu_j \xi_j \otimes \xi_j.$$

Note that each state ξ_j may not necessarily be a pure state, and is usually a mixed state. The SWAP TEST, performed additionally to this random permutation, will ensure that every ξ_j must be actually close to some pure state. This is nevertheless not enough: we want to ensure that each ξ_j is close to some Choi-Jamiołkowski state. To have this desirable property, we now assume that each pair of registers $(\mathsf{S}_j, \mathsf{S}_j')$ initially contains an EPR pair, and that the verifier initially holds the registers $\mathsf{S}_1, \ldots, \mathsf{S}_N$ and receives only, additionally to M, the registers $\mathsf{S}_1', \ldots, \mathsf{S}_N'$ as witness. This assumption is the only part where we need (a constant number of) shared EPR pairs, and removing it is the last obstacle that prevents us from proving the result $\mathrm{QMA} = \mathrm{QMA}_1$. To make use of this assumption, we further device a test called the SPACE RESTRICTION TEST that restricts the Hilbert space corresponding to the registers $(\mathsf{S}_1, \mathsf{S}_1', \mathsf{S}_2, \mathsf{S}_2')$ in which the verifier expects to receive the copies of the Choi-Jamiołkowski state. The assumption of a constant number of prior-shared EPR pairs is then tactically used with this SPACE RESTRICTION TEST to finally ensure that each ξ_j must be close to some legal Choi-Jamiołkowski state.

2.3 Final Protocol

The final protocol of the verifier in a QMA system of perfect completeness with a constant number of shared EPR pairs is given in Figure 2. Actually, Figure 2 presents a slightly simplified exposition of our final protocol; the complete description will appear in Section 6 (see Figure 6 in the proof of Theorem 2).

Let us briefly describe the protocol step by step, focusing on what happens when the prover is honest. At the end of Step 1, i.e., just after receiving a witness from the prover, the state in $(\mathsf{M}, \mathsf{S}_1, \mathsf{S}_1', \ldots, \mathsf{S}_N, \mathsf{S}_N')$ is given by

$$|w\rangle_{\mathsf{M}} \otimes |J(W_q)\rangle_{(\mathsf{S}_1,\mathsf{S}_1')} \otimes \cdots \otimes |J(W_q)\rangle_{(\mathsf{S}_N,\mathsf{S}_N')}.$$

When none of the two executions of the DISTILLATION PROCEDURE fails in Step 2, the state in $(\mathsf{R}_1,\mathsf{R}_2,\mathsf{S}_1,\mathsf{S}_1',\ldots,\mathsf{S}_N,\mathsf{S}_N')$ becomes

$$|\chi_p\rangle_{\mathsf{R}_1} \otimes |\chi_p\rangle_{\mathsf{R}_2} \otimes |J(W_q)\rangle_{(\mathsf{S}_1,\mathsf{S}_1')} \otimes \cdots \otimes |J(W_q)\rangle_{(\mathsf{S}_N,\mathsf{S}_N')},$$

at the end of this step. Step 3 just permutes the N pairs of registers $(\mathsf{S}_1, \mathsf{S}_1'), \ldots, (\mathsf{S}_N, \mathsf{S}_N')$ uniformly at random, which does not change the state at all. The SPACE RESTRICTION TEST in Step 4 forces each of the two-qubit states in $(\mathsf{S}_1, \mathsf{S}_1')$ and $(\mathsf{S}_2, \mathsf{S}_2')$ to be in the subspace spanned by $|\Phi^-\rangle$ and $|\Psi^+\rangle$ (as the state must be in this subspace if it is a product of the desirable Choi-Jamiołkowski states), which does not change the state either. Then the SWAP TEST in Step 5 never fails, since the registers $(\mathsf{S}_1, \mathsf{S}_1')$ and $(\mathsf{S}_2, \mathsf{S}_2')$ contain the identical pure state. Finally, Step 6 performs the REFLECTION

Verifier's QMA Protocol for Achieving Perfect Completeness with N Prior-Shared EPR Pairs (Simplified)

1. Store the particles of the shared N EPR pairs in $(\mathsf{S}_1, \ldots, \mathsf{S}_N)$. Receive a quantum witness in registers $(\mathsf{M}, \mathsf{S}'_1, \ldots, \mathsf{S}'_N)$.
2. Execute the DISTILLATION PROCEDURE twice in sequence, both using a state in M. Accept if any of the two executions fails, and continue otherwise, with storing the two generated single-qubit states in R_1 and R_2.
3. Permute the N pairs of registers $(\mathsf{S}_1, \mathsf{S}'_1), \ldots, (\mathsf{S}_N, \mathsf{S}'_N)$ uniformly at random.
4. Perform the SPACE RESTRICTION TEST. That is, test if the state in $(\mathsf{S}_j, \mathsf{S}'_j)$ is in the space spanned by $\{|\Phi^-\rangle, |\Psi^+\rangle\}$, for each $j \in \{1, 2\}$. Reject if not so, and continue otherwise.
5. Perform the SWAP TEST between $(\mathsf{S}_1, \mathsf{S}'_1)$ and $(\mathsf{S}_2, \mathsf{S}'_2)$. Reject if it fails, and continue otherwise.
6. Perform the REFLECTION SIMULATION TEST with $(\mathsf{R}_1, \mathsf{R}_2, \mathsf{S}_1, \mathsf{S}'_1, \mathsf{S}_2, \mathsf{S}'_2)$ as input. Accept if this returns "accept", and reject otherwise.

Figure 2: Slightly simplified description of the verifier's QMA protocol for achieving perfect completeness with N pre-shared EPR pairs. The complete description appears as Figure 6 in Section 6.

SIMULATION TEST, which must result in acceptance with certainty, as the value q was chosen appropriately so that the associated Hermitian operator with this REFLECTION SIMULATION TEST has an eigenvalue exactly $1/2$.

Rough Sketch of Soundness Analysis.

Here we give a very rough sketch of the soundness analysis for a no-instance case. The rigorous analysis can be found in Section 6.

Without loss of generality, it is assumed that the original QMA system has soundness exponentially close to 0. Then, if none of the two executions of the DISTILLATION PROCEDURE fails, whatever witness has been received in Step 1, the state generated in $(\mathsf{R}_1, \mathsf{R}_2)$ after Step 2 must be exponentially close to

$$|\chi_0\rangle_{\mathsf{R}_1} \otimes |\chi_0\rangle_{\mathsf{R}_2} = |0\rangle_{\mathsf{R}_1} \otimes |0\rangle_{\mathsf{R}_2}$$

(and the probability that the DISTILLATION PROCEDURE fails is actually exponentially small in this case). This implies that the state in $(\mathsf{R}_1, \mathsf{R}_2)$ is almost unentangled with the state in $(\mathsf{S}_1, \mathsf{S}'_1, \ldots, \mathsf{S}_N, \mathsf{S}'_N)$.

As the random permutation in Step 3 makes the state in $(\mathsf{S}_1, \mathsf{S}'_1, \ldots, \mathsf{S}_N, \mathsf{S}'_N)$ symmetric, from the quantum de Finetti theorem, the reduced state in $(\mathsf{R}_1, \mathsf{R}_2, \mathsf{S}_1, \mathsf{S}'_1, \mathsf{S}_2, \mathsf{S}'_2)$ after Step 3 must be close to the state of the form

$$(|0\rangle\langle 0|)^{\otimes 2} \otimes \Big(\sum_j \mu_j \xi_j^{\otimes 2}\Big).$$

A key property is that the reduced state in $(\mathsf{S}_1, \mathsf{S}_2)$ is exponentially close to the totally mixed state $(I/2)^{\otimes 2}$, which is guaranteed by the facts that each state in S_j for $j \in \{1, \ldots N\}$ was originally a half of the shared EPR pair, that the two executions of the DISTILLATION PROCEDURE disturbed the state by an amount at most exponentially small, and that the state $(I/2)^{\otimes N}$ in $(\mathsf{S}_1, \ldots, \mathsf{S}_N)$ is invariant under random permutation.

Now one can show that (stated here informally) if the probability of rejection is very small in the SPACE RESTRICTION TEST in Step 4 (otherwise the dishonest prover is caught with some reasonable probability in this Step 4), the state in $(\mathsf{R}_1, \mathsf{R}_2, \mathsf{S}_1, \mathsf{S}'_1, \mathsf{S}_2, \mathsf{S}'_2)$ at the end of Step 4 is sufficiently close to a state of the form

$$(|0\rangle\langle 0|)^{\otimes 2} \otimes \Big(\sum_j \mu'_j \xi'^{\otimes 2}_j\Big),$$

where ξ'_j is a mixture of the desirable Choi-Jamiołkowski states.

Now the SWAP TEST in Step 5 intuitively requires that each ξ'_j must be close to some pure state, and thus, if the probability of rejection is again very small in Step 5 (otherwise the dishonest prover is caught with some reasonable probability in this Step 5), the state in $(\mathsf{R}_1, \mathsf{R}_2, \mathsf{S}_1, \mathsf{S}'_1, \mathsf{S}_2, \mathsf{S}'_2)$ at the end of Step 5 must be sufficiently close to a state of the form

$$(|0\rangle\langle 0|)^{\otimes 2} \otimes \Big[\sum_j \mu''_j (|J(W_{a_j})\rangle\langle J(W_{a_j})|)^{\otimes 2}\Big]$$

which is a mixture of states of the desired form.

For each state of the form

$$|0\rangle^{\otimes 2} \otimes |J(W_{a_j})\rangle^{\otimes 2} = |\chi_0\rangle^{\otimes 2} \otimes |J(W_{a_j})\rangle^{\otimes 2},$$

however, we know that the REFLECTION SIMULATION TEST in Step 6 rejects with sufficiently large probability (shown to be exactly $1/16$) irrelevant to the value a_j, and thus, the verifier can reject with probability close to $1/16$ even when the verification procedure reaches Step 6 with very high probability.

3. PROOF IDEA OF THEOREM 4

This section gives an overview of the proof of Theorem 4 (more precisely, of the formal statement of this result, Theorem 25), which proves the inclusion $\mathrm{QIP}(m) \subseteq \mathrm{QIP}_1(m+1)$, for each $m \geq 2$. For simplicity, here we assume that the number m of messages is odd (the case with even number of messages can be proved with essentially the same argument), and completeness and soundness are $2/3$ and $1/3$, respectively, in the original quantum interactive proof system.

The basic idea is again to simulate the REFLECTION PROCEDURE associated with the original m-message quantum interactive proof system.

Fix an input x and the transformations of the prover P on x in the original m-message quantum interactive proof system. This time, we consider that the register M in the REFLECTION PROCEDURE described in Figure 1 contains all the qubits the prover P can access in the original system (i.e., all the private qubits of the prover and all the message qubits that are used for communications). We further consider that the register A contains all the private qubits of the verifier in the original system. Now, if we replace V_x in

Figure 1 by the unitary transformation U derived from the original quantum interactive proof system when the verifier communicates with P on input x, the REFLECTION PROCEDURE described in Figure 1 can be viewed as first applying U by performing a forward simulation of the communications with P, then applying a phase-flip with respect to the accepting states, and further applying $U^\dagger$ by performing a backward simulation of the communications with P to confirm if the entire state *does not* go back to a legal initial state.

Hence, if there is a strategy for a prover that can convince the verifier with probability exactly $1/2$ in the original system, then this specific REFLECTION PROCEDURE with such a prover must result in acceptance with certainty, from the property of the REFLECTION PROCEDURE. Fortunately, if the number m of messages is at least two, it is not hard for an all powerful prover to arbitrarily decrease the accepting probability, and thus, this essentially achieves the perfect completeness when the input is a yes-instance. On the other hand, for any no-instance, no prover can convince the verifier with probability more than $1/3$. This implies that the above specific REFLECTION PROCEDURE must result in rejection with some constant probability (actually with probability at least $1/9$), again from the property of the REFLECTION PROCEDURE. Therefore, this basically establishes a quantum interactive proof system of perfect completeness, as desired.

There are two problems in this construction. One is that a dishonest prover may not be so cooperative that a backward simulation forms $U^\dagger$ as required (i.e., a prover may behave during the backward simulation differently from the inverse of what he/she behaved during the forward simulation). The other is that the number of messages increases from m to $2m-1$, and thus, it is less communication-efficient than the existing construction of achieving perfect completeness in quantum interactive proofs due to Kitaev and Watrous [KW00].

Modified Reflection Procedure.

Both of the two problems mentioned above originate from the fact that the REFLECTION PROCEDURE involves one application of U and one application of $U^\dagger$. Now we modify the procedure so that it involves one application of $U^\dagger$ only (and no application of U is required), which simultaneously settles both of the two problems.

To do this, at the beginning, one expects to receive a state just after Step 1 of the REFLECTION PROCEDURE, and then performs on this state two tests, called REFLECTION TEST and INVERTIBILITY TEST, respectively, with equal probability without revealing which test the prover is undergoing. In the REFLECTION TEST, one simply performs Steps 2–4 of the REFLECTION PROCEDURE (i.e., one first applies the appropriate phase-flip and then applies $U^\dagger$) to finish the simulation of it. In the INVERTIBILITY TEST, one apply just $U^\dagger$ without performing the phase-flip and checks if the entire state *does* go back to a legal initial state of the original REFLECTION PROCEDURE. We call the resulting procedure the MODIFIED REFLECTION PROCEDURE, a precise description of which will be given in Subsection 7.1. The idea of making use of the INVERTIBILITY TEST originally appeared in Ref. [KKMV09] when achieving perfect completeness in quantum multi-prover interactive proofs, but the test was used only after the forward simulation of the protocol in their original construction, and was not for the purpose of reducing the number of messages.

As is clear from the construction above, the MODIFIED REFLECTION PROCEDURE requires only one application of $U^\dagger$ as desired. Thus, the quantum interactive proof system that simulates this MODIFIED REFLECTION PROCEDURE involves only m messages as required (for an even m, it involves $m+1$ messages, as the original system starts with a turn for a verifier, while the verifier in the constructed system needs to receive a witness before his/her first turn). Moreover, for any yes-instance, the honest prover clearly has only to cooperate with the verifier to perform the backward simulation of the original REFLECTION PROCEDURE and can convince the verifier with certainty. On the other hand, for any no-instance, the original REFLECTION PROCEDURE would have rejected with high probability, if the proper $U^\dagger$ were performed. Thus, if the backward simulation in the MODIFIED REFLECTION PROCEDURE were properly performed, the REFLECTION TEST of it could reject with high probability as it properly simulates the original REFLECTION PROCEDURE. In contrast, if the backward simulation were not proper in the MODIFIED REFLECTION PROCEDURE, then the INVERTIBILITY TEST of it would result in rejection with high probability, as it essentially forces the prover to perform a proper backward simulation of the original REFLECTION PROCEDURE. Indeed, as will be proved in Subsection 7.1, if one starts with a REFLECTION PROCEDURE that rejects with probability at least ε for every possible witness, the resulting MODIFIED REFLECTION PROCEDURE rejects with probability at least $\varepsilon/4$ no matter which witness is received (the proof of Proposition 30 essentially proves this). Hence, the soundness can be shown as well in the MODIFIED REFLECTION PROCEDURE.

4. PRELIMINARIES

Throughout this paper, let $\mathbb{N}$ and $\mathbb{Z}^+$ denote the sets of positive and nonnegative integers, respectively, and let $\Sigma = \{0,1\}$ denote the binary alphabet set. A function $f\colon \mathbb{Z}^+ \to \mathbb{N}$ is *polynomially bounded* if there exists a polynomial-time deterministic Turing machine that outputs $1^{f(n)}$ on input 1^n. A function $f\colon \mathbb{Z}^+ \to [0,1]$ is *negligible* if, for every polynomially bounded function $g\colon \mathbb{Z}^+ \to \mathbb{N}$, it holds that $f(n) < 1/g(n)$ for all but finitely many values of n.

Quantum Fundamentals.

We assume the reader is familiar with the quantum formalism, including pure and mixed quantum states, density operators, measurements, trace norm, fidelity, as well as the quantum circuit model (see Refs. [NC00, KSV02], for instance). Here we summarize some notations and properties that are used in this paper.

For each $k \in \mathbb{N}$, let $\mathbb{C}(\Sigma^k)$ denote the 2^k-dimensional complex Hilbert space whose standard basis vectors are indexed by the elements in Σ^k. In this paper, all Hilbert spaces are complex and have dimension a power of two. For a Hilbert space $\mathcal{H}$, let $I_{\mathcal{H}}$ denote the identity operator over $\mathcal{H}$, and let $\mathbf{D}(\mathcal{H})$ be the set of density operators over $\mathcal{H}$. For a quantum register R, let $|0\rangle_{\mathsf{R}}$ denote the state in which all the qubits in R are in state $|0\rangle$. As usual, denote the two single-qubit states in $\mathbb{C}(\Sigma)$ that form the *Hadamard basis* by

$$|+\rangle = \frac{1}{\sqrt{2}}(|0\rangle + |1\rangle), \quad |-\rangle = \frac{1}{\sqrt{2}}(|0\rangle - |1\rangle),$$

and the four two-qubit states in $\mathbb{C}(\Sigma^2)$ that form the *Bell basis* by

$$|\Phi^+\rangle = \frac{1}{\sqrt{2}}(|00\rangle + |11\rangle), \quad |\Phi^-\rangle = \frac{1}{\sqrt{2}}(|00\rangle - |11\rangle),$$
$$|\Psi^+\rangle = \frac{1}{\sqrt{2}}(|01\rangle + |10\rangle), \quad |\Psi^-\rangle = \frac{1}{\sqrt{2}}(|01\rangle - |10\rangle),$$

respectively. Let

$$H = \frac{1}{\sqrt{2}}\begin{pmatrix} 1 & 1 \\ 1 & -1 \end{pmatrix}, \quad X = \begin{pmatrix} 0 & 1 \\ 1 & 0 \end{pmatrix}, \quad Z = \begin{pmatrix} 1 & 0 \\ 0 & -1 \end{pmatrix}$$

denote the Hadamard and Pauli operators. For convenience, we may identify a unitary operator with the unitary transformation it induces. In particular, for a unitary operator U, the induced unitary transformation is also denoted by U.

For a linear operator A, the *trace norm* of A is defined by

$$\|A\|_{\mathrm{tr}} = \mathrm{tr}\sqrt{A^\dagger A}.$$

For two quantum states ρ and σ, the *trace distance* between them is defined by

$$D(\rho, \sigma) = \frac{1}{2}\|\rho - \sigma\|_{\mathrm{tr}},$$

and the *fidelity* between them is defined by

$$F(\rho, \sigma) = \mathrm{tr}\sqrt{\sqrt{\rho}\sigma\sqrt{\rho}}.$$

A special case of the trace distance is the *statistical difference* between two probability distributions μ and ν, which is defined by

$$\mathrm{SD}(\mu, \nu) = D(\mu, \nu)$$

by viewing probability distributions as special cases of quantum states with diagonal density operators. We will use the following important properties of the trace distance and fidelity.

LEMMA 6. *Let μ_ρ and μ_σ be the probability distributions derived from two quantum states ρ and σ, respectively, by performing an arbitrary identical measurement. Then,*

$$\mathrm{SD}(\mu_\rho, \mu_\sigma) \leq D(\rho, \sigma).$$

LEMMA 7 ([SR02, NS03]). *For any quantum states ρ, σ, and ξ,*

$$F(\rho, \sigma)^2 + F(\sigma, \xi)^2 \leq 1 + F(\rho, \xi).$$

For any unitary transformation U acting over the two-dimensional Hilbert space $\mathcal{H} = \mathbb{C}(\Sigma)$ (i.e., the single-qubit space), the *Choi-Jamiołkowski state* of U is the two-qubit state in $\mathcal{H} \otimes \mathcal{H} = \mathbb{C}(\Sigma^2)$ defined by

$$|J(U)\rangle = (I \otimes U)|\Phi^+\rangle.$$

In fact, the Choi-Jamiołkowski state can be defined for any admissible (and not limited to unitary) transformation and any finite-dimensional Hilbert space, using the Choi-Jamiołkowski representation [Jam72, Cho75], but which is unnecessary in this paper.

The Finite Quantum de Finetti Theorem.

For $N \in \mathbb{N}$ and quantum registers $\mathsf{Q}_1, \ldots, \mathsf{Q}_N$, each consisting of k qubits, an N-partite quantum state ρ in $(\mathsf{Q}_1, \ldots, \mathsf{Q}_N)$ is said to be *symmetric* if ρ is invariant under any permutation over the registers $\mathsf{Q}_1, \ldots, \mathsf{Q}_N$.

The *finite quantum de Finetti theorem* [KR05, CKMR07] provides a very useful property that the reduced m-partite state of any N-partite symmetric state when tracing out the last $N - m$ subsystems must be close to a mixture of m-fold product states. This paper uses the following bound proved in Ref. [CKMR07].

THEOREM 8 (FINITE QUANTUM DE FINETTI THEOREM). *For $N, k \in \mathbb{N}$, let $\mathsf{Q}_1, \ldots, \mathsf{Q}_N$ be quantum registers each consisting of k qubits, and let ρ be an N-partite symmetric state in $(\mathsf{Q}_1, \ldots, \mathsf{Q}_N)$. For any $m \in \mathbb{N}$ satisfying $m < N$ and the m-partite reduced state $\rho^{(m)}$ of ρ in $(\mathsf{Q}_1, \ldots, \mathsf{Q}_m)$, there exist $C \in \mathbb{N}$, a set $\{\xi_j\}_{j \in \{1,\ldots,C\}}$ of k-qubit states, and an associated probability distribution $\{\mu_j\}_{j \in \{1,\ldots,C\}}$ such that*

$$D\left(\rho^{(m)}, \sum_{j=1}^{C} \mu_j \xi_j^{\otimes m}\right) \leq \frac{2^{2k+1}m}{N}.$$

Polynomial-Time Uniformly Generated Families of Quantum Circuits.

Following conventions, we define quantum Merlin-Arthur proof systems in terms of quantum circuits. In particular, we use the following notion of polynomial-time uniformly generated families of quantum circuits.

A family $\{Q_x\}$ of quantum circuits is *polynomial-time uniformly generated* if there exists a deterministic procedure that, on every input x, outputs a description of Q_x and runs in time polynomial in $|x|$. It is assumed that the circuits in such a family are composed of gates in some reasonable, universal, finite set of quantum gates. Furthermore, it is assumed that the number of gates in any circuit is not more than the length of the description of that circuit. Therefore Q_x must have size polynomial in $|x|$. For convenience, we may identify a circuit Q_x with the unitary operator it induces.

Throughout this paper, we assume a gate set with which the Hadamard and any classical reversible transformations can be exactly implemented. Note that this assumption is satisfied by many standard gate sets such as the Shor basis [Sho96] consisting of the Hadamard, controlled-i-phase-shift, and Toffoli gates, and the gate set consisting of the Hadamard, Toffoli, and NOT gates [Shi02, Aha03]. Moreover, as the Hadamard transformation in some sense can be viewed as a quantum analogue of the classical operation of flipping a fair coin, our assumption would be the most natural quantum correspondence to the tacit classical assumption in randomized complexity theory that fair coins and perfect logical gates are available. Hence we believe that our condition is very reasonable and not restrictive. Note that, with a gate set satisfying this assumption, any transformation corresponding to a Clifford group operator is exactly implementable. In particular, the controlled-phase-flip transformation Z can be exactly realized by using an ancilla qubit prepared in state $|-\rangle = \frac{1}{\sqrt{2}}(|0\rangle - |1\rangle)$ (by applying a NOT and an Hadamard in sequence to $|0\rangle$) and performing a CNOT with this ancilla as the target.

Since non-unitary and unitary quantum circuits are equivalent in computational power [AKN98], it is sufficient to treat only unitary quantum circuits, which justifies the above definition. Nevertheless, for readability, most procedures in this paper will be described using intermediate projective measurements and unitary operations conditioned on the outcome of the measurements. All of these intermediate measurements can be deferred to the end of the procedure by a standard technique so that the procedure becomes implementable with a unitary circuit.

Quantum Interactive Proof Systems.

Now we review the model of quantum interactive proof systems.

A quantum interactive proof system is a communication model between two players called a *quantum verifier* V and a *quantum prover* P, both of whom receive a common input $x \in \Sigma^*$. Fix the input x. Let V and P be quantum registers corresponding to the private spaces of V and P, respectively, and let M be a quantum register corresponding to the message space that is used to exchange messages between V and P. One of the qubits in V, which is private to V, is designated as the *output qubit*. At the beginning, all the qubits in V and M are initialized to state $|0\rangle$, while the quantum state in P can be arbitrarily prepared by P. Then V and P together run a protocol that consists of alternating turns of the verifier and of the prover. The first turn is for the verifier if the total number of turns is even, and it is for the prover otherwise, whereas the last turn is always for the prover. At each turn of the verifier, V applies some unitary transformation implementable with a polynomial-size quantum circuit to the state in (V, M), and then sends the register M to P. At each turn of the prover, P applies some unitary transformation to the state in (P, M), and then sends M to V. After the last turn, the verifier V further applies some unitary transformation implementable with a polynomial-size quantum circuit to the state in (V, M), and then measures the output qubit in the standard basis. V accepts if this measurement results in $|1\rangle$ and rejects otherwise.

Formally, for any function $m \colon \mathbb{Z}^+ \to \mathbb{N}$ that is polynomially bounded, an *m-message polynomial-time quantum verifier* is a polynomial-time computable mapping $V \colon \Sigma^* \to \Sigma^*$. For each input $x \in \Sigma^*$, $V(x)$ is interpreted as describing a series $\{V_{x,j}\}_{j \in \{1,\ldots,\lceil (m(|x|)+1)/2 \rceil\}}$ of quantum circuits acting over the same number of qubits as well as a partition of the qubits on which these circuits act into registers V and M, where $\{V_{x,j}\}$ is a polynomial-time uniformly generated family of quantum circuits explained before (in particular, every circuit $V_{x,j}$ is composed of gates in some reasonable, universal, finite set of quantum gates). For any polynomially bounded function $m \colon \mathbb{Z}^+ \to \mathbb{N}$, an *$m$-message quantum prover* is a mapping P that simply maps an input binary string $x \in \Sigma^*$ to a series $\{P_{x,j}\}_{j \in \{1,\ldots,\lfloor (m(|x|)+1)/2 \rfloor\}}$ of unitary transformations as well as a partition of the qubits on which these unitary transformations act into registers M and P. It is always assumed that V and P are *compatible* (i.e., the register M is common for V and P) when they are associated with the same quantum interactive proof system.

Given an input x, an m-message polynomial-time quantum verifier V, and an m-message quantum prover P, let Q_x be the unitary transformation induced from V and P, acting over the space corresponding to $(\mathsf{V}, \mathsf{M}, \mathsf{P})$:

$$Q_x = (V_{x,(m(|x|)+1)/2} \otimes I_{\mathcal{P}})(I_{\mathcal{V}} \otimes P_{x,(m(|x|)+1)/2}) \cdots \cdots (V_{x,1} \otimes I_{\mathcal{P}})(I_{\mathcal{V}} \otimes P_{x,1})$$

if $m(|x|)$ is odd, while

$$Q_x = (V_{x,(m(|x|)/2)+1} \otimes I_{\mathcal{P}}) \times (I_{\mathcal{V}} \otimes P_{x,m(|x|)/2})(V_{x,m(|x|)/2} \otimes I_{\mathcal{P}}) \cdots \cdots (I_{\mathcal{V}} \otimes P_{x,1})(V_{x,1} \otimes I_{\mathcal{P}})$$

if $m(|x|)$ is even, where $\mathcal{V}$ and $\mathcal{P}$ are the Hilbert spaces corresponding to V and P, respectively. When communicating with the prover P who prepares the initial state $\rho \in \mathbf{D}(\mathcal{P})$, the verifier V accepts the input x if the measurement of the designated output qubit in V in the standard basis results in $|1\rangle$ at the end of the protocol after having applied the unitary transformation Q_x to the initial state $|0\rangle\langle 0|_{(\mathsf{V},\mathsf{M})} \otimes \rho$ in $(\mathsf{V}, \mathsf{M}, \mathsf{P})$.

Formally, the class $\mathrm{QIP}(m, c, s)$ of problems having m-message quantum interactive proof systems with completeness c and soundness s is defined as follows. For generality, throughout this paper, we use promise problems [ESY84] rather than languages when defining complexity classes.

Definition 9. *Given a polynomially bounded function $m \colon \mathbb{Z}^+ \to \mathbb{N}$ and functions $c, s \colon \mathbb{Z}^+ \to [0, 1]$ satisfying $c > s$, a promise problem $A = (A_{\mathrm{yes}}, A_{\mathrm{no}})$ is in $\mathrm{QIP}(m, c, s)$ iff there exists an m-message polynomial-time quantum verifier V such that, for every input x:*

(Completeness) *if $x \in A_{\mathrm{yes}}$, there exist an m-message quantum prover P and the initial state ρ_x of P that make V accept x with probability at least $c(|x|)$,*

(Soundness) *if $x \in A_{\mathrm{no}}$, for any m-message quantum prover P' and any initial state ρ'_x of P' prepared, V accepts x with probability at most $s(|x|)$.*

The class $\mathrm{QIP}(m)$ of problems having m-message quantum interactive proof systems is defined as follows.

Definition 10. *Given a polynomially bounded function $m \colon \mathbb{Z}^+ \to \mathbb{N}$, a promise problem $A = (A_{\mathrm{yes}}, A_{\mathrm{no}})$ is in $\mathrm{QIP}(m)$ iff A is in $\mathrm{QIP}(m, 1 - \varepsilon, \varepsilon)$ for some negligible function $\varepsilon \colon \mathbb{Z}^+ \to [0, 1]$.*

Similarly, the class $\mathrm{QIP}_1(m)$ of problems having m-message quantum interactive proof systems of perfect completeness is defined as follows.

Definition 11. *Given a polynomially bounded function $m \colon \mathbb{Z}^+ \to \mathbb{N}$, a promise problem $A = (A_{\mathrm{yes}}, A_{\mathrm{no}})$ is in $\mathrm{QIP}_1(m)$ iff A is in $\mathrm{QIP}(m, 1, \varepsilon)$ for some negligible function $\varepsilon \colon \mathbb{Z}^+ \to [0, 1]$.*

Finally, as quantum Merlin-Arthur proof systems are nothing but one-message quantum interactive proof systems, the classes QMA and QMA_1 of problems having quantum Merlin-Arthur proof systems and those of perfect completeness are simply defined as follows, respectively.

Definition 12. *A promise problem $A = (A_{\mathrm{yes}}, A_{\mathrm{no}})$ is in QMA iff A is in $\mathrm{QIP}(1, 1 - \varepsilon, \varepsilon)$ for some negligible function $\varepsilon \colon \mathbb{Z}^+ \to [0, 1]$.*

Definition 13. *A promise problem $A = (A_{\mathrm{yes}}, A_{\mathrm{no}})$ is in QMA_1 iff A is in $\mathrm{QIP}(1, 1, \varepsilon)$ for some negligible function $\varepsilon \colon \mathbb{Z}^+ \to [0, 1]$.*

Quantum Merlin-Arthur Proof Systems with Shared EPR Pairs.

We further introduce another variant of quantum Merlin-Arthur proof systems in which Arthur and Merlin initially share some copies of the EPR pair $|\Phi^+\rangle$. If Arthur and Merlin are allowed to share k EPR pairs initially, the resulting systems are called *quantum Merlin-Arthur proof systems with k shared EPR pairs*, or *k-EPR QMA proof systems* in short. Notice that this model is actually equivalent to a special case of two-message quantum interactive proof systems in which the first transformation of a verifier is just to create k copies of the EPR pairs (and k halves of these EPR pairs are sent to a prover as the first message).

Formally, the class $\mathrm{QMA}^{k\text{-EPR}}(c,s)$ of problems having quantum Merlin-Arthur proof systems with k shared EPR pairs with completeness c and soundness s is defined as follows.

DEFINITION 14. *Given a polynomially bounded function $k\colon \mathbb{Z}^+ \to \mathbb{N}$ and functions $c, s\colon \mathbb{Z}^+ \to [0,1]$ satisfying $c > s$, a promise problem $A = (A_{\mathrm{yes}}, A_{\mathrm{no}})$ is in $\mathrm{QMA}^{k\text{-EPR}}(c,s)$ iff A has a two-message quantum interactive proof system with completeness c and soundness s in which, for every input x, the first transformation of the associated quantum verifier is just to create $k(|x|)$ copies of EPR pairs and the first message from the verifier consists only of the $k(|x|)$ halves of these EPR pairs.*

We further define the class $\mathrm{QMA}^{\text{const-EPR}}$ of problems having quantum Merlin-Arthur proof systems with a constant number of shared EPR pairs with constant gap between completeness and soundness and the class $\mathrm{QMA}_1^{\text{const-EPR}}$ of problems having those of perfect completeness with constant soundness error as follows.

DEFINITION 15. *A promise problem $A = (A_{\mathrm{yes}}, A_{\mathrm{no}})$ is in $\mathrm{QMA}^{\text{const-EPR}}$ iff A is in $\mathrm{QMA}^{k\text{-EPR}}(2/3, 1/3)$ for some constant $k \in \mathbb{N}$.*

DEFINITION 16. *A promise problem $A = (A_{\mathrm{yes}}, A_{\mathrm{no}})$ is in $\mathrm{QMA}_1^{\text{const-EPR}}$ iff A is in $\mathrm{QMA}^{k\text{-EPR}}(1, 1/2)$ for some constant $k \in \mathbb{N}$.*

REMARK 1. *Definitions 15 and 16 are equivalent to the seemingly most conservative definitions*

$$\mathrm{QMA}^{\text{const-EPR}} \stackrel{\text{def}}{=} \bigcup_{k\in\mathbb{N}, 0\le s<c\le 1} \mathrm{QMA}^{k\text{-EPR}}(c,s)$$

$$\mathrm{QMA}_1^{\text{const-EPR}} \stackrel{\text{def}}{=} \bigcup_{k\in\mathbb{N}, s\in[0,1)} \mathrm{QMA}^{k\text{-EPR}}(1,s)$$

of these classes, for repeating the associated system with each of these classes constant times can achieve arbitrarily large constant gap between completeness and soundness (in the two-sided error case, one first achieves sufficiently large completeness via a parallel repetition followed by a threshold value computation, and then achieves desirably small soundness via another parallel repetition of the obtained large-completeness system, without decreasing the completeness too much).

5. REFLECTION PROCEDURE

We start with presenting a very simple base procedure, which we call the REFLECTION PROCEDURE, that forms a very base of our protocols to be constructed – basically, our protocols aim to simulate this base procedure with several suitable modifications.

Let $\mathcal{H}$ be some Hilbert space, and consider two decompositions of $\mathcal{H}$ into $\mathcal{X}_0 \oplus \mathcal{X}_1$ and $\mathcal{Y}_0 \oplus \mathcal{Y}_1$ for subspaces $\mathcal{X}_0$, $\mathcal{X}_1$, $\mathcal{Y}_0$, and $\mathcal{Y}_1$ of $\mathcal{H}$. Let Δ_j be the projection over $\mathcal{H}$ onto the subspace $\mathcal{X}_j$ and let Π_j be that onto $\mathcal{Y}_j$, for each $j \in \{0,1\}$.

Let U be some unitary transformation acting over $\mathcal{H}$, and let M be the Hermitian operator over $\mathcal{H}$ defined by

$$M = \Delta_0 U^\dagger \Pi_0 U \Delta_0.$$

Suppose that M has an eigenvalue $\lambda > 0$ and consider the eigenstate (i.e., the normalized eigenvector) $|\phi_0\rangle$ corresponding to λ. Then, $M|\phi_0\rangle = \lambda|\phi_0\rangle$, and thus,

$$\Delta_0|\phi_0\rangle = \frac{1}{\lambda}\Delta_0 M|\phi_0\rangle = \frac{1}{\lambda}M|\phi_0\rangle = |\phi_0\rangle.$$

Define the four states $|\psi_0\rangle$, $|\psi_1\rangle$, $|\xi_0\rangle$, and $|\xi_1\rangle$ in $\mathcal{H}$ as follows:

$$|\psi_0\rangle = \frac{\Pi_0 U|\phi_0\rangle}{\|\Pi_0 U|\phi_0\rangle\|}, \quad |\psi_1\rangle = \frac{\Pi_1 U|\phi_0\rangle}{\|\Pi_1 U|\phi_0\rangle\|},$$

$$|\xi_0\rangle = \frac{\Delta_0 U^\dagger|\psi_0\rangle}{\|\Delta_0 U^\dagger|\psi_0\rangle\|}, \quad |\xi_1\rangle = \frac{\Delta_1 U^\dagger|\psi_0\rangle}{\|\Delta_1 U^\dagger|\psi_0\rangle\|}.$$

Then, $\|\Pi_0 U|\phi_0\rangle\| = \|\Pi_0 U \Delta_0|\phi_0\rangle\| = \sqrt{\langle\phi_0|M|\phi_0\rangle} = \sqrt{\lambda}$, and thus, $\|\Pi_1 U|\phi_0\rangle\| = \sqrt{1-\lambda}$. It follows that

$$\begin{aligned}\|\Delta_0 U^\dagger|\psi_0\rangle\| &= \frac{1}{\sqrt{\lambda}}\|\Delta_0 U^\dagger \Pi_0 U|\phi_0\rangle\| \\ &= \frac{1}{\sqrt{\lambda}}\|\Delta_0 U^\dagger \Pi_0 U \Delta_0|\phi_0\rangle\| = \frac{1}{\sqrt{\lambda}}\|M|\phi_0\rangle\| = \sqrt{\lambda},\end{aligned}$$

and thus, $\|\Delta_1 U^\dagger|\psi_0\rangle\| = \sqrt{1-\lambda}$. Hence,

$$\begin{aligned}|\xi_0\rangle &= \frac{1}{\sqrt{\lambda}}\Delta_0 U^\dagger|\psi_0\rangle = \frac{1}{\lambda}\Delta_0 U^\dagger \Pi_0 U|\phi_0\rangle \\ &= \frac{1}{\lambda}\Delta_0 U^\dagger \Pi_0 U \Delta_0|\phi_0\rangle = \frac{1}{\lambda}M|\phi_0\rangle = |\phi_0\rangle.\end{aligned}$$

This implies that

$$\begin{aligned}U^\dagger|\psi_0\rangle &= \sqrt{\lambda}|\xi_0\rangle + \sqrt{1-\lambda}|\xi_1\rangle, \\ U^\dagger|\psi_1\rangle &= \sqrt{1-\lambda}|\xi_0\rangle - \sqrt{\lambda}|\xi_1\rangle,\end{aligned}$$

which was the crucial property analyzed by Marriott and Watrous [MW05] to develop their space-efficient QMA amplification technique.

It follows that

$$\begin{aligned}U^\dagger(-\Pi_0 + \Pi_1)U|\phi_0\rangle &= U^\dagger(-\sqrt{\lambda}|\psi_0\rangle + \sqrt{1-\lambda}|\psi_1\rangle) \\ &= (1-2\lambda)|\xi_0\rangle - 2\sqrt{\lambda(1-\lambda)}|\xi_1\rangle,\end{aligned}$$

and thus, when M has an eigenvalue $1/2$, the corresponding eigenstate (which is necessarily in $\mathcal{X}_0$) must be transformed into a state in $\mathcal{X}_1$ after the following process: one first applies U to $|\phi_0\rangle$, next flips the phase of states in $\mathcal{Y}_0$ (i.e., applies the unitary transformation $-\Pi_0 + \Pi_1$), and then applies $U^\dagger$. This property can be used to test if M has an eigenvalue $1/2$, which is summarized in Figure 3.

PROPOSITION 17. *Suppose that the Hermitian operator $M = \Delta_0 U^\dagger \Pi_0 U \Delta_0$ has an eigenvalue $1/2$. Then there exists a quantum state given in Step 1 of the* REFLECTION PROCEDURE *such that the procedure results in acceptance with certainty.*

Reflection Procedure

1. Receive a quantum register Q. Reject if the state in Q does not belong to the subspace corresponding to the projection Δ_0, and otherwise apply U to Q.
2. Perform a phase-flip (i.e., multiply -1 in phase) if the state in Q belongs to the subspace corresponding to the projection Π_0.
3. Apply $U^\dagger$ to Q.
4. Reject if the state in Q belongs to the subspace corresponding to Δ_0, and accept otherwise.

Figure 3: The Reflection Procedure.

PROOF. Consider the case where the eigenstate of M with its corresponding eigenvalue $1/2$ is received in Q in Step 1. Then the claim is immediate from the argument above. □

PROPOSITION 18. *For any $\varepsilon \in (0, \frac{1}{2}]$, suppose that none of the eigenvalues of the Hermitian operator $M = \Delta_0 U^\dagger \Pi_0 U \Delta_0$ is in the interval $\left(\frac{1}{2} - \varepsilon, \frac{1}{2} + \varepsilon\right)$. Then, for any quantum state given in Step 1 of the* REFLECTION PROCEDURE, *the procedure results in rejection with probability at least $4\varepsilon^2$.*

PROOF. Let $|\psi\rangle$ be any state received in Q in Step 1. Without loss of generality, one can assume that $|\psi\rangle$ is in $\mathcal{X}_0$ (as otherwise either rejected in Step 1 or projected onto a state in $\mathcal{X}_0$).

For the Hilbert space $\mathcal{H}$, there always exists an orthonormal basis such that all the basis states of it are eigenstates of M, and thus, the state $|\psi\rangle$ can be necessarily written as $|\psi\rangle = \sum_{j=1}^{d} \alpha_j |\phi_j\rangle$ for $d = \dim \mathcal{X}_0 \leq \dim \mathcal{H}$, where each $|\phi_j\rangle$ is an eigenstate of M in $\mathcal{X}_0$ and $\sum_{j=1}^{d} |\alpha_j|^2 = 1$.

From the analysis above, every eigenstate $|\phi_j\rangle$ of M in $\mathcal{X}_0$ with corresponding eigenvalue $\lambda_j > 0$ must satisfy that

$$\Delta_0 U^\dagger (-\Pi_0 + \Pi_1) U |\phi_j\rangle = (1 - 2\lambda_j)|\phi_j\rangle.$$

On the other hand, for every eigenstate $|\phi_j\rangle$ of M in $\mathcal{X}_0$ with corresponding eigenvalue $\lambda_j = 0$, it holds that

$$\|\Pi_0 U|\phi_j\rangle\| = \|\Pi_0 U \Delta_0 |\phi_j\rangle\| = \sqrt{\langle \phi_j | M | \phi_j\rangle} = 0,$$

which implies $\Pi_1 U|\phi_j\rangle = U|\phi_j\rangle$, and thus

$$\Delta_0 U^\dagger (-\Pi_0 + \Pi_1) U |\phi_j\rangle = \Delta_0 |\phi_j\rangle = |\phi_j\rangle = (1 - 2\lambda_j)|\phi_j\rangle.$$

Therefore,

$$\Delta_0 U^\dagger (-\Pi_0 + \Pi_1) U |\psi\rangle = \sum_{j=1}^{d} \alpha_j (1 - 2\lambda_j)|\phi_j\rangle,$$

and thus, the probability of rejection is at least

$$\sum_{j=1}^{d} |\alpha_j|^2 (1 - 2\lambda_j)^2 \geq 4\varepsilon^2 \sum_{j=1}^{d} |\alpha_j|^2 = 4\varepsilon^2,$$

as claimed. □

6. $\mathrm{QMA} \subseteq \mathrm{QMA}_1^{\text{const-EPR}} \subseteq \mathrm{QIP}_1(2)$

The goal of this section is to prove Theorem 2. In Subsection 6.1 we first describe building blocks, before presenting the proof in Subsection 6.2.

6.1 Building Blocks

6.1.1 Encoding Accepting Probability in Phase

Let V be the verifier of a certain QMA system. Consider the quantum circuit V_x of V when the input is x, which acts over a pair of two registers A of $v(|x|)$ qubits and M of $m(|x|)$ qubits, for some polynomially bounded functions $v, m \colon \mathbb{Z}^+ \to \mathbb{N}$. The circuit V_x expects to receive a quantum witness of $m(|x|)$ qubits in register M, and uses the $v(|x|)$ qubits in A as its work qubits. The Hilbert spaces associated with A and M are denoted by $\mathcal{A}$ and $\mathcal{M}$, respectively.

For an input x, let p_x be the maximum acceptance probability of the verifier V in this QMA system. Then, as pointed out by Marriott and Watrous [MW05], p_x corresponds to the maximum eigenvalue of the Hermitian operator

$$M_x = \Pi_{\mathrm{init}} V_x^\dagger \Pi_{\mathrm{acc}} V_x \Pi_{\mathrm{init}},$$

where Π_{init} is the projection onto the subspace spanned by states in which all the qubits in A are in state $|0\rangle$, and Π_{acc} is that onto the subspace spanned by accepting states of this QMA system. Let $|w_x\rangle$ be the eigenstate (i.e., eigenvector) of M_x corresponding to the eigenvalue p_x. A crucial analysis of Ref. [MW05] (which essentially follows from the arguments in Section 5) is that

$$\Pi_{\mathrm{init}} V_x^\dagger \Pi_{\mathrm{acc}} V_x (|0\rangle_{\mathsf{A}} \otimes |w_x\rangle_{\mathsf{M}}) = p_x |0\rangle_{\mathsf{A}} \otimes |w_x\rangle_{\mathsf{M}},$$
$$\Pi_{\mathrm{init}} V_x^\dagger \Pi_{\mathrm{rej}} V_x (|0\rangle_{\mathsf{A}} \otimes |w_x\rangle_{\mathsf{M}}) = (1 - p_x) |0\rangle_{\mathsf{A}} \otimes |w_x\rangle_{\mathsf{M}},$$

where $\Pi_{\mathrm{rej}} = I_{\mathcal{A} \otimes \mathcal{M}} - \Pi_{\mathrm{acc}}$ is the projection onto the subspace spanned by rejecting states of this QMA system.

Let $p = p_x^2/(2p_x^2 - 2p_x + 1)$. Using the property explained above, if one copy of $|w_x\rangle$ is given, one can generate with high probability the state

$$|\chi_p\rangle = \frac{1}{\sqrt{2p_x^2 - 2p_x + 1}} \left[(1 - p_x)|0\rangle + p_x|1\rangle\right]$$

as follows. One uses a single-qubit register R in addition to A and M, where one sets $|w_x\rangle$ in M, and initializes all the qubits in A and R to state $|0\rangle$. First, one performs a forward simulation of the original system over A and M (i.e., applies V_x to (A, M)), and flips the qubit in R if the content of (A, M) corresponds to an accepting state of the original system (i.e., applies the unitary transformation $X \otimes \Pi_{\mathrm{acc}} + I \otimes \Pi_{\mathrm{rej}}$ to (R, A, M)). One then performs a backward simulation of the original system over A and M (i.e., applies $V_x^\dagger$ to (A, M)). Now one measures all the qubits in A in the computational basis. If no $|1\rangle$ is measured (i.e., if the state is projected with respect to Π_{init}, which happens with probability $2p_x^2 - 2p_x + 1$), the unnormalized state in the system must be

$$\begin{aligned} &|0\rangle_{\mathsf{R}} \otimes (1 - p_x)|0\rangle_{\mathsf{A}} \otimes |w_x\rangle_{\mathsf{M}} + |1\rangle_{\mathsf{R}} \otimes p_x|0\rangle_{\mathsf{A}} \otimes |w_x\rangle_{\mathsf{M}} \\ &\quad = \left[(1 - p_x)|0\rangle + p_x|1\rangle\right]_{\mathsf{R}} \otimes |0\rangle_{\mathsf{A}} \otimes |w_x\rangle_{\mathsf{M}}, \end{aligned}$$

and thus, the desired state is successfully generated in R. We call this procedure the DISTILLATION PROCEDURE, which is summarized in Figure 4.

Distillation Procedure

Input: a single-qubit register R, a $v(|x|)$-qubit register A, and an $m(|x|)$-qubit register M.

Output: a single-qubit register R or a symbol $\perp$.

1. Apply V_x to (A, M).
2. Flip the qubit in R if the content of (A, M) corresponds to an accepting state of the original system.
3. Apply $V_x^\dagger$ to (A, M).
4. Measures all the qubits in A in the computational basis. If any of these measurements result in $|1\rangle$, output $\perp$, otherwise output R.

Figure 4: The Distillation Procedure.

6.1.2 *Multiplicatively Adjusting Accepting Probabilities*

For a real number $a \in [0,1]$, let W_a be the unitary transformation defined by

$$W_a = \begin{pmatrix} \sqrt{1-a} & \sqrt{a} \\ \sqrt{a} & -\sqrt{1-a} \end{pmatrix}.$$

Given a unitary transformation W_p for some real number $p \in \left[\frac{1}{2}, 1\right]$, we construct another unitary transformation U and an appropriate projection operator Π_0 acting over two qubits so that the probability $\|\Pi_0 U|00\rangle\|^2$ exactly equals 1/2.

Suppose that one can apply another unitary transformation W_q, for some real number $q \in [0,1]$, and define the unitary transformation U and projection operator Π_0 by

$$U = W_p \otimes W_q, \quad \Pi_0 = |11\rangle\langle 11|.$$

Then, clearly, $\|\Pi_0 U|00\rangle\|^2 = pq$, and thus, this probability equals 1/2 if and only if $pq = 1/2$. This in particular implies that there exists a real number $q \in [0,1]$ that achieves the adjusted accepting probability exactly 1/2 when $p \geq 1/2$, but no $q \in [0,1]$ can make it exactly equal to 1/2 when $p < 1/2$.

6.1.3 *Simulating Unitaries with Choi-Jamiołkowski States*

In this subsection, we consider the case where the aforementioned unitary transformation W_a itself is not available, but only the copies of its Choi-Jamiołkowski state $|J(W_a)\rangle = (I \otimes W_a)|\Phi^+\rangle$ are available.

Note that one copy of the Choi-Jamiołkowski state $|J(W_a)\rangle$ can be used to simulate one application of W_a (the simulation succeeds with probability 1/4). More precisely, the simulation of W_a is done as follows. Suppose one wants to apply W_a to the qubit in some single-qubit register R_1, while the state $|J(W_a)\rangle$ is available in $(\mathsf{R}_2, \mathsf{R}_2')$, for some single-qubit registers R_2 and R_2'. Then one measures the state in $(\mathsf{R}_1, \mathsf{R}_2)$ in the Bell basis. If this results in $|\Phi^+\rangle$, the application of W_a succeeds, and the desired state is available in the register R_2' (which can be verified via an argument similar to the analysis of seminal quantum teleportation).

Actually, when one wants to apply W_a to the specific state $|0\rangle$, there is a more efficient way than the simulation just explained above. A key observation is that, for any real number $a \in [0,1]$, the unitary transformation W_a in the last subsection can be written as

$$W_a = \begin{pmatrix} \sqrt{1-a} & \sqrt{a} \\ \sqrt{a} & -\sqrt{1-a} \end{pmatrix} = \sqrt{1-a}Z + \sqrt{a}X,$$

and thus, the state $|\chi_a\rangle$ is given by

$$|\chi_a\rangle = W_a|0\rangle = \sqrt{1-a}|0\rangle + \sqrt{a}|1\rangle,$$

while the Choi-Jamiołkowski state of W_a is given by

$$\begin{aligned} |J(W_a)\rangle &= \sqrt{1-a}|J(Z)\rangle + \sqrt{a}|J(X)\rangle \\ &= \sqrt{1-a}|\Phi^-\rangle + \sqrt{a}|\Psi^+\rangle. \end{aligned}$$

Hence, given one copy of the Choi-Jamiołkowski state $|J(W_a)\rangle$, one can easily generate the state $|\chi_a\rangle = W_a|0\rangle$ in the first qubit by applying the following unitary transformation T to $|J(W_a)\rangle$:

$$T\colon |\Phi^-\rangle \mapsto |00\rangle,\ |\Psi^-\rangle \mapsto |01\rangle,\ |\Psi^+\rangle \mapsto |10\rangle,\ |\Phi^+\rangle \mapsto |11\rangle$$

(note that this T can be realized by first applying the CNOT transformation using the first qubit as the control, then applying the Hadamard transformation H and the NOT transformation X in this order to the first qubit, and finally applying CNOT again using the first qubit as the control).

6.1.4 *Simulating the Reflection Procedure with Choi-Jamiołkowski States*

Now we consider simulating the Reflection Procedure with given two copies of $|\chi_p\rangle = W_p|0\rangle$ and two copies of a Choi-Jamiołkowski state $|J(W_q)\rangle$, where p and q are real numbers in $[0,1]$. The procedure basically follows the Reflection Procedure with taking the register Q to be a two-qubit register, the initial state $|\phi_0\rangle$ to be $|00\rangle$, the projection Δ_0 to be $|00\rangle\langle 00|$, and the underlying unitary U and projection Π_0 to be $W_p \otimes W_q$ and $|11\rangle\langle 11|$, as defined in Subsection 6.1.2. Thus, to precisely perform the Reflection Procedure in Figure 3 in this setting, we need to apply each of $W_p = W_p^\dagger$ and $W_q = W_q^\dagger$ twice. Fortunately, each of the first applications of W_p and W_q is to the $|0\rangle$ state, and thus, one may simply replace these applications by just using a given copy of $|\chi_p\rangle$ and generating $|\chi_q\rangle$ from a copy of $|J(W_q)\rangle$, respectively. The second applications of these unitaries can be probabilistically simulated by using the Choi-Jamiołkowski states $|J(W_p)\rangle$ and $|J(W_q)\rangle$, where one creates $|J(W_p)\rangle$ from a copy of $|\chi_p\rangle$. This leads to the procedure called Reflection Simulation Test described in Figure 5.

Now we analyze the properties of this simulation.

Proposition 19. *The* Reflection Simulation Test *accepts with certainty if the state in the input register* $(\mathsf{R}_1, \mathsf{R}_2, \mathsf{S}_1, \mathsf{S}_1', \mathsf{S}_2, \mathsf{S}_2')$ *is* $|\chi_p\rangle^{\otimes 2} \otimes |J(W_q)\rangle^{\otimes 2}$ *for some real numbers* $p, q \in [0,1]$ *satisfying* $pq = 1/2$.

Proof. The claim is almost obvious. With $|\chi_p\rangle$ in R_1 and $|J(W_q)\rangle$ in $(\mathsf{S}_1, \mathsf{S}_1')$ for such p and q, Step 1 in the Reflection Simulation Test creates the state

$$U|00\rangle = \left(\sqrt{1-p}|0\rangle + \sqrt{p}|1\rangle\right)_{\mathsf{R}_1} \otimes \left(\sqrt{1-q}|0\rangle + \sqrt{q}|1\rangle\right)_{\mathsf{S}_1}$$

in $(\mathsf{R}_1, \mathsf{S}_1)$, since the application of T generates the state $|\chi_q\rangle$ in S_1. As the application of $T^\dagger$ in Step 3 generates the

Reflection Simulation Test

Input: single-qubit registers R_1, R_2, S_1, S'_1, S_2, and S'_2.

Output: "accept" or "reject".

1. Receive six single-qubit registers R_1, R_2, S_1, S'_1, S_2, and S'_2.
   Apply the unitary transformation T to the state in $(\mathsf{S}_1, \mathsf{S}'_1)$.
   Prepare $|0\rangle$ in a single-qubit register R'_2.
2. Perform a phase-flip (i.e., multiply -1 in phase) if $(\mathsf{R}_1, \mathsf{S}_1)$ contains 11.
3. Try to simulate Step 3 of the REFLECTION PROCEDURE by performing the following:
   Apply $T^\dagger$ to the state in $(\mathsf{R}_2, \mathsf{R}'_2)$. Measure the states in $(\mathsf{R}_1, \mathsf{R}_2)$ and $(\mathsf{S}_1, \mathsf{S}_2)$ in the Bell basis. Continue if both of these two measurements result in $|\Phi^+\rangle$, and accept otherwise (accept with giving up due to failure of the simulation).
4. Reject if $(\mathsf{R}'_2, \mathsf{S}'_2)$ contains 00, and accept otherwise.

Figure 5: The Reflection Simulation Test, which tries to simulate the Reflection Procedure using Choi-Jamiołkowski states.

Choi-Jamiołkowski state $|J(W_p)\rangle$ in $(\mathsf{R}_2, \mathsf{R}'_2)$, one succeeds in Step 3 with probability $(1/4)^2 = 1/16$ in applying both of $W_p^\dagger = W_p$ and $W_q^\dagger = W_q$, which successfully simulates $U^\dagger$ with generating the desired state in $(\mathsf{R}'_2, \mathsf{S}'_2)$. Hence, the simulation of the REFLECTION PROCEDURE succeeds with probability 1/16, in which case the test necessarily results in acceptance as in the analysis in Section 5, since $(|00\rangle\langle 00|U^\dagger \Pi_0 U|00\rangle\langle 00|)|00\rangle = \|\Pi_0 U|00\rangle\|^2|00\rangle = \frac{1}{2}|00\rangle$. On the other hand, if any of measurements in Step 3 fails in measuring $|\Phi^+\rangle$, the test just stops and accepts with giving up. Therefore, the test must result in acceptance with certainty. □

PROPOSITION 20. *The* REFLECTION SIMULATION TEST *results in rejection with probability* 1/16 *if the state in the input register* $(\mathsf{R}_1, \mathsf{R}_2, \mathsf{S}_1, \mathsf{S}'_1, \mathsf{S}_2, \mathsf{S}'_2)$ *is* $|0\rangle^{\otimes 2} \otimes |J(W_q)\rangle^{\otimes 2}$ *for any real number* $q \in [0, 1]$.

PROOF. With $|0\rangle$ in R_1 and $|J(W_q)\rangle$ in $(\mathsf{S}_1, \mathsf{S}'_1)$, Step 1 in the REFLECTION SIMULATION TEST creates the state

$$|0\rangle_{\mathsf{R}_1} \otimes |\chi_q\rangle_{\mathsf{S}_1}$$

in $(\mathsf{R}_1, \mathsf{S}_1)$. For this state given, Step 2 in the REFLECTION SIMULATION TEST does not change the state in $(\mathsf{R}_1, \mathsf{S}_1)$ at all. As $|0\rangle = |\chi_0\rangle$, the application of $T^\dagger$ in Step 3 generates the Choi-Jamiołkowski state $|J(W_0)\rangle$ in $(\mathsf{R}_2, \mathsf{R}'_2)$, and thus, one succeeds in Step 3 with probability $(1/4)^2 = 1/16$ in applying both of $W_0^\dagger = W_0$ and $W_q^\dagger = W_q$. If such an event occurs, the state in $(\mathsf{R}'_2, \mathsf{S}'_2)$ becomes $|0\rangle_{\mathsf{R}'_2} \otimes |0\rangle_{\mathsf{S}'_2}$, and thus, the test results in rejection with certainty.

Taking it into account that the test just stops and accepts with giving up when any of measurements in Step 3 fails in measuring $|\Phi^+\rangle$, the test results in rejection with probability 1/16 in total. □

6.2 Proof of Theorem 2

Now we are ready to prove Theorem 2.

PROOF OF THEOREM 2. Let $A = (A_{\rm yes}, A_{\rm no})$ be in QMA and let V be the verifier of the corresponding QMA system. Without loss of generality, one can assume that both completeness and soundness errors are exponentially small in this QMA system.

For an input x, the quantum circuit V_x of the verifier V acts over a pair of two registers A of $v(|x|)$ qubits and M of $m(|x|)$ qubits, for some polynomially bounded functions $v, m \colon \mathbb{Z}^+ \to \mathbb{N}$. This can be interpreted as V_x expecting to receive a quantum witness $|w\rangle$ of $m(|x|)$ qubits in register M, and using the $v(|x|)$ qubits in A as its work qubits. By Refs. [Shi02, Aha03], one can further assume that the quantum circuit V_x for any input x consists of only the Hadamard, Toffoli, and NOT gates. As pointed out by Marriott and Watrous [MW05], the maximum acceptance probability p_x of V with input x corresponds to the maximum eigenvalue of the Hermitian operator

$$M_x = \Pi_{\rm init} V_x^\dagger \Pi_{\rm acc} V_x \Pi_{\rm init},$$

where $\Pi_{\rm init}$ is the projection onto the subspace spanned by states in which all the qubits in A are in state $|0\rangle$, and $\Pi_{\rm acc}$ is the projection onto the space spanned by the accepting states of V. From this verifier V, we shall construct a protocol for the verifier W of another QMA system in which W shares N EPR pairs a priori with a prover communicating with, where N is a constant that is a power of two.

Our basic strategy is to try to perform the REFLECTION SIMULATION TEST using V_x. Fix an input x, and let

$$p = \frac{p_x^2}{2p_x^2 - 2p_x + 1}.$$

Let $\mathsf{S}_1, \ldots, \mathsf{S}_N$ be single-qubit registers which store the particles of the shared EPR pairs. In addition to M, W receives N single-qubit registers $\mathsf{S}'_1, \ldots, \mathsf{S}'_N$. W expects to receive in M the state $|w_x\rangle$ that is the eigenstate (i.e., eigenvector) of M_x corresponding to the eigenvalue p_x, and to receive states in $\mathsf{S}'_1, \ldots, \mathsf{S}'_N$ such that the state in $(\mathsf{S}_j, \mathsf{S}'_j)$ forms $|J(W_q)\rangle$ for each $j \in \{1, \ldots, N\}$, for q satisfying

$$pq = \frac{p_x^2}{2p_x^2 - 2p_x + 1} q = \frac{1}{2}.$$

In addition to A, W prepares three single-qubit registers B, R_1, and R_2. All the qubits in A, B, R_1, and R_2 are initialized to the $|0\rangle$ state.

First, W performs the DISTILLATION PROCEDURE twice in sequence, first with $(\mathsf{R}_1, \mathsf{A}, \mathsf{M})$ as input, and second with $(\mathsf{R}_2, \mathsf{A}, \mathsf{M})$ as input. If any of these two runs of the DISTILLATION PROCEDURE outputs a symbol $\perp$, the simulation fails, and thus accept with giving up. If not failed, then W chooses two indices r_1 and r_2 from the set $\{1, \ldots, N\}$ uniformly at random. If $r_2 = 1$, W accepts with giving up. Otherwise W swaps the registers $(\mathsf{S}_1, \mathsf{S}'_1)$ and $(\mathsf{S}_{r_1}, \mathsf{S}'_{r_1})$ if $r_1 \geq 2$, and further swaps $(\mathsf{S}_2, \mathsf{S}'_2)$ and $(\mathsf{S}_{r_2}, \mathsf{S}'_{r_2})$ if $r_2 \geq 3$. Afterwards, W never touches the registers $(\mathsf{S}_j, \mathsf{S}'_j)$ for $j \geq 3$, and thus this process essentially has the same effect as performing a random permutation over the registers $(\mathsf{S}_1, \mathsf{S}'_1), \ldots, (\mathsf{S}_N, \mathsf{S}'_N)$. W then performs the SPACE RESTRICTION TEST by checking if the state in $(\mathsf{S}_j, \mathsf{S}'_j)$ is in the space spanned by $\{|\Phi^-\rangle, |\Psi^+\rangle\}$, for each $j \in \{1, 2\}$, and further performs the SWAP TEST between $(\mathsf{S}_1, \mathsf{S}'_1)$ and $(\mathsf{S}_2, \mathsf{S}'_2)$ (using the register B as the control). Finally, W performs the REFLECTION

Verifier's QMA Protocol for Achieving Perfect Completeness with N Prior-Shared EPR Pairs

1. Store the particles of the shared N EPR pairs in $(\mathsf{S}_1, \ldots, \mathsf{S}_N)$. Receive an $(m(|x|)+N)$-qubit quantum witness in $(\mathsf{M}, \mathsf{S}'_1, \ldots, \mathsf{S}'_N)$, where the first $m(|x|)$ qubits of the witness are in M, and the $(m(|x|)+j)$-th qubit of the witness is in S_j, for $j \in \{1, \ldots, N\}$.
   Prepare $|0\rangle$ in each of the three single-qubit registers B, R_1 and R_2, and $|0\rangle^{\otimes v(|x|)}$ in a $v(|x|)$-qubit register A, which corresponds to the private space of the original verifier.

2. Execute the DISTILLATION PROCEDURE with $(\mathsf{R}_1, \mathsf{A}, \mathsf{M})$ as input. Accept if this outputs $\perp$, and continue otherwise. Execute the DISTILLATION PROCEDURE again, this time using $(\mathsf{R}_2, \mathsf{A}, \mathsf{M})$ as input. Accept if this outputs $\perp$, and continue otherwise.

3. Choose two integers r_1 and r_2 from $\{1, \ldots, N\}$ uniformly at random. Accept if $r_2 = 1$ (accept with giving up due to failure of simulation), and continue otherwise. Swap the registers $(\mathsf{S}_1, \mathsf{S}'_1)$ and $(\mathsf{S}_{r_1}, \mathsf{S}'_{r_1})$ if $r_1 \geq 2$, and further swap the registers $(\mathsf{S}_2, \mathsf{S}'_2)$ and $(\mathsf{S}_{r_2}, \mathsf{S}'_{r_2})$ if $r_2 \geq 3$.

4. Perform the SPACE RESTRICTION TEST to check if the state in $(\mathsf{S}_j, \mathsf{S}'_j)$ is in the space spanned by $\{|\Phi^-\rangle, |\Psi^+\rangle\}$, for each $j \in \{1, 2\}$. Reject if not so, and continue otherwise.
   That is, perform the following for each $j \in \{1, 2\}$: Apply the unitary transformation T defined by
   $$T\colon |\Phi^-\rangle \mapsto |00\rangle, |\Psi^-\rangle \mapsto |01\rangle, |\Psi^+\rangle \mapsto |10\rangle, |\Phi^+\rangle \mapsto |11\rangle$$
   to the state in $(\mathsf{S}_j, \mathsf{S}'_j)$. Reject if S'_j contains 1, and apply $T^\dagger$ to the state in $(\mathsf{S}_j, \mathsf{S}'_j)$ to continue otherwise.

5. Perform the SWAP TEST between $(\mathsf{S}_1, \mathsf{S}'_1)$ and $(\mathsf{S}_2, \mathsf{S}'_2)$. Reject if it fails, and continue otherwise.
   That is, apply H to B, swap $(\mathsf{S}_1, \mathsf{S}'_1)$ and $(\mathsf{S}_2, \mathsf{S}'_2)$ if B contains 1, apply H to B again, and reject if B contains 1, and continue otherwise.

6. Perform the REFLECTION SIMULATION TEST with $(\mathsf{R}_1, \mathsf{R}_2, \mathsf{S}_1, \mathsf{S}'_1, \mathsf{S}_2, \mathsf{S}'_2)$ as input. Accept if this returns "accept", and reject otherwise.

Figure 6: Verifier's QMA protocol for achieving perfect completeness with N pre-shared EPR pairs.

SIMULATION TEST with $(\mathsf{R}_1, \mathsf{R}_2, \mathsf{S}_1, \mathsf{S}'_1, \mathsf{S}_2, \mathsf{S}'_2)$ as input. The protocol is summarized in Figure 6. Notice that this protocol is exactly implementable when the Hadamard and any classical reversible transformations can be performed exactly.

For the completeness, suppose that x is in $A_{\rm yes}$. Let $p = \frac{p_x^2}{2p_x^2 - 2p_x + 1}$. The honest Merlin sets his shares of the N EPR pairs in single-qubit registers $\mathsf{S}'_1, \ldots, \mathsf{S}'_N$, and applies W_q to each qubit in $(\mathsf{S}'_1, \ldots, \mathsf{S}'_N)$ to create the state $|J(W_q)\rangle$ in $(\mathsf{S}_j, \mathsf{S}'_j)$, for $j \in \{1, \ldots, N\}$, where q satisfies $pq = 1/2$ (such a q always exists when $p_x \geq 1/2$, which is ensured by the completeness condition of the original QMA system). He also prepares $|w_x\rangle$ in M, and sends the $(m(|x|)+N)$-qubit state in $(\mathsf{M}, \mathsf{S}'_1, \ldots, \mathsf{S}'_N)$ as a witness. Then, conditioned on the first application of the DISTILLATION PROCEDURE not outputting $\perp$, the state $|\chi_p\rangle = W_p|0\rangle$ is generated in R_1, and $|0\rangle^{\otimes v(|x|)} \otimes |w_x\rangle$ is left in (A, M), and thus, the state $|\chi_p\rangle$ is generated also in R_2 when the second application of the DISTILLATION PROCEDURE does not output $\perp$. Conditioned on the chosen r_2 not being 1 in Step 3, the protocol continues and the state remains the same after this step. When continued, the SPACE RESTRICTION TEST in Step 4 clearly never rejects and does not change the state at all, as the state in $(\mathsf{S}_j, \mathsf{S}'_j)$ is $|J(W_q)\rangle = \sqrt{1-q}|\Phi^-\rangle + \sqrt{q}|\Psi^+\rangle$ for each $j \in \{1, 2\}$. Furthermore, the SWAP TEST never fails in Step 5 and it does not change the state at all (and thus, the protocol never results in rejection in this step). Therefore, the state in $(\mathsf{R}_1, \mathsf{R}_2, \mathsf{S}_1, \mathsf{S}'_1, \mathsf{S}_2, \mathsf{S}'_2)$ is $|\chi_p\rangle^{\otimes 2} \otimes |J(W_q)\rangle^{\otimes 2}$, when entering Step 6. Hence, from Proposition 19, the REFLECTION SIMULATION TEST results in acceptance with certainty, when the protocol reaches Step 6. As rejections can happen only in Steps 4, 5, and 6, this proves the perfect completeness.

Now for the soundness, suppose that x is in $A_{\rm no}$. Let $\mathcal{R}_j$, $\mathcal{S}_j$, and $\mathcal{S}'_j$ denote the Hilbert spaces associated with the quantum registers R_j, S_j, and S'_j, for each j, respectively.

As the soundness error of the original QMA system is exponentially small, whatever state the register M contains, the probability that the first application of the DISTILLATION PROCEDURE outputs $\perp$ is exponentially small. Moreover, conditioned on this not outputting $\perp$, the state generated in R_1 is exponentially close to $|0\rangle$ (in trace distance). Similarly, whatever state left in M after the first application of the DISTILLATION PROCEDURE, the probability that the second application of the DISTILLATION PROCEDURE outputs $\perp$ is exponentially small, and the state generated in R_2 is exponentially close to $|0\rangle$. Hence, the state in $(\mathsf{R}_1, \mathsf{R}_2, \mathsf{S}_1, \mathsf{S}'_1, \ldots, \mathsf{S}_N, \mathsf{S}'_N)$ when entering Step 2 must be exponentially close to $(|0\rangle\langle 0|)^{\otimes 2} \otimes \rho$ for some $2N$-qubit state ρ such that the reduced state $\mathrm{tr}_{\mathcal{S}'_1 \otimes \cdots \otimes \mathcal{S}'_N} \rho$ is equal to the N-qubit totally mixed state $(I/2)^{\otimes N}$.

As Step 3 essentially has the same effect as performing a random permutation over the registers $(\mathsf{S}_1, \mathsf{S}'_1), \ldots, (\mathsf{S}_N, \mathsf{S}'_N)$ for the purpose of computing the reduced state in $(\mathsf{S}_1, \mathsf{S}'_1, \mathsf{S}_2, \mathsf{S}'_2)$, from the finite quantum de Finetti theorem (Theorem 8), the state in $(\mathsf{R}_1, \mathsf{R}_2, \mathsf{S}_1, \mathsf{S}'_1, \mathsf{S}_2, \mathsf{S}'_2)$ after Step 3 has trace distance at most $\frac{2^6}{N}$ to the state

$$\sigma = (|0\rangle\langle 0|)^{\otimes 2} \otimes \Bigl(\sum_j \mu_j \xi_j^{\otimes 2}\Bigr)$$

for some two-qubit states ξ_j, where $\sum_j \mu_j = 1$, if the state in $(\mathsf{R}_1, \mathsf{R}_2, \mathsf{S}_1, \mathsf{S}'_1, \ldots, \mathsf{S}_N, \mathsf{S}'_N)$ were $(|0\rangle\langle 0|)^{\otimes 2} \otimes \rho$ when entering Step 3 and if $r_2 \neq 1$ (here we are taking the randomness over the choices of r_1 and r_2 into account). By letting $\tau = \sum_j \mu_j \xi_j^{\otimes 2}$, this in particular implies that for the reduced state $\mathrm{tr}_{\mathcal{S}'_1 \otimes \mathcal{S}'_2} \tau$ and the two-qubit totally mixed state $(I/2)^{\otimes 2}$,

$$D\Bigl(\mathrm{tr}_{\mathcal{S}'_1 \otimes \mathcal{S}'_2} \tau, \Bigl(\frac{I}{2}\Bigr)^{\otimes 2}\Bigr) \leq \frac{2^6}{N}$$

holds, since $\mathrm{tr}_{\mathcal{S}'_1 \otimes \cdots \otimes \mathcal{S}'_N} \rho = (I/2)^{\otimes N}$. Taking it into account that the protocol enters Step 3 with probability exponentially close to 1 with the state in $(\mathsf{R}_1, \mathsf{R}_2, \mathsf{S}_1, \mathsf{S}'_1, \ldots, \mathsf{S}_N, \mathsf{S}'_N)$

being exponentially close to $(|0\rangle\langle 0|)^{\otimes 2} \otimes \rho$ in trace distance, we conclude that the protocol enters Step 4 with probability exponentially close to $1 - \frac{1}{N}$ with the state in $(\mathsf{R}_1, \mathsf{R}_2, \mathsf{S}_1, \mathsf{S}'_1, \mathsf{S}_2, \mathsf{S}'_2)$ having trace distance at most $\frac{2^6}{N} + \varepsilon$ to σ for some exponentially small ε.

Now from Proposition 21 which will be found below and proved in the end of this section, the protocol results in rejection with probability at least $\min\{\frac{2^7}{N}, \frac{1}{16} - 15(\frac{2^6}{N})^{\frac{1}{8}}\}$ if the state in $(\mathsf{R}_1, \mathsf{R}_2, \mathsf{S}_1, \mathsf{S}'_1, \mathsf{S}_2, \mathsf{S}'_2)$ were σ when entering Step 4. Hence, using Lemma 6, the protocol results in rejection with probability at least $\min\{\frac{2^6}{N} - \varepsilon, \frac{1}{16} - \frac{2^6}{N} - \varepsilon - 15(\frac{2^6}{N})^{\frac{1}{8}}\}$, when entering Step 4. As the protocol enters Step 4 with probability exponentially close to $1 - \frac{1}{N}$, by taking $N = 2^{70}$, the protocol results in rejection with probability at least

$$\left(1 - \frac{1}{2^{69}}\right) \cdot \min\left\{\frac{1}{2^{65}}, \frac{1}{16} - \frac{1}{2^{63}} - \frac{15}{2^8}\right\} \geq \frac{1}{2^{66}}.$$

This proves the inclusion

$$\mathrm{QMA} \subseteq \mathrm{QMA}^{2^{70}\text{-EPR}}\left(1, 1 - \frac{1}{2^{66}}\right).$$

Now for any constant $s \in (0, 1)$, one can achieve soundness s simply by repeating this proof system t times in parallel for some appropriate constant t, as the system is a special case of two-message quantum interactive proof systems, for which parallel repetition works perfectly [KW00]. This completes the proof. □

Finally, we prove the following proposition.

PROPOSITION 21. *When entering Step 4 of the protocol described in Figure 6, suppose that the state in* $(\mathsf{R}_1, \mathsf{R}_2, \mathsf{S}_1, \mathsf{S}'_1, \mathsf{S}_2, \mathsf{S}'_2)$ *were of the form* $(|0\rangle\langle 0|)^{\otimes 2} \otimes \tau$ *where* $\tau = \sum_j \mu_j \xi_j^{\otimes 2}$ *for some two-qubit states* ξ_j *and real numbers* $\mu_j \in [0, 1]$ *satisfying* $\sum_j \mu_j = 1$, *such that the reduced state of* τ *in* $(\mathsf{S}_1, \mathsf{S}_2)$ *has trace distance at most* δ *to the two-qubit totally mixed state* $(I/2)^{\otimes 2}$ *for some* δ *satisfying* $\frac{1}{16} - 15\delta^{\frac{1}{8}} > 0$. *Then the protocol results in rejection with probability at least* $\min\{2\delta, \frac{1}{16} - 15\delta^{\frac{1}{8}}\}$.

To prove Proposition 21, we first show two propositions that are special cases of Proposition 21.

PROPOSITION 22. *Let* $\mathcal{W}$ *be the two-dimensional space spanned by* $|\Phi^-\rangle$ *and* $|\Psi^+\rangle$. *When entering Step 4 of the protocol described in Figure 6, suppose that the state in* $(\mathsf{R}_1, \mathsf{R}_2, \mathsf{S}_1, \mathsf{S}'_1, \mathsf{S}_2, \mathsf{S}'_2)$ *were of the form* $(|0\rangle\langle 0|)^{\otimes 2} \otimes \tau$ *where* $\tau = \sum_j \mu_j (|\psi_j\rangle\langle\psi_j|)^{\otimes 2}$ *for some two-qubit states* $|\psi_j\rangle \in \mathcal{W}$ *and real numbers* $\mu_j \in [0, 1]$ *satisfying* $\sum_j \mu_j = 1$, *such that the reduced state of* τ *in* $(\mathsf{S}_1, \mathsf{S}_2)$ *has trace distance at most* δ *to the two-qubit totally mixed state* $(I/2)^{\otimes 2}$ *for some* $\delta < 2^{-9}$. *Then the protocol results in rejection with probability at least* $\frac{1}{16} - (2\delta)^{\frac{1}{2}}$.

The following lemma is essential for the proof of Proposition 22.

LEMMA 23. *For each* $j \in \{1, 2\}$, *let* $\mathcal{S}_j$ *and* $\mathcal{S}'_j$ *be two-dimensional complex Hilbert spaces* $\mathbb{C}(\Sigma)$, *and let* $\mathcal{W}_j$ *be the two-dimensional subspace of* $\mathcal{S}_j \otimes \mathcal{S}'_j$ *spanned by* $|\Phi^-\rangle$ *and* $|\Psi^+\rangle$. *Let* ρ *be any four-qubit state in* $\mathbf{D}(\mathcal{W}_1 \otimes \mathcal{W}_2) \subseteq \mathbf{D}(\mathcal{S}_1 \otimes \mathcal{S}'_1 \otimes \mathcal{S}_2 \otimes \mathcal{S}'_2)$ *that is a mixture of two-fold product pure states* $|\zeta_j\rangle^{\otimes 2}$ *in* $\mathcal{W}_1 \otimes \mathcal{W}_2$ *and such that* $D(\mathrm{tr}_{\mathcal{S}'_1 \otimes \mathcal{S}'_2} \rho, (I/2)^{\otimes 2}) \leq \varepsilon$. *Then there exists a four-qubit state* σ *that is a mixture of two-fold products* $|J(W_{a_j})\rangle^{\otimes 2}$ *of a Choi-Jamiołkowski state, for real numbers* $a_j \in [0, 1]$, *such that* $D(\rho, \sigma) \leq (2\varepsilon)^{\frac{1}{2}}$.

PROOF. As ρ is a mixture of two-fold product pure states in $\mathcal{W}_1 \otimes \mathcal{W}_2$, it must be written as

$$\rho = \sum_j \mu_j (|\zeta_j\rangle\langle\zeta_j|)^{\otimes 2},$$

where $|\zeta_j\rangle^{\otimes 2} \in \mathcal{W}_1 \otimes \mathcal{W}_2$, $\mu_j \in [0, 1]$ for each j, and $\sum_j \mu_j = 1$. Without loss of generality, one may assume that

$$|\zeta_j\rangle = \alpha_j |\Phi^-\rangle + \beta_j e^{i\theta_j} |\Psi^+\rangle$$

for each j, where α_j and β_j are real numbers in $[0, 1]$ satisfying $\alpha_j^2 + \beta_j^2 = 1$, and θ_j is a real number in $[0, 2\pi)$. For each j, let $a_j = \beta_j^2$, and define the two-qubit pure state $|\eta_j\rangle$ as

$$\begin{aligned}|\eta_j\rangle &= \alpha_j |\Phi^-\rangle + \beta_j |\Psi^+\rangle \\ &= \sqrt{1 - a_j} |\Phi^-\rangle + \sqrt{a_j} |\Psi^+\rangle = |J(W_{a_j})\rangle.\end{aligned}$$

Now take the four-qubit state σ as

$$\sigma = \sum_j \mu_j (|\eta_j\rangle\langle\eta_j|)^{\otimes 2}.$$

We shall show that this σ has the desired property. For this purpose, we prove two claims.

CLAIM 1. $D\left(\mathrm{tr}_{\mathcal{S}'_1 \otimes \mathcal{S}'_2} \rho, (I/2)^{\otimes 2}\right) \geq 2 \sum_j \mu_j \alpha_j^2 \beta_j^2 \sin^2 \theta_j$.

PROOF. Noticing that

$$\begin{aligned}|\zeta_j\rangle &= \frac{1}{\sqrt{2}} \left[\alpha_j (|00\rangle - |11\rangle) + \beta_j e^{i\theta_j} (|01\rangle + |10\rangle)\right] \\ &= \frac{1}{\sqrt{2}} \big[(\alpha_j |0\rangle + \beta_j e^{i\theta_j} |1\rangle) \otimes |0\rangle \\ &\qquad + e^{i\theta_j} (\beta_j |0\rangle - \alpha_j e^{-i\theta_j} |1\rangle) \otimes |1\rangle\big],\end{aligned}$$

the reduced state $\mathrm{tr}_{\mathcal{S}'_1 \otimes \mathcal{S}'_2} \rho$ is the mixture of the following four states

$$\begin{aligned}&(\alpha_j |0\rangle + \beta_j e^{i\theta_j} |1\rangle) \otimes (\alpha_j |0\rangle + \beta_j e^{i\theta_j} |1\rangle), \\ &(\alpha_j |0\rangle + \beta_j e^{i\theta_j} |1\rangle) \otimes (\beta_j |0\rangle - \alpha_j e^{-i\theta_j} |1\rangle), \\ &(\beta_j |0\rangle - \alpha_j e^{-i\theta_j} |1\rangle) \otimes (\alpha_j |0\rangle + \beta_j e^{i\theta_j} |1\rangle), \\ &(\beta_j |0\rangle - \alpha_j e^{-i\theta_j} |1\rangle) \otimes (\beta_j |0\rangle - \alpha_j e^{-i\theta_j} |1\rangle)\end{aligned}$$

with equal probability 1/4 for each, which can be expressed as a density matrix by

$$\frac{1}{4} \begin{pmatrix} 1 & -2i\alpha_j\beta_j s_j & -2i\alpha_j\beta_j s_j & -4\alpha_j^2\beta_j^2 s_j^2 \\ 2i\alpha_j\beta_j s_j & 1 & 4\alpha_j^2\beta_j^2 s_j^2 & -2i\alpha_j\beta_j s_j \\ 2i\alpha_j\beta_j s_j & 4\alpha_j^2\beta_j^2 s_j^2 & 1 & -2i\alpha_j\beta_j s_j \\ -4\alpha_j^2\beta_j^2 s_j^2 & 2i\alpha_j\beta_j s_j & 2i\alpha_j\beta_j s_j & 1 \end{pmatrix},$$

where s_j is the shorthand of $\sin\theta_j$. Let us denote the difference between $\mathrm{tr}_{\mathcal{S}'_1 \otimes \mathcal{S}'_2} \rho$ and $(I/2)^{\otimes 2}$ by A (i.e., $A = \mathrm{tr}_{\mathcal{S}'_1 \otimes \mathcal{S}'_2} \rho - (I/2)^{\otimes 2}$). In order to find the eigenvalues of $2A$, we solve the characteristic equation $|2A - \lambda I| = 0$. Straightforward calculations show that the four solutions of the equation $|2A - \lambda I| = 0$ are given by $-2\sum_j \mu_j \alpha_j^2 \beta_j^2 s_j^2$

(two-fold) and $2\sum_j \mu_j\alpha_j^2\beta_j^2 s_j^2 \pm 2\left|\sum_j \mu_j\alpha_j\beta_j s_j\right|$. This implies that

$$D\left(\mathrm{tr}_{S_1'\otimes S_2'}\rho, \left(\frac{I}{2}\right)^{\otimes 2}\right) = \frac{1}{2}\mathrm{tr}\sqrt{A^\dagger A}$$

$$= \frac{1}{2}\left[2\sum_j \mu_j\alpha_j^2\beta_j^2 s_j^2 + \left(\sum_j \mu_j\alpha_j^2\beta_j^2 s_j^2 + \left|\sum_j \mu_j\alpha_j\beta_j s_j\right|\right)\right.$$
$$\left. + \left|\sum_j \mu_j\alpha_j^2\beta_j^2 s_j^2 - \left|\sum_j \mu_j\alpha_j\beta_j s_j\right|\right|\right]$$
$$= \sum_j \mu_j\alpha_j^2\beta_j^2 s_j^2 + \max\left\{\sum_j \mu_j\alpha_j^2\beta_j^2 s_j^2, \left|\sum_j \mu_j\alpha_j\beta_j s_j\right|\right\},$$

which is at least $2\sum_j \mu_j\alpha_j^2\beta_j^2 s_j^2$. This completes the proof of the claim. □

CLAIM 2. *Let $\{\mu_j\}$ be a probability distribution, and $\{c_j\}$ be a set of real numbers. If $\sum_j \mu_j c_j^2 \leq \delta$, it holds that $\sum_j \mu_j|c_j| \leq \delta^{\frac{1}{2}}$.*

PROOF. By the Cauchy-Schwarz inequality, we have

$$\sum_j \mu_j|c_j| = \sum_j \sqrt{\mu_j}\cdot\sqrt{\mu_j}|c_j|$$
$$\leq \left(\sum_j \mu_j\right)^{\frac{1}{2}}\left(\sum_j \mu_j|c_j|^2\right)^{\frac{1}{2}} \leq \delta^{\frac{1}{2}},$$

as claimed. □

Now we bound $D(\rho,\sigma)$. Notice that

$$D(\rho,\sigma) \leq \sum_j \mu_j D\left((|\zeta_j\rangle\langle\zeta_j|)^{\otimes 2}, (|\eta_j\rangle\langle\eta_j|)^{\otimes 2}\right)$$
$$= \sum_j \mu_j\sqrt{1-\left(|\langle\zeta_j|\eta_j\rangle|^2\right)^2}.$$

Since

$$\left(|\langle\zeta_j|\eta_j\rangle|^2\right)^2 = \left(|\alpha_j^2 + \beta_j^2 e^{-i\theta_j}|^2\right)^2$$
$$= \left((\alpha_j^2+\beta_j^2\cos\theta_j)^2 + (\beta_j^2\sin\theta_j)^2\right)^2$$
$$= (1-2\alpha_j^2\beta_j^2\sin^2\theta_j)^2,$$

we have

$$\sqrt{1-\left(|\langle\zeta_j|\eta_j\rangle|^2\right)^2} = 2|\alpha_j\beta_j\sin\theta_j|\sqrt{1-\alpha_j^2\beta_j^2\sin^2\theta_j}$$
$$\leq 2|\alpha_j\beta_j\sin\theta_j|.$$

Therefore,

$$D(\rho,\sigma) \leq 2\sum_j \mu_j|\alpha_j\beta_j\sin\theta_j|.$$

By Claim 1, the assumption $D(\mathrm{tr}_{S_1'\otimes S_2'}\rho, (I/2)^{\otimes 2}) \leq \varepsilon$ implies that

$$\sum_j \mu_j\alpha_j^2\beta_j^2\sin^2\theta_j \leq \frac{\varepsilon}{2}.$$

By Claim 2, this implies that $D(\rho,\sigma) \leq 2(\frac{\varepsilon}{2})^{\frac{1}{2}} = (2\varepsilon)^{\frac{1}{2}}$, which completes the proof of Lemma 23. □

PROOF OF PROPOSITION 22. Let $\sigma = (|0\rangle\langle 0|)^{\otimes 2}\otimes\tau$. From Lemma 23, there exists a quantum state τ' that is a mixture of two-fold products $|J(W_{a_j})\rangle^{\otimes 2}$ of a Choi-Jamiołkowski state, for real numbers $a_j \in [0,1]$, such that, for $\sigma' = (|0\rangle\langle 0|)^{\otimes 2}\otimes\tau'$,

$$D(\sigma,\sigma') \leq (2\delta)^{\frac{1}{2}}.$$

From Proposition 20, the REFLECTION SIMULATION TEST results in rejection with probability $\frac{1}{16}$ if the quantum state in $(\mathsf{R}_1,\mathsf{R}_2,\mathsf{S}_1,\mathsf{S}_1',\mathsf{S}_2,\mathsf{S}_2')$ were σ'. By Lemma 6, this implies that the REFLECTION SIMULATION TEST results in rejection with probability at least $\frac{1}{16}-(2\delta)^{\frac{1}{2}}$ if the state in $(\mathsf{R}_1,\mathsf{R}_2,\mathsf{S}_1,\mathsf{S}_1',\mathsf{S}_2,\mathsf{S}_2')$ were σ. Note that σ is never rejected in Step 4 and passes the Swap-Test in Step 5 with certainty, and the state is not changed at all in these two steps. Hence, if the state in $(\mathsf{R}_1,\mathsf{R}_2,\mathsf{S}_1,\mathsf{S}_1',\mathsf{S}_2,\mathsf{S}_2')$ were σ when entering Step 4, the protocol results in rejection with probability at least $\frac{1}{16}-(2\delta)^{\frac{1}{2}}$, as claimed. □

We next show the following proposition, which is more general than Proposition 22, but still is a special case of Proposition 21.

PROPOSITION 24. *Let $\mathcal{W}$ be the two-dimensional space spanned by $|\Phi^-\rangle$ and $|\Psi^+\rangle$. When entering Step 4 of the protocol described in Figure 6, suppose that the state in $(\mathsf{R}_1,\mathsf{R}_2,\mathsf{S}_1,\mathsf{S}_1',\mathsf{S}_2,\mathsf{S}_2')$ were of the form $(|0\rangle\langle 0|)^{\otimes 2}\otimes\tau$ where $\tau = \sum_j \mu_j\xi_j^{\otimes 2}$ for some two-qubit states $\xi_j \in \mathbf{D}(\mathcal{W})$ and real numbers $\mu_j \in [0,1]$ satisfying $\sum_j \mu_j = 1$, such that the reduced state of τ in $(\mathsf{S}_1,\mathsf{S}_2)$ has trace distance at most δ to the two-qubit totally mixed state $(I/2)^{\otimes 2}$ for some δ satisfying $\frac{1}{16}-10\delta^{\frac{1}{4}} > 0$. Then the protocol results in rejection with probability at least $\min\{2\delta, \frac{1}{16}-10\delta^{\frac{1}{4}}\}$.*

PROOF. Let $\sigma = (|0\rangle\langle 0|)^{\otimes 2}\otimes\tau$. Note that σ is never rejected in Step 4, and the state is not changed at all in this step.

Fix a positive constant $\gamma_1 \in (0,1)$, and let S be the set of indices j defined by

$$S = \{j : \mathrm{tr}\xi_j^{\,2} \geq 1-\gamma_1\}.$$

Notice that the inequality $\mathrm{tr}\xi_j^{\,2} \geq 1-\gamma_1$ implies that the maximum eigenvalue of the Hermitian matrix ξ_j is at least $1-\gamma_1$, and thus, for each $j \in S$, there exist a two-qubit pure state $|\psi_j\rangle \in \mathcal{W}$, a two-qubit state $\nu_j \in \mathbf{D}(\mathcal{W})$, and a real number $\lambda_j \in [1-\gamma_1, 1]$ such that

$$\xi_j = \lambda_j|\psi_j\rangle\langle\psi_j| + (1-\lambda_j)\nu_j.$$

This implies that

$$\left\|\xi_j - |\psi_j\rangle\langle\psi_j|\right\|_{\mathrm{tr}} = \left\|\lambda_j|\psi_j\rangle\langle\psi_j| + (1-\lambda_j)\nu_j - |\psi_j\rangle\langle\psi_j|\right\|_{\mathrm{tr}}$$
$$= (1-\lambda_j)\left\|\nu_j - |\psi_j\rangle\langle\psi_j|\right\|_{\mathrm{tr}},$$

which further implies that

$$D(\xi_j, |\psi_j\rangle\langle\psi_j|) \leq (1-\lambda_j)D(\nu_j, |\psi_j\rangle\langle\psi_j|) \leq 1-\lambda_j \leq \gamma_1.$$

Fix another positive constant $\gamma_2 \in (0,1)$.

If $\sum_{j\in S}\mu_j < 1-\gamma_2$, the SWAP TEST in Step 5 results in rejection with probability greater than $\frac{1}{2}\gamma_1\gamma_2$.

On the other hand, if $\sum_{j\in S}\mu_j \geq 1-\gamma_2$, the state σ has trace distance at most $2\gamma_1+\gamma_2$ to the state $\sigma' = (|0\rangle\langle 0|)^{\otimes 2} \otimes \tau'$, where

$$\tau' = \frac{1}{\sum_{j\in S}\mu_j}\sum_{j\in S}\mu_j(|\psi_j\rangle\langle\psi_j|)^{\otimes 2}$$

and the reduced state of τ' in $(\mathsf{S}_1, \mathsf{S}_2)$ has trace distance at most $\delta + 2\gamma_1 + \gamma_2$ to $(I/2)^{\otimes 2}$.

Indeed,

$$\begin{aligned}
\|\tau - \tau'\|_{\mathrm{tr}} &= \Big\|\sum_j \mu_j\xi_j^{\otimes 2} - \tau'\Big\|_{\mathrm{tr}} \\
&\le \Big\|\sum_j \mu_j\xi_j^{\otimes 2} - \Big(\sum_{j\in S}\mu_j(|\psi_j\rangle\langle\psi_j|)^{\otimes 2} + \sum_{j\notin S}\mu_j\xi_j^{\otimes 2}\Big)\Big\|_{\mathrm{tr}} \\
&\quad + \Big\|\Big(\sum_{j\in S}\mu_j(|\psi_j\rangle\langle\psi_j|)^{\otimes 2} + \sum_{j\notin S}\mu_j\xi_j^{\otimes 2}\Big) - \tau'\Big\|_{\mathrm{tr}} \\
&\le \sum_{j\in S}\mu_j\|\xi_j^{\otimes 2} - (|\psi_j\rangle\langle\psi_j|)^{\otimes 2}\|_{\mathrm{tr}} \\
&\quad + \Big\|\sum_{j\notin S}\mu_j\xi_j^{\otimes 2} - \Big(\frac{1}{\sum_{j\in S}\mu_j} - 1\Big)\sum_{j\in S}\mu_j(|\psi_j\rangle\langle\psi_j|)^{\otimes 2}\Big\|_{\mathrm{tr}} \\
&\le \sum_{j\in S}\mu_j\Big(\|\xi_j^{\otimes 2} - |\psi_j\rangle\langle\psi_j|\otimes\xi_j\|_{\mathrm{tr}} \\
&\qquad + \||\psi_j\rangle\langle\psi_j|\otimes\xi_j - (|\psi_j\rangle\langle\psi_j|)^{\otimes 2}\|_{\mathrm{tr}}\Big) \\
&\quad + \Big(1 - \sum_{j\in S}\mu_j\Big)\Big\|\frac{1}{\sum_{j\notin S}\mu_j}\sum_{j\notin S}\mu_j\xi_j^{\otimes 2} - \tau'\Big\|_{\mathrm{tr}} \\
&\le 2\sum_{j\in S}\mu_j\|\xi_j - |\psi_j\rangle\langle\psi_j|\|_{\mathrm{tr}} \\
&\quad + \Big(1 - \sum_{j\in S}\mu_j\Big)\Big\|\frac{1}{\sum_{j\notin S}\mu_j}\sum_{j\notin S}\mu_j\xi_j^{\otimes 2} - \tau'\Big\|_{\mathrm{tr}},
\end{aligned}$$

and thus,

$$\begin{aligned}
D(\sigma, \sigma') &= D(\tau, \tau') \\
&\le 2\sum_{j\in S}\mu_j D(\xi_j, |\psi_j\rangle\langle\psi_j|) \\
&\quad + \Big(1 - \sum_{j\in S}\mu_j\Big) D\Big(\frac{1}{\sum_{j\notin S}\mu_j}\sum_{j\notin S}\mu_j\xi_j^{\otimes 2}, \tau'\Big) \\
&\le 2\gamma_1 + \gamma_2.
\end{aligned}$$

As the reduced state of τ in $(\mathsf{S}_1, \mathsf{S}_2)$ has trace distance at most δ to $(I/2)^{\otimes 2}$, it follows that the reduced state of τ' in $(\mathsf{S}_1, \mathsf{S}_2)$ has trace distance at most $\delta + 2\gamma_1 + \gamma_2$ to $(I/2)^{\otimes 2}$. Now from Proposition 22, the protocol results in rejection with probability at least $\frac{1}{16} - [2(\delta + 2\gamma_1 + \gamma_2)]^{\frac{1}{2}}$ if the state in $(\mathsf{R}_1, \mathsf{R}_2, \mathsf{S}_1, \mathsf{S}'_1, \mathsf{S}_2, \mathsf{S}'_2)$ were σ' when entering Step 4. Hence, from Lemma 6, the protocol results in rejection with probability at least $\frac{1}{16} - 2\gamma_1 - \gamma_2 - [2(\delta + 2\gamma_1 + \gamma_2)]^{\frac{1}{2}}$ if the state in the registers $(\mathsf{R}_1, \mathsf{R}_2, \mathsf{S}_1, \mathsf{S}'_1, \mathsf{S}_2, \mathsf{S}'_2)$ were σ when entering Step 4.

Overall, taking $\gamma_1 = \gamma_2 = 2\delta^{\frac{1}{2}}$, the protocol results in rejection with probability at least

$$\begin{aligned}
&\min\Big\{2\delta, \frac{1}{16} - 6\delta^{\frac{1}{2}} - \big[2\big(\delta + 6\delta^{\frac{1}{2}}\big)\big]^{\frac{1}{2}}\Big\} \\
&\quad \ge \min\Big\{2\delta, \frac{1}{16} - 6\delta^{\frac{1}{2}} - 4\delta^{\frac{1}{4}}\Big\} \ge \min\Big\{2\delta, \frac{1}{16} - 10\delta^{\frac{1}{4}}\Big\},
\end{aligned}$$

if the state in $(\mathsf{R}_1, \mathsf{R}_2, \mathsf{S}_1, \mathsf{S}'_1, \mathsf{S}_2, \mathsf{S}'_2)$ were σ when entering Step 4. This completes the proof. □

Now we are ready to prove Proposition 21.

Proof of Proposition 21. Let $\sigma = (|0\rangle\langle 0|)^{\otimes 2} \otimes \tau$. Let $\mathcal{W}$ be the two-dimensional space spanned by $|\Phi^-\rangle$ and $|\Psi^+\rangle$, and let

$$\Pi_{\mathcal{W}} = |\Phi^-\rangle\langle\Phi^-| + |\Psi^+\rangle\langle\Psi^+|$$

be the projection onto $\mathcal{W}$.

Fix a constant $\gamma \in (0, 1)$.

If $\mathrm{tr}\Pi_{\mathcal{W}}^{\otimes 2}\tau < 1 - \gamma$, Step 4 results in rejection with probability greater than γ.

On the other hand, if $\mathrm{tr}\Pi_{\mathcal{W}}^{\otimes 2}\tau \ge 1 - \gamma$, we claim that the state σ has trace distance at most $\sqrt{\gamma}$ to the state $\sigma' = (|0\rangle\langle 0|)^{\otimes 2} \otimes \tau'$, where

$$\tau' = \sum_j \mu'_j \xi'^{\otimes 2}_j$$

with

$$\mu'_j = \frac{1}{\mathrm{tr}\Pi_{\mathcal{W}}^{\otimes 2}\tau}(\mathrm{tr}\Pi_{\mathcal{W}}\xi_j)^2\mu_j, \quad \xi'_j = \frac{1}{\mathrm{tr}\Pi_{\mathcal{W}}\xi_j}\Pi_{\mathcal{W}}\xi_j\Pi_{\mathcal{W}},$$

for each j, and the reduced state of τ' in $(\mathsf{S}_1, \mathsf{S}_2)$ has trace distance at most γ to $(I/2)^{\otimes 2}$. Note that $\mu'_j \in [0, 1]$ and $\xi'_j \in \mathbf{D}(\mathcal{W})$ for each j, and $\sum_j \mu'_j = 1$.

Let $\mathcal{S}$ be the 2^4-dimensional Hilbert space $\mathbb{C}(\Sigma^4)$ associated with the quantum register $(\mathsf{S}_1, \mathsf{S}'_1, \mathsf{S}_2, \mathsf{S}'_2)$ and let $\mathcal{T}$ be another 2^4-dimensional Hilbert space $\mathbb{C}(\Sigma^4)$. Consider any purification $|\psi\rangle \in \mathcal{S} \otimes \mathcal{T}$ of $\tau \in \mathbf{D}(\mathcal{S})$, and define an eight-qubit pure state $|\psi'\rangle \in \mathcal{S} \otimes \mathcal{T}$ by

$$|\psi'\rangle = \frac{1}{\|(\Pi_{\mathcal{W}}^{\otimes 2} \otimes I_{\mathcal{T}})|\psi\rangle\|}(\Pi_{\mathcal{W}}^{\otimes 2} \otimes I_{\mathcal{T}})|\psi\rangle.$$

Then, $|\psi'\rangle$ is a purification of τ', since

$$\begin{aligned}
&\mathrm{tr}_{\mathcal{T}}|\psi'\rangle\langle\psi'| \\
&= \frac{1}{\|(\Pi_{\mathcal{W}}^{\otimes 2} \otimes I_{\mathcal{T}})|\psi\rangle\|^2}\mathrm{tr}_{\mathcal{T}}(\Pi_{\mathcal{W}}^{\otimes 2} \otimes I_{\mathcal{T}})|\psi\rangle\langle\psi|(\Pi_{\mathcal{W}}^{\otimes 2} \otimes I_{\mathcal{T}}) \\
&= \frac{1}{\mathrm{tr}\Pi_{\mathcal{W}}^{\otimes 2}\mathrm{tr}_{\mathcal{T}}|\psi\rangle\langle\psi|}\Pi_{\mathcal{W}}^{\otimes 2}(\mathrm{tr}_{\mathcal{T}}|\psi\rangle\langle\psi|)\Pi_{\mathcal{W}}^{\otimes 2} \\
&= \frac{1}{\mathrm{tr}\Pi_{\mathcal{W}}^{\otimes 2}\tau}\Pi_{\mathcal{W}}^{\otimes 2}\tau\Pi_{\mathcal{W}}^{\otimes 2} = \tau',
\end{aligned}$$

where the last equality follows from the fact that

$$\begin{aligned}
\tau' &= \sum_j \frac{1}{\mathrm{tr}\Pi_{\mathcal{W}}^{\otimes 2}\tau}(\mathrm{tr}\Pi_{\mathcal{W}}\xi_j)^2\mu_j\Big(\frac{1}{\mathrm{tr}\Pi_{\mathcal{W}}\xi_j}\Pi_{\mathcal{W}}\xi_j\Pi_{\mathcal{W}}\Big)^{\otimes 2} \\
&= \frac{1}{\mathrm{tr}\Pi_{\mathcal{W}}^{\otimes 2}\tau}\sum_j \mu_j(\Pi_{\mathcal{W}}\xi_j\Pi_{\mathcal{W}})^{\otimes 2} = \frac{1}{\mathrm{tr}\Pi_{\mathcal{W}}^{\otimes 2}\tau}\Pi_{\mathcal{W}}^{\otimes 2}\tau\Pi_{\mathcal{W}}^{\otimes 2}.
\end{aligned}$$

Therefore, by using the fact that

$$D\big(|\psi\rangle\langle\psi|, |\psi'\rangle\langle\psi'|\big) = \sqrt{1 - |\langle\psi|\psi'\rangle|^2}$$

holds for any pure states $|\psi\rangle$ and $|\psi'\rangle$ (which is ensured by calculating eigenvalues of the Hermitian matrix $|\psi\rangle\langle\psi| - |\psi'\rangle\langle\psi'|$),

$$\begin{aligned}
D(\sigma, \sigma') &= D(\tau, \tau') \\
&\le D\big(|\psi\rangle\langle\psi|, |\psi'\rangle\langle\psi'|\big) \\
&= \sqrt{1 - |\langle\psi|\psi'\rangle|^2} \\
&= \sqrt{1 - \|(\Pi_{\mathcal{W}}^{\otimes 2} \otimes I_{\mathcal{T}})|\psi\rangle\|^2} = \sqrt{1 - \mathrm{tr}\Pi_{\mathcal{W}}^{\otimes 2}\tau} \le \sqrt{\gamma}.
\end{aligned}$$

As the reduced state of τ in $(\mathsf{S}_1, \mathsf{S}_2)$ has trace distance at most δ to $(I/2)^{\otimes 2}$, it follows that the reduced state of τ' in $(\mathsf{S}_1, \mathsf{S}_2)$ has trace distance at most $\delta + \sqrt{\gamma}$ to $(I/2)^{\otimes 2}$. Now from Proposition 24, the protocol results in rejection with probability at least $\min\{2(\delta + \sqrt{\gamma}), \frac{1}{16} - 10(\delta + \sqrt{\gamma})^{\frac{1}{4}}\}$ if the state in $(\mathsf{R}_1, \mathsf{R}_2, \mathsf{S}_1, \mathsf{S}'_1, \mathsf{S}_2, \mathsf{S}'_2)$ were σ' when entering Step 4. Hence, Lemma 6 implies that the protocol results in rejection with probability at least $\min\{2(\delta + \sqrt{\gamma}) - \sqrt{\gamma}, \frac{1}{16} - \sqrt{\gamma} - 10(\delta + \sqrt{\gamma})^{\frac{1}{4}}\}$ if the state in $(\mathsf{R}_1, \mathsf{R}_2, \mathsf{S}_1, \mathsf{S}'_1, \mathsf{S}_2, \mathsf{S}'_2)$ were σ when entering Step 4.

Overall, taking $\gamma = 2\delta$, the protocol results in rejection with probability at least

$$\min\Big\{2\delta, 2\delta + (2\delta)^{\frac{1}{2}}, \frac{1}{16} - (2\delta)^{\frac{1}{2}} - 10\big[\delta + (2\delta)^{\frac{1}{2}}\big]^{\frac{1}{4}}\Big\}$$
$$\geq \min\Big\{2\delta, \frac{1}{16} - (2\delta)^{\frac{1}{2}} - 10(3\delta^{\frac{1}{2}})^{\frac{1}{4}}\Big\}$$
$$\geq \min\Big\{2\delta, \frac{1}{16} - 15\delta^{\frac{1}{8}}\Big\},$$

if the state in $(\mathsf{R}_1, \mathsf{R}_2, \mathsf{S}_1, \mathsf{S}'_1, \mathsf{S}_2, \mathsf{S}'_2)$ were σ when entering Step 4. This completes the proof. □

7. $\mathrm{QIP}(m) \subseteq \mathrm{QIP}_1(m+1)$

Now we show that any m-message QIP system with two-sided bounded error can be converted into an $(m+1)$-message QIP system with one-sided error of perfect completeness, for any $m \geq 2$.

THEOREM 25. *For any polynomially bounded function $m\colon \mathbb{Z}^+ \to \mathbb{N}$ and polynomial-time computable functions $c, s\colon \mathbb{Z}^+ \to [0,1]$ satisfying $m \geq 2$ and $c - s \geq 1/p$ for some polynomially bounded function $p\colon \mathbb{Z}^+ \to \mathbb{N}$,*

$$\mathrm{QIP}(m, c, s) \subseteq \mathrm{QIP}\Big(m+1, 1, 1 - \frac{(c-s)^2}{16}\Big).$$

If m is an odd-valued function whose values are at least three, we can show a stronger statement that any m-message QIP system with two-sided bounded error can be converted into another m-message QIP system with one-sided error of perfect completeness.

THEOREM 26. *For any polynomially bounded odd-valued function $m\colon \mathbb{Z}^+ \to 2\mathbb{N}+1$ and polynomial-time computable functions $c, s\colon \mathbb{Z}^+ \to [0,1]$ satisfying $m \geq 3$ and $c - s \geq 1/p$ for some polynomially bounded function $p\colon \mathbb{Z}^+ \to \mathbb{N}$,*

$$\mathrm{QIP}(m, c, s) \subseteq \mathrm{QIP}\Big(m, 1, 1 - \frac{(c-s)^2}{16}\Big).$$

REMARK 2. *In fact, in Theorems 25 and 26, it is sufficient for the claims that the functions c and s satisfy $c - s \geq 2^{-p}$ for some polynomially bounded function $p\colon \mathbb{Z}^+ \to \mathbb{N}$.*

With the perfect parallel repetition theorem for general quantum interactive proofs [Gut09], the following corollaries immediately follow.

COROLLARY 27. *For any polynomially bounded functions $m, p\colon \mathbb{Z}^+ \to \mathbb{N}$ and polynomial-time computable functions $c, s\colon \mathbb{Z}^+ \to [0,1]$ satisfying $m \geq 2$ and $c - s \geq 1/q$ for some polynomially bounded function $q\colon \mathbb{Z}^+ \to \mathbb{N}$,*

$$\mathrm{QIP}(m, c, s) \subseteq \mathrm{QIP}(m+1, 1, 2^{-p}).$$

COROLLARY 28. *For any polynomially bounded odd-valued function $m\colon \mathbb{Z}^+ \to 2\mathbb{N}+1$, polynomially bounded function $p\colon \mathbb{Z}^+ \to \mathbb{N}$, and polynomial-time computable functions $c, s\colon \mathbb{Z}^+ \to [0,1]$ satisfying $m \geq 3$ and $c - s \geq 1/q$ for some polynomially bounded function $q\colon \mathbb{Z}^+ \to \mathbb{N}$,*

$$\mathrm{QIP}(m, c, s) \subseteq \mathrm{QIP}(m, 1, 2^{-p}).$$

7.1 Modified Reflection Procedure

The REFLECTION PROCEDURE in Section 5 involves one application of U and one application of $U^\dagger$. Here we modify the procedure so that it involves one application of $U^\dagger$ only (and no application of U is required).

To do this, one expects to receive a state just after Step 1 of the REFLECTION PROCEDURE, and performs two tests, called REFLECTION TEST and INVERTIBILITY TEST, respectively, with equal probability without revealing which test the prover is undergoing. In the REFLECTION TEST, we simply perform Steps 2–4 of the REFLECTION PROCEDURE to finish the simulation of it, whereas in the INVERTIBILITY TEST, we apply $U^\dagger$ without performing the phase-flip to check that the state received was a legal state that can appear just after Step 1 of the REFLECTION PROCEDURE. The idea of making use of the INVERTIBILITY TEST has originally appeared in Ref. [KKMV09] when achieving perfect completeness in quantum multi-prover interactive proofs. From another viewpoint, the modification here may be considered as applying the "halving technique" in Ref. [KKMV09] to the REFLECTION PROCEDURE, the technique originally used to reduce the number of turns by (almost) half in quantum multi-prover interactive proofs. We will take this view when analyzing the soundness of this procedure in Proposition 30 below. The procedure is summarized in Figure 7.

PROPOSITION 29. *Suppose that the Hermitian operator $M = \Delta_0 U^\dagger \Pi_0 U \Delta_0$ has an eigenvalue $1/2$. Then there exists a quantum state given in Step 1 of the* MODIFIED REFLECTION PROCEDURE *such that the procedure results in acceptance with certainty.*

PROOF. The proof is almost straightforward. Let $|\psi^*\rangle$ be an eigenvector of M corresponding to its eigenvalue $1/2$, and consider the case where the state $U|\psi^*\rangle$ is received in Q in Step 1.

If the REFLECTION TEST is performed, this essentially simulates the original REFLECTION PROCEDURE with its received state being $|\psi^*\rangle$. As in the case of Proposition 17, the procedure results in acceptance with certainty in this case.

On the other hand, if the INVERTIBILITY TEST is performed, this produces the state $U^\dagger U|\psi^*\rangle = |\psi^*\rangle$ when entering Step 3.2. As $|\psi^*\rangle$ is an eigenvector of M with its corresponding eigenvalue $1/2$, it holds that

$$\Delta_0|\psi^*\rangle = 2\Delta_0 M|\psi^*\rangle = 2M|\psi^*\rangle = |\psi^*\rangle,$$

and thus, Step 3.2 results in acceptance with certainty.

Hence, given the state $U|\psi^*\rangle$ in Step 1, the procedure results in acceptance with certainty, and the claim follows. □

PROPOSITION 30. *For any $\varepsilon \in (0, \frac{1}{2}]$, suppose that none of the eigenvalues of the Hermitian operator $M = \Delta_0 U^\dagger \Pi_0 U \Delta_0$ is in the interval $\big(\frac{1}{2} - \varepsilon, \frac{1}{2} + \varepsilon\big)$. Then, for any quantum state given in Step 1 of the* MODIFIED REFLECTION PROCEDURE, *the procedure results in rejection with probability at least ε^2.*

Modified Reflection Procedure

1. Receive a quantum register Q. Flip a fair coin, and proceed to the REFLECTION TEST in Step 2 if it results in "Heads", and proceed to the INVERTIBILITY TEST in Step 3 if it results in "Tails".

2. (REFLECTION TEST)
Perform the following:

   2.1 Perform a phase-flip (i.e., multiply -1 in phase) if the state in Q belongs to the subspace corresponding to the projection Π_0.

   2.2 Apply $U^\dagger$ to Q.

   2.3 Reject if the state in Q belongs to the subspace corresponding to the projection Δ_0, and accept otherwise.

3. (INVERTIBILITY TEST)
Perform the following:

   3.1 Apply $U^\dagger$ to Q.

   3.2 Accept if the state in Q belongs to the subspace corresponding to Δ_0, and reject otherwise.

Figure 7: The Modified Reflection Procedure.

PROOF. The proof is similar to the proofs of Lemmas 4.1 and 5.1 in Ref. [KKMV09]. Let $|\psi\rangle$ be any state received in Q in Step 1. Denote the unitary transformation $U^\dagger(-\Pi_0+\Pi_1)$ by V, and let

$$|\alpha\rangle = \frac{\Delta_1 V|\psi\rangle}{\|\Delta_1 V|\psi\rangle\|}, \quad |\beta\rangle = \frac{\Delta_0 U^\dagger|\psi\rangle}{\|\Delta_0 U^\dagger|\psi\rangle\|}.$$

Then

$$\begin{aligned}\|\Delta_1 V|\psi\rangle\| &= \frac{1}{\|\Delta_1 V|\psi\rangle\|}\left|\langle\psi|V^\dagger\Delta_1 V|\psi\rangle\right| \\ &= F\big(|\alpha\rangle\langle\alpha|, V|\psi\rangle\langle\psi|V^\dagger\big) = F\big(V^\dagger|\alpha\rangle\langle\alpha|V, |\psi\rangle\langle\psi|\big),\end{aligned}$$

and thus, the probability p_1 of acceptance when the REFLECTION TEST is performed is given by

$$p_1 = F\big(V^\dagger|\alpha\rangle\langle\alpha|V, |\psi\rangle\langle\psi|\big)^2.$$

Similarly, the probability p_2 of acceptance when the INVERTIBILITY TEST is performed is given by

$$p_2 = F\big(U|\beta\rangle\langle\beta|U^\dagger, |\psi\rangle\langle\psi|\big)^2.$$

Hence, the probability $p_{\rm acc}$ of acceptance when the received state in Step 1 was $|\psi\rangle$ is given by

$$\begin{aligned}p_{\rm acc} &= \frac{1}{2}(p_1+p_2) \\ &= \frac{1}{2}\Big(F\big(V^\dagger|\alpha\rangle\langle\alpha|V, |\psi\rangle\langle\psi|\big)^2 + F\big(U|\beta\rangle\langle\beta|U^\dagger, |\psi\rangle\langle\psi|\big)^2\Big).\end{aligned}$$

It follows from Lemma 7 that

$$\begin{aligned}p_{\rm acc} &\leq \frac{1}{2}\Big(1 + F\big(V^\dagger|\alpha\rangle\langle\alpha|V, U|\beta\rangle\langle\beta|U^\dagger\big)\Big) \\ &= \frac{1}{2}\Big(1 + F\big(|\alpha\rangle\langle\alpha|, VU|\beta\rangle\langle\beta|U^\dagger V^\dagger\big)\Big).\end{aligned}$$

Now notice that $|\beta\rangle$ is a state in $\mathcal{X}_0$, and thus,

$$\|\Delta_1 VU|\beta\rangle\|^2 \leq 1 - 4\varepsilon^2,$$

since $\|\Delta_0 VU|\beta\rangle\|^2 \geq 4\varepsilon^2$ from the analysis on the REFLECTION PROCEDURE in the proof of Proposition 18. Hence, using $\Delta_1|\alpha\rangle = |\alpha\rangle$,

$$\begin{aligned}F\big(|\alpha\rangle\langle\alpha|, VU|\beta\rangle\langle\beta|U^\dagger V^\dagger\big) &= \left|\langle\alpha|VU|\beta\rangle\right| \\ &= \left|\langle\alpha|\Delta_1 VU|\beta\rangle\right| \leq \left\|\Delta_1 VU|\beta\rangle\right\| \leq \sqrt{1-4\varepsilon^2},\end{aligned}$$

and thus,

$$p_{\rm acc} \leq \frac{1}{2} + \frac{\sqrt{1-4\varepsilon^2}}{2} \leq \frac{1}{2} + \frac{1-2\varepsilon^2}{2} = 1 - \varepsilon^2.$$

Therefore, the procedure results in rejection with probability at least ε^2, as claimed. □

7.2 Perfectly Rewindable QIPs

Here we introduce the notion of *perfectly rewindable* QIP systems. The concept of perfectly rewindable systems was originally introduced for quantum multi-prover interactive proofs in Ref. [KKMV09], and the notion here is the single-prover version of it as a special case.

DEFINITION 31. *Given a polynomially bounded function $m\colon \mathbb{Z}^+ \to \mathbb{N}$ and a function $s\colon \mathbb{Z}^+ \to [0,1]$ satisfying $s < \frac{1}{2}$, a promise problem $A = \{A_{\rm yes}, A_{\rm no}\}$ has a perfectly rewindable m-message quantum interactive proof system with soundness s iff there exists an m-message polynomial-time quantum verifier V such that, for every input x:*

(Perfect Rewindability) *if $x \in A_{\rm yes}$, there exists an m-message quantum prover P such that the maximum probability that V accepts x when communicating with P is exactly $1/2$, where the maximum is taken over all possible initial states ρ_x of P,*

(Soundness) *if $x \in A_{\rm no}$, for any m-message quantum prover P' and any initial state ρ'_x of P' prepared, V accepts x with probability at most $s(|x|)$.*

Note that in the perfect rewindability property we first fix the transformations of the prover, and then maximize over all legal initial states, which hence have a fixed dimension. We first show how to modify any general QIP system to a perfectly rewindable one without changing the number of messages.

LEMMA 32. *Let $m\colon \mathbb{Z}^+ \to \mathbb{N}$ be a polynomially bounded function and let $c, s\colon \mathbb{Z}^+ \to [0,1]$ be polynomial-time computable functions satisfying $c - s \geq 1/p$ for some polynomially bounded function $p\colon \mathbb{Z}^+ \to \mathbb{N}$. Then, any promise problem $A = (A_{\rm yes}, A_{\rm no})$ in ${\rm QIP}(m, c, s)$ has a perfectly rewindable m-message quantum interactive proof system with soundness $\frac{1}{2} - \frac{c-s}{4}$.*

PROOF. Let $A = (A_{\rm yes}, A_{\rm no})$ be a problem in ${\rm QIP}(m, c, s)$ and let V be the corresponding m-message quantum verifier. We first modify V to obtain another m-message quantum verifier V' that witnesses the inclusion

$$A \in {\rm QIP}\Big(m, \frac{1}{2} + \frac{c-s}{4}, \frac{1}{2} + \frac{c-s}{4}\Big).$$

This can be done via a standard technique as follows. Fix an input x. The new verifier V' behaves in a manner exactly same as V, except for the acceptance condition. If

$c(|x|)+s(|x|) \geq 1$, V' accepts with probability $\frac{1}{c(|x|)+s(|x|)}$ when the final state in the system would make V accept (and reject otherwise). Thus, V' accepts $x \in A_{\mathrm{yes}}$ with probability at least

$$\frac{c(|x|)}{c(|x|)+s(|x|)} = \frac{1}{2}\Big(1 + \frac{c(|x|)-s(|x|)}{c(|x|)+s(|x|)}\Big),$$

while accepts $x \in A_{\mathrm{no}}$ with probability at most

$$\frac{s(|x|)}{c(|x|)+s(|x|)} = \frac{1}{2}\Big(1 - \frac{c(|x|)-s(|x|)}{c(|x|)+s(|x|)}\Big).$$

Similarly, if $c(|x|)+s(|x|) < 1$, letting $\varepsilon(|x|) = 1 - c(|x|)$ and $\delta(|x|) = 1 - s(|x|)$, V' rejects with probability $\frac{1}{\varepsilon(|x|)+\delta(|x|)} = \frac{1}{2-c(|x|)-s(|x|)}$ when the final state in the system would make V reject (and accept otherwise). Thus, V' rejects $x \in A_{\mathrm{yes}}$ with probability at most

$$\begin{aligned}\frac{\varepsilon(|x|)}{\varepsilon(|x|)+\delta(|x|)} &= \frac{1}{2}\Big(1 - \frac{\delta(|x|)-\varepsilon(|x|)}{\varepsilon(|x|)+\delta(|x|)}\Big)\\ &= \frac{1}{2}\Big(1 - \frac{c(|x|)-s(|x|)}{2-c(|x|)-s(|x|)}\Big),\end{aligned}$$

while V' rejects $x \in A_{\mathrm{no}}$ with probability at least

$$\begin{aligned}\frac{\delta(|x|)}{\varepsilon(|x|)+\delta(|x|)} &= \frac{1}{2}\Big(1 + \frac{\delta(|x|)-\varepsilon(|x|)}{\varepsilon(|x|)+\delta(|x|)}\Big)\\ &= \frac{1}{2}\Big(1 + \frac{c(|x|)-s(|x|)}{2-c(|x|)-s(|x|)}\Big).\end{aligned}$$

Taking it into account that, with a given finite-size gate set available for the verifier, it may not be possible to accept with probability exactly $\frac{1}{c(|x|)+s(|x|)}$ in the case $c(|x|)+s(|x|) \geq 1$, or to reject with probability exactly $\frac{1}{\varepsilon(|x|)+\delta(|x|)} = \frac{1}{2-c(|x|)-s(|x|)}$ in the case $c(|x|)+s(|x|) < 1$, we actually consider another verifier V'' who approximately performs the transformations of V' with sufficient accuracy, where the transformations of V'' are exactly implementable with the given finite-size gate set available for the verifier. As both $c(|x|)+s(|x|)$ and $2-c(|x|)-s(|x|)$ are at most $2-\frac{1}{p}$, the bounds obtained above are sufficient to claim that the m-message system with the verifier V'' has completeness $\frac{1}{2}+\frac{c-s}{4}$ and soundness $\frac{1}{2}-\frac{c-s}{4}$.

The rest of the proof is essentially the same as the proof of Lemma 3.2 in Ref. [KKMV09]. We further modify V'' to construct another m-message quantum verifier W for a perfectly rewindable proof system for A. The new verifier W prepares a single-qubit register B in addition to the register V which corresponds to the space used by V''. The qubit in B is initialized to $|0\rangle$. W behaves exactly in the same manner as V'' does, except that, in addition to all actions V'' would do, W also sends B to the prover in the last message from the verifier and receives B from the prover in the last message from the prover. As for the final decision, W accepts if and only if the content of V would make V'' accept *and* B contains 1. Notice that W accepts only if V'' would accept, and thus, the soundness is obviously at most $\frac{1}{2}+\frac{c-s}{4}$.

For perfect rewindability, we slightly modify the protocol of the honest prover in the case $x \in A_{\mathrm{yes}}$. Given a protocol of the honest prover P in the system with V'' and an initial state $|\psi_{\mathrm{init}}\rangle$ in the system with V'' that achieves the maximal acceptance probability $p_{\max}$ when V'' communicating with this P, we construct a protocol of the honest prover Q in the system with W as follows. Q uses $|\psi_{\mathrm{init}}\rangle$ as the initial state and behaves exactly in the same manner as P does, except that, upon receiving the last message from W, Q applies to the qubit in B the one-qubit unitary transformation U satisfying

$$U\colon |0\rangle \mapsto \sqrt{1-\frac{1}{2p_{\max}}}|0\rangle + \sqrt{\frac{1}{2p_{\max}}}|1\rangle,$$

in addition to all what the original P would do. From the construction it is obvious that the maximum accepting probability of W when communicating with Q is exactly equal to $\frac{1}{2}$ and that this maximum is achieved when Q uses $|\psi_{\mathrm{init}}\rangle$ as the initial state. Finally, as the transformations of V'' are exactly implementable with the given finite-size gate set available for the verifier, so are the transformations of W. □

REMARK 3. *In fact, in Lemma 32, it is sufficient for the claim that the functions c and s satisfy $c - s \geq 2^{-p}$ for some polynomially bounded function $p\colon \mathbb{Z}^+ \to \mathbb{N}$.*

7.3 Proofs of Theorems 25 and 26

Now we are ready to show Theorems 25 and 26. First we prove Theorem 26, assuming that m is an odd-valued function and $m \geq 3$. The case of general m is proved in the same manner as this special case, except that the number of messages increases by one when $m(|x|)$ is even, which gives Theorem 25.

PROOF OF THEOREM 26. As m is an odd-valued function and $m \geq 3$, there is a polynomially bounded function $r\colon \mathbb{Z}^+ \to \mathbb{N}$ such that $m = 2r+1$. Let $A = (A_{\mathrm{yes}}, A_{\mathrm{no}})$ be in $\mathrm{QIP}(2r+1, c, s)$. Then from Lemma 32, A has a perfectly rewindable $(2r+1)$-message quantum interactive proof system with soundness $\frac{1}{2}-\frac{c-s}{4}$. Let V be the verifier of this perfectly rewindable $(2r+1)$-message quantum interactive proof system. We construct another $(2r+1)$-message quantum verifier W of a new quantum interactive proof system for A.

Fix an input x. Let V be the quantum register consisting of private qubits used by the original verifier V, and let M be the quantum register consisting of qubits used for communications in the original proof system. Let $V_{x,j}$ be the jth transformation of V, for each $j \in \{1, \ldots, r(|x|)+1\}$, acting over (V, M). The new verifier W uses the same registers V and M as the original verifier V. W first receives the two registers V and M, expecting that the state in (V, M) forms what V would have after the last message from a prover had been received in the original proof system. W then performs one of the two tests, called REFLECTION TEST and INVERTIBILITY TEST, chosen uniformly at random. In the REFLECTION TEST, W first performs a phase-flip if the state in (V, M) would cause V to accept when the last transformation $V_{x,r(|x|)+1}$ of V was performed, and then moves to a backward simulation of the original system. W accepts when the backward simulation *does not* produce a legal initial state of the original system. In the INVERTIBILITY TEST, W just immediately moves to a backward simulation of the original system. This time, W accepts when the backward simulation *does* produce a legal initial state of the original system. The exact protocol is described in Figure 8. Notice that the number of messages in this system is indeed

$$1+1+2(r(|x|)-1)+1 = 2r(|x|)+1 = m(|x|).$$

Verifier's Protocol for Achieving Perfect Completeness (Odd-Number-Message Case)

1. Receive quantum registers V and M.
2. Choose $b \in \{0,1\}$ uniformly at random. If $b=0$, move to the Reflection Test described in Step 3, while if $b=1$, move to the Invertibility Test described in Step 4.
3. (Reflection Test)
   - 3.1 Apply $V_{x,r(|x|)+1}$ to the state in (V,M). Perform a phase-flip (i.e., multiply -1 in phase) if the content of (V,M) corresponds to an accepting state of the original system. Apply $V_{x,r(|x|)+1}^{\dagger}$ to the state in (V,M), and send M to the prover.
   - 3.2 For $j=r(|x|)$ down to 2, do the following: Receive M from the prover. Apply $V_{x,j}^{\dagger}$ to the state in (V,M), and send M to the prover.
   - 3.3 Receive M from the prover. Apply $V_{x,1}^{\dagger}$ to the state in (V,M). Reject if all the qubits in V are in state $|0\rangle$, and accept otherwise.
4. (Invertibility Test)
   - 4.1 Send M to the prover.
   - 4.2 For $j=r(|x|)$ down to 2, do the following: Receive M from the prover. Apply $V_{x,j}^{\dagger}$ to the state in (V,M), and send M to the prover.
   - 4.3 Receive M from the prover. Apply $V_{x,1}^{\dagger}$ to the state in (V,M). Accept if all the qubits in V are in state $|0\rangle$, and reject otherwise.

Figure 8: Verifier's protocol for achieving perfect completeness with $m=2r+1$.

For the completeness, suppose that x is in A_{yes}.

As the original system was perfectly rewindable, there exists a $(2r+1)$-message quantum prover P in the original system such that the maximum probability that V accepts x when communicating with this P is exactly $1/2$, where the maximum is taken over all possible initial states of P. Let P be the quantum register consisting of the private qubits of this P, and let $P_{x,j}$ be the jth transformation of P, for each $j\in\{1,\dots,r(|x|)+1\}$, acting over (M,P). Let $|\psi_x^*\rangle$ be an optimal initial state in (M,P) with which P achieves the accepting probability $1/2$ (note that P possesses the message register M at the beginning of the protocol, and that there always exists an optimal initial state that is pure).

Denote the Hilbert spaces associated with V, M, and P by $\mathcal{V}$, $\mathcal{M}$, and $\mathcal{P}$, respectively. Since the first action is done by P in this original proof system, one can assume without loss of generality that $P_{x,1}=I_{\mathcal{M}\otimes\mathcal{P}}$ (i.e., the first transformation of P may be regarded as a part of preparing the initial state). Taking this into account, define the unitary transformation Q_x acting over $(\mathsf{V},\mathsf{M},\mathsf{P})$ by

$$Q_x=\bigl(V_{x,r(|x|)+1}\otimes I_{\mathcal{P}}\bigr)\bigl(I_{\mathcal{V}}\otimes P_{x,r(|x|)+1}\bigr)\cdots$$
$$\cdots\bigl(V_{x,2}\otimes I_{\mathcal{P}}\bigr)\bigl(I_{\mathcal{V}}\otimes P_{x,2}\bigr)\bigl(V_{x,1}\otimes I_{\mathcal{P}}\bigr),$$

and further define the Hermitian matrix M_x by

$$M_x=\Pi_{\mathrm{init}}Q_x^{\dagger}\Pi_{\mathrm{acc}}Q_x\Pi_{\mathrm{init}},$$

where Π_{init} is the projection onto the subspace spanned by states in which all the qubits in V are in state $|0\rangle$, and Π_{acc} is that onto the subspace spanned by accepting states of the original system. Then the quantum state $|\phi_x^*\rangle$ in $(\mathsf{V},\mathsf{M},\mathsf{P})$ defined as $|\phi_x^*\rangle=|0\rangle_{\mathsf{V}}\otimes|\psi_x^*\rangle_{(\mathsf{M},\mathsf{P})}$ is the eigenvector of M_x with its corresponding eigenvalue $1/2$, since

$$\max_{|\phi\rangle\in\mathcal{V}\otimes\mathcal{M}\otimes\mathcal{P}}\langle\phi|M_x|\phi\rangle=\max_{|\psi\rangle\in\mathcal{M}\otimes\mathcal{P}}\|\Pi_{\mathrm{acc}}Q_x(|0\rangle\otimes|\psi\rangle)\|^2$$
$$=\|\Pi_{\mathrm{acc}}Q_x(|0\rangle\otimes|\psi_x^*\rangle)\|^2=\langle\phi_x^*|M_x|\phi_x^*\rangle=\frac{1}{2}.$$

Now, with a $(2r+1)$-message quantum prover R in the constructed system who prepares the state

$$|\xi_x^*\rangle=\bigl(V_{x,r(|x|)+1}^{\dagger}\otimes I_{\mathcal{P}}\bigr)Q_x|\phi_x^*\rangle$$

in $(\mathsf{V},\mathsf{M},\mathsf{P})$ as an initial state and applies $R_{x,1}=I_{\mathcal{M}\otimes\mathcal{P}}$ and $R_{x,j}=P_{x,r(|x|)-j+3}$ for each $j\in\{2,\dots,r(|x|)+1\}$, the constructed protocol may be viewed as performing the Modified Reflection Procedure with its underlying quantum register $\mathsf{Q}=(\mathsf{V},\mathsf{M},\mathsf{P})$, unitary transformation

$$U=\bigl(V_{x,r(|x|)+1}^{\dagger}\otimes I_{\mathcal{P}}\bigr)Q_x,$$

and projection operators

$$\Delta_0=\Pi_{\mathrm{init}},$$
$$\Pi_0=\bigl(V_{x,r(|x|)+1}^{\dagger}\otimes I_{\mathcal{P}}\bigr)\Pi_{\mathrm{acc}}\bigl(V_{x,r(|x|)+1}\otimes I_{\mathcal{P}}\bigr).$$

As the associated Hermitian operator

$$M=\Delta_0U^{\dagger}\Pi_0U\Delta_0=\Pi_{\mathrm{init}}Q_x^{\dagger}\Pi_{\mathrm{acc}}Q_x\Pi_{\mathrm{init}}=M_x$$

has an eigenvalue $1/2$ with its corresponding eigenvector $|\phi_x^*\rangle=|0\rangle_{\mathsf{V}}\otimes|\psi_x^*\rangle_{(\mathsf{M},\mathsf{P})}$, from Proposition 29, the protocol results in acceptance with certainty with this prover R and the initial state

$$|\xi_x^*\rangle=\bigl(V_{x,r(|x|)+1}^{\dagger}\otimes I_{\mathcal{P}}\bigr)Q_x|\phi_x^*\rangle=U|\phi_x^*\rangle,$$

which shows the perfect completeness.

Now for the soundness, suppose that x is in A_{no}.

Let R be any $(2r+1)$-message quantum prover of the constructed system, and let R be the quantum register consisting of the private qubits of R. Suppose that R applies the unitary transformation $R_{x,j}$ to the state in (M,R) as the jth transformation of R, for each $j\in\{1,\dots,r(|x|)+1\}$.

Define the unitary transformation Q_x acting over $(\mathsf{V},\mathsf{M},\mathsf{R})$ by

$$Q_x=\bigl(V_{x,r(|x|)+1}\otimes I_{\mathcal{R}}\bigr)\bigl(I_{\mathcal{V}}\otimes R_{x,2}^{\dagger}\bigr)\cdots$$
$$\cdots\bigl(V_{x,2}\otimes I_{\mathcal{R}}\bigr)\bigl(I_{\mathcal{V}}\otimes R_{x,r(|x|)+1}^{\dagger}\bigr)\bigl(V_{x,1}\otimes I_{\mathcal{R}}\bigr),$$

where $\mathcal{R}$ is the Hilbert space associated with the register R. Then the constructed protocol may be viewed as performing the Modified Reflection Procedure with its underlying quantum register $\mathsf{Q}=(\mathsf{V},\mathsf{M},\mathsf{R})$, unitary transformation

$$U=\bigl(V_{x,r(|x|)+1}^{\dagger}\otimes I_{\mathcal{R}}\bigr)Q_x,$$

and projection operators

$$\Delta_0=\Pi_{\mathrm{init}},$$
$$\Pi_0=\bigl(V_{x,r(|x|)+1}^{\dagger}\otimes I_{\mathcal{R}}\bigr)\Pi_{\mathrm{acc}}\bigl(V_{x,r(|x|)+1}\otimes I_{\mathcal{R}}\bigr).$$

The associated Hermitian operator of this MODIFIED REFLECTION PROCEDURE is given by

$$M_x = \Delta_0 U^\dagger \Pi_0 U \Delta_0 = \Pi_{\mathrm{init}} Q_x^\dagger \Pi_{\mathrm{acc}} Q_x \Pi_{\mathrm{init}}.$$

Consider the following $(2r+1)$-message quantum prover P' in the original system: P' uses R as a register consisting of his/her private qubits, and applies $I_{\mathcal{M}\otimes\mathcal{R}}$ as his/her first transformation, and $R^\dagger_{x,r(|x|)-j+3}$ as his/her jth transformation, for $j \in \{2,\dots,r(|x|)+1\}$. Then, from the soundness property of the original system, no matter which state P' initially prepares, the accepting probability is at most $\frac{1}{2} - \frac{c(|x|)-s(|x|)}{4}$, which implies that all the eigenvalues of M_x is at most $\frac{1}{2} - \frac{c(|x|)-s(|x|)}{4}$. Hence, from Proposition 30, the constructed protocol results in rejection with probability at least $\frac{(c(|x|)-s(|x|))^2}{16}$, which ensures the soundness $1 - \frac{(c-s)^2}{16}$.

Finally, the protocol given in Figure 8 slightly deviates from the standard form of quantum interactive proof systems in that the length of the first message from a prover is different from the lengths of other messages, which may be easily modified into a standard-form system that has exactly the same number of messages and completeness and soundness parameters. □

Now we prove Theorem 25. The proof is essentially the same as the proof of Theorem 26, and we analyze the case where the number of messages is even.

PROOF OF THEOREM 25. Let $A = (A_{\mathrm{yes}}, A_{\mathrm{no}})$ be in $\mathrm{QIP}(m,c,s)$. Then from Lemma 32, A has a perfectly rewindable m-message quantum interactive proof system with soundness $\frac{1}{2} - \frac{c-s}{4}$. Let V be the verifier of this perfectly rewindable m-message quantum interactive proof system. We construct an $(m+1)$-message quantum verifier W of a new quantum interactive proof system for A. The construction is essentially the same as that in the proof of Theorem 26.

Fix an input x. Suppose that $m(|x|) \geq 2$ is even, and write $m(|x|) = 2r(|x|)$ for some $r(|x|) \in \mathbb{N}$ (the proof of Theorem 26 already shows the case where $m(|x|)$ is odd). The exact protocol is described in Figure 9, where the only difference from the protocol in Figure 8 lies in the condition of judging whether the state is initialized or not – now a state is a legal initial state only when all the qubits in both of V and M must be in state $|0\rangle$. Notice that the number of messages in this system is indeed

$$1 + 1 + 2(r(|x|)-1) + 1 = 2r(|x|) + 1 = m(|x|) + 1.$$

The analysis on this protocol is essentially the same as that in the proof of Theorem 26, and is omitted. □

7.4 Cases with Quantum Multi-Prover Interactive Proofs

With essentially the same arguments discussed in this section, we can show similar properties even for quantum multi-prover interactive proof systems. The model of quantum multi-prover interactive proofs we use is that in the most general setting (i.e., both of a verifier and provers use quantum computation and communications, and provers can share arbitrary entanglement of arbitrarily large size). Let $\mathrm{QMIP}(k,m,c,s)$ be the class of problems having m-turn quantum k-prover interactive proof systems with completeness c and soundness s. See Ref. [KKMV09] for rigorous definitions of the quantum multi-prover model and resulting complexity classes. Here we give only the statements of theorems, as proofs of those theorems are essentially same as Theorems 25 and 26. Note that these theorems give a more communication-efficient way of achieving perfect completeness in quantum multi-prover interactive proofs than the original method presented in Ref. [KKMV09], where the number of turns increases by a factor of three.

THEOREM 33. *For any polynomially bounded functions $k, m\colon \mathbb{Z}^+ \to \mathbb{N}$ and polynomial-time computable functions $c, s\colon \mathbb{Z}^+ \to [0,1]$ satisfying $m \geq 2$ and $c - s \geq 1/p$ for some polynomially bounded function $p\colon \mathbb{Z}^+ \to \mathbb{N}$,*

$$\mathrm{QMIP}(k,m,c,s) \subseteq \mathrm{QMIP}\Big(k, m+1, 1, 1 - \frac{(c-s)^2}{16}\Big).$$

THEOREM 34. *For any polynomially bounded function $k\colon \mathbb{Z}^+ \to \mathbb{N}$, polynomially bounded odd-valued function $m\colon \mathbb{Z}^+ \to 2\mathbb{N}+1$, and polynomial-time computable functions $c, s\colon \mathbb{Z}^+ \to [0,1]$ satisfying $m \geq 3$ and $c - s \geq 1/p$ for some polynomially bounded function $p\colon \mathbb{Z}^+ \to \mathbb{N}$,*

$$\mathrm{QMIP}(k,m,c,s) \subseteq \mathrm{QMIP}\Big(k, m, 1, 1 - \frac{(c-s)^2}{16}\Big).$$

Verifier's Protocol for Achieving Perfect Completeness (Even-Number-Message Case)

1. Receive quantum registers V and M.
2. Choose $b \in \{0,1\}$ uniformly at random. If $b = 0$, move to the REFLECTION TEST described in Step 3, while if $b = 1$, move to the INVERTIBILITY TEST described in Step 4.
3. (REFLECTION TEST)
   - 3.1 Apply $V_{x,r(|x|)+1}$ to the state in (V, M). Perform a phase-flip (i.e., multiply -1 in phase) if the content of (V, M) corresponds to an accepting state of the original system. Apply $V^\dagger_{x,r(|x|)+1}$ to the state in (V, M), and send M to the prover.
   - 3.2 For $j = r(|x|)$ down to 2, do the following: Receive M from the prover. Apply $V^\dagger_{x,j}$ to the state in (V, M), and send M to the prover.
   - 3.3 Receive M from the prover. Apply $V^\dagger_{x,1}$ to the state in (V, M). Reject if all the qubits in (V, M) are in state $|0\rangle$, and accept otherwise.
4. (INVERTIBILITY TEST)
   - 4.1 Send M to the prover.
   - 4.2 For $j = r(|x|)$ down to 2, do the following: Receive M from the prover. Apply $V^\dagger_{x,j}$ to the state in (V, M), and send M to the prover.
   - 4.3 Receive M from the prover. Apply $V^\dagger_{x,1}$ to the state in (V, M). Accept if all the qubits in (V, M) are in state $|0\rangle$, and reject otherwise.

Figure 9: Verifier's protocol for achieving perfect completeness with $m(|x|) = 2r(|x|)$.

REMARK 4. *Similar to the single-prover case, in fact, it is sufficient for the claims in Theorems 33 and 34 that the functions c and s satisfy $c - s \geq 2^{-p}$ for some polynomially bounded function $p\colon \mathbb{Z}^+ \to \mathbb{N}$.*

8. ACKNOWLEDGEMENTS

The authors are grateful to Richard Cleve for useful discussions, and to an anonymous reviewer for helpful comments on improving some parameters in the proof of Theorem 2. This work is supported by the Grant-in-Aid for Scientific Research (A) No. 24240001 of the Japan Society for the Promotion of Science and the Grant-in-Aid for Scientific Research on Innovative Areas No. 24106009 of the Ministry of Education, Culture, Sports, Science and Technology in Japan. HK also acknowledges support from the Grant-in-Aid for Scientific Research (B) No. 21300002 of the Japan Society for the Promotion of Science. HN also acknowledges support from the Grant-in-Aids for Scientific Research (A) Nos. 21244007 and 23246071 of the Japan Society for the Promotion of Science and the Grant-in-Aid for Young Scientists (B) No. 22700014 of the Ministry of Education, Culture, Sports, Science and Technology in Japan.

9. REFERENCES

[AALV09] Dorit Aharonov, Itai Arad, Zeph Landau, and Umesh Vazirani. The detectability lemma and quantum gap amplification [extended abstract]. In *Proceedings of the 41st Annual ACM Symposium on Theory of Computing*, pages 417–426, 2009.

[AALV11] Dorit Aharonov, Itai Arad, Zeph Landau, and Umesh Vazirani. The 1D area law and the complexity of quantum states: A combinatorial approach. In *52nd Annual IEEE Symposium on Foundations of Computer Science*, pages 324–333, 2011.

[Aar09] Scott Aaronson. On perfect completeness for QMA. *Quantum Information and Computation*, 9(1–2):0081–0089, 2009.

[AE11] Dorit Aharonov and Lior Eldar. On the complexity of commuting local Hamiltonians, and tight conditions for topological order in such systems. In *52nd Annual IEEE Symposium on Foundations of Computer Science*, pages 334–343, 2011.

[Aha03] Dorit Aharonov. A simple proof that Toffoli and Hadamard are quantum universal. arXiv.org e-Print archive, arXiv:quant-ph/0301040, 2003.

[AKN98] Dorit Aharonov, Alexei Kitaev, and Noam Nisan. Quantum circuits with mixed states. In *Proceedings of the Thirtieth Annual ACM Symposium on Theory of Computing*, pages 20–30, 1998.

[ALM+98] Sanjeev Arora, Carsten Lund, Rajeev Motwani, Madhu Sudan, and Mario Szegedy. Proof verification and the hardness of approximation problems. *Journal of the ACM*, 45(3):501–555, 1998.

[AS98] Sanjeev Arora and Shmuel Safra. Probabilistic checking of proofs: A new characterization of NP. *Journal of the ACM*, 45(1):70–122, 1998.

[Bab85] László Babai. Trading group theory for randomness. In *Proceedings of the Seventeenth Annual ACM Symposium on Theory of Computing*, pages 421–429, 1985.

[Bra06] Sergey Bravyi. Efficient algorithm for a quantum analogue of 2-SAT. arXiv.org e-Print archive, arXiv:quant-ph/0602108, 2006.

[BSW11] Salman Beigi, Peter Shor, and John Watrous. Quantum interactive proofs with short messages. *Theory of Computing*, 7:101–117 (Article 7), 2011.

[Cho75] Man-Duen Choi. Completely positive linear maps on complex matrices. *Linear Algebra and its Applications*, 10(3):285–290, 1975.

[CKMR07] Matthias Christandl, Robert König, Graeme Mitchison, and Renato Renner. One-and-a-half quantum de Finetti theorems. *Communications in Mathematical Physics*, 273(2):473–498, 2007.

[ESY84] Shimon Even, Alan L. Selman, and Yacov Yacobi. The complexity of promise problems with applications to public-key cryptography. *Information and Control*, 61(2):159–173, 1984.

[Gro96] Lov K. Grover. A fast quantum mechanical algorithm for database search. In *Proceedings of the Twenty-Eighth Annual ACM Symposium on the Theory of Computing*, pages 212–219, 1996.

[GSU11] Sevag Gharibian, Jamie Sikora, and Sarvagya Upadhyay. QMA variants with polynomially many provers. arXiv.org e-Print archive, arXiv:1108.0617 [quant-ph], 2011.

[Gut09] Gustav Gutoski. *Quantum Strategies and Local Operations*. PhD thesis, David R. Cheriton School of Computer Science, University of Waterloo, 2009. arXiv:1003.0038 [quant-ph].

[GZ11] Oded Goldreich and David Zuckerman. Another proof that BPP $\subseteq$ PH (and more). In Oded Goldreich, editor, *Studies in Complexity and Cryptography, Miscellanea on the Interplay between Randomness and Computation*, volume 6650 of *Lecture Notes in Computer Science*, pages 40–53. Springer-Verlag, 2011. Electronic Colloquium on Computational Complexity, Report TR97-045, 1997.

[Jam72] Andrzej Jamiołkowski. Linear transformations which preserve trace and positive semidefiniteness of operators. *Reports on Mathematical Physics*, 3(4):275–278, 1972.

[JJUW11] Rahul Jain, Zhengfeng Ji, Sarvagya Upadhyay, and John Watrous. QIP = PSPACE. *Journal of the ACM*, 58(6):Article 30, 2011.

[JKNN12] Stephen P. Jordan, Hirotada Kobayashi, Daniel Nagaj, and Harumichi Nishimura. Achieving perfect completeness in classical-witness quantum Merlin-Arthur proof systems. *Quantum Information and Computation*, 12(5–6):0461–0471, 2012.

[Kit99] Alexei Yu. Kitaev. Quantum NP. Talk at the 2nd Workshop on Algorithms in Quantum Information Processing, DePaul University, Chicago, January 1999.

[KKMV09] Julia Kempe, Hirotada Kobayashi, Keiji Matsumoto, and Thomas Vidick. Using entanglement in quantum multi-prover interactive proofs. *Computational Complexity*, 18(2):273–307, 2009.

[Kni96] Emanuel Knill. Quantum randomness and nondeterminism. Technical Report LAUR-96-2186, Los Alamos National Laboratory, 1996. arXiv.org e-Print archive, arXiv:quant-ph/9610012.

[KR05] Robert König and Renato Renner. A de Finetti representation for finite symmetric quantum states. *Journal of Mathematical Physics*, 46(12):122108, 2005.

[KSV02] Alexei Yu. Kitaev, Alexander H. Shen, and Mikhail N. Vyalyi. *Classical and Quantum Computation*, volume 47 of *Graduate Studies in Mathematics*. American Mathematical Society, 2002.

[Kup09] Greg Kuperberg. How hard is it to approximate the Jones polynomial? arXiv.org e-print archive, arXiv:0908.0512 [quant-ph], 2009.

[KW00] Alexei Kitaev and John Watrous. Parallelization, amplification, and exponential time simulation of quantum interactive proof systems. In *Proceedings of the Thirty-Second Annual ACM Symposium on Theory of Computing*, pages 608–617, 2000.

[MW05] Chris Marriott and John Watrous. Quantum Arthur-Merlin games. *Computational Complexity*, 14(2):122–152, 2005.

[NC00] Michael A. Nielsen and Isaac L. Chuang. *Quantum Computation and Quantum Information.* Cambridge University Press, 2000.

[NS03] Ashwin Nayak and Peter Shor. Bit-commitment-based quantum coin flipping. *Physical Review A*, 67(1):012304, 2003.

[NWZ09] Daniel Nagaj, Pawel Wocjan, and Yong Zhang. Fast amplification of QMA. *Quantum Information and Computation*, 9(11–12):1053–1068, 2009.

[Shi02] Yaoyun Shi. Both Toffoli and Controlled-NOT need little help to do universal quantum computing. *Quantum Information and Computation*, 3(1):084–092, 2002.

[Sho96] Peter W. Shor. Fault-tolerant quantum computation. In *37th Annual Symposium on Foundations of Computer Science*, pages 56–65, 1996.

[SR02] Robert W. Spekkens and Terry Rudolph. Degrees of concealment and bindingness in quantum bit commitment protocols. *Physical Review A*, 65(1):012310, 2002.

[Vya03] Mikhail N. Vyalyi. QMA = PP implies that PP contains PH. Electronic Colloquium on Computational Complexity, Report TR03-021, 2003.

[Wat00] John Watrous. Succinct quantum proofs for properties of finite groups. In *41st Annual Symposium on Foundations of Computer Science*, pages 537–546, 2000.

[Wat03] John Watrous. PSPACE has constant-round quantum interactive proof systems. *Theoretical Computer Science*, 292(3):575–588, 2003.

[Wat09a] John Watrous. Quantum computational complexity. In Robert A. Meyers, editor, *Encyclopedia of Complexity and Systems Science*, pages 7174–7201. Springer-Verlag, 2009.

[Wat09b] John Watrous. Zero-knowledge against quantum attacks. *SIAM Journal on Computing*, 39(1):25–58, 2009.

[ZF87] Stathis Zachos and Martin Fürer. Probabilistic quantifiers vs. distrustful adversaries. In *Foundations of Software Technology and Theoretical Computer Science, Seventh Conference*, volume 287 of *Lecture Notes in Computer Science*, pages 443–455, 1987.

Active Self-Assembly of Algorithmic Shapes and Patterns in Polylogarithmic Time*

Damien Woods[1,2] Ho-Lin Chen[1,2,7] Scott Goodfriend[3]
Nadine Dabby[4] Erik Winfree[1,4,5,6] Peng Yin[1,5,6,8]
[1]Computer Science, [2]Center for Mathematics of Information, [3]Chemical Engineering,
[4]Computation and Neural Systems, [5]Bioengineering, [6]Center for Biological Circuit Design,
California Institute of Technology, Pasadena, CA 91125, USA

Present addresses: [7]Department of Electrical Engineering, National Taiwan University, Taiwan
[8]Wyss Institute for Biologically Inspired Engineering, 3 Blackfan Circle, Boston, MA 02445, USA

woods@caltech.edu, holinc@gmail.com, goodfriend.scott@gmail.com,
ndabby@caltech.edu, winfree@caltech.edu, peng_yin@hms.harvard.edu

ABSTRACT

We describe a computational model for studying the complexity of self-assembled structures with active molecular components. Our model captures notions of growth and movement ubiquitous in biological systems. The model is inspired by biology's fantastic ability to assemble biomolecules that form systems with complicated structure and dynamics, from molecular motors that walk on rigid tracks and proteins that dynamically alter the structure of the cell during mitosis, to embryonic development where large scale complicated organisms efficiently grow from a single cell. Using this active self-assembly model, we show how to efficiently self-assemble shapes and patterns from simple monomers. For example we show how to grow a line of monomers in time and number of monomer states that is merely logarithmic in its length. Our main results show how to grow arbitrary connected two-dimensional geometric shapes and patterns in expected time polylogarithmic in the size of the shape plus roughly the time required to run a Turing machine deciding whether or not a given pixel is in the shape. We do this while keeping the number of monomer types logarithmic in shape size, plus monomers required by the Kolmogorov complexity of the shape or pattern. This work thus highlights the fundamental efficiency advantage of active self-assembly over passive self-assembly and motivates experimental effort to construct active molecular self-assembly systems.

Categories and Subject Descriptors

F.1.1 [**Computation by abstract devices**]: Models of Computation—Computability theory

Keywords

Self-assembly; model of computation; molecular programming; reconfigurable robotics

1 Introduction

One of the main inspirations for our model comes from biology. Embryonic development showcases the capability of molecules to compute efficiently. A human zygote cell contains within it a program that encodes the geometric structure of an organism with roughly 10^{14} cells, that have a wide variety of forms and roles, with each such cell containing up to tens of thousands of proteins and other molecules with their own intricate arrangement and functions. Early stages of embryonic development demonstrate exponential growth rates in the number of cells over time, showing remarkable time efficiency. Not only this, but the developmental path from a single cell to a functioning organism is an intricately choreographed, and incredibly robust, temporal and spatial manufacturing process that operates at the molecular scale. Development is possibly the most impressive example of the ubiquitous process of molecular self-assembly, where relatively simple components (such as nucleic and amino acids, lipids, carbohydrates) organize themselves into larger systems with extremely complicated structure and dynamics (cells, organs, humans).

Molecular programming, where nanoscale engineering is thought of as a programming task, provides our second motivation. The field has progressed to the stage where we can design and synthesize a range of programable self-assembling molecular systems, all with relatively simple laboratory techniques. For example, short DNA strands that form 'tiles' can be self-assembled into DNA tile crystals [6] that are algorithmically patterned into counters and Sierpinski triangles. This form of *passive self-assembly* is theoretically capable of growing arbitrarily complex algorithmically described shapes and patterns. DNA origami can be used to create uniquely addressable shapes and patterns upon which objects can be localized within six nanometer resolution [4]. These systems are static, in the sense that after formation their structure is essentially fixed. However, DNA nanotechnology has seen increased interest in the fabrication of *active* nanostructures that have the ability to dynamically change their structure. Examples include DNA-based walkers, reconfigurable DNA origami, and molecular motors that transition between a small number of discrete states. In these systems the interplay between structure and dynamics leads to behaviors and capabilities not seen in static structures.

Here we suggest a model to motivate engineering of molecular structures that have complicated active dynamics of the kind seen in living biomolecular systems. Our model combines features seen in passive DNA-based tile self-assembly, molecular motors and other active systems, molecular circuits that evolve according to well-mixed chemical kinetics, and even

*Supported by NSF grants CCF-1219274, CCF-1162589, and 0832824—the Molecular Programming Project, an NSF Graduate Fellowship, and The Caltech Center for Biological Circuit Design. Many thanks to Niles Pierce and Patrick Mullen for valuable discussions.

ITCS'13, January 9–12, 2013, Berkeley, California, USA.
ACM 978-1-4503-1859-4/13/01.

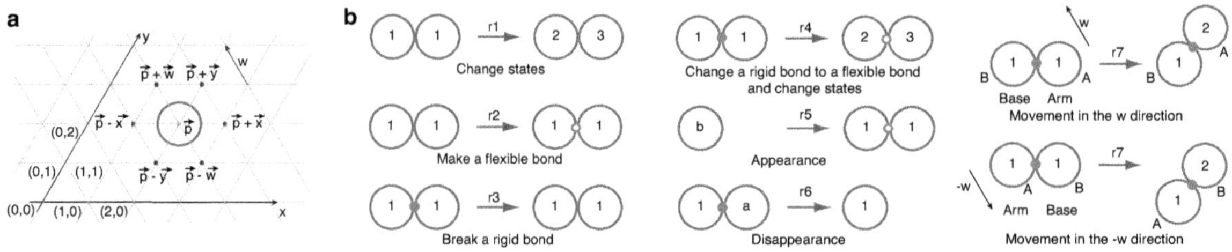

Figure 1: (a) A monomer in the triangular grid coordinate system. (b) Example monomer interaction rules. The movement rule ($r7$) nondeterministically applies one of two possible symmetric movements. When a movement rule is applied, any monomers attached to the arm are pushed along with it.

reaction-diffusion systems. The model is designed to capture the interplay between molecular structure and dynamics. In our model, simple molecular components form assemblies that can grow and shrink. Individual components can undergo state changes and move relative to each other.

The model consists of a two-dimensional grid of monomers, as shown in Figure 1. A specified set of rules, or a program, directs adjacent monomers to interact in a pairwise fashion. Monomers have internal states, and a pair of adjacent monomers can change their state with a single rule application. Monomers can appear and disappear from the grid. So far, the model can be thought of as a cellular automaton of a certain kind (rules are applied asynchronously and can be nondeterministic, and there is a notion of a growth front). An additional rule type allows monomers to move relative to each other. The movement rule is locally applied but propagates movement throughout the system in a very non-local fashion. This geometric and mechanical feature distinguishes our model, the *nubot* model, from previous molecular models and cellular automata, and crucially underlies its construction efficiency. The system evolves as a continuous time Markov process, with rules being applied to the grid asynchronously and in parallel analogous to standard chemical kinetics, modeling the distributed nature of molecular reactions.

The model can carry out local state changes on a grid, so it can easily simulate Turing machines, walkers, and cellular automata-like systems. We show examples of other simple programs such as robotic molecular arms that can move distance n in expected time $O(\log n)$, something that can not be done by cellular automata. By using a combination of monomer movement, appearance, and state change we show how to build a line of monomers in time that is merely logarithmic in the length of the line, something that is impossible in the (passive) abstract tile assembly model [1]. We go on to efficiently build a counter, that counts from 0 to n, within time and number of monomer states that are both logarithmic in n. We build on these results to show that the model is capable of building wide classes of shapes exponentially faster than passive self-assembly. We show how to build a computable shape of size $n \times n$ in time polylogarithmic in n, plus roughly the time needed to simulate a Turing machine that computes whether or not a given pixel is in the final shape. Our constructions are not only time efficient, but efficient in terms of their program-size: requiring at most polylogarithmic monomer types in terms of shape size, plus that required by the Kolmogorov complexity of the shape.

For shapes that have short algorithmic descriptions, but require a lot of time and space to compute their pixels, the previous computable shape construction necessarily requires (temporary) growth beyond the shape boundary. One can ask if there are interesting structures that we can build efficiently, but yet keep all growth confined within the boundary. It turns out that colored patterns, where the color of each pixel in the pattern is computable by a polynomial time Turing machine, can be computed extremely efficiently in this way. More precisely, we show that $n \times n$ colored patterns are computable in expected time $O(\log^{\ell+1} n)$ and using $O(s + \log n)$ states, where each pixel's color is computable by a program-size s Turing machine that runs in polynomial time in the length of the binary description of pixel indices (specifically, in time $O(\log^{\ell} n)$ where ℓ is $O(1)$). This entire construction is initiated by a single monomer and is carried out using only local information and in an entirely distributed and asynchronous fashion.

Our results are related to theoretical work in passive self-assembly [1, 6], chemical reaction networks [5], cellular automata, Lindenmayer systems [3] and reconfigurable robotics [2]—each such model sharing a subset of our active self-assembly model's features. In particular, reconfigurable modular robots with a similar long-range motion primitive to ours can achieve arbitrary reconfiguration in time logarithmic in shape size [2], so it will be interesting to compare such models to ours. Our constructions serve to show that exponentially large complicated shapes and patterns can be fabricated in polynomial time and using a linear number of states, besides the states that are required by the Kolmogorov complexity of the shape or pattern. Thus the model illustrates the power of active local growth along with non-local movement. We hope that the model can serve as the basis of further investigation into the computational properties of active self-assembly.

References

1. Leonard M. Adleman, Qi Cheng, Ashish Goel, and Ming-Deh Huang. Running time and program size for self-assembled squares. In *STOC 2001, pp 740–748.*
2. Greg Aloupis, Sébastien Collette, Erik D. Demaine, Stefan Langerman, Vera Sacristán, and Stefanie Wuhrer. Reconfiguration of cube-style modular robots using $O(\log n)$ parallel moves. In *Algorithms and Computation*, pages 342–353. Springer, 2008.
3. Aristid Lindenmayer. Mathematical models for cellular interactions in development I. Filaments with one-sided inputs. *J. Theor. Biol.*, 18(3):280–299, 1968.
4. Paul WK Rothemund. Folding DNA to create nanoscale shapes and patterns. *Nature*, 440(7082):297–302, 2006.
5. David Soloveichik, Matthew Cook, Erik Winfree, and Jehoshua Bruck. Computation with finite stochastic chemical reaction networks. *Natural Computing*, 7(4):615–633, 2008.
6. Erik Winfree, Furong Liu, Lisa Wenzler, and Nadrian C. Seeman. Design and self-assembly of two-dimensional DNA crystals. *Nature*, 394:539–544, 1998.

An Equational Approach to Secure Multi-Party Computation *

Daniele Micciancio
University of California, San Diego
daniele@cs.ucsd.edu

Stefano Tessaro†
Massachusetts Institute of Technology
tessaro@csail.mit.edu

ABSTRACT

We present a novel framework for the description and analysis of secure computation protocols that is at the same time mathematically rigorous and notationally lightweight and concise. The distinguishing feature of the framework is that it allows to specify (and analyze) protocols in a manner that is largely independent of time, greatly simplifying the study of cryptographic protocols. At the notational level, protocols are described by systems of mathematical equations (over domains), and can be studied through simple algebraic manipulations like substitutions and variable elimination. We exemplify our framework by analyzing in detail two classic protocols: a protocol for secure broadcast, and a verifiable secret sharing protocol, the second of which illustrates the ability of our framework to deal with probabilistic systems, still in a purely equational way.

Categories and Subject Descriptors

F.0 [**Theory**]: General; C.2.0 [**Computer Systems Organization**]: Computer-Communication Networks—*General*

General Terms

Theory

Keywords

Cryptography, Multi-Party Computation, Universal Composability

*This material is based on research sponsored by DARPA under agreement numbers FA8750-11-C-0096 and FA8750-11-2-0225. The U.S. Government is authorized to reproduce and distribute reprints for Governmental purposes notwithstanding any copyright notation thereon. The views and conclusions contained herein are those of the authors and should not be interpreted as necessarily representing the official policies or endorsements, either expressed or implied, of DARPA or the U.S. Government.

†Partially supported by NSF grant CCF-1018064.

ITCS'13, January 9–12, 2013, Berkeley, California, USA.

1. INTRODUCTION

Secure multiparty computation (MPC) is a cornerstone of theoretical cryptography, and a problem that is attracting increasingly more attention in practice too due to the pervasive use of distributed applications over the Internet and the growing popularity of computation outsourcing. The area has a long history, dating back to the seminal work of Yao [29] in the early 1980s, and a steady flow of papers contributing extensions and improvements that lasts to the present day (starting with the seminal works [12, 6, 3] introducing general protocols, and followed by literally hundreds of papers). But it is fair to say that MPC has yet to deliver its full load of potential benefits both to the applied and theoretical cryptography research communities. In fact, large portions of the research community still see MPC as a highly specialized research area, where only the top experts can read and fully understand the highly technical research papers routinely published in mainstream crypto conferences. Two main obstacles have kept, so far, MPC from becoming a more widespread tool to be used both in theoretical and applied cryptography: the prohibitive computational cost of executing many MPC protocols, and the inherent complexity of the models used to describe the protocols themselves. Much progress has been made in improving the efficiency of the first protocols [29, 12, 6] in a variety of models and with respect to several complexity measures, even leading to concrete implementations (cf. e.g. [19, 4, 17, 7, 24, 11]). However, the underlying models to describe and analyze security properties are still rather complex.

What makes MPC harder to model than traditional cryptographic primitives like encryption, is the inherently distributed nature of the security task being addressed: there are several distinct and mutually distrustful parties trying to perform a joint computation, in such a way that even if some parties deviate from the protocol, the protocol still executes in a robust and secure way.

The difficulty of properly modeling secure distributed computation is well recognized within the cryptographic community, and documented by several definitional papers attempting to improve the current state of the art [22, 9, 10, 23, 2, 18, 15, 20]. Unfortunately, the current state of the art is still pretty sore, with definitional/modeling papers easily reaching encyclopedic page counts, setting a very high barrier of entry for most cryptographers to contribute or actively follow the developments in MPC research. Moreover, most MPC papers are written in a semi-formal style reflecting an uncomfortable trade-off between the desire of giving to the subject the rigorous treatment it deserves and the

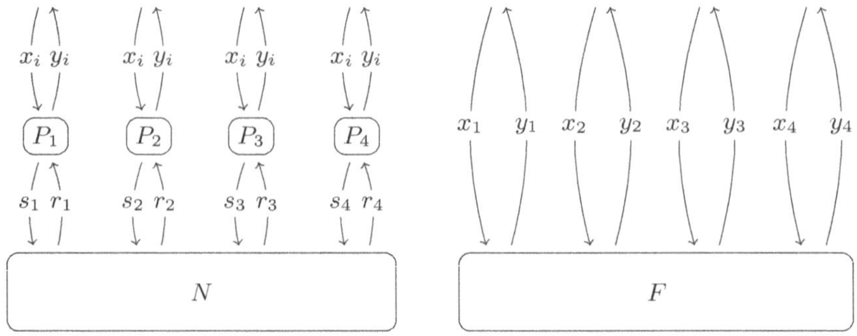

Figure 1: A multiparty protocol $P_1, \ldots, P_4$ with communication network N (left) implementing a functionality F (right).

implicit acknowledgment that this is just not feasible using the currently available formalisms (and even more so, within the page constraints of a typical conference or even journal publication.) At the other end, recent attempts to introduce abstractions [20] are too high level to deliver a precise formal language for protocol specification. The goal of this paper is to drastically change this state of affairs, by putting forward a model for the study of MPC protocols that is both concise, rigorous, and still firmly rooted in the intuitive ideas that pervade most past work on secure computation and most cryptographers know and love.

1.1 The simulation paradigm

Let us recall the well known and established simulation paradigm that underlies essentially all MPC security definitions. Cryptographic protocols are typically described by several component programs $P_1, \ldots, P_n$ executed by n participating parties, interconnected by a communication network N, and usually rendered by a diagram similar to the one in Figure 1 (left): each party receives some input x_i from an external environment, and sends/receives messages s_i, r_i from the network. Based on the external inputs x_i, and the messages s_i, r_i transmitted over the network N, each party produces some output value y_i which is returned to the outside world as the visible output of running the protocol. The computational task that the protocol is trying to implement is described by a single monolithic program F, called the "ideal functionality", which has the same input/output interface as the system consisting of $P_1, \ldots, P_n$ and N, as shown in Figure 1 (right). Conceptually, F is executed by a centralized entity that interacts with the individual parties through their local input/output interfaces x_i/y_i, and processes the data in a prescribed and trustworthy manner. A protocol $P_1, \ldots, P_n$ correctly implements functionality F in the communication model provided by N if the two systems depicted in Figure 1 (left and right) exhibit the same input/output behavior.

Of course, this is not enough for the protocol to be secure. In a cryptographic context, some parties can get corrupted, in which case an adversary (modeled as part of the external execution environment) gains direct access to the parties' communication channels s_i, r_i and is not bound to follow the instructions of the protocol programs P_i. Figure 2 (left) shows an execution where P_3 and P_4 are corrupted. The simulation paradigm postulates that whatever can be achieved by a concrete adversary attacking the protocol, can also be achieved by an idealized adversary S (called the simulator) attacking the ideal functionality F. In Figure 2 (right), the simulator takes over the role of P_3 and P_4, communicating for them with the ideal functionality, and recreating the attack of a real adversary by emulating an interface that exposes the network communication channels of P_3 and P_4. The protocol $P_1, \ldots, P_n$ securely implements functionality F if the systems described on the left and right of Figure 2 are functionally equivalent: no adversary (environment) connecting to the external channels $x_1, y_1, x_2, y_2, s_3, r_3, s_4, r_4$ can (efficiently) determine if it is interacting with the system described in Figure 2 (left) or the one in Figure 2 (right). In other words, anything that can be achieved corrupting a set of parties in a real protocol execution, can also be emulated by corrupting the same set of parties in an idealized execution where the protocol functionality F is executed by a trusted party in a perfectly secure manner.

This is a very powerful idea, inspired by the seminal work on zero knowledge proof systems [13], and embodied in many subsequent papers about MPC. But, of course, as much as evocative the diagrams in Figure 2 may be, they fall short of providing a formal definition of security. In fact, a similar picture can be drawn to describe essentially any of the secure multiparty computation models proposed so far at a very abstract level, but the real work is in the definition of what the blocks and communication links connecting them actually represent. Traditionally, building on classical work from computational complexity on interactive proof systems, MPC is formalized by modeling each block by an interactive Turing machine (ITM), a venerable model of sequential computation extended with some "communication tapes" used to model the channels connecting the various blocks. Unfortunately, this only provides an adequate model for the local computation performed by each component block, leaving out the most interesting features that distinguish MPC from simpler cryptographic tasks: computation is distributed and the concurrent execution of all ITMs needs to be carefully orchestrated. In a synchronous communication environment, where local computations proceed in lockstep through a sequence of rounds, and messages are exchanged only between rounds, this is relatively easy. But in asynchronous communication environments like the Internet, dealing with concurrency is a much trickier business. The standard approach to

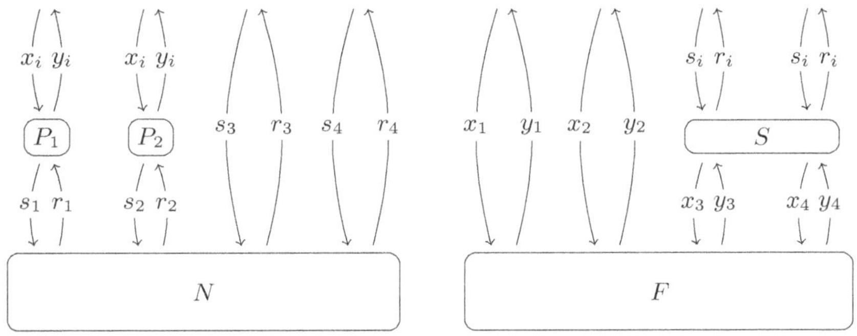

Figure 2: Simulation based security. The protocol $P_1, \ldots, P_4$ is a secure implementation of functionality F if the system (left) exposed to an adversary that corrupts a subset of parties (say P_3 and P_4) is indistinguishable from the one system (right) recreated by a simulator S interacting with F.

deal with concurrency in asynchronous distributed systems is to use nondeterminism: a system does not describe a single behavior, but a set of possible behaviors corresponding to all possible interleavings and message delivery orders. But nondeterminism is largely incompatible with cryptography, as it allows to break any cryptographic function by nondeterministically guessing the value of a secret key. As a result, cryptographic models of concurrent execution resort to an adversarially and adaptively chosen, but deterministic, message delivery order: whenever a message is scheduled for transmission between two component, it is simply queued and an external scheduling unit (which is also modeled as part of the environment) is notified about the event. While providing a technically sound escape route from the dangers of mixing nondeterministic concurrency with cryptography, this approach has several shortcomings:

- Adding a scheduler further increases the complexity of the system, making simulation based proofs of security even more technical.
- It results in a system that in many respects seems overspecified: as the goal is to design a robust system that exhibits the prescribed behavior in any execution environment, it would seem more desirable to abstract the scheduling away, rather than specifying it in every single detail of a fully sequential ordering of events.
- Finally, the intuitive and appealing idea conveyed by the diagrams in Figure 2 is in a sense lost, as the system is now more accurately described by a collection of isolated components all connected exclusively to the external environment that orchestrates their executions by scheduling the messages.

1.2 Our work

In this paper we describe a model of distributed computation that retains the simplicity and intuitiveness conveyed by the diagrams in Figures 1 and 2, and still it is both mathematically rigorous and concise. In other words, we seek a model where the components P_i, N, F, S occurring in the description and analysis of a protocol, and the systems obtained interconnecting them, can be given a simple and precise mathematical meaning. The operation of composing systems together should also be well defined, and satisfy a number of useful and intuitive properties, e.g., the result of connecting several blocks together does not depend on the order in which the connections are made. (Just as we expect the meaning of a diagram to be independent of the order in which the diagram was drawn.) Finally, it should provide a solid foundation for equational reasoning, in the sense that equivalent systems can be replaced by equivalent systems in any context.

Within such a framework, the proof that protocols can be composed together should be as simple as the following informal argument. (In fact, given the model formally defined in the rest of the paper, the following is actually a rigorous proof that our definition satisfies a universal composability property.) Say we have a protocol $P_1, \ldots, P_n$ securely implementing ideal functionality F using a communication network N, and also a protocol $Q_1, \ldots, Q_n$ in the F-hybrid model (i.e., an idealized model where parties can interact through functionality F) that securely implements functionality G. The security of the second protocol is illustrated in Figure 3.

Then, the protocol obtained simply by connecting P_i and Q_i together is a secure implementation of G, in the standard communication model N. Moreover, the simulator showing that the composed protocol is secure is easily obtained simply by composing the simulators for the two component protocols. In other words, we want to show that an adversary attacking the real system described in Figure 4 (left) is equivalent to the composition of the simulators attacking the ideal functionality G as described in Figure 4 (right).

This is easily shown by transforming Figure 4 (left) to Figure 4 (right) in two steps, going through the hybrid system described in Figure 5. Specifically, first we use the security of P_i to replace the system described in Figure 2 (left) with the one in Figure 2 (right). This turns the system in Figure 4 (left) into the equivalent one in Figure 5. Next we use the security of Q_i to substitute the system in Figure 3 (left) with the one in Figure 3 (right). This turns Figure 5 into Figure 4 (right).

While the framework proposed in this paper allows to work with complex distributed systems with the same simplicity as the informal reasoning described in this section, it is quite powerful and flexible. For example, it allows to model not only protocols that are universally composable, but also protocols that retain their security only when used

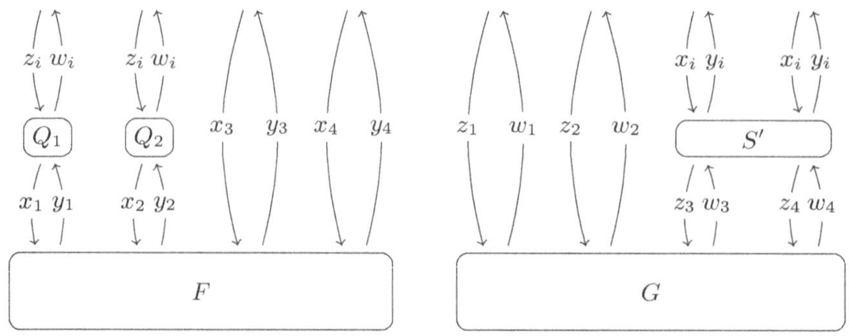

Figure 3: A protocol Q_i implementing G in the F-hybrid model.

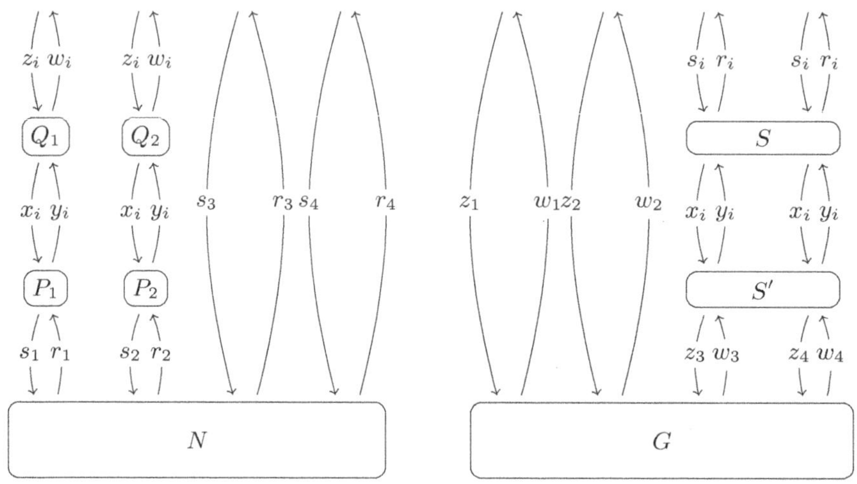

Figure 4: Protocol composition. Security is proved using a hybrid argument.

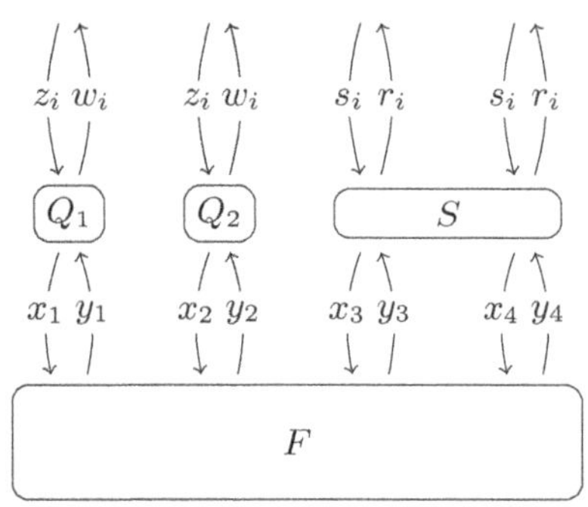

Figure 5: Hybrid system to prove the security of the composed protocol.

in restricted contexts. For simplicity, in this paper we focus on *perfectly secure* protocols against *unbounded* adversaries, as this already allows us to describe interesting protocols that illustrate the most important feature of our framework: the ability to design and analyze protocols without explicitly resorting to the notion of time and sequential scheduling of messages. Moreover, within the framework of universally composability, it is quite common to design perfectly secure protocols in a hybrid model that offers idealized versions of the cryptographic primitives, and then resorting to computationally secure cryptographic primitives only to realize the hybrid model. So, a good model for the analysis of perfect or statistical security can already be a useful and usable aid for the design of more general computationally secure protocols. Natively extending our framework to statistically or computationally secure protocols is also an attractive possibility. We consider the perfect/statistical/computational security dimension as being mostly orthogonal to the issues dealt with in this paper, and we believe the model described here offers a solid basis for extensions in that direction.

1.3 Techniques

In order to realize our vision, we introduce a computational model in which security proofs can be carried out without explicitly dealing with the notion of time. Formally, we associate to each communication channel connecting two components the set of all possible "channel histories", partially ordered according to their information content or temporal ordering. The simplest example is the set of all finite sequences M^* of messages from some underlying message space, ordered according to the prefix ordering relation. The components of the system are then modeled as functions mapping input histories to output histories. The functions are subject to some natural conditions, e.g., monotonicity: receiving more input values can only results in more output values being produced. Under appropriate technical conditions on the ordered sets associated to the communication channels, and the functions modeling the computations performed by the system components, this results in a well behaved framework, where components can be connected together, even forming loops, and always resulting in a unique and well defined function describing the input/output behavior of the whole system. Previous approaches to model interactive systems, such as Kahn networks [16] and Maurer's random systems [21], can indeed be seen as special cases of our general process model.[1] The resulting model is quite powerful, allowing even to model probabilistic computation as a special case. However, the simplicity of the model has a price: all components of the system must be monotone with respect to the information ordering relation. For example, if a program P on input messages x_1, x_2 outputs $P(x_1, x_2) = (y_1, y_2, y_3)$, then on input x_1, x_2, x_3 it can only output a sequence of messages that extends (y_1, y_2, y_3) with more output. In other words, P cannot "go back in time" and change y_1, y_2, y_3. While this is a very natural and seemingly innocuous restriction, it also means that the program run by P cannot perform operations of the form "if no input message has been received yet, then send y". This is because if an input message is received at a later point, P cannot go back in time and not send y.

It is our thesis that these time dependent operations make cryptographic protocols harder to understand and analyze, and therefore should be avoided whenever possible.

Organization.

The rest of the paper is organized as follows. In Section 2 we present our framework for the description and analysis of concurrent processes, and illustrate the definitions using a toy example. Next, we demonstrate the applicability of the framework by carefully describing and analyzing two classic cryptographic protocols: secure broadcast (in Section 3) and verifiable secret sharing (in Section 4). The secure broadcast protocol in Section 3 is essentially the one of Bracha, and only uses deterministic functions. Our modular analysis of the protocol illustrates the use of subprotocols that are not universally composable. The verifiable secret sharing protocol analyzed in Section 4 provides an example of randomized protocol.

[1]For the readers well versed in the subject, we remark that our model can be regarded as a generalization of Kahn networks where the channel behaviors are elements of arbitrary partially ordered sets (or, more precisely, domains) rather than simple sequences of messages. This is a significant generalization that allows to deal with probabilistic computations and intrinsically nondeterministic systems seamlessly, without incurring into the Brock-Ackerman anomaly and similar problems.

2. PROCESSES, COMPOSITION, AND SECURE COMPUTATION

In this section we introduce our mathematical framework for the description and analysis of distributed systems. We start with a high level description of our approach, which will be sufficient to apply our framework and to follow the proofs. We then give more foundational details justifying soundness of our approach. Finally, we provide security definitions for protocols in our framework.

2.1 Processes and systems

Our framework models (asynchronous and reactive) processes and systems with one or more input and output *channels* as mathematical functions mapping input histories to output histories. Before introducing more formal definitions, let us illustrate this concept with a simple example. Consider a deterministic process with one input and one output channels, which receives as input a sequence of messages, $x[1], \ldots, x[k]$, where each $x[k]$ is (or can be parsed as) an integer. The process receives the messages sequentially, one at a time, and in order to make the process finite one may assume that the process will accept only the first n messages. Upon receiving each input message $x[i]$, the process increments the value and immediately outputs $x[i]+1$. It is not hard to model the process in terms of a function mapping input to output sequences: The input and output of the function modeling the process are the set $\mathbb{Z}^{\leq n}$ of integer sequences of length at most n, and the process is described by the function $\mathrm{F}\colon \mathbb{Z}^{\leq n} \to \mathbb{Z}^{\leq n}$ mapping each input sequence $x \in \mathbb{Z}^k$ (for some $k \leq n$) to the output sequence $y \in \mathbb{Z}^k$ of the same length defined by the equations $y[i] = x[i]+1$ (for $i = 1, \ldots, k$). There are multiple ways one can possibly describe such a function. We describe the process in equational form as in Figure 6 (top). In the example, the first line assigns names to the function, input and output variables, while the remaining lines are equations that define the value of the output variables in terms of the input variables. Each variable ranges over a specific set ($x, y \in \mathbb{Z}^{\leq n}$), but for simplicity we often leave the specification of this set implicit, as it is usually clear from the context. By convention, all variables that appear in the equations, but not as part of the input or output variables, are considered *local/internal* variables, whose only purpose is to help defining the value of the output variables in terms of the input variables. Free index variables (e.g., i, j) are universally quantified (over appropriate ranges) and used to compactly describe sets of similar equations.

Processes as monotone functions.

In general, the reason we define a process F as a function mapping sequences to sequences[2] (rather than, say, as a function $f(x) = x+1$ applied to each incoming message x) is that it allows to describe the most general type of (e.g., stateful, reactive) process, whose output is a function of all messages received as input during the execution of the protocol. (Note that we do not need to model state explicitly.) Also, such functions can describe processes with multiple input and output channels by letting inputs and outputs be *tuples* of message sequences. However, clearly, not any such function mapping input to output sequences can be a valid

[2]Here we use sequences just as a concrete example. Our framework uses more general structures, namely domains.

$$
\begin{aligned}
&\mathrm{F}(x) = y: \\
&\quad y[i] = x[i] + 1 \qquad (1 \le i \le |x|)
\end{aligned}
$$

$$
\begin{aligned}
&\mathrm{G}(y) = (z, w): \\
&\quad z = y \\
&\quad w = y
\end{aligned}
$$

$$
\begin{aligned}
&\mathrm{H}(z) = x: \\
&\quad x[1] = 1 \\
&\quad x[j+1] = z[j] \qquad (j \le \min\{|z|, n-1\})
\end{aligned}
$$

Figure 6: Some simple processes.

$$
\begin{aligned}
&[\mathrm{G} \mid \mathrm{H}](y) = (w, x): \\
&\quad z = y \\
&\quad w = y \\
&\quad x[1] = 1 \\
&\quad x[j+1] = z[j] \qquad (j < n)
\end{aligned}
$$

$$
\begin{aligned}
&[\mathrm{G} \mid \mathrm{H}](y) = (w, x): \\
&\quad w = y \\
&\quad x[1] = 1 \\
&\quad x[j+1] = y[j] \qquad (j < n)
\end{aligned}
$$

Figure 7: Process composition.

process. To capture valid functions representing a process, input and output sets are endowed with a partial ordering relation $\le$, where $x \le y$ means that y is a possible *future* of x. (In the case of sequences of messages, $\le$ is the standard prefix partial ordering relation, where $x \le y$ if $y = x|z$ for some other sequence z, and $x|z$ is the concatenation of the two sequences.) Functions describing processes should be naturally restricted to monotone functions, i.e., functions such that $x \le y$ implies $\mathrm{F}(x) \le \mathrm{F}(y)$. In our example, this simply means that if on input a sequence of messages x, $\mathrm{F}(x)$ is produced as output, upon receiving additional messages z, the output sequence can only get longer, i.e., $\mathrm{F}(y) = \mathrm{F}(x|z) = \mathrm{F}(x)|z'$ for some z'. In other words, once the messages $\mathrm{F}(x)$ are sent out, the process cannot change its mind and set the output to a sequence that does not start with $\mathrm{F}(x)$.

Note that so far we only discussed an example of a *deterministic* process. Below, after introducing some further foundational tools, we will see that probabilistic processes are captured in the same way by letting the function output be a *distribution* over sequences, rather than a single sequence of symbols.

Further examples and notational conventions.

In the examples, $|x|$ denotes the length of a sequence x, and we use array notation $x[i]$ to index the elements of a sequence. Figure 6 gives two more examples of processes that further illustrate notational conventions. Process G, in Figure 6 (middle), simply duplicates the input y (as usual in $\mathbb{Z}^{\le n}$) and copies the input messages to two different output channels z and w. When input or output values are tuples, we usually give separate names to each component of the tuple. As before, all variables take values in $\mathbb{Z}^{\le n}$ and the output values are defined by a set of equations that express the output in terms of the input. Finally, process $\mathrm{H}(z)$ takes as input a sequence $z \in \mathbb{Z}^{\le n}$, and outputs the message 1 followed by the messages z received as input, possibly truncated to a prefix $z[< n]$ of length at most $n-1$, so that the output sequence x has length at most n.

Process composition.

Processes are *composed* in the expected way, connecting some output variables to other input variables. Here we use the convention that variable *names* are used to implicitly specify how different processes are meant to be connected together.[3] Composing two processes together yields, in turn, another process, which is obtained simply combining all the equations. We often refer to the resulting process as a *system* to stress its structure as a composition of basic processes. However, it should be noted that both a process and a system are objects of the same mathematical type, namely monotone functions described by systems of equations. For example, the result of composing G and H from Figure 6 yields the process (G | H) shown in Figure 7 (top), with input y and output (w, x), where $w = y$ replicates the input to make it externally visible. We use the convention that by default processes are connected by private channels, not visible outside of the system. This is modeled by turning their common input/output variables into local ones, not part of the input or output of the composed system. Of course, one can always either override this convention by explicitly listing such common input/output variables as part of the output, or bypass it by duplicating the value of a variable as done for example by process G. This is just a syntactical convention, and several other choices are possible, including never hiding variables during process composition and introducing a special projection operator to hide internal variables.

Since processes formally define functions (from input to output variables), and equations are just a syntactic method to specify functions, equations can be simplified without affecting the process. Simplifications are easily performed by substitution and variable elimination. For example, using the first equation $z = y$, one can substitute y for z, turning the last equation in the system into $x[i+1] = y[i]$. At this point, the local variable z is no longer used anywhere, and its defining equation can be removed from the system. The result is shown in Figure 7 (bottom). We remark that the two systems of equations shown in Figure 7 define the *same* process: they have the same input and output variables, and the equations define precisely the same function.

Feedback loops and recursive equations.

Now consider the composition of all three processes F,G,H from Figure 6. Composition can be performed one pair at a time, and in any order, e.g., as [[F | G] | H] or [F | [G | H]]. Given the appropriate mathematical definitions, it can be easily shown that the result is the same, independent from the order of composition. (This is clear at the syntactic level, where process composition is simply defined by combining all the equations together. But associativity of composition can also be proved at the semantic level, where the objects being combined are functions.) So, we write [F | G | H] to denote the result of composing multiple processes together, shown in Figure 8 (top). When studying multi-party compu-

[3]We stress that this is just a notational convention, and there are many other syntactical mechanisms that can be used to specify the "wiring" in more or less explicit ways.

$$
\begin{aligned}
&[\mathrm{F} \mid \mathrm{G} \mid \mathrm{H}]() = w\colon \\
&\quad y[i] = x[i] + 1 && (i \leq n) \\
&\quad z = y \\
&\quad w = y \\
&\quad x[1] = 1 \\
&\quad x[j+1] = z[j] && (j < n)
\end{aligned}
$$

$$
\begin{aligned}
&[\mathrm{F} \mid \mathrm{G} \mid \mathrm{H}]() = w\colon \\
&\quad w[1] = 2 \\
&\quad w[j+1] = w[j] + 1 && (j < n)
\end{aligned}
$$

Figure 8: Example of recursive process.

tation protocols, one is naturally led to consider collections of processes, e.g., $\mathrm{P}_1, \ldots, \mathrm{P}_n$, corresponding to the individual programs run by each participant. Given a collection $\{\mathrm{P}_i\}_i$ and a subset of indices $I \subseteq \{1, \ldots, n\}$, we write P_I to denote the composition of all P_i with $i \in I$. Similarly, we use x_A or $x[A]$ to denote a vector indexed by $i \in A$. As a matter of notation, we also use x^A to denote the $|A|$-dimensional vector indexed by $i \in A$ with all components set equal to x.

The system $[\mathrm{F} \mid \mathrm{G} \mid \mathrm{H}]$ has no inputs, and only one output w. More interestingly, the result of composing all three processes yields a recursive system of equations, where y is a function of x, x is a function of z and z is a function of y. Before worrying about solving the recursion, we can simplify the system. A few substitutions and variable eliminations yield the system in Figure 8 (bottom). The system consists of a single, recursively defined output variable w. The recursive definition of w is easy to solve, yielding $w[i] = i + 1$ for $i \leq n$.

2.2 Foundations: Domain theory and probabilistic processes

So far, equations have been treated in an intuitive and semi-formal way: in fact, obtaining an intuitive lightweight framework is one of our main objectives. But for the approach to be sound, it is important that the equations and the variable symbols manipulated during the design and analysis of a system be given a precise mathematical meaning. Also, we want to consider a more general model of processes where inputs and outputs are not restricted to simple sequences of messages, but can be more complex objects, including probability distributions. This requires us to introduce some further formal tools.

The standard framework to give a precise meaning to our equations is that of *domain theory*, a well established area of computer science developed decades ago to give a solid foundation to functional programming languages [27, 26, 14, 28, 1]. Offering a full introduction to domain theory is beyond the scope of this paper, but in order to reassure the reader that our framework is sound, we recall the most basic notions and illustrate how they apply to our setting.

Domains and partial orders.

Domains are a special kind of partially ordered set satisfying certain technical properties. We recall that a partially ordered set (or poset) $(X; \leq)$ is a set X together with a reflexive, transitive and antisymmetric relation $\leq$. We use posets to model the set of possible histories (or behaviors) of communication channels, with the partial order relation corresponding to temporal evolution. For example, a channel that allows the transmission of an arbitrary number of messages from a basic set M (and that preserves the order of transmitted messages) can be modeled by the poset $(M^*; \leq)$ of finite sequences of elements of M together with the prefix partial ordering relation $\leq$. A *chain* $x_1 \leq x_2 \leq \ldots \leq x_n$ represents a sequence of observations at different points in time.[4] In this paper we will extensively use an even simpler poset $M_\perp$, consisting of the base set M extended with a special "bottom" element $\perp$, and the flat partial order where $x \leq y$ if and only if $x = \perp$ or $x = y$. The poset $M_\perp$ is used to model a communication channel that allows the transmission of a single message from M, with the special value $\perp$ representing a state in which no message has been sent yet.

The Scott topology and continuity.

Posets can be endowed with a natural topology, called the *Scott topology*, that plays an important role in many definitions. In the case of posets $(X; \leq)$ with no infinite chains, closed sets can be simply defined as sets $C \subseteq X$ that are downward closed, i.e., if $x \in O$ and $y \leq x$, then $y \in C$. Intuitively, a set is closed if it contains all possible "pasts" that lead to a current set of events. Open sets are defined as usual as the complements of closed sets. It is easy to see that the standard (topological[5]) definition of continuous function $f\colon X \to Y$ (according to the Scott topology on posets with no infinite chains) boils down to requiring that f is monotone, i.e., for all $x, y \in X$, if $x \leq y$ in X, then $f(x) \leq f(y)$ in Y. In the case of posets with infinite chains, such as $(M^*; \leq)$, definitions are slightly more complex, and require the definition of limits of infinite chains. For any poset $(X; \leq)$ and subset $A \subseteq X$, $x \in X$ is an upper bound on A if $x \geq a$ for all $a \in A$. The value x is called the least upper bound of A if it is an upper bound on A, and any other upper bound y satisfies $x \leq y$. Informally, if $A = \{a_i \mid i = 1, 2, \ldots\}$ is a chain $a_1 \leq a_2 \leq a_3 \leq \ldots$, and A admits a least upper bound (denoted $\bigvee A$), then we think of $\bigvee A$ as the limit of the monotonically increasing sequence A. (In our setting, where the partial order models temporal evolution, the limit corresponds to the value of the variable describing the entire channel history once the protocol has finished executing.) All Scott domains (and all posets used in this paper) are complete partial orders (or CPO), i.e., posets such that all chains $A \subseteq X$ admit a least upper bound. CPOs have a minimal element $\perp = \bigvee \emptyset$, which satisfies $\perp \leq x$ for all $x \in X$. Closed sets $C \subseteq X$ of arbitrary CPOs X are defined by requiring C to be also closed under limits, i.e., for any chain $Z \subseteq C$ it must be $\bigvee Z \in C$. (Open sets are always defined as the complement of closed sets.) Similarly, continuous functions between CPOs $f\colon X \to Y$ should preserve limits, i.e., any chain $Z \subseteq X$ must satisfy $f(\bigvee Z) = \bigvee f(Z)$.

As an example, we see that $(M^*; \leq)$ is not a CPO. We can define infinite chains A of successively longer strings (e.g., take $x_i = 0^i$ for $M = \{0, 1\}$) such that no limit in M^* exists for this chain. However, note that such a chain always

[4]Domain theory usually resorts to the (related, but more general) notion of *directed set*. But not much is lost by restricting the treatment to chains, which are perhaps more intuitive to use in our setting.

[5]We recall that a function $f\colon X \to Y$ between two topological spaces is continuous if the preimage $f^{-1}(O)$ of any open set $O \subset Y$ is also open.

defines an infinite string $x^* \in M^\infty$ which is such that $y \leq x^*$ holds for all $y \in A$. Therefore, the poset $(M^* \cup M^\infty; \leq)$ is a CPO.[6] This CPO can be used to model processes taking input and output sequences of arbitrary length.

Later on, we often use generalizations of the above limit notion, called the *join* and the *meet*, respectively. For a set $Z \subseteq X$, let $Z^\uparrow = \{z' \in X : \forall z \in Z : z \leq z'\}$ be the set of upper bounds on Z. An element $z^* \in Z^\uparrow$ such that $z^* \leq z$ for all $z \in Z^\uparrow$, if it exists, is called the *join* of Z and denoted $\bigvee Z$. The set $Z^\downarrow$ and the *meet* $\bigwedge Z$ are defined symmetrically.

Equational descriptions and fixed points.

We can now provide formal justification for our equational approach given above. Note that CPOs can be combined in a variety of ways, using common set operations, while preserving the CPO structure. For example, the cartesian product $A \times B$ of two CPOs is a CPO with the component-wise partial ordering relation. Using cartesian products, one can always describe every valid system of equations (as informally used in the previous paragraphs to define a process or a system) as the definition of a function f of the form

$$f(z) = g(z, x) \quad \text{where} \quad x = h(z, x) \qquad (1)$$

for some internal variable x and bivariate continuous[7] functions $h(z, x)$ and $g(z, x)$. An important property of CPOs is that every continuous function $f: X \to X$ admits a least fixed point, i.e., a minimal $x \in X$ such that $f(x) = x$, which can be obtained by taking the limit of the chain $\perp \leq f(\perp) \leq \ldots \leq f^n(\perp) \leq \ldots$, and admits an intuitive operational interpretation: starting from the initial value $x = \perp$, one keeps updating the value $x \leftarrow f(x)$ until the computation stabilizes.

Least fixed points are used to define the solution to recursive equations as (1) above as follows, and to show that it is always defined, proving soundness of our approach. For any fixed z, the function $h_z(x) = h(z, x)$ is also continuous, and maps X to itself. So, it admits a least fixed point $x_z = \bigvee_i h_z^i(\perp)$. The function defined by (1) is precisely $f(z) = g(z, x_z)$ where x_z is the least fixed point of $h_z(x) = h(x, z)$. It is a standard exercise to show that the function $f(z)$ so defined is a continuous function of z.

Scott domains are a special class of CPOs satisfying a number of additional properties (technically, they are algebraic bounded complete CPOs), that are useful for the full development of the theory. As most of the concepts used in this paper can be fully described in terms of CPOs, we do not introduce additional definitions, and refer the reader to any introductory textbook on domain theory for a formal treatment of the subject.

Probabilistic processes.

So far, our theory does not support yet the definition of processes with probabilistic behavior. Intuitively, we want to define a process as a continuous map from elements of a CPO X to probability *distributions* over some CPO Y. We will now discuss how to define the set $D(Y)$ of such probability distributions, which turns out to be a CPO. Our approach follows [25].

Let $O(X)$ be the open sets of X, and $B(X)$ the Borel algebra of X, i.e., the smallest σ-algebra that contains $O(X)$. We recall that a probability distribution over a set X is a function $p: B(X) \to [0, 1]$ that is countably additive and has total mass $p(X) = 1$. The set of probability distributions over a CPO X, denoted $D(X)$, is a CPO according to the partial order relation such that $p \leq q$ if and only if $p(A) \leq q(A)$ for all open sets $A \in O(X)$. This partial order on probability distributions $D(X)$ captures precisely the natural notion of evolution of a probabilistic process: the probability of a closed set can only decrease as the system evolves and probability mass "escapes" from it into the future. A probabilistic process P with input in X and output in Y is described by a continuous functions from X to $D(Y)$ that on input an element $x \in X$ produces an output probability distribution $\mathrm{P}(x) \in D(Y)$ over the set Y.

While these mathematical definitions may seem somehow arbitrary and complicated, we reassure the reader that they correspond precisely to the common notion of probabilistic computation. For example, any function $\mathrm{P}: X \to D(Y)$ can be uniquely extended to take as input probability distributions. The resulting function $\hat{\mathrm{P}}: D(X) \to D(Y)$, on input a distribution D_X, produces precisely what one could expect: the output probability distribution $D_Y = \hat{\mathrm{P}}(D_X)$ is obtained by first sampling $x \leftarrow D_X$ according to the input distribution, and then sampling the output according to $y \leftarrow \mathrm{P}(x)$. Moreover, the result $\hat{\mathrm{P}}: D(X) \to D(Y)$ is continuous according to the standard topology of $D(X)$ and $D(Y)$.

The fact that a distribution $D_X \in D(X)$ and a function $f: X \to D(Y)$ can be combined to obtain an output distribution D_Y allows to extend our equational treatment of systems to probabilistic computations. A probabilistic system is described by a set of equations similar to (1), except that h is a continuous function from $Z \times X$ to $D(X)$, and we write the equation in the form $x \leftarrow h(z, x)$ to emphasize that $h(z, x)$ is a probability distribution to sample from, rather than a single value. For any fixed z, the function $h_z(x) = h(z, x)$ is continuous, and it can be extended to a continuous function $\hat{h}_z: D(X) \to D(X)$. The least fixed point of this function is a probability distribution $D_z \in D(X)$, and function f maps the value z to the distribution $g(z, D_z)$.

Formally, the standard mathematical tool to give the equations a precise meaning is the use of monads, where $\leftarrow$ corresponds to the monad "bind" operation. We reassure the reader that this is all standard, well studied in the context of category theory and programming language design, both in theory and practice, e.g., as implemented in mainstream functional programming languages like Haskell. Rigorous mathematical definitions to support the definition of systems of probabilistic equations can be easily given within the framework of domain theory, but no deep knowledge of the theory is necessary to work with the equations, just like knowledge of denotational semantics is not needed to write working computer programs.

2.3 Secure multi-party computation and composability

So far, we have developed a domain-theoretic framework to define processes, their composition, and their asynchronous interaction. We still need to define what it means for such

[6] In fact, usually, one can define M^∞ to be exactly the set of limits of infinite chains from M^*.

[7] Continuity for bivariate functions is defined regarding f as an univariate function with domain $Z \times X$.

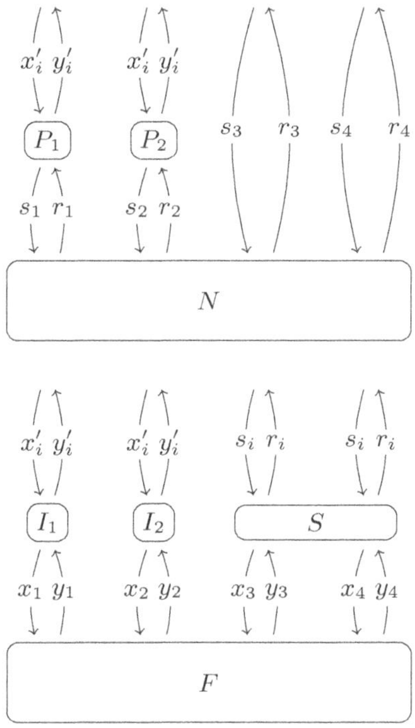

Figure 9: The protocol $(P_1,\ldots,P_4)$ securely implements interface $(I_1,\ldots,I_4)$ to functionality F in the communication model N.

a system to implement a multi-party protocol, and what it means for such a protocol to securely implement some functionality. Throughout this section, we give definitions in the deterministic case for simplicity. The definitions extend naturally to probabilistic processes by letting the output be a probability distribution over (the product of) the output sets.

We model secure multi-party computation along the lines described in the introduction. A secure computation task is modeled by an n-party functionality F that maps n inputs $(x_1,\ldots,x_n)$ to n outputs $(y_1,\ldots,y_n)$ in the deterministic case, or to a distribution on a set of n outputs in the probabilistic case. Each input or output variable is associated to a specific domain X_i/Y_i, and F is a continuous function $F\colon (X_1\times\cdots\times X_n)\to(Y_1\times\cdots\times Y_n)$, typically described by a system of domain equations. Each pair X_i/Y_i corresponds to the input and output channels used by user i to access the functionality. We remark that, within our framework, even if F is a (pure) mathematical function, it still models a reactive functionality that can receive inputs and produce outputs asynchronously in multiple rounds.

Sometimes, one knows in advance that F will be used within a certain context. (For example, in the next section we will consider a multicast channel that is always used for broadcast, i.e., in a context where the set of recipients is always set to the entire group of users.) In these settings, for efficiency reasons, it is useful to consider protocols that do not implement the functionality F directly, but only the use of F within the prescribed context. We formalize this usage by introducing the notion of a protocol implementing an *interface* to a functionality. An interface is a collection of continuous functions $I_i\colon X'_i\times Y_i\to X_i\times Y'_i$, where X'_i, Y'_i are the input and output domain of the interface. Combining the interface $I = I_1 \mid \ldots \mid I_n$ with the functionality F, yields a system $(F \mid I)$ with inputs $X'_1,\ldots,X'_n$ and outputs $Y'_1,\ldots,Y'_n$ that offers a limited access to F. The standard definition of (universally composable) security corresponds to setting I to the trivial interface where $X'_i = X_i$, $Y'_i = Y_i$ and each I_i to the identity function offering direct access to F.

Ideal functionalities can be used both to describe protocol problems, and underlying communication models. Let $N\colon S_1\times\ldots\times S_n\to R_1\times\ldots\times R_n$ be an arbitrary ideal functionality. One may think of N as modeling a communication network where user i sends $s_i\in S_i$ and receives $r_i\in R_i$, but all definitions apply to arbitrary N.

A protocol implementing an interface I to functionality F in the communication model N is a collection of functions $P_1,\ldots,P_n$ where $P_i\colon X'_i\times R_i\to Y'_i\times S_i$. We consider the execution of protocol P in a setting where an adversary can corrupt a subset of the participants. The set of corrupted players $A\subseteq\{1,\ldots,n\}$ must belong to a given family $\mathcal{A}$ of allowable sets, e.g., all sets of size less than $n/2$ in case security is to be guaranteed only for honest majorities. We can now define security.

Definition 1. *Protocol P securely implements interface I to functionality F in the communication model N if for any allowable set $A\in\mathcal{A}$ with complement $H=\{1,\ldots,n\}\setminus A$, there is a simulator $S\colon S_A\times Y_A\to X_A\times R_A$ such that the systems $(P_H \mid N)$ and $(S \mid I_H \mid F)$ are equivalent, i.e., they define the same function.*

$(P_H \mid N)$ is called the real system, and corresponds to an execution of the protocol in which the users in A are corrupted, while those in H are honest and follow the protocol. It is useful to illustrate this system with a diagram. See Figure 9 (top). We see from the diagram that the real system has inputs X'_H, S_A and outputs Y'_H, R_A. In the ideal setting, when the adversary corrupts the users in A, we are left with the system $I_H \mid F$ because corrupted users are not bound to use the intended interface I. This system $I_H \mid F$ has inputs X'_H, X_A and outputs Y'_H, Y_A. In order to turn this system into one with the same inputs and outputs as the real one, we need a simulator of type $S\colon S_A\times Y_A\to X_A\times R_A$. When we compose S with $I_H \mid F$ we get a system $(S \mid I_H \mid F)$ with the same input and output variables as the real system $(P_H \mid N)$. See Figure 9 (bottom). For the protocol to be secure, the two systems must be equivalent, showing that any attack that can be carried out on the real system by corrupting the set A can be simulated on the ideal system through the simulator.

When composing protocols together, N is not a communication network, but an ideal functionality representing a hybrid model. In this setting, we say that protocol P accesses N through interface $J=(J_1,\ldots,J_n)$ if each party runs a program of the form $P_i = J_i \mid P'_i$. If this is the case, we say that P securely implements interface I to functionality F through interface J to communication model N.

Composition theorems in our framework come essentially for free, and their proof easily follow from the general properties of systems of equations. For example, we have the following rather general composition theorem.

Theorem 1. *Assume P securely implements interface I to F in the communication model N, and $Q = Q' \mid I$ securely*

$\text{BCAST}(x) = (y_1, \ldots, y_n)$:
$y_i = x \quad (1 \le i \le n)$

$\text{WCAST}(x', w) = (y'_1, \ldots, y'_n)$:
$y'_i = x' \wedge w[i] \quad (1 \le i \le n)$

$\text{NET}(s_1, \ldots, s_n) = (r_1, \ldots, r_n)$:
$r_i[j] = s_j[i] \quad (1 \le i, j \le n)$

$\text{DEALER}(x) = (x', w)$:
$w[i] = \top \quad (1 \le i \le n)$
$x' = x$

$\text{PLAYER[i]}(y'_i, r_i) = (y_i, s_i)$: $\quad (1 \le i \le n)$
$s_i[j] = y'_i \vee t_1(r_i[1], \ldots, r_i[n]) \quad (1 \le j \le n)$
$y_i = t_2(r_i[1], \ldots, r_i[n])$

Figure 10: The Broadcast functionality and protocol.

implements G through interface I to F, then the composed protocol $Q' \mid P$ securely implements G in the communication model N.

The simple proof is similar to the informal argument presented in the introduction, and it is left to the reader as an exercise. The composition theorem is easily extended in several ways, e.g., by considering protocols Q that only implement a given interface J to G, and protocols P that use N through some given interface J'.

3. SECURE BROADCAST

In this section we provide, as a simple case study, the analysis of a secure broadcast protocol (similar to Bracha's reliable broadcast protocol [8]), implemented on an asynchronous point-to-point network. We proceed in two steps. In the first step, we build a weak broadcast protocol, that provides consistency, but does not guarantee that all parties terminate with an output. In the second step, we use the weak broadcast protocol to build a protocol achieving full security. We present the two steps in reverse order, first showing how to strengthen a weak broadcast protocol, and then implementing the weak broadcast on a point-to-point network.

3.1 Building broadcast from weak broadcast

In this section we build a secure broadcast protocol on top of a weak broadcast channel and a point to point communication network. The broadcast, weak broadcast, and communication network are described in Figure 10. The broadcast functionality (BCAST) receives a message x from a dealer, and sends a copy $y_i = x$ to each player. The weak broadcast channel (WCAST) allows a dishonest dealer to specify (using a boolean vector $w \in \{\bot, \top\}^n$) which subset of the players will receive the message. Notice that the functionality WCAST described in Figure 10 is in fact a multicast channel, that allows the sender to transmit a message to any subset of players of its choice. We call it a weak broadcast, rather than multicast, because we will not use (or implement) this functionality at its full power: the honest dealer in our protocol will always set all $w_i = \top$, and use WCAST as a broadcast channel $\text{BCAST}(x) = \text{WCAST}(x, \top^n)$. The auxiliary inputs w_i are used only to capture the extra power given to a dishonest dealer that, by not following the protocol, may restrict the delivery of the message x to a subset of the players. This will be used in the next section to provide a secure implementation of WCAST on top of a point to point communication network.

The broadcast protocol is very simple and it is also shown in Figure 10. The dealer simply uses WCAST to transmit its input message x to all n players by setting $w[i] = \top$ for all $1 \le i \le n$. The players have then access to a network functionality NET to exchange messages among themselves. The program run by the players makes use to two threshold functions t_1 and t_2 each taking n inputs, which are assumed to satisfy, for every admissible set of corrupted players $A \subseteq \{1, \ldots, n\}$ and complementary set $H = \{1, \ldots, n\} \setminus A$, input vector u, and value x, the following properties: $t_1(u[A], (x)^H) = t_2(u[A], (x)^H) = x$ (i.e., if all honest players agree on x, then t_1, t_2 output x irrespective of the other values), and $t_1((\bot)^A, u[H]) \ge t_2((\top)^A, u[H])$ (i.e., for any set of values provided by the honset players, t_1 is always bigger than t_2 regardless of the other values). It is easy to see that the threshold functions $t_i(u) = \bigvee_{|S|=k_i} \bigwedge_{j \in S} u_j$ satisfy these properties provided $|A| < k_1 \le k_2 - |A| \le n - 2|A|$, which in particular requires $n \ge 3|A| + 1$.

In the security analysis, we distinguish two cases, depending on whether the dealer is corrupt or not.

Honest dealer.

First we consider the simple case where the adversary corrupts a set of players $A \subset \{1, \ldots, n\}$, and the dealer behaves honestly. Let $H = \{1, \ldots, n\} \setminus A$ be the set of honest players. An execution of the protocol when players in A are corrupted is described by the system (DEALER | PLAYER[H] | WCAST | NET) with input (x, s_A) and output (y_H, y'_A, r_A) depicted in Figure 11 (top). Note that in this (and the following) figures, double arrows and boxes denote parallel processes and channels. Combining the defining equations of DEALER, PLAYER[h] for $h \in H$, WCAST and NET, and introducing the auxiliary variables $u_h = x \vee t_1(s_A[h], s_H[h])$ for all $h \in H$, we get that for any $1 \le i, j \le n$, and $h \in H$ the following holds:

$$\begin{aligned}
r_j[i] &= s_i[j] \\
y'_i &= x' \wedge w[i] = x \wedge \top = x \\
s_h[i] &= y'_h \vee t_1(r_h[1], \ldots, r_h[n]) \\
&= x \vee t_1(s_A[h], s_H[h]) = u_h \\
y_h &= t_2(r_h[1], \ldots, r_h[n]) \\
&= t_2(s_A[h], s_H[h]) = t_2(s_A[h], u_H) \\
u_h &= x \vee t_1(s_A[h], s_H[h]) = x \vee t_1(s_A(h), u_H) .
\end{aligned}$$

The last equation $u_h = x \vee t_1(s_A(h), u_H)$ provides a recursive definition of u_H, which can be easily solved by an iterative least fix point computation: starting from $u_H^{(0)} = \bot^H$, we get $u_H^{(1)} = (x \vee t_1(s_A(h), u_H^{(0)}))^H = x^H$, and then again $u_H^{(2)} = (x \vee t_1(s_A(h), u_H^{(1)}))^H = x^H$. Therefore the least fix point is $u_H = x^H$. Substituting $u_H = x^H$ in the previous equations, and using the properties of t_2, we see that the system of equations defined by (DEALER | PLAYER[H] | WCAST | NET) is equivalent to

$$\begin{aligned}
r_a &= (s_A[a], x^H) && (a \in A) \\
y'_a &= x && (a \in A) \\
y_h &= t_2(s_A[h], x^H) = x && (h \in H)
\end{aligned} \qquad (2)$$

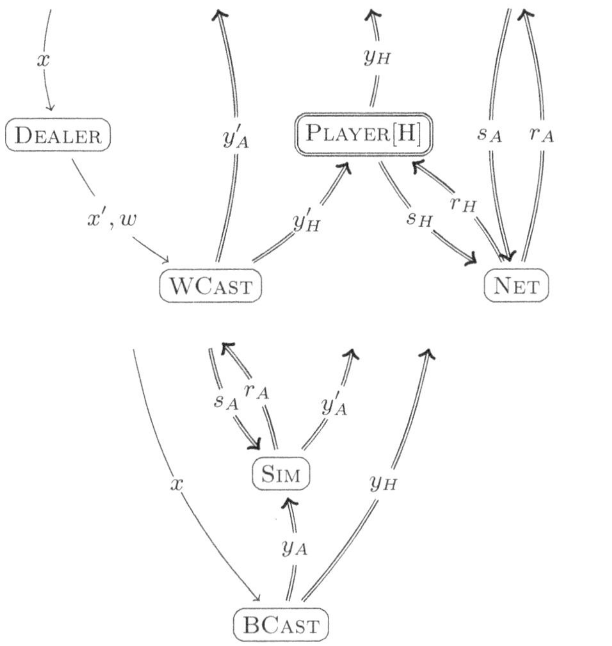

Figure 11: Security of broadcast protocol when the dealer is honest. Real world execution above. Simulated attack in the ideal world below.

We now show that an equivalent system can be obtained by combining the ideal functionality BCAST with a simulator SIM as in Figure 11 (bottom). The simulator takes (y_A, s_A) as input, and must output (y'_A, r_A) such that (SIM| BCAST) is equivalent to the system (DEALER| PLAYER[H] | WCAST| NET) specified by the last set of equations. The simulator is given in Figure 12 (left). It is immediate to verify that combining the equations of the simulator SIM with the equations $y_i = x$ of the ideal broadcast functionality, and eliminating local variables, yields a system of equations identical to (2).

Dishonest dealer.

We now consider the case where both the dealer and a subset of players A are corrupted. As before, let $H = \{1, \ldots, n\} \setminus A$ be the set of honest players. The system corresponding to a real execution of the protocol when DEALER

$\mathrm{SIM}(y_A, s_A) = (y'_A, r_A)$:

$$
\begin{aligned}
& r_A[a] = s_a[A] && (a \in A) \\
& r_A[h] = y_A && (h \in H) \\
& y'_A = y_A
\end{aligned}
$$

$\mathrm{SIM}'(x', w, y_A, s_A) = (x, r_A, y'_A)$:

$$
\begin{aligned}
& u_h = (x' \wedge w[h]) \vee t_1(s_A[h], u_H) && (h \in H) \\
& x = t_2(s_A[h], u_H) && (h = \min H) \\
& y'_a = x' \wedge w[a] && (a \in A) \\
& r_a[A] = s_A[a] && (a \in A) \\
& r_a[H] = u_H && (a \in A)
\end{aligned}
$$

Figure 12: Simulators for the broadcast protocol when the dealer is honest (top) or dishonest (bottom).

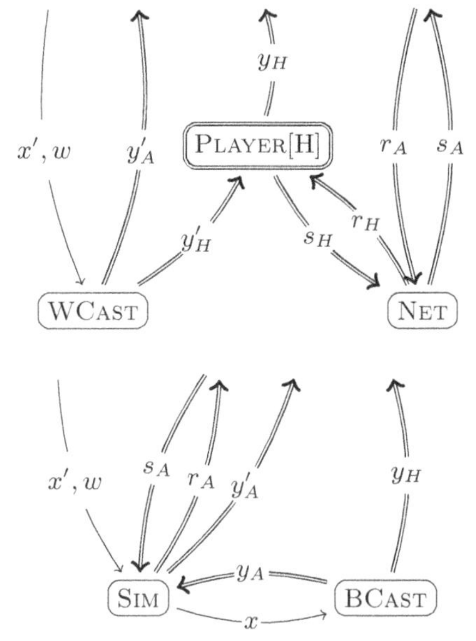

Figure 13: Security of broadcast protocol when the dealer is corrupted. Real world execution above. Simulated attack in the ideal world below.

and PLAYER[A] are corrupted is (PLAYER[H] | WCAST| NET), mapping (x', w, s_A) to (y_H, r_A, y'_A). (See Figure 13 (top).) Using the defining equations of PLAYER[H], WCAST and NET, and introducing auxiliary variables

$$u_h = y'_h \vee t_1(r_h[1], \ldots, r_h[n])$$

for $h \in H$, we get the following set of equations:

$$
\begin{aligned}
y_h &= t_2(r_h[A], r_h[H]) \\
&\quad = t_2(s_A[h], u_H) && (h \in H) \\
y'_a &= x' \wedge w[a] && (a \in A) \\
r_a[A] &= s_A[a] && (a \in A) \\
r_a[H] &= u_H \\
u_h &= (x' \wedge w[h]) \vee t_1(s_A[h], u_H) && (h \in H)
\end{aligned}
\tag{3}
$$

This time the simulator SIM' takes input (x', w, y_A, s_A) and outputs (x, r_A, y'_A). (See Figure 13 (bottom).) With these inputs and outputs, the simulator can directly set all variables except y_h just as in the real system (3). The simulator can also compute the value y_h, but it cannot set y_h directly because this variable is defined by the ideal functionality as $y_h = x$. We will prove that all variables y_h defined by (3) take the same value. It follows that the simulator can set $x = y_h$ for any $h \in H$, and the system (BCAST,SIM') will be equivalent to (3) (and therefore to (PLAYER[H] | WCAST| NET)). The code of the simulator is given in Figure 12 (right), where $x = y_h$ is arbitrarily selected using the smallest index $h = \min H$. (Any other choice of h would have been fine.)

It remains to prove that all y_h take the same value. By antisymmetry, it is enough to show that $y_i \le y_j$ for all $i, j \in H$. These easily follows from the assumptions on t_1, t_2.

In fact, by monotonicity, we have

$$y_i = t_2(s_A[i], u_H) \leq t_2(\top^A, u_H) \leq t_1(\bot^A, u_H) \leq t_1(s_A[j], u_H) \leq u_j \ .$$

It immediately follows that

$$y_j = t_2(s_A[j], u_H) \geq t_2(s_A[j], (y_i)^H) = y_i \ .$$

3.2 Weak broadcast

In this section we show how to implement the weak broadcast functionality WCast given in Figure 10 to be used within the BCast protocol discussed in the previous section, and analyze is security. We recall that WCast is a multicast functionality connecting a dealer to n other parties, which allows the dealer to send a message x' to a subset of the parties specified by a vector $w \in \{\bot, \top\}^n$. We stress that we do not need a secure implementation of WCast in its full generality, as our higher level broadcast protocol (BCast) uses WCast is a rather restricted way: it always set $w = (\top)^n$ and transmits x' to all parties. Accordingly, we give a protocol that securely implements this interface to WCast. Formally, the dealer's interface Int takes only x' as external input, and passes it along with $w = \top^n$ to the ideal functionality. The other parties have unrestricted access to the ideal functionality, and their interface is the identity function (or empty system of equations).

We implement interface Int to WCast on top of a point-to-point communication network similar to the Net functionality described in Figure 10, with the only difference that here also the dealer can send messages. The protocol is very simple: the dealer transmit the input x' to all parties, and the parties retransmit the message to each other. Each party sets its output using a threshold function of the messages received by the other parties. The equations corresponding to the network Net', interface Int, and protocol programs Dealer, Player[1],...,Player[n] are given in Figure 14. For reference, we have also repeated the definition of BCast from Figure 10. The function t is assumed to satisfy the following properties: $t(u[A], (x)^H) = x$ (i.e., if all honest parties agree on x, then the output is x), and, moreover, for all vectors u, u' with $u[H] = u'[H]$, we have $t(u) = t(u')$ or $t(u) = \bot$. It is easy to see that the threshold function $t(u) = \bigvee_{|S|=k} \bigwedge_{j \in S} u_j$ satisfies both properties for $k \geq \frac{n+|A|+1}{2}$. Namely, take any two vectors u, u' with $u[H] = u'[H]$, assume that there exist sets S and S' such that $u_j = x$ for all $j \in S$ and $u'_j = y$ all $j \in S'$. Then, since $|S \cap S' \cap H| \geq 2k - n - |A| > 0$, and hence $x = y$.

As usual, we consider two cases in the proof of security, depending on whether the dealer is corrupted or not.

Dishonest dealer.

It is convenient to consider the case when the dealer is dishonest first, as some of the derived equations will be useful in the honest dealer case too. Beside the dealer, the players in $A \subseteq \{1, \dots, n\}$ are corrupted, and we let $H = \{1, \dots, n\} \setminus A$ be the set of honest players. We consider the real-world system (Player[H] | Net') consisting of the honest participants and the network Net'. This is a system with input (s'_0, s'_A) and output (y'_H, r'_A) described by the defining equations of Player[h] for $h \in H$ and Net' given in Figure 14. We use these equations to express each output variable of the system in terms of the input variables. For y'_h ($h \in H$)

WCast$(x', w) = (y'_1, \dots, y'_n)$:
$$y'_i = x' \wedge w[i] \qquad (1 \leq i \leq n)$$

Int:
$$w = \top^n$$

Net'$(s'_0, \dots, s'_n) = (r'_1, \dots, r'_n)$:
$$r'_i[j] = s'_j[i] \qquad (1 \leq i \leq n; 0 \leq j \leq n)$$

Dealer$(x') = (s'_0)$:
$$s'_0[i] = x' \qquad (1 \leq i \leq n)$$

Player[i]$(r'_i) = (y'_i, s'_i)$:
$$s'_i[j] = r'_i[0] \qquad (1 \leq i \leq n) \ (1 \leq j \leq n)$$
$$y'_i = t(r'_i[1], \dots, r'_i[n])$$

Figure 14: Weak broadcast functionality and protocol.

we have

$$\begin{aligned} y'_h &= t(r'_h[1], \dots, r'_h[n]) \\ &= t(s'_1[h], \dots, s'_n[h]) \\ &= t(s'_A[h], s'_H[h]) \\ &= t(s'_A[h], r'_H[0]) = t(s'_A[h], s'_0[H]). \end{aligned}$$

For the other output variables $r'_A[i]$ we distinguish two cases, depending on whether $i \in A$. For $a \in A$, we immediately get $r'_A[a] = s'_a[A]$. For $h \in H$, we have $r'_A[h] = s'_h[A] = (r'_h[0])^A = (s'_0[h])^A$. The resulting system is given by the following equations

$$r'_A[a] = s'_a[A] \qquad (a \in A) \qquad (4)$$
$$r'_A[h] = (s'_0[h])^A \qquad (h \in H) \qquad (5)$$
$$y'_h = t(s'_A[h], s'_0[H]) \qquad (h \in H) \qquad (6)$$

We now turn to the simulator. Recall that the simulator should turn the system defined by WCast into one equivalent to the real world system. To this end, the simulator should take s'_0, s'_A and y'_A as input (from the external environment and ideal functionality respectively), and output x', w (to the ideal functionality) and r'_A (to the external environment). Notice that the simulator has all the inputs necessary to compute the values defined by the real system, and in fact can set r'_A using just those equations. The only difficulty is that the simulator cannot set y'_h directly, but has only indirect control over its value through the ideal functionality and the variables x', w. From the properties of function t, we know that all $y'_h = t(s'_A[h], s'_0[H])$ take either the same value or $\bot$. So, the simulator can set x' to this common value, and use w to force some y'_h to $\bot$ as appropriate. The simulator Sim' is given in Figure 15 (bottom). It is easy to verify that (Sim' | WCast) is equivalent to the real system.

Honest dealer.

In this case, we first consider the real-world system

(Dealer | Player[H] | Net')

consisting of the dealer, the honest participants (where $H \subseteq \{1, \dots, n\}$), and the network Net'. The corrupted parties are given by the set $A = \{1, \dots, n\} \setminus H$. This is a system with input (x', s'_A) and output (y'_H, r'_A) described by

$$\begin{aligned}
&\textsc{Sim}(y'_A, s'_A) = (r'_A):\\
&\quad r'_A[a] = s'_a[A] && (a \in A)\\
&\quad r'_A[h] = y'_A && (h \in H)
\end{aligned}$$

$$\begin{aligned}
&\textsc{Sim}'(y'_A, s'_0, s'_A) = (x', w, r'_A):\\
&\quad r'_A[a] = s'_a[A] && (a \in A)\\
&\quad r'_A[h] = (s'_0[h])^A && (h \in H)\\
&\quad x' = \textstyle\bigvee_{h\in H} t(s'_A[h].s'_0[H])\\
&\quad w[h] = (t(s'_A[h], s'_0[H]) > \bot) && (h \in H)
\end{aligned}$$

Figure 15: Simulators for the weak broadcast protocol. Honest dealer case (top) and dishonest dealer case (bottom).

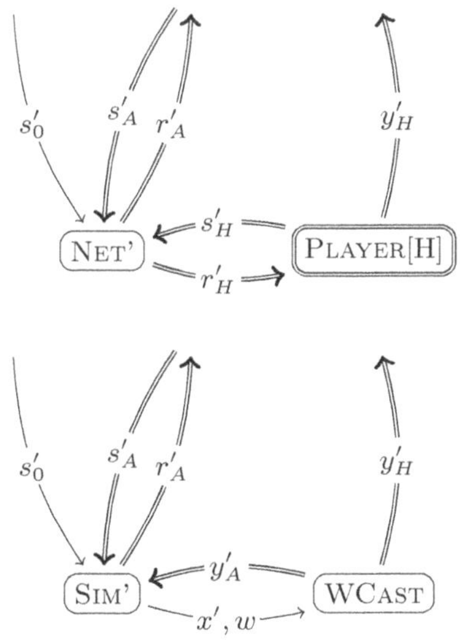

Figure 16: Security of the weak multicast protocol, when the dealer is dishonest. Real world execution above. Simulated attack in the ideal world below.

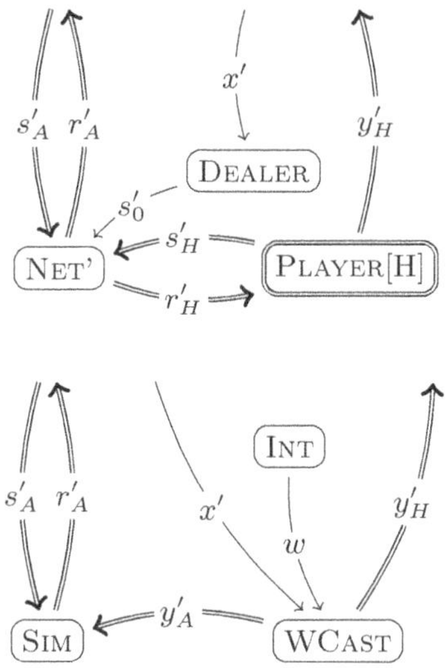

Figure 17: Security of the weak multicast protocol, when the dealer is honest. Real world execution above. Simulated attack in the ideal world below.

the defining equations of DEALER, PLAYER[h] for $h \in H$, and NET' given in Figure 14. Notice that this is a superset of the equations for the real-world system (PLAYER[H] | NET') considered in the dishonest dealer case. So, equations (4), (5) and (6) are still valid. Adding the equations from DEALER and using the properties of t we get that $y'_h = t(s'_A[h], s'_0[H]) = t(s'_A[h], (x)^H) = x$. Similarly, for $h \in H$, we have $r'_A[h] = (s'_0[h])^A = (x)^A$. Finally, we know from (4) that $r'_A[a] = s'_a[A]$. Combining the equations together, we get the following real system:

$$\begin{aligned}
y'_h &= x' && (h \in H)\\
r'_A[a] &= s'_a[A] && (a \in A)\\
r'_A[h] &= (x')^A && (h \in H)
\end{aligned}$$

We now move to the simulator. Recall that the simulator should turn the systen defined by WCAST and INT into one equivalent to the real world system. To this end, the simulator should take y'_A and s'_A as input (from the ideal functionality and external environment respectively), and output r'_A. Notice that $y'_h = x'$ in the real system is defined just as in the equations for the ideal functionality WCAST when combined with the (honest) dealer interface INT. (In fact, $y'_a = x'$ also for $a \in A$.) The other variables r'_A can be easily set by the simulator as shown in Figure 15 (top). It is immediate to check that (SIM | INT | WCAST) is equivalent to the real world system.

4. VERIFIABLE SECRET SHARING

Let $\mathbb{F}_t[X]$ be the set of all polynomials of degree at most t over a finite field $\mathbb{F}$ such that[8] $\{0, 1, \dots, n\} \subseteq \mathbb{F}$. We consider the n-party *verifiable secret sharing (VSS)* functionality that takes as input from a *dealer* a degree-t polynomial $\mathsf{p} \in \mathbb{F}_t[X]$ and, for all $1 \le i \le n$, outputs the evaluation $\mathsf{p}(i)$ to the

[8]This assumption is not really necessary; we could replace $\{0, 1, \dots, n\}$ with $\{0, x_1, \dots, x_n\}$ for any n distinct field elements $x_1, \dots, x_n$.

$$\mathrm{VSS}(\mathsf{p}) = (p_1, \ldots, p_n)$$
$$p_i = \mathsf{p}(i) \qquad (1 \le i \le n)$$

$$\textsc{Graph}(G_1, ..., G_n) = G:$$
$$G[i,j] = G_i[j] \qquad (1 \le i, j \le n)$$

$$\textsc{Net'}(s') = (r'_1, \ldots, r'_n):$$
$$r'_i = s'[i] \qquad (1 \le i \le n)$$

$$\textsc{Dealer}(\mathsf{p}) = s':$$
$$\mathsf{f} \leftarrow \mathcal{P}_t(\mathsf{p})$$
$$s'[i] = (\mathsf{f}(\cdot, i), \mathsf{f}(i, \cdot)) \qquad (1 \le i \le n)$$

$$\textsc{Player}[i](r'_i, G, r_i) = (p_i, s_i, G_i): \qquad (1 \le i \le n)$$
$$(\mathsf{g}_i, \mathsf{h}_i) = r'_i$$
$$s_i[j] = \mathsf{g}_i(j) \qquad (1 \le j \le n)$$
$$G_i[j] = \mathsf{eq}(r_i[j], \mathsf{h}_i(j)) \qquad (1 \le j \le n)$$
$$\mathsf{o}_i = \bigvee_{\substack{C \subseteq \{1,\ldots,n\} \\ |C| \ge n-t}} [\mathsf{clique}_C(G) \wedge \mathsf{interpolate}_{C,t}(r_i)]$$
$$p_i = \mathsf{o}_i(0)$$

Figure 18: The VSS functionality and protocol.

i-th party. The formal definition of VSS: $\mathbb{F}_t[X]_\perp \mapsto \mathbb{F}_\perp^n$ is given in Figure 18 (top), where by convention $\perp(x) = \perp$ for all x.

We devise a protocol implementing the VSS functionality on top of a point-to-point network functionality NET defined as in the previous section that allows the n parties to exchange elements from $\mathbb{F}$, and two other auxiliary functionalities. The protocol is based on the one by [5]. Even though its complexity is exponential in n, we have chosen to present this protocol due to its simplicity. The first auxiliary functionality (GRAPH) grants all parties access to the adjacency matrix of an n-vertex directed graph (with loops), where each party $i \in \{1, \ldots, n\}$ can add outgoing edges to vertex i, but not to any other vertex $j \neq i$. Formally, GRAPH: $\{\perp, \top\}^n \times \cdots \times \{\perp, \top\}^n \to \{\perp, \top\}^{n \times n}$ is given in Figure 18. Setting $G[i,j] = \top$ is interpreted as including an edge from i to j in the graph. GRAPH can be immediately implemented using n copies of a broadcast functionality, where a different party acts as the sender in each copy. We also assume the availability of an additional unidirectional network functionality NET': $(\mathbb{F}_t[X]_\perp^2)^n \to (\mathbb{F}_t[X]_\perp^2)^n$ that allows the VSS dealer to send to each party a pair of polynomials of degree at most t. See Figure 18.

The VSS protocol.

We turn to the actual protocol securely implementing the VSS functionality. We first define some auxiliary functions. For any subset $C \subseteq \{1, \ldots, n\}$, let $\mathsf{clique}_C : \{\perp, \top\}^{n \times n} \to \{\perp, \top\}$ be the function $\mathsf{clique}_C(G) = \bigwedge_{i,j \in C} G[i,j]$. This function is clearly monotone, and tests if C is a clique in G. For any set A, we equip the set $A_\perp$ with a monotone equality-test function $\mathsf{eq} : A_\perp \times A_\perp \to \{\perp, \top\}$ where $\mathsf{eq}(x,y) \equiv (x = y \neq \perp)$. Monotonicity follows from the fact that all the pairs (x,x) such that $\mathsf{eq}(x,y) = \top$ are maximal elements in $A_\perp \times A_\perp$.

For any $S \subseteq \{1, \ldots, n\}$ of size $|S| \ge t+1$, and $r \in \mathbb{F}_b^n$, let $\mathsf{interpolate}_S(r) \in \mathbb{F}_t[X]_\perp$ be the (unique) polynomial $\mathsf{h} \in \mathbb{F}_t[X]$ such that $\mathsf{h}(S) = r[S]$ if such polynomial exists, and $\mathsf{interpolate}_S(r) = \perp$ otherwise. For $C \subseteq \{1, \ldots, n\}$, define also a monotone function $\mathsf{interpolate}_{C,t} : \mathbb{F}_\perp{}^n \to \mathbb{F}_t[Y]_\perp^\top$ where $\mathsf{interpolate}_{C,t}(r) = \bigvee\{\mathsf{interpolate}_S(r) \colon S \subseteq C, |S| = |C| - t\}$. Notice that $\mathsf{interpolate}_{C,t}(r) = \perp$ if no interpolating polynomial exists, while $\mathsf{interpolate}_{C,t}(r) = \top$ if there are multiple solutions. Note that if $n \ge 4t+1$ and $|C| \ge n-t$, then $\top$ never occurs: Indeed, let $S, S' \subseteq C$ be such that $|S| = |S|' = |C| - t$, and such that both $\mathsf{interpolate}_S(r)$ and $\mathsf{interpolate}_{S'}(r)$ differ from $\perp$. Since $|S \cap S'| \ge |C| - 2t \ge n - 3t \ge t+1$, we must have $\mathsf{interpolate}_S(r) = \mathsf{interpolate}_{S'}(r)$ by the fact that two degree t polynomials agreeing at $t+1$ points are necessarily equal. For future reference, this is summarized by the following lemma.

LEMMA 1. *Let n, t be such that $n \ge 4t+1$, and let $C \subseteq \{1, \ldots, n\}$ be such that $|C| \ge n-t$. Then $\mathsf{interpolate}_{C,t}(r) \neq \top$ for all $r \in \mathbb{F}_\perp^n$.*

In the following, denote as $\mathbb{F}_t[X,Y]$ the set of polynomials $\mathsf{f} = \mathsf{f}(X,Y)$ in $\mathbb{F}[X,Y]$ with degree at most t in each variable X and Y. For any $\mathsf{p} \in \mathbb{F}_t[X]_\perp$, let $\mathcal{P}_t(\mathsf{p})$ the (uniform distribution over the) set of bivariate polynomials $\mathsf{f} = \mathsf{f}(X,Y) \in \mathbb{F}_t[X,Y]_\perp$ of degree at most t in X and Y such that $\mathsf{f}(\cdot, 0) = \mathsf{p}$. (By convention, if $\mathsf{p} = \perp$, then $\mathcal{P}_t(\mathsf{p}) = \{\perp\}$.)

The protocol consists of a dealer DEALER which, on input a polynomial p, first chooses a random bivariate polynomial f in $\mathcal{P}_t(\mathsf{p})$. (This is the only random choice of the entire protocol.) For all $i \in \{1, \ldots, n\}$, it sends the two polynomials $\mathsf{g}_i = \mathsf{f}(\cdot, i)$ and $\mathsf{h}_i = \mathsf{f}(i, \cdot)$ to player i, with the usual convention that if $\mathsf{f} = \perp$, then $f(\cdot, i) = f(i, \cdot) = \perp$. The players then determine whether the polynomials they received are consistent. This is achieved by having each honest party i send $\mathsf{g}_i(j)$ to player j, who, in turn, checks consistency with $\mathsf{h}_j(i)$. (Note that if the polynomials are correct, then $\mathsf{g}_i(j) = \mathsf{h}_j(i) = \mathsf{f}(j,i)$.) If the consistency check is successful, player j raises the entry $G[j,i]$ to $\top$. Each honest party i then waits for a clique $C \subseteq \{1, \ldots, n\}$ of size (at least) $n-t$ to appear in the directed graph defined by G, and computes the polynomial $\mathsf{o}_i \in \mathbb{F}_t[X]_\perp^\top$ obtained interpolating the values $\mathsf{g}_j(i)$ received from other parties. (Here $\top$ represents an error condition meaning that multiple interpolating polynomials were found, and should not really occur in actual executions, as we will show.) As soon as such a polynomial is found, the honest party terminates with output $p_i = \mathsf{o}_i(0)$. A formal specification is given in Figure 18.

In the following, we turn to proving security of the protocol. The analysis consists of two cases.

Honest dealer security.

We start by analyzing the security of the above protocol in the case where the dealer is honest. For all $A \subseteq \{1, \ldots, n\}$ where $|A| = t$ and $n \ge 4t+1$, define $H = \{1, \ldots, n\} \setminus A$. When the players in the set A are corrupted (and thus the players in H are honest), an execution of the VSS protocol with honest dealer is given by the system (DEALER | PLAYER[H] | NET' | NET | GRAPH) with inputs p, s_A, G_A and outputs $r_D[A], r_A, G, p_H$ given in Figure 19.

We proceed by combining all the equations together, and simplifying the result, until we obtain a system of equations that can be easily simulated. We use the above definition of the system to obtain the following equations describing (DEALER | PLAYER[H] | NET' | NET | GRAPH): For any $1 \le i, j \le n$, and any $h \in H, a \in A$, we have

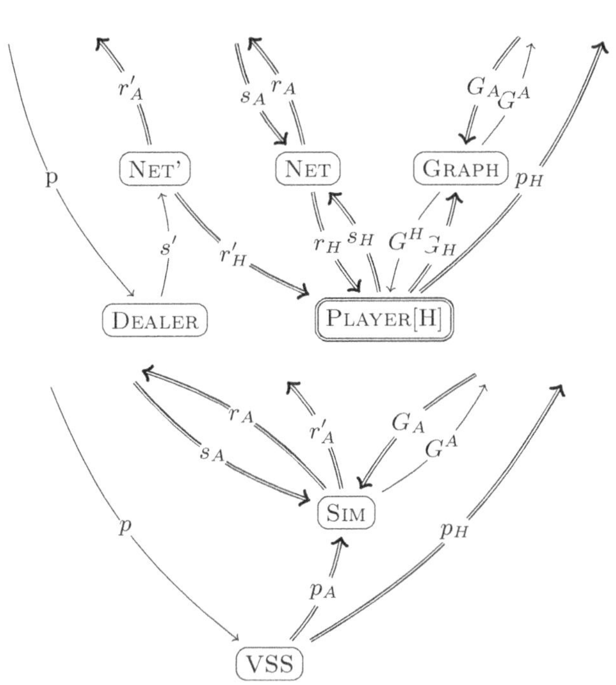

Figure 19: Security of the VSS protocol when the dealer is honest. Real world execution above. Simulated attack in the ideal world below.

$$
\begin{aligned}
\mathsf{f} &\stackrel{\$}{\leftarrow} \mathcal{P}_t(\mathsf{p}) \\
r'_i &= (\mathsf{f}(\cdot,i),\mathsf{f}(i,\cdot)) \\
r_i[h] &= \mathsf{f}(i,h) \\
r_i[a] &= s_a[i] \\
G[h,j] &= \mathsf{eq}(r_h[j],\mathsf{f}(h,j)) \\
G[a,j] &= G_a[j] \\
\mathsf{o}_h &= \bigvee_{\substack{C\subseteq\{1,\dots,n\}\\ |C|\geq n-t}} [\mathsf{clique}_C(G)\wedge \mathsf{interpolate}_{C,t}(r_h)] \\
p_h &= \mathsf{o}_h(0)\ .
\end{aligned}
$$

For convenience, some easy simplifications have already been made: First g_i and h_i have been replaced by $\mathsf{f}(\cdot,i)$ and $\mathsf{f}(i,\cdot)$, respectively. Second, we used the facts that $r'_i = s'[i]$ and $r_i[h] = s_h[i] = \mathsf{f}(i,h)$ for all $h \in H$ and all $i \in \{1,\dots,n\}$ by the definitions of the network functionalities NET' and NET. Finally, we have set values for $G[\cdot,\cdot]$ according to the protocol specification (for honest players) and the inputs G_a of players $a \in A$.

In order to further simplify the system, we claim that $p_h = \mathsf{p}(h)$ for $h \in H$. If $\mathsf{p} = \bot$, then this is easy to see because $\mathsf{f} = \bot$ and $G[h,j] = \mathsf{eq}(r_h[j],\bot) = \bot$. Therefore, we necessarily have $\mathsf{clique}_C(G) = \bot$ for all $C \subseteq \{1,\dots,n\}$ with $|C| \geq n-t$, since $|C \cap H| \geq n-2t > 0$. So, we only need to prove the claim for $\mathsf{p} \neq \bot$. Notice that the equations $G[h,j] = \mathsf{eq}(r_h[j],\mathsf{f}(h,j))$, depending on whether $j = h' \in H$ or $j = a \in A$, can be replaced by the set of equations

$$
\begin{aligned}
G[h,h'] &= \mathsf{eq}(r_h[h'],\mathsf{f}(h,h')) = \mathsf{eq}(\mathsf{f}(h,h'),\mathsf{f}(h,h')) = \top \\
G[h,a] &= \mathsf{eq}(r_h[a],\mathsf{f}(h,a)) = \mathsf{eq}(s_a[h],\mathsf{f}(h,a))\ .
\end{aligned}
$$

This in particular implies that $C = H$ is a clique of size at least $n-t$ in the graph defined by G, i.e., we have $\mathsf{clique}_H(G) = \top$ by the above. Also, since $r_h[h'] = \mathsf{f}(h,h')$, we necessarily have

$$\mathsf{o}_h \geq \mathsf{clique}_H(G) \wedge \mathsf{interpolate}_{H,t}(r_h) = \top \wedge \mathsf{f}(h,\cdot) = \mathsf{f}(h,\cdot)$$

by Lemma 1. Now, let $S \subseteq C$ be any sets such that $|C| \geq n-t$ and $|S| = |C|-t \geq n-2t$. Since $\mathsf{o}_h(h') = \mathsf{f}(h,h')$ for all $h' \in H$ and $|S \cap H| \geq n-3t \geq t+1$, we have $\mathsf{interpolate}_S(r_h) \geq \mathsf{f}(h,\cdot)$, and, by Lemma 1, $\mathsf{interpolate}_S(r_h) = \mathsf{f}(h,\cdot)$. This proves that $\mathsf{o}_h = \mathsf{interpolate}_{C,t}(r_h) = \mathsf{f}(h,\cdot)$, and $p_h = \mathsf{o}_h(0) = \mathsf{f}(h,0) = \mathsf{p}(h)$.

Summarizing, the real system is described by the following set of equations:

$$
\begin{aligned}
\mathsf{f} &\stackrel{\$}{\leftarrow} \mathcal{P}_t(\mathsf{p}) \\
r'_a &= (\mathsf{f}(\cdot,a),\mathsf{f}(a,\cdot)) \\
r_a[a'] &= s_{a'}[a] \\
r_a[h] &= f(a,h) \\
G[h,h'] &= (\mathsf{p} > \bot) \\
G[h,a] &= \mathsf{eq}(s_a[h],\mathsf{f}(h,a)) \\
G[a,j] &= G_a[j] \\
p_h &= \mathsf{p}(h)\ .
\end{aligned}
$$

Notice that this is exactly how p_h is defined by the VSS functionality. So, in order to prove security, it is enough to give a simulator SIM that on input p_A, s_A, G_A, outputs G, r_A and r'_A as defined in the above system of equations. See Figure 19 (bottom).

The problem faced by the simulator is that it cannot test $\mathsf{p} > \bot$ and generate f as in the equations because it does not know the value of p, rather it only has partial information $p_A = \mathsf{p}(A)$. The first condition $\mathsf{p} > \bot$ is easy to check because it is equivalent to $p_a = \mathsf{p}(a) > \bot$ for any $a \in A$. In order to complete the simulation, we observe that the equations only depend on the $2t$ polynomials $f(\cdot,A)$ and $f(A,\cdot)$. The next lemma shows that, given $\mathsf{p}(A)$, the polynomials $\mathsf{f}(\cdot,A)$ and $\mathsf{f}(A,\cdot)$ are statistically independent from p, and their distribution can be easily sampled.

LEMMA 2. *Let $\mathsf{p} \in \mathbb{F}_t[X]$, let $\mathsf{f} \stackrel{\$}{\leftarrow} \mathcal{P}_t(\mathsf{p})$, and for all $a \in A$, let $\mathsf{g}_a = \mathsf{f}(\cdot,a)$ and $\mathsf{h}_a = \mathsf{f}(a,\cdot)$. The conditional distribution of $(\mathsf{g}_a,\mathsf{h}_a)_{a\in A}$ given $\mathsf{p}(A)$ is statistically independent of p, and it can be generated by the following algorithm Samp(p_A): first pick random polynomials $\mathsf{h}_a \in \mathbb{F}_t[Y]$ independently and uniformly at random subject to the constraint $\mathsf{h}_a(0) = p_a$. Then, pick $\mathsf{g}_a \in \mathbb{F}_t[X]$, also independently and uniformly at random, subject to the constraint $\mathsf{g}_a(A) = \mathsf{h}_A(a)$.*

Using the algorithm from the lemma, we obtain the following simulator SIM:

$$\begin{aligned}
&\textsc{Sim}(p_A, s_A, G_A) = (G^A, r_A, r'_A):\\
&\quad (\mathsf{g}_A, \mathsf{h}_A) \leftarrow \text{Samp}(p_A)\\
&\quad r'_A = (\mathsf{g}_A, \mathsf{h}_A)\\
&\quad r_a[h] = \mathsf{h}_a(h) && (h \in H, a \in A)\\
&\quad r_a[a'] = s_{a'}[a] && (a, a' \in A)\\
&\quad G[h,h'] = \textstyle\bigvee_{a\in A}(p_a > \bot) && (h, h' \in H)\\
&\quad G[h,a] = \mathsf{eq}(s_a[h], \mathsf{g}_a(h)) && (h \in H, a \in A)\\
&\quad G[a,j] = G_a[j] && (a \in A, 1 \le j \le n)
\end{aligned}$$

As usual, if $\mathsf{p} = \bot$, then $p_A = \bot^A$ and by convention $\text{Samp}(p_A) = \{\bot, \bot\}$.

Dishonest dealer security.

We now look at the case where the dealer is not honest. As above, for all $A \subseteq \{1,\ldots,n\}$ where $|A| = t$ and $n \ge 4t+1$, define $H = \{1,\ldots,n\} \setminus A$. When the players in the set A are corrupted (and thus the players in H are honest), an execution of the VSS protocol with dishonest dealer is given by the system (PLAYER[H] | NET' | NET | GRAPH) with inputs s', r_A, G_A, and outputs r'_A, s_A, p_H and G^A. As above, we start with an equational description of the system, and will simplify it below into a form where the construction of a corresponding simulator becomes obvious. For all $i, j \in \{1,\ldots,n\}$, $h, h' \in H$, and $a \in A$, we have

$$\begin{aligned}
(\mathsf{g}_h, \mathsf{h}_h) &= s'[h]\\
r'_a &= s'[a]\\
r_i[h] &= \mathsf{g}_h(i)\\
r_i[a] &= s_a[i]\\
G[h,h'] &= \mathsf{eq}(\mathsf{g}_{h'}(h), \mathsf{h}_h(h'))\\
G[h,a] &= \mathsf{eq}(s_a[h], \mathsf{h}_h(a))\\
G[a,j] &= G_a[j]\\
\mathsf{o}_h &= \bigvee_{\substack{C\subseteq\{1,\ldots,n\}\\|C|\ge n-t}} [\mathsf{clique}_C(G) \wedge \mathsf{interpolate}_{C,t}(r_h)]\\
p_h &= \mathsf{o}_h(0)\,.
\end{aligned}$$

Notice that we have already undertaken several easy simplification steps, defining variables which are part of the output as a function of the system inputs and of auxiliary variables g_H, h_H, o_H, and r_H. Specifically, to obtain the above equations starting from the original system specification, we have used $r_i[j] = s_j[i]$, where $s_h[i] = \mathsf{g}_h(i)$, together with $r'_i = s'[i]$ and the definition of $G[h,i]$, distinguishing between the cases $i = a \in A$ and $i = h' \in H$.

Recall that in order to prove security, we need to give a simulator SIM with input s', G_A, s_A, p_A and output r'_A, r_A, G^A and p such that (VSS | SIM) is equivalent to the above system. (See Figure 20.) Notice that in the system describing a real execution, all variables except p_h (and intermediate value o_h) are defined as functions of the inputs given to the simulator. So, SIM can set all these variables just as in the system describing the real execution. The only difference between a real execution and a simulation is that the simulator is not allowed to set p_h directly. Rather, it should specify a polynomial $\mathsf{p} \in \mathbb{F}_t[X]_\bot$, which implicitly defines $p_h = \mathsf{p}(h)$ through the equations of the ideal VSS functionality. In other words, in order to complete the description of the simulator we need to show that SIM can determine such a polynomial p based on its inputs s', G_A, s_A, p_A such that $\mathsf{p}(h)$ equals p_h as defined by the above system of equations.

Before defining p, we recall the following lemma whose simple proof is standard and omitted:

LEMMA 3. *Let S be such that $|S| \ge t+1$ and let $\{\mathsf{g}_h, \mathsf{h}_h\}_{h\in S}$ be a set of $2 \cdot |S|$ polynomials of degree t. Then, $\mathsf{g}_h(h') = \mathsf{h}_{h'}(h)$ for all $h, h' \in S$ holds if and only if there exists a unique polynomial $\mathsf{f} \in \mathbb{F}_t[X,Y]$ such that $\mathsf{f}(\cdot,h) = \mathsf{g}_h$ and $\mathsf{f}(h,\cdot) = \mathsf{h}_h$ for all $h \in S$.*

For $T \subseteq H$, $|T| \ge t+1$, define $\mathsf{interpolate2}_T(s')$ to be the (unique) polynomial $\mathsf{f} \in \mathbb{F}_t[X,Y]$ such that $\mathsf{f}(\cdot,h) = \mathsf{g}_h$ and $\mathsf{f}(h,\cdot) = \mathsf{h}_h$ for all $h \in T$ (if it exists), and $\bot$ otherwise or if $s'[h] = \bot$ for some $h \in T$. Also, given $C \subseteq \{1,\ldots,n\}$, define

$$\mathsf{interpolate2}_C(s') = \bigvee\{\mathsf{interpolate2}_S(s') \;:\; S \subseteq C, |S| \ge |C| - t\}\,.$$

Note that since $|C| \ge n-t$ and $n \ge 4t+1$, $\mathsf{interpolate2}_C(s') \ne \top$. Indeed, for any two $S, S' \subseteq C$ such that $\mathsf{interpolate2}_S(s')$ and $\mathsf{interpolate2}_{S'}(s')$ differ from $\bot$, we have $|S \cap S'| \ge t+1$ and hence $\mathsf{interpolate2}_S(s') = \mathsf{interpolate2}_{S\cap S'}(s') = \mathsf{interpolate2}_{S'}(s')$ by Lemma 3. We finally define the polynomial $\mathsf{p} = \widetilde{f}(\cdot, 0)$, where

$$\widetilde{f} = \bigvee_{\substack{C\subseteq\{1,\ldots,n\}\\|C|\ge n-t}} \mathsf{clique}_C(G) \wedge \mathsf{interpolate2}_C(s')\,. \qquad (7)$$

We first prove that $\mathsf{p} < \top$: To this end, assume that $\mathsf{p} \ne \bot$. Then, $\widetilde{f} \ne \bot$, and there must exist $C \subseteq \{1,\ldots,n\}$ such that $\mathsf{clique}_C(G) = \top$. Let $S = C \cap H$. Note that for all $h, h' \in S$, since $G[h,h'] = \top$, it must be that $\mathsf{h}_h(h') = \mathsf{g}_{h'}(h)$. Therefore, since $|S| \ge n - 2t > 2t+1$, by Lemma 3, there exists a unique polynomial f_C such that $\mathsf{f}(\cdot,h) = \mathsf{g}_h$ and $\mathsf{f}(h,\cdot) = \mathsf{h}_h$ for all $h \in S$, and by the above

$$\mathsf{f}_C = \mathsf{interpolate2}_C(s') = \mathsf{interpolate2}_{C\cap H}(s')\,.$$

Now assume that there exist two such cliques C and C', with $S = C \cap H$ and $S' = C' \cap H$. Then, since

$$\begin{aligned}
|S \cap S'| &= |S| + |S'| - |S \cup S'|\\
&\ge 2(|C| - |A|) - |H| \ge n - 3|A| \ge t+1\,,
\end{aligned}$$

by Lemma 3, we necessarily have $\mathsf{f}_C = \mathsf{f}_{C'} = \widetilde{\mathsf{f}}$.

Finally, it is easy to see that $\mathsf{p}(h) = p_h$ for all $h \in H$. Namely, if there exists $C \subseteq \{1,\ldots,n\}$ with $\mathsf{clique}_C(G) = \top$, then $r_h[h'] = \mathsf{g}_{h'}(h) = \widetilde{\mathsf{f}}(h,h')$ for all $h' \in C \cap H$, and therefore $\mathsf{o}_h = \mathsf{interpolate}_C(r_h) = \mathsf{interpolate}_{C\cap H}(r_h) = \mathsf{f}(h,\cdot)$, and thus $p_h = \mathsf{o}_h(0) = \widetilde{\mathsf{f}}(h,0) = \mathsf{p}(h)$.

We therefore conclude that the real system is equivalent to (SIM | VSS) where SIM is the simulator defined by the following equations:

$$\begin{aligned}
&\textsc{Sim}(s', G_A, s_A, p_A) = (r'_A, r_A, G^A, \mathsf{p}):\\
&\quad r'_a = s'[a] && (a \in A)\\
&\quad r_a[h] = \mathsf{g}_h(a) && (h \in H, a \in A)\\
&\quad r_a[a'] = s_{a'}[a] && (a, a' \in A)\\
&\quad G[h,h'] = \mathsf{eq}(\mathsf{g}_{h'}(h), \mathsf{h}_h(h')) && (h, h' \in H)\\
&\quad G[h,a] = \mathsf{eq}(s_a[h], \mathsf{h}_h(a)) && (a \in A, h \in H)\\
&\quad G[a,j] = G_a[j] && (a \in A, 1 \le j \le n)\\
&\quad \widetilde{\mathsf{f}} = \textstyle\bigvee_{\substack{C\subseteq\{1,\ldots,n\}\\|C|\ge n-t}} \mathsf{clique}_C(G) \wedge \mathsf{interpolate2}_C(s')\\
&\quad \mathsf{p} = \widetilde{\mathsf{f}}(\cdot, 0)
\end{aligned}$$

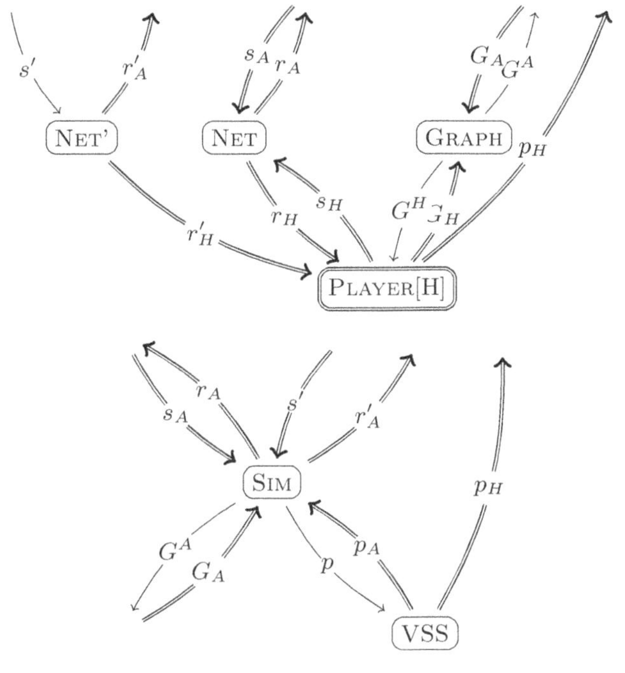

Figure 20: Security of the VSS protocol when the dealer is dishonest. Real world execution above. Simulated attack in the ideal world below.

5. CONCLUSIONS

Recognizing the inherent hardness of delivering security proofs for complex cryptographic protocols that are both precise and intuitive within existing security frameworks, we have presented a new framework to study the security of multi-party computations based on equational descriptions of interactive processes. Our framework allows a simple and intuitive, yet completely formal, description of interactive processes via sets of equations, and its foundations rely on tools from domain theory. Beyond its simplicity, our framework completely avoids explicit addressing of non-determinism within cryptographic security proofs, making security proofs a matter of simple equational manipulations over precise mathematical structures. As a case study, we have presented simple security analyses of (variants of) two classical asynchronous protocols within our framework, Bracha's broadcast protocol [8] and the Ben-Or, Canetti, Goldreich VSS protocol [5].

We are convinced that our work will open up the avenue to several directions for future work. First off, while the results in this paper are presented for the special case of perfect security, a natural next step is to extend the framework to statistical and even computational security. Moreover, while the expressiveness of our framework (i.e., the monotonicity restrictions on protocols) remains to be thoroughly investigated, most distributed protocols we examined so far seemed to admit a representation within our framework, possibly after minor modifications which often resulted in a simpler protocol description. For this reason, our thesis is that this holds true for *all* protocols of interest, and that non-monotonicity, as a source of unnecessary complexity and proof mistakes, should be avoided whenever possible.

6. REFERENCES

[1] S. Abramsky and A. Jung. *Handbook of Logic in Computer Science*, volume III, chapter Domain theory, pages 1–168. Oxford University Press, 1994.

[2] Michael Backes, Birgit Pfitzmann, and Michael Waidner. A general composition theorem for secure reactive systems. In *TCC 2004*, volume 2951 of *Lecture Notes in Computer Science*, pages 336–354, 2004.

[3] Donald Beaver and Shafi Goldwasser. Multiparty computation with faulty majority. In *CRYPTO '89*, volume 435 of *Lecture Notes in Computer Science*, pages 589–590, 1989.

[4] Assaf Ben-David, Noam Nisan, and Benny Pinkas. FairplayMP: a system for secure multi-party computation. In *ACM Conference on Computer and Communications Security*, pages 257–266, 2008.

[5] Michael Ben-Or, Ran Canetti, and Oded Goldreich. Asynchronous secure computation. In *STOC*, pages 52–61, 1993.

[6] Michael Ben-Or, Shafi Goldwasser, and Avi Wigderson. Completeness theorems for non-cryptographic fault-tolerant distributed computation (extended abstract). In *STOC '88*, pages 1–10, 1988.

[7] Peter Bogetoft, Dan Lund Christensen, Ivan Damgård, Martin Geisler, Thomas P. Jakobsen, Mikkel Krøigaard, Janus Dam Nielsen, Jesper Buus Nielsen, Kurt Nielsen, Jakob Pagter, Michael I. Schwartzbach, and Tomas Toft. Secure multiparty computation goes live. In *Financial Cryptography (FC 2009)*, volume 5628 of *Lecture Notes in Computer Science*, pages 325–343, 2009.

[8] Gabriel Bracha. An asynchronous [(n-1)/3]-resilient consensus protocol. In *PODC '84*, pages 154–162, 1984.

[9] Ran Canetti. Security and composition of multiparty cryptographic protocols. *J. Cryptology*, 13(1):143–202, 2000.

[10] Ran Canetti. Universally composable security: A new paradigm for cryptographic protocols. In *FOCS '01*, pages 136–145, 2001.

[11] Ivan Damgård, Marcel Keller, E. Larraia, C. Miles, and Nigel P. Smart. Implementing aes via an actively/covertly secure dishonest-majority mpc protocol. *IACR Cryptology ePrint Archive*, 2012.

[12] Oded Goldreich, Silvio Micali, and Avi Wigderson. How to play any mental game or a completeness theorem for protocols with honest majority. In *STOC '87*, pages 218–229, 1987.

[13] Shafi Goldwasser, Silvio Micali, and Charles Rackoff. The knowledge complexity of interactive proof systems. *SIAM J. Comput.*, 18(1):186–208, 1989.

[14] Carl A. Gunter. *Semantics of programming languages - structures and techniques*. Foundations of computing. MIT Press, 1993.

[15] Dennis Hofheinz and Victor Shoup. Gnuc: A new universal composability framework. *IACR Cryptology ePrint Archive*, 2011.

[16] G. Kahn. The semantics of a simple language for parallel programming. In J. L. Rosenfeld, editor, *Information processing*, pages 471–475, Stockholm, Sweden, Aug 1974. North Holland, Amsterdam.

[17] Vladimir Kolesnikov and Thomas Schneider. A practical universal circuit construction and secure evaluation of private functions. In *Financial Cryptography (FS 2008)*, volume 5143 of *Lecture Notes in Computer Science*, pages 83–97, 2008.

[18] Ralf Küsters. Simulation-based security with inexhaustible interactive turing machines. In *19th IEEE Computer Security Foundations Workshop, (CSFW-19 2006)*, pages 309–320, 2006.

[19] Dahlia Malkhi, Noam Nisan, Benny Pinkas, and Yaron Sella. Fairplay - secure two-party computation system. In *USENIX Security Symposium*, pages 287–302, 2004.

[20] Ueli Maurer and Renato Renner. Abstract cryptography. In *Innovations in Computer Science - ICS 2010*, pages 1–21, 2011.

[21] Ueli M. Maurer. Indistinguishability of random systems. In *EUROCRYPT 2002*, volume 2332 of *Lecture Notes in Computer Science*, pages 110–132, 2002.

[22] Silvio Micali and Phillip Rogaway. Secure computation (abstract). In *CRYPTO '91*, volume 576 of *Lecture Notes in Computer Science*, pages 392–404, 1991.

[23] Birgit Pfitzmann and Michael Waidner. A model for asynchronous reactive systems and its application to secure message transmission. In *IEEE Symposium on Security and Privacy*, pages 184–, 2001.

[24] Benny Pinkas, Thomas Schneider, Nigel P. Smart, and Stephen C. Williams. Secure two-party computation is practical. In *ASIACRYPT 2009*, volume 5912 of *Lecture Notes in Computer Science*, pages 250–267, 2009.

[25] N. Saheb-Djahromi. Cpo's of measures for nondeterminism. *Theor. Comput. Sci.*, 12:19–37, 1980.

[26] D. A. Schmidt. *Denotational Semantics.* Allyn and Bacon, 1986.

[27] J. E. Stoy. *Denotational Semantics: The Scott-Strachey Approach to Programming Language Theory.* MIT Press, 1977.

[28] Glynn Winskel. *The formal semantics of programming languages - an introduction.* Foundation of computing series. MIT Press, 1993.

[29] Andrew Chi-Chih Yao. Protocols for secure computations (extended abstract). In *FOCS '82*, pages 160–164, 1982.

Publicly Verifiable Proofs of Sequential Work

Mohammad Mahmoody[*]
Computer Science Department, Cornell University
Ithaca, NY, USA
mohammad@cs.cornell.edu

Tal Moran[†]
School of Computer Science, Interdisciplinary Center (IDC)
Herzliya, Israel
talm@idc.ac.il

Salil Vadhan[‡]
School of Engineering & Applied Sciences and Center for Research on Computation and Society, Harvard University
Cambridge, MA, USA
salil@seas.harvard.edu

ABSTRACT

We construct a publicly verifiable protocol for proving computational work based on collision-resistant hash functions and a new plausible complexity assumption regarding the existence of "inherently sequential" hash functions. Our protocol is based on a novel construction of time-lock puzzles. Given a sampled "puzzle" $\mathcal{P} \xleftarrow{\$} \mathbf{D}_n$, where n is the security parameter and $\mathbf{D}_n$ is the distribution of the puzzles, a corresponding "solution" can be generated using N evaluations of the sequential hash function, where $N > n$ is another parameter, while any feasible adversarial strategy for generating valid solutions must take at least as much time as $\Omega(N)$ *sequential* evaluations of the hash function after receiving $\mathcal{P}$. Thus, valid solutions constitute a "proof" that $\Omega(N)$ parallel time elapsed since $\mathcal{P}$ was received. Solutions can be publicly and efficiently verified in time $\text{poly}(n) \cdot \text{polylog}(N)$. Applications of these "time-lock puzzles" include noninteractive timestamping of documents (when the distribution over the possible documents corresponds to the puzzle distribution $\mathbf{D}_n$) and universally verifiable CPU benchmarks.

Our construction is secure in the standard model under complexity assumptions (collision-resistant hash functions and inherently sequential hash functions), and makes black-box use of the underlying primitives. Consequently, the corresponding construction in the random oracle model is secure unconditionally. Moreover, as it is a public-coin protocol, it can be made non-interactive in the random oracle model using the Fiat-Shamir Heuristic.

Our construction makes a novel use of "depth-robust" directed acyclic graphs—ones whose depth remains large even after removing a constant fraction of vertices—which were previously studied for the purpose of complexity lower bounds. The construction bypasses a recent negative result of Mahmoody, Moran, and Vadhan (CRYPTO '11) for time-lock puzzles in the random oracle model, which showed that it is impossible to have time-lock puzzles like ours in the random oracle model if the puzzle generator also computes a solution together with the puzzle.

Categories and Subject Descriptors

F.1.2 [**COMPUTATION BY ABSTRACT DEVICES**]: Modes of Computation—*Parallelism, Relativized computation*; K.6.5 [**MANAGEMENT OF COMPUTING AND INFORMATION SYSTEMS**]: Security and Protection—*Unauthorized access*

General Terms

Theory, Security

Keywords

Time-Lock Puzzles, Proofs of Work, Timestamping, Depth Robust Graphs

1. INTRODUCTION

A *timestamping scheme* is a mechanism for proving that a document was created before a certain time in the past. Timestamping schemes have variety of applications, including the resolution of intellectual property disputes (e.g., an inventor may timestamp her invention to prevent future patent challenges) and providing evidence of predictive powers (e.g., a stock analyst could prove that she correctly predicted stock price changes before they occurred).

We say a timestamping scheme is *noninteractive* if generating a timestamp does not require communication with a third party. This is a desirable property, both because it makes timestamping easily scalable (multiple parties generating timestamps do not interfere with each other), and it allows parties to hide the fact that they are generating a timestamp; this might be crucial in some scenarios (e.g., an inventor may not wish to reveal the fact that she has a new invention).

[*]Research supported in part by NSF Award CCF-0746990, AFOSR Award FA9550-10-1-0093, and DARPA and AFRL under contract FA8750-11-2- 0211.

[†]Work done in part while at the Harvard Center for Research on Computation and Society.

[‡]Supported in part by NSF grant CCF-1116616. Work done in part while on leave as a Visiting Researcher at Microsoft Research SVC and as a Visiting Scholar at Stanford University.

A natural cryptographic approach to timestamping is via *proofs of work*—use computational effort invested as a measure of time elapsed. For example, if a party wants to be able to issue future proofs that she knows a document D at time t_0, then starting at time t_0, she starts to evaluate a "moderately hard" function g on document D. If we know that g takes time $\approx N$ to evaluate, then the value $g(D)$ can be considered a "proof" that D was known N time units in the past.

Note that here we need both an upper bound and a lower bound on the complexity of computing g—an adversary should not be able to evaluate g on D much more quickly than an honest party following the specified algorithm for g. In addition, we would like verifying $y = g(D)$ (given D and y) to be done much more efficiently than evaluating g on D from scratch.

These (initial) goals can be achieved by taking $g = f^{-1}$ for a very strong one-way permutation $f : \{0,1\}^n \to \{0,1\}^n$, where we take the security parameter to be $n = \log N$. Given a document $D \in \{0,1\}^n$, the proof of work $f^{-1}(D)$ can be computed by brute force in time approximately $2^n = N$. Such a proof can be verified very quickly (e.g., in time $\text{poly}(n) = \text{poly}(\log N)$). Moreover, it is a plausible assumption that any efficient[1] algorithm for inverting f will require time $\Omega(2^n) = \Omega(N)$, at least on a uniformly random document $D \xleftarrow{\$} \{0,1\}^n$. (If D is not uniformly distributed, then we can heuristically apply this construction to a hash of D, or even apply a publicly known deterministic randomness extractor tailored to the distribution $\mathbf{D}_n$ from which D is sampled.)

One deficiency of the aforementioned construction is that, while it certifies that N units of computational effort were invested after receiving D, this need not correspond to clock time, because an adversary could parallelize its computational efforts (e.g., by using a bot-net to try many preimages at once). Thus, we would like to have proofs of work that are inherently sequential, i.e., even a massively parallel effort to evaluate $g(D)$ would still take time close to N. (Of course, "time" is still relative to single-core CPU speed, which may differ between the honest party and the adversary, but this gap should be easier to gauge and control than what can be achieved by massive parallelism.)

Based on ideas from [CLSY93, RSW96], Jerschow and Mauve [JM10] proposed the following timestamping function which is conjectured to be secure against parallel attack: $g(D) = 2^{2^D} \pmod N$, for an RSA integer N whose factors are kept secret. A verifier who *already knows* the secret factorization of N can check the computation efficiently using the "shortcut" $2^{2^D} \equiv 2^{(2^D \bmod \varphi(N))} \pmod N$; if $|N| \approx |D|$, this shortcut gives an exponential speed-up. The security of this scheme is based on the conjecture that modular exponentiation is an inherently sequential task without knowing the factorization of N.

Time-Lock Puzzles. The idea of using modular exponentiation as a proof of sequential work was first proposed by Cai, Lipton, Sedgewick and Yao [CLSY93], in the context of CPU benchmarks, and by Rivest, Shamir and Wagner [RSW96] in the context of *time-lock puzzles*. In a time-lock puzzle protocol, solving a puzzle should take approximately N time (even for a massively parallel solver), while generating the puzzle and verifying the solution should take considerably less. Thus, one can think of a time-lock puzzle as an interactive proof of sequential work and view a solution to the puzzle as a proof that at least roughly N time units have elapsed since the prover received the puzzle.

When used as a timestamping scheme, however, modular exponentiation has a serious drawback: the verifier must know and keep secret the factorization of the modulus. In practice, this means that the timestamper must decide in advance which verifiers to target. Moreover, if a verifier's secret key ever leaks, all timestamps using the corresponding public key can no longer be trusted.

To construct *publicly verifiable* timestamping schemes from time-lock puzzles, we employ *public-coin* time-lock puzzles and interpret the document D as the coin tosses generating the puzzle $\mathcal{P}$.

Generic Proofs of Work via Efficient Arguments. Suppose we are given an inherently sequential function family: $\{f_\mathcal{P} : \{0,1\}^n \mapsto \{0,1\}^n\}_{\mathcal{P}\in\{0,1\}^{\text{poly}(n)}}$, meaning that the t-fold composition $f^t_\mathcal{P}(0^n)$ takes parallel time $\Omega(t)$ for a uniformly random $\mathcal{P} \xleftarrow{\$} \{0,1\}^{\text{poly}(n)}$. A natural attempt to construct a proof of work is to use simple iteration of f: the prover chooses a function $f_\mathcal{P}$ from the family (determined by the puzzle $\mathcal{P}$) and begins with an initial fixed value $x_0 = 0^n$. In iteration i, the prover computes $x_i = f_\mathcal{P}(x_{i-1}) = f^i_\mathcal{P}(x_0)$. Assuming that every adversary that outputs $f^t_\mathcal{P}(x)$ must run in time $\Omega(t)$, sending x_t to the verifier constitutes a proof of $\Omega(t)$ work. We can make the verification time polylogarithmic in t by using an efficient (public-coin) argument system to prove that x_t was computed correctly. Efficient argument systems can be constructed based on collision-resistant hash functions [Kil92, Mic00, BG08] and can be made noninteractive in the ROM.

This approach appears conceptually simple, but hides complexity in the construction of the argument system: existing schemes all make use of complex Probabilistically Checkable Proofs (PCPs), and this appears to be an inherent property of efficient argument systems [RV10]. In contrast, the constants hidden in the asymptotic notation of our constructions are very small (see Theorem 3.7 for the parameters). A second drawback of the generic scheme is that it is non-black-box (a proof that x_t was "computed correctly" necessarily uses the code of the algorithm computing f). As well as being of theoretical interest, a black-box construction has practical advantages: the implementation can be made in a modular way, changing the underlying sequential function can be done easily and it may even be replaced with a hardware module (or a corresponding physical assumption).

1.1 Our Results

In this paper, following Mahmoody et. al [MMV11], we study proofs of work (in the spirit of Dwork, Goldberg, Naor, and Wee [DN92,DGN03,DNW05]) and noninteractive timestamping.

Time-Lock Puzzles and Noninteractive Timestamping. Our main result is the first black-box construction of a time-lock puzzle (secure against parallel attack) with a public-coin puzzle generator. As described above, this implies a publicly verifiable, noninteractive timestamping scheme. Our construction relies on the existence of collision-

[1]Here the adversary is assumed to be uniform, because a non-uniform attacker can in fact invert a one-way permutation in time 2^{cn} for some constant $c < 1$ [Hel80, FN99, DTT10].

resistant hash functions and a new assumption that *sequential* hash functions exist; these are functions where it is infeasible to find any "hash chain" of length N in time $\ll N$, even if the adversary enjoys massive parallel computing power (see Definition 3.2 for a formalization). Note that both assumptions hold in the random oracle model.

The following theorem states our main result informally; see Theorem 3.7 for a formal statement.

THEOREM 1.1 (MAIN RESULT—INFORMAL). *Given any family of collision-resistant hash functions $\mathcal{CH}$ and any family of sequential hash functions $\mathcal{SH}$ we construct a time-lock puzzle scheme that is secure for a puzzle distribution* $\mathbf{D}$ *assuming that $\mathcal{CH}$ and $\mathcal{SH}$ are both secure when their index s is sampled from the same distribution* $\mathbf{D}$.

The verification time for our time-lock puzzle (and the corresponding timestamping scheme) can be poly-logarithmic in the time it takes to solve the puzzle, and the soundness time-gap (the ratio between the running time of the honest solver and that of a successful adversarial solver) is bounded by a constant. That is, our honest solver evaluates the hash function N times, and any adversary whose solution is accepted by an honest verifier must have used time proportional to $c \cdot N$ *sequential* evaluations of the hash function for a constant c. Our construction is fully black box (in the terminology of [RTV04]). After the puzzle is generated non-interactively, the verification process for both the time-lock puzzle and corresponding timestamping scheme are interactive protocols (a noninteractive timestamping scheme may still have an interactive verification stage). However, since our construction is fully black box, it is unconditionally secure in the random oracle model, and in this model we can make the verification noninteractive using the Fiat-Shamir Heuristic.

Universally Verifiable Benchmarks. Cai et al. [CLSY93] suggested using proofs of work for running "uncheatable" benchmarks. Their idea is that a vendor can prove a supercomputer's performance by having it run a proof of work that is timed by the verifier. The soundness of the proof-of-work protocol would guarantee that vendors couldn't cheat by optimizing their code or modifying it in some other way. Cai et al. proposed using exponentiation modulo an RSA integer as the candidate function. This has the drawback, however, of being verifier-specific (since only the verifier who generated the modulus and knows the secret factorization can trust the results). Using our time-lock puzzle construction, combined with a public randomness beacon, this benchmark can be made "universally verifiable": the randomness beacon would be used as the puzzle generator (assuming that the beacon's output in the next time period cannot be predicted by the vendor), and the vendor would publish the solution. Since there is no secret information, anyone can verify the results of the benchmark.

Combinatorial Tools. Our construction involves a novel use of *depth-robust* graphs: these are directed acyclic graphs on N vertices with low degree (e.g. polylog N) whose depth remains $\Omega(N)$ even after removing any constant fraction of vertices. To prove that it has done a lot of computational work, our prover constructs a labeling of the vertices of a depth-robust graph G where each vertex v should be labeled with $u_v = H_{\mathcal{P}}(u_{v_1}, \ldots, u_{v_d})$, where $v_1, \ldots, v_d$ are all vertices that have edges pointing to v, $\mathcal{P}$ is the puzzle, and H is a family of sequential hash-functions. (This is well-defined and can be computed with $O(N)$ hash evaluations due to the acyclicity of G.) It then sends the verifier a short commitment to this labeling through a Merkle tree (see Section C) computed using a collision-resistant hash function. During the verification, the prover is then asked to reveal the labels of a few randomly chosen vertices v along with their in-neighbors, and the verifier checks that $u_v = H_{\mathcal{P}}(u_{v_1}, \ldots, u_{v_d})$ holds for each such vertex v. Intuitively, if the prover can pass this check for a large fraction of vertices v, due to depth-robustness of G, the labeling constructed by the prover must have a hash chain of length $\Omega(N)$, and the prover must have used time proportional to $\Omega(N)$ sequential evaluations of the hash function.

Depth-robust graphs were investigated in the 70's and 80's, motivated by efforts to prove lower-bounds on circuit complexity and Turing machine time [EGS75, Val77, PR80, Sch82, Sch83]. We use a construction of Erdős, Graham and Szemerédi [EGS75], which involves a recursive use of constant-degree expander graphs. For different settings of parameters, depth-robust graphs are related to matrix rigidity and the "grate" property of graphs, defined by Valiant [Val77]. As far as we know, our work is the first "positive" use of depth-robust graphs.

In the *random oracle model* (ROM), we assume that all parties have oracle access to a public random function $\mathcal{O}: \{0,1\}^* \to \{0,1\}^n$ (where n is the security parameter). The ROM provides us with a clean and convenient way of lower-bounding both the total work invested by a party (namely the number of oracle queries) and the parallel time invested (the number of rounds of adaptivity in oracle queries). For this measure of computation time, it can be easily shown that a random oracle is sequential (a proof appears in Section A). Since our constructions make only black-box use of the hash functions, they are *unconditionally* secure in the ROM.

Although random oracles do not exist in the real world, a common heuristic for instantiating protocols in the random-oracle model is to replace the oracle with a cryptographic hash function (e.g., SHA-256) [BR93, FS86a]. While no concrete hash-function can satisfy all the properties of an ideal random oracle (in fact, there are examples of schemes that are provably insecure for *any* instantiation of the oracle by a concrete hash function [CGH04, GT03]), it seams reasonable to conjecture that these functions are highly sequential.

1.2 Related Work

Timestamping. While physical timestamps have been in use for many years (e.g., having a notary public physically stamp a document) their introduction to the digital realm, by Haber and Stornetta [HS91], was more recent. Haber and Stornetta's main idea relies on a *Timestamping Service* (TSS): a trusted third party that is responsible for generating and managing the timestamps. Further work in this direction has improved communication and computational complexity, and allowed the use of an *untrusted* TSS (for examples, see [ABSW01, BHS92, BdM91, BdM93, BL98, BLLV98, BLS00]). The state-of-the-art schemes using third-party Timestamping Services are efficient, can give very precise timestamps and even hide the contents of a document that is stamped, but necessarily reveal the fact that a party is stamping *some* document.

The first construction of a *noninteractive* timestamping

scheme was given by Moran, Shaltiel and Ta-Shma [MSTS09], in the Bounded Storage Model (BSM). In the BSM, parties have limited storage space, and there exists a source that periodically broadcasts huge random strings to all parties. (The strings are large enough that no party can store more than a constant fraction of a string in every time period.) To generate a timestamp on a document at time t, the stamper uses the document to select a subset of the random string at time t and stores that subset. At every time period, verifiers store a small random subset of the random string. To prove that a timestamp is valid, the stamper proves that her stored subset is consistent with the values stored by the verifier.

Proofs of Work. Dwork and Naor [DN92] originally suggested using proofs of work as a "pricing mechanism" to fight SPAM and other denial-of-service (DoS) attacks. (They proposed that a sender of an email message would provide a proof of work related to the message, making mass emailing more expensive.) For fighting SPAM, requiring the proof of work to be sequential is pointless: an attacker who is trying to generate multiple messages can generate the proofs for each message in parallel. On the other hand, they do care about preventing amortization attacks: computing the proof for n messages in a batch should require approximately n times the work as computing the proof for a single message. Dwork, Naor and Wee [DNW05] later considered a proof of work that is memory-bound rather than CPU-bound; this is preferable as the variance between CPU speeds is much larger than the variance between memory access times.

Hash Graphs. The work of [DNW05] also makes use of "hash graphs". Dwork et al. use their hash graph G to have the adversary (who provides the proof of work) to generate a random-looking table T (which is larger than the cache size and will be used as a pointer-jumping table in the proof-of-work protocol) by computing the hash labels of G using a random oracle and taking the label of the output nodes as T. The crucial property of the hash graph G is that the adversary should not be able to compute T by accessing the main memory only "a few" times and is forced to encounter many cache misses. The hash graph G of [DNW05] is constructed by concatenating two subgraph DAGs: G_1 and G_2 (where inputs of G_2 are the outputs of G_1) as follows. The DAG G_1 is a super-concentrator (from [PTC77]) which is a sparse graph with high connectivity: for any set S of s input nodes and any set T of s outputs nodes there are s vertex disjoint paths from S to T. The graph G_2 is a shallow DAG (of logarithmic depth) which is robust in the following sense: by removing any "small fraction" of the nodes of G_2 (together with their incident edges), still a "large fraction" of the inputs remain connected to a "large fraction" of the outputs. Thus, at a high level, [DNW05] also uses some robust DAGs as we do in this work but with a different notion of robustness; their graphs are shallow and are robust against losing connectivity of input and outputs, while our graphs have large depth and preserve (most of) this depth even after removing some fraction of the nodes.

Non-Parallelizable Proofs of Work. Although the inherent sequentiality property is not very useful against SPAM, inherently sequential proofs of work *can* be useful as a countermeasure against DoS attacks in other cases. With this use in mind, several proof-of-work constructions (called "client puzzles" in this context) have been suggested. These include an improvement in the efficiency of Rivest et al.'s modular-exponentiation-based construction [RSW96] (by Karame and Capkun [KC10]), but also constructions based on different "structural" assumptions with conjectured security against parallel attacks: Tritilanunt et al. [TBFN07] constructed proofs of work based on the hardness of solving subset-sum problems and assuming that the LLL algorithm [LLL82] for finding the shortest vectors in lattices is *optimal* and *inherently sequential*. Jerschow and Mauve [JM11] constructed proofs of work under the assumption that computing square roots modulo a prime is an inherently sequential task. Both constructions are public coin, but they achieve only a polynomial time-gap between puzzle generation and solution.

To the best of our knowledge, the only construction based on general unstructured assumptions is the recent construction of Mahmoody, Moran and Vadhan [MMV11] in the random oracle model. However, that construction only achieves a linear time-gap between puzzle generation and solution and, similar to the modular-exponentiation-based constructions, is not public coin.

Bypassing a Lower-Bound. Mahmoody, Moran and Vadhan considered time-lock puzzles in the random oracle model [MMV11] and proved that for a large class of time-lock puzzles, a large gap between generation/verification time and time to solve the puzzle is not possible. This class of time-lock puzzles include those in which the verifier does *not* query the oracle, which includes as a special case puzzles in which the generator produces a solution (sent to the verifier) together with the puzzle itself. For any such puzzle, they show that if it requires t oracle queries to generate the puzzle, the puzzle can be solved in t adaptive rounds of queries (with only a polynomial overhead in the total number of queries compared to the honest solver). We bypass the lower-bound of [MMV11] by constructing a verifier that does indeed query the oracle, and in fact our construction gives a time-lock puzzle with a super-polynomial gap between solution and verification times.

2. TIME-LOCK PUZZLES AND TIMESTAMPING, FORMAL DEFINITIONS

In this section we formalize the notion of time-lock puzzles and its relation to proofs of work.

DEFINITION 2.1. *A* time-lock puzzle *is a game between three parties* (Gen, Sol, Ver) *who receive the common input* 1^n *for security parameter* n *and* $N = \text{poly}(n) > n$ *as the "complexity of the puzzle" and act as follows.*

1. *The puzzle generator* Gen *generates a "puzzle"* $\mathcal{P}$.
2. *The puzzle solver* Sol *receives the puzzle* $\mathcal{P}$ *and outputs some "solution"* $\mathcal{S}$ *in time* $N \cdot \text{poly}(n)$ *(where* $\text{poly}(n)$ *here is independent of* N*).*
3. *The verifier* Ver *receives the puzzle* $\mathcal{P}$ *and a solution* $\mathcal{S}$ *and either accepts or rejects. (This step could be noninteractive or through interaction with* Sol*—see the discussion below).*

We require the following properties. The exact definition of the running time function **Time**$(\cdot)$ *and its parallel variant* **ParTime**$(\cdot)$ *depend on the underlying computational model.*

- **Completeness.** *In an honest execution* Ver *accepts with probability* $1 - \text{negl}(n)$.

- **(Parallel) η-Soundness.** *The (parallel) η-soundness property asserts that every non-uniform adversary $\widehat{\mathsf{Sol}}$ that runs in* parallel *time that is slightly smaller than the time of the honest solver ($\mathbf{ParTime}(\widehat{\mathsf{Sol}}) < \eta \cdot \mathbf{Time}(\mathsf{Sol})$) will fail to convince* Ver *with more than negligible probability (i.e., the probability that the output of $\widehat{\mathsf{Sol}}$ is accepted by* Ver *is negligible). We allow the total work $\mathbf{Time}(\widehat{\mathsf{Sol}})$ to be much larger than $\mathbf{Time}(\mathsf{Sol})$ (as long as it is at most polynomial in the security parameter).*

Time Gap. For our applications, we are interested in time-lock puzzles where there is a time-gap between solving a puzzle (honestly or maliciously) and time it takes to verify a solution.

On Parallel Soundness. Intuitively, this guarantees that a successful $\widehat{\mathsf{Sol}}$, after receiving the puzzle, must have invested almost as much computational effort in terms of parallel-time complexity, as the honest solver Sol does in terms of its running time (η measures the "slowdown factor" of the honest solver compared to the parallel-time of the adversary—when $\eta = 1$ the adversary cannot solve any faster than the honest solver even with massive parallelism, while when $\eta = 1/2$ the adversary can run in half the time of the honest solver).

Note that we allow the adversary to perform arbitrary polynomial-time preprocessing before receiving the puzzle. For simplicity, we omit this from the definition above. However, our proof of security holds for a *non-uniform* adversary; in particular, this means we allow the adversary to receive arbitrary "advice" (that does not depend on the input, $\mathcal{P}$); any preprocessing done before receiving $\mathcal{P}$ can simply be treated as advice.

Interactive Verification. As we mentioned in Definition 2.1, the verification of the puzzle solution may be interactive (i.e., consist of an interactive protocol between the verifier and a "prover" who has access to the secret state of the puzzle solver Sol). The time-lock puzzles we construct in this paper have interactive verifiers. However, since their verification protocols are all public-coin, they can be made noninteractive in the random-oracle model by applying the Fiat-Shamir transformation.

Public vs. Secret Verification. Since the puzzle generator and the verifier in Definition 2.1 do not share any secret information, this definition guarantees that puzzles are "publicly verifiable": the verification protocol can be executed by any interested party. This property is especially useful for noninteractive time-lock puzzles: the solution and proof are both strings and can be easily published. The public verifiability means that anyone who receives the proof can verify it, without needing to trust any third parties. One can also consider an alternative definition of time-lock puzzles in which the puzzle generator and verifier do share secret information. This is the case, for example, in the repeated-squaring based puzzle of Rivest et al. [RSW96] (the secret information is the factorization of the modulus). The alternative definition is strictly weaker, and limits verification to parties that know the secret.

Timestamping Documents. Now we discuss how our results in the context of time-lock puzzles can be used for noninteractively timestamping documents. The type of timestamps we deal with are *relative* timestamps: that is, if Alice produces a d-timestamp of a document D at time T then she is claiming that she "knew" the document at time $T-d$. While relative timestamps can be used to construct absolute timestamps (e.g., by continuously computing d-timestamps for larger and larger d), they may also have direct applications. For example, suppose Alice believes she has solved a hard research problem, but is hesitant to publish before completely verifying her result. She can compute a one-week relative timestamp of her solution and store it; if, at some later time, Bob claims to have solved the problem, Alice has one week in which she can prove that she had a solution first. Our definition of security for timestamping is based on the following intuition: if Bob receives a previously unknown document D' at time T_0, then at time $T_0 + d$ he should not be able to produce a d'-timestamp of D' for any d' such that $d' \gg d$.

DEFINITION 2.2. *A noninteractive timestamping scheme is a protocol between a stamper,* Stamp *and a verifier,* Ver. *The protocol has two phases: In the* stamping *phase, the stamper receives an input document D and a duration d and computes the timestamp $\mathcal{S} = \mathsf{Stamp}(D, d)$. In the* verification *phase, the stamper communicates with the verifier. The stamper sends $(D, d, \mathcal{S})$ to the verifier and proves that $\mathcal{S}$ is a valid d-timestamp of D (this may be done using an interactive protocol). We also demand the following properties (where n is the security parameter).*

- **Completeness.** *We require a timestamping scheme to satisfy two completeness properties:*
  - *When parties execute the game honestly* Ver *accepts with probability $1 - \mathrm{negl}(n)$.*
  - *The honest stamper can compute $\mathsf{Stamp}(D, d)$ in d time.*
- **η-Soundness** *The soundness of the scheme is parameterized by $\eta \leq 1$ (measuring how much the adversary can cheat on the claimed timestamp duration) and by $\mathbf{D}$, the distribution of documents to be stamped. Consider the following game between an adversary* **Adv** *and* Ver*:*
  1. **Adv** *receives a document $D \xleftarrow{\$} \mathbf{D}$.*
  2. **Adv** *generates $(\mathcal{S}, d)$ and sends $(D, d, \mathcal{S})$ to the verifier* Ver.
  3. Ver *and* **Adv** *engage in the verification phase, after which* Ver *either accepts or rejects.*

  We say the timestamp scheme is η-sound with respect to document distribution $\mathbf{D}$ if for every non-uniform adversary **Adv** *of size $\mathrm{poly}(n)$ and whose parallel time (including the verification phase) is $\mathbf{ParTime}(\mathbf{Adv}) < \eta \cdot d$, the probability that* **Adv** *wins in the security game (by causing the verifier to accept) is negligible. (Note that, as in Definition 2.1, we allow the the adversary to perform arbitrary preprocessing before receiving the document to timestamp.)*

Timestamping Using Time-Lock Puzzles. Given an η-sound time-lock puzzle (Gen, Sol, Ver), we can envision (Sol, Ver) as defining a timestamping scheme that is η-sound against documents in the distribution generated by Gen. That is, when Bob receives a document D at time T and wants to timestamp it for duration d, he treats D as the puzzle and "solves" it for parameter N such that $\mathbf{Time}(\mathcal{S}) = N \cdot \text{poly}(n) = d$ to obtain the timestamp $\mathcal{S}$. The η-soundness of the time-lock puzzle guarantees that no adversary running in parallel time less than $\eta \cdot \mathbf{ParTime}(\mathsf{Sol})$ can convince the verifier to accept a valid timestamp.

The distribution $\mathbf{D}$ models the uncertainty about the documents to be timestamped. Any document D such that $\Pr[D \xleftarrow{\$} \mathbf{D}] \geq 1/\text{poly}(n)$ (where n is the security parameter) can be thought of as a "typical" document that the adversary can "guess" in advance. Therefore, it is reasonable to restrict ourselves to distributions that satisfy $\Pr[D \xleftarrow{\$} \mathbf{D}] \leq 1/\text{poly}(n)$ for every D and every polynomial $\text{poly}(n)$; namely, the distribution $\mathbf{D}$ has super-logarithmic min-entropy. It is plausible to assume we have a family of hash functions $\mathcal{CH}$ and $\mathcal{SH}$ that are simultaneously secure for all index distributions with super-logarithmic min-entropy (they exist in the random oracle model). Our timestamping scheme will then inherit this property.

Security in the Presence of Auxiliary Information. Note that in Theorem 1.1, the distribution $\mathbf{D}$ of the documents is the same as the index distribution of the used hash functions. The distribution $\mathbf{D}$ could capture the uncertainty of the adversary about the document D *conditioned on* the auxiliary information of the adversary about the document. Thus, if we want to guarantee the security of our scheme under *any* auxiliary information (e.g., knowing only half of the document), as long as there is $\omega(\log n)$ bits of uncertainty about the final version of the document, we can construct secure timestamping schemes under the assumption that the used hash functions are also secure under any index distribution with super-logarithmic min-entropy.

Timestamping for Unknown Duration. A desirable feature of a timestamping scheme is to allow the stamper to perform its job *without* knowing the time period d in advance. A simple trick (that decreases η by a small constant factor) is as follows: The stamper iteratively generates timestamps for $d = 1, 2, \ldots, 2^i, \ldots$ and always keeps the last generated timestamp as the current timestamp. It is easy to see that this scheme achieves $\eta' \geq \eta/4$. Our time-lock puzzle (using the specific construction of depth-robust graphs from Section B) construction satisfies an even stronger property, making it particularly suited for timestamping documents without knowing the duration in advance. In our construction, for $d_2 > d_1$, the computation $\mathsf{Sol}_{d_1}(P)$ is a prefix of the computation $\mathsf{Sol}_{d_2}(P)$; thus, it is possible to run the stamper continuously, generating timestamps of increasing duration and without paying the constant factor in η.

3. CONSTRUCTING TIME-LOCK PUZZLES

In this section we prove our main result which is a new construction of publicly verifiable time-lock puzzle based on sequential hash functions and collision-resistant hash functions.

3.1 Outline and High-Level Ideas

The high-level idea is to force the solver to compute a labeling of a DAG G as a "hash-graph" in which each node is labeled with the hash of its in-neighbors' labels. The soundness of of our construction will rely on a computational assumption about the hashes—namely that they are inherently *sequential* (see Definition 3.2 below for a formalization). The sequentiality of the hash functions ensures that any adversary that can output the label of an endpoint of a correct path in the graph must spend time at least proportional to the length of the path (i.e., there are no "shortcuts"). To check a proposed solution to the puzzle, the verifier will test random nodes in the graph and check if they were computed correctly. We use an underlying DAG that has a special combinatorial property called *depth-robustness*: in any large subset of the nodes of the hash-graph there is a "long" path (see Definition 3.6). To achieve η-soundness with η arbitrarily close to one we employ a modified version of the depth-robust DAGs constructed by Erdős, Graham, and Szemerédi [EGS75] (see Section B).

If too many nodes in the graph are badly labeled (i.e., their labels are not the hash of their in-neighbors' labels) the verifier will reject the solution with high probability. Thus, if the verifier accepts we can use the combinatorial property of the graph to conclude that there must be a long path consisting of nodes that were "correctly" computed, and from the sequential property of the hash it will follow that the solver must have spent a "long" time performing the computation.

Finally, to reduce the communication and verification time, instead of sending the labeling of the entire graph, the solver will commit to the graph labeling and send only the commitment to the verifier. When the verifier challenges the solver on a specific node in the graph, the solver will send the label of that node and the labels of its in-neighbors, and will prove that these are consistent with the commitment. An efficient commitment scheme with all of the required properties is the Merkle tree, which can be constructed based on any collision-resistant hash function.

3.2 Formal Definitions

In this subsection we provide the formal definitions required for stating and proving our theorems. First, we formally define the notion of a sequential function. We first describe the security game.

Construction 3.1. *We define a sequential function family by means of a game between an adversary and a challenger. Let n denote the security parameter. For every n and $m = m(n) \geq n$, let $H = \{h_s \colon \{0,1\}^m \mapsto \{0,1\}^n\}$ be a family of functions mapping m bits to n bits. The game is defined with respect to a distribution $\mathbf{D}_n$ defined over the indices of H. Both parties receive as inputs n, m and a "sequence-length" parameter N.*

1. *The challenger samples $s \xleftarrow{\$} \mathbf{D}_n$ as the index of the hash function and sends s to the adversary.*
2. *The adversary sends back some string y.*
3. *Then (after y is received by challenger) the adversary sends back a sequence $y_0, \ldots, y_N = y$.*

The adversary wins if for all $i \in [N]$ it holds that $h_s(y_{i-1})$ is a contiguous substring of y_i.

Definition 3.2 (Sequential Functions). *Let $\tau(n)$ be $0 < \tau(n) < \text{poly}(n)$, $H = \left\{h_s \colon \{0,1\}^{m(n)} \mapsto \{0,1\}^n\right\}$ be a* *family of (non-expanding) functions, and* $D = \{\mathbf{D}_n\}_{n\in\mathbb{N}}$ *be a family of distributions over the indexes* $s \in \{0,1\}^{\text{poly}(n)}$ *of* H. *The family* H *is called* τ-sequential *against* $\mathbf{D}$ *iff for every* $N = \text{poly}(n)$ *and every adversary* **Adv** *of the following form, the probability that* **Adv** *wins in the game of Construction 3.1 over common inputs* n *is* $\text{negl}(n)$*: the adversary* **Adv** *is a circuit of total size* $\text{poly}(n, N)$*, but the depth of this circuit till sending over* y *(in Step 2) is at most* $\tau \cdot N$.

The sequentiality parameter τ determines the level of confidence one has in the sequential nature of H and is always at most $t(n)$, where $t(n)$ is the time it takes to call $H(\cdot)$ on an input to get an n-bit output. On an extreme point, for a particular function H, one might believe that getting a sequence of length N really needs N sequential evaluations of the function resulting in $\tau(n) = t(n)$.

Our construction also employs a family of collision-resistant hash functions. We use the following generalized definition that holds with respect to particular distributions over the index:

DEFINITION 3.3 (COLLISION-RESISTANT HASHING). *Let* $H = \{h_s\colon \{0,1\}^{2n} \mapsto \{0,1\}^n\}$ *be a family of shrinking functions and let* $\mathbf{D}_n$ *be a distribution over the indexes of* H *for security parameter* n. *We call* H collision resistant *against* $\mathbf{D} = \{\mathbf{D}_n\}$ *iff for every non-uniform adversary* **Adv** *of size* $\text{poly}(n)$*, if we choose* $s \xleftarrow{\$} \mathbf{D}_n$ *and let* $(x_1, x_2) = \mathbf{Adv}(s)$*, then it holds that* $\Pr[h_s(x_1) = h_s(x_2) \wedge x_1 \neq x_2] \leq \text{negl}(n)$.

DEFINITION 3.4 (DIRECTED ACYCLIC GRAPHS). *A* directed acyclic graph *(or DAG for short)* $G = (V_G, E_G)$ *is a directed graph whose vertices* V_G *can be renamed as* $V_G = \{1, \ldots, N\}$*—called the* topological order*—such that for every directed edge* $(i,j) \in E_G$ *it holds that* $i < j$. *We assume that our DAGs are always given in topological order. For any vertex* $j \in [N]$ *we call* $\text{IN}(j) = \{i \mid (i,j) \in E_G\}$ *the* in-neighbors *of the node* j *and call* $d_{\text{in}}(j) = |\text{IN}(j)|$ *the* in-degree *of the vertex* j. *We say* G *is of* in-degree d *if* $d_{\text{in}}(j) \leq d$ *for all* $j \in V_G$. *We call a family* $\{G_N\}$ *of DAGs where* G_N *has* N *vertices and in-degree* d_N explicit *if for any given* $i \in [N]$ *and* $j \in [d_N]$ *one can compute in time* $\text{polylog}(N)$ *the index of the* j*-th in-neighbor of the node* i.

REMARK 3.5. *For simplicity we always assume that there is an extra redundant node* 0 *(not counted in the number of vertices) such that for every* $j \in [N]$ *there are* $d - d_{\text{in}}(j)$ *multiple edges from the node* 0 *to the node* j *to make the in-degrees of every* $j \in [N]$ *exactly equal to* d.

DEFINITION 3.6 (DEPTH ROBUSTNESS). *For* $\alpha \in [0,1]$ *and* $\beta \in [0, \alpha]$*, we call a DAG* $G = (V_G, E_G)$ *an* (α, β)-depth-robust *graph iff every induced subgraph* H *of* G *whose number of vertices is at least* $|V_H| \geq \alpha \cdot |V_G|$ *includes a path with at least* $\beta \cdot |V_G|$ *many vertices.*

3.3 The Main Theorem

In this section we describe and prove our main result about the existence of time-lock puzzles based on collision-resistant and sequential hash functions. As discussed above, this implies the existence of timestamping protocols (a formal proof appears in Section 2).

Used Hash Functions. Let $\mathcal{CH} = \{ch\colon \{0,1\}^{2n} \mapsto \{0,1\}^n\}$ be a family of collision resistant hash functions against index distribution $\mathbf{D}$ and let $\mathcal{SH} = \{sh\colon \{0,1\}^m \mapsto \{0,1\}^n\}$ for $m = \omega(n \cdot \log^3 n)$ be a τ-sequential function against the same index distribution $\mathbf{D}$. Let $t_{ch}(n)$ denote the time required for an honest user to evaluate $ch(x)$ for $ch \in \mathcal{CH}$ when $ch(x) \in \{0,1\}^n$, and similarly, let $t_{sh}(n)$ be the time required for an honest user to evaluate an input for function $sh \in \mathcal{SH}$ with output in $\{0,1\}^n$. When clear from the context, we drop the index n and use names t_{sh}, t_{ch}, etc.

THEOREM 3.7 (MAIN RESULT). *Let* n *be the security parameter,* $N = \text{poly}(n)$*, and* $k = \omega(\log n)$. *Suppose* $\mathcal{CH}$ *and* $\mathcal{SH}$ *as described above are sequential and collision-resistant hash functions with respect to index distribution* $\mathbf{D}$ *and let* $\beta < 1$ *be any constant. Then there exists a time-lock puzzle as follows:*

- **Generation.** *The puzzle generator* Gen *simply outputs a sample* $\mathcal{P} \xleftarrow{\$} \mathbf{D}$.
- **Solving.** *The honest solver* Sol *runs in time* $(t_{ch} + t_{sh} + \text{polylog}(N)) \cdot N$ *to generate the puzzle solution.*
- **Verification.** *To answer the verifier's challenges, the solver is only required to lookup the answers from a table generated during solving the puzzle (no need for additional computation). This only takes linear time over the answer size which is* $k \cdot (m+n)$. *The* interactive *verifier* Ver *only asks* k *public-coin challenges, and to verify the received answer it runs in time at most* $O(k) \cdot (t_{sh} + t_{ch} \cdot \log^3 N + \text{polylog}(N))$.
- **Completeness.** *When the honest solver* Sol *interacts with the verifier* Ver*,* Ver *accepts with probability* 1.
- **Soundness.** *No malicious solver* $\widehat{\mathsf{Sol}}$ *computed by a circuit of size* $\text{poly}(n, N)$ *is able to make* Ver *accept with probability more than* $\text{negl}(n)$ *if* $\widehat{\mathsf{Sol}}$*'s circuit has depth* $\tau \cdot N \cdot \beta$ *till sending the puzzle solution. (Recall that* $\mathcal{SH}$ *is* τ*-sequential.)*

REMARK 3.8 (BALANCING HASHING TIMES). *It is easy to see that the soundness of Theorem 3.7 as stated implies* η*-parallel-soundness for* $\eta \geq \tau\beta/(t_{ch} + t_{sh})$ *Thus we obtain* $\eta = \tau\beta/(t_{ch} + t_{sh})$*. Thus, on this extreme the advantage of the adversary relative to the honest solver, depends on the ratio between* τ*, the lower bound on the (average) time it takes the adversary to compute the sequential hash function* sh*, and* $t_{sh} + t_{ch}$*, the total time an honest party needs to evaluate* sh *once and* ch *once (where* ch *is the collision-resistant hash function). Since the adversary can always use the honest algorithm to compute* sh*, therefore it holds that* $\tau \leq t_{sh}$. *Thus, if* $t_{ch} \approx t_{sh}$ *(as would be the case, for example, if we used SHA-256 for both purposes), the adversary potentially could get a factor* ≈ 2 *advantage—even if the function is perfectly sequential* $(\tau = t_{sh})$. *A possible way to deal with this problem is by using the iterated function* sh^k *as the sequential function (where* $sh^i(x) = sh(sh^{i-1}(x))$*). Since any length-*$N$ *hash-chain of* sh^k *contains a length-*$(k \cdot N)$ *hash-chain for* sh*, it follows that* $\tau(sh^k) \geq k \cdot \tau(sh)$. *At the same time,* $t_{sh^k} = k \cdot t_{sh}$. *By increasing* k*, we can make the ratio* $\tau/(t_{sh} + t_{ch})$ *arbitrarily close to* τ/t_{sh} *(which is the best we can hope for). However, we pay for this increase by also increasing the computation time for the honest verifier; thus as* k *gets larger, the time-gap for the puzzle (the difference between the work done by the honest solver and the honest verifier) becomes smaller.*

We describe our construction using an interactive verifier in a hybrid model with access to an ideal commitment functionality Com that remains hiding against selective opening (the commitment scheme allows a short commitment to a set of blocks $(u_1, \ldots, u_n)$, and later allows the prover to selectively open block u_j for every $j \in [N]$). We then replace the ideal commitment with a commitment scheme using Merkle tree based on the collision-resistant hash function $\mathcal{CH}$. If a single evaluation of the hash function takes time t_{ch}, then commitment to N blocks using Com can be done in time $t_{ch} \cdot N$ and verification in time $t_{ch} \cdot \log N$ (see Section C for details). Algorithms 1 and 2 describes the honest solver and Algorithm 3 describes the corresponding verifier.

Algorithm 1 Honest solver Sol solving puzzle $\mathcal{P}$ using sequential hash family sh indexed with $\mathcal{P}$ and output length n, and a DAG G of in-degree d and N vertices given in topological order.

Initially assign the hash label $u_0 = 0^n$ to the extra redundant node (see Remark 3.5).
for $v \in \{1, \ldots, N\}$ **do** {Compute the hash-labels corresponding to the nodes of G}
  Suppose $v_1 \leq \cdots \leq v_d$ are the in-neighbors of v, and let u_{v_i} be the hash-label of v_i.
  Set $u_v = sh_{\mathcal{P}}(u_{v_1}, \ldots, u_{v_d})$.

Algorithm 2 Honest solver Sol answering a challenge for the generated solution c.

Receive a set of challenge nodes $\{v_1 \leq \ldots \leq v_k\}$ from the verifier.
for $i \in \{1, \ldots, k\}$ **do**
  Open the commitments to u_{v_i} and u_v for all $v \in \mathrm{IN}(v_i)$.

Algorithm 3 Verifier of a solution for the puzzle $\mathcal{P}$ using sequential hash family sh and the DAG G of N vertices in topological order and in-degree d.

Receive the commitment c (supposedly for the hash labels $(u_1, u_2, \ldots, u_N)$) from the solver.
Randomly choose k nodes $v_1, \ldots, v_k$ from $[N] = V_G$ and send them to the solver.
for $i \in \{1, \ldots, k\}$ **do**
  Verify the commitment openings of u_{v_i} and u_v for all $v \in \mathrm{IN}(v_i)$.
  Verify $u_{v_i} = sh_{\mathcal{P}}(u_{v_{(1,i)}}, \ldots, u_{v_{(d,i)}})$ where $v_{(1,i)} \leq \cdots \leq v_{(d,i)}$ are the in-neighbors of v_i.

CONSTRUCTION 3.9 (TIME-LOCK PUZZLE). *Given $n, N \in \mathbb{N}$ an explicit DAG G of N vertices and in-degree d, the time-lock puzzle $\Pi_{n,N}$ is as follows.*

- *The puzzle generator* Gen *outputs $\mathcal{P} \xleftarrow{\$} \mathbf{D}_n$.*
- *The puzzle solver* Sol *executes Algorithms 1 and 2, and the puzzle verifier* Ver *executes Algorithm 3.*

3.4 Proving Theorem 3.7

To prove Theorem 3.7, we feed Construction 3.9 with the following type of depth-robust graphs.

LEMMA 3.10 (EXPLICIT DEPTH-ROBUST GRAPHS). *For all constants $\beta < \alpha$ and all N there is an explicit family of (α, β)-depth robust graphs with N vertices and in-degree $O(\log^3 N)$.*

The proof of Lemma 3.10 is based on the ideas from [EGS75] and is presented in Section B

We now prove Theorem 3.7 by analyzing the properties of Construction 3.9 when instantiated by depth-robust graphs specified in Lemma 3.10.

Completeness. Clearly if the puzzle solver and the verifier follow Algorithms 1, 2, and 3, then the verifier accepts with probability one.

Running Times. The following lemma can be verified by inspecting Algorithms 1, 2, and 3, and the Merkle commitment algorithms of Section C. These bounds imply the bounds of Theorem 3.7 when substituting $d = O(\log^3 N)$ which is the degree of the DAG G we will use (according to Lemma 3.10).

LEMMA 3.11. *The running time of the parties in Construction 3.9 is as follows.*

- **Generation.** *The puzzle generator* Gen *simply outputs a sample string from $\mathbf{D}_n$.*
- **Honest Solver.** *The solver, in its first round of action simply calls* $\mathbf{Adv}_1$ *and returns its output directly as the puzzle solution. To generate the hash labels, the solver* Sol *first constructs the DAG G in time $N \cdot \mathrm{polylog}(N)$ and then evaluates the sequential hash $sh(\cdot)$ N times for the vertices of G (over inputs of length $d \cdot n$ and outputs of length n). To commit to the hash labels, the solver evaluates the collision-resistant hash function $ch(\cdot)$ at most $N/2 + N/4 + \cdots \leq N$ times over inputs of length $2n$ and outputs of length n. Therefore, if calling $sh(\cdot)$ takes time t_{sh} and calling $ch(\cdot)$ takes time t_{ch}, the total running time of* Sol *will be $(t_{sh} + t_{ch} + \mathrm{polylog}\, N) \cdot N$.*
- **Verifier.** *To answer each of the k challenges asked by the verifier, the solver (now playing as a prover) needs to send $2 \cdot (d+1) \cdot \log N$ strings of length n (which are computed already) to the verifier. Also, for each of these k challenges, the verifier first constructs the relevant part of G in time $\mathrm{polylog}(N)$, and then it evaluates the sequential hash $sh(\cdot)$ (in time t_{sh}) and evaluates $ch(\cdot)$ $2 \cdot (d+1) \cdot \log N$ times all in parallel time t_{ch} (see Algorithm 7).*

Parallel Soundness of Construction 3.9. The following lemma shows that by using an explicit (α, β)-depth robust graphs G for constants $\beta < \alpha$ from Lemma 3.10 in Construction 3.9, we can derive the soundness property stated in Theorem 3.7.

LEMMA 3.12. *Suppose the DAG G used in Construction 3.9 is (α, β)-depth-robust for some constants $0 < \beta < \alpha < 1$. Then any malicious solver who is a circuit of size $\mathrm{poly}(n, N)$ and depth at most $\tau \cdot N \cdot \beta$ till returning the puzzle solution is able to make the verifier accept with at most $\mathrm{negl}(n)$ probability.*

We first finish the proof of Theorem 3.7 using Lemma 3.12 and then will prove Lemma 3.12.

Concluding Theorem 3.7. Since we have $k = \omega(\log n)$ Theorem 3.7 follows as a corollary from Lemmas 3.10, 3.11, and 3.12, because **(1)** it holds that $d = O(\log^3 N)$ and **(2)** for $k = \omega(\log n)$ and $\alpha = 1-\Omega(1)$ it holds that $\alpha^k = \mathrm{negl}(n)$.

We first outline the proof of Lemma 3.12 and then will present the formal proof.

Outline of Proof of Lemma 3.12. Roughly speaking, for the committed labeling $u_1, \ldots, u_N$ by the adversary **Adv**, we call a node $i \in [N]$ a good node if its hash label is indeed equal to the hash of the labels of its in-neighbors. If the number of good nodes is at most $\alpha \cdot N$, then the probability that the adversary can convince the verifier is at most $\alpha^k + \mathrm{negl}(n)$. On the other hand, if the number of good nodes are more than $\alpha \cdot N$ then there should be path consisting of at least $\beta \cdot N$ many good nodes. The latter path, however, corresponds to a "chain" of queries, and the sequential property of $sh(\cdot)$ ensures that to generate such a chain the adversary must run in time proportional to the length of the chain.

More formally, the proof is by a reduction showing how to use an adversary that breaks η-soundness (i.e., can convince a verifier to accept a solution while working in "small" parallel time) to break the sequential soundness of sh (i.e., produce a "long" hash chain in "small" parallel time) as follows. Given an adversary **Adv** who breaks soundness of the time-lock puzzle scheme, we run **Adv** until it outputs the commitment c. We then execute $O(N)$ verification sessions using $O(N)$ copies of **Adv**. In each of these verification sessions we emulate a verifier that queries different vertices of the DAG, with the hope that after this stage we gather the labeling of "many" vertices of the DAG. The main challenges of the proof of soundness lie in the analysis of this reduction. Since **Adv** succeeds in convincing the verifier to accept with non-negligible probability, at most a constant fraction of the extracted labels can be "bad" (i.e., don't correspond to a hash of their in-neighbors' labels). Thus, by the depth-robustness property of the graph G, there must be a long path of good vertices in G. This path is exactly the hash-chain we are looking for.

3.5 Formal Proof of Lemma 3.12

In the following we start by assuming (for sake of contradiction) that there is an adversary $\mathbf{Adv}_1$ who breaks the parallel-soundness of Construction 3.9 with probability at least $\varepsilon_1 \geq 1/\mathrm{poly}(n)$ (when using a $(\alpha, \beta)-$depth-robust graph of degree $O(\log^3 N)$), has circuit size $\mathrm{poly}(n, N)$ and depth $\tau \cdot N \cdot \beta$ till sending the puzzle solution. Then we will show how to turn this adversary into another adversary that either breaks the sequential property of $sh(\cdot)$ or the binding property of the commitment (which by Lemma C.1 implies breaking the collision resistance of ch).

LEMMA 3.13 (EXTRACTING A CHAIN). *Suppose $\mathbf{Adv}_1$ is an adversary who convinces the verifier of Algorithm 3 with probability at least $\varepsilon_1 = \varepsilon_1' + \alpha^k$. Then there is an algorithm $\mathbf{Adv}_2$ (described in Algorithm 4) who executes $\ell = 2nN/\varepsilon_1'$ copies of $\mathbf{Adv}_1$, and then evaluates $sh(\cdot)$ $O(\ell \cdot k)$ times (and makes an additional $O(\ell \cdot k \cdot d)$ executions of the commitment scheme's verification algorithm) and $\Pr[E] \geq \varepsilon_1'/3$ where E is the event that: $\mathbf{Adv}_2$ breaks the binding of $\mathsf{Com}(\cdot)$ or its view has a chain of length βN in $sh(\cdot)$. Note that assuming $\varepsilon_1' > 1/\mathrm{poly}(n)$, the running time of $\mathbf{Adv}_2$ is only $\mathrm{poly}(n, N)$ times that of $\mathbf{Adv}_1$.*

Using Lemma 3.13 to Conclude Lemma 3.12. After obtaining the adversary $\mathbf{Adv}_2$ we can break the assumption that $sh(\cdot)$ is τ-sequential (which is a contradiction) as follows. The adversary $\mathbf{Adv}_2$ will simply forward the puzzle solution c of $\mathbf{Adv}_1$ (i.e., the Merkle-commitment string) as the label of the last node of the chain. Then, later on, suppose $\mathbf{Adv}_2$ has access to a set of hash labels $u_1, \ldots, u_N$ such that there is a chain of length at least $\beta \cdot N$ planted in them. Then, by Lemma 3.13, $\mathbf{Adv}_2$ is able to find a path $\overrightarrow{\mathsf{PT}}$ of length at least $\beta \cdot N$ in G whose labels are all accepted during the verification phase. This means that the revealed labels along the paths that connect the nodes of $\overrightarrow{\mathsf{PT}}$ to the root of the Merkle-tree are all extracted successfully. $\mathbf{Adv}_2$ will simply return the labels of $\overrightarrow{\mathsf{PT}}$ followed by the labels of the nodes connecting the last node of $\overrightarrow{\mathsf{PT}}$ to the root (which is c). Therefore, **Adv** is able to win in the security game of Construction 3.1 with non-negligible probability by finding a chain of depth $\beta \cdot N$ in depth $< \tau \cdot \beta \cdot N$ till sending c. This violates the assumption that $sh(\cdot)$ is τ-sequential.

Algorithm 4 Either find a collision or extract a $\beta \cdot N$-chain, by using oracle access to an adversary $\mathbf{Adv}_1$ who convinces the interactive verifier with probability $\varepsilon_1 = \varepsilon_1' + \alpha^k$.

1: Run $\mathbf{Adv}_1$ over a random puzzle $\mathcal{P} \xleftarrow{\$} \{0,1\}^n$ and random coins rand_2 and receive some commitment $c \in \{0,1\}^n$. At this moment save the state of the adversary $\mathbf{Adv}_1$ since we are going to execute $\mathbf{Adv}_1$ in many "different branches" *in parallel* by feeding many different challenge messages to $\mathbf{Adv}_1$ and asking it to open those commitments. We cannot afford to use standard "rewinding" since we want to keep the depth of the circuit of $\mathbf{Adv}_2$ close to that of $\mathbf{Adv}_1$.
2: Let $\delta = \varepsilon_1'/(2N)$ and $\ell = n/\delta$.
3: For all $j \in [\ell]$ choose a random subset $S_j \subset [N]$ of size $|S_j| = k$ (possibly with repetitions).
4: **for** all $j \in [\ell]$ **do**
5: Ask $\mathbf{Adv}_1$ to open the nodes in the challenge set S_j with respect to the commitment c.
6: After receiving decommitments for $(d+1) \cdot k \cdot \ell$ many nodes in $[N]$ (possibly with repetitions), run Merkle verification algorithm for all of them.
7: If two different openings for the same label are both accepted by the verifier, return a collision in ch according to Lemma C.1.
8: Let H be an empty graph with the same vertex set as that of G. For every challenge node v (from the set of all k challenges) that passes the Merkle verification, let $v_1, \ldots, v_d$ be the in-neighbors of v_i in G. Add the edges $(v_1, v), \ldots, (v_d, v)$ to the graph H.
9: Search for a the longest path $\overrightarrow{\mathsf{PT}}$ in the graph H and return the labels of the nodes of $\overrightarrow{\mathsf{PT}}$ continued with the $\log(N)$ labels of the nodes of the Merkle-tree decommitment connecting the last node of $\overrightarrow{\mathsf{PT}}$ to the root.

PROOF OF LEMMA 3.13. The running time of $\mathbf{Adv}_2$ is at most $O(Nn/\varepsilon_1') = \mathrm{poly}(N, n)$ times more that that of $\mathbf{Adv}_2$

(without considering the final verification). So we only need to prove the existence of the long chain in $sh(\cdot)$ in the view of $\mathbf{Adv}_2$, assuming that $\mathbf{Adv}_2$ did not break the binding property of $\mathsf{Com}(\cdot)$.

Since $\mathbf{Adv}_1$ succeeds in convincing the verifier with probability at least ε_1, by an averaging argument, with probability at least $\varepsilon_1'/2$ over the choices of the puzzle $\mathcal{P}$ and the randomness of $\mathbf{Adv}_1$ (i.e., rand_2), $\mathbf{Adv}_1$ will have at least a chance of $\alpha^k + \varepsilon_1'/2$ (over the randomness of the challenge message) to convince the verifier. In the following we assume that the sampled $\mathcal{P}$ and rand_2 in Step 1 of Algorithm 4 have this property. We will show that in this case, $\mathbf{Adv}_2$ succeeds in finding a (long enough) chain with probability at least 9/10, leading to a total probability of success at least $(\varepsilon_1'/2)\cdot(9/10) > \varepsilon_1'/3$.

Suppose W is the event that $\mathbf{Adv}_1$ succeeds answering a random challenge set S of k nodes. Call a node $i \in [N]$ a *heavy* node if $\Pr[i \in S \text{ and } W] \geq \delta = \varepsilon_1'/(2N)$ for a random challenge set S of size k. Call a node $i \in [N]$ *light* if it is not heavy. Let $\mathcal{HV}$ be the set of heavy nodes and $\mathcal{LT}$ be the set of light nodes. We claim that the number of heavy nodes is at least $\alpha \cdot N$. Otherwise $\mathbf{Adv}_1$ is able to answer a random challenge $S \subset [N]$ of k nodes correctly only with probability:

$$\begin{aligned}\Pr_S[W] &\leq \Pr_S[W \text{and } S \subset \mathcal{HV}] + \Pr_S[W \text{and } S \cap \mathcal{LT} \neq \varnothing] \\ &< \alpha^k + \sum_{i\in\mathcal{LT}} \Pr[W \text{and } i \in S] \leq \alpha^k + N\cdot\delta\end{aligned}$$

which is at most $\alpha^k + \varepsilon_1'/2$ as opposed to our assumption. On the other hand, since $\mathbf{Adv}_2$ chooses ℓ random challenge sets S_j of size k, for every heavy node $i \in [N]$, the probability that for some $j \in [\ell]$ $\mathbf{Adv}_1$ can successfully decommit to all of the nodes in S_j while it includes $i \in S_j$ is at least $1-(1-\delta)^\ell > 1-e^{-n} > 1-2^{-n}$. Therefore, by a union bound, with probability at least $1-2^{-n}\cdot N > 1-2^{-\Omega(n)}$ for every heavy node v, the adversary will decommit successfully (at some point) into some hash label for v and also some hash labels for the in-neighbors of v. When the latter holds we call v a good node, and call the (successfully opened) hash labels of v and its in-neighbors some *extracted* hash labels (note that potentially we might extract different hash labels for v in different branches of executing $\mathbf{Adv}_1$ over some challenge set S).

Note that we can safely assume that for all $i \in [N]$ all the extracted hash labels for the node $i \in [N]$ (either extracted as the label of a sampled node in a challenge set, or as the label of an in-neighbor of a sampled node) are identical. The reason is that otherwise we would have broken the binding property of $\mathsf{Com}(\cdot)$.

Therefore with probability at least $1-2^{-\Omega(n)}$, we get at least $\alpha\cdot N$ good nodes (with some extracted hash label for them and also for their in-neighbors) and also it holds that all the extracted hash labels are consistent (i.e., equal for the same node). By the (α,β)-depth-robustness of G, the set of good nodes will have an induced path $\overrightarrow{\mathsf{PT}}$ of size at least $\beta\cdot N$. For every node $v \in \overrightarrow{\mathsf{PT}}$, let w_v be equal to the string $(u_{v_1},\ldots,u_{v_d})$ where $v_1 \leq \cdots \leq v_d$ are the in-neighbors of v. Since $\overrightarrow{\mathsf{PT}}$ includes only good nodes that have passed the verification of the verifier, it holds that $sh_{\mathcal{P}}(w_v) = u_v$ where u_v is the extracted hash label of v. Hence, the sequence $(w_v)_{v\in\overrightarrow{\mathsf{PT}}}$ makes a chain of size $\beta\cdot N$. Thus, conditioned on the quality of the sampled $(\mathcal{P},\mathsf{rand}_2)$ as discussed above, with probability $(1-2^{-\Omega(n)}) > 9/10$ the adversary $\mathbf{Adv}_2$ gets a chain of size at least $\beta\cdot N + \log N > \beta\cdot N$ (including the nodes connecting $\overrightarrow{\mathsf{PT}}$ to the root of the Merkle tree). □

4. OPEN QUESTIONS

Using Time-Lock Puzzles to Achieve Fairness. One motivation for studying time-lock puzzles, and timed assumptions in general, is that they can be used to solve problems that are provably impossible in the standard model. For example, Boneh and Naor showed that *timed commitments* (ones that can be opened without the key in certain amount of time, but not faster) can be used to perform fair coin flipping [BN00], which was previously shown by Cleve to be impossible in the standard model [Cle86]. Boneh and Naor construct timed commitments based on the same assumption used by Rivest et al. [RSW96] to construct time-lock puzzles (the inherent sequentiality of exponentiation). Briefly, their coin-flipping protocol is as follows: Alice chooses a random bit b_a and sends $\mathsf{Com}(b_a)$ to Bob, where Com is a timed commitment. Bob chooses a random bit b_b and sends b_b to Alice. Alice verifies that b_b arrived fast enough (so Bob could not have forced open her commitment), and then opens the commitment. The result of the coin-flip is $b_a \oplus b_b$. The "timed" part of the commitment is used if Alice aborts before opening her commitment. In that case, Bob can spend a moderate amount of time to force-open the commitment and recover b_a without Alice's help. For this protocol to work, the time it takes to force open a commitment must be more than the maximum network latency. On the other hand, for efficiency, the time it takes to honestly open a commitment should be short as possible.

Mahmoody et al. [MMV11] showed that, in the random oracle model, timed commitments with a large time-gap (between the forced opening and an honest opening) cannot be constructed, hence we cannot use black-box constructions to implement them in the standard model. A natural approach would be to replace the timed commitment in the coin-flipping protocol with our proof of work: Alice sends a puzzle P to Bob, Bob sends a random bit-vector b_2, then Alice sends a bit-vector b_1 and proves it is the solution to the puzzle P. The result is taken to be $b_1 \cdot b_2$. This would be less efficient than using timed commitments, since Alice has to solve the puzzle even in an honest execution, but she can do the work offline, leaving the online phase of the protocol efficient. Unfortunately, this protocol is insecure: the soundness of our proof of work ensures that Alice spends time proportional to the honest solver, but still she may convince Bob to accept an incorrect solution b_1. An interesting open question is whether fair secure computation (and in particular fair coin flipping) is possible based on black-box sequentiality assumptions.

Necessity of Depth-Robust Graphs. The efficiency and security of our construction is tightly tied to the parameters of depth-robust graph constructions: graphs with lower degree give more efficient solutions, while graphs with higher robustness (the lower bound on the length of the longest path remaining after some of the vertices are removed) give us puzzles with smaller adversarial advantage. An interesting open question is whether the converse also holds: do time-lock puzzles with better parameters also imply the existence of depth-robust graphs with better parameters?

Space Complexity of the Solver. In our construction of time stamping and time-lock puzzles for time N, the solver keeps the hash labels of a graph of N vertices. Is there any other solution that uses $o(N)$ storage? Or is there any inherent reason that $\Omega(N)$ storage is necessary?

APPENDIX

A. TIME-LOCK PUZZLES IN THE RANDOM ORACLE MODEL

Our construction for Theorem 3.7 makes *black-box* use of sequential hash functions and collision-resistant hash functions. Both primitives can be easily constructed with unconditional security in the random oracle model (when time-complexity is measured by the number of oracle queries rather than computational effort) for every index distribution with super-logarithmic min-entropy. As a consequence, in this model we get unconditionally secure time-lock puzzles and time stamping schemes for any puzzle and/or document distribution with super-logarithmic min-entropy. Moreover, we can obtain time stamping protocols for any document distribution of super-logarithmic min-entropy.

More formally, in the random oracle model we model $\mathbf{Time}(\cdot)$ as the number of oracle queries and $\mathbf{ParTime}(\cdot)$ as the number of *rounds* of oracle queries. However, in the random oracle model (ROM), we can get stronger results: our construction is noninteractive and unconditionally secure. We prove the following theorem.

THEOREM A.1 (MAIN RESULT IN ROM). *Theorem 3.7 holds relative to any random oracle mapping $\{0,1\}^*$ to $\{0,1\}^n$ unconditionally for any distribution $\mathbf{D}$ of the messages with min-entropy $\omega(\log n)$. Moreover the verification of the scheme is noninteractive (i.e., no challenge is sent from the verifier to the puzzle solver).*

We prove Theorem A.1 by proving the following lemma, and using Fiat-Shamir transformation [FS86b] in the random oracle model.

LEMMA A.2. *Suppose $\mathbf{D} = \mathbf{D}_n$ is a distribution with min-entropy at least $\omega(\log n)$. Then relative to a random oracle from $\{0,1\}^*$ to $\{0,1\}^n$, there are efficient hash functions $\mathcal{CH}, \mathcal{SH}$ such that $\mathcal{CH}$ is collision resistant according to Definition 3.3 and $\mathcal{SH}$ is sequential according to Definition 3.2.*

A.1 Unconditional Interactive Construction in the ROM

In this subsection we prove Lemma A.2.

Implementing Hash Functions $sh(\cdot)$ and $ch(\cdot)$. For puzzle distributions of super-logarithmic mi-entropy, we pad the puzzle to become of size $|\mathcal{P}| \geq n$, and we use a random oracle of the same security parameter $\mathcal{O}\colon \{0,1\}^* \mapsto \{0,1\}^n$ as follows. The sequential hash function indexed by the puzzle $\mathcal{P}$, denoted $sh_{\mathcal{P}}(\cdot)$ is defined as follows: $sh_{\mathcal{P}}(x) = \mathcal{O}(\mathcal{P}, 0, x)$. To get the collision resistant hash function, we use $ch_{\mathcal{P}}(x) = \mathcal{O}(\mathcal{P}, 1, x)$ to map $2n$ bit strings to n bits.

Note that since our adversaries in this work always ask $\text{poly}(n) < 2^{o(n)}$ queries to $\mathcal{O}$, at the time $\mathcal{P} \stackrel{\$}{\leftarrow} \mathbf{D}$ is sampled, (except with $\text{negl}(n)$ probability) no query with prefix $\mathcal{P}$ is asked to $\mathcal{O}$ and therefore we can safely assume that both oracles $sh(\cdot)$ and $ch(\cdot)$ are completely random even conditioned on the $\text{poly}(n)$ preprocessing queries asked by the adversary. Therefore, to prove Lemma A.2 we just need to prove that random oracles can be *directly* used to get sequential and collision-resistant hash functions.

First we recall the well-known fact that a random oracle is collision-resistant.

LEMMA A.3 (RANDOM ORACLE IS COLLISION-RESISTANT). *Suppose $ch(\cdot)$ is a random oracle from $\{0,1\}^*$ to $\{0,1\}^n$. Then any adversary who asks at most $2^{o(n)}$ queries to $ch(\cdot)$ is able to find a collision $x \neq x', ch(x) = ch(x')$ with probability at most $2^{-\Omega(n)}$.*

Second we prove that the $sh(\cdot)$ is indeed a sequential function.

DEFINITION A.4. *A* chain *of length r relative to the oracle $sh(\cdot)$ is a sequence of strings $w_0, w_1 \ldots, w_r$ such that $sh(w_{i-1})$ is a (contiguous) substring of w_i for all $i \in [r]$.*

LEMMA A.5 (RANDOM ORACLE IS SEQUENTIAL). *Suppose $sh(\cdot)$ mapping $\{0,1\}^*$ to $\{0,1\}^n$. Then, no adversary with oracle access to $sh(\cdot)$ can break the η-sequential of $sh(\cdot)$ according to Definition 3.2 for any $\eta < 1$ and any $N = 2^{o(n)}$.*

PROOF. We prove the following claim.

CLAIM A.6. *Then and suppose A is an oracle algorithm who asks $2^{o(n)}$ queries of length at most $2^{o(n)}$ to $sh(\cdot)$ in $r-1$ adaptive rounds. The probability that A's queries include a chain of length r is at most $2^{-\Omega(n)}$.*

We first show how to conclude Lemma A.5 using Claim A.6. Suppose $\mathbf{Adv}$ is an adversary with oracle access to $sh(\cdot)$ who can break the sequential property of $sh(\cdot)$ according to Definition 3.2. By Claim A.6, the view of $\mathbf{Adv}$ after sending y as the last node the chain (in Construction 3.1) does not have any chain of length at least N. If $\mathbf{Adv}$ outputs any chain of length at least N ending at y, implies that $\mathbf{Adv}$ asks a total of $2^{o(n)}$ queries and inverts $sh(\cdot)$ over some y' in its view such that $sh(y')$ is not called by $\mathbf{Adv}$ (at the time y' was already in the view of $\mathbf{Adv}$). It is easy to see that, such inversion of a random oracle can succeed only with probability $2^{o(n)}$ when $sh(\cdot)$ is a random oracle.

Now, we prove Claim A.6. Suppose A has asked the queries $x_1, \ldots, x_\ell$ so far and is about to ask a new round of queries $y_1 \ldots, y_q$. We claim that with probability $1-2^{-\Omega(n)}$ the new queries $y_1, \ldots, y_q$ can only be the *last* nodes in any new chain in the view of A. Since the total number of queries of A is $2^{o(n)}$ we only need to prove the latter claim for one of the new queries, $y_i \in \{y_1, \ldots, y_q\}$ and the claim follows by a union bound. Let $X = \{x_1, \ldots, x_\ell, y_1, \ldots, y_{i-1}, y_{i+1}, \ldots, y_q\}$ be all the queries of A asked (or about to be asked) so far other than y_i. The total number of (contiguous) substrings of length n among all the elements of X is at most $2^{o(n)} \cdot 2^{o(n)} \leq 2^{o(n)}$ (because all those queries are of length $2^{o(n)}$ any substring is determined by choosing two points in the string). Since the answer to $sh(y_i)$ is a random string of length n, this answer will be different from all the contiguous substrings of the elements of X with probability at least $1 - 2^{-n}2^{o(n)} = 1 - 2^{-\Omega(n)}$.

Therefore, with probability at least $1 - 2^{-\Omega(n)}$ the length of the longest chain in the view of A can increase in each rounds of adaptive queries of A only by one (except with probability $2^{-\Omega(n)}$). Thus (by induction) the probability that A can output a chain of length r in $r-1$ rounds of queries is at most $2^{o(n)} \cdot 2^{-\Omega(n)} = 2^{-\Omega(n)}$. □

Lemmas A.5 and A.3 together Lemma A.2, which in turn proves our Theorem A.1 for the case of interactive verification.

A.2 Noninteractive Verification Using the Fiat-Shamir Transformation

In the random oracle model, by using the Fiat-Shamir transformation of Lemma A.7 we can remove the challenge message of the verifier in Construction 3.9 to make the verification completely noninteractive and obtain Theorem A.1.

Similarly to the previous subsection, here also we assume w.l.o.g. that the oracle $\mathcal{O}$ is completely random at the time the puzzle $\mathcal{P} \xleftarrow{\$} \mathbf{D}$ is chosen and given to the adversary. This is because we can pad all queries to $\mathcal{O}$ with $(\mathcal{P}, 3)$ and apply a similar argument to that of the sequential and collision hash functions $\mathcal{SH}, \mathcal{CH}$ above based on the $\omega(\log n)$ min-entropy of $\mathbf{D}$.

The following transformation is due to Fiat and Shamir [FS86a] and shows how to remove interaction from public-coin protocols in the random oracle model. For completeness, here we prove a special case in which there is only four messages exchanged, while we are interested in (almost) preserving the adaptivity of the adversary.

Lemma A.7 (Fiat-Shamir Transformation). *Suppose (P, V) is two party protocol using a random oracle $\mathcal{O}$ of output length n as follows.*

- *The protocol has only 4 messages: v_1, p_1, v_2, p_2 where v_1 and v_2 are public-coin messages of V and V does not use any private randomness to make her final decision.*
- *We have $|v_1| = n$ and $|v_2| \le \ell \cdot n$.*
- *The verifier rejects its interaction with probability $1-\varepsilon$ against* any *prover $\widehat{P}$ who:*
  1. *$\widehat{P}$ asks a total of q queries to the random oracle $\mathcal{O}$.*
  2. *$\widehat{P}$ has at most r rounds of adaptivity in its queries.*

Suppose (P', V') is a two-message *protocol defined based on (P, V) as follows: The second message v_2 of V is removed from the protocol and instead the oracle answers to the following queries are used $\mathcal{O}(v_1, p_1, 1), \mathcal{O}(v_1, p_1, 2), \ldots, \mathcal{O}(v_1, p_1, \ell)$. (Note that the number of obtained random bits this way will be exactly $n \cdot \ell = |v_2|$.) This randomness is used by the parties and the two messages of the prover (p_1, p_2) are sent together. Then it holds that any adversary $\widehat{P'}$ who interacts with V' and asks $q' = q/\ell$ number of queries to $\mathcal{O}$ and has at most $r' = r-1$ rounds of adaptivity is able to convince V' with probability at most $\varepsilon' = \varepsilon \cdot q$.*

Proof. For sake of contradiction suppose $\widehat{P'}$ is an adversary who interacts with V', asks at most $q' = q/\ell$ queries to $\mathcal{O}$, has at most $r' = r-1$ rounds of adaptivity, and is able to convince V' with probability $\varepsilon' > \varepsilon \cdot q$. We show how to get an adversary $\widehat{P}$ who interacts with V, asks at most $q' \cdot \ell = q$ oracle queries, has at most r rounds of adaptivity and is able to make V accept with probability at least $\varepsilon'/q = \varepsilon$, which is a contradiction.

First we modify $\widehat{P'}$ as follows.

- $\widehat{P'}$ never asks any query twice.
- $\widehat{P'}$ always asks the queries $\mathcal{O}(v_1, p_1, 1), \mathcal{O}(v_1, p_1, 2), \ldots, \mathcal{O}(v_1, p_1, \ell)$ before sending (p_1, p_2) in one round of adaptivity, if not asked already.
- If $\widehat{P'}$ makes any query of the form $\mathcal{O}(v_1', p_1', j)$ for any p_1' and $j \in [\ell]$, it also asks all the other queries $\{\mathcal{O}(v_1', p_1', i) \mid i \in [\ell], i \neq j\}$ in the same round of adaptivity. (Note that $\mathcal{O}(v_1', p_1', j)$ might be asked when v_1 is not known or p_1 is not decided yet).

The above changes might increase the total queries of $\widehat{P'}$ by a factor of ℓ and might add one round of adaptive queries to $\widehat{P'}$. The adversary $\widehat{P}$ works as follows:

1. When $\widehat{P'}$ asks for v_1, receive v_1 from V and forward it to $\widehat{P'}$.
2. Choose $i \xleftarrow{\$} [q]$ at random.
3. Emulate the execution of $\widehat{P'}$ by preserving the adaptivity of the queries as follows.
   (a) When $\widehat{P'}$ asks its i-th query $\mathcal{O}(y)$, if y is *not* of the form (v_1, p_1', j) for some $(p_1', j \in [\ell])$ then abort. Otherwise do the following:
      i. Send p_1' back to V as the first message of the prover and receive v_2.
      ii. Use v_2 to answer the query $\mathcal{O}(y)$ as well as all of $\{\mathcal{O}(v_1', p_1', i) \mid i \in [\ell], i \neq j\}$ that are going to be asked in the same round of adaptivity.
   (b) When the emulation of $\widehat{P'}$ is finished, suppose (p_1, p_2) is the generated message. If p_1 is different from p_1' (which was part of y) abort, otherwise send p_2 to V.

We claim that with probability $1/q$ over the random choice of $i \xleftarrow{\$} [q]$ the game above is a perfect emulation of the game in which $\widehat{P'}$ interacts with V'. The reason is that with probability $1/q$ the emulating adversary $\widehat{P}$ guesses the actual query $\mathcal{O}(v_1, p_1, 1)$ of $\widehat{P'}$ correctly, in which case since v_2 is completely random, we get a perfect emulation of the game of interaction between $\widehat{P'}$ and V' in the random oracle model (where a particular oracle query is answered using fresh randomness). Thus the emulation above leads to the accept of V with probability at least $\varepsilon' \cdot 1/q = \varepsilon$, while the number of rounds of oracle queries asked by $\widehat{P}$ is at most r. □

B. EXPLICIT CONSTRUCTIONS OF DEPTH ROBUST GRAPHS

In this section we prove Lemma 3.10 by showing how to obtain explicit (α, β)-depth robust graphs for constants $\alpha, \beta < 1$ that can be arbitrarily close to 1. Erdős, Graham and Szemerédi [EGS75] constructed (α, β)-depth robust graphs for some constants $0 < \beta < \alpha < 1$ based on a recursive use of constant-degree expanders. This construction can be made explicit using any explicit family of such expanders.

THEOREM B.1 ([EGS75]). *There exists an explicit family* $\{G_N\}$ *of DAGs with* N *vertices and in-degree* $d = O(\log N)$ *that is* (α, β)*-depth-robust for some* constants $0 < \beta < \alpha < 1$.

Using the proof of [EGS75] one can obtain, e.g., $\alpha = 99/100, \beta = 1/100$, but by minor modifications to the construction of [EGS75] one can obtain constants (α, β) that are arbitrarily close to 1 at the cost of larger degrees $\log^2 N$. For sake of completeness, in Section B we describe this construction. Our construction follows that of [EGS75] closely, with the difference that we use denser expanding graphs in the recursive construction.

DEFINITION B.2 (EXPANDING GRAPHS). *A bipartite graph* $G = (V_1, V_2, E)$, $|V_1| = |V_2| = M$ *is* A*-expanding if for every* $S_1 \subseteq V_1$ *and* $S_2 \subseteq V_2$ *such that* $|S_1| = |S_2| = \lceil M/A \rceil$ *there is an edge from* S_1 *to* S_2.

We use explicit constructions of A-expanding graphs of [RVW00, RVW01].

CONSTRUCTION B.3. *For simplicity suppose the number of vertices of our graph* G *is a power of two* $N = 2^t$, *and let* $\gamma = \varepsilon/\log N = \varepsilon/t$ *for arbitrarily small constant* ε. *We use the following recursive construction to get* $G = G_t$. *Let* G_1 *be a two-vertex graph with an edge between them. Informally,* G_{i+1} *consists of two identical copies of* G_i *connected with the edges of a bipartite* $(1/\gamma)$*-expanding graph. Formally,* $G_{i+1} = ((L_{i+1}, R_{i+1}), E_{i+1})$, *where* $L_{i+1} = \{1, \ldots, 2^i\}$, $R_{i+1} = \{2^i + 1, \ldots, 2^{i+1}\}$ *and the edges are*

$$E_{i+1} := E_i \cup \left\{(u + 2^i, v + 2^i) \mid (u, v) \in E_i\right\} \cup E'_{i+1} ,$$

where $G' = ((L, R), E'_{i+1})$ *is an explicit* $(1/\gamma)$*-expanding graph for* $L = \{1, 2, \ldots, 2^i\}$ *and* $R = \{2^i + 1, \ldots, 2^{i+1}\}$.

Degrees and Explicitness. The explicit expanding graphs we used in Construction B.3 to connect the two copies of G_i are all of in-degree $\widetilde{O}(\log N) < \log^2 N$ for large enough N. Since the depth of the recursion is $\lceil \log N \rceil$, the total in-degree of the final graph is at most $\widetilde{O}(\log^2 N) < \log^3 N$ for large enough N. The explicitness of our constructed graph follows from the explicitness of the expanding graphs used. In particular, given any node $v \in [N] = [2^t]$ let $v - 1 = (b_t, \ldots, b_1)$ where b_i is the i-th bit of the binary representation of $v - 1$. To know the list of in-neighbors of v in $G = G_t$ we will consider every $i \in [t]$ such that $b_i = 1$. The fact that $b_i = 1$ means that in the construction of G_i, the node v has been in the set R_i and we should find the list of the vertices L_i that are connected to it. The list of in-neighbors of v in G_i (which are due to the edges of the expanding graphs planted in G_i) can be computed in time polylog N (due to explicitness of G_i). Suppose the latter list is $\{v_1, \ldots, v_\ell\}$ where the binary representation of the numbers $v_j - 1$ (for all $j \in [\ell]$) have $i - 1$ bits. To get the index of v_j as a node in G we can take $u_j = 1 + (b_t, \ldots, b_{i+1}, 0, (v_j - 1))$. To find out all the in-neighbors of v in G we just have to go over all $i \in \lceil \log N \rceil$ and extract the in-neighbors as above.

Depth-Robustness. We now prove the depth-robustness of the DAG of Construction B.3.

LEMMA B.4. *For every* i *and* $\alpha \in (0, 1)$, *the graph* G_i *is* $(\alpha, \alpha - i\gamma)$*-depth-robust, and since* $\gamma = \varepsilon/\log N$, *the final graph* $G = G_{\log N}$ *is* $(\alpha, \alpha - \varepsilon)$*-depth-robust for every* $\alpha \in (0, 1)$.

PROOF. The proof is by induction over i. For $i = 1$, G_i consists of two vertices, and is trivially (α, α) depth-robust for all $\alpha \in (0, 1)$. Assuming the hypothesis holds for i, consider the graph $G_{i+1} = ((L_{i+1}, R_{i+1}), E_{i+1})$.

Fix an arbitrary $\alpha \in (0, 1)$. Suppose we select a subset S of the nodes of G_{i+1} of size at least $\alpha \cdot 2^{i+1}$ and call them "good" nodes. Let $\delta 2^i$ be the number of good nodes $S_L \subseteq S$ in L_{i+1}. Since the total number of good nodes is $\alpha 2^{i+1}$, there must be at least $(2\alpha - \delta)2^i$ good nodes $S_R \subseteq S$ in R_{i+1}. Below, by the length $|P|$ of a path P we denote the number of vertices in it.

By the induction hypothesis, there exists a path $P_L \subseteq S_L$ of good nodes such that $|P_L| \geq (\delta - i\gamma)2^i$. In the same way, there exists a path $P_R \subseteq S_R$ such that $|P_R| \geq (2\alpha - \delta - i\gamma)2^i$.

We must show that there exists a path $P \subseteq S_L \cup S_R = S$ such that $|P| \geq (\alpha - (i+1)\gamma)2^{i+1}$. If $\delta \leq 2\gamma$, then we can simply set $P = P_R$, since in this case $|P_R| \geq (2\alpha - (i+2)\gamma)2^i \geq (\alpha - (i+1)\gamma)2^{i+1}$. On the other hand if $\delta \geq 2\alpha - 2\gamma$, then in the same way we can set $P = P_L$. Otherwise, consider the set $\widehat{P}_R \subseteq P_R$ consisting of the first $\lceil \gamma 2^i \rceil$ nodes on P_R and the set $\widehat{P}_L \subseteq P_L$ consisting of the last $\lceil \gamma 2^i \rceil$ nodes on P_L. Since G_{i+1} contains a $(1/\gamma)$-expanding graph between the nodes of L_{i+1} and R_{i+1}, and given that $|\widehat{P}_L| = |\widehat{P}_R| = \lceil \gamma 2^i \rceil$, there exists an edge $(v_L, v_R) \in E_{i+1}$ going from $\widehat{P}_L$ to $\widehat{P}_R$. We define our new path P by connecting (most of) the paths P_L and P_R together with the edge (v_L, v_R) as follows: P is defined to be the nodes in P_L up to the node v_L, concatenated with the nodes of P_R starting from the node v_R. This way the number of vertices in P is at least

$$\begin{aligned}|P| &\geq |P_R| - (\lceil \gamma 2^i \rceil - 1) + |P_L| - (\lceil \gamma 2^i \rceil - 1) \\ &> (\delta - i\gamma + 2\alpha - \delta - i\gamma)2^i - 2\gamma 2^i = (\alpha - (i+1)\gamma)2^{i+1} .\end{aligned}$$

□

C. COMMITMENTS BY MERKLE TREES

Algorithm 5 shows how a Merkle tree is computed as a commitment to a set of strings with the possibility of opening the commitment to each string separately. Algorithm 6 describes how the opening is performed. To verify the decommitment of Algorithm 6 the receiver simply verifies the corresponding hash evaluations according to Algorithm 7. For simplicity, in this section we assume that the N strings being committed to are indexed by $\{0, 1, \ldots, N - 1\}$ (rather than $[N]$), but when we use the Merkle commitment we might choose to index the strings with $[N]$.

The following lemma asserts that if the family of hash functions $\mathcal{CH}$ from which $ch(\cdot)$ is sampled is collision resistant, then the commitment scheme based on the Merkle tree is binding. It can be shown that the commitment using Merkle trees has some strong hiding properties as well, but here we are only concerned with the binding property of such efficient commitments.

LEMMA C.1. *Suppose* **Adv** *is an adversary who sends a a Merkle-commitment string* $c \in \{0, 1\}^n$, *then send some* $i \in [N]$, *and finally Merkle-decommit successfully into* two different *values* $u_i \neq u'_i$ *(as the* i*-th string). Then there is*

Algorithm 5 (Merkle Commitment) For a hash function $ch\colon \{0,1\}^{2n} \mapsto \{0,1\}^n$ and N strings $u_0, \ldots, u_{N-1}$ from $u_i \in \{0,1\}^n$ the Merkle tree is computed as follows.

1: Let $t = \lceil \log N \rceil$, and define $u_i = 0^n$ for $N \le i < 2^t$.
2: **for** $i \in \{0, \ldots, 2^t - 1\}$ **do**
3: set $c_i^t = u_i$.
4: **for** $j \in \{t, t-1, \ldots 1\}$ **do** {compute $(j-1)$-th "layer" of the Merkle tree}
5: **for** $i \in \{0, 1, \ldots, 2^{j-1} - 1\}$ **do**
6: Let $c_i^{j-1} = ch(c_{2i}^j, c_{2i+1}^j)$
7: Output $c = c_0^0$ as the commitment string.

Algorithm 6 (Merkle Opening) For a hash function $ch\colon \{0,1\}^{2n} \mapsto \{0,1\}^n$ and as the Merkle commitment $c \in \{0,1\}^n$ for $N = 2^t$ strings of length n, the opening algorithm is as follows.

1: Receive some index $i \in \{0, \ldots, 2^t - 1\}$ as the index of the string to be opened.
2: Output u_i as the decommitment value.
3: To help the verifier verify the decommitment u_i, let $i = (b_t, \ldots, b_1)$ be the binary representation of i (i.e., $i = \sum_{j \in [t]} b_j 2^{j-1}$) and do the following.
4: **for** $j \in \{t, \ldots, 1\}$ **do**
5: Output the two strings $\overline{c}_0^j = c^j_{(b_t, \ldots b_{t-j+2}, 0)}$ and $\overline{c}_1^j = c^j_{(b_t, \ldots b_{t-j+2}, 1)}$ (from the j-th layer). (Note that one of $c^t_{(b_t, \ldots, b_2, 0)}$ and $c^t_{(b_t, \ldots, b_2, 1)}$ is simply equal the decommitted value u_i.)

Algorithm 7 (Merkle Verification) For a hash function $ch\colon \{0,1\}^{2n} \mapsto \{0,1\}^n$ and a received $c \in \{0,1\}^n$ as the Merkle commitment of $N = 2^t$ strings of length n, the verifying algorithm is as follows.

1: Send the index $i \in \{0, \ldots, 2^t - 1\}$ (i.e., the index of the string desired to be decommitted) to the opener of Algorithm 6 and let $i = (b_t, \ldots, b_1)$ be the binary representation of i.
2: Receive u_i as the decommitment value, and also receive the strings $\overline{c}_0^j$ and $\overline{c}_1^j$ for all $j \in [t]$.
3: Verify that $u_i = \overline{c}^t_{b_1}$.
4: Define $b_{t+1} = 0$ and $\overline{c}_0^0 = c$ (where c is the commitment string received before).
5: For all $j \in \{t, \ldots, 1\}$ (can be done in parallel) verify that $ch(\overline{c}_0^j, \overline{c}_1^j) = \overline{c}^{j-1}_{b_{t-j+2}}$.

---

an adversary **Adv**′ *who executes* **Adv** *as a black-box, asks* $O(\log N)$ *more queries to* $ch(\cdot)$*, and finds a collision:* $x \neq x', ch(x) = ch(x')$.

Proof. Let $t = \lceil \log N \rceil$. Suppose **Adv** is able to decommitment successfully into two different strings $u_i \neq u'_i$ as the i-th string with respect to the *same* commitment string c. For $j \in [t]$ let $\overline{c}_0^j$ and $\overline{c}_1^j$ be the pair of strings provided by **Adv** as the two needed strings from the j-th layer of the Merkle tree when decommitting to u_i, and similarly let $\overline{c'}_0^j$ and $\overline{c'}_1^j$ be the corresponding strings for u'_i. Define $\overline{c}_0^0 := c$ and $\overline{c'}_0^0 := c$. Since $\overline{c}^t_{b_1} = u_i \neq u'_i = \overline{c'}^t_{b_1}$, if we take j to be the smallest element in $[t]$ that $\overline{c}^j_{b_{t-j+1}} \neq \overline{c'}^j_{b_{t-j+1}}$, it holds that $ch(x) = \overline{c}^{j-1}_{b_{t-j+2}} = ch(x')$ for $x = (\overline{c}_0^j, \overline{c}_1^j) \neq (\overline{c'}_0^j, \overline{c'}_1^j) = x'$. **Adv**′ is able to find such colliding pair by computing the relevant $2t$ hash labels $ch(\cdot)$. □

D. ACKNOWLEDGMENTS

We thank the anonymous CRYPTO 2011 reviewers of our previous paper [MMV11], whose comments led us to investigate the topics in this paper. We also thank Moni Naor, Leslie Valiant, and Avi Wigderson for pointers to relevant work and Yuval Ishai for helpful discussions. Finally, we thank the anonymous ITCS 2013 reviewers for their helpful comments.

E. REFERENCES

[ABSW01] A. Ansper, A. Buldas, M. Saarepera, and J. Willemson, *Improving the availability of time-stamping services*, Information Security and Privacy, 6th Australasian Conference, ACISP, 2001, pp. 360–375.

[BdM91] J. Benaloh and M. de Mare, *Efficient broadcast time-stamping*, Tech. Report 1, Clarkson University Department of Mathematics and Computer Science, August 1991.

[BdM93] J. C. Benaloh and M. de Mare, *One-way accumulators: A decentralized alternative to digital sinatures (extended abstract)*, EUROCRYPT, 1993, pp. 274–285.

[BG08] Boaz Barak and Oded Goldreich, *Universal arguments and their applications*, SIAM J. Comput. **38** (2008), no. 5, 1661–1694.

[BHS92] D. Bayer, S. Haber, and W. S. Stornetta, *Improving the efficiency and reliability of digital time-stamping*, Sequences II: Methods in Communication, Security and Computer Science (R. M. Capocelli et al., ed.), Springer-Verlag, 1992, pp. 329–334.

[BL98] A. Buldas and P. Laud, *New linking schemes for digital time-stamping*, Information Security and Cryptology, 1998, pp. 3–13.

[BLLV98] A. Buldas, P. Laud, H. Lipmaa, and J. Villemson, *Time-stamping with binary linking schemes*, CRYPTO, 1998, pp. 486–501.

[BLS00] A. Buldas, H. Lipmaa, and B. Schoenmakers, *Optimally efficient accountable time-stamping*, Public Key Cryptography, 2000, pp. 293–305.

[BN00] Dan Boneh and Moni Naor, *Timed commitments*, CRYPTO (Mihir Bellare, ed.),

Lecture Notes in Computer Science, vol. 1880, Springer, 2000, pp. 236–254.

[BR93] Mihir Bellare and Phillip Rogaway, *Random Oracles are Practical: A Paradigm for Designing Efficient Protocols*, ACM Conference on Computer and Communications Security, 1993, pp. 62–73.

[CGH04] Ran Canetti, Oded Goldreich, and Shai Halevi, *The random oracle methodology, revisited*, J. ACM **51** (2004), no. 4, 557–594.

[Cle86] Richard Cleve, *Limits on the security of coin flips when half the processors are faulty (extended abstract)*, STOC, ACM, 1986, pp. 364–369.

[CLSY93] Jin-yi Cai, Richard J. Lipton, Robert Sedgewick, and Andrew Chi-Chih Yao, *Towards uncheatable benchmarks*, Structure in Complexity Theory Conference, 1993, pp. 2–11.

[DGN03] Cynthia Dwork, Andrew Goldberg, and Moni Naor, *On memory-bound functions for fighting spam*, CRYPTO (Dan Boneh, ed.), Lecture Notes in Computer Science, vol. 2729, Springer, 2003, pp. 426–444.

[DN92] Cynthia Dwork and Moni Naor, *Pricing via processing or combatting junk mail*, Crypto '92, 1992, LNCS No. 740, pp. 139–147.

[DNW05] Cynthia Dwork, Moni Naor, and Hoeteck Wee, *Pebbling and proofs of work*, CRYPTO (Victor Shoup, ed.), Lecture Notes in Computer Science, vol. 3621, Springer, 2005, pp. 37–54.

[DTT10] Anindya De, Luca Trevisan, and Madhur Tulsiani, *Time space tradeoffs for attacks against one-way functions and PRGs*, Advances in Cryptology - CRYPTO 2010, 30th Annual Cryptology Conference, Santa Barbara, CA, USA, August 15-19, 2010. Proceedings (Tal Rabin, ed.), Lecture Notes in Computer Science, vol. 6223, Springer, 2010, pp. 649–665.

[EGS75] Paul Erdős, Ronald L. Graham, and Endre Szemerédi, *On sparse graphs with dense long paths*, Computers & Mathematics with Applications **1** (1975), 365–369.

[FN99] Fiat and Naor, *Rigorous time/space trade-offs for inverting functions*, SICOMP: SIAM Journal on Computing **29** (1999).

[FS86a] Fiat and Shamir, *How to prove yourself: Practical solutions to identification and signature problems*, CRYPTO: Proceedings of Crypto, 1986.

[FS86b] A. Fiat and A. Shamir, *How to Prove Yourself: Practical Solutions to Identification and Signature Problems*, Crypto '86, 1986, LNCS No. 263, pp. 186–194.

[GT03] Shafi Goldwasser and Yael Tauman, *On the (in)security of the fiat-shamir paradigm*, Proc. 44th FOCS, IEEE, 2003.

[Hel80] Martin E. Hellman, *A cryptanalytic time-memory trade-off*, IEEE Transactions on Information Theory **26** (1980), no. 4, 401–406.

[HS91] Stuart Haber and W. Scott Stornetta, *How to time-stamp a digital document*, J. Cryptology **3** (1991), no. 2, 99–111.

[JM10] Y.I. Jerschow and M. Mauve, *Offline submission with rsa time-lock puzzles*, Computer and Information Technology (CIT), 2010 IEEE 10th International Conference on, 29 2010-july 1 2010, pp. 1058–1064.

[JM11] Yves Igor Jerschow and Martin Mauve, *Non-parallelizable and non-interactive client puzzles from modular square roots*, ARES 2011: Proceedings of thc 6th International Conference on Availability, Reliability and Security, August 2011.

[KC10] Ghassan Karame and Srdjan Capkun, *Low-cost client puzzles based on modular exponentiation*, ESORICS (Dimitris Gritzalis, Bart Preneel, and Marianthi Theoharidou, eds.), Lecture Notes in Computer Science, vol. 6345, Springer, 2010, pp. 679–697.

[Kil92] Joe Kilian, *A note on efficient zero-knowledge proofs and arguments (extended abstract)*, STOC, ACM, 1992, pp. 723–732.

[LLL82] Lenstra, Lenstra, and Lovasz, *Factoring polynomials with rational coefficients*, MATHANN: Mathematische Annalen **261** (1982).

[Mic00] Silvio Micali, *Computationally sound proofs*, SIAM J. Comput. **30** (2000), no. 4, 1253–1298.

[MMV11] Mohammad Mahmoody, Tal Moran, and Salil P. Vadhan, *Time-lock puzzles in the random oracle model*, CRYPTO (Phillip Rogaway, ed.), Lecture Notes in Computer Science, vol. 6841, Springer, 2011, pp. 39–50.

[MSTS09] Tal Moran, Ronen Shaltiel, and Amnon Ta-Shma, *Non-interactive timestamping in the bounded storage model*, J. Cryptology **22** (2009), no. 2, 189–226.

[PR80] Wolfgang J. Paul and Rüdiger Reischuk, *On alternation ii. a graph theoretic approach to determinism versus nondeterminism*, Acta Inf. **14** (1980), 391–403.

[PTC77] Wolfgang J. Paul, Robert Endre Tarjan, and James R. Celoni, *Space bounds for a game on graphs*, Mathematical Systems Theory **10** (1977), 239–251.

[RSW96] Ronald L. Rivest, Adi Shamir, and David A. Wagner, *Time-lock puzzles and timed-release crypto*, Tech. Report MIT/LCS/TR-684, MIT, February 1996.

[RTV04] Omer Reingold, Luca Trevisan, and Salil P. Vadhan, *Notions of reducibility between cryptographic primitives.*, Theory of Cryptography, First Theory of Cryptography Conference, TCC 2004, Lecture Notes in Computer Science, vol. 2951, Springer, 2004, pp. 1–20.

[RV10] Guy N. Rothblum and Salil P. Vadhan, *Are PCPs inherent in efficient arguments?*, Computational Complexity **19** (2010), no. 2, 265–304.

[RVW00] Reingold, Vadhan, and Wigderson, *Entropy waves, the zig-zag graph product, and new constant-degree expanders and extractors*,

FOCS: IEEE Symposium on Foundations of Computer Science (FOCS), 2000.

[RVW01] ———, *Entropy waves, the zig-zag graph product, and new constant-degree expanders and extractors*, ECCCTR: Electronic Colloquium on Computational Complexity, technical reports, 2001.

[Sch82] Georg Schnitger, *A family of graphs with expensive depth reduction*, Theor. Comput. Sci. **18** (1982), 89–93.

[Sch83] ———, *On depth-reduction and grates*, FOCS, IEEE, 1983, pp. 323–328.

[TBFN07] Suratose Tritilanunt, Colin Boyd, Ernest Foo, and Juan Manuel González Nieto, *Toward non-parallelizable client puzzles*, CANS (Feng Bao, San Ling, Tatsuaki Okamoto, Huaxiong Wang, and Chaoping Xing, eds.), Lecture Notes in Computer Science, vol. 4856, Springer, 2007, pp. 247–264.

[Val77] Leslie G. Valiant, *Graph-theoretic arguments in low-level complexity*, MFCS (Jozef Gruska, ed.), Lecture Notes in Computer Science, vol. 53, Springer, 1977, pp. 162–176.

On the Power of Nonuniformity in Proofs of Security

Kai-Min Chung
Cornell University
Ithaca, NY, USA
chung@cs.cornell.edu

Mohammad Mahmoody*
Cornell University
Ithaca, NY, USA
mohammad@cs.cornell.edu

Huijia Lin†
MIT and Boston University
Cambridge, MA, USA
huijia@csail.mit.edu

Rafael Pass‡
Cornell University
Ithaca, NY, USA
rafael@cs.cornell.edu

ABSTRACT

Nonuniform proofs of security are common in cryptography, but traditional black-box separations consider only uniform security reductions. In this paper, we initiate a formal study of the power and limits of nonuniform black-box proofs of security. We first show that a known protocol (based on the existence of one-way permutations) that uses a nonuniform proof of security, and it *cannot* be proven secure through a uniform security reduction. Therefore, nonuniform proofs of security are indeed provably more powerful than uniform ones.

We complement this result by showing that many known black-box separations in the uniform regime actually do extend to the nonuniform regime. We prove our results by providing general techniques for extending certain types of black-box separations to handle nonuniformity.

Categories and Subject Descriptors

F.1.3 [**COMPUTATION BY ABSTRACT DEVICES**]: Complexity Measures and Classes—*Relations among complexity measures*

*Supported in part by NSF Award CNS-1217821.

†Supported by DARPA grant FA8750-11-2-0225 and NSF grant CCF-1018064.

‡Supported in part by a Alfred P. Sloan Fellowship, Microsoft New Faculty Fellowship, NSF Award CNS-1217821, NSF CAREER Award CCF-0746990, AFOSR YIP Award FA9550-10-1-0093, and DARPA and AFRL under contract FA8750-11-2- 0211. The views and conclusions contained in this document are those of the authors and should not be interpreted as representing the official policies, either expressed or implied, of the Defense Advanced Research Projects Agency or the US Government

ITCS'13, January 9–12, 2013, Berkeley, California, USA.

Keywords

Black-Box Separations, Proofs of Security, Nonuniformity

1. INTRODUCTION

Most of cryptography relies on unproved hardness assumptions, such as the existence of one-way functions and one-way permutations, the hardness of factoring, etc. Understanding the minimal assumptions needed for proving the security of cryptographic tasks is thus of fundamental importance. Understanding *barriers* to such proofs of security has been an active line of research in the last decades since the seminal work of Impagliazzo and Rudich [37]. Their work demonstrates barriers to providing a "black-box construction" of key-agreement from one-way permutations—a black-box construction of a primitive $\mathcal{Q}$ (e.g., key-agreement) uses a primitive $\mathcal{P}$ (e.g., one-way permutations) as an oracle, while the specific details of the implementation of $\mathcal{P}$ is ignored by the construction; additionally, the proof of security is also black-box in the sense that the security reduction only uses the presumed attacker to $\mathcal{Q}$ as a black-box in order to violate the security of $\mathcal{P}$. Subsequently, many other black-box separations between cryptographic primitives have been established (e.g., [1, 10, 25, 25, 26, 38, 53, 55]); this paradigm has also been used to demonstrate lower bounds on the *efficiency* of black-box constructions (e.g., [5,6,13,22,32,39,41]). Very recently, several works [24,47,48] demonstrated barriers to proofs of security that apply even when the construction is non-black-box (that is, the implementation of $\mathcal{Q}$ may use the code of $\mathcal{P}$ instead of just treating it as an oracle) as long as just the proof of security is black-box.

The result of [37] and its follow-ups, however, suffer from the following restriction: They rule out only constructions with *uniform* proofs of security—that is, the "security reduction" is a uniform polynomial-time algorithm. In contrast, some quite commonly used techniques in cryptography make use of *nonuniformity* in the proof of the security (see e.g., [29–31, 36, 42]). For example, a common technique is to use a hybrid argument that involves nonuniformly fixing some "prefix" of the experiment to be the "best possible" value for the reduction. This may be thought of as a mild form of non-black-box access to the code (of the primitive and the adversary) by the security reduction. In some cases, initial nonuniform proofs of security were eventually made uniform. A celebrated example is the result of of [35], making the security reduction of the pseudorandom generator construction of [36] uniform (see [27] for more examples), but in general it is not clear whether nonuniformity makes proofs of security more powerful or not, leaving open the following question:

> *Are nonuniform proofs of security inherently more powerful than uniform ones, or can any nonuniform proof of security be made uniform?*

A closely related question is whether (known) barriers for uniform security extend to the nonuniform regime:

> *Do (known) black-box separations handling uniform security reductions extend to handle also nonuniform security reductions?*

In this work we address the above two questions. We answer the first question affirmatively—showing that a known protocol (specifically, the non-malleable commitment of [42], which is based on the existence of one-way permutations) that uses a nonuniform black-box proof of security cannot be proven secure using a uniform black-box proof of security. Thus, assuming the existence of one-way permutations, nonuniform proofs of security are provably more powerful than uniform ones.

Regarding the second question, we show that, although in general black-box separations for the uniform regime do not extend to uniform regime, many *known* black-box separations for the uniform regime actually do extend to the nonuniform regime. We prove our results by providing general techniques for extending certain types of black-box separations to handle nonuniformity. But before further explaining our result, we need to formally define nonuniform proofs of security.

1.1 Formalizing Nonuniform Proofs of Security

Let us start by recalling the formalization of a black-box proofs of security from [49]. In a black-box proof of security for a cryptographic scheme Q based on some cryptographic assumption P, a security proof S^A is an efficient oracle Turing machine that uses any adversary A who breaks Q as an oracle and breaks the security of P; we use the terms "security proof" or "security reduction" interchangeably. In a *black-box construction* [49] the implementation of the new primitive Q uses a implementation of the primitive P as an oracle, and the security reduction also may only access P as an oracle.

In order to allow the security reduction to be nonuniform, an initial approach would be to allow the security reduction S to be a nonuniform circuit (rather than an efficient Turing machine). More formally, we may extend the definition of a black-box security reduction to the nonuniform setting by requiring the existence of an efficient *circuit* S that for every adversary A breaking the security of Q, S^A breaks P. This "naive" way of defining a nonuniform proof of security, however, does not capture known nonuniform proof techniques where, for instance, the security reduction fixes some "prefix" of a computation to its "best value".[1] The reason is that for such nonuniform proofs of security, the nonuniform advice (i.e., the "best value" fixed by the reduction) can depend on the adversary A. Thus, such use of nonuniform advice may be viewed as a limited form of non-black-box use of the adversary. To also capture such techniques, we instead allow the nonuniform advice to be selected as a function of the adversary A and P.

DEFINITION 1.1 (GENERAL CONSTRUCTIONS). *A (general)* construction *of the primitive $\mathcal{Q}$ from another primitive $\mathcal{P}$ is consists of the following:*

- **Construction Mapping Q.** *There exists a mapping $Q(\cdot)$ such that: if P is an efficient implementation for $\mathcal{P}$, $Q(P)$ is an efficient implementation for $\mathcal{Q}$.*
- **Nonuniform Proof of Security.** *For every (computationally unbounded) adversary A breaking the security of the efficient construction $Q(P)$, there is a polynomial-size circuit S (which may depend on A and Q) such that S^A breaks the security of P.*

DEFINITION 1.2 (FULLY BLACK-BOX CONSTRUCTIONS). *A* fully black-box construction *of the primitive $\mathcal{Q}$ from another primitive $\mathcal{P}$ consists of:*

- **Black-box Construction Q.** *For every (computationally unbounded) oracle P implementing $\mathcal{P}$, Q^P implements $\mathcal{Q}$.*
- **Nonuniform Proof of Security.** *For every (computationally unbounded) oracle P implementing $\mathcal{P}$ and every (computationally unbounded) adversary A breaking the security of Q^P (as an implementation of $\mathcal{Q}$), there exists a polynomial-size security reduction S (which may depending on A and P) such that $S^{P,A}$ breaks the security of P as an implementation of $\mathcal{P}$.*

The above way of treating nonuniform proofs of security is closely related to a notion considered in [3, 43, 52] in the context of hardness amplification, and Lu [43] in the context of constructions of pseudorandom generators from one-way functions; however, as far as we know, no general treatment of non-uniformity in the context of black-box separations exists.

Before describing our results, let us briefly mention the work of Koblitz an Menezes [40] which argues that it is "unnatural and undesirable" to use non-uniform proof of security for "practice-oriented" cryptography. We do not take a stand on this claim; however, in our opinion, due to the extensive use of nonuniform proofs of security in the current cryptographic literature, we believe it is of crucial importance to understand the power and limitations of such techniques in a precise and formal way.

1.2 Our Results

1.2.1 Separating the power of uniform and nonuniform security reductions

Our first results shows a separation between the power of uniform and nonuniform proofs of security.

THEOREM 1.3 (INFORMALLY STATED). *There exists a construction C of commitments from one-way permutations with a nonuniform security reduction such that: the existence of a uniform security reduction for C means that the one-way permutation in use is efficiently invertible. Thus, nonuniform proofs of security are provably more powerful than uniform ones.*

[1] In fact, known black-box separations for the uniform regime easily extend also to this "naive" nonuniform setting.

As mentioned earlier, the commitment scheme we consider is not an artificial one—it is the actual non-malleable commitment scheme constructed in [42].[2] To prove the above theorem, we show that the recent framework of [47]—which proves barriers to cryptographic constructions using uniform security reductions—can be extended to rule security proofs for commitment schemes of the above type. Interestingly, as we shall shortly see, the actual result proven in [47] indeed extends to the nonuniform regime, but we can still use this framework for our separation.

Related Work. The work of Backes and Unruh [4] compares the power of uniform and non-uniform security reductions (the former are called *constructive* proofs in [4]). They present a cryptographic protocol Π, assuming some new (and very strong) complexity-theoretic objects, such that security of Π cannot be based on the collision-resistance of a class of hash functions using a uniform security reduction, but can be proven secure using a non-uniform security reductions; the authors also argue that using non-standard assumption may be needed to establish such a separation result. In contrast, our Theorem 1.3 is unconditional (and is additionally demonstrated for a natural scheme already appearing the literature).

1.2.2 Handling nonuniform reductions in fully black-box constructions

As mentioned, following the seminal work of Impagliazzo and Rudich [37] there has been a large body of work proving barriers to providing a "black-box construction" of various tasks from various primitives. Ten years after the work of [37], using a "reconstruction technique," Gennaro and Trevisan [23] (in the context of studying the efficiency of the black-box constructions) showed that a random permutation $P\colon \{0,1\}^n \mapsto \{0,1\}^n$ with overwhelming probability is *nonuniformly-hard* to invert. We first observe that the result of [23] can be used to directly extend the original result of [37] to rule out black-box constructions of key-agreement from one-way permutations also with respect to nonuniform proofs of security. This follows since: **(1)** [37] show how to break all key-agreement protocols through a *single* inefficient but $\mathrm{poly}(n)$-query attack, and **(2)** [23] show that any fixed computationally unbounded algorithm that gets $\mathrm{poly}(n)$ bits of advice about the random permutation P and may ask $\mathrm{poly}(n)$ queries to P, has negligible probability of inverting P; thus, if a black-box construction with a nonuniform security proof had existed, we could use the $\mathrm{poly}(n)$-query attacker A^P of [37] in conjunction with the nonuniform security reduction S to obtain a fixed computationally unbounded algorithm S' that inverts a random permutation P by getting $\mathrm{poly}(n)$ bits of advice about P and asking only $\mathrm{poly}(n)$-queries to it (contradicting [23]).

The "reconstruction technique" of [23] has subsequently been employed in several other black-box separation results [21, 32, 33] and by the same argument these results also extend to the nonuniform setting.

In this work, we also establish new black-box separations results in the non-uniform setting, and a primitive that we focus on is the families of collision-resistant hash functions. We note that although nonuniform hardness results have been proved also for other (idealized forms of) cryptographic primitives [14], as far as we know, no nonuniform hardness result have been proved for families of collision-resistant hash functions, leaving open the question of whether there exists a black-box construction of a key-agreement protocol from families of collision-resistant hash functions with a nonuniform proof of security. (It is well-known that in the uniform setting, the separation of [37] easily extends to hash functions.) We start by proving such a separation also in the nonuniform setting.

THEOREM 1.4. *There is no fully black-box construction of key-agreement protocols from families of collision-resistant hash functions even with a nonuniform proof of security.*

Since public-key encryption and oblivious transfer both imply key-agreement in a black-box way [25], Theorem 1.4 extends to separate families of collision-resistant hash functions from those primitives as well. Our proof proceeds by proving a nonuniform hardness lower bound for families of collision-resistant hash functions, and next relying on the above proof template sketched for the case of one-way permutations.

THEOREM 1.5 (NONUNIFORM COLLISION RESISTANCE). *Let the function $h\colon \{0,1\}^k \times \{0,1\}^m \mapsto \{0,1\}^n$ be chosen uniformly at random and $k \geq 4n, m > n$. Then with $1 - \mathrm{negl}(n)$ probability h will be $2^{n/10}$-secure as a collision-resistant hash function family $\{h_K : K \in \{0,1\}^k\}$. Namely, any circuit of size $2^{n/10}$ with h gates can find collision in h for at most $2^{n/10}$ fraction of the keys $K \in \{0,1\}^k$.*

The proof of Theorem 1.5 follows by a simple counting argument and an application of a lemma due to Unruh [54] (see Lemma 4.2). The proof extends to any *family* version of natural cryptographic primitives.

By applying Theorem 1.5 we also extend some earlier lower bounds [5, 22] on the *efficiency* of black-box constructions from families of collision-resistant hash functions to the nonuniform regime.

THEOREM 1.6. (Efficiency of constructions using FCRHs.)

1. *Any fully black-box construction $G\colon \{0,1\}^\ell \mapsto \{0,1\}^{\ell+k}$ of PRGs from families of collision-resistant hash functions with a nonuniform security reduction needs $\Omega(k/\log n)$ oracle calls to FCRHs.*

2. *Any fully black-box construction of digital signatures from FCRHs with a nonuniform security reduction and for messages of length at least n bits and needs $\Omega(n)$ oracle calls to FCRHs.*

1.2.3 Handling nonuniform reductions in general constructions

In recent years, new types of black-box separations have emerged. These types of separation apply even to non-black-box constructions, but still only rule out black-box proofs of security: Following the works of Brassard [11] and Akavia et al [2], demonstrating limitations of "NP-hard Cryptography",[3] Pass [46] and Pass, Tseng and Venkitasubramaniam [48] demonstrate that under certain (new) complexity

[2] [42] also provide a construction of a non-malleable commitment based on one-way functions; our separation does not seem to apply to this protocol.

[3] See also the results of Feigenbaum and Fortnow [18] and the result of Bogdanov and Trevisan [8] that demonstrate limitations of NP-hard cryptography for *restricted* types of reductions.

theoretic assumptions, various cryptographic tasks cannot be based on *one-way functions* using a black-box security reduction, even if the protocol uses the one-way function in a non-black-box way. Very recently, two independent works demonstrate similar types of lower bounds, but this time ruling our security reductions to a *general* set of intractability assumptions: Pass [47] demonstrates unconditional lower bounds on the possibility of using black-box reductions to prove the security of several primitives (e.g., Schnorr's identification scheme, commitment scheme secure under weak notions of selective opening, Chaum Blind signatures, etc) based on any "bounded-round" intractability assumption (where the challenger uses an a-priori bounded number of rounds, but is otherwise unbounded). Gentry and Wichs [24] provides a lower bound (assuming the existence of strong pseudorandom generators) on the possibility of using black-box security reductions to prove soundness of "succinct non-interactive arguments" (SNARGs) based on any "falsifiable" assumption (where the challenger is computationally bounded). Both of the above-mentioned work fall into the "meta-reduction" paradigm of Boneh and Venkatesan [9], which was previously used to prove separations for restricted types of reductions (see e.g., [12, 20, 34]).

As with the literature on fully black-box separations, the results of [24, 47] are only proved in the context of uniform security reductions. Here, we show that these results actually do extend to the nonuniform regime as well.

THEOREM 1.7 (INFORMALLY STATED). *The separations results of [24, 47] hold also when considering nonuniform black-box proofs of security.*

2. PRELIMINARIES

2.1 Notation

For any Boolean string x, by $|x|$ we denote the length of x. By $[k]$ we denote the set $\{1, \ldots, k\}$. We use bold letters (e.g., $\mathbf{x}$) when referring to random variables. By $x \xleftarrow{\$} \mathbf{x}$ we mean that x is sampled according to the distribution of the random variable $\mathbf{x}$. We use calligraphic letters (e.g., $\mathcal{S}$) to denote sets (e.g., events over random variables) and cryptographic primitives (e.g., one-way function). We use sans-serif letters (e.g., NP) to denote complexity classes. For a set $\mathcal{S}$, by $\mathbf{U}_\mathcal{S}$ we mean the random variable with uniform distribution over $\mathcal{S}$, and by $x \xleftarrow{\$} \mathcal{S}$ we mean $x \xleftarrow{\$} \mathbf{U}_\mathcal{S}$. By the *support* of the random variable $\mathbf{y}$, represented by $\mathrm{Supp}(\mathbf{y})$, we mean $\{y \mid \Pr[\mathbf{y} = y] > 0\}$. For jointly distributed random variables $(\mathbf{x}, \mathbf{y})$, and for any $y \in \mathrm{Supp}(\mathbf{y})$, the conditional distribution $(\mathbf{x} \mid y)$ is the random variable $\mathbf{x}$ conditioned on $\mathbf{y} = y$.

When we say that an event parameterized by n occurs with negligible probability, denoted by $\mathrm{negl}(n)$, we mean that it occurs with probability $n^{-\omega(1)}$, and we say it happens with overwhelming probability if it happens with probability $1 - \mathrm{negl}(n)$. We call two random variables $\mathbf{x}, \mathbf{y}$ (or their corresponding distributions) over the support set $\mathcal{S}$ ε-close if their statistical distance, defined as $\Delta(\mathbf{x}, \mathbf{y}) = \frac{1}{2} \cdot \sum_{s \in \mathcal{S}} |\Pr[\mathbf{x} = s] - \Pr[\mathbf{y} = s]|$, is at most ε. We call an algorithm D an ε-distinguisher between the random variables $\mathbf{x}$ and $\mathbf{y}$ if $|\Pr[D(\mathbf{x}) = 1] - \Pr[D(\mathbf{y}) = 1]| \geq \varepsilon$. It is easy to see that if there is any D that ε-distinguishes between $\mathbf{x}$ and $\mathbf{y}$, then $\Delta(\mathbf{x}, \mathbf{y}) \geq \varepsilon$.

We use the term *efficient* for any *probabilistic* algorithm that runs in polynomial time over its input length. By the *size* of a circuit we refer to the number of bits that is required to describe it. So the number of circuits of size k will be at most 2^k.

2.2 Intractability Assumptions and Security Reductions

We recall the definition of an intractability assumption from [47] (see also [15, 24, 33, 45, 50]).

DEFINITION 2.1 (INTRACTABILITY ASSUMPTIONS). *A* intractability assumption $\mathcal{C}$ *is a two party game between a* challenger Chal *and an adversary* Adv *where both parties get* 1^n *as common input and* Chal *at the end outputs accept or reject. Any intractability assumption* $\mathcal{C}$ *has a* security threshold $\tau_\mathcal{C}$ *assigned to it which is a constant in the interval* $[0, 1)$. *We say that an interactive algorithm* Adv breaks $\mathcal{C}$, *if* Adv *(over the common input* 1^n*) can make* Chal *accept with probability* $\tau_\mathcal{C} + \varepsilon(n)$ *for a nonnegligible function* $\varepsilon(n)$. *When the adversary wins with probability* $\tau_\mathcal{C} + \varepsilon$ *we say that he has won the game with* advantage ε. *We say that* $\mathcal{C}$ *can be* uniformly (resp. nonuniformly) broken *if there is a PPT (resp.* $\mathrm{poly}(n)$*-sized circuit)* Adv *that breaks* $\mathcal{C}$. *A* falsifiable *assumption is an intractability assumption where* Chal *is polynomial-time in the length of the messages it receives. A* bounded-round *assumption is an intractability assumption where the game between* $\mathcal{C}$ *and* Adv *has a fixed* $\mathrm{poly}(n)$ *number of rounds.*

Cryptographic Primitives. A cryptographic primitive is a syntactical requirement over a set of algorithms performing some cryptographic task. For example if $\mathcal{P}$ denotes the primitive one-way permutation, then it simply requires some algorithm P that computes some (hopefully one-way) permutation. We call (a computationally unbounded) oracle P an *implementation* of the primitive $\mathcal{P}$, if P satisfies the syntactical requirements of $\mathcal{P}$ (when all composed in one algorithm). We say an algorithm P *efficiently* implements $\mathcal{P}$ if it implements $\mathcal{P}$ and runs in polynomial time. We always assume that the algorithm P implementing the primitive $\mathcal{P}$ takes as its first input 1^n (and if it is efficient, it will run in time $\mathrm{poly}(n, |x|)$ where x is the main input). In most primitives the security parameter n can be related to the input length. For example in case of one-way function, n is usually taken to be equal to the input length, or for the case of PKE, it could be the length of the random seed used in the key-generation.

The security of (the efficient implementations of) almost all cryptographic primitives can be modeled as an intractability assumption. For instance, the security game of signature schemes is falsifiable, but it is not bounded-round, since the adversary is allowed to choose the number of received signatures before trying to forge one; soundness of a constant-round interactive argument, on the other hand, is a bounded-round assumption, but not falsifiable since checking whether an attacker succeeds is not efficient. The security threshold is usually either 0 (e.g., inverting a one-way function) or 1/2 (e.g., distinguishing a PRG from a uniform string).

DEFINITION 2.2 (CRYPTOGRAPHIC PRIMITIVES). *A cryptographic primitive* $\mathcal{P}$ *is a tuple* $(\mathcal{F}_\mathcal{P}, \mathcal{R}_\mathcal{P})$ *where every* $P \in$

$\mathcal{F}_\mathcal{P}$ is a function implementing P, and $\mathcal{R}_\mathcal{P}$ is a relation whose first component is always in $\mathcal{F}_\mathcal{P}$. When $(P, A) \in \mathcal{R}_\mathcal{P}$, we say that the "adversary" A breaks P (as an implementation of $\mathcal{P}$). By P_n we denote the implementation P restricted to the security parameter n. We restrict ourself to "natural" primitives where the security of any implementation P of $\mathcal{P}$ is defined through an intractability game with security threshold $\tau_\mathcal{P}$ that only depends on $\mathcal{P}$.

In the following, we formalize the definition of cryptographic constructions (fully black-box and general) and security reductions (uniform and non-uniform) separately. Formal variants of Definitions 1.2 and 1.1 can be obtained directly from these definitions.

DEFINITION 2.3 (CRYPTOGRAPHIC CONSTRUCTIONS). *A (general)* construction *of the primitive $\mathcal{Q}$ from another primitive $\mathcal{P}$ is a mapping $Q(\cdot)$ such that: if P is an efficient implementation for $\mathcal{P}$, $Q(P)$ is an efficient implementation for $\mathcal{Q}$. A* black-box construction *is a particular form of construction such that: $Q(P)$ is defined through an efficient (uniform) oracle machine Q accessing P only as an oracle, and Q^P is an implementation for $\mathcal{Q}$ for* any *(possibly inefficient) implementation P of $\mathcal{P}$.*

We might use the terms "non-black-box" and "general" (constructions) interchangeably.

DEFINITION 2.4 (SECURITY REDUCTIONS). *We say that a (general or black-box) construction Q of a primitive $\mathcal{Q}$ from another primitive $\mathcal{P}$ has a* nonuniform *(black-box) security reduction, if for every implementations P for $\mathcal{P}$ and $Q(P)$ for $\mathcal{Q}$, and every adversary A such that A_n breaks $Q_n(P)$ (over security parameter n) with advantage $\varepsilon \geq 1/\operatorname{poly}(n)$, there is a $\operatorname{poly}(n/\varepsilon)$-sized* oracle circuit *$S$ (whose code might depend on (P, A)) such that S^{P,A_n} breaks the security of P_m for some polynomially related security parameter $m = n^{\Theta(1)}$. A* uniform *security reduction is defined similarly by requiring the code of $S^{P,A_n}(1^n, 1^{1/\varepsilon})$ to be uniform and independent of the choices of the oracles (P, A).*

We might use the terms "security reduction" and "proof of security" interchangeably.

One can potentially define non-black-box proofs of security as well, but throughout this paper security reductions are always black-box.

REMARK 2.5. *The reason that we allow the security reduction S to call A only over a single security parameter n (which is polynomially related to $m = n^{\Theta(1)}$) is that here we work with the "almost-everywhere" notion of security (where any infinite–but arbitrarily sparse–sequence of security parameters $\{n_1 < n_2 \ldots\}$ over which A "wins" shall be transformed into a sequence of security parameters $\{m_1 < m_2 \ldots\}$ over which P is broken).*

The formal definition of a general construction of a primitive $\mathcal{Q}$ from another primitive together $\mathcal{P}$ with a non-uniform security reduction (i.e. the formalized form of Definition 1.1) can be obtained directly from Definitions 2.3 and 2.4. For the case of black-box constructions, we employ the following terminology whose uniform variant is due to [49].

DEFINITION 2.6 (FULLY BLACK-BOX CONSTRUCTIONS). *A* fully *black-box construction of a primitive $\mathcal{Q}$ from another primitive $\mathcal{P}$ consists of a black-box construction Q of $\mathcal{Q}$ from $\mathcal{P}$ together with a (uniform or nonuniform) black-box security reduction for this construction.*

For every fixed efficient implementation P of a primitive $\mathcal{P}$, and every (black-box or non-black-box) construction Q of primitive $\mathcal{Q}$ from $\mathcal{P}$, a black-box reduction of the security of $Q(P)$ to that of P can usually be modeled as an intractability assumption. Thus, intractability assumptions allow us to model the (uniform or nonuniform) proofs of security for cryptographic constructions directly (regardless of whether the construction is black-box or not).

Note that any intractably assumption $\mathcal{C} = (\mathsf{Chal}, \mathsf{Adv})$ can be considered as a cryptographic primitive $\widetilde{\mathcal{C}}$ such that: the set of implementations of $\widetilde{\mathcal{C}}_n$ (over security parameter n) only contains the empty function, and the security of $\widetilde{\mathcal{C}}_n$ is defined based on the interactive game $(\mathsf{Chal}, \mathsf{Adv})$ over security parameter n. Based on this perspective, the following definition formalizes what it means to base a cryptographic primitive on such a primitive.

DEFINITION 2.7 (REDUCTIONS TO ASSUMPTIONS). *We say that a cryptographic primitive $\mathcal{Q}$ can be based on a intractability assumption $\mathcal{C} = (\mathsf{Chal}, \mathsf{Adv})$ through a uniform (resp. non-uniform) black-box reduction iff there exists a construction of $\mathcal{Q}$ from $\mathcal{P} = \widetilde{\mathcal{C}}$ with a uniform (resp. non-uniform) security reduction.*

Refuting the possibility of basing a cryptographic primitive $\mathcal{Q}$ on any (falsifiable/bounded round/general) intractability assumption through a uniform (resp. non-uniform) black-box reduction immediately rules out the possibility of basing $\mathcal{Q}$ on a large class of natural cryptographic primitives (whose security for efficient implementations are of the form of intractability assumptions) for uniform (resp. nonuniform) black-box security reductions.

2.3 Special Soundness and Witness Hiding

We assume the reader is familiar with the notions Witness Indistinguishability and Commitment schemes. We refer the reader to [28] for formal definitions.

Special Soundness. Recall that a three-round public-coin interactive proof is said to be *special-sound*, if a valid witness to the statement x can be efficiently computed from any two accepting proof-transcripts of x which have the same first message but different second messages. [47] considers a relaxation of this notion—referred to as *computational special-soundness*—where **(a)** the number of communication rounds is any constant (instead of just three), **(b)** the extractor may need a polynomial number of accepting transcripts (instead of just two), and **(c)** extraction need only succeed if the transcripts are generated by communicating with a computationally-bounded prover (see Section 4 for a formal definition). All traditional constant-round public-coin proofs of knowledge protocols (such as [7, 29, 31, 51], as well as instantiations of [7, 29] using statistically-hiding commitments) satisfy this property, and continue to do so also under parallel repetition. We say that a computationally special-sound protocol has a *large challenge space* if the length of the verifier challenge is $\omega(\log n)$ on common inputs of length n.

DEFINITION 2.8 (COMPUTATIONAL SPECIAL-SOUNDNESS). *Let (P, V) be a k-round (where k is a constant) public-coin* *interactive argument for the language $L \in \mathsf{NP}$ with witness relation R_L. (P, V) is said to be* computationally special-sound *if there exists a polynomial $m(\cdot)$, and a polynomial-time extractor machine X, such that for every polynomial-time deterministic machine P^*, and every polynomial $p(\cdot)$, there exists a negligible function $\mu(\cdot)$ such that the following holds for every $x \in L$ and every auxiliary input z for P^*. Let $\vec{T} = (T_1, T_2, \ldots T_{p(|x|)})$ denote transcripts in $p(|x|)$ random executions between $P^*(x, z)$ and $V(x)$ where V uses the same randomness for the first $k-2$ messages (thus, the first $k-1$ messages are the same in all transcripts). Then, the probability (over the randomness used to generate $\vec{T}$) that:*

1. *$\vec{T}$ contains a set of $m(|x|)$ accepting transcripts with different round $k-1$ messages; and*
2. *$X(\vec{T})$ does not output a witness $w \in R_L(x)$*

is smaller than $\mu(|x|)$. We say that a computationally special-sound protocol has a large challenge space *if the length of the verifier challenge is $\omega(\log n)$ on common inputs of length n.*

Witness Hiding. A desirable property of interactive proofs is that they "hide" the witness used by the prover. We will consider a very weak notion of sequential witness hiding: roughly speaking, a protocol is said to be weakly sequential witness hiding if no polynomial time attacker can always recover the witness for any statement that it hear polynomially many sequential proofs of.

Definition 2.9 (Breaking Weak Witness Hiding). *Let (P, V) be an argument for the language L with witness relation R_L. We say that (a potentially unbounded) A* breaks weak $\ell(\cdot)$-sequential witness hiding of (P, V) *with respect to R_L if for every $n \in \mathbb{N}$, $x \in L \cap \{0,1\}^n$, and $w \in R_L(x)$, A wins in the following experiment with probability 1: Let $A(x)$ sequentially communicate with $P(x, w)$ $\ell(n)$ times; A is said to win if it outputs a witness w' such that $w' \in R_L(x)$. (P, V) is called* weakly $\ell(\cdot)$-sequentially witness hiding *w.r.t R_L if no polynomial time algorithm A breaks weak $\ell(\cdot)$-sequential witness hiding of (P, V) w.r.t R_L.*

Let us now state the uniform separation result of [47]:

Theorem 2.10 (Main Result of [47]). *Let (P, V) be a computationally-special-sound argument with large challenge space for the language L with a unique witness relation R_L, and let $\mathcal{C}$ be an $r(\cdot)$-round assumption where $r(\cdot)$ is a polynomial. If for every polynomial $\ell(\cdot)$ there exists a black-box security reduction S for basing weak $\ell(\cdot)$-sequential witness hiding of (P, V) w.r.t R_L on intractability assumption $\mathcal{C}$ w.r.t threshold $\tau_{\mathcal{C}}$, then there exists an efficient algorithm B such that $B(1^n)$ breaks $\mathcal{C}$ w.r.t. $\tau_{\mathcal{C}}$ with advantage $\varepsilon(n)$ for a nonnegligible $\varepsilon(n)$.*

Pass [47] shows how Theorem 2.10 can be used to separate several well-known cryptographic protocols/primitive (e.g., Schnorr's identification scheme, commitment scheme secure under weak notions of selective opening) from any intractability assumption w.r.t. uniform black-box reductions. It directly follows that if Theorem 2.10 is extended to the nonuniform setting, then these corollaries also extend to the nonuniform setting. We refer the reader to [47] for more details on these corollaries.

3. SEPARATING UNIFORM AND NONUNIFORM SECURITY REDUCTIONS

In this section, we demonstrate that a commitment scheme from [42] (LPV), which is proven secure based on the existence of one-way permutations through a *nonuniform* black-box proof of security, cannot be based on any bounded-round falsifiable assumptions through a uniform black-box proof of security; in particular, it cannot be based on the existence of one-way permutations using a uniform black-box proof of security. As such, we separate the power of nonuniform and uniform black-box proofs of security (assuming the existence of one-way permutations). Let us start by reviewing the LPV protocol.

The LPV protocol is a non-malleable commitment scheme [16], where the committer and the receiver receive as common input a security parameter n and an identity id of some length $\ell(n)$. To commit to a value v, committer and the receiver proceeds in three stages. In Stage 1, the receiver sends a random string $s \in \{0,1\}^n$. Then in Stage 2, the committer commits to v by sending string c using a non-interactive perfectly binding commitment scheme com. Finally, in Stage 3, the committer proves that either c is a valid commitment to v or it knows the pre-image of s through a one-way permutation f (that is, that it knows a string r such that $f(r) = s$). More specifically, the witness relation used is defined as follows: witness relation $R_L = \{((s, c), y) \mid f(y) = s \text{ or } c = \mathsf{com}(y; r) \text{ for some } r\}$. This is proved using $4\ell(n)$ invocations of a 3-round public-coin WI special-sound (WISSP) argument. Messages in these WISSP arguments are scheduled according to a special scheduling based on id that guarantees that there exist at least $2\ell(n)$ sequential WISSP arguments in the protocol. Our result will only rely on this fact, and thus for simplicity of exposition, below we outline our result w.r.t. a simplified protocol consisting of 2ℓ sequential WISSP arguments in Stage 3.[4] We refer to this protocol as $(C, R)_\ell$.

The following lemma is shown in [42].

Lemma 3.1 ([42]). *Let ℓ be any polynomial. Assuming the existence of one-way permutations, $(C, R)_\ell$ is perfectly binding and computationally hiding with a nonuniform black-box proof of security.*

To highlight the power of nonuniformity in security reductions, let us briefly sketch a proof of this lemma. Fix a polynomial ℓ. Assume that there is an adversary A (w.l.o.g. deterministic) that breaks the hiding property of the LPV protocol $(C, R)_\ell$; that is, for two values v_0, v_1, the adversary A after receiving a commitment to one of the values chosen at random, can guess with inverse polynomial probability which value it has received a commitment to. We now demonstrate the existence of a nonuniform reduction R that with black-box access to A breaks the computational hiding property of the perfectly binding commitment com. Since A is deterministic, the first message s that it sends is fixed. Thus the reduction R can receive as a nonuniform advice the pre-image r of s through the OWP f (i.e, a string r such that $f(r) = s$). Then, after receiving a com commitment c to one of the two values v_0, v_1 chosen at random, it can use the adversary A to guess which value it receives a commitment to by forwarding c to A and simulating all the WISSP

[4]It is easy to see that the same argument applies also to the original LPV protocol.

arguments using r as a fake witness; finally, it outputs A's guess. It follows from the witness indistinguishability property of the WISSP argument that R^A has inverse polynomial advantage in guessing whether it received a commitment to v_0 or v_1.

Let us now turn to showing the impossibility of basing the hiding property of the LPV protocol on any bounded-round falsifiable assumptions through a *uniform* black-box proof of security.

THEOREM 3.2. *Let $\mathcal{C}$ be an $r(\cdot)$-round falsifiable assumption where $r(\cdot)$ is a polynomial. If for every polynomial $\ell(\cdot)$ there exists an efficient black-box security reduction S for basing the hiding property of $\langle C, R\rangle_\ell$ on assumption $\mathcal{C}$ w.r.t threshold $\tau_\mathcal{C}$, then there exists an efficient algorithm B and a polynomial $p(\cdot)$ such that for infinitely many $n \in N$, $B(1^n)$ breaks $\mathcal{C}$ with advantage $1/p(n)$.*

Here, we provide an outline of the proof. See the full version for a full proof.

3.1 Outline of the Proof of Theorem 3.2

At first sight, it would seem that Theorem 3.2 directly follows from Theorem 2.10: At a very high-level, the LPV protocol simply consists of many sequentially repeated special-sound arguments (that are also constant-round and public coin) for the statement (s, c) defined by the messages in Stage 1 and 2. Additionally, demonstrating hiding, at the very least implies that these protocols are weakly $l(n)$-sequentially witness hiding (or else, the committed value can be completely recovered!).

However, this approach does not go through as Theorem 2.10 only provides a separation in the case of *unique witness languages*, whereas R_L admits two witnesses for every statement. To get around this problem, we consider a unique witness relation $R_{L'}$ for which every statement (s, c) only has one unique witness that is the unique committed value in c.

But if we change the language, the proofs in Stage 3 of the protocol are no longer special-sound for the witness relation $R_{L'}$, since for a specific instance (s, c), it might be easy to invert s and therefore the value extracted from a WISSP argument (in Stage 3 of the LPV protocol) might be the pre-image r instead of the committed value, violating the (computational) special soundness property for $R_{L'}$. We resolve the problem by observing that, in fact, the proof of the Theorem 2.10, when restricted to falsifiable bounded-round assumption (as opposed to general bounded-round assumption) in [47] itself is black-box and uniform[5]. Roughly speaking, theorem 2.10 states that if (P, V) is computationally special-sound for a unique witness language L, then it is impossible to base the sequential witness hiding property on any bound-round falsifiable assumptions through uniform black-box security reduction. This is proven by showing that for any (public-coin, constant-round) interactive protocol (P, V), if there is a uniform black-box security reduction S for basing its sequential witness hiding property for $R_{L'}$ on any bounded-round falsifiable assumption, then there is a *uniform meta reduction* M that with black-box access to S can violate the computational special-soundness of (P, V) w.r.t. $R_{L'}$. In our context, since (P, V) is a special-sound proof for R_L (as opposed to $R_{L'}$), this meta reduction may either violate computational special-soundness of (P, V) w.r.t. R_L, or may output a pre-image r to s. However, as long as s is chosen at random by M, we can thus use such an M to invert a random string s through f (assuming that computational special-soundness of (P, V) for R_L holds). See Section 3 for the detailed proof.

Let us briefly comment on the why the above proof sketch does not extend to nonuniform proofs of security (whereas as we shall see in Section 4.1, the main theorem of [47] does). The problem is that if the reduction S is nonuniform, it may get as nonuniform advice the string s (or some function of it); this means that in the above proof, M can no longer choose the string s uniformly at random (since S would notice this). Indeed, in the actual nonuniform proof of security of LPV, the reduction does get the pre-image of s as nonuniform advice.

[5]In fact, the proof of Theorem 2.10 as stated in [47] in actually *nonuniform*, but for the special case that the intractability assumption is falsifiable, the proof is uniform.

4. REFUTING NONUNIFORM REDUCTIONS TO INTRACTABILITY ASSUMPTIONS

In this section we prove Theorem 1.7.

4.1 Extending Theorem 2.10 to Nonuniform Security Reductions

Here we show how to extend Theorem 2.10 to handle nonuniform proofs of security. Pass showed how Theorem 2.10 can be used to prove that certain well known cryptographic protocols/primitive (e.g., Schnorr's identification scheme, commitment scheme secure under weak notions of selective opening) can not be based on any bounded-round intractability assumption through a black-box proof of security. It follows that all corollaries of [47] also extend to the nonuniform regime.

THEOREM 4.1. *Let (P, V) be a computationally-special-sound argument with large challenge space for the language L with a unique witness relation R_L, and let $\mathcal{C}$ be an $r(\cdot)$-round assumption where $r(\cdot)$ is a polynomial. If for every polynomial $\ell(\cdot)$ there exists a nonuniform black-box security reduction S for basing weak $\ell(\cdot)$-sequential witness hiding of (P, V) w.r.t R_L on intractability assumption $\mathcal{C}$ w.r.t threshold $\tau_\mathcal{C}$, then there exists an nonuniform polynomial-time algorithm B and a polynomial $p(\cdot)$ such that for infinitely many $n \in N$, $B(1^n)$ breaks $\mathcal{C}$ with advantage $1/p(n)$.*

Note that in Theorem 4.1 we consider also nonuniform security reductions S, but the conclusion is slightly weaker than the conclusion of Theorem 2.10: the machine B breaking the assumption $\mathcal{C}$ is no longer uniform, but it now is a nonuniform polynomial-time algorithms.

In the following we outline the proof of Theorem 4.1. See the full version of the paper for the full proof.

4.1.1 Outline of the Proof of Theorem 4.1

Let us start by briefly outlining the high-level approach used in the result of [47] and explain why handling nonuniform proofs of security becomes an issue. Assume there exists a security reduction S (and for now, assume that S is uniform) such that S^A breaks the assumption $\mathcal{C}$ whenever A breaks weak sequential witness hiding of a (computationally) special-sound argument (P, V) for a language with unique witnesses. We want to use S to directly break $\mathcal{C}$ *without the help of* A. So, (following the paradigm of [9]), the goal will be to efficiently emulate A for S (i.e., we will construct a "meta-reduction" M which uses the underlying reduction S to break $\mathcal{C}$). We consider a particular computationally unbounded oracle A that after hearing an appropriate number of proofs using (P, V) (acting as a verifier) simply outputs a witness to the statement proved. The idea is to "extract" out the witness that A is supposed to provide S by "rewinding" S—since (P, V) is computationally special-sound, S, intuitively, must know a witness for all statements x that it proves to A. (There are several obstacles in formalizing this approach. The main one is that the reduction S is not a "stand-alone" prover—it might *rewind and reset* the oracle A, so it is no longer clear that it needs to "know" a witness for x in order to convince A of x. It is here that the proof of [47] relies on the fact that there are multiple proofs being provided by S; this gives the meta-reduction more opportunities to rewind S, which enables extraction even if S "nests" its queries to A in an arbitrary way. We refer the reader to [47] for further details.

Let us point out a crucial component in the above proof: To succeed in its emulation of S, it is imperative that whenever A is acting as a verifier, it chooses fresh random coins to generate its messages, even in case A is rewound (technically, this is achieved by letting A generate its messages by applying a random function to its queries). This is needed to ensure that M can "rewind" S (in order to extract out a witness), sending it new verifier messages, while ensuring that S provides an answer back with the same probability as if S communicated with A. In other words, to ensure that M succeeds in extracting witnesses from S, we require A's verification message to have essentially "full entropy", or else S may be able to notice that it is being rewound, and may abort its computation. In the context of nonuniform reductions, we can no longer guarantee that A's answers have high entropy: S gets a nonuniform advice string as a function of A, and thus the conditional entropy of the answers of A drops. Our approach for getting around this problem is that: although the conditional entropy of A's answers drops (once S gets its nonuniform advice), for all but a polynomial number of "bad" queries to A, the answers to the remaining "good" queries will still have high enough entropy. In fact, by an argument due to Unruh [54], it can be shown that the conditional distribution of answers to "good" queries is statistically close to the original distribution of A.

LEMMA 4.2 (INFORMAL VARIANT OF [54]). *Suppose A is a randomized oracle, and suppose S is an oracle algorithm that gets as input a non-uniform (polynomial-size) advice z as function of (the description of) A, and then asks polynomially many queries to A. Then there is a "pre-sampling" algorithm* Samp *that given z samples s query-answers of A (according to their true distribution based on A), and the view of $S^A(z(A))$ is $1/\operatorname{poly}(n)$-close in another experiment in which S is given z, then* $\mathsf{Samp}(z)$ *samples a partial domain of A, then A gets* resampled *on every other point other than the outputs of* $\mathsf{Samp}(z)$*, and finally $S(z)$ gets executed with oracle access to the (newly sampled) A.*

If the reduction S had only queried these "good" queries (that are *not* presampled by Samp), we would already be done. But, S may of course ask also "bad" queries (i.e. the ones presampled by $\mathsf{Samp}(\cdot)$). To deal with this, we present a *nonuniform meta reduction M*—M receives as a nonuniform advice the set of "bad" queries (which may depend on the nonuniform advice of S), and for each of these queries, the answer that A actually would provide. M can then perfectly emulate "bad" queries (using its nonuniform advice), and as before emulate good queries (in a statistically close manner) by using rewindings. As a conclusion we get that the existence of a security reduction S can be used to break the intractability assumption $\mathcal{C}$ in *nonuniform polynomial time*.

4.2 Succinct Non-Interactive Arguments

In this section we show how to extend a result of Gentry and Wichs [24] on the impossibility of basing succinct non-interactive arguments (SNARGs) for NP on any falsifiable assumption to the nonuniform regime. We start by recalling the formal definition of SNARGs.

A succinct non-interactive argument system Π consists of three efficient algorithms (G, P, V): The generation algorithm G on input security parameter 1^n outputs a common reference string crs and a private verification state priv. The prover algorithm P on input crs, a statement $x \in \{0,1\}^n$ and a witness w outputs a proof π. The verifier algorithm V on input priv, x, and π outputs a bit $b \in \{0,1\}$ represents whether V accepts or rejects the proof π for x.

DEFINITION 4.3 (SUCCINCT NONINTERACTIVE ARGUMENTS). *$\Pi = (G, P, V)$ is a succinct non-interactive argument (SNARG) for an* NP *language L with relation R_L if following holds. (Below $|x| = n$ and by negligible we mean* $\operatorname{negl}(n)$.*)*

- **Completeness:** *For every $(x, w) \in R_L$ the probability that the verifier V rejects in the following experiment is negligible: (i) $(\mathsf{crs}, \mathsf{priv}) \leftarrow G(1^n)$, (ii) $\pi \leftarrow P(\mathsf{crs}, x, w)$, and (iii) $b \leftarrow V(\mathsf{priv}, x, \pi)$.*
- **(Adaptive) Soundness:** *For every efficient cheating prover P^*, the probability that the verifier V accepts in the following experiment is negligible: (i) $(\mathsf{crs}, \mathsf{priv}) \leftarrow G(1^n)$, (ii) P^* on input crs outputs both a statement x and a proof π, and (iii) $b \leftarrow V(\mathsf{priv}, x, \pi)$.*
- **Succinctness:** *The length of a proof $\pi \leftarrow P(\mathsf{crs}, x, w)$ generated by the prover is $n^{o(1)}$.*

We mention that for the simplicity of exposition, in the above definition, we restrict the length of statements to be the same as the security parameter n, and define the succinctness property by $|\pi| \le n^{o(1)}$. Our extension of the results of [24] holds for the general definition in [24] as well. We now recall the formal result of [24].

THEOREM 4.4 ([24]). *Assuming the existence of subexponentially hard one-way functions, for any SNARG $\Pi = (G, P, V)$ that satisfies the completeness and succinctness properties, the adaptive soundness of Π can not be based on any falsifiable assumption $\mathcal{C}$ through a* uniform *black-box reduction, unless $\mathcal{C}$ can already be broken (nonuniformly).*

Note that Theorem 4.4 only rules out *uniform* black-box security proof of adaptive soundness. Our goal is to extend the theorem to also rules out *nonuniform* black-box security proof. Towards this goal, we note that core of the proof of Theorem 4.4 in [24] is the construction of two adversarial provers, and we identify the key properties of the two adversarial provers that are needed by us.[6]

[6]Lemma 4.1 in [24] is stated only w.r.t. *efficient* distinguishers (indicating them to be uniform), but since it assumes the

LEMMA 4.5 (LEMMA 4.1 IN [24]). *Assuming the existence of sub-exponentially hard pseudorandom generators, for any SNARG system* $\Pi = (G, P, V)$ *that satisfies the completeness and succinctness properties, there exist two adversarial provers* A *and* B *that satisfy the following properties.*

- *A breaks the adaptive soundness of Π but is inefficient, whereas B is efficient.*
- *A and B are computationally indistinguishable in the following sense: for any polynomial-sized circuit family $\{D_n\}$ it holds that*

$$\left|\Pr[D_n^A = 1] - \Pr[D_n^B = 1]\right| = \mathrm{negl}(n).$$

- *Both A and B are randomized and* stateless *and use fresh independent randomness to generate answers to distinct queries (which are the* crs*'s).*

The third property allows us to view A (resp., B) as a deterministic algorithm that given any query $q = \mathsf{crs}$, access fresh randomness $RO(q)$ and returns $A(q, RO(q))$ (resp., $B(q, RO(q))$). We can think of $RO(\cdot)$ as a random oracle with long enough outputs length[7]. More explicitly, by $A[RO]$ we emphasize on the fact that A is using the sampled random oracle $RO \xleftarrow{\$} \mathbf{RO}$.

We are ready to extend Theorem 4.4 to rules out *nonuniform* black-box security proof.

THEOREM 4.6. *Assuming the existence of sub-exponentially hard pseudorandom generators, for any SNARG system* $\Pi = (G, P, V)$ *that satisfies the completeness and succinctness properties, the adaptive soundness of* Π *can not be based on any falsifiable assumption* $\mathcal{C}$ *through a* nonuniform *black-box reduction, unless* $\mathcal{C}$ *can already be broken (nonuniformly).*

Recall that $\mathbf{RO}$ denotes the distribution of random oracles, and for any partial length preserving function F suppose $\mathbf{RO}[F]$ denotes the distribution of random oracles with pre-sampled part F.

To prove Theorem 4.6 we again use Lemma 4.2 an a careful hybrid argument similar to the proof of Theorem 4.1. See the full version of the paper for the full proof.

5. REFUTING NONUNIFORM REDUCTIONS FOR FULLY-BLACK-BOX CONSTRUCTIONS

In this section we prove our results of Theorems 1.4, 1.5, and 1.6. We start by proving Theorem 1.5 and then will prove Theorems 1.4 and 1.6 based on that.

We also show how the techniques used in the proofs of these theorems can be used to obtain different proofs of nonuniform hardness for other primitives such as one-way permutations as well as extending known black-box separations in the uniform regime to the nonuniform regime.

Nonuniform Collision-Resistance of Random Hashing and Beyond. Here we prove Theorem 1.5 about the nonuniform hardness of random functions as families of collision-resistant hash functions. In fact we prove the following stronger theorem:

THEOREM 5.1 (NONUNIFORM COLLISION RESISTANCE). *Let the function* $\mathbf{h}\colon [K] \times [M] \mapsto [N]$ *be chosen uniformly at random. If for* $d, t \in \mathbb{N}$ *it holds that* $dN^3 < 2t^5 K$, *then for every t-query adversary A with d bits of advice z that may depend on h:* $A^h(i, z)$ *can find a collision pair for the hash function* $h_i(\cdot) = h(i, \cdot)$ *with probability at most* $3t^2/N$ *over the choice of* $h \xleftarrow{\$} \mathbf{h}, i \xleftarrow{\$} [K]$ *and the randomness of A.*

Instead of proving Theorem 5.1, in fact we prove a more general lemma about the non-uniform hardness of *families* of ideal primitives, if the ideal primitive is already (uniformly) secure against bounded-query adversaries.

LEMMA 5.2 (HARDNESS OF FAMILIES OF PRIMITIVES). *Suppose* $\mathbf{O}$ *is a randomized oracle such that any computationally unbounded t-query adversary A "wins" in the "game"* $A^{\mathbf{O}}$ *only with probability at most* ε *where the notion of winning only depends on the transcript of* $A^{\mathbf{O}}$. *Suppose* FO *is another randomized oracle which consists of* $K = 2^k$ *independent samples* $O_1, \ldots, O_K$ *from* $\mathbf{O}$ *accessed through a k-bit prefix to the queries. We define* $A^{\mathsf{FO}}(i)$ *wins iff the transcript of the interaction of A with O_i indicates a win for A. Suppose A also receives d bits of advice z about the oracle* FO. *Then for any such advice function, and any* $s \leq K$:

$$\Pr_{i \xleftarrow{\$} [K], \mathsf{FO} \xleftarrow{\$} \mathsf{FO}} [A^{\mathsf{FO}}(i, z(\mathsf{FO}))\ wins] \leq \varepsilon + s/K + \sqrt{td/2s}.$$

The high level idea behind the proof of Lemma 5.2 is to use Lemma 4.2 as follows. Each sampled oracle O_i could be considered as an answer returned by a random oracle over domain $[K]$. By Lemma 5.2 the oracle answers to most of the indexes in $[K]$ remain statistically close to uniform, even given a "small" advice about all of $\mathsf{FO} = [O_1, \ldots, O_K]$. So for a "typical" $i \xleftarrow{\$} [K]$, the job of the adversary to win against O_i is just as hard as the case there were no advice.

See the full version of the paper for a formal proof of Lemma 5.2 and how to derive Lemma 5.1 from it.

A Lemma for Ruling Out Nonuniform Security Reductions. Variants of the following lemma in the *uniform* regime has been used in some previous work [5, 13, 44].

LEMMA 5.3. *Let* $\mathcal{P}$ *and* $\mathcal{Q}$ *be two cryptographic primitives and* $\mathcal{P}$ *has security threshold zero and let* $\mathbf{O}$ *be a randomized oracle. Suppose the following two holds:*

1. *For* any *black-box construction* $Q^{\mathbf{O}}$ *of* $\mathcal{Q}$ *from* $\mathbf{O}$ *there is an adversary* Adv *who asks* $q(n)$ *oracle queries to* $\mathbf{O}$ *and breaks the security of* $Q_n^{\mathbf{O}}$ *(over security parameter* n*) with non-negligible probability* $\varepsilon > 1/\mathrm{poly}(n)$.
2. *There exists a black-box construction* $P^{\mathbf{O}}$ *of* $\mathcal{P}$ *from* $\mathbf{O}$ *such that for any* $m = n^{\Theta(1)}$ *any* $\mathrm{poly}(n)(q(n)+1)$*-query adversary T who receives* $\mathrm{poly}(n)$ *bits of advice about* $\mathbf{O}$ *can break* $P_m^{\mathbf{O}}$ *only with negligible probability* $\mathrm{negl}(n)$.

Then there is no black-box construction of $\mathcal{Q}$ *from* $\mathcal{P}$ *even with a nonuniform proof of security. Moreover, to rule out constructions in which* Q_n *only calls* P_n, *we only need to consider* $m = n$ *in second condition above.*

subset-membership problem to be non-uniformly hard, the very same proof given for Lemma 4.1 handles nonuniform distinguishers as well, so we state and use this lemma in this form.

[7]By padding the queries q appropriately, we can assume w.l.o.g that $RO(\cdot)$ is length preserving.

See the full version of the paper for a proof of Lemma 5.3.

Proving Theorems 1.4 and 1.6. Here we prove Theorems 1.4 and 1.6. Roughly speaking Theorem 1.4 can be concluded from Theorem 5.1 similar to the way we used the result of [23] to extend the result of [37] to the nonuniform regime. Formal proof is as follows. In the rest of this section we prove Theorem 1.4. In the following we prove Theorem 1.4.

PROOF OF THEOREM 1.4. We employ Lemma 5.3 as follows. We let the randomized oracle $\mathbf{O}$ be the random oracle. Theorem 5.1 shows that there is a construction of FCRHs relative to $\mathbf{O}$ such that any adversary T who gets $2^{o(n)}$ bits of advice about $\mathbf{O}$ and asks $2^{o(n)}$ queries to it can break it only with advantage $2^{-\Omega(n)}$. This would imply the second requirement of Lemma 5.3 with $q(n) = \mathrm{poly}(n) \leq 2^{n/10}$.

We also use the following result which is the main step toward separating one-way functions from key-agreement proved in [37] and provides us with the adversary Adv as needed for the first condition of Lemma 5.3.

LEMMA 5.4. *Suppose Π is a key-agreement protocol in which Alice and Bob each ask n oracle queries to the random oracle $O \xleftarrow{\$} \mathbf{RO}$, and they agree on a key with probability $1 - \mathrm{negl}(n)$. There is a computationally unbounded adversary Adv who only accesses the public messages sent between Alice and Bob, asks at most $\mathrm{poly}(n)$ oracle queries to O, and finds the key with probability $1 - 1/n^2$.*

Since both conditions of Lemma 5.3 are satisfied, Theorem 1.4 follows immediately.

□

Now we prove Theorem 1.6.

PROOF OF THEOREM 1.6. We will first prove Theorem 1.6 for PRGs and then will prove it for the case o digital signatures.

Part 1: Pseudorandom Generators. Suppose on the contrary that $G\colon \{0,1\}^\ell \mapsto \{0,1\}^{\ell+k}$ is a black-box construction of PRGs that stretches its input by k and $p = \lambda(n) \cdot (k/\log n)$ oracle queries while $1/\mathrm{poly}(n) \leq \lambda(n) \leq o(1)$. In this case we again use $\mathbf{O}$ to denote a random oracle, but we use a slightly different construction of FCRHs h (to be used as $\mathcal{H}$) relative to $\mathbf{O}$. Given any query (z, x) where $z \in \{0,1\}^{4n}$ and $x \in \{0,1\}^{2n}$ to choose the n-bit output we choose the last $r = \min \log^2 n, \frac{\log n}{10\lambda(n)} = \omega(\log n)$ bits of y uniformly at random, and we copy the $n - \frac{\log n}{\lambda(n)}$ first bits of x as the $n - \frac{\log n}{\lambda(n)}$ first bits of the output y.

Note that any adversary breaking collision resistance of h has to find a collision for the last r bits of h as well, so as a mental experiment we pretend that the output length of h is $r \leq \log^2 n$ Since $\mathrm{poly}(n) \cdot 2^{\log^2 n} \leq \mathrm{poly}(n) \cdot 2^{4n}$, Theorem 5.1 proves that the construction $\mathbf{h} = h^{\mathbf{O}}$ is non-uniformly secure in the sense that any $\mathrm{poly}(n)$ query attacker with $\mathrm{poly}(n)$ bits of advice about $\mathbf{O}$ can find a collision in $h^{\mathbf{O}}$ only with negligible probability. This shows that the second requirement of Lemma 5.3 holds for $q(n) = \mathrm{poly}(n)$.

LEMMA 5.5 ([22]). *There is an adversary Adv who asks no queries to $\mathbf{O}$ but is able to distinguish the output of $G(U_\ell)$ from $U_{\ell+k}$ with advantage $1/4$.*

We provide a proof for sake of completeness.

PROOF. The total number of random bits used in the computation of $G^h(\mathbf{U}_\ell)$ is $\ell + p \cdot \frac{\log n}{10\lambda(n)} < \ell + k$ (where $\mathbf{U}_\ell$ is a random string of length ℓ). Therefore the support set of the function $G^h(\mathbf{U}_\ell)$ has size at most $2^{\ell+k-1}$. The latter implies that a computationally unbounded adversary is able to distinguish between $G^h(\mathbf{U}_\ell)$ and $\mathbf{U}_{\ell+k}$ with advantage at least $1/4$ (by outputting 1 whenever the given y is in the support of $G^h(\mathbf{U}_\ell)$ and outputting 0 elsewhere). □

The attacker Adv of Lemma 5.5 satisfies the first requirement of Lemma 5.3. Therefore, the first part of Theorem 1.6 follows directly from Lemma 5.3.

Part 2: Signature Schemes. Now we prove the second part of Theorem 1.6. Suppose for sake of contradiction that D is a black-box construction of digital signatures for message space $\{0,1\}^n$ using $o(n)$ queries to $\mathcal{H}_n$. We use the same construction h for $\mathcal{H}_n$ as that of the proof of Theorem 1.4; namely a random FCRHs with key length $4n$, input length $2n$, and output length $2n$. By Theorem 5.1, $h^{\mathbf{O}}$ is $2^{n/10}$ secure, even if the adversary gets $2^{n/10}$ bits of advice about $\mathbf{O}$. Thus we obtain the first requirement of Lemma 5.3 for any $q(n) = 2^{o(n)}$.

LEMMA 5.6 ([5]). *For any construction of digital signatures D for message space $\{0,1\}^n$ in the random oracle model in which the key-generation, signing, and verification algorithms ask p oracle queries can be broken with advantage $1/\mathrm{poly}(n)$ by an adversary Adv who asks $\mathrm{poly}(n)2^{O(p)}$ oracle queries.*

Lemma 5.6 shows that if D asks only $o(n)$ many queries to $\mathcal{H}_n$, then Adv can break it with $q(n) = 2^{o(n)}$ queries. This implies that the first requirement of Lemma 5.3 holds as well and so Lemma 5.3 implies the second part of Theorem 1.6 directly.

6. REFERENCES

[1] Takahiro Matsuda 0002 and Kanta Matsuura. On black-box separations among injective one-way functions. In Yuval Ishai, editor, *TCC*, volume 6597 of *Lecture Notes in Computer Science*, pages 597–614. Springer, 2011.

[2] Adi Akavia, Oded Goldreich, Shafi Goldwasser, and Dana Moshkovitz. On basing one-way functions on np-hardness. In *Proceedings of the 38th Annual ACM Symposium on Theory of Computing (STOC)*, pages 701–710, 2006.

[3] Sergei Artemenko and Ronen Shaltiel. Lower bounds on the query complexity of nonuniform and adaptive reductions showing hardness amplification. *Electronic Colloquium on Computational Complexity (ECCC)*, 18:16, 2011.

[4] Michael Backes and Dominique Unruh. Limits of constructive security proofs. In Josef Pieprzyk, editor, *ASIACRYPT*, volume 5350 of *Lecture Notes in Computer Science*, pages 290–307. Springer, 2008.

[5] Boaz Barak and Mohammad Mahmoody-Ghidary. Lower bounds on signatures from symmetric primitives. In *IEEE Symposium on Foundations of Computer Science (FOCS)*, 2007.

[6] Boaz Barak and Mohammad Mahmoody-Mahmoody. Merkle puzzles are optimal - an $O(n^2)$-query attack on any key exchange from a random oracle. In Shai Halevi, editor, *Advances in Cryptology - CRYPTO 2009, 29th Annual International Cryptology Conference, Santa Barbara, CA, USA, August 16-20, 2009. Proceedings*, volume 5677 of *Lecture Notes in Computer Science*, pages 374–390. Springer, 2009.

[7] Manuel Blum. How to prove a theorem so no one else can claim it. In *Proceedings of the International Congress of Mathematicians*, pages 1444–1451, 1987.

[8] Andrej Bogdanov and Luca Trevisan. On worst-case to average-case reductions for np problems. *SIAM Journal on Computing*, 36(4):1119–1159, 2006.

[9] Boneh and Venkatesan. Breaking RSA may not be equivalent to factoring. In *EUROCRYPT: Advances in Cryptology: Proceedings of EUROCRYPT*, 1998.

[10] Dan Boneh, Periklis A. Papakonstantinou, Charles Rackoff, Yevgeniy Vahlis, and Brent Waters. On the Impossibility of Basing Identity Based Encryption on Trapdoor Permutations. In *FOCS*, pages 283–292, 2008.

[11] Gilles Brassard. Relativized cryptography. In *Proceedings of the 20th Annual Symposium on Foundations of Computer Science (FOCS)*, pages 383–391. IEEE Computer Society, 1979.

[12] Emmanuel Bresson, Jean Monnerat, and Damien Vergnaud. Separation results on the "one-more" computational problems. In Tal Malkin, editor, *CT-RSA*, volume 4964 of *Lecture Notes in Computer Science*, pages 71–87. Springer, 2008.

[13] Dana Dachman-Soled, Yehuda Lindell, Mohammad Mahmoody, and Tal Malkin. On black-box complexity of optimally-fair coin-tossing. In *Theory of Cryptography Conference - TCC 2011*, 2011.

[14] Anindya De, Luca Trevisan, and Madhur Tulsiani. Time space tradeoffs for attacks against one-way functions and PRGs. In Tal Rabin, editor, *Advances in Cryptology - CRYPTO 2010, 30th Annual Cryptology Conference, Santa Barbara, CA, USA, August 15-19, 2010. Proceedings*, volume 6223 of *Lecture Notes in Computer Science*, pages 649–665. Springer, 2010.

[15] Yevgeniy Dodis, Roberto Oliveira, and Krzysztof Pietrzak. On the generic insecurity of the full domain hash. *Lecture Notes in Computer Science*, pages 449–??, 2005.

[16] Danny Dolev, Cynthia Dwork, and Moni Naor. Nonmalleable cryptography. *SIAM Journal on Computing*, 30(2):391–437 (electronic), 2000. Preliminary version in STOC 1991.

[17] Danny Dolev, Cynthia Dwork, and Moni Naor. Nonmalleable cryptography. *SIAM Journal on Computing*, 30(2):391–437, 2000.

[18] Joan Feigenbaum and Lance Fortnow. Random-self-reducibility of complete sets. *SIAM Journal on Computing*, 22(5):994–1005, 1993.

[19] Amos Fiat and Adi Shamir. How to prove yourself: practical solutions to identification and signature problems. In *Proceedings on Advances in cryptology—CRYPTO '86*, pages 186–194, London, UK, 1987. Springer-Verlag.

[20] Marc Fischlin and Dominique Schröder. On the impossibility of three-move blind signature schemes. In Henri Gilbert, editor, *EUROCRYPT*, volume 6110 of *Lecture Notes in Computer Science*, pages 197–215. Springer, 2010.

[21] Gennaro, Gertner, and Katz. Lower bounds on the efficiency of encryption and digital signature schemes. In *STOC: ACM Symposium on Theory of Computing (STOC)*, 2003.

[22] Rosario Gennaro, Yael Gertner, Jonathan Katz, and Luca Trevisan. Bounds on the efficiency of generic cryptographic constructions. *SIAM J. Comput.*, 35(1):217–246, 2005.

[23] Rosario Gennaro and Luca Trevisan. Lower Bounds on the Efficiency of Generic Cryptographic constructions. In *FOCS*, pages 305–313, 2000.

[24] Craig Gentry and Daniel Wichs. Separating succinct non-interactive arguments from all falsifiable assumptions. In Lance Fortnow and Salil P. Vadhan, editors, *STOC*, pages 99–108. ACM, 2011.

[25] Yael Gertner, Sampath Kannan, Tal Malkin, Omer Reingold, and Mahesh Viswanathan. The Relationship between Public Key Encryption and Oblivious transfer. In *FOCS*, pages 325–335, 2000.

[26] Yael Gertner, Tal Malkin, and Omer Reingold. On the Impossibility of Basing Trapdoor Functions on Trapdoor Predicates. In *FOCS*, pages 126–135, 2001.

[27] Oded Goldreich. A uniform-complexity treatment of encryption and zero-knowledge. *Journal of Cryptology*, 6(1):21–53, 1993.

[28] Oded Goldreich. *Foundations of Cryptography: Basic Applications.* Cambridge University Press, 2004.

[29] Oded Goldreich, Silvio Micali, and Avi Wigderson. Proofs that yield nothing but their validity or all languages in NP have zero-knowledge proof systems. *Journal of the ACM*, 38(1):691–729, 1991.

[30] Oded Goldreich and Yair Oren. Definitions and properties of zero-knowledge proof systems. *Journal of Cryptology*, 7(1):1–32, 1994.

[31] Shafi Goldwasser, Silvio Micali, and Charles Rackoff. The knowledge complexity of interactive proof systems. *SIAM Journal on Computing*, 18(1):186–208, 1989.

[32] Iftach Haitner, Jonathan J. Hoch, Omer Reingold, and Gil Segev. Finding collisions in interactive protocols – A tight lower bound on the round complexity of statistically-hiding commitments. In *Proceedings of the 47th Annual Symposium on Foundations of Computer Science (FOCS)*. IEEE Computer Society, 2007.

[33] Iftach Haitner and Thomas Holenstein. On the (im)possibility of key dependent encryption. In Omer Reingold, editor, *Theory of Cryptography, 6th Theory of Cryptography Conference, TCC 2009, San Francisco, CA, USA, March 15-17, 2009. Proceedings*, volume 5444 of *Lecture Notes in Computer Science*, pages 202–219. Springer, 2009.

[34] Iftach Haitner, Alon Rosen, and Ronen Shaltiel. On the (im)possibility of arthur-merlin witness hiding protocols. In *Theory of Cryptography, Fourth Theory of Cryptography Conference, TCC 2009*, 2009.

[35] Johan Håstad. Pseudo-random generators under uniform assumptions. In *Proceedings of the 22nd*

Annual ACM Symposium on Theory of Computing (STOC), pages 387–394, 1990.

[36] Russell Impagliazzo, Leonid A. Levin, and Michael Luby. Pseudo-random generation from one-way functions. In *Proceedings of the 21st Annual ACM Symposium on Theory of Computing (STOC)*, pages 12–24, 1989.

[37] Russell Impagliazzo and Steven Rudich. Limits on the provable consequences of one-way permutations. In *Proceedings of the 21st Annual ACM Symposium on Theory of Computing (STOC)*, pages 44–61. ACM Press, 1989.

[38] Jonathan Katz, Dominique Schröder, and Arkady Yerukhimovich. Impossibility of blind signatures from one-way permutations. In Yuval Ishai, editor, *TCC*, volume 6597 of *Lecture Notes in Computer Science*, pages 615–629. Springer, 2011.

[39] Jeong Han Kim, Daniel R. Simon, and Prasad Tetali. Limits on the efficiency of one-way permutation-based hash functions. In *Proceedings of the 40th Annual Symposium on Foundations of Computer Science (FOCS)*, pages 535–542, 1999.

[40] Neal Koblitz and Alfred Menezes. Another look at non-uniformity. *IACR Cryptology ePrint Archive*, 2012:359, 2012. informal publication.

[41] Lin, Trevisan, and Wee. On hardness amplification of one-way functions. In *Theory of Cryptography Conference (TCC), LNCS*, volume 2, 2005.

[42] Huijia Lin, Rafael Pass, and Muthuramakrishnan Venkitasubramaniam. Concurrent non-malleable commitments from any one-way function. In Ran Canetti, editor, *TCC*, volume 4948 of *Lecture Notes in Computer Science*, pages 571–588. Springer, 2008.

[43] Chi-Jen Lu. On the security loss in cryptographic reductions. In Antoine Joux, editor, *EUROCRYPT*, volume 5479 of *Lecture Notes in Computer Science*, pages 72–87. Springer, 2009.

[44] Mohammad Mahmoody and Rafael Pass. The curious case of non-interactive commitments - on the power of black-box vs. non-black-box use of primitives. In Reihaneh Safavi-Naini and Ran Canetti, editors, *CRYPTO*, volume 7417 of *Lecture Notes in Computer Science*, pages 701–718. Springer, 2012.

[45] Moni Naor. On cryptographic assumptions and challenges. *Lecture Notes in Computer Science*, 2729:96–109, 2003.

[46] Rafael Pass. Parallel repetition of zero-knowledge proofs and the possibility of basing cryptography on NP-hardness. In *IEEE Conference on Computational Complexity*, pages 96–110. IEEE Computer Society, 2006.

[47] Rafael Pass. Limits of provable security from standard assumptions. In Lance Fortnow and Salil P. Vadhan, editors, *Proceedings of the 43rd ACM Symposium on Theory of Computing, STOC 2011, San Jose, CA, USA, 6-8 June 2011*, pages 109–118. ACM, 2011.

[48] Rafael Pass, Wei-Lung Dustin Tseng, and Muthuramakrishnan Venkitasubramaniam. Towards non-black-box lower bounds in cryptography. In Yuval Ishai, editor, *Theory of Cryptography - 8th Theory of Cryptography Conference, TCC 2011, Providence, RI, USA, March 28-30, 2011. Proceedings*, volume 6597 of *Lecture Notes in Computer Science*, pages 579–596. Springer, 2011.

[49] Omer Reingold, Luca Trevisan, and Salil P. Vadhan. Notions of reducibility between cryptographic primitives. In *Theory of Cryptography, First Theory of Cryptography Conference, TCC 2004*, volume 2951 of *Lecture Notes in Computer Science*, pages 1–20. Springer, 2004.

[50] Guy N. Rothblum and Salil P. Vadhan. Are PCPs inherent in efficient arguments? *Computational Complexity*, 19(2):265–304, 2010.

[51] Claus-Peter Schnorr. Efficient signature generation by smart cards. *J. Cryptology*, 4(3):161–174, 1991.

[52] Ronen Shaltiel and Emanuele Viola. Hardness amplification proofs require majority. *SIAM J. Comput*, 39(7):3122–3154, 2010.

[53] Daniel R. Simon. Finding Collisions on a One-Way Street: Can Secure Hash Functions Be Based on General Assumptions? In *EUROCRYPT*, pages 334–345, 1998.

[54] Dominique Unruh. Random oracles and auxiliary input. In Alfred Menezes, editor, *CRYPTO*, volume 4622 of *Lecture Notes in Computer Science*, pages 205–223. Springer, 2007.

[55] Yevgeniy Vahlis. Two Is a Crowd? A Black-Box Separation of One-Wayness and Security under Correlated Inputs. In *TCC*, pages 165–182, 2010.

Fast Reductions from RAMs to Delegatable Succinct Constraint Satisfaction Problems

[Extended Abstract]*

Eli Ben-Sasson†
Technion and MIT
eli@cs.technion.ac.il

Alessandro Chiesa‡
MIT
alexch@csail.mit.edu

Daniel Genkin†
Technion
danielg3@cs.technion.ac.il

Eran Tromer†
Tel Aviv University
tromer@cs.tau.ac.il

ABSTRACT

Succinct arguments for NP are proof systems that allow a weak verifier to retroactively check computation done by a powerful prover. Constructions of such protocols prove membership in languages consisting of *very large yet succinctly-represented constraint satisfaction problems* that, alas, are unnatural in the sense that the problems that arise in practice are not in such form.

For general computation tasks, the most natural representation is typically as random-access machine (RAM) algorithms, because such a representation can be obtained very efficiently by applying a compiler to code written in a high-level programming language. Thus, understanding the efficiency of reductions from RAM computations to other NP-complete problem representations for which succinct arguments (or proofs) are known is a prerequisite to a more complete understanding of the applicability of these arguments.

Existing succinct argument constructions rely either on circuit satisfiability or (in PCP-based constructions) on algebraic constraint satisfaction problems. In this paper, we present new and more efficient reductions from RAM (and parallel RAM) computations to both problems that (a) preserve succinctness (i.e., do not "unroll" the computation of a machine), (b) preserve zero-knowledge and proof-of-knowledge properties, and (c) enjoy fast and highly-parallelizable algorithms for transforming a witness for the RAM computation into a witness for the corresponding problem. These additional properties are typically not considered in "classical" complexity theory but are often required or very desirable in the application of succinct arguments.

Fulfilling all these efficiency requirements poses significant technical challenges, and we develop a set of tools (both unconditional and leveraging computational assumptions) for generically and efficiently structuring and arithmetizing RAM computations for use in succinct arguments. More generally, our results can be applied to proof systems for NP relying on the aforementioned problem representations; these include various zero-knowledge proof constructions.

*See [7] for the full version.

†The research leading to these results has received funding from the European Community's Seventh Framework Programme (FP7/2007-2013) under grant agreement number 240258.

‡This work was supported by the Check Point Institute for Information Security, by the Israeli Ministry of Science and Technology, and by the Israeli Centers of Research Excellence I-CORE program (center 4/11).

ITCS'13, January 9–12, 2013, Berkeley, California, USA.

Categories and Subject Descriptors

F.0 [**Theory of Computation**]: General; F.1 [**Theory of Computation**]: Computation by abstract devices—*relations between models, reducibility and completeness*

General Terms

Theory

Keywords

delegation of computation, succinct arguments, random-access machines, probabilistically checkable proofs, zero-knowledge proofs

1. INTRODUCTION

Cryptographic protocols offering integrity and confidentiality for general computation are much needed, e.g., for attaining secure cloud computing and reducing trust in execution platforms. Work in cryptography has focused, for instance, on the problems of *computing on encrypted data* [37, 39, 38, 19, 41, 40], *computing on authenticated data* [36], *delegation of computation* [46, 34, 25, 3, 21, 58], *delegation of memory and streams* [28, 24], *non-interactive zero-knowledge proofs* [52, 51, 1, 48, 50, 49], *succinct arguments* [61, 71, 5, 14, 29, 47, 16, 15], *succinct arguments with preprocessing* [50, 66, 35], and *proof-carrying data* [22, 23].

Each such cryptographic protocol "supports" a specific problem representation. For example, constructions of fully-homomorphic encryption schemes and delegation protocols work with evaluation of circuits; constructions of non-interactive zero-knowledge proofs often work with satisfiability of circuits; PCP-based succinct argument constructions work with constraint-satisfaction problems having a strong combinatorial or algebraic flavor (e.g., coloring problems over certain hypergraphs or whether there are low-degree polynomials with a certain set of roots).

However, problem representations such as the above are unnatural for the envisioned applications. While the circuit model may be convenient for highly-structured computational tasks (e.g., computing Fourier transforms or statistics on numerical data), it is not convenient in general; this is even more true for problem representations with strong combinatorial or algebraic structure. In the real world, the problems that we are interested in arise in the form of *algorithms* written in high-level programming languages such as C or Java.

In principle, this gap is not a problem: circuit evaluation is a complete problem for P, circuit satisfiability is a complete problem for NP, and so on. We can thus rely on generic polynomial-time reductions for transforming algorithms into the problem representations we need. However, the envisioned applications often deal with *very large* computations, and thus *the efficiency of such reductions is paramount* — reductions with only "polynomial-time" efficiency are not efficient enough.

The following question is thus of fundamental interest:

> **Informal Question:** How can we *generically and efficiently* transform algorithms written in high-level programming languages into the problem representations required by the underlying cryptographic protocols?

Ultimately, the hope is to develop a toolset for efficiently reducing the correctness of computation of algorithms to a variety of popular problem representations. Achieving this hope would bestow great flexibility to protocols that benefit from these reductions, because our ability to easily program algorithms would translate into the ability to easily *and efficiently* "program" less natural problem representations such as circuits or polynomials.

1.1 Random-Access Machine Computations

Existing compilers do a splendid job at reducing algorithms expressed in a high-level programming language to a sequence of basic instructions for a variety of computer architectures. Correct execution of such instructions, given the semantic specification of the architecture, is trivially and tightly reducible to the correct execution of a *random-access machine* (RAM) [26, 2]. Thus, RAM computations are a natural starting point to choose for reductions. More precisely, we consider the following constraint satisfaction problem: the **bounded-halting problem** on a two-tape random-access machine M, denoted $\mathrm{BH}_{\mathsf{RAM}}(M)$, is the language of all triples $(\mathtt{x}, T, S)$ such that there is a witness $\mathtt{w}$ for which $M(\mathtt{x}, \mathtt{w})$ accepts within T time steps[1] and using at most S memory cells.[2] The language $\mathrm{BH}_{\mathsf{RAM}}$ is the one induced by all quadruples $(M, \mathtt{x}, T, S)$ such that $(\mathtt{x}, \mathtt{w})$ is in $\mathrm{BH}_{\mathsf{RAM}}(M)$. Thus, thanks to compiler technology, focusing on $\mathrm{BH}_{\mathsf{RAM}}$ as a starting point for reductions comes at essentially no loss in efficiency.

We model the RAMs we use as realistic reduced-instruction-set computers (RISCs) as opposed to the traditional simpler, but less realistic, accumulator-based architectures with arbitrary-length memory cells used in complexity theory. Doing so will give us a more accurate understanding of the cost of reducing compiled programs into other problem representations. Concretely, a RAM is specified by a tuple (w, k, δ), potentially depending on the input size $|\mathtt{x}|$, where w is the *register width* (which also dictates the width of every memory cell), k is the number of local (i.e., non-memory) registers, and δ is the *transition function* (which is a boolean circuit that, when given random-access to memory, maps the k registers to their new values); note that $|\delta| \geq kw$ since δ takes as input the kw bits making up the registers.[3]

1.2 Our Focus: Succinct Arguments for NP

While there are many cryptographic protocols for which efficient reductions from $\mathrm{BH}_{\mathsf{RAM}}$ are desirable, we choose to focus on the problem of constructing efficient reductions from $\mathrm{BH}_{\mathsf{RAM}}$ for *proof systems for* NP. Also, we seek reductions that preserve zero-knowledge and proof-of-knowledge properties, since both properties are often those that make a proof system interesting to begin with.

Furthermore, we seek reductions that work even for proof systems for NP that are *succinct* [61, 71, 5], i.e., in which the verifier can check membership in a given language L in a way that is *much* faster than by directly verifying the validity of a witness. Such proof systems cannot be statistically sound (under plausible complexity-theoretic assumptions [18, 42, 45, 92]) so that one must settle for *argument systems* [20] (i.e., proof systems with only *computational* soundness). Constructing efficient reductions for succinct argument systems for NP is particularly important because such proof systems enable many useful protocols for delegating computation and, moreover, are most likely to deal with extremely large computations — and thus here efficient reductions are particularly needed.

Reductions and efficiency. Suppose that we have a succinct argument system (P, V) for an NP-complete language L and a reduction from $\mathrm{BH}_{\mathsf{RAM}}$ to L. For concreteness, suppose that L is circuit satisfiability (CSAT). Let us elaborate on the impact that the efficiency of the reduction has on the efficiency of the resulting argument system (P', V') for $\mathrm{BH}_{\mathsf{RAM}}$.

The prover P' uses the reduction to transform a membership question of the form "is $(\mathtt{x}, T, S)$ in $\mathrm{BH}_{\mathsf{RAM}}(M)$?" to one of the form "is the circuit C satisfiable?" and then invokes P. The verifier V' *also* uses the reduction in order to then invoke V.

To specify the question "is $(\mathtt{x}, T, S)$ in $\mathrm{BH}_{\mathsf{RAM}}(M)$?" we only need $O(|M| + |\mathtt{x}| + \log(T))$ bits, but the constraint sat-

[1] We do not employ the logarithmic-cost criterion [26] but instead count the number of machine state transitions.

[2] For now we assume that $|\mathtt{x}|, |\mathtt{w}| \leq T$; in Section 2.3 we show how to remove these restrictions. Furthermore, $S \leq T$ holds always; and ensuring that M does not use addresses much larger than S can be done via a sparse memory representation; see [84, Lemma 1].

[3] In "natural" RAMs, both $|\delta|$ and kw are $O(\log T)$. However, they will generally be significantly larger than $1 \cdot \log T$ depending on how "rich" the architecture of the machine is (e.g., how many different instructions are there, which arithmetic instructions are available, and so on). This is why we want to explicitly keep track of these parameters.

isfaction problem it describes (i.e., the correct execution of $M(\mathtt{x}, \mathtt{w})$, for some witness $\mathtt{w}$, for at most T steps) is much larger: it has size that is $\Omega(T)$. In a succinct argument, the verifier V' is weak, so he is only allowed to run in time that is $\mathsf{poly}(|M| + |\mathtt{x}| + \log(T))$ (and up to a polynomial in the security parameter). Thus, the reduction cannot "unroll" the computation of M and perform operations on it (e.g., by explicitly laying out a circuit of size $\Omega(T)$ encoding constraints, say, for each step of computation), since that would require $\Omega(T)$ time and make V' too slow, but must instead implicitly convert the *large yet succinctly-represented* constraint satisfaction problem described by $(M, \mathtt{x}, T, S)$ into a succinct representation of a question of the form "is C in satisfiable?", i.e., the reduction should in fact be from $\mathrm{BH}_{\mathsf{RAM}}$ to *succinct* CSAT (sCSAT). Thus, succinctness of the reduction is a property that we must ensure in order for it to work for succinct arguments.

But even if succinct, a reduction could still be very inefficient because it could blow up the size of the constraint satisfaction problem, e.g., by outputting a (succinct description of a) circuit of size $O(T^2)$; this would cause P' to invoke P on a much larger instance than the original computation. Thus, we seek reductions where the blowup in the size of the problem is as small as possible.

Additionally, the prover is also responsible for converting a witness $\mathtt{w}$ for the question "is $(\mathtt{x}, T, S)$ in $\mathrm{BH}_{\mathsf{RAM}}(M)$?" into a corresponding assignment of the circuit. The efficiency of this mapping is *also* critical. And because witnesses may themselves be as large as T, we shall seek reductions where this mapping is not only very fast but also *highly parallelizable*.

To preserve proof of knowledge, we shall also want that recovering a witness for $(M, \mathtt{x}, T, S)$ from a valid assignment of C can be done in polynomial-time, though we are not particularly interested in making this "inverse map" very efficient.[4] This requirement makes the reduction a *Levin* reduction.

Comparison with traditional reductions. Naturally, investigating the above question will benefit from insights from complexity theory, where the study of reductions between different computational problems is a basic tool. Nonetheless, the reductions we seek are different from the traditional ones in two ways. First, as already explained, we want reductions between *uniform and succinct* models of computation. Second, reductions need not have information-theoretic guarantees, but only *computational* ones. That is, computational reductions (when appropriately defined) will generally suffice. This relaxation may allow for simpler or more efficient reductions. (In this paper we will in fact see such an example.)

2. OVERVIEW OF RESULTS

In principle we may have to worry about reducing $\mathrm{BH}_{\mathsf{RAM}}$ to numerous and quite different problems, in order to cover as many argument system constructions as possible. Fortunately, it turns out that almost all succinct argument constructions rely either on *circuit satisfiability* or *algebraic constraint satisfaction problems*. Thus, in this paper, we concentrate on the two concrete goals of reducing $\mathrm{BH}_{\mathsf{RAM}}$ to both of these problems. We next describe each goal in more detail and our results for it in the next two subsections (Section 2.1 and Section 2.2 respectively). In both situations, preserving succinctness and minimizing the blowup in size of the constraint satisfaction problem will present significant challenges. Some of these will be overcome by *leveraging nondeterminism* as a resource.

2.1 Programming circuits: from $\mathrm{BH}_{\mathsf{RAM}}$ to circuit satisfaction

Circuit satisfiability is the language of all satisfiable boolean circuits. Its *succinct* version replaces each circuit by a (potentially much smaller) circuit descriptor. Here we consider the uniform formulation of this language. Informally:

DEFINITION 1 (sCSAT). *For a family of circuit descriptors $\Phi = \{\phi_{T,S}\}_{T,S\in\mathbb{N}}$, $\mathrm{sCSAT}(\Phi)$ is the language of $(\mathtt{x}, T, S)$ such that there exists $\mathtt{w}$ for which $C(\mathtt{x}, \mathtt{w})$ accepts,[5] where C is the circuit described by $\phi_{T,S}$.[6] The language sCSAT is the set of all $(\Phi, \mathtt{x}, T, S)$ such that $(\mathtt{x}, T, S) \in \mathrm{sCSAT}(\Phi)$.*

Reducing from $\mathrm{BH}_{\mathsf{RAM}}$ to sCSAT benefits many zero-knowledge argument systems, including [52, 51, 1, 48, 50, 49, 66, 35, 15].[7] Our first goal is:

> GOAL #1: EFFICIENTLY PROGRAM CIRCUITS. Namely, reduce $\mathrm{BH}_{\mathsf{RAM}}$ to sCSAT with a succinct Levin reduction that is as tight as possible (both in terms of circuit size and efficiency of the witness map).

Prior work toward Goal #1. Leveraging the fact that (multi-tape) Turing machines can sort in quasilinear time [87], Gurevich and Shelah [53, Theorem 2] showed that nondeterministic random-access machine computations can be simulated by nondeterministic (multi-tape) Turing machine computations with only polylogarithmic overhead. Combining this with the result of Pippenger and Fischer [80] that any T-step multi-tape Turing machine computation can be performed by an oblivious two-tape Turing machine in $\Theta(T \log T)$ steps, and the fact that the computation of an oblivious Turing machine (say with two tapes) in T' steps can be reduced to a circuit of size $\Theta(T')$, we deduce that there is a quasilinear-time reduction from random-access machines to circuits.

This reduction path already tells us that "random-access machines have small boolean circuits" and, from an asymptotic standpoint, already allows to efficiently program circuits for the purpose of, e.g., running zero-knowledge proofs [52, 51, 1, 48, 50, 49]. This reduction path, however, does not explicitly address the requirement of succinctness (though plausibly could be made to) or studies the efficiency of converting the witness $\mathtt{w}$ into a satisfying assignment; further, it

[4]Concretely, the efficiency of the witness recovery map affects the efficiency of security reductions relying on proof of knowledge and thus, ultimately, affects the size of the security parameter used to invoke the proof system.

[5]Once again, we assume for now that $|\mathtt{x}|, |\mathtt{w}| \leq T$; in Section 2.3 we show how to remove these restrictions.

[6]A circuit descriptor is an algorithm that, given as input a gate number of C, outputs information about the type of the gate, which gates are its inputs, which gates are its outputs, and so on. See [77] for a precise definition.

[7]Not all these arguments are succinct, and thus not all benefit from the succinctness of the reduction; but, of course, all do benefit from the efficiency of the reduction (i.e., the blow up in circuit size and how fast an assignment for the circuit can be computed).

hides large constants because it goes through (two) Turing machine reductions. A more efficient reduction was given by Robson [84], whose proof yields (when cast in our notation) a $\Theta(T\cdot(\log S+wk)\cdot\log S)$ reduction from random-access machines to boolean formulas. However, Robson also did not address succinctness or study the efficiency of converting the witness.

Our results toward Goal #1. Our first theorem addresses Goal #1:

THEOREM 1. *There are functions* $(\mathsf{p},\mathsf{w}_1,\mathsf{w}_2)$ *such that, for every random-access machine* M *(with register width* w*, number of registers* k*, and transition function* δ*) and instance* $(\mathtt{x},T,S)$*,*

SYNTAX: $\Phi=\{\phi_{T,S}\}_{T,S\in\mathbb{N}}=\mathsf{p}(M)$ *is a uniform family of circuit descriptors.*

SOUNDNESS: $(\mathtt{x},T,S)\in \mathrm{BH}_{\mathsf{RAM}}(M)$ *if and only if* $(\mathtt{x},T,S)\in \mathrm{sCSAT}(\Phi)$.

WITNESS REDUCTIONS:

- *if* $\mathtt{w}$ *is a witness to* $(\mathtt{x},T,S)\in \mathrm{BH}_{\mathsf{RAM}}(M)$ *then* $\mathsf{w}_1(M,\mathtt{x},T,S,\mathtt{w})$ *is a witness to* $(\mathtt{x},T,S)\in \mathrm{sCSAT}(\Phi)$*;*
- *if* $\mathtt{w}'$ *is a witness to* $(\mathtt{x},T,S)\in \mathrm{sCSAT}(\Phi)$ *then* $\mathsf{w}_2(M,\mathtt{x},T,S,\mathtt{w}')$ *is a witness to* $(\mathtt{x},T,S)\in \mathrm{BH}_{\mathsf{RAM}}(M)$.

EFFICIENCY:

- $\mathsf{p}(M)$ *runs in linear time.*
- $\phi_{T,S}$ *can be generated in* $O(|\delta|+\log T)$ *time and describes a circuit of size* $O(|\delta|+(\log S+w)\cdot\log S)\cdot T$ *with* $O(kw+(\log S+w)\cdot\log S)\cdot T$ *variables.*
- $\mathsf{w}_1(M,\mathtt{x},T,S,\mathtt{w})$ *runs in time* $O(kw+(\log S+w)\log S)\cdot T$ *and space* $O(kw+(\log S+w)\log S)\cdot S$*, or in parallel time* $O((\log S)^2)$ *when given the transcript of computation of* M *on* $(\mathtt{x},\mathtt{w})$.
- $\mathsf{w}_2(M,\mathtt{x},T,S,\mathtt{w}')$ *runs in linear time.*

Note that p is run by both the prover and (succinct) verifier, while the witness map w_1 is run only by the prover. (And the inverse witness map w_2 ensures proof of knowledge is preserved, and is usually only invoked in security reductions.)

In terms of blowup in the size of the problem, our Theorem 1 provides a modest improvement over the one of Robson [84]. More importantly, however, unlike Robson's result, our Theorem 1 provides a *succinct* reduction with a witness map w_1 that is very efficient (in both time *and* space) and is highly parallelizable. (Also see Section 2.3 for how computational assumptions can improve further the space complexity of w_1.) Our main technique for proving Theorem 1 is the use of routing networks together with nondeterminism, and our proof strategy builds on and simplifies Robson's.

For example, the succinctness property and the efficiency of the witness map w_1 from our Theorem 1 have been used in an essential way by Bitansky and Chiesa [16]. Concretely, they defined a *complexity-preserving* multiprover interactive proof (MIP) [6] to be one where, to check that a random-access machine M non-deterministically accepts an input $\mathtt{x}$ within T time steps and using at most S memory cells, each MIP prover runs in time $(|M|+T)\cdot\mathsf{polylog}(T)$ and space $(|M|+|\mathtt{x}|+S)\cdot\mathsf{polylog}(T)$ and the MIP verifier runs in time $(|M|+|\mathtt{x}|)\cdot\mathsf{polylog}(T)$ — these complexities are optimal up to polylogarithmic factors. Bitansky and Chiesa showed how to use Theorem 1 to construct a complexity-preserving one-round MIP of knowledge, and used it to construct "complexity-preserving" succinct arguments from standard assumptions.

2.2 Programming polynomials: from $\mathrm{BH}_{\mathsf{RAM}}$ to algebraic constraint satisfaction

Probabilistically-checkable proofs (PCPs) [4] are perhaps the starkest examples of powerful proof systems that rely on unnatural problem representations: typically, they are constructed for constraint satisfaction problems having a strong combinatorial or algebraic flavor. All known PCP-based succinct argument constructions [61, 71, 5, 30, 22, 14, 29, 47] inherit these problem representations. Unlike studying reductions to (succinct) circuit satisfiability, though, studying reductions to problems used in PCP constructions is not as well-defined a problem, because these problems are different from each other. Which one should we pick as a target?

Because not all PCP constructions are equally efficient (e.g., some do not have a succinct verifier, some have long proofs, and so on), we focus on problems for which there are PCPs where the prover and verifier running times are sate of the art. Following a line of work on PCPs with short proofs [4, 81, 55, 44, 12, 9, 11, 10, 69], Ben-Sasson et al. [8] constructed PCPs with "quasi-optimal" prover and verifier running time (and both highly parallelizable); their PCPs are constructed using algebraic (rather than combinatorial) techniques, and involve testing proximity and checking properties of univariate (rather than multivariate) polynomials. Concretely, they construct PCPs for a *succinct algebraic constraint satisfaction problem* (sACSP) that is informally defined as follows:

DEFINITION 2 (sACSP). *For a tuple of families* $\mathsf{par}=(\mathbf{F},\mathbf{H},\mathbf{N},\mathbf{P},\mathbf{I})$ *where*

- $\mathbf{F}=\{\mathbb{F}_{T,S}\}_{T,S\in\mathbb{N}}$ *and each* $\mathbb{F}_{T,S}$ *is a finite field of characteristic 2,*
- $\mathbf{H}=\{H_{T,S}\}_{T,S\in\mathbb{N}}$ *and each* $H_{T,S}$ *is a subspace of* $\mathbb{F}_{T,S}$*,*
- $\mathbf{N}=\{\vec{N}_{T,S}\}_{T,S\in\mathbb{N}}$ *and each* $\vec{N}_{T,S}=(N_{T,S,1},\ldots,N_{T,S,|\vec{N}_{T,S}|})$ *is a vector of* neighbor polynomials,
- $\mathbf{P}=\{P_{T,S}\}_{T,S\in\mathbb{N}}$ *and each* $P_{T,S}$ *is a multivariate* constraint polynomial,
- $\mathbf{I}=\{\vec{I}_{T,S}\}_{T,S\in\mathbb{N}}$ *and each* $\vec{I}_{T,S}=(I_{T,S,1},\ldots,I_{T,S,T})$ *is a vector of subspaces each contained in* $H_{T,S}$*,*
- $\deg P_{T,S}(x,x^{|H_{T,S}|\cdot\deg(N_{T,S,1})},\ldots,x^{|H_{T,S}|\cdot\deg(N_{T,S,|\vec{N}_T|})})$ *is at most* $|\mathbb{F}_{T,S}|/4$*,*

$\mathrm{sACSP}(\mathsf{par})$ *is the language of all* $(\mathtt{x},T,S)$ *such that, for a univariate polynomial* A *of degree at most* $|H_{T,S}|$*, it holds that* $P_{T,S}(\alpha,A(N_{T,S,1}(\alpha)),\ldots,A(N_{T,S,|\vec{N}_T|}(\alpha)))=0$ *for all* $\alpha\in H_{T,S}$ *and* $\mathtt{x}=A|_{I_{T,S,|\mathtt{x}|}}$*. The language* sACSP *is then defined as the set of all* $(\mathsf{par},\mathtt{x},T,S)$ *such that* $(\mathtt{x},T,S)\in\mathrm{sACSP}(\mathsf{par})$.[8]

As mentioned, reducing $\mathrm{BH}_{\mathsf{RAM}}$ to sACSP benefits all existing PCP-based succinct argument constructions. Thus, our second goal is:

[8]To ensure succinctness, the field is represented via an irreducible polynomial of the appropriate degree over $\mathbb{F}_2$, subspaces via a basis and an offset, and polynomials via arithmetic circuits.

Goal #2: Efficiently program PCP-friendly polynomials. Namely, reduce BH_{RAM} to sACSP with a succinct Levin reduction that is as tight as possible (both in terms of circuit size and efficiency of the witness map).

Prior work toward Goal #2 Reductions from "non-algebraic" satisfaction problems to algebraic satisfaction problems are common in the PCP literature, where this process is known as *arithmetization*. Typically, the measure of how "large" is an algebraic constraint satisfaction problem is the field size (i.e., this metric is analogous to circuit size). Most arithmetizations in the PCP literature do *not* preserve succinctness and, moreover, are also quite expensive in terms of field size; for example, [54, Chapter 5] shows how to arithmetize circuits, but with a *cubic* blow up and with a reduction that does not preserve succinctness.

To the best of the authors' knowledge, the only arithmetizations that have taken succinctness into account are those of [4] and [10]. Babai et al. [4] study a (succinct) reduction from *pointer machines* (concretely, those of Schönhage [88], which in turn generalize Kolmogorov–Uspenskiĭ machines [62, 63]); however, even if pointer machines can simulate random-access machines with only polylogarithmic overhead [53], the reduction of Babai et al. is not of quasilinear efficiency and, more importantly, generates an algebraic constraint satisfaction problem for multivariate polynomials for which, unlike sACSP as defined above, PCPs as efficient are those of Ben-Sasson et al. [8] are not known. Ben-Sasson et al. [10] study a (succinct) reduction from *Turing machines* to a problem that is very similar to (and inspired the definition of) sACSP. Once again, because Turing machines can simulate random-access machines with only polylogarithmic overhead [53, Theorem 2], the result of [10] could yield a reduction from BH_{RAM} to sACSP with quasilinear field size. However, this reduction path goes through two Turing machine reductions (the first to simulate the random-access machine and the second in their proof) and the field size depends *exponentially* on the (constant but large) number of states of the (second) Turing machine. A simple application of the techniques in [10] to circumvent the use of Turing machines only yields a reduction with *quadratic* field size. Additionally, the efficiency of converting the witness $\mathtt{w}$ into a suitable low-degree polynomial was not studied in [10].

Is there a "direct" reduction from BH_{RAM} to sACSP that, e.g., does not run into the inefficiencies of Turing machines and allows for a fast transformation of the witness?

Our results toward Goal #2 For a given random-access machine M, we introduce an additional complexity measure: we say that M has degree d if the (total) degree of its transition function δ, when viewed as an arithmetic circuit over $\mathbb{F}_2$, is at most d. Note that d is incomparable to both the state size kw and the size $|\delta|$ of the transition function as a boolean circuit; typically, $d = O(\log T)$.

Our second theorem addresses Goal #2:

Theorem 2. *There are functions* $(\mathsf{p}, \mathsf{w}_1, \mathsf{w}_2)$ *such that, for every random-access machine* M *(with register width* w*, number of registers* k*, and transition function* δ *with degree* d*) and instance* $(\mathtt{x}, T, S)$*,*

Syntax: $\mathsf{par} = (\mathbf{F}, \mathbf{H}, \mathbf{N}, \mathbf{P}, \mathbf{I}) = \mathsf{p}(M)$ *is a parameter choice for* sACSP.

Soundness: $(\mathtt{x}, T, S) \in \text{BH}_{\text{RAM}}(M)$ *if and only if* $(\mathtt{x}, T, S) \in$ sACSP(par).

Witness reductions:

- *if* $\mathtt{w}$ *is a witness to* $(\mathtt{x}, T, S) \in \text{BH}_{\text{RAM}}(M)$ *then* $\mathsf{w}_1(M, \mathtt{x}, T, S, \mathtt{w})$ *is one to* $(\mathtt{x}, T, S) \in$ sACSP(par);
- *if* A *is a witness to* $(\mathtt{x}, T, S) \in$ sACSP(par) *then* $\mathsf{w}_2(M, \mathtt{x}, T, S, A)$ *is one to* $(\mathtt{x}, T, S) \in \text{BH}_{\text{RAM}}(M)$.

Efficiency:

- $\mathsf{p}(M)$ *runs in linear time.*
- $|\mathbb{F}_{T,S}| = O((\log T + kw) \cdot \log T \cdot d) \cdot T$.
- *a basis-and-offset representation for* $H_{T,S}$ *can be generated in* $O(\log |\mathbb{F}_{T,S}|)$ *field operations.*
- $\vec{N}_{T,S}$ *has* $O(\log S + kw)$ *affine functions, and each can be generated in* $O(\log |\mathbb{F}_{T,S}|)$ *field operations.*
- $P_{T,S}$ *has size* $O(|\delta| + \log |\mathbb{F}_{T,S}|)$ *and can be generated in* $O(|\delta| + (\log |\mathbb{F}_{T,S}|)^2 \log \log |\mathbb{F}_{T,S}|)$ *field operations.*
- *a basis and offset for each affine subspace in* $\vec{I}_{T,S}$ *can be generated in* $O(\log |\mathbb{F}_{T,S}|)$ *field operations.*
- $\mathsf{w}_1(M, \mathtt{x}, T, S, \mathtt{w})$ *runs in time* $O(|\mathbb{F}_{T,S}|(\log |\mathbb{F}_{T,S}|)^2)$*, or in parallel time* $O((\log |\mathbb{F}_{T,S}|)^2)$ *when given the transcript of computation of* M *on* $(\mathtt{x}, \mathtt{w})$.
- $\mathsf{w}_2(M, \mathtt{x}, T, S, A)$ *runs in time* $O(|\mathbb{F}_{T,S}|(\log |\mathbb{F}_{T,S}|)^2)$*, or in parallel time* $O((\log |\mathbb{F}_{T,S}|)^2)$.

(As mentioned, all polynomials are represented via arithmetic circuits.)

As before, p is run by both the prover and (succinct) verifier, while w_1 is run only by the prover. (And w_2 ensures proof of knowledge is preserved, and is typically invoked only in security reductions.)

Our Theorem 2 thus provides a succinct reduction from BH_{RAM} to sACSP with small overhead and with a witness map w_1 that is very efficient in time (and is highly parallelizable). Unlike in Theorem 1, however, the witness map in Theorem 2 requires space $\Omega(|\mathbb{F}_{T,S}|) = \Omega(T)$ regardless of the space complexity of the machine M. While the space complexity of the witness map in Theorem 1 is dominated by the space needed to solve a routing problem of size $O(S)$, the space complexity of the witness reduction in Theorem 2 is dominated by the space needed to solve a univariate interpolation problem on a $\Omega(|\mathbb{F}_{T,S}|)$-size domain that, when solved with an FFT, requires $\Omega(|\mathbb{F}_{T,S}|)$ space. This inefficiency in terms of space complexity appears inherent.

The main techniques for proving Theorem 2 are the use of routing networks together with nondeterminism (as in Theorem 1), the use of novel arithmetization techniques (including further development of the computational properties of *linearized polynomials* [65, Section 2.5] used in [10]), and additive FFTs [68].

Our reduction from Theorem 2 has been used by Ben-Sasson et al. [8] to construct a PCP system for random-access machine computations where, to check that a random-access machine M non-deterministically accepts an input $\mathtt{x}$ within T time steps, the PCP prover runs in sequential time $(|M| + T) \cdot \mathsf{polylog}(T)$ (or parallel time $O((\log T)^2)$ when given a transcript of computation) and the PCP verifier runs in sequential time $(|M| + |\mathtt{x}|) \cdot \mathsf{polylog}(T)$ (or parallel time $O((\log T)^2)$); Ben-Sasson et al. then used these to construct a variant of universal arguments [5] with similar efficiency. In both cases, both the prover and verifier are highly parallelizable but the space complexity of the prover remains

$\Omega(T)$. See [8] for more details and open problems in this direction.

2.3 Extensions

Parallel RAMs Our results can be used in a simple and black-box way to also handle *parallel RAMs* (PRAMs) [32] and obtain completely analogous results for these. Essentially, a PRAM can be reduced to a corresponding (sequential) RAM in the trivial fashion (by round-robin instruction-by-instruction simulation on a single processor, swapping the registers to memory at each switch). This simple reduction preserves parallelism in the following sense: the transcript of the sequential RAM can still be generated in parallel time essentially equal to that of the original PRAM. One can then invoke our results for sequential RAMs, which themselves have low parallel time complexity.

Non-determinism and computational assumptions Theorem 1 and Theorem 2 provide unconditional guarantees. A natural question is whether by using computational assumptions one can obtain more efficient reductions. Let us discuss an example where this is the case.

Even if Theorem 1 ensures that the witness map can be computed in time and space that are close to those of the original machine M, it may still be not so efficient to run the witness map, e.g., when the space used by M is large only for a short period of time. While one can conceive of more sophisticated proofs to Theorem 1 that take into account additional information about the memory usage of M, a simpler "more dynamic" approach can be based on collision-resistant hash functions. The lemma is the following:

LEMMA 1. *Let $\mathcal{F} = \{f_\rho\}_\rho$ be a collision-resistant hash-function family. There exist functions $(\mathsf{p}, \mathsf{w}_1, \mathsf{w}_2, \mathsf{t}, \mathsf{s})$ such that for every random-access machine M:*

SYNTAX: *For every seed $\rho \in \{0,1\}^*$, $\mathsf{p}(\rho, M)$ is a random-access machine.*

WITNESS REDUCTIONS:

- *For every seed $\rho \in \{0,1\}^*$, instance $(\mathtt{x}, T, S)$, and $\mathtt{w}$, if $\mathtt{w}$ is a witness to $(\mathtt{x}, T, S) \in \mathrm{BH}_{\mathsf{RAM}}(M)$ then $\mathsf{w}_1(\rho, M, \mathtt{x}, T, S, \mathtt{w})$ is a witness to $(\mathtt{x}, \mathsf{t}(\rho, M, T, S), \mathsf{s}(\rho, M, T, S)) \in \mathrm{BH}_{\mathsf{RAM}}(\mathsf{p}(\rho, M))$.*
- *With high probability over ρ, if a witness $\mathtt{w}'$ for $(\mathtt{x}, \mathsf{t}(\rho, M, T, S), \mathsf{s}(\rho, M, T, S)) \in \mathrm{BH}_{\mathsf{RAM}}(\mathsf{p}(\rho, M))$ can be efficiently generated, then a witness $\mathtt{w}$ for $(\mathtt{x}, T, S) \in \mathrm{BH}_{\mathsf{RAM}}(M)$ can be efficiently extracted from it (so that, in particular, such a witness exists). Formally, for every polynomial-size circuit family $\{C_\kappa\}_{\kappa \in \mathbb{N}}$ and sufficiently large $\kappa \in \mathbb{N}$,*

$$\Pr_{\rho \leftarrow \{0,1\}^\kappa}\left[\begin{array}{c} \mathsf{w}_2(\rho, M, \mathtt{x}, T, S, \mathtt{w}') \text{ is not a witness to} \\ (\mathtt{x}, T, S) \in \mathrm{BH}_{\mathsf{RAM}}(M) \text{ and } \mathtt{w}' \text{ is witness to} \\ (\mathtt{x}, \mathsf{t}(\rho, M, T, S), \mathsf{s}(\rho, M, T, S)) \in \mathrm{BH}_{\mathsf{RAM}}(\mathsf{p}(\rho, M)) \end{array} \middle| \, (\mathtt{x}, 1^T, S, \mathtt{w}') \leftarrow C_\kappa(\rho)\right] < \mathsf{negl}(\kappa) \enspace .$$

EFFICIENCY:

- *$\mathsf{p}(\rho, M)$ runs in linear time.*
- *$\mathsf{w}_1(\rho, M, \mathtt{x}, T, S, \mathtt{w})$ runs in time $T \cdot \mathsf{poly}(|\rho| + \log S)$ and space that "mirrors" that used by $M(\mathtt{x}, \mathtt{w})$ (i.e., the number of non-zero memory cells in the i-th block of $\mathsf{poly}(|\rho| + \log S)$ steps of w_1 is equal to that at step i of $M(\mathtt{x}, \mathtt{w})$ times $\mathsf{poly}(|\rho| + \log S)$).*
- *$\mathsf{w}_2(\rho, M, \mathtt{x}, T, S, \mathtt{w}')$ runs in linear time.*
- *$\mathsf{t}(\rho, M, T, S) = T \cdot \log S \cdot \mathsf{poly}(|\rho|)$.*
- *$\mathsf{s}(\rho, M, T, S) = \mathsf{poly}(|\rho|)$.*

The important efficiency features of Lemma 1 are that the space complexity of $\mathsf{p}(\rho, M)$ is a fixed polynomial in $|\rho|$ and the witness map w_1 has space complexity that "mirrors" that of the computation of M on $(\mathtt{x}, \mathtt{w})$; in particular, even if M has large space complexity for a short period of time, w_1 will not have space complexity that is large for the entire computation (as was the case in Theorem 1).

Lemma 1 is in fact an immediate consequence of *online memory checking* [17] via Merkle trees [70]: $\mathsf{p}(\rho, M)$ stores memory in "untrusted storage" by dynamically maintaining the root of a Merkle tree over it; essentially, every load instruction of M is replaced by a *secure load*, consisting of a sequence of instructions verifying an alleged value, and every store instruction of M is replaced by a corresponding *secure store*, which appropriately updates the root of the Merkle tree, stored in a register.[9]

The new machine $\mathsf{p}(\rho, M)$ from Lemma 1 can then be plugged back into Theorem 1 to obtain a reduction to sCSAT where the space complexity of the witness map mirrors that of M.[10] As another application, Lemma 1 was used by Bitansky et al. [15] as an essential component to the construction of *complexity-preserving* non-interactive succinct arguments of knowledge.[11]

Note that the above application of collision-resistant hash functions crucially leverages nondeterminism as a resource and requires any proof system proving correctness of computation about the new machine $\mathsf{p}(\rho, M)$ to have a proof-of-knowledge property. We find it an interesting open question to further investigate the power of computational reductions to simplify or obtain results that cannot be achieved with only unconditional reductions.

Handling large non-uniform inputs So far we have assumed that $|\mathtt{x}|, |\mathtt{w}| \leq T$ when considering an instance $(M, \mathtt{x}, T, S)$ and witness $\mathtt{w}$. What happens when this is not the case? For instance, $\mathtt{x}$ or $\mathtt{w}$ (or both) may represent large databases and, if M has random-access to its two inputs, then T could potentially be *much smaller* than $|\mathtt{x}|$ or $|\mathtt{w}|$. (E.g., M may run binary search on $\mathtt{x}$ or $\mathtt{w}$.) Naively setting $T' = \max\{T, |\mathtt{x}|, |\mathtt{w}|\}$ as a new time bound and then considering the new instance $(M', \mathtt{x}, T', S)$, where M' has sequential-access to its inputs and simulates M, does *not* take advantage of the fact that T is much smaller than T'.

We now explain how to handle large inputs. Concretely, we show how an instance $(M, \mathtt{x}, T, S)$ and witness $\mathtt{w}$ can be modified to a new instance $(M', \mathtt{x}', T', S')$ and witness $\mathtt{w}'$

[9] When M does not read from the witness tape, *universal one-way hash functions* [73, 86] are in fact enough [17]; when M does read from the witness tape, collision-resistant hash functions are generally required.

[10] In fact, because the space complexity of $\mathsf{p}(\rho, M)$ is so low, one can at this point also use the trivial reduction from RAMs to circuits. In a sense, collision-resistant hash functions can thus be interpreted as an alternative to routing techniques as far as memory consistency is concerned.

[11] Indeed, it seems that the recursive composition and bootstrapping techniques of Bitansky et al. [15] cannot be performed on the circuit obtained in the proof of Theorem 1. The result of [15] is an example of an application that we know how to achieve only via a reduction with only computational guarantees.

where $|\mathtt{x}'|, |\mathtt{w}'| \le T'$ and, crucially, $T' = \tilde{O}(T)$ (perhaps up to polynomial factors in a security parameter). Thus, the restriction that $|\mathtt{x}|, |\mathtt{w}| \le T$ essentially comes without loss of generality. Let us begin by explaining how to handle the case in which $\mathtt{w}$ is large.

Say that we have an instance $(M, \mathtt{x}, T, S)$ where M has random-access to a (large) witness $\mathtt{w}$. Construct a new instance $(M', \mathtt{x}', T', S')$ where M has sequential-access to a new witness $\mathtt{w}'$ as follows:

- The new machine $M'(\tilde{\mathtt{x}}, \tilde{\mathtt{w}})$ parses $\tilde{\mathtt{w}}$ as a sequence of address-value pairs $((a_1, v_1), \ldots, (a_\ell, v_\ell))$, stores these pairs in addresses $0, \ldots, \ell - 1$ in memory, checks that they are sorted by the a_i (halting to reject if they are not sorted or if it finds any duplicate a_i) and then simulates $M(\mathtt{x}, \cdot)$ as follows. When $M(\mathtt{x}, \cdot)$ wishes to read location a of the witness, M' binary searches addresses $0, \ldots, \ell - 1$ for a pair whose first coordinate is a; if M' finds some pair of the form (a, v), it returns v to M, otherwise it halts and rejects. At the end of the simulation, M' accepts if and only if M does. Of course, M' can use addresses above ℓ to maintain M's memory during the simulation (along with any other state necessary to carry out the simulation).
- Define $\mathtt{w}'$ to be the (sorted) concatenation of the locations (and corresponding values) of $\mathtt{w}$ accessed by M when running on inputs $(\mathtt{x}, \mathtt{w})$; deducing $\mathtt{w}'$ can be done in time $\tilde{O}(T)$ by running M on $(\mathtt{x}, \mathtt{w})$ and then sorting by location.
- Define $\mathtt{x}' := \mathtt{x}$, $T' := O(T \log T)$, $S' := S + T$. In fact, letting ℓ be the number of locations of $\mathtt{w}$ accessed by M when running on inputs $(\mathtt{x}, \mathtt{w})$, if ℓ is known, one can define the better values $T' := O(T \log \ell)$, $S' := S + \ell$. (Note that $\ell \le T$ but ℓ could be much smaller than T.)

In other words, we replace the full (long) witness $\mathtt{w}$ with a "sparse" (short) partial copy $\mathtt{w}'$ that includes only those parts of $\mathtt{w}$ that are actually used during the computation of M on $(\mathtt{x}, \mathtt{w})$. Thus, in sum, we can "shrink" a long witness into one of length at most T and consider a new instance that takes this new witness as input. Then we can, e.g., invoke Theorem 1 or Theorem 2 to reduce the new instance (and witness).

If $\mathtt{x}$ is large, we can combine the previous solution approach with collision-resistant hash functions;[12] this will be another example of gaining efficiency in reductions though computational assumptions. First, someone trusted (e.g., the verifier) computes a short Merkle hash $\sigma_\mathtt{x}$ of $\mathtt{x}$; this operation takes $|\mathtt{x}| \cdot \mathsf{poly}(\kappa)$ time and needs to be performed only once and for all for the input $\mathtt{x}$. Now $\mathtt{x}$ can be kept somewhere untrusted (e.g., the verifier can give $\mathtt{x}$ to the prover). Later on, any given machine M can be reduced to another machine M' that has oracle access to its witness and works as follows: on input $(\sigma_\mathtt{x}, \tilde{\mathtt{w}})$, M parses its witness $\tilde{\mathtt{w}}$ as a pair $(\tilde{\mathtt{x}}, \mathtt{w})$ where $\tilde{\mathtt{x}}$ is a datastructure such that $\tilde{\mathtt{x}}_i$ is a bit (allegedly, $\mathtt{x}_i$) together with a Merkle authentication path (allegedly, the authentication path for $\mathtt{x}_i$); M' simply simulates M with the modification that, whenever M needs to access $\mathtt{x}_i$, M' will read $\tilde{\mathtt{x}}_i$ and verify it against $\sigma_\mathtt{x}$. We thus can construct a new instance $(M', \mathtt{x}', T', S')$ and witness $\mathtt{w}'$ where $\mathtt{x}' := \sigma_\mathtt{x}$ is short and $T' := T \cdot \mathsf{poly}(\kappa)$ and $S' = S$. However, now $|\mathtt{w}'| = |\mathtt{x}| \cdot \mathsf{poly}(\kappa) + |\mathtt{w}|$. But to deal with this we can use the transformation for large witnesses discussed above.[13]

[12] In fact here *universal one-way hash functions* [73, 86] suffice.

Overall, we have shown that the restriction that $|\mathtt{x}|, |\mathtt{w}| \le T$ essentially comes without any loss in generality or efficiency, and thus the reductions presented in this paper can also handle the cases in which $\mathtt{x}$ or $\mathtt{w}$ (or both) are large.

Reductions from other models. We have already noted that, because many problems arising in practice are algorithmic in nature and are written in high-level programming languages, it is convenient to use $\mathrm{BH}_{\mathsf{RAM}}$ as a starting point for reductions. For those occasions in which one is interested to use another model of computation as a starting point, one can always, e.g., write in C an interpreter for that model of computation and then compile it — after all, random-access machines are a powerful model of computation and can simulate other classical models of computation with little overhead [56, 78, 31, 83, 60, 85].

3. OPEN PROBLEMS

Leveraging the expressive power of combinatorial and algebraic properties of graphs and polynomials, in this paper we have developed tools for efficiently embedding generic computation of programs into the satisfiability of circuits and into algebraic constraint satisfaction problems. We believe that a deeper understanding of the efficiency (and inefficiency) of reductions from $\mathrm{BH}_{\mathsf{RAM}}$ to these problems, as well as other problems used in other protocols, is an important and exciting research direction. We list here several intriguing questions that our work leaves unanswered.

Arithmetizing RAMs with less overhead Our Theorem 1 gives a reduction from $\mathrm{BH}_{\mathsf{RAM}}$ to sCSAT with a circuit of size $O(|\delta| + (\log S + w) \cdot \log S) \cdot T$; in contrast, our Theorem 2 gives a reduction from $\mathrm{BH}_{\mathsf{RAM}}$ to sACSP with a field of size $O((\log T + kw) \cdot \log T \cdot d) \cdot T$. When $S = T$, the latter result is more expensive by "two $\log T$ factors": the degree d of the transition function δ, typically $\Omega(\log T)$, appears as a multiplicative factor in the field size; and each field element requires $\log |\mathbb{F}_{T,S}| \ge \log T$ bits to represent. Furthermore, when $S < T$, the $\log S$ factors in the former result are replaced by $\log T$ factors. While we conjecture that Theorem 1 is essentially tight, determining whether the additional $\log T$ factors to reduce from $\mathrm{BH}_{\mathsf{RAM}}$ to sACSP are inherent remains a challenging problem.

Programming deterministic models The reductions presented in this paper are inherently *non-deterministic*: they leverage non-determinism as a resource in order to gain efficiency by "enlarging" the witness. Indeed, many techniques used in this paper can be distilled into the paradigm of carefully choosing what additional information we should "put in the witness" because it is much faster to verify its goodness rather than to generate such information from scratch. Thus, even when M does not read any witness, our, e.g., Theorem 1 reduces $\mathrm{BH}_{\mathsf{RAM}}(M)$ to a circuit *satisfaction* prob-

[13] This last step is actually not needed if all the verifier wanted was to not have to keep around $\mathtt{x}$ and does not mind a machine running in time $\max\{|\mathtt{x}| \cdot \mathsf{poly}(\kappa), T\}$. Also, a similar strategy can handle the (potentially rarer) case in which $|M|$ is large (e.g., when it encodes some nonuniform program).

lem (that has a witness) and not a circuit *evaluation* one (that has no witness).

Our reliance on non-determinism for efficiency appears necessary: nondeterministic models of computation are quite robust under quasilinear-time reductions [79, 88, 53, 67, 57, 72] but reductions with such efficiency are not believed to exist for deterministic ones. Injecting non-determinism means that, unfortunately, our reductions cannot be used to benefit protocols that do not support nondeterminism; such protocols include all existing schemes for delegating polynomial-time functions, such as [46, 34, 25, 3, 21, 58]. Many of these protocols require a circuit or Turing machine representation, and the best (deterministic) reductions from random-access machine computations to (deterministic) circuit or Turing machine computations have a cost of $\Omega(T^2)$; such a cost is large for long computations, which are precisely the ones that we are likely to delegate. Thus, the applicability of proof systems that do *not* support nondeterminism is limited in the sense that they cannot benefit from the great efficiency benefits that nondeterminism brings to reductions.

While for sufficiently structured problems one can carry out careful circuit design with great efficiency gains [27], it is an interesting question whether reducing arbitrary random-access machines to "weaker" models of computation without the use of nondeterminism is bound to be expensive. Answering this question may be hard as it is related to circuit lower bounds.

Programming circuits for FHE Existing constructions of fully-homomorphic encryption [37] require a function to be represented as a circuit in order for it to be homomorphically evaluated on an encrypted input. The fact that our reductions leverage nondeterminism seems to imply that they cannot be used to efficiently program circuits for homomorphic evaluation either. Indeed, given only a random-access machine M and an encryption c of an input $\mathbf{x}$, it is not clear how to obtain an encryption of an assignment to the corresponding (succinctly-described) circuit generated by our reduction, without spending time that is at least quadratic in the running time of M on $\mathbf{x}$;[14] with such a slow transformation, one might as well have used the trivial quadratic (but deterministic) reduction from random-access machines to circuits. Thus, we do not know of any approach that is able to homomorphically evaluate a random-access machine in sub-quadratic time.[15]

While the aforementioned problem can be alleviated by exploiting the fact that the algorithms arising in practice are not "worst-case" [33], we believe it is an important open problem to either find a solution that can homomorphically evaluate an arbitrary random-access machine in, say, quasi-linear time, or show that such a solution is unlikely to exist. Until then, the applicability of fully-homomorphic encryption may be limited to sufficiently structured problems (i.e., those that are naturally represented as circuits) or algorithms with special properties (e.g., use little memory).

Other starting points and other targets? While we have argued that $\mathrm{BH}_{\mathsf{RAM}}$ is a natural starting point due to the ease with which high-level programming languages can be reduced to it, there may be other powerful models of computation that are perhaps better suited to run certain kinds of algorithms. We have already mentioned one such example, parallel RAMs, that in fact we can already support using the results of this paper. What other models of computation (not easily supported by RAMs or parallel RAMs) provide useful starting points? Conversely, we have focused on reducing $\mathrm{BH}_{\mathsf{RAM}}$ to sCSAT and sACSP; which other underlying problem representations urgently need efficient reductions?

4. PROOF STRATEGY

We prove Theorem 2 in two steps and the first step of our proof will yield a proof to Theorem 1. Concretely, we identify a convenient "stepping-stone" problem (similar to those used in [90, 11, 10]) that is a class of *succinct graph coloring problems* (sGCP). Roughly, an instance of sGCP consists of a coloring problem over a known (yet succinctly-represented) graph topology: each vertex in the graph has a corresponding coloring constraint (that can easily be deduced from the identity of the vertex) and this coloring constraint only involves the colors of the vertex itself and its neighbors. For comparison, sACSP can in fact be viewed as sGCP with the addition of certain algebraic constraints. Informally:

DEFINITION 3 (sGCP). *For a tuple of families* $\mathsf{par} = (\mathbf{V}, \mathbf{\Gamma}, \mathbf{K}, \mathbf{W})$ *where*

- $\mathbf{V} = \{V_{T,S}\}_{T,S\in\mathbb{N}}$ *and each* $V_{T,S}$ *is a vertex set,*
- $\mathbf{\Gamma} = \{\vec{\Gamma}_{T,S}\}_{T,S\in\mathbb{N}}$ *and each* $\vec{\Gamma}_{T,S} = (\Gamma_{T,S,1}, \dots, \Gamma_{T,S,|\vec{\Gamma}_{T,S}|})$ *is a vector of neighbor functions,*
- $\mathbf{K} = \{K_{T,S}\}_{T,S\in\mathbb{N}}$ *and each* $K_{T,S}$ *is a color constraint function,*
- $\mathbf{W} = \{\vec{W}_{T,S}\}_{T,S\in\mathbb{N}}$ *and each* $\vec{W}_{T,S} = (W_{T,S,1}, \dots, W_{T,S,T})$ *is a vector of vertex sets each contained in* $V_{T,S}$,

sGCP(par) *is the language of all* $(\mathbf{x}, T, S)$ *such that, for some coloring* C *of the vertices* $V_{T,S}$*, it holds that* $K_{T,S}(v, C(\Gamma_{T,S,1}(v)), \dots, C(\Gamma_{T,S,|\vec{\Gamma}_{T,S}|}(v))) = 0$ *for all* $v \in V_{T,S}$ *and* $\mathbf{x} = C|_{W_{T,S,|\mathbf{x}|}}$*. The language* sGCP *is then defined as the set of all* $(\mathsf{par}, \mathbf{x}, T, S)$ *such that* $(\mathbf{x}, T, S) \in$ sGCP(par).[16]

Our proof of Theorem 2 consists of the following two steps:

Step 1: from $\mathrm{BH}_{\mathsf{RAM}}$ to sGCP by "localizing & structuring" constraints. In this step we translate the constraints that determine correctness of computation of a given random-access machine M to a graph coloring problem over a graph with special topology (i.e., to some choice $(\mathbf{V}, \mathbf{\Gamma}, \mathbf{K}, \mathbf{W})$ of parameters for sGCP). This is where we tame the global and unstructured nature of the RAM's memory access operations, which can reach arbitrarily across memory and need

[14] Indeed, it is not clear how one would obtain, in less than quadratic time, an encryption of the transcript of the computation of M on $\mathbf{x}$, which is required in order to (homomorphically) solve the routing problem.

[15] A natural attempt would be to convert the given RAM into an *oblivious RAM* [43] in order to hide the information leaked by (logical) memory accesses, and then evaluate the transition function of the resulting "processor" under fully-homomorphic encryption in order to hide the registers and the oblivious RAM's secrets. However, in order to efficiently satisfy the processor's (oblivious) memory accesses, the evaluator needs to know the requested addresses, and these are produced in encrypted form. Thus, one needs an encryption scheme that lets the evaluator decrypt (correctly-computed) addresses and nothing else; no technique is known for this implausible-sounding goal.

[16] To ensure succinctness, vertex sets are represented via circuits that can output their elements and functions are represented via boolean circuits that compute them.

to be consistent with values stored arbitrarily long ago, by showing how to efficiently capture these by coloring constraints. The choice of topology and the fact that coloring constraints are local provides key properties that are used in the next step, during the process of arithmetization.

Step 2: from sGCP to sACSP by arithmetizing constraints. In this step we translate the choices of parameters for sGCP obtained in Step 1 to corresponding algebraic constraints in a finite field (i.e., to some choices of parameters $(\mathbf{F}, \mathbf{H}, \mathbf{N}, \mathbf{P}, \mathbf{I})$ for sACSP).

As mentioned, any sGCP problem easily induces a corresponding sCSAT problem: consider the boolean circuit that verifies (in parallel) all of the coloring constraints, and then takes the conjunction of all of these verification results; the succinctness of sGCP ensures that this boolean circuit can be represented succinctly. Thus, the reduction from sGCP to sCSAT is trivial and comes with no overhead. In the next two subsections (Section 4.1 and Section 4.2), we respectively discuss our proof strategy for Step 1, which will imply a proof to Theorem 1, and then Step 2, which together with Step 1 will imply Theorem 2.

4.1 Step 1: From BH_{RAM} To sGCP By Localizing & Structuring Constraints

The constraints that determine correctness of computation of a given random-access machine M can be divided into *code-consistency* constraints (i.e., did the machine correctly execute the correct instruction at every time step?) and *memory-consistency* constraints (i.e., did the machine load a value equal to the last stored value at the same address, every time it read from memory?). Our goal is to express these via a choice $(\mathbf{V}, \mathbf{\Gamma}, \mathbf{K}, \mathbf{W})$ of parameters for sGCP (see Definition 3) such that the underlying graph topology has certain special properties (to be discussed later). Let us fix a time bound T and let us temporarily fix the space bound S to be equal to T.

Given a time-ordered transcript of computation (i.e., a list of states of M) it is easy to locally check the code-consistency constraints: one can do so one at a time, considering pairs of adjacent states, by using the transition function δ of M. Furthermore, given a memory-ordered transcript of computation (i.e., a transcript of computation ordered by address, breaking ties using the timestamps) it is also easy to locally check the memory-consistency constraints: one can do so again one at a time, considering pairs of adjacent states, by ensuring that when a load follows a store at the same address the same value that was stored is loaded. The main difficulty, faced in every simulation result for machines with powerful memory models [4, 53, 84], is how to efficiently ensure that the time-ordered transcript and the memory-ordered transcript are encoding the same computation; the one technique that has been used to do so in all these results is various forms of *nondeterministic sorting*. Essentially, one relies on some mechanism that can verify that one list is either a sorting or a permutation of the other list [75, 87, 89].

In our case, we have several additional requirements: the mechanism must preserve succinctness, allow for a fast witness map, and have the appropriate structure to allow for an efficient arithmetization. (Let us temporarily ignore this last requirement of efficient arithmetization — we will address it in the next step in Section 4.2.) As the mechanism for nondeterministic sorting, we rely on a *routing network* with good algorithmic properties: *Beneš networks*. A Beneš network of size T is a graph with $O(\log T)$ columns, each with T vertices, that can route T elements from the first column to the last column, according to any given permutation, with no congestion. Here "route" simply means that intermediate columns receive a packet and either forward it to the "up neighbor" or "down neighbor" of the next column. Crucially, these routing decisions can be efficiently computed (and then treated as colors) in time linear in the size of the graph [13, 91, 76, 64] or in parallel time $O((\log T)^2)$ [74].

We can then define $\mathbf{V}$ and $\mathbf{\Gamma}$ to encode a family of Beneš networks of the appropriate size and define $\mathbf{K}$ to be a family of coloring constraints that verifies code-consistency, memory-consistency, or routing constraints depending on whether the colors to be verified are on the first column, last column, or middle columns of the appropriate Beneš network. Additional care is required to appropriately define a family of vertex sets $\mathbf{W}$ that takes care of consistency of the transcript with the input x. (Indeed, not only do we need to ensure via constraints that some valid computation occurred, but we must also establish that this computation had something to do with the specific input at hand.)

When the space bound S is not equal to T, however, the above simplistic approach is not efficient enough because the Beneš network has $O(T \log T)$ vertices and we can only afford graphs of size $O(T \log S)$. To tackle this problem, Robson [84] devises a system of checkpoints to ensure that he never has to sort a list much larger than S; his construction of a CNF formula, however, is further complicated by the fact that he is simulating a machine where the memory cells can store arbitrarily large values and thus must resort to an amortization scheme on top of his system of checkpoints.

We use a simpler approach. Concretely, we first transform M into a new machine M' that runs M with the twist that, every S steps of computation of M are preceded and followed by reading all S memory cells in order, *twice* in a row. (Note that the running time of M' is at most three times that of M.) The memory accesses of M', due to their special pattern, can be routed with a permutation that exhibits strong *locality*: essentially, no state needs to be routed more than $2S$ far from its position in the time ordered transcript, since every memory address is accessed at least once in every $2S$ steps. This observation raises the hope of leveraging "shallower" routing networks that can route only sufficiently local permutations. Such routing networks do exist [59]. In fact, in our case, the permutations that we need to route enjoy additional properties besides their locality and it suffices to consider the subnetwork consisting of the first $O(\log S)$ columns of the Beneš network — essentially, this subnetwork consists of T/S Beneš networks of size $O(S)$, and thus we still benefit from the algorithmic results for Beneš networks.

Overall, we reduce BH_{RAM} to a sGCP over a certain family of "shallow" Beneš networks. Formalizing the above intuition involves many technical details, including some imposed by the requirement that all of the above must be able to be expressed succinctly and imposing other coloring constraints not discussed above. As stated above, doing so yields a proof to Theorem 1.

4.2 Step 2: From sGCP To sACSP By Arithmetizing Constraints

Our second step is to efficiently arithmetize the sGCP problem on the graphs obtained in the first step. That is, we need to map the choice of parameters $(\mathbf{V}, \mathbf{\Gamma}, \mathbf{K}, \mathbf{W})$, where $(\mathbf{V}, \mathbf{\Gamma})$ encodes a family of shallow Beneš networks, to a choice of parameters $(\mathbf{F}, \mathbf{H}, \mathbf{N}, \mathbf{P}, \mathbf{I})$ for sACSP (see Definition 2) with as small a field size as possible while at the same time preserving succinctness. This process is quite delicate because one runs the risk of obtaining high-degree polynomials that are either not sparse or do not have small arithmetic circuits, or, worse, have a degree that is *too* high thereby forcing us to make the field size too large. Building on the initial work of Ben-Sasson et al. [10], we develop a set of algebraic tools that leverages the additive structure of subspaces of finite fields to tackle various problems that arise during arithmetization; many of these insights leverage the computational properties of *linearized polynomials* [65, Section 2.5].

At high level, we have two subtasks:

1. **Graph Arithmetization.** While the definition of sGCP does not impose any constraints on the vertex set family $\mathbf{V}$ and neighbor function family $\mathbf{\Gamma}$, the definition of sACSP imposes algebraic constraints on the vertex set family $\mathbf{H}$ and the neighbor function family $\mathbf{N}$. Namely, each vertex set $H_{T,S} \in \mathbf{H}$ must be a *subspace* of the field $\mathbb{F}_{T,S}$ and each vector of neighbor functions $\vec{N}_{T,S} \in \mathbf{N}$ must be a vector of (univariate) *polynomials* over $\mathbb{F}_{T,S}$. Thus, we need a way to efficiently arithmetize a shallow Beneš network: find $H_{T,S}$ and $\vec{N}_{T,S}$ such that the the graph induced by $(H_{T,S}, \vec{N}_{T,S})$ contains as a subgraph a shallow Beneš network of size T and $O(\log S)$ columns, where $H_{T,S}$ is as small as possible and $\vec{N}_{T,S}$ contains as few low-degree polynomials as possible.

   For this subtask we recall a routing network whose algebraic properties have been studied before by Polishchuk and Spielman [81], Ben-Sasson and Sudan [11], and Ben-Sasson et al. [9, 10]: *De Bruijn graphs.* When cast in our language, Ben-Sasson et al. [11] showed how to arithmetize a De Bruijn graph of size T (having $O(T \log T)$ vertices) with an affine subspace $H_{T,S}$ of size $O(T \log T)$ and a constant number of degree-1 polynomials in $\vec{N}_{T,S}$.

   Unfortunately, we do not know if an analogous result holds for the shallow Beneš networks constructed in our first step. Nonetheless, these can still be embedded in De Bruijn graphs of size T, so that Beneš networks benefit from the aforementioned result of Ben-Sasson and Sudan as well. Crucially, the algorithmic properties of Beneš networks carry over to De Bruijn graphs.

2. **Constraints Arithmetization.** Once again, while the definition of sGCP does not impose any constraints on the color constraint function family $\mathbf{K}$, the definition of sACSP requires that the constraint function family $\mathbf{P}$ be a family of (multivariate) polynomials where, essentially, for each $P_{T,S} \in \mathbf{P}$ all variables but the first have low degree. How to map $\mathbf{K}$ to $\mathbf{P}$? Doing so is the most delicate part of our reduction from sGCP to sACSP, so let us briefly discuss it next.

Storing coloring information A witness to the sACSP problem is an *assignment polynomial* $A \colon \mathbb{F}_{T,S} \to \mathbb{F}_{T,S}$ of degree at most $|H_{T,S}|$. Such a polynomial A can be interpreted as assigning a "color" to each field element in $\mathbb{F}_{T,S}$, and thus A can be thought of as a "low-degree coloring function". A first difficulty is about how we should store coloring information A in a way that it can be efficiently retrieved by the constraint polynomial $P_{T,S} \in \mathbf{P}$. Concretely, suppose that we have a coloring function $C \colon V_{T,S} \to \{0,1\}^c$, assigning a color of c bits to each vertex in the De Bruijn graph, that is a witness to the sGCP problem (and, for simplicity, assume that $c \le \log |\mathbb{F}_{T,S}|$). A natural approach would be to ensure that the bit string $C(v)$ is stored in the bit representation of $A(\Phi(v))$, where Φ is the function that embeds the vertex set $V_{T,S}$ of the De Bruijn graph into the field (guaranteed by the graph arithmetization discussed above). Such an economical "packing", however, has the problem that retrieving any given bit from $A(\Phi(v))$ requires a *projection polynomial* that has degree $\Omega(T)$; when the projection polynomial is composed with A, which also has degree $\Omega(T)$, we obtain a variable with degree $\Omega(T^2)$ — far too expensive.

To avoid this problem, we in fact use not just *one* De Bruijn graph but instead create c *copies* of the De Bruijn graph in $\mathbb{F}_{T,S}$. That is, we do not set $H_{T,S} = \Phi(V_{T,S})$ but instead consider an "extended vertex set" $\hat{V}_{T,S} := \bigcup_{j=1}^{c} (\Phi(V_{T,S}) + \theta_j)$ where $(\theta_j)_{j=1}^{c}$ is a vector of c (fixed) affine shifts of $\Phi(V_{T,S})$ chosen so that, $\forall j,k \in [c]$, $(\Phi(V_{T,S}) + \theta_j) \cap (\Phi(V_{T,S}) + \theta_k) = \emptyset$ and $\hat{V}_{T,S}$ is contained in a subspace of size $O(c \cdot |\Phi(V_{T,S})|)$. We can then store the i-th bit that C associates with the vertex $v \in V_{T,S}$ on the field element $\Phi(v) + \theta_i$, i.e., we ensure that $A(\Phi(v) + \theta_i) = C(v)_i$. Now no projection polynomials are needed to retrieve any given bit of a color because field elements store single bits. Overall, $H_{T,S}$ can (roughly) be set to be equal to $\hat{V}_{T,S}$ and $\vec{N}_{T,S}$ can (roughly) be set to equal to the $c \cdot O(1)$ degree-1 polynomials obtained by considering all the c shifts of the $O(1)$ degree-1 polynomials induced by the embedding Φ.

Having ensured that color information can be retrieved efficiently let us briefly discuss the construction of the constraint polynomial $P_{T,S} \in \mathbf{P}$, which will constrain the values of a candidate-witness low-degree polynomials, starting from the boolean circuit $K_{T,S} \in \mathbf{K}$.

Building the constraint polynomial The boolean circuit $K_{T,S}$ takes as input the current vertex $v \in V_{T,S}$ together with the colors assigned to the vertices in its "neighborhood", namely, to $\Gamma_{T,S,1}(v), \ldots, \Gamma_{T,S,|\vec{\Gamma}_{T,S}|}(v)$. The constraint polynomial $P_{T,S}$ takes as input $\Phi(v)$ together with the colors that A assigns to the field elements in its neighborhood, namely, the colors that A assigns to $N_{T,S,1}(\Phi(v)), \ldots, N_{T,S,|\vec{N}_T|}(\Phi(v))$.

Intuitively, $P_{T,S}$ has to evaluate $K_{T,S}$ as part of its computation. Yet, $P_{T,S}$ only has access to $\Phi(v)$, but not to v, so that $P_{T,S}$ must compute the bits of v himself in order to pass them on to $K_{T,S}$. We show that, *given* the bit representation of $\Phi(v)$, computing v amounts to only evaluating a collection of (easy-to-compute) multilinear polynomials. Furtermore, in this case it is not a problem to use (high-degree) projection polynomials to deduce the bits of $\Phi(v)$ starting from $\Phi(v)$ because (i) these are not composed with A, and (ii) despite being high-degree they can be shown to be sparse (since they are *linearized polynomials* [65, Section 2.5]).

Another issue is that the embedding of the De Bruijn graph mentioned earlier is not perfect: while a De Bruijn graph has out-degree 2 the embedding Φ requires $O(1)$ edges inside the field. We do not know a priori which of the neighbors of $\Phi(v)$ are "true" (i.e., are images of neighbors of v

in the De Bruijn graph), and thus $P_{T,S}$ needs to figure out which are the colors in the neighborhood of $\Phi(v)$ that should be forwarded to $K_{T,S}$ as inputs. We observe that, given the bit representation of $\Phi(v)$ (which $P_{T,S}$ already computes for the reasons explained in the previous paragraph) it is possible to use constant-degree *multiplexer polynomials* to select which are the true neighbors of $\Phi(v)$.

There are additional issues, requiring careful arithmetization, needed for the final construction of $P_{T,S}$. For example, we need a small arithmetic circuit for an *alternator polynomial*: namely, a polynomial that, given two subspaces $V, W \subseteq \mathbb{F}_{T,S}$ with $V \subseteq W$, is equal to 1 on V but vanishes everywhere on $W - V$. Such a polynomial is useful because it allows to "turn on" a given constraint on the subspace V but to specifically turn off the same constraint everywhere on $V - W$ (where another constraint can be turned on). An alternator polynomial has degree $|W|$, which is very large; nonetheless, we show how to make a small arithmetic circuit for it, even if the polynomial itself is not sparse.

In summary Once again, formalizing the above intuition involves many technical details, mostly having to do with keeping track of how expensive it is to convert, represent, and access the very large objects involved, as well as enforcing consistency with the input $\mathtt{x}$ (by appropriately defining the family of vector of subspaces $\mathbf{I}$). Overall, we obtain a choice of parameters $(\mathbf{F}, \mathbf{H}, \mathbf{N}, \mathbf{P}, \mathbf{I})$ for sACSP where $|H_{T,S}| = O(cT \log T)$, $\vec{N}_{T,S}$ contains $O(c)$ degree-1 polynomials, and $P_{T,S}$ has degree $|H_{T,S}|$ and total degree $\deg(K_{T,S})$ in the other variables. These settings allow us to choose a field $\mathbb{F}_{T,S}$ of size $O(cT \log T \deg(K_{T,S}))$. In Step 1, $c = \log T + kw$ and $\deg(K_{T,S}) = d$ (i.e., the degree of the transition function of M), as claimed in Theorem 2. The efficiency properties of converting the witness follow from routing algorithms on De Bruijn graphs (discussed in Step 1) and additive-FFT techniques [68].

5. REFERENCES

[1] M. Abe and S. Fehr. Perfect NIZK with adaptive soundness. In *TCC '07: Proceedings of the 4th Theory of Cryptography Conference on Theory of Cryptography*, pages 118–136, Berlin, Heidelberg, 2007. Springer-Verlag.

[2] D. Angluin and L. G. Valiant. Fast probabilistic algorithms for hamiltonian circuits and matchings. In *Proceedings on 9th Annual ACM Symposium on Theory of Computing*, STOC '77, pages 30–41, 1977.

[3] B. Applebaum, Y. Ishai, and E. Kushilevitz. From secrecy to soundness: Efficient verification via secure computation. In *Proceedings of the 37th International Colloquium on Automata, Languages and Programming*, ICALP '10, pages 152–163, 2010.

[4] L. Babai, L. Fortnow, L. A. Levin, and M. Szegedy. Checking computations in polylogarithmic time. In *Proceedings of the 23rd Annual ACM Symposium on Theory of Computing*, STOC '91, pages 21–32, 1991.

[5] B. Barak and O. Goldreich. Universal arguments and their applications. *SIAM Journal on Computing*, 38(5):1661–1694, 2008. Preliminary version appeared in CCC '02. We reference the version available online at `http://www.wisdom.weizmann.ac.il/~oded/PS/ua-rev3.ps`.

[6] M. Ben-Or, S. Goldwasser, J. Kilian, and A. Wigderson. Multi-prover interactive proofs: how to remove intractability assumptions. In *Proceedings of the 20th Annual ACM Symposium on Theory of Computing*, STOC '88, pages 113–131, 1988.

[7] E. Ben-Sasson, A. Chiesa, D. Genkin, and E. Tromer. Fast reductions from RAMs to delegatable succinct constraint satisfaction problems, 2012. Cryptology ePrint Archive, Report 2012/071.

[8] E. Ben-Sasson, A. Chiesa, D. Genkin, and E. Tromer. On the concrete-efficiency threshold of probabilistically-checkable proofs, 2012. Electronic Colloquium on Computational Complexity, TR12-045.

[9] E. Ben-Sasson, O. Goldreich, P. Harsha, M. Sudan, and S. Vadhan. Robust PCPs of proximity, shorter PCPs and applications to coding. In *Proceedings of the 26th Annual ACM Symposium on Theory of Computing*, STOC '04, pages 1–10, 2004.

[10] E. Ben-Sasson, O. Goldreich, P. Harsha, M. Sudan, and S. Vadhan. Short PCPs verifiable in polylogarithmic time. In *Proceedings of the 20th Annual IEEE Conference on Computational Complexity*, CCC '05, pages 120–134, 2005.

[11] E. Ben-Sasson and M. Sudan. Short PCPs with polylog query complexity. *SIAM Journal on Computing*, 38(2):551–607, 2008. Preliminary version appeared in STOC '05.

[12] E. Ben-Sasson, M. Sudan, S. Vadhan, and A. Wigderson. Randomness-efficient low degree tests and short pcps via epsilon-biased sets. In *Proceedings of the 35th Annual ACM Symposium on Theory of Computing*, STOC '03, pages 612–621, 2003.

[13] V. E. Beneš. *Mathematical theory of connecting networks and telephone traffic*. New York, Academic Press, 1965.

[14] N. Bitansky, R. Canetti, A. Chiesa, and E. Tromer. From extractable collision resistance to succinct non-interactive arguments of knowledge, and back again. Cryptology ePrint Archive, Report 2011/443, 2011.

[15] N. Bitansky, R. Canetti, A. Chiesa, and E. Tromer. Recursive composition and bootstrapping for SNARKs and proof-carrying data. Cryptology ePrint Archive, Report 2011/95, 2012.

[16] N. Bitansky and A. Chiesa. Succinct arguments from multi-prover interactive proofs and their efficiency benefits. In *Proceedings of the 32nd Annual International Cryptology Conference on Advances in Cryptology*, CRYPTO '12, 2012.

[17] M. Blum, W. Evans, P. Gemmell, S. Kannan, and M. Naor. Checking the correctness of memories. In *Proceedings of the 32nd Annual Symposium on Foundations of Computer Science*, FOCS '91, pages 90–99, 1991.

[18] R. B. Boppana, J. Håstad, and S. Zachos. Does co-NP have short interactive proofs? *Information Processing Letters*, 25(2):127–132, 1987.

[19] Z. Brakerski, C. Gentry, and V. Vinod. (leveled) fully homomorphic encryption without bootstrapping. In *Proceedings of the 4th Symposium on Innovations in Theoretical Computer Science*, ITCS '12, pages 309–325, 2012.

[20] G. Brassard, D. Chaum, and C. Crépeau. Minimum

disclosure proofs of knowledge. *Journal of Computer and System Sciences*, 37(2):156–189, 1988.

[21] R. Canetti, B. Riva, and G. N. Rothblum. Two 1-round protocols for delegation of computation. Cryptology ePrint Archive, Report 2011/518, 2011.

[22] A. Chiesa and E. Tromer. Proof-carrying data and hearsay arguments from signature cards. In *Proceedings of the 1st Symposium on Innovations in Computer Science*, ICS '10, pages 310–331, 2010.

[23] A. Chiesa and E. Tromer. Proof-carrying data: Secure computation on untrusted platforms (high-level description). *The Next Wave: The National Security Agency's review of emerging technologies*, 19(2):40–46, 2012.

[24] K.-M. Chung, Y. Kalai, F.-H. Liu, and R. Raz. Memory delegation. In *Proceedings of the 31st Annual International Cryptology Conference*, CRYPTO '11, pages 151–168, 2011.

[25] K.-M. Chung, Y. Kalai, and S. Vadhan. Improved delegation of computation using fully homomorphic encryption. In *Proceedings of the 30th Annual International Cryptology Conference*, CRYPTO '10, pages 483–501, 2010.

[26] S. A. Cook and R. A. Reckhow. Time-bounded random access machines. In *Proceedings of the 4th Annual ACM Symposium on Theory of Computing*, STOC '72, pages 73–80, 1972.

[27] G. Cormode, M. Mitzenmacher, and J. Thaler. Practical verified computation with streaming interactive proofs. In *Proceedings of the 4th Symposium on Innovations in Theoretical Computer Science*, ITCS '12, pages 90–112, 2012.

[28] G. Cormode, J. Thaler, and K. Yi. Verifying computations with streaming interactive proofs. ECCC, 2010. Available at `http://eccc.hpi-web.de/report/2010/159/`.

[29] I. Damgård, S. Faust, and C. Hazay. Secure two-party computation with low communication. In *Proceedings of the 9th International Conference on Theory of Cryptography*, TCC '12, pages 54–74, 2012.

[30] G. Di Crescenzo and H. Lipmaa. Succinct NP proofs from an extractability assumption. In *CiE '08*, pages 175–185, 2008.

[31] P. W. Dymond and M. Tompa. Speedups of deterministic machines by synchronous parallel machines. In *STOC '83*, pages 336–343, 1983.

[32] F. E. Fich. The complexity of computation on the parallel random access machine. In *[82]*, pages 843–899, 1993.

[33] C. Fletcher, M. van Dijk, and S. Devadas. Compilation techniques for efficient encrypted computation. Cryptology ePrint Archive, Report 2012/266, 2012.

[34] R. Gennaro, C. Gentry, and B. Parno. Non-interactive verifiable computing: outsourcing computation to untrusted workers. In *Proceedings of the 30th Annual International Cryptology Conference*, CRYPTO '10, pages 465–482, 2010.

[35] R. Gennaro, C. Gentry, B. Parno, and M. Raykova. Quadratic span programs and succinct NIZKs without PCPs. Cryptology ePrint Archive, Report 2012/215, 2012.

[36] R. Gennaro and D. Wichs. Fully homomorphic message authenticators. Cryptology ePrint Archive, Report 2012/290, 2012.

[37] C. Gentry. Fully homomorphic encryption using ideal lattices. In *Proceedings of the 41st Annual ACM Symposium on Theory of Computing*, pages 169–178, 2009.

[38] C. Gentry and S. Halevi. Fully homomorphic encryption without squashing using depth-3 arithmetic circuits. In *Proceedings of the IEEE 52nd Annual Symposium on Foundations of Computer Science*, FOCS' 11, pages 107–109, 2011.

[39] C. Gentry and S. Halevi. Implementing Gentry's fully-homomorphic encryption scheme. In *Proceedings of the 29th Annual International Conference on the Theory and Applications of Cryptographic Techniques*, EUROCRYPT '11, pages 129–148, 2011.

[40] C. Gentry, H. Shai, and N. P. Smart. Better bootstrapping in fully homomorphic encryption. In *PKC '12*, pages 1–16, 2012.

[41] C. Gentry, H. Shai, and N. P. Smart. Fully homomorphic encryption with polylog overhead. In *EUROCRYPT '12*, pages 465–482, 2012.

[42] O. Goldreich and J. Håstad. On the complexity of interactive proofs with bounded communication. *Information Processing Letters*, 67(4):205–214, 1998.

[43] O. Goldreich and R. Ostrovsky. Software protection and simulation on oblivious RAMs. *Journal of the ACM*, 43:431–473, May 1996.

[44] O. Goldreich and M. Sudan. Locally testable codes and pcps of almost-linear length. *Journal of the ACM*, 53:558–655, July 2006. Preliminary version in STOC '02.

[45] O. Goldreich, S. Vadhan, and A. Wigderson. On interactive proofs with a laconic prover. *Computational Complexity*, 11(1/2):1–53, 2002.

[46] S. Goldwasser, Y. T. Kalai, and G. N. Rothblum. Delegating computation: interactive proofs for muggles. In *STOC '08: Proceedings of the 40th Annual ACM Symposium on Theory of Computing*, pages 113–122, New York, NY, USA, 2008. ACM.

[47] S. Goldwasser, H. Lin, and A. Rubinstein. Delegation of computation without rejection problem from designated verifier CS-proofs. Cryptology ePrint Archive, Report 2011/456, 2011.

[48] J. Groth. Linear algebra with sub-linear zero-knowledge arguments. In *CRYPTO '09*, pages 192–208, 2009.

[49] J. Groth. Short non-interactive zero-knowledge proofs. In *Proceedings of the 16th International Conference on the Theory and Application of Cryptology and Information Security*, ASIACRYPT '10, pages 341–358, 2010.

[50] J. Groth. Short pairing-based non-interactive zero-knowledge arguments. In *ASIACRYPT '10*, pages 321–340, 2010.

[51] J. Groth, R. Ostrovsky, and A. Sahai. Non-interactive zaps and new techniques for NIZK. In *Proceedings of the 26th Annual International Conference on Advances in Cryptology*, CRYPTO '06, pages 97–111, 2006.

[52] J. Groth, R. Ostrovsky, and A. Sahai. Perfect

non-interactive zero knowledge for NP. In *EUROCRYPT '06*, pages 339–358, 2006.

[53] Y. Gurevich and S. Shelah. Nearly linear time. In *Logic at Botik '89, Symposium on Logical Foundations of Computer Science*, pages 108–118, 1989.

[54] P. Harsha. *Robust PCPs of Proximity and Shorter PCPs*. PhD thesis, MIT, EECS, September 2004.

[55] P. Harsha and M. Sudan. Small PCPs with low query complexity. *Computational Complexity*, 9(3–4):157–201, Dec 2000. Preliminary version in STACS '91.

[56] J. Hopcroft, W. Paul, and L. Valiant. On time versus space. *Journal of the ACM*, 24(2):332–337, 1977.

[57] N. D. Jones. Constant time factors do matter. In *Proceedings of the 25th Annual ACM Symposium on Theory of Computing*, STOC '93, pages 602–611, 1993.

[58] Y. Kalai, R. Raz, and R. Rothblum. Where delegation meets Einstein. Isaac Newton Institute for Mathematical Sciences, Formal and Computational Cryptographic Proofs, 2012.

[59] R. Kannan. The KR-Beneš network: A control-optimal rearrangeable permutation network. *IEEE Transactions on Computers*, 54(5):534–544, 2005.

[60] J. Katajainen, J. van Leeuwen, and M. Penttonen. Fast simulation of Turing machines by random access machines. *SIAM Journal on Computing*, 17(1):77–88, 1988.

[61] J. Kilian. A note on efficient zero-knowledge proofs and arguments. In *STOC '92*, pages 723–732, 1992.

[62] A. N. Kolmogorov. To the definition of an algorithm. *Uspekhi Matematicheskikh Nauk*, 8(4):175–176, 1953.

[63] A. N. Kolmogorov and V. A. Uspenskiĭ. To the definition of an algorithm. *Uspekhi Matematicheskikh Nauk*, 13(4):3–28, 1958. In Russian. English translation in in AMS Translations, ser. 2, vol. 21 (1963), 217–245.

[64] F. T. Leighton. *Introduction to parallel algorithms and architectures: array, trees, hypercubes*. Morgan Kaufmann Publishers Inc., San Francisco, CA, USA, 1992.

[65] R. Lidl and H. Niederreiter. *Finite Fields*. Cambridge University Press, Cambridge, UK, second edition edition, 1997.

[66] H. Lipmaa. Progression-free sets and sublinear pairing-based non-interactive zero-knowledge arguments. In *TCC '12*, pages 169–189, 2012.

[67] M. C. Loui and D. R. Luginbuhl. Optimal on-line simulations of tree machines by random access machines. *SIAM Journal on Computing*, 21(5):959–971, 1992.

[68] T. Mateer. *Fast Fourier Transform algorithms with applications*. PhD thesis, Clemson University, 2008.

[69] O. Meir. Combinatorial pcps with short proofs. In *CCC '12*, 2012.

[70] R. C. Merkle. A certified digital signature. In *CRYPTO '89*, pages 218–238, 1989.

[71] S. Micali. Computationally sound proofs. *SIAM Journal on Computing*, 30(4):1253–1298, 2000. Preliminary version appeared in FOCS '94.

[72] A. V. Naik, K. W. Regan, and D. Sivakumar. On quasilinear-time complexity theory. In *Proceedings of the 11th Annual Symposium on Theoretical Aspects of Computer Science*, STACS '94, pages 325–349, 1994.

[73] M. Naor and M. Yung. Universal one-way hash functions and their cryptographic applications. In *STOC '89*, pages 33–43, 1989.

[74] D. Nassimi and S. Sahni. Parallel algorithms to set up the Beneš permutation network. *IEEE Transactions on Computers*, 31(2):148–154, 1982.

[75] Y. P. Ofman. A universal automaton. *Transactions of the Moscow Mathematical Society*, 14:200–215, 1965.

[76] D. C. Opferman and N. T. Tsao-Wu. On a class of rearrangeable switching networks - part i: Control algorithm. *Bell System Technical Journal*, 50(5):1579–1600, 1971.

[77] C. H. Papadimitriou. *Computational Complexity*. Addison-Wesley, Reading, MA, USA, 1994.

[78] W. J. Paul. *Komplexitätstheorie*. Teubner, Stuttgart, Germany, 1978.

[79] W. J. Paul and R. Reischuk. On time versus space II. In *Proceedings of the 20th Annual Symposium on Foundations of Computer Science*, FOCS '79, pages 298–306, 1979.

[80] N. Pippenger and M. J. Fischer. Relations among complexity measures. *Journal of the ACM*, 26:361–381, April 1979.

[81] A. Polishchuk and D. A. Spielman. Nearly-linear size holographic proofs. In *STOC '94*, pages 194–203, 1994.

[82] J. H. Reif. *Synthesis of parallel algorithms*. Morgan Kaufman, San Mateo, CA, USA, 1993.

[83] J. M. Robson. Fast probabilistic RAM simulation of single tape turing machine computations. *Information and Control*, 63(1-2):67–87, 1986.

[84] J. M. Robson. An O(T log T) reduction from RAM computations to satisfiability. *Theoretical Computer Science*, 82(1):141–149, May 1991.

[85] J. M. Robson. Deterministic simulation of a single tape turing machine by a random access machine in sub-linear time. *Information and Computation*, 99(1):109–121, 1992.

[86] J. Rompel. One-way functions are necessary and sufficient for secure signatures. In *STOC '90*, pages 387–394, 1990.

[87] C.-P. Schnorr. Satisfiability is quasilinear complete in NQL. *Journal of the ACM*, 25:136–145, January 1978.

[88] A. Schönhage. Storage modification machines. *SIAM Journal on Computing*, 9(3):490–508, 1980.

[89] R. E. Stearns and H. B. I. Hunt. On the complexity of the satisfiability problem and the structure of NP. Technical Report 82-21, State University of New York at Albany, Computer Science Department, 1986.

[90] R. Venkatesan and L. Levin. Random instances of a graph coloring problem are hard. In *Proceedings of the 20th Annual ACM Symposium on Theory of Computing*, STOC '88, pages 217–222, 1988.

[91] A. Waksman. A permutation network. *Journal of the ACM*, 15(1):159–163, 1968.

[92] H. Wee. On round-efficient argument systems. In *Proceedings of the 32nd International Colloquium on Automata, Languages and Programming*, ICALP '05, pages 140–152, 2005.

Resource-based Corruptions and the Combinatorics of Hidden Diversity

Juan Garay
AT&T Labs – Research
Florham Park, NJ
garay@research.att.com

David Johnson
AT&T Labs – Research
Florham Park, NJ
dsj@research.att.com

Aggelos Kiayias
National and Kapodistrian University of Athens
Athens, Greece
aggelos@kiayias.com

Moti Yung
Google Inc. and Columbia University
New York, NY
moti@cs.columbia.edu

ABSTRACT

In the setting of cryptographic protocols, the corruption of a party has traditionally been viewed as a simple, uniform and atomic operation, where the adversary decides to get control over a party and this party immediately gets corrupted. In this paper, motivated by the fact that different players may require different resources to get corrupted, we put forth the notion of *resource-based corruptions*, where the adversary must invest some resources in order to corrupt a player.

If the adversary has full information about the system configuration then resource-based corruptions would provide no fundamental difference from the standard corruption model. However, in a resource "anonymous" setting, in the sense that such configuration is hidden from the adversary, much is to be gained in terms of efficiency and security.

We showcase the power of such *hidden diversity* in the context of secure multiparty computation (MPC) with resource-based corruptions and prove that anonymity it can effectively be used to circumvent known impossibility results. Specifically, if OPT is the corruption budget that violates the completeness of MPC (the case when half or more of the players are corrupted), we show that if hidden diversity is available, the completeness of MPC can be made to hold against an adversary with as much as a $B \cdot OPT$ budget, for any constant $B > 1$. This result requires a suitable choice of parameters (in terms of number of players and their hardness to corrupt), which we provide and further prove other tight variants of the result when the said choice is not available. Regarding efficiency gains, we show that hidden diversity can be used to force the corruption threshold to drop from $1/2$ to $1/3$, in turn allowing the use of much more efficient (information-theoretic) MPC protocols.

We achieve the above through a series of technical contributions:

- The modeling of the corruption process in the setting of cryptographic protocols through *corruption oracles* as well as the introduction of a notion of reduction to relate such oracles;
- the abstraction of the corruption game as a combinatorial problem and its analysis; and, importantly,
- the formulation of the notion of *inversion effort preserving* (IEP) functions which is a type of direct-sum property, and the property of *hardness indistinguishability*. While hardness indistinguishability enables the dissociation of parties' identities and the resources needed to corrupt them, IEP enables the discretization of adversarial work into corruption tokens,

all of which may be of independent interest.

Categories and Subject Descriptors

C.2.0 [**COMPUTER-COMM. NETWORKS**]: Security and Protection; E.3 [**DATA ENCRYPTION**]: Public key cryptosystems; G.2.1 [**DISCRETE MATHEMATICS**]: Combinatorics—*Combinatorial algorithms*

Keywords

Cost of corruption, secure multi-party computation, combinatorial analysis, exact hardness, hardness amplification.

1. INTRODUCTION

The notion of computing in the presence of an adversary which controls or gets access to parts of the system is at the heart of modern cryptography. This paradigm has given rise to cryptosystems and protocols which achieve general tasks in the presence of powerful adversaries. A prime example of the paradigm are "completeness theorems" which show that a distributed cryptographic protocol exists where an adversary controlling any minority of the parties, cannot prevent the secure computation of any efficient functionality defined over their inputs [22]. Similar secure multiparty computation (MPC) results hold over secure channels (and no additional cryptography) with an adversary controlling less than a third of the parties [5, 9]. Furthermore, these results are tight in the sense that when the adversary controls more parties there are functionalities that cannot be securely implemented.

In the works thus far however, the corruption of a party has been viewed as a simple, uniform and atomic operation where the adversary decides to corrupt a party and this party gets corrupted. The only limit the adversary has is on the number of individual party's corruptions and restrictions on when and how it can corrupt.

In this paper we are motivated by the fact that different players may require different resources to get corrupted. Indeed, the price paid for penetrating one organization, measured for example by the amount of money that a corrupt employee might have demanded, may differ from the cost of getting into another organization. Another example of a more cryptographic nature is when two organizations employ different password policies, or utilize VPN's relying on cryptosystems of different strengths. Taking such real world considerations into account gives rise to the notion we put forth of *resource-based corruption*, where the adversary must invest certain resources in order to corrupt a party. The initiation of the study of corruption models which describe situations like the above is our first contribution.

In a setting where the adversary has full information about a system, resource-based corruptions provide no fundamental divergence from the logic of the standard corruption model. The adversary, given an initial corruption budget, will target the largest subset of the system that it can afford and if such subset if large enough, the disruption of various security properties will ensue (as it follows from, e.g., [10]). The interesting case thus arises when the parties act on the system "anonymously" from the point of view of the adversary, in the sense that the association of parties' names and the individual corruption resources they require remains hidden. In this way, it seems plausible that a portion of the corruption budget will have to be wasted to learn the system configuration. Our second contribution is thus the investigation of the quantitative effect of this type of hidden diversity in the context of resource-based corruptions.

The problem the adversary faces can be abstracted as the following combinatorial game. The adversary is given a number of balls ("corruption tokens") and is faced with a sequence of buckets with the objective to fill a certain fraction of them. While it knows all the bucket sizes, it does not know their correspondence to the individual buckets in the sequence. If OPT is the minimum number of balls required to fill a given percentage of the buckets had the adversary been privy to the correspondence between the buckets and their sizes, how many balls as a function of OPT would be required if such hidden diversity is provided? We analyze this setting as "the combinatorics of hidden diversity" and show a number of results concerning the initial partial knowledge given to the adversary and the strategies it can apply. The analysis leads to corruption strategies (algorithms) and corruption impossibilities (lower bounds), under various cases of partial knowledge and size parameters.

Most importantly, we prove that the "value of hidden diversity" can be *unbounded!* Specifically, for any B there are ways to choose buckets' sizes so that the required resources needed by the adversary to reach its target would be $B \cdot OPT$, i.e., an arbitrarily high inflation of the required corruption budget (the cryptographic implications of this are shown below).

To realize the abstractions made above—including the combinatorial game for corruptions—we introduce a formal framework where there is a special entity called a *corruption oracle* that mediates the adversary's corruption capability. We describe a variety of natural corruption oracles and introduce a notion of reduction between them that makes the translation between different corruption games that an adversary might choose feasible. In particular this allows us to capture and quantify the setting where corruptions occur due to the inversion of computationally hard problem instances (what we call "computational corruptions").

Our third contribution is the study of the sufficient conditions under which such computational corruptions can be abstracted as token-based corruptions. First, we formulate the notion of *Inversion Effort Preserving* (IEP) functions, which, at a high level, postulates a complexity lower bound on the problem of solving (inverting) multiple instances simultaneously as a function of the sum of the complexities of solving those instances individually. This notion is a type of generalized direct-sum property. Such direct-sum properties have been studied in other contexts such as communication complexity and complexity of quadratic forms (see, e.g., [16, 27, 15]) and also relate to the notion of hardness amplification [38, 25]. We show that the IEP property holds for random functions as well as exponentiation maps in idealized models such as the random oracle model [3] and the generic group model (e.g., [37]), respectively; we also provide evidence that it holds in the computational model under complexity of factoring assumptions. Second, we formulate the notion of *hardness indistinguishability* which, essentially, expresses the inability of the adversary to distinguish between two or more inversion instances of different complexity. We express this property in the statistical sense, something that facilitates our reductions between corruption models. Effectively, the former notion (IEP) enables the discretization and token abstraction of the computational effort against a sequence of problems, while the latter (indistinguishability) provides the uncertainty the adversary faces while deciding its corruption budget allocation. In turn, these two notions rely on the hardness of the inversion problem of a function when measured in an *exact* sense, a notion we also formalize, investigate and relate to past notions.

Putting everything together, we show how hidden diversity in the context of resource-based corruptions enables us to get around impossibility results. Going back to our motivating example of secure multiparty computation, the impossibility result states that when the adversary has corruption resources sufficient to control half the players, many functionalities have to be given up. Specifically we prove the following (informally stated):

Let OPT be the optimal corruption budget for which the completeness of MPC is violated. Assuming hidden diversity, there exist configurations such that:

- For any B, the completeness of MPC holds against any adversary with less than $B \cdot OPT$ corruption budget assuming a sufficient number n of players (where $n = \Omega(\log(\frac{1}{\epsilon}) \cdot B)$, and ϵ is the probability of error).
- The above assumes the hardness of individual corruptions is not bounded. If, on the other hand, a bound M is imposed, the completeness of MPC holds against any

adversary with less than $\sim (\frac{\sqrt{M}}{\log(\frac{1}{\epsilon})}) \cdot OPT$ corruption budget assuming $n \geq \sqrt{M}$.

These results are expressed formally in Theorems 3.3 and 3.6, respectively. In addition, we provide evidence that the above results are essentially tight. For example, for the second formulation above, when the adversary's budget reaches an amount $\sim \sqrt{M} \cdot OPT$, there is a strategy that always corrupts half the players (Corollary 3.5).

Another way to exploit hidden diversity that we consider is to improve the efficiency of the implementation of MPC (as opposed to increasing the corruption budget the protocol can tolerate). We prove that, assuming the same OPT corruption budget, hidden diversity can force the corruption threshold to drop from 1/2 to 1/3, in turn allowing the use of much more efficient (information-theoretic) MPC protocols (see Theorem 3.7).

The above results demonstrate that there exist settings of player diversity that can be quite beneficial from a security standpoint if the diversity is appropriately hidden. This opens up the possibility for further investigation of the benefits of hidden diversity in various settings where a specific player configuration is assumed (or even can be imposed). We emphasize that our results are relevant in the a setting where (at least some) party corruptions require effort from the adversary; this captures a wide range of attacks, from cryptographic- (e.g., an offline dictionary attack against a password file) to system-based (e.g., a brute force search against address space layout randomization). Evidently, the relevance of our corruption model is conditional to particular system setups (but this is also the case for the setting where corruptions happen "for free" as well as any other conceivable corruption model).

Related work. To our knowledge, this is the first time that hidden diversity in terms of corruption effort is identified and used as a mechanism to boost security guarantees. This can be juxtaposed with results in the theory of cryptography that showed how other types of adversarial uncertainty can be beneficial, perhaps the closest one of which is (sender) anonymity. For example, it has been shown that variants of an anonymous channel can be used to implement unconditionally secure point-to-point channels and a broadcast channel [17, 26], as well as more efficient natural secure computation tasks, such as private information retrieval (PIR) [26]. It is worth noting that assuming sender-anonymity by itself does not fundamentally change the feasibility barriers of secure protocol design, while hidden diversity can circumvent the MPC impossibility results in the resource-based corruption setting.

With respect to resource-based corruptions, the notion of general adversary structures [24], where the adversary can choose different sets of players to corrupt from a collection of possible choices, not necessarily determined by their size, can be cast as an instance of resource-based corruption for an appropriate adversary budget and players' corruption thresholds. The two models, in fact, can be shown to be equivalent; the resource-based corruption model, however, is the one that enables us to reason about hidden diversity which is our main focus.

There is also related work regarding the "lower-bounding" of adversarial effort, including the notion of "moderately hard functions" to fight spam [14], cryptographic key escrow [36, 1], time-lock puzzles and timed-release cryptography (e.g., [33, 6, 20]), and resource fairness [19]. We note that in most such applications, however, the common theme is relating work to time, and thus crafting problems whose solution is hard to parallelize, which is not our concern here. In terms of measuring adversarial effort, our approach is along the same lines as *precise* zero-knowledge [30] where the knowledge gained by a player is measured in terms of its actual computation.

In an independent development, Bellare, Ristenpart and Tessaro [2] recently introduced the notion of *multi-instance* (MI) security, which relates to the notion of IEP functions introduced here. In settings where it is computationally feasible for instances to be compromised ("inverted," in our parlance), such as password-based cryptography, the application where the notion is showcased, it is shown that security can be amplified linearly in the number of instances in the random oracle (RO) model under a proper modeling. Such modeling, called "left-or-right xor" (LORX), is introduced in [2], aiming to capture the level of multi-instance security of a cryptographic primitive (encryption in that paper) with respect to indistinguishability-type challenges. In contrast, and in line with our objectives, the IEP property captures the multi-instance hardness behavior of one-way functions, and, as opposed to LORX, is cast as an intrinsic complexity characteristic that expresses the rate of hardness growth as a function of the number of instances.

As we already mentioned above, the notion of IEP functions also bears some resemblance to hardness amplification and direct-product theorems [38, 25]; we elaborate in more detail on such relation in the full version of the paper [18]. Finally, similar notions to the notion of exact hardness that we put forth in this paper have been considered in the literature; see Section 4.1 and [18] for a comparison to another "more refined than asymptotic" measure of inversion difficulty considered by Haitner, Harnik and Reingold [23].

Organization of the paper. The rest of the paper is organized as follows. In Section 2 we introduce the notion of resource-based corruptions, corruption oracles and reductions between them. In Section 3, we present the combinatorial analysis that allows us to prove the gains of hidden diversity at an abstract, "token" level. Finally, in Section 4 we give the definitions of exact hardness, IEP and hardness indistinguishability, which enable the application of the results to the computational-corruption setting. Candidate instantiations of the Section 4 definitions are presented in Appendix A. Some of the proofs, comparisons to related notions, as well as additional analysis and constructions, are presented in the full version of the paper [18]. We first introduce some basic notation.

Notation. We use $\lambda \in \mathbb{N}$ to denote the security parameter. All quantities are assumed to be functions of λ unless otherwise noted. Let X, Y be random variables with range in $\{0, 1\}$. We write $X \overset{\epsilon}{\approx} Y$ if we have that $|\mathbf{Pr}[X = 1] - \mathbf{Pr}[Y = 1]| < \epsilon$.

2. RESOURCE-BASED CORRUPTIONS

A main goal of this paper is to formulate the cost for an adversary to "corrupt" parties running a cryptographic protocol, in contrast to the traditional approach where the adversary gains control of parties for free. We will be modelling this process in what nowadays is the widely accepted method to formulate the security of a protocol carrying out a given task: the "trusted-party paradigm" [22]. Recall that in this paradigm, the protocol execution is compared with an ideal process where the outputs are computed by a trusted party that sees all the inputs. A protocol is then said to securely carry out a given task if running the protocol with a realistic adversary amounts to "emulating" the ideal process with the appropriate trusted party. In the perhaps most developed version of the paradigm, due to Canetti [7], the task of distinguishing between the two experiments is assigned to an entity (a polynomial-time interactive Turing machine [ITM]) called *the environment*, and denoted by $\mathcal{Z}$, which is also in charge of producing the inputs for and receiving the outputs from both executions. Besides $\mathcal{Z}$, the other basic entities (also ITMs) involved in the real-world execution are n players $P_1, ..., P_n$, and an adversary $\mathcal{A}$. We will be using a variant of this formulation, similar to [19], meant to capture synchronous communication and exact running-time bounds[1].

2.1 Corruption Oracles and Security Definition

We model the corruption process, under different costs, by the addition of a new entity (ITM) to the real-world execution, which we call the *corruption oracle* ($\mathcal{C}$), and whose essential purpose is to interact with adversary $\mathcal{A}$ and manage its corruption capability. In more detail, the two basic principles in $\mathcal{C}$'s operation are as follows:

- $\mathcal{C}$ is initialized with a random tape and the number of players $n \in \mathbb{N}$ involved in the system. It may return some information about the players to the adversary $\mathcal{A}$.
- For each player P_i, $\mathcal{A}$ may engage $\mathcal{C}$ in a simple (corruption) protocol, call it ρ_i, to determine whether player P_i gets corrupted. The adversary is free to schedule many such corruption protocols concurrently (either statically for a static adversary or dynamically for an adaptive one). If the protocol terminates with $\mathcal{C}$ accepting, then player P_i is declared corrupted, meaning that $\mathcal{A}$ has access to P_i's internal state, and is able to impersonate P_i in all of its subsequent interactions (for a malicious $\mathcal{A}$).

We consider communication with the corruption oracle as part of the adversary's basic step of (significant) computation (see Section 4.1). For succinctness, sometimes we will refer to the adversary $\mathcal{A}$ interacting with corruption oracle $\mathcal{C}$ as $\mathcal{A}^{\mathcal{C}}$. Following [7], we will use the notation $\text{EXEC}_{\pi,\mathcal{A}^{\mathcal{C}},\mathcal{Z}}$ to denote the (binary) distribution ensemble describing $\mathcal{Z}$'s output after interacting with adversary $\mathcal{A}$ running with corruption oracle $\mathcal{C}$, and players running protocol π.

In the ideal process we will model the corruption capability as follows. We consider a "wrapper" functionality $\mathcal{W}^{\mathcal{C}}(\mathcal{F})$ that for any functionality $\mathcal{F}$ and corruption oracle $\mathcal{C}$, "traps" the corruption requests directed to a party participating in it; all other messages and requests it immediately passes to the functionality. This will allow us to provide a corruption interface that is compatible with the corruption-oracle modeling of the real world. In more detail, for each party P_i involved in $\mathcal{F}$ the wrapper $\mathcal{W}^{\mathcal{C}}(\mathcal{F})$ initializes the corruption oracle and considers all parties as "uncorrupted." Mimicking the behavior of the real-world adversary attacking parties, $\mathcal{S}$ can submit corruption messages for party P_i following the protocol ρ_i to $\mathcal{W}^{\mathcal{C}}(\mathcal{F})$, who maintains the state of the corruption oracle. If, at some point, $\mathcal{C}$ terminates the execution of one of the ρ_i protocols and accepts, then $\mathcal{W}^{\mathcal{C}}(\mathcal{F})$ sets the party P_i status to "corrupted," issues a (standard) corruption message for P_i, (CORRUPT, P_i), to $\mathcal{F}$, and returns the functionality's response, namely, the party's internal state as kept by the functionality, back to $\mathcal{S}$. In addition, we note that once a party is corrupted, the ideal adversary is typically allowed to "re-write" the corrupted party's internal state; $\mathcal{W}^{\mathcal{C}}(\cdot)$ ignores such messages while the party is uncorrupted. Let $\text{EXEC}_{\mathcal{W}^{\mathcal{C}}(\mathcal{F}),\mathcal{S},\mathcal{Z}}$ denote the (binary) distribution ensemble describing $\mathcal{Z}$'s output after interacting with adversary $\mathcal{S}$ and the ideal protocol for $\mathcal{W}^{\mathcal{C}}(\mathcal{F})$ as specified above.

We now proceed to more formally specify how the two executions—real and ideal—would be indistinguishable to the environment. The typical order of quantifiers in simulation-based security definitions ($\forall\mathcal{A}\exists\mathcal{S}\forall\mathcal{Z}$) allows the ideal-world adversary to depend on the real-world adversary that it simulates, but it should be independent of the environment. Following [19], we use a slight weakening of this definition, which is appropriate for the setting of adversaries restricted to performing a specific number of steps of the computation. Specifically, let t denote the number of steps taken by the adversary, for t a monotonically increasing arithmetic function; we consider the "compound" ITM $\langle\mathcal{Z},\mathcal{A}\rangle$ (namely, two ITMs, interacting with each other and possibly with other ITMs in a well-defined manner, treated as a single entity) as being t-bounded. (This refinement will become useful when capturing corruptions as computational effort—cf. Section 4.)

DEFINITION 2.1. *For a given t, a protocol π is said to* securely realize a functionality $\mathcal{F}$ against t-bounded adversaries and corruption oracle $\mathcal{C}$, *if for all $\mathcal{A}$ there exists an ideal-world adversary $\mathcal{S}$, running in time $t+p$, such that for all $\mathcal{Z}$ with $\langle\mathcal{Z},\mathcal{A}\rangle$ being t-bounded,*

$$\text{EXEC}_{\pi,\mathcal{A}^{\mathcal{C}},\mathcal{Z}} \overset{\epsilon}{\approx} \text{EXEC}_{\mathcal{W}^{\mathcal{C}}(\mathcal{F}),\mathcal{S},\mathcal{Z}},$$

where ϵ is some negligible function and p some polynomial.

Next, we introduce the notion of *safety* for a corruption oracle.

DEFINITION 2.2. *For a given t, we say a corruption oracle $\mathcal{C}$ is* t-safe *if for all functionalities $\mathcal{F}$ (including those that guarantee fairness and output delivery to all honest parties), there is a protocol π that securely realizes $\mathcal{F}$ against t-bounded adversaries and $\mathcal{C}$.*

If a corruption oracle is t-safe for all t, then we call it simply safe. For example, it can be derived from [22, 8] that the standard (traditional) corruption oracle allowing less than $1/2$ of the players to be corrupted (to be denoted below as $\mathcal{C}^{\text{std}}_{\frac{1}{2}}$) is safe. Further, in case we want to be explicit about the parameters involved in the proof of safety, we will say that a corruption oracle $\mathcal{C}$ is (t,γ)-safe if it holds that the above definition is satisfied with a simulation that may fail with probability at most $1-\gamma$.

2.2 Cost Measures and Relations between Corruption Oracles

Next, we will start by capturing two cost measures for corruptions, namely, the traditional one (i.e., no cost) and the

[1]We note that these formulations are in fact more powerful than needed for this paper, as we will be focusing on stand-alone protocol execution.

"token" based (i.e., discretized) measure, defining corruption oracles for them, which will already enable us to establish the power of hidden diversity at an abstract level; later on (Section 4) we will provide the final "translation" by presenting the computational-based measure. In addition, we will define the "blinded" version of such oracles (which, looking forward, will effectively model the hardness indistinguishability of functions put forth in Section 4.1), and establish the relations between them.

Standard cryptographic corruption. In this case the corruption oracle is initialized with a threshold $\alpha \in (0,1)$, and maintains a counter ctr initially set to 0. The oracle provides the number of players n to the adversary. The corruption protocol ρ_i consists of a single message $(\textsc{Corrupt}, P_i)$ that is to be transmitted by the adversary to the oracle. Given such a message, the oracle checks whether $\mathsf{ctr}+1 < \lceil \alpha \cdot n \rceil$, and in this case declares player P_i corrupted (with the effect described above) and increases ctr by 1. We denote this corruption oracle by $\mathcal{C}^{\mathsf{std}}_{\alpha}$. For secure multi-party computation applications, typical values of α are $\frac{1}{2}$ (i.e., honest majority), $\frac{1}{3}$ and $1-\frac{1}{n}$ (i.e., at least one honest player).

Token-based corruption. In this case the corruption oracle is initialized with a vector $\overline{s} \in \mathbb{N}^n$ ($\overline{s}$ for bucket "sizes") and a threshold k (total number of tokens); the threshold of player P_i is the value s_i. The oracle gives to $\mathcal{A}$ the vector $\overline{s}$, and maintains counters $\mathsf{ctr}_1, \ldots, \mathsf{ctr}_n$ initially set to 0. Protocol ρ_i here consists of messages of the form $(\textsc{Corrupt}, P_i, v)$ sent by $\mathcal{A}$. The oracle checks that $v + \sum_i \mathsf{ctr}_i \le k$, and in this case it increases counter ctr_i by v; if it happens that $\mathsf{ctr}_i \ge s_i$, then player P_i gets corrupted. We will denote the token-based corruption oracle by $\mathcal{C}^{\mathsf{tk}}_{\overline{s},k}$.

Blinded token-based corruption. This corruption oracle, denoted by $\mathcal{C}^{\mathsf{btk}}_{\overline{s},k}$, is identical to $\mathcal{C}^{\mathsf{tk}}_{\overline{s},k}$ in operation with the following difference: whenever the adversary submits a $(\textsc{Corrupt}, P_i, v)$ message, the oracle performs the update operations on player $P_{p(i)}$ where p is a secret random permutation that is selected initially and maintained by the corruption oracle. Otherwise, the blinded token-based corruption oracle behaves as the token-based corruption oracle. Given that this oracle has a private state (permutation p), for technical reasons (to be revealed later) we will also consider a "leaky" version of this corruption oracle that is parameterized by an ITM L and operates on the private permutation p. In this leaky version, the adversary $\mathcal{A}$ may submit a special request given which the corruption oracle will run L on its internal state and return its output to $\mathcal{A}$. We will denote the leaky version of this corruption oracle by $\mathcal{C}^{\mathsf{btk},L}_{\overline{s},k}$.

We now set out to study the relations between corruption oracles defined above. Our main tool is the following definition.

Definition 2.3. *Fix some $\epsilon > 0$ and arithmetic function t. Given two corruption oracles $\mathcal{C}_1$ and $\mathcal{C}_2$, we say that $\mathcal{C}_2$* dominates $\mathcal{C}_1$ with error ϵ and complexity t, *denoted $\mathcal{C}_1 \le^t_\epsilon \mathcal{C}_2$, provided the following holds: for $n \in \mathbb{N}$ and any n-party protocol π, for any $\mathcal{A}$, there is an adversary $\mathcal{B}$, running in time $t+p$, such that for all $\mathcal{Z}$ with $\langle \mathcal{Z}, \mathcal{A}\rangle$ being t-bounded,*

$$\mathrm{EXEC}_{\pi,\mathcal{A}^{\mathcal{C}_1},\mathcal{Z}} \overset{\epsilon}{\approx} \mathrm{EXEC}_{\pi,\mathcal{B}^{\mathcal{C}_2},\mathcal{Z}},$$

where p is some polynomial.

The main intuition behind this definition is that if $\mathcal{C}_2$ dominates $\mathcal{C}_1$ and an adversary is given a choice between the two, it may always opt for the former. The way we will employ the above relation in our exposition is that if $\mathcal{C}_2$ dominates $\mathcal{C}_1$ and it happens that $\mathcal{C}_2$ is safe, then $\mathcal{C}_1$ is also safe. More specifically, if $\mathcal{C}_2$ is (t,γ)-safe and we have that $\mathcal{C}_1 \le^t_\epsilon \mathcal{C}_2$, then we have that $\mathcal{C}_1$ is $(t, \gamma-\epsilon)$-safe. It is easy to see that the relation $\le^t_\epsilon$ is reflexive and transitive and thus constitutes a preorder for any choice of the parameters t, ϵ.

Another easy observation is that $\mathcal{C}^{\mathsf{std}}_{\gamma_1} \le^t_\epsilon \mathcal{C}^{\mathsf{std}}_{\gamma_2}$ provided that $\gamma_1 \le \gamma_2$, independently of the values t, ϵ. This stems from the fact that the power of the adversary can only potentially increase in the corruption oracle of the right-hand side. When the relation $\le^t_\epsilon$ holds for any function t, we will write $\le_\epsilon$.

From token-based corruptions to standard corruptions. Let $\mathcal{A}$ be any adversary that interacts with $\mathcal{C}^{\mathsf{X}}_{\overline{s},k}$ for some $\overline{s} = (s_1, \ldots, s_n) \in \mathbb{N}^n, k \in \mathbb{N}$ and $\mathsf{X} \in \{\mathsf{tk}, \mathsf{btk}\}$. For some $\alpha \in (0,1)$ and complexity t, we denote by $\mathsf{bad}^t_{\mathsf{X}}[\overline{s}, k, \alpha]$ the supremum of the probability of the event that the number of corrupted players reaches $\lceil \alpha \cdot n \rceil$ in the execution of $M^{\mathcal{C}^{\mathsf{X}}_{\overline{s},k}}$, where M is any t-bounded ITM. We have the following :

Lemma 2.4. *For any $n, k \in \mathbb{N}, \overline{s} \in \mathbb{N}^n, \alpha \in (0,1)$ and arithmetic function t, we have that $\mathcal{C}^{\mathsf{X}}_{\overline{s},k} \le^t_\epsilon \mathcal{C}^{\mathsf{std}}_{\alpha}$, where $\epsilon \le \mathsf{bad}^t_{\mathsf{X}}[\overline{s}, k, \alpha]$ and $\mathsf{X} \in \{\mathsf{tk}, \mathsf{btk}\}$.*

Proof. The description of $\mathcal{B}$ is based on $\mathcal{A}$. Specifically, $\mathcal{B}$ will simulate the corruption oracle $\mathcal{C}^{\mathsf{X}}_{\overline{s},k}$ for $\mathcal{A}$ and whenever a player is corrupted according to the corruption oracle it will pass the corresponding corruption message to its own corruption oracle $\mathcal{C}^{\mathsf{std}}_{\alpha}$. The only problem that may occur in the simulation is when the corruption oracle of $\mathcal{B}$ rejects its corruption request for a certain player while the corresponding player is expected to be corrupted by $\mathcal{A}$. Using the fact that $\mathbf{Pr}[X|\neg B] = \mathbf{Pr}[Y|\neg B]$ implies that $|\mathbf{Pr}[X] - \mathbf{Pr}[Y]| \le \mathbf{Pr}[B]$ for any three events X, Y, B over the same probability space yields the proof, by taking X to be the output of $\mathcal{A}$'s execution, Y to be the output of $\mathcal{B}$'s execution, and B the probability that $\mathcal{A}$ is able to successfully corrupt a player while $\mathcal{B}$ is denied. ☐

This lemma would be most useful in case ϵ is negligible (cf. next section).

3. THE COMBINATORICS OF HIDDEN DIVERSITY

In this section we will use the relations we established between the corruption oracles in the previous section in order to derive cryptographic safety bounds at a purely combinatorial level. In particular we will provide bounds for the "bad" event (Lemma 2.4) and negative results—for the adversary—showing how the blinded version of corruption oracles remains safe for ranges of parameters that are unsafe in the regular case, hence demanding from the adversary a substantially higher "budget" to achieve its goal.

We defined two types of token-based corruption oracles, regular and blinded, which are specified by two parameters: $\overline{s}, k$. Let $OPT_\alpha(\overline{s})$ be the minimal number of tokens that need to be invested in order to corrupt a set of players of size at least $\lceil \alpha n \rceil$ in the token-based corruption oracle model, i.e., $OPT_\alpha(\overline{s}) = \min\{k : \exists C \subseteq \{1,\ldots,n\}$ with $|C| \geq \lceil \alpha n \rceil$ and $\sum_{i\in C} s_i = k\}$. Based on this definition, Lemma 2.4, and our observation that $\mathcal{C}^{\mathsf{std}}_{1/2}$ is safe, we have the following.

THEOREM 3.1. *For any $n \geq 2$, and $\overline{s} \in \mathbb{Z}^n$, the corruption oracle $\mathcal{C}^{\mathsf{tk}}_{\overline{s},k}$ is safe for any $k < OPT_{1/2}(\overline{s})$ and unsafe for any $k \geq OPT_{1/2}(\overline{s})$.*

PROOF. First, regarding cryptographic safety, we observe that as long as $k < OPT_{\frac{1}{2}}(\overline{s})$, it holds that an honest majority of players is always guaranteed. Due to the results of [22], it follows that a protocol can be constructed for any functionality $\mathcal{F}$. On the flip side, if $k \geq OPT_{\frac{1}{2}}(\overline{s})$ this means that there exists a set of players C for which it holds that $k \geq \sum_{i\in C} s_i$ and $|C| \geq \lceil \frac{n}{2} \rceil$. It follows that by corrupting this set of players it is impossible to realize all functionalities (this follows from the impossibility result of Cleve [10]). □

Next, we demonstrate how the blinded token-based corruption oracle remains safe for ranges of parameters that are unsafe in the regular case.

Balls and buckets. The problem at hand can be rephrased as the following game:An adversary wishes to distribute balls (corresponding to corruption tokens) to n buckets, so as to fill at least $\lceil \alpha n \rceil$ of them for some given $\alpha \in (0,1)$. The sizes of the buckets are given in the form of a vector $\overline{s} \in \mathbb{Z}^n$. If the adversary has full information about the buckets, it can achieve its goal by investing $OPT_\alpha(\overline{s})$ balls. Given the characteristics of the $\mathcal{C}^{\mathsf{btk}}_{\overline{s},k}$ oracle, we are interested in the case where the adversary does not know the correspondence between buckets and $\overline{s}$ so it may have to waste a certain number of balls to reach the $\lceil \alpha n \rceil$ threshold. Specifically, we assume that there is a hidden random permutation π that re-labels the buckets so the adversary knows $\overline{s}^\pi = (s_{\pi(1)},\ldots,s_{\pi(n)})$. We note that it should be the case that $\overline{s}$ includes at least 2 different sizes, since otherwise the hidden permutation would not stall the adversary in any way. Specifically, the cardinality of the set $\{s \mid \exists i : s = s_i\}$ is bigger than 1.

3.1 Increased Security from Hidden Diversity

We first consider the case when there are no restrictions on the number of sizes or their values.

THEOREM 3.2. *For any α, $0 < \alpha < 1$, constants $B > 1$ and $\epsilon < 2^{-4}$ and for any $n \geq \log(1/\epsilon)\cdot\max\{1/\alpha,(4B-2)/(1-\alpha)\}$, there exists a vector $\overline{s} \in \mathbb{Z}^n$ such that any adversary that is given $\overline{s}^\pi$ for a random permutation π, and has fewer than $B\cdot OPT_\alpha(\overline{s})$ balls, has probability less than ϵ of filling $\lceil \alpha n \rceil$ buckets.*

PROOF. For a c, $0 < c \leq \alpha$, to be specified later, our instance will have $\lceil cn \rceil$ buckets of size $\lceil \alpha n \rceil + 1$, $\lceil \alpha n \rceil - \lceil cn \rceil$ buckets of size 1, and $n - \lceil \alpha n \rceil$ buckets of size $(\lceil cn \rceil + 2)B\lceil \alpha n \rceil$. An optimal solution will consist of the $\lceil \alpha n \rceil$ smallest buckets, and will have total size $(\lceil cn \rceil + 1)\lceil \alpha n \rceil$. This implies that we cannot afford to fill any of the largest buckets if we are to use fewer than $B\cdot OPT_\alpha(\overline{s}) = B(\lceil cn \rceil + 1)\lceil \alpha n \rceil$ balls, and any algorithm that fills $\lceil \alpha n \rceil$ buckets must find and fill all the buckets of size $\lceil \alpha n \rceil + 1$.

But now note that the only way the adversary can tell whether a bucket has this size or one of the larger ones is to place $\lceil \alpha n \rceil + 1$ balls in the bucket. Thus, if the adversary is to use no more than $B(\lceil cn \rceil + 1)\lceil \alpha n \rceil$ balls, it can test no more than $B(\lceil cn \rceil + 1)$ buckets with size exceeding 1, of which there are $n - \lceil \alpha n \rceil + \lceil cn \rceil$. The probability of finding all $\lceil cn \rceil$ of the mid-size buckets is then at most

$$\binom{n-\lceil \alpha n \rceil}{B(\lceil cn \rceil + 1) - \lceil cn \rceil} \Big/ \binom{n-\lceil \alpha n \rceil + \lceil cn \rceil}{B(\lceil cn \rceil + 1)}.$$

Setting $X = n - \lceil \alpha n \rceil$ and $Y = B(\lceil cn \rceil + 1) - \lceil cn \rceil$, this is equal to

$$\binom{X}{Y} \Big/ \binom{X+\lceil cn \rceil}{Y+\lceil cn \rceil}$$

$$= \frac{(Y+1)(Y+2)\cdots(Y+\lceil cn \rceil)}{(X+1)(X+2)\cdots(X+\lceil cn \rceil)},$$

which we will be able to argue is sufficiently small if we can chose $c > 0$ such that, say, $Y + \lceil cn \rceil \leq (X + \lceil cn \rceil)/2$. This requires that $B\lceil cn \rceil + B < (n - \lceil \alpha n \rceil + \lceil cn \rceil)/2$, or $(2B-1)\lceil cn \rceil \leq n - \lceil \alpha n \rceil - 2B$. which will be true so long as $(2B-1)(cn+1) \leq n(1-\alpha) - 1 - 2B$, or $(2B-1)(cn) \leq n(1-\alpha) - 4B$, or $c \leq (1-\alpha)/(2B-1) - 4B/(n(2B-1))$. It is easy to see that our bound on n implies also that $n > 8B/(1-\alpha)$ hence all we need for $Y + \lceil cn \rceil < (X + \lceil cn \rceil)/2$ is that $c \leq (1-\alpha)/(4B-2)$. By our construction, we also need $c \leq \alpha$, so it suffices to set $c = \min\{\alpha, (1-\alpha)/(4B-2)\}$.

Given that $Y + \lceil cn \rceil < (X + \lceil cn \rceil)/2$, we then have that $(Y+i)/(X+i) \leq 1/2$ for $1 \leq i\lceil cn \rceil$, and hence the probability of success is at most

$$\frac{(Y+1)(Y+2)\cdots(Y+\lceil cn \rceil)}{(X+1)(X+2)\cdots(X+\lceil cn \rceil)} < (1/2)^{\lceil cn \rceil} \leq (1/2)^{cn}.$$

Setting $(1/2)^{cn} = \epsilon$ and solving for n yields the claimed result. □

The above theorem implies the following result.

COROLLARY 3.3. *For any $B > 1$ and $\epsilon < 2^{-4}$, and for any $n \geq \log(1/\epsilon)(8B-4)$, there exists a vector $\overline{s} \in \mathbb{Z}^n$ such that the corruption oracle $\mathcal{C}^{\mathsf{btk}}_{\overline{s},k}$ is $(1-\epsilon)$-safe provided that $k < B\cdot OPT_{1/2}(\overline{s})$.*

PROOF. We show that $\mathcal{C}^{\mathsf{btk}}_{\overline{s},k} \leq_\epsilon \mathcal{C}^{\mathsf{std}}_{n,\frac{1}{2}}$ for the choice of parameters $n, \overline{s}, k$ of the previous theorem. Cryptographic safety will follow then immediately due to Theorem 3.1.

In order to prove the reduction between the corruption oracles we need to provide an adversary $\mathcal{B}$ operating with $\mathcal{C}^{\mathsf{std}}_{n,1/2}$ for any adversary $\mathcal{A}$ operating with $\mathcal{C}^{\mathsf{btk}}_{\overline{s},k}$. $\mathcal{B}$ will simply simulate the corruption oracle of $\mathcal{A}$ and submit the corruption requests to $\mathcal{C}^{\mathsf{std}}_{n,1/2}$ whenever a corruption with $\mathcal{C}^{\mathsf{btk}}_{\overline{s},k}$ takes place. The simulator will fail with probability at most $\mathsf{bad}_{\mathsf{btk}}[\overline{s},k,1/2]$ from Lemma 2.4. Due to the previous theorem we can bound the probability by ϵ, which completes the proof. □

The above results require arbitrarily large bucket sizes (components of $\overline{s}$). In real applications, it is plausible that there might be some upper bound M on the maximum size. We now show how an adversary can exploit this (and other restrictions), and what level of safety may remain.

Consider the following algorithm $H2$ that is a hybrid between two simple bucket-filling strategies: one that continuously picks an empty bucket and fills it, and one that layers balls horizontally across all buckets. Let $M' = \lfloor\sqrt{M}\rfloor$. Algorithm $H2$ proceeds in two basic steps: (1) While less than $\lceil\alpha n\rceil$ buckets are full and there is an unfull bucket containing fewer than M' balls, choose one with the fewest balls and place a ball in it. (2) While less than $\lceil\alpha n\rceil$ buckets are full, pick an unfull bucket and add balls until it is filled to capacity.

Let $H2_\alpha(\overline{s})$ denote the worst-case number of balls that $H2$ must place in order to fill $\lceil\alpha n\rceil$ buckets. The following upper bound on the behavior of $H2$ is proved in the full version of the paper ([18], Section B.3.4.)

THEOREM 3.4. *For $0 < \alpha < 1, n \in \mathbb{N}$ and any $\overline{s} \in \mathbb{Z}^n$ with maximum size M, $\frac{H2_\alpha(\overline{s})}{OPT_\alpha(\overline{s})} \leq 1 + \frac{\sqrt{M}}{\alpha}$.*

COROLLARY 3.5. *For any $n > 1$, $M > 0$, and any $\overline{s} \in \mathbb{Z}^n$ with maximum level M, the corruption oracle $\mathcal{C}^{\mathsf{btk}}_{\overline{s},k}$ is unsafe whenever $k \geq (1 + 2\sqrt{M}) \cdot OPT_{1/2}(\overline{s})$.*

PROOF. The proof follows as a direct application of the previous theorem. Specifically, we have that due to the previous theorem there is an adversarial strategy that needs at most $1 + 2\sqrt{M}$ balls to fill $\lceil\frac{1}{2} \cdot n\rceil$ buckets. It follows that with this strategy an adversary can corrupt $\lceil\frac{1}{2} \cdot n\rceil$ players always and as we argued in Theorem 3.1, it follows that the corruption oracle is unsafe. □

The above relation between the maximum bucket size and unsafety is essentially tight—once the number of corruption tokens drops below $\sqrt{M}$ by a fixed fraction there exist $\overline{s}$ with maximum size M where with high probability the adversary will fail to fill the target number of buckets. In [18] we show the following.

THEOREM 3.6. *For any $\epsilon > 0$ and any $M \geq 8$, $n > 4$ with $\lceil\sqrt{M}\rceil$ dividing n, there is an $\overline{s} \in \mathbb{Z}^n$ with maximum size M, such that the corruption oracle $\mathcal{C}^{\mathsf{btk}}_{\overline{s},k}$ is $(1 - \epsilon)$-safe provided that $k < \delta \cdot \sqrt{M} \cdot OPT_{1/2}(\overline{s})$ where $\delta = \min\left(2/45, (4/15)/\log(1/\epsilon)\right)$.*

It is worth noting that this theorem becomes trivial if $\delta < 1/\sqrt{M}$, since in that case we would be given fewer than $OPT_{1/2}(\overline{s})$ balls and so even the unblinded corruption oracle would be safe. This in turn implies that the theorem is only meaningful for $\epsilon > 2^{-(4/15)\sqrt{M}}$.

The above results about the cryptographic safety of the blinded token-based corruption oracle are all proved using systems $\overline{s}$ that have three distinct sizes. The fact that we use more than two sizes turns out to be necessary. For systems with just two sizes, we show in [18] that there is an adversarial strategy that violates cryptographic safety given just $2 \cdot OPT_{1/2}(\overline{s})$ corruption tokens; this bound turns out to be tight.

3.2 Increased Efficiency from Hidden Diversity

Next, we explore the question whether hidden diversity can be used to relax the computational effort in secure multiparty computation (MPC). Consider an adversary that is given $k < OPT_{1/2}(\overline{s})$ corruption tokens. Recall that the corruption oracle $\mathcal{C}^{\mathsf{tk}}_{\overline{s},k}$ is safe for exactly this range of adversarial resources, i.e., fully secure MPC can be achieved under computational assumptions [22, 31, 8]. The problem we investigate in this section is what potential benefits can be reaped in the hidden diversity setting assuming the same level of adversarial resources. In [18] we show the following.

THEOREM 3.7. *For any $\beta > 0$, there are constants $N > 1$ and $a < 1$, such that for any $n > N$, there is a vector $\overline{s} \in \mathbb{Z}^n$ with $\mathcal{C}^{\mathsf{btk}}_{\overline{s},k} \leq_{a^n} \mathcal{C}^{\mathsf{std}}_{1/4+\beta}$, provided that $k \leq OPT_{1/2}(\overline{s})$.*

Thus, if we choose $\beta = 1/3 - 1/4 = 1/12$ and an instance $\overline{s}$ with sufficiently large n, an adversary will have probability less than ϵ of corrupting $1/3$ or more participants, where "sufficiently large" here again grows proportionally with $\log(1/\epsilon)$. This result can be used to extend the application domain of information-theoretic protocols for fully secure MPC such as those of [5, 12], which are typically much more efficient than the cryptographic ones, but that in the regular corruption model only tolerate a rate of corruptions less than $1/3$.

The full version of the paper contains additional results in the blinded balls-and-buckets model, including adversarial strategies that bound how much the previous result can be extended and an examination of the case where the number of buckets n is bounded but not the maximum size M [18].

4. COMPUTATIONAL CORRUPTIONS

In this last section we turn to capturing and quantifying the setting where corruptions occur due to the inversion of computationally hard problem instances (what we call "computational corruptions"), and study the sufficient conditions under which such corruptions can be abstracted out as token-based corruptions. We start by defining the corresponding corruption oracles. First, the computational corruption oracle captures the setting where the adversary can corrupt a player by "breaking in," specifically by solving an instance of a computational problem that is otherwise unrelated to the cryptographic protocol (for example, this would be the case when the adversary's offline attack against a cryptographic authentication protocol succeeds). The *blinded* computational corruption oracle extends the above to the setting where the adversary cannot determine the correspondence between players and the instances that need to be solved for a break-in to occur.

Computational corruption oracle. The oracle is initialized with the description of functions $f_1, \ldots, f_n$ and samples $x_1, \ldots, x_n$ from the functions' respective domains. Subsequently, it provides to the adversary the vector $(y_1, \ldots, y_n)$, where $y_i = f_i(x_i)$. The corruption protocol ρ_i here consists of messages of the form $(\text{CORRUPT}, P_i, x)$ provided by $\mathcal{A}$; if it happens that $y_i = f_i(x)$, then player P_i gets corrupted[2]. We denote this oracle by $\mathcal{C}^{\mathsf{cc}}_{\overline{f}}$, where $\overline{f} = (f_1, \ldots, f_n)$.

Blinded computational corruption oracle. This case is similar to computational corruption with the difference that in addition, the corruption oracle is initialized with a random permutation p. The oracle provides to $\mathcal{A}$ the vector $(y_{p(1)}, \ldots, y_{p(n)})$. The corruption protocol messages are as in the case of $\mathcal{C}^{\mathsf{cc}}_{\overline{f}}$. We denote this corruption oracle by $\mathcal{C}^{\mathsf{bcc}}_{\overline{f}}$.

[2]As stated, the corruption protocol is an abstract version of a potentially more complex interaction where, for example, y_i is the public-key of player P_i and corruption takes place by getting ahold of the secret key x_i via running some algorithm against y_i and then authenticating on behalf of P_i.

We will be considering this definition in the setting when the functions $\overline{f}$ are hardness indistinguishable.

Next, we introduce the two notions that play a fundamental role in the complexity interpretation of resource-based corruptions.

4.1 Hardness Indistinguishability and Inversion Effort Preserving Functions

Both notions are related to the hardness of the inversion problem of a function when measured in an *exact* sense. We start by explaining this notion of hardness first.

4.1.1 Exact hardness

Consider any function $f : X \to Y$, where $X = \cup_{\lambda \in \mathbb{N}} X_\lambda$, $Y = \cup_{\lambda \in \mathbb{N}} Y_\lambda$. In what follows, if λ is clear from the context, we may denote X_λ and Y_λ by simply X and Y, respectively.

An inversion algorithm for f with success $p(\lambda)$ in time $t(\lambda)$, is a non-uniform algorithm $\mathcal{A}$ that for any λ, receives input $f(x)$ where x is uniformly distributed over X_λ and returns a value that belongs in $f^{-1}(f(x))$ with probability at least $p(\lambda)$ while being restricted to read at most $t(\lambda)$ symbols of its advice string and run for at most $t(\lambda)$ steps. We write $\mathcal{A}_t$ to denote $\mathcal{A}$ restricted on performing only t steps of computation and reading only t symbols of its advice string (for any λ). We then denote the success probability of $\mathcal{A}$, namely, $\mathbf{Pr}[\mathcal{A}_t(f(x)) \in f^{-1}(f(x))]$, by $p_{\mathcal{A},t}(\lambda)$. For simplicity, in the sequel we may drop λ from $p_{\mathcal{A},t}(\lambda)$.

We remark that the restriction on the number of steps may only bind a specific operation, which would be computational significant compared to the others (such as, for example, modular exponentiation). At times we may specify the input distribution to be other than the uniform distribution over X; e.g., we may consider some $X' \subseteq X$ and let x be distributed uniformly over X'. Unless otherwise noted we will assume that the uniform over X is used.

We are now ready to introduce *exact hardness*, a notion which will later on allow us to compare functions according to their inversion difficulty. In a nutshell, the exact hardness of a function, parameterized by ϵ, is the number of steps that necessarily needs to be surpassed in order to achieve probability of success at least ϵ. More formally:

DEFINITION 4.1. *For any $\epsilon \in (0,1)$ and a function $f : X \to Y$, we define the* exact hardness of f with probability ϵ *to be the maximum $H \in \mathbb{N}$ such that for any $\mathcal{A}$ and $t \leq H$, it holds that $p_{\mathcal{A},t} < \epsilon$. For each $\lambda \in \mathbb{N}$, we denote the maximum such H by $H_{f,\epsilon}(\lambda)$.*

Notions of similar nature have been considered in the literature; a salient difference is that exact hardness fixes ϵ, and then calls for the largest possible t for which the function remains hard to invert. Also, observe that, by definition, there is a (non-uniform) algorithm $\mathcal{A}$ that performs a number of steps $t = H_{f,\epsilon}(\lambda) + 1$ with a similarly sized advice string and satisfies $p_{\mathcal{A},t}(\lambda) \geq \epsilon$ for all λ. This holds since if there was no such algorithm, then $H_{f,\epsilon}$ would not be the maximum possible for that particular value of λ.

Similar notions to the notion of exact hardness that we put forth in this paper have been considered in the literature. Notably, Nissan and Wigderson [32] define the hardness of a Boolean function as the largest size of the circuit whose bias is still bounded by the inverse of its size. In our setting, we are interested in fixing the bound of success to a certain level ϵ and maximizing with respect to that (as opposed to allowing ϵ to vary as the inverse of the circuit size). Bellare and Rogaway [4] define a function to be (t,ϵ)-secure if there is no "t-inverter" (an algorithm bounded by t in number of steps and size) with success probability at least ϵ. Put in this latter context, our notion of exact hardness can be defined by fixing ϵ and calling for the largest possible t for which the function remains (t,ϵ)-secure. Another "more refined than asymptotic" measure of inversion difficulty has been considered by Haitner, Harnik and Reingold [23]; we explore its relation to exact hardness in more detail in the full version of the paper [18].

Next, we show two basic properties of our notion of exact hardness. Specifically, we show that exact hardness is monotonically increasing in the probability of inversion success ϵ, and that there is a natural upper bound for exact hardness that stems from the fact that any function over a finite domain can be subjected to a brute-force attack.

PROPOSITION 4.2. *Let $f : X \to Y$ be any function. For any $\lambda \in \mathbb{N}$ we have:*

1. *For any $0 < \epsilon \leq \epsilon'$, it holds that $H_{f,\epsilon}(\lambda) \leq H_{f,\epsilon'}(\lambda)$.*
2. *For any $\epsilon > 0$, $H_{f,\epsilon}(\lambda) \leq \lceil \epsilon \cdot |X_\lambda| \rceil$.*

PROOF. We drop λ for notational simplicity. For the first property, assume for the sake of contradiction that $\epsilon \leq \epsilon'$ and $H_{f,\epsilon} > H_{f,\epsilon'}$. Consider now an algorithm $\mathcal{A}$ running in $t \leq H_{f,\epsilon}$ steps. It follows that it has probability of success less than $\epsilon \leq \epsilon'$. As a result any algorithm $\mathcal{A}$ running in time at most $H_{f,\epsilon}$ has probability of success less than ϵ'. This contradicts that $H_{f,\epsilon'}$ is the maximum integer with this property.

For the second property, we consider the basic step to be the operation of reading a pair (x,y) and an element y' from the respective tapes they reside in, and testing whether $y = y'$. Now let $z \geq 1$ be an integer function and consider a family of advice strings that contain pairs of the type (x_i, y_i), $i = 1, \ldots, z$, that belong to the graph of f following a lexicographic ordering. Consider now the algorithm $\mathcal{A}$ that, given y, scans the advice string, and if it finds (x_i, y_i) such that $y = y_i$ it returns x_i. It is easy to see that the number of steps that $\mathcal{A}$ takes is z (in the worst case—without loss of generality we can assume that $\mathcal{A}$ always takes that many steps). The success probability of $\mathcal{A}$ is $\frac{z}{|X|}$, since the desired output x is selected at random from all inputs.

Recall now that no algorithm running $H_{f,\epsilon}$ steps can have probability of success at least ϵ. If, for the sake of contradiction, we assume that for sufficiently large values of the security parameter it holds that $\lceil \epsilon \cdot |X| \rceil < H_{f,\epsilon}$, it follows that $H_{f,\epsilon} \geq \lceil \epsilon \cdot |X| \rceil + 1$; thus, setting $z = \lceil \epsilon \cdot |X| \rceil + 1$, we have that $\mathcal{A}$ performs $z \leq H_{f,\epsilon}$ operations and has success probability of success $\frac{z}{|X|} > \epsilon$, which is a contradiction. □

It is worth noting that in the specification of $H_{f,\epsilon}$ there is no presumption of a "minimal hardness" for the inversion problem of the function f; rather, $H_{f,\epsilon}$ is meant to capture the intrinsic property of f that corresponds to the minimum computational effort (measured in basic operations depending on the computational model) that is required to invert the function with a certain probability of success. If one assumes that this value is sufficiently high, then the function would be presumed to be one-way. To this end, we now show the basic relations between exact hardness and one-wayness. Specifically, for one-wayness we have that for any ϵ that is bounded away from 0 by an inverse polynomial, the exact hardness of the function to beat ϵ should exceed any polynomial function. Similarly, for *weak* one-way functions, we have that there is some threshold, which is an inverse polynomial away from 1, that in order to be reached the exact hardness should exceed any polynomial function.

PROPOSITION 4.3. *Let $f : X \to Y$ be a polynomial-time computable function. Then:*

1. *f is a one-way function if and only if $\forall c_1, c_2 : \epsilon = \lambda^{-c_1}$ implies $H_{f,\epsilon}(\lambda) > \lambda^{c_2}$ for sufficiently large λ.*
2. *f is a weak one-way function if and only if $\exists c_1\ \forall c_2 : \epsilon = 1 - \lambda^{-c_1}$ implies $H_{f,\epsilon}(\lambda) > \lambda^{c_2}$ for sufficiently large λ.*

PROOF. The proofs of the two statements are similar so we only prove the first one. For the forward direction, we assume that the function is one-way and $\exists c_1, c_2$ for which if $\epsilon = \lambda^{-c_1}$, then $H_{f,\epsilon} \leq \lambda^{c_2}$. Then we have that there is some algorithm that runs in $\lambda^{c_2} + 1$ steps (which is a polynomial in λ) and has success probability at least λ^{-c_1} for infinitely many λ. This contradicts one-wayness.

For the backward direction, consider an algorithm $\mathcal{A}$ that attempts to invert f and runs in λ^{c_2} steps. Also let λ^{c_1} be any polynomial. Now suppose that the probability of inversion success is at least λ^{-c_1} for infinitely many choices of λ (i.e., the function f fails to be one-way). This contradicts the fact that $H_{f,\epsilon} > \lambda^{c_2}$, which states that in order to reach probability of success λ^{-c_1} one has to exceed λ^{c_2} steps. □

It is natural to ask how easy is to calculate $H_{f,\epsilon}$ for a function f. Evidently, any inversion algorithm for f provides an upper bound for exact hardness, while any lower bound argument on the complexity of the inversion problem of f is a lower bound for $H_{f,\epsilon}$. While finding a formula for $H_{f,\epsilon}$ might be hard for a given function f, for certain functions in idealized computational models, such as random functions [3] or exponentiation maps in the generic group model (e.g., [37]), obtaining exact formulae is in fact possible; we provide such results in Appendix A. Furthermore, under cryptographic assumptions, reasonable ranges for $H_{f,\epsilon}$ can be stated; we do so for factoring-related assumptions also in Appendix A.

4.1.2 The IEP property

Next, we consider the setting where instead of just one, a *set* of functions are to be inverted, and would like, in particular, to have a measure for their "combined" hardness, as a function of the functions' individual hardnesses.

DEFINITION 4.4. *Let $\epsilon > 0, n \in \mathbb{N}$ and τ be a monotonically increasing function. We say a sequence of functions $\{f_i\}_{i=1,\ldots,n}$ is τ-inversion effort preserving (τ-IEP) if for any subset $S = \{i_1, \ldots, i_m\} \subseteq [n]$, it holds that $H_{f^S,\epsilon} \geq \tau(\sum_{i \in S} H_{f_i,\epsilon})$, where $f^S(x_1, \ldots, x_m) \stackrel{\text{def}}{=} \langle f_{i_1}(x_1), \ldots, f_{i_k}(x_m)\rangle$.*

Note that, trivially, $H_{f^{[n]},\epsilon} \geq \max_i H_{f_i,\epsilon}$, since any algorithm that inverts a sequence of instances will have to spend at least as much time as the time needed to invert the most difficult one. Nevertheless, it is not guaranteed that the work performed for the solution of any single instance cannot be used to speed up the solution of other instances. Essentially, the IEP property above says that the speed-up that can occur is lower bounded by a value that is determined by the sum of the individual exact-hardness functions, calibrated by a given function (τ). In the extreme case, if τ is the identity function, then the instances have to be solved entirely independently and there is no algorithm that can proceed towards solving a subset of the instances simultaneously with a joint strategy.

Our IEP property is related to the notions of direct sum and direct product in complexity-theoretic models. A direct sum result holds in a model for a problem if solving one instance x of a problem costs c, then when given k independent instances $x_1, ..., x_k$, no significant gain is achievable and the model requires about ck cost to solve all instances. A direct product result, on the other hand, holds if a fixed probability p to solve a single instance correctly is given, then the probability of solving a m-vector of instances drops exponentially with m (as in, for example, Yao's "concatenation lemma" [38]). We provide further context on this relation in [18].

The IEP property can be proven to hold in idealized models such as the random oracle model or the generic group model (we demonstrate this in Appendix A); furthermore, it is reasonable to assume that it holds for standard cryptographic functions such as multiplication of primes, provided that a suitably function τ is chosen (also Appendix A).

4.1.3 Hardness indistinguishability

To introduce this notion, we define first the notion of *indistinguishability* between two functions. At a high level, it is the realization of this property that will provide the hiding of the functions' hardness, "blinding" the adversary as to what functions to attack first.

DEFINITION 4.5. *For $\epsilon > 0$, two functions $f_1 : X_1 \to Y_1, f_2 : X_2 \to Y_2$ are statistically indistinguishable if the random variables $f_1(x_1), f_2(x_2)$ have statistical distance less than ϵ when x_i is uniformly drawn from X_i, for $i = 1, 2$.*

We observe that for all but at most an ϵ fraction of $y_2 \in f_2(X_2)$ it holds that there is some x_1 with $f_1(x_1) = y_2$. The above definition is particularly interesting to us in the setting where, say, $H_{f_1,\epsilon} < H_{f_2,\epsilon}$ for some ϵ; i.e., the functions behave differently with respect to the exact hardness of the inversion problem. In such case we will talk about *hardness indistinguishability*. Given that an instance can be solved almost always in more than one way, hardness indistinguishability ensures that the hardness level can be *equivocated*[3].

The definition extends to the case of a sequence of functions in a straightforward way. We will call a sequence of functions indistinguishable when every pair of functions is indistinguishable. We give two constructions of such functions, one generic (that requires the extension of the function's outputs) and one more efficient that depends on dense public-key cryptosystems [35]. Note that since indistinguishability is required in the statistical sense, there is no need to

[3]This property becomes handy when designing simulators for reductions between corruption models (cf. Section 4.2). We note that the reason for considering statistical as opposed to computational indistinguishability is that the former provides to the simulator the ability to "equivocate" even when the adversary is able to invert some of the functions, as we allow in our corruption model.

consider how the decision problem's computational complexity amortizes over a sequence of indistinguishable instances (as it is unattainable except with probability ϵ).

Our first construction is general and relies on the existence of *regular* one-way functions see e.g., [21].

Construction #1. Let $f_1 : X_1 \to Y_1$ and $f_2 : X_2 \to Y_2$ be any two regular functions with exact hardness $H_{f_i,\epsilon}$ for $i = 1, 2$. We define the functions f_1', f_2' as follows $f_1' : X_1 \times Y_2 \to Y_1 \times Y_2$ and $f_2' : Y_1 \times X_2 \to Y_1 \times Y_2$ so that $f_1'(x_1, y_2) = (f_1(x_1), y_2)$ and $f_2'(y_1, x_2) = (y_1, f_2(x_2))$. Observe that $H_{f_i',\epsilon} = H_{f_i,\epsilon}$ for $i = 1, 2$. Moreover the domains of f_1', f_2' are efficiently sampleable (assuming those of f_1, f_2 are). The proof of the following proposition is straightforward.

PROPOSITION 4.6. *For any regular f_1, f_2, the functions f_1', f_2' defined as above are (perfectly) hardness indistinguishable.*

The above approach generalizes easily to a sequence of functions (at the expense of increasing linearly the length of the domain and range elements).

Construction #2. A more efficient way to construct indistinguishable functions is using *dense one-way functions* along the lines of dense public-key cryptosystems of [35, 34]. Specifically, a one-way function is called dense if its output is statistically indistinguishable from a random string of a certain length. More formally, if f is the function, it holds that $f(x)$ is statistically close to $\{0, 1\}^k$ for some suitable k when x is uniformly distributed. In order to show hardness indistinguishability, given a sequence of dense one-way functions, each function output can be padded with random bits so that all of them match the length of the longest one. Based on the density property, the functions modified as above are pairwise statistically indistinguishable.

We now briefly sketch how a dense one-way function can be constructed. Given a function $f : X \to Y$ (for simplicity assume it is an injection), a dense one way function can be derived by applying a strong randomness extractor that is also collision resistant (see [13]). Specifically, if Ext is such an extractor, we have that $f'(r, x) = (r, \mathsf{Ext}(r, f(x)))$ is a dense one-way function. Indeed, since Ext is a strong extractor and r is a uniformly random seed, it holds that the output of f' is almost uniformly distributed (provided Ext has suitable length). On the other hand, given the collision resistance property of Ext any inversion algorithm against f' can be turned to an algorithm inverting f, hence, f' is a one-way function of exact hardness not much less than that of f. We omit further details.

In Appendix A we study and give bounds for the exact hardness, IEP property and hardness indistinguishability of several candidate functions, namely, random functions, exponentiation maps in the generic group model, and integer multiplication.

4.2 From Computational Corruptions to Token based Corruptions

We now have the tools to consider the relation between the computational corruption oracle and the token-based corruption oracle. Connecting the two relies on whether the computation effort invested by the adversary against corrupting players can be abstracted as discrete token investments. The notion of IEP functions introduced above plays a crucial role here.

THEOREM 4.7. *Let $\epsilon > 0$ and τ a monotonically increasing invertible function. Given a τ-IEP sequence of functions $f_1, \ldots, f_n$, we have that for any t there exist $\overline{s}, k, L$ such that*

$$\mathcal{C}^{\mathsf{cc}}_{\overline{f}} \leq^t_\epsilon \mathcal{C}^{\mathsf{tk}}_{\overline{s},k} \quad \text{and} \quad \mathcal{C}^{\mathsf{bcc}}_{\overline{f}} \leq^t_\epsilon \mathcal{C}^{\mathsf{btk},L}_{\overline{s},k},$$

where $\overline{s} = (s_1, \ldots, s_n)$ is such that $s_i = H_{f_i,\epsilon}$ for $i = 1, \ldots, n$ and $k = \lceil \tau^{-1}(t) \rceil$, and where $L(p)$ operates so that it returns $(y_{p(1)}, \ldots, y_{p(n)})$ with $y_i = f(x_i)$ and x_i a randomly selected input of f_i.

PROOF. We first consider the relation between computational corruption and token-based corruption. The adversary $\mathcal{B}$ will simulate $\mathcal{A}$ as well as the corruption oracle $\mathcal{C}^{\mathsf{cc}}_{\overline{f}}$. During the simulation, $\mathcal{B}$ operates exactly as $\mathcal{A}$ with the following modification: when $\mathcal{A}$ submits a corruption request $(\textsc{Corrupt}, P_i, x)$, $\mathcal{B}$ submits $(\textsc{Corrupt}, P_i, s_i)$ to the corruption oracle.

Corruption requests $(\textsc{Corrupt}, P_i, x)$ for which it holds that $f_i(x) \neq y_i$ are ignored by $\mathcal{B}$.

The only divergence in the simulation is when it may happen that $\mathcal{A}$ issues a corruption request that is granted while the corresponding corruption request of $\mathcal{B}$ is denied. Suppose this happens with probability at least ϵ. This means that $\mathcal{B}$ has used all its tokens $\lceil \tau^{-1}(t) \rceil$, i.e., the set of players C corrupted by $\mathcal{A}$ satisfies that $\sum_{i \in C} s_i > \lceil \tau^{-1}(t) \rceil \geq \tau^{-1}(t)$. Note that since $\mathcal{A}$ manages to corrupt the set of players C with probability at least ϵ it follows that it runs for at least $\tau(\sum_{i \in C} H_{f_i,\epsilon}) + 1$ steps due to the τ-IEP property, i.e., $t \geq \tau(\sum_{i \in C} H_{f_i,\epsilon}) + 1 > \tau(\sum_{i \in C} s_i)$, which is a contradiction.

Regarding the relation of blinded computational corruption and leaky blinded token-based corruption we construct $\mathcal{B}$ as follows. When $\mathcal{B}$ receives $\overline{s}$ from its corruption oracle $\mathcal{C}^{\mathsf{btk},L}_{\overline{s},k}$ it requests to obtain the leak $(y_{p(1)}, \ldots, y_{p(n)})$ and returns this to the adversary $\mathcal{A}$. Otherwise the simulation and proof proceeds in the same fashion as before. □

We next consider the potential advantage that is given by the leaking capability of the leaky blinded-token corruption oracle. We have the following:

THEOREM 4.8. *Let $\epsilon > 0, n, k \in \mathbb{N}, \overline{s} \in \mathbb{N}^n$ be parameters. Given any sequence of statistically indistinguishable functions $\overline{f} = \langle f_1, \ldots, f_n \rangle$ we have $\mathcal{C}^{\mathsf{btk},L}_{\overline{s},k} \leq_{n \cdot \epsilon} \mathcal{C}^{\mathsf{btk}}_{\overline{s},k}$, where L is defined as in Theorem 4.7 and ϵ is an upper bound on the pairwise statistical distances for the sequence $\overline{f}$.*

PROOF. Basically, $\mathcal{B}$ will simulate $\mathcal{A}$ as well as the leak that is received by $\mathcal{A}$. The only issue in the simulation is that $\mathcal{B}$ is not privy to the permutation of its corruption oracle and it will still need to simulate the leak. $\mathcal{B}$ utilizes the sampler for the *hardest* of the $f_1, \ldots, f_n$ functions to obtain n instances $y_1, \ldots, y_n$. The simulator then provides $(y_1, \ldots, y_n)$ to $\mathcal{A}$. The simulator proceeds as follows: whenever the adversary submits a corruption message to the corruption oracle with a certain number of tokens the simulator passes through this request to its own corruption oracle. Due to the fact that the sampling done is at a distance at most ϵ away from regular operation for each pair of functions the behavior of $\mathcal{A}$ cannot result in a change of more than $n \cdot \epsilon$ in the execution experiment. □

With the above results we conclude that under the proper assumptions (namely IEP and hardness indistinguishability) the (blinded) token-based corruption oracle is an accurate abstraction of the (blinded) computational corruption oracle. It then follows from the results of Section 3 that the blinded computational corruption oracle remains t-safe even for values of t that far exceed the computational cost needed to corrupt a majority of player instances, thus establishing the value of the hidden diversity in the computational corruption setting.

5. SUMMARY AND DIRECTIONS FOR FUTURE RESEARCH

Adversaries in modern cryptography have thus far been allowed to "corrupt" parties for free. In this paper, motivated by the fact that different parties may require different resources to get corrupted, we put forth the notion of *resource-based corruptions*, where the adversary must invest some resources in order to corrupt parties. We further showed that in a resource *anonymous* setting (where "anonymous" is in the sense that such resource configuration is hidden from the adversary) much is to be gained in terms of efficiency and security.

We achieved the above through a series of technical contributions. These include the modeling of the corruption process in the setting of cryptographic protocols through *corruption oracles* as well as the introduction of a notion of reduction to relate such oracles; the abstraction of the corruption game as a combinatorial problem and its analysis; and, finally, the formulation of the notion of *inversion effort preserving* (IEP) functions and the property of *hardness indistinguishability*, which we apply to natural cryptographic candidates. An immediate next step is to expand the pool of such candidates.

In showing the advantages of hidden diversity, we have mainly shown that *there exist* instances where it provides significant benefits both in terms of security and efficiency. In the real world, however, systems may or may not mimic these instances and the potential benefits of hidden diversity may vary depending on the diversity distribution that actually exists. Investigating such benefits in a setting where corruption diversity follows a given probability distribution is an interesting research direction. Furthermore, one may consider the setting where a designer intervenes and is allowed to design the system taking diversity into account. This poses the problem of choosing the required corruption effort (bucket sizes), subject to a cost function. Can hidden diversity allow us to reduce cost, or increase security for a given level of expenditure? This is the subject of current research.

6. ACKNOWLEDGEMENTS

The authors are grateful to Ran Gelles, Arjen Lenstra and Alexander May for valuable comments. The work of Aggelos Kiayias was partly supported by EU projects CODAMODA and RECUP.

7. REFERENCES

[1] Mihir Bellare and Shafi Goldwasser. Verifiable partial key escrow. In Richard Graveman, Philippe A. Janson, Clifford Neumann, and Li Gong, editors, *ACM Conference on Computer and Communications Security*, pages 78–91. ACM, 1997.

[2] Mihir Bellare, Thomas Ristenpart, and Stefano Tessaro. Multi-instance security and its application to password-based cryptography. In Reihaneh Safavi-Naini and Ran Canetti, editors, *CRYPTO*, volume 7417 of *Lecture Notes in Computer Science*, pages 312–329. Springer, 2012.

[3] Mihir Bellare and Phillip Rogaway. Random oracles are practical: A paradigm for designing efficient protocols. In *ACM Conference on Computer and Communications Security*, pages 62–73, 1993.

[4] Mihir Bellare and Phillip Rogaway. The exact security of digital signatures - how to sign with rsa and rabin. In *EUROCRYPT*, pages 399–416, 1996.

[5] Michael Ben-Or, Shafi Goldwasser, and Avi Wigderson. Completeness theorems for non-cryptographic fault-tolerant distributed computation (extended abstract). In Janos Simon, editor, *STOC*, pages 1–10. ACM, 1988.

[6] Dan Boneh and Moni Naor. Timed commitments. In Mihir Bellare, editor, *CRYPTO*, volume 1880 of *Lecture Notes in Computer Science*, pages 236–254. Springer, 2000.

[7] Ran Canetti. Universally composable security: A new paradigm for cryptographic protocols. In *Cryptology ePrint Archive, Report 2000/067*, December 2005. Latest version at `http://eprint.iacr.org/2000/067/`.

[8] Ran Canetti, Uriel Feige, Oded Goldreich, and Moni Naor. Adaptively secure multi-party computation. In Miller [31], pages 639–648.

[9] David Chaum, Claude Crépeau, and Ivan Damgard. Multiparty unconditionally secure protocols. In *Proceedings of the twentieth annual ACM symposium on Theory of computing*, STOC '88, pages 11–19, New York, NY, USA, 1988. ACM.

[10] Richard Cleve. Limits on the security of coin flips when half the processors are faulty (extended abstract). In Juris Hartmanis, editor, *STOC*, pages 364–369. ACM, 1986.

[11] Don Coppersmith. Modifications to the number field sieve. *J. Cryptology*, 6(3):169–180, 1993.

[12] Ivan Damgård, Yuval Ishai, and Mikkel Krøigaard. Perfectly secure multiparty computation and the computational overhead of cryptography. In Henri Gilbert, editor, *EUROCRYPT*, volume 6110 of *Lecture Notes in Computer Science*, pages 445–465. Springer, 2010.

[13] Yevgeniy Dodis. On extractors, error-correction and hiding all partial information. In *Theory and Practice in Information-Theoretic Security, 2005. IEEE Information Theory Workshop on*, pages 74 –79, oct. 2005.

[14] Cynthia Dwork and Moni Naor. Pricing via processing or combatting junk mail. In Ernest F. Brickell, editor, *CRYPTO*, volume 740 of *Lecture Notes in Computer Science*, pages 139–147. Springer, 1992.

[15] Tomás Feder, Eyal Kushilevitz, Moni Naor, and Noam Nisan. Amortized communication complexity. *SIAM J. Comput.*, 24(4):736–750, 1995.

[16] Ephraim Feig and Shmuel Winograd. On the direct

sum conjecture. *Linear Algebra and its Applications*, 63(0):193 – 219, 1984.

[17] Matthias Fitzi, Juan A. Garay, Ueli M. Maurer, and Rafail Ostrovsky. Minimal complete primitives for secure multi-party computation. *J. Cryptology*, 18(1):37–61, 2005.

[18] Juan A. Garay, David Johnson, Aggelos Kiayias, and Moti Yung. Resource-based corruptions and the combinatorics of hidden diversity. *IACR Cryptology ePrint Archive*, 2012:556, 2012.

[19] Juan A. Garay, Philip D. MacKenzie, Manoj Prabhakaran, and Ke Yang. Resource fairness and composability of cryptographic protocols. *J. Cryptology*, 24(4):615–658, 2011.

[20] Juan A. Garay and Carl Pomerance. Timed fair exchange of standard signatures (Extended Abstract). In Rebecca N. Wright, editor, *Financial Cryptography*, volume 2742 of *Lecture Notes in Computer Science*, pages 190–207. Springer, 2003.

[21] Oded Goldreich, Hugo Krawczyk, and Michael Luby. On the existence of pseudorandom generators. *SIAM J. Comput.*, 22(6):1163–1175, 1993.

[22] Oded Goldreich, Silvio Micali, and Avi Wigderson. How to play any mental game or a completeness theorem for protocols with honest majority. In Alfred V. Aho, editor, *STOC*, pages 218–229. ACM, 1987.

[23] Iftach Haitner, Danny Harnik, and Omer Reingold. Efficient pseudorandom generators from exponentially hard one-way functions. In Michele Bugliesi, Bart Preneel, Vladimiro Sassone, and Ingo Wegener, editors, *ICALP (2)*, volume 4052 of *Lecture Notes in Computer Science*, pages 228–239. Springer, 2006.

[24] Martin Hirt and Ueli M. Maurer. Player simulation and general adversary structures in perfect multiparty computation. *J. Cryptology*, 13(1):31–60, 2000.

[25] Russell Impagliazzo, Ragesh Jaiswal, Valentine Kabanets, and Avi Wigderson. Uniform direct product theorems: Simplified, optimized, and derandomized. *SIAM J. Comput.*, 39(4):1637–1665, 2010.

[26] Yuval Ishai, Eyal Kushilevitz, Rafail Ostrovsky, and Amit Sahai. Cryptography from anonymity. In *FOCS*, pages 239–248. IEEE Computer Society, 2006.

[27] Mauricio Karchmer, Ran Raz, and Avi Wigderson. Super-logarithmic depth lower bounds via the direct sum in communication complexity. *Computational Complexity*, 5(3/4):191–204, 1995.

[28] Arjen K. Lenstra, Hendrik W. Lenstra Jr., Mark S. Manasse, and John M. Pollard. The number field sieve. In Harriet Ortiz, editor, *STOC*, pages 564–572. ACM, 1990.

[29] Hendrik W. Lenstra. Factoring integers with elliptic curves. *The Annals of Mathematics*, 126(3):649–673, Nov. 1987.

[30] Silvio Micali and Rafael Pass. Local zero knowledge. In Jon M. Kleinberg, editor, *STOC*, pages 306–315. ACM, 2006.

[31] Gary L. Miller, editor. *Proceedings of the Twenty-Eighth Annual ACM Symposium on the Theory of Computing, Philadelphia, Pennsylvania, USA, May 22-24, 1996.* ACM, 1996.

[32] Noam Nisan and Avi Wigderson. Hardness vs randomness. *J. Comput. Syst. Sci.*, 49(2):149–167, 1994.

[33] Ron Rivest, Adi Shamir, and David Wagner. Timed-lock puzzles and timed-release crypto. In *MIT/LCS/TR-684*, 1996.

[34] Alfredo De Santis, Giovanni Di Crescenzo, and Giuseppe Persiano. Necessary and sufficient assumptions for non-iterative zero-knowledge proofs of knowledge for all np relations. In Ugo Montanari, José D. P. Rolim, and Emo Welzl, editors, *ICALP*, volume 1853 of *Lecture Notes in Computer Science*, pages 451–462. Springer, 2000.

[35] Alfredo De Santis and Giuseppe Persiano. Zero-knowledge proofs of knowledge without interaction (extended abstract). In *FOCS*, pages 427–436. IEEE Computer Society, 1992.

[36] Adi Shamir. Partial key escrow: A new approach to software key escrow. In *Key Escrow Conference*, 1995.

[37] Victor Shoup. Lower bounds for discrete logarithms and related problems. In *EUROCRYPT*, pages 256–266, 1997.

[38] Andrew Chi-Chih Yao. Theory and applications of trapdoor functions (extended abstract). In *FOCS*, pages 80–91. IEEE Computer Society, 1982.

APPENDIX

A. CANDIDATE IEP AND HARDNESS INDISTINGUISHABLE FUNCTIONS

In this section we study and give bounds for the exact hardness, the IEP property and hardness indistinguishability of three natural cryptographic candidates: random functions, discrete logarithm in the generic group model, and factorization. We note that all the functions we present here can be used in conjunction with constructions #1 and #2 given in Section 4.1.3 to derive hardness indistinguishable functions.

A.1 Random Functions

We first consider the notion of exact hardness and argue that for the inversion problem of a function that is modeled as a random oracle [3], we can calculate exactly the expression for exact hardness. In this model, we only count queries to the random oracle as the basic computational operation, and thus all complexity measures are expressed in terms of such queries.

PROPOSITION A.1. *Let $\epsilon > 0$ and $f : [2^\lambda] \to [2^\lambda]$ be modelled as a random oracle. Then $H_{f,\epsilon}(\lambda) = \epsilon \cdot 2^\lambda - 1$.*

PROOF. When f is modelled as a random oracle the probability $\mathbf{Pr}[\mathcal{A}_t(f(x)) \in f^{-1}(f(x))]$ is taken over all possible choices of x (uniformly selected from $[2^\lambda]$) and the choices of f (thought as a random table with 2^λ entries). Any algorithm that queries f will have probability $(q+1)2^{-\lambda}$ of returning the inverse of the input value $y = f(x)$ if it is allowed q queries. To see this consider the following: if $\mathcal{A}$ asks q distinct queries and finds the inverse among them it can return it for a probability of success equal to 1; otherwise, any $\mathcal{A}$ no matter which strategy it follows will have at best a $\frac{1}{n-q}$ chance of succeeding. Note that if $\mathcal{A}$ is repeating some queries the probability of success would be worse, but this is something we can assume without loss of generality that it does not happen given that there is no restriction in space for $\mathcal{A}$. The statement of the proposition now follows since the probability of success is $q2^{-\lambda} + (1 - q2^{-\lambda})(1/(2^{\lambda} - q)) = (q+1)2^{-\lambda}$ by requiring this probability to be less than ϵ and considering a query to f as the basic computational step. □

We now study the inversion-effort-preserving property of random oracles. We show that if the functions are modeled as independent random oracles, then no speed up is possible for such set of instances.

PROPOSITION A.2. *For $n > 0$, the sequence of functions $\{f_i\}_{i=1,\ldots,n}$ with $f_i : [2^{\lambda}] \to [2^{\lambda}]$ is IEP assuming each one of them is modelled as a random oracle.*

PROOF. We will use the fact that querying function f_i gives no information about function f_j for $j \neq i$. As in Proposition A.1, the inversion of function f_i can succeed with probability $(q_i + 1)2^{-\lambda}$ as long as q_i queries are made. Also as before, any algorithm inverting f_i with probability ϵ requires $\epsilon \cdot 2^{\lambda} - 1$ queries to f_i. We will show that any algorithm running in $t = n\epsilon \cdot 2^{\lambda} - n$ steps cannot invert all of the functions with probability greater than ϵ. We argue as follows. At the end of any execution at the specified number of steps t we can build a table of size q_i for each function f_i; we have that $\sum_{i=1}^{n} q_i \leq t$. By conditioning on the subset A of the functions for which a good query has been made, we obtain that the probability of success can be upper-bounded by the expression

$$\sum_{A \subseteq [n]} \prod_{i \in A} \frac{q_i}{2^{\lambda}} \cdot \prod_{i \notin A} (1 - \frac{q_i}{2^{\lambda}}) \cdot \prod_{i \notin A} \frac{1}{2^{\lambda} - q_i}$$

$$= \sum_{A \subseteq [n]} \frac{\prod_{i \in A} q_i}{2^{\lambda n}} = \frac{\prod_{i=1}^{n} (q_i + 1)}{2^{\lambda n}} \leq \left(\frac{n + \sum_{i=1}^{n} q_i}{n \cdot 2^{\lambda}} \right)^n$$

where the last inequality follows from the arithmetic and geometric means inequality. Now applying the bound $\sum_{i=1}^{n} q_i \leq t = n\epsilon \cdot 2^{\lambda} - n$ and the fact that $\epsilon^n \leq \epsilon$ we bound the probability by ϵ. The result on $H_{f^S,\epsilon}$ (cf. Definition 4.4) now immediately follows. □

A.2 Discrete Logarithm

We now consider the exact hardness of discrete logarithms in the generic group model (see, e.g., [37]). In this setting, any algorithm $\mathcal{A}$ solving the discrete logarithm is given the encodings of two group elements, $\sigma(1)$ and $\sigma(x)$, where $\sigma : \mathbb{Z}_q \to S$ is a random permutation. Here q is a prime number that is λ-bits.

$\mathcal{A}$ aims to discover x but has no way to internally emulate the group operation. Instead, the algorithm operates with access to an oracle that takes input (r, s) and returns the value $\sigma(r + sx)$; we measure those oracle calls as the basic steps taken by the algorithm.

We denote all the queries of $\mathcal{A}$ to the oracle by $Q_{\mathcal{A}}$. A key observation used in [37] is that as long as it holds that $r + sx = r' + s'x \bmod q$ for two queries $(r, s), (r', s')$ to the oracle, it is possible to reconstruct x. The second key observation is that if this event does not occur then $\mathcal{A}$'s behavior is independent of x. It follows that the success of algorithm $\mathcal{A}$ in solving the discrete logarithm problem is bounded by the probability that $r + sx = r' + s'x$ or $y = x$ for some $(r, s), (r', s') \in Q_{\mathcal{A}}$, where x is uniformly distributed over $\mathbb{Z}_q$ and y is some arbitrarily distributed value (in this setting, y would capture the output of $\mathcal{A}$). If the algorithm performs k queries then we have that the probability of success is bounded by $(\binom{k}{2} + 1)/q$ (this stems from the fact that the k queries can be thought of lines over a plane that determine $\binom{k}{2}$ cut points—the probability of equality amounts to hitting one of those cut points). Based on this we state the following.

PROPOSITION A.3. *Let $\epsilon > 0$ and q be a λ-bit prime number. Suppose $f : \mathbb{Z}_q \to S$ is the exponentiation function over a generic multiplicative group. Then $H_{f,\epsilon} \geq \sqrt{2q\epsilon}$.*

PROOF. The proof follows from the argument presented above (due to [37]). Suppose $H_{f,\epsilon} < T = \sqrt{2q\epsilon}$. This means that there is an algorithm that in T steps achieves a probability of success ϵ. But we observe that T is such that $(\binom{T}{2} + 1)/q < \epsilon$, hence a contradiction following the above arguments (assuming $T \geq 2$). □

Next, we consider the IEP property in the same setting. We consider the solution of n independent instances of the discrete-logarithm problem over n groups. Each group is assumed to have a separate encoding of elements σ_i that is independently selected. Specifically, an algorithm $\mathcal{A}$ is given the pairs $(\sigma_i(1), \sigma(x_i))$ for $i = 1, \ldots, n$ and aims to produce the vector $(x_1, \ldots, x_n)$. $\mathcal{A}$ is allowed to access an oracle that accepts queries of the form (i, r, s) and returns $\sigma_i(r + sx_i)$.

PROPOSITION A.4. *Let $\epsilon > 0$, $n > 0$ and q be a prime λ-bit number. Suppose $f^{[n]} : (\mathbb{Z}_q)^n \to S_1 \times \ldots \times S_n$ is the coordinate-wise exponentiation function over a sequence of n generic multiplicative groups. Then $H_{f^{[n]},\epsilon} \geq \sqrt{2n \cdot \epsilon^{1/n} \cdot q}$.*

PROOF. Suppose that $H_{f^{(n)},\epsilon} < T = \lceil \sqrt{2n\epsilon^{1/n} q} \rceil$. This means that there is an algorithm $\mathcal{A}$ that in T steps has probability of success at least ϵ. Define by t_i the number of queries posed to the i-th oracle by $\mathcal{A}$. Then it holds that $\sum_{i=1}^{n} t_i = T$ since we count only oracle queries in the running time of $\mathcal{A}$. We let C_i be the event that a collision has occurred at the i-th oracle. Now let $B \subseteq [n]$ be the set of groups over which the event C_i takes place, i.e., for all i, $i \in B$ if and only if C_i is true. Assuming this conditioning we know that the probability of success of algorithm $\mathcal{A}$ is at most $(1/q)^{n-|B|}$ since it essentially has to guess all the other queries. Furthermore, the probability of event B happening is the probability that we get a collision; given the independence of the group encodings this is $\prod_{i \in B} \binom{t_i}{2}/q$. So overall we have that the probability is bounded by

$$q^{-n} \cdot \sum_{B \subseteq [n]} \prod_{i \in B} \binom{t_i}{2} = q^{-n} \cdot \prod_{i=1}^{n} (\binom{t_i}{2} + 1)$$

$$\leq (n \cdot q)^{-n} (n + \sum_{i=1}^{n} \binom{t_i}{2})^n,$$

where the last inequality follows from the geometric-arithmetic means inequality. Observe now that $\sum_{i=1}^{n} \binom{t_i}{2} = \frac{1}{2} \cdot (\sum_{i=1}^{n} t_i^2 - T) < T(T-1)/2$. From this we obtain that the probability of success ϵ is strictly bounded by $(T^2/2qn)^n$. This is a contradiction since $(T^2/2qn)^n \geq \epsilon$ by definition of T. □

COROLLARY A.5. *Let $\epsilon > 0, n > 0$, and q be a λ-bit prime number. Suppose $f_i : \mathbb{Z}_q \to S_i$ is the exponentiation function over a generic multiplicative group S_i. Then the set of functions $\{f_i\}_{i=1,\ldots,n}$ is τ-IEP for $\tau(\cdot) = (\cdot)^{1/2}$.*

PROOF. By definition we need to show that for any subset $S \subseteq [n]$ we have that $H_{f^S,\epsilon} \geq \tau(\sum_{i\in S} H_{f_i,\epsilon})$. Using Propositions A.3 and A.4 we have that

$$H_{f^S,\epsilon} \geq \sqrt{|S|} \cdot \sqrt{2q\epsilon^{1/n}} \geq$$

$$\sqrt{|S|} \cdot \max_{i\in S} H_{f_i,\epsilon} \geq (\sum_{i\in S} H_{f_i,\epsilon})^{1/2},$$

which completes the proof. □

A.3 Factoring

The complexity to factor an integer N with the best known algorithm (the number field sieve [28]) takes time on the order of $L[1/3, 1.9229]$, where

$$L[\alpha, \beta] = \exp((\beta + o(1))(\log N)^{\alpha}(\log\log N)^{1-\alpha}),$$

and was improved to $L[1/3, 1.902]$ by Coppersmith [11]. Assuming that this result matches the complexity of the factoring problem, this will provide bounds for the exact hardness of the multiplication function. Specifically, if P_λ is the set of all λ-bit prime numbers, we have that if $f_{\mathsf{mult}} : \mathsf{P}_\lambda \times \mathsf{P}_\lambda \to \mathbb{N}$ with $f_{\mathsf{mult}}(p, q) = p \cdot q$, then for any ϵ,

$$\epsilon \cdot L(1/3, 1.902) \leq H_{f,\epsilon} \leq \epsilon \cdot L(1/2, \sqrt{2}) \qquad (1)$$

According to the above statement, the exact hardness of factoring is a subexponential function that is bounded from below by a time complexity that is derived from the running time of the number field sieve algorithm. We note that a similar assumption was made in [4] when stating the "exact security" of the RSA function. The upper bound in the statement is derived from Lenstra's elliptic curve factorization algorithm [29]. This algorithm is suitable for expressing an upper bound in the form above since it is an algorithm that repetitively picks an elliptic curve and a point on it, and then tests whether the group law holds by calculating a scalar of the point. The complexity of the algorithm is determined by the fact that after picking around $L(1/2, \sqrt{2})$ curves, then with very high probability a "bad" curve will be found. As a result, if we wish to succeed with probability ϵ, we should sample about $\epsilon \cdot L(1/2, \sqrt{2})$ curves.

Regarding the IEP property, it was shown in [11] that it is possible to amortize cost when factoring n integers and there exists an algorithm with expected time complexity $L[1/3, 2.0068]+n \cdot L[1/3, 1.6386]$. Under the assumption that Coppersmith's algorithm (and small optimizations thereof) is the best possible when trying to factor simultaneously a sequence of moduli, one might be willing to assume that if $f^{[n]}$ is the function that multiplies n pairs of primes to the corresponding moduli, the following lower bound would hold true:

$$H_{f^{[n]},\epsilon} \geq \epsilon \cdot n \cdot L[1/3, \sqrt{2}]. \qquad (2)$$

From the above two assumptions, the τ-IEP property for factoring is satisfied by letting $\tau(x) = e^{(\ln x)^{2/3}}$. This holds due to the fact that for any n, ϵ, we have that $\epsilon \cdot n \cdot L(1/3, \sqrt{2}) \geq \tau(\epsilon \cdot n \cdot L(1/2, \sqrt{2}))$.

Time Hierarchies for Sampling Distributions

Thomas Watson
University of California, Berkeley
Berkeley, CA, USA
tom@cs.berkeley.edu

ABSTRACT

We show that "a little more time gives a lot more power to sampling algorithms." We prove that for every constant $k \geq 2$, every polynomial time bound t, and every polynomially small ϵ, there exists a family of distributions on k elements that can be sampled exactly in polynomial time but cannot be sampled within statistical distance $1 - 1/k - \epsilon$ in time t. This implies the following general time hierarchy for sampling distributions on arbitrary-size domains such as $\{0,1\}^n$: For every polynomial time bound t and every constant $\epsilon > 0$, there exists a family of distributions that can be sampled exactly in polynomial time but cannot be sampled within statistical distance $1 - \epsilon$ in time t.

Our proof involves reducing the problem to a communication problem over a certain type of noisy channel. To solve the latter problem we use a type of list-decodable code for a setting where there is no bound on the number of errors but each error gives more information than an erasure. This type of code can be constructed using certain known traditional list-decodable codes, but we give a new construction that is elementary, self-contained, and tailored to this setting.

Categories and Subject Descriptors

F.1.3 [**Computation by Abstract Devices**]: Complexity Measures and Classes—*Complexity hierarchies*

Keywords

Time Hierarchies; Sampling; Distributions

1. INTRODUCTION

The most commonly studied computational problems in theoretical computer science are *search problems*, where there is a relation specifying which outputs are acceptable, and the goal is to find any acceptable output. Another important type of computational problem is *sampling problems*, where the goal is for the output to be distributed according to (or at least statistically close to) a specified probability distribution.

Sampling problems have received much attention in the algorithms community. For example, there has been substantial work on algorithms for sampling graph colorings [16], independent sets [34, 41], matchings [25, 26], lattice tilings [33, 45], knapsack solutions [35], linear extensions of partial orders [7, 45], factored numbers [2, 27], DNF solutions [29], eulerian tours [8], stable marriages [5], words from context-free languages [20], chemical isomers [17], points on algebraic varieties [9], contingency tables [28, 11], and spanning trees [38, 44, 30]. In the complexity community, historically most research has focused on search problems (and the special case of decision problems). However, there has been a surge of interest in complexity-theoretic results that accord sampling problems a status as first-class computational problems [18, 43, 1, 32, 12, 42, 4]. Many of those works focus on proving lower bounds for explicit sampling problems on restricted models of computation.

In the context of sampling problems, we revisit the genesis of complexity theory. In their seminal paper, Hartmanis and Stearns [23] proved a *time hierarchy theorem* for decision problems, showing that there are decision problems that are solvable by deterministic algorithms running in time t but not by deterministic algorithms running in time a little less than t. This is often considered the first result in complexity theory. We study the corresponding question for sampling problems. First, observe that there is a trivial time hierarchy for exact sampling: In time t, an algorithm can produce a particular output with probability $1/2^t$, which clearly cannot be done in time less than t. The interesting question is whether a *robust* time hierarchy can be proved, showing that there exists a distribution family that can be sampled in time t, but that algorithms running in time a little less than t cannot even come close to sampling (in statistical distance). We succeed in proving such a hierarchy theorem, showing that algorithms running in a sufficiently smaller amount of time cannot sample the distribution within a statistical distance that is any constant less than 1. This is a corollary to our main theorem, which is a quantitatively tight result for distributions on constant-size domains, showing that algorithms running in a sufficiently smaller amount of time cannot sample the distribution much better than the trivial statistical distance achieved by the uniform distribution. Our results can be summarized as "a little more time gives a lot more power to sampling algorithms."

There are several proofs of time hierarchy theorems for nondeterministic algorithms and other models of computation [10, 39, 46, 14], but these proofs do not directly carry over to our setting. On the surface, our setting may seem more closely related to the long-standing open problem of proving a hierarchy for polynomial-time randomized algorithms solving decision problems. The chief difficulty in the latter setting is that an algorithm must satisfy the "promise" of having bounded error on every input, and it is not known how to guarantee this while diagonalizing against a randomized algorithm that may not have bounded error. There is a beautiful line of research that circumvents this obstacle by working in slightly-nonuniform or average-case settings [3, 13, 19, 15, 36, 21, 40, 37, 31, 24]. Our setting is intrinsically different because there is no "promise" that could be violated: Whatever algorithm we consider, it is guaranteed to sample some family of distributions. We have fundamentally different issues to address.

1.1 Results

We start with our definitions. We let $[k] = \{1, \ldots, k\}$ and let $\mathbb{N}$ denote the set of positive integers. For distributions D, D' on $[k]$, recall that the statistical distance is defined as $|D - D'| = \max_{S \subseteq [k]} |\Pr_D(S) - \Pr_{D'}(S)|$. Our results hold for any reasonable uniform model of computation; for concreteness we may assume the model is Turing machines with access to unbiased independent coin flips.

For a function $k : \mathbb{N} \to \mathbb{N}$, we define a *k-family* to be a sequence $D = (D_1, D_2, D_3, \ldots)$ where D_n is a distribution on $[k(n)]$. For a function $\delta : \mathbb{N} \to [0, 1]$, we say a randomized algorithm A *δ-samples* a k-family D if when given n as input, A outputs an element $A(n) \in [k(n)]$ such that the output distribution satisfies $|A(n) - D_n| \leq \delta(n)$. For a function $t : \mathbb{N} \to \mathbb{N}$, we say that A *runs in time t* if for all $n \in \mathbb{N}$, A always halts in at most $t(n)$ steps when given n as input.[1] We define

$$\textsc{SampTime}_{k,\delta}(t)$$

to be the class of k-families δ-sampled by algorithms running in time t.[2]

THEOREM 1. *For every constant $k \geq 2$ and every constant $c \geq 1$,*

$$\textsc{SampTime}_{k,0}(\text{poly}(n)) \not\subseteq \textsc{SampTime}_{k,1-1/k-\epsilon}(t)$$

where $\epsilon(n) = 1/n^c$ and $t(n) = n^c$.

COROLLARY 1. *For every function $k(n) \geq \omega(1)$ and every constant $c \geq 1$,*

$$\textsc{SampTime}_{k,0}(\text{poly}(n)) \not\subseteq \textsc{SampTime}_{k,1-\epsilon}(t)$$

where $\epsilon = 1/c$ and $t(n) = n^c$.

PROOF OF COROLLARY 1. We explain how Theorem 1 implies Corollary 1 by the contrapositive. Supposing $k(n)$ and c are a counterexample to Corollary 1, we claim that k' and c' are a counterexample to Theorem 1 where $k' = c' = c+1$. A family $D \in \textsc{SampTime}_{k',0}(\text{poly}(n))$ can be viewed as being in $\textsc{SampTime}_{k,0}(\text{poly}(n))$ (since $[k'] \subseteq [k(n)]$ for all but finitely many n) and thus also in $\textsc{SampTime}_{k,1-1/c}(n^c)$. Now to get a $\textsc{SampTime}_{k',1-1/k'-1/n^{c'}}(n^{c'})$ algorithm for D, we just run the $\textsc{SampTime}_{k,1-1/c}(n^c)$ algorithm except that if it outputs a value $> k'$ then we output k' instead. This modification does not cause the statistical distance to go up. Thus the new algorithm runs in time $n^c + O(1)$, and for all but finitely many n it samples a distribution within statistical distance $1 - 1/c \leq 1 - 1/k' - 1/n^{c'}$ from D_n. □

[1] We measure the running time here as a function of the value of the input, not the bit length of the input. Alternatively, we could view the input as the string 1^n and measure the running time as a function of the bit length.

[2] If we write something such as $\textsc{SampTime}_{O(\log n),1/2-1/\text{poly}(n)}(\text{poly}(n))$, we formally mean the union of $\textsc{SampTime}_{k,\delta}(t)$ over all functions of the form $k = O(\log n)$, $\delta = 1/2 - 1/\text{poly}(n)$, and $t = \text{poly}(n)$.

1.2 Discussion

Our definition of k-families is "unary", since there is one distribution for each n. We could alternatively define a k-family to be a function mapping bit strings of length n to distributions on $[k(n)]$ (for all n). This would more realistically model algorithmic sampling problems, but our hierarchy results are stronger with the unary definition (since a "non-unary" hierarchy follows by just ignoring all but one input of each length). Also, in average-case complexity (see [6]), unary sampling arises naturally: The random input to an algorithm is often modeled as coming from an efficiently samplable distribution on $\{0,1\}^n$ (or $[2^n]$, in our notation) for all n. This can be viewed as a secondary motivation for our results.

For Corollary 1 it may seem like it would be cleaner to omit the domain size k from the complexity classes and just say, for example, that the domain is always $\{0,1\}^*$. However, this would make the corollary true for trivial reasons: A poly(n)-time samplable distribution could be supported on bit strings of length $> t(n)$, whereas a t-time samplable distribution must be supported on bit strings of length $\leq t(n)$. Corollary 1 is only meaningful when the domain size is at most 2^t.

Note that the $1 - 1/k - \epsilon$ statistical distance bound in Theorem 1 is tight since the theorem becomes false if $\epsilon = 0$. This is because the uniform distribution (which is samplable in constant time) is within statistical distance $1 - 1/k$ from every distribution on $[k]$. We mention that our proofs of Theorem 1 and Corollary 1 relativize, and that they carry through without change for quantum algorithms instead of classical randomized algorithms.

We give the intuition for Theorem 1 in Section 2. We give the formal proof of Theorem 1 in Section 3. One key ingredient in the proof is a certain type of code, which we construct in Section 4.

2. INTUITION FOR THEOREM 1

Recall that the original deterministic time hierarchy of [23] is proved by diagonalization: A separate input length n_i is reserved for each algorithm A_i running in the smaller time bound, and an algorithm running in the larger time bound is designed which, when given an input of length n_i, simulates A_i and outputs the opposite answer. In our setting, Brouwer's fixed point theorem gives a barrier to using this "direct complementation" strategy: Suppose we design an algorithm running in the larger time bound which takes n_i and simulates $A_i(n_i)$ any number of times (drawing samples from the distribution $A_i(n_i)$ as a black box) and then performs some computation and produces an output. This algorithm would implement a continuous function from distributions on $[k]$ to distributions on $[k]$,[3] where the input to the function represents the distribution $A_i(n_i)$. This function would have a fixed point, so there would be some distribution, which $A_i(n_i)$ might sample, that would cause the diagonalizing algorithm to produce exactly the same distribution. The trivial time hierarchy for exact sampling mentioned in the introduction gets around this by exploiting the fact that $A_i(n_i)$ cannot be an arbitrary distribution; it must be "discretized". However, the latter observation cannot be used to get a robust time hierarchy with a nonnegligible statistical distance gap. Another potential way to bypass the fixed point barrier would be to argue that A_i cannot sample anything close to a fixed point, but it is not clear how to make this approach work.

Since a straightforward direct complementation does not work, we take as a starting point the *delayed diagonalization* technique introduced by Žák [46]. This technique can be used to prove a time hierarchy for solving decision problems with almost any uniform model of computation that is syntactic (meaning there is no promise to be satisfied). The idea is to space out the n_i's so that n_{i+1} is exponentially larger than n_i, and use all the input lengths from n_i to $n_{i+1}-1$ to diagonalize against the ith algorithm A_i. On inputs of length $n \in \{n_i, \ldots, n_{i+1}-2\}$ the diagonalizing algorithm copies the behavior of A_i on inputs of length $n+1$, and on inputs of length $n = n_{i+1}-1$ the diagonalizing algorithm "does the opposite" of A_i on inputs of length n_i (by brute force). Thus A_i cannot agree with the diagonalizing algorithm for all $n \in \{n_i, \ldots, n_{i+1}-1\}$ or we would obtain a contradiction.

The delayed diagonalization technique leads to a straightforward proof of the $k=2$ case of Theorem 1, as follows. Let us use $D = (D_1, D_2, \ldots)$ to denote the k-family 0-sampled by A_i (the algorithm we are diagonalizing against) and $D^* = (D_1^*, D_2^*, \ldots)$ to denote the k-family 0-sampled by our diagonalizing algorithm. We can let $D^*_{n_{i+1}-1}$ be concentrated entirely on the least likely outcome of D_{n_i}, say $M \in [2]$.[4] (This is where delayed diagonalization has an advantage over direct diagonalization: On input $n_{i+1}-1$ the diagonalizing algorithm has enough time to determine M with certainty by brute force, which breaks the "continuity barrier" that applies to methods that merely sample D_{n_i}.) Now for $n = (n_{i+1}-2), \ldots, n_i$, by induction we may assume that $\Pr_{D^*_{n+1}}(M) \geq 1-\epsilon(n+1)/2$ and thus $\Pr_{D_{n+1}}(M) \geq 1/2+\epsilon(n+1)/2$ (assuming $|D_{n+1}-D^*_{n+1}| \leq 1/2-\epsilon(n+1)$). By sampling from D_{n+1} many times and taking the majority outcome, we can ensure that $\Pr_{D^*_n}(M) \geq 1-\epsilon(n)/2$. In the end we have $\Pr_{D^*_{n_i}}(M) \geq 1-\epsilon(n_i)/2$ while $\Pr_{D_{n_i}}(M) \leq 1/2$, which gives a contradiction if $|D_{n_i}-D^*_{n_i}| \leq 1/2-\epsilon(n_i)$.

This simple argument breaks down when $k \geq 3$. Suppose we let $D^*_{n_{i+1}-1}$ be concentrated on $M \in [k]$, the least likely outcome of D_{n_i}. If $D_{n_{i+1}-1}$ is uniform on $\{1, \ldots, k-1\}$ then this would be consistent with any $M \in \{1, \ldots, k-1\}$, since $D_{n_{i+1}-1}$ would simultaneously have statistical distance $1-1/(k-1) \ll 1-1/k$ from the distributions concentrated on such M's. Note that it is impossible to have statistical distance $< 1-1/k$ from the distributions concentrated on *all* possible M's, so $D_{n_{i+1}-1}$ would be forced to reveal *some* information about the correct M, namely it must rule out at least one value.

Here is the first idea we use to fix this problem. Instead of using a single input n_i to "close the cycle" and obtain a contradiction, suppose we reserve m inputs $n_i, n_i+1, \ldots, n_i+m-1$ and let M_α be the least likely outcome of $D_{n_i+\alpha}$ for $\alpha \in \{0, 1, \ldots, m-1\}$. Suppose that on these inputs, our diagonalizing algorithm could somehow obtain (with high probability) a list of m candidates for the sequence $M_0, M_1, \ldots, M_{m-1}$, where at least one candidate is correct. Then we could have $D^*_{n_i+\alpha}$ put most of its probability mass on the αth value from the αth candidate sequence. If the αth candidate sequence is the correct one, then we get $\Pr_{D^*_{n_i+\alpha}}(M_\alpha) \geq 1-\epsilon(n_i+\alpha)/2$ while $\Pr_{D_{n_i+\alpha}}(M_\alpha) \leq 1/k$, which gives a contradiction if $|D_{n_i+\alpha}-D^*_{n_i+\alpha}| \leq 1-1/k-\epsilon(n_i+\alpha)$.

How do we get a small list of candidates? For some input n_i^* exponentially larger than n_i, suppose we encode the message $M_0, M_1, \ldots, M_{m-1}$ in some way as $\gamma \in [k]^\ell$ and use a block of ℓ inputs $n_i^*, n_i^*+1, \ldots, n_i^*+\ell-1$ to "declare" the codeword γ, by having $D^*_{n_i^*+j-1}$ be concentrated entirely on γ_j for $j \in [\ell]$.[5] Then we are faced with the following communication problem over a noisy channel: For some smaller inputs $n < n_i^*$, we would like to recover the original message so we can "retransmit" it to even smaller inputs (until it eventually reaches the inputs $n_i, n_i+1, \ldots, n_i+m-1$). Our only way to get information about the message is by sampling from the distributions $D_{n_i^*+j-1}$ (for $j \in [\ell]$), which only weakly reflect the transmitted codeword (under the assumption that A_i $(1-1/k-\epsilon)$-samples D^*). Thus the algorithm A_i being diagonalized against serves as a noisy channel for transmitting the message from larger inputs to smaller inputs.

As noted above, it is information-theoretically impossible to uniquely recover the original message when $k \geq 3$, but provided we use a suitable encoding we may be able to recover a small list of candidates. Then for each candidate in the list we could use a disjoint block of ℓ inputs to retransmit the encoding of that candidate message. More precisely, suppose there exists a small set S of messages containing the correct one, such that by sampling from $D_{n_i^*+j-1}$ (for $j \in [\ell]$) we can discover S with high probability. Then for each message in S we could have a block of ℓ inputs (that are polynomially smaller than n_i^*) "declare" the codeword corresponding to that message. Then on even smaller inputs, the diagonalizing algorithm could sample from D on the inputs in a particular block to recover a small list of candidates for the message encoded by that block. This leads to a tree structure.[6] Each node in the tree attempts to transmit a codeword to its children, after attempting to receive a codeword from its parent by simulating A_i to get samples from D, and running some sort of list-decoder. Each node can see "which child it is" and interpret this as advice specifying which message on the list it is responsible for encoding and transmitting (the hth child is responsible for the lexicographically h^{th} smallest message). The inputs $n_i, n_i+1, \ldots, n_i+m-1$ are the leaves of the tree. The

[3] In general we would talk about $[k(n_i)]$, but recall that k is a constant in Theorem 1.

[4] M might seem like unusual notation here, but it is convenient in the formal proof, and it stands for "message".

[5] For notational reasons, it turns out to be more convenient for us to use 0-based indexing for the sequence of M_α's and 1-based indexing for the coordinates of the codeword γ.

[6] The paper [40] uses a similar tree of input lengths but for a different reason.

final overall list corresponds to these leaves; input $n_i + \alpha$ would get the αth message of the overall list. So α specifies a path down the tree, and there must be some path along which the original message is faithfully transmitted. Provided the tree has height logarithmic in n_i and the list at each node has constant size, the overall list would have size polynomial in n_i, and for every input the diagonalizing algorithm would only need to get polynomially many samples from D on polynomially larger inputs, and would thus run in polynomial time.

However, there are complications with implementing the above idea. It is too much to hope that when a codeword is transmitted over the channel, we can recover a unique set S of candidate messages with high probability. To cut to the chase, what we will be able to guarantee is that there exists a fixed set S of $k-1$ messages (where S depends on the distributions of D on the block we are trying to receive from) such that we can get a random set of messages T which, with high probability, contains the correct message and is contained in S. We have no further control over the distribution of T. When $k = 3$ this is not a problem: Suppose we use the advice to specify whether the correct message is lexicographically first or last in S. The child corresponding to the correct advice will get $T = S$ with some probability, and with the remaining probability T will contain only the correct message, and in either case the child knows what the correct message is. The child corresponding to the wrong advice may output garbage, but it does not matter.

The above argument does not generalize to $k \geq 4$. For example, when $k = 4$ and the correct message is the middle message in S, if we get $|T| = 2$ then we do not know whether the correct message is the first or second message in T. We now describe the key idea to solve this problem. For each message in S, consider the probability it is in T. By the pigeonhole principle, using a constant amount of advice we can identify a significant "gap" in these probabilities, so that every message in S has probability either above the gap or below the gap. By taking a certain number of samples of T and intersecting these sets, the probabilities go down exponentially in the number of samples, so the probabilities below the gap become vanishingly small while the probabilities above the gap remain very close to 1. Then by a union bound over the messages in S, we find that with high probability the intersection of our sampled sets T equals T^*, the set of messages in S with probabilities above the gap (which includes the correct message). As described above, since we get the unique set T^* with high probability, we can retransmit the correct codeword provided we know which message of T^* is the correct one. The branching factor of the tree becomes k^2 because the advice needs to specify which of k possible "gaps" to use (and thus how many samples of T to take) as well as the lexicographic index of the correct message within T^*.[7]

We now explain the decoding process in more detail. Suppose we are trying to receive the codeword $\gamma \in [k]^\ell$ transmitted by some block of inputs $n, \ldots, n+\ell-1$. Then for $j \in [\ell]$, $\Pr_{D^*_{n+j-1}}(\gamma_j)$ is close to 1 (assuming we are on the "good" path down the tree) and thus $\Pr_{D_{n+j-1}}(\gamma_j)$ is somewhat larger than $1/k$ (since we are assuming for contradiction that A_i $(1-1/k-\epsilon)$-samples D^*). There is some other value $\kappa_j \in [k]$ such that $\Pr_{D_{n+j-1}}(\kappa_j) < 1/k$. Hence if we repeatedly sample from D_{n+j-1} and let $\rho_j \subseteq [k]$ be the set of values that occur with frequency at least slightly greater than $1/k$ in the empirical distribution, then with high probability we get $\gamma_j \in \rho_j \subseteq [k]\backslash\kappa_j$. In general we will not get a unique ρ_j with high probability, since under D_{n+j-1} some symbols might occur with probability very close to the threshold used in defining ρ_j. We view $\rho = \rho_1 \cdots \rho_\ell$ as the received word. There is no bound on the number of "errors" here, but each error is more informative than an erasure ($\rho_j = [k]$ would correspond to an erasure). We need a construction of a list-decodable error-correcting code for this non-traditional setting (which is related to the notion of "list-recovery" from the list-decoding literature). Our list-decoder is deterministic, but since ρ is random, the list of messages T is also random. With high probability, $T \subseteq S$ where S is the list of messages for the received word $[k]\backslash\kappa_1 \cdots [k]\backslash\kappa_\ell$.

By a fairly simple reduction to the traditional setting of list-decoding, one can use certain known constructions (such as [22]) to handle our non-traditional setting. We provide a direct, self-contained construction which is tailored to this setting and is much simpler than the known traditional constructions.

We now discuss our code construction. The codeword for a message is defined by interpreting the message as a bit string[8] and evaluating all possible surjections $f : \{0,1\}^{k-1} \to [k]$ on all possible sets of $k-1$ coordinates of the bit string. It can be shown that this code is list-decodable in principle (with list size $k-1$) by using the following lemma: For every set of k distinct bit strings of the same length, there exist $k-1$ coordinates on which they remain distinct. Our polynomial-time list-decoder uses this lemma in an iterative way, building and pruning a set of candidate strings of increasing lengths until it has arrived at the correct set of messages.

3. PROOF OF THEOREM 1

As sketched in Section 2, the $k = 2$ case of Theorem 1 is a simple application of delayed diagonalization and estimation by repeated sampling. Henceforth we assume $k \geq 3$. We start by describing a few ingredients we use in the proof.

We need a construction of a code for the following model of error-correction. Codewords are length-ℓ strings over the alphabet $[k]$, and each coordinate of a codeword can be corrupted to a subset of $[k]$ containing the correct symbol. More formally, we say a codeword $\gamma \in [k]^\ell$ is *consistent* with a received word[9] $\rho \in (\mathcal{P}([k]))^\ell$ if $\gamma_j \in \rho_j$ for all $j \in [\ell]$. A traditional erasure corresponds to the case $\rho_j = [k]$, but in our model of error-correction that is forbidden: ρ_j must be a strict subset of $[k]$, so each coordinate of the received word is more informative than an erasure. The tradeoff is that, unlike in traditional error-correction settings, we do not assume any upper bound on the number of "errors". We give an elementary construction of a list-decodable code for this setting.

THEOREM 2. *For every constant $k \geq 3$ there exists a polynomial-time encodable code $C : \{0,1\}^m \to [k]^\ell$ where*

[7]We actually only need a branching factor of $(k-1)^2$, but for simplicity we round it up to k^2 in the proof.

[8]In the formal proof we actually use m to denote the bit length of the message, rather than the length of the sequence over $[k]$.

[9]Recall that $\mathcal{P}([k])$ denotes the power set of $[k]$.

Define $d = \lceil \max(2^c, 3k \log_2 k) \rceil$

For $i \in \mathbb{N}$ define:

$$n_i = \begin{cases} \text{a sufficiently large constant power of 2} & \text{if } i = 1 \\ n_{i-1}^{d^{(\log_2 n_{i-1})+1}} & \text{if } i > 1 \end{cases}$$

$$m_i = \lceil \log_2 k^{(k^2)^{\log_2 n_i}} \rceil$$

$$\ell_i = \Theta(m_i^{k-1}), \text{ the codeword length from Theorem 2 for messages of length } m_i$$

$$C_i = \{0,1\}^{m_i} \to [k]^{\ell_i}, \text{ the code from Theorem 2}$$

$$\mathrm{Dec}_i = \text{the list-decoder from Theorem 2}$$

For $i \in \mathbb{N}$, $b \in \{0, 1, \ldots, \log_2 n_i\}$, $\alpha \in \{0, 1, \ldots, (k^2)^{(\log_2 n_i)-b} - 1\}$, $j \in [\ell_i]$ define:

$$n_{i,b} = n_i^{d^b}$$

$$n_{i,b,\alpha} = \begin{cases} n_{i,b} + \alpha & \text{if } b = 0 \\ n_{i,b} + \alpha \ell_i & \text{if } b > 0 \end{cases}$$

$$n_{i,b,\alpha,j} = \begin{cases} \text{undefined} & \text{if } b = 0 \\ n_{i,b,\alpha} + j - 1 & \text{if } b > 0 \end{cases}$$

$$N_{i,b,\alpha} = \begin{cases} \{n_{i,b,\alpha}\} & \text{if } b = 0 \\ \{n_{i,b,\alpha,1}, \ldots, n_{i,b,\alpha,\ell_i}\} & \text{if } b > 0 \end{cases}$$

Figure 1: Notation for Algorithm 1

$\ell = \Theta_k(m^{k-1})$ such that the following holds. For every received word $\rho \in (\mathcal{P}([k]))^\ell$ with $\rho_j \neq [k]$ for all $j \in [\ell]$, there are at most $k-1$ messages $\mu \in \{0,1\}^m$ whose codeword $C(\mu)$ is consistent with ρ; moreover, the list of all such μ can be found in polynomial time given ρ.

As mentioned in Section 2, an alternative version of Theorem 2 (that is adequate for our purpose) can be derived from sophisticated off-the-shelf components (such as [22]). In Section 4 we give a thorough discussion of the above model of error-correction, describe the alternative construction, and give our self-contained proof of Theorem 2.

Now let $A_1, A_2, A_3, \ldots$ be an enumeration of all randomized algorithms that run in time t and always output an element of $[k]$. We use a procedure Estimate(A_i, n, ζ, η) which returns a vector $(\pi_1, \pi_2, \ldots, \pi_k) \in [0,1]^k$ such that

(i) with probability at least $1-\eta$, $|\pi_\kappa - \Pr(A_i(n) = \kappa)| \leq \zeta$ for all $\kappa \in [k]$, and

(ii) with probability 1, $\pi_1 + \pi_2 + \cdots + \pi_k = 1$.

In other words, it returns a distribution that probably approximates the distribution of $A_i(n)$. If $\zeta, \eta > 0$ then by a standard Chernoff bound, Estimate(A_i, n, ζ, η) can be implemented in time $O\big(t(n) \cdot \frac{1}{\zeta^2} \log \frac{1}{\eta}\big)$ by simulating $A_i(n)$ $O\big(\frac{1}{\zeta^2} \log \frac{1}{\eta}\big)$ times and taking the empirical distribution.[10] Also, Estimate$(A_i, n, 0, 0)$ can be implemented in time $O(t(n) \cdot 2^{t(n)})$.

Algorithm 1 0-samples a k-family $D^* = (D_1^*, D_2^*, \ldots)$, and we argue below that it runs in time poly(n). Thus $D^* \in \textsc{SampTime}_{k,0}(\text{poly}(n))$. We need to show that $D^* \notin \textsc{SampTime}_{k,1-1/k-\epsilon}(t)$. Suppose for contradiction there exists an i such that A_i $(1 - 1/k - \epsilon)$-samples D^*. Let $D = (D_1, D_2, \ldots)$ be the k-family that is 0-sampled by A_i. We have $|D_n - D_n^*| \leq 1 - 1/k - \epsilon(n)$ for all n.

[10] We are ignoring the logarithmic factor time overhead usually associated with simulating an algorithm using a universal algorithm.

The parameters used in Algorithm 1 are defined in Figure 1. We use the inputs from n_i through $n_{i+1} - 1$ to diagonalize against A_i. The parameters create a tree structure out of the inputs. The tree is a full tree with branching factor k^2 and depth $\log_2 n_i$, with the leaves at level $b = 0$ and the root at level $b = \log_2 n_i$. Thus the number of leaves is $(k^2)^{\log_2 n_i}$. Each node of the tree has a contiguous block of inputs associated to it. Each leaf's block only consists of a single input, but each internal node's block has ℓ_i inputs, which represent the coordinates of codewords under the code C_i. Level b of the tree starts at input $n_{i,b} = n_i^{d^b}$. There are $(k^2)^{(\log_2 n_i)-b}$ nodes across level b, indexed by $\alpha \in \{0, 1, \ldots, (k^2)^{(\log_2 n_i)-b} - 1\}$, and their blocks of inputs $N_{i,b,\alpha}$ are consecutive from left to right across the level. Writing α in base k^2 allows us to interpret α as specifying a path down the tree from the root to the current node. The input n_1 is an unspecified constant power of 2, which just needs to be large enough so the blocks $N_{i,b,\alpha}$ are all disjoint and $\log_2 n_1 > 1$. There exists such an n_1 since $d \geq 3k \log_2 k$. Hence line 1 of Algorithm 1 will find unique values i, b, α (if they exist).

The reason we use message length $m_i = \lceil \log_2 k^{(k^2)^{\log_2 n_i}} \rceil$ is because messages represent sequences of length $(k^2)^{\log_2 n_i}$ over the alphabet $[k]$ (one symbol for each leaf of the tree). We assume there is a canonical way of interconverting between sequences of length $(k^2)^{\log_2 n_i}$ over $[k]$ and messages in $\{0,1\}^{m_i}$. It is most convenient for us to use 0-based indexing for the sequences $M_0, M_1, \ldots, M_{(k^2)^{\log_2 n_i}-1}$ and 1-based indexing for the messages $\mu = \mu_1 \cdots \mu_{m_i}$, codewords $C(\mu) = C(\mu)_1 \cdots C(\mu)_{\ell_i}$, and received words $\rho = \rho_1 \cdots \rho_{\ell_i}$.

In general, each block of inputs $N_{i,b,\alpha}$ attempts to "receive" an encoded message via a noisy channel from its parent block and "send" the re-encoded message to its children blocks. Lines 3–24 are the *receiving phase*, and lines 25–32 are the *sending phase*. The receiving is different at the root ($b = \log_2 n_i$) because the algorithm generates the message directly without receiving it over a noisy channel. The sending is different at the leaves ($b = 0$) because instead of send-

Algorithm 1: Diagonalizing algorithm for Theorem 1

Input: $n \in \mathbb{N}$
Output: an element of $[k]$

find i, b, α such that $n \in N_{i,b,\alpha}$
if such values do not exist **then** halt and output an arbitrary element of $[k]$

if $b = \log_2 n_i$ **then**
  foreach $\alpha' \in \{0, 1, \ldots, (k^2)^{\log_2 n_i} - 1\}$ **do**
    let $(\pi_1^{\alpha'}, \ldots, \pi_k^{\alpha'}) = \text{Estimate}(A_i, n_{i,0,\alpha'}, 0, 0)$
    let $M_{\alpha'} = \arg\min_{\kappa \in [k]}(\pi_\kappa^{\alpha'})$ (breaking ties arbitrarily)
  end
  convert the sequence $M_0, M_1, \ldots, M_{(k^2)^{\log_2 n_i} - 1}$ to a bit string $\mu \in \{0,1\}^{m_i}$
else
  write α in base k^2: $\alpha = \sum_{\tau=0}^{(\log_2 n_i)-b-1} \alpha_\tau (k^2)^\tau$ where $\alpha_\tau \in \{0, 1, \ldots, k^2 - 1\}$
  write α_0 in base k: $\alpha_0 = (q-1)k + (h-1)$ where $q, h \in [k]$
  let $\alpha' = \sum_{\tau=0}^{(\log_2 n_i)-b-2} \alpha_{\tau+1} (k^2)^\tau$
  let $Q = \left(1/\epsilon(n_{i,b+1})\right)^{4q+2}$
  foreach $r \in [Q]$ **do**
    foreach $j' \in [\ell_i]$ **do**
      let $n' = n_{i,b+1,\alpha',j'}$
      let $(\pi_1^{j'}, \ldots, \pi_k^{j'}) = \text{Estimate}(A_i, n', \epsilon(n')/4, \eta)$ where $\eta = \epsilon(n_{i,b+1})/4\ell_i Q$
      let $\rho_{j'} = \{\kappa \in [k] \ : \ \pi_\kappa^{j'} \geq 1/k + \epsilon(n')/4\}$
    end
    let $T_r = \text{Dec}_i(\rho) \subseteq \{0,1\}^{m_i}$ where $\rho = \rho_1 \cdots \rho_{\ell_i} \in (\mathcal{P}([k]))^{\ell_i}$
  end
  if $|T_1 \cap \cdots \cap T_Q| < h$ **then** halt and output an arbitrary element of $[k]$
  let μ be the lexicographically h^{th} smallest element of $T_1 \cap \cdots \cap T_Q$
end

if $b = 0$ **then**
  convert μ to a sequence $M_0, M_1, \ldots, M_{(k^2)^{\log_2 n_i} - 1}$ over $[k]$
  halt and output M_α
else
  compute $C_i(\mu)$
  find j such that $n = n_{i,b,\alpha,j}$
  halt and output $C_i(\mu)_j$
end

ing, the algorithm uses the message to attempt to deliver the coup de grâce and ensure that A_i fails to $(1-1/k-\epsilon)$-sample D^* if it has not already failed somewhere along the chain of "transmissions". The following claim is the heart of the analysis. It shows that there exists a path down the tree along which the original message μ^* (generated by the root) is faithfully transmitted.

CLAIM 1. *For every $b \in \{0,1,\ldots,\log_2 n_i\}$ there exists an $\alpha \in \{0,1,\ldots,(k^2)^{(\log_2 n_i)-b}-1\}$ such that for every $n \in N_{i,b,\alpha}$, with probability $\geq 1-\epsilon(n)/2$ Algorithm 1 reaches the sending phase (lines 25–32) and the μ computed in the receiving phase (lines 3–24) equals μ^* (the message generated by the root of the tree on line 8).*

CLAIM 2. *Algorithm 1 runs in time* poly(n).

We now show how to finish the proof of Theorem 1 given these claims. By Claim 2, D^* is in $\text{SAMPTIME}_{k,0}(\text{poly}(n))$. Consider the good α from Claim 1 for $b=0$. On input $n=n_{i,0,\alpha}$, with probability $\geq 1-\epsilon(n)/2$ Algorithm 1 reaches the sending phase and the μ computed in the receiving phase equals μ^*. Thus the sequence $M_0, M_1, \ldots, M_{(k^2)^{\log_2 n_i}-1}$ found on line 26 is the same as the sequence generated by the root of the tree on lines 4–7. Hence we have $M_\alpha = \arg\min_{\kappa\in[k]}(\Pr_{D_n}(\kappa))$ and in particular $\Pr_{D_n}(M_\alpha) \leq 1/k$. Since $\Pr_{D_n^*}(M_\alpha) \geq 1-\epsilon(n)/2$, this contradicts the fact that $|D_n - D_n^*| \leq 1-1/k-\epsilon(n)$ (which follows from our contradiction assumption). This finishes the proof of Theorem 1. All that remains is to prove Claim 1 and Claim 2.

PROOF OF CLAIM 1. By induction on $b=\log_2 n_i,\ldots,0$. The base case $b=\log_2 n_i$ is trivial by the definition of μ^* (with $\alpha=0$ and with probability 1, in fact). Now assume $b<\log_2 n_i$ and the claim holds for $b+1$. Let $\alpha' \in \{0,1,\ldots,(k^2)^{(\log_2 n_i)-b-1}-1\}$ be the good α from the induction hypothesis. For each $n' \in N_{i,b+1,\alpha'}$, say $n' = n_{i,b+1,\alpha',j'}$, the induction hypothesis says that on input n', with probability $\geq 1-\epsilon(n')/2$ Algorithm 1 reaches the sending phase and the μ computed in the receiving phase equals μ^*. Since $b+1>0$, by lines 28–32 this implies that $D^*_{n'}$ puts $\geq 1-\epsilon(n')/2$ probability mass on $C_i(\mu^*)_{j'}$. Since $|D_{n'}-D^*_{n'}| \leq 1-1/k-\epsilon(n')$, we find that $D_{n'}$ puts $\geq 1/k+\epsilon(n')/2$ probability mass on $C_i(\mu^*)_{j'}$.

We show that there exist $q,h\in[k]$ such that $\alpha=(k^2)\alpha'+\alpha_0$ satisfies the desired properties, where $\alpha_0=(q-1)k+(h-1)$. For any such α, suppose $n\in N_{i,b,\alpha}$ and consider Algorithm 1 on input n. Note that α' computed on line 12 is indeed the α' from the induction hypothesis, and the block $N_{i,b+1,\alpha'}$ is the parent of the block $N_{i,b,\alpha}$ in the tree.

Now consider lines 15–19. For any $j'\in[\ell_i]$, let us denote $n'=n_{i,b+1,\alpha',j'}$, and let us define $\kappa_{j'}$ to be the least likely outcome of $D_{n'}$ (breaking ties arbitrarily). Then $D_{n'}$ puts $\geq 1/k+\epsilon(n')/2$ probability mass on $C_i(\mu^*)_{j'}$ and $<1/k$ probability mass on $\kappa_{j'}$. Hence with probability $\geq 1-\eta$ over the estimation on line 17,

$$\pi^{j'}_{C_i(\mu^*)_{j'}} \;\geq\; (1/k+\epsilon(n')/2)-\epsilon(n')/4 \;=\; 1/k+\epsilon(n')/4$$

and $\pi^{j'}_{\kappa_{j'}} < 1/k+\epsilon(n')/4$ and thus

$$C_i(\mu^*)_{j'} \;\in\; \rho_{j'} \;\subseteq\; [k]\backslash\kappa_{j'}. \tag{1}$$

Note that with probability 1 we have $\rho_{j'}\neq[k]$ for all j' and thus ρ is a valid received word. For any $r\in[Q]$, let E_r be the event (depending on the randomness of lines 15–19) that Equation (1) holds for all j' (in the rth iteration of the loop on line 14). We have

$$\Pr(E_r) \;\geq\; (1-\eta)^{\ell_i} \;\geq\; 1-\eta\ell_i. \tag{2}$$

Now define

$$S \;=\; \text{Dec}_i\big([k]\backslash\kappa_1 \;\cdots\; [k]\backslash\kappa_{\ell_i}\big) \;\subseteq\; \{0,1\}^{m_i}$$

and note that $|S|\leq k-1$. Conditioned on E_r, we have $\mu^*\in T_r\subseteq S$ (since $C_i(\mu^*)$ is consistent with ρ, and all codewords consistent with ρ are also consistent with $[k]\backslash\kappa_1\;\cdots\;[k]\backslash\kappa_{\ell_i}$). Note that for different r's, T_r conditioned on E_r are independent and identically distributed. For each $\sigma\in S$ let us define p_σ to be the probability that $\sigma\in T_r$ conditioned on E_r. Note that $p_{\mu^*}=1$ and since $|S|\leq k-1$, by the pigeonhole principle there exists a $q\in[k]$ such that for every $\sigma\in S$, either $p_\sigma\geq\exp\big(-(\epsilon^*)^{4q+4}\big)$ or $p_\sigma<\exp\big(-(\epsilon^*)^{4q}\big)$ where $\epsilon^*=\epsilon(n_{i,b+1})$. We fix this value of q and the corresponding value $Q=(1/\epsilon^*)^{4q+2}$. For each $\sigma\in S$, we have

$$\Pr\big(\sigma\in T_1\cap\cdots\cap T_Q \;\big|\; E_1\cap\cdots\cap E_Q\big) \;=\; (p_\sigma)^Q$$

and we have either

$$(p_\sigma)^Q \;\geq\; \exp\big(-(\epsilon^*)^2\big) \;\geq\; 1-\epsilon(n)/4k$$

or

$$(p_\sigma)^Q \;<\; \exp\big(-(1/\epsilon^*)^2\big) \;\leq\; \epsilon(n)/4k$$

regardless of which $n\in N_{i,b,\alpha}$ we are considering.[11] Defining

$$T^* \;=\; \{\sigma\in S \;:\; (p_\sigma)^Q>1/2\},$$

by a union bound over $\sigma\in S$ we find that

$$\Pr\big((T_1\cap\cdots\cap T_Q)=T^* \;\big|\; E_1\cap\cdots\cap E_Q\big) \;\geq\; 1-\epsilon(n)/4. \tag{3}$$

Since $(p_{\mu^*})^Q=1>1/2$, we have $\mu^*\in T^*$. Now we fix $h\in[k]$ to be such that μ^* is the lexicographically h^{th} smallest element of T^*. Then when $(T_1\cap\cdots\cap T_Q)=T^*$, we have $|T_1\cap\cdots\cap T_Q|\geq h$ and so Algorithm 1 reaches the sending phase, and the μ computed in the receiving phase equals μ^*, as desired. Thus for every $n\in N_{i,b,\alpha}$ where $\alpha=(k^2)\alpha'+(q-1)k+(h-1)$ we have

$$\begin{aligned}
&\Pr\big(\text{Algorithm 1 reaches the sending phase with } \mu=\mu^*\big)\\
\geq\;& \Pr\big((T_1\cap\cdots\cap T_Q)=T^*\big)\\
\geq\;& \Pr\big(E_1\cap\cdots\cap E_Q\big)\cdot\\
&\Pr\big((T_1\cap\cdots\cap T_Q)=T^* \;\big|\; E_1\cap\cdots\cap E_Q\big)\\
\geq\;& (1-\eta\ell_i Q)\cdot(1-\epsilon(n)/4)\\
\geq\;& 1-\epsilon(n)/2
\end{aligned}$$

where the next-to-last line follows by Inequality (2) and Inequality (3), and the last line follows by $\eta\ell_i Q=\epsilon(n_{i,b+1})/4\leq\epsilon(n)/4$ (where η is as on line 17 of Algorithm 1). This finishes the proof of Claim 1. □

PROOF OF CLAIM 2. Line 1 can be done in poly(n) time by direct computation. If $b=\log_2 n_i$ then

$$n \;\geq\; n_i^{d^{\log_2 n_i}} \;=\; 2^{n_i^{\log_2 d}\log_2 n_i} \;\geq\; 2^{n_i^c\log_2 n_i}$$

[11] We can assume without loss of generality that c is large enough in terms of k for these inequalities to hold (recall that $\epsilon(n)=1/n^c$).

since $d \geq 2^c$, and so the number of iterations on line 4 is $\text{polylog}(n)$ and the computation on line 5 takes time $O(t(n_i) \cdot 2^{t(n_i)}) = O(n_i^c \cdot 2^{n_i^c}) \leq \text{poly}(n)$. Suppose $b < \log_2 n_i$. Lines 10–13 are simple calculations, and $Q \leq \left(1/\epsilon(n^d)\right)^{4k+2} \leq \text{poly}(n)$ since $n_{i,b+1} = n_{i,b}^d \leq n^d$. We also have $m_i, \ell_i \leq \text{poly}(n_i) \leq \text{poly}(n)$ and so the loops on lines 14 and 15 have $\text{poly}(n)$ iterations. For lines 16 and 17, we have $n' \leq n_{i,b}^{d^2} \leq n^{d^2}$ and $\epsilon(n')/4 \geq 1/\text{poly}(n)$ and $\eta \geq 1/\text{poly}(n) \geq 1/\exp(\text{poly}(n))$ and so the Estimate procedure takes time $\text{poly}(n)$. The list-decoding on line 20 takes time $\text{poly}(m_i) \leq \text{poly}(n)$. The sending phase (lines 25–32) trivially takes time $\text{poly}(n)$ since C_i is polynomial-time encodable. Overall, the running time is $\text{poly}(n)$. □

4. LIST-DECODING FROM UBIQUITOUS INFORMATIVE ERRORS

In Section 4.1 we discuss the model of error-correction used in the proof of Theorem 1. Then in Section 4.2 we give our self-contained proof of Theorem 2.

4.1 Discussion of the Error-Correction Model

Recall that in our model of error-correction, the received word is $\rho \in (\mathcal{P}([k]))^\ell$ where each $\rho_j \neq [k]$, and the goal is to find the list of all messages whose codeword $\gamma \in [k]^\ell$ is consistent with ρ in the sense that $\gamma_j \in \rho_j$ for all $j \in [\ell]$.

We first remark that in this setting, it can be assumed without loss of generality that $|\rho_j| = k-1$ for all $j \in [\ell]$ (since we can always enlarge each coordinate of the received word to a superset of size $k-1$, then find all the relevant messages, and then output only those messages whose codeword is consistent with the original received word). However, the way we have described the code is more convenient for our application.

Our setting is related to the notion of "list-recoverable" codes which has been studied in the list-decoding literature. In list-recovery, each coordinate of the received word is a set of symbols, but there are several differences from our setting. We allow each coordinate of the received word to be as large as possible without becoming an erasure, whereas in list-recovery each coordinate is usually restricted to be a fairly small set. Also, sometimes in list-recovery a small fraction of coordinates of the received word are allowed to violate the size restriction and become erasures. Also, in list-recovery the correct codeword is sometimes only guaranteed to agree with *many* coordinates of the received word, whereas we assume it agrees with *all* coordinates.

A simple application of the probabilistic method shows that if we drop the requirement that the encoding and list-decoding can be done in polynomial time, then there exist codes for our model with list size $k-1$ (where k is the alphabet size) and codeword length $\ell = \Theta(m)$ (where m is the message length and the hidden constant depends on k). In other words, there exist codes with $\ell = \Theta(m)$ such that for every set of k codewords, there exists a coordinate on which each element of $[k]$ appears exactly once among the k codewords. We are not aware of explicit constructions of such codes with $\ell = \Theta(m)$, but the polynomial length in Theorem 2 is good enough for our purpose.

For our application in Theorem 1, we do not need the list size to be $k-1$, as long as it is a constant depending on k. Such codes for our setting follow from certain known constructions of traditional list-decodable codes. Recall that a code is said to be (β, L)-list-decodable if for every received word in $[k]^\ell$, there are at most L codewords at relative Hamming distance $\leq \beta$, and the list of all such codewords can be found in polynomial time. Every $(1 - 1/(k-1), L)$-list-decodable code is also list-decodable under our model with list size $(k-1)L$: Given a received word $\rho \in (\mathcal{P}([k]))^\ell$ where each $|\rho_j| = k-1$, we can form new "received words" $\rho^{(1)}, \ldots, \rho^{(k-1)}$ by letting $\rho^{(g)} \in [k]^\ell$ consist of the gth smallest symbol in each coordinate of ρ. Since a codeword consistent with ρ must have relative Hamming distance $\leq 1 - 1/(k-1)$ from some $\rho^{(g)}$, running the traditional list-decoder on each $\rho^{(g)}$ will reveal all the codewords consistent with ρ.

For a traditional list-decodable code construction to be used for our application via the above connection, there are several properties it should satisfy: (i) It should work for constant-size alphabets (some constructions only work for large alphabets). (ii) It should work for *every* constant-size alphabet (some constructions require the alphabet to be a finite field). (iii) The list size should be a constant depending on the alphabet size (some constructions have list size polynomial in the message length). Property (iii) is crucial, but in some cases violations of (i) and (ii) may be fixable by concatenation with a brute-force code.

The construction of Guruswami and Indyk [22], which uses expanders and spectral techniques, satisfies all these properties and is (β, L)-list-decodable with $L = O\left(1/(1-1/k-\beta)^3\right)$ assuming $\beta < 1 - 1/k$. Taking $\beta = 1 - 1/(k-1)$, the list size is $O(k^6)$, which becomes $O(k^7)$ after applying the reduction from our setting. The list-decoder is randomized, but that is not a problem for our application in the proof of Theorem 1. Thus the result of [22] yields an alternative version of Theorem 2 that is sufficient for our application. This alternative construction has the following advantages: The codeword length is $\Theta(m)$, and the encoding and list-decoding can be done in linear time. But it has the following disadvantages: The list size is $O(k^7)$ rather than the optimal $k-1$, the list-decoder is randomized, and the proof is much more complicated than our proof of Theorem 2. Although it is convenient to use this off-the-shelf machinery, our code construction demonstrates that such machinery is overkill and that elementary techniques suffice.

4.2 Proof of Theorem 2

Before giving our construction of a code C satisfying the properties in Theorem 2, we give a key lemma.

4.2.1 A Combinatorial Lemma

For a set S and number a, we let $\binom{S}{a}$ denote the set of all subsets of S of size a. For a string $\sigma \in \{0,1\}^b$ and $i \in [b]$ and $I \subseteq [b]$, we let σ_i denote the ith bit of σ, and we let σ_I denote the length-$|I|$ string consisting of the bits of σ indexed by I.

LEMMA 1. *For all $1 \leq a \leq b$ and every set of distinct strings $\sigma^1, \ldots, \sigma^a \in \{0,1\}^b$, there exists an $I \in \binom{[b]}{a-1}$ such that $\sigma_I^1, \ldots, \sigma_I^a \in \{0,1\}^{a-1}$ are distinct.*

PROOF. By induction on a, with $a = 1$ and $a = 2$ being trivial. Suppose $a \geq 3$. By the induction hypothesis there exists an $I' \in \binom{[b]}{a-2}$ such that $\sigma_{I'}^1, \ldots, \sigma_{I'}^{a-1}$ are distinct. If $\sigma_{I'}^a$ is different from each of $\sigma_{I'}^1, \ldots, \sigma_{I'}^{a-1}$ then we can take an arbitrary $I \supseteq I'$ of size $a-1$. Otherwise, $\sigma_{I'}^a = \sigma_{I'}^h$ for

Algorithm 2: List-decoder for Theorem 2

Input: $\rho \in (\mathcal{P}([k]))^\ell$ with $\rho_{I,f} \neq [k]$ for all I, f
Output: set of all $\mu \in \{0,1\}^m$ such that $C(\mu)$ is consistent with ρ

1 let $S_{k-1} = \mathrm{List}(\rho, [k-1])$
2 **foreach** $n = k, \ldots, m$ **do**
3   suppose $S_{n-1} = \{\sigma^1, \ldots, \sigma^{|S_{n-1}|}\} \subseteq \{0,1\}^{n-1}$
4   find an $I \in \binom{[n-1]}{k-2}$ such that $\sigma_I^1, \ldots, \sigma_I^{|S_{n-1}|}$ are distinct
5   let $S_n = \left\{ s \in \{0,1\}^n \;:\; s_{[n-1]} \in S_{n-1} \text{ and } s_{I\cup\{n\}} \in \mathrm{List}(\rho, I \cup \{n\}) \right\}$
6 **end**
7 output the set of all $\mu \in S_m$ such that $C(\mu)$ is consistent with ρ

exactly one $h \in [a-1]$. Since $\sigma^a \neq \sigma^h$, there exists an $i \in [b]\backslash I'$ such that $\sigma_i^a \neq \sigma_i^h$, and we can take $I = I' \cup \{i\}$. □

It is not difficult to see that the $a-1$ bound in Lemma 1 is tight (there do not always exist $a-2$ coordinates on which a distinct bit strings remain distinct).

4.2.2 Code Construction

We now give our construction of the code C for an arbitrary constant $k \geq 3$ and message length $m \geq k$. By convention we use the notation $\mu \in \{0,1\}^m$ for messages, $\gamma \in [k]^\ell$ for codewords, and $\rho \in (\mathcal{P}([k]))^\ell$ for received words.

Let us define Surj_k to be the set of all surjections $f : \{0,1\}^{k-1} \to [k]$. The coordinates of a codeword are indexed by $\binom{[m]}{k-1} \times \mathrm{Surj}_k$, in other words by pairs I, f where I is a subset of $[m]$ of size $k-1$ and $f : \{0,1\}^{k-1} \to [k]$ is a surjection. We let $\ell = \left|\binom{[m]}{k-1} \times \mathrm{Surj}_k\right| = \Theta(m^{k-1})$, and we define the code $C : \{0,1\}^m \to [k]^\ell$ by

$$C(\mu) \;=\; \big(f(\mu_I)\big)_{I\in\binom{[m]}{k-1},\; f\in\mathrm{Surj}_k}.$$

In other words, the I, f coordinate of the codeword is the evaluation of f on the bits of the message indexed by I. Encoding can clearly be done in polynomial time.

It just remains to exhibit a polynomial-time list-decoder for C. Let us fix an arbitrary received word $\rho \in (\mathcal{P}([k]))^\ell$ with $\rho_{I,f} \neq [k]$ for all I, f. We need to show that there are at most $k-1$ messages whose codewords are consistent with ρ, and that moreover, these messages can be found in polynomial time given ρ.

For each $I \in \binom{[m]}{k-1}$ we define $\mathrm{List}(\rho, I)$ to be the set of all $\sigma \in \{0,1\}^{k-1}$ such that $f(\sigma) \in \rho_{I,f}$ for all $f \in \mathrm{Surj}_k$. Note that the set $\mathrm{List}(\rho, I)$ can be found efficiently given ρ and I by trying all possibilities.

Observation 1. *If $\mu \in \{0,1\}^m$ is such that $C(\mu)$ is consistent with ρ, then for all $I \in \binom{[m]}{k-1}$, $\mu_I \in \mathrm{List}(\rho, I)$.*

Lemma 2. *For all $I \in \binom{[m]}{k-1}$, $|\mathrm{List}(\rho, I)| \leq k-1$.*

Proof. Consider any set of k distinct strings $\sigma^1, \ldots, \sigma^k \in \{0,1\}^{k-1}$. There exists an $f \in \mathrm{Surj}_k$ with the property that $\{f(\sigma^1), \ldots, f(\sigma^k)\} = [k]$. Therefore since $\rho_{I,f} \neq [k]$ there exists an $h \in [k]$ such that $f(\sigma^h) \notin \rho_{I,f}$, which implies that $\sigma^h \notin \mathrm{List}(\rho, I)$. □

Now to see that C is list-decodable in principle, suppose for contradiction that there are k distinct messages $\mu^1, \ldots, \mu^k$ whose codewords are all consistent with ρ. Applying Lemma 1 with $a = k$ and $b = m$, there exists an $I \in \binom{[m]}{k-1}$ such that $\mu_I^1, \ldots, \mu_I^k$ are distinct. But for all $h \in [k]$, we have $\mu_I^h \in \mathrm{List}(\rho, I)$ by Observation 1. Thus $\mathrm{List}(\rho, I) \geq k$, which contradicts Lemma 2. Hence for our arbitrary received word ρ, there are at most $k-1$ messages whose codewords are consistent with ρ. Algorithm 2 finds this list of messages in polynomial time given ρ. The correctness of the algorithm follows immediately from the following claim and line 7 of the algorithm.

Claim 3. *For all $n = (k-1), \ldots, m$, the following three properties hold: $S_n \subseteq \{0,1\}^n$, $|S_n| \leq k-1$, and for every $\mu \in \{0,1\}^m$ such that $C(\mu)$ is consistent with ρ we have $\mu_{[n]} \in S_n$.*

Proof. By induction on n. The base case $n = k-1$ is immediate from Lemma 2 and Observation 1, so assume $n \geq k$ and the claim holds for $n-1$. By the induction hypothesis, $|S_{n-1}| \leq k-1$ and so line 4 of the algorithm will succeed by Lemma 1 (with $a = |S_{n-1}|$ and $b = n-1$).

We now verify the three properties of S_n. The property $S_n \subseteq \{0,1\}^n$ is immediate. To see that $|S_n| \leq k-1$, suppose for contradiction that there are k distinct strings $s^1, \ldots, s^k \in S_n$. Then since $|\mathrm{List}(\rho, I \cup \{n\})| \leq k-1$ (by Lemma 2) and $s_{I\cup\{n\}}^h \in \mathrm{List}(\rho, I \cup \{n\})$ for all $h \in [k]$, there must exist $h_1 \neq h_2$ such that $s_{I\cup\{n\}}^{h_1} = s_{I\cup\{n\}}^{h_2}$. Since $s_{[n-1]}^{h_1}, s_{[n-1]}^{h_2} \in S_{n-1}$ and $s_I^{h_1} = s_I^{h_2}$, we must have $s_{[n-1]}^{h_1} = s_{[n-1]}^{h_2} = \sigma^h$ for some h. But now $s_{[n-1]}^{h_1} = s_{[n-1]}^{h_2}$ and $s_n^{h_1} = s_n^{h_2}$, which contradicts our assumption that s^{h_1} and s^{h_2} are distinct. Thus we have verified that $|S_n| \leq k-1$. To verify the third property, consider an arbitrary $\mu \in \{0,1\}^m$ such that $C(\mu)$ is consistent with ρ. By the induction hypothesis, $\mu_{[n-1]} \in S_{n-1}$, and by Observation 1, $\mu_{I\cup\{n\}} \in \mathrm{List}(\rho, I \cup \{n\})$. By line 5 of the algorithm, this means that $\mu_{[n]} \in S_n$. □

We now discuss the running time of the algorithm. Line 4 can be implemented in polynomial time since an efficient algorithm for finding I can be gleaned from the proof of Lemma 1 (or less elegantly, since k is a constant, we can just try all possible subsets of size $k-2$). Line 5 can be implemented efficiently by looking at each string in S_{n-1} and considering extending it with each possible symbol in $[k]$ and checking whether the $I \cup \{n\}$ coordinates form a string in $\mathrm{List}(\rho, I \cup \{n\})$. Line 7 runs in polynomial time since C is efficiently encodable and consistency is easy to check.

Since our list-decoding algorithm is correct and runs in polynomial time, this completes the proof of Theorem 2.

5. ACKNOWLEDGMENTS

I thank Oded Goldreich, Luca Trevisan, and anonymous reviewers for helpful comments.

This material is based upon work supported by the National Science Foundation Graduate Research Fellowship under Grant No. DGE-0946797 and by the National Science Foundation under Grant No. CCF-1017403.

6. REFERENCES

[1] S. Aaronson. The equivalence of sampling and searching. In *Proceedings of the 6th International Computer Science Symposium in Russia*, pages 1–14, 2011.

[2] E. Bach. How to generate factored random numbers. *SIAM Journal on Computing*, 17(2):179–193, 1988.

[3] B. Barak. A probabilistic-time hierarchy theorem for slightly non-uniform algorithms. In *Proceedings of the 6th International Workshop on Randomization and Computation*, pages 194–208, 2002.

[4] C. Beck, R. Impagliazzo, and S. Lovett. Large deviation bounds for decision trees and sampling lower bounds for AC^0-circuits. In *Proceedings of the 53rd Symposium on Foundations of Computer Science (to appear)*, 2012.

[5] N. Bhatnagar, S. Greenberg, and D. Randall. Sampling stable marriages: Why spouse-swapping won't work. In *Proceedings of the 19th ACM Symposium on Discrete Algorithms*, pages 1223–1232, 2008.

[6] A. Bogdanov and L. Trevisan. Average-case complexity. *Foundations and Trends in Theoretical Computer Science*, 2(1), 2006.

[7] R. Bubley and M. Dyer. Faster random generation of linear extensions. *Discrete Mathematics*, 201(1-3):81–88, 1999.

[8] P. Chebolu, M. Cryan, and R. Martin. Exact counting of Euler tours for generalized series-parallel graphs. *Journal of Discrete Algorithms*, 10:110–122, 2012.

[9] M. Cheraghchi and A. Shokrollahi. Almost-uniform sampling of points on high-dimensional algebraic varieties. In *Proceedings of the 26th International Symposium on Theoretical Aspects of Computer Science*, pages 277–288, 2009.

[10] S. Cook. A hierarchy for nondeterministic time complexity. *Journal of Computer and System Sciences*, 7(4):343–353, 1973.

[11] M. Cryan, M. Dyer, and D. Randall. Approximately counting integral flows and cell-bounded contingency tables. *SIAM Journal on Computing*, 39(7):2683–2703, 2010.

[12] A. De and T. Watson. Extractors and lower bounds for locally samplable sources. *ACM Transactions on Computation Theory*, 4(1), 2012.

[13] L. Fortnow and R. Santhanam. Hierarchy theorems for probabilistic polynomial time. In *Proceedings of the 45th IEEE Symposium on Foundations of Computer Science*, pages 316–324, 2004.

[14] L. Fortnow and R. Santhanam. Robust simulations and significant separations. In *Proceedings of the 38th International Colloquium on Automata, Languages and Programming*, pages 569–580, 2011.

[15] L. Fortnow, R. Santhanam, and L. Trevisan. Hierarchies for semantic classes. In *Proceedings of the 37th ACM Symposium on Theory of Computing*, pages 348–355, 2005.

[16] A. Frieze and E. Vigoda. A survey on the use of Markov chains to randomly sample colorings. In *Combinatorics, Complexity, and Chance*. Oxford University Press, 2007.

[17] L. A. Goldberg and M. Jerrum. Randomly sampling molecules. *SIAM Journal on Computing*, 29(3):834–853, 1999.

[18] O. Goldreich, S. Goldwasser, and A. Nussboim. On the implementation of huge random objects. *SIAM Journal on Computing*, 39(7):2761–2822, 2010.

[19] O. Goldreich, M. Sudan, and L. Trevisan. From logarithmic advice to single-bit advice. *Studies in Complexity and Cryptography*, pages 109–113, 2011.

[20] V. Gore, M. Jerrum, S. Kannan, Z. Sweedyk, and S. Mahaney. A quasi-polynomial-time algorithm for sampling words from a context-free language. *Information and Computation*, 134(1):59–74, 1997.

[21] D. Grigoriev, E. Hirsch, and K. Pervyshev. Time hierarchies for cryptographic function inversion with advice. Technical Report TR05-076, Electronic Colloquium on Computational Complexity, 2005.

[22] V. Guruswami and P. Indyk. Linear time encodable and list decodable codes. In *Proceedings of the 35th ACM Symposium on Theory of Computing*, pages 126–135, 2003.

[23] J. Hartmanis and R. Stearns. On the computational complexity of algorithms. *Transactions of the American Mathematical Society*, 117:285–306, 1965.

[24] D. Itsykson. Structural complexity of AvgBPP. *Annals of Pure and Applied Logic*, 162(3):213–223, 2010.

[25] M. Jerrum and A. Sinclair. Approximating the permanent. *SIAM Journal on Computing*, 18(6):1149–1178, 1989.

[26] M. Jerrum, A. Sinclair, and E. Vigoda. A polynomial-time approximation algorithm for the permanent of a matrix with nonnegative entries. *Journal of the ACM*, 51(4):671–697, 2004.

[27] A. Kalai. Generating random factored numbers, easily. *Journal of Cryptology*, 16(4):287–289, 2003.

[28] R. Kannan, P. Tetali, and S. Vempala. Simple Markov-chain algorithms for generating bipartite graphs and tournaments. *Random Structures and Algorithms*, 14(4):293–308, 1999.

[29] R. Karp, M. Luby, and N. Madras. Monte-Carlo approximation algorithms for enumeration problems. *Journal of Algorithms*, 10(3):429–448, 1989.

[30] J. Kelner and A. Madry. Faster generation of random spanning trees. In *Proceedings of the 50th IEEE Symposium on Foundations of Computer Science*, pages 13–21, 2009.

[31] J. Kinne and D. van Melkebeek. Space hierarchy results for randomized and other semantic models. *Computational Complexity*, 19(3):423–475, 2010.

[32] S. Lovett and E. Viola. Bounded-depth circuits cannot sample good codes. *Computational Complexity*, 21(2):245–266, 2012.

[33] M. Luby, D. Randall, and A. Sinclair. Markov chain

algorithms for planar lattice structures. *SIAM Journal on Computing*, 31(1):167–192, 2001.

[34] M. Luby and E. Vigoda. Fast convergence of the Glauber dynamics for sampling independent sets. *Random Structures and Algorithms*, 15(3-4):229–241, 1999.

[35] B. Morris and A. Sinclair. Random walks on truncated cubes and sampling 0-1 knapsack solutions. *SIAM Journal on Computing*, 34(1):195–226, 2004.

[36] K. Pervyshev. Time hierarchies for computations with a bit of advice. Technical Report TR05-054, Electronic Colloquium on Computational Complexity, 2005.

[37] K. Pervyshev. On heuristic time hierarchies. In *Proceedings of the 22nd IEEE Conference on Computational Complexity*, pages 347–358, 2007.

[38] J. Propp and D. Wilson. How to get a perfectly random sample from a generic Markov chain and generate a random spanning tree of a directed graph. *Journal of Algorithms*, 27(2):170–217, 1998.

[39] J. Seiferas, M. Fischer, and A. Meyer. Separating nondeterministic time complexity classes. *Journal of the ACM*, 25(1):146–167, 1978.

[40] D. van Melkebeek and K. Pervyshev. A generic time hierarchy with one bit of advice. *Computational Complexity*, 16(2):139–179, 2007.

[41] E. Vigoda. A note on the Glauber dynamics for sampling independent sets. *Electronic Journal of Combinatorics*, 8(1), 2001.

[42] E. Viola. Extractors for circuit sources. In *Proceedings of the 52nd IEEE Symposium on Foundations of Computer Science*, pages 220–229, 2011.

[43] E. Viola. The complexity of distributions. *SIAM Journal on Computing*, 41(1):191–218, 2012.

[44] D. Wilson. Generating random spanning trees more quickly than the cover time. In *Proceedings of the 28th ACM Symposium on Theory of Computing*, pages 296–303, 1996.

[45] D. Wilson. Mixing times of lozenge tiling and card shuffling Markov chains. *Annals of Applied Probability*, 14(1):274–325, 2004.

[46] S. Žák. A Turing machine time hierarchy. *Theoretical Computer Science*, 26:327–333, 1983.

Properties and Applications of Boolean Function Composition

Avishay Tal
Weizmann Institute of Science
Rehovot, Israel
avishay.tal@weizmann.ac.il

ABSTRACT

For Boolean functions $f : \{0,1\}^n \to \{0,1\}$ and $g : \{0,1\}^m \to \{0,1\}$, the function composition of f and g denoted by $f \circ g : \{0,1\}^{nm} \to \{0,1\}$ is the value of f on n inputs, each of them is the calculation of g on a distinct set of m Boolean variables. Motivated by previous works that achieved some of the best separations between complexity measures such as *sensitivity, block-sensitivity, degree, certificate complexity* and *decision tree complexity* we show that most of these complexity measures behave multiplicatively under composition. We use this multiplicative behavior to establish several applications.

First, we give a negative answer for Adam Kalai's question from [MOS04]: *"Is it true that every Boolean function $f : \{0,1\}^n \to \{0,1\}$ with degree as a polynomial over the reals (denoted by* $\deg(f)$*) at most $n/3$, has a restriction fixing $2n/3$ of its variables under which f becomes a parity function?"* This question was motivated by the problem of learning juntas as it suggests a simple algorithm, faster than that of Mossel et al. We give a counterexample for the question using composition of functions strongly related to the Walsh-Hadamard code. In fact, we show that for every constants $\epsilon, \delta > 0$ there are (infinitely many) Boolean functions $f : \{0,1\}^n \to \{0,1\}$ such that $\deg(f) \leq \epsilon \cdot n$ and under any restriction fixing less than $(1-\delta) \cdot n$ variables, f does not become a parity function.

Second, we show that for composition, the *block sensitivity* (denoted by bs) property has an unusual behavior - namely that $\mathrm{bs}(f \circ g)$ can be larger than $\mathrm{bs}(f) \cdot \mathrm{bs}(g)$. We show that the ratio between these two has a strong connection to the integrality gap of the *Set Packing* problem. In addition, we obtain the best known separation between *block-sensitivity* and *certificate complexity* (denoted by C) giving infinitely many functions f such that $\mathrm{C}(f) \geq \mathrm{bs}(f)^{\log(26)/\log(17)} = \mathrm{bs}(f)^{1.149\ldots}$.

Last, we present a factor 2 improvement of a result by Nisan and Szegedy [NS94], by showing that for all Boolean functions $\mathrm{bs}(f) \leq \deg(f)^2$.

ITCS'13, January 9–12, 2013, Berkeley, California, USA.

Categories and Subject Descriptors

F.1.3 [**Computation by Abstract Devices**]: Complexity Measures and Classes—*Relations among complexity measures*

General Terms

Theory

Keywords

Boolean functions, block sensitivity, certificate complexity, decision tree complexity

1. INTRODUCTION

Complexity measures such as *decision tree complexity, certificate complexity, block sensitivity, sensitivity* and *degree as a polynomial* study the low-level complexity of Boolean functions. The decision tree complexity of a Boolean function f, denoted by $\mathrm{D}(f)$, is the minimal number of bits needed to be read from the input in order to be certain of the value of f. Other measures mentioned above are relaxations of this measure. Their study has found many applications in other fields of complexity such as communication complexity, circuit lower bounds, quantum computation and concurrent computation. In this regime complexity refers to a more combinatorial property than computational. We say that two measures M and N are *polynomially related* if there are constants c_1 and c_2 such that for any Boolean function f we have $M(f) = O(N(f)^{c_1})$ and $N(f) = O(M(f)^{c_2})$. In a beautiful line of works, most of these features were proven to be *polynomially related.* In particular [BI87] showed that the deterministic decision tree complexity is at most quadratic in the non-deterministic decision tree complexity (usually called *certificate complexity*). After proving many such relations for different complexity measures, a natural question to ask is whether these inequalities are tight? One way to show tightness is to construct examples for which the gap is tight, for instance provide infinitely many fs such that $M(f) = \Omega(N(f)^{c_1})$.

As in most cases, using the right tool for the job is essential. In this paper we demonstrate the power of quite a simple tool, Boolean function composition (in short BFC), to prove several results on old and new complexity measures of Boolean functions. BFC is defined for any two Boolean functions $f : \{0,1\}^n \to \{0,1\}$ and $g : \{0,1\}^m \to \{0,1\}$ as a function $f \circ g : \{0,1\}^{nm} \to \{0,1\}$ whose value is the value of f on n inputs, each of them is the calculation of g on an independent set of m bits. The tool of BFC was used in several previous works to exhibit separations [1] between complexity measures of Boolean functions mentioned above. Generating separations is a very natural application of BFC as many of these complexity measures behave multiplicatively when composing two functions. Namely, for most complexity measures mentioned above $M(f \circ g) \leq M(f) \cdot M(g)$ and under some simple conditions on f and g equality holds. Using this property, one can get a series of functions, $\{f^k\}_{k\in\mathbb{N}}$ (where powering is defined as repeated composition of f to itself) with polynomial gaps between two such complexity measures from any specific function f with the slightest gap between the two complexities. To demonstrate this, say that you are given a function f with $M(f) = 2$ and $N(f) = 4$ where M and N behave multiplicatively under composition. This automatically gives a quadratic separation between the two as $\forall k \in \mathbb{N} \,.\, N(f^k) = 4^k = (2^k)^2 = (M(f^k))^2$.

1.1 Our Results and Techniques

One motivating question for our study was posed by Adam Kalai in [MOS04]. We give an equivalent form of it (the equivalence easily follows from the discussion in [MOS04]):

Question 1.1 *Is it true that for any Boolean function g on n bits which has degree as a polynomial over the reals (denoted $\deg(f)$) at most $n/3$, there is a restriction fixing at most $2/3n$ bits under which g becomes a parity function?*

The question, interesting on its own, gives as an immediate application a learning algorithm for the *junta* problem if true. In short, in the junta learning problem one wants to learn a Boolean function defined over N variables that depends only on an unknown subset of size $n \ll N$ of them. A positive answer for A. Kalai's question gives a roughly $N^{2/3n}$ algorithm for the problem improving Mossel et al. analysis of roughly $N^{n\omega/(\omega+1)}$, where $\omega < 2.374$ is the matrix multiplication exponent. Recent work of [Val12] actually gives a roughly $N^{0.61n}$ learning algorithm for this problem, removing motivation from the possible application.

Let the *minimal restriction size* of g, denoted by $\mathrm{mr}(g)$, be the minimal number of bits needed to be fixed in order for g to become a parity function. We show that the answer to A. Kalai's question is a strong *no* as we demonstrate infinitely many Boolean functions with small degree over the reals, and high minimal restriction size.

Theorem 1 *For any $\epsilon > 0$ and $\delta > 0$ there are infinitely many integers n and Boolean functions $f : \{0,1\}^n \to \{0,1\}$ such that $\deg(f) \leq \epsilon \cdot n$ and $\mathrm{mr}(f) \geq (1-\delta) \cdot n$.*

The proof of this theorem relies on two important ingredients, one of them is a Boolean function derived from the Walsh-Hadamard code with $\mathrm{mr}(f) = n - o(n)$ and degree $n/2$. The second is the behavior of the minimal restriction size and the degree under composition. We show that $\mathrm{mr}(f \circ g) \geq \mathrm{mr}(f) \cdot \mathrm{mr}(g)$, while $\deg(f \circ g) = \deg(f) \cdot \deg(g)$. Combining the two together gives Theorem 1.

We introduce several definitions in order to describe the next problem.

[1] A separation between two complexities measures M, N is an infinite sequence of functions $\{f_i\}_{i\in\mathbb{N}}$ for which $M(f_i) = \omega(N(f_i))$ as $i \to \infty$. We say a separation is a polynomial separation if $M(f_i) = \Omega(N(f_i)^c)$ for some constant $c > 1$.

Definition 1.2 (Sensitivity, Block Sensitivity) *For $i \in \{0,\ldots,n-1\}$ denote by e_i the vector whose ith coordinate is 1 and the rest are zeros.*

The sensitivity *of a Boolean function $f : \{0,1\}^n \to \{0,1\}$ on a point x, $\mathrm{sens}(f,x)$, is the number of coordinates $i \in \{0,1\ldots,n-1\}$ such that $f(x) \neq f(x \oplus e_i)$. The* sensitivity *of f, $\mathrm{sens}(f)$, is the maximal $\mathrm{sens}(f,x)$ over all xs.*

The block sensitivity *of f on x, $\mathrm{bs}(f,x)$, is the maximal number of disjoint blocks $B_1,\ldots,B_k \subseteq \{0,1,\ldots,n-1\}$ such that flipping each B_i flips f's value, i.e. $f(x) \neq f(x \oplus \bigoplus_{j\in B_i} e_j)$. The* block sensitivity *of f, $\mathrm{bs}(f)$, is the maximal $\mathrm{bs}(f,x)$ over all xs.*

Definition 1.3 (Certificate Complexity) *Let $f : \{0,1\}^n \to \{0,1\}$ be a Boolean function and $x \in \{0,1\}^n$, a* certificate *for f on x is a set of variables $S \subseteq \{0,1,\ldots,n-1\}$ such that any $y \in \{0,1\}^n$ satisfying $x_i = y_i$ for all $i \in S$ has $f(y) = f(x)$.*

The certificate complexity *of f on x is the size of the minimal such certificate. The* certificate complexity *of f, $\mathrm{C}(f)$, is the maximal $\mathrm{C}(f,x)$ over all xs. The* minimal certificate *for f, $\mathrm{C}_{\min}(f)$, is the minimal $\mathrm{C}(f,x)$ over all xs.*

In [Ver10] Elad Verbin noted that (under some condition) $\mathrm{bs}(f^k) \geq \mathrm{bs}(f)^k$, asking whether the converse $\mathrm{bs}(f^k) \leq \mathrm{bs}(f)^k$ is true. This may seem natural, as choosing a complexity measure M to be one of *sensitivity, certificate complexity, decision tree complexity* or *degree* we have $M(f \circ g) \leq M(f) \cdot M(g)$. We answer this question by giving infinitely many examples for which $\mathrm{bs}(f^2) \geq 1.26 \cdot \mathrm{bs}(f)^2$. The main ingredient in the analysis of block sensitivity of BFC is the integer program representation of the problem. We show several interesting results using this perspective. We Introduce two "new" complexity measures: *fractional block sensitivity* (denoted by fbs) which corresponds to the linear relaxation of the problem and *fractional certificate complexity* (denoted by FC) which corresponds to the dual linear program (see Section 5.1 for the exact formulations as an integer and linear program). We show that both measures are the same, and serve as an intermediate measure between block sensitivity and certificate complexity.

Theorem 2 *Let $f : \{0,1\}^n \to \{0,1\}$ and $x \in \{0,1\}^n$ then*

$$\mathrm{bs}(f,x) \leq \mathrm{fbs}(f,x) = \mathrm{FC}(f,x) \leq \mathrm{C}(f,x)$$

Actually, the "new" complexity measures are equal, up to a constant factor, to the randomized certificate complexity defined by Aaronson in [Aar03]. The next theorem shows the important role of fractional block sensitivity in the analysis of block-sensitivity of BFC.

Theorem 3 *Let $f : \{0,1\}^n \to \{0,1\}$, $g : \{0,1\}^m \to \{0,1\}$ be Boolean functions, then $\mathrm{bs}(f \circ g) \leq \mathrm{fbs}(f) \cdot \mathrm{bs}(g)$.*

In fact, we show that this is tight in some weak sense. We then obtain and analyze, using this theorem, the best known separation between block sensitivity and certificate complexity.

Surprisingly, the third application demonstrates that BFC can be used to tighten upper bounds. In particular, we give an improved upper bound to a result by [NS94]:

Theorem 4 *Let f be a Boolean function, then $\mathrm{bs}(f) \leq \deg(f)^2$.*

1.2 Related Work

In [BI87] the decision tree complexity, $D(f)$, was polynomially related to $C(f)$ as $C(f) \leq D(f) \leq C(f)^2$. Saks and Wigderson used BFC in [SW86] to give polynomial separations between $C(f)$, $D(f)$ and the *Randomized Decision Tree complexity*. In [Nis89], Nisan defined block-sensitivity and showed that $\mathrm{bs}(f) \leq C(f) \leq \mathrm{bs}(f) \cdot \mathrm{sens}(f)$. In [WZ89] BFC was used to give separations between $\mathrm{sens}(f)$ and $C_{\min}(f)$, and the behavior of $C_{\min}$ and sens with respect to composition was analyzed. They gave examples also considered to be the best separations till this work between block-sensitivity and certificate complexity, though the analysis was missing from their work as they didn't even consider block-sensitivity. In [NS94], the degree of a Boolean function as a polynomial over the reals was related to other complexity measures such as bs, C and D. There, it was shown that $\mathrm{bs}(f) \leq 2\deg(f)^2$. In addition, they used BFC to give a separation between sensitivity and degree showing an infinite family $\{f_i\}_{i \in \mathbb{N}}$, such that $\mathrm{sens}(f) = \deg(f)^{\log_2(3)}$. In [NW94], an example by Kushilevitz, using BFC once again, established a better separation between sensitivity and degree. This was used to show a separation between the communication complexity of a Boolean function and the log-rank of the associated matrix. De Wolf and Buhrman gave an excellent survey of the field in [BdW02] with some new unpublished results. Aaronson introduced the notion of *randomized* and *quantum certificate complexity* (denoted RC and QC respectively) in [Aar03] and gave separations between these complexities, block sensitivity and certificate complexity using BFC. Our use of strong duality to show equality between fbs and FC resembles his argument that $QC(f) = \Theta(\sqrt{RC(f)})$. Other works in quantum complexity area used BFC as a crucial tool, in particular using Ambainis's *quantum adversary method* (see [Amb03], [HLS07]).

2. PRELIMINARIES

We use indices starting from 0 instead of 1, mainly because it makes more sense in section 4. We shall denote the set $\{0, 1, \dots, n-1\}$ by $[n]$. For a set $S \subseteq [n]$, we shall denote 1_S as the characteristic vector of the set S, i.e. $(1_S)_i = 1$ iff $i \in S$. For an n-dimensional vector space over the field F, the standard basis is denoted by $\{e_i\}_{i \in [n]}$ where e_i denotes the vector with a 1 in the ith coordinate and zeros elsewhere.

f, g will usually denote Boolean functions. n, m will usually denote the number of variables of a Boolean function. ρ, τ will usually denote restrictions to Boolean functions.

Definition 2.1 (Boolean Function Restriction) *For a partial assignment $\rho : [n] \to \{0, 1, *\}$ and a Boolean function $f : \{0,1\}^n \to \{0,1\}$ the restriction of f to ρ, $f|_\rho$ is defined as $f|_\rho(x) = f(y)$ where*

$$y_i = \begin{cases} x_i & \rho(i) = * \\ \rho(i) & \rho(i) \in \{0,1\} \end{cases}$$

for $i \in [n]$. We say that ρ fixes the variables x_i with $\rho(i) \in \{0,1\}$. The size of ρ, denoted by $|\rho|$, is the number of fixed variables.

The function $f|_\rho$ is defined as a function with n variables, but actually only the non-fixed variables are relevant.

2.1 Complexity Measures for Boolean Functions

After defining sensitivity, block sensitivity and certificate complexity in the introduction, we formally define other complexity measures which we will discuss in this paper.

Definition 2.2 (Degree) *The degree of a Boolean function f, $\deg(f)$, is the degree of the unique multivariate multi-linear polynomial over the reals which agrees with f on $\{0,1\}^n$.*

Similarly one can define the degree of a Boolean function over the field $\mathbb{F}_2$.

Definition 2.3 (Decision Tree, [BdW02]) *A* deterministic decision tree *is a rooted ordered binary tree T. Each internal node of T is labeled with a variable x_i and each leaf is labeled with a value 0 or 1. Given an input $x \in \{0,1\}^n$, the tree is evaluated as follows. Start at the root. If this is a leaf then stop. Otherwise, query the variable x_i that labels the root. If $x_i = 0$, then recursively evaluate the left subtree, if $x_i = 1$ then recursively evaluate the right subtree. The output of the tree is the value (0 or 1) of the leaf that is reached eventually. Note that an input x deterministically determines the leaf, and thus the output, that the procedure ends up in. We say a decision tree computes f if its output equals $f(x)$, for all $x \in \{0,1\}^n$.* The decision tree complexity *of f, $D(f)$, is the minimal depth of a decision tree computing f.*

Definition 2.4 (Minimal Restriction Size) *A Boolean function f is a* parity function *(or affine over $\mathbb{F}_2$) if we can write*

$$f(x) = c + \sum_{i \in S} x_i \pmod 2$$

for some $S \subseteq [n]$ and $c \in \{0,1\}$.

The minimal restriction size *of a Boolean function f,* $\mathrm{mr}(f)$, *is the minimal size of a restriction ρ for which $f|_\rho$ is a parity function.*

Note that $C_{\min}(f) \geq \mathrm{mr}(f)$ as any certificate induces a restriction under which f is constant and in particular a parity function. We introduce the following notation.

Definition 2.5 *For a Boolean function f, $z \in \{0,1\}$ and a measure $M \in \{\mathrm{sens}, \mathrm{bs}, C\}$ we denote by*

$$M^z(f) \triangleq \max_{x : f(x) = z} M(f, x)$$

2.2 Discrete Fourier Transform

In this section we briefly describe the discrete Fourier transform of Boolean functions - giving notations and stating known facts about it. For a more thorough introduction to the field we suggest the first chapters in O'Donnell's book/blog ([O'D12]).

A discrete Fourier transform is a representation of a Boolean function as a polynomial. Let $f : \{0,1\}^n \to \{0,1\}$. It is convenient to consider f as a function from $\{\pm 1\}^n$ to $\{\pm 1\}$ using the mapping $b \mapsto (-1)^b$, which is equivalent to the linear mapping $b \mapsto 1 - 2b$ restricted to $\{0,1\}$. More formally, we define $F : \{-1,1\}^n \to \{-1,1\}$ by

$$F(x_0, \dots, x_{n-1}) = 1 - 2 \cdot f\left(\frac{1-x_0}{2}, \frac{1-x_1}{2}, \dots, \frac{1-x_{n-1}}{2}\right).$$

Using this representation, one can define inner product of Boolean functions as $< f, g >= 1/2^n \cdot \sum_{x\in\{-1,1\}^n} f(x)\cdot g(x)$ where all operations are done in $\mathbb{R}$. For any $S \subseteq [n]$ the S-Fourier character is defined as $\chi_S(x) \triangleq \prod_{i\in S} x_i$. The Fourier characters form an orthonormal basis for the vector space of functions mapping $\{\pm 1\}^n \to \mathbb{R}$. The Fourier transform of F is the representation of F as a linear combination in this basis:

$$F(x) = \sum_{S\subseteq[n]} \chi_S(x)\cdot \hat{F}(S),$$

where the coefficient $\hat{F}(S)$ is called the S-Fourier coefficient of F. Note that this represents F as a multilinear polynomial. By orthonormality of the characters,

$$\begin{aligned}\hat{f}(S) \triangleq \hat{F}(S) &= \langle \chi_S, F\rangle \\ &= 1/2^n \cdot \sum_{x\in\{-1,1\}^n} \chi_S(x)\cdot F(x) \\ &= 1/2^n \cdot \sum_{x\in\{0,1\}^n} (-1)^{\sum_{i\in S} x_i}\cdot(-1)^{f(x)} \\ &= E_{x\in_R\{0,1\}^n}((-1)^{\sum_{i\in S} x_i}\cdot(-1)^{f(x)}) \quad (1)\end{aligned}$$

The following fact relates the Fourier coefficients of a Boolean function and its restriction.

Fact 2.6 *Let $f : \{0,1\}^n \to \{0,1\}$, $i \in [n]$, $c \in \{0,1\}$ and $S \subseteq [n] - \{i\}$, then the S-Fourier coefficient of the restricted function $\widehat{(f|_{x_i=c})}(S)$ is equal to $\hat{f}(S) + (-1)^c\cdot \hat{f}(S\cup\{i\})$*

Thus, the largest (in absolute value) Fourier coefficient of $f|_{x_i=c}$ is at most twice the largest Fourier coefficient of f. Induction gives as an immediate corollary the following:

Corollary 2.7 *Let $f : \{0,1\}^n \to \{0,1\}$, and ρ be a restriction fixing k variables, then*

$$\|\widehat{f|_\rho}\|_\infty \le \|\hat{f}\|_\infty \cdot 2^k$$

The next fact relates the Fourier transform of a Boolean function and the Fourier transform of the function composed with a linear transformation.

Fact 2.8 *Let $f : \{0,1\}^n \to \{0,1\}$ and $A \in (\mathbb{F}_2)^{n\times m}$ then the composition $f\circ A : \{0,1\}^m \to \{0,1\}$ has Fourier spectrum $\widehat{f\circ A}(T) = \sum_{S:A^t\cdot 1_S = 1_T} \hat{f}(S)$, $\forall T \subseteq [m]$ where matrix-vector multiplication is over $\mathbb{F}_2$.*

Proof. Expressing $(f\circ A)$ using the Fourier transform of f

$$\begin{aligned}(f\circ A)(x) &= f(A(x)) = \sum_{S\subseteq[n]} \hat{f}(S)\cdot(-1)^{1_S^t\cdot(A\cdot x)} \\ &= \sum_{S\subseteq[n]} \hat{f}(S)\cdot(-1)^{(A^t\cdot 1_S)^t\cdot x} \\ &= \sum_{T\subseteq[m]} (-1)^{(1_T)^t\cdot x}\cdot \sum_{S:A^t\cdot 1_S=1_T} \hat{f}(S)\end{aligned}$$

In the last equality we used the fact that when multiplying A by a vector over the field $\mathbb{F}_2$ the result must be a Boolean vector. □

As a special case if $A \in (\mathbb{F}_2)^{n\times n}$ is invertible, then the Fourier spectrum of f and $f\circ A$ are a (linear) permutation of one another.

2.3 Function Composition

Definition 2.9 (Function Composition) *Let $f : \{0,1\}^n \to \{0,1\}$ and $g : \{0,1\}^m \to \{0,1\}$, then the function composition of f and g, $f\circ g : \{0,1\}^{nm} \to \{0,1\}$ is defined as follows:*

$$\begin{aligned}(f\circ g)\left(x_0^0, x_1^0, \ldots, x_{m-1}^{n-1}\right) = \\ f\left(g\left(x_0^0, x_1^0, \ldots, x_{m-1}^0\right), \ldots, g\left(x_0^{n-1}, x_1^{n-1}\ldots, x_{m-1}^{n-1}\right)\right)\end{aligned}$$

Definition 2.10 (Function Powering) *Let $f : \{0,1\}^n \to \{0,1\}$ and $k \in \mathbb{N}$, then the kth power of f denoted by f^k is defined recursively by $f^1 \triangleq f$ and $f^k \triangleq f\circ(f^{k-1})$ for $k > 1$.*

Definition 2.11 (Good Form) *For $f : \{0,1\}^n \to \{0,1\}$, $M \in \{\text{sens}, \text{bs}, \text{C}\}$ [2] and $z \in \{0,1\}$ we say that f is in (M,z)-*good form *if $f(z^n) = z$ and $M(f, z^n) = M(f)$.*

Remark 2.12 *Any function can be transformed to an (M,z)-good form by applying*

$$\tilde{f}(x) = f(b)\oplus z\oplus f(x\oplus b\oplus z^n)$$

for $b \in \{0,1\}^n$ which maximizes the measure M (i.e. $M(f,b) = M(f)$). This transformation does not change the measures $\text{sens}, \text{bs}, \text{C}, \text{C}_{\min}, \text{mr}, \text{D}$ and $\deg$ of the Boolean function. This definition is useful as functions in M-good form have a better lower bound on measure M of their composition.

3. FUNCTION COMPOSITION PROPERTIES

The following basic lemma relates complexity measures of functions and their compositions. Properties 5 and 9 were previously proven in [WZ89].

Lemma 3.1 (Function Composition Properties) *Let $f : \{0,1\}^n \to \{0,1\}$ and $g : \{0,1\}^m \to \{0,1\}$ be Boolean functions, then the following holds:*

1. $\deg(f\circ g) = \deg(f)\cdot\deg(g)$
2. $\text{D}(f\circ g) = \text{D}(f)\cdot\text{D}(g)$
3. $\text{C}(f\circ g) \le \text{C}(f)\cdot\text{C}(g)$
4. *for $z \in \{0,1\}$, if $f(z^n) = g(z^m) = z$ then* $\text{C}(f\circ g, z^{nm}) \ge \text{C}(f, z^n)\cdot\text{C}(g, z^m)$
5. $\text{sens}(f\circ g) \le \text{sens}(f)\cdot\text{sens}(g)$
6. *for $z \in \{0,1\}$, if $f(z^n) = g(z^m) = z$ then* $\text{sens}(f\circ g, z^{nm}) \ge \text{sens}(f, z^n)\cdot\text{sens}(g, z^m)$
7. *for $z \in \{0,1\}$, if $f(z^n) = g(z^m) = z$ then* $\text{bs}(f\circ g, z^{nm}) \ge \text{bs}(f, n^z)\cdot\text{bs}(g, z^m)$
8. $\text{mr}(f\circ g) \ge \text{mr}(f)\cdot\text{C}_{\min}(g)$ *$(\ge \text{mr}(f)\cdot\text{mr}(g))$*
9. $\text{C}_{\min}(f\circ g) \ge \text{C}_{\min}(f)\cdot\text{C}_{\min}(g)$

In particular for $M \in \{\text{bs}, \text{sens}, \text{C}\}$ if f, g are in (M,z) good form $M(f\circ g) \ge M(f)\cdot M(g)$.

[2] And also for $M \in \{\text{fbs}, \text{FC}\}$ which we define later

Proof. We will use in the proofs of these properties the following notations:

$$(f \circ g)\left(x_0^0, x_1^0, \ldots, x_{m-1}^{n-1}\right) = f\left(g\left(x_0^0, x_1^0, \ldots, x_{m-1}^0\right), \ldots, g\left(x_0^{n-1}, x_1^{n-1} \ldots, x_{m-1}^{n-1}\right)\right)$$

x^i will denote the m-bit input to g, $(x_0^i, \ldots, x_{m-1}^i)$. We will sometime abuse notation and denote by x^i as the set of variables $\{x_j^i\}_{j\in[m]}$. $y_0, \ldots, y_{n-1}$ will denote the input variables to f. We will refer to $g(x^i)$ as g_i.

1. $\deg(f \circ g) = \deg(f) \cdot \deg(g)$. It is obvious that $\deg(f \circ g) \leq \deg(f) \cdot \deg(g)$. In the other direction, taking a maximal monomial in f, $c \cdot \prod_{i\in T} y_i$ and a maximal monomial in g, $d \cdot \prod_{j\in S} x_j$, the monomial $c \cdot d^{|T|} \cdot \prod_{i\in T, j\in S} x_j^i$ is in the expansion of $f \circ g$ and there is no way canceling it out. Hence, there is a monomial with degree $|T| \cdot |S| = \deg(f) \cdot \deg(g)$ and coefficient $c \cdot d^{|T|} \neq 0$ in $f \circ g$ expansion.

2. $\mathrm{D}(f \circ g) = \mathrm{D}(f) \cdot \mathrm{D}(g)$. We start by showing $\mathrm{D}(f \circ g) \leq \mathrm{D}(f) \cdot \mathrm{D}(g)$. Given optimal decision trees for f and g we construct a decision tree for $f \circ g$. We transform the decision tree for f to a decision tree for $f \circ g$ by replacing each inspection of y_i by a decision tree of depth $\mathrm{D}(g)$ on x^i. This gives a decision tree for $f \circ g$ of depth at most $\mathrm{D}(g) \cdot \mathrm{D}(f)$.

   For the other direction, we use an analogous characterization for the decision tree complexity called the *Adversary Argument* (see [AB09], chapter 12). The decision tree complexity of a Boolean function is the maximal d such that there is a way to answer any less than d adaptively chosen queries in such a way that the answers do not determine f's value. We call this the *f-Adversarial strategy.*

   We describe an adversarial strategy for $f \circ g$. When asked about a variable x_j^i such that less than $\mathrm{D}(g)$ variables of x^i were examined up till this point, we will answer according to the g-adversarial strategy, leaving the value of g_i undetermined. Whenever we must determine the value of g_i (i.e. after at least $\mathrm{D}(g)$ queries on variables in x^i), we will pick the value for g_i according to the value we would have given y_i in an f-adversarial strategy. The decision is not certain until at least $\mathrm{D}(f)$ of the g_is were determined. Thus, the decision tree complexity is at least $\mathrm{D}(f) \cdot \mathrm{D}(g)$.

3. $\mathrm{C}(f \circ g) \leq \mathrm{C}(f) \cdot \mathrm{C}(g)$. Let $x \in \{0,1\}^{nm}$ be an input maximizing $\mathrm{C}(f \circ g)$, and let $y \in \{0,1\}^n$ be the intermediate values $y_i = g(x^i)$. f has a certificate S for y of size $\mathrm{C}(f, y) \leq \mathrm{C}(f)$, and g has certificates T_i for each x^i of size $\mathrm{C}(g, x^i) \leq \mathrm{C}(g)$. By definition, the union of certificates $\cup_{i\in S} T_i$ is a certificate for $f \circ g$ at input x: any input $\tilde{x}$ agreeing with x on the certificate has $g(\tilde{x}^i) = g(x^i)\ \forall i \in S$ and since S is a certificate for f we conclude that $(f \circ g)(\tilde{x}) = (f \circ g)(x)$.

4. for $z \in \{0,1\}$, if $f(z^n) = g(z^m) = z$ then $\mathrm{C}(f \circ g, z^{nm}) \geq \mathrm{C}(f, z^n) \cdot \mathrm{C}(g, z^m)$. We show this property for $z = 0$, the case $z = 1$ is similar. Consider the shortest certificate for f on 0^{nm} and assume by contradiction that its size is strictly less than $\mathrm{C}(f, 0^n) \cdot \mathrm{C}(g, 0^m)$. This means that for at most $\mathrm{C}(f, 0^n) - 1$ of $i \in [n]$ the certificate contains $\mathrm{C}(g, 0^m)$ variables or more from x^i. The value of g_i for x^i with less than $\mathrm{C}(g, 0^m)$ variables in the certificate is undetermined under the restriction the certificate induces, since otherwise g would have a shorter certificate on 0^m. This means that the value of g_i is determined for at most $\mathrm{C}(f, 0^n) - 1$ different $i \in [n]$, which shows that the value of $f \circ g$ is undetermined under the restriction the certificate induces, in contradiction to the assumption.

5. $\mathrm{sens}(f \circ g) \leq \mathrm{sens}(f) \cdot \mathrm{sens}(g)$. Let x be an input maximizing $\mathrm{sens}(f \circ g)$ and let $y_i = g(x^i)$ be the intermediate values. Any sensitive coordinate x_j^i must be a sensitive coordinate for g on input x^i, and y_i must be a sensitive coordinate for f on input $(y_0, \ldots, y_{n-1})$. Hence, there are at most $\mathrm{sens}(f) \cdot \mathrm{sens}(g)$ sensitive coordinates for $f \circ g$.

6. for $z \in \{0,1\}$, if $f(z^n) = g(z^m) = z$ then $\mathrm{sens}(f \circ g, z^{nm}) \geq \mathrm{sens}(f, z^n) \cdot \mathrm{sens}(g, z^m)$. We show this property for $z = 0$, the case $z = 1$ is similar. Choosing the input $x = 0^{nm}$, the assumption on g gives that the intermediate values $y_i = g(x^i) = 0$. Since $y = 0$, there are $\mathrm{sens}(f, 0^n)$ many y_is for which if we change their value, the value of $f \circ g$ will change. For each such y_i there are $\mathrm{sens}(g, 0^m)$ variables of x^i such that changing their value from 0 to 1 changes y_i from 0 to 1, and then changing the value of $f \circ g$ from 0 to 1.

7. for $z \in \{0,1\}$, if $f(z^n) = g(z^m) = z$ then $\mathrm{bs}(f \circ g, z^{nm}) \geq \mathrm{bs}(f, n^z) \cdot \mathrm{bs}(g, z^m)$. We show this property for $z = 0$, the case $z = 1$ is similar. Choosing the input $x = 0^{nm}$, the assumption on g gives that the intermediate values $y_i = g(x^i) = 0$. For $i \in [n]$, pick $\mathrm{bs}(g, 0^m)$ disjoint subsets for each set of variables x^i that flips g's value on the 0^m input, denote them by $T_1^i, T_2^i, \ldots, T_{\mathrm{bs}(g,0^m)}^i$. Let $B_1, \ldots, B_{\mathrm{bs}(f,0^n)} \subseteq [n]$ be a maximal set of sensitive blocks for f on input 0^n. For $k = 1, \ldots, \mathrm{bs}(f, 0^n)$, and $\ell = 1, \ldots, \mathrm{bs}(g, 0^m)$ put $A_{k,\ell} \triangleq \cup_{i\in B_k} T_\ell^i$. This defines $\mathrm{bs}(f, 0^n) \cdot \mathrm{bs}(g, 0^m)$ disjoint subsets of $\{0,1\}^{nm}$ that flips the value of $f \circ g$ on 0^{nm}.

8. $\mathrm{mr}(f \circ g) \geq \mathrm{mr}(f) \cdot \mathrm{C}_{\min}(g)$. Let $\rho : [nm] \to \{0, 1, *\}$ be a restriction fixing at most $\mathrm{mr}(f) \cdot \mathrm{C}_{\min}(g) - 1$ variables. In at most $\mathrm{mr}(f) - 1$ of the sets x^i, ρ fixes $\mathrm{C}_{\min}(g)$ or more variables. Hence, under the restriction at least $n - \mathrm{mr}(f) + 1$ of the g_is are nonconstants. Assume by contradiction that the function $(f \circ g)|\rho$ is affine over $\mathbb{F}_2$. Let $\tau : \{0, 1, \ldots, n-1\} \to \{0, 1, *\}$ be the induced restriction of ρ on f, i.e.

$$\tau_i = \begin{cases} * & \rho \text{ does not set the value of } g(x^i) \\ 0 & \rho \text{ sets the value of } g(x^i) \text{ to } 0 \\ 1 & \rho \text{ sets the value of } g(x^i) \text{ to } 1 \end{cases} .$$

For every nonconstant g_i pick two assignments ϕ_i^0, ϕ_i^1 for x^i agreeing with ρ under which g equals 0 and 1 respectively. For g_i that is fixed under ρ pick any two assignments ϕ_i^0, ϕ_i^1 agreeing with ρ. For a bit $b \in \mathbb{F}_2$ and two vectors $u, v \in \mathbb{F}_2^m$ define $\mathrm{MUX}_b(u, v) \triangleq (1 - b) \cdot u \oplus b \cdot v$. The bit b chooses between two vectors, if $b = 0$ the output is u and if $b = 1$ the output is v. For constant vectors u, v, $\mathrm{MUX}_b(u, v)$ is affine over $\mathbb{F}_2$ as a function of b. Let

$$h(x_0, \ldots, x_{n-1}) = ((f \circ g)|_\rho)(y_0, \ldots, y_{n-1})$$

where $y_i = \mathrm{MUX}_{x_i}(\phi_i^0, \phi_i^1)$. h is affine over $\mathbb{F}_2$ as a composition of affine transformations. Furthermore, h equals $f|_\tau$ and hence $f|_\tau$ is affine, and we reach a contradiction as τ fixes less than $\mathrm{C}_{\min}(f)$ variables.

9. $\mathrm{C}_{\min}(f \circ g) \geq \mathrm{C}_{\min}(f) \cdot \mathrm{C}_{\min}(g)$. As in 8, fixing less than $\mathrm{C}_{\min}(f) \cdot \mathrm{C}_{\min}(g)$ variables guarantees that at least $n - (\mathrm{C}_{\min}(f) - 1)$ of the g_is are nonconstant and thus $f \circ g$ is nonconstant.

□

Using Lemma 3.1 it is easy to generate polynomial separations between two complexity measures. Let $M \in \{\deg, \mathrm{D}, \mathrm{C}, \mathrm{sens}\}$ and $N \in \{\deg, \mathrm{D}, \mathrm{C}, \mathrm{sens}, \mathrm{bs}, \mathrm{mr}, \mathrm{C}_{\min}\}$ be two complexity measures and suppose we are given a function f, such that $M(f) < N(f)$. If $N \in \{\mathrm{sens}, \mathrm{bs}, \mathrm{C}\}$, we can assume WLOG that f is in $(N, 0)$ good form. Then, taking powers of this function gives infinitely many examples such that $M(f^k) \leq M(f)^k$ and $N(f^k) \geq N(f)^k$ for $k \in \mathbb{N}$. This is a polynomial separation as

$$N(f^k) \geq N(f)^k = M(f)^{k \cdot \frac{\log N(f)}{\log M(f)}} \geq M(f^k)^{\frac{\log N(f)}{\log M(f)}} .$$

Remark 3.2 *Note that for $f = \mathrm{OR}_n$ and $g = \mathrm{AND}_n$ the sensitivity, block-sensitivity and certificate complexity of $f \circ g$ is n. This shows that being in M-good form is necessary to achieve $M(f \circ g) \geq M(f) \cdot M(g)$.*

4. A. KALAI'S QUESTION

In this section we give a negative answer for Question 1.1. First, we construct a function based on the Walsh-Hadamard code. Then, we take powers of this function showing that this is a counterexample for the question.

4.1 Boolean Functions from The Walsh-Hadamard Code

Example 4.1 *Let $n \in \mathbb{N}$, we define $\mathrm{WHIP_n} : \{0,1\}^{2^{2n}} \to \{0,1\}$ as follows. Denote by $\mathrm{IP_n} : \{0,1\}^{2n} \to \{0,1\}$ the Boolean function defined as:*

$$\mathrm{IP_n}(y_0, y_1, \ldots, y_{2n-1}) = y_0 \cdot y_1 + \ldots + y_{2n-2} \cdot y_{2n-1} \pmod 2 .$$

For a non-negative integer k, denote by k_i the i'th least significant bit of k in its binary representation. Let $\mathrm{WH} \in (\mathbb{F}_2)^{2n \times 2^{2n}}$ be the matrix defined as $\mathrm{WH}_{i,k} = k_i$ for $i \in [2n], k \in [2^{2n}]$. Finally, we define $\mathrm{WHIP_n}$ as:

$$\mathrm{WHIP_n}(x) = \mathrm{IP_n}(\mathrm{WH} \cdot x)$$

where the matrix vector multiplication $\mathrm{WH} \cdot x$ is done over $\mathbb{F}_2$.

This example is a degree 2 polynomial over $\mathbb{F}_2$. Yet, as the next theorem states, f requires a lot of variables to be fixed in order to become a parity function i.e. a degree 1 function over $\mathbb{F}_2$.

Theorem 4.2 $\deg(\mathrm{WHIP_n}) = 2^{2n-1}$ *and* $\mathrm{mr}(\mathrm{WHIP_n}) = 2^{2n} - 2^n$.

In order to prove Theorem 4.2 we prove several lemmas first, showing the role of WH and $\mathrm{IP_n}$ in the construction. In the following proofs it is convenient to associate a restriction with an affine vector subspace.

Definition 4.3 *Let $\rho : [m] \to \{0, 1, *\}$ be a restriction, then the inputs that agrees with ρ form an affine subspace of $(\mathbb{F}_2)^m$ defined by $v_\rho + V_\rho$ where $V_\rho = \mathrm{span}\{e_i : \rho(i) = *\}$ and $(v_\rho)_i = 1$ iff $\rho(i) = 1$ and 0 elsewhere.*

Lemma 4.4 (The "Role" of WH) *For $S \subseteq [2^{2n}]$, let $V = \mathrm{span}(\{e_k\}_{k \in S})$ be a linear subspace of $(\mathbb{F}_2)^{2^{2n}}$ then $|S| = \dim(V) \leq 2^{\dim(\mathrm{WH}(V))}$.*

PROOF. Let $d = \dim(\mathrm{WH}(V))$, and let $U \subseteq (\mathbb{F}_2)^{2n}$ be the orthogonal complement of $\mathrm{WH}(V)$ (with respect to the natural bilinear form $B(x, y) = x^t \cdot y$ over $\mathbb{F}_2$). Fix some basis $\{u_j\}_{j \in [2n-d]}$ for U. For any $k \in S$ we have that $\mathrm{WH}(e_k) \perp U$, thus

$$\forall\, j \in [2n-d] \; , \; 0 = \sum_{i=0}^{2n-1} (u_j)_i \cdot (\mathrm{WH} \cdot e_k)_i = \sum_{i=0}^{2n-1} (u_j)_i \cdot k_i \, .$$

So each $k \in S$ is a solution to a system of $2n - d$ linearly independent linear equations in its binary representation as an integer. Thus, the number of such indices is at most 2^d. □

We state some slight variant of a known property of $\mathrm{IP_n}$ whose proof is given in Appendix A.

Lemma 4.5 *Let $A \subseteq (\mathbb{F}_2)^{2n}$ be an affine subspace of dimension d defined by $v_A + \mathrm{span}\{v_0, v_1, \ldots, v_{d-1}\}$. If $\mathrm{IP_n}|_A(x_0, x_1, \ldots, x_{d-1}) \triangleq \mathrm{IP_n}(v_A + \sum_{i \in [d]} x_i \cdot v_i)$ is a parity function, then $d \leq n$.*

This property is essential to achieve the next lemma.

Lemma 4.6 (The "Role" of $\mathrm{IP_n}$) *Let $f = \mathrm{IP_n} \circ A$ where $A \in (F_2)^{2n \times m}$ is a linear transformation. Let ρ be a restriction, under which $\mathrm{IP_n} \circ A$ is a parity function, then $\dim(A(V_\rho)) \leq n$.*

PROOF. Denote by $V' = v_\rho + V_\rho$, $U = A(V_\rho)$, $u_\rho = A(v_\rho)$ and let $d = \dim(A(V_\rho))$. We write $U = A(V_\rho)$ as $\mathrm{span}\{u_0, u_1, \ldots, u_{d-1}\}$ where $\{u_i\}_{i \in [d]}$ are linearly independent vectors in $(\mathbb{F}_2)^{2n}$. For $i \in [d]$, fix $v_i \in V_\rho$ to be some arbitrary preimage of u_i by the mapping A. We have

$$\begin{aligned} \mathrm{IP_n}|_U(x_0, \ldots, x_{d-1}) &= \mathrm{IP_n}(u_\rho + \sum_{i \in [d]} u_i \cdot x_i) \\ &= (\mathrm{IP_n} \circ A)(v_\rho + \sum_{i \in [d]} v_i \cdot x_i) \\ &= f|_\rho(v_\rho + \sum_{i \in [d]} v_i \cdot x_i) \, . \end{aligned}$$

Using our assumption on $f|_\rho$, this shows that $\mathrm{IP_n}|_U$ is a parity function and by Lemma 4.5 this gives $d \leq n$. □

We are ready to prove Theorem 4.2.

PROOF. First, we show that $\deg(\mathrm{WHIP_n}) = 2^{2n-1}$. By Fact 2.8 the nonzero Fourier coefficients of $\mathrm{WHIP_n}$ are $\mathrm{WH}^t \cdot 1_S$ for $S \subseteq [2n]$. Opening this up gives that the nonzero Fourier coefficients are the sets

$$\left\{ k \in [2^{2n}] \;\middle|\; \bigoplus_{i \in S} k_i = 1 \right\}$$

for $S \subseteq [2n]$. The size of each such set is either 0 for $S = \emptyset$ or 2^{2n-1} otherwise, hence the degree of $\mathrm{WHIP_n}$ over the reals is 2^{2n-1}.

Next, we show $\mathrm{mr}(\mathrm{WHIP_n}) \geq 2^{2n} - 2^n$. Let ρ be a restriction under which $\mathrm{WHIP_n}$ becomes a parity function. By Lemma 4.6, $\dim(\mathrm{WH}(V_\rho)) \leq n$. Using Lemma 4.4 we have $\dim(V_\rho) \leq 2^n$, hence ρ fixes at least $2^{2n} - 2^n$ variables.

On the other hand, there's a restriction fixing $2^{2n} - 2^n$ variables that makes $\mathrm{WHIP_n}$ a constant, by fixing $x_k = 0$ for any k such that $(k_0, k_2, \ldots, k_{2n-2}) \neq 0^n$. □

Remark 4.7 *The matrix used in the construction of Example 4.1 is the transpose of the encoding matrix of the Walsh-Hadamard error correcting code (alternatively, the parity-check matrix for the Hamming code). The above construction can be generalized to use any ϵ-biased sample space instead of the Walsh-Hadamard code, resulting in similar guarantees on the minimal restriction size and degree. Actually, as the Walsh-Hadamard code is an ϵ-biased sample space with $\epsilon = 0$ it can viewed as a special case of this generalization. We discuss this in Appendix B*

4.2 Counterexample for A. Kalai's Question

We combine Theorem 4.2 and Property 8 from Lemma 3.1 to get a counterexample for A. Kalai's question.

Theorem (Theorem 1, restated) *For any $\epsilon > 0$ and $\delta > 0$ there exists infinitely many integers N and Boolean functions $f : \{0,1\}^N \to \{0,1\}$ such that $\deg(f) \leq \epsilon \cdot N$ and $\mathrm{mr}(f) \geq (1-\delta) \cdot N$. In particular, for $\epsilon = \delta < 1/3$ this answers A. Kalai's question.*

PROOF. Put $m = \lceil \log_2(\frac{1}{\epsilon}) \rceil$ and choose any integer $n \geq \log_2(\frac{m}{\delta})$ (equivalently $\delta \geq m/2^n$). Take the function g to be $(\mathrm{WHIP_n})^m$. g is defined over $N \triangleq 2^{2nm}$ variables. Applying Property 1 from Lemma 3.1 gives $\deg(g) = (2^{2n-1})^m = 2^{2nm} \cdot 1/2^m \leq \epsilon \cdot N$. On the other hand, applying Property 8 from the same lemma gives

$$\begin{aligned} \mathrm{mr}(g) &\geq \mathrm{mr}(\mathrm{WHIP_n})^m \\ &= 2^{2nm} \cdot \left(1 - \frac{1}{2^n}\right)^m \\ &\underset{\text{Bernoulli}}{\geq} N \cdot \left(1 - \frac{m}{2^n}\right) \\ &\geq N \cdot (1-\delta) \ . \ \square \end{aligned}$$

4.3 Polynomial Separations between Degree and Minimal Restriction Size

We demonstrate an infinite family of functions with a polynomial separation between deg and mr

Claim 4.8 *There are infinitely many Boolean functions f such that $\mathrm{mr}(f) \geq 2/3 \cdot \deg(f)^{log_2 3} = 2/3 \cdot \deg(f)^{1.58\ldots}$.*

PROOF. The function

$$f(x_0, x_1, x_2, x_3) = (x_0 + x_1) \cdot (x_2 + x_3) + x_0 + x_2 \pmod 2$$

defined over $\{0,1\}^4$ has $\deg(f) = 2$, $\mathrm{C_{min}}(f) = 3$, $\mathrm{mr}(f) = 2$. Applying Lemma 3.1, $g = f^k$ has $\deg(g) = 2^k$ and

$$\begin{aligned} \mathrm{mr}(g) &\geq \mathrm{mr}(f) \cdot \mathrm{C_{min}}(f^{k-1}) \\ &\geq \mathrm{mr}(f) \cdot \mathrm{C_{min}}(f)^{k-1} \\ &= 2 \cdot 3^{k-1} \\ &= 2/3 \cdot \deg(g)^{log_2 3} \ . \end{aligned}$$

□

Note that these functions are not counterexamples for A. Kalai's question as their minimal restriction size is less than $2/3n$.

5. BLOCK-SENSITIVITY OF FUNCTION COMPOSITION

One may note that a natural bound is missing from Lemma 3.1: "$\mathrm{bs}(f \circ g) \leq \mathrm{bs}(f) \cdot \mathrm{bs}(g)$". While this bound may seem reasonable at first glance, it turns out to be false, as we demonstrate next.

We first show that block sensitivity is actually a subcase of the NP-Complete problem *Set Packing*. The maximal gap between $\mathrm{bs}(f \circ g)$ and $\mathrm{bs}(f) \cdot \mathrm{bs}(g)$ is closely related to the integrality gap between the value of the integer program (IP) for Set Packing and the value of its standard linear relaxation. The linear program (LP) gives tight upper bounds on $\mathrm{bs}(f \circ g)$. The integer/linear programming approach shed interesting light on the problem of block-sensitivity, relating it to a relaxed version which we call *Fractional Block Sensitivity*. In fact, $\mathrm{bs}(f) \leq \mathrm{C}(f)$ is just a corollary of LP duality.

We use the IP/LP formulation of block sensitivity to analyze the powers of a previously known example, demonstrating the gaps between $\mathrm{bs}(f)^2$ and $\mathrm{bs}(f^2)$.

5.1 Block Sensitivity as a Special Case of Set Packing

The problem of (unweighted) *Set Packing* is the following. Given sets $B_0, B_1, \ldots, B_{k-1} \subseteq [n]$ find the largest collection of sets not intersecting. This seems familiar, as the block sensitivity of $f : \{0,1\}^n \to \{0,1\}$ on a given $x \in \{0,1\}^n$ is exactly that problem, where the sets are $B \subseteq [n]$ such that $f(x \oplus 1_B) \neq f(x)$. WLOG, we can consider only subsets minimal to inclusion. Consider the following integer program for Set Packing:

$$\begin{aligned} \max \quad & \textstyle\sum_{j=0}^{k-1} w_j \\ \text{s.t.} \quad & \textstyle\sum_{j: i \in B_j} w_j \leq 1 \quad \forall i \in [n] \\ & w_j \in \{0,1\} \qquad\quad \forall j \in [k] \end{aligned} \qquad (\mathrm{IP(bs(f))})$$

The variable w_j equals 1 iff we choose B_j to our collection. Note that the first constraint states that each coordinate is covered at most once. The linear relaxation of this problem is:

$$\begin{aligned} \max \quad & \textstyle\sum_{j=0}^{k-1} w_j \\ \text{s.t.} \quad & \textstyle\sum_{j: i \in B_j} w_j \leq 1 \quad \forall i \in [n] \\ & w_j \geq 0 \qquad\qquad \forall j \in [k] \end{aligned} \qquad (\mathrm{LP(bs(f))})$$

Next, we define the *Fractional Block Sensitivity* which captures the value of this linear program.

Definition 5.1 (Fractional Block Sensitivity) *Let $f : \{0,1\}^n \to \{0,1\}$ be a Boolean function, and $x \in \{0,1\}^n$, then the* Fractional Block Sensitivity $\mathrm{fbs}(f,x)$ *of f on x, is the maximal sum of non-negative weights assigned to a collection of blocks, $B_0, \ldots, B_{k-1} \subseteq [n]$ such that for each B_j, $f(x) \neq f(x \oplus 1_{B_j})$ and each coordinate $i \in [n]$ is contained by blocks with total weight at most 1 (relaxed disjointness). The fractional block sensitivity of f, $\mathrm{fbs}(f)$, is $\max_x \mathrm{fbs}(f,x)$.*

The *dual* program for Set Packing is the well known *Set Cover* problem. With our notations, the dual program can be written as

$$\begin{array}{lll} \min & \sum_{i=0}^{n-1} u_i & \\ \text{s.t.} & \sum_{i:i\in B_j} u_i \geq 1 & \forall j \in [k] \\ & u_i \geq 0 & \forall i \in [n] \end{array} \qquad \text{(Dual LP)}$$

Replacing the constraint $u_i \geq 0$ with $u_i \in \{0,1\}$ defines an IP we call the *"dual integer program"*. In fact, this integer program exactly captures the notion of certificate complexity.

Lemma 5.2 *The value of the dual IP is* $\mathrm{C}(f,x)$.

PROOF. The set of coordinates i having $u_i = 1$ are a certificate for f on x, and vice versa, for any certificate $S \subseteq [n]$ for f on x the values $u_i = (1_S)_i$ form a feasible solution for the integer program whose value equals the certificate size. □

In order to capture the value of Dual LP we define the *Fractional Certificate Complexity*.

Definition 5.3 (Fractional Certificate Complexity) *Let $f : \{0,1\}^n \to \{0,1\}$ be a Boolean function, and $x \in \{0,1\}^n$, then the* Fractional Certificate Complexity $\mathrm{FC}(f,x)$ *of f on x, is the minimal sum of weights assigned to $i \in [n]$, such that for each y such that $f(x) \neq f(y)$, we have $\sum_{i:x_i\neq y_i} \mathrm{weight}(i)$ is at least 1. The fractional certificate complexity of f, $\mathrm{FC}(f)$, is $\max_x \mathrm{FC}(f,x)$.*

As both the primal and dual programs are feasible, *strong duality* states that the optimal values of both LPs are equal. This gives the next theorem.

Theorem (Theorem 2) *Let $f : \{0,1\}^n \to \{0,1\}$ and $x \in \{0,1\}^n$ then*

$$\mathrm{bs}(f,x) \leq \mathrm{fbs}(f,x) = \mathrm{FC}(f,x) \leq \mathrm{C}(f,x)$$

And, of course, the same inequality holds when taking the maximum over all $x \in \{0,1\}^n$.

5.1.1 Fractional Certificate Complexity is Randomized Certificate Complexity

The "new" measure we defined is actually the same measure up to a constant as the *randomized certificate complexity* defined by Aaronson in [Aar03]:

Definition 5.4 (Randomized Certificate Complexity) A randomized verifier *for input x is a randomized algorithm that, on input y to f, (i) accepts with probability* 1 *if $y = x$, and (ii) rejects with probability at least $1/2$ if $f(y) \neq f(x)$. (If $y \neq x$ but $f(y) = f(x)$, the acceptance probability can be arbitrary.) Then $\mathrm{RC}(f,x)$ is the minimum expected number of queries used by a randomized verifier for x, and $\mathrm{RC}(f)$ is the maximum of $\mathrm{RC}(f,x)$ over all x.*

Claim 5.5 $\mathrm{RC}(f,x) = \Theta(\mathrm{FC}(f,x))$.

We use in the proof the variant of nonadaptive randomized certificate, also defined in [Aar03]

Definition 5.6 (Nonadaptive Randomized Certificate Complexity) *Call a randomized verifier for x nonadaptive if, on input y , it queries each y_i with independent probability λ_i, and rejects if and only if it encounters a disagreement with x. Let $\mathrm{RC}_{\mathrm{na}}(f,x)$ be the minimum of $\sum_{i\in[n]} \lambda_i$ over all nonadaptive verifiers for x.*

Aaronson showed adaptiveness does not help much as: $\mathrm{RC}(f,x) = \Theta(\mathrm{RC}_{\mathrm{na}}(f,x))$. Our proof follows some of his lines.

PROOF. We show that $\mathrm{RC}_{\mathrm{na}}(f,x) = \Theta(\mathrm{FC}(f,x))$. Let $u_0,\ldots,u_{n-1}$ be the weights for the minimal fractional certificate for f on x. By minimality, each u_i is at most 1. Then taking $\lambda_i = u_i$ for $i \in [n]$ gives a non-adaptive verifier such that if $f(x) \neq f(y)$ we have

$$\begin{aligned} \Pr(\text{The verifier accepts } y) &= \prod_{i\in[n]:x_i\neq y_i} (1-\lambda_i) \\ &\leq \prod_{i\in[n]:x_i\neq y_i} e^{-\lambda_i} \\ &= e^{-\sum_{i\in[n]:x_i\neq y_i} \lambda_i} \\ &\leq e^{-1} \end{aligned}$$

where the last inequality is by the definition of a fractional certificate. Thus, $\mathrm{RC}_{\mathrm{na}}(f,x) \leq \mathrm{FC}(f,x)$.

For the second direction, given an optimal non-adaptive verifier with probabilities λ_i take $u_i = 2\lambda_i$. For y such that $f(x) \neq f(y)$ the probability of finding a disagreement is at least half, thus

$$1/2 \leq \Pr(\text{The verifier rejects } y) \underset{\text{UB}}{\leq} \sum_{i:x_i\neq y_i} \lambda_i$$

This gives in turn, $\sum_{i:x_i\neq y_i} u_i \geq 1$ which shows that the u_is are a fractional certificate for x. Thus, we have $\mathrm{FC}(f,x) \leq 2\mathrm{RC}_{\mathrm{na}}(f,x)$. □

5.1.2 Previous Results Regarding Set Cover and Set Packing

As Set Cover and Set Packing are fundamental optimization problems, much research was done on them. We survey some of the results and their connections to our discussion.

First, we note that Nisan's result that $\mathrm{C}(f) \leq \mathrm{bs}(f) \cdot \mathrm{sens}(f)$ ([Nis89]) can be viewed as a special (unweighted) case of the primal-dual approximation algorithm for Set Cover in [BYE81].

Second, [CL10] showed that the integrality gap of Set Packing is no bigger than $\ell - 1 + 1/\ell$ for ℓ being the size of the largest set. This bound is tight for infinitely many ℓs using Fano-plane examples. As $\ell \leq \mathrm{sens}(f)$ this gives

$$\mathrm{fbs}(f) \leq \mathrm{bs}(f) \cdot (\mathrm{sens}(f) - 1 + 1/\mathrm{sens}(f)) .$$

Fano-planes gives examples for which $\mathrm{fbs}(f,x) = \mathrm{bs}(f,x) \cdot (\ell - 1 + 1/\ell)$ for arbitrary large ℓs and a specific x. However, as fbs and bs are defined as the maximum over all xs, our attempts to find functions with arbitrary large gaps between bs and fbs have failed so far.

Last, [Lov75] showed that the integrality gap of Set Cover (i.e. the ratio between C and FC) is at most $H_t = \sum_{i=1}^{t} 1/i \approx \ln(t)$ where $t = \max_i |\{B_j \mid i \in B_j\}|$ in our notations. Note that for example for MAJ_n on 0^n, $t = \Theta(2^n/\sqrt{n})$, so this does not imply a logarithmic factor between C and FC. Indeed, we will give an example with a polynomial gap between the two.

5.2 Upper Bounding The Block Sensitivity of BFC

With the IP/LP perspective of block-sensitivity we have the proper tools to prove the next theorem, giving an upper bound on the block-sensitivity of the composition of Boolean functions.

Theorem (Theorem 3, restated) *Let* $f : \{0,1\}^n \to \{0,1\}$, $g : \{0,1\}^m \to \{0,1\}$ *be Boolean functions, then* $\mathrm{bs}(f \circ g) \le \mathrm{fbs}(f) \cdot \mathrm{bs}(g)$. *Moreover, this inequality is weakly tight in the following sense: for g such that* $\mathrm{bs}^0(g) = \mathrm{bs}^1(g)$ *we have that* $\mathrm{bs}(f \circ g) \ge \mathrm{fbs}(f) \cdot \mathrm{bs}(g) - 2^n$.

The theorem shows that if f is some fixed function and we take a sequence of functions $\{g_i\}_{i\in\mathbb{N}}$ such that $\mathrm{bs}^0(g_i) = \mathrm{bs}^1(g_i)$ for all $i \in \mathbb{N}$ and $\lim_{i\to\infty} \mathrm{bs}(g_i) = \infty$ then the ratio between $\mathrm{bs}(f \circ g_i)/\mathrm{bs}(g_i)$ tends to $\mathrm{fbs}(f)$ as $i \to \infty$.

Proof. Let $x = (x^i_j)_{i\in[n],j\in[m]}$ be an input to $f \circ g$. We formulate $\mathrm{bs}(f \circ g, x)$ as an integer program. Let $y \in \{0,1\}^n$ be the input to f that x induces, i.e. $y_i = g(x^i)$ for $i \in [n]$. Denote the minimal sensitive blocks for f on y by $B_0, B_1, \dots, B_{k-1}$. The key observation is this: a set is a minimal sensitive block for $f \circ g$ on x iff it is a collection of minimal sensitive blocks for several g_is, where the g_is that participate in the collection form a minimal sensitive block for f. Thus, in a collection of disjoint minimal sensitive blocks for $f \circ g$, there can be at most $\mathrm{bs}(g, x^i)$ sets intersecting each x^i. The problem of calculating $\mathrm{bs}(f \circ g, x)$ reduces to finding the maximal number of B_js such that each y_i is covered at most $\mathrm{bs}(g, x^i)$ times. Any feasible solution for this problem can be transformed into a collection of disjoint blocks flipping $f \circ g$ value on x and vice versa. The formulation of this problem in terms of integer programming is:

$$\begin{aligned} \max \quad & \textstyle\sum_{j=0}^{k-1} w_j \\ \text{s.t.} \quad & \textstyle\sum_{j: i\in B_j} w_j \le \mathrm{bs}(g, x^i) \quad \forall i \in [n] \\ & w_j \in \{0, 1, \dots, \mathrm{bs}(g)\} \quad \forall j \in [k] \end{aligned} \qquad \text{(IP(bs(fg)))}$$

Relaxing this to an LP gives

$$\begin{aligned} \max \quad & \textstyle\sum_{j=0}^{k-1} w_j \\ \text{s.t.} \quad & \textstyle\sum_{j: i\in B_j} w_j \le \mathrm{bs}(g, x^i) \quad \forall i \in [n] \\ & w_j \ge 0 \quad \forall j \in [k] \end{aligned} \qquad \text{(LP(bs(fg)))}$$

Observing the constraints, any feasible solution for the linear program LP(bs(fg)) where each w_j is divided by $\mathrm{bs}(g)$ is a feasible solution for the LP for $\mathrm{fbs}(f, y)$. Thus,

$$\begin{aligned} \mathrm{fbs}(f, y) &\ge \frac{\mathrm{OPT}(LP(bs(fg)))}{\mathrm{bs}(g)} \\ &\ge \frac{OPT(IP(bs(fg)))}{\mathrm{bs}(g)} = \frac{\mathrm{bs}(f \circ g, x)}{\mathrm{bs}(g)} . \end{aligned}$$

Rearranging this gives $\mathrm{bs}(f \circ g, x) \le \mathrm{fbs}(f, y) \cdot \mathrm{bs}(g)$. Taking x which maximizes $\mathrm{bs}(f \circ g)$ gives the desired upper bound.

For the tightness part, let $p^0, p^1 \in \{0,1\}^m$ be points achieving the maximal $\mathrm{bs}^0(g), \mathrm{bs}^1(g)$ respectively, and let y be the point achieving the maximal $\mathrm{fbs}(f)$. Consider the block sensitivity of $f \circ g$ on the point $x = (x^i_j)_{i\in[n],j\in[m]}$ where $x^i = p^{y_i}$. Note that the additive gap between IP(bs(fg)) and LP(bs(fg)) is at most k. Indeed, if the optimal values of the LP are w^*_j, then $w_j = \lfloor w^*_j \rfloor$ is a feasible solution for the IP with value at least $\mathrm{OPT}(LP(bs(fg))) - k$. Our choice of x gives $\mathrm{bs}(g, x^i) = \mathrm{bs}(g)$ for all $i \in [n]$, hence the value of LP(bs(fg)) is exactly $\mathrm{bs}(g)$ times the value of LP(bs(f)) as the constraints are equivalent up to the constant factor $\mathrm{bs}(g)$. Hence,

$$\begin{aligned} \mathrm{fbs}(f) \cdot \mathrm{bs}(g) &= \mathrm{OPT}(LP(bs(fg))) \\ &\le \mathrm{OPT}(IP(bs(fg))) + k \\ &= \mathrm{bs}(f \circ g, x) + k \\ &\le \mathrm{bs}(f \circ g) + k . \end{aligned}$$

As $k \le 2^n$ this completes the proof. □

The behavior of fbs with respect to composition resembles that of sens and C.

Claim 5.7 *Let* $f : \{0,1\}^n \to \{0,1\}$ *and* $g : \{0,1\}^m \to \{0,1\}$ *be Boolean functions, then (i)* $\mathrm{fbs}(f \circ g) \le \mathrm{fbs}(f) \cdot \mathrm{fbs}(g)$ *and (ii) For* $z \in \{0,1\}$ *if* $f(z^n) = g(z^m) = z$ *then* $\mathrm{fbs}(f \circ g, z^{nm}) \ge \mathrm{fbs}(f, z^n) \cdot \mathrm{fbs}(g, z^m)$

We defer the proof to Appendix C.

5.3 Analysis of an Example

In order to demonstrate the analysis of block sensitivity of composed Boolean functions we present the next example.

Example 5.8 *Let f be a function on 6 variables defined by:*

$$f = \mathrm{MAJ}(x_0 \oplus x_1 \oplus x_3, x_0 \oplus x_2 \oplus x_4, x_1 \oplus x_2 \oplus x_5) .$$

The example above has $\mathrm{bs}(f, x) = 4$, $\forall x \in \{0,1\}^6$ and $\mathrm{C}(f) = 5$. It was actually presented in [BSW86] and its composition was analyzed in [WZ89] and [Aar03]. It was considered the best separation between bs and C, but the analysis of this function composition was wrong claiming that $\mathrm{bs}(f^k) = \mathrm{bs}(f)^k$. As we shall see, $\mathrm{bs}(f^2) = 18 > 16 = \mathrm{bs}(f)^2$ and in general:

Lemma 5.9 *For* $k \ge 1$: $\mathrm{bs}(f^{k+1}) = \lfloor 4.5 \cdot \mathrm{bs}(f^k) \rfloor$ *and this value is achieved on any input.*

Proof. Let $\{x^i_j\}_{i\in[6],j\in[6^k]}$ be an input for $f^{k+1} = f \circ f^k$ and let $y_i = f(x^i)$. The minimal sensitive blocks of f at any point are, up to indices name change:

$$\{0\}, \{1\}, \{2\}, \{3,4\}, \{3,5\}, \{4,5\} .$$

The optimal solution for the linear program for $\mathrm{fbs}(f)$ on y is $(1, 1, 1, 0.5, 0.5, 0.5)$ respectively. Consider the IP for $\mathrm{bs}(f \circ f^k, x)$ as in Theorem 3. By induction $\mathrm{bs}(f^k, x^i) = \mathrm{bs}(f^k)$. Put weights $\mathrm{bs}(f^k)$ on each set $\{i\}$ for $i = 0, 1, 2$, $\lfloor \mathrm{bs}(f^k)/2 \rfloor$ on each of the sets $\{3,4\}, \{3,5\}$ and $\lceil \mathrm{bs}(f^k)/2 \rceil$ on the set $\{4,5\}$. This is a feasible solution for the IP, as any $i \in [6]$ was covered at most $\mathrm{bs}(f^k)$ times. The solution size is $\lfloor \mathrm{bs}(f^k) \cdot 4.5 \rfloor$, and as Theorem 3 gives $\mathrm{bs}(f^{k+1}) \le \mathrm{fbs}(f) \cdot \mathrm{bs}(f^k) = 4.5 \cdot \mathrm{bs}(f^k)$, this is optimal. □

For k large enough, using Lemma 5.9, we derive $\mathrm{bs}(f^k) \approx 0.8877 \cdot 4.5^k$. This shows that for k large enough and $g = f^k$, the ratio $\mathrm{bs}(g^2)/\mathrm{bs}(g)^2 \approx 1/0.8877 > 1.126$. Claim 5.7 gives $\mathrm{fbs}(f^k) = 4.5^k$, so there is a small 1.126 factor separating $\mathrm{bs}(f^k)$ from $\mathrm{fbs}(f^k)$. The next claim, proven in Appendix D, shows that this constant factor is no coincidence.

Claim 5.10 *Let* $f : \{0,1\}^n \to \{0,1\}$ *then for any integer k the ratio* $\mathrm{fbs}(f^k)/\mathrm{bs}(f^k)$ *is at most* $c(n)$ *i.e. independent of k.*

5.4 Block Sensitivity and Certificate Complexity Separation

As we demonstrated above the example considered to have the best separation between block-sensitivity and certificate-complexity has a smaller separation than what was previously claimed: $\mathrm{C}(f^k) = 5^k = \Theta(\mathrm{bs}(f^k)^{\log(5)/\log(4.5)}) = \Theta(\mathrm{bs}(f^k)^{1.07\ldots})$. The best separation we could find uses a composition of a symmetric function, and was previously presented in [Aar03]. Our analysis is slightly better than that of Aaronson since we use a (C, 0)-good form of the function.

Example 5.11 *Consider the symmetric function on 29 variables whose value is 1 iff the weight of the input* $\|x\| = \sum_{i=1}^{29} x_i$ *is in* $\{13, 14, 15, 16\}$.

This function has certificate complexity 26, achieved on inputs of weight 13, 14, 15, 16, as we need to expose at least $29 - 3$ coordinates to convince that $f(x) = 1$. The sensitivity of the function is 17, achieved on inputs of weight 12 or 17. The block sensitivity of the function is also 17, achieved on inputs of weight 12 or 17 using 17 blocks of size 1, or on inputs of weight 13 or 16 using 13 blocks of size 1 in addition to 4 blocks of size 4. One can check that the fractional block sensitivity of f is also 17. Take $\tilde{f}$ to be a (C, 0) good form of f, as in Remark 2.12. Lemma 3.1 gives $\forall k \in \mathbb{N} : \mathrm{C}(\tilde{f}^k) = \mathrm{C}(\tilde{f})^k = 26^k$, while Claim 5.7 gives $\forall k \in \mathbb{N} : \mathrm{fbs}(\tilde{f}^k) \leq 17^k$. Hence,

$$\mathrm{C}(\tilde{f}^k) \geq \mathrm{fbs}(\tilde{f}^k)^{\log(26)/\log(17)} \geq \mathrm{bs}(\tilde{f}^k)^{\log(26)/\log(17)}$$

6. IMPROVING NISAN-SZEGEDY BOUND

The last application shows that function composition can prove not only separations between complexity measures but even tighten relations between them. Nisan and Szegedy showed that:

Theorem 6.1 ([NS94]) *Let f be a Boolean function, then* $\mathrm{bs}(f) \leq 2\deg(f)^2$.

We improve their result by a factor 2:

Theorem (Theorem 4, restated) *Let f be a Boolean function, then* $\mathrm{bs}(f) \leq \deg(f)^2$.

Proof. Assume by contradiction that there exists a Boolean function f for which $\mathrm{bs}(f) \geq \deg(f)^2 + 1$. WLOG f is in (bs, 0) good form. Let $d \triangleq \deg(f) \geq 1$ and take $g = f^{2d^2}$. By Property 1 of Lemma 3.1 $\deg(g) = d^{2d^2}$. By Property 7

$$\begin{aligned} \mathrm{bs}(g) &\geq (d^2+1)^{2d^2} \\ &= (d^2)^{2d^2} \cdot \left(1 + \frac{1}{d^2}\right)^{2d^2} \\ &\geq^3 (d^{2d^2})^2 \cdot 2^2 \\ &= \deg(g)^2 \cdot 4 \end{aligned}$$

and this is a contradiction to Theorem 6.1 □

This improves as a corollary another relation between complexity measures:

Corollary 6.2 ([Mid04])

$$\mathrm{C}(f) \leq \mathrm{D}(F) \leq \mathrm{bs}(f) \cdot \deg(f) \leq \deg(f)^3$$

Remark 6.3 *The method used in Theorem 4 shows that for any two complexity measures M, N where* $M \in \{\mathrm{sens}, \mathrm{bs}, \mathrm{fbs}, \mathrm{C}, \mathrm{C}_{\min}, \mathrm{mr}, \deg, \mathrm{D}\}$ *and* $N \in \{\mathrm{sens}, \mathrm{fbs}, \mathrm{C}, \deg, \mathrm{D}\}$, *a relation of the form* $M(f) \leq N(f)^{\alpha+o(1)}$ *can be tighten to* $M(f) \leq N(f)^{\alpha}$.

7. DISCUSSION

In this paper we saw some applications and interesting questions regarding function composition.

BFC most natural use is to generate asymptotic separations based on a constant (even small) size examples for which two complexity measures differ. Hence, possible further work will be to get better separations by finding better examples. This can be done using computer search. More surprisingly, BFC can help tighten relations between complexity measures as in Theorem 4. Can this technique be used to tighten other relations?

BFC fails to separate complexity measures which behave similarly to composition. In particular, this technique fails to separate bs from fbs as proven in Claim 5.7. An interesting question is whether or not $\mathrm{bs}(f) = \Theta(\mathrm{fbs}(f))$, a negative answer will need to use different techniques than composition. A possible approach may involve the integrality gap shown in Section 5, perhaps using examples closely related to Fano-planes as in [CL10]. Answering this question may shed light on other questions such as bs vs. C.

Another interesting matter raised by Example 4.1 is of the connection between codes and Boolean functions. In particular, it will be interesting to see what more can we learn from this connection.

8. ACKNOWLEDGEMENTS

I thank Benjamin Eliot Klein for lots of support and advice; my advisor, Ran Raz, for guidance and encouragement; Igor Shinkar for his proof of Lemma B.1 and Gregory Valiant for helpful discussions. I also thank the anonymous referees for helpful comments.

9. REFERENCES

[Aar03] S. Aaronson. Quantum certificate complexity. In *IEEE Conference on Computational Complexity*, pages 171–178, 2003.

[AB09] S. Arora and B. Barak. *Computational complexity: a modern approach.* Cambridge University Press, 2009.

[Amb03] Andris Ambainis. Polynomial degree vs. quantum query complexity. In *FOCS*, pages 230–239, 2003.

[BdW02] H. Buhrman and R. de Wolf. Complexity measures and decision tree complexity: a survey. *Theor. Comput. Sci.*, 288(1):21–43, 2002.

[BI87] M. Blum and R. Impagliazzo. Generic oracles and oracle classes (extended abstract). In *FOCS*, pages 118–126, 1987.

[BKS+10] B. Barak, G. Kindler, R. Shaltiel, B. Sudakov, and A. Wigderson. Simulating independence: New constructions of condensers, ramsey graphs, dispersers, and extractors. *J. ACM*, 57(4), 2010.

[BSW86] S. Bublitz, U. Schürfeld, and I. Wegener. Properties of complexity measures for prams and wrams. *Theor. Comput. Sci.*, 48(3):53–73, 1986.

[BYE81] R. Bar-Yehuda and S. Even. A linear-time approximation algorithm for the weighted vertex cover problem. *J. Algorithms*, 2(2):198–203, 1981.

[CL10] Y. H. Chan and L. C. Lau. On linear and semidefinite programming relaxations for hypergraph matching. In *SODA*, pages 1500–1511, 2010.

[HLS07] Peter Høyer, Troy Lee, and Robert Spalek. Negative weights make adversaries stronger. In *STOC*, pages 526–535, 2007.

[Lov75] L. Lovasz. On the ratio of optimal integral and fractional covers. *Discrete Mathematics*, 13(4):383 – 390, 1975.

[Mid04] G. Midrijanis. Exact quantum query complexity for total boolean functions. *arXiv:quant-ph/0403168v2*, 2004.

[MOS04] E. Mossel, R. O'Donnell, and R. A. Servedio. Learning functions of k relevant variables. *J. Comput. Syst. Sci.*, 69(3):421–434, 2004.

[Nis89] N. Nisan. Crew prams and decision trees. In *STOC*, pages 327–335, 1989.

[NN93] J. Naor and M. Naor. Small-bias probability spaces: Efficient constructions and applications. *SIAM J. on Computing*, 22(4):838–856, 1993.

[NS94] N. Nisan and M. Szegedy. On the degree of Boolean functions as real polynomials. *Computational Complexity*, 4:301–313, 1994.

[NW94] N. Nisan and A. Wigderson. On rank vs. communication complexity. In *FOCS*, pages 831–836, 1994.

[O'D12] R. O'Donnell. Analysis of boolean functions. http://analysisofbooleanfunctions.org/, 2012.

[SW86] Michael E. Saks and Avi Wigderson. Probabilistic boolean decision trees and the complexity of evaluating game trees. In *FOCS*, pages 29–38, 1986.

[Val12] Gregory Valiant. Finding correlations in subquadratic time, with applications to learning parities and juntas with noise. *Electronic Colloquium on Computational Complexity (ECCC)*, 19:6, 2012.

[Ver10] E. Verbin. comments on my philomath project: Sensitivity versus block-sensitivity. S. Aaronson blog, http://www.scottaaronson.com/blog/?p=453, 2010.

[WZ89] I. Wegener and L. Zádori. A note on the relations between critical and sensitive complexity. *Elektronische Informationsverarbeitung und Kybernetik*, 25(8/9):417–421, 1989.

APPENDIX

A. PROPERTIES OF THE IP FUNCTION

The next lemma states a well known property of $\mathrm{IP_n}$ which we later use to prove Lemma 4.5. We include the proof for completeness.

Lemma A.1 *Denote by* $\mathrm{IP_n} : \{0,1\}^{2n} \to \{0,1\}$ *the Boolean function defined as:*

$$\mathrm{IP_n}(y_0, y_1, \ldots, y_{2n-1}) = y_0 \cdot y_1 + \ldots + y_{2n-2} \cdot y_{2n-1} \pmod 2 .$$

Then, every Fourier coefficient of $\mathrm{IP_n}$ *is of magnitude* 2^{-n}.

Proof. Let S be a subset of $\{0,1\}^{2n}$. Using Equation (1) the S-Fourier coefficient of $\mathrm{IP_n}$ is equal to

$$\widehat{\mathrm{IP_n}}(S) = E_{y \in_R \{0,1\}^{2n}} \left((-1)^{\mathrm{IP_n}(y)} \cdot (-1)^{\sum_{i=0}^{2n-1} S_i \cdot y_i} \right)$$

where S_i is the indicator that $i \in S$. Now we may write

$$\widehat{\mathrm{IP_n}}(S) = E_{y \in_R \{0,1\}^{2n}} \left(\prod_{i=0}^{n-1} (-1)^{y_{2i} \cdot y_{2i+1} + S_{2i} \cdot y_{2i} + S_{2i+1} \cdot y_{2i+1}} \right)$$

and as the different multiplicands are probabilistically independent, we can replace expectation and product. Thus, $\widehat{\mathrm{IP_n}}(S) = \prod_{i=0}^{n-1} E\left((-1)^{y_{2i} \cdot y_{2i+1} + S_{2i} \cdot y_{2i} + S_{2i+1} \cdot y_{2i+1}}\right)$. It can be checked by complete enumeration that the expectancy of each multiplicand is either $1/2$ or $-1/2$, hence $|\widehat{\mathrm{IP_n}}(S)| = 2^{-n}$. □

We are ready to prove Lemma 4.5.

Lemma (Lemma 4.5, restated) *Let* $A \subseteq (\mathbb{F}_2)^{2n}$ *be an affine subspace of dimension* d *defined by* $v_A + \mathrm{span}\{v_0, \ldots, v_{d-1}\}$. *If* $\mathrm{IP_n}|_A(x_0, x_1, \ldots, x_{d-1}) \triangleq \mathrm{IP_n}(v_A + \sum_{i \in [d]} x_i \cdot v_i)$ *is a parity function, then* $d \leq n$.

Proof. Let T be a change of basis matrix mapping $v_i \mapsto e_i$ for $i \in [d]$. If $v_A = \vec{0}$, obviously $T(v_A) = \vec{0}$, else we can assume WLOG that $v_A \notin \mathrm{span}\{v_i : i \in [d]\}$ and since v_A is linearly independent of them we can demand that $T(v_A) = e_d$. Write $\mathrm{IP_n} = (\mathrm{IP_n} \circ T^{-1}) \circ T$, and denote $\mathrm{IP_n} \circ T^{-1}$ by $\tilde{\mathrm{IP}}_\mathrm{n}$. As $\tilde{\mathrm{IP}}_\mathrm{n}$ is a composition of $\mathrm{IP_n}$ with an invertible linear transformation, Fact 2.8 gives that its Fourier spectrum is a (linear) permutation of the Fourier spectrum of $\mathrm{IP_n}$, hence every coefficient is of magnitude 2^{-n}. Let $\tau : [2n] \to \{0, 1, *\}$ be the restriction defined by:

$$\tau(i) = \begin{cases} * & i \in [d] \\ T(v_A)_i & otherwise \end{cases} .$$

If $\mathrm{IP_n}|_A$ is a parity function then so is $\tilde{\mathrm{IP}}_\mathrm{n}|_\tau$ as

$$\begin{aligned} \tilde{\mathrm{IP}}_\mathrm{n}|_\tau(x_0, \ldots, x_{2n-1}) &= \tilde{\mathrm{IP}}_\mathrm{n}(T(v_A) + \sum_{i \in [d]} x_i \cdot e_i) \\ &= \mathrm{IP_n}(v_A + \sum_{i \in [d]} x_i \cdot v_i) . \end{aligned}$$

According to Corollary 2.7 the maximal Fourier coefficient of $\tilde{\mathrm{IP}}_\mathrm{n}|_\tau$ is at most the maximal Fourier coefficient of $\tilde{\mathrm{IP}}_\mathrm{n}$ times 2^{2n-d}, hence at most 2^{n-d}. As $\tilde{\mathrm{IP}}_\mathrm{n}|_\tau$ becomes parity, there is one Fourier coefficient of magnitude 1, giving $d \leq n$. □

Remark A.2 *Lemma 4.5 shows in particular that* $\mathrm{IP_n}$ *restricted to any* $n+1$ *dimension affine subspace is nonconstant. This property is called being an* affine disperser for dimension $n+1$. *In fact, any affine disperser for dimension* $n+1$ *doesn't become a parity function under any restriction to an affine subspace of dimension* $n+2$. *Thus, our property is almost identical to being an affine disperser for dimension* $n+1$. *The fact that* $\mathrm{IP_n}$ *is an affine disperser is regarded to Ben-Sasson, Hoory, Rosenman, Vadhan and Wigderson (in an unpublished manuscript, mentioned in [BKS+ 10]).*

B. GENERALIZATION TO EPSILON-BIASED SETS

In the construction of Example 4.1 we can replace the WH matrix by a matrix associated with any ϵ-biased sample space as follows. Let $\mathcal{C} \subseteq \mathbb{F}_2{}^{2n}$, we say $\mathcal{C}$ is a an *ϵ-biased sample space* if for any nonzero linear functional $\Phi : (\mathbb{F}_2)^{2n} \to \mathbb{F}_2$ the expectancy of $E_{v \in_R \mathcal{C}}(\Phi(v))$ is in the range $[1/2-\epsilon, 1/2+\epsilon]$. ϵ-biased sets where first defined and constructed in [NN93], following a sequence of works giving better constructions.

Putting an order on the set $\mathcal{C} = \{\mathcal{C}_1, \ldots, \mathcal{C}_m\}$ it is convenient to think of an ϵ-biased set as a $2n \times m$ matrix over $\mathbb{F}_2$ where each XOR of a nonempty subset of rows gives a row with $m \cdot (1/2 \pm \epsilon)$ ones. Let $A \in (\mathbb{F}_2)^{2n \times m}$ be the matrix associated with the sample space $\mathcal{C}$, then A naturally defines a (linear) mapping $A : (\mathbb{F}_2)^m \to (\mathbb{F}_2)^{2n}$. The composition of the mappings $f = \mathrm{IP_n} \circ A$ gives a construction with similar properties to that of Example 4.1.

We begin with the following lemma which is analogous to Lemma 4.4

Lemma B.1 *The bitwise* OR *of n rows in an ϵ-biased matrix with m columns has at most $m - m \cdot (1-2^{-n}) \cdot (1-2\epsilon)$ zeros.*

The proof of Lemma B.1 is due to Igor Shinkar.

PROOF. We may assume WLOG that A is an ϵ-biased matrix of size $n \times m$. Let

$$\mathrm{NZ} = \{j \in [m] : \exists i \in [n] : A_{i,j} = 1\}$$

be the set of nonzero columns. For a fixed $j \in \mathrm{NZ}$, let I be a set chosen uniformly at random from the nonempty subsets of $[n]$ then

$$\Pr_I \left(\bigoplus_{i \in I} A_{i,j} = 1 \right) = \frac{2^{n-1}}{2^n - 1}$$

Let $w_I(j) = \bigoplus_{i \in I} A_{i,j}$ and denote by $\|w_I\|_1 = \sum_{j \in [m]} w_I(j)$ where the sum is over the reals. By the definition of ϵ-biased sets, for all choices of I we have $\|w_I\|_1 \geq m \cdot (1/2 - \epsilon)$. This gives

$$m \cdot (1/2 - \epsilon) \leq E_I(\|w_I\|_1) = \frac{2^{n-1}}{2^n - 1} \cdot |\mathrm{NZ}| \; .$$

Rearranging this we have

$$|\mathrm{NZ}| \geq m \cdot \frac{2^n - 1}{2^{n-1}} \cdot (1/2 - \epsilon) = m \cdot (1 - 2^{-n}) \cdot (1 - 2\epsilon) \; .$$

As the set of zero coordinates is $[m] - \mathrm{NZ}$ its size is at most $m - m \cdot (1-2^{-n}) \cdot (1-2\epsilon)$. □

Claim B.2 *Let $f = \mathrm{IP_n} \circ A$ where A is a $2n \times m$ ϵ-biased matrix then $\deg(f) = m \cdot (1/2 \pm \epsilon)$ and $\mathrm{mr}(f) \geq m \cdot (1 - 2^{-n}) \cdot (1 - 2\epsilon)$*

PROOF. The proof closely follows the lines of the proof of Theorem 4.2. By Fact 2.8 any nonzero Fourier coefficient subset characteristic vector is the XOR of a nonempty subset of rows in A. By definition the subsets are of size $m \cdot (1/2 \pm \epsilon)$, hence the degree of f over the reals is $m \cdot (1/2 \pm \epsilon)$.

Let ρ be a restriction under which f is parity, and let d be the dimension of $A(V_\rho)$, then by Lemma 4.6 $d \leq n$. Let $U = A(V_\rho)^\perp$, we have that $\dim(U) = 2n - d$. Since performing an invertible linear transformation on the rows of A preserves the property of being a an ϵ-biased matrix, we may assume WLOG that the image of $A(V_\rho)$ is $\mathrm{span}\{e_0, e_1, \ldots, e_{d-1}\}$ and thus $U = \mathrm{span}\{e_d, e_{d+1}, \ldots, e_{2n-1}\}$. Let k be a variable not fixed by ρ, then $A \cdot e_k \perp U$. Equivalently, the kth column in A has $2n - d$ zeros in the last $2n - d$ entries, hence it is a zero of the bitwise OR of the last $2n - d$ rows of A. As $d \leq n$ it is a zero entry in the bitwise OR of the last n rows. By Lemma B.1 the number of such variables is at most $m - m \cdot (1 - 2^{-n}) \cdot (1 - 2\epsilon)$ which completes the proof. □

C. FRACTIONAL BLOCK SENSITIVITY OF FUNCTION COMPOSITION

We repeat and prove the next claim.

Claim (Claim 5.7, restated) *Let $f : \{0,1\}^n \to \{0,1\}$ and $g : \{0,1\}^m \to \{0,1\}$ be Boolean functions, then (i) $\mathrm{fbs}(f \circ g) \leq \mathrm{fbs}(f) \cdot \mathrm{fbs}(g)$ and (ii) For $z \in \{0,1\}$ if $f(z^n) = g(z^m) = z$ then $\mathrm{fbs}(f \circ g, z^{nm}) \geq \mathrm{fbs}(f, z^n) \cdot \mathrm{fbs}(g, z^m)$*

PROOF. For the first part, we show that $\mathrm{FC}(f \circ g) \leq \mathrm{FC}(f) \cdot \mathrm{FC}(g)$ (which is equivalent to $\mathrm{fbs}(f \circ g) \leq \mathrm{fbs}(f) \cdot \mathrm{fbs}(g)$). Let $x = (x^i_j)_{i \in [n], j \in [m]}$ be an input for $f \circ g$ and let $y \in \{0,1\}^n$ be the intermediate values, $y_i = g(x^i)$. Let $T_i : [m] \to \mathbb{R}^+$ be a minimal fractional certificate for g on x^i i.e. a collection of weights for the variables $\{x^i_j\}_{j \in [m]}$. Let $S : [n] \to \mathbb{R}^+$ be a minimal fractional certificate for f on y. We show that the weights $R : [n] \times [m] \to \mathbb{R}^+$ defined by $R(i,j) = S(i) \cdot T_i(j)$ are a fractional certificate for $f \circ g$. Let $x' = (x'^i_j)_{i \in [n], j \in [m]}$ such that $(f \circ g)(x) \neq (f \circ g)(x')$ and let y' be the intermediate values for x' i.e. $y'_i = g(x'^i_j)$. Since $f(y) \neq f(y')$ we have $\sum_{i : y_i \neq y'_i} S(i) \geq 1$ and since each T_i is a certificate we have:

$$\forall i : y_i \neq y'_i . \sum_{j : x^i_j \neq x'^i_j} T_i(j) \geq 1 \; .$$

Thus,

$$\begin{aligned} \sum_{i,j : x^i_j \neq x'^i_j} R(i,j) &\geq \sum_{i : y_i \neq y'_i} \sum_{j : x^i_j \neq x'^i_j} R(i,j) \\ &= \sum_{i : y_i \neq y'_i} \left(S(i) \cdot \sum_{j : x^i_j \neq x'^i_j} T_i(j) \right) \\ &\geq \sum_{i : y_i \neq y'_i} S(i) \geq 1 \; , \end{aligned}$$

showing that R is a fractional certificate for $f \circ g$. The total weight of R is

$$\sum_{i,j} R(i,j) = \sum_i \left(S(i) \cdot \sum_j T_i(j) \right) \leq \mathrm{FC}(f) \cdot \mathrm{FC}(g) \; .$$

For the second part, we show that $\mathrm{fbs}(f \circ g, z^{nm}) \geq \mathrm{fbs}(f, z^n) \cdot \mathrm{fbs}(g, z^m)$. Put $x = z^{nm}$ as the input for $f \circ g$. As $g(z^m) = z$, the intermediate values $y_i = g(x^i) = z$. Let $\{B_k\}_k$ be minimal blocks which are sensitive for f on z^n, let $\{u_k\}_k$ be optimal weights for these blocks achieving $\mathrm{fbs}(f, z^n)$. For $i \in [n]$ let $\{T^i_\ell\}_\ell$ be minimal blocks which are sensitive for g on $x^i = z^m$, and let $\{v^i_\ell\}_\ell$ be optimal weights (independent of i) for these blocks achieving $\mathrm{fbs}(g, z^m)$.

We show that the sets $A_{k,\ell} = \cup_{i \in B_k} T^i_\ell$ with weights $w_{k,\ell} = u_k \cdot v_\ell$ are "relaxed disjoint". For any coordinate (i,j) the sum of weights for blocks containing this coordinate is at most 1 as

$$\begin{aligned}\sum_{k,\ell:(i,j)\in A_{k,\ell}} w_{k,\ell} &= \sum_{k:i\in B_k}\sum_{\ell:j\in T^i_\ell} w_{k,\ell}\\ &= \sum_{k:i\in B_k}\left(u_k\cdot\sum_{\ell:j\in T^i_\ell} v_\ell\right)\\ &\le \sum_{k:i\in B_k} u_k \le 1\,.\end{aligned}$$

The total weight assigned to the sets $A_{k,\ell}$ is $\sum_{k,\ell} w_{k,\ell} = \mathrm{fbs}(f, z^n)\cdot\mathrm{fbs}(g, z^m)$. As this is a feasible solution for fractional block sensitivity linear program we conclude that

$$\mathrm{fbs}(f\circ g, z^{nm}) \ge \mathrm{fbs}(f, z^n)\circ\mathrm{fbs}(g, z^m)\,. \quad \square$$

D. GAPS BETWEEN BLOCK SENSITIVITY AND FRACTIONAL BLOCK SENSITIVITY OF COMPOSED FUNCTIONS

In this section we prove Claim 5.10. In the proof we use the next lemmas and the following definition.

Definition D.1 *Let $f : \{0,1\}^n \to \{0,1\}$, we say f is monotone increasing (decreasing) if $x \ge y$ pointwise implies $f(x) \ge f(y)$ ($f(x) \le f(y)$). We say that f is monotone if either cases hold.*

Lemma D.2 ([Nis89]) *Let $f : \{0,1\}^n \to \{0,1\}$ be a monotone function then $\mathrm{sens}(f) = \mathrm{bs}(f) = \mathrm{C}(f)$.*

Lemma D.3 ([Nis89]) *Let $f : \{0,1\}^n \to \{0,1\}$ be a Boolean function, and $z \in \{0,1\}$ then $\mathrm{C}^z(f) \le \mathrm{bs}^z(f)\cdot \mathrm{sens}^{1-z}(f)$.*

Lemma D.4 *Let f and g be Boolean functions, then $\mathrm{bs}^z(f\circ g) \ge \mathrm{bs}^z(f)\circ\min_{z'\in\{0,1\}}(\mathrm{bs}^{z'}(g))$*

PROOF. Let p^0 and p^1 be the inputs maximizing $\mathrm{bs}^0(g)$ and $\mathrm{bs}^1(g)$ respectively and let y be the input maximizing $\mathrm{bs}^z(f)$. Take the input $x = (x^0||x^1||\dots||x^{n-1})$ where $x^i = p^{y_i}$ and consider the block sensitivity of $f\circ g$ on this input. f has $\mathrm{bs}^z(f)$ many disjoint blocks on y and each block can be expanded into at least $\min(\mathrm{bs}^0(g), \mathrm{bs}^1(g))$ disjoint sensitive blocks for $f\circ g$ on x. $\square$

Lemma D.5 *Let f, g be Boolean functions such that f is not monotone and let $z \in \{0,1\}$, then*

1. *$\mathrm{bs}(f) \ge 2$*
2. *$\mathrm{bs}^z(f\circ g) \ge \mathrm{bs}(g)$*
3. *$\mathrm{fbs}^z(f\circ g) \ge \mathrm{fbs}(g)$*
4. *The sequence $\{\mathrm{bs}^z(f^\ell)\}_{\ell\in\mathbb{N}}$ is monotone increasing and tends to infinity.*

PROOF. 1. Any function with $\mathrm{bs}(f) = 1$ is either $f(x) = x_i$ or $f(x) = 1 - x_i$ for some i. Either functions are monotone, hence any non-monotone function has $\mathrm{bs}(f) \ge 2$.

2. Let $z' \in \{0,1\}$ be such that $\mathrm{bs}^{z'}(g) = \mathrm{bs}(g)$. Since f is not monotone, there is an input $y = y(z', z)$ and a bit $i \in [n]$ such that $y_i = z'$ and changing y_i from $z' \to 1-z'$ makes a $z \to 1-z$ change in the output of f.

   Let p^0 and p^1 be inputs maximizing $\mathrm{bs}^0(g)$ and $\mathrm{bs}^1(g)$ respectively, and take the input $x = (x^0||x^1||\dots||x^{n-1})$ where $x^i = p^{y_i}$. First, $(f\circ g)(x) = f(y) = z$. Second, by our choice of i, changing each sensitive block of g on x^i changes the value of $f\circ g$ and we have $\mathrm{bs}(g, x^i) = \mathrm{bs}(g)$ such sensitive blocks.

3. The bound on $\mathrm{fbs}^z(f\circ g)$ can be proven similarly.

4. By Property 2 $\mathrm{bs}^z(f^{\ell+1}) \ge \mathrm{bs}(f^\ell) \ge \mathrm{bs}^z(f^\ell)$. It remains to show that the sequence diverges. Combining Property 2 above and Lemma D.4 gives that for any $k\in\mathbb{N}$:

$$\begin{aligned}\mathrm{bs}^z(f^{2k}) &\underset{\text{Lemma D.4}}{\ge} \mathrm{bs}^z(f^2)\cdot\min_{z'\in\{0,1\}}(\mathrm{bs}^{z'}(f^{2k-2}))\\ &\underset{\text{Prop. 2}}{\ge} \mathrm{bs}(f)\cdot\min_{z'\in\{0,1\}}(\mathrm{bs}^{z'}(f^{2k-2}))\,.\end{aligned}$$

   Induction gives $\mathrm{bs}^z(f^{2k}) \ge \mathrm{bs}(f)^k$ which in turn is at least 2^k by Property 1.

$\square$

Claim (Claim 5.10, restated) *Let $f : \{0,1\}^n \to \{0,1\}$ then for integer $\ell\in\mathbb{N}$ the ratio $\mathrm{fbs}(f^\ell)/\mathrm{bs}(f^\ell)$ is at most $c(n) = 25\cdot n^2\cdot 2^n$ i.e. independent of ℓ.*

PROOF. If f is monotone then f^ℓ is monotone and by D.2 we have that $\mathrm{bs}(f^\ell) = \mathrm{C}(f^\ell)$. Hence, in this case, $\mathrm{fbs}(f^\ell) = \mathrm{bs}(f^\ell)$, and we can assume that f is not monotone for the rest of the proof.

Let $z \in \{0,1\}$. Denote by $r^z_\ell \triangleq \left(\frac{\mathrm{bs}^z(f^\ell)}{\mathrm{fbs}^z(f^\ell)}\right)$ and $r_\ell \triangleq \min(r^0_\ell, r^1_\ell)$. We show that r_ℓ is a lower bound on the ratio $\mathrm{bs}(f^\ell)/\mathrm{fbs}(f^\ell)$. Let $z' \in \{0,1\}$ such that $\mathrm{fbs}^{z'}(f^\ell) = \mathrm{fbs}(f^\ell)$, then we have

$$\frac{\mathrm{bs}(f^\ell)}{\mathrm{fbs}(f^\ell)} = \frac{\mathrm{bs}(f^\ell)}{\mathrm{fbs}^{z'}(f^\ell)} \ge \frac{\mathrm{bs}^{z'}(f^\ell)}{\mathrm{fbs}^{z'}(f^\ell)} = r^{z'}_\ell \ge r_\ell\,.$$

By Lemma D.5,4, there exists a minimal $m\in\mathbb{N}$ such that $\mathrm{bs}(f^m) \ge 2\cdot 2^n$. Then, by Lemma D.5,2 for any $z\in\{0,1\}$ we have $\mathrm{bs}^z(f^{m+1}) \ge 2\cdot 2^n$. On the other hand, since m is the minimal such integer, using Theorem 3 gives

$$\mathrm{bs}^z(f^{m+1}) \le \mathrm{bs}(f^{m+1}) \le \mathrm{fbs}(f^2)\cdot\mathrm{bs}(f^{m-1}) \le n^2\cdot 2\cdot 2^n\,.$$

By Lemma D.3 and Theorem 2 we have for all $\ell\in\mathbb{N}$:

$$\begin{aligned}\mathrm{fbs}^z(f^\ell) &\underset{\text{Thm 2}}{\le} \mathrm{C}^z(f^\ell)\\ &\underset{\text{Lemma D.3}}{\le} \mathrm{bs}^z(f^\ell)\cdot\mathrm{sens}^{1-z}(f^\ell)\\ &\le \mathrm{bs}^z(f^\ell)\cdot\mathrm{bs}^{1-z}(f^\ell)\end{aligned}$$

In particular, for $\ell \le m+1$ we have

$$\begin{aligned}r^z_\ell = \frac{\mathrm{bs}^z(f^\ell)}{\mathrm{fbs}^z(f^\ell)} &\ge \frac{1}{\mathrm{bs}^{1-z}(f^\ell)}\\ &\underset{\text{Lemma D.5,4}}{\ge} \frac{1}{\mathrm{bs}^{1-z}(f^{m+1})} \ge \frac{1}{2^n\cdot 2\cdot n^2}\,.\end{aligned}$$

Next, we show that for $\ell \ge m+1$:

$$r_{\ell+1} \ge r_\ell\cdot(1 - 2^{-1-\lfloor\frac{l-(m+1)}{2}\rfloor})\,.$$

This will finish the proof as it gives a global lower bound on all r_ℓs for $\ell \ge m+1$:

$$r_\ell \ge r_{m+1}\cdot\prod_{i=1}^{\infty}(1-2^{-i})^2 \ge r_{m+1}\cdot 0.08 \ge \frac{1}{2^n\cdot 25\cdot n^2}\,.$$

Let $x = (x^0||x^1||\dots||x^{n-1})$ be the input maximizing $\text{fbs}^z(f \circ f^\ell)$. Let y be the intermediate values in the composition $f \circ f^\ell$ i.e. $y_i = f^\ell(x^i)$. For p^0, p^1 which maximizes $\text{bs}^0(f^\ell)$, $\text{bs}^1(f^\ell)$ respectively, take $\tilde{x} = (\tilde{x}^0||\tilde{x}^1||\dots||\tilde{x}^{n-1})$ to be an input such that $\tilde{x}^i = p^{y_i}$. Let $B_0, \dots, B_{k-1}$ be the minimal sensitive blocks for f on y, then the value of $\text{fbs}(f^{\ell+1})$ is the optimal value for the following linear program

$$\begin{array}{lll} \max & \sum_{j=0}^{k-1} w_j & \\ \text{s.t.} & \sum_{j:i\in B_j} w_j \le \text{fbs}(f^\ell, x^i) & \text{for all } i \in [n] \\ & w_j \ge 0 & \text{for all } j \in [k] \end{array}$$

Denoting the optimal weights by w_j^*, and taking $w_j = \lfloor w_j^* \cdot r_\ell \rfloor$ gives

$$\forall i \in [n] : \sum_{j:i\in B_j} w_j \le \text{bs}(f^\ell, \tilde{x}^i) \ .$$

Thus, $\{w_j\}_{j\in[k]}$ a feasible solution for the block sensitivity integer program for $\text{bs}(f \circ f^\ell, \tilde{x})$. As $(f \circ f^\ell)(\tilde{x}) = z$, this shows that

$$\text{bs}^z(f^{\ell+1}) \ge \text{fbs}^z(f^{\ell+1}) \cdot r_\ell - 2^n \ ,$$

hence the ratio

$$r^z_{\ell+1} = \frac{\text{bs}^z(f^{\ell+1})}{\text{fbs}^z(f^{\ell+1})} \ge r_\ell - \frac{2^n}{\text{fbs}^z(f^{\ell+1})} \ .$$

For z' which minimizes $r^{z'}_\ell$ we have

$$\begin{aligned} r^z_{\ell+1} &\ge r_\ell - \frac{2^n}{\text{fbs}^z(f^{\ell+1})} \\ &= r_\ell \left(1 - \frac{2^n}{\text{fbs}^z(f^{\ell+1})} \cdot \frac{\text{fbs}^{z'}(f^\ell)}{\text{bs}^{z'}(f^\ell)}\right) \\ &\underset{\text{Lemma D.5,3}}{\ge} r_\ell \left(1 - \frac{2^n}{\text{bs}^{z'}(f^\ell)}\right) \end{aligned}$$

Previous lemmas gives

$$\begin{aligned} \text{bs}^{z'}(f^\ell) &\underset{\text{Lemma D.4}}{\ge} \text{bs}^{z'}(f^{\ell-(m+1)}) \cdot \min_{b\in\{0,1\}} (\text{bs}^b(f^{m+1})) \\ &\underset{\text{Lemma D.5,4}}{\ge} 2^{\lfloor \frac{\ell-(m+1)}{2} \rfloor} \cdot (2 \cdot 2^n) \ . \end{aligned}$$

Thus $r_{\ell+1} \ge r_\ell \cdot (1 - 2^{-1-\lfloor \frac{\ell-(m+1)}{2} \rfloor})$, which completes the proof. $\square$

Pseudo-partitions, Transversality and Locality: A Combinatorial Characterization for the Space Measure in Algebraic Proof Systems*

Ilario Bonacina
Dipartimento di Informatica
Sapienza Università di Roma
via Salaria, 113
Rome, Italy
bonacina@di.uniroma1.it

Nicola Galesi
Dipartimento di Informatica
Sapienza Università di Roma
via Salaria, 113
Rome, Italy
galesi@di.uniroma1.it

ABSTRACT

We devise a new combinatorial framework for proving space lower bounds in algebraic proof systems like Polynomial Calculus (PC) and Polynomial Calculus with Resolution (PCR). Our method can be thought as a Spoiler-Duplicator game, which is capturing boolean reasoning on polynomials instead that clauses as in the case of Resolution. Hence, for the first time, we move the problem of studying the space complexity for algebraic proof systems in the range of 2-players games, as is the case for Resolution.

A very simple case of our method allows us to obtain all the currently known space lower bounds for PC/PCR (CT_n, PHP^m_n, BIT-PHP^m_n, XOR-PHP^m_n). The way our method applies to all these examples explains how and why all the known examples of space lower bounds for PC/PCR are an application of the method originally given by [1] that holds for set of contradictory polynomials having high degree. Our approach unifies in a clear way under a common combinatorial framework and language the proofs of the space lower bounds known so far for PC/PCR.

More importantly, using our approach in its full potentiality, we answer to the open problem [1, 30] of proving space lower bounds in Polynomial Calculus and Polynomials Calculus with Resolution for the polynomial encoding of randomly chosen k-CNF formulas. Our result holds for $k \geqslant 4$. Then, as proved for Resolution in [9], also in PC and in PCR refuting a random k-CNF over n variables requires high space measure of the order of $\Omega(n)$. Our method also applies to the Graph-PHP^m_n, which is a PHP^m_n defined over a constant (left) degree bipartite expander graph. We develop a common language for the two examples.

*Both authors were supported by the project "The Limits of Theorem Proving" granted by John Templeton Foundation.

ITCS'13, January 9–12, 2013, Berkeley, California, USA.

Categories and Subject Descriptors

F.2.2 [**Analysis of Algorithms and Problem Complexity**]: Non Numerical Algorithms and Problems—*Complexity of Proof Procedures*; F.4.1 [**Mathematical Logic and Formal Languages**]: Mathematical Logic—*Mechanical Theorem Proving,Proof Theory*

General Terms

Theory

Keywords

Proof Complexity, Space Complexity, Polynomial Calculus, Resolution,Random k-CNF Formulae

1. INTRODUCTION

Proof complexity is a research field initiated by Cook and Reckhow [23] that studies the complexity of proving (alternatively refuting) propositional tautologies (alternatively contradictions) in different logical propositional proof systems. The historical motivation for investigating the complexity of proofs is the P vs. NP question. A proof system S is said to be *polynomially bounded* if there exists a polynomial p such that for every tautology $x \in TAUT$ there is a proof $\pi(x)$ in S of size at most $p(|x|)$. As observed in [23], one way of establishing co-NP$\neq$ NP , and hence P$\neq$ NP would be to prove that there are no polynomially bounded proof systems. One suggested approach to this problem is that of studying proof limits in always stronger proof systems. But proving that NP $\neq$ co-NP showing incrementally that examples of proof systems are not polynomially bounded seems unlikely. Rarely a universal statement is proved by proving all its instances. Nevertheless proving these lower bounds we may hope to uncover hidden computational hardness assumptions and then try to reduce the conjecture to some more approachable problem [34]. This is what is known as the *Cook's Program* in Proof Complexity. Among the most studied proof systems there are the logical systems of Resolution [41, 15] and algebraic proof systems like Polynomial Calculus [22] or Polynomial Calculus with Resolution [1].

1.1 High-level Motivations

1.1.1 Theoretical investigation of Space measure

As remarked by Razborov [39], proof complexity plays the same role in the field of feasible proofs of the role played by the Boolean Circuits/Turing Machine in the field of efficient computations. Hence *Proof Size* in Proof Complexity should be view as *Circuit-Size/Running-Time* in circuit complexity. It is then no surprise that, as for efficient computations we consider *memory occupation* as a measure of efficiency, a notion of *Proof Space Measure* was introduced also for proof systems ([28, 1]) and since then studied and investigated in depth in this field, especially for resolution ([28, 1, 9, 27, 12, 13, 36, 37, 30] among many others). As seen there is a vast bibliography on the space measure for the system of resolution. On the other hand Polynomial Calculus, though being a very well-studied proof systems when considering the size and degree complexity of a proof [22, 19, 20, 40, 38, 10, 33, 2, 32, 31], is still at the beginning of the investigation of the space measure [1, 30]. The reason being that current lower bounds techniques for Resolution space do not hold for algebraic systems that deal with polynomials.

The main motivation of our work is to contribute to the development of the theoretical study of the space complexity measure for propositional proof systems and specifically in algebraic proof systems. We design a new combinatorial framework for proving space lower bounds in algebraic systems like Polynomial Calculus (PC) and Polynomial Calculus with Resolution (PCR). Our approach unifies in a clear way under a common combinatorial framework the proofs of *all* the space lower bounds known so far for PC/PCR (CT_n, PHP^m_n, BIT-PHP^m_n, XOR-PHP^m_n). Moreover we answer to the open problem [1, 30] of proving space lower bounds in PC and PCR for the polynomial encoding of randomly chosen k-CNF formulas.

1.1.2 Finite Model Theory and Proof Complexity

Atserias [3] discovered a very interesting connection between the fields of finite model theory and propositional proof complexity. This connection was capturing the following informal reasoning: if a formula is hard to refute in Resolution, then for a bounded player should be hard to distinguish it from a satisfiable formula. This was the base for the result that encodings of combinatorial principles as propositional tautologies are hard-to-prove could serve for logical non-expressibility result via combinatorial games. The second link between finite model theory and propositional proof complexity is the tight connection between the number of pebbles needed by the an adversary (Duplicator) to win the existential-pebble game and the concept of width in Resolution. Two crucial facts relate pebble games to resolution proof complexity measures. First Feder and Vardi [29], observed that the satisfiability problem of a k-CNF formula can be identified with the homomorphism problem on relational structures. Then existential-pebble games provide a purely combinatorial characterization of resolution width. Second Ben-Sasson and Galesi [9] invented a 2-player Matching Game to study space lower bounds in Resolution k-CNF formulas. The Matching Game is essentially an existential pebble game which indeed was used by Atserias [3] to establish the connection between Finite Model Theory and Proof Complexity. The main observation is that winning strategies for the adversary in the Matching Game can be described in terms of a class of homomorphisms characterizing Duplicator winning strategies in Ehrenfeucht-Fraïssé games. As an application of this combinatorial characterization Atserias [3] and Atserias and Dalmau [4] got the impressive result relating the space and the width in resolution showing that space is lower bounded by width.

Our work can be view as a first step towards a 2-players game characterization for algebraic systems, i.e. dealing with polynomials, instead that with clauses. Our main definition (k-extendibility) characterizes the winning strategies for an adversary as a class of combinatorial objects. While for resolution the class of homomorphism is in fact a class of partial bounded boolean assignments, in our case we have *Admissible Configurations*, which are pairs containing a partition of a subset of the variables (*pseudo-partitions*) and a whole class of assignments fulfilling some locality properties (*local modifiability*). Our main definition should also be compared with the definition, given by Esteban, et al. in [27] of wining strategies for getting space lower bounds in $Res(k)$, that is a Resolution system on k-DNF.

1.1.3 SAT-Solvers and Theorem Provers

The *satisfiability* problem and the study of complexity measure related to SAT-solvers and theorem provers have recently been matter of research in proof complexity. From a proof complexity point of view an interesting feature of the modern SAT-solvers is that they are still based on the Davis-Putnam-Logemann-Loveland or DPLL procedure [26, 25] augmented with clause learning [6, 35] or similar techniques. It is well-known that the DPLL algorithm applied on UNSAT formulas produce a (tree-like) resolution refutations of that formula. This is the reason why there is a growing interests in studying (theoretically) the complexity of logical proof systems SAT-solver algorithms [6, 5, 18, 11, 17]. Indeed studying the complexity of proofs in such systems allows to understand the potential and limitations of such algorithms for SAT-solving or theorem proving.

It is well-known that the main problems of modern SAT-solvers is that of rapidly accessing huge amount of informations. Then one of the main bottleneck for these algorithms is represented by the memory occupation.

In proof complexity studying (theoretically, but driven by concrete applied industrial problems) proof size and proof space, one wants to understand how the resources of time and space are linked and how they can be optimized. We could say that the final aim might be that of studying theoretically the limit of applied SAT-solver algorithms and hopefully that of finding some theoretical results indicating how to overcome applied problems (see [6, 5, 18, 11, 17] among many other works in the area).

Polynomial Calculus (PC) is a proof systems having its algebraic base on the Gröbner Basis Algorithm. Then PC is surely one of the proof systems that have some hope of producing new insights onto the field of SAT-solvers. For instance Clegg et al., [22] showed an algorithm (based on Gröbner Algorithm) to find in polynomial time in the minimal degree required, a PC refutation of a set of polynomials. For this reason at that time there was quite some hope polynomial calculus could give raise to better SAT-solvers than those based on Resolution. There are PC-based solvers such as PolyBoRi [16], but in general they seem to be an order of magnitude slower than state-of-the-art solvers.

Our work contributes to better understand theoretically

the space measure in Polynomial Calculus. We think that our discrete combinatorial framework of the space in algebraic proof systems might open the way to better understand how to encode polynomials and devise algorithms (Theorem provers or SAT-solvers) working on polynomials but using discrete combinatorial concepts.

1.2 Contributions and Innovations

The first contribution of this work is a new method for proving space lower bounds in PCR and PCR. In our approach is not anymore a structural property of the formula (to have high initial degree) that allow one to get lower bounds. But is a semantic argument, similar to that used in Resolution. It is known [4] that in Resolution "space is lower bounded by the width" and hence width lower bounds imply space lower bounds. This connection is obtained by a characterization of the width and the space through winning strategies of the adversary in a Spoiler-Duplicator k-existential game. The definition of k-extendibility characterizes how long an adversary (Duplicator) can answer to a player (Spoiler) downloading polynomials into the memory without falling into a contradiction. This idea is close to the one used in Resolution both in the characterization of the space by Asterias and Dalmau [4] or by Esteban et al. in [27] where they independently introduced the notion of k-dynamical satisfiability to study space lower bounds in Resolution or $Res(k)$.

Given a CNF to be refuted we want to find a combinatorial characterization of the winning strategies of the adversary. In the case of Resolution these winning strategies are families $\mathcal{F}$ of of bounded-domain partial assignments (bounded-domain partial homomorphism in the language of Atserias [3, 4]) which preserve two properties: (1) closure under sub-assignments; and (2) assignments in $\mathcal{F}$ with not too big domain, can be extended to bounded-domain new assignments, still in $\mathcal{F}$, which do not create a contradiction in the unsatisfiable CNF to refute.

In our case, instead of having families of bounded-domain assignments, we have families $\mathcal{F}$ of pairs formed by two elements: (1) partitions of subsets of the variables of bounded-cardinality (*pseudo-partitions* $\mathcal{Q}$, see Definition 8); and (2) families of assignments which have a locality property over elements of the pseudo-partition ($\mathcal{Q}$-locally modifiable, see Definition 12). As in the case of Resolution these families (1) are closed under restrictions; and (2) have an extendibility property for "small"-cardinality pseudo-partitions (condition 3 of k-extendibility, see Definition 14).

The definition of k-extendibility (see Definition 14) is one of our main new concepts and encloses the core of our lower bound proof in Theorem 1. This definition should be compared with definition of winning strategies for the Duplicator in the paper by Atserias and Dalmau [4] (Definition 2) or definition about winning strategies (Definition 28) in the paper by Esteban et al. [27]. k-extendibility is one of the main innovation of our work, since it reduce space lower bounds for algebraic systems to winning strategies for combinatorial games as happening for the case of Resolution.

Our Main Theorem (Theorem 1) places a precise link between finding a k-extendible family for an unsatisfiable CNF and the space needed to refute its translation as a set of polynomials in PC or PCR. We state it here, even if we have not clarified precisely the notion of k-extendibility, to give an idea of the kind of relationship we provide between the notion of k-extendibility and space lower bounds.

> MAIN THEOREM: Let ϕ be a contradictory set of polynomials in $\mathbb{F}[V]$ and I a proper ideal in that ring. Suppose that there exists a non-empty k-extendible family of admissible configurations $\mathcal{F}$ for ϕ with respect to I. Then $Sp(\phi \vdash 1) \geqslant k/4$.

The second contribution of the paper is the following: our Main Theorem allow us to re-obtain under unique combinatorial framework and technique all the known space lower bound for PC/PCR known so far. All these lower bounds are obtained by the Main Theorem showing concrete examples of extendible families of admissible configurations of the right dimension. It is worth to mention, in our opinion, that the way we obtain these lower bounds is using only a limited part of the strength of the definition of k-extendibility. We discuss this issues in more details in the next subsection. Here is sufficient to say that in the winning strategies we provide for the known cases, we use only a very specific type of pseudo-partitions: they are subsets of a fixed (full) partition of the variables. Here we state our version of the resuls obtained in [30, 1] (see Section 4):

- $Sp(CT_n \vdash 1) \geqslant n/4$,
- $Sp(PHP_n^m \vdash 1) \geqslant n/4$,
- $Sp(XPHP_n^m \vdash 1) \geqslant (n-1)/4$,
- $Sp(BPHP_n^m \vdash 1) \geqslant n/8$.

We recall that in the case of $XPHP_n^m$ the original result in [30] is that $Sp(XPHP_n^m \vdash 1) \geqslant n/4$, so, only in this case, we obtain almost the same lower bound but not exactly the same.

As a third, and probably main contribution, we answer to the open problem [1, 30] of proving space lower bound for random k-CNF in PC/PCR. In this case we use our Main Theorem in its full potential. In building a $\Omega(n)$-extendible family of admissible configurations for a random k-CNF it is no longer sufficient to look only at *full* partitions of the variables, but we really have to deal with pseudo-partitions. One combinatorial ingredient of the construction of this family of configurations is the Matching Game of Ben-Sasson and Galesi [9] (simplified in [3]). But differently from their case, where they deal only with *matchings* in bipartite graphs, here we have to handle *multiple* matchings in bipartite graphs. Hence we extend the Matching Game to the case of multiple matchings.

Dealing with multiple matchings instead of matchings implies that to prove the required expansion property we need left degree at least 4 in the incidence bipartite graph associated to a random k-CNF. Our result (Theorem 9) then hold for $k \geqslant 4$ (see also next subsection).

> SPACE LOWER BOUND FOR RANDOM k-CNF: Let $k \geqslant 4$ be any integer, $\epsilon > 0$ any constant and $\Delta \geqslant 1$. Let $F \sim \mathcal{F}(n, \Delta, k)$ be a random k-CNF over n variables and Δn clauses. There exists a constant $c = c_{k,\Delta,\epsilon}$, $c \geqslant 1$, such that with high probability $Sp(F \vdash 1) \geqslant \frac{n}{4c}$.

Finally we prove an analogous result, and this is our fourth contribution, for the so-called Graph-Pigeonhole principle, which is a Pigeonhole principle defined over an expander bipartite graph with constant left degree. Also this theorem (Theorem 11) is proved through the techniques used to prove the result for random k-CNF.

> SPACE LOWER BOUND FOR $\mathcal{G}$-PHP: There exists a constant degree $d \geqslant 3$ bipartite graph $\mathcal{G} = (U \cup V, E)$ with $|U| = n+1$ and $|V| = n$, such that $Sp(\mathcal{G} - PHP \vdash 1) \geqslant \Omega(n/d)$.

1.3 Main Ideas, Notions and Techniques

To explain our approach to the problem we start by describing a high level proof of the main theorem, which is common to all space lower bound proofs known so far, also in Resolution.

The proofs of the space lower bound theorem are usually based on the following idea: inductively for each memory configuration $\mathcal{C}_i$, find a bounded boolean function M_i (in the case of PC/PCR a 2-CNF such that its number of clauses $|M_i|$ is less than $2Sp(\mathcal{C}_i)$) which implies the memory configuration $\mathcal{C}_i$. Such proofs include always two key ingredients: (1) a Locality Lemma ([14, 28, 1, 9, 30]) that informally says that if a configuration $\mathcal{C}_i$ is satisfiable, then it will be satisfied by an M_i properly bounded in the space of $\mathcal{C}_i$; (2) a combinatorial property that allows to keep the memory configuration still satisfiable by a M_i when we download an axiom (both logical or belonging to the formula to refute) in the memory configuration and the space used is still not too much.

One important issue in the Locality Lemma for PCR of [1] and [30] is that the 2-CNF M_i should be formed by distinct variables. It turns out that in the lower bound argument it is important to keep a sort of *independence* of the variables mentioned in the 2-CNF. In our approach this independence is realized through the elements of the pseudo-partition. We require that the variables in the 2-CNF all belongs to different elements of some pseudo-partition associated to the 2-CNF. Moreover we also require a *transversality* of the 2-CNF with respect to the pseudo-partition. That is we require that at most one variable for element of the partition can be hit in the 2-CNF. We consider the following two definitions, that are central to our work: *Transversal set* (see Definition 9) and *Transversal 2-CNF* (see Definition 15).

If a 2-CNF M implies a memory configuration $\mathcal{C}$, this means that every assignment satisfying M also satisfy $\mathcal{C}$. In our case we filter the assignments satisfying M by a k-extendible family of assignments associated to the pseudo-partition. We then use only that filtered set of assignments to satisfy the memory configuration $\mathcal{C}$.

Our Locality Lemma (Lemma 3) will then keep into account this dependence from the psuedo-partition and from the associated class of locally modifiable assignments. It is important to notice that the main strength and feature of our argument is that the pseudo-partition – and consequently the associated class of locally modifiable assignments – change dynamically with the proofs from one memory configuration to another.

At this point, for the reader who knows the proofs of space lower bound theorem in [1, 30], should be clear that while in their case, what is really modeling the space measure is the number of distinct variables mentioned in the 2-CNF (divided by 2), in our case what is important is the number of elements in the pseudo-partitions (divided by 2). This means that while an adversary can find admissible configurations associated to the memory configurations where the number of elements in the pseudo-partitions are keep bounded, then the memory configuration will be still implied by a proper 2-CNF.

Informally speaking, the proof of the Main Theorem goes as follows: suppose that we have a k-extendible family for P and, by contradiction, that the space to refute P is $< k/4$. We show, by induction on the number of memory configurations $\mathcal{C}_i$, that we are able to inductively maintain the following properties (see proof of Theorem 1 for the formal statement):

There exists a pseudo-partition $\mathcal{Q}^i$, a 2CNF M^i transversal to $\mathcal{Q}^i$ and a family of assignments $\mathcal{H}^i$, locally modifiable to $\mathcal{Q}^i$, such that the following holds:

1. *$(\mathcal{Q}^i, \mathcal{H}^i)$ is k-extendible family,*
2. *M^i satisfies $\mathcal{C}^i$ with respect $(\mathcal{Q}^i, \mathcal{H}^i)$,*
3. *$|M^i|$ is bounded by a function of the number of distinct monomials appearing in $\mathcal{C}_i$.*

In the case of an axiom download we maintain the properties by k-extendibility. This property guarantees us that if the pseudo-partition has cardinality strictly smaller than k then for each axiom we are still able to find another admissible configuration that satisfies that axiom through its associated set of locally modifiable assignments and has a most one element more in the pseudo-partition. Hence under the hypothesis that the space is $< k/4$, using $k-$extendibility, we can maintain the inductive property.

Similarly in the case of an erasure of some polynomial from the memory we maintain the inductive property by the Locality Lemma and by the closure by restrictions of the k-extendible family provided by the hypothesis of the Theorem. So we obtain the contradiction that the final configuration is satisfiable.

Let's se now how we can apply the Main Theorem to particular families. First of all we notice that the Main Theorem does not rely on the degree of the monomials in the set of polynomials to refute. This is an essential feature to get lower bounds for the space of refuting families of polynomials with small degree. But the theorem applies also to cases in which initials monomials are of high degree (as in the case of PHP^m_n), but giving in this form slightly worse results of what is currently known (see Section 4 for details). We discuss the example of the PigeonHole Principle to introduce our applications.

PHP^m_n is defined over the variables are x_{ij} for all $i \in [m]$ and $j \in [n]$. The axioms in PHP^m_n are: (1) $\neg x_{ij} \vee \neg x_{i'j}$ for all $i \neq i'$ and for all $j \in [n]$; (2) $x_{i1} \vee x_{i2} \vee \ldots \vee x_{in}$ for all $i \in [m]$.

As *full* partition we choose $\mathcal{P} = \{P_1, \ldots, P_n\}$, where $P_j = \{x_{ij} \mid i \in [m]\}$. Informally speaking we define $\mathcal{F}$ as the family of admissible configurations defined by all the pairs $(\mathcal{Q}, \mathcal{H})$ such that $\mathcal{Q} \subseteq \mathcal{P}$ and $\mathcal{H}$ is the family of all the injective assignments of some pigeons into the holes named in $\cup\mathcal{Q}$.

The family $\mathcal{F}$ defined above is n-extendible for PHP^m_n (see Section 4 for all the technical details for this result). We discuss our approach with this example in hand. The main point in the argument [1] was that assuming (by contradiction) that the space used is small, then each time we download a high degree axiom in the memory, we are sure to find at least two *new* variables we can use to build a new 2-CNF that implies the new memory configuration. In our case, instead, we have that axioms of high degree are *transversal* to each element of the *full* partition of the variables. Since the space is (by contradiction) small, then we are able to find two elements of the partition where two find (in each of them) a new variable that we can use to form our new 2-CNF that implies the new memory configuration. As one can notice, this is easy in the case the PHP_n^m, since the axioms are of high degree and then, defining the proper partition, they hit all the element of the partition. Under the assumption the space is small, this guarantees us to find always new elements of the partitions where to pick new variables. Moreover we can satisfy the *small axioms* basically by definition of the family $\mathcal{F}$.

As a matter of fact the same reasoning, that is *fixing a constant full partition of the variables*, is valid to get the lower bounds also for $BPHP_n^m$ and $XPHP_n^m$, which do not have high initial degree. In this sense these cases are an application of the method used by [1] for CT_n and PHP_n^m. This is since the particular syntactical properties of these encodings.

If, as in the case of random k-CNF or of the Graph-PHP, we do not have high degree initial axioms, then this reasoning is not valid anymore. Fixing a full partition at the beginning is not useful anymore. We need another way of capturing the idea that "small space memory configurations can be satisfied by 2-CNF". The way we implement this is as follows:

- We use the (multiple) matching game to identify at each step of the proofs what are the variables involved in a possible 2-CNF that implies the memory configuration. This is not new, since Ben-Sasson and Galesi in [9] where doing exactly this for Resolution. But instead of multiple matchings they had simple matchings and instead of 2-CNF they have assignments (i.e. 1-CNF).
- We handle, by the mechanism of the pseudo-partition and admissible configurations, the changing of the variables involved from one memory configuration to the other as modeled by the multiple Matching Game. Hence pseudo-partitions and the associated families of locally modifiable assignments might change in passing from one memory configuration to the sequent one.

In particular for random k-CNF and the Graph-PHP we dynamically maintain a property, the (r, s)-*double matching property* (see below and Definition 18), that allows us to identify dynamically for each memory configuration a set of initial clauses we are satisfying (in addition to the actual memory configuration). Moreover we can keep that set of initial clauses satisfied by using variables that we can consider "independent" and we capture this notion of independence by using pseudo-partitions and locally modifiable families of assignments.

> (r, s)-DOUBLE MATCHING PROPERTY: Let $r \leqslant s$, $\mathcal{G} = (U \cup V, E)$ a bipartite graph and $A \subseteq U$ of size at most $r \leqslant s$ and $B \subseteq V \cap N_{\mathcal{G}}(A)$. We say that $(\mathcal{G}, A, B)$ has the (r, s)-*double matching property* if for every $C \subseteq U \backslash A$, if $|C| = s - |A|$ then there exists a 2-matching of C into $V \backslash B$.

The idea behind this definition is to focus on the extension of an existing multiple matching, i.e. how in the Matching Game Duplicator can continue the game, hiding all the details on how Spoiler and Duplicator arrived to that configuration of the game but focusing only on the current configuration. In the previous definition the sets A and B play the role of the actual configuration of the game: we are not interested in how is constructed the multiple matching inside the sets A and B (and we inductively construct that multiple matching) to extend. The aim of that definition is to guarantee Duplicator that no matters how he and Spoiler arrived to a configuration, Duplicator can always make his move. Clearly this is a game very close to the Matching Game developed in [9, 3]. See Section 5 for all the details of how we succeed to use this game on a bipartite graph to obtain an $\Omega(n)$-extendible family for the Random k-CNF and Graph-PHP. The only detail of that construction we want to focus is the definition of expansion we need to dynamically maintain the (r, s)-double matching property. That is a stronger notion of expansion than the ones usually used (see [9, 3]) because we need to provide the existence of a *multiple* matchings (actually double matchings). The precise notion of expansion we use is the following (Definition 7).

> (s, ϵ)-BIPARTITE EXPANSION: Let $\mathcal{G} = (U \cup V, E)$ a bipartite graph. We say that $\mathcal{G}$ is an (s, ϵ)-*bipartite expander* if
>
> $$\forall A \subseteq U,\ |A| \leqslant s \longrightarrow |N_{\mathcal{G}}(A)| \geqslant (2 + \epsilon)|A|.$$

Due to this stronger requirement on the expansion we obtain our lower bound for random k-CNF for $k \geqslant 4$.

1.4 Organization

The paper is organized as follows: Section 2 contains all the preliminary definitions on algebraic proof systems, partial assignments and graph properties we need in the paper. Section 3 starts with the definition of our main concepts of *pseudo-partitons*, *local modifiability* and *k-extendibility*, then includes The Locality Lemma in Subsection 3.2 and finally its last Subsection 3.3 is entirely devoted to the proof of our Main Theorem on space lower bounds. Section 4 includes as an application of our method the proofs of all the previously known space lower bounds for PC/PCR. Section 5 contains the proof of the lower bounds for random k-CNF and for the Graph Pigeonhole Principle. Last Section deals with future research questions opened by our work.

2. PRELIMINARY DEFINITIONS

We denote by x a Boolean variable. A literal l is either a variable or its negation. A clause $C = (l_1 \vee \ldots \vee l_k)$ is a disjunction of literals. We think of clauses as sets, so that the ordering of the literals is irrelevant and no literals are repeated. A clause containing at most k literals is called a k-clause. A CNF formula $\phi = C_1 \wedge \ldots \wedge C_m$ is a conjunction of clauses. We will think of CNF formulas as sets of clauses. A k-CNF formula is a CNF formula consisting of k-clauses. A clause C is a clause over a set of variables V if the set of variables it mentions is a subset of V . We similarly define CNFs over V.

We use the standard notation $Var(\phi)$ to denote the set of the variables mentioned in the formula ϕ.

2.1 Algebraic Proof systems and Space Measure in Proof Complexity

Polynomial Calculus (PC) is a refutational system defined in [22], and based on the ring $\mathbb{F}[x_1, \ldots, x_n]$ of polynomials. Given $p \in \mathbb{F}[x_1, \ldots, x_n]$ we always consider equations of the form $p = 0$, and we simply denote them as p. The equations are intended to hold on $\{0,1\}^n$ thus the system contains the following logical axioms:

$$x_i^2 - x_i, \quad i \in [n] \ \textit{(Boolean Axioms)}.$$

Moreover it has two rules. For any $\alpha, \beta \in \mathbb{F}$, p, q polynomials and variable x:

$$\frac{p \quad q}{\alpha p + \beta q} \ \textit{(Linear Combination)}, \qquad \frac{p}{xp} \ \textit{(Multiplication)}.$$

A PC proof of a polynomial g from a set of initial polynomials $f_1, \ldots, f_m$ (denoted by $f_1, \ldots, f_m \vdash g$) is a sequence of polynomials where each one is either an initial one, a logical axiom, or it is obtained applying one of the rules to previously derived polynomials. A PC refutation is a proof of the polynomial 1.

PC is a complete proof system, in the sense that a polynomial g has a PC proof from a set of polynomials E iff $g(\vec{x}) = 0$ for every $\vec{x} \in \{0,1\}^n$ which is a common root of E. Moreover E has no common $\{0,1\}$ solutions (we call E contradictory) iff $1 \in \mathit{Span}(E \cup \{x_i^2 - x_i\}_{i \in [n]})$. Completeness of PC comes as a corollary of Hilbert's Nullstellensatz (see [24]) and from complete algorithms based on Gröebner bases [22].

We remark here that when we work in Polynomial Calculus, we implicitly assume that the polynomials $\{x_i^2 - x_i\}_{i \in [n]}$ are always included in the set of initial polynomials.

Given a PC proof Π, the *degree* of Π, $deg(\Pi)$, is the maximal degree of a polynomial in the proof; the *size* of Π, $S(\Pi)$, is the number of monomials in the proof, the *length* of Π, $|\Pi|$, is the number of lines in the proof.

Following what done in [28, 1] for studying space complexity in Resolution and general sequential proof systems, we view a proof in PC as similar to a non-deterministic Turing machine computation, with a working memory where all derivation steps are saved and a special read-only input tape from which the initials polynomials being refuted (the axioms) can be downloaded. Thus the length of a proof is essentially the time of the computation while the space measures the memory consumption. Following [1] we have:

Definition 1. (MEMORY CONFIGURATION) A *Memory Configuration* is a set of polynomials. Given $\{f_1, \ldots, f_m\}$ a set of initials polynomials and a polynomial g, a PC proof Π of $f_1, \ldots, f_m \vdash g$ can be view as sequence of memory configurations $\Pi = \{\mathcal{C}_0, \ldots, \mathcal{C}_l\}$ such that: $\mathcal{C}_0 = \varnothing$, $\mathcal{C}_l$ contains g and for all $i \in [l]$, $\mathcal{C}_i$ is obtained by $\mathcal{C}_{i-1}$ by one of the following three rules:

Axiom Download $\mathcal{C}_i = \mathcal{C}_{i-1} \cup \{p\}$, where p is some initial polynomial $f_j \in F$ or some boolean axiom.

Inference Adding $\mathcal{C}_i = \mathcal{C}_{i-1} \cup \{p\}$, where p is some polynomial inferred by using one of the rule of the calculus applied on polynomials occurring in $\mathcal{C}_{i-1}$.

Erasure $\mathcal{C}_i = \mathcal{C}_{i-1} \backslash \{p\}$, for some $p \in \mathcal{C}_{i-1}$.

Following [1] we define the the *space* measure for PC.

Definition 2. (SPACE MEASURE) The *space* of a PC memory configuration $\mathcal{C}$, $Sp(\mathcal{C})$ is the number of distinct monomials occurring in $\mathcal{C}$. The space of a PC proof Π, $Sp(\Pi)$), is the maximal space of a memory configuration in Π. The space of proving g from $\{f_1 \ldots, f_m\}$ in PC,

$$Sp(\{f_1 \ldots, f_m\} \vdash g),$$

is the minimal space over all possible PC proofs of g from $\{f_1 \ldots, f_m\}$.

The standard polynomial translation tr of CNF formulas into polynomials is defined as follows:

$$tr(x) = x \qquad tr(\neg x) = (1 - x) \qquad tr(\bigvee_{i=1}^{n} l_i) = \prod_{i=1}^{n} tr(l_i)$$

When we refer to PC refutations of some family of CNF formulas we always mean refutations of the family of polynomial translation of the CNF formulas.

Polynomial Calculus with Resolution (PCR) [1] is a refutational system which extends PC to polynomials in the ring $\mathbb{F}[x_1, \ldots, x_n, \bar{x}_1, \ldots, \bar{x}_n]$, where $\bar{x}_1, \ldots, \bar{x}_n$ are new formal variables. PCR includes the axioms and rules of PC plus a new set of logical axioms defined by

$$1 - x_i - \bar{x}_i \quad i \in [n]$$

to force $\bar{x}$ variables to have the opposite values of x variables. The standard polynomial translation tr of CNF formulas into polynomials in $\mathbb{F}[x_1, \ldots, x_n, \bar{x}_1, \ldots, \bar{x}_n]$ is the following:

$$tr(x) = x \qquad tr(\neg x) = \bar{x} \qquad tr(\bigvee_{i=1}^{n} l_i) = \prod_{i=1}^{n} tr(l_i)$$

When we refer to PCR refutations of some family of CNF formulas we always mean refutations of the family of polynomial obtained by the translation above applied to the CNFs.

We extend to PCR the definitions of proof, refutation, degree, size and length and space given for PC. Observe that using the linear transformation $\bar{x} \mapsto 1 - x$, any PCR refutation can be converted into a PC refutation without increasing the degree. As noticed above such transformation could cause an exponential increase in size. When in the next we refer to space we omit to say if we are in PC or PCR.

2.2 Partial Assignments

Let V be a set of variables, we say that an application $\alpha : V \longrightarrow \{0, 1, \star\}$ is a *partial (boolean) assignment* over V. The *domain* of α is $dom(\alpha) = \alpha^{-1}(\{0,1\})$. If $x \in dom(\alpha)$ we say that α is *assigning* a value to x.

We denote with $\varnothing$ the empty set and the partial assignment with empty domain, i.e. the assignment mapping each variable to $\star$. It will be clear from the context if we are talking about sets or assignments.

Given two partial assignments α and β such that $\alpha(x) = \beta(x)$ for each $x \in dom(\alpha) \cap dom(\beta)$. We define the partial assignment $\alpha \cup \beta$:

$$\alpha \cup \beta(x) = \begin{cases} \alpha(x) & \text{if } x \in dom(\alpha), \\ \beta(x) & \text{if } x \in dom(\beta), \\ \star & \text{otherwise.} \end{cases}$$

We say that a partial assignment β *extends* another partial assignment α if $dom(\alpha) \subseteq dom(\beta)$ and for all $x \in dom(\alpha)$, $\beta(x) = \alpha(x)$. We write $\alpha \subseteq \beta$.

Given a partial assignment α and $A \subseteq V$ we define the restriction $\alpha\restriction_A$:

$$\alpha\restriction_A(x) = \begin{cases} \alpha(x) & \text{if } x \in A, \\ \star & \text{otherwise.} \end{cases}$$

Given a clause C (or a polynomial P) we can substitute each variable x appearing in C (or P) with the value α is assigning to x, if $x \in dom(\alpha)$, or leave x untouched if $x \notin dom(\alpha)$. We denote the result of this operation with $\alpha(C)$.

If $x \notin dom(\alpha)$ we emphasize that $\alpha(x^2 - x) = x^2 - x \neq 0$.

Definition 3. ($\models$ FOR FORMULAS) Let C be a boolean formula and α a partial assignment over the variables appearing in C. We say that α *models* C, $\alpha \models C$ if $\alpha(C) = 1$.

Let $\mathcal{A}$ be a family of partial assignments, $\mathcal{A} \models C$ if for each $\alpha \in \mathcal{A}$ $\alpha \models C$.

If we are in PCR, i.e. we have a set of variables V and $\overline{V} = \{\overline{x} \mid x \in V\}$, and α is a partial assignment over V we can define clearly a partial assignment α^* over $V \cup \overline{V}$ extending α such that if $x \in dom(\alpha)$ then $\alpha^*(x + \overline{x} - 1) = 0$. Clearly is possible to do that defining

$$\alpha^*(\overline{x}) = \begin{cases} 1 - \alpha(x) & \text{if } x \in dom(\alpha), \\ \star & \text{otherwise.} \end{cases}$$

In the following we *always* suppose we are working with partial assignments over $V \cup \overline{V}$ of this sort. We do that referring explicitly only to the variables in V but every time we have a partial assignment α over V we implicitly are referring to the assignment α^*.

Definition 4. ($\models_I$ FOR POLYNOMIALS) Let V a set of variables and $\mathbb{F}[V]$ a ring of polynomials. Let I be a proper ideal in $\mathbb{F}[V]$ and p be a polynomial in $\mathbb{F}[V]$ and α a partial assignment. We say that α *models* p, $\alpha \models_I p$ if $\alpha(p) \in I$. If I it's clear from the context we'll omit the subscript.

Let $\mathcal{A}$ be a family of partial assignments, $\mathcal{A} \models_I p$ if for each $\alpha \in \mathcal{A}$ $\alpha \models_I p$. Analogously if we have a family of polynomials.

OBSERVATION 1. *Let V a set of variables and $\mathbb{F}[V]$ a ring of polynomials. Let I be a proper ideal in $\mathbb{F}[V]$, $P \subset \mathbb{F}[V]$ a set of polynomials and α a partial assignment. If $\alpha \models_I P$ then $\alpha \models_I Span(P)$. So in particular if P is a contradictory set of polynomials we have that for every partial assignment α and for every proper ideal I $\alpha \not\models_I P$.*

Definition 5. Let V a set of variables and $\mathbb{F}[V]$ a ring of polynomials. Let I be a proper ideal in $\mathbb{F}[V]$ and α a partial assignment we'll say that α *respects* I if

$$\forall p \in I \quad \alpha(p) \in I.$$

It's clear that partial boolean assignments respect the proper ideal $Span(\{x_i^2 - x_i, x_i + \overline{x_i} - 1\}_{i=1,\dots,n})$.

2.3 Graph properties and notations

Let $\mathcal{G} = (U \cup V, E)$ be a bipartite graph of left degree at most d.

Definition 6. (MULTIPLE MATCHING) Consider a bipartite graph $\mathcal{G} = (U \cup V, E)$ be a bipartite graph and $\pi \subseteq E$. Let $\pi(u) = \{v \in V \mid (u, v) \in \pi\}$. We say that π is a *matching* of $A \subseteq U$ if

1. $\pi \subseteq A \times V$,
2. for every u and u' in A $\pi(u)$ and $\pi(u')$ are disjoint non-empty sets.

If for every $u \in A$ $|\pi(u)| = 2$ we say that π is a 2-*matching* of A. If for every $u \in A$ $|\pi(u)| \geqslant 2$ we say that π is a *multiple matching* of A.

Given a set $A \subseteq U$ of nodes, we define $\pi(A) = \{\pi(u) \mid u \in A\}$ and we denote by $\cup\pi(A)$ the set of variables in $\pi(A)$.

We use the following notion of expansion on bipartite graphs.

Definition 7. ((s, ϵ)-BIPARTITE EXPANSION) Let $\mathcal{G} = (U \cup V, E)$ a bipartite graph. We say that $\mathcal{G}$ is an (s, ϵ)-*bipartite expander* if

$$\forall A \subseteq U,\ |A| \leqslant s \longrightarrow |N_{\mathcal{G}}(A)| \geqslant (2 + \epsilon)|A|.$$

Notice that our expansion factor is $(2 + \epsilon)$ instead than the usual $(1 + \epsilon)$.

We use the standard notation $N_{\mathcal{G}}(A)$ to indicate the neighborhood of A in the graph $\mathcal{G}$. We use the following application of Hall's Theorem proved in [1] (Corollary 4.16).

LEMMA 1 ([1]). *Let $\mathcal{G} = (U \cup V, E)$ be a bipartite graph. For every set $A \subseteq U$, if $|N_{\mathcal{G}}(A)| \geqslant 2|A|$, then there is a 2-matching of U in V.*

Notice that we have that if $A \subseteq U$ is the smallest set such that we cannot find a 2-matching of A in $\mathcal{G}$, then we have that $|N_{\mathcal{G}}(A)| < 2|A|$. Moreover if $\mathcal{G} = (U \cup V, E)$ is a (s, ϵ)-bipartite expander then, from the previous lemma, every subset of U of size at most s admit a 2-matching.

2.3.1 The Matching Game

If a bipartite graph $\mathcal{G} = (U \cup V, E)$ is such that $|V| > |U|$, then there is no perfect matching of U into V. Ben-Sasson and Galesi [9] introduced a 2-player game *the Matching Game* to prove this claim, using "limited space". The two players are a Prover and a Disprover. Prover tries to prove that there is no matching from U to V, and Disprover tries to prove that such a matching exists. Each player has k fingers. In each round of the game, Prover may place a finger over an uncovered node in U or remove a finger from a covered node in U. If Prover places a finger over node $u \in U$, Disprover must place her corresponding finger over an uncovered node in $N_{\mathcal{G}}(u)$. If Prover removes a finger from a node in U, Disprover must remove her corresponding finger from V. The game is over when Disprover is not able to answer to a move of the Prover. In that case, we say that Prover wins the game. If Disprover can make the game go on forever, we say that Disprover wins the game. Notice that at every non-final round, the fingers placed on U determine a partial matching of U into V. The goal of Disprover is to maintain a partial matching forever. The Matching Game was used by Atserias in [3] where he gave a more compact treatment of main properties. In Section 5 we extend the Matching Game to deal with *multiple matchings* in bipartite graphs instead that simply matchings. We refer to the notation developed in [3].

3. A COMBINATORIAL FRAMEWORK FOR SPACE LOWER BOUNDS

In this section we consider fixed a set V of variables, a ring of polynomials $\mathbb{F}[V]$, a contradictory set of polynomials ϕ included in $\mathbb{F}[V]$ and a proper ideal I in $\mathbb{F}[V]$.

3.1 k-extendibility: preserving axioms satisfiability

Let V be the set of variables appearing in some contradictory set of polynomials ϕ. We start introducing the main notions we use in the paper.

Definition 8. (PSEUDO-PARTITION) A *pseudo-partition* on a set of variables V is a collection of *disjoint* sets $\mathcal{Q} = \{Q_1, \ldots, Q_t\}$, such that each $Q_i \subseteq V$. We use the notation $\cup\mathcal{Q}$ to denote the set of variables occurring in all elements of $\mathcal{Q}$.

Definition 9. (TRANSVERSAL SET) Let $\mathcal{Q} = \{Q_1, \ldots, Q_t\}$ be a pseudo-partition over V. We say that a set $A \subseteq V$ of variables is *transversal* to $\mathcal{Q}$ if $\forall Q_i \in \mathcal{Q}\ |Q_i \cap A| \leqslant 1$.

We now introduce a class of *relevant* assignments with respect to pseudo-partitions. In the rest of the paper we are going to deal always with assignments from this class. First we need some notations.

Definition 10. Let $\mathcal{H}$ be family of assignments all with domain B, and let $A \subseteq B$. We define $\mathcal{H}{\restriction_A} = \{\alpha{\restriction_A} \mid \alpha \in \mathcal{H}\}$. If we have that $\mathcal{Q}$ is a pseudo-partition s.t. $\cup\mathcal{Q} \subseteq B$ we'll write $\mathcal{H}{\restriction_\mathcal{Q}}$ to indicate $\mathcal{H}{\restriction_{\cup\mathcal{Q}}}$

Definition 11. Let A and B be two families of partial assignments such that for each $\alpha \in A$ and $\beta \in B$ $dom(\alpha) \cap dom(\beta) = \varnothing$, then we define

$$A \times B = \{\alpha \cup \beta \mid \alpha \in A,\ \beta \in B\}.$$

Definition 12. ($\mathcal{Q}$-LM FAMILY OF ASSIGNMENTS) Let $\mathcal{Q} = \{Q_1, \ldots, Q_t\}$ be a pseudo-partition over V and $H_1, \ldots, H_t$ families of partial assignments such that the domain of every partial assignments in H_i is Q_i. A family of assignments $\mathcal{H} = H_1 \times \ldots \times H_t$ is *$\mathcal{Q}$-locally-modifiable* (we abbreviate by *$\mathcal{Q}$-lm*) with respect to I if and only if:

1. $\forall H_i \in \{H_1, \ldots, H_t\}$ $\forall \alpha \in H_i$ α is respecting I,

2. $\forall Q_i \in \mathcal{Q}$ $\forall x \in Q_i$ $\exists \alpha_0, \alpha_1 \in H_i$ such that $\alpha_1(x) = 1$ and $\alpha_0(x) = 0$.

The main properties of a set $\mathcal{H}$ of $\mathcal{Q}$-lm assignments are made up to guarantee a sort of independence of the assignments in each element of the pseudo-partition $\mathcal{Q}$.

We now give one easy example of a locally modifiable class of assignments to illustrate better our definition. We use the polynomial ring $\mathbb{F}[x, y, z, w]$ and the proper ideal $I = Span(x^2 - x, y^2 - y, z^2 - z)$.

Assume to have a pseudo-partition $\mathcal{Q} = \{\{x, y\}, \{z\}\}$ and let us describe $\mathcal{H}$ as a table. Let H_{xy} and H_z the followings:

$H_{xy} =$

x	y
0	0
1	1

and $H_z =$

z
0
1

.

So $\mathcal{H} = H_{xy} \times H_z$ is the following class of assignments:

$\mathcal{H} =$

x	y	z
0	0	1
1	1	1
0	0	0
1	1	0

.

Notice that we when required that each block of the product has to be respectful with respect to the ideal I, we automatically have that the full family $\mathcal{H}$ is respectful of I.

We are interested in (partial) assignments with domain transversal to a pseudo-partition $\mathcal{Q}$, i.e. assigning at most one variable in each element of $\mathcal{Q}$. According to Definition 9 we call this kind of assignments *transversal* to a pseudo-partition $\mathcal{Q}$. One useful observation is the following:

OBSERVATION 2. *Let $\mathcal{Q}$ be a pseudo-partition and α a partial assignment over the variables $\cup\mathcal{Q}$ transversal to $\mathcal{Q}$. Let $\mathcal{H}$ be $\mathcal{Q}$-lm with respect to I. Then there exists a $\beta \in \mathcal{H}$ that extends α.*

PROOF. Let $\delta \in \mathcal{H}$ be an assignment such that $A_\delta = \{x \in dom(\alpha) \mid \alpha(x) \neq \delta(x)\}$ has the minimal size among all the possible assignments in $\mathcal{H}$. If, by contradiction, $A_\delta \neq \varnothing$ we can find a variable $x \in A_\delta$. Let $Q_x \in \mathcal{Q}$ the only element in $\mathcal{Q}$ containing x: we can decompose $\mathcal{H}$ as $\mathcal{H}' \times H_x$, where H_x is a family of assignments with domain Q_x and respecting the properties of the definition of $\mathcal{Q}$-lm family.

By property 2 of $\mathcal{Q}$-lm family we can find an assignment $\beta \in H_x$ such that $\alpha(x) = \beta(x)$. By definition of $\mathcal{Q}$-lm family we have that $\delta' = \beta \cup \delta{\restriction_{\mathcal{Q}\setminus\{Q_x\}}}$ is in $\mathcal{H}$ but $A_{\delta'}$ has size one less than A_δ. In fact we have that β is not assigning a value to any of the variables of $dom(\alpha)$ except for x because α is transversal to $\mathcal{Q}$. For the minimality of A_δ this is absurd, so we must have that $A_\delta = \varnothing$. □

Notice that in the previous proof we have not used property (1) of the definition of $\mathcal{Q}$-lm family: we'll require that property later.

Pseudo-partitions and locally modifiable families of assignments are combinatorial objects that will play central role in our main theorem. To manage them together we introduce the notion of admissible configurations.

Definition 13. (ADMISSIBLE CONFIGURATION) Let V be a set of variables. An *admissible configuration* with respect to I is a pair $(\mathcal{Q}, \mathcal{H})$ such that: (1) $\mathcal{Q}$ is a pseudo-partition over V and (2) $\mathcal{H}$ is $\mathcal{Q}$-lm with respect to I.

Notice that the configuration $(\varnothing, \{\varnothing\})$ is admissible. The next Observation and Lemma are about basic properties of admissible configurations below the operations of restriction and extension.

OBSERVATION 3. *If $\mathcal{Q}' \subseteq Q$ and $(\mathcal{Q}, \mathcal{H})$ is an admissible configuration, then $(\mathcal{Q}', \mathcal{H}{\restriction_{\mathcal{Q}'}})$ is an admissible configuration.*

The next Lemma is one of the tool we use to extend locally-modifiable families of assignments. It captures the way we can build a class of locally-modifiable assignments starting from assignments local to a set of variables. In the next, in all examples of formulas for which we need to build a family of locally modifiable assignments, we are going to use this easy lemma.

LEMMA 2. *Let $(\mathcal{Q},\mathcal{H})$ be an admissible configuration. Let A be a subset of the variables $V\backslash \cup \mathcal{Q}$ and Σ be a family of assignments $\{A\}$-lm with respect to I. Then $(\mathcal{Q}\cup\{A\},\mathcal{H}\times\Sigma)$ is an admissible configuration.*

Moreover, given a set of polynomials P over the variables V such that $\mathcal{H} \models_I P$ or such that $\Sigma \models_I P$, then $\mathcal{H}\times\Sigma \models_I P$.

PROOF. Clearly $\mathcal{Q} \cup \{A\}$ is a pseudo-partition, and it's easy to see that $\mathcal{H} \times \Sigma$ is $\mathcal{Q} \cup \{A\}$-lm with respect to I: this follows from associativity of $\times$.

To show the second part of the Lemma, let's choose $\beta \in \mathcal{H}$ and $\gamma \in \Sigma$, so that $\alpha = \beta \cup \gamma \in \mathcal{H} \times \Sigma$. If $\mathcal{H} \models_I P$ then we have that $\alpha(P) = \gamma(\beta(P)) \in I$, because by hypothesis $\beta(P) \in I$ and γ respects I (by property (1) of local modifiability). If $\Sigma \models_I P$ we obtain that $\mathcal{H} \times \Sigma \models_I P$ by induction over $|\mathcal{Q}|$, where $\mathcal{Q}$ is the pseudo-partition associated to $\mathcal{H}$. □

The next definition is our main definition and encloses the core of our lower bound proof in Theorem 1. This definition should be compared with definition of winning strategies for the Duplicator in the paper by Atserias and Dalmau [4] (Definition 2) or definition about winning strategies (Definition 28) in the paper by Esteban et al. [27].

Definition 14. (k-EXTENDIBILITY) A non-empty family $\mathcal{F}$ of admissible configurations is *k-extendible* for ϕ with respect to I if and only if for every $(\mathcal{Q},\mathcal{H}) \in \mathcal{F}$ the following conditions hold:

1. $|\mathcal{Q}| \leqslant k$,
2. $\forall \mathcal{Q}' \subseteq \mathcal{Q}\ \ (\mathcal{Q}', \mathcal{H}\upharpoonright_{\mathcal{Q}'}) \in \mathcal{F}$.
3. if $|\mathcal{Q}| < k$, then $\forall p \in \phi\ \exists A \subseteq V\backslash \cup \mathcal{Q}\ \exists \Sigma\ \{A\}$-lm with respect to I such that:
   (a) $(\mathcal{Q} \cup \{A\}, \mathcal{H} \times \Sigma) \in \mathcal{F}$
   (b) $\mathcal{H} \times \Sigma \models_I p$, i.e $\forall \alpha \in \mathcal{H} \times \Sigma\ \alpha(p) \in I$.

We observe that if in the property (2) of the previous definition we choose $\mathcal{Q}' = \varnothing$ we have, as a special case, that $(\varnothing, \{\varnothing\}) \in \mathcal{F}$. Moreover we notice that in property (3) when $\mathcal{H} \models_I a$ then it is sufficient to choose $A = \varnothing$ and $\Sigma = \{\varnothing\}$. The interesting case is when $\mathcal{H} \not\models_I a$: in this case we must have that $A \neq \varnothing$ (or equivalently that $\Sigma \neq \{\varnothing\}$). This is a key point in the proof of main theorem.

3.2 Locality Lemma for 2CNFs over Admissible Configurations

Let us first introduce the main notions for the Locality Lemma. Given a formula ψ in the variables V and a pseudo-partition $\mathcal{Q}$ over V, we denote by $\mathcal{Q}_\psi$ the elements of the partition $\mathcal{Q}$ hit by $Var(\psi)$, i.e. $\mathcal{Q}_\psi = \{Q_i \in \mathcal{Q} \mid Q_i \cap Var(\psi) \neq \varnothing\}$. In particular we'll use this notation for formulas M that are 2CNFs.

According to Definition 9 we give the definition of *Transversal* 2CNF.

Definition 15. (TRANSVERSAL 2CNF) Let $\mathcal{Q}$ be a pseudo-partition over the variables V and M be a 2CNF in the variables V. We say that M is a *2CNF transversal to* $\mathcal{Q}$ iff

1. $Var(M) \subseteq \cup\mathcal{Q}$,
2. each variable in $Var(M)$ appears in exactly one literal in M,
3. $Var(M)$ is a transversal set to $\mathcal{Q}$ and moreover $\mathcal{Q}_M = \mathcal{Q}$, i.e. for each $A \in Q\ |Var(M) \cap A| = 1$.

We required that $\mathcal{Q}_M = \mathcal{Q}$ to simplify some following notations and proofs. We use the notation $|M|$ for the number of clauses in M.

Let us consider the following symbol $\models_I^{(\mathcal{Q},\mathcal{H})}$ defined only if $(\mathcal{Q},\mathcal{H})$ is an admissible configuration.

Definition 16. Let $\mathcal{Q}$ be a pseudo-partition over V, M a 2CNF and P a set of polynomials. We say that $M \models_I^{(\mathcal{Q},\mathcal{H})} P$ if and only if M is transversal to $\mathcal{Q}$, $\mathcal{H}$ is $\mathcal{Q}$-lm with respect to I and

$$\forall \alpha \in \mathcal{H}\ (\alpha \models M \longrightarrow \alpha \models_I P).$$

We observe that $M \models_I^{(\mathcal{Q},\mathcal{H})} P$ means that we are forcing ourselves to use assignments of domain $\cup\mathcal{Q}$ to satisfy M. So our definition is not simply saying that $\forall \alpha\ (\alpha \models M \longrightarrow \alpha \models_I P)$.

LEMMA 3 (LOCALITY LEMMA). *Let P be a set of polynomials, $\mathcal{Q}$ a pseudo-partition and $\mathcal{H}$ a $\mathcal{Q}$-lm family of assignments. Let M be a 2CNF transversal to $\mathcal{Q}$. If $M \models_I^{(\mathcal{Q},\mathcal{H})} P$, then there exists a pseudo-partition $\mathcal{Q}' \subseteq \mathcal{Q}$ and there exists a 2CNF M' transversal to $\mathcal{Q}'$ such that:*

- $M' \models_I^{(\mathcal{Q}',\mathcal{H}\upharpoonright_{\mathcal{Q}'})} P$ *and*
- $|M'| \leqslant 2Sp(P)$[1].

PROOF. Let us consider the bipartite graph $\mathcal{G} = (U \cup V, E)$, where U is the set of distinct monomials appearing in P, V is the set of clauses appearing in M and we have that $(m, C) \in E$ if and only if $Var(m) \cap \mathcal{Q}_C \neq \varnothing$. Let us choose a maximal set $\Gamma \subseteq U$ such that $|N_\mathcal{G}(\Gamma)| \leqslant 2|\Gamma|$. By Lemma 1, we have that $\overline{\Gamma} = V\backslash\Gamma$ admit a 2-matching into $U\backslash N_\mathcal{G}(\Gamma)$. Let $\pi = \{(m_i, C_{i,1}), (m_i, C_{i,2})\}$ be that 2-matching.

Let us see now how to construct the 2CNF M'. For each edge in π we choose a variable $x_{i,j}$, where $j = 1,2$, such that $x_{i,j} \in Var(m_i) \cap \mathcal{Q}_{C_{1,j}}$ and we consider $sat_{i,j} \in \{0,1\}$ such that every assignment that maps $x_{i,j}$ into $sat_{i,j}$ maps the monomial m_i to 0. Let us choose also the variables $y_{i,j} \in Var(C_{i,j})\backslash\mathcal{Q}_{x_{i,j}}$: we'll use later these variables. Let

$$M' = N_\mathcal{G}(\Gamma) \cup \{(x_{i,1}^{sat_{i,1}} \vee x_{i,2}^{sat_{i,2}}) \mid i \in \overline{\Gamma}\}.$$

Let $\mathcal{Q}'$ be $\mathcal{Q}\upharpoonright_{M'}$. Clearly we have that $\mathcal{Q}'$ is a pseudo-partition and that M' is a 2CNF transversal to $\mathcal{Q}'$. We set $\mathcal{H}' = \mathcal{H}\upharpoonright_{\mathcal{Q}'}$. We have that $|M'| \leqslant 2Sp(P)$, indeed:

$$|M'| = |N_\mathcal{G}(\Gamma)| + |\overline{\Gamma}| \leqslant 2|\Gamma| + |\overline{\Gamma}| \leqslant 2(|\Gamma| + |\overline{\Gamma}|) = 2Sp(P).$$

The only part of the lemma remaining to prove is that $M' \models_I^{(\mathcal{Q}',\mathcal{H}')} P$. So let $\alpha \in \mathcal{H}'$ such that $\alpha \models M'$: we have to prove that $\alpha \models_I P$. The strategy to do this is to find a $\beta \in \mathcal{H}$ st

- $\beta \models_I M$,
- $\beta(m) = \alpha(m)$ for each monomial m appearing in P.

Before going into the construction of β, let us suppose we have such a β and see how we conclude from that. We have by hypothesis that $M \models_I^{(\mathcal{H},\mathcal{Q})} P$, so, from the first property,

[1]We recall that $Sp(P)$ is the number of distinct monomials appearing in P.

we have that $\beta \models P$. By the second property we have that α and β are coincident on the monomials in P so we must have that $\alpha \models P$.

Let us go into the construction of β. We have that $\mathcal{H}{\restriction}_{\mathcal{Q}\setminus\mathcal{Q}'}$ is $(\mathcal{Q}\setminus\mathcal{Q}')$-lm and we have that exists a γ transversal to $\mathcal{Q}\setminus\mathcal{Q}'$ such that $\alpha\cup\gamma \models M$ (because M is transversal). We observe that we can choose γ such that $Var(\gamma) \subseteq \mathcal{Q}\setminus\mathcal{Q}'$. Then, by Observation 2, we have that exists $\tilde{\gamma} \in \mathcal{H}{\restriction}_{\mathcal{Q}\setminus\mathcal{Q}'}$ such that $\tilde{\gamma} \supseteq \gamma$. If we set $\beta = \alpha \cup \tilde{\gamma}$ we have by definition that $\beta \in \mathcal{H}$ and clearly $\beta \models M$.

Let us prove that $\beta(m) = \alpha(m)$ for each monomial m appearing in P. For each m_i with $i \in \overline{\Gamma}$ we have that $\alpha(m) = 0$, then clearly $\beta(m_i) = 0$ (because $\beta \supseteq \alpha$). Let us consider now the case $m \in \Gamma$. If $\alpha(m) \neq \beta(m)$ we must have that β is assigning some variable from m, so we must have that exists $y_{i,j}$ such that $\mathcal{Q}_{y_{i,j}} \cap Var(m) \neq \emptyset$. This is absurd because we have that $\mathcal{Q}_{y_{i,j}} \subseteq Q_{C_{i,j}}$, and then $Q_{C_{i,j}} \cap Var(m) \neq \emptyset$, so we should have the edge $(m, C_{i,j})$ in $\mathcal{G}$, but by construction $m \in \Gamma$ and $C_{i,j} \notin N_{\mathcal{G}}(\Gamma)$. □

3.3 Space Lower Bound Theorem

Let us consider the following straightforward observation.

OBSERVATION 4. *Let $\mathcal{Q}$ be a pseudo-partition over V, $\mathcal{H}$ $\mathcal{Q}$-locally modifiable, M a 2CNF transversal to $\mathcal{Q}$, P a set of polynomials, and p a polynomial. If $M \models_I^{(\mathcal{Q},\mathcal{H})} P$ and $\mathcal{H} \models_I p$, then $M \models_I^{(\mathcal{Q},\mathcal{H})} P \cup \{p\}$.*

THEOREM 1 (MAIN THEOREM). *Let ϕ be a contradictory set of polynomials in $\mathbb{F}[V]$ and I a proper ideal in that ring. Suppose that there exists a non-empty k-extendible family of admissible configurations $\mathcal{F}$ for ϕ with respect to I. Then the $Sp(\phi \vdash 1) \geqslant k/4$.*

PROOF. Let $\Pi = C_1, \ldots, C_s$ be a refutation of ϕ in PCR. Assume by contradiction that $Sp(\Pi) < k/4$. We prove by induction on i that there exists a pseudo-partition $\mathcal{Q}^i$, a 2CNF M^i transversal[2] to $\mathcal{Q}^i$ and a family of assignments $\mathcal{H}^i$, $\mathcal{Q}^i$-lm such that the followings hold:

1. $M_i \models_I^{(\mathcal{Q}^i,\mathcal{H}^i)} C_i$,
2. $|M_i| \leqslant 2Sp(C_i)$,
3. $(\mathcal{Q}^i, \mathcal{H}^i) \in \mathcal{F}$.

Before proving the statement by induction on i, we show that the inductive hypothesis leads to a contradiction. The inductive property (1) implies that every memory configuration can be mapped into I (if $M_i = \emptyset$ we must have that $C_i \subseteq I$). This is impossible since the last one contains the polynomial 1 so we must have that $1 \in I$ but by hypothesis I is proper.

For the base case we set: $\mathcal{Q}^0 = \emptyset$, $M^0 = \emptyset$ and $\mathcal{H}^0 = \{\emptyset\}$. (1) follows since for an assignment satisfy a memory configuration is an universal statement about the polynomials in that configuration. So the empty assignment satisfy the empty memory configuration. (2) follows since $|M^0| = Sp(C_0) = 0$; (3) follows since by definition $(\emptyset, \{\emptyset\}) \in \mathcal{F}$.

For the inductive case we distinguish three cases according with the rules to modify the memory.

[2]Remember that by definitions of transversal 2CNF this means that $\mathcal{Q}^i = \mathcal{Q}_{M^i}$.

In the ERASURE case, we apply the Locality Lemma with $M = M^i$, $\mathcal{Q} = \mathcal{Q}^i$, $\mathcal{H} = \mathcal{H}^i$ and $P = C_{i+1}$ to get $\mathcal{Q}'$ and M' satisfying the conclusions of the Lemma. We set $M^{i+1} = M'$, $\mathcal{Q}^{i+1} = \mathcal{Q}'$, $\mathcal{H}^{i+1} = \mathcal{H}^i{\restriction}_{\mathcal{Q}'}$, (1) then follows by the point (1) of the Locality Lemma. (2) follows from the point (2) of the Locality Lemma. (3) follows from the property 2 of the definition of k-extendibility.

In the INFERENCE ADDING case, we set $\mathcal{Q}^{i+1} = \mathcal{Q}^i$, $M^{i+1} = M^i$ and $\mathcal{H}^{i+1} = \mathcal{H}^i$. The result follows since C_{i+1} is a subset of the ideal generated by C_i and $\mathcal{H}^i \models_I Span(C_i)$ (by Observation 1). Clearly we have $Sp(C_i) < Sp(C_{i+1})$.

In the AXIOM DOWNLOAD case, i.e. $C_{i+1} = C_i \cup \{a\}$ with $a \in \phi$. We distinguish two cases: $\mathcal{H}^i \models_I a$ and $\mathcal{H}^i \not\models_I a$.

If $\mathcal{H}^i \models_I a$, then we set $\mathcal{Q}^{i+1} = \mathcal{Q}^i$, $M^{i+1} = M^i$ and $\mathcal{H}^{i+1} = \mathcal{H}^i$. We have now that (1) follows by Observation 4, (2) since $Sp(C_i) < Sp(C_{i+1})$ and (3) immediately from the setting.

Assume now that $\mathcal{H}^i \not\models_I a$. We claim that $|\mathcal{Q}^i| < k - 1$. We know that $|M^i| \leqslant 2Sp(C_i)$, and, by the assumption, that $Sp(C_i) < k/4 - 1$ (the -1 is since at step $i + 1$ we are downloading and axiom more into the memory). Since M^i is a transversal 2CNF to $\mathcal{Q}^i$, then $|\mathcal{Q}^i| = 2|M^i|$ and hence $|\mathcal{Q}^i| < k - 4 < k - 1$. By the claim, we can use the extendibility property of $\mathcal{F}$ on $(\mathcal{Q}^i, \mathcal{H}^i)$ and a, to conclude that there exist a $(\mathcal{Q}^i \cup \{A\}, \mathcal{H}^i \times \Sigma) \in \mathcal{F}$, such that: $\mathcal{H}^i \times \Sigma \models_I a$.

From $\mathcal{H}^i \not\models_I a$ we conclude that $\Sigma \neq \{\emptyset\}$. We can moreover suppose Σ is such that maximizes the number of initial polynomials in ϕ mapped by $\mathcal{H}^i \times \Sigma$ in I. Let us call $\tilde{\phi}$ this set of polynomials such that $\mathcal{H}^i \times \Sigma \models_I \tilde{\phi}$. Clearly $a \in \tilde{\phi}$. By Observation 1 we can't have that $\mathcal{H}^i \times \Sigma \models_I \phi$, because ϕ is contradictory and I is proper.

So we must have that $\tilde{\phi}$ is a proper subset of ϕ, then there exists a polynomial $b \in \phi$ such that $\mathcal{H} \times \Sigma \not\models_I b$. Observe that $|\mathcal{Q}^i \cup \{A\}| < k$ (since $|\mathcal{Q}^i| < k - 1$), hence we can apply the extendibility property for a second time on $(\mathcal{Q} \cup \{A\}, \mathcal{H}^i \times \Sigma)$ and b. We then have a pair $(\mathcal{Q}^i \cup \{A\} \cup \{B\}, \mathcal{H} \times \Sigma \times \Sigma') \in \mathcal{F}$ such that $\mathcal{H}^i \times \Sigma \times \Sigma' \models_I b$. We can't have that $\Sigma' = \{\emptyset\}$ because $\mathcal{H}^i \times \Sigma \not\models_I b$.

Now we are ready to set our new parameters: $\mathcal{Q}^{i+1} = \mathcal{Q}^i \cup \{A\} \cup \{B\}$, $\mathcal{H}^{i+1} = \mathcal{H}^i \times \Sigma \times \Sigma'$. To form M^{i+1} we choose two *new* variables $x \in A$ and $y \in B$. Hence $M^{i+1} = M^i \wedge (x \vee y)$.

Property $M_{i+1} \models_I^{(\mathcal{Q}^{i+1},\mathcal{H}^{i+1})} C_i \cup \{a\}$, holds since, by applying twice Lemma 2, $\mathcal{H}^{i+1} \models C_i$ and $\mathcal{H}^{i+1} \models_I a$ (because $a \in \tilde{\phi}$). Property (2) follows since $|M^{i+1}| = |M^i| + 1 \leqslant 2Sp(C_i) + 2 = 2Sp(C_{i+1})$. (3) follows by contruction. □

4. KNOWN SPACE LOWER BOUNDS: AN UNIFIED FRAMEWORK

In this section we show how to re-obtain the known results given for CT_n and PHP_n^m by Alekhnovich et al. in [1] and the results for $BPHP_n^m$ and $XPHP_n^m$ given by Filmus et al. in [30]. Currently these are the only space known lower bounds for algebraic systems. As we see, all these cases fall into a very easy application of our main theorem. The main point in all these examples is that we do not need real pseudo-partitions that are changing from one memory configuration to the next one. In all these cases pseudo-partitions are subsets of one *full* partition of the variables fixed one for all and not changing along the proof. Hence in these cases characterizing the k-extendible family of assignment will coincide with the problem of finding an appropriate full partition of the variables to use. As we will see in the next section for random k-CNF or the Graph-PHP_n this will be not anymore the case.

Our main theorem does not depend on the degree of the monomials in the set of polynomials to refute. This is an essential feature to get lower bounds for the space of refuting families of polynomials with small degree. Our Main Theorem applies also to cases in which initials monomials are of high degree (as in the case of the pigeon hole principle or the case of complete contradictions), but giving slightly worse results of what is currently known. To get the best possible lower bound we tune our Theorem in order to apply it in his full strength also to such cases.

According to Definition 9 we introduce the notion of transversal monomial.

Definition 17. (TRANSVERSAL MONOMIAL) We say that a monomial m is *transversal* to a pseudo-partition $\mathcal{Q}$ if $Var(m)$ is a transversal set to $\mathcal{Q}$ and moreover for each $A \in \mathcal{Q}$ $|Var(m) \cap A| = 1$.

THEOREM 2. *Let $\phi = \psi \cup \mu$ a contradictory set of polynomials. Suppose that:*

1. *exists a non-empty k-extendible family of admissible configurations $\mathcal{F}$ for ψ with respect to the ideal $I = \{0\}$ and*
2. *every polynomial in μ is* monomial *at least k variables which is transversal to each pseudo-partition named in $\mathcal{F}$.*

Then, $Sp(\phi \vdash 1) \geqslant k/4$.

PROOF. The proof is the same of the Main Theorem. We use the very same notations used before. The only part we have to show is how to prove the induction properties when we download an axiom from μ. So let $\mathcal{C}_{i+1} = \mathcal{C}_i \cup \{m\}$ with $m \in \mu$.

We already noticed that $|Q^i| < k - 1$, then we have that exists a variable x in $Var(m)$ not in $\cup\mathcal{Q}^i$ by property (2). Then we can find $(\mathcal{Q}^i \cup \{A\}, \mathcal{H}^i \times \Sigma) \in \mathcal{F}$ such that, $\mathcal{H}^i \models_I x^2 - x$. Since $x \notin \cup\mathcal{Q}^i$ we must have that $x \in A$. We have that $|\mathcal{Q}^i \cup \{A\}| < k$ then again we can find a variable $y \in Var(m)$ but not in $\cup\mathcal{Q}^i \cup A$. Reasoning exactly as above we use the k-extendibility again obtaining the pair $(\mathcal{Q}^i \cup \{A\} \cup \{B\}, \mathcal{H}^i \times \Sigma \times \Sigma') \in \mathcal{F}$ and exactly as above we have that $y \in B$.

We set $\mathcal{Q}^{i+1} = \mathcal{Q}^i \cup \{A\} \cup \{B\}$, $\mathcal{H}^{i+1} = \mathcal{H}^i \times \Sigma \times \Sigma'$ and

$$M^{i+1} = M^i \wedge (x^{sat_x(m)} \vee y^{sat_y(m)}),$$

where $sat_x(m)$ e $sat_y(m)$ are the values we can give to x or y respectively to set m to zero. □

4.1 The case of CT_n

CT_n is a contradiction in the variables $x_1, \ldots, x_n$. We recall that the axioms of CT_n are *all* the possible clauses in the above n variables of width n. We choose the full partition $\mathcal{P} = \{P_1, \ldots, P_n\}$, where $P_i = \{x_i\}$. This is a trivial special case of the Theorem 2. Following the notations of that Theorem we set $I = \{0\}$, ψ all the logical axioms and $\mu = CT_n$. Then we choose as a family $\mathcal{F}$ the pairs $(\mathcal{Q}, \mathcal{H})$ where $\mathcal{Q} \subseteq \mathcal{P}$ and $\mathcal{H}$ *all* the possible partial assignments with domain $\cup\mathcal{Q}$.

PROPOSITION 1. *The family $\mathcal{F}$ is n-extendible for ψ with respect to I.*

PROOF. The restriction part is clear. The extension part goes as follows: let $a \in \psi$ and $(\mathcal{Q}, \mathcal{H}) \in \mathcal{F}$. We have that $Var(a) = \{x_i\}$. If $x_i \in \cup\mathcal{Q}$ we clearly have that $\mathcal{H} \models_I a$. If $x_i \notin \cup\mathcal{Q}$ we set $\Sigma = \{x_i \mapsto 0, x_i \mapsto 1\}$. By applying Lemma 2 have that $(\mathcal{Q} \cup \{P_i\}, \mathcal{H} \times \Sigma)$ is an admissible configuration and clearly $\mathcal{H} \times \Sigma$ are *all* the possible partial assignments with domain $\cup\mathcal{Q} \cup P_i$, so $(\mathcal{Q} \cup \{P_i\}, \mathcal{H} \times \Sigma) \in \mathcal{F}$. To conclude we observe that $\mathcal{H} \times \Sigma \models_I a$. □

THEOREM 3 ([1]). *$Sp(CT_n \vdash 1) \geqslant n/4$.*

PROOF. We proved that the family $\mathcal{F}$ is n-extendible for ψ and it's easy to see that $\mu = CT_n$ satisfy the requests of the Theorem 2. The result follows. □

We observe that for CT_n is possible to apply directly the Main Result (Theorem 1) but, it's easy to see, in that manner we obtain as lower bound $n/8$. The Theorem 2 allows us to re-obtain exactly the known lower bound.

4.2 The case of PHP_n^m

The variables are x_{ij} for all $i \in [m]$ and $j \in [n]$. The axioms in PHP_n^m are:

1. $\neg x_{ij} \vee \neg x_{i'j}$ for all $i \neq i'$ and for all $j \in [n]$;
2. $x_{i1} \vee x_{i2} \vee \ldots \vee x_{in}$ for all $i \in [m]$.

As global partition we choose $\mathcal{P} = \{P_1, \ldots, P_n\}$, where $P_j = \{x_{ij} \mid i \in [m]\}$. We want to apply again Theorem 2, so we use the ideal $I = \{0\}$. As ψ we choose all the logical axioms plus all the axioms in (1). As μ we choose all the axioms in (2).

We define $\mathcal{F}$ as the family of all the pairs $(\mathcal{Q}, \mathcal{H})$ such that $\mathcal{Q} \subseteq \mathcal{P}$ and $\mathcal{H}$ is the family of all the partial assignments of domain $\cup\mathcal{Q}$ satisfying the axioms in ψ having variables in $\cup\mathcal{Q}$.

PROPOSITION 2. *The family $\mathcal{F}$ is n-extendible for ψ with respect to I.*

PROOF. The restriction part is clear. The extension part goes as follows: let $a \in \psi$ and $(\mathcal{Q}, \mathcal{H}) \in \mathcal{F}$, with $|\mathcal{Q}| < n$. We have that there exists exactly *one* $P_j \in \mathcal{P}$ such that $Var(a) \cap P_j \neq \varnothing$. If $P_j \in \mathcal{Q}$ we clearly have that $\mathcal{H} \models_I a$. If $P_j \notin \mathcal{Q}$ we set as Σ the family of assignments with domain P_j verifying all the axioms in ψ having variables in P_j. By Lemma 2 we have that $(\mathcal{Q} \cup \{P_j\}, \mathcal{H} \times \Sigma)$ is an admissible configuration, so it's easy to see that $(\mathcal{Q} \cup \{P_j\}, \mathcal{H} \times \Sigma) \in \mathcal{F}$ and by construction $\mathcal{H} \times \Sigma \models_I a$. □

THEOREM 4 ([1]). *$Sp(PHP_n^m \vdash 1) \geqslant n/4$.*

PROOF. We proved that the family $\mathcal{F}$ is n-extendible for ψ and it's easy to see that μ satisfy the requests of the Corollary 2. The result follows. □

Similarly with what we say about CT_n, it is possible to apply directly the Main Result (Theorem 1) also to PHP_n^m but in that manner we obtain as lower bound $n/8$. We wrote the Theorem2 to re-obtain exactly the known space lower bound for PHP_n^m.

4.3 The case of $BPHP^m_n$

The *Bit Pigeon-Hole Principle* is the formalization of the Pigeon-Hole principle that uses variables x_{ij} with $i \in [m]$ and $j \in [\log n]$. The intuitive meaning of the variable $x_{ij} = 1$ is "the pigeon i goes to some hole h and the j-th bit of a binary representation of h is 1". Similarly for $x_{ij} = 0$.

The axioms of $BPHP^m_n$ are clauses telling us that two pigeons i and i' can't go into the same hole h because they differ on the some bit of the binary representation of h. More formally for each hole $h \in [n]$ we consider the binary expansion of h, $(\epsilon^h_1, \ldots, \epsilon^h_{\log(n)})_2$. If we define $B^h_{i,i'} = \bigvee_{j=1}^{\log(n)} (x_{ij} \neq \epsilon^h_j \vee x_{i'j} \neq \epsilon^h_j)$, then

$$BPHP^m_n := \left\{B^h_{i,i'} \mid h \in [n], i \neq i' \in [m]\right\}$$

is a contradiction for $m > n$. We choose a global partition of the variables $\mathcal{P} = \{P_1, \ldots, P_m\}$ where $P_i = \{x_{ij} \mid j \in [\log n]\}$. Our strategy is to apply the Main Result (Theorem 1) using the ideal $I = Span(\{x_i^2 - x_i, x_i + \overline{x_i} - 1\}_{i=1,\ldots,n})$.

Given a hole $h = (\epsilon^h_1, \ldots, \epsilon^h_{\log(n)})_2$ we define the hole $\overline{h} = (1 - \epsilon^h_1, \ldots, 1 - \epsilon^h_{\log(n)})_2$. We observe that we have a natural partition of the holes $\mathcal{S} = \{S_1, \ldots, S_{n/2}\}$, where each $S_j = \{h, \overline{h}\}$ for some hole h.

We'll use the notation $\{i \mapsto h\}$ where $i \in [m]$ and $h \in [n]$, referring to a partial assignment α with domain P_i and such that $\alpha(x_{ij}) = \epsilon^h_j$.

We are now ready to define the family $\mathcal{F}$. An admissible configuration $(\mathcal{Q}, \mathcal{H})$ is in $\mathcal{F}$ if and only if:

1. $|\mathcal{Q}| \leqslant n/2$,
2. for each $A \in \mathcal{Q}$ there exists $i, i' \in [m]$ such that $A = P_i \cup P_{i'}$, we say that the pigeons i and i' are mentioned into $\mathcal{Q}$,
3. $$\mathcal{H} = \bigtimes_{A \in \mathcal{Q}} H_A,$$
   where if $A = P_i \cup P_{i'}$, $H_A = \{\{i \mapsto h_A, i' \mapsto \overline{h_A}\}, \{i \mapsto \overline{h_A}, i' \mapsto h_A\}\}$ and moreover $\{\{h_A, \overline{h_A}\} \mid A \in \mathcal{Q}\} \subseteq \mathcal{S}$.

PROPOSITION 3. *$\mathcal{F}$ is $n/2$-extendible for to $BPHP^m_n$.*

PROOF. The restriction part is obvious. Let us see the extension part: let $(\mathcal{Q}, \mathcal{H}) \in \mathcal{F}$ such that $|\mathcal{Q}| < n/2$ and a an axiom. If $\mathcal{H} \models_I a$ we are done. So suppose that $\mathcal{H} \not\models_I a$, this implies that $a = B^h_{i,i'}$ with at lest one pigeon between i and i' not mentioned in $\mathcal{Q}$. If this is not the case it's easy to see that $\mathcal{H} \models_I B^h_{i,i'}$. If both i and $i'$are not mentioned into $\mathcal{Q}$ we put $A_{i,i'} = P_i \cup P_{i'}$. If only one of them is not mentioned into $\mathcal{Q}$, wlog i is not mentioned into $\mathcal{Q}$, we want to find another pigeon not mentioned into $\mathcal{Q}$. We have that the pigeons mentioned in $\mathcal{Q}$ are strictly less than n and by hypothesis we have $m > n$ pigeons so we can find another pigeon i'' not mentioned into $\mathcal{Q}$. In this case we put $A_{i,i''} = P_i \cup P_{i''}$. The assignments in $\mathcal{H}$ are naming strictly less than $n/2$ elements of the partition of the holes $\mathcal{S}$ (because the number of elements in $\mathcal{S}$ named in $\mathcal{H}$ equals $|\mathcal{Q}|$). So we can find an $\{h, \overline{h}\} \in \mathcal{S}$ not used by $\mathcal{H}$. Let $\alpha_{i,j} = \{i \mapsto h, j \mapsto \overline{h}\}$ and $\overline{\alpha}_{i,j} = \{i \mapsto h, j \mapsto \overline{h}\}$, then $\Sigma_{i,j} = \{\alpha_{i,j}, \overline{\alpha}_{i,j}\}$ for $j = i', i''$.

CLAIM 1. *For $j = i', i''$ we have that $\Sigma_{i,j}$ is $\{A_{i,j}\}$-lm with respect to I.*

PROOF. Let x be a variable in $A_{i,j}$, we have that $\alpha_{i,j}(x) = 0$ if and only if $\overline{\alpha}_{i,j}(x) = 1$. This is by definition of $\alpha_{i,j}$ and $\overline{\alpha}_{i,j}$ and by the particular form of the partition of the holes $\mathcal{S}$ we chose. ☐

By Lemma 2 we obtain that $(\mathcal{Q} \cup \{A_{i,j}\}, \mathcal{H} \times \Sigma_{i,j})$ is an admissible configuration. It's straightforward to see that in both cases of $j = i'$ and $j = i''$, $(\mathcal{Q} \cup \{A_{i,j}\}, \mathcal{H} \times \Sigma_{i,j}) \in \mathcal{F}$ and $\mathcal{H} \times \Sigma_{i,j} \models_I B^h_{i,i'}$.

THEOREM 5 ([30]). *$Sp(BPHP^m_n \vdash 1) \geqslant n/8$.*

PROOF. By the previous Proposition and the Main Theorem. ☐

4.4 The case of $XPHP^m_n$

Quoting [30] we start recalling what is the *XOR pigeon-hole principle formula $XPHP^m_n$*. $XPHP^m_n$ has propositional variables $x_{i,j}$ for each $i \in [0, m)$ and $j \in [0, n]$[3]. We think of $[0, m)$ as a set of pigeons and $[0, n]$ as a set of hole indicators. Each pigeon i gives a 0 or 1 value to every hole indicator j, recorded in the variable $x_{i,j}$.

The hole indicators indicate assignments of pigeons to holes indirectly: a pigeon $i \in [0, m)$ is assigned to a hole $j \in [0, n)$ when $x_{i,j} \not\equiv x_{i,j+1}$ is true, that is when $x_{i,j}$ and $x_{i,j+1}$ have different truth values. This assignment need not be unique: the formula will only ensure that each pigeon is assigned to an odd number of holes.

The formula $XPHP^m_n$ asserts the following:

1. Every pigeon gives different values to the first and last hole indicators. That is, for each $i \in [0, m)$, $x_{i,0} \not\equiv x_{i,n}$:
   $$x_{i,0} \vee x_{i,n}$$
   $$\neg x_{i,0} \vee \neg x_{i,n}$$
2. At most one pigeon is assigned to any given hole. That is, for all distinct $i, i' \in [0, m)$ and all $j \in [0, n)$, $(x_{i,j} \equiv x_{i,j+1}) \vee (x_{i',j} \equiv x_{i',j+1})$:
   $$x_{i,j} \vee \neg x_{i,j+1} \vee x_{i',j} \vee \neg x_{i',j+1}$$
   $$\neg x_{i,j} \vee x_{i,j+1} \vee \neg x_{i',j} \vee x_{i',j+1}$$
   $$x_{i,j} \vee \neg x_{i,j+1} \vee \neg x_{i',j} \vee x_{i',j+1}$$
   $$\neg x_{i,j} \vee x_{i,j+1} \vee x_{i',j} \vee \neg x_{i',j+1}$$

$XPHP^m_n$ is the conjunction of all the previous clauses so $XPHP^m_n$ is a 4-CNF and for $m > n$ it is a contradiction. To see this notice that, by condition (1), for each pigeon $i \in [0, m)$ there must be at least one hole $j \in [0, n)$ for which i gives different values to indicators j and $j + 1$; say that such a j is assigned to i. Since $n < m$, by the pigeonhole principle there must be some pair of distinct pigeons which are assigned the same hole. But this contradicts condition (2).

We fix the partition of the variables $\mathcal{P} = \{P_0, \ldots, P_{m-1}\}$, where $P_i = \{x_{i,j} \mid j \in [0, n)\}$, and the ideal $I = Span(\{x_i^2 - x_i, x_i + \overline{x_i} - 1\}_{i=1,\ldots,n})$. We are now ready to define the family $\mathcal{F}$. An admissible configuration $(\mathcal{Q}, \mathcal{H})$ is in $\mathcal{F}$ if and only if:

1. $|\mathcal{Q}| \leqslant n - 1$,
2. $\mathcal{Q} \subseteq \mathcal{P}$, if $P_i \in \mathcal{Q}$ we say that the pigeon i is named in $\mathcal{Q}$,

[3] Recall that $[0, m) = \{0, \ldots, m - 1\}$ and $[0, n] = \{0, \ldots, n\}$.

3. Let $H_{i,j} = \{i \mapsto j\} = \{\alpha_{i,j}, \beta_{i,j}\}$, where $dom(\alpha_{i,j}) = dom(\beta_{i,j}) = P_i$,

$$\alpha_{i,j}(x_{i,j'}) = \begin{cases} 0 & \text{if } j' \leqslant j \\ 1 & \text{otherwise} \end{cases}$$

and $\beta_{i,j}(x_{i,j'}) = 1 - \alpha_{i,j}(x_{i,j'})$.

Then $\mathcal{H} = \times_{P_i \in \mathcal{Q}} H_{i,j}$ and the holes j named in all the $H_{i,j}$ are distinct, i.e $\mathcal{H}$ is made up injective assignments over the pigeon named in $\mathcal{Q}$.

Proposition 4. *The family $\mathcal{F}$ defined above is $(n-1)$-extendible of $XPHP_n^m$.*

Proof. The restriction part is clear. Let us focus on the extension part. Let $(\mathcal{Q}, \mathcal{H}) \in \mathcal{F}$ with $|\mathcal{Q}| < n - 2$ and a an initial axiom in $XPHP_n^m$.

Let us suppose first that $a = (x_{i,j} \equiv x_{i,j+1}) \vee (x_{i',j} \equiv x_{i',j+1})$. If both P_i and P_i' are in $\mathcal{Q}$ by definition $\mathcal{H} \models_I a$. So w.l.o.g. suppose that $P_i \notin \mathcal{Q}$. We have that $\mathcal{H}$ is made up of an injective assignment of at most $n-2$ pigeons, so we can find a hole h different from j not assigned. We define $\Sigma = \{i \mapsto h\}$. By Lemma 2 we have that $(\mathcal{Q} \cup \{P_i\}, \mathcal{H} \times \Sigma)$ is an admissible configuration and it's straightforward to see that $(\mathcal{Q} \cup \{P_i\}, \mathcal{H} \times \Sigma) \in \mathcal{F}$ and $\mathcal{H} \times \Sigma \models_I a$.

Similarly if $a = (x_{i,0} \not\equiv x_{i,n})$ we proceed as before assigning the pigeon i somewhere if needed. ☐

Theorem 6. *([30]) $Sp(XPHP_n^m \vdash 1) \geqslant (n-1)/4$.*

Proof. By the previous Proposition and the Main Theorem. ☐

This is only slightly worse than the result obtained in [30].

5. THE CASE OF RANDOM FORMULAS AND GRAPH-PHP

We prove that to refute random k-CNF formulas over n variables (and the Graph-PHP) it will be required high space in PC/PCR. We are going to construct a family of $\Omega(n)$-extendible admissible configurations for random k-CNF, $k \geqslant 4$. The main tool we use is a variation of the *Matching Game* (see Section 2.3.1) which was devised in [9] to prove space lower bound for random k-CNF in Resolution. It was also used in [3] to prove indefinability of random k-CNF in certain fragments of first order logic. Differently from these cases, here we are dealing with *double* matchings in a bipartite graph, instead of simply matchings. This is making some difference in the argument. Nevertheless the proofs of the main properties are essentially similar to that of [9, 3], except for small details which are due mainly to the fact that the invariant property (the (r,s)-double matching property we define next) deals with double matchings.

Definition 18. ((r,s)-double matching property) Let $r \leqslant s$, $\mathcal{G} = (U \cup V, E)$ a bipartite graph and $A \subseteq U$ of size at most $r \leqslant s$ and $B \subseteq V \cap N_{\mathcal{G}}(A)$. We say that $(\mathcal{G}, A, B)$ has the *(r,s)-double matching property* if for every $C \subseteq U \backslash A$, if $|C| = s - |A|$ then there exists a 2-matching of C into $V \backslash B$.

Observation 5. *Let $\mathcal{G} = (U \cup V, E)$ be a bipartite graph that is a (s,ϵ)-bipartite expander, then $(\mathcal{G}, \varnothing, \varnothing)$ has the (s,s)-double matching property.*

Proof. It follow immediately from the expansion property and Lemma 1. ☐

Lemma 4 (extension lemma). *Let $\mathcal{G} = (U \cup V, E)$ be a bipartite graph of left degree at most d that is a (s,ϵ)-bipartite expander. Let $A \subseteq U$ and $B \subseteq V$ two sets such that $(\mathcal{G}, A, B)$ has the (r,s)-double matching property with*

$$r \leqslant \frac{\epsilon s}{d^2(d-1)+\epsilon}$$

and $|A| < r$.

For each $u \in U \backslash A$ there exists two distinct nodes $v, v' \in N_{\mathcal{G}}(u) \cap (V \backslash B)$ such that $(\mathcal{G}, A \cup \{u\}, B \cup \{v, v'\})$ has the (r,s)-double matching property.

Proof. Let $N_{\mathcal{G}}(u) \cap (V \backslash B) = \{v_1, \ldots, v_l\}$. Clearly we have that $l \leqslant d$ because $\mathcal{G}$ has left degree at most d and $l \geqslant 2$ because of the (r,s)-double matching property on $(\mathcal{G}, A, B)$.

Let $A' = A \cup \{u\}$ and $B^{ij} = B \cup \{v_i, v_j\}$ with $v_i \neq v_j$. We note that $|A'| \leqslant r$ because $|A| < r$ and $|A'| = |A| + 1$. Let us suppose for sake of contradiction that for every pair of distinct indexes $i, j \in \{1, \ldots, l\}$, $(\mathcal{G}, A', B^{ij})$ has not the (r,s)-double matching property. This means that for every $i \neq j$ we have a set $C^{ij} \subseteq U \backslash A'$ that does not admit a 2-matching into $V \backslash B^{ij}$ s.t. $|C^{ij}| = s - |A'|$. Let $D^{ij} \subseteq C^{ij}$ not admitting a 2-matching into $V \backslash B^{ij}$ of minimal size. Then, by Lemma 1, we have that

$$|N_{\mathcal{G}}(D^{ij}) \cap (V \backslash B^{ij})| < 2|D^{ij}|,$$

so we obtain that

$$(2+\epsilon)|D^{ij}| \leqslant |N_{\mathcal{G}}(D^{ij})| = |N_{\mathcal{G}}(D^{ij}) \cap (V \backslash B^{ij})| + |N_{\mathcal{G}}(D^{ij}) \cap B^{ij}| < 2|D^{ij}| + |B^{ij}|,$$

where the first inequality came from the expansion property of $\mathcal{G}$ since $|D^{ij}| \leqslant s - |A'| < s$. From this chain of inequalities we obtain immediately that

$$|B^{ij}| > \epsilon |D^{ij}|,$$

and, using the fact that $B^{ij} \subseteq N_{\mathcal{G}}(A')$, we have that $|B^{ij}| \leqslant d|A'|$. Putting all this inequalities together we have that

$$d|A'| > \epsilon |D^{ij}|.$$

Claim 2. *$\bigcup_{i \neq j} D^{ij} \cup \{u\}$ does not admit a 2-matching into $V \backslash B$.*

Proof. To prove this suppose by contradiction that there exists a 2-matching $\pi \subseteq E$ of that set into $V \backslash B$. Let $\pi(u) = \{v_h, v_k\}$. We have that $\pi(D^{hk}) \cap \pi(u) \neq \varnothing$, in fact $\pi(D^{hk}) \subseteq V \backslash B$ and, by construction, $\pi(D^{hk}) \nsubseteq V \backslash B^{hk}$. So we must have that $\pi(D^{hk}) \cap \{v_h, v_k\} \neq \varnothing$. We reach a contradiction observing that $u \notin D^{hk}$ so we obtain two elements mapped by π in the same element. ☐

We have that $\bigcup_{ij} D^{ij} \cup \{u\} \subseteq U \backslash A$ and $(\mathcal{G}, A, B)$ by hypothesis has the double matching property, so we must have that

$$\left| \bigcup_{ij} D_{ij} \cup \{u\} \right| > s - |A|$$

so we have that there exists a pair of indexes i, j such that $|D^{ij}| > \frac{s-|A'|}{l(l-1)} \geqslant \frac{s-|A'|}{d(d-1)}$.

So we have obtained that

$$d|A'| > \epsilon \frac{s - |A'|}{d(d-1)}.$$

And from this we obtain that

$$|A'| > \frac{\epsilon s}{d^2(d-1)+\epsilon} = r.$$

But this is a contradiction by hypothesis.

LEMMA 5 (RETRACTION LEMMA). *Let $\mathcal{G} = (U \cup V, E)$ be a bipartite graph of left degree at most d that is a (s,ϵ)-bipartite expander. Let $A \subseteq U$ and $B \subseteq V$ two sets such that $(\mathcal{G}, A, B)$ has the (r,s)-double matching property. If $u \in A$ and $L \subseteq N_{\mathcal{G}}(u) \cap B$ such that $|L| \geqslant 2$ and $B \backslash L \subseteq N_{\mathcal{G}}(A \backslash \{u\})$ and*

$$r \leqslant \frac{\epsilon s}{d+\epsilon},$$

then $(\mathcal{G}, A\backslash\{u\}, B\backslash L)$ has the (r,s)-double matching property.

PROOF. Let $A' = A\backslash\{u\}$ and $B' = B\backslash L$. Clearly $|A'| \leqslant r$ and $B' \subseteq N_{\mathcal{G}}(A')$. Let $C \subseteq U\backslash A'$ of size $s - |A'|$. We have two cases: or $u \in C$ or $u \notin C$.

$\underline{u \in C}$: In this case we have that $C\backslash\{u\} \subseteq U\backslash A$, and has size $s - |A'| - 1 = s - |A|$, then we have that there exists a 2-matching of $C\backslash\{u\}$ into $V\backslash B$. We have now by hypothesis that $|L| \geqslant 2$ so we can find (u, v) and (u, w) in $\{u\} \times L$. So we can extend the 2-matching found for $C\backslash\{u\}$ to a 2-matching of C.

$\underline{u \notin C}$: We have that for every $w \in C$ there exists a 2-matching of $C\backslash\{w\} \subseteq U\backslash A$ into $V\backslash B \subseteq V\backslash B'$. Then if C is not 2-matchable into $V\backslash B'$ it follows that C is not 2-matchable of minimal size. Using Lemma 1 we have that

$$|N_{\mathcal{G}}(C) \cap (V\backslash B')| < 2|C|,$$

and, using the fact that $\mathcal{G}$ is an (s,ϵ)-bipartite expander, and that $|C| = s - |A'| \leqslant s$,

$$(2+\epsilon)|C| \leqslant |N_{\mathcal{G}}(C)| < 2|C| + |B'|.$$

So $|B'| > \epsilon|C|$. We have now that $|C| = s - |A'|$, and $|B'| \leqslant d|A'|$, so we obtain

$$|A'| > \frac{\epsilon s}{d+\epsilon} \geqslant r.$$

A contradiction. □

5.1 Random *k-CNF*

Let n,m and k be positive natural numbers and let $X = \{x_1, \ldots, x_n\}$ be a set of variables. Let $\mathcal{F}(n,m,k)$ be the set of all k-CNF formulas on X with exactly m clauses each defined on k literals on distinct variables. Alternatively, $\mathcal{F}(n,m,k)$ can be described as the result of repeating m times independently the following experiment: choose exactly k variables from X, and negate each variable independently with probability 1/2. We will use this interpretation whenever it is convenient. The ratio m/n is denoted by Δ, and is called the clause density. Usually, Δ is fixed to a constant and therefore is determined by n . We are interested in studying the asymptotic properties of a randomly chosen formula $F \sim \mathcal{F}(n,m,k)$ as n approaches to infinity. It is well known that when the clause density exceeds a certain constant θ_k that only depends on k, a randomly chosen formula is almost surely unsatisfiable. We are interested only in the region in which F is unsatisfiable with high probability, then we always consider fixed $\Delta >> \theta_k$, then $\mathcal{F}(n,m,k)$ can be made dependent only on n, Δ and k and denoted as $\mathcal{F}(n,\Delta,k)$

Let $F = \bigwedge_{i=1}^{\Delta n} C_k \sim \mathcal{F}(n,\Delta,k)$ be a random k-CNF. Let us consider the associated bipartite graph $\mathcal{G}_F = (U \cup V, E)$ where U is the set of clauses appearing in F and V is the underlying set of variables appearing in F. As in [9, 3] we put $(C,x) \in E$ if the variable x is appearing in some literal of C. We observe that the graph $\mathcal{G}_F$ has left degree k. It is a well-known result (see [21, 7, 14, 9, 3] among several others) that if $F \sim \mathcal{F}(n,\Delta,k)$, then $\mathcal{G}_F$ is a good expander (at least when the expansion factor is $(1+\epsilon)$). Since in this work we are dealing with 2-matchings, we are interested in an expansion factor of $(2+\epsilon)$ (see Definition 7). Nevertheless we are able to prove that also in this case $\mathcal{G}_F$ is a good expander, provided $k \geqslant 4$. We comment on the case $k = 3$ in the conclusions. The proof of next theorem is standard and can be found for instance in [9]. Our proof contains exactly the same calculations with the only difference that to deal with an expansion factor of $(2+\epsilon)$ in $\mathcal{G}_F$ we need to have $k \geqslant 4$.

THEOREM 7 ([21, 7, 9, 14]). *For any $k \geqslant 4$ and any constant ϵ with $0 < \epsilon < k-3$, there is a constant $\kappa = \kappa_{k,\epsilon}$ such that if $F \sim \mathcal{F}(n,\Delta,k)$, then with high probability $\mathcal{G}_F$ is a (s,ϵ)-bipartite expander, with $s = \frac{\kappa \cdot n}{\Delta^{\frac{1+\epsilon}{k-3-\epsilon}}}$.*

PROOF. The same proof given in [9] works exactly in our context substituting each occurrence of $(1+\epsilon)$ with $(2+\epsilon)$ and the condition $k \geqslant 3$ with $k \geqslant 4$. □

Let us suppose that the graph $\mathcal{G}$ is an (s,ϵ)-bipartite expander. Notice that for all k and s,

$$\tilde{r} = \min\left\{s, \frac{\epsilon s}{k+\epsilon}, \frac{\epsilon s}{k^2(k-1)+\epsilon}\right\} = \frac{\epsilon s}{k^2(k-1)+\epsilon}.$$

Let $I = Span(\{x_i^2 - x_i, x_i + \overline{x_i} - 1\}_{i=1,\ldots,n})$. We define the family $\mathcal{F}$ as follow: an admissible configuration $(\mathcal{Q},\mathcal{H})$ is in $\mathcal{F}$ is and only if there exists a 2-matching π of some $A \subseteq U$ such that:

1. $|A| \leqslant \tilde{r}$,
2. $(\mathcal{G}, A, \cup\pi(A))$ has the $(\tilde{r}, s)$-double matching property,
3. $\mathcal{Q} = \pi(A) = \{\pi(C) \mid C \in A\}$,
4. for each clause $C \in A$ $\mathcal{H}{\restriction}_{\pi(C)} \models_I C$.

We have that $(\mathcal{G}, \varnothing, \varnothing)$ has the $(\tilde{r}, s)$-double matching property so $(\varnothing, \{\varnothing\}) \in \mathcal{F}$ and this family is non-empty.

THEOREM 8. *The family $\mathcal{F}$ defined above is $\tilde{r}$-extendible.*

PROOF. Suppose we have a pair $(\mathcal{Q},\mathcal{H}) \in \mathcal{F}$, i.e. we have the properties (1), (2), (3) and (4) listed above. Clearly we have that $|\mathcal{Q}| \leqslant \tilde{r}$, because $\mathcal{Q} = \{\pi(C) \mid C \in A\}$, so $|\mathcal{Q}| = |A|$ and, by (1), $|A| \leqslant \tilde{r}$.

To prove the restriction property suppose we have a $\mathcal{Q}' \subseteq \mathcal{Q}$: we have to prove that $(\mathcal{Q}', \mathcal{H}{\restriction}_{\mathcal{Q}'}) \in \mathcal{F}$. Let $A' = \{C \in A \mid \pi(C) \in \mathcal{Q}'\}$, $\pi' = \pi \restriction_{A'}$ the 2-matching obtained as a restriction of π over A' and $\mathcal{H}' = \mathcal{H}{\restriction}_{\mathcal{Q}'}$. (1) is true since $|A'| \leqslant |A| \leqslant \tilde{r}$. (3) is true since $\mathcal{Q}' = \pi'(A')$. (4) follows since $\pi = \pi'$ over A' and for all $C \in A'$, $\pi(C) \in \mathcal{Q}'$ and then we have $\mathcal{H}'{\restriction}_{\pi'(C)} \models C$ for each $C \in A'$. The difficult part is to prove (2), i.e. that $(\mathcal{G}, A', \cup\pi'(A'))$ has the $(\tilde{r}, s)$-double matching property. We remove one by one the clauses $C \in A \backslash A'$ by applying for each such C the *retraction* Lemma 5 with $u = C$ and $L = \pi(C)$. It is straightforward to see that such L fulfills the hypothesis of retraction Lemma 5.

To prove the extension property for the family $\mathcal{F}$, let us suppose that $|\mathcal{Q}| < \tilde{r}$ and that we have an axiom a.

As usual we need to distinguish the case of $\mathcal{H} \models_I a$ (in this case we don't have anything to do) or $\mathcal{H} \not\models_I a$. This second case corresponds to $a = C$ a clause $C \notin A$.

By Lemma 4 we can find a two distinct vertexes $v, v' \in V \backslash \cup\pi(A)$ such that $v, v' \in N_{\mathcal{G}}(C)$ and $(\mathcal{G}, A \cup \{C\}, \cup\pi(A) \cup \{v, v'\})$ has the $(\tilde{r}, s)$-double matching property. So we define $A' = A \cup \{C\}$ and $\pi' = \pi \cup \{(C, v), (C, v')\}$. And we define $\mathcal{Q}' = \mathcal{Q} \cup \{\{v, v'\}\} = \pi'(A')$. The only thing left is to construct the new family of assignments $\mathcal{H}'$. To do this first we define a family $\Sigma = \{\gamma, \overline{\gamma}\}$ such that

- $dom(\gamma) = dom(\overline{\gamma}) = \{v, v'\}$,
- $\gamma(v) = sat_C(v)$ and $\gamma(v') = 1 - sat_C(v')$. Where $sat_C(x)$ is the boolean value we have to set the variable x to satisfy C.
- $\overline{\gamma}(v) = 1 - sat_C(v)$ and $\overline{\gamma}(v') = sat_C(v')$.

Then we define $\mathcal{H}' = \mathcal{H} \times \Sigma$.

By Lemma 2 we have that $(\mathcal{Q}', \mathcal{H}')$ is an admissible configuration. It is straightforward to see that for $(\mathcal{Q}', \mathcal{H}') \in \mathcal{F}$ and by construction $\Sigma \models_I C$ so $\mathcal{H} \times \Sigma \models_I C$. □

In this versions of the work we are not interested in improving constants, so we omit detailed calculations that will instead follow in a subsequent version of the paper.

THEOREM 9. *Let $k \geqslant 4$ be any integer, $\epsilon > 0$ any constant and $\Delta \geqslant 1$. Let $F \sim \mathcal{F}(n, \Delta, k)$. There exists a constant $c = c_{k,\Delta,\epsilon}$, $c \geqslant 1$, such that with high probability*

$$Sp(F \vdash 1) \geqslant \frac{n}{4c}.$$

PROOF. Theorem 7 tells us that with high probability $\mathcal{G}_F$ is a (s, ϵ)-expander, with $s = \frac{\kappa \cdot n}{\Delta^{\frac{1+\epsilon}{k-3-\epsilon}}}$. Using definition of $\tilde{r}$ we have that there exists a a constant $c = c_{k,\Delta,\epsilon}$ such that with high probability the family of admissible configurations of Theorem 8 is $(\frac{n}{c})$-extendible family for F. The result then follows by the Main Theorem (Theorem 1). □

5.2 Graph-PHP

We recall the definition of the *Graph PigeonHole Principle* in order to fix the notations we'll use. Let $\mathcal{G} = (U \cup V, E)$ a bipartite graph and U and V two disjoint sets of size respectively $n+1$ and n. Clearly there is no perfect matching from U to V. This combinatorial principle is expressed as a conjunction over the variables $W = \{x_{u,v} \mid (u, v) \in E\}$. Intuitively setting the variable $x_{u,v}$ to 1 means that the pigeon $u \in U$ is mapped to $v \in V$. For every $u \in U$ let

$$P_u = \bigvee_{v:(u,v)\in E} x_{u,v}$$

and for all $(u, w) \in E$ and $(v, w) \in E$ let

$$H_w^{u,v} = \neg x_{u,w} \vee \neg x_{v,w}.$$

$\mathcal{G}$-PHP is the conjunction of all the previous clauses. We observe that if $\mathcal{G}$ has left degree d then $\mathcal{G}$-PHP is a d-CNF.

According with the general strategy we fix the partition $\mathcal{P} = \{H_1, \ldots, H_n\}$, where $H_j = \{x_{ij} \mid (i,j) \in E\}$, i.e. we are partitioning the variables according to the hole they are referring. Let us start with a notation we'll use: suppose we have a (multiple) matching π of a set $A \subseteq U$. For every $u \in A$ we call

$$var(\pi)(u) = \bigcup_{i \in \pi(u)} H_j$$

and for each $B \subseteq A$

$$var(\pi)(B) = \{var(\pi)(u) \mid u \in B\}.$$

Let us suppose that the graph $\mathcal{G}$ is an (s, ϵ)-bipartite expander with left degree d and let

$$\tilde{r} = \min\left\{s, \frac{\epsilon s}{d+\epsilon}, \frac{\epsilon s}{d^2(d-1)+\epsilon}\right\} = \frac{\epsilon s}{d^2(d-1)+\epsilon}.$$

We use the ideal I generated by $\{H_w^{u,v}\} \cup \{x_i^2 - x_i, x_i + \overline{x_i} - 1\}_{i=1,\ldots,n}$. We want now to construct a family $\mathcal{F}$ that is $\tilde{r}$-extendible with respect to I.

The family $\mathcal{F}$ is defined as follow: an admissible configuration $(\mathcal{Q}, \mathcal{H}) \in \mathcal{F}$ if and only if there exists a 2-matching π of some $A \subseteq U$ st

1. $|A| \leqslant \tilde{r}$,
2. $(\mathcal{G}, A, \cup\pi(A))$ has the $(\tilde{r}, s)$-double matching property,
3. $\mathcal{Q} = var(\pi)(A)$,
4. for each $u \in A$ $\mathcal{H}\restriction_{var(\pi)(u)} \models_I P_u$ and $\mathcal{H}\restriction_{var(\pi)(u)}$ respects I.

As noticed for the random kCNF we have that $(\emptyset, \{\emptyset\}) \in \mathcal{F}$ so the family we defined is non-empty.

Formally the definition of this family is very close to the definition we had for the random k-CNF, but the ideal used is different so the proof that the family above is well defined and $\tilde{r}$-extendible is somehow different from the proof we provided for the random formulas.

THEOREM 10. *The family $\mathcal{F}$ defined above is $\tilde{r}$-extendible.*

PROOF. Let us suppose we have a pair $(\mathcal{Q}, \mathcal{H}) \in \mathcal{F}$, i.e. we have the properties (1), (2), (3) and (4) listed above. Clearly we have that $|\mathcal{Q}| \leqslant \tilde{r}$, because $|\mathcal{Q}| = |A|$ and, by (1), $|A| \leqslant \tilde{r}$.

To prove the restriction property suppose we have a $\mathcal{Q}' \subseteq \mathcal{Q}$: we have to prove that $(\mathcal{Q}', \mathcal{H}\restriction_{\mathcal{Q}'}) \in \mathcal{F}$. Let $A' = \{u \in A \mid var(\pi)(u) \in \mathcal{Q}'\}$ and $\pi' = \pi\restriction_{A'}$ the 2-matching obtained as a restriction of π over A'. Clearly we have that $|A'| \leqslant |A| \leqslant \tilde{r}$, $\mathcal{Q}' = var(\pi')(A')$ and $\mathcal{H}\restriction_{var(\pi')(u)} \models_I P_u$ for each $u \in A'$. The difficult part is to prove that $(\mathcal{G}, A', \pi'(A'))$ has the $(\tilde{r}, s)$-double matching property. We remove one by one the vertices $u \in A \backslash A'$ by applying for each such u Lemma 5 with and $L = \pi(u)$. It is straightforward to see that such L fulfills the hypothesis of Lemma 5.

To prove the extension property let's suppose that $|\mathcal{Q}| < \tilde{r}$ and that we have an axiom a. As usual we need to distinguish two cases: $\mathcal{H} \models_I a$ (i.e we have nothing to do) or $\mathcal{H} \not\models_I a$, i.e. $a = P_u$ for some $u \in U \backslash A$. By Lemma 4 we can find two distinct vertexes $v, v' \in N_G(u)$ not in $\cup\pi(A)$ such that $(\mathcal{G}, A \cup \{u\}, \cup\pi(A) \cup \{v, v'\})$ has the $(\tilde{r}, s)$-double matching property. So we define $A' = A \cup \{u\}$ and $\pi' = \pi \cup \{(u, v), (u, v')\}$. And we define $\mathcal{Q}' = \mathcal{Q} \cup \{H_v \cup H_{v'}\} =$

$var(\pi')(A')$. We have now to construct the new family of assignments $\mathcal{H}'$. To do this first we define a family of partial assignments Σ as the set of all assignments of domain $H_v \cup H_{v'}$ extending $\{x_{u,v} \mapsto 1, x_{u,v'} \mapsto 0\}$, or extending $\{x_{u,v} \mapsto 0, x_{u,v'} \mapsto 1\}$, and satisfying all the axioms $H_v^{ww'}$ and $H_{v'}^{ww'}$ (i.e. all the axioms stating the injectivity on the holes v and v'). We observe that the assignments we put in Σ respect I. Then we define $\mathcal{H}' = \mathcal{H} \times \Sigma$. By Lemma 2 we have that $(\mathcal{Q}', \mathcal{H}')$ is an admissible configuration. Moreover it's straightforward to see that $(\mathcal{Q}', \mathcal{H}') \in \mathcal{F}$ and by construction $\mathcal{H} \times \Sigma \models_I P_u$, as by construction the assignments in Σ map u somewhere. □

THEOREM 11. *There exists a constant degree $d \geqslant 3$ bipartite graph $\mathcal{G} = (U \cup V, E)$ with $|U| = n + 1$ and $|V| = n$, such that $Sp(\mathcal{G}\text{-}PHP \vdash 1) \geqslant \Omega(n/d)$.*

PROOF. We proceed as in [9]. A similar proof to that Ben-Sasson in his thesis [8] (Theorem 2.46) prove that there exists a degree d bipartite graph $\mathcal{G} = (U \cup V, E)$ with $|U| = n+1$ and $|V| = n$ which is a $(\Omega(n/d), 7d/8-2)$-expander (it is sufficient to set $\epsilon = 7d/8-2$ in his proof for his calculations to work with our expansion factor of $(2+\epsilon)$). The Theorem then follows using definition of $\tilde{r}$, previous Theorem 10 and Main Theorem 1. □

6. OPEN PROBLEMS

We think that our result on the space in PC/PCR can open the way to a more precise characterization of the space, and we do not exclude the degree, of PC/PCR proofs in terms of 2-Player games like variants of the existential pebble games for Resolution like Ehrenfeucht-Fraïssé games. We find very attractive the idea that, as was done in Resolution by Atserias and Dalmau in [4], to find a precise combinatorial characterization of the degree and proving some relations between space and degree, similar to the one between width and space for Resolution. We think that our work and our notion of k-extendibility is a first step in this directions. So far there is no results that seems to exclude that "space might be lower bounded by degree" in PC/PCR. As was done for random k-CNF for DATALOG by Asterias [3], our game characterizationof boolean reasoning with polynomials can suggest non-expressibility results in stronger logic appropriate to this kind of reasoning.

To work in this direction it might be useful to prove lower bounds for other classes of tautologies for which we know to require high degree. In particular we think to Tseitin Tautologies (Beame et al. in [19] proves that they require high degree) and Linear ordering principle on Graphs GOP_n (Galesi and Lauria [31] recently proved they require high degree in PC/PCR) or GT_n. We think that our technique could work also for this case provided we have the right definition of graph underlying the principle.

Another issue concern the possibilities of using a similar characterization of the space to try prove space lower bounds in other more powerful systems. Nothing for instance is known about space complexity in Cutting Planes and Lovasz-Schriver proof systems. We think that also in this case our work can be a starting point to try to come up with similar ideas to prove space lower bounds in these systems.

Another natural open problem arising form our work is to study the variable space for PC/PCR for all the principles we prove space lower bounds for. We think that the same steps of [1] together with our approach based on transversality and pseudo-partitions one can hopefully prove quadratic lower bounds for variable space in all these cases.

An important problem missing in this work is the case of random 3-CNFs. This case seems quite interesting for the following reasons: on one hand 3-CNFs are certainly hard to prove. On the other hand since with our Multiple Matching Game we are dealing with double matchings it seems not easy to keep hardness and expansion properties of the bipartite graph induced by the 3-CNF. It might be possible that the analysis of the case of random 3-CNF might require some new technique to prove the stronger expansion property we need in this work.

7. ACKNOWLEDGEMENTS

The authors are greatly grateful to Roberto Grossi and to the Department of Computer Science of the University of Pisa for the very kind hospitality they offer. Part of this work was done while Nicola Galesi was visiting Roberto Grossi at the University of Pisa. We would thank Massimo Lauria, Jacob Nordström, Eli BenSasson, Mladen Mikša and Mark Vinals Perez for reading carefully the paper and pointing out to us several interesting comments and minor mistakes. Their comments together with the very helpful comments coming from the anonymous referees of the Conference ITCS allowed us that greatly improve the paper and its readability.

We also want to thanks Jacob Nordström, Mladen Mikša and Mark Vinals Perez for inspiring comments about future research directions in a work afternoon in Rome during the Workshop "Limits of Theorem Proving".

8. REFERENCES

[1] Michael Alekhnovich, Eli Ben-Sasson, Alexander A. Razborov, and Avi Wigderson. Space complexity in propositional calculus. *SIAM J. Comput.*, 31(4):1184–1211, 2002.

[2] Michael Alekhnovich and Alexander A. Razborov. Lower bounds for polynomial calculus: Non-binomial case. In *42nd Annual Symposium on Foundations of Computer Science*, pages 190–199, 2001.

[3] Albert Atserias. On sufficient conditions for unsatisfiability of random formulas. *Journal of ACM*, 51(2):281–311, 2004. A preliminary version appeared in the Proceedings of the 17th IEEE Symposium on Logic in Computer Sience (LICS), pagine 325–334, 2002.

[4] Albert Atserias and Víctor Dalmau. A combinatorial characterization of resolution width. *J. Comput. Syst. Sci.*, 74(3):323–334, 2008.

[5] Albert Atserias, J. Fichte, and M. Thurley. Clause-learning algorithms with many restarts and bounded-width resolution. *Theory and Applications of Satisfiability Testing-SAT 2009*, pages 114–127, 2009.

[6] Paul Beame, Henry A. Kautz, and Ashish Sabharwal. Towards understanding and harnessing the potential of clause learning. *J. Artif. Intell. Res. (JAIR)*, 22:319–351, 2004.

[7] Paul Beame and Toniann Pitassi. Simplified and improved resolution lower bounds. In *37th Annual*

Symposium on Foundations of Computer Science, pages 274 – 282. IEEE, 1996.

[8] Eli Ben-sasson. *Expansion in Proof Complexity.* PhD thesis, Hebrew University, 2001.

[9] Eli Ben-Sasson and Nicola Galesi. Space complexity of random formulae in resolution. *Random Struct. Algorithms*, 23(1):92–109, 2003.

[10] Eli Ben-Sasson and Russell Impagliazzo. Random CNFs are hard for the polynomial calculus. In *40th Annual Symposium on Foundations of Computer Science*, pages 415–421, 1999.

[11] Eli Ben-Sasson and Jan Johannsen. Lower bounds for width-restricted clause learning on small width formulas. *Theory and Applications of Satisfiability Testing–SAT 2010*, pages 16–29, 2010.

[12] Eli Ben-Sasson and Jakob Nordström. A space hierarchy for k-dnf resolution. *Electronic Colloquium on Computational Complexity (ECCC)*, 16(047), 2009.

[13] Eli Ben-Sasson and Jakob Nordström. Understanding space in resolution: Optimal lower bounds and exponential trade-offs. *Electronic Colloquium on Computational Complexity (ECCC)*, 16(034), 2009.

[14] Eli Ben-Sasson and Avi Wigderson. Short proofs are narrow - resolution made simple. *J. ACM*, 48(2):149–169, 2001.

[15] Archie Blake. *Canonical Expressions in Boolean Algebra.* PhD thesis, University of Chicago, 1938.

[16] Michael Brickenstein and Alexander Dreyer. Polybori: A framework for gröbner-basis computations with boolean polynomials. *J. Symb. Comput*, 44(9):1326–1345, 2009.

[17] Sam Buss, Maria Luisa Bonet, and Jan Johannsen. Improved separations of regular resolution from clause learning proof systems. *Submitted*, 2012.

[18] Sam Buss, Jan Hoffman, and Jan Johannsen. Resolution trees with lemmas - resolution refinements that characterize dll-algorithms with clause learning. *Logical Methods in Computer Science*, 4,:4:13, 2008.

[19] Samuel R. Buss, Dima Grigoriev, Russell Impagliazzo, and Toniann Pitassi. Linear gaps between degrees for the polynomial calculus modulo distinct primes. *J. Comput. Syst. Sci.*, 62(2):267–289, 2001.

[20] Samuel R. Buss, Russell Impagliazzo, Jan Krajíček, Pavel Pudlák, Alexander A. Razborov, and Jiří Sgall. Proof complexity in algebraic systems and bounded depth frege systems with modular counting. *Computational Complexity*, 6(3):256–298, 1997.

[21] Vasek Chvátal and Endre Szemerédi. Many hard examples for resolution. *J. ACM*, 35(4):759–768, 1988.

[22] Matthew Clegg, Jeff Edmonds, and Russell Impagliazzo. Using the Gröebner basis algorithm to find proofs of unsatisfiability. In *Proceedings of the Twenty-Eighth Annual ACM Symposium on the Theory of Computing*, pages 174–183, 1996.

[23] Stephen A. Cook and Robert A. Reckhow. The relative efficiency of propositional proof systems. *Journal of Symbolic Logic*, 44:36–50, 1979.

[24] David Cox, John Little, and Donal O'Shea. *Ideals, Varieties, and Algorithms : An Introduction to Computational Algebraic Geometry and Commutative Algebra, 3rd edition.* Springer, 2007.

[25] Martin Davis, George Logemann, and Donald Loveland. A machine program for theorem-proving. *Commun. ACM*, 5:394–397, July 1962.

[26] Martin Davis and Hilary Putnam. A computing procedure for quantification theory. *J. ACM*, 7:201–215, July 1960.

[27] Juan Luis Esteban, Nicola Galesi, and Jochen Messner. On the complexity of resolution with bounded conjunctions. *Theor. Comput. Sci.*, 321(2-3):347–370, 2004.

[28] Juan Luis Esteban and Jacobo Torán. Space bounds for resolution. *Information and Computation*, 171(1):84–97, 2001.

[29] Tomás Feder and Moshe Y. Vardi. The computational structure of monotone monadic snp and constraint satisfaction: A study through datalog and group theory. *SIAM J. Comput.*, 28(1):57–104, 1998.

[30] Yuval Filmus, Massimo Lauria, Jakob Nordström, Neil Thapen, and Noga Zewi. Space complexity in polynomial calculus. In *IEEE Conference on Computational Complexity 2012*, 2012. To appear.

[31] Nicola Galesi and Massimo Lauria. On the automatizability of polynomial calculus. *Theory of Computing Systems*, 47(2):491–506, 2010.

[32] Nicola Galesi and Massimo Lauria. Optimality of size-degree trade-offs for polynomial calculus. *ACM Transactions on Computational Logic*, 12(1):??, 2010. To appear.

[33] Russell Impagliazzo, Pavel Pudlák, and Jiří Sgall. Lower bounds for the polynomial calculus and the gröbner basis algorithm. *Computational Complexity*, 8(2):127–144, 1999.

[34] Jan Krajíček. Propositional proof complexity i. 2009.

[35] Joao P. Marques-Silva and Karem A. Sakallah. Grasp—a new search algorithm for satisfiability. In *Proceedings of the IEEE/ACM International Conference on Computer-Aided Design (ICCAD '96),*, pages 220–227, 1996.

[36] Jakob Nordström. Narrow proofs may be spacious: separating space and width in resolution. In *STOC*, pages 507–516, 2006.

[37] Jakob Nordström and Johan Håstad. Towards an optimal separation of space and length in resolution. In *STOC*, pages 701–710, 2008.

[38] Pavel Pudlák and Jiří Sgall. Algebraic models of computation and interpolation for algebraic proof systems. *DIMACS series in Theoretical Computer Science*, 39:279–296, 1998.

[39] Alexander Razborov. Pseudorandom generators hard for k-dnf resolution and polynomial calculus resolution. *Manuscript availbale at author's webpage*, 2003.

[40] Alexander A. Razborov. Lower bounds for the polynomial calculus. *Computational Complexity*, 7(4):291–324, 1998.

[41] J. A. Robinson. A machine-oriented logic based on the resolution principle. *J. ACM*, 12:23–41, January 1965.

Competing Provers Protocols for Circuit Evaluation*

Gillat Kol
Weizmann Institute

Ran Raz
Weizmann Institute

ABSTRACT

Let C be a (fan-in 2) Boolean circuit of size s and depth d, and let x be an input for C. Assume that a verifier that knows C but doesn't know x can access the low degree extension of x at one random point. Two competing provers try to convince the verifier that $C(x) = 0$ and $C(x) = 1$, respectively, and assume that one of the provers is honest.

For any $r \geq 1$, we give an r rounds protocol with communication complexity $d^{\frac{1}{r}} polylog(s)$ that convinces the verifier in the correct value of $C(x)$ (with small probability of error). In particular, when we allow only one round, the protocol exchanges $d \cdot polylog(s)$ bits, and when we allow $r = O\left(\frac{log(d)}{loglog(s)}\right)$ rounds, the protocol exchanges only $polylog(s)$ bits.

Moreover, the complexity of the verifier and honest provers in this protocol is $poly(s)$, and if in addition the circuit is $log(s)$-space uniform, the complexity of the verifier is $d^{\frac{1}{r}} polylog(s)$.[1]

The protocol is obtained by combining the *delegation protocol* of Goldwasser, Kalai and Rothblum [5] and the *competing provers protocols* of Feige and Kilian [3] and some new techniques. We suggest two applications of these results:

Delegating computation to competing clouds: The main motivation behind the protocol of [5] was *delegating computation* to a cloud. Using our new protocol, a verifier can delegate computation to two (or more) competing clouds. If at least one of the clouds is reliable the verifier can trust that the computation is correct (with high probability). The advantage over the protocol of [5] is that the communication complexity and the number of rounds in our protocol are significantly lower.

Communication complexity with competing provers, and circuit lower bounds: Aaronson and Wigderson [1] suggested the model of communication complexity with competing provers, where two competing provers try to convince two players that $f(x, y) = 0$ and $f(x, y) = 1$, respectively, where x is an input held by the first player and y is an input held by the second player. By scaling down the competing provers protocols of [3], they showed that strong enough lower bounds for the communication complexity of f, in this model, imply lower bounds for the computational complexity of f.

Our results strengthen this connection. More precisely, we show that if f can be computed by a Boolean circuit of size s and depth d then for any $r \geq 1$ there is an r rounds protocol for f, in this model, with communication complexity $d^{\frac{1}{r}} polylog(s)$. This can be viewed as a possible direction towards proving circuit lower bounds. For instance, in order to prove $f \notin \mathcal{NC}$, it suffices to show that any one round protocol for f, in this model, requires the exchange of $\omega(polylog(n))$ bits. This gives a relatively simple combinatorial property that implies strong circuit lower bounds.

*Research supported by the Israel Science Foundation (ISF).

[1] We have learnt that a result similar to ours for the case $r = 1$, as well as the motivation of delegating computation to competing clouds, was independently obtained by Canetti, Riva and Rothblum [2].

ITCS'13, January 9–12, 2012, Berkeley, California, USA.

Categories and Subject Descriptors

F.2.0 [**Theory of Computation**]: Analysis of Algorithms and Problem Complexity—*General*

Keywords

Interactive Proofs, Delegating Computation, Competing Provers, Communication Complexity, Circuit Lower Bound

1. INTRODUCTION

The model of *refereed games,* or, *interactive proofs with competing provers,* was first introduced by Feige, Shamir and Tennenholtz [4]. Informally, given a language L and an input x, an efficient verifier interacts (that is, exchanges private messages) with two computationally-unbounded provers in order to decide whether or not $x \in L$. One prover tries to convince the verifier that $x \in L$, while the other prover tries to convince the verifier that $x \notin L$. (The assumption is that the prover who is right is honest and follows the protocol, while the other is untrusted). The seminal paper of Feige and Kilian [3] shows that the class of languages with a *single round* refereed games is exactly PSPACE, and the class of languages with $poly(n)$ rounds refereed games is exactly EXP.

Let C be a (fan-in 2) Boolean circuit of size s and depth d, and let x be an input for C. Assume that a verifier that knows C but doesn't know x can access the low degree extension of x at one random point. The verifier tries to decide whether or not x satisfies C. Two competing provers try to convince the verifier that $C(x) = 0$ and $C(x) = 1$, respectively, and, as before, assume that one of the provers is honest.

Problems of this type in the model of *interactive proofs with a single prover* were studied in [6, 5]. In particular, the beautiful paper of Goldwasser, Kalai and Rothblum [5] gives a protocol where the prover convinces the verifier in the correct value of $C(x)$ (with small probability of error), and where the number of rounds and the communication complexity are both $d \cdot polylog(s)$, and the complexity of the prover is $poly(s)$. Moreover, maybe the most interesting aspect of their protocol is that if in addition one assumes that the circuit C is $log(s)$-space uniform, the complexity of the verifier in the protocol is $d \cdot polylog(s)$. That is, the complexity of the verifier may be significantly smaller than the size of the circuit. In other words, the computation was delegated to the prover, while the verifier is still convinced that the computation is correct.

1.1 Our Results

As before, let C be a (fan-in 2) Boolean circuit of size s and depth d, and let x be an input for C. Assume that a verifier that knows C but doesn't know x can access the low degree extension of x at one random point. Two competing provers try to convince the verifier that $C(x) = 0$ and $C(x) = 1$, respectively.

For any $r \geq 1$, we give an r rounds protocol with communication complexity $d^{\frac{1}{r}} polylog(s)$ that convinces the verifier in the correct value of $C(x)$ (with small probability of error). In particular, when we allow only one round, the protocol exchanges $d \cdot polylog(s)$ bits, and when we allow $r = O\left(\frac{log(d)}{loglog(s)}\right)$ rounds, the protocol exchanges only $polylog(s)$ bits.

Moreover, the complexity of the verifier and (honest) provers in this protocol is $poly(s)$, and if in addition the circuit is $log(s)$-space uniform, the complexity of the verifier is $d^{\frac{1}{r}} polylog(s)$.

The protocol is obtained by combining the *delegation protocol* of Goldwasser, Kalai and Rothblum [5] and the *competing provers protocols* of Feige and Kilian [3], together with some new techniques.

We have learnt that a result similar to ours for the case $r = 1$, as well as the motivation of delegating computation to competing clouds, was independently obtained by Canetti, Riva and Rothblum [2].

1.2 Delegating Computation to Competing Clouds

As mentioned above, the main motivation behind the protocol of Goldwasser, Kalai and Rothblum [5] was delegating computation to a cloud: Consider the case of log-space uniform circuits. As mentioned above, the complexity of the verifier in this case is relatively small, assuming that she has access to the low degree extension of x at a random point. Moreover, even if the verifier doesn't have access to the low degree extension of x (but rather knows x), she can compute the low degree extension of x at a random point by herself in almost linear time, which can be significantly smaller than the size of the circuit. Thus, the computation was delegated to the prover, while the verifier is convinced (with high probability) that the computation was performed correctly.

Using our new protocol, a verifier can delegate computation to two (or more) competing clouds, viewing each cloud as a separate prover. If at least one of the clouds is reliable, the verifier will be able to identify the correct answer and trust that the computation is correct (with high probability). The advantage over the protocol of [5] is that the communication complexity and the number of rounds in our protocol are significantly lower.

1.3 Communication Complexity with Competing Provers and Circuit Lower Bounds

Aaronson and Wigderson [1] suggested the model of communication complexity with two competing provers.

Recall that the standard setting of communication complexity involves two separated, computationally-unbounded players, Alice and Bob, each holding a private n-bit input string. Assume that Alice holds $x \in \{0,1\}^n$ and Bob holds $y \in \{0,1\}^n$. Let $f : \{0,1\}^{2n} \to \{0,1\}$ be a Boolean function known to both Alice and Bob, and let $x \circ y \in \{0,1\}^{2n}$ denote the concatenation of x and y. The players' mutual goal is to compute $f(x \circ y)$ with the least amount of communication between them.

In the model of communication complexity with competing provers the players may communicate, via private channels, with two provers *that are assumed to know f, as well as both x and y*. The two provers try to convince the players that $f(x \circ y) = 0$ and $f(x \circ y) = 1$, respectively. The *communication complexity* of a protocol is the total number of bits exchanged between all the parties (players and provers). In this paper we are interested in both the number of rounds and the communication complexity of the suggested protocols.

By scaling down the competing provers protocols of [3], Aaronson and Wigderson showed that strong enough lower bounds for the communication complexity of f, in this model, imply lower bounds for the computational complexity of f. More precisely, they show that for any language $L \in \mathsf{P}$ there are protocols in this model with poly-logarithmic rounds and communication complexity, and for any language $L \in \mathsf{LOGSPACE}$ there are one-round protocols with poly-logarithmic communication complexity.

Our results strengthen this connection and relates the communication complexity of f in this model to the circuit complexity of f.

More precisely, our results imply that if f can be computed by a Boolean circuit of size s and depth d then for any $r \geq 1$ there is an r rounds protocol for f, in this model, with communication complexity $d^{\frac{1}{r}} polylog(s)$. In particular, as before, when we allow only one round, the protocol exchanges $d \cdot polylog(s)$ bits, and when we allow $r = O\left(\frac{log(d)}{loglog(s)}\right)$ rounds, the protocol exchanges only $polylog(s)$ bits.

This can be viewed as a possible direction towards proving circuit lower bounds. For instance, in order to prove $f \notin \mathcal{NC}$, it suffices to show that any one-round protocol for f, in this model, requires the exchange of $\omega(polylog(n))$ bits. The one-round case is very appealing as it gives a relatively simple combinatorial condition that implies strong circuit lower bounds.

We also consider the model of communication complexity with one prover, where a single prover tries to convince the players that $f(x, y) = 1$. We observe that the result of [5] (combined with the approach of [1]) implies a connection between the communication complexity of f in this model and the circuit complexity of f. More precisely, their result implies that if f can be computed by a Boolean circuit of size s and depth d, then there are protocols for f, in this model, with $d \cdot polylog(s)$ rounds and the exchange of $d \cdot polylog(s)$ bits.

2. OUR SETTINGS

We study the query complexity and communication complexity settings in the presence of (untrusted) provers. In this section we present the formal settings used in the paper.

We start by reviewing the standard query and communication complexity settings (Subsection 2.1). We present a generalized framework for interaction between players and provers, called *general communication protocols* (Subsection 2.2). We describe the settings for query and communication complexity with provers (Subsections 2.3 and 2.4). Finally, we discuss the relations between query and communication complexity with provers (Subsection 2.5).

Let $\mathcal{F}_n$ be the set of Boolean functions on n bits, $\mathcal{F}_n = \{f \mid f : \{0,1\}^n \rightarrow \{0,1\}\}$.

2.1 Query and Communication Complexity

2.1.1 Query Complexity

In the query complexity setting, we are given a function $f \in \mathcal{F}_n$ and an input $x \in \{0,1\}^n$. We are then asked to compute $f(x)$ by reading the least number of bits from x.

2.1.2 Communication Complexity

The communication complexity setting involves two separated, computationally-unbounded players, Alice and Bob, that attempt to evaluate a function $f \in \mathcal{F}_{2n}$ known to both. Alice receives a private n-bit string x, and Bob receives a private n-bit string y. Let $x \circ y \in \{0,1\}^{2n}$ denote the concatenation of the strings x and y. The goal is for one of the players (for concreteness, say Alice) to compute and output $f(x \circ y)$, with the least amount of communication between them.

2.2 General Communication Protocols

We consider the setting in which a set of players and provers, each holding a private input (bit-string), communicate. A general communication protocol (GCP) prescribes a probabilistic strategy to each participant. During the execution of the protocol, any player may exchange messages (bit-strings) with any of the other players or provers through a private channel. We assume that there is no communication among provers.

At the end of the protocol the first player must output a value in $\{0, 1, \perp\}$. Informally speaking, this value should be the result of the evaluation of a Boolean function on the participants' inputs. A 0 or 1 output is interpreted as the actual value of the function, while $\perp$ indicates that one of the provers did not follow his prescribed strategy.

A GCP proceeds in *rounds*. Each round consists of three sets of messages sent in the following order (messages may be empty):

1. Players send questions: Each player sends a message (question) to each of the provers.
2. Provers reply: Each prover sends a message (answer) to each of the players.
3. Players interact: Each player sends a message to each of the other players, according to some pre-specified order.

The *communication complexity* of a GCP is defined as the maximal number of bits exchanged by all the involved parties (provers and players) in any execution. An (r, c)-GCP is a GCP with at most r rounds, and communication complexity at most c.

2.3 Query and Communication Complexity with Provers

Next, we formally define the settings used in the paper. We define two variants of the query complexity model, called QCP and QCCP, as well as the two variants of the communication complexity model, called CCP and CCCP.

In the CCP and CCCP models, the players attempt to compute the value of a function $f \in \mathcal{F}_{2n}$ on an input $x \circ y \in \{0,1\}^{2n}$. We assume that the prover(s) know both x and y, while Alice only has x, and Bob only has y.

In the QCP and QCCP models, the player attempts to compute the value of a function $f \in \mathcal{F}_n$ on an input $x \in \{0,1\}^n$. We assume that the prover(s) have the input x, *while the player has an oracle access to a (possibly a more "elaborated") version of x.* That is, the player has access to a string $y = g(x)$, where g is a function that possibly "stretches" x. We mention that in this paper $g(x)$ will always be the low-degree extension of x (see Subsection 2.4).

In the QCP model, we require the player to output one of the values $f(x)$ or $\perp$ with probability at least $1-\epsilon$, regardless of the behavior of the prover (that is, the player is only allowed to make a mistake with probability at most ϵ). If the prover is truthful (i.e., follows the prescribed strategy), we require the player to always output $f(x)$. The requirements for the CCP model are similar.

In the QCCP model, we assume that at least one of the provers is truthful (i.e., follows the prescribed strategy), and require the player to output $f(x)$ with probability at least $1 - \epsilon$, regardless of the behavior of the other prover. Note that, without loss of generality, we may assume that one prover tries to convince the player that $f(x) = 1$, while the other tries to convince the player that $f(x) = 0$. The requirements for the CCCP model are similar.

For the rest of the section let $\epsilon \in [0, 1]$, $n, r, c, q, \ell \in \mathbb{N}$, $\mathbb{F}$ be a field, and $g : \{0,1\}^n \rightarrow \mathbb{F}^\ell$.

DEFINITION 1 (QCP). $\mathsf{QCP}_{\epsilon,g}(r, c, q)$ *is the set of functions $f \in \mathcal{F}_n$ that can be computed by an (r, c)-GCP between a player and a prover, in the following sense: The prover is given an input $x \in \{0,1\}^n$, while the player is given the input $y = g(x)$.*

For any strategy of the prover, a player who follows the protocol reads at most q symbols from y and, with probability at least $1 - \epsilon$, outputs either $f(x)$ or $\perp$. If the prover also follows the protocol, then the player always outputs $f(x)$.

DEFINITION 2 (CCP). $\mathsf{CCP}_{\epsilon}(r, c)$ *is the set of functions $f \in \mathcal{F}_{2n}$, that can be computed by an (r, c)-GCP between two players, Alice and Bob, and a prover, in the following sense:*

Alice is given an input $x \in \{0,1\}^n$ and Bob is given an input $y \in \{0,1\}^n$, while the prover is given the input $x \circ y$.

If both players follow the protocol, then for any strategy of the prover, with probability at least $1-\epsilon$, Alice outputs either $f(x \circ y)$ or $\perp$. If the prover also follows the protocol, then Alice always outputs $f(x \circ y)$.

DEFINITION 3 (QCCP). *$\mathsf{QCCP}_{\epsilon,g}(r,c,q)$ is the set of functions $f \in \mathcal{F}_n$, that can be computed by an (r,c)-GCP between a player and a pair of provers, in the following sense: Both provers are given (the same) input $x \in \{0,1\}^n$, while the player is given the input $y = g(x)$.*

Assume that for any fixed f and x, one of the provers, whose identity maybe unknown to the player, always follows the protocol. That is, this prover runs the probabilistic strategy prescribed to him by the protocol. Then, for any strategy of the other prover, a player who follows the protocol reads at most q symbols from y and, with probability at least $1-\epsilon$, outputs $f(x)$.

DEFINITION 4 (CCCP). *$\mathsf{CCCP}_{\epsilon}(r,c)$ is the set of functions $f \in \mathcal{F}_{2n}$, that can be computed by an (r,c)-GCP between two players, Alice and Bob, and a pair of provers, in the following sense: Alice is given the input $x \in \{0,1\}^n$ and Bob is given the input $y \in \{0,1\}^n$, while both provers are given $x \circ y$.*

Assume that for any fixed f, x and y, one of the provers, whose identity maybe unknown to the players, always follows the protocol. That is, this prover runs the probabilistic strategy prescribed to him by the protocol. For any strategy of the other prover, if both players follow the protocol, Alice outputs $f(x \circ y)$ with probability at least $1-\epsilon$.

2.4 Low Degree Extension (LDE)

Recall that in the QCP and QCCP models, the prover(s) have an input x, while the player has access to $y = g(x)$. As mentioned before, in this paper, $g(x)$ is always the low-degree extension of x. In this subsection we define the function $g(x) = \mathsf{LDE}(x)$, that maps x to its low-degree extension.

Let $\mathbb{H} = \{0,...,h-1\}$ be a set and $\mathbb{F} = \{0,...,p-1\}$ be a field satisfying $h \le p \in \mathbb{N}$. Recall that the Low-Degree Extension (LDE) of a function $x : \mathbb{H}^m \to \mathbb{F}$ is the unique m variate polynomial $\tilde{x} : \mathbb{F}^m \to \mathbb{F}$ that agrees with x on $\mathbb{H}^m$ (i.e., $\tilde{x}\mid_{\mathbb{H}^m} = x$), and has degree at most $h-1$ in each of its m variables.

We sometimes refer to x and $\tilde{x}$ as truth table strings instead of functions. More precisely, we identify x with the vector in $\mathbb{F}^{h^m}$ whose j^{th} coordinate is $x(h_j)$, where h_j is the jth element in the lexicographic ordering of $\mathbb{H}^m$. Similarly, we identify $\tilde{x}$ with the vector in $\mathbb{F}^{p^m}$ whose j^{th} coordinate is $\tilde{x}(p_j)$, where p_j is the jth element in the lexicographic ordering of $\mathbb{F}^m$.

Let $s \in \mathbb{N}$. We define a set $\mathbb{H}_s = \{0,...,h_s-1\}$ and a field $\mathbb{F}_s = \{0,...,p_s-1\}$ satisfying $h_s \le p_s \in \mathbb{N}$. Let $h_s = \lceil log(s) \rceil$. Let $m_s \in \mathbb{N}$ be the minimal such that $h_s^{m_s} \ge s$. Let $\mathbb{F}_s$ be the field of smallest size satisfying $p_s \ge 12 m_s h_s^3$. Note that $h_s, p_s \le polylog(s)$, $m_s = O\left(\frac{log(s)}{loglog(s)}\right)$ and $s \le h_s^{m_s}, p_s^{m_s} \le poly(s)$.

For $n < s \in \mathbb{N}$, we define the function $\mathsf{LDE}_s : \{0,1\}^n \to \mathbb{F}_s^{p_s^{m_s}}$ as follows: Given $x \in \{0,1\}^n$, we pad x with 1's to get an $h_s^{m_s}$-size string $x' \in \mathbb{F}_s^{h_s^{m_s}}$. That is, x' is defined by: $\forall i \in [n] : x'_i = x_i$, and $\forall i \in \{n+1,...,h_s^{m_s}\} : x'_i = 1$. We remark that we pad x with 1's and not with 0's to make the proof of Lemma 13 (below) simpler. Finally, we define $\mathsf{LDE}_s(x)$ to be the low-degree extension $\tilde{x}'$ of x'.

2.5 Connection Between Query and Communication Complexity with Provers

The following observation made by [1] shows that results for the query complexity model (with $g(x) = \mathsf{LDE}_s(x)$) imply analogous results for the communication complexity model. More precisely, in the communication complexity setting, any point in the low degree extension of the concatenated input $x \circ y$, can be computed by the players by the exchange of a single field element.

Let S be a set, and let $c \in \mathbb{N}$. Consider the simple generalization of the standard communication complexity setting that allows Alice and Bob to exchange symbols from the set S (instead of just bits). We denote by $\mathsf{CC}_S(c)$ the class of all functions $f : \{0,1\}^{2n} \to S$ that can be computed by having Alice and Bob exchange at most c elements of S.

PROPOSITION 5 ([1]). Fix $n, s \in \mathbb{N}$, $s > 2n$, and $z \in \mathbb{F}_s^{m_s}$. Let $f : \{0,1\}^{2n} \to \mathbb{F}_s$ be given by $f(x \circ y) = (\mathsf{LDE}_s(x \circ y))(z)$. Then, $f \in \mathsf{CC}_{\mathbb{F}_s}(1)$.

The proof of Proposition 5 follows easily by the fact that low degree extension is a linear function.

We say that a QCP or a QCCP protocol is *non-adaptive* if the queries to $y = g(x)$ made by the player only depend on the player's random string. We mention that protocols presented in this paper are non-adaptive.

The following is an easy corollary of the above proposition.

COROLLARY 6. Let $f \in \mathcal{F}_{2n}$, $r, c, q, s \in \mathbb{N}$, $2n < s$, and $\epsilon \in [0,1]$.

1. Assume $f \in \mathsf{QCP}_{\epsilon,\mathsf{LDE}_s}(r,c,q)$, with a non-adaptive protocol. Then $f \in \mathsf{CCP}_{\epsilon}(r, c + O(q \cdot log(s)))$.
2. *Assume $f \in \mathsf{QCCP}_{\epsilon,\mathsf{LDE}_s}(r,c,q)$, with a non-adaptive* protocol. Then $f \in \mathsf{CCCP}_{\epsilon}(r, c + O(q \cdot log(s)))$.

COROLLARY 7. *In the above CCP and CCCP protocols for f, the players exchange c bits with the prover(s), and $O(q \cdot log(s))$ bits among themselves.*

3. OUR RESULTS

Let $\mathcal{F}_{s,d}$ be the set of all functions $f \in \mathcal{F}_{2n}$ that have an $s(n)$ size, $d(n)$ depth, Boolean circuit of fan-in 2. The main result of this paper is that functions in $\mathcal{F}_{s,d}$ can be computed with low query and communication cost in the QCCP model, and therefore (due to Corollary 6) with low communication cost in the CCCP model.

The first theorem claims that in the QCP and CCP models, $d \cdot polylog(s)$ communication bits suffice in order to compute any $f \in \mathcal{F}_{s,d}$ with high probability. The QCP part of the theorem is a restatement of the main theorem of [5], while the CCP part of it follows as in Corollary 6.

REMARK 1. *In all the protocols below, the players and honest provers run in time at most $poly(s)$.*

THEOREM 8 ([5]). *Let $f \in \mathcal{F}_{s,d}$ and $\epsilon = \frac{1}{log(s)}$. Then, there exists a field $\mathbb{F}$ of size $poly(d, log(s))$ and a function*[2]

[2]The function g is a low degree extension with different parameters than the ones we have here.

$g : \{0,1\}^n \to \mathbb{F}^{poly(s)}$, *such that,*

$$f \in \mathsf{QCP}_{\epsilon,g}\left(d \cdot polylog\left(s\right), d \cdot polylog\left(s\right), 1\right)$$

and

$$f \in \mathsf{CCP}_{\epsilon}\left(d \cdot polylog\left(s\right), d \cdot polylog\left(s\right)\right).$$

Our next theorem shows that the computation of $f \in \mathcal{F}_{s,d}$ can be done with even lower communication complexity in the competing provers models. The theorem offers a trade-off between the number of rounds and the communication complexity of the protocol. Namely, for every $r \in \mathbb{N}$, there is a protocol that computes f with high probability, and only requires r rounds and $d^{\frac{1}{r}} polylog\left(s\right)$ communication bits.

THEOREM 9 **(Main)**. *Let $f \in \mathcal{F}_{s,d}$ and $\epsilon = \frac{1}{log(s)}$. $\forall r \in \mathbb{N}$ it holds that*

$$f \in \mathsf{QCCP}_{\epsilon,\mathsf{LDE}_s}\left(r, d^{\frac{1}{r}} polylog\left(s\right), 1\right)$$

and

$$f \in \mathsf{CCCP}_{\epsilon}\left(r, d^{\frac{1}{r}} polylog\left(s\right)\right).$$

The next two theorems are easy corollaries of Theorem 9 that are obtained by taking r to extreme values. Theorem 10 takes r to be 1, and claims that f can be computed by the exchange of $d \cdot polylog\left(s\right)$ bits and *with only a single communication round.* Theorem 11 shows that by choosing $r = O\left(\frac{log(d)}{loglog(s)}\right)$ we can reduce the communication complexity of the protocol to $polylog\left(s\right)$ at the price of having $O\left(\frac{log(d)}{loglog(s)}\right)$ rounds.

THEOREM 10. *Let $f \in \mathcal{F}_{s,d}$ and $\epsilon = \frac{1}{log(s)}$.* Then,

$$f \in \mathsf{QCCP}_{\epsilon,\mathsf{LDE}_s}\left(\mathbf{1}, d \cdot polylog\left(s\right), 1\right)$$

and

$$f \in \mathsf{CCCP}_{\epsilon}\left(\mathbf{1}, d \cdot polylog\left(s\right)\right).$$

THEOREM 11. *Let $f \in \mathcal{F}_{s,d}$ and $\epsilon = \frac{1}{log(s)}$.* Then,

$$f \in \mathsf{QCCP}_{\epsilon,\mathsf{LDE}_s}\left(O\left(\frac{log(d)}{loglog(s)}\right), polylog\left(s\right), 1\right),$$

$$f \in \mathsf{CCCP}_{\epsilon}\left(O\left(\frac{log(d)}{loglog(s)}\right), polylog\left(s\right)\right).$$

The next theorem claims that if f is given by a $log\left(s\right)$-space uniform circuit of size s and depth d, then the player(s) in Theorem 9 can be very efficient and run in time $d^{\frac{1}{r}} polylog\left(s\right)$.

THEOREM 12. *Let $f \in \mathcal{F}_{s,d}$ with a $log\left(s\right)$-**space uniform circuit**, and let $\epsilon = \frac{1}{log(s)}$. $\forall r \in \mathbb{N}$ the claim of* Theorem 9 holds with players that run in time $d^{\frac{1}{r}} polylog\left(s\right)$ (and honest provers that run in time $poly\left(s\right)$), and error 2ϵ.

4. PRELIMINARIES

Fix a size s depth d circuit C, and an input x for C. Set $\epsilon = \frac{1}{log(s)}$. From now on, we omit the sub-s and write $\mathbb{H}$, $\mathbb{F}$, h, p, m instead of $\mathbb{H}_s$, $\mathbb{F}_s$, h_s, p_s, m_s. We enumerate the layers of C such that layer 0 is the output layer and layer d is the input layer. Note that since s is the number of wires in C, the number of gates in each of the layers cannot exceed s.

We add gates to each of the layers of C, so that each will contain exactly $h^m > s$ gates. We label the gates in every layer by elements of $\mathbb{H}^m$. The gates added to every layer i ($i \in \{0, ..., d\}$), are all "special" gates that always return 1. The fact that every layer contains such a gate makes the proof of Lemma 13 (below) simpler.

We associate with every layer $i \in \{0, ..., d\}$ the vector $V_i \in \mathbb{F}^{h^m}$ that consists of the values of the layer's gates when C is evaluated on x. That is, for $j \in [h^m]$, the jth coordinate of V_i is the value, when C is evaluated on x, of the gate in layer i whose label is the jth element in the lexicographic ordering of $\mathbb{H}^m$. We denote by $\tilde{V}_i \in \mathbb{F}^{p^m}$ the low-degree extension of V_i.

We may assume, without loss of generality, that the output layer, layer 0, originally consists of a single gate whose label is now 0^m. The player's task can now be rephrased as computing $\tilde{V}_0\left(0^m\right)$.

Let $I = \{0, ..., d\}$ and $L = \{0, ..., 2m\}$. Given a set A and an element $a \in A$, we denote $A_{-a} = A \backslash \{a\}$. Let $\phi \in \mathbb{F}^0$ be the unique zero-coordinates vector. Whenever we say that a curve or a polynomial is of degree k, we mean that it is of degree at most k. A line is a degree 1 curve.

5. REDUCING COMPUTATION OF LAYER I TO LAYER $I+1$

In this section we follow the lines of [5] and show that the problem of computing $\tilde{V}_i$ on a point in $\mathbb{F}^m$ can be reduced to the task of computing $\tilde{V}_{i+1}$ on two points in $\mathbb{F}^m$, using a sum-check protocol.

5.1 $\tilde{V}_i$ is a Quadratic Polynomial in the Values of V_{i+1}

Let $i \in I_{-d}$. The next lemma claims that $\tilde{V}_i$ is a degree-2 polynomial in the values of V_{i+1}. The reason is that since $\tilde{V}_i$ is the low-degree extension of V_i, for every $z \in \mathbb{F}^m$, the value $\tilde{V}_i\left(z\right)$ is a linear combination of the values of V_i on $\mathbb{H}^m$. That is, it is a linear combination of the values of the gates of layer i. In addition, the value of a gate in layer i is a degree-2 polynomial in the values of its two children in layer $i+1$.

LEMMA 13. *For every $i \in I_{-d}$, there exists a function $\beta_i : \mathbb{F}^m \times \left(\mathbb{H}^m\right)^2 \to \mathbb{F}$ that does not depend on the input x to the circuit, such that:*

1. $\forall z \in \mathbb{F}^m$:
$$\tilde{V}_i\left(z\right) = \sum_{w_0, w_1 \in \mathbb{H}^m} \beta_i\left(z, w_0, w_1\right) V_{i+1}\left(w_0\right) V_{i+1}\left(w_1\right).$$

2. For every fixed $w_0, w_1 \in \mathbb{H}^m$, and every $j \in [m]$, the function $\beta_i\left(z_1 ... z_m, w_0, w_1\right)$ is a polynomial of degree at most $h-1$ in z_j.

Proof Fix $i \in I_{-d}$ and let $z \in \mathbb{F}^m$. The value $\tilde{V}_i\left(z\right)$ can be written as

$$\tilde{V}_i\left(z\right) = \sum_{p \in \mathbb{H}^m} \beta'\left(z, p\right) \cdot V_i\left(p\right),$$

where $\beta'\left(z, p\right) : \mathbb{F}^m \times \mathbb{H}^m \to \mathbb{F}$ is the following $2m$-variables function

$$\beta'(z,p)=\prod_{j=1}^{m}\prod_{q_j\in\mathbb{H}\setminus\{p_j\}}(z_j-q_j)\cdot(p_j-q_j)^{-1}.$$

Note that for every $j\in[m]$ and every fixed $p_0\in\mathbb{H}^m$, the function $\beta'(z_1...z_m,p_0)$ is a degree $h-1$ polynomial in z_j.

The value of gate $p\in\mathbb{H}^m$ in layer i depends on the values of its two child gates in layer $i+1$. Recall that every layer of C contains at least one "special" gate, that returns 1 on every input. Conclude that there exists a function $c:(\mathbb{H}^m)^3\to\mathbb{F}$ (c depends on the circuit C) such that

$$V_i(p)=\sum_{w_0,w_1\in\mathbb{H}^m}c(p,w_0,w_1)V_{i+1}(w_0)V_{i+1}(w_1).$$

For example, if gate p in layer i is an OR gate whose children are gates $w_0,w_1\in\mathbb{H}^m$ in layer $i+1$, and gate $w^*\in\mathbb{H}^m$ in layer $i+1$ is a gate that always returns 1, then

$$V_i(p)=V_{i+1}(w_0)V_{i+1}(w^*)+V_{i+1}(w_1)V_{i+1}(w^*)$$
$$-V_{i+1}(w_0)V_{i+1}(w_1).$$

Putting it all together,

$$\tilde{V}_i(z)=$$

$$\sum_{p\in\mathbb{H}^m}\beta'(z,p)\cdot\left(\sum_{w_0,w_1\in\mathbb{H}^m}c(p,w_0,w_1)V_{i+1}(w_0)V_{i+1}(w_1)\right)=$$

$$\sum_{w_0,w_1\in\mathbb{H}^m}\left(\sum_{p\in\mathbb{H}^m}\beta'(z,p)\cdot c(p,w_0,w_1)\right)V_{i+1}(w_0)V_{i+1}(w_1).$$

Finally, we denote

$$\beta_i(z,w_0,w_1)=\sum_{p\in\mathbb{H}^m}\beta'(z,p)\cdot c(p,w_0,w_1),$$

and get

$$\tilde{V}_i(z)=\sum_{w_0,w_1\in\mathbb{H}^m}\beta_i(z,w_0,w_1)V_{i+1}(w_0)V_{i+1}(w_1).$$

Since $\beta'(z_1...z_m,p)$ is of degree at most $h-1$ in z_j for every $j\in[m]$, it is also the case that β_i is of degree at most $h-1$ in z_j.

5.2 Computing $\tilde{V}_i$ Given $\tilde{V}_{i+1}$ by Sum-Check

Let $i\in I_{-d}$. The following lemma shows that for every $z\in\mathbb{F}^m$, verifying a claimed value for $\tilde{V}_i(z)$ can be done by a sum-check protocol that only requires the values of $\tilde{V}_{i+1}$ on two points in $\mathbb{F}^m$.

LEMMA 14. *For every $i\in I_{-d}$, there exists a function $\tilde{\beta}_i:(\mathbb{F}^m)^3\to\mathbb{F}$ that does not depend on the input x to the circuit, such that the function $\Phi_i:(\mathbb{F}^m)^3\to\mathbb{F}$ given by*

$$\Phi_i(z,w_0,w_1)=\tilde{\beta}_i(z,w_0,w_1)\tilde{V}_{i+1}(w_0)\tilde{V}_{i+1}(w_1)$$

satisfies:

1. $\forall z\in\mathbb{F}^m:\tilde{V}_i(z)=\sum_{w_0,w_1\in\mathbb{H}^m}\Phi_i(z,w_0,w_1)$.
2. Φ_i is of degree at most $2(h-1)$ in each of its $3m$ variables.

Proof Fix $i\in I_{-d}$, let $z,w_0,w_1\in\mathbb{F}^m$, and let $\beta_i:\mathbb{F}^m\times(\mathbb{H}^m)^2\to\mathbb{F}$ be the function promised by Lemma 13. We denote by $\tilde{\beta}_i:(\mathbb{F}^m)^3\to\mathbb{F}$ the low-degree extension of $\beta_i(z,w_0,w_1)$ with respect to w_0 and w_1. That is, fix $z\in\mathbb{F}^m$, and let $\beta_{i,z}:\mathbb{H}^{2m}\to\mathbb{F}$ be given by $\beta_{i,z}(w_0,w_1)=\beta_i(z,w_0,w_1)$. Let $\tilde{\beta}_{i,z}:\mathbb{F}^{2m}\to\mathbb{F}$ be the low-degree extension of $\beta_{i,z}$. Finally, let $\tilde{\beta}_i(z,w_0,w_1)=\tilde{\beta}_{i,z}(w_0,w_1)$.

Due to Lemma 13, it holds that

$$\forall z\in\mathbb{F}^m:\tilde{V}_i(z)=\sum_{w_0,w_1\in\mathbb{H}^m}\Phi_i(z,w_0,w_1).$$

Furthermore, $\Phi_i(z,w_0,w_1)$ is of low-degree in each of its $3m$ variables: Let $z=z_1...z_m$, $w_0=w_{0,1}...w_{0,m}$, $w_1=w_{1,1}...w_{1,m}$, and fix $j\in[m]$. Since $\tilde{\beta}_i$ is the low-degree extension of β_i (with respect to w_0 and w_1), it is of degree at most $h-1$ in $w_{0,j}$ and $w_{1,j}$. Since $\tilde{V}_{i+1}$ is a low-degree extension of V_{i+1}, it is of degree at most $h-1$ in each of its m variables. Conclude that Φ_i is of degree at most $2(h-1)$ in $w_{0,j}$ and $w_{1,j}$.

Fix $w_0,w_1\in\mathbb{H}^m$. Using Lemma 13, the function $\beta_i(z_1...z_m,w_0,w_1)$ is a polynomial of degree $h-1$ in z_j. Again, using the fact that $\tilde{\beta}_i$ is the low-degree extension of β_i, it holds that $\tilde{\beta}_i(z,w_0,w_1)$ is a linear combination of the values $\beta_i(z,w_0',w_1')$ ($w_0',w_1'\in\mathbb{H}^m$) with coefficients that depend only on w_0,w_1,w_0',w_1' (and are independent of z).

For every $w_0',w_1'\in\mathbb{H}^m$, the value $\beta_i(z,w_0',w_1')$ is a polynomial of degree at most $h-1$ in z_j. Thus, any linear combination of these values, and in particular $\tilde{\beta}_i(z,w_0,w_1)$, is a polynomial of degree at most $h-1$ in z_j. Conclude that Φ_i is of degree at most $h-1$ in z_j.

For $i\in I_{-d}$, let Φ_i be the function defined in Lemma 14. For every $i\in I_{-d},\ell\in L$, we define the partial-sum function $\Phi_{i,\ell}(z,x):\mathbb{F}^m\times\mathbb{F}^\ell\to\mathbb{F}$ as follows:

$$\Phi_{i,\ell}(z,x_1...x_\ell)=\sum_{x_{\ell+1},...,x_{2m}\in\mathbb{H}}\Phi_i(z,x_1...x_{2m}).$$

Note that $\Phi_{i,\ell}(z_1...z_m,x_1...x_\ell)$ is of degree at most $2(h-1)$ in each of its $m+\ell$ variables, and that

$$\tilde{V}_i(z)=\Phi_{i,0}(z,\phi)\qquad(1)$$

$$\Phi_i(z,w_0,w_1)=\Phi_{i,2m}(z,w_0\circ w_1).\qquad(2)$$

Also observe that a sum-check protocol can be used to reduce the computation of $\tilde{V}_i(z)=\Phi_{i,0}(z,\phi)$ to the computation of $\Phi_i(z,w_0,w_1)=\Phi_{i,2m}(z,w_0\circ w_1)$. Since $\tilde{\beta}_i$ does not depend on the input to the circuit x, the player can compute $\Phi_{i,2m}(z,w_0\circ w_1)$ by herself given $\tilde{V}_{i+1}(w_0)$ and $\tilde{V}_{i+1}(w_1)$. In other words, the evaluation of $\tilde{V}_i$ on z can be reduced, by a sum-check protocol, to the computation of $\tilde{V}_{i+1}$ on the pair of points $w_0,w_1\in\mathbb{F}^m$.

6. ONE ROUND PROTOCOL

In this section we prove Theorem 10. Namely, we show that for any $f\in\mathcal{F}_{s,d}$ it holds that $f\in\mathsf{QCCP}_{\epsilon,\mathsf{LDE}_s}(1,d\cdot polylog(s),1)$ where $\epsilon=\frac{1}{log(s)}$. We describe a protocol that given a size s depth d circuit C on n bits, and an input $x\in\{0,1\}^n$, outputs $C(x)$ with probability at least $1-\epsilon$. The protocol consists of a *single round*, requires the exchange of $d \cdot polylog(s)$ bits, and makes a single query to $\tilde{x} = \mathsf{LDE}_s(x)$.

The protocol consists of three steps: (*i*) The player sends questions to the provers (Subsection 6.1). (*ii*) The provers reply (Subsection 6.2). (*iii*) Using the provers' answers, the player decides on the value of $C(x)$ (Subsection 6.4). Subsection 6.3 contains observations that are used in Subsection 6.4 in order to show the correctness of the player's decision.

We assume that one of the provers claims that $C(x) = 1$, while the other claims $C(x) = 0$. Otherwise, if both claim that $C(x) = b$ ($b \in \{0,1\}$), then since at least one of the provers is truthful, it must be the case that indeed $C(x) = b$. In the protocol below we assume that the player knows the identity of the prover claiming that $C(x) = 1$ (we call him P_1), and the identity of the prover claiming that $C(x) = 0$ (we call him P_0). This assumption is justified as the player may require each prover to add his claimed value for $C(x)$ to his reply message.

For the rest of the section let $\beta \in \mathbb{F} \backslash \mathbb{H}$ be an arbitrary element.

REMARK 2 (**functions representation**). *During the execution of the protocol, the participants exchange a set of curves and polynomials. Each of the exchanged curves is of degree (at most) h. Each exchanged polynomial is either of the form $F(r) = \tilde{V}_i(Z(r))$ ($i \in I$) or of the form $F(r,t) = \Phi_{i,\ell}(Z(r), X(t))$ ($i \in I_{-d}, \ell \in L$), where $Z(r) : \mathbb{F} \to \mathbb{F}^m$ and $X(t) : \mathbb{F} \to \mathbb{F}^\ell$ are two previously exchanged degree-h curves. In other words, the exchanged polynomials are all restrictions of $\tilde{V}_i$ and $\Phi_{i,\ell}$ to degree h curves.*

The polynomial $\tilde{V}_i(z)$ is of degree at most $h-1$ in each of its m variables, as it is the low-degree extension of V_i. The polynomial $\Phi_{i,\ell}(z, x_1 ... x_\ell)$ is of degree at most $2(h-1)$ in each of its $m+\ell$ variables (see Subsection 5.2). Therefore, each exchanged polynomial is of total degree at most $h \cdot 2(h-1) \cdot (m+\ell) < 6mh^2$. We require each such polynomial to be sent in a canonical representation, *as a sequence of at most $6mh^2$ coefficients. Curves will be sent as sequences of polynomials.*

6.1 The Player's Questions

For every $i \in I_{-d}, \ell \in L$, the player constructs a degree-h curve $C_{i,\ell} : \mathbb{F} \to \mathbb{F}^\ell$, and a line $D_{i,\ell} : \mathbb{F} \to \mathbb{F}^\ell$. For every $i \in I$, the player constructs a degree-2 curve $Z_i : \mathbb{F} \to \mathbb{F}^m$, and a point $z_i \in \mathbb{F}^m$. The curves Z_i ($i \in I$) and $C_{i,\ell}$ ($i \in I_{-d}, \ell \in L$) are given to P_1, while the points z_i ($i \in I$) and the lines $D_{i,\ell}$ ($i \in I_{-d}, \ell \in L$) are given to P_0.

Let $Z_0 : \mathbb{F} \to \mathbb{F}^m$ be the constant 0^m curve. That is, $\forall r \in \mathbb{F} : Z_0(r) = 0^m$. Randomly select $\zeta_0 \in_R \mathbb{F} \backslash \{0,1\}$. Set $z_0 = Z_0(\zeta_0) = 0^m$.

Recall that $\beta \in \mathbb{F} \backslash \mathbb{H}$ is an arbitrary element. For $i = 0, ..., d-1$ we construct the additional needed curves and points in the following order:

The curves $(C_{i,\ell})_{\ell \in L}$ and $(D_{i,\ell})_{\ell \in L}$ are constructed recursively.

- **Construct** $C_{i,0}, D_{i,0}$**:** Define $C_{i,0}, D_{i,0} : \mathbb{F} \to \mathbb{F}^0$ by $\forall t \in \mathbb{F} : C_{i,0}(t) = D_{i,0}(t) = \phi$.
- **Construct** $C_{i,\ell}$ **given** $D_{i,\ell-1}$ ($\ell \in L_{-0}$)**:**
Randomly select $\delta_{i,\ell-1} \in_R \mathbb{F} \backslash \{0\}$ and set $a_{i,\ell-1} = D_{i,\ell-1}(\delta_{i,\ell-1})$.
Let $C_{i,\ell}$ be a *random* degree-h curve satisfying $\forall \alpha \in \mathbb{H} : C_{i,\ell}(\alpha) = a_{i,\ell-1} \circ \alpha$, chosen as follows: Randomly select $c_{i,\ell} \in_R \mathbb{F}^\ell$, and let $C_{i,\ell}$ be the degree-h curve satisfying $\forall \alpha \in \mathbb{H} : C_{i,\ell}(\alpha) = a_{i,\ell-1} \circ \alpha$ and $C_{i,\ell}(\beta) = c_{i,\ell}$.
- **Construct** $D_{i,\ell}$ **given** $C_{i,\ell}$ ($\ell \in L_{-0}$)**:**
Randomly select $\gamma_{i,\ell} \in_R \mathbb{F} \backslash \mathbb{H}$.
Let $D_{i,\ell}$ be a *random* line satisfying $D_{i,\ell}(0) = C_{i,\ell}(\gamma_{i,\ell})$, chosen as follows: Randomly select $d_{i,\ell} \in_R \mathbb{F}^\ell$, and let $D_{i,\ell}$ be the line satisfying $D_{i,\ell}(0) = C_{i,\ell}(\gamma_{i,\ell})$ and $D_{i,\ell}(1) = d_{i,\ell}$.

The curve Z_{i+1} is constructed as follows. Randomly select $\delta_{i,2m} \in_R \mathbb{F} \backslash \{0\}$ and set $a_{i,2m} = D_{i,2m}(\delta_{i,2m})$. Denote $a_{i,2m} = w_{i,0} \circ w_{i,1}$ where $w_{i,0}, w_{i,1} \in \mathbb{F}^m$. Let Z_{i+1} be a *random* degree-2 curve satisfying $Z_{i+1}(0) = w_{i,0}$ and $Z_{i+1}(1) = w_{i,1}$, chosen as follows: Randomly select $w_{i+1} \in_R \mathbb{F}^m$, and let Z_{i+1} be the degree-2 curve satisfying $Z_{i+1}(0) = w_{i,0}$, $Z_{i+1}(1) = w_{i,1}$ and $Z_{i+1}(2) = w_{i+1}$.

The point z_{i+1} is selected as follows. Randomly select $\zeta_{i+1} \in_R \mathbb{F} \backslash \{0,1\}$. Set $z_{i+1} = Z_{i+1}(\zeta_{i+1})$.

6.2 The Provers' Answers

P_1*'s reply*

For $i \in I_{-d}, \ell \in L_{-0}$, denote by $T^*_{i,\ell} : \mathbb{F} \times \mathbb{F} \to \mathbb{F}$ the polynomial $T^*_{i,\ell}(r,t) = \Phi_{i,\ell}(Z_i(r), C_{i,\ell}(t))$. For $i \in I_{-0}$, denote by $U^*_i : \mathbb{F} \to \mathbb{F}$ the polynomial $U^*_i(r) = \tilde{V}_i(Z_i(r))$.

P_1 replies with a set of polynomials $T_{i,\ell} : \mathbb{F} \times \mathbb{F} \to \mathbb{F}$ ($i \in I_{-d}, \ell \in L_{-0}$), and a set of polynomials $U_i : \mathbb{F} \to \mathbb{F}$ ($i \in I_{-0}$). The honest P_1 should reply with $T_{i,\ell} = T^*_{i,\ell}$ and $U_i = U^*_i$.

P_0*'s reply*

For $i \in I_{-d}, \ell \in L$, denote by $Q^*_{i,\ell} : \mathbb{F} \to \mathbb{F}$ the polynomial $Q^*_{i,\ell}(t) = \Phi_{i,\ell}(z_i, D_{i,\ell}(t))$.

P_0 replies with a set of polynomials $Q_{i,\ell} : \mathbb{F} \to \mathbb{F}$ ($i \in I_{-d}, \ell \in L$). The honest P_0 should reply with $Q_{i,\ell} = Q^*_{i,\ell}$.

6.3 Propositions

This subsection contains propositions that will be useful in the analysis of the player's decision in Subsection 6.4. Propositions 1 and 2 claim that the information given to P_1 by the player is independent of the pairs of values $(\zeta_i, \gamma_{i,\ell})$. Propositions 3 and 4 claim that the information given to P_0 by the player is independent of the values $\delta_{i,\ell}$.

Denote by I_1 and I_0 the random variables describing the information given to P_1 and P_0 (respectively): $I_1 = \left((Z_i)_{i \in I}, (C_{i,\ell})_{i \in I_{-d}, \ell \in L}\right)$, and $I_0 = \left((z_i)_{i \in I}, (D_{i,\ell})_{i \in I_{-d}, \ell \in L}\right)$. In the proofs below, whenever we say "object" we mean a field element, point or curve selected by the player while constructing the questions to the provers.

PROPOSITION 1. *Let $i \in I_{-d}, \ell \in L_{-0}$. $\gamma_{i,\ell}$ is independent of I_1. That is, $\gamma_{i,\ell}$ is uniformly distributed in $\mathbb{F} \backslash \mathbb{H}$, even given I_1.*

Proof Let X be a random variable consisting of all the curves $Z_{i'}$ and $C_{i',\ell'}$ selected by the player *before* $\gamma_{i,\ell}$ is selected. Let Y be a random variable consisting of all the curves $Z_{i'}$ and $C_{i',\ell'}$ selected *after* $\gamma_{i,\ell}$. Clearly, $\gamma_{i,\ell}$ is selected independently of X. We will show that Y is independent of the pair $(X, \gamma_{i,\ell})$. This implies that I_1 is independent of $\gamma_{i,\ell}$.

The curve $D_{i,\ell}$ was selected to be a *random* line satisfying $D_{i,\ell}(0) = C_{i,\ell}(\gamma_{i,\ell})$. Therefore, for every fixed $\delta \in \mathbb{F}\setminus\{0\}$, the value $D_{i,\ell}(\delta)$ is uniformly distributed in $\mathbb{F}^{\ell}$, even given all the objects selected before $D_{i,\ell}$. In particular, $a_{i,\ell} = D_{i,\ell}(\delta_{i,\ell})$ is uniformly distributed in $\mathbb{F}^{\ell}$, even given all objects selected before $D_{i,\ell}$.

The player can select all the objects selected *after* $D_{i,\ell}$ by only knowing $a_{i,\ell}$. Since $a_{i,\ell}$ is uniformly distributed in $\mathbb{F}^{\ell}$, even given all objects selected before $D_{i,\ell}$, it holds that the objects selected after $D_{i,\ell}$ are independent of all objects selected before $D_{i,\ell}$. In particular, Y is independent of the pair $(X, \gamma_{i,\ell})$.

PROPOSITION 2. *Let $i \in I_{-d}, \ell \in L_{-0}$. ζ_i is independent of the pair $(I_1, \gamma_{i,\ell})$. That is, ζ_i is uniformly distributed in $\mathbb{F}\setminus\{0,1\}$, even given $(I_1, \gamma_{i,\ell})$. Furthermore, ζ_d is independent of I_1.*

Proof Clearly, ζ_i is uniformly distributed, even given all the previously selected objects. In addition, all the objects selected after ζ_i (and after z_i was set) are independent of all the objects selected up-to ζ_i (including ζ_i).

PROPOSITION 3. *Let $i \in I_{-d}, \ell \in L_{-2m}$. $\delta_{i,\ell}$ is independent of I_0. That is, $\delta_{i,\ell}$ is uniformly distributed in $\mathbb{F}\setminus\{0\}$, even given I_0.*

Proof Let X be a random variable consisting of all the points $z_{i'}$ and curves $D_{i',\ell'}$ selected by the player *before* $\delta_{i,\ell}$ is selected. Let Y be a random variable consisting of all the points $z_{i'}$ and curves $D_{i',\ell'}$ selected *after* $\delta_{i,\ell}$. Clearly, $\delta_{i,\ell}$ is selected independently of X. We will show that Y is independent of the pair $(X, \delta_{i,\ell})$. This implies that I_0 is independent of $\delta_{i,\ell}$.

The curve $C_{i,\ell+1}$ was selected to be a *random* degree-h curve satisfying $\forall\alpha \in \mathbb{H} : C_{i,\ell+1}(\alpha) = a_{i,\ell} \circ \alpha$. Therefore, for every fixed $\gamma \in \mathbb{F}\setminus\mathbb{H}$, the value $C_{i,\ell+1}(\gamma)$ is uniformly distributed in $\mathbb{F}^{\ell+1}$, even given all objects selected before $C_{i,\ell+1}$. In particular, $C_{i,\ell+1}(\gamma_{i,\ell+1})$ is uniformly distributed in $\mathbb{F}^{\ell+1}$, even given all objects selected before $C_{i,\ell+1}$.

The player can select all the objects selected after $C_{i,\ell+1}$ by only knowing $C_{i,\ell+1}(\gamma_{i,\ell+1})$. Since $C_{i,\ell+1}(\gamma_{i,\ell+1})$ is uniformly distributed in $\mathbb{F}^{\ell+1}$, even given all objects selected before $C_{i,\ell+1}$, it holds that the objects selected after $C_{i,\ell+1}$ are independent of all objects selected before $C_{i,\ell+1}$. In particular, Y is independent of the pair $(X, \delta_{i,\ell})$.

PROPOSITION 4. *Let $i \in I_{-d}$. $\delta_{i,2m}$ is independent of I_0. That is, $\delta_{i,2m}$ is uniformly distributed in $\mathbb{F}\setminus\{0\}$, even given I_0.*

Proof Clearly, $\delta_{i,2m}$ is uniformly distributed, even given all the previously selected objects. In addition, all the objects selected after z_{i+1} are independent of all the objects selected up-to z_{i+1} (including z_{i+1}). Therefore, it suffices to show that z_{i+1} itself is independent of all the objects selected up-to $\delta_{i,2m}$ (including $\delta_{i,2m}$).

The curve Z_{i+1} was selected to be a *random* degree-2 curve satisfying $Z_{i+1}(0) = w_{i,0}$ and $Z_{i+1}(1) = w_{i,1}$. Therefore, for every fixed $\zeta \in \mathbb{F}\setminus\{0,1\}$, the value $Z_{i+1}(\zeta)$ is uniformly distributed in $\mathbb{F}^m$, even given all the objects selected before Z_{i+1}. In particular, $z_{i+1} = Z_{i+1}(\zeta_{i+1})$ is uniformly distributed in $\mathbb{F}^m$, even given all the objects selected up-to $\delta_{i,2m}$ (including $\delta_{i,2m}$).

Let $i \in I_{-d}, \ell \in L_{-2m}$. Proposition 5 shows that if P_1 responds with the correct polynomial $T_{i,\ell+1}$, then the player can compute by herself the correct value of $Q_{i,\ell}(\delta_{i,\ell})$.

PROPOSITION 5. *Let $i \in I_{-d}, \ell \in L_{-2m}$. It hold that*

$$\sum_{\alpha\in\mathbb{H}} T^*_{i,\ell+1}(\zeta_i, \alpha) = Q^*_{i,\ell}(\delta_{i,\ell}).$$

Proof

$$\begin{aligned}
\sum_{\alpha\in\mathbb{H}} T^*_{i,\ell+1}(\zeta_i, \alpha) &= \sum_{\alpha\in\mathbb{H}} \Phi_{i,\ell+1}(Z_i(\zeta_i), C_{i,\ell+1}(\alpha)) \\
&= \sum_{\alpha\in\mathbb{H}} \Phi_{i,\ell+1}(z_i, a_{i,\ell} \circ \alpha) \\
&= \Phi_{i,\ell}(z_i, a_{i,\ell}) \\
&= \Phi_{i,\ell}(z_i, D_{i,\ell}(\delta_{i,\ell})) \\
&= Q^*_{i,\ell}(\delta_{i,\ell}).
\end{aligned}$$

Fix strategies for P_1 and P_0. Formally, a strategy for P_1 is a probabilistic algorithm that gets the sets of curves Z_i and $C_{i,\ell}$ as inputs, and outputs the sets of polynomials $T_{i,\ell}$ and U_i. A strategy for P_0 is a probabilistic algorithm that gets the set of points z_i and set of curves $D_{i,\ell}$ as inputs, and outputs the set of polynomials $Q_{i,\ell}$. For the rest of the section probabilities will be taken over P_1's random string R_1, P_0's random string R_0, and the player's random string.

We call each of the polynomials sent by the provers a "reply polynomial". The player's decision protocol checks the correctness of the reply polynomials in a pre-determined order. Let F be a reply polynomial. Denote by E_F the event that F is the first incorrect reply polynomial checked by the protocol. That is, E_F is the event that all the reply polynomials checked prior to F are correct, but F is incorrect.

PROPOSITION 6. *Let F be a reply polynomial sent by P_1. Let X be a random variable that is independent of the pair (I_1, R_1). Then, X is independent of (I_1, R_1, I_{E_F}), where I_{E_F} is the random variable that gets the value 1 if E_F occurs, and 0 otherwise.*

The same holds when the parts of P_1 and P_0 are switched.

Proof Assume that E_F occurs with positive probability. P_1 is dishonest as he sent an incorrect polynomial F with positive probability. Since we assume that at least one prover is honest, it must be P_0. Therefore, all the reply polynomials sent by P_0 are correct. This implies that the event E_F depends solely on I_1 and R_1. That is, I_{E_F} is a function of I_1 and R_1. Since X is independent of (I_1, R_1), it is independent of (I_1, R_1, I_{E_F}).

6.4 The Player's Decision

First, the player queries $\tilde{x}(z_d)$ and denote the value by v_d. Note that $\tilde{x} = \mathsf{LDE}_s(x) = \tilde{V}_d$, and thus $v_d = \tilde{V}_d(z_d)$. Next, the player iterates over the layers of C, from the layer adjacent to the input layer (layer $i = d-1$), to the output layer (layer $i = 0$). The iteration that handles layer i (simply referred to as "iteration i") assumes that the variable v_{i+1}

is set to the value $\tilde{V}_{i+1}(z_{i+1})$. The goal of iteration i is to calculate the value $v_i = \tilde{V}_i(z_i)$. At the end of the loop the player returns v_0, which is, supposedly, $v_0 = \tilde{V}_0(z_0) = \tilde{V}_0(0^m) = C(x)$.

In order to compute v_i, iteration i proceeds in a series of "check steps" (tests), each designed to check the correctness of one of the reply polynomials for layer i. Let F be a reply polynomial, and let S_F be the check step designed to check F. If S_F succeeds, the protocol proceeds to the next check step. If S_F fails, the player outputs the value of $C(x)$ claimed by the prover that *did not* send F. The reason is that we assume that at least one of the provers is honest. Since F is incorrect, the prover that did not send F must be the honest one.

Recall that E_F denotes the event that F is the first incorrect reply polynomial checked by the protocol. Denote by C_F the event that all reply polynomials checked up-to F (including F) are correct. In order to prove Theorem 10 it suffices to show that for every reply polynomial F the following holds:

1. If C_F occurs, then S_F always succeeds.

2. If E_F occurs, then with probability at least $1-\epsilon$, S_F fails.

3. If all the reply polynomials are correct, then the player returns $C(x)$.

Next, we describe the check steps that compose iteration i, and show that each of them satisfies both (1) and (2). Assume for simplicity that the reply polynomial F depends on only one variable. The check step S_F does the following: It computes $F(\sigma)$, where $\sigma \in \mathbb{F}$ is a field element that cannot be predicted by the prover that sent F. It then compares $F(\sigma)$ against the supposed value of $F^*(\sigma)$ (this latter value is computed by earlier check steps). If F is correct then $F = F^*$, and the test succeeds. If F is incorrect, F and F^* are different low-degree polynomials. Thus, it is likely that $F(\sigma) \neq F^*(\sigma)$, and the test is likely to fail.

We assume by induction (on the layers i) that if all the reply polynomials checked by iterations $d-1, ..., i+1$ are correct, then at the beginning of iteration i it holds that $v_{i+1} = \tilde{V}_{i+1}(z_{i+1})$.

Check U_{i+1}.

Check $U_{i+1}(\zeta_{i+1}) = v_{i+1}$. ***If not, return*** 0.

If $C_{U_{i+1}}$ ***occurs:*** By assumption, $v_{i+1} = \tilde{V}_{i+1}(z_{i+1}) = \tilde{V}_{i+1}(Z_{i+1}(\zeta_{i+1})) = U^*_{i+1}(\zeta_{i+1})$. Since U_{i+1} is correct, the test passes.

If $E_{U_{i+1}}$ ***occurs:*** Using Propositions 2 and 6, ζ_{i+1} is uniformly distributed in $\mathbb{F}\setminus\{0,1\}$, even given I_1, R_1 and $E_{U_{i+1}}$. Since U_{i+1} only depends on I_1 and R_1, it holds that when $E_{U_{i+1}}$ occurs, ζ_{i+1} is uniformly distributed, even given U_{i+1}.

As explained above, $v_{i+1} = U^*_{i+1}(\zeta_{i+1})$. Since U_{i+1} is incorrect, $U_{i+1} \neq U^*_{i+1}$. Since both U_{i+1} and U^*_{i+1} are of degrees less than $6mh^2$ (see the remark regarding functions representation at the beginning of the section), $U_{i+1}(\zeta)$ can only agree with $U^*_{i+1}(\zeta)$ on less than $6mh^2$ elements $\zeta \in \mathbb{F}$.

Recall that when $E_{U_{i+1}}$ occurs, ζ_{i+1} is uniformly distributed in $\mathbb{F}\setminus\{0,1\}$, even given U_{i+1}, and get that the probability that $U_{i+1}(\zeta_{i+1}) = U^*_{i+1}(\zeta_{i+1}) = v_{i+1}$ is less than $\frac{6mh^2}{|\mathbb{F}\setminus\{0,1\}|}$. Since $|\mathbb{F}| \geq 12mh^3$, it holds that $\frac{6mh^2}{|\mathbb{F}\setminus\{0,1\}|} < \frac{6mh^2}{\frac{1}{2}|\mathbb{F}|} \leq \frac{1}{h} \leq \frac{1}{log(s)} = \epsilon$.

Check $Q_{i,2m}$.

Calculate the supposed value $\phi_{i,2m}$ *of* $\Phi_{i,2m}(z_i, a_{i,2m}) = \Phi_i(z_i, w_{i,0} \circ w_{i,1})$ *(see Equation 2) using* $U_{i+1}(0)$ *as* $\tilde{V}_{i+1}(w_{i,0})$ *and* $U_{i+1}(1)$ *as* $\tilde{V}_{i+1}(w_{i,1})$.

Check $Q_{i,2m}(\delta_{i,2m}) = \phi_{i,2m}$. ***If not, return*** 1.

If $C_{Q_{i,2m}}$ ***occurs:*** Since U_{i+1} is correct $U_{i+1}(0) = U^*_{i+1}(0) = \tilde{V}_{i+1}(Z_{i+1}(0)) = \tilde{V}_{i+1}(w_{i,0})$, and similarly $U_{i+1}(1) = \tilde{V}_{i+1}(w_{i,1})$. Thus, $\phi_{i,2m}$ is set to $\Phi_{i,2m}(z_i, a_{i,2m}) = \Phi_{i,2m}(z_i, D_{i,2m}(\delta_{i,2m})) = Q^*_{i,2m}(\delta_{i,2m})$. Since $Q_{i,2m}$ is correct, the test passes.

If $E_{Q_{i,2m}}$ ***occurs:*** Using Propositions 4 and 6, $\delta_{i,2m}$ is uniformly distributed in $\mathbb{F}\setminus\{0\}$, even given I_0, R_0 and $E_{Q_{i,2m}}$. Since $Q_{i,2m}$ only depends on I_0 and R_0, it holds that when $E_{Q_{i,2m}}$ occurs, $\delta_{i,2m}$ is uniformly distributed, even given $Q_{i,2m}$.

As explained above, $\phi_{i,2m}$ is set to $Q^*_{i,2m}(\delta_{i,2m})$. Since $Q_{i,2m}$ is incorrect, $Q_{i,2m} \neq Q^*_{i,2m}$. An argument similar to the one used in check step $S_{U_{i+1}}$ shows that the probability that $Q_{i,2m}(\delta_{i,2m}) = Q^*_{i,2m}(\delta_{i,2m}) = \phi_{i,2m}$ is less than ϵ.

Check $T_{i,2m}$.

Check $T_{i,2m}(\zeta_i, \gamma_{i,2m}) = Q_{i,2m}(0)$. ***If not, return*** 0.

If $C_{T_{i,2m}}$ ***occurs:***

$$T^*_{i,2m}(\zeta_i, \gamma_{i,2m}) = \Phi_{i,2m}(Z_i(\zeta_i), C_{i,2m}(\gamma_{i,2m}))$$

$$= \Phi_{i,2m}(z_i, D_{i,2m}(0)) = Q^*_{i,2m}(0).$$

Since $Q_{i,2m}$ and $T_{i,2m}$ are correct, the test passes.

If $E_{T_{i,2m}}$ ***occurs:*** Using Propositions 1, 2 and 6, the pair $(\zeta_i, \gamma_{i,2m})$ is uniformly distributed in $(\mathbb{F}\setminus\{0,1\}) \times (\mathbb{F}\setminus\mathbb{H})$, even given I_1, R_1 and $E_{T_{i,2m}}$. Since $T_{i,2m}$ only depends on I_1 and R_1, it holds that when $E_{T_{i,2m}}$ occurs, the pair $(\zeta_i, \gamma_{i,2m})$ is uniformly distributed, even given $T_{i,2m}$.

Since $Q_{i,2m}$ is correct but $T_{i,2m}$ is incorrect, it holds that $Q_{i,2m} = Q^*_{i,2m}$ and $T_{i,2m} \neq T^*_{i,2m}$. Using the Schwartz–Zippel Lemma, since both $T_{i,2m}$ and $T^*_{i,2m}$ are of total degree less than $6mh^2$ (see the remark regarding functions representation at the beginning of the section), $T_{i,2m}(\zeta, \gamma)$ can only agree with $T^*_{i,2m}(\zeta, \gamma)$ on less than $\frac{6mh^2}{|\mathbb{F}|}$-fraction of the points $(\zeta, \gamma) \in \mathbb{F}^2$.

Recall that when $E_{T_{i,2m}}$ occurs, the pair $(\zeta_i, \gamma_{i,2m})$ is uniformly distributed in $(\mathbb{F}\setminus\{0,1\}) \times (\mathbb{F}\setminus\mathbb{H})$, even given $T_{i,2m}$, and get that the probability that $T_{i,2m}(\zeta_i, \gamma_{i,2m}) = T^*_{i,2m}(\zeta_i, \gamma_{i,2m}) = Q^*_{i,2m}(0) = Q_{i,2m}(0)$ is less than $\frac{6mh^2 \cdot |\mathbb{F}|}{|(\mathbb{F}\setminus\{0,1\}) \times (\mathbb{F}\setminus\mathbb{H})|}$. Since $|\mathbb{F}| \geq 12mh^3$, it holds that $\frac{6mh^2 \cdot |\mathbb{F}|}{|(\mathbb{F}\setminus\{0,1\}) \times (\mathbb{F}\setminus\mathbb{H})|} < \frac{6mh^2 \cdot |\mathbb{F}|}{\frac{1}{2}|\mathbb{F}|^2} \leq \frac{1}{h} \leq \frac{1}{log(s)} = \epsilon$.

Check $Q_{i,2m-1}$.

Check $Q_{i,2m-1}(\delta_{i,2m-1}) = \sum_{\alpha \in \mathbb{H}} T_{i,2m}(\zeta_i, \alpha)$. ***If not, return*** 1.

If $C_{Q_{i,2m-1}}$ ***occurs:*** Using Proposition 5, since $T_{i,2m}$ and $Q_{i,2m-1}$ are correct, the test passes.

If $E_{Q_{i,2m-1}}$ ***occurs:*** Using Propositions 3 and 6, $\delta_{i,2m-1}$ is uniformly distributed in $\mathbb{F}\setminus\{0\}$, even given I_0, R_0 and $E_{Q_{i,2m-1}}$. Since $Q_{i,2m-1}$ only depends on I_0 and R_0, it holds that when $E_{Q_{i,2m-1}}$ occurs, $\delta_{i,2m-1}$ is uniformly distributed, even given $Q_{i,2m-1}$.

Using Proposition 5, since $T_{i,2m}$ is correct,

$$\sum_{\alpha\in\mathbb{H}} T_{i,2m}(\zeta_i,\alpha) = Q^*_{i,2m-1}(\delta_{i,2m-1}).$$

Since $Q_{i,2m-1}$ is incorrect, $Q_{i,2m-1} \neq Q^*_{i,2m-1}$. An argument similar to the one used in check step $S_{U_{i+1}}$ shows that the probability that $Q_{i,2m-1}(\delta_{i,2m-1}) = Q^*_{i,2m-1}(\delta_{i,2m-1}) = \sum_{\alpha\in\mathbb{H}} T_{i,2m}(\zeta_i,\alpha)$ is less than ϵ.

Repeat the last two steps to check $T_{i,2m-1}, Q_{i,2m-2}, \ldots, T_{i,1}, Q_{i,0}$.

Set $v_i = Q_{i,0}(\beta)$. Note that if $Q_{i,0}$ is correct then using Equation 1, $v_i = Q_{i,0}(\beta) = Q^*_{i,0}(\beta) = \Phi_{i,0}(z_i, D_{i,0}(\beta)) = \tilde{V}_i(z_i)$, and the induction hypothesis holds. In particular, if all reply polynomials are correct then $v_0 = \tilde{V}_0(z_0) = \tilde{V}_0(0^m) = C(x)$.

7. TRADE-OFF PROTOCOL

In this section we prove Theorem 9. We describe a protocol that given a size s depth d circuit C on n bits, and an input $x \in \{0,1\}^n$, outputs $C(x)$ with probability at least $1-\epsilon$. The new protocol uses the one-round protocol described in Section 6 as a building block. The new protocol consists of r rounds, requires the exchange of $d^{\frac{1}{r}} \cdot polylog(s)$ bits, and makes a single query to $\mathsf{LDE}_s(x)$.

Assume without loss of generality that $r \leq log(d)$ (otherwise, set $r = \lfloor log(d) \rfloor$). Set $k = 2\left\lceil d^{\frac{1}{r}} \right\rceil$. The new protocol consists of two stages. The goal of the first stage (Subsection 7.1) is to find two "close" layers $i', i'' \in I$ with $i' > i''$ and $i' - i'' \leq k$, such that the provers agree on a point on $\tilde{V}_{i'}$, but disagree on a point on $\tilde{V}_{i''}$. Note that such layers exist, as the provers agree on the input x for C (and thus on $\mathsf{LDE}_s(x) = \tilde{V}_d$), but disagree on the output $C(x)$ (and therefore on $\tilde{V}_0$).

Finding layers i' and i'' is done by running a version of a binary search that in every round partitions the search range into k (almost equal) intervals (instead of just two). Note that $r-1$ search rounds suffice in order to find such layers i' and i'' satisfying $i' - i'' \leq k$: Each search round reduces the range of indices searched by a factor of at least $\frac{k}{2}$. Thus, after $r-1$ rounds we are left with a range of at most

$$(d+1)\cdot\left(\frac{k}{2}\right)^{-(r-1)} = (d+1)\left(\left\lceil d^{\frac{1}{r}}\right\rceil\right)^{-(r-1)}$$

$$\leq 2d\left(d^{\frac{1}{r}}\right)^{-(r-1)} \leq 2d \cdot d^{\frac{1-r}{r}} = 2d^{\frac{1}{r}} \leq k.$$

Let C' a subcircuit composed of layers $i', \ldots, i''$ of C, and let $x' = \tilde{V}_{i'}$. The provers agree on a point on the input layer $\mathsf{LDE}_s(x') = \tilde{V}_{i'}$ of C', but disagree on a point on the output layer $\tilde{V}_{i''}$ of C'.

Stage 2 of the new protocol (Subsection 7.2) runs the one-round protocol described in Section 6 with C' and x' as inputs in order to determine which of the provers is truthful.

7.1 Stage 1: Search

First, the player constructs questions for the provers as in Subsection 6.1. That is, the player constructs the curves $C_{i,\ell}$, $D_{i,\ell}$ ($i \in I_{-d}, \ell \in L$), and the curves Z_i and points z_i ($i \in I$). For $i \in I$, let $U^*_i : \mathbb{F} \to \mathbb{F}$ be the function $U^*_i(r) = \tilde{V}_i(Z_i(r))$, and let $u^*_i \in \mathbb{F}$ be the value $u^*_i = \tilde{V}_i(z_i)$.

Next, the protocol proceeds in $r-1$ search rounds. In each round the player constructs a set of k indices $M \subseteq I$ (M contains indices that partition the remaining search range into almost equal parts). The player sends the curves Z_i ($i \in M$) to P_1, and the points z_i ($i \in M$) to P_0. P_1 replies with the functions $U_i : \mathbb{F} \to \mathbb{F}$ ($i \in M$), and P_0 replies with the values $u_i \in \mathbb{F}$ ($i \in M$). The honest P_1 should reply with $U_i = U^*_i$, and the honest P_0 should reply with $u_i = u^*_i$.

The goal of Stage 1 is to find two layers $i' > i'' \in I$, $i' - i'' \leq k$ such that $U_{i'}(\zeta_{i'}) = u_{i'}$, but $U_{i''}(\zeta_{i''}) \neq u_{i''}$. By comparing the values of $U_i(\zeta_i)$ and u_i ($i \in M$), the player decides on the smaller search range for the next round, until the desired layers i' and i'' are found.

Note that during the first round the player checks the provers agreement on the input and output layers. If $U_0(\zeta_0) = u_0$ (the provers agree on the output $C(x)$), then since at least one of the provers is truthful, the player outputs u_0. If $U_d(\zeta_d) \neq u_d$ (the provers disagree on a point in the low-degree extension $\tilde{x} = \tilde{V}_d$ of the input), the player queries $\tilde{x}(z_d)$. Since at least one of the provers is truthful, the queried value $\tilde{x}(z_d)$ is either $U_d(\zeta_d)$ or u_d. If $\tilde{x}(z_d) = U_d(\zeta_d)$, the player outputs 1. If $\tilde{x}(z_d) = u_d$, the player outputs 0.

7.2 Stage 2: Run the One-Round Protocol

Let C' be the circuit composed of layers $i', \ldots, i''$ of C. Run the one-round protocol on C' and $x' = V_i$, using the questions that were already constructed in Stage 1, and with the following changes. Return the obtained value.

- Instead of querying $\mathsf{LDE}_s(x')$ at the point $z_{i'}$, use the value $u_{i'}$.

- Instead of returning the computed value v_0 in the last step, return 0 if $v_0 = u_{i''}$ and 1 otherwise.

8. VERY EFFICIENT PLAYER

In this section we prove Theorem 12. That is, we assume in addition to the previous assumptions that the circuit C is $log(s)$-space uniform and show that in this case the player can run in time $d^{\frac{1}{r}} polylog(s)$.

First observe that each of the check steps of the protocol described in Section 6, excluding the check steps $S_{Q_{i,2m}}$ ($i \in I_{-d}$), can be preformed by the player in $polylog(s)$ time and without knowing the circuit C. The only check steps that require knowing the circuit C are the check steps $S_{Q_{i,2m}}$ ($i \in I_{-d}$), as explained next.

The check step $S_{Q_{i,2m}}$ ($i \in I_{-d}$) requires the player to compute the value $\Phi_i(z_i, w_{i,0}, w_{i,1})$ given the (supposed) values of $\tilde{V}_{i+1}(w_{i,0})$ and $\tilde{V}_{i+1}(w_{i,1})$. Recall that Φ_i was defined in Lemma 14 as $\Phi_i(z, w_0, w_1) = \tilde{\beta}_i(z, w_0, w_1)\tilde{V}_{i+1}(w_0)\tilde{V}_{i+1}(w_1)$. Therefore, in order to compute $\Phi_i(z_i, w_{i,0}, w_{i,1})$, the player needs to know $\tilde{\beta}_i(z_i, w_{i,0}, w_{i,1})$. Note that $\tilde{\beta}_i$ depends on the circuit C, and that for a general size s depth d circuit C, the evaluation of $\tilde{\beta}_i$ may be pricy and require $poly(s)$ time. Moreover, even in the case where the circuit C is $log(s)$-space uniform, the evaluation of $\tilde{\beta}_i$ by the player may require $poly(s)$ time.

The crucial observation is that in the case of a $log(s)$-space uniform circuit C, the function $\tilde{\beta}_i$ is computable in space $O(log(s))$. Note, that the inputs for the function $\tilde{\beta}_i$ are themselves of length $O(log(s))$. Hence, the function $\tilde{\beta}_i$ can be computed in space polynomial in the length of its inputs, that is $\tilde{\beta}_i \in \mathsf{PSPACE}$.

Recall that for every language in PSPACE, Feige and Kilian give a one-round competing provers protocol that only requires polynomial communication complexity [3]. Therefore, there is a one-round competing provers protocol that computes $\tilde{\beta}_i$, with communication complexity polynomial in the length of the inputs for $\tilde{\beta}_i$, that is, communication complexity of $polylog(s)$. Thus, the player cannot evaluate the function $\tilde{\beta}_i$ in time $polylog(s)$ by herself, but she can do that with the help of the two competing provers.

This naturally leads to an $r+2$ rounds protocol (rather than the r rounds protocol that we want). We start by describing the $r+2$ rounds protocol and then show how to collapse the last two rounds of the protocol to round r of the protocol.

REMARK 3. *We remark that when applying the competing provers protocol of Feige and Kilian for $log(s)$-space, the provers' running time may be super-polynomial in s, and thus not efficient enough for our purposes. Therefore, for the rest of the paper we consider an updated version of the Feige and Kilian protocol, obtained using our protocol, as follows. A similar approach was taken in [5].*

By Lemma 3.4.3 of [7], any $log(s)$-space language has a poly(s)-size polylog(s)-depth arithmetic circuit C, for which the associated functions $\tilde{\beta}_i$ have polylog(s)-size arithmetic circuits. Therefore, the following is a competing provers protocol for $log(s)$-space, with efficient parties: Given a $log(s)$-space language, the parties run our 1-round competing provers protocol with the circuit C. Observe that since C has poly(s)-size and polylog(s)-depth, the provers run in time $poly(s)$. In addition, since the associated functions $\tilde{\beta}_i$ have polylog(s)-size circuits, the player can evaluate $\tilde{\beta}_i$ by herself in polylog(s) time.

8.1 The $r+2$ Rounds Protocol

The first r rounds of the protocol run the r rounds of the protocol of Section 7, except for the player's decision that is still not made. In order to make her decision, the player needs to evaluate $\tilde{\beta}_i(z_i, w_{i,0}, w_{i,1})$ for each of the at most k layers $i \in \{i'', ..., i'-1\}$ that round r of the protocol considers (see Subsection 7.2).

In order to compute the needed values of $\tilde{\beta}_i(z_i, w_{i,0}, w_{i,1})$, the player sends in round $r+1$ the values $(z_i, w_{i,0}, w_{i,1})$ (for $i \in \{i'', ..., i'-1\}$) to both provers, and asks each prover to reply with the values of $\tilde{\beta}_i(z_i, w_{i,0}, w_{i,1})$ (for $i \in \{i'', ..., i'-1\}$). If the provers agree on all the values $\tilde{\beta}_i(z_i, w_{i,0}, w_{i,1})$, the player knows that these values are correct (because at least one of the provers is honest), and can proceed with her decision. If the provers disagree on one or more of the values $\tilde{\beta}_i(z_i, w_{i,0}, w_{i,1})$, the player picks one such value and applies in round $r+2$ the PSPACE protocol of Feige and Kilian in order to identify the correct value and decide which prover is honest.

Next, we show how to reduce the number of rounds from $r+2$ to r.

8.2 Collapsing Round $r+1$ to Round r

We now describe how to collapse round $r+1$ of the protocol to round r. We cannot just send all the values $(z_i, w_{i,0}, w_{i,1})$ (for $i \in \{i'', ..., i'-1\}$) to both provers at the beginning of round r, because this would give each prover additional information that may enable him to cheat in round r.

Note, however, that at the beginning of round r, the prover P_1 gets all the curves Z_i (for $i \in \{i'', ..., i'\}$). Hence, for $i \in \{i'', ..., i'-1\}$, the prover P_1 already knows the needed values of $w_{i,0}, w_{i,1}$ (since $Z_{i+1}(0) = w_{i,0}$ and $Z_{i+1}(1) = w_{i,1}$), as well as the curve Z_i that contains the point z_i. Thus, we can just ask P_1 for the values of $\tilde{\beta}_i(z_i', w_{i,0}, w_{i,1})$ for all the points z_i' on the image of Z_i.

In addition, at the beginning of round r, the prover P_0 gets all the points z_i as well as the curves $D_{i,2m}$ (for $i \in \{i'', ..., i'-1\}$). Hence, for $i \in \{i'', ..., i'-1\}$, the prover P_0 already knows the needed value of z_i, as well as the curve $D_{i,2m}$ that contains $w_{i,0} \circ w_{i,1}$ (since $D_{i,2m}(\delta_{i,2m}) = a_{i,2m} = w_{i,0} \circ w_{i,1}$). Thus, we can just ask P_0 for the values of $\tilde{\beta}_i(z_i, w_{i,0}' \circ w_{i,1}') = \tilde{\beta}_i(z_i, w_{i,0}', w_{i,1}')$ for all the points $w_{i,0}' \circ w_{i,1}'$ on the image of $D_{i,2m}$.

Denote by $A_i^*, B_i^* : \mathbb{F} \to \mathbb{F}$ the following restrictions of the function $\tilde{\beta}_i$ to curves: $A_i^*(t) = \tilde{\beta}_i(Z_i(t), w_{i,0}, w_{i,1})$ and $B_i^*(t) = \tilde{\beta}_i(z_i, D_{i,2m}(t))$ (for $i \in \{i'', ..., i'-1\}$). The new protocol asks P_1 to add to his reply message in round r the polynomials A_i^*, and asks P_0 to add to his reply message in round r the polynomials B_i^* (for $i \in \{i'', ..., i'-1\}$).

Suppose that P_1 replied with $A_i : \mathbb{F} \to \mathbb{F}$ and that P_0 replied with $B_i : \mathbb{F} \to \mathbb{F}$ (for $i \in \{i'', ..., i'-1\}$). Observe that $A_i^*(\zeta_i) = \tilde{\beta}_i(Z_i(\zeta_i), w_{i,0}, w_{i,1}) = \tilde{\beta}_i(z_i, w_{i,0}, w_{i,1})$ and that $B_i^*(\delta_{i,2m}) = \tilde{\beta}_i(z_i, D_{i,2m}(\delta_{i,2m})) = \tilde{\beta}_i(z_i, a_{i,2m}) = \tilde{\beta}_i(z_i, w_{i,0}, w_{i,1})$. If for every $i \in \{i'', ..., i'-1\}$ it holds that $A_i(\zeta_i) = B_i(\delta_{i,2m})$, the player may use the value $A_i(\zeta_i) = B_i(\delta_{i,2m})$ as $\tilde{\beta}_i(z_i, w_{i,0}, w_{i,1})$ and complete her decision protocol. Otherwise, she proceeds to round $r+2$.

Thus, we showed how to collapse round $r+1$ of the protocol to round r.

8.3 Collapsing Round $r+2$ to Round r

We now show how to collapse round $r+2$ to round r, resulting in an r rounds protocol. Round $r+2$ is only reached if there exists $j \in \{i'', ..., i'-1\}$ such that $A_j(\zeta_j) \neq B_j(\delta_{j,2m})$. In this case, in order to decide which of the provers is truthful, the player runs the one-round protocol of [3].

In round $r+2$, if reached, the player and provers run the one-round protocol of [3] in order to determine the value of $\tilde{\beta}_j(z_j, w_{j,0}, w_{j,1})$, for some $j \in \{i'', ..., i'-1\}$ and some $z_j, w_{j,0}, w_{j,1}$, where P_0 claims that the value is $B = B_j(\delta_{j,2m})$ and P_1 claims that the value is $A = A_j(\zeta_j)$. We would like to collapse round $r+2$ to round r, but the problem is that after the questions part of round r, the values of $j, z_j, w_{j,0}, w_{j,1}, A, B$ are still not all known to the player or the provers. Note, however, that the number of possibilities for these values is small from the point of view of each of the parties.

First note that j can take at most k values and A, B can each take at most $p = |\mathbb{F}|$ values. Also, after the questions part of round r, the player and P_1 already know $w_{j,0}, w_{j,1}$, and from the point of view of P_0 the element $w_{j,0} \circ w_{j,1}$ can take at most p values (as $w_{j,0} \circ w_{j,1}$ is on the image of $D_{j,2m}$, which is of size at most p). As for z_j, after the questions part of round r, the player and P_0 already know z_j, and from the point of view of P_1 the point z_j can take at most p values (as z_j is on the image of Z_j, which is of size at most p).

Let Λ be the set of all $\lambda = \left(j', z'_{j'}, w'_{j',0}, w'_{j',1}, A', B'\right)$, such that, $j' \in \{i'', ..., i'-1\}$, and $z'_{j'}$ is on the image of $Z_{j'}$, and $w'_{j',0} \circ w'_{j',1}$ is on the image of $D_{j',2m}$, and $A', B' \in \mathbb{F}$. For every $\lambda \in \Lambda$, let $\mathcal{Q}(\lambda) = (\mathcal{Q}_0(\lambda), \mathcal{Q}_1(\lambda))$ be independently chosen pair of questions for the Feige-Kilian protocol corresponding to λ (that is, for $\lambda = \left(j', z'_{j'}, w'_{j',0}, w'_{j',1}, A', B'\right)$, the Feige-Kilian protocol for evaluating $\tilde{\beta_{j'}}\left(z'_{j'}, w'_{j',0}, w'_{j',1}\right)$ when P_0 claims that the value is B' and P_1 claims that the value is A').

We can now collapse round $r+2$ to round r as follows. In the questions part of round r, in addition to the questions of the original protocol of Section 7, the player will send to P_0 the pair $(\lambda, \mathcal{Q}_0(\lambda))$, for every $\lambda = \left(j', z'_{j'}, w'_{j',0}, w'_{j',1}, A', B'\right) \in \Lambda$, such that, $z'_{j'} = z_{j'}$. In the same way, the player will send to P_1 the pair $(\lambda, \mathcal{Q}_1(\lambda))$, for every $\lambda = \left(j', z'_{j'}, w'_{j',0}, w'_{j',1}, A', B'\right) \in \Lambda$, such that, $\left(w'_{j',0}, w'_{j',1}\right) = (w_{j',0}, w_{j',1})$. Note that this doesn't give the provers additional information about the questions of the original protocol of Section 7, because each prover could have constructed by himself questions that are distributed the same as the additional questions that he got.

In the reply part of round r, the prover P_0 will send his reply for the question $\mathcal{Q}_0(\lambda)$ for the Feige-Kilian protocol corresponding to λ, for every pair $(\lambda, \mathcal{Q}_0(\lambda))$ that he got. This is in addition to the replies for the questions of the original protocol of Section 7, and in addition to the functions B_i (required in order to collapse round $r+1$ to round r, as discussed above). In the same way, the prover P_1 will send his reply for the question $\mathcal{Q}_1(\lambda)$ for the Feige-Kilian protocol corresponding to λ, for every pair $(\lambda, \mathcal{Q}_1(\lambda))$ that he got (this is in addition to the replies for the questions of the original protocol of Section 7, and in addition to the functions A_i). Denote the reply of P_0 for the question $\mathcal{Q}_0(\lambda)$ by $\mathcal{R}_0(\lambda)$, and denote the reply of P_1 for the question $\mathcal{Q}_1(\lambda)$ by $\mathcal{R}_1(\lambda)$.

The decision made by the player is as follows. If for every $i \in \{i'', ..., i'-1\}$ it holds that $A_i(\zeta_i) = B_i(\delta_{i,2m})$, the player may use the value $A_i(\zeta_i) = B_i(\delta_{i,2m})$ as $\tilde{\beta_i}(z_i, w_{i,0}, w_{i,1})$ and make her decision according to the decision part of the original protocol of Section 7. If for some $j \in \{i'', ..., i'-1\}$ it holds that $A_j(\zeta_j) \neq B_j(\delta_{j,2m})$, the player decides according to the decision part of the Feige-Kilian protocol corresponding to $\lambda = (j, z_j, w_{j,0}, w_{j,1}, A_j(\zeta_j), B_j(\delta_{j,2m}))$. This can be done since both provers have sent replies $\mathcal{R}_0(\lambda)$ and $\mathcal{R}_1(\lambda)$, respectively.

Thus, we obtained an r rounds protocol. Note that the size of Λ is $k \cdot polylog(s)$. Hence, the total communication of the new protocol is $d^{\frac{1}{r}} polylog(s)$, as required. Since the error of the original protocol of Section 7 is ϵ, and the error of the protocol of Feige and Kilian is negligible and in particular is smaller than $\frac{\epsilon}{|\Lambda|}$, the total error of the new protocol is at most 2ϵ (by the union bound).

8.4 Running Time of the Player

The running time of the player in the protocol described in the previous subsections is $d \cdot polylog(s)$, rather than the desired $d^{\frac{1}{r}} polylog(s)$. This is because in the original protocol of Section 7, the player generates for every layer $i \in I_{-d}$ the corresponding curves and points, at the beginning of the protocol, which takes time $d \cdot polylog(s)$. To reduce the running time of the player to $d^{\frac{1}{r}} polylog(s)$, note that the player only needs to generate the curves and points corresponding to layers $i \in I_{-d}$ that are actually used.

More precisely, define the questions corresponding to layer $i \in I_{-d}$ to be the set of curves $C_{i,\ell}$ and $D_{i,\ell}$ ($\ell \in L$), the curve Z_{i+1}, and the point z_{i+1}. Note that the questions for layer i can be generated independently of the questions for all the other layers.

We change the protocol, so that the player generates the questions corresponding to layer i only if and when layer i is used. That is, the questions corresponding to layer i are generated during round $r' \in [r]$ iff i is one of the k indices queried in round r'. Note that since only a total number of $O(r \cdot k) \leq O\left(log(d) \cdot d^{\frac{1}{r}}\right)$ indices are queried, the player only spends $d^{\frac{1}{r}} polylog(s)$ time constructing questions.

9. REFERENCES

[1] Scott Aaronson and Avi Wigderson. Algebrization: A new barrier in complexity theory. *TOCT*, 1(1), 2009.

[2] Ran Canetti, Ben Riva, and Guy N. Rothblum. Two protocols for delegation of computation. In *ICITS*, pages 37–61, 2012.

[3] Uriel Feige and Joe Kilian. Making games short (extended abstract). In *STOC*, pages 506–516, 1997.

[4] Uriel Feige, Adi Shamir, and Moshe Tennenholtz. The noisy oracle problem. In *CRYPTO*, pages 284–296, 1988.

[5] Shafi Goldwasser, Yael Tauman Kalai, and Guy N. Rothblum. Delegating computation: interactive proofs for muggles. In *STOC*, pages 113–122, 2008.

[6] Yael Tauman Kalai and Ran Raz. Interactive PCP. In *ICALP (2)*, pages 536–547, 2008.

[7] Guy N. Rothblum. Delegating computation reliably: Paradigms and constructions. In *Ph.D. Thesis - Massachusetts Institute of Technology, Dept. of Electrical Engineering and Computer Science*, 2009.

Catch Them if You Can: How to Serve Impatient Users

Marek Cygan
Institute of Informatics,
University of Warsaw,
Banacha 2, 02-097 Warszawa,
cygan@mimuw.edu.pl

Matthias Englert
Department of Computer
Science and DIMAP,
University of Warwick,
Coventry CV4 7AL,
englert@dcs.warwick.ac.uk

Anupam Gupta
Department of Computer
Science, Carnegie Mellon
University, Pittsburgh,
PA 15213
anupamg@cs.cmu.edu

Marcin Mucha
Institute of Informatics,
University of Warsaw,
Banacha 2, 02-097 Warszawa,
mucha@mimuw.edu.pl

Piotr Sankowski
Institute of Informatics,
University of Warsaw,
Banacha 2, 02-097 Warszawa,
sank@mimuw.edu.pl

ABSTRACT

Consider the following problem of *serving impatient users*: we are given a set of customers we would like to serve. We can serve at most one customer in each time step (getting value v_i for serving customer i). At the end of each time step, each as-yet-unserved customer i leaves the system independently with probability q_i, never to return. What strategy should we use to serve customers to maximize the expected value collected?

The standard model of competitive analysis can be applied to this problem: picking the customer with maximum value gives us half the value obtained by the optimal algorithm, and using a vertex weighted online matching algorithm gives us $1 - 1/e \approx 0.632$ fraction of the optimum. As is usual in competitive analysis, these approximations compare to the best value achievable by an clairvoyant adversary that knows all the coin tosses of the customers. Can we do better?

We show an upper bound of ≈ 0.648 if we compare our performance to such an clairvoyant algorithm, suggesting we cannot improve our performance substantially. However, these are pessimistic comparisons to a much stronger adversary: what if we compare ourselves to the optimal strategy for this problem, which does not have an unfair advantage? In this case, we can do much better: in particular, we give an algorithm whose expected value is at least 0.7 of that achievable by the optimal algorithm. This improvement is achieved via a novel rounding algorithm, and a non-local analysis.

Categories and Subject Descriptors

F.2.2 [**Theory of Computation**]: Nonnumerical Algorithms and Problems; G.2.2 [**Discrete Mathematics**]: Graph theory—*Graph algorithms*

General Terms

Algorithms, Theory

Keywords

online algorithms, stochastic models, bipartite matching, impatience

1. INTRODUCTION

The presence of impatient users is a common phenomenon in many contexts, and in this paper we initiate an algorithmic investigation of impatience. In particular, we consider the following problem of *serving impatient users*: we are given a set of n customers we would like to serve. At each time step, we look at the customers still in the system and choose one of them to serve: if we serve customer i, we get a value of v_i. This customer, once served, departs from the system—we serve each customer only once. Moreover, the customers are impatient: at the end of each time step, each customer still in the system may "time out". We model this timing-out process in a stochastic way. After every timestep each customer i decides to stay in the system independently with probability p_i, and leaves, never to return, with the remaining probability $1 - p_i$. (Hence, customer i remains in the system $T_i \sim \text{Geom}(p_i)$ time steps, or fewer, if she was served earlier.) Our goal: to devise a strategy for serving customers, so that we (approximately) maximize the expected total value obtained.

Not only is this problem interesting in its own right, it also focuses attention on a new set of unexplored problems lying in the intersection of queueing theory/stochastic processes and approximation algorithms. It combines elements from both disciplines: the population evolves according to a natural stochastic process, but the values v_i and probabilities p_i are chosen in a worst-case fashion and not drawn from some underlying distribution themselves. To the best of our knowledge, this problem has not been studied in either literature. However, we believe that the problem is worth studying as it tries to answer a very basic question: what shall we do next when options can disappear? How shall we trade-off the probability of timing-out of the client with its value? Should clients with high value and low impatience be served before clients with low value and high impatience?

We show in this paper that this question does not have a straight forward answer, and even understanding the case when all clients are identical is non-trivial.

From an algorithmic point of view, such a problem naturally lends itself to investigation in the competitive analysis framework, where we compare ourselves to an all-knowing "clairvoyant" adversary who knows the values of the timeouts T_i. A simple online algorithm is to ignore the probabilities p_i, and serve the remaining customer with the highest value v_i, and it is easy to show this is $\frac{1}{2}$-competitive even against the clairvoyant adversary (see Section 2 for proofs of claims in this paragraph). An example with two equal clients shows that in the case of non-stochastic adversarial timeouts, this greedy approach cannot get more then $\frac{1}{2}$ of the optimum. However, even in our much weaker stochastic model greedy is not better—we give an upper bound example of $\frac{1}{2} + \epsilon$, for any $\epsilon > 0$. We can do something better: we can model this process as an online bipartite matching problem with customers on one side, and time steps on the other, where at each timestep we only need to know which customers are still in the system: using the optimal results of Aggarwal et al. [1] for vertex-weighted online matching, we get a $(1 - 1/e)$-competitive algorithm.

However, these results make an unfair comparison to a clairvoyant adversary. Instead, we would like to level the playing field, and compare our algorithm to the best algorithm of its class. This would not be a concern if we could get much better competitive ratios against clairvoyant adversaries. However, our first result shows that this is not the case, even for the simplest setting where all the customers are identical.

Theorem 1.1 *There exist instances with n identical customers, where the optimal algorithm gets at most $0.648\ldots+\varepsilon$ times the value obtained by the optimal clairvoyant algorithm w.p. $1 - e^{-\Omega(\varepsilon^2 n)}$.*

However, if we compare ourselves to the optimal non-clairvoyant algorithm, our next result shows how to obtain a better approximation.

Theorem 1.2 *There is a randomized algorithm that for any instance I, obtains an expected value of at least $(1 - 1/(2e - 2)) \geq 0.709$ times an LP relaxation, and hence at least 70.9% of the non-clairvoyant optimum.*

Our algorithm is based on rounding a linear-programming relaxation of the problem. The naïve rounding of the LP solution gives only a $(1-1/e)$-approximation. The improved approximation is based on a novel rounding algorithm that moves LP value between the rounds, and hence avoid lower bounds on a purely local analysis.

1.1 Some Important Notation

In the paper, we will use "items" instead of "customers" or "users", and "picking items" will represent "serving users". Again, the value of item i is v_i, its survival probability is p_i. *Time* begins with $t = 0$, and hence the probability of i being alive at time t (a.k.a. *round* t) is p_i^t. A *clairvoyant* algorithm is one that knows the coin tosses of all the items (and hence when the item dies/disappears), a *non-clairvoyant* or *online* algorithm does not know in time t which items will be survive to round $t + 1$.

1.2 Related Work

There has been a significant body of work on stochastic optimization in the operations research community (see, e.g., [3]). The work from a worst-case analysis and approximation algorithms viewpoint is more recent, less than a decade old, starting with the work on two-stage stochastic covering problems [8, 16, 11, 17]. A prominent class of problems deals with situations where the input is given a set of random variables, the distributions of which are known up-front, but the actual realizations are only revealed upon the algorithm probing them; examples of these are stochastic knapsack [7] and stochastic matching [4]. The challenge in these problems is the hidden stochastic information, whereas our problem is a full-information problem, where the challenge is to cope with the stochastic departure of the clients, and the associated loss in value.

A line of work relevant to our problem is that on online bipartite matching, where vertices on one side are given up front, and vertices on the other side (and the edges between them) are revealed online. This started with the paper of Karp et al. [14] showing that this problem admits a $(1 - 1/e)$-competitive randomized algorithm, and this is the best possible. Aggarwal et al. [1] show the same optimal approximation guarantee for the case where the known vertices have weights, and one wants to maximize the weight of matched nodes. (The connection between this problem and our work is sketched in Section 2.) Better results are known for the case where each arriving vertex is an i.i.d. draw from a known distribution [10] or when the unknown vertices are chosen by an adversary but appear in random order [13, 15].

Another extensively studied related problem is *online bounded-delay buffer management*, which can be cast as vertex-weighted bipartite matching where each vertex is connected to a contiguous set of vertices on the other side. In contrast to our model (a) items arrive over time instead of all in the first step and (b) the deadline of items are known instead of being modelled by a (known) probability distribution. In particular, Chin and Fung [6] prove an upper bound of 4/5 on the competitive ratio of any randomized algorithm for this related problem. On the positive side, Chin et al. [5] gave a $(1 - 1/e)$-competitive randomized online algorithm for this related problem. Jeż [12] also gives a $(1 - 1/e)$-competitive randomized algorithm using different techniques. This later algorithm and proof can be easily adapted to handle our problem, even if items are not all available from the start but arrive online.

Our problem also bears some similarities to problems of serving clients with fixed service times and with impatient customers, that have been studied in the queuing theory and stochastic processes literature [2, 18]. However, the problems studied there have a different flavor, i.e., clients wait in fixed-order queues, but leave the queue according to some distribution. In such models one is interested in analyzing the average queuing time in the steady state of the system, and not the value collected from customers. The question of whom to serve next is not studied in these models.

2. SIMPLE SOLUTIONS

Lemma 2.1 *The greedy algorithm that always picks the item with highest value is $\frac{1}{2}$-competitive against a clairvoyant adversary, and even against a non-clairvoyant adversary it does not do better.*

Proof. We first observe that the value of the items picked by the clairvoyant adversary and not picked by the greedy algorithm cannot be higher then the total value gained by the greedy algorithm. This is because in every step, in which the adversary picks such an item, the greedy algorithm picks an item with at least the same value. Hence, $v(\mathsf{opt}) \leq v(\mathsf{opt} \setminus \mathsf{alg}) + v(\mathsf{alg}) \leq 2v(\mathsf{alg})$, where alg is the set of items picked by the greedy algorithm, opt is the set of items picked by the adversary, and $v(S)$ denotes the total value of items in set S. For the upper bound, consider two items with $p_1 = 1$, $v_1 = 1 + \epsilon$ and $p_2 = 0$, $v_2 = 1$. The greedy algorithm collects $1 + \varepsilon$ value, while an optimal non-clairvoyant algorithm collects $2 + \varepsilon$. ■

As the above proof shows, the greedy algorithm is non-optimal with respect to a non-clairvoyant adversary, even for two items. The following is easy to show.

Lemma 2.2 *The optimal online strategy for two items with values v_1 and v_2 and survival probabilities p_1 andp_2 is to pick item i maximizing $q_i v_i = (1 - p_i)v_i$.*

What this lemma says is that for two items we should minimize the expected lost value, which seems to be a reasonable strategy. One could hope that it is actually the optimal one. However, as the following theorem shows, it can perform arbitrarily bad (proof in Appendix A).

Theorem 2.3 *The strategy of always picking an item maximizing $q_i v_i = (1 - p_i)v_i$ does not guarantee a constant competitive ratio with respect to a non-clairvoyant adversary.*

Call an algorithm *ordering-based* if, for every instance, it follows a fixed ordering of items, i.e. it picks items in a fixed order, skipping over the ones that are no longer alive. An interesting consequence of the proof of Theorem 2.3 is the following.

Corollary 2.4 *There is no ordering-based algorithm that is optimal with respect to a non-clairvoyant adversary.*

Proof. Consider any instance with all $p_i \neq 0$. For any pair of items $(v_1, p_1), (v_2, p_2)$ it is possible, that at some point they are the only two items left (unless one of them is always picked in the first round). Therefore, any optimal ordering-based algorithm needs to always pick the item with highest $(1 - p_i)v_i$ first. It follows that if there existed an ordering based optimal algorithm, it would need to pick items in order of decreasing $(1 - p_i)v_i$ (except for, perhaps, the first item). The example used in the proof of Theorem 2.3 shows that this strategy is not optimal. ■

As mentioned in the introduction, it is possible to be $(1 - 1/e)$-competitive in the case when items are allowed to arrive at arbitrary timesteps. Even the following stronger statement holds.

Lemma 2.5 *Against a clairvoyant adversary, there is a $(1 - 1/e)$-competitive algorithm even in the case of adversarial arrivals and departures of items.*

This follows by [1], when we observe that our model can be interpreted as a vertex weighted bipartite matching problem, where vertices on one side correspond to time rounds, whereas vertices on the other side correspond to items. Moreover, since the algorithm in [1] does not need to know the values of the items before timesteps in which it can be picked, this reduction also works when the items arrive online.

3. AN UPPER BOUND AGAINST CLAIRVOYANT ADVERSARIES

Let us consider the case where there are n items, each with the same survival probability $p = \frac{k-1}{k}$ for an integer value k to be chosen later. (This parameter k will lie in $[n/2, n]$.) We will show that the best clairvoyant algorithm can pick $\approx k(1 + \ln \frac{n}{k})$ items with high probability. Since all items are identical, there is only one reasonable non-clairvoyant algorithm, which is to pick one of the remaining items at each time, and we show that this algorithm gets $\approx k(\ln(1 + \frac{n}{k}))$ items, again with high probability. Hence, the competitive ratio against the clairvoyant adversary is $\ln(1 + \frac{n}{k})/(1 + \ln \frac{n}{k})$, which is minimized for $k \approx n/1.84$, taking on value $0.64842\ldots$ This shows that the $(1 - 1/e)$-competitiveness given by the reduction to vertex-weighted online matching cannot be significantly improved unless we compare to a non-clairvoyant optimum.

3.1 Clairvoyant Algorithms

First, let us give a lower bound on the performance of a clairvoyant algorithm, which knows when the items die, and hence can choose items accordingly.

Theorem 3.1 *For any $k \in [n/2, n]$, and any constant $\varepsilon \in [0, 1]$, there exists a clairvoyant adversary that can pick $(1 - \varepsilon)(k - 1)(1 + \ln(n/k))$ items with probability at least $1 - n\,e^{-\Omega(\varepsilon^2 k)}$.*

Proof. Let $e_1, \ldots, e_n$ be the items in the order in which they die, i.e., e_1 dies first and e_n dies last. Ties between items dying in the same step are broken arbitrarily. Define $\ell = n - k(1 - \varepsilon)p(1 + \ln(n/k))$. At step $t \in [0, n - \lceil \ell \rceil]$, pick item $e_{t+\lceil \ell \rceil}$ (if alive). If all these items are alive, we can collect at least $n - \ell$ items. It remains to show that, with high probability, all items we are trying to pick are indeed alive at the time we pick them.

Fix any step $1 \leq t \leq n - \ell$. We need an upper bound on the probability of the bad event that at least $t + \ell$ items died in steps $0, \ldots, t - 1$. Let X_i be the indicator r.v. for the ith item dying in the first t steps, and let $X = \sum_{i=1}^{n} X_i$. It has expectation $\mathrm{E}[X] = n(1 - p^t)$, and we are interested in $\Pr[X \geq t + \ell]$. Equivalently, defining $\beta := \frac{t+\ell}{\mathrm{E}[X]} - 1$, we wish to upper bound $\Pr[X \geq (1 + \beta)\mathrm{E}[X]]$. To apply a Chernoff bound, we would like bounds for β and $\mathrm{E}[X]$.

Claim 3.2 *$\beta \cdot \mathrm{E}[X] \geq \varepsilon pk = \varepsilon(k - 1)$, for $k \leq n$.*

Proof. Substituting for β, ℓ and $\mathrm{E}[X] = n(1 - p^t)$ we get

$$\begin{aligned}
\beta \cdot \mathrm{E}[X] &= t + \ell - \mathrm{E}[X] \\
&= t + n - k(1 - \varepsilon)p(1 + \ln(n/k)) - n(1 - p^t) \\
&= t + np^t - kp(1 + \ln(n/k)) + \varepsilon kp(1 + \ln(n/k)) \\
&\geq \frac{\ln(-1/(n \ln p)) - 1}{\ln p} - kp(1 + \ln(n/k)) \\
&\quad + \varepsilon kp(1 + \ln(n/k)) \\
&\geq \varepsilon kp(1 + \ln(n/k)) \geq \varepsilon kp\ ,
\end{aligned}$$

where the third line follows from the fact that $t + np^t$ is minimized for $t = \ln(-1/(n \ln p))/\ln p$; the fourth line uses $-1/k = p - 1 \geq \ln p \geq 1 - 1/p = -1/(kp)$, where we replace $\ln p$ in the denominator by $-1/kp$ and the $\ln p$ in the numerator by $-1/k$. The last inequality follows from $k \leq n$. ■

Since $\mathrm{E}[X] = n(1-p^t) \leq n$ the claim also implies $\beta \geq \varepsilon(k-1)/n \geq \varepsilon/4$ (for $n \geq 4$).

We can now apply a Chernoff bound to get the desired upper bound on $\Pr[X \geq t + \ell]$, which is the probability that, in step t, we can pick the designated item.

$$\Pr[X \geq t+\ell] = \Pr[X \geq (1+\beta)\mathrm{E}[X]] \leq \exp\left(-\frac{\beta^2 \mathrm{E}[X]}{2+\beta}\right)$$
$$\leq \exp\left(-\frac{\beta\varepsilon(k-1)}{2+\beta}\right) \leq \exp\left(-\frac{\varepsilon^2(k-1)}{8+\varepsilon}\right),$$

where the last inequality follows since $\beta \geq \varepsilon/4$. Taking a union bound over the failure probability of at most n steps, completes the proof of Theorem 3.1. ■

3.2 Non-Clairvoyant Algorithm

Since the items are identical and each dies in a memoryless way, there is only one non-clairvoyant algorithm: pick an arbitrary item at each step. We now give bounds on its performance. Recall that $p = \frac{k-1}{k}$ for some $k \in \mathbb{Z}$. Here, we no long require that $k \geq \frac{n}{2}$.

Theorem 3.3 *For small enough* $\varepsilon > 0$

$$\Pr\left[\mathsf{alg} \geq \log_p \frac{k-1}{n+k-1} + \varepsilon k\right] \leq e^{-\Omega(\varepsilon^2 k)}$$

and

$$\Pr\left[\mathsf{alg} \leq \log_p \frac{k-1}{n+k-1} - \varepsilon k\right] \leq e^{-\Omega(\varepsilon^2 k)}.$$

Proof. Consider the following process. We start with a bin of n balls marked *alive* and $\frac{p}{1-p} = k-1$ balls marked *dead*. In each step, we first mark a single alive ball as dead. (If there are no alive balls to mark at the beginning of a step, we put an additional dead ball into the bin, and call it an *extra* dead ball.) After this, each ball in the bin (alive or dead) is removed from the bin with probability $1-p$, independently of each other and of past events. Let A_t, D_t and E_t be the number of alive balls, (non-extra) dead balls and extra dead balls, respectively, after t steps. Note that $A_0 = n$, $D_0 = \frac{p}{p-1}$ and $E_0 = 0$.

Consider now two sequences of random variables: $B_t = A_t + D_t$ and $C_t = D_t + E_t$. We can use A_t to model the behaviour of the optimum online algorithm for identical items as follows: we have $\mathrm{E}[\mathsf{alg}] = \mathrm{E}[T]$, where $T = \min\{t \mid A_t = 0\}$. Note that whenever $A_t > 0$, we have $E_t = 0$, and so $B_t > C_t$. Therefore

$$T \leq \min\{t \mid E_t > 0\} = \min\{t \mid C_t > B_t\},$$

and it is this last expression that we are going to bound.

First consider B_t. This does not include the extra balls, so for each of the $B_0 = n+k-1$ original balls, the probability of surviving t rounds is p^t independent of other balls, giving us $\mathrm{E}[B_t] = p^t B_0$. By a Chernoff bound, for any $0 < \varepsilon < 1$, and any value $\lambda \geq \mathrm{E}[B_t]$, we get

$$\Pr[B_t \geq (1+\varepsilon)\lambda] \leq e^{\frac{-\varepsilon^2\lambda}{3}}. \quad (3.1)$$

Now consider C_t. Here, a single new ball is added at the beginning of each step, and then each ball is removed with probability $1-p$. Since $C_0 = D_0 = \frac{p}{1-p}$, we have $\mathrm{E}[C_t] = p(1 + \mathrm{E}[C_{t-1}]) = C_0$ by a simple induction. Moreover, each C_t is actually a sum of $C_0 + t$ independent (but not identical) $\{0,1\}$ r.v.s: C_0 for the balls initially in the bin, and a single variable for each new ball. Again using a Chernoff bound, we get for any $0 < \varepsilon < 1$

$$\Pr[C_t \leq (1-\varepsilon)\mathrm{E}[C_t]] = \Pr[C_t \leq (1-\varepsilon)C_0] \leq e^{\frac{-\varepsilon^2 C_0}{2}}. \quad (3.2)$$

To get an estimate of $\min\{t \mid C_t > B_t\}$, let us first identify t_0 such that $\mathrm{E}[C_{t_0}] = \mathrm{E}[B_{t_0}]$. This is just

$$\frac{p}{1-p} = \left(n + \frac{p}{1-p}\right)p^{t_0}.$$

Using $p = 1 - \frac{1}{k}$, we get $\frac{p}{1-p} = k-1$ and consequently

$$t_0 = \log_p \frac{k-1}{n+k-1}.$$

Consider now $t \geq \lceil t_0 + 3k\varepsilon \rceil$, where $\varepsilon > 0$ is small. We have

$$\mathrm{E}[B_t] = B_0\, p^t \leq (k-1)p^{3k\varepsilon} = (k-1)\left(1 - \frac{1}{k}\right)^{3k\varepsilon}$$
$$\leq (k-1)e^{-3\varepsilon} \leq (k-1)(1-2\varepsilon)$$

for small enough ε. We now use the concentration bound for B_t from (3.1) to get

$$\Pr[B_t \geq (1-\varepsilon)(k-1)] \leq \Pr[B_t \geq (1+\varepsilon)(1-2\varepsilon)(k-1)]$$
$$\leq e^{\frac{-\varepsilon^2(1-2\varepsilon)(k-1)}{3}}$$

and that for C_t from (3.2) with $C_0 = k-1$ to get

$$\Pr[C_t \leq (1-\varepsilon)(k-1)] \leq e^{\frac{-\varepsilon^2(k-1)}{2}}.$$

This implies that

$$\Pr[\min\{t \mid C_t > B_t\} > t_0 + 3k\varepsilon] \leq e^{-\Omega(\varepsilon^2 k)}$$

and gives us the first claim.

An analogous reasoning leads to the second one. ■

Using the fact that $\ln p \leq -1/(kp) = -1/(k-1)$, we infer that the algorithm gets at most $(1+\varepsilon)(k-1)\ln(1+n/k)$ items with high probability. And combining with the result of Theorems 3.1, the competitive ratio of the algorithm versus the clairvoyant adversary is at most

$$\min_{k \in [n/2, n]} \frac{(1+\varepsilon)(k-1)\ln(1+n/k)}{(1-\varepsilon)(k-1)(1+\ln(n/k))}$$
$$= \min_{\alpha \in [1,2]} \frac{(1+\varepsilon)\ln(1+\alpha)}{(1-\varepsilon)(1+\ln\alpha)} \leq 0.64842\ldots + 3\varepsilon.$$

This is very close to the $(1-1/e) = 0.63212\ldots$ competitiveness, which shows we cannot improve the result substantially against clairvoyant adversaries. In the next section, however, we show that against the non-clairvoyant optimum, we can do significantly better.

4. AN LP-BASED ALGORITHM

Our algorithm is based on writing an LP relaxation for the problem which captures all non-clairvoyant algorithms, and then rounding it to guide the choices of the algorithm.

4.1 LP formulations and basic properties

Consider the following linear program $LP_x(I)$ for a given instance $I = (v, p)$.

$$\max \sum_{i,t} x_{it} v_i \qquad (LP_x(I))$$
$$\text{subject to} \quad \sum_t x_{it}/p_i^t \le 1 \qquad \forall i$$
$$\sum_i x_{it} \le 1 \qquad \forall t$$
$$x_{it} \ge 0$$

To begin, we claim this linear program is a feasible relaxation of the problem.

Lemma 4.1 *For any instance I of the problem, we have $\mathsf{opt}(I) \le \mathsf{opt}_{LP}(I)$, where $\mathsf{opt}(I)$ is the expected value of the optimal non-clairvoyant algorithm, and $\mathsf{opt}_{LP}(I)$ is the optimal value of $LP_x(I)$.*

Proof. Given any non-clairvoyant algorithm $\mathcal{A}$ with expected total value of V^* on I, we can obtain a feasible solution to $LP_x(I)$ with the same objective value. To do this, set x_{it} to the probability that the algorithm $\mathcal{A}$ picks item i in round t. Since x_{it} are probabilities, $\sum_i x_{it} \le 1$. Also, define y_{it} to be the probability of picking item i in round t *conditioned on item i being alive in round t*: hence $x_{it} = y_{it} \cdot p_i^t$. Since the algorithm can pick i in at most one round, we get $\sum_t y_{it} \le 1$. Finally, the expected value we get is precisely $\sum_{it} x_{it} v_i = V^*$. ■

As in the above proof, it will often be convenient to think of the linear program in terms of the y_{it} variables, so let us record this equivalent LP (called $LP_y(I)$) here:

$$\max \sum_{i,t} y_{it} p_i^t v_i \qquad (LP_y(I))$$
$$\text{subject to} \quad \sum_t y_{it} \le 1 \qquad \forall i$$
$$\sum_i y_{it} p_i^t \le 1 \qquad \forall t$$
$$y_{it} \ge 0$$

Lemma 4.2 *The integrality gap of this LP is at least $(1 - 1/2e)$: i.e., for every constant $\varepsilon > 0$, there are instances where $\mathsf{opt}(I) < (1 - \frac{1}{2e} + \varepsilon)\mathsf{opt}_{LP}(I)$.*

Proof. Consider the instance where we have n items, each with $v_i = 1$ and $p_i = \frac{1}{n}$. By setting $x_{i1} = \frac{1}{n}$, $x_{i2} = \frac{n-1}{n^2}$ and all other $x_{it} = 0$, we obtain a feasible solution to $LP_x(I)$ with value $2 - \frac{1}{n}$. However, any non-clairvoyant algorithm can get unit value in the first round, at most $1 - (1 - 1/n)^n$ expected value in the second round, and at most $1/n$ expected value in all subsequent rounds. For large enough n, this is at most $2 - 1/e + \varepsilon$, which gives us the claimed integrality gap. ■

This integrality gap example is interesting because it shows that no "local" reasoning based on the LP relaxation (i.e., one that considers a single round at a time) can beat the ratio of $1 - \frac{1}{e}$ with respect to non-clairvoyant algorithms. Later on we show how to sidestep this problem. We show how one can introduce interactions between rounds, and impose additional structural constraints on the solutions to $LP_x(I)$, which are not satisfied by the solution considered in the above proof.

Finally, we note that $LP_x(I)$ does not capture clairvoyant algorithms, which is a positive thing, otherwise due to the results of Section 3 we would not be able to obtain competitive ratios better than 0.648 using this LP.

Theorem 4.3 *There exists an instance I, such that the expected total value of an optimal clairvoyant algorithm is strictly larger than $\mathsf{opt}_{LP}(I)$.*

Proof. Consider an instance with two items: one with $v_1 = 1, p_1 = 0$, and the other with $v_2 = 2, p_2 = 1/2$. Here, the optimal clairvoyant algorithm picks item 2 in the first round if and only if it dies before the second round, yielding a value of 2.5. On the other hand, any solution to $LP_x(I)$ has an objective value of at most 2. This is because we have $x_{21} = 0$, $x_{11} + x_{21} \le 1$ and $x_{21} + 2x_{22} \le 1$ and the objective function is the sum of the left hand sides of these two inequalities. ■

4.2 Randomized Rounding: the First Try

The basic approach to rounding $LP_x(I)$ could be to assign each item i to round t using $y_{it} := x_{it}/p_i^t$'s as probabilities. When the algorithm is run, in round t we choose the highest value item that was assigned to this round (and is still alive). The expected total value of such items is equal to $\sum_i y_{it} p_i^t v_i$, exactly the contribution of round t to the objective function of $LP_x(I)$. Of course, we may not be able to obtain this much value—we can only pick one item each round, and more than one item assigned to round t might still be alive in round t. The following lemma gives some insight into the performance of this strategy.

Lemma 4.4 *Let n items have values $v_1 \ge v_2 \ge \ldots \ge v_n \ge 0$ and let the i-th item be available with probability π_i, independently of other items, where $\sum_{i=1}^n \pi_i \le 1$. Let X be the value of the highest valued available item, and 0 if there are no items available. Then*

$$\mathrm{E}[X] \ge \Pr[\textit{at least one item is available}] \cdot \frac{\sum_{i=1}^n \pi_i v_i}{\sum_{i=1}^n \pi_i}.$$

We will prove this lemma (in fact, a generalization of it) shortly, but let us first point out its implications. Adding in a zero value item v_{n+1} with a probability of being available of $\pi_{n+1} := 1 - \sum_{i=1}^n \pi_i$, and using the fact that the probability of at least one item being available is $1 - \prod_{i=1}^{n+1}(1 - \pi_i) \ge 1 - \exp(-\sum_{i=1}^{n+1} \pi_i) = 1 - 1/e$, Lemma 4.4 gives us the following corollary.

Corollary 4.5 *With v_i, π_i and X as defined in Lemma 4.4 we have $\mathrm{E}[X] \ge \left(1 - \frac{1}{e}\right) \sum_{i=1}^n \pi_i v_i$.*

Theorem 4.6 *The basic rounding scheme gives us expected value $\left(1 - \frac{1}{e}\right) \cdot \mathsf{opt}_{LP}(I)$, and hence $(1 - 1/e)$ times the expected value of the best non-clairvoyant algorithm. Moreover, this ratio is tight.*

Proof. To bound the competitive ratio, simply use Corollary 4.5 with availability probabilities set to $y_{it} p_i^t$. To show that it is tight, consider an instance I with n identical items and all $v_i = 1$ and all $p_i = 1$. One optimal solution to $LP_y(I)$

is $y_{it} = \frac{1}{n}$ for all $i = 1, \dots, n$ and $t = 1, \dots, n$. Rounding this solution using the basic rounding scheme puts us in a classic balls-and-bins scenario, where in expectation only a $\approx (1 - \frac{1}{e})$ fraction of the bins are non-empty which proves the claim. ■

This means we need to work harder to get an improvement over $(1 - 1/e)$, which we will do in the next section. But first, let us give the proof of Lemma 4.4.

4.2.1 *Proof of Lemma 4.4*

For the improved analysis in Section 4.3, it will be useful to prove a slightly more general result. Let n items have values $v_1 \geq v_2 \geq \cdots \geq v_n \geq 0$. Let $S_j = \{1, 2, \dots, j\}$. Fix a downwards closed family of subsets $\mathcal{I} \subset 2^{[n]}$. Consider the following process, which depends on the (v_i, π_i) values, and the family $\mathcal{I}$. Let the i-th item be *available* with probability π_i, independently of other items, and let A be the (random) set of available items. Pick a subset of the available items as follows: consider items in increasing order of indices, and *pick* item i if (a) it is available and (b) if $S_{i-1} \cap A$, the subset of available elements previously seen, lies in $\mathcal{I}$. (For instance, if $\mathcal{I}$ consists of all k-element subsets, then this process picks the top $k+1$ available elements with largest value—this is the context in which we will use the following lemma.)

Lemma 4.7 *Let V be the value and N be the cardinality of the set picked by the above process. Then*

$$\mathrm{E}[V] \geq \mathrm{E}[N] \cdot \frac{\sum_{i=1}^n \pi_i v_i}{\sum_{i=1}^n \pi_i}.$$

Proof. Define $\mathcal{B}_i$ as the event that $(S_{i-1} \cap A) \in \mathcal{I}$. Note that i is picked with probability $\pi_i \cdot \Pr[\mathcal{B}_i]$. Moreover, we have the monotonicity property that

$$\Pr[\mathcal{B}_i] \geq \Pr[\mathcal{B}_j] \qquad \forall i \leq j,$$

since $S_{j-1} \cap A \in \mathcal{I} \Rightarrow S_{i-1} \cap A \in \mathcal{I}$. Note that

$$\frac{\mathrm{E}[V]}{\mathrm{E}[N]} = \frac{\sum_{i=1}^n v_i \pi_i \Pr[\mathcal{B}_i]}{\sum_{i=1}^n \pi_i \Pr[\mathcal{B}_i]}. \tag{4.3}$$

We first consider the case where, for some k, $v_1 = \cdots = v_k = 1$ and $v_{k+1} = \cdots = v_n = 0$. We call these sequences of values *basic*. In this case,

$$\begin{aligned}\frac{\mathrm{E}[V]}{\mathrm{E}[N]} &= \frac{\sum_{i=1}^k \pi_i \Pr[\mathcal{B}_i]}{\sum_{i=1}^n \pi_i \Pr[\mathcal{B}_i]} \\ &= \frac{\sum_{i=1}^k \pi_i \Pr[\mathcal{B}_i]}{\sum_{i=1}^k \pi_i \Pr[\mathcal{B}_i] + \sum_{i'=k+1}^n \pi_{i'} \Pr[\mathcal{B}_{i'}]} \\ &\geq \frac{\sum_{i=1}^k \pi_i \Pr[\mathcal{B}_i]}{\sum_{i=1}^k \pi_i \Pr[\mathcal{B}_i] + \Pr[\mathcal{B}_k] \sum_{i'=k+1}^n \pi_{i'}} \\ &\geq \frac{\sum_{i=1}^k \pi_i \Pr[\mathcal{B}_k]}{\sum_{i=1}^k \pi_i \Pr[\mathcal{B}_k] + \Pr[\mathcal{B}_k] \sum_{i'=k+1}^n \pi_{i'}} \\ &= \frac{\sum_{i=1}^k \pi_i}{\sum_{i=1}^k \pi_i + \sum_{i'=k+1}^n \pi_{i'}},\end{aligned}$$

where the first inequality uses that $\Pr[\mathcal{B}_k] \geq \Pr[\mathcal{B}_{i'}]$ for all $i' > k$, and the second inequality uses the two facts that (a) $\Pr[\mathcal{B}_i] \geq \Pr[\mathcal{B}_k]$ for all $i \leq k$, and (b) reducing the numerator and denominator by the same value causes the fraction to decrease.

Let us look again at the inequality we proved for all basic sequences v_i:

$$\mathrm{E}[V] \geq \left(\sum_{i=1}^n \pi_i v_i\right) \cdot \frac{\mathrm{E}[N]}{\sum_{i=1}^n \pi_i},$$

Note that if we fix the π_i, then the last term is a constant and the other two: $\mathrm{E}[V]$ and $\sum_{i=1}^n \pi_i v_i$ are linear in v_i and non-negative. Therefore, the inequality extends to all non-negative linear combinations of basic sequences, and these are exactly the non-increasing sequences of values. ■

Proof of Lemma 4.4: Use Lemma 4.7 with $\mathcal{I} = \{\emptyset\}$. Hence the process picks the most valuable item, and the expected size $\mathrm{E}[N]$ is equal the probability that at least one item appears. (We note that alternatively, Lemma 4.4 can be proven via the concept of fair contention resolution due to Feige and Vondrak [9].) ■

4.3 Randomized Rounding: Second Time's the Charm

To improve on the previous analysis, the main idea is the following. We want a rounding procedure that takes advantage of a situation where none of the items assigned to some round are picked because none survived. In this case we allow picking, say, two items *during the next round.* (We will actually pick one of these items in this round, "borrowing" from the future.) We show that if we are allowed to take two items in a round with constant probability, then we can obtain more than a $(1 - 1/e)$ fraction of the LP value in expectation.

Note that conditioning on the event that in round $t-1$ no item was picked changes the probabilities for items being assigned to round t. However, we show that these events are positively correlated. In other words, knowing that no item was picked in round $t-1$ can only increase the probability that an item is assigned to round t and survives.

Another technical problem we face is that for some rounds it may be the case that we always pick some item (e.g., this happens in round 0). We artificially decrease the probabilities of assigning items to such rounds to ensure that even in these rounds, with constant probability, no item is picked.

4.3.1 *The Algorithm*

We first change the LP formulation slightly as follows: we add the constraint that for a special item i', $x_{i'0} = 1$. By iterating over all items i, each time adding a constraint $x_{i0} = 1$ to the linear program $LP_x(I)$, we select the best LP solution among all the n solutions considered. This does not alter the fact that the (new) LP optimum value is still an upper bound for $\mathsf{opt}(I)$.

Before we present the rounding, here is a thought experiment. The natural rounding algorithm would be to assign item i to round t with probability y_{it}, independently of the other items. Let $Y_{i,t}$ be an indicator variable corresponding to an item i being available in step t, i.e., i being assigned to round t and not dying before round t. (Note that the underlying sample space is given by the random allocations of items to rounds, and by the randomness of the items coin flips.) Also, let $\mathcal{A}_t = \{\sum_i Y_{i,t} = 0\}$ be the event that there are no items available in round t (they all either die before this round, or are assigned elsewhere).

Now for the actual algorithm: we preprocess all the probabilities so that for each round t we have $\Pr[\mathcal{A}_t] \geq Q$, where we set $Q = \frac{1}{2(e-1)} \approx 0.2909\ldots$ More precisely, for each round t we compute the greatest value of $\alpha_t \in (0,1]$ such that $\Pr[\mathcal{A}_t] = \prod_i (1 - \alpha_t\, y_{it}\, p_i^t) \geq Q$. Next, we randomly assign items to rounds so that item i is assigned to round t with probability $\alpha_t y_{it}$. (With probability $(1 - \sum_t \alpha_t y_{it})$, the item i remains unassigned).

When the algorithm is run, in round t we consider the available items in this round: those which were assigned to this round by the random process and are still alive. Among these, we pick the most valuable item. Moreover, for $t > 0$, if more than one item is available, and if no item was picked in round $t-1$, we also pick the second most valuable available item.

Note that this algorithm allows us to pick two items in some rounds, which is not allowed by our model. However, we can implement this as follows: if none of the items assigned to round t survived, we pick the most valuable item that was assigned to round $t+1$ and is still alive. Then, when round $t+1$ comes, we can pick an item again (if any survived), effectively picking two items in this round. Note that in this way we cannot do worse than actually picking two items in round $t+1$. We might do better though, if the item picked in round t were to die after that round. This brings us to a subtle technical issue: To know whether we can pick two items in round $t+2$, we need to know if any of the items assigned to round $t+1$ survived. However, we cannot know this if we picked an item assigned to round $t+1$ in round t, and then no other item survived until round $t+1$. When that happens, we flip a coin for this item and declare it alive/dead in round $t+1$ accordingly. We need to keep these technical issues in mind when analyzing the rounding algorithm.

4.3.2 Analysis

To analyze the algorithm, we need the following improvement over Lemma 4.4, where instead of picking the most valuable item in the round, we pick the two most valuable items (if possible). This is where we make use of the more general Lemma 4.7.

Lemma 4.8 *Let n items have values $v_1 \geq v_2 \geq \ldots \geq v_n \geq 0$ and let the i-th item be available with probability π_i, independently of other items, where $\sum_{i=1}^n \pi_i \leq 1$. Let X be the sum of the values of the two highest valued available item (or less if there are fewer items available). Then*

$$\mathrm{E}[X] \geq \left(2 - \frac{3}{e}\right) \sum_{i=1}^{n} \pi_i v_i.$$

Proof. To prove this, we use Lemma 4.7 with the family $\mathcal{I} = \{\emptyset, \{1\}, \{2\}, \ldots, \{n\}\}$, which ensures that we pick the two most valuable items. In this case $N = \min(Y, 2)$, where Y is the number of items available. It is easy to see that $\mathrm{E}[N]$ is maximized when all the π_i's are equal, in which case

$$\begin{aligned}
\mathrm{E}[N] &= \Pr[Y \geq 1] + \Pr[Y \geq 2] \\
&= 2 - 2\Pr[Y = 0] - \Pr[Y = 1] \\
&= 2 - 2\left(1 - \frac{1}{n}\right)^n - \left(1 - \frac{1}{n}\right)^{n-1} \geq 2 - 3/e,
\end{aligned}$$

where the inequality holds for all $n \geq 1$, which proves the lemma. The last step follows from Lemma B.1 (see Appendix B). ■

Recall that $Y_{i,t}$ is the probability that item i is available in round t (i.e., it is assigned to round t by the algorithm, and is actually alive in that round); $\mathcal{A}_t$ is the event that no items are available in round t.

Lemma 4.9 *The following facts hold true for the variables $Y_{i,t}$ and events $\mathcal{A}_t$:*

(a) $(Y_{i,t} \mid \mathcal{A}_{t-1}) = (Y_{i,t} \mid (Y_{i,t-1} = 0))$,

(b) $\Pr[Y_{i,t} = 1 \mid \mathcal{A}_{t-1}] = \frac{y_{i,t} p_i^t}{1 - y_{i,t-1} p_i^{t-1}} \geq \Pr[Y_{i,t} = 1]$,

(c) $Y_{i,t}$ for different items i are conditionally independent on $\mathcal{A}_{t-1}$.

Proof. Statement (a) is obvious, (b) follows from (a), and (c) is easy to verify using (b) and its joint version saying that the joint distribution of $Y_{i,t}$ and $Y_{j,t}$ conditioned on $\mathcal{A}_{t-1}$ is the same as their distribution conditioned on $Y_{i,t-1} + Y_{j,t-1} = 0$. ■

Theorem 4.10 *The rounding algorithm of Section 4.3.1 achieves a value of at least $(1 - \frac{1}{2(e-1)})\, LP_x(I)$, i.e., at least 70.9% of the optimum.*

Proof. By linearity of expectations we can analyze the contribution of each round separately and it is enough to prove that in each round we gain at least a $1 - Q$ fraction of its contribution to the objective function of the LP. Let $LP_t = \sum_i x_{it} v_i$. We consider two cases, $\alpha_t < 1$ and $\alpha_t = 1$.

Case I: $\alpha_t < 1$. In this case we know that $\Pr[\mathcal{A}_t] = Q$, and by Lemma 4.4 in round t we gain at least

$$(1 - \Pr[\mathcal{A}_t]) \cdot \frac{\sum_i v_i(\alpha_t\, y_{it}\, p_i^t)}{\sum_i (\alpha_t\, y_{it}\, p_i^t)} \geq (1-Q)\frac{\alpha_t\, LP_t}{\alpha_t} = (1-Q)\, LP_t.$$

Case II: $\alpha_t = 1$. We infer that $t > 0$, since we know that there exists an item i, such that $x_{i,0} = 1$, and consequently $\alpha_0 = 1 - Q$. Therefore with probability $\Pr[\mathcal{A}_{t-1}]$ we are eligible to pick two items in round t (since we picked no items in the previous timestep), and with probability $1 - \Pr[\mathcal{A}_{t-1}]$ we can pick only one item in round t. Let us denote by X_1 and X_2 the value of the most valuable and second most valuable item available in round t respectively. Note that the expected gain of the algorithm in round t equals $\mathrm{E}[X_1] + \mathrm{E}[X_2 | \mathcal{A}_{t-1}] \Pr[\mathcal{A}_{t-1}]$. As in our first approach, where we can always only pick one item, Corollary 4.5 implies that $\mathrm{E}[X_1] \geq (1 - 1/e) LP_t$. Moreover, by Lemma 4.8 we have $\mathrm{E}[X_1] + \mathrm{E}[X_2] = \mathrm{E}[X_1 + X_2] \geq (2 - 3/e) LP_t$. Observe, that it suffices to show $\mathrm{E}[X_2 | \mathcal{A}_{t-1}] \geq \mathrm{E}[X_2]$, to prove that the expected gain generated in round t is at least $(1-Q)LP_t$, since then

$$\begin{aligned}
&\mathrm{E}[X_1] + \mathrm{E}[X_2|\mathcal{A}_{t-1}] \Pr[\mathcal{A}_{t-1}] \geq \mathrm{E}[X_1] + \mathrm{E}[X_2] \Pr[\mathcal{A}_{t-1}] \\
&= \Pr[\mathcal{A}_{t-1}]\, \mathrm{E}[X_1 + X_2] + (1 - \Pr[\mathcal{A}_{t-1}]) \mathrm{E}[X_1] \\
&\geq \left(\Pr[\mathcal{A}_{t-1}]\left(2 - \frac{3}{e}\right) + (1 - \Pr[\mathcal{A}_{t-1}])\left(1 - \frac{1}{e}\right)\right) LP_t \\
&= \left(\Pr[\mathcal{A}_{t-1}]\left(1 - \frac{2}{e}\right) + \left(1 - \frac{1}{e}\right)\right) \\
&\geq LP_t \left(Q\left(1 - \frac{2}{e}\right) + \left(1 - \frac{1}{e}\right)\right) LP_t = (1-Q) LP_t\,.
\end{aligned}$$

Observe that by Lemma 4.9 when conditioning on $\mathcal{A}_{t-1}$ the probability that a given item is available in round t is increasing (property (b)) and the events of corresponding to different items being available in round t are still independent (property (c)). Therefore in order to prove $\mathrm{E}[X_2|\mathcal{A}_{t-1}] \geq \mathrm{E}[X_2]$ we can use the coupling technique. By standard arguments we can define an auxiliary probability space, such that when a set of items S is available in round t and $\mathcal{A}_{t-1}$ holds, then in the second probability space the set of available items S' is a superset of S. Therefore the second most valuable item in S' is at least as valuable as the second most valuable item in S and consequently $\mathrm{E}[X_2|\mathcal{A}_{t-1}] \geq \mathrm{E}[X_2]$.

Since both cases give us at least $(1-Q)\,LP_t$, the theorem follows. ∎

5. CONCLUSIONS

The presence of impatient users is an important aspect of many real-world processes, and we initiate an algorithmic investigation in this paper. In particular, we model the problem of serving impatient users to maximize the expected value accrued, where the impatience of the users is modeled by each user leaving the system based on an independent random Geometric random variable. The first approaches to solving this problem give only a $(1-1/e) \approx 0.63$ approximation, so our approach is to give a more careful rounding process that gets within a 0.709 factor of the non-clairvoyant optimum. We also show that any online algorithm can get only 0.64 factor of the clairvoyant optimum, so our algorithm's comparison to the non-clairvoyant optimum is not only fair but necessary. Several questions remain: can we close the gap between our approximation algorithms and the upper bounds? Can we give algorithms for the case of user arrivals? (For this last problem, it is not difficult to adapt the algorithm from [12] to give an improvement over $1-1/e$ when the survival probabilities are bounded away from 1.)

6. ACKNOWLEDGMENTS

We thank Marco Molinaro and Krzysztof Onak for many interesting discussions in the initial stages of this research. Moreover, the first, fourth and fifth author were partly supported by NCN grant N N206 567940. The fourth author was also supported by ERC StG project PAAl no. 259515. The second author was partly supported by EPSRC award EP/D063191/1 and EPSRC grant EP/F043333/1, while the third author was supported in part by NSF awards CCF-0964474 and CCF-1016799, and by a grant from the CMU-Microsoft Center for Computational Thinking.

7. REFERENCES

[1] G. Aggarwal, G. Goel, C. Karande, and A. Mehta. Online vertex-weighted bipartite matching and single-bid budgeted allocations. In *SODA*, pages 1253–1264, 2011.

[2] F. Baccelli and G. Hébuterne. *On Queues with Impatient Customers.* Rapports de recherche. Institut national de recherche en informatique et en automatique, 1981.

[3] J. R. Birge and F. Louveaux. *Introduction to stochastic programming.* Springer Series in Operations Research. Springer-Verlag, New York, 1997.

[4] N. Chen, N. Immorlica, A. R. Karlin, M. Mahdian, and A. Rudra. Approximating matches made in heaven. In *Proceedings of the 36th International Colloquium on Automata, Languages and Programming: Part I*, ICALP '09, pages 266–278, Berlin, Heidelberg, 2009. Springer-Verlag.

[5] F. Y. L. Chin, M. Chrobak, S. P. Y. Fung, W. Jawor, J. Sgall, and T. Tichý. Online competitive algorithms for maximizing weighted throughput of unit jobs. *Journal of Discrete Algorithms*, 4(2):255–276, 2006.

[6] F. Y. L. Chin and S. P. Y. Fung. Online scheduling with partial job values: Does timesharing or randomization help? *Algorithmica*, 37(3):149–164, 2003.

[7] B. C. Dean, M. X. Goemans, and J. Vondrák. Approximating the stochastic knapsack problem: The benefit of adaptivity. *Math. Oper. Res.*, 33(4):945–964, 2008.

[8] S. Dye, L. Stougie, and A. Tomasgard. The stochastic single resource service-provision problem. *Nav. Res. Logist.*, 50(8):869–887, 2003.

[9] U. Feige and J. Vondrák. The submodular welfare problem with demand queries. *Theory of Computing*, 6(1):247–290, 2010.

[10] J. Feldman, A. Mehta, V. S. Mirrokni, and S. Muthukrishnan. Online stochastic matching: Beating 1-1/e. In *FOCS*, pages 117–126, 2009.

[11] N. Immorlica, D. Karger, M. Minkoff, and V. Mirrokni. On the costs and benefits of procrastination: Approximation algorithms for stochastic combinatorial optimization problems. In *15th SODA*, pages 684–693, 2004.

[12] Ł. Jeż. One to rule them all: A general randomized algorithm for buffer management with bounded delay. In *ESA*, pages 239–250, 2011.

[13] C. Karande, A. Mehta, and P. Tripathi. Online bipartite matching with unknown distributions. In *STOC*, pages 587–596, 2011.

[14] R. M. Karp, U. V. Vazirani, and V. V. Vazirani. An optimal algorithm for on-line bipartite matching. In *STOC*, pages 352–358, 1990.

[15] M. Mahdian and Q. Yan. Online bipartite matching with random arrivals: an approach based on strongly factor-revealing lps. In *STOC*, pages 597–606, 2011.

[16] R. Ravi and A. Sinha. Hedging uncertainty: Approximation algorithms for stochastic optimization problems. In *10th IPCO*, pages 101–115, 2004.

[17] D. B. Shmoys and C. Swamy. An approximation scheme for stochastic linear programming and its application to stochastic integer programs. *J. ACM*, 53(6):978–1012, 2006.

[18] S. Zeltyn and A. Mandelbaum. Call centers with impatient customers: Many-server asymptotics of the m/m/i+ g queue. *Queueing Systems*, 51:361–402, 2005. 10.1007/s11134-005-3699-8.

APPENDIX

A. PROOF OF THEOREM 2.3

Proof of Theorem 2.3: Fix a large constant c. We will define an instance, for which the algorithm that always picks an item with the highest value of $q_i v_i$, obtains in expectation at most $\frac{2}{c}$ of the value obtained by the optimum online algorithm.

Take two sets of items: S_1 contains $n_1 = n$ items, each with value $v_1 = 1$ and survival probability $p_1 = 1 - \frac{1}{k_1}$ where $k_1 = n^{1/c^2}$. S_2 contains $n_2 = n^{1/(2c)}$ items, each with value $v_2 = c$ and survival probability $p_2 = 1 - \frac{1}{k_2}$ where $k_2 = ck_1 = cn^{1/c^2}$.

Consider first the algorithm which always picks an item with the highest value of $q_i v_i$. Note that this value is the same for both sets, so by perturbing it slightly, we can make the algorithm pick elements from set S_1 until none are left. How many elements will be picked from S_1. By Theorem 3.3 w.h.p. they will end after about

$$\log_{p_1} \frac{n_1}{k_1} \approx n^{1/c^2} \ln n$$

steps. Note that by this time, the expected number of elements of S_2 that are still alive is 1, so this algorithm does not profit from these elements.

Consider now the algorithm that picks elements from S_2 as long as possible. Using Theorem 3.3 again we get that it picks about

$$\log_{p_2} \frac{n_2}{k_2} \approx n^{1/c^2} \ln n \left(\frac{1}{2} - \frac{1}{c}\right)$$

elements. For large c this is almost half of the elements picked by the first algorithm, but the values of elements in S_2 are c, which gives the claim. ∎

B. EXPLANATION FOR THE PROOF OF LEMMA 4.8

Lemma B.1 *For all positive integers n*

$$2\left(1 - \frac{1}{n}\right)^n + \left(1 - \frac{1}{n}\right)^{n-1} \leq \frac{3}{e}.$$

Proof. The claim can easily be verified for $n = 1, 2$. To prove it for larger values of n we show that the left-hand side of the claim is an increasing function of n for $n \geq 2$. The claim follows, since the right-hand side is the limit of the left-hand side as $n \to \infty$.

Let us define $x = \frac{1}{n}$ and let $f(x)$ be the value of the left-hand side of the claim. Then $x \in (0, 1]$ and

$$f(x) = 2(1-x)^{\frac{1}{x}} + (1-x)^{\frac{1}{x}-1} = (1-x)^{\frac{1}{x}} \left(2 + \frac{1}{1-x}\right).$$

We need to show that $f'(x) < 0$ for $x \in (0, \frac{1}{2}]$. By differentiating we obtain

$$f'(x) = (1-x)^{\frac{1}{x}} \frac{-3x - 3\ln(1-x) + 2x\ln(1-x)}{x^2(1-x)}.$$

By using the Taylor expansion

$$-\ln(1-x) = \sum_{n=1}^{\infty} \frac{x^n}{n}$$

we see that the numerator in the expression for $f'(x)$ is equal to

$$-\frac{x^2}{2} + \sum_{n=4}^{\infty} x^n \left(\frac{3}{n} - \frac{2}{n-1}\right).$$

Since for $n \geq 4$ we have

$$0 < \frac{3}{n} - \frac{2}{n-1} \leq 0.1$$

we can upper-bound this expression by

$$-\frac{x^2}{2} + \frac{x^4}{10(1-x)} = \frac{x^2(x^2 + 5x - 5)}{10(1-x)},$$

which is negative in the interval $(0, \frac{3\sqrt{5}-5}{2}) \supseteq (0, \frac{1}{2}]$ and hence $f'(x)$ is negative as well, which ends the proof. ∎

Instance-Sensitive Robustness Guarantees for Sequencing with Unknown Packing and Covering Constraints*

[Extended Abstract]

Nicole Megow†
Institut für Mathematik
Technische Universität Berlin
Straße des 17. Juni 136
10623 Berlin, Germany
nmegow@math.tu-berlin.de

Julián Mestre‡
School of Information Technologies
SIT Building, J12
The University of Sydney
NSW 2006, Australia
mestre@it.usyd.edu.au

ABSTRACT

Sequencing problems with an unknown covering or packing constraint appear in various applications, e.g., in real-time computing environments with uncertain run-time availability. A sequence is called α-robust when, for any possible constraint, the maximal or minimal prefix of the sequence that satisfies the constraint is at most a factor α from an optimal packing or covering. It is known that the covering problem always admits a 4-robust solution, and there are instances for which this factor is tight. For the packing variant no such constant robustness factor is possible in general.

In this work we address the fact that many problem instances may allow for a much better robustness guarantee than the pathological worst case instances. We aim for more meaningful, instance-sensitive performance guarantees. We present an algorithm that constructs for each instance a solution with a robustness factor arbitrarily close to optimal. This implies nearly optimal solutions for previously studied problems such as the universal knapsack problem and for universal scheduling on an unreliable machine. The crucial ingredient and main result is a nearly exact feasibility test for dual-value sequencing with a given target function. We show that deciding exact feasibility is strongly $\mathcal{NP}$-hard, and thus, our test is best possible, unless $\mathcal{P}$=$\mathcal{NP}$.

We hope that the idea of instance-sensitive performance guarantees inspires to revisit other optimization problems and design algorithm tailored to perform well for each individual instance.

*Supported by the German Science Foundation (DFG) with grant ME 3825/2.

†Supported by DFG grant ME 3825/1.

‡Supported by an ARC grant DE130101664.

Categories and Subject Descriptors

F.2 [**Analysis of Algorithms and Problem Complexity**]: Nonnumerical Algorithms and ProblemsSequencing and scheduling; F.1.2 [**Modes of Computation**]: Online computation

General Terms

Algorithms

Keywords

sequencing, instance-sensitive worst-case guarantee, robustness factor, universal solution, knapsack

1. INTRODUCTION

We study two complementary variants of a general *dual-value sequencing problem*, one with an unknown covering constraint, the other one with an unknown packing constraint. In both cases, we want to find a universal sequence of good quality for all realizations of the unknown constraint. Such problems find applications in real-time computing environments with uncertain run-time availability such as medical diagnosis systems, automated trading systems, and game-playing programs [1]. In particular, dual-value sequencing with an unknown covering constraint has been identified as a core subproblem when *scheduling on an unreliable machine* [7] and in the context of *online flow-time scheduling* [2].

In a geometric interpretation of the dual-value sequencing problem (see Figure 1), we are asked to linearly arrange a given set of rectangles defined by positive values x_j and y_j along the positive x-axis. In the covering variant, a solution is called α-robust, for some $\alpha \geq 1$, if, for all values $t > 0$, the total sum of y-values of rectangles covering the interval $[0, t]$ is within a factor α of the least possible total y-value of such a cover. In the packing variant, a solution is called α-robust, for some $\alpha \leq 1$, if the total sum of y-values of rectangles that can be packed into the interval $[0, t]$ is within a factor α of a maximum packing. In both cases we call α the *robustness factor* of the solution.

For the packing variant there are instances that do not admit solutions with constant robustness factor. A simple example is a two-item instance with one small square and one huge square. For the covering variant, Epstein *et al.* [7]

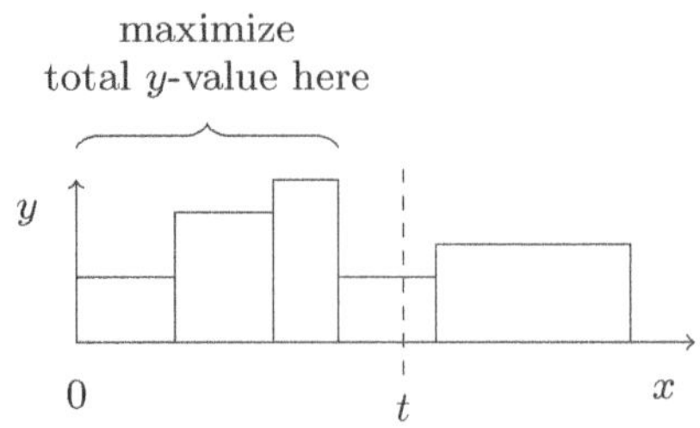

(a) packing constraint

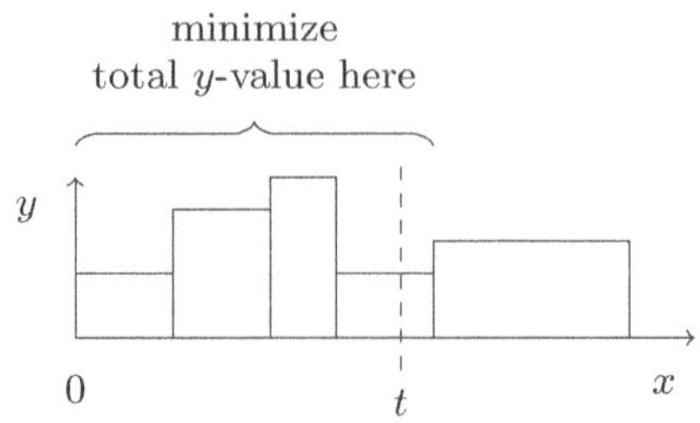

(b) covering constraint

Figure 1: Geometric interpretation of the dual-value sequencing problem.

designed an algorithm that returns a 4-robust solution, and showed that there are instances with optimal robustness factor arbitrarily close to 4. Notice that these are absolute bounds over *all* possible instances. Clearly many instances admit a much better robustness factor than the overall worst case. For example, the simple instance for the packing variant requires items with very large ratio of maximum and minimum weight. Also the instance with optimal robustness factor close to 4 in the covering version [7] is highly structured, it uses items with exponentially large values, and is arguably very unlikely to occur in practice. To address such limitations in the meaningfulness of a general performance guarantee, we propose to find solutions with the best robustness factor on an instance-by-instance basis. For a given input instance (a set of items), we are interested in the robustness factor achievable for this particular instance instead of over all possible instances. We call our approach *instance-sensitive robustness guarantees.*

Our main contributions are polynomial time approximation schemes that find for any instance a solution with nearly optimal robustness factor for the packing and the covering variants of the dual-value sequencing problem.

Our approach of approximating an (unknown) instance-sensitive guarantee allows us to circumvent pathological instances while still maintaining a worst-case perspective. It is worth noting that this approach can be applied to other optimization problems where a (large) absolute approximation or competitive ratio has been found to be tight for a certain subclass of instances. As our work shows, it may still be possible to get better solutions by focusing on instances-sensitive guarantees. It is worth noting that this approach has been pursued, albeit not in a systematic way, in other contexts such as low-distortion embeddings of metrics into geometric spaces, e.g., in [6], subset selection problems [14], and earliest arrival network flows [9]. We hope that our work stimulates further research on instance-sensitive worst-case guarantees for other combinatorial optimization problems.

Overview of our results.

We give nearly optimal instance-sensitive performance guarantees for dual-value sequencing with an unknown packing and covering constraint. Our main contribution is a polynomial time approximation scheme (PTAS) that constructs for any instance and any $\epsilon > 0$ a solution with a robustness factor within $1+\epsilon$ of the optimal factor for the input instance. For the covering problem, this contrasts a previous algorithm that achieves a factor of 4 for all instances [7]. For the packing variant, this is, to the best of our knowledge, the first positive result for general instances. Our algorithm also computes the unknown optimal robustness factor for a given instance up to any desired accuracy. These results imply directly instance-dependent (nearly) optimal solutions for universal scheduling on an unreliable machine to minimize $\sum w_j f(C_j)$, for non-negative, non-decreasing cost functions f, and for determining universal or incremental knapsack solutions.

The crucial ingredient of our algorithm, and the main result of the paper, is an approximate feasibility test for *dual-value sequencing with a given target function.* For a given instance J and a function $Z : \mathbb{R}^+ \to \mathbb{R}^+$, the task is to decide, if there is a sequence of rectangles such that, for any $t > 0$, the total sum of y-values of rectangles whose x-values cover (can be packed in) the interval $[0, t]$ is at most (least) $Z(t)$. Our *approximate* feasibility test outputs, for a given target function $Z(t)$ and a precision parameter $\epsilon > 0$, a sequence that achieves for any covering/packing constraint t a total y-value which is not more than a factor $1 + \epsilon$ above/below $Z(t)$, or reports that there is no sequence with a value above/below $Z(t)$ for all t. We believe that this result is of independent interest. On the negative side, we show that deciding exact feasibility for dual-value sequencing with an *arbitrary* target function is strongly $\mathcal{NP}$-hard.

The high-level idea behind our approximate feasibility test is as follows. First, the target curve $Z(t)$ is replaced with a simpler step function $\tilde{Z}$ that approximates it. Then, dynamic programming is used to assign some items with "large" y-value to each step. The remaining gaps are filled with "small" items by allowing a carefully limited fractional assignment in which such items can be split across several steps. Finally, this fractional solution is converted into a proper sequence at the expense of a small multiplicative violation of the target curve. A major hurdle in carrying out this plan is the large number of steps in $\tilde{Z}$ which prohibits to guess the placement of all large items in one shot. Instead, each DP state stores the large items in only a constant number of steps; global consistency is achieved through a careful recursive definition of the state values.

We note that standard rounding techniques for knapsack problems do not seem to be amenable to our problem: A round-off error of the y-value of an item could be at the same time negligible with respect to a tall step and prohibitive with respect to a short step; similarly it is not clear how to round the x-value without potentially significantly affecting the robustness factor of the instance. For this reason, our algorithm works directly with the input values and avoids any rounding.

Related work.

Our work falls broadly in the field of optimization under uncertainty, in particular *robust optimization* in an *online* environment, and it builds on the concepts of *universal solutions* [7, 13] and *incremental solutions* [15, 16].

The notion of α-robustness was introduced by Hassin and Rubinstein [11] in the context of cardinality-robust solutions for maximum independent set problems. A related knapsack variant with an uncertain *cardinality bound* has been studied recently in [14]. It has been shown that any knapsack instance I admits a $\nu(I)$-robust solution, where $\nu(I)$ is the rank of the knapsack system corresponding to I [11], and it is $\mathcal{NP}$-hard to decide if a given instance admits an improved or even optimal robustness factor [14]. On the positive side, there is an FPTAS that finds solutions with nearly optimal robustness factor [14]. We note that these results do not apply to our problem. Their setting is somewhat simpler than ours since it is really a subset selection problem: Once a feasible set of items has been chosen, the optimal sequence is to order them by decreasing profit.

Other robust variants of the knapsack problem have been studied extensively from various perspectives, see, e.g., [3–5, 19]. These models differ from ours as the uncertainty lies typically in item sizes and/or profits and the task is to find a fixed subset that is feasible in all scenarios. Closest to our work is a size-robust knapsack variant in which only the knapsack capacity underlies uncertainty, which has been studied in [4] from a computational point of view.

In the *universal knapsack problem* we ask for robust solutions in a different sense: Given a set of items with non-negative sizes and profits, the task is to find a permutation that maximizes the total profit of items that fully fit into the knapsack for an unknown capacity. This problem is exactly dual-value sequencing with an unknown packing constraint. The notion of incremental solutions differs from universal solutions in the limited (constant) number of scenarios for the uncertain capacity constraint. The *incremental knapsack problem* has been studied in [10]. The authors give an FPTAS for approximating the optimal robustness factor for the special case of proportional profits.

Universal sequencing on an unreliable machine refers to scheduling problems in which a given set of jobs is to be executed on a machine that may unpredictably change its processing speed or becomes fully unavailable for periods of time. The goal is to find a sequencing of the jobs that performs well under any machine behavior with respect to some cost function. The problem of minimizing $\sum_{j\in J} w_j f(C_j)$, for non-negative, non-decreasing cost functions f, has been studied in [7]. The authors propose an algorithm (with polynomial running time) that constructs a permutation that is $(4+\epsilon)$-robust for all machine behaviors. Interestingly, the solution is the same universal sequence independently of the cost function f. This result is tight, even when the particular cost function is fixed. To obtain this universal sequencing result, Epstein et al. [7] relate the problem of universally scheduling on an unreliable machine to *sequencing to minimize the remaining weight in the system*, which corresponds to the covering variant of dual-value sequencing with a cost function expressed on the reverse sequence. This problem also plays a role in online flow-time scheduling [2].

Other related problems occur in real-time systems where the available computing time is uncertain and the output quality for each job improves as the spent execution time increases. Incremental problem-solving techniques, in particular, *contract algorithms* [1, 18, 20], play an important role. However, these problems differ from ours since multiple copies of a job can be scheduled for different durations and the evaluation function that is based on the computation time that has been spent on each job.

Outline of the paper.

In Section 2 we define the two problems of dual-value sequencing with uncertain covering and with uncertain packing constraints. We also state our main results and their relation to scheduling on an unreliable machine and the universal knapsack problem. In Section 3 we describe the general algorithmic framework for our PTAS for the dual-value sequencing problem. Here we focus on the covering variant. The key routine within the PTAS is an approximate feasibility test for the dual-value sequencing problem with given target function which we provide in Section 4. This key result is best possible since deciding feasibility is $\mathcal{NP}$-hard as we show in Section 5. In Section 6 we argue how the main results can be obtained for the problem with an unknown packing constraint. We conclude with open problems and an outlook in Section 7.

2. FORMAL STATEMENT OF OUR PROBLEMS AND MAIN RESULTS

2.1 Problem definitions

An instance of a dual-value sequencing problem is a set of items $J = \{1, \ldots, n\}$ with two values $x_j > 0$ and $y_j \geq 1$. Let $x(J') = \sum_{j\in J'} x_j$ and $y(J') = \sum_{j\in J'} y_j$, for any $J' \subseteq J$. We denote by $X = x(J)$ and $Y = y(J)$. For two functions F and G of t we use the shorthand notation $F \leq G$ to denote $F(t) \leq G(t)$ for all t. For a function F of t and for a scalar α, we use $\alpha \cdot F$ to denote the function mapping t to $\alpha F(t)$.

The problem of *dual-value sequencing with an uncertain covering constraint* is to minimize the cost function of accumulated y-value for any covering constraint on the x-values. More precisely, we define for a given sequence π the cost function:

$$Y^\pi(t) = \min_{j : x(\pi(\{1,\ldots,j\})) \geq t} y(\pi(\{1, \ldots, j\})).$$

A point-wise lower bound is $Y^*(t) = \min_\pi Y^\pi(t)$. In general there is no sequence that satisfies $Y^\pi = Y^*$. Instead, our goal is to find a sequence π such that the maximum deviation from Y^* is minimized. A sequence π is *α-robust* if $Y^\pi \leq \alpha \cdot Y^*$. A sequence is *optimal-robust* if it obtains a best possible (or optimal) robustness factor for J:

$$\alpha^*(J) = \min_\pi \max_t \frac{Y^\pi(t)}{Y^*(t)}.$$

The variant with *an uncertain packing constraint* is to maximize the cost function of accumulated y-value for any packing constraint on the x-values. For a sequence π, we define

$$\bar{Y}^\pi(t) = \max_{j : x(\pi(\{1,\ldots,j\})) \leq t} y(\pi(\{1, \ldots, j\})),$$

and let $\bar{Y}^*(t) = \max_\pi \bar{Y}^\pi(t)$ denote the function of upper bounds for all packing constraints. A sequence π is α-robust if $\bar{Y}^\pi \geq \alpha \cdot \bar{Y}^*$. A sequence is optimal-robust if it obtains an optimal robustness factor for J:

$$\alpha^*(J) = \max_{\pi} \min_{t} \frac{\bar{Y}^{\pi}(t)}{\bar{Y}^*(t)}.$$

2.2 Main results

We efficiently find a nearly optimal-robust sequence for both the covering and packing variants.

THEOREM 1. *Given an instance J of the dual-value sequencing problem, there are polynomial time approximation schemes that compute, for any $\epsilon > 0$, a $(1+\epsilon)\cdot\alpha^*(J)$-robust covering solution and a $(1-\epsilon)\cdot\alpha^*(J)$-robust packing solution, respectively. The algorithms also compute the exact value of $\alpha^*(J)$ up to an accuracy factor of $1+\epsilon$.*

Dual-value sequencing with an uncertain covering constraint was identified as a key subproblem of universal sequencing on an unreliable machine with the objective of minimizing $\sum_{j\in J} w_j f(C_j)$ for non-decreasing, non-negative cost functions f [7]. In particular, there is a one-to-one correspondence of performance guarantees for any instance [7, Lemma 1]. Thus, our new algorithm implies directly the following nearly optimal instance-sensitive results.

COROLLARY 1. *There is a PTAS for approximating instance-wise the best possible competitive ratio for universal sequencing to minimize $\sum_{j\in J} w_j f(C_j)$ for all machine behaviors and all non-decreasing, nonnegative functions f simultaneously.*

Dual-value sequencing with uncertain packing constraint is precisely the universal knapsack problem with x-values as item sizes and y-values as profits.

COROLLARY 2. *There is a PTAS for approximating the optimal robustness factor for the universal knapsack problem.*

3. PTAS FOR DUAL-VALUE SEQUENCING WITH COVERING CONSTRAINT

For a given dual-value sequencing instance J, we know neither the optimal robustness factor $\alpha^*(J)$ nor the function Y^*. In fact, even computing a single point of Y^* is a knapsack problem by itself and its space complexity (number of different values) of Y^* can be exponential on the number of items [17]. Therefore, we use a simplified approximation of Y^* depending on the parameter $\epsilon > 0$ which we compute as follows. Let t_i^* be the smallest value such that $Y^*(t_i^*) \geq (1+\epsilon')^i$. Using an FPTAS for knapsack [12], we can find in polynomial time values $t_i \in [t_i^*, t_{i+1}^*)$. We define a new curve $Z^*(t) = (1+\epsilon')^{i+1}$ for $t \in [t_{i-1}, t_i)$, which satisfies $Y^* \leq Z^* \leq (1+\epsilon')^2 \cdot Y^*$.

Our algorithm now does a binary search on the robustness factor by testing feasibility for multiples of the curve Z^*. The crucial ingredient of our approximation scheme is an approximate feasibility test that outputs, for a given target function Z and a precision parameter $\epsilon > 0$, a sequence π such that $Y^{\pi} \leq (1+\epsilon)\cdot Z$, or reports that there is no π^* such that $Y^{\pi^*} \leq Z$. We provide such a test in Section 4, but now we show how to use it to approximate the optimal robustness factor.

THEOREM 2. *Given an instance J, $\epsilon > 0$ and a $(1+\epsilon)$-approximate feasibility test, there is a PTAS that computes a $(1+\epsilon)\cdot\alpha^*(J)$-robust solution for dual-value sequencing with an unknown covering constraint. Furthermore, the algorithm computes a value α with $\alpha^*(J) \leq \alpha \leq (1+\epsilon)\cdot\alpha^*(J)$.*

PROOF. Let $\epsilon' = \epsilon/8$. First, we compute an approximation of $Y^*(t)$ such that $Y^* \leq Z^* \leq (1+\epsilon')^2 \cdot Y^*$ as described above. Then we perform binary search for $\alpha^*(J)$ in the interval $[1,4]$ up to the desired level of accuracy. In iteration $i \in \{1,2,\ldots\}$ we test α_i, the mid-point of the current pinning interval, by running the approximate feasibility test with accuracy parameter ϵ' on the target function $Z_i = \alpha_i \cdot Z^*$. After $k = \lceil \log 3/\epsilon' \rceil$ iterations the length of the search interval for $\alpha^*(J)$ has reduced to ϵ'. We consider three cases.

(a) Suppose that all feasibility tests were positive. In this case, $1 \leq \alpha^*(J) \leq \alpha_k \leq 1+\epsilon'$, and thus, the solution sequence returned in last iteration is $(1+\epsilon')\cdot\alpha^*(J)$-robust. Let $\alpha = \alpha_k$.

(b) Suppose that all feasibility tests returned a negative answer. In this case we know that $4-\epsilon' \leq \alpha_k < \alpha^*(J)$. Algorithm DOUBLE in [7] is guaranteed to return a solution with robustness $4+\epsilon'$ in polynomial time. We let this be our final solution and set $\alpha = 4$.

(c) In the remaining case, let i denote the last iteration that returned a positive answer and let i' denote the last iteration with a negative answer. Then $\alpha^*(J) \in [\alpha_{i'}, \alpha_i]$ and $\alpha_i \leq (1+\epsilon')\alpha^*(J)$. Let $\alpha = \alpha_i$. The sequence π returned in iteration i satisfies

$$\begin{aligned} Y^{\pi} &\leq (1+\epsilon')\cdot\alpha\cdot Z^* \leq (1+\epsilon')^2\cdot\alpha^*(J)\cdot Z^* \\ &\leq (1+\epsilon')^4\cdot\alpha^*(J)\cdot Y^*. \end{aligned}$$

In all cases, our choice of ϵ' guarantees that the computed sequence is $(1+\epsilon)\cdot\alpha^*(J)$-robust for all $\epsilon < 4$. Furthermore, the value α approximates the optimal robustness factor arbitrarily well, i.e., $\alpha^*(J) \leq \alpha \leq (1+\epsilon)\cdot\alpha^*(J)$. □

Together with Theorem 3 in Section 4 this implies the covering result stated in Theorem 1.

4. A NEARLY EXACT FEASIBILITY TEST FOR A GIVEN TARGET FUNCTION

In this section we show that there is an approximate feasibility test for the covering variant of the dual-value sequencing problem with a given target curve.

THEOREM 3. *For any fixed $\epsilon > 0$, there is polynomial time approximate feasibility test for the dual-value sequencing problem with a given target curve Z that either reports that there is no π^* such that $Y^{\pi^*} \leq Z$, or it outputs a permutation π such that $Y^{\pi} \leq (1+\epsilon)\cdot Z$.*

In order to describe our algorithm we need to introduce the concept of *fractional sequencing* where we allow items to be split into smaller proportional items; more precisely, an item (x_j, y_j) can be split into items $(x_j^1, y_j^1), \ldots, (x_j^a, y_j^a)$ such that $x_j = x_j^1 + x_j^2 + \cdots + x_j^a$ and $x_j/y_j = x_j^1/y_j^1 = \cdots = x_j^a/y_j^a$. We will use $\tilde{\pi}$ to denote a fractional sequencing of a set of items J.

Algorithm 1 APPROXIMATE FEASIBILITY TEST(J, Z, ϵ)

1. Simplify Z into a step function $\widetilde{Z}$ such that $\widetilde{Z} \leq (1+\epsilon) \cdot Z$
2. Try to find a restricted fractional sequencing $\hat{\pi}$ such that $Y^{\hat{\pi}} \leq (1+\epsilon) \cdot \widetilde{Z}$
3. **if** $\hat{\pi}$ was found **then**
4. Compute a sequencing π such that $Y^{\pi} \leq Y^{\hat{\pi}}$
5. **return** π
6. **else**
7. **return** "Z is not attainable"

Figure 2: Algorithm to approximately test feasibility

At a very high level, our algorithm consists of three steps: First, the input target curve Z is simplified into a step function $\widetilde{Z}$ where the steps are powers of $(1+\epsilon)$ such that $\widetilde{Z} \leq (1+\epsilon)Z$; second, we attempt to find a fractional sequencing $\hat{\pi}$ such that $Y^{\hat{\pi}} \leq (1+\epsilon) \cdot \widetilde{Z}$ having the property that no "large" item is split and the splitting of the remaining items obeys further restrictions (details of these restrictions are given in Section 4.2); third, from $\hat{\pi}$ we compute a proper (non-fractional) sequencing π such that $Y^{\pi} \leq (1+\epsilon) \cdot Y^{\hat{\pi}}$. If Step 2 fails, we will get a certificate showing that there is no π such that $Y^{\pi} \leq \widetilde{Z}$. Otherwise, the algorithm is guaranteed to output a solution π such that $Y^{\pi} \leq (1+\epsilon)^3 \cdot Z$. The pseudo-code for the algorithm is given in Figure 2

The next three subsections explain how each of these steps is carried out. The final subsection provides the proof of Theorem 3.

4.1 Simplifying the input target curve

As a first step in the development of our algorithm we simplify the target curve Z by turning it into a step function[1]. Let t_i be the smallest value such that $Z(t_i) \geq (1+\epsilon)^i$. We define a new curve $\widetilde{Z}(t) = (1+\epsilon)^i$ for $t \in [t_{i-1}, t_i)$. Clearly $\widetilde{Z} \leq (1+\epsilon) \cdot Z$, as desired. We consider Z to be part of the input, so computing the t_i values is trivial (in contrast to the similar approximation of the unknown curve Y^* in Section 3).

We call $[t_{i-1}, t_i)$ the ith step of $\widetilde{Z}$. Given a (perhaps fractional) sequencing, we say that an item j *is assigned to step* i, if when linearly arranging the items in the interval $[0, x(J)]$ according to the sequencing, the left endpoint of j (viewed as a rectangle) belongs to the ith step.

We say an item j is *large* for step i if $y_j > (1+\epsilon)^i/\ell$, where ℓ is set to ϵ^{-2}. Similarly, we say an item j is *medium* for step i if $y_j \in [(1+\epsilon)^i/\ell^2, (1+\epsilon)^i/\ell]$, and *small* if $y_j < (1+\epsilon)^i/\ell^2$. We denote by L_i, M_i, and S_i the set of large, medium, and small items for step i respectively. For brevity we may omit the particular step when we refer to large, medium, or small items in a high level description whenever the step in question is clear from the context.

4.2 Computing a fractional sequencing

Our aim is to find a fractional sequencing such that (i) at most one new item is split per step and (ii) such an item is not large for that step. By at most one new split item per step, we mean that at most one item can be split for the first time in this step. The total number of items that appear fractionally in the ith step is then bounded by i. We show that if there is a proper (non-fractional) sequencing π such that $Y^{\pi} \leq \widetilde{Z}$ then we can find such a fractional solution $\hat{\pi}$ where $Y^{\hat{\pi}} \leq (1+\epsilon) \cdot \widetilde{Z}$.

To find such a restricted fractional sequencing we develop a dynamic programming algorithm (DP) that assigns large (and some medium) items to steps such that (ii) is guaranteed. Based on this assignment we construct a partially fractional sequence $\hat{\pi}$ with the desired properties (i) and (ii).

Our DP states are defined by a tuple $[i, A_i, A_{i-1}, \ldots, A_{i-k}, B]$, where $A_j \subseteq M_j \cup L_j$ for $j = i-k, \ldots, i$ and $B \subseteq M_i \cup L_i$ are disjoint sets. A state can either be invalid, or valid; for the latter case we associate a finite value $T[i, A_i, A_{i-1}, \ldots, A_{i-k}, B] \geq t_i$. We set $k = \log_{1+\epsilon} \ell$, so that $(1+\epsilon)^i = \ell(1+\epsilon)^{i-k}$. The index i ranges from $k+1$ to $i_{\max} = \lceil \log_{1+\epsilon} y(J) \rceil$. Notice that with this choice of k we have the property that $S_i \cup M_i = S_{i+k}$ for all steps i.

We say that a proper or fractional sequencing *follows* the DP state $[i, A_i, \ldots, A_{i-k}, B]$ if the items in A_j are assigned to step j for $j = i, \ldots, i-k$ and items in B are assigned to step $i-k-1$ or earlier without splitting any item in $A_i \cup \cdots \cup A_{i-k} \cup B$.

The high level idea behind a DP state $[i, A_i, \ldots, A_{i-k}, B]$ is as follows. If the state is invalid, then we have a certificate that there is no proper solution π that follows the state and satisfies $Y^{\pi}(t) \leq \widetilde{Z}(t)$ for all $t \in [0, t_i]$. If the state is valid, then we will be able to produce a partial fractional solution that spans at least $[0, t_i]$ and follows the state such that the gaps left by the items $A_i \cup \cdots \cup A_{i-k} \cup B$ can be filled using items in S_i while staying under the curve $\widetilde{Z}$ during $[0, t_i]$. Furthermore, $T[i, A_i, \ldots, A_{i-k}, B]$ is the smallest total x-value of such a solution among a certain subset of solutions that includes all proper partial solutions. We spend the rest of this section formalizing this high level description.

To verify if a DP state is valid we will fill the gaps left between the large and medium items by fractionally assigning small items (details follow below). To that end, let $FK(J', x')$ be the minimum possible total y-value that we would observe in a (unrestricted) fractional solution to the knapsack-type problem where we are allowed to use items from $J' \subseteq \{1, \ldots, n\}$ and we want to cover a total x-value of x'. Notice that such a minimum value solution is achieved by a greedy algorithm that packs items in non-decreasing ra-

[1]We describe here the feasibility test for an arbitrary target function. When using it as a subroutine for the approximation scheme in Section 3, then we omit this first simplification step since the input is already a step function.

tio of $\frac{y_j}{x_j}$ for $j \in J'$, with perhaps the last item being packed fractionally.

Formal definition of DP states.

First consider a state $[k+1, A_{k+1}, \ldots, A_1, \emptyset]$. Let $Q = A_{k+1} \cup \cdots \cup A_1$. We will build a partial sequencing of items Q and fill possibly remaining gaps in each step using items in $S_{k+1} \setminus Q$, which are small in step $k+1$, as follows. First we assign the items in A_1. If $x(A_1) < t_1$, we fill the gap until t_1 using items in $S_{k+1} \setminus Q$. This is done by greedily choosing the items with the best $\frac{y_j}{x_j}$ ratio first and possibly splitting a single item at t_1. If there are not sufficiently many items in $S_{k+1} \setminus Q$ to fill the gap until t_1, or if the total y-value assigned to the first step exceeds $1+\epsilon$, then we stop and mark the state as invalid. Otherwise we continue with A_2; we place all items in A_2 in step 2 and again fill any eventual gap until t_2. This continues until either the state is declared invalid or we are done sequencing A_{k+1}. Let τ_{k+1} denote the x-span of the current partial sequencing, i.e., the total x-value of all items assigned so far. If all items A_j start in step j for $j = 1, \ldots, k+1$ and the total accumulated y-value of $A_1 \cup \cdots \cup A_j$ and the small, possibly split items is at most $(1+\epsilon)^j$ for $j = 1, \ldots, k+1$, then we declare the state valid and set $T[k+1, A_{k+1}, \ldots, A_1, \emptyset] = \tau_{k+1}$. Notice that the T-value of the DP state can equal t_i (if there was a gap in the last step) or be strictly larger than t_i (if the last item in A_k sticks beyond t_i). Otherwise, the value of the state is declared in invalid.

Now consider a state $[i, A_i, \ldots, A_{i-k}, B]$ for $i > k+1$. Then we define

$$T[i, A_i, \ldots, A_{i-k}, B] = \min_{A', B'} \tau, \qquad (1)$$

where $[i-1, A_{i-1}, \ldots, A_{i-1-k}, A', B']$ is a valid DP state, and

$$\tau = \max\left\{t_i, T[i-1, A_{i-1}, \ldots, A_{i-k}, A', B'] + x(A_i)\right\},$$

provided that

$$x(S_i \setminus Q) \geq \tau - x(Q)$$

and

$$y(Q) + \mathrm{FK}(S_i \setminus Q, \tau - x(Q)) \leq (1+\epsilon)^i,$$

where $Q = A_i \cup \cdots \cup A_{i-k} \cup B$.

This last condition guarantees that the gaps left after assigning Q can be filled greedily using items in $S_i \setminus Q$ while keeping the accumulated y-value under $(1+\epsilon)^i$.

Feasibility condition.

Now suppose that there is a valid state $[i_{\max}, A_{i_{\max}}, \ldots, A_{i_{\max}-k}, B]$. In this case, we say the DP is *feasible.* The next lemma shows that if there is a proper solution that stays under $\widetilde{Z}$ then the DP is feasible.

LEMMA 1. *If there is a sequence π^* such that $Y^{\pi^*} \leq \widetilde{Z}$, then the DP is feasible.*

PROOF. Let A_i be the set of medium and large items assigned to step i in π^*. Let $B = (A_1 \cup \cdots \cup A_{i-k-1}) \setminus S_i$ and $B' = (A_1 \cup \cdots \cup A_{i-k-2}) \setminus S_{i-1}$. Let τ_i^* be the maximum of t_i and the rightmost point of items in A_i. We show by induction the state $[i, A_i, \ldots, A_{i-k}, B]$ is valid; furthermore, $T[i, A_i, \ldots, A_{i-k}, B] \leq \tau_i^*$.

The base case is $i = k+1$. Let $Q = A_{k+1} \cup \cdots \cup A_1$. Consider the following transformation to π: First, we linearly arrange the items (viewed as rectangles) according to π; second we remove all items not in Q, while keeping Q in place; third, for $j = 1, \ldots, k$, we slide items A_j as much to the left as possible without leaving their assigned step; forth, we greedily and fractionally fill the gaps in $[0, t_{k+1}]$ using items in $S_{i+1} \setminus Q$. Originally, those gaps used to be filled with items in $S_{i+1} \setminus Q$ and were larger before the shifting was performed. Since the original solution stayed under $\widetilde{Z}$ in $[0, t_i]$, so does the new partial fractional solution. Therefore, the state $[k+1, A_{k+1}, \ldots, A_1, \emptyset]$ is valid and $T[k+1, A_{k+1}, \ldots, A_1, \emptyset] \leq \tau_{k+1}^*$.

For the recursive step, $i > k+1$, let $Q = A_i \cup \cdots \cup A_{i-k} \cup B$. First we note that assuming $T[i-1, A_{i-1}, \ldots, A_{i-1-k}, B'] \leq \tau_{i-1}^*$, we can conclude that $T[i, A_i, \ldots, A_{i-k}, B] \leq \tau_i^*$ by (1), provided the state is indeed valid. As we did before, suppose we remove all items not in Q and we fractionally fill the gaps using items in $S_{k+1} \setminus Q$. Clearly the y-value accumulated at τ_i^* cannot be more than before, which was at most $(1+\epsilon)^i$ by virtue of $Y^{\pi^*} \leq \widetilde{Z}$. In other words,

$$y(Q) + \mathrm{FK}(S_i \setminus Q, \tau_i^* - x(Q)) \leq (1+\epsilon)^i,$$

so the test in (1) is successful and thus the state is valid and $T[i, A_i, \ldots, A_{i-k}, B] \leq \tau_i^*$.

This holds for all i, and in particular for $i_{\max}$; so it follows that the DP is feasible. □

Extracting a fractional solution.

If the DP is feasible then there must be a chain of states

$$\begin{aligned}
\tau_{k+1} &= T[k+1, A_{k+1}, \ldots, A_1, \emptyset] \\
\tau_{k+2} &= T[k+2, A_{k+2}, \ldots, A_2, B_{k+2}] \\
&\vdots \\
\tau_{i_{\max}} &= T[i_{\max}, A_{i_{\max}}, \ldots, A_{i_{\max}-k}, B_{i_{\max}}]
\end{aligned}$$

such that each one attains the minimum in (1) for the next state, where $B_i = (A_{i-k-1} \cup \cdots \cup A_1) \setminus S_i$.

Notice that such a chain of states specifies a sequence of disjoint sets $A_1, \ldots, A_{i_{\max}}$. Given this sequence, we build a fractional solution as follows. First we assign items in A_i to $[\tau_{i-1}, \tau_{i-1} + x(A)]$ for $i = 1, \ldots, i_{\max}$. Then, we fill the gaps using the remaining non-large items in a greedy fashion: When trying to fill a gap in step i we choose a yet-unassigned item j minimizing $\frac{y_j}{x_j}$ with $y_j \leq (1+\epsilon)^i/\ell$, that is, we restrict ourselves to items that are not large in the current step. We call this algorithm RESTRICTED FRACTIONAL KNAPSACK (RFK) because we restrict the set of items we can used in each step and we fix some items (the large and medium items in each step chosen by the chain of DP states) in advance. Notice that by this construction of the solution, an item can only be split at the end of a step and that such an item cannot be large in that step. We denote this solution as $\hat{\pi}$.

LEMMA 2. *If the DP is feasible then* RFK *produces a fractional solution $\hat{\pi}$ such that $Y^{\hat{\pi}} \leq (1+\epsilon) \cdot \widetilde{Z}$. Furthermore, in $\hat{\pi}$ at most one new item is split per step and such an item is not large in that step.*

PROOF. First we argue that the algorithm indeed produces a solution when the DP is feasible. Notice that this is not immediately obvious since the algorithm may not have enough non-large items to fill the gaps left after assigning the items in $A_1, \ldots, A_{i_{\max}}$. Suppose, for the sake of contradiction that the algorithm cannot fill the gap at some step i, and this is the first time this happens. Let $Q = A_i \cup \cdots \cup A_{i-k} \cup B_i$. By the definition of $T[i, A_i, \ldots, A_{i-k}, B_i]$ we are guaranteed that $x(S_i \setminus Q) \geq \tau_i - x(Q)$. Since RFK successfully filled the gaps up to step $i-1$ and it is allowed to use in step i any item in $(S_i \cup M_i) \setminus Q$, it can fill also the gap in step i. We have reached a contradiction, so RFK can fill all gaps.

The fact that at most one non-large new item can be split at each step follows directly from the definition of RFK. It only remains to show that the fractional solution stays below $(1+\epsilon)\cdot\widetilde{Z}$. We show this by induction on the number of steps.

Our base case is the first state in the chain of feasible states, $T[k+1, A_{k+1}, \ldots, A_1, \emptyset]$. Let $Q = A_{k+1} \cup \cdots \cup A_1$. Notice that the procedure used to establish the validity of the state places items $A_1, \ldots, A_{k+1}$ in the same place as RFK; however, it uses items in $S_{k+1} \setminus Q$ to fill the gaps, while RFK is allowed to use items $(S_1 \cup M_1) \setminus Q = S_{k+1} \setminus Q$ in step 1, and items $S_{k+2} \setminus Q$ in step 2, etc. In other words, the greedy procedure used to establish the validity of $[k+1, A_{k+1}, \ldots, A_1, \emptyset]$ is more restricted than RFK in its choice of items to fill the gaps. Therefore, the accumulated y-value by RFK is less than the accumulated y-value by the procedure defining the state, which in turn is guaranteed to be stay below $\widetilde{Z}$ in $[0, \tau_{k+1}]$.

For the inductive case (step $i > k+1$) we show that $Y^{\hat{\pi}}(\tau_i) \leq (1+\epsilon)^{i+1}$, assuming that the property holds for earlier steps. Let $Q = A_i \cup \cdots \cup A_{i-k} \cup B_i$. By inductive hypothesis, it follows that $Y^{\hat{\pi}}(\tau_{i-k-1}) \leq (1+\epsilon)^{i-k}$. Notice that $\hat{\pi}$ places $A_{i-k} \cup \cdots \cup A_i$ in the interval $[\tau_{i-k-1}, \tau_i]$ and fills any eventual gap with items that are not large at each step. As we argued in the base case, the procedure used to define $T[i, A_i, \ldots, A_{i-k}, B_i]$ uses a greedy algorithm to fill these gaps with items in S_i and that such an algorithm is more restricted than RFK in its choice of items during the interval $[\tau_{i-k-1}, \tau_i]$. It follows that the total gain in y-value by RFK to fill the gaps in $[\tau_{i-k-1}, \tau_i]$ is at most the gain of the greedy procedure to fill the gaps in $[0, \tau_i]$, which is at most $FK(S_i \setminus Q, \tau_i - x(Q))$. Therefore,

$$\begin{aligned} Y^{\hat{\pi}}(\tau_i) &\leq (1+\epsilon)^{i-k} + y(Q \setminus B_i) + FK(S_i \setminus Q, \tau_i - x(Q)) \\ &\leq (1+\epsilon)^i/\ell + y(Q) + FK(S_i \setminus Q, \tau_i - x(Q)) \\ &\leq \epsilon^2(1+\epsilon)^i + (1+\epsilon)^i \\ &= (1+\epsilon)^{i+1} \end{aligned}$$

where the second to last inequality follows from the facts that $T[i, A_i, \ldots, A_{i-k}, B_i]$ is a valid state and $\ell = \epsilon^{-2}$. $\square$

4.3 Turning a fractional solution into a feasible sequence

Suppose we obtained a fractional solution $\hat{\pi}$ as described in Lemma 2. Now we show how to turn it into a proper sequence by increasing the accumulate y-value by at most a factor $1+\epsilon$.

LEMMA 3. *For a given a fractional solution $\hat{\pi}$ such that $Y^{\hat{\pi}} \leq (1+\epsilon)\cdot\widetilde{Z}$, having at most one new split item per step and only for items that are not large, let π be the proper solution that orders the items by their first occurrence in $\hat{\pi}$. Then $Y^{\pi} \leq (1+\epsilon)^2 \cdot \widetilde{Z}$.*

PROOF. Consider some $t \in [t_{i-1}, t_i)$ in step i. We show that when going from $\hat{\pi}$ to π, the increase in the accumulated y-value at t is bounded by $\epsilon \cdot (1+\epsilon)^i = \epsilon \cdot \widetilde{Z}(t)$. Only items that were split in $\hat{\pi}$ and that where partially assigned in steps $1, 2, \ldots, i-1$ may contribute additional y-volume to this increase. We know that there is at most one new split item per step and that such an item is not large in the respective steps, i.e., the new split item in step a has y-value at most $(1+\epsilon)^a$. Therefore, the total increase in the accumulated y-value in step i is at most $\sum_{a=1}^{i-1}(1+\epsilon)^a/\ell \leq (1+\epsilon)^i/(\epsilon\ell)$. Since $\ell = \epsilon^{-2}$, we have that π satisfies $Y^{\pi}(t) \leq (1+\epsilon)^i + (1+\epsilon)^i/(\epsilon\ell) = (1+\epsilon)^2 \cdot \widetilde{Z}(t)$ for any t in step i, and thus for all t. $\square$

4.4 Summarizing the feasibility test and proof of Theorem 2

In summary, our approximate feasibility test proceeds as follows. First, we simplify the target curve and compute $\widetilde{Z} \leq (1+\epsilon)Z$, for a given $\epsilon > 0$. Then we run the DP. If the DP is not feasible, then by Lemma 1 it follows that the instance is not feasible, so we can report so. Otherwise, if the DP is feasible, then by Lemma 2 we can find a fractional solution whose accumulated y-value stays below $(1+\epsilon)\cdot\widetilde{Z}$. Finally, this fractional solution can be turned into a proper sequencing π at the cost of an additional factor $(1+\epsilon)$ using Lemma 3. Thus, π satisfies $Y^{\pi} \leq (1+\epsilon)^3 \cdot Z$. Adjusting the parameter ϵ according to the desired accuracy of the test, proves one part of the claim of Theorem 3.

It remains to show that the running time of the algorithm is for any fixed $\epsilon > 0$ is polynomial in the input encoding. Rounding the target function, which we assume to be encoded polynomially in the dual-value sequencing instance J, requires polynomial time since we have to solve at most $\log_{1+\epsilon} y(J)$ knapsack problems each with running time $\mathcal{O}(n^3/\epsilon)$ [12]. The computational effort for our DP is $\mathcal{O}(\log_{1+\epsilon} y(J) n^{(k+2)\ell^2})$. To see that, observe that by definition there can fit at most ℓ^2 large and medium items in each step. In each state we store the large-and-medium-item assignment for $k+1$ steps, and we have in total $\log_{1+\epsilon} y(J)$ steps. To compute the value of a DP state of the form $[i, *]$ we need to inspect all compatible states of the form $[i-1, *]$, which involved trying all possible choices of medium and large items for step $i-k-1$. With our choices of $k = \log_{1+\epsilon} \ell$ and $\ell = 1/\epsilon^2$, the total running time is polynomial in the input encoding of J for any fixed $\epsilon > 0$. This concludes the proof of the covering part of Theorem 3. $\square$

5. HARDNESS OF TESTING EXACT FEASIBILITY FOR A GIVEN TARGET FUNCTION

In this section we show that the $(1+\epsilon)$-approximate feasibility test in Theorem 3 is best possible. We prove that the problem of deciding exact feasibility for a given target curve is strongly $\mathcal{NP}$-hard.

THEOREM 4. *Given an instance of the dual-value sequencing problem with a given target curve T it is strongly $\mathcal{NP}$-hard to decide if there is a sequence π with $Y(t)^{\pi} \leq T(t)$ for all t. This is true even in the case of proportional values and when the encoding length of the target function is linear in the remaining input.*

PROOF. The proof is by reduction from 3-PARTITION: given a set of integers $\{a_1, \ldots, a_{3n}\}$, does there exist a partition into triples such each triplet add up to the same value A. It is well known that this problem is strongly $\mathcal{NP}$-hard even when all integers are in the range $(A/4, A/2)$ [8]. We consider only 3-partition instances having this property.

Given an instance of 3-partition, we build a dual-value sequencing instance where each number a_j induces an item with values $x_j = y_j = a_j$. The target function is set to $T(t) = A\left\lceil \frac{t}{A} \right\rceil$. It is worth pointing out that in this case the target curve T is given to us explicitly and its complexity is linear on the number of items.

It is easy to see that there is a sequence π of all items such that $Y(t)^\pi \leq T(t)$, for any $t \geq 0$, if and only if the 3-partition instance admits a partition into triples adding up to A. □

6. DUAL-VALUE SEQUENCING WITH AN UNKNOWN PACKING CONSTRAINT

In this section we argue that the methods and results in Sections 3, 4, and 5 can be obtained similarly for dual-value sequencing with unknown packing constraint.

To obtain a PTAS, we again first approximate the *lower bound* function $\bar{Y}^*$ by a step function. Let t_i^* be the *largest* value such that $Y^*(t_i) \leq (1+\epsilon)^i$. Using an FPTAS for knapsack, we can find in polynomial time values $t_i \in [t_{i-1}^*, t_i^*]$. We define $Z^*(t) = (1+\epsilon)^{i-1}$ for $t \in [t_i, t_{i+1})$. This step function lies *below* $\bar{Y}^*$; more precisely, $(1-\epsilon)^2\bar{Y}^*(t) \leq Z(t) \leq \bar{Y}^*(t)$. Again, we combine a binary search for $\alpha^*(J)$ with an approximate feasibility test for a given target function. Such a test returns for a given function Z either a sequence π with $\bar{Y}^\pi(t) \geq (1-\epsilon) \cdot Z(t)$, for all t, or it states that there is no π^* that satisfies $\bar{Y}^\pi(t) \geq Z(t)$ for all t.

To adopt the method in Section 4 for obtaining the approximate test for target function Z, we basically replace the minimization criterion by a maximization criterion: Let $FK(J', x')$ denote now the *maximum* possible total y-value in a fractional solution when packing items from $J' \subseteq \{1, \ldots, n\}$ into an interval of length x'. This maximum value is achieved by a greedy algorithm that packs items in *non-increasing* order of ratios y_j/x_j for $j \in J'$, with perhaps the last item being packed fractionally. With a DP we assign large and medium items to steps without splitting them, and we fill the gaps by greedily packing small items according to the maximized ratio y_j/x_j. This allows to argue similarly to Lemma 1 that the DP must be infeasible if there is no sequence π^* such that $Y^{\pi^*}(t) \geq Z(t)$ for all t. On the other hand, if the DP is feasible, then there is a fractional solution $\hat{\pi}$ with $\bar{Y}^{\hat{\pi}} \geq (1-\epsilon) \cdot Z$, with at most one new split item per step and such item is not large in this step. Now, we derive from $\hat{\pi}$ a proper solution π by sequencing items in order of their *last* occurrence in $\hat{\pi}$. Similarly to the proof of Lemma 3, we can show that this transformation from $\hat{\pi}$ to π decreases the total y-value accumulated by time t by at most $\epsilon \cdot (1+\epsilon)^i \leq \epsilon \cdot Z(t)$ for t in step i, i.e., $t \in [t_i, t_{i+1})$. This gives the following result.

THEOREM 5. *There is an approximate feasibility test for the dual-value sequencing problem with a given target curve Z that either reports that there is no π^* such that $\bar{Y}^{\pi^*}(t) \geq Z(t)$, for all t, or it outputs a permutation π such that $\bar{Y}^\pi(t) \geq (1-\epsilon) \cdot Z(t)$, for all t, for any given $\epsilon > 0$ in polynomial time.*

In terms of approximation Theorem 5 is best possible since testing exact feasibility is $\mathcal{NP}$-hard.

THEOREM 6. *Given an instance of the dual-value sequencing problem with a given target curve T it is strongly $\mathcal{NP}$-hard to decide if there is a sequence π with $Y(t)^\pi \geq T(t)$ for all t. This is true even in the case of proportional values and when the encoding length of the target function is linear in the remaining input.*

PROOF. The proof is nearly identical to the proof of Theorem 4. Given an instance of 3-partition in the same notation, we construct the same dual-value sequencing instance and define the slightly modified target function $T(t) = A\left\lfloor \frac{t}{A} \right\rfloor$. Again, it is easy to see that there is a sequence π of all items such that $Y(t)^\pi \geq T(t)$, for any $t \geq 0$, if and only if the 3-partition instance admits a partition into triples adding up to A. □

We embed the test in the binary search framework. Observe that in the packing variant of dual-value sequencing, there is no upper bound on the robustness factor for all instances (as it was 4 in the covering variant). However, for each instance J holds the upper bound $\alpha^*(J) \leq y(J)$. And this robustness factor is achieved by an arbitrary sequence. Thus, we can run a standard binary search for $\alpha^*(J) \in [1, y(J)]$ such that in iteration $i \in \{1, 2, \ldots\}$ with α_i we run the approximate feasibility test with given accuracy parameter ϵ and target function $Z_i(t) = \alpha_i \in Z^*(t)$. After $k = \lceil \log y(J)/\epsilon \rceil$ iterations the length of the search interval for $\alpha^*(J)$ has reduced to ϵ. Notice that k is polynomial in the encoding length of instance J, and we can conclude with the same argumentation as in the proof of Theorem 2.

THEOREM 7. *There is a PTAS that computes a $(1-\epsilon) \cdot \alpha^*(J)$-robust solution for dual-value sequencing with an unknown packing constraint problem. Furthermore, the algorithm computes a value α with $(1-\epsilon)\alpha^*(J) \leq \alpha \leq \alpha^*(J)$.*

Combined with Theorem 2 this concludes the proof of Theorem 1.

7. CONCLUDING REMARKS

We leave as an open problem to determine the complexity of finding an optimal-robust solution for an arbitrary instance of the dual-value sequencing problem. We conjecture that the problem is at least $\mathcal{NP}$-hard—notice that it is not even clear that the problem belongs to $\mathcal{NP}$ or co-$\mathcal{NP}$.

Admittedly, our techniques are strongly tailored to the sequencing problem at hand. However, we feel that our idea of approximating an (unknown) instance-sensitive guarantee does have greater applicability. We hope that our work inspires others to revisit optimization problems where an absolute approximation or competitive ratio has been found to be tight for a certain subclass of instances. For such problems, it may still be possible to improve upon these absolute guarantees by focusing on instances-sensitive guarantees.

8. REFERENCES

[1] S. Angelopoulos and A. López-Ortiz. Interruptible algorithms for multi-problem solving. In *Proceedings of IJCAI*, pages 380–386, 2009.

[2] L. Becchetti, S. Leonardi, A. Marchetti-Spaccamela, and K. Pruhs. Online weighted flow time and deadline scheduling. *Journal of Discrete Algorithms*, 4(3):339–352, 2006.

[3] D. Bertsimas and M. Sim. The price of robustness. *Operation Research*, 52(1):35–53, 2004.

[4] P. C. Bouman, J. M. van den Akker, and J. A. Hoogeveen. Recoverable robustness by column generation. In *Proceedings of ESA*, pages 215–226, 2011.

[5] C. Büsing, A. M. C. A. Koster, and M. Kutschka. Recoverable robust knapsacks: the discrete scenario case. *Optimization Letters*, 5(3):379–392, 2011.

[6] M. Bădoiu, K. Dhamdhere, A. Gupta, Y. Rabinovich, H. Räcke, R. Ravi, and A. Sidiropoulos. Approximation algorithms for low-distortion embeddings into low-dimensional spaces. In *Proceedings of SODA*, pages 119–128, 2005.

[7] L. Epstein, A. Levin, A. Marchetti-Spaccamela, N. Megow, J. Mestre, M. Skutella, and L. Stougie. Universal sequencing on a single unreliable machine. *SIAM Journal on Computing*, 41(3):565–586, 2012.

[8] M. R. Garey and D. S. Johnson. *Computers and Intractability, A Guide to the Theory of NP-Completeness*. W.H. Freeman and Company, 1979.

[9] M. Groß, J.-P. W. Kappmeier, D. R. Schmidt, and M. Schmidt. Approximating earliest arrival flows in arbitrary networks. In *Proceedings of ESA*, pages 551–562, 2012.

[10] J. Hartline and A. Sharp. An incremental model for combinatorial maximization problems. In *Proceedings of WEA*, pages 36–48, 2006.

[11] R. Hassin and S. Rubinstein. Robust matchings. *SIAM Journal on Discrete Mathematics*, 15(4):530–537, 2002.

[12] O. H. Ibarra and C. E. Kim. Fast approximation algorithms for the knapsack and sum of subset problems. *Journal of the ACM*, 22(4):463–468, 1975.

[13] L. Jia, G. Lin, G. Noubir, R. Rajaraman, and R. Sundaram. Universal approximations for tsp, steiner tree, and set cover. In *Proceedings of STOC*, pages 386–395, 2005.

[14] N. Kakimura, K. Makino, and K. Seimi. Computing knapsack solutions with cardinality robustness. In *Proceedings of ISAAC*, pages 693–702, 2011.

[15] G. Lin, C. Nagarajan, R. Rajaraman, and D. P. Williamson. A general approach for incremental approximation and hierarchical clustering. *SIAM Journal on Computing*, 39(8):3633–3669, 2010.

[16] R. Mettu and G. Plaxton. The online median problem. *SIAM Journal on Computing*, 32(3):816–832, 2003.

[17] C. H. Papadimitriou and M. Yannakakis. On the approximability of trade-offs and optimal access of web sources. In *Proceedings of FOCS*, pages 86–92, 2000.

[18] S. J. Russell and S. Zilberstein. Composing real-time systems. In *Proceedings of IJCAI*, pages 212–217, 1991.

[19] G. Yu. On the max-min 0-1 knapsack problem with robust optimization applications. *Operations Research*, 44(2):407–415, 1996.

[20] S. Zilberstein, F. Charpillet, and P. Chassaing. Optimal sequencing of contract algorithms. *Annals of Mathematics and Artificial Intelligence*, 39:1–18, 2003.

Robust Optimization in the Presence of Uncertainty

Joachim M. Buhmann
Department of Computer Science,
ETH Zurich,
Zurich, Switzerland
jbuhmann@inf.ethz.ch

Matúš Mihalák
Department of Computer Science,
ETH Zurich,
Zurich, Switzerland
mmihalak@inf.ethz.ch

Rastislav Šrámek
Department of Computer Science,
ETH Zurich,
Zurich, Switzerland
rsramek@inf.ethz.ch

Peter Widmayer
Department of Computer Science,
ETH Zurich,
Zurich, Switzerland
widmayer@inf.ethz.ch

ABSTRACT

We study optimization in the presence of uncertainty such as noise in measurements, and advocate a novel approach of tackling it. The main difference to any existing approach is that we do not assume any knowledge about the nature of the uncertainty (such as for instance a probability distribution). Instead, we are given several instances of the same optimization problem as input, and, assuming they are typical w.r.t. the uncertainty, we make use of it in order to compute a solution that is good for the sample instances as well as for future (unknown) typical instances.

We demonstrate our approach for the case of two typical input instances. We first propose a measure of similarity of instances with respect to an objective. This concept allows us to assess whether instances are indeed typical. Based on this concept, we then choose a solution randomly among all solutions that are near-optimum for both instances. We show that the exact notion of near-optimum is intertwined with the proposed measure of similarity. Furthermore, we will show that our measure of similarity also allows us to derive formal statements about the expected quality of the computed solution: If the given instances are not similar, or are too noisy, our approach will detect this. We demonstrate for a few optimization problems and real world data that our approach works well not only in theory, but also in practice.

Categories and Subject Descriptors

F.2.2 [**Analysis of Algorithms and Problem Complexity**]: Nonnumerical Algorithms and Problems; I.2.6 [**Artificial Intelligence**]: Learning

Keywords

Optimization; Uncertainty; Noise; Robustness; Instance similarity

1. INTRODUCTION

Inaccuracy and uncertainty of data in input instances of optimization problems are a curse, but a reality. How can we even hope to solve a problem optimally if the input data are noisy? So much for the traditional opinion.

In this paper, we argue that the opposite is often true: Uncertainty can be a blessing that allows us to reach meaningful solutions. In reality, it is mostly an illusion that input data are accurate or that solutions can be implemented accurately. For instance, edge weights of a graph might represent travel time measurements. A shortest path from a start vertex to a target is used to indicate the fastest trip, but might turn out not to be the best choice if the trip is taken in the future, or if the measurements were noisy. For real world problems, this dilemma questions the standard approach of optimizing for a certain objective: Why should it be best to find an optimum solution for an input instance whose data come from measurements that we cannot realistically assume to be exact? And, on the same note: What should the computational goal be in this case?

Viewed from a machine learning perspective, optimization under uncertainty pursues the conflicting goals of optimizing an objective function while keeping the result statistically robust. Optimization must naturally adapt solutions to the last detail, and therefore to fluctuations in the data. That objective is the reason why solutions need mathematical regularization to avoid over-fitting.

In this paper, we advocate an approach that attempts to extract information from data, to eliminate noise, and thereby to reach a typical and robust solution rather than a solution that is geared far too strongly towards a noisy input. Our approach has the following four key properties: (1) It is based on a few input samples only (at least two), (2) it needs no tweaking of parameters, (3) it needs no knowledge on probability distributions of input instances, whether systematic (like travel times that depend on weather) or random, and (4) it provides a self-assessment of how typical and meaningful its solution is. We reach our goal through a notion of *information with respect to an objective*, through a measure that we call the problem-based similarity of instances. Our approach at the same time provides for a purely algorithmic justification of a pioneering information theoretic method [1, 2], as well as for a refinement of this method for optimization problems that exhibit structure in the solution space. This approach reflects the understanding that averaging over fluctuating solutions with near optimal objective function values promises to stabilize the optimization process. Both strategies together, optimization and fluctuation averaging, enhance the predictive value of solutions in the sense that optimized, stable solutions should also yield good objective function values on new problem instances. In this sense, we interpret optimization under uncertainty as a prediction problem.

For a few examples of optimization problems, we demonstrate what it means to use our approach in solving their uncertain versions. It turns out that on one hand, interesting algorithmic problems arise. On the other hand, we get solutions that tend to be only a few percentage points from optimum for real world input instances, and that are better than any competing method that we could imagine.

Related work.

Noisy inputs received attention in a variety of ways. *Stochastic optimization* [3, 4] investigates the fortunate situation in which a distribution of input data is known, and it mostly aims at the optimum in expectation. *Info-gap decision theory* is peculiar in that it models uncertainty as an information gap rather than a probability [5]. *Robust optimization* [6] explicitly describes the uncertainty that is inherent in the input data. In the discrete version, we get a discrete set of input instances for which the structure of a solution must be chosen (such as a path from start to target vertex), and after this choice, one of the given instances is revealed as the true one. A worst case perspective in which an adversary will reveal the worst possible instance, given the chosen solution, is far too pessimistic for real world situations. *Recoverable robust optimization* [7] pursues this approach one step further and allows the algorithm to modify the proposed solution after the true instance has been revealed. This adaptation enables us to at least generate a feasible solution in all cases, while for robust optimization in general, feasibility cannot be guaranteed. *Optimization for stable inputs* attempts to understand when and how small changes in the input data affect the solution [8, 9, 10, 11, 12, 13]. *Regret minimization and online learning* focuses on finding a good solution in an online setting, revealing one input after another, assuming an arbitrary adversary [14]. Here, for a meaningful analysis, necessarily more instances are needed.

2. A BIRD'S EYE VIEW OF OUR APPROACH

Generator.

We are given two input instances of an optimization problem. The two instances are related in an unknown way, like two travel time measurements of the same set of routes at different times. We will consider them to be generated by some abstract *generator*. Given both generated instances, the goal is to compute a good solution for the next (unknown) generated instance. The generator induces noise that we do not know how to predict or eliminate. Specifically, we do not postulate any characteristics of the noise (such as additive, Gaussian, or independent on different parts of the input instance). We assume that the generated instances have the same structure, and differ only in measured values (e.g., for an optimization problem on graphs, the structure of the graph is the same, but edge weights may differ).

Optimization problems.

In our setting, an *uncertain minimization problem* is given by $(\mathcal{I}, S, c)$, where $\mathcal{I}$ is the set of all instances (e.g., all edge-weighted graphs of the same topology), S is the set of all feasible solutions of any instance $I \in \mathcal{I}$, i.e., we assume that a solution $s \in S$ is a feasible solution for every instance $I \in \mathcal{I}$ (e.g., all simple paths from vertex s to vertex t), and $c(s, I)$ is the cost of solution $s \in S$ in an instance $I \in \mathcal{I}$ (e.g., the sum of the edge-weights in instance I along a path s). Note that the set of instances as well as the set of feasible solutions can have infinite size, for instance if we allow arbitrary weights and solutions are points in continuous space. Given an instance I of a (standard) minimization problem, the goal is to find a feasible solution s^* of minimum cost $c(s^*, I)$; we call such a solution a *minimum* of I. The goal of our approach for an *uncertain* minimization problem, however, is to find a feasible solution that is close to optimum for a typical instance of the given minimization problem. We define an *uncertain maximization problem* analogously, and by *optimization* we refer to either minimization or maximization. Note that in our definition, we only look at a class of instances of fixed size. Whenever we argue about problem complexity, we will therefore consider the union of problems of all topologies and sizes, as usual.

Two instances.

By looking at a single input instance we cannot hope to separate the noise from the information: the input could be fully determined by noise and we would not be able to tell that it is so. We therefore assume that several instances are given as input – these instances are considered to be representative, typical instances of the problem. In this paper we explain our approach for two instances.

Example.

Consider the problem of driving from town s to town t in the road network $G = (V, E)$ of Figure 1a. The path through a_2 and b_2 is a highway, while the other edges are local roads. The edge weights in Figures 1b and 1c are driving times. Driving on the highway is usually fast. Due to maintenance, however, edges a_2 and b_2 are prone to traffic jams. A feasible solution is an s-t path. In total, there are eleven s-t paths (the nine paths using at least partially the highway, and the two paths through local roads c_1 and c_2). An optimum solution is a path of smallest driving time. In case of no traffic jam the highway is the (only) optimum solution. We focus our investigation on the situation where congestion appears. Figures 1b and 1c are two instances I_1 and I_2 for two consecutive days where congestion appears

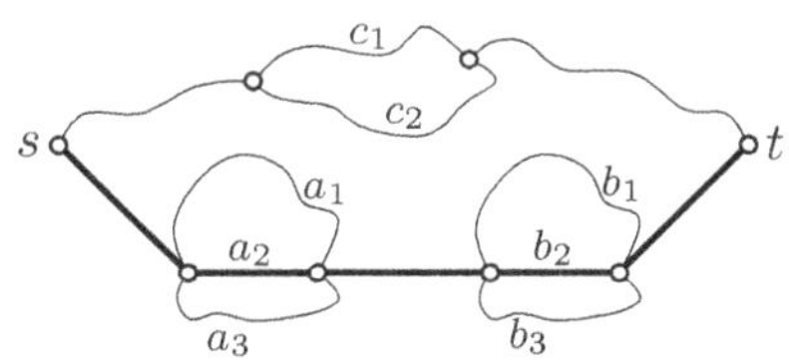

(a) A road network

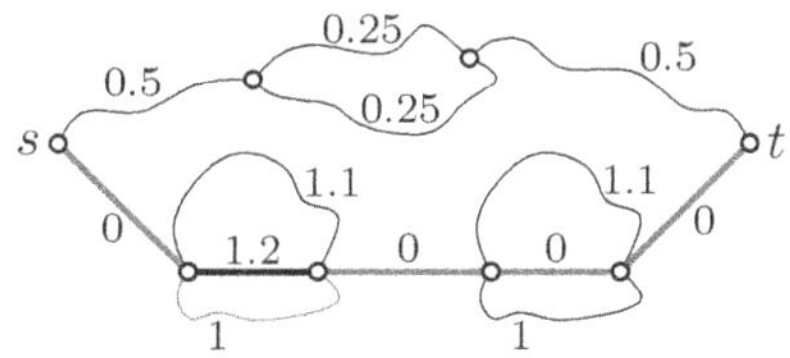

(b) Instance I_1 and its optimum path

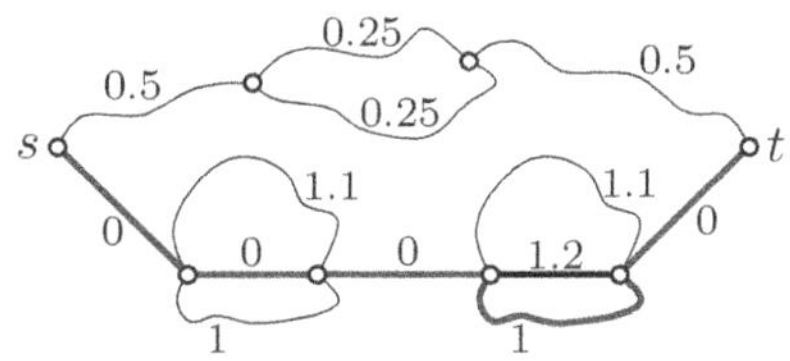

(c) Instance I_2 and its optimum path

Figure 1: A fastest path from s to t

on the first and the second part of the highway, respectively. The question is now how to drive on the third day.

Similarity of instances.

Given two typical instances, we aim at extracting the relevant information and at discarding the irrelevant noise. Since we lack any other knowledge, we look for common features with respect to the goal of close to optimum solutions. We define closeness to optimum by means of an *approximation ratio* ρ: A near optimum solution for an instance I is a *ρ-approximate solution*, i.e., a solution $s \in \mathcal{S}$ with $\text{cost}(s, I) \leq \rho \cdot \text{cost}(s^*, I)$, where $s^* \in \mathcal{S}$ is an optimum solution for instance I. The appropriate ρ is problem and generator dependent and unknown to us. We will call the set of all ρ-approximate solutions of an instance I a *ρ-approximation set of* I, and denote it by $A_\rho(I)$.

Thus, the common features of instances I_1 and I_2 (with respect to our optimization goal) are feasible solutions that lie in the intersection $A_\rho(I_1) \cap A_\rho(I_2)$ of the respective ρ-approximation sets. While one might further investigate the structure of this intersection to capture the information contained in it, we will see that already the number of solutions in this intersection provides a considerable amount of information. Naturally, we expect that for approximation ratio close to 1, the approximation sets, and in particular their intersection, even for unrelated instances, tend to be small, while for approximation ratio far from 1, they tend to be large. When the size of the intersection of both approximation sets is farthest from this expectation, we learn the most from it. Therefore, we choose the value of ρ accordingly. The following definition summarizes this intuition.

Definition 1 (Problem-based instance similarity). *Let I_1 and I_2 be two input instances of an uncertain combinatorial optimization problem $\mathcal{P} = (\mathcal{I}, \mathcal{S}, c)$. For a given ρ, let $A_\rho(I_1)$ and $A_\rho(I_2)$ be ρ-approximation sets for I_1 and I_2. Further, let $es(\rho, a, b)$ be the expected size of the intersection of two ρ-approximation sets of sizes a and b of two arbitrary instances $I_a, I_b \in \mathcal{I}$, respectively, where the expectation is over all approximation sets of the respective sizes, using the uniform probability distribution. Then, the expression*

$$U_\rho(I_1, I_2) := \frac{|A_\rho(I_1) \cap A_\rho(I_2)|}{es(\rho, |A_\rho(I_1)|, |A_\rho(I_2)|)} \qquad (1)$$

is the unexpected similarity of I_1 and I_2 at value ρ *(with respect to the optimization problem $\mathcal{P}$), and the expression*

$$U(I_1, I_2) := \max_\rho U_\rho(I_1, I_2) \qquad (2)$$

is the unexpected similarity of I_1 and I_2 *with respect to the optimization problem $\mathcal{P}$.*

We call $U(I_1, I_2)$ the *unexpected similarity* due to the fact that we normalize the absolute similarity, expressed as the number of solutions in $A_\rho(I_1) \cap A_\rho(I_2)$, with the expected similarity, expressed as the expected size of the intersection. Note that $U(I_1, I_2) \geq 1$ as we can always set ρ so that both approximation sets contain all solutions. The usage of the uniform probability distribution in the definition of the expected intersection follows the Laplace's principle of indifference, as we do not have further information about the generator.

Example (continued).

In our examples in Figures 1b and 1c, the optimum paths for the two instances are different, but both have the same travel time, namely 1. For $\rho = 1.1$ we get two paths in $A_\rho(I_1)$, namely the path through a_3 and b_2 and the path through a_1 and b_2. Similarly, $A_\rho(I_2)$ contains paths through a_2 and b_3 and through a_2 and b_1. These approximation sets have no path in common. For $\rho = 1.2$, only the highway through a_2 and b_2 is in both $A_\rho(I_1)$ and $A_\rho(I_2)$. Observe that $\rho = 1.2$ is the smallest value for which $A_\rho(I_1) \cap A_\rho(I_2) \neq \emptyset$. This may appear to be a natural choice of ρ: Pick the smallest ρ for which $A_\rho(I_1) \cap A_\rho(I_2) \neq \emptyset$. Then, pick a path from the intersection $A_\rho(I_1) \cap A_\rho(I_2)$ – the highway in our case. In our example, this path is risky: It will reach a cost of 2.4 if traffic jams appear in both parts of the highway. Instead, one should also consider to drive on the local roads only (the paths through c_1 and c_2), resulting in a driving time of 1.25. We will see that our method will choose $\rho = 1.25$ as the approximation ratio that maximizes $U_\rho(I_1, I_2)$.

Computing a solution.

We choose a solution from the intersection of the two approximation sets uniformly at random. In the absence of any knowledge about the generator, this is a natural choice following Laplace's principle of indifference. Naturally, we want to choose ρ so that the chance of getting a good solution is maximized.

Choosing ρ.

When the two instances are indeed similar, they have many good solutions in common. Some solutions in the intersection $A_\rho(I_1) \cap A_\rho(I_2)$, however, are present simply because ρ is large. Let us call such solutions *expected*. The good solutions are then the ones in addition to the expected ones – the *unexpected* solutions. Now the goal is to find the

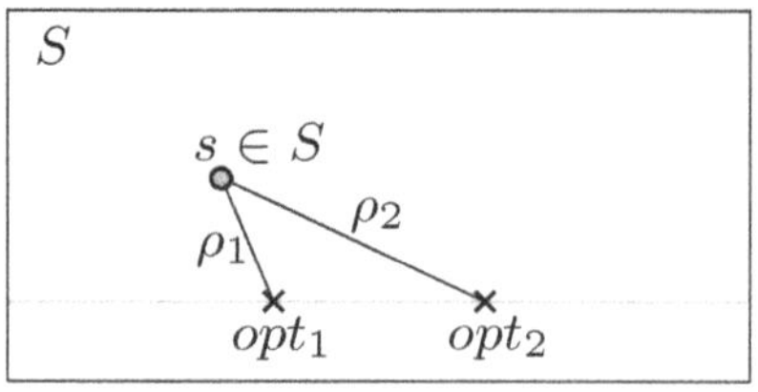

(a) Placing a solution s

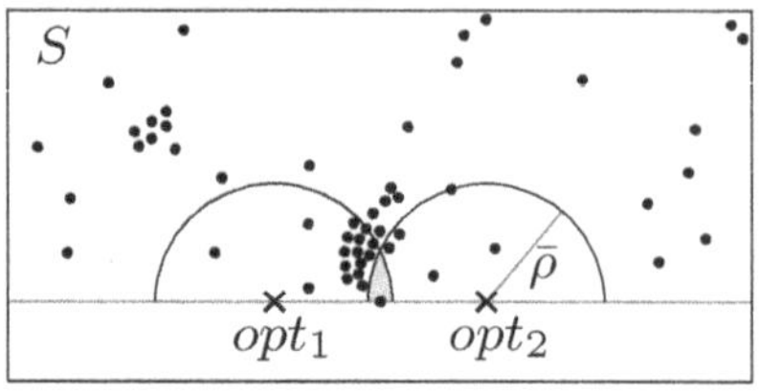

(b) $A_{\bar{\rho}}(I_1) \cap A_{\bar{\rho}}(I_2)$

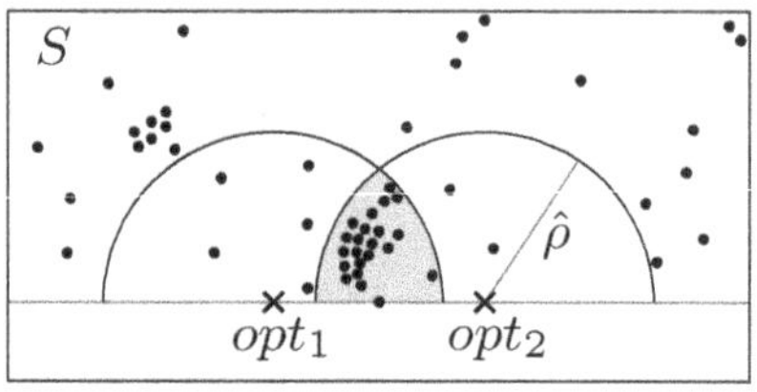

(c) $A_{\hat{\rho}}(I_1) \cap A_{\hat{\rho}}(I_2)$

Figure 2: Approximation sets for similar instances I_1 and I_2. (a): We place the respective optimum solutions opt_1 and opt_2 on a horizontal line at an arbitrary distance. Each remaining point $s \in S$ is then placed above the horizontal line at distance ρ_1 from opt_1 and ρ_2 from opt_2, where ρ_1 and ρ_2 are the corresponding approximation factors that solution s achieves. (b) and (c): Examples of approximation sets $A_\rho(I_i)$, $i = 1, 2$, $\rho = \bar{\rho}, \hat{\rho}$. Warning: distances between solution points other than those to opt_i are meaningless.

value of ρ that will maximize the proportion of good (unexpected) solutions in the intersection, since this maximizes the chances to draw a good solution at random. Figure 2 illustrates these ideas.

We have no direct way of counting the number of unexpected solutions in $A_\rho(I_1) \cap A_\rho(I_2)$, but we can try to compute an expectation of the size of the intersection of any two *feasible approximation sets* A and B of the same sizes as $A_\rho(I_1)$ and $A_\rho(I_2)$, respectively. Here, a feasible approximation set X is a subset of S which is a ρ'-approximation set of I' for some instance I' and some value ρ'.

Given ρ and the sizes $|A_\rho(I_1)| =: k(\rho)$ and $|A_\rho(I_2)| =: l(\rho)$, let $es(\rho, k(\rho), l(\rho))$ denote the expected size of the intersection of two feasible approximation sets A and B of sizes $k(\rho)$ and $l(\rho)$, respectively. If the intersection of $A_\rho(I_1)$ and $A_\rho(I_2)$ is larger than the expected number $es(\rho, k(\rho), l(\rho))$, then it contains some unexpected solutions.

Denoting the number of unexpected solutions in the intersection with $u(\rho)$, we want to find ρ that maximizes $\frac{u(\rho)}{u(\rho)+es(\rho,k(\rho),l(\rho))}$. This is the same as maximizing the ratio

$$\frac{u(\rho) + es(\rho, k(\rho), l(\rho))}{es(\rho, k(\rho), l(\rho))} = \frac{|A_\rho(I_1) \cap A_\rho(I_2)|}{es(\rho, k(\rho), l(\rho))} = U_\rho. \quad (3)$$

Thus, the value of ρ that maximizes the chances of picking a good solution is the same as the value that defines the unexpected similarity of instances.

Example (continued).
Recall that the first non-empty intersection $A_\rho(I_1) \cap A_\rho(I_2)$ appears for $\rho = 1.2$ and contains the path through a_2 and b_2. The unexpected similarity is $U_{1.2} = \frac{1}{6219/87^2} \approx 1.217$ (one can check this for instance by brute-force enumeration). For $\rho = 1.25$, the approximation sets get larger by the two paths through c_1 and c_2. The unexpected similarity is then $U_{1.25} = \frac{3}{71307/177^2} \approx 1.318$. Tedious calculations show that this value maximizes U_ρ. We therefore pick one of the three s-t paths from the intersection $A_{1.25}(I_1) \cap A_{1.25}(I_2)$ uniformly at random, arguably a good choice, which balances (i) the quality and (ii) the robustness, i.e., respectively, the cost of travelling and the risk of travelling too long (if the congestion appears on both parts on the highway).

Self-assessment.
If the unexpected similarity is near 1.0, we know that the two instances are not unusually similar. This limit may be because the noise level is very high, or the instances are actually unrelated. On the other hand, if the unexpected similarity is large, then the instances are similar, i.e., the noise level is low and the intersection contains good solutions for a third instance, generated by the same generator. Unexpected similarity is thus at the same time the key to choosing a good solution with the highest probability, and the measure of the expected quality of the chosen solution. Both are rare properties among known generalization and prediction methods.

Recapitulation of the general approach

For an uncertain optimization problem $(\mathcal{I}, S, c)$, proceed as follows:

1. Determine the domains $\mathcal{F}_k$ of feasible approximation sets of size k.
2. Provide a mathematical analysis or an algorithm $ALG_{\mathbb{E}}$ that computes the expected size of the intersection of two approximation sets of given sizes k and l.
3. Provide an algorithm $ALG_\cap$ that computes the size of the intersection $A_\rho(I_1) \cap A_\rho(I_2)$, given ρ and two instances I_1 and I_2.
4. Find (smallest) ρ^* that maximizes the unexpected similarity U_ρ, using $ALG_{\mathbb{E}}$ and $ALG_\cap$.
5. Provide an algorithm ALG_{rand} that picks a random solution from the intersection $A_{\rho^*}(I_1) \cap A_{\rho^*}(I_2)$.

In Section 3 we discuss in more detail what it means to follow this approach, and in particular how to determine the expectation in point 2.

A prototypic example

We expect our method to exceed the performance of other optimization methods, when the set of good solutions that have stable cost over all or most instances is large enough not to be completely hidden in the noise, but there is a certain number of unstable solutions with wildly differing costs which might out-perform the stable solutions with low probability. When the cost of a large number of solutions is very random, a few of them might sometimes eclipse the true, stable solutions. Usual combinatorial optimization methods go straight for the single solution that minimizes the cost, often missing the truly optimal solutions in the process.

In the following we give a concrete example of a very simple instance generator which illustrates such a situation. We consider an uncertain minimization problem $(\mathcal{I}, S, c)$, with a set of solutions $S = G \cup B$, $|G| =: g \ll b := |B|$, and a cost function $c(s, I) \in \{1, \hat{\rho}, 2\}$, $1 < \hat{\rho} < 2$, for every instance I and every solution s. An instance I is generated with the following random process. The cost of every solution $s \in G$ is $\hat{\rho}$ (always). The cost of a solution $s \in B$ is 1 with probability p and 2 with probability $(1-p)$. We set $\hat{\rho}$ and p such that $\hat{\rho}$, the cost of $s \in G$ is smaller than $2-p$, the expected cost of $s \in B$.

In this setting, the obvious "optimization goal" is to find a solution $s \in G$. How can we achieve this goal, given two instances generated by the above process? We will demonstrate that our approach does well with regard to this goal. To quantify this performance, we compare our approach with two natural competitors: given two instances I_1 and I_2, (i) the `Average` method averages the costs of every solution and selects the solution $s \in S$ with the smallest average cost; (ii) the `FirstIntersection` method chooses the smallest ρ for which $A_\rho(I_1)$ and $A_\rho(I_2)$ intersect, and selects a solution from the respective intersection (if the intersection contains more than one solution).

Let b_1, b_2 be the number of solutions from B with cost 1 in I_1 and I_2, respectively, and let b_x be the number of solutions that have cost 1 in both I_1 and I_2. For appropriately set values of g, b, and p it follows that our approach selects $s \in G$ with higher probability than `Average` and `FirstIntersection`. Roughly speaking, both `Average` and `FirstIntersection` selects $s \in G$ only if $b_x = 0$, which happens with an extremely small probability $(1-p)^b$. On the other hand, our approach maximizes the unexpected similarity for $\rho = \hat{\rho}$ with high probability and then selects a solution $s \in G$ with probability at least, but usually much more than, $\frac{g}{g+b}$.

3. PROPERTIES OF UNEXPECTED SIMILARITY

In this section we investigate the unexpected similarity. Computing the unexpected similarity is not straightforward. One of the difficulties lies in the computation of the denominator – the expected size of an intersection of two approximation sets. If each set of feasible solutions is a *feasible approximation set*, i.e., ρ'-approximation set for some instance I' and some value ρ', we can calculate the expected size of the intersection easily, as the following theorem shows. In the following, we denote by $\mathcal{F}_x$ the set of all feasible approximation sets of size x.

THEOREM 1. *Let $P = (\mathcal{I}, S, c)$ be an optimization problem with the property that for any subset A of the set of all feasible solutions S there exists an input instance I and value ρ' such that $A_{\rho'}(I) = A$. Then, the unexpected similarity of two instances $I_1, I_2 \in \mathcal{I}$ at value ρ is*

$$U_\rho = \frac{|S||A_\rho(I_1) \cap A_\rho(I_2)|}{|A_\rho(I_1)||A_\rho(I_2)|}. \tag{4}$$

PROOF. Let $|A_\rho(I_1)| = k$ and $|A_\rho(I_2)| = l$. As every subset A of S is a ρ'-approximation set of some instance I, we get that $\mathcal{F}_k$ and $\mathcal{F}_l$ are the sets of all subsets of S of size k and l, respectively. Therefore, $\mathbb{E}_{A \in \mathcal{F}_k, B \in \mathcal{F}_l} |A \cap B|$ is the expected overlap of two randomly chosen subsets A and B of S of size k and l, respectively, which amounts to $l\frac{k}{|S|}$, and the claim follows. □

As an example, the problem of clustering data points [1] satisfies this property.

When not every subset $A \subseteq S$ is a feasible approximation set, the situation is more complicated, and there is no general recipe for how to compute the expected size of the intersection. Still, the right-hand side of Equation (4) is in some cases an upper bound on the unexpected similarity, as we will later argue. Whenever $|A_\rho(I_1)| = |A_\rho(I_2)|$, this expression may be close to the real value of the unexpected similarity.

The following equality will prove to be useful in arguing about the expected size of the intersection of two unrelated feasible approximation sets.

LEMMA 2. *The expected size of the intersection of two approximation sets $A \in \mathcal{F}_k$, $B \in \mathcal{F}_l$ for the uniform probability distribution is*

$$\frac{1}{|\mathcal{F}_k||\mathcal{F}_l|} \sum_{\substack{F_1 \in \mathcal{F}_k \\ F_2 \in \mathcal{F}_l}} |F_1 \cap F_2| = \frac{1}{|\mathcal{F}_k||\mathcal{F}_l|} \sum_{s \in S} |\{F \in \mathcal{F}_k | s \in F\}| \cdot |\{F \in \mathcal{F}_l | s \in F\}|.$$

PROOF. It is easy to see that $\sum_{\substack{F_1 \in \mathcal{F}_k \\ F_2 \in \mathcal{F}_l}} |F_1 \cap F_2| = \sum_{s \in S} |\{F \in \mathcal{F}_k | s \in F\}| \cdot |\{F \in \mathcal{F}_l | s \in F\}|$ simply by summing up in two different ways. □

We now show that in some cases the expression in Equation (4) provides an upper bound on U_ρ.

THEOREM 3. *Let $P = (\mathcal{I}, S, c)$ be an optimization problem. If $|A_\rho(I_1)| = |A_\rho(I_2)|$ for a given ρ, then*

$$U_\rho \leq \frac{|S||A_\rho(I_1) \cap A_\rho(I_2)|}{|A_\rho(I_1)||A_\rho(I_2)|}. \tag{5}$$

PROOF. Define $k := |A_\rho(I_1)| = |A_\rho(I_2)|$. Recall that $\mathcal{F}_k$ is the collection of all feasible approximation sets that consist of k feasible solutions. Substituting k for $|A_\rho(I_1)|$ and $|A_\rho(I_2)|$, we can calculate the expected size of the intersection as:

$$\frac{1}{|\mathcal{F}_k|^2} \sum_{\substack{F_1 \in \mathcal{F}_k \\ F_2 \in \mathcal{F}_k}} |F_1 \cap F_2| \stackrel{(a)}{=} \frac{1}{|\mathcal{F}_k|^2} \sum_{s \in S} |\{F \in \mathcal{F}_k | s \in F\}|^2 \stackrel{(b)}{\geq} \sum_{s \in S} \frac{k^2 |\mathcal{F}_k|^2}{|\mathcal{F}_k|^2 |S|^2} = \frac{k^2}{|S|} = \frac{|A_\rho(I_1)||A_\rho(I_2)|}{|S|} \tag{6}$$

Equality (a) follows from Lemma 2. Inequality (b) is due to the fact that the sum of squares of positive numbers $\sum_i^n a_i^2$ subject to $\sum_i^n a_i = A$ is minimized when for all i, $a_i = A/n$. Here, obviously, $\sum_s |\{F \in \mathcal{F}_k | s \in F\}| = k|\mathcal{F}_k|$.

Dividing the expression $|A_\rho(I_1) \cap A_\rho(I_2)|$ by the obtained lower bound on the expected size of an intersection, we obtain the claimed upper bound on the unexpected similarity.

□

From the proof of Theorem 3 we immediately see that Equation (4) holds whenever every feasible solution $s \in S$

is part of the same number of approximation sets $\mathcal{F}_k$. Generalizing this observation, we obtain a lower bound on the unexpected similarity, as follows.

THEOREM 4. *Let a be a constant such that for each feasible solution s of some optimization problem $P = (\mathcal{I}, S, c)$ it holds that $|\{F \in \mathcal{F}_k | s \in F\}| \leq ak|\mathcal{F}_k|/|S|$. Then,*

$$U_\rho \geq \frac{|S||A_\rho(I_1) \cap A_\rho(I_2)|}{a|A_\rho(I_1)||A_\rho(I_2)|} \tag{7}$$

PROOF. The proof is similar to the proof of Theorem 3. The sum of contributions of a single feasible solution is maximized when $1/a$ of the feasible solutions are in the maximum number of approximation sets and the rest of the feasible solutions is in no approximation set. □

If instead of the best case situation in the proof of Theorem 3 we consider the worst case, we get a lower bound on U_ρ that is smaller by a factor $|S|$ as compared with the derived upper bound of Theorem 3.

THEOREM 5. *Let $P = (\mathcal{I}, S, c)$ be an optimization problem. Then,*

$$U_\rho \geq \frac{|A_\rho(I_1) \cap A_\rho(I_2)|}{|A_\rho(I_1)||A_\rho(I_2)|} \tag{8}$$

PROOF. We can construct an (artificial) optimization problem where all but one feasible solution can only lie in a single approximation set of some fixed size k and the one last solution is contained in all approximation sets. Then the expected size of the intersection attains the lower bound that results from the most uneven division of feasible solutions into approximation sets. □

The missing factor $|S|$ in the lower bound would for small $|A_\rho(I_1)|$ and $|A_\rho(I_2)|$ often dominate the whole expression and leaving it out makes for an extremely large gap between the upper and the lower bound. This shows that the step of deriving the appropriate specific formula or algorithm to calculate the expected size of the intersection is a necessary component of the approach unless it is possible to show that for a concrete problem, the upper bound is sufficient. One could hope that many typical combinatorial optimization problems have solution spaces which are uniform, i.e., the constant a from Theorem 4 should be low and the upper bound should be reasonably tight.

To the end, we point out an interesting property of our approach. Given two instances I_1 and I_2, where the (unique) optimum solution of I_1 equals the (unique) optimum solution of I_2, then assuming the instances are typical, one would pick the common optimum solution as a good robust solution for the optimization problem. This is what our method usually does as well. In the case when every subset $F \subseteq S$ of solutions is a feasible approximation set, it is always the case, because $U_1 \geq U_\rho$ for every $\rho > 1$, as $U_1 = \frac{1}{1 \cdot 1}|S| \geq \frac{\min\{|A_\rho(I_1)|, |A_\rho(I_2)|\}}{|A_\rho(I_1)| \cdot |A_\rho(I_2)|}|S| \geq U_\rho$.

PROPOSITION 6. *Let I_1 and I_2 be two instances of an uncertain optimization problem such that $s \in S$ is a unique optimum solution in I_1 and a unique optimum solution in I_2. Then $U_1(I_1, I_2) \geq U_\rho(I_1, I_2)$ for every $\rho \geq 1$. Moreover, our method chooses s as the solution.*

4. FINDING A SUB-ARRAY OF MAXIMUM SUM

The classical textbook optimization problem MAXIMUM-SUBARRAYSUM takes an array $(a_1, a_2, \ldots, a_n)$ of n integers and asks for a contiguous sub-array for which the sum of its elements is maximum. A linear time solution of the problem is attributed to Jay Kadane [15]. Despite its general importance, finding the k best sub-arrays has been studied only recently [16, 17, 18]. The optimal algorithm runs in time $O(n + k)$.

Uncertain optimization.

In the uncertain optimization version of this problem, we are given I_1 and I_2, two integer arrays of size n each. The set of all feasible solutions consists of all the $\frac{n(n+1)}{2} + 1$ sub-arrays, including the empty sub-array whose sum is zero. Given an approximation ratio ρ, in order to determine U_ρ we need to compute: (i) the size of the intersection $A_\rho(I_1) \cap A_\rho(I_2)$, and (ii) the expected size of the intersection $A \cap B$ of any two feasible approximation sets A and B of sizes $|A| = |A_\rho(I_1)|$ and $|B| = |A_\rho(I_2)|$.

The size of the intersection.

The size of the intersection $A_\rho(I_1) \cap A_\rho(I_2)$ can be computed as follows. First, note that from a given approximation ratio ρ, a threshold $t = \rho \cdot OPT_I$ for the sub-array sum approximation follows immediately from the optimum OPT_I of a given instance I. We scan through the array and maintain for scanning position j an auxiliary array $aux_j[i]$ of sub-array sums of elements from position i to j. It is not necessary to maintain this explicitly, since at each position in the scan we only need to know how many of the entries of aux are greater than t. Therefore, instead of updating all entries in aux when a new position with element x is scanned, we decrease the threshold by x. It is then enough to maintain a data structure that supports a query for the number of elements above a threshold, in addition to the insertion of new elements. A balanced search tree with aggregates at inner vertices can service both in time $O(\log n)$. This allows us to compute the size of an approximation set for a given value of ρ in time $O(n \log n)$. The intersection of two approximation sets can be found similarly, by maintaining a 2-dimensional range tree with aggregates at inner vertices, and by querying it with a 2-dimensional threshold at each scan position. Hence, we proved the following theorem.

THEOREM 7. *Let I_1 and I_2 be two arrays of size n. Given ρ, the size of the intersection of the ρ-approximation sets $A_\rho(I_1)$ and $A_\rho(I_2)$ can be found in time $O(n \log^2 n)$.*

The expected size of the intersection.

Here we face the problem that not every set of sub-arrays is a feasible approximation set, and thus we cannot use Theorem 1. To see this, consider an example with the set of sub-arrays $F = \{(a, c), (b, d)\}$, where $a < b < c < d$ are array positions and (i, j) denotes the sub-array from position i to position j. Recall that a sub-array (i, j) is in an approximation set A_ρ if and only if $a_i + \ldots + a_j \geq \rho \cdot \text{opt}$. Thus, F cannot be a feasible approximation set: it would also need to contain one or both of the sub-arrays (a, d) and (b, c).

In the technical report [19] we derive an asymptotic substitute for the exact expected intersection size, given the sizes of the feasible approximation sets, as expressed in the following theorem.

THEOREM 8. *The expected size of an intersection of two randomly picked feasible approximation sets of sizes k and l on two arrays of length n each equals*

$$\frac{4k^2l^2 - 2kl}{2k + 2l - 3} \cdot \frac{1}{n^2} + O(n^{-3}). \quad (9)$$

An experimental evaluation with real world data.

Our problem has a natural interpretation when array elements are price differences, such as day-to-day stock price fluctuations: A maximum sub-array is then a single best interval of buying, keeping and selling a stock (where instead of the price difference, we naturally took the ratio of stock prices, calculated as maximum sub-array sum for logarithms of factors). We thus based our experiments on the historical daily prices of a variety of stock indices (BEL-20, Dow Jones, Hang Seng, Nikkei, AEX, CAC-40, DAX, Eurotop100, FTSE100, JSX, Nasdaq, AS30, RTSIndex, and SMI) from 1999 to 2010, adjusted for inflation [20].

In an attempt to assess how well our approach works in comparison with potential competing approaches, we came up with a number of algorithms that, when provided with two instances, return a (hopefully good) sub-array. We then evaluated the sum of this predicted sub-array on a third instance. The first algorithm, denoted by RANDOM, picks a random sub-array and is used simply to illustrate that the results of following algorithms are not caused by excessive growth of the markets. The less naïve algorithm PICKONE randomly chooses one of the input instances and returns an optimum solution for this instance. Algorithm AVERAGE averages the two instances day by day and returns an optimum sub-array for the averaged instance. Algorithm UPPERBOUND maximizes the upper bound on U_ρ given by Theorem 3 and picks a random solution from the generated intersection. Algorithm FIRSTINTERSECTION finds the smallest ρ that results in a non-empty approximation set intersection and returns a random solution from it (in case there is more than one). Algorithm ASYMPTOTIC is similar to UPPERBOUND, but uses the asymptotic estimate given by Theorem 8 for the expectation in U_ρ to choose the correct approximation ratio. Finally, algorithm OPTIMALOFFLINE returns a sub-array that maximizes the average gain over all instances of the given year – the best one one can possibly get.

We considered each year as a separate class of instances, and we used each pair of input instances as an input to each algorithm. We then evaluated the output of the algorithm on all (different) instances from that year. Table 1(a) shows the average loss (over all years) of each method when compared to the algorithm OPTIMALOFFLINE, where ρ was determined by checking values with a step size of 0.01. Algorithm ASYMPTOTIC performs best here at 87% of the optimal off-line algorithm. In Table 1(b) we used only those pairs of instances that had unexpected similarity higher than 5.0, and we evaluated those on all third instances of the same year. This choice corresponds to the idea that instance pairs of low unexpected similarity have little predictive capability. We chose 5.0 so that roughly 50% of all triples of instances were left after the filtering (6048 out of 12012). Choosing higher threshold would decrease the number of chosen triples and thus the relevancy of our results. The performance of ASYMPTOTIC increased to 96% of the optimum off-line solution. Note that all other algorithms (except RANDOM) benefit from the instance similarity calculated by our method as well. It is, however, that the performance of ASYMPTOTIC increases the most.

Algorithm	loss vs. opt	% of opt
RANDOM	24.14	4.4%
PICKONE	4.21	83.3%
AVERAGE	4.02	84.0%
UPPERBOUND	4.26	83.1%
FIRSTINTERSECTION	3.44	86.3%
ASYMPTOTIC	3.33	86.8%
OPTIMALOFFLINE	0.0	100.0%

(a) Instances with arbitrary unexpected similarity

Algorithm	loss vs. opt	% of opt
RANDOM	27.79	4.4%
PICKONE	2.22	92.4%
AVERAGE	2.13	92.7%
UPPERBOUND	1.40	95.2%
FIRSTINTERSECTION	1.31	95.5%
ASYMPTOTIC	1.16	96.0%
OPTIMALOFFLINE	0.0	100.0%

(b) Instances with unexpected similarity larger than 5.0

Table 1: Comparison of optimization methods

5. CONCLUSION

Further experiments

We have demonstrated on two optimization problems that our proposed optimization methodology performs well – on the available data it performed the best among the natural algorithmic competitors. We have performed few more experiments and reported about them in the technical report [19], where we treat two more problems for our optimization method – the shortest path problem and the minimum spanning tree problem. Obviously, the framework requires more experiments with real data.

Variations of the framework

Our proposed optimization methodology in the presence of noise should be understood as a framework that is open to variations. In the following, we point out some of the most immediate questions that need to be addressed.

How exactly should we choose approximation sets?

We should study optimizing the size of the intersection for a variety of choices of approximation sets. It may be useful to pick approximation sets parametrized by their size k instead of quality ρ. We chose to optimize ρ because this leads to some pleasant properties. For instance, a feasible solution belongs to the approximation set only because of its quality, regardless of other solutions. But it might be worth giving up pleasant properties for others, and for computational ease. Furthermore, we chose a single value of ρ for both instances. It might be worth to study what happens for two independent approximation factors ρ_1 and ρ_2, or two independent sizes k_1 and k_2.

In our normalization, we took all topologically different approximation sets to be equally likely. We might, however, have expectations about the generated instances. For shortest paths in a traffic network, for instance, we might expect edge weights to lie in some fixed range. Expectations like these might be factored into the expected size of the approximation set intersection.

Are all solutions in the intersection created equal?

Our method expects all solutions in the best approximation set intersection to be equally desirable (e.g., equally good for a third, unknown instance). In some cases, it might be useful to choose the solution based on some problem specific criterion.

Will more input lead to better results?

We studied two input instances because they are the minimum number necessary to distinguish information from noise. The extension to multiple instances is not immediately obvious. In general, there are two approaches when we have more than two instances at hand: (i) looking at the intersection of all instances and its expectation, or (ii) looking at all intersections between all pairs, triples, etc. of the instances. While the second approach extracts the maximum amount of information from the instances, it seems it could lead to over-fitting and would be extremely computationally difficult.

Can we find efficient algorithmic solutions?

Even though it appears that our approach leads to high-quality solutions, it does not lead to efficient algorithms easily. Quite the opposite: It generates a family of algorithmic problems, namely to compute the intersection size of approximation sets, and to pick a solution at random from this set. Ideally, we would want to avoid the explicit computation of the set, and get hold of a random solution from it more directly. For some problems, such as the MAXIMUM-SUBARRAYSUM, the intersection can be found efficiently. In many cases, though, the sizes of the approximation sets are exponential. The problem of exact counting is often computationally hard, even if the underlying problems themselves are solvable in polynomial time. A way out may be to resort to approximation algorithms for these counting and enumeration problems.

Problem-based similarity beyond optimization

An interesting side-result that we did not focus on in this paper is the expressiveness of instance similarity U. For example, consider the problem of computing a shortest path between vertices s and t in a graph G. Having two instances I_1 and I_2 of this problem, one may attempt to measure the similarity of these instances using the usual statistical tools – e.g., the correlation coefficient. If the instances differ "a lot" only in the edge-weights of very "heavy" edges that are never used in any nearly-shortest path, then the unexpected similarity of these two instances will regard these instances to be very similar, whereas the correlation coefficient will tell the opposite. At the same time, if the computational goal was a maximum matching, the unexpected similarity would regard the two instances as significantly different. This example highlights the need for a measure of *similarity of instances with respect to a computational goal.* We therefore believe that the unexpected similarity may prove to be useful also outside of the proposed framework. For example, Table 1 suggests that inputs that are very similar, measured according to the *unexpected similarity*, yield good results not only for our, but also for other optimization methods.

And finally

In spite of the need to study all the mentioned variations (and more), we believe that the proposed approach has the potential to provide a solid theoretical foundation of practical value for optimization in the presence of unknown noise.

6. ACKNOWLEDGMENTS

This work has been partially supported by the Swiss National Science Foundation (SNF) under the grant number 200021_138117/1, and by the EU FP7/2007-2013, under grant agreement no. 288094 (project eCOMPASS).

7. REFERENCES

[1] Joachim M. Buhmann. Information theoretic model validation for clustering. In *IEEE International Symposium on Information Theory (ISIT)*, 2010.

[2] Joachim M. Buhmann. Context sensitive information: Model validation by information theory. In *Proceedings of the Third Mexican Conference on Pattern Recognition (MCPR)*, volume 6718 of *LNCS*, pages 12–21. Springer, 2011.

[3] J.J. Schneider and S. Kirkpatrick. *Stochastic Optimization.* Springer, 2007.

[4] Peter Kall and János Mayer. *Stochastic Linear Programming: Models, Theory, and Computation.* Springer Verlag, 2005.

[5] Y. Ben-Haim. *Info-gap decision theory: decisions under severe uncertainty.* Academic, 2006.

[6] Aharon Ben-Tal, Laurent El Ghaoui, and Arkadi Nemirovski. *Robust Optimization.* Princeton Series in Applied Mathematics. Princeton University Press, October 2009.

[7] Christian Liebchen, Marco E. Lübbecke, Rolf H. Möhring, and Sebastian Stiller. The concept of recoverable robustness, linear programming recovery, and railway applications. In Ravindra K. Ahuja, Rolf H. Möhring, and Christos D. Zaroliagis, editors, *Robust and Online Large-Scale Optimization*, volume 5868 of *Lecture Notes in Computer Science*, pages 1–27. Springer, 2009.

[8] Yonatan Bilu and Nathan Linial. Are stable instances easy? In Andrew Chi-Chih Yao, editor, *Proceedings of the First Symposium on Innovations in Computer Science (ICS)*, pages 332–341. Tsinghua University Press, 2010.

[9] Davide Bilò, Michael Gatto, Luciano Gualà, Guido Proietti, and Peter Widmayer. Stability of networks in stretchable graphs. In Shay Kutten and Janez Zerovnik, editors, *SIROCCO*, volume 5869 of *Lecture Notes in Computer Science*, pages 100–112. Springer, 2009.

[10] Michael Gatto and Peter Widmayer. On robust online scheduling algorithms. *J. Scheduling*, 14(2):141–156, 2011.

[11] Matúš Mihalák, Marcel Schöngens, Rastislav Šrámek, and Peter Widmayer. On the complexity of the metric TSP under stability considerations. In Ivana Černá, Tibor Gyimóthy, Juraj Hromkovič, Keith G. Jeffery, Rastislav Kráľovič, Marko Vukolic, and Stefan Wolf, editors, *SOFSEM*, volume 6543 of *Lecture Notes in Computer Science*, pages 382–393. Springer, 2011.

[12] Yonatan Bilu, Amit Daniely, Nati Linial, and Michael Saks. On the practically interesting instances of MAXCUT. *CoRR*, abs/1205.4893, 2012.

[13] Amit Daniely, Nati Linial, and Michael Saks. Clustering is difficult only when it does not matter. *CoRR*, abs/1205.4891, 2012.

[14] Nicolò Cesa-Bianchi and Gábor Lugosi. *Prediction, Learning, and Games*. Cambridge University Press, 2006.

[15] Jon Bentley. Programming pearls: algorithm design techniques. *Commun. ACM*, 27:865–873, September 1984.

[16] Fredrik Bengtsson and Jingsen Chen. Efficient algorithms for k maximum sums. *Algorithmica*, 46(1):27–41, 2006.

[17] Sung Eun Bae and Tadao Takaoka. Improved algorithms for the k-maximum subarray problem. *The Computer Journal*, 49(3):358–374, 2006.

[18] Chih-Huai Cheng, Kuan-Yu Chen, Wen-Chin Tien, and Kun-Mao Chao. Improved algorithms for the maximum-sums problems. *Theoretical Computer Science*, 362(1-3):162–170, 2006.

[19] Joachim M. Buhmann, Matúš Mihalák, Rastislav Šrámek, and Peter Widmayer. Optimization in the presence of uncertainty. Technical Report 755, Institute of Theoretical Computer Science, ETH Zurich, 2012. Available online at `http://www.inf.ethz.ch/research/disstechreps/techreports`.

[20] Market rates online. `http://www.marketratesonline.com`.

Sorting Noisy Data with Partial Information

Konstantin Makarychev
Microsoft Research

Yury Makarychev*
TTIC

Aravindan Vijayaraghavan
CMU

ABSTRACT

In this paper, we propose two semi-random models for the Minimum Feedback Arc Set Problem and present approximation algorithms for them. In the first model, which we call the Random Edge Flipping model, an instance is generated as follows. We start with an arbitrary acyclic directed graph and then randomly flip its edges (the adversary may later un-flip some of them). In the second model, which we call the Random Backward Edge model, again we start with an arbitrary acyclic graph but now add new random backward edges (the adversary may delete some of them). For the first model, we give an approximation algorithm that finds a solution of cost $(1+\delta)\,\text{opt-cost} + n\,\text{polylog}\ n$, where opt-cost is the cost of the optimal solution. For the second model, we give an approximation algorithm that finds a solution of cost $O(\text{planted-cost}) + n\,\text{polylog}\ n$, where planted-cost is the cost of the planted solution.

Additionally, we present an approximation algorithm for semi-random instances of Minimum Directed Balanced Cut.

Categories and Subject Descriptors

F.2 [**Theory of Computation**]: Analysis of Algorithms

Keywords

Minimum Feedback Arc Set, semi-random model, average-case analysis, approximation algorithm

1. INTRODUCTION

The Minimum Feedback Arc Set (FAS) problem is one of the most basic optimization problems in the context of directed graphs. The problem asks to find the minimum set of edges (arcs) whose removal makes a given graph a directed acyclic graph (DAG). As any directed acyclic graph can be topologically sorted, this is equivalent to finding an ordering of the vertices, which minimizes the number of backward edges (according to the ordering).

Definition 1.1 *Given a directed graph $G(V,E)$ and a vertex ordering $\pi : V \to \{1,\dots,n\}$, we say that an edge (arc) $(u,v) \in E$ is a forward edge w.r.t π if $\pi(u) < \pi(v)$; otherwise, we say that the edge is a backward edge w.r.t. π.*

Definition 1.2 *The Minimum Feedback Arc Set problem is as follows. Given a directed graph $G = (V,E)$, find a vertex ordering $\pi : V \to \{1,\dots,n\}$ that minimizes the number of backward edges w.r.t. π. The value of the problem equals the number of backward edges w.r.t. the optimal ordering.*

The history of the problem dates back to as early as 1957, when Unger [Ung57] considered it in his paper on asynchronous logical feedback networks. The interest in FAS stems from its numerous applications in simplifying the analysis of feedback systems (removing feedback loops) [Ung57, SR61], finding inconsistencies and cyclic dependencies [You63], and ranking based on pairwise information [KS63, ACN08]. It is the complementary problem of the Maximum Acyclic Subgraph [BS90, CMM07, GMR08], which asks to find the largest acyclic graph (w.r.t. the number of edges) in a given digraph.

The problem has been extensively studied in the literature. Karp [Kar72] showed that the problem is NP-hard in 1972, and Kann [Kan92] showed that the problem is APX-hard in 1992. Furthermore, Guruswami, Manokaran, and Raghavendra [GMR08] showed that there is no constant factor approximation for FAS, assuming the Unique Games Conjecture. In their seminal paper, Leighton and Rao [LR99] gave the first polylogarithmic approximation algorithm for the problem with approximation factor $O(\log^2 n)$. This result was later improved by Seymour [Sey95], who used a clever divide and conquer approach to get an approximation factor of $O(\log n \log\log n)$. His technique was generalized by Even, Naor, Rao, and Schieber to a more general family of ordering problems by the method of spreading-metrics [ENRS00]. Several researchers studied the special case of tournaments, directed graphs in which every pair of vertices is connected by a directed edge [ACN08, CFR06, KMS07]; Kenyon-Mathieu and Schudy gave a polynomial-time approximation scheme (PTAS) for FAS in tournaments [KMS07]. To summarize, despite our best efforts we only know polylogarithmic approximation algorithms for the problem, and, assuming the Unique Games Conjecture, we cannot get a constant factor approximation for worst-case instances.

*Supported in part by NSF CAREER grant CCF-1150062.

ITCS'13, January 9–12, 2013, Berkeley, California, USA.

However, our primary interest in such optimization problems comes from many different applications they arise in. The instances that we encounter in the real world are not worst-case instances. Besides, instances that are produced in hardness reductions are often contrived, and we are unlikely to encounter them in practice. Also it may be too hard, if not impossible, to design an algorithm that gives a good approximation guarantee for every instance of FAS. This motivates the study of the average-case complexity of the problem.

Question 1 *Can we design algorithms with better provable approximation guarantees for realistic average-case models for the Minimum Feedback Arc Set problem?*

Braverman and Mossel [BM08] studied the problem of *sorting in the presence of random noise.* The problem corresponds to FAS on tournaments with random noise. In their random model, the instance is generated as follows. There is a planted (complete) ordering of the vertices. An edge is added between every pair of vertices: the edge is directed to respect the ordering with probability $\frac{1}{2}+\varepsilon$ and it is directed against the ordering with probability $\frac{1}{2}-\varepsilon$. Braverman and Mossel show that with high probability, we can find the optimal ordering, and the optimal ordering is at most $O(n)$ far from the planted ordering (in ℓ_1 distance). This result requires that we have *complete* (but noisy) information; that is, the digraph must be a tournament. The result does not apply to more general instances of FAS.

In this paper, we propose and study two new semi-random models for FAS, which we believe capture many properties of real world instances. We develop new algorithms for semi-random instances of FAS which give $(1+\delta)$ and constant factor approximations in these two models (see below for the precise statements). In the process, we also develop a constant factor approximations for a natural semi-random model for Minimum Directed Balanced Cut.

Our models are geared towards the two chief applications of FAS: noisy topological sorting and breaking cyclic dependencies. In both of these semi-random models, a semi-random instance can be seen as an acyclic digraph (a FAS instance with cost 0), augmented with random noise.

1.1 Semi-random Models

We now describe the two semi-random models for FAS that we study in this paper.

Our first semi-random model is called the *Random Edge Flipping model.* It models the problem of topological sorting in the presence of a noisy oracle. Imagine there is a unknown ordering of all vertices in a set V. We are given a set of comparisons between some pairs of vertices. However, the comparisons are noisy: with some probability $\varepsilon > 0$, the comparison does not agree with the ordering (we assume that the noise is independent for different pairs of vertices). Our goal is to find an ordering which is consistent with as many comparisons as possible. We represent all comparisons by directed edges between vertices. The FAS instance given by the obtained digraph on V defines a semi-random instance in the Random Edge Flipping model.

Let us consider an example in the rank aggregation setting to illustrate why this model seems to capture many real world instances. Suppose that we need to rank web pages (or movies etc.) for a recommendation system. We are given comparisons between some (but not all) of the pairs of web pages, based on the user feedback[1]. It is natural to assume that there is a true underlying order among these web pages, and our goal is to find it. The pairwise comparisons that we see are likely to be noisy perturbations of the true ordering. Note that it is unrealistic to expect that we have comparisons for all pairs of web pages.

This motivates the following formal definition for our first semi-random model:

Definition 1.3 (Random Edge Flipping Model) *We are given a set of vertices V of size n, and a parameter ε. A semi-random instance of the Random Edge Flipping model is generated as follows.*

1. *Adversary chooses a directed acyclic graph on V, i.e. she chooses a set of edges E so that $G(V,E)$ is acyclic.*
2. *Every edge in E is flipped (its direction is reversed) with probability ε independently at random. The set of flipped edges is denoted by E_R.*
3. *The adversary chooses a subset of edges in E_R (possibly empty) and un-flips them (restores the original direction).*

Our second semi-random model for FAS is called the *Random Backward Edge* model. Informally speaking, the instance consists of an adversarial directed acyclic graph and a set of random backward edges, i.e. random edges directed opposite to the ordering. The planted solution to FAS consists of these random backward edges. Our goal is to find a solution whose cost is comparable to the cost of the planted solution.

Definition 1.4 (Random Backward Edge Model) *We are given a set of vertices V of size n, and a parameter ε. A semi-random instance of the Random Backward Edge model is generated as follows.*

1. *The adversary chooses an ordering π of V.*
2. *Nature adds a random set of backward edges to G: for every pair (u,v) with $\pi(u) > \pi(v)$, nature adds an edge (u,v) to G with probability ε. The choices for all edges are independent. The set of random edges is denoted by E_R.*
3. *The adversary adds an arbitrary set of forward edges w.r.t. π. She also removes some set (possibly empty) of backward edges added by nature.*

(Note that this model is stronger than a model where the adversary first adds forward edges, and nature then adds random backward edges).

This model tries to capture settings where FAS is used to remove cyclic dependencies (or feedback loops) in a system. As an example, imagine we need to schedule a set of jobs on a machine. There are dependencies between jobs described by a digraph: a directed edge from job i to job j indicates that job i needs to be executed before job j. A valid schedule is an ordering of these jobs. Ideally, jobs can be ordered in a way that satisfies all dependencies. However, some cyclic dependencies may arise due to some random unlikely events. So the dependency graph consists of

[1]As an aside, see [Saa77, Saa08] on why pairwise comparisons are often preferred to comparisons between several objects at once.

a digraph (which encodes "genuine" dependencies) and random edges (which encode "accidental" dependencies). Our second model captures such instances.

1.2 Our Results

In this paper, we obtain the following results.

Informal Theorem 1 *For every $\delta > 0$, there is a polynomial-time algorithm that given a semi-random instance G of FAS in the Random Edge Flipping model (with noise probability $\varepsilon < 1/4$), finds a feedback arc set of cost at most $(1+\delta)\,\text{opt-cost} + n \operatorname{polylog} n$ w.h.p., where opt-cost is the cost of the optimal solution in G.*

The formal statement of this theorem is given in Theorem 2.2.

Informal Theorem 2 *There is a polynomial-time algorithm that given a semi-random instance G of FAS in the Random Backward Edge model, finds a feedback arc set of cost at most $O(\text{planted-cost}) + n \operatorname{polylog} n$ w.h.p., where planted-cost is the number of random edges added at step 2 (in other words, it is the cost of the planted solution in G after step 2).*

The formal statement of this theorem is given in Theorem 3.5.

Note that in the first model the approximation additive term is much smaller than the cost of the planted solution if $\varepsilon\Delta \gg \operatorname{polylog} n$ (where Δ is the average degree of G). In the second model, the approximation additive term is much smaller than the number of random backward edges in E_R if $\varepsilon \gg \operatorname{polylog} n/n$.

There is an important difference between our results for the first and second models. In our result for the first model, we compare the performance of our algorithm with the cost of the *optimal* solution for FAS. Thus we get a true $1+\delta$ approximation scheme (with an extra additive approximation term) for FAS. In the second model, we compare the performance of our algorithm with the cost of the *planted* solution. The algorithm gives a true approximation only if the cost of the planted solution is close to the cost of the optimal solution (which we believe should be the case for real-world instances).

1.3 Related Work on Semi-random Models

Over the last two decades, there has been extensive research on average-case complexity of many important combinatorial optimization problems. Many algorithms has been proposed for random and semi-random models. In random models, an instance is chosen from a fixed probabilistic distribution of instances (of given size), and the adversary has no influence on the choice. Random models have been studied in the context of graph partitioning problems [BLCS87, DF86, Bop87, JS93, DI98, CK99, McS01, CO06], Graph Coloring [AK94, BS95, AKS99], Minimum Steiner Tree [KMSPT86], Densest Subgraph [BCC+10] and other problems. On a more related note, Newman [New04] studied random models for Maximum Acyclic Subgraph, the complementary problem of FAS, and showed how semi-definite programming relaxations have integrality gap at most 1.64 for these instances with high probability.

In semi-random models, an instance is generated in a series of steps: some of them are random and some are adversarial. Because of that, semi-random instances may have much more structure then completely random instances. Research on semi-random models was initiated by Blum and Spencer [BS95], who introduced and investigated semi-random models for k-coloring. Later Feige and Kilian [FK98] studied a robust semi-random model for Minimum Bisection, and Feige and Krauthgamer [FK00] studied a semi-random model for Maximum Clique. In all these models, the algorithm can actually exactly find the planted solution. Recently, Kenyon-Mathieu and Schudy [MS10] considered a semi-random model for Correlation Clustering on complete graphs, for which they designed a PTAS.

Most related to our current work are recent results by Kolla, Makarychev and Makarychev [KMM11] on semi-random instances of Unique Games and by Makarychev, Makarychev and Vijayaraghavan [MMV12] on semi-random instances of graph partitioning problems. The algorithms for these models find a solution whose cost is within a constant factor of the cost of randomly added/corrupted edges (as in our second model); in these models, it is not possible to find the planted solution even information theoretically.

1.4 Techniques

The general approach of both our algorithms for semi-random instances of FAS are influenced by [KMM11] and [MMV12]. At a very high level, this approach can be outlined as follows. We write an SDP relaxation[2] for the problem and find a small family of representative SDP solutions. Now for a fixed planted solution, we show that every *fixed* feasible SDP solution is far from the optimal SDP solution unless it has certain structural properties. Finally, using the union bound and the fact that there are much fewer representative SDP solutions than semi-random instances, we prove that *every* feasible SDP solution is far from the optimal SDP solution unless it has the required structural properties. Thus the optimal solution has these structural properties w.h.p.

However, techniques from [KMM11] and [MMV12] deal with metric SDP relaxations and are not directly applicable to FAS. In our algorithm for the first model, the Random Edge Flipping model, we introduce a novel SDP relaxation for FAS. Roughly speaking, we start with a very basic LP relaxation for the problem, in which we have an LP variable x_{uv} for every pair of vertices. Given an ordering π of V, the intended solution corresponding to π is defined by: $x_{uv} = 1$ if $\pi(u) > \pi(v)$, $x_{uv} = 0$, otherwise. We require that $x_{uv} + x_{vu} = 1$ and $0 \le x_{uv} \le 1$. The objective function is to minimize $\sum_{(u,v)\in E} x_{uv}$. Clearly, this LP is a relaxation. However, it is a very weak relaxation since the optimal value is always equal to 0 — just consider the solution in which $x_{uv} = 0$ if there is an edge from u to v, $x_{uv} = 1$ if there is an edge from v to u, and $x_{uv} = 1/2$ otherwise (in this example, we assume that if G contains (u,v) then it does not contain (v,u)). Now we strengthen this LP by SDP constraints. We introduce two SDP variables $L(u)$ and $R(u)$ for every vertex u. We require that $x_{uv} = \langle L(u), R(v)\rangle$, and all vectors $L(u)$ and $R(u)$ have length $\sqrt{\lceil \log_2 n \rceil}$. We obtain an SDP relaxation. Note that this relaxation is very unusual — it is not even clear right away what the intended values of vectors $L(u)$ and $R(v)$ are! We show that for almost all randomly flipped edges (u,v), $x_{uv} \equiv \langle L(u), R(v)\rangle \ge 1-\delta$ in the optimal SDP solution w.h.p. So first we remove all edges (u,v) with $x_{uv} \ge 1-\delta$. We obtain an instance with less than $\text{opt-cost}/(\log n \log\log n)$ backward edges. Then we just run

[2] To obtain some of their results, [KMM11] and [MMV12] use C-SDP or local SDP relaxations.

the "off-the-shelf" algorithm for FAS by Seymour [Sey95] and get a linear ordering.

It is interesting that we get a true approximation algorithm for the Random Edge Flipping model: we compare the cost of the solution with the cost of the optimal solution. That is different from results for Unique Games [KMM11], graph partitioning problems [MMV12] and our second model — all of them compare the cost of the solution with the cost of the planted solution.

Our algorithm for the second model, the Random Backward Edge model, reduces the problem to the Minimum Directed Balanced Cut problem using the reduction of Leighton and Rao [LR99]. Recall that Minimum Directed Balanced Cut asks to cut a directed graph G into two balanced pieces S and T so as minimize the number of directed edges going from S to T. In our paper, we present a constant factor approximation algorithm for a natural semi-random model for this problem (see Definition 3.3 for details). Then we use a slightly modified reduction of Leighton and Rao: we find an approximate directed balanced cut (S,T) in the graph, then recursively solve the problem on induced subinstances on S and T, and finally we combine the obtained solutions. Since our algorithm for Minimum Directed Balanced Cut gives a constant factor approximation, the cost of the directed cut performed in the first level of recursion is at most $O(|E_R|)$ ($|E_R|$ is the number of random edges). We show that the total costs of cuts performed in consecutive levels of recursion go down geometrically (roughly speaking). Thus the total cost of the obtained solution is $O(|E_R|)$. In fact, we slightly change the reduction of Leighton and Rao [LR99]: we stop the recursion once a subinstance contains fewer that $n/(\log n \log\log n)$ vertices and then run the algorithm of Seymour [Sey95]; we do that, roughly speaking, because we pay some small additive penalty every time we find a directed balanced cut. Our algorithm for Minimum Directed Balanced Cut resembles the algorithm for Minimum Balanced Cut (undirected) from [MMV12]. We use the same iterative approach: in iteration t we solve an SDP for the problem, preprocess the graph (remove "heavy vertices") and then remove all edges that are "longer" then a threshold value $\delta_t = 2^{-t}$. The key difference is that we have to use a directed distance on the graph, and remove edges that are longer than δ with respect to this directed distance. Some properties of directed metrics are quite different from properties of regular undirected metrics. For example, two balls of radius 0 with distinct centers may overlap; because of that it is more difficult to remove non-overlapping balls from a directed metric space. We overcome these difficulties by introducing an additional preprocessing step (which we run in every iteration) that either returns a good directed balanced cut in the graph or finds a large subset of the graph where the directed metric is well approximated with an undirected metric (up to an additive error of $\Theta(\delta)$).

Further Applications of Our Techniques. In follow-up research, we showed how to use methods developed in this paper to solve semi-random instances of the Correlation Clustering Problem.

2. RANDOM EDGE FLIPPING MODEL

We set some notation that we use in this section. Denote by $F^{\pi,G} = \{(u,v) \in E : \pi(u) < \pi(v)\}$ the set of forward edges in the graph G w.r.t. the ordering $\pi : V \to \{1,\dots,n\}$. Denote by $B^{\pi,G} = \{(u,v) \in E : \pi(u) > \pi(v)\}$ the set of backward edges. For a set of directed edges E', we denote the set of reversed edges by $\text{reverse}(E') = \{(v,u) : (u,v) \in E'\}$. Finally, let $D = O(\log n \log\log n)$ be the approximation ratio of Seymour's algorithm [Sey95] for Minimum Feedback Arc Set.

In the Random Edge Flipping model, the adversary picks an arbitrary directed acyclic graph $G_0 = (V, E_0)$. Then the nature picks a random subset of edges $E_R \subset E_0$: the nature independently adds every edge $(u,v) \in E_0$ to E_R with the same probability ε. Finally, the adversary may replace each edge $(u,v) \in E_R$ with the edge (v,u), remove it, keep it unchanged, or even add an edge (v,u) without removing (u,v). Additionally, the adversary can add an arbitrary set of forward edges. The model is captured in the following definition.

Definition 2.1 *Let $G_0 = (V, E_0)$ be an acyclic directed graph. Let π be an ordering $V \to [n]$ consistent with G_0 (that is, an ordering such that all edges of G_0 are forward edges w.r.t. G_0). We define a random set of graphs $SR(G_0, \varepsilon)$ as follows: Let E_R be a random subset of E_0 such that every edge $(u,v) \in E_0$ belongs to E_R with probability ε (random choices for all edges are independent). Then $G = (V,E) \in SR(G_0,\varepsilon)$ if for each edge $(u,v) \in E_0 \,\Delta\, E$, $(u,v) \in E_R$, $(v,u) \in E_R$, or $(u,v) \in F^{\pi,G}$.*

In other words, $G = (V,E) \in SR(G_0,\varepsilon)$ if $E_0 \setminus E_R \subset F^{\pi,G}$, and $B^{\pi,G} \subset \text{reverse}(E_R)$.

Note that the definition given above defines a slightly more general model than the one discussed in the introduction. In this model, the adversary may add extra edges which are consistent with the ordering π at the final step.

Theorem 2.2 *There exists a polynomial-time approximation algorithm satisfying the following condition. For every directed acyclic graph $G_0 = (V, E_0)$ on n vertices with the average degree $\Delta = 2|E_0|/|V|$, every $\varepsilon \in (0, 1/4)$, every $\delta \in (0,1)$ with probability $1-o(1)$ given any graph $G = (V,E)$ in $SR(G_0,\varepsilon)$, the algorithm returns an ordering $\pi : V \to [n]$ of cost at most $(1+\delta)OPT + O_\delta(n \log^5 n \log\Delta\,(\log\log n)^3)$, where OPT is the cost of the optimal solution; the hidden constant in $O_\delta(\cdot)$ may depend on δ.*

Remark 2.3 *We can replace the condition $\varepsilon \in (0, 1/4)$ with $\varepsilon \in (0, \varepsilon_0)$ for any $\varepsilon_0 < 1/2$. We chose $\varepsilon_0 = 1/4$ to slightly simplify the proof. However, almost the same proof works for every $\varepsilon_0 < 1/2$.*

In the analysis, we assume that $\delta \leq 1/2$ (otherwise, we may replace δ with $\delta' = 1/2$).

SDP Relaxation. We use a novel SDP relaxation for this problem. The SDP is based on the following observation. For every n, there exists a collection of vectors

$$L^*(1), \dots, L^*(n) \text{ and } R^*(1), \dots, R^*(n)$$

of length $M = \sqrt{\lceil \log_2 n \rceil}$ such that

$$\langle L^*(i), R^*(j) \rangle = \begin{cases} 0, & \text{if } i \leq j; \\ 1, & \text{if } i > j. \end{cases}$$

We show that such vectors exist in Lemma 2.5. This lets us use the following intended solution. Every ordering of the vertices $\pi : V \to [n]$ corresponds to the collection of vectors

$L^\pi(u) = L^*(\pi(u))$ and $R^\pi(v) = R^*(\pi(v))$. Note, that the number of backward edges equals

$$|B^{\pi,G}| = \sum_{(u,v)\in E} \mathbf{1}(\pi(u) > \pi(v)) = \sum_{(u,v)\in E} \langle L^\pi(u), R^\pi(v)\rangle,$$

here $\mathbf{1}(\cdot)$ denotes the indicator function. The vectors $L^\pi(u)$ and $R^\pi(v)$ satisfy the constraints

$$\|L^\pi(u)\|^2 = \|R^\pi(v)\|^2 = M^2,$$

$$\langle L^\pi(u), R^\pi(v)\rangle \in \{0,1\} \tag{1}$$

and

$$\langle L^\pi(u), R^\pi(v)\rangle + \langle L^\pi(v), R^\pi(u)\rangle = 1$$

for every $u, v \in V$. We relax the constraints (1) and obtain the following SDP.

$$\mathbf{min} \sum_{(u,v)\in E} \langle L(u), R(v)\rangle$$

subject to: for all $u, v \in V$,

$$\begin{aligned} \langle L(u), R(v)\rangle + \langle L(v), R(u)\rangle &= 1 & (2)\\ \|L(u)\|^2 = \|R(v)\|^2 &= M^2 & (3)\\ \langle L(u), R(v)\rangle &\in [0,1] & (4)\end{aligned}$$

The variables of the SDP are $2n$ vectors $L(u)$ and $R(v)$, $u, v \in V$. We can also add the triangle inequality constraints $\langle L(v), R(w)\rangle \le \langle L(u), R(v)\rangle + \langle L(v), R(w)\rangle$, but we do not need them in this algorithm.

We denote the optimal value of the Minimum Feedback Arc Set Problem by OPT, and the optimal value of the SDP by SDP. If π is the optimal ordering of the vertices, then

$$\begin{aligned} OPT &= \sum_{(u,v)\in E} \mathbf{1}(\pi(u) > \pi(v))\\ &= \sum_{(u,v)\in E} \langle L^\pi(u), R^\pi(v)\rangle \ge SDP. \end{aligned}$$

Hence, $SDP \le OPT$.

Algorithm. The algorithm solves the SDP relaxation, removes all edges $(u,v) \in E$ with $\langle L(u), R(v)\rangle \ge (1-\delta)$, and then runs an "off-the-shelf" algorithm for the Minimum Feedback Arc Set problem.

Input: a directed graph $G = (V, E)$ on n vertices, parameter $\delta \in (0,1)$

Output: an ordering of vertices $\pi_{ALG} : V \to [n]$

1. Solve the SDP and obtain a collection of vectors $L(u)$, $R(u)$ for $u \in V$.
2. Remove all edges $(u,v) \in E$ with $\langle L(u), R(v)\rangle \ge 1-\delta$. Let E_δ^+ be the set of the remaining edges, i.e., let
$$E_\delta^+ = \{(u,v) \in E : \langle L(u), R(v)\rangle < 1-\delta\}.$$
3. Run the algorithm of Seymour on the instance (V, E_δ^+) and obtain an ordering $\pi_{ALG} : V \to [n]$.
4. Return π_{ALG}.

ANALYSIS. The proof relies on the following lemma, which implies that the cost of the optimal solution for the graph (V, E_δ^+) is small.

Lemma 2.4 *Let $G_0 = (V, E_0)$ be an acyclic graph on n vertices with the average degree $\Delta = 2|E_0|/|V|$, and let $\pi : V \to \{1,\dots,n\}$ be a "planted" ordering such that G_0 does not have backward edges w.r.t. π. Then, for every $\varepsilon \in (0, 1/4)$, every $\delta \in (0,1)$ and $D_1, D_2 \ge 1$ satisfying $D_2 \ge C_\delta n D_1^2 \log^2 n \log\Delta$ (where C_δ is a parameter depending only on δ) with probability $1-o(1)$ the set $SR(G_0,\varepsilon)$ satisfies the following property $\star$: For every $G = (V,E) \in SR(G_0,\varepsilon)$, for every feasible (not necessarily optimal) SDP solution $L(u)$, $R(v)$ with SDP value at most OPT,*

$$|B^{\pi,G} \cap E_\delta^+| \le (|B^{\pi,G}|/D_1 + D_2),$$

where $E_\delta^+ = \{(u,v) \in E : \langle L(u), R(v)\rangle < 1-\delta\}$ is the set of short edges w.r.t. the SDP solution.

We prove the lemma in Section 2.1. Let $\pi : V \to \{1,\dots,n\}$ be a "planted" ordering i.e., an ordering such that all edges in G_0 are forward edges. We show that the algorithm returns a solution of cost at most

$$(1+4\delta)OPT + O_\delta(n\log^5 n \log\Delta\,(\log\log n)^3)$$

assuming that the property $\star$ holds with

$$\begin{aligned} D_1 &= \delta^{-1}D = \Omega(\delta^{-1}\log n \log\log n)\\ D_2 &= C_\delta n D_1^2 \log^2 n \log\Delta = O_\delta(n\log^4 n \log\Delta(\log\log n)^2). \end{aligned}$$

Recall, that $D = O(\log n \log\log n)$ is the approximation ratio of Seymour's algorithm. We first bound the number of edges removed at the second step. Write,

$$\sum_{(u,v)\in E} \langle L(u), R(v)\rangle = SDP \le OPT.$$

We remove edges $(u,v) \in E$ with $\langle L(u), R(v)\rangle \ge (1-\delta)$, thus we remove at most $(1-\delta)^{-1}OPT \le (1+2\delta)OPT$ edges.

By our assumption the property $\star$ holds which means that the optimal solution for the remaining graph (V, E_δ^+) has cost at most $|B^{\pi,G}|/D_1 + D_2$. The approximation ratio of Seymour's algorithm is D, thus, the number of backward edges in E_δ^+ with respect to the ordering π_{ALG} returned by the algorithm is at most

$$D\times\Big(\frac{|B^{\pi,G}|}{D_1} + D_2\Big) \le \delta|B^{\pi,G}| + O(n\log^5 n\log\Delta(\log\log n)^3).$$

The total number of backward edges is at most

$$(1+2\delta)OPT + \delta|B^{\pi,G}| + O(n\log^5 n\log\Delta(\log\log n)^3).$$

We now show that

$$|B^{\pi,G}| \le (1+2\delta)OPT + O(n\log^5 n\log\Delta(\log\log n)^3),$$

which concludes the proof. Indeed, let $L'(u)$, $R'(v)$ be the "integral" SDP solution corresponding to the optimal solution. This solution satisfies the conditions of Lemma 2.4. Now, E_δ^+ is the set of forward edges in the optimal solution. Hence, $|B^{\pi,G}| - OPT \le |B^{\pi,G} \cap E_\delta^+| \le \delta|B^{\pi,G}| + D_2$, and $|B^{\pi,G}| \le (1-\delta)^{-1}(OPT + D_2) \le (1+2\delta)(OPT + D_2)$. □

2.1 Proofs

Lemma 2.5 *For every natural $n > 0$, there exists a collection of vectors $L(1),\dots,L(n)$, $R(1),\dots,R(n)$ of length $\sqrt{\lceil\log_2 n\rceil}$ such that $\langle L(i), R(j)\rangle = \mathbf{1}(i > j)$.*

PROOF. Without loss of generality we may assume that n is a power of 2: otherwise, we construct $n' = 2^{\lceil \log_2 n \rceil}$ vectors $L(i)$ and $R(j)$, and then pick the first n vectors. Consider the complete binary tree T of depth $\log_2 n$ with leafs labeled with numbers $1, \dots, n$ from left to right. The coordinates of the vectors $L(1), \dots, L(n)$ and $R(1), \dots, R(n)$ correspond to the internal nodes of the tree. We denote the x-th coordinate of $L(i)$ by $L_x(i)$ and the x-th coordinate of $R(j)$ by $R_x(j)$. We let $L_x(i) = 1$, if the number i lies in the subtree rooted at the right child of x; and $L_x(i) = 0$, otherwise. Similarly, we let $R_x(j) = 1$, if the number j lies in the subtree rooted at the left child of x; and $R_x(j) = 0$, otherwise. Let P_i be the path from the root to the leaf i. Observe, that $L_x(i) = 0$ and $R_x(i) = 0$ if $x \notin P_i$. Hence, $\|L(i)\|^2 \le \text{length}(P_i) = \log_2 n$ and $\|R(i)\|^2 \le \text{length}(P_i) = \log_2 n$. By definition, $\langle L(i), R(j)\rangle = \sum_{x \in T} L_x(i) R_x(j)$. Hence, $\langle L(i), R(j)\rangle$ equals the number of x's such that i is in the right subtree of x and j is in the left subtree of x. If $i > j$, then there is exactly one such x — the least common ancestor of i and j. If $i \le j$, then clearly there are no such x.

Finally, we pick two vectors A and B orthogonal to all vectors $L(i)$, $R(j)$ and each other (we do this by appending all vectors with two extra coordinates). We add to each $L(i)$ a multiple of A and to each $R(j)$ a multiple of B so that the length of all vectors $L(i)$ and $R(j)$ is exactly $\sqrt{\lceil \log_2 n \rceil}$. Since A is orthogonal to all $R(j)$'s and B is orthogonal to all $L(i)$'s the inner products $\langle L(i), R(j)\rangle$ do not change. □

Remark 2.6 *The bound on the lengths of the vectors in the lemma above is nearly optimal. We can show that the lengths must be at least $\Omega(\sqrt{\log n})$ to satisfy $\langle L(i), R(j)\rangle = 1(i > j)$. The proof follows from [CMM07]. But, we omit the details here.*

We now show that the set of feasible vector solutions to the SDP can be approximated by a much smaller family of representative SDP solutions.

Lemma 2.7 *For every graph $G = (V, E)$ on n vertices ($V = \{1, \dots, n\}$) with the average degree $\Delta = 2|E|/|V|$, real $M \ge 1$, and $\gamma \in (0, 1)$, there exists a set of matrices $\mathcal{W}$ of size at most $|\mathcal{W}| \le \exp(O(\frac{nM^4 \log \Delta}{2\gamma^2} + n \log n))$ such that: for every collection of vectors $L(1), \dots, L(n)$, $R(1), \dots R(n)$ with $\|L(i)\| = M$, $\|R(j)\| = M$ and $\langle L(i), R(j)\rangle \in [0, 1]$, there exists $W \in \mathcal{W}$ satisfying for every $(i, j) \in E$:*

$$w_{ij} \le \langle L(i), R(j)\rangle \le w_{ij} + \gamma;$$

$$w_{ij} \in [0, 1].$$

PROOF. We use the following easy corollary of Grothendieck's inequality: For every set of vectors $L(i)$, $R(j)$ of length M, there exists a set of random variables $X_1, \dots, X_n$, $Y_1, \dots, Y_n$ taking values in the set $\{-\widetilde{M}, \widetilde{M}\}$ (where $\widetilde{M} = \sqrt{K_G} M \le \sqrt{2} M$, and K_G is Grothendieck's constant), such that

$$\mathbb{E}[X_i Y_j] = \langle L(i), R(j)\rangle$$

for every i, j. We refer the reader to [AMMN05] (see Lemma 2.3) and [Mak08] (see Theorem 2.8) for more details. Consider $T = 8M^4\gamma^{-2} \ln \Delta$ independent copies of $X_1, \dots, X_n$, $Y_1, \dots, Y_n$. We denote the variables in the t-th copy by $X_i(t)$ and $Y_j(t)$. Let $Z_{ij}(t) = X_i(t) Y_j(t)$. Then, $\mathbb{E} Z_{ij}(t) = \mathbb{E}[X_i Y_j] = \langle L(i), R(j)\rangle$ and $Z_{ij}(t) \in \{-\widetilde{M}^2, \widetilde{M}^2\}$. By the Chernoff bound, for fixed i and j,

$$\begin{aligned}
\Pr\left(\left|\frac{1}{T}\sum_{t=1}^{T} Z_{ij}(t) - \langle L(i), R(j)\rangle\right| \ge \gamma\right) &\le 2e^{-\frac{T\gamma^2}{2M^4}} \\
&\le 2e^{-\ln \Delta} \\
&= \frac{2}{\Delta}.
\end{aligned}$$

Hence, there exists a sample $X_i^*(t)$, $Y_j^*(t)$ such that the condition $|\frac{1}{T}\sum_{t=1}^{T} Z_{ij}(t) - \langle L(i), R(j)\rangle| \le \gamma$ holds for all but n edges $(i, j) \in E$. Using this observation we define a set of matrices $\mathcal{W}_1$:

$$\mathcal{W}_1 = \Big\{\frac{1}{T}\sum_{t=1}^{T} X(t) \otimes Y(t) : X(t), Y(t) \in \{-\widetilde{M}, \widetilde{M}\}^n\Big\}.$$

Above, $X(t) \otimes Y(t)$ is the rank 1 matrix with entries $(X(t) \otimes Y(t))_{ij} = X_i(t) Y_j(t)$. The set $\mathcal{W}_1$ has at most 2^{2nT} elements — this is the number of ways to pick $2T$ vectors $X(t), Y(t) \in \{-\widetilde{M}, \widetilde{M}\}^n$. As we just have shown using the probabilistic method, for every sequence of vectors $L(i)$, $R(j)$ satisfying the conditions of the lemma, there exists a matrix $W \in \mathcal{W}_1$ such that the condition $|\langle L(i), R(j)\rangle - w_{ij}| \le \gamma$ holds for all but n edges $(i, j) \in E$. Now we need to truncate all entries of matrices $W \in \mathcal{W}_1$ so that they are in the range $[0, 1]$ and shift them so that $w_{ij} \le \langle L(i), R(j)\rangle$. Let

$$h(W)_{ij} = \begin{cases} w_{ij} - \gamma, & \text{if } w_{ij} - \gamma \in [0, 1]; \\ 0, & \text{if } w_{ij} - \gamma < 0; \\ 1, & \text{if } w_{ij} - \gamma > 1. \end{cases}$$

Since $\langle L(i), R(j)\rangle \in [0, 1]$, if $|\langle L(i), R(j)\rangle - w_{ij}| \le \gamma$, then $h(W)_{ij} \le \langle L(i), R(j)\rangle \le h(W)_{ij} + 2\gamma$ ($\diamond$). Let $\mathcal{W}_2 = h(\mathcal{W}_1)$. Clearly, $|\mathcal{W}_2| \le |\mathcal{W}_1| = 2^{2nT}$.

We are almost done. We only need to take care of n edges for which ($\diamond$) does not hold. For each matrix $W \in \mathcal{W}_2$, we add to the set $\mathcal{W}$ the matrix W and all matrices W' that differ from W in at most n positions and whose entries at those positions are multiples of γ in the range $[0, 1 - \gamma]$. There are at most $(n^2)^n$ ways to pick at most n positions (for $n > 1$), and there are $\lceil 1/\gamma \rceil^n$ ways to pick the new values for them. So for every matrix $W \in \mathcal{W}$, we add at most $\exp(2n \ln n + n \ln \lceil 1/\gamma \rceil)$ new matrices to $\mathcal{W}$. Then,

$$|\mathcal{W}| \le 2^{2nT} \cdot e^{2n \ln n + n \ln \lceil 1/\gamma \rceil} = e^{O(\frac{nM^4 \log \Delta}{\gamma^2} + n \log n)}.$$

□

2.2 Proof of Lemma 2.4

PROOF OF LEMMA 2.4. Let $\mathcal{W}$ be the set of matrices for G_0 as in Lemma 2.7 with $\gamma = \delta/(2D_1)$ and $M^2 = \lceil \log_2 n \rceil$. We show that if the property $\star$ is violated then there exists a matrix W in the set $\mathcal{W}$ satisfying the condition

$$2 \sum_{(u,v) \in E_R} w_{uv} \ge \sum_{(u,v) \in E_0 \setminus E_R} w_{uv} + \delta D_2. \qquad (5)$$

We call such matrix W a witness. Note that E_R constitutes only an ε fraction of the edge set E. We then argue that a fixed matrix W is a witness with exponentially small probability. Using the union bound over all $W \in \mathcal{W}$, we conclude that such witness $W \in \mathcal{W}$ exists with probability $o(1)$, and, hence, the property $\star$ is violated with probability $o(1)$.

I. Assume that $\star$ is violated. Pick one of the graphs $G = (V, E) \in SR(G_0, \varepsilon)$ for which the number of backward edges in E_δ^+ with respect to the ordering π is greater than $(|B^{\pi,G}|/D_1 + D_2)$. Denote by $F = F^{\pi,G} \subset E$ the set of forward edges with respect to π, and by $B = B^{\pi,G} \subset E$ the set of backward edges. Then, $E_0 \setminus E_R \subset F$ and $B \subset \text{reverse}(E_R)$.

Let $L(u)$, $R(v)$ be the SDP solution. We know that

$$SDP \leq OPT \leq |B|,$$

thus

$$\sum_{(u,v)\in E} \langle L(u), R(v)\rangle = \sum_{(u,v)\in F} \langle L(u), R(v)\rangle + \sum_{(v,u)\in B} \langle L(v), R(u)\rangle \leq \sum_{(v,u)\in B} 1.$$

Consequently,

$$\sum_{(v,u)\in B} \langle L(u), R(v)\rangle = \sum_{(v,u)\in B} (1 - \langle L(v), R(u)\rangle) \geq \sum_{(u,v)\in F} \langle L(u), R(v)\rangle.$$

The first equality follows from the SDP constraint

$$\langle L(u), R(v)\rangle + \langle L(v), R(u)\rangle = 1.$$

We now obtain another lower bound on the left hand side. Recall, that we assumed that $|E_\delta^+ \cap B| \geq (|B|/D_1 + D_2)$. For each $(v, u) \in E_\delta^+$, we have $\langle L(v), R(u)\rangle < (1 - \delta)$ (by definition of E_δ^+) and $\langle L(u), R(v)\rangle \geq \delta$. Hence,

$$\sum_{(v,u)\in B} \langle L(u), R(v)\rangle \geq \delta(|B|/D_1 + D_2).$$

Therefore,

$$2\sum_{(v,u)\in B} \langle L(u), R(v)\rangle \geq \sum_{(u,v)\in F} \langle L(u), R(v)\rangle + \delta\Big(\frac{|B|}{D_1} + D_2\Big).$$

Since $E_0 \setminus E_R \subset F$,

$$2\sum_{(v,u)\in B} \langle L(u), R(v)\rangle \geq \sum_{(u,v)\in E_0\setminus E_R} \langle L(u), R(v)\rangle + \delta\Big(\frac{|B|}{D_1} + D_2\Big).$$

Pick $W \in \mathcal{W}$ such that $w_{uv} \leq \langle L(u), R(v)\rangle \leq w_{uv} + \gamma$ for $(u, v) \in E_0$. We rewrite the inequality above in terms of W,

$$2\sum_{(v,u)\in B} (w_{uv} + \gamma) \geq \sum_{(u,v)\in E_0\setminus E_R} w_{uv} + \delta\Big(\frac{|B|}{D_1} + D_2\Big).$$

Thus,

$$\begin{aligned} 2\sum_{(v,u)\in B} w_{uv} &\geq \sum_{(u,v)\in E_0\setminus E_R} w_{uv} + \delta\Big(\frac{|B|}{D_1} + D_2\Big) - 2\gamma|B| \\ &= \sum_{(u,v)\in E_0\setminus E_R} w_{uv} + \delta D_2. \end{aligned}$$

Finally, using $B \subset \text{reverse}(E_R)$, we obtain the desired inequality

$$2\sum_{(u,v)\in E_R} w_{uv} \geq \sum_{(u,v)\in E_0\setminus E_R} w_{uv} + \delta D_2. \qquad (6)$$

II. We now estimate the probability (over the choice of the random set E_R) that a fixed matrix $W \in \mathcal{W}$ is a witness i.e., satisfies (5). Define a random variable X_{uv}: $X_{uv} = 2$, if $(u, v) \in E_R$ and $X_{uv} = -1$, otherwise. Then $\mathbb{E}X_{uv} = 2\varepsilon - (1 - \varepsilon) = 3\varepsilon - 1 < -\varepsilon$. Condition (5) can be rewritten as follows

$$S \equiv \sum_{(u,v)\in E_0} w_{uv} X_{uv} \geq \delta D_2 \equiv \lambda_1.$$

We denote the left hand side by S, the right hand side by λ_1, we also let $\lambda_2 = \varepsilon \sum_{(u,v)\in E_0} w_{uv}$. We have

$$\mathbb{E}[S] = \sum_{(u,v)\in E_0} w_{uv}\mathbb{E}[X_{uv}] \leq -\varepsilon \sum_{(u,v)\in E_0} w_{uv} = -\lambda_2.$$

and

$$\begin{aligned} \text{Var}[S] &= \sum_{(u,v)\in E_0} w_{uv}^2 \,\text{Var}[X_{uv}] = 9\varepsilon(1 - \varepsilon) \sum_{(u,v)\in E_0} w_{uv}^2 \\ &\leq 9\varepsilon \sum_{(u,v)\in E_0} w_{uv} = 9\lambda_2. \end{aligned}$$

By the Bernstein inequality,

$$\begin{aligned} \Pr(S \geq \lambda_1) &= \Pr(S - \mathbb{E}S \geq \lambda_1 + \lambda_2) \\ &\leq \exp\Big(-\frac{(\lambda_1 + \lambda_2)^2}{2\,\text{Var}[S] + 2(\lambda_1 + \lambda_2)}\Big) \\ &\leq \exp(-C(\lambda_1 + \lambda_2)) \leq \exp(-C\delta D_2), \end{aligned}$$

for $C = 1/20$. By Lemma 2.7,

$$\begin{aligned} |\mathcal{W}| &\leq \exp\Big(O\big(\frac{nM^4 \log\Delta}{2\gamma^2} + n\log n\big)\Big) \\ &= \exp\Big(O_\delta\big(n\, D_1^2 \log^2 n \log\Delta\big)\Big). \end{aligned}$$

Hence, by the union bound (since $D_2 \geq C_\delta n D_1^2 \log^2 n \log\Delta$), there exists a witness $W \in \mathcal{W}$ with probability at most $o(e^{-n})$. $\square$

3. RANDOM BACKWARD EDGE MODEL

3.1 Minimum Feedback Arc Set

We reduce the Minimum Feedback Arc Set problem to the Minimum Directed Balanced Cut problem. Recall that in the Minimum Directed Balanced Cut problem, we are given a directed graph G and our goal is to find a balanced cut (S, T) in G so as to minimize the number of edges going from S to T. The reduction, which was introduced by Leighton and Rao [LR99] for worst-case instances of FAS, works as follows. Consider an instance G of FAS. Let $\pi : V \to [n]$ be an optimal solution for FAS. Let OPT be its cost. Note that there is a directed bisection cut in G of cost at most OPT. Specifically, let $S = \{u : \pi(u) > n/2\}$ and $T = \{u : \pi(u) \leq n/2\}$. Then every edge from S to T is a backward edge (w.r.t. π); thus, the total number of edges from S to T is at most OPT.

The reduction approximately finds a directed balanced cut (S', T') in G, then recursively solves subinstances of FAS on the induced graphs $G[S']$ and $G[T']$. Finally, it concatenates solutions for $G[T']$ and $G[S']$ (so that every vertex in T' lies to the left of every vertex in S'). Note that, for any one level of the recursion tree defined by this procedure, OPT is an upper bound on the total sum of the optimal solution costs of all the Directed Balanced Cut problems on it. Hence, this reduction gives an $O(\alpha_{MDBC} \log n)$ approximation algorithm for worst case instances of FAS, where α_{MDBC} is the approximation factor for Minimum Directed Balanced Cut, since the depth of the recursion is $O(\log n)$, and the cost of all cuts we perform at one level of recursion is at most $\alpha_{MDBC} \cdot OPT$. If we use the SDP algorithm of Agarwal, Charikar, Makarychev, and Makarychev [ACMM05], then $\alpha_{MDBC} = O(\sqrt{\log n})$; if we use the LP algorithm of Leighton and Rao [LR99], then $\alpha_{MDBC} = O(\log n)$.

In this paper, we present a constant factor approximation algorithm for semi-random instances of the Minimum Directed Balanced Cut problem. Then we adapt the reduction to work with this algorithm.

Definition 3.1 *We say that (S,T) is a partition of V if $V = S \cup T$ and $S \cap T = \varnothing$. A partition (S,T) is b-balanced if $|S| \geq b|V|$, $|T| \geq b|V|$ (where $b \in [0,1/2]$). A partition (S,T) is a bisection of V if $||S| - |T|| \leq 1$. We say that a cut (S,T) in a graph $G = (V,E)$ is b-balanced if (S,T) is a b-balanced partition of V; similarly, a cut (S,T) is a bisection cut if (S,T) is a bisection partition of V.*

We say that a directed edge (u,v) is cut by a directed cut (S,T) if $u \in S$ and $t \in V$ (note that if $u \in T$ and $v \in S$ then the edge is not cut). The cost of a cut (S,T) in a directed graph G is the number of edges in G cut by (S,T). We denote the cost of (S,T) by $\text{cost}(S,T)$. Given a set of edges E, we denote the number of edges in E cut by (S,T) by $\text{cost}_E(S,T)$.

Definition 3.2 *Let V be a set of vertices and $\varepsilon > 0$. Construct a random set E_R of directed edges as follows. Choose every pair $(u,v) \in V \times V$ independently with probability ε and add it to E_R. We say that E_R is an ε-random set of edges.*

Our algorithm proceeds by considering semi-random instances of Minimum Directed Balanced Cut, defined recursively based on the partitioning in the previous steps. This motivates the definition of the following semi-random family of graphs.

Definition 3.3 *Let V be a set of vertices and $\varepsilon > 0$. Let E_R be an ε-random set of edges. Define the random family of graphs $\mathsf{SRD}(V,E_R)$ by $\mathsf{SRD}(V,E_R) =$*

$$\{H = (U,E_H) : U \subset V,\ (S,T) \text{ is a bisection of } U \text{ and } E_H \cap (S \times T) \subset E_R\}.$$

In other words, graphs $\mathsf{SRD}(V,E_R)$ are those graphs H that can be obtained as follows. Choose a subset $U \subset V$ and a bisection (S,T) of U. Then choose a set of edges $E_1 \subset E_R \cap (S \times T)$ and a set of edges $E_2 \subset (S \times S) \cup (T \times S) \cup (T \times T)$. Finally, let $H = (U, E_1 \cup E_2)$.

We call graphs in the family $\mathsf{SRD}(V,E_R)$ semi-random directed graphs.

We present an approximation algorithm for the Minimum Directed Balanced Cut problem in semi-random directed graphs in the following theorem.

Theorem 3.4 *There is a randomized polynomial-time algorithm for the Minimum Directed Balanced Cut problem that does the following. Let V be a set of vertices, $\varepsilon > 0$, and E_R be an ε-random set of edges. With probability at least $1 - e^{-cn}$ over E_R, for every graph $H = (U,E_H) \in \mathsf{SRD}(V,E_R)$, the algorithm given H finds a b-balanced cut (S',T') of H such that*

$$\text{cost}(S',T') \leq C \max(\varepsilon|U|^2, g(n)),$$

where $g(n) = n\sqrt{\log n}(\log\log n)^2$, and $c > 0$, $C > 0$ and $b > 0$ are some absolute constants.

We will prove this theorem in the next subsection. We show now how to get a constant factor approximation for semi-random instances of FAS using this algorithm. While we follow essentially the same reduction as in the worst-case, from FAS to Minimum Directed Balanced Cut (except that we stop recursing when the instance size is roughly $O(n/\log n)$), we only lose a constant factor in the approximation guarantee for semi-random instances, because the total cost we incur in each level of the recursion goes down geometrically.

Theorem 3.5 *There is a randomized polynomial-time algorithm for semi-random instances of the Minimum Feedback Arc Set problem that does the following. Let V be a set of vertices, $\varepsilon > 0$, and E_R be an ε-random set of edges. Then with probability $1 - o(1)$ over E_R, for every vertex ordering π and every directed graph G in which all backward edges w.r.t. π belong to E_R, the algorithm given G finds an ordering π' such that G has at most $O(\varepsilon n^2 + (\log n)^{3/2}(\log\log n)^3 n)$ backward edges w.r.t. π'.*

Proof. We may assume that $\varepsilon > (\log n)^{3/2}(\log\log n)^3/n$; as otherwise we let $\varepsilon' = (\log n)^{3/2}(\log\log n)^3 n$ and let $E'_R \supset E_R$. We use the recursive approach that we outlined above. Let π be the planted solution for FAS on G. First, we observe that for every $U \subset V$, $G[U] \in \mathsf{SRD}(V,E_R)$. Indeed, let T be the set of the first $\lceil |U|/2 \rceil$ elements of U w.r.t. π and and S be the set of the last $\lfloor |U|/2 \rfloor$ elements of U w.r.t. π. Note that all edges from S to T are backward edges in the planted solution and therefore they belong to E_R. Hence $G[U] \in \mathsf{SRD}(V,E_R)$ and we can apply Theorem 3.4 to $G[U]$.

We write a recursive procedure that given a set $U \subset V$ finds a linear ordering of vertices in U.

1. If $|U| \leq n/(\log n \log\log n)$ the algorithm applies the algorithm of Seymour [Sey95] to the induced graph $G[U]$ and returns the obtained ordering of U.
2. If $|U| > n/(\log n \log\log n)$, the algorithm finds an approximate directed balanced cut (S',T') using the algorithm from Theorem 3.4. Then it recursively finds linear orderings $\pi_{T'}$ for T' and $\pi_{S'}$ for S'. It returns the concatenation of orderings $\pi_{T'}$ and $\pi_{S'}$.

Let us bound the cost of the solution returned by the algorithm. Consider its recursion tree. We charge every backward edge (u,v) to the node of the recursion tree where we separate u and v.

First consider leaf nodes of the recursion tree. Let us prove that with probability $1 - e^{-\Omega(n/\sqrt{\log n})}$, for every subset U of size $\Theta(n/(\log n \log\log n))$ the induced graph $G[U]$ contains at most $2\varepsilon|U|^2$ edges from E_R. There are $e^{O(n/\log n)}$ sets U of size $\Theta(n/(\log n \log\log n))$. For each U, the induced graph $G[U]$ contains at most $\varepsilon|U|^2$ edges from E_R in expectation. Thus by Chernoff's bound, $G[U]$ contains at most $2\varepsilon|U|^2$ edges from E_R with probability $1 - e^{-\Omega(\varepsilon|U|^2)} = 1 - e^{-\Omega(n/\sqrt{\log n})}$. By the union bound, we get that with probability $1 - e^{-\Omega(n/\sqrt{\log n})}$ all subgraphs $G[U]$ contain at most $2\varepsilon|U|^2$ random edges.

Since the set U for every leaf of the recursion tree has size $|U| = \Theta(n/(\log n \log\log n))$, we get that $G[U]$ contains at most $2\varepsilon|U|^2 = O\left(\frac{\varepsilon n}{\log n \log\log n}\right)|U|$ edges (w.h.p. for all leaf nodes). Therefore, the algorithm of Seymour finds a solution of cost at most $O(\varepsilon n)\cdot|U|$ in $G[U]$. So the total cost charged to all leaf nodes is at most $O(\varepsilon n)\cdot\sum|U| = O(\varepsilon n^2)$.

Now consider internal nodes of the recursion tree. An internal node pays for edges from S' to T' in $G[U]$. By Theorem 3.4, the total number of such edges is at most $C\max(\varepsilon|U|^2, g(n)) \le C(\varepsilon|U|^2 + g(n))$. Since sizes of sets U decrease geometrically in the recursion, the sum of $C\varepsilon|U|^2$ over all internal nodes of the recursion tree is at most $O(\varepsilon n^2)$. The sum of all terms $g(n)$ is at most $g(n)\cdot O(\log n \log\log n)$ since there are $O(\log n \log\log n)$ nodes in the recursion tree.

We get that w.h.p. the cost of the solution is

$$O(\varepsilon|U|^2 + g(n)\log n \log\log n).$$

□

4. PROOF OF THEOREM 3.4

4.1 Proof Overview

Our algorithm is similar to the algorithm for undirected Minimum Balanced Cut from [MMV12]. It iteratively removes edges and vertices from the graph H. It starts with $H_0 = H$. Then it iteratively constructs a sequence of subgraphs $H_0 \supset H_1 \supset H_2 \supset \dots$. In iteration t, the algorithm solves an SDP relaxation for the Minimum Directed Balanced Cut problem in H_t, performs some preprocessing by removing some vertices from H_t and then cuts some edges in the remaining graph. In the obtained graph H_{t+1}, the number of edges from E_R drops by a constant factor (compared to H_t). After at most $O(\log\log n)$ rounds, the algorithm gets a graph with at most $\varepsilon|U|^2/\sqrt{\log n}$ edges from E_R. Then it finds a balanced directed cut in this graph using the algorithm of Agarwal, Charikar, Makarychev, and Makarychev [ACMM05].

The SDP that we solve in each iteration (given in Section 4.2) defines a "directed distance" on the vertices. We show that the edges from E_R get successively "sparsified" by a constant factor in the subgraphs H_t as mentioned above, that follows from Theorem 4.6 (Structutal Theorem): after the preprocessing step, most of the edges from E_R are "longer" (according to this directed distance) than a certain threshold $\delta_t = 2^{-t}$ (at most $O(\delta_t^2)$ fraction of the edges are longer than δ_t). However, the use of the directed distance (as opposed to an undirected distance in [MMV12]) introduces some difficulties, which we handle by performing a preprocessing step (see Lemma 4.3) at the start of each iteration. This ensures that the directed distance from the SDP at step t can be well approximated by an undirected distance (up to an additive error of δ_t) in the remaining graph. Now, we can use the ideas from [MMV12] to identify the vertices to remove, and edges to cut to obtain H_{t+1}.

4.2 SDP relaxation

We now describe the SDP relaxation for Minimum Directed Balanced Cut. Our algorithm will iteratively construct a sequence of subgraphs $H = H_0 \supset H_1 \supset H_2 \supset \dots$. The SDP will be a relaxation for the following problem: find a bisection (S,T) of U that minimizes the number of cut edges in a given set $E' \subset E_H$. In iteration i, E' will be the set of edges in the graph H_i.

We have a unit vector variable $\bar{u}$ for every vertex $u \in U$. We also have a special unit vector $\bar{v}_0$. Denote by $d(u,v)$ the directed distance ([ACMM05]):

$$d(u,v) = \|\bar{u} - \bar{v}\|^2 + 2\langle \bar{v}_0, \bar{u} - \bar{v}\rangle.$$

We write an SDP relaxation as follows. subject to: for every $u, v, w \in U$,

$$\frac{1}{2}\sum_{u,v\in U}\|\bar{u}-\bar{v}\|^2 \ge |U|^2 - 1 \quad (7)$$

$$\|\bar{u}-\bar{v}\|^2 + \|\bar{v}-\bar{w}\|^2 \ge \|\bar{u}-\bar{w}\|^2 \quad (8)$$

$$d(u,v) \ge 0 \quad (9)$$

We denote this SDP relaxation by SDP(U, E'). We denote the value of the optimal SDP solution by sdp-cost(U, E'). The constraints of the SDP define an undirected distance between the vertices (given by $\|\bar{u}-\bar{v}\|^2$), that is referred to as the ℓ_2^2 metric. Further, $d(u,v)$ defines a directed distance (directed semi-metric, to be precise) between the vertices (see Lemma 4.2 for details).

Suppose that (S,T) is a bisection of U. Then in the intended solution, we assign $\bar{u} = \bar{v}_0$ if $u \in S$ and $\bar{u} = -\bar{v}_0$ if $u \in T$. Note that only edges (u,v) that go from S to T contribute to the objective function. And for every such edge (u,v), we have $\frac{1}{8}d(u,v) = 1$. Thus the objective function equals $\text{cost}_{E'}(S,T)$. Thus sdp-cost$(U,E') \le \text{cost}_{E'}(S,T)$.

Definition 4.1 *Given an SDP solution on U, we define directed balls* $\text{Ball}^+(u,r)$ *and* $\text{Ball}^-(u,r)$ *as follows*

$$\text{Ball}^+(u,r) = \{v : d(u,v) \le r\}$$

and

$$\text{Ball}^-(u,r) = \{v : d(v,u) \le r\}.$$

Let $\text{Ball}^0(u,r) = \{v : \|\bar{u}-\bar{v}\|^2 \le r\}$. *The width of a subset $M \subset U$ is* $\text{width}(M) = \max_{u,v\in M}\langle \bar{v}_0, \bar{u}-\bar{v}\rangle$. *The ℓ_2^2-diameter of a set M is* $\text{diam}(M) = \max_{u,v\in M}\|\bar{u}-\bar{v}\|^2$.

Lemma 4.2 *Consider the directed distance function $d(u,v)$ defined by a feasible solution to* SDP(U,E').

1. *The function $d(u,v)$ defines a directed semi-metric on U. That is, $d(u,v) \ge 0$ and $d(u,v) + d(v,w) \ge d(u,w)$.*
2. *For every u and v in U,*
$$4\langle \bar{v}_0, \bar{u}-\bar{v}\rangle \le d(u,v) \le 2\|\bar{u}-\bar{v}\|^2.$$
3. *Suppose that M is a subset of U of width w then for every $u, v \in M$, we have $\|\bar{u}-\bar{v}\|^2 - 2w \le d(u,v) \le \|\bar{u}-\bar{v}\|^2 + 2w$.*
4. *If* $\text{width}(M) \le w$ *(as in part 3), then for $u \in M$,*
$$\text{Ball}^0(u,r/2)\cap M \subset \text{Ball}^+(u,r)\cap M \subset \text{Ball}^0(u,r+2w)\cap M,$$
and
$$\text{Ball}^0(u,r/2)\cap M \subset \text{Ball}^-(u,r)\cap M \subset \text{Ball}^0(u,r+2w)\cap M.$$

PROOF. 1. The condition $d(u,v) \geq 0$ is ensured by an SDP constraint. Then $d(u,v)+d(v,w) = \|\bar{u}-\bar{v}\|^2+2\langle\bar{v}_0,\bar{u}-\bar{v}\rangle+\|\bar{v}-\bar{w}\|^2+2\langle\bar{v}_0,\bar{v}-\bar{w}\rangle \geq \|\bar{u}-\bar{w}\|^2+2\langle\bar{v}_0,\bar{u}-\bar{w}\rangle = d(u,w)$.

2. We have, $4\langle\bar{v}_0,\bar{u}-\bar{v}\rangle = d(u,v) - d(v,u) \leq d(u,v) \leq d(u,v) + d(v,u) = 2\|\bar{u}-\bar{v}\|^2$.

3. The inequality immediately follows from the definition of $d(u,v)$:

$$d(u,v) = \|\bar{u}-\bar{v}\|^2 + 2\langle\bar{v}_0,\bar{u}-\bar{v}\rangle \leq \|\bar{u}-\bar{v}\|^2 + 2\,\mathrm{width}(M).$$

$$d(u,v) = \|\bar{u}-\bar{v}\|^2 + 2\langle\bar{v}_0,\bar{u}-\bar{v}\rangle \geq \|\bar{u}-\bar{v}\|^2 - 2\,\mathrm{width}(M).$$

4. If $v \in \mathrm{Ball}^0(u,r/2)$, then $\|\bar{u}-\bar{v}\|^2 \leq r/2$, and, consequently, $d(u,v) \leq r$ (by item 2). If $v \in \mathrm{Ball}^+(u,r) \cap M$, then $d(u,v) \leq r$ and $u,v \in M$. Thus, by item 3, $\|\bar{u}-\bar{v}\|^2 \leq d(u,v) + 2w \leq r + 2w$. □

4.3 Preprocessing

The directed semi-metric $d(u,v)$ defined by a feasible SDP solution has two components: the undirected ℓ_2^2 component $\|\bar{u}-\bar{v}\|^2$ and the projection of $u-v$ on to v_0. Here, we show how to preprocess the graph, so that in the remaining graph, the directed semi-metric $d(u,v)$ can be approximated well by the undirected ℓ_2^2 distance. The preprocessing algorithm is motivated by the following observation: edges (u,v) whose distance $d(u,v)$ has a large contribution from the projection $\langle\bar{v}_0,\bar{u}-\bar{v}\rangle$, can be separated cheaply by looking at their projections on $\bar{v}_0$. We now describe the preprocessing step, along with its guarantees.

Lemma 4.3 *There is an algorithm that given a $H'(U',E')$, a parameter $\delta > 0$ and an SDP solution $\{\bar{u}\}$ of cost* sdp-cost *does the following. Either it finds a 0.1-balanced cut in H' of cost $O(\text{sdp-cost}/\delta)$, or it partitions U' into sets L, C, and R such that*

1. *each of the sets L and R contains at most $|U'|/10$ vertices;*
2. *the total cost of directed cuts (R,C), (C,L) and (R,L) is $O(\text{sdp-cost}/\delta)$,*
3. $\mathrm{width}(C) \leq \delta/8$.

PROOF. We run the following algorithm.

Preprocessing Algorithm

Input: Graph $H(U',E')$, parameter $\delta > 0$ and a feasible SDP solution $\{\bar{u}\}$, as in Lemma 4.3.
Output: A directed balanced cut or a partition of U' into three sets L, C, and R.

1. Let μ be the median of the set $\{\langle\bar{v}_0,\bar{u}\rangle : u \in U'\}$.
2. Let $L_\tau = \{u \in U : \langle\bar{v}_0,\bar{u}\rangle < \mu - \tau\}$, $C_\tau = \{u \in U : |\langle\bar{v}_0,\bar{u}\rangle - \mu| \leq \tau\}$, and $R_\tau = \{u \in U : \langle\bar{v}_0,\bar{u}\rangle > \mu + \tau\}$.
3. Choose $\tau \in (0,\delta/16)$ that minimizes the total cost of directed cuts (R_τ,C_τ), (C_τ,L_τ) and (R_τ,L_τ).
4. If $|L_\tau| > |U'|/10$ return the cut $(C_\tau \cup R_\tau, L_\tau)$; if $|R_\tau| > |U'|/10$ return the cut $(R_\tau, C_\tau \cup L_\tau)$.
5. Otherwise, return sets $L = L_\tau$, $C = C_\tau$, and $R = R_\tau$.

Note that if the algorithm outputs a directed cut, the side of the cut that equals L_τ or R_τ contains at least $|U'|/10$ vertices, and the other side, which equals $L_\tau \cup C_\tau$ or $R_\tau \cup C_\tau$, contains at least $|U'|/2$ vertices since $|L_\tau \cup C_\tau| \geq |\{u \in U : \langle\bar{v}_0,\bar{u}\rangle \leq \mu\}| \geq |U'|/2$ (by the definition of μ); similarly, $|R_\tau \cup C_\tau| \geq |U'|/2$. Therefore, the cut is 0.1-balanced. If the algorithm outputs sets L, C, and R then condition (1) clearly holds.

Now we will prove that if the algorithm outputs a directed cut then its cost is at most $32\,\text{sdp-cost}/\delta$, and if the algorithm outputs sets L, C, R then condition (2) holds. To this end, we show that the total cost of cuts (R_τ,C_τ), (C_τ,L_τ) and (R_τ,L_τ) is at most $32\,\text{sdp-cost}/\delta$. Suppose that we choose τ uniformly at random from $(0,\delta/16)$. Consider an edge $(u,v) \in E'$. We compute the probability that (u,v) is cut by one of the directed cuts (C_τ,L_τ) and (R_τ,L_τ). If $\langle\bar{v}_0,u\rangle \leq \langle\bar{v}_0,v\rangle$ then the edge (u,v) cannot be cut. If $\langle\bar{v}_0,u\rangle \geq \langle\bar{v}_0,v\rangle$ then the probability that (u,v) is cut is at most $\langle\bar{v}_0,\bar{u}-\bar{v}\rangle/(\delta/16) \leq 4d(u,v)/\delta$ (by Lemma 4.2). Since $\frac{1}{8}\sum_{(u,v)\in E_H} d(u,v) \leq \text{sdp-cost}$, the expected total number of cut edges is at most $32\,\text{sdp-cost}/\delta$. Thus for the optimal value of $\tau \in (0,\delta)$, the total number of cut edges is also at most $32\,\text{sdp-cost}/\delta$.

Finally, $\mathrm{width}(C) = \max_{u,v\in C}(\langle\bar{v}_0,\bar{u}\rangle - \langle\bar{v}_0,\bar{v}\rangle) \leq (\mu + \delta/16) - (\mu - \delta/16) = \delta/8$. □

4.4 Heavy Vertices and Geometric Expansion

In this subsection, we first remind the definitions of *heavy vertices* and *geometric expansion* from [MMV12] and state some related results from [MMV12]. Then we describe the heavy vertex removal procedure for directed graphs (which is a modification of the vertex removal procedure for undirected graphs from [MMV12]).

Definition 4.4 *Let U be a set of vertices, and $M \subseteq U$. Suppose that $\{\bar{u}\}$ is a feasible SDP solution. We say that a vertex $u \in M$ is δ–heavy in M if $|\mathrm{Ball}^0(u,\delta) \cap M| \geq \delta^2|U|$. We denote the set of all heavy vertices by $\mathsf{Hv}_\delta(M)$. (Note that the set of heavy vertices depends on the SDP solution.)*

Definition 4.5 *(Geometric Expansion) A graph $H = (U,E_H)$ satisfies the geometric expansion property with cut value X at scale δ if for every feasible SDP solution $\{\bar{u}\}$ and every subset of vertices $M \subseteq U$ satisfying $\mathsf{Hv}_\delta(M) = \varnothing$ w.r.t $\{\bar{u}\}$,*

$$|\{(u,v) \in E \cap (M \times M) : \|\bar{u}-\bar{v}\|^2 \leq \delta/2\}| \leq 2\delta^2 X.$$

A graph $H = (U,E_H)$ satisfies the geometric expansion property with cut value X up to scale δ^* if it satisfies the geometric expansion property for every $\delta \in [\delta^*,1] \cap \{2^{-t} : t \in \mathbb{N}_{\geq 0}\}$.

We will also use the following theorem, which is a simple variant of Theorem 5.1 proved in [MMV12]. (We omit the proof of Theorem 4.6 in this paper.)

Theorem 4.6 *Let V be a set of vertices of size n, $\varepsilon \in (0,1)$, and $D > 2$. Let E_R be an ε-random set of edges. Then with probability $1 - 2^{-\Omega(n)}$ the random set $\mathsf{SRD}(V,E_R)$ satisfies the following property: every graph $H = (U,E_H) \in \mathsf{SRD}(V,E_R)$ is geometrically expanding with cut cost*

$$X = C\max\{\varepsilon^2|U|,\ nD(\log^2 D)\}$$

up to scale $1/\sqrt{D}$.

Now we present a procedure that removes heavy vertices from a graph. This procedure is similar to the Heavy Vertex Removal Lemma from [MMV12].

Lemma 4.7 *There exists a polynomial-time algorithm that given sets $U' \subset U$, a feasible SDP solution $\{\bar{u}\}$, and a subset $M \subseteq U'$ of width $w \leq \delta/4$, finds a set of vertices $M' \subset M$ and a partition of $M \setminus M'$ into disjoint sets $Z_1, \dots, Z_k$ (for some $k \geq 0$) such that*

- *the set M' does not contain any δ–heavy vertices (i.e., $\mathsf{Hv}_\delta(M') = \varnothing$) w.r.t. the SDP solution $\{\bar{u}\}$.*
- *$|Z_i| \leq \frac{3}{4}|U|$ for each set Z_i;*
- *for every two vertices u^* and v^* in M, we have*

$$\Pr(\exists i \text{ s.t. } u^* \in Z_i \text{ and } v^* \notin Z_1 \cup \dots \cup Z_i) \leq$$
$$\leq C\Big(\delta^{-1} + \delta^{-2}\,\frac{\mathbb{E}[|M \setminus M'|]}{|U|}\Big) d(u^*, v^*).$$

PROOF. We use the following algorithm. If $\delta \geq 1/128$, we run the algorithm with $\delta' = 1/128$.

Heavy Vertices Removal Procedure

Input: a set of vertices U, a subset $M \subseteq U$, an SDP solution $\{\bar{u}\}$, a parameter $\delta \in (0, 1/128]$;
Output: a set $M' \subseteq M$, partition $M \setminus M' = Z_1 \cup \dots Z_k$ (for some $k \geq 0$);

- while $(\mathsf{Hv}_\delta(M) \neq \varnothing)$
  - Connect heavy vertices in M at ℓ_2^2 distance at most 8δ with an undirected edge and denote the new set of undirected edges by A; that is,
  $$A = \{(u,v) \in \mathsf{Hv}_\delta(M) \times \mathsf{Hv}_\delta(M) : \|\bar{u} - \bar{v}\|^2 \leq 8\delta\}.$$
  - Break undirected graph $(\mathsf{Hv}_\delta(M), A)$ into connected components.
  - Pick a random $r \in [2\delta, 3\delta)$.
  - *Remove components of small diameter:* For each connected component Q with
  $$\operatorname{diam}(Q) \equiv \max_{u,v \in Q} \|\bar{u} - \bar{v}\|^2 \leq 1/8,$$
  let
  $$B_Q = \bigcup_{u \in Q} \text{Ball}^+(u, r) \cap M$$
  $$= \{v \in M : \exists u \in Q \text{ s.t. } d(u,v) \leq r\}.$$
  Denote the set of all connected components of diameter at most $1/8$ by $\mathcal{Q}$.
  - *Remove a maximal independent set:* In the remaining set $\mathsf{Hv}_\delta(M) \setminus \bigcup_{Q \in \mathcal{Q}} Q$ find a maximal independent set I (this is done independently of the random variable r, e.g., using a deterministic greedy algorithm). For each $u \in I$, let $B_u = \text{Ball}^+(u, r) \cap M$.
  - Remove sets B_Q and B_u from M:
  $$M = M \setminus \Big(\bigcup_{U \in \mathcal{U}} B_U \cup \bigcup_{u \in S} B_u\Big);$$
- Let sets $Z_1, \dots, Z_k$ be the sets that we removed from M (in the order in which we removed them).
- **return** $M' = M$ and sets $\{Z_i\}$.

ANALYSIS. It is clear that the algorithm always terminates in polynomial-time (since at every step at least one vertex is removed). When the algorithm terminates $\mathsf{Hv}_\delta(M) = \varnothing$ by the condition of the "while" loop. In order to bound the size of sets Z_i, we prove that the ℓ_2^2-diameter of every set Z_i is at most $1/4$. Each set Z_i is either equal to some B_u or some B_Q. Every set B_u removed from M at one of the iterations is contained in $\text{Ball}^+(u, 3\delta) \cap M \subset \text{Ball}^0(u, 3\delta + 2w) \cap M$ by Lemma 4.2; thus its ℓ_2^2-diameter is at most $6\delta + 4w \leq 1/4$. Every set B_Q is contained in $\bigcup_{u \in Q} \text{Ball}^+(u, 3\delta) \cap M \subset \bigcup_{u \in Q} \text{Ball}^0(u, 3\delta + 2w) \cap M$. Since the ℓ_2^2-diameter of Q is at most $1/8$, the ℓ_2^2-diameter of Q is at most $1/8 + 6\delta + 4w < 1/4$. We get that for every Z_i:

$$\sum_{u,v \in U} \|\bar{u} - \bar{v}\|^2 \leq (|U|^2 - |Z_i|^2) \cdot \underbrace{\max_{u,v \in U} \|\bar{u} - \bar{v}\|^2}_{\text{at most } 4} + |Z_i|^2 \cdot \underbrace{\max_{u,v \in Z_i} \|\bar{u} - \bar{v}\|^2}_{\text{at most } 1/4} \leq 4|U|^2 - \frac{15}{4}|Z_i|^2.$$

By the SDP spreading constraint, the left hand side is greater than or equal to $2(|U|^2 - 1)$, thus $|Z_i|^2 \leq (8|U|^2 + 8)/15$, and $|Z_i| \leq \frac{3}{4}|U|$ (when $|U| \geq 5$). Now we verify the third item of the lemma. Fix two vertices u^* and v^*; and consider one iteration of the algorithm. We may assume that the algorithm first picks the independent set I and a collection of connected components $\mathcal{Q}$, and only then chooses random $r \in [2\delta, 3\delta)$. Observe, that the ℓ_2^2-distance between (SDP vectors corresponding to) any two vertices in I is at least 8δ (because I is an independent set), the ℓ_2^2-distance between every two sets in $\mathcal{Q}$ is at least 8δ (otherwise, these two sets would form one connected component), and the ℓ_2^2-distance between every $Q \in \mathcal{Q}$ and $u \in I$ is at least 8δ (again because Q is a connected component, and $u \notin Q$). Thus, u^* may belong to at most one $\bigcup_{u \in Q} \text{Ball}^0(u, 4\delta)$ or $\text{Ball}^0(u, 4\delta)$. By Lemma 4.2, $\text{Ball}^+(u, 3\delta) \subset \text{Ball}^0(u, 4\delta)$ (since $w < \delta/2$), thus u^* may belong to at most one $\bigcup_{u \in Q} \text{Ball}^+(u, 3\delta)$ or $\text{Ball}^+(u, 3\delta)$. If $u^* \in \text{Ball}^+(u, 3\delta) \cap M$ and $v^* \in M$, then

$$\begin{aligned}
\Pr(u^* \in \text{Ball}^+(u, r),\ v^* \notin \text{Ball}(u, r)) &= \Pr(d(u, u^*) \leq r \leq d(u, v^*)) \\
&\leq \Pr(d(u, u^*) \leq r \leq d(u, u^*) + d(u^*, v^*)) \\
&\leq \frac{d(u^*, v^*)}{3\delta}.
\end{aligned}$$

Of course, if $u^* \notin \text{Ball}^+(u, 3\delta)$, then

$$\Pr(u^* \in \text{Ball}^+(u, r),\ v^* \notin \text{Ball}^+(u, r)) \leq$$
$$\leq \Pr(u^* \in \text{Ball}^+(u, r)) = 0.$$

The same statements hold if we replace $u \in I$ with $Q \in \mathcal{Q}$. Thus, at one iteration, the probability that u^* belongs to a removed ball but v^* does not belong to the same ball (and v^* was not removed previously) is at most $O(d(u,v)/\delta)$. Denote by T the number of iterations of the algorithm. Then, the probability that u^* is cut from M at one iteration and v^* is not cut from M at this or prior iteration is $O(\delta^{-1}\mathbb{E}[T] d(u,v))$.

We now prove that at every iteration but possibly the last, the algorithm removes at least $\Omega(\delta|U|)$ vertices from

M. Thus, $\mathbb{E}[T] \le 1 + O(\mathbb{E}|M' \setminus M|/(\delta|U|))$, and the third item of Lemma 4.7 follows. Observe, that if $I = \varnothing$, then the algorithm terminates. If $I \ne \varnothing$, there exists at least one connected component L with $\operatorname{diam}(L) \ge 1/8$. The maximal independent set in L must contain at least $\Omega(\delta^{-1})$ vertices, since for every edge $(u, v) \in A$, $\|\bar{u} - \bar{v}\|^2 \le 8\delta$. Thus, $|I| \ge \Omega(\delta^{-1})$. Since each $u \in I$ is δ-heavy and $r \ge 2\delta$, $|B_u| \ge |\operatorname{Ball}^+(u, 2\delta) \cap M| \ge |\operatorname{Ball}^0(u, \delta) \cap M| \ge \delta^2|U|$. Hence (using the fact that sets B_u are disjoint),

$$\left|\bigcup_{u \in I} B_u\right| = \sum_{u \in S} |B_u| \ge \Omega(\delta|U|).$$

□

Now we combine Lemma 4.7 and Lemma 4.3 and obtain the following lemma.

Lemma 4.8 *There is a polynomial-time algorithm that given a graph $H(U, E_H)$, its subgraph $H'(U', E')$ and a feasible SDP solution $\{\bar{u}\}$ of cost at most* sdp-cost = sdp-cost(U, E'), *partition U' into three sets S^*, T^* and U'' satisfying the following conditions:*

- *The set U'' does not contain any δ-heavy vertices w.r.t. $\{\bar{u}\}$ ($\mathsf{Hv}_\delta(U'') = \varnothing$).*
- $|S^*| \le 0.9|U|$ *and* $|T^*| \le 0.9|U|$.
- *The total cost of directed cuts (S^*, U''), (S^*, T^*) and (U'', T^*) is at most*

$$C\Big(\delta^{-1} + \delta^{-2}\,\frac{\mathbb{E}[|U \setminus U'|]}{|U|}\Big) \cdot \text{sdp-cost}.$$

Proof. We run the algorithm from Lemma 4.3. If the algorithm returns a directed balanced cut in (U, E') of cost $O(\text{sdp-cost}/\delta)$, we let (S^*, T^*) be this cut, and let $U'' = \varnothing$. The first condition trivially holds since $U'' = \varnothing$. The second and third conditions hold by Lemma 4.3. Otherwise, the algorithm returns three sets L, C and R. We run the algorithm from Lemma 4.7 on $M = C$ and get a partition of M into a set M' and a family of sets $Z_1, \dots, Z_k$.

We consider two cases. First, assume that $|R \cup Z_1 \cup \cdots \cup Z_k| \le 0.9|U|$. Then we let $S^* = R \cup Z_1 \cup \cdots \cup Z_k$, $T^* = L$ and $U'' = M'$. The first property holds by Lemma 4.7. By our assumption, $|S^*| \le 0.9|U|$; by Lemma 4.3, $|T^*| = |L^*| < 0.1|U''| < 0.9|U|$. It follows from Lemmas 4.3 and 4.7 that the total cost of cuts (S^*, U''), (S^*, T^*) and (U'', T^*) is $O\Big(\delta^{-1} + \delta^{-2}\,\frac{\mathbb{E}[|U' \setminus U''|]}{|U|}\Big) \cdot \text{sdp-cost}$.

Now let us assume that $|R \cup Z_1 \cup \cdots \cup Z_k| > 0.9|U|$. We find the last index i such that $|R \cup Z_1 \cup \cdots \cup Z_i| \le 0.9|U|$. Let $S^* = R \cup Z_1 \cup \dots Z_i$, $T^* = C \cup L \cup Z_{i+1} \cup \cdots \cup Z_k$ and $U'' = \varnothing$. The first property trivially holds since $U'' = \varnothing$. We verify that the second property holds. By our choice of i, $|S^*| \le 0.9|U|$. Since $|S^* \cup Z_{i+1}| > 0.9|U|$ and $|Z_{i+1}| < 0.75|U_i|$, we have $|S^*| > 0.15|U|$, and therefore $|T^*| = |U'| - |S^*| < 0.85|U|$. Finally, it follows from Lemmas 4.3 and 4.7 that the cost of the cut (S^*, T^*) is at most $O\Big(\delta^{-1} + \delta^{-2}\,\frac{\mathbb{E}[|U' \setminus U''|]}{|U|}\Big) \cdot$ sdp-cost. □

4.5 Algorithm for Minimum Directed Balanced Cut

Now we are ready to present our algorithm.

Input: a graph $H(U, E_H)$;
Output: a directed balanced cut (S', T');

- Let $t = 0$, $H_0 = H$, $U_0 = U$, $E_0 = E_H$.
- while ($\delta_t \ge (\log n)^{-1/4}$) do
  - A. Let $\delta = \delta_t = 2^{-t}$.
  - B. Solve the SDP relaxation SDP(U, E_t) for the Minimum Directed Balanced Cut.
  - C. Run the algorithm from Lemma 4.8, and obtain sets $S_{t+1} = S^*$, $T_{t+1} = T^*$ and $U_{t+1} = U''$.
  - D. Consider the induced graph $H_t[U_{t+1}]$. Remove all edges $(u, v) \in H_t[U_{t+1}]$ with $d(u, v) \ge \delta_t/4$. Denote the obtained graph by $H_{t+1} = (U_{t+1}, E_{t+1})$.
  - E. Let $t = t + 1$.
- Find a directed 0.1-balanced cut (S^{**}, T^{**}) in the graph (U, E_t) using the algorithm of Agarwal, Charikar, Makarychev and Makarychev [ACMM05].
- Let $A_1 = S_1$, …, $A_t = S_t$, $A_{t+1} = S^{**} \cap U_t$, $A_{t+2} = T^{**} \cap U_t$, $A_{t+3} = T_1$, …, $A_{2t+2} = T_t$.
- Find the last j^* s.t. $\sum_{i=1}^{j^*} |A_j| < 0.95|U|$.
- Let $S' = \bigcup_{i=1}^{j^*} A_i$ and $T' = \bigcup_{i=j^*+1}^{2t+2} A_i$.
- **return** (S', T')

Analysis. By Theorem 4.6, graph $(U, E_R \cap (U \times U))$ is geometrically expanding with cut value

$$X = C \max\{\varepsilon^2|U|, n\sqrt{\log n}(\log^2 \log n)\}$$

up to scale $(\log n)^{-1/4}$. Consider iteration t of the algorithm. By Lemma 4.8, the set U'_{t+1} contains no δ_t-heavy vertices. Therefore, by the definition of geometric expansion, there are at most $2\delta_t^2 X$ edges $(u, v) \in E_R \cap (U' \times U')$ with $\|\bar{u} - \bar{v}\|^2 \le \delta_t/2$. Note that if $\|\bar{u} - \bar{v}\|^2 > \delta_t/2$ then

$$d(u, v) \ge \|\bar{u} - \bar{v}\|^2 - 2\operatorname{width}(U') \ge \delta_t/4.$$

Thus at step D, we remove all but at most $2\delta_t^2 X$ random edges from H_t. That is, $|E_R \cap E_{t+1}| \le \delta_t^2 X$. Therefore, sdp-cost$(U, E_{t+1}) \le 2\delta_t^2 X$.

Now we bound the cost of the cut. Note that the total number of edges cut at step C — edges that go from S_{t+1} and T_{t+1}, from S_{t+1} to U_{t+1}, or from U_{t+1} to T_{t+1} — is at most $O\Big((\delta_t X + \frac{\mathbb{E}[|U_t \setminus U_{t+1}|]}{|U|})X\Big)$. Since $\sum_t \delta_t < 2$, and $\sum_t \mathbb{E}[|U_t \setminus U_{t+1}|]/\,|U| < 1$, we get that the total number of edges cut at step C in all iterations is $O(X)$. We cut at most sdp-cost$(U, E_i)/(\delta_t/4) = O(\delta_t X)$ edges at step D in one iteration; and we cut at most $O(X)$ edges in total all iterations. Finally, we bound the cost of $(S**, T^**)$. The planted cut (S, T) in U cuts at most $|E_t \cap E_R| \le \delta_t^2 X$ edges in E_t. Thus (here, $\delta_t < (\log n)^{-1/4}$)

$$\begin{aligned}\operatorname{cost}_{E_t}(S^{**}, T^{**}) &\le O(\sqrt{\log n}) \operatorname{cost}_{E_t}(S, T)\\ &\le O(\sqrt{\log n})\delta_t^2 X = O(X).\end{aligned}$$

Finally, we verify that the cut (S', T') is balanced. By our choice of j^*, $|S'| < 0.95|U|$. Since $|A_i| \leq 0.9|U|$ for all i,

$$|T'| = |U| - |S| = |U| - \left(\sum_{i=1}^{j^*+1} |A_i|\right) + |A_{j^*+1}|$$
$$\leq |U| - 0.95|U| + 0.9|U| = 0.95|U|.$$

□

5. REFERENCES

[ACMM05] Amit Agarwal, Moses Charikar, Konstantin Makarychev, and Yury Makarychev. $O(\sqrt{\log n})$ approximation algorithms for Min UnCut, Min 2CNF Deletion, and directed cut problems. In *Proceedings of the Thirty-Seventh Annual ACM Symposium on Theory of Computing*, pages 573–581, 2005.

[ACN08] Nir Ailon, Moses Charikar, and Alantha Newman. Aggregating inconsistent information: Ranking and clustering. *J. ACM*, 55(5):23:1–23:27, November 2008.

[AK94] Noga Alon and Nabil Kahale. A spectral technique for coloring random 3-colorable graphs. In *Proceedings of the Twenty-Sixth ACM Symposium on Theory of Computing*, pages 346–355, 1994.

[AKS99] Noga Alon, Michael Krivelevich, and Benny Sudakov. List coloring of random and pseudo-random graphs. *Combinatorica*, 19:453–472, 1999.

[AMMN05] Noga Alon, Konstantin Makarychev, Yury Makarychev, and Assaf Naor. Quadratic forms on graphs. *Invent. Math*, 163:486–493, 2005.

[BCC$^+$10] Aditya Bhaskara, Moses Charikar, Eden Chlamtac, Uriel Feige, and Aravindan Vijayaraghavan. Detecting high log-densities: an $O(n^{1/4})$ approximation for densest k-subgraph. In *Proceedings of the 42nd ACM Symposium on Theory of Computing*, pages 201–210, 2010.

[BLCS87] Thang Nguyen Bui, F. Thomson Leighton, Soma Chaudhuri, and Michael Sipser. Graph bisection algorithms with good average case behavior. *Combinatorica*, 7:171–191, June 1987.

[BM08] Mark Braverman and Elchanan Mossel. Noisy sorting without resampling. In *Proceedings of the Nineteenth Annual ACM-SIAM Symposium on Discrete Algorithms*, pages 268–276, 2008.

[Bop87] Ravi B. Boppana. Eigenvalues and graph bisection: An average-case analysis. In *28th Annual Symposium on Foundations of Computer Science*, pages 280–285, 1987.

[BS90] Bonnie Berger and Peter W. Shor. Approximation alogorithms for the maximum acyclic subgraph problem. In *Proceedings of the First Annual ACM-SIAM Symposium on Discrete Algorithms*, pages 236–243, 1990.

[BS95] Avrim Blum and Joel Spencer. Coloring random and semi-random k-colorable graphs. *J. Algorithms*, 19:204–234, September 1995.

[CFR06] Don Coppersmith, Lisa Fleischer, and Atri Rudra. Ordering by weighted number of wins gives a good ranking for weighted tournaments. In *Proceedings of the Seventeenth Annual ACM-SIAM Symposium on Discrete Algorithm*, pages 776–782, 2006.

[CK99] Anne Condon and Richard Karp. Algorithms for graph partitioning on the planted partition model. In *Randomization, Approximation, and Combinatorial Optimization. Algorithms and Techniques*, volume 1671 of *Lecture Notes in Computer Science*, pages 221–232. Springer Berlin / Heidelberg, 1999.

[CMM07] Moses Charikar, Konstantin Makarychev, and Yury Makarychev. On the advantage over random for maximum acyclic subgraph. In *Proceedings of the 48th Annual IEEE Symposium on Foundations of Computer Science*, pages 625–633, 2007.

[CO06] Amin Coja-Oghlan. A spectral heuristic for bisecting random graphs. *Random Structures & Algorithms*, 29(3):351–398, 2006.

[DF86] M. E. Dyer and A. M. Frieze. Fast solution of some random NP-hard problems. In *27th Annual Symposium on Foundations of Computer Science*, pages 331–336, 1986.

[DI98] Tassos Dimitriou and Russell Impagliazzo. Go with the winners for graph bisection. In *Proceedings of the Ninth Annual ACM-SIAM Symposium on Discrete Algorithms*, pages 510–520, 1998.

[ENRS00] Guy Even, Joseph Seffi Naor, Satish Rao, and Baruch Schieber. Divide-and-conquer approximation algorithms via spreading metrics. *J. ACM*, 47(4):585–616, July 2000.

[FK98] Uriel Feige and Joe Kilian. Heuristics for finding large independent sets, with applications to coloring semi-random graphs. In *Proceedings of the 39th Annual Symposium on Foundations of Computer Science*, pages 674 –683, 1998.

[FK00] Uriel Feige and Robert Krauthgamer. Finding and certifying a large hidden clique in a semirandom graph. *Random Struct. Algorithms*, 16:195–208, March 2000.

[GMR08] Venkatesan Guruswami, Rajsekar Manokaran, and Prasad Raghavendra. Beating the random ordering is hard: Inapproximability of maximum acyclic subgraph. In *Proceedings of the 49th Annual IEEE Symposium on Foundations of Computer Science*, pages 573–582, 2008.

[JS93] Mark Jerrum and Gregory Sorkin. Simulated annealing for graph bisection. In *Proceedings of the 34th Annual IEEE Symposium on Foundations of Computer Science*, pages 94–103, 1993.

[Kan92] V. Kann. *On the Approximability of NP-complete Optimization Problems.* PhD thesis, Department of Numerical Analysis and Computing Science, Royal Institute of Technology, Stockholm, 1992.

[Kar72] R. Karp. Reducibility among combinatorial problems. In R. Miller and J. Thatcher, editors, *Complexity of Computer Computations*, pages 85–103. Plenum Press, 1972.

[KMM11] Alexandra Kolla, Konstantin Makarychev, and Yury Makarychev. How to play unique games against a semi-random adversary: Study of semi-random models of unique games. In *Proceedings of the 52nd Annual Symposium on Foundations of Computer Science*, pages 443–452, 2011.

[KMS07] Claire Kenyon-Mathieu and Warren Schudy. How to rank with few errors. In *Proceedings of the Thirty-Ninth Annual ACM Symposium on Theory of Computing*, pages 95–103, 2007.

[KMSPT86] Ludek Kucera, Alberto Marchetti-Spaccamela, Marco Protasi, and Maurizio Talamo. Near optimal algorithms for finding minimum steiner trees on random graphs. In *Mathematical Foundations of Computer Science*, pages 501–511, London, UK, UK, 1986. Springer-Verlag.

[KS63] John G. Kemeny and J. Laurie Snell. *Mathematical models in the social sciences.* Blaisdell Publ., 1963.

[LR99] Tom Leighton and Satish Rao. Multicommodity max-flow min-cut theorems and their use in designing approximation algorithms. *J. ACM*, 46:787–832, November 1999.

[Mak08] Konstantin Makarychev. *Quadratic Forms on Graphs and Their Applications.* PhD thesis, Department of Computing Science, Princeton, University, Princeton, NJ, USA, 2008.

[McS01] Frank McSherry. Spectral partitioning of random graphs. In *Proceedings of the 42nd IEEE Symposium on Foundations of Computer Science*, pages 529–537, 2001.

[MMV12] Konstantin Makarychev, Yury Makarychev, and Aravindan Vijayaraghavan. Approximation algorithms for semi-random graph partitioning problems. In *Proceedings of the 44th symposium on Theory of Computing*, pages 367–384, 2012.

[MS10] Claire Mathieu and Warren Schudy. Correlation clustering with noisy input. In *Proceedings of the Twenty-First Annual ACM-SIAM Symposium on Discrete Algorithms*, pages 712–728, 2010.

[New04] Alantha Newman. Cuts and orderings: On semidefinite relaxations for the linear ordering problem. In Klaus Jansen, Sanjeev Khanna, JosÃl'D.P. Rolim, and Dana Ron, editors, *Approximation, Randomization, and Combinatorial Optimization. Algorithms and Techniques*, volume 3122 of *Lecture Notes in Computer Science*, pages 195–206. Springer Berlin Heidelberg, 2004.

[Saa77] Thomas L Saaty. A scaling method for priorities in hierarchical structures. *Journal of Mathematical Psychology*, 15(3):234 – 281, 1977.

[Saa08] Thomas L. Saaty. Relative measurement and its generalization in decision making: Why pairwise comparisons are central in mathematics for the measurement of intangible factors – the analytic hierarchy/network process. *Revista de la Real Academia de Ciencias Exactas, Físicas y Naturales. Serie A: Matemáticas (RACSAM)*, 102(2):251–318, 2008.

[Sey95] Paul D. Seymour. Packing directed circuits fractionally. *Combinatorica*, 15(2):281–288, 1995.

[SR61] S. Seshu and M.B. Reed. *Linear graphs and electrical networks.* Addison-Wesley series in the engineering science. Addison-Wesley Pub. Co., 1961.

[Ung57] Stephen H. Unger. *A Study of Asynchronous Logical Feedback Networks.* Technical report. Research Laboratory of Electronics, Massachusetts Inst. of Technology, 1957.

[You63] D. Younger. Minimum feedback arc sets for a directed graph. *IEEE Transactions on Circuit Theory*, 10(2):238 – 245, jun 1963.

New Affine-Invariant Codes from Lifting

Alan Guo
CSAIL
MIT
Cambridge, MA
aguo@mit.edu

Swastik Kopparty
Dept. of Computer Science &
Dept. of Mathematics
Rutgers University
Piscataway, NJ
swastik.kopparty@rutgers.edu

Madhu Sudan
Microsoft Research New
England
Cambridge, MA
madhu@mit.edu

ABSTRACT

In this work we explore error-correcting codes derived from the "lifting" of "affine-invariant" codes. Affine-invariant codes are simply linear codes whose coordinates are a vector space over a field and which are invariant under affine-transformations of the coordinate space. Lifting takes codes defined over a vector space of small dimension and lifts them to higher dimensions by requiring their restriction to every subspace of the original dimension to be a codeword of the code being lifted. While the operation is of interest on its own, this work focusses on new ranges of parameters that can be obtained by such codes, in the context of local correction and testing. In particular we present four interesting ranges of parameters that can be achieved by such lifts, all of which are new in the context of affine-invariance and some may be new even in general. The main highlight is a construction of high-rate codes with sublinear time decoding. The only prior construction of such codes is due to Kopparty, Saraf and Yekhanin [33]. All our codes are extremely simple, being just lifts of various parity check codes (codes with one symbol of redundancy), and in the final case, the lift of a Reed-Solomon code.

We also present a simple connection between certain lifted codes and lower bounds on the size of "Nikodym sets". Roughly, a Nikodym set in $\mathbb{F}_q^m$ is a set S with the property that every point has a line passing through it which is almost entirely contained in S. While previous lower bounds on Nikodym sets were roughly growing as $q^m/2^m$, we use our lifted codes to prove a lower bound of $(1-o(1))q^m$ for fields of constant characteristic.

Categories and Subject Descriptors

E.4 [**Coding and Information Theory**]: Error Control Codes

Keywords

affine-invariance; lifting; locally correctible codes; locally testable codes; Nikodym sets; property testing

1. INTRODUCTION

In this work we explore the "locality properties" of some highly symmetric codes constructed by "lifting" "affine-invariant" codes. We describe these terms below.

1.1 Basic terminology and background

We start with some standard coding theory preliminaries. Let $\mathbb{F}_q$ denote the finite field of cardinality q and for any finite set D, let $\{D \to \mathbb{F}_q\}$ denote the set of all functions from D to $\mathbb{F}_q$. In this work, a code on coordinate set D is a set of functions $\mathcal{F} \subseteq \{D \to \mathbb{F}_q\}$. A code $\mathcal{F}$ is said to be linear if it forms a vector space over $\mathbb{F}_q$, i.e., if for every $f, g \in \mathcal{F}$ and $\alpha \in \mathbb{F}_q$ the function $\alpha f + g \in \mathcal{F}$. We refer to $N = |D|$ as the length of the code. A second parameter of interest is the dimension of the code which is the dimension of $\mathcal{F}$ as a vector space. The dual of a code $\mathcal{F}$, denoted $\mathcal{F}^\perp$, is the set of functions $\{g : D \to \mathbb{F}_q | \langle f, g\rangle = 0 \; \forall f \in \mathcal{F}\}$, where $\langle f, g\rangle = \sum_{x\in D} f(x)g(x)$ denotes the standard inner product of vectors. Let $\mathrm{wt}(f) = |\{x \in D | f(x) \neq 0\}|$ denote the weight of f. Let $\delta(f, g) = |\{x \in D | f(x) \neq g(x)\}|/|D|$ denote the (normalized Hamming) distance between f and g. (So $\delta(f, g) = \mathrm{wt}(f - g)/|D|$.) We say f is δ-close to g if $\delta(f, g) \leq \delta$ and δ-far otherwise. We say f is δ-close to $\mathcal{F}$ if there exists $g \in \mathcal{F}$ that is δ-close to f and δ-far otherwise. We say $\mathcal{F}$ is a code of distance δ if every pair of distinct codewords in $\mathcal{F}$ are δ-far from each other. We use $\delta(\mathcal{F})$ to denote the maximum δ such that $\mathcal{F}$ is a code of distance δ.

In this work we explore some aspects of affine-invariant codes. In such codes the domain D is a vector space $\mathbb{F}_{q^n}^m$, i.e., an m-dimensional vector space over the n-dimensional extension field of the range $\mathbb{F}_q$. Let $Q = q^n$ and let $\mathbb{F}_Q$ denote the field of size Q. We say a function $A : \mathbb{F}_Q^m \to \mathbb{F}_Q^m$ is an affine function if $A(x) = M \cdot x + b$ for some matrix $M \in \mathbb{F}_Q^{m\times m}$ and vector $b \in \mathbb{F}_Q^m$. We say A is an affine permutation if M is invertible. A code $\mathcal{F} \subseteq \{\mathbb{F}_Q^m \to \mathbb{F}_q\}$ is said to be affine-invariant if for every affine permutation function $A : \mathbb{F}_Q^m \to \mathbb{F}_Q^m$ and for every $f \in \mathcal{F}$ the function $f \circ A$ given by $(f \circ A)(x) = f(A(x))$ is also in $\mathcal{F}$.[1]

[1]In some of the earlier works invariance is defined with respect to all affine functions and not just permutations. In the full version [23] we show that the two notions are equivalent and so we use invariance with respect to permutations in this paper.

Affine-invariant codes are of interest to us because they exhibit, under natural and almost necessary conditions, very good locality properties: they tend to be locally testable and locally correctible. We introduce these notions below. We say a code $\mathcal{F}$ is (k,δ)-locally correctible ((k,δ)-LCC) if there exists a probabilistic algorithm CORR that, given $x \in D$ and oracle access to a function $f : D \to \mathbb{F}_q$ which is δ-close to some $g \in \mathcal{F}$, makes at most k queries to f and outputs $g(x)$ with probability at least 2/3. We say that $\mathcal{F}$ is (k,ϵ,δ)-locally testable ((k,ϵ,δ)-LTC) if $\mathcal{F}$ is a code of distance δ and there exists a probabilistic algorithm TEST that, given oracle access to $f : D \to \mathbb{F}_q$, makes at most k queries to f and accepts $f \in \mathcal{F}$ with probability one, while rejecting f that is τ-far from $\mathcal{F}$ with probability at least $\epsilon \cdot \tau$.

1.2 This work: Motivation and Results

As noted above affine-invariant lead naturally to locally decodable codes and locally testable codes. In this work we use a certain lifting operation to exhibit codes with very good locality. We start by defining the lifting operation. For a function $f : \mathbb{F}_Q^m \to \mathbb{F}_q$ and set $S \subseteq \mathbb{F}_Q^m$ let $f|_S$ denote the restriction of f to the domain S.

DEFINITION 1.1 (LIFTING). *For a code $\mathcal{F} \subseteq \{\mathbb{F}_Q^t \to \mathbb{F}_q\}$, and integer $m \geq t$, its m-dimensional lift $\mathrm{Lift}_m(\mathcal{F}) \subseteq \{\mathbb{F}_Q^m \to \mathbb{F}_q\}$ is the code consisting of all $f : \mathbb{F}_Q^m \to \mathbb{F}_q$ such that $f|_V \in \mathcal{F}$ for every t-dimensional affine subspace V.*

(Note that the definition above assumes some canonical way to equate t-dimensional subspaces of $\mathbb{F}_Q^m$ with $\mathbb{F}_Q^t$. But for affine-invariant families $\mathcal{F}$ the exact correspondence does not matter as long as the map is an isomorphism.)

The lift is a very natural operation on affine-invariant codes, and builds long codes from shorter ones. Indeed, lifts may be interpreted as the basic operation that leads to the construction of "(Generalized) Reed-Muller" codes, codes formed by m-variate polynomials over $\mathbb{F}_q$ of total degree at most d: Such codes are the "lifts" of t-variate polynomials of degree at most d, for $t = \lceil \frac{d+1}{q-q/p} \rceil$ where p is the characteristic of q. (This follows from the "characterization" of polynomials as proven in [30].) While the locality properties (testability and correctability) of Reed-Muller codes are well-studied [36, 3, 4, 35, 1, 30, 27, 10, 26], they are essentially the only rich class of symmetric codes that are well-studied. The only other basic class of symmetric codes that are studied seem to be sparse ones, i.e., ones with few codewords.

In this work we explore the lifting of codes as a means to building rich new classes of *dense* symmetric codes. (In Theorems 1.2 - 1.5 below we describe some of the codes we obtain this way, and contrast them with known results.) Along the way we also initiate a systematic study of lifts of codes. Lifts of codes were introduced first in [7], who explored it to prove negative results — specifically, to build "symmetric LDPC codes" that are not testable. (Their definition was more restrictive than ours, and also somewhat less clean.) Our work is the first to explore positive use of lifts.

We remark that all codes constructed by lifting have relative distance of at least Q^{-t} and are $(Q^t, Q^{-t}/3)$-LCC's and $(Q^t, \Omega(Q^{-2t}), Q^{-t})$-LTC's. The local correctability follows directly from their definition, while the local testability is a consequence of the main result of [31, Theorem 2.9]. (See also Proposition 2.10.) This general feature suffices for three of our code construction, while in the fourth case we have to analyze the decodability a little more carefully.

An example.

Let q be a power of 2, let $d = (1-\delta)q$ and let us consider the lift of the set of all univariate polynomials over $\mathbb{F}_q$ of degree at most d to $\mathbb{F}_q^2$. Explicitly, we mean the code $\mathcal{F}$ consisting of all functions $f : \mathbb{F}_q^2 \to \mathbb{F}_q$ such that the restriction of f to any line of $\mathbb{F}_q^2$ is a univariate polynomial of degree at most d. $\mathcal{F}$ is an affine-invariant linear space.

By construction, it is clear that $\mathcal{F}$ has a lot of local structure; this leads to a simple local-correction algorithm for $\mathcal{F}$ based on picking random lines and performing noisy univariate polynomial interpolation (i.e., Reed-Solomon decoding). We will show that in fact $\mathcal{F}$ also has large dimension (when δ is small). This leads to a high-rate locally correctable code.

Which functions $f : \mathbb{F}_q^2 \to \mathbb{F}_q$ lie in $\mathcal{F}$? We will give an answer to this question later in the paper, in terms of the polynomial representation $f(X,Y) = \sum_{0 \leq i,j < q} a_{ij} X^i Y^j$. Here since we are interested in showing that $\dim \mathcal{F}$ is large, it will suffice for us to show that there are many linearly independent elements in $\mathcal{F}$. To do this, we will study when a monomial $g(X,Y) = X^i Y^j$ is in $\mathcal{F}$. Note that if we restrict g to a line $\ell(T) = (\alpha_1 T + \alpha_0, \beta_1 T + \beta_0)$, we get the function

$$\begin{aligned} g|_\ell(T) &= (\alpha_1 T + \alpha_0)^i (\beta_1 T + \beta_0)^j \\ &= \sum_{r \leq i} \sum_{s \leq j} \alpha_1^r \alpha_0^{i-r} \beta_1^s \beta_0^{j-s} \binom{i}{r} \binom{j}{s} T^{r+s}. \end{aligned}$$

This function will equal a univariate polynomial of degree at most d at all points of $\mathbb{F}_q$ if, when we reduce it mod $T^q - T$, we see no monomials of degree $> d$. Reducing the above polynomial mod $T^q - T$ amounts to replacing T^{r+s} in the above expression with $T^{r+s \pmod{^*} q}$ (where $a \pmod{^*} q) = 0$ if $a = 0$ and $a \pmod{^*} q) = b \in \{1, \ldots, q-1\}$ if $a \neq 0$ and $a = b \pmod{q-1}$). This will happen if i, j satisfy the following criterion: for every $r \leq i, s \leq j$, if $\binom{i}{r} \neq 0 \mod 2$ and $\binom{j}{s} \neq 0 \mod 2$, then $r + s \pmod{^*} q) \leq d$. Via Lucas' theorem (which gives a characterization of when $\binom{a}{b} = 0 \mod 2$, we deduce that the monomial $X^i Y^j$ is in $\mathcal{F}$ if (i,j) lies in the set:

$$S = \{(i,j) \mid \forall r \leq_2 i, j \leq_2 s, r + s \pmod{^*} q) \leq d\},$$

where $a \leq_2 b$ means that set of coordinates that equal 1 in the binary representation of a is a subset of the set of coordinates that equal 1 in the binary representation of b. Finally, an analysis of the set S shows that its size is $\geq (1-\epsilon_\delta) \cdot q^2$, where $\epsilon_\delta \to 0$ as $\delta \to 0$. Thus the dimension of $\mathcal{F}$ is at least $(1-\epsilon_\delta) \cdot q^2$.

We will formally treat this example in greater generality in a later section. Before that, we will build up the theory of lifts of multivariate codes. In Proposition 2.2 we will see that affine-invariant codes are completely characterized by (and in fact spanned by) the monomials in the code; thus the dimension of the code above exactly equals $|S|$.

The constructions.

For simplicity most codes are described for the case of fields of characteristic two, while the construction does generalize to other fields. (The main exception is in Theorem 1.3 where the code is later applied in other cases, so we describe the more general result.) The codes in the first three theorems below are obtained by the lifting of the parity-check code. By making appropriate choices of Q and t we get codes with different locality (and distance). The fourth code works over large fields only and is obtained by lifting the Reed-Solomon code.

Our first code has constant locality k, for k being a power of 2. If the length of the code is N (in our setting $N = Q^m$), then the code has dimension $\Omega_k((\log N)^k)$.

THEOREM 1.2. *For every positive integer t and $k = 2^t$, there exists a constant $c_k > 0$ such that for every positive integer m and $N = 2^m$, there exists a binary code of length N, dimension at least $c_k(\log N)^{k-2}$ which is a $(k-1, k^{-1}/3)$-LCC, and a $(k, \Omega(k^{-2}), k^{-1})$-LTC.*

To contrast this with other known codes, essentially the only symmetric binary code known in this regime is the Reed-Muller code, which has dimension $\Omega((\log N)^{\log k})$ for locality k. Thus our code has significantly greater dimension in this regime. Our results are also asymptotically optimal for affine-invariant codes, by a result of Ben-Sasson and Sudan [9] which shows that any affine-invariant code with such local correctability or testability must have dimension $(\log N)^{k+O(1)}$.

For local correctability, these codes asymptotically match the performance of best-known codes, which would be obtained by taking Generalized Reed-Muller codes over a field of size roughly k and then composing it with some binary code. Our codes are simpler to describe and the symmetry comes without any loss of parameters. Furthermore, for really small constants, say $k = 4$ or $k = 8$, these codes seem to be better than previously known locally correctible codes.

Our next two codes consider relatively large locality (growing with N). The advantage with these codes is that the redundancy (the difference between the length and the dimension) grows exceedingly slowly. The first of these two codes considers the setting where the locality is N^ϵ for some positive (but tiny) ϵ. In such cases, we get codes of dimension $N - N^{1-\epsilon'}$ where $\epsilon' > 0$ if $\epsilon > 0$. Thus the dimension is extremely close to the length.

THEOREM 1.3. *For every $\epsilon > 0$ and prime p, there exists $\epsilon' > 0$ such that for infinitely many N, there is a p-ary code of length N, dimension $N - N^{1-\epsilon'}$ which is a $(N^\epsilon, N^{-\epsilon}/3)$-LCC and a $(N^\epsilon, \Omega(N^{-2\epsilon}), N^{-\epsilon})$-LTC.*

The codes from Theorem 1.3 are not new. These codes, and in particular their exact dimension are well-known in the literature in combinatorics [11, 38]. Their locality was first noted by Yekhanin [39] who noticed in particular that they are LCCs. Our main contribution is to note that these are (naturally) obtained from lifts. In the process we get that these are affine-invariant codes and so are also LTCs, a fact that was not known before. Finally, our bounds while cruder, give better asymptotic sense of the redundancy of these codes (and in particular note that the redundancy is sublinear in the code length).

We remark that these codes have very poor distance and very poor error-correcting capability. However, in the context of applications such as constructions of PCPs (probabilistically checkable proofs, see e.g., [2]) one does not need distance or error-correction capability per se. All one seems to need is the local correction and decoding capability. So the theorem above motivates the search for extremely efficient PCPs, where the difference between the length of the PCP and the length of the classical proof is sublinear, while allowing for sublinear query complexity. Such a result, if at all possible, would really be transformative in the use of PCPs as a positive concept. We also note that these codes play a useful role in giving lower bounds on the size of Nikodym sets — we will elaborate on this shortly.

Next, we consider codes of locality $\Omega(N)$, so linear in the length of the code. This range of parameters was motivated by the recent result of Barak et al. [5] who used such codes (with additional properties that we are not yet able to prove) to build "small-set expanders" with many "large eigenvalues". We won't describe the application here, but instead turn to the parameters they sought. They wanted codes of length N with locality ϵN and dimension $N - \text{poly}(\log N)$. The codes they used were Reed-Muller codes. By exploring lifts we are able to suggest some alternate codes. These codes do have slightly better dimension, though unfortunately, the improvement is not asymptotically significant (and certainly not close to any known limits). Nevertheless we report the codes below.

THEOREM 1.4. *For every $\epsilon > 0$ and for infinitely many N, there is a binary code of length N, that has dimension $N - O_\epsilon((\log N)^{\log 1/\epsilon})$, which is a $(\epsilon N, \frac{1}{3}(\epsilon N)^{-1})$-LCC and a $(\epsilon N, \Omega((\epsilon N)^{-2}), (\epsilon N)^{-1})$-LTC.*

We note that Barak et al. also require the codes to be "absolutely testable", a strong notion of testability that we do not achieve in this work. Indeed, it is unclear if the codes as described above will turn out to be absolutely testable. In followup work to ours, Haramaty et al. [25], do show that some codes constructed by the above principle (but not all) are absolutely testable. The dimensions of their codes are somewhere between those of Barak et al. and those from the above theorem (so are still of no asymptotic significance).

Finally, we describe the most interesting choice of parameters. Our final code has locality N^δ for arbitrarily small $\delta > 0$, while achieving dimension $(1-\epsilon)N$ for arbitrarily small $\epsilon > 0$. While the dimension of this code is smaller than that of the codes of Theorem 1.4, it corrects a constant positive fraction of errors.

THEOREM 1.5. *For every $\epsilon, \delta > 0$ there exists $\tau > 0$ such that for infinitely many N, there is a q-code of length N over $\mathbb{F}_Q$, for $Q \approx N^\delta$, of dimension $(1-\epsilon)N$ which is a (N^δ, τ)-LCC, for some $q \approx N^\delta$.*

Till 2010, no codes achieving such a range of parameters were known. In particular no code was known that achieved dimension greater than $N/2$ while achieving $o(N)$ locality to correct constant fraction of errors. In 2010, Kopparty et al. [33] introduced what they called the "multiplicity codes" which manage to overcome the rate 1/2 barrier. Other than their codes, no other constructions were known that achieved the parameters of Theorem 1.5 and our construction provides the first alternate. We remark that while qualitatively our theorem matches theirs, the behavior of τ as a function of ϵ and δ is much worse in our construction. Nevertheless for concrete values of N, ϵ and δ our construction actually seems to perform quite well. Also, whereas in the basic codes of [33] are over larger alphabets than N, our codes are naturally over much smaller alphabets. (Of course, one can always use concatenation to reduce alphabet sizes, but such operations do result in a loss in concrete settings of parameters.)

Theorems 1.2-1.5 are proved in Section 3. While each of the codes above may be of interest on their own, the underlying phenomenon, of constructing codes with interesting parameters by lifting shorter codes is an important one. Given our belief that lifting is an important operation that deserves study, we also do some systematic analysis of lifts. In particular in this work we show that lifting of a base code essentially preserves distance. This preservation is not exact and we give examples proving this fact.

Bounds on the size of Nikodym sets.

One of the applications of our results is to bounding, from below, the size of "Nikodym sets" over finite fields (of small characteristic). We define this concept before describing our results.

A set $N \subseteq \mathbb{F}_q^m$ is said to be a *Nikodym set* if every point x has a line passing through it such that all points of the line, except possibly the point x itself, are elements of N. More precisely, N is a Nikodym set if for every $x \in \mathbb{F}_q^m$ there exists $y \in \mathbb{F}_q^m \setminus \{\mathbf{0}\}$ such that $\{x + ty | t \in \mathbb{F}_q^*\} \subseteq N$.

Nikodym sets are closely related to "Kakeya sets" — the latter contain a line in every direction, while the former contain almost all of a line through every point. A lower bound for Kakeya sets was proved by Dvir [12] using the polynomial method and further improved by using "method of multiplicities " by Saraf and Sudan [37] and Dvir et al. [13]. Kakeya sets have seen applications connecting its study to the study of randomness extractors, esp. [14, 15]. Arguably Nikodym sets are about as natural in this connection as Kakeya sets.

Previous lower bounds on Kakeya sets were typically also applicable to Nikodym sets and led to bounds of the form $|N| \geq (1 - o(1))q^m/2^m$ where the $o(1)$ term goes to zero as $q \to \infty$[2]. In particular previous lower bounds failed to separate the growth of Nikodym sets from those of Kakeya sets. In this work we present a simple connection (see Proposition 4.1) that shows that existence of (high-rate) affine-invariant codes that are lifts of non-trivial univariate codes yield (large) lower bounds on the size of Nikodym sets. Using this connection we significantly improve the known lower bound on the size of Nikodym sets over fields of constant characteristic.

THEOREM 1.6. *For every prime p, and every integer m, there exists $\epsilon = \epsilon(p, m) > 0$ such that for every finite field $\mathbb{F}_q$ of characteristic p, if $N \subseteq \mathbb{F}_q^m$ is a Nikodym set, then $|N| \geq q^m - q^{(1-\epsilon)m}$. In particular if $q \to \infty$, then $|N| \geq (1 - o(1)) \cdot q^m$.*

Thus whereas previous lower bounds on the size of Nikodym sets allowed for the possibility that the density of the Nikodym sets vanishes as m grows, ours show that Nikodym sets occupy almost all the space. One way to view our results is that they abstract the polynomial method in a more general way, and thus lead to stronger lower bounds (in some cases).

Previous work on affine-invariance.

The study of invariance, and in particular affine-invariance, in property testing was initiated by Kaufman and Sudan [31] and there have been many subsequent works [9, 21, 22, 20, 32, 29, 6, 7, 28, 8, 24]. Most of the works, with the exceptions of [32, 29], study the broad class with the aim of characterizing all the testable properties. The exceptions, Kaufman and Wigderson [32] and Kaufman and Lubotzky [29], are the few that attempt to find new codes using invariance. While the performance of their codes is very good, unfortunately they do not seem to lead to local testability and the performance is too good to be locally decodable (or locally correctible). Our work seems to be the first in this context to explore new codes that do guarantee some locality properties.

A second, more technical, point of departure is that our work refocusses attention on invariance of "multivariate properties". Since the work of [31] most subsequent works focussed on univariate properties. While this study seemed to be without loss of generality, for the purpose of constructions it seems necessary to go back to the multivariate setting. One specific contribution in this direction is that we show that invariance under general affine-transformations and under affine-permutations lead to the same set of properties (see the full version [23]).

[2]In the $m = 2$ case, better bounds are known for Nikodym sets [16, 34].

Organization.

In Section 2 we present some of the background material on affine-invariant codes and present some extensions in the multivariate setting. In Section 3 we describe our codes and analyze them. In Section 4 we describe our application to lower bounding Nikodym sets. In Section 5 we describe how distance of lifted codes behave. Some of the technical proofs are deferred to the appendix.

2. PRELIMINARIES

In this section we describe some basic aspects of affine-invariant properties, specifically their degree sets. We mention in particular the fact that the size of degree sets determines the dimension of a given affine-invariant code. Finally we conclude by relating the degree set of a base code to the degree set of a lifted code. In later sections we will use this relationship to lower bound the size of the degree set of lifted codes, and thus lower bound their dimension. We note that the results of this section are described for general q (and not for the special case of $q = 2$). Proofs are omitted but can be found in the full version [23].

For a function $f : \mathbb{F}_Q^m \to \mathbb{F}_q$, we associate with it the unique polynomial in $\mathbb{F}_Q[x_1, \ldots, x_m]$ of degree at most $Q-1$ in each variable that evaluates to f. (We abuse notation by using the same notation to refer to a function and the associated polynomial.) For $\mathbf{d} = \langle d_1, \ldots, d_m \rangle$ and $\mathbf{x} = \langle x_1, \ldots, x_m \rangle$, let $\mathbf{x}^{\mathbf{d}}$ denote the monomial $\prod_{i=1}^m x_i^{d_i}$. For a function $f = \sum_{\mathbf{d}} c_{\mathbf{d}} \mathbf{x}^{\mathbf{d}}$, let its support, denoted $\text{supp}(f)$, be the set of degrees with non-zero coefficients in f, i.e., $\text{supp}(f) = \{\mathbf{d} \mid c_{\mathbf{d}} \neq 0\}$.

DEFINITION 2.1 (DEGREE SET). *For a code $\mathcal{F} \subseteq \{\mathbb{F}_Q^m \to \mathbb{F}_q\}$, its degree set, denoted $\text{Deg}(\mathcal{F})$, is the set $\text{Deg}(\mathcal{F}) = \cup_{f \in \mathcal{F}} \text{supp}(f)$. For a set $D \subseteq \{0, \ldots, Q-1\}^m$, let its code, denoted $\text{Fam}(\mathcal{F})$ be the set $\text{Fam}(\mathcal{F}) = \{f : \mathbb{F}_Q^m \to \mathbb{F}_q \mid \text{supp}(f) \subseteq D\}$.*

For an affine-invariant code, its degree set uniquely determines the code and in particular the following proposition holds.

PROPOSITION 2.2. *For linear affine-invariant codes* $\mathcal{F} \subseteq \{\mathbb{F}_Q^m \to \mathbb{F}_q\}$, *we have* $\text{Fam}(\text{Deg}(\mathcal{F})) = \mathcal{F}$.

Our reason to study the degree sets is that the size of the degree set gives the dimension of a code exactly.

PROPOSITION 2.3. *For a linear affine-invariant code* $\mathcal{F} \subseteq \{\mathbb{F}_Q^m \to \mathbb{F}_q\}$, *we have the dimension of* $\mathcal{F}$ *equals* $|\text{Deg}(\mathcal{F})|$.

Next we attempt to describe how the degree set of a lifted code can be determined from the degree set of a base code. We start by mentioning a simple property of degree sets that will be quite useful in our analysis.

Let $(\text{mod}^* Q)$ denote the operation that maps non-negative integers to the set $\{0, \ldots, Q-1\}$ as given by $a \pmod{^* Q} = 0$ if $a = 0$ and $a \pmod{^* Q} = b \in \{1, \ldots, Q-1\}$ if $a \neq 0$ and $a = b \pmod{Q-1}$. (Note that if $a \pmod{^* Q} = b$, then $x^a = x^b \pmod{x^Q - x}$.)

For $Q = q^n$ and $\mathbf{e}, \mathbf{d} \in \{0, \ldots, Q-1\}^n$, we say that $\mathbf{e}$ is a q-shift of $\mathbf{d}$ if there exists j such that for every i, we have $e_i = q^j \cdot d_i \pmod{^* Q}$. Note that $\mathbf{e}$ is a q-shift of $\mathbf{d}$ if and only if $\mathbf{d}$ is a q-shift of $\mathbf{e}$.

PROPOSITION 2.4. *Let* $\mathcal{F} \subseteq \{\mathbb{F}_Q^m \to \mathbb{F}_q\}$ *be a linear affine-invariant code and let* $D = \text{Deg}(\mathcal{F})$ *be its degree set. Then* D *is* q*-shift closed, i.e., if* $\mathbf{d} \in D$ *and* $\mathbf{e}$ *is a* q*-shift of* $\mathbf{d}$ *then* $\mathbf{e} \in D$.

We now turn to identifying the degree sets of lifted codes. We start with the case of lifts of univariate codes, which are somewhat simpler to describe. The lifts of multivariate codes come from the same principles, but are messier to describe.

It turns out that the structure of the degree set (not every set D is the degree set of an affine-invariant code) is strongly influenced by the base p representation of its members, where p is the characteristic of q, the alphabet of our codes. We start with some notions related to such representations. For non-negative integers a and b, let $a^{(0)}, a^{(1)}, \ldots,$ and $b^{(0)}, b^{(1)}, \ldots,$ be their base p expansion, i.e., $0 \leq a^{(i)}, b^{(i)} < p$, $a = \sum_i a^{(i)} p^i$ and $b = \sum_i b^{(i)} p^i$. We say a is in the p-shadow of b, denoted $a \leq_p b$, if $a^{(i)} \leq b^{(i)}$ for every i. We extend the notion to vectors coordinate-wise. So for, $\mathbf{e}, \mathbf{d} \in \mathbb{Z}^n$, we say $\mathbf{e} \leq_p \mathbf{d}$ if $e_i \leq_p d_i$ for all $i \in [n]$.

DEFINITION 2.5. *For a set* $D \subseteq \{0, \ldots, Q-1\}$, *its* m*th lift, denoted* $\text{Lift}_m(D)$ *is the set of* $\mathbf{d} \in \{0, \ldots, Q-1\}^m$ *such that for all, for all* $\mathbf{e} \leq_p \mathbf{d}$, *we have* $\sum_{i=1}^m e_i \pmod{^* Q} \in D$.

The following proposition makes the implied connection between lifts of codes and their degree sets explicit. We note that this proposition is implicit in [7].

PROPOSITION 2.6. *For every linear affine-invariant code* $\mathcal{F} \subseteq \{\mathbb{F}_Q \to \mathbb{F}_q\}$, *and for every* $m \geq 1$, *we have*

$$\underset{m}{\text{Lift}}(\text{Deg}(\mathcal{F})) = \text{Deg}(\underset{m}{\text{Lift}}(\mathcal{F})).$$

We now extend the above definition and proposition to the case where the code being lifted is itself a multivariate one.

To this end we extend some of the notations from the previous parts to matrices. For matrices $\mathbf{A}, \mathbf{B} \in \mathbb{Z}^{n \times \ell}$ we say $\mathbf{A} \leq_p \mathbf{B}$ if $(\mathbf{A})_{ij} \leq_p (\mathbf{B})_{ij}$ for every pair $(i, j) \in [n] \times [\ell]$.

Next, we extend the notion to compare vectors to elements and matrices to vectors. For $\mathbf{e} \in \mathbb{Z}^\ell$ and $d \in \mathbb{Z}$ we say $\mathbf{e} \leq_p d$ if for every $\mathbf{f} \leq_p \mathbf{e}$ we have $\sum_{i \in [\ell]} f_i \leq_p d$. (This notion corresponds to the support of $(1 + \sum_{i=1}^\ell x_i)^d$: $\mathbf{x}^\mathbf{e}$ appears with a non-zero coefficient only if $\mathbf{e} \leq_p d$.) Extending to matrices and vectors, $\mathbf{A} \in \mathbb{Z}^{n \times \ell}$ with rows $(\mathbf{A})_j \in \mathbb{Z}^\ell$ and $\mathbf{d} = \langle d_1, \ldots, d_n \rangle \in \mathbb{Z}^n$ we say $\mathbf{A} \leq_p \mathbf{d}$ if $(\mathbf{A})_j \leq_p d_j$ for every $j \in [n]$.

Finally, we need one more piece of notation before defining the degree sets of multivariate lifts. For matrix $\mathbf{A} \in \mathbb{Z}^{n \times \ell}$, let $\Sigma(\mathbf{A}) \in \mathbb{Z}^\ell$ denote its row sum given by $\Sigma(\mathbf{A})_j = \sum_{i=1}^n (\mathbf{A})_{ij}$.

We are now ready to define the lifts of multivariate degree sets.

DEFINITION 2.7 (DEGREE SETS OF LIFTS). *For a set* $D \subseteq \{0, \ldots, Q-1\}^t$, *its* m*th lift, denoted* $\text{Lift}_m(D)$, *is the set of* $\mathbf{d} \in \{0, \ldots, Q-1\}^m$ *such that, for all* $\mathbf{E} \in \mathbb{Z}^{m \times t} \leq_p \mathbf{d}$, *we have* $\Sigma(\mathbf{E}) \pmod{^* Q} \in D$.

The following proposition is the multivariate analog of Proposition 2.6.

PROPOSITION 2.8. *For every linear affine-invariant code* $\mathcal{F} \subseteq \{\mathbb{F}_Q^t \to \mathbb{F}_q\}$, *and for every* $m \geq t$, *we have*

$$\underset{m}{\text{Lift}}(\text{Deg}(\mathcal{F})) = \text{Deg}(\underset{m}{\text{Lift}}(\mathcal{F})).$$

The definition of $\text{Lift}_m(D)$ is somewhat cumbersome and not easy to work with. However in the upcoming sections we will try to gain some combinatorial insights about it to derive bounds on the dimension of the codes of interest.

Finally, before concluding we mention explicitly the locality properties of lifted codes. We start with a simple observation.

PROPOSITION 2.9. *Let* $\mathcal{F} \subsetneq \{\mathbb{F}_Q^m \to \mathbb{F}_q\}$ *be a linear affine-invariant code. The* $\delta(\mathcal{F}) \geq 2 \cdot Q^{-m}$.

PROPOSITION 2.10. *Let* $\mathcal{F} \subsetneq \{\mathbb{F}_Q^t \to \mathbb{F}_q\}$ *be a linear affine-invariant code. Let* $\mathcal{L} = \text{Lift}_m(\mathcal{F})$ *be its* m*-ary lift. Then* $\mathcal{L}$ *is a* $(Q^t - 1, \frac{1}{3}Q^{-t})$*-LCC and a* $(Q^t, \Omega(Q^{-2t}), Q^{-t})$*-LTC.*

3. CONSTRUCTIONS

3.1 Codes of constant locality

In this section we prove Theorem 1.2 which promised binary codes of locality k and length N with dimension $\Omega_k(\log N)^{k-2}$.

The Code.

Fix $k = Q = 2^\ell$ and $N = 2^{m\ell}$. Let $\mathcal{F}_1 \subseteq \{\mathbb{F}_Q \to \mathbb{F}_2\}$ be the code given by $\{f : \mathbb{F}_Q \to \mathbb{F}_2 \mid \sum_{\alpha \in \mathbb{F}_Q} f(\alpha) = 0\}$. Let $\mathcal{L}_1 = \text{Lift}_m(\mathcal{F}_1)$. In what follows we verify that $\mathcal{L}_1$ has the properties claimed in Theorem 1.2.

We start with some obvious aspects.

PROPOSITION 3.1. $\mathcal{L}_1$ *is a binary code of length* N *and a* $(k-1, k^{-1}/3)$*-LCC and a* $(k, \Omega(k^{-2}), k^{-1})$*-LTC.*

PROOF. The length is immediate from the construction. The local correctability and testability follow from Proposition 2.10. □

The main aspect to be verified is the dimension of $\mathcal{L}_1$. We first describe the degree set of $\mathcal{F}_1$.

CLAIM 3.2. $\text{Deg}(\mathcal{F}_1) = \{0, \ldots, Q-2\}$.

PROOF. Write $f : \mathbb{F}_Q \to \mathbb{F}_2$ as $f(x) = \sum_{d=0}^{Q-1} f_d x^d$. Then $\sum_{\alpha \in \mathbb{F}_Q} f(\alpha) = \sum_{\alpha \in \mathbb{F}_Q} \sum_{d=0}^{Q-1} f_d \alpha^d = \sum_{d=0}^{Q-1} f_d \left(\sum_{\alpha \in \mathbb{F}_Q} \alpha^d\right) = -f_{Q-1}$ where we have used the fact that $\sum_{\alpha \in \mathbb{F}_Q} \alpha^d = -1$ if $d = Q-1$ and is equal to 1 otherwise. Therefore $f \in \mathcal{F}_1$ if and only if $\deg(f) < Q-1$. □

Remark: Note that the proof above applies without change to the case of the range being $\mathbb{F}_q$, for any q, provided $\mathbb{F}_Q$ extends $\mathbb{F}_q$.

The next claim interprets the definition of $\text{Lift}_m(D)$ in our setting.

CLAIM 3.3. *$\mathbf{d} \in \{0, \ldots, Q-1\}^m$ is contained in $\text{Deg}(\mathcal{L}_1)$ if and only if for every $\mathbf{e} \leq_2 \mathbf{d}$ we have $\sum_{i=1}^m e_i \pmod{^*\, Q} \neq Q-1$.*

PROOF. Follows immediately by applying Proposition 2.6 to Claim 3.2. □

Given the claim, it is simple to get a lower bound on the dimension of our code.

LEMMA 3.4. *The dimension of $\mathcal{L}_1$ is at least $\binom{m}{Q-2}$.*

PROOF. For $S \subseteq [m]$ let $\mathbf{d}_S$ denote the vector that is one on coordinates from S and zero outside. It is clear that for $|S| \leq Q-2$, $\mathbf{d}_S \in \text{Lift}_m(\text{Deg}(\mathcal{F}_1))$ and there are at least $\binom{m}{Q-2}$ such sets. □

PROOF OF THEOREM 1.2. Theorem 1.2 follows Proposition 3.1 and Lemma 3.4 and plugging the values of m and Q from the construction. Specificalle we have that the dimension of the code is at least $\binom{m}{Q-2} \geq \frac{1}{k^{k-2}k!}(\log N)^{k-2}$. So the theorem follows for $c_k = \frac{1}{k^{k-2}k!}$. □

3.2 Codes of sublinear locality

Next we turn to Theorem 1.3, which asserts the existence of codes of locality N^ϵ with dimension $N - N^{1-\epsilon'}$.

The Code.

Given $\epsilon > 0$ and prime p, let $m = \lceil 1/\epsilon \rceil$. Let ℓ be an integer such that $p^{m\ell} \geq N$. Let $Q = p^\ell$. Let $\mathcal{F}_2 \subseteq \{\mathbb{F}_Q \to \mathbb{F}_p\}$ be the code $\{f : \mathbb{F}_Q \to \mathbb{F}_p \mid \sum_{\alpha \in \mathbb{F}_Q} f(\alpha) = 0\}$. Let $\mathcal{L}_2 = \text{Lift}_m(\mathcal{F}_2)$.

As usual we get the following proposition.

PROPOSITION 3.5. *$\mathcal{F}_2$ is a p-ary code of length at least N and locality at most N^ϵ. Specifically it is a $(N^\epsilon, \Omega(N^{-\epsilon}))$-LCC and a $(N^\epsilon, \Omega(N^{-2\epsilon}), N^{-\epsilon})$-LTC.*

We now turn to the task of analyzing the dimension of this code. We first describe the degree sets of $\mathcal{F}_2$ and $\mathcal{L}_2$.

CLAIM 3.6. $\text{Deg}(\mathcal{F}_2) = \{0, \ldots, Q-2\}$. *Moreover, $\mathbf{d} \in \{0, \ldots, Q-1\}^m$ is in $\text{Deg}(\mathcal{L}_2)$ if and only if,] for all $\mathbf{e} \leq_p \mathbf{d}$ we have $\sum_i e_i \pmod{^*\, Q} \neq Q-1$.*

PROOF. The first part follows from the proof of Claim 3.2 (see the remark following the proof). The second part follows immediately from Proposition 2.8. □

LEMMA 3.7. *The dimension of $\mathcal{L}_2$ is at least $N - N^{1-\epsilon'}$ for some $\epsilon' = \Omega(2^{-2/\epsilon})$.*

PROOF. Let $D = \text{Deg}(\mathcal{F}_2)$. Let $\mathbf{e} = \langle e_1, \ldots, e_m \rangle$ and $e_i^{(0)}, e_i^{(1)}, \ldots, e_i^{(\ell-1)}$ denote the p-ary expansion of e_i.

CLAIM 3.8. *If there exists integer $s \in \{0, \ldots, \ell-1\}$ such that for every $i \in [m]$ and every $j \in [1 + \lceil \log m \rceil]$ we have $e_i^{(s+j \pmod{\ell})} = 0$, then $\mathbf{e} \in \text{Lift}_m(D)$.*

PROOF. Recall, by Proposition 2.4 that $\mathbf{e} \in \text{Lift}_m(D)$ if and only if $\mathbf{e}' \in D$ for every $\mathbf{e}'$ that is a p-shift of $\mathbf{e}$. Thus without loss of generality we can assume (by shifting $\mathbf{e}$ appropriately), that the block of zeroes are the most significant digits in the e_i's. (i.e., $s = \ell - \lceil \log m \rceil - 2$.)

With this assumption, we now have $e_i < p^{\ell - \log m - 1} < Q/(pm) < (Q-1)/m$. We thus conclude that for every $\mathbf{f} \leq_2 \mathbf{e}$, $\sum_{i=1}^m f_i \leq \sum_{i=1}^m e_i < Q-1$ and so (by Claim 3.6) $\mathbf{e} \in \text{Lift}_m(D)$. □

The lemma follows by an easy counting argument. Let $t = 1 + \lceil \log m \rceil$. We partition the set $[\ell]$ into ℓ/t blocks of t successive integers each. For each such block the number of possible assignments of digits that do not make the entire block zero in each e_i is $p^{mt} - 1$. Thus the total number of vectors $\mathbf{e}$ that do not have any of these blocks set to zero is $(p^{mt} - 1)^{\ell/t} = p^{m\ell}(1 - p^{-mt})^{\ell/t} \approx p^{m\ell} e^{\ell/(tp^{mt})} = p^{m\ell(1 - \Omega(1/mtp^{mt}))} = N^{1-\epsilon'}$ for $\epsilon' = 1/(mtp^{mt})$. Recalling that $\epsilon = 1/m$, we have $\epsilon' = \Omega(p^{-2/\epsilon})$. The lemma follows by noting that if $\mathbf{e} \notin \text{Lift}_m(D)$ then in each of these blocks it must be non-zero somewhere (by Claim 3.8 above).

PROOF OF THEOREM 1.3. Theorem 1.3 follows immediately from Proposition 3.5 and Lemma 3.7. □

3.3 Codes of linear locality

Finally, we prove Theorem 1.4, which claims codes of locality ϵN with dimension $N - \text{poly}\log N$. This construction is different from the previous two in that here we lift a multivariate code, whereas in both previous constructions we lifted univariate codes.

The Code.

Let $\ell = \lceil \log 1/\epsilon \rceil$ (so that $2^{-\ell} \leq \epsilon$). Let $Q = 2^\ell$. For integer m let $N = 2^{m\ell}$ and let $t = m-1$. Let $\mathcal{F}_3 \subseteq \{\mathbb{F}_Q^t \to \mathbb{F}_2\}$ be given by $\mathcal{F}_3 = \{f : \mathbb{F}_Q^t \to \mathbb{F}_2 \mid \sum_{\alpha \in \mathbb{F}_Q^t} f(\alpha) = 0\}$. Let $\mathcal{L}_3 = \text{Lift}_m(\mathcal{F}_3)$.

PROPOSITION 3.9. *$\mathcal{L}_3$ is a code of block length N with locality ϵN. Specifically, it is a $(\epsilon N, \frac{1}{3}(\epsilon N)^{-1})$-LCC and a $(\epsilon N, (\epsilon N) - 2, (\epsilon N)^{-1})$-LTC.*

The proposition below asserts that every degree except the vector that is $Q-1$ in every coordinate is in the degree set of $\mathcal{F}_3$. (Here $(Q-1)^t$ denotes the t-tuple all of whose entries is $Q-1$, rather than $(Q-1)$ exponentiated to the t-th power).

PROPOSITION 3.10. $\text{Deg}(\mathcal{F}_3) = \{0, \ldots, Q-1\}^t - \{(Q-1)^t\}$.

PROOF. Write $f : \mathbb{F}_Q^t \to \mathbb{F}_2$ as $f(\mathbf{x}) = \sum_{\mathbf{d} \in \{0, \ldots, Q-1\}^t} f_{\mathbf{d}} \mathbf{x}^{\mathbf{d}}$. Then $\sum_{\alpha \in \mathbb{F}_Q^t} f(\alpha) = \sum_{\alpha \in \mathbb{F}_Q^t} \sum_{\mathbf{d}} f_{\mathbf{d}} \mathbf{x}^{\mathbf{d}} = \sum_{\mathbf{d}} f_{\mathbf{d}} \left(\sum_{\alpha \in \mathbb{F}_Q^t} \alpha^{\mathbf{d}}\right) =$

$\sum_{\mathbf{d}} f_{\mathbf{d}} \prod_{i=1}^{t} \left(\sum_{\alpha \in \mathbb{F}_Q} \alpha^{d_i}\right) = (-1)^t f_{(Q-1)^t}$ where we have used the fact that $\sum_{\alpha \in \mathbb{F}_Q} \alpha^d = -1$ if $d = Q-1$ and is equal to 0 otherwise. Therefore $f \in \mathcal{F}_3$ if and only if $f_{(Q-1)^t} = 0$. □

While in general degree sets of lifts of multivariate families are not easy to characterize, in this particular case we have a clean characterization of the degree set.

Given $\mathbf{e} = \langle e_1, \ldots, e_m \rangle$ let $e_i^{(j)}$ denote the jth bit in the binary expansion of e_i. Let $M(\mathbf{e})$ denote the $m \times \ell$ matrix with entries $M(\mathbf{e})_{i,j} = e_i^{(j)}$.

LEMMA 3.11. *$\mathbf{e} \in \mathrm{Lift}_m(\mathrm{Deg}(\mathcal{F}_3))$ if and only if there exists a column in $M(\mathbf{e})$ with at least two zeroes.*

PROOF. As in the proof of Lemma 3.7 we have that $\mathbf{e} \in \mathrm{Lift}_m(\mathrm{Deg}(\mathcal{F}_3))$ if and only if $2\mathbf{e} \pmod{^*} Q) \in \mathrm{Lift}_m(\mathrm{Deg}(\mathcal{F}_3))$. So without loss of generality we can assume that $\mathbf{e}$ is shifted so that the two zeroes are in the most significant bits. Thus we have that $m-2$ of the e_i's, say $e_1, \ldots, e_{m-2}$, are at most $Q-1$ and the remaining two are at most $Q/2 - 1$. We thus have that $\sum_{i=1}^m e_i < (m-1)Q - 1$. Using this and applying Proposition 2.8 it is easy to verify that $\mathbf{e}$ is not in $\mathrm{Lift}_m(\mathrm{Deg}(\mathcal{F}_3))$. □

The following lemma now follows by simple counting.

LEMMA 3.12. *The dimension of $\mathcal{L}_3$ is $2^{m\ell} - (m+1)^\ell$.*

PROOF OF THEOREM 1.4. Follows by plugging in the values for the parameters, specifically by setting $\ell = \log 1/\epsilon$ and $m = (\log N / \log 1/\epsilon)$. We get that the dimension of $\mathcal{L}_3$ is $N - (1 + \log N / \log 1/\epsilon)^{\log 1/\epsilon}$. □

We remark that the construction in [5] is very close in parameters. In their construction (i.e., the Reed-Muller codes) the matrix $M(\mathbf{e})$ must have at least $\ell + 1$ zeroes. Since any such matrix must have two zeroes in a single column it follows that every matrix their construction admits is also admissible in ours, while our allow for other matrices also. However the difference between the length and dimension is at most a constant factor (depending on ℓ). (More precisely, the dimension of their code is $2^{m\ell} - \sum_{i=0}^{\ell} \binom{m\ell}{i} \approx 2^{m\ell} - (em)^\ell$.) Of course, for their application the code needs to have much better local testability than given here. But the local testability given here is just what follows immediately from the definition and previous works, and it is quite possible that better bounds can be achieved by more careful examination of this code.

3.4 High-rate high-error LCCs

Finally, we prove Theorem 1.5. This construction is a departure from the others in that the code is not binary, and the code being lifted is not the parity check code. Finally the decoding algorithm is a bit more complex to explain, though even this algorithm is by now folklore.

The code itself is a generalization of the classical multivariate polynomial code. Here we consider the set of all functions $f : \mathbb{F}_q^m \to \mathbb{F}_q$ such that the restriction of f to any line has degree d. As is well known, every multivariate polynomial of degree at most d is such a function. The remarkable fact is that if q has small characteristic, then there are many more such functions.

The Code.

Recall that we are given δ, ϵ and some N_0 and we wish a code of length $N \geq N_0$ of dimension $(1-\epsilon)N$ and locality N^δ. Let $m = \lceil 1/\delta \rceil$ and s be such that $Q = 2^s \geq N_0^\delta$. Let $b = 1 + \lceil \log m \rceil$ and $c = \lceil b 2^{bm} \log 1/\epsilon \rceil$. Let $\gamma = 2^{-c}$ and $\tau = \gamma/6$ (so that $6\tau \leq \gamma \leq \epsilon^{-(1+\lceil \log m \rceil) 2^{m(1+\lceil \log m \rceil)}}$ and let $d = (1 - 2^{-c})Q$. Let $\mathcal{F}_4 = \{f : \mathbb{F}_Q \to \mathbb{F}_Q \mid \deg(f) \leq d\}$. Let $\mathcal{L}_4 = \mathrm{Lift}_m(\mathcal{F}_4)$. In words, it is the set of all degree m-variate functions that have degree at most d when restricted to a line.

Decoding.

The general idea for decoding $\mathcal{L}_4$ is the same as that for multivariate polynomials, and in particular the algorithm from Gemmell et al. [18].

Given $f : \mathbb{F}_Q^m \to \mathbb{F}_Q$ that is τ-close to $p \in \mathcal{L}_4$ and $\mathbf{a} \in \mathbb{F}_Q^m$, the decoding algorithm works as follows: Pick a random $\mathbf{b} \in \mathbb{F}_Q^m$ and let $h : \mathbb{F}_Q \to \mathbb{F}_Q$ be given by $h(t) = f(\mathbf{a} + t\mathbf{b})$. Compute, using a Reed-Solomon decoder (see, for instance, [19, Appendix]), a polynomial $g \in \mathbb{F}_Q[t]$ of degree at most d such that $\delta(h, g) < \gamma/2$. Output $g(0)$.

LEMMA 3.13. *$\mathcal{L}_4$ is a code of block length N with locality N^δ. Specifically, it is a $(N^\delta, \gamma/6)$-LCC.*

PROOF. Let $L = \{\mathbf{a} + t\mathbf{b} \mid t \in \mathbb{F}_Q - \{0\}\}$ be the line through $\mathbf{a}$ with slope $\mathbf{b}$. We first claim that with probability at least $2/3$, the line L contains fewer that $\gamma/2$ fraction errors (i.e., points $t \neq 0$ such $h(t) \neq p|_L(t)$).

CLAIM 3.14. *For every $\mathbf{a}$, $\Pr_{\mathbf{b}}[\delta(h, p|_L) \geq \gamma/2] < 2\tau/\gamma$.*

The above claim follows easily from an application of Markov's inequality. Next we note that if the fraction of errors on L is less than $\gamma/2$ then the decoder satisfies $g = p|_L$ and so outputs $g(0) = p|_L(0) = p(\mathbf{a})$ as desired. □

Next we turn to the analysis of the dimension of $\mathcal{L}_4$ which is similar to the analysis of $\mathcal{L}_2$. First we note the obvious fact.

PROPOSITION 3.15. $\mathrm{Deg}(\mathcal{F}_4) = \{0, \ldots, d\}$. *Moreover, $\mathbf{d} \in \{0, \ldots, Q-1\}^m$ is in $\mathrm{Deg}(\mathcal{L}_4)$ if and only if for all $\mathbf{e} \leq_2 \mathbf{d}$ we have $\sum_{i=1}^m e_i \pmod{^*} Q) \in \{0, \ldots, d\}$.*

LEMMA 3.16. *The dimension of $\mathcal{L}_4$ is at least $(1-\epsilon)N$.*

PROOF. For non-negative integer b, let $b^{(j)}$ denote its binary expansion so that $b = \sum_j b^{(j)} 2^j$. Recall $d = (1 - 2^{-c})Q$. Letting $d^{(j)}$ denoting its binary expansion, we note an integer $e \in \{0, \ldots, Q-1\}$ is at most d if (and only if) one of the bits $e^{(s-c)}, \ldots, e^{(s-1)}$ is zero. We use this to reason about $\mathrm{Deg}(\mathcal{L}_4)$.

Let $\mathbf{d} = \langle d_1, \ldots, d_m \rangle$ and let $d_i^{(j)}$ denote the jth bit in the binary expansion of d_i.

CLAIM 3.17. *Let $b = 1 + \lceil \log m \rceil$. If there exists $j \in \{s-c, \ldots, s-b\}$ such that for every $i \in [m]$ and every $\ell \in \{0, \ldots, b-1\}$ we have $d_i^{(j+\ell)} = 0$, then $\mathbf{d} \in \mathrm{Deg}(\mathcal{L}_4)$.*

PROOF. Let $\mathbf{e} = \langle e_1, \ldots, e_m \rangle \leq_2 \mathbf{d}$ and let $e = \sum_{i=1}^m e_i \pmod{^*} Q)$. We claim that $e^{(j+b-1)} = 0$, which suffices to show that $e \leq d$. Let $\bar{e}_i = 2^{s-(j+b)} e_i \pmod{^*} Q)$ for all $i \in [m]$, and let $\bar{e} = \sum_{i=1}^m \bar{e}_i \pmod{^*} Q)$. For every $i \in [m]$ and every

$k \in [s]$, $e_i^{(k)} = \overline{e}_i^{(k+s-(j+b) \pmod s)}$ and similarly $e^{(k)} = \overline{e}^{(k+s-(j+b) \pmod s)}$. Therefore it suffices to show that $\overline{e}^{(s-1)} = 0$ or equivalently $\overline{e} < 2^{s-1}$. By our assumption on $\mathbf{d}$, $e_i^{(j+\ell)} = 0$ for all $\ell \in \{0, \ldots, b-1\}$, so $\overline{e}_i^{(k)} = 0$ for all $k \in \{s-b, \ldots, s-1\}$ and thus $\overline{e}_i < 2^{s-b}$ for all $i \in [m]$. By our choice of b, $m \le 2^{b-1}$, and thus $\sum_{i=1}^{m} \overline{e}_i < m2^{s-b} \le 2^{s-1}$. □

We now consider picking $\mathbf{d}$ at random. By partitioning the c most significant bits into disjoint blocks of b bits each, we get that any such block is all zero with probability at least 2^{-mb}. Thus the probability there exists a block which is all zero is at least $1-(1-2^{-mb})^{c/b} \ge 1-e^{-c/(b2^{mb})}$. By choice of c we have that $c/(b2^{mb}) \ge \ln(1/\epsilon)$ and so $e^{-c/(b2^{mb})} \le \epsilon$ and thus the dimension is lower bounded by $(1-\epsilon)N$.

Proof of Theorem 1.5. Follows immediately from Lemmas 3.13 and 3.16. □

We remark that the construction of this section is somewhat contrary to folk belief, which tends to suggest that generalized Reed-Muller codes (evaluations of m-variate polynomials of degree at most d) are equivalently defined by requiring that their restriction to lines are Reed-Solomon codewords (evaluations of univariate degree d polynomials). As pointed out earlier this folk statement is true only with some restrictions on d and Q, and our construction benefits by violating the restrictions. While the fact that there exist functions that are not degree d polynomials, for $d \ge Q - Q/p$, which are degree d polynomials on every line has been known for a while [17], presumably it was suspected that the effect on the dimension of the lifted family was negligible. Fortunately for this work, this presumption turned out to be false.

We also give below an example of some concrete setting of parameters for which this construction works.

Example 3.18. *For every $N = 2^{2n}$, for $n \ge 7$, there exists a code of length N over the alphabet $\mathbb{F}_{2^n}$ of dimension $.77N$ that is decodable from 0.26% fraction errors with $\sqrt{N}$ queries*

The example is obtained by setting $c = 6$, $m = 2$ and $Q = 2^n$ in the construction. The fraction of errors is $2^{-6}/6 \approx 0.26\%$. The rate follows from the following claim.

Claim 3.19. *The dimension of the code is at least $((4^c - (5/4)3^c + 1/4)/4^c)N$.*

While the error-correction rate of the code is smaller than that in [33], it does seem to start working at much smaller lengths and with much smaller alphabet sizes.

4. NIKDOYM SETS

A *Nikodym set* $N \subseteq \mathbb{F}_q^m$ is a set such that for all $x \in \mathbb{F}_q^m$, there exists $y \in \mathbb{F}_q^m$ such that the punctured line $\{x + ty \mid t \in \mathbb{F}_q \setminus \{0\}\} \subseteq N$.

The following proposition strengthens and generalizes the result usually obtained via the polynomial method [12].

Proposition 4.1. *If $\mathcal{L} \subset \{\mathbb{F}_q^m \to \mathbb{F}_q\}$ is the lift of some univariate linear affine-invariant family $\mathcal{F} \subsetneq \{\mathbb{F}_q \to \mathbb{F}_q\}$, and $N \subseteq \mathbb{F}_q^m$ is a Nikodym set, then $|N| \ge \dim \mathcal{L}$.*

Proof. Suppose for sake of contradiction that $|N| < \dim \mathcal{L}$. Then there exists nonzero $f \in \mathcal{L}$ such that $f|_N \equiv 0$. Let $x \in \mathbb{F}_q^m$. Then there is $y \in \mathbb{F}_q^m$ such that $x + ty \in N$ for every $t \in \mathbb{F}_q \setminus \{0\}$. Define $g(t) = f(x + ty)$. By definition of $\mathcal{L}$, we have $g \in \mathcal{F}$, and moreover $\mathcal{F}$ is a nontrivial, so by Proposition 2.9, either $g = 0$ or $\mathrm{wt}(g) \ge 2$. But $g(t) = 0$ for every $t \ne 0$, hence $g = 0$, and in particular $f(x) = g(0) = 0$. Since x was arbitrary, this shows that f is identically zero, a contradiction. □

We are now ready to prove Theorem 1.6.

Proof of Theorem 1.6. Follows immediately by applying Proposition 4.1 to the code $\mathcal{L}$ obtained from Theorem 1.3, i.e. the family of f taking values in $\mathbb{F}_p$ whose restrictions to lines are polynomials of degree at most $q-2$. □

For comparison, the bound obtained by the polynomial method is $\binom{m+q-2}{m} \approx q^m/m!$, which can be improved to $q^m/2^m$ using the method of multiplicities. Other work on finite field Nikodym sets by Li [34] as well as Feng, Li, and Shen [16] obtain lower bounds that beat the standard polynomial method bound for $m = 2$. In particular, [16] obtains a bound of $q^2 - q^{3/2} - q$, which is actually better than our bound for two dimensions, which is $q^2 - O(q^{\log_2 3/4})$ for characteristic two. Moreover, their bound applies to q of any characteristic. However, our bounds are the best known and the only ones achieving $q^m(1-o(1))$ for $m \ge 3$.

5. GENERAL INVESTIGATION OF LIFTING

The codes of the previous section simply picked some basic codes and lifted them to derive long codes of reasonable distance and interesting local testability and decodability. To go beyond this setting, we feel it is important to pick basic codes of possibly high distance and then lift them, and this could improve the performance of such codes. As may be observed from the previous section most of the work needed to analyze lifted codes is devoted to determining their dimension, and this can be a function of the exact code chosen. Features such as distance, decodability, and testability seem to follow more generically. In this section, we examine the simplest of these properties, namely the distance of the lifted code and prove some basic facts.

Theorem 5.1. *Let $\mathcal{F} \subseteq \{\mathbb{F}_Q^t \to \mathbb{F}_q\}$ and $\mathcal{L} = \mathrm{Lift}_m(\mathcal{F})$ for some $m \ge t$. We have the following:*

1. *$\delta(\mathcal{L}) \le \delta(\mathcal{F})$.*
2. *$\delta(\mathcal{L}) \ge \delta(\mathcal{F}) - Q^{-t}$.*
3. *If $Q \in \{2,3\}$ and $\delta(\mathcal{F}) > Q^{-t}$ then $\delta(\mathcal{L}) \ge \delta(\mathcal{F})$.*

5.1 Proof of Theorem 5.1

We divide the proof of Theorem 5.1 into several parts. We start by proving that distance does not increase under lifting (Theorem 5.1, Part 1).

Lemma 5.2. *Let $\mathcal{F} \subseteq \{\mathbb{F}_Q^t \to \mathbb{F}_q\}$ be a linear affine-invariant code with lift $\mathcal{L} = \mathrm{Lift}_m(\mathcal{F})$. Then $\delta(\mathcal{L}) \le \delta(\mathcal{F})$.*

Proof. By induction, it suffices to show the assertion for the case $m = t+1$. Let $f \in \mathcal{F}$ and let $\delta = \delta(f, 0)$. Let $\mathbf{x} = \langle x_1, \ldots, x_t \rangle$. Now consider the function $g(\mathbf{x}, y) = f(\mathbf{x})$.

Clearly we have $\delta(g,0)=\delta$. We claim that $g \in \mathcal{L}$, which completes the proof. To do so we will show that $g|_H \in \mathcal{F}$ for every t-dimensional affine subspace $H \subseteq \mathbb{F}_Q^m$. Fix such a subspace H and let $A: \mathbb{F}_Q^t \to \mathbb{F}_Q^m$ be an affine map whose image is H (such a map does exist). Note that $g|_H(\mathbf{z}) = f(A(\mathbf{z})_1, \ldots, A(\mathbf{z})_t)$. Thus if we let $A': \mathbb{F}_Q^t \to \mathbb{F}_Q^t$ be the affine map given by the projection of A to its first t coordinates, we have that $g|_H = f \circ A'$. By [23, Theorem A.1], $f \circ A' \in \mathcal{F}$ and so we have $g \in \mathcal{F}$ as claimed. (Note that we need to use [23, Theorem A.1] since A' need not be an affine permutation but it is an affine transformation.) $\square$

Next we prove Part 3 of Theorem 5.1 which asserts that the distance of non-trivial binary codes does not decrease with lifting.

LEMMA 5.3. *If $\mathcal{F} \subseteq \{\mathbb{F}_2^t \to \mathbb{F}_2\}$ has distance $\delta(\mathcal{F}) > \frac{1}{2^t}$, then $\delta(\mathrm{Lift}_m(\mathcal{F})) \geq \delta(\mathcal{F})$ for all $m \geq t$.*

We prove the above lemma by stating and proving the following stronger lemma first.

LEMMA 5.4. *For all $m \geq 2$, if $\delta > \frac{1}{2^{m-1}}$ and $f: \mathbb{F}_2^m \to \mathbb{F}_2$ such that $0 < \Pr_{x \in \mathbb{F}_2^m}[f(x) \neq 0] < \delta$, then there exists an $(m-1)$-dimensional affine subspace $H \subsetneq \mathbb{F}_2^m$ such that $0 < \Pr_{x \in H}[f(x) \neq 0] < \delta$.*

PROOF. We proceed by induction on m. The base case $m=2$ is straightforward to verify.

Now suppose $m > 2$ and our assertion holds for $m-1$. Let H_0, H_1 be the affine subspaces given by $x_m = 0$ and $x_m = 1$ respectively. Let δ_0, δ_1 denote $\delta(f|_{H_0}, 0), \delta(f|_{H_1}, 0)$ respectively. Note that $\delta > \delta(f,0) = (\delta_0 + \delta_1)/2$. If both $\delta_0, \delta_1 > 0$, then by averaging we have $0 < \delta_i < \delta$ and so $H = H_i$ does the job. Otherwise, suppose w.l.o.g. that $\delta_1 = 0$. Note that $0 < \delta_0 < 2\delta$ and $2\delta > \frac{1}{2^{m-2}}$. Thus, by the induction hypothesis, there exists an $(m-2)$-dimensional affine subspace $H_0' \subset H_0$ such that $0 < \delta(f|_{H'}, 0) < 2\delta$. Let $H_1' = \{(a_1, \ldots, a_{m-1}, 1) \in \mathbb{F}_2^m \mid (a_1, \ldots, a_{m-1}, 0) \in H_0'\}$ be the translate of H_0' in H_1, and note that $\delta(f|_{H_1'}, 0) = 0$. Let $H = H_0' \cup H_1'$. Then H is an $(m-1)$-dimensional subspace of $\mathbb{F}_2^m$ such that $0 < \delta(f|_H, 0) = (\delta(f|_{H_0'}, 0) + \delta(f|_{H_1'}, 0))/2 < \delta$. $\square$

PROOF OF LEMMA 5.3. We prove the lemma by induction on $m-t$. Indeed the inductive step is straightforward since $\mathrm{Lift}_m(\mathcal{F}) = \mathrm{Lift}_m(\mathrm{Lift}_{m-1}(\mathcal{F}))$ and by induction both lifts on the RHS have smaller value of $m-t$ and so the distance does not reduce in either step. The main case is thus the base case with $m = t+1$.

Suppose $f \in \mathrm{Lift}_m(\mathcal{F}) \subsetneq \{\mathbb{F}_2^m \to \mathbb{F}_2\}$ such that $0 < \delta(f,0) < \delta(\mathcal{F})$. By Lemma 5.4, there exists an $(m-1)$-dimensional affine subspace $H \subset \mathbb{F}_2^m$ such that $0 < \delta(f|_H, 0) \leq \delta(f,0) < \delta$, contradicting the fact that $f|_H \in \mathcal{F}$. $\square$

A similar approach works for $q=3$, thus we have the following.

LEMMA 5.5. *If $\mathcal{F} \subseteq \{\mathbb{F}_3^t \to \mathbb{F}_3\}$ has distance $\delta(\mathcal{F}) > \frac{1}{3^t}$, then $\delta(\mathrm{Lift}_m(\mathcal{F})) \geq \delta(\mathcal{F})$ for all $m \geq t$.*

Again, we prove this by stating and proving the following analogue of Lemma 5.4.

LEMMA 5.6. *For all $m \geq 2$, if $f: \mathbb{F}_3^m \to \mathbb{F}_3$ such that $\delta(f,0) \geq \frac{1}{3^{m-1}}$, then there exists an $(m-1)$-dimensional affine subspace $H \subset \mathbb{F}_3^m$ such that $0 < \delta(f|_H, 0) \leq \delta(f,0)$.*

PROOF. Let $\delta = \delta(f,0)$. We proceed by induction on m. For the base case $m=2$, $\delta \geq \frac{1}{3}$. Suppose $f = f(x,y)$ and consider $f|_{y=i}$ for $i \in \mathbb{F}_3$. If $f|_{y=i}$ is not identically zero for all $i \in \mathbb{F}_3$, then by averaging there is some $i \in \mathbb{F}_3$ for which $0 < \Pr_{x \in \mathbb{F}_3}[f(x,i) \neq 0] \leq \delta$. Otherwise, w.l.o.g. suppose $f|_{y=2} \equiv 0$. Further, w.l.o.g. suppose $f|_{y=0} \not\equiv 0$ and $f(0,0) \neq 0$. Now, if $\delta \geq \frac{2}{3}$, then the line $H = \{(x,y) \in \mathbb{F}_3^2 \mid x = 0\}$ does the job, since $0 < \Pr_{y \in \mathbb{F}_3}[f(0,y) \neq 0] \leq \frac{2}{3} \leq \delta$. If $\delta < \frac{2}{3}$, then there must exist some $a, b \in \mathbb{F}_3$ and $c \in \{0,1\}$ such that $f(a,c) \neq 0$ and $f(b, 1-c) = 0$. Then the line $H = \{(a,c), (b, 1-c), (2b-a, 2)\}$ does the job, since $0 < \Pr_{(x,y) \in H}[f(x,y) \neq 0] = \frac{1}{3} \leq \delta$.

Now suppose $m > 2$ and the assertion holds for $m-1$. For $i \in \mathbb{F}_3$, let H_i be the hyperplane cut out by $x_m = i$ and let $\delta_i = \delta(f|_{H_i}, 0)$. Then $\delta_1 + \delta_2 + \delta_3 = 3\delta$. If $\delta_i > 0$ for all $i \in \mathbb{F}_3$, then by simple averaging for some $i \in \mathbb{F}_3$ we have $0 < \delta_i \leq \delta$, so assume w.l.o.g. $\delta_2 = 0$ and $\delta_0 \geq \delta_1$. First suppose $\delta_0 \geq \frac{1}{3^{m-2}}$. Then, by the inductive hypothesis, there exists an $(m-2)$-dimensional affine subspace $H \subset H_0$ such that $0 < \delta(f|_H, 0) \leq \delta_1$. Let $H^{(0)}$ be defined by the linear equations $\sum_{i=1}^m a_i x_i - a_0 = 0$ and $x_m = 0$ for some $\langle a_0, \ldots, a_m \rangle \in \mathbb{F}_3^{m+1}$. For each $i, j \in \mathbb{F}_3$, let $H^{(i)} + j \subset H_1$ denote the affine subspace defined by $\sum_{i=1}^m a_i x_i - a_0 = j$ and $x_m = i$. By averaging, for some $i \in \mathbb{F}_3$, $\delta(f|_{H^{(1)}+i}, 0) \leq \delta_2$. Take $H = H^{(0)} \cup (H^{(1)} + i) \cup (H^{(2)} + 2i)$. Then $0 < \delta(f|_H, 0) \leq \delta$. Otherwise, suppose $\frac{1}{3^{m-2}} > \delta_0$, so $\delta_0, \delta_1 \leq \frac{2}{3^{m-1}}$. There exists $H^{(0)} \subset H_0$ be an $(m-2)$-dimensional affine subspace such that $\delta(f|_{H^{(0)}}, 0) = \frac{1}{3^{m-1}}$. To see this, let $a, b \in H_0$ such that $f(a), f(b)$ are nonzero, and suppose a and b differ in the k-th coordinate. Then take $H^{(0)}$ defined by $x_k = a_k$ and $x_m = 0$. Again, for $i, j \in \mathbb{F}_3$ let $H^{(j)} + i$ be the $(m-2)$-dimensional affine subspace defined by $x_k = a_k + i$ and $x_m = j$. Since $\delta_2 \leq \frac{2}{3^{m-2}}$, there is $i \in \mathbb{F}_3$ such that $f|_{H^{(1)}+i} \equiv 0$. Then, taking $H = H^{(0)} \cup (H^{(1)} + i) \cup (H^{(2)} + 2i)$, we have $0 < \delta(f|_H, 0) = \frac{1}{3^{m-1}} \leq \delta$. $\square$

PROOF OF LEMMA 5.5. We prove the lemma by induction on $m-t$. The inductive step is straightforward since $\mathrm{Lift}_m(\mathcal{F}) = \mathrm{Lift}_m(\mathrm{Lift}_{m-1}(\mathcal{F}))$ and by induction both lifts on the RHS have smaller value of $m-t$ and so the distance does not reduce in either step. The main case is thus the base case with $m = t+1$.

Suppose $f \in \mathrm{Lift}_m(\mathcal{F}) \subsetneq \{\mathbb{F}_3^m \to \mathbb{F}_3\}$ such that $0 < \delta(f,0) < \delta(\mathcal{F})$. If $\delta(f,0) \geq \frac{1}{3^{m-1}}$, then, by Lemma 5.6, there exists an $(m-1)$-dimensional affine subspace $H \subset \mathbb{F}_3^m$ such that $0 < \delta(f|_H, 0) \leq \delta(f,0) < \delta(\mathcal{F})$, contradicting the fact that $f|_H \in \mathcal{F}$. If $\delta(f,0) < \frac{1}{3^{m-1}}$, then there are at most two points $a, b \in \mathbb{F}_3^m$ such that $f(a), f(b)$ are nonzero. Let $i \in [m]$ such that $a_i \neq b_i$ and let H be the hyperplane defined by $x_i = a_i$. Then $f|_H$ is nonzero only on a, so $0 < \delta(f|_H) = \frac{1}{3^{m-1}} < \delta(\mathcal{F})$, again contradicting the fact that $f|_H \in \mathcal{F}$. $\square$

For general $q > 3$, we have the following.

LEMMA 5.7. *If $\mathcal{F} \subseteq \{\mathbb{F}_Q^t \to \mathbb{F}_q\}$ has distance $\delta(\mathcal{F}) = \delta$, then $\delta(\mathrm{Lift}_m(\mathcal{F})) > \delta - \frac{1-\delta}{Q^t - 1}$.*

PROOF. Fix a non-zero $f \in \mathrm{Lift}_m(\mathcal{F})$ and let $\tau = \delta(f,0)$. Fix $a \in \mathbb{F}_Q^m$ such that $f(a) \neq 0$. Now let A be a t-dimensional affine subspace containing a chosen uniformly at random from all such subspaces. Let $X(A) = |\{x \in A \mid f(x) \neq 0\}|$ be the random variable denoting the number of non-zero points of f on A. Since A samples every point of $\mathbb{F}_Q^n - \{a\}$ uniformly, we have

$$\mathbb{E}_A[X(A)] = 1 + \frac{\tau Q^m - 1}{Q^m - 1}(Q^t - 1) < 1 + \tau(Q^t - 1).$$

Therefore there must exist a t-dimensional subspace A containing a with $X(A) < \tau(Q^t - 1) + 1$. Since $f|_A$ is a non-zero function in $\mathcal{F}$, we have $\tau(Q^t - 1) + 1 \geq \delta Q^t$ and thus we conclude that $\tau \geq \delta - \frac{1-\delta}{Q^t - 1}$. In other words every non-zero function in $\mathcal{F}$ is non-zero on $\delta - \frac{1-\delta}{Q^t-1}$ fraction of the points, as asserted. □

Finally we mention examples which show that, in some senses the gaps in Theorem 5.1, Parts 2 and 3 are inherent.

First note that if $\mathcal{F} = \{F_Q^t \to \mathbb{F}_q\}$ then $\text{Lift}_m(\mathcal{F}) = \{\mathbb{F}_Q^m \to \mathbb{F}_q\}$ whose distance is Q^{-m}, and so some loss in the distance is inherent in Part 2 of Theorem 5.1. However, one could hope that if $\mathcal{F} \subsetneq \{F_Q^t \to \mathbb{F}_q\}$ then its distance is preserved by lifting (as in Part 3 of Theorem 5.1). Unfortunately (actually fortunately, since this is where the rate improvement of codes in Theorem 1.2 comes from) even this hope is not true. If one takes $\mathcal{F}$ to be the binary code with degree set being all weight one integers, then its lift contains all the weight one integers as well as some integers of weight greater than one. The code consisting of only weight one integers in its degree set has distance exactly 1/2 while codes that have rate greater than these must have distance strictly smaller than 1/2 (by the Plotkin bound). This suggests that distances can reduce under lifts. A search reveals that the code $\mathcal{F} \subseteq \{\mathbb{F}_4 \to \mathbb{F}_2\}$ with degree set $\text{Deg}(\mathcal{F}) = \{0, 1, 2\}$ has distance 1/2 while its lift $\mathcal{L} = \text{Lift}_2(\mathcal{F})$ has distance 3/8.

Acknowledgments

We would like to thank Sergey Yekhanin for introducing us to the projective space codes which led to the parameter settings of Section 3.2. We would like to thank Elad Haramaty for clarifying discussions on the relationship between the definition of lifting in [6] and in this work. The first author was supported supported in part by NSF grants CCF-0829672, CCF-1065125, CCF-6922462, and an NSF Graduate Research Fellowship.

6. REFERENCES

[1] Noga Alon, Tali Kaufman, Michael Krivelevich, Simon Litsyn, and Dana Ron. Testing Reed-Muller codes. *IEEE Transactions on Information Theory*, 51(11):4032–4039, 2005.

[2] Sanjeev Arora and Boaz Barak. *Computational Complexity: A Modern Approach.* Cambridge, 2009.

[3] Sanjeev Arora, Carsten Lund, Rajeev Motwani, Madhu Sudan, and Mario Szegedy. Proof verification and the hardness of approximation problems. *Journal of the ACM*, 45(3):501–555, May 1998.

[4] Sanjeev Arora and Madhu Sudan. Improved low degree testing and its applications. *Combinatorica*, 23(3):365–426, 2003. Preliminary version in Proceedings of ACM STOC 1997.

[5] Boaz Barak, Parikshit Gopalan, Johan Håstad, Raghu Meka, Prasad Raghavendra, and David Steurer. Making the long code shorter, with applications to the unique games conjecture. *CoRR*, abs/1111.0405, 2011.

[6] Eli Ben-Sasson, Elena Grigorescu, Ghid Maatouk, Amir Shpilka, and Madhu Sudan. On sums of locally testable affine invariant properties. *Electronic Colloquium on Computational Complexity (ECCC)*, 18:79, 2011.

[7] Eli Ben-Sasson, Ghid Maatouk, Amir Shpilka, and Madhu Sudan. Symmetric LDPC codes are not necessarily locally testable. In *IEEE Conference on Computational Complexity*, pages 55–65. IEEE Computer Society, 2011.

[8] Eli Ben-Sasson, Noga Ron-Zewi, and Madhu Sudan. Sparse affine-invariant linear codes are locally testable. *Electronic Colloquium on Computational Complexity (ECCC)*, 19:49, 2012.

[9] Eli Ben-Sasson and Madhu Sudan. Limits on the rate of locally testable affine-invariant codes. *Electronic Colloquium on Computational Complexity (ECCC)*, 17:108, 2010.

[10] Arnab Bhattacharyya, Swastik Kopparty, Grant Schoenebeck, Madhu Sudan, and David Zuckerman. Optimal testing of Reed-Muller codes. In *FOCS*, pages 488–497. IEEE Computer Society, 2010.

[11] Pier Vittorio Ceccherini and J. W. P. Hirschfeld. The dimension of projective geometry codes. *Discrete Mathematics*, 106-107:117–126, 1992.

[12] Zeev Dvir. On the size of Kakeya sets in finite fields. *Journal of the American Mathematical Society*, (to appear), 2008. Article electronically published on June 23, 2008.

[13] Zeev Dvir, Swastik Kopparty, Shubhangi Saraf, and Madhu Sudan. Extensions to the method of multiplicities, with applications to kakeya sets and mergers. In *FOCS*, pages 181–190. IEEE Computer Society, 2009.

[14] Zeev Dvir and Amir Shpilka. An improved analysis of linear mergers. *Computational Complexity*, 16(1):34–59, 2007.

[15] Zeev Dvir and Avi Wigderson. Kakeya sets, new mergers, and old extractors. *SIAM J. Comput.*, 40(3):778–792, 2011.

[16] Chunrong Feng, Liangpan Li, and Jian Shen. Some inequalities in functional analysis, combinatorics, and probability theory. *Electr. J. Comb.*, 17(1), 2010.

[17] Katalin Friedl and Madhu Sudan. Some improvements to total degree tests. In *Proceedings of the 3rd Annual Israel Symposium on Theory of Computing and Systems*, pages 190–198, Washington, DC, USA, 4-6 January 1995. IEEE Computer Society. Corrected version available online at `http://people.csail.mit.edu/madhu/papers/friedl.ps`.

[18] Peter Gemmell, Richard Lipton, Ronitt Rubinfeld, Madhu Sudan, and Avi Wigderson. Self-testing/correcting for polynomials and for approximate functions. In *Proceedings of the Twenty Third Annual ACM Symposium on Theory of Computing*, pages 32–42, New Orleans, Louisiana, 6-8 May 1991.

[19] Peter Gemmell and Madhu Sudan. Highly resilient correctors for multivariate polynomials. *Information Processing Letters*, 43(4):169–174, September 1992.

[20] Oded Goldreich and Tali Kaufman. Proximity oblivious testing and the role of invariances. *Electronic*

Colloquium on Computational Complexity (ECCC), 17:58, 2010.

[21] Elena Grigorescu, Tali Kaufman, and Madhu Sudan. 2-transitivity is insufficient for local testability. In *IEEE Conference on Computational Complexity*, pages 259–267, 2008.

[22] Elena Grigorescu, Tali Kaufman, and Madhu Sudan. Succinct representation of codes with applications to testing. In *Proceedings of RANDOM-APPROX 2009*, volume 5687 of *Lecture Notes in Computer Science*, pages 534–547. Springer, 2009.

[23] Alan Guo, Swastik Kopparty, and Madhu Sudan. New affine-invariant codes from lifting. *CoRR*, abs/1208.5413v2, 2012. Also appears as *ECCC TR 12-149*.

[24] Alan Guo and Madhu Sudan. Some closure features of locally testable affine-invariant properties. *Electronic Colloquium on Computational Complexity (ECCC)*, 19:48, 2012.

[25] Elad Haramaty, Noga Ron-Zewi, and Madhu Sudan. Absolutely sound testing of lifted codes. Manuscript, November 2012.

[26] Elad Haramaty, Amir Shpilka, and Madhu Sudan. Optimal testing of multivariate polynomials over small prime fields. In Rafail Ostrovsky, editor, *IEEE 52nd Annual Symposium on Foundations of Computer Science, FOCS 2011, Palm Springs, CA, USA, October 22-25, 2011*, pages 629–637. IEEE, 2011.

[27] Charanjit S. Jutla, Anindya C. Patthak, Atri Rudra, and David Zuckerman. Testing low-degree polynomials over prime fields. *Random Struct. Algorithms*, 35(2):163–193, 2009.

[28] Tali Kaufman and Shachar Lovett. Testing of exponentially large codes, by a new extension to weil bound for character sums. *Electronic Colloquium on Computational Complexity (ECCC)*, 17:65, 2010.

[29] Tali Kaufman and Alexander Lubotzky. Edge transitive ramanujan graphs and symmetric ldpc good codes. In Howard J. Karloff and Toniann Pitassi, editors, *STOC*, pages 359–366. ACM, 2012.

[30] Tali Kaufman and Dana Ron. Testing polynomials over general fields. *SIAM Journal of Computing*, 36(3):779–802, 2006.

[31] Tali Kaufman and Madhu Sudan. Algebraic property testing: The role of invariance. *Electronic Colloquium on Computational Complexity (ECCC)*, 14(111), 2007.

[32] Tali Kaufman and Avi Wigderson. Symmetric LDPC codes and local testing. In Andrew Chi-Chih Yao, editor, *ICS*, pages 406–421. Tsinghua University Press, 2010.

[33] Swastik Kopparty, Shubhangi Saraf, and Sergey Yekhanin. High-rate codes with sublinear-time decoding. In Lance Fortnow and Salil P. Vadhan, editors, *STOC*, pages 167–176. ACM, 2011.

[34] Liangpan Li. On the size of Nikodym sets in finite fields. *ArXiv e-prints*, March 2008.

[35] Ran Raz and Shmuel Safra. A sub-constant error-probability low-degree test, and a sub-constant error-probability PCP characterization of NP. In *Proceedings of the Twenty-Ninth Annual ACM Symposium on Theory of Computing*, pages 475–484, New York, NY, 1997. ACM Press.

[36] Ronitt Rubinfeld and Madhu Sudan. Robust characterizations of polynomials with applications to program testing. *SIAM Journal on Computing*, 25(2):252–271, April 1996.

[37] Shubhangi Saraf and Madhu Sudan. Improved lower bound on the size of Kakeya sets over finite fields. *ArXiv e-prints*, August 2008.

[38] K.J.C. Smith. On the p-rank of the incidence matrix of points and hyperplanes in a finite projective geometry. *Journal of Combinatorial Theory*, 7(2):122–129, 1969.

[39] Sergey Yekhanin. Personal communication, April 2011.

H-wise Independence

Ishay Haviv
School of Computer Science
The Academic College of Tel Aviv-Yaffo
Tel Aviv 61083, Israel

Michael Langberg*
Dept. of Mathematics and Computer Science
The Open University of Israel
Raanana 43107, Israel

ABSTRACT

For a hypergraph H on the vertex set $\{1, \ldots, n\}$, a distribution $D = (D_1, \ldots, D_n)$ over $\{0,1\}^n$ is *H-wise independent* if every restriction of D to indices which form an edge in H is uniform. This generalizes the notion of k-wise independence obtained by taking H to be the complete n vertex k-uniform hypergraph. This generalization was studied by Schulman (STOC 1992), who presented constructions of H-wise independent distributions that are *linear*, i.e., the samples are strings of inner products (over $\mathbb{F}_2$) of a fixed set of vectors with a uniformly chosen random vector.

Let $\ell(H)$ denote the minimum possible size of a sample space of a uniform H-wise independent distribution. The ℓ parameter is well understood for the special case of k-wise independence. In this work we study the notion of H-wise independence and the ℓ parameter for general graphs and hypergraphs. For graphs, we show how the ℓ parameter relates to standard graph parameters (e.g., clique number, chromatic number, Lovász theta function, minrank). We derive algorithmic and hardness results for this parameter as well as an explicit construction of graphs G for which $\ell(G)$ is exponentially smaller than the size of the sample space of any linear G-wise independent distribution. For hypergraphs, we study the problem of testing whether a given distribution is H-wise independent, generalizing results of Alon et al. (STOC 2007).

Categories and Subject Descriptors

F.1.2 [**Theory of Computation**]: Models of Computation—*probabilistic computation*; G.2.2 [**Discrete Mathematics**]: Graph Theory

Keywords

Derandomization, k-wise independence, H-wise independence

*Work supported in part by ISF grant 480/08 and by the Open University of Israel's research fund (grant no. 46114).

1. INTRODUCTION

In the past decades, the study of randomized algorithms has become a wide and rich field of research in theoretical computer science. Whereas randomization was found useful in many algorithmic applications, many efforts were made to understand the true role of randomness in computation. In many cases, it was shown that algorithms that use randomness can be deterministically simulated, i.e., derandomized.

In general, randomized algorithms can be viewed as two-step algorithms: in the first step, a sample point, consisting of n random unbiased coins, is chosen according to the uniform distribution, and in the second step a deterministic algorithm is applied to the input and to the random coins from the first step. In many randomized algorithms the assumption that the random string of coins is chosen uniformly from all the 2^n possible random strings is not crucial for the analysis. Namely, it might suffice to take the random choice from a much smaller sample space. If it is possible to efficiently generate the elements of the smaller sample space then one can reduce the amount of randomness used by the algorithm. When the sample space is small enough, it is possible to deterministically apply the second step of the algorithm to every element in this space, and to decide according to the majority. Among other applications, this approach was found useful for derandomizing parallel algorithms, in which applying the deterministic algorithm with distinct samples can be done in parallel (see, e.g., [23, 3, 29, 30]). Therefore, research on the size of sample spaces with some randomness properties is motivated from theoretical and practical points of view.

The most fundamental type of randomness is *pairwise independence*, which means that every two coins are independent. It is well-known that a sample space of size $O(n)$ suffices in order to pick n pairwise independent unbiased coins. This was found useful in many applications, e.g., in constructions of efficient hashing schemes (for more applications see the survey of Luby and Wigderson [31]). The notion of pairwise independence is naturally generalized to k-wise independence for $k \geq 3$, in which the distribution on every induced k bit locations of the random string is uniform. It was shown by Chor et al. [13] that every uniform k-wise independent distribution over n bit strings has sample space of size $\Omega(n^{\lfloor \frac{k}{2} \rfloor})$. Alon, Babai and Itai [3] extended this lower bound to the non-uniform case and gave a construction, which is based on BCH codes, of a uniform k-wise independent distribution matching this bound. This means that k-wise independent sample spaces of size polynomial in n are only possible for constant k.

Several approaches were presented in the literature in order to overcome the lower bound of [13, 3]. One idea was to consider a sample space of non-polynomial size and to use a conditional expectation technique in order to choose a good sample (instead of iterating over all the samples). This was used in [33, 8] to prove that certain problems lie in the complexity class NC. Another approach was taken by Naor and Naor [34] who introduced the notion of *almost* k-wise independence. Here, the restriction of the samples to k coordinates should only be statistically close to a uniform distribution for some statistical distance parameter ε. It was shown in [34] (see also [4]) that the size of the sample space of such distributions can be significantly smaller than that of k-wise independent distributions and that almost k-wise independent distributions suffice for many applications (for more applications see, e.g., [1, 11]).

In this work we study some other method, originally considered by Schulman [36], to overcome the lower bound on the size of sample spaces of k-wise independent distributions (see also [27]). To illustrate this method, let us look at the following very simple example. It is well-known that for an n vertex graph $G = (V, E)$ a random cut has expected size $\frac{|E|}{2}$, since every two adjacent vertices are in distinct sides of the cut with probability $\frac{1}{2}$. Moreover, the same argument holds even if the cut partition is not chosen from a uniform distribution over all the 2^n partitions but from a pairwise independent distribution. However, the pairwise independence requirement might be in certain cases much stronger than what is really needed. Indeed, in order to have expected cut size $\frac{|E|}{2}$ all we need is a distribution over $\{0,1\}^n$ in which the coordinates corresponding to *adjacent* vertices are independent. We say that such a distribution is *G-wise independent*, and this is the notion of randomness considered in this paper. Notice that the randomness property required from the sample space depends on the input graph. It can be seen that a G-wise independent distribution might have much smaller sample space than a pairwise independent distribution. For example, it can be observed that if the graph G is a cycle or is k-colorable for some constant k, a sample space of constant size suffices. The notion of G-wise independence is naturally extended to hypergraphs, where restrictions to indices which form an edge in the hypergraph should be uniform.

DEFINITION 1.1 (H-WISE INDEPENDENCE; $\ell(H)$). *For an n vertex hypergraph $H = ([n], E)$, we say that a distribution $D = (D_1, \ldots, D_n)$ over $\{0,1\}^n$ is* H-wise independent *if for every edge $\{i_1, \ldots, i_k\} \in E$ all strings in $\{0,1\}^k$ are equally likely to occur in the restriction $(D_{i_1}, \ldots, D_{i_k})$. A distribution D is* uniform H-wise independent *if it is H-wise independent, and in addition it is uniform over a sample space Ω (i.e., choosing an element from Ω uniformly at random yields the distribution D). In this setting, Ω may be considered as a* multiset *of vectors in $\{0,1\}^n$. Let $\ell(H)$ denote the minimum possible size of a sample space Ω of a uniform H-wise independent distribution over $\{0,1\}^n$.*

For example, for the 8-cycle C_8 it holds that $\ell(C_8) = 4$ as one can define the distribution $D = (D_1, D_2, \ldots, D_8)$ to be uniform over $\Omega = \{00000000, 01010101, 10101010, 11111111\}$. Here for each edge $\{i, i+1\}$ in C_8 it holds that D_i and D_{i+1} are independent, where the indices are taken modulo 8. For the complete n vertex k-uniform hypergraph $K_n^{(k)}$ we get the special case of k-wise independence, for which the ℓ-value is known as stated below.

THEOREM 1.2 ([13, 3]). *For any k, $\ell(K_n^{(k)}) = \Theta(n^{\lfloor \frac{k}{2} \rfloor})$.*

The parameter given in Definition 1.1 measures the amount of randomness required by a randomized algorithm in order to handle a *specific* hypergraph instance H, thus its study may have implications on *per-instance* analysis of derandomization. In addition, Schulman presented in [36] several concrete applications motivating constructions of H-wise independent distributions. The applications of [36] include testing VLSI circuits, coding for burst errors on noisy channels, and derandomization of the algorithmic Lovász local lemma (see [32] for a recent progress on the latter). We note that one can also formulate a variant of the ℓ parameter which generalizes *almost* k-wise independence, but in this work we take a first step in this line of research and concentrate on perfect independence.

The approach taken by Schulman [36] for constructing H-wise independent distributions for a k-uniform hypergraph H is based on constructions of vectors over $\mathbb{F}_2$ with certain linear independence requirements. Namely, consider a multiset of m-dimensional vectors $\{v_i\}_{i=1}^n$ such that every set of vectors corresponding to an edge in H is linearly independent. Let D be the distribution defined by $D = (\langle w, v_1 \rangle, \ldots, \langle w, v_n \rangle)$, where w is uniformly chosen from $\mathbb{F}_2^m$ and $\langle \cdot, \cdot \rangle$ represents the inner product operator in $\mathbb{F}_2^m$. We refer to such distributions as *linear*. It is not hard to verify that D is a uniform H-wise independent distribution whose sample space has size 2^m, implying that $\ell(H) \le 2^m$. Schulman [36] applied a simple probabilistic argument, which assigns uniformly chosen random vectors to vertices in the hypergraph H, to obtain the following bounds on ℓ.

THEOREM 1.3 ([36]). *Every k-uniform hypergraph $H = (V, E)$ satisfies $\ell(H) \le 2^{k+1} \cdot |E|$. If every vertex of H belongs to at most Δ edges then $\ell(H) \le 2^{k+1} \cdot \Delta$. If every edge of H intersects at most $\bar{\Delta}$ edges then $\ell(H) \le 2^{k+1} \cdot e\bar{\Delta}$, where e is the natural logarithm constant.*

1.1 Our Contribution

In this paper we study several aspects of H-wise independence and the ℓ parameter given in Definition 1.1. Our contribution is two-fold. We first perform an extensive study of the ℓ parameter for graphs (i.e., 2-uniform hypergraphs), tying ℓ to several well-studied graph parameters. We then turn to address hypergraphs H, and focus our study on the problem of *testing* H-wise independence.

1.1.1 The ℓ Parameter of Graphs

We start with the special case of graphs and show how the ℓ parameter relates to several classical graph parameters. Denoting by $\omega(G)$ and $\chi(G)$ the maximum size of a clique in a graph G and the chromatic number of G respectively, we show that

$$\omega(G) \le \ell(G) \le O(\chi(G)). \qquad (1)$$

It is not difficult to observe that both the upper and lower bounds in (1) can be tight, as is achieved by the n vertex complete graph K_n. Indeed, a K_n-wise independent distribution is pairwise independent, and the minimum possible size of a sample space of such uniform distribution is known to be $\Theta(n)$ [13, 3]. We turn to focus on the potential slackness in the upper bound of (1) and show that there are graphs whose ℓ parameter is significantly smaller than their chromatic number. Specifically, we present an explicit construction of a graph family for which the chromatic number is exponential in the ℓ parameter. This gap is proven to be optimal as stated below.

THEOREM 1.4. *For every graph G, $\ell(G) \geq \Omega(\log \chi(G))$. Moreover, for every sufficiently large n there exists an explicit construction of an n vertex graph for which this bound is tight.*

The proof of Theorem 1.4 is based on a theorem due to Frankl and Rödl [18] which confirmed a 250$ conjecture of Erdös [16] regarding the size of families of subsets of $\{1, 2, \ldots, n\}$ with no two subsets intersecting at exactly $\frac{n}{4}$ elements (see Theorem 3.4).

Theorem 1.4 and its proof are used to obtain a couple of consequences. First, we show that there are graphs G for which $\ell(G)$ is exponentially smaller than the size of the sample space of any *linear* G-wise independent distribution. This means that for certain graphs G the approach taken by Schulman in [36] for constructing G-wise independent distributions inherently leads to a significant loss in the size of the sample space. Second, we obtain the following two *negative* computational results. (a) The problem of deciding, given a graph G, whether there is a uniform G-wise independent distribution with sample space of size ℓ is NP-complete for every constant ℓ divisible by 4 (see Theorem 3.13; notice that the size of the sample space is always divisible by 4 unless G is edgeless). This follows from a characterization of the ℓ parameter in terms of graph homomorphisms and a result of Hell and Nešetřil on the hardness of a problem called H-coloring [21]. (b) Applying known hardness results on the chromatic number of a graph [14, 15], we derive that it is impossible to approximate the ℓ parameter of an n vertex graph in polynomial time to within a factor of $\Omega(\log\log n)$ assuming a certain variant of the Unique Games Conjecture of [25] (see Corollary 3.14).

A somewhat related graph parameter is the *Shannon capacity* of graphs, introduced by Shannon in [37]. The Shannon capacity of a graph G is defined as

$$c(G) = \lim_{k\to\infty} \sqrt[k]{\alpha(G^k)},$$

where $\alpha(G)$ stands for the independence number of G and G^k is what is known as the k-fold strong graph product of G with itself. This graph parameter, studied in the context of information theory, measures the effective size of an alphabet in zero-error communication over a noisy channel represented by the graph. Unfortunately, the behavior of the Shannon capacity of graphs in general is far from being well understood. Even the Shannon capacity of very simple graphs, such as the cycle of length 7, is not known. Therefore, upper and lower bounds on the Shannon capacity of graphs are of interest. It can be seen that the Shannon capacity of a graph satisfies $\alpha(G) \leq c(G) \leq \chi(\overline{G})$, or, equivalently, $\omega(G) \leq c(\overline{G}) \leq \chi(G)$. However, there are tighter upper bounds on the Shannon capacity. One well-known and tractable upper bound is due to Lovász [28], known as the *Lovász ϑ-function* (see Definition 2.3). In this work we show that $\ell(G)$ is bounded from below by the ϑ-function of the complement graph $\overline{G}$ implying that

$$\omega(G) \leq c(\overline{G}) \leq \vartheta(\overline{G}) \leq \ell(G) \leq O(\chi(G)).$$

Using the above connections between the ℓ parameter, the Lovász ϑ-function and the chromatic number, we employ the semidefinite programming algorithm of Karger, Motwani and Sudan [22] for graph coloring to obtain the *positive* algorithmic result stated below.[1]

THEOREM 1.5. *For every ℓ there exists a polynomial-time randomized algorithm that given an n vertex graph G satisfying $\ell(G) = \ell$ finds a linear G-wise independent distribution with sample space of size $\tilde{O}(n^{1-\frac{3}{\ell+1}})$.*

Another upper bound on the Shannon capacity, called *minrank*, was introduced by Haemers in [20] (see Definition 2.4). The minrank and the Lovász ϑ-function tend to behave quite differently and are known to be incomparable [19]. Nevertheless, similarly to the case of the ϑ-function, we relate the ℓ parameter to the minrank and obtain that

$$\omega(G) \leq c(\overline{G}) \leq \text{minrk}_{\mathbb{R}}(\overline{G}) \leq \ell(G) + 1 \leq O(\chi(G)),$$

where $\text{minrk}_{\mathbb{R}}$ stands for the minrank parameter over the reals.

1.1.2 Testing H-wise Independence

We now turn to study the problem of *testing* whether a given distribution over $\{0,1\}^n$ is H-wise independent for a general n vertex k-uniform hypergraph H.[2] The goal is to develop an algorithm that given samples drawn from a distribution over $\{0,1\}^n$ with high probability accepts H-wise independent distributions and rejects distributions which are δ-far in statistical distance from any H-wise independent distribution. We study the dependence of the number of queries required by such an algorithm on the hypergraph H. Previously this problem was addressed only for the special case of $H = K_n^{(k)}$, i.e., testing k-wise independence [5, 2, 35].

DEFINITION 1.6. *Let H be an n vertex hypergraph, and fix some $\delta \in (0,1)$. An algorithm A is a δ-tester for H-wise independence with sample complexity q if for every distribution D over $\{0,1\}^n$, given an access to q independently chosen samples from D,*

- *if D is H-wise independent then A accepts with probability at least $\frac{2}{3}$, and*
- *if D is δ-far from any H-wise independent distribution then A accepts with probability at most $\frac{1}{3}$.*

The approach taken in the literature for testing k-wise independence is based on calculating the *biases* of the drawn samples on all sets of at most k bits. Since the biases measure the imbalance of exclusive-or on these sets, k-wise independent distributions are expected to have biases close to 0. However, for distributions that are far from k-wise independence, it was proved by Alon, Goldreich and Mansour [5] that at least one of these biases is expected to be bounded away from 0. Their analysis implies that there is a tester

[1] The $\tilde{O}$ and $\tilde{\Omega}$ notations are used to hide poly-logarithmic factors.

[2] Throughout the discussion, for ease of presentation, k is assumed to be a fixed constant and thus we do not explicitly state the (usually exponential) dependence of our expressions on k.

for k-wise independence over $\{0,1\}^n$ with sample complexity $O(n^{2k})$. In a paper of Alon, Andoni, Kaufman, Matulef, Rubinfeld and Xie [2] the analysis was improved using Fourier transform techniques and led to an upper bound of $\widetilde{O}(n^k)$ on the sample complexity.

Considering k-wise independence as H-wise independence, where H is the complete n vertex k-uniform hypergraph $K_n^{(k)}$ with edge set $E_n^{(k)}$, the improved results of [2] can be stated in terms of the edge set size $|E_n^{(k)}|$. Namely, the tester of [2] for testing $K_n^{(k)}$-wise independence has sample complexity of $\widetilde{O}(|E_n^{(k)}|)$. In this work, we address general hypergraphs H, and present a tester for H-wise independence with sample complexity proportional to the number of edges in H. Our tester follows the line of that presented in [2] and calculates the biases of the samples on all subsets of edges in H. See Section 4.1 for details.

THEOREM 1.7. *For every $\delta > 0$, k, and an n vertex k-uniform hypergraph $H = ([n], E)$ there exists a δ-tester for H-wise independence with sample complexity $\widetilde{O}(|E|)$.*

As for a lower bound on the sample complexity, it was implicitly shown in [5] that any tester of k-wise independence requires at least $\Omega(n^{k/4})$ queries. This followed from the observation that sample spaces of too small support must be far from k-wise independence. In [2, 38], a lower bound of $\Omega(\frac{1}{\delta} \cdot n^{\frac{k-1}{2}})$ was shown for $\delta = O(1/n)$ by studying the typical distance of a random uniform distribution from k-wise independence. Using our terminology and stating these results in terms of the edge set $E_n^{(k)}$ of the complete hypergraph $K_n^{(k)}$, one gets lower bounds of $\Omega(|E_n^{(k)}|^{1/4})$ [5] and $\Omega(\frac{1}{\delta} \cdot \sqrt{|E_n^{(k)}|/n})$ [2] accordingly.

In this work, we employ the techniques of [5, 2] aiming in obtaining a lower bound of $\Omega(\sqrt{|E|})$ for testing H-wise independence of general hypergraphs H with edge set E. We present two incomparable results. Fitting the analysis of [2] to our setting, for small values of $\delta = O(1/n)$, we present a lower bound of $\Omega(\frac{1}{\delta} \cdot \sqrt{|E|/n}) \geq \Omega(\sqrt{|E|})$. For general δ, we enhance the techniques of [5] and show that any tester of H-wise independence must query at least $\Omega(\sqrt{\frac{n^k}{n^{k/2}+|\overline{E}|}})$ samples, where $|\overline{E}|$ is the number of non-edges of H. It is not hard to verify that the latter lower bound is at its best $\Omega(|E|^{1/4})$, as achieved by very dense hypergraphs H, and is much weaker for sparser hypergraphs. See Section 4.2 for details.

THEOREM 1.8. *For every n vertex k-uniform hypergraph $H = ([n], E)$, δ-testing H-wise independence requires sample complexity $\Omega\left(\frac{1}{\delta} \cdot \sqrt{\frac{|E|}{n}}\right)$ if $\delta = O(\frac{1}{n})$ and $\Omega(\sqrt{\frac{n^k}{|\overline{E}|+n^{k/2}}})$ if $\delta \leq \frac{1}{2}$ and k is even. The same holds for an odd k replacing k by $k-1$ in the bound.*

1.2 Outline

The paper is organized as follows. In Section 2 we gather all the definitions on distributions, graphs and Fourier transform needed in the paper. In Section 3 we present our results on the ℓ parameter of graphs and derive some algorithmic and hardness results. Finally, in Section 4 we prove upper and lower bounds on the sample complexity of testing H-wise independence for a general hypergraph H.

2. PRELIMINARIES

2.1 General

We denote by $[n]$ the set $\{1, 2, \ldots, n\}$. The *Hamming weight* of a vector $x \in \mathbb{F}_2^n$ is the number of its nonzero entries, and the *Hamming distance* between $x, y \in \mathbb{F}_2^n$, denoted $\text{dist}_H(x, y)$, is the number of positions at which x and y differ. A probability distribution D over $\{0,1\}^n$ is a function $D : \{0,1\}^n \to [0,1]$ satisfying $\sum_{x\in\{0,1\}^n} D(x) = 1$. The *support* of D is defined as $\text{support}(D) = \{x \in \{0,1\}^n \mid D(x) \neq 0\}$. Let $U_{\{0,1\}^n}$ denote the uniform distribution defined by $U_{\{0,1\}^n}(x) = \frac{1}{2^n}$ for every $x \in \{0,1\}^n$. The *statistical distance* between two distributions D_1 and D_2 over $\{0,1\}^n$ is defined by $\Delta(D_1, D_2) = \frac{1}{2} \cdot \sum_{x\in\{0,1\}^n} |D_1(x) - D_2(x)| = \max_{S\subset\{0,1\}^n} D_1(S) - D_2(S)$. The *min-entropy* of a distribution D is defined as $-\log_2 \max_{x\in\{0,1\}^n} D(x)$. For a distribution $D = (D_1, \ldots, D_n)$ over $\{0,1\}^n$, the *bias* of D on a (non-empty) set $S \subseteq [n]$ is defined as

$$\begin{aligned} \text{bias}_S(D) &= \Pr[\oplus_{i\in S} D_i = 0] - \Pr[\oplus_{i\in S} D_i = 1] \\ &= 2 \cdot \Pr[\oplus_{i\in S} D_i = 0] - 1. \end{aligned}$$

For an n vertex hypergraph H the distance of a distribution D from H-wise independence, denoted $\Delta(D, \mathfrak{D}_{H-wise})$, is defined as the minimum of $\Delta(D, D')$ over all H-wise independent distributions D' (see Definition 1.1). We say that D is δ-far from H-wise independence if $\Delta(D, \mathfrak{D}_{H-wise}) \geq \delta$.

For a set system E we denote by $\tilde{E}$ the set of all non-empty subsets of sets in E, i.e.,

$$\tilde{E} = \{S \mid |S| \geq 1 \text{ and } \exists T \in E,\ S \subseteq T\}.$$

It is easy to see that for a hypergraph H with edge set E, H-wise independence can be represented as a requirement on the biases on the sets in $\tilde{E}$. This is stated below.

LEMMA 2.1. *For every n vertex hypergraph $H = ([n], E)$ and a distribution D over $\{0,1\}^n$, D is H-wise independent if and only if $\text{bias}_S(D) = 0$ for every $S \in \tilde{E}$.*

2.2 Graphs

Let us recall several standard notions in graph theory. For a graph $G = (V, E)$, the independence number, denoted $\alpha(G)$, is the maximum size of a subset of V containing no adjacent vertices. The clique number, denoted $\omega(G)$, is the maximum size of a subset of V in which every two vertices are adjacent. A k-coloring of G is a function $c : V \to [k]$ for which $\{x, y\} \in E$ implies $c(x) \neq c(y)$. The chromatic number of G, denoted $\chi(G)$, is the minimum k for which G is k-colorable.

A *homomorphism* from a graph $G_1 = (V_1, E_1)$ to a graph $G_2 = (V_2, E_2)$ is a function $f : V_1 \to V_2$ which preserves edges, that is, $\{x, y\} \in E_1$ implies $\{f(x), f(y)\} \in E_2$. It is easy to see that if there is a homomorphism from G_1 to G_2 then $\chi(G_1) \leq \chi(G_2)$. A similar property is satisfied by the ℓ parameter (see Definition 1.1), as stated below.

LEMMA 2.2. *For every two graphs $G_1 = ([n_1], E_1)$ and $G_2 = ([n_2], E_2)$, if there is a homomorphism from G_1 to G_2 then $\ell(G_1) \leq \ell(G_2)$.*

PROOF. Let $f : [n_1] \to [n_2]$ be a homomorphism from G_1 to G_2 and let $D = (D_1, \ldots, D_{n_2})$ be a G_2-wise independent distribution uniform on a multiset of size ℓ. Consider the distribution of $D' = (D_{f(1)}, \ldots, D_{f(n_1)})$. Since f preserves edges, D' is G_1-wise independent, hence $\ell(G_1) \le \ell$. $\Box$

We define below the Lovász ϑ-function of a graph [28]. Note that the ϑ-value of a graph is known to be equal to a graph parameter known as the *strict vector chromatic number* of the complement $\overline{G}$ of G [22] (for many other equivalent definitions see [26]). It is well-known that the ϑ-value of a graph bounds its independence number from above, i.e., $\alpha(G) \le \vartheta(G)$, and can be calculated in polynomial time using semidefinite programming.

DEFINITION 2.3. *An* orthonormal representation *of a graph* $G = (V, E)$ *is an assignment of a unit vector* a_v *in a Euclidean space to each vertex* $v \in V$ *such that* $\langle a_u, a_v \rangle = 0$ *for every distinct* u *and* v *satisfying* $\{u, v\} \notin E$. *The* ϑ*-value of a graph* G*, denoted by* $\vartheta(G)$*, is equal to the minimum over all unit vectors* d *and all orthonormal representations* $(a_v)_{v \in V}$ *of* G *of* $\max_{v \in V} \frac{1}{\langle d, a_v \rangle^2}$.

We now define the minrank parameter of a graph (over $\mathbb{R}$) which was introduced in [20]. We note that studying the minrank parameter over finite fields is motivated by a problem called index coding, as was shown by Bar-Yossef et al. [6].

DEFINITION 2.4. *Let* $A = (a_{ij})$ *be an* n *by* n *real matrix. We say that* A represents *an* n *vertex graph* $G = ([n], E)$ *if* $a_{ii} \ne 0$ *for all* i*, and* $a_{ij} = 0$ *for every distinct* i *and* j *satisfying* $\{i, j\} \notin E$. *The* minrank *of a graph* G *over* $\mathbb{R}$ *is defined as* $\mathrm{minrk}_{\mathbb{R}}(G) = \min\{\mathrm{rank}_{\mathbb{R}}(A) \mid A \text{ represents } G\}$.

2.3 Fourier Transform

The set of functions from $\{0,1\}^n$ to $\mathbb{R}$ is a 2^n-dimensional vector space in which the inner product of two elements f and g is defined by $\langle f, g \rangle = \frac{1}{2^n} \cdot \sum_{x \in \{0,1\}^n} f(x) \cdot g(x)$. For every set $S \subseteq [n]$ let $\chi_S : \{0,1\}^n \to \{-1, 1\}$ be the function defined by $\chi_S(x) = (-1)^{\sum_{i \in S} x_i}$. The set $\{\chi_S \mid S \subseteq [n]\}$ is known to be an orthonormal basis of the vector space, hence every function $f : \{0,1\}^n \to \mathbb{R}$ can be represented as $f = \sum_{S \subseteq [n]} \hat{f}(S) \cdot \chi_S$. The coefficients in this representation satisfy $\hat{f}(S) = \langle f, \chi_S \rangle$ and are called the *Fourier coefficients* of f. Observe that if D is a distribution over $\{0,1\}^n$ then $\mathrm{bias}_S(D) = 2^n \cdot \widehat{D}(S)$.

For every real $p \ge 1$ the p-norm of f is defined by

$$\|f\|_p = \left(\frac{1}{2^n} \cdot \sum_{x \in \{0,1\}^n} |f(x)|^p \right)^{1/p}.$$

For $p = \infty$, $\|f\|_\infty = \max_{x \in \{0,1\}^n} |f(x)|$. Parseval's equality is the standard name of the relation $\|f\|_2^2 = \sum_{S \subseteq [n]} \hat{f}(S)^2$ which easily follows from the orthogonality of the basis. Observe that for two distributions D_1 and D_2 over $\{0,1\}^n$, $\Delta(D_1, D_2) = 2^{n-1} \cdot \|D_1 - D_2\|_1$. The following well-known hyper-contractive inequality will be used.

THEOREM 2.5 (BECKNER-BONAMI INEQUALITY [7, 10]). *Let* $f : \{0,1\}^n \to \mathbb{R}$ *be a function that is a linear combination of* $\{\chi_S \mid |S| \le k\}$. *Then, for every even* $p > 2$, $\|f\|_p \le (p-1)^{k/2} \cdot \|f\|_2$.

The *convolution* $f * g$ of two functions f and g is the function defined by $(f * g)(x) = \frac{1}{2^n} \cdot \sum_{y \in \{0,1\}^n} f(y) \cdot g(x \oplus y)$ where $\oplus$ denotes the bit-wise addition, and is known to satisfy $\widehat{f * g} = \hat{f} \cdot \hat{g}$. A special case of Young's inequality says that $\|f * g\|_\infty \le \|f\|_\infty \cdot \|g\|_1$.

3. THE ℓ PARAMETER OF GRAPHS

In this section we study the ℓ parameter (see Definition 1.1) for the special case of graphs and show how it relates to several graph parameters. We start with a definition of a graph family G_ℓ whose properties will be used in our proofs. The graphs G_ℓ will be *extremal* with respect to our ℓ parameter.

DEFINITION 3.1. *For an* ℓ *divisible by 4, the graph* G_ℓ *is defined as follows. Its vertex set consists of all the vectors in* $\{0,1\}^\ell$ *with Hamming weight* $\frac{\ell}{2}$. *Two such vectors* u, v *are adjacent if they represent independent distributions, i.e., for every* $(\alpha, \beta) \in \{0,1\}^2$ *the number of indices* i *for which* $(u_i, v_i) = (\alpha, \beta)$ *is* $\frac{\ell}{4}$.

Observe that for every graph G and every ℓ divisible by 4, the following two statements are equivalent: (a) There exists a uniform G-wise independent distribution with sample space of size ℓ. (b) There exists a homomorphism from G to G_ℓ. This equivalence follows from the natural correspondence between a uniform G-wise independent distribution with sample space of size ℓ and the homomorphism from G to G_ℓ that maps every vertex to the ℓ-dimensional vector in G_ℓ representing its distribution, where the ith coordinate corresponds to the ith sample (an isolated vertex is mapped arbitrarily). This gives the following alternative characterization of the ℓ parameter of graphs. To justify the restriction on ℓ stated below, we note that $\ell(G)$ is always divisible by 4 unless G is edgeless.

CLAIM 3.2. *For every non-edgeless graph* G*,* $\ell(G)$ *is the smallest* ℓ *divisible by 4 for which there exists a homomorphism from* G *to* G_ℓ.

Using Lemma 2.2, we analyze the ℓ-parameter of G_ℓ:

LEMMA 3.3. *For every* ℓ *divisible by 4,* $\ell(G_\ell) \le \ell$. *Moreover, if there exists a graph* G *for which* $\ell(G) = \ell$ *then* $\ell(G_\ell) = \ell$.

PROOF. Let $n = \binom{\ell}{\ell/2}$. Consider the distribution $D = (D_1, \ldots, D_n)$ over $\{0,1\}^n$ in which D_i is exactly the distribution of support size ℓ implied by the ℓ-vector corresponding to the ith vertex of G_ℓ. Now, for each edge $\{i, j\}$ of G_ℓ it holds that D_i and D_j are independent. Thus, $\ell(G_\ell) \le \ell$. Moreover, let G be any graph for which $\ell(G) = \ell$ then by Lemma 2.2 and Claim 3.2 it holds that $\ell = \ell(G) \le \ell(G_\ell)$. $\Box$

We turn to estimate the chromatic number of G_ℓ. We need the following theorem due to Frankl and Rödl [18] that confirmed a conjecture of Erdös [16].

THEOREM 3.4 ([18]). *There exists an absolute constant* $c < 1$ *such that for every* n *divisible by 4 and every family* $\mathfrak{F}$ *of subsets of* $[n]$ *without* $F, F' \in \mathfrak{F}$ *such that* $|F \cap F'| = \frac{n}{4}$*, it holds that* $|\mathfrak{F}| \le 2^{cn}$.

LEMMA 3.5. *For every* ℓ *divisible by 4,* $\chi(G_\ell) = 2^{\Theta(\ell)}$.

PROOF. On one hand, it is obvious that $\chi(G_\ell) \le |V(G_\ell)| = \binom{\ell}{\ell/2} < 2^\ell$. On the other hand, observe that the vertices in every independent set of G_ℓ are the characteristic vectors of subsets of $[\ell]$ such that no two of them have intersection size $\frac{\ell}{4}$. To see this, observe that the characteristic vectors of every two subsets of $[\ell]$ of size $\frac{\ell}{2}$ that intersect at exactly $\frac{\ell}{4}$ elements must represent independent distributions. Hence, Theorem 3.4 implies that $\alpha(G_\ell) \le 2^{c\ell}$ for some $c < 1$, which implies that $\chi(G_\ell) \ge \frac{|V(G_\ell)|}{\alpha(G_\ell)} \ge \frac{\binom{\ell}{\ell/2}}{2^{c\ell}} = \frac{2^{(1-o(1))\ell}}{2^{c\ell}} = 2^{\Omega(\ell)}$. □

Now, our lower and upper bounds on the ℓ parameter of graphs in terms of their chromatic number follow easily.

THEOREM 3.6. *For every graph G, $\Omega(\log\chi(G)) \le \ell(G) \le O(\chi(G))$. Moreover, there are explicit constructions of graphs attaining the upper and lower bounds for every sufficiently large number of vertices.*

PROOF. Observe that for every graph G, the function that maps every vertex to its color in an optimal coloring is a homomorphism from G to $K_{\chi(G)}$. This is because every two adjacent vertices in G are mapped to two distinct colors. By Lemma 2.2 and Theorem 1.2, $\ell(G) \le \ell(K_{\chi(G)}) = O(\chi(G))$, and, as mentioned before, this bound is tight for the n vertex complete graph.

For the lower bound, apply Claim 3.2 to obtain that every graph G with $\ell(G) = \ell$ satisfies $\chi(G) \le \chi(G_\ell) < 2^\ell$. By Lemma 3.3 and Lemma 3.5, the lower bound is attained at the graph family G_ℓ which satisfies $\ell(G_\ell) \le \ell$ and $\chi(G_\ell) = 2^{\Theta(\ell)}$. □

As a consequence of Theorem 3.6, we show below that there are graphs G for which $\ell(G)$, the minimum size of the sample space of a uniform G-wise independent distribution, is exponentially smaller than that of any *linear* G-wise independent distribution.

COROLLARY 3.7. *For every sufficiently large n, there is an n vertex graph G for which $\ell(G) \le O(\log n)$ whereas any linear G-wise independent distribution has sample space of size at least $n^{\Omega(1)}$.*

PROOF. Recall that for a graph $G = ([n], E)$, a G-wise independent distribution is linear if it can be represented as $(\langle w, v_1\rangle, \ldots, \langle w, v_n\rangle)$ where the v_i's are fixed vectors in $\mathbb{F}_2^m$ for some m and w is uniformly chosen from $\mathbb{F}_2^m$. In this case the size of the sample space is 2^m. Observe that the assignment of every vertex i to the corresponding vector v_i is a 2^m-coloring of G. Indeed, if two vertices i and j are adjacent then the vectors v_i and v_j must be distinct. This implies that the chromatic number of G is bounded from above by the size of the sample space of any linear G-wise independent distribution. Since the construction in Theorem 3.6 gives us an n vertex graph G with $\ell(G) \le O(\log n)$ and $\chi(G) \ge n^{\Omega(1)}$ the result follows. □

The following lemma relates the Lovász ϑ-function of a graph (see Definition 2.3) to the ℓ parameter. Since every graph G satisfies $\vartheta(G) \ge \alpha(G)$ [28], the lemma implies that for every graph G, $\ell(G) \ge \omega(G)$.

LEMMA 3.8. *For every graph G, $\ell(G) \ge \vartheta(\overline{G})$.*

PROOF. Consider a uniform G-wise independent distribution over $\{0,1\}^n$ with sample space of size ℓ, and let B denote an ℓ by n Boolean matrix whose columns represent the vertex distributions. Namely, the G-wise independent distribution is obtained by choosing a row uniformly at random from B. For every vertex v of G let b_v denote the column of B indexed by the vertex v. Now, for every vertex v define the unit ℓ-dimensional vector

$$a_v = \frac{1}{\sqrt{\ell}} \cdot ((-1)^{(b_v)_1}, (-1)^{(b_v)_2}, \ldots, (-1)^{(b_v)_\ell}).$$

Observe that $(a_v)_{v\in V}$ is an orthonormal representation of the complement $\overline{G}$ of G, since for every two vertices u, v which are adjacent in G,

$$\langle a_u, a_v\rangle = \frac{1}{\ell} \cdot (\ell - 2 \cdot \mathrm{dist}_H(b_u, b_v)) = 0.$$

Choosing $d = (1, 0, \ldots, 0)$ we obtain that

$$\vartheta(\overline{G}) \le \max_{v\in V} \frac{1}{\langle d, a_v\rangle^2} = \ell.$$

□

REMARK 3.9. *It was shown in [22] that there are n vertex graphs G satisfying $\vartheta(\overline{G}) = 3$ and $\chi(G) \ge n^{\Omega(1)}$. By Theorem 3.6, this implies that there are n vertex graphs G for which $\vartheta(\overline{G}) = 3$ and $\ell(G) = \Omega(\log n)$. In addition, a result of [17] implies that there are n vertex graphs G for which $\omega(G) < 2^{\sqrt{\log n}}$ and $\ell(G) > n/2^{O(\sqrt{\log n})}$.*

We apply Lemma 3.8 to obtain the following algorithmic corollary.

COROLLARY 3.10. *For every $\ell \ge 4$ there exists a randomized polynomial-time algorithm that given an n vertex graph G satisfying $\ell(G) = \ell$ finds a linear G-wise independent distribution with sample space of size $\widetilde{O}(n^{1-\frac{3}{\ell+1}})$.*

PROOF. It was proved by Karger, Motwani and Sudan [22] that there exists a randomized polynomial-time algorithm that given an n vertex graph G such that $\vartheta(\overline{G}) \le \vartheta$ for some $\vartheta \ge 2$ finds a coloring of G that uses $\widetilde{O}(n^{1-\frac{3}{\vartheta+1}})$ colors. Consider the algorithm that given an n vertex graph G satisfying $\ell(G) = \ell$ applies the algorithm of [22] to obtain a coloring of G. By Lemma 3.8, $\vartheta(\overline{G}) \le \ell$, hence this coloring uses at most $N = \widetilde{O}(n^{1-\frac{3}{\ell+1}})$ colors. Denote the coloring by $c : [n] \to [N]$ and assume without loss of generality that $N = 2^k - 1$ for some integer k. Assign each color i to a (distinct) nonzero vector v_i in $\mathbb{F}_2^k$ and let the algorithm output the uniform distribution over the strings $(\langle w, v_{c(1)}\rangle, \ldots, \langle w, v_{c(n)}\rangle)$ where w is uniformly chosen from $\mathbb{F}_2^k$. Observe that every two adjacent vertices i, j are assigned by c to distinct colors, and that this implies that the inner products $\langle w, v_{c(i)}\rangle$ and $\langle w, v_{c(j)}\rangle$ are independent. Therefore, the distribution that our algorithm outputs is a linear G-wise independent distribution, and its sample space is of size $2^k = N + 1 = \widetilde{O}(n^{1-\frac{3}{\ell+1}})$. □

REMARK 3.11. *For the special case of $\ell = 4$ one can use Claim 3.2 to show that $\ell(G) = 4$ if and only if G is 3-colorable. Thus, the best known polynomial-time algorithm for coloring 3-colorable graphs [12, 24] implies that there exists a polynomial-time algorithm that given an n vertex graph G satisfying $\ell(G) = 4$ finds a linear G-wise independent distribution with sample space of size $\widetilde{O}(n^{0.2038})$.*

We now relate the minrank parameter (see Definition 2.4) to the ℓ parameter.

LEMMA 3.12. *For every graph G, $\ell(G) \geq \mathrm{minrk}_{\mathbb{R}}(\overline{G}) - 1$.*

PROOF. It can be assumed that G contains no isolated vertices, since such vertices do not affect $\ell(G)$ nor $\mathrm{minrk}_{\mathbb{R}}(\overline{G})$. Consider a uniform G-wise independent distribution over $\{0,1\}^n$ with sample space of size ℓ, and let B denote an ℓ by n Boolean matrix whose columns represent the vertex distributions. Notice that the inner product over $\mathbb{R}$ of every two columns of B that correspond to adjacent vertices in G equals $\frac{\ell}{4}$ and that the inner product over $\mathbb{R}$ of every column of B with itself equals $\frac{\ell}{2}$. Let J_n denote the all-one n by n matrix and define $A = B^T \cdot B - \frac{\ell}{4} \cdot J_n$. Observe that every entry in the diagonal of A equals $\frac{\ell}{4}$, whereas every entry corresponding to an edge of G (i.e., a non-edge of $\overline{G}$) equals 0. This implies that the matrix A represents $\overline{G}$, hence

$$\begin{aligned}\mathrm{minrk}_{\mathbb{R}}(\overline{G}) &\leq \mathrm{rank}_{\mathbb{R}}(A)\\ &\leq \mathrm{rank}_{\mathbb{R}}(B^T \cdot B) + \mathrm{rank}_{\mathbb{R}}(\frac{\ell}{4} \cdot J_n) \leq \ell + 1.\end{aligned}$$

□

We turn to show some hardness results on the ℓ parameter.

THEOREM 3.13. *For every constant $\ell \geq 4$ divisible by 4, the problem of deciding whether for an input graph G there exists a uniform G-wise independent distribution with sample space of size ℓ is* NP*-complete.*

PROOF. It is clear that the problem in the statement lies in NP. For NP-hardness, we employ a result of Hell and Nešetřil [21] on the hardness of the H-coloring problem, in which given an input graph G the goal is to decide whether there is a homomorphism from G to the fixed graph H. It was shown in [21] that this problem is NP-hard whenever H is not bipartite and does not contain a loop. The graph G_ℓ (see Definition 3.1) clearly does not contain a loop and we observe that it is not bipartite. To see this, let u_1, u_2, u_3 be the three vectors consisting of $\frac{\ell}{4}$ concatenated copies of $(0,0,1,1)$, $(0,1,0,1)$ and $(0,1,1,0)$ respectively, and notice that these vectors form a triangle in G_ℓ. Therefore, the result of [21] implies that deciding whether for an input graph G there is a homomorphism from G to G_ℓ, i.e., there exists a uniform G-wise independent distribution with sample space of size ℓ, is NP-hard. □

Finally, we observe that hardness of approximating the ℓ parameter can be derived from known hardness results on the chromatic number of a graph. It was shown in [14, 15] that assuming a certain variant of the Unique Games Conjecture of [25], it is NP-hard to decide whether the chromatic number of an n vertex input graph is at most some constant or at least $\Omega(\log^c n)$ for some constant $c > 0$. Combining this with Theorem 3.6 implies the following corollary.

COROLLARY 3.14. *Assuming the variant of the Unique Games Conjecture from [14, 15], there exists a constant $c > 0$ for which approximating $\ell(G)$ for an n vertex input graph G to within a factor of $c \cdot \log\log n$ is* NP*-hard.*

4. TESTING H-WISE INDEPENDENCE

In this section we present our results on the problem of testing H-wise independence. Recall that the goal is to develop an algorithm which given samples from a distribution distinguishes H-wise independent distributions from those that are δ-far from any H-wise independent distribution (see Definition 1.6). We turn to prove upper and lower bounds on the sample complexity of such an algorithm for a general k-uniform hypergraph H, extending results of [5, 2]. We note that for ease of presentation, k is assumed to be a fixed constant and thus we do not explicitly state the (usually exponential) dependence of our expressions on k.

4.1 Upper Bound

A natural way to test H-wise independence is to pick samples from the input distribution and to calculate the biases of the samples on every $S \in \tilde{E}$, where $\tilde{E}$ is the set of all non-empty subsets of edges in H. This is a generalization of the tester presented in [2] for testing k-wise independence. If the distribution is H-wise independent the biases are expected to be close to 0. For the analysis, one has to show that if the distribution is far from H-wise independence then at least one of these biases will be far away from 0 with high probability, and thus one may be able to identify this scenario via multiple queries.

The question of estimating the statistical distance of a general distribution from the class of k-wise independent distributions was first addressed in [5]. It was shown there that every distribution X over $\{0,1\}^n$ with $|\mathrm{bias}_S(X)| = \varepsilon$ for some $S \subseteq [n]$ can be modified to another distribution Y over $\{0,1\}^n$ such that $\mathrm{bias}_S(Y) = 0$, the other biases do not increase (in absolute value), and the statistical distance between X and Y is at most ε. Applying this argument iteratively to every S such that $1 \leq |S| \leq k$ implies that for every distribution X there exists a k-wise independent distribution Y such that $\Delta(X,Y) \leq n^k \cdot \max_{1 \leq |S| \leq k} |\mathrm{bias}_S(X)|$. A similar approach can be useful for estimating the distance of a general distribution from the class of H-wise independent distributions for some k-uniform hypergraph H. Here, the modification of [5] should be applied only to every $S \in \tilde{E}$, since if $\mathrm{bias}_S(Y) = 0$ for every such S then Y is H-wise independent (see Lemma 2.1). Hence, for every distribution X there exists some H-wise independent distribution Y such that $\Delta(X,Y) \leq |\tilde{E}| \cdot \max_{S \in \tilde{E}} |\mathrm{bias}_S(X)|$. As will be clear from our analysis (and that of [2]), this result implies a tester for H-wise independence with query complexity $O(|\tilde{E}|^2)$. We improve on this below.

The bound of [5] on the statistical distance of a distribution from k-wise independence was improved in [2]. The high level idea was to approximate a general distribution X by a function Y all of whose Fourier coefficients $\widehat{Y}(S)$ for non-empty S of size at most k are zeros. This was done by defining Y to satisfy $\widehat{Y}(S) = 0$ whenever $1 \leq |S| \leq k$ and $\widehat{Y}(S) = \widehat{X}(S)$ otherwise. If Y would be a distribution then it must be k-wise independent, and one can prove using Parseval's equality that $\Delta(X,Y) \leq n^{k/2} \cdot \max_{1 \leq |S| \leq k} |\mathrm{bias}_S(X)|$. This significantly improves upon the bound of [5]. However, it is definitely possible that the function Y is not a distribution, since its values might be negative. In order to overcome this difficulty the approach taken in [5] was to replace the function Y by a convex combination of Y and some k-wise independent distributions. Two types of k-wise independent distributions were used for this goal: the uniform distribution $U_{\{0,1\}^n}$ (whose support size is 2^n) which handled the negative values of points with relatively small magnitude; and the economical k-wise independent distributions of [3] (whose support size is roughly $n^{\lfloor \frac{k}{2} \rfloor}$) which handled the negative values of points with relatively large magnitude.

Here we employ the techniques of [2] and generalize their bound. For a k-uniform hypergraph H, given a distribution X our goal is to find some H-wise independent distribution close to X. To do so, we consider the function Y whose Fourier coefficients are identical to the ones of X, besides the coefficients corresponding to some $S \in \tilde{E}$ for which we require $\widehat{Y}(S) = 0$. Then, in order to make Y a distribution, we take a convex combination of Y with certain H-wise independent distributions. To handle the points of small magnitude we take, as in [2], the uniform distribution $U_{\{0,1\}^n}$ over n bit strings, whereas to handle the points of large magnitude we take uniform H-wise distributions of sample space of size $\ell(H)$. Finally, we apply the upper bound on $\ell(H)$ of Schulman [36] (Theorem 1.3) and obtain an upper bound on the distance of X from H-wise independence in terms of the number of edges in H and $\max_{S\in\tilde{E}} |\text{bias}_S(X)|$ generalizing that of [2].

Lemma 4.1. *For every n vertex k-uniform hypergraph $H = ([n], E)$ and a distribution D over $\{0,1\}^n$,*

$$\begin{aligned}\Delta(D, \mathfrak{D}_{H-wise}) &\le O(\log^{k/2}|\tilde{E}|) \cdot \sqrt{\sum_{S\in\tilde{E}} |bias_S(D)|^2} \\ &\le O(|\tilde{E}|^{1/2} \cdot \log^{k/2}|\tilde{E}|) \cdot \max_{S\in\tilde{E}} |bias_S(D)|.\end{aligned}$$

Proof. Let D be a distribution over $\{0,1\}^n$, and write $D = D_1 + D_2$ where $D_1, D_2 : \{0,1\}^n \to \mathbb{R}$ are the functions whose Fourier coefficients satisfy

$$\widehat{D_1}(S) = \begin{cases} 0 & \text{if } S \in \tilde{E} \\ \widehat{D}(S) & \text{o.w.} \end{cases}, \quad \widehat{D_2}(S) = \begin{cases} \widehat{D}(S) & \text{if } S \in \tilde{E} \\ 0 & \text{o.w.} \end{cases}$$

Denote $b_1 = \sum_{S\in\tilde{E}} |\text{bias}_S(D)|$ and $b_2 = \sqrt{\sum_{S\in\tilde{E}} |\text{bias}_S(D)|^2}$, and observe that $b_2 \le b_1 \le \sqrt{|\tilde{E}|} \cdot b_2$ (the right hand side follows from Cauchy-Schwarz inequality). For some λ to be determined later, we consider a partition of $\{0,1\}^n$ into two sets: the set $Z = \{z \in \{0,1\}^n \mid D_2(z) \ge \frac{\lambda \cdot b_2}{2^n}\}$ of *heavy* points and the set $\{0,1\}^n \setminus Z$ of *light* points. Let U_z be a uniform H-wise independent distribution over $\{0,1\}^n$ whose sample space contains z and has size $\ell(H)$. Such a distribution can be obtained by taking some optimal uniform H-wise independent distribution and xoring its samples with a fixed vector in order to include z in the support. Define a function $D' : \{0,1\}^n \to \mathbb{R}$ by

$$D'(x) = \frac{D_1(x) + \frac{\lambda \cdot b_2}{2^n} + w \cdot \sum_{z\in Z} U_z(x)}{1 + \lambda b_2 + w \cdot |Z|},$$

where $w = \frac{\ell(H) \cdot b_1}{2^n}$. We claim that the function D' represents a distribution, i.e., its values on $\{0,1\}^n$ are non-negative and sum to 1. Since $\widehat{D_1}(\phi) = 2^{-n}$, it can be seen that $\sum_x D'(x) = 1$, so we turn to show that D' is non-negative on light and heavy points separately:

1. Assume that x is light, i.e., $D_2(x) < \frac{\lambda \cdot b_2}{2^n}$. By the definition of D',

$$D'(x) \ge \frac{D_1(x) + \frac{\lambda \cdot b_2}{2^n}}{1 + \lambda b_2 + w \cdot |Z|} = \frac{D(x) - D_2(x) + \frac{\lambda \cdot b_2}{2^n}}{1 + \lambda b_2 + w \cdot |Z|} \ge 0.$$

2. Assume that x is heavy, i.e., $D_2(x) \ge \frac{\lambda \cdot b_2}{2^n}$, and observe that

$$\begin{aligned} D'(x) &\ge \frac{D_1(x) + w \cdot U_x(x)}{1 + \lambda b_2 + w \cdot |Z|} = \frac{D_1(x) + \frac{w}{\ell(H)}}{1 + \lambda b_2 + w \cdot |Z|} \\ &= \frac{D(x) - D_2(x) + \frac{b_1}{2^n}}{1 + \lambda b_2 + w \cdot |Z|} \ge 0, \end{aligned}$$

where the last inequality holds since any $x \in \{0,1\}^n$ satisfies

$$|D_2(x)| = |\sum_{S\in\tilde{E}} \widehat{D}(S)\chi_S(x)| \le \sum_{S\in\tilde{E}} |\widehat{D}(S)| = 2^{-n} \cdot b_1.$$

Moreover, by Lemma 2.1, the distribution D' is H-wise independent as $\text{bias}_S(D') = 2^n \cdot \widehat{D'}(S)$ is a linear combination of $\widehat{D_1}(S)$ and the $\widehat{U_z}(S)$ which are all zeros for any $S \in \tilde{E}$.

Now, apply Cauchy-Schwarz inequality and Parseval's equality to get that

$$\begin{aligned}\|D - D_1\|_1 &= 2^{-n} \cdot \sum_{x\in\{0,1\}^n} |D(x) - D_1(x)| \\ &\le 2^{-n/2} \cdot \sqrt{\sum_{x\in\{0,1\}^n} |D(x) - D_1(x)|^2} = 2^{-n} \cdot b_2.\end{aligned}$$

In addition, by the triangle inequality and the fact that the statistical distance between two distributions is always at most 1, we get that

$$\begin{aligned}\|D_1 - D'\|_1 &\le \lambda \cdot b_2 \|D' - U_{\{0,1\}^n}\|_1 + w \sum_{z\in Z} \|D' - U_z\|_1 \\ &\le 2^{-n+1} \cdot (\lambda \cdot b_2 + w \cdot |Z|).\end{aligned}$$

This implies that

$$\begin{aligned}\Delta(D, \mathfrak{D}_{H-wise}) &\le 2^{n-1} \cdot (\|D - D_1\|_1 + \|D_1 - D'\|_1) \\ &\le \frac{b_2}{2} + \lambda \cdot b_2 + w \cdot |Z|.\end{aligned}$$

It remains to present an upper bound on the number $|Z|$ of heavy points. For this purpose we use the Beckner-Bonami hyper-contractive inequality (Theorem 2.5; [7, 10]). Since Parseval's equality implies that $\|\frac{2^n}{b_2} \cdot D_2\|_2 = 1$, we get that for every even $p > 2$,

$$\begin{aligned}\frac{|Z|}{2^n} &= \Pr_{x\in\{0,1\}^n}\left[D_2(x) \ge \frac{\lambda \cdot b_2}{2^n}\right] \\ &\le \Pr_{x\in\{0,1\}^n}\left[\left|\frac{2^n}{b_2} \cdot D_2(x)\right| \ge \lambda\right] \\ &\le \frac{\|\frac{2^n}{b_2} \cdot D_2\|_p^p}{\lambda^p} \le \frac{(p-1)^{pk/2}}{\lambda^p}.\end{aligned}$$

Finally, we choose the parameters $p = \log(\ell(H) \cdot \sqrt{|\tilde{E}|})$ (which can be assumed to be even) and $\lambda = 2p^{k/2}$ and obtain that

$$|Z| \le 2^n \cdot \left(\frac{p^{k/2}}{\lambda}\right)^p \le \frac{2^n}{\ell(H) \cdot \sqrt{|\tilde{E}|}}.$$

Combining this with the above bound we get

$$\Delta(D, \mathfrak{D}_{H-wise}) \leq \frac{b_2}{2} + \lambda \cdot b_2 + \frac{\ell(H) \cdot b_1}{2^n} \cdot |Z| \leq b_2(\frac{3}{2} + \lambda).$$

By Theorem 1.3, $\ell(H) \leq 2^{k+1} \cdot |E|$, so it follows that

$$\Delta(D, \mathfrak{D}_{H-wise}) \leq O(\log^{k/2} |\tilde{E}|) \cdot b_2.$$

□

Equipped with Lemma 4.1, we are ready to prove our upper bound on the sample complexity of testing H-wise independence.

THEOREM 4.2. *For every $\delta > 0$ and an n vertex k-uniform hypergraph $H = ([n], E)$ there exists a δ-tester for H-wise independence with sample complexity $O\left(\frac{|E| \cdot \log^{k+1} |E|}{\delta^2}\right)$.*

PROOF. Following [2], consider the tester which draws a set Q of $q = O\left(\frac{|\tilde{E}| \cdot \log^{k+1} |\tilde{E}|}{\delta^2}\right)$ independent samples from the input distribution D and accepts if and only if $|\text{bias}_S(Q)| < \delta'$ for every $S \in \tilde{E}$ where $\delta' = \frac{c \cdot \delta}{|\tilde{E}|^{1/2} \cdot \log^{k/2} |\tilde{E}|}$ for a certain absolute constant c.

Assume that D is H-wise independent. By the Chernoff bound, the probability that $|\text{bias}_S(Q)| \geq 2\delta'$ is at most $e^{-\Omega(q\delta'^2)} \leq \frac{1}{3|\tilde{E}|}$, so by the union bound the probability that the tester rejects is at most $\frac{1}{3}$. On the other hand, assume that $\Delta(D, \mathfrak{D}_{H-wise}) \geq \delta$, so by Lemma 4.1 (for a certain choice of c) there exists some $S \in \tilde{E}$ such that $|\text{bias}_S(D)| \geq 2\delta'$. For this S, by the Chernoff bound,

$$\begin{aligned}\Pr\left[|\text{bias}_S(Q)| < \delta'\right] &\leq \Pr\left[|\text{bias}_S(Q) - \text{bias}_S(D)| \geq \delta'\right] \\ &\leq e^{-\Omega(q\delta'^2)} \leq \frac{1}{3},\end{aligned}$$

and with such probability the tester accepts. Since $|\tilde{E}| \leq 2^k \cdot |E|$ the result follows. □

4.2 Lower Bounds

A standard method to prove lower bounds on the sample complexity of testing algorithms is to present two input distributions, such that one of them should be accepted and the other one should be rejected, however it is impossible to distinguish one from another with few samples. We turn to show a lower bound for testing H-wise independence using this method. To this end, we present a lower bound on the min-entropy of any H-wise independent distribution. Our bound, depending on the number $|\overline{E}|$ of non-edges of H, is given in the following lemma and generalizes a statement of [5] on k-wise independence.

LEMMA 4.3. *For every even k and every n vertex k-uniform hypergraph $H = ([n], E)$, every H-wise independent distribution over $\{0,1\}^n$ has min-entropy at least*

$$\log_2\left(\frac{n^k}{2^{2k} \cdot |\overline{E}| + (k/2)^k \cdot n^{k/2}}\right).$$

The same holds for an odd k replacing k by $k-1$ in the bound.

PROOF. We prove the lemma for an even k, and it can be similarly proven for an odd k. Let $D = (D_1, \ldots, D_n)$ be some H-wise independent distribution and assume without loss of generality that the all-zero string has the maximum probability according to D (otherwise xor D with the string that has maximum probability). Define $Z_i = D_i - \frac{1}{2}$ and apply the generalized Chebyshev inequality to obtain

$$\begin{aligned}\Pr[D = (0, \ldots, 0)] &= \Pr\left[\sum_{i=1}^{n} D_i = 0\right] \\ &\leq \Pr\left[|\sum_{i=1}^{n} Z_i| \geq \frac{n}{2}\right] \leq \frac{\mathbf{E}\left[(\sum_{i=1}^{n} Z_i)^k\right]}{(n/2)^k}.\end{aligned}$$

Write $\mathbf{E}\left[(\sum_{i=1}^{n} Z_i)^k\right] = \sum_{i_1,\ldots,i_k \in [n]} \mathbf{E}\left[Z_{i_1} \cdots Z_{i_k}\right]$ and consider a term $Z_{i_1} \cdots Z_{i_k}$ for which $\{i_1, \ldots, i_k\}$ is an edge in H or a subset of an edge in H. Observe that if there is at least one index i_j that appears exactly once in this term then the expectation of this term contributes 0 to the sum. Indeed, in this case $\mathbf{E}\left[Z_{i_1} \cdots Z_{i_k}\right] = \mathbf{E}\left[Z_{i_j}\right] \cdot \mathbf{E}\left[\Pi_{h \neq j} Z_{i_h}\right] = 0$. Therefore, the only terms which might have positive contribution to the sum are the ones that correspond to a subset of a non-edge, whose number is smaller than $\binom{2k-1}{k} \cdot |\overline{E}| < 2^{2k} \cdot |\overline{E}|$, and the ones in which each index appears at least twice, whose number is smaller than $\binom{n}{k/2} \cdot (k/2)^k < (k/2)^k \cdot n^{k/2}$. Observe that every term in the sum contributes at most $\frac{1}{2^k}$ since for every i, $|Z_i| \leq \frac{1}{2}$. Hence, we conclude that the maximum probability of a string according to the distribution D is at most

$$\frac{\frac{1}{2^k} \cdot (2^{2k} \cdot |\overline{E}| + (k/2)^k \cdot n^{k/2})}{(n/2)^k} = \frac{2^{2k} \cdot |\overline{E}| + (k/2)^k \cdot n^{k/2}}{n^k},$$

and we are done. □

Equipped with Lemma 4.3 we are ready to prove the following lower bound.

THEOREM 4.4. *For every even k, n vertex k-uniform hypergraph H and $\delta \leq \frac{1}{2}$, δ-testing H-wise independence requires at least $\Omega(\sqrt{\frac{n^k}{|\overline{E}|+n^{k/2}}})$ samples from the distribution. The same holds for an odd k replacing k by $k-1$ in the bound.*

PROOF. We prove the theorem for an even k, and it can be similarly proven for an odd k. Denote $z = \frac{n^k}{2^{2k} \cdot |\overline{E}| + (k/2)^k \cdot n^{k/2}}$, let A be a tester which makes at most $q = o(\sqrt{z})$ queries, and consider the following two distributions: the uniform distribution $U_{\{0,1\}^n}$ and a uniform distribution D_Q over some uniformly chosen set $Q \subseteq \{0,1\}^n$ of $\frac{z}{2}$ strings. Whereas the former is clearly H-wise independent distribution, it turns out that the latter is $\frac{1}{2}$-far from any such distribution. Indeed, by Lemma 4.3 any H-wise independent distribution D has min-entropy at least $\log_2 z$, hence

$$\begin{aligned}\Delta(D, D_Q) &\geq \Pr[D \in \{0,1\}^n \setminus \text{support}(D_Q)] \\ &\geq 1 - \frac{|\text{support}(D_Q)|}{z} = \frac{1}{2}.\end{aligned}$$

By the birthday paradox, all the q strings queried by A from either $U_{\{0,1\}^n}$ or D_Q are distinct with probability $1 - o(1)$, and hence A cannot distinguish between the two with probability bounded away from $\frac{1}{2}$. This contradicts the fact that A δ-tests H-wise independence. □

Our next lower bound holds for $\delta = O(\frac{1}{n})$ and employs a proof technique used in [2] for a lower bound on the sample complexity of testing k-wise independence. At the heart of its proof lies the following lemma (to be proven at the end of this section) which gives a lower bound on the distance of a random uniform distribution from H-wise independence.

LEMMA 4.5. *There exists a constant $c > 0$ such that for every n vertex k-uniform hypergraph $H = ([n], E)$ and $\delta > 0$ such that $\delta \leq \frac{1}{2n}$ the following holds. If D_Q is a uniform distribution over some uniformly chosen multiset $Q \subseteq \{0,1\}^n$ of size $z = \frac{2^k \cdot |E|}{\delta^2 \cdot n}$ then almost surely $\Delta(D_Q, \mathfrak{D}_{H-wise}) \geq c \cdot \delta$.*

THEOREM 4.6. *For every n vertex k-uniform hypergraph $H = ([n], E)$ and $\delta = O(\frac{1}{n})$, δ-testing H-wise independence requires at least $\Omega\left(\frac{1}{\delta} \cdot \sqrt{\frac{|E|}{n}}\right)$ samples from the distribution.*

PROOF. Define $z = \frac{c^2 \cdot 2^k \cdot |E|}{\delta^2 \cdot n}$ for some $\delta \leq \frac{c}{2n}$, where c is the constant from Lemma 4.5. Let A be a tester which makes at most $q = o(\sqrt{z})$ queries, and consider the following two distributions: the uniform distribution $U_{\{0,1\}^n}$ and a uniform distribution D_Q over some uniformly chosen multiset $Q \subseteq \{0,1\}^n$ of z strings. Whereas the former is clearly H-wise independent distribution, by Lemma 4.5 the latter is almost surely δ-far from any such distribution. By the birthday paradox, all the strings queried by A from either $U_{\{0,1\}^n}$ or D_Q are distinct with probability $1 - o(1)$, and hence A cannot distinguish between the two with probability bounded away from $\frac{1}{2}$. This contradicts the fact that A δ-tests H-wise independence. □

We need the following concentration result.

THEOREM 4.7 (BERNSTEIN'S INEQUALITY [9]). *Consider independent real-valued random variables $X_1, \ldots, X_z$ such that $|X_i| \leq C$ for all $1 \leq i \leq z$. Let $\mu = \sum_{i=1}^{z} \mathbf{E}[X_i]$ and $\sigma^2 = \frac{1}{z} \cdot \sum_{i=1}^{z} \mathbf{Var}[X_i]$. Then, for any $t > 0$,*

$$\Pr\left[|\sum_{i=1}^{z} X_i - \mu| > zt\right] \leq e^{-\frac{zt^2}{2\sigma^2 + 2Ct/3}}.$$

PROOF OF LEMMA 4.5. Let D be some H-wise independent distribution over $\{0,1\}^n$ with minimum statistical distance from D_Q, and define $f_Q = D_Q - D$. Notice that by Lemma 2.1 for every $S \in \tilde{E}$, $\widehat{f_Q}(S) = \widehat{D_Q}(S)$ and that $\Delta(D_Q, \mathfrak{D}_{H-wise}) = 2^{n-1} \cdot \|f_Q\|_1$. Let $g_Q, h_Q : \{0,1\}^n \to \mathbb{R}$ be the functions defined by

$$\widehat{g_Q}(S) = \begin{cases} \widehat{f_Q}(S) & \text{if } S \in \tilde{E} \\ 0 & \text{o.w.} \end{cases}, \qquad h_Q = f_Q * g_Q.$$

Observe that $\widehat{h_Q}(S) = \widehat{f_Q}(S)^2$ if $S \in \tilde{E}$ and $\widehat{h_Q}(S) = 0$ otherwise.

We now prove that

1. for some $c' > 0$, $\|h_Q\|_\infty \geq c' \cdot \frac{|\tilde{E}|}{2^{2n} \cdot z}$ almost surely, and
2. for some $c'' > 0$, $\|g_Q\|_\infty \leq \frac{c''}{2^n} \cdot \sqrt{\frac{n \cdot |\tilde{E}|}{z}}$ almost surely.

By the union bound both (1) and (2) hold almost surely. Therefore, by Young's inequality, we obtain that for some $c > 0$ almost surely

$$\Delta(D_Q, \mathfrak{D}_{H-wise}) = 2^{n-1} \cdot \|f_Q\|_1 \geq 2^{n-1} \cdot \frac{\|h_Q\|_\infty}{\|g_Q\|_\infty} \geq c \cdot \delta,$$

where for the last inequality we used $|\tilde{E}| \leq 2^k \cdot |E|$.

Proof of Item (1).
First, observe that $\|h_Q\|_\infty = h_Q(0)$, since for every $x \in \{0,1\}^n$,

$$\begin{aligned} |h_Q(x)| &= |\sum_{S \in \tilde{E}} \widehat{h_Q}(S) \chi_S(x)| \leq \sum_{S \in \tilde{E}} |\widehat{h_Q}(S)| \\ &= \sum_{S \in \tilde{E}} \widehat{h_Q}(S) = h_Q(0). \end{aligned}$$

This implies that $\|h_Q\|_\infty = h_Q(0) = \sum_{S \in \tilde{E}} \widehat{f_Q}(S)^2$, where for every $S \in \tilde{E}$,

$$\widehat{f_Q}(S) = \widehat{D_Q}(S) = \frac{1}{2^n} \cdot \sum_{y \in Q} D_Q(y) \cdot \chi_S(y) = \frac{1}{2^n z} \cdot \sum_{y \in Q} \chi_S(y). \quad (2)$$

A calculation of the expectation and the variance of $\|h_Q\|_\infty$ (similar to the calculation in [2]) implies that

$$\mathbf{E}_Q[\|h_Q\|_\infty] = \frac{|\tilde{E}|}{2^{2n} z} \cdot \left(1 - \frac{z-1}{2^n - 1}\right) \quad \text{and}$$

$$\mathbf{Var}_Q[\|h_Q\|_\infty] = \frac{2|\tilde{E}|}{2^{4n} z^2}(1 - o(1)).$$

By Chebyshev's inequality, it follows that almost surely

$$\|h_Q\|_\infty \geq c' \cdot \mathbf{E}_Q[\|h_Q\|_\infty]$$

for some constant $c' > 0$, and we are done.

Proof of Item (2).
Fix $x \in \{0,1\}^n$, and define the function Y_x by $Y_x(y) = \sum_{S \in \tilde{E}} \chi_S(x + y)$. Using (2) we observe that

$$\begin{aligned} g_Q(x) &= \sum_{S \in \tilde{E}} \widehat{f_Q}(S) \chi_S(x) \\ &= \frac{1}{2^n z} \cdot \sum_{S \in \tilde{E}} \sum_{y \in Q} \chi_S(x + y) = \frac{1}{2^n z} \cdot \sum_{y \in Q} Y_x(y). \end{aligned}$$

Notice that the random variables $\{Y_x(y)\}_{y \in Q}$ are independent and satisfy $|Y_x(y)| \leq |\tilde{E}|$. In addition, since the expectation of $\chi_S(y)$ over a random uniformly chosen y for a non-empty S is 0, it can be observed that $\mathbf{E}_y[Y_x(y)] = 0$ and that $\mathbf{Var}_y[Y_x(y)] = |\tilde{E}|$. Define $t = 2 \cdot \sqrt{\frac{n|\tilde{E}|}{z}}$ and notice that $t \leq 1$ by the definition of z and the assumption on δ. Apply Bernstein's inequality (Theorem 4.7) to get that

$$\begin{aligned} \Pr\left[|g_Q(x)| > \frac{t}{2^n}\right] &= \Pr\left[|\sum_{y \in Q} Y_x(y)| > zt\right] \\ &\leq e^{-\frac{zt^2}{2|\tilde{E}| + 2|\tilde{E}|t/3}} \leq e^{-\frac{zt^2}{3|\tilde{E}|}} = o(2^{-n}). \end{aligned}$$

By the union bound, $|g_Q(x)| \leq \frac{t}{2^n}$ for every $x \in \{0,1\}^n$ almost surely, hence for some constant $c'' > 0$, almost surely $\|g_Q\|_\infty \leq \frac{c''}{2^n} \cdot \sqrt{\frac{n|\tilde{E}|}{z}}$. □

5. ACKNOWLEDGMENTS

We would like to thank Leonard Schulman and Adi Shraibman for helpful discussions and Ning Xie for clarifications on [2].

6. REFERENCES

[1] N. Alon. A parallel algorithmic version of the local lemma. *Random Struct. Algorithms*, 2(4):367–378, 1991. Preliminary version in FOCS'91.

[2] N. Alon, A. Andoni, T. Kaufman, K. Matulef, R. Rubinfeld, and N. Xie. Testing k-wise and almost k-wise independence. In *STOC*, pages 496–505, 2007.

[3] N. Alon, L. Babai, and A. Itai. A fast and simple randomized parallel algorithm for the maximal independent set problem. *J. Algorithms*, 7(4):567–583, 1986.

[4] N. Alon, O. Goldreich, J. Håstad, and R. Peralta. Simple construction of almost k-wise independent random variables. *Random Struct. Algorithms*, 3(3):289–304, 1992. Preliminary version in FOCS'90.

[5] N. Alon, O. Goldreich, and Y. Mansour. Almost k-wise independence versus k-wise independence. *Inf. Process. Lett.*, 88(3):107–110, 2003.

[6] Z. Bar-Yossef, Y. Birk, T. S. Jayram, and T. Kol. Index coding with side information. In *FOCS*, pages 197–206, 2006.

[7] W. Beckner. Inequalities in Fourier analysis. *Ann. of Math.*, 102:159–182, 1975.

[8] B. Berger and J. Rompel. Simulating $(\log^c n)$-wise independence in NC. *J. ACM*, 38(4):1026–1046, 1991. Preliminary version in FOCS'89.

[9] S. Bernstein. *The Theory of Probabilities*. Gostehizdat Publishing House, Moscow, 1946.

[10] A. Bonami. Étude des coefficients de Fourier des fonctions de $L^p(G)$. *Annales de l'Institut Fourier*, 20(2):335–402, 1970.

[11] J. Boyar, G. Brassard, and R. Peralta. Subquadratic zero-knowledge. *J. ACM*, 42(6):1169–1193, 1995. Preliminary version in FOCS'91.

[12] E. Chlamtac. Approximation algorithms using hierarchies of semidefinite programming relaxations. In *FOCS*, pages 691–701, 2007.

[13] B. Chor, O. Goldreich, J. Håstad, J. Friedman, S. Rudich, and R. Smolensky. The bit extraction problem of t-resilient functions. In *FOCS*, pages 396–407, 1985.

[14] I. Dinur, E. Mossel, and O. Regev. Conditional hardness for approximate coloring. *SIAM J. Comput.*, 39(3):843–873, 2009. Preliminary version in STOC'06.

[15] I. Dinur and I. Shinkar. On the conditional hardness of coloring a 4-colorable graph with super-constant number of colors. In *APPROX-RANDOM*, pages 138–151, 2010.

[16] P. Erdös. Problems and results in graph theory and combinatorial analysis. In *Proceedings of the Fifth British Combinatorial Conference*, pages 169–192, 1975.

[17] U. Feige. Randomized graph products, chromatic numbers, and the Lovász ϑ-function. *Combinatorica*, 17(1):79–90, 1997. Preliminary version in STOC'95.

[18] P. Frankl and V. Rödl. Forbidden intersections. *Trans. Amer. Math. Soc.*, 300(1):259–286, 1987.

[19] W. Haemers. On some problems of Lovász concerning the Shannon capacity of a graph. *IEEE Trans. Inform. Theory*, 25(2):231–232, 1979.

[20] W. Haemers. An upper bound for the Shannon capacity of a graph. In *Algebraic methods in graph theory, Vol. I, II (Szeged, 1978)*, volume 25 of *Colloq. Math. Soc. János Bolyai*, pages 267–272. North-Holland, Amsterdam, 1981.

[21] P. Hell and J. Nešetřil. On the complexity of H-coloring. *J. Comb. Theory, Ser. B*, 48(1):92–110, 1990.

[22] D. R. Karger, R. Motwani, and M. Sudan. Approximate graph coloring by semidefinite programming. *J. ACM*, 45(2):246–265, 1998. Preliminary version in FOCS'94.

[23] R. M. Karp and A. Wigderson. A fast parallel algorithm for the maximal independent set problem. *J. ACM*, 32(4):762–773, 1985. Preliminary version in STOC'84.

[24] K. Kawarabayashi and M. Thorup. Combinatorial coloring of 3-colorable graphs. In *FOCS*, 2012. To appear.

[25] S. Khot. On the power of unique 2-prover 1-round games. In *STOC*, pages 767–775, 2002.

[26] D. E. Knuth. The sandwich theorem. *Electronic J. Combinatorics*, 1:1, 1994.

[27] D. Koller and N. Megiddo. Constructing small sample spaces satisfying given constraints. *SIAM J. Discrete Math.*, 7(2):260–274, 1994. Preliminary version in STOC'93.

[28] L. Lovász. On the Shannon capacity of a graph. *IEEE Trans. Inform. Theory*, 25(1):1–7, 1979.

[29] M. Luby. A simple parallel algorithm for the maximal independent set problem. *SIAM J. Comput.*, 15(4):1036–1053, 1986.

[30] M. Luby. Removing randomness in parallel computation without a processor penalty. *J. Comput. System Sci.*, 47(2):250–286, 1993.

[31] M. Luby and A. Wigderson. Pairwise independence and derandomization. *Foundations and Trends in Theoretical Computer Science*, 1(4), 2005.

[32] R. A. Moser. A constructive proof of the Lovász local lemma. In *STOC*, pages 343–350, 2009.

[33] R. Motwani, J. Naor, and M. Naor. The probabilistic method yields deterministic parallel algorithms. *J. Comput. System Sci.*, 49(3):478–516, 1994. Preliminary version in FOCS'89.

[34] J. Naor and M. Naor. Small-bias probability spaces: Efficient constructions and applications. *SIAM J. Comput.*, 22(4):838–856, 1993. Preliminary version in STOC'90.

[35] R. Rubinfeld and N. Xie. Testing non-uniform k-wise independent distributions over product spaces. In *ICALP (1)*, pages 565–581, 2010.

[36] L. J. Schulman. Sample spaces uniform on neighborhoods. In *STOC*, pages 17–25, 1992.

[37] C. E. Shannon. The zero error capacity of a noisy channel. *Institute of Radio Engineers, Transactions on Information Theory*, IT-2(September):8–19, 1956.

[38] N. Xie. Personal communication, 2012.

Sparse Extractor Families for All the Entropy

Andrej Bogdanov*
Dept. of Computer Science and Engineering and
Institute for Theoretical CS and Communications
Chinese University of Hong Kong
andrejb@cse.cuhk.edu.hk

Siyao Guo†
Dept. of Computer Science and Engineering
Chinese University of Hong Kong
syguo@cse.cuhk.edu.hk

ABSTRACT

We consider the problem of extracting entropy by sparse transformations, namely functions with a small number of overall input-output dependencies. In contrast to previous works, we seek extractors for essentially all the entropy without any assumption on the underlying distribution beyond a min-entropy requirement.

We give two simple constructions of *sparse extractor families*. These are collections of sparse functions such that for any distribution X on inputs of sufficiently high min-entropy, the output of most functions from the collection on input X is statistically close to uniform.

For strong extractor families (i.e., functions in the family do not take additional randomness) we give upper and lower bounds on the sparsity that are tight up to a constant factor for a wide range of min-entropies. We then prove that for some min-entropies weak extractor families can achieve better sparsity.

We show how this construction can be used towards more efficient parallel transformation of (non-uniform) one-way functions into pseudorandom generators. More generally, sparse extractor families can be used instead of pairwise independence in various randomized or nonuniform settings where preserving sparsity or locality (i.e., parallelism) is of interest.

Categories and Subject Descriptors

F.2 [**Theory of Computation**]: Analysis of Algorithms and Problem Complexity

*Work supported by grants RGC GRF CUHK410309 and CUHK410111.

†Part of the research leading to these results has received funding from the European Research Council under the European Union's Seventh Framework Programme (FP/2007-2013) / ERC Grant Agreement n. 307952.

Keywords

randomness extraction, parallel cryptography, random matrices

1. INTRODUCTION

Randomness extractors [19, 23], have numerous applications in complexity theory and cryptography. For example, in computational complexity they are used to isolate satisfying assignments of boolean formulas [27] and in constructing pseudorandom generators for space-bounded computation [18, 22]. One notable use in cryptography is in the construction of pseudorandom generators from one-way functions [12, 11, 26].

In many applications of extractors, including the above ones, it is important that the extractors recover essentially all the entropy of the input distribution. A popular choice in such scenarios is to instantiate the extractor by a pairwise independent hash function family [4, 13]. Pairwise independent functions are appealing because they have a variety of implementations, ranging from very simple ones [7] to very efficient ones [14].

Mansour, Nisan, and Tiwari [16] observed that pairwise independent hash functions must be "dense" in the sense that a typical output in a typical function in the family must depend on a linear number of inputs. Therefore in terms of the number of input-output dependencies, pairwise independent functions are quite complex. Motivated by an application to parallel cryptography, Bogdanov and Rosen [5] gave one way to bypass this barrier in the context of hardness amplification of "local" functions.

In this work we study sparse extractors for all the entropy, namely extractors with a small number of overall input-output dependencies. We consider the more general notion of sparse extractor families. An *extractor family* for distributions of min-entropy k over $\{0,1\}^n$ with error ε is a distribution H on functions $\{0,1\}^n \times \{0,1\}^s \to \{0,1\}^m$ where $m \leq s + k$ such that for every distribution X over $\{0,1\}^n$ of min-entropy k, the statistical distance between $(H, H(X, U_s))$ and (H, U_m) is at most ε (where U_s and U_m are uniformly random). The extractor family is *strong* if $s = 0$, i.e. H does not take any additional randomness beyond X.

Without the sparsity restriction extractors and extractor families are essentially the same object, as the randomness used to choose an extractor from the family can be included in the seed. Once we take sparsity into consideration, however, extractor families allow for more flexibility. This advantage is especially pronounced in the case of strong extractors: Any single strong extractor in which some output bit depends only on ℓ input bits cannot extract from a source that fixes all those ℓ bits. In contrast, we show strong extractor families can achieve much better sparsity.

In this work we prove three results regarding sparse extractor families. First we give a simple construction of sparse extractor families for all the entropy. Then we show that the sparsity of our construction is optimal up to constant factors for a wide range of the min-entropy parameter. Finally, we show that an equally simple construction of weak extractor families achieves better sparsity. Thus when sparsity is required, weak extractors can provably outperform strong ones.

We also show our weak extractor family gives a somewhat improved nonuniform construction of local pseudorandom generators from local one-way functions, based on works of Haitner, Reingold, and Vadhan [11] and Vadhan and Zheng [26]. In general our results can be useful in randomized or nonuniform settings where hashing is used and obtaining or preserving a small number of input-output dependencies (i.e., parallelism) is of interest.

1.1 Our results

Let $h\colon \{0,1\}^n \to \{0,1\}^m$ be a function. We say output j of h *depends* on input i if there exists assignments $x, x' \in \{0,1\}^n$ that differ only in the ith coordinate such that $h(x)_j \neq h(x')_j$. We say h is *s-sparse* if the number of input-output pairs (i,j) such that output j depends on input i is at most s, and h is *ℓ-local* if every output j depends on at most ℓ inputs i.

THEOREM 1. *Let K be a sufficiently large constant and n,k,m,δ be parameters such that $1 \le m \le k \le n$, and $0 < \delta < 1$. Let $H(x) = Mx$, where M is an $m \times n$ matrix over $GF(2)$ where each entry equals 1 independently with probability*

$$p = \min\left\{\frac{1}{m} \cdot \log\frac{m}{\delta} \ln\frac{Kn}{m}, \frac{1}{2}\right\}.$$

Then H is a strong extractor family for min-entropy k with error at most $1/2\sqrt{\delta + K \cdot 2^{-k+m}}$.

By a large deviation bound, all but an δ-fraction of H are $O(nmp)$-sparse. The best error that any extractor can attain is $\Omega(\sqrt{2^{-k+m}})$, which is achieved by a pairwise independent hash function family [21], which has sparsity $\Omega(mn)$. Theorem 1 shows the sparsity can be reduced dramatically at the cost of increasing the error by a little. For example if we set $\delta = 2^{-k+m}$, we obtain a $O(n \log m \log(n/m))$ sparse strong extractor family whose error is within a constant factor of optimal.

Our main negative result shows that this sparsity is necessary for a large range of values of k and when δ is constant.

THEOREM 2. *Suppose $n^{0.99} \le m \le n/6$. There exists a distribution $\mathcal{D}$ over distributions $\overline{X}$ on $\{0,1\}^n$ of min-entropy $1.5m$ each so that for every function $h\colon \{0,1\}^n \to \{0,1\}^m$ of sparsity $0.001n \log m \log(2n/m)$, the expected statistical distance between $h(\overline{X})$ and the uniform distribution over $\{0,1\}^m$ is at least $1 - e^{-m^{\Omega(1)}}$.*

Applying Yao's minimax principle or just take the covex combination of distributions $\overline{X}$ as the bad distribution, we conclude that the sparsity in Theorem 1 is optimal up to constant factor for this range of parameters. By a union bound the sparsity in Theorem 1 cannot be improved even if the extractor is weak but uses m^α bits of seed for a sufficiently small constant α. However, if we do not restrict the length of the seed, our next result shows that the sparsity can be improved for certain parameter settings:

THEOREM 3. *Let K be a sufficiently large constant and n,k,c,m be parameters such that $1 \le k \le n$, $1 \le s < m$ and $c > 1$. Let $H\colon \{0,1\}^n \times \{0,1\}^s \to \{0,1\}^m$ be given by $H(x,r) = Mx + Br$, where M is an $m \times n$ random matrix in which each entry equals 1 independently with probability*

$$p = \min\left\{\frac{K}{m} \cdot \ln\frac{n}{\ln c}, \frac{1}{2}\right\},$$

and B is an $m \times s$ $(m > s)$ matrix of full rank over $GF(2)$ where every set of at most $m/2K$ rows is linearly independent. Then H is an extractor family for min-entropy k with error $1/2\sqrt{c \cdot 2^{-k-s+m}}$.

The construction of $O(m)$-sparse matrices B with the desired properties is a well studied problem in the theory of low density parity check codes [9, 24]. Capalbo et al. [6] give an explicit construction with $s = \alpha m$ for some constant $\alpha < 1$ and every m, which is optimal up to the choice of the constant α. Instantiating Theorem 3 with this matrix, and setting $c = 2$, we obtain a family of $O(n \log n)$ sparse extractors with error $O(\sqrt{2^{-k-s+m}})$, which is optimal up to constant factor. (If $m = k + s - O(1)$, the output contains almost all the entropy from the source plus all the entropy invested by the seed and the error is an arbitrarily small constant.) By using a larger value of c, we can reduce the sparsity at the cost of increasing the error. In particular, if $c = 2^{\beta n}$ where $\beta < 1$ is a constant, the sparsity can be reduced to $O(n)$. (However to keep the error $1/2\sqrt{c \cdot 2^{-k-s+m}}$ smaller than 1, the entropy loss $k + s - m$ has to be larger than βn.)

We observe that using the randomized encoding of Applebaum et al. [1], these extractors can be made to have constant locality at the cost of increasing the seed length r to $O(n \log n)$ bits.

For certain parameters the weak extractor family from Theorem 3 bypasses the limitation on strong extractor families from Theorem 2. For example, for constant statistical distance and $m = n^{0.99}$ Theorem 2 implies that for a strong extractor to produce even a constant fraction of the entropy a sparsity of $\Omega(n(\log n)^2)$ is necessary, while Theorem 3 says that an $O(n \log n)$-sparse weak extractor family can extract all but $O(1)$ bits of entropy.

Local pseudorandom generators from local one-way functions. The construction of pseudorandom generators from one-way functions of Håstad et al. [12] does not in general preserve locality. Haitner, Reingold, and Vadhan [11] gave a construction that is more efficient and can be implemented in NC^1. Recently Vadhan and Zheng [26] gave an even simpler variant of this construction. In combination with the "compiler" of Applebaum, Ishai, and Kushilevitz [2], one obtains a generic locality-preserving transformation of one-way functions into pseudorandom generators.

Applying the generic transformation of Applebaum et al. may have an adverse effect on seed length, which grows quadratically. However, the construction of Vadhan and Zheng is extremely simple; it is obtained by applying extractor to a sequence of "blocks", each of which inherits the locality of the one-way function f. Instantiating the extractor by the construction from Theorem 3, we obtain a transformation of *nonuniform* one-way functions into nonuniform pseudorandom generators that preserves output locality logarithmic in the size of the adversary with the same seed length as the one obtained by Vadhan and Zheng. Using an additional idea of Applebaum et al., the transformation can be made to preserve constant output locality at the expense of increasing the seed length. We describe this application in Section 5 (see Proposition 9).

1.2 Related work

Sparse extractors for restricted sources. Motivated by certain applications, Zhou and Bruck [29] show that low density random matrices can efficiently extract random bits from some restricted noisy sources, such as bit fixing sources and Markov sources. Our Theorem 1 shows that essentially the same construction extracts from arbitrary sources of given min-entropy.

Extractors in NC^0. Applebaum, Ishai and Kushilevitz [3] give a weak extractor in NC^0 (with sparsity $O(n)$) that works for min-entropy $k = (1 - O(1))n$, but suffers $\Omega(n)$ entropy loss. Our extractor family from Theorem 3 matches these parameters. The construction from [3] does not appear to extend to distributions of smaller min-entropy or allow for smaller entropy loss, while ours does. However, they provide a single extractor that works for all distributions, while we only give an extractor family.

Locally computable extractors. A *locally computable extractor* [15, 25] is an extractor in which after the seed is fixed, the output as a whole depends on a small number of input bits. Such extractors are used to implement private-key encryption in the bounded storage model [17]. We observe that the notions of locally computable extractors and sparse extractor families are fundamentally different. This is best illustrated in the regime in which we extract all the entropy, which is of main interest in this work. A lower bound of Vadhan [25] shows that when the output length m is linear in the min-entropy k, then even after the seed is fixed the output of the extractor as a whole must depend on at least a linear fraction of the input. Thus $o(n)$-locally computable extractors are not possible when $m = \Omega(k)$.

The locally computable extractors of Lu [15] and De and Trevisan [8] are also sparse, but they extract only a fixed root of the min-entropy k. This is sufficient for bounded storage cryptography, but not for the application we describe in Section 5.

1.3 Our proofs

Bogdanov and Rosen [5] proved a quantitatively weaker version of Theorem 1 that achieves sparsity $O(n(\log n)^3)$ instead of the optimal $O(n(\log m)\log(n/m))$. (They did not attempt to determine the dependence on m but their proof gives sparsity $O(n(\log m)\log(n/m)^2)$.) In their proof, H is viewed as a collection of boolean functions $(h_1, \ldots, h_m)$, where $h_i\colon \{0,1\}^n \to \{0,1\}$. They show that for most choices of h_1, conditioning on $h_1(x)$ reduces the min-entropy k of x by at most $1 + 1/\mathrm{poly}(k)$ bits (unless k is very small), and so this bit extraction can be applied iteratively for m steps.

One drawback of this argument is that as i gets larger and the min-entropy of x conditioned on $h_1(x), \ldots, h_{i-1}(x)$ becomes smaller, the density of the functions h_i must keep increasing (as required by our lower bound). To achieve our optimal (up to constant) sparsity, we must analyze the effect of all the functions $h_1, \ldots, h_m$ simultaneously.

To do this, we upper bound the probability that two samples x, x' collide under h, that is the probability that $h(x + x') = 0$. For a fixed pair (x, x'), each entry $h_i(x + x')$ of $h(x+x')$ is biased towards zero. We can think of $h_i(x+x')$ as a random variable that takes value zero with some probability $p(x, x')$, and is unbiased otherwise. Intuitively, our analysis shows that the unbiased components of this distribution dominate in collisions. Several technical complications arise in the formal argument. One useful tool that allows us to analyze the case when most of the components of $h(x + x')$ are unbiased is Hölder's inequality.

To give an idea of our proof of Theorem 2, let us make the simplifying assumption that h is ℓ-local, where $\ell = \gamma(n/m)\log m \log(n/m)$, and *linear*. We give a heuristic argument why we expect the output of h to be far from uniform. Let X be the p-biased distribution over $\{0,1\}^n$ (each bit takes value 1 independently with probability p) and p is chosen so that $H(p) = m/n$, where $H(p)$ is the binary entropy of p. Then the distribution X has Shannon entropy m. However, every output bit of $h(X)$ is $(1 - 2p)^\ell$-biased, and we chose the parameters so that $(1-2p)^\ell = m^{-\Omega(\gamma)}$. By choosing γ small enough, we can ensure that every output bit of h has, say, $m^{-1/2}$ bits of *entropy deficiency*, so by the sub-additivity of Shannon entropy $h(X)$ has $m^{1/2}$ fewer bits of entropy than a uniformly random variable over $\{0,1\}^m$. So $h(X)$ does not "look" random in terms of Shannon entropy.

To turn this heuristic argument into a proof we need to handle several issues, the most interesting of which is replacing entropy deficiency by statistical distance from the uniform distribution. One advantage of measuring entropy deficiency is that entropy is subadditive, which allows us to ignore the dependencies between the various outputs of $h(X)$ in the above argument. In contrast, to obtain a good lower bound on statistical distance we must take into account these dependencies. One of the tools we use is a recent deviation bound of Gavinsky et al. [10]. To extend the analysis from linear functions to general ones we apply an elegant idea of Viola [28] of shifting X by a random offset.

We establish Theorem 3 by a relatively straightforward probabilistic calculation.

1.4 Open problems

In terms of seed length our extractor families are quite poor. For example the size of the family H in Theorem 1 is exponential in n. By a standard probabilistic argument it can be shown that a random sample of H of size $O(n/\varepsilon^2)$ is as effective as the whole family while incurring an additional penalty of only ε in statistical distance. Therefore there is no existential obstacle to sparse extractor families with short seed. It remains to see if such families can be found efficiently.

For weak sparse extractors, our work leaves open two questions. First, we do not know if the sparsity of our weak extractors is the best possible. Second, we do not know what is the minimal size of a sparse weak extractor family. It could be that even a family of size 1, i.e. a single sparse weak extractor, is sufficient. Such an extractor could be used to improve uniform constructions of local pseudorandom generators from local one-way functions.

2. PROOF OF THEOREM 1

To prove Theorem 1 it is sufficient to show that for every set S of size 2^k, the statistical distance between $(H, H(X))$ and (H, U) is at most $1/2\sqrt{\delta + O(2^{-k+m})}$, where X is chosen at random from S and U is uniformly random. In fact we will show for every $x_0 \in S$,

$$\Pr_{H,X}[H(X) = H(x_0)] \le \frac{1 + \delta + O(2^{-k+m})}{2^m}$$

from where

$$\Pr_{H,X,X'}[H(X) = H(X')] \le \max_{x_0 \in S} \Pr_{H,X}[H(X) = H(x_0)] \le \frac{1 + \delta + O(2^{-k+m})}{2^m}$$

where X and X' are independent samples from S. This is sufficient to establish Theorem 1 using the relation between collision probability and statistical distance from Claim 10 in Appendix A.

PROOF. When $p = 1/2$ the analysis is standard, so we will assume that $p = \frac{1}{m} \cdot \log(m/\delta) \ln(15n/m) < 1/2$. Since entries of M are chosen independently from each other, for any $y \in \{0,1\}^n$, we have

$$\Pr_H[H(y) = 0] = \Pr_a[\langle a, y\rangle = 0]^m = \Big(\frac{1 + (1-2p)^{|y|}}{2}\Big)^m = \frac{1}{2^m}\sum_{i=0}^{m} \tbinom{m}{i}(1-2p)^{i|y|}$$

Here $a \sim \{0,1\}^m$ is chosen from the p-biased distribution. Let S_0 be the set $\{x_0 + x \colon x \in S\}$. Then

$$\Pr_{H,X}[H(X) = H(x_0)] = \Pr_{H,y\sim S_0}[H(y) = 0] = \mathrm{E}_{y\sim S_0}\Big[\frac{1}{2^m}\sum_{i=0}^{m}\tbinom{m}{i}(1-2p)^{i|y|}\Big] = \frac{1}{2^m}\sum_{i=0}^{m}\tbinom{m}{i}\,\mathrm{E}_{y\sim S_0}[(1-2p)^{i|y|}]$$

Let $a_i = \mathrm{E}_{y\sim S_0}[(1-2p)^{i|y|}]$. We now upper bound the sum $\sum_{i=0}^{m}\binom{m}{i}a_i$ by $1 + \delta + O(2^{-k+m})$. We will consider two cases: When i is small – specifically, $i \le k/(2\log(m/\delta))$, we show that a_i decreases at a rate faster than $(m/\delta)^{-i}$, so the sum is dominated by the term $i = 0$. When i is large, we want to bound both a_i and $\binom{m}{i}$ by its largest possible value. To achieve this, we have to further split the large i's into "mildly large" and "very large" ones and apply the argument to each summation separately. The resulting contribution is $O(2^{-k+m})$. Notice that, in the case $m \le k/(2\log(m/\delta))$, we need not consider the contribution of large i's thus we can improve p to be $\frac{1}{k}\cdot\log(m/\delta)\ln(15n/k)$ by using the same analysis for small i's.

The small i's. We show that if $i \le k/(2\log(m/\delta))$, then $a_i \le (m/\delta)^{-1.8i}$ and therefore

$$\sum_{i=0}^{k/(2\log(m/\delta))}\tbinom{m}{i}a_i \le (1 + (m/\delta)^{-1.8})^m \le e^{\delta^{1.8}/m^{0.8}} \le 1 + \delta.$$

To bound a_i we apply Hölder's inequality, which says that for every $B \ge 1$:

$$a_i = \mathrm{E}_{y\sim S_0}[(1-2p)^{i|y|}] = \frac{1}{|S|}\sum_{y\in\{0,1\}^n} 1_{y\in S_0}\cdot(1-2p)^{i|y|} \le \frac{1}{|S|}|S|^{1-1/B}\sum_{y\in\{0,1\}^n}\big((1-2p)^{Bi|y|}\big)^{1/B}.$$

The last expression can be simplified to give

$$a_i \le \Big(\frac{(1 + (1-2p)^{Bi})^n}{|S|}\Big)^{1/B} \le \Big(\frac{(1 + e^{-2piB})^n}{|S|}\Big)^{1/B}.$$

We choose $B = k/(2i\log(m/\delta))$, which is at least one because $i \le k/(2\log(m/\delta))$. By our choice of p, it follows that $2piB \ge \ln(15n/m)$ and so

$$a_i \le \Big(\frac{(1 + m/15n)^n}{|S|}\Big)^{1/B} \le \Big(\frac{e^{m/15}}{2^k}\Big)^{1/B} \le \Big(\frac{e^{k/15}}{2^k}\Big)^{1/B} \le (2^{-0.9})^{k/B} = (m/\delta)^{-1.8i}.$$

The large i's. We have that

$$a_i = \mathrm{E}_{y\sim S_0}[(1-2p)^{i|y|}] \le \frac{1}{|S|}\sum_{y\in\{0,1\}^n}(1-2p)^{i|y|} = \frac{(1 + (1-2p)^i)^n}{|S|} \le \frac{(1 + e^{-2pi})^n}{|S|}. \tag{1}$$

When $i \ge m/4$, the last expression is at most $(1 + e^{-pm/2})^n/|S|$. By our choice of p, $pm/2 \ge 1/2\log m\ln(15n/m)$. Optimizing for $\log m$, it can be calculated that this expression is at least $\ln n$ when n is sufficiently large. It then follows that

$$a_i \le \frac{(1 + 1/n)^n}{|S|} \le e2^{-k}$$

and so

$$\sum_{i=m/4}^{m}\tbinom{m}{i}a_i \le 2^m \cdot e2^{-k} = e2^{-k+m}.$$

Finally, we handle the i's in the range $k/(2\log(m/\delta)) < i < m/4$. Using (1) and the lower bound on i, we have that

$$a_i \le \frac{(1 + m/15n)^n}{|S|} \le \frac{e^{m/15}}{|S|} \le 2^{0.1m-k}$$

and so

$$\sum_{k/(2\log(m/\delta))<i<m/4}\tbinom{m}{i}a_i \le 2^{0.1m-k}\sum_{i=0}^{m/4}\tbinom{m}{i} \le 2^{0.1m-k}\cdot 2^{H(1/4)m+O(1)} \le 2^{-k+m+O(1)},$$

where H is the binary entropy function, and $H(1/4) \le 0.9$. □

3. PROOF OF THEOREM 2

Let distribution $\overline{X}$ be a truncated variant of the p-biased distribution X where p is chosen so that $H(p) = 2m/n$ and $p \le 1/2$. The distribution $\mathcal{D}$ on distributions is defined as follows. Choose y uniformly from $\{0,1\}^n$ and output $y + \overline{X}$. To prove Theorem 2, we will show for most choices of y, there exists a statistical test T_y that distinguishes $h(y+\overline{X})$ from the uniform distribution U and then argue the expected statistical distance over choice of y between $h(y+\overline{X})$ and U is large. We will define T_y shortly for $y \in \{0,1\}^n$ and first argue that for most choice of y, T_y distinguishes $h(y+X)$ from U. Then we will show how to define $\overline{X}$ of min-entropy $1.5m$ in a way that X and $\overline{X}$ are statistically close. Finally, we conclude that the expected statistical distance over choice of y between $h(y+\overline{X})$ and U is at least $1-e^{-m^{\Omega(1)}}$.

The following bounds on p are obtained by plugging in $H(p)=2m/n$ in Lemma 11 in Appendix B:

$$\frac{m}{3n\log_2(n/m)} \le p \le \frac{2m}{n\log_2(n/2m)}. \qquad (2)$$

Now suppose h has sparsity $(m/2p)\beta\log m$, where β is a sufficiently small constant, say $\beta=0.08$. Notice this β also satisfies $n \le m^{1+2\beta}$ (since by assumption $m \ge n^{0.99}$). Partition the inputs of h' into two sets H and L, where H contains those inputs that participate in at least $m^{2-6\beta}/pn$ outputs of h', and L contains the rest. By Markov's inequality (using the assumption $n \le m^{1+2\beta}$), H has size at most $m^{8\beta}\beta\log k$. For $x \in \{0,1\}^n$, let x_0 and x_1 denote its projections onto H and L, respectively. For every $y \in \{0,1\}^n$, we define the statistical test

$$T_y = \{z \in \{0,1\}^m : \exists x_0, \Delta(h(x_0,y_1),z) \le 1/2 - m^{-\beta}/4\}$$

where$\Delta(a,b)$ is relative Hamming distance between the strings a and b, i.e. the fraction of positions in which they differ.

CLAIM 4. *For sufficiently large k, $\Pr_X[h(X+y) \in T_y] \ge 1-e^{-m^{3\beta}/2}$ for at a least $1-e^{-m^{3\beta}/2}$ values of $y \in \{0,1\}^n$.*

In the proof we will need the following fact about Boolean functions $f\colon \{0,1\}^d \to \{0,1\}$

$$\Pr_{X,Y}[f(X+Y) \ne f(Y)] \le \tfrac{1}{2} - \tfrac{1}{2}(1-2p)^d \qquad (3)$$

where Y is uniformly distributed in $\{0,1\}^n$, and X is chosen independently from the p-biased distribution on $\{0,1\}^n$. This fact follows easily by Fourier analysis [20] and was also used by Viola [28] in a context related to ours. We will use it to show that when h is md sparse, the expected relative hamming distance between $h(X+Y)$ and $h(Y)$ is at most $1/2(1-(1-2p)^d)$.

We will also use the following result of Gavinsky et al. [10]. Boolean-valued random variables $Z_1,\ldots,Z_m$ form a *read t family* if there exist independent Boolean-valued random variables $X_1,\ldots,X_n$ so that every Z_j depends on at most t of the X_i's. Gavinsky et al. show that for every such read-t family and every $\varepsilon>0$,

$$\Pr[Z \ge \mathrm{E}[Z]+\varepsilon m] \le e^{-2\varepsilon^2 m/t}. \qquad (4)$$

where $Z = Z_1+\cdots+Z_m$.

PROOF OF CLAIM 4. We will show that for every choice of x_0,y_0, with probability $1-e^{-\Omega(m^{1-\beta})}$ over the choice of x_1,y_1, $h(x+y)=h(x_0+y_0,x_1+y_1)$ is in T_y. Fix x_0,y_0 and consider the function $h^{x_0+y_0}(x_1)=h(x_0+y_0,x_1)$. Let $Z=Z_1+\cdots+Z_m$, where

$$Z_i = \begin{cases} 1, & \text{if } h_i^{x_0+y_0}(x_1+y_1) \ne h_i^{x_0+y_0}(y_1), \\ 0, & \text{otherwise.} \end{cases}$$

Suppose $h_i^{x_0+y_0}$ depends on d_i inputs for $1 \le i \le m$, by (3) we have

$$\mathrm{E}[Z_i] \le 1/2(1-(1-2p)^{d_i}).$$

By linearity of expectation and $\sum_{i=1}^m d_i \le (m/2p)\beta\log m$,

$$\mathrm{E}[Z] \le m/2(1-(1-2p)^{\beta\log m/2p}) \le m(1/2-m^{-\beta}/2).$$

Now we apply tail bound (4) to $Z_1,\ldots,Z_m$ with $t=m^{2-6\beta}/pn$ and $\varepsilon = m^{-\beta}/4$ to obtain

$$\Pr[Z \ge m(1/2-m^{-\beta}/4)] \le e^{-2\varepsilon^2 m/(m^{2-6\beta}/pn)} \le e^{-m^{3\beta}}$$

where we used the estimate (2) to lower bound pn. Hence,

$$\Pr_{x_1,y_1}[\Delta(h_{x_0+y_0}(y_1),h_{x_0+y_0}(x_1+y_1)) \le 1/2-m^{-\beta}/4] \ge 1-e^{-m^{3\beta}}.$$

It follows that

$$\begin{aligned}\Pr_{x,y}&[h(x+y)\in T_y] \\ &\ge \mathrm{E}_{x_0,y_0}\left[\Pr_{x_1,y_1}[\Delta(h_{x_0+y_0}(y_1),h_{x_0+y_0}(x_1+y_1)) \le 1/2-m^{-\beta}/4]\right] \\ &\ge 1-e^{-m^{3\beta}}.\end{aligned}$$

Applying Markov's inequality, we conclude that for at least $1-e^{-m^{3\beta}/2}$ choices of y,

$$\mathrm{E}_X[h(X+y)\in T_y] \ge 1-e^{-m^{3\beta}/2}. \quad \square$$

CLAIM 5. *For any fixed $y \in \{0,1\}^n$, with probability $1-2^{-\Omega(m^{1-2\beta})}$ over the choice of a uniform $U \sim \{0,1\}^m$, U is not in T_y.*

PROOF. Since H has size at most $m^{8\beta}\beta\log k$, the range of $h'(x_0,y_1)$ has at most $2^{m^{8\beta}\beta\log m}$ elements. For every such element $h(x_0,y_1)$, the probability that U is within distance $m/2-m^{1-\beta}/4$ to $h(x_0,y_1)$ can be computed by Chernoff bounds to be at most $2^{-\Omega(m^{1-2\beta})}$. Taking a union bound over all such $h(x_0,y_1)$, we obtain

$$\Pr[U\in T_y] \le 2^{m^{8\beta}\beta\log m}2^{-\Omega(m^{1-2\beta})} = 2^{-\Omega(m^{1-2\beta})}$$

as long as $\beta < 1/10$ and m is sufficiently large. $\square$

From these two claims, it follows that for $1-e^{-m^{3\beta}/2}$ choices of y,

$$\begin{aligned}&\Pr_X[h(X+y)\in T_y] - \Pr_U[U\in T_y] \\ &\ge 1-1-e^{-m^{3\beta}/2} - 2^{-\Omega(m^{1-2\beta})}. \end{aligned} \qquad (5)$$

To finish the proof, we show how to replace X with another variable $\overline{X}$ of min-entropy at least $1.5m$ that is statistically close to it. We define $\overline{X}$ as follows: First, choose X from the p-biased distribution. If the Hamming weight of X is at least $0.9pn$, set $\overline{X}=X$. Otherwise, let $\overline{X}$ be uniformly random in $\{0,1\}^n$. We prove the following claim in Appendix C:

CLAIM 6. *$\overline{X}$ has min-entropy at least $1.5m$.*

Clearly the same conclusion holds for the distribution $\overline{X}+y$. The statistical distance between X and $\overline{X}$ is at most the probability that X has Hamming weight less than $0.9pn$, which is at most $\exp(-\Omega(pn))$ by Chernoff bounds. Using the lower bound (2) this is at most $\exp(-\Omega(m/\log(n/m))) = \exp(-m^{\Omega(1)})$ (since $m \geq n^{-0.99}$). Applying the triangle inequality, for all y satisfying (5) we have

$$\Pr_{\overline{X}}[h(\overline{X}+y) \in T_y] - \Pr_U[U \in T_y] \geq 1 - e^{-m^{\Omega(1)}}.$$

We conclude that the expected statistical distance between $h(\overline{X}+y)$ and U_m for a random choice of y is at least $(1 - e^{-m^{\Omega(1)}})(1 - e^{-m^{\Omega(1)}}) = 1 - e^{-m^{\Omega(1)}}$.

4. PROOF OF THEOREM 3

As in the proof of Theorem 1, it is sufficient to show for every set S of size 2^k and every x_0 in S and r_0 in $\{0,1\}^s$,

$$\Pr_{M,X,R}[MX + BR = Mx_0 + Br_0] \leq \frac{1 + (1/\delta) \cdot 2^{-k-s+m}}{2^m}$$

where the probability is taken over the random matrix M, X chosen uniformly from S and R chosen uniformly from $\{0,1\}^s$.

Assume that $p \leq 1/2$. Let S_0 be the set $\{x + x_0 : x \in S\}$. Let Y be a random element from S_0 and M_i, B_i denote the ith row of M and B. Then

$$\begin{aligned}
&\Pr_{M,X,R}[MX + BR = Mx_0 + Br_0] \\
&= \Pr_{M,X,R}[M(X + x_0) = B(R + r_0)] \\
&= \Pr_{M,Y,R}[MY = BR] \\
&= \mathrm{E}_{M,Y,R}[\prod_{i=1}^{m} \frac{1 + (-1)^{M_i Y + B_i R}}{2}] \\
&= \frac{1}{2^m} \sum_{T \subseteq [m]} \mathrm{E}_{M,Y,R}[(-1)^{\sum_{i\in T} M_i Y + B_i R}] \\
&= \frac{1}{2^m} \sum_{T \subseteq [m]} \mathrm{E}_{M,Y}[(-1)^{\sum_{i\in T} M_i Y}]\, \mathrm{E}_R[(-1)^{\sum_{i\in T} B_i R}].
\end{aligned}$$

Since any $t = m/2K$ rows of B are linearly independent, for every nonempty T of size at most t, $\sum_{i\in T} B_i \neq 0$ and so $\mathrm{E}[(-1)^{\sum_{i\in T} B_i R}] = 0$. On the other hand for every T of size at least t we have

$$\begin{aligned}
&\mathrm{E}_{M,Y}[(-1)^{\sum_{i\in T} M_i Y}] \\
&= \frac{1}{2^k} \sum_{y \in S_0} \mathrm{E}_M[(-1)^{\sum_{i\in T} M_i y}] = \frac{1}{2^k} \sum_{y\in S_0} (1-2p)^{|y|\cdot|T|} \\
&\leq \frac{1}{2^k} \sum_{y \in \{0,1\}^n} (1-2p)^{t|y|} \leq \frac{1}{2^k}(1 + (1-2p)^t)^n \\
&\leq \frac{e^{ne^{-2pt}}}{2^k}.
\end{aligned}$$

Since B has full rank, the condition $\sum_{i\in T} B_i = 0$ is satisfied for at most 2^{m-s} sets T. Hence,

$$\begin{aligned}
&\sum_{T\subseteq[m]} \mathrm{E}_{M,Y}[(-1)^{\sum_{i\in T} M_i Y}]\, \mathrm{E}_R[(-1)^{\sum_{i\in T} B_i R}] \\
&= 1 + \sum_{T:|T|>t} \mathrm{E}_{M,Y}[(-1)^{\sum_{i\in T} M_i y}]\, \mathrm{E}_R[(-1)^{\sum_{i\in T} B_i s}] \\
&\leq 1 + \sum_{T:|T|>t} \frac{e^{ne^{-2pt}}}{2^k} |\mathrm{E}_R[(-1)^{\sum_{i\in T} B_i R}]| \\
&\leq 1 + 2^{m-s} \cdot \frac{e^{ne^{-2pt}}}{2^k} = 1 + \frac{e^{ne^{-2pt}}}{2^{s+k-m}}.
\end{aligned}$$

Plugging in $t = \frac{m}{2K}$ and $p = \frac{K}{m} \cdot \ln \frac{n}{\ln c}$ we get the desired bound.

5. LOCAL PSEUDORANDOM GENERATORS FROM LOCAL ONE-WAY FUNCTIONS

A sequence of correlated random variables $X_1, \dots, X_m$ taking values in $\{0,1\}^n$ has (s,ε) *conditional pseudo-min-entropy* r if for every $1 \leq i \leq m$, there exists a random variable Y_i jointly distributed with $X_1, \dots, X_{i-1}$ such that the min-entropy of Y conditioned on any choice of $X_1, \dots, X_{i-1}$ is at least r and for every circuit D of size s,

$$\left|\Pr[D(X_i) \mid X_1, \dots, X_{i-1}] - \Pr[D(Y_i) \mid X_1, \dots, X_{i-1}]\right| \leq \varepsilon.$$

Vadhan and Zheng [26] give the following construction of conditional pseudo-min-entropy sequences from a one-way function $f\colon \{0,1\}^n \to \{0,1\}^n$. Let $z_i, 1 \leq i \leq t$ be the random strings

$$z_i = {}_{o_i}\lfloor f(x_{i1}) \circ x_{i1} \circ \cdots \circ f(x_{ik}) \circ x_{ik} \rfloor_{n-o_i}$$

where $1 \leq o_i \leq n$ is an offset, $x_{i1}, \dots, x_{ik}$ are random strings, and ${}_f\lfloor y \rfloor_\ell$ denotes truncating the first f and last ℓ bits of y respectively. Let $X_j = z_{1j} z_{2j} \dots z_{tj}$, where z_{ij} denotes the jth bit of z_i. Vadhan and Zheng prove the following theorem (we state it in the nonuniform setting).

THEOREM 7 (VADHAN AND ZHENG). *Suppose $f\colon \{0,1\}^n \to \{0,1\}^n$ is computable by a circuit of size* $\mathrm{poly}(n)$ *and is hard to invert on a $1/s$ fraction of inputs by circuits of size s. There exists offsets $o_1, \dots, o_t$ such that for every ε, $X_1, \dots, X_m$ has $(s^{\Omega(1)}/\mathrm{poly}(n\varepsilon), \varepsilon)$ conditional pseudo-min-entropy at least $t(1/2 + \Omega((\log s)/n))$ where $k = O(n/\log s)$, $t = O((n/\log s)^2 \log^2 n \log(1/\varepsilon))$ and $m = 2(k-1)n$.*

The following claim was proved in the uniform setting by Haitner, Reingold, and Vadhan. We need a nonuniform version of it, whose proof is analogous. We include it at the end of this section for completeness.

CLAIM 8. *Suppose $X_1, \dots, X_m$ (where X_i takes values in $\{0,1\}^t$) has (T,ε_1) conditional pseudo-min-entropy α. Let H be an extractor family for min-entropy α with error ε_2 so that every function in H is computable in size T_0. Then with probability at least $1/2$ over the choice of H the distribution $(H(X_1, R_1), \dots, H(X_m, R_m))$ is $(T - mT_0, m\varepsilon_1 + 2m^2\varepsilon_2)$-pseudorandom where $R_1, \dots, R_m \sim \{0,1\}^r$.*

Instantiating Claim 8 with the function family from Theorem 3 where we set the output length of function to be $t(1/2 + \Omega((\log s)/n)) + r$ and let d be the entropy loss. We obtain the following consequence for the function

$$G(x_{11}, \dots, x_{tk}, r_1, \dots, r_m) = (H(X_1, r_1), \dots, H(X_m, r_m)).$$

PROPOSITION 9. *Suppose $f\colon \{0,1\}^n \to \{0,1\}^n$ is an ℓ-local function computable by a circuit of size* $\mathrm{poly}(n)$ *and is hard to invert on a $1/s$ fraction of inputs by circuits of size s. With probability at least $1/2$ over the choice of H,*

$$G\colon \{0,1\}^{nkt+mr} \to \{0,1\}^{nkt(1+\Omega(\frac{\log s}{n}))+mr}$$

is an $O(\ell \cdot (nkt \ln(t/\ln c)))$-sparse, $(s^{\Omega(1)}/\mathrm{poly}(n\varepsilon), \mathrm{poly}(n)(\varepsilon + \sqrt{c} \cdot 2^{-d/2}))$ pseudorandom generator where $k = O(n/\log s)$, $m = 2(k-1)n$ and $t = O((n/\log s)^2 \log^2 n \log(1/\varepsilon))$.

A pairwise independent function family with the same entropy loss would give a pseudorandom generator of average sparsity $O(\ell \cdot t)$ (i.e., the number of input bits that every output depends on) and security $(s^{\Omega(1)}/\text{poly}(n\varepsilon), \text{poly}(n)(\varepsilon + 2^{-d/2}))$. Our construction improves the average sparsity to $O(\ell \cdot \ln(t/\ln c))$ with only increasing the error by a factor of $\sqrt{c}$. In paricular, by letting $c = O(1)$ we can achieve optimal error with average sparsity $O(\ell \cdot \ln t) = O(\ell \cdot \log n)$ and optimal average sparsity $O(\ell)$ can be obtained by letting $c = 2^{\Omega(t)}$.

We can improve the locality of G at the expense of increasing its input and output length by the factor of $O(\ln(t/\ln c))$ (which can be upper bounded by $O(\log n)$) via the following transformation of Applebaum, Ishai, and Kushilevitz. For every output of G, which is obtained by applying a sparse linear transformation to some X_j and therefore has the form

$$X_{jk_1} + \cdots + X_{jk_i}$$

introduce auxiliary new inputs $r_{j3}, r_{j4}, \ldots, r_{j(i-1)}$ for G and replace its corresponding output by the tuple

$$(X_{jk_1}+X_{jk_2}+r_{j3}, r_{j3}+X_{jk_3}+r_{j4}, \ldots, r_{j_{i-1}}+X_{jk_{i-1}}+X_{jk_i}).$$

Call this new function G'. Applebaum et al. show that if G is $(s^{\Omega(1)}, s^{-\Omega(1)})$-pseudorandom, so is G'. Since every bit of X_j comes either from some input x_i or from some output $f(x_i)$, it follows that if f has locality ℓ, then G' has locality 3ℓ. This transformation can also improve the locality of pseudorandom generators which is obtained by instantiating pairwise independent function family. However the input and output length will be increased by a fact of $\Omega(t)$ (which is typically$\Omega(\ n^2)$) via the same transformation.

Proof of Claim 8. Let Y_i be the conditional min-entropy model for X_i. We consider the hybrid distributions $X^{(i)} = (H(X_1, R_1), \ldots, H(X_{i-1}, R_{i-1}), H(X_i, R_i), U_{i+1}, \ldots, U_m)$ and $Y^{(i)} = (H(X_1, R_1), \ldots, H(X_{i-1}, R_{i-1}), H(Y_i, R_i), U_{i+1}, \ldots, U_m)$ where $U_1, \ldots, U_m$ are uniformly random and independent. By the definition of conditional pseudo-min-entropy, for every i the distributions $X^{(i)}$ and $Y^{(i)}$ are $(T - mT_0, \varepsilon_1)$-indistinguishable. Because $\mathcal{H}$ is an extractor family, the distributions $(H, H(Y_i, R_i) \mid X_1, \ldots, X_{i-1})$ and (H, U_i) are within statistical distance ε_2 for any choice of $X_1, \ldots, X_{i-1}$. It follows that $(H, Y^{(i)})$ and $(H, X^{(i-1)})$ are within statistical distance at most ε_2, so by Markov's inequality $Y^{(i)}$ and $X^{(i-1)}$ are within statistical distance $2m\varepsilon_2$ with probability at least $1 - 1/2m$ over the choice of H. By a union bound, with probability at least $1/2$ over the choice of H, $Y^{(i)}$ and $X^{(i-1)}$ are $2m\varepsilon_2$-statistically close for all i. For such a choice of H, by the triangle inequality $X^{(m)}$ is $(T - mT_0, m\varepsilon_1 + 2m^2\varepsilon_2)$ indistinguishable from $X^{(0)}$. Since $X^{(m)} = (H(X_1 R_1), \ldots, H(X_m, R_m))$ and $X^{(0)}$ is the uniform distribution, we obtain the desired conclusion. □

Acknowledgments

We would like to thank Rafail Ostrovsky for asking about the existence of a local analogue to hash functions in the context of randomness extraction. We also thank Elchanan Mossel, Oded Regev, Alon Rosen, and Sidharth Jaggi for helpful discussions and the anonymous reviewers for useful comments.

6. REFERENCES

[1] B. Applebaum, Y. Ishai, and E. Kushilevitz. Cryptography in nc0. In *Foundations of Computer Science, 2004. Proceedings. 45th Annual IEEE Symposium on*, pages 166–175. IEEE, 2004.

[2] B. Applebaum, Y. Ishai, and E. Kushilevitz. Cryptography in nc0. In *Foundations of Computer Science, 2004. Proceedings. 45th Annual IEEE Symposium on*, pages 166–175. IEEE, 2004.

[3] B. Applebaum, Y. Ishai, and E. Kushilevitz. On pseudorandom generators with linear stretch in nc 0. *Approximation, Randomization, and Combinatorial Optimization. Algorithms and Techniques*, pages 260–271, 2006.

[4] C. Bennett, G. Brassard, and J. Robert. Privacy amplification by public discussion. *SIAM journal on Computing*, 17:210, 1988.

[5] A. Bogdanov and A. Rosen. Input locality and hardness amplification. *Theory of Cryptography*, pages 1–18, 2011.

[6] M. R. Capalbo, O. Reingold, S. P. Vadhan, and A. Wigderson. Randomness conductors and constant-degree lossless expanders. In *Proceedings of the 34th Annual ACM Symposium on Theory of Computing*, pages 659–668, 2002.

[7] J. Carter and M. Wegman. Universal classes of hash functions. *Journal of computer and system sciences*, 18(2):143–154, 1979.

[8] A. De and L. Trevisan. Extractors using hardness amplification. *Approximation, Randomization, and Combinatorial Optimization. Algorithms and Techniques*, pages 462–475, 2009.

[9] R. Gallager. Low-density parity-check codes. *IRE Transactions on Information Theory*, 8(1):21–28, 1962.

[10] D. Gavinsky, S. Lovett, M. Saks, and S. Srinivasan. A tail bound for read-k families of functions. *Arxiv preprint arXiv:1205.1478*, 2012.

[11] I. Haitner, O. Reingold, and S. Vadhan. Efficiency improvements in constructing pseudorandom generators from one-way functions. In *Proceedings of the 42nd ACM symposium on Theory of computing*, pages 437–446. ACM, 2010.

[12] J. Håstad, R. Impagliazzo, L. Levin, and M. Luby. A pseudorandom generator from any one-way function. *SIAM J. Comput.*, 28(4):1364–1396, 1999.

[13] R. Impagliazzo, L. Levin, and M. Luby. Pseudo-random generation from one-way functions. In *Proceedings of the twenty-first annual ACM symposium on Theory of computing*, pages 12–24. ACM, 1989.

[14] Y. Ishai, E. Kushilevitz, R. Ostrovsky, and A. Sahai. Cryptography with constant computational overhead. In *Proceedings of the 40th annual ACM symposium on Theory of computing*, pages 433–442. ACM, 2008.

[15] C. Lu. Encryption against storage-bounded adversaries from on-line strong extractors. *Journal of Cryptology*, 17(1):27–42, 2004.

[16] Y. Mansour, N. Nisan, and P. Tiwari. The computational complexity of universal hashing. *Theoretical Computer Science*, 107(1):121–133, 1993.

[17] U. Maurer. Conditionally-perfect secrecy and a

provably-secure randomized cipher. *Journal of Cryptology*, 5(1):53–66, 1992.

[18] N. Nisan. Pseudorandom generators for space-bounded computation. *Combinatorica*, 12(4):449–461, 1992.

[19] N. Nisan and D. Zuckerman. Randomness is linear in space. In *Symposium on Theory of Computing*, pages 235–244. Citeseer, 1993.

[20] R. O'Donnell. Hardness amplification within np. In *Proceedings of the thiry-fourth annual ACM symposium on Theory of computing*, pages 751–760. ACM, 2002.

[21] J. Radhakrishnan and A. Ta-Shma. Tight bounds for depth-two superconcentrators, 1997.

[22] R. Raz and O. Reingold. On recycling the randomness of states in space bounded computation. In *Proceedings of the thirty-first annual ACM symposium on Theory of computing*, pages 159–168. ACM, 1999.

[23] R. Shaltiel. Recent developments in explicit constructions of extractors. *Current Trends in Theoretical Computer Science: Algorithms and complexity*, 1:189, 2004.

[24] M. Sipser and D. Spielman. Expander codes. *Information Theory, IEEE Transactions on*, 42(6):1710–1722, 1996.

[25] S. Vadhan. On constructing locally computable extractors and cryptosystems in the bounded storage model. *Advances in Cryptology-CRYPTO 2003*, pages 61–77, 2003.

[26] S. Vadhan and J. Zheng. Characterizing pseudoentropy and simplifying pseudorandom generator constructions. Technical Report TR11-141, Electronic Colloquium on Computational Complexity, 2011.

[27] L. Valiant and V. Vazirani. Np is as easy as detecting unique solutions. *Theoretical Computer Science*, 47:85–93, 1986.

[28] E. Viola. The complexity of constructing pseudorandom generators from hard functions. *Computational Complexity*, 13(3):147–188, 2005.

[29] H. Zhou and J. Bruck. Linear extractors for extracting randomness from noisy sources. In *Information Theory Proceedings (ISIT), 2011 IEEE International Symposium on*, pages 1738–1742. IEEE, 2011.

APPENDIX

A. STATISTICAL DISTANCE VERSUS COLLISION PROBABILITY

Here we give a standard bound of the statistical distance of the distributions $(H, H(X))$ and (H, U) in terms of the collision probability of H. The proof is very well known when the distribution over H is uniform. In our application, however, it is not, so we include the proof for completeness.

CLAIM 10. *Let H be a distribution on functions from $\{0,1\}^n$ to $\{0,1\}^m$, X be a distribution over $\{0,1\}^n$ and U be the uniform distribution over $\{0,1\}^m$. The statistical distance between $(H, H(X))$ and (H, U) is at most*

$$\frac{1}{2}\sqrt{2^k \Pr_{H,X,X'}[H(X) = H(X')] - 1}.$$

where X and X' are independent samples from the same distribution.

PROOF. We upper bound the ℓ_1 distance, which is twice the statistical distance:

$$\begin{aligned}
&\ell_1((H, h(X)), (H, U)) \\
&= \sum_{h,b} \left|\Pr_{H,X}[H = h \wedge H(X) = b] - \Pr_H[H = h]2^{-m}\right| \\
&= \sum_{h,b} \sqrt{\Pr_H[H = h]} \cdot \sqrt{\Pr_H[H = h]}\left|\Pr_X[h(X) = b] - 2^{-m}\right| \\
&\leq \sqrt{\sum_{h,b} \Pr_H[H = h]} \cdot \\
&\sqrt{\sum_{h,b} \Pr_h[H = h]\left(\Pr_{H,X}[H(X) = b] - 2^{-m}\right)^2} \\
&= \sqrt{2^m} \cdot \sqrt{\Pr_{H,X,X'}[H(X) = H(X')] - 2^{-m}} \\
&= \sqrt{2^m \Pr_{H,X,X'}[H(X) = H(X')] - 1}.
\end{aligned}$$

□

B. BOUNDS ON THE INVERSE OF ENTROPY

LEMMA 11. *For every $p \in (0, 1/2]$,*

$$\frac{H(p)}{6\log_2 2/H(p)} \leq p \leq \frac{H(p)}{\log_2 1/H(p)}.$$

The upper bound on p follows from the inequality $H(p) \geq p\log_2 1/p$. Applying twice we obtain

$$\frac{1}{p} \geq \frac{1}{H(p)}\log_2\frac{1}{p} \geq \frac{1}{H(p)}\log_2\Big(\frac{1}{H(p)}\log_2\frac{1}{p}\Big) \geq \frac{1}{H(p)}\log_2\frac{1}{H(p)}$$

because $1/p \geq 2$. For the lower bound, we apply $H(p) \leq 2p\log_2 1/p$ twice to obtain

$$\frac{1}{p} \leq \frac{2}{H(p)}\log_2\frac{1}{p} \leq \frac{2}{H(p)}\log_2\Big(\frac{2}{H(p)}\log_2\frac{1}{p}\Big).$$

Now $2/H(p) \geq (1/p)\log_2(1/p) \geq \sqrt{\log_2(1/p)}$, which is true for every $p \in (0, 1]$. Therefore

$$\frac{1}{p} \leq \frac{2}{H(p)}\log_2\Big(\frac{8}{H(p)^3}\Big) = \frac{6}{H(p)}\log_2\Big(\frac{2}{H(p)}\Big).$$

C. PROOF OF CLAIM 6

The maximum probability in $\overline{X}$ is attained by those strings in $\{0,1\}^n$ that have Hamming weight exactly $0.9pn$. Let a be such a string. Then

$$\begin{aligned}
\Pr[\overline{X} = a] &\leq \Pr[X = a] + \Pr[U = a] \\
&= p^{0.9pn}(1-p)^{1.1(1-p)n} + 2^{-n} \\
&\leq 2^{-nH(p)} \cdot p^{-0.1pn} + 2^{-n} \\
&= 2^{-nH(p)} \cdot 2^{0.1p\log_2(1/p)n} + 2^{-n} \\
&\leq 2^{-nH(p)} \cdot 2^{0.1nH(p)} + 2^{-n} \\
&= 2^{-0.9nH(p)} + 2^{-n} \\
&= 2^{-1.8m} + 2^{-n} \leq 2^{-1.5m}.
\end{aligned}$$

On the Power of Conditional Samples in Distribution Testing

Sourav Chakraborty
Chennai Mathematical Institute (CMI)
Plot No. H1 SIPCOT IT Park
Padur PO, Siruseri - 603103
Tamil Nadu, India
sourav@cmi.ac.in

Eldar Fischer
Faculty of Computer Science
Technion – Israel Institute of Technology
Haifa 32000, Israel
eldar@cs.technion.ac.il

Yonatan Goldhirsh
Faculty of Computer Science
Technion – Israel Institute of Technology
Haifa 32000, Israel
jongold@cs.technion.ac.il

Arie Matsliah
IBM Research and Faculty of Computer Science
Technion – Israel Institute of Technology
Haifa 32000, Israel
arie.matsliah@gmail.com

ABSTRACT

In this paper we define and examine the power of the *conditional sampling* oracle in the context of distribution-property testing. The conditional sampling oracle for a discrete distribution μ takes as input a subset $S \subset [n]$ of the domain, and outputs a random sample $i \in S$ drawn according to μ, conditioned on S (and independently of all prior samples). The conditional-sampling oracle is a natural generalization of the ordinary sampling oracle in which S always equals $[n]$.

We show that with the conditional-sampling oracle, testing uniformity, testing identity to a known distribution, and testing any label-invariant property of distributions is easier than with the ordinary sampling oracle. On the other hand, we also show that for some distribution properties the sample complexity remains near-maximal even with conditional sampling.

Categories and Subject Descriptors

F.1.2 [**Modes of Computation**]: Probabilistic computation; F.2.2 [**Nonnumerical Algorithms and Problems**]: Computations on discrete structures; G.3 [**Probability and Statistics**]: Probabilistic algorithms

General Terms

Theory, Algorithms

Keywords

Distribution testing, conditional samples, statistical approximation

1. INTRODUCTION

In the last decade several works have investigated the problem of testing various properties of huge data sets, that can be represented as an unknown distribution from which independent samples can be taken. In *distribution-property testing*, the goal is to distinguish the case where the samples come from a distribution that has a certain property $\mathcal{P}$, from the case where the samples come from a distribution that is far, in the variation distance, from any distribution that has the property $\mathcal{P}$ (the variation distance between two distributions μ and μ' over a common set B is $\frac{1}{2}\sum_{i\in B}|\Pr_\mu[i]-\Pr_{\mu'}[i]|$, which is equal to the maximum difference in probability between the distributions for any possible event). In the traditional setting no access is provided to the distribution apart from the ability to take samples, and the two cases should be distinguished using as few samples as possible.

There are several natural distribution properties that were studied in this context: testing whether a distribution is uniform [8], testing identity between distributions (taking samples from both) [4, 11], testing whether a joint distribution is independent (a product of two distributions) [3] and more. Some useful general techniques have also been designed to obtain nearly tight lower bounds on various distribution-property testing problems [13]. Other tightly related works study the problems of estimating various measures of distributions, such as entropy [2, 9] or support size [12].

Most attention has been given to testing properties of distributions over very large (discrete) domains, where the need for sublinear time and sample complexities is vital. Distribution-property testers with a sublinear sample complexity are motivated by problems from various areas, such as physics, cryptography, statistics, computational learning theory, property testing of graphs and sequences and streaming algorithms (see the overview in [11] for a comprehensive list of references). Indeed, in many of the aforementioned works testers have been designed with sublinear sample (and time) complexity, that is often of the form n^α, where n is the size of the domain and α is a positive constant smaller than 1.

While most previous works are focused on the ordinary sampling oracle, other stronger oracles were considered too. A major reason is that the number of required samples, while sublinear, is still very large in the original model. The most notable example is the oracle from [2], that also allows querying the exact probability weight of any element from the domain. Another research direction involved restricting the problem further, for example by adding the promise of the distribution being monotone [5].

In this work we study the problem of testing several distribution properties in an unrestricted setting while providing for a stronger oracle, that can be thought of as more natural than the one of [2] in some situations. Namely, we allow the samples obtained from the unknown distribution to be conditioned over specified subsets of the domain. In our setting, we assume that a sampling oracle to the unknown distribution μ over the discrete domain $[n] = \{1, \ldots, n\}$ is provided, that allows us to sample random (according to μ) elements conditioned on any specified subset $S \subseteq [n]$. If the original distribution is described by the probabilities $p_1, \ldots, p_n$ (where the probability for obtaining $i \in [n]$ is p_i), then when restricting to S the probability of sampling $i \in [n]$ is $p_i/(\sum_{j \in S} p_j)$ if $i \in S$ and 0 otherwise (see the formal definition of the model and corresponding testers in Section 2).

In various scenarios, conditional samples can be obtained naturally, or come at a low cost relative to that of extracting any sample – see some illustrating examples in Section 1.1. This leads to the following natural question: can we reduce the sample complexity of distribution-property testers using conditional samples?

Indeed, conditional sampling is more powerful than the traditional model: We show that with conditional samples, several natural distribution properties, such as uniformity, can be tested in constant time (compared to $\widetilde{\Theta}(\sqrt{n})$ unconditional samples even for uniformity [8, 3]). The most general result of this paper (Section 4) is that any label-invariant property of distributions (a symmetric property in the terminology of [13]) can be tested using $\text{poly}(\log n)$ conditional samples.[1]

On the other hand, there are properties for which testing remains almost as hard as possible even with conditional samples: We show a property of distributions that requires at least $\Omega(n)$ conditional samples to test (Section 7).

Another feature that makes conditional-samples interesting is that in contrast to the testers using ordinary samples, which are non-adaptive by definition, adaptivity (and the algorithmic aspect of testing) in the conditional-sampling model plays an important role. For instance, the aforementioned task of testing uniformity, while still possible with a much better sampling complexity than in the traditional model, cannot be done non-adaptively with a constant number of samples (Section 6.2).

[1]For an l-variate function f, we say that $f(\alpha_1, \ldots, \alpha_l) = \text{poly}(g_1(\alpha_1, \ldots, \alpha_l), \ldots, g_k(\alpha_1, \ldots, \alpha_l))$ if there exists a k-variate polynomial $p(x_1, \ldots, x_k)$ such that $f \leq p(g_1, \ldots, g_k)$ for all values of $\alpha_1, \ldots, \alpha_l$ in their respective domains.

Before we move to some motivating examples, let us address the concern of whether arbitrary conditioning is realistic: While the examples below do relate to arbitrary conditioning, sometimes one would like the conditioning to be more restricted, in some sense describable by fewer than the n bits required to describe the conditioning set S. In fact, many of our algorithms require less than that. For example, the adaptive uniformity test takes only unconditional samples and samples conditioned on a constant size set, so the description size per sample is in fact $O(\log n)$, as there are $n^{O(1)}$ possibilities. The adaptive general label invariant property tester takes only samples conditioned to dyadic intervals of $[n]$, so here the description size is $O(\log n)$ as well. The non-adaptive tests do require general conditioning, as they pick uniformly random sets of prescribed sizes.

1.1 Some more motivating examples

Lottery machines

The *gravity pick lottery machine* is the most common lottery machine used worldwide to pick random numbers. A set B of balls, each marked with a unique number $i \in \mathbb{N}$, are dropped into the machine while it is spinning, and after a certain amount of time the machine allows a single ball to drop out. Ensuring that such a machine is fair is an important real-life problem.[2]

Suppose that, given a machine and a set of balls, we wish to test them for being fair. Specifically, we would like to distinguish between the following cases:

- The machine picks a ball uniformly at random. That is, for any subset $B' \subseteq B$ of balls dropped into the machine, and for each $i \in B'$, the probability that the machine picks i is $1/|B'|$;
- The distribution according to which the machine picks a ball is ϵ-far from uniform (where $\epsilon > 0$ is some fixed constant, and the distance we consider is the standard variation distance defined above).

Suppose furthermore that we wish to distinguish between those cases as quickly as possible, and in particular, within few activations of the machine. Compare the following solutions.

We can use the uniformity tester [8] for this task. Obtaining each sample from the underlying distribution requires one activation of the machine (with the entire set B), and we can complete the test using $\widetilde{\Theta}(\sqrt{|B|})$ activations.

Alternatively, using the algorithm we present in Section 3.1, with conditional samples we can complete the test using $O(1)$ activations only (the number of activations only has a polynomial dependency on ϵ and is logarithmic in the confidence parameter). Assuming that the drawing probabilities depend only on the physical characteristics of every ball separately, a conditional sample here corresponds to activating the machine with a specific subset of the balls rather than the entire set B.

This is for testing uniformity. Using the algorithm from Section 4, we could also test for any label-invariant property with $\text{poly}(\log |B|)$ activations, which would allow us for

[2]As was demonstrated in the the Pennsylvania Lottery scandal, see e.g. `http://en.wikipedia.org/w/index.php?title=1980_Pennsylvania_Lottery_scandal&oldid=496671681`

example to give an estimation of the actual distance of the distribution from being uniform.

Asymmetric communication scenarios

Suppose that two computers A and B are linked with an asymmetric communication link, in which transmitting information in one of the directions (say from A to B) is much easier than in the other direction (consider e.g. a spacecraft traveling in remote space, with limited energy, computational power and transmitting capability; actually numerous examples of asymmetric communications also exist here on earth). Now assume that B has access to some large data that can be modeled as collection of samples coming from an unknown distribution μ, while A wants to learn or test some properties of μ. We could simulate the standard testing algorithms by sending a request to B whenever a random sample from μ is needed. Assuming that the most important measure of efficiency is how much information is sent by B, it would translate to the sample complexity of the simulated algorithm.

However, if B can also produce conditional samples (for example if it has nearly unlimited cost-free access to samples from the distribution), then any property that is significantly easier to test with conditional samples can be tested with fewer resources here.

Political polls

We mention these here because the modern-day practice of polling actually uses conditional sampling. Rather than taking a random sample of all willing potential participants, the polling population is usually first divided to groups according to common traits, and then each such group is polled separately before the results are re-integrated into the final prediction[3].

1.2 Informal description of results

In all sample-complexity upper bounds listed below there is a hidden factor of $\log(\delta^{-1})$, where δ is the maximal failure probability of the tester. Also, all lower bounds are for a fixed (and not so small) ϵ. The results are summarized in Table 1.

Adaptive testing

The first result we prove here is that uniformity, and more generally identity to any distribution that is very close to uniform in the ℓ_∞ norm, can be tested (adaptively) with $\text{poly}(\epsilon^{-1})$ conditional samples (Theorem 3.1.1 and Theorem 3.1.2, respectively). This is done by capturing (for far distributions) both "light" and "heavy" elements in the same small set and then conditioning over it. Our next result is that identity to any known distribution can be tested adaptively with $\text{poly}(\log^\star n, \epsilon^{-1})$ conditional samples, where n is the size of the domain (Theorem 3.2.1). This uses the uniformity result with the bucketing technique of [3] together with a recursive argument.

Our most general result is that any label-invariant (i.e. invariant under permutations of the domain) property of distributions can be tested adaptively with $\text{poly}(\log n, \epsilon^{-1})$ conditional samples (Theorem 4.0.1). In fact, we go further to prove the following stronger result: $\text{poly}(\log n, \epsilon^{-1}, \log(\delta^{-1}))$ conditional samples taken from μ are enough to compute a distribution μ' that is ϵ-close to μ up to some permutation of the domain $[n]$ (Theorem 4.0.3). For showing this we construct an *explicit persistent sampler* that could be interesting in itself. Essentially we construct a way to simulate (unconditional) samples from a distribution $\tilde{\mu}$ that is close to μ, and for which we can also provide exact probability queries like the oracle of [2]. This explicit persistent sampler also leads to an algorithm for testing whether two unknown distributions, accessible by conditional samples, are isomorphic[4] (Theorem 4.0.2).

Adaptive	
Upper bounds	
Uniformity	$\text{poly}(\epsilon^{-1})$
Identity to known dist.	$\text{poly}(\log^\star n, \epsilon^{-1})$
Any label-invariant prop.	$\text{poly}(\log n, \epsilon^{-1})$
Lower bounds	
Uniformity and identity	—
Any label-invariant prop.	$\Omega(\sqrt{\log\log n})$
General properties	$\Omega(n)$
Non-adaptive	
Upper bounds	
Uniformity	$\text{poly}(\log n, \epsilon^{-1})$
Identity to known dist.	$\text{poly}(\log n, \epsilon^{-1})$
Any label-invariant prop.	—
Lower bounds	
Uniformity and identity	$\Omega(\log\log n)$
Any label-invariant prop.	(follows uniformity)
General properties	(follows adaptive)

Table 1: Summary of results.

Non-adaptive testing

We prove that uniformity can be tested non-adaptively with $\text{poly}(\log n, \epsilon^{-1})$ conditional samples. Here too the tester enjoys a certain degree of tolerance, in the sense that it is possible to test identity with any distribution that is close enough to uniform (Theorems 5.1.1 and 5.1.2). This is by first proving (through bucketing) that a portion of the "total difference" of μ from being uniform is in relatively equal-probability members of $[n]$, and then trying to capture just a few of them in a random set of an appropriate size. We also prove (from the uniformity test through standard bucketing arguments) that identity to any known distribution can be tested non-adaptively with $\text{poly}(\log n, \epsilon^{-1})$ conditional samples (Theorem 5.2.1).

Lower bounds

As already mentioned in the introduction, adaptivity is useful when we have access to conditional sampling. We demonstrate this by proving that testing uniformity non-adaptively requires $\Omega(\log\log n)$ conditional samples, for some fixed $\epsilon > 0$ (Theorem 6.2.1). We also prove that the tester for any label-invariant property (from our main result) cannot be improved to work with a constant number of conditional samples: There is a label invariant property which requires

[3]This use of conditional samples can actually spark much debate, as in this opinion piece by Dick Morris: `http://www.dickmorris.com/why-the-ny-times-poll-is-wrong/`

[4]Two distributions μ, μ' over the domain $[n]$ are *isomorphic* if there is some permutation $\pi : [n] \to [n]$ such that $\mu = \mu' \circ \pi$.

$\Omega(\sqrt{\log\log n})$ samples to test, whether adaptively or not (Theorem 6.3.1). Our third lower bound shows that for some properties conditional samples do not help much: There are distribution properties that cannot be tested (adaptively) with $o(n)$ conditional samples (Theorem 7.0.1). The first two lower bounds are through a special adaptation of Yao's method, while the last one is through a reduction to general properties of Boolean strings, of which maximally untestable examples are known.

About the gaps in the bounds

We believe that, for non-adaptive uniformity testing, the upper bound is closer in the truth, in that the actual complexity would be close to logarithmic in n. A more careful analysis of the lower bound construction would be a good starting point towards narrowing the gap. We also believe that the correct lower bound for adaptive testing of general label-invariant properties is higher than our achieved one. Additionally we believe that an examination of the methods of [13] should allow us to construct label-invariant properties for which testing in the traditional (unconditioned) sampling model is nearly useless.

1.3 Recent developments

Independently, Cannone et. al. [6] formulated the model of distribution testing with conditional samples as well. Cannone et. al. consider the uniformity testing and identity testing problems in the adaptive setting, giving $\mathrm{poly}(\epsilon^{-1})$ upper bounds for both. Another main result given by Cannone et. al. is a $\mathrm{poly}(\log n, \epsilon^{-1})$ adaptive test for identity between two unknown distributions (where samples may be obtained from both), using what they call an "EVAL oracle". Such an oracle is given some element $i \in [n]$ and should return a good estimate of the probability of i, while allowed to fail for some small fixed subset of $[n]$. This notion is somewhat reminiscent of the notion of an explicit persistent sampler used in Section 4. For the results appearing both in [6] and in here, the corresponding algorithms and proofs are for the most part considerably different.

2. PRELIMINARIES

2.1 The conditional distribution testing model

Let μ be a distribution over $[n] \triangleq \{1,\dots,n\}$, its probabilities denoted by $p_1,\dots,p_n$, where $p_i = \Pr_\mu[i]$. We will also write $\mu(i)$ for $\Pr_\mu[i]$ where we deal with more then one distribution. The distribution μ is not known to the algorithm explicitly, and may only be accessed by drawing samples. A conditional distribution testing algorithm may submit any set $A \subseteq \{1,\dots,n\}$ and receive a sample $i \in A$ that is drawn according to μ conditioned on A (and independent of any previous samples).

Thus when a sample is drawn according to μ conditioned on A, the probability of getting j is $\Pr[j|A] = p_j/(\sum_{i\in A} p_i)$ for $j \in A$ and 0 for $j \notin A$. If $\sum_{i\in A} p_i = 0$ then we assume (somewhat arbitrarily) that the algorithm obtains a uniformly drawn member of A.

We measure *farness* using the variation distance: We say that μ is ϵ*-far* from a property $\mathcal{P}$ of distributions over $[n]$, if for every μ' that satisfies $\mathcal{P}$ and is described by $p'_1,\dots,p'_n$ we have $d(\mu,\mu') = \frac{1}{2}\sum_{i=1}^n |p_i - p'_i| \geq \epsilon$.

We will consider two types of conditional distribution testing algorithms. Non-adaptive testers, which must decide the sets to sample from before getting any samples, and adaptive testers, which have no such restriction.

DEFINITION 2.1.1 (NON-ADAPTIVE TESTER). *A* non-adaptive distribution tester for a property $\mathcal{P}$ with conditional sample complexity $t : \mathbb{R}\times\mathbb{R}\times\mathbb{N} \to \mathbb{N}$ *is a randomized algorithm that receives $\epsilon,\delta > 0$, $n \in \mathbb{N}$ and a conditional sampling oracle to a distribution μ over $[n]$ and operates as follows.*

1. *The algorithm generates a sequence of $t \leq t(\epsilon,\delta,n)$ sets $A_1,\dots,A_t \subseteq [n]$ (possibly with repetitions).*
2. *It calls the conditional oracle t times with $A_1,\dots,A_t$ respectively, and receives $j_1,\dots,j_t$, where every j_i is drawn according to the distribution μ conditioned on A_i, independently of $j_1,\dots,j_{i-1}$ and any other history.*
3. *Based on the received elements $j_1,\dots,j_t$ and its internal coin tosses, the algorithm accepts or rejects the distribution μ.*

If μ satisfies $\mathcal{P}$ then the algorithm must accept with probability at least $1-\delta$, and if μ is ϵ-far from $\mathcal{P}$ then the algorithm must reject with probability at least $1-\delta$.

DEFINITION 2.1.2 (ADAPTIVE TESTER). *An* adaptive distribution tester for a property $\mathcal{P}$ with conditional sample complexity $t : \mathbb{R}\times\mathbb{R}\times\mathbb{N} \to \mathbb{N}$ *is a randomized algorithm that receives $\epsilon,\delta > 0$, $n \in \mathbb{N}$ and a conditional sampling oracle to a distribution μ over $[n]$ and operates as follows.*

1. *For $i \in \{1,\dots,t\}$, at the ith phase the algorithm generates a set $A_i \subseteq [n]$ (based on $j_1,\dots,j_{i-1}$ and its internal coin tosses), and calls the conditional oracle with A_i to receive an element j_i, drawn according to the distribution μ conditioned on A_i, independently of $j_1,\dots,j_{i-1}$ and any other history.*
2. *Based on the received elements $j_1,\dots,j_t$ and its internal coin tosses, the algorithm accepts or rejects the distribution μ.*

If μ satisfies $\mathcal{P}$ the algorithm must accept with probability at least $1-\delta$, and if μ is ϵ-far from $\mathcal{P}$ the algorithm must reject with probability at least $1-\delta$.

As is standard in the field of property testing, the primary measure of efficiency of these testers is their sample complexity.

2.2 Tools from previous works

Our algorithms will make use of the Identity Tester of Batu et. al. [3] (though it is important to note that this result is used mainly as a "primitive" and can be replaced in the sequel with making enough samples to fully approximate the distribution).

THEOREM 2.2.1 (IDENTITY TESTER). *There is an algorithm T for testing identity between an unknown distribution μ' and a known distribution μ, both over $[n]$, with (ordinary) sample complexity $\tilde{O}(\sqrt{n}\mathrm{poly}(\epsilon^{-1})\log(\delta^{-1}))$. Namely, T accepts with probability $1-\delta$ if $\mu' = \mu$ and rejects with probability $1-\delta$ if μ' is ϵ-far from μ.*

We will also use the following inequality, which appears as Theorem A.1.11 and Theorem A.1.13 in [1]:

LEMMA 2.2.2. *Let $p_1, \ldots, p_n \in [0,1]$, $X_1, \ldots, X_n$ be fully independent random variables with $\Pr[X_i = 1 - p_i] = p_i$ and $\Pr[X_i = -p_i] = 1 - p_i$, and let $p = \frac{1}{n}\sum_{i=1}^{n} p_i$ and $X = \sum_{i=1}^{n} X_i$. Then $\Pr[|X| > a] < 2\exp(-a^2/2pn)$.*

When using this lemma we interpret $X+pn = \sum_{i=1}^{n}(X_i+p_i)$ as the number of successes in n independent trials where the probability of success in the ith trial is p_i.

Bucketing

Bucketing is a general tool, introduced in [4, 3], that decomposes any explicitly given distribution into a collection of distributions that are almost uniform. In this section we recall the bucketing technique and the lemmas (from [4, 3]) that we will need for our proofs.

DEFINITION 2.2.3. *Given a distribution μ over $[n]$, and $M \subseteq [n]$ such that $\mu(M) > 0$, the* restriction *$\mu \restriction_M$ is the distribution over M with $\mu \restriction_M (i) = \mu(i)/\mu(M)$ (this is the the same as the conditioning of μ on B, only here we also change the domain).*

Given a partition $\mathcal{M} = \{M_0, M_1, \ldots, M_k\}$ of $[n]$, we denote by $\mu_{\langle \mathcal{M} \rangle}$ the distribution over $\{0\} \cup [k]$ in which we set $\mu_{\langle \mathcal{M} \rangle}(i) = \mu(M_i)$. This is the coarsening *of μ according to $\mathcal{M}$.*

DEFINITION 2.2.4. *Given an explicit distribution μ over $[n]$, Bucket$(\mu, [n], \epsilon)$ is a procedure that generates a partition $\{M_0, M_1, \ldots, M_k\}$ of the domain $[n]$, where $k = \frac{\log n}{\log(1+\epsilon)} < \frac{2}{\epsilon}\log(n)$. This partition satisfies the following conditions:*

- *$M_0 = \{j \in [n] \mid \mu(j) < \frac{1}{n}\}$;*
- *$M_i = \left\{j \in [n] \mid \frac{(1+\epsilon)^{i-1}}{n} \le \mu(j) < \frac{(1+\epsilon)^i}{n}\right\}$, for all $i \in [k]$.*

LEMMA 2.2.5 (LEMMA 8 IN [3]). *Let μ be a distribution over $[n]$ and let $\{M_0, M_1, \ldots, M_k\} \leftarrow$ Bucket$(\mu, [n], \epsilon)$. Then for all $i \in [k]$, $\|\mu \restriction_{M_i} - U \restriction_{M_i}\|_\infty \le \epsilon/n$.*

LEMMA 2.2.6 (LEMMA 6 IN [3]). *Let μ, μ' be two distributions over $[n]$ and let $\mathcal{M} = \{M_0, M_1, \ldots, M_k\}$ be a partition of $[n]$. If $\|\mu \restriction_{M_i} - \mu' \restriction_{M_i}\|_1 \le \epsilon_1$ for every $i \in [k]$ and $\|\mu_{\langle \mathcal{M} \rangle} - \mu_{\langle \mathcal{M} \rangle}\|_1 \le \epsilon_2$, then $\|\mu - \mu'\|_1 \le \epsilon_1 + \epsilon_2$. Furthermore, $\|\mu - \mu'\|_1 \le \sum_{0 \le i \le k} \mu(M_i)\|\mu \restriction_{M_i} - \mu' \restriction_{M_i}\| + \epsilon_2$.*

We reproduce the proof to obtain the "furthermore" claim:

PROOF. This results from the following.

$$\|\mu - \mu'\|_1 = \sum_{0 \le i \le k} \sum_{j \in M_i} |\mu(j) - \mu'(j)|$$

$$= \sum_{0 \le i \le k} \sum_{j \in M_i} |\mu(M_i)\mu \restriction_{M_i} (j) - \mu'(M_i)\mu' \restriction_{M_i} (j)|$$

$$\le \sum_{0 \le i \le k} \sum_{j \in M_i} |\mu(M_i)\mu \restriction_{M_i} (j) - \mu(M_i)\mu' \restriction_{M_i} (j)|$$

$$+ \sum_{0 \le i \le k} \sum_{j \in M_i} |\mu(M_i)\mu' \restriction_{M_i} (j) - \mu'(M_i)\mu' \restriction_{M_i} (j)|$$

$$= \sum_{0 \le i \le k} \sum_{j \in M_i} \mu(M_i)|\mu \restriction_{M_i} (j) - \mu' \restriction_{M_i} (j)|$$

$$+ \sum_{0 \le i \le k} \sum_{j \in M_i} \mu' \restriction_{M_i} (j)|\mu(M_i) - \mu'(M_i)|$$

$$= \sum_{0 \le i \le k} \mu(M_i) \sum_{j \in M_i} \|\mu \restriction_{M_i} (j) - \mu' \restriction_{M_i} (j)\|_1$$

$$+ \sum_{0 \le i \le k} |\mu(M_i) - \mu'(M_i)|$$

$$\le \sum_{0 \le i \le k} \mu(M_i) \sum_{j \in M_i} \|\mu \restriction_{M_i} (j) - \mu' \restriction_{M_i} (j)\|_1 + \epsilon_2$$

This provides the "furthermore" claim. To obtain from the above the original claim note that

$$\sum_{0 \le i \le k} \mu(M_i) \sum_{j \in M_i} \|\mu \restriction_{M_i} (j) - \mu' \restriction_{M_i} (j)\|_1$$

$$\le \sum_{0 \le i \le k} \mu(M_i)\epsilon_1 = \epsilon_1.$$

□

3. ADAPTIVE TESTING FOR UNIFORMITY AND IDENTITY

In the following we formulate our testing algorithms to have a polynomial dependence on $\log(\delta^{-1})$. To make it linear we can first run the algorithm $100\log(\delta^{-1})$ times with a fixed $\frac{1}{3}$ error bound and then take the majority vote.

3.1 Testing for uniformity

THEOREM 3.1.1. *There is an (adaptive) algorithm testing uniformity using $\mathrm{poly}(\epsilon^{-1}, \log(\delta^{-1}))$ conditional samples independently of n.*

In fact we will prove something slightly stronger, which will prove useful in next sections:

THEOREM 3.1.2 (NEAR UNIFORMITY TESTER). *Let μ be a known distribution over $[n]$ such that $\|\mu - U_n\|_\infty < \frac{\epsilon}{100n}$. Identity with μ can be tested using $\mathrm{poly}(\epsilon^{-1}, \log(\delta^{-1}))$ conditional samples by an adaptive algorithm.*

Let μ' be the unknown distribution that is to be sampled from.

ALGORITHM 3.1.3. *(Near Uniformity Tester) The algorithm receives μ, ϵ, δ and n and operates as follows.*

1. *Take S to be $k = (6/\epsilon)\log(\delta^{-1})$ independent samples according to μ' (unconditioned).*
2. *Take U to be k members of $\{1, \ldots, n\}$ chosen uniformly at random.*
3. *Invoke the Identity Tester of Theorem 2.2.1 to check whether $\mu' \restriction_{U \cup S}$ is $\frac{\epsilon^2}{600\log(\delta^{-1})}$-close to $\mu \restriction_{U \cup S}$ over $U \cup S$ with bounded error probability $\delta/3$, and answer as the tester did.*

LEMMA 3.1.4. *The sample complexity of Algorithm 3.1.3 is $\mathrm{poly}(\epsilon^{-1}, \log(\delta^{-1}))$.*

PROOF. The algorithm draws k samples, and then invokes the closeness tester on a set of size $2k$ and an error parameter polynomial in ϵ^{-1}. Since the sample complexity of the closeness tester is polynomial in the support size and error parameter, and $k = (6/\epsilon)\log(\delta^{-1})$, the total sample complexity of Algorithm 3.1.3 is $\text{poly}(\epsilon^{-1}, \log(\delta^{-1}))$. □

LEMMA 3.1.5. *If $d(\mu, \mu') = 0$ then Algorithm 3.1.3 accepts with probability at least $1 - \delta$.*

PROOF. If $\|\mu - \mu'\|_1 = 0$ then $\|\mu \restriction_{U\cup S} - \mu' \restriction_{U\cup S}\|_1 = 0$ and then the algorithm will accept if the closeness tester does, which will happen with probability at least $1 - \frac{\delta}{3}$. □

Let the individual probabilities for the distribution μ be denoted by $p_1, \ldots, p_n$ and the probabilities for the distribution μ' denoted by $p'_1, \ldots, p'_n$. We first note that

$$2d(\mu, \mu') = \|\mu - \mu'\|_1$$

$$= \sum_{i=1}^{n} |p_i - p'_i| = 2 \sum_{p'_i < p_i} (p_i - p'_i) = 2 \sum_{p'_i > p_i} (p'_i - p_i)$$

Assume from now on that this distance is at least 2ϵ (which corresponds to variation distance at least ϵ).

LEMMA 3.1.6. *With probability at least $1 - \delta/3$ we have an $i \in S$ for which $(p'_i - p_i) \geq \frac{\epsilon}{2n}$.*

PROOF. Clearly $\sum_{p_i < p'_i < p_i + \epsilon/2n} (p'_i - p_i) < \frac{1}{2}\epsilon$. Therefore:

$$\sum_{p'_i \geq p_i + \epsilon/2n} p'_i > \sum_{p'_i \geq p_i + \epsilon/2n} (p'_i - p_i)$$

$$= \sum_{p'_i > p_i} (p'_i - p_i) - \sum_{p_i < p'_i < p_i + \epsilon/2n} (p'_i - p_i) > \frac{1}{2}\epsilon$$

This means that after $(6/\epsilon)\log(\delta^{-1})$ samples, with probability at least $1 - \delta/3$ we will get an i with such a p'_i into S. □

LEMMA 3.1.7. *With probability at least $1 - \delta/3$ we have an $i \in U$ for which $p'_i < p_i$.*

PROOF. Note that $\sum_{p'_i < p_i} (p_i - p'_i) \leq |\{i : p'_i < p_i\}| \cdot \max\{p_i\}$. Now since $\max_i\{p_i\} < (1 + \frac{\epsilon}{100})\frac{1}{n}$ there are at least $(\epsilon/2)n$ such i. A uniformly random choice of $(6/\epsilon)\log(\delta^{-1})$ indexes will get one with probability at least $1 - \delta/3$. □

LEMMA 3.1.8. *When both events above occur, $\mu' \restriction_{U\cup S}$ is at least $\frac{\epsilon^2}{600\log(\delta^{-1})}$-far from $\mu \restriction_{U\cup S}$ over $U \cup S$.*

PROOF. Note that $|S \cup U| = 2k = 2 \cdot (6/\epsilon)\log(\delta^{-1})$, and that the two events above mean that there are i and j in this set such that $p'_i \geq \frac{1+\epsilon/2}{1+\epsilon/100} p'_j$. Denoting the conditional probabilities $q_i = p_i/\mu(S \cup U)$ and $q'_i = p'_i/\mu'(S \cup U)$, we note that we obtain $q'_i \geq \frac{1+\epsilon/2}{1+\epsilon/100} q'_j$, while both q_i and q_j are bounded between $\frac{1-\epsilon/100}{1+\epsilon/100}\frac{1}{2k}$ and $\frac{1+\epsilon/100}{1-\epsilon/100}\frac{1}{2k}$. Therefore, either $q'_i > q_i + \frac{\epsilon}{40k}$ or $q'_j < q_j - \frac{\epsilon}{40k}$. Either way, $d(\mu \restriction_{U\cup S}, \mu' \restriction_{U\cup S}) > \frac{\epsilon}{100k}$, which concludes the proof. □

This concludes the soundness proof, as the last step of the algorithm checks the closeness of $\mu' \restriction_{U\cup S}$ to $\mu \restriction_{U\cup S}$ with this approximation parameter. Thus we obtain:

LEMMA 3.1.9. *Let μ be a known probability distribution over $[n]$. Then if $\|\mu - U_n\|_\infty < \frac{\epsilon}{100n}$ and $d(\mu, \mu') > \epsilon$ then Algorithm 3.1.3 rejects with probability at least $1 - \delta$.*

PROOF. Follows from a union bound for the events of Lemma 3.1.6 and Lemma 3.1.7, and the failure probability of the test invoked in the last step of the algorithm. □

3.2 Testing identity to a known distribution

Recall that if we define $\log^{(0)}(n) = n$ and by induction $\log^{(k+1)}(n) = \log(\log^{(k)}(n))$, then the $\log^\star$ function is defined by $\log^\star(n) = \min\{k : \log^{(k)}(n) \leq 1\}$.

THEOREM 3.2.1. *Identity with a known distribution can be tested using $\text{poly}(\log^\star n, \epsilon^{-1}, \log(\delta^{-1}))$ conditional samples by an adaptive algorithm.*

Let μ be the known distribution and μ' be the unknown distribution that is accessed by sampling. The following is an algorithm for testing identity to the known distribution μ over $[n]$. In the initial run we feed it $m = n$, but in the recursive runs it keeps track of m as the "original n".

ALGORITHM 3.2.2. *(Identity Test) The algorithm receives ϵ, δ, n, m and μ, operating as follows.*

0. *If $n \leq \left(\frac{400\log(1/\epsilon)}{\epsilon}\log^\star m\right)^3$ then perform a brute-force test: Take $100\log(1/\delta)\epsilon^{-2}n^2\log n$ samples to write a distribution $\tilde{\mu}$ that is $\frac{\epsilon}{2}$-close to μ' (with probability $1-\delta$); if $d(\tilde{\mu}, \mu) \leq \frac{\epsilon}{2}$ then ACCEPT and otherwise REJECT.*

1. *$\mathcal{M} = \{M_0, M_1, \ldots, M_k\} \leftarrow \text{Bucket}(\mu, [n], \frac{\epsilon}{200\log^\star m})$.*

2. *Sample $r = 4\epsilon^{-1}\log^\star(m)\log(\delta^{-1})$ elements from μ'. Let $M_{i_1}, \ldots, M_{i_r}$ be the buckets where these elements lie.*

3. *For every bucket $M_{i_1}, \ldots, M_{i_r}$ use the Near Uniformity Test (Theorem 3.1.2) for the distributions $\mu \restriction_{M_{i_j}}, \mu' \restriction_{M_{i_j}}$ to test whether $\|\mu \restriction_{M_{i_j}} - \mu' \restriction_{M_{i_j}}\|_1 \geq \frac{\epsilon}{2\log^\star m}$ with error bound $\frac{\delta\epsilon}{12\log^\star(m)\log(\delta^{-1})}$.*

4. *If for any i_j we have $\|\mu \restriction_{M_{i_j}} - \mu' \restriction_{M_{i_j}}\|_1 \geq \frac{\epsilon}{2\log^\star m}$ then REJECT.*

5. *Else recursively test whether $\|\mu_{\langle\mathcal{M}\rangle} - \mu'_{\langle\mathcal{M}\rangle}\|_1 \leq \epsilon\left(1 - \frac{1}{\log^\star m}\right)$ with error bound $\frac{\delta}{3}$. If not then REJECT else ACCEPT.*

First, we bounds the number of recursion levels that can occur.

LEMMA 3.2.3. *Algorithm 3.2.2 never enters more than $2\log^\star(n)$ recursion levels from the initial $n = m$ call.*

PROOF. Note that in the first $2\log^\star(n)$ recursion levels distance parameter that is passed is always lower bounded by $\epsilon\left(1 - \frac{1}{\log^\star n}\right)^{2\log^\star(n)} > \frac{\epsilon}{e^2}$, so we will prove the bound on the number of levels even if this is the distance parameter that is used in all but the first level. If $\log(n) \leq \left(\frac{400\log(1/\epsilon)}{\epsilon}\log^\star m\right)$ then after at most one recursion level the test goes to the brute force procedure in Step 0 and ends. Otherwise, note that the recursive call now receives $n' \leq \frac{400e^2 \log(n) \log^\star(m)}{\epsilon} \leq \log^3(n)$, and that call itself will make a recursive call with $n'' \leq \frac{1200e^2 \log\log(n) \log^\star(m)}{\epsilon} \leq \log n$ (unless it already terminated for some other reason). This is sufficient for the bound. □

LEMMA 3.2.4. *If $d(\mu, \mu') = 0$ then Algorithm 3.2.2 accepts with probability at least $1 - \delta$.*

PROOF. The base case where $n \leq \left(\frac{400 \log(1/\epsilon)}{\epsilon} \log^\star m\right)^3$ is clear. Otherwise, if $\|\mu - \mu'\|_1 = 0$ then for all buckets M_i we have $\|\mu \restriction_{M_i} - \mu' \restriction_{M_i}\|_1 = 0$ and $\|\mu_{\langle \mathcal{M} \rangle} - \mu'_{\langle \mathcal{M} \rangle}\|_1 = 0$. From Lemma 2.2.5 we know that $\|\mu \restriction_{M_i} - U \restriction_{M_i}\|_\infty \leq \frac{\epsilon}{200 \log^\star m} \cdot \frac{1}{n} \leq \frac{\epsilon'}{100n}$, where ϵ' is the distance parameter fed to the Near Uniformity Tester, and hence the Near Uniformity tester (Theorem 3.1.2) is applicable and will accept with probability $1 - \frac{\delta\epsilon}{12 \log^\star(m) \log(\delta^{-1})}$. Taking the union bound over the number of samples taken and the probability of failure for the recursive call gives us the desired bound. □

For soundness we need the following lemma.

LEMMA 3.2.5. *If $\|\mu - \mu'\|_1 \geq \epsilon$ then for any t at least one of the following two will happen:*

1. $\sum_{\{i : \|\mu \restriction_{M_i} - \mu' \restriction_{M_i}\|_1 \geq \epsilon/2t\}} \mu(M_i) \geq \epsilon/2t$
2. $\|\mu_{\langle \mathcal{M} \rangle} - \mu'_{\langle \mathcal{M} \rangle}\|_1 \geq \epsilon(1 - 1/t)$

PROOF. Recall Lemma 2.2.6:

$$\|\mu - \mu'\|_1$$

$$\leq \sum_{0 \leq i \leq k} \mu(M_i) \sum_{j \in M_i} \|\mu \restriction_{M_i}(j) - \mu' \restriction_{M_i}(j)\|_1$$

$$+ \|\mu_{\langle \mathcal{M} \rangle} - \mu'_{\langle \mathcal{M} \rangle}\|_1$$

Thus if $\|\mu_{\langle \mathcal{M} \rangle} - \mu'_{\langle \mathcal{M} \rangle}\|_1 < \epsilon(1 - 1/t)$ and additionally $\sum_{\{i : \|\mu \restriction_{M_i} - \mu' \restriction_{M_i}\|_1 \geq \epsilon/2t\}} \mu(M_i) < \epsilon/2t$ then we obtain the bound $\|\mu - \mu'\|_1 < \epsilon$, a contradiction. □

LEMMA 3.2.6. *If $d(\mu, \mu') > \epsilon$ then Algorithm 3.1.3 rejects with probability at least $1 - \delta$.*

PROOF. The base case of $n \leq \left(\frac{400 \log(1/\epsilon)}{\epsilon} \log^\star m\right)^3$ is clear. Refer now to Lemma 3.2.5, taking $t = \log^\star m$. Assume that we are in the first case of the lemma, that is $\sum_{\{i : \|\mu \restriction_{M_i} - \mu' \restriction_{M_i}\|_1 \geq \epsilon/2t\}} \mu(M_i) \geq \epsilon/2t$. therefore, the probability of sampling an index for which the test in Line 3 should reject is at least $\frac{\epsilon}{2 \log^\star m}$. This implies that the probability that one of the sampled elements is such is at least $\delta/3$, and since the probability that all calls to the Near Uniformity Test fail is at most $\delta/3$ as well, we accept with probability at most $2\delta/3$.

Now assuming that we are in the second case of Lemma 3.2.5, by the induction hypothesis we reject with probability at least $\delta/3$. Thus the overall error probability is at most δ. □

LEMMA 3.2.7. *The sample complexity of Algorithm 3.2.2 is* $\text{poly}(\log^\star n, \epsilon^{-1}, \log(\delta^{-1}))$.

PROOF. If $n \leq \left(\frac{400 \log(1/\epsilon)}{\epsilon} \log^\star m\right)^3$ then it is polynomial in ϵ and $\log^\star m$, and so is the result of substituting it in the number of queries of the brute force check of Step 0, $q_b(\epsilon, \delta, n) = 100 \log(1/\delta) \epsilon^{-2} n^2 \log n$. For analyzing the sample complexity when the above does not hold for $m = n$, let $q(\epsilon, \delta, n)$ denote the sample complexity of the algorithm. By the algorithm's definition, we have the following formula, where q_u is the sample complexity of the Near Uniformity Tester:

$$q(\epsilon, \delta, n, m) \leq \Bigg(4\epsilon^{-1} \log^\star(m) \log(\delta^{-1})$$

$$\cdot \left(1 + q_u\left(\frac{\epsilon}{2 \log^\star m}, \frac{\delta\epsilon}{12 \log^\star(m) \log(\delta^{-1})}, n\right)\right)\Bigg)$$

$$+ q\left(\epsilon\left(1 - \frac{1}{\log^\star m}\right), \frac{\delta}{3}, \frac{400 \log(n) \log^\star(m)}{\epsilon}, m\right)$$

According to Lemma 3.2.3, after at most $2 \log^\star n$ recursion levels from the initial $n = m$, the right hand side is now within the realm of the brute force check, and we get another summand, which can be bounded by $q_b(\epsilon/e^2, \delta \cdot 3^{-2 \log^\star n}, \left(\frac{400 \log(1/\epsilon)}{\epsilon} \log^\star n\right)^3)$, which is in turn bounded by $\text{poly}(\log^\star n, \epsilon^{-1}, \log(\delta^{-1}))$. Therefore:

$$q(\epsilon, \delta, n, n) \leq \Bigg(8\epsilon^{-1} (\log^\star n)^2 \log(\delta^{-1})$$

$$\cdot \left(1 + q_u\left(\frac{\epsilon}{2e^2 \log^\star n}, \frac{\epsilon \cdot \delta \cdot 3^{-2 \log^\star n}}{40e^2 (\log^\star n)^2 \log(\delta^{-1})}, n\right)\right)\Bigg)$$

$$+ \text{poly}(\log^\star n, \epsilon^{-1}, \log(\delta^{-1}))$$

Since by Lemma 3.1.4, the Near Uniformity Tester has sample complexity polynomial in the distance parameter and polylogarithmic in the error bound, we obtain the statement of the lemma. □

4. TESTING ANY LABEL-INVARIANT PROPERTY

We show here the following "universal testing" theorem for label-invariant properties.

THEOREM 4.0.1. *Every label-invariant property of distributions can be tested using* $\text{poly}(\log n, \epsilon^{-1}, \log(\delta^{-1}))$ *adaptive conditional samples.*

The same tools used to prove Theorem 4.0.1 also allow us to develop a tester in the unknown-unknown setting.

THEOREM 4.0.2. *Isomorphism between two unknown distributions can be tested using* $\text{poly}(\log n, \epsilon^{-1}, \log(\delta^{-1}))$ *adaptive conditional samples.*

Both theorems are in fact a direct corollary of the following learning result.

THEOREM 4.0.3. *There exist an adaptive algorithm that uses* $\text{poly}(\log n, \epsilon^{-1}, \log(\delta^{-1}))$ *conditional samples to output a distribution $\tilde{\mu}$ over $[n]$, so that with probability at least $1-\delta$ some permutation of $\tilde{\mu}$ will be ϵ-close to μ.*

To derive Theorem 4.0.1, use Theorem 4.0.3 to obtain a distribution $\tilde{\mu}$ that is $\epsilon/2$-close to a permutation of μ, and then accept μ if and only if $\tilde{\mu}$ is $\epsilon/2$-close to the tested property.

To derive Theorem 4.0.2, use Theorem 4.0.3 to obtain two distributions $\tilde{\mu_1}, \tilde{\mu_2}$ such that $\tilde{\mu_1}$ is $\epsilon/3$-close to a permutation of μ_1 and $\tilde{\mu_2}$ is $\epsilon/3$-close to a permutation of μ_2, and then accept if and only if $\tilde{\mu_1}$ is $\epsilon/3$-close to some permutation of $\tilde{\mu_2}$

The main idea of the proof of Theorem 4.0.3 is to use a bucketing, and try to approximate the number of members of every bucket, which allows us to construct an approximate distribution. However, there are some roadblocks, and in the foremost the fact that we cannot really query the value $\mu(i)$. Instead we will construct a way to approximate the distribution, and then go further to simulate the approximated distribution instead of the original.

In all the following we assume that n is a power of 2, as otherwise we can "pad" the probability space with additional zero-probability members.

4.1 Bucketing and approximations

We need a bucketing that also goes into smaller probabilities than those needed for the other sections.

DEFINITION 4.1.1. *Given an explicit distribution μ over $[n]$, Bucket'$(\mu, [n], \epsilon)$ is a procedure that generates a partition $\{M_0, M_1, \ldots, M_k\}$ of the domain $[n]$, where we set $k = \frac{\log n \log(\epsilon^{-1})}{\log^2(1+\epsilon)}$. This partition satisfies the following conditions:*

- $M_0 = \{j \in [n] \mid \mu(j) < \frac{\epsilon}{n}\}$;
- $M_i = \left\{j \in [n] \mid \frac{(1+\epsilon)^{i-1}}{n}\epsilon \le \mu(j) < \frac{(1+\epsilon)^i}{n}\epsilon\right\}$, *for all* $i \in [k]$.

In the rest of this section, bucketing will always refer to this version. Also, from here on we fix ϵ and $k = \frac{\log n \log(\epsilon^{-1})}{\log^2(1+\epsilon)}$ as above (as well as mostly ignore floor and ceiling signs). We also assume that ϵ is small enough, say smaller than $\frac{1}{100}$.

Suppose that we have $m_0, \ldots, m_k$, where $m_i = |M_i|$ is the size of the i'th set in the bucketing of a distribution μ. Then we can use these to construct a distribution that is guaranteed to be close to some permutation of μ.

DEFINITION 4.1.2. *Given $m_0, \ldots, m_k$ for which it holds that $\sum_{j=0}^k m_j = n$ and ϵ, the* tentative distribution *over $[n]$ is the one constructed according to the following.*

- *Set $r_1, \ldots, r_n$ so that $|\{i : r_i = 0\}| = m_0$ and $|\{i : r_i = \frac{(1+\epsilon)^{j-1}}{n}\epsilon\}| = m_j$ for every $1 \le j \le k$ (the order of $r_1, \ldots, r_n$ is arbitrary).*
- *Set a distribution $\tilde{\mu}$ over $[n]$ by setting $\mu(i)$ equal to $r_i / \sum_{j=1}^n r_i$.*

To gain some intuition, note the following.

OBSERVATION 4.1.3. *If $M_0, \ldots, M_k$ is the bucketing of μ and $\tilde{\mu}$ is the tentative distribution according to the bucket sizes $m_0 = |M_0|, \ldots, m_k = |M_k|$, then $\tilde{\mu}$ is 2ϵ-close to some permutation of μ.*

PROOF. We assume that we have already permuted $\tilde{\mu}$ so that each $\tilde{\mu}(i)$ refers to an r_i set according to the bucket M_j satisfying $i \in M_j$ (such a permutation is possible because here we used the actual sizes of the buckets).

We recall that the distance is in particular equal to the sum $\sum_{\{i:\tilde{\mu}(i)<\mu(i)\}}(\mu(i) - \tilde{\mu}(i))$. Referring to the r_i of the definition above, we note that in this case we have that $\sum_{i=0}^n r_i \le \sum_{i=0}^n \mu(i) = 1$ and hence $\tilde{\mu}(i) \ge r_i$. For $i \notin M_0$, this means that $\tilde{\mu}(i) \ge (1-\epsilon)\mu(i)$. For the rest we just note that $\sum_{i \in M_0} \mu(i) \le \epsilon$. Together we get the required bound. $\square$

The above observation essentially states that it is enough to find the numbers $m_0, \ldots, m_k$ associated with μ. However, the best we can hope for is to somehow estimate the size, or total probability, of every bucket. The following shows that this is in fact sufficient.

DEFINITION 4.1.4. *Given $\alpha_0, \ldots, \alpha_k$ for which holds the equation $\sum_{j=0}^k \alpha_j = 1$, the* bucketization *thereof is the sequence of integers $\hat{m}_0, \ldots, \hat{m}_k$ defined by the following.*

- *For any $1 \le j \le k$ let $\hat{m}_j$ be the integer closest to $n\alpha_k$ (where an "exact half" is arbitrarily rounded down).*
- *If $\sum_{j=1}^k \hat{m}_j > n$, then decrease the $\hat{m}_j$ until they sum up to n, each time picking j to be the smallest index for which $\hat{m}_j > 0$ and decreasing that quantity by 1.*
- *Finally set $\hat{m}_0 = n - \sum_{j=1}^k \hat{m}_j$.*

We say that the bucketization has failed *if in the second step we had to decrease any $\hat{m}_j$ for which $\frac{(1+\epsilon)^{j-1}}{n}\epsilon \ge \frac{\epsilon}{k}$.*

LEMMA 4.1.5. *Suppose that $m_0, \ldots, m_k$, $\alpha_0, \ldots, \alpha_k$ are such that :*

- $\sum_{j=0}^k m_j = n$
- $\sum_{j=1}^k m_j \frac{(1+\epsilon)^{j-1}}{n}\epsilon \le 1$
- $\sum_{j=0}^k \alpha_j = 1$
- $|m_j - \alpha_j| \frac{(1+\epsilon)^{j-1}}{n}\epsilon < \frac{\epsilon}{2k}$ *for all* $1 \le j \le k$

and let $\hat{m}_0, \ldots, \hat{m}_k$ be the bucketization of $\alpha_0, \ldots, \alpha_k$. Then $\hat{m}_0, \ldots, \hat{m}_k$ are all well defined (the bucketization process did not fail), and additionally if $\tilde{\mu}$ is the tentative distribution according to $m_0, \ldots, m_k$ and $\hat{\mu}$ is the tentative distribution according to $\hat{m}_0, \ldots, \hat{m}_k$, then the distance between $\hat{\mu}$ and $\tilde{\mu}$ (after some permutation) is at most 4ϵ.

PROOF. First thing to note is that $m_j = \hat{m}_j$ for all j for which $\frac{(1+\epsilon)^{j-1}}{n}\epsilon \ge \frac{\epsilon}{k}$, before the decreasing step, so there will be no need to decrease these values and the bucketization will not fail.

For all other $j \ge 1$, before decreasing some of the $\hat{m}_j$ we have that $|m_j - \hat{m}_j| \frac{(1+\epsilon)^{j-1}}{n}\epsilon < \frac{\epsilon}{k}$ (if $\frac{(1+\epsilon)^{j-1}}{n}\epsilon \le \frac{\epsilon}{k}$ then the distance is not more than doubled by the rounding, and otherwise it follows from $|\alpha_j - \hat{m}_j| \le 1$). Since the bucketization did not fail, the decreasing step only affects values $\hat{m}_j$ for which $\frac{(1+\epsilon)^{j-1}}{n}\epsilon < \frac{\epsilon}{k}$, and the total required decrease in them was by not more than k (as the rounding in the first step of the bucketization added no more than

1 to each value), we obtain the total bound $\sum_{j=1}^{k}|m_j - \hat{m}_j|\frac{(1+\epsilon)^{j-1}}{n}\epsilon \leq 3\epsilon$.

Let r_i denote the corresponding values in the definition of $\tilde{\mu}$ being the tentative distribution according to $m_0, \ldots, m_k$, and $\hat{r}_i$ be the analog values in the definition of $\hat{\mu}$ being the tentative distribution according to $\hat{m}_0, \ldots, \hat{m}_k$. By what we already know about $\sum_{j=1}^{k}|m_j - \hat{m}_j|\frac{(1+\epsilon)^{j-1}}{n}$ we have in particular $\sum_{i=1}^{n}\hat{r}_i = \sum_{i=1}^{n} r_i \pm 3\epsilon$. Combined with the known bounds on $\sum_{i=1}^{n} r_i$, we can conclude by finding a permutation for which we can bound $\sum_{i=1}^{n}|r_i - \hat{r}_i|$ by 3ϵ, which will give the 4ϵ bound on the distribution distance $\frac{1}{2}\sum_{i=1}^{n}|\tilde{\mu}(i) - \hat{\mu}(i)|$.

The permutation we take is the one that maximizes the number of i's for which $r_i = \hat{r}_i$; for the value $\frac{(1+\epsilon)^{j-1}}{n}\epsilon$ we can find $\min\{m_i, \hat{m}_i\}$ such i's (for every $1 \leq j \leq k$), and the hypothetical worst case is that whenever $r_i \neq \hat{r}_i$ one of them is zero (sometimes the realizable worst case is in fact not as bad as the hypothetical one). Thus we obtain the $\sum_{j=1}^{k}|m_j - \hat{m}_j|\frac{(1+\epsilon)^{j-1}}{n}\epsilon \leq 3\epsilon$ bound leading to the 4ϵ bound on the distribution distance. □

A problem still remains, in that sampling from μ will not obtain a value α_j close enough to the required $m_j\frac{(1+\epsilon)^{j-1}}{n}\epsilon$. The variations in the $\mu(i)$ inside the bucket M_j itself could be higher than the $\frac{\epsilon}{2k}$ that we need here. In the next subsection we will construct not only a "bucket identifying" oracle, but tie it with a sampler that will simulate the approximate distribution rather than the original μ.

4.2 Ratio trees and reconstituted distributions

The main driving force in our algorithm is a way to estimate the ratio between the distribution weight of two disjoint sets. To make it into a weight oracle for a value $i \in [n]$, we will use successive partitions of $[n]$, through a fixed binary tree. Remember that here n is assumed to be a power of 2.

We first define how to "reconstruct" a distribution from a tree with ratios, and afterward show how to put the ratios there.

DEFINITION 4.2.1. *Let T be a (full) balanced binary tree with n leaves labeled by $[n]$. Let U be the set of non-leaf nodes of the tree, and assume that we have a function $\alpha : U \to [0,1]$. For $u \in U$ denote by $L(u)$ the set of leaves that are descendants of the left child of u, and by $R(u)$ the leaves that are descendants of the right child of u.*

The reconstituted distribution *according to α is the distribution $\tilde{\mu}$ that is calculated for every $i \in [n]$ as follows:*

- *Let $u_1, \ldots, u_{\log(n)+1}$ be the root to leaf path for i (so in particular $u_{\log(n)+1} = i$).*
- *For ever $1 \leq j \leq \log n$, set $p_j = \alpha(u_j)$ if i is a descendant of the left child of u_j (that is if $i \in L(u_j)$), and otherwise set $p_j = 1 - \alpha(u_j)$.*
- *Set $\tilde{\mu}(i) = \prod_{j=1}^{\log n} p_j$.*

For intuition, note the following trivial observation.

OBSERVATION 4.2.2. *If for a distribution μ we set $\alpha(u) = \frac{\mu(L(u))}{\mu(L(u))+\mu(R(u))}$, using an arbitrary value (say $\frac{1}{2}$) for the case where $\mu(L(u)) + \mu(R(u)) = 0$, then the reconstituted distribution $\tilde{\mu}$ is identical to μ.*

However, we cannot know the values $\frac{\mu(L(u))}{\mu(L(u))+\mu(R(u))}$. The best we can do the the following.

DEFINITION 4.2.3. *An (ϵ, δ)-ratio estimator for T and a distribution μ is an algorithm A that given a non-leaf vertex $u \in U$ outputs a number r, such that with probability $1 - \delta$ we have that $\frac{\mu(L(v))}{\mu(L(v))+\mu(R(v))} - \epsilon \leq r \leq \frac{\mu(L(v))}{\mu(L(v))+\mu(R(v))} + \epsilon$.*

ALGORITHM 4.2.4. *(Ratio Estimator) The estimator algorithm is given a balanced binary tree T with n leaves, a non-leaf vertex $u \in U$ and parameters ϵ, δ. It also has conditional sample access to a distribution μ.*

1. *Sample $t = 2\epsilon^{-2}\log(\delta^{-1})$ elements according to the distribution $\mu\restriction_{L(u)\cup R(u)}$, and let s be the number of samples that are in $L(u)$.*
2. *Return the ratio $\frac{s}{t}$ of the samples that are in $L(u)$ to the total number of samples.*

LEMMA 4.2.5. *For any ϵ, δ Algorithm 4.2.4 is an (ϵ, δ)-ratio estimator for T and μ which uses $t = 2\epsilon^{-2}\log(\delta^{-1})$ non-adaptive conditional samples from μ.*

PROOF. The number of samples used is immediate. Let us now proceed to show that this is indeed an (ϵ, δ)-ratio estimator. The expected value of $\frac{s}{t}$ is $\frac{\mu(L(u))}{\mu(L(u))+\mu(R(u))}$.

By Chernoff's inequality, the probability that $\frac{s}{t}$ deviates from its expected value by an additive term of more than ϵ is at most $2\exp(-2\epsilon^2 \cdot t)$. By our choice of t we obtain the statement. □

If we could "populate" the entire tree T (through the function α) by values that do not deviate by much from the corresponding ratios, then we would be able to create an estimate for μ that is good for most values.

DEFINITION 4.2.6. *The function $\alpha : U \to [0,1]$ is called* ϵ-fine *if $|\alpha(u) - \frac{\mu(L(u))}{\mu(L(u))+\mu(R(u))}| \leq (\frac{\epsilon}{2\log(n)})^2$ for every $u \in U$.*

We call a distribution $\tilde{\mu}$ ϵ-fine *if there exists a set B such that $\mu(B) \leq \epsilon$, and additionally $\tilde{\mu}(i) = (1 \pm \epsilon)\mu(i)$ for every $i \in [n] \setminus B$.*

LEMMA 4.2.7. *If α is ϵ-fine then the reconstituted distribution $\tilde{\mu}$ is ϵ-fine.*

PROOF. To define the set B, for every i consider the $p_1, \ldots, p_{\log n}$ that are set as per Definition 4.2.1, and set $i \in B$ if and only if there exist some p_j that is smaller than $\frac{\epsilon}{2\log(n)}$. Next, denote by $q_1, \ldots, q_k$ the "intended" values, that is $q_j = \frac{\mu(L(u_j))}{\mu(L(u_j))+\mu(R(u_j))}$ if $i \in L(u_j)$ and $q_j = \frac{\mu(R(u_j))}{\mu(L(u_j))+\mu(R(u_j))}$ otherwise. Noting that p_j does not deviates from q_j by more than $(\frac{\epsilon}{2\log(n)})^2$, an induction over $\log n$ (the height of T) gives that $1 - \mu(B)$ is at least $(1 - \frac{\epsilon}{\log n})^{\log n} > 1 - \epsilon$.

For $i \in [n] \setminus B$, we note that in this case $p_j = (1 \pm \frac{\epsilon}{2\log n})q_j$, and hence $\tilde{\mu}(i) = \prod_{j=1}^{\log n} p_j = (1 \pm \frac{\epsilon}{2\log n})^{\log n}\prod_{j=1}^{\log n} q_j = (1 \pm \epsilon)\mu(i)$. □

We should note here that it is not hard to prove that an ϵ-fine distribution $\tilde{\mu}$ is of distance not more than 4ϵ from the original μ. However, we will in fact refer to yet another distribution which will be easier to estimate, so we will show closeness to it instead.

DEFINITION 4.2.8. *Given an ϵ-fine distribution $\tilde{\mu}$ and its respective set B, its* ϵ-trimmed distribution $\overline{\mu}$ *is a distribution over $[n] \cup \{0\}$ defined by the following.*

- *For $i \in B \cup \{i : \tilde{\mu}(i) < \frac{\epsilon}{n}\}$ we set $\overline{\mu}(i) = 0$. For such i we also set $j_i = 0$.*
- *For all other $i \in [n]$ we set j_i to be the largest integer for which $\frac{(1+\epsilon)^{j_i-1}}{n}\epsilon \leq \tilde{\mu}(i)$, and set $\overline{\mu}(i) = \frac{(1+\epsilon)^{j_i-1}}{n}\epsilon$.*
- *Finally set $\overline{\mu}(0) = 1 - \sum_{i=1}^{n} \overline{\mu}(i)$; note that $\overline{\mu}(i) \leq \tilde{\mu}(i)$ for all $1 \leq i \leq n$ and hence $\overline{\mu}(0) \geq 0$.*

The ϵ-renormalized distribution $\hat{\mu}$ *over $[n]$ is just the conditioning $\overline{\mu} \upharpoonright_{[n]}$.*

It is important to know that the renormalized distribution is in fact (a permutation of) the tentative distribution according to $m_0, \ldots, m_k$, where for $0 \leq j \leq k$ we set $m_j = |\{i : j_i = j\}|$.

LEMMA 4.2.9. *The renormalized distribution $\hat{\mu}$ corresponding to an ϵ-fine distribution $\tilde{\mu}$ is 4ϵ-close to μ.*

PROOF. First we consider the trimmed distribution $\overline{\mu}$, and its distance from μ (when we extend it by setting $\mu(0) = 0$). Recalling that this variation distance is equal to the sum $\sum_{\{i:\overline{\mu}(i)<\mu(i)\}}(\mu(i) - \overline{\mu}(i))$, we partition the set of relevant i's into two subsets.

- For those i that are in B (for which $\overline{\mu}(i) = 0$), the total difference is $\mu(B) \leq \epsilon$.
- For any other i for which $\overline{\mu}(i) < \mu(i)$, note that $\overline{\mu}(i) \geq \frac{1}{1+\epsilon}\tilde{\mu}(i) \geq \frac{1-\epsilon}{1+\epsilon}\mu(i) > (1-3\epsilon)\mu(i)$. This means that the sum over differences for all such i is bounded by 3ϵ.
- We never have $\overline{\mu}(0) < \mu(0)$.

Thus the distance between $\overline{\mu}$ and μ is not more than 4ϵ. As for $\hat{\mu}$, the sum of differences over i for which $\hat{\mu}(i) < \mu(i)$ is only made smaller (the conditioning only increases the probability for every $i > 0$), and so the 4ϵ bound remains. □

4.3 Distribution samplers and learning

For our learning algorithm we need to not only sample from the distribution μ, but to be able to "report" $\mu(i)$ for every i thus sampled. This we cannot do, but it turns out that we can sample from a close distribution $\tilde{\mu}$ while reporting $\tilde{\mu}(i)$. In fact we will sample from a distribution that in itself will be drawn from the following distribution over distributions.

DEFINITION 4.3.1. *The* (ϵ, δ)-condensation *of μ is the distribution over ϵ-fine distributions (with respect to μ) that is defined by the following process.*

- *Let T be a (full) balanced binary tree whose leaves are labeled by $[n]$, and U be its set of internal nodes.*
- *For every $u \in U$, let $\alpha(u)$ be the (randomized) result of running the corresponding $((\frac{\epsilon}{2\log(n)})^2, \delta)$-Ratio Estimator (Algorithm 4.2.4), when conditioned on this result indeed being of distance not more than $(\frac{\epsilon}{2\log(n)})^2$ from $\frac{\mu(L(u_j))}{\mu(L(u_j))+\mu(R(u_j))}$. This is done independently for every u.*
- *The drawn distribution $\tilde{\mu}$ is the reconstituted distribution according to T and α*

The algorithm that we define next is an explicit persistent sampler: It is explicit in that it relays information about $\tilde{\mu}(i)$ along with i, and persistent in that it simulates (with high probability) a sequence of s independent samples from the same $\tilde{\mu}$.

DEFINITION 4.3.2. *Given a distribution over distributions, a* (δ, s)-explicit persistent sampler *is an algorithm that can be run up to s times (and during each run may store information to be used in subsequent runs), that in every run returns a pair (i, η). It must satisfy that with probability at least $1-\delta$, the i's for all s runs are independent samples of a single distribution $\tilde{\mu}$ that in itself was drawn according to the distribution over distributions, and every output pair (i, η) satisfies $\eta = \tilde{\mu}(i)$.*

ALGORITHM 4.3.3. *(Persistent Sampler) The algorithm is given parameters ϵ, δ and s, and has conditional sample access to a distribution μ.*

1. *On the initial run, set T to be a full balanced binary tree with n leaves labeled by $[n]$. Let w denote the root vertex and U denote the set of non-leaf vertices. α is initially unset.*
2. *On all runs, set $u_1 = w$, and repeat the following for $l = 1, \ldots, \log n$.*
   (a) *If $\alpha(u_l)$ is not set yet, set it to the result of the $((\frac{\epsilon}{2\log(n)})^2, \frac{\delta}{s\log n})$-Ratio Estimator (refer to Algorithm 4.2.4); run it independently of prior runs.*
   (b) *Independently of any prior choices, and without sampling from μ, with probability $\alpha(u_l)$ set u_{l+1} to be the left child of u_l and $p_l = \alpha(u_l)$, and with probability $1 - \alpha(u_l)$ set u_{l+1} to be the right child of u_l and $p_l = 1 - \alpha(u_l)$.*
   (c) *Set i to be the label of the leaf $u_{\log n}$ and $\eta = \prod_{l=1}^{k} p_l$. Return i and η.*

LEMMA 4.3.4. *For any ϵ, δ and s, Algorithm 4.3.3 is a (δ, s)-explicit persistent sampler for the $(\epsilon, \frac{\delta}{s\log n})$-condensation of μ. It uses a total of $2^5 \cdot \epsilon^{-4}\log^5 n \cdot \log(s\delta^{-1}\log n)$ many adaptive conditional samples from μ to output a sample.*

PROOF. Calculating the number of samples is straightforward (but note that these are adaptive now). During s runs, by the union bound with probability at least $1-\delta$ all of the calls to the $((\frac{\epsilon}{2\log(n)})^2, \frac{\delta}{s\log n})$-Ratio Estimator produced results that are not more than $(\frac{\epsilon}{2\log(n)})^2$-away from the actual rations.

Conditioned on the above event, the algorithm acts the same as the algorithm that first chooses for every $u \in U$ the value $\alpha(u)$ according to a run of the $((\frac{\epsilon}{2\log(n)})^2, \frac{\delta}{s\log n})$-Ratio Estimator conditioned on it being successful, and only then traverses the tree T for every required sample. The latter algorithm is identical to picking a distribution $\tilde{\mu}$ according to the $(\epsilon, \frac{\delta}{s\log n})$-condensation of μ, and then (explicitly) sampling from it. □

This is almost sufficient to learn the distribution. The next step would be to estimate the size of a bucket of the ϵ-fine distribution $\tilde{\mu}$ by explicit sampling (i.e. getting the samples along with their probabilities). However, Lemma 4.1.5 requires an approximation not of $\tilde{\mu}(M_j)$ (where M_j is a bucket of $\tilde{\mu}$) but rather of $|M_j|\frac{(1+\epsilon)^{j-1}}{n}\epsilon$. In other words, we really need to approximate $\overline{\mu}(M_j)$, where $\overline{\mu}$ is the corresponding trimmed distribution.

Therefore we define the following explicit sampler for an ϵ-trimmed distribution. We "bend" the definition a little, as this sampler will not be able to provide the corresponding probability for $i = 0$.

ALGORITHM 4.3.5. *(Trimming Sampler) The algorithm is given parameters ϵ, δ and s, and has conditional sample access to a distribution μ.*

1. *Run the Persistent Sampler (Algorithm 4.3.3) with parameters ϵ, δ and s to obtain i and η; additionally retain $p_1, \ldots, p_{\log n}$ as calculated during the run of the Persistent Sampler.*
2. *If there exists l for which $p_l < \frac{\epsilon}{2\log(n)}$ then return "0".*
3. *If $\eta < \frac{\epsilon}{n}$ then return "0".*
4. *Otherwise, let j be the largest integer for which it holds that $\frac{(1+\epsilon)^{j-1}}{n}\epsilon \leq \eta$, and set $\eta' = \frac{(1+\epsilon)^{j-1}}{n}\epsilon$.*
5. *With probability $1 - \eta'/\eta$ return "0", and with probability η'/η return (i, j) (where j corresponds to $\overline{\mu}(i) = \eta'$).*

The following observation is now easy.

OBSERVATION 4.3.6. *The trimming sampler (refer to Algorithm 4.3.5) is a (δ, s)-persistent sampler, and explicit whenever the returned sample is not 0, for the distribution over distributions that results from taking the ϵ-trimming of an ϵ-fine distribution $\tilde{\mu}$ and its corresponding B that was drawn according to the $(\epsilon, \frac{\delta}{s\log n})$-condensation of μ. The algorithm uses in total $2^5 \cdot \epsilon^{-4}\log^5 n \cdot \log(s\delta^{-1}\log n)$ many adaptive conditional samples from μ to output a sample.*

PROOF. The number of samples is inherited from Algorithm 4.3.3 as no other samples are taken. The algorithm switches the return value to "0" whenever $i \in B$ (as defined in the proof of Lemma 4.2.7), and otherwise returns "0" exactly according to the corresponding conditional probability difference for i between $\tilde{\mu}$ (as in the definition of a reconstituted distribution) and $\overline{\mu}$ (as in the definition of the corresponding trimmed distribution). Finally, whenever the returned sample is $i > 0$ the algorithm clearly returns the corresponding j_i (see Definition 4.2.8). □

We are now ready to present the algorithm providing Theorem 4.0.3.

ALGORITHM 4.3.7. *(Distribution Approximation) The algorithm is given parameters ϵ, δ, and has conditional sample access to a distribution μ.*

1. *Set $s = 2^{12}\epsilon^{-4}\log^2(n)\log(\delta^{-1})$, and $k = \frac{\log n \log(8\epsilon^{-1})}{\log^2(1+\epsilon/8)}$ (the number of buckets in an $\epsilon/8$-bucketing of a distribution over $[n]$).*
2. *Take s samples through the $(\epsilon/8, \delta/2, s)$-Trimming Sampler.*
3. *Denote by s_0 the number of times that the sampler returned "0", and for $1 \leq j \leq k$ denote by s_j the number of times that the sampler returned (i, j) for any i.*
4. *Let $m'_0, \ldots, m'_k$ be the bucketization of the sequence $\alpha_0 = \frac{s_0}{s}, \ldots, \alpha_k = \frac{s_k}{s}$.*
5. *Return the tentative distribution according to the sequence $m'_0, \ldots, m'_k$.*

LEMMA 4.3.8. *The Distribution Approximation algorithm (Algorithm 4.3.7) will with probability at least $1 - \delta$ return a distribution that is ϵ-close to a permutation of μ. This is performed using at most $\tilde{O}(\epsilon^{-8}\log^7 n \log^2(\delta^{-1}))$ conditional samples.*

PROOF. The number of samples is immediate from the algorithm statement and Observation 4.3.6.

By Observation 4.3.6, with probability at least $1 - \delta/2$ all samples of the Trimming Sampler will be from one $\epsilon/8$-trimming of some $\epsilon/8$-fine distribution $\overline{\mu}$. Set $m_0 = |\{1 \leq i \leq n : \overline{\mu}(i) = i\}|$ and for $1 \leq j \leq k$ set $m_j = |\{i : \overline{\mu}(i) = \frac{(1+\epsilon)^{j-1}}{n}\epsilon\}|$. Recall that the $\epsilon/8$-renormalized distribution corresponding to $\overline{\mu}$ is in fact the tentative distribution according to $m_0, \ldots, m_k$. By Lemma 4.2.9, this distribution is $\epsilon/2$-close to μ.

Note now that for every $1 \leq j \leq k$ the expectation of α_j is exactly $m_j\frac{(1+\epsilon/8)^{j-1}}{n}\epsilon/8$. By virtue of a Chernoff bound and the union bound, our choice of s implies that with probability $1-\delta/2$ (conditioned on the previous event) we in fact get values that satisfy $|m_j - \alpha_j|\frac{(1+\epsilon/8)^{j-1}}{n}\epsilon/8 < \frac{\epsilon/8}{2k}$ for every $1 \leq j \leq k$. This satisfies the assertions of Lemma 4.1.5, and thus the tentative distribution according to $m'_0, \ldots, m'_k$ will be $\epsilon/2$-close to the tentative distribution according to $m_0, \ldots, m_k$, and hence will be ϵ-close to μ. □

Note that if we were to use this algorithm for testing purposes, the dependence on δ^{-1} can be made logarithmic by setting it to 1/3 and repeating the algorithm $\log(\delta^{-1})$ times, taking majority.

5. NON-ADAPTIVE TESTING FOR UNIFORMITY AND IDENTITY

In this section we return to the definition of bucketing introduced in the preliminaries (Definition 2.2.4).

5.1 Testing uniformity

THEOREM 5.1.1. *Testing uniformity can be done using* poly$(\log n, \epsilon^{-1}, \log(\delta^{-1}))$ *non-adaptive conditional samples.*

Again, we will actually prove the following stronger statement:

THEOREM 5.1.2 (NEAR UNIFORMITY TESTER). *Let μ be a known distribution over $[n]$. If $\|\mu - U_n\|_\infty < \epsilon/8n$ then identity with μ can be tested using* poly$(\log n, \epsilon^{-1}, \log(\delta^{-1}))$ *conditional samples by a non-adaptive algorithm.*

To simplify analysis and presentation, the algorithm will succeed with probability 2/3. This can be amplified to $1 - \delta$ by the standard technique of repeating it for $\log(\delta^{-1})$ times and taking the majority vote. This obviously incurs a multiplicative factor of $\log(\delta^{-1})$ in the sample complexity.

ALGORITHM 5.1.3. *The algorithm is given n, ϵ and μ, and has nonadaptive conditional sample access to μ'.*

1. *For $\lceil \log(28800\epsilon^{-6}\log^5(n)) \rceil \le j \le \lceil \log(n) \rceil$, set U_j to be a uniformly random set of $\min\{n, 2^j\}$ indices.*
2. *For every U_j, perform $16\epsilon^{-2}\log^2(n)$ conditional samples, and if the same index was drawn twice, REJECT.*
3. *Uniformly pick a random set U of $1980\epsilon^{-6}\log^5(n)$ elements, and invoke the Identity Tester of Theorem 2.2.1 to test whether $\mu' \restriction_U = \mu \restriction_U$ or $d(\mu' \restriction_U, \mu \restriction_U) > \frac{\epsilon}{24|U|}$ with success probability $\frac{19}{20}$.*
4. *ACCEPT unless any of the above testers rejected.*

LEMMA 5.1.4. *If $d(\mu, \mu') = 0$ then Algorithm 3.1.3 accepts with probability at least 2/3.*

PROOF. Since $\|\mu - U_n\|_\infty < \epsilon/8n$, the probability that an element will be drawn twice in the jth iteration of Line 2 is at most $\binom{16\epsilon^{-2}\log^2(n)}{2} \cdot \left(\frac{1+\epsilon/8}{1-\epsilon/8}\right)^2 \cdot 2^{-2j}$. Summation over all values of j gives us less than 1/9.

Since $\mu = \mu'$, $\mu' \restriction_U = \mu \restriction_U$ for any $U \subseteq [n]$, and the probability that Line 3 rejects is at most 1/9. This obtains the error bound in the lemma. □

The following is immediate from the algorithm statement and Theorem 2.2.1:

LEMMA 5.1.5. *The sample complexity of Algorithm 3.2.2 is* $\mathrm{poly}(\log n, \epsilon^{-1})$.

PROOF. This follows from the number of samples used in Lines 2 and 3 and the fact that Line 2 is iterated at most $\log n$ times. □

In the following we assume that $d(\mu, \mu') > \epsilon$.

Let the sets $M_1, M_2, \ldots, M_k$ be the bucketing of μ and let $M'_1, M'_2, \ldots, M'_k$ be the bucketing of μ' with $\epsilon/3$. Denote the individual probabilities by $p_1, \ldots, p_n$ and $p'_1, \ldots, p'_n$ respectively.

LEMMA 5.1.6. *$|M'_0 \cup M'_1| \ge \epsilon n$ and there exists $2 < j \le k$ such that $|M'_j| \ge \frac{\epsilon^2 n}{24(1+\epsilon/3)^j \log n}$*

PROOF. Note that $[n] = M_0 \cup M_1$ by our requirement from μ. Now following Lemma 3.1.7, $\sum_{p'_i < p_i}(p_i - p'_i) \le |\{i : p'_i < p_i\}| \cdot \max\{p_i\}$. Now since $\max_i\{p_i\} < (1+\epsilon/8)\frac{1}{n}$ there are at least $(\epsilon/2)n$ such i.

For the second part we will adapt the proof of Lemma 3.1.6. Clearly $\sum_{p_i < p'_i < p_i + 11\epsilon/12n}(p'_i - p_i) < \frac{11}{12}\epsilon$. Therefore:

$$\sum_{p'_i \ge p_i + 11\epsilon/12n} p'_i > \sum_{p'_i \ge p_i + 11\epsilon/12n} (p'_i - p_i)$$

$$= \sum_{p'_i > p_i} (p'_i - p_i) - \sum_{p_i < p'_i < p_i + 11\epsilon/12n} (p'_i - p_i) > \frac{1}{12}\epsilon$$

Since $p_i \ge \frac{1-\epsilon/8}{n}$, we know that the p'_i in the left hand side have (assuming $\epsilon < 1/10$)

$$p'_i \ge \frac{1-\epsilon/8}{n} + \frac{11\epsilon}{12n} = \frac{1 + 19\epsilon/24}{n} \ge \frac{(1+\epsilon/3)^2}{n}$$

and therefore all these p'_is are in buckets M'_j for $2 < j \le k$.

Since $k = \frac{\log n}{\log(1+\epsilon/3)}$, there exists some $2 < j \le k$ such that $\mu'(M'_j) = \frac{\epsilon \log(1+\epsilon/3)}{4 \log n}$. By the definition of the buckets this gives $|M'_j| \ge \frac{\epsilon \log(1+\epsilon/3)}{4\log n} \cdot \frac{n}{(1+\epsilon/3)^j} > \frac{\epsilon^2 n}{24(1+\epsilon/3)^j \log n}$. □

LEMMA 5.1.7. *Given a set B of size l, a set U containing a uniformly random choice of $\min\{n, \frac{3n}{l}\}$ indices will with probability more than $\frac{19}{20}$ contain a member of B.*

PROOF. The probability is lower bounded by the probability for $3n/l$ indexes chosen uniformly and independently with repetitions from $[n]$ to intersect B, which is $1 - (1 - l/n)^{\frac{3n}{l}} \ge \frac{19}{20}$. □

LEMMA 5.1.8. *Let μ be a known distribution over $[n]$. If $\|\mu - U_n\|_\infty < \epsilon/8n$ and $d(\mu, \mu') > \epsilon$ then Algorithm 3.1.3 rejects with probability at least 2/3.*

PROOF. We partition into cases according to the j guaranteed by Lemma 5.1.6.

If $(1+\frac{\epsilon}{3})^j \le 40\epsilon^{-4}\log^4 n$, then $|M'_j| \ge \frac{\epsilon^6}{960 \log^5 n} n$, so by Lemma 5.1.7 with probability $\frac{19}{20}$ the set U in Line 3 will contain a member h of M'_j. Note that $j > 2$ and therefore $\mu'(h) \ge \frac{(1+\epsilon/3)^2}{n}$. By the first part of Lemma 5.1.6 with probability $\frac{19}{20}$ (actually much more than that) we will also sample an element $l \in M'_0 \cup M'_1$. Thus we have $\mu'(h) \ge (1+\epsilon/3)\mu'(l)$, and also $\mu' \restriction_U (h) \ge (1+\epsilon/3)\mu' \restriction_U (l)$, while both $\mu \restriction_U (h)$ and $\mu \restriction_U (l)$ are restricted between $\frac{1-\epsilon/8}{1+\epsilon/8}\frac{1}{|U|}$ and $\frac{1+\epsilon/8}{1-\epsilon/8}\frac{1}{|U|}$. Therefore, either $\mu' \restriction_U (h) > \mu \restriction_U (h) + \frac{\epsilon}{12|U|}$ or $\mu' \restriction_U (l) < \mu \restriction_U (l) - \frac{\epsilon}{12|U|}$. Either way $d(\mu' \restriction_U, \mu \restriction_U) > \frac{\epsilon}{24|U|}$, which will be identified by the tester of Theorem 2.2.1 with probability $\frac{19}{20}$. Thus in total we get a rejection probability greater than $\frac{7}{9}$.

Otherwise, let i be such that the value 2^i is between $\min\{n, 720\epsilon^{-2}\log n(1+\frac{\epsilon}{3})^j\}$ and $2\min\{n, 720\epsilon^{-2}\log n(1+\frac{\epsilon}{3})^j\}$ (recall the lower bound on $(1+\frac{\epsilon}{3})^j$). In that case the U_i in Line 2 will with probability at least $\frac{19}{20}$ contain a member a of M'_j. Additionally, the expected value of $\mu'(U_i)$ is $\min\{1, \frac{2^i}{n}\} \le \min\{1, \frac{1440}{n}\epsilon^{-2}(1+\frac{\epsilon}{3})^j \log n\}$, thus by Markov's inequality, with probability at least $\frac{8}{9}$ we will have $\mu'(U_i) \le \min\{1, \frac{14400}{n}\epsilon^{-2}(1+\frac{\epsilon}{3})^j \log n\}$. Therefore, $\mu' \restriction_{U_i} (a) \ge \frac{\epsilon^2}{14400(1+\epsilon/3)\log n}$. Thus the expected number of times a is sampled is at least $\frac{\log n}{125}$ and therefore by Lemma 2.2.2 with probability $1 - 2\exp(-\frac{\log n}{250})$ we will sample a at least twice. Thus in total we get a rejection probability greater than $\frac{7}{9}$ for $n > 2^{253}$ (this lower bound can be traded for a higher degree polynomial dependence on $\log n$). □

5.2 Testing identity to a known distribution

THEOREM 5.2.1. *Identity to a known distribution can be tested using* $\mathrm{poly}(\log n, \epsilon^{-1}, \log(\delta^{-1}))$ *non-adaptive conditional samples.*

Let μ be the known distribution and μ' be the unknown distribution that is accessed by sampling. The following is an algorithm for testing identity with the known distribution μ over $[n]$:

ALGORITHM 5.2.2. *(Identity Test) The algorithm receives ϵ, δ, n and μ and operates as follows.*

1. *Let $\mathcal{M} = \{M_0, M_1, \ldots, M_k\} \leftarrow Bucket(\mu, [n], \frac{\epsilon}{8})$.*

2. *For each bucket $M_1, \ldots, M_k$ test using the Nonadaptive Near Uniformity Test (Theorem 5.1.2) to check whether $\|\mu \restriction_{M_j} - \mu' \restriction_{M_j}\|_1 \geq \epsilon/2$ with the error bound $\frac{\delta \log(1+\epsilon/8)}{2 \log n}$, rejecting immediatly if any test rejects.*

3. *Invoke the Identity Tester of Theorem 2.2.1 to test if $\|\mu_{\langle \mathcal{M} \rangle} - \mu'_{\langle \mathcal{M} \rangle}\|_1 \leq \epsilon/2$ with error bound $\delta/2$, answering as the test does.*

LEMMA 5.2.3. *If $d(\mu, \mu') = 0$ then Algorithm 5.2.2 accepts with probability at least $1 - \delta$.*

PROOF. In this case, for all buckets $\|\mu \restriction_{M_j} - \mu' \restriction_{M_j}\|_1 = 0$ and $\|\mu_{\langle \mathcal{M} \rangle} - \mu'_{\langle \mathcal{M} \rangle}\|_1 = 0$, and thus by the union bound we obtain the statement. □

LEMMA 5.2.4. *The sample complexity of Algorithm 3.2.2 is* $\text{poly}(\log n, \epsilon^{-1}, \log(\delta^{-1}))$.

PROOF. We invoke the Nonadaptive Near Uniformity Test $\frac{\log n}{\log(1+\epsilon/8)}$ times, and invoke the Closeness Tester with a distribution of support size $\frac{\log n}{\log(1+\epsilon/8)}$. Therefore by Lemma 5.1.5 and Theorem 2.2.1 we obtain the bound in the statement. □

LEMMA 5.2.5. *If $d(\mu, \mu') > \epsilon$, then Algorithm 5.2.2 rejects with probability at least $1 - \delta$.*

PROOF. Assume that the test accepted. If no error was made, then by Lemma 2.2.6 we have that $d(\mu, \mu') \leq \epsilon$. By the union bound the probability of error is at most δ. □

6. LOWER BOUNDS FOR LABEL INVARIANT PROPERTIES

In this section we prove two sample complexity lower bounds for testing label-invariant distribution properties in our model. The first is for testing uniformity, and applies to non-adaptive algorithms. The second bound is for testing whether a distribution is uniform over some subset $U \subseteq \{1, \ldots, n\}$ of size exatcly 2^{2k} for some k, and applies to general (adaptive) algorithms.

The analysis as it is written relies on the particular behavior of our model when conditioning on a set of probability zero, but this can be done away with: Instead of a distribution μ with probabilities $p_1, \ldots, p_n$ over $[n]$, we can replace it with the $o(1)$-close distribution $\hat{\mu}$ with probabilities $\hat{p_1}, \ldots, \hat{p_i}$ where $\hat{p_i} = \frac{1}{n^2} + (1 - \frac{1}{n})p_i$. The same analysis of why an algorithm will fail to correctly respond to μ will pass on to $\hat{\mu}$, which has no zero probability sets.

6.1 Preliminary definitions

We start with some definitions that are common to both lower bounds.

First, an informal reminder of Yao's method for proving impossibility results for general randomized algorithms: Suppose that there is a fixed distribution over "positive" inputs (inputs that should be accepted) and a distribution over "negative" inputs, so that no deterministic algorithm of the prescribed type can distinguish between the two distributions. That is, suppose that for every such algorithm, the difference in the acceptance probability over both input distributions is $o(1)$. This will mean that no randomized algorithm can distinguish between these distributions as well, and hence for every possible randomized algorithm there is a positive instance and a negative instance so that it cannot be correct for both of them.

In our case an "input" is a distribution μ over $\{1, \ldots, n\}$, and so a "distribution over inputs" is in fact a distribution over distributions. To see why a distribution over distributions cannot be replaced with just a single "averaged distribution", consider the following example. Assume that an algorithm takes two independent samples from a distribution μ over $\{1, 2\}$. If μ is with probability $\frac{1}{2}$ the distribution always giving 1, and with probability $\frac{1}{2}$ the distribution always giving 2, then the two samples will be either $(1, 1)$ or $(2, 2)$, each with probability $\frac{1}{2}$. This can never be the case if we had used a fixed distribution for μ, rather than a distribution over distributions.

What it means to be a deterministic version of our testers will be defined below; as with other settings, these result from fixing in advance the results of the coin tosses of the randomized testers. The following are the two distributions over distributions that we will use to prove lower bounds (and a third which will simply be "pick the uniform distribution over $\{1, \ldots, n\}$ with probability 1").

DEFINITION 6.1.1. *Given a set $U \subseteq \{1, \ldots, n\}$, we define the* U-distribution *to be the uniform distribution over U, that is we set $p_i = 1/|U|$ if $i \in U$ and $p_i = 0$ otherwise.*

The even uniblock distribution *over distributions is defined by the following:*

1. *Uniformly choose an integer k such that $\frac{1}{8} \log n \leq k \leq \frac{3}{8} \log n$.*

2. *Uniformly (from all possible such sets) pick a set $U \subseteq \{1, \ldots, n\}$ of size exactly 2^{2k}.*

3. *The output distribution μ over $\{1, \ldots, n\}$ is the U-distribution (as defined above).*

The odd uniblock distribution *over distributions is defined by the following:*

1. *Uniformly choose an integer k such that $\frac{1}{8} \log n \leq k \leq \frac{3}{8} \log n$.*

2. *Uniformly (from all possible such sets) pick a set $U' \subseteq \{1, \ldots, n\}$ of size exactly 2^{2k+1}.*

3. *The output distribution μ over $\{1, \ldots, n\}$ is the U'-distribution.*

Finally, we also identify the uniform distribution *as a distribution over distributions that picks with probability 1 the uniform distribution over $\{1, \ldots, n\}$.*

For these to be useful for Yao arguments, we first note their farness properties.

OBSERVATION 6.1.2. *Any distribution over $[n]$ that may result from the even uniblock distribution over distributions is $\frac{1}{2}$-far from the uniform distribution over $\{1, \ldots, n\}$, as well as $\frac{1}{2}$-far from any distribution that may result from the odd uniblock distribution over distributions.*

PROOF. This follows directly from a variation distance calculation. Specifically, the variation distance between a uniform distribution over U and (a permutation of) a uniform distribution over V with $|V| \geq |U|$ (which is minimized when we make the permutation such that $U \subseteq V$) is

$(|V| - |U|)/|V|$. In our case we always have $|V| \geq 2|U|$, and hence the lower bound. $\square$

All throughout this section we consider properties that are label-invariant (such as the properties of being in the support of the distributions defined above). This allows us to simplify the analysis of our algorithms.

First, some technical definitions.

DEFINITION 6.1.3. *Given $A_1, \ldots, A_r \subseteq \{1, \ldots, n\}$, define the* atoms generated by $A_1, \ldots, A_r$ *to be all sets of the type $\bigcap_{j=1}^{r} C_j$ where every C_j is one of A_j or $\{1, \ldots, n\} \setminus A_j$. In other words, these are the minimal (by containment) non-empty sets that can be created by boolean operations over $A_1, \ldots, A_r$. The family of all such atoms is called the* partition *generated by $A_1, \ldots, A_r$; when $r = 0$ that partition includes the one set $\{1, \ldots, n\}$.*

Given $A_1, \ldots, A_r$ and $j_1, \ldots, j_r$ where $j_i \in A_i$ for all i, the r-configuration *of $j_1, \ldots, j_r$ is the information for any $1 \leq l, k \leq r$ of whether $j_k \in A_l$ (or equivalently, which is the atom that contains j_k) and whether $j_k = j_l$.*

The label-invariance of all properties discussed in this section will allow us to "simplify" our algorithms prior to proving lower bounds. We next define a simplified version of a non-adaptive algorithm.

DEFINITION 6.1.4. *A* core non-adaptive distribution tester *is a non-adaptive distribution tester, that in its last phase bases its decision to accept or reject only on the $t(\epsilon)$-configuration of its received samples and on its internal coin tosses.*

For a core non-adaptive tester, fixing the values of the internal "coins" in advance gives a very simple deterministic counterpart (for use in Yao arguments): The algorithm now consists of a sequence of fixed sets $A_1, \ldots, A_{t(\epsilon)}$, followed by a function assigning to every possible $t(\epsilon)$-configuration a decision to accept or reject.

We note that indeed in the non-adaptive setting we only need to analyze core algorithms:

OBSERVATION 6.1.5. *A non-adaptive testing algorithm for a label-invariant property can be converted to a corresponding core algorithm with the same sample complexity.*

PROOF. We start with the original algorithm, but choose a uniformly random permutation σ of $\{1, \ldots, n\}$ and have the algorithm act on the correspondingly permuted input distribution, rather than the original one. That is, every set A_i that the algorithm conditions on is converted to $\{\sigma(k) : k \in A_i\}$, while instead of j_i the algorithm receives $\sigma^{-1}(j_i)$. This clearly preserves the guaranteed bounds on the error probability if the property is label-invariant.

To conclude, note that due to the random permutation, all outcomes for $j_1, \ldots, j_t$ that satisfy a given configuration are equally likely, and hence can be simulated using internal coin tosses once the configuration itself is made known to the algorithm. $\square$

For an adaptive algorithm, the definition will be more complex. In fact we will need to set aside some "external" coin tosses, so that also the "deterministic" counterpart will have a probabilistic element. But it will be a manageable one.

DEFINITION 6.1.6. *A* core adaptive distribution tester *is an adaptive distribution tester, that acts as follows.*

- *In the i'th phase, based only on the internal coin tosses and the configuration of the sets $A_1, \ldots, A_{i-1}$ and the sequence $j_1, \ldots, j_{i-1}$, the algorithm assigns a number k_A for every atom A that is generated by $A_1, \ldots, A_{i-1}$, between 0 and $|A \setminus \{j_1, \ldots, j_{i-1}\}|$, where not all such numbers are 0. Additionally the algorithm provides $K_i \subseteq \{1, \ldots, i-1\}$.*
- *A set $B_i \subseteq \{1, \ldots, n\} \setminus \{j_1, \ldots, j_{i-1}\}$ is drawn uniformly among all such sets whose intersection with every atom A as above is of size k_A, and A_i is set to $B_i \cup \{j_k : k \in K_i\}$. The random draw is done independently of prior draws and the algorithm's own internal coins, and A_i is not revealed to the algorithm (however, the algorithm will be able to calculate the sizes of the atoms in the partition generated by $A_1 \ldots, A_i$ using the $i-1$-configuration, and the numbers provided based on it and the internal coin tosses).*
- *A sample j_i is drawn according to μ conditioned over A_i, independently of all other draws. j_i is not revealed to the algorithm, but the new i-configuration is revealed (in other words, the new information that the algorithm receives is whether $j_i \in A_k$ and whether $j_i = j_k$ for each $k < i$).*
- *After $t(\epsilon)$ such phases, the algorithm bases its decision to accept or reject only on the t-configuration of its received samples and on its internal coin tosses.*

Note that also a "deterministic" version of the above algorithm acts randomly, but only in a somewhat "oblivious" manner. The sets A_i will still be drawn at random, but the decisions that the algorithm is allowed to make about them (through the k_A numbers and the K_i sets) as well as the final decision whether to accept or reject will all be deterministic. This is since a deterministic version fixes the algorithm's internal coins and only them.

Also for adaptive algorithms we need to analyze only the respective core algorithms.

OBSERVATION 6.1.7. *An adaptive testing algorithm for a label-invariant property can be converted to a corresponding core algorithm with the same sample complexity.*

PROOF. Again we use a uniformly random permutation σ of $\{1, \ldots, n\}$. Regardless of how the original set A_i was chosen, now it will be chosen uniformly at random among all sets satisfying the same intersection sizes with the atoms of the partition generated by $A_1, \ldots, A_{i-1}$ and the same membership relations with $j_1, \ldots, j_{i-1}$. Hence the use of a uniformly drawn set based on the k_A numbers and K_i is justified, and since σ is not revealed to the algorithm, the particular resulting set A_i is not revealed.

Also, the probability for a particular value of j_i now can depend only on the resulting i-configuration, and hence it is sufficient to reveal only the configuration to the algorithm – the algorithm can then use internal coin tosses to simulate the actual value of j_i (uniformly drawing it from all values satisfying the same configuration). The same goes for the decision whether to accept or reject in the end.

To further illustrate the last point, note that the analysis does not change even if we assume that at every phase, after choosing A_i we also draw a new random permutation, chosen uniformly at random among all those that preserve $j_1, \dots, j_{i-1}$ and the atoms of $A_1, \dots, A_i$ (but can "reshuffle" each atom internally). Then the "position inside its atom" of j_i will be completely uniform among those of the same configuration (if the configuration makes it equal to a previous j_k then there is only one choice for j_i anyway). □

6.2 Uniformity has no constant sample non-adaptive test

THEOREM 6.2.1. *Testing uniformity requires using at least $\Omega(\log\log n)$ non-adaptive conditional samples (for some fixed ϵ).*

To prove this lower bound, we show that for any fixed t and large enough n, no deterministic non-adaptive algorithm can distinguish with probability $\frac{1}{3}$ between the case where the input distribution is the uniform one (with probability 1), and the case where the input distribution is drawn according to the even uniblock distribution over distributions. Recall that such a deterministic algorithm is in fact given by fixed sets $A_1, \dots, A_t \subseteq \{1, \dots, n\}$ and a fixed acceptance criteria based on the t-configuration of the obtained samples (to see this, take a core non-adaptive testing algorithm and arbitrarily fix its internal coins).

We now analyze the performance of a deterministic non-adaptive tester against the even uniblock distribution. Asymptotic expressions are for a fixed t and an increasing n.

DEFINITION 6.2.2. *We call a set $A \subseteq \{1, \dots, n\}$* large *if $|A| > n2^{\sqrt{\log n}}/|U|$, where U is the set chosen in the construction of the even uniblock distribution. We call A* small *if $|A| < n2^{-\sqrt{\log n}}/|U|$.*

LEMMA 6.2.3. *With probability at least $1 - \frac{2^{t+2}}{\sqrt{\log n}}$ over the choice of U, all atoms in the partition generated by $A_1, \dots, A_t$ are either large or small.*

PROOF. There is a fixed number of at most 2^t atoms. An atom A is neither large nor small if $n2^{-\sqrt{\log n}} \le |A||U| \le n2^{\sqrt{\log n}}$. $|U| = 2^{2k}$ where $\frac{1}{8}\log n \le k \le \frac{3}{8}\log n$ uniformly. Therefore, for a fixed A, there are at most $\sqrt{\log n}$ values of k which will make it neither large nor small. Since the range of k is of size $\frac{1}{4}\log n$, we get that with probability at most $\frac{4}{\sqrt{\log n}}$ A is neither large nor small. Taking the union bound over all atoms gives the statement of the lemma. □

LEMMA 6.2.4. *With probability at least $1 - 2^{t-\sqrt{\log n}}$, no small atom intersects U.*

PROOF. Given a fixed k, for any small set A the probability of it intersecting U is clearly bounded by $2^{-\sqrt{\log n}}$. We can now conclude the proof by union-bounding over all small atoms, whose number is bounded by 2^t. □

LEMMA 6.2.5. *With probability $1 - \exp(t - t^2)$, for every large atom A, we have $|A \cap U| = \left(1 \pm \frac{t}{2\sqrt{\log n/4}}\right)|A| \cdot |U|/n$.*

PROOF. This is by a large deviations inequality followed by a union bound over all atoms. Note first that if instead of U we had a uniformly random sequence $u_1, \dots, u_{2^{2k}}$ (chosen with possible repetitions), then this would have been covered by Lemma 2.2.2. However, U is a random set of fixed size instead. For this we appeal to Section 6 of [10], where it is proved that moving from a Binomial to a Hypergeometric distribution (which corresponds to choosing the set U with the fixed size) only makes the distribution more concentrated. The rest follows by the fact that A is large enough. □

Now we can take $t \le \frac{1}{4}\log\log n$ and put forth the following lemma, which implies that the uniblock distribution over distributions is indeed indistinguishable by a deterministic non-adaptive core algorithm from the uniform distribution using only t samples.

LEMMA 6.2.6. *For $t \le \frac{1}{4}\log\log n$, with probability $1 - o(1)$, the distribution over $\{1, \dots, n\}$ obtained from the uniblock distribution over distributions, is such that the resulting distribution over the configurations of $j_1, \dots, j_t$ is $o(1)$-close in the variation distance to the distribution over configurations resulting from the uniform distribution over $[n]$.*

PROOF. With probability $1 - o(1)$ all of the events in Lemmas 6.2.3, 6.2.4 and 6.2.5 occur. We prove that in this case the two distributions over configurations are $o(1)$-close. Recall that the uniform distribution over the set U (resulting from the uniblock distribution) is called the *U-distribution*. The lemma follows from the following:

- A sample taken from a set A_i that contains only small atoms will be uniform from this set (and independent of all others), both for the uniform distribution and the U-distribution. For the U-distribution it follows from U not intersecting A_i at all (recall that in our model, a conditional sample with a set of empty weight returns a uniformly random element from that set).

- A sample taken from a set A_i that contains some large atom will not be identical to any other sample with probability $1 - o(1)$ for both distributions. This follows from the birthday paradox: Setting A to be the large atom contained in A_i, recall that $|A \cap U| = \left(1 \pm \frac{\log\log n/4}{2\sqrt{\log n/4}}\right)|A| \cdot |U|/n$. This quantity is at least $\omega(\log^2 \log n)$. Thus for a fixed i the probability for a collision with any other j is $o(1/\log\log n)$ (regardless of whether A_j contains a large atom), and hence with probability $1 - o(1)$ there will be no collision for any i for which A_i contains a large atom.

- For a set A_i containing a large atom, the distribution over the algebra of the events $j_i \in A_k$ (which corresponds to the distribution over the atom in the partition generated by $A_1, \dots, A_t$ containing j_i) are $o(1)$ close for both distributions. To show this we analyze every atom A generated by $A_1, \dots, A_t$ that is contained in A_i separately. If A is small, then for the uniform distribution, j_i will not be in it with probability $1 - o(1)$ (a small atom is in particular of size $o(|A_i|)$ since A_i contains a large atom as well), while for the U-distribution this is with probability 1 (recall that we conditioned on the event of U not intersecting any small atom). If A is large, then we have $|A \cap U| = \left(1 \pm \frac{\log\log(n)/4}{2\sqrt{\log n/4}}\right)|A| \cdot |U|/n$, implying that the probabilities for $j_i \in A$ for the U-distribution and the uniform one are only $o(1)$ apart.

The items above allow us to conclude the proof. They mean that for both the $|U|$-distribution (conditioned on the events in Lemmas 6.2.3, 6.2.4 and 6.2.5) and the uniform distribution, the resulting distributions over configurations are $o(1)$-close to the one resulting by setting the following:

1. For every i for which A_i is small, uniformly pick $j_i \in A_i$ independently of all other random choices; write down the equalities between these samples and the atoms to which these samples belong.

2. For every i for which A_i is large, write j_i as having no collisions with any other sample; then pick the atom containing j_i from all atoms contained in A_i according to their relative sizes, in a manner independent of all other random choices.

□

Lemma 6.2.6 allows us to conclude the argument by Yao's method.

LEMMA 6.2.7. *All non-adaptive algorithms taking at most $t \leq \frac{1}{4}\log\log n$ conditional samples will fail to distinguish the uniform distribution from the even uniblock distribution over distributions (which are all $\frac{1}{2}$-far from uniform) with any probability more than $o(1)$.*

PROOF. By Observation 6.1.5 it is enough to consider core non-adaptive algorithms, and by Yao's argument it is enough to consider deterministic ones.

For any deterministic non-adaptive core algorithm (characterized by $A_1, \ldots, A_t$ and a function assigning a decision to every possible configuration), the even uniblock distribution with probability $1-o(1)$ will choose a U-distribution, which in turn will induce a distribution over configurations that is $o(1)$-close to that induced by the uniform distribution over $\{1, \ldots, n\}$. This means that if we look at the distribution over configurations caused by the even uniblock distribution over distributions itself, it will also be $o(1)$-close to the one induced by the uniform distribution. Therefore the acceptance probabilities of the algorithm for both distributions over distributions are $o(1)$-close. □

It would be interesting to make the bound on the number of samples into a power of $\log n$, possibly by trying to analyze the sets A_i in themselves rather than through their generated partition.

6.3 A label-invariant property with no constant sample adaptive test

THEOREM 6.3.1. *There exists a label invariant property such that any adaptive testing algorithm for it must use at least $\Omega(\sqrt{\log\log n})$ conditional samples (for some ϵ).*

The property will be that of the distribution being the possible result of the even uniblock distribution over distributions. In other words, it is the property of being equal to the U-distribution over some set U of size 2^{2k} for some $\frac{1}{8}\log n \leq k \leq \frac{3}{8}\log n$.

We show that no "deterministic" adaptive core algorithm can distinguish between the even and odd uniblock distributions using $o(\sqrt{\log\log n})$ samples, while by Observation 6.1.2 a proper $\frac{1}{2}$-test must distinguish between these. Considering such algorithms, we first note that they can be represented by decision trees, where each node of height i corresponds to an $i-1$-configuration of the samples made so far. An internal node describes a new sample, through the numbers k_A provided for every atom A of $A_1, \ldots, A_i$ (where the atoms are labeled by their operations, as the A_i themselves are not revealed to the algorithm), and the set K_i (all these parameters could be different for different nodes of height i). A leaf is labeled with an accept or reject decision.

The basic ideas of the analysis are similar to those of the previous subsection, but the analysis itself is more complex because we have to consider the "partition generated by the samples so far" in every step of the algorithm.

First thing to note is that there are not too many nodes in the decision tree.

OBSERVATION 6.3.2. *The number of nodes in a decision tree corresponding to a t-sample algorithm is less than $t2^{2t^2}$.*

PROOF. A configuration can be described by assigning each of the i samples with a vector of length $2i$ indicating which sets do they belong to and which of the other samples are they equal to. This gives an $i \times 2i$ binary matrix, where every possible i-configuration for i samples corresponds to some such matrix. That gives us at most 2^{2i^2} possible i-configurations. Summing for all $i \leq t$ gives the bound in the statement. □

From now on we will always assume that n is larger than an appropriate fixed constant. For the analysis, we consider two input distributions as being drawn at once, one according to the even uniblock distribution and the other according to the odd uniblock distribution. We first choose $\frac{1}{8}\log n \leq k \leq \frac{3}{8}\log n$ uniformly at random, and then uniformly choose a set U of size 2^{2k} and a set U' of size 2^{2k+1}. We then set μ to be the U-distribution and μ' to be the U'-distribution.

We will now show that the fixed decision tree accepts with almost the same probability when given either μ or μ', which will allow us to conclude the proof using Yao's argument. We start with a notion of "large" and "small" similar to the one used for non-adaptive algorithms, only here we need it for the numbers themselves.

DEFINITION 6.3.3. *We call a number b* large *with respect to U if $b > n2^{\sqrt{\log n}}/|U|$. We call b* small *with respect to U if $b < n2^{-\sqrt{\log n}}/|U|$. We make the analogous definitions with respect to U'.*

LEMMA 6.3.4. *With probability at least $1 - \frac{t2^{3t^2+2}}{\sqrt{\log n}}$, all "$k_A$" numbers appearing in the decision tree are either small with respect to both U and U', or large with respect to both U and U'.*

PROOF. By Observation 6.3.2 the total of different "k_A" numbers is no more than $t2^{3t^2}$ (the number of nodes times 2^t – the bound on the size of the partition generated by $A_1, \ldots, A_i$ in every node). We can conclude similarly to the proof of Lemma 6.2.3 that since $|U|$ and $|U'|$ differ by a factor of 2, there are at most $\sqrt{\log n}$ values of k for which some fixed number k_A will not be either large with respect to both or small with respect to both. The bound in the statement then follows by union bound. □

From now on we assume that the event of Lemma 6.3.4 has occurred, and fix k (that is, the following will hold not only for the entire distributions, but also for the conditioning on every specific k for which the event of Lemma 6.3.4 is satisfied). The following lemma is analogous to the non-adaptive counterparts Lemma 6.2.4 and Lemma 6.2.5, but here it is proved by induction for every node that is reached while running the decision tree over the distribution drawn according to either μ or μ', where the inductive argument requires both statements to hold. This lemma will essentially be used as a warm-up, since the final proof will refer to the proof and not just the statement of the lemma.

LEMMA 6.3.5. *Assuming $t \leq \sqrt{\frac{1}{32}\log\log n}$ and conditioned on that the events of Lemma 6.3.4 have occurred, for every $1 \leq i \leq t$, with probability at least $1 - \frac{2^{t+1}}{\sqrt{\log n}}$, the following occur.*

- *All small atoms in the partition generated by the sets $A_1, \ldots, A_i$ contain no members of either U or U' outside (possibly) $\{j_1, \ldots, j_{i-1}\}$.*
- *For every large atom B in the partition generated by $A_1, \ldots, A_i$, we have both $|B \cap U| = \left(1 \pm \frac{i}{2\sqrt{\log n/4}}\right)|B| \cdot |U|/n$ and $|B \cap U'| = \left(1 \pm \frac{i}{2\sqrt{\log n/4}}\right)|B| \cdot |U'|/n$.*

PROOF. We shall prove the lemma not only conditioned on the event of Lemma 6.3.4, but also conditioned on any fixed $|U|$ (and $|U'| = 2|U|$) for which Lemma 6.3.4 is satisfied. We assume by induction that this occurs for the atoms in the partition generated by $A_1, \ldots, A_{i-1}$ with probability at least $1 - \frac{2^i}{\sqrt{\log n}}$, and prove it for $A_1, \ldots, A_i$ with probability at least $1 - \frac{2^{i+1}}{\sqrt{\log n}}$. Recall that the way A_i is generated, the algorithm in fact specifies how many members of it will appear in $A \setminus \{j_1, \ldots, j_{i-1}\}$ for every atom A of the partition generated by $A_1, \ldots, A_{i-1}$ (while specifying exactly which of $j_1, \ldots, j_{i-1}$ will appear in it), and then the actual set is drawn uniformly at random from those that satisfy it.

We show the conclusion of the lemma to hold even if U and U' are held fixed (as long as they satisfy the induction hypothesis and their sizes satisfy the assertion of Lemma 6.3.4). Let B be an atom of $A_1, \ldots, A_i$ and let A be the atom of $A_1, \ldots, A_{i-1}$ so that $B \subseteq A$. We have several cases to consider, conditioned on the fact that the event in the statement does occur for $i-1$.

- If A is small, then so is B. By the induction hypothesis $A \setminus \{j_1, \ldots, j_{i-1}\}$ has no members of U or U', and hence so does B. This happens with (conditional) probability 1.
- If A is large but B is small, by the induction hypothesis both $|A \cap U| = \left(1 \pm \frac{(i-1)}{2\sqrt{\log n/4}}\right)|A| \cdot |U|/n$ and $|A \cap U'| = \left(1 \pm \frac{(i-1)}{2\sqrt{\log n/4}}\right)|A| \cdot |U'|/n$. When this happens, as $B \setminus \{j_1, \ldots, j_{i-1}\}$ is in fact chosen uniformly from all subsets of $A \setminus \{j_1, \ldots, j_{i-1}\}$ of the same size (either k_A or $|A \setminus \{j_1, \ldots, j_{i-1}\}| - k_A$), and since B is small, we can use a union bound to see that no member of either U or U' is taken into B with probability $1 - 2^{1-\sqrt{\log n}}$.
- If B is large (and hence so is A), then again by the induction hypothesis both $|A \cap U| = \left(1 \pm \frac{(i-1)}{2\sqrt{\log n/4}}\right)|A| \cdot |U|/n$ and $|A \cap U'| = \left(1 \pm \frac{(i-1)}{2\sqrt{\log n/4}}\right)|A| \cdot |U'|/n$. We also note that since B is large we have in particular $t \leq \frac{1/2}{2\sqrt{\log n/4}}|B|$. We can now use a large deviation inequality (as in Lemma 6.2.5) to conclude the bounds for $|B \cap U|$ and $|B \cap U'|$ with probability $1 - 2\exp(-2^{\sqrt{\log n}/2-2})$.

Thus in all cases the statement will not hold with probability at most $\frac{1}{\sqrt{\log n}}$ for n large enough. By taking the union bound over all possibilities for B (up to 2^i events in total) we get that with probability $1 - \frac{2^i}{\sqrt{\log n}}$ the statement of the lemma holds for $A_1, \ldots, A_i$, conditioned on the event occurring for $A_1, \ldots, A_{i-1}$. A union bound with the event of the induction hypothesis happening for $A_1, \ldots, A_{i-1}$ gives the required bound. □

We now prove the lemma showing the indistinguishability of μ from μ' whenever $t \leq \sqrt{\frac{1}{32}\log\log n}$, conditioned on the event of Lemma 6.3.4. We assume without loss of generality that the decision tree of the algorithm is full and balanced, which means that the algorithm will always take t samples even if its output was already determined before they were taken.

LEMMA 6.3.6. *Assuming that $t \leq \sqrt{\frac{1}{32}\log\log n}$ and that the event of Lemma 6.3.4 has occurred, consider the resulting distributions of which of the leaves of the algorithm was reached. These two distributions, under μ compared to under μ', are at most $\frac{2^{3t+1}}{\sqrt{\log n}}$ apart from each other.*

PROOF. The proof is reminiscent of the proof of Lemma 6.2.6 above, but requires more cases to be considered, as well as induction over the height of the node. Denoting this height by i, we shall prove by induction that the distributions over which of the height i nodes was reached, under μ compared to μ', are only are at most $1 - \frac{2^{3i+1}}{\sqrt{\log n}}$ apart from each other.

We shall use the induction hypothesis that the corresponding distributions over the node of height $i-1$ (the parent of the node that we consider now) are at most $1 - \frac{2^{3i-2}}{\sqrt{\log n}}$ apart, and then show that the variation distance between the distributions determining the transition from a particular parent to the child node is no more than $\frac{2^{3i}}{\sqrt{\log n}}$, which when added to the difference in the distributions over the parent nodes gives required bound.

The full induction hypothesis will include not only the bound on the distributions of the parent nodes, but also a host of other assumptions, that we prove along to occur with probability at least $1 - \frac{2^{3i+1}}{\sqrt{\log n}}$. In particular, instead of using the statement of Lemma 6.3.5, we essentially re-prove it here. So the induction hypothesis also includes that all of the events proved during the inductive proof of Lemma 6.3.5 hold here with respect to $A_1, \ldots, A_{i-1}$. Also, as in the proof of Lemma 6.3.5, the conditional probability of them not holding for $A_1, \ldots, A_i$ is at most $\frac{2^i}{\sqrt{\log n}}$ (by the union bound done there for every atom generated by $A_1, \ldots, A_i$ of the event of the hypothesis failing for any single atom A). Therefore, we assume that additionally the inductive hypothesis used in the proof of Lemma 6.3.5 has occurred for $A_1, \ldots, A_i$, and prove that with probability at least $1 - \frac{2^{2i}}{\sqrt{\log n}}$

all other assertions of the inductive hypothesis occur as well as that the variation distance between the distributions over the choice of the child node is at most $\frac{2^{2i}}{\sqrt{\log n}}$. By a union bound argument (and for the variation distance, a "common large probability event" argument), this will give us the $1-\frac{2^{3i}}{\sqrt{\log n}}$ bound that we need for the induction. Recall that the choice of child node depends deterministically on the question of which atom of $A_1,\ldots,A_i$ contains the obtained sample j_i, so in fact we will bound the distance between the distributions of the atom in which j_i has landed.

Additionally, we define by induction over i the following notion: An index i is called *smallish* if all the "k_A" numbers relating to it are small, and additionally K_i contains only smallish indexes (recall that $K_i \subseteq \{1,\ldots,i-1\}$). A final addition to our induction hypothesis is that with probability at least $1-\frac{2^{3i-2}}{\sqrt{\log n}}$, in addition to all our other assertions, the following occur for every $i' < i$.

- The sample $j_{i'}$ is in U or respectively U' if and only if i' is not smallish (note that the assignment of smallish indexes depends on the parent node).

- If i' is not smallish but all its corresponding "k_A" numbers are small, then $j_{i'}$ is equal to some j_l where l is a non-smallish index smaller than i'.

- If there exists a large "k_A" number for i', then $j_{i'}$ is not equal to j_l for any $l < i'$, and additionally $j_{i'}$ lies in some atom A' for which the corresponding $k_{A'}$ is not small (it is allowed that $A' = A$).

We now work for every possible parent node of height $i-1$ separately. Note that we restrict our attention to nodes whose corresponding $(i-1)$-configurations satisfy the induction hypothesis. Recall that we assume that the induction hypothesis in the proof of Lemma 6.3.5 has occurred for $A_1,\ldots,A_i$, and aim for a $\frac{2^{2i}}{\sqrt{\log n}}$ "failure probability" bound. We separate to cases according to the nature of $A_1,\ldots,A_i$.

- A sample taken from a set A_i, where i is smallish, will be uniform and independent of other samples, for both the U-distribution and the U'-distribution. Moreover, this j_i in itself will not be a member of U or respectively U'. This is since $A_i \setminus \{j_k : k \in K_i\}$ does not intersect U or U', while using the induction hypothesis for $\{j_k : k \in K_i\}$ (so also A_i does not intersect U or U'). So conditioned on the entire induction hypothesis for $i-1$ and the hypothesis in the proof of Lemma 6.3.5 for $A_1,\ldots,A_i$, all assertions for i will occur with probability 1, and the distributions for selecting the height i node given this particular parent node are identical under either μ or μ'.

- A sample taken from a set A_i, where the k_A numbers are all small but i is not smallish, will be a member of U or respectively U', chosen uniformly (and independently) from $\{j_k : k \in K'_i\}$, where K'_i denotes the (non-empty) set of all non-smallish indexes in K_i. This is since $\{j_k : k \in K'_i\}$ is exactly the set of members of U or respectively of U' in A_i (by the hypothesis for $A_1,\ldots,A_i$ there will be no member of U or U' in $A_i \setminus \{j_k : k \in K_i\}$, and the rest follows from the induction hypothesis concerning smallish indexes). Again the assertions for i follow with probability 1 (conditioned on the above hypotheses), and the distributions for selecting the height i node are identical.

- If a sample is taken from A_i where at least one of the k_A numbers is not small, then the following occur.
  - Since A_i in particular contains the atom A, and both $|A\cap U| = \left(1 \pm \frac{i}{2\sqrt{\log n}/4}\right)|A|\cdot|U|/n$ and $|A \cap U'| = \left(1 \pm \frac{i}{2\sqrt{\log n}/4}\right)|A|\cdot|U'|/n$ by the assertion over $A_1,\ldots,A_i$ relating to Lemma 6.3.5, we note that in particular $i = o(\frac{1}{\sqrt{\log n}}|A_i \cap U|)$ and $i = o(\frac{1}{\sqrt{\log n}}|A_i \cap U'|)$, so with probability less than $\frac{1}{\sqrt{\log n}}$ (for n larger than some constant) we will get under either μ or μ' a sample that is identical to a prior one.
  - By the assertion over $A_1,\ldots,A_i$, an atom B inside A_i for which the corresponding k_B is small will not contain a member of U or U', and so j_i will not be in such an atom (in the preceding item we have already established that there are members of U and respectively U' in A_i).
  - By the assertion over $A_1,\ldots,A_i$, for every large atom B inside A_i we have both that $|B\cap U| = \left(1 \pm \frac{i}{2\sqrt{\log n}/4}\right)|B|\cdot|U|/n$ and that $|B\cap U'| = \left(1 \pm \frac{i}{2\sqrt{\log n}/4}\right)|B|\cdot|U'|/n$, implying that $\frac{|B\cap U|}{|U|} = \left(1 \pm \frac{i}{2\sqrt{\log n}/5}\right)\frac{|B\cap U'|}{|U'|}$ (for large enough n). Also, every small atom C inside A_i contains no members of U or U', so summing over all atoms of A_i we obtain $\frac{|A_i\cap U|}{|U|} = \left(1 \pm \frac{i}{2\sqrt{\log n}/5}\right)\frac{|A_i\cap U'|}{|U'|}$, and thus for every atom B of A_i (large or small) we finally have $\frac{|B\cap U|}{|A_i\cap U|} = \left(1 \pm \frac{i}{2\sqrt{\log n}/6}\right)\frac{|B\cap U'|}{|A_i\cap U'|}$ (for small atoms both sides are zero).

  Te final thing to note is that $\frac{|B\cap U|}{|A_i\cap U|}$ and respectively $\frac{|B\cap U'|}{|A_i\cap U'|}$ equal the probabilities of obtaining a sample from B under μ and respectively μ'. Summing over all atoms contained in A_i (of which there are 2^{i-1}) we obtain a difference over these distributions that is bounded by $\frac{2^i}{\sqrt{\log n}}$, which satisfies the requirements (also after conditioning on that the events related to the rest of the induction hypothesis have occurred).

Having covered all cases, this completes the proof that the inductive hypothesis follows to i, and thus the proof of the lemma. □

Now we can conclude the argument by Yao's method to prove the following lemma that implies the theorem.

LEMMA 6.3.7. *All adaptive algorithms taking at most* $t \le \sqrt{\frac{1}{32}\log\log n}$ *conditional samples will fail to distinguish the even uniblock distribution over distributions from the odd one (whose outcomes are always* $\frac{1}{2}$*-far from those of the even distribution) with any probability more than* $o(1)$.

PROOF. By Observation 6.1.7 it is enough to consider only core adaptive algorithms, and then by Yao's argument it is enough to consider "deterministic" ones (the quote marks are because the external coin tosses are retained as per the definitions above). We now consider the decision tree of such an algorithm, and feed to it either μ or μ' that are drawn as per the definition above. With probability at least $1-\frac{t2^{3t^2+2}}{\sqrt{\log n}}=1-o(1)$ the event of Lemma 6.3.4 has occurred, and conditioned on this event (or even if we condition on particular U and U'), Lemma 6.3.6 provides that the variation distance between the resulting distributions over the leafs is at most $\frac{2^{3t+1}}{\sqrt{\log n}}=o(1)$. In particular this bounds the difference between the (conditional) probabilities of the event of reaching an accepting leaf of the algorithm.

Since we have an $o(1)$ difference when conditioned on a $1-o(1)$ probability event, we also have an $o(1)$ difference on the unconditioned probability of reaching an accepting leaf under μ compared to μ'. This means that the algorithm cannot distinguish between the two corresponding distributions over distributions. □

7. A LOWER BOUND FOR TESTING GENERAL PROPERTIES OF DISTRIBUTIONS

For properties that are not required to be label-invariant, near-maximal non-testability could happen also when conditional samples are allowed.

THEOREM 7.0.1. *Some properties of distributions on $[n]$ require $\Omega(n)$ conditional samples to test (adaptive or not).*

We assume n is even. To prove Theorem 7.0.1 we reduce the problem of testing general $n/2$-bit binary string properties $P\subseteq\{0,1\}^{n/2}$ to the problem of testing properties of distributions over $[n]$ with conditional samples. The reduction is probabilistic, succeeding with probability $1-o(1)$, and only incurs an additional $O(1)$ factor in the query complexity, that is, each conditional sample made by the distribution tester is translated into (expected) $O(1)$ queries to the input binary string $x\in\{0,1\}^{n/2}$. Then the lower bound follows by the existence of hard-to-test properties $P\subseteq\{0,1\}^{n/2}$ that require $\Omega(n)$ queries to test (see e.g. [7]).

7.1 The Reduction

We start with a few definitions. A string $y\in\{0,1\}^n$ is *balanced* if it has the same number of 0s and 1s (in particular we assume here that n is even). For $x\in\{0,1\}^{n/2}$, let $b(x)\in\{0,1\}^n$ be the string obtained by concatenating x with its bitwise complement (in which each original bit of x is flipped). Clearly $b(x)$ is balanced for all x.

For a property $P\subseteq\{0,1\}^{n/2}$, define $b(P)\subseteq\{0,1\}^n$ as $b(P)\triangleq\{b(x):x\in P\}$.

OBSERVATION 7.1.1. *For all $x,y\in\{0,1\}^{n/2}$, $d(x,y)=d(b(x),b(y))$.*

PROOF. Follows from the fact that if x and y differ in $d(x,y)\cdot\frac{n}{2}$ entries, then $b(x)$ and $b(y)$ differ in $d(x,y)\cdot n$ entries. □

OBSERVATION 7.1.2. *For all P and $\epsilon>0$, ϵ-testing $b(P)$ requires at least as many queries as ϵ-testing P.*

PROOF. This is since we can simulate the tester for $b(P)$ also for a non balanced string $x\in\{0,1\}^{n/2}$, where a query for an index $i\le n/2$ would return x_i and for $i>n/2$ the query would return $1-x_{i-n/2}$. □

Next, for every balanced string $x\in\{0,1\}^n$ we define a distribution μ_x on $[n]$ as follows:

- If $x_i=0$ then $\mu_x(i)=\frac{1}{2n}$;
- if $x_i=1$ then $\mu_x(i)=\frac{3}{2n}$.

Note that since x is balanced μ_x is indeed a distribution as $\sum_{i=1}^n\mu_x(i)=1$.

Extending this definition further, for every property $P\subseteq\{0,1\}^{n/2}$ we define a property $\mathcal{P}_P$ of distributions over $[n]$ as follows:

$$\mathcal{P}_P\triangleq\{\mu_x:x\in b(P)\}.$$

OBSERVATION 7.1.3. *For all $x,y\in\{0,1\}^{n/2}$, it holds that $d(b(x),b(y))=2\cdot d(\mu_{b(x)},\mu_{b(y)})$, where the first distance refers to the normalized Hamming distance between binary strings, and the second is the variation distance between distributions.*

PROOF. This follows by direct calculation. □

Theorem 7.0.1 follows by the following extension of Observation 7.1.2:

LEMMA 7.1.4. *For all P and $\epsilon>0$, if ϵ-testing P with success probability $3/5$ requires at least q queries, then $\epsilon/2$-testing $\mathcal{P}_P$ with success probability $2/3$ requires at least $q/100$ conditional samples.*

PROOF. By Observation 7.1.3, for all $x\in\{0,1\}^{n/2}$, if $x\in P$ then $\mu_{b(x)}\in\mathcal{P}_P$, and if $d(x,P)>\epsilon$ then $d(\mu_{b(x)},\mathcal{P}_P)>\epsilon/2$. Now we show how to reduce the task of testing P to testing $\mathcal{P}_P$. Let T be a tester for $\mathcal{P}_P$ making at most $q/100$ conditional samples. Given an oracle access to the input string $x\in\{0,1\}^{n/2}$, which is to be tested for membership in P, we simulate each conditional sample $\emptyset\ne Q\subseteq[n]$ to $\mu_{b(x)}$ made by T as follows:

Sampler.

1. Pick $i\in Q$ uniformly at random. If $i\le n/2$ query x_i and set $v_i\leftarrow x_i$. Else, query $x_{i-n/2}$ and set $v_i\leftarrow 1-x_{i-n/2}$.
2. If $v_i=1$, output i.
3. Else, with probability $1/3$ output i, and with the remaining probability go to Step 1.

It is clear that whenever Sampler outputs i with $v_i=1$, then i is distributed uniformly among all indices $\{j\in Q:v_j=1\}$. Same is true for i such that $v_i=0$. So, to convince ourselves that Sampler simulates conditional samples correctly, we only need to prove that the ratio between the probability of outputting i with $v_i=1$ and the probability of outputting i with $v_i=0$ is correct.

Let $q_1\triangleq|\{i\in Q:v_i=1\}|$ and $q_0\triangleq|\{i\in Q:v_i=0\}|$. According to our distribution $\mu_b(x)$, the distribution of indices in Q corresponding to the conditional sample is as follows:

- $\Pr[i]=\frac{3}{3q_1+q_0}$ if $v_i=1$.

- $\Pr[i] = \frac{1}{3q_1+q_0}$ if $v_i = 0$.

In particular, the probability of selecting i such that $v_i = 1$ is $3q_1/q_0$ times the probability of selecting i with $v_i = 0$.

Let us now analyze what is the probability with which Sampler outputs (eventually) an index $i \in Q$ with $v_i = 1$, and with $v_i = 0$, respectively. At every round, an index i with $v_i = 1$ is output with probability $\frac{q_1}{q_1+q_0}$, and an index i with $v_i = 0$ is output with probability $\frac{q_0}{3(q_1+q_0)}$. With the remaining probability (of $\frac{2q_0}{3(q_1+q_0)}$) no index is output, and the process repeats independently of all previous rounds. Hence the ratio of the probability of outputting i such that $v_i = 1$ to the probability of outputting i with $v_i = 0$ is $3q_1/q_0$, as required. Note also that the expected number of rounds (and so queries to x) per one execution of Sampler is $(1 - \frac{2q_0}{3(q_1+q_0)})^{-1} \leq 3$.

The last ingredient in the reduction is a counter for total queries, that makes sure that the number of queries to x does not exceed q (the lower bound). If so, the reduction fails. Since Sampler is called at most $q/100$ times (the query complexity of T), a $3/100 < 1/15$ bound on the failure probability follows by Markov's inequality, and we are done (the bound on the success probability follows even if we assume that the distribution tester "magically" guesses the correct answer whenever the reduction to the string property fails). $\square$

8. ACKNOWLEDGEMENTS

The research leading to these results has received funding from the European Union's - Seventh Framework Programme [FP7/2007-2013] under grant agreement nÂř 202405 (PROPERTY TESTING).

9. REFERENCES

[1] N. Alon and J. H. Spencer. *The probabilistic method.* Wiley-Interscience Series in Discrete Mathematics and Optimization. John Wiley & Sons Inc., Hoboken, NJ, third edition, 2008.

[2] T. Batu, S. Dasgupta, R. Kumar, and R. Rubinfeld. The complexity of approximating the entropy. *SIAM J. Comput.*, 35(1):132–150, 2005.

[3] T. Batu, L. Fortnow, E. Fischer, R. Kumar, R. Rubinfeld, and P. White. Testing random variables for independence and identity. In B. Werner, editor, *Proceedings of the 42nd Annual Symposium on Foundations of Computer Science (FOCS-01)*, pages 442–451, Los Alamitos, CA, Oct. 14–17 2001.

[4] T. Batu, L. Fortnow, R. Rubinfeld, W. D. Smith, and P. White. Testing closeness of discrete distributions. *CoRR*, abs/1009.5397, 2010. Extended abstract appeared in the proceedings of the 41st Annual Symposium on Foundations of Computer Science (FOCS-00), pages 259–269.

[5] T. Batu, R. Kumar, and R. Rubinfeld. Sublinear algorithms for testing monotone and unimodal distributions. In *Proceedings of the 36th Annual ACM Symposium on Theory of Computing*, pages 381–390, New York, 2004.

[6] C. Cannone, D. Ron, and R. Servedio. Testing probability distributions using conditional samples. *Electronic Colloquium on Computational Complexity (ECCC)*, 2012. TR12-155.

[7] O. Goldreich, S. Goldwasser, and D. Ron. Property testing and its connection to learning and approximation. *J. ACM*, 45(4):653–750, 1998.

[8] O. Goldreich and D. Ron. On testing expansion in bounded-degree graphs. In O. Goldreich, editor, *Studies in Complexity and Cryptography*, volume 6650 of *Lecture Notes in Computer Science*, pages 68–75. Springer, 2011.

[9] S. Guha, A. McGregor, and S. Venkatasubramanian. Sublinear estimation of entropy and information distances. *ACM Transactions on Algorithms*, 5(4), 2009.

[10] W. Hoeffding. Probability inequalities for sums of bounded random variables. *J. Amer. Statist. Assoc.*, 58:13–30, 1963.

[11] R. Levi, D. Ron, and R. Rubinfeld. Testing properties of collections of distributions. In B. Chazelle, editor, *Proceedings of the 1st Symposium on Innovations in Computer Science (ICS-10)*, pages 179–194, Beijing, China, Jan. 5–7 2010.

[12] S. Raskhodnikova, D. Ron, A. Shpilka, and A. Smith. Strong lower bounds for approximating distribution support size and the distinct elements problem. *SIAM J. Comput.*, 39(3):813–842, 2009.

[13] P. Valiant. Testing symmetric properties of distributions. *SIAM J. Comput.*, 40(6):1927–1968, 2011.

Author Index

www.ingramcontent.com/pod-product-compliance
Ingram Content Group UK Ltd.
Pitfield, Milton Keynes, MK11 3LW, UK
UKHW051417290926
15471UKWH00009B/1645

9 781450 320870